D0204221

[redacted]

PJ 4731 .B53 O94 1989 v.3
Owens, John Joseph, 1918-
Analytical key to the Old Testament

Analytical Key
to the Old Testament

Analytical Key to the Old Testament

John Joseph Owens

Volume 3

Ezra–Song of Solomon

BAKER BOOK HOUSE
Grand Rapids, Michigan 49516

VNYS PJ 4731 .B53
O94 1989 v.3 c.1
lkvn18

Copyright © 1991 by Baker Books
a division of Baker Book House Company
P.O. Box 6287, Grand Rapids, MI 49516-6287

ISBN: 0-8010-6715-4

Fifth printing, March 2000

Printed in the United States of America

All rights reserved. No part of this publication may be reproduced, stored in a retrieval system, or transmitted in any form or by any means, electronic, mechanical, photocopying, recording, or otherwise, without prior permission from Baker Book House.

Biblia Hebraica Stuttgartensia © 1967/77 by Deutsche Bibelgesellschaft, Stuttgart, and used by permission. The English Bible text in this publication is adapted from the RSV Bible, and used by permission of the Division of Education and Ministry, the National Council of the Churches of Christ in the U.S.A.

Library of Congress Cataloging-in-Publication Data
(Revised for vol. 3)

Owens, John Joseph, 1918–
Analytical key to the Old Testament.

English and Hebrew.
"The English Bible text in this publication is adapted from the RSV Bible"—T.p. verso.
Contents: —v. 3. Ezra–Song of Solomon—v. 4. Isaiah–Malachi.
1. Bible. O.T.—Study. 2. Hebrew language—Inflection. 3. Hebrew language—Parts of speech. I. Bible. O.T. Hebrew. 1989. II. Bible. O.T. English. Owens. 1989. III. Title.
PJ4731.B53094 1989 221.4'4 89-437
ISBN 0-8010-6713-8 (v. 4)

For information about academic book, resources for Christian leaders, and all new releases available from Baker Book House, visit our web site:

http://www.bakerbooks.com

To

Mary Frances

my wife and best friend
whose consistent Christian life and love
have guided, inspired, and sustained me

Contents

Preface	ix
Abbreviations	xi
Ezra	1
Nehemiah	47
Esther	109
Job	143
Psalms	259
Proverbs	521
Ecclesiastes	611
Song of Solomon	645

Preface

Translation is the art of transferring the thoughts expressed in one language and culture to the syntax, style, and words of a different language and culture. Much more is involved than the simple replacement of one Hebrew word with an English word. Even though there are many excellent translations, the original text and/or a translation must be interpreted for an understanding of the form, style, nuance, and context of the author. This analytical key seeks to provide the basic elements necessary for valid interpretation. Since it is very difficult to transfer one linguistic, sociological, religious context into a completely different milieu, it is imperative to examine the specific "building blocks" of the original writing in order to establish distinct boundaries of meaning.

This key is intended to assist the person who knows some Hebrew but has not retained interpretive or grammatical discernment. The user of this volume must supplement this information with his/her own interpretive skill. For instance, the use of a Hiph'il form when a Qal form is available is an important nuance. Since there are no such things as absolute synonyms, one must be alert to the specific grammatical structures utilized in the text.

It is the task of students, pastors, and theologians to interpret the biblical text for untrained readers. From a translation, one cannot be positive that the innuendos of the Hebrew text are properly understood. The interpreter should be alert to such things as the verbal structures, the presence or absence of the definite article, the construct relationships as distinguished from the adjectival construction, and the waw conjunctives and/or consecutives.

Since the conjunction as prefixed to an imperfect may take two different written forms, this phenomenon is regularly noted (the simple conjunction is noted as "conj." and the more complex form as "consec.").

Scholars disagree about the conjunction prefixed to a perfect. In earlier times, some interpreters reasoned that if the imperfect had two forms of a conjunction, it is only logical that the perfect could have two forms. However, the biblical text uses only one form for the conjunction. Therefore, this volume identifies the conjunction + perfect as "conj." It is the task of the interpreter to ascertain the syntax and meaning of these grammatical facts.

This key seeks to provide complete grammatical and lexicographical information for each word of the entire canon. Each form has been identified. The presence of definite articles, prepositions, and conjunctions is noted. Nouns are clearly explained as to usage and relationship. Each grammatical explanation provides the reader with information that must be used in defining the various shades of meaning.

Accuracy has been attempted throughout in such forms as construct relationships. Any noun with a pronominal suffix forms a construct relationship. A pronominal suffix with a verb forms a verb/direct object construction. No special note is taken of these.

The use of nouns/substantives/adjectives with the construct usage is indicated. Also, the definite article has been indicated only when it is grammatically present. Many translators have inserted or omitted articles due to linguistic considerations. Since it is the biblical text which is the object of interpretation, it is important to know what the original writers used or did not use.

This volume provides for each word the page number of the standard Hebrew-English dictionary (Francis Brown, S. R. Driver, and Charles A. Briggs, *A Hebrew and English Lexicon of the Old Testament* [Oxford: Clarendon, 1975]) on which that word's explanation begins.

This volume follows the Hebrew text chapter/verse by chapter/verse. Upon finding the desired chapter/verse, the reader can locate the term desired by following the Hebrew text at the left of the column.

The Hebrew text is the best complete Ben Asher text available (K. Ellinger and W. Rudolph, eds., *Biblia Hebraica Stuttgartensia* [Stuttgart: Württembergische Bibelanstalt, 1977]). When there has been an insoluble difficulty in the text, a variant reading may be provided from better translations or grammars.

If the student has difficulty in following the biblical Hebrew text, he/she can identify the desired form from the English translation provided at the conclusion of each entry. Generally, the English translation will follow the Revised Standard Version. However, at times there will be a more literal translation to assist in identifying the elements of the Hebrew text.

Sample Entry

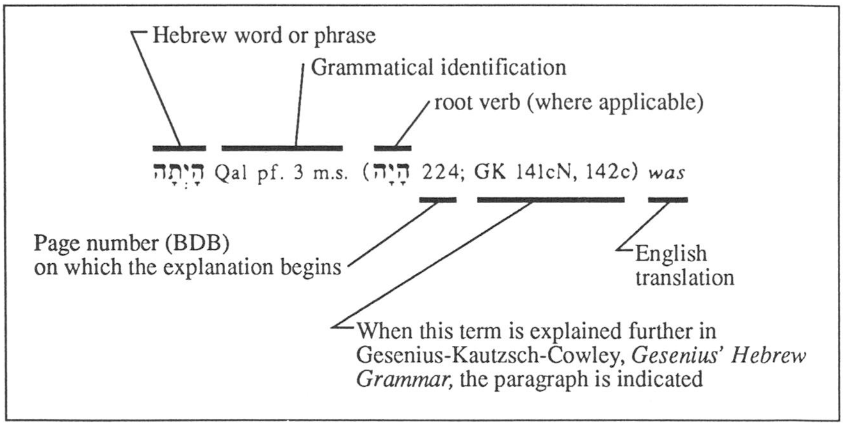

Abbreviations

abs.	absolute
abstr.	abstract
acc.	accusative
act.	active
adj.	adjective
adv.	adverb
advers.	adversative
apoc.	apocopated
art.	article
BH	Biblia Hebraica
BHK	Biblia Hebraica Kittel
c.	common
card.	cardinal
cf.	compare
coh.	cohortative
coll.	collective
cond.	conditional
conj.	conjunctive
consec.	consecutive
crpt.	corrupt
cstr.	construct
def.	definite, defective
defect.	defective
dei.	deity
del.	delete
demons.	demonstrative
dir.	direct
du.	dual
dub.	dubious
encl.	enclitic
epen.	epenthetic
exclam.	exclamatory
f.	feminine
fig.	figurative
gen.	genitive, generic, gentilic
gent.	gentilic
Ges.	Gesenius
Gk.	Greek
GK	Gesenius-Kautzsch
Heb.	Hebrew
Hi.	Hiph'il
Hith.	Hithpa'el
Ho.	Hoph'al
hypoth.	hypothetical
impf.	imperfect
impv.	imperative
indecl.	indeclinable
indef.	indefinite
inf.	infinitive
infra	below
intens.	intensive
interj.	interjection
interr.	interrogative
juss.	jussive
K	Kethiv
lit.	literal
loc.	locale
LXX	Septuagint
m.	masculine
mlt.	many
mng.	meaning
ms(s).	manuscript(s)
n.	noun
neg.	negative
Ni.	Niph'al
num.	numeral
obj.	object
ord.	ordinal
p.	plural
part.	particle
pass.	passive
paus.	pausal
pers.	personal
pf.	perfect
Pi.	Pi'el
pleon.	(full) pleonastic
poss.	possible
pr.	proper, pronoun
prb.	probable
prep.	preposition
pron.	pronoun
ptc.	participle
Pu.	Pu'al
Q	Qere
rd.	read(s)
redupl.	reduplicated
rel.	relative
Rob.	Robinson
RSV	Revised Standard Version
s.	singular
Sam.Pent.	Samaritan Pentateuch
segh.	segholate
sf.	suffix
subst.	substantive
supra	above
Syr.	Syriac
T.	Targum
temp.	temporal
tr.	transposed
txt.	text or textual
V	Vulgate
v.	vide or see
vol.	voluntative
Vul.	Vulgate
>	omits
<	adds
+	adds
Θ	Theodotion
Σ	Symmachus

Ezra

1:1

וּבִשְׁנַת conj.-prep.-n.f.s. cstr. (1040) *in the year of*

אַחַת adj. num. f.s. (25) *first*

לְכוֹרֶשׁ prep.-pr.n. (468) *Cyrus*

מֶלֶךְ n.m.s. cstr. (I 572) *king of*

פָּרַס pr.n. (828) *Persia*

לִכְלוֹת prep.-Qal inf.cstr. (כָּלָה 477) *that might be accomplished*

דְּבַר־יהוה n.m.s. cstr. (182)-pr.n. (217) *the word of Yahweh*

מִפִּי prep.-n.m.s. cstr. (804) *by the mouth of*

יִרְמְיָה pr.n. (941) *Jeremiah*

הֵעִיר Hi. pf. 3 m.s. (עוּר I 734) *stirred up*

יהוה pr.n. (217) *Yahweh*

אֶת־רוּחַ dir.obj.-n.f.s. cstr. (924) *the spirit of*

כֹּרֶשׁ v.supra *Cyrus*

מֶלֶךְ־פָּרַס v.supra-v.supra *king of Persia*

וַיַּעֲבֶר־קוֹל consec.-Hi. impf. 3 m.s. (עָבַר 716) -n.m.s. (876) *so that he made a proclamation*

בְּכָל־מַלְכוּתוֹ prep.-n.m.s. cstr. (481)-n.f.s.-3 m.s. sf. (574) *throughout all his kingdom*

וְגַם־בְּמִכְתָּב conj.-adv. (168)-prep.-n.m.s. (508) *and also put it in writing*

לֵאמֹר prep.-Qal inf.cstr. (55) *(saying)*

1:2

כֹּה אָמַר adv. (462)-Qal pf. 3 m.s. (55) *thus says*

כֹּרֶשׁ pr.n. (468) *Cyrus*

מֶלֶךְ n.m.s. cstr. (I 572) *king of*

פָּרַס pr.n. (828) *Persia*

כֹּל מַמְלְכוֹת n.m.s. cstr. (481)-n.f.p. cstr. (575) *all the kingdoms of*

הָאָרֶץ def.art.-n.f.s. (75) *the earth*

נָתַן לִי Qal pf. 3 m.s. (678)-prep.-1 c.s. sf. *has given me*

יהוה pr.n. (217) *Yahweh*

אֱלֹהֵי הַשָּׁמַיִם n.m.p. cstr. (43)-def.art.-n.m. du. paus. (1029) *the God of heaven*

וְהוּא־פָקַד conj.-pers.pr. 3 m.s. (214)-Qal pf. 3 m.s. (823) *and he has charged*

עָלַי prep.-1 c.s. sf. *me*

לִבְנוֹת־לוֹ prep.-Qal inf.cstr. (בָּנָה 124)-prep.-3 m.s. sf. *to build him*

בַּיִת n.m.s. (108) *a house*

בִּירוּשָׁלַםִ prep.-pr.n. (436) *at Jerusalem*

אֲשֶׁר בִּיהוּדָה rel. (81)-prep.-pr.n. (397) *which is in Judah*

1:3

מִי־בָכֶם interr. (566)-prep.-2 m.p. sf. *whoever is among you*

מִכָּל־עַמּוֹ prep.-n.m.s. cstr. (481)-n.m.s.-3 m.s. sf. (I 766) *of all his people*
יְהִי Qal impf. 3 m.s. apoc. (הָיָה 224) *may be*
אֱלֹהָיו n.m.p.-3 m.s. sf. (43) *his God*
עִמּוֹ prep.-3 m.s. sf. *with him*
וְיַעַל conj.-Qal impf. 3 m.s. apoc.vol. (עָלָה 748) *and let him go up*
לִירוּשָׁלַםִ prep.-pr.n. (436) *to Jerusalem*
אֲשֶׁר בִּיהוּדָה rel. (81)-prep.-pr.n. (397) *which is in Judah*
וְיִבֶן conj.-Qal impf. 3 m.s. apoc.vol. (בָּנָה 124) *and rebuild*
אֶת־בֵּית יהוה dir.obj.-n.m.s. cstr. (108)-pr.n. (217) *the house of Yahweh*
אֱלֹהֵי n.m.p. cstr. (43) *the God of*
יִשְׂרָאֵל pr.n. (975) *Israel*
הוּא pers.pr. 3 m.s. (214) *he is*
הָאֱלֹהִים def.art.-n.m.p. (43) *the God*
אֲשֶׁר בִּירוּשָׁלָםִ rel. (81)-prep.-pr.n. paus. (436) *who is in Jerusalem*

1:4

וְכָל־הַנִּשְׁאָר conj.-n.m.s. cstr. (481)-def.art.-Ni. ptc. (שָׁאַר I 983) *and each survivor*
מִכָּל־הַמְּקֹמוֹת prep.-v.supra-def.art.-n.m.p. (879) *in every place*
אֲשֶׁר הוּא גָר־ rel. (81)-pers.pr. 3 m.s. (214)-Qal act.ptc. (or Qal pf. 3 m.s. גור I 157) *which he sojourns*
שָׁם adv. (1027) *there*
יְנַשְּׂאוּהוּ Pi. impf. 3 m.s.-3 m.s. sf. (נָשָׂא 669) *let him be assisted*
אַנְשֵׁי מְקֹמוֹ n.m.p. cstr. (35)-n.m.s.-3 m.s. sf. (879) *by the men of his place*
בְּכֶסֶף prep.-n.m.s. (494) *with silver*
וּבְזָהָב conj.-prep.-n.m.s. (262) *and gold*
וּבִרְכוּשׁ conj.-prep.-n.m.s. (940) *with goods*
וּבִבְהֵמָה conj.-prep.-n.f.s. (96) *and with beasts*
עִם־הַנְּדָבָה prep.-def.art.-n.f.s. (621) *besides freewill offerings*
לְבֵית prep.-n.m.s. cstr. (108) *for the house of*
הָאֱלֹהִים def.art.-n.m.p. (43) *God*
אֲשֶׁר בִּירוּשָׁלָםִ rel. (81)-prep.-pr.n. (436) *which is in Jerusalem*

1:5

וַיָּקוּמוּ consec.-Qal impf. 3 m.p. (קוּם 877) *then rose up*
רָאשֵׁי הָאָבוֹת n.m.p. cstr. (910)-def.art.-n.m.p. (3) *the heads of the fathers*
לִיהוּדָה prep.-pr.n. (397) *of Judah*
וּבִנְיָמִן conj.-pr.n. (122) *and Benjamin*
וְהַכֹּהֲנִים conj.-def.art.-n.m.p. (463) *and the priests*
וְהַלְוִיִּם conj.-def.art.-adj. gent. m.p. (II 532) *and the Levites*
לְכֹל prep.-n.m.s. (481) *every one*
הֵעִיר Hi. pf. 3 m.s. (עוּר I 734) *had stirred*
הָאֱלֹהִים def.art.-n.m.p. (43) *God*
אֶת־רוּחוֹ dir.obj.-n.f.s.-3 m.s. sf. (924) *whose spirit*
לַעֲלוֹת prep.-Qal inf.cstr. (עָלָה 748) *to go up*
לִבְנוֹת prep.-Qal inf.cstr. (בָּנָה 124) *to rebuild*
אֶת־בֵּית יהוה dir.obj.-n.m.s. cstr. (108)-pr.n. (217) *the house of Yahweh*
אֲשֶׁר בִּירוּשָׁלָםִ rel. (81)-prep.-pr.n. (436) *which is in Jerusalem*

1:6

וְכָל־סְבִיבֹתֵיהֶם conj.-n.m.s. cstr. (481)-subst. f.p. -3 m.p. sf. (686) *and all who were about them*
חִזְּקוּ בִידֵיהֶם Pi. pf. 3 c.p. (חָזַק 304)-prep.-n.f. du.-3 m.p. sf. (388) *aided them (strengthened their hands)*
בִּכְלֵי־כֶסֶף prep.-n.m.p. cstr. (479)-n.m.s. (494) *with vessels of silver*
בַּזָּהָב prep.-def.art.-n.m.s. (262) *with gold*
בָּרְכוּשׁ prep.-def.art.-n.m.s. (940) *with goods*
וּבַבְּהֵמָה conj.-prep.-def.art.-n.f.s. (96) *with beasts*
וּבַמִּגְדָּנוֹת conj.-prep.-def.art.-n.f.p. (550) *and with costly wares*
לְבַד prep.-n.m.s. as prep. (94) *besides*
עַל־כָּל־הִתְנַדֵּב prep.-n.m.s. (481)-Hith. pf. 3 m.s. (or Hith. inf.cstr. נָדַב 621) *all that was freely offered*

1:7

וְהַמֶּלֶךְ conj.-def.art.-n.m.s. (I 572) *and the king*
כּוֹרֶשׁ pr.n. (468) *Cyrus*
הוֹצִיא Hi. pf. 3 m.s. (יָצָא 422) *brought out*
אֶת־כְּלֵי dir.obj.-n.m.p. cstr. (479) *the vessels of*
בֵית־יהוה n.m.s. cstr. (108)-pr.n. (217) *the house of Yahweh*
אֲשֶׁר הוֹצִיא rel. (81)-v.supra *which had carried away*
נְבוּכַדְנֶצַּר pr.n. (613) *Nebuchadnezzar*
מִירוּשָׁלַםִ prep.-pr.n. (436) *from Jerusalem*
וַיִּתְּנֵם consec.-Qal impf. 3 m.s.-3 m.p. sf. (נָתַן 678) *and placed them*
בְּבֵית אֱלֹהָיו prep.-n.m.s. cstr. (108)-n.m.p.-3 m.s. sf. (43) *in the house of his gods*

1:8

וַיּוֹצִיאֵם consec.-Hi. impf. 3 m.s.-3 m.p. sf. (יָצָא 422) *and brought them*
כּוֹרֶשׁ pr.n. (468) *Cyrus*
מֶלֶךְ פָּרַס n.m.s. cstr. (I 572)-pr.n. (828) *king of Persia*
עַל־יַד prep.-n.f.s. cstr. (388) *in charge of*
מִתְרְדָת pr.n. (609) *Mithredath*
הַגִּזְבָּר def.art.-n.m.s. (159) *the treasurer*
וַיִּסְפְּרֵם consec.-Qal impf. 3 m.s.-3 m.p. sf. (סָפַר 707) *who counted them out*
לְשֵׁשְׁבַּצַּר prep.-pr.n. (1058) *to Sheshbazzar*
הַנָּשִׂיא def.art.-n.m.s. (I 672) *the prince*
לִיהוּדָה prep.-pr.n. (397) *of Judah*

1:9

וְאֵלֶּה conj.-demons.adj. c.p. (41) *and these*
מִסְפָּרָם n.m.s.-3 m.p. sf. (708) *the number of them*
אֲגַרְטְלֵי זָהָב n.m.p. cstr. (173)-n.m.s. (262) *basins of gold*
שְׁלֹשִׁים num. p. (1026) *thirty*
אֲגַרְטְלֵי־כֶסֶף v.supra-n.m.s. (494) *basins of silver*
אָלֶף n.m.s. (48) *a thousand*
מַחֲלָפִים n.m.p. (322) *knives (censers)*
תִּשְׁעָה וְעֶשְׂרִים num. f. (1077)-conj.-num. p. (797) *twenty-nine*

1:10

כְּפוֹרֵי זָהָב n.m.p. cstr. (499)-n.m.s. (262) *bowls of gold*
שְׁלֹשִׁים num. p. (1026) *thirty*
כְּפוֹרֵי כֶסֶף v.supra-n.m.s. (494) *bowls of silver*
מִשְׁנִים n.m.p. (1041) *of a second sort*
אַרְבַּע num. (916) *four*
מֵאוֹת n.f.p. (547) *hundred*
וַעֲשָׂרָה conj.-num. f. (796) *and ten*
כֵּלִים אֲחֵרִים n.m.p. (479)-adj. m.p. (29) *other vessels*
אָלֶף n.m.s. paus. (48) *a thousand*

1:11

כָּל־כֵּלִים n.m.s. cstr. (481)-n.m.p. (479) *all vessels*
לַזָּהָב prep.-def.art.-n.m.s. (262) *of gold*
וְלַכֶּסֶף conj.-prep.-def.art.-n.m.s. (494) *and of silver*
חֲמֵשֶׁת אֲלָפִים num. f. cstr. (331)-n.m.p. (48) *five thousand*
וְאַרְבַּע מֵאוֹת conj.-num. (916)-n.f.p. (547) *and four hundred*
הַכֹּל def.art.-n.m.s. (481) *all*

הֶעֱלָה Hi. pf. 3 m.s. (עָלָה 748) *did bring up*
שֵׁשְׁבַּצַּר pr.n. (1058) *Sheshbazzar*
עִם הֵעָלוֹת prep.-Ni. inf.cstr. (עָלָה 748) *when were brought up*
הַגּוֹלָה def.art.-n.f.s. (163) *the exiles*
מִבָּבֶל prep.-pr.n. (93) *from Babylonia*
לִירוּשָׁלָ͏ִם prep.-pr.n. paus. (436) *to Jerusalem*

2:1

וְאֵלֶּה conj.-demons.adj. c.p. (41) *now these were*
בְּנֵי הַמְּדִינָה n.m.p. cstr. (119)-def.art.-n.f.s. (193) *the people of the province*
הָעֹלִים def.art.-Qal act.ptc. m.p. (עָלָה 748) *who came up out*
מִשְּׁבִי הַגּוֹלָה prep.-n.m.s. cstr. (985)-def.art.-n.f.s. (163) *of the captivity of those exiles*
אֲשֶׁר הֶגְלָה rel. (81)-Hi. pf. 3 m.s. (גָּלָה 162) *whom ... had carried captive*
נְבוּכַדְנֶצּוּר pr.n. (613) *Nebuchadnezzar*
מֶלֶךְ־בָּבֶל n.m.s. cstr. (I 572)-pr.n. (93) *the king of Babylon*
לְבָבֶל prep.-pr.n. (93) *to Babylonia*
וַיָּשׁוּבוּ consec.-Qal impf. 3 m.p. (שׁוּב 996) *they returned*
לִירוּשָׁלַ͏ִם prep.-pr.n. (436) *to Jerusalem*
וִיהוּדָה conj.-pr.n. (397) *and Judah*
אִישׁ לְעִירוֹ n.m.s. (35)-prep.-n.f.s.-3 m.s. sf. (746) *each to his own town*

2:2

אֲשֶׁר־בָּאוּ rel. (81)-Qal pf. 3 c.p. (בּוֹא 97) *they came*
עִם־זְרֻבָּבֶל prep.-pr.n. (279) *with Zerubbabel*
יֵשׁוּעַ pr.n. (221) *Jeshua*
נְחֶמְיָה pr.n. (637) *Nehemiah*
שְׂרָיָה pr.n. (976) *Seraiah*
רְעֵלָיָה pr.n. (947) *Reelaiah*
מָרְדֳּכַי pr.n. (598) *Mordecai*
בִּלְשָׁן pr.n. (119) *Bilshan*
מִסְפָּר pr.n. (709) *Mispar*
בִּגְוַי pr.n. (94) *Bigvai*
רְחוּם pr.n. (933) *Rehum*
בַּעֲנָה pr.n. (128) *Baanah*
מִסְפַּר n.m.s. cstr. (708) *the number of*
אַנְשֵׁי n.m.s. cstr. (35) *the men of*
עַם יִשְׂרָאֵל n.m.s. cstr. (I 766)-pr.n. (975) *the people of Israel*

2:3

בְּנֵי פַרְעֹשׁ n.m.p. cstr. (119)-pr.n. (II 829) *the sons of Parosh*
אַלְפַּיִם n.m. du. (48) *two thousand*

מֵאָה n.f.s. (547) ***one hundred***
שִׁבְעִים וּשְׁנָיִם num. p. (988)-conj.-num. m. paus. (1040) ***and seventy-two***

2:4

בְּנֵי שְׁפַטְיָה n.m.p. cstr. (119)-pr.n. (1049) ***the sons of Shephatiah***
שְׁלֹשׁ מֵאוֹת num. m. cstr. (1025)-n.f.p. (547) ***three hundred***
שִׁבְעִים וּשְׁנָיִם num. p. (988)-conj.-num. m. paus. (1040) ***and seventy-two***

2:5

בְּנֵי אָרַח n.m.p. cstr. (119)-pr.n. (73) ***the sons of Arah***
שְׁבַע מֵאוֹת num. m. cstr. (I 987)-n.f.p. (547) ***seven hundred***
חֲמִשָּׁה וְשִׁבְעִים num. f. (331)-conj.-num. p. (988) ***and seventy-five***

2:6

בְּנֵי־פַחַת מוֹאָב n.m.p. cstr. (119)-pr.n. (809) ***the sons of Pahath-moab***
לִבְנֵי יֵשׁוּעַ prep.-v.supra-pr.n. (221) ***the sons of Jeshua***
יוֹאָב pr.n. (222) ***Joab***
אַלְפַּיִם n.m. du. (48) ***two thousand***
שְׁמֹנֶה מֵאוֹת num. (1032)-n.f.p. (547) ***eight hundred***
וּשְׁנֵים עָשָׂר conj.-num. (1040)-num. (797) ***and twelve***

2:7

בְּנֵי עֵילָם n.m.p. cstr. (119)-pr.n. (II 743) ***the sons of Elam***
אֶלֶף n.m.s. (48) ***one thousand***
מָאתַיִם n.f. du. (547) ***two hundred***
חֲמִשִּׁים num. p. (332) ***fifty***
וְאַרְבָּעָה conj.-num. f. (916) ***and four***

2:8

בְּנֵי זַתּוּא n.m.p. cstr. (119)-pr.n. (285) ***the sons of Zattu***
תְּשַׁע מֵאוֹת num. cstr. (1077)-v.supra ***nine hundred***
וְאַרְבָּעִים conj.-num. p. (917) ***forty***
וַחֲמִשָּׁה conj.-num. f. (331) ***and five***

2:9

בְּנֵי זַכָּי v.supra-pr.n. (269) ***the sons of Zaccai***
שְׁבַע מֵאוֹת num. cstr. (988)-v.supra ***seven hundred***
וְשִׁשִּׁים conj.-num. p. (995) ***and sixty***

2:10

בְּנֵי בָנִי n.m.p. cstr. (119)-pr.n. (125) ***the sons of Bani***
שֵׁשׁ מֵאוֹת num. (995)-v.supra ***six hundred***
אַרְבָּעִים וּשְׁנָיִם num. p. (917)-conj.-num. paus. (1040) ***and forty-two***

2:11

בְּנֵי בֵבָי n.m.p. cstr. (119)-pr.n. (93) ***the sons of Bebai***
שֵׁשׁ מֵאוֹת num. (995)-v.supra ***six hundred***
עֶשְׂרִים וּשְׁלֹשָׁה num. p. (797)-conj.-num. f. (1025) ***and twenty-three***

2:12

בְּנֵי עַזְגָּד v.supra-pr.n. (739) ***the sons of Azgad***
אֶלֶף n.m.s. (48) ***one thousand***
מָאתַיִם n.f. du. (547) ***two hundred***
עֶשְׂרִים וּשְׁנָיִם num. p. (797)-conj.-num. paus. (1040) ***and twenty-two***

2:13

בְּנֵי אֲדֹנִיקָם v.supra-pr.n. (12) ***the sons of Adonikam***
שֵׁשׁ מֵאוֹת num. (995)-v.supra ***six hundred***
שִׁשִּׁים וְשִׁשָּׁה num. p. (995)-conj.-num. f. (995) ***sixty-six***

2:14

בְּנֵי בִגְוָי n.m.p. cstr. (119)-pr.n. (94) ***the sons of Bigvai***
אַלְפַּיִם num. m. du. (48) ***two thousand***
חֲמִשִּׁים num. p. (332) ***fifty***
וְשִׁשָּׁה conj.-num. f. (995) ***six***

2:15

בְּנֵי עָדִין v.supra-pr.n. (II 726) ***the sons of Adin***
אַרְבַּע מֵאוֹת num. (916)-v.supra ***four hundred***
חֲמִשִּׁים num. p. (332) ***fifty***
וְאַרְבָּעָה conj.-num. f. (916) ***four***

2:16

בְּנֵי־אָטֵר v.supra-pr.n. (32) ***the sons of Ater***
לִיחִזְקִיָּה prep.-pr.n. (306) ***of Hezekiah***
תִּשְׁעִים num. p. (1077) ***ninety***
וּשְׁמֹנָה conj.-num. f. (1032) ***eight***

2:17

בְּנֵי בֵצָי v.supra-pr.n. (130) ***the sons of Bezai***

שְׁלֹשׁ מֵאוֹת num. cstr. (1025)-v.supra *three hundred*
עֶשְׂרִים num. p. (797) *twenty*
וּשְׁלֹשָׁה conj.-num. f. (1025) *three*

2:18

בְּנֵי יוֹרָה n.m.p. cstr. (119)-pr.n. (435) *the sons of Jorah*
מֵאָה n.f.s. (547) *one hundred*
וּשְׁנֵים עָשָׂר conj.-num. (1040)-num. (797) *and twelve*

2:19

בְּנֵי חָשֻׁם v.supra-pr.n. (365) *the sons of Hashum*
מָאתַיִם n.f. du. (547) *two hundred*
עֶשְׂרִים וּשְׁלֹשָׁה num. p. (797)-conj.-num. f. (1025) *twenty-three*

2:20

בְּנֵי גִבָּר v.supra-pr.n. (150) *the sons of Gibbar*
תִּשְׁעִים num. p. (1077) *ninety*
וַחֲמִשָּׁה conj.-num. f. (331) *five*

2:21

בְּנֵי בֵית־לָחֶם n.m.p. cstr. (119)-pr.n. (111) *the sons of Bethlehem*
מֵאָה n.f.s. (547) *one hundred*
עֶשְׂרִים num. p. (797) *twenty*
וּשְׁלֹשָׁה conj.-num. f. (1025) *three*

2:22

אַנְשֵׁי נְטֹפָה n.m.p. cstr. (35)-pr.n. (643) *the men of Netophah*
חֲמִשִּׁים וְשִׁשָּׁה num. p. (332)-conj.-num. f. (995) *fifty-six*

2:23

אַנְשֵׁי עֲנָתוֹת n.m.p. cstr. (35)-pr.n. (779) *the men of Anathoth*
מֵאָה n.f.s. (547) *one hundred*
עֶשְׂרִים וּשְׁמֹנָה num. p. (797)-conj.-num. f. (1032) *twenty-eight*

2:24

בְּנֵי עַזְמָוֶת n.m.p. cstr. (119)-pr.n. (740; 112) *the sons of Azmaveth*
אַרְבָּעִים num. p. (917) *forty*
וּשְׁנָיִם conj.-num. paus. (1040) *two*

2:25

בְּנֵי קִרְיַת עָרִים n.m.p. cstr. (119)-pr.n. (900) *the sons of Kiriatharim*
כְּפִירָה pr.n. (499) *Chepirah*
וּבְאֵרוֹת conj.-pr.n. (92) *and Beeroth*
שְׁבַע מֵאוֹת num. cstr. (988)-n.f.p. (547) *seven hundred*
וְאַרְבָּעִים conj.-num. p. (917) *and forty*
וּשְׁלֹשָׁה conj.-num. f. (1025) *three*

2:26

בְּנֵי הָרָמָה n.m.p. cstr. (119)-pr.n. (928) *the sons of Ramah*
וָגָבַע conj.-pr.n. (148) *and Geba*
שֵׁשׁ מֵאוֹת num. (995)-n.f.p. (547) *six hundred*
עֶשְׂרִים num. p. (797) *twenty*
וְאֶחָד conj.-num. (25) *one*

2:27

אַנְשֵׁי מִכְמָס n.m.p. cstr. (35)-pr.n. (485) *the men of Michmas*
מֵאָה n.f.s. (547) *one hundred*
עֶשְׂרִים num. p. (797) *twenty*
וּשְׁנָיִם conj.-num. paus. (1040) *two*

2:28

אַנְשֵׁי בֵית־אֵל n.m.p. cstr. (35)-pr.n. (110) *the men of Bethel*
וְהָעָי conj.-def.art.-pr.n. (743) *and Ai*
מָאתַיִם n.f. du. (547) *two hundred*
עֶשְׂרִים num. p. (797) *twenty*
וּשְׁלֹשָׁה conj.-num. f. (1025) *three*

2:29

בְּנֵי נְבוֹ n.m.p. cstr. (119)-pr.n. (I 612) *the sons of Nebo*
חֲמִשִּׁים num. p. (332) *fifty*
וּשְׁנָיִם conj.-num. paus. (1040) *two*

2:30

בְּנֵי מַגְבִּישׁ v.supra-pr.n. (150) *the sons of Magbish*
מֵאָה n.f.s. (547) *one hundred*
חֲמִשִּׁים num. p. (332) *fifty*
וְשִׁשָּׁה conj.-num. f. (995) *six*

2:31

בְּנֵי עֵילָם אַחֵר v.supra-pr.n. (II 743)-adj. (29) *the sons of the other Elam*
אֶלֶף n.m.s. (48) *one thousand*
מָאתַיִם n.f. du. (547) *two hundred*
חֲמִשִּׁים num. p. (332) *fifty*

וְאַרְבָּעָה conj.-num. f. (916) *four*

2:32

בְּנֵי חָרִם v.supra-pr.n. (356) *the sons of Harim*
שְׁלֹשׁ מֵאוֹת num. cstr. (1025)-n.f.p. (547) *three hundred*
וְעֶשְׂרִים conj.-num. p. (797) *twenty*

2:33

בְּנֵי־לֹד n.m.p. cstr. (119)-pr.n. (528) *the sons of Lod*
חָדִיד pr.n. (292) *Hadid*
וְאוֹנוֹ conj.-pr.n. (20) *and Ono*
שְׁבַע מֵאוֹת num. cstr. (988)-v.supra *seven hundred*
עֶשְׂרִים num. p. (797) *twenty*
וַחֲמִשָּׁה conj.-num. f. (331) *five*

2:34

בְּנֵי יְרֵחוֹ v.supra-pr.n. (437) *the sons of Jericho*
שְׁלֹשׁ מֵאוֹת num. cstr. (1025)-n.f.p. (547) *three hundred*
אַרְבָּעִים num. p. (917) *forty*
וַחֲמִשָּׁה conj.-num. f. (331) *five*

2:35

בְּנֵי סְנָאָה n.m.p. cstr. (119)-pr.n. (702) *the sons of Senaah*
שְׁלֹשֶׁת num. f. cstr. (1025) *three*
אֲלָפִים n.m.p. (48) *thousand*
וְשֵׁשׁ מֵאוֹת conj.-num. (995)-n.f.p. (547) *and six hundred*
וּשְׁלֹשִׁים conj.-num. p. (1026) *and thirty*

2:36

הַכֹּהֲנִים def.art.-n.m.p. (463) *the priests*
בְּנֵי יְדַעְיָה n.m.p. cstr. (119)-pr.n. (396) *the sons of Jedaiah*
לְבֵית יֵשׁוּעַ prep.-n.m.s. cstr. (108)-pr.n. (221) *of the house of Jeshua*
תְּשַׁע מֵאוֹת num. cstr. (1077)-n.f.p. (547) *nine hundred*
שִׁבְעִים num. p. (988) *seventy*
וּשְׁלֹשָׁה conj.-num. f. (1025) *three*

2:37

בְּנֵי אִמֵּר n.m.p. cstr. (119)-pr.n. (57) *the sons of Immer*
אֶלֶף n.m.s. (48) *one thousand*
חֲמִשִּׁים num. p. (332) *fifty*
וּשְׁנָיִם conj.-num. paus. (1040) *two*

2:38

בְּנֵי פַשְׁחוּר v.supra-pr.n. (832) *the sons of Pashhur*
אֶלֶף n.m.s. (48) *one thousand*
מָאתַיִם n.f. du. (547) *two hundred*
אַרְבָּעִים num. p. (917) *forty*
וְשִׁבְעָה conj.-num. f. (988) *seven*

2:39

בְּנֵי חָרִם v.supra-pr.n. (356) *the sons of Harim*
אֶלֶף n.m.s. (48) *one thousand*
וְשִׁבְעָה עָשָׂר conj.-num. f. (988)-num. (797) *and seventeen*

2:40

הַלְוִיִּם def.art.-adj. gent. (II 532) *the Levites*
בְּנֵי־יֵשׁוּעַ n.m.p. cstr. (119)-pr.n. (221) *the sons of Jeshua*
וְקַדְמִיאֵל conj.-pr.n.(870) *and Kadmiel*
לִבְנֵי הוֹדַוְיָה prep.-v.supra-pr.n. (217; 392) *of the sons of Hodaviah*
שִׁבְעִים num. p. (988) *seventy*
וְאַרְבָּעָה conj.-num. f. (916) *four*

2:41

הַמְשֹׁרְרִים def.art.-Polel ptc. (שִׁיר 1010) *the singers*
בְּנֵי אָסָף n.m.p. cstr. (119)-pr.n. (63) *the sons of Asaph*
מֵאָה n.f.s. (547) *one hundred*
עֶשְׂרִים num. p. (797) *twenty*
וּשְׁמֹנָה conj.-num. f. (1032) *eight*

2:42

בְּנֵי הַשֹּׁעֲרִים v.supra-def.art.-n.m.p. (1045) *the sons of the gate-keepers*
בְּנֵי־שַׁלּוּם v.supra-pr.n. (1024) *the sons of Shallum*
בְּנֵי־אָטֵר v.supra-pr.n. (32) *the sons of Ater*
בְּנֵי־טַלְמוֹן v.supra-pr.n. (379) *the sons of Talmon*
בְּנֵי־עַקּוּב v.supra-pr.n. (784) *the sons of Akkub*
בְּנֵי חֲטִיטָא v.supra-pr.n. (310) *the sons of Hatita*
בְּנֵי שֹׁבָי v.supra-pr.n. (986) *the sons of Shobai*
הַכֹּל def.art.-n.m.s. (481) *in all*
מֵאָה n.f.s. (547) *one hundred*
שְׁלֹשִׁים num. p. (1026) *thirty*
וְתִשְׁעָה conj.-num. f. (1077) *nine*

2:43

הַנְּתִינִים def.art.-n.m.p. (682) *(Nethinim) the temple servants*
בְנֵי־צִיחָא v.supra-pr.n. (851) *the sons of Ziha*
בְנֵי־חֲשׂוּפָא v.supra-pr.n. (362) *the sons of Hasupha*
בְּנֵי טַבָּעוֹת v.supra-pr.n. (371) *the sons of Tabbaoth*

2:44

בְּנֵי־קֵרֹס n.m.p. cstr. (119)-pr.n. (902) *the sons of Keros*
בְּנֵי־סִיעֲהָא v.supra-pr.n. (696) *the sons of Siaha*
בְּנֵי פָדוֹן v.supra-pr.n. (804) *the sons of Padon*

2:45

בְּנֵי־לְבָנָה v.supra-pr.n. (526) *the sons of Lebanah*
בְנֵי־חֲגָבָה v.supra-pr.n. (290) *the sons of Haggabah*
בְּנֵי עַקּוּב v.supra-pr.n. (784) *the sons of Akkub*

2:46

בְּנֵי־חָגָב v.supra-pr.n. (II 290) *the sons of Hagab*
בְּנֵי־שַׁמְלַי v.supra-pr.n. (969) *the sons of Shamlai*
בְּנֵי חָנָן v.supra-pr.n. (336) *the sons of Hanan*

2:47

בְּנֵי־גִדֵּל v.supra-pr.n. (153) *the sons of Giddel*
בְּנֵי־גַחַר v.supra-pr.n. (161) *the sons of Gahar*
בְּנֵי רְאָיָה v.supra-pr.n. (909) *the sons of Reaiah*

2:48

בְּנֵי־רְצִין v.supra-pr.n. (954) *the sons of Rezin*
בְּנֵי־נְקוֹדָא v.supra-pr.n. (667) *the sons of Nekoda*
בְּנֵי גַזָּם v.supra-pr.n. (160) *the sons of Gazzam*

2:49

בְּנֵי־עֻזָּא v.supra-pr.n. (739) *the sons of Uzza*
בְנֵי־פָסֵחַ v.supra-pr.n. (820) *the sons of Paseah*
בְּנֵי בֵסָי v.supra-pr.n. (126) *the sons of Besai*

2:50

בְּנֵי־אַסְנָה v.supra-pr.n. (62) *the sons of Asnah*
בְנֵי־מְעִינִים v.supra-pr.n. (589) *the sons of Meunim*
בְּנֵי נְפִיסִים v.supra-pr.n. (656) *the sons of Nephisim*

2:51

בְּנֵי־בַקְבּוּק v.supra-pr.n. (132) *the sons of Bakbuk*
בְּנֵי־חֲקוּפָא v.supra-pr.n. (349) *the sons of Hakupha*
בְּנֵי חַרְחוּר v.supra-pr.n. (359) *the sons of Harhur*

2:52

בְּנֵי־בַצְלוּת n.m.p. cstr. (119)-pr.n. (130) *the sons of Bazluth*
בְּנֵי־מְחִידָא v.supra-pr.n. (563) *the sons of Mehida*
בְּנֵי חַרְשָׁא v.supra-pr.n. (361) *the sons of Harsha*

2:53

בְּנֵי־בַרְקוֹס v.supra-pr.n. (140) *the sons of Barkos*
בְּנֵי־סִיסְרָא v.supra-pr.n. (696) *the sons of Sisera*
בְּנֵי־תָמַח v.supra-pr.n. (1069) *the sons of Temah*

2:54

בְּנֵי נְצִיחַ v.supra-pr.n. (664) *the sons of Neziah*
בְּנֵי חֲטִיפָא v.supra-pr.n. (310) *the sons of Hatipha*

2:55

בְּנֵי עַבְדֵי v.supra-n.m.p. cstr. (713) *the sons of the servants of*
שְׁלֹמֹה pr.n. (1024) *Solomon*
בְּנֵי־סֹטַי n.m.p. cstr. (119)-pr.n. (691) *the sons of Sotai*
בְּנֵי־הַסֹּפֶרֶת v.supra-pr.n. (709) *the sons of Hassophereth*
בְּנֵי פְרוּדָא v.supra-pr.n. (825) *the sons of Peruda*

2:56

בְּנֵי־יַעְלָה v.supra-pr.n. (419) *the sons of Jaalah*
בְנֵי־דַרְקוֹן v.supra-pr.n. (204) *the sons of Darkon*
בְּנֵי גִדֵּל v.supra-pr.n. (153) *the sons of Giddel*

2:57

בְּנֵי שְׁפַטְיָה n.m.p. cstr. (119)-pr.n. (1049) *the sons of Shephatiah*
בְנֵי־חַטִּיל v.supra-pr.n. (310) *the sons of Hattil*
בְּנֵי פֹּכֶרֶת הַצְּבָיִים v.supra-pr.n. (810) *the sons of Pochereth-hazzebaim*
בְּנֵי אָמִי v.supra-pr.n. (51) *the sons of Ami*

2:58

כָּל־הַנְּתִינִים n.m.s. cstr. (481)-def.art.-n.m.p. (682) *all the temple servants (Nethinim)*

וּבְנֵי עַבְדֵי conj.-v.supra-n.m.p. cstr. (713) *and the sons of the servants of*

שְׁלֹמֹה pr.n. (1024) *Solomon*

שְׁלֹשׁ מֵאוֹת num. (1025)-n.f.p. (547) *three hundred*

תִּשְׁעִים וּשְׁנָיִם num. p. (1077)-conj.-num. paus. (1040) *and ninety-two*

2:59

וְאֵלֶּה conj.-demons.adj. c.p. (41) *and these*

הָעֹלִים def.art.-Qal act.ptc. m.p. (עָלָה 748) *who came up*

מִתֵּל מֶלַח prep.-pr.n. (1068) *from Tel-melah*

תֵּל חַרְשָׁא pr.n. (1068) *Tel-harsha*

כְּרוּב pr.n. (I 500) *Cherub*

אַדָּן pr.n. (11) *Addan*

אִמֵּר pr.n. (57) *Immer*

וְלֹא יָכְלוּ conj.-neg.-Qal pf. 3 c.p. (יָכֹל 407) *though they could not*

לְהַגִּיד prep.-Hi. inf.cstr. (נָגַד 616) *prove*

בֵּית־אֲבוֹתָם n.m.s. cstr. (108)-n.m.p.-3 m.p. sf. (3) *their fathers' house*

וְזַרְעָם conj.-n.m.s.-3 m.p. sf. (282) *or their descent*

אִם מִיִּשְׂרָאֵל hypoth.part. (49)-prep.-pr.n. (975) *whether to Israel*

הֵם pers.pr. 3 m.p. (241) *they*

2:60

בְּנֵי־דְלָיָה n.m.p. cstr. (119)-pr.n. (195) *the sons of Delaiah*

בְנֵי־טוֹבִיָּה v.supra-pr.n. (375) *the sons of Tobiah*

בְּנֵי נְקוֹדָא v.supra-pr.n. (667) *the sons of Nekoda*

שֵׁשׁ מֵאוֹת num. (995)-n.f.p. (547) *six hundred*

חֲמִשִּׁים וּשְׁנָיִם num. p. (332)-conj.-num. paus. (1040) *and fifty-two*

2:61

וּמִבְּנֵי conj.-prep.-n.m.p. cstr. (119) *also, of the sons of*

הַכֹּהֲנִים def.art.-n.m.p. (463) *the priests*

בְּנֵי חֳבַיָּה v.supra-pr.n. (285) *the sons of Habaiah*

בְּנֵי הַקּוֹץ v.supra-def.art.-pr.n. (881) *the sons of Hakkoz*

בְּנֵי בַרְזִלַּי v.supra-pr.n. (137) *the sons of Barzillai*

אֲשֶׁר לָקַח rel. (81)-Qal pf. 3 m.s. (542) *who had taken*

מִבְּנוֹת prep.-n.f.p. cstr. (I 123) *from the daughters of*

בַּרְזִלַּי pr.n. (137) *Barzillai*

הַגִּלְעָדִי def.art.-pr.n. gent. (167) *the Gileadite*

אִשָּׁה n.f.s. (61) *a wife*

וַיִּקָּרֵא consec.-Ni. impf. 3 m.s. (894) *and was called*

עַל־שְׁמָם prep.-n.m.s.-3 m.p. sf. (1027) *by their name*

2:62

אֵלֶּה בִּקְשׁוּ demons.adj. c.p. (41)-Pi. pf. 3 c.p. (134) *these sought*

כְּתָבָם n.m.s.-3 m.p. sf. (508; GK 131r) *their registration*

הַמִּתְיַחְשִׂים def.art.-Hith. ptc. m.p. (405) *among those enrolled in the genealogies*

וְלֹא נִמְצָאוּ conj.-neg.-Ni. pf. 3 c.p. paus. (מָצָא 592) *but they were not found*

וַיְגֹאֲלוּ consec.-Pu. impf. 3 m.p. (גָּאַל II 146) *and so they were excluded as unclean*

מִן־הַכְּהֻנָּה prep.-def.art.-n.f.s. (464) *from the priesthood*

2:63

וַיֹּאמֶר consec.-Qal impf. 3 m.s. (55) *and told*

הַתִּרְשָׁתָא def.art.-n.m.s. (1077) *the governor (Tirshatha)*

לָהֶם prep.-3 m.p. sf. *them*

אֲשֶׁר לֹא־יֹאכְלוּ rel. (81)-neg.-Qal impf. 3 m.p. (37) *that they were not to partake*

מִקֹּדֶשׁ הַקֳּדָשִׁים prep.-n.m.s. cstr. (871)-def.art.-n.m.p. (871) *of the most holy food*

עַד עֲמֹד כֹּהֵן prep. (III 723)-Qal inf.cstr. (763)-n.m.s. (463) *until there should be a priest to consult*

לְאוּרִים prep.-n.m.p. (22) *Urim*

וּלְתֻמִּים conj.-prep.-n.m.p. (1070) *and Thummim*

2:64

כָּל־הַקָּהָל n.m.s. cstr. (481)-def.art.-n.m.s. (874) *the whole assembly*

כְּאֶחָד prep.-num. (25) *together*

אַרְבַּע num. (916) *four*

רִבּוֹא n.f.s. (914) *ten thousand*

אַלְפַּיִם n.m. du. (II 48) *two thousand*

שְׁלֹשׁ־מֵאוֹת num. cstr. (1025)-n.f.p. (547) *three hundred*

שִׁשִּׁים num. p. (995) *and sixty*

2:65

מִלְּבַד prep.-prep.-n.m.s. (II 94) *besides*
עַבְדֵיהֶם n.m.p.-3 m.p. sf. (713) *their menservants*
וְאַמְהֹתֵיהֶם conj.-n.f.p.-3 m.p. sf. (51) *and maidservants*
אֵלֶּה demons.adj. c.p. (41) *of these*
שִׁבְעַת num. f.s. cstr. (988) *seven*
אֲלָפִים n.m.p. (48) *thousand*
שְׁלֹשׁ מֵאוֹת num. cstr. (1025)-n.f.p. (547) *three hundred*
שְׁלֹשִׁים num. p. (1026) *thirty*
וְשִׁבְעָה conj.-num. f. (988) *and seven*
וְלָהֶם conj.-prep.-3 m.p. sf. *and they had*
מְשֹׁרְרִים Polel ptc. m.p. (שִׁיר 1010) *male singers*
וּמְשֹׁרְרוֹת conj.-Polel ptc. f.p. (1010) *and female singers*
מָאתָיִם nf. du. (547) *two hundred*

2:66

סוּסֵיהֶם n.m.p.-3 m.p. sf. (692) *their horses*
שְׁבַע num. cstr. (988) *seven*
מֵאוֹת n.f.p. (547) *hundred*
שְׁלֹשִׁים num. p. (1026) *thirty*
וְשִׁשָּׁה conj.-num. f. (995) *and six*
פִּרְדֵיהֶם n.m.p.-3 m.p. sf. (825) *and their mules*
מָאתַיִם n.f. du. (547) *two hundred*
אַרְבָּעִים num. p. (917) *forty*
וַחֲמִשָּׁה conj.-num. f. (331) *and five*

2:67

גְּמַלֵּיהֶם n.m.p.-3 m.p. sf. (168) *their camels*
אַרְבַּע num. (916) *four*
מֵאוֹת n.f.p. (547) *hundred*
שְׁלֹשִׁים num. p. (1026) *thirty*
וַחֲמִשָּׁה conj.-num. f. (331) *and five*
חֲמֹרִים n.m.p. (331) *and their asses*
שֵׁשֶׁת num. f. cstr. (995) *six*
אֲלָפִים n.m.p. (48) *thousand*
שְׁבַע מֵאוֹת num. cstr. (988)-n.f.p. (547) *seven hundred*
וְעֶשְׂרִים conj.-num. p. (797) *and twenty*

2:68

וּמֵרָאשֵׁי conj.-prep.-n.m.p. cstr. (910) *and some of the heads of*
הָאָבוֹת def.art.-n.m.p. (3) *the families*
בְּבוֹאָם prep.-Qal inf.cstr.-3 m.p. sf. (בּוֹא 97) *when they came*
לְבֵית יהוה prep.-n.m.s. cstr. (108)-pr.n. (217) *to the house of Yahweh*
אֲשֶׁר בִּירוּשָׁלָם rel. (81)-prep.-pr.n. paus. *which is in Jerusalem*
הִתְנַדְּבוּ Hith. pf. 3 c.p. (נָדַב 621) *made freewill offerings*
לְבֵית הָאֱלֹהִים prep.-n.m.s. cstr. (108)-def.art. -n.m.p. (43) *for the house of God*
לְהַעֲמִידוֹ prep.-Hi. inf.cstr.-3 m.s. sf. (עָמַד 763) *to erect it*
עַל־מְכוֹנוֹ prep.-n.m.s.-3 m.s. sf. (467) *on its site*

2:69

כְּכֹחָם prep.-n.m.s.-3 m.p. sf. (470) *according to their ability*
נָתְנוּ Qal pf. 3 c.p. (נָתַן 678) *they gave*
לְאוֹצַר prep.-n.m.s. cstr. (68) *to the treasury of*
הַמְּלָאכָה def.art.-n.f.s. (521) *the work*
זָהָב n.m.s. (262) *gold*
דַּרְכְּמוֹנִים n.m.p. (204) *darics*
שֵׁשׁ־רִבֹּאוֹת num. (995)-n.f.p. (914; GK 97g) *six ten thousand*
וָאֶלֶף conj.-n.m.s. (48) *and one thousand*
וְכֶסֶף conj.-n.m.s. (494) *and silver*
מָנִים n.m.p. (584) *minas*
חֲמֵשֶׁת אֲלָפִים num. f. cstr. (331)-n.m.p. (48) *five thousand*
וְכָתְנֹת conj.-n.f.p. cstr. (509) *and garments of*
כֹּהֲנִים n.m.p. (463) *priests*
מֵאָה n.f.s. (547) *one hundred*

2:70

וַיֵּשְׁבוּ consec.-Qal impf. 3 m.p. (יָשַׁב 442) *and lived*
הַכֹּהֲנִים def.art.-n.m.p. (463) *the priests*
וְהַלְוִיִּם conj.-def.art.-n.m.p. (II 532) *and the Levites*
וּמִן־הָעָם conj.-prep.-def.art.-n.m.s. (I 766) *and some of the people*
וְהַמְשֹׁרְרִים conj.-def.art.-Polel ptc. m.p. (שִׁיר 1010) *and the singers*
וְהַשּׁוֹעֲרִים conj.-def.art.-n.m.p. (1045) *and the gatekeepers*
וְהַנְּתִינִים conj.-def.art.-n.m.p. (682) *and the temple servants (Nethinim)*
בְּעָרֵיהֶם prep.-n.f.p.-3 m.p. sf. (746) *in their towns*
וְכָל־יִשְׂרָאֵל conj.-n.m.s. cstr. (481)-pr.n. (975) *and all Israel*
בְּעָרֵיהֶם v.supra *in their towns*

3:1

וַיִּגַּע consec.-Qal impf. 3 m.s. (619) *when came*

הַחֹדֶשׁ הַשְּׁבִיעִי def.art.-n.m.s. (II 294)-def.art. -num. ord. (988) *the seventh month*
וּבְנֵי יִשְׂרָאֵל conj.-n.m.p. cstr. (119)-pr.n. (975) *and the sons of Israel*
בֶּעָרִים prep.-def.art.-n.f.p. (746) *in the towns*
וַיֵּאָסְפוּ consec.-Ni. impf. 3 m.p. (אָסַף 62) *and were gathered*
הָעָם def.art.-n.m.s. (I 766) *the people*
כְּאִישׁ אֶחָד prep.-n.m.s. (35)-num. (25) *as one man*
אֶל־יְרוּשָׁלָֽם prep.-n.m.s. paus. (436) *to Jerusalem*

3:2

וַיָּקָם consec.-Qal impf. 3 m.s. (קוּם 877) *then arose*
יֵשׁוּעַ pr.n. (221) *Jeshua*
בֶּן־יוֹצָדָק n.m.s. cstr. (119)-pr.n. (221) *the son of Jozadak*
וְאֶחָיו conj.-n.m.p.-3 m.s. sf. (26) *with his brothers*
הַכֹּהֲנִים def.art.-n.m.p. (463) *the priests*
וּזְרֻבָּבֶל conj.-pr.n. (279) *and Zerubbabel*
בֶּן־שְׁאַלְתִּיאֵל v.supra-pr.n. (982) *the son of Shealtiel*
וְאֶחָיו v.supra *with his kinsmen*
וַיִּבְנוּ consec.-Qal impf. 3 m.p. (בָּנָה 124) *and they built*
אֶת־מִזְבַּח dir.obj.-n.m.s. cstr. (258) *the altar of*
אֱלֹהֵי n.m.p. cstr. (43) *the God of*
יִשְׂרָאֵל pr.n. (975) *Israel*
לְהַעֲלוֹת prep.-Hi. inf.cstr. (עָלָה 748) *to offer*
עָלָיו prep.-3 m.s. sf. *upon it*
עֹלוֹת n.f.p. (II 750) *burnt offerings*
כַּכָּתוּב prep.-def.art.-Qal pass.ptc. (כָּתַב 507) *as it is written*
בְּתוֹרַת prep.-n.f.s. cstr. (435) *in the law of*
מֹשֶׁה pr.n. (602) *Moses*
אִישׁ־הָאֱלֹהִים n.m.s. cstr. (35)-def.art.-n.m.p. (43) *the man of God*

3:3

וַיָּכִינוּ consec.-Hi. impf. 3 m.p. (כּוּן I 465) *and they set*
הַמִּזְבֵּחַ def.art.-n.m.s. (258) *the altar*
עַל־מְכוֹנֹתָיו prep.-n.f.p.-3 m.s. sf. (467) *in its place*
כִּי בְּאֵימָה conj.-prep.-n.f.s. (33; GK 147a) *for fear*
עֲלֵיהֶם prep.-3 m.p. sf. *upon them*
מֵעַמֵּי prep.-n.m.p. cstr. (I 766; GK 124q) *because of the peoples of*
הָאֲרָצוֹת def.art.-n.f.p. (75) *the lands*
וַיַּעַל consec.-Hi. impf. 3 m.p. (עָלָה 748) *and they offered*
עָלָיו prep.-3 m.s. sf. *upon it*
עֹלוֹת n.f.p. (II 750) *burnt offerings*
לַיהוה prep.-pr.n. (217) *to Yahweh*
עֹלוֹת v.supra *burnt offerings*
לַבֹּקֶר prep.-def.art.-n.m.s. (133) *morning*
וְלָעָרֶב conj.-prep.-def.art.-n.m.s. (787) *and evening*

3:4

וַיַּעֲשׂוּ consec.-Qal impf. 3 m.p. (עָשָׂה I 793) *and they kept*
אֶת־חַג הַסֻּכּוֹת dir.obj.-n.m.s. cstr. (290)-def. art.-n.f.p. (697) *the feast of booths*
כַּכָּתוּב prep.-def.art.-Qal pass.ptc. (507) *as it is written*
וְעֹלַת conj.-n.f.s. cstr. (II 750) *and burnt offerings*
יוֹם בְּיוֹם n.m.s. (398)-prep.-v.supra *daily*
בְּמִסְפָּר prep.-n.m.s. (708) *by number*
כְּמִשְׁפַּט prep.-n.m.s. cstr. (1048) *according to the ordinance*
דְּבַר־יוֹם בְּיוֹמוֹ n.m.s. cstr. (182)-v.supra-v.supra *as each day required*

3:5

וְאַחֲרֵיכֵן conj.-prep.-adv. (485) *and after that*
עֹלַת תָּמִיד n.f.s. cstr. (II 750)-n.m.s. (556) *the continual burnt offerings*
וְלֶחֳדָשִׁים conj.-prep.-def.art.-n.m.p. (II 294) *and at the new moon*
וּלְכָל־מוֹעֲדֵי conj.-prep.-n.m.s. cstr. (481)-n.m.p. cstr. (417) *and at all the appointed feasts of*
יהוה pr.n. (217) *Yahweh*
הַמְקֻדָּשִׁים def.art.-Pu. ptc. m.p. (קָדַשׁ 872) *which had been consecrated*
וּלְכֹל conj.-prep.-n.m.s. cstr. (481) *and of every one who*
מִתְנַדֵּב נְדָבָה Hith. ptc. (נָדַב 621)-n.f.s. (621) *made a freewill offering*
לַיהוה prep.-pr.n. (217) *to Yahweh*

3:6

מִיּוֹם אֶחָד prep.-n.m.s. (398)-num. (25; GK 134p) *from the first day*
לַחֹדֶשׁ prep.-def.art.-n.m.s. (II 294) *of the ... month*
הַשְּׁבִיעִי def.art.-num. ord. (988) *seventh*
הֵחֵלּוּ Hi. pf. 3 c.p. (חָלַל III 320) *they began*
לְהַעֲלוֹת prep.-Hi. inf.cstr. (עָלָה 748) *to offer*

עֹלוֹת n.f.p. (II 750) *burnt offerings*
לַיהוה prep.-pr.n. (217) *to Yahweh*
וְהֵיכַל conj.-n.m.s. cstr. (228) *but the temple of*
יהוה pr.n. (217) *Yahweh*
לֹא יֻסָּד neg.-Pu. pf. 3 m.s. paus. (יָסַד 413) *was not yet founded*

3:7

וַיִּתְּנוּ־ consec.-Qal impf. 3 m.p. (נָתַן 678) *so they gave*
כֶּסֶף n.m.s. (494) *money*
לַחֹצְבִים prep.-def.art.-Qal act.ptc. m.p. (חָצַב 345) *to the masons*
וְלֶחָרָשִׁים conj.-prep.-def.art.-n.m.p. (360) *and the carpenters*
וּמַאֲכָל conj.-n.m.s. (38) *and food*
וּמִשְׁתֶּה conj.-n.m.s. (1059) *and drink*
וָשֶׁמֶן conj.-n.m.s. (1032) *and oil*
לַצִּדֹנִים prep.-def.art.-adj. gent. p. (851) *to the Sidonians*
וְלַצֹּרִים conj.-prep.-def.art.-adj. gent. (863) *and the Tyrians*
לְהָבִיא prep.-Hi. inf.cstr. (בּוֹא 97) *to bring*
עֲצֵי אֲרָזִים n.m.p. cstr. (781)-n.m.p. (72) *cedar trees*
מִן־הַלְּבָנוֹן prep.-def.art.-pr.n. (526) *from Lebanon*
אֶל־יָם prep.-n.m.s. (410) *to the sea*
יָפוֹא pr.n. (421) *to Joppa*
כְּרִשְׁיוֹן prep.-n.m.s. cstr. (957) *according to the grant of*
כּוֹרֶשׁ pr.n. (468) *Cyrus*
מֶלֶךְ־פָּרַס n.m.s. cstr. (I 572)-pr.n. (828) *the king of Persia*
עֲלֵיהֶם prep.-3 m.p. sf. *unto them*

3:8

וּבַשָּׁנָה הַשֵּׁנִית conj.-prep.-def.art.-n.f.s. (1040) -def.art.-num. ord. f. (1041) *now in the second year*
לְבוֹאָם prep.-Qal inf.cstr.-3 m.p. sf. (בּוֹא 97) *of their coming*
אֶל־בֵּית הָאֱלֹהִים prep.-n.m.s. cstr. (108)-def.art. -n.m.p. (43) *to the house of God*
לִירוּשָׁלַםִ prep.-pr.n. (436) *at Jerusalem*
בַּחֹדֶשׁ הַשֵּׁנִי prep.-def.art.-n.m.s. (II 294)-def. art.-num. ord. m. (1041) *in the second month*
הֵחֵלּוּ Hi. pf. 3 c.p. (חָלַל III 320) *made a beginning*
זְרֻבָּבֶל pr.n. (279) *Zerubbabel*
בֶּן־שְׁאַלְתִּיאֵל n.m.s. cstr. (119)-pr.n. (982) *the son of Shealtiel*
וְיֵשׁוּעַ conj.-pr.n. (221) *and Jeshua*
בֶּן־יוֹצָדָק v.supra-pr.n. (221) *the son of Jozadak*
וּשְׁאָר אֲחֵיהֶם conj.-n.m.s. cstr. (984)-n.m.p.-3 m.p. sf. (26) *together with the rest of their brethren*
הַכֹּהֲנִים def.art.-n.m.p. (463) *the priests*
וְהַלְוִיִּם conj.-def.art.-adj. gent. p. (II 532) *and the Levites*
וְכָל־הַבָּאִים conj.-n.m.s. cstr. (481)-def.art.-Qal act.ptc. m.p. (בּוֹא 97) *and all who had come*
מֵהַשְּׁבִי prep.-def.art.-n.m.s. (985) *from the captivity*
יְרוּשָׁלַםִ pr.n. (436) *to Jerusalem*
וַיַּעֲמִידוּ consec.-Hi. impf. 3 m.p. (עָמַד 763) *they appointed*
אֶת־הַלְוִיִּם dir.obj.-v.supra *the Levites*
מִבֶּן עֶשְׂרִים שָׁנָה prep.-n.m.s. cstr. (119)-num. p. (797)-n.f.s. (1040) *from twenty years old*
וָמַעְלָה conj.-subst.-loc.he (751) *and upwards*
לְנַצֵּחַ prep.-Pi. inf.cstr. (נָצַח 663) *to have the oversight*
עַל־מְלֶאכֶת prep.-n.f.s. cstr. (521) *of the work of*
בֵּית־יהוה n.m.s. cstr. (108)-pr.n. (217) *the house of Yahweh*

3:9

וַיַּעֲמֹד consec.-Qal impf. 3 m.s. (763) *and stood*
יֵשׁוּעַ pr.n. (221) *Jeshua*
בָּנָיו n.m.p.-3 m.s. sf. (119) *with his sons*
וְאֶחָיו conj.-n.m.p.-3 m.s. sf. (26) *and his kinsmen*
קַדְמִיאֵל pr.n. (870) *Kadmiel*
וּבָנָיו conj.-v.supra *and his sons*
בְּנֵי־יְהוּדָה n.m.p. cstr. (119)-pr.n. (397) *the sons of Judah*
כְּאֶחָד prep.-num. (25) *together*
לְנַצֵּחַ prep.-Pi. inf.cstr. (נָצַח 663) *to take the oversight*
עַל־עֹשֵׂה prep.-Qal act.ptc. m.s. cstr. (I 793) *of the workmen of*
הַמְּלָאכָה def.art. n.f.s. (521) *the work*
בְּבֵית הָאֱלֹהִים prep.-n.m.s. cstr. (108)-def.art. -n.m.p. (43) *the house of God*
בְּנֵי חֵנָדָד n.m.p. cstr. (119)-pr.n. (337) *the sons of Henadad*
בְּנֵיהֶם n.m.p.-3 m.p. sf. (119) *their sons*
וַאֲחֵיהֶם conj.-n.m.p.-3 m.p. sf. (26) *and their kinsmen*
הַלְוִיִּם def.art.-adj. gent. (II 532) *the Levites*

3:10

וְיִסְּדוּ conj.-Pi. pf. 3 c.p. (יָסַד 413) *and when laid the foundation*
הַבֹּנִים def.art.-Qal act.ptc. m.p. (בָּנָה 124) *the builders*
אֶת־הֵיכַל יהוה dir.obj.-n.m.s. cstr. (228)-pr.n. (217) *of the temple of Yahweh*
וַיַּעֲמִידוּ consec.-Hi. impf. 3 m.p. (763) *came forward*
הַכֹּהֲנִים def.art.-n.m.p. (463) *the priests*
מְלֻבָּשִׁים Pu. ptc. m.p. (לָבַשׁ 527) *arrayed*
בַּחֲצֹצְרוֹת prep.-def.art.-n.f.p. (348) *with trumpets*
וְהַלְוִיִּם conj.-def.art.-adj. gent. p. (II 532) *and the Levites*
בְּנֵי־אָסָף n.m.p. cstr. (119)-pr.n. (63) *the sons of Asaph*
בַּמְצִלְתַּיִם prep.-def.art.-n.f. du. (853) *with cymbals*
לְהַלֵּל prep.-Pi. inf.cstr. (הָלַל II 237) *to praise*
אֶת־יהוה dir.obj.-pr.n. (217) *Yahweh*
עַל־יְדֵי דָּוִיד prep.-n.f. du. cstr. (388)-pr.n. (187) *according to the directions of David*
מֶלֶךְ־יִשְׂרָאֵל n.m.s. cstr. (I 572)-pr.n. (975) *king of Israel*

3:11

וַיַּעֲנוּ consec.-Qal impf. 3 m.p. (עָנָה IV 777) *and they sang responsively*
בְּהַלֵּל prep.-Pi. inf.cstr. (הָלַל II 237) *praising*
וּבְהוֹדֹת conj.-prep.-Hi. inf.cstr. (יָדָה 392) *and giving thanks*
ליהוה prep.-pr.n. (217) *to Yahweh*
כִּי טוֹב conj. (471)-adj. m.s. (II 373) *for he is good*
כִּי־לְעוֹלָם conj. (471)-prep.-n.m.s. (761) *for for ever*
חַסְדּוֹ n.m.s.-3 m.s. sf. (338) *his steadfast love*
עַל־יִשְׂרָאֵל prep.-pr.n. (975) *toward Israel*
וְכָל־הָעָם conj.-n.m.s. cstr. (481)-def.art.-n.m.s. (I 766) *and all the people*
הֵרִיעוּ Hi. pf. 3 c.p. (רוּעַ 929) *shouted*
תְרוּעָה גְדוֹלָה n.f.s. (929)-adj. f.s. (152) *with a great shout*
בְּהַלֵּל prep.-Pi. inf.cstr. (II 237) *when they praised*
ליהוה prep.-pr.n. (217) *Yahweh*
עַל הוּסַד prep.-Ho. inf.cstr. (יָסַד 413) *because of the founding of*
בֵּית־יהוה n.m.s. cstr. (108)-v.supra *the house of Yahweh*

3:12

וְרַבִּים conj.-adj. m.p. (I 912) *but many*
מֵהַכֹּהֲנִים prep.-def.art.-n.m.p. (463) *of the priests*
וְהַלְוִיִּם conj.-def.art.-adj. gent. p. (II 532) *and Levites*
וְרָאשֵׁי conj.-n.m.p. cstr. (910) *and heads of*
הָאָבוֹת def.art.-n.m.p. (3) *the fathers*
הַזְּקֵנִים def.art.-adj. m.p. (278) *old men*
אֲשֶׁר רָאוּ rel. (81)-Qal pf. 3 c.p. (רָאָה 906) *who had seen*
אֶת־הַבַּיִת הָרִאשׁוֹן dir.obj.-def.art.-n.m.s. (108) -def.art.-adj. m.s. (911) *the first house*
בְּיָסְדוֹ prep.-Qal inf.cstr.-3 m.s. sf. (יָסַד 413) *when it was founded*
זֶה הַבַּיִת demons.adj. m.s. (260)-def.art.-n.m.s. (108; GK 126aa) *this is the house*
בְּעֵינֵיהֶם prep.-n.f. du.-3 m.p. sf. (744) *in their eyes*
בֹּכִים Qal act.ptc. m.p. (בָּכָה 113) *weeping*
בְּקוֹל גָּדוֹל prep.-n.m.s. (876)-adj. m.s. (152) *with a loud voice*
וְרַבִּים conj.-adj. m.p. (I 912) *though many*
בִּתְרוּעָה prep.-n.f.s. (929) *with a shout*
בְשִׂמְחָה prep.-n.f.s. (970) *with joy*
לְהָרִים prep.-Hi. inf.cstr. (רוּם 926) *raised*
קוֹל n.m.s. (876) *a voice*

3:13

וְאֵין הָעָם conj.-neg. cstr. (II 34)-def.art.-n.m.s. (I 766) *so that the people could not*
מַכִּירִים Hi. ptc. m.p. (נָכַר 647) *distinguish*
קוֹל n.m.s. cstr. (876) *the sound of*
תְּרוּעַת הַשִּׂמְחָה n.f.s. cstr. (929)-def.art.-n.f.s. (970) *the joyful shout*
לְקוֹל prep.-v.supra *from the sound of*
בְּכִי הָעָם n.m.s. cstr. (113)-v.supra *the people's weeping*
כִּי הָעָם conj. (471)-v.supra *for the people*
מְרִיעִים Hi. ptc. m.p. (רוּעַ 929) *shouted*
תְּרוּעָה גְדוֹלָה n.f.s. (929)-adj. f.s. (152) *with a great shout*
וְהַקּוֹל conj.-def.art.-n.m.s. (876) *and the sound*
נִשְׁמַע Ni. pf. 3 m.s. (1033) *was heard*
עַד־לְמֵרָחוֹק prep.-prep.-prep.-adj. (935) *afar*

4:1

וַיִּשְׁמְעוּ consec.-Qal impf. 3 m.p. (1033) *now when heard*
צָרֵי n.m.p. cstr. (III 865) *the adversaries of*
יְהוּדָה pr.n. (397) *Judah*
וּבִנְיָמִן conj.-pr.n. (122) *and Benjamin*

כִּי־בְנֵי conj. (471)-n.m.p. cstr. (119) *that the sons of*
הַגּוֹלָה def.art.-n.f.s. (163) *the exile*
בּוֹנִים Qal act.ptc. m.p. (בָּנָה 124) *were building*
הֵיכָל n.m.s. (228) *a temple*
לַיהוה prep.-pr.n. (217) *to Yahweh*
אֱלֹהֵי n.m.p. cstr. (43) *the God of*
יִשְׂרָאֵל pr.n. (975) *Israel*

4:2

וַיִּגְּשׁוּ consec.-Qal impf. 3 m.p. (נָגַשׁ 620) *and they approached*
אֶל־זְרֻבָּבֶל prep.-pr.n. (279) *Zerubbabel*
וְאֶל־רָאשֵׁי conj.-prep.-n.m.p. cstr. (910) *and the heads of*
הָאָבוֹת def.art.-n.m.p. (3) *the fathers*
וַיֹּאמְרוּ consec.-Qal impf. 3 m.p. (55) *and said*
לָהֶם prep.-3 m.p. sf. *to them*
נִבְנֶה Qal impf. 1 c.p.-apoc.-coh.he? (בָּנָה 124) *let us build*
עִמָּכֶם prep.-2 m.p. sf. *with you*
כִּי כָכֶם conj. (471)-prep.-2 m.p. sf. *for as you*
נִדְרוֹשׁ Qal impf. 1 c.p. (דָּרַשׁ 205) *we worship*
לֵאלֹהֵיכֶם prep.-n.m.p.-2 m.p. sf. (43) *your God*
וְלֹא conj.-neg. (Q rd. וְלוֹ conj.-prep.-3 m.s. sf.) *and to him*
אֲנַחְנוּ זֹבְחִים pers.pr. 1 c.p. (59)-Qal act.ptc. m.p. (256) *we have been sacrificing*
מִימֵי prep.-n.m.p. cstr. (398) *ever since the days of*
אֵסַר חַדֹּן pr.n. (64) *Esar-haddon*
מֶלֶךְ אַשּׁוּר n.m.s. cstr. (I 572)-pr.n. (78) *king of Assyria*
הַמַּעֲלֶה def.art.-Hi. ptc. (עָלָה 748) *who brought*
אֹתָנוּ dir.obj.-1 c.p. sf. *us*
פֹּה adv. (805) *here*

4:3

וַיֹּאמֶר לָהֶם consec.-Qal impf. 3 m.s. (55) -prep.-3 m.p. sf. *but said to them*
זְרֻבָּבֶל pr.n. (279) *Zerubbabel*
וְיֵשׁוּעַ conj.-pr.n. (221) *and Jeshua*
וּשְׁאָר conj.-n.m.s. cstr. (984) *and the rest of*
רָאשֵׁי n.m.p. cstr. (910) *the heads of*
הָאָבוֹת def.art.-n.m.p. (3) *the fathers*
לְיִשְׂרָאֵל prep.-pr.n. (975) *in Israel*
לֹא־לָכֶם neg.-prep.-2 m.p. sf. *not to you*
וָלָנוּ conj.-prep.-1 c.p. sf. *but to us*
לִבְנוֹת prep.-Qal inf.cstr. (בָּנָה 124) *in building*
בַּיִת n.m.s. (108) *a house*
לֵאלֹהֵינוּ prep.-n.m.p.-1 c.p. sf. (43) *to our God*
כִּי אֲנַחְנוּ conj. (471)-pers.pr. 1 c.p. (59) *but we*
יַחַד adv. (403) *together*
נִבְנֶה Qal impf. 1 c.p. (124) *will build*
לַיהוה prep.-pr.n. (217) *to Yahweh*
אֱלֹהֵי יִשְׂרָאֵל n.m.p. cstr. (43)-pr.n. (975) *the God of Israel*
כַּאֲשֶׁר צִוָּנוּ prep.-rel. (81)-Pi. pf. 3 m.s.-1 c.p. sf. (צָוָה 845) *as has commanded us*
הַמֶּלֶךְ def.art.-n.m.s. (I 572) *King*
כּוֹרֶשׁ pr.n. (468) *Cyrus*
מֶלֶךְ־פָּרָס n.m.s. cstr. (I 572)-pr.n. (828) *the king of Persia*

4:4

וַיְהִי consec.-Qal impf. 3 m.s. (הָיָה 224) *then were*
עַם־הָאָרֶץ n.m.s. cstr. (I 766)-def.art.-n.f.s. (75) *the people of the land*
מְרַפִּים Pi. ptc. m.p. (רָפָה 951) *letting drop*
יְדֵי n.f. du. cstr. (388) *the hands of*
עַם־יְהוּדָה v.supra-pr.n. (397) *the people of Judah*
וּמְבַלְּהִים conj.-Pi. ptc. m.p. (בָּלָה 117; Q וּמְבַהֲלִים from בָּהַל 96) *and were wearing out* (Q – *and were making afraid*)
אוֹתָם dir.obj.-3 m.p. sf. *them*
לִבְנוֹת prep.-Qal inf.cstr. (בָּנָה 124) *to build*

4:5

וְסֹכְרִים conj.-Qal act.ptc. m.p. (II 698) *and hiring*
עֲלֵיהֶם prep.-3 m.p. sf. *against them*
יוֹעֲצִים Qal act.ptc. m.p. (יָעַץ 419) *counselors*
לְהָפֵר prep.-Hi. inf.cstr. (פָּרַר I 830) *to frustrate*
עֲצָתָם n.f.s.-3 m.p. sf. (420) *their purpose*
כָּל־יְמֵי n.m.s. cstr. (481)-n.m.p. cstr. (398) *all the days of*
כּוֹרֶשׁ pr.n. (468) *Cyrus*
מֶלֶךְ פָּרַס n.m.s. cstr. (I 572)-pr.n. (828) *king of Persia*
וְעַד־מַלְכוּת conj.-prep. (III 723)-n.f.s. cstr. (574) *even until the reign of*
דָּרְיָוֶשׁ pr.n. (201) *Darius*
מֶלֶךְ־פָּרָס v.supra-v.supra *king of Persia*

4:6

וּבְמַלְכוּת conj.-prep.-n.f.s. cstr. (574) *and in the reign of*
אֲחַשְׁוֵרוֹשׁ pr.n. (31) *Ahasuerus*
בִּתְחִלַּת prep.-n.f.s. cstr. (321) *in the beginning of*
מַלְכוּתוֹ n.f.s.-3 m.s. sf. (574) *his reign*
כָּתְבוּ Qal pf. 3 c.p. (507) *they wrote*
שִׂטְנָה n.f.s. (I 966) *an accusation*

עַל־יָשְׁבֵי prep.-Qal act.ptc. m.p. cstr. (יָשַׁב 442) *against the inhabitants of*
יְהוּדָה pr.n. (397) *Judah*
וִירוּשָׁלָֽם conj.-pr.n. paus. (436) *and Jerusalem*

4:7

וּבִימֵי conj.-prep.-n.m.p. cstr. (398) *and in the days of*
אַרְתַּחְשַׁשְׂתָּא pr.n. (77) *Artaxerxes*
כָּתַב Qal pf. 3 m.s. (507) *wrote*
בִּשְׁלָם pr.n. (143) *Bishlam*
מִתְרְדָת pr.n. (609) *Mithredath*
טָבְאֵל pr.n. (370) *Tabeel*
וּשְׁאָר conj.-n.m.s. cstr. (984) *and the rest of*
כְּנָוֺתָו n.f.p.-3 m.s. sf. (490) *their associates*
עַל־אַרְתַּחְשַׁשְׂתְּא prep.-v.supra *to Artaxerxes*
מֶלֶךְ פָּרָס n.m.s. cstr. (I 572)-pr.n. (828) *king of Persia*
וּכְתָב הַנִּשְׁתְּוָן conj.-n.m.s. cstr. (508)-def.art. -n.m.s. (677) *the writing of the letter*
כָּתוּב Qal pass.ptc. (507) *was written*
אֲרָמִית adv. (74) *in Aramaic*
וּמְתֻרְגָּם conj.-Qal pass.ptc. (תִּרְגֵּם 1076; GK 55h) *and translated*
אֲרָמִית v.supra (GK 1c) *in Aramaic*

4:8

רְחוּם pr.n. (1113) *Rehum*
בְּעֵל־טְעֵם n.m.s. cstr. (1085)-n.m.s. (1094) *commander*
וְשִׁמְשַׁי conj.-pr.n. (1116) *and Shimshai*
סָפְרָא n.m.s.-def.art. (1104) *the scribe*
כְּתַבוּ Peal pf. 3 m.p. (1098) *wrote*
אִגְּרָה חֲדָה n.f.s. (1078)-adj. f.s. (1079) *a letter*
עַל־יְרוּשְׁלֶם prep.-pr.n. paus. (436; 1096) *against Jerusalem*
לְאַרְתַּחְשַׁשְׂתְּא prep.-pr.n. (77) *to Artaxerxes*
מַלְכָּא n.m.s.-def.art. (1100) *the king*
כְּנֵמָא adv. (1097) *as follows*

4:9

אֱדַיִן adv. (1078) *then*
רְחוּם pr.n. (1113) *Rehum*
בְּעֵל־טְעֵם v. 4:8 *the commander*
וְשִׁמְשַׁי conj.-pr.n. (1116) *Shimshai*
סָפְרָא n.m.s.-def.art. (1104) *the scribe*
וּשְׁאָר conj.-n.m.s. cstr. (1114) *and the rest of*
כְּנָוָתְהוֹן n.m.p.-3 m.p. sf. (1097) *their associates*
דִּינָיֵא pr.n. gent. (1088) *the judges (Dinaites)*
וַאֲפַרְסַתְכָיֵא conj.-pr.n. gent. (1082) *and the governors*
טַרְפְּלָיֵא pr.n. gent. (1094) *the officials*
אֲפָרְסָיֵא pr.n. gent. (1082) *the Persians (secretaries)*
אַרְכְּוָי pr.n. gent. (1083) *the men of Erech*
בָבְלָיֵא adj. gent. p.-def.art. (1084) *the Babylonians*
שׁוּשַׁנְכָיֵא pr.n. gent. p. (1114) *the men of Susa*
דֶּהָוֵא pr.n. gent. (1087) *the Dehaites* (Q דֶּהָיֵא *that is)*
עֵלְמָיֵא pr.n. gent. p. (1106) *the Elamites*

4:10

וּשְׁאָר conj.-n.m.s. cstr. (1114) *and the rest of*
אֻמַּיָּא n.f.p.-def.art. (1081) *the nations*
דִּי הַגְלִי rel. (1087)-Haphel pf. 3 m.s. (גְּלָא 1086) *whom deported*
אָסְנַפַּר pr.n. (1082) *Osnappar*
רַבָּא adj. m.s.-def.art. (1112) *the great*
וְיַקִּירָא conj.-adj. m.s.-def.art. (1096) *and noble*
וְהוֹתֵב conj.-Haphel pf. 3 m.s. (יְתִב 1096) *and settled*
הִמּוֹ pers.pr. 3 m.p. (1090) *(them)*
בְּקִרְיָה prep.-n.f.s. (1111) *in the cities*
דִּי שָׁמְרָיִן mark of gen. (1087)-pr.n. (1116) *of Samaria*
וּשְׁאָר v.supra *and in the rest of*
עֲבַר־נַהֲרָה n.m.s. cstr. (1105)-n.m.s.-def.art. (1102) *Beyond the River*
וּכְעֶנֶת conj.-adv. (1107) *and now*

4:11

דְּנָה demons.pr. (1088) *this is*
פַּרְשֶׁגֶן n.m.s. cstr. (1109) *copy of*
אִגַּרְתָּא n.f.s.-def.art. (1078) *the letter*
דִּי שְׁלַחוּ rel. (1087)-Peal pf. 3 m.p. (שְׁלַח 1115) *that they sent*
עֲלוֹהִי prep.-3 m.s. sf. *(to him)*
עַל־אַרְתַּחְשַׁשְׂתְּא prep.-pr.n. (77) *to Artaxerxes*
מַלְכָּא n.m.s.-def.art. (1100) *the king*
עַבְדָיךְ n.m.p.-2 m.s. sf. (1105) *your servants*
אֱנָשׁ n.m.s. cstr. (1081) *men of*
עֲבַר־נַהֲרָה n.m.s. cstr. (1105)-n.m.s.-def.art. (1102) *Beyond the River*
וּכְעֶנֶת conj.-adv. (1107) *and now*

4:12

יְדִיעַ Peal pass.ptc. (Peil) (1095) *known*
לֶהֱוֵא Peal impf. 3 m.s. (הֲוָא 1089) *be it*
לְמַלְכָּא prep.-n.m.s.-def.art. (1100) *to the king*
דִּי יְהוּדָיֵא rel. (1087)-pr.n. gent. p.-def.art. (1095) *that the Jews*
דִּי סְלִקוּ rel. (1087)-Peal pf. 3 m.p. (סְלִק 1104) *who came up*

The King's Library

מִן־לְוָתָךְ prep.-prep.-2 m.s. sf. (1099) *from you*

עֲלֶינָא prep.-1 c.p. sf. *to us*

אֲתוֹ Peal pf. 3 m.p. (אֲתָה 1083) *have gone*

לִירוּשְׁלֶם prep.-pr.n. (1096) *to Jerusalem*

קִרְיְתָא n.f.s.-def.art. (1111) *the city*

מָרָדְתָּא adj. f.s.-def.art. (1101) *rebellious*

וּבִאישְׁתָּא conj.-adj. f.s.-def.art. (1084) *and wicked*

בָּנַיִן Peal ptc. p. (בְּנָה 1084) *they are rebuilding*

וְשׁוּרַיָּ conj.-n.m.p.-def.art. (1114) *and the walls*

אַשְׁכְלִלוּ Shaphal pf. 3 m.s. (prb.rd. שַׁכְלִילוּ ; 1097 כְּלַל) *they are finishing*

וְאֻשַּׁיָּא conj.-n.m.p.-def.art. (1083) *and the foundations*

יַחִיטוּ Haphel impf. 3 m.p. (חוט 1092) *they are repairing*

4:13

כְּעַן adv. (1107) *now*

יְדִיעַ Peal ptc.pass. (יְדַע 1095) *known*

לֶהֱוֵא Peal impf. 3 m.s. (הֲוָא 1089) *be it*

לְמַלְכָּא prep.-n.m.s.-def.art. (1100) *to the king*

דִּי הֵן rel. (1087)-conj. (1090) *that if*

קִרְיְתָא דָךְ n.f.s.-def.art. (1111)-demons.pr. f. (1088) *this city*

תִּתְבְּנֵא Hithpeal impf. 3 f.s. (בְּנָה 1084) *is rebuilt*

וְשׁוּרַיָּה conj.-n.m.p.-def.art. (1114) *and the walls*

יִשְׁתַּכְלְלוּן Ishtaphel impf. 3 m.p. (כְּלַל 1097) *finished*

מִנְדָּה־ n.f.s. (1101) *tribute*

בְלוֹ n.m.s. (1084) *custom*

וַהֲלָךְ conj.-n.m.s. (1090) *or toll*

לָא יִנְתְּנוּן neg.-Peal impf. 3 m.p. (נְתַן 1103) *they will not pay*

וְאַפְּתֹם מַלְכִים conj.-n.f.s. cstr. (1082)-n.m.p. (1100) *the royal revenue*

תְּהַנְזִק Haphel impf. 3 f.s. (נְזַק 1102) *will be impaired*

4:14

כְּעַן v.4:13 *now*

כָּל־קֳבֵל דִּי־ n.m.s. (1097)-subst. as prep. (1110)-rel. (1087) *because*

מְלַח הֵיכְלָא n.m.s. cstr. (1100)-n.m.s.-def.art. (1090) *the salt of the palace*

מְלַחְנָא Peal pf. 1 c.p. (מְלַח 1100) *we eat*

וְעַרְוַת מַלְכָּא conj.-n.f.s. cstr. (1107)-n.m.s. -def.art. (1100) *and the king's dishonor*

לָא אֲרִיךְ neg.-adj. vb. (1082) *it is not fitting*

לַנָא prep.-1 c.p. sf. *for us*

לְמֶחֱזֵא prep.-Peal inf. (חֲזָה 1092) *to witness*

עַל־דְּנָה prep.-demons. (1088) *therefore*

שְׁלַחְנָא Peal pf. 1 c.p. (שְׁלַח 1115) *we send*

וְהוֹדַעְנָא conj.-Haphel pf. 1 c.p. (יְדַע 1095) *and inform*

לְמַלְכָּא prep.-v.supra *the king*

4:15

דִּי יְבַקַּר conj. (1087)-Pael impf. 3 m.s. (בְּקַר 1085) *in order that search may be made*

בִּסְפַר־ prep.-n.m.s. cstr. (1104) *in the book of*

דָּכְרָנַיָּא n.m.p.-def.art. (1088) *the records*

דִּי אֲבָהָתָךְ mark of gen. (1087)-n.m.p.-2 m.s. sf. (1078) *of your fathers*

וּתְהַשְׁכַּח conj.-Haphel impf. 2 m.s. (שְׁכַח 1115) *and you will find*

בִּסְפַר v.supra *in the book of*

דָּכְרָנַיָּא v.supra *the records*

וְתִנְדַּע conj.-Peal impf. 2 m.s. (יְדַע 1095) *and learn*

דִּי קִרְיְתָא דָךְ conj. (1087)-n.f.s.-def.art. (1111) -demons. f. (1088) *that this city*

קִרְיָא מָרָדָא n.f.s. (1111)-adj. f.-def.art. (1101) *a rebellious city*

וּמְהַנְזְקַת conj.-Haphel ptc. f.s. cstr. (נְזַק 1102) *hurtful to*

מַלְכִין n.m.p. (1100) *kings*

וּמְדִנָן conj.-n.f.p. (1088) *and provinces*

וְאֶשְׁתַּדּוּר conj.-n.m.s. (1114) *and that sedition*

עָבְדִין Peal ptc. m.p. (עֲבַד 1104) *was stirred up*

בְּגַוַּהּ prep.-n.m.s.-3 f.s. sf. (1086) *in it*

מִן־יוֹמָת עָלְמָא prep.-n.m.s. cstr. (1095)-n.m.s. -def.art. (1106) *from of old*

עַל־דְּנָה prep.-demons.pr. (1088) *that was why*

קִרְיְתָא דָךְ n.f.s.-def.art. (1111)-demons.pr. f. (1088) *this city*

הָחָרְבַת Hophal pf. 3 f.s. (חֲרַב 1093) *was laid waste*

4:16

מְהוֹדְעִין Haphel ptc. m.p. (יְדַע 1095) *make known*

אֲנַחְנָה pers.pr. 1 c.p. (1081) *we*

לְמַלְכָּא prep.-n.m.s.-def.art. (1100) *to the king*

דִּי הֵן conj. (1087)-conj. (1090) *that if*

קִרְיְתָא דָךְ n.f.s.-def.art. (1111)-demons.pr. f.s. (1088) *this city*

תִּתְבְּנֵא Hithpeal impf. 3 f.s. (בְּנָה 1084) *is rebuilt*

וְשׁוּרַיַּהּ conj.-n.m.p.-def.art. (1114) *and its walls*

יִשְׁתַּכְלְלוּן Ishtaphal impf. 3 m.p. (כְּלַל 1097) *finished*

לְקֳבֵל דְּנָה prep.-subst. as prep. (1110)-demons.pr. (1088) *then*
חֲלָק n.m.s. (1093) *possession*
בַּעֲבַר נַהֲרָא prep.-n.m.s. cstr. (1105)-n.m.s. -def.art. (1102) *beyond the river*
לָא אִיתַי לָךְ neg.-part. (1080)-prep.-2 m.s. sf. *you will have no*

4:17

פִּתְגָמָא n.m.s.-def.art. (1109) *the answer*
שְׁלַח Peal pf. 3 m.s. (1115) *sent*
מַלְכָּא n.m.s.-def.art. (1100) *the king*
עַל־רְחוּם prep.-pr.n. (1113) *to Rehum*
בְּעֵל־טְעֵם n.m.s. cstr. (1085)-n.m.s. (1094) *the commander*
וְשִׁמְשַׁי conj.-pr.n. (1116) *and Shimshai*
סָפְרָא n.m.s.-def.art. (1104) *the scribe*
וּשְׁאָר conj.-n.m.s. cstr. (1114) *and the rest of*
כְּנָוָתְהוֹן n.m.p.-3 m.p. sf. (1097) *their associates*
דִּי יָתְבִין rel. (1087)-Peal ptc. m.p. (יְתִב 1096) *who live*
בְּשָׁמְרָיִן prep.-pr.n. (1116) *in Samaria*
וּשְׁאָר v.supra *and the rest of*
עֲבַר־נַהֲרָה n.m.s. cstr. (1105)-n.m.s.-def.art. (1102) *Beyond the River*
שְׁלָם וּכְעֶת n.m.s. (1116)-conj.-adv. (1107) *greeting and now*

4:18

נִשְׁתְּוָנָא n.m.s.-def.art. (1103) *the letter*
דִּי שְׁלַחְתּוּן rel. (1087)-Peal pf. 2 m.p. (שְׁלַח 1115) *which you sent*
עֲלֶינָא prep.-1 c.p. sf. *to us*
מְפָרַשׁ קֱרִי Pa. ptc.pass. (פְּרַשׁ 1109)-Peil pf. 3 m.s. (קְרָא 1111) *has been plainly read*
קָדָמָי prep.-1 c.s. sf. paus. (1110) *before me*

4:19

וּמִנִּי conj.-prep.-1 c.s. sf. (1100) *and from me*
שִׂים Peil pf. 3 m.s. (שׂוּם 1113) *was made*
טְעֵם n.m.s. (1094) *a decree*
וּבַקַּרוּ conj.-Pael pf. 3 m.p. (בְּקַר 1085) *and search has been made*
וְהַשְׁכַּחוּ conj.-Haphel pf. 3 m.p. (שְׁכַח 1115) *and it has been found*
דִּי קִרְיְתָא דָךְ conj. (1087)-n.f.s.-def.art. (1111) -demons.pr. f.s. (1088) *that this city*
מִן־יוֹמָת עָלְמָא prep.-n.m.p. cstr. (1095) -n.m.s.-def.art. (1106) *from of old*
עַל־מַלְכִין prep.-n.m.p. (1100) *against kings*
מִתְנַשְּׂאָה Hithpeal ptc. f.s. (נְשָׂא 1103) *has risen*
וּמְרַד conj.-n.m.s. (1101) *and that rebellion*
וְאֶשְׁתַּדּוּר conj.-n.m.s. (1114) *and sedition*
מִתְעֲבֶד־בַּהּ Hithpeal ptc. (עֲבַד 1104)-prep.-3 f.s. sf. *have been made in it*

4:20

וּמַלְכִין conj.-n.m.p. (1100) *and kings*
תַּקִּיפִין adj. m.p. (1118) *mighty*
הֲווֹ Peal pf. 3 m.p. (הֲוָא 1089) *have been*
עַל־יְרוּשְׁלֶם prep.-pr.n. (1096) *over Jerusalem*
וְשַׁלִּיטִין conj.-adj. m.p. (1115) *who ruled*
בְּכֹל prep.-n.m.s. cstr. (1097) *over the whole*
עֲבַר נַהֲרָה n.m.s. cstr. (1105)-n.m.s.-def.art. (1102) *Beyond the River*
וּמִדָּה conj.-n.f.s. (1101) *and tribute*
בְלוֹ n.m.s. (1084) *custom*
וַהֲלָךְ conj.-n.m.s. (1090) *and toll*
מִתְיְהֵב לְהוֹן Hithpeal ptc. (יְהַב 1095)-prep.-3 m.p. sf. *were paid (to them)*

4:21

כְּעַן adv. (1107) *therefore*
שִׂימוּ טְעֵם Peal impv. 2 m.p. (שׂוּם 1113)-n.m.s. (1094) *make a decree*
לְבַטָּלָא prep.-Peal inf. (בְּטֵל 1084) *that be made to cease*
גֻּבְרַיָּא אִלֵּךְ n.m.p.-def.art. (1086)-demons.pr. p. (1080) *these men*
וְקִרְיְתָא דָךְ conj.-n.f.s.-def.art. (1111)-demons.pr. f.s. (1088) *and that this city*
לָא תִתְבְּנֵא neg.-Hithpeal impf. 3 f.s. (בְּנָה 1084) *not be rebuilt*
עַד־מִנִּי prep. (1105)-prep.-1 c.s. sf. *until by me*
טַעְמָא n.m.s.-def.art. (1094) *a decree*
יִתְּשָׂם Hithpeal impf. 3 m.s. (שׂוּם 1113) *is made*

4:22

וּזְהִירִין הֱווֹ conj.-Peil ptc. m.p. (זְהַר 1091)-Peal impv. 2 m.p. (הֲוָא 1089) *and take care*
שָׁלוּ n.f.s. (1115) *to be slack*
לְמֶעְבַּד עַל־דְּנָה prep.-Peal inf. (עֲבַד 1104)-prep. -demons.pr. (1088) *in this matter*
לְמָה prep.-interr. (1099) *why*
יִשְׂגֵּא Peal impf. 3 m.s. (שְׂגָא 1113) *should grow*
חֲבָלָא n.m.s.-def.art. (1092) *damage*
לְהַנְזָקַת prep.-Haphel inf.cstr. (נְזִק 1102) *to the hurt of*
מַלְכִין n.m.p. (1100) *the king(s)*

4:23

אֱדַיִן adv. (1078) *then*
מִן־דִּי prep.-conj. (1087) *when*
פַּרְשֶׁגֶן n.m.s. cstr. (1109) *the copy of*

נִשְׁתְּוָנָא n.m.s.-def.art. (1103) *the letter*
דִּי אַרְתַּחְשַׁשְׂתְּא gen. (1087)-pr.n. (1083) *of Artaxerxes*
מַלְכָּא n.m.s.-def.art. (1100) *King*
קֱרִי Peil pf. 3 m.s. (קְרָא 1111) *was read*
קֳדָם־רְחוּם prep. (1110)-pr.n. (1113) *before Rehum*
וְשִׁמְשַׁי conj.-pr.n. (1116) *and Shimshai*
סָפְרָא n.m.s.-def.art. (1104) *the scribe*
וּכְנָוָתְהוֹן conj.-n.m.s.-3 m.p. sf. (1097) *and their associates*
אֲזַלוּ Peal pf. 3 m.p. (אֲזַל 1079) *they went*
בִבְהִילוּ prep.-n.f.s. (1084) *in haste*
לִירוּשְׁלֶם prep.-pr.n. (1096) *at Jerusalem*
עַל־יְהוּדָיֵא prep.-pr.n. gent. p.-def.art. (1095) *to the Jews*
וּבַטִּלוּ conj.-Pael pf. 3 m.p. (בְּטֵל 1084) *and made cease*
הִמּוֹ pers.pr. 3 m.p. (1090) *them*
בְּאֶדְרָע prep.-n.f.s. (1089) *by force*
וְחָיִל conj.-n.m.s. paus. (1093) *and power*

4:24

בֵּאדַיִן prep.-adv. (1078) *then*
בְּטֵלַת Peal pf. 3 f.s. (בְּטֵל 1084) *stopped*
עֲבִידַת n.f.s. cstr. (1105) *the work on*
בֵּית־אֱלָהָא n.m.s. cstr. (1084)-n.m.s.-def.art. (1080) *the house of God*
דִּי בִּירוּשְׁלֶם rel. (1087)-prep.-pr.n. (1096) *which is in Jerusalem*
וַהֲוָת בָּטְלָא conj.-Peal pf. 3 f.s. (הֲוָא 1089)-Peal ptc. f.s. (בְּטֵל 1084) *and it ceased*
עַד שְׁנַת prep. (1105) n.f.s. cstr. (1116) *until the year (of)*
תַּרְתֵּין n.m.s. (1118) *two*
לְמַלְכוּת prep.-n.f.s. cstr. (1100) *of the reign of*
דָּרְיָוֶשׁ pr.n. (1089) *Darius*
מֶלֶךְ־פָּרָס n.m.s. cstr. (1100)-pr.n. (1108) *king of Persia*

5:1

וְהִתְנַבִּי conj.-Hith. pf. 3 m.s. (נָבָא 612; Q נביא) *now prophesied*
חַגַּי pr.n. (291) *Haggai*
נְבִיָּאה n.m.s.-def.art. (1101) *the prophet*
וּזְכַרְיָה conj.-pr.n. (1091) *and Zechariah*
בַר־עִדּוֹא n.m.s. cstr. (1085)-pr.n. (723) *the son of Iddo*
נְבִיַּיָּא n.m.p.-def.art. (1101) *the prophets*
עַל־יְהוּדָיֵא prep. (1106)-pr.n. gent.-def.art. (1095) *to the Jews*
דִּי בִיהוּד rel. (1087)-prep.-pr.n. (1095) *who were in Judah*
וּבִירוּשְׁלֶם conj.-prep.-pr.n. (1096) *and Jerusalem*
בְּשֻׁם אֱלָהּ prep.-n.m.s. cstr. (1116)-n.m.s. cstr. (1080) *in the name of the God of*
יִשְׂרָאֵל pr.n. (1096) *Israel*
עֲלֵיהוֹן prep.-3 m.p. sf. *who was over them*

5:2

בֵּאדַיִן prep.-adv. (1078) *then*
קָמוּ Peal pf. 3 m.p. (קוּם 1110) *arose*
זְרֻבָּבֶל pr.n. (1091 & 279) *Zerubbabel*
בַּר־שְׁאַלְתִּיאֵל n.m.s. cstr. (1085)-pr.n. (982) *the son of Shealtiel*
וְיֵשׁוּעַ conj.-pr.n. (1096 & 221) *and Jeshua*
בַּר־יוֹצָדָק n.m.s. cstr. (1085)-pr.n. (221) *the son of Jozadak*
וְשָׁרִיו conj.-Pa. pf. 3 m.p. (שְׁרָא 1117) *and began*
לְמִבְנֵא prep.-Pe. inf. (בְּנָה 1084) *to build*
בֵּית אֱלָהָא n.m.s. cstr. (1084)-pr.n.-def.art. (1080) *the house of God*
דִּי בִירוּשְׁלֶם rel. (1087)-prep.-pr.n. (1096) *which is in Jerusalem*
וְעִמְּהוֹן conj.-prep.-3 m.p. sf. (1107) *and with them*
נְבִיַּיָּא n.m.p.-def.art. (1101) *the prophets*
דִּי־אֱלָהָא gen.-n.m.s.-def.art. (1080) *of God*.
מְסָעֲדִין Pa. ptc. m.p. (עֲבַד 1104) *helping*
לְהוֹן prep.-3 m.p. sf. *them*

5:3

בֵּהּ־זִמְנָא prep.-3 m.s. sf.-n.m.s.-def.art. (1091) *at the same time*
אֲתָא Pe. pf. 3 m.s. (אֲתָה 1083) *came*
עֲלֵיהוֹן prep.-3 m.p. sf. *to them*
תַּתְּנַי pr.n. (1118) *Tattenai*
פַּחַת n.m.s. cstr. (1108) *governor of*
עֲבַר־נַהֲרָה n.m.s. cstr. (1105)-n.m.s.-def.art. (1102) *Beyond the River*
וּשְׁתַר בּוֹזְנַי conj.-pr.n. (1117) *and Shethar-bozenai*
וּכְנָוָתְהוֹן conj.-n.m.p.-3 m.p. sf. (1097) *and their associates*
וְכֵן conj.-adv. (1097) *and thus*
אָמְרִין Pe. ptc. m.p. (אֲמַר 1081) *spoke*
לְהֹם prep.-3 m.p. sf. *to them*
מַן־שָׂם interr. (1100)-Pe. pf. 3 m.s. (שׂוּם 1113) *who gave*
לְכֹם prep.-2 m.p. sf. *to you*
טְעֵם n.m.s. (1094) *a decree*
בַּיְתָא דְנָה n.m.s.-def.art. (1084)-demons.adj. (1088) *this house*
לִבְּנֵא prep.-Pe. inf. (בְּנָה 1084) *to build*

וְאֻשַּׁרְנָא דְנָה conj.-n.m.s. (1083)-demons.adj. (1088) *and this structure*
לְשַׁכְלָלָה prep.-Shaph. inf. (כְּלַל 1097) *to finish*

5:4

אֱדַיִן כְּנֵמָא adv. (1078)-adv. (1097) *also this*
אֲמַרְנָא Pe. pf. 1 c.p. (אֲמַר 1081) *we asked*
לְהֹם prep.-3 m.p. sf. *them*
מַן־אִנּוּן interr. (1100)-pers.pr. 3 m.p. (1081) *who are they*
שְׁמָהָת n.m.p. cstr. (1116) *the names of*
גֻּבְרַיָּא n.m.p.-def.art. (1086) *the men*
דִּי־דְנָה rel. (1087)-demons.adj. (1088) *who this*
בִנְיָנָא n.m.s.-def.art. (1084) *building*
בָּנַיִן Pe. act.ptc. m.p. (בְּנָה 1084) *are building*

5:5

וְעֵין conj.-n.f.s. cstr. (1105) *but the eye of*
אֱלָהֲהֹם n.m.s.-3 m.p. sf. (1080) *their God*
הֲוָת Pe. pf. 3 f.s. (הֲוָא 1089) *was*
עַל־שָׂבֵי prep. (1106)-Pe. ptc. m.p. cstr. (שִׂיב 1114) *upon the elders of*
יְהוּדָיֵא pr.n. gent. m.p.-def.art. (1095) *the Jews*
וְלָא־בַטִּלוּ conj.-neg.-Pa. pf. 3 m.p. (בְּטֵל 1084) *and they did not stop*
הִמּוֹ pers.pr. 3 m.p. (1090) *them*
עַד־טַעְמָא adv. (1105)-n.m.s.-def.art. (1094) *until the report*
לְדָרְיָוֶשׁ prep.-pr.n. (1089) *(to) Darius*
יְהָךְ Pe. impf. 3 m.s. (הֲלַךְ 1090) *should reach*
וֶאֱדַיִן conj.-adv. (1078) *and then*
יְתִיבוּן Haph. impf. 3 m.p. (תּוּב 1117) *be returned*
נִשְׁתְּוָנָא n.m.s.-def.art. (1103) *by letter*
עַל־דְּנָה prep.-demons.adj. (1088) *concerning it*

5:6

פַּרְשֶׁגֶן n.m.s. cstr. (1109) *the copy of*
אִגַּרְתָּא n.f.s.-def.art. (1078) *the letter*
דִּי־שְׁלַח rel. (1087)-Pe. pf. 3 m.s. (שְׁלַח 1115) *which sent*
תַּתְּנַי pr.n. (1118) *Tattenai*
פַּחַת n.m.s. cstr. (1108) *the governor of*
עֲבַר־נַהֲרָה n.m.s. cstr. (1105)-n.m.s.-def.art. (1102) *Beyond the River*
וּשְׁתַר בּוֹזְנַי conj.-pr.n. (1117) *and Shethar-bozenai*
וּכְנָוָתֵהּ conj.-n.m.p.-3 m.s. sf. (1097) *and his associates*
אֲפַרְסְכָיֵא pr.n. gent. (1082; אֲפַרְסַתְכָיֵא) *the governors*

דִּי בַּעֲבַר נַהֲרָה rel. (1087)-prep.-n.m.s. cstr. (1105)-n.m.s.-def.art. (1102) *who were in Beyond the River*
עַל־דָּרְיָוֶשׁ prep.-pr.n. (1089) *to Darius*
מַלְכָּא n.m.s.-def.art. (1100) *the king*

5:7

פִּתְגָמָא n.m.s.-def.art. (1109) *the report*
שְׁלַחוּ Pe. pf. 3 c.p. (שְׁלַח 1115) *they sent*
עֲלוֹהִי prep.-3 m.s. sf. *to him*
וְכִדְנָה conj.-prep.-demons.adj. (1088) *and as follows*
כְּתִיב Peil pf. 3 m.s. (כְּתַב 1098) *was written*
בְּגַוֵּהּ prep.-n.m.s.-3 m.s. sf. (1086) *in which (midst)*
לְדָרְיָוֶשׁ prep.-pr.n. (1089) *to Darius*
מַלְכָּא n.m.s.-def.art. (1100) *the king*
שְׁלָמָא כֹלָּא n.m.s.-def.art. (1116)-n.m.s.-def.art. (1097) *all peace*

5:8

יְדִיעַ לֶהֱוֵא Pe. pass.ptc. (יְדַע 1095)-Pe. impf. 3 m.s. (הֲוָא 1089) *be it known*
לְמַלְכָּא prep.-n.m.s.-def.art. (1100) *to the king*
דִּי־אֲזַלְנָא conj.-Pe. pf. 1 c.p. (אֲזַל 1079) *that we went*
לִיהוּד prep.-pr.n. (1095) *to Judah*
מְדִינְתָּא n.f.s.-def.art. (1088) *the province*
לְבֵית prep.-n.m.s. cstr. (1084) *to the house of*
אֱלָהָא רַבָּא n.m.s.-def.art. (1080)-adj. m.s.-def.art. (1112) *the great God*
וְהוּא conj.-pers.pr. 3 m.s. (1090) *and it*
מִתְבְּנֵא Hithpe. ptc. (בְּנָה 1084) *being built*
אֶבֶן גְּלָל n.f.s. (1078)-n.m.s. (1086) *rolling stone*
וְאָע conj.-n.m.s. (1082) *and timber*
מִתְּשָׂם Hithpe. ptc. (שׂוּם 1113) *is laid*
בְּכֻתְלַיָּא prep.-n.m.p.-def.art. (1098) *in the walls*
וַעֲבִידְתָּא דָךְ conj.-n.f.s.-def.art. (1105)-demons. adj. (1088) *and this work*
אָסְפַּרְנָא adv. (1082) *diligently*
מִתְעַבְדָא Hithpe. ptc. f.s. (עֲבַד 1104) *goes on*
וּמַצְלַח conj.-Haph. ptc. (צְלַח 1109) *and prospers*
בְּיֶדְהֹם prep.-n.f.s.-3 m.p. sf. (1094) *in their hands*

5:9

אֱדַיִן adv. (1078) *then*
שְׁאֵלְנָא Pe. pf. 1 c.p. (שְׁאֵל 1114) *we asked*
לְשָׂבַיָּא אִלֵּךְ prep.-Pe. ptc. m.p.-def.art. (שִׂיב 1114)-demons.adj. m.p. (1080) *to those elders*
כְּנֵמָא adv. (1097) *as follows*

אֲמַרְנָא Pe. pf. 1 c.p. (אֲמַר 1081) *we spoke*
לְהֹם prep.-3 m.p. sf. *to them*
מַן־שָׂם interr. (1100)-Pe. pf. 3 m.s. (שׂוּם 1113) *who gave*
לְכֹם prep.-2 m.p. sf. *to you*
טְעֵם n.m.s. (1094) *a decree*
בַּיְתָא דְנָה n.m.s.-def.art. (1084)-demons.adj. m.s. (1088) *this house*
לְמִבְנְיָה prep.-Pe. inf. (בְּנָה 1084) *to build*
וְאֻשַּׁרְנָא דְנָה conj.-n.m.s.-def.art. (1083)-demons. adj. m.s. (1088) *and this structure*
לְשַׁכְלָלָה prep.-Shaphel inf. (כְּלַל 1097) *to finish*

5:10

וְאַף conj.-conj. (1082) *also*
שְׁמָהָתְהֹם n.m.p.-3 m.p. sf. (1116) *their names*
שְׁאֵלְנָא Pe. pf. 1 c.p. (שְׁאֵל 1114) *we asked*
לְהֹם prep.-3 m.p. sf. *to them*
לְהוֹדָעוּתָךְ prep.-Ha. inf.-2 m.s. sf. (יְדַע 1095) *for your information*
דִּי נִכְתֻּב conj.-Pe. impf. 1 c.p. (כְּתַב 1098) *that we might write*
שֻׁם־גֻּבְרַיָּא n.m.s. cstr. (1116)-n.m.p.-def.art. (1086) *the names of the men*
דִּי בְרָאשֵׁיהֹם rel.-prep.-n.m.p.-3 m.p. sf. (1112) *at their head*

5:11

וּכְנֵמָא conj.-adv. (1097) *and this*
פִתְגָמָא n.m.s.-def.art. (1109) *the word*
הֲתִיבוּנָא Haph. pf. 3 m.p.-1 c.p. sf. (תּוּב 1117) *which they replied to us*
לְמֵמַר Pe. inf. (אֲמַר 1081) *to say*
אֲנַחְנָא pers.pr. 1 c.p. (1081) *we*
הִמּוֹ pers.pr. 3 m.p. as nominative (1090) *are*
עַבְדוֹהִי n.m.p.-3 m.s. sf. (1105) *his servants*
דִּי־אֱלָהּ gen. (1087)-n.m.s. cstr. (1080) *of the God of*
שְׁמַיָּא n.m.p.-def.art. (1116) *the heavens*
וְאַרְעָא conj.-n.f.s.-def.art. (1083) *and the earth*
וּבָנַיִן conj.-Pe. act.ptc. m.p. (בְּנָה 1084) *and are building*
בַּיְתָא n.m.s.-def.art. (1084) *the house*
דִּי־הֲוָא rel. (1087)-Pe. pf. 3 m.s. (הֲוָא 1089) *that was*
בְנֵה Pi. pass.ptc. (בְּנָה 1084) *built*
מִקַּדְמַת דְּנָה prep.-n.f.s. cstr. (1110)-demons.adj. f.s. (1088) *ago*
שְׁנִין שַׂגִּיאָן n.f.p. (1116)-adj. f.p. (1113) *many years*
וּמֶלֶךְ conj.-n.m.s. (1100) *and the king*
לְיִשְׂרָאֵל prep.-pr.n. gent. (1096) *of Israel*
רַב adj. m.s. (1112) *great*
בְּנָהִי Pe. pf. 3 m.s.-3 m.s. sf. (בְּנָה 1084) *built it*
וְשַׁכְלְלֵהּ conj.-Shaphel pf. 3 m.s.-3 m.s. sf. (כְּלַל 1097) *and finished (it)*

5:12

לָהֵן conj. (1099, II) *but*
מִן־דִּי prep. (1100)-conj. (1087) *because*
הַרְגִּזוּ Ha. pf. 3 m.p. (רְגַז 1112) *had angered*
אֲבָהָתַנָא n.m.p.-1 c.p. sf. (1078) *our fathers*
לֶאֱלָהּ prep.-n.m.s. cstr. (1080) *the God of*
שְׁמַיָּא n.m.p.-def.art. (1116) *heaven*
יְהַב Pe. pf. 3 m.s. (1095) *he gave*
הִמּוֹ pr. 3 c.p. (1090) *them*
בְּיַד prep.-n.f.s. cstr. (1094) *into the hand of*
נְבוּכַדְנֶצַּר pr.n. (1102) *Nebuchadnezzar*
מֶלֶךְ־בָּבֶל n.m.s. cstr. (1100)-pr.n. (1084) *king of Babylon*
כַּסְדָּיָא pr.n.gent.-def.art. (1098) *the Chaldean*
וּבַיְתָה דְנָה conj.-n.m.s.-def.art. (1084) -demons.adj. (1088) *this house*
סַתְרֵהּ Pe. pf. 3 m.s.-3 m.s. sf. (סְתַר II 1104) *he destroyed*
וְעַמָּה conj.-n.m.s.-def.art. (1107) *and the people*
הַגְלִי Ha. pf. 3 m.s. (גְּלָא 1086) *carried away*
לְבָבֶל prep.-pr.n. loc. (1084) *to Babylonia*

5:13

בְּרַם adv. (1085) *however*
בִּשְׁנַת חֲדָה prep.-n.f.s. cstr. (1116)-adj. (1079) *in the first year*
לְכוֹרֶשׁ prep.-pr.n. (1096) *of Cyrus*
מַלְכָּא n.m.s.-def.art. (1100) *the king*
דִּי בָבֶל gen. (1087)-pr.n. (1084) *of Babylon*
כּוֹרֶשׁ pr.n. (1096) *Cyrus*
מַלְכָּא n.m.s.-def.art. (1100) *the king*
שָׂם טְעֵם Pe. pf. 3 m.s. (שׂוּם 1113)-n.m.s. (1094) *made a decree*
בֵּית־אֱלָהָא n.m.s. cstr. (1084)-n.m.s.-def.art. (1080) *house of God*
דְנָה demons.adj. m.s. (1088) *this*
לִבְּנֵא Pe. inf. (בְּנָה 1084) *to build*

5:14

וְאַף conj.-conj. (1082) *also*
מָאנַיָּא n.m.p.-def.art. (1099) *the vessels*
דִּי־בֵית־אֱלָהָא gen. (1087)-n.m.s. cstr. (1084) -n.m.s.-def.art. (1080) *of the house of God*
דִּי דַהֲבָה gen. (1087) n.m.s.-def.art. (1087) *of gold*
וְכַסְפָּא conj.-n.m.s.-def.art. (1097) *and silver*

דִּי נְבוּכַדְנֶצַּר rel. (1087)-pr.n. (1102) *which Nebuchadnezzar*
הַנְפֵּק Ha. pf. 3 m.s. (נְפַק 1103) *had taken*
מִן־הֵיכְלָא prep.-n.m.s.-def.art. (1090) *out of the temple*
דִּי בִירוּשְׁלֶם rel. (1087)-prep.-pr.n. loc. (1096) *that was in Jerusalem*
וְהֵיבֵל conj.-Ha. pf. 3 m.s. (יְבַל 1094) *and brought*
הִמּוֹ pr. 3 m.p. (1090) *(them)*
לְהֵיכְלָא prep.-n.m.s.-def.art. (1090) *into the temple*
דִּי בָבֶל gen. (1087)-pr.n. loc. (1084) *of Babylon*
הַנְפֵּק Ha. pf. 3 m.s. (נְפַק 1103) *took out*
הִמּוֹ v.supra *(them)*
כּוֹרֶשׁ pr.n. (1096) *Cyrus*
מַלְכָּא n.m.s.-def.art. (1100) *the king*
מִן־הֵיכְלָא prep.-n.m.s.-def.art. (1090) *out of the temple*
דִּי בָבֶל gen. (1087)-pr.n. (1084) *of Babylon*
וִיהִיבוּ conj.-Peil pf. 3 m.p. (יְהַב 1095) *and they were delivered*
לְשֵׁשְׁבַּצַּר prep.-pr.n. (1058) *to Sheshbazzar*
שְׁמֵהּ n.m.s.-3 m.s. sf. (1116) *his name*
דִּי פֶחָה rel. (1087)-n.m.s. (1108) *whom governor*
שָׂמֵהּ Pe. pf. 3 m.s.-3 m.s. sf. (שׂוּם 1113) *he had made (him)*

5:15

וַאֲמַר־לֵהּ conj.-Pe. pf. 3 m.s. (1081)-prep.-3 m.s. sf. *and he said to him*
אֵלֶּה demons.pr. p. (1080; K אֵלֶּה; Q אֵל) *these*
מָאנַיָּא n.m.p.-def.art. (1099) *vessels*
שֵׂא Pe. impv. 2 m.s. (נְשָׂא 1103) *take*
אֵזֶל־אֲחֵת Pe. impv. 2 m.s. (אֲזַל 1079)-Ha. impv. 2 m.s. (נְחַת 1102) *go, put*
הִמּוֹ pr. 3 c.p. (1090) *them*
בְּהֵיכְלָא prep.-n.m.s.-def.art. (1090) *in the temple*
דִּי בִירוּשְׁלֶם rel. (1087)-prep.-pr.n. loc. (1096) *which is in Jerusalem*
וּבֵית אֱלָהָא conj.-n.m.s. cstr. (1084)-n.m.s.-def.art. (1080) *and the house of God*
יִתְבְּנֵא Hithpe. impf. 3 m.s. (בְּנָה 1084) *let be rebuilt*
עַל־אַתְרֵהּ prep.-n.m.s.-3 m.s. sf. (1083) *on its site*

5:16

אֱדַיִן adv. (1078) *then*
שֵׁשְׁבַּצַּר דֵּךְ pr.n. (1058)-demons.pr. m.s. (1088) *this Sheshbazzar*
אֲתָא Pe. pf. 3 m.s. (אֲתָה 1083) *came*
יְהַב Pe. pf. 3 m.s. (יְהַב 1095) *laid*
אֻשַּׁיָּא n.m.p.-def.art. (1083) *the foundations*
דִּי־בֵית gen. (1087)-n.m.s. cstr. (1084) *of the house of*
אֱלָהָא n.m.s.-def.art. (1080) *God*
דִּי בִירוּשְׁלֶם rel. (1087)-prep.-pr.n. (1096) *which is in Jerusalem*
וּמִן־אֱדַיִן conj.-prep. (1100)-adv. (1078) *and from that time*
וְעַד־כְּעַן conj.-prep. (1105)-adv. (1107) *until now*
מִתְבְּנֵא Hithpe. ptc. (בְּנָה 1084) *it has been in building*
וְלָא שְׁלִם conj.-neg. (1098)-Pe. ptc.pass. (שְׁלַם 1115) *and it is not yet finished*

5:17

וּכְעַן conj.-adv. (1107) *and now*
הֵן conj. (1090) *if*
עַל־מַלְכָּא prep. (1106)-n.m.s.-def.art. (1100) *to the king*
טָב adj. m.s. (1094) *it seem good*
יִתְבַּקַּר Hithpa. impf. 3 m.s. (בְּקַר 1085) *let search be made*
בְּבֵית prep.-n.m.s. cstr. (1084) *in the house of*
גִּנְזַיָּא n.m.p.-def.art. (1086) *the treasures*
דִּי־מַלְכָּא gen. (1087)-n.m.s.-def.art. (1100) *of the king*
תַּמָּה adv. (1118) *there*
דִּי בְּבָבֶל rel. (1087)-prep.-pr.n. loc. (1084) *in Babylon*
הֵן conj. (1090) *whether*
אִיתַי part. (1080) *there is*
דִּי־מִן־כּוֹרֶשׁ rel. (1087)-prep. (1100)-pr.n. (1096) *by Cyrus*
מַלְכָּא n.m.s.-def.art. (1100) *the king*
שִׂים טְעֵם Peil pf. 3 m.s. (שׂוּם 1113)-n.m.s. (1094) *a decree was issued*
לְמִבְנֵא prep.-Pe. inf. (בְּנָה 1084) *for the building of*
בֵּית־אֱלָהָא־דֵךְ n.m.s. cstr. (1084)-n.m.s.-def.art. (1080)-demons.pr. m.s. (1088) *this house of God*
בִּירוּשְׁלֶם prep.-pr.n. loc. (1096) *in Jerusalem*
וּרְעוּת conj.-n.f.s. cstr. (1113) *and the pleasure of*
מַלְכָּא v.supra *the king*
עַל־דְּנָה prep. (1106)-demons.pr. c. (1088) *in this matter*
יִשְׁלַח Pe. impf. 3 m.s. (שְׁלַח 1115) *let send*
עֲלֶינָא prep.-1 c.p. sf. (1106) *us*

6:1

בֵּארַיִן prep.-adv. (1078) *then*
דָּרְיָוֶשׁ pr.n. (1089) *Darius*
מַלְכָּא n.m.s.-def.art. (1100) *the king*
שָׂם Pe. pf. 3 m.s. (שׂוּם 1113) *made*
טְעֵם n.m.s. (1094) *a decree*
וּבַקַּרוּ conj.-Pa. pf. 3 m.p. (בְּקַר 1085) *search was made*
בְּבֵית prep.-n.m.s. cstr. (1084) *in the house of*
סִפְרַיָּא n.m.p.-def.art. (1104) *books*
דִּי גִנְזַיָּא conj. (1087)-n.m.p.-def.art. (1086) *where the documents*
מְהַחֲתִין Ha. ptc.pass. m.p. (נְחַת 1102) *were deposited (stored)*
תַּמָּה adv. (1118) *there*
בְּבָבֶל prep.-pr.n. loc. (1084) *in Babylonia*

6:2

וְהִשְׁתְּכַח conj.-Hithpe. pf. 3 m.s. (שְׁכַח 1115) *was found*
בְּאַחְמְתָא prep.-pr.n. loc. (1079) *in Ecbatana*
בְּבִירְתָא prep.-n.f.s.-def.art. (1084) *in the capital (castle)*
דִּי בְּמָדַי rel. (1087)-prep.-pr.n. terr. (1099) *which in Media*
מְדִינְתָּה n.f.s.-def.art. (1088) *the province*
מְגִלָּה חֲדָה n.f.s. (1086)-adj. f.s. (1079) *a scroll*
וְכֵן־כְּתִיב conj.-adv. (1097)-Peil pf. 3 m.s. (כְּתַב 1098) *and thus it was written*
בְּגַוַּהּ prep.-n.m.s.-3 f.s. sf. (1086) *on which (in its midst)*
דִּכְרוֹנָה n.m.s.-def.art. (1088) *the record*

6:3

בִּשְׁנַת חֲדָה prep.-n.f.s. cstr. (1116)-adj. f.s. (1079) *in the first year*
לְכוֹרֶשׁ prep.-pr.n. (1096) *of Cyrus*
מַלְכָּא n.m.s.-def.art. (1100) *the king*
כּוֹרֶשׁ v.supra *Cyrus*
מַלְכָּא v.supra *the king*
שָׂם טְעֵם Pe. pf. 3 m.s. (1113)-n.m.s. (1094) *issued a decree*
בֵּית־אֱלָהָא n.m.s. cstr. (1084)-n.m.s.-def.art. (1080) *the house of God*
בִּירוּשְׁלֶם prep.-pr.n. loc. (1096) *in Jerusalem*
בַּיְתָא n.m.s.-def.art. (1084) *the house*
יִתְבְּנֵא Hithpe. impf. 3 m.s. (בְּנָה 1084) *let be rebuilt*
אֲתַר n.m.s. (1083) *place*
דִּי־דָבְחִין rel. (1087)-Pe. act.ptc. m.p. (דְּבַח 1087) *where are offered*
דִּבְחִין n.m.p. (1087) *sacrifices*
וְאֻשּׁוֹהִי conj.-n.m.p.-3 m.s. sf. (1083) *and its foundations*
מְסוֹבְלִין Po. pass.ptc. m.p. (סְבַל 1103) *(be) raised*
רוּמֵהּ n.m.s.-3 m.s. sf. (1112) *its height*
אַמִּין שִׁתִּין n.f.p. (1081)-n. indeclin. (1114) *sixty cubits*
פְּתָיֵהּ n.m.s.-3 m.s. sf. (1109) *its breadth*
אַמִּין שִׁתִּין v.supra-v.supra *sixty cubits*

6:4

נִדְבָּכִין n.m.p. (1102) *courses*
דִּי־אֶבֶן gen. (1087)-n.f.s. (1078) *of stone*
גְּלָל n.m.s. (1086) *rolling*
תְּלָתָא n.f.s. (1118) *three*
וְנִדְבָּךְ conj.-n.m.s. (1102) *and ... course*
דִּי־אָע gen. (1087)-n.m.s. (1082) *of timber*
חֲדַת n.f.s. (1079; of adj. 1092) *one* or *new*
וְנִפְקְתָא conj.-n.f.s.-def.art. (1103) *and the outlay (cost)*
מִן־בֵּית prep. (1100)-n.m.s. cstr. (1084) *from the house of*
מַלְכָּא n.m.s.-def.art. (1100) *the king*
תִּתְיְהִב Hithpe. impf. 3 f.s. (יְהַב 1095) *be given (paid)*

6:5

וְאַף conj.-conj. (1082) *and also*
מָאנֵי n.m.p. cstr. (1099) *the vessels of*
בֵית־אֱלָהָא n.m.s. cstr. (1084)-n.m.s.-def.art. (1080) *the house of God*
דִּי דַהֲבָה gen. (1087)-n.m.s.-def.art. (1087) *of gold*
וְכַסְפָּא conj.-n.m.s.-def.art. (1097) *and silver*
דִּי נְבוּכַדְנֶצַּר rel. (1087)-pr.n. (1102) *which Nebuchadnezzar*
הַנְפֵּק Haph. pf. 3 m.s. (נְפַק 1103) *took out*
מִן־הֵיכְלָא prep. (1100)-n.m.s.-def.art. (1090) *of the temple*
דִּי־בִירוּשְׁלֶם rel. (1087)-prep.-pr.n. (1096) *that is in Jerusalem*
וְהֵיבֵל conj.-Haph. pf. 3 m.s. (יְבַל 1094) *and brought*
לְבָבֶל prep.-pr.n. loc. (1084) *to Babylon*
יַהֲתִיבוּן Haph. impf. 3 m.p. (תּוּב 1117) *be restored*
וִיהָךְ conj.-Pe. impf. 3 m.s. (הֲלַךְ 1090) *and be brought back*
לְהֵיכְלָא prep.-n.m.s.-def.art. (1090) *to the temple*
דִּי־בִירוּשְׁלֶם v.supra-v.supra *which is in Jerusalem*
לְאַתְרֵהּ prep.-n.m.s.-3 m.s. sf. (1083) *to its place*

וְתַחֵת Haph. impf. 2 m.s. (נְחַת 1102) *you shall put*

בְּבֵית אֱלָהָא prep.-v.supra-v.supra *in the house of God*

6:6

כְּעַן adv. (1107) *now*

תַּתְּנַי pr.n. (1118) *Tattenai*

פַּחַת n.m.s. cstr. (1108) *governor of*

עֲבַר־נַהֲרָה n.m.s. cstr. (1105)-n.m.s.-def.art. (1102) *Beyond the River*

שְׁתַר בּוֹזְנַי pr.n. (1117) *Shethar-bozenai*

וּכְנָוָתְהוֹן conj.-n.m.p.-3 m.p. sf. (1097) *and their associates*

אֲפַרְסְכָיֵא pr.n. gent. (1082) *the generals (governors)*

דִּי rel. (1087) *who are*

בַּעֲבַר נַהֲרָה prep.-v.supra-v.supra *Beyond the River*

רַחִיקִין adj. p. (1113) *far*

הֲווֹ Pe. impv. 2 m.p. (הֲוָא 1089) *be*

מִן־תַּמָּה prep. (1100)-adv. (1118) *from there*

6:7

שְׁבֻקוּ Pe. impv. 2 m.p. (שְׁבַק 1114) *let alone*

לַעֲבִידַת prep.-n.f.s. cstr. (1105) *the work on*

בֵּית־אֱלָהָא n.m.s. cstr. (1084)-n.m.s.-def.art. (1080) *the house of God*

דֵךְ demons.adj. (1088) *this*

פַּחַת n.m.s. cstr. (1108) *the governor of*

יְהוּדָיֵא pr.n. gent.-def.art. (1095) *the Jews*

וּלְשָׂבֵי conj.-prep.-Pe. ptc. m.p. cstr. as subst. (1114 שִׂיב) *and the elders of*

יְהוּדָיֵא v.supra *the Jews*

בֵּית־ n.m.s. cstr. (1084) *house of*

אֱלָהָא דֵךְ n.m.s.-def.art. (1080)-demons.adj. (1088) *this ... God*

יִבְנוֹן Pe. impf. 3 m.s. (בְּנָה 1084) *let ... rebuild*

עַל־אַתְרֵהּ prep. (1106)-n.m.s.-3 m.s. sf. (1083) *on its site*

6:8

וּמִנִּי conj.-prep.-1 c.s. sf. (1100) *and by me*

שִׂים Peil pf. 3 m.s. (שׂוּם 1113) *is made*

טְעֵם n.m.s. (1094) *a decree*

לְמָא prep.-interr. (1099) *regarding what*

דִּי־תַעַבְדוּן rel. (1087)-Pe. impf. 2 m.p. (עֲבַד 1104) *you shall do*

עִם־שָׂבֵי prep. (1107)-Pe. ptc. m.p. cstr. as subst. (שִׂיב 1114) *for ... elders of*

יְהוּדָיֵא pr.n. m.p.-def.art. (1095) *the Jews*

אִלֵּךְ demons.pr. p. (1080) *these*

לְמִבְנֵא prep.-Pe. inf. (בְּנָה 1084) *for the rebuilding of*

בֵּית־אֱלָהָא n.m.s. cstr. (1084)-n.m.s.-def.art. (1080) ... *house of God*

דֵךְ demons.adj. (1088) *this*

וּמִנִּכְסֵי conj.-prep.-n.m.p. cstr. (1103) *and from the property of*

מַלְכָּא n.m.s.-def.art. (1100) *the king*

דִּי מִדַּת gen. (1087)-n.f.s. cstr. (1101) *the tribute of*

עֲבַר נַהֲרָה n.m.s. cstr. (1105)-n.m.s.-def.art. (1102) *Beyond the River*

אָסְפַּרְנָא adv. (1082) *in full (thoroughly)*

נִפְקְתָא n.f.s.-def.art. (1103) *the outlay*

תֶּהֱוֵא Pe. impf. 3 f.s. (הֲוָא 1089) *is to be*

מִתְיַהֲבָא Hithpe. ptc. f.s. (יְהַב 1095) *paid*

לְגֻבְרַיָּא prep.-n.m.p.-def.art. (1086) *to ... men*

אִלֵּךְ demons.adj. p. (1080) *these*

דִּי־לָא לְבַטָּלָא rel. (1087)-neg.-prep.-Pa. inf. (1084 בְּטֵל) *without delay (not made to cease)*

6:9

וּמָה conj.-interr. (1099) *and whatever*

חַשְׁחָן n.f.p. (1093) *is needed*

וּבְנֵי תוֹרִין conj.-n.m.p. cstr. (בַּר I 1085)-n.m.p. (1117) *and young bulls*

וְדִכְרִין conj.-n.m.p. (1088) *rams*

וְאִמְּרִין conj.-n.m.p. (1081) *or sheep*

לַעֲלָוָן prep.-n.f.p. (1106) *for burnt offerings*

לֶאֱלָהּ שְׁמַיָּא prep.-n.m.s. cstr. (1080)-n.m.p. -def.art. (1116) *to the God of heaven*

חִנְטִין n.f.p. (1093) *wheat*

מְלַח n.m.s. (1100) *salt*

חֲמַר n.m.s. (1093) *wine*

וּמְשַׁח conj.-n.m.s. (1101) *or oil*

כְּמֵאמַר part.-n.m.s. cstr. (1081) *as required (the word of)*

כָּהֲנַיָּא n.m.p.-def.art. (1096) *the priests*

דִּי־בִירוּשְׁלֶם rel. (1087)-prep.-pr.n. loc. (1096) *at Jerusalem*

לֶהֱוֵא Pe. impf. 3 m.s. (הֲוָא 1089) *let that be*

מִתְיְהֵב Hithpe. ptc. m.s. (יְהַב 1095) *given*

לְהֹם prep.-3 m.p. sf. *to them*

יוֹם בְּיוֹם n.m.s. (1095)-prep.-v.supra *day by day*

דִּי־לָא שָׁלוּ conj. (1087)-neg. (1098)-n.f.s. (1115) *without fail*

6:10

דִּי־לֶהֱוֺן conj. (1087)-Pe. impf. 3 m.p. (הֲוָא 1089) *that they may*

מְהַקְרְבִין Haph. act.ptc. p. (קְרֵב 1111) *offer*

נִיחוֹחִין n.m.p. (1102) *pleasing sacrifices*
לֶאֱלָהּ שְׁמַיָּא prep.-n.m.s. cstr. (1080)-n.m.p. -def.art. (1116) *to the God of heaven*
וּמְצַלַּיִן conj.-Pa. ptc. m.p. (צְלָא 1109) *and pray*
לְחַיֵּי prep.-adj. p. cstr. (1092) *for the life of*
מַלְכָּא n.m.s.-def.art. (1100) *the king*
וּבְנוֹהִי conj.-n.m.p.-3 m.s. sf. (1085) *and his sons*

6:11

וּמִנִּי conj.-prep.-1 c.s. sf. (1100) *also I*
שִׂים Peil pf. 3 m.s. (שׂוּם 1113) *make*
טְעֵם n.m.s. (1094) *a decree*
דִּי כָל־אֱנָשׁ conj. (1087)-n.m.s. cstr. (1097)-n.m.s. (1081) *that any one*
דִּי יְהַשְׁנֵא rel. (1087)-Haph. impf. 3 m.s. (שְׁנָא 1116) *alters*
פִּתְגָמָא דְנָה n.m.s.-def.art. (1100)-demons.adj. (1088) *this edict*
יִתְנְסַח Hithpe. impf. 3 m.s. (נְסַח 1103) *shall be pulled out*
אָע n.m.s. (1082) *a beam*
מִן־בַּיְתֵהּ prep. (1100)-n.m.s.-3 m.s. sf. (1084) *out of his house*
וּזְקִיף conj.-Pe. ptc.pass. (זְקַף 1091) *and lifted up*
יִתְמְחֵא Hithpa. impf. 3 m.s. (מְחָא 1099) *he shall be impaled*
עֲלֹהִי prep.-3 m.s. sf. (1106) *upon it*
וּבַיְתֵהּ conj.-n.m.s.-3 m.s. sf. (1084) *and his house*
נְוָלוּ n.f.s. (1102) *a dunghill*
יִתְעֲבֵד Hithpe. impf. 3 m.s. (עֲבַד 1104) *shall be made*
עַל־דְּנָה prep. (1100)-demons.pr. (1088) *(on account of this)*

6:12

וֵאלָהָא conj.-n.m.s.-def.art. (1080) *and the God*
דִּי שַׁכִּן rel. (1087)-Pa. pf. 3 m.s. (שְׁכַן 1115) *who has caused to dwell*
שְׁמֵהּ n.m.s.-3 m.s. sf. (1116) *his name*
תַּמָּה adv. (1118) *there*
יְמַגַּר Pa. impf. 3 m.s. (מְגַר 1099) *may overthrow*
כָּל־מֶלֶךְ n.m.s. cstr. (1097)-n.m.s. (1100) *any king*
וְעַם conj.-n.m.s. (1107) *or people*
דִּי יִשְׁלַח rel. (1087) Pe. impf. 3 m.s. (1115) *that shall put forth*
יְדֵהּ n.f.s.-3 m.s. sf. (1094) *his hand*
לְהַשְׁנָיָה prep.-Haph. inf. (שְׁנָא 1116) *to alter*
לְחַבָּלָה prep.-Pa. inf. (חֲבַל 1091) *(or) to destroy*
בֵּית־אֱלָהָא n.m.s. cstr. (1084)-n.m.s.-def.art. (1080) ... *house of God*
דֵךְ demons.pr. (1088) *this*

דִּי בִירוּשְׁלֶם rel. (1087)-prep.-pr.n. loc. (1096) *which is in Jerusalem*
אֲנָה דָרְיָוֶשׁ pers.pr. 1 c.s. (1081)-pr.n. (1089) *I Darius*
שָׂמֶת Pe. pf. 1 c.s. (שׂוּם 1113) *make*
טְעֵם n.m.s. (1094) *a decree*
אָסְפַּרְנָא adv. (1082) *with all diligence*
יִתְעֲבִד Hithpe. impf. 3 m.s. (עֲבַד 1104) *let it be done*

6:13

אֱדַיִן adv. (1078) *then*
תַּתְּנַי pr.n. (1118) *Tattenai*
פַּחַת n.m.s. cstr. (1108) *governor of*
עֲבַר־נַהֲרָה n.m.s. cstr. (1105)-n.m.s.-def.art. (1102) *Beyond the River*
שְׁתַר בּוֹזְנַי pr.n. (1117) *Shethar-bozenai*
וּכְנָוָתְהוֹן conj.-n.m.p.-3 m.p. sf. (1097) *and their associates*
לָקֳבֵל דִּי־ prep.-subst. (1110)-conj. (1087) *according to (as)*
שְׁלַח Pe. pf. 3 m.s. (שְׁלַח 1115) *sent*
דָּרְיָוֶשׁ pr.n. (1089) *Darius*
מַלְכָּא n.m.s.-def.art. (1100) *the king*
כְּנֵמָא adv. (1097) *accordingly*
אָסְפַּרְנָא adv. (1082) *with all diligence*
עֲבַדוּ Pe. pf. 3 c.p. (עֲבַד 1104) *did*

6:14

וְשָׂבֵי conj.-Pe. ptc. p. cstr. (שִׂיב 1114) *and the elders of*
יְהוּדָיֵא pr.n. p.-def.art. (1095) *the Jews*
בָּנַיִן Pe. act.ptc. p. (בְּנָה 1084) *built*
וּמַצְלְחִין conj.-Haph. ptc. p. (צְלַח 1109) *and prospered*
בִּנְבוּאַת prep.-n.f.s. cstr. (1102) *through the prophesying of*
חַגַּי pr.n. (1092) *Haggai*
נְבִיָּאה n.m.s.-def.art. (1101) *the prophet*
וּזְכַרְיָה conj.-pr.n. (1091) *and Zechariah*
בַּר־עִדּוֹא n.m.s. cstr. (1085)-pr.n. (723) *the son of Iddo*
וּבְנוֹ conj.-Pe. pf. 3 m.p. (בְּנָה 1084) *they built*
וְשַׁכְלִלוּ conj.-Shaph. pf. 3 m.p. (כְּלַל 1097) *and finished*
מִן־טַעַם prep. (1100)-n.m.s. cstr. (1094) *by command of*
אֱלָהּ n.m.s. cstr. (1080) *the God of*
יִשְׂרָאֵל pr.n. (1096) *Israel*
וּמִטְּעֵם conj.-prep. (1100)-n.m.s. cstr. (1094) *and by decree of*
כּוֹרֶשׁ pr.n. (1096) *Cyrus*

וְדָרְיָוֶשׁ conj.-pr.n. (1089) *and Darius*
וְאַרְתַּחְשַׁשְׂתְּא conj.-pr.n. (1083) *and Artaxerxes*
מֶלֶךְ פָּרָס n.m.s. cstr. (1100)-pr.n. terr. (1108) *king of Persia*

6:15

וְשֵׁיצִיא conj.-Shaph. pf. 3 m.s. (1115) *and was finished*
בַּיְתָה דְנָה n.m.s.-def.art. (1084)-demons.adj. (1088) *this house*
עַד יוֹם prep. (1105)-n.m.s. (1095) *on ... day*
תְּלָתָה n.f.s. (1118) *third*
לִירַח אֲדָר prep.-n.m.s. (1096)-pr.n. (1078) *of the month of Adar*
דִּי־הִיא rel. (1087)-pr. f.s. (1090) *in (which it)*
שְׁנַת־שֵׁת n.f.s. cstr. (1116)-n.m.s. (1114) *the sixth year*
לְמַלְכוּת prep.-n.f.s. cstr. (1100) *of the reign of*
דָּרְיָוֶשׁ pr.n. (1089) *Darius*
מַלְכָּא n.m.s.-def.art. (1100) *the king*

6:16

וַעֲבַדוּ conj.-Pe. pf. 3 m.p. (**עֲבַד** 1104) *and celebrated (made)*
בְנֵי־יִשְׂרָאֵל n.m.p. cstr. (1085)-pr.n. (1096) *the people of Israel*
כָּהֲנַיָּא n.m.p.-def.art. (1096) *the priests*
וְלֵוָיֵא conj.-pr.n. gent. p.-def.art. (1099) *and the Levites*
וּשְׁאָר conj.-n.m.s. cstr. (1114) *and the rest of*
בְּנֵי־גָלוּתָא n.m.p. cstr. (1085)-n.f.s.-def.art. (1086) *the sons of the exile*
חֲנֻכַּת n.f.s. cstr. (1093) *the dedication of*
בֵּית־אֱלָהָא n.m.s. cstr. (1084)-n.m.s.-def.art. (1080) ... *house of God*
דְנָה demons.adj. (1088) *this*
בְּחֶדְוָה prep.-n.f.s. (1092) *with joy*

6:17

וְהַקְרִבוּ conj.-Haph. pf. 3 cm.p. (**קְרֵב** 1111) *they offered*
לַחֲנֻכַּת prep.-n.f.s. cstr. (1093) *at the dedication of*
בֵּית־אֱלָהָא n.m.s. cstr. (1084)-n.m.s.-def.art. (1080) ... *house of God*
דְנָה demons.adj. (1088) *this*
תּוֹרִין מְאָה n.m.p. (1117)-n.f.s. (1099) *one hundred bulls*
דִּכְרִין מָאתַיִן n.m.p. (1088)-n.f. du. (1099) *two hundred rams*
אִמְּרִין n.m.p. (1081) *lambs*
אַרְבַּע מְאָה n.m.s. (1112)-n.f.s. (1099) *four hundred*
וּצְפִירֵי עִזִּין conj.-n.m.s. cstr. (1110)-n.f.p. (1107) *and he-goats*
לְחַטָּיָא prep.-n.f.s. (1092) *as a sin offering*
עַל־כָּל־יִשְׂרָאֵל prep. (1106)-n.m.s. cstr. (1096) *for all Israel*
תְּרֵי־עֲשַׂר n.m.s. cstr. (1118)-n.m.s. (1108) *twelve*
לְמִנְיָן prep.-n.m.s. cstr. (1101) *according to the number of*
שִׁבְטֵי יִשְׂרָאֵל n.m.p. cstr. (1114)-pr.n. (1096) *the tribes of Israel*

6:18

וַהֲקִימוּ conj.-Haph. pf. 3 c.p. (**קוּם** 1110) *and they set*
כָהֲנַיָּא n.m.p.-def.art. (1096) *the priests*
בִּפְלֻגָּתְהוֹן prep.-n.f.s.-3 m.p. sf. (1108) *in their divisions*
וְלֵוָיֵא conj.-n.m.p.-def.art. (1099) *and the Levites*
בְּמַחְלְקָתְהוֹן prep.-n.f.p.-3 m.p. sf. (1093) *in their courses*
עַל־עֲבִידַת prep. (1106)-n.f.s. cstr. (1105) *for the service of*
אֱלָהָא n.m.s.-def.art. (1080) *God*
דִּי בִירוּשְׁלֶם rel. (1087)-prep.-pr.n. loc. (1096) *at Jerusalem*
כִּכְתָב conj. (1096)-n.m.s. cstr. (1098) *as it is written in*
סְפַר מֹשֶׁה n.m.s. cstr. (1104)-pr.n. (1101) *the book of Moses*

6:19

וַיַּעֲשׂוּ consec.-Qal impf. 3 m.p. (**עָשָׂה** I 793) *and kept*
בְנֵי־הַגּוֹלָה n.m.p. cstr. (119)-def.art.-n.f.s. (163) *the returned exiles*
אֶת־הַפָּסַח dir.obj.-def.art.-n.m.s. (820) *the passover*
בְּאַרְבָּעָה עָשָׂר prep.-num. f.s. (916)-n.m.s. (797) *on the fourteenth*
לַחֹדֶשׁ prep.-def.art.-n.m.s. (294) *of the ... month*
הָרִאשׁוֹן def.art.-adj. m.s. (911) *first*

6:20

כִּי הִטַּהֲרוּ conj. (471)-Hith. pf. 3 c.p. (**טָהֵר** 372) *had purified themselves*
הַכֹּהֲנִים def.art.-n.m.p. (463) *the priests*
וְהַלְוִיִּם conj.-def.art.-n.m.p. (532) *and the Levites*
כְּאֶחָד prep.-adj. num. (25) *together*
כֻּלָּם n.m.s.-3 m.p. sf. (481) *all of them*
טְהוֹרִים adj. m.p. (373) *were clean*

וַיִּשְׁחֲטוּ consec.-Qal impf. 3 m.p. (שָׁחַט 1006) *so they killed*
הַפָּסַח def.art.-n.m.s. (820) *the passover*
לְכָל־בְּנֵי prep.-n.m.s. cstr. (481)-n.m.p. cstr. (119) *all of the sons of*
הַגּוֹלָה def.art.-n.f.s. (163) *exile*
וְלַאֲחֵיהֶם conj.-prep.-n.m.p.-3 m.p. sf. (26) *for their fellow*
הַכֹּהֲנִים def.art.-n.m.p. (463) *priests*
וְלָהֶם conj.-prep.-3 m.p. sf. *and for themselves*

6:21

וַיֹּאכְלוּ consec.-Qal impf. 3 m.p. (אָכַל 37) *and it was eaten by*
בְּנֵי־יִשְׂרָאֵל n.m.p. cstr. (119)-pr.n. (975) *the people of Israel*
הַשָּׁבִים def.art.-Qal act.ptc. m.p. (שׁוּב 996) *who had returned*
מֵהַגּוֹלָה prep.-def.art.-n.f.s. (163) *from exile*
וְכֹל הַנִּבְדָּל conj.-n.m.s. cstr. (481)-def.art.-Ni. ptc. m.s. (בָּדַל 95) *and also by every one who had separated themselves*
מִטֻּמְאַת prep.-n.f.s. cstr. (380) *from the pollutions of*
גּוֹיֵ־הָאָרֶץ n.m.p. cstr. (156)-def.art.-n.f.s. (75; GK 8k) *the peoples of the land*
אֲלֵהֶם prep.-3 m.p. sf. (39) *themselves (unto them)*
לִדְרֹשׁ prep.-Qal inf.cstr. (205) *to worship*
לַיהוה prep.-pr.n. (217) *Yahweh*
אֱלֹהֵי n.m.p. cstr. (43) *the God of*
יִשְׂרָאֵל pr.n. (975) *Israel*

6:22

וַיַּעֲשׂוּ consec.-Qal impf. 3 m.p. (עָשָׂה I 793) *and they kept*
חַג־מַצּוֹת n.m.s. cstr. (290)-n.f.p. (595) *the feast of unleavened bread*
שִׁבְעַת יָמִים n.f.s. cstr. (988)-n.m.p. (398) *seven days*
בְּשִׂמְחָה prep.-n.f.s. (970) *with joy*
כִּי שִׂמְּחָם conj. (471)-Pi. pf. 3 m.s.-3 m.p. sf. (970 שָׂמַח) *for ... had made them joyful*
יהוה pr.n. (217) *Yahweh*
וְהֵסֵב conj.-Hi. pf. 3 m.s. (סָבַב 685) *and had turned*
לֵב n.m.s. cstr. (524) *the heart of*
מֶלֶךְ־אַשּׁוּר n.m.s. cstr. (572)-pr.n. (78) *the king of Assyria*
עֲלֵיהֶם prep.-3 m.p. sf. (752) *to them*
לְחַזֵּק prep.-Pi. inf.cstr. (304) *so that he strengthened*
יְדֵיהֶם n.f.p.-3 m.p. sf. (388) *their hands*
בִּמְלֶאכֶת prep.-n.f.s. cstr. (521) *in the work of*
בֵּית־הָאֱלֹהִים n.m.s. cstr. (108)-def.art.-n.m.p. (43) *the house of God*
אֱלֹהֵי יִשְׂרָאֵל n.m.p. cstr. (43)-pr.n. (975) *the God of Israel*

7:1

וְאַחַר conj.-prep. (29) *now after*
הַדְּבָרִים הָאֵלֶּה def.art.-n.m.p. (182)-def.art. -demons.adj. c.p. (41) *this (these words)*
בְּמַלְכוּת prep.-n.f.s. cstr. (574) *in the reign of*
אַרְתַּחְשַׁסְתְּא pr.n. (77) *Artaxerxes*
מֶלֶךְ־ n.m.s. cstr. (572) *king of*
פָּרָס pr.n. (828) *Persia*
עֶזְרָא pr.n. (740) *Ezra*
בֶּן־שְׂרָיָה n.m.s. cstr. (119)-pr.n. (976) *the son of Seraiah*
בֶּן־עֲזַרְיָה v.supra-pr.n. (741) *the son of Azariah*
בֶּן־חִלְקִיָּה v.supra-pr.n. (324) *the son of Hilkiah*

7:2

בֶּן־שַׁלּוּם v.supra-pr.n. (1024) *son of Shallum*
בֶּן־צָדוֹק v.supra-pr.n. (843) *son of Zadok*
בֶּן־אֲחִיטוּב v.supra-pr.n. (26) *son of Ahitub*

7:3

בֶּן־אֲמַרְיָה v.supra-pr.n. (57) *son of Amariah*
בֶּן־עֲזַרְיָה v.supra-pr.n. (741) *son of Azariah*
בֶּן־מְרָיוֹת v.supra-pr.n. (599) *son of Meraioth*

7:4

בֶּן־זְרַחְיָה v.supra-pr.n. (280) *son of Zerahiah*
בֶּן־עֻזִּי v.supra-pr.n. (739) *son of Uzzi*
בֶּן־בֻּקִּי v.supra-pr.n. (131) *son of Bukki*

7:5

בֶּן־אֲבִישׁוּעַ v.supra-pr.n. (4) *son of Abishua*
בֶּן־פִּינְחָס v.supra-pr.n. (810) *son of Phinehas*
בֶּן־אֶלְעָזָר v.supra-pr.n. (46) *son of Eleazar*
בֶּן־אַהֲרֹן v.supra-pr.n. (14) *son of Aaron*
הַכֹּהֵן הָרֹאשׁ def.art.-n.m.s. (463)-def.art.-n.m.s. (910) *the chief priest*

7:6

הוּא עֶזְרָא demons.adj. m.s. (214)-pr.n. (740) *this Ezra*
עָלָה Qal pf. 3 m.s. (748) *went up*
מִבָּבֶל prep.-pr.n. loc. (93) *from Babylonia*
וְהוּא־סֹפֵר conj.-pers.pr. 3 m.s. (214)-n.m.s. (708) *and he was a ... scribe*
מָהִיר adj. m.s. (555) *skilled*

בְּתוֹרַת מֹשֶׁה prep.-n.f.s. cstr. (435)-pr.n. (602) *in the law of Moses*
אֲשֶׁר־נָתַן rel. (81)-Qal pf. 3 m.s. (678) *which ... had given*
יהוה pr.n. (217) *Yahweh*
אֱלֹהֵי יִשְׂרָאֵל n.m.p. cstr. (43)-pr.n. (975) *the God of Israel*
וַיִּתֶּן־לוֹ consec.-Qal impf. 3 m.s. (נָתַן 678) -prep.-3 m.s. sf. *and granted him*
הַמֶּלֶךְ def.art.-n.m.s. (572) *the king*
כְּיַד־יהוה prep.-n.f.s. cstr. (388)-pr.n. (217) *for the hand of Yahweh*
אֱלֹהָיו n.m.p.-3 m.s. sf. (43) *his God*
עָלָיו prep.-3 m.s. sf. *was upon him*
כֹּל בַּקָּשָׁתוֹ n.m.s. cstr. (481)-n.m.s.-3 m.s. sf. (135) *all that he asked*

7:7

וַיַּעֲלוּ consec.-Qal impf. 3 m.p. (עָלָה 748) *and there went up*
מִבְּנֵי־יִשְׂרָאֵל prep.-n.m.p. cstr. (119)-pr.n. (975) *some of the people of Israel*
וּמִן־הַכֹּהֲנִים conj.-prep.-def.art.-n.m.p. (463) *and some of the priests*
וְהַלְוִיִּם conj.-def.art.-n.m.p. (532) *and Levites*
וְהַמְשֹׁרְרִים conj.-def.art.-Polel ptc. m.p. (שִׁיר 1010) *the singers*
וְהַשֹּׁעֲרִים conj.-def.art.-n.m.p. (1045) *and gatekeepers*
וְהַנְּתִינִים conj.-def.art.-n.m.p. (682) *and the temple servants*
אֶל־יְרוּשָׁלָם prep. (39)-pr.n. (436) *to Jerusalem*
בִּשְׁנַת־שֶׁבַע prep.-n.f.s. cstr. (1040)-num. m.s. (988) *in the seventh year*
לְאַרְתַּחְשַׁסְתְּא prep.-pr.n. (77) *of Artaxerxes*
הַמֶּלֶךְ def.art.-n.m.s. (572) *the king*

7:8

וַיָּבֹא consec.-Qal impf. 3 m.s. (בּוֹא 97) *and he came to*
יְרוּשָׁלַם pr.n. (436) *Jerusalem*
בַּחֹדֶשׁ prep.-def.art.-n.m.s. (294) *in the ... month*
הַחֲמִישִׁי def.art.-num.ord. (332) *fifth*
הִיא demons. f.s. (214) *which was*
שְׁנַת n.f.s. cstr. (1040) *the ... year*
הַשְּׁבִיעִית def.art.-num.ord. f.s. (988) *seventh*
לַמֶּלֶךְ prep.-def.art.-n.m.s. (572) *of the king*

7:9

כִּי בְּאֶחָד conj. (471)-prep.-adj. m.s. (25) *for on the first day*
לַחֹדֶשׁ prep.-def.art.-n.m.s. (294) *of the ... month*
הָרִאשׁוֹן def.art.-num.ord. m.s. (911) *first*
הוּא יְסֻד demons.adj. m.s. (214)-n.m.s. cstr. (414) *that was the foundation of*
הַמַּעֲלָה def.art.-n.f.s. (752) *the going up*
מִבָּבֶל prep.-pr.n. (93) *from Babylonia*
וּבְאֶחָד conj.-v.supra *and on the first day*
לַחֹדֶשׁ prep.-def.art.-n.m.s. (294) *of the ... month*
הַחֲמִישִׁי def.art.-num.ord. m. (332) *fifth*
בָּא Qal pf. 3 m.s. (בּוֹא 97) *he came*
אֶל־יְרוּשָׁלַם prep.-pr.n. (436) *to Jerusalem*
כְּיַד־אֱלֹהָיו prep.-n.f.s. cstr. (388)-n.m.p.-3 m.s. sf. (43) *for the ... hand of his God*
הַטּוֹבָה def.art.-adj. f.s. (373) *good*
עָלָיו prep.-3 m.s. sf. (752) *was upon him*

7:10

כִּי עֶזְרָא conj. (471)-pr.n. (740) *for Ezra*
הֵכִין Hi. pf. 3 m.s. (כּוּן 465) *had set*
לְבָבוֹ n.m.s.-3 m.s. sf. (523) *his heart*
לִדְרוֹשׁ prep.-Qal inf.cstr. (דָּרַשׁ 205) *to study*
אֶת־תּוֹרַת dir.obj.-n.f.s. cstr. (435) *the law of*
יהוה pr.n. (217) *Yahweh*
וְלַעֲשֹׂת conj.-prep.-Qal inf.cstr. (עָשָׂה I 793) *and to do it*
וּלְלַמֵּד conj.-prep.-Pi. inf.cstr. (לָמַד 540) *and to teach*
בְּיִשְׂרָאֵל prep.-pr.n. (975) *in Israel*
חֹק n.m.s. (349) *statutes*
וּמִשְׁפָּט conj.-n.m.s. (1048) *and ordinances*

7:11

וְזֶה conj.-demons.adj. m.s. (260) *this*
פַּרְשֶׁגֶן n.m.s. cstr. (832) *the copy of*
הַנִּשְׁתְּוָן def.art.-n.m.s. (677) *the letter*
אֲשֶׁר נָתַן rel. (81)-Qal pf. 3 m.s. (678) *which ... gave*
הַמֶּלֶךְ def.art.-n.m.s. (572) *the king*
אַרְתַּחְשַׁסְתְּא pr.n. (77) *Artaxerxes*
לְעֶזְרָא prep.-pr.n. (740) *to Ezra*
הַכֹּהֵן def.art.-n.m.s. (463) *the priest*
הַסֹּפֵר def.art.-n.m.s. (708) *the scribe*
סֹפֵר Qal act.ptc. m.s. (סָפַר 707) *learned (writing)*
דִּבְרֵי n.m.p. cstr. (182) *in the matters of*
מִצְוֹת־יהוה n.f.p. cstr. (846)-pr.n. (217) *the commandments of Yahweh*
וְחֻקָּיו conj.-n.m.p.-3 m.s. sf. (349) *and his statutes*
עַל־יִשְׂרָאֵל prep.-pr.n. (975) *for Israel*

7:12

אַרְתַּחְשַׁסְתְּא pr.n. (77; GK 1c) *Artaxerxes*

מֶלֶךְ n.m.s. cstr. (572) *king of*
מַלְכַיָּא n.m.p.-def.art. (Aramaic; 1100) *kings*
לְעֶזְרָא prep.-pr.n. (1105) *to Ezra*
כָהֲנָא n.m.s.-def.art. (1096) *the priest*
סָפַר n.m.s. cstr. (1104) *the scribe of*
דָתָא n.f.s.-def.art. (1089) *the law*
דִּי־אֱלָהּ gen. (1087)-n.m.s. cstr. (1080) *of the God of*
שְׁמַיָּא n.m.p.-def.art. (1116) *the heavens*
גְּמִיר Pe. ptc.pass. as adj. (גְּמַר 1086) *perfect*
וּכְעֶנֶת conj.-adv. (1107) *and now*

7:13

מִנִּי prep.-1 c.s. sf. (1100) *from me*
שִׂים Peil pf. 3 m.s. (שׂוּם 1113) *is made*
טְעֵם n.m.s. (1094) *a decree*
דִּי conj. (1087) *that*
כָל־מִתְנַדַּב n.m.s. cstr. (1097)-Hithpa. ptc. (נְדַב 1102) *any volunteer*
בְּמַלְכוּתִי prep.-n.f.s.-1 c.s. sf. (1100) *in my kingdom*
מִן־עַמָּה prep. (1100)-n.m.s.-def.art. (1107) *of the people*
יִשְׂרָאֵל pr.n. (1096) *Israel*
וְכָהֲנוֹהִי conj.-n.m.p.-3 m.s. sf. (1096) *or their priests*
וְלֵוָיֵא conj.-n.m.p. gent.-def.art. (1099) *or Levites*
לִמְהָךְ prep.-Pe. inf. (הֲלַךְ 1090) *to go*
לִירוּשְׁלֶם prep.-pr.n. loc. (1096) *to Jerusalem*
עִמָּךְ prep.-2 m.s. sf. (1107) *with you*
יְהָךְ Pe. impf. 3 m.s. (הֲלַךְ 1090) *may go*

7:14

כָּל־קֳבֵל דִּי n.m.s. cstr. (1097)-conj. (1110)-conj. (1087) *for*
מִן־קֳדָם prep. (1100)-prep. (1110) *from before*
מַלְכָּא n.m.s.-def.art. (1100) *the king*
וְשִׁבְעַת conj.-n.f.s. cstr. (1114) *and seven of*
יָעֲטֹהִי n.m.p.-3 m.s. sf. (1096) *his counselors*
שְׁלִיחַ Pe. pass.ptc. (שְׁלַח 1115) *are sent*
לְבַקָּרָא prep.-Pa. inf. (בְּקַר 1085) *to make inquiries*
עַל־יְהוּד prep. (1106)-pr.n. (1095) *about Judah*
וְלִירוּשְׁלֶם conj.-prep.-pr.n. (1096) *and Jerusalem*
בְּדָת prep.-n.f.s. cstr. (1089) *according to the law of*
אֱלָהָךְ n.m.s.-2 m.s. sf. (1080) *your God*
דִּי בִידָךְ rel. (1087)-prep.-n.f.s.-2 m.s. sf. (1094) *which is in your hand*

7:15

וּלְהֵיבָלָה conj.-prep.-Haph. inf. (יְבַל 1094) *and also to convey*
כְּסַף n.m.s. (1097) *silver*
וּדְהַב conj.-n.m.s. (1087) *and gold*
דִּי־מַלְכָּא rel. (1087)-n.m.s.-def.art. (1100) *which the king*
וְיָעֲטוֹהִי conj.-n.m.p.-3 m.s. sf. (1096) *and his counselors*
הִתְנַדַּבוּ Hith.pa. pf. 3 m.p. (נְדַב 1102) *have freely offered*
לֶאֱלָהּ prep.-n.m.s. cstr. (1080) *to the God of*
יִשְׂרָאֵל pr.n. (1096) *Israel*
דִּי בִירוּשְׁלֶם rel.-prep.-pr.n. (1096) *whose ... in Jerusalem*
מִשְׁכְּנֵהּ n.m.s.-3 m.s. sf. (1115) *dwelling*

7:16

וְכֹל conj.-n.m.s. cstr. (1097) *with all of*
כְּסַף n.m.s. (1097) *silver*
וּדְהַב conj.-n.m.s. (1087) *and gold*
דִּי תְהַשְׁכַּח rel. (1087)-Haph. impf. 2 m.s. (שְׁכַח 1115) *which you shall find*
בְּכֹל prep.-n.m.s. cstr. (1097) *in the whole*
מְדִינַת n.f.s. cstr. (1088) *province of*
בָּבֶל pr.n. (1084) *Babylonia*
עִם הִתְנַדָּבוּת prep. (1107)-Hithpa. inf. (נְדַב 1102) *with the freewill offerings of*
עַמָּא n.m.s.-def.art. (1107) *the people*
וְכָהֲנַיָּא conj.-n.m.p.-def.art. (1096) *and the priests*
מִתְנַדְּבִין Hithpa. ptc. m.p. (נְדַב 1102) *vowed willingly*
לְבֵית prep.-n.m.s. cstr. (1084) *for the house of*
אֱלָהֲהֹם n.m.s.-3 m.p. sf. (1080) *their God*
דִּי בִירוּשְׁלֶם rel. (1087)-prep.-pr.n. (1096) *which is in Jerusalem*

7:17

כָּל־קֳבֵל דְּנָה n.m.s. cstr. (1097)-prep. (1110) -demons.pr. (1088) *then*
אָסְפַּרְנָא adv. (1082) *with all diligence*
תִקְנֵא Pe. impf. 2 m.s. (קְנָא 1111) *you shall buy*
בְּכַסְפָּא דְנָה prep.-n.m.s.-def.art. (1097)-demons. adj. c. (1088) *with this money*
תּוֹרִין n.m.p. (1117) *bulls*
דִּכְרִין n.m.p. (1088) *rams*
אִמְּרִין n.m.p. (1081) *lambs*
וּמִנְחָתְהוֹן conj.-n.f.p.-3 m.p. sf. (1101) *with their cereal offerings*
וְנִסְכֵּיהוֹן conj.-n.m.p.-3 m.p. sf. (1103) *and their drink offerings*

וּתְקָרֵב conj.-Pa. impf. 2 m.s. (קְרֵב 1111) *and you shall offer*
הִמּוֹ pr. 3 p. (1090) *them*
עַל־מַדְבְּחָה prep. (1106)-n.m.s.-def.art. (1087) *upon the altar*
דִּי בֵּית gen. (1087)-n.m.s. cstr. (1084) *of the house of*
אֱלָהֲכֹם n.m.s.-2 m.p. sf. (1080) *your God*
דִּי בִירוּשְׁלֶם rel. (1087)-prep.-pr.n. (1096) *which is in Jerusalem*

7:18

וּמָה conj.-interr. (1099) *whatever*
דִּי עֲלָיךְ rel. (1087)-prep.-2 m.s. sf. (1106) *to you*
וְעַל־אֶחָיךְ conj.-prep.-n.m.p.-2 m.s. sf. (1079) *and your brethren*
יֵיטַב Pe. impf. 3 m.s. (יְטַב 1095) *seems good*
בִּשְׁאָר prep.-n.m.s. cstr. (1114) *with the rest of*
כַּסְפָּא n.m.s.-def.art. (1097) *the silver*
וְדַהֲבָה conj.-n.m.s.-def.art. (1087) *and gold*
לְמֶעְבַּד prep.-Pe. inf. (עֲבַד 1104) *to do*
כִּרְעוּת prep.-n.f.s. cstr. (1113) *according to the will of*
אֱלָהֲכֹם n.m.s.-2 m.p. sf. (1080) *your God*
תַּעַבְדוּן Pe. impf. 2 m.p. (עֲבַד 1104) *you may do*

7:19

וּמָאנַיָּא conj.-n.m.p.-def.art. (1099) *the vessels*
דִּי־מִתְיַהֲבִין rel. (1087)-Hithpe. ptc. m.p. (יְהַב 1095) *that have been given*
לָךְ prep.-2 m.s. sf. *to you*
לְפָלְחָן prep.-n.m.s. cstr. (1108) *for the service of*
בֵּית n.m.s. cstr. (1084) *the house of*
אֱלָהָךְ n.m.s.-2 m.s. sf. (1080) *your God*
הַשְׁלֵם Haph. impv. 2 m.s. (שְׁלֵם 1115) *you shall deliver (render in full)*
קֳדָם אֱלָהּ prep. (1110)-n.m.s. cstr. (1080) *before the God of*
יְרוּשְׁלֶם pr.n. (1096) *Jerusalem*

7:20

וּשְׁאָר conj.-n.m.s. cstr. (1114) *and the remainder of*
חַשְׁחוּת n.f. coll. cstr. (1093) *the things needed for*
בֵּית n.m.s. cstr. (1084) *the house of*
אֱלָהָךְ n.m.s.-2 m.s. sf. (1080) *your God*
דִּי יִפֶּל־לָךְ rel. (1087)-Pe. impf. 3 m.s. (נְפַל 1103)-prep.-2 m.s. sf. *which you have occasion (will fall to you)*
לְמִנְתַּן prep.-Pe. inf. (נְתַן 1103) *to provide*
תִּנְתֵּן Pe. impf. 2 m.s. (נְתַן 1103) *you may provide*
מִן־בֵּית prep.-n.m.s. cstr. (1084) *out of the house of*
גִּנְזֵי n.m.p. cstr. (1086) *the treasures of*
מַלְכָּא n.m.s.-def.art. (1100) *the king*

7:21

וּמִנִּי conj.-prep.-1 c.s. sf. *and from me*
אֲנָה pers.pr. 1 c.s. (1081) *I*
אַרְתַּחְשַׁסְתְּא pr.n. (1083) *Artaxerxes*
מַלְכָּא n.m.s.-def.art. (1100) *the king*
שִׂים Peil pf. 3 m.s. (שׂוּם 1113) *is made*
טְעֵם n.m.s. (1094) *a decree*
לְכֹל prep.-n.m.s. cstr. (1097) *to all*
גִּזַּבְרַיָּא n.m.p.-def.art. (1086) *the treasurers*
דִּי בַּעֲבַר rel. (1087)-prep.-n.m.s. cstr. (1105) *which in Beyond*
נַהֲרָה n.m.s.-def.art. (1102) *the River*
דִּי כָל־דִּי conj. (1087)-n.m.s. (1097)-rel. (1087) *whatever*
יִשְׁאֲלֶנְכוֹן Pe. impf. 3 m.s.-2 m.p. sf. (שְׁאֵל 1114) *requires of you*
עֶזְרָא pr.n. (1105) *Ezra*
כָהֲנָה n.m.s.-def.art. (1096) *the priest*
סָפַר n.m.s. cstr. (1104) *the scribe of*
דָּתָא n.f.s.-def.art. (1089) *the law*
דִּי־אֱלָהּ gen. (1087)-n.m.s. cstr. (1080) *of the God of*
שְׁמַיָּא n.m.p.-def.art. (1116) *the heaven*
אָסְפַּרְנָא adv. (1082) *with all diligence*
יִתְעֲבֵד Hithpe. impf. 3 m.s. (עֲבַד 1104) *be it done*

7:22

עַד־כְּסַף prep. (1105)-n.m.s. (1097) *up to silver*
כַּכְּרִין n.f.p. (1098) *talents*
מְאָה n.f.s. (1099) *a hundred*
וְעַד־חִנְטִין conj.-v.supra-n.f.p. (1093) *wheat*
כֹּרִין n.m.p. (1096) *cors*
מְאָה v.supra *a hundred*
וְעַד־חֲמַר v.supra-n.m.s. (1093) *and wine*
בַּתִּין n.m.p. (1085) *baths*
מְאָה v.supra *a hundred*
וְעַד־בַּתִּין v.supra-v.supra *and baths*
מְשַׁח n.m.s. (1101) *oil*
מְאָה v.supra *a hundred*
וּמְלַח conj.-n.m.s. (1100) *and salt*
דִּי־לָא כְתָב rel. (1087)-neg.-n.m.s. (1098) *without prescribing how much*

7:23

כָּל־דִּי n.m.s. (1097)–conj. (1087) *whatever*
מִן־טַעַם prep. (1100)–n.m.s. cstr. (1094) *is commanded by*
אֱלָהּ n.m.s. cstr. (1080) *the God of*
שְׁמַיָּא n.m.p.–def.art. (1116) *heaven*
יִתְעֲבֵד Hithpe. impf. 3 m.s. (עֲבַד 1104) *let it be done*
אַדְרַזְדָּא adv. (1079) *in full*
לְבֵית prep.–n.m.s. cstr. (1084) *for the house of*
אֱלָהּ n.m.s. cstr. (1084) *the God of*
שְׁמַיָּא v.supra *heaven*
דִּי־לְמָה conj. (1087)–prep.–interr. (1099) *lest*
לֶהֱוֵא Pe. impf. 3 m.s. (הֲוָא 1089) *be*
קְצַף n.m.s. (1111) *wrath*
עַל־מַלְכוּת prep. (1106)–n.f.s. cstr. (1100) *against the realm of*
מַלְכָּא n.m.s.–def.art. (1100) *the king*
וּבְנוֹהִי conj.–n.m.p.–3 m.s. sf. (1085) *and his sons*

7:24

וּלְכֹם conj.–prep.–2 m.p. sf. *also you*
מְהוֹדְעִין Haph. act.ptc. m.p. (יְדַע 1095) *we notify*
דִּי כָל־כָּהֲנַיָּא conj. (1087)–n.m.s. cstr. (1097) –n.m.p.–def.art. (1096) *upon any of the priests*
וְלֵוָיֵא conj.–n.m.p.–def.art. (1099) *and Levites*
זַמָּרַיָּא n.m.p.–def.art. (1091) *the singers*
תָרָעַיָּא n.m.p.–def.art. (1118) *the door-keepers*
נְתִינַיָּא n.m.p.–def.art. (1103) *the temple servants*
וּפָלְחֵי conj.–Pe. ptc. m.p. cstr. (פְּלַח 1108) *and servants of*
בֵּית n.m.s. cstr. (1084) ... *house of*
אֱלָהָא n.m.s.–def.art. (1080) *God*
דְנָה demons.adj. (1088) *this*
מִנְדָּה n.f.s. (1101) *tribute*
בְלוֹ n.m.s. (1084) *custom*
וַהֲלָךְ conj.–n.m.s. (1090) *or toll*
לָא שַׁלִּיט neg.–adj. (1115) *it shall not be lawful*
לְמִרְמֵא prep.–Pe. inf. (רְמָא 1113) *to impose tribute*
עֲלֵיהֹם prep.–3 m.p. sf. (1106) *upon them*

7:25

וְאַנְתְּ conj.–pers.pr. 2 m.s. (1082) *and you*
עֶזְרָא pr.n. (1105) *Ezra*
כְּחָכְמַת prep.–n.f.s. cstr. (1093) *according to the wisdom of*
אֱלָהָךְ n.m.s.–2 m.s. sf. (1080) *your God*
דִּי־בִידָךְ rel. (1087)–prep.–n.f.s.–2 m.s. sf. (1094) *which is in your hand*
מֶנִּי Pa. impv. 2 m.s. (מְנָה 1101) *appoint*
שָׁפְטִין Pe. ptc. m.p. as n.m.p. (1117) *judges (magistrates)*
וְדַיָּנִין conj.–Pe. ptc. m.p. as n.m.p. (דִּין 1088) *and judges*
דִּי־לֶהֱוֺן rel. (1087)–Pe. impf. 3 m.p. (הֲוָא 1089) *who may*
דָּאנִין Pe. ptc. m.p. (דִּין 1088) *judge*
לְכָל־ prep.–n.m.s. cstr. (1097) *all*
עַמָּה n.m.s.–def.art. (1107) *the people*
דִּי בַּעֲבַר rel. (1087)–prep.–n.m.s. cstr. (1105) *in Beyond*
נַהֲרָה n.m.s.–def.art. (1102) *the River*
לְכָל־יָדְעֵי prep.–n.m.s. cstr. (1097)–Pe. act.ptc. m.p. cstr. (יְדַע 1095) *all such as know*
דָּתֵי n.f.p. (cstr.?) (1089) *laws of*
אֱלָהָךְ n.m.s.–2 m.s. sf. (1080) *your God*
וְדִי לָא יָדַע conj.–rel. (1087)–neg.–Pe. act.ptc. (1095 יְדַע) *and those who do not know*
תְּהוֹדְעוּן Haph. impf. 2 m.p. (יְדַע 1095) *you shall teach*

7:26

וְכָל־ conj.–n.m.s. (1097) *and all*
דִּי־לָא לֶהֱוֵא conj. (1097)–neg.–Pe. impf. 3 m.s. (1089 הֲוָא) *who will not*
עָבֵד Pe. act.ptc. (עֲבַד 1104) *obey*
דָתָא n.f.s.–def.art. (1089) *the law*
דִּי־אֱלָהָךְ gen. (1087)–n.m.s.–2 m.s. sf. (1080) *of your God*
וְדָתָא conj.–v.supra *and the law*
דִּי מַלְכָּא gen. (1087)–n.m.s.–def.art. (1100) *of the king*
אָסְפַּרְנָא adv. (1082) *strictly*
דִּינָה n.m.s.–def.art. (1088) *judgment*
לֶהֱוֵא Pe. impf. 3 m.s. (הֲוָא 1089) *let be*
מִתְעֲבֵד Hithpe. ptc. (עֲבַד 1104) *executed*
מִנֵּהּ prep.–3 m.s. sf. (1100) *upon him*
הֵן conj. (1090) *whether*
לְמוֹת prep.–n.m.s. (1099) *for death*
הֵן לִשְׁרֹשׁוּ v.supra–prep.–n.f.s. (1117) *for banishment*
הֵן־לַעֲנָשׁ v.supra–prep.–n.m.s. cstr. (1107) *whether for confiscation of*
נִכְסִין n.m.p. (1103) *his goods (property)*
וְלֶאֱסוּרִין conj.–prep.–n.m.p. (1082) *or for imprisonment*

7:27

בָּרוּךְ Qal pass.ptc. (138) *blessed be*
יהוה pr.n. (217) *Yahweh*
אֱלֹהֵי n.m.p. cstr. (43) *the God of*
אֲבוֹתֵינוּ n.m.p.–1 c.p. sf. (3) *our fathers*

אֲשֶׁר נָתַן rel. (81)–Qal pf. 3 m.s. (678) *who put*
כָּזֹאת prep.–demons.adj. f.s. (260) *such a thing as this*
בְּלֵב prep.–n.m.s. cstr. (524) *into the heart of*
הַמֶּלֶךְ def.art.–n.m.s. (572) *the king*
לְפָאֵר prep.–Pi. inf.cstr. (פָּאַר 802) *to beautify*
אֶת־בֵּית dir.obj.–n.m.s. cstr. (108) *the house of*
יהוה pr.n. (217) *Yahweh*
אֲשֶׁר בִּירוּשָׁלָםִ rel. (81)–prep.–pr.n. (436) *which is in Jerusalem*

7:28

וְעָלַי conj.–prep.–1 c.s. sf. *and to me*
הִטָּה־חֶסֶד Hi. pf. 3 m.s. (נָטָה 639)–n.m.s. (338) *who extended his steadfast love*
לִפְנֵי prep.–n.m.p. cstr. (815) *before*
הַמֶּלֶךְ def.art.–n.m.s. (572) *the king*
וְיוֹעֲצָיו conj.–Qal act.ptc. m.p.–3 m.s. sf. (יָעַץ 419) *and his counselors*
וּלְכָל־ conj.–prep.–n.m.s. cstr. (481) *and before all of*
שָׂרֵי n.m.p. cstr. (978) *the officers of*
הַמֶּלֶךְ def.art.–n.m.s. (572) *the king*
הַגִּבֹּרִים def.art.–adj. m.p. (150) *mighty*
וַאֲנִי conj.–pers.pr. 1 c.s. (58) *I*
הִתְחַזַּקְתִּי Hith. pf. 1 c.s. (חָזַק 305) *took courage*
כְּיַד־ prep.–n.f.s. cstr. (388) *for the hand of*
יהוה pr.n. (217) *Yahweh*
אֱלֹהַי n.m.p.–1 c.s. sf. (43) *my God*
עָלַי prep.–1 c.s. sf. *upon me*
וָאֶקְבְּצָה consec.–Qal impf. 1 c.s. (קָבַץ 867; GK 49e) *and I gathered*
מִיִּשְׂרָאֵל prep.–pr.n. (975) *from Israel*
רָאשִׁים n.m.p. (910) *leading men*
לַעֲלוֹת prep.–Qal inf.cstr. (עָלָה 748) *to go up*
עִמִּי prep.–1 c.s. sf. *with me*

8:1

וְאֵלֶּה conj.–demons.adj. c.p. (41) *these*
רָאשֵׁי n.m.p. cstr. (910) *the heads of*
אֲבֹתֵיהֶם n.m.p.–3 m.p. sf. (3) *their fathers*
וְהִתְיַחְשָׂם conj.–Hithpa. inf.cstr.–3 m.p. sf. (405; GK 64i) *this is the genealogy of those*
הָעֹלִים def.art.–Qal act.ptc. m.p. (עָלָה 748) *who went up*
עִמִּי prep.–1 c.s. sf. *with me*
בְּמַלְכוּת prep.–n.f.s. cstr. (574) *in the reign of*
אַרְתַּחְשַׁסְתְּא pr.n. (77) *Artaxerxes*
הַמֶּלֶךְ def.art.–n.m.s. (572) *the king*
מִבָּבֶל prep.–pr.n. (93) *from Babylonia*

8:2

מִבְּנֵי prep.–n.m.p. cstr. (119) *of the sons of*
פִּינְחָס pr.n. (810) *Phinehas*
גֵּרְשֹׁם pr.n. (177) *Gershom*
מִבְּנֵי v.supra *of the sons of*
אִיתָמָר pr.n. (16) *Ithamar*
דָּנִיֵּאל pr.n. (193) *Daniel*
מִבְּנֵי v.supra *of the sons of*
דָּוִיד pr.n. (187) *David*
חַטּוּשׁ pr.n. (310) *Hattush*

8:3

מִבְּנֵי v.supra *of the sons of*
שְׁכַנְיָה pr.n. (1016) *Shecaniah*
מִבְּנֵי v.supra *of the sons of*
פַרְעֹשׁ pr.n. (829) *Parosh*
זְכַרְיָה pr.n. (272) *Zechariah*
וְעִמּוֹ conj.–prep.–3 m.s. sf. *with whom*
הִתְיַחֵשׂ Hith. inf.cstr. (405) *were registered*
לִזְכָרִים prep.–v.supra *to Zechariah*
מֵאָה n.f.s. (547) *a hundred*
וַחֲמִשִּׁים conj.–num. m.p. (332) *and fifty*

8:4

מִבְּנֵי prep.–n.m.p. cstr. (119) *of the sons of*
פַּחַת מוֹאָב pr.n. (809) *Pahath-moab*
אֶלְיְהוֹעֵינַי pr.n. (41) *Eliehoenai*
בֶּן־ n.m.s. cstr. (119) *son of*
זְרַחְיָה pr.n. (280) *Zerahiah*
וְעִמּוֹ conj.–prep.–3 m.s. sf. *and with him*
מָאתַיִם n.f. du. (547) *two hundred*
הַזְּכָרִים def.art.–n.m.p. (271) *men*

8:5

מִבְּנֵי prep.–n.m.p. cstr. (119) *of the sons of*
שְׁכַנְיָה pr.n. (1016) *Shecaniah*
בֶּן־ n.m.s. cstr. (119) *son of*
יַחֲזִיאֵל pr.n. (303) *Jahaziel*
וְעִמּוֹ conj.–prep.–3 m.s. sf. *and with him*
שְׁלֹשׁ num. m.s. (1025) *three*
מֵאוֹת n.f.p. (547) *hundred*
הַזְּכָרִים def.art.–n.m.p. (271) *men*

8:6

וּמִבְּנֵי conj.–prep.–n.m.p. cstr. (119) *of the sons of*
עָדִין pr.n. (726) *Adin*
עֶבֶד pr.n. (714) *Ebed*
בֶּן־ n.m.s. cstr. (119) *son of*
יוֹנָתָן pr.n. (220) *Jonathan*
וְעִמּוֹ conj.–prep.–3 m.s. sf. *and with him*
חֲמִשִּׁים num. m.p. (332) *fifty*

הַזְּכָרִים def.art.-n.m.p. (271) *men*

8:7

וּמִבְּנֵי conj.-v.supra *and of the sons of*
עֵילָם pr.n. (743) *Elam*
יְשַׁעְיָה pr.n. (447) *Jeshaiah*
בֶּן־ n.m.s. cstr. (119) *son of*
עֲתַלְיָה pr.n. (800) *Athaliah*
וְעִמּוֹ v.supra *and with him*
שִׁבְעִים num. m.p. (988) *seventy*
הַזְּכָרִים v.supra *men*

8:8

וּמִבְּנֵי v.supra *and of the sons of*
שְׁפַטְיָה pr.n. (1049) *Shephatiah*
זְבַדְיָה pr.n. (256) *Zebadiah*
בֶּן־ v.supra *son of*
מִיכָאֵל pr.n. (567) *Michael*
וְעִמּוֹ v.supra *and with him*
שְׁמֹנִים num. m.p. (1033) *eighty*
הַזְּכָרִים v.supra *men*

8:9

מִבְּנֵי v.supra *of the sons of*
יוֹאָב pr.n. (222) *Joab*
עֹבַדְיָה pr.n. (715) *Obadiah*
בֶּן־ v.supra *son of*
יְחִיאֵל pr.n. (313) *Jehiel*
וְעִמּוֹ v.supra *and with him*
מָאתַיִם n.f. du. (547) *two hundred*
וּשְׁמֹנָה conj.-num. f.s. (1032) *and eight*
עָשָׂר num. m.s. (797) *ten*
הַזְּכָרִים v.supra *men*

8:10

וּמִבְּנֵי v.supra *and of the sons of*
שְׁלוֹמִית pr.n. (1025) *Shelomith*
בֶּן־ v.supra *son of*
יוֹסִפְיָה pr.n. (415) *Josiphiah*
וְעִמּוֹ v.supra *and with him*
מֵאָה n.f.s. (547) *a hundred*
וְשִׁשִּׁים conj.-num. m.p. (995) *and sixty*
הַזְּכָרִים v.supra *men*

8:11

וּמִבְּנֵי v.supra *and of the sons of*
בֵּבַי pr.n. (93) *Bebai*
זְכַרְיָה pr.n. (272) *Zechariah*
בֶּן־ v.supra *son of*
בֵּבָי pr.n. paus. (93) *Bebai*
וְעִמּוֹ v.supra *and with him*
עֶשְׂרִים num. m.p. (797) *twenty*
וּשְׁמֹנָה conj.-num. f.s. (1032) *and eight*
הַזְּכָרִים v.supra *men*

8:12

וּמִבְּנֵי v.supra *and of the sons of*
עַזְגָּד pr.n. (739) *Azgad*
יוֹחָנָן pr.n. (220) *Johanan*
בֶּן־ v.supra *son of*
הַקָּטָן pr.n. (882) *Hakkatan*
וְעִמּוֹ v.supra *and with him*
מֵאָה n.f.s. (547) *a hundred*
וַעֲשָׂרָה conj.-num. f.s. (797) *and ten*
הַזְּכָרִים v.supra *men*

8:13

וּמִבְּנֵי v.supra *and of the sons of*
אֲדֹנִיקָם pr.n. (12) *Adonikam*
אַחֲרֹנִים adj. f.p. (30) *those who came later*
וְאֵלֶּה conj.-demons.adj. c.p. (41) *and these*
שְׁמוֹתָם n.m.p.-3 m.p. sf. (1027) *their names*
אֱלִיפֶלֶט pr.n. (45) *Eliphelet*
יְעִיאֵל pr.n. (48) *Jeuel (Jeiel)*
וּשְׁמַעְיָה conj.-pr.n. (1035) *Shemaiah*
וְעִמָּהֶם conj.-prep.-3 m.p. sf. *and with them*
שִׁשִּׁים num. m.p. (996) *sixty*
הַזְּכָרִים v.supra *men*

8:14

וּמִבְּנֵי v.supra *and of the sons of*
בִּגְוַי pr.n. (94) *Bigvai*
עוּתַי pr.n. (736) *Uthai*
וְזַבּוּד conj.-pr.n. (256) *Zaccur (Zabbud)*
וְעִמּוֹ v.supra *and with him*
שִׁבְעִים num. m.p. (988) *seventy*
הַזְּכָרִים v.supra *men*

8:15

וָאֶקְבְּצֵם consec.-Qal impf. 1 c.s.-3 m.p. sf. (קָבַץ 867) *I gathered them*
אֶל־הַנָּהָר prep.-def.art.-n.m.s. (625) *to the river*
הַבָּא def.art.-Qal act.ptc. (בּוֹא 97) *that runs*
אֶל־אַהֲוָא prep.-pr.n. loc. (13) *to Ahava*
וַנַּחֲנֶה consec.-Qal impf. 1 c.p. (חָנָה 333) *and we encamped*
שָׁם adv. (1027) *there*
יָמִים שְׁלֹשָׁה n.m.p. (398)-num. f.s. (1025) *three days*
וָאָבִינָה consec.-Qal impf. 1 c.s. (בִּין 106) *as I reviewed*
בָעָם prep.-def.art.-n.m.s. (766) *the people*
וּבַכֹּהֲנִים conj.-prep.-def.art.-n.m.p. (463) *and the priests*

וּמִבְּנֵי conj.-prep.-n.m.p. cstr. (119) *and of the sons of*
לֵוִי pr.n. (532) *Levi*
לֹא־מָצָאתִי neg.-Qal pf. 1 c.s. (מָצָא 592) *I found none*
שָׁם adv. (1027) *there*

8:16

וָאֶשְׁלְחָה consec.-Qal impf. 1 c.s. (שָׁלַח 1018) *then I sent*
לֶאֱלִיעֶזֶר prep.-pr.n. (45) *for Eliezer*
לַאֲרִיאֵל prep.-pr.n. (72) *Ariel*
לִשְׁמַעְיָה prep.-pr.n. (1035) *Shemaiah*
וּלְאֶלְנָתָן conj.-prep.-pr.n. (46) *Elnathan*
וּלְיָרִיב conj.-prep.-pr.n. (937) *Jarib*
וּלְאֶלְנָתָן v.supra *Elnathan*
וּלְנָתָן conj.-prep.-pr.n. (681) *Nathan*
וְלִזְכַרְיָה conj.-prep.-pr.n. (272) *Zechariah*
וְלִמְשֻׁלָּם conj.-prep.-pr.n. (1024) *Meshullam*
רָאשִׁים n.m.p. (910) *leading men*
וּלְיוֹיָרִיב conj.-prep.-pr.n. (220) *and for Joiarib*
וּלְאֶלְנָתָן v.supra *and Elnathan*
מְבִינִים Hi. ptc. m.p. (בִּין 106) *men of insight*

8:17

וָאֲוַצֶּאה consec.-Pi. impf. 1 c.s. (צָוָה 845) *and I sent* (Q וָאֲצַוֶּה)
אוֹתָם dir.obj.-3 m.p. sf. *them*
עַל־אִדּוֹ prep.-pr.n. (9) *to Iddo*
הָרֹאשׁ def.art.-n.m.s. (910) *the leading man*
בְּכָסִפְיָא prep.-pr.n. loc. (494) *at Casiphia*
הַמָּקוֹם def.art.-n.m.p. (879) *the place*
וָאָשִׂימָה consec.-Qal impf. 1 c.s. (שִׂים 962) *and I set*
בְּפִיהֶם prep.-n.m.s.-3 m.p. sf. (804) *in their mouth*
דְּבָרִים n.m.p. (182) *words*
לְדַבֵּר prep.-Pi. inf.cstr. (דָּבַר 180) *to speak*
אֶל־אִדּוֹ prep.-v.supra *to Iddo*
אָחִיו n.m.s.-3 m.s. sf. (26; LXX p.) *his brother*
הַנְּתוּנִים def.art.-n.m.p. (682) *the temple servants*
בְּכָסִפְיָא prep.-v.supra *at Casiphia*
הַמָּקוֹם def.art.-n.m.s. (879) *the place*
לְהָבִיא־לָנוּ prep.-Hi. inf.cstr.-prep.-1 c.p. sf. *to send us*
מְשָׁרְתִים Pi. ptc. m.p. (שָׁרַת 1058) *ministers*
לְבֵית prep.-n.m.s. cstr. (108) *for the house of*
אֱלֹהֵינוּ n.m.p.-1 c.p. sf. (43) *our God*

8:18

וַיָּבִיאוּ consec.-Hi. impf. 3 m.p. (בּוֹא 97) *and they brought*
לָנוּ prep.-1 c.p. sf. *us*
כְּיַד־ prep.-n.f.s. cstr. (388) *by the ... hand of*
אֱלֹהֵינוּ n.m.p.-1 c.p. sf. (43) *our God*
הַטּוֹבָה def.art.-adj. f.s. (373) *good*
עָלֵינוּ prep.-1 c.p. sf. *upon us*
אִישׁ n.m.s. cstr. (35) *a man of*
שֶׂכֶל n.m.s. (968) *discretion*
מִבְּנֵי prep.-n.m.p. cstr. (119) *of the sons of*
מַחְלִי pr.n. (563) *Mahli*
בֶּן־לֵוִי n.m.s. cstr. (119)-pr.n. (532) *the son of Levi*
בֶּן־יִשְׂרָאֵל v.supra-pr.n. (975) *son of Israel*
וְשֵׁרֵבְיָה conj.-pr.n. (1055) *namely Sherebiah*
וּבָנָיו conj.-n.m.p.-3 m.s. sf. (119) *with his sons*
וְאֶחָיו conj.-n.m.p.-3 m.s. sf. (26) *and kinsmen*
שְׁמֹנָה עָשָׂר num. f.s. (1032)-num. m.s. (797) *eighteen*

8:19

וְאֶת־חֲשַׁבְיָה conj.-dir.obj.-pr.n. (364) *also Hashabiah*
וְאִתּוֹ conj.-prep.-3 m.s. sf. (II 85) *and with him*
יְשַׁעְיָה pr.n. (447) *Jeshaiah*
מִבְּנֵי prep.-n.m.p. cstr. (119) *of the sons of*
מְרָרִי pr.n. (601) *Merari*
אֶחָיו n.m.p.-3 m.s. sf. (26) *his kinsmen*
וּבְנֵיהֶם conj.-n.m.p.-3 m.p. sf. (119) *and their sons*
עֶשְׂרִים num. m.p. (797) *twenty*

8:20

וּמִן־הַנְּתִינִים conj.-prep.-def.art.-n.m.p. (682) *and of the temple servants*
שֶׁנָּתַן rel. (979)-Qal pf. 3 m.s. (678) *whom had set apart*
דָּוִיד pr.n. (187) *David*
וְהַשָּׂרִים conj.-def.art.-n.m.p. (978) *and the officials*
לַעֲבֹדַת prep.-n.f.s. cstr. (715) *for the service of*
הַלְוִיִּם def.art.-n.m.p. (532) *the Levites*
נְתִינִים n.m.p. (682) *temple servants*
מָאתַיִם n.f. du. (547) *two hundred*
וְעֶשְׂרִים conj.-num. m.p. (797) *and twenty*
כֻּלָּם n.m.s.-3 m.p. sf. (481) *these all*
נִקְּבוּ Ni. pf. 3 c.p. (נָקַב 666) *were mentioned*
בְשֵׁמוֹת prep.-n.m.p. (1027) *by name*

8:21

וָאֶקְרָא consec.-Qal impf. 1 c.s. (קָרָא 894) *then I proclaimed*
שָׁם adv. (1027) *there*
צוֹם n.m.s. (847) *a fast*

עַל־הַנָּהָר prep.-def.art.-n.m.s. (625) *at the river*
אַהֲוָא pr.n. (13) *Ahava*
לְהִתְעַנּוֹת prep.-Hith. inf.cstr. (עָנָה 776) *that we might humble ourselves*
לִפְנֵי prep.-n.m.p. cstr. (815) *before*
אֱלֹהֵינוּ n.m.p.-1 c.p. sf. (43) *our God*
לְבַקֵּשׁ prep.-Pi. inf.cstr. (בָּקַשׁ 134) *to seek*
מִמֶּנּוּ prep.-3 m.s. sf. *from him*
דֶּרֶךְ יְשָׁרָה n.m.s. cstr. (202)-adj. f.s. (449) *a straight way*
לָנוּ prep.-1 c.p. sf. *for ourselves*
וּלְטַפֵּנוּ conj.-prep.-n.m. coll.-1 c.p. sf. (381) *and for our children*
וּלְכָל־ conj.-prep.-n.m.s. cstr. (481) *and for all of*
רְכוּשֵׁנוּ n.m.s.-1 c.p. sf. (940) *our goods*

8:22

כִּי בֹשְׁתִּי conj. (471)-Qal pf. 1 c.s. (בּוֹשׁ 101) *for I was ashamed*
לִשְׁאוֹל prep.-Qal inf.cstr. (שָׁאַל 981) *to ask*
מִן־הַמֶּלֶךְ prep.-def.art.-n.m.s. (I 572) *the king*
חַיִל n.m.s. (298) *a band of soldiers*
וּפָרָשִׁים conj.-n.m.p. (832) *and horsemen*
לְעָזְרֵנוּ prep.-Qal inf.cstr.-1 c.p. sf. (עָזַר 740) *to protect us*
מֵאוֹיֵב prep.-Qal act.ptc. (אָיַב 33) *against the enemy*
בַּדָּרֶךְ prep.-def.art.-n.m.s. (202) *on our way*
כִּי־אָמַרְנוּ conj. (471)-Qal pf. 1 c.p. (אָמַר 55) *since we had told*
לַמֶּלֶךְ prep.-def.art.-n.m.s. (I 572) *the king*
לֵאמֹר prep.-Qal inf.cstr. (55) *(saying)*
יַד־ n.f.s. cstr. (388) *the hand of*
אֱלֹהֵינוּ n.m.p.-1 c.p. sf. (43) *our God*
עַל־כָּל־ prep. (752)-n.m.s. cstr. (481) *upon all that*
מְבַקְשָׁיו Pi. ptc. m.p.-3 m.s. sf. (בָּקַשׁ 134) *seek him*
לְטוֹבָה prep.-adj. f.s. (373) *for good*
וְעֻזּוֹ conj.-n.m.s.-3 m.s. sf. (738) *and his power*
וְאַפּוֹ conj.-n.m.s.-3 m.s. sf. (60) *and his wrath*
עַל כָּל־ prep. (752)-n.m.s. cstr. (481) *against all that*
עֹזְבָיו Qal act.ptc. m.p.-3 m.s. sf. (עָזַב 736) *forsake him*

8:23

וַנָּצוּמָה consec.-Qal impf. 1 c.p. (צוּם 847) *so we fasted*
וַנְּבַקְשָׁה consec.-Pi. impf. 1 c.p. (בָּקַשׁ 134) *and besought*
מֵאֱלֹהֵינוּ prep.-n.m.p.-1 c.p. sf. (43) *our God*
עַל־זֹאת prep.-demons.adj. f.s. (260) *for this*
וַיֵּעָתֵר consec.-Ni. impf. 3 m.s. (עָתַר 801; GK 51n) *and he listened to ... entreaty (he was entreated)*
לָנוּ prep.-1 c.p. sf. *for us*

8:24

וָאַבְדִּילָה consec.-Hi. impf. 1 c.s. (בָּדַל 95) *then I set apart*
מִשָּׂרֵי prep.-n.m.p. cstr. (978) *of the leaders of*
הַכֹּהֲנִים def.art.-n.m.p. (463) *priests*
שְׁנֵים עָשָׂר num. m.p. (1040)-num. m.s. (797) *twelve*
לְשֵׁרֵבְיָה prep.-pr.n. (1055) *Sherebiah*
חֲשַׁבְיָה pr.n. (365) *Hashabiah*
וְעִמָּהֶם conj.-prep.-3 m.p. sf. *and with them*
מֵאֲחֵיהֶם prep.-n.m.p.-3 m.p. sf. (26) *of their kinsmen*
עֲשָׂרָה num. f.s. (796) *ten*

8:25

וָאֶשְׁקוֹלָה consec.-Qal impf. 1 c.s. (שָׁקַל 1053) *and I weighed out*
לָהֶם prep.-3 m.p. sf. *to them*
אֶת־הַכֶּסֶף dir.obj.-def.art.-n.m.s. (494) *the silver*
וְאֶת־הַזָּהָב conj.-dir.obj.-def.art.-n.m.s. (262) *and the gold*
וְאֶת־הַכֵּלִים conj.-dir.obj.-def.art.-n.m.p. (479) *and the vessels*
תְּרוּמַת n.f.s. cstr. (929) *the offering for*
בֵּית־ n.m.s. cstr. (108) *the house of*
אֱלֹהֵינוּ n.m.p.-1 c.p. sf. (43) *our God*
הַהֵרִימוּ def.art.-as rel.pr. (GK 138i)-Hi. pf. 3 c.p. (רוּם 926) *which ... had offered*
הַמֶּלֶךְ def.art.-n.m.s. (I 572) *the king*
וְיֹעֲצָיו conj.-Qal act.ptc. m.p.-3 m.s. sf. (יָעַץ 419) *and his counselors*
וְשָׂרָיו conj.-n.m.p.-3 m.s. sf. (978) *and his lords*
וְכָל־יִשְׂרָאֵל conj.-n.m.s. cstr. (481)-pr.n. (975) *and all Israel*
הַנִּמְצָאִים def.art.-Ni. ptc. m.p. (מָצָא 592; GK 93oo) *there present*

8:26

וָאֶשְׁקֲלָה consec.-Qal impf. 1 c.s. (שָׁקַל 1053) *I weighed out*
עַל־יָדָם prep.-n.f.s.-3 m.p. sf. (388) *into their hand*
כֶּסֶף n.m.s. (494) *silver*
כִּכָּרִים n.f.p. (503) *talents*

שֵׁשׁ־מֵאוֹת num. m.s. (995)-n.f.p. (547) *six hundred*
וַחֲמִשִּׁים conj.-num. m.p. (332) *and fifty*
וּכְלֵי־כֶסֶף conj.-n.m.p. cstr. (479)-n.m.s. (494) *and silver vessels*
מֵאָה n.f.s. (547) *a hundred*
לְכִכָּרִים prep.-v.supra *of weight (talents)*
זָהָב n.m.s. (262) *gold*
מֵאָה כִכָּר n.f.s. (547)-n.f.s. (503) *a hundred talents*

8:27

וּכְפֹרֵי זָהָב conj.-n.m.p. cstr. (499)-n.m.s. (262) *and bowls of gold*
עֶשְׂרִים num. m.p. (797) *twenty*
לַאֲדַרְכֹנִים prep.-n.m.p. (204) *darics*
אָלֶף num. m.s. (48) *a thousand*
וּכְלֵי conj.-n.m.p. cstr. (479) *and vessels of*
נְחֹשֶׁת n.m.s. (638) *bronze*
מֻצְהָב Ho. ptc. (צָהֵב 843) *bright*
טוֹבָה adj. f.s. (373) *fine*
שְׁנַיִם num. m.p. (1040) *two*
חֲמוּדֹת n.f.p. (326) *as precious*
כַּזָּהָב prep.-def.art.-n.m.s. (262) *as gold*

8:28

וָאֹמְרָה consec.-Qal impf. 1 c.s. (אָמַר 55) *and I said*
אֲלֵהֶם prep.-3 m.p. sf. *to them*
אַתֶּם pers.pr. 2 m.p. (61) *you are*
קֹדֶשׁ n.m.s. (871) *holy*
לַיהוה prep.-pr.n. (217) *to Yahweh*
וְהַכֵּלִים conj.-def.art.-n.m.p. (479) *and the vessels*
קֹדֶשׁ n.m.s. (871) *are holy*
וְהַכֶּסֶף conj.-def.art.-n.m.s. (494) *and the silver*
וְהַזָּהָב conj.-def.art.-n.m.s. (262) *and the gold*
נְדָבָה n.f.s. (621) *a freewill offering*
לַיהוה prep.-pr.n. (217) *to Yahweh*
אֱלֹהֵי n.m.p. cstr. (43) *the God of*
אֲבֹתֵיכֶם n.m.p.-2 m.p. sf. (3) *your fathers*

8:29

שִׁקְדוּ Qal impv. 2 m.p. (שָׁקַד 1052) *guard*
וְשִׁמְרוּ conj.-Qal impv. 2 m.p. (שָׁמַר 1036) *and keep*
עַד־תִּשְׁקְלוּ prep. (III 723)-Qal impf. 2 m.p. (שָׁקַל 1053) *until you weigh*
לִפְנֵי שָׂרֵי prep.-n.m.p. cstr. (815)-n.m.p. cstr. (978) *before the chief*
הַכֹּהֲנִים def.art.-n.m.p. (463) *priests*
וְהַלְוִיִּם conj.-def.art.-n.m.p. (532) *and the Levites*
וְשָׂרֵי־ conj.-v.supra *and the heads of*
הָאָבוֹת def.art.-n.m.p. (3) *the fathers*
לְיִשְׂרָאֵל prep.-pr.n. (975) *in Israel*
בִּירוּשָׁלָ͏ִם prep.-pr.n. loc. (436) *at Jerusalem*
הַלִּשְׁכוֹת def.art.-n.f.p. (545; GK 127g) *the chambers*
בֵּית n.m.s. cstr. (108) *house of*
יהוה pr.n. (217) *Yahweh*

8:30

וְקִבְּלוּ conj.-Pi. pf. 3 c.p. (קָבַל 867) *so ... took over*
הַכֹּהֲנִים def.art.-n.m.p. (463) *the priests*
וְהַלְוִיִּם conj.-def.art.-n.m.p. (532) *and the Levites*
מִשְׁקַל n.m.s. cstr. (1054; GK 92g) *the weight of*
הַכֶּסֶף def.art.-n.m.s. (494) *the silver*
וְהַזָּהָב conj.-def.art.-n.m.s. (262) *and the gold*
וְהַכֵּלִים conj.-def.art.-n.m.p. (479) *and the vessels*
לְהָבִיא prep.-Hi. inf.cstr. (בּוֹא 97) *to bring*
לִירוּשָׁלַ͏ִם prep.-pr.n. loc. (436) *to Jerusalem*
לְבֵית prep.-n.m.s. cstr. (108) *to the house of*
אֱלֹהֵינוּ n.m.p.-1 c.p. sf. (43) *our God*

8:31

וַנִּסְעָה consec.-Qal impf. 1 c.p. (נָסַע 652) *then we departed*
מִנְּהַר prep.-n.m.s. cstr. (625) *from the river (of)*
אַהֲוָא pr.n. loc. (13) *Ahava*
בִּשְׁנֵים עָשָׂר prep.-num. m.s. (1040)-num. m.s. (797) *on the twelfth (day)*
לַחֹדֶשׁ prep.-def.art.-n.m.s. (294) *of the ... month*
הָרִאשׁוֹן def.art.-adj. m.s. (911) *first*
לָלֶכֶת prep.-Qal inf.cstr. (הָלַךְ 229) *to go*
יְרוּשָׁלָ͏ִם pr.n. loc. (436) *(to) Jerusalem*
וְיַד־ conj.-n.f.s. cstr. (388) *and the hand of*
אֱלֹהֵינוּ n.m.p.-1 c.p. sf. (43) *our God*
הָיְתָה Qal pf. 3 f.s. (הָיָה 224) *was*
עָלֵינוּ prep.-1 c.p. sf. *upon us*
וַיַּצִּילֵנוּ consec.-Hi. impf. 3 m.s.-1 c.p. sf. (נָצַל 664) *and he delivered us*
מִכַּף prep.-n.f.s. cstr. (496) *from the hand of*
אוֹיֵב Qal act.ptc. m.s. (אָיַב 33) *the enemy*
וְאוֹרֵב conj.-Qal act.ptc. as n. coll. (אָרַב 70) *and ambushes*
עַל־הַדָּרֶךְ prep. (752)-def.art.-n.m.s. (202) *by the way*

8:32

וַנָּבוֹא consec.-Qal impf. 1 c.p. (בּוֹא 97) *then we came*
יְרוּשָׁלָ͏ִם pr.n. loc. (436) *to Jerusalem*

וַנֵּשֶׁב consec.-Qal impf. 1 c.p. (יָשַׁב 442) *and we remained*
שָׁם adv. (1027) *there*
יָמִים שְׁלֹשָׁה n.m.p. (398)-num. f.s. (1025) *three days*

8:33

וּבַיּוֹם conj.-prep.-def.art.-n.m.s. (398) *and on the ... day*
הָרְבִיעִי def.art.-num. ord. (917) *fourth*
נִשְׁקַל Ni. pf. 3 m.s. (שָׁקַל 1053) *were weighed*
הַכֶּסֶף def.art.-n.m.s. (494) *the silver*
וְהַזָּהָב conj.-def.art.-n.m.s. (262) *and the gold*
וְהַכֵּלִים conj.-def.art.-n.m.p. (479) *and the vessels*
בְּבֵית prep.-n.m.s. cstr. (108) *within the house of*
אֱלֹהֵינוּ n.m.p.-1 c.p. sf. (43) *our God*
עַל־יַד prep. (752)-n.f.s. cstr. (388) *into the hands of*
מְרֵמוֹת pr.n. (599) *Meremoth*
בֶּן־ n.m.s. cstr. (119) *son of*
אוּרִיָּה pr.n. (22) *Uriah*
הַכֹּהֵן def.art.-n.m.s. (463) *the priest*
וְעִמּוֹ conj.-prep.-3 m.s. sf. *and with him*
אֶלְעָזָר pr.n. (46) *Eleazar*
בֶּן־ v.supra *son of*
פִּינְחָס pr.n. (810) *Phinehas*
וְעִמָּהֶם conj.-prep.-3 m.p. sf. *and with them*
יוֹזָבָד pr.n. (220) *Jozabad*
בֶּן־יֵשׁוּעַ v.supra-pr.n. (221) *the son of Jeshua*
וְנוֹעַדְיָה conj.-pr.n. (418) *and Noadiah*
בֶּן־בִּנּוּי v.supra-pr.n. (125) *the son of Binnui*
הַלְוִיִּם def.art.-n.m.p. (532) *the Levites*

8:34

בְּמִסְפָּר prep.-n.m.s. (708) *in count*
בְּמִשְׁקָל prep.-n.m.s. (1054) *in weight*
לַכֹּל prep.-def.art.-n.m.s. (481) *to the whole*
וַיִּכָּתֵב consec.-Ni. impf. 3 m.s. (כָּתַב 507) *and was recorded*
כָּל־הַמִּשְׁקָל n.m.s. cstr. (481)-def.art.-n.m.s. (1054) *the weight of everything*
בָּעֵת הַהִיא prep.-def.art.-n.f.s. (773)-def.art. -demons.adj. f.s. (214) *at that time*

8:35

הַבָּאִים def.art.-Qal act.ptc. m.p. (בּוֹא 97) *those who had come*
מֵהַשְּׁבִי prep.-def.art.-n.m.s. (985) *from captivity*
בְנֵי־הַגּוֹלָה n.m.p. cstr. (119)-def.art.-n.f.s. (163) *the returned exiles*
הִקְרִיבוּ Hi. pf. 3 c.p. (קָרַב 897) *offered*
עֹלוֹת n.f.p. (750) *burnt offerings*
לֵאלֹהֵי prep.-n.m.p. cstr. (43) *to the God of*
יִשְׂרָאֵל pr.n. (975) *Israel*
פָּרִים n.m.p. (83) *bulls*
שְׁנֵים־עָשָׂר n.m.p. (1040)-n.m.s. (797) *twelve*
עַל־כָּל־ prep.-n.m.s. cstr. (481) *for all*
יִשְׂרָאֵל pr.n. (975) *Israel*
אֵילִים n.m.p. (17) *rams*
תִּשְׁעִים num. m.p. (1077) *ninety*
וְשִׁשָּׁה conj.-num. f.s. (995) *and six*
כְּבָשִׂים n.m.p. (461) *lambs*
שִׁבְעִים num. m.p. (988) *seventy*
וְשִׁבְעָה conj.-num. f.s. (987) *and seven*
צְפִירֵי n.m.p. cstr. (862) *rams for*
חַטָּאת n.f.s. (308) *sin-offering*
שְׁנֵים עָשָׂר num. m.p. (1040)-n.m.s. (797) *twelve*
הַכֹּל def.art.-n.m.s. (481) *all*
עוֹלָה n.f.s. (750) *a burnt offering*
לַיהוה prep.-pr.n. (217) *to Yahweh*

8:36

וַיִּתְּנוּ consec.-Qal impf. 3 m.p. (נָתַן 678) *they also delivered*
אֶת־דָּתֵי dir.obj.-n.f.p. cstr. (206) *the commissions of*
הַמֶּלֶךְ def.art.-n.m.s. (572) *the king*
לַאֲחַשְׁדַּרְפְּנֵי prep.-n.m.p. cstr. (31) *to the satraps of*
הַמֶּלֶךְ v.supra *the king*
וּפַחֲווֹת conj.-n.m.p. cstr. (808) *and to the governors of*
עֵבֶר n.m.s. cstr. (719) *Beyond*
הַנָּהָר def.art.-n.m.s. (625) *the River*
וְנִשְּׂאוּ conj.-Pi. pf. 3 c.p. (669; GK 112rr) *and they aided*
אֶת־הָעָם dir.obj.-def.art.-n.m.s. (766) *the people*
וְאֶת־בֵּית־ conj.-dir.obj.-n.m.s. cstr. (108) *and the house of*
הָאֱלֹהִים def.art.-n.m.p. (43) *God*

9:1

וּכְכַלּוֹת conj.-prep.-Pi. inf.cstr. (כָּלָה 477) *and as the completion of*
אֵלֶּה demons.adj. c.p. (41) *these things*
נִגְּשׁוּ Ni. pf. 3 c.p. (נָגַשׁ 620) *approached*
אֵלַי prep.-1 c.s. sf. *(unto) me*
הַשָּׂרִים def.art.-n.m.p. (978) *the officials*
לֵאמֹר prep.-Qal inf.cstr. (55) *and said*
לֹא־נִבְדְּלוּ neg.-Ni. pf. 3 c.p. (בָּדַל 95) *have not separated themselves*
הָעָם def.art.-n.m.s. (766) *the people*
יִשְׂרָאֵל pr.n. (975) *Israel*

וְהַכֹּהֲנִים conj.-def.art.-n.m.p. (463) *and the priests*
וְהַלְוִיִּם conj.-def.art.-n.m.p. (532) *and the Levites*
מֵעַמֵּי prep.-n.m.p. cstr. (766) *from the peoples of*
הָאֲרָצוֹת def.art.-n.f.p. (75) *the lands*
כְּתוֹעֲבֹתֵיהֶם prep.-n.f.p.-3 m.p. sf. (1072) *with their abominations*
לַכְּנַעֲנִי prep.-def.art.-pr.n. gent. (489) *from the Canaanites*
הַחִתִּי def.art.-pr.n. gent. (366) *the Hittites*
הַפְּרִזִּי def.art.-pr.n. gent. (827) *the Perizzites*
הַיְבוּסִי def.art.-pr.n. gent. (101) *the Jebusites*
הָעַמֹּנִי def.art.-pr.n. gent. (770) *the Ammonites*
הַמֹּאָבִי def.art.-pr.n. gent. (555) *the Moabites*
הַמִּצְרִי def.art.-pr.n. gent. (596) *the Egyptians*
וְהָאֱמֹרִי conj.-def.art.-pr.n. gent. (57) *and the Amorites*

9:2

כִּי־נָשְׂאוּ conj. (471)-Qal pf. 3 c.p. (נָשָׂא 669) *for they have taken*
מִבְּנֹתֵיהֶם prep.-n.f.p.-3 m.p. sf. (123) *some of their daughters*
לָהֶם prep.-3 m.p. sf. *for themselves*
וְלִבְנֵיהֶם conj.-prep.-n.m.p.-3 m.p. sf. (119) *and for their sons*
וְהִתְעָרְבוּ conj.-Hith. pf. 3 c.p. (עָרַב II 786) *and they have mixed themselves (exchanged pledges)*
זֶרַע n.m.s. cstr. (282) *the seed of*
הַקֹּדֶשׁ def.art.-n.m.s. (871) *holiness*
בְּעַמֵּי prep.-n.m.p. cstr. (766) *with the peoples of*
הָאֲרָצוֹת def.art.-n.f.p. (75) *the lands*
וְיַד conj.-n.f.s. cstr. (388) *and the hand of*
הַשָּׂרִים def.art.-n.m.p. (978) *the officials*
וְהַסְּגָנִים conj.-def.art.-n.m.p. (688) *and the rulers*
הָיְתָה Qal pf. 3 f.s. (הָיָה 224) *has been*
בַּמַּעַל הַזֶּה prep.-def.art.-n.m.s. (591)-def.art.-demons.adj. m.s. (260) *in this faithlessness*
רִאשׁוֹנָה adj. f.s. (911) *foremost*

9:3

וּכְשָׁמְעִי conj.-prep.-Qal inf.cstr.-1 c.s. sf. (שָׁמַע 1033) *and when I heard*
אֶת־הַדָּבָר הַזֶּה dir.obj.-def.art.-n.m.s. (182)-def.art.-demons.adj. m.s. (260) *this (word)*
קָרַעְתִּי Qal pf. 1 c.s. (קָרַע 902) *I rent*
אֶת־בִּגְדִי dir.obj.-n.m.s.-1 c.s. sf. (93) *my garments*
וּמְעִילִי conj.-n.m.s.-1 c.s. sf. (591) *and my mantle*
וָאֶמְרְטָה consec.-Qal impf. 1 c.s. (מָרַט 598) *then I made bare*
מִשְּׂעַר רֹאשִׁי prep.-n.m.s. cstr. (972)-n.m.s.-1 c.s. sf. (910) *from the hair of my head*
וּזְקָנִי conj.-n.m.s.-1 c.s. sf. (278) *and my beard*
וָאֵשְׁבָה consec.-Qal impf. 1 c.s. (יָשַׁב 442) *then I sat*
מְשׁוֹמֵם Po'el ptc. m.s. (שָׁמֵם 1030) *appalled*

9:4

וְאֵלַי conj.-prep.-1 c.s. sf. (39) *then unto me*
יֵאָסְפוּ Ni. impf. 3 m.p. (אָסַף 62) *were gathered*
כֹּל חָרֵד n.m.s. (481)-adj. m.s. (353) *all who trembled*
בְּדִבְרֵי prep.-n.m.p. cstr. (182) *at the words of*
אֱלֹהֵי־ n.m.p. cstr. (43) *the God of*
יִשְׂרָאֵל pr.n. (975) *Israel*
עַל מַעַל prep. (752)-n.m.s. cstr. (591) *because of the faithlessness of*
הַגּוֹלָה def.art.-n.f.s. (163) *the returned exiles*
וַאֲנִי conj.-pers.pr. 1 c.s. (58) *while I*
יֹשֵׁב Qal act.ptc. m.s. (יָשַׁב 442) *sat*
מְשׁוֹמֵם Po'el ptc. m.s. (שָׁמֵם 1030) *appalled*
עַד לְמִנְחַת prep. (III 723)-prep.-n.f.s. cstr. (585) *until the offering of*
הָעָרֶב def.art.-n.m.s. paus. (787) *the evening*

9:5

וּבְמִנְחַת conj.-prep.-v.supra *and at the sacrifice of*
הָעֶרֶב def.art.-n.m.s. (787) *the evening*
קַמְתִּי Qal pf. 1 c.s. (קוּם 877) *I rose*
מִתַּעֲנִיתִי prep.-n.f.s.-1 c.s. sf. (777) *from my fasting*
וּבְקָרְעִי conj.-prep.-Qal inf.cstr.-1 c.s. sf. (קָרַע 902) *and with my rending*
בִּגְדִי n.m.s.-1 c.s. sf. (93) *my garments*
וּמְעִילִי conj.-n.m.s.-1 c.s. sf. (591) *and my mantle*
וָאֶכְרְעָה consec.-Qal impf. 1 c.s. (כָּרַע 502) *and fell*
עַל־בִּרְכַּי prep.-n.f.p.-1 c.s. sf. (139) *upon my knees*
וָאֶפְרְשָׂה consec.-Qal impf. 1 c.s. (פָּרַשׂ 831) *and spread out*
כַפַּי n.f.p.-1 c.s. sf. (496) *my hands*
אֶל־יהוה prep.-pr.n. (217) *to Yahweh*
אֱלֹהָי n.m.p.-1 c.s. sf. (43) *my God*

9:6

וָאֹמְרָה consec.-Qal impf. 1 c.s. (אָמַר 55) *saying*
אֱלֹהַי n.m.p.-1 c.s. sf. (43) *O my God*
בֹּשְׁתִּי Qal pf. 1 c.s. (בּוֹשׁ 101) *I am ashamed*

וְנִכְלַמְתִּי conj.-Ni. pf. 1 c.s. (כָּלַם 483) *and blush (am humiliated)*
לְהָרִים prep.-Hi. inf.cstr. (רוּם 926) *to raise*
אֱלֹהַי n.m.p.-1 c.s. sf. (43) *O my God*
פָּנַי n.m.p.-1 c.s. sf. (815) *my face*
אֵלֶיךָ prep.-2 m.s. sf. *to thee*
כִּי עֲוֹנֹתֵינוּ conj. (471)-n.m.p.-1 c.p. sf. (730) *for our iniquities*
רָבוּ Qal pf. 3 c.p. (רָבָה 915) *have risen (are great)*
לְמַעְלָה prep.-subst.-loc.he as adv. (751) *upwards*
רֹאשׁ n.m.s. (910; GK 22s) *a head*
וְאַשְׁמָתֵנוּ conj.-n.f.s.-1 c.p. sf. (80) *and our guilt*
גָדְלָה Qal pf. 3 f.s. (גָּדַל 152) *has mounted up (become great)*
עַד לַשָּׁמָיִם prep. (723)-prep.-def.art.-n.m. du. (1029) *to the heavens*

9:7

מִימֵי prep.-n.m.p. cstr. (398) *from the days of*
אֲבֹתֵינוּ n.m.p.-1 c.p. sf. (3) *our fathers*
אֲנַחְנוּ pers.pr. 1 c.p. (59) *we*
בְּאַשְׁמָה prep.-n.f.s. (80) *in ... guilt*
גְדֹלָה adj. f.s. (152) *great*
עַד הַיּוֹם prep. (723)-def.art.-n.m.s. (398) *to ... day*
הַזֶּה def.art.-demons.adj. m.s. (260) *this*
וּבַעֲוֹנֹתֵינוּ conj.-prep.-n.m.p.-1 c.p. sf. (730) *and for our iniquities*
נִתַּנּוּ Ni. pf. 1 c.p. (נָתַן 678) *have been given*
אֲנַחְנוּ v.supra *we*
מְלָכֵינוּ n.m.p.-1 c.p. sf. (572) *our kings*
כֹהֲנֵינוּ n.m.p.-1 c.p. sf. (463) *our priests*
בְּיַד prep.-n.f.s. cstr. (388) *into the hand of*
מַלְכֵי n.m.p. cstr. (572) *the kings of*
הָאֲרָצוֹת def.art.-n.f.p. (75) *the lands*
בַּחֶרֶב prep.-def.art.-n.f.s. (352) *to the sword*
בַּשְּׁבִי prep.-def.art.-n.m.s. (985) *to captivity*
וּבַבִּזָּה conj.-prep.-def.art.-n.f.s. (103) *to plundering*
וּבְבֹשֶׁת פָּנִים conj.-prep.-n.f.s. cstr. (102)-n.m.p. (815) *and to utter shame*
כְּהַיּוֹם הַזֶּה prep.-def.art.-n.m.s. (398)-def.art. -demons.adj. m.s. (260) *as at this day*

9:8

וְעַתָּה conj.-adv. (773) *but now*
כִּמְעַט־רֶגַע prep.-subst. cstr. (589)-n.m.s. (921) *for a brief moment (as the littleness of the moment)*
הָיְתָה Qal pf. 3 f.s. (הָיָה 224) *has been*
תְחִנָּה n.f.s. (I 337) *favor*
מֵאֵת יהוה prep.-dir.obj.-pr.n. (217) *by Yahweh*
אֱלֹהֵינוּ n.m.p.-1 c.p. sf. (43) *our God*
לְהַשְׁאִיר prep.-Hi. inf.cstr. (שָׁאַר 983) *to leave*
לָנוּ prep.-1 c.p. sf. *us*
פְּלֵיטָה n.f.s. (812) *a remnant*
וְלָתֶת־לָנוּ conj.-prep.-Qal inf.cstr. (נָתַן 678) -prep.-1 c.p. sf. *and to give us*
יָתֵד n.f.s. (450) *a secure hold (a peg or tent-pin)*
בִּמְקוֹם prep.-n.m.s. cstr. (879) *within the place of*
קָדְשׁוֹ n.m.s.-3 m.s. sf. (871) *his holiness*
לְהָאִיר prep.-Hi. inf.cstr. (אוֹר 21) *that ... may brighten*
עֵינֵינוּ n.f.p.-1 c.p. sf. (744) *our eyes*
אֱלֹהֵינוּ n.m.p.-1 c.p. sf. (43) *our God*
וּלְתִתֵּנוּ conj.-prep.-Qal inf.cstr.-1 c.p. sf. (נָתַן 678) *and grant us*
מִחְיָה n.f.s. (313) *a reviving*
מְעַט subst. (589) *little*
בְּעַבְדֻתֵנוּ prep.-n.f.s.-1 c.p. sf. (715) *in our bondage*

9:9

כִּי־עֲבָדִים conj. (471)-n.m.p. (713) *for bondmen*
אֲנַחְנוּ pers.pr. 1 c.p. (59) *we*
וּבְעַבְדֻתֵנוּ conj.-prep.-n.f.s.-1 c.p. sf. (715) *yet in our bondage*
לֹא עֲזָבָנוּ neg.-Qal pf. 3 m.s.-1 c.p. sf. (עָזַב 736) *has not forsaken us*
אֱלֹהֵינוּ n.m.p.-1 c.p. sf. (43) *our God*
וַיַּט־עָלֵינוּ consec.-Hi. impf. 3 m.s. (נָטָה 639) -prep.-1 c.p. sf. *but has extended to us*
חֶסֶד n.m.s. (338) *steadfast love*
לִפְנֵי prep.-n.m.p. cstr. (815) *before*
מַלְכֵי n.m.p. cstr. (572) *the kings of*
פָרַס pr.n. terr. (828) *Persia*
לָתֶת־לָנוּ prep.-Qal inf.cstr. (נָתַן 678)-prep.-1 c.p. sf. *to grant us*
מִחְיָה n.f.s. (313) *some reviving*
לְרוֹמֵם prep.-Polel inf.cstr. (רוּם 926) *to set up*
אֶת־בֵּית dir.obj.-n.m.s. cstr. (108) *the house of*
אֱלֹהֵינוּ n.m.p.-1 c.p. sf. (43) *our God*
וּלְהַעֲמִיד conj.-prep.-Hi. inf.cstr. (עָמַד 763) *and to repair*
אֶת־חָרְבֹתָיו dir.obj.-n.f.p.-3 m.s. sf. (352) *its ruins*
וְלָתֶת־לָנוּ conj.-prep.-Qal inf.cstr. (נָתַן 678) -prep.-1 c.p. sf. *and to give us*
גָדֵר n.m.s. (154) *protection (a wall)*
בִּיהוּדָה prep.-pr.n. loc. (397) *in Judea*
וּבִירוּשָׁלָם conj.-prep.-pr.n. (436) *and Jerusalem*

9:10

וְעַתָּה conj.-adv. (773) *and now*
מַה־נֹּאמַר interr. (552)-Qal impf. 1 c.p. (אָמַר 55) *what shall we say*
אֱלֹהֵינוּ n.m.p.-1 c.p. sf. (43) *O our God*
אַחֲרֵי־זֹאת prep. (29)-demons.adj. f.s. (260) *after this*
כִּי עָזַבְנוּ conj. (471)-Qal pf. 1 c.p. (עָזַב 736) *for we have forsaken*
מִצְוֺתֶיךָ n.f.p.-2 m.s. sf. (846) *thy commandments*

9:11

אֲשֶׁר צִוִּיתָ rel. (81)-Pi. pf. 2 m.s. (צָוָה 845) *which thou didst command*
בְּיַד prep.-n.f.s. cstr. (388) *by the hand of*
עֲבָדֶיךָ n.m.p.-2 m.s. sf. (713) *thy servants*
הַנְּבִיאִים def.art.-n.m.p. (611) *the prophets*
לֵאמֹר prep.-Qal inf.cstr. (55) *saying*
הָאָרֶץ def.art.-n.f.s. (75) *the land*
אֲשֶׁר אַתֶּם rel. (81)-pers.pr. 2 m.s. (61) *which you*
בָּאִים Qal act.ptc. m.p. (בּוֹא 97) *are entering*
לְרִשְׁתָּהּ prep.-Qal inf.cstr.-3 f.s. sf. (יָרַשׁ 439) *to take possession of it*
אֶרֶץ n.f.s. cstr. (75) *a land of*
נִדָּה n.f.s. (622) *impurity*
הִיא adj. f.s. (214) *it is*
בְּנִדַּת prep.-n.f.s. cstr. (622) *with pollutions of*
עַמֵּי n.m.p. cstr. (766) *the peoples of*
הָאֲרָצוֹת def.art.-n.f.p. (75) *the lands*
בְּתוֹעֲבֹתֵיהֶם prep.-n.f.p.-3 m.p. sf. (1072) *with their abominations*
אֲשֶׁר מִלְאוּהָ rel. (81)-Pi. pf. 3 c.p.-3 f.s. sf. (מָלֵא 570) *which have filled it*
מִפֶּה אֶל־פֶּה prep.-n.m.s. (804)-prep.-v.supra *from end to end*
בְּטֻמְאָתָם prep.-n.f.s.-3 m.p. sf. (380) *with their uncleanness*

9:12

וְעַתָּה conj.-adv. (773) *therefore*
בְּנוֹתֵיכֶם n.f.p.-2 m.p. sf. (123) *your daughters*
אַל־תִּתְּנוּ neg. (39)-Qal impf. 2 m.p. (נָתַן 678) *give not*
לִבְנֵיהֶם prep.-n.m.p.-3 m.p. sf. (119) *to their sons*
וּבְנוֹתֵיהֶם conj.-n.f.p.-3 m.p. sf. (123) *neither their daughters*
אַל־תִּשְׂאוּ neg.-Qal impf. 2 m.p. (נָשָׂא 669) *take*
לִבְנֵיכֶם prep.-n.m.p.-2 m.p. sf. (119) *for your sons*
וְלֹא־תִדְרְשׁוּ conj.-neg.-Qal impf. 2 m.p. (דָּרַשׁ 205) *and never seek*
שְׁלֹמָם n.m.s.-3 m.p. sf. (1022) *their peace*
וְטוֹבָתָם conj.-n.f.s.-3 m.p. sf. (375) *or prosperity*
עַד־עוֹלָם prep.-n.m.s. (761) *(ever)*
לְמַעַן prep.-subst. as prep. (775) *that*
תֶּחֶזְקוּ Qal impf. 2 m.p. (חָזַק 304) *you may be strong*
וַאֲכַלְתֶּם conj.-Qal pf. 2 m.p. (אָכַל 37) *and eat*
אֶת־טוּב dir.obj.-n.m.s. cstr. (375) *the good of*
הָאָרֶץ def.art.-n.f.s. (75) *the land*
וְהוֹרַשְׁתֶּם conj.-Hi. pf. 2 m.p. (יָרַשׁ 439) *and leave it for an inheritance*
לִבְנֵיכֶם prep.-n.m.p.-2 m.p. sf. (119) *to your children*
עַד־עוֹלָם prep. (723)-n.m.s. (761) *for ever*

9:13

וְאַחֲרֵי conj.-prep. (29) *and after*
כָּל־הַבָּא n.m.s. cstr. (481)-def.art.-Qal act.ptc. (97 בּוֹא) *all that has come*
עָלֵינוּ prep.-1 c.p. sf. *upon us*
בְּמַעֲשֵׂינוּ prep.-n.m.p.-1 c.p. sf. (795) *for our ... deeds*
הָרָעִים def.art.-adj. m.p. (948) *evil*
וּבְאַשְׁמָתֵנוּ conj.-prep.-n.f.s.-1 c.p. sf. (80) *and for our ... guilt*
הַגְּדֹלָה def.art.-adj. f.s. (152) *great*
כִּי אַתָּה conj. (471)-pers.pr. 2 m.s. (61) *seeing that thou*
אֱלֹהֵינוּ n.m.p.-1 c.p. sf. (43) *our God*
חָשַׂכְתָּ Qal pf. 2 m.s. (חָשַׂךְ 362) *hast punished*
לְמַטָּה prep.-adv. (641) *downwards (less)*
מֵעֲוֺנֵנוּ prep.-n.m.s.-1 c.p. sf. (730) *than our iniquities*
וְנָתַתָּה conj.-Qal pf. 2 m.s. (נָתַן 678) *and hast given*
לָנוּ prep.-1 c.p. sf. *us*
פְּלֵיטָה n.f.s. (812) *a remnant*
כָּזֹאת prep.-demons.adj. f.s. (260) *as this*

9:14

הֲנָשׁוּב interr.-Qal impf. 1 c.p. (שׁוּב 996) *shall we ... again*
לְהָפֵר prep.-Hi. inf.cstr. (פָּרַר 830) *break*
מִצְוֺתֶיךָ n.f.p.-2 m.s. sf. (846) *thy commandments*
וּלְהִתְחַתֵּן conj.-prep.-Hith. inf.cstr. (חָתַן 368) *and intermarry*
בְּעַמֵּי prep.-n.m.p. cstr. (766) *with the peoples of*
הַתֹּעֵבוֹת def.art.-n.f.p. (1072) ... *abominations*
הָאֵלֶּה def.art.-demons.adj. c.p. (41) *these*

הֲלוֹא תֶאֱנַף־ interr.-neg.-Qal impf. 2 m.s. (אָנַף 60) *wouldst thou not be angry*
בָּנוּ prep.-1 c.p. sf. *with us*
עַד־כַּלֵּה prep. (723)-Pi. inf.cstr. (כָּלָה 478; GK 75aa) *till thou wouldst consume us*
לְאֵין prep.-neg. (II 34) *so that there should be no*
שְׁאֵרִית n.f.s. (984) *remnant*
וּפְלֵיטָה conj.-n.f.s. (812) *or escape*

9:15

יהוה pr.n. (217) *O Yahweh*
אֱלֹהֵי n.m.p. cstr. (43) *God of*
יִשְׂרָאֵל pr.n. (975) *Israel*
צַדִּיק adj. m.s. (843) *art just*
אַתָּה pers.pr. 2 m.s. (61) *thou*
כִּי־נִשְׁאַרְנוּ conj. (471)-Ni. pf. 1 c.p. (שָׁאַר 983) *for we are left*
פְלֵיטָה n.f.s. (812) *that has escaped*
כְּהַיּוֹם prep.-def.art.-n.m.s. (398) *as at ... day*
הַזֶּה def.art.-demons.adj. m.s. (260) *this*
הִנְנוּ demons.part.-1 c.p. sf. (243) *behold, we*
לְפָנֶיךָ prep.-n.m.p.-2 m.s. sf. (815) *before thee*
בְּאַשְׁמָתֵינוּ prep.-n.f.s.-1 c.p. sf. (80) *in our guilt*
כִּי אֵין conj. (471)-neg. (34) *for none can*
לַעֲמוֹד prep.-Qal inf.cstr. (עָמַד 763) *stand*
לְפָנֶיךָ v.supra *before thee*
עַל־זֹאת prep. (752)-demons.adj. f.s. (260) *because of this*

10:1

וּכְהִתְפַּלֵּל conj.-prep.-Hith. inf.cstr. (פָּלַל 813) *while ... prayed*
עֶזְרָא pr.n. (740) *Ezra*
וּכְהִתְוַדֹּתוֹ conj.-prep.-Hith. inf.cstr.-3 m.s. sf. (392 יָדָה) *and made confession*
בֹּכֶה Qal inf.cstr. (בָּכָה 113) *weeping*
וּמִתְנַפֵּל conj.-Hith. ptc. (נָפַל 656) *and casting himself down*
לִפְנֵי prep.-n.m.p. cstr. (815) *before*
בֵּית n.m.s. cstr. (108) *the house of*
הָאֱלֹהִים def.art.-n.m.p. (43) *God*
נִקְבְּצוּ Ni. pf. 3 c.p. (קָבַץ 867) *were gathered*
אֵלָיו prep.-3 m.s. sf. *to him*
מִיִּשְׂרָאֵל prep.-pr.n. (975) *out of Israel*
קָהָל n.m.s. (874) *a ... assembly*
רַב־מְאֹד adj. m.s. (912)-adv. (547) *very great*
אֲנָשִׁים n.m.p. (35) *men*
וְנָשִׁים conj.-n.f.p. (61) *and women*
וִילָדִים conj.-n.m.p. (409) *and children*
כִּי־בָכוּ conj. (471)-Qal pf. 3 c.p. (בָּכָה 113) *for ... wept*
הָעָם def.art.-n.m.s. (766) *the people*
הַרְבֵּה־בֶכֶה Hi. inf.abs. (רָבָה 915)-n.m.s. (113) *bitterly*

10:2

וַיַּעַן consec.-Qal impf. 3 m.s. apoc. (עָנָה 772) *and ... answered*
שְׁכַנְיָה pr.n. (1016) *Shecaniah*
בֶן־יְחִיאֵל n.m.s. cstr. (119)-pr.n. (313) *the son of Jehiel*
מִבְּנֵי prep.-n.m.p. cstr. (119) *of the sons of*
עֵולָם pr.n. (743) *Elam*
וַיֹּאמֶר consec.-Qal impf. 3 m.s. (55) *and said*
לְעֶזְרָא prep.-pr.n. (740) *Ezra*
אֲנַחְנוּ pers.pr. 1 c.p. (59) *we*
מָעַלְנוּ Qal pf. 1 c.p. (מָעַל 591) *have broken faith*
בֵּאלֹהֵינוּ prep.-n.m.p.-1 c.p. sf. (43) *with our God*
וַנֹּשֶׁב consec.-Hi. impf. 1 c.p. (יָשַׁב 442) *and have married*
נָשִׁים n.f.p. (61) *women*
נָכְרִיּוֹת adj. f.p. (648) *foreign*
מֵעַמֵּי prep.-n.m.p. cstr. (766) *from the peoples of*
הָאָרֶץ def.art.-n.f.s. (75) *the land*
וְעַתָּה conj.-adv. (773) *but even now*
יֵשׁ־מִקְוֶה subst. (441)-n.m.s. (876) *there is hope*
לְיִשְׂרָאֵל prep.-pr.n. (975) *for Israel*
עַל־זֹאת prep. (752)-demons.adj. f.s. (260) *in spite of this*

10:3

וְעַתָּה conj.-adv. (773) *therefore*
נִכְרָת־ Qal impf. 1 c.p. (כָּרַת 503) *let us make (cut)*
בְּרִית n.f.s. (136) *a covenant*
לֵאלֹהֵינוּ prep.-n.m.p.-1 c.p. sf. (43) *with our God*
לְהוֹצִיא prep.-Hi. inf.cstr. (יָצָא 422) *to put away*
כָּל־נָשִׁים n.m.s. cstr. (481)-n.f.p. (61) *all of the women*
וְהַנּוֹלָד conj.-def.art.-Ni. ptc. m.s. (יָלַד 408) *and the ones born*
מֵהֶם prep.-3 m.p. sf. *of them*
בַּעֲצַת prep.-n.f.s. cstr. (420) *according to the counsel of*
אֲדֹנָי n.m.p.-1 c.s. sf. (10) *my lord*
וְהַחֲרֵדִים conj.-def.art.-verb.adj. m.p. (353) *and of those who tremble*
בְּמִצְוַת prep.-n.f.s. cstr. (846) *at the commandment of*

אֱלֹהֵינוּ n.m.p.–1 c.p. sf. (43) *our God*
וְכַתּוֹרָה conj.–prep.–def.art.–n.f.s. (435) *and according to the law*
יֵעָשֶׂה Ni. impf. 3 m.s. vol. (עָשָׂה 793; GK 75,l) *let it be done*

10:4

קוּם Qal impv. 2 m.s. (877) *arise*
כִּי־עָלֶיךָ conj. (471)–prep.–2 m.s. sf. *for to you*
הַדָּבָר def.art.–n.m.s. (182) *the task*
וַאֲנַחְנוּ conj.–pers.pr. 1 c.p. (59) *and we*
עִמָּךְ prep.–2 m.s. sf. paus. *with you*
חֲזַק Qal impv. 2 m.s. (חָזַק 304) *be strong*
וַעֲשֵׂה conj.–Qal impv. 2 m.s. (עָשָׂה 793) *and do it*

10:5

וַיָּקָם consec.–Qal impf. 3 m.s. (קוּם 877) *then arose*
עֶזְרָא pr.n. (740) *Ezra*
וַיַּשְׁבַּע consec.–Hi. impf. 3 m.s. (שָׁבַע 989) *and made ... take oath*
אֶת־שָׂרֵי dir.obj.–n.m.p. cstr. (978) *the leaders of*
הַכֹּהֲנִים def.art.–n.m.p. (463) *the priests*
הַלְוִיִּם def.art.–n.m.p. (532) *the Levites*
וְכָל־ conj.–n.m.s. cstr. (481) *and all of*
יִשְׂרָאֵל pr.n. (975) *Israel*
לַעֲשׂוֹת prep.–Qal inf.cstr. (עָשָׂה 793) *that they would do*
כַּדָּבָר prep.–def.art.–n.m.s. (182) *according to ... word*
הַזֶּה def.art.–demons.adj. m.s. (260) *this*
וַיִּשָּׁבֵעוּ consec.–Ni. impf. 3 m.p. paus. (שָׁבַע 989) *so they took the oath*

10:6

וַיָּקָם consec.–Qal impf. 3 m.s. (קוּם 877) *then withdrew*
עֶזְרָא pr.n. (740) *Ezra*
מִלִּפְנֵי prep.–prep.–n.m.p. cstr. (815) *from before*
בֵּית n.m.s. cstr. (108) *the house of*
הָאֱלֹהִים def.art.–n.m.p. (43) *God*
וַיֵּלֶךְ consec.–Qal impf. 3 m.s. (הָלַךְ 229) *and went*
אֶל־לִשְׁכַּת prep.–n.f.s. cstr. (545) *to the chamber of*
יְהוֹחָנָן pr.n. (220) *Jehohanan*
בֶּן־אֶלְיָשִׁיב n.m.s. cstr. (119)–pr.n. (46) *the son of Eliashib*
וַיֵּלֶךְ consec.–Qal impf. 3 m.s. (הָלַךְ 229) *and went*
שָׁם adv. (1027) *there*
לֶחֶם n.m.s. (536) *bread*
לֹא־אָכַל neg.–Qal pf. 3 m.s. (37) *neither eating*
וּמַיִם conj.–n.m.p. (565) *nor water*
לֹא־שָׁתָה neg.–Qal pf. 3 m.s. (1059) *drinking*
כִּי מִתְאַבֵּל conj. (471)–Hith. ptc. (אָבַל 5) *for he was mourning*
עַל־מַעַל prep.–n.m.s. cstr. (591) *over the faithlessness of*
הַגּוֹלָה def.art.–n.f.s. (163) *the exiles*

10:7

וַיַּעֲבִירוּ consec.–Hi. impf. 3 m.p. (עָבַר 716) *and they proclaimed*
קוֹל n.m.s. (877) *a voice*
בִּיהוּדָה prep.–pr.n. loc. (397) *throughout Judah*
וִירוּשָׁלַםִ conj.–pr.n. (436) *and Jerusalem*
לְכֹל prep.–n.m.s. cstr. (481) *to all of*
בְּנֵי n.m.p. cstr. (119) *sons of*
הַגּוֹלָה def.art.–n.f.s. (163) *the exile*
לְהִקָּבֵץ prep.–Ni. inf.cstr. (קָבַץ 867) *that they should assemble*
יְרוּשָׁלָםִ pr.n. (436) *at Jerusalem*

10:8

וְכֹל אֲשֶׁר conj.–n.m.s. (481)–rel. (81) *and that if any one*
לֹא־יָבוֹא neg.–Qal impf. 3 m.s. (בּוֹא 97) *did not come*
לִשְׁלֹשֶׁת prep.–num. f.s. cstr. (1025) *within three*
הַיָּמִים def.art.–n.m.p. (398) *days*
כַּעֲצַת prep.–n.f.s. cstr. (420) *by order of*
הַשָּׂרִים def.art.–n.m.p. (978) *the officials*
וְהַזְּקֵנִים conj.–def.art.–n.m.p. (278) *and the elders*
יָחֳרַם Ho. impf. 3 m.s. (חָרַם 355) *should be forfeited*
כָּל־רְכוּשׁוֹ n.m.s. cstr. (481)–n.m.s.–3 m.s. sf. (940) *all his property*
וְהוּא conj.–pers.pr. 3 m.s. (214) *and he himself*
יִבָּדֵל Ni. impf. 3 m.s. (בָּדַל 95) *banned*
מִקְּהַל prep.–n.m.s. cstr. (874) *from the congregation of*
הַגּוֹלָה def.art.–n.f.s. (163) *the exiles*

10:9

וַיִּקָּבְצוּ consec.–Ni. impf. 3 m.p. (קָבַץ 867) *then were assembled*
כָל־אַנְשֵׁי־ n.m.s. cstr. (481)–n.m.p. cstr. (35) *all the men of*
יְהוּדָה pr.n. (397) *Judah*
וּבִנְיָמִן conj.–pr.n. (122) *and Benjamin*
יְרוּשָׁלַםִ pr.n. (436) *at Jerusalem*

לִשְׁלֹ֫שֶׁת prep.-num. f.s. cstr. (1025) *within the three*
הַיָּמִים def.art.-n.m.p. (398) *days*
הוּא pers.pr. 3 m.s. (227) *it was*
חֹדֶשׁ n.m.s. (294) *month*
הַתְּשִׁיעִי def.art.-num.ord. m. (1077) *the ninth*
בְּעֶשְׂרִים prep.-num. m.p. (797) *on the twentieth*
בַּחֹדֶשׁ prep.-def.art.-n.m.s. (294) *of the month*
וַיֵּשְׁבוּ consec.-Qal impf. 3 m.p. (יָשַׁב 442) *and sat*
כָל־הָעָם n.m.s. cstr. (481)-def.art.-n.m.s. (766) *all the people*
בִּרְחוֹב prep.-n.f.s. cstr. (932) *in the open square of*
בֵּית n.m.s. cstr. (108) *the house of*
הָאֱלֹהִים def.art.-n.m.p. (43) *God*
מַרְעִידִים Hi. ptc. m.p. (רָעַד 944) *trembling*
עַל־הַדָּבָר prep.-def.art.-n.m.s. (182) *because of this matter*
וּמֵהַגְּשָׁמִים conj.-prep.-def.art.-n.m.p. (177) *and because of the heavy rain*

10.10

וַיָּקָם consec.-Qal impf. 3 m.s. (קוּם 877) *and stood up*
עֶזְרָא pr.n. (740) *Ezra*
הַכֹּהֵן def.art.-n.m.s. (463) *the priest*
וַיֹּאמֶר consec.-Qal impf. 3 m.s. (אָמַר 55) *and said*
אֲלֵהֶם prep.-3 m.p. sf. *to them*
אַתֶּם pers.pr. 2 m.p. (61) *you*
מְעַלְתֶּם Qal pf. 2 m.p. (מָעַל 591) *have trespassed*
וַתֹּשִׁיבוּ consec.-Hi. impf. 2 m.p. (יָשַׁב 442) *and married*
נָשִׁים n.f.p. (61) *women*
נָכְרִיּוֹת adj. f.p. (648) *foreign*
לְהוֹסִיף prep.-Hi. inf.cstr. (יָסַף 414) *and so increased*
עַל־אַשְׁמַת prep.-n.f.s. cstr. (80) *the guilt of*
יִשְׂרָאֵל pr.n. (975) *Israel*

10:11

וְעַתָּה conj.-adv. (773) *now then*
תְּנוּ Qal impv. 2 m.p. (נָתַן 678) *make*
תוֹדָה n.f.s. (392) *confession*
ליהוה prep.-pr.n. (217) *to Yahweh*
אֱלֹהֵי־ n.m.p. cstr. (43) *the God of*
אֲבֹתֵיכֶם n.m.p.-2 m.p. sf. (3) *your fathers*
וַעֲשׂוּ conj.-Qal impv. 2 m.p. (עָשָׂה 793) *and do*
רְצוֹנוֹ n.m.s.-3 m.s. sf. (953) *his will*
וְהִבָּדְלוּ conj.-Ni. impv. 2 m.p. (בָּדַל 95) *and separate yourselves*
מֵעַמֵּי prep.-n.m.p. cstr. (766) *from the people of*
הָאָרֶץ def.art.-n.f.s. (75) *the land*
וּמִן־הַנָּשִׁים conj.-prep.-def.art.-n.f.p. (61) *and from the wives*
הַנָּכְרִיּוֹת def.art.-adj. f.p. (648) *foreign*

10:12

וַיַּעֲנוּ consec.-Qal impf. 3 m.p. (עָנָה 772) *then answered*
כָל־ n.m.s. cstr. (481) *all of*
הַקָּהָל def.art.-n.m.s. (874) *the assembly*
וַיֹּאמְרוּ consec.-Qal impf. 3 m.p. (55) *and said*
קוֹל גָּדוֹל n.m.s. (876)-adj. m.s. (152) *with a loud voice*
כֵּן adv. (485) *it is so*
כִּדְבָרְךָ prep.-n.m.p.-2 m.s. sf. (182) *according to your words*
עָלֵינוּ prep.-1 c.p. sf. *to us*
לַעֲשׂוֹת prep.-Qal inf.cstr. (עָשָׂה 793) *to do*

10:13

אֲבָל adv. (6) *but*
הָעָם def.art.-n.m.s. (766) *the people*
רָב adj. m.s. (912) *are many*
וְהָעֵת conj.-def.art.-n.f.s. (773; GK 141d) *and the time*
גְּשָׁמִים n.m.p. (177) *of heavy rain*
וְאֵין כֹּחַ conj.-neg. (II 34)-n.m.s. (470) *and we cannot*
לַעֲמוֹד prep.-Qal inf.cstr. (עָמַד 763) *stand*
בַּחוּץ prep.-def.art.-n.m.s. (299) *in the open*
וְהַמְּלָאכָה conj.-def.art.-n.f.s. (521) *and the work*
לֹא־לְיוֹם neg.-prep.-def.art.- (398) *is not for ... day*
אֶחָד num. m.s. (25) *one*
וְלֹא לִשְׁנַיִם conj.-neg.-prep.-num. m. (104) *or for two*
כִּי־הִרְבִּינוּ conj. (471)-Hi. pf. 1 c.p. (רָבָה 915) *for we have greatly*
לִפְשֹׁעַ prep.-Qal inf.cstr. (פָּשַׁע 833) *transgressed*
בַּדָּבָר הַזֶּה prep.-def.art.-n.m.s. (182)-def.art. -demons.adj. m.s. (260) *in this matter*

10:14

יַעֲמְדוּ־נָא Qal impf. 3 m.p. (עָמַד 763)-part.of entreaty (609) *let ... stand*
שָׂרֵינוּ n.m.p.-1 c.p. sf. (978) *our officials*
לְכָל־ prep.-n.m.s. cstr. (481) *for the whole*
הַקָּהָל def.art.-n.m.s. (874) *assembly*

וְכֹל אֲשֶׁר conj.-n.m.s. (481)-rel. (81) *and all*
בְּעָרֵינוּ prep.-n.f.p.-1 c.p. sf. (746; GK 127i) *in our cities*
הַהֹשִׁיב def.art.-Hi. inf.cstr. (יָשַׁב 442; GK 138i) *who have taken*
נָשִׁים n.f.p. (61) *wives*
נָכְרִיּוֹת adj. f.p. (648) *foreign*
יָבֹא Qal impf. 3 m.s. (בּוֹא 97) *come*
לְעִתִּים prep.-n.m.p. (773) *at ... times*
מְזֻמָּנִים Pu. ptc. m.p. (זָמַן 273) *appointed*
וְעִמָּהֶם conj.-prep.-3 m.p. sf. *and with them*
זִקְנֵי־ adj. m.p. cstr. (278) *the elders of*
עִיר וָעִיר n.f.s. (746)-conj.-v.supra *every city*
וְשֹׁפְטֶיהָ conj.-Qal act.ptc. m.p.-3 f.s. sf. (שָׁפַט 1047) *and its judges*
עַד לְהָשִׁיב adv. (723)-prep.-Hi. inf.cstr. (שׁוּב 996) *until ... be averted*
חֲרוֹן אַף־ n.m.s. cstr. (354)-n.m.s. cstr. (60) *the fierce wrath of*
אֱלֹהֵינוּ n.m.p.-1 c.p. sf. (43) *our God*
מִמֶּנּוּ prep.-1 c.p. sf. *from us*
עַד לַדָּבָר הַזֶּה prep. (723)-prep.-def.art.-n.m.s. (182)-def.art.-demons.adj. m.s. (260) *over this matter*

10:15

אַךְ adv. (36) *only*
יוֹנָתָן pr.n. (220) *Jonathan*
בֶּן־עֲשָׂהאֵל n.m.s. cstr. (119)-pr.n. (795) *the son of Asahel*
וְיַחְזְיָה conj.-pr.n. (303) *and Jahzeiah*
בֶן־תִּקְוָה v.supra-pr.n. (876) *the son of Tikvah*
עָמְדוּ Qal pf. 3 c.p. (763) *opposed* (lit. *stood*)
עַל־זֹאת prep. (752)-demons.adj. f.s. (260) *against this*
וּמְשֻׁלָּם conj.-pr.n. (1024) *and Meshullam*
וְשַׁבְּתַי conj.-pr.n. (992) *and Shabbethai*
הַלֵּוִי def.art.-n.m.s. (532) *the Levite*
עֲזָרֻם Qal pf. 3 c.p.-3 m.p. sf. (עָזַר 740) *supported them*

10:16

וַיַּעֲשׂוּ־כֵן consec.-Qal impf. 3 m.p. (עָשָׂה 793)-adv. (485) *then ... did so*
בְּנֵי הַגּוֹלָה n.m.p. cstr. (119)-def.art.-n.f.s. (163) *the returned exiles*
וַיִּבָּדְלוּ consec.-Ni. impf. 3 m.p. (בָּדַל 95) *and selected*
עֶזְרָא pr.n. (740) *Ezra*
הַכֹּהֵן def.art.-n.m.s. (463) *the priest*
אֲנָשִׁים n.m.p. (35) *men*
רָאשֵׁי n.m.p. cstr. (910) *heads of*
הָאָבוֹת def.art.-n.m.p. (3) *the fathers*
לְבֵית prep.-n.m.s. cstr. (108) *of the house of*
אֲבֹתָם n.m.p.-3 m.p. sf. (3) *their fathers*
וְכֻלָּם conj.-n.m.s.-3 m.p. sf. (481) *and each of them*
בְּשֵׁמוֹת prep.-n.m.p. (1027) *by name*
וַיֵּשְׁבוּ consec.-Qal impf. 3 m.p. (יָשַׁב 442) *and they sat down*
בְּיוֹם אֶחָד prep.-n.m.s. (398)-num. (25) *on the first day*
לַחֹדֶשׁ prep.-def.art.-n.m.s. (294) *of the ... month*
הָעֲשִׂירִי def.art.-num.ord. (798) *tenth*
לְדַרְיוֹשׁ prep.-Qal inf.cstr. (דָּרַשׁ 205; GK 45g) *to examine*
הַדָּבָר def.art.-n.m.s. (182) *the matter*

10:17

וַיְכַלּוּ consec.-Pi. impf. 3 m.p. (כָּלָה 477) *and they had come to the end*
בַכֹּל prep.-def.art.-n.m.s. (481) *of all*
אֲנָשִׁים n.m.p. (35; GK 127cN) *men*
הַהֹשִׁיבוּ def.art. as rel. (206; GK 138i)-Hi. pf. 3 c.p. (יָשַׁב 442) *who had married*
נָשִׁים n.f.p. (61) *women*
נָכְרִיּוֹת adj. f.p. (648) *foreign*
עַד יוֹם אֶחָד prep. (723)-n.m.s. (398)-num. (25) *by the first day*
לַחֹדֶשׁ prep.-def.art.-n.m.s. (294) *of the ... month*
הָרִאשׁוֹן def.art.-adj. m.s. (911) *first*

10:18

וַיִּמָּצֵא consec.-Ni. impf. 3 m.s. (מָצָא 592) *were found*
מִבְּנֵי prep.-n.m.p. cstr. (119) *of the sons of*
הַכֹּהֲנִים def.art.-n.m.p. (463) *the priests*
אֲשֶׁר הֹשִׁיבוּ rel. (81)-Hi. pf. 3 c.p. (יָשַׁב 442) *who had married*
נָשִׁים n.f.p. (61) *(wives) women*
נָכְרִיּוֹת adj. f.p. (648) *foreign*
מִבְּנֵי v.supra *of the sons of*
יֵשׁוּעַ pr.n. (221) *Jeshua*
בֶּן־יוֹצָדָק n.m.s. cstr. (119)-pr.n. (221) *the son of Jozadak*
וְאֶחָיו conj.-n.m.p.-3 m.s. sf. (26) *and his brethren*
מַעֲשֵׂיָה pr.n. (796) *Maaseiah*
וֶאֱלִיעֶזֶר conj.-pr.n. (45) *and Eliezer*
וְיָרִיב conj.-pr.n. (937) *and Jarib*
וּגְדַלְיָה conj.-pr.n. (153) *and Gedaliah*

10:19

וַיִּתְּנוּ יָדָם consec.-Qal impf. 3 m.p. (נָתַן 678) -n.f.s.-3 m.p. sf. (388) *and they pledged themselves (and they gave their hand)*
לְהוֹצִיא prep.-Hi. inf.cstr. (יָצָא 422) *to put away*
נְשֵׁיהֶם n.f.p.-3 m.p. sf. (61) *their wives*
וַאֲשֵׁמִים conj.-adj. m.p. (79) *and guilty*
אֵיל־צֹאן n.m.s. cstr. (17)-n.f.s. (838) *a ram of a flock*
עַל־אַשְׁמָתָם prep.-n.f.s.-3 m.p. sf. (80) *for their guilt*

10:20

וּמִבְּנֵי conj.-prep.-n.m.p. cstr. (119) *of the sons of*
אִמֵּר pr.n. (57) *Immer*
חֲנָנִי pr.n. (337) *Hanani*
וּזְבַדְיָה conj.-pr.n. (256) *and Zebadiah*

10:21

וּמִבְּנֵי conj.-prep.-n.m.p. cstr. (119) *of the sons of*
חָרִם pr.n. (356) *Harim*
מַעֲשֵׂיָה pr.n. (796) *Maaseiah*
וְאֵלִיָּה conj.-pr.n. (45) *Elijah*
וּשְׁמַעְיָה conj.-pr.n. (1035) *Shemaiah*
וִיחִיאֵל conj.-pr.n. (313) *Jehiel*
וְעֻזִּיָּה conj.-pr.n. (739) *and Uzziah*

10:22

וּמִבְּנֵי conj.-prep.-n.m.p. cstr. (119) *of the sons of*
פַּשְׁחוּר pr.n. (832) *Pashhur*
אֶלְיוֹעֵינַי pr.n. (41) *Elioenai*
מַעֲשֵׂיָה pr.n. (796) *Maaseiah*
יִשְׁמָעֵאל pr.n. (1035) *Ishmael*
נְתַנְאֵל pr.n. (682) *Nethanel*
יוֹזָבָד pr.n. (220) *Jozabad*
וְאֶלְעָשָׂה conj.-pr.n. (46) *and Elasah*

10:23

וּמִן־הַלְוִיִּם conj.-prep.-def.art.-n.m.p. (532) *of the Levites*
יוֹזָבָד pr.n. (220) *Jozabad*
וְשִׁמְעִי conj.-pr.n. (1035) *Shimei*
וְקֵלָיָה conj.-pr.n. (877) *Kelaiah*
הוּא demons.adj. m.s. (214) *that is*
קְלִיטָא pr.n. (886) *Kelita*
פְּתַחְיָה pr.n. (836) *Pethahiah*
יְהוּדָה pr.n. (397) *Judah*
וֶאֱלִיעֶזֶר conj.-pr.n. (45) *and Eliezer*

10:24

וּמִן־הַמְשֹׁרְרִים conj.-prep.-def.art.-Po. ptc. m.p. (1010 שִׁיר) *of the singers*
אֶלְיָשִׁיב pr.n. (46) *Eliashib*
וּמִן־הַשֹּׁעֲרִים conj.-prep.-def.art.-n.m.p. (1045) *of the gatekeepers*
שַׁלֻּם pr.n. (1024) *Shallum*
וָטֶלֶם conj.-pr.n. (378) *Telem*
וְאוּרִי conj.-pr.n. (22) *and Uri*

10:25

וּמִיִּשְׂרָאֵל conj.-prep.-pr.n. (975) *and of Israel*
מִבְּנֵי prep.-n.m.p. cstr. (119) *of the sons of*
פַרְעֹשׁ pr.n. (829) *Parosh*
רַמְיָה pr.n. (941) *Ramiah*
וְיִזִּיָּה conj.-pr.n. (633) *Izziah*
וּמַלְכִּיָּה conj.-pr.n. (575) *Malchijah*
וּמִיָּמִן conj.-pr.n. (568) *Mijamin*
וְאֶלְעָזָר conj.-pr.n. (46) *Eleazar*
וּמַלְכִּיָּה conj.-pr.n. (575) *Malchijah*
וּבְנָיָה conj.-pr.n. (125) *and Benaiah*

10:26

וּמִבְּנֵי conj.-prep.-n.m.p. cstr. (119) *of the sons of*
עֵילָם pr.n. (743) *Elam*
מַתַּנְיָה pr.n. (682) *Mattaniah*
זְכַרְיָה pr.n. (272) *Zechariah*
וִיחִיאֵל conj.-pr.n. (313) *Jehiel*
וְעַבְדִּי conj.-pr.n. (751) *Abdi*
וִירֵמוֹת conj.-pr.n. (438) *Jeremoth*
וְאֵלִיָּה conj.-pr.n. (45) *and Elijah*

10:27

וּמִבְּנֵי conj.-prep.-n.m.p. cstr. (119) *of the sons of*
זַתּוּא pr.n. (285) *Zattu*
אֶלְיוֹעֵנַי pr.n. (41) *Elioenai*
אֶלְיָשִׁיב pr.n. (46) *Eliashib*
מַתַּנְיָה pr.n. (682) *Mattaniah*
וִירֵמוֹת conj.-pr.n. (438) *Jeremoth*
וְזָבָד conj.-pr.n. (256) *Zabad*
וַעֲזִיזָא conj.-pr.n. (739) *and Aziza*

10:28

וּמִבְּנֵי conj.-prep.-n.m.p. cstr. (119) *of the sons of*
בֵּבָי pr.n. (93) *Bebai*
יְהוֹחָנָן pr.n. (220) *Jehohanan*
חֲנַנְיָה pr.n. (337) *Hananiah*
זַבַּי pr.n. (256) *Zabbai*
עַתְלָי pr.n. (800) *Athlai*

10:29

וּמִבְּנֵי conj.-prep.-n.m.p. cstr. (119) *of the sons of*
בָּנִי pr.n. (125) *Bani*
מְשֻׁלָּם pr.n. (1024) *Meshullam*
מַלּוּךְ pr.n. (576) *Malluch*
וַעֲדָיָה conj.-pr.n. (726) *Adaiah*
יָשׁוּב pr.n. (1000) *Jashub*
וּשְׁאָל conj.-pr.n. (982) *and Sheal*
יְרָמוֹת pr.n. (438; Q וְרָמוֹת conj.-pr.n. 928) *Jeremoth*

10:30

וּמִבְּנֵי conj.-prep.-n.m.p. cstr. (119) *of the sons of*
פַּחַת מוֹאָב pr.n. (809) *Pahath-moab*
עַדְנָא pr.n. (726) *Adna*
וּכְלָל conj.-pr.n. (483) *and Chelal*
בְּנָיָה pr.n. (125) *Benaiah*
מַעֲשֵׂיָה pr.n. (796) *Maaseiah*
מַתַּנְיָה pr.n. (682) *Mattaniah*
בְצַלְאֵל pr.n. (130) *Bezalel*
וּבִנּוּי conj.-pr.n. (125) *and Binnui*
וּמְנַשֶּׁה conj.-pr.n. (586) *and Manasseh*

10:31

וּבְנֵי conj.-n.m.p. cstr. (119) *and the sons of*
חָרִם pr.n. (356) *Harim*
אֱלִיעֶזֶר pr.n. (45) *Eliezer*
יִשִּׁיָּה pr.n. (674) *Isshijah*
מַלְכִּיָּה pr.n. (575) *Malchijah*
שְׁמַעְיָה pr.n. (1035) *Shemaiah*
שִׁמְעוֹן pr.n. (1035) *Shimeon*

10:32

בִּנְיָמִן pr.n. (122) *Benjamin*
מַלּוּךְ pr.n. (576) *Malluch*
שְׁמַרְיָה pr.n. (1037) *Shemariah*

10:33

מִבְּנֵי prep.-n.m.p. cstr. (119) *of the sons of*
חָשֻׁם pr.n. (365) *Hashum*
מַתְּנַי pr.n. (682) *Mattenai*
מַתַּתָּה pr.n. (683) *Mattattah*
זָבָד pr.n. (256) *Zabad*
אֱלִיפֶלֶט pr.n. (45) *Eliphelet*
יְרֵמַי pr.n. (438) *Jeremai*
מְנַשֶּׁה pr.n. (586) *Manasseh*
שִׁמְעִי pr.n. (1035) *Shimei*

10:34

מִבְּנֵי prep.-n.m.p. cstr. (119) *of the sons of*
בָנִי pr.n. (125) *Bani*
מַעֲדַי pr.n. (588) *Maadai*
עַמְרָם pr.n. (771) *Amram*
וְאוּאֵל conj.-pr.n. (15) *and Uel*

10:35

בְּנָיָה pr.n. (125) *Benaiah*
בֵדְיָה pr.n. (95) *Bedeiah*
כְּלֻהִי pr.n. (479) *Cheluhi*

10:36

וַנְיָה pr.n. (255) *Vaniah*
מְרֵמוֹת pr.n. (599) *Meremoth*
אֶלְיָשִׁיב pr.n. (46) *Eliashib*

10:37

מַתַּנְיָה pr.n. (682) *Mattaniah*
מַתְּנַי pr.n. (682) *Mattenai*
וְיַעֲשָׂו conj.-pr.n. (795) *and Jaasu*

10:38

וּבָנִי conj.-pr.n. (125) *and Bani*
וּבִנּוּי conj.-pr.n. (125) *and Binnui*
שִׁמְעִי pr.n. (1035) *Shimei*

10:39

וְשֶׁלֶמְיָה conj.-pr.n. (1025) *and Shelemiah*
וְנָתָן conj.-pr.n. (681) *and Nathan*
וַעֲדָיָה conj.-pr.n. (726) *and Adaiah*

10:40

מַכְנַדְבַי pr.n. (569) *Machnadebai*
שָׁשַׁי pr.n. (1058) *Shashai*
שָׁרָי pr.n. (1056) *Sharai*

10:41

עֲזַרְאֵל pr.n. (741) *Azarel*
וְשֶׁלֶמְיָהוּ conj.-pr.n. (1025) *and Shelemiah*
שְׁמַרְיָה pr.n. (1037) *Shemariah*

10:42

שַׁלּוּם pr.n. (1024) *Shallum*
אֲמַרְיָה pr.n. (57) *Amariah*
יוֹסֵף pr.n. (415) *Joseph*

10:43

מִבְּנֵי prep.-n.m.p. cstr. (119) *of the sons of*
נְבוֹ pr.n. (612) *Nebo*
יְעִיאֵל pr.n. (418) *Jeiel*
מַתִּתְיָה pr.n. (682) *Mattithiah*

זָבָד pr.n. (256) *Zabad*
זְבִינָא pr.n. (259) *Zebina*
יַדַּו pr.n. (392; Q יַדַּי) *Jaddai*
וְיוֹאֵל conj.-pr.n. (222) *and Joel*
בְּנָיָה pr.n. (125) *Benaiah*

10:44

כָּל־אֵלֶּה n.m.s. cstr. (481)-demons.adj. c.p. (41) *all these*
נָשְׂאוּ Qal pf. 3 c.p. (נָשָׂא 669) *had married*
נָשִׁים n.f.p. (61) *wives*
נָכְרִיּוֹת adj. f.p. (648) *foreign*
וְיֵשׁ conj.-subst. (441) *and there are*
מֵהֶם prep.-3 m.p. sf. *from them*
נָשִׁים v.supra *wives*
וַיָּשִׂימוּ consec.-Qal impf. 3 m.p. (שִׂים 962) *and they placed*
בָּנִים n.m.p. (119) *children*

Nehemiah

1:1

דִּבְרֵי נְחֶמְיָה n.m.p. cstr. (182)-pr.n. (637) *the words of Nehemiah*

בֶּן־חֲכַלְיָה n.m.s. cstr. (119)-pr.n. (314) *the son of Hacaliah*

וַיְהִי consec.-Qal impf. 3 m.s. (**הָיָה** 224) *now it happened*

בְחֹדֶשׁ־כִּסְלֵו prep.-n.m.s. cstr. (294)-pr.n. (493) *Chislev*

שְׁנַת עֶשְׂרִים n.f.s. cstr. (1040)-num. p. (797) *in the twentieth year*

וַאֲנִי הָיִיתִי conj.-pers.pr. 1 c.s. (58)-Qal pf. 1 c.s. (224 **הָיָה**) *as I was*

בְּשׁוּשַׁן prep.-pr.n. (II 1004) *in Susa*

הַבִּירָה def.art.-n.f.s. (108) *the fortress*

1:2

וַיָּבֹא חֲנָנִי consec.-Qal impf. 3 m.s. (**בּוֹא** 97) -pr.n. (337) *that Hanani came*

אֶחָד מֵאַחַי num. (25)-prep.-n.m.p.-1 c.s. sf. (26) *one of my brethren*

הוּא וַאֲנָשִׁים pers.pr. 3 m.s. (214)-conj.-n.m.p. (35) *he and certain men*

מִיהוּדָה prep.-pr.n. (397) *out of Judah*

וָאֶשְׁאָלֵם consec.-Qal impf. 1 c.s.-3 m.p. sf. (**שָׁאַל** 981) *and I asked them*

עַל־הַיְּהוּדִים prep.-adj. gent. m.p. (I 397) *concerning the Jews*

הַפְּלֵיטָה def.art.-n.f.s. (812) *that survived*

אֲשֶׁר־נִשְׁאֲרוּ rel. (81)-Ni. pf. 3 c.p. (**שָׁאַר** 983) *who had escaped*

מִן־הַשֶּׁבִי prep.-def.art.-n.m.s. (985) *exile*

וְעַל־יְרוּשָׁלָםִ conj.-prep.-pr.n. (436) *and concerning Jerusalem*

1:3

וַיֹּאמְרוּ לִי consec.-Qal impf. 3 m.p. (**אָמַר** 55)-prep.-1 c.s. sf. *and they said to me*

הַנִּשְׁאָרִים def.art.-Ni. ptc. m.p. (**שָׁאַר** 983) *the survivors*

אֲשֶׁר־נִשְׁאֲרוּ rel. (81)-Ni. pf. 3 c.p. (**שָׁאַר** 983) *who remained*

מִן־הַשְּׁבִי prep.-def.art.-n.m.s. (985) *from exile*

שָׁם בַּמְּדִינָה adv. (1027)-prep.-def.art.-n.f.s. (193) *there in the province*

בְּרָעָה גְדֹלָה prep.-n.f.s. (949)-adj. f.s. (152) *in great trouble*

וּבְחֶרְפָּה conj.-prep.-n.f.s. (357) *and shame*

וְחוֹמַת יְרוּשָׁלַםִ conj.-n.f.s. cstr. (327)-pr.n. (436) *and the wall of Jerusalem*

מְפֹרָצֶת Pu. ptc. f.s. (**פָּרַץ** I 829) *is broken down*

וּשְׁעָרֶיהָ conj.-n.m.p.-3 f.s. sf. (1044) *and its gates*

נִצְּתוּ בָאֵשׁ Ni. pf. 3 c.p. (יָצַת 428)-prep.-def. art.-n.f.s. (77) *are destroyed by fire*

1:4

וַיְהִי כְּשָׁמְעִי consec.-Qal impf. 3 m.s. (הָיָה 224)-prep.-Qal inf.cstr.-1 c.s. sf. (שָׁמַע 1033) *when I heard*

אֶת־הַדְּבָרִים הָאֵלֶּה dir.obj.-def.art.-n.m.p. (182) -def.art.-demons.adj. c.p. (41) *these words*

יָשַׁבְתִּי Qal pf. 1 c.s. (יָשַׁב 442) *I sat down*

וָאֶבְכֶּה consec.-Qal impf. 1 c.s. (בָּכָה 113) *and wept*

וָאֶתְאַבְּלָה יָמִים consec.-Hith. impf. 1 c.s. (אָבַל 5)-n.m.p. (398) *and mourned for days*

וָאֱהִי צָם consec.-Qal impf. 1 c.s. (הָיָה 224)-Qal act.ptc. (צוּם 847) *and I continued fasting*

וּמִתְפַּלֵּל conj.-Hith. ptc. (פָּלַל 813) *and praying*

לִפְנֵי אֱלֹהֵי הַשָּׁמָיִם prep.-n.m.p. cstr. (815)-n.m.p. cstr. (43)-def.art.-n.m. du. paus. (1029) *before the God of heaven*

1:5

וָאֹמַר consec.-Qal impf. 1 c.s. (אָמַר 55) *and I said*

אָנָּא יהוה interj. (58)-pr.n. (217) *Ah, now O Yahweh*

אֱלֹהֵי הַשָּׁמַיִם n.m.p. cstr. (43)-n.m. du. (1029) *God of heaven*

הָאֵל הַגָּדוֹל def.art.-n.m.s. (42)-def.art.-adj. m.s. (152) *the great ... God*

וְהַנּוֹרָא conj.-def.art.-Ni. ptc. (יָרֵא 431) *and terrible*

שֹׁמֵר הַבְּרִית Qal act.ptc. (שָׁמַר 1036)-def.art. -n.f.s. (136) *who keeps covenant*

וָחֶסֶד conj.-n.m.s. (338) *and steadfast love*

לְאֹהֲבָיו prep.-Qal act.ptc. m.p.-3 m.s. sf. (אָהַב 12) *with those who love him*

וּלְשֹׁמְרֵי מִצְוֹתָיו conj.-prep.-Qal act.ptc. m.p. cstr. (שָׁמַר 1036)-n.f.p.-3 m.s. sf. (846) *and keep his commandments*

1:6

תְּהִי נָא Qal impf. 3 f.s. (הָיָה 224)-part.of entreaty (609) *let be*

אָזְנְךָ־קַשֶּׁבֶת n.f.s.-2 m.s. sf. (23)-adj. f.s. (904) *thy ear ... attentive*

וְעֵינֶיךָ פְתֻחוֹת conj.-n.f.p.-2 m.s. sf. (744)-Qal pass.ptc. f.p. (פָּתַח I 834) *and thy eyes open*

לִשְׁמֹעַ prep.-Qal inf.cstr. (שָׁמַע 1033) *to hear*

אֶל־תְּפִלַּת עַבְדְּךָ prep.-n.f.s. cstr. (813)-n.m.s.-2 m.s. sf. (713) *the prayer of thy servant*

אֲשֶׁר אָנֹכִי מִתְפַּלֵּל rel. (81)-pers.pr. 1 c.s. (59) -Hith. ptc. (פָּלַל 813) *which I now pray*

לְפָנֶיךָ prep.-n.m.p.-2 m.s. sf. (815) *before thee*

הַיּוֹם יוֹמָם וָלַיְלָה def.art.-n.m.s. (398)-adv. (401) -conj.-n.m.s. (538) *today day and night*

עַל־בְּנֵי יִשְׂרָאֵל prep.-n.m.p. cstr. (119)-pr.n. (975) *for the people of Israel*

עֲבָדֶיךָ n.m.p.-2 m.s. sf. (713) *thy servants*

וּמִתְוַדֶּה conj.-Hith. ptc. (יָדָה 392) *confessing*

עַל־חַטֹּאות prep.-n.f.p. cstr. (308) *the sins of*

בְּנֵי־יִשְׂרָאֵל v.supra-v.supra *the people of Israel*

אֲשֶׁר חָטָאנוּ לָךְ rel. (81)-Qal pf. 1 c.p. (חָטָא 306)-prep.-2 m.s. sf. paus. *which we have sinned against thee*

וַאֲנִי וּבֵית־אָבִי conj.-pers.pr. 1 c.s. (58)-conj. -n.m.s. cstr. (108)-n.m.s.-1 c.s. sf. (3) *Yea, I and my father's house*

חָטָאנוּ v.supra *(we) have sinned*

1:7

חֲבֹל חָבַלְנוּ לָךְ Qal inf.cstr. used as abs. (חָבַל II 287)-Qal pf. 1 c.p. (II 287)-prep.-2 m.s. sf. paus. *we have acted very corruptly against thee*

וְלֹא־שָׁמַרְנוּ conj.-neg.-Qal pf. 1 c.p. (שָׁמַר 1036) *and have not kept*

אֶת־הַמִּצְוֹת dir.obj.-def.art.-n.f.p. (846) *the commandments*

וְאֶת־הַחֻקִּים conj.-dir.obj.-def.art.-n.m.p. (349) *the statutes*

וְאֶת־הַמִּשְׁפָּטִים conj.-dir.obj.-def.art.-n.m.p. (1048) *and the ordinances*

אֲשֶׁר צִוִּיתָ rel. (81)-Pi. pf. 2 m.s. (צָוָה 845) *which thou didst command*

אֶת־מֹשֶׁה עַבְדֶּךָ dir.obj.-pr.n. (602)-n.m.s.-2 m.s. sf. (713) *thy servant Moses*

1:8

זְכָר־נָא Qal impv. 2 m.s. (זָכַר 269)-part.of entreaty (609) *remember*

אֶת־הַדָּבָר dir.obj.-def.art.-n.m.s. (182) *the word*

אֲשֶׁר צִוִּיתָ rel. (81)-Pi. pf. 2 m.s. (צָוָה 845) *which thou didst command*

אֶת־מֹשֶׁה dir.obj.-pr.n. (602) *Moses*

עַבְדְּךָ n.m.s.-2 m.s. sf. (713) *thy servant*

לֵאמֹר prep.-Qal inf.cstr. (55) *saying*

אַתֶּם תִּמְעָלוּ pers.pr. 2 m.p. (61)-Qal impf. 2 m.p. (מָעַל 591) *if you are unfaithful*

אֲנִי אָפִיץ pers.pr. 1 c.s. (58)-Hi. impf. 1 c.s. (פּוּץ 806) *I will scatter*

אֶתְכֶם בָּעַמִּים dir.obj.-2 m.p. sf.-prep.-def.art. -n.m.p. (I 766) *you among the peoples*

1:9

וְשַׁבְתֶּם אֵלַי conj.-Qal pf. 2 m.p. (שׁוּב 996) -prep.-1 c.s. sf. *but if you return to me*

וּשְׁמַרְתֶּם מִצְוֹתַי conj.-Qal pf. 2 m.p. (שָׁמַר 1036)-n.f.p.-1 c.s. sf. (846) *and keep my commandments*

וַעֲשִׂיתֶם אֹתָם conj.-Qal pf. 2 m.p. (עָשָׂה I 793)-dir.obj.-3 m.p. sf. *and do them*

אִם־יִהְיֶה hypoth.part. (49)-Qal impf. 3 m.s. (הָיָה 224) *though be*

נִדַּחֲכֶם Ni. ptc.-2 m.p. sf. (נָדַח 623) *your dispersed ones*

בִּקְצֵה הַשָּׁמַיִם prep.-n.m.s. cstr. (892)-def.art. -n.m. du. (1029) *under the farthest skies*

מִשָּׁם אֲקַבְּצֵם prep.-adv. (1027)-Pi. impf. 1 c.s.-3 m.p. sf. (קָבַץ 867) *I will gather them thence*

וַהֲבוֹאתִים conj.-Hi. pf. 1 c.s.-3 m.p. sf. (בּוֹא 97) *and bring them*

אֶל־הַמָּקוֹם prep.-def.art.-n.m.s. (879) *to the place*

אֲשֶׁר בָּחַרְתִּי rel. (81) Qal pf. 1 c.s. (בָּחַר 103) *which I have chosen*

לְשַׁכֵּן אֶת־שְׁמִי prep.-Pi. inf.cstr. (שָׁכֵן 1014) -dir.obj.-n.m.s.-1 c.s. sf. (1027) *to make my name dwell*

שָׁם adv. (1027) *there*

1:10

וְהֵם עֲבָדֶיךָ conj.-pers.pr. 3 m.p. (241)-n.m.p.-2 m.s. sf. (713) *they are thy servants*

וְעַמֶּךָ conj.-n.m.s.-2 m.s. sf. (I 766) *and thy people*

אֲשֶׁר פָּדִיתָ rel. (81)-Qal pf. 2 m.s. (פָּדָה 804) *whom thou hast redeemed*

בְּכֹחֲךָ הַגָּדוֹל prep.-n.m.s.-2 m.s. sf. (470)-def. art.-adj. m.s. (152) *by thy great power*

וּבְיָדְךָ הַחֲזָקָה conj.-prep.-n.f.s.-2 m.s. sf. (388) -def.art.-adj. f.s. (305) *and by thy strong hand*

1:11

אָנָּא אֲדֹנָי interj. (58)-n.m.p.-1 c.s. sf. (10) *ah now O Lord*

תְּהִי נָא Qal impf. 3 f.s. apoc. (הָיָה 224)-part.of entreaty (609) *let be*

אָזְנְךָ־קַשֶּׁבֶת n.f.s.-2 m.s. sf. (23)-adj. f.s. (904) *thy ear attentive*

אֶל־תְּפִלַּת עַבְדְּךָ prep.-n.f.s. cstr. (813)-n.m.s.-2 m.s. sf. (713) *to the prayer of thy servant*

וְאֶל־תְּפִלַּת עֲבָדֶיךָ conj.-v.supra-v.supra-n.m.p.-2 m.s. sf. (713) *and to the prayer of thy servants*

הַחֲפֵצִים def.art.-adj. m.p. (343) *who delight*

לְיִרְאָה אֶת־שְׁמֶךָ prep.-Qal inf.cstr. (יָרֵא 431) -dir.obj.-n.m.s.-2 m.s. sf. paus. (1027) *to fear thy name*

וְהַצְלִיחָה־נָּא conj.-Hi. impv. 2 m.s. (צָלַח II 852) -part.of entreaty (609) *and give success*

לְעַבְדְּךָ prep.-n.m.s.-2 m.s. sf. (713) *to thy servant*

הַיּוֹם def.art.-n.m.s. (398) *today*

וּתְנֵהוּ לְרַחֲמִים conj.-Qal impv. 2 m.s.-3 m.s. sf. (678 נָתַן)-prep.-n.m.p. (933) *and grant him mercy*

לִפְנֵי הָאִישׁ הַזֶּה prep.-n.m.p. cstr. (815)-def.art. -n.m.s. (35)-def.art.-demons.adj. m.s. (260) *in the sight of this man*

וַאֲנִי הָיִיתִי conj.-pers.pr. 1 c.s. (58)-Qal pf. 1 c.s. (224 הָיָה) *now I was*

מַשְׁקֶה n.m.s. (I 1052) *cupbearer*

לַמֶּלֶךְ prep.-def.art.-n.m.s. (I 572) *to the king*

2:1

וַיְהִי בְּחֹדֶשׁ נִיסָן consec.-Qal impf. 3 m.s. (הָיָה 224)-prep.-n.m.s. cstr. (I 294)-pr.n. (644) *in the month of Nisan*

שְׁנַת עֶשְׂרִים n.f.s. cstr. (1040)-num. p. (797) *in the twentieth year*

לְאַרְתַּחְשַׁסְתְּא prep.-pr.n. (77) *of Artaxerxes*

הַמֶּלֶךְ def.art.-n.m.s. (I 572) *the king*

יַיִן לְפָנָיו n.m.s. (406)-prep.-n.m.p.-3 m.s. sf. (815) *when wine was before him*

וָאֶשָּׂא אֶת־הַיַּיִן conj.-Qal impf. 1 c.s. (נָשָׂא 669) -dir.obj.-def.art.-n.m.s. (406) *I took up the wine*

וָאֶתְּנָה לַמֶּלֶךְ consec.-Qal impf. 1 c.s. (נָתַן 678) -prep.-def.art.-n.m.s. (I 572) *and gave it to the king*

וְלֹא־הָיִיתִי רַע conj.-neg.-Qal pf. 1 c.s. (הָיָה 224)-adj. m.s. (I 948) *now I had not been sad*

לְפָנָיו prep.-n.m.p.-3 m.s. sf. (815) *in his presence*

2:2

וַיֹּאמֶר לִי consec.-Qal impf. 3 m.s. (אָמַר 55) -prep.-1 c.s. sf. *and said to me*

הַמֶּלֶךְ def.art.-n.m.s. (I 572) *the king*

מַדּוּעַ פָּנֶיךָ adv. (396)-n.m.p.-2 m.s. sf. (815) *why is your face*

רָעִים adj. m.p. (I 948) *sad*

וְאַתָּה conj.-pers.pr. 2 m.s. (61) *seeing you*

אֵינְךָ חוֹלֶה neg.-2 m.s. sf. (II 34)-Qal act.ptc. (I 317 **חָלָה**) *are not sick*

אֵין זֶה כִּי־אִם neg. (II 34)-demons.adj. m.s. (260) -conj. (471)-hypoth.part. (49) *this nothing else but*

רֹעַ לֵב n.m.s. cstr. (947)-n.m.s. (524) *sadness of the heart*

וָאִירָא הַרְבֵּה מְאֹד consec.-Qal impf. 1 c.s. (**יָרֵא** 431)-Hi. inf.abs. (**רָבָה** I 915)-adv. (547) *then I was very much afraid*

2:3

וָאֹמַר לַמֶּלֶךְ consec.-Qal impf. 1 c.s. (**אָמַר** 55) -prep.-def.art.-n.m.s. (I 572) *I said to the king*

הַמֶּלֶךְ לְעוֹלָם יִחְיֶה def.art.-v.supra-prep.-n.m.s. (761)-Qal impf. 3 m.s. (**חָיָה** 310) *let the king live for ever*

מַדּוּעַ לֹא־יֵרְעוּ פָנַי adv. (396)-neg.-Qal impf. 3 m.p. (**רָעַע** 949; GK 67dd)-n.m.p.-1 c.s. sf. (815) *why should not my face be sad*

אֲשֶׁר הָעִיר rel. (81)-def.art.-n.f.s. (746) *when the city*

בֵּית־קִבְרוֹת אֲבֹתַי n.m.s. cstr. (108)-n.m.p. cstr. (868)-n.m.p.-1 c.s. sf. (3) *the place of my fathers' sepulchres*

חֲרֵבָה adj. f.s. (351) *lies waste*

וּשְׁעָרֶיהָ conj.-n.m.p.-3 f.s. sf. (1044) *and its gates*

אֻכְּלוּ בָאֵשׁ Pu. pf. 3 c.p. (**אָכַל** 37)-prep.-def.art. -n.f.s. (77) *have been destroyed by fire*

2:4

וַיֹּאמֶר לִי consec.-Qal impf. 3 m.s. (**אָמַר** 55)-prep.-1 c.s. sf. *then said to me*

הַמֶּלֶךְ def.art.-n.m.s. (I 572) *the king*

עַל־מַה־זֶּה prep.-interr. (552)-demons.adj. m.s. (260) *for what*

אַתָּה מְבַקֵּשׁ pers.pr. 2 m.s. (61)-Pi. ptc. (**בָּקַשׁ** 134) *do you make request*

וָאֶתְפַּלֵּל consec.-Hith. impf. 1 c.s. (**פָּלַל** 813) *so I prayed*

אֶל־אֱלֹהֵי הַשָּׁמָיִם prep.-n.m.p. cstr. (43)-def.art. -n.m. du. paus. (1029) *to the God of heaven*

2:5

וָאֹמַר consec.-Qal impf. 1 c.s. (**אָמַר** 55) *and I said*

לַמֶּלֶךְ prep.-def.art.-n.m.s. (I 572) *to the king*

אִם־עַל־הַמֶּלֶךְ hypoth.part. (49)-prep.-def.art. -n.m.s. (I 572) *if to the king*

טוֹב Qal act.ptc. (**טוֹב** I 373) *it pleases*

וְאִם־יִיטַב עַבְדְּךָ conj.-v.supra-Qal impf. 3 m.s. (405 **יָטַב**)-n.m.s.-2 m.s. sf. (713) *and if your servant has found favor*

לְפָנֶיךָ prep.-n.m.p.-2 m.s. sf. (815) *in your sight*

אֲשֶׁר תִּשְׁלָחֵנִי rel. (81)-Qal impf. 2 m.s.-1 c.s. sf. (**שָׁלַח** 1018) *that you send me*

אֶל־יְהוּדָה prep.-pr.n. (397) *to Judah*

אֶל־עִיר קִבְרוֹת אֲבֹתַי prep.-n.f.s. cstr. (746) -n.m.p. cstr. (868)-n.m.p.-1 c.s. sf. (3) *to the city of my fathers' sepulchres*

וְאֶבְנֶנָּה conj.-Qal impf. 1 c.s.-3 f.s. sf. (**בָּנָה** 124) *that I may rebuild it*

2:6

וַיֹּאמֶר לִי consec.-Qal impf. 3 m.s. (**אָמַר** 55) -prep.-1 c.s. sf. *and said to me*

הַמֶּלֶךְ def.art.-n.m.s. (I 572) *the king*

וְהַשֵּׁגַל conj.-def.art.-n.f.s. (993) *and the queen*

יוֹשֶׁבֶת אֶצְלוֹ Qal act.ptc. f.s. (**יָשַׁב** 442)-prep.-3 m.s. sf. (I 69) *sitting beside him*

עַד־מָתַי יִהְיֶה prep. (III 723)-adv. (607)-Qal impf. 3 m.s. (**הָיָה** 224) *how long will be*

מַהֲלָכֲךָ n.m.s.-2 m.s. sf. (237) *your journey*

וּמָתַי תָּשׁוּב conj.-v.supra-Qal impf. 2 m.s. sf. (996 **שׁוּב**) *and when will you return*

וַיִּיטַב consec.-Qal impf. 3 m.s. (**יָטַב** 405) *so it pleased*

לִפְנֵי־הַמֶּלֶךְ prep.-n.m.p. cstr. (815)-def.art.-n.m.s. (I 572) *the king*

וַיִּשְׁלָחֵנִי consec.-Qal impf. 3 m.s.-1 c.s. sf. (**שָׁלַח** 1018) *to send me*

וָאֶתְּנָה לוֹ consec.-Qal impf. 1 c.s. (**נָתַן** 678) -prep.-3 m.s. sf. *and I set him*

זְמָן n.m.s. (273) *a time*

2:7

וָאוֹמַר לַמֶּלֶךְ consec.-Qal impf. 1 c.s. (**אָמַר** 55; GK 68g)-prep.-def.art.-n.m.s. (I 572) *and I said to the king*

אִם־עַל־הַמֶּלֶךְ hypoth.part. (49)-prep.-def. art.-n.m.s. (I 572) *if unto the king*

טוֹב adj. m.s. (II 373) *it is pleasing*

אִגְּרוֹת יִתְּנוּ־לִי n.f.p. (8)-Qal impf. 3 m.p. (**נָתַן** 678)-prep.-1 c.s. sf. *let letters be given to me*

עַל־פַּחֲווֹת prep.-n.m.p. (808) *to the governors*

עֵבֶר הַנָּהָר n.m.s. cstr. (719)-def.art.-n.m.s. (625) *of Beyond the River*

אֲשֶׁר יַעֲבִירוּנִי rel. (81)-Hi. impf. 3 m.p.-1 c.s. sf. (**עָבַר** 716) *that they may let me pass through*

עַד אֲשֶׁר־אָבוֹא prep. (III 723)-v.supra-Qal impf. 1 c.s. (**בּוֹא** 97) *until I come*

אֶל־יְהוּדָה prep.-pr.n. (397) *to Judah*

2:8

וְאִגֶּרֶת conj.-n.f.s. (8) *and a letter*

אֶל־אָסָף prep.-pr.n. (63) *to Asaph*

שֹׁמֵר הַפַּרְדֵּס Qal act.ptc. (1036)-def.art.-n.m.s. (825) *the keeper of the forest*

אֲשֶׁר לַמֶּלֶךְ rel. (81)-prep.-def.art.-n.m.s. (I 572) *of the king*

אֲשֶׁר יִתֶּן־לִי v.supra-Qal impf. 3 m.s. (נָתַן 678) -prep.-1 c.s. sf. *that he may give me*

עֵצִים n.m.p. (781) *timber*

לְקָרוֹת Pi. inf.cstr. (קָרָה 900) *to make beams*

אֶת־שַׁעֲרֵי הַבִּירָה dir.obj.-n.m.p. cstr. (1044)-def. art.-n.f.s. (108) *for the gates of the fortress*

אֲשֶׁר־לַבַּיִת v.supra-prep.-def.art.-n.m.s. (108) *of the temple*

וּלְחוֹמַת הָעִיר conj.-prep.-n.f.s. cstr. (327)-def. art.-n.f.s. (746) *and for the wall of the city*

וְלַבַּיִת conj.-prep.-def.art.-n.m.s. (108) *and for the house*

אֲשֶׁר־אָבוֹא אֵלָיו v.supra-Qal impf. 1 c.s. (בּוֹא 97)-prep.-3 m.s. sf. *which I shall occupy*

וַיִּתֶּן־לִי הַמֶּלֶךְ consec.-Qal impf. 3 m.s. (נָתַן 678)-prep.-1 c.s. sf.-def.art.-n.m.s. (I 572) *and the king granted me*

כְּיַד־אֱלֹהַי prep.-n.f.s. cstr. (388)-n.m.p.-1 c.s. sf. (43) *for the ... hand of my God*

הַטּוֹבָה def.art.-adj. f.s. (II 373) *good*

עָלָי prep.-1 c.s. sf. paus. *was upon me*

2:9

וָאָבוֹא consec.-Qal impf. 1 c.s. (בּוֹא 97) *then I came*

אֶל־פַּחֲווֹת prep.-n.m.p. cstr. (808) *to the governors of*

עֵבֶר הַנָּהָר n.m.s. cstr. (719)-def.art.-n.m.s. (625) *Beyond the River*

וָאֶתְּנָה לָהֶם consec.-Qal impf. 1 c.s. (נָתַן 678) -prep.-3 m.p. sf. *and gave them*

אֵת אִגְּרוֹת הַמֶּלֶךְ dir.obj.-n.f.p. cstr. (8)-def. art.-n.m.s. (I 572) *the king's letters*

וַיִּשְׁלַח עִמִּי consec.-Qal impf. 3 m.s. (1018) -prep.-1 c.s. sf. (767) *now ... had sent with me*

הַמֶּלֶךְ v.supra *the king*

שָׂרֵי חַיִל n.m.p. cstr. (978)-n.m.s. (298) *officers of the army*

וּפָרָשִׁים conj.-n.m.p. (832) *and horsemen*

2:10

וַיִּשְׁמַע consec.-Qal impf. 3 m.s. (1033) *but when ... heard*

סַנְבַלַּט הַחֹרֹנִי pr.n. (702)-def.art.-adj. gent. (357, 111) *Sanballat the Horonite*

וְטוֹבִיָּה הָעֶבֶד conj.-pr.n. (375)-def.art.-n.m.s. (713) *and Tobiah the servant*

הָעַמֹּנִי def.art.-adj. gent. (770) *the Ammonite*

וַיֵּרַע לָהֶם consec.-Qal impf. 3 m.s. (רָעַע 949)-prep.-3 m.p. sf. *it displeased them*

רָעָה גְּדֹלָה n.f.s. (949)-adj. f.s. (152) *greatly*

אֲשֶׁר־בָּא אָדָם rel. (81)-Qal pf. 3 m.s. (בּוֹא 97)-n.m.s. (9) *that some one had come*

לְבַקֵּשׁ טוֹבָה prep.-Pi. inf.cstr. (בָּקַשׁ 134)-n.f.s. (375) *to seek the welfare*

לִבְנֵי יִשְׂרָאֵל prep.-n.m.p. cstr. (119)-pr.n. (975) *of the children of Israel*

2:11

וָאָבוֹא consec.-Qal impf. 1 c.s. (בּוֹא 97) *so I came*

אֶל־יְרוּשָׁלִָם prep.-pr.n. (436) *to Jerusalem*

וָאֱהִי־שָׁם consec.-Qal impf. 1 c.s. (הָיָה 224) -adv. (1027) *and was there*

יָמִים שְׁלֹשָׁה n.m.p. (398)-num. f.s. (1025) *three days*

2:12

וָאָקוּם לַיְלָה consec.-Qal impf. 1 c.s. (קוּם 877) -n.m.s. (538) *then I arose in the night*

אֲנִי וַאֲנָשִׁים pers.pr. 1 c.s. (58)-conj.-n.m.p. (35) *I and ... men*

מְעַט עִמִּי adv. (589; GK 131e)-prep.-1 c.s. sf. (767) *a few ... with me*

וְלֹא־הִגַּדְתִּי conj.-neg.-Hi. pf. 1 c.s. (נָגַד 616) *and I told no*

לְאָדָם prep.-n.m.s. (9) *one*

מָה אֱלֹהַי נֹתֵן interr. (552; GK 137c)-n.m.p.-1 c.s. sf. (43)-Qal act.ptc. (נָתַן 678) *what my God had put*

אֶל־לִבִּי prep.-n.m.s.-1 c.s. sf. (524) *into my heart*

לַעֲשׂוֹת prep.-Qal inf.cstr. (עָשָׂה I 793) *to do*

לִירוּשָׁלִָם prep.-pr.n. (436) *for Jerusalem*

וּבְהֵמָה אֵין עִמִּי conj.-n.f.s. (96)-neg. (II 34) -v.supra *and there was no beast with me*

כִּי אִם־הַבְּהֵמָה conj. (474)-def.art.-v.supra *but the beast*

אֲשֶׁר אֲנִי רֹכֵב בָּהּ rel. (81)-v.supra-Qal act.ptc. (938 רָכַב)-prep.-3 f.s. sf. *on which I rode*

2:13

וָאֵצְאָה consec.-Qal impf. 1 c.s. (יָצָא 422) *I went out*

בְשַׁעַר־הַגַּיא prep.-n.m.s. cstr. (1044)-def.art. -n.m.s. (161) *by the Valley Gate*

לַיְלָה n.m.s. (538) *by night*

וְאֶל־פְּנֵי עֵין הַתַּנִּין conj.-prep.-n.m.p. cstr. (815) -n.f.s. cstr. (II 745)-def.art.-n.m.p. (1072) *to the Jackal's Well*

וְאֶל־שַׁעַר הָאַשְׁפֹּת conj.-prep.-n.m.s. cstr. (1044) -def.art.-n.m.p. (1046) *and to the Dung Gate*

וָאֱהִי שֹׂבֵר consec.-Qal impf. 1 c.s. (הָיָה 224) -Qal act.ptc. (שָׂבַר I 960) *and I inspected*

בְּחוֹמֹת יְרוּשָׁלַםִ prep.-n.f.p. cstr. (327)-pr.n. (436) *the walls of Jerusalem*

אֲשֶׁר־הֵמפְּרוּצִים rel. (81)-pers.pr. 3 m.p. (241; GK 5n)-Qal pass.ptc. m.p. (פָּרַץ I 829; Q הֵם פְּרוּצִים) *which were broken down*

וּשְׁעָרֶיהָ conj.-n.m.p.-3 f.s. sf. (1044) *and its gates*

אֻכְּלוּ בָאֵשׁ Pu. pf. 3 c.p. (אָכַל 37)-prep.-def.art. -n.f.s. (77) *which had been destroyed by fire*

2:14

וָאֶעֱבֹר consec.-Qal impf. 1 c.s. (עָבַר 716) *then I went on*

אֶל־שַׁעַר הָעַיִן prep.-n.m.s. cstr. (1044)-def.art. -n.m.s. (II 745) *to the Fountain Gate*

וְאֶל־בְּרֵכַת הַמֶּלֶךְ conj.-prep.-n.f.s. cstr. (140) -def.art.-n.m.s. (I 572) *and to the King's Pool*

וְאֵין־מָקוֹם conj.-neg. (II 34)-n.m.s. (879) *but there was no place*

לַבְּהֵמָה prep.-def.art.-n.f.s. (96) *for the beast*

לַעֲבֹר תַּחְתָּי prep.-Qal inf.cstr. (עָבַר 716) -prep.-1 c.s. sf. paus. (1065) *that was under me to pass*

2:15

וָאֱהִי עֹלֶה consec.-Qal impf. 1 c.s. (הָיָה 224) -Qal act.ptc. (עָלָה 748) *then I went up*

בַנַּחַל prep.-def.art.-n.m.s. (636) *by the valley*

לַיְלָה n.m.s. (538) *in the night*

וָאֱהִי שֹׂבֵר v.supra-Qal act.ptc. (שָׂבַר I 960) *and inspected*

בַּחוֹמָה prep.-def.art.-n.f.s. (327) *the wall*

וָאָשׁוּב וָאָבוֹא consec.-Qal impf. 1 c.s. (שׁוּב 996) -consec.-Qal impf. 1 c.s. (בּוֹא 97) *and I turned back and entered*

בְּשַׁעַר הַגַּיְא prep.-n.m.s. cstr. (1044)-def.art. -n.m.s. (161) *by the Valley Gate*

וָאָשׁוּב v.supra *and so returned*

2:16

וְהַסְּגָנִים conj.-def.art.-n.m.p. (688) *and the officials*

לֹא יָדְעוּ neg.-Qal pf. 3 c.p. (יָדַע 393) *did not know*

אָנָה הָלַכְתִּי adv.-he locale (33)-Qal pf. 1 c.s. (229 הָלַךְ) *where I had gone*

וּמָה אֲנִי עֹשֶׂה conj.-interr. (552)-pers.pr. 1 c.s. (58)-Qal act.ptc. (עָשָׂה I 793) *or what I was doing*

וְלַיְּהוּדִים conj.-prep.-def.art.-adj. gent. m.p. (397) *and the Jews*

וְלַכֹּהֲנִים conj.-prep.-def.art.-n.m.p. (463) *the priests*

וְלַחֹרִים conj.-prep.-def.art.-n.m.p. (II 359) *the nobles*

וְלַסְּגָנִים conj.-prep.-def.art.-n.m.p. (688) *the officials*

וּלְיֶתֶר עֹשֵׂה הַמְּלָאכָה conj.-prep.-n.m.s. cstr. (451)-Qal act.ptc. m.s. cstr. (עָשָׂה I 793) -def.art.-n.f.s. (521) *and the rest that were to do the work*

עַד־כֵּן לֹא הִגַּדְתִּי prep. (III 723)-adv. (485)-neg. -Hi. pf. 1 c.s. (נָגַד 616) *and I had not yet told*

2:17

וָאוֹמַר אֲלֵהֶם consec.-Qal impf. 1 c.s. (אָמַר 55)-prep.-3 m.p. sf. *then I said to them*

אַתֶּם רֹאִים pers.pr. 2 m.p. (61)-Qal act.ptc. m.p. (906 רָאָה) *you see*

הָרָעָה def.art.-n.f.s. (949) *the trouble*

אֲשֶׁר אֲנַחְנוּ בָהּ rel. (81)-pers.pr. 1 c.p. (59)-prep. -3 f.s. sf. *we are in*

אֲשֶׁר יְרוּשָׁלַםִ v.supra-pr.n. (436) *how Jerusalem*

חֲרֵבָה adj. f.s. (II 351) *lies in ruins*

וּשְׁעָרֶיהָ conj.-n.m.p.-3 f.s. sf. (1044) *and its gates*

נִצְּתוּ בָאֵשׁ Ni. pf. 3 c.p. (יָצַת 428)-prep. -def.art.-n.f.s. (77) *burned with fire*

לְכוּ וְנִבְנֶה Qal impv. 2 m.p. (הָלַךְ 229)-conj.-Qal impf. 1 c.p. (בָּנָה 124) *come, let us build*

אֶת־חוֹמַת יְרוּשָׁלַםִ dir.obj.-n.f.s. cstr. (327)-pr.n. (436) *the wall of Jerusalem*

וְלֹא־נִהְיֶה עוֹד conj.-neg.-Qal impf. 1 c.p. (הָיָה 224)-adv. (728) *that we may no longer be*

חֶרְפָּה n.f.s. (357) *a reproach*

2:18

וָאַגִּיד לָהֶם consec.-Hi. impf. 1 c.s. (נָגַד 616) -prep.-3 m.p. sf. *and I told them*

אֶת־יַד אֱלֹהַי dir.obj.-n.f.s. cstr. (388)-n.m.p.-1 c.s. sf. (43) *of the hand of my God*

אֲשֶׁר־הִיא טוֹבָה עָלַי rel. (81)-pers.pr. 3 f.s. (214)-adj. f.s. (II 373)-prep.-1 c.s. sf. *which had been upon me for good*

וְאַף־דִּבְרֵי הַמֶּלֶךְ conj.-conj. (II 64)-n.m.p. cstr. (182)-def.art.-n.m.s. (I 572) *and also of the words of the king*

אֲשֶׁר אָמַר־לִי v.supra-Qal pf. 3 m.s. (55)-prep.-1 c.s. sf. *which he said to me*

וַיֹּאמְרוּ consec.-Qal impf. 3 m.p. (אָמַר 55) *and they said*

נָקוּם וּבָנִינוּ Qal impf. 1 c.p. (קוּם 877)-conj.-Qal pf. 1 c.p. (בָּנָה 124) *let us rise up and build*

וַיְחַזְּקוּ consec.-Pi. impf. 3 m.p. (חָזַק 304) *so they strengthened*

יְדֵיהֶם n.f.p.-3 m.p. sf. (388) *their hands*

לַטּוֹבָה prep.-def.art.-adj. f.s. (II 373) *for the good work*

2:19

וַיִּשְׁמַע סַנְבַלַּט consec.-Qal impf. 3 m.s. (1033) -pr.n. (702) *but when Sanballat heard*

הַחֹרֹנִי def.art.-adj. gent. (357, 111) *the Horonite*

וְטֹבִיָּה הָעֶבֶד conj.-pr.n. (375)-def.art.-n.m.s. (713) *and Tobiah the servant*

הָעַמּוֹנִי def.art.-adj. gent. (770) *the Ammonite*

וְגֶשֶׁם הָעַרְבִי conj.-pr.n. (I 177)-def.art.-adj. gent. (787) *and Geshem the Arab*

וַיַּלְעִגוּ לָנוּ consec.-Hi. impf. 3 c.p. (לָעַג 541) -prep.-1 c.p. sf. *they derided us*

וַיִּבְזוּ עָלֵינוּ consec.-Qal impf. 3 c.p. (בָּזָה 102) -prep.-1 c.p. sf. *and despised us*

וַיֹּאמְרוּ consec.-Qal impf. 3 m.p. (אָמַר 55) *and said*

מָה־הַדָּבָר הַזֶּה interr. (552)-def.art.-n.m.s. (182)-def.art.-demons.adj. m.s. (260) *what is this thing*

אֲשֶׁר אַתֶּם עֹשִׂים rel. (81)-pers.pr. 2 m.p. (61) -Qal act.ptc. m.p. (עָשָׂה I 793) *that you are doing*

הַעַל הַמֶּלֶךְ interr.part.-prep.-def.art.-n.m.s. (I 572) *are ... against the king*

אַתֶּם מֹרְדִים v.supra-Qal act.ptc. m.p. (מָרַד 597) *you rebelling*

2:20

וָאָשִׁיב אוֹתָם דָּבָר consec.-Hi. impf. 1 c.s. (שׁוּב 996)-dir.obj.-3 m.p. sf.-n.m.s. (182) *then I replied to them*

וָאוֹמַר לָהֶם consec.-Qal impf. 1 c.s. (אָמַר 55)-prep.-3 m.p. sf. *(and said to them)*

אֱלֹהֵי הַשָּׁמַיִם n.m.p. cstr. (43)-def.art.-n.m. du. (1029) *the God of heaven*

הוּא יַצְלִיחַ לָנוּ pers.pr. 3 m.s. (214)-Hi. impf. 3 m.s. (צָלַח II 852)-prep.-1 c.p. sf. *(he) will make us prosper*

וַאֲנַחְנוּ עֲבָדָיו conj.-pers.pr. 1 c.p. (59)-n.m.p.-3 m.s. sf. (713) *and we his servants*

נָקוּם וּבָנִינוּ Qal impf. 1 c.p. (קוּם 877)-conj.-Qal pf. 1 c.p. (בָּנָה 124) *will arise and build*

וְלָכֶם אֵין־חֵלֶק conj.-prep.-2 m.p. sf.-neg. (II 34)-n.m.s. (324) *but you have no portion*

וּצְדָקָה conj.-n.f.s. (842) *or right*

וְזִכָּרוֹן conj.-n.m.s. (272) *or memorial*

בִּירוּשָׁלָֽם prep.-pr.n. paus. (436) *in Jerusalem*

3:1

וַיָּקָם consec.-Qal impf. 3 m.s. (קוּם 877) *then rose up*

אֶלְיָשִׁיב pr.n. (46) *Eliashib*

הַכֹּהֵן הַגָּדוֹל def.art.-n.m.s. (463)-def.art.-adj. m.s. (152) *the high priest*

וְאֶחָיו conj.-n.m.p.-3 m.s. sf. (26) *with his brethren*

הַכֹּהֲנִים def.art.-n.m.p. (463) *the priests*

וַיִּבְנוּ consec.-Qal impf. 3 m.p. (בָּנָה 124) *and they built*

אֶת־שַׁעַר הַצֹּאן dir.obj.-n.m.s. cstr. (1044) -def.art.-n.f.s. (838) *the Sheep Gate*

הֵמָּה קִדְּשׁוּהוּ pers.pr. 3 m.p. (241)-Pi. pf. 3 c.p.-3 m.s. sf. (קָדַשׁ 872) *they consecrated it*

וַיַּעֲמִידוּ consec.-Hi. impf. 3 m.p. (עָמַד 763) *and set*

דַּלְתֹתָיו n.f.p.-3 m.s. sf. (195) *its doors*

וְעַד־מִגְדַּל הַמֵּאָה conj.-prep. (III 723)-n.m.s. cstr. (153)-def.art.-n.f.s. (547) *as far as the Tower of the Hundred*

קִדְּשׁוּהוּ v.supra *they consecrated it*

עַד מִגְדַּל חֲנַנְאֵל v.supra-v.supra-pr.n. (337) *as far as the Tower of Hananel*

3:2

וְעַל־יָדוֹ conj.-prep.-n.f.s.-3 m.s. sf. (388) *and next to him*

בָנוּ Qal pf. 3 c.p. (בָּנָה 124) *built*

אַנְשֵׁי יְרֵחוֹ n.m.p. cstr. (35)-pr.n. (437) *the men of Jericho*

וְעַל־יָדוֹ v.supra-v.supra *and next to him*

בָּנָה Qal pf. 3 m.s. (124) *built*

זַכּוּר pr.n. (271) *Zaccur*

בֶּן־אִמְרִי n.m.s. cstr. (119)-pr.n. (57) *the son of Imri*

3:3

וְאֶת שַׁעַר הַדָּגִים conj.-dir.obj.-n.m.s. cstr. (1044) -def.art.-n.m.p. (185) *and the Fish Gate*

בָּנוּ Qal pf. 3 c.p. (בָּנָה 124) *built*

בְּנֵי הַסְּנָאָה n.m.p. cstr. (119)-def.art.-pr.n. (702) *Hassenaah*

הֵמָּה קֵרוּהוּ pers.pr. 3 m.p. (241)-Pi. pf. 3 c.p.-3 m.s. sf. (קָרָה 900) *they laid its beams*

וַיַּעֲמִידוּ consec.-Hi. impf. 3 m.p. (עָמַד 763) *and set*

דַּלְתֹתָיו n.f.p.-3 m.s. sf. (195) *its doors*

מַנְעוּלָיו n.m.p.-3 m.s. sf. (653) *its bolts*

וּבְרִיחָיו conj.-n.m.p.-3 m.s. sf. (138) *and its bars*

3:4

וְעַל־יָדָם conj.-prep.-n.f.s.-3 m.p. sf. (388) *and next to them*

הֶחֱזִיק Hi. pf. 3 m.s. (חָזַק 304) *repaired*

מְרֵמוֹת pr.n. (599) *Meremoth*

בֶּן־אוּרִיָּה n.m.s. cstr. (119)-pr.n. (22) *the son of Uriah*

בֶּן־הַקּוֹץ v.supra-dir.obj.-pr.n. (881) *son of Hakkoz*

וְעַל־יָדָם v.supra-v.supra *and next to them*

הֶחֱזִיק v.supra *repaired*

מְשֻׁלָּם בֶּן־בֶּרֶכְיָה pr.n. (1024)-v.supra-pr.n. (140) *Meshullam the son of Berechiah*

בֶּן־מְשֵׁיזַבְאֵל v.supra-pr.n. (604) *son of Meshezabel*

וְעַל־יָדָם v.supra-v.supra *and next to them*

הֶחֱזִיק v.supra *repaired*

צָדוֹק בֶּן־בַּעֲנָא pr.n. (843)-v.supra-pr.n. (128) *Zadok the son of Baana*

3:5

וְעַל־יָדָם conj.-prep.-n.f.s.-3 m.p. sf. (388) *and next to them*

הֶחֱזִיקוּ Hi. pf. 3 c.p. (חָזַק 304) *repaired*

הַתְּקוֹעִים def.art.-adj. gent. m.p. (1075) *the Tekoites*

וְאַדִּירֵיהֶם conj.-adj. m.p.-3 m.p. sf. (12) *but their nobles*

לֹא־הֵבִיאוּ neg.-Hi. pf. 3 c.p. (בּוֹא 97) *did not put*

צַוָּרָם n.m.s.-3 m.p. sf. (צַוָּאר 848) *their necks*

בַּעֲבֹדַת אֲדֹנֵיהֶם prep.-n.f.s. cstr. (715)-n.m.p.-3 m.p. sf. (10) *to the work of their lords*

3:6

וְאֶת שַׁעַר הַיְשָׁנָה conj.-dir.obj.-n.m.s. cstr. (1044)-def.art.-adj. f.s. (445) *and the Old Gate*

הֶחֱזִיקוּ Hi. pf. 3 c.p. (חָזַק 304) *repaired*

יוֹיָדָע בֶּן־פָּסֵחַ pr.n. (220)-n.m.s. cstr. (119)-pr.n. (820) *Joiada the son of Paseah*

וּמְשֻׁלָּם בֶּן־בְּסוֹדְיָה conj.-pr.n. (1024)-v.supra -pr.n. (126) *and Meshullam the son of Besodeiah*

הֵמָּה קֵרוּהוּ pers.pr. 3 m.p. (241)-Pi. pf. 3 c.p.-3 m.s. sf. (קָרָה 900) *they laid its beams*

וַיַּעֲמִידוּ consec.-Hi. impf. 3 m.p. (עָמַד 763) *and set*

דַּלְתֹתָיו n.f.p.-3 m.s. sf. (195) *its doors*

וּמַנְעֻלָיו n.m.p.-3 m.s. sf. (653) *its bolts*

וּבְרִיחָיו conj.-n.m.p.-3 m.s. sf. (138) *and its bars*

3:7

וְעַל־יָדָם conj.-prep.-n.f.s.-3 m.p. sf. (388) *and next to them*

הֶחֱזִיק Hi. pf. 3 m.s. (חָזַק 304) *repaired*

מְלַטְיָה הַגִּבְעֹנִי pr.n. (572)-def.art.-adj. gent. (149) *Melatiah the Gibeonite*

וְיָדוֹן הַמֵּרֹנֹתִי conj.-pr.n. (193)-def.art.-adj. gent. (599) *and Jadon the Meronothite*

אַנְשֵׁי גִבְעוֹן n.m.p. cstr. (35)-pr.n. (149) *the men of Gibeon*

וְהַמִּצְפָּה conj.-def.art.-pr.n. (859) *and of Mizpah*

לְכִסֵּא פַּחַת prep.-n.m.s. cstr. (490)-n.m.s. cstr. (808) *under the jurisdiction of the governor of*

עֵבֶר הַנָּהָר n.m.s. cstr. (719)-def.art.-n.m.s. (625) *Beyond the River*

3:8

עַל־יָדוֹ prep.-n.f.s.-3 m.s. sf. (388) *next to them*

הֶחֱזִיק Hi. pf. 3 m.s. (חָזַק 304) *repaired*

עֻזִּיאֵל בֶּן־חַרְהֲיָה pr.n. (739)-n.m.s. cstr. (119) -pr.n. (354) *Uzziel the son of Harhaiah*

צוֹרְפִים Qal act.ptc. m.p. (צָרַף 864; GK 124o,128v) *goldsmiths*

וְעַל־יָדוֹ v.supra-v.supra *next to him*

הֶחֱזִיק v.supra *repaired*

חֲנַנְיָה pr.n. (337) *Hananiah*

בֶּן־הָרַקָּחִים n.m.s. cstr. (119)-def.art.-n.m.p. (955) *the son of perfumers*

וַיַּעַזְבוּ consec.-Qal impf. 3 m.p. (עָזַב II 738) *and they restored*

יְרוּשָׁלַםִ pr.n. (436) *Jerusalem*

עַד חוֹמָה הָרְחָבָה prep. (III 723)-n.f.s. 327)-def. art.-adj. f.s. (932) *as far as the Broad Wall*

3:9

וְעַל־יָדָם conj.-prep.-n.f.s.-3 m.p. sf. (388) *and next to them*

הֶחֱזִיק Hi. pf. 3 m.s. (חָזַק 304) *repaired*
רְפָיָה בֶן־חוּר pr.n. (951)-n.m.s. cstr. (119)-pr.n. (II 301) *Rephaiah the son of Hur*
שַׂר חֲצִי n.m.s. cstr. (978)-n.m.s. cstr. (345) *ruler of half of*
פֶּלֶךְ יְרוּשָׁלָםִ n.m.s. cstr. (813)-pr.n. (436) *the district of Jerusalem*

3:10

וְעַל־יָדָם conj.-prep.-n.f.s.-3 m.p. sf. (388) *and next to them*
הֶחֱזִיק Hi. pf. 3 m.s. (חָזַק 304) *repaired*
יְדָיָה בֶן־חֲרוּמַף pr.n. (393)-n.m.s. cstr. (119)-pr.n. (354) *Jedaiah the son of Harumaph*
וְנֶגֶד בֵּיתוֹ conj.-prep. (617)-n.m.s.-3 m.s. sf. (108) *opposite his house*
וְעַל־יָדוֹ v.supra-n.f.s.-3 m.s. sf. (388) *and next to him*
הֶחֱזִיק v.supra *repaired*
חַטּוּשׁ בֶּן־חֲשַׁבְנְיָה pr.n. (310)-v.supra-pr.n. (364) *Hattush the son of Hashabneiah*

3:11

מִדָּה שֵׁנִית n.f.s. (I 551)-adj. f. (1041) *another section*
הֶחֱזִיק Hi. pf. 3 m.s. (חָזַק 304) *repaired*
מַלְכִּיָּה בֶן־חָרִם pr.n. (575)-n.m.s. cstr. (119)-pr.n. (356) *Malchijah the son of Harim*
וְחַשּׁוּב conj.-pr.n. (363) *and Hasshub*
בֶּן־פַּחַת מוֹאָב n.m.s. cstr. (119)-pr.n. (809) *the son of Pahath-moab*
וְאֵת מִגְדַּל הַתַּנּוּרִים conj.-dir.obj.-n.m.s. cstr. (153)-def.art.-n.m.p. (1072) *and the Tower of the Ovens*

3:12

וְעַל־יָדוֹ conj.-prep.-n.f.s.-3 m.s. sf. (388) *and next to him*
הֶחֱזִיק Hi. pf. 3 m.s. (חָזַק 304) *repaired*
שַׁלּוּם בֶּן־הַלּוֹחֵשׁ pr.n. (1024)-n.m.s. cstr. (119) -def.art.-pr.n. (538) *Shallum the son of Hallohesh*
שַׂר חֲצִי n.m.s. cstr. (978)-n.m.s. cstr. (345) *ruler of half of*
פֶּלֶךְ יְרוּשָׁלָםִ n.m.s. cstr. (813)-pr.n. paus. (436) *the district of Jerusalem*
הוּא וּבְנוֹתָיו pers.pr. 3 m.s. (214)-conj.-n.f.p.-3 m.s. sf. (I 123) *he and his daughters*

3:13

אֵת שַׁעַר הַגַּיְא dir.obj.-n.m.s. cstr. (1044) -def.art.-n.m.s. (161) *the Valley Gate*
הֶחֱזִיק Hi. pf. 3 m.s. (304) *repaired*
חָנוּן pr.n. (337) *Hanun*
וְיֹשְׁבֵי זָנוֹחַ conj.-Qal act.ptc. m.p. cstr. (יָשַׁב 442)-pr.n. (276) *and the inhabitants of Zanoah*
הֵמָּה בָנוּהוּ pers.pr. 3 m.p. (241)-Qal pf. 3 c.p.-3 m.s. sf. (בָּנָה 124) *they rebuilt it*
וַיַּעֲמִידוּ consec.-Hi. impf. 3 m.p. (עָמַד 763) *and set*
דַּלְתֹתָיו n.f.p.-3 m.s. sf. (195) *its doors*
מַנְעֻלָיו n.m.p.-3 m.s. sf. (653) *its bolts*
וּבְרִיחָיו conj.-n.m.p.-3 m.s. sf. (138) *and its bars*
וְאֶלֶף אַמָּה conj.-n.m.s. cstr. (48)-n.f.s. (52) *and a thousand cubits*
בַּחוֹמָה prep.-def.art.-n.f.s. (327) *of the wall*
עַד שַׁעַר הָשְׁפוֹת prep. (III 723)-n.m.s. cstr. (1044)-def.art.-n.m.s. (1046; GK 35d) *as far as the Dung Gate*

3:14

וְאֵת שַׁעַר הָאַשְׁפּוֹת conj.-dir.obj.-n.m.s. cstr. (1044)-def.art.-n.m.s. (1046) *and the Dung Gate*
הֶחֱזִיק Hi. pf. 3 m.s. (304) *repaired*
מַלְכִּיָּה בֶן־רֵכָב pr.n. (575)-n.m.s. cstr. (119)-pr.n. (939) *Malchijah the son of Rechab*
שַׂר פֶּלֶךְ n.m.s. cstr. (978)-n.m.s. cstr. (813) *ruler of the district of*
בֵּית־הַכָּרֶם pr.n. (111) *Beth-haccherem*
הוּא יִבְנֶנּוּ pers.pr. 3 m.s. (214)-Qal impf. 3 m.s.-3 m.s. sf. (בָּנָה 124) *he rebuilt it*
וְיַעֲמִיד conj.-Hi. impf. 3 m.s. (עָמַד 763) *and set*
דַּלְתֹתָיו n.f.p.-3 m.s. sf. (195) *its doors*
מַנְעֻלָיו n.m.p.-3 m.s. sf. (653) *its bolts*
וּבְרִיחָיו conj.-n.m.p.-3 m.s. sf. (138) *and its bars*

3:15

וְאֵת שַׁעַר הָעַיִן conj.-dir.obj.-n.m.s. cstr. (1044) -def.art.-n.f.s. (II 745) *and the Fountain Gate*
הֶחֱזִיק Hi. pf. 3 m.s. (304) *repaired*
שַׁלּוּן בֶּן־כָּל־חֹזֶה pr.n. (1024)-n.m.s. cstr. (119) -pr.n. (480) *Shallun the son of Colhozeh*
שַׂר פֶּלֶךְ n.m.s. cstr. (978)-n.m.s. cstr. (813) *ruler of the district of*
הַמִּצְפָּה def.art.-pr.n. (859) *Mizpah*
הוּא יִבְנֶנּוּ pers.pr. 3 m.s. (214)-Qal impf. 3 m.s.-3 m.s. sf. (בָּנָה 124) *he rebuilt it*
וִיטַלְלֶנּוּ conj.-Pi. impf. 3 m.s.-3 m.s. sf. (טָלַל II 378) *and covered it*
וְיַעֲמִידוּ conj.-Hi. impf. 3 m.p. (עָמַד 763; Q-3 m.s.) *and set*

דַּלְתֹתָיו n.f.p.-3 m.s. sf. (195) *its doors*
מַנְעֻלָיו n.m.p.-3 m.s. sf. (653) *its bolts*
וּבְרִיחָיו conj.-n.m.p.-3 m.s. sf. (138) *and its bars*
וְאֵת חוֹמַת בְּרֵכַת conj.-dir.obj.-n.f.s. cstr. (327) -n.f.s. cstr. (140) *and the wall of the Pool of*
הַשֶּׁלַח def.art.-pr.n. (III 1019) *Shelah*
לְגַן־הַמֶּלֶךְ prep.-n.m.s. cstr. (171)-def.art.-n.m.s. (I 572) *of the king's garden*
וְעַד־הַמַּעֲלוֹת conj.-prep. (III 723)-def.art.-n.f.p. (752) *as far as the stairs*
הַיּוֹרְדוֹת def.art.-Qal act.ptc. f.p. (יָרַד 432) *that go down*
מֵעִיר דָּוִיד prep.-n.f.s. cstr. (746)-pr.n. (187) *from the City of David*

3:16

אַחֲרָיו הֶחֱזִיק prep.-3 m.s. sf. (29)-Hi. pf. 3 m.s. (304) *after him repaired*
נְחֶמְיָה בֶן־עַזְבּוּק pr.n. (637)-n.m.s. cstr. (119)-pr.n. (739) *Nehemiah the son of Azbuk*
שַׂר חֲצִי n.m.s. cstr. (978)-n.m.s. cstr. (345) *ruler of half of*
פֶּלֶךְ בֵּית־צוּר n.m.s. cstr. (813)-pr.n. (112) *the district of Beth-zur*
עַד־נֶגֶד prep. (III 723)-prep. (617) *to a point opposite*
קִבְרֵי דָוִיד n.m.p. cstr. (868)-pr.n. (187) *the sepulchres of David*
וְעַד־הַבְּרֵכָה הָעֲשׂוּיָה conj.-v.supra-def.art.-n.f.s. (140)-def.art.-Qal pass.ptc. f.s. (עָשָׂה I 793) *to the artificial pool*
וְעַד בֵּית הַגִּבֹּרִים conj.-v.supra-n.m.s. cstr. (108) -def.art.-adj. m.p. (150) *and to the house of the mighty men*

3:17

אַחֲרָיו הֶחֱזִיקוּ prep.-3 m.p. sf. (29)-Hi. pf. 3 c.p. (304 חָזַק) *after him repaired*
הַלְוִיִּם def.art.-adj. m.p. (532) *the Levites*
רְחוּם בֶּן־בָּנִי pr.n. (933)-n.m.s. cstr. (119)-pr.n. (125) *Rehum the son of Bani*
עַל־יָדוֹ prep.-n.f.s.-3 m.s. sf. (388) *next to him*
הֶחֱזִיק Hi. pf. 3 m.s. (304) *repaired*
חֲשַׁבְיָה pr.n. (364) *Hashabiah*
שַׂר־חֲצִי־פֶלֶךְ n.m.s. cstr. (978)-n.m.s. cstr. 345)-n.m.s. cstr. (813) *ruler of half the district of*
קְעִילָה pr.n. (890) *Keilah*
לְפִלְכּוֹ prep.-n.m.s.-3 m.s. sf. (813) *for his district*

3:18

אַחֲרָיו הֶחֱזִיקוּ prep.-3 m.s. sf. (29)-Hi. pf. 3 c.p. (304) *after him repaired*
אֲחֵיהֶם n.m.p.-3 m.p. sf. (26) *their brethren*
בַּוַּי בֶּן־חֵנָדָד pr.n. (100)-n.m.s. cstr. (119)-pr.n. (337) *Bavvai the son of Henadad*
שַׂר חֲצִי פֶּלֶךְ n.m.s. cstr. (978)-n.m.s. cstr. (345)-n.m.s. cstr. (813) *ruler of half the district of*
קְעִילָה pr.n. (890) *Keilah*

3:19

וַיְחַזֵּק consec.-Pi. impf. 3 m.s. (חָזַק 304) *repaired*
עַל־יָדוֹ prep.-n.f.s.-3 m.s. sf. (388) *next to him*
עֵזֶר בֶּן־יֵשׁוּעַ pr.n. (II 740)-n.m.s. cstr. (119)-pr.n. (221) *Ezer the son of Jeshua*
שַׂר הַמִּצְפָּה n.m.s. cstr. (978)-def.art.-pr.n. (859) *ruler of Mizpah*
מִדָּה שֵׁנִית n.f.s. (I 551)-adj. f.s. (1041) *another section*
מִנֶּגֶד עֲלֹת prep.-prep. (617)-Qal inf.cstr. (עָלָה 748) *opposite the ascent to*
הַנֶּשֶׁק def.art.-n.m.s. (676) *the armory*
הַמִּקְצֹעַ def.art.-n.m.s. (893) *at the Angle*

3:20

אַחֲרָיו הֶחֱרָה prep.-3 m.s. sf. (29)-Hi. pf. 3 m.s. (354 חָרָה) *after him burned with zeal*
הֶחֱזִיק Hi. pf. 3 m.s. (304) *repaired*
בָּרוּךְ בֶּן־זַבַּי pr.n. (140)-n.m.s. cstr. (119)-pr.n. (256) *Baruch the son of Zabbai*
מִדָּה שֵׁנִית n.f.s. (551)-adj. f.s. (1041) *another section*
מִן־הַמִּקְצוֹעַ prep.-def.art.-n.m.s. (893) *from the Angle*
עַד־פֶּתַח prep. (III 723)-n.m.s. cstr. (835) *to the door of*
בֵּית אֶלְיָשִׁיב n.m.s. cstr. (108)-pr.n. (46) *the house of Eliashib*
הַכֹּהֵן הַגָּדוֹל def.art.-n.m.s. (463)-def.art.-adj. m.s. (152) *the high priest*

3:21

אַחֲרָיו הֶחֱזִיק prep.-3 m.s. sf. (29)-Hi. pf. 3 m.s. (304) *after him repaired*
מְרֵמוֹת בֶּן־אוּרִיָּה pr.n. (599)-n.m.s. cstr. (119) -pr.n. (22) *Meremoth the son of Uriah*
בֶּן־הַקּוֹץ v.supra-def.art.-pr.n. (881) *son of Hakkoz*
מִדָּה שֵׁנִית n.f.s. (I 551)-adj. f.s. (1041) *another section*

מִפֶּתַח prep.-n.m.s. cstr. (835) *from the door of*
בֵּית אֶלְיָשִׁיב n.m.s. cstr. (108)-pr.n. (46) *the house of Eliashib*
וְעַד־תַּכְלִית conj.-v.supra-n.f.s. cstr. (479) *to the end of*
בֵּית אֶלְיָשִׁיב v.supra-v.supra *the house of Eliashib*

3:22

וְאַחֲרָיו הֶחֱזִיקוּ conj.-prep.-3 m.s. sf. (29)-Hi. pf. 3 c.p. (304) *after him repaired*
הַכֹּהֲנִים def.art.-n.m.p. (463) *the priests*
אַנְשֵׁי הַכִּכָּר n.m.p. cstr. (35)-def.art.-n.f.s. (503) *the men of the Round*

3:23

אַחֲרָיו הֶחֱזִיק prep.-3 m.s. sf. (29)-Hi. pf. 3 m.s. (304) *after them repaired*
בִּנְיָמִן וְחַשּׁוּב pr.n. (122)-conj.-pr.n. (363) *Benjamin and Hasshub*
נֶגֶד בֵּיתָם prep. (617)-n.m.s.-3 m.p. sf. (108) *opposite their house*
אַחֲרָיו הֶחֱזִיק v.supra-v.supra *after them repaired*
עֲזַרְיָה בֶן־מַעֲשֵׂיָה pr.n. (741)-n.m.s. cstr. (119)-pr.n. (796) *Azariah the son of Maaseiah*
בֶּן־עֲנָנְיָה v.supra-pr.n. (778) *son of Ananiah*
אֵצֶל בֵּיתוֹ prep. (I 69)-n.m.s.-3 m.s. sf. (108) *beside his own house*

3:24

אַחֲרָיו הֶחֱזִיק prep.-3 m.s. sf. (29)-Hi. pf. 3 m.s. (304) *after him repaired*
בִּנּוּי בֶּן־חֵנָדָד pr.n. (125)-n.m.s. cstr. (119)-pr.n. (337) *Binnui the son of Henadad*
מִדָּה שֵׁנִית n.f.s. (I 551)-adj. f.s. (1041) *another section*
מִבֵּית עֲזַרְיָה prep.-n.m.s. cstr. (108)-pr.n. (741) *from the house of Azariah*
עַד־הַמִּקְצוֹעַ prep. (III 723)-def.art.-n.m.s. (893) *to the Angle*
וְעַד־הַפִּנָּה conj.-v.supra-def.art.-n.f.s. (819) *and to the corner*

3:25

פָּלָל בֶּן־אוּזַי pr.n. (813)-n.m.s. cstr. (119)-pr.n. (17) *Palal the son of Uzai*
מִנֶּגֶד הַמִּקְצוֹעַ prep.-prep. (617)-def.art.-n.m.s. (893) *opposite the Angle*
וְהַמִּגְדָּל conj.-def.art.-n.m.s. (153) *and the tower*
הַיּוֹצֵא def.art.-Qal act.ptc. (יָצָא 422) *projecting*
מִבֵּית הַמֶּלֶךְ הָעֶלְיוֹן prep.-n.m.s. cstr. (108)-def. art.-n.m.s. (I 572)-def.art.-adj. m.s. (751) *from the upper house of the king*
אֲשֶׁר לַחֲצַר הַמַּטָּרָה rel. (81)-prep.-n.m.s. cstr. (I 346)-def.art.-n.f.s. (643) *at the court of the guard*
אַחֲרָיו prep.-3 m.s. sf. (29) *after him*
פְּדָיָה בֶן־פַּרְעֹשׁ pr.n. (804)-n.m.s. cstr. (119)-pr.n. (II 829) *Pedaiah the son of Parosh*

3:26

וְהַנְּתִינִים conj.-def.art.-n.m.p. (682) *and the Nethinim*
הָיוּ יֹשְׁבִים Qal pf. 3 c.p. (הָיָה 224)-Qal act.ptc. m.p. (יָשַׁב 442) *were living*
בָּעֹפֶל prep.-def.art.-n.m.s. (I 779) *on Ophel (the mound)*
עַד נֶגֶד prep. (III 723)-prep. (617) *opposite*
שַׁעַר הַמַּיִם n.m.s. cstr. (1044)-def.art.-n.m.p. (565) *the Water Gate*
לַמִּזְרָח prep.-def.art.-n.m.s. (280) *on the east*
וְהַמִּגְדָּל הַיּוֹצֵא conj.-def.art.-n.m.s. (153)-def.art. -Qal act.ptc. (יָצָא 422) *and the projecting tower*

3:27

אַחֲרָיו הֶחֱזִיקוּ prep.-3 m.s. sf. (29)-Hi. pf. 3 c.p. (304 חָזַק) *after him repaired*
הַתְּקֹעִים def.art.-adj. gent. m.p. (1075) *the Tekoites*
מִדָּה שֵׁנִית n.f.s. (I 551)-adj. f.s. (1041) *another section*
מִנֶּגֶד הַמִּגְדָּל הַגָּדוֹל prep.-prep. (617)-def.art. -n.m.s. (153)-def.art.-adj. m.s. (152) *opposite the great ... tower*
הַיּוֹצֵא def.art.-Qal act.ptc. (יָצָא 422) *projecting*
וְעַד חוֹמַת הָעֹפֶל conj.-prep. (III 723)-n.f.s. cstr. (327)-def.art.-n.m.s. (I 779) *as far as the wall of Ophel*

3:28

מֵעַל שַׁעַר הַסּוּסִים prep.-prep.-n.m.s. cstr. (1044) -def.art.-n.m.p. (692) *above the Horse Gate*
הֶחֱזִיקוּ הַכֹּהֲנִים Hi. pf. 3 c.p. (חָזַק 304)-def.art. -n.m.p. (463) *the priests repaired*
אִישׁ לְנֶגֶד בֵּיתוֹ n.m.s. (35)-prep.-prep. (617) -n.m.s.-3 m.s. sf. (108) *each one opposite his own house*

3:29

אַחֲרָיו prep.-3 m.s. sf. (29) *after him*

הֶחֱזִיק צָדוֹק Hi. pf. 3 m.s. (304)-pr.n. (843) *Zadok repaired*

בֶּן־אִמֵּר n.m.s. cstr. (119)-pr.n. (57) *the son of Immer*

נֶגֶד בֵּיתוֹ prep. (617)-n.m.s.-3 m.s. sf. (108) *opposite his own house*

וְאַחֲרָיו הֶחֱזִיק conj.-v.supra-v.supra *and after him repaired*

שְׁמַעְיָה בֶן־שְׁכַנְיָה pr.n. (1035)-v.supra-pr.n. (1016) *Shemaiah the son of Shecaniah*

שֹׁמֵר Qal act.ptc. (שָׁמַר 1036) *the keeper of*

שַׁעַר הַמִּזְרָח n.m.s. cstr. (1044)-def.art.-n.m.s. (280) *the East Gate*

3:30

אַחֲרַי הֶחֱזִיק prep.-1 c.s. sf. (29; many אַחֲרָיו) -Hi. pf. 3 m.s. (304) *after him repaired*

חֲנַנְיָה בֶן־שֶׁלֶמְיָה pr.n. (337)-n.m.s. cstr. (119) -pr.n. (1025) *Hananiah the son of Shelemiah*

וְחָנוּן בֶּן־צָלָף conj.-pr.n. (337)-v.supra-pr.n. (854) *and Hanun the ... son of Zalaph*

הַשִּׁשִּׁי def.art.-adj. m.s. (995) *sixth*

מִדָּה שֵׁנִי n.f.s. (551)-adj. m.s. (1041; שֵׁנִית) *another section*

אַחֲרָיו הֶחֱזִיק prep.-3 m.s. sf. (29)-v.supra *after him repaired*

מְשֻׁלָּם בֶּן־בֶּרֶכְיָה pr.n. (1024)-v.supra-pr.n. (140) *Meshullam the son of Berechiah*

נֶגֶד נִשְׁכָּתוֹ prep. (617)-n.f.s.-3 m.s. sf. (675) *opposite his chamber*

3:31

אַחֲרַי הֶחֱזִיק prep.-1 c.s. sf. (29; rd. אַחֲרָיו)-Hi. pf. 3 m.s. (304) *after him repaired*

מַלְכִּיָּה בֶּן־הַצֹּרְפִי pr.n. (575)-n.m.s. cstr. (119) -def.art.-n.m. coll. (864; GK 128v) *Malchijah the son of the goldsmiths*

עַד־בֵּית הַנְּתִינִים prep. (III 723)-n.m.s. cstr. (108)-def.art.-n.m.p. (682) *as far as the house of the Nethinim*

וְהָרֹכְלִים conj.-def.art.-Qal act.ptc. m.p. (רָכַל 940) *and of the merchants*

נֶגֶד שַׁעַר הַמִּפְקָד prep. (617)-n.m.s. cstr. (1044)-def.art.-n.m.s. (824) *opposite the Muster Gate*

וְעַד עֲלִיַּת הַפִּנָּה conj.-prep. (III 723)-n.f.s. cstr. (751)-def.art.-n.f.s. (819) *and to the upper chamber of the corner*

3:32

וּבֵין עֲלִיַּת הַפִּנָּה conj.-prep. (107)-n.f.s. cstr. (751)-def.art.-n.f.s. (819) *and between the upper chamber of the corner*

לְשַׁעַר הַצֹּאן prep.-n.m.s. cstr. (1044)-def.art. -n.f.s. (838) *and the Sheep Gate*

הֶחֱזִיקוּ הַצֹּרְפִים Hi. pf. 3 c.p. (חָזַק 304)-def.art. -Qal act.ptc. m.p. (צָרַף 864) *the goldsmiths repaired*

וְהָרֹכְלִים conj.-def.art.-Qal act.ptc. m.p. (רָכַל 940) *and the merchants*

3:33 (Eng.4:1)

וַיְהִי כַּאֲשֶׁר consec.-Qal impf. 3 m.s. (הָיָה 224)-prep.-rel. (81) *now when*

שָׁמַע סַנְבַלַּט Qal pf. 3 m.s. (1033)-pr.n. (702) *Sanballat heard*

כִּי־אֲנַחְנוּ בוֹנִים conj. (471)-pers.pr. 1 c.p. (59)-Qal act.ptc. m.p. (בָּנָה 124) *that we were building*

אֶת־הַחוֹמָה dir.obj.-def.art.-n.f.s. (327) *the wall*

וַיִּחַר לוֹ consec.-Qal impf. 3 m.s. (חָרָה 354) -prep.-3 m.s. sf. *he was angry*

וַיִּכְעַס הַרְבֵּה consec.-Qal impf. 3 m.s. (כָּעַס 494)-Hi. inf.abs. (רָבָה I 915) *and greatly enraged*

וַיַּלְעֵג consec.-Hi. impf. 3 m.s. (לָעַג 541) *and he ridiculed*

עַל־הַיְּהוּדִים prep.-def.art.-adj. gent. m.p. (I 397) *the Jews*

3:34

וַיֹּאמֶר consec.-Qal impf. 3 m.s. (55) *and he said*

לִפְנֵי אֶחָיו prep.-n.m.p. cstr. (815)-n.m.p.-3 m.s. sf. (26) *in the presence of his brethren*

וְחֵיל שֹׁמְרוֹן conj.-n.m.s. cstr. (298)-pr.n. (1037) *and of the army of Samaria*

וַיֹּאמֶר v.supra *(and he said)*

מָה הַיְּהוּדִים הָאֲמֵלָלִים interr. (552)-def.art.-adj. gent. m.p. (I 397)-def.art.-adj. m.p. (51) *these feeble Jews*

עֹשִׂים Qal act.ptc. m.p. (עָשָׂה I 793) *are doing*

הֲיַעַזְבוּ לָהֶם interr.part.-Qal impf. 3 m.p. (עָזַב I 736)-prep.-3 m.p. sf. (some rd. לֵאלֹהִים) *will they forsake them (God)?*

הֲיִזְבָּחוּ interr.part.-Qal impf. 3 m.p. paus. (זָבַח 256) *will they sacrifice?*

הַיְכַלּוּ בַיּוֹם interr.part.-Pi. impf. 3 m.p. (כָּלָה I 477)-prep.-def.art.-n.m.s. (398) *will they finish up in a day?*

הַיְחַיּוּ interr.part.-Pi. impf. 3 m.p. (חָיָה 310) *will they revive*

אֶת־הָאֲבָנִים dir.obj.-def.art.-n.f.p. (6) *the stones*

מֵעֲרֵמוֹת הֶעָפָר prep.-n.f.p. cstr. (790)-def.art. -n.m.s. (779) *out of the heaps of rubbish*
וְהֵמָּה שְׂרוּפוֹת conj.-pers.pr. 3 m.p. (241)-Qal pass.ptc. f.p. (שָׂרַף 976) *and they the burned ones*

3:35

וְטוֹבִיָּה הָעַמֹּנִי conj.-pr.n. (375)-def.art.-adj. gent. (770) *and Tobiah the Ammonite*
אֶצְלוֹ prep.-3 m.s. sf. (I 69) *was by him*
וַיֹּאמֶר consec.-Qal impf. 3 m.s. (55) *and he said*
גַּם אֲשֶׁר־הֵם בּוֹנִים adv. (168)-rel. (81)-pers.pr. 3 m.p. (241)-Qal act.ptc. m.p. (בָּנָה 124) *Yes, what they are building*
אִם־יַעֲלֶה שׁוּעָל hypoth.part. (49)-Qal impf. 3 m.s. (עָלָה 748)-n.m.s. (I 1043) *if a fox goes up*
וּפָרַץ conj.-Qal pf. 3 m.s. (I 829) *he will break down*
חוֹמַת אַבְנֵיהֶם n.f.s. cstr. (327)-n.f.p.-3 m.p. sf. (6) *their stone wall*

3:36

שְׁמַע Qal impv. 2 m.s. (שָׁמַע 1033) *hear*
אֱלֹהֵינוּ n.m.p.-1 c.p. sf. (43) *O our God*
כִּי־הָיִינוּ בוּזָה conj. (471)-Qal pf. 1 c.p. (הָיָה 224)-n.f.s. (100) *for we are despised*
וְהָשֵׁב conj.-Hi. impv. 2 m.s. (שׁוּב 996) *turn back*
חֶרְפָּתָם n.f.s.-3 m.p. sf. (352) *their taunt*
אֶל־רֹאשָׁם prep.-n.m.s.-3 m.p. sf. (910) *upon their own heads*
וּתְנֵם conj.-Qal impv. 2 m.s.-3 m.p. sf. (נָתַן 678) *and give them up*
לְבִזָּה prep.-n.f.s. (103) *to be plundered*
בְּאֶרֶץ שִׁבְיָה prep.-n.f.s. cstr. (75)-986) *in a land where they are captives*

3:37

וְאַל־תְּכַס conj.-neg.-Pi. impf. 2 m.s. (כָּסָה 491) *do not cover*
עַל־עֲוֹנָם prep.-n.m.s.-3 m.p. sf. (730) *their guilt*
וְחַטָּאתָם conj.-n.f.s.-3 m.p. sf. (308) *and their sin*
מִלְּפָנֶיךָ prep.-prep.-n.m.p.-2 m.s. sf. (815) *from thy sight*
אַל־תִּמָּחֶה neg.-Ni. impf. 2 m.s. (מָחָה 562) *let not be blotted out*
כִּי הִכְעִיסוּ conj. (471)-Hi. pf. 3 c.p. (כָּעַס 494) *for they have provoked*
לְנֶגֶד הַבּוֹנִים prep.-prep. (617)-def.art.-Qal act.ptc. m.p. (בָּנָה 124) *before the builders*

3:38 (Eng.4:6)

וַנִּבְנֶה consec.-Qal impf. 1 c.p. (בָּנָה 124) *so we built*
אֶת־הַחוֹמָה dir.obj.-def.art.-n.f.s. (327) *the wall*
וַתִּקָּשֵׁר consec.-Ni. impf. 3 f.s. (קָשַׁר 905) *and was joined together*
כָּל־הַחוֹמָה n.m.s. cstr. (481)-v.supra *all the wall*
עַד־חֶצְיָהּ prep. (III 723)-n.m.s.-3 f.s. sf. (345) *to half its height*
וַיְהִי לֵב לָעָם consec.-Qal impf. 3 m.s. (הָיָה 224) -n.m.s. (524)-prep.-def.art.-n.m.s. (I 766) *for the people had a mind*
לַעֲשׂוֹת prep.-Qal inf.cstr. (עָשָׂה I 793) *to work*

4:1 (Eng.4:7)

וַיְהִי כַּאֲשֶׁר שָׁמַע consec.-Qal impf. 3 m.s. (הָיָה 224)-prep.-rel. (81)-Qal pf. 3 m.s. (1033) *but when ... heard*
סַנְבַלַּט וְטוֹבִיָּה pr.n. (702)-conj.-pr.n. (375) *Sanballat and Tobiah*
וְהָעַרְבִים conj.-def.art.-adj. gent. m.p. (787) *and the Arabs*
וְהָעַמֹּנִים conj.-def.art.-adj. gent. m.p. (770) *and the Ammonites*
וְהָאַשְׁדּוֹדִים conj.-def.art.-adj. gent. m.p. (78) *and the Ashdodites*
כִּי־עָלְתָה conj. (471)-Qal pf. 3 f.s. (עָלָה 748) *that was going forward*
אֲרוּכָה n.f.s. (74) *the repairing*
לְחֹמוֹת יְרוּשָׁלַםִ prep.-n.f.p. cstr. (327)-pr.n. (436) *of the walls of Jerusalem*
כִּי־הֵחֵלּוּ conj. (471)-Hi. pf. 3 c.p. (חָלַל III 320) *and that were beginning*
הַפְּרֻצִים def.art.-Qal pass.ptc. m.p. (פָּרַץ I 829) *the breaches*
לְהִסָּתֵם prep.-Ni. inf.cstr. (סָתַם 711) *to be closed*
וַיִּחַר לָהֶם מְאֹד consec.-Qal impf. 3 m.s. (חָרָה 354)-prep.-3 m.p. sf.-adv. (547) *and they were very angry*

4:2

וַיִּקְשְׁרוּ כֻלָּם יַחְדָּו consec.-Qal impf. 3 m.p. (קָשַׁר 905)-n.m.s.-3 m.p. sf. (481)-adv. (403) *and they all plotted together*
לָבוֹא prep.-Qal inf.cstr. (בּוֹא 97) *to come*
לְהִלָּחֵם prep.-Ni. inf.cstr. (לָחַם 535) *to fight*
בִּירוּשָׁלָ͏ִם prep.-pr.n. paus. (436) *against Jerusalem*
וְלַעֲשׂוֹת לוֹ conj.-prep.-Qal inf.cstr. (עָשָׂה I 793)-prep.-3 m.s. sf. *and to cause in it*
תּוֹעָה n.f.s. (1073) *confusion*

4:3

וַנִּתְפַּלֵּל consec.-Hith. impf. 1 c.p. (פָּלַל 813) *and we prayed*

אֶל־אֱלֹהֵינוּ prep.-n.m.p.-1 c.p. sf. (43) *to our God*

וַנַּעֲמִיד consec.-Hi. impf. 1 c.p. (עָמַד 763; GK 49eN,53n) *and set*

מִשְׁמָר n.m.s. (1038) *a guard*

עֲלֵיהֶם prep.-3 m.p. sf. *against them*

יוֹמָם וָלַיְלָה adv. (401)-conj.-n.m.s. (538) *day and night*

מִפְּנֵיהֶם prep.-n.m.p.-3 m.p. sf. (815) *from before them*

4:4 (Eng.4:10)

וַיֹּאמֶר יְהוּדָה consec.-Qal impf. 3 m.s. (55)-pr.n. (397) *but Judah said*

כָּשַׁל Qal pf. 3 m.s. (505) *is failing*

כֹּחַ הַסַּבָּל n.m.s. cstr. (470)-def.art.-n.m.s. (688) *the strength of the burden-bearers*

וְהֶעָפָר הַרְבֵּה conj.-def.art.-n.m.s. (779)-Hi. inf.abs. (רָבָה I 915) *and there is much rubbish*

וַאֲנַחְנוּ לֹא נוּכַל conj.-pers.pr. 1 c.p. (59)-neg. -Qal impf. 1 c.p. (יָכֹל 407) *and we are not able*

לִבְנוֹת בַּחוֹמָה prep.-Qal inf.cstr. (בָּנָה 124)-prep. (GK 119m)-def.art.-n.f.s. (327) *to build on the wall*

4:5

וַיֹּאמְרוּ צָרֵינוּ consec.-Qal impf. 3 m.p. (אָמַר 55) -n.m.p.-1 c.p. sf. (III 865) *and our enemies said*

לֹא יֵדְעוּ neg.-Qal impf. 3 m.p. (יָדַע 393) *they will not know*

וְלֹא יִרְאוּ conj.-neg.-Qal impf. 3 m.p. (רָאָה 906) *and will not see*

עַד אֲשֶׁר־נָבוֹא prep. (III 723)-rel. (81)-Qal impf. 1 c.p. (בּוֹא 97) *till we come*

אֶל־תּוֹכָם prep.-n.m.s.-3 m.p. sf. (1063) *into the midst of them*

וַהֲרַגְנוּם conj.-Qal pf. 1 c.p.-3 m.p. sf. (הָרַג 246) *and kill them*

וְהִשְׁבַּתְנוּ conj.-Hi. pf. 1 c.p. (שָׁבַת 991) *and stop*

אֶת־הַמְּלָאכָה dir.obj.-def.art.-n.f.s. (521) *the work*

4:6

וַיְהִי כַּאֲשֶׁר־בָּאוּ consec.-Qal impf. 3 m.p. (הָיָה 224)-prep.-rel. (81)-Qal pf. 3 c.p. (בּוֹא 97) *when ... came*

הַיְּהוּדִים def.art.-adj. gent. m.p. (397) *the Jews*

הַיֹּשְׁבִים def.art.-Qal act.ptc. m.p. (יָשַׁב 442) *who lived*

אֶצְלָם prep.-3 m.p. sf. (I 69) *by them*

וַיֹּאמְרוּ לָנוּ consec.-Qal impf. 3 m.p. (אָמַר 55) -prep.-1 c.p. sf. *they said to us*

עֶשֶׂר פְּעָמִים num. (796)-n.f.p. (821) *ten times*

מִכָּל־הַמְּקֹמוֹת prep.-n.m.s. cstr. (481)-def.art. -n.m.p. (879) *from all the places*

אֲשֶׁר תָּשׁוּבוּ עָלֵינוּ rel. (81)-Qal impf. 2 m.p. (996 שׁוּב)-prep.-1 c.p. sf. *which you return against us*

4:7

וָאַעֲמִיד consec.-Hi. impf. 1 c.s. (עָמַד 763) *so I stationed*

מִתַּחְתִּיּוֹת prep.-adj. f.p. (1066) *in the lowest parts*

לַמָּקוֹם prep.-def.art.-n.m.s. (879) *of the space*

מֵאַחֲרֵי לַחוֹמָה prep.-prep. (29)-prep.-def. art.-n.f.s. (327) *behind the wall*

בַּצְּחִחִיים prep.-def.art.-n.m.p. (850) *in open places*

וָאַעֲמִיד v.supra *I stationed*

אֶת־הָעָם dir.obj.-def.art.-n.m.s. (I 766) *the people*

לְמִשְׁפָּחוֹת prep.-n.f.p. (1046) *according to their families*

עִם־חַרְבֹתֵיהֶם prep.-n.f.p.-3 m.p. sf. (352) *with their swords*

רָמְחֵיהֶם n.m.p.-3 m.p. sf. (942) *their spears*

וְקַשְּׁתֹתֵיהֶם conj.-n.f.p.-3 m.p. sf. (905; GK 20h) *and their bows*

4:8

וָאֵרֶא consec.-Qal impf. 1 c.s. (רָאָה 906) *and I looked*

וָאָקוּם consec.-Qal impf. 1 c.s. (קוּם 877) *and arose*

וָאֹמַר consec.-Qal impf. 1 c.s. (אָמַר 55) *and said*

אֶל־הַחֹרִים prep.-def.art.-n.m.p. (II 359) *to the nobles*

וְאֶל־הַסְּגָנִים conj.-prep.-def.art.-n.m.p. (688) *and to the officials*

וְאֶל־יֶתֶר הָעָם v.supra-n.m.s. cstr. (451)-def.art. -n.m.s. (I 766) *and to the rest of the people*

אַל־תִּירְאוּ neg.-Qal impf. 2 m.p. (יָרֵא 431) *do not be afraid*

מִפְּנֵיהֶם prep.-n.m.p.-3 m.p. sf. (815) *of them*

אֶת־אֲדֹנָי dir.obj.-n.m.p.-1 c.s. sf. (10) *the Lord*

הַגָּדוֹל וְהַנּוֹרָא def.art.-adj. m.s. (152)-conj.-def. art.-Ni. ptc. m.s. (יָרֵא 431) *the great and terrible*

זְכֹרוּ Qal impv. 2 m.p. (זָכַר 269) *remember*

וְהִלָּחֲמוּ conj.-Ni. impv. 2 m.p. (לָחַם 535) *and fight*

עַל־אֲחֵיכֶם prep.-n.m.p.-2 m.p. sf. (26) *for your brethren*

בְּנֵיכֶם n.m.p.-2 m.p. sf. (119) *your sons*

וּבְנֹתֵיכֶם conj.-n.f.p.-2 m.p. sf. (I 123) *your daughters*

נְשֵׁיכֶם n.f.p.-2 m.p. sf. (61) *your wives*

וּבָתֵּיכֶם conj.-n.m.p.-2 m.p. sf. (108) *and your homes*

4:9 (Eng.4:15)

וַיְהִי כַּאֲשֶׁר־שָׁמְעוּ consec.-Qal impf. 3 m.s. (הָיָה 224)-prep.-rel. (81)-Qal pf. 3 c.p. (שָׁמַע 1033) *when ... heard*

אוֹיְבֵינוּ Qal act.ptc. m.p.-1 c.p. sf. (אָיַב 33) *our enemies*

כִּי־נוֹדַע לָנוּ conj. (471)-Ni. pf. 3 m.s. (יָדַע 393) -prep.-1 c.p. sf. *that it was known to us*

וַיָּפֶר הָאֱלֹהִים consec.-Hi. impf. 3 m.s. (פָּרַר I 830; GK 67x)-def.art.-n.m.p. (43) *and that God had frustrated*

אֶת־עֲצָתָם dir.obj.-n.f.s.-3 m.p. sf. (420) *their plan*

וַנָּשָׁב כֻּלָּנוּ consec.-Qal impf. 1 c.p. (שׁוּב 996; GK 49eN)-n.m.s.-1 c.p. sf. (481) *we all returned*

אֶל־הַחוֹמָה prep.-def.art.-n.f.s. (327) *to the wall*

אִישׁ אֶל־מְלַאכְתּוֹ n.m.s. (35)-prep.-n.f.s.-3 m.s. sf. (521) *each to his work*

4:10

וַיְהִי consec.-Qal impf. 3 m.s. (הָיָה 224) *and it was*

מִן־הַיּוֹם הַהוּא prep.-def.art.-n.m.s. (398)-def.art. -demons.adj. m.s. (214) *from that day on*

חֲצִי נְעָרַי n.m.s. cstr. (345)-n.m.p.-1 c.s. sf. (654) *half of my servants*

עֹשִׂים בַּמְּלָאכָה Qal act.ptc. m.p. (עָשָׂה I 793) -prep.-def.art.-n.f.s. (521) *worked on construction*

וְחֶצְיָם conj.-n.m.s.-3 m.p. sf. (345) *and half of them*

מַחֲזִיקִים Hi. ptc. m.p. (חָזַק 304) *holding*

וְהָרְמָחִים conj.-def.art.-n.m.p. (942) *the spears*

הַמָּגִנִּים def.art.-n.m.p. (171) *shields*

וְהַקְּשָׁתוֹת conj.-def.art.-n.f.p. (905) *bows*

וְהַשִּׁרְיֹנִים conj.-def.art.-n.m.p. (1056) *and coats of mail*

וְהַשָּׂרִים conj.-def.art.-n.m.p. (978) *and the leaders*

אַחֲרֵי כָּל־בֵּית יְהוּדָה prep. (29)-n.m.s. cstr. (481) -n.m.s. cstr. (108)-pr.n. (397) *behind all the house of Judah*

4:11

הַבּוֹנִים def.art.-Qal act.ptc. m.p. (בָּנָה 124) *who were building*

בַּחוֹמָה prep.-def.art.-n.f.s. (327) *on the wall*

וְהַנֹּשְׂאִים conj.-def.art.-Qal act.ptc. m.p. (נָשָׂא 669) *those who carried*

בַּסֶּבֶל prep.-def.art.-n.m.s. (687) *burdens*

עֹמְשִׂים Qal act.ptc. m.p. (עָמַשׂ - עָמַס 770) *were laden*

בְּאַחַת יָדוֹ prep.-n.f.s. cstr. 25)-n.f.s.-3 m.s. sf. (388) *with one hand*

עֹשֶׂה בַמְּלָאכָה Qal act.ptc. (עָשָׂה I 793)-prep. -def.art.-n.f.s. (521) *labored on the work*

וְאַחַת conj.-v.supra *and with the other*

מַחֲזֶקֶת הַשָּׁלַח Hi. ptc. f.s. (חָזַק 304)-def.art. -n.m.s. paus. (I 1019) *held his weapon*

4:12 (Eng.4:18)

וְהַבּוֹנִים conj.-def.art.-Qal act.ptc. m.p. (בָּנָה 124) *and the builders*

אִישׁ חַרְבּוֹ n.m.s. (35)-n.f.s.-3 m.s. sf. (352) *each with his sword*

אֲסוּרִים Qal pass.ptc. m.p. (אָסַר 63; GK 116kN) *girded*

עַל־מָתְנָיו prep.-n.m. du.-3 m.s. sf. (608) *at his side*

וּבוֹנִים conj.-Qal act.ptc. m.p. (בָּנָה 124) *while he built*

וְהַתּוֹקֵעַ conj.-def.art.-Qal act.ptc. (תָּקַע 1075) *and the man who sounded*

בַּשּׁוֹפָר prep.-def.art.-n.m.s. (1051) *the trumpet*

אֶצְלִי prep.-1 c.s. sf. (I 69) *beside me*

4:13

וָאֹמַר אֶל־הַחֹרִים consec.-Qal impf. 1 c.s. (אָמַר 55)-prep.-def.art.-n.m.p. (II 359) *and I said to the nobles*

וְאֶל־הַסְּגָנִים conj.-prep.-def.art.-n.m.p. (688) *and to the officials*

וְאֶל־יֶתֶר הָעָם v.supra-n.m.s. cstr. (451)-def.art. -n.m.s. (I 766) *and to the rest of the people*

הַמְּלָאכָה הַרְבֵּה def.art.-n.f.s. (521)-Hi. inf.abs. (I 915 רָבָה) *the work is great*

וּרְחָבָה conj.-adj. f.s. (932) *and widely spread*

וַאֲנַחְנוּ נִפְרָדִים conj.-pers.pr. 1 c.p. (59)-Ni. ptc. m.p. (פָּרַד 825) *and we are separated*
עַל־הַחוֹמָה prep.-def.art.-n.f.s. (327) *on the wall*
רְחוֹקִים אִישׁ מֵאָחִיו adj. m.p. (935)-n.m.s. (35) -prep.-n.m.s.-3 m.s. sf. (26) *far from one another*

4:14

בִּמְקוֹם אֲשֶׁר prep.-n.m.s. cstr. (879)-rel. (81) *in the place where*
תִּשְׁמְעוּ Qal impf. 2 m.p. (שָׁמַע 1033) *you hear*
אֶת־קוֹל הַשּׁוֹפָר dir.obj.-n.m.s. cstr. (876)-def. art.-n.m.s. (1051) *the sound of the trumpet*
שָׁמָּה תִּקָּבְצוּ אֵלֵינוּ adv.-loc.he (1027)-Ni. impf. 2 m.p. (קָבַץ 867)-prep.-1 c.p. sf. *rally to us there*
אֱלֹהֵינוּ n.m.p.-1 c.p. sf. (43) *our God*
יִלָּחֶם לָנוּ Ni. impf. 3 m.s. (לָחַם 535)-prep.-1 c.p. sf. *will fight for us*

4:15 (Eng.4:21)

וַאֲנַחְנוּ עֹשִׂים conj.-pers.pr. 1 c.p. (59)-Qal act.ptc. m.p. (עָשָׂה I 793) *so we labored*
בַּמְּלָאכָה prep.-def.art.-n.f.s. (521) *at the work*
וְחֶצְיָם conj.-n.m.s.-3 m.p. sf. (345) *and half of them*
מַחֲזִיקִים Hi. ptc. m.p. (חָזַק 304) *held*
בָּרְמָחִים prep.-def.art.-n.m.p. (942) *the spears*
מֵעֲלוֹת הַשַּׁחַר prep.-Qal inf.cstr. (עָלָה 748)-def. art.-n.m.s. (1007) *from the break of dawn*
עַד צֵאת הַכּוֹכָבִים prep. (III 723)-Qal inf.cstr. (422 יָצָא)-def.art.-n.m.p. (456) *till the stars came out*

4:16

גַּם בָּעֵת הַהִיא adv. (168)-prep.-def.art.-n.f.s. (773)-def.art.-demons.adj. f.s. (214) *also at that time*
אָמַרְתִּי Qal pf. 1 c.s. (אָמַר 55) *I said*
לָעָם prep.-def.art.-n.m.s. (I 766) *to the people*
אִישׁ וְנַעֲרוֹ n.m.s. (35)-conj.-n.m.s.-3 m.s. sf. (654) *every man and his servant*
יָלִינוּ Qal impf. 3 m.p. (לִין I 533) *let pass the night*
בְּתוֹךְ יְרוּשָׁלָ͏ִם prep.-n.m.s. cstr. (1063)-pr.n. paus. (436) *within Jerusalem*
וְהָיוּ־לָנוּ conj.-Qal pf. 3 c.p. (הָיָה 224)-prep.-1 c.p. sf. *that they may be for us*
הַלַּיְלָה def.art.-n.m.s. (538) *by night*
מִשְׁמָר n.m.s. (1038) *a guard*
וְהַיּוֹם conj.-def.art.-n.m.s. (398) *and by day*
מְלָאכָה n.f.s. (521) *may labor*

4:17 (Eng.4:23)

וְאֵין אֲנִי וְאַחַי conj.-neg. (II 34; GK 152n)-pers. pr. 1 c.s. (58)-conj.-n.m.p.-1 c.s. sf. (26) *so neither I nor my brethren*
וּנְעָרַי conj.-n.m.p.-1 c.s. sf. (654) *nor my servants*
וְאַנְשֵׁי הַמִּשְׁמָר conj.-n.m.p. cstr. (35)-def.art. -n.m.s. (1038) *nor the men of the guard*
אֲשֶׁר אַחֲרַי rel. (81)-prep.-1 c.s. sf. (29) *who followed me*
אֵין־אֲנַחְנוּ neg. (II 34)-pers.pr. 1 c.p. (59) *none of us*
פֹּשְׁטִים בְּגָדֵינוּ Qal act.ptc. m.p. (פָּשַׁט 832) -n.m.p.-1 c.p. sf. (93) *took off our clothes*
אִישׁ שִׁלְחוֹ n.m.s. (35)-n.m.s.-3 m.s. sf. (I 1019) *each his weapon*
הַמָּיִם def.art.-n.m.p. paus. (565) *the water*

5:1

וַתְּהִי consec.-Qal impf. 3 f.s. (הָיָה 224) *now there arose*
צַעֲקַת n.f.s. cstr. (858) *a ... outcry of*
הָעָם def.art.-n.m.s. (I 766) *the people*
וּנְשֵׁיהֶם conj.-n.f.p.-2 m.p. sf. (61) *and of their wives*
גְּדוֹלָה adj. f.s. (152) *great*
אֶל־אֲחֵיהֶם הַיְּהוּדִים prep.-n.m.p.-3 m.p. sf. (26)-def.art.-adj. gent. m.p. (397) *against their Jewish brethren*

5:2

וְיֵשׁ אֲשֶׁר אֹמְרִים conj.-subst. (441)-rel. (81)-Qal act.ptc. m.p. (אָמַר 55) *for there were those who said*
בָּנֵינוּ וּבְנֹתֵינוּ n.m.p.-1 c.p. sf. (119)-conj.-n.f.p.-1 c.p. sf. (I 123) *with our sons and our daughters*
אֲנַחְנוּ רַבִּים pers.pr. 1 c.p. (59)-adj. m.p. (I 912) *we are many*
וְנִקְחָה דָגָן conj.-Qal impf. 1 c.p.-vol.he (לָקַח 542)-n.m.s. (186) *let us get grain*
וְנֹאכְלָה conj.-Qal impf. 1 c.p.-vol.he (אָכַל 37) *that we may eat*
וְנִחְיֶה conj.-Qal impf. 1 c.p. (חָיָה 310) *and keep alive*

5:3

וְיֵשׁ אֲשֶׁר אֹמְרִים conj.-subst. (441)-rel. (81)-Qal act.ptc. m.p. (אָמַר 55) *there were also those who said*
שְׂדֹתֵינוּ n.m.p.-1 c.p. sf. (961) *our fields*
וּכְרָמֵינוּ conj.-n.m.p.-1 c.p. sf. (501) *our vineyards*

וּבָתֵּינוּ conj.-n.m.p.-1 c.p. sf. (108) *and our houses*
אֲנַחְנוּ עֹרְבִים pers.pr. 1 c.p. (59)-Qal act.ptc. m.p. (II 786) *we are mortgaging*
וְנִקְחָה דָגָן conj.-Qal impf. 1 c.p.-vol.he (לָקַח 542)-n.m.s. (186) *to get grain*
בָּרָעָב prep.-def.art.-n.m.s. (944) *because of the famine*

5:4

וְיֵשׁ אֲשֶׁר אֹמְרִים conj.-subst. (441)-rel. (81)-Qal act.ptc. m.p. (אָמַר 55) *and there were those who said*
לָוִינוּ כֶסֶף Qal pf. 1 c.p. (לָוָה II 531)-n.m.s. (494) *we have borrowed money*
לְמִדַּת הַמֶּלֶךְ prep.-n.f.s. cstr. (II 551)-def.art. -n.m.s. (I 572) *for the king's tax*
שְׂדֹתֵינוּ n.m.p.-1 c.p. sf. (961) *upon our fields*
וּכְרָמֵינוּ conj.-n.m.p.-1 c.p. sf. (501) *and our vineyards*

5:5

וְעַתָּה conj.-adv. (773) *and now*
כִּבְשַׂר אַחֵינוּ prep.-n.m.s. cstr. (142)-n.m.p.-1 c.p. sf. (26) *as the flesh of our brethren*
בְּשָׂרֵנוּ n.m.s.-1 c.p. sf. (142) *our flesh*
כִּבְנֵיהֶם prep.-n.m.p.-3 m.p. sf. (119) *as their children*
בָּנֵינוּ n.m.p.-1 c.p. sf. (119) *our children*
וְהִנֵּה conj.-interj. (243) *and yet*
אֲנַחְנוּ כֹבְשִׁים pers.pr. 1 c.p. (59)-Qal act.ptc. m.p. (כָּבַשׁ 461) *we are forcing*
אֶת־בָּנֵינוּ dir.obj.-n.m.p.-1 c.p. sf. (119) *our sons*
וְאֶת־בְּנֹתֵינוּ conj.-dir.obj.-n.f.p.-1 c.p. sf. (I 123) *and our daughters*
לַעֲבָדִים prep.-n.m.p. (713) *to be slaves*
וְיֵשׁ מִבְּנֹתֵינוּ conj.-subst. (441)-prep.-n.f.p.-1 c.p. sf. (I 123) *and some of our daughters*
נִכְבָּשׁוֹת Ni. ptc. f.p. (כָּבַשׁ 461) *have already been enslaved*
וְאֵין לְאֵל יָדֵנוּ conj.-neg. (II 34)-prep.-n.m.s. cstr. (II 42)-n.f.s.-1 c.p. sf. (388) *but it is not in our power*
וּשְׂדֹתֵינוּ conj.-n.m.p.-1 c.p. sf. (961) *and our fields*
וּכְרָמֵינוּ conj.-n.m.p.-1 c.p. sf. (501) *and our vineyards*
לַאֲחֵרִים prep.-adj. m.p. (29) *to others*

5:6

וַיִּחַר לִי מְאֹד consec.-Qal impf. 3 m.s. (חָרָה 354)-prep.-1 c.s. sf.-adv. (547) *I was very angry*
כַּאֲשֶׁר שָׁמַעְתִּי prep.-rel. (81)-Qal pf. 1 c.s. (שָׁמַע 1033) *when I heard*
אֶת־זַעֲקָתָם dir.obj.-n.f.s.-3 m.p. sf. (277) *their outcry*
וְאֵת הַדְּבָרִים הָאֵלֶּה conj.-dir.obj.-def.art.-n.m.p. (182)-def.art.-demons.adj. c.p. (41) *and these words*

5:7

וַיִּמָּלֵךְ לִבִּי עָלַי consec.-Ni. impf. 3 m.s. (מָלַךְ II 576)-n.m.s.-1 c.s. sf. (524)-prep.-1 c.s. sf. *I took counsel with myself*
וָאָרִיבָה consec.-Qal impf. 1 c.s. (רִיב 936) *and I brought charges*
אֶת־הַחֹרִים dir.obj.-def.art.-n.m.p. (II 359) *against the nobles*
וְאֶת־הַסְּגָנִים conj.-dir.obj.-def.art.-n.m.p. (688) *and the officials*
וָאֹמְרָה לָהֶם consec.-Qal impf. 1 c.s. (אָמַר 55)-prep.-3 m.p. sf. *and I said to them*
מַשָּׁא n.m.s. (673) *interest*
אִישׁ־בְּאָחִיו n.m.s. (35)-prep.-n.m.s.-3 m.s. sf. (26) *each from his brother*
אַתֶּם נֹשְׁאִים pers.pr. 2 m.p. (61)-Qal act.ptc. m.p. (I 673) *you are exacting*
וָאֶתֵּן עֲלֵיהֶם consec.-Qal impf. 1 c.s. (נָתַן 678) -prep.-3 m.p. sf. *and I held against them*
קְהִלָּה גְדוֹלָה n.f.s. (875)-adj. f.s. (152) *a great assembly*

5:8

וָאֹמְרָה לָהֶם consec.-Qal impf. 1 c.s. (אָמַר 55)-prep.-3 m.p. sf. *and I said to them*
אֲנַחְנוּ קָנִינוּ pers.pr. 1 c.p. (59)-Qal pf. 1 c.p. (קָנָה 888) *we have bought back*
אֶת־אַחֵינוּ הַיְּהוּדִים dir.obj.-n.m.p.-1 c.p. sf. (26) -def.art.-adj. gent. m.p. (397) *our Jewish brethren*
הַנִּמְכָּרִים def.art.-Ni. ptc. m.p. (מָכַר 569) *who have been sold*
לַגּוֹיִם prep.-def.art.-n.m.p. (156) *to the nations*
כְּדֵי בָנוּ prep.-ssubst. cstr. (191)-prep.-1 c.p. sf. *as far as we are able*
וְגַם־אַתֶּם תִּמְכְּרוּ conj.-adv. (168)-pers.pr. 2 m.p. (61)-Qal impf. 2 m.p. (מָכַר 569) *but you even sell*
אֶת־אֲחֵיכֶם dir.obj.-n.m.p.-2 m.p. sf. (26) *your brethren*
וְנִמְכְּרוּ־לָנוּ conj.-Ni. pf. 3 c.p. (מָכַר 569)-prep.-1 c.p. sf. *that they may be sold to us*
וַיַּחֲרִישׁוּ consec.-Hi. impf. 3 m.p. (חָרַשׁ II 361) *they were silent*

וְלֹא מָצְאוּ דָּבָר conj.-neg.-Qal pf. 3 c.p. (מָצָא 592)-n.m.s. (182) *and could not find a word to say*

5:9

וָיֹּאמַר consec.-Qal impf. 1 c.s. (אָמַר 55) *so I said*
לֹא־טוֹב neg.-adj. m.s. (II 373) *is not good*
הַדָּבָר def.art.-n.m.s. (182) *the thing*
אֲשֶׁר־אַתֶּם עֹשִׂים rel. (81)-pers.pr. 2 m.s. (61) -Qal act.ptc. m.p. (עָשָׂה I 793) *that you are doing*
הֲלוֹא interr.part.-neg. *not?*
בְּיִרְאַת אֱלֹהֵינוּ prep.-n.f.s. cstr. (432)-n.m.p.-1 c.p. sf. (43) *in the fear of our God*
תֵּלֵכוּ Qal impf. 2 m.p. paus. (הָלַךְ 229) *ought you to walk*
מֵחֶרְפַּת הַגּוֹיִם prep.-n.f.s. cstr. (357)-def.art. -n.m.p. (156) *to prevent the taunts of the nations*
אוֹיְבֵינוּ Qal act.ptc. m.p.-1 c.p. sf. (אָיַב 33) *our enemies*

5:10

וְגַם־אֲנִי conj.-adv. (168)-pers.pr. 1 c.s. (58) *moreover I*
אַחַי וּנְעָרַי n.m.p.-1 c.s. sf. (26)-conj.-n.m.p.-1 c.s. sf. (654) *my brethren and my servants*
נֹשִׁים בָּהֶם Qal act.ptc. m.p. (נָשָׁה I 674)-prep.-3 m.p. sf. *are lending them*
כֶּסֶף וְדָגָן n.m.s. (494)-conj.-n.m.s. (186) *money and grain*
נַעַזְבָה־נָּא Qal impf. 1 c.p.-vol.he (עָזַב I 736) -part.of entreaty (609) *let us leave off*
אֶת־הַמַּשָּׁא הַזֶּה dir.obj.-def.art.-n.m.s. (673) *this interest*

5:11

הָשִׁיבָה נָא לָהֶם Hi. impv. 2 m.s.-vol.he (שׁוּב 996)-part.of entreaty (609)-prep.-3 m.p. sf. *return to them*
כְּהַיּוֹם prep.-def.art.-n.m.s. (398) *this very day*
שְׂדֹתֵיהֶם n.m.p.-3 m.p. sf. (961) *their fields*
כַּרְמֵיהֶם n.m.p.-3 m.p. sf. (501) *their vineyards*
זֵיתֵיהֶם n.m.p.-3 m.p. sf. (268) *their olive orchards*
וּבָתֵּיהֶם conj.-n.m.p.-3 m.p. sf. (108) *and their houses*
וּמְאַת הַכֶּסֶף conj.-n.f.s. cstr. (547)-def.art.-n.m.s. (494) *and the hundredth of money*
וְהַדָּגָן conj.-def.art.-n.m.s. (186) *grain*
הַתִּירוֹשׁ def.art.-n.m.s. (440) *wine*
וְהַיִּצְהָר conj.-def.art.-n.m.s. (I 844) *and oil*
אֲשֶׁר אַתֶּם נֹשִׁים rel. (81)-pers.pr. 2 m.p. (61)-Qal act.ptc. m.p. (נָשָׁה I 674) *which you have been exacting*
בָּהֶם prep.-3 m.p. sf. *of them*

5:12

וַיֹּאמְרוּ consec.-Qal impf. 3 m.p. (אָמַר 55) *then they said*
נָשִׁיב Hi. impf. 1 c.p. (שׁוּב 996) *we will restore*
וּמֵהֶם conj.-prep.-3 m.p. sf. *and from them*
לֹא נְבַקֵּשׁ neg.-Pi. impf. 1 c.p. (בָּקַשׁ 134) *we not require*
כֵּן נַעֲשֶׂה adv. (485)-Qal impf. 1 c.p. (עָשָׂה I 793) *thus we will do*
כַּאֲשֶׁר אַתָּה אוֹמֵר prep.-rel. (81)-pers.pr. 2 m.s. (61)-Qal act.ptc. (אָמַר 55) *as you say*
וָאֶקְרָא אֶת־הַכֹּהֲנִים consec.-Qal impf. 1 c.s. (894) -dir.obj.-def.art.-n.m.p. (463) *and I called the priests*
וָאַשְׁבִּיעֵם לַעֲשׂוֹת consec.-Hi. impf. 1 c.s.-3 m.p. sf. (שָׁבַע 989)-prep.-Qal inf.cstr. (עָשָׂה I 793) *and took an oath of them to do*
כַּדָּבָר הַזֶּה prep.-def.art.-n.m.s. (182)-def.art. -demons.adj. m.s. (260) *according to this word*

5:13

גַּם־חָצְנִי adv. (168)-n.m.s.-1 c.s. sf. (346) *also my lap (bosom)*
נָעַרְתִּי Qal pf. 1 c.s. (נָעַר II 654) *I shook out*
וָאֹמְרָה consec.-Qal impf. 1 c.s. (אָמַר 55) *and I said*
כָּכָה יְנַעֵר adv. (462)-Pi. impf. 3 m.s. (נָעַר II 654) *so may ... shake out*
הָאֱלֹהִים def.art.-n.m.p. (43) *God*
אֶת־כָּל־הָאִישׁ dir.obj.-n.m.s. cstr. (481)-def. art.-n.m.s. (35) *every man*
אֲשֶׁר לֹא־יָקִים rel. (81)-neg.-Hi. impf. 3 m.s. (קוּם 877) *who does not perform*
אֶת־הַדָּבָר הַזֶּה dir.obj.-def.art.-n.m.s. (182)-def. art.-demons.adj. m.s. (260) *this promise*
מִבֵּיתוֹ prep.-n.m.s.-3 m.s. sf. (108) *from his house*
וּמִיגִיעוֹ conj.-prep.-n.m.s.-3 m.s. sf. (388) *and from his labor*
וְכָכָה יִהְיֶה conj.-v.supra-Qal impf. 3 m.s. (הָיָה 224) *so may he be*
נָעוּר וָרֵק Qal pass.ptc. (II 654)-conj.-adj. m.s. (938) *shaken out and empty*
וַיֹּאמְרוּ consec.-Qal impf. 3 m.p. (אָמַר 55) *and said*

כָּל־הַקָּהָל n.m.s. cstr. (481)-def.art.-n.m.s. (874) *all the assembly*
אָמֵן adv. (53) *Amen*
וַיְהַלְלוּ consec.-Pi. impf. 3 m.p. (הָלַל II 237) *and praised*
אֶת־יהוה dir.obj.-pr.n. (217) *Yahweh*
וַיַּעַשׂ הָעָם consec.-Qal impf. 3 m.s. (עָשָׂה I 793)-def.art.-n.m.s. (I 766) *and the people did*
כַּדָּבָר הַזֶּה prep.-def.art.-v.supra-v.supra *as they had promised*

5:14

גַּם מִיּוֹם adv. (168)-prep.-n.m.s. (398) *moreover from the time*
אֲשֶׁר־צִוָּה אֹתִי rel. (81)-Pi. pf. 3 m.s. (צָוָה 845)-dir.obj.-1 c.s. sf. *that I was appointed*
לִהְיוֹת פֶּחָם prep.-Qal inf.cstr. (הָיָה 224)-n.m.s. -3 m.p. sf. (808; GK 91e) *to be their governor*
בְּאֶרֶץ יְהוּדָה prep.-n.f.s. cstr. (75)-pr.n. (397) *in the land of Judah*
מִשְּׁנַת עֶשְׂרִים prep.-n.f.s. cstr. (1040)-num. p. (797) *from the twentieth year*
וְעַד שְׁנַת שְׁלֹשִׁים וּשְׁתַּיִם conj.-prep. (III 723)-v.supra-num. p. (1026)-conj.-num. f. (1040) *to the thirty-second year*
לְאַרְתַּחְשַׁסְתְּא prep.-pr.n. (77) *of Artaxerxes*
הַמֶּלֶךְ def.art.-n.m.s. (I 572) *the king*
שָׁנִים שְׁתֵּים עֶשְׂרֵה n.f.p. (1040)-num. f. (1040)-num. 797) *twelve years*
אֲנִי אַחַי pers.pr. 1 c.s. (58)-n.m.p.-1 c.s. sf. (26) *I and my brethren*
לֶחֶם הַפֶּחָה n.m.s. cstr. (536)-def.art.-n.m.s. (808) *the food allowance of the governor*
לֹא אָכַלְתִּי neg.-Qal pf. 1 c.s. (אָכַל 37) *I did not eat*

5:15

וְהַפַּחוֹת הָרִאשֹׁנִים conj.-def.art.-n.m.p. (808)-def. art.-adj. m.p. (911) *the former governors*
אֲשֶׁר־לְפָנַי rel. (81)-prep.-n.m.p.-1 c.s. sf. (815) *who were before me*
הִכְבִּידוּ עַל־הָעָם Hi. pf. 3 c.p. (כָּבֵד 457)-prep. -def.art.-n.m.s. (I 766) *laid heavy burdens upon the people*
וַיִּקְחוּ מֵהֶם consec.-Qal impf. 3 m.p. (לָקַח 542)-prep.-3 m.p. sf. *and took from them*
בְּלֶחֶם וָיַיִן prep.-n.m.s. (536)-conj.-n.m.s. (406) *food and wine*
אַחַר כֶּסֶף־שְׁקָלִים prep. (29)-n.m.s. cstr. (494) -n.m.p. (1053) *besides ... shekels of silver*
אַרְבָּעִים num. p. (917) *forty*

גַּם נַעֲרֵיהֶם adv. (168)-n.m.p.-3 m.p. sf. (654) *even their servants*
שָׁלְטוּ עַל־הָעָם Qal pf. 3 c.p. (שָׁלַט 1020)-prep. -def.art.-n.m.s. (I 766) *lorded it over the people*
וַאֲנִי לֹא־עָשִׂיתִי כֵן conj.-pers.pr. 1 c.s. (58)-neg. -Qal pf. 1 c.s. (עָשָׂה I 793)-adv. (485) *but I did not do so*
מִפְּנֵי יִרְאַת אֱלֹהִים prep.-n.m.p. cstr. (815)-n.f.s. cstr. (432)-n.m.p. (43) *because of the fear of God*

5:16

וְגַם בִּמְלֶאכֶת conj.-adv. (168)-prep.-n.f.s. cstr. (521) *also ... to the work on*
הַחוֹמָה הַזֹּאת def.art.-n.f.s. (327)-def.art. -demons.adj. f.s. (260) *this wall*
הֶחֱזַקְתִּי Hi. pf. 1 c.s. (חָזַק 304) *I held*
וְשָׂדֶה לֹא קָנִינוּ conj.-n.m.s. (961)-neg.-Qal pf. 1 c.p. (קָנָה 888) *and we acquired no land*
וְכָל־נְעָרַי conj.-n.m.s. cstr. (481)-n.m.p.-1 c.p. sf. (654) *and all my servants*
קְבוּצִים שָׁם Qal pass.ptc. m.p. (קָבַץ 867)-adv. (1027) *were gathered there*
עַל־הַמְּלָאכָה prep.-def.art.-n.f.s. (521) *for the work*

5:17

וְהַיְּהוּדִים conj.-def.art.-adj. gent. p. (397) *Jews*
וְהַסְּגָנִים conj.-def.art.-n.m.p. (688) *and officials*
מֵאָה וַחֲמִשִּׁים אִישׁ n.f.s. (547)-conj.-num. p. (332)-n.m.s. (35) *a hundred and fifty men*
וְהַבָּאִים אֵלֵינוּ conj.-def.art.-Qal act.ptc. m.p. (בּוֹא 97)-prep.-1 c.p. sf. *who came to us*
מִן־הַגּוֹיִם prep.-def.art.-n.m.p. (156) *from the nations*
אֲשֶׁר־סְבִיבֹתֵינוּ rel. (81)-adv.-1 c.p. sf. (686) *which were about us*
עַל־שֻׁלְחָנִי prep.-n.m.s.-1 c.s. sf. (1020) *at my table*

5:18

וַאֲשֶׁר הָיָה conj.-rel. (81)-Qal pf. 3 m.s. (224) *now that which was*
נַעֲשֶׂה Ni. ptc. (עָשָׂה I 793) *prepared*
לְיוֹם אֶחָד prep.-n.m.s. (398)-num. m.s. (25) *for one day*
שׁוֹר אֶחָד n.m.s. (1004)-v.supra *one ox*
צֹאן שֵׁשׁ־בְּרֻרוֹת n.f.s. (838)-num. (995)-Qal pass.ptc. f.p. (בָּרַר 140) *six choice sheep*
וְצִפֳּרִים conj.-n.f.p. (861) *likewise fowls*

נַעֲשׂוּ־לִי Ni. pf. 3 c.p. (עָשָׂה I 793)-prep.-1 c.s. sf. *were prepared for me*

וּבֵין עֲשֶׂרֶת יָמִים conj.-prep. (107)-num. f. cstr. (796)-n.m.p. (398) *and every ten days*

בְּכָל־יַיִן prep.-n.m.s. cstr. (481)-n.m.s. (406) *with all wine*

לְהַרְבֵּה prep.-Hi. inf.abs. (רָבָה I 915) *in abundance*

וְעִם־זֶה conj.-prep.-demons.adj. m.s. (260) *yet with all this*

לֶחֶם הַפֶּחָה n.m.s. cstr. (536)-def.art.-n.m.s. (808) *the food allowance of the governor*

לֹא בִקַּשְׁתִּי neg.-Pi. pf. 1 c.s. (בָּקַשׁ 134) *I did not demand*

כִּי־כָבְדָה conj. (471)-Qal pf. 3 f.s. (כָּבֵד 457) *because was heavy*

הָעֲבֹדָה def.art.-n.f.s. (715) *the servitude*

עַל־הָעָם הַזֶּה prep.-def.art.-n.m.s. (I 766)-def. art.-demons.adj. m.s. (260) *upon this people*

5:19

זָכְרָה־לִּי Qal impv. 2 m.s.-vol.he (זָכַר 269) -prep.-1 c.s. sf. *remember for me*

אֱלֹהַי n.m.p.-1 c.s. sf. (43) *O my God*

לְטוֹבָה prep.-n.f.s. (375) *for good*

כֹּל אֲשֶׁר־עָשִׂיתִי n.m.s. (481)-rel. (81)-Qal pf. 1 c.s. (עָשָׂה I 793) *all that I have done*

עַל־הָעָם הַזֶּה prep.-def.art.-n.m.s. (I 766)-def. art.-demons.adj. m.s. (260) *for this people*

6:1

וַיְהִי כַאֲשֶׁר consec.-Qal impf. 3 m.s. (הָיָה 224) -prep.-rel. (81) *now when*

נִשְׁמַע Ni. pf. 3 m.s. (שָׁמַע 1033) *it was reported*

לְסַנְבַלַּט prep.-pr.n. (702) *to Sanballat*

וְטוֹבִיָּה conj.-pr.n. (375) *and Tobiah*

וּלְגֶשֶׁם conj.-prep.-pr.n. (I 177) *and to Geshem*

הָעַרְבִי def.art.-adj. gent. (787) *the Arab*

וּלְיֶתֶר אֹיְבֵינוּ conj.-prep.-n.m.s. cstr. (451)-Qal act.ptc. m.p.-1 c.p. sf. (אָיַב 33) *and to the rest of our enemies*

כִּי בָנִיתִי conj. (471)-Qal pf. 1 c.s. (בָּנָה 124) *that I had built*

אֶת־הַחוֹמָה dir.obj.-def.art.-n.f.s. (327) *the wall*

וְלֹא־נוֹתַר בָּהּ conj.-neg.-Ni. pf. 3 m.s. (יָתַר 451) -prep.-3 f.s. sf. *and that there was no ... left*

פָּרֶץ n.m.s. paus. (829) *breach*

גַּם עַד־הָעֵת הַהִיא adv. (168)-prep. (III 723)-def. art.-n.f.s. (773)-def.art.-demons.adj. f.s. (214) *although up to that time*

דְּלָתוֹת n.f.p. (195) *doors*

לֹא־הֶעֱמַדְתִּי neg.-Hi. pf. 1 c.s. (עָמַד 763) *I have not set up*

בַּשְּׁעָרִים prep.-def.art.-n.m.p. (1044) *in the gates*

6:2

וַיִּשְׁלַח consec.-Qal impf. 3 m.s. (שָׁלַח 1018) *sent*

סַנְבַלַּט pr.n. (702) *Sanballat*

וְגֶשֶׁם conj.-pr.n. (I 177) *and Geshem*

אֵלַי לֵאמֹר prep.-1 c.s. sf.-prep.-Qal inf.cstr. (55 אָמַר) *to me, saying*

לְכָה Qal impv. 2 m.s.-vol.he (הָלַךְ 229) *come*

וְנִוָּעֲדָה יַחְדָּו conj.-Ni. impf. 1 c.p.-vol.he (יָעַד 416)-adv. (403) *and let us meet together*

בַּכְּפִירִים prep.-def.art.-n.m.p. (499) *in the villages*

בְּבִקְעַת אוֹנוֹ prep.-n.f.s. cstr. (132)-pr.n. (20) *in the plain of Ono*

וְהֵמָּה חֹשְׁבִים conj.-pers.pr. 3 m.p. (241)-Qal act.ptc. m.p. (חָשַׁב 362) *but they intended*

לַעֲשׂוֹת לִי רָעָה prep.-Qal inf.cstr. (עָשָׂה I 793)-prep.-1 c.s. sf.-n.f.s. (949) *to do me harm*

6:3

וָאֶשְׁלְחָה עֲלֵיהֶם consec.-Qal impf. 1 c.s. (שָׁלַח 1018)-prep.-3 m.p. sf. *and I sent to them*

מַלְאָכִים n.m.p. (521) *messengers*

לֵאמֹר prep.-Qal inf.cstr. (אָמַר 55) *saying*

מְלָאכָה גְדוֹלָה n.f.s. (521)-adj. f.s. (152) *a great work*

אֲנִי עֹשֶׂה pers.pr. 1 c.s. (58)-Qal act.ptc. (עָשָׂה I 793) *I am doing*

וְלֹא אוּכַל לָרֶדֶת conj.-neg.-Qal impf. 1 c.s. (יָכֹל 407)-prep.-Qal inf.cstr. (יָרַד 432) *I cannot come down*

לָמָּה תִשְׁבַּת הַמְּלָאכָה prep.-interr. (552)-Qal impf. 3 f.s. (שָׁבַת 991)-def.art.-n.f.s. (521) *why should the work stop*

כַּאֲשֶׁר אַרְפֶּהָ prep.-rel. (81)-Hi. impf. 1 c.s.-3 f.s. sf. (רָפָה 951) *while I leave it*

וְיָרַדְתִּי אֲלֵיכֶם conj.-Qal pf. 1 c.s. (יָרַד 432) -prep.-2 m.p. sf. *and come down to you*

6:4

וַיִּשְׁלְחוּ אֵלַי consec.-Qal impf. 3 m.p. (שָׁלַח 1018)-prep.-1 c.s. sf. *and they sent to me*

כַּדָּבָר הַזֶּה prep.-def.art.-n.m.s. (182)-def. art.-demons.adj. m.s. (260) *in this way*

אַרְבַּע פְּעָמִים num. cstr. (916)-n.f.p. (821) *four times*

וָאָשִׁיב אוֹתָם consec.-Hi. impf. 1 c.s. (שׁוּב 996) -dir.obj.-3 m.p. sf. *and I answered them*

כַּדָּבָר הַזֶּה v.supra-v.supra *in the same manner*

6:5

וַיִּשְׁלַח אֵלַי consec.-Qal impf. 3 m.s. (1018) -prep.-1 c.s. sf. *sent to me*

סַנְבַלַּט pr.n. (702) *Sanballat*

כַּדָּבָר הַזֶּה prep.-def.art.-n.m.s. (182)-def.art. -demons.adj. m.s. (260) *in the same way*

פַּעַם חֲמִישִׁית n.f.s. (821)-num. f.s. (332) *for the fifth time*

אֶת־נַעֲרוֹ dir.obj.-n.m.s.-3 m.s. sf. (654) *his servant*

וְאִגֶּרֶת פְּתוּחָה conj.-n.f.s. (8)-Qal pass.ptc. f.s. (I 834 פָּתַח) *with an open letter*

בְּיָדוֹ prep.-n.f.s.-3 m.s. sf. (388) *in his hand*

6:6

כָּתוּב בָּהּ Qal pass.ptc. (507)-prep.-3 f.s. sf. *in it was written*

בַּגּוֹיִם prep.-def.art.-n.m.p. (156) *among the nations*

נִשְׁמָע Ni. ptc. (שָׁמַע 1033) *it is reported*

וְגַשְׁמוּ conj.-pr.n. (I 177; GK 90k) *also Gashmu*

אֹמֵר Qal act.ptc. (אָמַר 55) *saying*

אַתָּה וְהַיְּהוּדִים pers.pr. 2 m.s. (61)-conj.-def.art. -adj. gent. p. (397) *that you and the Jews*

חֹשְׁבִים לִמְרוֹד Qal act.ptc. m.p. (חָשַׁב 362) -prep.-Qal inf.cstr. (מָרַד 597) *intend to rebel*

עַל־כֵּן אַתָּה בוֹנֶה prep.-adv. (485)-pers.pr. 2 m.s. (61)-Qal act.ptc. (בָּנָה 124) *that is why you are building*

הַחוֹמָה def.art.-n.f.s. (327) *the wall*

וְאַתָּה הֹוֶה conj.-v.supra-Qal act.ptc. (הָוָה 217) *and you wish to become*

לָהֶם לְמֶלֶךְ prep.-3 m.p. sf.-prep.-n.m.s. (I 572) *their king*

כַּדְּבָרִים הָאֵלֶּה prep.-def.art.-n.m.p. (182)-def.art. -demons.adj. c.p. (41) *according to this report*

6:7

וְגַם־נְבִיאִים conj.-adv. (168)-n.m.p. (611) *and also prophets*

הֶעֱמַדְתָּ Hi. pf. 2 m.s. (עָמַד 763) *you have set up*

לִקְרֹא עָלֶיךָ prep.-Qal inf.cstr. (קָרָא 894)-prep. -2 m.s. sf. *to proclaim concerning you*

בִירוּשָׁלַםִ prep.-pr.n. (436) *in Jerusalem*

לֵאמֹר prep.-Qal inf.cstr. (55) *saying*

מֶלֶךְ בִּיהוּדָה n.m.s. (I 572)-prep.-pr.n. (397) *there is a king in Judah*

וְעַתָּה יִשָּׁמַע conj.-adv. (773)-Ni. impf. 3 m.s. (1033 שָׁמַע) *and now it will be reported*

לַמֶּלֶךְ prep.-def.art.-n.m.s. (I 572) *to the king*

כַּדְּבָרִים הָאֵלֶּה prep.-def.art.-n.m.p. (182)-def.art. -demons.adj. c.p. (41) *according to these words*

וְעַתָּה לְכָה v.supra-Qal impv. 2 m.s.-vol.he (הָלַךְ 229) *so now come*

וְנִוָּעֲצָה יַחְדָּו conj.-Ni. impf. 1 c.p.-vol.he (יָעַץ 419)-adv. (403) *and let us take counsel together*

6:8

וָאֶשְׁלְחָה אֵלָיו consec.-Qal impf. 1 c.s. (שָׁלַח 1018)-prep.-3 m.s. sf. *then I sent to him*

לֵאמֹר prep.-Qal inf.cstr. (55) *saying*

לֹא נִהְיָה neg.-Ni. pf. 3 m.s. (הָיָה 224) *it has not been*

כַּדְּבָרִים הָאֵלֶּה prep.-def.art.-n.m.p. (182)-def.art. -demons.adj. c.p. (41) *according to these words*

אֲשֶׁר אַתָּה אוֹמֵר rel. (81)-pers.pr. 2 m.s. (61)-Qal act.ptc. (55) *as you say*

כִּי מִלִּבְּךָ conj. (471)-prep.-n.m.s.-2 m.s. sf. (524) *for out of your own mind*

אַתָּה בוֹדָאם v.supra-Qal act.ptc.-3 m.p. sf. (בָּדָא 94; GK 23c,74i) *you are inventing them*

6:9

כִּי כֻלָּם מְיָרְאִים conj. (471)-n.m.s.-3 m.p. sf. (481)-Pi. ptc. m.p. (יָרֵא 431) *for they all wanted to frighten*

אוֹתָנוּ dir.obj.-1 c.p. sf. *us*

לֵאמֹר prep.-Qal inf.cstr. (55) *thinking*

יִרְפּוּ יְדֵיהֶם Qal impf. 3 m.p. (רָפָה 951)-n.f.p.-3 m.p. sf. (388) *their hands will drop*

מִן־הַמְּלָאכָה prep.-def.art.-n.f.s. (521) *from the work*

וְלֹא תֵעָשֶׂה conj.-neg.-Ni. impf. 3 f.s. (עָשָׂה I 793) *and it will not be done*

וְעַתָּה conj.-adv. (773) *but now*

חַזֵּק Pi. impv. 2 m.s. (חָזַק 304) *strengthen thou*

אֶת־יָדָי dir.obj.-n.f.p.-1 c.s. sf. paus. (388) *my hands*

6:10

וַאֲנִי־בָאתִי conj.-pers.pr. 1 c.s. (58)-Qal pf. 1 c.s. (97 בּוֹא) *now when I went*

בֵּית שְׁמַעְיָה n.m.s. cstr. (108)-pr.n. (1035) *into the house of Shemaiah*

בֶּן־דְּלָיָה n.m.s. cstr. (119)-pr.n. (195) *the son of Delaiah*

בֶּן־מְהֵיטַבְאֵל v.supra-pr.n. (406) *son of Mehetabel*

וְהוּא עָצוּר conj.-pers.pr. 3 m.s. (214)-Qal pass.ptc. (עָצַר 783) *who was shut up*

וַיֹּאמֶר consec.-Qal impf. 3 m.s. (55) *and he said*

נִוָּעֵד Ni. impf. 1 c.p. (יָעַד 416) *let us meet together*

אֶל־בֵּית הָאֱלֹהִים prep.-n.m.s. cstr. (108)-def.art.-n.m.p. (43) *in the house of God*

אֶל־תּוֹךְ הַהֵיכָל prep.-n.m.s. cstr. (1063)-def.art.-n.m.s. (228) *with the temple*

וְנִסְגְּרָה conj.-Qal impf. 1 c.p.-vol.he (סָגַר 688) *and let us close*

דַּלְתוֹת הַהֵיכָל n.f.p. cstr. (195)-v.supra *the doors of the temple*

כִּי בָּאִים לְהָרְגֶךָ conj. (471)-Qal act.ptc. m.p. (בּוֹא 97; GK 144i)-prep.-Qal inf.cstr.-2 m.s. sf. (הָרַג 246) *for they are coming to kill you*

וְלַיְלָה conj.-n.m.s. (538) *and at night*

בָּאִים לְהָרְגֶךָ v.supra-v.supra *they are coming to kill you*

6:11

וָאֹמְרָה consec.-Qal impf. 1 c.s. (אָמַר 55) *but I said*

הַאִישׁ כָּמוֹנִי יִבְרָח interr.part. (GK 100m)-n.m.s. (35) -prep.-1 c.s. sf.-Qal impf. 3 m.s. (בָּרַח 137) *should such a man as I flee?*

וּמִי כָמוֹנִי conj.-interr. (566)-v.supra *and who such as I*

אֲשֶׁר־יָבוֹא rel. (81)-Qal impf. 3 m.s. (בּוֹא 97) *could go*

אֶל־הַהֵיכָל prep.-def.art.-n.m.s. (228) *into the temple*

וָחָי conj.-adj. m.s. paus. or Qal pf. 3 m.s. (חָיָה 311 or 310) *and live*

לֹא אָבוֹא neg.-Qal impf. 1 c.s. (בּוֹא 97) *I will not go in*

6:12

וָאַכִּירָה consec.-Hi. impf. 1 c.s. (נָכַר I 647) *and I understood*

וְהִנֵּה לֹא־אֱלֹהִים conj.-interj. (243)-neg.-n.m.p. (43) *and saw that God had not*

שְׁלָחוֹ Qal pf. 3 m.s.-3 m.s. sf. (שָׁלַח 1018) *sent him*

כִּי הַנְּבוּאָה conj. (471)-def.art.-n.f.s. (612) *but the prophecy*

דִּבֶּר עָלַי Pi. pf. 3 m.s. (180)-prep.-1 c.s. sf. *he had pronounced against me*

וְטוֹבִיָּה conj.-pr.n. (375) *because Tobiah*

וְסַנְבַלַּט conj.-pr.n. (702) *and Sanballat*

שְׂכָרוֹ Qal pf. 3 m.s.-3 m.s. sf. (שָׂכַר 968) *had hired him*

6:13

לְמַעַן שָׂכוּר הוּא prep. (775)-Qal pass.ptc. (שָׂכַר 968)-pers.pr. 3 m.s. (214) *for this purpose he was hired*

לְמַעַן־אִירָא v.supra-Qal impf. 1 c.s. (יָרֵא 431) *that I should be afraid*

וְאֶעֱשֶׂה־כֵּן conj.-Qal impf. 1 c.s. (עָשָׂה I 793)-adv. (485) *and act in this way*

וְחָטָאתִי conj.-Qal pf. 1 c.s. (חָטָא 306) *and I would sin*

וְהָיָה לָהֶם conj.-Qal pf. 3 m.s. (224)-prep.-3 m.p. sf. *and it was to them*

לְשֵׁם רָע prep.-n.m.s. (1027)-adj. m.s. (948) *an evil name*

לְמַעַן יְחָרְפוּנִי conj. (775)-Pi. impf. 3 m.p.-1 c.s. sf. (חָרַף 357) *in order to taunt me*

6:14

זָכְרָה אֱלֹהַי Qal impv. 2 m.s.-vol.he (זָכַר 269)-n.m.p.-1 c.s. sf. (43) *remember, O my God*

לְטוֹבִיָּה prep.-pr.n. (375) *Tobiah*

וּלְסַנְבַלַּט conj.-prep.-pr.n. (702) *and Sanballat*

כְּמַעֲשָׂיו אֵלֶּה prep.-n.m.p.-3 m.s. sf. (795)-demons.adj. c.p. (41) *according to these things that they did*

וְגַם לְנוֹעַדְיָה conj.-adv. (168)-prep.-pr.n. (418) *and also Noadiah*

הַנְּבִיאָה def.art.-n.f.s. (612) *the prophetess*

וּלְיֶתֶר הַנְּבִיאִים conj.-prep.-n.m.s. cstr. (451)-def. art.-n.m.p. (611) *and the rest of the prophets*

אֲשֶׁר הָיוּ מְיָרְאִים אוֹתִי rel. (81)-Qal pf. 3 c.p. (224)-Pi. ptc. m.p. (יָרֵא 431)-dir.obj.-1 c.s. sf. *who wanted to make me afraid*

6:15

וַתִּשְׁלַם הַחוֹמָה consec.-Qal impf. 3 f.s. (שָׁלַם 1022)-def.art.-n.f.s. (327) *so the wall was finished*

בְּעֶשְׂרִים וַחֲמִשָּׁה prep.-num. p. (797)-conj.-num. f.s. (331) *on the twenty-fifth (day)*

לֶאֱלוּל prep.-pr.n. (47) *of Elul*

לַחֲמִשִּׁים וּשְׁנַיִם יוֹם prep.-num. p. (332)-conj.-num. m. (1040)-n.m.s. (398) *in fifty-two days*

6:16

וַיְהִי כַּאֲשֶׁר שָׁמְעוּ consec.-Qal impf. 3 m.s. (הָיָה 224)-prep.-rel. (81)-Qal pf. 3 c.p. (שָׁמַע 1033) *and when heard*

כָּל־אוֹיְבֵינוּ n.m.s. cstr. (481)-Qal act.ptc. m.p.-1 c.p. sf. (אָיַב 33) *all our enemies*

וַיִּרְאוּ consec.-Qal impf. 3 m.p. (יָרֵא 431) *were afraid*

כָּל־הַגּוֹיִם n.m.s. cstr. (481)-def.art.-n.m.p. (156) *all the nations*

אֲשֶׁר סְבִיבֹתֵינוּ rel. (81)-adv.-1 c.p. sf. (686) *round about us*

וַיִּפְּלוּ מְאֹד consec.-Qal impf. 3 m.p. (נָפַל 656)-adv. (547) *and fell greatly*

בְּעֵינֵיהֶם prep.-n.f.p.-3 m.p. sf. (744) *in their own esteem*

וַיֵּדְעוּ consec.-Qal impf. 3 m.p. (יָדַע 393) *for they perceived*

כִּי מֵאֵת אֱלֹהֵינוּ conj. (471)-prep.-prep. (II 85) -n.m.p.-1 c.p. sf. (43) *that with the help of our God*

נֶעֶשְׂתָה הַמְּלָאכָה Ni. pf. 3 f.s. (עָשָׂה I 793) -def.art.-n.f.s. (521) *that ... work had been accomplished*

הַזֹּאת def.art.-demons.adj. f.s. (260) *this*

6:17

גַּם בַּיָּמִים הָהֵם adv. (168)-prep.-def.art.-n.m.p. (398)-def.art.-demons.adj. m.p. (241) *moreover in those days*

מַרְבִּים Hi. ptc. m.p. (רָבָה I 915) *sent many*

חֹרֵי יְהוּדָה n.m.p. cstr. (II 359)-pr.n. (397) *the nobles of Judah*

אִגְּרֹתֵיהֶם n.f.p.-3 m.p. sf. (8) *their letters*

הוֹלְכוֹת עַל־טוֹבִיָּה Qal act.ptc. f.p. (הָלַךְ 229)-prep.-pr.n. (375) *to Tobiah*

וַאֲשֶׁר לְטוֹבִיָּה conj.-rel. (81)-prep.-pr.n. (375) *and Tobiah's letters*

בָּאוֹת אֲלֵיהֶם Qal act.ptc. f.p. (בּוֹא 97)-prep.-3 m.p. sf. *came to them*

6:18

כִּי־רַבִּים conj. (471)-adj. m.p. (I 912) *for many*

בִּיהוּדָה prep.-pr.n. (397) *in Judah*

בַּעֲלֵי שְׁבוּעָה לוֹ n.m.p. cstr. (I 127)-n.f.s. (989) -prep.-3 m.s. sf. *were bound by oath to him*

כִּי־חָתָן הוּא conj. (471)-n.m.s. (368)-pers.pr. 3 m.s. (214) *because he was son-in-law*

לִשְׁכַנְיָה prep.-pr.n. (1016) *of Shecaniah*

בֶן־אָרַח n.m.s. cstr. (119)-pr.n. (73) *the son of Arah*

וִיהוֹחָנָן בְּנוֹ conj.-pr.n. (220)-n.m.s.-3 m.s. sf. (119) *and his son Jehohanan*

לָקַח Qal pf. 3 m.s. (542) *had taken as his wife*

אֶת־בַּת־מְשֻׁלָּם dir.obj.-n.f.s. cstr. (I 123)-pr.n. (1024) *the daughter of Meshullam*

בֶּן בֶּרֶכְיָה v.supra-pr.n. (140) *the son of Berechiah*

6:19

גַּם טוֹבֹתָיו adv. (168)-n.f.p.-3 m.s. sf. (375) *also his good deeds*

הָיוּ אֹמְרִים Qal pf. 3 c.p. (הָיָה 224)-Qal act.ptc. m.p. (אָמַר 55) *they spoke of*

לְפָנַי prep.-n.m.p.-1 c.s. sf. (815) *in my presence*

וּדְבָרַי הָיוּ conj.-n.m.p.-1 c.s. sf. (182)-v.supra *and my words were*

מוֹצִיאִים לוֹ Hi. ptc. m.p. (יָצָא 422)-prep.-3 m.s. sf. *being reported to him*

אִגְּרוֹת n.f.p. (8) *and letters*

שָׁלַח טוֹבִיָּה Qal pf. 3 m.s. (1018)-pr.n. (375) *Tobiah sent*

לְיָרְאֵנִי prep.-Qal act.ptc.-1 c.s. sf. (יָרֵא 431) *to make me afraid*

7:1

וַיְהִי כַּאֲשֶׁר consec.-Qal impf. 3 m.s. (הָיָה 224)-prep.-rel. (81) *now when*

נִבְנְתָה הַחוֹמָה Ni. pf. 3 f.s. (בָּנָה 124)-def.art. -n.f.s. (327) *the wall had been built*

וָאַעֲמִיד consec.-Hi. impf. 1 c.s. (עָמַד 763) *and I had set up*

הַדְּלָתוֹת def.art.-n.f.p. (195) *the doors*

וַיִּפָּקְדוּ consec.-Ni. impf. 3 m.p. (פָּקַד 823) *and had been appointed*

הַשּׁוֹעֲרִים def.art.-n.m.p. (1045) *the gatekeepers*

וְהַמְשֹׁרְרִים conj.-def.art.-Polel ptc. m.p. (שִׁיר 1010) *the singers*

וְהַלְוִיִּם conj.-def.art.-adj. gent. m.p. (II 532) *and the Levites*

7:2

וָאֲצַוֶּה consec.-Pi. impf. 1 c.s. (צָוָה 845) *I gave charge*

אֶת־חֲנָנִי אָחִי dir.obj.-pr.n. (337)-n.m.s.-1 c.s. sf. (26) *Hanani my brother*

וְאֶת־חֲנַנְיָה conj.-dir.obj.-pr.n. (337) *and Hananiah*

שַׂר הַבִּירָה n.m.s. cstr. (978)-def.art.-n.f.s. (108) *the governor of the castle*

עַל־יְרוּשָׁלָםִ prep.-pr.n. (436) *over Jerusalem*

כִּי־הוּא conj. (471)-pers.pr. 3 m.s. (214) *for he was*

כְּאִישׁ אֱמֶת prep. (GK 118x)-n.m.s. cstr. (35)-n.f.s. (54) *indeed (more) a man of faith*

וְיָרֵא אֶת־הָאֱלֹהִים conj.-Qal act.ptc. (431)-dir. obj.-def.art.-n.m.p. (43) *and God-fearing*

מֵרַבִּים prep.-adj. m.p. (I 912) *than many*

7:3

וַיֹּאמַר לָהֶם consec.-Qal impf. 1 c.s. (אָמַר 55)-prep.-3 m.p. sf. *and I said to them*

לֹא יִפָּתְחוּ neg.-Ni. impf. 3 m.p. (פָּתַח I 834) *let not be opened*

שַׁעֲרֵי יְרוּשָׁלַםִ n.m.p. cstr. (1044)-pr.n. (436) *the gates of Jerusalem*

עַד־חֹם הַשֶּׁמֶשׁ prep. (III 723)-n.m.s. cstr. (328) -def.art.-n.f.s. (1039) *until the sun is hot*

וְעַד הֵם עֹמְדִים conj.-v.supra-pers.pr. 3 m.p. (241)-Qal act.ptc. m.p. (עָמַד 763) *and while they are still standing*

יָגִיפוּ הַדְּלָתוֹת Hi. impf. 3 m.p. (גּוּף 157)-def.art. -n.f.p. (195) *let them shut the doors*

וֶאֱחֹזוּ conj.-Qal impv. 2 m.p. (אָחַז 28) *and bar*

וְהַעֲמֵיד מִשְׁמְרוֹת conj.-Hi. inf.abs. (עָמַד 763)-n.f.p. (1038) *appoint guards*

יֹשְׁבֵי יְרוּשָׁלַםִ Qal act.ptc. m.p. cstr. (יָשַׁב 442) -pr.n. (436) *from among the inhabitants of Jerusalem*

אִישׁ בְּמִשְׁמָרוֹ n.m.s. (35)-prep.-n.m.s.-3 m.s. sf. (1038) *each to his station*

וְאִישׁ נֶגֶד בֵּיתוֹ conj.-v.supra-prep. (617)-n.m.s.-3 m.s. sf. (108) *and each opposite his own house*

7:4

וְהָעִיר conj.-def.art.-n.f.s. (746) *and the city*

רַחֲבַת יָדַיִם adj. f.s. cstr. (932)-n.f. du. (388) *wide*

וּגְדוֹלָה conj.-adj. f.s. (152) *and large*

וְהָעָם מְעַט conj.-def.art.-n.m.s. (I 766)-subst. (589) *but the people were few*

בְּתוֹכָהּ prep.-n.m.s.-3 f.s. sf. (1063) *within it*

וְאֵין בָּתִּים conj.-neg. (II 34)-n.m.p. (108) *and no houses*

בְּנוּיִם Qal pass.ptc. m.p. (בָּנָה 124) *had been built*

7:5

וַיִּתֵּן אֱלֹהַי consec.-Qal impf. 3 m.s. (נָתַן 678) -n.m.p.-1 c.s. sf. (43) *then my God put it*

אֶל־לִבִּי prep.-n.m.s.-1 c.s. sf. (524) *into my mind*

וָאֶקְבְּצָה consec.-Qal impf. 1 c.s. (קָבַץ 867) *and I gathered*

אֶת־הַחֹרִים dir.obj.-def.art.-n.m.p. (II 359) *the nobles*

וְאֶת־הַסְּגָנִים conj.-dir.obj.-def.art.-n.m.p. (688) *and the officials*

וְאֶת־הָעָם conj.-dir.obj.-def.art.-n.m.s. (I 766) *and the people*

לְהִתְיַחֵשׂ prep.-Hith. inf.cstr. (יָחַשׂ 405) *to be enrolled by genealogy*

וָאֶמְצָא סֵפֶר consec.-Qal impf. 1 c.s. (מָצָא 592) -n.m.s. cstr. (706) *and I found the book of*

הַיַּחַשׂ def.art.-n.m.s. (405) *genealogy*

הָעוֹלִים def.art.-Qal act.ptc. m.p. (עָלָה 748) *of those who came up*

בָּרִאשׁוֹנָה prep.-def.art.-adj. f.s. (911) *at the first*

וָאֶמְצָא consec.-v.supra *and I found*

כָּתוּב בּוֹ Qal pass.ptc. (כָּתַב 507)-prep.-3 m.s. sf. *written in it*

7:6

אֵלֶּה demons.adj. c.p. (41) *these were*

בְּנֵי הַמְּדִינָה n.m.p. cstr. (119)-def.art.-n.f.s. (193) *the people of the province*

הָעֹלִים def.art.-Qal act.ptc. m.p. (עָלָה 748) *who came up*

מִשְּׁבִי הַגּוֹלָה prep.-n.m.s. cstr. (985)-def.art.-n.f.s. (163) *out of the captivity of those exiles*

אֲשֶׁר הֶגְלָה rel. (81)-Hi. pf. 3 m.s. (גָּלָה 162) *whom ... had carried into exile*

נְבוּכַדְנֶצַּר pr.n. (613) *Nebuchadnezzar*

מֶלֶךְ בָּבֶל n.m.s. cstr. (I 572)-pr.n. (93) *the king of Babylon*

וַיָּשׁוּבוּ consec.-Qal impf. 3 m.p. (שׁוּב 996) *they returned*

לִירוּשָׁלַםִ prep.-pr.n. (436) *to Jerusalem*

וְלִיהוּדָה conj.-prep.-pr.n. (397) *and Judah*

אִישׁ לְעִירוֹ n.m.s. (35)-prep.-n.f.s.-3 m.s. sf. (746) *each to his town*

7:7

הַבָּאִים def.art.-Qal act.ptc. m.p. (בּוֹא 97) *they came*

עִם־זְרֻבָּבֶל prep. (767)-pr.n. (279) *with Zerubbabel*

יֵשׁוּעַ pr.n. (221) *Jeshua*

נְחֶמְיָה pr.n. (637) *Nehemiah*

עֲזַרְיָה pr.n. (741) *Azariah*

רַעַמְיָה pr.n. (947) *Raamiah*

נַחֲמָנִי pr.n. (637) *Nahamani*

מָרְדֳּכַי pr.n. (598) *Mordecai*

בִּלְשָׁן pr.n. (119) *Bilshan*

מִסְפֶּרֶת pr.n. (709) *Mispereth*

בִּגְוַי pr.n. (94) *Bigvai*

נְחוּם pr.n. (637) *Nehum*

בַּעֲנָה pr.n. (128) *Baanah*

מִסְפַּר אַנְשֵׁי n.m.s. cstr. (708)-n.m.p. cstr. (35) *the number of the men of*

עַם יִשְׂרָאֵל n.m.s. cstr. (I 766)-pr.n. (975) *the people of Israel*

7:8

בְּנֵי פַרְעֹשׁ n.m.p. cstr. (119)–pr.n. (II 829) *the sons of Parosh*
אַלְפַּיִם n.m. du. (48) *two thousand*
מֵאָה n.f.s. (547) *a hundred*
וְשִׁבְעִים וּשְׁנָיִם conj.–num. p. (988)–conj.–num. paus. (1040) *and seventy-two*

7:9

בְּנֵי שְׁפַטְיָה n.m.p. cstr. (119)–pr.n. (1049) *the sons of Shephatiah*
שְׁלֹשׁ מֵאוֹת num. cstr. (1025)–n.f.p. (547) *three hundred*
שִׁבְעִים וּשְׁנָיִם num. p. (988)–conj.–num. paus. (1040) *and seventy-two*

7:10

בְּנֵי אָרַח n.m.p. cstr. (119)–pr.n. (73) *the sons of Arah*
שֵׁשׁ מֵאוֹת num. (995)–n.f.p. (547) *six hundred*
חֲמִשִּׁים וּשְׁנָיִם num. p. (332)–conj.–num. paus. (1040) *and fifty-two*

7:11

בְּנֵי־פַחַת מוֹאָב n.m.p. cstr. (119)–pr.n. (809) *the sons of Pahath-moab*
לִבְנֵי יֵשׁוּעַ prep.–v.supra–pr.n. (221) *namely the sons of Jeshua*
וְיוֹאָב conj.–pr.n. (222) *and Joab*
אַלְפַּיִם n.m. du. (48) *two thousand*
וּשְׁמֹנֶה מֵאוֹת conj.–num. (1032)–n.f.p. (547) *eight hundred*
שְׁמֹנָה עָשָׂר num. f. (1032)–num. (797) *eighteen*

7:12

בְּנֵי עֵילָם n.m.p. cstr. (119)–pr.n. (II 743) *the sons of Elam*
אֶלֶף מָאתַיִם n.m.s. (48)–n.f. du. (547) *a thousand two hundred*
חֲמִשִּׁים וְאַרְבָּעָה num. p. (332)–conj.–num. f. (916) *and fifty-four*

7:13

בְּנֵי זַתּוּא n.m.p. cstr. (119)–pr.n. (285) *the sons of Zattu*
שְׁמֹנֶה מֵאוֹת num. m. (1032)–n.f.p. (547) *eight hundred*
אַרְבָּעִים וַחֲמִשָּׁה num. p. (917)–conj.–num. f. (331) *and forty-five*

7:14

בְּנֵי זַכָּי n.m.p. cstr. (119)–pr.n. (269) *the sons of Zaccai*
שְׁבַע מֵאוֹת num. m. cstr. (I 987)–n.f.p. (547) *seven hundred*
וְשִׁשִּׁים conj.–num. p. (995) *and sixty*

7:15

בְּנֵי בִנּוּי n.m.p. cstr. (119)–pr.n. (125) *the sons of Binnui*
שֵׁשׁ מֵאוֹת num. (995)–n.f.p. (547) *six hundred*
אַרְבָּעִים וּשְׁמֹנָה num. p. (917)–conj.–num. f. (1032) *and forty-eight*

7:16

בְּנֵי בֵבָי n.m.p. cstr. (119)–pr.n. (93) *the sons of Bebai*
שֵׁשׁ מֵאוֹת num. (995)–n.f.p. (547) *six hundred*
עֶשְׂרִים וּשְׁמֹנָה num. p. (797)–conj.–num. f. (1032) *and twenty-eight*

7:17

בְּנֵי עַזְגָּד n.m.p. cstr. (119)–pr.n. (739) *the sons of Azgad*
אַלְפַּיִם n.m. du. (48) *two thousand*
שְׁלֹשׁ מֵאוֹת num. m. cstr. (1025)–n.f.p. (547) *three hundred*
עֶשְׂרִים וּשְׁנָיִם num. p. (797)–conj.–num. du. paus. (1040) *and twenty-two*

7:18

בְּנֵי אֲדֹנִיקָם n.m.p. cstr. (119)–pr.n. (12) *the sons of Adonikam*
שֵׁשׁ מֵאוֹת num. (995)–n.f.p. (547) *six hundred*
שִׁשִּׁים וְשִׁבְעָה num. p. (995)–conj.–num. f. (I 987) *and sixty-seven*

7:19

בְּנֵי בִגְוָי n.m.p. cstr. (119)–pr.n. (94) *the sons of Bigvai*
אַלְפַּיִם n.m. du. (48) *two thousand*
שִׁשִּׁים וְשִׁבְעָה num. p. (995)–conj.–num. f. (I 987) *and sixty-seven*

7:20

בְּנֵי עָדִין n.m.p. cstr. (119)–pr.n. (II 726) *the sons of Adin*
שֵׁשׁ מֵאוֹת num. (995)–n.f.p. (547) *six hundred*
חֲמִשִּׁים וַחֲמִשָּׁה num. p. (332)–conj.–num. f. (331) *and fifty-five*

7:21

בְּנֵי־אָטֵר n.m.p. cstr. (119)-pr.n. (32) ***the sons of Ater***
לְחִזְקִיָּה prep.-pr.n. (306) ***namely of Hezekiah***
תִּשְׁעִים וּשְׁמֹנָה num. p. (1077)-conj.-num. f. (1032) ***ninety-eight***

7:22

בְּנֵי חָשֻׁם n.m.p. cstr. (119)-pr.n. (365) ***the sons of Hashum***
שְׁלֹשׁ מֵאוֹת num. cstr. (1025)-n.f.p. (547) ***three hundred***
עֶשְׂרִים וּשְׁמֹנָה num. p. (797)-conj.-num. f. (1032) ***and twenty-eight***

7:23

בְּנֵי בֵצָי n.m.p. cstr. (119)-pr.n. (130) ***the sons of Bezai***
שְׁלֹשׁ מֵאוֹת num. cstr. (1025)-n.f.p. (547) ***three hundred***
עֶשְׂרִים וְאַרְבָּעָה num. p. (797)-conj.-num. f. (916) ***and twenty-four***

7:24

בְּנֵי חָרִיף n.m.p. cstr. (119)-pr.n. (358) ***the sons of Hariph***
מֵאָה n.f.s. (547) ***a hundred***
שְׁנֵים עָשָׂר num. (1040)-num. (797) ***and twelve***

7:25

בְּנֵי גִבְעוֹן n.m.p. cstr. (119)-pr.n. (149) ***the sons of Gibeon***
תִּשְׁעִים וַחֲמִשָּׁה num. p. (1077)-conj.-num. f. (331) ***ninety-five***

7:26

אַנְשֵׁי בֵית־לֶחֶם n.m.p. cstr. (35)-pr.n. (111) ***the men of Bethlehem***
וּנְטֹפָה conj.-pr.n. (643) ***and Netophah***
מֵאָה n.f.s. (547) ***a hundred***
שְׁמֹנִים וּשְׁמֹנָה num. p. (1033)-conj.-num. f. (1032) ***and eighty-eight***

7:27

אַנְשֵׁי עֲנָתוֹת n.m.p. cstr. (35)-pr.n. (779) ***the men of Anathoth***
מֵאָה n.f.s. (547) ***a hundred***
עֶשְׂרִים וּשְׁמֹנָה num. p. (797)-conj.-num. f. (1032) ***and twenty-eight***

7:28

אַנְשֵׁי בֵית־עַזְמָוֶת n.m.p. cstr. (35)-pr.n. (112) ***the men of Beth-azmaveth***
אַרְבָּעִים וּשְׁנָיִם num. p. (917)-conj.-num. du. paus. (1040) ***forty-two***

7:29

אַנְשֵׁי קִרְיַת יְעָרִים n.m.p. cstr. (35)-pr.n. (900) ***the men of Kiriath-jearim***
כְּפִירָה pr.n. (499) ***Chephirah***
וּבְאֵרוֹת conj.-pr.n. (92) ***and Beeroth***
שְׁבַע מֵאוֹת num. cstr. (I 987)-n.f.p. (547) ***seven hundred***
אַרְבָּעִים וּשְׁלֹשָׁה num. p. (917)-conj.-num. f. (1025) ***and forty-three***

7:30

אַנְשֵׁי הָרָמָה n.m.p. cstr. (35)-def.art.-pr.n. (928) ***the men of Ramah***
וָגָבַע conj.-pr.n. paus. (148) ***and Geba***
שֵׁשׁ מֵאוֹת num. (995)-n.f.p. (547) ***six hundred***
עֶשְׂרִים וְאֶחָד num. p. (797)-conj.-num. (25) ***and twenty-one***

7:31

אַנְשֵׁי מִכְמָס n.m.p. cstr. (35)-pr.n. (485) ***the men of Michmas***
מֵאָה n.f.s. (547) ***a hundred***
וְעֶשְׂרִים וּשְׁנָיִם conj.-num. p. (797)-conj.-num. du. paus. (1040) ***and twenty-two***

7:32

אַנְשֵׁי בֵית־אֵל n.m.p. cstr. (35)-pr.n. (110) ***the men of Bethel***
וְהָעָי conj.-def.art.-pr.n. (743) ***and Ai***
מֵאָה n.f.s. (547) ***a hundred***
עֶשְׂרִים וּשְׁלֹשָׁה num. p. (797)-conj.-num. f. (1025) ***twenty-three***

7:33

אַנְשֵׁי נְבוֹ אַחֵר n.m.p. cstr. (35)-pr.n. (I 612)-adj. m.s. (29) ***the men of the other Nebo***
חֲמִשִּׁים וּשְׁנָיִם num. p. (332)-conj.-num. du. paus. (1040) ***fifty-two***

7:34

בְּנֵי עֵילָם אַחֵר n.m.p. cstr. (119)-pr.n. (II 743)-adj. m.s. (29) ***the sons of the other Elam***
אֶלֶף n.m.s. (48) ***a thousand***
מָאתַיִם n.f. du. (547) ***two hundred***
חֲמִשִּׁים וְאַרְבָּעָה num. p. (332)-conj.-num. f. (916) ***and fifty-four***

7:35

בְּנֵי חָרִם n.m.p. cstr. (119)-pr.n. (356) ***the sons of Harim***

שְׁלֹשׁ מֵאוֹת num. cstr. (1025)-n.f.p. (547) ***three hundred***

וְעֶשְׂרִים conj.-num. p. (797) ***and twenty***

7:36

בְּנֵי יְרֵחוֹ n.m.p. cstr. (119)-pr.n. (437) ***the sons of Jericho***

שְׁלֹשׁ מֵאוֹת num. cstr. (1025)-n.f.p. (547) ***three hundred***

אַרְבָּעִים וַחֲמִשָּׁה num. p. (917)-conj.-num. f. (331) ***and forty-five***

7:37

בְּנֵי־לֹד n.m.p. cstr. (119)-pr.n. (528) ***the sons of Lod***

חָדִיד pr.n. (292) ***Hadid***

וְאוֹנוֹ conj.-pr.n. (20) ***and Ono***

שְׁבַע מֵאוֹת num. cstr. (I 987)-n.f.p. (547) ***seven hundred***

וְעֶשְׂרִים וְאֶחָד conj.-num. p. (797)-conj.-num. (25) ***and twenty-one***

7:38

בְּנֵי סְנָאָה n.m.p. cstr. (119)-pr.n. (702) ***the sons of Senaah***

שְׁלֹשֶׁת אֲלָפִים num. f. cstr. (1025)-n.m. du. (48) ***three thousand***

תְּשַׁע מֵאוֹת num. cstr. (1077)-n.f.p. (547) ***nine hundred***

וּשְׁלֹשִׁים conj.-num. p. (1026) ***and thirty***

7:39

הַכֹּהֲנִים def.art.-n.m.p. (463) ***the priests***

בְּנֵי יְדַעְיָה n.m.p. cstr. (119)-pr.n. (396) ***the sons of Jedaiah***

לְבֵית יֵשׁוּעַ prep.-n.m.s. cstr. (108)-pr.n. (221) ***namely the house of Jeshua***

תְּשַׁע מֵאוֹת num. cstr. (1077)-n.f.p. (547) ***nine hundred***

שִׁבְעִים וּשְׁלֹשָׁה num. p. (988)-conj.-num. f. (1025) ***and seventy-three***

7:40

בְּנֵי אִמֵּר n.m.p. cstr. (119)-pr.n. (57) ***the sons of Immer***

אֶלֶף n.m.s. (48) ***a thousand***

חֲמִשִּׁים וּשְׁנָיִם num. p. (332)-conj.-num. du. paus. (1040) ***and fifty-two***

7:41

בְּנֵי פַשְׁחוּר n.m.p. cstr. (119)-pr.n. (832) ***the sons of Pashhur***

אֶלֶף n.m.s. (48) ***a thousand***

מָאתַיִם n.f. du. (547) ***two hundred***

אַרְבָּעִים וְשִׁבְעָה num. p. (917)-conj.-num. f. (I 987) ***and forty-seven***

7:42

בְּנֵי חָרִם n.m.p. cstr. (119)-pr.n. (356) ***the sons of Harim***

אֶלֶף n.m.s. (48) ***a thousand***

שִׁבְעָה עָשָׂר num. f. (I 987)-num. (797) ***and seventeen***

7:43

הַלְוִיִּם def.art.-adj. m.p. (532) ***the Levites***

בְּנֵי־יֵשׁוּעַ n.m.p. cstr. (119)-pr.n. (221) ***the sons of Jeshua***

לְקַדְמִיאֵל prep.-pr.n. (870) ***namely of Kadmiel***

לִבְנֵי לְהוֹדְוָה prep.-v.supra-prep.-pr.n. (217) ***of the sons of Hodevah***

שִׁבְעִים וְאַרְבָּעָה num. p. (988)-conj.-num. f. (916) ***seventy-four***

7:44

הַמְשֹׁרְרִים def.art.-Polel ptc. m.p. (שִׁיר 1010) ***the singers***

בְּנֵי אָסָף n.m.p. cstr. (119)-pr.n. (63) ***the sons of Asaph***

מֵאָה n.f.s. (547) ***a hundred***

אַרְבָּעִים וּשְׁמֹנָה num. p. (917)-conj.-num. f. (1032) ***and forty-eight***

7:45

הַשֹּׁעֲרִים def.art.-n.m.p. (1045) ***the gatekeepers***

בְּנֵי־שַׁלּוּם n.m.p. cstr. (119)-pr.n. (1024) ***the sons of Shallum***

בְּנֵי־אָטֵר v.supra-pr.n. (32) ***the sons of Ater***

בְּנֵי־טַלְמֹן v.supra-pr.n. (379) ***the sons of Talmon***

בְּנֵי־עַקּוּב v.supra-pr.n. (784) ***the sons of Akkub***

בְּנֵי חֲטִיטָא v.supra-pr.n. (310) ***the sons of Hatita***

בְּנֵי שֹׁבָי v.supra-pr.n. (986) ***the sons of Shobai***

מֵאָה n.f.s. (547) ***a hundred***

שְׁלֹשִׁים וּשְׁמֹנָה num. p. (1026)-conj.-num. f. (1032) ***and thirty-eight***

7:46

הַנְּתִינִים def.art.-n.m.p. (682) ***the Nethinim (temple servants)***

בְּנֵי־צִחָא n.m.p. cstr. (119)-pr.n. (851) *the sons of Ziha*
בְּנֵי־חֲשֻׂפָא v.supra-pr.n. (362) *the sons of Hasupha*
בְּנֵי טַבָּעוֹת v.supra-pr.n. (371) *the sons of Tabbaoth*

7:47
בְּנֵי־קֵירֹס n.m.p. cstr. (119)-pr.n. (902) *the sons of Keros*
בְּנֵי־סִיעָא v.supra-pr.n. (696) *the sons of Sia*
בְּנֵי פָדוֹן v.supra-pr.n. (804) *the sons of Padon*

7:48
בְּנֵי־לְבָנָה n.m.p. cstr. (119)-pr.n. (526) *the sons of Lebana*
בְּנֵי־חֲגָבָה v.supra-pr.n. (290) *the sons of Hagaba*
בְּנֵי שַׁלְמָי v.supra-pr.n. paus. (969) *the sons of Shamai*

7:49
בְּנֵי־חָנָן n.m.p. cstr. (119)-pr.n. (336) *the sons of Hanan*
בְּנֵי־גִדֵּל v.supra-pr.n. (153) *the sons of Giddel*
בְּנֵי־גָחַר v.supra-pr.n. (161) *the sons of Gahar*

7:50
בְּנֵי־רְאָיָה n.m.p. cstr. (119)-pr.n. (909) *the sons of Reaiah*
בְּנֵי־רְצִין v.supra-pr.n. (954) *the sons of Rezin*
בְּנֵי נְקוֹדָא v.supra-pr.n. (667) *the sons of Nekoda*

7:51
בְּנֵי־גַזָּם n.m.p. cstr. (119)-pr.n. (160) *the sons of Gazzam*
בְּנֵי־עֻזָּא v.supra-pr.n. (739) *the sons of Uzza*
בְּנֵי פָסֵחַ v.supra-pr.n. (820) *the sons of Paseah*

7:52
בְּנֵי־בֵסָי n.m.p. cstr. (119)-pr.n. (126) *the sons of Besai*
בְּנֵי־מְעוּנִים v.supra-pr.n. (589) *the sons of Meunim*
בְּנֵי נְפוּשְׁסִים v.supra-pr.n. (656) *the sons of Nephushesim*

7:53
בְּנֵי־בַקְבּוּק n.m.p. cstr. (119)-pr.n. (132) *the sons of Bakbuk*
בְּנֵי־חֲקוּפָא v.supra-pr.n. (349) *the sons of Hakupha*
בְּנֵי חַרְחוּר v.supra-pr.n. (359) *the sons of Harhur*

7:54
בְּנֵי־בַצְלִית n.m.p. cstr. (119)-pr.n. (130) *the sons of Bazlith*
בְּנֵי־מְחִידָא v.supra-pr.n. (563) *the sons of Mehida*
בְּנֵי חַרְשָׁא v.supra-pr.n. (361) *the sons of Harsha*

7:55
בְּנֵי־בַרְקוֹס n.m.p. cstr. (119)-pr.n. (140) *the sons of Barkos*
בְּנֵי־סִיסְרָא v.supra-pr.n. (696) *the sons of Sisera*
בְּנֵי־תָמַח v.supra-pr.n. paus. (1069) *the sons of Temah*

7:56
בְּנֵי נְצִיחַ n.m.p. cstr. (119)-pr.n. (664) *the sons of Neziah*
בְּנֵי חֲטִיפָא v.supra-pr.n. (310) *the sons of Hatipha*

7:57
בְּנֵי עַבְדֵי שְׁלֹמֹה n.m.p. cstr. (119)-n.m.p. cstr. (713)-pr.n. (1024) *the sons of Solomon's servants*
בְּנֵי־סוֹטַי v.supra-pr.n. (691) *the sons of Sotai*
בְּנֵי־סוֹפֶרֶת v.supra-pr.n. (709) *the sons of Sophereth*
בְּנֵי פְרִידָא v.supra-pr.n. (825) *the sons of Perida*

7:58
בְּנֵי־יַעְלָא n.m.p. cstr. (119)-pr.n. (II 419) *the sons of Jaala*
בְּנֵי־דַרְקוֹן v.supra-pr.n. (204) *the sons of Darkon*
בְּנֵי גִדֵּל v.supra-pr.n. (153) *the sons of Giddel*

7:59
בְּנֵי שְׁפַטְיָה n.m.p. cstr. (119)-pr.n. (1049) *the sons of Shephatiah*
בְּנֵי־חַטִּיל v.supra-pr.n. (310) *the sons of Hattil*
בְּנֵי פֹּכֶרֶת הַצְּבָיִים v.supra-pr.n. (810) *the sons of Pochereth-hazzebaim*
בְּנֵי אָמוֹן v.supra-pr.n. (51) *the sons of Amon*

7:60

כָּל־הַנְּתִינִים n.m.s. cstr. (481)-def.art.-n.m.p. (682) *all the Nethinim (temple servants)*

וּבְנֵי עַבְדֵי שְׁלֹמֹה conj.-v.supra-n.m.p. cstr. (713) -pr.n. (1024) *and the sons of Solomon's servants*

שְׁלֹשׁ מֵאוֹת num. cstr. (1025)-n.f.p. (547) *three hundred*

תִּשְׁעִים וּשְׁנָיִם num. p. (1077)-conj.-num. du. paus. (1040) *and ninety-two*

7:61

וְאֵלֶּה הָעוֹלִים conj.-demons.adj. c.p. (41)-def.art. -Qal act.ptc. m.p. (עָלָה 748) *those who came up*

מִתֵּל מֶלַח prep.-pr.n. (1068) *from Tel-melah*

תֵּל חַרְשָׁא pr.n. (1068) *Tel-harsha*

כְּרוּב pr.n. (500) *Cherub*

אַדּוֹן pr.n. (11, 500) *Addon*

וְאִמֵּר conj.-pr.n. (57) *and Immer*

וְלֹא יָכְלוּ conj.-neg.-Qal pf. 3 c.p. (יָכֹל 407) *but they could not*

לְהַגִּיד prep.-Hi. inf.cstr. (נָגַד 616) *prove*

בֵּית־אֲבוֹתָם n.m.s. cstr. (108)-n.m.p.-3 m.p. sf. (3) *their fathers' houses*

וְזַרְעָם conj.-n.m.s.-3 m.p. sf. (282) *nor their descent*

אִם מִיִּשְׂרָאֵל הֵם hypoth.part. (49)-prep.-pr.n. (975)-pers.pr. 3 m.p. (241) *whether they belonged to Israel*

7:62

בְּנֵי־דְלָיָה n.m.p. cstr. (119)-pr.n. (195) *the sons of Delaiah*

בְנֵי־טוֹבִיָּה v.supra-pr.n. (375) *the sons of Tobiah*

בְּנֵי נְקוֹדָא v.supra-pr.n. (667) *the sons of Nekoda*

שֵׁשׁ מֵאוֹת num. (995)-n.f.p. (547) *six hundred*

וְאַרְבָּעִים וּשְׁנָיִם conj.-num. p. (917)-conj.-num. du. paus. (1040) *and forty-two*

7:63

וּמִן־הַכֹּהֲנִים conj.-prep.-def.art.-n.m.p. (463) *also of the priests*

בְּנֵי חֳבַיָּה n.m.p. cstr. (119)-pr.n. (285) *the sons of Hobaiah*

בְּנֵי הַקּוֹץ v.supra-def.art.-pr.n. (881) *the sons of Hakkoz*

בְּנֵי בַרְזִלַּי v.supra-pr.n. (137) *the sons of Barzillai*

אֲשֶׁר לָקַח rel. (81)-Qal pf. 3 m.s. (542) *who had taken*

מִבְּנוֹת בַּרְזִלַּי prep.-n.f.p. cstr. (I 123)-pr.n. (137) *of the daughters of Barzillai*

הַגִּלְעָדִי def.art.-adj. gent. (167) *the Gileadite*

אִשָּׁה n.f.s. (61) *a wife*

וַיִּקָּרֵא consec.-Ni. impf. 3 m.s. (קָרָא 894) *and was called*

עַל־שְׁמָם prep.-n.m.s.-3 m.p. sf. (1027) *by their name*

7:64

אֵלֶּה בִּקְשׁוּ demons.adj. c.p. (41)-Pi. pf. 3 c.p. (134 בָּקַשׁ) *these sought*

כְּתָבָם n.m.s.-3 m.p. sf. (508) *their registration*

הַמִּתְיַחְשִׂים def.art.-Hith. ptc. m.p. (יָחַשׂ 405; GK 64i) *among the enrolled*

וְלֹא נִמְצָא conj.-neg.-Ni. pf. 3 m.s. or ptc. (מָצָא 592) *but it was not found*

וַיְגֹאֲלוּ consec.-Pu. impf. 3 m.p. (גָּאַל II 146) *so they were excluded*

מִן־הַכְּהֻנָּה prep.-def.art.-n.f.s. (464) *from the priesthood*

7:65

וַיֹּאמֶר הַתִּרְשָׁתָא לָהֶם consec.-Qal impf. 3 m.s. (55)-def.art.-n.m.s. (1077)-prep.-3 m.p. sf. *the governor told them*

אֲשֶׁר לֹא־יֹאכְלוּ rel. (81)-neg.-Qal impf. 3 m.p. (37 אָכַל) *that they were not to partake*

מִקֹּדֶשׁ הַקֳּדָשִׁים prep.-n.m.s. cstr. (871)-def.art. -n.m.p. (871) *of the most holy food*

עַד עֲמֹד הַכֹּהֵן prep. (III 723)-Qal inf.cstr. (עָמַד 763)-def.art.-n.m.s. (463) *until a priest should arise*

לְאוּרִים וְתוּמִּים prep.-n.m.p. (22)-conj.-n.m.p. (1070) *with Urim and Thummim*

7:66

כָּל־הַקָּהָל n.m.s. cstr. (481)-def.art.-n.m.s. (874) *the whole assembly*

כְּאֶחָד prep.-num. (25) *together*

אַרְבַּע רִבּוֹא אַלְפַּיִם num. (916)-n.f.s. (914; GK 23i)-n.m. du. (48) *forty-two thousand*

שְׁלֹשׁ־מֵאוֹת num. cstr. (1025)-n.f.p. (547) *three hundred*

וְשִׁשִּׁים conj.-num. p. (995) *and sixty*

7:67

מִלְּבַד עַבְדֵיהֶם prep.-prep.-n.m.s. (94)-n.m.p.-3 m.p. sf. (713) *besides their menservants*

וְאַמְהֹתֵיהֶם conj.-n.f.p.-3 m.p. sf. (51) *and maidservants*
אֵלֶּה שִׁבְעַת אֲלָפִים demons.adj. c.p. (41)-num. f. cstr. (I 987)-n.m.p. (48) *of whom there were seven thousand*
שְׁלֹשׁ מֵאוֹת num. cstr. (1025)-n.f.p. (547) *three hundred*
שְׁלֹשִׁים וְשִׁבְעָה num. p. (1026)-conj.-num. f. (I 987) *and thirty-seven*
וְלָהֶם מְשֹׁרְרִים conj.-prep.-3 m.p. sf.-Polel ptc. m.p. (שִׁיר 1010) *and they had male singers*
וּמְשֹׁרְרוֹת conj.-Polel ptc. f.p. (שִׁיר 1010) *and female singers*
מָאתַיִם n.f. du. (547) *two hundred*
וְאַרְבָּעִים וַחֲמִשָּׁה conj.-num. p. (917)-conj.-num. f. (331) *and forty-five*

7:68

גְּמַלִּים n.m.p. (168) *camels*
אַרְבַּע מֵאוֹת num. (916)-n.f.p. (547) *four hundred*
שְׁלֹשִׁים וַחֲמִשָּׁה num. p. (1026)-conj.-num. f. (331) *and thirty-five*
חֲמֹרִים n.m.p. (331) *asses*
שֵׁשֶׁת אֲלָפִים num. f. cstr. (995)-n.m.p. (48) *six thousand*
שְׁבַע מֵאוֹת num. cstr. (I 987)-n.f.p. 547) *seven hundred*
וְעֶשְׂרִים conj.-num. p. (797) *and twenty*

7:69

וּמִקְצָת רָאשֵׁי הָאָבוֹת conj.-prep.-n.f.s. cstr. (892) -n.m.p. cstr. (910)-def.art.-n.m.p. (3) *now some of the heads of fathers' houses*
נָתְנוּ Qal pf. 3 c.p. (נָתַן 678) *gave*
לַמְּלָאכָה prep.-def.art.-n.f.s. (521) *to the work*
הַתִּרְשָׁתָא נָתַן def.art.-n.m.s. (1077)-Qal pf. 3 m.s. (678) *the governor gave*
לָאוֹצָר prep.-def.art.-n.m.s. (69) *to the treasury*
זָהָב דַּרְכְּמֹנִים n.m.s. (262)-n.m.p. (204) *darics of gold*
אֶלֶף n.m.s. (48) *a thousand*
מִזְרָקוֹת חֲמִשִּׁים n.m.p. (284)-num. p. (332) *fifty basins*
כָּתְנוֹת כֹּהֲנִים n.f.p. cstr. (509)-n.m.p. (463) *priests' garments*
שְׁלֹשִׁים num. p. (1026) *thirty*
וַחֲמֵשׁ מֵאוֹת conj.-num. cstr. (331)-n.f.p. (547) *and five hundred*

7:70

וּמֵרָאשֵׁי הָאָבוֹת conj.-prep.-n.m.p. cstr. (910) -def.art.-n.m.p. (3) *and some of the heads of fathers' houses*
נָתְנוּ Qal pf. 3 c.p. (נָתַן 678) *gave*
לְאוֹצַר הַמְּלָאכָה prep.-n.m.s. cstr. (69)-def.art. -n.f.s. (521) *into the treasury of the work*
זָהָב דַּרְכְּמוֹנִים n.m.s. (262)-n.m.p. (204) *darics of gold*
שְׁתֵּי רִבּוֹת num. f. cstr. (1040)-n.f.p. (914) *twenty thousand*
וְכֶסֶף מָנִים conj.-n.m.s. (494)-n.m.p. (584) *and minas of silver*
אֲלָפַיִם n.m. du. (48) *two thousand*
וּמָאתָיִם n.f. du. paus. (547) *and two hundred*

7:71

וַאֲשֶׁר נָתְנוּ conj.-rel. (81)-Qal pf. 3 c.p. (נָתַן 678) *and what ... gave*
שְׁאֵרִית הָעָם n.f.s. cstr. (984)-def.art.-n.m.s. (I 766) *the rest of the people*
זָהָב דַּרְכְּמוֹנִים n.m.s. (262)-n.m.p. (204) *darics of gold*
שְׁתֵּי רִבּוֹא num. f. cstr. (1040)-n.f.s. (914; GK 23i) *twenty thousand*
וְכֶסֶף מָנִים conj.-n.m.s. (494)-n.m.p. (584) *and minas of silver*
אַלְפָּיִם n.m. du. paus. (48) *two thousand*
וְכָתְנֹת כֹּהֲנִים conj.-n.f.p. cstr. (509)-n.m.p. (463) *and priests' garments*
שִׁשִּׁים וְשִׁבְעָה num. p. (995)-conj.-num. f. (I 987) *sixty-seven*

7:72

וַיֵּשְׁבוּ consec.-Qal impf. 3 m.p. (יָשַׁב 442) *so lived*
הַכֹּהֲנִים def.art.-n.m.p. (463) *the priests*
וְהַלְוִיִּם conj.-def.art.-adj. gent. m.p. (532) *the Levites*
וְהַשּׁוֹעֲרִים conj.-def.art.-n.m.p. (1045) *the gatekeepers*
וְהַמְשֹׁרְרִים conj.-def.art.-Polel ptc. m.p. (שִׁיר 1010) *the singers*
וּמִן־הָעָם conj.-prep.-def.art.-n.m.s. (I 766) *some of the people*
וְהַנְּתִינִים conj.-def.art.-n.m.p. (682) *the temple servants (Nethinim)*
וְכָל־יִשְׂרָאֵל conj.-n.m.s. cstr. (481)-pr.n. (975) *and all Israel*
בְּעָרֵיהֶם prep.-n.f.p.-3 m.p. sf. (746) *in their towns*

וַיִּגַּע consec.-Qal impf. 3 m.s. (נָגַע 619) *and when had come*
הַחֹדֶשׁ הַשְּׁבִיעִי def.art.-n.m.s. (I 294)-def.art.-num. ord. (988) *the seventh month*
וּבְנֵי יִשְׂרָאֵל conj.-n.m.p. cstr. (119)-pr.n. (975) *and the children of Israel*
בְּעָרֵיהֶם prep.-n.f.p.-3 m.p. sf. (746) *in their towns*

8:1

וַיֵּאָסְפוּ consec.-Ni. impf. 3 m.p. (אָסַף 62) *and gathered*
כָל־הָעָם n.m.s. cstr. (481)-def.art.-n.m.s. (I 766) *all the people*
כְּאִישׁ אֶחָד prep.-n.m.s. (35)-num. (25) *as one man*
אֶל־הָרְחוֹב prep.-def.art.-n.f.s. (I 932) *into the square*
אֲשֶׁר לִפְנֵי שַׁעַר־הַמָּיִם rel. (81)-prep.-n.m.p. cstr. (815)-n.m.s. cstr. (1044)-def.art.-n.m.p. paus. (565) *before the Water Gate*
וַיֹּאמְרוּ consec.-Qal impf. 3 m.p. (55) *and they told*
לְעֶזְרָא prep.-pr.n. (740) *Ezra*
הַסֹּפֵר def.art.-n.m.s. (708) *the scribe*
לְהָבִיא prep.-Hi. inf.cstr. (בּוֹא 97) *to bring*
אֶת־סֵפֶר dir.obj.-n.m.s. cstr. (706) *the book of*
תּוֹרַת מֹשֶׁה n.f.s. cstr. (435)-pr.n. (602) *the law of Moses*
אֲשֶׁר־צִוָּה יהוה rel. (81)-Pi. pf. 3 m.s. (צָוָה 845)-pr.n. (217) *which Yahweh had given*
אֶת־יִשְׂרָאֵל dir.obj.-pr.n. (975) *to Israel*

8:2

וַיָּבִיא consec.-Hi. impf. 3 m.s. (בּוֹא 97; GK 74,l) *and brought*
עֶזְרָא הַכֹּהֵן pr.n. (740)-def.art.-n.m.s. (463) *Ezra the priest*
אֶת־הַתּוֹרָה dir.obj.-def.art.-n.f.s. (435) *the law*
לִפְנֵי הַקָּהָל prep.-n.m.p. cstr. (815)-def.art.-n.m.s. (874) *before the assembly*
מֵאִישׁ וְעַד־אִשָּׁה prep.-n.m.s. (35)-conj.-prep. (III 723)-n.f.s. (61) *both men and women*
וְכֹל מֵבִין לִשְׁמֹעַ conj.-n.m.s. (481)-Hi. ptc. (בִּין 106)-prep.-Qal inf.cstr. (שָׁמַע 1033) *and all who could hear with understanding*
בְּיוֹם אֶחָד prep.-n.m.s. cstr. (398)-num. (25) *on the first day*
לַחֹדֶשׁ הַשְּׁבִיעִי prep.-def.art.-n.m.s. (294)-def. art.-num. ord. (988) *of the seventh month*

8:3

וַיִּקְרָא־בוֹ consec.-Qal impf. 3 m.s. (קָרָא 894) -prep.-3 m.s. sf. *and he read from it*
לִפְנֵי הָרְחוֹב prep.-n.m.p. cstr. (815)-def.art.-n.f.s. (932) *facing the square*
אֲשֶׁר לִפְנֵי שַׁעַר־הַמַּיִם rel. (81)-v.supra-n.m.s. cstr. (1044)-def.art.-n.m.p. (565) *before the Water Gate*
מִן־הָאוֹר prep.-def.art.-n.m.s. (21) *from early morning*
עַד־מַחֲצִית הַיּוֹם prep. (III 723)-n.f.s. cstr. (345)-def.art.-n.m.s. (398) *until midday*
נֶגֶד הָאֲנָשִׁים prep. (617)-dof.art.-n.m.p. (35) *in the presence of the men*
וְהַנָּשִׁים conj.-def.art.-n.f.p. (61) *and the women*
וְהַמְּבִינִים conj.-def.art.-Hi. ptc. m.p. (בִּין 106) *and those who could understand*
וְאָזְנֵי כָל־הָעָם conj.-n.f.p. cstr. (23)-n.m.s. cstr. (481)-def.art.-n.m.s. (I 766) *and the ears of all the people*
אֶל־סֵפֶר הַתּוֹרָה prep.-n.m.s. cstr. (706)-def.art. -n.f.s. (435) *to the book of the law*

8:4

וַיַּעֲמֹד consec.-Qal impf. 3 m.s. (עָמַד 763) *and stood*
עֶזְרָא הַסֹּפֵר pr.n. (740)-def.art.-n.m.s. (708) *Ezra the scribe*
עַל־מִגְדַּל־עֵץ prep.-n.m.s. cstr. (153)-n.m.s. (781) *on a wooden pulpit*
אֲשֶׁר עָשׂוּ rel. (81)-Qal pf. 3 c.p. (עָשָׂה I 793) *which they had made*
לַדָּבָר prep.-def.art.-n.m.s. (182) *for the purpose*
וַיַּעֲמֹד consec.-Qal impf. 3 m.s. (763) *and stood*
אֶצְלוֹ prep.-3 m.s. sf. (I 69) *beside him*
מַתִּתְיָה pr.n. (682) *Mattithiah*
וְשֶׁמַע conj.-pr.n. (1034) *Shema*
וַעֲנָיָה conj.-pr.n. (777) *Anaiah*
וְאוּרִיָּה conj.-pr.n. (22) *Uriah*
וְחִלְקִיָּה conj.-pr.n. (324) *Hilkiah*
וּמַעֲשֵׂיָה conj.-pr.n. (796) *and Maaseiah*
עַל־יְמִינוֹ prep.-n.f.s.-3 m.s. sf. (I 411) *on his right hand*
וּמִשְּׂמֹאלוֹ conj.-prep.-n.m.s.-3 m.s. sf. (969) *and on his left hand*
פְּדָיָה pr.n. (804) *Pedaiah*
וּמִישָׁאֵל conj.-pr.n. (567) *Mishael*
וּמַלְכִּיָּה conj.-pr.n. (575) *Malchiah*
וְחָשֻׁם conj.-pr.n. (365) *Hashum*
וְחַשְׁבַּדָּנָה conj.-pr.n. (364) *Hashbaddanah*
זְכַרְיָה pr.n. (272) *Zechariah*
מְשֻׁלָּם pr.n. (1024) *and Meshullam*

8:5

וַיִּפְתַּח consec.-Qal impf. 3 m.s. (פָּתַח I 834) *and opened*

עֶזְרָא pr.n. (740) *Ezra*

הַסֵּפֶר def.art.-n.m.s. (706) *the book*

לְעֵינֵי כָל־הָעָם prep.-n.f.p. cstr. (744)-n.m.s. cstr. (481)-def.art.-n.m.s. (I 766) *in the sight of all the people*

כִּי־מֵעַל כָּל־הָעָם conj. (471)-prep.-prep.-n.m.s. cstr. (481)-v.supra *for above all the people*

הָיָה Qal pf. 3 m.s. (224) *he was*

וּכְפִתְחוֹ conj.-prep.-n.m.s.-3 m.s. sf. (835) *and when he opened it*

עָמְדוּ Qal pf. 3 c.p. (עָמַד 763) *stood*

כָל־הָעָם v.supra-v.supra *all the people*

8:6

וַיְבָרֶךְ עֶזְרָא consec.-Pi. impf. 3 m.s. (בָּרַךְ 138)-pr.n. (740) *and Ezra blessed*

אֶת־יהוה dir.obj.-pr.n. (217) *Yahweh*

הָאֱלֹהִים הַגָּדוֹל def.art.-n.m.p. (43)-def.art.-adj. m.s. (152) *the great God*

וַיַּעֲנוּ כָל־הָעָם consec.-Qal impf. 3 m.p. (עָנָה I 772)-n.m.s. cstr. (481)-def.art.-n.m.s. (I 766) *and all the people answered*

אָמֵן אָמֵן adv. (53)-v.supra *Amen, Amen*

בְּמֹעַל יְדֵיהֶם prep.-n.m.s. cstr. (751)-n.f.p.-3 m.p. sf. (388) *lifting up their hands*

וַיִּקְּדוּ consec.-Qal impf. 3 m.p. (קָדַד I 869) *and they bowed*

וַיִּשְׁתַּחֲוֻ consec.-Hith. impf. 3 m.p. (שָׁחָה 1005) *and worshiped*

ליהוה prep.-pr.n. (217) *Yahweh*

אַפַּיִם אָרְצָה n.m. du. (60)-n.f.s.-dir.he (75) *their faces to the ground*

8:7

וְיֵשׁוּעַ conj.-pr.n. (221) *also Jeshua*

וּבָנִי conj.-pr.n. (125) *Bani*

וְשֵׁרֵבְיָה conj.-pr.n. (1055) *Sherebiah*

יָמִין pr.n. (II 412) *Jamin*

עַקּוּב pr.n. (784) *Akkub*

שַׁבְּתַי pr.n. (992) *Shabbethai*

הוֹדִיָּה pr.n. (217) *Hodiah*

מַעֲשֵׂיָה pr.n. (796) *Maaseiah*

קְלִיטָא pr.n. (886) *Kelita*

עֲזַרְיָה pr.n. (741) *Azariah*

יוֹזָבָד pr.n. (220) *Jozabad*

חָנָן pr.n. (336) *Hanan*

פְּלָאיָה pr.n. (811) *Pelaiah*

וְהַלְוִיִּם conj.-def.art.-adj. gent. m.p. (532) *and the Levites*

מְבִינִים Hi. ptc. m.p. (בִּין 106) *causing to understand*

אֶת־הָעָם dir.obj.-def.art.-n.m.s. (I 766) *the people*

לַתּוֹרָה prep.-def.art.-n.f.s. (435) *the law*

וְהָעָם conj.-v.supra *while the people*

עַל־עָמְדָם prep.-n.m.s.-3 m.p. sf. (765) *in their standing place*

8:8

וַיִּקְרְאוּ consec.-Qal impf. 3 m.p. (קָרָא 894) *and they read*

בַסֵּפֶר prep.-def.art.-n.m.s. (706) *from the book*

בְּתוֹרַת הָאֱלֹהִים prep.-n.f.s. cstr. (435)-def.art.-n.m.p. (43) *from the law of God*

מְפֹרָשׁ Pu. ptc. m.s. (פָּרַשׁ I 831) *clearly (made distinct)*

וְשׂוֹם שֶׂכֶל conj.-Qal inf.abs. (שִׂים 962)-n.m.s. (968; GK 2t) *and they gave the sense*

וַיָּבִינוּ consec.-Qal impf. 3 m.p. (בִּין 106) *so that they understood*

בַּמִּקְרָא prep.-def.art.-n.m.s. (896) *the reading*

8:9

וַיֹּאמֶר נְחֶמְיָה consec.-Qal impf. 3 m.s. (55)-pr.n. (637) *and Nehemiah said*

הוּא הַתִּרְשָׁתָה pers.pr. 3 m.s. (214)-def.art.-n.m.s. (1077) *who was the governor*

וְעֶזְרָא הַכֹּהֵן conj.-pr.n. (740)-def.art.-n.m.s. (463) *and Ezra the priest*

הַסֹּפֵר def.art.-n.m.s. (708) *the scribe*

וְהַלְוִיִּם conj.-def.art.-adj. gent. m.p. (532) *and the Levites*

הַמְּבִינִים def.art.-Hi. ptc. m.p. (בִּין 106) *who taught*

אֶת־הָעָם dir.obj.-def.art.-n.m.s. (I 766) *the people*

לְכָל־הָעָם prep.-n.m.s. cstr. (481)-v.supra *to all the people*

הַיּוֹם def.art.-n.m.s. (398) *this day*

קָדֹשׁ־הוּא adj.m.s. (872)-pers.pr. 3 m.s. (214) *it is holy*

ליהוה אֱלֹהֵיכֶם prep.-pr.n. (217)-n.m.p.-2 m.p. sf. (43) *to Yahweh your God*

אַל־תִּתְאַבְּלוּ neg.-Hith. impf. 2 m.p. (אָבַל 5) *do not mourn*

וְאַל־תִּבְכּוּ conj.-neg.-Qal impf. 2 m.p. (בָּכָה 113) *or do not weep*

כִּי בוֹכִים conj. (471)-Qal act.ptc. m.p. (בָּכָה 113) *for wept*

כָּל־הָעָם n.m.s. cstr. (481)-def.art.-n.m.s. (I 766) *all the people*
כְּשָׁמְעָם prep.-Qal inf.cstr.-3 m.p. sf. (שָׁמַע 1033) *when they heard*
אֶת־דִּבְרֵי הַתּוֹרָה dir.obj.-n.m.p. cstr. (182)-def. art.-n.f.s. (435) *the words of the law*

8:10

וַיֹּאמֶר לָהֶם consec.-Qal impf. 3 m.s. (55) -prep.-3 m.p. sf. *then he said to them*
לְכוּ אִכְלוּ Qal impv. 2 m.p. (הָלַךְ 229)-Qal impv. 2 m.p. (אָכַל 37) *go, eat*
מַשְׁמַנִּים n.m.p. (1032) *the fat*
וּשְׁתוּ conj.-Qal impv. 2 m.p. (שָׁתָה 1059) *and drink*
מַמְתַקִּים n.m.p. (609; GK 85gN) *sweet wine*
וְשִׁלְחוּ מָנוֹת conj.-Qal impv. 2 m.p. (שָׁלַח 1018)-n.f.p. (584) *and send portions*
לְאֵין נָכוֹן לוֹ prep. (GK 152v,155n)-neg. (II 34)-Ni. ptc. (כּוּן I 465)-prep.-3 m.s. sf. *to him for whom nothing is prepared*
כִּי־קָדוֹשׁ הַיּוֹם conj. (471)-adj. m.s. (872; GK 128p)-def.art.-n.m.s. (398) *for this day is holy*
לַאֲדֹנֵינוּ prep.-n.m.p.-1 c.p. sf. (10) *to our Lord*
וְאַל־תֵּעָצֵבוּ conj.-neg.-Ni. impf. 2 m.p. (עָצַב I 780) *and do not be grieved*
כִּי־חֶדְוַת יהוה conj. (471)-n.f.s. cstr. (292)-pr.n. (217) *for the joy of Yahweh*
הִיא מָעֻזְּכֶם pers.pr. 3 f.s. (214)-n.m.s.-2 m.p. sf. (731) *is your strength*

8:11

וְהַלְוִיִּם מַחְשִׁים conj.-def.art.-adj. gent. m.p. (532)-Hi. ptc. m.p. (חָשָׁה 364) *so the Levites stilled*
לְכָל־הָעָם prep.-n.m.s. cstr. (481)-def.art.-n.m.s. (I 766) *all the people*
לֵאמֹר prep.-Qal inf.cstr. (אָמַר 55) *saying*
הַסּוּ Qal impv. 2 m.p. (הַס 245 interj.; GK 105a) *be quiet*
כִּי הַיּוֹם קָדֹשׁ conj. (471)-def.art.-n.m.s. (398) -adj. m.s. (972) *for this day is holy*
וְאַל־תֵּעָצֵבוּ conj.-neg.-Ni. impf. 2 m.p. paus. (I 780 עָצַב) *do not be grieved*

8:12

וַיֵּלְכוּ כָל־הָעָם consec.-Qal impf. 3 m.p. (הָלַךְ 229)-n.m.s. cstr. (481)-def.art.-n.m.s. (I 766) *and all the people went*
לֶאֱכֹל prep.-Qal inf.cstr. (אָכַל 37) *to eat*
וְלִשְׁתּוֹת conj.-prep.-Qal inf.cstr. (שָׁתָה 1059) *and drink*
וּלְשַׁלַּח מָנוֹת conj.-prep.-Pi. inf.cstr. (שָׁלַח 1018)-n.f.p. (584) *and to send portions*
וְלַעֲשׂוֹת שִׂמְחָה גְדוֹלָה conj.-prep.-Qal inf.cstr. (I 793 עָשָׂה)-n.f.s. (970)-adj. f.s. (152) *and to make great rejoicing*
כִּי הֵבִינוּ conj. (471)-Hi. pf. 3 c.p. (בִּין 106) *because they had understood*
בַּדְּבָרִים prep.-def.art.-n.m.p. (182) *the words*
אֲשֶׁר הוֹדִיעוּ לָהֶם rel. (81)-Hi. pf. 3 c.p. (יָדַע 393)-prep.-3 m.p. sf. *that were declared to them*

8:13

וּבַיּוֹם הַשֵּׁנִי conj.-prep.-def.art.-n.m.s. (398)-def. art.-num. ord. (1041) *on the second day*
נֶאֶסְפוּ Ni. pf. 3 c.p. (אָסַף 62) *came together*
רָאשֵׁי הָאָבוֹת n.m.p. cstr. (910)-def.art.-n.m.p. (3) *the heads of the fathers*
לְכָל־הָעָם prep.-n.m.s. cstr. (481)-def.art.-n.m.s. (I 766) *of all the people*
הַכֹּהֲנִים def.art.-n.m.p. (463) *with the priests*
וְהַלְוִיִּם conj.-def.art.-adj. gent. m.p. (532) *and the Levites*
אֶל־עֶזְרָא הַסֹּפֵר prep.-pr.n. (740)-def.art.-n.m.s. (708) *to Ezra the scribe*
וּלְהַשְׂכִּיל conj.-prep.-Hi. inf.cstr. (שָׂכַל 968) *in order to study*
אֶל־דִּבְרֵי הַתּוֹרָה prep.-n.m.p. cstr. (182)-def.art. -n.f.s. (435) *the words of the law*

8:14

וַיִּמְצְאוּ consec.-Qal impf. 3 m.p. (מָצָא 592) *and they found (it)*
כָּתוּב Qal pass.ptc. (כָּתַב 507) *written*
בַּתּוֹרָה prep.-def.art.-n.f.s. (435) *in the law*
אֲשֶׁר צִוָּה יהוה rel. (81)-Pi. pf. 3 m.s. (צָוָה 845) -pr.n. (217) *that Yahweh had commanded*
בְּיַד־מֹשֶׁה prep.-n.f.s. cstr. (388)-pr.n. (602) *by the hand of Moses*
אֲשֶׁר יֵשְׁבוּ v.supra-Qal impf. 3 m.p. (יָשַׁב 442) *that should dwell*
בְנֵי־יִשְׂרָאֵל n.m.p. cstr. (119)-pr.n. (975) *the people of Israel*
בַּסֻּכּוֹת prep.-def.art.-n.f.p. (697) *in booths*
בֶּחָג prep.-def.art.-n.m.s. (290) *during the feast*
בַּחֹדֶשׁ הַשְּׁבִיעִי prep.-def.art.-n.m.s. (294)-def. art.-num. ord. (988) *of the seventh month*

8:15

וַאֲשֶׁר יַשְׁמִיעוּ conj.-rel. (81)-Hi. impf. 3 m.p. (1033 שָׁמַע) *and that they should publish*

וְיַעֲבִירוּ קוֹל conj.-Hi. impf. 3 m.p. (עָבַר 716) -n.m.s. (876) *and proclaim*

בְּכָל־עָרֵיהֶם prep.-n.m.s. cstr. (481)-n.f.p.-3 m.p. sf. (746) *in all their towns*

וּבִירוּשָׁלַםִ conj.-prep.-pr.n. (436) *and in Jerusalem*

לֵאמֹר prep.-Qal inf.cstr. (אָמַר 55) *(saying)*

צְאוּ הָהָר Qal impv. 2 m.p. (יָצָא 422)-def.art. -n.m.s. (249) *go out to the hills*

וְהָבִיאוּ conj.-Hi. impv. 2 m.p. (בּוֹא 97) *and bring*

עֲלֵי־זַיִת n.m.p. cstr. (750)-n.m.s. (268) *branches of olive*

וַעֲלֵי־עֵץ שֶׁמֶן conj.-v.supra-n.m.s. cstr. (781) -n.m.s. (1032) *and branches of oil trees*

וַעֲלֵי הֲדַס v.supra-n.m.s. (213) *myrtle*

וַעֲלֵי תְמָרִים v.supra-n.m.p. (I 1071) *palm*

וַעֲלֵי עֵץ עָבֹת v.supra-v.supra-adj. m.s. (721) *and other leafy trees*

לַעֲשֹׂת סֻכֹּת prep.-Qal inf.cstr. (עָשָׂה I 793) -n.f.p. (697) *to make booths*

כַּכָּתוּב prep.-def.art.-Qal pass.ptc. (כָּתַב 507) *as it is written*

8:16

וַיֵּצְאוּ הָעָם consec.-Qal impf. 3 m.p. (יָצָא 422)-def.art.-n.m.s. (I 766) *so the people went out*

וַיָּבִיאוּ consec.-Hi. impf. 3 m.p. (בּוֹא 97) *and brought*

וַיַּעֲשׂוּ לָהֶם consec.-Qal impf. 3 m.p. (עָשָׂה I 793)-prep.-3 m.p. sf. *and made for themselves*

סֻכּוֹת n.f.p. (697) *booths*

אִישׁ עַל־גַּגּוֹ n.m.s. (35)-prep.-n.m.s.-3 m.s. sf. (150) *each on his roof*

וּבְחַצְרֹתֵיהֶם conj.-prep.-n.f.p.-3 m.p. sf. (I 346) *and in their courts*

וּבְחַצְרוֹת conj.-prep.-n.f.p. cstr. (I 346) *and in the courts of*

בֵּית הָאֱלֹהִים n.m.s. cstr. (108)-def.art.-n.m.p. (43) *the house of God*

וּבִרְחוֹב conj.-prep.-n.f.s. cstr. (I 932) *and in the square at*

שַׁעַר הַמַּיִם n.m.s. cstr. (1044)-def.art.-n.m.p. (565) *the Water Gate*

וּבִרְחוֹב v.supra *and in the square at*

שַׁעַר אֶפְרָיִם v.supra-pr.n. (68) *the Gate of Ephraim*

8:17

וַיַּעֲשׂוּ consec.-Qal impf. 3 m.p. (עָשָׂה I 793) *and made*

כָל־הַקָּהָל n.m.s. cstr. (481)-def.art.-n.m.s. (874) *all the assembly*

הַשָּׁבִים def.art.-Qal act.ptc. m.p. (שׁוּב 996) *who had returned*

מִן־הַשְּׁבִי prep.-def.art.-n.m.s. (985) *from the captivity*

סֻכּוֹת n.f.p. (697) *booths*

וַיֵּשְׁבוּ בַסֻּכּוֹת consec.-Qal impf. 3 m.p. (יָשַׁב 442)-prep.-def.art.-v.supra *and dwelt in the booths*

כִּי לֹא־עָשׂוּ conj. (471)-neg.-Qal pf. 3 c.p. (עָשָׂה I 793) *for had not done*

מִימֵי יֵשׁוּעַ prep.-n.m.p. cstr. (398)-pr.n. (221) *from the days of Jeshua*

בִּן־נוּן n.m.s. cstr. (119)-pr.n. (630) *the son of Nun*

כֵּן adv. (485) *so*

בְּנֵי יִשְׂרָאֵל n.m.p. cstr. (119)-pr.n. (975) *the people of Israel*

עַד הַיּוֹם הַהוּא prep. (III 723)-def.art.-n.m.s. (398)-def.art.-demons.adj. m.s. (214) *to that day*

וַתְּהִי שִׂמְחָה גְּדוֹלָה consec.-Qal impf. 3 f.s. (הָיָה 224)-n.f.s. (970)-adj. f.s. (152) *and there was ... great rejoicing*

מְאֹד adv. (547) *very*

8:18

וַיִּקְרָא consec.-Qal impf. 3 m.s. (קָרָא 894) *and he read*

בְּסֵפֶר prep.-n.m.s. cstr. (706) *from the book of*

תּוֹרַת הָאֱלֹהִים n.f.s. cstr. (435)-def.art.-n.m.p. (43) *the law of God*

יוֹם בְּיוֹם n.m.s. (398)-prep.-v.supra *day by day*

מִן־הַיּוֹם הָרִאשׁוֹן prep.-def.art.-v.supra-def. art.-adj. m.s. (911) *from the first day*

עַד הַיּוֹם הָאַחֲרוֹן prep. (III 723)-v.supra-def.art. -adj. m.s. (30) *to the last day*

וַיַּעֲשׂוּ־חָג consec.-Qal impf. 3 m.p. (עָשָׂה I 793)-n.m.s. (290) *they kept the feast*

שִׁבְעַת יָמִים n.f.s. cstr. (I 987)-n.m.p. (398) *seven days*

וּבַיּוֹם הַשְּׁמִינִי conj.-prep.-def.art.-n.m.s. (398) -def.art.-num. ord. (1033) *and on the eighth day*

עֲצֶרֶת כַּמִּשְׁפָּט n.f.s. (783)-prep.-def.art.-n.m.s. (1048) *a solemn assembly according to the ordinance*

9:1

וּבְיוֹם conj.-prep.-n.m.s. (398) *now on the ... day*
עֶשְׂרִים וְאַרְבָּעָה num. p. (797)-conj.-num. f. (916) *the twenty-fourth*
לַחֹדֶשׁ הַזֶּה prep.-def.art.-n.m.s. (294)-def.art.-demons.adj. m.s. (260) *of this month*
נֶאֶסְפוּ Ni. pf. 3 c.p. (אָסַף 62) *were assembled*
בְנֵי־יִשְׂרָאֵל n.m.p. cstr. (119)-pr.n. (975) *the people of Israel*
בְּצוֹם prep.-n.m.s. (847) *with fasting*
וּבְשַׂקִּים conj.-prep.-n.m.p. (974) *and in sackcloth*
וַאֲדָמָה עֲלֵיהֶם conj.-n.f.s. (9)-prep.-3 m.p. sf. *and with earth upon them*

9:2

וַיִּבָּדְלוּ consec.-Ni. impf. 3 m.p. (בָּדַל 95) *and separated themselves*
זֶרַע יִשְׂרָאֵל n.m.s. cstr. (282)-pr.n. (975) *the Israelites*
מִכֹּל בְּנֵי נֵכָר prep.-n.m.s. cstr. (481)-n.m.p. cstr. (119)-n.m.s. (648) *from all foreigners*
וַיַּעַמְדוּ consec.-Qal impf. 3 m.p. (עָמַד 763) *and stood*
וַיִּתְוַדּוּ consec.-Hith. impf. 3 m.p. (יָדָה 392) *and confessed*
עַל־חַטֹּאתֵיהֶם prep.-n.f.p.-3 m.p. sf. (308) *their sins*
וַעֲוֹנוֹת אֲבוֹתֵיהֶם conj.-n.m.p. cstr. (730)-n.m.p.-3 m.p. sf. (3) *and the iniquities of their fathers*

9:3

וַיָּקוּמוּ consec.-Qal impf. 3 m.p. (קוּם 877) *and they stood up*
עַל־עָמְדָם prep.-n.m.s.-3 m.p. sf. (765) *in their place*
וַיִּקְרְאוּ בְּסֵפֶר consec.-Qal impf. 3 m.p. (894)-prep.-n.m.s. cstr. (706) *and read from the book of*
תּוֹרַת יהוה n.f.s. cstr. (435)-pr.n. (217) *the law of Yahweh*
אֱלֹהֵיהֶם n.m.p.-3 m.p. sf. (43) *their God*
רְבִעִית הַיּוֹם num. adj. f. cstr. (917)-def.art.-n.m.s. (398) *for a fourth of the day*
וּרְבִעִית מִתְוַדִּים conj.-v.supra-Hith. ptc. m.p. (392 יָדָה) *for another fourth they made confession*
וּמִשְׁתַּחֲוִים conj.-Hith. ptc. m.p. (שָׁחָה 1005) *and worshiped*
לַיהוה אֱלֹהֵיהֶם prep.-pr.n. (217)-n.m.p.-3 m.p. sf. (43) *Yahweh their God*

9:4

וַיָּקָם consec.-Qal impf. 3 m.s. (קוּם 877) *and stood*
עַל־מַעֲלֵה הַלְוִיִּם prep.-n.m.s. cstr. (752)-def.art.-adj. gent. m.p. (532) *upon the stairs of the Levites*
יֵשׁוּעַ pr.n. (221) *Jeshua*
וּבָנִי conj.-pr.n. (125) *Bani*
קַדְמִיאֵל pr.n. (870) *Kadmiel*
שְׁבַנְיָה pr.n. (987) *Shebaniah*
בֻּנִּי pr.n. (125) *Bunni*
שֵׁרֵבְיָה pr.n. (1055) *Sherebiah*
בָּנִי v.supra *Bani*
כְנָנִי pr.n. (487) *and Chenani*
וַיִּזְעֲקוּ consec.-Qal impf. 3 m.p. (זָעַק 277) *and they cried*
בְּקוֹל גָּדוֹל prep.-n.m.s. (876)-adj. m.s. (152) *with a loud voice*
אֶל־יהוה prep.-pr.n. (217) *to Yahweh*
אֱלֹהֵיהֶם n.m.p.-3 m.p. sf. (43) *their God*

9:5

וַיֹּאמְרוּ הַלְוִיִּם consec.-Qal impf. 3 m.p. (55)-def.art.-adj. gent. m.p. (532) *then the Levites said*
יֵשׁוּעַ v.supra *Jeshua*
וְקַדְמִיאֵל v.supra *Kadmiel*
בָּנִי v.supra *Bani*
חֲשַׁבְנְיָה pr.n. (364) *Hashabneiah*
שֵׁרֵבְיָה v.supra *Sherebiah*
הוֹדִיָּה pr.n. (217) *Hodiah*
שְׁבַנְיָה v.supra *Shebaniah*
פְתַחְיָה pr.n. (836) *Pethahiah*
קוּמוּ בָּרְכוּ Qal impv. 2 m.p. (קוּם 877)-Pi. impv. 2 m.p. (בָּרַךְ 138) *stand up and bless*
אֶת־יהוה אֱלֹהֵיכֶם dir.obj.-pr.n. (217)-n.m.p.-2 m.p. sf. (43) *Yahweh your God*
מִן־הָעוֹלָם prep.-def.art.-n.m.s. (761) *from everlasting*
עַד־הָעוֹלָם prep. (III 723)-v.supra *to everlasting*
וִיבָרְכוּ conj.-Pi. impf. 3 m.p. (בָּרַךְ 138) *blessed be*
שֵׁם כְּבוֹדֶךָ n.m.s. cstr. (1027)-n.m.s.-2 m.s. sf. (458) *thy glorious name*
וּמְרוֹמַם conj.-Polal ptc. m.s. (רוּם 926) *which is exalted*
עַל־כָּל־בְּרָכָה prep.-n.m.s. cstr. (481)-n.f.s. (139) *above all blessing*
וּתְהִלָּה conj.-n.f.s. (239) *and praise*

9:6

אַתָּה־הוּא pers.pr. 2 m.s. (61)-pers.pr. 3 m.s. (214) *thou art he*

יהוה לְבַדֶּךָ pr.n. (217)-prep.-n.m.s.-2 m.s. sf. (94) *Yahweh thou alone*

אַתָּ עָשִׂיתָ pers.pr. 2 m.s. (61)-Qal pf. 2 m.s. (I 793 עָשָׂה) *thou hast made*

אֶת־הַשָּׁמַיִם dir.obj.-def.art.-n.m. du. (1029) *heaven*

שְׁמֵי הַשָּׁמַיִם n.m.p. cstr. (1029)-v.supra *the heaven of heavens*

וְכָל־צְבָאָם conj.-n.m.s. cstr. (481)-n.m.s.-3 m.p. sf. (838) *with all their host*

הָאָרֶץ def.art.-n.f.s. (75) *the earth*

וְכָל־אֲשֶׁר עָלֶיהָ conj.-v.supra-rel. (81)-prep.-3 f.s. sf. *and all that is on it*

הַיַּמִּים def.art.-n.m.p. (410) *the seas*

וְכָל־אֲשֶׁר בָּהֶם v.supra-v.supra-prep.-3 m.p. sf. *and all that is in them*

וְאַתָּה מְחַיֶּה conj.-v.supra-Pi. ptc. m.s. (חָיָה 310) *and thou preservest*

אֶת־כֻּלָּם dir.obj.-n.m.s.-3 m.p. sf. (481) *all of them*

וּצְבָא הַשָּׁמַיִם conj.-n.m.s. cstr. (838)-def.art.-n.m. du. (1029) *and the host of heaven*

לְךָ מִשְׁתַּחֲוִים prep.-2 m.s. sf.-Hith. ptc. m.p. (1005 שָׁחָה) *worships thee*

9:7

אַתָּה־הוּא v.supra-v.supra *thou art he*

יהוה הָאֱלֹהִים v.supra-v.supra *Yahweh God*

אֲשֶׁר בָּחַרְתָּ rel. (81)-Qal pf. 2 m.s. (בָּחַר 103) *who didst choose*

בְּאַבְרָם prep.-pr.n. (4) *Abram*

וְהוֹצֵאתוֹ conj.-Hi. pf. 2 m.s.-3 m.s. sf. (יָצָא 422) *and who didst bring him forth*

מֵאוּר כַּשְׂדִּים prep.-pr.n. (III 22)-pr.n. (505) *out of Ur of the Chaldeans*

וְשַׂמְתָּ שְּׁמוֹ conj.-Qal pf. 2 m.s. (שִׂים 962)-n.m.s.-3 m.s. sf. (1027) *and gave him the name*

אַבְרָהָם pr.n. (4) *Abraham*

9:8

וּמָצָאתָ conj.-Qal pf. 2 m.s. (מָצָא 592) *and thou didst find*

אֶת־לְבָבוֹ dir.obj.-n.m.s.-3 m.s. sf. (523) *his heart*

נֶאֱמָן לְפָנֶיךָ Ni. ptc. (אָמַן 52)-prep.-n.m.p.-2 m.s. sf. (815) *faithful before thee*

וְכָרוֹת עִמּוֹ conj.-Qal inf.abs. (כָּרַת 503)-prep.-3 m.s. sf. (767) *and didst make with him*

הַבְּרִית def.art.-n.f.s. (136) *the covenant*

לָתֵת prep.-Qal inf.cstr. (נָתַן 678) *to give*

אֶת־אֶרֶץ הַכְּנַעֲנִי dir.obj.-n.f.s. cstr. (75)-def.art.-adj. gent. (I 489) *the land of the Canaanite*

הַחִתִּי def.art.-adj. gent. (366) *the Hittite*

הָאֱמֹרִי def.art.-adj. gent. (57) *the Amorites*

וְהַפְּרִזִּי conj.-def.art.-adj. gent. (827) *the Perizzite*

וְהַיְבוּסִי conj.-def.art.-adj. gent. (101) *the Jebusite*

וְהַגִּרְגָּשִׁי conj.-def.art.-adj. gent. (173) *the Girgashite*

לָתֵת v.supra *to give*

לְזַרְעוֹ prep.-n.m.s.-3 m.s. sf. (282) *to his descendants*

וַתָּקֶם consec.-Hi. impf. 2 m.s. (קוּם 877) *and thou hast fulfilled*

אֶת־דְּבָרֶיךָ dir.obj.-n.m.p.-2 m.s. sf. (182) *thy promise*

כִּי צַדִּיק אָתָּה conj. (471)-adj. m.s. (843)-pers.pr. 2 m.s. paus. (61) *for thou art righteous*

9:9

וַתֵּרֶא consec.-Qal impf. 2 m.s. (רָאָה 906) *and thou didst see*

אֶת־עֳנִי אֲבֹתֵינוּ dir.obj.-n.m.s. cstr. (777)-n.m.p.-1 c.p. sf. (3) *the affliction of our fathers*

בְּמִצְרָיִם prep.-pr.n. paus. (595) *in Egypt*

וְאֶת־זַעֲקָתָם conj.-dir.obj.-n.f.s.-3 m.p. sf. (277) *and their cry*

שָׁמַעְתָּ Qal pf. 2 m.s. (שָׁמַע 1033) *thou didst hear*

עַל־יַם־סוּף prep.-n.m.s. cstr. (410)-n.m.s. (I 693) *at the Red Sea (sea of reeds)*

9:10

וַתִּתֵּן אֹתֹת consec.-Qal impf. 2 m.s. (נָתַן 678)-n.m.p. (16) *and didst perform signs*

וּמֹפְתִים conj.-n.m.p. (68) *and wonders*

בְּפַרְעֹה prep.-pr.n. (829) *against Pharaoh*

וּבְכָל־עֲבָדָיו conj.-prep.-n.m.s. cstr. (481)-n.m.p.-3 m.s. sf. (713) *and all his servants*

וּבְכָל־עַם אַרְצוֹ v.supra-n.m.s. cstr. (I 766)-n.f.s.-3 m.s. sf. (75) *and all the people of his land*

כִּי יָדַעְתָּ conj. (471)-Qal pf. 2 m.s. (יָדַע 393) *for thou knewest*

כִּי הֵזִידוּ עֲלֵיהֶם v.supra-Hi. pf. 3 c.p. (זיד 267)-prep.-3 m.p. sf. *that they acted insolently against them*

וַתַּעַשׂ־לְךָ consec.-Qal impf. 2 m.s. (עָשָׂה I 793)-prep.-2 m.s. sf. *and thou didst get thee*

שֵׁם n.m.s. (1027) *a name*

כְּהַיּוֹם הַזֶּה prep.-def.art.-n.m.s. (398)-def.art. -demons.adj. m.s. (260) *as it is to this day*

9:11

וְהַיָּם בָּקַעְתָּ conj.-def.art.-n.m.s. (410)-Qal pf. 2 m.s. (בָּקַע 131) *and thou didst divide the sea*
לִפְנֵיהֶם prep.-n.m.p.-3 m.p. sf. (815) *before them*
וַיַּעַבְרוּ consec.-Qal impf. 3 m.p. (עָבַר 716) *so that they went through*
בְתוֹךְ־הַיָּם prep.-n.m.s. cstr. (1063)-def.art.-n.m.s. (410) *the midst of the sea*
בַּיַּבָּשָׁה prep.-def.art.-n.f.s. (387) *on dry land*
וְאֶת־רֹדְפֵיהֶם conj.-dir.obj.-Qal act.ptc. m.p.-3 m.p. sf. (רָדַף 922) *and their pursuers*
הִשְׁלַכְתָּ Hi. pf. 2 m.s. (שָׁלַךְ 1020) *thou didst cast*
בִמְצוֹלֹת prep.-n.f.p. (846) *into the depths*
כְּמוֹ־אֶבֶן conj. (455)-n.f.s. (6) *as a stone*
בְּמַיִם עַזִּים prep.-n.m.p. (565)-adj. m.p. (738) *into mighty waters*

9:12

וּבְעַמּוּד עָנָן conj.-prep.-n.m.s. cstr. (765)-n.m.s. (777) *by a pillar of cloud*
הִנְחִיתָם Hi. pf. 2 m.s.-3 m.p. sf. (נָחָה 634) *thou didst lead them*
יוֹמָם adv. (401) *in the day*
וּבְעַמּוּד אֵשׁ v.supra-n.f.s. (77) *and by a pillar of fire*
לַיְלָה n.m.s. (538) *in the night*
לְהָאִיר לָהֶם prep.-Hi. inf.cstr. (אוֹר 21)-prep.-3 m.p. sf. *to light for them*
אֶת־הַדֶּרֶךְ dir.obj.-def.art.-n.m.s. (202) *the way*
אֲשֶׁר יֵלְכוּ־בָהּ rel. (81)-Qal impf. 3 m.p. (הָלַךְ 229)-prep.-3 f.s. sf. *in which they should go*

9:13

וְעַל הַר־סִינַי conj.-prep.-n.m.s. cstr. (249)-pr.n. (696) *upon Mount Sinai*
יָרַדְתָּ Qal pf. 2 m.s. (יָרַד 432) *thou didst come down*
וְדַבֵּר conj.-Pi. inf.cstr. (דָּבַר 180) *and speak*
עִמָּהֶם prep.-3 m.p. sf. *with them*
מִשָּׁמָיִם prep.-n.m. du. paus. (1029) *from heaven*
וַתִּתֵּן לָהֶם consec.-Qal impf. 2 m.s. (נָתַן 678) -prep.-3 m.p. sf. *and give them*
מִשְׁפָּטִים יְשָׁרִים n.m.p. (1048)-adj. m.p. (449; GK 132d) *right ordinances*
וְתוֹרוֹת אֱמֶת conj.-n.f.p. cstr. (435)-n.f.s. (54) *and true laws*
חֻקִּים n.m.p. (349) *statutes*

וּמִצְוֹת טוֹבִים conj.-n.f.p. (846)-adj. m.p. (II 373) *and good commandments*

9:14

וְאֶת־שַׁבַּת קָדְשְׁךָ inf.cstr.dir.obj.-n.f.s. cstr. (992)-n.m.s.-2 m.s. sf. (871) *and thy holy sabbath*
הוֹדַעְתָּ לָהֶם Hi. pf. 2 m.s. (יָדַע 393)-prep.-3 m.p. sf. *thou didst make known to them*
וּמִצְווֹת conj.-n.f.p. (846) *and commandments*
וְחֻקִּים conj.-n.m.p. (349) *and statutes*
וְתוֹרָה conj.-n.f.s. (435) *and a law*
צִוִּיתָ לָהֶם Pi. pf. 2 m.s. (צָוָה 845)-prep.-3 m.p. sf. *thou didst make known to them*
בְּיַד מֹשֶׁה prep.-n.f.s. cstr. (388)-pr.n. (602) *by the hand of Moses*
עַבְדֶּךָ n.m.s.-2 m.s. sf. (713) *thy servant*

9:15

וְלֶחֶם מִשָּׁמַיִם conj.-n.m.s. (536)-prep.-n.m. du. (1029) *and bread from heaven*
נָתַתָּה לָהֶם Qal pf. 2 m.s. (נָתַן 678)-prep.-3 m.p. sf. *thou didst give them*
לִרְעָבָם prep.-n.m.s.-3 m.p. sf. (944) *for their hunger*
וּמַיִם מִסֶּלַע conj.-n.m.p. (565)-prep.-n.m.s. (700) *and water from the rock*
הוֹצֵאתָ לָהֶם Hi. pf. 2 m.s. (יָצָא 422)-v.supra *bring forth for them*
לִצְמָאָם prep.-n.m.s.-3 m.p. sf. (854) *for their thirst*
וַתֹּאמֶר לָהֶם consec.-Qal impf. 2 m.s. (אָמַר 55)-v.supra *and thou didst tell them*
לָבוֹא prep.-Qal inf.cstr. (בּוֹא 97) *to go in*
לָרֶשֶׁת אֶת־הָאָרֶץ prep.-Qal inf.cstr. (יָרַשׁ 439) -dir.obj.-def.art.-n.f.s. (75) *to possess the land*
אֲשֶׁר־נָשָׂאתָ rel. (81)-Qal pf. 2 m.s. (נָשָׂא 669) *which thou had lifted up*
אֶת־יָדְךָ dir.obj.-n.f.s.-2 m.s. sf. (388) *thy hand*
לָתֵת לָהֶם prep.-Qal inf.cstr. (נָתַן 678)-v.supra *to give them*

9:16

וְהֵם וַאֲבֹתֵינוּ conj.-pers.pr. 3 m.p. (241)-conj. -n.m.p.-1 c.p. sf. (3) *but they and our fathers*
הֵזִידוּ Hi. pf. 3 c.p. (זִיד 267) *acted presumptuously*
וַיַּקְשׁוּ אֶת־עָרְפָּם consec.-Hi. impf. 3 m.p. (קָשָׁה I 904)-dir.obj.-n.m.s.-3 m.p. sf. (791) *and stiffened their neck*

וְלֹא שָׁמְעוּ conj.-neg.-Qal pf. 3 c.p. (שָׁמַע 1033) *and did not obey*

אֶל־מִצְוֹתֶיךָ prep.-n.f.p.-2 m.s. sf. (846) *thy commandments*

9:17

וַיְמָאֲנוּ consec.-Pi. impf. 3 m.p. (מָאַן 549) *and they refused*

לִשְׁמֹעַ prep.-Qal inf.cstr. (שָׁמַע 1033) *to obey*

וְלֹא־זָכְרוּ conj.-neg.-Qal pf. 3 c.p. (זָכַר 269) *and were not mindful*

נִפְלְאֹתֶיךָ Ni. ptc. f.p.-2 m.s. sf. (פָּלָא 810) *of the wonders*

אֲשֶׁר עָשִׂיתָ עִמָּהֶם rel. (81)-Qal pf. 2 m.s. (עָשָׂה I 793)-prep.-3 m.p. sf. *which thou didst perform among them*

וַיַּקְשׁוּ אֶת־עָרְפָּם consec.-Hi. impf. 3 m.p. (קָשָׁה 904)-dir.obj.-n.m.s.-3 m.p. sf. (791) *but they stiffened their neck*

וַיִּתְּנוּ־רֹאשׁ consec.-Qal impf. 3 m.p. (נָתַן 678) -n.m.s. (910) *and appointed a leader*

לָשׁוּב לְעַבְדֻתָם prep.-Qal inf.cstr. (שׁוּב 996) -prep.-n.f.s.-3 m.p. sf. (715) *to return to their bondage*

בְּמִרְיָם prep.-n.m.s.-3 m.p. sf. (598; LXX ἐν Αἰγύπτῳ) *in Egypt*

וְאַתָּה אֱלוֹהַּ conj.-pers.pr. 2 m.s. (61)-n.m.s. (42) *but thou art a God*

סְלִיחוֹת n.f.p. (699) *of abundant forgiveness*

חַנּוּן וְרַחוּם adj. m.s. (337)-conj.-adj. m.s. (933) *gracious and merciful*

אֶרֶךְ־אַפַּיִם adj. m.s. cstr. (74)-n.m. du. (I 60) *slow to anger*

וְרַב־וְחֶסֶד conj.-adj. m.s. cstr. (I 912)-n.m.s. (338) *and abounding in steadfast love*

וְלֹא עֲזַבְתָּם conj.-neg.-Qal pf. 2 m.s.-3 m.p. sf. (I 736 עָזַב) *and didst not forsake them*

9:18

אַף כִּי־עָשׂוּ לָהֶם conj. (II 64)-conj. (471)-Qal pf. 3 c.p. (עָשָׂה I 793)-prep.-3 m.p. sf. *even when they had made for themselves*

עֵגֶל מַסֵּכָה n.m.s. cstr. (722)-n.f.s. (I 651) *a molten calf*

וַיֹּאמְרוּ consec.-Qal impf. 3 m.p. (אָמַר 55) *and said*

זֶה אֱלֹהֶיךָ demons.adj. m.s. (260)-n.m.p.-2 m.s. sf. (43) *this is your God*

אֲשֶׁר הֶעֶלְךָ rel. (81)-Hi. pf. 3 m.s.-2 m.s. sf. (עָלָה 748) *who brought you up*

מִמִּצְרָיִם prep.-pr.n. paus. (595) *out of Egypt*

וַיַּעֲשׂוּ consec.-Qal impf. 3 m.p. (עָשָׂה I 793) *and had committed*

נֶאָצוֹת גְּדֹלוֹת n.f.p. (611)-adj. f.p. (152) *great blasphemies*

9:19

וְאַתָּה conj.-pers.pr. 2 m.s. (61) *and thou*

בְּרַחֲמֶיךָ הָרַבִּים prep.-n.m.p.-2 m.s. sf. (933) -def.art.-adj. m.p. (I 912) *in thy great mercies*

לֹא עֲזַבְתָּם neg.-Qal pf. 2 m.s.-3 m.p. sf. (עָזַב I 736) *didst not forsake them*

בַּמִּדְבָּר prep.-def.art.-n.m.s. (184) *in the wilderness*

אֶת־עַמּוּד הֶעָנָן dir.obj.-n.m.s. cstr. 765)-def. art.-n.m.s. (777) *the pillar of the cloud*

לֹא־סָר מֵעֲלֵיהֶם neg.-Qal pf. 3 m.s. (סוּר 693) -prep.-3 m.p. sf. *did not depart from them*

בְּיוֹמָם prep.-adv. (401) *by day*

לְהַנְחֹתָם prep.-Hi. inf.cstr.-3 m.p. sf. (נָחָה 634) *to lead them*

בְּהַדֶּרֶךְ prep.-def.art.-n.m.s. (202) *in the way*

וְאֶת־עַמּוּד הָאֵשׁ conj.-dir.obj.-v.supra-def. art.-n.f.s. (77) *nor the pillar of fire*

בְּלַיְלָה prep.-n.m.s. (538) *by night*

לְהָאִיר לָהֶם prep.-Hi. inf.cstr. (אוֹר 21)-prep.-3 m.p. sf. *which lighted for them*

וְאֶת־הַדֶּרֶךְ conj.-dir.obj.-def.art.-n.m.s. (202) *the way*

אֲשֶׁר יֵלְכוּ־בָהּ rel. (81)-Qal Qal impf. 3 m.p. (229 הָלַךְ)-prep.-3 f.s. sf. *by which they should go*

9:20

וְרוּחֲךָ הַטּוֹבָה conj.-n.f.s.-2 m.s. sf. (924)-def.art. -adj. f.s. (II 373) *thy good Spirit*

נָתַתָּ Qal pf. 2 m.s. (נָתַן 678) *thou gavest*

לְהַשְׂכִּילָם prep.-Hi. inf.cstr.-3 m.p. sf. (שָׂכַל 968) *to instruct them*

וּמַנְךָ conj.-n.m.s.-2 m.s. sf. (I 577) *and thy manna*

לֹא־מָנַעְתָּ neg.-Qal pf. 2 m.s. (מָנַע 586) *didst not withhold*

מִפִּיהֶם prep.-n.m.s.-3 m.p. sf. (804) *from their mouth*

וּמַיִם נָתַתָּה conj.-n.m.p. (565)-Qal pf. 2 m.s. (נָתַן 678) *and gavest ... water*

לָהֶם לִצְמָאָם prep.-3 m.p. sf.-prep.-n.m.s.-3 m.p. sf. (854) *to them for their thirst*

9:21

וְאַרְבָּעִים שָׁנָה conj.-num. p. (917)-n.f.s. (1040) *forty years*

כִּלְכַּלְתָּם Pilpel pf. 2 m.s.-3 m.p. sf. (כּוּל 465) *didst thou sustain them*

בַּמִּדְבָּר prep.-def.art.-n.m.s. (184) *in the wilderness*

לֹא חָסֵרוּ neg.-Qal pf. 3 c.p. paus. (חָסֵר 341) *and they lacked nothing*

שַׂלְמֹתֵיהֶם n.f.p.-3 m.p. sf. (971) *their clothes*

לֹא בָלוּ neg.-Qal pf. 3 c.p. (בָּלָה 115) *did not wear out*

וְרַגְלֵיהֶם n.f.p.-3 m.p. sf. (919) *and their feet*

לֹא בָצֵקוּ neg.-Qal pf. 3 c.p. paus. (בָּצֵק 130) *did not swell*

9:22

וַתִּתֵּן לָהֶם consec.-Qal impf. 2 m.s. (נָתַן 678) -prep.-3 m.p. sf. *and thou didst give them*

מַמְלָכוֹת n.f.p. (575) *kingdoms*

וַעֲמָמִים conj.-n.m.p. (I 766) *and peoples*

וַתַּחְלְקֵם לְפֵאָה consec.-Qal impf. 2 m.s.-3 m.p. sf. (חָלַק 323)-prep.-n.f.s. (802) *and didst allot to them every corner*

וַיִּירְשׁוּ consec.-Qal impf. 3 m.p. (יָרַשׁ 439) *so they took possession*

אֶת־אֶרֶץ סִיחוֹן dir.obj.-n.f.s. cstr. (75)-pr.n. (695) *the land of Sihon*

וְאֶת־אֶרֶץ conj.-v.supra-v.supra *and the land of*

מֶלֶךְ חֶשְׁבּוֹן n.m.s. cstr. (I 572)-pr.n. (II 363) *the king of Heshbon*

וְאֶת־אֶרֶץ עוֹג v.supra-v.supra-pr.n. (728) *and the land of Og*

מֶלֶךְ־הַבָּשָׁן v.supra-def.art.-pr.n. (143) *king of Bashan*

9:23

וּבְנֵיהֶם conj.-n.m.p.-3 m.p. sf. (119) *and their descendants*

הִרְבִּיתָ Hi. pf. 2 m.s. (רָבָה I 915) *thou didst multiply*

כְּכֹכְבֵי הַשָּׁמָיִם prep.-n.m.p. cstr. (456)-def.art. -n.m. du. paus. (1029) *as the stars of heaven*

וַתְּבִיאֵם consec.-Hi. impf. 2 m.s.-3 m.p. sf. (בּוֹא 97) *and thou didst bring them*

אֶל־הָאָרֶץ prep.-def.art.-n.f.s. (75) *into the land*

אֲשֶׁר־אָמַרְתָּ rel. (81)-Qal pf. 2 m.s. (אָמַר 55) *which thou hadst told*

לַאֲבֹתֵיהֶם prep.-n.m.p.-3 m.p. sf. (3) *their fathers*

לָבוֹא לָרֶשֶׁת prep.-Qal inf.cstr. (בּוֹא 97)-prep. -Qal inf.cstr. (יָרַשׁ 439) *to enter and possess*

9:24

וַיָּבֹאוּ הַבָּנִים consec.-Qal impf. 3 m.p. (בּוֹא 97)-def.art.-n.m.p. (119) *so the descendants went in*

וַיִּירְשׁוּ אֶת־הָאָרֶץ consec.-Qal impf. 3 m.p. (יָרַשׁ 439)-dir.obj.-def.art.-n.f.s. (75) *and possessed the land*

וַתַּכְנַע לִפְנֵיהֶם consec.-Hi. impf. 2 m.s. (כָּנַע 488)-prep.-n.m.p.-3 m.p. sf. (815) *and thou didst subdue before them*

אֶת־יֹשְׁבֵי הָאָרֶץ dir.obj.-Qal act.ptc. m.p. cstr. (442 יָשַׁב)-def.art.-n.f.s. (75) *the inhabitants of the land*

הַכְּנַעֲנִים def.art.-adj. gent. m.p. (I 489) *the Canaanites*

וַתִּתְּנֵם בְּיָדָם consec.-Qal impf. 2 m.s.-3 m.p. sf. (נָתַן 678)-prep.-n.f.s.-3 m.p. sf. (388) *and didst give them into their hands*

וְאֶת־מַלְכֵיהֶם conj.-dir.obj.-n.m.p.-3 m.p. sf. (I 572) *with their kings*

וְאֶת־עַמְמֵי הָאָרֶץ v.supra-n.m.p. cstr. (I 766) -v.supra *and the peoples of the land*

לַעֲשׂוֹת בָּהֶם prep.-Qal inf.cstr. (עָשָׂה I 793) -prep.-3 m.p. sf. *that they might do with them*

כִּרְצוֹנָם prep.-n.m.s.-3 m.p. sf. (953) *as they would*

9:25

וַיִּלְכְּדוּ consec.-Qal impf. 3 m.p. (לָכַד 539) *and they captured*

עָרִים בְּצֻרוֹת n.f.p. (746)-Qal pass.ptc. f.p. (בָּצַר 130) *fortified cities*

וַאֲדָמָה שְׁמֵנָה conj.-n.f.s. (9)-adj. f.s. (1032) *and a rich land*

וַיִּירְשׁוּ בָּתִּים consec.-Qal impf. 3 m.p. (יָרַשׁ 439)-n.m.p. (108) *and took possession of houses*

מְלֵאִים־כָּל־טוּב adj. m.p. (570)-n.m.s. cstr. (481)-n.m.s. (375) *full of all good things*

בֹּרוֹת חֲצוּבִים n.m.p. (92)-Qal pass.ptc. m.p. (חָצַב 345) *cisterns hewn out*

כְּרָמִים n.m.p. (501) *vineyards*

וְזֵיתִים conj.-n.m.p. (268) *olive orchards*

וְעֵץ מַאֲכָל conj.-n.m.s. cstr. (781)-n.m.s. (38) *and fruit (food) trees*

לָרֹב prep.-n.m.s. (914) *in abundance*

וַיֹּאכְלוּ consec.-Qal impf. 3 m.p. (אָכַל 37) *so they ate*

וַיִּשְׂבְּעוּ consec.-Qal impf. 3 m.p. (שָׂבַע 959) *and were filled*

וַיַּשְׁמִינוּ consec.-Hi. impf. 3 m.p. (שָׁמֵן 1031) *and became fat*

וַיִּתְעַדְּנוּ consec.-Hith. impf. 3 m.p. (עָדַן 726) *and delighted themselves*

בְּטוּבְךָ הַגָּדוֹל prep.-n.m.s.-2 m.s. sf. (375)-def. art.-adj. m.s. (152) *in thy great goodness*

9:26

וַיַּמְרוּ consec.-Hi. impf. 3 m.p. (מָרָה 598) *nevertheless they were disobedient*

וַיִּמְרְדוּ בָּךְ consec.-Qal impf. 3 m.p. (מָרַד 597)-prep.-2 m.s. sf. paus. *and rebelled against thee*

וַיַּשְׁלִכוּ consec.-Hi. impf. 3 m.p. (שָׁלַךְ 1020) *and they cast*

אֶת־תּוֹרָתְךָ dir.obj.-n.f.s.-2 m.s. sf. (435) *thy law*

אַחֲרֵי גַוָּם prep. (29)-n.m.s.-3 m.p. sf. (156) *behind their back*

וְאֶת־נְבִיאֶיךָ conj.-dir.obj.-n.m.p.-2 m.s. sf. (611) *and thy prophets*

הָרָגוּ Qal pf. 3 c.p. paus. (הָרַג 246) *killed*

אֲשֶׁר־הֵעִידוּ בָם rel. (81)-Hi. pf. 3 c.p. (עוּד 729) -prep.-3 m.p. sf. *who had warned them*

לַהֲשִׁיבָם אֵלֶיךָ prep.-Hi. inf.cstr.-3 m.p. sf. (שׁוּב 996)-prep.-2 m.s. sf. *in order to turn them back to thee*

וַיַּעֲשׂוּ consec.-Qal impf. 3 m.p. (עָשָׂה I 793) *and they committed*

נֶאָצוֹת גְּדוֹלֹת n.f.p. (611)-adj. f.p. (152) *great blasphemies*

9:27

וַתִּתְּנֵם consec.-Qal impf. 2 m.s.-3 m.p. sf. (נָתַן 678) *therefore thou didst give them*

בְּיַד צָרֵיהֶם prep.-n.f.s. cstr. (388)-n.m.p. (865) *into the hand of their enemies*

וַיָּצֵרוּ לָהֶם consec.-Hi. impf. 3 m.p. (צָרַר I 864)-prep.-3 m.p. sf. *who made them suffer*

וּבְעֵת צָרָתָם conj.-prep.-n.f.s. cstr. (773)-n.f.s.-3 m.p. sf. (I 865) *and in the time of their suffering*

יִצְעֲקוּ אֵלֶיךָ Qal impf. 3 m.p. (צָעַק 858)-prep.-2 m.s. sf. *they cried to thee*

וְאַתָּה מִשָּׁמַיִם conj.-pers.pr. 2 m.s. (61)-prep. -n.m. du. (1029) *and thou from heaven*

תִּשְׁמָע Qal impf. 2 m.s. paus. (שָׁמַע 1033) *didst hear*

וּכְרַחֲמֶיךָ הָרַבִּים conj.-prep.-n.m.p.-2 m.s. sf. (933)-def.art.-adj. m.p. (I 912) *and according to thy great mercies*

תִּתֵּן לָהֶם Qal impf. 2 m.s. (נָתַן 678)-prep.-3 m.p. sf. *thou didst give them*

מוֹשִׁיעִים Hi. ptc. m.p. (יָשַׁע 446) *saviors*

וְיוֹשִׁיעוּם conj.-Hi. impf. 3 m.p.-3 m.p. sf. (יָשַׁע 446) *who saved them*

מִיַּד צָרֵיהֶם prep.-n.f.s. cstr. (388)-n.m.p.-3 m.p. sf. (III 865) *from the hand of their enemies*

9:28

וּכְנוֹחַ לָהֶם conj.-prep.-Qal inf.cstr. (נוּחַ 628) -prep.-3 m.p. sf. *but after they had rest*

יָשׁוּבוּ לַעֲשׂוֹת רַע Qal impf. 3 m.p. (שׁוּב 996) -prep.-Qal inf.cstr. (עָשָׂה I 793)-n.m.s. (948) *they did evil against*

לְפָנֶיךָ prep.-n.m.p.-2 m.s. sf. (815) *before thee*

וַתַּעַזְבֵם consec.-Qal impf. 2 m.s.-3 m.p. sf. (עָזַב I 736) *and thou didst abandon them*

בְּיַד אֹיְבֵיהֶם prep.-n.f.s. cstr. (388)-Qal act.ptc. m.p.-3 m.p. sf. (אָיַב 33) *to the hand of their enemies*

וַיִּרְדּוּ בָהֶם consec.-Qal impf. 3 m.p. (רָדָה I 921)-prep.-3 m.p. sf. *so that they had dominion over them*

וַיָּשׁוּבוּ consec.-Qal impf. 3 m.p. (שׁוּב 996) *yet when they turned*

וַיִּזְעָקוּךָ consec.-Qal impf. 3 m.p.-2 m.s. sf. (זָעַק 277) *and cried to thee*

וְאַתָּה מִשָּׁמַיִם conj.-pers.pr. 2 m.s. (61)-prep. -n.m. du. (1029) *thou from heaven*

תִּשְׁמַע Qal impf. 2 m.s. (שָׁמַע 1033) *didst hear*

וְתַצִּילֵם conj.-Hi. impf. 2 m.s.-3 m.p. sf. (נָצַל 664) *and thou didst deliver them*

כְּרַחֲמֶיךָ prep.-n.m.p.-2 m.s. sf. (933) *according to thy mercies*

רַבּוֹת עִתִּים adj. f.p. (I 912)-n.f.p. (773) *many times*

9:29

וַתָּעַד בָּהֶם consec.-Hi. impf. 2 m.s. (עוּד 729) -prep.-3 m.p. sf. *and thou didst warn them*

לַהֲשִׁיבָם prep.-Hi. inf.cstr. (שׁוּב 996)-3 m.p. sf. *in order to turn them back*

אֶל־תּוֹרָתֶךָ prep.-n.f.s.-2 m.s. sf. (435) *to thy law*

וְהֵמָּה הֵזִידוּ conj.-pers.pr. 3 m.p. (241)-Hi. pf. 3 c.p. (זִיד 267) *yet they acted presumptuously*

וְלֹא־שָׁמְעוּ conj.-neg.-Qal pf. 3 c.p. (שָׁמַע 1033) *and did not obey*

לְמִצְוֹתֶיךָ prep.-n.f.p.-2 m.s. sf. (846) *thy commandments*

וּבְמִשְׁפָּטֶיךָ conj.-prep.-n.m.p.-2 m.s. sf. (1048) *but against thy ordinances*

חָטְאוּ־בָם Qal pf. 3 c.p. (חָטָא 306)-prep.-3 m.p. sf. *sinned against them*

אֲשֶׁר־יַעֲשֶׂה אָדָם rel. (81)-Qal impf. 3 m.s. (I 793)-n.m.s. (9) *which a man should do*

וְחָיָה בָהֶם conj.-Qal pf. 3 m.s. (310)-prep.-3 m.p. sf. *and live by them*

וַיִּתְּנוּ consec.-Qal impf. 3 m.p. (נָתַן 678) *and turned*

כָתֵף סוֹרֶרֶת n.f.s. (509)-Qal act.ptc. f.s. (סָרַר 710) *a stubborn shoulder*

וְעָרְפָּם conj.-n.m.s.-3 m.p. sf. (791) *and their neck*

הִקְשׁוּ Hi. pf. 3 c.p. (קָשָׁה 904) *stiffened*

וְלֹא שָׁמֵעוּ conj.-neg.-Qal pf. 3 c.p. paus. (שָׁמַע 1033) *and would not obey*

9:30

וַתִּמְשֹׁךְ עֲלֵיהֶם consec.-Qal impf. 2 m.s. (מָשַׁךְ 604)-prep.-3 m.p. sf. *thou didst bear with them*

שָׁנִים רַבּוֹת n.f.p. (1040)-adj. f.p. (I 912) *many years*

וַתָּעַד בָּם consec.-Hi. impf. 2 m.s. (עוּד 729) -prep.-3 m.p. sf. *and didst warn them*

בְּרוּחֲךָ prep.-n.f.s.-2 m.s. sf. (924) *by thy Spirit*

בְּיַד־נְבִיאֶיךָ prep.-n.f.s. cstr. (388)-n.m.p.-2 m.s. sf. (611) *through the hand of thy prophets*

וְלֹא הֶאֱזִינוּ conj.-neg.-Hi. pf. 3 c.p. (אָזַן 24) *yet they would not give ear*

וַתִּתְּנֵם consec.-Qal impf. 2 m.s.-3 m.p. sf. (נָתַן 678) *therefore thou didst give them*

בְּיַד עַמֵּי הָאֲרָצֹת v.supra-n.m.p. cstr. (I 766)-def. art.-n.f.p. (75) *into the hand of the peoples of the lands*

9:31

וּבְרַחֲמֶיךָ הָרַבִּים conj.-prep.-n.m.p.-2 m.s. sf. (933)-def.art.-adj. m.p. (I 912) *nevertheless in thy great mercies*

לֹא־עֲשִׂיתָם כָּלָה neg.-Qal pf. 2 m.s.-3 m.p. sf. (I 793 עָשָׂה)-n.f.s. (478) *thou didst not make an end of them*

וְלֹא עֲזַבְתָּם conj.-neg.-Qal pf. 2 m.s.-3 m.p. sf. (I 736 עָזַב) *or forsake them*

כִּי אֵל־חַנּוּן conj. (471)-n.m.s. (42)-adj. m.s. (337) *for a gracious God*

וְרַחוּם אָתָּה conj.-adj. m.s. (933)-pers.pr. 2 m.s. paus. (61) *and merciful thou art*

9:32

וְעַתָּה אֱלֹהֵינוּ conj.-adv. (773)-n.m.p.-1 c.p. sf. (43) *now therefore our God*

הָאֵל הַגָּדוֹל def.art.-n.m.s. (42)-def.art.-adj. m.s. (152) *the great God*

הַגִּבּוֹר וְהַנּוֹרָא def.art.-n.m.s. (150)-conj.-def.art. -Ni. ptc. m.s. (יָרֵא 431) *and mighty and terrible*

שׁוֹמֵר הַבְּרִית Qal act.ptc. (שָׁמַר 1036)-def.art. -n.f.s. (136) *who keepest covenant*

וְהַחֶסֶד conj.-def.art.-n.m.s. (338) *and steadfast love*

אַל־יִמְעַט neg.-Qal impf. 3 m.s. (מָעַט 589) *let not seem little*

לְפָנֶיךָ prep.-n.m.p.-2 m.s. sf. (815) *to thee*

אֵת כָּל־הַתְּלָאָה dir.obj.-n.m.s. cstr. (481)-def.art. -n.f.s. (521) *all the hardship*

אֲשֶׁר־מְצָאַתְנוּ rel. (81)-Qal pf. 3 f.s.-1 c.p. sf. (592 מָצָא) *that has come upon us*

לִמְלָכֵינוּ prep.-n.m.p.-1 c.p. sf. (I 572) *upon our kings*

לְשָׂרֵינוּ prep.-n.m.p.-1 c.p. sf. (978) *our princes*

וּלְכֹהֲנֵינוּ conj.-prep.-n.m.p.-1 c.p. sf. (463) *our priests*

וְלִנְבִיאֵנוּ conj.-prep.-n.m.p.-1 c.p. sf. (611) *our prophets*

וְלַאֲבֹתֵינוּ conj.-prep.-n.m.p.-1 c.p. sf. (3) *our fathers*

וּלְכָל־עַמֶּךָ conj.-prep.-n.m.s. cstr. (481)-n.m.s.-2 m.s. sf. paus. (I 766) *and all thy people*

מִימֵי מַלְכֵי אַשּׁוּר prep.-n.m.p. cstr. (388)-n.m.p. cstr. (I 572)-pr.n. (78) *since the time of the kings of Assyria*

עַד הַיּוֹם הַזֶּה prep. (III 723)-def.art.-n.m.s. (398)-def.art.-demons.adj. m.s. (260) *until this day*

9:33

וְאַתָּה צַדִּיק conj.-pers.pr. 2 m.s. (61)-adj. m.s. (843) *yet thou hast been just*

עַל כָּל־הַבָּא עָלֵינוּ prep.-n.m.s. cstr. (481)-def. art.-Qal act.ptc. (בּוֹא 97)-prep.-1 c.p. sf. *in all that has come upon us*

כִּי־אֱמֶת עָשִׂיתָ conj. (471)-n.f.s. (54)-Qal pf. 2 m.s. (עָשָׂה I 793) *for thou hast dealt faithfully*

וַאֲנַחְנוּ הִרְשָׁעְנוּ conj.-pers.pr. 1 c.p. (59)-Hi. pf. 1 c.p. (רָשַׁע 957) *and we have acted wickedly*

9:34

וְאֶת־מְלָכֵינוּ conj.-dir.obj.-n.m.p.-1 c.p. sf. (I 572) *our kings*

שָׂרֵינוּ n.m.p.-1 c.p. sf. (978) *our princes*
כֹּהֲנֵינוּ n.m.p.-1 c.p. sf. (463) *our priests*
וַאֲבֹתֵינוּ conj.-n.m.p.-1 c.p. sf. (3) *and our fathers*
לֹא עָשׂוּ neg.-Qal pf. 3 c.p. (עָשָׂה I 793) *have not kept*
תּוֹרָתֶךָ n.f.s.-2 m.s. sf. (435) *thy law*
וְלֹא הִקְשִׁיבוּ conj.-neg.-Hi. pf. 3 c.p. (קָשַׁב 904) *or heeded*
אֶל־מִצְוֹתֶיךָ prep.-n.f.p.-2 m.s. sf. (846) *thy commandments*
וּלְעֵדְוֹתֶיךָ conj.-prep.-n.f.p.-2 m.s. sf. (730) *and thy warnings*
אֲשֶׁר הַעִידֹתָ בָּהֶם rel. (81)-Hi. pf. 2 m.s. (עוּד 729)-prep.-3 m.p. sf. *which thou didst give them*

9:35

וְהֵם בְּמַלְכוּתָם conj.-pers.pr. 3 m.p. (241)-prep.-n.f.s.-3 m.p. sf. (574) *and they in their kingdom*
וּבְטוּבְךָ הָרָב conj.-prep.-n.m.s.-2 m.s. sf. (375)-def.art.-adj. m.s. (I 912) *and in thy great goodness*
אֲשֶׁר־נָתַתָּ לָהֶם rel. (81)-Qal pf. 2 m.s. (נָתַן 678)-prep.-3 m.p. sf. *which thou gavest them*
וּבְאֶרֶץ הָרְחָבָה conj.-prep.-n.f.s. (75; GK 126x)-def.art.-adj. f.s. (I 932) *in the large land*
וְהַשְּׁמֵנָה conj.-def.art.-adj. f.s. (1032) *and rich*
אֲשֶׁר־נָתַתָּ לִפְנֵיהֶם rel. (81)-Qal pf. 2 m.s. (נָתַן 678)-prep.-n.m.p.-3 m.p. sf. (815) *which thou didst set before them*
לֹא עֲבָדוּךָ neg.-Qal pf. 3 c.p.-2 m.s. sf. (עָבַד 712) *they did not serve thee*
וְלֹא־שָׁבוּ conj.-neg.-Qal pf. 3 c.p. (שׁוּב 996) *and they did not turn*
מִמַּעַלְלֵיהֶם הָרָעִים prep.-n.m.p.-3 m.p. sf. (760)-def.art.-adj. m.p. (I 948) *from their wicked works*

9:36

הִנֵּה אֲנַחְנוּ interj. (243)-pers.pr. 1 c.p. (59) *behold, we are*
הַיּוֹם def.art.-n.m.s. (398) *this day*
עֲבָדִים n.m.p. (713) *slaves*
וְהָאָרֶץ conj.-def.art.-n.f.s. (75) *in the land*
אֲשֶׁר־נָתַתָּה rel. (81)-Qal pf. 2 m.s. (נָתַן 678) *that thou gavest*
לַאֲבֹתֵינוּ prep.-n.m.p.-1 c.p. sf. (3) *to our fathers*
לֶאֱכֹל prep.-Qal inf.cstr. (אָכַל 37) *to enjoy (eat)*
אֶת־פִּרְיָהּ dir.obj.-n.m.s.-3 f.s. sf. (826) *its fruit*
וְאֶת־טוּבָהּ conj.-v.supra-n.m.s.-3 f.s. sf. (375) *and its good gifts*
הִנֵּה אֲנַחְנוּ v.supra-v.supra *behold, we are*
עֲבָדִים עָלֶיהָ n.m.p. (713)-prep.-3 f.s. sf. *slaves to it*

9:37

וּתְבוּאָתָהּ מַרְבָּה conj.-n.f.s.-3 f.s. sf. (100)-Hi. ptc. f.s. (רָבָה I 915) *and its rich yield*
לַמְּלָכִים prep.-def.art.-n.m.p. (I 572) *to the kings*
אֲשֶׁר־נָתַתָּה עָלֵינוּ rel. (81)-Qal pf. 2 m.s. (נָתַן 678)-prep.-1 c.p. sf. *whom thou hast set over us*
בְּחַטֹּאותֵינוּ prep.-n.f.p.-1 c.p. sf. (308) *because of our sins*
וְעַל גְּוִיֹּתֵינוּ conj.-prep.-n.f.p.-1 c.p. sf. (156) *and over our bodies*
מֹשְׁלִים Qal act.ptc. m.p. (מָשַׁל 605) *they have power*
וּבִבְהֶמְתֵּנוּ conj.-prep.-n.f.s.-1 c.p. sf. (96) *and over our cattle*
כִּרְצוֹנָם prep.-n.m.s.-3 m.p. sf. (953) *at their pleasure*
וּבְצָרָה גְדוֹלָה conj.-prep.-n.f.s. (865)-adj. f.s. (152) *and in great distress*
אֲנָחְנוּ pers.pr. 1 c.p. paus. (59) *we are*

10:1 (Eng.9:38)

וּבְכָל־זֹאת conj.-prep.-n.m.s. cstr. (481)-demons.adj. f.s. (260) *because of all this*
אֲנַחְנוּ pers.pr. 1 c.p. (59) *we*
כֹּרְתִים אֲמָנָה Qal act.ptc. m.p. (כָּרַת 503)-n.f.s. (53) *make a firm covenant*
וְכֹתְבִים conj.-Qal act.ptc. m.p. (כָּתַב 507) *and write it*
וְעַל־הֶחָתוּם conj.-prep.-def.art.-Qal pass.ptc. (367 חָתַם) *and under the seal*
שָׂרֵינוּ n.m.p.-1 c.p. sf. (978) *our princes*
לְוִיֵּנוּ adj. gent. m.p.-1 c.p. sf. (532) *our Levites*
כֹּהֲנֵינוּ n.m.p.-1 c.p. sf. (463) *our priests*

10:2 (Eng.10:1)

וְעַל הַחֲתוּמִים conj.-prep.-def.art.-Qal pass.ptc. m.p. (חָתַם 367) *and under the seals*
נְחֶמְיָה pr.n. (637) *Nehemiah*
הַתִּרְשָׁתָא def.art.-n.m.s. (1077) *the governor*
בֶּן־חֲכַלְיָה n.m.s. cstr. (119)-pr.n. (314) *the son of Hacaliah*
וְצִדְקִיָּה conj.-pr.n. (843) *and Zedekiah*

10:3

שְׂרָיָה pr.n. (976) *Seraiah*

עֲזַרְיָה pr.n. (741) *Azariah*
יִרְמְיָה pr.n. (941) *Jeremiah*

10:4
פַּשְׁחוּר pr.n. (832) *Pashhur*
אֲמַרְיָה pr.n. (57) *Amariah*
מַלְכִּיָּה pr.n. (575) *Malchijah*

10:5
חַטּוּשׁ pr.n. (310) *Hattush*
שְׁבַנְיָה pr.n. (987) *Shebaniah*
מַלּוּךְ pr.n. (576) *Malluch*

10:6
חָרִם pr.n. (356) *Harim*
מְרֵמוֹת pr.n. (599) *Meremoth*
עֹבַדְיָה pr.n. (715) *Obadiah*

10:7
דָּנִיֵּאל pr.n. (193) *Daniel*
גִּנְּתוֹן pr.n. (171) *Ginnethon*
בָּרוּךְ pr.n. (140) *Baruch*

10:8
מְשֻׁלָּם pr.n. (1024) *Meshullam*
אֲבִיָּה pr.n. (4) *Abijah*
מִיָּמִן pr.n. (568) *Mijamin*

10:9
מַעַזְיָה pr.n. (589) *Maaziah*
בִּלְגַּי pr.n. (114) *Bilgai*
שְׁמַעְיָה pr.n. (1035) *Shemaiah*
אֵלֶּה הַכֹּהֲנִים demons.adj. c.p. (41)–def.art.–n.m.p. (463) *these are the priests*

10:10 (Eng.10:9)
וְהַלְוִיִּם conj.–def.art.–adj. gent. m.p. (532) *and the Levites*
וְיֵשׁוּעַ conj.–pr.n. (221) *Jeshua*
בֶּן־אֲזַנְיָה n.m.s. cstr. (119)–pr.n. (24) *the son of Azaniah*
בִּנּוּי pr.n. (125) *Binnui*
מִבְּנֵי חֵנָדָד prep.–n.m.p. cstr. (119)–pr.n. (337) *of the sons of Henedad*
קַדְמִיאֵל pr.n. (870) *Kadmiel*

10:11
וַאֲחֵיהֶם conj.–n.m.p.–3 m.p. sf. (26) *and their brethren*
שְׁבַנְיָה pr.n. (987) *Shebaniah*
הוֹדִיָּה pr.n. (217) *Hodiah*
קְלִיטָא pr.n. (886) *Kelita*
פְּלָאיָה pr.n. (811) *Pelaiah*
חָנָן pr.n. (336) *Hanan*

10:12
מִיכָא pr.n. (567) *Mica*
רְחוֹב pr.n. (932) *Rehob*
חֲשַׁבְיָה pr.n. (364) *Hashabiah*

10:13
זַכּוּר pr.n. (271) *Zaccur*
שֵׁרֵבְיָה pr.n. (1055) *Sherebiah*
שְׁבַנְיָה pr.n. (987) *Shebaniah*

10:14
הוֹדִיָּה pr.n. (217) *Hodiah*
בָּנִי pr.n. (125) *Bani*
בְּנִינוּ pr.n. (125) *Beninu*

10:15
רָאשֵׁי הָעָם n.m.p. cstr. (910)–def.art.–n.m.s. (I 766) *the chiefs of the people*
פַּרְעֹשׁ pr.n. (829) *Parosh*
פַּחַת מוֹאָב pr.n. (809) *Pahath-moab*
עֵילָם pr.n. (II 743) *Elam*
זַתּוּא pr.n. (285) *Zattu*
בָּנִי pr.n. (125) *Bani*

10:16
בֻּנִּי pr.n. (125) *Bunni*
עַזְגָּד pr.n. (739) *Azgad*
בֵּבָי pr.n. (93) *Bebai*

10:17
אֲדֹנִיָּה pr.n. (11) *Adonijah*
בִגְוַי pr.n. (94) *Bigvai*
עָדִין pr.n. (II 726) *Adin*

10:18
אָטֵר pr.n. (32) *Ater*
חִזְקִיָּה pr.n. (306) *Hezekiah*
עַזּוּר pr.n. (741) *Azzur*

10:19
הוֹדִיָּה pr.n. (217) *Hodiah*
חָשֻׁם pr.n. (365) *Hashum*
בֵּצָי pr.n. (130) *Bezai*

10:20
חָרִיף pr.n. (358) *Hariph*
עֲנָתוֹת pr.n. (779) *Anathoth*
נֵובָי pr.n. (626) *Nebai*

10:21

מַגְפִּיעָשׁ pr.n. (550) *Magpiash*
מְשֻׁלָּם pr.n. (1024) *Meshullam*
חֵזִיר pr.n. (306) *Hezir*

10:22

מְשֵׁיזַבְאֵל pr.n. (604) *Meshezabel*
צָדוֹק pr.n. (843) *Zadok*
יַדּוּעַ pr.n. (396) *Jaddua*

10:23

פְּלַטְיָה pr.n. (812) *Pelatiah*
חָנָן pr.n. (336) *Hanan*
עֲנָיָה pr.n. (777) *Anaiah*

10:24

הוֹשֵׁעַ pr.n. (448) *Hoshea*
חֲנַנְיָה pr.n. (337) *Hananiah*
חַשּׁוּב pr.n. (363) *Hasshub*

10:25

הַלּוֹחֵשׁ def.art.-pr.n. (538) *Hallohesh*
פִּלְחָא pr.n. (812) *Pilha*
שׁוֹבֵק pr.n. (990) *Shobek*

10:26

רְחוּם pr.n. (933) *Rehum*
חֲשַׁבְנָה pr.n. (364) *Hashabnah*
מַעֲשֵׂיָה pr.n. (796) *Maaseiah*

10:27

וַאֲחִיָּה conj.-pr.n. (26) *and Ahiah*
חָנָן pr.n. (336) *Hanan*
עָנָן pr.n. (II 778) *Anan*

10:28

מַלּוּךְ pr.n. (576) *Malluch*
חָרִם pr.n. (356) *Harim*
בַּעֲנָה pr.n. (128) *Baanah*

10:29

וּשְׁאָר הָעָם conj.-n.m.s. cstr. (984)-def.art.-n.m.s. (I 766) *the rest of the people*
הַכֹּהֲנִים def.art.-n.m.p. (463) *the priests*
הַלְוִיִּם def.art.-adj. gent. m.p. (532) *the Levites*
הַשּׁוֹעֲרִים def.art.-n.m.p. (1045) *the gatekeepers*
הַמְשֹׁרְרִים def.art.-Polel ptc. m.p. (שִׁיר 1010) *the singers*
הַנְּתִינִים def.art.-n.m.p. (682) *the temple servants (Nethinim)*
וְכָל־הַנִּבְדָּל conj.-n.m.s. cstr. (481)-def.art.-Ni. ptc. m.s. (בָּדַל 95) *and all who separated themselves*
מֵעַמֵּי הָאֲרָצוֹת prep.-n.m.p. cstr. (I 766)-def.art. -n.f.p. (75) *from the peoples of the lands*
אֶל־תּוֹרַת הָאֱלֹהִים prep.-n.f.s. cstr. (435)-def. art.-n.m.p. (43) *to the law of God*
נְשֵׁיהֶם n.f.p.-3 m.p. sf. (61) *their wives*
בְּנֵיהֶם n.m.p.-3 m.p. sf. (119) *their sons*
וּבְנֹתֵיהֶם conj.-n.f.p.-3 m.p. sf. (I 123) *and their daughters*
כֹּל יוֹדֵעַ n.m.s. cstr. (481)-Qal act.ptc. (יָדַע 393) *all who have knowledge*
מֵבִין Hi. ptc. (בִּין 106) *and understanding*

10:30 (Eng.10:29)

מַחֲזִיקִים Hi. ptc. m.p. (חָזַק 304) *who join*
עַל־אֲחֵיהֶם prep.-n.m.p.-3 m.p. sf. (26) *with their brethren*
אַדִּירֵיהֶם adj. m.p.-3 m.p. sf. (12) *their nobles*
וּבָאִים בְּאָלָה conj.-Qal act.ptc. m.p. (בּוֹא 97) -prep.-n.f.s. (46) *and enter into a curse*
וּבִשְׁבוּעָה conj.-prep.-n.f.s. (989) *and an oath*
לָלֶכֶת prep.-Qal inf.cstr. (הָלַךְ 229) *to walk*
בְּתוֹרַת הָאֱלֹהִים prep.-n.f.s. cstr. (435)-def. art.-n.m.p. (43) *in God's law*
אֲשֶׁר נִתְּנָה rel. (81)-Pi. pf. 3 f.s. (נָתַן 678) *which was given*
בְּיַד מֹשֶׁה prep.-n.f.s. cstr. (388)-pr.n. (602) *by the hand of Moses*
עֶבֶד־הָאֱלֹהִים n.m.s. cstr. (713)-v.supra *the servant of God*
וְלִשְׁמוֹר conj.-prep.-Qal inf.cstr. (שָׁמַר 1036) *and to observe*
וְלַעֲשׂוֹת conj.-prep.-Qal inf.cstr. (עָשָׂה I 793) *and to do*
אֶת־כָּל־מִצְוֹת יהוה dir.obj.-n.m.s. cstr. (481) -n.f.p. cstr. (846)-pr.n. (217) *all the commandments of Yahweh*
אֲדֹנֵינוּ n.m.p.-1 c.p. sf. (10) *our Lord*
וּמִשְׁפָּטָיו conj.-n.m.p.-3 m.s. sf. (1048) *and his ordinances*
וְחֻקָּיו conj.-n.m.p.-3 m.s. sf. (349) *and his statutes*

10:31

וַאֲשֶׁר לֹא־נִתֵּן conj.-rel. (81)-neg.-Qal impf. 1 c.p. (נָתַן 678) *and we will not give*
בְּנֹתֵינוּ n.f.p.-1 c.p. sf. (I 123) *our daughters*
לְעַמֵּי הָאָרֶץ prep.-n.m.p. cstr. (I 766)-def.art. -n.f.s. (75) *to the peoples of the land*

וְאֶת־בְּנֹתֵיהֶם conj.-dir.obj.-n.f.p.-3 m.p. sf. (I 123) *or their daughters*
לֹא נִקַּח neg.-Qal impf. 1 c.p. (לָקַח 542) *we will not take*
לְבָנֵינוּ prep.-n.m.p.-1 c.p. sf. (119) *for our sons*

10:32

וְעַמֵּי הָאָרֶץ conj.-n.m.p. cstr. (I 766)-def.art. -n.f.s. (75) *and the peoples of the land*
הַמְבִיאִים def.art.-Hi. ptc. m.p. (בּוֹא 97) *who bring in*
אֶת־הַמַּקָּחוֹת dir.obj.-def.art.-n.f.p. (544) *wares*
וְכָל־שֶׁבֶר conj.-n.m.s. cstr. (481)-n.m.s. (III 991) *or any grain*
בְּיוֹם הַשַּׁבָּת prep.-n.m.s. cstr. (398)-def.art.-n.f.s. (992) *on the sabbath day*
לִמְכּוֹר prep.-Qal inf.cstr. (מָכַר 569) *to sell*
לֹא־נִקַּח מֵהֶם neg.-Qal impf. 1 c.p. (לָקַח 542) -prep.-3 m.p. sf. *we will not buy from them*
בַּשַּׁבָּת prep.-def.art.-n.f.s. (992) *on the sabbath*
וּבְיוֹם קֹדֶשׁ conj.-prep.-n.m.s. cstr. (398)-n.m.s. (871) *or on a holy day*
וְנִטֹּשׁ conj.-Qal impf. 1 c.p. (נָטַשׁ 643) *and we will forego*
אֶת־הַשָּׁנָה הַשְּׁבִיעִית dir.obj.-def.art.-n.f.s. (1040)-def.art.-num. f. ord. (988) *the seventh year*
וּמַשָּׁא conj.-n.m.s. (673) *and the exaction (of debt)*
כָּל־יָד n.m.s. cstr. (481)-n.f.s. (388) *every*

10:33

הֶעֱמַדְנוּ עָלֵינוּ Hi. pf. 1 c.p. (עָמַד 763)-prep.-1 c.p. sf. *we lay upon ourselves*
מִצְוֹת n.f.p. (846) *the obligation*
לָתֵת עָלֵינוּ prep.-Qal inf.cstr. (נָתַן 678)-v.supra *to charge ourselves*
שְׁלִשִׁית הַשֶּׁקֶל num. adj. f. cstr. (1026)-def.art. -n.m.s. (1053) *with the third part of a shekel*
בַּשָּׁנָה prep.-def.art.-n.f.s. (1040) *yearly*
לַעֲבֹדַת prep.-n.f.s. cstr. (715) *for the service of*
בֵּית אֱלֹהֵינוּ n.m.s. cstr. (108)-n.m.p.-1 c.p. sf. (43) *the house of our God*

10:34 (Eng.10:33)

לְלֶחֶם הַמַּעֲרֶכֶת prep.-n.m.s. cstr. (536)-def.art. -n.f.s. (790) *for the showbread*
וּמִנְחַת הַתָּמִיד conj.-n.f.s. cstr. (585)-def.art. -n.m.s. (556) *the continual cereal offering*
וּלְעוֹלַת הַתָּמִיד conj.-prep.-n.f.s. cstr. (I 750) -v.supra *the continual burnt offering*
הַשַּׁבָּתוֹת def.art.-n.f.p. (992) *the sabbaths*
הֶחֳדָשִׁים def.art.-n.m.p. (I 294) *the new moons*
לַמּוֹעֲדִים prep.-def.art.-n.m.p. (417) *the appointed feasts*
וְלַקֳּדָשִׁים conj.-prep.-def.art.-n.m.p. (871) *the holy things*
וְלַחַטָּאוֹת conj.-prep.-def.art.-n.f.p. (308) *and the sin offerings*
לְכַפֵּר עַל־יִשְׂרָאֵל prep.-Pi. inf.cstr. (כָּפַר 497) -prep.-pr.n. (975) *to make atonement for Israel*
וְכֹל מְלֶאכֶת conj.-n.m.s. cstr. (481)-n.f.p. cstr. (521) *and for all the work of*
בֵּית־אֱלֹהֵינוּ n.m.s. cstr. (108)-n.m.p.-1 c.p. sf. (43) *the house of our God*

10:35

וְהַגּוֹרָלוֹת conj.-def.art.-n.m.p. (174) *and lots*
הִפַּלְנוּ Hi. pf. 1 c.p. (נָפַל 656) *we have cast*
עַל־קֻרְבַּן הָעֵצִים prep.-n.m.s. cstr. (898)-def. art.-n.m.p. (781) *for the wood offering*
הַכֹּהֲנִים def.art.-n.m.p. (463) *the priests*
הַלְוִיִּם def.art.-adj. gent. m.p. (532) *the Levites*
וְהָעָם conj.-def.art.-n.m.s. (I 766) *and the people*
לְהָבִיא prep.-Hi. inf.cstr. (בּוֹא 97) *to bring*
לְבֵית אֱלֹהֵינוּ prep.-n.m.s. cstr. (108)-n.m.p.-1 c.p. sf. (43) *into the house of our God*
לְבֵית־אֲבֹתֵינוּ prep.-v.supra-n.m.p.-1 c.p. sf. (3) *according to our fathers' houses*
לְעִתִּים מְזֻמָּנִים prep.-n.m.p. (773)-Pu. ptc. m.p. (273 זָמַן) *at times appointed*
שָׁנָה בְשָׁנָה n.f.s. (1040)-prep.-v.supra *year by year*
לְבַעֵר prep.-Pi. inf.cstr. (בָּעַר 128) *to burn*
עַל־מִזְבַּח prep.-n.m.s. cstr. (258) *upon the altar of*
יהוה אֱלֹהֵינוּ pr.n. (217)-n.m.p.-1 c.p. sf. (43) *Yahweh our God*
כַּכָּתוּב prep.-def.art.-Qal pass.ptc. (כָּתַב 507) *as it is written*
בַּתּוֹרָה prep.-def.art.-n.f.s. (435) *in the law*

10:36

וּלְהָבִיא conj.-prep.-Hi. inf.cstr. (בּוֹא 97) *and to bring*
אֶת־בִּכּוּרֵי אַדְמָתֵנוּ dir.obj.-n.m.p. cstr. (114) -n.f.s.-1 c.p. sf. (9) *the first fruits of our ground*
וּבִכּוּרֵי כָּל־פְּרִי conj.-v.supra-n.m.s. cstr. (481) -n.m.s. cstr. (826) *and the first fruits of all fruit of*
כָּל־עֵץ v.supra-n.m.s. (781) *every tree*

שָׁנָה בְשָׁנָה n.f.s. (1040)–prep.–v.supra *year by year*

לְבֵית יהוה prep.–n.m.s. cstr. (108)–pr.n. (217) *to the house of Yahweh*

10:37

וְאֶת־בְּכֹרוֹת conj.–dir.obj.–n.m.p. cstr. (114) *also the first-born of*

בָּנֵינוּ וּבְהֶמְתֵּינוּ n.m.p.–1 c.p. sf. (119)–conj.–n.f.p.–1 c.p. sf. (96) *our sons and of our cattle*

כַּכָּתוּב prep.–def.art.–Qal pass.ptc. (כָּתַב 507) *as it is written*

בַּתּוֹרָה prep.–def.art.–n.f.s. (435) *in the law*

וְאֶת־בְּכוֹרֵי בְקָרֵינוּ conj.–dir.obj.–n.m.p. cstr. 114)–n.m.p.–1 c.p. sf. (133; GK 123aN) *and the firstlings of our herds*

וְצֹאנֵינוּ conj.–n.f.p.–1 c.p. sf. (838) *and of our flocks*

לְהָבִיא prep.–Hi. inf.cstr. (בּוֹא 97) *to bring*

לְבֵית אֱלֹהֵינוּ prep.–n.m.s. cstr. (108)–n.m.p.–1 c.p. sf. (43) *to the house of our God*

לַכֹּהֲנִים prep.–def.art.–n.m.p. (463) *to the priests*

הַמְשָׁרְתִים def.art.–Pi. ptc. m.p. (שָׁרַת 1058) *who minister*

בְּבֵית אֱלֹהֵינוּ prep.–v.supra–v.supra *in the house of our God*

10:38

וְאֶת־רֵאשִׁית conj.–dir.obj.–n.f.s. cstr. (912) *and the first of*

עֲרִיסֹתֵינוּ n.f.p.–1 c.p. sf. (791) *our coarse meal*

וּתְרוּמֹתֵינוּ conj.–n.f.p.–1 c.p. sf. (929) *and our contributions*

וּפְרִי כָל־עֵץ conj.–n.m.s. cstr. (826)–n.m.s. cstr. (481)–n.m.s. (781) *and the fruit of every tree*

תִּירוֹשׁ n.m.s. (440) *the wine*

וְיִצְהָר conj.–n.m.s. (I 844) *and the oil*

נָבִיא Hi. impf. 1 c.p. (בּוֹא 97) *we will bring*

לַכֹּהֲנִים prep.–def.art.–n.m.p. (463) *to the priests*

אֶל־לִשְׁכוֹת prep.–n.f.s. cstr. (545) *to the chambers of*

בֵּית־אֱלֹהֵינוּ n.m.s. cstr. (108)–n.m.p.–1 c.p. sf. (43) *the house of our God*

וּמַעְשַׂר אַדְמָתֵנוּ conj.–n.m.s. cstr. 798)–n.f.s.–1 c.p. sf. (9) *and the tithes from our ground*

לַלְוִיִּם prep.–dir.obj.–adj. gent. m.p. (532) *to the Levites*

וְהֵם הַלְוִיִּם conj.–pers.pr. 3 m.p. (241)–v.supra *for it is the Levites*

הַמְעַשְּׂרִים def.art.–Pi. ptc. m.p. (עָשַׂר 797) *who collect the tithes*

בְּכֹל עָרֵי עֲבֹדָתֵנוּ prep.–n.f.p. cstr. (746)–n.f.s.–1 c.p. sf. (715) *in all our towns of service*

10:39

וְהָיָה הַכֹּהֵן conj.–Qal pf. 3 m.s. (224)–def.art.–n.m.s. (463) *and the priest shall be*

בֶּן־אַהֲרֹן n.m.s. cstr. (119)–pr.n. (14) *the son of Aaron*

עִם־הַלְוִיִּם prep.–def.art.–adj. gent. m.p. (532) *with the Levites*

בַּעְשֵׂר הַלְוִיִּם prep.–Pi. inf.abs. (עָשַׂר 797; GK 53k)–v.supra *when the Levites receive the tithes*

וְהַלְוִיִּם יַעֲלוּ conj.–v.supra–Hi. impf. 3 m.p. (עָלָה 748) *and the Levites shall bring up*

אֶת־מַעֲשַׂר הַמַּעֲשֵׂר dir.obj.–n.m.s. cstr. (798)–def.art.–n.m.s. (798) *the tithe of the tithes*

לְבֵית אֱלֹהֵינוּ prep.–n.m.s. cstr. (108)–n.m.p.–1 c.p. sf. (43) *to the house of our God*

אֶל־הַלְּשָׁכוֹת prep.–def.art.–n.f.p. (545) *to the chambers*

לְבֵית הָאוֹצָר prep.–n.m.s. cstr. (108)–def.art.–n.m.s. (69) *to the storehouse*

10:40

כִּי אֶל־הַלְּשָׁכוֹת conj. (471)–prep.–def.art.–n.f.p. (545) *for to the chambers*

יָבִיאוּ Hi. impf. 3 m.p. (בּוֹא 97) *shall bring*

בְנֵי־יִשְׂרָאֵל n.m.p. cstr. (119)–pr.n. (975) *the people of Israel*

וּבְנֵי הַלֵּוִי conj.–v.supra–def.art.–pr.n. (532) *and the sons of Levi*

אֶת־תְּרוּמַת הַדָּגָן dir.obj.–n.f.s. cstr. (929)–def.art.–n.m.s. (186) *the contribution of grain*

הַתִּירוֹשׁ def.art.–n.m.s. (440) *wine*

וְהַיִּצְהָר conj.–def.art.–n.m.s. (I 844) *and oil*

וְשָׁם conj.–adv. (1027) *and there*

כְּלֵי הַמִּקְדָּשׁ n.m.p. cstr. (479)–def.art.–n.m.s. (874) *the vessels of the sanctuary*

וְהַכֹּהֲנִים conj.–def.art.–n.m.p. (463) *and the priests*

הַמְשָׁרְתִים def.art.–Pi. ptc. m.p. (שָׁרַת 1058) *that minister*

וְהַשּׁוֹעֲרִים conj.–def.art.–n.m.p. (1045) *and the gatekeepers*

וְהַמְשֹׁרְרִים conj.–def.art.–Polel ptc. m.p. (שִׁיר 1010) *and the singers*

וְלֹא נַעֲזֹב conj.–neg.–Qal impf. 1 c.p. (עָזַב I 736) *we will not neglect*

אֶת־בֵּית אֱלֹהֵינוּ dir.obj.–n.m.s. cstr. (108)–n.m.p.–1 c.p. sf. (43) *the house of our God*

11:1

וַיֵּשְׁבוּ consec.-Qal impf. 3 m.p. (יָשַׁב 442) *now lived*

שָׂרֵי־הָעָם n.m.p. cstr. (978)-def.art.-n.m.s. (I 766) *the leaders of the people*

בִּירוּשָׁלָ͏ִם prep.-pr.n. (436) *in Jerusalem*

וּשְׁאָר הָעָם conj.-n.m.s. cstr. (984)-v.supra *and the rest of the people*

הִפִּילוּ גוֹרָלוֹת Hi. pf. 3 c.p. (נָפַל 656)-n.m.p. (174) *cast lots*

לְהָבִיא prep.-Hi. inf.cstr. (בּוֹא 97) *to bring*

אֶחָד מִן־הָעֲשָׂרָה num. (25)-prep.-def.art.-num. f. (796) *one out of ten*

לָשֶׁבֶת prep.-Qal inf.cstr. (יָשַׁב 442) *to live*

בִּירוּשָׁלַ͏ִם prep.-pr.n. (436) *in Jerusalem*

עִיר הַקֹּדֶשׁ n.f.s. cstr. (746)-def.art.-n.m.s. (871) *the holy city*

וְתֵשַׁע הַיָּדוֹת conj.-num. cstr. (1077)-def.art. -n.f.p. (388) *while nine tenths*

בֶּעָרִים prep.-def.art.-n.f.p. (746) *in the towns*

11:2

וַיְבָרְכוּ הָעָם consec.-Pi. impf. 3 m.p. (בָּרַךְ 138)-def.art.-n.m.s. (I 766) *and the people blessed*

לְכֹל הָאֲנָשִׁים prep.-n.m.s. cstr. (481)-def.art. -n.m.p. (35) *all the men*

הַמִּתְנַדְּבִים def.art.-Hith. ptc. m.p. (נָדַב 621) *who willingly offered*

לָשֶׁבֶת prep.-Qal inf.cstr. (יָשַׁב 442) *to live*

בִּירוּשָׁלָ͏ִם prep.-pr.n. paus. (436) *in Jerusalem*

11:3

וְאֵלֶּה conj.-demons.adj. c.p. (41) *these are*

רָאשֵׁי הַמְּדִינָה n.m.p. cstr. (910)-def.art.-n.f.s. (193) *the chiefs of the province*

אֲשֶׁר יָשְׁבוּ rel. (81)-Qal pf. 3 c.p. (יָשַׁב 442) *who lived*

בִּירוּשָׁלָ͏ִם prep.-pr.n. paus. (436) *in Jerusalem*

וּבְעָרֵי יְהוּדָה conj.-prep.-n.f.p. cstr. (746)-pr.n. (397) *but in the towns of Judah*

יָשְׁבוּ v.supra *lived*

אִישׁ בַּאֲחֻזָּתוֹ n.m.s. (35)-prep.-n.f.s.-3 m.s. sf. (28) *every one on his property*

בְּעָרֵיהֶם prep.-n.f.p.-3 m.p. sf. (746) *in their towns*

יִשְׂרָאֵל pr.n. (975) *Israel*

הַכֹּהֲנִים def.art.-n.m.p. (463) *the priests*

וְהַלְוִיִּם conj.-def.art.-adj. gent. m.p. (532) *the Levites*

וְהַנְּתִינִים conj.-def.art.-n.m.p. (682) *the temple servants (Nethinim)*

וּבְנֵי עַבְדֵי שְׁלֹמֹה conj.-n.m.p. cstr. (119)-n.m.p. cstr. (713)-pr.n. (1024) *and the descendants of Solomon's servants*

11:4

וּבִירוּשָׁלַ͏ִם conj.-prep.-pr.n. (436) *and in Jerusalem*

יָשְׁבוּ Qal pf. 3 c.p. (יָשַׁב 442) *lived*

מִבְּנֵי יְהוּדָה prep.-n.m.p. cstr. (119)-pr.n. (397) *certain of the sons of Judah*

וּמִבְּנֵי בִנְיָמִן conj.-v.supra-pr.n. (122) *and of the sons of Benjamin*

מִבְּנֵי יְהוּדָה v.supra-v.supra *of the sons of Judah*

עֲתָיָה pr.n. (800) *Athaiah*

בֶּן־עֻזִּיָּה n.m.s. cstr. (119)-pr.n. (739) *the son of Uzziah*

בֶּן־זְכַרְיָה v.supra-pr.n. (272) *son of Zechariah*

בֶּן־אֲמַרְיָה v.supra-pr.n. (57) *son of Amariah*

בֶּן־שְׁפַטְיָה v.supra-pr.n. (1049) *son of Shephatiah*

בֶּן־מַהֲלַלְאֵל v.supra-pr.n. (239) *son of Mahalalel*

מִבְּנֵי־פָרֶץ v.supra-pr.n. (II 829) *of the sons of Perez*

11:5

וּמַעֲשֵׂיָה conj.-pr.n. (796) *and Maaseiah*

בֶּן־בָּרוּךְ n.m.s. cstr. (119)-pr.n. (140) *the son of Baruch*

בֶּן־כָּל־חֹזֶה v.supra-pr.n. (480) *son of Col-hozeh*

בֶּן־חֲזָיָה v.supra-pr.n. (303) *son of Hazaiah*

בֶּן־עֲדָיָה v.supra-pr.n. (726) *son of Adaiah*

בֶּן־יוֹיָרִיב v.supra-pr.n. (220) *son of Joiarib*

בֶּן־זְכַרְיָה v.supra-pr.n. (272) *son of Zechariah*

בֶּן־הַשִּׁלֹנִי v.supra-def.art.-adj. gent. (1018) *son of the Silonite*

11:6

כָּל־בְּנֵי־פֶרֶץ n.m.s. cstr. (481)-n.m.p. cstr. (119) -pr.n. (II 829) *all the sons of Perez*

הַיֹּשְׁבִים def.art.-Qal act.ptc. m.p. (יָשַׁב 442) *who lived*

בִּירוּשָׁלָ͏ִם prep.-pr.n. (436) *in Jerusalem*

אַרְבַּע מֵאוֹת num. (916)-n.f.p. (547) *four hundred*

שִׁשִּׁים וּשְׁמֹנָה num. p. (995)-conj.-num. f. (1032) *and sixty-eight*

אַנְשֵׁי־חָיִל n.m.p. cstr. (35)-n.m.s. paus. (298) *valiant men*

11:7

וְאֵלֶּה conj.-demons.adj. c.p. (41) *and these are*

בְּנֵי בִנְיָמִן n.m.p. cstr. (119)-pr.n. (122) *the sons of Benjamin*
סַלֻּא pr.n. (699) *Sallu*
בֶּן־מְשֻׁלָּם n.m.s. cstr. (119)-pr.n. (1024) *the son of Meshullam*
בֶּן־יוֹעֵד v.supra-pr.n. (222) *son of Joed*
בֶּן־פְּדָיָה v.supra-pr.n. (804) *son of Pedaiah*
בֶּן־קוֹלָיָה v.supra-pr.n. (877) *son of Kolaiah*
בֶּן־מַעֲשֵׂיָה v.supra-pr.n. (796) *son of Maaseiah*
בֶּן־אִיתִיאֵל v.supra-pr.n. (87) *son of Ithiel*
בֶּן־יְשַׁעְיָה v.supra-pr.n. (447) *son of Jeshaiah*

11:8

וְאַחֲרָיו conj.-prep.-3 m.s. sf. (29) *and after him*
גַּבַּי סַלָּי pr.n. (146) *Gabbai Sallai*
תְּשַׁע מֵאוֹת num. (1077)-n.f.p. (547) *nine hundred*
עֶשְׂרִים וּשְׁמֹנָה num. p. (797)-conj.-num. f. (1032) *and twenty-eight*

11:9

וְיוֹאֵל conj.-pr.n. (222) *and Joel*
בֶּן־זִכְרִי n.m.s. cstr. (119)-pr.n. (271) *the son of Zichri*
פָּקִיד עֲלֵיהֶם n.m.s. (824)-prep.-3 m.p. sf. *their overseer*
וִיהוּדָה conj.-pr.n. (397) *and Judah*
בֶּן־הַסְּנוּאָה v.supra-def.art.-pr.n. (703) *the son of Hassenuah*
עַל־הָעִיר prep.-def.art.-n.f.s. (746) *over the city*
מִשְׁנֶה n.m.s. (1041) *second*

11:10

מִן־הַכֹּהֲנִים prep.-def.art.-n.m.p. (463) *of the priests*
יְדַעְיָה pr.n. (396) *Jedaiah*
בֶּן־יוֹיָרִיב n.m.s. cstr. (119)-pr.n. (220) *the son of Joiarib*
יָכִין pr.n. (467) *Jachin*

11:11

שְׂרָיָה pr.n. (976) *Seraiah*
בֶּן־חִלְקִיָּה n.m.s. cstr. (119)-pr.n. (324) *the son of Hilkiah*
בֶּן־מְשֻׁלָּם v.supra-pr.n. (1024) *son of Meshullam*
בֶּן־צָדוֹק v.supra-pr.n. (843) *son of Zadok*
בֶּן־מְרָיוֹת v.supra-pr.n. (599) *son of Meraioth*
בֶּן־אֲחִיטוּב v.supra-pr.n. (26) *son of Ahitub*
נְגִד בֵּית הָאֱלֹהִים n.m.s. cstr. (617)-n.m.s. cstr. (108)-def.art.-n.m.p. (43) *ruler of the house of God*

11:12

וַאֲחֵיהֶם conj.-n.m.p.-3 m.p. sf. (26) *and their brethren*
עֹשֵׂי הַמְּלָאכָה Qal act.ptc. m.p. cstr. (עָשָׂה I 793)-def.art.-n.f.s. (521) *who did the work*
לַבַּיִת prep.-def.art.-n.m.s. (108) *of the house*
שְׁמֹנֶה מֵאוֹת num. (1032)-n.f.p. (547) *eight hundred*
עֶשְׂרִים וּשְׁנָיִם num. p. (797)-num. du. paus. (1040) *and twenty-two*
וַעֲדָיָה conj.-pr.n. (726) *and Adaiah*
בֶּן־יְרֹחָם n.m.s. cstr. (119)-pr.n. (934) *the son of Jeroham*
בֶּן־פְּלַלְיָה v.supra-pr.n. (813) *son of Pelaliah*
בֶּן־אַמְצִי v.supra-pr.n. (55) *son of Amzi*
בֶּן־זְכַרְיָה v.supra-pr.n. (272) *son of Zechariah*
בֶּן־פַּשְׁחוּר v.supra-pr.n. (832) *son of Pashhur*
בֶּן־מַלְכִּיָּה v.supra-pr.n. (575) *son of Malchijah*

11:13

וְאֶחָיו conj.-n.m.p.-3 m.s. sf. (26) *and his brethren*
רָאשִׁים n.m.p. (910) *heads*
לְאָבוֹת prep.-n.m.p. (3) *of the fathers*
מָאתַיִם n.f. du. (547) *two hundred*
אַרְבָּעִים וּשְׁנָיִם num. p. (917)-conj.-num. du. paus. (1040) *and forty-two*
וַעֲמַשְׁסַי conj.-pr.n. (772) *and Amashsai*
בֶּן־עֲזַרְאֵל n.m.s. cstr. (119)-pr.n. (741) *the son of Azarel*
בֶּן־אַחְזַי v.supra-pr.n. (28) *son of Ahzai*
בֶּן־מְשִׁלֵּמוֹת v.supra-pr.n. (1024) *son of Meshillemoth*
בֶּן־אִמֵּר v.supra-pr.n. (57) *son of Immer*

11:14

וַאֲחֵיהֶם conj.-n.m.p.-3 m.p. sf. (26) *and their brethren*
גִּבּוֹרֵי חַיִל n.m.p. cstr. (150)-n.m.s. (298) *mighty men of valor*
מֵאָה n.f.s. (547) *a hundred*
עֶשְׂרִים וּשְׁמֹנָה num. p. (797)-conj.-num. f. (1032) *and twenty-eight*
וּפָקִיד עֲלֵיהֶם conj.-n.m.s. (824)-prep.-3 m.p. sf. *their overseer*
זַבְדִּיאֵל pr.n. (256) *Zabdiel*
בֶּן־הַגְּדוֹלִים v.supra-def.art.-pr.n. (153) *the son of Haggedolim*

11:15

וּמִן־הַלְוִיִּם conj.-prep.-def.art.-adj. gent. m.p. (532) *and of the Levites*

שְׁמַעְיָה 1035) *Shemaiah*
בֶּן־חַשּׁוּב n.m.s. cstr. (119)-pr.n. (363) *the son of Hasshub*
בֶּן־עַזְרִיקָם v.supra-pr.n. (741) *son of Azrikam*
בֶּן־חֲשַׁבְיָה v.supra-pr.n. (364) *son of Hashabiah*
בֶּן־בּוּנִּי v.supra-pr.n. (125) *son of Bunni*

11:16

וְשַׁבְּתַי conj.-pr.n. (992) *and Shabbethai*
וְיוֹזָבָד conj.-pr.n. (220) *and Jozabad*
עַל־הַמְּלָאכָה prep.-def.art.-n.f.s. (521) *over the ... work*
הַחִיצֹנָה def.art.-adj. f.s. (300) *outside*
לְבֵית הָאֱלֹהִים prep.-n.m.s. cstr. (108)-def.art.-n.m.p. (43) *of the house of God*
מֵרָאשֵׁי הַלְוִיִּם prep.-n.m.p. cstr. (910)-def.art.-adj. gent. m.p. (532) *of the chiefs of the Levites*

11:17

וּמַתַּנְיָה conj.-pr.n. (682) *and Mattaniah*
בֶּן־מִיכָה n.m.s. cstr. (119)-pr.n. (567) *son of Mica*
בֶּן־זַבְדִּי v.supra-pr.n. (256) *son of Zabdi*
בֶּן־אָסָף v.supra-pr.n. (63) *son of Asaph*
רֹאשׁ הַתְּחִלָּה n.m.s. cstr. (910)-def.art.-n.f.s. (321) *who was the leader to begin*
יְהוֹדֶה Hi. impf. 3 m.s. (יָדָה 392; GK 53q) *the thanksgiving*
לַתְּפִלָּה prep.-def.art.-n.f.s. (813) *in prayer*
וּבַקְבֻּקְיָה conj.-pr.n. (132) *and Bakbukiah*
מִשְׁנֶה pr.n. (1041) *second*
מֵאֶחָיו prep.-n.m.p.-3 m.s. sf. (26) *among his brethren*
וְעַבְדָּא conj.-pr.n. (715) *and Abda*
בֶּן־שַׁמּוּעַ n.m.s. cstr. (119)-pr.n. (1035) *the son of Shammua*
בֶּן־גָּלָל v.supra-pr.n. (III 165) *son of Galal*
בֶּן־יְדִיתוּן v.supra-pr.n. (393) *son of Jeduthun*

11:18

כָּל־הַלְוִיִּם n.m.s. cstr. (481)-def.art.-adj. gent. m.p. (532) *all the Levites*
בְּעִיר הַקֹּדֶשׁ prep.-n.f.s. cstr. (746)-def.art.-n.m.s. (871) *in the holy city*
מָאתַיִם n.f. du. (547) *two hundred*
שְׁמֹנִים וְאַרְבָּעָה num. p. (1033)-conj.-num. f. (916) *and eighty-four*

11:19

וְהַשּׁוֹעֲרִים conj.-def.art.-n.m.p. (1045) *the gatekeepers*
עַקּוּב pr.n. (784) *Akkub*
טַלְמוֹן pr.n. (379) *Talmon*
וַאֲחֵיהֶם conj.-n.m.p.-3 m.p. sf. (26) *and their brethren*
הַשֹּׁמְרִים def.art.-Qal act.ptc. m.p. (שָׁמַר 1036) *who kept watch*
בַּשְּׁעָרִים prep.-def.art.-n.m.p. (1044) *at the gates*
מֵאָה n.f.s. (547) *a hundred*
שִׁבְעִים וּשְׁנָיִם num. p. (988)-conj.-num. du. paus. (1040) *and seventy-two*

11:20

וּשְׁאָר יִשְׂרָאֵל conj.-n.m.s. cstr. (984)-pr.n. (975) *and the rest of Israel*
הַכֹּהֲנִים def.art.-n.m.p. (463) *of the priests*
הַלְוִיִּם def.art.-adj. gent. m.p. (532) *of the Levites*
בְּכָל־עָרֵי יְהוּדָה prep.-n.m.s. cstr. (481)-n.f.p. cstr. (746)-pr.n. (397) *in all the towns of Judah*
אִישׁ בְּנַחֲלָתוֹ n.m.s. (35)-prep.-n.f.s.-3 m.s. sf. (635) *every one in his inheritance*

11:21

וְהַנְּתִינִים conj.-def.art.-n.m.p. (682) *but the temple servants (Nethinim)*
יֹשְׁבִים Qal act.ptc. m.p. (יָשַׁב 442) *lived*
בָּעֹפֶל prep.-def.art.-n.m.s. (I 779) *on Ophel (the mound)*
וְצִיחָא conj.-pr.n. (851) *and Ziha*
וְגִשְׁפָּא conj.-pr.n. (177) *and Gishpa*
עַל־הַנְּתִינִים prep.-def.art.-v.supra *over the temple servants*

11:22

וּפְקִיד הַלְוִיִּם conj.-n.m.s. cstr. (824)-def.art.-adj. gent. m.p. (532) *the overseer of the Levites*
בִּירוּשָׁלַםִ prep.-pr.n. (436) *in Jerusalem*
עֻזִּי pr.n. (739) *Uzzi*
בֶּן־בָּנִי n.m.s. cstr. (119)-pr.n. (125) *the son of Bani*
בֶּן־חֲשַׁבְיָה v.supra-pr.n. (364) *son of Hashabiah*
בֶּן־מַתַּנְיָה v.supra-pr.n. (682) *son of Mattaniah*
בֶּן־מִיכָא v.supra-pr.n. (567) *son of Mica*
מִבְּנֵי אָסָף prep.-n.m.p. cstr. (119)-pr.n. (63) *of the sons of Asaph*
הַמְשֹׁרְרִים def.art.-Polel ptc. m.p. (שִׁיר 1010) *the singers*
לְנֶגֶד מְלֶאכֶת prep.-prep. (617)-n.f.s. cstr. (521) *over the work of*
בֵּית־הָאֱלֹהִים n.m.s. cstr. (108)-def.art.-n.m.p. (43) *the house of God*

11:23

כִּי־מִצְוַת הַמֶּלֶךְ conj. (471)–n.f.s. cstr. (846)–def. art.–n.m.s. (I 572) *for a command from the king*

עֲלֵיהֶם prep.–3 m.p. sf. *concerning them*

וַאֲמָנָה conj.–n.f.s. (53) *and a settled provision*

עַל־הַמְשֹׁרְרִים prep.–def.art.–Polel ptc. m.p. (שִׁיר 1010) *for the singers*

דְּבַר־יוֹם בְּיוֹמוֹ n.m.p. cstr. (182)–n.m.s. (398) –prep.–v.supra–3 m.s. sf. *as every day required*

11:24

וּפְתַחְיָה conj.–pr.n. (836) *and Pethahiah*

בֶּן־מְשֵׁיזַבְאֵל n.m.s. cstr. (119)–pr.n. (604) *the son of Meshezabel*

מִבְּנֵי־זֶרַח prep.–n.m.p. cstr. (119)–pr.n. (II 280) *of the sons of Zerah*

בֶּן־יְהוּדָה v.supra–pr.n. (397) *the son of Judah*

לְיַד הַמֶּלֶךְ prep.–n.f.s. cstr. (388)–def.art.–n.m.s. (I 572) *at the king's hand*

לְכָל־דָּבָר prep.–n.m.s. cstr. (481)–n.m.s. (182) *in all matters*

לָעָם prep.–def.art.–n.m.s. (I 766) *concerning the people*

11:25

וְאֶל־הַחֲצֵרִים conj.–prep.–def.art.–n.m.p. (II 347) *and as for the villages*

בִּשְׂדֹתָם prep.–n.m.p.–3 m.p. sf. (961) *with their fields*

מִבְּנֵי יְהוּדָה prep.–n.m.p. cstr. (119)–pr.n. (397) *some of the people of Judah*

יָשְׁבוּ Qal pf. 3 c.p. (יָשַׁב 442) *lived*

בְּקִרְיַת הָאַרְבַּע prep.–pr.n. (n.f.s. cstr. 900; def.art.–num. 916; 900) *in Kiriath-arba*

וּבְנֹתֶיהָ conj.–n.f.p.–3 f.s. sf. (I 123) *and its villages*

וּבְדִיבֹן conj.–prep.–pr.n. (192) *and in Dibon*

וּבְנֹתֶיהָ v.supra *and its villages*

וּבִיקַּבְצְאֵל conj.–prep.–pr.n. (868) *and in Jekabzeel*

וַחֲצֵרֶיהָ conj.–n.m.p.–3 f.s. sf. (II 347) *and its villages*

11:26

וּבְיֵשׁוּעַ conj.–prep.–pr.n. (221) *and in Jeshua*

וּבְמוֹלָדָה conj.–prep.–pr.n. (409) *and in Moladah*

וּבְבֵית פָּלֶט conj.–prep.–pr.n. paus. (112) *and Beth-pelet*

11:27

וּבַחֲצַר שׁוּעָל conj.–prep.–pr.n. (347) *in Hazar-shual*

וּבִבְאֵר שֶׁבַע conj.–prep.–pr.n. (92) *and in Beer-sheba*

וּבְנֹתֶיהָ conj.–n.f.p.–3 f.s. sf. (I 123) *and its villages*

11:28

וּבְצִקְלַג conj.–prep.–pr.n. (862) *in Ziklag*

וּבִמְכֹנָה conj.–prep.–pr.n. (569) *in Meconah*

וּבִבְנֹתֶיהָ conj.–prep.–n.f.p.–3 f.s. sf. (I 123) *and its villages*

11:29

וּבְעֵין רִמּוֹן conj.–prep.–pr.n. (745) *in En-rimmon*

וּבְצָרְעָה conj.–prep.–pr.n. (864) *in Zorah*

וּבְיַרְמוּת conj.–prep.–pr.n. (438) *in Jarmuth*

11:30

זָנֹחַ pr.n. (276) *Zanoah*

עֲדֻלָּם pr.n. (726) *Adullam*

וְחַצְרֵיהֶם conj.–n.m.p.–3 m.p. sf. (II 347) *and their villages*

לָכִישׁ pr.n. (540) *Lachish*

וּשְׂדֹתֶיהָ conj.–n.m.p.–3 f.s. sf. (961) *and its fields*

עֲזֵקָה pr.n. (740) *and Azekah*

וּבְנֹתֶיהָ conj.–n.f.p.–3 f.s. sf. (I 123) *and its villages*

וַיַּחֲנוּ consec.–Qal impf. 3 m.p. (חָנָה 333) *so they encamped*

מִבְּאֵר־שֶׁבַע prep.–pr.n. (92) *from Beer-sheba*

עַד־גֵּיא־הִנֹּם prep. (III 723)–n.m.s. cstr. (161)–pr.n. (244) *to the valley of Hinnom*

11:31

וּבְנֵי בִנְיָמִן conj.–n.m.p. cstr. (119)–pr.n. (122) *the people of Benjamin*

מִגָּבַע prep.–pr.n. (148) *from Geba*

מִכְמָשׂ pr.n. (485) *at Michmash*

וְעַיָּה conj.–pr.n. (743) *Aija*

וּבֵית־אֵל conj.–pr.n. (110) *Bethel*

וּבְנֹתֶיהָ conj.–n.f.p.–3 f.s. sf. (I 123) *and its villages*

11:32

עֲנָתוֹת pr.n. (779) *Anathoth*

נֹב pr.n. (611) *Nob*

עֲנָנְיָה pr.n. (778) *Ananiah*

11:33

חָצוֹר pr.n. (347) *Hazor*
רָמָה pr.n. (II 928) *Ramah*
גִּתָּיִם pr.n. (388) *Gittaim*

11:34

חָדִיד pr.n. (292) *Hadid*
צְבֹעִים pr.n. (840) *Zeboim*
נְבַלָּט pr.n. (615) *Neballat*

11:35

לֹד pr.n. (528) *Lod*
וְאוֹנוֹ conj.-pr.n. (20) *and Ono*
גֵּי הַחֲרָשִׁים n.m.s. cstr. (161)-def.art.-n.m.p. (360) *the valley of craftsmen*

11:36

וּמִן־הַלְוִיִּם conj.-prep.-def.art.-adj. gent. m.p. (532) *and of the Levites*
מַחְלְקוֹת יְהוּדָה n.f.p. cstr. (324)-pr.n. (397) *certain divisions in Judah*
לְבִנְיָמִין prep.-pr.n. (122) *were joined to Benjamin*

12:1

וְאֵלֶּה conj.-demons.adj. c.p. (41) *now these are*
הַכֹּהֲנִים def.art.-n.m.p. (463) *the priests*
וְהַלְוִיִּם conj.-def.art.-adj. gent. m.p. (532) *and the Levites*
אֲשֶׁר עָלוּ rel. (81)-Qal pf. 3 c.p. (עָלָה 748) *who came up*
עִם־זְרֻבָּבֶל prep. (767)-pr.n. (279) *with Zerubbabel*
בֶּן־שְׁאַלְתִּיאֵל n.m.s. cstr. (119)-pr.n. (982) *the son of Shealtiel*
וְיֵשׁוּעַ conj.-pr.n. (221) *and Jeshua*
שְׂרָיָה pr.n. (976) *Seraiah*
יִרְמְיָה pr.n. (941) *Jeremiah*
עֶזְרָא pr.n. (740) *Ezra*

12:2

אֲמַרְיָה pr.n. (57) *Amariah*
מַלּוּךְ pr.n. (576) *Malluch*
חַטּוּשׁ pr.n. (310) *Hattush*

12:3

שְׁכַנְיָה pr.n. (1016) *Shecaniah*
רְחֻם pr.n. (933) *Rehum*
מְרֵמֹת pr.n. (599) *Meremoth*

12:4

עִדּוֹא pr.n. (723) *Iddo*
גִּנְּתוֹי pr.n. (171) *Ginnethoi*
אֲבִיָּה pr.n. (4) *Abijah*

12:5

מִיָּמִין pr.n. (568) *Mijamin*
מַעַדְיָה pr.n. (588) *Maadiah*
בִּלְגָּה pr.n. (114) *Bilgah*

12:6

שְׁמַעְיָה pr.n. (1035) *Shemaiah*
וְיוֹיָרִיב conj.-pr.n. (220) *Joiarib*
יְדַעְיָה pr.n. (396) *Jedaiah*

12:7

סַלּוּ pr.n. (699) *Sallu*
עָמוֹק pr.n. (771) *Amok*
חִלְקִיָּה pr.n. (324) *Hilkiah*
יְדַעְיָה pr.n. (396) *Jedaiah*
אֵלֶּה demons.adj. c.p. (41) *these were*
רָאשֵׁי הַכֹּהֲנִים n.m.p. cstr. (910)-def.art.-n.m.p. (463) *the chiefs of the priests*
וַאֲחֵיהֶם conj.-n.m.p.-3 m.p. sf. (26) *and of their brethren*
בִּימֵי יֵשׁוּעַ prep.-n.m.p. cstr. (398)-pr.n. (221) *in the days of Jeshua*

12:8

וְהַלְוִיִּם conj.-def.art.-adj. gent. m.p. (532) *and the Levites*
יֵשׁוּעַ pr.n. (221) *Jeshua*
בִּנּוּי pr.n. (125) *Binnui*
קַדְמִיאֵל pr.n. (870) *Kadmiel*
שֵׁרֵבְיָה pr.n. (1055) *Sherebiah*
יְהוּדָה pr.n. (397) *Judah*
מַתַּנְיָה pr.n. (682) *Mattaniah*
עַל־הֻיְּדוֹת prep.-n.f.p. (392) *of the songs of thanksgiving*
הוּא וְאֶחָיו pers.pr. 3 m.s. (214)-conj.-n.m.p.-3 m.s. sf. (26) *he and his brethren*

12:9

וּבַקְבֻּקְיָה conj.-pr.n. (132) *and Bakbukiah*
וְעֻנּוֹ conj.-pr.n. (777) *and Unno*
אֲחֵיהֶם n.m.p.-3 m.p. sf. (26) *their brethren*
לְנֶגְדָּם prep.-prep.-3 m.p. sf. (617) *opposite them*
לְמִשְׁמָרוֹת prep.-n.f.p. (1038) *in the service*

12:10

וְיֵשׁוּעַ conj.-pr.n. (221) *and Jeshua*
הוֹלִיד Hi. pf. 3 m.s. (יָלַד 408) *was the father*
אֶת־יוֹיָקִים dir.obj.-pr.n. (220) *Joiakim*
וְיוֹיָקִים conj.-v.supra *and Joiakim*

הוֹלִיד v.supra *was the father*
אֶת־אֶלְיָשִׁיב dir.obj.-pr.n. (46) *Eliashib*
וְאֶלְיָשִׁיב conj.-v.supra *and Eliashib*
אֶת־יוֹיָדָע dir.obj.-pr.n. (220) *of Joiada*

12:11
וְיוֹיָדָע conj.-pr.n. (220) *and Joiada*
הוֹלִיד Hi. pf. 3 m.s. (יָלַד 408) *was the father*
אֶת־יוֹנָתָן dir.obj.-pr.n. (220) *of Jonathan*
וְיוֹנָתָן conj.-v.supra *and Jonathan*
הוֹלִיד v.supra *was the father*
אֶת־יַדּוּעַ dir.obj.-pr.n. (396) *of Jaddua*

12:12
וּבִימֵי יוֹיָקִים conj.-prep.-n.m.p. cstr. (398)-pr.n. (220) *and in the days of Joiakim*
הָיוּ כֹּהֲנִים Qal pf. 3 c.p. (הָיָה 224)-n.m.p. (463) *were priests*
רָאשֵׁי הָאָבוֹת n.m.p. cstr. (910)-def.art.-n.m.p. (3) *heads of fathers*
לִשְׂרָיָה prep.-pr.n. (976) *of Seraiah*
מְרָיָה pr.n. (599) *Meraiah*
לְיִרְמְיָה prep.-pr.n. (941) *of Jeremiah*
חֲנַנְיָה pr.n. (337) *Hananiah*

12:13
לְעֶזְרָא prep.-pr.n. (740) *of Ezra*
מְשֻׁלָּם pr.n. (1024) *Meshullam*
לַאֲמַרְיָה prep.-pr.n. (57) *of Amariah*
יְהוֹחָנָן pr.n. (220) *Jehohanan*

12:14
לִמְלוּכִי prep.-pr.n. (576) *of Malluchi*
יוֹנָתָן pr.n. (220) *Jonathan*
לִשְׁבַנְיָה prep.-pr.n. (987) *of Shebaniah*
יוֹסֵף pr.n. (415) *Joseph*

12:15
לְחָרִם prep.-pr.n. (356) *of Harim*
עַדְנָא pr.n. (726) *Adna*
לִמְרָיוֹת prep.-pr.n. (599) *of Meraioth*
חֶלְקָי pr.n. (324) *Helkai*

12:16
לְעִדִּיא prep.-pr.n. (723) *of Iddo*
זְכַרְיָה pr.n. (272) *Zechariah*
לְגִנְּתוֹן prep.-pr.n. (171) *of Ginnethon*
מְשֻׁלָּם pr.n. (1024) *Meshullam*

12:17
לַאֲבִיָּה prep.-pr.n. (4) *of Abijah*
זִכְרִי pr.n. (271) *Zichri*
לְמִנְיָמִין prep.-pr.n. (568) *of Miniamin*
לְמוֹעַדְיָה prep.-pr.n. (588) *of Moadiah*
פִּלְטָי pr.n. (812) *Piltai*

12:18
לְבִלְגָּה prep.-pr.n. (114) *of Bilgah*
שַׁמּוּעַ pr.n. (1035) *Shammua*
לִשְׁמַעְיָה prep.-pr.n. (1035) *of Shemaiah*
יְהוֹנָתָן pr.n. (220) *Jehonathan*

12:19
וּלְיוֹיָרִיב conj.-prep.-pr.n. (220) *of Joiarib*
מַתְּנַי pr.n. (682) *Mattenai*
לִידַעְיָה prep.-pr.n. (396) *of Jedaiah*
עֻזִּי pr.n. (739) *Uzzi*

12:20
לְסַלַּי prep.-pr.n. (699) *of Sallai*
קַלָּי pr.n. paus. (887) *Kallai*
לְעָמוֹק prep.-pr.n. (771) *of Amok*
עֵבֶר pr.n. (II 720) *Eber*

12:21
לְחִלְקִיָּה prep.-pr.n. (324) *of Hilkiah*
חֲשַׁבְיָה pr.n. (364) *Hashabiah*
לִידַעְיָה prep.-pr.n. (396) *of Jedaiah*
נְתַנְאֵל pr.n. (682) *Nethanel*

12:22
הַלְוִיִּם def.art.-adj. gent. m.p. (532) *as for the Levites*
בִּימֵי אֶלְיָשִׁיב prep.-n.m.p. cstr. (398)-pr.n. (46) *in the days of Eliashib*
יוֹיָדָע pr.n. (220) *Joiada*
וְיוֹחָנָן conj.-pr.n. (220) *Johanan*
וְיַדּוּעַ conj.-pr.n. (396) *and Jaddua*
כְּתוּבִים Qal pass.ptc. m.p. (כָּתַב 507) *there were recorded*
רָאשֵׁי אָבוֹת n.m.p. cstr. (910)-n.m.p. (3) *the heads of fathers*
וְהַכֹּהֲנִים conj.-def.art.-n.m.p. (463) *also the priests*
עַל־מַלְכוּת prep.-n.f.s. cstr. (574) *until the reign of*
דָּרְיָוֶשׁ pr.n. (201) *Darius*
הַפָּרְסִי def.art.-adj. gent. (828) *the Persian*

12:23
בְּנֵי לֵוִי n.m.p. cstr. (119)-pr.n. (532) *the sons of Levi*
רָאשֵׁי הָאָבוֹת n.m.p. cstr. (910)-def.art.-n.m.p. (3) *heads of fathers*

כְּתוּבִים Qal pass.ptc. m.p. (כָּתַב 507) *were written*
עַל־סֵפֶר prep.-n.m.s. cstr. (706) *in the book of*
דִּבְרֵי הַיָּמִים n.m.p. cstr. (182)-def.art.-n.m.p. (398) *the Chronicles*
וְעַד־יְמֵי יוֹחָנָן conj.-prep. (III 723)-n.m.p. cstr. (398)-pr.n. (220) *until the days of Johanan*
בֶּן־אֶלְיָשִׁיב n.m.s. cstr. (119)-pr.n. (46) *the son of Eliashib*

12:24

וְרָאשֵׁי הַלְוִיִּם conj.-n.m.p. cstr. (910)-def.art.-adj. gent. m.p. (532) *and the chiefs of the Levites*
חֲשַׁבְיָה pr.n. (364) *Hashabiah*
שֵׁרֵבְיָה pr.n. (1055) *Sherebiah*
וְיֵשׁוּעַ conj.-pr.n. (221) *and Jeshua*
בֶּן־קַדְמִיאֵל n.m.s. cstr. (119)-pr.n. (870) *the son of Kadmiel*
וַאֲחֵיהֶם conj.-n.m.p.-3 m.p. sf. (26) *with their brethren*
לְנֶגְדָּם prep.-prep.-3 m.p. sf. (617) *over against them*
לְהַלֵּל prep.-Pi. inf.cstr. (הָלַל II 237) *to praise*
לְהוֹדוֹת prep.-Hi. inf.cstr. (יָדָה 392) *and to give thanks*
בְּמִצְוַת דָּוִיד prep.-n.f.s. cstr. (846)-pr.n. (187) *according to the commandment of David*
אִישׁ־הָאֱלֹהִים n.m.s. cstr. (35)-def.art.-n.m.p. (43) *the man of God*
מִשְׁמָר n.m.s. (1038) *watch*
לְעֻמַּת מִשְׁמָר prep.-n.f.s. cstr. as prep. (769)-v.supra *corresponding to watch*

12:25

מַתַּנְיָה pr.n. (682) *Mattaniah*
וּבַקְבֻּקְיָה conj.-pr.n. (132) *Bakbukiah*
עֹבַדְיָה pr.n. (715) *Obadiah*
מְשֻׁלָּם pr.n. (1024) *Meshullam*
טַלְמוֹן pr.n. (379) *Talmon*
עַקּוּב pr.n. (784) *Akkub*
שֹׁמְרִים שׁוֹעֲרִים Qal act.ptc. m.p. (שָׁמַר 1036)-n.m.p. (1045) *were gatekeepers*
מִשְׁמָר n.m.s. (1038) *guard*
בַּאֲסֻפֵּי הַשְּׁעָרִים prep.-n.m.p. cstr. (63)-def.art. -n.m.p. (1044) *at the storehouses of the gates*

12:26

אֵלֶּה demons.adj. c.p. (41) *these were*
בִּימֵי יוֹיָקִים prep.-n.m.p. cstr. (398)-pr.n. (220) *in the days of Joiakim*

בֶּן־יֵשׁוּעַ n.m.s. cstr. (119)-pr.n. (221) *the son of Jeshua*
בֶּן־יוֹצָדָק v.supra-pr.n. (221) *son of Jozadak*
וּבִימֵי נְחֶמְיָה conj.-v.supra-pr.n. (637) *and in the days of Nehemiah*
הַפֶּחָה def.art.-n.m.s. (808) *the governor*
וְעֶזְרָא conj.-pr.n. (740) *and of Ezra*
הַכֹּהֵן def.art.-n.m.s. (463) *the priest*
הַסּוֹפֵר def.art.-n.m.s. (708) *the scribe*

12:27

וּבַחֲנֻכַּת conj.-prep.-n.f.s. cstr. (335) *and at the dedication of*
חוֹמַת יְרוּשָׁלַםִ n.f.s. cstr. (327)-pr.n. (436) *the wall of Jerusalem*
בִּקְשׁוּ Pi. pf. 3 c.p. (בָּקַשׁ 134) *they sought*
אֶת־הַלְוִיִּם dir.obj.-def.art.-adj. gent. m.p. (532) *the Levites*
מִכָּל־מְקוֹמֹתָם prep.-n.m.s. cstr. (481)-n.m.p.-3 m.p. sf. (879) *in all their places*
לַהֲבִיאָם prep.-Hi. inf.cstr.-3 m.p. sf. (בּוֹא 97) *to bring them*
לִירוּשָׁלָםִ prep.-pr.n. paus. (436) *to Jerusalem*
לַעֲשֹׂת prep.-Qal inf.cstr. (עָשָׂה I 793) *to celebrate*
חֲנֻכָּה n.f.s. (335) *the dedication*
וְשִׂמְחָה conj.-n.f.s. (970) *with gladness*
וּבְתוֹדוֹת conj.-prep.-n.f.p. (392) *with thanksgivings*
וּבְשִׁיר conj.-prep.-n.m.s. (1010) *and with singing*
מְצִלְתַּיִם n.f. du. (853) *with cymbals*
נְבָלִים n.m.p. (II 614) *harps*
וּבְכִנֹּרוֹת conj.-prep.-n.m.p. (490) *and lyres*

12:28

וַיֵּאָסְפוּ consec.-Ni. impf. 3 m.p. (אָסַף 62) *and gathered together*
בְּנֵי הַמְשֹׁרְרִים n.m.p. cstr. (119)-def.art.-Polel ptc. m.p. (שִׁיר 1010) *the sons of the singers*
וּמִן־הַכִּכָּר conj.-prep.-def.art.-n.f.s. (503) *and from the circuit*
סְבִיבוֹת יְרוּשָׁלַםִ prep. (686)-pr.n. (436) *round Jerusalem*
וּמִן־חַצְרֵי conj.-prep.-n.m.p. cstr. (II 347) *and from the villages of*
נְטֹפָתִי adj. gent. (643) *the Netophathites*

12:29

וּמִבֵּית הַגִּלְגָּל conj.-prep.-pr.n. (111) *also from Beth-gilgal*
וּמִשְּׂדוֹת גֶּבַע conj.-prep.-n.m.p. cstr. (961)-pr.n. (148) *and from the region of Geba*

וְעַזְמָוֶת conj.-pr.n. (112) *and Azmaveth*
כִּי חֲצֵרִים conj. (471)-n.m.p. (II 347) *for villages*
בָּנוּ לָהֶם Qal pf. 3 c.p. (בָּנָה 124)-prep.-3 m.p. sf. *had built for themselves*
הַמְשֹׁרְרִים def.art.-Polel ptc. m.p. (שִׁיר 1010) *the singers*
סְבִיבוֹת יְרוּשָׁלָ‍ִם prep. (686)-pr.n. (436) *around Jerusalem*

12:30

וַיִּטַּהֲרוּ consec.-Hith. impf. 3 m.p. (טָהֵר 372) *and purified themselves*
הַכֹּהֲנִים def.art.-n.m.p. (463) *the priests*
וְהַלְוִיִּם conj.-def.art.-adj. gent. m.p. (532) *and the Levites*
וַיְטַהֲרוּ consec.-Pi. impf. 3 m.p. (טָהֵר 372) *and they purified*
אֶת־הָעָם dir.obj.-def.art.-n.m.s. (I 766) *the people*
וְאֶת־הַשְּׁעָרִים conj.-dir.obj.-def.art.-n.m.p. (1044) *and the gates*
וְאֶת־הַחוֹמָה conj.-dir.obj.-def.art.-n.f.s. (327) *and the wall*

12:31

וָאַעֲלֶה consec.-Qal impf. 1 c.s. (עָלָה 748) *then I brought up*
אֶת־שָׂרֵי יְהוּדָה dir.obj.-n.m.p. cstr. (978)-pr.n. (397) *the princes of Judah*
מֵעַל לַחוֹמָה prep.-prep. (752)-prep.-def.art. -n.f.s. (327) *upon the wall*
וָאַעֲמִידָה consec.-Hi. impf. 1 c.s. (עָמַד 763) *and I appointed*
שְׁתֵּי תוֹדֹת גְּדוֹלֹת num. f. cstr. (1040)-n.f.p. (392)-adj. f.p. (152) *two great companies*
וְתַהֲלֻכֹת conj.-n.f.p. (237) *and processions*
לַיָּמִין prep.-def.art.-n.f.s. (I 411) *to the right*
מֵעַל לַחוֹמָה v.supra-v.supra *upon the wall*
לְשַׁעַר הָאַשְׁפֹּת prep.-n.m.s. cstr. (1044)-def. art.-n.m.p. (1046) *to the Dung Gate*

12:32

וַיֵּלֶךְ אַחֲרֵיהֶם consec.-Qal impf. 3 m.s. (הָלַךְ 229)-prep.-3 m.p. sf. (29) *and went after them*
הוֹשַׁעְיָה pr.n. (448) *Hoshaiah*
וַחֲצִי conj.-n.m.s. cstr. (345) *and half of*
שָׂרֵי יְהוּדָה n.m.p. cstr. (978)-pr.n. (397) *the princes of Judah*

12:33

וַעֲזַרְיָה conj.-pr.n. (741) *and Azariah*
עֶזְרָא pr.n. (740) *Ezra*
וּמְשֻׁלָּם conj.-pr.n. (1024) *and Meshullam*

12:34

יְהוּדָה pr.n. (397) *Judah*
וּבִנְיָמִן conj.-pr.n. (122) *Benjamin*
וּשְׁמַעְיָה conj.-pr.n. (1035) *Shemaiah*
וְיִרְמְיָה conj.-pr.n. (941) *and Jeremiah*

12:35

וּמִבְּנֵי הַכֹּהֲנִים conj.-prep.-n.m.p. cstr. (119) -def.art.-n.m.p. (463) *and certain of the priests' sons*
בַּחֲצֹצְרוֹת prep.-n.f.p. (348) *with trumpets*
זְכַרְיָה pr.n. (272) *Zechariah*
בֶּן־יוֹנָתָן n.m.s. cstr. (119)-pr.n. (220) *the son of Jonathan*
בֶּן־שְׁמַעְיָה v.supra-pr.n. (1035) *son of Shemaiah*
בֶּן־מַתַּנְיָה v.supra-pr.n. (682) *son of Mattaniah*
בֶּן־מִיכָיָה v.supra-pr.n. (567) *son of Micaiah*
בֶּן־זַכּוּר v.supra-pr.n. (271) *son of Zaccur*
בֶּן־אָסָף v.supra-pr.n. (63) *son of Asaph*

12:36

וְאֶחָיו conj.-n.m.p.-3 m.s. sf. (26) *and his kinsmen*
שְׁמַעְיָה pr.n. (1035) *Shemaiah*
וַעֲזַרְאֵל conj.-pr.n. (741) *Azarel*
מִלֲלַי pr.n. (576) *Milalai*
גִּלֲלַי pr.n. (165) *Gilalai*
מָעַי pr.n. (590) *Maai*
נְתַנְאֵל pr.n. (682) *Nethanel*
וִיהוּדָה conj.-pr.n. (397) *and Judah*
חֲנָנִי pr.n. (337) *Hanani*
בִּכְלֵי־שִׁיר prep.-n.m.p. cstr. (479)-n.m.s. cstr. (1010) *with the musical instruments of*
דָּוִיד pr.n. (187) *David*
אִישׁ הָאֱלֹהִים n.m.s. cstr. (35)-def.art.-n.m.p. (43) *the man of God*
וְעֶזְרָא conj.-pr.n. (740) *and Ezra*
הַסּוֹפֵר def.art.-n.m.s. (708) *the scribe*
לִפְנֵיהֶם prep.-n.m.p.-3 m.p. sf. (815) *before them*

12:37

וְעַל שַׁעַר הָעַיִן conj.-prep.-n.m.s. cstr. (1044) -def.art.-n.f.s. (744) *at the Fountain Gate*
וְנֶגְדָּם conj.-prep.-3 m.p. sf. (617) *straight before them*
עָלוּ Qal pf. 3 c.p. (עָלָה 748) *they went up*
עַל־מַעֲלוֹת prep.-n.f.p. cstr. (752) *by the stairs of*

עִיר דָּוִיד n.f.s. cstr. (746)-pr.n. (187) *the city of David*
בַּמַּעֲלֶה prep.-def.art.-n.m.s. (751) *at the ascent*
לַחוֹמָה prep.-def.art.-n.f.s. (327) *of the wall*
מֵעַל לְבֵית דָּוִיד prep.-prep.-prep.-n.m.s. cstr. (108)-v.supra *above the house of David*
וְעַד שַׁעַר הַמַּיִם conj.-prep. (III 723)-n.m.s. cstr. (1044)-def.art.-n.m.p. (565) *to the Water Gate*
מִזְרָח n.m.s. (280) *on the east*

12:38

וְהַתּוֹדָה הַשֵּׁנִית conj.-def.art.-n.f.s. (392)-def. art.-num. ord. f. (1041) *the other company of those who gave thanks*
הַהוֹלֶכֶת def.art.-Qal act.ptc. f.s. (הָלַךְ 229) *went*
לְמוֹאל prep.-subst. (I 557) *in the opposite direction*
וַאֲנִי אַחֲרֶיהָ conj.-pers.pr. 1 c.s. (58)-prep.-3 f.s. sf. (29) *and I followed them*
וַחֲצִי הָעָם conj.-n.m.s. cstr. (345)-def.art.-n.m.s. (I 766) *with half of the people*
מֵעַל לְהַחוֹמָה prep.-prep.-prep.-def.art.-n.f.s. (327) *upon the wall*
מֵעַל לְמִגְדַּל הַתַּנּוּרִים prep.-prep.-prep.-n.m.s. cstr. (153)-def.art.-n.m.p. (1072) *above the Tower of the Ovens*
וְעַד הַחוֹמָה הָרְחָבָה conj.-prep. (III 723)-def.art. -n.f.s. (327)-def.art.-adj. f.s. (I 932) *to the Broad Wall*

12:39

וּמֵעַל לְשַׁעַר־אֶפְרַיִם conj.-prep.-prep.-prep. -n.m.s. cstr. (1044)-pr.n. (68) *and above the Gate of Ephraim*
וְעַל־שַׁעַר הַיְשָׁנָה conj.-prep.-v.supra -def.art.-adj. f.s. (445) *and by the Old Gate*
וְעַל־שַׁעַר הַדָּגִים v.supra-v.supra-def.art.-n.m.p. (185) *and by the Fish Gate*
וּמִגְדַּל חֲנַנְאֵל conj.-n.m.s. cstr. (153)-pr.n. (337) *and the Tower of Hananel*
וּמִגְדַּל הַמֵּאָה v.supra-def.art.-n.f.s. (547) *and the Tower of the Hundred*
וְעַד שַׁעַר הַצֹּאן conj.-prep. (III 723)-v.supra -def.art.-n.f.s. (838) *to the Sheep Gate*
וְעָמְדוּ conj.-Qal pf. 3 c.p. (עָמַד 763) *and they came to a halt*
בְּשַׁעַר הַמַּטָּרָה prep.-v.supra-def.art.-n.f.s. (643) *at the Gate of the Guard*

12:40

וַתַּעֲמֹדְנָה consec.-Qal impf. 3 f.p. (עָמַד 763) *so stood*
שְׁתֵּי הַתּוֹדֹת num. f. cstr. (1040)-def.art.-n.f.p. (392) *both companies of those who gave thanks*
בְּבֵית הָאֱלֹהִים prep.-n.m.s. cstr. (108)-def.art. -n.m.p. (43) *in the house of God*
וַאֲנִי conj.-pers.pr. 1 c.s. (58) *and I*
וַחֲצִי הַסְּגָנִים conj.-n.m.s. cstr. (345)-def.art. -n.m.p. (688) *and half of the officials*
עִמִּי prep.-1 c.s. sf. (767) *with me*

12:41

וְהַכֹּהֲנִים conj.-def.art.-n.m.p. (463) *and the priests*
אֶלְיָקִים pr.n. (45) *Eliakim*
מַעֲשֵׂיָה pr.n. (796) *Maaseiah*
מִנְיָמִין pr.n. (568) *Miniamin*
מִיכָיָה pr.n. (567) *Micaiah*
אֶלְיוֹעֵינַי pr.n. (41) *Elioenai*
זְכַרְיָה pr.n. (272) *Zechariah*
חֲנַנְיָה pr.n. (337) *Hananiah*
בַּחֲצֹצְרוֹת prep.-n.f.p. (348) *with trumpets*

12:42

וּמַעֲשֵׂיָה conj.-pr.n. (796) *and Maaseiah*
וּשְׁמַעְיָה conj.-pr.n. (1035) *and Shemaiah*
וְאֶלְעָזָר conj.-pr.n. (46) *Eleazar*
וְעֻזִּי conj.-pr.n. (739) *Uzzi*
וִיהוֹחָנָן conj.-pr.n. (220) *Jehohanan*
וּמַלְכִּיָּה conj.-pr.n. (575) *Malchijah*
וְעֵילָם conj.-pr.n. (II 743) *Elam*
וָעָזֶר conj.-pr.n. paus. (740) *and Ezer*
וַיַּשְׁמִיעוּ consec.-Hi. impf. 3 m.p. (שָׁמַע 1033) *and sang*
הַמְשֹׁרְרִים def.art.-Polel ptc. m.p. (שִׁיר 1010) *the singers*
וְיִזְרַחְיָה conj.-pr.n. (280) *with Jezrahiah*
הַפָּקִיד def.art.-n.m.s. (824) *as their leader*

12:43

וַיִּזְבְּחוּ consec.-Qal impf. 3 m.p. (זָבַח 256) *and they offered*
בַּיּוֹם־הַהוּא prep.-def.art.-n.m.s. (398)-def.art. -demons.adj. m.s. (214) *that day*
זְבָחִים גְּדוֹלִים n.m.p. (257)-adj. m.p. (152) *great sacrifices*
וַיִּשְׂמָחוּ consec.-Qal impf. 3 m.p. (שָׂמַח 970) *and rejoiced*
כִּי הָאֱלֹהִים conj. (471)-def.art.-n.m.p. (43) *for God*
שִׂמְּחָם Pi. pf. 3 m.s.-3 m.p. sf. (שָׂמַח 970) *had made them rejoice*

שִׂמְחָה גְדוֹלָה n.f.s. (970)-adj. f.s. (152) *with great joy*
וְגַם הַנָּשִׁים conj.-adv. (168)-def.art.-n.f.p. (61) *and also the women*
וְהַיְלָדִים conj.-def.art.-n.m.p. (409) *and children*
שָׂמֵחוּ Qal pf. 3 c.p. paus. (שָׂמַח 970) *rejoiced*
וַתִּשָּׁמַע consec.-Ni. impf. 3 f.s. (שָׁמַע 1033) *and was heard*
שִׂמְחַת יְרוּשָׁלַםִ n.f.s. cstr. (970)-pr.n. (436) *the joy of Jerusalem*
מֵרָחוֹק prep.-n.m.s. (935) *afar off*

12:44

וַיִּפָּקְדוּ consec.-Ni. impf. 3 m.p. (פָּקַד 823) *were appointed*
בַּיּוֹם הַהוּא prep.-def.art.-n.m.s. (398)-def.art. -demons.adj. m.s. (214) *on that day*
אֲנָשִׁים n.m.p. (35) *men*
עַל־הַנְּשָׁכוֹת prep.-def.art.-n.f.p. (675) *over the chambers*
לָאוֹצָרוֹת prep.-def.art.-n.m.p. (69) *for the stores*
לַתְּרוּמוֹת prep.-def.art.-n.f.p. (929) *the contributions*
לָרֵאשִׁית prep.-n.f.s. (912) *the first fruits*
וְלַמַּעַשְׂרוֹת conj.-prep.-def.art.-n.m.p. (798) *and the tithes*
לִכְנוֹס בָּהֶם prep.-Qal inf.cstr. (כָּנַס 488)-prep.-3 m.p. sf. *to gather into them*
לִשְׂדֵי הֶעָרִים prep.-n.m.p. cstr. (961)-def.art. -n.f.p. (746) *according to the fields of the towns*
מְנָאוֹת הַתּוֹרָה n.f.p. cstr. (584; GK 95n)-def. art.-n.f.s. (435) *the portions required by the law*
לַכֹּהֲנִים prep.-def.art.-n.m.p. (463) *for the priests*
וְלַלְוִיִּם conj.-prep.-def.art.-adj. gent. m.p. (532) *and for the Levites*
כִּי שִׂמְחַת יְהוּדָה conj. (471)-n.f.s. cstr. (970) -pr.n. (397) *for the joy of Judah*
עַל־הַכֹּהֲנִים prep.-def.art.-n.m.p. (463) *over the priests*
וְעַל־הַלְוִיִּם conj.-v.supra-v.supra *and the Levites*
הָעֹמְדִים def.art.-Qal act.ptc. m.p. (עָמַד 763) *who ministered*

12:45

וַיִּשְׁמְרוּ consec.-Qal impf. 3 m.p. (שָׁמַר 1036) *and they performed*
מִשְׁמֶרֶת אֱלֹהֵיהֶם n.f.s. cstr. (1038)-n.m.p.-3 m.p. sf. (43) *the service of their God*
וּמִשְׁמֶרֶת הַטָּהֳרָה conj.-v.supra-def.art.-n.f.s. (372) *and the service of purification*
וְהַמְשֹׁרְרִים conj.-def.art.-Polel ptc. m.p. (שִׁיר 1010) *and the singers*
וְהַשֹּׁעֲרִים conj.-def.art.-n.m.p. (1045) *and the gatekeepers*
כְּמִצְוַת דָּוִיד prep.-n.f.s. cstr. (846)-pr.n. (187) *according to the command of David*
שְׁלֹמֹה בְנוֹ pr.n. (1024)-n.m.s.-3 m.s. sf. (119) *Solomon his son*

12:46

כִּי־בִימֵי דָוִיד conj. (471)-prep.-n.m.p. cstr. (398)-pr.n. (187) *for in the days of David*
וְאָסָף conj.-pr.n. (63) *and Asaph*
מִקֶּדֶם prep.-n.m.s. (869) *of old*
רָאשֵׁי הַמְשֹׁרְרִים n.m.s. cstr. (910)-def.art.-Polel ptc. m.p. (שִׁיר 1010) *there was a chief of the singers*
וְשִׁיר־תְּהִלָּה conj.-n.m.s. cstr. (1010)-n.f.s. (239) *and songs of praise*
וְהֹדוֹת לֵאלֹהִים conj.-Hi. inf.cstr. (יָדָה 392) -prep.-n.m.p. (43) *and thanksgiving to God*

12:47

וְכָל־יִשְׂרָאֵל conj.-n.m.s. cstr. (481)-pr.n. (975) *and all Israel*
בִּימֵי זְרֻבָּבֶל prep.-n.m.p. cstr. (398)-pr.n. (279) *in the days of Zerubbabel*
וּבִימֵי נְחֶמְיָה conj.-v.supra-pr.n. (637) *and in the days of Nehemiah*
נֹתְנִים Qal act.ptc. m.p. (נָתַן 678) *gave*
מְנָיוֹת n.f.p. cstr. (584; GK 95n) *the ... portions for*
הַמְשֹׁרְרִים def.art.-Polel ptc. m.p. (שִׁיר 1010) *the singers*
וְהַשֹּׁעֲרִים conj.-def.art.-n.m.p. (1045) *and the gatekeepers*
דְּבַר־יוֹם בְּיוֹמוֹ n.m.s. cstr. (182)-n.m.s. (398) -prep.-n.m.s.-3 m.s. sf. (398) *daily*
וּמַקְדִּשִׁים conj.-Hi. ptc. m.p. (קָדַשׁ 872) *and they set apart*
לַלְוִיִּם prep.-def.art.-adj. gent. m.p. (532) *for the Levites*
וְהַלְוִיִּם conj.-def.art.-v.supra *and the Levites*
מַקְדִּשִׁים v.supra *set apart*
לִבְנֵי אַהֲרֹן prep.-n.m.p. cstr. (119)-pr.n. (14) *for the sons of Aaron*

13:1

בַּיּוֹם הַהוּא prep.-def.art.-n.m.s. (398)-def.art. -demons.adj. m.s. (214) *on that day*

נִקְרָא Ni. ptc. (**קָרָא** 894) *it was read*
בְּסֵפֶר מֹשֶׁה prep.-n.m.s. cstr. (706)-pr.n. 602) *from the book of Moses*
בְּאָזְנֵי הָעָם prep.-n.f.p. cstr. (23)-def.art.-n.m.s. (766) *in the hearing of the people*
וְנִמְצָא conj.-Ni. ptc. (**מָצָא** 592) *and was found*
כָּתוּב בּוֹ Qal pass.ptc. (**כָּתַב** 507)-prep.-3 m.s. sf. *written in it*
אֲשֶׁר לֹא־יָבוֹא rel. (81)-neg.-Qal impf. 3 m.s. (97 **בּוֹא**) *that should not enter*
עַמֹּנִי adj. gent. (770) *an Ammonite*
וּמוֹאָבִי conj.-adj. gent. (555) *a Moabite*
בִּקְהַל הָאֱלֹהִים prep.-n.m.s. cstr. (874)-def.art. -n.m.p. (43) *into the assembly of God*
עַד־עוֹלָם prep. (III 723)-n.m.s. (761) *ever*

13:2

כִּי לֹא קִדְּמוּ conj. (471)-neg.-Pi. pf. 3 c.p. (**קָדַם** 869) *for they did not meet*
אֶת־בְּנֵי יִשְׂרָאֵל dir.obj.-n.m.p. cstr. (119)-pr.n. (975) *the children of Israel*
בַּלֶּחֶם prep.-def.art.-n.m.s. (536) *with bread*
וּבַמָּיִם conj.-prep.-def.art.-n.m.p. paus. (565) *and water*
וַיִּשְׂכֹּר עָלָיו consec.-Qal impf. 3 m.s. (**שָׂכַר** 968) -prep.-3 m.s. sf. *but hired against them*
אֶת־בִּלְעָם dir.obj.-pr.n. (I 118) *Balaam*
לְקַלְלוֹ prep.-Pi. inf.cstr.-3 m.s. sf. (**קָלַל** 886) *to curse them*
וַיַּהֲפֹךְ אֱלֹהֵינוּ consec.-Qal impf. 3 m.s. (**הָפַךְ** 245)-n.m.p.-1 c.p. sf. (43) *yet our God turned*
הַקְּלָלָה def.art.-n.f.s. (887) *the curse*
לִבְרָכָה prep.-n.f.s. (139) *into a blessing*

13:3

וַיְהִי כְּשָׁמְעָם consec.-Qal impf. 3 m.s. (**הָיָה** 224)-prep.-Qal inf.cstr.-3 m.p. sf. (**שָׁמַע** 1033) *when (the people) heard*
אֶת־הַתּוֹרָה dir.obj.-def.art.-n.f.s. (435) *the law*
וַיַּבְדִּילוּ consec.-Hi. impf. 3 m.p. (**בָּדַל** 95) *they separated*
כָל־עֵרֶב n.m.s. cstr. (481)-n.m.s. (I 786) *all of the mixed company*
מִיִּשְׂרָאֵל prep.-pr.n. (975) *from Israel*

13:4

וְלִפְנֵי מִזֶּה conj.-prep.-n.m.p. cstr. (815)-prep. -demons.adj. m.s. (260) *now before this*
אֶלְיָשִׁיב pr.n. (46) *Eliashib*
הַכֹּהֵן def.art.-n.m.s. (463) *the priest*
נָתוּן בְּלִשְׁכַּת Qal pass.ptc. (**נָתַן** 678)-prep.-n.f.s. cstr. (545) *who was appointed over the chambers of*
בֵּית־אֱלֹהֵינוּ n.m.s. cstr. (108)-n.m.p.-1 c.p. sf. (43) *the house of our God*
קָרוֹב לְטוֹבִיָּה adj. m.s. (898)-prep.-pr.n. (375) *who was connected with Tobiah*

13:5

וַיַּעַשׂ לוֹ consec.-Qal impf. 3 m.s. (**עָשָׂה** I 793) -prep.-3 m.s. sf. *prepared for him*
לִשְׁכָּה גְדוֹלָה n.f.s. (545)-adj. f.s. (152) *a large chamber*
וְשָׁם הָיוּ conj.-adv. (1027)-Qal pf. 3 c.p. (**הָיָה** 224) *and there they had been*
לְפָנִים prep.-n.m.p. (815) *previously*
נֹתְנִים Qal act.ptc. m.p. (**נָתַן** 678) *putting*
אֶת־הַמִּנְחָה dir.obj.-def.art.-n.f.s. (585) *the offering*
הַלְּבוֹנָה def.art.-n.f.s. (I 526) *the frankincense*
וְהַכֵּלִים conj.-def.art.-n.m.p. (479) *the vessels*
וּמַעְשַׂר הַדָּגָן conj.-n.m.s. cstr. (798)-def.art. -n.m.s. (186) *and the tithes of grain*
הַתִּירוֹשׁ def.art.-n.m.s. (440) *wine*
וְהַיִּצְהָר conj.-def.art.-n.m.s. (I 844) *and oil*
מִצְוַת הַלְוִיִּם n.f.s. cstr. (846)-def.art.-adj. gent. m.p. (532) *by commandment to the Levites*
וְהַמְשֹׁרְרִים conj.-def.art.-Polel ptc. m.p. (**שִׁיר** 1010) *singers*
וְהַשֹּׁעֲרִים conj.-def.art.-n.m.p. (1045) *the gatekeepers*
וּתְרוּמַת הַכֹּהֲנִים conj.-n.f.s. cstr. (929)-def.art. -n.m.p. (463) *and the contributions for the priests*

13:6

וּבְכָל־זֶה conj.-prep.-n.m.s. cstr. (481)-demons.adj. m.s. (260) *and while this (was taking place)*
לֹא הָיִיתִי neg.-Qal pf. 1 c.s. (**הָיָה** 224) *I was not*
בִּירוּשָׁלָם prep.-pr.n. (436) *in Jerusalem*
כִּי בִּשְׁנַת conj. (471)-prep.-n.f.s. cstr. (1040) *for in the ... year of*
שְׁלֹשִׁים וּשְׁתַּיִם num. p. (1026)-conj.-num. f. du. (1040) *thirty-second*
לְאַרְתַּחְשַׁסְתְּא prep.-pr.n. (77) *Artaxerxes*
מֶלֶךְ־בָּבֶל n.m.s. cstr. (I 572)-pr.n. (93) *king of Babylon*
בָּאתִי Qal pf. 1 c.s. (**בּוֹא** 97) *I went*
אֶל־הַמֶּלֶךְ prep.-def.art.-n.m.s. (I 572) *to the king*
וּלְקֵץ יָמִים conj.-prep.-n.m.s. cstr. (893)-n.m.p. (398) *and after some time*

נִשְׁאַלְתִּי Ni. pf. 1 c.s. (שָׁאַל 981) *I asked leave*
מִן־הַמֶּלֶךְ prep.-def.art.-v.supra *of the king*

13:7

וָאָבוֹא consec.-Qal impf. 1 c.s. (בּוֹא 97) *and I came*
לִירוּשָׁלָ͏ִם prep.-pr.n. (436) *to Jerusalem*
וָאָבִינָה consec.-Qal impf. 1 c.s. (בִּין 106) *and I then discovered*
בָרָעָה prep.-def.art.-n.f.s. (949) *the evil*
אֲשֶׁר עָשָׂה rel. (81)-Qal pf. 3 m.s. (I 793) *that ... had done*
אֶלְיָשִׁיב pr.n. (46) *Eliashib*
לְטוֹבִיָּה prep.-pr.n. (375) *for Tobijah*
לַעֲשׂוֹת לוֹ prep.-Qal inf.cstr. (עָשָׂה I 793) -prep.-3 m.s. sf. *preparing for him*
נִשְׁכָּה n.f.s. (675) *a chamber*
בְּחַצְרֵי prep.-n.m.p. cstr. (I 346) *in the courts of*
בֵּית הָאֱלֹהִים n.m.s. cstr. (108)-def.art.-n.m.p. (43) *the house of God*

13:8

וַיֵּרַע לִי מְאֹד consec.-Qal impf. 3 m.s. (רָעַע 949; GK 67p)-prep.-1 c.s. sf.-adv. (547) *and I was very angry*
וָאַשְׁלִיכָה consec.-Hi. impf. 1 c.s. (שָׁלַךְ 1020) *and I threw out*
אֶת־כָּל־כְּלֵי dir.obj.-n.m.s. cstr. (481)-n.m.p. cstr. (479) *all the furniture of*
בֵית־טוֹבִיָּה n.m.s. cstr. (108)-pr.n. (375) *the house of Tobijah*
הַחוּץ def.art.-n.m.s. (299) *out*
מִן־הַלִּשְׁכָּה prep.-def.art.-n.f.s. (545) *of the chamber*

13:9

וָאֹמְרָה consec.-Qal impf. 1 c.s. (אָמַר 55) *then I gave orders*
וַיְטַהֲרוּ consec.-Pi. impf. 3 m.p. (טָהֵר 372; GK 165a) *and they cleansed*
הַלְּשָׁכוֹת def.art.-n.f.p. (545) *the chambers*
וָאָשִׁיבָה שָּׁם consec.-Qal impf. 1 c.s. (שׁוּב 996) -adv. (1027) *and I brought back thither*
כְּלֵי בֵּית הָאֱלֹהִים n.m.p. cstr. (479)-n.m.s. cstr. (108)-def.art.-n.m.p. (43) *the vessels of the house of God*
אֶת־הַמִּנְחָה dir.obj.-def.art.-n.f.s. (585) *with the offering*
וְהַלְּבוֹנָה conj.-def.art.-n.f.s. (I 526) *and the frankincense*

13:10

וָאֵדְעָה consec.-Qal impf. 1 c.s. (יָדַע 393) *I also found out*
כִּי־מְנָיוֹת הַלְוִיִּם conj. (471)-n.f.p. cstr. (584) -def.art.-adj. gent. m.p. (532) *that the portions of the Levites*
לֹא נִתָּנָה neg.-Ni. pf. 3 f.s. (נָתַן 678) *had not been given*
וַיִּבְרְחוּ consec.-Qal impf. 3 m.p. (בָּרַח 137) *so that ... had fled*
אִישׁ־לְשָׂדֵהוּ n.m.s. (35)-prep.-n.m.s.-3 m.s. sf. (961) *each to his field*
הַלְוִיִּם v.supra *the Levites*
וְהַמְשֹׁרְרִים conj.-def.art.-Polel ptc. m.p. (שִׁיר 1010) *and the singers*
עֹשֵׂי הַמְּלָאכָה Qal act.ptc. m.p. cstr. (עָשָׂה I 793)-def.art.-n.f.s. (521) *who did the work*

13:11

וָאָרִיבָה consec.-Qal impf. 1 c.s. (רִיב 936) *so I remonstrated*
אֶת־הַסְּגָנִים dir.obj.-def.art.-n.m.p. (688) *with the officials*
וָאֹמְרָה pr.n.Qal impf. 1 c.s. (אָמַר 55) *and I said*
מַדּוּעַ נֶעֱזַב adv. (396)-Ni. pf. 3 m.s. (עָזַב I 736) *why is forsaken*
בֵּית־הָאֱלֹהִים n.m.s. cstr. (108)-def.art.-n.m.p. (43) *the house of God*
וָאֶקְבְּצֵם consec.-Qal impf. 1 c.s.-3 m.p. sf. (קָבַץ 867) *and I gathered them together*
וָאַעֲמִדֵם consec.-Hi. impf. 1 c.s.-3 m.p. sf. (עָמַד 763) *and I set them*
עַל־עָמְדָם prep.-n.m.s.-3 m.p. sf. (765) *in their stations*

13:12

וְכָל־יְהוּדָה conj.-n.m.s. cstr. (481)-pr.n. (397) *then all Judah*
הֵבִיאוּ Hi. pf. 3 c.p. (בּוֹא 97) *brought*
מַעְשַׂר הַדָּגָן n.m.s. cstr. (798)-def.art.-n.m.s. (186) *the tithe of the grain*
וְהַתִּירוֹשׁ conj.-def.art.-n.m.s. (440) *wine*
וְהַיִּצְהָר conj.-def.art.-n.m.s. (I 844) *and oil*
לָאוֹצָרוֹת prep.-def.art.-n.m.p. (69) *into the storehouses*

13:13

וָאוֹצְרָה consec.-Hi. impf. 1 c.s. (אָצַר 69; GK 53g,n) *and I appointed as treasurers*
עַל־אוֹצָרוֹת prep.-n.m.p. (69) *over the storehouses*
שֶׁלֶמְיָה pr.n. (1025) *Shelemiah*

הַכֹּהֵן def.art.-n.m.s. (463) ***the priest***
וְצָדוֹק conj.-pr.n. (843) ***and Zadok***
הַסּוֹפֵר def.art.-n.m.s. (708) ***the scribe***
וּפְדָיָה conj.-pr.n. (804) ***and Pedaiah***
מִן־הַלְוִיִּם prep.-def.art.-adj. gent. m.p. (532) ***of the Levites***
וְעַל־יָדָם conj.-prep.-n.f.s.-3 m.p. sf. (388) ***and as their assistant***
חָנָן pr.n. (336) ***Hanan***
בֶּן־זַכּוּר n.m.s. cstr. (119)-pr.n. (271) ***the son of Zaccur***
בֶּן־מַתַּנְיָה v.supra-pr.n. (682) ***son of Mattaniah***
כִּי נֶאֱמָנִים conj. (471)-Ni. ptc. m.p. (אָמַן 52) ***for faithful***
נֶחְשָׁבוּ Ni. pf. 3 c.p. paus. (חָשַׁב 362) ***they were counted***
וַעֲלֵיהֶם conj.-prep. (II 752)-3 m.p. sf. ***and upon them***
לַחֲלֹק prep.-Qal inf.cstr. (חָלַק 323) ***to distribute***
לַאֲחֵיהֶם prep.-n.m.p.-3 m.p. sf. (26) ***to their brethren***

13:14

זָכְרָה־לִּי Qal impv. 2 m.s. (זָכַר 270)-prep.-1 c.s. sf. ***remember me***
אֱלֹהַי n.m.p.-1 c.s. sf. (43) ***O my God***
עַל־זֹאת prep.-demons.adj. f.s. (260) ***concerning this***
וְאַל־תֶּמַח conj.-neg.-Qal impf. 2 m.s.(מָחָה 562) ***and wipe not out***
חֲסָדַי n.m.p.-1 c.s. sf. (338) ***my good deeds***
אֲשֶׁר עָשִׂיתִי rel. (81)-Qal pf. 1 c.s. (עָשָׂה I 793) ***that I have done***
בְּבֵית אֱלֹהַי prep.-n.m.s. cstr. (108)-n.m.p.-1 c.s. sf. (43) ***for the house of my God***
וּבְמִשְׁמָרָיו conj.-prep.-n.m.p.-3 m.s. sf. (1038) ***and for his service***

13:15

בַּיָּמִים הָהֵמָּה prep.-def.art.-n.m.p. (398)-def.art.-demons.adj. m.p. (241) ***in those days***
רָאִיתִי Qal pf. 1 c.s. (רָאָה 906) ***I saw***
בִיהוּדָה prep.-pr.n. (397) ***in Judah***
דֹרְכִים־גִּתּוֹת Qal act.ptc. m.p. (דָּרַךְ 201)-n.f.p. (I 387) ***men treading wine presses***
בַּשַּׁבָּת prep.-def.art.-n.f.s. (992) ***on the sabbath***
וּמְבִיאִים הָעֲרֵמוֹת conj.-Hi. ptc. m.p. (בּוֹא 97)-def.art.-n.f.p. (790) ***and bringing in heaps of grain***
וְעֹמְסִים conj.-Qal act.ptc. m.p. (עָמַס 770) ***and loading (them)***
עַל־הַחֲמֹרִים prep.-def.art.-n.m.p. (II 331) ***on asses***
וְאַף־יַיִן conj.-adv. (II 64)-n.m.s. (406) ***and also wine***
עֲנָבִים n.m.p. (772) ***grapes***
וּתְאֵנִים conj.-n.f.p. (1061) ***and figs***
וְכָל־מַשָּׂא conj.-n.m.s. cstr. (481)-n.m.s. (I 672) ***and all kinds of burden***
וּמְבִיאִים v.supra ***which they brought***
יְרוּשָׁלָםִ pr.n. (436) ***into Jerusalem***
בְּיוֹם הַשַּׁבָּת prep.-n.m.s. cstr. (398)-def.art.-n.f.s. (992) ***on the sabbath day***
וָאָעִיד consec.-Hi. impf. 1 c.s. (עוּד 729) ***and I warned (them)***
בְּיוֹם prep.-n.m.s. cstr. (398) ***on the day when***
מִכְרָם צָיִד Qal inf.cstr.-3 m.p. sf. (מָכַר 569)-n.m.s. paus. II 845) ***they sold food***

13:16

וְהַצֹּרִים conj.-def.art.-adj. gent. m.p. (863) ***and men of Tyre***
יָשְׁבוּ בָהּ Qal pf. 3 c.p. (יָשַׁב 442)-prep.-3 f.s. sf. ***who lived in it (the city)***
מְבִיאִים Hi. ptc. m.p. (בּוֹא 97) ***brought in***
דָּאג n.m.s. (185; GK 9b) ***fish***
וְכָל־מֶכֶר conj.-n.m.s. cstr. (481)-n.m.s. (569) ***and all kinds of wares***
וּמֹכְרִים conj.-Qal act.ptc. m.p. (מָכַר 569) ***and sold (them)***
בַּשַּׁבָּת prep.-def.art.-n.f.s. (992) ***on the sabbath***
לִבְנֵי יְהוּדָה prep.-n.m.p. cstr. (119)-pr.n. (397) ***to the people of Judah***
וּבִירוּשָׁלָםִ conj.-prep.-pr.n. (436) ***and in Jerusalem***

13:17

וָאָרִיבָה consec.-Qal impf. 1 c.s. (רִיב 936) ***then I remonstrated***
אֶת חֹרֵי יְהוּדָה dir.obj.-n.m.p. cstr. (II 359)-pr.n. (397) ***with the nobles of Judah***
וָאֹמְרָה לָהֶם consec.-Qal impf. 1 c.s. (אָמַר 55)-prep.-3 m.p. sf. ***and said to them***
מָה־הַדָּבָר הָרָע הַזֶּה interr. (552)-def.art.-n.m.s. (182)-def.art.-adj. m.s. (I 948)-def.art.-demons.adj. m.s. (260) ***what is this evil thing***
אֲשֶׁר אַתֶּם עֹשִׂים rel. (81)-pers.pr. 2 m.p. (61)-Qal act.ptc. m.p. (עָשָׂה I 793) ***which you are doing***
וּמְחַלְּלִים conj.-Pi. ptc. m.p. (חָלַל III 320) ***profaning***

אֶת־יוֹם הַשַּׁבָּת dir.obj.-n.m.s. cstr. (398) -def.art.-n.f.s. (992) ***the sabbath day***

13:18

הֲלוֹא כֹה interr.part.-neg.-adv. (462) ***did not in this way***
עָשׂוּ אֲבֹתֵיכֶם Qal pf. 3 c.p. (עָשָׂה I 793) -n.m.p.-2 m.p. sf. (3) ***your fathers act***
וַיָּבֵא אֱלֹהֵינוּ consec.-Hi. impf. 3 m.s. (בּוֹא 97)-n.m.p.-1 c.p. sf. (43) ***and did not our God bring***
עָלֵינוּ prep.-1 c.p. sf. ***on us***
אֵת כָּל־הָרָעָה הַזֹּאת dir.obj.-n.m.s. cstr. (481) -def.art.-n.f.s. (949)-def.art.-demons.adj. f.s. (260) ***all this evil***
וְעַל הָעִיר הַזֹּאת conj.-prep.-def.art.-n.f.s. (746) -def.art.-demons.adj. f.s. (260) ***and on this city***
וְאַתֶּם מוֹסִיפִים conj.-pers.pr. 2 m.p. (61)-Hi. ptc. m.p. (יָסַף 414) ***yet you add more***
חָרוֹן n.m.s. (354) ***wrath***
עַל־יִשְׂרָאֵל prep.-pr.n. (975) ***upon Israel***
לְחַלֵּל אֶת־הַשַּׁבָּת prep.-Pi. inf.cstr. (חָלַל III 320)-dir.obj.-def.art.-n.f.s. (992) ***by profaning the sabbath***

13:19

וַיְהִי כַּאֲשֶׁר consec.-Qal impf. 3 m.s. (הָיָה 224)-prep.-rel. (81) ***when it began***
צָלְלוּ Qal pf. 3 c.p. (צָלַל III 853) ***to be dark***
שַׁעֲרֵי יְרוּשָׁלַםִ n.m.p. cstr. (1044)-pr.n. (436) ***the gates of Jerusalem***
לִפְנֵי הַשַּׁבָּת prep.-n.m.p. cstr. (815)-def.art.-n.f.s. (992) ***before the sabbath***
וָאֹמְרָה consec.-Qal impf. 1 c.s. (אָמַר 55) ***I commanded***
וַיִּסָּגְרוּ הַדְּלָתוֹת consec.-Ni. impf. 3 m.p. (סָגַר 688)-def.art.-n.f.p. (195) ***that the doors should be shut***
וָאֹמְרָה v.supra ***and gave orders***
אֲשֶׁר לֹא יִפְתָּחוּם rel. (81)-neg.-Qal impf. 3 m.p.-3 m.p. sf. (פָּתַח I 834) ***that they should not be opened***
עַד אַחַר הַשַּׁבָּת prep. (III 723)-prep. (29)-def. art.-n.f.s. (992) ***until after the sabbath***
וּמִנְּעָרַי conj.-prep.-n.m.p.-1 c.s. sf. (654) ***and some of my servants***
הֶעֱמַדְתִּי Hi. pf. 1 c.s. (עָמַד 763) ***I set***
עַל־הַשְּׁעָרִים prep.-def.art.-n.m.p. (1044) ***over the gates***
לֹא־יָבוֹא neg.-Qal impf. 3 m.s. (בּוֹא 97) ***that one would not bring in***
מַשָּׂא n.m.s. (I 672) ***a burden***
בְּיוֹם הַשַּׁבָּת prep.-n.m.s. cstr. (398)-v.supra ***on the sabbath day***

13:20

וַיָּלִינוּ consec.-Qal impf. 3 m.p. (לִין 533) ***then lodged***
הָרֹכְלִים def.art.-Qal act.ptc. m.p. (רָכַל 940) ***the merchants***
וּמֹכְרֵי conj.-Qal act.ptc. m.p. cstr. (מָכַר 569) ***and sellers of***
כָל־מִמְכָּר n.m.s. cstr. (481)-pr.n. (569) ***all kinds of wares***
מִחוּץ לִירוּשָׁלָםִ prep.-n.m.s. (299)-prep.-pr.n. paus. (436) ***outside Jerusalem***
פַּעַם וּשְׁתָּיִם n.f.s. (821)-conj.-num. f. paus. (1040) ***once or twice***

13:21

וָאָעִידָה consec.-Hi. impf. 1 c.s. (עוּד 729) ***but I warned***
בָהֶם prep.-3 m.p. sf. ***them***
וָאֹמְרָה אֲלֵיהֶם consec.-Qal impf. 1 c.s. (אָמַר 55)-prep.-3 m.p. sf. ***and said to them***
מַדּוּעַ אַתֶּם לֵנִים adv. (396)-pers.pr. 2 m.p. (61) -Qal act.ptc. m.p. (לִין 533; GK 73f) ***why do you lodge***
נֶגֶד הַחוֹמָה prep. (617)-def.art.-n.f.s. (327) ***before the wall***
אִם־תִּשְׁנוּ hypoth.part. (49)-Qal impf. 2 m.p. (III 1040 שָׁנָה) ***if you do so again***
יָד אֶשְׁלַח בָּכֶם n.f.s. (388)-Qal impf. 1 c.s. (שָׁלַח 1018)-prep.-2 m.p. sf. ***I will lay hands on you***
מִן־הָעֵת הַהִיא prep.-def.art.-n.f.s. (773)-def. art.-demons.adj. f.s. (214) ***from that time***
לֹא־בָאוּ neg.-Qal pf. 3 c.p. (בּוֹא 97) ***they did not come***
בַּשַּׁבָּת prep.-def.art.-n.f.s. (992) ***on the sabbath***

13:22

וָאֹמְרָה consec.-Qal impf. 1 c.s. (אָמַר 55) ***and I commanded***
לַלְוִיִּם prep.-def.art.-adj. gent. m.p. (532) ***the Levites***
אֲשֶׁר יִהְיוּ מִטַּהֲרִים rel. (81)-Qal impf. 3 m.p. (224 הָיָה)-Hith. ptc. m.p. (טָהֵר 372) ***that they should purify themselves***
וּבָאִים conj.-Qal act.ptc. m.p. (בּוֹא 97) ***and come***
שֹׁמְרִים הַשְּׁעָרִים Qal act.ptc. m.p. (שָׁמַר 1036) -def.art.-n.m.p. (1044) ***and guard the gates***
לְקַדֵּשׁ prep.-Pi. inf.cstr. (קָדַשׁ 872) ***to keep holy***

אֶת־יוֹם הַשַּׁבָּת dir.obj.-n.m.s. cstr. (398)-def. art.-n.f.s. (992) *the sabbath day*
גַּם־זֹאת adv. (168)-demons.adj. f.s. (260) *this also*
זָכְרָה־לִּי Qal impv. 2 m.s. (זָכַר 269)-prep.-1 c.s. sf. *remember in my favor*
אֱלֹהַי n.m.p.-1 c.s. sf. (43) *O my God*
וְחוּסָה עָלַי conj.-Qal impv. 2 m.s.-vol.he (חוּס 299)-prep.-1 c.s. sf. *and spare me*
כְּרֹב חַסְדֶּךָ prep.-n.m.s. cstr. (913)-n.m.s.-2 m.s. sf. (338) *according to the greatness of thy steadfast love*

13:23

גַּם בַּיָּמִים הָהֵם adv. (168)-prep.-def.art.-n.m.p. (398)-def.art.-demons.adj. m.s. (241) *in those days also*
רָאִיתִי Qal pf. 1 c.s. (רָאָה 906) *I saw*
אֶת־הַיְּהוּדִים dir.obj.-def.art.-adj. gent. m.p. (I 397) *the Jews*
הֹשִׁיבוּ Hi. pf. 3 c.p. (יָשַׁב 442) *who had married*
נָשִׁים n.f.p. (61) *women*
אַשְׁדֳּודִיּוֹת adj. gent. f.p. (78) *of Ashdod*
עַמֳּונִיּוֹת adj. gent. f.p. (770) *Ammon*
מוֹאֲבִיּוֹת adj. gent. f.p. (555) *and Moab*

13:24

וּבְנֵיהֶם חֲצִי conj.-n.m.p.-3 m.p. (119)-n.m.s. (345) *and half of their children*
מְדַבֵּר Pi. ptc. (דָּבַר 180) *spoke*
אַשְׁדּוֹדִית adv. (78; GK 2w) *the language of Ashdod*
וְאֵינָם מַכִּירִים conj.-neg.-3 m.p. sf. (II 34)-Hi. ptc. m.p. (נָכַר 647) *and none could recognize*
לְדַבֵּר יְהוּדִית prep.-Pi. inf.cstr. (דָּבַר 180)-adj. gent. f. (I 397; GK 2a) *to speak the language of Judah*
וְכִלְשׁוֹן עַם וָעָם conj.-prep.-n.f.s. cstr. (546) -n.m.s. (I 766)-conj.-v.supra paus. *but the language of each people*

13:25

וָאָרִיב עִמָּם consec.-Qal impf. 1 c.s. (רִיב 936) -prep.-3 m.p. sf. (767) *and I contended with them*
וָאֲקַלְלֵם consec.-Pi. impf. 1 c.s.-3 m.p. sf. (קָלַל 886) *and cursed them*
וָאַכֶּה מֵהֶם consec.-Hi. impf. 1 c.s. (נָכָה 645) -prep.-3 m.p.sf. *and beat some of them*
אֲנָשִׁים n.f.p. (61) *women*
וָאֶמְרְטֵם consec.-Qal impf. 1 c.s.-3 m.p. sf. (מָרַט 598) *and pulled out their hair*
וָאַשְׁבִּיעֵם consec.-Hi. impf. 1 c.s.-3 m.p. sf. (שָׁבַע 989) *and I made them take oath*
בֵּאלֹהִים prep.-n.m.p. (43) *by God*
אִם־תִּתְּנוּ hypoth.part. (49)-Qal impf. 2 m.p. (נָתַן 678) *you shall not give*
בְנֹתֵיכֶם n.f.p.-2 m.p. sf. (I 123) *your daughters*
לִבְנֵיהֶם prep.-n.m.p.-3 m.p. sf. (119) *to their sons*
וְאִם־תִּשְׂאוּ conj.-v.supra-Qal impf. 2 m.p. (נָשָׂא 669) *or you shall not take*
מִבְּנֹתֵיהֶם prep.-n.f.p.-3 m.p. sf. (I 123) *of their daughters*
לִבְנֵיכֶם prep.-n.m.p.-2 m.p. sf. (119) *for your sons*
וְלָכֶם conj.-prep.-2 m.p. sf. *or for yourselves*

13:26

הֲלוֹא עַל־אֵלֶּה interr.part.-neg.-prep.-demons. adj. c.p. (41) *did not on account of these*
חָטָא־שְׁלֹמֹה Qal pf. 3 m.s. (306)-pr.n. (1024) *Solomon sin*
מֶלֶךְ יִשְׂרָאֵל n.m.s. cstr. (I 572)-pr.n. (975) *king of Israel*
וּבַגּוֹיִם הָרַבִּים conj.-prep.-def.art.-n.m.p. (156) -def.art.-adj. m.p. (I 912) *among the many nations*
לֹא־הָיָה neg.-Qal pf. 3 m.s. (224) *there was not*
מֶלֶךְ n.m.s. (I 572) *a king*
כָּמֹהוּ adv.-3 m.s. sf. (455) *like him*
וְאָהוּב conj.-Qal pass.ptc. (אָהַב 12) *beloved*
לֵאלֹהָיו prep.-n.m.p.-3 m.s. sf. (43) *by his God*
הָיָה v.supra *he was*
וַיִּתְּנֵהוּ אֱלֹהִים consec.-Qal impf. 3 m.s.-3 m.s. sf. (נָתַן 678)-n.m.p. (43) *and God made him*
מֶלֶךְ n.m.s. (I 572) *king*
עַל־כָּל־יִשְׂרָאֵל prep.-n.m.s. cstr. (481)-pr.n. (975) *over all Israel*
גַּם־אוֹתוֹ הֶחֱטִיאוּ adv. (168)-dir.obj.-3 m.s. sf.-Hi. pf. 3 c.p. (חָטָא 306) *nevertheless made even him to sin*
הַנָּשִׁים הַנָּכְרִיּוֹת def.art.-n.f.p. (61)-def.art.-adj. f.p. (648) *foreign women*

13:27

וְלָכֶם הֲנִשְׁמַע conj.-prep.-2 m.p. sf.-interr.part. -Qal impf. 1 c.p. (שָׁמַע 1033) *shall we then listen to you*
לַעֲשֹׂת prep.-Qal inf.cstr. (עָשָׂה I 793) *and do*
אֵת כָּל־הָרָעָה הַגְּדוֹלָה הַזֹּאת dir.obj.-n.m.s. cstr. (481)-def.art.-n.f.s. (949)-def.art.-adj. f.s. (152)-def.art.-demons.adj. f.s. (260) *all this great evil*

לִמְעֹל בֵּאלֹהֵינוּ prep.-Qal inf.cstr. (מָעַל 591) -prep.-n.m.p.-1 c.p. sf. (43) *and act treacherously against our God*

לְהֹשִׁיב prep.-Hi. inf.cstr. (יָשַׁב 442) *by marrying*

נָשִׁים נָכְרִיּוֹת n.f.p. (61)-adj. f.p. (648) *foreign women*

13:28

וּמִבְּנֵי יוֹיָדָע conj.-prep.-n.m.p. cstr. (119)-pr.n. (220) *and one of the sons of Jehoiada*

בֶּן־אֶלְיָשִׁיב n.m.s. cstr. (119)-pr.n. (46) *the son of Eliashib*

הַכֹּהֵן הַגָּדוֹל def.art.-n.m.s. (463)-def.art.-adj. m.s. (152) *the high priest*

חָתָן n.m.s. (368) *the son-in-law*

לְסַנְבַלַּט prep.-pr.n. (702) *of Sanballat*

הַחֹרֹנִי def.art.-adj. gent. (111) *the Horonite*

וָאַבְרִיחֵהוּ consec.-Hi. impf. 1 c.s.-3 m.s. sf. (בָּרַח 137) *therefore I chased him*

מֵעָלָי prep.-prep.-1 c.s. sf. paus. *from me*

13:29

זָכְרָה לָהֶם Qal impv. 2 m.s.-vol.he (זָכַר 269) -prep.-3 m.p. sf. *remember them*

אֱלֹהָי n.m.p.-1 c.s. sf. paus. (43) *O my God*

עַל גָּאֳלֵי הַכְּהֻנָּה prep.-n.m.p. cstr. (146)-def.art. -n.f.s. (464) *because they have defiled the priesthood*

וּבְרִית הַכְּהֻנָּה conj.-n.f.s. cstr. (136)-v.supra *and the covenant of the priesthood*

וְהַלְוִיִּם conj.-def.art.-adj. gent. m.p. (532) *and the Levites*

13:30

וְטִהַרְתִּים conj.-Pi. pf. 1 c.s.-3 m.p. sf. (טָהֵר 372) *thus I cleansed them*

מִכָּל־נֵכָר prep.-n.m.s. cstr. (481)-n.m.s. (648) *from everything foreign*

וָאַעֲמִידָה consec.-Hi. impf. 1 c.s. (עָמַד 763) *and I established*

מִשְׁמָרוֹת n.f.p. (1038) *the duties*

לַכֹּהֲנִים prep.-def.art.-n.m.p. (463) *of the priests*

וְלַלְוִיִּם conj.-prep.-def.art.-adj. gent. m.p. (532) *and Levites*

אִישׁ בִּמְלַאכְתּוֹ n.m.s. (35)-prep.-n.f.s.-3 m.s. sf. (521) *each in his work*

13:31

וּלְקֻרְבַּן הָעֵצִים conj.-prep.-n.m.s. cstr. (898)-def. art.-n.m.p. (781) *and for the wood offering*

בְּעִתִּים מְזֻמָּנוֹת prep.-n.f.p. (773)-Pu. ptc. f.p. (273) *at appointed times*

וְלַבִּכּוּרִים conj.-prep.-def.art.-n.m.p. (114) *and for the first fruits*

זָכְרָה־לִּי Qal impv. 2 m.s.-vol.he (זָכַר 269) -prep.-1 c.s. sf. *remember me*

אֱלֹהַי n.m.p.-1 c.s. sf. (43) *O my God*

לְטוֹבָה prep.-n.f.s. (375) *for good*

Esther

1:1

וַיְהִי consec.-Qal impf. 3 m.s. (הָיָה 224) *and it was*

בִּימֵי אֲחַשְׁוֵרוֹשׁ prep.-n.m.p. cstr. (398)-pr.n. (31) *in the days of Ahasuerus*

הוּא אֲחַשְׁוֵרוֹשׁ pers.pr. 3 m.s. (214)-v.supra *he was Ahasuerus*

הַמֹּלֵךְ def.art.-Qal act.ptc. (מָלַךְ 573) *who reigned*

מֵהֹדּוּ prep.-pr.n. (213) *from India*

וְעַד־כּוּשׁ conj.-prep. (III 723)-pr.n. (I 468) *to Ethiopia (Cush)*

שֶׁבַע וְעֶשְׂרִים num. (I 987)-conj.-num. p. (797) *and twenty-seven*

וּמֵאָה conj.-n.f.s. (547) *and one hundred*

מְדִינָה n.f.s. (193) *provinces*

1:2

בַּיָּמִים הָהֵם prep.-def.art.-n.m.p. (398)-def.art.-demons.adj. m.p. (241) *in those days*

כְּשֶׁבֶת הַמֶּלֶךְ prep.-Qal inf.cstr. (יָשַׁב 442)-def.art.-n.m.s. (I 572) *when King ... sat*

אֲחַשְׁוֵרוֹשׁ pr.n. (31) *Ahasuerus*

עַל כִּסֵּא prep.-n.m.s. cstr. (490) *on the throne of*

מַלְכוּתוֹ n.f.s.-3 m.s. sf. (574) *his kingdom*

אֲשֶׁר בְּשׁוּשַׁן rel. (81)-prep.-pr.n. (1004) *in Susa*

הַבִּירָה def.art.-n.f.s. (108) *the capital*

1:3

בִּשְׁנַת שָׁלוֹשׁ prep.-n.f.s. cstr. (1040)-num. (1025) *in the third year*

לְמָלְכוֹ prep.-Qal inf.cstr.-3 m.s. sf. (מָלַךְ II 573) *of his reign*

עָשָׂה מִשְׁתֶּה Qal pf. 3 m.s. (I 793)-n.m.s. (1059) *he gave a banquet*

לְכָל־שָׂרָיו prep.-n.m.s. cstr. (481)-n.m.p.-3 m.s. sf. (978) *for all his princes*

וַעֲבָדָיו conj.-n.m.p.-3 m.s. sf. (713) *and servants*

חֵיל פָּרַס n.m.s. cstr. (298)-pr.n. (828) *the army of Persia*

וּמָדַי conj.-pr.n. (552) *and Media*

הַפַּרְתְּמִים def.art.-n.m.p. (832) *the nobles*

וְשָׂרֵי הַמְּדִינוֹת conj.-n.m.p. cstr. (978)-def.art.-n.f.p. (193) *and governors of the provinces*

לְפָנָיו prep.-n.m.p.-3 m.s. sf. (815) *being before him*

1:4

בְּהַרְאֹתוֹ prep.-Hi. inf.cstr.-3 m.s. sf. (רָאָה 906) *while he showed*

אֶת־עֹשֶׁר dir.obj.-n.m.s. cstr. (799) *the riches of*

כְּבוֹד מַלְכוּתוֹ n.m.s. cstr. (458)-n.f.s.-3 m.s. sf. (574) *his royal glory*

וְאֶת־יְקָר conj.-dir.obj.-n.m.s. (430; GK 93ww) *and the splendor*

תִּפְאֶרֶת גְּדוּלָּתוֹ n.f.s. cstr. (802)-n.f.s.-3 m.s. sf. (153) *and pomp of his majesty*

יָמִים רַבִּים n.m.p. (398)-adj. m.p. (I 912) *for many days*

שְׁמוֹנִים num. p. (1033) *eighty*

וּמְאַת conj.-n.f.s. cstr. (547) *and a hundred of*

יוֹם n.m.s. (398) *days*

1:5

וּבִמְלוֹאת conj.-prep.-Qal inf.cstr. (מָלֵא 569; GK 74h) *and when were completed*

הַיָּמִים הָאֵלֶּה def.art.-n.m.p. (398)-def.art. -demons.adj. c.p. (41) *these days*

עָשָׂה הַמֶּלֶךְ Qal pf. 3 m.s. (I 793)-def.art.-n.m.s. (I 572) *the king gave*

לְכָל־הָעָם prep.-n.m.s. cstr. (481)-def.art.-n.m.s. (I 766) *for all the people*

הַנִּמְצְאִים def.art.-Ni. ptc. m.p. (מָצָא 592) *present*

בְּשׁוּשַׁן prep.-pr.n. (II 1004) *in Susa*

הַבִּירָה def.art.-n.f.s. (108) *the capital*

לְמִגָּדוֹל וְעַד־קָטָן prep.-prep.-adj. m.s. (152)-conj. -prep.-adj. m.s. (I 881) *both great and small*

מִשְׁתֶּה n.m.s. (1059) *a banquet*

שִׁבְעַת יָמִים num. f. cstr. (I 987)-n.m.p. (398) *seven days*

בַּחֲצַר prep.-n.m.s. cstr. (I 346) *in the court of*

גִּנַּת n.f.s. cstr. (171) *the garden of*

בִּיתַן הַמֶּלֶךְ n.m.s. cstr. (113)-def.art.-n.m.s. (I 572) *the king's palace*

1:6

חוּר כַּרְפַּס n.m.s. cstr. (I 301)-n.m.s. (502) *white stuff of fine linen (?)*

וּתְכֵלֶת אָחוּז conj.-n.f.s. (1067)-Qal pass. ptc. (28) *and blue hangings caught up*

בְּחַבְלֵי־בוּץ prep.-n.m.p. cstr. (286)-n.m.s. (101) *with cords of byssus*

וְאַרְגָּמָן conj.-n.m.s. (71) *and purple*

עַל־גְּלִילֵי כֶסֶף prep.-n.m.p. cstr. (II 165)-n.m.s. (494) *to silver rods*

וְעַמּוּדֵי שֵׁשׁ conj.-n.m.p. cstr. (765)-n.m.s. (II 1010) *and marble pillars*

מִטּוֹת זָהָב n.f.p. cstr. (641)-n.m.s. (262) *couches of gold*

וָכֶסֶף conj.-n.m.s. (494) *and silver*

עַל רִצְפַת prep.-n.f.s. cstr. (954) *on a pavement of*

בַּהַט־וָשֵׁשׁ n.m.s. (96)-conj.-n.m.s. (II 1010) *porphyry and marble*

וְדַר conj.-n.m.s. (204) *pearl*

וְסֹחָרֶת conj.-n.f.s. paus. (695) *and precious stones*

1:7

וְהַשְׁקוֹת conj.-Hi. inf.cstr. (שָׁקָה 1052) *and drinks were served*

בִּכְלֵי זָהָב prep.-n.m.p. cstr. (479)-n.m.s. (262) *in golden goblets*

וְכֵלִים מִכֵּלִים שׁוֹנִים conj.-n.m.p. (479)-prep. -v.supra-Qal act.ptc. m.p. (שָׁנָה I 1039) *goblets of different kinds*

וְיֵין מַלְכוּת conj.-n.m.s. cstr. (406)-n.f.s. (574) *and the royal wine*

רָב adj. m.s. (I 912) *there was much*

כְּיַד הַמֶּלֶךְ prep.-n.f.s. cstr. (388)-def.art.-n.m.s. (I 572) *according to the bounty of the king*

1:8

וְהַשְּׁתִיָּה conj.-def.art.-n.f.s. (1059) *and drinking*

כַדָּת prep.-def.art.-n.f.s. (206) *according to the law*

אֵין אֹנֵס neg. (II 34)-Qal act.ptc. (אָנַס 60) *no one was compelled*

כִּי־כֵן conj. (471)-adv. (485) *for thus*

יִסַּד הַמֶּלֶךְ Pi. pf. 3 m.s. (יָסַד 413)-def.art.-n.m.s. (I 572) *the king had given orders*

עַל כָּל־רַב prep.-n.m.s. cstr. (481)-n.m.s. cstr. (II 913) *to all the officials of*

בֵּיתוֹ n.m.s.-3 m.s. sf. (108) *his palace*

לַעֲשׂוֹת prep.-Qal inf.cstr. (עָשָׂה I 793) *to do*

כִּרְצוֹן prep.-n.m.s. cstr. (953) *according to the desire of*

אִישׁ־וָאִישׁ n.m.s. (35)-conj.-v.supra *every man*

1:9

גַּם וַשְׁתִּי adv. (168)-pr.n. (255) *also Vashti*

הַמַּלְכָּה def.art.-n.f.s. (573) *the queen*

עָשְׂתָה מִשְׁתֵּה Qal pf. 3 f.s. (עָשָׂה I 793)-n.m.s. cstr. (1059) *gave a banquet for*

נָשִׁים n.f.p. (61) *the women*

בֵּית הַמַּלְכוּת n.m.s. cstr. (108)-def.art.-n.f.s. (574) *in the palace of the kingdom*

אֲשֶׁר לַמֶּלֶךְ rel. (81)-prep.-def.art.-n.m.s. (I 572) *which belonged to King*

אֲחַשְׁוֵרוֹשׁ pr.n. (31) *Ahasuerus*

1:10

בַּיּוֹם הַשְּׁבִיעִי prep.-def.art.-n.m.s. (398)-def.art. -num. ord. (988) *on the seventh day*

בְּטוֹב prep.-Qal inf.cstr. (טוֹב I 373) *when was merry*
לֵב־הַמֶּלֶךְ n.m.s. cstr. (524)-def.art.-n.m.s. (I 572) *the heart of the king*
בַּיָּיִן prep.-def.art.-n.m.s. paus. (406) *with wine*
אָמַר Qal pf. 3 m.s. (55) *he commanded*
לִמְהוּמָן prep.-pr.n. (54) *Mehuman*
בִּזְּתָא pr.n. (103) *Biztha*
חַרְבוֹנָא pr.n. (353) *Harbona*
בִּגְתָא pr.n. (94) *Bigtha*
וַאֲבַגְתָא conj.-pr.n. (1) *and Abagtha*
זֵתַר pr.n. (285) *Zethar*
וְכַרְכַּס conj.-pr.n. (501) *and Carkas*
שִׁבְעַת הַסָּרִיסִים num. f. cstr. (I 987)-dir.obj. -n.m.p. (710) *the seven eunuchs*
הַמְשָׁרְתִים def.art.-Pi. ptc. m.p. (שָׁרַת 1058) *who served*
אֶת־פְּנֵי dir.obj.-n.m.p. cstr. (815) *in the presence of*
הַמֶּלֶךְ אֲחַשְׁוֵרוֹשׁ def.art.-n.m.s. (I 572)-pr.n. (31) *King Ahasuerus*

1:11

לְהָבִיא prep.-Hi. inf.cstr. (בּוֹא 97) *to bring*
אֶת־וַשְׁתִּי הַמַּלְכָּה dir.obj.-pr.n. (255)-def.art. -n.f.s. (573) *Queen Vashti*
לִפְנֵי הַמֶּלֶךְ prep.-n.m.p. cstr. (815)-def.art.-n.m.s. (I 572) *before the king*
בְּכֶתֶר מַלְכוּת prep.-n.m.s. cstr. (509)-n.f.s. (574) *with her royal crown*
לְהַרְאוֹת prep.-Hi. inf.cstr. (רָאָה 906) *to show*
הָעַמִּים וְהַשָּׂרִים def.art.-n.m.p. (I 766)-conj. -def.art.-n.m.p. (978) *the peoples and the princes*
אֶת־יָפְיָהּ dir.obj.-n.m.s.-3 f.s. sf. (421) *her beauty*
כִּי־טוֹבַת conj. (471)-adj. f.s. cstr. (II 373) *for was fair of*
מַרְאֶה הִיא n.m.s. (909)-pers.pr. 3 f.s. (214) *appearance she*

1:12

וַתְּמָאֵן consec.-Pi. impf. 3 f.s. (מָאֵן 549) *but refused*
הַמַּלְכָּה וַשְׁתִּי def.art.-n.f.s. (573)-pr.n. (255) *Queen Vashti*
לָבוֹא prep.-Qal inf.cstr. (בּוֹא 97) *to come*
בִּדְבַר הַמֶּלֶךְ prep.-n.m.s. cstr. (182)-def.art.-n.m.s. (I 572) *at the king's command*
אֲשֶׁר בְּיַד הַסָּרִיסִים rel. (81)-prep.-n.f.s. cstr. (388)-def.art.-n.m.p. (710) *by the eunuchs*
וַיִּקְצֹף הַמֶּלֶךְ consec.-Qal impf. 3 m.s. (קָצַף 893)-v.supra *at this the king was ... enraged*
מְאֹד adv. (547) *very*
וַחֲמָתוֹ conj.-n.f.s.-3 m.s. sf. (404) *and his anger*
בָּעֲרָה בוֹ Qal pf. 3 f.s. (בָּעַר 128)-prep.-3 m.s. sf. *burned within him*

1:13

וַיֹּאמֶר הַמֶּלֶךְ consec.-Qal impf. 3 m.s. (55)-def. art.-n.m.s. (I 572) *then the king said*
לַחֲכָמִים prep.-def.art.-adj. m.p. (314) *to the wise men*
יֹדְעֵי הָעִתִּים Qal act.ptc. m.p. cstr. (יָדַע 393) -def.art.-n.f.p. (773) *who knew the times*
כִּי־כֵן conj. (471)-adv. (485) *for it was thus*
דְּבַר הַמֶּלֶךְ n.m.s. cstr. (182)-def.art.-n.m.s. (I 572) *the king's procedure*
לִפְנֵי כָּל־יֹדְעֵי prep.-n.m.p. cstr. (815)-n.m.s. cstr. (481)-v.supra *toward all who were versed in*
דָּת וָדִין n.f.s. (206)-conj.-n.m.s. (192) *law and judgment*

1:14

הַקָּרֹב אֵלָיו def.art.-adj. m.s. (898)-prep.-3 m.s. sf. *the men next to him*
כַּרְשְׁנָא pr.n. (503) *Carshena*
שֵׁתָר pr.n. (1060) *Shethar*
אַדְמָתָא pr.n. (10) *Admatha*
תַרְשִׁישׁ pr.n. (II 1076) *Tarshish*
מֶרֶס pr.n. (599) *Meres*
מַרְסְנָא pr.n. (599) *Marsena*
מְמוּכָן pr.n. (577) *Memucan*
שִׁבְעַת שָׂרֵי n.f.s. cstr. (I 987)-n.m.p. cstr. (978) *seven princes of*
פָּרַס וּמָדַי pr.n. (828)-conj.-pr.n. (552) *Persia and Media*
רֹאֵי פְּנֵי הַמֶּלֶךְ Qal act.ptc. m.p. cstr. (רָאָה 906)-n.m.p. cstr. (815)-def.art.-n.m.s. (I 572) *who saw the king's face*
הַיֹּשְׁבִים רִאשֹׁנָה def.art.-Qal act.ptc. m.p. (יָשַׁב 442)-adv. f. (911) *and who sat first*
בַּמַּלְכוּת prep.-def.art.-n.f.s. (574) *in the kingdom*

1:15

כְּדָת prep.-n.f.s. (206) *according to the law*
מַה־לַּעֲשׂוֹת interr. (552)-prep.-Qal inf.cstr. (I 793 עָשָׂה) *what is to be done*
בַּמַּלְכָּה וַשְׁתִּי prep.-def.art.-n.f.s. (573)-pr.n. (255) *to Queen Vashti*
עַל אֲשֶׁר לֹא־עָשְׂתָה prep.-rel. (81)-neg.-Qal pf. 3 f.s. (עָשָׂה I 793) *because she has not performed*
אֶת־מַאֲמַר dir.obj.-n.m.s. cstr. (57) *the command of*

הַמֶּלֶךְ אֲחַשְׁוֵרוֹשׁ def.art.-n.m.s. (I 572)-pr.n. (31) *King Ahasuerus*
בְּיַד הַסָּרִיסִים prep.-n.f.s. cstr. (388)-def.art. -n.m.p. (710) *by the eunuchs*

1:16

וַיֹּאמֶר מְומֻכָן consec.-Qal impf. 3 m.s. (55)-pr.n. (577) *then Memucan said*
לִפְנֵי הַמֶּלֶךְ prep.-n.m.p. cstr. (815)-def.art.-n.m.s. (I 572) *in presence of the king*
וְהַשָּׂרִים conj.-def.art.-n.m.p. (978) *and the princes*
לֹא עַל־הַמֶּלֶךְ לְבַדּוֹ neg.-prep.-v.supra-prep. -n.m.s.-3 m.s. sf. (II 94) *not only to the king*
עָוְתָה Qal pf. 3 f.s. (עָוָה 731) *has done wrong*
וַשְׁתִּי הַמַּלְכָּה pr.n. (255)-def.art.-n.f.s. (573) *Queen Vashti*
כִּי עַל־כָּל־הַשָּׂרִים conj. (471)-prep.-n.m.s. cstr. (481)-def.art.-n.m.p. (978) *but also to all the princes*
וְעַל־כָּל־הָעַמִּים pr.n.prep.-v.supra-def.art.-n.m.p. (I 766) *and all the peoples*
אֲשֶׁר בְּכָל־מְדִינוֹת rel. (81)-prep.-v.supra-n.f.p. cstr. (193) *who are in all the provinces of*
הַמֶּלֶךְ אֲחַשְׁוֵרוֹשׁ v.supra-pr.n. (31) *King Ahasuerus*

1:17

כִּי־יֵצֵא conj. (471)-Qal impf. 3 m.s. (יָצָא 422) *for will be made known*
דְבַר־הַמַּלְכָּה n.m.s. cstr. (182)-def.art.-n.f.s. (573) *this deed of the queen*
עַל־כָּל־הַנָּשִׁים prep.-n.m.s. cstr. (481)-def.art. -n.f.p. (61) *to all women*
לְהַבְזוֹת prep.-Hi. inf.cstr. (בָּזָה 102) *causing them to look with contempt*
בַּעְלֵיהֶן n.m.p.-3 f.p. sf. (127; GK 93m) *upon their husbands*
בְּעֵינֵיהֶן prep.-n.f.p.-3 f.p. sf. (744) *in their eyes*
בְּאָמְרָם prep.-Qal inf.cstr.-3 m.p. sf. (אָמַר 55) *since they will say*
הַמֶּלֶךְ אֲחַשְׁוֵרוֹשׁ def.art.-n.m.s. (I 572)-pr.n. (31) *King Ahasuerus*
אָמַר לְהָבִיא Qal pf. 3 m.s. (55)-prep.-Hi. inf.cstr. (בּוֹא 97) *commanded to be brought*
אֶת־וַשְׁתִּי הַמַּלְכָּה dir.obj.-pr.n. (255)-def.art. -n.f.s. (573) *Queen Vashti*
לְפָנָיו prep.-n.m.p.-3 m.s. sf. (815) *before him*
וְלֹא־בָאָה conj.-neg.-Qal pf. 3 f.s. (בּוֹא 97) *and she did not come*

1:18

וְהַיּוֹם הַזֶּה conj.-def.art.-n.m.s. (398)-def.art. -demons.adj. m.s. (260) *this very day*
תֹּאמַרְנָה Qal impf. 3 f.p. (אָמַר 55) *will be telling*
שָׂרוֹת n.f.p. cstr. (I 979) *the ladies of*
פָּרַס־וּמָדַי pr.n. (828)-conj.-pr.n. (552) *Persia and Media*
אֲשֶׁר שָׁמְעוּ rel. (81)-Qal pf. 3 c.p. (שָׁמַע 1033) *who have heard*
אֶת־דְּבַר הַמַּלְכָּה dir.obj.-n.m.s. cstr. (182)-def. art.-n.f.s. (573) *of the queen's behavior*
לְכֹל שָׂרֵי הַמֶּלֶךְ prep.-n.m.s. cstr. (481)-n.m.p. cstr. (978)-def.art.-n.m.s. (I 572) *to all the king's princes*
וּכְדַי conj.-prep.-subst. (191) *and there will be in plenty*
בִּזָּיוֹן n.m.s. (102) *contempt*
וָקָצֶף conj.-n.m.s. (I 893) *and wrath*

1:19

אִם־עַל־הַמֶּלֶךְ hypoth.part. (49)-prep.-def.art. -n.m.s. (I 572) *if unto the king*
טוֹב adj. m.s. (II 373) *it please*
יֵצֵא Qal impf. 3 m.s. (יָצָא 422) *let go forth*
דְבַר־מַלְכוּת n.m.s. cstr. (182)-n.f.s. (574) *a royal order*
מִלְּפָנָיו prep.-prep.-n.m.p.-3 m.s. sf. (815) *from him*
וְיִכָּתֵב conj.-Ni. impf. 3 m.s. vol. (כָּתַב 507) *and let it be written*
בְּדָתֵי prep.-n.f.p. cstr. (206) *among the laws of*
פָרַס־וּמָדַי pr.n. (828)-conj.-pr.n. (552) *the Persians and the Medes*
וְלֹא יַעֲבוֹר conj.-neg.-Qal impf. 3 m.s. (עָבַר 716) *so that it may not be altered*
אֲשֶׁר לֹא־תָבוֹא rel. (81)-neg.-Qal impf. 3 f.s. (97 בּוֹא) *that ... is to come no more*
וַשְׁתִּי pr.n. (255) *Vashti*
לִפְנֵי הַמֶּלֶךְ prep.-n.m.p. cstr. (815)-def.art.-n.m.s. (I 572) *before King*
אֲחַשְׁוֵרוֹשׁ pr.n. (31) *Ahasuerus*
וּמַלְכוּתָהּ conj.-n.f.s.-3 f.s. sf. (574) *and her royal position*
יִתֵּן הַמֶּלֶךְ Qal impf. 3 m.s. (נָתַן 678)-def.art. -n.m.s. (I 572) *let the king give*
לִרְעוּתָהּ prep.-n.f.s.-3 f.s. sf. (I 946) *to another than she*
הַטּוֹבָה מִמֶּנָּה def.art.-adj. f.s. (II 373)-prep.-3 f.s. sf. *who is better than she*

1:20

וְנִשְׁמַע conj.-Ni. pf. 3 m.s. (שָׁמַע 1033) *so let be heard*

פִּתְגָם הַמֶּלֶךְ n.m.s. cstr. (834)-def.art.-n.m.s. (I 572) *the decree by the king*

אֲשֶׁר־יַעֲשֶׂה rel. (81)-Qal impf. 3 m.s. (עָשָׂה I 793) *which he will make*

בְּכָל־מַלְכוּתוֹ prep.-n.m.s. cstr. (481)-n.f.s.-3 m.s. sf. (574) *throughout all his kingdom*

כִּי רַבָּה הִיא conj. (471)-adj. f.s. (I 912)-pers.pr. 3 f.s. (214) *vast as it is*

וְכָל־הַנָּשִׁים conj.-v.supra-def.art.-n.f.p. (61) *and all women*

יִתְּנוּ יְקָר Qal impf. 3 m.p. (נָתַן 678)-adj. m.s. (429) *will give honor*

לְבַעְלֵיהֶן prep.-n.m.p.-3 f.p. sf. (127; GK 93m) *to their husbands*

לְמִגָּדוֹל וְעַד־קָטָן prep.-prep.-adj. m.s. (152)-conj. -prep. (III 723)-adj. m.s. (881) *high and low*

1:21

וַיִּיטַב הַדָּבָר consec.-Qal impf. 3 m.s. (יָטַב 405) -def.art.-n.m.s. (182) *this advice pleased (was good)*

בְּעֵינֵי הַמֶּלֶךְ prep.-n.f.p. cstr. (744)-def.art.-n.m.s. (I 572) *in the eyes of the king*

וְהַשָּׂרִים conj.-def.art.-n.m.p. (978) *and the princes*

וַיַּעַשׂ הַמֶּלֶךְ consec.-Qal impf. 3 m.s. (עָשָׂה I 793)-v.supra *and the king did*

כִּדְבַר מְמוּכָן prep.-n.m.s. cstr. (182)-pr.n. (577) *as Memucan proposed*

1:22

וַיִּשְׁלַח consec.-Qal impf. 3 m.s. (שָׁלַח 1018) *and he sent*

סְפָרִים n.m.p. (706) *letters*

אֶל־כָּל־מְדִינוֹת prep.-n.m.s. cstr. (481)-n.f.p. cstr. (193) *to all the provinces of*

הַמֶּלֶךְ def.art.-n.m.s. (I 572) *the king*

אֶל־מְדִינָה וּמְדִינָה prep.-n.f.s. (193)-conj.-v.supra *to every province*

כִּכְתָבָהּ prep.-n.m.s.-3 f.s. sf. (508) *in its own script*

וְאֶל־עַם וָעָם conj.-prep.-n.m.s. (I 766)-conj. -v.supra *and to every people*

כִּלְשׁוֹנוֹ prep.-n.f.s.-3 m.s. sf. (546) *in its own language*

לִהְיוֹת כָּל־אִישׁ prep.-Qal inf.cstr. (הָיָה 224) -n.m.s. cstr. (481)-n.m.s. (35) *that every man be*

שֹׂרֵר Qal act.ptc. (שָׂרַר 979) *lord*

בְּבֵיתוֹ prep.-n.m.s.-3 m.s. sf. (108) *in his own house*

וּמְדַבֵּר conj.-Pi. ptc. (דָּבַר 180) *and speak*

כִּלְשׁוֹן עַמּוֹ prep.-n.f.s. cstr. (546)-n.m.s.-3 m.s. sf. (766) *according to the language of his people*

2:1

אַחַר הַדְּבָרִים הָאֵלֶּה prep. (29)-def.art.-n.m.p. (182)-def.art.-demons.adj. c.p. (41) *after these things*

כְּשֹׁךְ prep.-Qal inf.cstr. (שָׁכַךְ 1013) *when had abated*

חֲמַת הַמֶּלֶךְ n.f.s. cstr. (404)-def.art.-n.m.s. (I 572) *the anger of King*

אֲחַשְׁוֵרוֹשׁ pr.n. (31) *Ahasuerus*

זָכַר Qal pf. 3 m.s. (269) *he remembered*

אֶת־וַשְׁתִּי dir.obj.-pr.n. (255) *Vashti*

וְאֵת אֲשֶׁר־עָשָׂתָה conj.-dir.obj.-rel. (81)-Qal pf. 3 f.s. paus. (עָשָׂה I 793) *and what she had done*

וְאֵת אֲשֶׁר־נִגְזַר v.supra-v.supra-Ni. pf. 3 m.s. (גָּזַר 160) *and what had been decreed*

עָלֶיהָ prep.-3 f.s. sf. *against her*

2:2

וַיֹּאמְרוּ consec.-Qal impf. 3 m.p. (אָמַר 55) *then said*

נַעֲרֵי־הַמֶּלֶךְ n.m.p. cstr. (654)-def.art.-n.m.s. (I 572) *the king's servants*

מְשָׁרְתָיו Pi. ptc. m.p.-3 m.s. sf. (שָׁרַת 1058) *who attended him*

יְבַקְשׁוּ Pi. impf. 3 m.p. (בָּקַשׁ 134) *let be sought out*

לַמֶּלֶךְ prep.-def.art.-v.supra *for the king*

נְעָרוֹת בְּתוּלוֹת n.f.p. (655)-n.f.p. (143) *young virgins*

טוֹבוֹת מַרְאֶה adj. f.p. cstr. (II 373)-n.m.s. (909) *beautiful*

2:3

וְיַפְקֵד הַמֶּלֶךְ conj.-Hi. impf. 3 m.s. apoc. (פָּקַד 823) *and let the king appoint*

פְּקִידִים n.m.p. (824) *officers*

בְּכָל־מְדִינוֹת prep.-n.m.s. cstr. (481)-n.f.p. cstr. (193) *in all the provinces of*

מַלְכוּתוֹ n.f.s.-3 m.s. sf. (574) *his kingdom*

וְיִקְבְּצוּ conj.-Qal impf. 3 m.p. (קָבַץ 867) *and let be gathered*

אֶת־כָּל־נַעֲרָה־בְתוּלָה dir.obj.-v.supra-n.f.s. (655) -n.f.s. (143) *all the young virgins*

טוֹבַת מַרְאֶה adj. f.s. (II 373)-v.supra *beautiful*

אֶל־שׁוּשַׁן prep.-pr.n. (II 1004) *in Susa*
הַבִּירָה def.art.-n.f.s. (108) *the capital*
אֶל־בֵּית הַנָּשִׁים prep.-n.m.s. cstr. (108)-def.art.-n.f.p. (61) *to the harem*
אֶל־יַד הֵגֶא prep.-n.f.s. cstr. (388)-pr.n. (211) *under custody of Hegai*
סְרִיס הַמֶּלֶךְ n.m.s. cstr. (710)-def.art.-n.m.s. (I 572) *the king's eunuch*
שֹׁמֵר הַנָּשִׁים Qal act.ptc. (1036)-def.art.-v.supra *who is in charge of the women*
וְנָתוֹן conj.-Qal inf.abs. (נָתַן 678) *let be given*
תַּמְרוּקֵיהֶן n.m.p.-3 f.p. sf. (600) *their ointments*

2:4

וְהַנַּעֲרָה conj.-def.art.-n.f.s. (655) *and the maiden*
אֲשֶׁר תִּיטַב rel. (81)-Qal impf. 3 f.s. (יָטַב 405) *who pleases*
בְּעֵינֵי הַמֶּלֶךְ prep.-n.f.p. cstr. (744)-def.art.-n.m.s. (I 572) *in the eyes of the king*
תִּמְלֹךְ Qal impf. 3 f.s. vol. (מָלַךְ 573) *let her reign*
תַּחַת וַשְׁתִּי prep. (1065)-pr.n. (255) *instead of Vashti*
וַיִּיטַב הַדָּבָר consec.-Qal impf. 3 m.s. (יָטַב 405)-def.art.-n.m.s. (182) *this thing pleased*
בְּעֵינֵי הַמֶּלֶךְ v.supra-v.supra *in the eyes of the king*
וַיַּעַשׂ כֵּן consec.-Qal impf. 3 m.s. (עָשָׂה I 793)-adv. (485) *and he did so*

2:5

אִישׁ יְהוּדִי n.m.s. (35)-adj. gent. (I 397) *a Jew*
הָיָה בְּשׁוּשַׁן Qal pf. 3 m.s. (224)-prep.-pr.n. (II 1004) *was in Susa*
הַבִּירָה def.art.-n.f.s. (108) *the capital*
וּשְׁמוֹ מָרְדֳּכַי conj.-n.m.s.-3 m.s. sf. (1027)-pr.n. (598) *whose name was Mordecai*
בֶּן יָאִיר n.m.s. cstr. (119)-pr.n. (22) *the son of Jair*
בֶּן־שִׁמְעִי v.supra-pr.n. (1035) *son of Shimei*
בֶּן־קִישׁ v.supra-pr.n. (885) *son of Kish*
אִישׁ יְמִינִי n.m.s. cstr. (35)-adj. gent. (II 412) *a Benjaminite*

2:6

אֲשֶׁר הָגְלָה rel. (81)-Ho. pf. 3 m.s. (גָּלָה 162) *who had been carried away*
מִירוּשָׁלַיִם prep.-pr.n. (436) *from Jerusalem*
עִם־הַגֹּלָה prep. (767)-def.art.-n.f.s. (163) *among the captives*
אֲשֶׁר הָגְלְתָה v.supra-Ho. pf. 3 f.s. (גָּלָה 162) *carried away*
עִם יְכָנְיָה v.supra-pr.n. (220) *with Jeconiah*
מֶלֶךְ־יְהוּדָה n.m.s. cstr. (I 572)-pr.n. (397) *king of Judah*
אֲשֶׁר הֶגְלָה v.supra-Hi. pf. 3 m.s. (גָּלָה 162) *whom ... had carried away*
נְבוּכַדְנֶאצַּר pr.n. (613) *Nebuchadnezzar*
מֶלֶךְ בָּבֶל v.supra-pr.n. (93) *king of Babylon*

2:7

וַיְהִי אֹמֵן consec.-Qal impf. 3 m.s. (הָיָה 224)-Qal act.ptc. (אָמַן I 52) *he had brought up*
אֶת־הֲדַסָּה dir.obj.-pr.n. (213) *Hadassah*
הִיא אֶסְתֵּר pers.pr. 3 f.s. (214)-pr.n. (64) *that is Esther*
בַּת־דֹּדוֹ n.f.s. cstr. (I 123)-n.m.s.-3 m.s. sf. (187) *the daughter of his uncle*
כִּי אֵין לָהּ אָב conj. (471)-neg. (II 34)-prep.-3 f.s. sf.-n.m.s. (3) *for she had neither father*
וָאֵם conj.-n.f.s. (51) *nor mother*
וְהַנַּעֲרָה conj.-def.art.-n.f.s. (655) *the maiden*
יְפַת־תֹּאַר adj. f.s. cstr. (421)-n.m.s. (1061) *beautiful*
וְטוֹבַת מַרְאֶה conj.-adj. f.s. cstr. (II 373)-n.m.s. (909) *and lovely*
וּבְמוֹת אָבִיהָ conj.-prep.-Qal inf.cstr. (מוּת 559)-n.m.s.-3 f.s. sf. (3) *and when her father died*
וְאִמָּהּ conj.-n.f.s.-3 f.s. sf. (51) *and her mother*
לְקָחָהּ מָרְדֳּכַי Qal pf. 3 m.s.-3 f.s. sf. (לָקַח 542)-pr.n. (598) *Mordecai took her*
לוֹ לְבַת prep.-3 m.s. sf.-prep.-n.f.s. (I 123) *as his own daughter*

2:8

וַיְהִי בְּהִשָּׁמַע consec.-Qal impf. 3 m.s. (הָיָה 224)-prep.-Ni. inf.cstr. (שָׁמַע 1033) *so when were proclaimed*
דְּבַר־הַמֶּלֶךְ n.m.s. cstr. (182)-def.art.-n.m.s. (I 572) *the king's order*
וְדָתוֹ conj.-n.f.s.-3 m.s. sf. (206) *and his edict*
וּבְהִקָּבֵץ conj.-prep.-Ni. inf.cstr. (קָבַץ 867) *and when were gathered*
נְעָרוֹת רַבּוֹת n.f.p. (655)-adj. f.p. (I 912) *many maidens*
אֶל־שׁוּשַׁן prep.-pr.n. (II 1004) *in Susa*
הַבִּירָה def.art.-n.f.s. (108) *the capital*
אֶל־יַד הֵגָי prep.-n.f.s. cstr. (388)-pr.n. (211) *in custody of Hegai*
וַתִּלָּקַח אֶסְתֵּר consec.-Ni. impf. 3 f.s. (לָקַח 542)-pr.n. (64) *Esther also was taken*
אֶל־בֵּית הַמֶּלֶךְ prep.-n.m.s. cstr. (108)-def.art.-n.m.s. (I 572) *into the king's palace*

אֶל־יַד הֵגַי v.supra-v.supra-v.supra *in custody of Hegai*
שֹׁמֵר הַנָּשִׁים Qal act.ptc. (1036)-def.art.-n.f.p. (61) *who had charge of the women*

2:9

וַתִּיטַב הַנַּעֲרָה consec.-Qal impf. 3 f.s. (יָטַב 405)-def.art.-n.f.s. (655) *and the maiden pleased*
בְעֵינָיו prep.-n.f.p.-3 m.s. sf. (744) *in his eyes*
וַתִּשָּׂא חֶסֶד לְפָנָיו consec.-Qal impf. 3 f.s. (נָשָׂא 669)-n.m.s. (338)-prep.-n.m.p.-3 m.s. sf. (815) *and won his favor*
וַיְבַהֵל consec.-Pi. impf. 3 m.s. (בָּהַל 96) *and he quickly provided*
אֶת־תַּמְרוּקֶיהָ dir.obj.-n.m.p.-3 f.s. sf. (600) *with her ointments*
וְאֶת־מָנוֹתֶהָ conj.-dir.obj.-n.f.p.-3 f.s. sf. (584) *and her portion of food*
לָתֶת לָהּ prep.-Qal inf.cstr. (נָתַן 678)-prep.-3 f.s. sf. *to give her*
וְאֵת שֶׁבַע הַנְּעָרוֹת conj.-dir.obj.-num. m. cstr. (I 987)-def.art.-n.f.p. (655) *and with seven maids*
הָרְאֻיוֹת def.art.-Qal pass.ptc. f.p. (רָאָה 906; GK 75v) *chosen*
לָתֶת־לָהּ prep.-Qal inf.cstr. (נָתַן 678)-prep.-3 f.s. sf. *to give to her*
מִבֵּית הַמֶּלֶךְ prep.-n.m.s. cstr. (108)-def.art.-n.m.s. (I 572) *from the king's palace*
וַיְשַׁנֶּהָ consec.-Pi. impf. 3 m.s.-3 f.s. sf. (שָׁנָה I 1039) *and assigned her*
וְאֶת־נַעֲרוֹתֶיהָ conj.-dir.obj.-n.f.p.-3 f.s. sf. (655) *and her maids*
לְטוֹב prep.-adj. m.s. cstr. (II 373) *to the best place in*
בֵּית הַנָּשִׁים n.m.s. cstr. (108)-def.art.-n.f.p. (61) *the harem*

2:10

לֹא־הִגִּידָה אֶסְתֵּר neg.-Hi. pf. 3 f.s. (נָגַד 616) -pr.n. (64) *Esther had not made known*
אֶת־עַמָּהּ dir.obj.-n.m.s.-3 f.s. sf. (I 766) *her people*
וְאֶת־מוֹלַדְתָּהּ conj.-dir.obj.-n.f.s.-3 f.s. sf. (409) *or kindred*
כִּי מָרְדֳּכַי conj. (471)-pr.n. (598) *for Mordecai*
צִוָּה עָלֶיהָ Pi. pf. 3 m.s. (צָוָה 845)-prep.-3 f.s. sf. *had charged her*
אֲשֶׁר לֹא־תַגִּיד rel. (81)-neg.-Hi. impf. 3 f.s. (נָגַד 616) *not to make it known*

2:11

וּבְכָל־יוֹם וָיוֹם conj.-prep.-n.m.s. cstr. (481; GK 123c)-n.m.s. (398)-conj.-v.supra *and every day*
מָרְדֳּכַי pr.n. (598) *Mordecai*
מִתְהַלֵּךְ Hith. ptc. (הָלַךְ 229) *walked*
לִפְנֵי חֲצַר prep.-n.m.p. cstr. (815)-n.m.s. cstr. (I 346) *in front of the court of*
בֵּית־הַנָּשִׁים n.m.s. cstr. (108)-def.art.-n.f.p. (61) *the harem*
לָדַעַת prep.-Qal inf.cstr. (יָדַע 393) *to learn*
אֶת־שְׁלוֹם אֶסְתֵּר dir.obj.-n.m.s. cstr. (1022)-pr.n. (64) *the welfare of Esther*
וּמַה־יֵּעָשֶׂה בָּהּ conj.-interr. (552)-Ni. impf. 3 m.s. (עָשָׂה I 793)-prep.-3 f.s. sf. *and what would be done to her*

2:12

וּבְהַגִּיעַ conj.-prep.-Hi. inf.cstr. (נָגַע 619) *now when came*
תֹּר נַעֲרָה n.m.s. cstr. (I 1064)-n.f.s. (655) *the turn for a maiden*
וְנַעֲרָה conj.-n.f.s. (655) *and a maiden*
לָבוֹא אֶל־הַמֶּלֶךְ prep.-Qal inf.cstr. (בּוֹא 97) -prep.-def.art.-n.m.s. (I 572) *to go in to King*
אֲחַשְׁוֵרוֹשׁ pr.n. (31) *Ahasuerus*
מִקֵּץ הֱיוֹת לָהּ prep.-n.m.s. (893)-Qal inf.cstr. (224 הָיָה)-prep.-3 f.s. sf. *after being*
כְּדָת הַנָּשִׁים prep.-n.f.s. cstr. (206)-def.art.-n.f.p. (61) *under the regulations for the women*
שְׁנֵים עָשָׂר חֹדֶשׁ n.m.s. (1040)-num. (797)-n.m.s. (294) *twelve months*
כִּי כֵּן יִמְלְאוּ conj. (471)-adv. (485)-Qal impf. 3 m.p. (מָלֵא 569) *for thus they fulfil*
יְמֵי מְרוּקֵיהֶן n.m.p. cstr. (398)-n.m.p.-3 f.p. sf. (599) *the regular period of their beautifying*
שִׁשָּׁה חֳדָשִׁים num. f. (995)-n.m.p. (I 294) *six months*
בְּשֶׁמֶן הַמֹּר prep.-n.m.s. cstr. (1032)-def.art. -n.m.s. (600) *with oil of myrrh*
וְשִׁשָּׁה חֳדָשִׁים conj.-v.supra-v.supra *and six months*
בַּבְּשָׂמִים prep.-def.art.-n.m.p. (141) *with spices*
וּבְתַמְרוּקֵי הַנָּשִׁים conj.-prep.-n.m.p. cstr. (600) -def.art.-n.f.p. (61) *and ointments for women*

2:13

וּבָזֶה conj.-prep.-demons.adj. (260) *when*
הַנַּעֲרָה def.art.-n.f.s. (655) *the maiden*
בָּאָה אֶל־הַמֶּלֶךְ Qal pf. 3 f.s. (בּוֹא 97)-prep. -def.art.-n.m.s. (I 572) *went in to the king*

אֶת כָּל־אֲשֶׁר תֹּאמַר dir.obj.-n.m.s. (481)-rel. (81)-Qal impf. 3 f.s. (אָמַר 55) *whatever she desired*

יִנָּתֵן לָהּ Ni. impf. 3 m.s. (נָתַן 678)-prep.-3 f.s. sf. *was given to her*

לָבוֹא עִמָּהּ prep.-Qal inf.cstr. (בּוֹא 97)-prep.-3 f.s. sf. (767) *to take with her*

מִבֵּית הַנָּשִׁים prep.-n.m.s. cstr. (108)-def.art.-n.f.p. (61) *from the harem*

עַד־בֵּית הַמֶּלֶךְ prep. (III 723)-v.supra-v.supra *to the king's palace*

2:14

בָּעֶרֶב prep.-def.art.-n.m.s. (787) *in the evening*

הִיא בָאָה pers.pr. 3 f.s. (214)-Qal pf. 3 f.s. (בּוֹא 97) *she went*

וּבַבֹּקֶר conj.-prep.-def.art.-n.m.s. (133) *and in the morning*

הִיא שָׁבָה v.supra-Qal pf. 3 f.s. (שׁוּב 996) *she came back*

אֶל־בֵּית הַנָּשִׁים prep.-n.m.s. cstr. (108)-def. art.-n.f.p. (61) *to the ... harem*

שֵׁנִי num. ord. (1041) *second*

אֶל־יַד שַׁעַשְׁגַז prep.-n.f.s. cstr. (388)-pr.n. (1045) *in custody of Shaashgaz*

סְרִיס הַמֶּלֶךְ n.m.s. cstr. (710)-def.art.-n.m.s. (I 572) *the king's eunuch*

שֹׁמֵר הַפִּילַגְשִׁים Qal act.ptc. (1036)-def.art.-n.f.p. (811) *who was in charge of the concubines*

לֹא־תָבוֹא עוֹד neg.-Qal impf. 3 f.s. (בּוֹא 97) -adv. (728) *she did not go in again*

אֶל־הַמֶּלֶךְ prep.-def.art.-n.m.s. (I 572) *to the king*

כִּי אִם־חָפֵץ בָּהּ conj. (471)-hypoth.part. (49)-Qal pf. 3 m.s. (342)-prep.-3 f.s. sf. *unless ... delighted in her*

הַמֶּלֶךְ v.supra *the king*

וְנִקְרְאָה בְשֵׁם conj.-Ni. pf. 3 f.s. (קָרָא 894)-prep. -n.m.s. (1027) *and she was summoned by name*

2:15

וּבְהַגִּיעַ conj.-prep.-Hi. inf.cstr. (נָגַע 619) *when ... came*

תֹּר־אֶסְתֵּר n.m.s. cstr. (I 1064)-pr.n. (64) *the turn for Esther*

בַּת־אֲבִיחַיִל n.f.s. cstr. (I 123)-pr.n. (4) *the daughter of Abihail*

דֹּד מָרְדֳּכַי n.m.s. cstr. (187)-pr.n. (598) *the uncle of Mordecai*

אֲשֶׁר לָקַח־לוֹ rel. (81)-Qal pf. 3 m.s. (542)-prep. -3 m.s. sf. *who had adopted as his own*

לְבַת prep.-n.f.s. (I 123) *daughter*

לָבוֹא prep.-Qal inf.cstr. (בּוֹא 97) *to go in*

אֶל־הַמֶּלֶךְ prep.-def.art.-n.m.s. (I 572) *to the king*

לֹא בִקְשָׁה דָּבָר neg.-Pi. pf. 3 f.s. (בָּקַשׁ 134)-n.m.s. (182) *she asked for nothing*

כִּי אִם אֶת־אֲשֶׁר conj. (471)-hypoth.part. (49) -dir.obj.-rel. (81) *except what*

יֹאמַר הֵגַי Qal impf. 3 m.s. (אָמַר 55)-pr.n. (211) *Hegai advised*

סְרִיס־הַמֶּלֶךְ n.m.s. cstr. (710)-def.art.-n.m.s. (I 572) *the king's eunuch*

שֹׁמֵר הַנָּשִׁים Qal act.ptc. (1036)-def.art.-n.f.p. (61) *who had charge of the women*

וַתְּהִי אֶסְתֵּר consec.-Qal impf. 3 f.s. (הָיָה 224)-pr.n. (64) *now Esther was*

נֹשֵׂאת חֵן Qal act.ptc. f.s. cstr. (נָשָׂא 669)-n.m.s. (336) *finding favor*

בְּעֵינֵי כָּל־רֹאֶיהָ prep.-n.f.p. cstr. (744)-n.m.s. cstr. (481)-Qal act.ptc. m.p.-3 f.s. sf. (רָאָה 906) *in the eyes of all who saw her*

2:16

וַתִּלָּקַח אֶסְתֵּר consec.-Ni. impf. 3 f.s. (לָקַח 542)-pr.n. (64) *and when Esther was taken*

אֶל־הַמֶּלֶךְ prep.-def.art.-n.m.s. (I 572) *to King*

אֲחַשְׁוֵרוֹשׁ pr.n. (31) *Ahasuerus*

אֶל־בֵּית מַלְכוּתוֹ prep.-n.m.s. cstr. (108)-n.f.s.-3 m.s. sf. (574) *into his royal palace*

בַּחֹדֶשׁ הָעֲשִׂירִי prep.-def.art.-n.m.s. (I 294)-def. art.-num. ord. (798) *in the tenth month*

הוּא־חֹדֶשׁ טֵבֵת pers.pr. 3 m.s. (214)-v.supra -pr.n. (372) *which is the month of Tebeth*

בִּשְׁנַת־שֶׁבַע prep.-n.f.s. cstr. (1040)-num. (I 987) *in the seventh year*

לְמַלְכוּתוֹ prep.-n.f.s.-3 m.s. sf. (574) *of his reign*

2:17

וַיֶּאֱהַב הַמֶּלֶךְ consec.-Qal impf. 3 m.s. (אָהַב 12)-def.art.-n.m.s. (I 572) *the king loved*

אֶת־אֶסְתֵּר dir.obj.-pr.n. (64) *Esther*

מִכָּל־הַנָּשִׁים prep.-n.m.s. cstr. (481)-def.art.-n.f.p. (61) *more than all the women*

וַתִּשָּׂא־חֵן consec.-Qal impf. 3 f.s. (נָשָׂא 669) -n.m.s. (336) *and she found grace*

וָחֶסֶד conj.-n.m.s. (338) *and favor*

לְפָנָיו prep.-n.m.p.-3 m.s. sf. (815) *in his sight*

מִכָּל־הַבְּתוּלֹת v.supra-def.art.-n.f.p. (143) *more than all the virgins*

וַיָּשֶׂם consec.-Qal impf. 3 m.s. (שִׂים 962) *so that he set*

כֶּתֶר־מַלְכוּת n.m.s. cstr. (509)-n.f.s. (574) *the royal crown*

בְּרֹאשָׁהּ prep.-n.m.s.-3 f.s. sf. (910) *on her head*

וַיַּמְלִיכֶהָ consec.-Hi. impf. 3 m.s.-3 f.s. sf. (מָלַךְ 573) *and made her queen*
תַּחַת וַשְׁתִּי prep. (1065)-pr.n. (255) *instead of Vashti*

2:18

וַיַּעַשׂ הַמֶּלֶךְ consec.-Qal impf. 3 m.s. (עָשָׂה I 793)-def.art.-n.m.s. (I 572) *then the king gave*
מִשְׁתֶּה גָדוֹל n.m.s. (1059)-adj. m.s. (152) *a great banquet*
לְכָל־שָׂרָיו prep.-n.m.s. cstr. (481)-n.m.p.-3 m.s. sf. (978) *to all his princes*
וַעֲבָדָיו conj.-n.m.p.-3 m.s. sf. (713) *and servants*
אֵת מִשְׁתֵּה אֶסְתֵּר dir.obj.-n.m.s. cstr. (1059)-pr.n. (64) *it was Esther's banquet*
וַהֲנָחָה conj.-n.f.s. (629) *and a holiday-making*
לַמְּדִינוֹת prep.-def.art.-n.f.p. (193) *to the provinces*
עָשָׂה Qal pf. 3 m.s. (I 793) *he granted*
וַיִּתֵּן מַשְׂאֵת consec.-Qal impf. 3 m.s. (נָתַן 678)-n.f.s. (673) *and gave gifts*
כְּיַד הַמֶּלֶךְ prep.-n.f.s. cstr. (388)-v.supra *with royal liberality*

2:19

וּבְהִקָּבֵץ conj.-prep.-Ni. inf.cstr. (קָבַץ 867) *when were gathered together*
בְּתוּלוֹת n.f.p. (143) *the virgins*
שֵׁנִית num. ord. f. (1041) *a second time*
וּמָרְדֳּכַי conj.-pr.n. (598) *and Mordecai*
יֹשֵׁב Qal act.ptc. (יָשַׁב 442) *was sitting*
בְּשַׁעַר־הַמֶּלֶךְ prep.-n.m.s. cstr. (1044)-def.art. -n.m.s. (I 572) *at the king's gate*

2:20

אֵין אֶסְתֵּר מַגֶּדֶת neg. (II 34)-pr.n. (64)-Hi. ptc. f.s. (נָגַד 616) *now Esther had not made known*
מוֹלַדְתָּהּ n.f.s.-3 f.s. sf. (409) *her kindred*
וְאֶת־עַמָּהּ conj.-dir.obj.-n.m.s.-3 f.s. sf. (I 766) *or her people*
כַּאֲשֶׁר צִוָּה prep.-rel. (81)-Pi. pf. 3 m.s. (צָוָה 845) *as had charged*
עָלֶיהָ prep.-3 f.s. sf. *her*
מָרְדֳּכַי pr.n. (598) *Mordecai*
וְאֶת־מַאֲמַר מָרְדֳּכַי conj.-dir.obj.-n.m.s. cstr. (57) -v.supra *and the command of Mordecai*
אֶסְתֵּר עֹשָׂה pr.n. (64)-Qal act.ptc. f.s. (עָשָׂה I 793) *Esther did*
כַּאֲשֶׁר הָיְתָה prep.-rel. (81)-Qal pf. 3 f.s. (הָיָה 224) *just as when she was*

בְאָמְנָה אִתּוֹ prep.-n.f.s. (53)-prep.-3 m.s. sf. (II 85) *brought up by him*

2:21

בַּיָּמִים הָהֵם prep.-def.art.-n.m.p. (398)-def.art. -demons.adj. m.p. (241) *in those days*
וּמָרְדֳּכַי יֹשֵׁב conj.-pr.n. (598)-Qal act.ptc. (יָשַׁב 442) *as Modecai was sitting*
בְּשַׁעַר־הַמֶּלֶךְ prep.-n.m.s. cstr. (1044)-def.art. -n.m.s. (I 572) *at the king's gate*
קָצַף Qal pf. 3 m.s. (893) *became angry*
בִּגְתָן וָתֶרֶשׁ pr.n. (94)-conj.-pr.n. (1076) *Bigthan and Teresh*
שְׁנֵי־סָרִיסֵי num. m.p. cstr. (1040)-n.m.p. cstr. (710) *two of the eunuchs of*
הַמֶּלֶךְ def.art.-n.m.s. (I 572) *the king*
מִשֹּׁמְרֵי הַסַּף prep.-Qal act.ptc. m.p. cstr. (1036) -def.art.-n.m.s. (II 706) *who guarded the threshold*
וַיְבַקְשׁוּ consec.-Pi. impf. 3 m.p. (בָּקַשׁ 134) *and sought*
לִשְׁלֹחַ יָד prep.-Qal inf.cstr. (1018)-n.f.s. (388) *to lay hands*
בַּמֶּלֶךְ אֲחַשְׁוֵרֹשׁ prep.-def.art.-n.m.s. (I 572)-pr.n. (31) *on King Ahasuerus*

2:22

וַיִּוָּדַע הַדָּבָר consec.-Ni. impf. 3 m.s. (יָדַע 393) -def.art.-n.m.s. (182) *and this came to the knowledge of*
לְמָרְדֳּכַי prep.-pr.n. (598) *of Mordecai*
וַיַּגֵּד consec.-Hi. impf. 3 m.s. (נָגַד 616) *and he told it*
לְאֶסְתֵּר הַמַּלְכָּה prep.-pr.n. (64)-def.art.-n.f.s. (573) *to Queen Esther*
וַתֹּאמֶר אֶסְתֵּר consec.-Qal impf. 3 f.s. (אָמַר 55)-v.supra *and Esther told*
לַמֶּלֶךְ prep.-def.art.-n.m.s. (I 572) *to the king*
בְּשֵׁם מָרְדֳּכָי prep.-n.m.s. cstr. (1027)-pr.n. paus. (598) *in the name of Mordecai*

2:23

וַיְבֻקַּשׁ הַדָּבָר consec.-Pu. impf. 3 m.s. (בָּקַשׁ 134)-def.art.-n.m.s. (182) *when the affair was investigated*
וַיִּמָּצֵא consec.-Ni. impf. 3 m.s. (מָצָא 592) *and was found*
וַיִּתָּלוּ שְׁנֵיהֶם consec.-Ni. impf. 3 m.p. (תָּלָה 1067)-num.-3 m.p. sf. (1040) *both of them were hanged*
עַל־עֵץ prep.-n.m.s. (781) *on the gallows*

וַיִּכָּתֵב consec.-Ni. impf. 3 m.s. (כָּתַב 507) *and it was recorded*
בְּסֵפֶר prep.-n.m.s. cstr. (706) *in the book of*
דִּבְרֵי הַיָּמִים n.m.p. cstr. (182)-def.art.-n.m.p. (398) *the Chronicles*
לִפְנֵי הַמֶּלֶךְ prep.-n.m.p. cstr. (815)-def.art.-n.m.s. (I 572) *in the presence of the king*

3:1

אַחַר הַדְּבָרִים הָאֵלֶּה prep. (29)-def.art.-n.m.p. (182)-def.art.-demons.adj. c.p. (41) *after these things*
גִּדַּל Pi. pf. 3 m.s. (גָּדַל 152) *promoted*
הַמֶּלֶךְ אֲחַשְׁוֵרוֹשׁ def.art.-n.m.s. (I 572)-pr.n. (31) *King Ahasuerus*
אֶת־הָמָן dir.obj.-pr.n. (243) *Haman*
בֶּן־הַמְּדָתָא n.m.s. cstr. (119)-pr.n. (241) *the son of Hammedatha*
הָאֲגָגִי def.art.-adj. gent. (8) *the Agagite*
וַיְנַשְּׂאֵהוּ consec.-Pi. impf. 3 m.s.-3 m.s. sf. (נָשָׂא 669) *and advanced him*
וַיָּשֶׂם consec.-Qal impf. 3 m.s. (שִׂים 962) *and set*
אֶת־כִּסְאוֹ dir.obj.-n.m.s.-3 m.s. sf. (490) *his seat*
מֵעַל כָּל־הַשָּׂרִים prep.-prep. (752)-n.m.s. cstr. (481)-def.art.-n.m.p. (978) *above all the princes*
אֲשֶׁר אִתּוֹ rel. (81)-prep.-3 m.s. sf. (II 85) *who were with him*

3:2

וְכָל־עַבְדֵי הַמֶּלֶךְ conj.-n.m.s. cstr. (481)-n.m.p. cstr. (713)-def.art.-n.m.s. (I 572) *and all the king's servants*
אֲשֶׁר־בְּשַׁעַר הַמֶּלֶךְ rel. (81)-prep.-n.m.s. cstr. (1044)-v.supra *who were at the king's gate*
כֹּרְעִים Qal act.ptc. m.p. (כָּרַע 502) *bowed down*
וּמִשְׁתַּחֲוִים conj.-Hith. ptc. m.p. (1005 שָׁחָה) *and did obeisance*
לְהָמָן prep.-pr.n. (243) *to Haman*
כִּי־כֵן conj. (471)-adv. (485) *for so*
צִוָּה־לוֹ Pi. pf. 3 m.s. (צָוָה 845)-prep.-3 m.s. sf. *had commanded concerning him*
הַמֶּלֶךְ def.art.-n.m.s. (I 572) *the king*
וּמָרְדֳּכַי conj.-pr.n. (598) *but Mordecai*
לֹא יִכְרַע neg.-Qal impf. 3 m.s. (כָּרַע 502) *did not bow down*
וְלֹא יִשְׁתַּחֲוֶה conj.-neg.-Hith. impf. 3 m.s. (1005 שָׁחָה) *and did not do obeisance*

3:3

וַיֹּאמְרוּ consec.-Qal impf. 3 m.p. (אָמַר 55) *then said*
עַבְדֵי הַמֶּלֶךְ n.m.p. cstr. (713)-def.art.-n.m.s. (I 572) *the king's servants*
אֲשֶׁר־בְּשַׁעַר הַמֶּלֶךְ rel. (81)-prep.-n.m.s. cstr. (1044)-v.supra *who were at the king's gate*
לְמָרְדֳּכָי prep.-pr.n. paus. (598) *to Mordecai*
מַדּוּעַ adv. (396) *why*
אַתָּה עוֹבֵר pers.pr. 2 m.s. (61)-Qal act.ptc. (עָבַר 716) *do you transgress*
אֵת מִצְוַת הַמֶּלֶךְ dir.obj.-n.f.s. cstr. (846)-v.supra *the king's command*

3:4

וַיְהִי בְּאָמְרָם אֵלָיו consec.-Qal impf. 3 m.s. (הָיָה 224)-prep.-Qal inf.cstr.-3 m.p. sf. (אָמַר 55)-prep.-3 m.s. sf. *and when they spoke to him*
יוֹם וָיוֹם n.m.s. (398)-conj.-v.supra *day after day*
וְלֹא שָׁמַע אֲלֵיהֶם conj.-neg.-Qal pf. 3 m.s. (1033)-prep.-3 m.p. sf. *and he would not listen to them*
וַיַּגִּידוּ לְהָמָן consec.-Hi. impf. 3 m.p. (נָגַד 616)-prep.-pr.n. (243) *they told Haman*
לִרְאוֹת prep.-Qal inf.cstr. (רָאָה 906) *in order to see*
הֲיַעַמְדוּ interr.part.-Qal impf. 3 m.p. (עָמַד 763) *whether would avail*
דִּבְרֵי מָרְדֳּכַי n.m.p. cstr. (182)-pr.n. (598) *Mordecai's words*
כִּי־הִגִּיד לָהֶם conj. (471)-Hi. pf. 3 m.s. (נָגַד 616)-prep.-3 m.p. sf. *for he had told them*
אֲשֶׁר־הוּא יְהוּדִי rel. (81; GK 157c)-pers.pr. 3 m.s. (214)-adj. gent. (I 397) *that he was a Jew*

3:5

וַיַּרְא הָמָן consec.-Qal impf. 3 m.s. (רָאָה 906)-pr.n. (243) *and when Haman saw*
כִּי־אֵין מָרְדֳּכַי כֹּרֵעַ conj. (471)-neg. (II 34)-pr.n. (598)-Qal act.ptc. (כָּרַע 502) *that Mordecai did not bow down*
וּמִשְׁתַּחֲוֶה לוֹ conj.-Hith. ptc. (שָׁחָה 1005)-prep.-3 m.s. sf. *or do obeisance to him*
וַיִּמָּלֵא הָמָן consec.-Ni. impf. 3 m.s. (מָלֵא 569)-pr.n. (243) *Haman was filled*
חֵמָה n.f.s. (404) *with fury*

3:6

וַיִּבֶז בְּעֵינָיו consec.-Qal impf. 3 m.s. (בָּזָה 102)-prep.-n.f.p.-3 m.s. sf. (744) *but he disdained (despised in his eyes)*

לִשְׁלֹחַ יָד prep.-Qal inf.cstr. (שָׁלַח 1018)-n.f.s. (388) *to lay hands*
בְּמָרְדֳּכַי prep.-pr.n. (598) *on Mordecai*
לְבַדּוֹ prep.-n.m.s.-3 m.s. sf. (94) *alone*
כִּי־הִגִּידוּ לוֹ conj. (471)-Hi. pf. 3 c.p. (נָגַד 616)-prep.-3 m.s. sf. *so as they had made known to him*
אֶת־עַם מָרְדֳּכַי dir.obj.-n.m.s. cstr. (I 766) -v.supra *the people of Mordecai*
וַיְבַקֵּשׁ הָמָן consec.-Pi. impf. 3 m.s. (בָּקַשׁ 134)-pr.n. (243) *Haman sought*
לְהַשְׁמִיד prep.-Hi. inf.cstr. (שָׁמַד 1029) *to destroy*
אֶת־כָּל־הַיְּהוּדִים dir.obj.-n.m.s. cstr. (481)-def. art.-adj. gent. m.p. (I 397) *all the Jews*
אֲשֶׁר בְּכָל־מַלְכוּת rel. (81)-prep.-v.supra-n.f.s. cstr. (574) *throughout the whole kingdom of*
אֲחַשְׁוֵרוֹשׁ pr.n. (31) *Ahasuerus*
עַם מָרְדֳּכָי n.m.s. cstr. paus. (I 766)-v.supra *the people of Mordecai*

3:7

בַּחֹדֶשׁ הָרִאשׁוֹן prep.-def.art.-n.m.s. (I 294)-def. art.-adj. m.s. (911) *in the first month*
הוּא־חֹדֶשׁ נִיסָן demons.adj. m.s. (214)-v.supra -pr.n. (644) *which is the month of Nisan*
בִּשְׁנַת שְׁתֵּים עֶשְׂרֵה prep.-n.f.s. cstr. (1040)-num. (1040)-num. (797) *in the twelfth year*
לַמֶּלֶךְ אֲחַשְׁוֵרוֹשׁ prep.-def.art.-n.m.s. (I 572) -pr.n. (31) *of King Ahasuerus*
הִפִּיל פּוּר Hi. pf. 3 m.s. (נָפַל 656)-n.m.s. (807) *they cast Pur*
הוּא הַגּוֹרָל demons.adj. m.s. (214)-def.art.-n.m.s. (174) *that is the lot*
לִפְנֵי הָמָן prep.-n.m.p. cstr. (815)-pr.n. (243) *before Haman*
מִיּוֹם לְיוֹם prep.-n.m.s. (398)-prep.-v.supra *day after day*
וּמֵחֹדֶשׁ לְחֹדֶשׁ conj.-prep.-n.m.s. (I 294)-prep. -v.supra *and month after month*
שְׁנֵים־עָשָׂר num. (1040)-num. (797) *(till) the twelfth*
הוּא־חֹדֶשׁ אֲדָר v.supra-v.supra-pr.n. (12) *which is the month of Adar*

3:8

וַיֹּאמֶר הָמָן consec.-Qal impf. 3 m.s. (אָמַר 55) -pr.n. (243) *then Haman said*
לַמֶּלֶךְ אֲחַשְׁוֵרוֹשׁ prep.-def.art.-n.m.s. (I 572) -pr.n. (31) *to King Ahasuerus*
יֶשְׁנוֹ עַם־אֶחָד subst.-3 m.s. sf. (441; GK 100oN)-n.m.s. (I 766)-adj. (25) *there is a certain people*
מְפֻזָּר Pu. ptc. (פָּזַר 808) *scattered abroad*
וּמְפֹרָד conj.-Pu. ptc. (פָּרַד 825) *and dispersed*
בֵּין הָעַמִּים prep. (107)-def.art.-n.m.p. (I 766) *among the peoples*
בְּכֹל מְדִינוֹת prep.-n.m.s. cstr. (481)-n.f.p. cstr. (193) *in all the provinces of*
מַלְכוּתֶךָ n.f.s.-2 m.s. sf. (574) *your kingdom*
וְדָתֵיהֶם conj.-n.f.p.-3 m.p. sf. (206) *and their laws*
שֹׁנוֹת Qal act.ptc. f.p. (שָׁנָה I 1039) *are different*
מִכָּל־עָם prep.-n.m.s. cstr. (481)-n.m.s. paus. (I 766) *from those of every other people*
וְאֶת־דָּתֵי הַמֶּלֶךְ conj.-dir.obj.-n.f.p. cstr. (206) -def.art.-n.m.s. (I 572) *and the king's laws*
אֵינָם עֹשִׂים neg.-3 m.p. sf. (II 34)-Qal act.ptc. m.p. (עָשָׂה I 793) *they do not keep*
וְלַמֶּלֶךְ conj.-prep.-def.art.-v.supra *so for the king*
אֵין־שֹׁוֶה neg. (II 34)-Qal act.ptc. (שָׁוָה 1000) *it is not an equivalent (profit)*
לְהַנִּיחָם prep.-Hi. inf.cstr.-3 m.p. sf. (נוּחַ 628) *to tolerate them*

3:9

אִם־עַל־הַמֶּלֶךְ hypoth.part. (49)-prep.-def.art. -n.m.s. (I 572) *if to the king*
טוֹב adj. (II 373) *it is pleasing*
יִכָּתֵב Ni. impf. 3 m.s. (כָּתַב 507) *let it be decreed*
לְאַבְּדָם prep.-Pi. inf.cstr.-3 m.p. sf. (אָבַד 1) *that they be destroyed*
וַעֲשֶׂרֶת אֲלָפִים conj.-num. f. cstr. (796)-n.m.p. (48) *and ten thousand*
כִּכַּר־כֶּסֶף n.f.s. cstr. (503)-n.m.s. (494) *talents of silver*
אֶשְׁקוֹל Qal impf. 1 c.s. (שָׁקַל 1053) *I will pay*
עַל־יְדֵי prep.-n.f.p. cstr. (388) *into the hands of*
עֹשֵׂי הַמְּלָאכָה Qal act.ptc. m.p. cstr. (עָשָׂה I 793)-def.art.-n.f.s. (521) *those who have change of the business*
לְהָבִיא prep.-Hi. inf.cstr. (בּוֹא 97) *that they may put it*
אֶל־גִּנְזֵי הַמֶּלֶךְ prep.-n.m.p. cstr. (170)-def.art. -n.m.s. (I 572) *into the king's treasuries*

3:10

וַיָּסַר הַמֶּלֶךְ consec.-Qal impf. 3 m.s. (סוּר 693) -def.art.-n.m.s. (I 572) *so the king took*

אֶת־טַבַּעְתּוֹ dir.obj.-n.f.s.-3 m.s. sf. (371) *his signet ring*
מֵעַל יָדוֹ prep.-prep. (II 752)-n.f.s.-3 m.s. sf. (388) *from his hand*
וַיִּתְּנָהּ consec.-Qal impf. 3 m.s.-3 f.s. sf. (נָתַן 678) *and gave it*
לְהָמָן prep.-pr.n. (243) *to Haman*
בֶּן־הַמְּדָתָא n.m.s. cstr. (119)-pr.n. (241) *the son of Hammedatha*
הָאֲגָגִי def.art.-adj. gent. (8) *the Agagite*
צֹרֵר הַיְּהוּדִים Qal act.ptc. cstr. (צָרַר II 865)-def. art.-adj. gent. m.p. (397) *the enemy of the Jews*

3:11

וַיֹּאמֶר הַמֶּלֶךְ consec.-Qal impf. 3 m.s. (אָמַר 55)-def.art.-n.m.s. (I 572) *and the king said*
לְהָמָן prep.-pr.n. (243) *to Haman*
הַכֶּסֶף def.art.-n.m.s. (494) *the money*
נָתוּן לָךְ Qal pass.ptc. (נָתַן 678)-prep.-2 m.s. sf. paus. *is given to you*
וְהָעָם conj.-def.art.-n.m.s. (I 766) *the people also*
לַעֲשׂוֹת בּוֹ prep.-Qal inf.cstr. (עָשָׂה I 793) -prep.-3 m.s. sf. *to do with them*
כַּטּוֹב בְּעֵינֶיךָ prep.-def.art.-adj. m.s. (II 373) -prep.-n.f.p.-2 m.s. sf. (744) *as it seems good in your eyes*

3:12

וַיִּקָּרְאוּ consec.-Ni. impf. 3 m.p. (קָרָא 894) *then were summoned*
סֹפְרֵי הַמֶּלֶךְ n.m.p. cstr. (708)-def.art.-n.m.s. (I 572) *the king's secretaries*
בַּחֹדֶשׁ הָרִאשׁוֹן prep.-def.art.-n.m.s. (I 294)-def. art.-adj. m.s. (911) *of the first month*
בִּשְׁלוֹשָׁה עָשָׂר יוֹם בּוֹ prep.-num. f.s. (1025) -num. (797)-n.m.s. (398)-prep.-3 m.s. sf. *on the thirteenth day of it*
וַיִּכָּתֵב consec.-Ni. impf. 3 m.s. (כָּתַב 507) *and was written*
כְּכָל־אֲשֶׁר־צִוָּה הָמָן prep.-n.m.s. (481)-rel. (81)-Pi. pf. 3 m.s. (צָוָה 845)-pr.n. (243) *according to all that Haman commanded*
אֶל אֲחַשְׁדַּרְפְּנֵי־הַמֶּלֶךְ prep.-n.m.p. cstr. (31)-def. art.-n.m.s. (I 572) *to the king's satraps*
וְאֶל־הַפַּחוֹת conj.-prep.-def.art.-n.m.p. (808) *and to the governors*
אֲשֶׁר עַל־מְדִינָה וּמְדִינָה rel. (81)-prep.-n.f.s. (193)-conj.-v.supra *over all the provinces*
וְאֶל־שָׂרֵי עַם וָעָם conj.-prep.-n.m.p. cstr. (978) -n.m.s. (I 766)-conj.-v.supra *and to the princes of all the peoples*
מְדִינָה וּמְדִינָה v.supra-conj.-v.supra *to every province*
כִּכְתָבָהּ prep.-n.m.s.-3 f.s. sf. (508) *in its own script*
וְעַם וָעָם conj.-v.supra-conj.-v.supra *and every people*
כִּלְשׁוֹנוֹ prep.-n.f.s.-3 m.s. sf. (546) *in its own language*
בְּשֵׁם הַמֶּלֶךְ prep.-n.m.s. cstr. (1027)-def.art. -n.m.s. (I 572) *in the name of King*
אֲחַשְׁוֵרֹשׁ pr.n. (31) *Ahasuerus*
נִכְתָּב Ni. ptc. (כָּתַב 507) *it was written*
וְנֶחְתָּם conj.-Ni. ptc. (or pf. 3 m.s.) (חָתַם 367) *and sealed*
בְּטַבַּעַת הַמֶּלֶךְ prep.-n.f.s. cstr. (371)-v.supra *with the king's ring*

3:13

וְנִשְׁלוֹחַ conj.-Ni. inf.abs. (שָׁלַח 1018; GK 113z) *and were sent*
סְפָרִים n.m.p. (706) *letters*
בְּיַד הָרָצִים prep.-n.f.s. cstr. (388)-def.art.-Qal act.ptc. m.p. (רוּץ 930) *by couriers*
אֶל־כָּל־ prep.-n.m.s. cstr. (481) *to all of*
מְדִינוֹת הַמֶּלֶךְ n.f.p. cstr. (193)-def.art.-n.m.s. (I 572) *the king's provinces*
לְהַשְׁמִיד prep.-Hi. inf.cstr. (שָׁמַד 1029) *to destroy*
לַהֲרֹג prep.-Qal inf.cstr. (הָרַג 246) *to slay*
וּלְאַבֵּד conj.-prep.-Pi. inf.cstr. (אָבַד 1) *and to annihilate*
אֶת־כָּל־הַיְּהוּדִים dir.obj.-n.m.s. cstr. (481)-def. art.-adj. gent. m.p. (397) *all Jews*
מִנַּעַר וְעַד־זָקֵן prep.-n.m.s. (655)-conj.-prep. (III 723)-adj. m.s. (278) *young and old*
טַף וְנָשִׁים n.m.s. (381)-conj.-n.f.p. (61) *children and women*
בְּיוֹם אֶחָד prep.-n.m.s. (398)-adj. m.s. (25) *in one day*
בִּשְׁלוֹשָׁה עָשָׂר prep.-num. f. (1025)-num. (797) *the thirteenth day*
לְחֹדֶשׁ שְׁנֵים־עָשָׂר prep.-n.m.s. (I 294)-num. (1040)-num. (797) *of the twelfth month*
הוּא־חֹדֶשׁ אֲדָר pers.pr. 3 m.s. (214)-v.supra-pr.n. (12) *which is the month of Adar*
וּשְׁלָלָם לָבוֹז conj.-n.m.s.-3 m.p. sf. (1021)-prep. -Qal inf.cstr. (בָּזַז 102) *and to plunder their goods*

3:14

פַּתְשֶׁגֶן הַכְּתָב n.m.s. cstr. (837)-def.art.-n.m.s. (508) *a copy of the document*

לְהִנָּתֵן prep.-Ni. inf.cstr. (נָתַן 678) *was to be issued*
דָּת n.f.s. (206) *as a decree*
בְּכָל־מְדִינָה וּמְדִינָה prep.-n.m.s. cstr. (481)-n.f.s. (193)-conj.-v.supra *in every province*
גָּלוּי Qal pass.ptc. (גָּלָה 162) *by proclamation*
לְכָל־הָעַמִּים prep.-v.supra-def.art.-n.m.p. (I 766) *to all the peoples*
לִהְיוֹת עֲתִדִים prep.-Qal inf.cstr. (הָיָה 224)-adj. m.p. (800) *to be ready*
לַיּוֹם הַזֶּה prep.-def.art.-n.m.s. (398)-def.art. -demons.adj. m.s. (260) *for that day*

3:15

הָרָצִים def.art.-Qal act.ptc. m.p. (רוּץ 930) *the couriers*
יָצְאוּ Qal pf. 3 c.p. (יָצָא 422) *went out*
דְּחוּפִים Qal pass.ptc. m.p. (דָּחַף 191) *in haste*
בִּדְבַר הַמֶּלֶךְ prep.-n.m.s. cstr. (182)-def.art.-n.m.s. (I 572) *by order of the king*
וְהַדָּת conj.-def.art.-n.f.s. (206) *and the decree*
נִתְּנָה Pi. pf. 3 f.s. (נָתַן 678) *was issued*
בְּשׁוּשַׁן prep.-pr.n. (1004) *in Susa*
הַבִּירָה def.art.-n.f.s. (108) *the capital*
וְהַמֶּלֶךְ וְהָמָן conj.-def.art.-n.m.s. (I 572)-conj. -pr.n. (243) *and the king and Haman*
יָשְׁבוּ Qal pf. 3 c.p. (יָשַׁב 442) *sat down*
לִשְׁתּוֹת prep.-Qal inf.cstr. (שָׁתָה 1059) *to drink*
וְהָעִיר conj.-def.art.-n.f.s. (746) *but the city*
שׁוּשָׁן pr.n. (1004) *Susa*
נָבוֹכָה Ni. pf. 3 f.s. (בּוּךְ 100) *was perplexed*

4:1

וּמָרְדֳּכַי יָדַע conj.-pr.n. (598)-Qal pf. 3 m.s. (393) *when Mordecai learned*
אֶת־כָּל־אֲשֶׁר נַעֲשָׂה dir.obj.-n.m.s. cstr. (481)-rel. (81)-Ni. pf. 3 m.s. (עָשָׂה I 793) *all that had been done*
וַיִּקְרַע מָרְדֳּכַי consec.-Qal impf. 3 m.s. (קָרַע 902)-v.supra *Mordecai rent*
אֶת־בְּגָדָיו dir.obj.-n.m.p.-3 m.s. sf. (93) *his clothes*
וַיִּלְבַּשׁ שַׂק consec.-Qal impf. 3 m.s. (לָבַשׁ 527)-n.m.s. (974) *and put on sackcloth*
וָאֵפֶר conj.-n.m.s. (68) *and ashes*
וַיֵּצֵא consec.-Qal impf. 3 m.s. (יָצָא 422) *and went out*
בְּתוֹךְ הָעִיר prep.-n.m.s. cstr. (1063)-def.art.-n.f.s. (746) *into the midst of the city*
וַיִּזְעַק consec.-Qal impf. 3 m.s. (זָעַק 277) *and cried out*
זְעָקָה גְדֹלָה n.f.s. (277)-adj. f.s. (152) *a loud cry*
וּמָרָה conj.-adj. f.s. (I 600) *and bitter*

4:2

וַיָּבוֹא consec.-Qal impf. 3 m.s. (בּוֹא 97) *he went*
עַד לִפְנֵי שַׁעַר־הַמֶּלֶךְ prep. (III 723)-prep.-n.m.p. cstr. (815)-n.m.s. cstr. (1044)-def.art.-n.m.s. (I 572) *up to the entrance of the king's gate*
כִּי אֵין לָבוֹא conj. (471)-neg. (II 34)-prep.-Qal inf.cstr. (בּוֹא 97; GK 114,l) *for no one might enter*
אֶל־שַׁעַר הַמֶּלֶךְ prep.-v.supra-v.supra *the king's gate*
בִּלְבוּשׁ שָׂק prep.-n.m.s. cstr. (528)-n.m.s. paus. (974) *clothed with sackcloth*

4:3

וּבְכָל־מְדִינָה וּמְדִינָה conj.-prep.-n.m.s. cstr. (481) -n.f.s. (193)-conj.-v.supra *and in every province*
מְקוֹם אֲשֶׁר n.m.s. cstr. (879)-rel. (81) *wherever*
דְּבַר־הַמֶּלֶךְ n.m.s. cstr. (182)-def.art.-n.m.s. (I 572) *the king's command*
וְדָתוֹ conj.-n.f.s.-3 m.s. sf. (206) *and his decree*
מַגִּיעַ Hi. ptc. (נָגַע 619) *came*
אֵבֶל גָּדוֹל n.m.s. (5)-adj. m.s. (152) *great mourning*
לַיְּהוּדִים prep.-def.art.-adj. gent. m.p. (397) *among the Jews*
וְצוֹם וּבְכִי conj.-n.m.s. (847)-conj.-n.m.s. (113) *with fasting and weeping*
וּמִסְפֵּד conj.-n.m.s. (704) *and lamenting*
שַׂק וָאֵפֶר n.m.s. (974)-conj.-n.m.s. (68) *in sackcloth and ashes*
יֻצַּע Ho. impf. 3 m.s. (יָצַע 426) *were spread*
לָרַבִּים prep.-def.art.-adj. m.p. (I 912) *for many*

4:4

וַתָּבוֹאינָה consec.-Qal impf. 3 f.p. (בּוֹא 97) *when came*
נַעֲרוֹת אֶסְתֵּר n.f.p. cstr. (655)-pr.n. (64) *Esther's maids*
וְסָרִיסֶיהָ conj.-n.m.p.-3 f.s. sf. (710) *and her eunuchs*
וַיַּגִּידוּ לָהּ consec.-Hi. impf. 3 m.p. (נָגַד 616) -prep.-3 f.s. sf. *and told her*
וַתִּתְחַלְחַל consec.-Hithpalp. impf. 3 f.s. (חוּל I 296) *and writhed (in anxiety)*
הַמַּלְכָּה def.art.-n.f.s. (573) *the queen*
מְאֹד adv. (547) *deeply*
וַתִּשְׁלַח בְּגָדִים consec.-Qal impf. 3 f.s. (שָׁלַח 1018)-n.m.p. (93) *she sent garments*
לְהַלְבִּישׁ prep.-Hi. inf.cstr. (לָבַשׁ 527) *to clothe*

אֶת־מָרְדֳּכָי dir.obj.-pr.n. (598) *Mordecai*
וּלְהָסִיר שַׂקּוֹ conj.-prep.-Hi. inf.cstr. (סוּר 693) -n.m.s.-3 m.s. sf. (974) *so that he might take off his sackcloth*
מֵעָלָיו prep.-prep.-3 m.s. sf. *from upon him*
וְלֹא קִבֵּל conj.-neg.-Pi. pf. 3 m.s. (קָבַל 867) *but he would not accept them*

4:5

וַתִּקְרָא אֶסְתֵּר consec.-Qal impf. 3 f.s. (קָרָא 894) -pr.n. (64) *then Esther called*
לַהֲתָךְ prep.-pr.n. (251) *for Hathach*
מִסָּרִיסֵי הַמֶּלֶךְ prep.-n.m.p. cstr. (710)-def.art. -n.m.s. (I 572) *one of the king's eunuchs*
אֲשֶׁר הֶעֱמִיד rel. (81)-Hi. pf. 3 m.s. (עָמַד 763) *who stood*
לְפָנֶיהָ prep.-n.m.p.-3 f.s. sf. (815) *before her*
וַתְּצַוֵּהוּ consec.-Pi. impf. 3 f.s.-3 m.s. sf. (צָוָה 845) *and she ordered him*
עַל־מָרְדֳּכָי prep. (II 752)-pr.n. paus. (598) *unto Mordecai*
לָדַעַת prep.-Qal inf.cstr. (יָדַע 393) *to learn*
מַה־זֶּה interr. (552)-demons.adj. m.s. (260) *what this was*
וְעַל־מַה־זֶּה conj.-v.supra-v.supra-v.supra *and why it was*

4:6

וַיֵּצֵא הֲתָךְ consec.-Qal impf. 3 m.s. (יָצָא 422) -pr.n. (251) *Hathach went out*
אֶל־מָרְדֳּכָי prep.-pr.n. paus. (598) *to Mordecai*
אֶל־רְחוֹב הָעִיר prep.-n.f.s. cstr. (I 932)-def. art.-n.f.s. (746) *in the open square of the city*
אֲשֶׁר לִפְנֵי rel. (81)-prep.-n.m.p. cstr. (815) *in front of*
שַׁעַר־הַמֶּלֶךְ n.m.s. cstr. (1044)-def.art.-n.m.s. (I 572) *the king's gate*

4:7

וַיַּגֶּד־לוֹ consec.-Hi. impf. 3 m.s. (נָגַד 616) -prep.-3 m.s. sf. *and ... told him*
מָרְדֳּכַי pr.n. (598) *Mordecai*
אֵת כָּל־אֲשֶׁר dir.obj.-n.m.s. (481)-rel. (81) *all that*
קָרָהוּ Qal pf. 3 m.s.-3 m.s. sf. (קָרָה 899) *had happened to him*
וְאֵת פָּרָשַׁת הַכֶּסֶף conj.-dir.obj.-n.f.s. cstr. (831) -def.art.-n.m.s. (494) *and the exact sum of money*
אֲשֶׁר אָמַר הָמָן rel. (81)-Qal pf. 3 m.s. (55)-pr.n. (243) *that Haman had promised*
לִשְׁקוֹל prep.-Qal inf.cstr. (שָׁקַל 1053) *to pay*
עַל־גִּנְזֵי הַמֶּלֶךְ prep.-n.m.p. cstr. (170)-def.art. -n.m.s. (I 572) *into the king's treasuries*
בַּיְּהוּדִים prep.-def.art.-adj. gent. m.p. (397) *of the Jews*
לְאַבְּדָם prep.-Pi. inf.cstr.-3 m.p. sf. (אָבַד 1) *for their destruction*

4:8

וְאֶת־פַּתְשֶׁגֶן conj.-dir.obj.-n.m.s. cstr. 837) *and a copy of*
כְּתָב־הַדָּת n.m.s. cstr. (508; GK 93ww)-def. art.-n.f.s. (206) *the written decree*
אֲשֶׁר־נִתַּן rel. (81)-Ni. pf. 3 m.s. (נָתַן 678) *issued*
בְּשׁוּשָׁן prep.-pr.n. paus. (1004) *in Susa*
לְהַשְׁמִידָם prep.-Hi. inf.cstr.-3 m.p. sf. (שָׁמַד 1029) *for their destruction*
נָתַן לוֹ Qal pf. 3 m.s. (678)-prep.-3 m.s. sf. *gave to him*
לְהַרְאוֹת prep.-Hi. inf.cstr. (רָאָה 906) *that he might show*
אֶת־אֶסְתֵּר dir.obj.-pr.n. (64) *to Esther*
וּלְהַגִּיד לָהּ conj.-prep.-Hi. inf.cstr. (נָגַד 616) -prep.-3 f.s. sf. *and explain it to her*
וּלְצַוּוֹת עָלֶיהָ conj.-prep.-Pi. inf.cstr. (צָוָה 845)-prep.-3 f.s. sf. *and charge her*
לָבוֹא prep.-Qal inf.cstr. (בּוֹא 97) *to go*
אֶל־הַמֶּלֶךְ prep.-def.art.-n.m.s. (I 572) *to the king*
לְהִתְחַנֶּן־לוֹ prep.-Hith. inf.cstr. (חָנַן I 335) -prep.-3 m.s. sf. *to make supplication to him*
וּלְבַקֵּשׁ מִלְּפָנָיו conj.-prep.-Pi. inf.cstr. (בָּקַשׁ 134)-prep.-prep.-n.m.p.-3 m.s. sf. (815) *and entreat him*
עַל־עַמָּהּ prep.-n.m.s.-3 f.s. sf. (I 766) *for her people*

4:9

וַיָּבוֹא הֲתָךְ consec.-Qal impf. 3 m.s. (בּוֹא 97)-pr.n. (251) *and Hathach went*
וַיַּגֵּד לְאֶסְתֵּר consec.-Hi. impf. 3 m.s. (נָגַד 616)-prep.-pr.n. (64) *and told Esther*
אֵת דִּבְרֵי מָרְדֳּכָי dir.obj.-n.m.p. cstr. (182)-pr.n. paus. (598) *what Mordecai had said*

4:10

וַתֹּאמֶר אֶסְתֵּר consec.-Qal impf. 3 f.s. (אָמַר 55)-pr.n. (64) *then Esther spoke*
לַהֲתָךְ prep.-pr.n. (251) *to Hathach*
וַתְּצַוֵּהוּ consec.-Pi. impf. 3 f.s.-3 m.s. sf. (צָוָה 845) *and gave him a message*
אֶל־מָרְדֳּכָי prep.-pr.n. paus. (598) *for Mordecai*

4:11

כָּל־עַבְדֵי הַמֶּלֶךְ n.m.s. cstr. (481)-n.m.p. cstr. (713)-def.art.-n.m.s. (I 572) *all the king's servants*

וְעַם־מְדִינוֹת conj.-n.m.s. cstr. (I 766)-n.f.p. cstr. (193) *and the people of the provinces of*

הַמֶּלֶךְ v.supra *the king*

יוֹדְעִים אֲשֶׁר Qal act.ptc. m.p. (יָדַע 393)-rel. (81) *know that*

כָּל־אִישׁ וְאִשָּׁה n.m.s. cstr. (481)-n.m.s. (35) -conj.-n.f.s. (61) *any man or woman*

אֲשֶׁר יָבוֹא־ rel. (81)-Qal impf. 3 m.s. (בּוֹא 97) *who goes*

אֶל־הַמֶּלֶךְ prep.-v.supra *to the king*

אֶל־הֶחָצֵר הַפְּנִימִית prep.-def.art.-n.m.s. (I 346) -def.art.-adj. f.s. (819) *inside the inner court*

אֲשֶׁר לֹא־יִקָּרֵא rel. (81)-neg.-Ni. impf. 3 m.s. (894 קָרָא) *without being called*

אַחַת דָּתוֹ adj. f.s. (25)-n.f.s.-3 m.s. sf. (206) *there is but one law*

לְהָמִית prep.-Hi. inf.cstr. (מוּת 559) *to be put to death*

לְבַד מֵאֲשֶׁר prep.-n.m.s. (94)-prep.-rel. (81) *except one to whom*

יוֹשִׁיט־לוֹ Hi. impf. 3 m.s. (יָשַׁט 445)-prep.-3 m.s. sf. *holds out to him*

הַמֶּלֶךְ def.art.-n.m.s. (I 572) *the king*

אֶת־שַׁרְבִיט הַזָּהָב dir.obj.-n.m.s. cstr. (987)-def. art.-n.m.s. (262) *the golden scepter*

וְחָיָה conj.-Qal pf. 3 m.s. (חָיָה 310) *that he may live*

וַאֲנִי לֹא נִקְרֵאתִי conj.-pers.pr. 1 c.s. (58)-neg. -Ni. pf. 1 c.s. (קָרָא 894) *and I have not been called*

לָבוֹא prep.-Qal inf.cstr. (בּוֹא 97) *to come in*

אֶל־הַמֶּלֶךְ prep.-v.supra *to the king*

זֶה שְׁלוֹשִׁים יוֹם demons.adj. m.s. (260)-num. p. (1026)-n.m.s. (398) *these thirty days*

4:12

וַיַּגִּידוּ consec.-Hi. impf. 3 m.p. (נָגַד 616) *and they told*

לְמָרְדֳּכָי prep.-pr.n. paus. (598) *Mordecai*

אֵת דִּבְרֵי אֶסְתֵּר dir.obj.-n.m.p. cstr. (182)-pr.n. (64) *what Esther had said*

4:13

וַיֹּאמֶר מָרְדֳּכַי consec.-Qal impf. 3 m.s. (אָמַר 55)-pr.n. (598) *then Mordecai told*

לְהָשִׁיב prep.-Hi. inf.cstr. (שׁוּב 996) *to return*

אֶל־אֶסְתֵּר prep.-pr.n. (64) *to Esther*

אַל־תְּדַמִּי neg.-Pi. impf. 2 f.s. (דָּמָה I 197) *think not*

בְנַפְשֵׁךְ prep.-n.f.s.-2 f.s. sf. (659) *in yourself*

לְהִמָּלֵט prep.-Ni. inf.cstr. (מָלַט 572) *that you will escape*

בֵּית־הַמֶּלֶךְ n.m.s. cstr. (108)-def.art.-n.m.s. (I 572) *in the king's palace*

מִכָּל־הַיְּהוּדִים prep.-n.m.s. cstr. (481)-def.art.-adj. gent. m.p. (397) *more than all the other Jews*

4:14

כִּי אִם־הַחֲרֵשׁ תַּחֲרִישִׁי conj. (471)-hypoth.part. (49)-Hi. inf.abs. (חָרַשׁ II 361)-Hi. impf. 2 f.s. (חָרַשׁ II 361) *for if you keep silence*

בָּעֵת הַזֹּאת prep.-def.art.-n.f.s. (773)-def.art. -demons.adj. f.s. (260) *at such a time as this*

רֶוַח וְהַצָּלָה n.m.s. (926)-conj.-n.f.s. (665) *relief and deliverance*

יַעֲמוֹד Qal impf. 3 m.s. (עָמַד 763) *will rise*

לַיְּהוּדִים prep.-def.art.-adj. gent. m.p. (397) *for the Jews*

מִמָּקוֹם אַחֵר prep.-n.m.s. (879)-adj. m.s. (29) *from another quarter*

וְאַתְּ conj.-pers.pr. 2 f.s. (61) *but you*

וּבֵית־אָבִיךְ conj.-n.m.s. cstr. (108)-n.m.s.-2 f.s. sf. (3) *and your father's house*

תֹּאבֵדוּ Qal impf. 2 m.p. (אָבַד 1) *will perish*

וּמִי יוֹדֵעַ conj.-interr. (566)-Qal act.ptc. (יָדַע 393) *and who knows*

אִם־לְעֵת כָּזֹאת hypoth.part. (49)-prep.-n.f.s. (773)-prep.-demons. adj. f.s. (260) *whether for such a time as this*

הִגַּעַתְּ Hi. pf. 2 f.s. (נָגַע 619) *you have come*

לַמַּלְכוּת prep.-def.art.-n.f.s. (574) *to the kingdom*

4:15

וַתֹּאמֶר אֶסְתֵּר consec.-Qal impf. 3 f.s. (אָמַר 55)-pr.n. (64) *then Esther told (them)*

לְהָשִׁיב prep.-Hi. inf.cstr. (שׁוּב 996) *to return*

אֶל־מָרְדֳּכָי prep.-pr.n. paus. (598) *to Mordecai*

4:16

לֵךְ כְּנוֹס Qal impv. 2 m.s. (הָלַךְ 249)-Qal impv. 2 m.s. (כָּנַס 488) *go, gather*

אֶת־כָּל־הַיְּהוּדִים dir.obj.-n.m.s. cstr. (481)-def. art.-adj. gent. m.p. (397) *all the Jews*

הַנִּמְצְאִים def.art.-Ni. ptc. m.p. (מָצָא 592) *to be found*

בְּשׁוּשָׁן prep.-pr.n. (1004) *in Susa*

וְצוּמוּ עָלַי conj.-Qal impv. 2 m.p. (צוּם 847) -prep.-1 c.s. sf. *and hold a fast on my behalf*

וְאַל־תֹּאכְלוּ conj.-neg.-Qal impf. 2 m.p. (אָכַל 37) *and neither eat*

וְאַל־תִּשְׁתּוּ v.supra-Qal impf. 2 m.p. (שָׁתָה 1059) *nor drink*

שְׁלֹשֶׁת יָמִים num. f. cstr. (1025)-n.m.p. (398) *for three days*

לַיְלָה וָיוֹם n.m.s. (538)-conj.-n.m.s. (398) *night or day*

גַּם־אֲנִי adv. (168)-pers.pr. 1 c.s. (58) *also I*

וְנַעֲרֹתַי conj.-n.f.p.-1 c.s. sf. (655) *and my maids*

אָצוּם כֵּן Qal impf. 1 c.s. (צוּם 847)-adv. (485) *will fast as you do*

וּבְכֵן אָבוֹא conj.-prep.-adv. (485)-Qal impf. 1 c.s. (בּוֹא 97) *and then I will go*

אֶל־הַמֶּלֶךְ prep.-def.art.-n.m.s. (I 572) *to the king*

אֲשֶׁר לֹא־כַדָּת rel. (81)-neg.-prep.-def.art.-n.f.s. (206) *though it is against the law*

וְכַאֲשֶׁר אָבַדְתִּי conj.-prep.-rel. (81)-Qal pf. 1 c.s. (1 אָבַד) *and if I perish*

אָבָדְתִּי v.supra paus. *I perish*

4:17

וַיַּעֲבֹר מָרְדֳּכָי consec.-Qal impf. 3 m.s. (עָבַר 716)-pr.n. paus. (598) *Mordecai then went away*

וַיַּעַשׂ consec.-Qal impf. 3 m.s. (עָשָׂה I 793) *and did*

כְּכֹל prep.-n.m.s. (481) *everything*

אֲשֶׁר־צִוְּתָה rel. (81)-Pi. pf. 3 f.s. (צָוָה 845) *as ... had ordered*

עָלָיו prep.-3 m.s. sf. *him*

אֶסְתֵּר pr.n. (64) *Esther*

5:1

וַיְהִי consec.-Qal impf. 3 m.s. (הָיָה 224) *and it was*

בַּיּוֹם הַשְּׁלִישִׁי prep.-def.art.-n.m.s. (398)-def. art.-num. ord. (1026) *on the third day*

וַתִּלְבַּשׁ אֶסְתֵּר consec.-Qal impf. 3 f.s. (לָבַשׁ 527)-pr.n. (64) *Esther put on the ... robe*

מַלְכוּת n.f.s. (574) *royal*

וַתַּעֲמֹד consec.-Qal impf. 3 f.s. (עָמַד 763) *and stood*

בַּחֲצַר prep.-n.m.s. cstr. (I 346) *in the court of*

בֵּית־הַמֶּלֶךְ n.m.s. cstr. (108)-def.art.-n.m.s. (I 572) *the king's palace*

הַפְּנִימִית def.art.-adj. f.s. (819) *inner*

נֹכַח בֵּית הַמֶּלֶךְ prep. (647)-v.supra-v.supra *opposite the king's hall*

וְהַמֶּלֶךְ יוֹשֵׁב conj.-v.supra-Qal act.ptc. (יָשַׁב 442) *the king was sitting*

עַל־כִּסֵּא מַלְכוּתוֹ prep.-n.m.s. cstr. (490)-n.f.s.-3 m.s. sf. (574) *on his royal throne*

בְּבֵית הַמַּלְכוּת prep.-n.m.s. cstr. (108)-def.art. -n.f.s. (574) *inside the palace*

נֹכַח פֶּתַח הַבָּיִת v.supra-n.m.s. cstr. (835)-def. art.-n.m.s. paus. (108) *opposite the entrance to the palace*

5:2

וַיְהִי כִרְאוֹת consec.-Qal impf. 3 m.s. (הָיָה 224) -prep.-Qal inf.cstr. (רָאָה 906) *and when ... saw*

הַמֶּלֶךְ def.art.-n.m.s. (I 572) *the king*

אֶת־אֶסְתֵּר הַמַּלְכָּה dir.obj.-pr.n. (64)-def.art. -n.f.s. (573) *Queen Esther*

עֹמֶדֶת בֶּחָצֵר Qal act.ptc. f.s. (עָמַד 763)-prep. -def.art.-n.m.s. (I 346) *standing in the court*

נָשְׂאָה חֵן Qal pf. 3 f.s. (נָשָׂא 669)-n.m.s. (336) *she found favor*

בְּעֵינָיו prep.-n.f.p.-3 m.s. sf. (744) *in his sight*

וַיּוֹשֶׁט הַמֶּלֶךְ consec.-Hi. impf. 3 m.s. (יָשַׁט 445) -def.art.-n.m.s. (I 572) *and the king held out*

לְאֶסְתֵּר prep.-pr.n. (64) *to Esther*

אֶת־שַׁרְבִיט הַזָּהָב dir.obj.-n.m.s. cstr. (987)-def. art.-n.m.s. (262) *the golden scepter*

אֲשֶׁר בְּיָדוֹ rel. (81)-prep.-n.f.s.-3 m.s. sf. (388) *that was in his hand*

וַתִּקְרַב אֶסְתֵּר consec.-Qal impf. 3 f.s. (קָרַב 897)-pr.n. (64) *then Esther approached*

וַתִּגַּע consec.-Qal impf. 3 f.s. (נָגַע 619) *and touched*

בְּרֹאשׁ הַשַּׁרְבִיט prep.-n.m.s. cstr. (910)-def. art.-n.m.s. (987) *the top of the scepter*

5:3

וַיֹּאמֶר לָהּ consec.-Qal impf. 3 m.s. (אָמַר 55)-prep.-3 f.s. sf. *and said to her*

הַמֶּלֶךְ def.art.-n.m.s. (I 572) *the king*

מַה־לָּךְ interr. (552)-prep.-2 f.s. sf. *what is it*

אֶסְתֵּר הַמַּלְכָּה pr.n. (64)-def.art.-n.f.s. (573) *Queen Esther*

וּמַה־בַּקָּשָׁתֵךְ conj.-interr. (552)-n.m.s.-2 f.s. sf. (135) *what is your request*

עַד־חֲצִי הַמַּלְכוּת prep. (III 723)-n.m.s. cstr. (345)-def.art.-n.f.s. (574) *to the half of the kingdom*

וְיִנָּתֵן לָךְ conj.-Ni. impf. 3 m.s. (נָתַן 678)-prep.-2 f.s. sf. *it shall be given you*

5:4

וַתֹּאמֶר אֶסְתֵּר consec.-Qal impf. 3 f.s. (אָמַר 55)-pr.n. (64) *and Esther said*

אִם־עַל־הַמֶּלֶךְ hypoth.part. (49)-prep.-def.art. -n.m.s. (I 572) *if unto the king*
טוֹב adj. m.s. (II 373) *it please*
יָבוֹא Qal impf. 3 m.s. (בּוֹא 97) *let come*
הַמֶּלֶךְ וְהָמָן def.art.-n.m.s. (I 572)-conj.-pr.n. (243) *the king and Haman*
הַיּוֹם def.art.-n.m.s. (298) *this day*
אֶל־הַמִּשְׁתֶּה prep.-def.art.-n.m.s. (1059) *to a dinner*
אֲשֶׁר־עָשִׂיתִי לוֹ rel. (81)-Qal pf. 1 c.s. (עָשָׂה I 793)-prep.-3 m.s. sf. *that I have prepared for him*

5:5

וַיֹּאמֶר הַמֶּלֶךְ consec.-Qal impf. 3 m.s. (אָמַר 55)-def.art.-n.m.s. (I 572) *then said the king*
מַהֲרוּ אֶת־הָמָן Pi. impv. 2 m.p. (מָהַר 554)-dir. obj.-pr.n. (243) *bring Haman quickly*
לַעֲשׂוֹת prep.-Qal inf.cstr. (עָשָׂה I 793) *that we may do*
אֶת־דְּבַר אֶסְתֵּר dir.obj.-n.m.s. cstr. (182)-pr.n. (64) *the word of Esther*
וַיָּבֹא consec.-Qal impf. 3 m.s. (בּוֹא 97) *so came*
הַמֶּלֶךְ וְהָמָן def.art.-n.m.s. (I 572)-conj.-pr.n. (243) *the king and Haman*
אֶל־הַמִּשְׁתֶּה prep.-def.art.-n.m.s. (1059) *to the dinner*
אֲשֶׁר־עָשְׂתָה אֶסְתֵּר rel. (81)-Qal pf. 3 f.s. (עָשָׂה I 793)-pr.n. (64) *that Esther had prepared*

5:6

וַיֹּאמֶר הַמֶּלֶךְ consec.-Qal impf. 3 m.s. (אָמַר 55)-def.art.-n.m.s. (I 572) *and the king said*
לְאֶסְתֵּר prep.-pr.n. (64) *to Esther*
בְּמִשְׁתֵּה הַיַּיִן prep.-n.m.s. cstr. (1059)-def.art. -n.m.s. (406) *as they were drinking wine*
מַה־שְּׁאֵלָתֵךְ interr. (552)-n.f.s.-2 f.s. sf. (982) *what is your petition*
וְיִנָּתֵן לָךְ conj.-Ni. impf. 3 m.s. (נָתַן 678)-prep.-2 f.s. sf. *it shall be granted you*
וּמַה־בַּקָּשָׁתֵךְ conj.-v.supra-n.m.s.-2 f.s. sf. (135) *and what is your request*
עַד־חֲצִי הַמַּלְכוּת prep. (III 723)-n.m.s. cstr. (345) -def.art.-n.f.s. (574) *even to the half of my kingdom*
וְתֵעָשׂ conj.-Ni. impf. 3 f.s. apoc. (עָשָׂה I 793) *and it shall be fulfilled*

5:7

וַתַּעַן אֶסְתֵּר consec.-Qal impf. 3 f.s. (עָנָה I 772)-pr.n. (64) *but Esther answered*
וַתֹּאמַר consec.-Qal impf. 3 f.s. (אָמַר 55) *and said*
שְׁאֵלָתִי n.f.s.-1 c.s. sf. (982) *my petition*
וּבַקָּשָׁתִי conj.-n.m.s.-1 c.s. sf. (135) *and my request*

5:8

אִם־מָצָאתִי חֵן hypoth.part. (49)-Qal pf. 1 c.s. (592)-n.m.s. (336) *if I have found favor*
בְּעֵינֵי הַמֶּלֶךְ prep.-n.f.p. cstr. (744)-def.art.-n.m.s. (I 572) *in the sight of the king*
וְאִם־עַל־הַמֶּלֶךְ conj.-v.supra-prep.-v.supra *and if unto the king*
טוֹב adj. m.s. (II 373) *it pleases*
לָתֵת prep.-Qal inf.cstr. (נָתַן 678) *to grant*
אֶת־שְׁאֵלָתִי dir.obj.-n.f.s.-1 c.s. sf. (982) *my petition*
וְלַעֲשׂוֹת conj.-prep.-Qal inf.cstr. (עָשָׂה I 793) *and fulfil*
אֶת־בַּקָּשָׁתִי dir.obj.-n.m.s.-1 c.s. sf. (135) *my request*
יָבוֹא Qal impf. 3 m.s. (בּוֹא 97) *let come*
הַמֶּלֶךְ וְהָמָן def.art.-n.m.s. (I 572)-conj.-pr.n. (243) *the king and Haman*
אֶל־הַמִּשְׁתֶּה prep.-def.art.-n.m.s. (1059) *to the dinner*
אֲשֶׁר אֶעֱשֶׂה לָהֶם rel. (81)-Qal impf. 1 c.s. (עָשָׂה I 793)-prep.-3 m.p. sf. *which I will prepare for them*
וּמָחָר conj.-adv. (563) *and tomorrow*
אֶעֱשֶׂה Qal impf. 1 c.s. (עָשָׂה I 793) *I will do*
כִּדְבַר הַמֶּלֶךְ prep.-n.m.s. cstr. (182)-v.supra *as the king has said*

5:9

וַיֵּצֵא הָמָן consec.-Qal impf. 3 m.s. (יָצָא 422) -pr.n. 243) *and Haman went out*
בַּיּוֹם הַהוּא prep.-def.art.-n.m.s. (398)-def.art. -demons.adj. m.s. (214) *that day*
שָׂמֵחַ adj. m.s. (970) *joyful*
וְטוֹב לֵב conj.-adj. m.s. cstr. (II 373)-n.m.s. (524) *and glad of heart*
וְכִרְאוֹת הָמָן conj.-prep.-Qal inf.cstr. (רָאָה 906)-pr.n. (243) *but when Haman saw*
אֶת־מָרְדֳּכַי dir.obj.-pr.n. (598) *Mordecai*
בְּשַׁעַר הַמֶּלֶךְ prep.-n.m.s. cstr. (1044)-def. art.-n.m.s. (I 572) *in the king's gate*
וְלֹא־קָם conj.-neg.-Qal pf. 3 m.s. (קוּם 877) *that he neither rose*
וְלֹא־זָע conj.-neg.-Qal pf. 3 m.s. (זוּעַ 266) *nor trembled*
מִמֶּנּוּ prep.-3 m.s. sf. *before him*

וַיִּמָּלֵא הָמָן consec.-Ni. impf. 3 m.s. (מָלֵא 569) -pr.n. (243) *Haman was filled*
עַל־מָרְדֳּכַי prep.-pr.n. (598) *against Mordecai*
חֵמָה n.f.s. (404) *with wrath*

5:10

וַיִּתְאַפַּק הָמָן consec.-Hith. impf. 3 m.s. (אָפַק 67)-pr.n. (243) *Haman restrained himself*
וַיָּבוֹא אֶל־בֵּיתוֹ consec.-Qal impf. 3 m.s. (בּוֹא 97)-prep.-n.m.s.-3 m.s. sf. (108) *and went to his house*
וַיִּשְׁלַח consec.-Qal impf. 3 m.s. (שָׁלַח 1018) *and he sent*
וַיָּבֵא consec.-Hi. impf. 3 m.s. (בּוֹא 97) *and fetched*
אֶת־אֹהֲבָיו dir.obj.-Qal act.ptc. m.p.-3 m.s. sf. (12 אָהַב) *his friends*
וְאֶת־זֶרֶשׁ אִשְׁתּוֹ conj.-dir.obj.-pr.n. (284)-n.f.s.-3 m.s. sf. (61) *and his wife Zeresh*

5:11

וַיְסַפֵּר לָהֶם consec.-Pi. impf. 3 m.s. (סָפַר 707) -prep.-3 m.p. sf. *and ... recounted to them*
הָמָן pr.n. (243) *Haman*
אֶת־כְּבוֹד עָשְׁרוֹ dir.obj.-n.m.s. cstr. (458)-n.m.s.-3 m.s. sf. (799) *the splendor of his riches*
וְרֹב בָּנָיו conj.-n.m.s. cstr. (913)-n.m.p.-3 m.s. sf. (119) *the number of his sons*
וְאֵת כָּל־אֲשֶׁר conj.-dir.obj.-n.m.s. (481)-rel. (81) *and all which*
גִּדְּלוֹ הַמֶּלֶךְ Pi. pf. 3 m.s.-3 m.s. sf. (גָּדַל 152)-def. art.-n.m.s. (I 572) *the king had made him great*
וְאֵת אֲשֶׁר נִשְּׂאוֹ conj.-dir.obj.-v.supra-Pi. pf. 3 m.s.-3 m.s. sf. (נָשָׂא 669) *and how he had advanced him*
עַל־הַשָּׂרִים prep.-def.art.-n.m.p. (978) *above the princes*
וְעַבְדֵי הַמֶּלֶךְ conj.-n.m.p. cstr. (713)-def.art. -n.m.s. (I 572) *and the servants of the king*

5:12

וַיֹּאמֶר הָמָן consec.-Qal impf. 3 m.s. (אָמַר 55) -pr.n. (243) *and Haman added*
אַף לֹא־הֵבִיאָה conj. (II 64)-neg.-Hi. pf. 3 f.s. (97 בּוֹא) *even ... let no one come*
אֶסְתֵּר הַמַּלְכָּה pr.n. (64)-def.art.-n.f.s. (573) *Queen Esther*
עִם־הַמֶּלֶךְ prep. (767)-def.art.-n.m.s. (I 572) *with the king*
אֶל־הַמִּשְׁתֶּה prep.-def.art.-n.m.s. (1059) *to the banquet*
אֲשֶׁר־עָשָׂתָה rel. (81)-Qal pf. 3 f.s. (עָשָׂה I 793) *she prepared*
כִּי אִם־אוֹתִי conj. (471)-hypoth.part. (49)-dir. obj.-1 c.s. sf. *but myself*
וְגַם־לְמָחָר conj.-adv. (168)-prep.-adv. (563) *and tomorrow*
אֲנִי קְרוּא־לָהּ pers.pr. 1 c.s. (58)-Qal pass.ptc. (894 קָרָא)-prep.-3 f.s. sf. *I am invited by her*
עִם־הַמֶּלֶךְ prep. (767)-def.art.-n.m.s. (I 572) *with the king*

5:13

וְכָל־זֶה conj.-n.m.s. cstr. (481)-demons.adj. m.s. (260) *yet all this*
אֵינֶנּוּ שֹׁוֶה לִי neg.-3 m.s. sf. (II 34)-Qal act.ptc. (I 1000 שָׁוָה)-prep.-1 c.s. sf. *does me no good*
בְּכָל־עֵת prep.-n.m.s. cstr. (481)-n.f.s. (773) *so long as*
אֲשֶׁר אֲנִי רֹאֶה rel. (81)-pers.pr. 1 c.s. (58)-Qal act.ptc. (רָאָה 906) *as I see*
אֶת־מָרְדֳּכַי dir.obj.-pr.n. (598) *Mordecai*
הַיְּהוּדִי def.art.-adj. gent. m.s. (397) *the Jew*
יוֹשֵׁב Qal act.ptc. (יָשַׁב 442) *sitting*
בְּשַׁעַר הַמֶּלֶךְ prep.-n.m.s. cstr. (1044)-def. art.-n.m.s. (I 572) *at the king's gate*

5:14

וַתֹּאמֶר לוֹ consec.-Qal impf. 3 f.s. (אָמַר 55)-prep.-3 m.s. sf. *then ... said to him*
זֶרֶשׁ אִשְׁתּוֹ pr.n. (284)-n.f.s.-3 m.s. sf. (61) *Zeresh his wife*
וְכָל־אֹהֲבָיו conj.-n.m.s. cstr. (481)-Qal act.ptc. m.p.-3 m.s. sf. (אָהַב 12) *and all his friends*
יַעֲשׂוּ־עֵץ Qal impf. 3 m.p. (עָשָׂה I 793)-n.m.s. (781) *let a gallows be made*
גָּבֹהַּ חֲמִשִּׁים אַמָּה adj. m.s. (147)-num. p. (332) -n.f.s. (52) *fifty cubits high*
וּבַבֹּקֶר conj.-prep.-def.art.-n.m.s. (133) *and in the morning*
אֱמֹר לַמֶּלֶךְ Qal impv. 2 m.s. (אָמַר 55)-prep. -def.art.-n.m.s. (I 572) *tell the king*
וְיִתְלוּ conj.-Qal impf. 3 m.p. (תָּלָה 1067) *and let be hanged*
אֶת־מָרְדֳּכַי dir.obj.-pr.n. (598) *Mordecai*
עָלָיו prep.-3 m.s. sf. *upon it*
וּבֹא־עִם־הַמֶּלֶךְ conj.-Qal impv. 2 m.s. (בּוֹא 97)-prep. (767)-def.art.-n.m.s. (I 572) *then go with the king*
אֶל־הַמִּשְׁתֶּה prep.-def.art.-n.m.s. (1059) *to the dinner*
שָׂמֵחַ adj. (970) *merrily*

וַיִּיטַב הַדָּבָר consec.-Qal impf. 3 m.s. (יָטַב 405) -def.art.-n.m.s. (182) *this counsel pleased*

לִפְנֵי הָמָן prep.-n.m.p. cstr. (815)-pr.n. (243) *before Haman*

וַיַּעַשׂ הָעֵץ consec.-Qal impf. 3 m.s. (עָשָׂה I 793)-def.art.-n.m.s. (781) *and he had the gallows made*

6:1

בַּלַּיְלָה הַהוּא prep.-def.art.-n.m.s. (538)-def. art.-demons.adj. m.s. (214) *on that night*

נָדְדָה שְׁנַת הַמֶּלֶךְ Qal pf. 3 f.s. (נָדַד 622)-n.f.s. cstr. (446)-def.art.-n.m.s. (I 572) *the king could not sleep*

וַיֹּאמֶר consec.-Qal impf. 3 m.s. (אָמַר 55) *and he gave orders*

לְהָבִיא prep.-Hi. inf.cstr. (בּוֹא 97) *to bring*

אֶת־סֵפֶר הַזִּכְרֹנוֹת dir.obj.-n.m.s. cstr. (706)-def. art.-n.m.p. (272) *the book of memorable deeds*

דִּבְרֵי הַיָּמִים n.m.p. cstr. (182)-def.art.-n.m.p. (398) *the chronicles*

וַיִּהְיוּ נִקְרָאִים consec.-Qal impf. 3 m.p. (הָיָה 224)-Ni. ptc. m.p. (קָרָא 894) *and they were read*

לִפְנֵי הַמֶּלֶךְ prep.-n.m.p. cstr. (815)-def.art.-n.m.s. (I 572) *before the king*

6:2

וַיִּמָּצֵא consec.-Ni. impf. 3 m.s. (מָצָא 592) *and it was found*

כָתוּב Qal pass.ptc. (כָּתַב 507) *written*

אֲשֶׁר הִגִּיד מָרְדֳּכַי rel. (81)-Hi. pf. 3 m.s. (נָגַד 616)-pr.n. (598) *how Mordecai had told*

עַל־בִּגְתָנָא prep. (II 752)-pr.n. (94) *about Bigthana*

וָתֶרֶשׁ conj.-pr.n. (1076) *and Teresh*

שְׁנֵי סָרִיסֵי num. p. cstr. (1040)-n.m.p. cstr. (710) *two of the eunuchs of*

הַמֶּלֶךְ def.art.-n.m.s. (I 572) *the king*

מִשֹּׁמְרֵי הַסַּף prep.-Qal act.ptc. m.p. cstr. (שָׁמַר 1036)-def.art.-n.m.s. (II 706) *of those who guarded the threshold*

אֲשֶׁר בִּקְשׁוּ rel. (81)-Pi. pf. 3 c.p. (בָּקַשׁ 134) *who had sought*

לִשְׁלֹחַ יָד prep.-Qal inf.cstr. (שָׁלַח 1018)-n.f.s. (388) *to lay hands*

בַּמֶּלֶךְ אֲחַשְׁוֵרוֹשׁ prep.-def.art.-n.m.s. (I 572) -pr.n. (31) *on King Ahasuerus*

6:3

וַיֹּאמֶר הַמֶּלֶךְ consec.-Qal impf. 3 m.s. (אָמַר 55)-def.art.-n.m.s. (I 572) *and the king said*

מַה־נַּעֲשָׂה interr. (552)-Ni. pf. 3 m.s. (עָשָׂה I 793) *what has been done*

יְקָר וּגְדוּלָּה n.m.s. (430)-conj.-n.f.s. (153) *honor or dignity*

לְמָרְדֳּכַי prep.-pr.n. (598) *for Mordecai*

עַל־זֶה prep.-demons.adj. m.s. (260) *for this*

וַיֹּאמְרוּ consec.-Qal impf. 3 m.p. (אָמַר 55) *then said*

נַעֲרֵי הַמֶּלֶךְ n.m.p. cstr. (654)-def.art.-n.m.s. (I 572) *the king's servants*

מְשָׁרְתָיו Pi. ptc. m.p.-3 m.s. sf. (שָׁרַת 1058) *who attended him*

לֹא־נַעֲשָׂה neg.-Ni. pf. 3 m.s. (עָשָׂה I 793) *has not been done*

עִמּוֹ prep.-3 m.s. sf. (767) *for him*

דָּבָר n.m.s. (182) *anything*

6:4

וַיֹּאמֶר הַמֶּלֶךְ consec.-Qal impf. 3 m.s. (אָמַר 55)-def.art.-n.m.s. (I 572) *and the king said*

מִי בֶחָצֵר interr. (566)-prep.-def.art.-n.m.s. (I 346) *who is in the court?*

וְהָמָן בָּא conj.-pr.n. (243)-Qal pf. 3 m.s. (בּוֹא 97) *now Haman had entered*

לַחֲצַר prep.-n.m.s. cstr. (I 346) *the court of*

בֵּית־הַמֶּלֶךְ n.m.s. cstr. (108)-def.art.-n.m.s. (I 572) *the king's palace*

הַחִיצוֹנָה def.art.-adj. f.s. (300) *the outer*

לֵאמֹר prep.-Qal inf.cstr. (55) *to speak*

לַמֶּלֶךְ prep.-def.art.-v.supra *to the king*

לִתְלוֹת prep.-Qal inf.cstr. (תָּלָה 1067) *about having ... hanged*

אֶת־מָרְדֳּכַי dir.obj.-pr.n. (598) *Mordecai*

עַל־הָעֵץ prep.-def.art.-n.m.s. (781) *on the gallows*

אֲשֶׁר־הֵכִין לוֹ rel. (81)-Hi. pf. 3 m.s. (כּוּן 465) -prep.-3 m.s. sf. *that he had prepared for him*

6:5

וַיֹּאמְרוּ consec.-Qal impf. 3 m.p. (אָמַר 55) *so ... told*

נַעֲרֵי הַמֶּלֶךְ n.m.p. cstr. (654)-def.art.-n.m.s. (I 572) *the king's servants*

אֵלָיו prep.-3 m.s. sf. *him*

הִנֵּה הָמָן עֹמֵד demons.part. (243)-pr.n. (243) -Qal act.ptc. (עָמַד 763) *behold, Haman is standing*

בֶּחָצֵר prep.-def.art.-n.m.s. (I 346) *in the court*

וַיֹּאמֶר הַמֶּלֶךְ consec.-Qal impf. 3 m.s. (55)-def. art.-n.m.s. (I 572) *and the king said*
יָבוֹא Qal impf. 3 m.s. (בּוֹא 97) *let him come in*

6:6

וַיָּבוֹא הָמָן consec.-Qal impf. 3 m.s. (בּוֹא 97) -pr.n. (243) *so Haman came in*
וַיֹּאמֶר לוֹ consec.-Qal impf. 3 m.s. (55)-prep.-3 m.s. sf. *and ... said to him*
הַמֶּלֶךְ def.art.-n.m.s. (I 572) *the king*
מַה־לַּעֲשׂוֹת interr. (552)-prep.-Qal inf.cstr. (I 793 עָשָׂה) *what shall be done*
בָּאִישׁ prep.-def.art.-n.m.s. (35) *to the man*
אֲשֶׁר הַמֶּלֶךְ rel. (81)-v.supra *to the man whom the king*
חָפֵץ Qal pf. 3 m.s. (342) *delights*
בִּיקָרוֹ prep.-n.m.s.-3 m.s. sf. (430) *to honor (him)*
וַיֹּאמֶר הָמָן consec.-Qal impf. 3 m.s. (55)-pr.n. (243) *and Haman said*
בְּלִבּוֹ prep.-n.m.s.-3 m.s. sf. (524) *to himself (in his heart)*
לְמִי יַחְפֹּץ prep.-interr. (566)-Qal impf. 3 m.s. (342 חָפֵץ) *whom would ... delight*
הַמֶּלֶךְ def.art.-n.m.s. (I 572) *the king*
לַעֲשׂוֹת יְקָר prep.-Qal inf.cstr. (עָשָׂה I 793) -n.m.s. (430) *to honor*
יוֹתֵר מִמֶּנִּי n.m.s. (452)-prep.-1 c.s. sf. *more than me*

6:7

וַיֹּאמֶר הָמָן consec.-Qal impf. 3 m.s. (55)-pr.n. (243) *and Haman said*
אֶל־הַמֶּלֶךְ prep.-def.art.-n.m.s. (I 572) *to the king*
אִישׁ אֲשֶׁר n.m.s. (35)-rel. (81) *for the man whom*
הַמֶּלֶךְ חָפֵץ v.supra-Qal pf. 3 m.s. (342) *the king delights*
בִּיקָרוֹ prep.-n.m.s.-3 m.s. sf. (430) *to honor (him)*

6:8

יָבִיאוּ Hi. impf. 3 m.p. (בּוֹא 97) *let be brought*
לְבוּשׁ מַלְכוּת n.m.s. cstr. (528)-n.f.s. (574) *royal robes*
אֲשֶׁר לָבַשׁ־בּוֹ rel. (81)-Qal pf. 3 m.s. (527) -prep.-3 m.s. sf. *which ... has worn*
הַמֶּלֶךְ def.art.-n.m.s. (I 572) *the king*
וְסוּס conj.-n.m.s. (692) *and a horse*
אֲשֶׁר רָכַב עָלָיו v.supra-Qal pf. 3 m.s. (938) -prep.-3 m.s. sf. *which ... has ridden*
הַמֶּלֶךְ v.supra *the king*
וַאֲשֶׁר נִתַּן conj.-v.supra-Ni. pf. 3 m.s. (נָתַן 678) *and which is set*
כֶּתֶר מַלְכוּת n.m.s. cstr. (509)-n.f.s. (574) *a royal crown*
בְּרֹאשׁוֹ prep.-n.m.s.-3 m.s. sf. (910) *on his head*

6:9

וְנָתוֹן conj.-Qal inf.abs. (נָתַן 678; GK 113z) *and let be handed over*
הַלְּבוּשׁ def.art.-n.m.s. (528) *the robes*
וְהַסּוּס conj.-dir.obj.-n.m.s. (692) *and the horse*
עַל־יַד־אִישׁ prep.-n.f.s. cstr. (388)-n.m.s. (35) *to the hand of a man*
מִשָּׂרֵי הַמֶּלֶךְ prep.-n.m.p. cstr. (978)-def.art. -n.m.s. (I 572) *one of the king's princes*
הַפַּרְתְּמִים def.art.-n.m.p. (832) *the nobles*
וְהִלְבִּישׁוּ conj.-Hi. pf. 3 c.p. (לָבַשׁ 527) *and let them array*
אֶת־הָאִישׁ dir.obj.-def.art.-n.m.s. (35) *the man*
אֲשֶׁר הַמֶּלֶךְ rel. (81)-v.supra *whom the king*
חָפֵץ Qal pf. 3 m.s. (342) *delights*
בִּיקָרוֹ prep.-n.m.s.-3 m.s. sf. (430) *to honor*
וְהִרְכִּיבֻהוּ conj.-Hi. pf. 3 c.p.-3 m.s. sf. (רָכַב 938) *and let them conduct him*
עַל־הַסּוּס prep.-def.art.-n.m.s. (692) *on horseback*
בִּרְחוֹב הָעִיר prep.-n.f.s. cstr. (932)-def.art.-n.f.s. (746) *through the open square of the city*
וְקָרְאוּ לְפָנָיו conj.-Qal pf. 3 c.p. (קָרָא 894)-prep. -n.m.p.-3 m.s. sf. (815) *proclaiming before him*
כָּכָה יֵעָשֶׂה adv. (462)-Ni. impf. 3 m.s. (עָשָׂה I 793) *thus shall it be done*
לָאִישׁ prep.-def.art.-n.m.s. (35) *to the man*
אֲשֶׁר הַמֶּלֶךְ rel. (81)-v.supra *whom the king*
חָפֵץ v.supra *delights*
בִּיקָרוֹ v.supra *to honor*

6:10

וַיֹּאמֶר הַמֶּלֶךְ consec.-Qal impf. 3 m.s. (55)-def. art.-n.m.s. (I 572) *then the king said*
לְהָמָן prep.-pr.n. (243) *to Haman*
מַהֵר Pi. impv. 2 m.s. (מָהַר I 554) *make haste*
קַח Qal impv. 2 m.s. (לָקַח 542) *take*
אֶת־הַלְּבוּשׁ dir.obj.-def.art.-n.m.s. (528) *the robes*
וְאֶת־הַסּוּס conj.-dir.obj.-def.art.-n.m.s. (692) *and the horse*
כַּאֲשֶׁר דִּבַּרְתָּ prep.-rel. (81)-Pi. pf. 2 m.s. (דָּבַר 180) *as you have said*
וַעֲשֵׂה־כֵן conj.-Qal impv. 2 m.s. (עָשָׂה I 793) -adv. (485) *and do so*
לְמָרְדֳּכַי prep.-pr.n. (598) *to Mordecai*
הַיְּהוּדִי def.art.-adj. gent. m.s. (397) *the Jew*
הַיּוֹשֵׁב def.art.-Qal act.ptc. (יָשַׁב 442) *who sits*

בְּשַׁעַר הַמֶּלֶךְ prep.-n.m.s. cstr. (1044)-v.supra *at the king's gate*
אַל־תַּפֵּל דָּבָר neg.-Hi. impf. 2 m.s. apoc. (נָפַל 656)-n.m.s. (182) *leave out nothing*
מִכֹּל אֲשֶׁר דִּבַּרְתָּ prep.-n.m.s. (481)-rel. (81)-Pi. pf. 2 m.s. (דָּבַר 180) *of all that you have mentioned*

6:11

וַיִּקַּח הָמָן consec.-Qal impf. 3 m.s. (לָקַח 542) -pr.n. (243) *so Haman took*
אֶת־הַלְּבוּשׁ dir.obj.-def.art.-n.m.s. (528) *the robes*
וְאֶת־הַסּוּס conj.-dir.obj.-def.art.-n.m.s. (692) *the horse*
וַיַּלְבֵּשׁ consec.-Hi. impf. 3 m.s. (לָבַשׁ 527) *and he arrayed*
אֶת־מָרְדֳּכָי dir.obj.-pr.n. paus. (598) *Mordecai*
וַיַּרְכִּיבֵהוּ consec.-Hi. impf. 3 m.s.-3 m.s. sf. (רָכַב 938) *and made him ride*
בִּרְחוֹב הָעִיר prep.-n.f.s. cstr. (932)-def.art.-n.f.s. (746) *through the open square of the city*
וַיִּקְרָא לְפָנָיו consec.-Qal impf. 3 m.s. (קָרָא 894) -prep.-n.m.p.-3 m.s. sf. (815) *proclaiming before him*
כָּכָה יֵעָשֶׂה adv. (462)-Ni. impf. 3 m.s. (עָשָׂה I 793) *thus shall it be done*
לָאִישׁ prep.-def.art.-n.m.s. (35) *to the man*
אֲשֶׁר הַמֶּלֶךְ rel. (81)-def.art.-n.m.s. (I 572) *whom the king*
חָפֵץ Qal pf. 3 m.s. (342) *delights*
בִּיקָרוֹ prep.-n.m.s.-3 m.s. sf. (430) *to honor*

6:12

וַיָּשָׁב מָרְדֳּכַי consec.-Qal impf. 3 m.s. (שׁוּב 996)-pr.n. (598) *then Mordecai returned*
אֶל־שַׁעַר הַמֶּלֶךְ prep.-n.m.s. cstr. (1044)-def. art.-n.m.s. (I 572) *to the king's gate*
וְהָמָן נִדְחַף conj.-pr.n. (243)-Ni. pf. 3 m.s. (דָּחַף 191) *but Haman hurried*
אֶל־בֵּיתוֹ prep.-n.m.s.-3 m.s. sf. (108) *to his house*
אָבֵל adj. m.s. (I 5) *mourning*
וַחֲפוּי רֹאשׁ conj.-Qal pass.ptc. m.s. cstr. (חָפָה 341)-n.m.s. (910) *and with his head covered*

6:13

וַיְסַפֵּר הָמָן consec.-Pi. impf. 3 m.s. (סָפַר 707) -pr.n. (243) *and Haman told*
לְזֶרֶשׁ אִשְׁתּוֹ prep.-pr.n. (284)-n.f.s.-3 m.s. sf. (61) *to Zeresh his wife*
וּלְכָל־אֹהֲבָיו conj.-prep.-n.m.s. cstr. (481)-Qal act.ptc. m.p.-3 m.s. sf. (אָהַב 12) *and all his friends*
אֵת כָּל־אֲשֶׁר dir.obj.-n.m.s. (481)-rel. (81) *everything that*
קָרָהוּ Qal pf. 3 m.s.-3 m.s. sf. (קָרָה 899) *had befallen him*
וַיֹּאמְרוּ לוֹ consec.-Qal impf. 3 m.p. (אָמַר 55)-prep.-3 m.s. sf. *then ... said to him*
חֲכָמָיו adj. m.p.-3 m.s. sf. (314) *his wise men*
וְזֶרֶשׁ conj.-v.supra *and Zeresh*
אִשְׁתּוֹ v.supra *his wife*
אִם מִזֶּרַע hypoth.part. (49)-prep.-n.m.s. cstr. (282) *if of the seed of*
הַיְּהוּדִים def.art.-adj. gent. m.p. (397) *of the Jews*
מָרְדֳּכַי pr.n. (598) *Mordecai*
אֲשֶׁר הַחִלּוֹתָ rel. (81)-Hi. pf. 2 m.s. (חָלַל III 320) *whom you have begun*
לִנְפֹּל prep.-Qal inf.cstr. (נָפַל 656) *to fall*
לְפָנָיו prep.-n.m.p.-3 m.s. sf. (815) *before him*
לֹא־תוּכַל לוֹ neg.-Qal impf. 2 m.s. (יָכֹל 407) -prep.-3 m.s. sf. *you will not prevail against him*
כִּי־נָפוֹל תִּפּוֹל conj. (471)-Qal inf.abs. (נָפַל 656) -Qal impf. 2 m.s. (נָפַל 656) *but you will surely fall*
לְפָנָיו v.supra *before him*

6:14

עוֹדָם מְדַבְּרִים adv.-3 m.p. sf. (728)-Pi. ptc. m.p. (דָּבַר 180) *while they were yet talking*
עִמּוֹ prep.-3 m.s. sf. (767) *with him*
וְסָרִיסֵי הַמֶּלֶךְ conj.-n.m.p. cstr. (710)-def. art.-n.m.s. (I 572) *the king's eunuchs*
הִגִּיעוּ Hi. pf. 3 c.p. (נָגַע 619) *arrived*
וַיַּבְהִלוּ consec.-Hi. impf. 3 m.p. (בָּהַל 96) *and in haste*
לְהָבִיא prep.-Hi. inf.cstr. (בּוֹא 97) *brought*
אֶת־הָמָן dir.obj.-pr.n. (243) *Haman*
אֶל־הַמִּשְׁתֶּה prep.-def.art.-n.m.s. (1059) *to the banquet*
אֲשֶׁר־עָשְׂתָה rel. (81)-Qal pf. 3 f.s. (עָשָׂה I 793) *that ... had prepared*
אֶסְתֵּר pr.n. (64) *Esther*

7:1

וַיָּבֹא consec.-Qal impf. 3 m.s. (בּוֹא 97) *so went in*
הַמֶּלֶךְ וְהָמָן def.art.-n.m.s. (I 572)-conj.-pr.n. (243) *the king and Haman*
לִשְׁתּוֹת prep.-Qal inf.cstr. (שָׁתָה 1059) *to feast*
עִם־אֶסְתֵּר prep. (767)-pr.n. (64) *with Esther*
הַמַּלְכָּה def.art.-n.f.s. (573) *Queen*

7:2

וַיֹּאמֶר הַמֶּלֶךְ consec.-Qal impf. 3 m.s. (55)-def. art.-n.m.s. (I 572) *and the king said*

לְאֶסְתֵּר prep.-pr.n. (64) *to Esther*

גַּם בַּיּוֹם הַשֵּׁנִי adv. (168)-prep.-def.art.-n.m.s. (398)-def.art.-num. ord. (1041) *again on the second day*

בְּמִשְׁתֵּה הַיַּיִן prep.-n.m.s. cstr. (1059)-def. art.-n.m.s. (406) *as they were drinking wine*

מַה־שְּׁאֵלָתֵךְ interr. (552)-n.f.s.-2 f.s. sf. (982) *what is your petition*

אֶסְתֵּר הַמַּלְכָּה pr.n. (64)-def.art.-n.f.s. (573) *Queen Esther*

וְתִנָּתֵן לָךְ conj.-Ni. impf. 3 f.s. (נָתַן 678)-prep.-2 f.s. sf. *and it shall be granted you*

וּמַה־בַּקָּשָׁתֵךְ conj.-interr. (552)-n.f.s.-2 f.s. sf. (135) *and what is your request*

עַד־חֲצִי הַמַּלְכוּת prep. (III 723)-n.m.s. cstr. (345)-def.art.-n.f.s. (574) *even to the half of my kingdom*

וְתֵעָשׂ conj.-Ni. impf. 3 f.s. apoc. (עָשָׂה I 793; GK 109f) *it shall be fulfilled*

7:3

וַתַּעַן consec.-Qal impf. 3 f.s. (עָנָה I 772) *then answered*

אֶסְתֵּר הַמַּלְכָּה pr.n. (64)-def.art.-n.f.s. (573) *Queen Esther*

וַתֹּאמַר consec.-Qal impf. 3 f.s. (אָמַר 55) *and said*

אִם־מָצָאתִי חֵן hypoth.part. (49)-Qal pf. 1 c.s. (592 מָצָא)-n.m.s. (336) *if I have found favor*

בְּעֵינֶיךָ prep.-n.f.p.-2 m.s. sf. (744) *in your sight*

הַמֶּלֶךְ def.art.-n.m.s. (I 572) *O King*

וְאִם־עַל־הַמֶּלֶךְ conj.-v.supra-prep.-v.supra *and if ... the king*

טוֹב adj. m.s. (II 373) *it pleases*

תִּנָּתֶן־לִי Ni. impf. 3 f.s. (נָתַן 678)-prep.-1 c.s. sf. *let be given me*

נַפְשִׁי n.f.s.-1 c.s. sf. (659) *my life*

בִּשְׁאֵלָתִי prep.-n.f.s.-1 c.s. sf. (982) *at my petition*

וְעַמִּי conj.-n.m.s.-1 c.s. sf. (I 766) *and my people*

בְּבַקָּשָׁתִי prep.-n.f.s.-1 c.s. sf. (135) *at my request*

7:4

כִּי נִמְכַּרְנוּ conj. (471)-Ni. pf. 1 c.s. (מָכַר 569) *for we are sold*

אֲנִי וְעַמִּי pers.pr. 1 c.s. (58)-conj.-n.m.s.-1 c.s. sf. (I 766) *I and my people*

לְהַשְׁמִיד prep.-Hi. inf.cstr. (שָׁמַד 1029) *to be destroyed*

לַהֲרוֹג prep.-Qal inf.cstr. (הָרַג 246) *to be slain*

וּלְאַבֵּד conj.-prep.-Pi. inf.cstr. (אָבַד 1) *and to be annihilated*

וְאִלּוּ conj.-conj. (47) *if*

לַעֲבָדִים prep.-n.m.p. (713) *as slaves*

וְלִשְׁפָחוֹת conj.-prep.-n.f.p. (1046) *and maid-servants*

נִמְכַּרְנוּ Ni. pf. 1 c.p. (מָכַר 569) *we had been sold*

הֶחֱרַשְׁתִּי Hi. pf. 1 c.s. (חָרַשׁ II 361) *I would have held my peace*

כִּי אֵין הַצָּר conj. (471)-neg. (II 34)-def.art. -n.m.s. (III 865) *for there is no affliction*

שֹׁוֶה Qal act.ptc. (שָׁוָה I 1000) *to be compared*

בְּנֵזֶק הַמֶּלֶךְ prep.-n.m.s. cstr. (634)-def.art.-n.m.s. (I 572) *with the loss to the king*

7:5

וַיֹּאמֶר consec.-Qal impf. 3 m.s. (55) *then said*

הַמֶּלֶךְ אֲחַשְׁוֵרוֹשׁ def.art.-n.m.s. (I 572)-pr.n. (31) *King Ahasuerus*

וַיֹּאמֶר v.supra *and said*

לְאֶסְתֵּר הַמַּלְכָּה prep.-pr.n. (64)-def.art.-n.f.s. (573) *to Queen Esther*

מִי הוּא זֶה interr. (566)-pers.pr. 3 m.s. (214) -demons.adj. m.s. (260) *who is he*

וְאֵי־זֶה הוּא conj.-interr.adv. (32; GK 137a) -v.supra-v.supra *and where is he*

אֲשֶׁר־מְלָאוֹ לִבּוֹ rel. (81)-Qal pf. 3 m.s.-3 m.s. sf. (569; GK 74g)-n.m.s.-3 m.s. sf. (524) *that would presume*

לַעֲשׂוֹת כֵּן prep.-Qal inf.cstr. (עָשָׂה I 793)-adv. (485) *to do this*

7:6

וַתֹּאמֶר־אֶסְתֵּר conj.-Qal impf. 3 f.s. (אָמַר 55) -pr.n. (64) *and Esther said*

אִישׁ צַר וְאוֹיֵב n.m.s. (35)-n.m.s. (III 865)-conj. -Qal act.ptc. (אָיַב 33) *a foe and enemy*

הָמָן הָרָע הַזֶּה pr.n. (243)-def.art.-adj. m.s. (I 948)-def.art.-demons.adj. m.s. (260) *this wicked Haman*

וְהָמָן נִבְעַת conj.-pr.n. (243)-Ni. pf. 3 m.s. (בָּעַת 129) *then Haman was in terror*

מִלִּפְנֵי הַמֶּלֶךְ prep.-prep.-n.m.p. cstr. (815)-def. art.-n.m.s. (I 572) *before the king*

וְהַמַּלְכָּה conj.-def.art.-n.f.s. (573) *and the queen*

7:7

וְהַמֶּלֶךְ קָם conj.-def.art.-n.m.s. (I 572)-Qal pf. 3 m.s. (קוּם 877) *and the king rose*

בַּחֲמָתוֹ prep.-n.f.s.-3 m.s. sf. (404) *in his wrath*

מִמִּשְׁתֵּה הַיַּיִן prep.-n.m.s. cstr. (1059)-def. art.-n.m.s. (406) *from the feast (of wine)*
אֶל־גִּנַּת הַבִּיתָן prep.-n.f.s. cstr. (171)-def. art.-n.m.s. (113) *into the palace garden*
וְהָמָן עָמַד conj.-pr.n. (243)-Qal pf. 3 m.s. (763) *but Haman stayed*
לְבַקֵּשׁ prep.-Pi. inf.cstr. (בָּקַשׁ 134) *to beg*
עַל־נַפְשׁוֹ prep.-n.f.s.-3 m.s. sf. (659) *his life*
מֵאֶסְתֵּר הַמַּלְכָּה prep.-pr.n. (64)-def.art.-n.f.s. (573) *from Queen Esther*
כִּי רָאָה conj. (471)-Qal pf. 3 m.s. (906) *for he saw*
כִּי־כָלְתָה אֵלָיו conj. (471)-Qal pf. 3 f.s. (כָּלָה I 477)-prep.-3 m.s. sf. *that was determined against him*
הָרָעָה def.art.-n.f.s. (949) *evil*
מֵאֵת הַמֶּלֶךְ prep.-prep. (II 85)-def.art.-n.m.s. (I 572) *by the king*

7:8

וְהַמֶּלֶךְ שָׁב conj.-def.art.-n.m.s. (I 572)-Qal pf. 3 m.s. (שׁוּב 996) *and the king returned*
מִגִּנַּת הַבִּיתָן prep.-n.f.s. cstr. (171)-def.art.-n.m.s. (113) *from the palace garden*
אֶל־בֵּית prep.-n.m.s. cstr. (108) *to the place where*
מִשְׁתֵּה הַיַּיִן n.m.s. cstr. (1059)-def.art.-n.m.s. (406) *they were drinking wine*
וְהָמָן נֹפֵל conj.-pr.n. (243)-Qal act.ptc. (נָפַל 656) *as Haman was falling*
עַל־הַמִּטָּה prep.-def.art.-n.f.s. (641) *on the couch*
אֲשֶׁר אֶסְתֵּר עָלֶיהָ rel. (81)-pr.n. (64)-prep.-3 f.s. sf. *where Esther was*
וַיֹּאמֶר הַמֶּלֶךְ consec.-Qal impf. 3 m.s. (55) -def.art.-n.m.s. (I 572) *and the king said*
הֲגַם לִכְבּוֹשׁ interr.part.-adv. (168)-prep.-Qal inf.cstr. (כָּבַשׁ 461; GK 114i) *will he even assault*
אֶת־הַמַּלְכָּה dir.obj.-def.art.-n.f.s. (573) *the queen*
עִמִּי prep.-1 c.s. sf. (767) *in my presence*
בַּבָּיִת prep.-def.art.-n.m.s. (108) *in my own house*
הַדָּבָר יָצָא def.art.-n.m.s. (182)-Qal pf. 3 m.s. (592) *as the words left*
מִפִּי הַמֶּלֶךְ prep.-n.m.s. cstr. (804)-def.art.-n.m.s. (I 572) *the mouth of the king*
וּפְנֵי הָמָן conj.-n.m.p. cstr. (815)-pr.n. (243) *Haman's face*
חָפוּ Qal pf. 3 c.p. (חָפָה 341) *they covered*

7:9

וַיֹּאמֶר חַרְבוֹנָה consec.-Qal impf. 3 m.s. (55) -pr.n. (353) *then said Harbona*
אֶחָד מִן־הַסָּרִיסִים num. (25)-prep.-def.art.-n.m.p. (710) *one of the eunuchs*
לִפְנֵי הַמֶּלֶךְ prep.-n.m.p. cstr. (815)-def.art.-n.m.s. (I 572) *in attendance on the king*
גַּם הִנֵּה־הָעֵץ adv. (168)-demons.part. (243)-def. art.-n.m.s. (781) *moreover, behold the gallows*
אֲשֶׁר־עָשָׂה הָמָן rel. (81)-Qal pf. 3 m.s. (I 793) -pr.n. (243) *which Haman has prepared*
לְמָרְדֳּכַי prep.-pr.n. (598) *for Mordecai*
אֲשֶׁר דִּבֶּר־טוֹב rel. (81)-Pi. pf. 3 m.s. (דָּבַר 180)-adj. m.s. (II 373) *whose word saved*
עַל־הַמֶּלֶךְ prep.-def.art.-n.m.s. (I 572) *the king*
עֹמֵד Qal act.ptc. (763) *is standing*
בְּבֵית הָמָן prep.-n.m.s. cstr. (108)-pr.n. (243) *in Haman's house*
גָּבֹהַּ adj. m.s. (147) *high*
חֲמִשִּׁים אַמָּה num. p. (332)-n.f.s. (52) *fifty cubits*
וַיֹּאמֶר הַמֶּלֶךְ consec.-Qal impf. 3 m.s. (55) -def.art.-n.m.s. (I 572) *and the king said*
תְּלֻהוּ עָלָיו Qal impv. 2 m.p.-3 m.s. sf. (תָּלָה 1067)-prep.-3 m.s. sf. *hang him on that*

7:10

וַיִּתְלוּ consec.-Qal impf. 3 m.p. (תָּלָה 1067) *so they hanged*
אֶת־הָמָן dir.obj.-pr.n. (243) *Haman*
עַל־הָעֵץ prep.-def.art.-n.m.s. (781) *on the gallows*
אֲשֶׁר־הֵכִין rel. (81)-Hi. pf. 3 m.s. (כּוּן 465) *which he had prepared*
לְמָרְדֳּכָי prep.-pr.n. paus. (598) *for Mordecai*
וַחֲמַת הַמֶּלֶךְ conj.-n.f.s. cstr. (404)-def.art.-n.m.s. (I 572) *then the anger of the king*
שָׁכָכָה Qal pf. 3 f.s. paus. (שָׁכַךְ 1013) *abated*

8:1

בַּיּוֹם הַהוּא prep.-def.art.-n.m.s. (398)-def. art.-demons.adj. m.s. (214) *on that day*
נָתַן Qal pf. 3 m.s. (678) *gave*
הַמֶּלֶךְ אֲחַשְׁוֵרוֹשׁ def.art.-n.m.s. (I 572)-pr.n. (31) *King Ahasuerus*
לְאֶסְתֵּר הַמַּלְכָּה prep.-pr.n. (64)-def.art.-n.f.s. (573) *to Queen Esther*
אֶת־בֵּית הָמָן dir.obj.-n.m.s. cstr. (108)-pr.n. (243) *the house of Haman*
צֹרֵר הַיְּהוּדִים Qal act.ptc. cstr. (צָרַר II 865) -def.art.-adj. gent. m.p. (397) *the enemy of the Jews*
וּמָרְדֳּכַי בָּא conj.-pr.n. (598)-Qal pf. 3 m.s. (בּוֹא 97) *and Mordecai came*

לִפְנֵי הַמֶּלֶךְ prep.-n.m.p. cstr. (815)-def.art.-n.m.s. (I 572) *before the king*

כִּי־הִגִּידָה אֶסְתֵּר conj. (471)-Hi. pf. 3 f.s. (נָגַד 616)-pr.n. (64) *for Esther had told*

מַה הוּא־לָהּ interr. (552; GK 137c)-pers.pr. 3 m.s. (214)-prep.-3 f.s. sf. *what he was to her*

8:2

וַיָּסַר הַמֶּלֶךְ consec.-Qal impf. 3 m.s. (סוּר 693) -def.art.-n.m.s. (I 572) *and the king took off*

אֶת־טַבַּעְתּוֹ dir.obj.-n.f.s.-3 m.s. sf. (371) *his signet ring*

אֲשֶׁר הֶעֱבִיר rel. (81)-Hi. pf. 3 m.s. (עָבַר 716) *which he had taken*

מֵהָמָן prep.-pr.n. (243) *from Haman*

וַיִּתְּנָהּ consec.-Qal impf. 3 m.s.-3 f.s. sf. (נָתַן 678) *and gave it*

לְמָרְדֳּכָי prep.-pr.n. paus. (598) *to Mordecai*

וַתָּשֶׂם אֶסְתֵּר consec.-Qal impf. 3 f.s. (שִׂים 962)-pr.n. (64) *and Esther set*

אֶת־מָרְדֳּכַי dir.obj.-pr.n. (598) *Mordecai*

עַל־בֵּית הָמָן prep.-n.m.s. cstr. (108)-pr.n. (243) *over the house of Haman*

8:3

וַתּוֹסֶף אֶסְתֵּר consec.-Hi. impf. 3 f.s. (יָסַף 414)-pr.n. (64) *and Esther again (added)*

וַתְּדַבֵּר consec.-Pi. impf. 3 f.s. (דָּבַר 180) *spoke*

לִפְנֵי הַמֶּלֶךְ prep.-n.m.p. cstr. (815)-def.art.-n.m.s. (I 572) *to the king*

וַתִּפֹּל consec.-Qal impf. 3 f.s. (נָפַל 656) *and she fell*

לִפְנֵי רַגְלָיו v.supra-n.f.p.-3 m.s. sf. (919) *at his feet*

וַתֵּבְךְּ consec.-Qal impf. 3 f.s. (בָּכָה 113) *and (with tears) wept*

וַתִּתְחַנֶּן־לוֹ consec.-Hith. impf. 3 f.s. (חָנַן I 335)-prep.-3 m.s. sf. *and besought him*

לְהַעֲבִיר prep.-Hi. inf.cstr. (עָבַר 716) *to avert*

אֶת־רָעַת dir.obj.-n.f.s. cstr. (949) *the evil design of*

הָמָן הָאֲגָגִי pr.n. (243)-def.art.-adj. gent. (8) *Haman the Agagite*

וְאֵת מַחֲשַׁבְתּוֹ conj.-dir.obj.-n.f.s.-3 m.s. sf. (364) *and the plot*

אֲשֶׁר חָשַׁב rel. (81)-Qal pf. 3 m.s. (362) *which he had devised*

עַל־הַיְּהוּדִים prep.-def.art.-adj. gent. m.p. (397) *against the Jews*

8:4

וַיּוֹשֶׁט הַמֶּלֶךְ consec.-Hi. impf. 3 m.s. (יָשַׁט 445) -def.art.-n.m.s. (I 572) *and the king held out*

לְאֶסְתֵּר prep.-pr.n. (64) *to Esther*

אֵת שַׁרְבִט הַזָּהָב dir.obj.-n.m.s. cstr. (987)-def. art.-n.m.s. (262) *the golden scepter*

וַתָּקָם אֶסְתֵּר consec.-Qal impf. 3 f.s. (קוּם 877)-pr.n. (64) *and Esther rose*

וַתַּעֲמֹד consec.-Qal impf. 3 f.s. (עָמַד 763) *and stood*

לִפְנֵי הַמֶּלֶךְ prep.-n.m.p. cstr. (815)-def.art.-n.m.s. (I 572) *before the king*

8:5

וַתֹּאמֶר consec.-Qal impf. 3 f.s. (אָמַר 55) *and she said*

אִם־עַל־הַמֶּלֶךְ hypoth.part. (49)-prep.-def.art. -n.m.s. (I 572) *if unto the king*

טוֹב adj. m.s. (II 373) *it please*

וְאִם־מָצָאתִי חֵן conj.-v.supra-Qal pf. 1 c.s. (מָצָא 592)-n.m.s. (336) *and if I have found favor*

לְפָנָיו prep.-n.m.p.-3 m.s. sf. (815) *before him*

וְכָשֵׁר הַדָּבָר conj.-Qal pf. 3 m.s. (506)-def.art. -n.m.s. (182) *and the thing seem right*

לִפְנֵי הַמֶּלֶךְ prep.-n.m.p. cstr. (815)-def.art.-n.m.s. (I 572) *before the king*

וְטוֹבָה אֲנִי conj.-adj. f.s. (II 373)-pers.pr. 1 c.s. (58) *and I be pleasing*

בְּעֵינָיו prep.-n.f.p.-3 m.s. sf. (744) *in his eyes*

יִכָּתֵב Ni. impf. 3 m.s. (כָּתַב 507) *let be written*

לְהָשִׁיב prep.-Hi. inf.cstr. (שׁוּב 996) *to revoke*

אֶת־הַסְּפָרִים dir.obj.-def.art.-n.m.p. (706) *the letters*

מַחֲשֶׁבֶת הָמָן n.f.s. cstr. (364)-pr.n. (243) *devised by Haman*

בֶּן־הַמְּדָתָא n.m.s. cstr. (119)-pr.n. (241) *the son of Hammedatha*

הָאֲגָגִי def.art.-adj. gent. (8) *the Agagite*

אֲשֶׁר כָּתַב rel. (81)-Qal pf. 3 m.s. (507) *which he wrote*

לְאַבֵּד prep.-Pi. inf.cstr. (אָבַד 1) *to destroy*

אֶת־הַיְּהוּדִים dir.obj.-def.art.-adj. gent. m.p. (397) *the Jews*

אֲשֶׁר בְּכָל־ rel. (81)-prep.-n.m.s. cstr. (481) *who are in all*

מְדִינוֹת הַמֶּלֶךְ n.f.p. cstr. (193)-v.supra *the provinces of the king*

8:6

כִּי אֵיכָכָה conj. (471)-adv. (32) *for how*

אוּכַל Qal impf. 1 c.s. (יָכֹל 407) *can I endure*

וְרָאִיתִי conj.-Qal pf. 1 c.s. (רָאָה 906) *to see*

בָּרָעָה prep.-def.art.-n.f.s. (949) *the calamity*
אֲשֶׁר־יִמְצָא rel. (81)-Qal impf. 3 m.s. (מָצָא 592) *that is coming*
אֶת־עַמִּי dir.obj.-n.m.s.-1 c.s. sf. (I 766) *to my people*
וְאֵיכָכָה אוּכַל conj.-v.supra-v.supra *or how can I endure*
וְרָאִיתִי v.supra *to see*
בְּאָבְדַן מוֹלַדְתִּי prep.-n.m.s. cstr. (2)-n.f.p.-1 c.s. sf. (409) *the destruction of my kindred*

8:7

וַיֹּאמֶר consec.-Qal impf. 3 m.s. (55) *then said*
הַמֶּלֶךְ אֲחַשְׁוֵרֹשׁ def.art.-n.m.s. (I 572)-pr.n. (31) *King Ahasuerus*
לְאֶסְתֵּר הַמַּלְכָּה prep.-pr.n. (64)-def.art.-n.f.s. (573) *to Queen Esther*
וּלְמָרְדֳּכַי conj.-prep.-pr.n. (598) *and to Mordecai*
הַיְּהוּדִי def.art.-adj. gent. m.s. (397) *the Jew*
הִנֵּה demons.part. (243) *behold*
בֵּית־הָמָן n.m.s. cstr. (108)-pr.n. (243) *the house of Haman*
נָתַתִּי Qal pf. 1 c.s. (נָתַן 678) *I have given*
לְאֶסְתֵּר prep.-pr.n. (64) *to Esther*
וְאֹתוֹ תָּלוּ conj.-dir.obj.-3 m.s. sf.-Qal pf. 3 c.p. (1067 תָּלָה) *and they have hanged him*
עַל־הָעֵץ prep.-def.art.-n.m.s. (781) *on the gallows*
עַל אֲשֶׁר־שָׁלַח יָדוֹ prep.-rel. (81)-Qal pf. 3 m.s. (1018)-n.f.s.-3 m.s. sf. (388) *because he would lay hands*
בַּיְּהוּדִיים prep.-def.art.-adj. gent. m.p. (397) *on the Jews*

8:8

וְאַתֶּם כִּתְבוּ conj.-pers.pr. 2 m.p. (61)-Qal impv. 2 m.p. (כָּתַב 507) *and you may write*
עַל־הַיְּהוּדִים prep.-def.art.-adj. gent. m.p. (397) *with regard to the Jews*
כַּטּוֹב prep.-def.art.-adj. m.s. (II 373) *as you please (as the good)*
בְּעֵינֵיכֶם prep.-n.f.p.-2 m.p. sf. (744) *in your eyes*
בְּשֵׁם הַמֶּלֶךְ prep.-n.m.s. cstr. (1027)-def.art. -n.m.s. (I 572) *in the name of the king*
וְחִתְמוּ conj.-Qal impv. 2 m.p. (חָתַם 367) *and seal*
בְּטַבַּעַת הַמֶּלֶךְ prep.-n.f.s. cstr. (371)-v.supra *with the king's ring*
כִּי־כְתָב conj. (471)-n.m.s. (508) *for an edict*
אֲשֶׁר־נִכְתָּב rel. (81)-Ni. ptc. (כָּתַב 507) *which is written*
בְּשֵׁם־הַמֶּלֶךְ prep.-n.m.s. cstr. (1027)-v.supra *in the name of the king*
וְנַחְתּוֹם conj.-Ni. inf.abs. (חָתַם 367; GK 63c,113z) *and sealed*
בְּטַבַּעַת הַמֶּלֶךְ v.supra-v.supra *with the king's ring*
אֵין לְהָשִׁיב neg. (II 34)-prep.-Hi. inf.cstr. (שׁוּב 996) *cannot be revoked*

8:9

וַיִּקָּרְאוּ consec.-Ni. impf. 3 m.p. (קָרָא 894) *so were summoned*
סֹפְרֵי־הַמֶּלֶךְ n.m.p. cstr. (708)-def.art.-n.m.s. (I 572) *the king's secretaries*
בָּעֵת־הַהִיא prep.-def.art.-n.f.s. (773)-def. art.-demons.adj. f.s. (214) *at that time*
בַּחֹדֶשׁ הַשְּׁלִישִׁי prep.-def.art.-n.m.s. (I 294) -def.art.-num. ord. (1026) *in the third month*
הוּא־חֹדֶשׁ סִיוָן demons.adj. m.s. (214)-v.supra -pr.n. (695) *which is the month of Sivan*
בִּשְׁלוֹשָׁה וְעֶשְׂרִים prep.-num. f.s. (1025) -conj.-num. p. (797) *on the twenty-third day*
בּוֹ prep.-3 m.s. sf. *on it*
וַיִּכָּתֵב consec.-Ni. impf. 3 m.s. (כָּתַב 507) *and it was written*
כְּכָל־אֲשֶׁר־צִוָּה prep.-n.m.s. (481)-rel. (81)-Pi. pf. 3 m.s. (צָוָה 845) *according to all that commanded*
מָרְדֳּכַי pr.n. (598) *Mordecai*
אֶל־הַיְּהוּדִים prep.-def.art.-adj. gent. m.p. (397) *concerning the Jews*
וְאֶל הָאֲחַשְׁדַּרְפְּנִים־ conj.-prep.-def.art.-n.m.p. (31) *to the satraps*
וְהַפַּחוֹת conj.-def.art.-n.m.p. (808) *and the governors*
וְשָׂרֵי הַמְּדִינוֹת conj.-n.m.p. cstr. (978)-def.art. -n.f.p. (193) *and the princes of the provinces*
אֲשֶׁר מֵהֹדּוּ rel. (81)-prep.-pr.n. (213) *from India*
וְעַד־כּוּשׁ conj.-prep. (III 723)-pr.n. (I 468) *to Ethiopia*
שֶׁבַע וְעֶשְׂרִים וּמֵאָה num. (I 987)-conj.-num. p. (797)-conj.-n.f.s. (547) *a hundred and twenty-seven*
מְדִינָה n.f.s. (193) *provinces*
מְדִינָה וּמְדִינָה v.supra-conj.-v.supra *to every province*
כִּכְתָבָהּ prep.-n.m.s.-3 f.s. sf. (508) *in its own script*
וְעַם וָעָם conj.-n.m.s. (I 766)-conj.-v.supra *and to every people*
כִּלְשֹׁנוֹ prep.-n.f.s.-3 m.s. sf. (546) *in its own language*

וְאֶל־הַיְּהוּדִים conj.-prep.-def.art.-adj. gent. m.p. (397) *and also to the Jews*
כִּכְתָבָם prep.-n.m.s.-3 m.p. sf. (508) *in their script*
וְכִלְשׁוֹנָם conj.-prep.-n.f.s.-3 m.p. sf. (546) *and their language*

8:10

וַיִּכְתֹּב consec.-Qal impf. 3 m.s. (כָּתַב 507) *and he wrote*
בְּשֵׁם הַמֶּלֶךְ prep.-n.m.s. cstr. (1027)-def.art. -n.m.s. (I 572) *in the name of King*
אֲחַשְׁוֵרֹשׁ pr.n. (31) *Ahasuerus*
וַיַּחְתֹּם consec.-Qal impf. 3 m.s. (חָתַם 367) *and sealed*
בְּטַבַּעַת הַמֶּלֶךְ prep.-n.f.s. cstr. (371)-v.supra *with the king's ring*
וַיִּשְׁלַח סְפָרִים consec.-Qal impf. 3 m.s. (שָׁלַח 1018)-n.m.p. (706) *and he sent letters*
בְּיַד הָרָצִים prep.-n.f.s. cstr. (388)-def.art.-Qal act.ptc. m.p. (רוּץ 930) *by couriers*
בַּסּוּסִים prep.-def.art.-n.m.p. (692) *on horses*
רֹכְבֵי הָרֶכֶשׁ Qal act.ptc. m.p. cstr. (רָכַב 938) -def.art.-n.m. coll. (940) *riding on swift horses*
הָאֲחַשְׁתְּרָנִים def.art.-adj. m.p. (31) *royal*
בְּנֵי הָרַמָּכִים n.m.p. cstr. (119)-def.art.-n.f.p. (942) *sons of the (royal) mares*

8:11

אֲשֶׁר נָתַן הַמֶּלֶךְ rel. (81)-Qal pf. 3 m.s. (678)-def. art.-n.m.s. (I 572) *by these the king allowed*
לַיְּהוּדִים prep.-def.art.-adj. gent. m.p. (397) *the Jews*
אֲשֶׁר בְּכָל־עִיר־וָעִיר v.supra-prep.-n.m.s. cstr. (481)-n.f.s. (746)-conj.-v.supra *who were in every city*
לְהִקָּהֵל prep.-Ni. inf.cstr. (קָהַל 874) *to gather*
וְלַעֲמֹד עַל־נַפְשָׁם conj.-prep.-Qal inf.cstr. (עָמַד 763)-prep.-n.f.s.-3 m.p. sf. (659) *and defend their lives*
לְהַשְׁמִיד prep.-Hi. inf.cstr. (שָׁמַד 1029) *to destroy*
וְלַהֲרֹג conj.-prep.-Qal inf.cstr. (הָרַג 246) *to slay*
וּלְאַבֵּד conj.-prep.-Pi. inf.cstr. (אָבַד 1) *and to annihilate*
אֶת־כָּל־חֵיל עַם dir.obj.-n.m.s. cstr. (481)-n.m.s. cstr. (298)-n.m.s. (I 766) *any armed force of any people*
וּמְדִינָה conj.-n.f.s. (193) *or province*
הַצָּרִים אֹתָם def.art.-Qal act.ptc. m.p. (צוּר III 849)-dir.obj.-3 m.p. sf. *that might attack them*
טַף וְנָשִׁים n.m. coll. (381)-conj.-n.f.p. (61) *with children and women*
וּשְׁלָלָם conj.-n.m.s.-3 m.p. sf. (1021) *and their goods*
לָבוֹז prep.-Qal inf.cstr. (בָּזַז 102) *to plunder*

8:12

בְּיוֹם אֶחָד prep.-n.m.s. (398)-num. (25) *upon one day*
בְּכָל־מְדִינוֹת prep.-n.m.s. cstr. (481)-n.f.p. cstr. (193) *throughout all the provinces of*
הַמֶּלֶךְ אֲחַשְׁוֵרוֹשׁ def.art.-n.m.s. (I 572)-pr.n. (31) *King Ahasuerus*
בִּשְׁלוֹשָׁה עָשָׂר prep.-num. f. (1025)-num. (797) *on the thirteen day*
לְחֹדֶשׁ שְׁנֵים־עָשָׂר prep.-n.m.s. (I 294)-num. (1040)-num. 9797) *of the twelfth month*
הוּא־חֹדֶשׁ אֲדָר demons.adj. m.s. (214)-n.m.s. (I 294)-pr.n. (12) *which is the month of Adar*

8:13

פַּתְשֶׁגֶן הַכְּתָב n.m.s. cstr. (837)-def.art.-n.m.s. (508) *a copy of what was written*
לְהִנָּתֵן דָּת prep.-Ni. inf.cstr. (נָתַן 678)-n.f.s. (206) *was to be issued as a decree*
בְּכָל־מְדִינָה וּמְדִינָה prep.-n.m.s. cstr. (481)-n.f.s. (193)-conj.-v.supra *in every province*
גָּלוּי לְכָל־הָעַמִּים Qal pass.ptc. (גָּלָה 162)-prep. -v.supra-def.art.-n.m.p. (I 766) *and by proclamation to all peoples*
וְלִהְיוֹת הַיְּהוּדִים conj.-prep.-Qal inf.cstr. (הָיָה 224)-def.art.-adj. gent. m.p. (397) *and the Jews were to be*
עֲתוּדִים adj. m.p. (800) *ready*
לַיּוֹם הַזֶּה prep.-def.art.-n.m.s. (398)-def.art. -demons.adj. m.s. (260) *on that day*
לְהִנָּקֵם prep.-Ni. inf.cstr. (נָקַם 667) *to avenge themselves*
מֵאֹיְבֵיהֶם prep.-Qal act.ptc. m.p.-3 m.p. sf. (אָיַב 33) *upon their enemies*

8:14

הָרָצִים def.art.-Qal act.ptc. m.p. (רוּץ 930) *so the couriers*
רֹכְבֵי הָרֶכֶשׁ Qal act.ptc. m.p. cstr. (רָכַב 938) -def.art.-n.m. coll. (940) *mounted on their ... horses*
הָאֲחַשְׁתְּרָנִים def.art.-adj. m.p. (31) *royal*
יָצְאוּ Qal pf. 3 c.p. (יָצָא 422) *rode out*

מְבֹהָלִים Pu. ptc. m.p. (בָּהַל 96) *in haste*
וּדְחוּפִים conj.-Qal pass.ptc. m.p. (דָּחַף 191) *urged*
בִּדְבַר הַמֶּלֶךְ prep.-n.m.s. cstr. (182)-def.art.-n.m.s. (I 572) *by the king's command*
וְהַדָּת conj.-def.art.-n.f.s. (206) *and the decree*
נִתְּנָה Ni. pf. 3 f.s. (נָתַן 678) *was issued*
בְּשׁוּשַׁן prep.-pr.n. (1004) *in Susa*
הַבִּירָה def.art.-n.f.s. (108) *the capital*

8:15

וּמָרְדֳּכַי conj.-pr.n. (598) *then Mordecai*
יָצָא Qal pf. 3 m.s. (422) *went out*
מִלִּפְנֵי הַמֶּלֶךְ prep.-prep.-n.m.p. cstr. (815)-def. art.-n.m.s. (I 572) *from the presence of the king*
בִּלְבוּשׁ מַלְכוּת prep.-n.m.s. cstr. (528)-n.f.s. (574) *in royal robes*
תְּכֵלֶת וָחוּר n.f.s. (1067)-conj.-n.m.s. (301) *of blue and white*
וַעֲטֶרֶת זָהָב גְּדוֹלָה conj.-n.f.s. cstr. (I 742)-n.m.s. (262)-adj. f.s. (152) *with a great golden crown*
וְתַכְרִיךְ conj.-n.m.s. (501) *and a mantle*
בּוּץ וְאַרְגָּמָן n.m.s. (101)-conj.-n.m.s. (71) *of fine linen and purple*
וְהָעִיר שׁוּשָׁן conj.-def.art.-n.f.s. (746)-pr.n. paus. (1004) *while the city of Susa*
צָהֲלָה Qal pf. 3 f.s. (צָהַל I 843) *shouted*
וְשָׂמֵחָה conj.-Qal pf. 3 f.s. (שָׂמַח 970) *and rejoiced*

8:16

לַיְּהוּדִים הָיְתָה prep.-def.art.-adj. gent. m.p. (397)-Qal pf. 3 f.s. (הָיָה 224) *the Jews had*
אוֹרָה n.f.s. (I 21) *light*
וְשִׂמְחָה conj.-n.f.s. (970) *and gladness*
וְשָׂשֹׂן conj.-n.m.s. (965) *and joy*
וִיקָר conj.-n.m.s. (430) *and honor*

8:17

וּבְכָל־מְדִינָה וּמְדִינָה conj.-prep.-n.m.s. cstr. (481)-n.f.s. (193)-conj.-v.supra *and in every province*
וּבְכָל־עִיר וָעִיר v.supra-n.f.s. (746)-conj.-v.supra *and in every city*
מְקוֹם אֲשֶׁר n.m.s. cstr. (879)-rel. (81) *wherever*
דְּבַר־הַמֶּלֶךְ n.m.s. cstr. (182)-def.art.-n.m.s. (I 572) *the king's command*
וְדָתוֹ conj.-n.f.s.-3 m.s. sf. (206) *and his edict*
מַגִּיעַ Hi. ptc. (נָגַע 619) *came*
שִׂמְחָה n.f.s. (970) *there was gladness*
וְשָׂשׂוֹן conj.-n.m.s. (965) *and joy*
לַיְּהוּדִים prep.-def.art.-adj. gent. m.p. (397) *among the Jews*
מִשְׁתֶּה n.m.s. (1059) *a feast*
וְיוֹם טוֹב conj.-n.m.s. (398)-adj. m.s. (II 373) *and a holiday*
וְרַבִּים conj.-adj. m.p. (I 912) *and many*
מֵעַמֵּי הָאָרֶץ prep.-n.m.p. cstr. (I 766)-def.art. -n.f.s. (75) *from the peoples of the country*
מִתְיַהֲדִים Hith. ptc. m.p. (יהד 397) *declared themselves Jews*
כִּי־נָפַל conj. (471)-Qal pf. 3 m.s. (656 *for had fallen*
פַּחַד־הַיְּהוּדִים n.m.s. cstr. 808)-def.art.-adj. gent. m.p. (397) *the fear of the Jews*
עֲלֵיהֶם prep.-3 m.p. sf. *upon them*

9:1

וּבִשְׁנֵים עָשָׂר חֹדֶשׁ conj.-prep.-num. (1040) -num. (797)-n.m.s. (I 294) *now in the twelfth month*
הוּא־חֹדֶשׁ אֲדָר demons.adj. m.s. (214)-v.supra -pr.n. (12) *which is the month of Adar*
בִּשְׁלוֹשָׁה עָשָׂר יוֹם בּוֹ prep.-num. f. (1025)-num. (797)-n.m.s. (398)-prep.-3 m.s. sf. *on the thirteenth day of the same*
אֲשֶׁר הִגִּיעַ rel. (81)-Hi. pf. 3 m.s. (נָגַע 619) *when were about*
דְּבַר־הַמֶּלֶךְ n.m.s. cstr. (182)-def.art.-n.m.s. (I 572) *the king's command*
וְדָתוֹ conj.-n.f.s.-3 m.s. sf. (206) *and his edict*
לְהֵעָשׂוֹת prep.-Ni. inf.cstr. (עָשָׂה I 793) *to be executed*
בַּיּוֹם prep.-def.art.-n.m.s. (398) *on the very day*
אֲשֶׁר שִׂבְּרוּ rel. (81)-Pi. pf. 3 c.p. (שָׂבַר II 960) *when hoped*
אֹיְבֵי הַיְּהוּדִים Qal act.ptc. m.p. cstr. (אָיַב 33) -def.art.-adj. gent. m.p. (397) *the enemies of the Jews*
לִשְׁלוֹט בָּהֶם prep.-Qal inf.cstr. (שָׁלַט 1020) -prep.-3 m.p. sf. *to get the mastery over them*
וְנַהֲפוֹךְ הוּא conj.-Ni. inf.abs. (הָפַךְ 245; GK 63c)-pers.pr. 3 m.s. (214) *but which had been changed*
אֲשֶׁר יִשְׁלְטוּ הַיְּהוּדִים rel. (81)-Qal impf. 3 m.p. (1020)-def.art.-adj. gent. m.p. (397) *when the Jews should get the mastery*
הֵמָּה בְּשֹׂנְאֵיהֶם pers.pr. 3 m.p. (241; GK 135aN) -prep.-Qal act.ptc. m.p.-3 m.p. sf. (שָׂנֵא 971) *they over their foes*

9:2

נִקְהֲלוּ הַיְּהוּדִים Ni. pf. 3 c.p. (קָהַל 874)-def. art.-adj. gent. m.p. (397) ***the Jews gathered***

בְּעָרֵיהֶם prep.-n.f.p.-3 m.p. sf. (746) ***in their cities***

בְּכָל־מְדִינוֹת prep.-n.m.s. cstr. (481)-n.f.p. cstr. (193) ***throughout all the provinces of***

הַמֶּלֶךְ אֲחַשְׁוֵרוֹשׁ def.art.-n.m.s. (I 572)-pr.n. (31) ***King Ahasuerus***

לִשְׁלֹחַ יָד prep.-Qal inf.cstr. (1018)-n.f.s. (388) ***to lay hands***

בִּמְבַקְשֵׁי רָעָתָם prep.-Pi. ptc. m.p. cstr. (בָּקַשׁ 134)-n.f.s.-3 m.p. sf. (949) ***on such as sought their hurt***

וְאִישׁ conj.-n.m.s. (35) ***and a man***

לֹא־עָמַד לִפְנֵיהֶם neg.-Qal pf. 3 m.s. (763) -prep.-n.m.p.-3 m.p. sf. (815) ***could not make a stand against them***

כִּי־נָפַל פַּחְדָּם conj. (471)-Qal pf. 3 m.s. (656) -n.m.s.-3 m.p. sf. (808) ***for the fear of them had fallen***

עַל־כָּל־הָעַמִּים prep.-n.m.s. cstr. (481)-def. art.-n.m.p. (I 766) ***upon all peoples***

9:3

וְכָל־שָׂרֵי conj.-n.m.s. cstr. (481)-n.m.p. cstr. (978) ***all the princes of***

הַמְּדִינוֹת def.art.-n.f.p. (193) ***the provinces***

וְהָאֲחַשְׁדַּרְפְּנִים conj.-def.art.-n.m.p. (31) ***and the satraps***

וְהַפַּחוֹת conj.-def.art.-n.m.p. (808) ***and the governors***

וְעֹשֵׂי הַמְּלָאכָה conj.-Qal act.ptc. m.p. cstr. (עָשָׂה I 793)-def.art.-n.f.s. (521) ***and the ... officials***

אֲשֶׁר לַמֶּלֶךְ rel. (81)-prep.-def.art.-n.m.s. (I 572) ***royal***

מְנַשְּׂאִים Pi. ptc. m.p. (נָשָׂא 669) ***also helped***

אֶת־הַיְּהוּדִים dir.obj.-def.art.-adj. gent. m.p. (397) ***the Jews***

כִּי־נָפַל conj. (471)-Qal pf. 3 m.s. (656) ***for ... had fallen***

פַּחַד־מָרְדֳּכַי n.m.s. cstr. (808)-pr.n. (598) ***the fear of Mordecai***

עֲלֵיהֶם prep.-3 m.p. sf. ***upon them***

9:4

כִּי־גָדוֹל conj. (471)-adj. m.s. (152) ***for was great***

מָרְדֳּכַי pr.n. (598) ***Mordecai***

בְּבֵית הַמֶּלֶךְ prep.-n.m.s. cstr. (108)-def.art.-n.m.s. (I 572) ***in the king's house***

וְשָׁמְעוֹ conj.-n.m.s.-3 m.s. sf. (1035) ***and his fame***

הוֹלֵךְ Qal act.ptc. (הָלַךְ 229) ***spread***

בְּכָל־הַמְּדִינוֹת prep.-n.m.s. cstr. (481)-def.art. -n.f.p. (193) ***throughout all the provinces***

כִּי־הָאִישׁ conj. (471)-def.art.-n.m.s. (35) ***for the man***

מָרְדֳּכַי pr.n. (598) ***Mordecai***

הוֹלֵךְ וְגָדוֹל v.supra-conj.-adj. m.s. (152) ***grew more and more powerful***

9:5

וַיַּכּוּ הַיְּהוּדִים consec.-Hi. impf. 3 m.p. (נָכָה 645)-def.art.-adj. gent. m.p. (397) ***so the Jews smote***

בְּכָל־אֹיְבֵיהֶם prep.-n.m.s. cstr. (481)-Qal act.ptc. m.p.-3 m.p. sf. (אָיַב 33) ***all their enemies***

מַכַּת־חֶרֶב n.f.s. cstr. (646)-n.f.s. (352) ***with the sword***

וְהֶרֶג וְאַבְדָן conj.-n.m.s. (247)-conj.-n.m.s. (2) ***slaughtering and destroying them***

וַיַּעֲשׂוּ consec.-Qal impf. 3 m.p. (עָשָׂה I 793) ***and they did***

בְשֹׂנְאֵיהֶם prep.-Qal act.ptc. m.p.-3 m.p. sf. (שָׂנֵא 971) ***to those who hated them***

כִּרְצוֹנָם prep.-n.m.s.-3 m.p. sf. (953) ***as they pleased***

9:6

וּבְשׁוּשַׁן conj.-prep.-pr.n. (1004) ***in Susa***

הַבִּירָה def.art.-n.f.s. (108) ***the capital***

הָרְגוּ הַיְּהוּדִים Qal pf. 3 c.p. (הָרַג 246)-def. art.-adj. gent. m.p. (397) ***the Jews slew***

וְאַבֵּד conj.-Pi. inf.abs. (אָבַד 1; GK 113z) ***and destroyed***

חֲמֵשׁ מֵאוֹת אִישׁ num. (331)-n.f.p. (547)-n.m.s. (35) ***five hundred men***

9:7

וְאֵת פַּרְשַׁנְדָּתָא conj. (GK 2r)-dir.obj.-pr.n. (832) ***and Parshandatha***

וְאֵת דַּלְפוֹן v.supra-pr.n. (196) ***and Dalphon***

וְאֵת אַסְפָּתָא v.supra-pr.n. (63) ***and Aspatha***

9:8

וְאֵת פּוֹרָתָא conj.-dir.obj.-pr.n. (807) ***and Poratha***

וְאֵת אֲדַלְיָא v.supra-pr.n. (9) ***and Adalia***

וְאֵת אֲרִידָתָא v.supra-pr.n. (71) ***and Aridatha***

9:9

וְאֵת פַּרְמַשְׁתָּא conj.-dir.obj.-pr.n. (828) ***and Parmashta***

וְאֵת אֲרִיסַי v.supra-pr.n. (1120) ***and Arisai***

וְאֵת אֲרִדַי v.supra-pr.n. (71) *and Aridai*
וְאֵת וַיְזָתָא v.supra-pr.n. (255) *and Vaizatha*

9:10

עֲשֶׂרֶת בְּנֵי הָמָן num. cstr. (796)-n.m.p. cstr. (119)-pr.n. (243) *the ten sons of Haman*
בֶּן־הַמְּדָתָא n.m.s. cstr. (119)-pr.n. (241) *the son of Hammedatha*
צֹרֵר הַיְּהוּדִים Qal act.ptc. cstr. (צָרַר II 865) -def.art.-adj. gent. m.p. (397) *the enemy of the Jews*
הָרָגוּ Qal pf. 3 c.p. paus. (הָרַג 246) *they slew*
וּבַבִּזָּה conj.-prep.-def.art.-n.f.s. (103) *but on the plunder*
לֹא שָׁלְחוּ neg.-Qal pf. 3 c.p. (שָׁלַח 1018) *they laid no*
אֶת־יָדָם dir.obj.-n.f.s.-3 m.p. sf. (388) *hand*

9:11

בַּיּוֹם הַהוּא prep.-def.art.-n.m.s. (398)-def.art. -demons.adj. m.s. (214) *that very day*
בָּא Qal pf. 3 m.s. (בּוֹא 97) *was reported*
מִסְפַּר הַהֲרוּגִים n.m.s. cstr. (708)-def.art.-Qal pass.ptc. m.p. (הָרַג 246) *the number of those slain*
בְּשׁוּשַׁן prep.-pr.n. (1004) *in Susa*
הַבִּירָה def.art.-n.f.s. (108) *the capital*
לִפְנֵי הַמֶּלֶךְ prep.-n.m.p. cstr. (815)-def.art.-n.m.s. (I 572) *to the king*

9:12

וַיֹּאמֶר הַמֶּלֶךְ consec.-Qal impf. 3 m.s. (אָמַר 55)-def.art.-n.m.s. (I 572) *and the king said*
לְאֶסְתֵּר הַמַּלְכָּה prep.-pr.n. (64)-def.art.-n.f.s. (573) *to Queen Esther*
בְּשׁוּשַׁן prep.-pr.n. (1004) *in Susa*
הַבִּירָה def.art.-n.f.s. (108) *the capital*
הָרְגוּ הַיְּהוּדִים Qal pf. 3 c.p. (הָרַג 246)-def. art.-adj. gent. m.p. (397) *the Jews have slain*
וְאַבֵּד conj.-Pi. inf.abs. (אָבַד 1) *(and destroying)*
חֲמֵשׁ מֵאוֹת אִישׁ num. cstr. (331)-n.f.p. (547) -n.m.s. (35) *five hundred men*
וְאֵת עֲשֶׂרֶת conj.-dir.obj.-num. f. cstr. (796) *and also the ten*
בְּנֵי־הָמָן n.m.p. cstr. (119)-pr.n. (243) *sons of Haman*
בִּשְׁאָר מְדִינוֹת prep.-n.m.s. cstr. (984)-n.f.p. cstr. (193) *in the rest of the provinces of*
הַמֶּלֶךְ def.art.-n.m.s. (I 572) *the king*
מֶה עָשׂוּ interr. (552)-Qal pf. 3 c.p. (עָשָׂה I 793) *what have they done*

וּמַה־שְּׁאֵלָתֵךְ conj.-interr. (552)-n.f.s.-2 f.s. sf. (982) *now what is your petition*
וְיִנָּתֵן לָךְ conj.-Ni. impf. 3 m.s. (נָתַן 678)-prep.-2 f.s. sf. *it shall be granted you*
וּמַה־בַּקָּשָׁתֵךְ עוֹד v.supra-n.m.s.-2 f.s. sf. (135) -adv. (728) *and what further is your request*
וְתֵעָשׂ conj.-Ni. impf. 3 f.s. (עָשָׂה I 793) *and it shall be fulfilled*

9:13

וַתֹּאמֶר אֶסְתֵּר consec.-Qal impf. 3 f.s. (אָמַר 55)-pr.n. (64) *and Esther said*
אִם־עַל־הַמֶּלֶךְ hypoth.part. (49)-prep.-def. art.-n.m.s. (I 572) *if it ... the king*
טוֹב adj. m.s. (II 373) *please*
יִנָּתֵן Ni. impf. 3 m.s. (נָתַן 678) *let be allowed*
גַּם־מָחָר adv. (168)-adv. (563) *also tomorrow*
לַיְּהוּדִים prep.-def.art.-adj. gent. m.p. (397) *the Jews*
אֲשֶׁר בְּשׁוּשַׁן rel. (81)-prep.-pr.n. (1004) *who are in Susa*
לַעֲשׂוֹת prep.-Qal inf.cstr. (עָשָׂה I 793) *to do*
כְּדָת הַיּוֹם prep.-n.f.s. cstr. (206)-def.art.-n.m.s. (398) *according to this day's edict*
וְאֵת עֲשֶׂרֶת conj.-dir.obj.-num. f. cstr. (796) *and the ten*
בְּנֵי־הָמָן n.m.p. cstr. (119)-pr.n. (243) *sons of Haman*
יִתְלוּ Qal impf. 3 m.p. (תָּלָה 1067) *let be hanged*
עַל־הָעֵץ prep.-def.art.-n.m.s. (781) *on the gallows*

9:14

וַיֹּאמֶר הַמֶּלֶךְ consec.-Qal impf. 3 m.s. (אָמַר 55)-def.art.-n.m.s. (I 572) *so the king commanded*
לְהֵעָשׂוֹת כֵּן prep.-NI. inf.cstr. (עָשָׂה I 793)-adv. (485) *this to be done*
וַתִּנָּתֵן דָּת consec.-Ni. 3 f.s. (נָתַן 678)-n.f.s. (206) *a decree was issued*
בְּשׁוּשָׁן prep.-pr.n. paus. (1004) *in Susa*
וְאֵת עֲשֶׂרֶת conj.-dir.obj.-num. f. cstr. (796) *and the ten*
בְּנֵי־הָמָן n.m.p. cstr. (119)-pr.n. (243) *sons of Haman*
תָּלוּ Qal pf. 3 c.p. (תָּלָה 1067) *were hanged*

9:15

וַיִּקָּהֲלוּ consec.-Ni. impf. 3 m.p. (קָהַל 874) *gathered also*
הַיְּהוּדִיִּים def.art.-adj. gent. m.p. (397) *the Jews*

אֲשֶׁר־בְּשׁוּשָׁן rel. (81)-prep.-pr.n. paus. (1004) *who were in Susa*
גַּם בְּיוֹם adv. (168)-prep.-n.m.s. cstr. (398) *also on the day of*
אַרְבָּעָה עָשָׂר num. f. (916)-num. (797) *the fourteenth*
לְחֹדֶשׁ אֲדָר prep.-n.m.s. cstr. (I 294)-pr.n. (12) *of the month of Adar*
וַיַּהַרְגוּ consec.-Qal impf. 3 m.p. (הָרַג 246) *and they slew*
בְשׁוּשָׁן prep.-pr.n. paus. (1004) *in Susa*
שְׁלֹשׁ מֵאוֹת אִישׁ num. (1025)-n.f.p. (547)-n.m.s. (35) *three hundred men*
וּבַבִּזָּה conj.-prep.-def.art.-n.f.s. (103) *but on the plunder*
לֹא שָׁלְחוּ neg.-Qal pf. 3 c.p. (שָׁלַח 1018) *they laid no*
אֶת־יָדָם dir.obj.-n.f.s.-3 m.p. sf. (388) *hands*

9:16

וּשְׁאָר הַיְּהוּדִים conj.-n.m.s. cstr. (984)-def.art.-adj. gent. m.p. (397) *now the other Jews*
אֲשֶׁר בִּמְדִינוֹת הַמֶּלֶךְ rel. (81)-prep.-n.f.p. cstr. (193)-def.art.-n.m.s. (I 572) *who were in the king's provinces*
נִקְהֲלוּ Ni. pf. 3 c.p. (קָהַל 874) *gathered*
וְעָמֹד עַל־נַפְשָׁם conj.-Qal inf.abs. (עָמַד 763; GK 113z)-prep.-n.f.s.-3 m.p. sf. (659) *to defend their lives*
וְנוֹחַ conj.-Qal inf.abs. (נוּחַ 628) *and got relief*
מֵאֹיְבֵיהֶם prep.-Qal act.ptc. m.p.-3 m.p. sf. (אָיַב 33) *from their enemies*
וְהָרֹג conj.-Qal inf.abs. (הָרַג 246; GK 113z) *and slew*
בְּשֹׂנְאֵיהֶם prep.-Qal act.ptc. m.p.-3 m.p. sf. (שָׂנֵא 971) *of those who hated them*
חֲמִשָּׁה וְשִׁבְעִים אָלֶף num. f. (331)-conj.-num. p. (988)-n.m.s. paus. (48) *seventy-five thousand*
וּבַבִּזָּה conj.-prep.-def.art.-n.f.s. (103) *but on the plunder*
לֹא שָׁלְחוּ neg.-Qal pf. 3 c.p. (שָׁלַח 1018) *they laid no*
אֶת־יָדָם dir.obj.-n.f.s.-3 m.p. sf. (388) *hands*

9:17

בְּיוֹם־שְׁלֹשָׁה עָשָׂר prep.-n.m.s. cstr. (398)-num. f. (1025)-num. (797) *this was on the thirteenth day*
לְחֹדֶשׁ אֲדָר prep.-n.m.s. cstr. (I 294)-pr.n. (12) *of the month of Adar*
וְנוֹחַ conj.-Qal inf.abs. (נוּחַ 628) *they rested*
בְּאַרְבָּעָה עָשָׂר בּוֹ prep.-num. f. (916)-num. (797)-prep.-3 m.s. sf. *on the fourteenth (day) of it*
וְעָשֹׂה אֹתוֹ conj.-Qal inf.abs. (עָשָׂה I 793)-dir.obj.-3 m.s. sf. *and made that*
יוֹם מִשְׁתֶּה n.m.s. cstr. (398)-n.m.s. (1059) *a day of feasting*
וְשִׂמְחָה conj.-n.f.s. (970) *and gladness*

9:18

וְהַיְּהוּדִים conj.-def.art.-adj. gent. m.p. (397) *but the Jews*
אֲשֶׁר־בְּשׁוּשָׁן rel. (81)-prep.-pr.n. paus. (1004) *who were in Susa*
נִקְהֲלוּ Ni. pf. 3 c.p. (קָהַל 874) *gathered*
בִּשְׁלֹשָׁה עָשָׂר בּוֹ prep.-num. f. (1025)-num. (797)-prep.-3 m.s. sf. *on the thirteenth (day) of it*
וּבְאַרְבָּעָה עָשָׂר בּוֹ conj.-prep.-num. f. (916)-num. (797)-prep.-3 m.s. sf. *and on the fourteenth of it*
וְנוֹחַ conj.-Qal inf.abs. (נוּחַ 628; GK 113z) *and rested*
בַּחֲמִשָּׁה עָשָׂר בּוֹ prep.-num. f. (331)-v.supra-v.supra *on the fifteenth day*
וְעָשֹׂה אֹתוֹ conj.-Qal inf.abs. (עָשָׂה I 793)-dir.obj.-3 m.s. sf. *making that*
יוֹם מִשְׁתֶּה n.m.s. cstr. (398)-n.m.s. (1059) *a day of feasting*
וְשִׂמְחָה conj.-n.f.s. (970) *and gladness*

9:19

עַל־כֵּן prep.-adv. (485) *therefore*
הַיְּהוּדִים הַפְּרָזִים def.art.-adj. gent. m.p. (397)-def.art.-n.m.p. (826) *the Jews of the villages*
הַיֹּשְׁבִים def.art.-Qal act.ptc. m.p. (יָשַׁב 442) *who live*
בְּעָרֵי הַפְּרָזוֹת prep.-n.f.p. cstr. (746)-def.art.-n.f.p. (826) *in the open towns*
עֹשִׂים Qal act.ptc. m.p. (עָשָׂה I 793) *hold*
אֵת יוֹם אַרְבָּעָה עָשָׂר dir.obj.-n.m.s. cstr. (398)-num. (797) *the fourteenth day*
לְחֹדֶשׁ אֲדָר prep.-n.m.s. cstr. (I 294)-pr.n. (12) *of the month of Adar*
שִׂמְחָה n.f.s. (970) *gladness*
וּמִשְׁתֶּה conj.-n.m.s. (1059) *and feasting*
וְיוֹם טוֹב conj.-n.m.s. (398)-adj. m.s. (II 373) *and holiday-making*
וּמִשְׁלוֹחַ מָנוֹת conj.-n.m.s. cstr. (1020)-n.f.p. (584) *on which they send choice portions*

אִישׁ לְרֵעֵהוּ n.m.s. (35)-prep.-n.m.s.-3 m.s. sf. (945) *to one another*

9:20

וַיִּכְתֹּב מָרְדֳּכַי consec.-Qal impf. 3 m.s. (כָּתַב 507)-pr.n. (598) *and Mordecai recorded*

אֶת־הַדְּבָרִים הָאֵלֶּה dir.obj.-def.art.-n.m.p. (182)-def.art.-demons.adj. c.p. (41) *these things*

וַיִּשְׁלַח consec.-Qal impf. 3 m.s. (שָׁלַח 1018) *and sent*

סְפָרִים n.m.p. (706) *letters*

אֶל־כָּל־הַיְּהוּדִים prep.-n.m.s. cstr. (481)-def. art.-adj. gent. m.p. (397) *to all the Jews*

אֲשֶׁר בְּכָל־מְדִינוֹת rel. (81)-prep.-v.supra-n.f.p. (193) *who were in all the provinces of*

הַמֶּלֶךְ אֲחַשְׁוֵרוֹשׁ def.art.-n.m.s. (I 572)-pr.n. (31) *King Ahasuerus*

הַקְּרוֹבִים def.art.-adj. m.p. (898) *both near*

וְהָרְחוֹקִים conj.-def.art.-adj. m.p. (935) *and far*

9:21

לְקַיֵּם עֲלֵיהֶם prep.-Pi. inf.cstr. (קוּם 877)-prep.-3 m.p. sf. *enjoining them*

לִהְיוֹת עֹשִׂים prep.-Qal inf.cstr. (הָיָה 224)-Qal act.ptc. m.p. (עָשָׂה I 793) *that they should keep*

אֵת יוֹם dir.obj.-n.m.s. cstr. (398) *the ... day*

אַרְבָּעָה עָשָׂר num. f. (916)-num. (797) *fourteenth*

לְחֹדֶשׁ אֲדָר prep.-n.m.s. cstr. (I 294)-pr.n. (12) *of the month Adar*

וְאֵת יוֹם־ conj.-dir.obj.-n.m.s. cstr. (398) *and also the ... day*

חֲמִשָּׁה עָשָׂר בּוֹ num. f. (331)-num. (797)-prep.-3 m.s. sf. *fifteenth ... of the same*

בְּכָל־שָׁנָה וְשָׁנָה prep.-n.m.s. cstr. (481)-n.f.s. (1040)-conj.-v.supra *year by year*

9:22

כַּיָּמִים prep.-def.art.-n.m.p. (398) *as the days*

אֲשֶׁר־נָחוּ בָהֶם rel. (81)-Qal pf. 3 c.p. (נוּחַ 628)-prep.-3 m.p. sf. *on which ... got relief*

הַיְּהוּדִים def.art.-adj. gent. m.p. (397) *the Jews*

מֵאוֹיְבֵיהֶם prep.-Qal act.ptc. m.p.-3 m.p. sf. (אָיַב 33) *from their enemies*

וְהַחֹדֶשׁ conj.-def.art.-n.m.s. (I 294) *and as the month*

אֲשֶׁר נֶהְפַּךְ לָהֶם v.supra-Ni. pf. 3 m.s. (הָפַךְ 245)-prep.-3 m.p. sf. *that had been turned for them*

מִיָּגוֹן prep.-n.m.s. (387) *from sorrow*

לְשִׂמְחָה prep.-n.f.s. (970) *into gladness*

וּמֵאֵבֶל conj.-prep.-n.m.s. (5) *and from mourning*

לְיוֹם טוֹב prep.-n.m.s. (398)-adj. m.s. (II 373) *into a holiday*

לַעֲשׂוֹת אוֹתָם prep.-Qal inf.cstr. (עָשָׂה I 793)-dir.obj.-3 m.p. sf. *that they should make them*

יְמֵי מִשְׁתֶּה n.m.p. cstr. (398)-n.m.s. (1059) *days of feasting*

וְשִׂמְחָה conj.-n.f.s. (970) *and gladness*

וּמִשְׁלוֹחַ מָנוֹת conj.-n.m.s. cstr. (1020)-n.f.p. (584) *for sending choice portions*

אִישׁ לְרֵעֵהוּ n.m.s. (35)-prep.-n.m.s.-3 m.s. sf. (945) *to one another*

וּמַתָּנוֹת conj.-n.f.p. (I 682) *and gifts*

לָאֶבְיוֹנִים prep.-def.art.-adj. m.p. (2) *to the poor*

9:23

וְקִבֵּל הַיְּהוּדִים consec.-Pi. pf. 3 m.s. (קָבַל 867; GK 145oN)-def.art.-adj. gent. m.p. (397; GK 124e) *so the Jews undertook*

אֵת אֲשֶׁר־הֵחֵלּוּ dir.obj.-rel. (81)-Hi. pf. 3 c.p. (III 320 חָלַל) *as they had begun*

לַעֲשׂוֹת prep.-Qal inf.cstr. (עָשָׂה I 793) *to do*

וְאֵת אֲשֶׁר־כָּתַב conj.-v.supra-v.supra-Qal pf. 3 m.s. (507) *and as ... had written*

מָרְדֳּכַי pr.n. (598) *Mordecai*

אֲלֵיהֶם prep.-3 m.p. sf. *to them*

9:24

כִּי הָמָן conj. (471)-pr.n. (243) *for Haman*

בֶּן־הַמְּדָתָא n.m.s. cstr. (119)-pr.n. (241) *the son of Hammedatha*

הָאֲגָגִי def.art.-adj. gent. (8) *the Agagite*

צֹרֵר כָּל־הַיְּהוּדִים Qal act.ptc. (צָרַר II 865)-n.m.s. cstr. (481)-def.art.-adj. gent. m.p. (397) *the enemy of all the Jews*

חָשַׁב Qal pf. 3 m.s. (362) *plotted*

עַל־הַיְּהוּדִים prep.-v.supra *against the Jews*

לְאַבְּדָם prep.-Pi. inf.cstr.-3 m.p. sf. (אָבַד 1) *to destroy them*

וְהִפִּיל conj.-Hi. pf. 3 m.s. (נָפַל 656) *and had cast*

פּוּר n.m.s. (807) *Pur (a lot)*

הוּא הַגּוֹרָל demons.adj.m.s. (214)-def.art.-n.m.s. (174) *that is the lot*

לְהֻמָּם prep.-Qal inf.cstr.-3 m.p. sf. (הָמַם 243) *to crush them*

וּלְאַבְּדָם conj.-prep.-Pi. inf.cstr.-3 m.p. sf. (אָבַד 1) *and destroy them*

9:25

וּבְבֹאָהּ conj.-prep.-Qal inf.cstr.-3 f.s. sf. (בּוֹא 97) *but when she (Esther) came*

לִפְנֵי הַמֶּלֶךְ prep.-n.m.p. cstr. (815)-def.art.-n.m.s. (I 572) *before the king*

אָמַר Qal pf. 3 m.s. (55) *he gave orders*

עִם־הַסֵּפֶר prep.-def.art.-n.m.s. (706) *in writing*

יָשׁוּב Qal impf. 3 m.s. (שׁוּב 996) *that should come*

מַחֲשַׁבְתּוֹ n.f.s.-3 m.s. sf. (364) *his plot*

הָרָעָה def.art.-adj. f.s. (I 948) *wicked*

אֲשֶׁר־חָשַׁב rel. (81)-Qal pf. 3 m.s. (362) *which he had devised*

עַל־הַיְּהוּדִים prep.-def.art.-adj. gent. m.p. (397) *against the Jews*

עַל־רֹאשׁוֹ prep.-n.m.s.-3 m.s. sf. (910) *upon his own head*

וְתָלוּ אֹתוֹ conj.-Qal pf. 3 c.p. (תָּלָה 1067)-dir.obj. -3 m.s. sf. *and that he ... should be hanged*

וְאֶת־בָּנָיו conj.-dir.obj.-n.m.p.-3 m.s. sf. (119) *and his sons*

עַל־הָעֵץ prep.-def.art.-n.m.s. (781) *on the gallows*

9:26

עַל־כֵּן קָרְאוּ prep.-adv. (485)-Qal pf. 3 c.p. (קָרָא 894) *therefore they called*

לַיָּמִים הָאֵלֶּה prep.-def.art.-n.m.s. (398)-def. art.-demons.adj. c.p. (41) *these days*

פוּרִים n.m.p. (807) *Purim (lots)*

עַל־שֵׁם הַפּוּר prep.-n.m.s. cstr. (1027)-def. art.-n.m.s. (807) *after the term Pur (lot)*

עַל־כֵּן v.supra *therefore*

עַל־כָּל־דִּבְרֵי prep.-n.m.s. cstr. (481)-n.m.p. cstr. (182) *because of all that was written in*

הָאִגֶּרֶת הַזֹּאת def.art.-n.f.s. (8)-def.art. -demons.adj. f.s. (260) *this letter*

וּמָה־רָאוּ conj.-interr. (552)-Qal pf. 3 c.p. (רָאָה 906) *and of what they had faced*

עַל־כָּכָה prep.-adv. (462) *in this matter*

וּמָה הִגִּיעַ conj.-v.supra-Hi. pf. 3 m.s. (נָגַע 619) *and of what had befallen*

אֲלֵיהֶם prep.-3 m.p. sf. *them*

9:27

קִיְּמוּ Pi. pf. 3 c.p. (קוּם 877) *ordained*

וְקִבְּלֻ conj.-Pi. pf. 3 c.p. (קָבַל 867) *and took it*

הַיְּהוּדִים def.art.-adj. gent. m.p. (397) *the Jews*

עֲלֵיהֶם prep.-3 m.p. sf. *upon themselves*

וְעַל־זַרְעָם conj.-prep.-n.m.s.-3 m.p. sf. (282) *and their descendants*

וְעַל כָּל־הַנִּלְוִים v.supra-n.m.s. cstr. (481)-def.art. -Ni. ptc. m.p. (לָוָה I 530) *and all who joined*

עֲלֵיהֶם v.supra *them*

וְלֹא יַעֲבוֹר conj.-neg.-Qal impf. 3 m.s. (עָבַר 716) *that without fail*

לִהְיוֹת עֹשִׂים prep.-Qal inf.cstr. (הָיָה 224)-Qal act.ptc. m.p. (עָשָׂה I 793) *they would keep*

אֵת שְׁנֵי הַיָּמִים הָאֵלֶּה dir.obj.-num. cstr. (1040) -def.art.-n.m.p. (398)-def.art.-demons.adj. c.p. (41) *these two days*

כִּכְתָבָם prep.-n.m.s.-3 m.p. sf. (508) *according to what was written*

וְכִזְמַנָּם conj.-prep.-n.m.s.-3 m.p. sf. (273) *and at the time appointed*

בְּכָל־שָׁנָה וְשָׁנָה prep.-n.m.s. cstr. (481)-n.f.s. (1040)-conj.-v.supra *every year*

9:28

וְהַיָּמִים הָאֵלֶּה conj.-def.art.-n.m.p. (398)-def.art. -demons.adj. c.p. (41) *that these days*

נִזְכָּרִים Ni. ptc. m.p. (זָכַר 269) *should be remembered*

וְנַעֲשִׂים conj.-Ni. ptc. m.p. (עָשָׂה I 793) *and kept*

בְּכָל־דּוֹר וָדוֹר prep.-n.m.s. cstr. (481)-n.m.s. (189) -conj.-v.supra *throughout every generation*

מִשְׁפָּחָה וּמִשְׁפָּחָה n.f.s. (1046)-conj.-v.supra *in every family*

מְדִינָה וּמְדִינָה n.f.s. (193)-conj.-v.supra *province*

וְעִיר וָעִיר conj.-n.f.s. (746)-conj.-v.supra *and city*

וִימֵי הַפּוּרִים הָאֵלֶּה conj.-n.m.p. cstr. (398)-def. art.-n.m.p. (807)-def.art.-demons.adj. c.p. (41) *and that these days of Purim*

לֹא יַעַבְרוּ neg.-Qal impf. 3 m.p. (עָבַר 716) *should never fall*

מִתּוֹךְ הַיְּהוּדִים prep.-n.m.s. cstr. (1063)-def. art.-adj. gent. m.p. (397) *into disuse among the Jews*

וְזִכְרָם conj.-n.m.s.-3 m.p. sf. (271) *nor should the commemoration of them*

לֹא־יָסוּף neg.-Qal impf. 3 m.s. (סוּף 692) *(not) cease*

מִזַּרְעָם prep.-n.m.s.-3 m.p. sf. (282) *among their descendants*

9:29

וַתִּכְתֹּב consec.-Qal impf. 3 f.s. (כָּתַב 507) *then wrote*

אֶסְתֵּר הַמַּלְכָּה pr.n. (64)-def.art.-n.f.s. (573) *Queen Esther*

בַת־אֲבִיחַיִל n.f.s. cstr. (I 123)-pr.n. (4) *the daughter of Abihail*

וּמָרְדֳּכַי conj.-pr.n. (598) *and Mordecai*
הַיְּהוּדִי def.art.-adj. gent. m.s. (397) *the Jew*
אֶת־כָּל־תֹּקֶף dir.obj.-n.m.s. cstr. (481)-1076) *full authority*
לְקַיֵּם prep.-Pi. inf.cstr. (קוּם 877) *confirming*
אֵת אִגֶּרֶת הַפּוּרִים dir.obj.-n.f.s. cstr. (8)-def. art.-n.m.p. (807) *the letter about Purim*
הַזֹּאת הַשֵּׁנִית def.art.-demons.adj. f.s. (260)-def. art.-num. ord. f. (1041) *this second*

9:30

וַיִּשְׁלַח consec.-Qal impf. 3 m.s. (שָׁלַח 1018) *and he sent*
סְפָרִים n.m.p. (706) *letters*
אֶל־כָּל־הַיְּהוּדִים prep.-n.m.s. cstr. (481)-def.art. -adj. gent. m.p. (397) *to all the Jews*
אֶל־שֶׁבַע וְעֶשְׂרִים prep.-num. (I 987)-conj.-num. p. (797) *to twenty-seven*
וּמֵאָה conj.-n.f.s. (547) *and a hundred*
מְדִינָה n.f.s. (193) *provinces*
מַלְכוּת אֲחַשְׁוֵרוֹשׁ n.f.s. cstr. (574)-pr.n. (31) *of the kingdom of Ahasuerus*
דִּבְרֵי שָׁלוֹם n.m.p. cstr. (182)-n.m.s. (1022) *in words of peace*
וֶאֱמֶת conj.-n.f.s. (54) *and truth*

9:31

לְקַיֵּם prep.-Pi. inf.cstr. (קוּם 877) *that should be observed*
אֶת־יְמֵי הַפֻּרִים הָאֵלֶּה dir.obj.-n.m.p. cstr. (398) -def.art.-n.m.p. (807)-def.art.-demons.adj. c.p. (41) *these days of Purim*
בִּזְמַנֵּיהֶם prep.-n.m.p.-3 m.p. sf. (273) *at their appointed seasons*
כַּאֲשֶׁר קִיַּם עֲלֵיהֶם prep.-rel. (81)-Pi. pf. 3 m.s. (877 קוּם)-prep.-3 m.p. sf. *as enjoined upon them*
מָרְדֳּכַי הַיְּהוּדִי pr.n. (598)-def.art.-adj. gent. m.s. (397) *Mordecai the Jew*
וְאֶסְתֵּר הַמַּלְכָּה conj.-pr.n. (64)-def.art.-n.f.s. (573) *and Queen Esther*
וְכַאֲשֶׁר קִיְּמוּ conj.-prep.-rel. (81)-Pi. pf. 3 c.p. (877 קוּם) *and as they had laid down*
עַל־נַפְשָׁם prep.-n.f.s.-3 m.p. sf. (659) *for themselves*
וְעַל־זַרְעָם conj.-v.supra-n.m.s.-3 m.p. sf. (282) *and for their descendants*
דִּבְרֵי הַצֹּמוֹת n.m.p. cstr. (182)-def.art.-n.m.p. (847) *with regard to their fasts*
וְזַעֲקָתָם conj.-n.f.s.-3 m.p. sf. (277) *and their lamenting*

9:32

וּמַאֲמַר אֶסְתֵּר conj.-n.m.s. cstr. (57)-pr.n. (64) *the command of Esther*
קִיַּם Pi. pf. 3 m.s. (קוּם 877) *fixed*
דִּבְרֵי הַפֻּרִים הָאֵלֶּה n.m.p. cstr. (182)-def.art. -n.m.p. (807)-def.art.-demons.adj. c.p. (41) *these practices of Purim*
וְנִכְתָּב conj.-Ni. ptc. (כָּתַב 507) *and it was recorded*
בַּסֵּפֶר prep.-def.art.-n.m.s. (706) *in writing*

10:1

וַיָּשֶׂם consec.-Qal impf. 3 m.s. (שִׂים 962) *and laid*
הַמֶּלֶךְ אֲחַשְׁ רֹשׁ def.art.-n.m.s. (I 572)-pr.n. (31) *King Ahasuerus*
מַס n.m.s. (I 586) *tribute*
עַל־הָאָרֶץ prep.-def.art.-n.f.s. (75) *on the land*
וְאִיֵּי הַיָּם conj.-n.m.p. cstr. (I 15)-def.art.-n.m.s. (410) *and on the coastlands of the sea*

10:2

וְכָל־מַעֲשֵׂה conj.-n.m.s. cstr. (481)-n.m.s. cstr. (795) *and all the acts of*
תָקְפּוֹ n.m.s.-3 m.s. sf. (1076) *his power*
וּגְבוּרָתוֹ conj.-n.f.s.-3 m.s. sf. (150) *and his might*
וּפָרָשַׁת conj.-n.f.s. cstr. (831) *and the full account of*
גְּדֻלַּת n.f.s. cstr. (153) *the high honor of*
מָרְדֳּכַי pr.n. (598) *Mordecai*
אֲשֶׁר גִּדְּלוֹ rel. (81)-Pi. pf. 3 m.s.-3 m.s. sf. (גָּדַל 152) *to which ... advanced him*
הַמֶּלֶךְ def.art.-n.m.s. (I 572) *the king*
הֲלוֹא־הֵם כְּתוּבִים interr.part.-neg.-pers.pr. 3 m.p. (241)-Qal pass.ptc. m.p. (כָּתַב 507) *are they not written*
עַל־סֵפֶר prep.-n.m.s. cstr. (706) *in the Book of*
דִּבְרֵי הַיָּמִים n.m.p. cstr. (182)-def.art.-n.m.p. (398) *the Chronicles*
לְמַלְכֵי מָדַי prep.-n.m.p. cstr. (I 572)-pr.n. (552) *of the kings of Media*
וּפָרָס conj.-pr.n. (828) *and Persia*

10:3

כִּי מָרְדֳּכַי conj. (471)-pr.n. (598) *for Mordecai*
הַיְּהוּדִי def.art.-adj. gent. m.s. (397) *the Jew*
מִשְׁנֶה n.m.s. (1041) *next in rank*
לַמֶּלֶךְ אֲחַשְׁוֵרוֹשׁ prep.-def.art. n.m.s. (I 572) -pr.n. (31) *to King Ahasuerus*
וְגָדוֹל conj.-adj. m.s. (152) *and he was great*
לַיְּהוּדִים prep.-def.art.-adj. gent. m.p. (397) *among the Jews*

וְרָצוּי conj.-Qal pass.ptc. (**רָצָה** 953) *and popular*
לְרֹב אֶחָיו prep.-n.m.s. cstr. (913)-n.m.p.-3 m.s. sf. (26) *with the multitude of his brethren*
דֹּרֵשׁ Qal act.ptc. (**דָּרַשׁ** 205) *for he sought*
טוֹב לְעַמּוֹ adj. m.s. (II 373)-prep.-n.m.s.-3 m.s. sf. (I 766) *the welfare of his people*
וְדֹבֵר שָׁלוֹם conj.-Qal act.ptc. (**דָּבַר** 180)-n.m.s. (1022) *and spoke peace*
לְכָל־זַרְעוֹ prep.-n.m.s. cstr. (481)-n.m.s.-3 m.s. sf. (282) *to all his people*

Job

1:1

אִישׁ n.m.s. (35) *a man*

הָיָה Qal pf. 3 m.s. (224) *there was*

בְּאֶרֶץ־ prep.-n.f.s. cstr. (75) *in the land of*

עוּץ pr.n. (734) *Uz* (LXX Αὐσίτιδι)

אִיּוֹב pr.n. (33; GK 155e,156b) *Job*

שְׁמוֹ n.m.s.-3 m.s. sf. (1027) *his name*

וְהָיָה conj.-Qal pf. 3 m.s. (224) *and was*

הָאִישׁ הַהוּא def.art.-n.m.s. (35)-def.art. -demons.adj. m.s. (214) *that man*

תָּם adj. m.s. (1070) *sound (blameless)* (LXX ἀληθινός, ἄμεμπτος)

וְיָשָׁר conj.-adj. m.s. (449) *and upright*

וִירֵא conj.-Qal act.ptc. cstr. (431; LXX θεοσεβής) *and one who feared*

אֱלֹהִים n.m.p. (43) *God*

וְסָר conj.-Qal act.ptc. (693 סוּר; LXX ἀπεχόμενος ἀπὸ παντὸς ... πράγματος)

מֵרָע prep.-n.m.s. (948) *from evil*

1:2

וַיִּוָּלְדוּ consec.-Ni. impf. 3 m.p. (408 יָלַד) *there were born*

לוֹ prep.-3 m.s. sf. *to him*

שִׁבְעָה בָנִים num. f.s. (988)-n.m.p. (119) *seven sons*

וְשָׁלוֹשׁ בָּנוֹת conj.-num. m.s. (1025)-n.f.p. (I 123) *and three daughters*

1:3

וַיְהִי consec.-Qal impf. 3 m.s. (224 הָיָה) *and ... was*

מִקְנֵהוּ n.m.s.-3 m.s. sf. (889) *his acquired possession*

שִׁבְעַת אַלְפֵי־צֹאן n.f.s. cstr. (988)-num. m.p. cstr. (48)-n.f.s. (838; GK 123a) *seven thousand sheep*

וּשְׁלֹשֶׁת אַלְפֵי גְמַלִּים conj.-n.f.s. cstr. (1025) -v.supra-n.m.p. (168) *three thousand camels*

וַחֲמֵשׁ מֵאוֹת conj.-num. m.s. cstr. (331)-n.f.p. cstr. (547) *and five hundred (of)*

צֶמֶד־בָּקָר n.m.s. cstr. (855)-n.m.s. (133) *yoke of oxen*

וַחֲמֵשׁ מֵאוֹת v.supra-v.supra *and five hundred*

אֲתוֹנוֹת n.f.p. (87; LXX νομάδις) *she-asses*

וַעֲבֻדָּה conj.-n.f.s. (715) *and servants*

רַבָּה מְאֹד adj. f.s. (I 912)-adv. (547; LXX+καὶ ἔργω μεγάλα ἦν αὐτῷ ἐπὶ τῆς γῆς) *very many*

וַיְהִי v.supra *so that ... was*

הָאִישׁ הַהוּא def.art.-n.m.s. (35)-def.art. -demons.adj. m.s. (214) *this man*

גָּדוֹל adj. m.s. (152) *great(er)*
מִכָּל־ prep.-n.m.s. cstr. (481) *than all*
בְּנֵי־קֶדֶם n.m.p. cstr. (119)-n.m.s. (869) *the people of the east*

1:4

וְהָלְכוּ conj.-Qal pf. 3 c.p. (229) *and ... used to go*
בָנָיו n.m.p.-3 m.s. sf. (119) *his sons*
וְעָשׂוּ conj.-Qal pf. 3 c.p. (עָשָׂה I 793) *and hold*
מִשְׁתֶּה n.m.s. (1059) *a feast*
בֵּית אִישׁ n.m.s. cstr. (108)-n.m.s. (35) *in the house of each*
יוֹמוֹ n.m.s.-3 m.s. sf. (398) *on his day*
וְשָׁלְחוּ conj.-Qal pf. 3 c.p. (1018; GK 112dd) *and they would send*
וְקָרְאוּ conj.-Qal pf. 3 c.p. (894) *and invite*
לִשְׁלֹשֶׁת prep.-num. f.s. cstr. (1025; GK 97c) *the three of*
אַחְיֹתֵיהֶם n.f.p.-3 m.p. sf. (27) *their sisters*
לֶאֱכֹל prep.-Qal inf.cstr. (אָכַל 37) *to eat*
וְלִשְׁתּוֹת conj.-prep.-Qal inf.cstr. (שָׁתָה 1059) *and drink*
עִמָּהֶם prep.-3 m.p. sf. *with them*

1:5

וַיְהִי כִּי consec.-Qal impf. 3 m.s. (הָיָה 224)-conj. (471) *and when*
הִקִּיפוּ Hi. pf. 3 c.p. (נָקַף II 668) *had completed their circuit*
יְמֵי הַמִּשְׁתֶּה n.m.p. cstr. (398)-def.art.-n.m.s. (1059) *the days of the feast*
וַיִּשְׁלַח אִיּוֹב consec.-Qal impf. 3 m.s. (1018)-pr.n. (33) *afterwards Job sent*
וַיְקַדְּשֵׁם consec.-Pi. impf. 3 m.s.-3 m.p. sf. (קָדַשׁ 872) *and consecrated them*
וְהִשְׁכִּים conj.-Hi. pf. 3 m.s. (שָׁכַם 1014; GK 112f; LXX ἀνιστάμενος) *that is he rose early*
בַּבֹּקֶר prep.-def.art.-n.m.s. (133) *in the morning*
וְהֶעֱלָה conj.-Hi. pf. 3 m.s. (עָלָה 748; GK 112f; LXX προσέφερεν) *and offered*
עֹלוֹת n.f.p. (750) *burnt offerings*
מִסְפַּר כֻּלָּם n.m.s. cstr. (I 708)-n.m.s.-3 m.p. sf. (481; GK 118h; LXX+καὶ μόσχον ἕνα περὶ ἁμαρτίας περὶ τῶν ψυχῶν αὐτῶν) *the number of them all*
כִּי אָמַר אִיּוֹב conj. (471)-Qal pf. 3 m.s. (55; GK 164d)-pr.n. (33) *for Job said*
אוּלַי adv. (II 19) *it may be that*
חָטְאוּ Qal pf. 3 c.p. (306) *have sinned*
בָנַי n.m.p.-1 c.s. sf. (119) *my sons*
וּבֵרְכוּ conj.-Pi. pf. 3 c.p. (138; LXX κακὰ ἐνενόησαν) *and cursed (blessed)*

אֱלֹהִים n.m.p. (43) *God*
בִּלְבָבָם prep.-n.m.s.-3 m.p. sf. (523; LXX ἐν τῇ διανοίᾳ αὐτῶν) *in their hearts*
כָּכָה adv. (462; LXX+οὖν) *thus*
יַעֲשֶׂה אִיּוֹב Qal impf. 3 m.s. (עָשָׂה I 793; GK 107e,112dd)-pr.n. (33) *Job did (repeatedly)*
כָּל־הַיָּמִים n.m.s. cstr. (481)-def.art.-n.m.p. (398) *continually (all the days)*

1:6

וַיְהִי הַיּוֹם consec.-Qal impf. 3 m.s. (הָיָה 224; GK 126s)-def.art.-n.m.s. (398) *now there was a day*
וַיָּבֹאוּ consec.-Qal impf. 3 m.p. (בּוֹא 97) *when came*
בְּנֵי הָאֱלֹהִים n.m.p. cstr. (119)-def.art.-n.m.p. (43; GK 128v; LXX οἱ ἄγγελοι τοῦ θεοῦ) *the sons of God*
לְהִתְיַצֵּב prep.-Hith. inf.cstr. (יָצַב 426) *to present themselves (take one's stand)*
עַל־יהוה prep. (II 752; GK 119cc)-pr.n. (217) *before (against) Yahweh*
וַיָּבוֹא consec.-Qal impf. 3 m.s. (בּוֹא 97) *and came*
גַם־הַשָּׂטָן adv. (168)-def.art.-n.m.s. (966; LXX ὁ διάβολος) *Satan (the adversary) also*
בְּתוֹכָם prep.-n.m.s.-3 m.p. sf. (1063) *among them*

1:7

וַיֹּאמֶר consec.-Qal impf. 3 m.s. (55) *then said*
יהוה pr.n. (217) *Yahweh*
אֶל־הַשָּׂטָן prep. (39)-def.art.-n.m.s. (966; LXX τῷ διαβόλῳ) *to the adversary*
מֵאַיִן prep.-adv. (32) *whence*
תָּבֹא Qal impf. 2 m.s. (97; GK 107h) *have you come?*
וַיַּעַן consec.-Qal impf. 3 m.s. (עָנָה I 792) *then answered*
הַשָּׂטָן v.supra *the adversary*
אֶת־יהוה dir.obj.-v.supra *Yahweh*
וַיֹּאמַר consec.-Qal impf. 3 m.s. (55) *then he said*
מִשּׁוּט prep.-Qal inf.cstr. (שׁוּט 1001) *from going to and fro*
בָּאָרֶץ prep.-def.art.-n.f.s. (75; LXX ὑπ᾽ οὐρανὸν) *on the earth*
וּמֵהִתְהַלֵּךְ conj.-prep.-Hith. inf.cstr. (הָלַךְ 229) *and from walking up and down*
בָּהּ prep.-3 f.s. sf. *on it*

1:8

וַיֹּאמֶר consec.-Qal impf. 3 m.s. (55) *and said*
יהוה pr.n. (217) *Yahweh*

אֶל־הַשָּׂטָן prep.-def.art.-n.m.s. (966; LXX>) *to the adversary*
הֲשַׂמְתָּ interr.-Qal pf. 2 m.s. (שִׂים 962) *have you set?*
לִבְּךָ n.m.s.-2 m.s. sf. (524) *your heart (your mind)*
עַל־עַבְדִּי prep. (II 752; some rd. אֶל)-n.m.s.-1 c.s. sf. (713; LXX κατὰ τοῦ παιδός μου) *on my servant*
אִיּוֹב pr.n. (33) *Job*
כִּי אֵין conj. (471) neg. cstr. (II 34) *that there is none*
כָּמֹהוּ subst.-3 m.s. sf. (453, 455) *like him*
בָּאָרֶץ prep.-def.art.-n.f.s. (75) *on the earth*
אִישׁ n.m.s. (35) *a man*
תָּם adj. m.s. (1070) *blameless*
וְיָשָׁר conj.-adj. m.s. (449) *and upright*
יְרֵא אֱלֹהִים Qal act.ptc. m.s. cstr. (431)-n.m.p. (43) *who fears God*
וְסָר conj.-Qal act.ptc. (סוּר 693) *and turns away*
מֵרָע prep.-n.m.s. (948) *from evil*

1:9

וַיַּעַן consec.-Qal impf. 3 m.s. (עָנָה I 772) *then answered*
הַשָּׂטָן def.art.-n.m.s. (966) *the adversary*
אֶת־יהוה dir.obj.-pr.n. (217) *Yahweh*
וַיֹּאמַר consec.-Qal impf. 3 m.s. (55) *(and said)*
הַחִנָּם interr.-adv. (336) *is it for nought?*
יָרֵא Qal act.ptc. m.s. (or Qal pf. 3 m.s.; יָרֵא 431) *is fearing*
אִיּוֹב pr.n. (33) *Job*
אֱלֹהִים n.m.p. (43) *God*

1:10

הֲלֹא־אַתָּ interr.-neg.-pers.pr. 2 m.s. (61) *have you not?*
שַׂכְתָּ Qal pf. 2 m.s. (שׂוּךְ I 962; some mss. סכת; LXX σὺ περιέφραξας) *put a hedge*
בַּעֲדוֹ prep.-3 m.s. sf. (126) *about him*
וּבְעַד־בֵּיתוֹ conj.-prep. (126)-n.m.s.-3 m.s. sf. (108) *and his house*
וּבְעַד v.supra *and (around)*
כָּל־אֲשֶׁר־לוֹ n.m.s. (481)-rel. (81)-prep.-3 m.s. sf. *all that he has*
מִסָּבִיב prep.-adv. (686) *on every side*
מַעֲשֵׂה n.m.s. cstr. (795) *the work of*
יָדָיו n.f.p.-3 m.s. sf. (388) *his hands*
בֵּרַכְתָּ Pi. pf. 2 m.s. (בָּרַךְ 138) *you have blessed*
וּמִקְנֵהוּ conj.-n.m.s.-3 m.s. sf. (889) *and his possessions*
פָּרַץ Qal pf. 3 m.s. (I 829) *have increased*
בָּאָרֶץ prep.-def.art.-n.f.s. (75) *in the land*

1:11

וְאוּלָם conj.-adv. (III 19) *but*
שְׁלַח־נָא Qal impv. 2 m.s. (1018)-part.of entreaty (609) *put forth now*
יָדְךָ n.f.s.-2 m.s. sf. (388) *your hand*
וְגַע conj.-Qal impv. 2 m.s. (נָגַע 619) *and touch*
בְּכָל־אֲשֶׁר־לוֹ prep.-n.m.s. (481)-rel. (81)-prep.-3 m.s. sf. *all that he has*
אִם־לֹא cond.part. (49)-neg. (after an oath, an emphatic affirmative)
עַל־פָּנֶיךָ prep.-n.m.p.-2 m.s. sf. (815) *to your face*
יְבָרְכֶךָּ Pi. impf. 3 m.s.-2 m.s. sf. (בָּרַךְ 138; LXX εὐλογήσει) *he will curse you*

1:12

וַיֹּאמֶר consec.-Qal impf. 3 m.s. (55) *and said*
יהוה pr.n. (217) *Yahweh*
אֶל־הַשָּׂטָן prep.-def.art.-n.m.s. (966) *to the adversary*
הִנֵּה demons.part. (243) *behold*
כָּל־אֲשֶׁר־לוֹ n.m.s. (481)-rel. (81)-prep.-3 m.s. sf. (LXX+δίδωμι) *all that he has*
בְּיָדֶךָ prep.-n.f.s.-2 m.s. sf. (388) *in your power*
רַק אֵלָיו adv. (956)-prep.-3 m.s. sf. *only upon himself*
אַל־תִּשְׁלַח neg. (39)-Qal impf. 2 m.s. (שָׁלַח 1018) *you may not put forth*
יָדֶךָ n.f.s.-2 m.s. sf. (388) *your hand*
וַיֵּצֵא consec.-Qal impf. 3 m.s. (יָצָא 422) *so went forth*
הַשָּׂטָן v.supra *the adversary*
מֵעִם פְּנֵי prep.-prep. (768)-n.m.p. cstr. (815) *from the presence of*
יהוה pr.n. (217) *Yahweh*

1:13

וַיְהִי הַיּוֹם consec.-Qal impf. 3 m.s. (הָיָה 224) -def.art.-n.m.s. (398; GK 126s) *now there was a day*
וּבָנָיו conj.-n.m.p.-3 m.s. sf. (119) *when both his sons*
וּבְנֹתָיו conj.-n.f.p.-3 m.s. sf. (I 123) *and his daughters*
אֹכְלִים Qal act.ptc. m.p. (אָכַל 37; LXX>) *were eating*
וְשֹׁתִים conj.-Qal act.ptc. m.p. (שָׁתָה 1059) *and drinking*
יַיִן n.m.s. (406) *wine*
בְּבֵית prep.-n.m.s. cstr. (108) *in the house of*

אֲחִיהֶם n.m.s.-3 m.p. sf. (26) *their brother*
הַבְּכוֹר def.art.-n.m.s. (114) *the first-born*

1:14

וּמַלְאָךְ conj.-n.m.s. (521) *and a messenger*
בָּא Qal pf. 3 m.s. (בּוֹא 97) *came*
אֶל־אִיּוֹב prep.-pr.n. (33) *to Job*
וַיֹּאמַר consec.-Qal impf. 3 m.s. (55) *and said*
הַבָּקָר def.art.-n.m.s. (133; GK 145c) *the oxen*
הָיוּ Qal pf. 3 c.p. (הָיָה 224; GK 116r,141i) *they were (used to be)*
חֹרְשׁוֹת Qal act.ptc. f.p. (חָרַשׁ I 360) *plowing*
וְהָאֲתֹנוֹת conj.-def.art.-n.f.p. (87; GK 122c) *and the she-asses*
רֹעוֹת Qal act.ptc. f.p. (רָעָה I 944) *feeding*
עַל־יְדֵיהֶם prep. (II 752)-n.f.p.-3 m.p. sf. (388; GK 119cc,135o; some ms. rd. יְדֵיהֶן) *beside them*

1:15

וַתִּפֹּל consec.-Qal impf. 3 f.s. (נָפַל 656) *and fell*
שְׁבָא pr.n. f. (985; GK 122i) *the Sabeans*
וַתִּקָּחֵם consec.-Qal impf. 3 f.s.-3 m.p. sf. (לָקַח 542; GK 135o) *and took them*
וְאֶת־הַנְּעָרִים conj.-dir.obj.-def.art.-n.m.p. (654) *and the servants*
הִכּוּ Hi. pf. 3 c.p. (נָכָה 645) *they slew*
לְפִי־חָרֶב prep.-n.m.s. cstr. (804)-n.f.s. paus. (352) *with the edge of the sword*
וָאִמָּלְטָה consec.-Ni. impf. 1 c.s.-dir.he? (מָלַט 572; GK 49e) *and I have escaped*
רַק־אֲנִי לְבַדִּי adv. (956)-pers.pr. 1 c.s. (58)-prep. -n.m.s.-1 c.s. sf. (94) *only I by myself*
לְהַגִּיד prep.-Hi. inf.cstr. (נָגַד 616) *to tell*
לָךְ prep.-2 m.s. sf. paus. *you*

1:16

עוֹד adv. (728; GK 116u) *while*
זֶה demons.adj. m.s. (260) *this one*
מְדַבֵּר Pi. ptc. (180; GK 164a) *was speaking*
וְזֶה conj.-demons.adj. m.s. (260; LXX ἕτερος ἄγγελος) *also another*
בָּא Qal pf. 3 m.s. (בּוֹא 97; or Qal act.ptc.; LXX+ πρὸς Ιωβ) *came*
וַיֹּאמַר consec.-Qal impf. 3 m.s. (55) *and said*
אֵשׁ אֱלֹהִים n.f.s. cstr. (77)-n.m.p. (43; LXX πῦρ) *the fire of God*
נָפְלָה Qal pf. 3 f.s. (נָפַל 656) *fell*
מִן־הַשָּׁמַיִם prep.-def.art.-n.m. du. (1029) *from heaven*
וַתִּבְעַר consec.-Qal impf. 3 f.s. (בָּעַר 128) *and burned up*
בַּצֹּאן prep.-def.art.-n.f.s. (838) *the sheep*
וּבַנְּעָרִים conj.-prep.-def.art.-n.m.p. (654; LXX καὶ τοὺς ποιμένας=וּבָרֹעִים) *and the servants*
וַתֹּאכְלֵם consec.-Qal impf. 3 f.s.-3 m.p. sf. (אָכַל 37; LXX+ὁμοίως) *and consumed them*
וָאִמָּלְטָה cf.v.15 consec.-Ni. impf. 1 c.s.-dir.he? (572; GK 49e) *and I have escaped*
רַק־אֲנִי לְבַדִּי adv. (956)-pers.pr. 1 c.s. (58)-prep. -n.m.s.-1 c.s. sf. (94) *only I by myself*
לְהַגִּיד לָךְ prep.-Hi. inf.cstr. (נָגַד 616)-prep.-2 m.s. paus. *to tell you*

1:17

עוֹד adv. (728) *while*
זֶה demons.adj. m.s. (260) *this one*
מְדַבֵּר Pi. ptc. (180) *was speaking*
וְזֶה conj.-demons.adj. m.s. (260; LXX ἕτερος ἄγγελος) *also another*
בָּא Qal pf. 3 m.s. (בּוֹא 97) *came*
וַיֹּאמַר consec.-Qal impf. 3 m.s. (55; LXX+πρὸς Ιωβ) *and said*
כַּשְׂדִּים pr.n. p. (505; LXX Οἱ ἱππεῖς) *the Chaldeans*
שָׂמוּ Qal pf. 3 c.p. (שִׂים 962) *formed*
שְׁלֹשָׁה num. f.s. (1025) *three*
רָאשִׁים n.m.p. (910) *companies*
וַיִּפְשְׁטוּ consec.-Qal impf. 3 m.p. (פָּשַׁט 832; LXX ἐκύκλωσαν) *and made a raid*
עַל־הַגְּמַלִּים prep.-def.art.-n.m.p. (168) *upon the camels*
וַיִּקָּחוּם consec.-Qal impf. 3 m.p.-3 m.p. sf. (לָקַח 542) *and took them*
וְאֶת־הַנְּעָרִים conj.-dir.obj.-def.art.-n.m.p. (654) *and the servants*
הִכּוּ Hi. pf. 3 c.p. (נָכָה 645) *they slew*
לְפִי־חָרֶב prep.-n.m.s. cstr. (804)-n.f.s. paus. (352) *with the edge of the sword*
וָאִמָּלְטָה consec.-Ni. impf. 1 c.s.-dir.he? (מָלַט 572) *and I have escaped*
רַק־אֲנִי לְבַדִּי adv. (956)-pers.pr. 1 c.s. (58)-prep. -n.m.s.-1 c.s. sf. (94) *only I by myself*
לְהַגִּיד לָךְ prep.-Hi. inf.cstr. (נָגַד 616)-prep.-2 m.s. sf. paus. *to tell you*

1:18

עַד adv. (III 723; many mss. rd. עוֹד; GK 116v) *while*
זֶה demons.adj. m.s. (260) *this one*
מְדַבֵּר Pi. ptc. (180) *was speaking*
וְזֶה conj.-v.supra *also another*
בָּא Qal pf. 3 m.s. (בּוֹא 97) *came*

וַיֹּאמַר consec.-Qal impf. 3 m.s. (55; LXX+τῷ Ιωβ) *and said*
בָּנֶיךָ n.m.p.-2 m.s. sf. (119) *your sons*
וּבְנוֹתֶיךָ conj.-n.f.p.-2 m.s. sf. (I 123) *and your daughters*
אֹכְלִים Qal act.ptc. m.p. (37) *were eating*
וְשֹׁתִים conj.-Qal act.ptc. m.p. (שָׁתָה 1059) *and drinking*
יַיִן n.m.s. (406; LXX>) *wine*
בְּבֵית prep.-n.m.s. cstr. (108) *in the house of*
אֲחִיהֶם n.m.s.-3 m.p. sf. (26) *their brother*
הַבְּכוֹר def.art.-n.m.s. (114) *the first-born*

1:19

וְהִנֵּה conj.-demons.part. (243) *and behold*
רוּחַ גְּדוֹלָה n.f.s. (924)-adj. f.s. (152) *a great wind*
בָּאָה Qal pf. 3 f.s. (בּוֹא 97) *came*
מֵעֵבֶר prep.-n.m.s. cstr. (I 719) *across*
הַמִּדְבָּר def.art.-n.m.s. (184) *the wilderness*
וַיִּגַּע consec.-Qal impf. 3 m.s. (נָגַע 619; some propose וַתִּגַּע; GK 145t) *and struck*
בְּאַרְבַּע prep.-num. m.s. cstr. (I 916) *the four of*
פִּנּוֹת n.f.p. cstr. (819; LXX>) *the corners of*
הַבַּיִת def.art.-n.m.s. (108) *the house*
וַיִּפֹּל consec.-Qal impf. 3 m.s. (נָפַל 656) *and it (the house) fell*
עַל־הַנְּעָרִים prep.-def.art.-n.m.p. (654; GK 122g; LXX ἐπὶ τὰ παιδία σου) *upon the young people*
וַיָּמוּתוּ consec.-Qal impf. 3 m.p. (מוּת 559; LXX καὶ ἐτελεύτησαν) *and they died*
וָאִמָּלְטָה consec.-Ni. impf. 1 c.s.-dir.he? (מָלַט 572) *and I have escaped*
רַק־אֲנִי לְבַדִּי adv. (956)-pers.pr. 1 c.s. (58)-prep.-n.m.s.-1 c.s. sf. (94) *only I by myself*
לְהַגִּיד לָךְ prep.-Hi. inf.cstr. (נָגַד 616)-prep.-2 m.s. sf. paus. *to tell you*

1:20

וַיָּקָם consec.-Qal impf. 3 m.s. (קוּם 877) *then arose*
אִיּוֹב pr.n. (33) *Job*
וַיִּקְרַע consec.-Qal impf. 3 m.s. (קָרַע 902) *and rent*
אֶת־מְעִלוֹ dir.obj.-n.m.s.-3 m.s. sf. (591) *his robe*
וַיָּגָז consec.-Qal impf. 3 m.s. (גָּזַז 159) *and shaved*
אֶת־רֹאשׁוֹ dir.obj.-n.m.s.-3 m.s. sf. (910) *his head*
וַיִּפֹּל consec.-Qal impf. 3 m.s. (נָפַל 656) *and fell*
אַרְצָה n.f.s.-dir.he (75) *toward the ground*
וַיִּשְׁתָּחוּ consec.-Hithpalel impf. 3 m.s. apoc. (1005 שָׁחָה) *and prostrated himself*

1:21

וַיֹּאמַר consec.-Qal impf. 3 m.s. (55) *and he said*
עָרֹם adj. m.s. (736; GK 118n) *naked*
יָצָתִי Qal pf. 1 c.s. (יָצָא 422; Q יצאתי; GK 23f,74k) *I came*
מִבֶּטֶן prep.-n.f.s. cstr. (105) *from the womb of*
אִמִּי n.f.s.-1 c.s. sf. (51) *my mother*
וְעָרֹם conj.-v.supra (GK 118n) *and naked*
אָשׁוּב Qal impf. 1 c.s. (שׁוּב 996) *shall I return (am about to)*
שָׁמָה adv.-dir.he (1027) *thither*
יהוה נָתַן pr.n. (217)-Qal pf. 3 m.s. (678) *Yahweh gave*
ויהוה לָקָח conj.-v.supra-Qal pf. 3 m.s. paus. (542; LXX+ὡς τῷ κυρίῳ ἔδοξεν, οὕτως καὶ ἔγενετο) *and Yahweh has taken away*
יְהִי Qal impf. 3 m.s. apoc.vol. (הָיָה 224) *let be*
שֵׁם יהוה n.m.s. cstr. (1027)-v.supra *the name of Yahweh*
מְבֹרָךְ Pu ptc. (בָּרַךְ 138) *blessed*

1:22

בְּכָל־זֹאת prep.-n.m.s. cstr. (481)-demons.adj. f.s. (260; LXX+τοῖς συμβεβηκόσιν αὐτῷ) *in all this*
לֹא־חָטָא neg.-Qal pf. 3 m.s. (306) *did not sin*
אִיּוֹב pr.n. (33; LXX+ἐναντίον τοῦ κυρίου) *Job*
וְלֹא־נָתַן conj.-neg.-Qal pf. 3 m.s. (678) *or charge*
תִּפְלָה n.f.s. (1074) *with wrong (moral unsavouriness)*
לֵאלֹהִים prep.-n.m.p. (43) *to God*

2:1

וַיְהִי consec.-Qal impf. 3 m.s. (הָיָה 224) *and then there was*
הַיּוֹם def.art.-n.m.s. (398) *the day*
וַיָּבֹאוּ consec.-Qal impf. 3 m.p. (בּוֹא 97) *when came*
בְּנֵי הָאֱלֹהִים n.m.p. cstr. (119)-def.art.-n.m.p. (43; GK 128v) *the sons of God*
לְהִתְיַצֵּב prep.-Hith. inf.cstr. (יָצַב 426; LXX παραστῆναι) *to present themselves (to take their stands)*
עַל־יהוה prep.-pr.n. (217) *before (against) Yahweh*
וַיָּבוֹא consec.-Qal impf. 3 m.s. (בּוֹא 97) *and came*
גַם־הַשָּׂטָן adv. (168)-def.art.-n.m.s. (966) *also the adversary*
בְּתֹכָם prep.-n.m.s.-3 m.p. sf. (1063) *among them*
לְהִתְיַצֵּב v.supra *to take a stand*

עַל־יהוה prep.-pr.n. (217) *against Yahweh*

2:2

וַיֹּאמֶר consec.-Qal impf. 3 m.s. (55) *and said*

יהוה pr.n. (217) *Yahweh*

אֶל־הַשָּׂטָן prep.-def.art.-n.m.s. (966) *to the adversary*

אֵי מִזֶּה interr.adv. (32)-prep.-demons.adj. m.s. (260) *whence*

תָּבֹא Qal impf. 2 m.s. (בּוֹא 97) *have you come*

וַיַּעַן consec.-Qal impf. 3 m.s. (עָנָה I 772) *and answered*

הַשָּׂטָן v.supra *the adversary*

אֶת־יהוה dir.obj.-pr.n. (217) *Yahweh*

וַיֹּאמַר consec.-Qal impf. 3 m.s. (55; LXX>) *and said*

מִשֻּׁט prep.-Qal inf.cstr. (שׁוּט 1001) *from going to and fro*

בָּאָרֶץ prep.-def.art.-n.f.s. (75) *on the earth*

וּמֵהִתְהַלֵּךְ conj.-prep.-Hith. inf.cstr. (הָלַךְ 229) *and from walking up and down*

בָּהּ prep.-3 f.s. sf. *on it*

2:3

וַיֹּאמֶר consec.-Qal impf. 3 m.s. (55) *and said*

יהוה pr.n. (217) *Yahweh*

אֶל־הַשָּׂטָן prep.-def.art.-n.m.s. (966) *to the adversary*

הֲשַׂמְתָּ לִבְּךָ interr.-Qal pf. 2 m.s. (שִׂים 962)-n.m.s.-2 m.s. sf. (524) *have you considered*

אֶל־עַבְדִּי prep.-n.m.s.-1 c.s. sf. (713; LXX τῷ θεράποντί μου) *my servant*

אִיּוֹב pr.n. (33) *Job*

כִּי אֵין conj. (471)-neg. (II 34) *that there is none*

כָּמֹהוּ subst.-3 m.s. sf. (453) *like him*

בָּאָרֶץ prep.-def.art.-n.f.s. (75) *on the earth*

אִישׁ תָּם n.m.s. (35)-adj. m.s. (1070; LXX ἄνθρωπος ἄκακος, ἀληθινός) *a man blameless*

וְיָשָׁר conj.-adj. m.s. (449; LXX ἄμεμπτος) *and upright*

יְרֵא אֱלֹהִים Qal act.ptc. m.s. cstr. (יָרֵא 431) -n.m.p. (43) *who fears God*

וְסָר conj.-Qal act.ptc. (סוּר 693) *and turns away*

מֵרָע prep.-n.m.s. (948) *from evil*

וְעֹדֶנּוּ conj.-subst.-3 m.s. sf. (728) *he still*

מַחֲזִיק Hi. ptc. (חָזַק 304) *holds fast*

בְּתֻמָּתוֹ prep.-n.f.s.-3 m.s. sf. (1070; LXX ἀκακίας) *his integrity*

וַתְּסִיתֵנִי consec.-Hi. impf. 2 m.s.-1 c.s. sf. (סוּת 694; GK 111,l) *although you moved me (instigate)*

בוֹ prep.-3 m.s. sf. *against him*

לְבַלְּעוֹ prep.-Pi. inf.cstr.-3 m.s. sf. (בָּלַע 118) *to destroy him*

חִנָּם adv. (336) *without cause*

2:4

וַיַּעַן consec.-Qal impf. 3 m.s. (עָנָה I 772) *then answered*

הַשָּׂטָן def.art.-n.m.s. (966) *the adversary*

אֶת־יהוה dir.obj.-pr.n. (217) *Yahweh*

וַיֹּאמַר consec.-Qal impf. 3 m.s. (55) *(and said)*

עוֹר n.m.s. (736) *skin*

בְּעַד־עוֹר subst. cstr. (126)-v.supra *for skin*

וְכֹל אֲשֶׁר conj.-n.m.s. (481)-rel. (81) *and everything which (belongs)*

לָאִישׁ prep.-def.art.-n.m.s. (35) *to the man*

יִתֵּן Qal impf. 3 m.s. (נָתַן 678) *he will give*

בְּעַד נַפְשׁוֹ subst. cstr. (126)-n.f.s.-3 m.s. sf. (659) *for his life*

2:5

אוּלָם adv. (19) *but*

שְׁלַח־נָא Qal impv. 2 m.s. (1018)-part.of entreaty (609) *put forth now*

יָדְךָ n.f.s.-2 m.s. sf. (388) *your hand*

וְגַע conj.-Qal impv. 2 m.s. (נָגַע 619) *and touch*

אֶל־עַצְמוֹ prep.-n.f.s.-3 m.s. sf. (782) *his bone*

וְאֶל־בְּשָׂרוֹ conj.-prep.-n.m.s.-3 m.s. sf. (142) *and his flesh*

אִם־לֹא cond.part. (49)-neg. (after an oath an emphatic affirmative)

אֶל־פָּנֶיךָ prep.-n.m.p.-2 m.s. sf. (815; some mss. rd. עַל־) *to your face*

יְבָרְכֶךָּ Pi. impf. 3 m.s.-2 m.s. sf. (בָּרַךְ 138; LXX εὐλογήσει) *he will curse you (or bless you)*

2:6

וַיֹּאמֶר consec.-Qal impf. 3 m.s. (55) *and said*

יהוה pr.n. (217) *Yahweh*

אֶל־הַשָּׂטָן prep.-def.art.-n.m.s. (966) *to the adversary*

הִנּוֹ demons.part.-3 m.s. sf. (243) LXX+ παραδίδωμι *behold, he*

בְּיָדֶךָ prep.-n.f.s.-2 m.s. sf. (388) *in your power*

אַךְ adv. (36) *only*

אֶת־נַפְשׁוֹ dir.obj.-n.f.s.-3 m.s. sf. (659) *his life*

שְׁמֹר Qal impv. 2 m.s. (1036) *spare (protect)*

2:7

וַיֵּצֵא consec.-Qal impf. 3 m.s. (יָצָא 422) *so went forth*

הַשָּׂטָן def.art.-n.m.s. (966) *the adversary*

מֵאֵת פְּנֵי יהוה prep.-prep. (II 85)-n.m.p. cstr. (815)-pr.n. (217) *from the presence of Yahweh*

וַיַּךְ consec.-Hi. impf. 3 m.s. (נָכָה 645) *and afflicted*

אֶת־אִיּוֹב dir.obj.-pr.n. (33) *Job*

בִּשְׁחִין prep.-n.m.s. (1006) *with sores*

רָע adj. m.s. (948) *loathsome*

מִכַּף prep.-n.f.s. cstr. (496) *from the sole of*

רַגְלוֹ n.f.s.-3 m.s. sf. (919) *his foot*

עַד קָדְקֳדוֹ prep. (III 723)-n.m.s.-3 m.s. sf. (869; Q וְעַד) *to the crown of his head*

2:8

וַיִּקַּח־לוֹ consec.-Qal impf. 3 m.s. (לָקַח 542) -prep.-3 m.s. sf. *and he took for himself*

חֶרֶשׂ n.m.s. (360) *a potsherd*

לְהִתְגָּרֵד prep.-Hith. inf.cstr. (גָּרַד 173; LXX ἵνα τὸν ἰχῶρα ξύῃ) *to scrape himself*

בּוֹ prep.-3 m.s. sf. *with it*

וְהוּא יֹשֵׁב conj.-pers.pr. 3 m.s. (214)-Qal act.ptc. (יָשַׁב 442) *and was sitting*

בְּתוֹךְ־הָאֵפֶר prep.-n.m.s. cstr. (1063)-def.art. -n.m.s. (68; LXX ἐπὶ τῆς κοπρίας; LXX+ ἔξω τῆς πόλεως) *among the ashes*

2:9

(LXX+χρόνου δὲ πολλοῦ προβεβηκότος)

וַתֹּאמֶר לוֹ consec.-Qal impf. 3 f.s. (55)-prep.-3 m.s. sf. *then said to him*

אִשְׁתּוֹ n.f.s.-3 m.s. sf. (61) *his wife*

עֹדְךָ adv.-2 m.s. sf. (728) *do you still*

מַחֲזִיק Hi. ptc. (חָזַק 304) *hold fast*

בְּתֻמָּתֶךָ prep.-n.f.s.-2 m.s. sf. (1070) *your integrity*

LXX+ in 2:9b

Ἰδοὺ ἀναμένω χρόνον ἔτι μικρὸν
προσδεχόμενος τὴν ἐλπίδα τῆς σωτηρίας μου;
ἰδοὺ γὰρ ἠφάνισταί σου τὸ μνημόσυνον ἀπὸ τῆς γῆς
υἱοὶ καὶ θυγατέρες, ἐμῆς κοιλίας ὠδῖνες καὶ πόνοι,
οὓς εἰς τὸ κενὸν ἐκοπίασα μετὰ μόχθων.
σύ τε αὐτὸς ἐν σαπρίᾳ σκωλήκων κάθησαι κιανυκτερεύων αἴθριος
κἀγὼ πλανῆτις καὶ λάτρις
τόπον ἐκ τόπου περιερχομένη καὶ οἰκίαν ἐξ οἰκίας
προσδεχομένη τὸν ἥλιον πότε δύσεται,
ἵνα ἀναπαύσωμαι τῶν μόχθων καὶ τῶν ὀδυνῶν, αἵ με νῦν συνέχουσιν.

בָּרֵךְ Pi. impv. 2 m.s. (138; GK 110f; LXX ἀλλὰ εἰπόν τι ῥῆμα) *curse (bless)*

אֱלֹהִים n.m.p. (43) *God*

וָמֻת conj.-Qal impv. 2 m.s. (מוּת 559; LXX καὶ τελεύτα; GK 110f) *and die*

2:10

LXX+ ὁ δὲ ἐμβλέψας

וַיֹּאמֶר consec.-Qal impf. 3 m.s. (55) *but he said*

אֵלֶיהָ prep.-3 f.s. sf. *to her*

כְּדַבֵּר prep.-Pi. inf.cstr. (180) *as would speak*

אַחַת הַנְּבָלוֹת num. f.s. cstr. (25)-def.art.-adj. f.p. (I 614) *one of the foolish women*

תְּדַבֵּרִי Pi. impf. 2 f.s. (180) *you speak*

גַּם adv. (168; GK 153) *yea*

אֶת־הַטּוֹב dir.obj.-def.art.-n.m.s. (III 375) *good*

נְקַבֵּל Pi. impf. 1 c.p. (קָבַל 867; LXX ἐδεξάμεθα) *we have been receiving*

מֵאֵת הָאֱלֹהִים prep.-prep.-def.art.-n.m.p. (43) *from God*

וְאֶת־הָרָע conj.-dir.obj.-def.art.-n.m.s. (948) *but the evil*

לֹא נְקַבֵּל neg.-v.supra (GK 150a; LXX οὐκ ὑποίσομεν) *shall we not receive*

בְּכָל־זֹאת prep.-n.m.s. cstr. (481)-demons.adj. f.s. (260; LXX+ τοῖς συμβεβηκόσιν αὐτῷ) *in all this*

לֹא־חָטָא neg.-Qal pf. 3 m.s. (306) *did not sin*

אִיּוֹב pr.n. (33) *Job*

בִּשְׂפָתָיו prep.-n.f.p.-3 m.s. sf. (973; LXX+ ἐναντίον τοῦ θεοῦ) *with his lips*

2:11

וַיִּשְׁמְעוּ consec.-Qal impf. 3 m.p. (שָׁמַע 1033) *now when ... heard*

שְׁלֹשֶׁת רֵעֵי num. f.s. cstr. (1025)-n.m.p. cstr. (945) *three friends of*

אִיּוֹב pr.n. (33; LXX αὐτοῦ) *Job*

אֵת כָּל־ dir.obj.-n.m.s. cstr. (481) *of all of*

הָרָעָה הַזֹּאת def.art.-n.f.s. (949)-def.art. -demons.adj. f.s. (260) *this evil*

הַבָּאָה def.art.-Qal act.ptc. f.s. (בּוֹא 97) *that had come*

עָלָיו prep.-3 m.s. sf. *upon him*

וַיָּבֹאוּ consec.-Qal impf. 3 m.p. (בּוֹא 97) *they came*

אִישׁ n.m.s. (35) *each*

מִמְּקֹמוֹ prep.-n.m.s.-3 m.s. sf. (879; LXX πρὸς αὐτόν) *from his own place*

אֱלִיפַז pr.n. (45) *Eliphaz (God is fine gold)*

הַתֵּימָנִי def.art.-gent.adj. (412; LXX ὁ Θαιμανων βασιλεὺς) *the Temanite*

וּבִלְדַּד conj.-pr.n. (115; LXX Βαλδαδ) *Bildad (Bel has loved)*

הַשּׁוּחִי def.art.-gent.adj. (1001; LXX ὁ Σαυχαίων τύραννος) *the Shuhite*

וְצוֹפַר conj.-pr.n. (862) *and Zophar*

הַנַּעֲמָתִי def.art.-gent.adj. (654; LXX ὁ Μιναίων βασιλεύς) *the Naamathite*

וַיִּוָּעֲדוּ consec.-Ni. impf. 3 m.p. (יָעַד 416) *and they made an appointment*

יַחְדָּו adv. (403) *together*

לָבוֹא prep.-Qal inf.cstr. (97; LXX+ καὶ) *to come*

לָנוּד־לוֹ prep.-Qal inf.cstr. (נוּד 626)-prep.-3 m.s. sf. *to condole with him*

וּלְנַחֲמוֹ conj.-prep.-Pi. inf.cstr.-3 m.s. sf. (נָחַם 636) *and to comfort him*

2:12

וַיִּשְׂאוּ consec.-Qal impf. 3 m.p. (נָשָׂא 669) *and when they lifted*

אֶת־עֵינֵיהֶם dir.obj.-n.f.p.-3 m.p. sf. (744) *their eyes*

מֵרָחוֹק prep.-n.m.s. (935) *from afar*

וְלֹא הִכִּירֻהוּ conj.-neg.-Hi. pf. 3 c.p.-3 m.s. sf. (647 נָכַר) *and they did not recognize him*

וַיִּשְׂאוּ קוֹלָם consec.-Qal impf. 3 m.p. (נָשָׂא 669)-n.m.s.-3 m.p. sf. (876; LXX φωνῇ μεγάλῃ) *and they raised their voices*

וַיִּבְכּוּ consec.-Qal impf. 3 m.p. (בָּכָה 113) *and wept*

וַיִּקְרְעוּ consec.-Qal impf. 3 m.p. (קָרַע 902) *and they rent*

אִישׁ n.m.s. (35) *each*

מְעִלוֹ n.m.s.-3 m.s. sf. (591) *his robe*

וַיִּזְרְקוּ consec.-Qal impf. 3 m.p. (זָרַק 284; LXX καὶ καταπασάμενοι) *and sprinkled*

עָפָר n.m.s. (779) *dust*

עַל־רָאשֵׁיהֶם prep.-n.m.p.-3 m.p. sf. (910; LXX>) *upon their heads*

הַשָּׁמָיְמָה def.art.-n.m. du.-dir.he (1029; LXX>) *toward heaven*

2:13

וַיֵּשְׁבוּ consec.-Qal impf. 3 m.p. (יָשַׁב 442) *and they sat*

אִתּוֹ prep.-3 m.s. sf. (II 85) *with him*

לָאָרֶץ prep.-def.art.-n.f.s. (75; LXX>) *on the ground*

שִׁבְעַת יָמִים num. f.s. cstr. (988)-n.m.p. (398) *seven days*

וְשִׁבְעַת לֵילוֹת conj.-v.supra-n.m.p. (538) *and seven nights*

וְאֵין־דֹּבֵר conj.-neg. cstr. (II 34)-Qal act.ptc. (180) *and no one spoke*

אֵלָיו prep.-3 m.s. sf. *to him*

דָּבָר n.m.s. (182; LXX>) *a word*

כִּי רָאוּ conj.-Qal pf. 3 c.p. (רָאָה 906) *for they saw*

כִּי־גָדַל conj. (471)-Qal pf. 3 m.s. (152) *that was great*

הַכְּאֵב def.art.-n.m.s. (456) *the pain*

מְאֹד adv. (547) *exceedingly*

3:1

אַחֲרֵי־כֵן prep. (29)-adv. (I 485) *after this*

פָּתַח Qal pf. 3 m.s. (I 834) *opened*

אִיּוֹב pr.n. (33) *Job*

אֶת־פִּיהוּ dir.obj.-n.m.s.-3 m.s. sf. (804) *his mouth*

וַיְקַלֵּל consec.-Pi. impf. 3 m.s. (קָלַל 886) *and cursed (made light of)*

אֶת־יוֹמוֹ dir.obj.-n.m.s.-3 m.s. sf. (398) *his day*

3:2

LXX+ λέγων

וַיַּעַן consec.-Qal impf. 3 m.s. (עָנָה I 772) *then answered*

אִיּוֹב pr.n. (33) *Job*

וַיֹּאמַר consec.-Qal impf. 3 m.s. (55; GK 68e) *and said*

3:3

יֹאבַד Qal impf. 3 m.s. (אָבַד 1; GK 29e,68d) *let perish*

יוֹם n.m.s. (398; GK 155i) *the day*

אִוָּלֶד בּוֹ Ni. impf. 1 c.s. (יָלַד 408; GK 107k) -prep.-3 m.s. sf. *wherein I was born*

וְהַלַּיְלָה conj.-def.art.-n.m.s. (538; GK 155f) *and the night*

אָמַר Qal pf. 3 m.s. (55) *(which) said*

הֹרָה גָבֶר Pu. pf. 3 m.s. (הָרָה I 247)-n.m.s. paus. (149; LXX Ἰδοὺ ἄρσεν) *a man-child is conceived*

3:4

הַיּוֹם הַהוּא def.art.-n.m.s. (398)-def.art. -demons.adj. m.s. (214; GK 141cN) *that day*

יְהִי Qal impf. 3 m.s. apoc.juss. (הָיָה 224) *let be*

חֹשֶׁךְ n.m.s. (365) *darkness*

אַל־יִדְרְשֵׁהוּ neg. (II 39)-Qal impf. 3 m.s.-3 m.s. sf. juss. (דָּרַשׁ 205) *may ... not seek it*

אֱלוֹהַּ n.m.s. (42) *God*

מִמָּעַל prep.-adv. (751) *above*

וְאַל־תּוֹפַע conj.-neg. (II 39)-Hi. impf. 3 f.s. (יָפַע 422) *nor shine*

עָלָיו prep.-3 m.s. sf. *upon it*
נְהָרָה n.f.s. (626) *light*

3:5
יִגְאָלֻהוּ Qal impf. 3 m.p.-3 m.s. sf. (גָּאַל I 145) *let claim (as kinsman) it*
חֹשֶׁךְ n.m.s. (365) *darkness*
וְצַלְמָוֶת conj.-n.m.s. (853; LXX σκιὰ θανάτου) *and deep darkness*
תִּשְׁכָּן־ Qal impf. 3 f.s. (שָׁכַן 1014) *let dwell*
עָלָיו prep.-3 m.s. sf. *upon it*
עֲנָנָה n.f.s. (778; GK 122t) *clouds*
יְבַעֲתֻהוּ Pi. impf. 3 m.p.-3 m.s. sf. (בָּעַת 129; LXX>) *let terrify it*
כִּמְרִירֵי יוֹם n.m.p. cstr. (485)-n.m.s. (398; LXX καταραθείη ἡ ἡμέρα) *blackness of day*

3:6
הַלַּיְלָה הַהוּא def.art.-n.m.s. (538)-def.art. -demons.adj. m.s. (214) *that night*
יִקָּחֵהוּ Qal impf. 3 m.s.-3 m.s. sf. (לָקַח 542) *let seize it*
אֹפֶל n.m.s. (66) *thick darkness*
אַל־יִחַדְּ neg. (II 39)-Qal impf. 3 m.s. apoc.juss. (II 292 חָדָה; GK 75r; LXX μὴ εἴη) *let it not rejoice*
בִּימֵי שָׁנָה prep.-n.m.p. cstr. (398)-n.f.s. (1040) *among days of a year*
בְּמִסְפַּר prep.-n.m.s. cstr. (708) *into a number of*
יְרָחִים n.m.p. (437) *months*
אַל־יָבֹא neg. (II 39)-Qal impf. 3 m.s. (בּוֹא 97) *let it not come*

3:7
הִנֵּה demons.part. (243; LXX ἀλλὰ) *yea*
הַלַּיְלָה הַהוּא def.art.-n.m.s. (538)-def.art. -demons.adj. m.s. (214) *that night*
יְהִי Qal impf. 3 m.s. apoc.juss. (הָיָה 224) *let ... be*
גַּלְמוּד adj. m.s. (166) *barren*
אַל־תָּבֹא neg. (39)-Qal impf. 3 f.s. (בּוֹא 97) *let not come*
רְנָנָה n.f.s. (943; LXX εὐφροσύνη μηδὲ χαρμονή) *a joyful cry*
בוֹ prep.-3 m.s. sf. *in it*

3:8
יִקְּבֻהוּ Qal impf. 3 m.p.-3 m.s. sf. (קָבַב II 866; GK 67g) *let those curse it*
אֹרְרֵי־ Qal act.ptc. m.p. cstr. (אָרַר 76) *who curse*
יוֹם n.m.s. (398) *a day*
הָעֲתִידִים def.art.-adj. m.p. (800) *who are skilled in*
עֹרֵר Polel inf.cstr. (עוּר I 734; GK 114m) *rousing up*
לִוְיָתָן n.m.s. (531; LXX κῆτος) *Leviathan*

3:9
יֶחְשְׁכוּ Qal impf. 3 m.p. (חָשַׁךְ 364) *let be dark*
כּוֹכְבֵי n.m.p. cstr. (456) *the stars of*
נִשְׁפּוֹ n.m.s.-3 m.s. sf. (676; LXX τῆς νυκτὸς ἐκείνης) *its days*
יְקַו־ Pi. impf. 3 m.s. apoc.juss. (קָוָה I 875) *let it hope*
לְאוֹר prep.-n.m.s. (21) *for light*
וָאַיִן conj.-neg. (II 34; GK 152k) *but have none*
וְאַל־יִרְאֶה conj.-neg. (II 39)-Qal impf. 3 m.s. -vol.he (רָאָה 906; GK 109aN) *nor let it see*
בְּעַפְעַפֵּי־ prep.-n.m.p. cstr. (733) *eyelids of*
שָׁחַר n.m.s. paus. (1007) *dawn*

3:10
כִּי לֹא סָגַר conj. (471)-neg.-Qal pf. 3 m.s. (688) *because it did not shut*
דַּלְתֵי n.f.p. cstr. (195) *the doors of*
בִטְנִי n.f.s.-1 c.s. sf. (105) *my womb*
וַיַּסְתֵּר consec.-Hi. impf. 3 m.s. (סָתַר 711; LXX ἀπήλλαξεν= וַיָּסַר) *nor hide*
עָמָל n.m.s. (765) *trouble*
מֵעֵינָי prep.-n.f.p.-1 c.s. paus. (744) *from my eyes*

3:11
לָמָּה לֹּא interr. (552)-neg. (GK 20f) *why not*
מֵרֶחֶם prep.-n.m.s. (933) *from a womb (at birth)*
אָמוּת Qal impf. 1 c.s. (מוּת 559) *did I die?*
מִבֶּטֶן prep.-n.f.s. (105) *from a womb*
יָצָאתִי Qal pf. 1 c.s. (יָצָא 422) *did I come forth*
וְאֶגְוָע conj.-Qal impf. 1 c.s. (גָּוַע 157; GK 152z; LXX+εὐθὺς) *and expire*

3:12
מַדּוּעַ adv. (396) *why*
קִדְּמוּנִי Pi. pf. 3 c.p.-1 c.s. sf. (קָדַם 869) *did ... receive me*
בִרְכָּיִם n.f. du. (139) *knees*
וּמַה־ conj.-interr. (552) *or why*
שָׁדַיִם n.m. du. (994) *breasts*
כִּי אִינָק conj. (471)-Qal impf. 1 c.s. (יָנַק 413) *that I should suck?*

3:13
כִּי־עַתָּה conj.-adv. (773) *for then*

שָׁכַבְתִּי Qal pf. 1 c.s. (שָׁכַב 1011; GK 106p) *I should have lain down*

וְאֶשְׁקוֹט conj.-Qal impf. 1 c.s. (שָׁקַט 1052) *and been quiet*

יָשַׁנְתִּי Qal pf. 1 c.s. (יָשֵׁן 445; GK 159dd) *I should have slept*

אָז adv. (23) *then*

יָנוּחַ לִי Qal impf. 3 m.s. (נוּחַ 628)-prep.-1 c.s. sf. *there would have been rest for me*

3:14

עִם־מְלָכִים prep. (767)-n.m.p. (I 572) *with kings*

וְיֹעֲצֵי conj.-Qal act.ptc. m.p. cstr. (יָעַץ 419) *and counselors of*

אָרֶץ n.f.s. paus. (75) *earth*

הַבֹּנִים def.art.-Qal act.ptc. m.p. (בָּנָה 124) *who are building*

חֳרָבוֹת n.f.p. (352) *ruins*

לָמוֹ prep.-3 m.p. sf. (LXX>) *for themselves*

3:15

אוֹ עִם־שָׂרִים conj. (14)-prep. (767)-n.m.p. (978) *or with princes*

זָהָב לָהֶם n.m.s. (262)-prep.-3 m.p. sf. (GK 155e; LXX+πολὺς) *who had gold*

הַמְמַלְאִים def.art.-Pi. ptc. m.p. (מָלֵא 569) *who filled*

בָּתֵּיהֶם n.m.p.-3 m.p. sf. (108) *their houses*

כָּסֶף n.m.s. paus. (494) *with silver*

3:16

אוֹ כְנֵפֶל conj. (14)-prep.-n.m.s. (658) *or as an abortion*

טָמוּן Qal pass.ptc. (טָמַן 380; LXX ἐκπορευόμενον ἐκ μήτρας μητρὸς) *hidden*

לֹא אֶהְיֶה neg.-Qal impf. 1 c.s. (הָיָה 224) *was I not*

כְּעֹלְלִים prep.-n.m.p. (760) *as infants*

לֹא־רָאוּ neg.-Qal pf. 3 c.p. (רָאָה 906) *that never see*

אוֹר n.m.s. (21) *light*

3:17

שָׁם רְשָׁעִים adv. (1027)-adj. m.p. (957) *there wicked ones*

חָדְלוּ Qal pf. 3 c.p. (חָדַל 292; GK 106,l; LXX ἐξέκαυσαν θυμὸν) cease

רֹגֶז n.m.s. (919) *raging*

וְשָׁם conj.-v.supra *and there*

יָנוּחוּ Qal impf. 3 m.p. (נוּחַ 628) *rest*

יְגִיעֵי כֹחַ adj. m.p. cstr. (388)-n.m.s. (470); LXX κατάκοποι τῷ σώματι) *the weary in strength*

3:18

יַחַד adv. (403) *together*

אֲסִירִים n.m.p. (64; LXX οἱ αἰώνιοι) *prisoners*

שַׁאֲנָנוּ Palel pf. 3 c.p. (983; GK 55d) *are at ease*

לֹא שָׁמְעוּ neg.-Qal pf. 3 c.p. (1033) *they hear not*

קוֹל n.m.s. cstr. (876) *a voice of*

נֹגֵשׂ Qal act.ptc. (נָגַשׂ 620) *a taskmaster*

3:19

קָטֹן adj. m.s. (882) *small*

וְגָדוֹל conj.-adj. m.s. (152) *and great*

שָׁם הוּא adv. (1027)-demons.adj. m.s. (214; GK 135aN) *are there*

וְעֶבֶד conj.-n.m.s. (713) *and a slave*

חָפְשִׁי adj. m.s. (344; LXX οὐ δεδοικὼς) *is free*

מֵאֲדֹנָיו prep.-n.m.p.-3 m.s. sf. (10) *from his master*

3:20

לָמָּה יִתֵּן interr. (552)-Qal impf. 3 m.s. (נָתַן 678; LXX δέδοται; S,T,V,LXX=יֻתַּן) *why is given*

לְעָמֵל prep.-n.m.s. (I 766) *to him that is in misery*

אוֹר n.m.s. (21) *light*

וְחַיִּים conj.-n.m.p. (313) *and life*

לְמָרֵי prep.-adj. m.p. cstr. (I 600) *to ones bitter in*

נָפֶשׁ n.f.s. (659; GK 128y) *soul*

3:21

הַמְחַכִּים def.art.-Pi. ptc. m.p. (חָכָה 314) *who long*

לַמָּוֶת prep.-def.art.-n.m.s. (560) *for death*

וְאֵינֶנּוּ conj.-neg.-3 m.s. sf. (II 34) *but it comes not*

וַיַּחְפְּרֻהוּ consec.-Qal impf. 3 m.p.-3 m.s. sf. (I 343) *and dig for it*

מִמַּטְמוֹנִים prep.-n.m.p. (380) *more than for hid treasures*

3:22

הַשְּׂמֵחִים def.art.-adj. m.p. (970) *who rejoice*

אֱלֵי־גִיל prep. (39)-n.m.s. (I 162) *exceedingly (unto joy)*

יָשִׂישׂוּ Qal impf. 3 m.p. (שׂוּשׂ 965; LXX (32a) περιχαρεῖς δὲ ἐγένοντο) *and are glad*

כִּי יִמְצְאוּ־ conj.-Qal impf. 3 m.p. (592) *when they find*

קָבֶר n.m.s. paus. (868) *a grave*

3:23

לְגֶבֶר prep.-n.m.s. (149) *to a man*

אֲשֶׁר־דַּרְכּוֹ rel. (81)-n.f.s.-3 m.s. sf. (202) *whose way*

נִסְתָּרָה Ni. pf. 3 f.s. paus. (סָתַר 711) *is hid*

וַיָּסֶךְ consec.-Qal impf. 3 m.s. (סוּךְ II 692) *and has hedged in*

אֱלוֹהַּ n.m.s. (42) *God*

בַּעֲדוֹ prep.-3 m.s. sf. (126) *whom*

3:24

כִּי־לִפְנֵי conj.-prep.-n.m.p. cstr. (815) *for before*

לַחְמִי n.m.s.-1 c.s. sf. (536) *my bread*

אַנְחָתִי n.f.s.-1 c.s. sf. (58) *my sighing*

תָבֹא Qal impf. 3 f.s. (בּוֹא 97) *comes*

וַיִּתְּכוּ consec.-Qal impf. 3 m.p. (נָתַךְ 677; GK 145p) *and are poured out*

כַּמַּיִם prep.-def.art.-n.m.p. (565) *like water*

שַׁאֲגֹתָי n.f.p.-1 c.s. sf. paus. (980; LXX συνεχόμενος φοβῷ) *my groanings*

3:25

כִּי פַחַד conj. (471)-n.m.s. (808) *for the object of dread*

פָּחַדְתִּי Qal pf. 1 c.s. (פָּחַד 808) *which I fear*

וַיֶּאֱתָיֵנִי consec.-Qal impf. 3 m.s.-1 c.s. sf. (אָתָה 87; GK 75u) *and it comes upon me*

וַאֲשֶׁר יָגֹרְתִּי conj.-rel. (81)-Qal pf. 1 c.s. (יָגֹר 388) *and what I dread*

יָבֹא לִי Qal impf. 3 m.s. (בּוֹא 97)-prep.-1 c.s. sf. *befalls me*

3:26

לֹא שָׁלַוְתִּי neg.-Qal pf. 1 c.s. (שָׁלָה I 1017) *I am not at ease*

וְלֹא־שָׁקַטְתִּי conj.-neg.-Qal pf. 1 c.s. (שָׁקַט 1052) *nor am I quiet*

וְלֹא־נָחְתִּי conj.-neg.-Qal pf. 1 c.s. (נוּחַ 628) *I have no rest*

וַיָּבֹא consec.-Qal impf. 3 m.s. (בּוֹא 97) *but comes*

רֹגֶז n.m.s. (919; LXX ὀργή) *trouble*

4:1

וַיַּעַן consec.-Qal impf. 3 m.s. (עָנָה I 772) *then answered*

אֱלִיפַז pr.n. (45) *Eliphaz*

הַתֵּימָנִי def.art.-gent.adj. (412) *the Temanite*

וַיֹּאמַר consec.-Qal impf. 3 m.s. (55) *(and said)*

4:2

הֲנִסָּה interr.part.-Pi. pf. 3 m.s. (נָסָה 650; LXX+ πολλάκις; cf. Aq.,Theod.,Sym.=הֲנִשָּׂא) *if one ventures*

דָבָר n.m.s. (182) *a word*

אֵלֶיךָ prep.-2 m.s. sf. *with you*

תִּלְאֶה Qal impf. 2 m.s. (לָאָה 521; GK 150m; LXX ἐν κόπῳ) *will you be offended (be impatient)*

וַעְצֹר conj.-Qal inf.cstr. (עָצַר 783; GK 28b; LXX ἰσχὺν) *and to restrain*

בְּמִלִּין prep.-n.f.p. (576; GK 87e; LXX+ σου) *in words*

מִי יוּכָל interr. (566)-Qal impf. 3 m.s. (יָכֹל 407) *who can*

4:3

הִנֵּה יִסַּרְתָּ demons.part. (243)-Pi. pf. 2 m.s. (יָסַר 415) *behold, you have instructed*

רַבִּים adj. m.p. (912) *many*

וְיָדַיִם רָפוֹת conj.-n.f. du. (388)-adj. f.p. (952; GK 132f) *and weak hands*

תְּחַזֵּק Pi. impf. 2 m.s. (חָזַק 304; GK 107e) *you have strengthened*

4:4

כּוֹשֵׁל Qal act.ptc. (כָּשַׁל 505) *him who was stumbling*

יְקִימוּן Hi. impf. 3 m.p. (קוּם 877) *have upheld*

מִלֶּיךָ n.m.p.-2 m.s. sf. (576) *your words*

וּבִרְכַּיִם conj.-n.f. du. (139) *and ... knees*

כֹּרְעוֹת Qal act.ptc. f.p. as adj. (כָּרַע 502) *feeble (tottering)*

תְּאַמֵּץ Pi. impf. 2 m.s. (אָמֵץ 54) *you have made firm*

4:5

כִּי עַתָּה conj. (471)-adv. (773) *but now*

תָּבוֹא Qal impf. 3 f.s. (בּוֹא 97; GK 11t,144b) *it (?) has come*

אֵלֶיךָ prep.-2 m.s. sf. *to you*

וַתֵּלֶא consec.-Qal impf. 2 m.s. (לָאָה 521; LXX+ καὶ) *and you are impatient*

תִּגַּע Qal impf. 3 f.s. (נָגַע 619) *it touches*

עָדֶיךָ prep.-2 m.s. sf. *you*

וַתִּבָּהֵל consec.-Ni. impf. 2 m.s. (בָּהַל 96; LXX σὺ δὲ ἐσπούδασας) *and you are dismayed*

4:6

הֲלֹא interr.-neg. *is not?*

יִרְאָתְךָ n.f.s.-2 m.s. sf. (432) *your fear*

כְּסְלָתֶךָ n.f.s.-2 m.s. sf. paus. (493; LXX ἐν ἀφροσύνῃ) *your confidence (your stupidity)*

תִּקְוָתְךָ n.f.s.-2 m.s. sf. (876) *your hope*

וְתֹם conj.-n.m.s. cstr. (1070; GK 143d) *and the integrity of*

דְּרָכֶיךָ n.m.p.-2 m.s. sf. (202) *your ways*

4:7

זְכָר־נָא Qal impv. 2 m.s. (269)-part.of entreaty (609) *remember now*

מִי הוּא interr. (566)-pers.pr. 3 m.s. (214; GK 136c) *who that was*

נָקִי adj. m.s. (667) *innocent*

אָבָד Qal pf. 3 m.s. paus. (1) *ever perished*

וְאֵיפֹה conj.-adv. (33) *and where*

יְשָׁרִים adj. m.p. (449) *upright ones*

נִכְחָדוּ Ni. pf. 3 c.p. paus. (כָּחַד 470) *were cut off*

4:8

כַּאֲשֶׁר prep.-rel. (81) *as*

רָאִיתִי Qal pf. 1 c.s. (רָאָה 906) *I have seen*

חֹרְשֵׁי Qal act.ptc. m.p. cstr. (חָרַשׁ I 360) *those who plow*

אָוֶן n.m.s. (19) *iniquity*

וְזֹרְעֵי conj.-Qal act.ptc. m.p. cstr. (זָרַע 281) *and who sow*

עָמָל n.m.s. (765) *trouble*

יִקְצְרֻהוּ Qal impf. 3 m.p.-3 m.s. sf. (קָצַר II 894) *reap the same*

4:9

מִנִּשְׁמַת prep.-n.f.s. cstr. (675) *by (from) the breath of*

אֱלוֹהַּ n.m.s. (42) *God*

יֹאבֵדוּ Qal impf. 3 m.p. paus. (אָבַד 1) *they perish*

וּמֵרוּחַ conj.-prep.-n.f.s. cstr. (294) *and by the blast of*

אַפּוֹ n.m.s.-3 m.s. sf. (I 60) *his anger*

יִכְלוּ Qal impf. 3 m.p. (כָּלָה I 477) *they are consumed*

4:10

שַׁאֲגַת n.f.s. cstr. (980) *a roar of*

אַרְיֵה n.m.s. (71) *a lion*

וְקוֹל conj.-n.m.s. cstr. (876) *and a voice of*

שָׁחַל n.m.s. paus. (1006) *a fierce lion*

וְשִׁנֵּי conj.-n.f.p. cstr. (1042) *and teeth of*

כְפִירִים n.m.p. (498) *young lions*

נִתָּעוּ Ni. pf. 3 c.p. (נָתַע 683) *are broken*

4:11

לַיִשׁ n.m.s. (I 539) *a strong lion*

אֹבֵד Qal act.ptc. (1) *perishes*

מִבְּלִי־טָרֶף prep.-neg. (115)-n.m.s. paus. (383) *for lack of prey*

וּבְנֵי conj.-n.m.p. cstr. (119) *and whelps of*

לָבִיא n.f.s. (522) *a lioness*

יִתְפָּרָדוּ Hith. impf. 3 m.p. paus. (פָּרַד 825; LXX+ ἀλλήλους) *are scattered*

4:12

וְאֵלַי conj.-prep.-1 c.s. sf. *now to me*

דָּבָר n.m.s. (182; LXX ἐν λόγοις σου; LXX+ ἀληθινὸν) *a word*

יְגֻנָּב Pu. impf. 3 m.s. paus. (גָּנַב 170; LXX οὐθὲν ἄν σοι τούτων κακὸν ἀπήντησεν) *was brought stealthily*

וַתִּקַּח consec.-Qal impf. 3 f.s. (לָקַח 542) *and received*

אָזְנִי n.f.s.-1 c.s. sf. (23) *my ear*

שֵׁמֶץ n.m.s. (1036) *a whisper*

מֶנְהוּ prep.-3 m.s. sf. paus. (GK 103i) *of it*

4:13

בִּשְׂעִפִּים prep.-n.m.p. (972; LXX φόβοι) *amid thoughts*

מֵחֶזְיֹנוֹת prep.-n.f.p. cstr. (303; LXX καὶ ἠχῷ) *from visions of*

לָיְלָה n.m.s. (538) *a night*

בִּנְפֹל prep.-Qal inf.cstr. (נָפַל 656) *when falls*

תַּרְדֵּמָה n.f.s. (922; LXX φόβος) *deep sleep*

עַל־אֲנָשִׁים prep.-n.m.p. (35) *on men*

4:14

פַּחַד n.m.s. (808) *dread*

קְרָאַנִי Qal pf. 3 m.s.-1 c.s. sf. (קָרָא II 896) *came upon me*

וּרְעָדָה conj.-n.f.s. (944) *and trembling*

וְרֹב conj.-n.m.s. cstr. (913) *and the great quantity of (all)*

עַצְמוֹתַי n.f.p.-1 c.s. sf. (I 782) *my bones*

הִפְחִיד Hi. pf. 3 m.s. (פָּחַד 808) *filled with dread*

4:15

וְרוּחַ conj.-n.m.s. (924) *a spirit*

עַל־פָּנַי prep.-n.m.p.-1 c.s. sf. (815) *past my face*

יַחֲלֹף Qal impf. 3 m.s. (חָלַף 322) *glided*

תְּסַמֵּר Pi. impf. 3 f.s. (סָמַר 702) *did bristle up*

שַׂעֲרַת n.f.s. cstr. (972; LXX τρίχες καὶ) *the hair of*

בְּשָׂרִי n.m.s.-1 c.s. sf. (142) *my flesh*

4:16

יַעֲמֹד Qal impf. 3 m.s. (עָמַד 763) *it stood still*
וְלֹא־אַכִּיר conj.-neg.-Hi. impf. 1 c.s. (נָכַר 647) *but I could not discern*
מַרְאֵהוּ n.m.s.-3 m.s. sf. (909) *its appearance*
תְּמוּנָה n.f.s. (568) *a form*
לְנֶגֶד עֵינָי prep.-prep. (617)-n.f.p.-1 c.s. sf. (744; LXX+ ἀλλ' ἤ) *before my eyes*
דְּמָמָה n.f.s. (199) *silence*
וָקוֹל conj.-n.m.s. (876) *but a voice*
אֶשְׁמָע Qal impf. 1 c.s. paus. (שָׁמַע 1033) *I heard*

4:17

הַאֱנוֹשׁ interr.-n.m.s. (60) *can mortal man*
מֵאֱלוֹהַּ prep.-n.m.s. (42; GK 133bN) *before (more than) God*
יִצְדָּק Qal impf. 3 m.s. paus. (צָדַק 842) *be righteous*
אִם מֵעֹשֵׂהוּ hypoth.part. (49)-prep.-Qal act.ptc.-3 m.s. sf. (עָשָׂה I 793; GK 150h) *is it possible ... before (more than) his Maker*
יִטְהַר־ Qal impf. 3 m.s. (טָהֵר 372; GK 107r) *can be pure(r)*
גָּבֶר n.m.s. paus. (149) *a man*

4:18

הֵן interj. (II 243; LXX εἰ) *even (behold)*
בַּעֲבָדָיו prep.-n.m.p.-3 m.s. sf. (713) *in his servants*
לֹא יַאֲמִין neg.-Hi. impf. 3 m.s. (אָמַן 52; GK 107f) *he puts no trust*
וּבְמַלְאָכָיו conj.-prep.-n.m.p.-3 m.s. sf. (521) *and his angels*
יָשִׂים תָּהֳלָה Qal impf. 3 m.s. (שׂוּם 962)-n.f.s. (1062) *he charges with error*

4:19

אַף conj. (64) *how much more*
שֹׁכְנֵי Qal act.ptc. m.p. cstr. (שָׁכַן 1014) *those who dwell in*
בָתֵּי־חֹמֶר n.m.p. cstr. (108)-n.m.s. (I 330) *houses of clay*
אֲשֶׁר־בֶּעָפָר rel. (81)-prep.-def.art.-n.m.s. (779) *in the dust*
יְסוֹדָם n.f.s.-3 m.p. sf. (414) *whose foundation*
יְדַכְּאוּם Pi. impf. 3 m.p.-3 m.p. sf. (דָּכָא 193; GK 144g; LXX,Targ. יְדַכְּאֻם) *who are crushed*
לִפְנֵי־עָשׁ prep.-n.m.p. cstr. (815)-n.m.s. (II 799) *before a moth*

4:20

מִבֹּקֶר prep.-n.m.s. (133) *between morning*
לָעֶרֶב prep.-def.art.-n.m.s. (787) *and evening*
יֻכַּתּוּ Ho. impf. 3 m.p. (כָּתַת 510; GK 29,l;67g,y) *they are destroyed*
מִבְּלִי מֵשִׂים prep.-neg. (115)-Hi. ptc. (שִׂים I 962) *without any regarding it*
לָנֶצַח prep.-n.m.s. (I 664) *for ever*
יֹאבֵדוּ Qal impf. 3 m.p. paus. (אָבַד 1) *they perish*

4:21

הֲלֹא־נִסַּע interr.-neg.-Ni. pf. 3 m.s. (נָסַע I 652; GK 150m; LXX ἐνεφύσησεν γὰρ αὐτοῖς) *if ... is plucked up*
יִתְרָם n.m.s.-3 m.p. sf. (II 452; LXX καὶ ἐξηράνθησαν) *their tent-cord*
בָּם prep.-3 m.p. sf. *within them*
יָמוּתוּ Qal impf. 3 m.p. (מוּת 559) *do they not die*
וְלֹא בְחָכְמָה conj.-neg.-prep.-n.f.s. (315) *and that without wisdom*

5:1

קְרָא־נָא Qal impv. 2 m.s. (894)-part.of entreaty (609) *call now*
הֲיֵשׁ עוֹנֶךָּ interr.-subst. (441)-Qal act.ptc. m.s.-2 m.s. sf. (עָנָה I 772; GK 61h,91d) *is there any one who will answer you*
וְאֶל־מִי conj.-prep.-interr. (566) *and to which*
מִקְּדֹשִׁים prep.-adj. m.p. (872) *of holy ones*
תִּפְנֶה Qal impf. 2 m.s. (פָּנָה 815) *will you turn*

5:2

כִּי־לֶאֱוִיל conj. (471)-prep.-adj. m.s. (17; GK 117n) *surely a fool*
יַהֲרָג־כָּעַשׂ Qal impf. 3 m.s. (הָרַג 246)-n.m.s. paus. (495; many mss. כָּעַס) *vexation kills*
וּפֹתֶה conj.-Qal act.ptc. (פָּתָה 834) *and a simple one*
תָּמִית Hi. impf. 3 f.s. (מוּת 559) ... *slays*
קִנְאָה n.f.s. (888) *jealousy*

5:3

אֲנִי־רָאִיתִי pers.pr. 1 c.s. (58)-Qal pf. 1 c.s. (רָאָה 906; GK 135a) *I have seen*
אֱוִיל n.m.s. (17) *a fool*
מַשְׁרִישׁ Hi. ptc. (שָׁרַשׁ 1057) *taking root*
וָאֶקּוֹב consec.-Qal impf. 1 c.s. (קָבַב II 866; LXX ἀλλ' ... ἐβρώθη=וְרָקַב) *but I cursed*
נָוֵהוּ n.m.s.-3 m.s. sf. (627) *his dwelling*
פִּתְאֹם adv. (837) *suddenly*

5:4

יִרְחֲקוּ Qal impf. 3 m.p. (רָחַק 934) *are far*
בָנָיו n.m.p.-3 m.s. sf. (119) *his sons*
מִיֶּשַׁע prep.-n.m.s. (447) *from safety*
וְיִדַּכְּאוּ conj.-Hith. impf. 3 m.p. (דָּכָא 193) *and they must let themselves be crushed*
בַשַּׁעַר prep.-def.art.-n.m.s. (1044) *in the gate*
וְאֵין מַצִּיל conj.-neg. cstr. (II 34)-Hi. ptc. (נָצַל 664) *and there is no one to deliver*

5:5

אֲשֶׁר קְצִירוֹ rel. (81)-n.m.s.-3 m.s. sf. (I 894) *his harvest*
רָעֵב adj. m.s. (944; LXX δίκαιοι) *hungry one*
יֹאכֵל Qal impf. 3 m.s. (אָכַל 37) *eats*
וְאֶל־מִצִּנִּים conj.-prep.-prep.-n.m.p. (856; GK 119e) *and even out of thorns* (lit. *and unto from thorns)*
יִקָּחֵהוּ Qal impf. 3 m.s.-3 m.s. sf. (לָקַח 542) *he takes it*
וְשָׁאַף conj.-Qal pf. 3 m.s. (I 983; LXX ἐκσιφωνισθείη) *and pant*
צַמִּים n.m.s. (855; Aq.,Sym.,Syr.,Vulg. צְמֵאִים *as thirsty ones) a snare*
חֵילָם n.m.s.-3 m.p. sf. (298) *their wealth*

5:6

כִּי לֹא־יֵצֵא conj. (471)-neg.-Qal impf. 3 m.s. (422 יָצָא) *for does not come*
מֵעָפָר prep.-n.m.s. (779) *from dust*
אָוֶן n.m.s. (19) *affliction*
וּמֵאֲדָמָה conj.-prep.-n.f.s. (9) *nor from ground*
לֹא־יִצְמַח neg.-Qal impf. 3 m.s. (855) *sprout*
עָמָל n.m.s. (765) *trouble*

5:7

כִּי־אָדָם conj.-n.m.s. (9) *for mankind*
לְעָמָל prep.-n.m.s. (765) *to trouble*
יוּלָּד Pu. pf. 3 m.s. (יָלַד 408) *is born*
וּבְנֵי־רֶשֶׁף conj.-n.m.p. cstr. (119)-n.m.s. (I 958; GK 128v,161a; LXX γυπὸς) *and sparks*
יַגְבִּיהוּ עוּף Hi. impf. 3 m.p. (גָּבַהּ 146)-Qal inf.cstr. (עוּף I 733) *fly upward*

5:8

אוּלָם adv. (19) *but*
אֲנִי pers.pr. 1 c.s. (58) *as for me*
אֶדְרֹשׁ Qal impf. 1 c.s. (דָּרַשׁ 205) *I would seek*
אֶל־אֵל prep.-n.m.s. (42; GK 107x) *God*
וְאֶל־אֱלֹהִים conj.-prep.-n.m.p. (43) *and to God*
אָשִׂים Qal impf. 1 c.s. (שִׂים 962) *would I commit*
דִּבְרָתִי n.f.s.-1 c.s. sf. (184) *my cause*

5:9

עֹשֶׂה Qal act.ptc. (I 793) *who does*
גְדֹלוֹת adj. f.p. (152) *great things*
וְאֵין חֵקֶר conj.-neg. cstr. (II 34)-n.m.s. (350) *and it is unsearchable*
נִפְלָאוֹת n.f.p. (Ni. ptc. f.p. פָּלָא 810; LXX καὶ ἐξαίσια) *and marvelous things*
עַד־אֵין מִסְפָּר prep. (III 723I)-neg. cstr. (II 34)-n.m.s. (708) *without number*

5:10

הַנֹּתֵן def.art.-Qal act.ptc. (678; GK 126b) *he gives*
מָטָר n.m.s. (564) *rain*
עַל־פְּנֵי־אָרֶץ prep.-n.m.p. cstr. (815)-n.f.s. paus. (75) *upon the earth*
וְשֹׁלֵחַ conj.-Qal act.ptc. (1018) *and sends*
מַיִם n.m.p. (565) *rain*
עַל־פְּנֵי חוּצוֹת v.supra-n.m.p. (299; LXX ἐπὶ τὴν ὑπ' οὐρανόν) *upon fields (outside)*

5:11

לָשׂוּם prep.-Qal inf.cstr. (I 962; LXX τὸν ποιοῦντα) *to set*
שְׁפָלִים adj. m.p. (1050) *lowly ones*
לְמָרוֹם prep.-n.m.s. (928) *on high*
וְקֹדְרִים conj.-Qal act.ptc. m.p. (קָדַר 871) *and mourners*
שָׂגְבוּ Qal pf. 3 c.p. (960) *are lifted*
יֶשַׁע n.m.s. (447) *to safety*

5:12

מֵפֵר Hi. ptc. (פָּרַר I 830) *he frustrates*
מַחְשְׁבוֹת n.f.p. cstr. (364) *devices of*
עֲרוּמִים adj. m.p. (791) *crafty ones*
וְלֹא־תַעֲשֶׂינָה conj.-neg.-Qal impf. 3 f.p. (עָשָׂה I 793; GK 166a) *and do not achieve*
יְדֵיהֶם n.f.p.-3 m.p. sf. (388) *their hands*
תּוּשִׁיָּה n.f.s. (444) *abiding success*

5:13

לֹכֵד Qal act.ptc. (לָכַד 539) *he captures*
חֲכָמִים adj. m.p. (314) *wise ones*
בְּעָרְמָם prep.-n.m.s. (791; GK 91e) *in their own craftiness*
וַעֲצַת conj.-n.f.s. cstr. (420) *and schemes of*
נִפְתָּלִים Ni ptc. m.p. (פָּתַל 836) *(tortuous) wily ones*
נִמְהָרָה Ni. pf. 3 f.s. paus. (מָהַר I 554) *are brought to a quick end*

5:14

יוֹמָם adv. (401) *in the daytime*

יְפַגְּשׁוּ־ Pi. impf. 3 m.p. (פָּגַשׁ 803) *they meet*

חֹשֶׁךְ n.m.s. (365) *darkness*

וְכַלַּיְלָה conj.-prep.-def.art.-n.m.s. (538; GK 118u) *and as in the night*

יְמַשְׁשׁוּ Pi. impf. 3 m.p. (מָשַׁשׁ 606) *they grope*

בַצָּהֳרָיִם prep.-def.art.-n.m.p. (I 843) *at noonday*

5:15

וַיֹּשַׁע consec.-Hi. impf. 3 m.s. (446) *but he saves*

מֵחֶרֶב prep.-n.f.s. (352; LXX ἐν πολέμῳ) *from a sword*

מִפִּיהֶם prep.-n.m.s.-3 m.p. sf. (804; LXX>) *from their mouth*

וּמִיַּד חָזָק conj.-prep.-n.f.s. cstr. (388)-adj. m.s. (305) *and from the hand of the mighty*

אֶבְיוֹן n.m.s. (2) *the needy*

5:16

וַתְּהִי consec.-Qal impf. 3 f.s. (הָיָה 224) *so there shall be*

לַדַּל prep.-def.art.-n.m.s. (195) *to the poor*

תִּקְוָה n.f.s. (876) *hope*

וְעֹלָתָה conj.-n.f.s. (732; GK 90g) *and injustice*

קָפְצָה Qal pf. 3 f.s. (קָפַץ 891) *shuts*

פִּיהָ n.m.s.-3 f.s. sf. (804) *her mouth*

5:17

הִנֵּה demons.part. (243; LXX,Syr.,Vulg.>) *behold*

אַשְׁרֵי n.m.p. cstr. (80) *happy is*

אֱנוֹשׁ n.m.s. (60) *a man*

יוֹכִחֶנּוּ Hi. impf. 3 m.s.-3 m.s. sf. (יָכַח 406) ... *reproves (him)*

אֱלוֹהַּ n.m.s. (42) *God*

וּמוּסַר שַׁדַּי conj.-n.m.s. cstr. (416)-n.m.s. (994) *therefore the chastening of the Almighty*

אַל־תִּמְאָס neg.-Qal impf. 2 m.s. paus. (מָאַס 549) *despise not*

5:18

כִּי הוּא conj. (471)-pers.pr. 3 m.s. (214) *for he himself*

יַכְאִיב Hi. impf. 3 m.s. (כָּאַב 456) *wounds*

וְיֶחְבָּשׁ conj.-Qal impf. 3 m.s. (חָבַשׁ 289) *so that he may bind*

יִמְחַץ Qal impf. 3 m.s. (מָחַץ 563) *he smites*

וְיָדָו conj.-n.f.p.-3 m.s. sf. (388; Q וְיָדָיו) *and his hands*

תִּרְפֶּינָה Qal impf. 3 f.p. (רָפָה 950; GK 75qq) *may heal*

5:19

בְּשֵׁשׁ צָרוֹת prep.-num. m. (995)-n.f.p. (865; LXX ἑξάκις ἐξ ἀναγκῶν) *from six troubles*

יַצִּילֶךָּ Hi. impf. 3 m.s.-2 m.s. sf. (נָצַל 664) *he will deliver you*

וּבְשֶׁבַע conj.-prep.-num. m. (988; GK 134s) *and in seven*

לֹא־יִגַּע neg.-Qal impf. 3 m.s. (נָגַע 619) *shall not touch*

בְּךָ prep.-2 m.s. sf. *you*

רָע n.m.s. (948) *evil*

5:20

בְּרָעָב prep.-n.m.s. (944) *in famine*

פָּדְךָ Qal pf. 3 m.s.-2 m.s. sf. (פָּדָה 804) *he will redeem you*

מִמָּוֶת prep.-n.m.s. (560) *from death*

וּבְמִלְחָמָה conj.-prep.-n.f.s. (536) *and in war*

מִידֵי prep.-n.f.p. cstr. (388) *from power of*

חָרֶב n.f.s. paus. (352) *a sword*

5:21

בְּשׁוֹט prep.-n.m.s. cstr. (1002; LXX ἀπὸ μάστιγος) *from a scourge of*

לָשׁוֹן n.f.s. (546) *a tongue*

תֵּחָבֵא Ni. impf. 2 m.s. (חָבָא 285) *you shall be hid*

וְלֹא־תִירָא conj.-neg.-Qal impf. 2 m.s. (יָרֵא 431) *and you shall not fear*

מִשֹּׁד prep.-n.m.s. (I 994) *destruction*

כִּי יָבוֹא conj.-Qal impf. 3 m.s. (בּוֹא 97) *when it comes*

5:22

לְשֹׁד prep.-n.m.s. (I 994) *at destruction*

וּלְכָפָן conj.-prep.-n.m.s. (495; LXX καὶ ἀνόμων) *and famine*

תִּשְׂחָק Qal impf. 2 m.s. (שָׂחַק 965) *you shall laugh*

וּמֵחַיַּת conj.-prep.-n.f.s. cstr. (I 312) *and the beasts of*

הָאָרֶץ def.art.-n.f.s. (75) *the earth*

אַל־תִּירָא neg.-Qal impf. 2 m.s. (יָרֵא; GK 109e) *you shall not fear*

5:23

כִּי עִם־אַבְנֵי conj. (471)-prep. (767)-n.m.p. cstr. (6; LXX>) *for with the stones of*

הַשָּׂדֶה def.art.-n.m.s. (961; LXX>) *the field*

בְרִיתֶךָ n.f.s.-2 m.s. sf. (136; LXX>) *your covenant*

וְחַיַּת conj.-n.f.s. cstr. (I 312) *and the beasts of*

הַשָּׂדֶה def.art.-n.m.s. (961) *the field*
הָשְׁלְמָה־ Ho. pf. 3 f.s. (שָׁלַם 1023) *shall be at peace*
לָךְ prep.-2 m.s. sf. paus. *with you*

5:24

וְיָדַעְתָּ conj.-Qal pf. 2 m.s. (יָדַע 393) *and you shall know*
כִּי־שָׁלוֹם conj. (471)-n.m.s. (1022) *safe*
אָהֳלֶךָ n.m.s.-2 m.s. sf. (13) *your tent*
וּפָקַדְתָּ conj.-Qal pf. 2 m.s. (פָּקַד 823) *and you shall inspect*
נָוְךָ n.m.s.-2 m.s. sf. (627) *your fold*
וְלֹא תֶחֱטָא conj.-neg.-Qal impf. 2 m.s. (חָטָא 306; GK 159g) *and miss nothing*

5:25

וְיָדַעְתָּ conj.-Qal pf. 2 m.s. (יָדַע 393) *and you shall know*
כִּי־רַב conj.-adj. m.s. (I 912) *are many*
זַרְעֶךָ n.m.s.-2 m.s. sf. (282) *your descendants*
וְצֶאֱצָאֶיךָ conj.-n.m.p.-2 m.s. sf. (425) *and your offspring*
כְּעֵשֶׂב prep.-n.m.s. cstr. (793) *as the grass of*
הָאָרֶץ def.art.-n.f.s. (75) *the earth*

5:26

תָּבוֹא Qal impf. 2 m.s. (בּוֹא 97) *you shall come*
בְכֶלַח prep.-n.m.s. (480) *in firm strength*
אֱלֵי־קָבֶר prep. (39)-n.m.s. (868) *to a grave*
כַּעֲלוֹת prep.-Qal inf.cstr. (עָלָה 748) *as comes up*
גָּדִישׁ n.m.s. (I 155) *a shock of grain*
בְּעִתּוֹ prep.-n.f.s.-3 m.s. sf. (773) *in its season*

5:27

הִנֵּה־ demons.part. (243) *lo*
זֹאת demons.adj. f.s. (260) *this*
חֲקַרְנוּהָ Qal pf. 1 c.p.-3 f.s. sf. (חָקַר 350) *we have searched out*
כֶּן־הִיא adv. (I 485)-demons.adj. f.s. (214; GK 20g) *it is true*
שְׁמָעֶנָּה Qal impv. 2 m.s.-3 f.s. sf. (שָׁמַע 1033; LXX ἃ ἀκηκόαμεν) *hear (it)*
וְאַתָּה conj.-pers.pr. 2 m.s. (61) *and you for yourself*
דַע־לָךְ Qal impv. 2 m.s. (יָדַע 393)-prep.-2 m.s. sf. paus. *know for yourself*

6:1

וַיַּעַן consec.-Qal impf. 3 m.s. (עָנָה I 772) *then answered*
אִיּוֹב pr.n. (33) *Job*
וַיֹּאמַר consec.-Qal impf. 3 m.s. (55) *(and said)*

6:2

לוּ conj. (530) *O that*
שָׁקוֹל יִשָּׁקֵל Qal inf.abs. (1053)-Ni. impf. 3 m.s. (1053 שָׁקַל; GK 113w) *were weighed*
כַּעְשִׂי n.m.s.-1 c.s. sf. (495) *my vexation*
וְהַיָּתִי conj.-n.f.s.-1 c.s. sf. (217; LXX τὰς δὲ ὀδύνας μου) *and my calamity*
בְּמֹאזְנַיִם prep.-n.m. du. (24) *in balances*
יִשְׂאוּ־ Qal impf. 3 m.p. (נָשָׂא 669; GK 144g; LXX ἆραι= יִשָּׂא) *they put*
יָחַד adv. paus. (403) *together*

6:3

כִּי־עַתָּה conj. (471)-adv. (773) *for then*
מֵחוֹל prep.-n.m.s. cstr. (297) *than sand of*
יַמִּים n.m.p. (410) *seas*
יִכְבָּד Qal impf. 3 m.s. paus. (כָּבֵד 457) *it would be heavier*
עַל־כֵּן prep.-adv. (485) *therefore*
דְּבָרַי n.m.p.-1 c.s. sf. (182) *my words*
לָעוּ Qal pf. 3 c.p. (לוּעַ II 534) *have been rash*

6:4

כִּי חִצֵּי conj.-n.m.p. cstr. (346) *for the arrows of*
שַׁדַּי n.m.s. (994) *the Almighty*
עִמָּדִי prep.-1 c.s. sf. (767; LXX ἐν τῷ σώματί μοῦ) *in (with) me*
אֲשֶׁר חֲמָתָם rel. (81)-n.f.s.-3 m.p. sf. (404) *their poison*
שֹׁתָה Qal act.ptc. f.s. (שָׁתָה 1059) *drinks*
רוּחִי n.f.s.-1 c.s. sf. (924; LXX μου τὸ αἷμα) *my spirit*
בִּעוּתֵי n.m.p. cstr. (130; LXX ὅταν ἄρξωμαι λαλεῖν) *the terrors of*
אֱלוֹהַּ n.m.s. (42; LXX>) *God*
יַעַרְכוּנִי Qal impf. 3 m.p.-1 c.s. sf. (עָרַךְ 789) *they arrange against me*

6:5

הֲיִנְהַק־ interr.-Qal impf. 3 m.s. (נָהַק 625; GK 150h) *does ... bray?*
פֶּרֶא n.m.s. (825) *a wild ass*
עֲלֵי־דֶשֶׁא prep. (752)-n.m.s. (206) *when he has (upon) grass*
אִם יִגְעֶה־ hypoth.part. (49)-Qal impf. 3 m.s. (171 גָּעָה) *or ... low*
שׁוֹר n.m.s. (1004) *an ox*

עַל־בְּלִילוֹ prep.-n.m.s.-3 m.s. sf. (117) *over his fodder*

6:6

הֲיֵאָכֵל interr.-Ni. impf. 3 m.s. (אָכַל 37) *can ... be eaten?*
תָּפֵל adj. m.s. (I 1074) *that which is tasteless*
מִבְּלִי־מֶלַח prep.-neg. (115)-n.m.s. (571) *without salt*
אִם־יֶשׁ־ hypoth.part. (49)-subst. (441) *or is there*
טַעַם n.m.s. (381) *any taste*
בְּרִיר prep.-n.m.s. cstr. (938) *in slime of*
חַלָּמוּת n.f.s. (321) *purslane*

6:7

מֵאֲנָה Pi. pf. 3 f.s. (מָאֵן 549; GK 106g; LXX οὐ δύναται) *refuses*
לִנְגּוֹעַ prep.-Qal inf.cstr. (נָגַע 619; GK 66b; LXX παύσασθαι) *to touch*
נַפְשִׁי n.f.s.-1 c.s. sf. (659) *my appetite*
הֵמָּה pers.pr. 3 m.p. (241; LXX βρόμον γὰρ ὁρῶ = וְהֵמָּה) *they*
כִּדְוֵי n.m.s. cstr. (188; LXX ὥσπερ ὀσμὴν λεόντος= כָּאֲרִי) *like disease in*
לַחְמִי n.m.s.-1 c.s. sf. (536) *my food*

6:8

מִי־יִתֵּן interr. (566)-Qal impf. 3 m.s. (נָתַן 678) *O that*
תָּבוֹא Qal impf. 3 f.s. (בּוֹא 97) *might come*
שֶׁאֱלָתִי n.f.s.-1 c.s. sf. (982; GK 95h) *my request*
וְתִקְוָתִי conj.-n.f.s.-1 c.s. sf. (876) *and my desire (hope)*
יִתֵּן Qal impf. 3 m.s. (נָתַן 678; GK 151d) *would grant*
אֱלוֹהַּ n.m.s. (42) *God*

6:9

וְיֹאֵל conj.-Hi. impf. 3 m.s. juss. (יָאַל II 383; GK 120d) *and that would he willing*
אֱלוֹהַּ n.m.s. (42) *God*
וִידַכְּאֵנִי conj.-Pi. impf. 3 m.s.-1 c.s. sf. (דָּכָא 193) *and he would crush me*
יַתֵּר Hi. impf. 3 m.s. apoc.juss. (נָתַר II 684) *that he would let loose*
יָדוֹ n.f.s.-3 m.s. sf. (388) *his hand*
וִיבַצְּעֵנִי conj.-Pi. impf. 3 m.s.-1 c.s. sf. (בָּצַע 130) *and that he would cut me off*

6:10

וּתְהִי־ conj.-Qal impf. 3 f.s. apoc.juss. (הָיָה 224; LXX εἴη δὲ μου πόλις τάφος) *and that ... would be*
עוֹד adv. (728) *yet*
נֶחָמָתִי n.f.s.-1 c.s. sf. (637) *my comfort*
וַאֲסַלְּדָה conj.-Pi. impf. 1 c.s.-vol.he (סָלַד 698; GK 108f) *and I would spring*
בְחִילָה prep.-n.f.s. (297) *in anguish*
לֹא יַחְמוֹל neg.-Qal impf. 3 m.s. (חמל 328; LXX ἐφ' ἧς ἐπὶ τειχέων ἡλλόμην ἐπ' αὐτῆς, οὐ μὴ φείσωμαι) *unsparing*
כִּי־לֹא כִחַדְתִּי conj.-neg.-Pi. pf. 1 c.s. (כָּחַד 470) *for I have not disowned*
אִמְרֵי n.m.p. cstr. (56; LXX ῥήματα ἅγια θεοῦ μου) *words of*
קָדוֹשׁ adj. m.s. (872) *the Holy One*

6:11

מַה־כֹּחִי interr. (552)-n.m.s.-1 c.s. sf. (470) *what is my strength*
כִּי־אֲיַחֵל conj. (471)-Pi. impf. 1 c.s. (יָחַל 403) *that I should wait*
וּמַה־קִּצִּי conj.-v.supra-n.m.s.-1 c.s. sf. (893; LXX μου ὁ χρόνος) *and what is my end*
כִּי־אַאֲרִיךְ נַפְשִׁי conj. (471)-Hi. impf. 1 c.s. (אָרַךְ 73)-n.f.s.-1 c.s. sf. (659) *that I should be patient*

6:12

אִם־כֹּחַ hypoth.part. (49)-n.m.s. cstr. (470; GK 141c,150f) *if strength of*
אֲבָנִים n.f.p. (6) *stones*
כֹּחִי n.m.s.-1 c.s. sf. (470) *my strength*
אִם־ v.supra *or is*
בְּשָׂרִי n.m.s.-1 c.s. sf. (142) *my flesh*
נָחוּשׁ adj. m.s. (639) *bronze*

6:13

הַאִם interr.-interr.part. (50; GK 150gN) *is it?*
אֵין עֶזְרָתִי neg. cstr. (II 34)-n.f.s.-1 c.s. sf. (740; LXX οὐκ ἐπ' αὐτῷ ἐπεποίθειν) *I have no hope (help)*
בִי prep.-1 c.s. sf. *in me*
וְתֻשִׁיָּה conj.-n.f.s. (444; LXX βοήθεια= וּתְשׁוּעָה) *and abiding success*
נִדְּחָה Ni. pf. 3 f.s. (נָדַח 623) *is driven*
מִמֶּנִּי prep.-1 c.s. sf. *from me*

6:14

לָמָּס prep.-def.art.-adj. m.s. (588; LXX ἀπείπατό με= לְמָשׁ) *to him who despaireth* (some rd. למאס 549; *he who withholds (refuses)*)

מֵרֵעֵהוּ prep.-n.m.s.-3 m.s. sf. (945; LXX>) *from his friend*

חָסֶד n.m.s. paus. (338) *kindness*

וְיִרְאַת conj.-n.f.s. cstr. (432; LXX ἐπισκοπή) *and the fear of*

שַׁדַּי n.m.s. (994) *the Almighty*

יַעֲזוֹב Qal impf. 3 m.s. (עָזַב I 736) *forsakes*

6:15

אַחַי n.m.p.-1 c.s. sf. (26) *my brethren*

בָּגְדוּ Qal pf. 3 c.p. (93) *are treacherous*

כְמוֹ־נָחַל adv. (455)-n.m.s. paus. (636) *as a torrent-bed*

כַּאֲפִיק נְחָלִים prep.-n.m.s. cstr. (67)-n.m.p. (636) *as a channel of torrent-beds*

יַעֲבֹרוּ Qal impf. 3 m.p. (716) *they pass away*

6:16

הַקֹּדְרִים def.art.-Qal act.ptc. m.p. (קָדַר 871; GK 126b; LXX διελαβοῦτο) *which are dark*

מִנִּי־קָרַח prep. (577; GK 90,l)-n.m.s. paus. (901; LXX>) *with ice*

עָלֵימוֹ prep.-3 m.p. sf. *over them*

יִתְעַלֶּם־ Hith. impf. 3 m.s. (עָלַם I 761) *hides itself*

שָׁלֶג n.m.s. paus. (1017) *snow*

6:17

בְּעֵת prep.-n.f.s. cstr. (773; GK 130d,155,l) *in time of*

יְזֹרְבוּ Pu. impf. 3 c.p. (זָרַב 279) *that they were scorched*

נִצְמָתוּ Ni. pf. 3 c.p. paus. (צָמַת 856) *they disappear (are annihilated)*

בְּחֻמּוֹ prep.-Qal inf.cstr.-3 m.s. sf. (חָמַם 328) *when it is hot*

נִדְעֲכוּ Ni. pf. 3 c.p. (דָּעַךְ 200) *they vanish (are made extinct)*

מִמְּקוֹמָם prep.-n.m.s.-3 m.p. sf. (879) *from their place*

6:18

יִלָּפְתוּ Ni. impf. 3 m.p. (לָפַת 542; LXX οὕτως κἀγὼ κατελείφθην ὑπὸ πάντων) *they turn aside (twist)*

אָרְחוֹת n.m.p. cstr. (73) *ways of* (some rd. *caravans)*

דַּרְכָּם n.m.s.-3 m.p. sf. (202) *their way (from their course)*

יַעֲלוּ Qal impf. 3 m.p. (עָלָה 748; LXX ἀπωλόμην δὲ καὶ ἔξοικος ἐγενόμην) *they go up*

בַתֹּהוּ prep.-def.art.-n.m.s. (1062) *into the waste*

וְיֹאבֵדוּ conj.-Qal impf. 3 m.p. (אָבַד 1) *and perish*

6:19

הִבִּיטוּ Hi. pf. 3 c.p. (נָבַט 613) *look*

אָרְחוֹת n.m.p. cstr. (73) *ways (caravans) of*

תֵּמָא pr.n. (1066) *Tema*

הֲלִיכֹת n.f.p. cstr. (237) *the travelers of*

שְׁבָא pr.n. (985) *Sheba*

קִוּוּ־לָמוֹ Pi. pf. 3 c.p. (קָוָה I 875)-prep.-3 m.p. sf. (GK 119s) *hope (for them)*

6:20

בֹּשׁוּ Qal pf. 3 c.p. (בּוֹשׁ 101) *they feel shame*

כִּי־בָטָח conj. (471)-Qal pf. 3 m.s. paus. (בָּטַח I 105; GK 145u) *because they were confident*

בָּאוּ Qal pf. 3 c.p. (בּוֹא 97; LXX οἱ ἐπὶ πόλεσιν καὶ χρήμασιν πεποιθότες) *they come*

עָדֶיהָ prep.-3 f.s. sf. (III 723; GK 135p) *thither*

וַיֶּחְפָּרוּ consec.-Qal impf. 3 m.p. paus. (חָפֵר II 344) *and are confounded*

6:21

כִּי־ conj. (471; or כֵּן 485) *such*

עַתָּה adv. (773) *now*

הֱיִיתֶם Qal pf. 2 m.p. (הָיָה 224; LXX+ ἀνελεημόνως) *you have become*

לֹא neg. (Q לוֹ; GK 152a; LXX μοι) *to him*

תִּרְאוּ Qal impf. 2 m.p. (רָאָה 906; GK 75t) *you see*

חֲתַת n.m.s. (369) *a terror*

וַתִּירָאוּ consec.-Qal impf. 2 m.p. (יָרֵא 431) *and are afraid*

6:22

הֲכִי־אָמַרְתִּי interr.-conj.-Qal pf. 1 c.s. (55) *have I said?*

הָבוּ לִי Qal impv. 2 m.p. (יָהַב 396; GK 69o) -prep.-1 c.s. sf. *give to me*

וּמִכֹּחֲכֶם conj.-prep.-n.m.s.-2 m.p. sf. (470) *or from your wealth*

שִׁחֲדוּ Qal impv. 2 m.p. (1005; GK 22p,64a) *offer a bribe*

בַּעֲדִי prep.-1 c.s. sf. (126) *for me*

6:23

וּמַלְּטוּנִי conj.-Pi. impv. 2 m.p.-1 c.s. sf. (מָלַט 572) *or deliver me*

מִיַּד־ prep.-n.f.s. cstr. (388) *from hand of*

צָר n.m.s. paus. (III 865) *an adversary*

וּמִיַּד conj.-v.supra *or from a hand of*

עָרִיצִים adj. m.p. (792) *oppressors*

תִּפְדּוּנִי Qal impf. 2 m.p.-1 c.s. sf. (פָּדָה 804) *ransom me*

6:24

הוֹרוּנִי Hi. impv. 2 m.p.-1 c.s. sf. (יָרָה 434) *teach me*

וַאֲנִי conj.-pers.pr. 1 c.s. (58) *and I on my part*

אַחֲרִישׁ Hi. impf. 1 c.s. (חָרַשׁ II 361) *will be silent*

וּמַה־ conj.-interr. (552) *and how*

שָׁגִיתִי Qal pf. 1 c.s. (שָׁגָה 993) *I have erred*

הָבִינוּ לִי Hi. impv. 2 m.p. (בִּין 106)-prep.-1 c.s. sf. *make me understand*

6:25

מַה־ interr. (552) *how*

נִמְרְצוּ Ni. pf. 3 c.p. (מָרַץ 599; LXX φαῦλα, some propose מָלַץ 576=*smooth* or *agreeable*) *sickened*

אִמְרֵי־ n.m.p. cstr. (56) *words of*

יֹשֶׁר n.m.s. (449) *uprightness*

וּמַה־ conj.-v.supra (GK 154a) *but what*

יוֹכִיחַ Hi. impf. 3 m.s. (יָכַח 406) *does ... reprove*

הוֹכֵחַ Hi. inf.abs. (יָכַח 406) *reproof*

מִכֶּם prep.-2 m.p. sf. (LXX οὐ γὰρ παρ' ὑμῶν ἰσχὺν αἰτοῦμαι) *from you*

6:26

הַלְהוֹכַח interr.-prep.-Hi. inf.cstr. (יָכַח 406; GK 65f,69v) *that you can reprove*

מִלִּים n.f.p. (576) *words*

תַּחְשֹׁבוּ Qal impf. 2 m.p. (חָשַׁב 362) *do you think*

וּלְרוּחַ conj.-prep.-n.f.s. (924; LXX οὐδὲ γὰρ ὑμῶν φθέγμα ῥήματος ἀνέξομαι) *and to wind*

אִמְרֵי נֹאָשׁ n.m.p. cstr. (56)-Ni. ptc. m.s. paus. (384 יָאַשׁ) *the speech of a despairing man*

6:27

אַף־ conj. (II 64) *indeed* (or n.m.s. I 60–*anger*)

עַל־יָתוֹם prep.-n.m.s. (450) *over the fatherless*

תַּפִּילוּ Hi. impf. 2 m.p. (נָפַל 656; LXX ἐπιπίπτετε) *would you cast*

וְתִכְרוּ conj.-Qal impf. 2 m.p. (כָּרָה II 500; LXX ἐνάλλεσθε) *and will you bargain*

עַל־רֵיעֲכֶם prep.-n.m.s.-2 m.p. sf. (II 945) *over your friend*

6:28

וְעַתָּה conj.-adv. (773) *but now*

הוֹאִילוּ Hi. impv. 2 m.p. (יָאַל 383; GK 120g) *be willing*

פְּנוּ־בִי Qal impv. 2 m.p. (פָּנָה 815)-prep.-1 c.s. sf. *look at me*

וְעַל־פְּנֵיכֶם conj.-prep.-n.m.p.-2 m.p. sf. (815) *for to your face*

אִם־אֲכַזֵּב hypoth.part. (49)-Pi. impf. 1 c.s. (כָּזַב 469) *I will not lie*

6:29

שֻׁבוּ־נָא Qal impv. 2 m.p. (שׁוּב 996)-part.of entreaty (609) *turn, I pray*

אַל־תְּהִי neg. (39)-Qal impf. 3 f.s. apoc.vol. (הָיָה 224) *let there not be*

עַוְלָה n.f.s. (732) *injustice*

וְשֻׁבִי עוֹד conj.-Qal impv. 2 m.p. (שׁוּב 996)-adv. (728) *turn again*

צִדְקִי־ n.m.s.-1 c.s. sf. (841) *my vindication (righteousness)*

בָהּ prep.-3 f.s. sf. *(to it)*

6:30

הֲיֵשׁ־ interr.subst. (441) *is there?*

בִּלְשׁוֹנִי prep.-n.f.s.-1 c.s. sf. (546) *on my tongue*

עַוְלָה n.f.s. (732) *wrong (injustice)*

אִם־חִכִּי interr.part. (50)-n.m.s.-1 c.s. sf. (335) *my palate?*

לֹא־יָבִין neg.-Qal impf. 3 m.s. (בִּין 106) *cannot ... discern?*

הַוּוֹת n.f.p. (217) *calamity*

7:1

הֲלֹא־צָבָא interr.-neg.-n.m.s. (838) *is not a hard service*

לֶאֱנוֹשׁ prep.-n.m.s. (60) *to man*

עֲלֵי־אָרֶץ prep.-n.f.s. paus. (75) *upon earth*

וְכִימֵי conj.-prep.-n.m.p. cstr. (398) *and like days of*

שָׂכִיר adj. m.s. (969) *a hireling*

יָמָיו n.m.p.-3 m.s. sf. (398) *his days*

7:2

כְּעֶבֶד prep.-n.m.s. (713; GK 155g) *like a slave*

יִשְׁאַף־ Qal impf. 3 m.s. (שָׁאַף I 983) *longs for*

צֵל n.m.s. (853) *a shadow*

וּכְשָׂכִיר conj.-prep.-adj. m.s. (969) *and like a hireling*

יְקַוֶּה Pi. impf. 3 m.s. (קָוָה I 875) *looks for*
פָּעֳלוֹ n.m.s.-3 m.s. sf. (821) *his wages*

7:3

כֵּן הָנְחַלְתִּי adv. (485)-Ho. pf. 1 c.s. (נָחַל 635; GK 121c; LXX ὑπέμεινα) *so I am allotted*
לִי prep.-1 c.s. sf. *to myself*
יַרְחֵי n.m.p. cstr. (I 437) *months of*
שָׁוְא n.m.s. (996) *emptiness*
וְלֵילוֹת conj.-n.m.p. cstr. (538) *and nights of*
עָמָל n.m.s. (765) *misery*
מִנּוּ־ Pi. pf. 3 c.p. (מָנָה 584; GK 144g; LXX δεδομέναι μοι εἰσιν) *are apportioned*
לִי prep.-1 c.s. sf. *to me*

7:4

אִם־שָׁכַבְתִּי hypoth.part. (49)-Qal pf. 1 c.s. (שָׁכַב 1011) *when I lie down*
וְאָמַרְתִּי conj.-Qal pf. 1 c.s. (55) *and I say*
מָתַי אָקוּם interr. (607)-Qal impf. 1 c.s. (קוּם 877; LXX ὡς δ' ἂν ἀναστῶ) *when shall I arise?*
וּמִדַּד־עָרֶב conj.-Pi. pf. 3 m.s. (מָדַד 551; GK 52a)-n.m.s. paus. (787) *but night is long* (lit. *evening is extended*)
וְשָׂבַעְתִּי conj.-Qal pf. 1 c.s. (שָׂבֵעַ 959) *and I am full of (sated)*
נְדֻדִים n.m.p. (622; GK 124f) *tossing*
עֲדֵי־נָשֶׁף prep. (III 723)-n.m.s. paus. (676) *till dawn*

7:5

לָבַשׁ Qal pf. 3 m.s. (527) *is clothed with*
בְשָׂרִי n.m.s.-1 c.s. sf. (142) *my flesh*
רִמָּה n.f.s. (942) *worms*
וְגִישׁ conj.-n.m.s. cstr. (159; Q וְגוּשׁ) *and clods of*
עָפָר n.m.s. (779) *dust*
עוֹרִי n.m.s.-1 c.s. sf. (736) *my skin*
רָגַע Qal pf. 3 m.s. (III 921) *hardens*
וַיִּמָּאֵס consec.-Ni. impf. 3 m.s. (מָאַס II 549) *and runs (flows afresh)*

7:6

יָמַי n.m.p.-1 c.s. sf. (398) *my days*
קַלּוּ Qal pf. 3 c.p. (קָלַל 886) *are swift(er)*
מִנִּי־אָרֶג prep. (577)-n.m.s. paus. (71; GK 133b) *than a loom*
וַיִּכְלוּ consec.-Qal impf. 3 m.p. (כָּלָה 477) *and come to an end*
בְּאֶפֶס תִּקְוָה prep.-n.m.s. cstr. (67)-n.f.s. (876) *without hope*

7:7

זְכֹר Qal impv. 2 m.s. (269) *remember*
כִּי־רוּחַ conj. (471)-n.f.s. (924) *is a breath*
חַיָּי n.m.p.-1 c.s. sf. (313) *my life*
לֹא־תָשׁוּב neg.-Qal impf. 3 f.s. (שׁוּב 996) *will never again*
עֵינִי n.f.s.-1 c.s. sf. (744) *my eye*
לִרְאוֹת prep.-Qal inf.cstr. (רָאָה 906) *see*
טוֹב n.m.s. (III 375) *good (prosperity)*

7:8 (LXX>)

לֹא־תְשׁוּרֵנִי neg.-Qal impf. 3 f.s.-1 c.s. sf. (שׁוּר II 1003) *will behold me no more*
עֵין רֹאִי n.f.s. cstr. (744)-Qal act.ptc. m.s.-1 c.s. sf. (רָאָה 906) *the eye of him who sees me*
עֵינֶיךָ n.f.p.-2 m.s. sf. (744) *your eyes*
בִּי prep.-1 c.s. sf. *on me*
וְאֵינֶנִּי conj.-neg.-1 c.s. sf. (II 34) *and I shall be gone (and an absence of me)*

7:9

כָּלָה Qal pf. 3 m.s. (I 477) *fades*
עָנָן n.m.s. (I 777; Targum עֲשַׁן) *a cloud*
וַיֵּלַךְ consec.-Qal impf. 3 m.s. (הָלַךְ 229; LXX ἀπ' οὐρανοῦ) *and vanishes*
כֵּן יוֹרֵד adv. (485)-Qal act.ptc. (יָרַד 432) *so he who goes down*
שְׁאוֹל n.f.s. (982; LXX εἰς ᾅδην) *to Sheol*
לֹא יַעֲלֶה neg.-Qal impf. 3 m.s. (עָלָה 748) *does not come up*

7:10

לֹא־יָשׁוּב neg.-Qal pf. 3 m.s. (שׁוּב 996) *he does not return*
עוֹד adv. (728) *again*
לְבֵיתוֹ prep.-n.m.s.-3 m.s. sf. (108) *to his house*
וְלֹא־יַכִּירֶנּוּ conj.-neg.-Hi. impf. 3 m.s.-3 m.s. sf. (נָכַר 647) *nor does ... know him*
עוֹד v.supra *any more*
מְקֹמוֹ n.m.s.-3 m.s. (879) *his place*

7:11

גַּם־אֲנִי adv. (168)-pers.pr. 1 c.s. (58) *therefore, I myself*
לֹא אֶחֱשָׂךְ neg.-Qal impf. 1 c.s. (חָשַׂךְ 362) *will not restrain*
פִּי n.m.s.-1 c.s. sf. (804) *my mouth*
אֲדַבְּרָה Pi. impf. 1 c.s.-vol.he (180) *let me speak*
בְּצַר prep.-n.m.s. cstr. (II 865) *in the anguish of*
רוּחִי n.f.s.-1 c.s. sf. (924) *my spirit*
אָשִׂיחָה Qal impf. 1 c.s.-vol.he (שִׂיחַ 967) *let me complain*

בְּמַר prep.-subst. m.s. cstr. (I 600) *in the bitterness of*
נַפְשִׁי n.f.s.-1 c.s. sf. (659) *my soul*

7:12
הֲיָם־אָנִי interr.-n.m.s. (410)-pers.pr. 1 c.s. (58) *am I a sea?*
אִם־תַּנִּין conj. (49)-n.m.s. (1072) *or a sea-monster*
כִּי־תָשִׂים conj. (471)-Qal impf. 2 m.s. (שִׂים 962) *that you set*
עָלַי prep.-1 c.s. sf. *over me*
מִשְׁמָר n.m.s. (1038) *a guard*

7:13
כִּי־אָמַרְתִּי conj. (471)-Qal pf. 1 c.s. (55; GK 112hh) *when I say*
תְּנַחֲמֵנִי Pi. impf. 3 f.s.-1 c.s. sf. (נָחַם 636) *will comfort me*
עַרְשִׂי n.f.s.-1 c.s. sf. (793) *my bed*
יִשָּׂא Qal impf. 3 m.s. (נָשָׂא 669; GK 119m) *will ease (lift up)*
בְשִׂיחִי prep.-n.m.s.-1 c.s. sf. (967) *my complaint*
מִשְׁכָּבִי n.m.s.-1 c.s. sf. (1012) *my couch*

7:14
וְחִתַּתַּנִי conj.-Pi. pf. 2 m.s.-1 c.s. sf. (חָתַת 369) *and you scare me*
בַחֲלֹמוֹת prep.-n.m.p. (321) *with dreams*
וּמֵחֶזְיֹנוֹת conj.-prep.-n.m.p. (303) *and with visions*
תְּבַעֲתַנִּי Pi. impf. 2 m.s.-1 c.s. sf. (בָּעַת 129; GK 58i,60d) *you terrify me*

7:15
וַתִּבְחַר consec.-Qal impf. 3 f.s. (בָּחַר 103) *so that ... would choose*
מַחֲנָק n.m.s. (338) *strangling*
נַפְשִׁי n.f.s.-1 c.s. sf. (659) *my soul (I myself)*
מָוֶת n.m.s. (560) *death*
מֵעַצְמוֹתָי prep.-n.f.p.-1 c.s. sf. paus. (I 782; GK 133b) *rather than my bones*

7:16
מָאַסְתִּי Qal pf. 1 c.s. (מָאַס 549) *I loathe (despise)*
לֹא־לְעֹלָם neg.-prep.-n.m.s. (761) *not for ever*
אֶחְיֶה Qal impf. 1 c.s. (חָיָה 310) *I would live*
חֲדַל מִמֶּנִּי Qal impv. 2 m.s. (חָדַל 292)-prep.-1 c.s. sf. *let me alone*
כִּי־הֶבֶל conj.-n.m.s. (I 210) *for a breath*
יָמָי n.m.p.-1 c.s. sf. paus. (398) *my days*

7:17
מָה־אֱנוֹשׁ interr. (552)-n.m.s. (60) *what is man?*
כִּי תְגַדְּלֶנּוּ conj. (471)-Pi. impf. 2 m.s.-3 m.s. sf. (152 גָּדַל) *that you make so much of him*
וְכִי־ conj.-conj. (471) *and that*
תָשִׁית Qal impf. 2 m.s. (שִׁית 1011) *you set*
אֵלָיו prep.-3 m.s. sf. *upon him*
לִבֶּךָ n.m.s.-2 m.s. sf. (524) *your heart*

7:18
וַתִּפְקְדֶנּוּ consec.-Qal impf. 2 m.s.-3 m.s. sf. (פָּקַד 823) *and you visit him*
לִבְקָרִים prep.-n.m.p. (133; GK 123c) *every morning*
לִרְגָעִים prep.-n.m.p. (921) *every moment*
תִּבְחָנֶנּוּ Qal impf. 2 m.s.-3 m.s. sf. (בָּחַן 103) *you test him*

7:19
כַּמָּה prep.-def.art.-interr. (553) *how long*
לֹא־תִשְׁעֶה neg.-Qal impf. 2 m.s. (שָׁעָה 1043) *will you not look*
מִמֶּנִּי prep.-1 c.s. sf. *away from me*
לֹא־תַרְפֵּנִי neg.-Hi. impf. 2 m.s.-1 c.s. sf. (רָפָה 951) *you do not forsake me*
עַד־בִּלְעִי prep. (III 723)-Qal inf.cstr.-1 c.s. sf. (118 בָּלַע) *till I swallow*
רֻקִּי n.m.s.-1 c.s. sf. (956; LXX+ ἐν ὀδύνῃ) *my spittle*

7:20
חָטָאתִי Qal pf. 1 c.s. (306; GK 159h) *I have sinned*
מָה אֶפְעַל interr. (552)-Qal impf. 1 c.s. (פָּעַל 821) *what do I do*
לָךְ prep.-2 m.s. sf. paus. *to you*
נֹצֵר Qal act.ptc. (נָצַר 665; LXX+ τὸν νοῦν) *O watcher*
הָאָדָם def.art.-n.m.s. (9) *of mankind*
לָמָה שַׂמְתַּנִי prep. (GK 102,l)-interr. (552)-Qal pf 2 m.s.-1 c.s. sf. (שִׂים 962) *why do you make me*
לְמִפְגָּע לָךְ prep.-n.m.s. (803)-prep.-2 m.s. sf. paus. *a mark for yourself*
וָאֶהְיֶה consec.-Qal impf. 1 c.s. (הָיָה 224) *and I have become*
עָלַי prep. (GK 119aa)-1 c.s. sf. (LXX ἐπὶ σοὶ) *for myself*
לְמַשָּׂא prep.-n.m.s. (I 672) *a burden*

7:21

וּמֶה לֹא־תִשָּׂא conj.-interr. (552; GK 37f) -neg.-Qal impf. 2 m.s. (נָשָׂא 669) *and why do you not pardon?*

פִּשְׁעִי n.m.s.-1 c.s. sf. (833) *my transgression*

וְתַעֲבִיר conj.-Hi. impf. 2 m.s. (עָבַר 716) *and take away*

אֶת־עֲוֺנִי dir.obj.-n.m.s.-1 c.s. sf. (730) *my iniquity*

כִּי־עַתָּה conj. (471)-adv. (773) *for now*

לֶעָפָר prep.-def.art.-n.m.s. (779) *on the dust*

אֶשְׁכָּב Qal impf. 1 c.s. paus. (שָׁכַב 1011) *I shall lie*

וְשִׁחַרְתַּנִי conj.-Pi. pf. 2 m.s.-1 c.s. sf. (שָׁחַר 1107; LXX ὀρθρίζων) *and you shall seek me*

וְאֵינֶנִּי conj.-subst.-1 c.s. sf. (II 34) *but I shall not be*

8:1

וַיַּעַן consec.-Qal impf. 3 m.s. (עָנָה I 772) *then answered*

בִּלְדַּד pr.n. (115) *Bildad*

הַשּׁוּחִי def.art.-pr.n. gent. (1001) *the Shuhite*

וַיֹּאמַר consec.-Qal impf. 3 m.s. (55) *(and said)*

8:2

עַד־אָן prep. (III 723)-adv. (33) *how long*

תְּמַלֶּל־ Pi impf. 2 m.s. (מָלַל I 576) *will you say*

אֵלֶּה demons.adj. c.p. (41) *these things*

וְרוּחַ כַּבִּיר conj.-n.f.s. cstr. (924)-adj. m.s. (460) *and a great wind*

אִמְרֵי־פִיךָ n.m.p. cstr. (56)-n.m.s.-2 m.s. sf. (804) *the words of your mouth*

8:3

הַאֵל interr.part.-n.m.s. (42) *does God*

יְעַוֵּת Pi. impf. 3 m.s. (עָוַת 736) *pervert*

מִשְׁפָּט n.m.s. (1048) *justice?*

וְאִם־שַׁדַּי conj.-conj. (49)-pr.n. (994) *or does the Almighty*

יְעַוֵּת־ v.supra *pervert*

צֶדֶק n.m.s. (841) *the right?*

8:4

אִם־בָּנֶיךָ hypoth.part. (49)-n.m.p.-2 m.s. sf. (119) *if your children*

חָטְאוּ־ Qal pf. 3 c.p. (חָטָא 306) *have sinned*

לוֹ prep.-3 m.s. sf. *against him*

וַיְשַׁלְּחֵם consec.-Pi. impf. 3 m.s.-3 m.p. sf. (שָׁלַח 1018) *and he has delivered them*

בְּיַד־פִּשְׁעָם prep.-n.f.s. cstr. (388)-n.m.s.-3 m.p. sf. (833) *into the power of their transgression*

8:5

אִם־אַתָּה hypoth.part. (49)-pers.pr. 2 m.s. (61) *if you (on your own part)*

תְּשַׁחֵר Pi. impf. 2 m.s. (שָׁחַר 1007) *seek eagerly*

אֶל־אֵל prep.-n.m.s. (42) *God*

וְאֶל־שַׁדַּי conj.-prep.-pr.n. (994) *and to the Almighty*

תִּתְחַנָּן Hith. impf. 2 m.s. (חָנַן I 335; GK 159r) *you make supplication*

8:6

אִם־זַךְ hypoth.part. (49; GK 159r)-adj. m.s. (269) *if pure*

וְיָשָׁר conj.-adj. m.s. (449) *and upright*

אָתָּה pers.pr. 2 m.s. paus. (61) *you*

כִּי־עַתָּה conj. (471)-adv. (773) *surely then*

יָעִיר Hi. impf. 3 m.s. (עוּר I 734; LXX δεήσεως ἐπακούσεταί σου) *he will rouse himself*

עָלֶיךָ prep.-2 m.s. sf. *for you*

וְשִׁלַּם conj.-Pi. pf. 3 m.s. (שָׁלֵם 1022) *and reward*

נְוַת n.m.s. cstr. (I 627) *with the habitation of*

צִדְקֶךָ n.m.s.-2 m.s. sf. (841) *your righteousness*

8:7

וְהָיָה conj. (GK 145u)-Qal pf. 3 m.s. (224) *and was*

רֵאשִׁיתְךָ n.f.s.-2 m.s. sf. (912) *your beginning*

מִצְעָר n.m.s. (I 859) *a small thing*

וְאַחֲרִיתְךָ conj.-n.f.s.-2 m.s. sf. (31) *and your latter part*

יִשְׂגֶּה Qal impf. 3 m.s. (שָׂגָה 960; GK 145u) *shall grow*

מְאֹד adv. (547) *exceedingly*

8:8

כִּי־שְׁאַל־נָא conj. (471)-Qal impv. 2 m.s. (981) -part.of entreaty (609) *for inquire, I pray you*

לְדֹר prep.-n.m.s. (189) *of ... ages*

רִישׁוֹן adj. m.s. (911) *former*

וְכוֹנֵן conj.-Polel impv. 2 m.s. (כּוּן I 465; poss.rd. וּבוֹנֵן) *and consider*

לְחֵקֶר prep.-n.m.s. cstr. (350) *the thing searched out by*

אֲבוֹתָם n.m.p.-3 m.p. sf. (3; LXX πατέρων) *their fathers*

8:9

כִּי־תְמוֹל conj. (471)-subst. (1069) *for of yesterday*

אֲנַחְנוּ pers.pr. 1 c.p. (59; GK 141d) *we*

וְלֹא נֵדָע conj.-neg.-Qal impf. 1 c.p. paus. (יָדַע 393) *and know nothing*

כִּי צֵל conj.-n.m.s. (853) *for a shadow*

יָמֵינוּ n.m.p.-1 c.p. sf. (398) *our days*

עֲלֵי־אָרֶץ prep.-n.f.s. paus. (75) *on earth*

8:10

הֲלֹא־הֵם interr.-neg.-pers.pr. 3 m.p. (241) *will they not?*

יוֹרוּךָ Hi. impf. 3 m.p.-2 m.s. sf. (יָרָה 434) *teach you*

יֹאמְרוּ לָךְ Qal impf. 3 m.p. (55)-prep.-2 m.s. sf. paus. (LXX καὶ ἀναγγελοῦσιν) *they say to you*

וּמִלִּבָּם conj.-prep.-n.m.s.-3 m.p. sf. (524; LXX>suffix) *and out of their heart*

יוֹצִאוּ Hi. impf. 3 m.p. (יָצָא 422) *they utter*

מִלִּים n.f.p. (576; GK 125c) *words*

8:11

הֲיִגְאֶה־ interr.-Qal impf. 3 m.s. (גָּאָה 144) *can ... grow*

גֹּמֶא n.m.s. (167) *papyrus*

בְּלֹא בִצָּה prep.-neg.-n.f.s. (130; GK 152aN; LXX+ה) *where there is no marsh*

יִשְׂגֶּה־ Qal impf. 3 m.s. (שָׂגָה 960; GK 75rr,150h) *can ... flourish*

אָחוּ n.m.s. coll. (28) *reeds*

בְלִי־מָיִם neg. (115)-n.m.p. (565; GK 152aN) *where there is no water*

8:12

עֹדֶנּוּ adv.-3 m.s. sf. (728) *while it*

בְאִבּוֹ prep.-n.m.s.-3 m.s. sf. (1) *in its flower (freshness)*

לֹא יִקָּטֵף neg.-Ni. impf. 3 m.s. (קָטַף 882) *it is not cut down*

וְלִפְנֵי conj.-prep.-n.m.p. cstr. (815) *and before*

כָל־חָצִיר n.m.s. cstr. (481)-n.m.s. (II 348) *any other plant*

יִיבָשׁ Qal impf. 3 m.s. paus. (יָבֵשׁ 386) *it withers*

8:13

כֵּן adv. (485) *such*

אָרְחוֹת n.m.p. cstr. (73; LXX τὰ ἔσχατα=אַחֲרִית) *the paths of*

כָּל־ n.m.s. cstr. (481) *all who*

שֹׁכְחֵי Qal act.ptc. m.p. cstr. (1013) *forget*

אֵל n.m.s. (42) *God*

וְתִקְוַת conj.-n.f.s. cstr. (876) *and the hope of*

חָנֵף adj. m.s. (338) *profane man*

תֹּאבֵד Qal impf. 3 f.s. (אָבַד 1) *shall perish*

8:14

אֲשֶׁר־יָקוֹט rel.-Qal impf. 3 m.s. (?קוט 876; GK 72r) *breaks in sunder (feels a loathing)*

כִּסְלוֹ n.m.s.-3 m.s. sf. (492) *whose confidence*

וּבֵית conj.-n.m.s. cstr. (108) *and a house of*

עַכָּבִישׁ n.m.s. (747) *a spider*

מִבְטַחוֹ n.m.s.-3 m.s. sf. (105; GK 93oo) *his trust*

8:15

יִשָּׁעֵן Ni. impf. 3 m.s. (שָׁעַן 1043) *he leans*

עַל־בֵּיתוֹ prep.-n.m.s.-3 m.s. sf. (108) *against his house*

וְלֹא יַעֲמֹד conj.-neg.-Qal impf. 3 m.s. (עָמַד 763) *but it does not stand*

יַחֲזִיק Hi. impf. 3 m.s. (חָזַק 304) *he lays hold*

בּוֹ prep.-3 m.s. sf. *of it*

וְלֹא יָקוּם conj.-neg.-Qal impf. 3 m.s. (קוּם 877) *but it does not endure*

8:16

רָטֹב הוּא adj. m.s. (936)-pers.pr. 3 m.s. (214) *he thrives (is moist, fresh)*

לִפְנֵי־ prep.-n.m.p. cstr. (815) *before*

שָׁמֶשׁ n.f.s. paus. (1039) *the sun*

וְעַל־גַּנָּתוֹ conj.-prep.-n.f.s.-3 m.s. sf. (171) *and over his garden*

יֹנַקְתּוֹ n.f.s.-3 m.s. sf. (413) *his shoots*

תֵצֵא Qal impf. 3 f.s. (יָצָא 422) *spread (go forth)*

8:17

עַל־גַּל prep.-n.m.s. (164) *about the stone-heap*

שָׁרָשָׁיו n.m.p.-3 m.s. sf. (1057) *his roots*

יְסֻבָּכוּ Pu. impf. 3 m.p. paus. (סָבַךְ 687) *are interwoven*

בֵּית אֲבָנִים n.m.s. cstr. (108; rd. בֵּין = *among*) -n.f.p. (6) *a house of stones*

יֶחֱזֶה Qal impf. 3 m.s. (חָזָה 302; LXX = יִחְיֶה *he lives*) *he sees*

8:18

אִם־יְבַלְּעֶנּוּ hypoth.part. (49)-Pi. impf. 3 m.s.-3 m.s. sf. (בָּלַע 118) *if he is destroyed*

מִמְּקוֹמוֹ prep.-n.m.s.-3 m.s. sf. (879) *from his place*

וְכִחֶשׁ בּוֹ conj.-Pi. pf. 3 m.s. (471; GK 29g,64g) -prep.-3 m.s. sf. *and he denies him*

לֹא רְאִיתִיךָ neg.-Qal pf. 1 c.s.-2 m.s. sf. (רָאָה 906) *I have never seen you*

8:19

הֶן־הוּא interj. (243)-demons.adj. m.s. (214; LXX ὅτι καταστροφὴ ἀσεβοῦς τοιαύτη) *behold, this*

מְשׂוֹשׂ דַּרְכּוֹ n.m.s. cstr. (965)-n.m.s.-3 m.s. sf. (202) *the joy of his way*

וּמֵעָפָר conj.-prep.-n.m.s. (779) *and out of the earth*

אַחֵר adj. m.s. (I 29; GK 145d) *other*

יִצְמָחוּ Qal impf. 3 m.p. paus. (צָמַח 855) *they will spring*

8:20

הֶן־אֵל interj. (243)-n.m.s. (42) *behold, God*

לֹא יִמְאַס־ neg.-Qal impf. 3 m.s. (מָאַס 549) *will not reject*

תָּם adj. m.s. (1070) *a blameless man*

וְלֹא־יַחֲזִיק conj.-neg.-Hi. impf. 3 m.s. (חָזַק 304) *nor take (strengthen)*

בְּיַד־מְרֵעִים prep.-n.f.s. cstr. (388)-Hi. ptc. m.p. (949 רָעַע) *the hand of evildoers*

8:21

עַד־ prep. (III 723; prb.rd. עֹד 728) *until (yet)*

יְמַלֵּה Pi. impf. 3 m.s. (מָלֵא 569; GK 23e,75pp; prb.rd. יְמַלֵּא) *he will fill*

שְׂחוֹק n.m.s. (966) *with laughter*

פִּיךָ n.m.s.-2 m.s. sf. (804) *your mouth*

וּשְׂפָתֶיךָ conj.-n.f. du.-2 m.s. sf. (973) *and your lips*

תְרוּעָה n.f.s. (929) *with shouting*

8:22

שֹׂנְאֶיךָ Qal act.ptc. m.p.-2 m.s. sf. (שָׂנֵא 971) *those who hate you*

יִלְבְּשׁוּ־ Qal impf. 3 m.p. (לָבַשׁ 527) *will be clothed*

בֹשֶׁת n.f.s. (102) *with shame*

וְאֹהֶל conj.-n.m.s. cstr. (13) *and the tent of*

רְשָׁעִים adj. m.p. (957) *the wicked*

אֵינֶנּוּ subst.-3 m.s. sf. (II 34) *will be no more*

9:1

וַיַּעַן consec.-Qal impf. 3 m.s. (עָנָה I 772) *then answered*

אִיּוֹב pr.n. (33) *Job*

וַיֹּאמַר consec.-Qal impf. 3 m.s. (55) *(and he said)*

9:2

אָמְנָם adv. (53) *truly*

יָדַעְתִּי Qal pf. 1 c.s. (יָדַע 393) *I know*

כִּי־כֵן conj.-adv. (485) *that it is so*

וּמַה־יִּצְדַּק conj.-interr. (552)-Qal impf. 3 m.s. (842 צָדַק) *but how can ... be just*

אֱנוֹשׁ n.m.s. (60) *a man*

עִם־אֵל prep. (767)-n.m.s. (42) *before God*

9:3

אִם־יַחְפֹּץ hypoth.part. (49)-Qal impf. 3 m.s. (342 חָפֵץ) *if one might wish*

לָרִיב prep.-Qal inf.cstr. (936) *to contend*

עִמּוֹ prep.-3 m.s. sf. *with him*

לֹא־יַעֲנֶנּוּ neg.-Qal impf. 3 m.s.-3 m.s. sf. (עָנָה I 772) *one could not answer him*

אַחַת num. f.s. (25) *once*

מִנִּי־אָלֶף prep. (577)-num. paus. (48) *in a thousand*

9:4

חֲכַם לֵבָב adj. m.s. cstr. (314)-n.m.s. (523) *a wise person in heart*

וְאַמִּיץ כֹּחַ conj.-adj. m.s. cstr. (55)-n.m.s. (470) *and mighty in strength*

מִי־הִקְשָׁה interr. (566)-Hi. pf. 3 m.s. (קָשָׁה 904) *who has hardened himself*

אֵלָיו prep.-3 m.s. sf. *against him*

וַיִּשְׁלָם consec.-Qal impf. 3 m.s. paus. (שָׁלֵם 1022) *and he succeeded*

9:5

הַמַּעְתִּיק def.art.-Hi. ptc. (עָתַק 801) *he who removes*

הָרִים n.m.p. (249) *mountains*

וְלֹא יָדָעוּ conj.-neg.-Qal pf. 3 c.p. paus. (יָדַע 393) *and they know it not*

אֲשֶׁר הֲפָכָם rel. (81)-(Qal pf. 3 m.s.-3 m.p. sf. (245 הָפַךְ) *which he overturns (them)*

בְּאַפּוֹ prep.-n.m.s.-3 m.s. sf. (I 60) *in his anger*

9:6

הַמַּרְגִּיז def.art.-Hi. ptc. (רָגַז 919) *who shakes*

אֶרֶץ n.f.s. (75) *earth*

מִמְּקוֹמָהּ prep.-n.m.s.-3 f.s. sf. (879) *out of its place*

וְעַמּוּדֶיהָ conj.-n.m.p.-3 f.s. sf. (765) *and its pillars*

יִתְפַלָּצוּן Hith. impf. 3 m.p. paus. (פָּלַץ 814; GK 54k) *tremble (shudder)*

9:7

הָאֹמֵר def.art.-Qal act.ptc. (אָמַר 55) *who commands*

לַחֶרֶס prep.-def.art.-n.m.s. (I 357) *the sun*

וְלֹא יִזְרָח conj.-neg.-Qal impf. 3 m.s. paus. (זָרַח 280; GK 109g,165a) *and it does not rise*

וּבְעַד כּוֹכָבִים conj.-prep. (126)-n.m.p. (456) *and (behind) the stars*

יַחְתֹּם Qal impf. 3 m.s. (חָתַם 367) *he seals up*

9:8

נֹטֶה Qal act.ptc. (639) *who stretched out*

שָׁמַיִם n.m. du. (1029) *the heavens*

לְבַדּוֹ prep.-n.m.s.-3 m.s. sf. (94) *alone*

וְדוֹרֵךְ conj.-Qal act.ptc. (דָּרַךְ 201) *and trampled*

עַל־בָּמֳתֵי prep.-n.f.p. cstr. (119; GK 87s) *upon the high places of*

יָם n.m.s. (410; some עָב 728; *the cloud*) *the sea*

9:9

עֹשֶׂה־ Qal act.ptc. (I 793) *who made*

עָשׁ n.f.s. (798; see עַיִשׁ 747) *Great Bear* (name of constellation)

כְּסִיל n.m.s. (II 493) *Orion*

וְכִימָה conj.-n.f.s. (465) *and Pleiades*

וְחַדְרֵי conj.-n.m.p. cstr. (293) *and chambers of*

תֵמָן n.f.s. (412) *south*

9:10

עֹשֶׂה Qal act.ptc. (I 793) *who does*

גְדֹלוֹת adj. f.p. (152) *great things*

עַד־אֵין חֵקֶר prep. (III 723)-subst. cstr. (II 34)-n.m.s. (350) *beyond understanding*

וְנִפְלָאוֹת conj.-n.f.p. (Ni. ptc. *Fla* 810) *and marvelous things*

עַד־אֵין מִסְפָּר v.supra-n.m.s. (I 708) *without number*

9:11

הֵן יַעֲבֹר interj. (243)-Qal impf. 3 m.s. (עָבַר 716) *lo, he passes*

עָלַי prep.-1 c.s. sf. *by me*

וְלֹא אֶרְאֶה conj.-neg.-Qal impf. 1 c.s. (רָאָה 906) *and I see him not*

וְיַחֲלֹף conj.-Qal impf. 3 m.s. (חָלַף 322) *and he moves on*

וְלֹא־אָבִין לוֹ conj.-neg.-Qal impf. 1 c.s. (בִּין 106; GK 117n) prep.-3 m.s. sf. *I do not perceive him*

9:12

הֵן יַחְתֹּף interj. (243)-Qal impf. 3 m.s. (חָתַף 368) *behold, he snatches away*

מִי יְשִׁיבֶנּוּ interr. (566)-Hi. impf. 3 m.s.-3 m.s. sf. (שׁוּב 996) *who can hinder him*

מִי־יֹאמַר v.supra-Qal impf. 3 m.s. (55) *who will say*

אֵלָיו prep.-3 m.s. sf. *to him*

מַה־תַּעֲשֶׂה interr. (552)-Qal impf. 2 m.s. (עָשָׂה I 793) *what do you do?*

9:13

אֱלוֹהַּ לֹא־יָשִׁיב n.m.s. (42)-neg.-Hi. impf. 3 m.s. (שׁוּב 996) *God will not turn back*

אַפּוֹ n.m.s.-3 m.s. sf. (I 60) *his anger*

תַּחְתָּו prep.-3 m.s. sf. (1065) *beneath him*

שָׁחֲחוּ Qal pf. 3 c.p. (שָׁחַח 1005) *bowed*

עֹזְרֵי Qal act.ptc. m.p. cstr. (עָזַר 740) *the helpers of*

רָהַב n.m.s. (923) *Rahab* (mythical sea monster)

9:14

אַף כִּי־אָנֹכִי conj. (II 64)-conj.-pers.pr. 1 c.s. (59) *how then ... I*

אֶעֱנֶנּוּ Qal impf. 1 c.s.-3 m.s. sf. (עָנָה I 772) *can I answer him*

אֶבְחֲרָה Qal impf. 1 c.s.-vol.he (בָּחַר 103) *let me choose*

דְבָרַי n.m.p.-1 c.s. sf. (182) *my words*

עִמּוֹ prep.-3 m.s. sf. *with him*

9:15

אֲשֶׁר אִם־ rel. (81; LXX>)-hypoth.part. (49; GK 159n,160a) *though*

צָדַקְתִּי Qal pf. 1 c.s. (צָדַק 842) *I am innocent*

לֹא אֶעֱנֶה neg.-Qal impf. 1 c.s. (עָנָה I 772; LXX οὐκ εἰσακούσεταί μου) *I cannot answer him*

לִמְשֹׁפְטִי prep.-n.m.s.-1 c.s. sf. (1048; GK 55b) *for my right*

אֶתְחַנָּן Hith. impf. 1 c.s. paus. (חָנַן I 335) *I must appeal for mercy*

9:16

אִם־קָרָאתִי hypoth.part. (49)-Qal pf. 1 c.s. (894) *if I summoned (called)*

וַיַּעֲנֵנִי consec.-Qal impf. 3 m.s.-1 c.s. sf. (עָנָה I 772) *and he answered me*

לֹא־אַאֲמִין neg.-Hi. impf. 1 c.s. (אָמַן 52) *I would not believe*

כִּי־יַאֲזִין conj.-Hi. impf. 3 m.s. (אָזַן 24; GK 111x) *that he was listening to*

קוֹלִי n.m.s.-1 c.s. sf. (876) *my voice*

9:17

אֲשֶׁר־בִּשְׂעָרָה rel. (81)–prep.–n.f.s. (973) *for with a tempest*

יְשׁוּפֵנִי Qal impf. 3 m.s.–1 c.s. sf. (שׁוּף 1003) *he crushes me*

וְהִרְבָּה conj.–Hi. pf. 3 m.s. (רָבָה I 915) *and he multiplies*

פְצָעַי n.m.p.–1 c.s. sf. (822) *my wounds*

חִנָּם adv. (336) *without cause*

9:18

לֹא־יִתְּנֵנִי neg.–Qal impf. 3 m.s.–1 c.s. sf. (נָתַן 678; GK 114m) *he will not let me*

הָשֵׁב Hi. inf.abs. (שׁוּב 996) *return*

רוּחִי n.f.s.–1 c.s. sf. (924) *my breath*

כִּי יַשְׂבִּעַנִי conj. (471)–Hi. impf. 3 m.s.–1 c.s. sf. (959 שָׂבַע) *but fills me (sates)*

מַמְּרֹרִים n.m.p. (601; GK 20h) *with bitter things*

9:19

אִם־לְכֹחַ hypoth.part. (49)–prep.–n.m.s. cstr. (470) *if a contest of (strength of)*

אַמִּיץ adj. m.s. (55) *mighty persons*

הִנֵּה demons.part. (243; GK 147b) *behold (him)*

וְאִם־לְמִשְׁפָּט conj.–v.supra–prep.–n.m.s. (1048) *if of justice*

מִי יוֹדִיעֵנִי interr. (566)–Hi. impf. 3 m.s.–1 c.s. sf. (יָעַד 416) *who can summon me*

9:20

אִם־אֶצְדָּק v.supra–Qal impf. 1 c.s. (צָדֵק 842) *though I am innocent*

פִּי יַרְשִׁיעֵנִי n.m.s.–1 c.s. sf. (804)–Hi. impf. 3 m.s.–1 c.s. sf. (רָשַׁע 957; GK 107x) *my own mouth would condemn me*

תָּם־אָנִי adj. m.s. (1070)–pers.pr. 1 c.s. (58) *(though) I am blameless*

וַיַּעְקְשֵׁנִי consec.–Hi. impf. 3 m.s.–1 c.s. sf. (עָקַשׁ 786; GK 53n) *he would prove me perverse (declare me crooked)*

9:21

תָּם־אָנִי v.supra–v.supra *I am blameless*

לֹא־אֵדַע neg.–Qal impf. 1 c.s. (יָדַע 393) *I regard not*

נַפְשִׁי n.f.s.–1 c.s. sf. (659) *myself*

אֶמְאַס Qal impf. 1 c.s. (מָאַס 549) *I loathe*

חַיָּי n.m.p.–1 c.s. sf. (313) *my life*

9:22

אַחַת הִיא num. f.s. (25)–demons.adj. f.s. (214; LXX>) *it is one*

עַל־כֵּן אָמַרְתִּי prep.–adv. (485)–Qal pf. 1 c.s. (55; GK 106i) *therefore I say*

תָּם וְרָשָׁע adj. m.s. (1070)–adj. m.s. (957) *blameless and wicked*

הוּא מְכַלֶּה pers.pr. 3 m.s. (214)–Pi. ptc. (כָּלָה 477) *he destroys*

9:23

אִם־שׁוֹט hypoth.part. (49)–n.m.s. (1002) *if calamity*

יָמִית Hi. impf. 3 m.s. (מוּת 559) *brings death*

פִּתְאֹם adv. (837) *suddenly*

לְמַסַּת prep.–n.f.s. cstr. (II 650; or I 588) *at the despair of*

נְקִיִּם adj. m.p. (667) *innocent ones*

יִלְעָג Qal impf. 3 m.s. paus. (לָעַג 541) *he mocks*

9:24

אֶרֶץ n.f.s. (75) *earth*

נִתְּנָה Ni. pf. 3 f.s. (נָתַן 678) *is given*

בְיַד־רָשָׁע prep.–n.f.s. cstr. (388)–adj. m.s. (957) *into the hand of the wicked*

פְּנֵי־ n.m.p. cstr. (815; LXX> supplied from Vss.) *the faces of*

שֹׁפְטֶיהָ Qal act.ptc. m.p.–3 f.s. sf. (שָׁפַט 1047) *its judges*

יְכַסֶּה Pi. impf. 3 m.s. (כָּסָה 491) *he covers*

אִם־לֹא hypoth.part. (49)–neg. *if it is not*

אֵפוֹא מִי־הוּא enclitic part. (66; GK 150,lN) –interr. (566)–demons.adj. m.s. (214) *then who is it?*

9:25

וְיָמַי conj.–n.m.p.–1 c.s. sf. (398) *and my days*

קַלּוּ Qal pf. 3 c.p. (קָלַל 886) *are swift(er)*

מִנִּי־רָץ prep.–Qal act.ptc. m.s. (רוּץ 930) *than a runner*

בָּרְחוּ Qal pf. 3 c.p. (בָּרַח 137) *they flee away*

לֹא־רָאוּ neg.–Qal pf. 3 c.p. (רָאָה 906) *they do not see*

טוֹבָה n.f.s. (375) *good things*

9:26

חָלְפוּ Qal pf. 3 c.p. (חָלַף 322) *they go by*

עִם־אֳנִיּוֹת prep. (767; GK 161aN)–n.f.p. cstr. (58) *with ships of*

אֵבֶה n.m.s. (3) *reed (papyrus)*

כְּנֶשֶׁר prep.–n.m.s. (676; GK 155g) *like an eagle*

יָטוּשׂ Qal impf. 3 m.s. (טוּשׂ 377) *swoops (rushes)*

עֲלֵי־אֹכֶל prep.–n.m.s. (38) *upon food*

9:27

אִם־אָמְרִי hypoth.part. (49)–Qal inf.cstr.–1 c.s. sf. (55; GK 159u; LXX εἴπω as Qal pf. 1 c.s.) *if I say*

אֶשְׁכְּחָה Qal impf. 1 c.s.–vol.he (שָׁכַח 1013) *I will forget*

שִׂיחִי n.m.s.–1 c.s. sf. (967) *my complaint*

אֶעֶזְבָה Qal impf. 1 c.s.–vol.he (עָזַב I 736) *I will put off*

פָנַי n.m.p.–1 c.s. sf. (815) *my (sad) countenance*

וְאַבְלִיגָה conj.–Hi. impf. 1 c.s.–vol.he (בָּלַג 114) *and I will be of good cheer*

9:28

יָגֹרְתִּי Qal pf. 1 c.s. (יָגֹר 388) *I am afraid*

כָל־עַצְּבֹתָי n.m.s. cstr. (481)–n.f.p.–1 c.s. sf. (781) *of all my suffering*

יָדַעְתִּי Qal pf. 1 c.s. (יָדַע 393) *I know*

כִּי־לֹא תְנַקֵּנִי conj.–neg.–Pi. impf. 2 m.s.–1 c.s. sf. (נָקָה 667) *you will not hold me innocent*

9:29

אָנֹכִי אֶרְשָׁע pers.pr. 1 c.s. (59)–Qal impf. 1 c.s. (957 רָשַׁע; GK 107n) *I am guilty*

לָמָּה־זֶּה prep.–interr. (552)–demons.adj. m.s. (260) *why then?*

הֶבֶל n.m.s. (210; LXX διὰ τί οὐκ ἀπέθανον = בל אָגְוַע) *in vain*

אִיגָע Qal impf. 1 c.s. (יָגַע 388) *do I labor?*

9:30

אִם־הִתְרָחַצְתִּי hypoth.part. (49; GK 159n)–Hith. pf. 1 c.s. (רָחַץ 934) *if I wash myself*

בְמוֹ־שָׁלֶג prep. (91)–n.m.s. (1017) *with snow*

וַהֲזִכּוֹתִי conj.–Hi. pf. 1 c.s. (זָכַךְ 269) *and cleanse*

בְּבֹר prep.–n.m.s. (II 141) *with lye*

כַּפָּי n.f.p.–1 c.s. sf. paus. (496) *my hands*

9:31

אָז בַּשַּׁחַת adv. (23)–prep.–def.art. (GK 126r) –n.f.s. (1001) *yet into the pit*

תִּטְבְּלֵנִי Qal impf. 2 m.s.–1 c.s. sf. (טָבַל I 371) *you will plunge me*

וְתִעֲבוּנִי conj.–Pi. pf. 3 c.p.–1 c.s. sf. (תָּעַב 1073) *and you will abhor me*

שַׂלְמוֹתָי n.f.p.–1 c.s. sf. (971) *my garments*

9:32

כִּי־לֹא־אִישׁ conj. (471)–neg.–n.m.s. (35; GK 116s,152d,166a) *for not a man*

כָּמֹנִי subst.–1 c.s. sf. (453) *as I am*

אֶעֱנֶנּוּ Qal impf. 1 c.s.–3 m.s. sf. (עָנָה I 772) *that I might answer him*

נָבוֹא Qal impf. 1 c.p. (בּוֹא 97) *that we should come*

יַחְדָּו adv. (403) *together*

בַּמִּשְׁפָּט prep.–def.art.–n.m.s. (1048) *to trial*

9:33

לֹא יֵשׁ־ neg. (LXX εἴθε = לוּ 530 *would that*) –subst. (441; GK 152d,166a) *there is no*

בֵּינֵינוּ prep.–1 c.p. sf. (107) *between us*

מוֹכִיחַ Hi. ptc. (יָכַח 406) *umpire*

יָשֵׁת Qal impf. 3 m.s. apoc.vol. (שִׁית 1011; GK 109i) *who might lay*

יָדוֹ n.f.s.–3 m.s. sf. (388) *his hand*

עַל־שְׁנֵינוּ prep.–n.m.p.–1 c.p. sf. (1040) *upon us both*

9:34

יָסֵר Hi. impf. 3 m.s. apoc.vol. (סוּר 693) *let him take away*

מֵעָלַי prep.–prep.–1 c.s. sf. (758) *from me*

שִׁבְטוֹ n.m.s.–3 m.s. sf. (986) *his rod*

וְאֵמָתוֹ conj.–n.f.s.–3 m.s. sf. (33) *and dread of him*

אַל־תְּבַעֲתַנִּי neg. (39)–Pi. impf. 3 f.s.–1 c.s. sf. (129 בָּעַת; GK 60d) *let not ... terrify me*

9:35

אֲדַבְּרָה Pi. impf. 1 c.s.–vol.he (דָּבַר 180) *let me speak*

וְלֹא אִירָאֶנּוּ conj.–neg.–Qal impf. 1 c.s.–3 m.s. sf. (יָרֵא 431) *that I might not fear him*

כִּי לֹא־כֵן conj. (471)–neg.–adv. (485) *for not so*

אָנֹכִי עִמָּדִי pers.pr. 1 c.s. (59)–prep.–1 c.s. sf. (767) *am I in myself*

10:1

נָקְטָה Qal pf. 3 f.s. (as if from נָקַט; however, 876 has Ni. pf. 3 f.s. קוּט; GK 67dd,72dd) *loathe*

נַפְשִׁי n.f.s.–1 c.s. sf. (659) *I myself*

בְּחַיָּי prep.–n.m.p.–1 c.s. sf. (313) *my life*

אֶעֶזְבָה Qal impf. 1 c.s.–vol.he (עָזַב 736) *let me loose*

עָלַי prep.–1 c.s. sf. (752) *upon me*

שִׂיחִי n.m.s.–1 c.s. sf. (967) *my complaint*

אֲדַבְּרָה Pi. impf. 1 c.s.–vol.he (דָּבַר 180) *let me speak*

בְּמַר prep.–adj. m.s. cstr. (I 600) *in the bitterness of*

נַפְשִׁי v.supra (LXX+συνεχόμενος) *my soul*

10:2

אֹמַר Qal impf. 1 c.s.-vol. (אָמַר 55) *let me say*
אֶל־אֱלוֹהַּ prep.-n.m.s. (42) *to God*
אַל־תַּרְשִׁיעֵנִי neg.-Hi. impf. 2 m.s.-1 c.s. sf. (רָשַׁע 957) *do not condemn me*
הוֹדִיעֵנִי Hi. impv. 2 m.s.-1 c.s. sf. (יָדַע 393) *make me know*
עַל מַה־ prep.-interr. (552) *why*
תְּרִיבֵנִי Qal impf. 2 m.s.-1 c.s. sf. (רִיב 936) *do you contend against me*

10:3

הֲטוֹב לְךָ interr.-adj. m.s. (II 373)-prep.-2 m.s. sf. *does it seem good to you*
כִּי־תַעֲשֹׁק conj. (471)-Qal impf. 2 m.s. (עָשַׁק 798) *that you oppress*
כִּי־תִמְאַס v.supra-Qal impf. 2 m.s. (מָאַס 549) *that you despise*
יְגִיעַ n.m.s. cstr. (388) *the work of*
כַּפֶּיךָ n.f.p.-2 m.s. sf. (496) *your hands*
וְעַל־עֲצַת conj.-prep.-n.f.s. cstr. (420) *and the designs of*
רְשָׁעִים adj. m.p. (957) *the wicked*
הוֹפָעְתָּ Hi. pf. 2 m.s. paus. (יָפַע 422) *you favor*

10:4

הַעֵינֵי interr.-n.f.p. cstr. (744) *eyes of?*
בָשָׂר n.m.s. (142) *flesh?*
לָךְ prep.-2 m.s. sf. paus. *to you*
אִם־כִּרְאוֹת hypoth.part. (49)-prep.-Qal inf.cstr. (906 רָאָה) *as seeing of?*
אֱנוֹשׁ n.m.s. (60) *a man?*
תִּרְאֶה Qal impf. 2 m.s. (רָאָה 906) *do you see?*

10:5

הֲכִימֵי interr.-prep.-n.m.p. cstr. (398) *as days of?*
אֱנוֹשׁ n.m.s. (60) *man?*
יָמֶיךָ n.m.p.-2 m.s. sf. (398) *are your days?*
אִם־שְׁנוֹתֶיךָ hypoth.part. (49)-n.f.p.-2 m.s. sf. (1040) *or are your years?*
כִּימֵי גָבֶר prep.-v.supra-n.m.s. paus. (149) *as man's years (days)*

10:6

כִּי־תְבַקֵּשׁ conj. (471)-Pi. impf. 2 m.s. (בָּקַשׁ 134) *that you seek out*
לַעֲוֹנִי prep.-n.m.s.-1 c.s. sf. (730) *my iniquity*
וּלְחַטָּאתִי conj.-prep.-n.f.s.-1 c.s. sf. (308) *and for my sin*
תִדְרוֹשׁ Qal impf. 2 m.s. (דָּרַשׁ 205) *you search*

10:7

עַל־דַּעְתְּךָ prep. (752)-n.f.s.-2 m.s. sf. (395; GK 119aaN) *in spite of your knowing*
כִּי־לֹא אֶרְשָׁע conj. (471)-neg.-Qal impf. 1 c.s. paus. (רָשַׁע 957) *that I am not guilty*
וְאֵין conj.-neg. (II 34) *and there is none*
מִיָּדְךָ prep.-n.f.s.-2 m.s. sf. (388) *out of your hand*
מַצִּיל Hi. ptc. m.s. (נָצַל 664) *to deliver*

10:8

יָדֶיךָ n.f.p.-2 m.s. sf. (388) *your hands*
עִצְּבוּנִי Pi. pf. 3 c.p.-1 c.s. sf. (עָצַב II 781) *fashioned me*
וַיַּעֲשׂוּנִי consec.-Qal impf. 3 m.p.-1 c.s. sf. (עָשָׂה I 793) *and made me*
יַחַד adv. (403) *together*
סָבִיב subst.as adv. (686; LXX μετὰ ταῦτα μεταβαλών = אַחַר סַבּוֹתָ) *round about*
וַתְּבַלְּעֵנִי consec.-Pi. impf. 2 m.s.-1 c.s. sf. (בָּלַע 118; GK 111e) *and you destroy (engulf) me*

10:9

זְכָר־נָא Qal impv. 2 m.s. (269)-part.of entreaty (609; LXX>) *remember, I pray thee*
כִּי־כַחֹמֶר conj.-prep.-def.art.-n.m.s. (I 330) *that like the clay*
עֲשִׂיתָנִי Qal pf. 2 m.s.-1 c.s. sf. (עָשָׂה I 793) *you made me*
וְאֶל־עָפָר conj.-prep.-n.m.s. (779) *and to dust*
תְּשִׁיבֵנִי Hi. impf. 2 m.s.-1 c.s. sf. (שׁוּב 996) *you will turn me again*

10:10

הֲלֹא כֶחָלָב interr.-neg.-prep.-def.art.-n.m.s. (316) *not like milk?*
תַּתִּיכֵנִי Hi. impf. 2 m.s.-1 c.s. sf. (נָתַךְ 677) *did you pour me out?*
וְכַגְּבִנָּה conj.-prep.-def.art.-n.f.s. (148) *and like cheese*
תַּקְפִּיאֵנִי Hi. impf. 2 m.s.-1 c.s. sf. (קָפָא 891) *you curdled me*

10:11

עוֹר וּבָשָׂר n.m.s. (736)-conj.-n.m.s. (142) *skin and flesh*
תַּלְבִּישֵׁנִי Hi. impf. 2 m.s.-1 c.s. sf. (לָבַשׁ 527) *you clothed me*
וּבַעֲצָמוֹת conj.-prep.-n.f.p. (782) *and with bones*
וְגִידִים conj.-n.m.p. (161) *and sinews*
תְּסֹכְכֵנִי Po'el impf. 2 m.s.-1 c.s. sf. (rd. תְּשֹׂכְכֵנִי from שָׂכַךְ II 968) *you did knit me together*

10:12

חַיִּים n.m.p. (313) *life*
וָחֶסֶד conj.-n.m.s. (338) *and steadfast love*
עָשִׂיתָ Qal pf. 2 m.s. (עָשָׂה I 793; LXX ἔθου) *you have granted*
עִמָּדִי prep.-1 c.s. sf. (767) *to me*
וּפְקֻדָּתְךָ conj.-n.f.s.-2 m.s. sf. (824) *and your care (visitation)*
שָׁמְרָה Qal pf. 3 f.s. (שָׁמַר 1036) *has preserved*
רוּחִי n.f.s.-1 c.s. sf. (924) *my spirit*

10:13

וְאֵלֶּה conj.-demons.adj. c.p. (41) *yet these things*
צָפַנְתָּ Qal pf. 2 m.s. (צָפַן 860) *you have hidden*
בִלְבָבֶךָ prep.-n.m.s.-2 m.s. sf. (523) *in your heart*
יָדַעְתִּי Qal pf. 1 c.s. (יָדַע 393) *I know*
כִּי־זֹאת conj. (471)-demons.adj. f.s. (260) *that this*
עִמָּךְ prep.-2 m.s. sf. paus. (767) *with you (your purpose)*

10:14

אִם־חָטָאתִי hypoth.part. (49)-Qal pf. 1 c.s. (חָטָא 306) *if I sin*
וּשְׁמַרְתָּנִי conj.-Qal pf. 2 m.s.-1 c.s. sf. (שָׁמַר 1036) *you mark me (preserve me)*
וּמֵעֲוֺנִי conj.-prep.-n.m.s.-1 c.s. sf. (730) *and of my iniquity*
לֹא תְנַקֵּנִי neg.-Pi. impf. 2 m.s.-1 c.s. sf. (נָקָה 667) *you do not acquit me*

10:15

אִם־רָשַׁעְתִּי hypoth.part. (49; GK 159ff)-Qal pf. 1 c.s. (רָשַׁע 957) *if I am wicked*
אַלְלַי לִי interj. (47)-prep.-1 c.s. sf. *woe to me*
וְצָדַקְתִּי conj.-Qal pf. 1 c.s. (צָדַק 842) *if I am righteous*
לֹא־אֶשָּׂא neg.-Qal impf. 1 c.s. (נָשָׂא 669) *I cannot lift up*
רֹאשִׁי n.m.s.-1 c.s. sf. (910) *my head*
שְׂבַע adj. m.s. cstr. (960) *being sated with*
קָלוֹן n.m.s. (885) *disgrace*
וּרְאֵה conj.-adj. m.s. cstr. (909; some rd. וּרְוֵה = *drenched with) and look upon*
עָנְיִי n.m.s.-1 c.s. sf. (777) *my affliction*

10:16

וְיִגְאֶה conj.-Qal impf. 3 m.s. (גָּאָה 144; GK 109h) *and if he lifts himself up*
כַּשַּׁחַל prep.-def.art.-n.m.s. (1006) *like the lion*
תְּצוּדֵנִי Qal impf. 2 m.s.-1 c.s. sf. (צוּד I 844) *you hunt me*
וְתָשֹׁב conj.-Qal impf. 2 m.s. (שׁוּב 996; GK 109h,120g) *and you again*
תִּתְפַּלָּא־ Hith. impf. 2 m.s. (פָּלָא 810) *work wonders*
בִי prep.-1 c.s. sf. *against me*

10:17

תְּחַדֵּשׁ Pi. impf. 2 m.s. (חָדַשׁ 293) *you renew*
עֵדֶיךָ n.m.p.-2 m.s. sf. (729) *your witnesses*
נֶגְדִּי prep.-1 c.s. sf. (617) *against me*
וְתֶרֶב conj.-Hi. impf. 2 m.s. (רָבָה I 915) *and increase (multiply)*
כַּעַשְׂךָ n.m.s.-2 m.s. sf. (495) *your vexation*
עִמָּדִי prep.-1 c.s. sf. (767) *toward me*
חֲלִיפוֹת n.f.p. (322; LXX ἐπήγαγες = תַּחֲלִיף) *changes*
וְצָבָא conj.-n.m.s. (838; GK 154aN; LXX πειρατήρια = צְבָאוֹת) *and a host*
עִמִּי prep.-1 c.s. sf. *with me*

10:18

וְלָמָּה conj.-prep.-interr. (552) *and why*
מֵרֶחֶם prep.-n.m.s. (933) *from a womb*
הֹצֵאתָנִי Hi. pf. 2 m.s.-1 c.s. sf. (יָצָא 422) *did you bring me forth?*
אֶגְוַע Qal impf. 1 c.s. (גָּוַע 157; GK 107n) *should I die*
וְעַיִן conj.-n.f.s. (744) *and an eye*
לֹא־תִרְאֵנִי neg.-Qal impf. 2 m.s.-1 c.s. sf. (רָאָה 906) *should not see me*

10:19

כַּאֲשֶׁר prep.-rel. (81) *as though*
לֹא־הָיִיתִי neg. Qal pf. 1 c.s. (הָיָה 224) *I had not been*
אֶהְיֶה Qal impf. 1 c.s. (הָיָה 224; GK 107n) *should I be*
מִבֶּטֶן prep.-n.f.s. (105) *from a womb*
לַקֶּבֶר prep.-def.art.-n.m.s. (868) *to the grave*
אוּבָל Ho. impf. 1 c.s. (יָבַל 384) *should I be carried*

10:20

הֲלֹא־מְעַט interr.-neg.-subst. (589) *are not few?*
יָמַי n.m.p.-1 c.s. sf. (398; LXX ὁ χρόνος τοῦ βίου μου) *my days*
יֶחְדָּל Qal impf. 3 m.s. juss. (חָדַל 292; Q-conj.-Qal impv. 2 m.s. וַחֲדַל) *let him cease*
יָשִׁית Qal impf. 3 m.s. juss. (שִׁית 1011; Q-conj.-Qal impv. 2 m.s. וְשִׁית; LXX ἔασον = שְׁעֵה) *let him direct (attention)*
מִמֶּנִּי prep.-1 c.s. sf. *from me*

וְאַבְלִיגָה conj.-Hi. impf. 1 c.s.-coh.he (בָּלַג 114) *and let me smile*
מְּעָט adv. paus. (589) *a little*

10:21

בְּטֶרֶם prep.-adv. (382) *before*
אֵלֵךְ Qal impf. 1 c.s. (הָלַךְ 229; GK 107c) *I go*
וְלֹא אָשׁוּב conj.-neg.-Qal impf. 1 c.s. (שׁוּב 996) *whence I shall not return*
אֶל־אֶרֶץ prep.-n.f.s. cstr. (75) *to a land of*
חֹשֶׁךְ n.m.s. (365) *gloom*
וְצַלְמָוֶת conj.-n.m.s. (853) *and deep darkness*

10:22

אֶרֶץ n.f.s. cstr. (75) *a land of*
עֵיפָתָה n.f.s.-dir.he (734; GK 90g) *darkness*
כְּמוֹ אֹפֶל adv. (455)-n.m.s. (66) *as darkness (gloom)*
צַלְמָוֶת n.m.s. (853) *deep darkness*
וְלֹא סְדָרִים conj.-neg.-n.m.p. (690; GK 152aN; LXX φέγγος) *without order (confusion)*
וַתֹּפַע consec.-Hi. impf. 3 f.s. or 2 m.s. (יָפַע 422) *and it shines*
כְּמוֹ־אֹפֶל v.supra-v.supra *as darkness*

11:1

וַיַּעַן consec.-Qal impf. 3 m.s. (עָנָה I 772) *then answered*
צֹפַר pr.n. (862) *Zophar*
הַנַּעֲמָתִי def.art.-adj.gent. (654) *the Naamathite*
וַיֹּאמַר consec.-Qal impf. 3 m.s. (אָמַר 55) *(and said)*

11:2

הֲרֹב interr.-n.m.s. cstr. (913; LXX ὁ τά πολλὰ) *a multitude of?*
דְּבָרִים n.m.p. (182) *words?*
לֹא יֵעָנֶה neg.-Ni. impf. 3 m.s. (עָנָה I 772) *should go unanswered?*
וְאִם־אִישׁ conj.-hypoth.part. (49)-n.m.s. cstr. (35) *and should a man of*
שְׂפָתַיִם n.f. du. (973; GK 128t) *talk (lips)*
יִצְדָּק Qal impf. 3 m.s. paus. (צָדֵק 842) *be vindicated?*

11:3

בַּדֶּיךָ n.m.p.-2 m.s. sf. (III 95) *your babble (idle talk)*
מְתִים n.m.p. (607) *men*
יַחֲרִישׁוּ Hi. impf. 3 m.p. (חָרַשׁ II 361) *should silence*
וַתִּלְעַג consec.-Qal impf. 2 m.s. (לָעַג 541; GK 111t) *and when you mock*
וְאֵין מַכְלִם conj.-neg. cstr. (II 34)-Hi. ptc. m.s. (483 כָּלַם) *shall no one shame (you)*

11:4

וַתֹּאמֶר consec.-Qal impf. 2 m.s. (אָמַר 55) *for you say*
זַךְ adj. m.s. (269) *pure*
לִקְחִי n.m.s.-1 c.s. sf. (544) *my doctrine*
וּבַר conj.-adj. m.s. (II 141) *and clean*
הָיִיתִי Qal pf. 1 c.s. (הָיָה 224) *I am*
בְעֵינֶיךָ prep.-n.f. du.-2 m.s. sf. (744; LXX ἐναντίον αὐτοῦ) *in your eyes*

11:5

וְאוּלָם conj.-adv. (III 19) *but*
מִי־יִתֵּן interr. (566)-Qal impf. 3 m.s. (נָתַן 678) *oh, that (who will grant)*
אֱלוֹהַּ n.m.s. (42) *God*
דַּבֵּר Pi. inf.cstr. (דָּבַר 180; GK 151b) *would speak*
וְיִפְתַּח conj.-Qal impf. 3 m.s. (פָּתַח I 834; GK 110i) *and that he would open*
שְׂפָתָיו n.f. du.-3 m.s. sf. (973) *his lips*
עִמָּךְ prep.-2 m.s. sf. paus. (767) *to you*

11:6

וְיַגֶּד־לְךָ conj.-Hi. impf. 3 m.s.-apoc.vol. (נָגַד 616; GK 110i)-prep.-2 m.s. sf. *and that he would tell you*
תַּעֲלֻמוֹת n.f.p. cstr. (761) *secrets of*
חָכְמָה n.f.s. (315) *wisdom*
כִּי־כִפְלַיִם conj. (471)-n.m. du. (495; GK 134rN) *for double*
לְתוּשִׁיָּה prep.-n.f.s. (444) *in sound wisdom*
וְדַע conj.-Qal impv. 2 m.s. (יָדַע 393) *and know*
כִּי־יַשֶּׁה conj.-Hi. impf. 3 m.s. (נָשָׁה II 674; if I 674-*lends (obligates) to you ...) allows a part ... to be forgotten*
לְךָ prep.-2 m.s. sf. *to you*
אֱלוֹהַּ n.m.s. (42) *God*
מֵעֲוֺנֶךָ prep.-n.m.s.-2 m.s. sf. paus. (730) *of your guilt*

11:7

הַחֵקֶר interr.-n.m.s. cstr. (350) *the deep things of*
אֱלוֹהַּ n.m.s. (42) *God*
תִּמְצָא Qal impf. 2 m.s. (מָצָא 592) *can you find out*
אִם עַד־תַּכְלִית conj. (49)-prep. (III 723)-n.f.s. cstr. (479) *or unto the end of*

שַׁדַּי pr.n. (994) *the Almighty*
תִּמְצָא v.supra *can you find out*

11:8

גָּבְהֵי n.m.p. cstr. (147) *heights of*
שָׁמַיִם n.m. du. (1029) *heaven*
מַה־תִּפְעָל interr. (552)-Qal impf. 2 m.s. paus. (821 פָּעַל) *what can you do?*
עֲמֻקָּה adj. f.s. (771) *deep(er)*
מִשְּׁאוֹל prep.-pr.n. (982) *than Sheol*
מַה־תֵּדָע interr. (552)-Qal impf. 2 m.s. paus. (393 יָדַע) *what can you know*

11:9

אֲרֻכָּה adj. f.s. (74) *long(er)*
מֵאֶרֶץ prep.-n.f.s. (75) *than earth*
מִדָּהּ n.f.s.-3 f.s. sf. (551; GK 91e) *its measure*
וּרְחָבָה conj.-adj. f.s. (I 932) *and broad(er)*
מִנִּי־יָם prep. (577)-n.m.s. (410) *than a sea*

11:10

אִם־יַחֲלֹף hypoth.part. (49)-Qal impf. 3 m.s. (322 חָלַף) *if he passes through*
וְיַסְגִּיר conj.-Hi. impf. 3 m.s. (סָגַר 688) *and imprisons*
וְיַקְהִיל conj.-Hi. impf. 3 m.s. (קָהַל 874) *and calls to judgment*
וּמִי conj.-interr. (566) *and who*
יְשִׁיבֶנּוּ Hi. impf. 3 m.s.-3 m.s. sf. (שׁוּב 996) *can hinder him*

11:11

כִּי־הוּא conj.-pers.pr. 3 m.s. (214) *for he*
יָדַע Qal pf. 3 m.s. (393) *knows*
מְתֵי־ n.m.p. cstr. (607; GK 128t) *men of*
שָׁוְא n.m.s. (996) *worthlessness*
וַיַּרְא־אָוֶן consec.-Qal impf. 3 m.s. (רָאָה 906) -n.m.s. (19) *when he sees iniquity*
וְלֹא יִתְבּוֹנָן conj.-neg.-Hithpolel impf. 3 m.s. paus. (בִּין 106) *will he not consider (it)*

11:12

וְאִישׁ נָבוּב conj.-n.m.s. (35)-Qal pass.ptc. (נָבַב 612) *but a hollow-minded man*
יִלָּבֵב Ni. impf. 3 m.s. (לָבַב I 525; GK 51g) *shall get a mind*
וְעַיִר conj.-n.m.s. cstr. (747; GK 131cN) *when a colt of*
פֶּרֶא n.m.s. (825) *a wild ass*
אָדָם n.m.s. (9) *a man*
יִוָּלֵד Ni. impf. 3 m.s. (יָלַד 408) *is born*

11:13

אִם־אַתָּה hypoth.part. (49)-pers.pr. 2 m.s. (61) *if you*
הֲכִינוֹתָ Hi. pf. 2 m.s. (כּוּן I 465; LXX καθαρὰν ἔθου = הֲזִכּוֹתָ) *set aright*
לִבֶּךָ n.m.s.-2 m.s. sf. (524) *your heart*
וּפָרַשְׂתָּ conj.-Qal pf. 2 m.s. (פָּרַשׂ 831) *and you will stretch out*
אֵלָיו prep.-3 m.s. sf. *toward him*
כַּפֶּךָ n.f.s.-2 m.s. sf. (496) *your hand*

11:14

אִם־אָוֶן hypoth.part. (49)-n.m.s. (19) *if iniquity*
בְּיָדְךָ prep.-n.f.s.-2 m.s. sf. (388) *in your hand*
הַרְחִיקֵהוּ Hi. impv. 2 m.p.-3 m.s. sf. (רָחַק 934) *put it far away*
וְאַל־תַּשְׁכֵּן conj.-neg.-Hi. impf. 3 f.s.-apoc.vol. (1014 שָׁכַן; LXX μὴ αὐλισθήτω = וְאַל־תִּשְׁכֹּן) *and let not ... dwell*
בְּאֹהָלֶיךָ prep.-n.m.p.-2 m.s. sf. (13) *in your tents*
עַוְלָה n.f.s. (732) *wickedness*

11:15

כִּי־אָז conj. (471)-adv. (23; GK 159ee) *surely then*
תִּשָּׂא Qal impf. 2 m.s. (נָשָׂא 669) *you will lift up*
פָנֶיךָ n.m.p.-2 m.s. sf. (815) *your face*
מִמּוּם prep.-n.m.s. (548; GK 119w) *without blemish*
וְהָיִיתָ conj.-Qal pf. 2 m.s. (הָיָה 224) *and you will be*
מֻצָק Ho. ptc. m.s. (יָצַק 427) *secure (firmly established)*
וְלֹא תִירָא conj.-neg.-Qal impf. 2 m.s. (יָרֵא 431) *and you will not fear*

11:16

כִּי־אַתָּה conj. (471)-pers.pr. 2 m.s. (214) *for you*
עָמָל n.m.s. (765) *(your) misery*
תִּשְׁכָּח Qal impf. 2 m.s. paus. (שָׁכַח 1013) *will forget*
כְּמַיִם prep.-n.m.p. (565) *as waters*
עָבְרוּ Qal pf. 3 c.p. (עָבַר 716) *that have passed away*
תִזְכֹּר Qal impf. 2 m.s. (זָכַר 269) *you will remember (it)*

11:17

וּמִצָּהֳרַיִם conj.-prep.-n.m.p. (I 843; GK 133e) *and than noonday*

יָקוּם Qal impf. 3 m.s. (קוּם 877; GK 108e) *will shine bright(er)*
חָלֶד n.m.s. paus. (317) *duration (of life)*
תָּעֻפָה n.f.s. (734; GK 48d,144c) *darkness*
כַּבֹּקֶר prep.-def.art.-n.m.s. (133) *like the morning*
תִּהְיֶה Qal impf. 3 f.s. (הָיָה 224) *will be*

11:18

וּבָטַחְתָּ conj.-Qal pf. 2 m.s. (בָּטַח 105) *and you will have confidence*
כִּי־יֵשׁ תִּקְוָה conj. (471)-subst. (441)-n.f.s. (876) *because there is hope*
וְחָפַרְתָּ conj.-Qal pf. 2 m.s. (חָפַר I 343) *and you will look around*
לָבֶטַח prep.-n.m.s. as adv. (I 105; LXX ἐκ δὲ μερίμνης καὶ φροντίδος ἀναφανεῖταί σοι εἰρήνη) *in safety (securely)*
תִּשְׁכָּב Qal impf. 2 m.s. paus. (שָׁכַב 1011) *you will sleep*

11:19

וְרָבַצְתָּ conj.-Qal pf. 2 m.s. (רָבַץ 918) *and you will lie down*
וְאֵין conj.-subst. cstr. (II 34) *and none*
מַחֲרִיד Hi. ptc. m.s. (חָרֵד 353) *will make (you) afraid*
וְחִלּוּ conj.-Pi. pf. 3 c.p. (חָלָה II 318) *and ... will entreat*
פָנֶיךָ n.m.p.-2 m.s. sf. (815) *your favor (face)*
רַבִּים adj. m.p. (I 912) *many*

11:20

וְעֵינֵי conj.-n.f.p. cstr. (744) *but eyes of*
רְשָׁעִים adj. m.p. (957) *wicked ones*
תִּכְלֶינָה Qal impf. 3 f.p. (כָּלָה I 477) *will fail*
וּמָנוֹס conj.-n.m.s. (631) *and escape*
אָבַד Qal pf. 3 m.s. (אָבַד 1) *will be lost*
מִנְהֶם prep.-3 m.p. sf. (GK 103i,m) *to them*
וְתִקְוָתָם conj.-n.f.s.-3 m.p. sf. (876) *and their hope*
מַפַּח־נָפֶשׁ n.m.s. cstr. (656)-n.f.s. paus. (659) *a breathing out of life (expiring)*

12:1

וַיַּעַן consec.-Qal impf. 3 m.s. (עָנָה I 772) *then answered*
אִיּוֹב pr.n. (33) *Job*
וַיֹּאמַר consec.-Qal impf. 3 m.s. (אָמַר 55) *(and said)*

12:2

אָמְנָם adv. (53) *no doubt (verily)*
כִּי אַתֶּם־ conj. (471)-pers.pr. 2 m.p. (61) *you (are)*
עָם n.m.s. paus. (I 766) *people*
וְעִמָּכֶם conj.-prep.-2 m.p. sf. (767) *and with you*
תָּמוּת Qal impf. 3 f.s. (מוּת 559) *will die*
חָכְמָה n.f.s. (315) *wisdom*

12:3

גַּם־לִי adv. (168)-prep.-1 c.s. sf. *but I have*
לֵבָב n.m.s. (523) *understanding (heart)*
כְּמוֹכֶם prep.-2 m.p. sf. (455) *as well as you*
לֹא־נֹפֵל neg.-Qal act.ptc. (656; GK 152d) *not inferior*
אָנֹכִי pers.pr. 1 c.s. (59) *I*
מִכֶּם prep.-2 m.p. sf. *to you*
וְאֶת־מִי־ conj.-prep. (II 85)-interr. (566) *and with whom*
אֵין neg. (II 34) *there is not*
כְּמוֹ־אֵלֶּה adv. (455)-demons.adj. c.p. (41) *such things as these*

12:4

שְׂחֹק n.m.s. (966) *a laughingstock*
לְרֵעֵהוּ prep.-n.m.p.-3 m.s. sf. (945) *to his friends*
אֶהְיֶה Qal impf. 1 c.s. (הָיָה 224; LXX-3 m.s.) *I am*
קֹרֵא Qal act.ptc. m.s. (קָרָא 894; GK 111u) *who call*
לֶאֱלוֹהַּ prep.-n.m.s. (42) *upon God*
וַיַּעֲנֵהוּ consec.-Qal impf. 3 m.s.-3 m.s. sf. (עָנָה I 772) *and he answered him*
שְׂחוֹק v.supra *a laughingstock*
צַדִּיק adj. m.s. (843) *a just man*
תָּמִים adj. m.s. (1071) *a blameless man*

12:5

לַפִּיד prep.-def.art.-n.m.s. (810) *for misfortune*
בּוּז n.m.s. (100) *there is contempt*
לְעַשְׁתּוּת prep.-n.f.s. cstr. (799) *in thought of*
שַׁאֲנָן adj. m.s. paus. (983) *one who is at ease*
נָכוֹן Ni. ptc. m.s. (כּוּן I 465) *it is ready (prepared)*
לְמוֹעֲדֵי prep.-Qal act.ptc. m.p. cstr. (יָעַד 588) *for those whose ... slip*
רָגֶל n.f.s. paus. (919) *feet*

12:6

יִשְׁלָיוּ Qal impf. 3 m.p. (שָׁלָה I 1017; GK 29t,75u) *are at peace*
אֹהָלִים n.m.p. (13) *tents*

לְשֹׁדְדִים prep.-Qal act.ptc. m.p. (שָׁדַד 994) *of robbers*
וּבַטֻּחוֹת conj.-n.f.p. (105; GK 124e) *and security*
לְמַרְגִּיזֵי prep.-Hi. ptc. m.p. cstr. (רָגַז 919) *to those who provoke*
אֵל n.m.s. (42) *God*
לַאֲשֶׁר prep.-rel. (81) *who*
הֵבִיא Hi. pf. 3 m.s. (בּוֹא 97) *bring*
אֱלוֹהַּ n.m.s. (42) *God*
בְּיָדוֹ prep.-n.f.s.-3 m.s. sf. (388) *in his hand*

12:7

וְאוּלָם conj.-adv. (III 19) *but*
שְׁאַל־נָא Qal impv. 2 m.s. (שָׁאַל 981)-part.of entreaty (609) *ask now*
בְהֵמוֹת n.f.p. (96; GK 145k) *beasts*
וְתֹרֶךָּ conj.-Hi. impf. 3 f.s.-2 m.s. sf. (יָרָה 434) *and let one (of them) teach you*
וְעוֹף conj.-n.m.s. cstr. (733) *also the bird of*
הַשָּׁמַיִם def.art.-n.m. du. (1029) *the air (heavens)*
וְיַגֶּד־לָךְ conj.-Hi. impf. 3 m.s.-apoc.vol. (נָגַד 616)-prep.-2 m.s. sf. paus. *and let it tell you*

12:8

אוֹ שִׂיחַ conj. (14)-Qal impv. 2 m.s. (שִׂיחַ 967) *or speak*
לָאָרֶץ prep.-def.art.-n.f.s. (75) *to the earth*
וְתֹרֶךָּ v.supra *and let it teach you*
וִיסַפְּרוּ conj.-Pi. impf. 3 m.p. (סָפַר 707) *and let ... declare*
לְךָ prep.-2 m.s. sf. *to you*
דְּגֵי הַיָּם n.m.p. cstr. (185)-def.art.-n.m.s. (410) *the fish of the sea*

12:9

מִי interr. (566) *who*
לֹא־יָדַע neg.-Qal pf. 3 m.s. (393) *does not know*
בְּכָל־אֵלֶּה prep.-n.m.s. cstr. (481)-demons.adj. c.p. (41) *among all these*
כִּי יַד־יהוה conj. (471)-n.f.s. cstr. (388)-pr.n. (217) *that the hand of Yahweh*
עָשְׂתָה Qal pf. 3 f.s. (עָשָׂה I 793) *has done*
זֹּאת demons.adj. f.s. (260) *this*

12:10

אֲשֶׁר בְּיָדוֹ rel. (81)-prep.-n.f.s.-3 m.s. sf. (388) *in his hand*
נֶפֶשׁ n.f.s. cstr. (659) *the life of*
כָּל־חָי n.m.s. cstr. (481)-adj. m.s. paus. (311) *every living thing*
וְרוּחַ conj.-n.f.s. cstr. (924) *and breath of*
כָּל־בְּשַׂר־אִישׁ v.supra-n.m.s. cstr. (142)-n.m.s. (35) *all mankind*

12:11

הֲלֹא־אֹזֶן interr.-neg.-n.f.s. (23) *does not an ear*
מִלִּין n.f.p. (576) *words*
תִּבְחָן Qal impf. 3 f.s. (בָּחַן 103) *try*
וְחֵךְ conj.-n.m.s. (335) *as a palate*
אֹכֶל n.m.s. (38) *food*
יִטְעַם־לוֹ Qal impf. 3 m.s. (טָעַם 380; GK 135i)-prep.-3 m.s. sf. *tastes*

12:12

בִּישִׁישִׁים prep.-adj. m.p. (450) *with aged ones*
חָכְמָה n.f.s. (315) *wisdom*
וְאֹרֶךְ יָמִים conj.-n.m.s. cstr. (73; GK 161a)-n.m.p. (398) *and in length of days*
תְּבוּנָה n.f.s. (108) *understanding*

12:13

עִמּוֹ prep.-3 m.s. sf. (767) *with him*
חָכְמָה v.supra *wisdom*
וּגְבוּרָה conj.-n.f.s. (150) *and might*
לוֹ prep.-3 m.s. sf. *he has (to him)*
עֵצָה n.f.s. (420) *counsel*
וּתְבוּנָה conj.-v.supra *and understanding*

12:14

הֵן יַהֲרוֹס hypoth.part. (243)-Qal impf. 3 m.s. (248 הָרַס; GK 159w) *if he tears down*
וְלֹא יִבָּנֶה conj.-neg.-Ni. impf. 3 m.s. (בָּנָה 124) *and none can rebuild*
יִסְגֹּר Qal impf. 3 m.s. (סָגַר 688) *if he shuts in*
עַל־אִישׁ prep.-n.m.s. (35) *a man*
וְלֹא יִפָּתֵחַ conj.-neg.-Ni. impf. 3 m.s. (פָּתַח I 834) *none can open*

12:15

הֵן יַעְצֹר hypoth.part. (243)-Qal impf. 3 m.s. (783 עָצַר; GK 159w) *if he withholds*
בַּמַּיִם prep.-def.art.-n.m.p. (565) *the waters*
וְיִבָשׁוּ conj.-Qal impf. 3 m.p. paus. (יָבֵשׁ I 386; GK 15c) *they dry up*
וִישַׁלְּחֵם conj.-Pi. impf. 3 m.s.-3 m.p. sf. (שָׁלַח 1018) *if he sends them out*
וְיַהַפְכוּ conj.-Qal impf. 3 m.p. (הָפַךְ 245) *and they overwhelm*
אָרֶץ n.f.s. paus. (75) *the land*

12:16

עִמּוֹ prep.-3 m.s. sf. (767) *with him*
עֹז n.m.s. (738) *strength*

וְתוּשִׁיָּה conj.–n.f.s. (444) *and sound wisdom*
לוֹ prep.–3 m.s. sf. *are his (to him)*
שֹׁגֵג Qal act.ptc. (שָׁגַג 992; some rd. שׁוֹגֶה) *a deceiver*
וּמַשְׁגֶּה conj.–Hi. ptc. (שָׁגָה 993) *and a misleader*

12:17
מוֹלִיךְ Hi. ptc. (הָלַךְ 229; GK 116s) *he leads*
יוֹעֲצִים Qal act.ptc. m.p. (יָעַץ 419) *counselors*
שׁוֹלָל adj. m.s. (1021; GK 118o) *stripped (barefoot)*
וְשֹׁפְטִים conj.–Qal act.ptc. m.p. (שָׁפַט 1047; GK 116s) *and judges*
יְהוֹלֵל Po'el impf. 3 m.s. (הָלַל II 237; GK 116x) *he makes fools*

12:18
מוּסַר n.m.s. cstr. (64) *bonds of*
מְלָכִים n.m.p. (I 572) *kings*
פִּתֵּחַ Pi. pf. 3 m.s. (פָּתַח I 834) *he looses*
וַיֶּאְסֹר consec.–Qal impf. 3 m.s. (אָסַר 63) *and binds*
אֵזוֹר n.m.s. (25) *a waistcloth*
בְּמָתְנֵיהֶם prep.–n.m. du.–3 m.p. sf. (608) *on their loins*

12:19
מוֹלִיךְ v.supra (GK 116s) *he leads*
כֹּהֲנִים n.m.p. (463) *priests*
שׁוֹלָל v.supra *stripped*
וְאֵתָנִים conj.–adj. m.p. (I 450) *and them that are firmly seated*
יְסַלֵּף Pi. impf. 3 m.s. (סָלַף 701; GK 116x) *he subverts*

12:20
מֵסִיר Hi. ptc. m.s. (סוּר 693; GK 116s) *he deprives of*
שָׂפָה n.f.s. (973) *speech*
לְנֶאֱמָנִים prep.–Ni. ptc. m.p. (אָמַן 52) *those who are trusted*
וְטַעַם conj.–n.m.s. cstr. (381) *and the discernment of*
זְקֵנִים adj. m.p. (278) *elders*
יִקָּח Qal impf. 3 m.s. paus. (לָקַח 542) *he takes away*

12:21
שׁוֹפֵךְ Qal act.ptc. (שָׁפַךְ 1049) *he pours*
בּוּז n.m.s. (II 100) *contempt*
עַל־נְדִיבִים prep.–adj. m.p. (622) *on princes*
וּמְזִיחַ conj.–n.m.s. cstr. (561) *and a belt of*
אֲפִיקִים n.m.p. (67; some rd. אָפִיק = *strong*) *channels (streams)*
רִפָּה Pi. pf. 3 m.s. (רָפָה 951) *he looses*

12:22
מְגַלֶּה Pi. ptc. (גָּלָה 162) *he uncovers*
עֲמֻקוֹת adj. f.p. (771) *deeps*
מִנִּי־חֹשֶׁךְ prep.–n.m.s. (365) *out of darkness*
וַיֹּצֵא consec.–Hi. impf. 3 m.s. (יָצָא 422) *and brings*
לָאוֹר prep.–def.art.–n.m.s. (21) *to light*
צַלְמָוֶת n.m.s. (853) *deep darkness*

12:23
מַשְׂגִּיא Hi. ptc. (שָׂגָא 960; many rd. מַשְׁגִּיא as Hi. ptc. of שָׁגָה 993 = *he leads astray*) *he makes great*
לַגּוֹיִם prep.–def.art.–n.m.p. (156) *the nations*
וַיְאַבְּדֵם consec.–Pi. impf. 3 m.s.–3 m.p. sf. (אָבַד 1) *and he destroys them*
שֹׁטֵחַ Qal act.ptc. (שָׁטַח 1008; GK 117n) *he enlarges*
לַגּוֹיִם v.supra (some rd. לְאֻמִּים) *nations*
וַיַּנְחֵם consec.–Hi. impf. 3 m.s.–3 m.p. sf. (נָחָה 634) *and leads them away*

12:24
מֵסִיר Hi. ptc. (סוּר 693) *he takes away*
לֵב n.m.s. (524) *understanding*
רָאשֵׁי n.m.p. cstr. (910; GK 128a) *(from) the chiefs of*
עַם־ n.m.s. cstr. (I 766; LXX>) *the people of*
הָאָרֶץ def.art.–n.f.s. (75) *the earth*
וַיַּתְעֵם consec.–Hi. impf. 3 m.s.–3 m.p. sf. (תָּעָה 1073) *and makes them wander*
בְּתֹהוּ prep.–n.m.s. (1062) *in a waste*
לֹא־דָרֶךְ neg.–n.m.s. paus. (202; GK 152u) *pathless*

12:25
יְמַשְׁשׁוּ־ Pi. impf. 3 m.p. (מָשַׁשׁ 606) *they grope*
חֹשֶׁךְ n.m.s. (365) *in the dark*
וְלֹא־אוֹר conj.–neg.–n.m.s. (21) *without light*
וַיַּתְעֵם v.supra (LXX πλανηθείησαν) *he makes them stagger*
כַּשִּׁכּוֹר prep.–def.art.–adj. m.s. (1016) *like a drunken man*

13:1
הֶן־כֹּל interj. (II 243)–n.m.s. (481; some mss.+ ταῦτα) *lo, all this*
רָאֲתָה Qal pf. 3 f.s. (רָאָה 906) *has seen*

עֵינִי n.f.s.-1 c.s. sf. (744) *my eye*
שָׁמְעָה Qal pf. 3 f.s. (שָׁמַע 1033) *has heard*
אָזְנִי n.f.s.-1 c.s. sf. (23) *my ear*
וַתָּבֶן־לָהּ consec.-Qal impf. 3 f.s. (בִּין 106) -prep.-3 f.s. sf. *and understood it*

13:2

כְּדַעְתְּכֶם prep.-n.f.s.-2 m.p. sf. (395) *what you know*
יָדַעְתִּי Qal pf. 1 c.s. (יָדַע 393) *I know*
גַּם־אָנִי adv. (168)-pers.pr. 1 c.s. paus. (58) *even I*
לֹא־נֹפֵל neg.-Qal act.ptc. (נָפַל 656) *not inferior*
אָנֹכִי מִכֶּם pers.pr. 1 c.s. (59)-prep.-2 m.p. sf. *I ... to you*

13:3

אוּלָם אֲנִי adv. (III 19)-pers.pr. 1 c.s. (58) *but I*
אֶל־שַׁדַּי prep.-pr.n. (994) *to the Almighty*
אֲדַבֵּר Pi. impf. 1 c.s. (דָּבַר 180) *would speak*
וְהוֹכֵחַ conj.-Hi. inf.abs. (יָכַח 406; GK 53k,113d) *and to argue my case*
אֶל־אֵל prep.-n.m.s. (42) *with God*
אֶחְפָּץ Qal impf. 1 c.s. paus. (חָפֵץ 342) *I desire*

13:4

וְאוּלָם אַתֶּם conj.-adv. (III 19)-pers.pr. 2 m.p. (61) *but as for you*
טֹפְלֵי־ Qal act.ptc. m.p. cstr. (טָפַל 381) *you whitewash (smear) with*
שָׁקֶר n.m.s. paus. (1055) *lies*
רֹפְאֵי Qal act.ptc. m.p. cstr. (רָפָא 950) *physicians of*
אֱלִל n.m.s. (47) *worthlessness*
כֻּלְּכֶם n.m.s.-2 m.p. sf. (481) *all of you*

13:5

מִי־יִתֵּן interr. (566)-Qal impf. 3 m.s. (נָתַן 678) *oh that*
הַחֲרֵשׁ תַּחֲרִישׁוּן Hi. inf.abs. (חָרַשׁ II 361)-Hi. impf. 2 m.p. (II 361) *you would keep absolutely silent*
וּתְהִי לָכֶם conj.-Qal impf. 3 f.s. (הָיָה 224) -prep.-2 m.p. sf. *and it would be your*
לְחָכְמָה prep.-n.f.s. (315) *wisdom*

13:6

שִׁמְעוּ־נָא Qal impv. 2 m.p. (1033)-part.of entreaty (609) *hear now*
תּוֹכַחְתִּי n.f.s.-1 c.s. sf. (407; LXX ἔλεγχον στόματός μου) *my reasoning*
וְרִבוֹת conj.-n.m.p. cstr. (936; LXX κρίσιν) *and pleadings of*
שְׂפָתַי n.f. du.-1 c.s. sf. (973) *my lips*
הַקְשִׁיבוּ Hi. impv. 2 m.p. (קָשַׁב 904) *listen to*

13:7

הַלְאֵל interr.-prep.-n.m.s. (42) *for God?*
תְּדַבְּרוּ Pi. impf. 2 m.p. (דָּבַר 180) *will you speak?*
עַוְלָה n.f.s. (732) *falsely*
וְלוֹ conj.-prep.-3 m.s. sf. (GK 150h) *and for him*
תְּדַבְּרוּ v.supra (LXX φθέγγεσθε) *will you speak?*
רְמִיָּה n.f.s. (I 941) *deceitfully*

13:8

הֲפָנָיו interr.-n.m.p.-3 m.s. sf. (815) *toward him?*
תִּשָּׂאוּן Qal impf. 2 m.p. (נָשָׂא 669) *will you show partiality?*
אִם־לָאֵל hypoth.part. (49)-prep.-def.art.-n.m.s. (42) *or for God?*
תְּרִיבוּן Qal impf. 2 m.p. (רִיב 936) *will you plead the case?*

13:9

הֲטוֹב interr.-adj. m.s. (II 373) *will it be well?*
כִּי־יַחְקֹר conj. (471)-Qal impf. 3 m.s. (חָקַר 350) *when he searches out*
אֶתְכֶם dir.obj.-2 m.p. sf. *you*
אִם־כְּהָתֵל conj. (49)-prep.-Hi. inf.cstr. (תָּלַל II 1068) *or as one deceives*
בֶּאֱנוֹשׁ prep.-n.m.s. (60) *a man?*
תְּהָתֵלּוּ Hi. impf. 2 m.p. (תָּלַל II 1068; GK 53q) *can you deceive*
בוֹ prep.-3 m.s. sf. *him*

13:10

הוֹכֵחַ יוֹכִיחַ Hi. inf.abs. (יָכַח 406)-Hi. impf. 3 m.s. (406) *he will surely rebuke*
אֶתְכֶם dir.obj.-2 m.p. sf. *you*
אִם־בַּסֵּתֶר hypoth.part. (49)-prep.-def.art.-n.m.s. (712) *if in secret*
פָּנִים תִּשָּׂאוּן n.m.p. (815)-Qal impf. 2 m.p. (נָשָׂא 669; Syr.,Sym.,Targ.,V פָּנָיו) *you show partiality*

13:11

הֲלֹא שְׂאֵתוֹ interr.-neg.-n.f.s.-3 m.s. sf. (673) *will not his majesty?*
תְּבַעֵת Pi. impf. 3 f.s. (בָּעַת 129) *terrify*
אֶתְכֶם dir.obj.-2 m.p. sf. *you*
וּפַחְדּוֹ conj.-n.m.s.-3 m.s. sf. (808) *and the dread of him*
יִפֹּל Qal impf. 3 m.s. (נָפַל 656) *fall*
עֲלֵיכֶם prep.-2 m.p. sf. *upon you*

13:12

זִכְרֹנֵיכֶם n.m.p.-2 m.p. sf. (272) *your memorial-sentences (maxims)*

מִשְׁלֵי־ n.m.p. cstr. (605) *proverbs of*

אֵפֶר n.m.s. (68) *ashes*

לְגַבֵּי־חֹמֶר prep.-n.m.p. cstr. (146)-n.m.s. (I 330) *defenses (bulwarks) of clay*

גַּבֵּיכֶם n.m.p.-2 m.p. sf. (146) *your defenses*

13:13

הַחֲרִישׁוּ מִמֶּנִּי Hi. impv. 2 m.p. (חָרַשׁ II 361) -prep.-1 c.s. sf. (GK 119ff; LXX>) *let me have silence*

וַאֲדַבְּרָה־אָנִי conj.-Pi. impf. 1 c.s.-vol.he (דָּבַר 180)-pers.pr. 1 c.s. (58) *and I want to speak*

וְיַעֲבֹר conj.-Qal impf. 3 m.s. vol. (עָבַר 716) *and let come*

עָלַי prep.-1 c.s. sf. *over me*

מָה interr. (552; GK 137c) *what may*

13:14

עַל־מָה אֶשָּׂא prep.-interr. (552; LXX>)-Qal impf. 1 c.s. (נָשָׂא 669) *why should I take*

בְשָׂרִי n.m.s.-1 c.s. sf. (142) *my flesh*

בְשִׁנָּי prep.-n.f.p.-1 c.s. sf. paus. (I 1042) *in my teeth*

וְנַפְשִׁי conj.-n.f.s.-1 c.s. sf. (659) *and my life*

אָשִׂים Qal impf. 1 c.s. (שִׂים 962) *should I put*

בְּכַפִּי prep.-n.f.s.-1 c.s. sf. (496) *in my hand*

13:15

הֵן יִקְטְלֵנִי interj. (243)-Qal impf. 3 m.s.-1 c.s. sf. (קָטַל 881) *behold he will slay me*

לֹא אֲיַחֵל neg.-Pi. impf. 1 c.s. (יָחַל 403; Q לוֹ *in him) I have no hope*

אַךְ־דְּרָכַי adv. (36)-n.m.p.-1 c.s. sf. (202; GK 153) *yet my ways*

אֶל־פָּנָיו prep.-n.m.p.-3 m.s. sf. (815) *to his face*

אוֹכִיחַ Hi. impf. 1 c.s. (יָכַח 406) *I will defend*

13:16

גַּם־הוּא־ adv. (168)-demons.adj. m.s. (214; LXX καὶ τοῦτο) *indeed this*

לִי לִישׁוּעָה prep.-1 c.s. sf.-prep.-n.f.s. (447) *to me salvation*

כִּי־לֹא לְפָנָיו conj. (471)-neg.-prep.-n.m.p.-3 m.s. sf. (815; GK 152e) *that not before him*

חָנֵף adj. m.s. (338) *a godless man*

יָבוֹא Qal impf. 3 m.s. (בּוֹא 97) *shall come*

13:17

שִׁמְעוּ שָׁמוֹעַ Qal impv. 2 m.p. (1033)-Qal inf.abs. (1033; GK 113r) *listen carefully*

מִלָּתִי n.f.s.-1 c.s. sf. (576) *to my words*

וְאַחֲוָתִי conj.-n.f.s.-1 c.s. sf. (296; LXX ἀναγγελῶ) *and my declaration*

בְּאָזְנֵיכֶם prep.-n.f.p.-2 m.p. sf. (23) *in your ears*

13:18

הִנֵּה־נָא interj. (243)-part.of entreaty (609) *behold*

עָרַכְתִּי Qal pf. 1 c.s. (עָרַךְ 789) *I have prepared*

מִשְׁפָּט n.m.s. (1048) *my case*

יָדַעְתִּי Qal pf. 1 c.s. (יָדַע 393) *I know*

כִּי־אֲנִי conj. (471)-pers.pr. 1 c.s. (58) *that I*

אֶצְדָּק Qal impf. 1 c.s. paus. (צָדַק 842) *shall be vindicated*

13:19

מִי־הוּא interr. (566)-pers.pr. 3 m.s. (214) *who is he who*

יָרִיב Qal impf. 3 m.s. (רִיב 936) *will contend*

עִמָּדִי prep.-1 c.s. sf. (767) *with me?*

כִּי־עַתָּה conj. (471)-adv. (773) *for then*

אַחֲרִישׁ Hi. impf. 1 c.s. (חָרַשׁ II 361) *I would be silent*

וְאֶגְוָע conj.-Qal impf. 1 c.s. paus. (גָּוַע 157) *and would die*

13:20

אַךְ־שְׁתַּיִם adv. (36)-n.f. du. (1040) *only two things*

אַל־תַּעַשׂ neg.-Qal impf. 2 m.s. apoc.vol. (עָשָׂה I 793) *do not do*

עִמָּדִי prep.-1 c.s. sf. (767) *with me*

אָז מִפָּנֶיךָ adv. (23)-prep.-n.m.p.-2 m.s. sf. (815) *then from your face*

לֹא אֶסָּתֵר neg.-Ni. impf. 1 c.s. (סָתַר 711) *I will not hide myself*

13:21

כַּפְּךָ n.f.s.-2 m.s. sf. (496) *your hand*

מֵעָלַי prep.-prep.-1 c.s. sf. *from me*

הַרְחַק Hi. impv. 2 m.s. (רָחַק 934; GK 29q,64h) *withdraw far*

וְאֵמָתְךָ conj.-n.f.s.-2 m.s. sf. (33) *and the dread of you*

אַל־תְּבַעֲתַנִּי neg.-Pi. impf. 3 f.s.-1 c.s. sf. (בָּעַת 129; GK 60d) *let not terrify me*

13:22

וּקְרָא conj.-Qal impv. 2 m.s. (894) *then call*

וְאָנֹכִי אֶעֱנֶה conj.-pers.pr. 1 c.s. (59)-Qal impf. 1 c.s. (עָנָה I 772) *and I will answer*
אוֹ־אֲדַבֵּר conj. (14)-Pi. impf. 1 c.s. (דָּבַר 180) *or let me speak*
וַהֲשִׁיבֵנִי conj.-Hi. impv. 2 m.s.-1 c.s. sf. (שׁוּב 996) *and do reply to me*

13:23

כַּמָּה prep.-def.art.-interr. (552) *how many*
לִי prep.-1 c.s. sf. *(to me) are my*
עֲוֹנוֹת n.f.p. (730) *iniquities*
וְחַטָּאוֹת conj.-n.f.p. (308) *and sins?*
פִּשְׁעִי n.m.s.-1 c.s. sf. (833) *my transgression*
וְחַטָּאתִי conj.-n.f.s.-1 c.s. sf. (308) *and my sin*
הֹדִיעֵנִי Hi. impv. 2 m.s.-1 c.s. sf. (יָדַע 393) *make me know*

13:24

לָמָּה־פָנֶיךָ prep.-interr. (552)-n.m.p.-2 m.s. sf. (815) *why ... your face*
תַסְתִּיר Hi. impf. 2 m.s. (סָתַר 711) *do you hide*
וְתַחְשְׁבֵנִי conj.-Qal impf. 2 m.s.-1 c.s. sf. (חָשַׁב 362) *and count me*
לְאוֹיֵב לָךְ prep.-Qal act.ptc. as n.m.s. (33) -prep.-2 m.s. sf. paus. *as your enemy?*

13:25

הֶעָלֶה נִדָּף interr.part. (GK 100n)-n.m.s. (750)-Ni. ptc. as n.m.s. (623) *a driven leaf?*
תַּעֲרוֹץ Qal impf. 2 m.s. (עָרַץ 791) *will you frighten?*
וְאֶת־קַשׁ יָבֵשׁ conj.-dir.obj.-n.m.s. (905)-adj. m.s. (386; GK 117c) *and dry chaff*
תִּרְדֹּף Qal impf. 2 m.s. (רָדַף 922) *will you pursue?*

13:26

כִּי־תִכְתֹּב conj. (471)-Qal impf. 2 m.s. (כָּתַב 507) *for you write*
עָלַי prep.-1 c.s. sf. *against me*
מְרֹרוֹת n.f.p. (601; GK 124e) *bitter things*
וְתוֹרִישֵׁנִי conj.-Hi. impf. 2 m.s.-1 c.s. sf. (יָרַשׁ 439) *and make me inherit*
עֲוֹנוֹת נְעוּרָי n.m.p. cstr. (730)-n.m.p.-1 c.s. sf. paus. (655) *the iniquities of my youth*

13:27

וְתָשֵׂם conj.-Qal impf. 2 m.s. apoc. (?) (שִׂים 962) *you put*
בַּסַּד prep.-def.art.-n.m.s. (690) *in the stocks*
רַגְלַי n.f.p.-1 c.s. sf. (919) *my feet*
וְתִשְׁמוֹר conj.-Qal impf. 2 m.s. (שָׁמַר 1036) *and you watch*
כָּל־אָרְחוֹתָי n.m.s. cstr. (481)-n.m.p.-1 c.s. sf. paus. (73; GK 93r) *all my paths*
עַל־שָׁרְשֵׁי prep.-n.m.p. cstr. (1057) *to the soles of*
רַגְלַי n.f.p.-1 c.s. sf. (919) *my feet*
תִּתְחַקֶּה Hith. impf. 2 m.s. paus. (חָקָה 348; GK 54f) *you set a bound*

13:28

וְהוּא conj.-pers.pr. 3 m.s. (214; GK 144p) *and he*
כְּרָקָב prep.-n.m.s. (955; LXX ἴσα ἀσκῷ) *like a rotten thing*
יִבְלֶה Qal impf. 3 m.s. (בָּלָה 115) *wastes away*
כְּבֶגֶד prep.-n.m.s. (93; GK 155h) *like a garment*
אֲכָלוֹ Qal pf. 3 m.s.-3 m.s. sf. (אָכַל 37) *that is ... eaten*
עָשׁ n.m.s. (II 799) *moth*

14:1

אָדָם n.m.s. (9) *man*
יְלוּד Qal pass.ptc. m.s. cstr. (יָלַד 408; GK 116,l) *that is born of*
אִשָּׁה n.f.s. (61) *a woman*
קְצַר יָמִים adj. m.s. cstr. (894)-n.m.p. (398) *of few days*
וּשְׂבַע־רֹגֶז conj.-adj. m.s. cstr. (960)-n.m.s. (919) *and full of trouble*

14:2

כְּצִיץ prep.-n.m.s. (I 847) *like a flower*
יָצָא Qal pf. 3 m.s. (422; GK 111s) *he comes forth*
וַיִּמָּל consec.-Qal impf. 3 m.s. paus. (מָלַל III 576) *and withers*
וַיִּבְרַח consec.-Qal impf. 3 m.s. (בָּרַח 137) *and he flees*
כַּצֵּל prep.-def.art.-n.m.s. (853) *like the shadow*
וְלֹא יַעֲמוֹד conj.-neg.-Qal impf. 3 m.s. (עָמַד 763) *and continues not*

14:3

אַף־עַל־זֶה conj. (II 64)-prep.-demons.adj. m.s. (260; GK 153) *yea, upon such a one*
פָּקַחְתָּ Qal pf. 2 m.s. (פָּקַח 824) *do you open*
עֵינֶךָ n.f. du.-2 m.s. sf. (744) *your eyes*
וְאֹתִי תָבִיא conj.-dir.obj.-1 c.s. sf.-Hi. impf. 2 m.s. (בּוֹא 97; LXX καὶ τοῦτον ἐποιήσας εἰσελθεῖν) *and me you bring*
בְמִשְׁפָּט prep.-n.m.s. (1048) *into judgment*
עִמָּךְ prep.-2 m.s. sf. paus. *with you?*

14:4

מִי־יִתֵּן interr. (566)–Qal impf. 3 m.s. (נָתַן 678; GK 151b) *who can?*
טָהוֹר adj. m.s. (373) *a clean thing*
מִטָּמֵא prep.–adj. m.s. (II 379) *out of an unclean?*
לֹא אֶחָד neg.–num. (25) *there is not one*

14:5

אִם חֲרוּצִים hypoth.part. (49)–Qal pass.part. m.p. (חָרַץ I 358) *if are determined*
יָמָיו n.m.p.–3 m.s. sf. (398) *his days*
מִסְפַּר־ n.m.s. cstr. (708) *the number of*
חֳדָשָׁיו n.m.p.–3 m.s. sf. (I 294) *his months*
אִתָּךְ prep.–2 m.s. sf. paus. (II 85) *is with you*
חֻקָּו n.m.p.–3 m.s. sf. (349; LXX εἰς χρόνον) *his bounds*
עָשִׂיתָ Qal pf. 2 m.s. (עָשָׂה I 793) *you have appointed*
וְלֹא יַעֲבוֹר conj.–neg.–Qal impf. 3 m.s. (עָבַר 716) *that he cannot pass*

14:6

שְׁעֵה Qal impv. 2 m.s. (שָׁעָה 1043) *look away*
מֵעָלָיו prep.–prep.–3 m.s. sf. *from him*
וְיֶחְדָּל conj.–Qal impf. 3 m.s. paus. (חָדַל 292; GK 109f) *that he may desist*
עַד־יִרְצֶה prep. (III 723)–Qal impf. 3 m.s. (רָצָה 953) *that he may enjoy*
כְּשָׂכִיר prep.–adj. m.s. (969) *like a hireling*
יוֹמוֹ n.m.s.–3 m.s. sf. (398) *his day*

14:7

כִּי יֵשׁ conj. (471)–subst. (441) *for there is*
לָעֵץ prep.–def.art.–n.m.s. (781) *for the tree*
תִּקְוָה n.f.s. (876) *hope*
אִם־יִכָּרֵת hypoth.part. (49)–Ni. impf. 3 m.s. (כָּרַת 503) *if it be cut down*
וְעוֹד conj.–adv. (728) *that again*
יַחֲלִיף Hi. impf. 3 m.s. (חָלַף 322) *it may show newness*
וְיֹנַקְתּוֹ conj.–n.f.s.–3 m.s. sf. (413) *and that its shoots*
לֹא תֶחְדָּל neg.–Qal impf. 3 f.s. paus. (חָדַל 292) *may not cease*

14:8

אִם־יַזְקִין hypoth.part. (49)–Hi. impf. 3 m.s. (זָקֵן 278) *though ... grow old*
בָּאָרֶץ prep.–def.art.–n.f.s. (75) *in the earth*
שָׁרְשׁוֹ n.m.s.–3 m.s. sf. (1057) *its root*
וּבֶעָפָר conj.–prep.–def.art.–n.m.s. (779) *and in the ground*
יָמוּת Qal impf. 3 m.s. (מוּת 559) *die*
גִּזְעוֹ n.m.s.–3 m.s. sf. (160) *its stump*

14:9

מֵרֵיחַ prep.–n.m.s. cstr. (926) *at a scent of*
מַיִם n.m.p. (565) *water*
יַפְרִחַ Hi. impf. 3 m.s. (פָּרַח I 827; GK 65e) *it will bud*
וְעָשָׂה conj.–Qal pf. 3 m.s. (I 793; GK 112m) *and put forth*
קָצִיר n.m. coll. (II 894) *branches*
כְּמוֹ־נָטַע prep.–n.m.s. paus. (642) *like a young plant*

14:10

וְגֶבֶר conj.–n.m.s. (149) *but a man*
יָמוּת Qal impf. 3 m.s. (מוּת 559; GK 111t) *dies*
וַיֶּחֱלָשׁ consec.–Qal impf. 3 m.s. paus. (חָלַשׁ 325; GK 111t; LXX ᾤχετο) *and is prostrate*
וַיִּגְוַע consec.–Qal impf. 3 m.s. (גָּוַע 157) *and breathes his last*
אָדָם n.m.s. (9) *man*
וְאַיּוֹ conj.–interr.adv. –3 m.s. sf. (32; LXX οὐκέτι ἔστιν) *and where is he?*

14:11

אָזְלוּ־מַיִם Qal pf. 3 c.p. (אָזַל 23)–n.m.p. (565) *waters fail*
מִנִּי־יָם prep.–n.m.s. (410) *from a lake*
וְנָהָר conj.–n.m.s. (625) *and a river*
יֶחֱרַב Qal impf. 3 m.s. (חָרֵב II 351) *wastes away*
וְיָבֵשׁ conj.–Qal pf. 3 m.s. (I 386) *and dries up*

14:12

וְאִישׁ שָׁכַב conj.–n.m.s. (35)–Qal pf. 3 m.s. (1011) *man lies down*
וְלֹא־יָקוּם conj.–neg.–Qal impf. 3 m.s. (קוּם 877) *and rises not again*
עַד־בִּלְתִּי prep. (III 723)–neg. (116) *till ... no more*
שָׁמַיִם n.m. du. (1029) *heavens*
לֹא יָקִיצוּ neg.–Hi. impf. 3 m.p. (קִיץ I 884) *they will not awake*
וְלֹא־יֵעֹרוּ conj.–neg.–Ni. impf. 3 m.p. (עוּר I 734) *or be roused*
מִשְּׁנָתָם prep.–n.f.s.–3 m.p. sf. (446) *out of his (their) sleep*

14:13

מִי יִתֵּן interr. (566)–Qal impf. 3 m.s. (נָתַן 678) *oh that*
בִּשְׁאוֹל prep.–n.f.s. (982) *in Sheol*

תַּצְפִּנֵנִי Hi. impf. 2 m.s.-1 c.s. sf. (צָפַן 860) *you would hide me*
תַּסְתִּירֵנִי Hi. impf. 2 m.s.-1 c.s. sf. (סָתַר 711) *you would conceal me*
עַד־שׁוּב prep. (III 723)-Qal inf.cstr. (שׁוּב 996) *until the turning back of*
אַפֶּךָ n.m.s.-2 m.s. sf. (I 60) *your wrath*
תָּשִׁית לִי Qal impf. 2 m.s. (שִׁית 1011)-prep.-1 c.s. sf. *you would appoint me*
חֹק n.m.s. (349) *a set time*
וְתִזְכְּרֵנִי conj.-Qal impf. 2 m.s.-1 c.s. sf. (זָכַר 269) *and remember me*

14:14

אִם־יָמוּת hypoth.part. (49)-Qal impf. 3 m.s. (מוּת 559) *if ... die*
גֶּבֶר n.m.s. (149) *a man*
הֲיִחְיֶה interr.part.-Qal impf. 3 m.s. (חָיָה 310) *may he live again?*
כָּל־יְמֵי n.m.s. cstr. (481)-n.m.p. cstr. (398) *all the days of*
צְבָאִי n.m.s.-1 c.s. sf. (838) *my service*
אֲיַחֵל Pi. impf. 1 c.s. (יָחַל 403) *I would wait*
עַד־בּוֹא prep. (III 723)-Qal inf.cstr. (בּוֹא 97) *till the coming of*
חֲלִיפָתִי n.f.s.-1 c.s. sf. (322) *my release*

14:15

תִּקְרָא Qal impf. 2 m.s. (קָרָא 894) *you would call*
וְאָנֹכִי conj.-pers.pr. 1 c.s. (59) *and I (on my part)*
אֶעֱנֶךָּ Qal impf. 1 c.s.-2 m.s. sf. (עָנָה I 772) *would answer you*
לְמַעֲשֵׂה prep.-n.m.s. cstr. (795) *for the work of*
יָדֶיךָ n.f.p.-2 m.s. sf. (388) *your hands*
תִכְסֹף Qal impf. 2 m.s. (כָּסַף 493) *you would long for*

14:16

כִּי־עַתָּה conj.-adv. (773) *for then*
צְעָדַי n.m.p.-1 c.s. sf. (857) *my steps*
תִּסְפּוֹר Qal impf. 2 m.s. (סָפַר 707) *you would number*
לֹא־תִשְׁמוֹר neg.-Qal impf. 2 m.s. (שָׁמַר 1036; LXX καὶ οὐ μὴ παρέλθῃ σε οὐδέν) *you would not keep watch*
עַל־חַטָּאתִי prep.-n.f.s.-1 c.s. sf. (308) *my sin*

14:17

חָתֻם Qal pass.ptc. (חָתַם 367) *sealed up*
בִּצְרוֹר prep.-n.m.s. (I 865) *in a bag*
פִּשְׁעִי n.m.s.-1 c.s. sf. (833) *my transgression*
וַתִּטְפֹּל consec.-Qal impf. 2 m.s. (טָפַל 381) *and you would cover*
עַל־עֲוֺנִי prep.-n.m.s.-1 c.s. sf. (730) *over my iniquity*

14:18

וְאוּלָם conj.-adv. (III 19) *but*
הַר־נוֹפֵל n.m.s. (249)-Qal act.ptc. (נָפַל 656) *a mountain falls*
יִבּוֹל Qal impf. 3 m.s. (נָבֵל 615; GK 66d; LXX διαπεσεῖται) *crumbles away*
וְצוּר conj.-n.m.s. (849) *and a rock*
יֶעְתַּק Qal impf. 3 m.s. (עָתַק) *is removed*
מִמְּקֹמוֹ prep.-n.m.s.-3 m.s. sf. (879) *from its place*

14:19

אֲבָנִים n.f.p. (6) *stones*
שָׁחֲקוּ Qal pf. 3 c.p. (שָׁחַק 1006) *wear away*
מַיִם n.m.p. (565) *waters*
תִּשְׁטֹף־ Qal impf. 3 f.s. (שָׁטַף 1009; GK 145k) *wash away*
סְפִיחֶיהָ n.m.p.-3 f.s. sf. (I 705; txt.dub.) *its outpourings*
עֲפַר־אָרֶץ n.m.s. cstr. (779)-n.f.s. paus. (75) *soil of earth*
וְתִקְוַת conj.-n.f.s. cstr. (876) *and hope of*
אֱנוֹשׁ n.m.s. (61) *man*
הֶאֱבַדְתָּ Hi. pf. 2 m.s. (אָבַד 1) *you destroy*

14:20

תִּתְקְפֵהוּ Qal impf. 2 m.s.-3 m.s. sf. (תָּקַף 1075) *you prevail against him*
לָנֶצַח prep.-n.m.s. (664) *for ever*
וַיַּהֲלֹךְ consec.-Qal impf. 3 m.s. (הָלַךְ 229) *and he passes*
מְשַׁנֶּה Pi. ptc. m.s. (שָׁנָה I 1039) *changes*
פָּנָיו n.m.p.-3 m.s. sf. (815) *his countenance*
וַתְּשַׁלְּחֵהוּ consec.-Pi. impf. 2 m.s.-3 m.s. sf. (1018 שָׁלַח) *and send him away*

14:21

יִכְבְּדוּ Qal impf. 3 m.p. (כָּבֵד 457) *come to honor*
בָנָיו n.m.p.-3 m.s. sf. (119) *his sons*
וְלֹא יֵדָע conj.-neg.-Qal impf. 3 m.s. paus. (יָדַע 393) *and he does not know it*
וְיִצְעֲרוּ conj.-Qal impf. 3 m.p. (צָעַר 858) *and they are brought low*
וְלֹא־יָבִין לָמוֹ conj.-neg.-Qal impf. 3 m.s. (בִּין 106)-prep.-3 m.p. sf. *and he perceives them not*

14:22

אַף־בְּשָׂרוֹ adv. (36)-n.m.s.-3 m.s. sf. (142; GK 153) *only his own body*
עָלָיו prep.-3 m.s. sf. *upon himself*
יִכְאָב Qal impf. 3 m.s. paus. (כָּאַב 456) *he feels the pain*
וְנַפְשׁוֹ conj.-n.f.s.-3 m.s. sf. (659) *and he himself*
עָלָיו prep.-3 m.s. sf. *for himself*
תֶּאֱבָל Qal impf. 3 f.s. paus. (אָבַל 1) *mourns*

15:1

וַיַּעַן consec.-Qal impf. 3 m.s. (עָנָה I 772) *then answered*
אֱלִיפַז pr.n. (45) *Eliphaz*
הַתֵּמָנִי def.art.-adj.gent. (412) *the Temanite*
וַיֹּאמַר consec.-Qal impf. 3 m.s. (אָמַר 55)

15:2

הֶחָכָם interr.part. (GK 10n)-adj. m.s. (314) *a wise man?*
יַעֲנֶה Qal impf. 3 m.s. (עָנָה I 772) *should answer?*
דַעַת־רוּחַ n.f.s. cstr. (395)-n.f.s. (924) *windy knowledge*
וִימַלֵּא conj.-Pi. impf. 3 m.s. (569) *and fill*
קָדִים n.m.s. (870) *east wind*
בִּטְנוֹ n.f.s.-3 m.s. sf. (105) *his body (himself)*

15:3

הוֹכֵחַ Hi. inf.abs. (יָכַח 406; GK 113h) *an arguing*
בְּדָבָר prep.-n.m.s. (182) *in talk*
לֹא יִסְכּוֹן neg.-Qal impf. 3 m.s. (סָכַן I 698) *which will not profit*
וּמִלִּים conj.-n.f.p. (576) *or words*
לֹא־יוֹעִיל בָּם neg.-Hi. impf. 3 m.s. (יָעַל I 418) -prep.-3 m.p. sf. *with which he can do no good*

15:4

אַף־אַתָּה conj. (II 64)-pers.pr. 2 m.s. (61) *but you*
תָּפֵר Hi. impf. 2 m.s. (פָּרַר I 830) *are doing away with*
יִרְאָה n.f.s. (432) *fear*
וְתִגְרַע conj.-Qal impf. 2 m.s. (גָּרַע 175) *and you are hindering*
שִׂיחָה n.f.s. (967) *meditation (complaint)*
לִפְנֵי־אֵל prep.-n.m.p. cstr. (815)-n.m.s. (42) *before God*

15:5

כִּי יְאַלֵּף conj. (471)-Pi. impf. 3 m.s. (אָלַף I 48) *for teaches*
עֲוֹנְךָ n.m.s.-2 m.s. sf. (730) *your iniquity*
פִיךָ n.m.s.-2 m.s. sf. (804) *your mouth*
וְתִבְחַר conj.-Qal impf. 2 m.s. (בָּחַר 103) *and you choose*
לְשׁוֹן n.f.s. cstr. (546) *the tongue of*
עֲרוּמִים adj. m.p. (791) *crafty ones*

15:6

יַרְשִׁיעֲךָ Hi. impf. 3 m.s.-2 m.s. sf. (רָשַׁע 957) *condemns you*
פִיךָ n.m.s.-2 m.s. sf. (804) *your own mouth*
וְלֹא־אָנִי conj.-neg.-pers.pr. 1 c.s. (58) *and not I*
וּשְׂפָתֶיךָ conj.-n.f.p.-2 m.s. sf. (973) *and your own lips*
יַעֲנוּ־ Qal impf. 3 m.p. (עָנָה I 772; GK 145u) *testify*
בָךְ prep.-2 m.s. sf. paus. *against you*

15:7

הֲרִאישׁוֹן אָדָם interr.-adj. m.s. cstr. (911)-n.m.s. (9) *the first man?*
תִּוָּלֵד Ni. impf. 2 m.s. (יָלַד 408; GK 121d) *were you born?*
וְלִפְנֵי conj.-prep.-n.m.p. cstr. (815; GK 150h) *or before*
גְבָעוֹת n.f.p. (148) *hills*
חוֹלָלְתָּ Polal pf. 2 m.s. paus. (חוּל I 296) *were you brought forth*

15:8

הַבְסוֹד interr.-prep.-n.m.s. cstr. (691) *in the council of*
אֱלוֹהַ n.m.s. (42) *God?*
תִּשְׁמָע Qal impf. 2 m.s. paus. (שָׁמַע 1033) *have you listened?*
וְתִגְרַע conj.-Qal impf. 2 m.s. (גָּרַע 175) *and do you limit*
אֵלֶיךָ prep.-2 m.s. sf. *to yourself*
חָכְמָה n.f.s. (315) *wisdom*

15:9

מַה־יָּדַעְתָּ interr. (552)-Qal pf. 2 m.s. (יָדַע 393) *what do you know*
וְלֹא־נֵדָע conj.-neg.-Qal impf. 1 c.s. (יָדַע 393) *that we do not know*
תָּבִין Qal impf. 2 m.s. (בִּין 106) *what do you understand*
וְלֹא־עִמָּנוּ conj.-neg.-prep.-1 c.p. sf. (767) *and not with us*
הוּא demons.adj. m.s. (214) *it*

15:10

גַּם־שָׂב adv. (168)-Qal act.ptc. (שִׂיב 966) *both the gray-haired*
גַּם־יָשִׁישׁ v.supra-adj. m.s. (450) *and aged*
בָּנוּ prep.-1 c.p. sf. *among us*
כַּבִּיר adj. m.s. (460; GK 131q) *older (greater)*
מֵאָבִיךָ prep.-n.m.s.-2 m.s. sf. (3) *than your father*
יָמִים n.m.p. (398; GK 131q) *in days*

15:11

הַמְעַט interr.-adv. (589) *too small?*
מִמְּךָ prep.-2 m.s. sf. *for you*
תַּנְחֻמוֹת n.m.p. cstr. (637) *the consolations of*
אֵל n.m.s. (42) *God*
וְדָבָר conj.-n.m.s. (182) *or a word*
לָאַט prep.-adv. (31) *gently*
עִמָּךְ prep.-2 m.s. sf. paus. *with you*

15:12

מַה־יִּקָּחֲךָ interr. (552)-Qal impf. 3 m.s.-2 m.s. sf. (לָקַח 542) *why does ... carry you away*
לִבֶּךָ n.m.s.-2 m.s. sf. (524) *your heart*
וּמַה־יִּרְזְמוּן conj.-v.supra-Qal impf. 3 m.p. (רָזַם 931; LXX ἐπήνεγκαν) *and why do ... flash*
עֵינֶיךָ n.f.p.-2 m.s. sf. (744) *your eyes*

15:13

כִּי־תָשִׁיב conj. (471)-Hi. impf. 2 m.s. (שׁוּב 996) *that you turn*
אֶל־אֵל prep.-n.m.s. (42) *against God*
רוּחֶךָ n.f.s.-2 m.s. sf. (924) *your spirit*
וְהֹצֵאתָ conj.-Hi. pf. 2 m.s. (יָצָא 422) *and you let go out*
מִפִּיךָ prep.-n.m.s.-2 m.s. sf. (804) *of your mouth*
מִלִּין n.f.p. (576; GK 125c) *such words*

15:14

מָה־אֱנוֹשׁ interr. (552)-n.m.s. (60) *what is man*
כִּי־יִזְכֶּה conj. (471)-Qal impf. 3 m.s. (זָכָה 269) *that he can be clean*
וְכִי־יִצְדַּק conj.-conj. (471)-Qal impf. 3 m.s. (צָדַק 842) *or that he can be righteous*
יְלוּד אִשָּׁה Qal pass.ptc. m.s. cstr. (יָלַד 408)-n.f.s. (61) *he that is born of a woman*

15:15

הֵן interj. (243) *behold*
בִּקְדֹשָׁו prep.-adj. m.p.-3 m.s. sf. (872) *in his holy ones*
לֹא יַאֲמִין neg.-Hi. impf. 3 m.s. (אָמַן 52) *he puts no trust*
וְשָׁמַיִם conj.-n.m. du. (1029) *and heavens*
לֹא־זַכּוּ neg.-Qal pf. 3 c.p. (זָכַךְ 269; GK 67cc) *are not clean*
בְעֵינָיו prep.-n.f.p.-3 m.s. sf. (744) *in his sight*

15:16

אַף כִּי־ conj. (II 64)-conj. (471) *how much less*
נִתְעָב Ni. ptc. m.s. (תָּעַב 1073; GK 116e) *one who is abominable*
וְנֶאֱלָח conj.-Ni. ptc. m.s. (אָלַח 47) *and corrupt*
אִישׁ־שֹׁתֶה n.m.s. (35)-Qal act.ptc. (שָׁתָה 1059) *a man who drinks*
כַמַּיִם prep.-def.art.-n.m.p. (565) *like water*
עַוְלָה n.f.s. (732) *iniquity*

15:17

אֲחַוְּךָ Pi. impf. 1 c.s.-2 m.s. sf. (חָוָה III 296; GK 75bb) *I will show you*
שְׁמַע־לִי Qal impv. 2 m.s. (1033)-prep.-1 c.s. sf. *hear me*
וְזֶה־חָזִיתִי conj.-demons.adj. m.s. (260)-Qal pf. 1 c.s. (חָזָה 302; GK 138h) *and what I have seen*
וַאֲסַפֵּרָה conj.-Pi. impf. 1 c.s.-vol.hc (סָפַר 707; GK 143d) *I will declare*

15:18

אֲשֶׁר־חֲכָמִים rel. (81)-adj. m.p. (314) *what wise men*
יַגִּידוּ Hi. impf. 3 m.p. (נָגַד 616) *have told*
וְלֹא כִחֲדוּ conj.-neg.-Pi. pf. 3 c.p. (כָּחַד 470) *and have not hidden*
מֵאֲבוֹתָם prep.-n.m.p.-3 m.p. sf. (3) *from their fathers*

15:19

לָהֶם לְבַדָּם prep.-3 m.p. sf.-prep.-n.m.s.-3 m.p. sf. (94) *to whom alone*
נִתְּנָה Ni. pf. 3 f.s. (נָתַן 678) *was given*
הָאָרֶץ def.art.-n.f.s. (75) *the land*
וְלֹא־עָבַר conj.-neg.-Qal pf. 3 m.s. (716) *and did not pass*
זָר Qal act.ptc. m.s. (זוּר I 266) *a stranger*
בְּתוֹכָם prep.-n.m.s.-3 m.p. sf. (1063) *among them*

15:20

כָּל־יְמֵי n.m.s. cstr. (481)-n.m.p. cstr. (398) *all the days of*
רָשָׁע adj. m.s. (957) *a wicked person*
הוּא pers.pr. 3 m.s. (214) *he*
מִתְחוֹלֵל Hithpolel ptc. m.s. (חוּל I 296) *writhes in pain*

וּמִסְפַּר conj.-n.m.s. cstr. (708; GK 146a) *and the number of*
שָׁנִים n.f.p. (1040) *years*
נִצְפְּנוּ Ni. pf. 3 c.p. (צָפַן 860) *they are stored up*
לֶעָרִיץ prep.-def.art.-adj. m.s. (792) *for the ruthless*

15:21

קוֹל־ n.m.s. cstr. (876) *sound of*
פְּחָדִים n.m.p. (808) *dread (error)*
בְּאָזְנָיו prep.-n.f.p.-3 m.s. sf. (23) *in his ears*
בַּשָּׁלוֹם prep.-def.art.-n.m.s. (1022; GK 118f) *in prosperity*
שׁוֹדֵד Qal act.ptc. (שָׁדַד 994) *a destroyer*
יְבוֹאֶנּוּ Qal impf. 3 m.s.-3 m.s. sf. (בּוֹא 97) *will come upon him*

15:22

לֹא־יַאֲמִין neg.-Hi. impf. 3 m.s. (אָמַן 52) *he does not believe*
שׁוּב Qal inf.cstr. (שׁוּב 996) *(that he will) return*
מִנִּי־חֹשֶׁךְ prep.-n.m.s. (365) *out of darkness*
וְצָפוּ conj.-Qal pass.ptc. (צָפָה I 859; GK 75v) *and destined (spied out)*
הוּא pers.pr. 3 m.s. (214) *he is*
אֱלֵי־חָרֶב prep. (39)-n.f.s. paus. (352) *for the sword*

15:23

נֹדֵד הוּא Qal act.ptc. (נָדַד I 622; LXX κατατέτακται δὲ)-pers.pr. 3 m.s. (214) *he wanders*
לַלֶּחֶם prep.-def.art.-n.m.s. (536; LXX εἰς σῖτα) *for bread*
אַיֵּה interr.adv. (32; GK 147c; LXX γυψίν) *where*
יָדַע Qal pf. 3 m.s. (393) *he knows*
כִּי־נָכוֹן conj. (471)-Ni. ptc. m.s. (כּוּן I 465) *that is ready*
בְּיָדוֹ prep.-n.f.s.-3 m.s. sf. (388; LXX στροβήσει) *at his hand*
יוֹם־חֹשֶׁךְ n.m.s. cstr. (398)-n.m.s. (365) *a day of darkness*

15:24

יְבַעֲתֻהוּ Pi. impf. 3 m.p.-3 m.s. sf. (בָּעַת 129) *terrify him*
צַר n.m.s. (II 865) *distress*
וּמְצוּקָה conj.-n.f.s. (848) *and anguish*
תִּתְקְפֵהוּ Qal impf. 3 f.s.-3 m.s. sf. (תָּקַף 1075) *it prevails against him*
כְּמֶלֶךְ prep.-n.m.s. (I 572) *like a king*
עָתִיד adj. m.s. (800) *prepared*
לַכִּידוֹר prep.-def.art.-n.m.s. (461) *for battle (the onset)*

15:25

כִּי־נָטָה conj. (471)-Qal pf. 3 m.s. (639) *because he has stretched forth*
אֶל־אֵל prep.-n.m.s. (42) *against God*
יָדוֹ n.f.s.-3 m.s. sf. (388) *his hand*
וְאֶל־שַׁדַּי conj.-prep.-pr.n. (994) *and to the Almighty*
יִתְגַּבָּר Hith. impf. 3 m.s. paus. (גָּבַר 149) *he bids defiance*

15:26

יָרוּץ Qal impf. 3 m.s. (רוּץ 930) *running*
אֵלָיו prep.-3 m.s. sf. *against him*
בְּצַוָּאר prep.-n.m.s. (848; LXX ὕβρει; some rd. κατὰ τοῦ θεοῦ) *stubbornly (with a neck)*
בַּעֲבִי prep.-n.m.p. cstr. (716; GK 128r) *the thickness of*
גַּבֵּי n.m.p. cstr. (146) *bosses of* (convex projection of shield)
מָגִנָּיו n.m.p.-3 m.s. sf. (171) *his shields*

15:27

כִּי־כִסָּה conj. (471)-Pi. pf. 3 m.s. (כָּסָה 491) *because he has covered*
פָנָיו n.m.p.-3 m.s. sf. (815) *his face*
בְּחֶלְבּוֹ prep.-n.m.s.-3 m.s. sf. (316) *with his fat*
וַיַּעַשׂ consec.-Qal impf. 3 m.s. (עָשָׂה I 793) *and gathered*
פִימָה n.f.s. (810) *fat (superabundance)*
עֲלֵי־כָסֶל prep.-n.m.s. paus. (492) *upon his loins*

15:28

וַיִּשְׁכּוֹן consec.-Qal impf. 3 m.s. (שָׁכַן 1014) *and has lived in*
עָרִים n.f.p. (746) *cities*
נִכְחָדוֹת Ni. ptc. f.p. (כָּחַד 470) *desolate*
בָּתִּים n.m.p. (108) *houses*
לֹא־יֵשְׁבוּ neg.-Qal impf. 3 m.p. (יָשַׁב 442) *which they should not inhabit*
לָמוֹ prep.-3 m.p. sf. *(in them)*
אֲשֶׁר הִתְעַתְּדוּ rel. (81)-Hith. pf. 3 c.p. (עָתַד I 800) *which were destined*
לְגַלִּים prep.-n.m.p. (164) *to become heaps of ruins*

15:29

לֹא־יֶעְשַׁר neg.-Qal impf. 3 m.s. (עָשַׁר 799) *he will not be rich*

וְלֹא־יָקוּם conj.-neg.-Qal impf. 3 m.s. (קוּם 877) *and will not endure*
חֵילוֹ n.m.s.-3 m.s. sf. (298) *his wealth*
וְלֹא־יִטֶּה conj.-neg.-Qal impf. 3 m.s. (נָטָה 639; LXX οὐ μὴ βάλῃ) *nor will he stretch out*
לָאָרֶץ prep.-def.art.-n.f.s. (75) *in the earth*
מִנְלָם n.m.s.-3 m.p. sf. (649; LXX σκιὰν) *their acquisition*

15:30

לֹא־יָסוּר neg.-Qal impf. 3 m.s. (סוּר 693) *he will not escape*
מִנִּי־חֹשֶׁךְ prep.-n.m.s. (365) *from darkness*
יֹנַקְתּוֹ n.f.s.-3 m.s. sf. (413) *his shoots*
תְּיַבֵּשׁ Pi. impf. 3 f.s. (יָבֵשׁ 386) *will dry up*
שַׁלְהֶבֶת n.f.s. (529) *a flame*
וְיָסוּר conj.-v.supra; LXX ἐκπέσοι) *and will depart*
בְּרוּחַ prep.-n.f.s. (924) *by a wind*
פִּיו n.m.s.-3 m.s. sf. (804; LXX αὐτοῦ τὸ ἄνθος) *his mouth*

15:31

אַל־יַאֲמֵן neg.-Hi. impf. 3 m.s. apoc.vol. (אָמַן 52) *let him not trust*
בַּשָּׁו prep.-def.art.-n.m.s. (996) *in emptiness*
נִתְעָה Ni. pf. 3 m.s. (תָּעָה 1073) *deceiving himself*
כִּי־שָׁוְא conj. (471)-v.supra *for emptiness*
תִּהְיֶה Qal impf. 3 f.s. (הָיָה 224) *will be*
תְמוּרָתוֹ n.f.s.-3 m.s. sf. (558; LXX+ἡ τομὴ αὐτοῦ) *his recompense*

15:32

בְּלֹא־יוֹמוֹ prep.-neg.-n.m.s.-3 m.s. sf. (398) *in not (before) his day*
תִּמָּלֵא Ni. impf. 3 f.s. (מָלֵא 569; LXX φθαρήσεται) *it will be paid in full*
וְכִפָּתוֹ conj.-n.f.s.-3 m.s. sf. (497) *and his branch*
לֹא רַעֲנָנָה neg.-adj. f.s. (947) *will not be green*

15:33

יַחְמֹס Qal impf. 3 m.s. (חָמַס 329) *he will shake off*
כַּגֶּפֶן prep.-def.art.-n.f.s. (172) *like the vine*
בִּסְרוֹ n.m.s.-3 m.s. sf. (126) *his unripe grape*
וְיַשְׁלֵךְ conj.-Hi. impf. 3 m.s. apoc. (שָׁלַךְ 1020) *and cast off*
כַּזַּיִת prep.-def.art.-n.m.s. (268) *like the olive tree*
נִצָּתוֹ n.f.s.-3 m.s. sf. (665) *his blossom*

15:34

כִּי־עֲדַת conj.-n.f.s. cstr. (II 417) *for the company of*
חָנֵף adj. m.s. (338) *the godless*
גַּלְמוּד adj. m.s. (166) *is barren*
וְאֵשׁ conj.-n.f.s. (77) *and fire*
אָכְלָה Qal pf. 3 f.s. (אָכַל 37) *consumes*
אָהֳלֵי־שֹׁחַד n.m.p. cstr. (13)-n.m.s. (1005) *tents of bribery*

15:35

הָרֹה Qal inf.abs. (הָרָה I 247) *conceiving*
עָמָל n.m.s. (765) *mischief*
וְיָלֹד conj.-Qal inf.abs. (יָלַד 408) *and bringing forth*
אָוֶן n.m.s. (19) *evil*
וּבִטְנָם conj.-n.f.s.-3 m.p. sf. (105) *and their heart (body)*
תָּכִין Hi. impf. 3 f.s. (כּוּן I 465; LXX ὑποίσει) *prepares*
מִרְמָה n.f.s. (941) *deceit*

16:1

וַיַּעַן consec.-Qal impf. 3 m.s. (עָנָה I 772) *then answered*
אִיּוֹב pr.n. (33) *Job*
וַיֹּאמַר consec.-Qal impf. 3 m.s. (אָמַר 55) *(and said)*

16:2

שָׁמַעְתִּי Qal pf. 1 c.s. (1033) *I have heard*
כְאֵלֶּה prep.-demons.adj. c.p. (41) *such things*
רַבּוֹת adj. f.p. (I 912) *many*
מְנַחֲמֵי Pi. ptc. m.p. cstr. (636) *comforters of*
עָמָל n.m.s. (765) *misery (trouble)*
כֻּלְּכֶם n.m.s.-2 m.p. sf. (481) *you all*

16:3

הֲקֵץ interr.-n.m.s. (893) *shall have an end?*
לְדִבְרֵי־רוּחַ prep.-n.m.p. cstr. (182)-n.f.s. (924) *windy words*
אוֹ מַה־ conj. (14; GK 150g)-interr. (552) *or what*
יַמְרִיצְךָ Hi. impf. 3 m.s.-2 m.s. sf. (מָרַץ 599) *provokes you (sickens)*
כִּי תַעֲנֶה conj. (471)-Qal impf. 2 m.s. (עָנָה I 772) *that you answer*

16:4

גַּם אָנֹכִי adv. (168)-pers.pr. 1 c.s. (59) *I also*
כָּכֶם prep.-2 m.p. sf. (GK 103,l) *as you do*

אֲדַבְּרָה Pi. impf. 1 c.s.-coh.he (דָּבַר 180; GK 108f) *could speak*
לוּ־יֵשׁ conj. (530)-subst. (441) *if it could be*
נַפְשְׁכֶם n.f.s.-2 m.p. sf. (659) *you*
תַּחַת נַפְשִׁי prep. (1065)-n.f.s.-1 c.s. sf. (659) *in my place*
אַחְבִּירָה Hi. impf. 1 c.s.-coh.he (חָבַר 287) *I could join together*
עֲלֵיכֶם prep.-2 m.p. sf. *against you*
בְּמִלִּים prep.-n.f.p. (576) *words*
וְאָנִיעָה conj.-Hi. impf. 1 c.s.-coh.he (נוּעַ 631) *and I could shake*
עֲלֵיכֶם v.supra *against you*
בְּמוֹ רֹאשִׁי prep. (91)-n.m.s.-1 c.s. sf. (910; GK 119q) *my head*

16:5

אֲאַמִּצְכֶם Pi. impf. 1 c.s.-2 m.p. sf. (אָמֵץ 54; GK 60f) *I could strengthen you*
בְּמוֹ־פִי prep. (91)-n.m.s.-1 c.s. sf. (804) *with my mouth*
וְנִיד conj.-n.m.s. cstr. (627) *and the solace of (motion of)*
שְׂפָתַי n.f.p.-1 c.s. sf. (973) *my lips*
יַחְשֹׂךְ Qal impf. 3 m.s. (חָשַׂךְ 364; LXX οὐ φείσομαι) *would assuage your pain*

16:6

אִם־אֲדַבְּרָה hypoth.part. (49)-Pi. impf. 1 c.s. -coh.he (דָּבַר 180; GK 108e,159ff) *if I speak*
לֹא־יֵחָשֵׂךְ neg.-Ni. impf. 3 m.s. (חָשַׂךְ 364) *is not assuaged*
כְּאֵבִי n.m.s.-1 c.s. sf. (456) *my pain*
וְאַחְדְּלָה conj.-Qal impf. 1 c.s.-coh.he (חָדַל 292; GK 63f) *and if I forbear*
מַה־מִּנִּי interr. (552)-prep.-1 c.s. sf. *how much of it ... me*
יַהֲלֹךְ Qal impf. 3 m.s. (הָלַךְ 229) *leaves*

16:7

אַךְ־עַתָּה adv. (36)-adv. (773) *surely now*
הֶלְאָנִי Hi. pf. 3 m.s.-1 c.s. sf. paus. (לָאָה 521; GK 75ee,144p) *he has worn me out (wearied)*
הֲשִׁמּוֹתָ Hi. pf. 2 m.s. (שָׁמֵם 1030; GK 53p) *you have made desolate*
כָּל־עֲדָתִי n.m.s. cstr. (481)-n.f.s.-1 c.s. sf. (II 417) *all my company*

16:8

וַתִּקְמְטֵנִי consec.-Qal impf. 2 m.s.-1 c.s. sf. (888) *and you have seized me*
לְעֵד prep.-n.m.s. (729) *for a witness*
הָיָה Qal pf. 3 m.s. (224) *it is*
וַיָּקָם consec.-Qal impf. 3 m.s. (קוּם 877) *and has risen up*
בִּי prep.-1 c.s. sf. *against me*
כַחֲשִׁי n.m.s.-1 c.s. sf. (471) *my leanness*
בְּפָנַי prep.-n.m.p.-1 c.s. sf. (815) *to my face*
יַעֲנֶה Qal impf. 3 m.s. (עָנָה I 772; GK 120c) *it testifies*

16:9

אַפּוֹ n.m.s.-3 m.s. sf. (I 60) *his wrath*
טָרַף Qal pf. 3 m.s. (382) *has torn*
וַיִּשְׂטְמֵנִי consec.-Qal impf. 3 m.s.-1 c.s. sf. (שָׂטַם 966; LXX χρησάμενος) *and he hated me*
חָרַק Qal pf. 3 m.s. (359) *he has gnashed*
עָלַי prep.-1 c.s. sf. *at me*
בְּשִׁנָּיו prep.-n.f.p.-3 m.s. sf. (1042; GK 118q) *his teeth*
צָרִי n.m.s.-1 c.s. sf. (865) *my adversary*
יִלְטוֹשׁ Qal impf. 3 m.s. (לָטַשׁ 538) *sharpens*
עֵינָיו n.f.p.-3 m.s. sf. (744) *his eyes*
לִי prep.-1 c.s. sf. *against me*

16:10

פָּעֲרוּ Qal pf. 3 c.p. (פָּעַר 822) *they have gaped*
עָלַי prep.-1 c.s. sf. *at me*
בְּפִיהֶם prep.-n.m.s.-3 m.p. sf. (804; GK 119q) *with their mouth*
בְּחֶרְפָּה prep.-n.f.s. (357; LXX ὀξεῖ) *insolently*
הִכּוּ Hi. pf. 3 c.p. (נָכָה 645) *they have struck*
לְחָיָי prep.-n.m. du.-1 c.s. sf. paus. (534) *upon the cheek*
יַחַד עָלַי adv. (403)-prep.-1 c.s. sf. *together against me*
יִתְמַלָּאוּן Hith. impf. 3 m.p. (מָלֵא 569) *they mass themselves*

16:11

יַסְגִּירֵנִי Hi. impf. 3 m.s.-1 c.s. sf. (סָגַר 688) *gives me up*
אֵל n.m.s. (42) *God*
אֶל עֲוִיל prep.-n.m.s. (732) *to the ungodly*
וְעַל־יְדֵי conj.-prep.-n.f.p. cstr. (388) *and into the hands of*
רְשָׁעִים adj. m.p. (957) *the wicked*
יִרְטֵנִי Qal impf. 3 m.s.-1 c.s. sf. (רָטָה 936) *he casts me (he wrings me out?)*

16:12

שָׁלֵו adj. m.s. (1017) *at ease*
הָיִיתִי Qal pf. 1 c.s. (הָיָה 224) *I was*

וַיְפַרְפְּרֵנִי consec.-Pilpel impf. 3 m.s.-1 c.s. sf. (I 830 פָּרַר) *and he broke me asunder*
וְאָחַז conj.-Qal pf. 3 m.s. (אָחַז 28; GK 112tt) *and he seized*
בְּעָרְפִּי prep.-n.m.s.-1 c.s. sf. (791; LXX τῆς κόμης) *by the neck*
וַיְפַצְפְּצֵנִי consec.-Pilpel impf. 3 m.s.-1 c.s. sf. (822 פָּצַץ) *and dashed me to pieces*
וַיְקִימֵנִי consec.-Hi. impf. 3 m.s.-1 c.s. sf. (קוּם 877) *and he set me up*
לוֹ prep.-3 m.s. sf. *for himself*
לְמַטָּרָה prep.-n.f.s. (643) *as a target*

16:13

יָסֹבּוּ Qal impf. 3 m.p. (סָבַב 685) *they surround*
עָלַי prep.-1 c.s. sf. *against me*
רַבָּיו n.m.p.-3 m.s. sf. (914; LXX λόγχαις) *his archers*
יְפַלַּח Pi. impf. 3 m.s. (פָּלַח 812) *he slashes open*
כִּלְיוֹתַי n.f.p.-1 c.s. sf. (480) *my kidneys*
וְלֹא יַחְמוֹל conj.-neg.-Qal impf. 3 m.s. (חָמַל 328) *and does not spare*
יִשְׁפֹּךְ Qal impf. 3 m.s. (שָׁפַךְ 1049) *he pours out*
לָאָרֶץ prep.-def.art.-n.f.s. (75) *on the ground*
מְרֵרָתִי n.f.s.-1 c.s. sf. (601; GK 95h) *my gall*

16:14

יִפְרְצֵנִי Qal impf. 3 m.s.-1 c.s. sf. (פָּרַץ I 829) *he breaks me*
פֶּרֶץ n.m.s. (829) *breach*
עַל־פְּנֵי־פָרֶץ prep.-n.m.p. cstr. (815)-v.supra paus. *upon breach*
יָרֻץ Qal impf. 3 m.s. (רוּץ 930) *he runs*
עָלַי prep.-1 c.s. sf. *upon me*
כְּגִבּוֹר prep.-n.m.s. (150; GK 126p) *like a warrior*

16:15

שַׂק n.m.s. (974) *sackcloth*
תָּפַרְתִּי Qal pf. 1 c.s. (תָּפַר 1074) *I have sewed*
עֲלֵי גִלְדִּי prep.-n.m.s.-1 c.s. sf. (162) *upon my skin*
וְעֹלַּלְתִּי conj.-Po'el pf. 1 c.s. (עָלַל III 760) *and have laid (thrust in)*
בֶעָפָר prep.-def.art.-n.m.s. (779) *in the dust*
קַרְנִי n.f.s.-1 c.s. sf. (901) *my strength (horn)*

16:16

פָּנַי n.m.p.-1 c.s. sf. (815; GK 44m) *my face*
חֳמַרְמְרָה Pe'al'al pf. pass. 3 m.p. (חָמַר IV 331; GK 55e; Q חמרמרו) *is red*
מִנִּי־בֶכִי prep.-n.m.s. (113) *with weeping*
וְעַל עַפְעַפַּי conj.-prep.-n.m. du.-1 c.s. sf. (733) *and on my eyelids*
צַלְמָוֶת n.m.s. (853) *deep darkness*

16:17

עַל לֹא־חָמָס prep.-neg.-n.m.s. (329; GK 152aN) *although there is no violence*
בְּכַפָּי prep.-n.f. du.-1 c.s. sf. paus. (496) *in my hands*
וּתְפִלָּתִי conj.-n.f.s.-1 c.s. sf. (813) *and my prayer*
זַכָּה adj. f.s. (269) *is pure*

16:18

אֶרֶץ n.f.s. (75) *O earth*
אַל־תְּכַסִּי neg.-Pi. impf. 2 f.s. (כָּסָה I 491) *cover not*
דָמִי n.m.s.-1 c.s. sf. (196) *my blood*
וְאַל־יְהִי conj.-neg.-Qal impf. 3 m.s. apoc. (הָיָה 224) *and let there not be*
מָקוֹם n.m.s. (879) *a resting place*
לְזַעֲקָתִי prep.-n.f.s.-1 c.s. sf. (277) *for my cry*

16:19

גַּם־עַתָּה adv. (168)-adv. (773) *even now*
הִנֵּה־ interj. (243) *behold*
בַשָּׁמַיִם prep.-def.art.-n.m. du. (1029) *in heaven*
עֵדִי n.m.s.-1 c.s. sf. (729) *my witness*
וְשָׂהֲדִי conj.-n.m.s.-1 c.s. sf. (962) *and he that vouches for me (my witness)*
בַּמְּרוֹמִים prep.-def.art.-n.m.p. (928; GK 124b) *on high (in the heights)*

16:20

מְלִיצַי Hi. ptc. m.p.-1 c.s. sf. (לִיץ 539; LXX ἀφίκοιτό μου ἡ δέησις) *scorn me*
רֵעָי n.m.p.-1 c.s. sf. paus. (945) *my friends*
אֶל־אֱלוֹהַ prep.-n.m.s. (42) *to God*
דָּלְפָה Qal pf. 3 f.s. (דָּלַף 196) *pours out (drops in) tears*
עֵינִי n.f.s.-1 c.s. sf. (744) *my eye*

16:21

וְיוֹכַח conj.-Hi. impf. 3 m.s. (יָכַח 406) *that he would maintain the right*
לְגֶבֶר prep.-n.m.s. (149) *of a man*
עִם־אֱלוֹהַּ prep. (767)-n.m.s. (42) *with God*
וּבֶן־אָדָם conj.-n.m.s. cstr. (119)-n.m.s. (9; some rd. וּבֵין) *and that of a man (son of man)*
לְרֵעֵהוּ prep.-n.m.s.-3 m.s. sf. (945) *with his neighbor*

16:22

כִּי־שְׁנוֹת conj.-n.f.p. cstr. (1040) *for when years of*

מִסְפָּר n.m.s. (708) *number (a few)*

יֶאֱתָיוּ Qal impf. 3 m.p. (אָתָה 87; GK 75u,145u) *have come*

וְאֹרַח conj.-n.m.s. (73) *and a way*

לֹא־אָשׁוּב neg.-Qal impf. 1 c.s. (שׁוּב 996) *whence I shall not return*

אֶהֱלֹךְ Qal impf. 1 c.s. (הָלַךְ 229; GK 69x) *I shall go*

17:1

רוּחִי n.f.s.-1 c.s. sf. (924) *my spirit*

חֻבָּלָה Pu. pf. 3 f.s. (חָבַל II 287) *is broken*

יָמַי n.m.p.-1 c.s. sf. (398) *my days*

נִזְעָכוּ Ni. pf. 3 c.p. paus. (זָעַךְ 276; cf. 200 דָּעַךְ; some rd. נִדְעָכוּ) *are extinct*

קְבָרִים n.m.p. (868; GK 124c) *graves*

לִי prep.-1 c.s. sf. *for me*

17:2

אִם־לֹא hypoth.part. (49)-neg. (50) *surely*

הֲתֻלִים n.m.p. (251) *mockery*

עִמָּדִי prep.--1 c.s. sf. (767) *about me*

וּבְהַמְּרוֹתָם conj.-prep.-Hi. inf.cstr.-3 m.p. sf. (598 מָרָה; GK 20h,75ff) *and on their provocation*

תָּלַן Qal impf. 3 f.s. (לוּן I 533; GK 73e) *dwells*

עֵינִי n.f.s.-1 c.s. sf. (744) *my eye*

17:3

שִׂימָה־נָּא Qal impv. 2 m.s.-vol.he (שִׂים 962) -part.of entreaty (609) *lay down (give i.e. a pledge)*

עָרְבֵנִי Qal impv. 2 m.s.-1 c.s. sf. (עָרַב II 786) *go surety for me*

עִמָּךְ prep.-2 m.s. sf. paus. *with yourself*

מִי הוּא interr. (566)-pers.pr. 3 m.s. (214) *who is there*

לְיָדִי prep.-n.f.s.-1 c.s. sf. (388) *for me*

יִתָּקֵעַ Ni. impf. 3 m.s. (תָּקַע 1075) *who will strike himself i.e. pledge himself*

17:4

כִּי־לִבָּם conj.-n.m.s.-3 m.p. sf. (524) *since their minds*

צָפַנְתָּ Qal pf. 2 m.s. (צָפַן 860) *you have closed*

מִשָּׂכֶל prep.-n.m.s. paus. (968) *to understanding*

עַל־כֵּן prep.-adv. (485) *therefore*

לֹא תְרֹמֵם neg.-Polel impf. 2 m.s. (רוּם 926; GK 72cc) *you will not let them triumph*

17:5

לְחֵלֶק prep.-n.m.s. (I 324) *for a share*

יַגִּיד Hi. impf. 3 m.s. (נָגַד 616) *he informs against*

רֵעִים n.m.p. (945) *friends*

וְעֵינֵי conj.-n.f. du. cstr. (744) *and the eyes of*

בָנָיו n.m.p.-3 m.s. sf. (119) *his children*

תִּכְלֶנָה Qal impf. 3 f.p. (כָּלָה I 477; GK 75w) *will fail*

17:6

וְהִצִּגַנִי conj.-Hi. pf. 3 m.s.-1 c.s. sf. (יָצַג 426) *he has made me*

לִמְשֹׁל prep.-n.m.s. cstr. (605; LXX θρύλημα) *a byword of*

עַמִּים n.m.p. (I 766) *peoples*

וְתֹפֶת conj.-n.f.s. (1064) *and a spitting*

לְפָנִים prep.-n.m.p. (815; LXX+αὐτοῖς) *in the face*

אֶהְיֶה Qal impf. 1 c.s. (הָיָה 224) *I become*

17:7

וַתֵּכַהּ consec.-Qal impf. 3 f.s. (כָּהָה I 462; GK 75p) *and has grown dim*

מִכַּעַשׂ prep.-n.m.s. (495) *from grief*

עֵינִי n.f.s.-1 c.s. sf. (744) *my eye*

וִיצֻרַי conj.-n.m.p.-1 c.s. sf. (428) *and my members*

כַּצֵּל prep.-def.art.-n.m.s. (853) *like a shadow*

כֻּלָּם n.m.s.-3 m.p. sf. (481) *all of them*

17:8

יָשֹׁמּוּ Qal impf. 3 m.p. (שָׁמֵם 1030) *are appalled*

יְשָׁרִים adj. m.p. (449) *upright men*

עַל־זֹאת prep.-demons.adj. f.s. (260) *at this*

וְנָקִי conj.-adj. m.s. (667) *and an innocent person*

עַל־חָנֵף prep.-adj. m.s. (338) *against a godless person*

יִתְעֹרָר Hithpolel impf. 3 m.s. (עוּר I 734) *stirs himself*

17:9

וְיֹאחֵז conj.-Qal impf. 3 m.s. (אָחַז 28) *yet holds*

צַדִּיק adj. m.s. (843) *a righteous one*

דַּרְכּוֹ n.m.s.-3 m.s. sf. (202) *to his way*

וּטֳהָר־יָדַיִם conj.-adj. m.s. cstr. (373; GK 10h)-n.f. du. (388) *and he that has clean hands*

יֹסִיף Hi. impf. 3 m.s. (יָסַף 414) *adds*

אֹמֶץ n.m.s. (55) *strength*

17:10

וְאוּלָם conj.-adv. (III 19) *but*

קֻלָּם n.m.s.-3 m.p. sf. (481; GK 135r) *all of them* (some rd. כֻּלְּכֶם)
תָּשֻׁבוּ וּבֹאוּ Qal impf. 2 m.p. (שׁוּב 996)-conj.-Qal impv. 2 m.p. (בּוֹא 97; GK 120e) *come on again*
נָא part.of entreaty (609)
וְלֹא־אֶמְצָא conj.-neg.-Qal impf. 1 c.s. (מָצָא 592) *and I shall not find*
בָכֶם prep.-2 m.p. sf. *among you*
חָכָם adj. m.s. (314) *a wise man*

17:11

יָמַי n.m.p.-1 c.s. sf. (398) *my days*
עָבְרוּ Qal pf. 3 c.p. (עָבַר 716) *are past*
זִמֹּתַי n.f.p.-1 c.s. sf. (273; LXX ἐν βρόμῳ) *my plans*
נִתְּקוּ Ni. pf. 3 c.p. (נָתַק 683) *are broken off*
מוֹרָשֵׁי n.m.p. cstr. (440; LXX τὰ ἄρθρα) *the desires of (possessions–cherished thoughts)*
לְבָבִי n.m.s.-1 c.s. sf. (523) *my heart*

17:12

לַיְלָה n.m.s. (538) *night*
לְיוֹם prep.-n.m.s. (398) *to day*
יָשִׂימוּ Qal impf. 3 m.p. (שִׂים 962) *they make*
אוֹר n.m.s. (21) *light*
קָרוֹב adj. m.s. (898) *near*
מִפְּנֵי־חֹשֶׁךְ prep.-n.m.p. cstr. (815)-n.m.s. (365) *to darkness*

17:13

אִם־אֲקַוֶּה hypoth.part. (49)-Pi. impf. 1 c.s. (קָוָה I 875) *if I look for*
שְׁאוֹל pr.n. f.s. (982) *Sheol*
בֵּיתִי n.m.s.-1 c.s. sf. (108) *as my house*
בַּחֹשֶׁךְ prep.-def.art.-n.m.s. (365) *in darkness*
רִפַּדְתִּי Pi. pf. 1 c.s. (רָפַד 951) *I spread*
יְצוּעָי n.m.p.-1 c.s. sf. paus. (426; GK 124b) *my couch*

17:14

לַשַּׁחַת prep.-def.art.-n.f.s. (1001; LXX θάνατον) *to the pit*
קָרָאתִי Qal pf. 1 c.s. (קָרָא 894) *I say*
אָבִי n.m.s.-1 c.s. sf. (3) *my father*
אָתָּה pers.pr. 2 m.s. paus. (61; LXX>) *you are*
אִמִּי n.f.s.-1 c.s. sf. (51) *my mother*
וַאֲחֹתִי conj.-n.f.s.-1 c.s. sf. (27) *or my sister*
לָרִמָּה prep.-def.art.-n.f.s. (942) *to the worm*

17:15

וְאַיֵּה conj.-interr.adv. (32) *and where*
אֵפוֹ enclitic part. (66) *then*
תִקְוָתִי n.f.s.-1 c.s. sf. (876) *my hope*
וְתִקְוָתִי conj.-v.supra (LXX ἢ τὰ ἀγαθά μου) *and my hope*
מִי יְשׁוּרֶנָּה interr. (566)-Qal impf. 3 m.s.-3 f.s. sf. (שׁוּר II 1003) *who will see it*

17:16

בַּדֵּי n.m.p. cstr. (II 94; LXX ἢ μετ᾽ ἐμοῦ) *bars of*
שְׁאֹל pr.n. f.s. (982) *Sheol*
תֵּרַדְנָה Qal impf. 3 f.p. (יָרַד 432; GK 47k) *will it (they) go down*
אִם־יַחַד hypoth.part. (49)-adv. (403) *together?*
עַל־עָפָר prep.-n.m.s. (779) *into dust*
נָחַת n.f.s. paus. (629; LXX καταβησόμεθα) *a rest (of death)*

18:1

וַיַּעַן consec.-Qal impf. 3 m.s. (עָנָה I 772) *then answered*
בִּלְדַּד pr.n. (115) *Bildad*
הַשֻּׁחִי def.art.-adj.gent. (1001) *the Shuhite*
וַיֹּאמַר consec.-Qal impf. 3 m.s. (אָמַר 55) *(and said)*

18:2

עַד־אָנָה prep. (III 723)-adv.-dir.he (33) *how long*
תְּשִׂימוּן Qal impf. 2 m.p. (שִׂים 962) *will you set*
קִנְצֵי n.m.p. cstr. (890; GK 130a; LXX οὐ παύσῃ) *snares for*
לְמִלִּין prep.-n.f.p. (576) *words*
תָּבִינוּ Qal impf. 2 m.p. (בִּין 106) *will you consider*
וְאַחַר conj.-prep. (29; LXX καὶ αὐτοί) *and afterwards*
נְדַבֵּר Pi. impf. 1 c.p. (דָּבַר 180) *we will speak*

18:3

מַדּוּעַ adv. (396) *why*
נֶחְשַׁבְנוּ Ni. pf. 1 c.p. (חָשַׁב 362) *are we counted*
כַבְּהֵמָה prep.-def.art.-n.f.s. (96) *like cattle*
נִטְמִינוּ Ni. pf. 1 c.p. (טָמָן 380; GK 75qq) *are we stupid*
בְּעֵינֵיכֶם prep.-n.f.p.-2 m.p. sf. (744; LXX ἐναντίον σου) *in your sight*

18:4

טֹרֵף Qal act.ptc. (טָרַף 382) *who tear*
נַפְשׁוֹ n.f.s.-3 m.s. sf. (659; GK 139f) *himself*
בְּאַפּוֹ prep.-n.m.s.-3 m.s. sf. (I 60) *in his anger*
הַלְמַעַנְךָ interr.-prep.-prep. (775)-2 m.s. sf. *for your sake?*

תֵּעָזַב Ni. impf. 3 f.s. (עָזַב I 736; GK 51n) *shall be forsaken*
אָרֶץ n.f.s. paus. (75) *the earth?*
וְיֶעְתַּק־ conj.-Qal impf. 3 m.s. (עָתַק 801; LXX ἢ καταστραφήσεται) *or removed*
צוּר n.m.s. (849; LXX ὄρη) *the rock*
מִמְּקֹמוֹ prep.-n.m.s.-3 m.s. sf. (879; LXX ἐκ θεμελίων) *out of its place*

18:5

גַּם אוֹר adv. (168)-n.m.s. cstr. (21) *yea, light of*
רְשָׁעִים adj. m.p. (957) *wicked ones*
יִדְעָךְ Qal impf. 3 m.s. (דָּעַךְ 200) *is put out*
וְלֹא־יִגַּהּ conj.-neg.-Qal impf. 3 m.s. (נָגַהּ 618) *and does not shine*
שְׁבִיב אִשּׁוֹ n.m.s. cstr. (985)-n.f.s.-3 m.s. sf. (77) *the flame of his fire*

18:6

אוֹר חָשַׁךְ n.m.s. (21)-Qal pf. 3 m.s. (חָשַׁךְ 364) *light is dark*
בְּאָהֳלוֹ prep.-n.m.s.-3 m.s. sf. (13) *in his tent*
וְנֵרוֹ conj.-n.m.s.-3 m.s. sf. (632) *and his lamp*
עָלָיו prep.-3 m.s. sf. *above him*
יִדְעָךְ Qal impf. 3 m.s. paus. (דָּעַךְ 200) *is put out*

18:7

יֵצְרוּ Qal impf. 3 m.p. (צָרַר I 864; GK 67dd) *are cramped*
צַעֲדֵי אוֹנוֹ n.m.p. cstr. (857)-n.m.s.-3 m.s. sf. (20; GK 135n) *his strong steps*
וְתַשְׁלִיכֵהוּ conj.-Hi. impv. 3 f.s.-3 m.s. sf. (שָׁלַךְ 1020; LXX σφάλαι δὲ αὐτοῦ) *and throw him down*
עֲצָתוֹ n.f.s.-3 m.s. sf. (420) *his own schemes*

18:8

כִּי־שֻׁלַּח conj.-Pu. pf. 3 m.s. (שָׁלַח 1018) *for he is cast*
בְּרֶשֶׁת prep.-n.f.s. (440) *into a net*
בְּרַגְלָיו prep.-n.f.p.-3 m.s. sf. (919) *by his own feet*
וְעַל שְׂבָכָה conj.-prep.-n.f.s. (959) *and on a network (lattice-work)*
יִתְהַלָּךְ Hith. impf. 3 m.s. (הָלַךְ 229; GK 54k; LXX ἑλεχθείη) *he walks*

18:9

יֹאחֵז Qal impf. 3 m.s. (אָחַז 28) *seizes*
בְּעָקֵב prep.-n.m.s. (784) *by the heel*
פָּח n.m.s. paus. (I 809) *a trap*
יַחֲזֵק Hi. impf. 3 m.s. apoc. (חָזַק 304) *lays hold*
עָלָיו prep.-3 m.s. sf. *of him*
צַמִּים n.m.s. (855) *a snare*

18:10

טָמוּן Qal pass.ptc. (טָמַן 380) *is hid*
בָּאָרֶץ prep.-def.art.-n.f.s. (75) *in the ground*
חַבְלוֹ n.m.s.-3 m.s. sf. (286) *his rope*
וּמַלְכֻּדְתּוֹ conj.-n.f.s.-3 m.s. sf. (540) *and his trap*
עֲלֵי נָתִיב prep. (II 752)-n.m.s. (677) *in the path*

18:11

סָבִיב adv. (686) *on every side*
בִּעֲתֻהוּ Pi. pf. 3 c.p.-3 m.s. sf. (בָּעַת 129) *frighten him*
בַּלָּהוֹת n.f.p. (117) *terrors*
וֶהֱפִיצֻהוּ conj.-Hi. pf. 3 c.p.-3 m.s. sf. (פּוּץ I 806) *and chase him*
לְרַגְלָיו prep.-n.f.p.-3 m.s. sf. (919) *at his heels (feet)*

18:12

יְהִי־רָעֵב Qal impf. 3 m.s. apoc. (הָיָה 224)-adj. m.s. (944; GK 109k) *is hunger-bitten*
אֹנוֹ n.m.s.-3 m.s. sf. (20) *his strength*
וְאֵיד conj.-n.m.s. (15) *and calamity*
נָכוֹן Ni. ptc. (כּוּן I 465) *is ready*
לְצַלְעוֹ prep.-n.m.s.-3 m.s. sf. (854) *for his stumbling*

18:13

יֹאכַל Qal impf. 3 m.s. (אָכַל 37) *it consumes*
בַּדֵּי עוֹרוֹ n.m.p. cstr. (94)-n.m.s.-3 m.s. sf. (736) *the limbs of his skin*
יֹאכַל v.supra *consumes*
בַּדָּיו n.m.p.-3 m.s. sf. (94) *his limbs*
בְּכוֹר n.m.s. cstr. (114) *the first-born of*
מָוֶת n.m.s. (560) *death*

18:14

יִנָּתֵק Ni. impf. 3 m.s. (נָתַק 683) *he is torn*
מֵאָהֳלוֹ prep.-n.m.s.-3 m.s. sf. (13) *from his tent*
מִבְטַחוֹ n.m.s.-3 m.s. sf. (105; LXX ἴασις) *the object of his confidence*
וְתַצְעִדֵהוּ conj.-Hi. impf. 3 f.s.-3 m.s. sf. (צָעַד 857) *and it makes him march*
לְמֶלֶךְ prep.-n.m.s. cstr. (I 572) *to the king of*
בַּלָּהוֹת n.f.p. (117) *terrors*

18:15

תִּשְׁכּוֹן Qal impf. 3 f.s. (שָׁכַן 1014) *it dwells*
בְּאָהֳלוֹ prep.-n.m.s.-3 m.s. sf. (13) *in his tent*

מִבְּלִי־לוֹ prep.-neg. (115)-prep.-3 m.s. sf. *which is none of his*
יְזֹרֶה Pu. impf. 3 m.s. (זָרָה 279) *is scattered*
עַל־נָוֵהוּ prep.-n.m.s.-3 m.s. sf. (627) *upon his habitation*
גָפְרִית n.f.s. (172) *brimstone*

18:16

מִתַּחַת prep.-adv. (1065) *beneath*
שָׁרָשָׁיו n.m.p.-3 m.s. sf. (1057) *his roots*
יִבָשׁוּ Qal impf. 3 m.p. paus. (יָבֵשׁ 386) *dry up*
וּמִמַּעַל conj.-prep.-adv. (751) *and above*
יִמַּל Qal impf. 3 m.s. (מָלַל III 576) *wither*
קְצִירוֹ n.m.s.-3 m.s. sf. (894) *his branches*

18:17

זִכְרוֹ־ n.m.s.-3 m.s. sf. (271) *his memory*
אָבַד Qal pf. 3 m.s. (1) *perishes*
מִנִּי־אָרֶץ prep.-n.f.s. paus. (75) *from the earth*
וְלֹא־שֵׁם לוֹ conj.-neg.-n.m.s. (1027)-prep.-3 m.s. sf. *and he has no name*
עַל־פְּנֵי־חוּץ prep.-n.m.p. cstr. (815)-n.m.s. (299) *in the street*

18:18

יֶהְדְּפֻהוּ Qal impf. 3 m.p.-3 m.s. sf. (הָדַף 213; GK 144g) *he is thrust*
מֵאוֹר prep.-n.m.s. (21) *from light*
אֶל־חֹשֶׁךְ prep.-n.m.s. (365) *into darkness*
וּמִתֵּבֵל conj.-prep.-n.f.s. (385) *and out of the world*
יְנִדֻּהוּ Hi. impf. 3 m.p.-3 m.s. sf. (נָדַד I 622; GK 144g) *is driven out*

18:19

לֹא נִין לוֹ neg.-n.m.s. (630)-prep.-3 m.s. sf. *he has no offspring*
וְלֹא נֶכֶד conj.-neg.-n.m.s. (645) *or descendant*
בְּעַמּוֹ prep.-n.m.s.-3 m.s. sf. (I 766) *among his people*
וְאֵין שָׂרִיד conj.-subst. cstr. (II 34)-n.m.s. (I 975) *and no survivor*
בִּמְגוּרָיו prep.-n.m.p.-3 m.s. sf. (158) *in his dwelling-places*

18:20

עַל־יוֹמוֹ prep.-n.m.s.-3 m.s. sf. (398; LXX ἐπ' αὐτῷ) *at his day*
נָשַׁמּוּ Ni. pf. 3 c.p. (שָׁמֵם 1030) *are appalled*
אַחֲרֹנִים adj. m.p. (30) *they of the west (they that come after)*
וְקַדְמֹנִים conj.-adj. m.p. (I 870) *and them of the east*
אָחֲזוּ Qal pf. 3 c.p. (אָחַז 28; LXX sg.) *seizes*
שָׂעַר n.m.s. paus. (I 972) *horror*

18:21

אַךְ־אֵלֶּה adv. (36)-demons.adj. c.p. (41) *surely these are*
מִשְׁכְּנוֹת n.m.p. cstr. (1015) *dwellings of*
עַוָּל n.m.s. (732) *the ungodly*
וְזֶה conj.-demons.adj. m.s. (260) *and this is*
מְקוֹם n.m.s. cstr. (879; GK 130d) *the place of*
לֹא־יָדַע־ neg.-Qal pf. 3 m.s. (393) *one who knows not*
אֵל n.m.s. (42) *God*

19:1

וַיַּעַן consec.-Qal impf. 3 m.s. (עָנָה I 772) *then answered*
אִיּוֹב pr.n. (33) *Job*
וַיֹּאמַר consec.-Qal impf. 3 m.s. (אָמַר 55) *(and said)*

19:2

עַד־אָנָה prep.-adv.-dir.he (33) *how long*
תּוֹגְיוּן Hi. impf. 2 m.p. (יָגָה I 387; GK 21d,75gg,oo) *will you torment*
נַפְשִׁי n.f.s.-1 c.s. sf. (659) *me*
וּתְדַכְּאוּנַנִי conj.-Pi. impf. 2 m.p.-1 c.s. sf. (דָּכָא 193; GK 60e) *and break me in pieces*
בְמִלִּים prep.-n.f.p. (576) *with words*

19:3

זֶה עֶשֶׂר demons.adj. m.s. (260)-num. m.s. (796) *these ten*
פְּעָמִים n.f.p. (821) *times*
תַּכְלִימוּנִי Hi. impf. 2 m.p.-1 c.s. sf. (כָּלַם 483) *you have cast reproach upon me*
לֹא־תֵבֹשׁוּ neg.-Qal impf. 2 m.p. (בּוֹשׁ 101) *are you not ashamed*
תַּהְכְּרוּ־ Hi. (or Qal) impf. 2 m.p. (הָכַר 229; GK 53n,120c; LXX ἐπίκεισθέ μοι) *that you wrong*
לִי prep.-1 c.s. sf. *me*

19:4

וְאַף־אָמְנָם conj.-conj. (II 64)-adv. (53) *and even if it be true*
שָׁגִיתִי Qal pf. 1 c.s. (שָׁגָה 993) *I have erred*
אִתִּי prep.-1 c.s. sf. (II 85) *with me*
תָּלִין Qal impf. 3 f.s. (לִין I 533) *remains*
מְשׁוּגָתִי n.f.s.-1 c.s. sf. (1000; LXX-no suffix) *my error*

19:5

אִם־אָמְנָם hypoth.part (49)–adv. (53) *if indeed*
עָלַי prep.–1 c.s. sf. *against me*
תַּגְדִּילוּ Hi. impf. 2 m.p. (גָּדַל 152) *you magnify yourselves*
וְתוֹכִיחוּ conj.–Hi. impf. 2 m.p. (יָכַח 406) *and you make an argument*
עָלַי v.supra *against me*
חֶרְפָּתִי n.f.s.–1 c.s. sf. (357) *my humiliation*

19:6

דְּעוּ־אֵפוֹ Qal impv. 2 m.p. (יָדַע 393)–enclitic part. (66) *know then*
כִּי־אֱלוֹהַּ conj. (471)–pr.n. (42) *that God*
עִוְּתָנִי Pi. pf. 3 m.s.–1 c.s. sf. (עָוַת 736) *has put me in the wrong*
וּמְצוּדוֹ conj.–n.m.s.–3 m.s. sf. (II 844) *and his net (hunting implement)*
עָלַי prep.–1 c.s. sf. *about me*
הִקִּיף Hi. pf. 3 m.s. (נָקַף II 668) *closed*

19:7

הֵן interj. (243; GK 159w) *behold*
אֶצְעַק Qal impf. 1 c.s. (צָעַק 858) *I cry out*
חָמָס n.m.s. (329) *violence*
וְלֹא אֵעָנֶה conj.–neg.–Ni. impf. 1 c.s. (עָנָה I 772; GK 63hN) *but I am not answered*
אֲשַׁוַּע Pi. impf. 1 c.s. (שָׁוַע 1002) *I call aloud*
וְאֵין conj.–subst. cstr. (II 34) *but there is no*
מִשְׁפָּט n.m.s. (1048) *justice*

19:8

אָרְחִי n.m.s.–1 c.s. sf. (73) *my way*
גָּדַר Qal pf. 3 m.s. (154) *he has walled up*
וְלֹא אֶעֱבוֹר conj.–neg.–Qal impf. 1 c.s. (עָבַר 716) *so that I cannot pass*
וְעַל נְתִיבוֹתַי conj.–prep.–n.f.p.–1 c.s. sf. (677) *and upon my paths*
חֹשֶׁךְ n.m.s. (365) *darkness*
יָשִׂים Qal impf. 3 m.s. (שִׂים 962) *he has set*

19:9

כְּבוֹדִי n.m.s.–1 c.s. sf. (458) *my glory*
מֵעָלַי prep.–prep.–1 c.s. sf. *from me*
הִפְשִׁיט Hi. pf. 3 m.s. (פָּשַׁט 832) *he has stripped*
וַיָּסַר consec.–Qal impf. 3 m.s. (סוּר 693) *and has taken*
עֲטֶרֶת n.f.s. cstr. (I 742) *the crown from*
רֹאשִׁי n.m.s.–1 c.s. sf. (910) *my head*

19:10

יִתְּצֵנִי Qal impf. 3 m.s.–1 c.s. sf. (נָתַץ 683) *he breaks me down*
סָבִיב adv. (686) *on every side*
וָאֵלַךְ consec.–Qal impf. 1 c.s. (הָלַךְ 229; GK 69p,x) *and I am gone*
וַיַּסַּע consec.–Hi. impf. 3 m.s. (נָסַע I 652) *and he pulled up*
כָּעֵץ prep.–def.art.–n.m.s. (781) *like a tree*
תִּקְוָתִי n.f.s.–1 c.s. sf. (876) *my hope*

19:11

וַיַּחַר consec.–Hi. impf. 3 m.s. (חָרָה 354) *and he has kindled*
עָלַי prep.–1 c.s. sf. *against me*
אַפּוֹ n.m.s.–3 m.s. sf. (I 60) *his wrath*
וַיַּחְשְׁבֵנִי consec.–Qal impf. 3 m.s.–1 c.s. sf. (חָשַׁב 362) *and counts me*
לוֹ כְצָרָיו prep.–3 m.s. sf.–prep.–n.m.p.–3 m.s. sf. (III 865; LXX ὥσπερ ἐχθρόν) *as his adversary*

19:12

יַחַד adv. (403) *together*
יָבֹאוּ Qal impf. 3 m.p. (בּוֹא 97) *come on*
גְדוּדָיו n.m.p.–3 m.s. sf. (I 151) *his troops*
וַיָּסֹלּוּ consec.–Qal impf. 3 m.p. (סָלַל 699) *and they have cast up*
עָלַי prep.–1 c.s. sf. *against me*
דַּרְכָּם n.m.s.–3 m.p. sf. (202) *their way*
וַיַּחֲנוּ consec.–Qal impf. 3 c.p. (חָנָה 333) *and they encamp*
סָבִיב adv. (686) *round about*
לְאָהֳלִי prep.–n.m.s.–1 c.s. sf. (13) *my tent*

19:13

אַחַי n.m.p.–1 c.s. sf. (26) *my brethren*
מֵעָלַי prep.–prep.–1 c.s. sf. *from me*
הִרְחִיק Hi. pf. 3 m.s. (רָחַק 934; LXX–pl.) *he has put far*
וְיֹדְעַי conj.–Qal act.ptc. m.p.–1 c.s. sf. (יָדַע 393) *and my acquaintances*
אַךְ־זָרוּ adv. (36)–Qal pf. 3 c.p. (זוּר I 266) *are wholly estranged*
מִמֶּנִּי prep.–1 c.s. sf. *from me*

19:14

חָדְלוּ Qal pf. 3 c.p. (חָדַל 292) *have failed (me)*
קְרוֹבָי adj. m.p.–1 c.s. sf. paus. (898) *those near me*
וּמְיֻדָּעַי conj.–Pu. ptc. m.p.–1 c.s. sf. (יָדַע 393) *and my acquaintances*

שְׁכֵחוּנִי Qal pf. 3 c.p.-1 c.s. sf. (שָׁכַח 1013) *have forgotten me*

19:15

גָּרֵי Qal act.ptc. m.p. cstr. (גּוּר I 157) *the guests of (in)*
בֵיתִי n.m.s.-1 c.s. sf. (108) *my house*
וְאַמְהֹתַי conj.-n.f.p.-1 c.s. sf. (51) *and my maidservants*
לְזָר prep.-Qal act.ptc. m.s. (זוּר I 266) *as a stranger*
תַּחְשְׁבֻנִי Qal impf. 2 m.p.-1 c.s. sf. (חָשַׁב 362; GK 60a) *count me*
נָכְרִי adj. m.s. (648) *an alien*
הָיִיתִי Qal pf. 1 c.s. (הָיָה 224) *I have become*
בְעֵינֵיהֶם prep.-n.f.p.-3 m.p. sf. (744) *in their eyes*

19:16

לְעַבְדִּי prep.-n.m.s.-1 c.s. sf. (713) *to my servant*
קָרָאתִי Qal pf. 1 c.s. (קָרָא 894) *I call*
וְלֹא יַעֲנֶה conj.-neg.-Qal impf. 3 m.s. (עָנָה I 772) *but he gives me no answer*
בְּמוֹ־פִי prep. (91)-n.m.s.-1 c.s. sf. (804) *with my mouth*
אֶתְחַנֶּן־ Hith. impf. 1 c.s. (חָנַן I 335) *I must beseech*
לוֹ prep.-3 m.s. sf. *him*

19:17

רוּחִי n.f.s.-1 c.s. sf. (924) *my spirit (I myself; my breath)*
זָרָה Qal pf. 3 f.s. (זוּר II 266) *is repulsive*
לְאִשְׁתִּי prep.-n.f.s.-1 c.s. sf. (61) *to my wife*
וְחַנֹּתִי conj.-Qal pf. 1 c.s. (חָנַן II 337; GK 67ee) *and I am loathsome*
לִבְנֵי prep.-n.m.p. cstr. (119) *to the sons of*
בִטְנִי n.f.s.-1 c.s. sf. (I 105) *my (mother's) womb*

19:18

גַּם־עֲוִילִים adv. (168)-n.m.p. (I 732) *even young children*
מָאֲסוּ בִי Qal pf. 3 c.p. (מָאַס 549)-prep.-1 c.s. sf. *despise me*
אָקוּמָה Qal impf. 1 c.s.-coh.he (קוּם 877; GK 108e,159e) *(if) I arise*
וַיְדַבְּרוּ־בִי consec.-Pi. impf. 3 m.p. (דָּבַר 180)-v.supra *they talk against me*

19:19

תִּעֲבוּנִי Pi. pf. 3 c.p.-1 c.s. sf. (תָּעַב 1073) *abhor me*

כָּל־מְתֵי n.m.s. cstr. (481)-n.m.p. cstr. (607) *all the men of*
סוֹדִי n.m.s.-1 c.s. sf. (691) *my circle of familiar friends*
וְזֶה־ conj.-demons.adj. m.s. (260; GK 138h) *and this one*
אָהַבְתִּי Qal pf. 1 c.s. (אָהַב 12) *whom I love*
נֶהְפְּכוּ־ Ni. pf. 3 c.p. (הָפַךְ 245) *have turned*
בִי prep.-1 c.s. sf. *against me*

19:20

בְּעוֹרִי prep.-n.m.s.-1 c.s. sf. (736) *to my skin*
וּבִבְשָׂרִי conj.-prep.-n.m.s.-1 c.s. sf. (142) *and to my flesh*
דָּבְקָה Qal pf. 3 f.s. (דָּבַק 179; LXX ἐσάπησαν) *cleave*
עַצְמִי n.f.s.-1 c.s. sf. (782) *my bones*
וָאֶתְמַלְּטָה consec.-Hith. impf. 1 c.s.-dir.he (מָלַט 572) *and I have escaped*
בְּעוֹר prep.-n.m.s. cstr. (736) *by the skin of*
שִׁנָּי n.f.p.-1 c.s. sf. (1042) *my teeth*

19:21

חָנֻּנִי Qal impv. 2 m.p.-1 c.s. sf. (חָנַן I 335) *have pity on me*
חָנֻּנִי v.supra *have pity on me*
אַתֶּם pers.pr. 2 m.p. (61) *you*
רֵעָי n.m.p.-1 c.s. sf. paus. (945) *my friends*
כִּי יַד־ conj. (471)-n.f.s. cstr. (388) *for the hand of*
אֱלוֹהַּ n.m.s. (42) *God*
נָגְעָה Qal pf. 3 f.s. (נָגַע 619) *has touched*
בִּי prep.-1 c.s. sf. *me*

19:22

לָמָּה prep.-interr. (552) *why*
תִּרְדְּפֻנִי Qal impf. 2 m.p.-1 c.s. sf. (רָדַף 922) *do you pursue me*
כְּמוֹ־אֵל prep. (455)-n.m.s. (42) *like God*
וּמִבְּשָׂרִי conj.-prep.-n.m.s.-1 c.s. sf. (142) *and with my flesh*
לֹא תִשְׂבָּעוּ neg.-Qal impf. 2 m.p. paus. (שָׂבַע 959) *you are not satisfied?*

19:23

מִי־יִתֵּן אֵפוֹ interr. (566)-Qal impf. 3 m.s. (נָתַן 678)-enclitic part. (66) *oh that*
וְיִכָּתְבוּן conj.-Ni. impf. 3 m.p. (כָּתַב 507; GK 151d) *were written*
מִלָּי n.f.p.-1 c.s. sf. paus. (576) *my words*
מִי־יִתֵּן v.supra *oh that*

בַּסֵּפֶר prep.-def.art.-n.m.s. (706; GK 126s) *in a book*

יֵחָקוּ conj.-Ho. impf. 3 m.p. (חָקַק 349; GK 53u,67y,151d) *they were inscribed*

19:24

בְּעֵט־ prep.-n.m.s. cstr. (741) *with a stylus of*

בַּרְזֶל n.m.s. (137) *iron*

וְעֹפֶרֶת conj.-n.m.s. (780) *and lead*

לָעַד prep.-n.m.s. (I 723) *for ever*

בַּצּוּר prep.-def.art.-n.m.s. (849) *in the rock*

יֵחָצְבוּן Ni. impf. 3 m.p. (חָצַב 345; GK 51m) *they were graven*

19:25

וַאֲנִי יָדַעְתִּי conj.-pers.pr. 1 c.s. (58)-Qal pf. 1 c.s. (יָדַע 393) *for I know*

גֹּאֲלִי Qal act.ptc.-1 c.s. sf. (גָּאַל I 145) *my redeemer*

חָי adj. m.s. paus. (311) *lives*

וְאַחֲרוֹן conj.-adj. m.s. (30; GK 118n) *and one coming after (me)*

עַל־עָפָר prep.-n.m.s. (779) *upon dust*

יָקוּם Qal impf. 3 m.s. (קוּם 877) *will stand (arise)*

19:26

וְאַחַר עוֹרִי conj.-prep. (29)-n.m.s.-1 c.s. sf. (736) *and after my skin*

נִקְּפוּ־ Pi. pf. 3 c.p. (נָקַף I 668; GK 119w) *which they have struck off*

זֹאת demons.adj. f.s. (260; GK 144g) *this!*

וּמִבְּשָׂרִי conj.-prep.-n.m.s.-1 c.s. sf. (142) *then from my flesh*

אֶחֱזֶה Qal impf. 1 c.s. (חָזָה 302) *I shall see*

אֱלוֹהַּ n.m.s. (42) *God*

19:27

אֲשֶׁר אֲנִי rel. (81)-pers.pr. 1 c.s. (58) *whom I*

אֶחֱזֶה־ v.supra *shall see*

לִי prep.-1 c.s. sf. *for myself*

וְעֵינַי conj.-n.f.p.-1 c.s. sf. (744) *and my eyes*

רָאוּ Qal pf. 3 c.p. (רָאָה 906) *shall see (have seen)*

וְלֹא־זָר conj.-neg.-Qal act.ptc. (זוּר I 266) *and not another (a stranger)*

כָּלוּ Qal pf. 3 c.p. (כָּלָה I 477) *faint (fail)*

כִלְיֹתַי n.f.p.-1 c.s. sf. (480) *my kidneys (as seat of emotion)*

בְּחֵקִי prep.-n.m.s.-1 c.s. sf. (300) *in my bosom (within me)*

19:28

כִּי תֹאמְרוּ conj. (471)-Qal impf. 2 m.p. (אָמַר 55) *if you say*

מַה־נִּרְדָּף־ interr. (552)-Qal impf. 1 c.p. (רָדַף 922) *how we will pursue*

לוֹ prep.-3 m.s. sf. (GK 117n) *him*

וְשֹׁרֶשׁ conj.-n.m.s. cstr. (1057) *and root of*

דָּבָר n.m.s. (182) *the matter*

נִמְצָא־ Ni. ptc. (מָצָא 592) *is found*

בִי prep.-1 c.s. sf. (many rd. 3 m.s. sf.) *in me*

19:29

גּוּרוּ לָכֶם Qal impv. 2 m.p. (גּוּר III 158)-prep.-2 m.p. sf. *be afraid (for yourselves)*

מִפְּנֵי־חֶרֶב prep.-n.m.p. cstr. (815)-n.f.s. (352) *of the sword*

כִּי־חֵמָה conj. (471)-n.f.s. (404; LXX θυμὸς γὰρ) *for wrath (brings)*

עֲוֹנוֹת n.f.p. cstr. (730; LXX ἐπ' ἀνόμους) *the punishment of*

חָרֶב n.f.s. paus. (352; LXX ἐπελεύσεται) *the sword*

לְמַעַן תֵּדְעוּן prep. (775)-Qal impf. 2 m.p. (יָדַע 393) *that you may know*

שַׁדִּין rel.-n.m.s. (192, see note; some see שַׁדַּי; Aq., Θ, Symm., Syr., V. rd. שַׁדִּין) *that there is judgment*

20:1

וַיַּעַן consec.-Qal impf. 3 m.s. (עָנָה I 772) *then answered*

צֹפַר pr.n. (862) *Zophar*

הַנַּעֲמָתִי def.art.-adj.gent. (654) *the Naamathite*

וַיֹּאמַר consec.-Qal impf. 3 m.s. (אָמַר 55) *(and said)*

20:2

לָכֵן prep.-adv. (485; LXX Οὐχ οὕτως) *therefore*

שְׂעִפַּי n.m.p.-1 c.s. sf. (972) *my thoughts*

יְשִׁיבוּנִי Hi. impf. 3 m.p.-1 c.s. sf. (שׁוּב 996) *answer me*

וּבַעֲבוּר conj.-prep.-prep. (721) *because of*

חוּשִׁי בִי Qal inf.cstr.-1 c.s. sf. (חוּשׁ 301)-prep.-1 c.s. sf. *my haste within me*

20:3

מוּסַר n.m.s. cstr. (416) *the correction of (which leadeth to)*

כְּלִמָּתִי n.f.s.-1 c.s. sf. (484) *my insult*

אֶשְׁמָע Qal impf. 1 c.s. paus. (שָׁמַע 1033) *I hear*

וְרוּחַ conj.-n.f.s. (924) *and a spirit*

מִבִּינָתִי prep.-n.f.s.-1 c.s. sf. (108; LXX omits sf.) *out of my understanding*
יַעֲנֵנִי Qal impf. 3 m.s.-1 c.s. sf. (עָנָה I 772) *answers me*

20:4

הֲזֹאת interr.-demons.adj. f.s. (260; GK 150e) *this?*
יָדַעְתָּ Qal pf. 2 m.s. (יָדַע 393) *do you know?*
מִנִּי־עַד prep.-n.m.s. (I 723) *from of old*
מִנִּי שִׂים prep.-Qal inf.cstr. (962) *since placing of*
אָדָם n.m.s. (9) *man*
עֲלֵי־אָרֶץ prep.-n.f.s. paus. (75) *upon earth*

20:5

כִּי רִנְנַת conj. (471)-n.f.s. cstr. (943) *that the exulting of*
רְשָׁעִים adj. m.p. (957) *the wicked*
מִקָּרוֹב prep.-adj. m.s. (898) *is short (of the briefest)*
וְשִׂמְחַת conj.-n.f.s. cstr. (970) *and the joy of*
חָנֵף adj. m.s. (338) *the godless*
עֲדֵי־רָגַע prep.-n.m.s. paus. (921) *but for a moment*

20:6

אִם־יַעֲלֶה hypoth.part. (49)-Qal impf. 3 m.s. (748 עָלָה) *though ... mount up*
לַשָּׁמַיִם prep.-def.art.-n.m.p. (1029) *to the heavens*
שִׂיאוֹ n.m.s.-3 m.s. sf. (673) *his height*
וְרֹאשׁוֹ conj.-n.m.s.-3 m.s. sf. (910) *and his head*
לָעָב prep.-def.art.-n.m.s. (728) *to the clouds*
יַגִּיעַ Hi. impf. 3 m.s. (נָגַע 619) *reach*

20:7

כְּגֶלֲלוֹ prep.-n.m.s.-3 m.s. sf. (165) *like his own dung*
לָנֶצַח prep.-n.m.s. (664) *for ever*
יֹאבֵד Qal impf. 3 m.s. (אָבַד 1) *he will perish*
רֹאָיו Qal act.ptc. m.p.-3 m.s. sf. (רָאָה 906) *those who have seen him*
יֹאמְרוּ Qal impf. 3 m.p. (אָמַר 55) *will say*
אַיּוֹ interr.adv.-3 m.s. sf. (32) *where is he?*

20:8

כַּחֲלוֹם prep.-n.m.s. (321) *like a dream*
יָעוּף Qal impf. 3 m.s. (עוּף 733) *he will fly away*
וְלֹא יִמְצָאוּהוּ conj.-neg.-Qal impf. 3 m.p.-3 m.s. sf. (מָצָא 592) *and they will not find him*

וְיֻדַּד conj.-Ho. impf. 3 m.s. (נָדַד I 622; LXX ἔπτη) *he will be chased away*
כְּחֶזְיוֹן prep.-n.m.s. cstr. (303) *like a vision of*
לָיְלָה n.m.s. (538) *the night*

20:9

עַיִן n.f.s. (744) *an eye*
שְׁזָפַתּוּ Qal pf. 3 f.s.-3 m.s. sf. (שָׁזַף 1004) *which saw him*
וְלֹא תוֹסִיף conj.-neg.-Hi. impf. 3 f.s. (יָסַף 414) *will see him no more*
וְלֹא־עוֹד conj.-neg.-adv. (728) *nor any more*
תְּשׁוּרֶנּוּ Qal impf. 3 f.s.-3 m.s. sf. (שׁוּר II 1003) *will (an eye) behold him*
מְקוֹמוֹ n.m.s.-3 m.s. sf. (879; GK 122,l) *his place*

20:10

בָּנָיו n.m.p.-3 m.s. sf. (119) *his children*
יְרַצּוּ Pi. impf. 3 m.p. (רָצָה 953; LXX ὀλέσαισαν) *will seek the favor of*
דַלִּים adj. m.p. (195) *poor ones*
וְיָדָיו conj.-n.f.p.-3 m.s. sf. (388) *and his hands*
תָּשֵׁבְנָה Hi. impf. 3 f.p. (שׁוּב 996; GK 72k) *will give back*
אוֹנוֹ n.m.s.-3 m.s. sf. (I 20) *his wealth*

20:11

עַצְמוֹתָיו n.f.p.-3 m.s. sf. (782) *his bones*
מָלְאוּ Qal pf. 3 c.p. (מָלֵא 569) *are full of*
עֲלוּמָו n.m.p.-3 m.s. sf. (761) *his youthful vigor*
וְעִמּוֹ conj.-prep.-3 m.s. sf. (767) *but with him*
עַל־עָפָר prep.-n.m.s. (779) *in dust*
תִּשְׁכָּב Qal impf. 3 f.s. (or 2 m.s.)(שָׁכַב 1011) *it will lie down*

20:12

אִם־תַּמְתִּיק hypoth.part. (49)-Hi. impf. 3 f.s. (608 מָתֹק; GK 159q) *though ... gives a sweet taste*
בְּפִיו prep.-n.m.s.-3 m.s. sf. (804) *in his mouth*
רָעָה n.f.s. (949) *wickedness*
יַכְחִידֶנָּה Hi. impf. 3 m.s.-3 f.s. sf. (כָּחַד 470) *though he hides it*
תַּחַת לְשׁוֹנוֹ prep. (1065)-n.f.s.-3 m.s. sf. (546) *under his tongue*

20:13

יַחְמֹל Qal impf. 3 m.s. (חָמַל 328) *though he spares (has compassion)*
עָלֶיהָ prep.-3 f.s. sf. *(over) it*
וְלֹא יַעַזְבֶנָּה conj.-neg.-Qal impf. 3 m.s.-3 f.s. sf. (עָזַב I 736) *he does not let it go*

וְיִמְנָעֶנָּה conj.-Qal impf. 3 m.s.-3 f.s. sf. (מָנַע 586) *and holds it*
בְּתוֹךְ חִכּוֹ prep.-n.m.s. cstr. (1063)-n.m.s.-3 m.s. sf. (335) *in his mouth*

20:14
לַחְמוֹ n.m.s.-3 m.s. sf. (536) *his food*
בְּמֵעָיו prep.-n.m.p.-3 m.s. sf. (588) *in his stomach*
נֶהְפָּךְ Ni. pf. 3 m.s. paus. (הָפַךְ 245; GK 159q) *is turned*
מְרוֹרַת n.f.s. cstr. (601) *gall of*
פְּתָנִים n.m.p. (837) *asps*
בְּקִרְבּוֹ prep.-n.m.s.-3 m.s. sf. (899) *within him*

20:15
חַיִל n.m.s. (298) *riches*
בָּלַע Qal pf. 3 m.s. (118) *he swallows down*
וַיְקִאֶנּוּ consec.-Qal impf. 3 m.s.-3 m.s. sf. (קִיא 883) *and vomits them up again*
מִבִּטְנוֹ prep.-n.f.s.-3 m.s. sf. (105) *out of his belly*
יֹרִשֶׁנּוּ Hi. impf. 3 m.s.-3 m.s. sf. (יָרַשׁ 439) *casts them out*
אֵל n.m.s. (42) *God*

20:16
רֹאשׁ־ n.m.s. cstr. (II 912) *poison of*
פְּתָנִים n.m.p. (837) *asps*
יִינָק Qal impf. 3 m.s. paus. (יָנַק 413) *he will suck*
תַּהַרְגֵהוּ Qal impf. 3 f.s.-3 m.s. sf. (הָרַג 246) *will kill him*
לְשׁוֹן n.f.s. cstr. (546) *the tongue of*
אֶפְעֶה n.m.s. (821) *a viper*

20:17
אַל־יֵרֶא neg.-Qal impf. 3 m.s. apoc. (רָאָה 906; GK 109e) *he will not look*
בִפְלַגּוֹת prep.-n.f.p. (811) *upon the rivers*
נַהֲרֵי n.m.p. cstr. (625) *streams of*
נַחֲלֵי n.m.p. cstr. (636; GK 130e) *torrents of*
דְּבַשׁ n.m.s. (185) *honey*
וְחֶמְאָה conj.-n.f.s. (326) *and curds*

20:18
מֵשִׁיב Hi. ptc. m.s. (שׁוּב 996; LXX εἰς κενὰ καὶ μάταια) *he will give back*
יָגָע n.m.s. (388) *the fruit of his toil*
וְלֹא יִבְלָע conj.-neg.-Qal impf. 3 m.s. paus. (בָּלַע 118) *and will not swallow it down*
כְּחֵיל prep.-n.m.s. cstr. (298) *from the profit of*
תְּמוּרָתוֹ n.f.s.-3 m.s. sf. (558) *his trading*

וְלֹא יַעֲלֹס conj.-neg.-Qal impf. 3 m.s. (עָלַס 763) *he will get no enjoyment*

20:19
כִּי־רִצַּץ conj. (471)-Pi. pf. 3 m.s. (רָצַץ 954) *for he has crushed*
עָזַב Qal pf. 3 m.s. (I 736; GK 154aN) *he has abandoned*
דַּלִּים adj. m.p. (195) *the poor*
בַּיִת n.m.s. (108) *a house*
גָּזַל Qal pf. 3 m.s. (159; GK 154aN) *he has seized*
וְלֹא יִבֶנֵהוּ conj.-neg.-Qal impf. 3 m.s.-3 m.s. sf. (בָּנָה 124) *which he did not build*

20:20
כִּי לֹא־יָדַע conj. (471)-neg.-Qal pf. 3 m.s. (393) *for did not know*
שָׁלֵו adj. m.s. (1017) *rest*
בְּבִטְנוֹ prep.-n.f.s.-3 m.s. sf. (105) *in his belly*
בַּחֲמוּדוֹ prep.-Qal pass.ptc.-3 m.s. sf. (חָמַד 326) *in which he delights*
לֹא יְמַלֵּט neg.-Pi. impf. 3 m.s. (מָלַט 572) *he will not save anything*

20:21
אֵין־שָׂרִיד subst. cstr. (II 34)-n.m.s. (I 975) *there was nothing left*
לְאָכְלוֹ prep.-Qal inf.cstr.-3 m.s. sf. (אָכַל 37) *after he had eaten*
עַל־כֵּן prep.-adv. (485) *therefore*
לֹא־יָחִיל neg.-Qal impf. 3 m.s. (חִיל 298; LXX οὐκ ἀνθήσει) *will not endure (is not firm)*
טוּבוֹ n.m.s.-3 m.s. sf. (375) *his prosperity*

20:22
בִּמְלֹאות prep.-Qal inf.cstr. (מָלֵא 569; GK 74h) *in the fulness of*
שִׂפְקוֹ n.m.s.-3 m.s. sf. (974) *his sufficiency*
יֵצֶר לוֹ Qal impf. 3 m.s. (צָרַר B 864; GK 118e)-prep.-3 m.s. sf. *he will be in straits*
כָּל־יַד n.m.s. cstr. (481)-n.f.s. cstr. (388) *all the force of*
עָמֵל n.m.s. (766) *a sufferer*
תְּבוֹאֶנּוּ Qal impf. 3 f.s.-3 m.s. sf. (בּוֹא 97) *will come upon him*

20:23
יְהִי לְמַלֵּא Qal impf. 3 m.s. apoc. (הָיָה 224)-prep.-Pi. inf.cstr. (569) *to fill full*
בִּטְנוֹ n.f.s.-3 m.s. sf. (105) *his belly*
יְשַׁלַּח־בּוֹ Pi. impf. 3 m.s. (שָׁלַח 1018)-prep.-3 m.s. sf. *he will send into him*

חֲרוֹן אַפּוֹ n.m.s. cstr. (354)–n.m.s.–3 m.s. sf. (I 60) *his fierce anger*

וְיַמְטֵר conj.–Hi. impf. 3 m.s. apoc. (מָטַר 565) *and rain (it)*

עָלֵימוֹ prep.–3 m.s. sf. (GK 103fN) *upon him*

בִּלְחוּמוֹ prep.–n.m.s.–3 m.s. sf. (535; LXX ὀδύνας) *into his (very) bowels*

20:24

יִבְרַח Qal impf. 3 m.s. (בָּרַח 137; GK 159c) *he will flee*

מִנֵּשֶׁק prep.–n.m.s. cstr. (676) *from a weapon of*

בַּרְזֶל n.m.s. (137) *iron*

תַּחְלְפֵהוּ Qal impf. 3 f.s.–3 m.s. sf. (חָלַף 322; GK 159c) *will strike him through*

קֶשֶׁת נְחוּשָׁה n.f.s. cstr. (905)–n.f.s. (639) *a bronze arrow*

20:25

שָׁלַף Qal pf. 3 m.s. (1025; LXX διεξέλθοι δὲ διὰ σώματος αὐτοῦ βέλος) *it is drawn forth*

וַיֵּצֵא consec.–Qal impf. 3 m.s. (יָצָא 422) *and comes out*

מִגֵּוָה prep.–n.f.s. (II 156) *of his body (from the back)*

וּבָרָק conj.–n.m.s. (140) *and lightning (fig.–of flashing arrow-head)*

מִמְּרֹרָתוֹ prep.–n.f.s.–3 m.s. sf. (601) *out of his gall*

יַהֲלֹךְ Qal impf. 3 m.s. (הָלַךְ 229; LXX, V rd. pl.) *come*

עָלָיו prep.–3 m.s. sf. *upon him*

אֵמִים n.f.p. (33) *terrors*

20:26

כָּל־חֹשֶׁךְ n.m.s. cstr. (481)–n.m.s. (365) *utter darkness*

טָמוּן Qal pass.ptc. (טָמַן 380) *is laid up (hidden)*

לִצְפּוּנָיו prep.–Qal pass.ptc. m.p.–3 m.s. sf. (צָפַן 860; LXX>) *for his treasures*

תְּאָכְלֵהוּ Qal impf. 3 f.s.–3 m.s. sf. (אָכַל 37; GK 68f; LXX κατέδεται) *will devour him*

אֵשׁ n.f.s. (77) *fire*

לֹא־נֻפָּח neg.–Pu. pf. 3 m.s. paus. (נָפַח 655; GK 145u,156f) *not blown upon*

יֵרַע Qal impf. 3 m.s. apoc. (רָעָה I 944) *will consume*

שָׂרִיד n.m.s. (I 975) *what is left*

בְּאָהֳלוֹ prep.–n.m.s.–3 m.s. sf. (13) *in his tent*

20:27

יְגַלּוּ Pi. impf. 3 m.p. (גָּלָה 162) *will reveal*

שָׁמַיִם n.m.p. (1029) *the heavens*

עֲוֹנוֹ n.m.s.–3 m.s. sf. (730) *his iniquity*

וְאֶרֶץ conj.–n.f.s. (75) *and the earth*

מִתְקוֹמָמָה Hithpolel ptc. f.s. (קוּם 877) *will rise up*

לוֹ prep.–3 m.s. sf. *against him*

20:28

יִגֶל Qal impf. 3 m.s. apoc.juss. (גָּלָה 162; LXX ἑλκύσαι) *will be carried away*

יְבוּל בֵּיתוֹ n.m.s. cstr. (385)–n.m.s.–3 m.s. sf. (108; LXX ἀπώλεια εἰς τέλος) *the possessions of his house*

נִגָּרוֹת Ni. ptc. f.p. (נָגַר 620) *dragged off*

בְּיוֹם prep.–n.m.s. cstr. (398) *in the day of*

אַפּוֹ n.m.s.–3 m.s. sf. (I 60) *his wrath*

20:29

זֶה demons.adj. m.s. (260) *this is*

חֵלֶק־ n.m.s. cstr. (324; GK 131c) *the portion of*

אָדָם רָשָׁע n.m.s. (9)–adj. m.s. (957) *a wicked man*

מֵאֱלֹהִים prep.–n.m.p. (43) *from God*

וְנַחֲלַת conj.–n.f.s. cstr. (635) *and the heritage of*

אִמְרוֹ n.m.s.–3 m.s. sf. (56; GK 135m) *his word*

מֵאֵל prep.–n.m.s. (42) *by God*

21:1

וַיַּעַן consec.–Qal impf. 3 m.s. (עָנָה I 772) *then answered*

אִיּוֹב pr.n. (33) *Job*

וַיֹּאמַר consec.–Qal impf. 3 m.s. (אָמַר 55) *(and said)*

21:2

שִׁמְעוּ שָׁמוֹעַ Qal impv. 2 m.p. (שָׁמַע 1033)–Qal inf.abs. (1033) *listen carefully*

מִלָּתִי n.f.s.–1 c.s. sf. (576) *to my words*

וּתְהִי־זֹאת conj.–Qal impf. 3 f.s. apoc.vol. (הָיָה 224)–demons.adj. f.s. (260) *and let this be*

תַּנְחוּמֹתֵיכֶם n.m.p.–2 m.p. sf. (637; LXX αὕτη ἡ παράκλησις) *your consolation*

21:3

שָׂאוּנִי Qal impv. 2 m.p.–1 c.s. sf. (נָשָׂא 669) *bear with me*

וְאָנֹכִי conj.–pers.pr. 1 c.s. (59) *and I myself*

אֲדַבֵּר Pi. impf. 1 c.s. (דָּבַר 180) *will speak*

וְאַחַר דַּבְּרִי conj.–adv. (29)–Pi. inf.cstr.–1 c.s. sf. (180) *and after I have spoken*

תַלְעִיג Hi. impf. 2 m.s. (לָעַג 541; LXX εἶτ' οὐ καταγελάσετέ μου) *mock on*

21:4

הֶאָנֹכִי interr.-pers.pr. 1 c.s. (59; GK 100n,135f, 143a) *as for me*
לְאָדָם prep.-n.m.s. (9) *against man?*
שִׂיחִי n.m.s.-1 c.s. sf. (967) *my complaint*
וְאִם־מַדּוּעַ conj.-hypoth.part. (49)-adv. (396; GK 150g) *why?*
לֹא־תִקְצַר neg.-Qal impf. 3 f.s. (קָצַר 894) *should not ... be short*
רוּחִי n.f.s.-1 c.s. sf. (924) *my spirit (breath)*

21:5

פְּנוּ־אֵלַי Qal impv. 2 m.p. (פָּנָה 815)-prep.-1 c.s. sf. *look at me*
וְהָשַׁמּוּ conj.-Hi. impv. 2 m.p. (שָׁמֵם 1030; GK 67v) *and be appalled*
וְשִׂימוּ יָד conj.-Qal impv. 2 m.s. (שִׂים 962) -n.f.s. (388) *and lay a hand*
עַל־פֶּה prep.-n.m.s. (804) *upon (your) mouth*

21:6

וְאִם־זָכַרְתִּי conj.-hypoth.part. (49)-Qal pf. 1 c.s. (269 זָכַר) *when I remember*
וְנִבְהָלְתִּי conj.-Ni. pf. 1 c.s. paus. (בָּהַל 96) *I am dismayed*
וְאָחַז conj.-Qal pf. 3 m.s. (28) *and seizes*
בְּשָׂרִי n.m.s.-1 c.s. sf. (142) *my flesh*
פַּלָּצוּת n.f.s. (814) *shuddering*

21:7

מַדּוּעַ adv. (396) *why?*
רְשָׁעִים adj. m.p. (957) *the wicked*
יִחְיוּ Qal impf. 3 m.p. (חָיָה 310) *do live?*
עָתְקוּ Qal pf. 3 c.p. (עָתַק 801) *they reach old age*
גַּם־גָּבְרוּ adv. (168)-Qal pf. 3 c.p. (גָּבַר 149; GK 117z) *and grow mighty*
חָיִל n.m.s. paus. (298) *in power*

21:8

זַרְעָם n.m.s.-3 m.p. sf. (282) *their children*
נָכוֹן Ni. ptc. m.s. (כּוּן 465) *are established*
לִפְנֵיהֶם עִמָּם prep.-n.m.p.-3 m.p. sf. (815) -prep.-3 m.p. sf. (767) *in their presence*
וְצֶאֱצָאֵיהֶם conj.-n.m.p.-3 m.p. sf. (425) *and their offspring*
לְעֵינֵיהֶם prep.-n.f. du.-3 m.p. sf. (744) *before their eyes*

21:9

בָּתֵּיהֶם n.m.p.-3 m.p. sf. (108) *their houses*
שָׁלוֹם n.m.s. (1022; GK 141cN; LXX εὐθηνοῦσιν) *are safe*
מִפָּחַד prep.-n.m.s. paus. (808; GK 119w; LXX+ οὐδαμοῦ) *from fear*
וְלֹא שֵׁבֶט conj.-neg.-n.m.s. cstr. (986) *and no rod of*
אֱלוֹהַּ n.m.s. (42) *God*
עֲלֵיהֶם prep.-3 m.p. sf. *upon them*

21:10

שׁוֹרוֹ n.m.s.-3 m.s. sf. (1004; LXX ἡ βοῦς αὐτῶν) *his bull*
עִבַּר Pi. pf. 3 m.s. (עָבַר 716) *breeds*
וְלֹא יַגְעִל conj.-neg.-Hi. impf. 3 m.s. (גָּעַל 171) *and does not cause (the cow) to reject as loathsome*
תְּפַלֵּט Pi. impf. 3 f.s. (פָּלַט 812) *calves*
פָּרָתוֹ n.f.s.-3 m.s. sf. (831) *his cow*
וְלֹא תְשַׁכֵּל conj.-neg.-Pi. impf. 3 f.s. (שָׁכֹל 1013) *and does not cast her calf*

21:11

יְשַׁלְּחוּ Pi. impf. 3 m.p. (שָׁלַח 1018) *they send forth*
כַּצֹּאן prep.-def.art.-n.f.s. (838) *like the flock*
עֲוִילֵיהֶם n.m.p.-3 m.p. sf. (732) *their little ones*
וְיַלְדֵיהֶם conj.-n.m.p.-3 m.p. sf. (409) *and their children*
יְרַקֵּדוּן Pi. impf. 3 m.p. (רָקַד 955; GK 52n) *dance*

21:12

יִשְׂאוּ Qal impf. 3 m.p. (נָשָׂא 669) *they sing (lift up)*
כְּתֹף prep.-n.m.s. (1074) *to the tambourine*
וְכִנּוֹר conj.-n.m.s. (490) *and lyre*
וְיִשְׂמְחוּ conj.-Qal impf. 3 m.p. (שָׂמַח 970) *and rejoice*
לְקוֹל עוּגָב prep.-n.m.s. cstr. (876)-n.m.s. (721) *to the sound of the pipe*

21:13

יְבַלּוּ Pi. impf. 3 m.p. (בָּלָה 115; Q יְכַלּוּ) *they spend (wear out)*
בַּטּוֹב prep.-def.art.-n.m.s. (III 375) *in prosperity*
יְמֵיהֶם n.m.p.-3 m.p. sf. (398) *their days*
וּבְרֶגַע conj.-prep.-n.m.s. (921; LXX ἐν δὲ ἀναπαύσει) *in a moment*
שְׁאוֹל n.f.s. (982) *to Sheol*
יֵחָתּוּ Qal impf. 3 m.p. (נָחַת 639; GK 21i,66f; LXX ἐκοιμήθησαν) *they go down*

21:14

וַיֹּאמְרוּ consec.-Qal impf. 3 m.p. (אָמַר 55) *then they say*

לָאֵל prep.-def.art.-n.m.s. (42) *to God*
ס֣וּר מִמֶּ֑נּוּ Qal impv. 2 m.s. (סוּר 693)-prep.-1 c.p. sf. *depart from us*
וְדַ֥עַת conj.-n.f.s. cstr. (395) *and the knowledge of*
דְּ֝רָכֶ֗יךָ n.m.p.-2 m.s. sf. (202) *your ways*
לֹ֣א חָפָֽצְנוּ neg.-Qal pf. 1 c.p. paus. (חָפֵץ 342) *we do not desire*

21:15

מַה־שַׁדַּ֥י interr. (552)-pr.n. (994) *what is the Almighty?*
כִּֽי־נַעַבְדֶ֑נּוּ conj. (471)-Qal impf. 1 c.p.-3 m.s. sf. (712 עָבַד) *that we should serve him*
וּמַה־נּ֝וֹעִ֗יל conj.-interr. (552)-Hi. impf. 1 c.p. (I 418 יָעַל) *and what profit do we get*
כִּ֣י נִפְגַּע־בּֽוֹ conj.-Qal impf. 1 c.p. (פָּגַע 803) -prep.-3 m.s. sf. *if we pray (encounter with request) to him*

21:16

הֵ֤ן interj. (243) *behold*
לֹ֣א בְיָדָ֣ם neg.-prep.-n.f.s.-3 m.p. sf. (388; LXX> לֹא) *not in their hand*
טוּבָ֑ם n.m.s.-3 m.p. sf. (375) *their prosperity*
עֲצַ֥ת n.f.s. cstr. (420) *the counsel of*
רְ֝שָׁעִ֗ים adj. m.p. (957) *the wicked*
רָ֣חֲקָה Qal pf. 3 f.s. (רָחַק 934; GK GK 106nN) *is far*
מֶֽנִּי prep.-1 c.s. sf. (GK 20f) *from me*

21:17

כַּמָּ֤ה prep.-def.art.-interr. (553; GK 150h) *how often*
נֵר־ n.m.s. cstr. (632) *the lamp of*
רְשָׁעִ֣ים adj. m.p. (957) *the wicked*
יִדְעָ֑ךְ Qal impf. 3 m.s. paus. (דָּעַךְ 200) *is put out*
וְיָבֹ֣א conj.-Qal impf. 3 m.s. (בּוֹא 97) *that comes*
עָלֵ֣ימוֹ prep.-3 m.p. sf. *upon them*
אֵידָ֑ם n.m.s.-3 m.p. sf. (15) *their calamity*
חֲ֝בָלִ֗ים n.m.p. (286) *pains*
יְחַלֵּ֥ק Pi. impf. 3 m.s. (חָלַק 323; LXX αὐτοὺς ἕξουσιν) *he distributes*
בְּאַפּֽוֹ prep.-n.m.s.-3 m.s. sf. (I 60) *in his anger*

21:18

יִ֭הְיוּ Qal impf. 3 m.p. (הָיָה 224) *they are*
כְּתֶ֣בֶן prep.-n.m.s. (1061) *like straw*
לִפְנֵי־ר֑וּחַ prep.-n.m.p. cstr. (815)-n.f.s. (924) *before wind*
וּ֝כְמֹ֗ץ conj.-prep.-n.m.s. (558) *and like chaff*
גְּנָבַ֥תּוּ Qal pf. 3 f.s.-3 m.s. sf. (גָּנַב 170) *carries it away*
סוּפָֽה n.f.s. (693) *storm-wind*

21:19

אֱ֭לוֹהַּ n.m.s. (42) *God*
יִצְפֹּן־ Qal impf. 3 m.s. (צָפַן 860) *stores up*
לְבָנָ֣יו prep.-n.m.p.-3 m.s. sf. (119) *for their sons*
אוֹנ֑וֹ n.m.s.-3 m.s. sf. (19) *their iniquity*
יְשַׁלֵּ֖ם Pi. impf. 3 m.s. (שָׁלַם 1022) *let him recompense it*
אֵלָ֣יו prep.-3 m.s. sf. *to themselves*
וְיֵדָֽע conj.-Qal impf. 3 m.s. paus. (יָדַע 393) *that they may know it*

21:20

יִרְא֣וּ Qal impf. 3 m.p. (רָאָה 906) *let ... see*
עֵינָ֣ו n.f. du.-3 m.s. sf. (744) *their own eyes*
כִּיד֑וֹ n.m.s.-3 m.s. sf. (475; hapax; ? פִּידוֹ 810) *their destruction*
וּמֵחֲמַ֖ת conj.-prep.-n.f.s. cstr. (404) *and of the wrath of*
שַׁדַּ֣י pr.n. (994) *the Almighty*
יִשְׁתֶּֽה Qal impf. 3 m.s. (שָׁתָה 1059) *let them drink*

21:21

כִּ֤י מַה־חֶפְצ֣וֹ conj. (471)-interr. (552)-n.m.s.-3 m.s. sf. (343; GK 37d) *for what do they care*
בְּבֵית֣וֹ prep.-n.m.s.-3 m.s. sf. (108) *for their houses*
אַחֲרָ֑יו prep.-3 m.s. sf. (29) *after them*
וּמִסְפַּ֖ר conj.-n.m.s. cstr. (708; GK 146a) *when the number of*
חֳדָשָׁ֣יו n.m.p.-3 m.s. sf. (294) *their months*
חֻצָּֽצוּ Pu. pf. 3 m.p. paus. (חָצַץ 346) *is cut off*

21:22

הַלְאֵ֥ל interr.-prep.-n.m.s. (42) *to God?*
יְלַמֶּד־ Pi. impf. 3 m.s. (לָמַד 540) *will any teach*
דָּ֑עַת n.f.s. paus. (395) *knowledge*
וְ֝ה֗וּא conj.-pers.pr. 3 m.s. (214; GK 142d) *seeing that he*
רָמִ֥ים Qal act.ptc. m.p. (רוּם 926; LXX φόνους) *those that are on high*
יִשְׁפּֽוֹט Qal impf. 3 m.s. (שָׁפַט 1047) *judges*

21:23

זֶ֗ה demons.adj. m.s. (260) *this one*
יָ֭מוּת Qal impf. 3 m.s. (מוּת 559) *dies*
בְּעֶ֣צֶם תֻּמּ֑וֹ prep.-n.f.s. cstr. (I 782)-n.m.s.-3 m.s. sf. (1070; GK 139g) *in full prosperity*

כֻּלֹּו n.m.s.-3 m.s. sf. (481) *all of them*
שַׁלְאֲנַן adj. m.s. (1016; 983) *at ease*
וְשָׁלֵיו conj.-adj. m.s. (1017) *and secure*

21:24

עֲטִינָיו n.m.p.-3 m.s. sf. (742; LXX τὰ δὲ ἔγκατα αὐτοῦ) *his pails*
מָלְאוּ Qal pf. 3 c.p. (מָלֵא 569) *are full of*
חָלָב n.m.s. (316; LXX στέατος=חֵלֶב) *milk*
וּמֹחַ conj.-n.m.s. cstr. (562) *and the marrow of*
עַצְמוֹתָיו n.f.p.-3 m.s. sf. (782) *his bones*
יְשֻׁקֶּה Pu. impf. 3 m.s. (שָׁקָה 1052) *is moist (watered)*

21:25

וְזֶה conj.-demons.adj. m.s. (260) *and another*
יָמוּת Qal impf. 3 m.s. (מוּת 559) *dies*
בְּנֶפֶשׁ מָרָה prep.-n.f.s. (659)-adj. f.s. (I 600; GK 119m) *in bitterness of soul*
וְלֹא־אָכַל conj.-neg.-Qal pf. 3 m.s. (37) *never having tasted*
בַּטּוֹבָה prep.-def.art.-n.f.s. (375) *of good*

21:26

יַחַד adv. (403) *alike (together)*
עַל־עָפָר prep.-n.m.s. (779) *in the dust*
יִשְׁכָּבוּ Qal impf. 3 m.p. paus. (שָׁכַב 1011) *they lie down*
וְרִמָּה conj.-n.f.s. (942) *and worms*
תְּכַסֶּה Pi. impf. 3 f.s. (כָּסָה 491) *cover*
עֲלֵיהֶם prep.-3 m.p. sf. *them*

21:27

הֵן interj. (243) *behold*
יָדַעְתִּי Qal pf. 1 c.s. (יָדַע 393) *I know*
מַחְשְׁבוֹתֵיכֶם n.f.p.-2 m.p. sf. (364) *your thoughts*
וּמְזִמּוֹת conj.-n.f.p. (273; GK 155k) *and schemes (wherewith)*
עָלַי prep.-1 c.s. sf. *against me*
תַּחְמֹסוּ Qal impf. 2 m.p. (חָמַס 329) *you do violence*

21:28

כִּי תֹאמְרוּ conj. (471)-Qal impf. 2 m.p. (אָמַר 55) *for you say*
אַיֵּה interr.adv. (32) *where is*
בֵית־נָדִיב n.m.s. cstr. (108)-adj. m.s. (622) *house of (the) prince*
וְאַיֵּה conj.-v.supra *and where*
אֹהֶל n.m.s. (13; some mss. >) *the tent*
מִשְׁכְּנוֹת n.m.p. cstr. (1015) *in which dwell*
רְשָׁעִים adj. m.p. (957) *wicked*

21:29

הֲלֹא שְׁאֶלְתֶּם interr.-neg.-Qal pf. 2 m.p. (שָׁאַל 981; GK 44d,64f) *have you not asked*
עוֹבְרֵי Qal act.ptc. m.p. cstr. (עָבַר 716) *those who travel*
דָרֶךְ n.m.s. paus. (202) *roads*
וְאֹתֹתָם conj.-n.f.p.-3 m.p. sf. (16) *and their testmony (signs)*
לֹא תְנַכֵּרוּ neg.-Pi. impf. 2 m.p. (נָכַר 647) *do you not accept?*

21:30

כִּי לְיוֹם conj. (471)-prep.-n.m.s. cstr. (398) *that in the day of*
אֵיד n.m.s. (15) *calamity*
יֵחָשֶׂךְ Ni. impf. 3 m.s. (חָשַׂךְ 362) *is spared*
רָע adj. m.s. (948) *wicked man*
לְיוֹם v.supra *in the day of*
עֲבָרוֹת n.f.p. (720) *wrath*
יוּבָלוּ Ho. impf. 3 m.p. paus. (יָבַל 384) *they are rescued*

21:31

מִי־יַגִּיד interr. (566)-Hi. impf. 3 m.s. (נָגַד 616) *who declares*
עַל־פָּנָיו prep.-n.m.p.-3 m.s. sf. (815) *to his face*
דַּרְכּוֹ n.m.s.-3 m.s. sf. (202) *his way*
וְהוּא־עָשָׂה conj.-pers.pr. 3 m.s. (214)-Qal pf. 3 m.s. (I 793) *for what he has done*
מִי יְשַׁלֶּם־לוֹ interr. (566)-Pi. impf. 3 m.s. (שָׁלַם 1022)-prep.-3 m.s. sf. *who requites him*

21:32

וְהוּא conj.-pers.pr. 3 m.s. (214) *when he*
לִקְבָרוֹת prep.-n.m.p. (868; GK 124c) *to (the) grave*
יוּבָל Ho. impf. 3 m.s. (יָבַל 384) *is borne*
וְעַל־גָּדִישׁ conj.-prep.-n.m.s. (II 155) *and over (his) tomb*
יִשְׁקוֹד Qal impf. 3 m.s. (שָׁקַד 1052) *watch is kept*

21:33

מָתְקוּ־ Qal pf. 3 c.p. (מָתַק 608) *are sweet*
לוֹ prep.-3 m.s. sf. *to him*
רִגְבֵי n.m.p. cstr. (918) *the clods of*
נָחַל n.m.s. paus. (636) *(the) valley*
וְאַחֲרָיו conj.-prep.-3 m.s. sf. (29) *after him*
כָּל־אָדָם n.m.s. cstr. (481)-n.m.s. (9) *all men*
יִמְשׁוֹךְ Qal impf. 3 m.s. (מָשַׁךְ 604) *follow*
וּלְפָנָיו conj.-prep.-n.m.p.-3 m.s. sf. (815) *and before him*

אֵין מִסְפָּר subst. cstr. (II 34)-n.m.s. paus. (708) *are innumerable*

21:34

וְאֵיךְ conj.-interr.adv. (32) *how then*
תְּנַחֲמוּנִי Pi. impf. 2 m.p.-1 c.s. sf. (נָחַם 636) *will you comfort me*
הָבֶל n.m.s. paus. as adv. (210) *vainly (to no purpose)*
וּתְשׁוּבֹתֵיכֶם conj.-n.f.p.-2 m.p. sf. (1000) *and of your answers*
נִשְׁאַר־ Ni. pf. 3 m.s. (שָׁאַר 983) *is left*
מָעַל n.m.s. paus. (591) *faithlessness*

22:1

וַיַּעַן consec.-Qal impf. 3 m.s. (עָנָה I 772) *then answered*
אֱלִיפַז pr.n. (45) *Eliphaz*
הַתֵּמָנִי def.art.-adj.gent. (412) *the Temanite*
וַיֹּאמַר consec.-Qal impf. 3 m.s. (55) *(and said)*

22:2

הַלְאֵל interr.-prep.-n.m.s. (42) *can ... to God?*
יִסְכָּן־ Qal impf. 3 m.s. (סָכַן I 698) *be of use*
גָּבֶר n.m.s. paus. (149) *a man*
כִּי־יִסְכֹּן conj. (471)-Qal impf. 3 m.s. (סָכַן I 698) *surely is of use*
עָלֵימוֹ prep.-3 m.s. sf. (GK 103fN) *to himself*
מַשְׂכִּיל Hi. ptc. m.s. as subst. (שָׂכַל 968) *he who is wise*

22:3

הַחֵפֶץ interr.-n.m.s. (343) *is it any pleasure*
לְשַׁדַּי prep.-pr.n. (994) *to the Almighty*
כִּי תִצְדָּק conj. (471)-Qal impf. 2 m.s. paus. (צָדַק 842) *if you are righteous*
וְאִם־בֶּצַע conj.-hypoth.part. (49)-n.m.s. (130) *or is it gain (to him)*
כִּי־תַתֵּם conj. (471)-Hi. impf. 2 m.s. (תָּמַם 1070; GK 67y) *if you make sound*
דְּרָכֶיךָ n.m.p.-2 m.s. sf. (202) *your ways*

22:4

הֲמִיִּרְאָתְךָ interr.-prep.-n.f.s.-2 m.s. sf. (432) *is it for your fear (of him)*
יֹכִיחֶךָ Hi. impf. 3 m.s.-2 m.s. sf. (יָכַח 406) *that he reproves you*
יָבוֹא Qal impf. 3 m.s. (בּוֹא 97) *he enters*
עִמְּךָ prep.-2 m.s. sf. (767) *with you*
בַּמִּשְׁפָּט prep.-def.art.-n.m.s. (1048) *into judgment*

22:5

הֲלֹא רָעָתְךָ interr.-neg.-n.f.s.-2 m.s. sf. (949) *is not your wickedness*
רַבָּה adj. f.s. (I 912) *great?*
וְאֵין־קֵץ conj.-subst. cstr. (II 34)-n.m.s. (893) *and there is no end*
לַעֲוֹנֹתֶיךָ prep.-n.m.p.-2 m.s. sf. (730) *to your iniquities*

22:6

כִּי־תַחְבֹּל conj. (471)-Qal impf. 2 m.s. (חָבַל I 286) *for you have exacted pledges of*
אַחֶיךָ n.m.p.-2 m.s. sf. (26) *your brothers*
חִנָּם adv. (336) *for nothing*
וּבִגְדֵי conj.-n.m.p. cstr. (93) *and garments of*
עֲרוּמִּים adj. m.p. (736) *the naked*
תַּפְשִׁיט Hi. impf. 2 m.s. (פָּשַׁט 832) *you have stripped*

22:7

לֹא־מַיִם neg.-n.m.p. (565; GK 152e) *no water*
עָיֵף adj. m.s. (746) *to the weary*
תַּשְׁקֶה Hi. impf. 2 m.s. (שָׁקָה 1052) *you have given to drink*
וּמֵרָעֵב conj.-prep.-adj. m.s. (944) *and from the hungry*
תִּמְנַע־ Qal impf. 2 m.s. (מָנַע 586) *you have withheld*
לָחֶם n.m.s. paus. (536) *bread*

22:8

וְאִישׁ conj.-n.m.s. (35) *and a man*
זְרוֹעַ לוֹ n.f.s. (283)-prep.-3 m.s. sf. *an arm to him (with power)*
הָאָרֶץ def.art.-n.f.s. (75) *the land*
וּנְשׂוּא פָנִים conj.-Qal pass.ptc. m.s. cstr. (נָשָׂא 669)-n.m.p. (815) *and the favored man (lifted of face)*
יֵשֶׁב בָּהּ Qal impf. 3 m.s. (יָשַׁב 442)-prep.-3 f.s. sf. *dwelt in it*

22:9

אַלְמָנוֹת n.f.p. (48) *widows*
שִׁלַּחְתָּ Pi. pf. 2 m.s. (שָׁלַח 1018) *you have sent away*
רֵיקָם adv. (938) *empty*
וּזְרֹעוֹת conj.-n.f.p. cstr. (283) *and arms of*
יְתֹמִים n.m.p. (450) *fatherless*
יְדֻכָּא Pu. impf. 3 m.s. (דָּכָא 193; GK 121b; LXX ἐκάκωσας) *were crushed*

22:10

עַל־כֵּן prep.-adv. (485) *therefore*
סְבִיבוֹתֶיךָ subst. p.-2 m.s. sf. (686) *around about you*
פַחִים n.m.p. (809) *snares*
וִיבַהֶלְךָ conj.-Pi. impf. 3 m.s.-2 m.s. sf. (בָּהַל 96) *and overwhelms you*
פַּחַד n.m.s. cstr. (808) *terror of*
פִּתְאֹם subst. (837) *suddenness*

22:11

אוֹ־חֹשֶׁךְ conj. (14)-n.m.s. (365; LXX τὸ φῶς σοι σκότος ἀπέβη) *or darkness*
לֹא־תִרְאֶה neg.-Qal impf. 2 m.s. (רָאָה 906) *(so that) you cannot see*
וְשִׁפְעַת־ conj.-n.f.s. cstr. (1051) *and a flood of*
מַיִם n.m.p. (565) *water*
תְּכַסֶּךָ Pi. impf. 3 f.s.-2 m.s. sf. (כָּסָה 491) *covers you*

22:12

הֲלֹא־אֱלוֹהַּ interr.-neg.-n.m.s. (42) *is not God?*
גֹּבַהּ שָׁמָיִם n.m.s. cstr. (147)-n.m.p. paus. (1029; GK 141c) *high in the heavens*
וּרְאֵה conj.-Qal impv. 2 m.s. (רָאָה 906; LXX ὕβρει) *and see*
רֹאשׁ כּוֹכָבִים n.m.s. cstr. (910)-n.m.p. (456) *the highest stars*
כִּי־רָמּוּ conj. (471)-Qal pf. 3 c.p. (רוּם 926; GK 20i,117h,158a) *how lofty they are (that they are high)*

22:13

וְאָמַרְתָּ conj.-Qal pf. 2 m.s. (55) *therefore you say*
מַה־יָּדַע interr. (552)-Qal pf. 3 m.s. (393) *what does ... know?*
אֵל n.m.s. (42) *God*
הַבְעַד עֲרָפֶל interr.-prep. (126)-n.m.s. (791) *through the deep darkness?*
יִשְׁפּוֹט Qal impf. 3 m.s. (שָׁפַט 1047) *can he judge?*

22:14

עָבִים n.m.p. (728) *thick clouds*
סֵתֶר־לוֹ n.m.s. (712)-prep.-3 m.s. sf. *a covering for him*
וְלֹא יִרְאֶה conj.-neg.-Qal impf. 3 m.s. (רָאָה 906) *so that he does not see*
וְחוּג שָׁמַיִם conj.-n.m.s. cstr. (295)-n.m.p. (1029) *and (the) vault of heaven*
יִתְהַלָּךְ Hith. impf. 3 m.s. paus. (הָלַךְ 229) *he walks on*

22:15

הַאֹרַח עוֹלָם interr.-n.m.s. cstr. (73)-n.m.s. (762) *to the old way?*
תִּשְׁמוֹר Qal impf. 2 m.s. (שָׁמַר 1036) *will you keep?*
אֲשֶׁר דָּרְכוּ rel. (81)-Qal pf. 3 c.p. (דָּרַךְ 201) *which have trod*
מְתֵי־אָוֶן n.m.p. cstr. (607)-n.m.s. (19) *wicked men*

22:16

אֲשֶׁר־קֻמְּטוּ rel. (81)-Pu. pf. 3 c.p. (קָמַט 888) *they were snatched away*
וְלֹא־עֵת conj.-neg.-n.f.s. (773) *before (and not) time*
נָהָר n.m.s. (625; GK 121d) *in a stream (river)*
יוּצַק Ho. impf. 3 m.s. (יָצַק 427) *was washed away (poured out)*
יְסוֹדָם n.m.s.-3 m.p. sf. (414) *their foundation*

22:17

הָאֹמְרִים def.art.-Qal act.ptc. m.p. (אָמַר 55) *they say*
לָאֵל prep.-def.art.-n.m.s. (42) *to God*
סוּר Qal impv. 2 m.s. (סוּר 693) *depart*
מִמֶּנּוּ prep.-1 c.p. sf. *from us*
וּמַה־יִּפְעַל conj.-interr. (552)-Qal impf. 3 m.s. (821 פָּעַל) *and what can ... do?*
שַׁדַּי pr.n. (994) *the Almighty*
לָמוֹ prep.-3 m.p. sf. (LXX ἡμῖν) *to them*

22:18

וְהוּא conj.-pers.pr. 3 m.s. (214) *yet he*
מִלֵּא Pi. pf. 3 m.s. (מָלֵא 569) *filled*
בָתֵּיהֶם n.m.p.-3 m.p. sf. (108) *their houses*
טוֹב n.m.s. (III 375) *with good things*
וַעֲצַת conj.-n.f.s. cstr. (420; GK 106nN) *but the counsel of*
רְשָׁעִים adj. m.p. (957) *the wicked*
רָחֲקָה Qal pf. 3 f.s. (רָחַק 934) *is far*
מֶנִּי prep.-1 c.s. sf. (LXX ἀπ' αὐτοῦ) *from me*

22:19

יִרְאוּ Qal impf. 3 m.p. (רָאָה 906; LXX ἰδόντες) *see*
צַדִּיקִים adj. m.p. (843) *the righteous*
וְיִשְׂמָחוּ conj.-Qal impf. 3 m.p. paus. (שָׂמַח 970) *and are glad*
וְנָקִי conj.-adj. m.s. (667) *and the innocent*

יִלְעַג־לָמוֹ Qal impf. 3 m.s. (לָעַג 541)-prep.-3 m.p. sf. *laugh them to scorn*

22:20

אִם־לֹא hypoth.part.-neg. (49) *surely*

נִכְחַד Ni. pf. 3 m.s. (כָּחַד 470; GK 149e) *are cut off*

קִימָנוּ n.m.s.-1 c.p. sf. (879; GK 91f; LXX ἡ ὑπόστασις αὐτῶν) *our adversaries*

וְיִתְרָם conj. n.m.s.-3 m.p. sf. (I 451) *and what they left*

אָכְלָה Qal pf. 3 f.s. (אָכַל 37) *has consumed*

אֵשׁ n.f.s. (77) *fire*

22:21

הַסְכֶּן־נָא Hi. impv. 2 m.s. (סָכַן 698; GK 110f)-part.of entreaty (609) *agree*

עִמּוֹ prep.-3 m.s. sf. *with him*

וּשְׁלָם conj.-Qal impv. 2 m.s. (1023) *and be at peace*

בָּהֶם prep.-3 m.p. sf. (GK 135p) *thereby*

תְּבוֹאַתְךָ Qal impf. 3 f.s.-2 m.s. sf. (בּוֹא 97; GK 48d) *will come to you*

טוֹבָה n.f.s. (375) *good*

22:22

קַח־נָא Qal impv. 2 m.s. (לָקַח 542)-part.of entreaty (609) *receive*

מִפִּיו prep.-n.m.s.-3 m.s. sf. (804) *from his mouth*

תּוֹרָה n.f.s. (435) *instruction*

וְשִׂים conj.-Qal impv. 2 m.s. (שִׂים 962) *and lay up*

אֲמָרָיו n.m.p.-3 m.s. sf. (56) *his words*

בִּלְבָבֶךָ prep.-n.m.s.-2 m.s. sf. (523) *in your heart*

22:23

אִם־תָּשׁוּב hypoth.part. (49)-Qal impf. 2 m.s. (996 שׁוּב; GK 159ff) *if you return*

עַד־שַׁדַּי prep. (III 723)-pr.n. (994) *to the Almighty*

תִּבָּנֶה Ni. impf. 2 m.s. (בָּנָה 124; LXX καὶ ταπεινώσῃς σεαυτὸν) *you will be built up*

תַּרְחִיק Hi. impf. 2 m.s. (רָחַק 934; GK 159ff) *if you remove*

עַוְלָה n.f.s. (732) *unrighteousness*

מֵאָהֳלֶךָ prep.-n.m.p.-2 m.s. sf. paus. (13) *from your tents*

22:24

וְשִׁית־ conj.-Qal impv. 2 m.s. (שִׁית 1011) *and put*

עַל־עָפָר prep.-n.m.s. (779) *in dust*

בָּצֶר n.m.s. paus. (I 131) *gold*

וּבְצוּר conj.-prep.-n.m.s. cstr. (849) *and among stones of*

נְחָלִים n.m.p. (636) *the torrent bed*

אוֹפִיר pr.n. (20) *(gold of) Ophir*

22:25

וְהָיָה conj.-Qal pf. 3 m.s. (224) *and is*

שַׁדַּי pr.n. (994) *the Almighty*

בְּצָרֶיךָ n.m.p.-2 m.s. sf. (I 131) *your gold*

וְכֶסֶף conj.-n.m.s. cstr. (494) *and silver of*

תּוֹעָפוֹת n.f.p. (419) *eminence*

לָךְ prep.-2 m.s. sf. paus. *to you*

22:26

כִּי־אָז conj. (471)-adv. (23) *then*

עַל־שַׁדַּי prep.-pr.n. (994) *in the Almighty*

תִּתְעַנָּג Hith. impf. 2 m.s. paus. (עָנַג 772) *you will delight yourself*

וְתִשָּׂא conj.-Qal impf. 2 m.s. (נָשָׂא 669) *and you will lift up*

אֶל־אֱלוֹהַּ prep.-n.m.s. (42) *to God*

פָּנֶיךָ n.m.p.-2 m.s. sf. (815) *your face*

22:27

תַּעְתִּיר Hi. impf. 2 m.s. (עָתַר I 801) *you will make your prayer*

אֵלָיו prep.-3 m.s. sf. *to him*

וְיִשְׁמָעֶךָ conj.-Qal impf. 3 m.s.-2 m.s. sf. paus. (1033 שָׁמַע) *and he will hear you*

וּנְדָרֶיךָ conj.-n.m.p.-2 m.s. sf. (623) *and your vows*

תְשַׁלֵּם Pi. impf. 2 m.s. (שָׁלַם 1022) *you will pay*

22:28

וְתִגְזַר־ conj.-Qal impf. 2 m.s. (גָּזַר *and you will decide (decree)*

אוֹמֶר n.m.s. (56) *a matter*

וְיָקָם לָךְ conj.-Qal impf. 3 m.s. (קוּם 877)-prep. -2 m.s. sf. paus. *and it will be established for you*

וְעַל־דְּרָכֶיךָ conj.-prep.-n.m.p.-2 m.s. sf. (202) *and on your ways*

נָגַהּ Qal pf. 3 m.s. (618) *will shine*

אוֹר n.m.s. (21) *light*

22:29

כִּי־הִשְׁפִּילוּ conj. (471)-Hi. pf. 3 c.p. (שָׁפֵל 1050) *and when they abased*

וַתֹּאמֶר consec.-Qal impf. 2 m.s. (אָמַר 55) *you said*

גֵּוָה n.f.s. (145; GK 23f) *proud (up!)*

וּשַׁח עֵינַיִם adj. m.s. cstr. (1006)–n.f. du. (744) *and lowly of eyes*
יוֹשִׁעַ Hi. impf. 3 m.s. (יָשַׁע 446) *he saves*

22:30

יְמַלֵּט Pi. impf. 3 m.s. (מָלַט 572) *he delivers*
אִי־נָקִי adv. (IV 33)–adj. m.s. (667; GK 152q) *him that is not innocent*
וְנִמְלַט conj.–Ni. pf. 3 m.s. (מָלַט 572) *and he is delivered*
בְּבֹר prep.–n.m.s. cstr. (141) *through the cleanness of*
כַּפֶּיךָ n.f.p.–2 m.s. sf. (496) *your hands*

23:1

וַיַּעַן consec.–Qal impf. 3 m.s. (עָנָה I 772) *then answered*
אִיּוֹב pr.n. (33) *Job*
וַיֹּאמַר consec.–Qal impf. 3 m.s. (אָמַר 55) *(and said)*

23:2

גַּם־הַיּוֹם adv. (168)–def.art.–n.m.s. (398; LXX καὶ δὴ οἶδα) *also today*
מְרִי n.m.s. (598) *rebellion*
שִׂחִי n.m.s.–1 c.s. sf. (967) *my complaint*
יָדִי n.f.s.–1 c.s. sf. (388; LXX ἡ χεὶρ αὐτοῦ) *my hand*
כָּבְדָה Qal pf. 3 f.s. (כָּבֵד 457) *is heavy*
עַל־אַנְחָתִי prep.–n.f.s.–1 c.s. sf. (58; GK 119aa) *in spite of my groaning*

23:3

מִי־יִתֵּן interr. (566)–Qal impf. 3 m.s. (נָתַן 678) *oh that*
יָדַעְתִּי Qal pf. 1 c.s. (יָדַע 393) *I knew*
וְאֶמְצָאֵהוּ conj.–Qal impf. 1 c.s.–3 m.s. sf. (מָצָא 4592; GK 120c) *where (that) I might find him*
אָבוֹא Qal impf. 1 c.s. (בּוֹא 97) *(that) I might come*
עַד־תְּכוּנָתוֹ prep. (III 723)–n.f.s.–3 m.s. sf. (467) *to his seat*

23:4

אֶעֶרְכָה Qal impf. 1 c.s.–vol.he (עָרַךְ 789) *I would lay (arrange)*
לְפָנָיו prep.–n.m.p.–3 m.s. sf. (815) *before him*
מִשְׁפָּט n.m.s. (1048; LXX ἐμαυτοῦ κρίμα) *my case*
וּפִי conj.–n.m.s.–1 c.s. sf. (804) *and my mouth*
אֲמַלֵּא Pi. impf. 1 c.s. (מָלֵא 569) *I would fill*
תוֹכָחוֹת n.f.p. (407) *with arguments*

23:5

אֵדְעָה Qal impf. 1 c.s.–vol.he (יָדַע 393) *I would know*
מִלִּים n.f.p. (576) *words*
יַעֲנֵנִי Qal impf. 3 m.s.–1 c.s. sf. (עָנָה I 772) *he would answer me*
וְאָבִינָה conj.–Qal impf. 1 c.s.–vol.he (בִּין 106) *and understand*
מַה־יֹּאמַר interr. (552)–Qal impf. 3 m.s. (אָמַר 55) *what he would say*
לִי prep.–1 c.s. sf. *to me*

23:6

הַבְּרָב־ interr.–prep.–n.m.s. cstr. (913; GK 100,l) *in the greatness of?*
כֹּחַ n.m.s. (470) *(his) power?*
יָרִיב Qal impf. 3 m.s. (רִיב 936) *would he contend?*
עִמָּדִי prep.–1 c.s. sf. *with me*
לֹא neg. (some rd. לֹא = לוֹ) *No*
אַךְ־הוּא adv. (36)–pers.pr. 3 m.s. (214) *surely he*
יָשִׂם בִּי Qal impf. 3 m.s. (שִׂים 962)–prep.–1 c.s. sf. *he would give (heed) to me*

23:7

שָׁם adv. (1027) *there*
יָשָׁר adj. m.s. (449) *an upright man*
נוֹכָח עִמּוֹ Ni. ptc. (יָכַח 406)–prep.–3 m.s. sf. *could reason with him*
וַאֲפַלְּטָה conj.–Pi. impf. 1 c.s.–vol.he (פָּלַט 812) *and I should be acquitted*
לָנֶצַח prep.–n.m.s. (664) *for ever*
מִשֹּׁפְטִי prep.–Qal act.ptc.–1 c.s. sf. (שָׁפַט 1047) *by my judge*

23:8

הֵן interj. (243) *behold*
קֶדֶם n.m.s. (869) *forward*
אֶהֱלֹךְ Qal impf. 1 c.s. (הָלַךְ 229) *I go*
וְאֵינֶנּוּ conj.–subst.–3 m.s. sf. (II 34; LXX καὶ οὐκέτι εἰμί) *but he is not there*
וְאָחוֹר conj.–subst. (30) *and backward*
וְלֹא־אָבִין conj.–neg.–Qal impf. 1 c.s. (בִּין 106) *but I cannot perceive*
לוֹ prep.–3 m.s. sf. *him*

23:9

שְׂמֹאול n.m.s. (969) *on the left hand*
בַּעֲשֹׂתוֹ prep.–Qal inf.cstr.–3 m.s. sf. (עָשָׂה I 793) *when he works*
וְלֹא־אָחַז conj.–neg.–Qal impf. 1 c.s. paus.= אֶחֱזֶה (אָחַז I 302; GK 109k) *but I cannot behold*

יַעְטֹף Qal impf. 3 m.s. (עָטַף 742) *he turns to*
יָמִין n.f.s. (411) *to the right hand*
וְלֹא אֶרְאֶה conj.-neg.-Qal impf. 1 c.s. (רָאָה 906) *but I cannot see (him)*

23:10

כִּי־יָדַע conj. (471)-Qal pf. 3 m.s. (393) *but he knows*
דֶּרֶךְ n.m.s. (202) *the way*
עִמָּדִי prep.-1 c.s. sf. (767) *with me (that I take)*
בְּחָנַנִי Qal impv. 2 m.s.-1 c.s. sf. (בָּחַן 103) *try me*
כַּזָּהָב prep.-def.art.-n.m.s. (262) *as gold*
אֵצֵא Qal impf. 1 c.s. (יָצָא 422) *I shall come forth*

23:11

בַּאֲשֻׁרוֹ prep.-n.f.s.-3 m.s. sf. (81; LXX ἐν ἐντάλμασιν αὐτοῦ) *to his steps*
אָחֲזָה Qal pf. 3 f.s. (אָחַז 28) *has held fast*
רַגְלִי n.f.s.-1 c.s. sf. (919) *my foot*
דַּרְכּוֹ n.m.s.-3 m.s. sf. (202) *his way*
שָׁמַרְתִּי Qal pf. 1 c.s. (שָׁמַר 1036) *I have kept*
וְלֹא־אָט conj.-neg.-Hi. impf. 1 c.s. apoc. paus. (639 נָטָה; GK 76c) *and have not turned aside*

23:12

מִצְוַת n.f.s. cstr. (846) *from the commandment of*
שְׂפָתָיו n.f.p.-3 m.s. sf. (973) *his lips*
וְלֹא אָמִישׁ conj.-neg.-Hi. impf. 1 c.s. (מוּשׁ I 559; GK 143d) *I have not departed*
מֵחֻקִּי prep.-n.m.s.-1 c.s. sf. (349; LXX ἐν δὲ κόλπῳ μου) *from my statute*
צָפַנְתִּי Qal pf. 1 c.s. (צָפַן 860) *I have treasured (hidden)*
אִמְרֵי־פִיו n.m.p. cstr. (56)-n.m.s.-3 m.s. sf. (804) *the words of his mouth*

23:13

וְהוּא conj.-pers.pr. 3 m.s. (214) *but he*
בְאֶחָד prep. (88)-adj. (25; GK 119i) *consists of oneness*
וּמִי יְשִׁיבֶנּוּ conj.-interr. (566)-Hi. impf. 3 m.s.-3 m.s. sf. (שׁוּב 996) *and who can turn him*
וְנַפְשׁוֹ conj.-n.f.s.-3 m.s. sf. (659) *and he himself*
אִוְּתָה Pi. pf. 3 f.s. (אָוָה 16) *desires*
וַיָּעַשׂ consec.-Qal impf. 3 m.s. paus. (עָשָׂה I 793) *that he does*

23:14 (LXX>)

כִּי יַשְׁלִים conj. (473,3c)-Hi. impf. 3 m.s. (שָׁלֵם 1022) *for he will complete*
חֻקִּי n.m.s.-1 c.s. sf. (349) *my decree (what he appoints for me)*
וְכָהֵנָּה conj.-prep.-def.art.-demons.adj. f.p. (241) *and such things*
רַבּוֹת adj. f.p. (I 912) *many*
עִמּוֹ prep.-3 m.s. sf. (767) *with him (in his mind)*

23:15

עַל־כֵּן prep.-adv. (485) *therefore*
מִפָּנָיו prep.-n.m.p.-3 m.s. sf. (815) *at his presence*
אֶבָּהֵל Ni. impf. 1 c.s. (בָּהַל 96) *I am terrified*
אֶתְבּוֹנֵן Hithpolel impf. 1 c.s. (בִּין 106) *when I consider*
וְאֶפְחַד conj.-Qal impf. 1 c.s. (פָּחַד 808) *I am in dread*
מִמֶּנּוּ prep.-3 m.s. sf. *of him*

23:16

וְאֵל conj.-n.m.s. (42) *and God*
הֵרַךְ Hi. pf. 3 m.s. (רָכַךְ 939; GK 67v) *has made faint (weak)*
לִבִּי n.m.s.-1 c.s. sf. (524) *my heart*
וְשַׁדַּי conj.-pr.n. (994) *and the Almighty*
הִבְהִילָנִי Hi. pf. 3 m.s.-1 c.s. sf. (בָּהַל 96) *has terrified me*

23:17

כִּי־לֹא נִצְמַתִּי conj. (471)-neg.-Ni. pf. 1 c.s. (856 צָמַת) *for I am not annihilated*
מִפְּנֵי־חֹשֶׁךְ prep.-n.m.p. cstr. (815)-n.m.s. (365) *by darkness*
וּמִפָּנַי conj.-prep.-n.m.p.-1 c.s. sf. (815) *and from my face*
כִּסָּה־ Pi. pf. 3 m.s. (כָּסָה I 491) *covers*
אֹפֶל n.m.s. (66) *thick darkness*

24:1

מַדּוּעַ adv. (396) *why*
מִשַּׁדַּי prep.-pr.n. (994; GK 121f) *by the Almighty*
לֹא־נִצְפְּנוּ neg.-Ni. pf. 3 c.p. (צָפַן 860) *are not kept (stored up)*
עִתִּים n.f.p. (773) *times*
וְיֹדְעוֹ conj.-Qal act.ptc. m.p.-3 m.s. sf. (יָדַע 393; Q וְיֹדְעָיו) *and why do those who know him*
לֹא־חָזוּ neg.-Qal pf. 3 c.p. (חָזָה 302; GK 75m) *never see*
יָמָיו n.m.p.-3 m.s. sf. (388) *his days*

24:2

גְּבֻלוֹת n.f.p. (148) *landmarks*

יַשִּׂיגוּ Hi. impf. 3 m.p. (נָשַׂג 673; I 690) *men remove*

עֵדֶר n.m.s. (727) *flocks*

גָּזְלוּ Qal pf. 3 c.p. (גָּזַל 159) *they seize*

וַיִּרְעוּ consec.-Qal impf. 3 m.p. (רָעָה I 944) *and pasture (them)*

24:3

חֲמוֹר n.m.s. cstr. (331) *the ass of*

יְתוֹמִים n.m.p. (450) *the fatherless*

יִנְהָגוּ Qal impf. 3 m.p. (נָהַג 624) *they drive away*

יַחְבְּלוּ Qal impf. 3 m.p. (חָבַל I 286) *they take for a pledge*

שׁוֹר n.m.s. cstr. (1004) *the ox of*

אַלְמָנָה n.f.s. (48) *a widow*

24:4

יַטּוּ Hi. impf. 3 m.p. (נָטָה 639) *they thrust off*

אֶבְיוֹנִים n.m.p. (2) *the poor*

מִדָּרֶךְ prep.-n.m.s. paus. (202) *from the road*

יַחַד adv. (403) *all*

חֻבְּאוּ Pu. pf. 3 c.p. (חָבָא 285) *are made to hide themselves*

עֲנִיֵּי־אָרֶץ n.m.p. cstr. (776)-n.f.s. (75) *the poor of the earth*

24:5

הֵן interj. (243) *behold*

פְּרָאִים n.m.p. (825; GK 118r) *wild asses*

בַּמִּדְבָּר prep.-def.art.-n.m.s. (184) *in the desert*

יָצְאוּ Qal pf. 3 c.p. (יָצָא 422) *they go forth*

בְּפָעֳלָם prep.-n.m.s.-3 m.p. sf. (821) *to their toil*

מְשַׁחֲרֵי Pi. ptc. m.p. cstr. (שָׁחַר 1007; GK 130a) *seeking of*

לַטָּרֶף prep.-def.art.-n.m.s. (383) *prey*

עֲרָבָה n.f.s. (787) *in the wilderness*

לוֹ לֶחֶם prep.-3 m.s. sf.-n.m.s. (536; GK 145m) *food to him*

לַנְּעָרִים prep.-def.art.-n.m.p. (654) *for the children*

24:6

בַּשָּׂדֶה prep.-def.art.-n.m.s. (961) *in the field*

בְּלִילוֹ n.m.s.-3 m.s. sf. (117; LXX πρὸ ὥρας οὐκ αὐτῶν ὄντα=בְּלִי לוֹ) *his fodder*

יִקְצִירוּ Hi. impf. 3 m.p. (קָצַר II 894; Q-Qal impf. 3 m.p.) *they gather*

וְכֶרֶם conj.-n.m.s. cstr. (501) *and the vineyard of*

רָשָׁע adj. m.s. (957) *the wicked man*

יְלַקֵּשׁוּ Pi. impf. 3 m.p. (לָקַשׁ 545) *they glean (despoil)*

24:7

עָרוֹם adj. m.s. (736) *naked*

יָלִינוּ Qal impf. 3 m.p. (לִין I 533; GK 118o) *they lie*

מִבְּלִי לְבוּשׁ prep.-neg. (115)-n.m.s. (528) *without clothing*

וְאֵין כְּסוּת conj.-subst.cstr. (II 34)-n.f.s. (592) *and have no covering*

בַּקָּרָה prep.-def.art.-n.f.s. (903) *in the cold*

24:8

מִזֶּרֶם prep.-n.m.s. cstr. (281) *with the rain of*

הָרִים n.m.p. (249) *the mountains*

יִרְטָבוּ Qal impf. 3 m.p. paus. (רָטַב 936) *they are wet*

וּמִבְּלִי conj.-prep.-neg. (115) *and for want of*

מַחְסֶה n.m.s. (340) *shelter*

חִבְּקוּ־ Pi. pf. 3 c.p. (חָבַק 287) *they cling to*

צוּר n.m.s. (849) *the rock*

24:9

יִגְזְלוּ Qal impf. 3 m.p. (גָּזַל I 159) *there are those who snatch*

מִשֹּׁד prep.-n.m.s. (II 994) *from the breast*

יָתוֹם n.m.s. (450) *the fatherless child*

וְעַל־עָנִי conj.-prep.-adj. m.s. (776) *and upon the poor*

יַחְבֹּלוּ Qal impf. 3 m.p. (חָבַל I 286) *they take in pledge*

24:10

עָרוֹם adj. m.s. (736; GK 118o) *naked*

הִלְּכוּ Pi. pf. 3 c.p. (הָלַךְ) *they go about*

בְּלִי לְבוּשׁ neg. (115)-n.m.s. (528; GK 152u) *without clothing*

וּרְעֵבִים conj.-adj. m.p. (944) *and hungry*

נָשְׂאוּ Qal pf. 3 c.p. (נָשָׂא 669) *they carry*

עֹמֶר n.m.s. (I 771) *the sheaves*

24:11

בֵּין־שׁוּרֹתָם prep. (107)-n.f.p.-3 m.p. sf. (1004) *among the olive rows*

יַצְהִירוּ Hi. impf. 3 m.p. (צָהַר 844) *they make oil*

יְקָבִים n.m.p. (428) *the wine presses*

דָּרְכוּ Qal pf. 3 c.p. (דָּרַךְ 201) *they tread*

וַיִּצְמָאוּ consec.-Qal impf. 3 m.p. paus. (צָמֵא 854) *but suffer thirst*

24:12

מֵעִיר prep.-n.f.s. (746) *from out of the city*
מְתִים n.m.p. (607; LXX οἴκων ἰδίων) *men*
יִנְאָקוּ Qal impf. 3 m.p. paus. (נָאַק 611) *groan*
וְנֶפֶשׁ־ conj.-n.f.s. cstr. (659) *and the soul of*
חֲלָלִים n.m.p. (I 319) *fatally wounded*
תְּשַׁוֵּעַ Pi. impf. 3 f.s. (שָׁוַע 1002) *cries for help*
וֶאֱלוֹהַּ conj.-n.m.s. (42) *yet God*
לֹא־יָשִׂים neg.-Qal impf. 3 m.s. (שִׂים 962) *pays no attention to*
תִּפְלָה n.f.s. (1074; Syr. rds. תְּפִלָּה 813=*prayer*) *unseemliness*

24:13

הֵמָּה pers.pr. 3 m.p. (241) *there are those*
הָיוּ Qal pf. 3 c.p. (הָיָה 224) *who are*
בְּמֹרְדֵי־ prep.-Qal act.ptc. m.p. cstr. (מָרַד 597) *among the rebellers against*
אוֹר n.m.s. (21) *the light*
לֹא־הִכִּירוּ neg.-Hi. pf. 3 c.p. (נָכַר I 647) *who are not acquainted with*
דְּרָכָיו n.m.p.-3 m.s. sf. (202) *its ways*
וְלֹא יָשְׁבוּ conj.-neg.-Qal pf. 3 c.p. (יָשַׁב 442; LXX ἐπορεύθησαν) *and do not stay*
בִּנְתִיבֹתָיו prep.-n.f.p.-3 m.s. sf. (677) *in its paths*

24:14

לָאוֹר prep.-def.art.-n.m.s. (21) *at the light*
יָקוּם Qal impf. 3 m.s. (קוּם 877) *rises*
רוֹצֵחַ Qal act.ptc. (רָצַח 953) *the murderer*
יִקְטָל־ Qal impf. 3 m.s. (קָטַל 881; GK 109k,120c) *that he may kill*
עָנִי adj. m.s. (776) *the poor*
וְאֶבְיוֹן conj.-adj. m.s. (2) *and needy*
וּבַלַּיְלָה conj.-prep.-def.art.-n.m.s. (538) *and in the night*
יְהִי Qal impf. 3 m.s. apoc. (הָיָה 224) *that he may be*
כַגַּנָּב prep.-def.art.-n.m.s. (170; GK 118x) *as the thief*

24:15

וְעֵין conj.-n.f.s. cstr. (744) *and the eye of*
נֹאֵף Qal act.ptc. (נָאַף 610) *the adulterer*
שָׁמְרָה Qal pf. 3 f.s. (שָׁמַר 1036) *waits for*
נֶשֶׁף n.m.s. (676) *the twilight*
לֵאמֹר prep.-Qal inf.cstr. (55) *saying*
לֹא־תְשׁוּרֵנִי neg.-Qal impf. 3 f.s.-1 c.s. sf. (שׁוּר 1003) *will not see me*
עָיִן n.f.s. paus. (744) *an eye*
וְסֵתֶר conj.-n.m.s. cstr. (712) *and a covering of*
פָּנִים n.m.p. (815) *face (disguise)*

יָשִׂים Qal impf. 3 m.s. (962) *he makes*

24:16

חָתַר Qal pf. 3 m.s. (369) *they (he) dig through*
בַּחֹשֶׁךְ prep.-def.art.-n.m.s. (365) *in the dark*
בָּתִּים n.m.p. (108) *houses*
יוֹמָם adv. (401) *by day*
חִתְּמוּ־לָמוֹ Pi. pf. 3 c.p. (חָתַם 367)-prep.-3 m.s. sf. *they shut themselves up*
לֹא־יָדְעוּ neg.-Qal pf. 3 c.p. (יָדַע 393) *they do not know*
אוֹר n.m.s. (21) *the light*

24:17

כִּי יַחְדָּו conj. (471)-adv. (403) *for together*
בֹּקֶר n.m.s. (133) *morning (is)*
לָמוֹ prep.-3 m.p. sf. *to them*
צַלְמָוֶת n.m.s. (853) *deep darkness*
כִּי־יַכִּיר conj.-Hi. impf. 3 m.s. (נָכַר I 647) *for they recognize (are acquainted with)*
בַּלְהוֹת n.f.p. cstr. (117) *terrors of*
צַלְמָוֶת v.supra *deep darkness*

24:18

קַל־הוּא adj. m.s. (886)-pers.pr. 3 m.s. (214) *they are swift*
עַל־פְּנֵי־מַיִם prep.-n.m.p. cstr. (815)-n.m.p. (565) *upon face of waters*
תְּקֻלַּל Pu. impf. 3 f.s. (קָלַל 886) *is cursed*
חֶלְקָתָם n.f.s.-3 m.p. sf. (I 324) *their portion*
בָּאָרֶץ prep.-def.art.-n.f.s. (75) *in the land*
לֹא־יִפְנֶה neg.-Qal impf. 3 m.s. (פָּנָה 815) *one does not face*
דֶּרֶךְ n.m.s. cstr. (202) *toward*
כְּרָמִים n.m.p. (501) *vineyards*

24:19

צִיָּה n.f.s. (851) *drought*
גַם־חֹם adv. (168)-n.m.s. (328; GK 161a) *even heat*
יִגְזְלוּ Qal impf. 3 m.p. (גָּזַל 159) *snatch away*
מֵימֵי־שֶׁלֶג n.m.p. cstr. (565)-n.m.s. (1017) *snow waters*
שְׁאוֹל pr.n. f.s. (982) *Sheol*
חָטָאוּ Qal pf. 3 c.p. paus. (חָטָא 306) *those who have sinned*

24:20

יִשְׁכָּחֵהוּ Qal impf. 3 m.s.-3 m.s. sf. (שָׁכַח 1013) *forgets him*
רֶחֶם n.m.s. (933) *a womb*
מְתָקוֹ Qal pf. 3 m.s.-3 m.s. sf. (מָתֹק 608; GK 145o) *sucks him*

רִמָּה n.f.s. (942) *a worm*
עוֹד לֹא־יִזָּכֵר adv. (728)-neg.-Ni. impf. 3 m.s. (269 **זָכַר**) *still is no longer remembered*
וַתִּשָּׁבֵר consec.-Ni. impf. 3 f.s. (**שָׁבַר** 990) *so is broken*
כָּעֵץ prep.-def.art.-n.m.s. (781) *like a tree*
עַוְלָה n.f.s. (732) *wickedness*

24:21

רֹעֶה Qal act.ptc. (**רָעָה** I 944) *they feed on*
עֲקָרָה adj. f.s. (785) *the barren woman*
לֹא תֵלֵד neg.-Qal impf. 3 f.s. (**יָלַד** 408) *childless*
וְאַלְמָנָה conj.-n.f.s. (40) *and to the widow*
לֹא יְיֵטִיב neg.-Hi. impf. 3 m.s. (**יָטַב** 405; GK 70d,116x) *they do not good*

24:22

וּמָשַׁךְ conj.-Qal pf. 3 m.s. (604) *yet he prolongs*
אַבִּירִים adj. m.p. (7) *mighty ones*
בְּכֹחוֹ prep.-n.m.s.-3 m.s. sf. (II 470) *by his power*
יָקוּם Qal impf. 3 m.s. (**קוּם** 877) *they rise up*
וְלֹא־יַאֲמִין conj.-neg.-Hi. impf. 3 m.s. (**אָמַן** I 52; GK 156f) *when they do not trust*
בַּחַיִּין prep.-def.art.-n.m.p. (313; GK 87e; LXX κατὰ τῆς ἑαυτοῦ ζωῆς) *in life*

24:23

יִתֶּן־לוֹ Qal impf. 3 m.s. (**נָתַן** 678)-prep.-3 m.s. sf. *he gives them*
לָבֶטַח prep.-n.m.s. (105) *security*
וְיִשָּׁעֵן conj.-Ni. impf. 3 m.s. (**שָׁעַן** 1043) *and they are supported*
וְעֵינֵיהוּ conj.-n.f. du.-3 m.s. sf. (744; GK 91,l) *and his eyes*
עַל־דַּרְכֵיהֶם prep.-n.m.p.-3 m.p. sf. (202) *upon their ways*

24:24

רוֹמּוּ Qal pf. 3 c.p. (**רָמַם** 942; GK 67m) *they are exalted*
מְּעַט adv. (589) *a little while*
וְאֵינֶנּוּ conj.-subst.-3 m.s. sf. (II 34) *and then are gone*
וְהֻמְּכוּ conj.-Ho. pf. 3 c.p. (**מָכַךְ** 568; GK 67y) *and they are brought low*
כַּכֹּל prep.-def.art.-n.m.s. (481; LXX ὥσπερ μολόχη) *like all*
יִקָּפְצוּן Ni. impf. 3 m.p. (**קָפַץ** 891; GK 51m) *they draw themselves together*

וּכְרֹאשׁ conj.-prep.-n.m.s. cstr. (910) *and like the heads of*
שִׁבֹּלֶת n.f.s. (II 987) *grain*
יִמָּלוּ Qal impf. 3 m.p. (**מָלַל** III 576) *they wither*

24:25

וְאִם־לֹא אֵפוֹ conj.-hypoth.part. (49)-neg. -enclitic part. (66; GK 150,lN) *if it is not so*
מִי יַכְזִיבֵנִי interr. (566)-Hi. impf. 3 m.s.-1 c.s. sf. (**כָּזַב** 469) *who will prove me a liar*
וְיָשֵׂם conj.-Qal impf. 3 m.s. apoc. (**שִׂים** 962) *and show*
לְאַל prep.-adv. of negation as subst. (39; GK 152a) *to nought*
מִלָּתִי n.f.s.-1 c.s. sf. (576) *my word*

25:1

וַיַּעַן consec.-Qal impf. 3 m.s. (**עָנָה** I 772) *then answered*
בִּלְדַּד pr.n. (115) *Bildad*
הַשֻּׁחִי def.art.-adj.gent. (1001) *the Shuhite*
וַיֹּאמַר consec.-Qal impf. 3 m.s. (**אָמַר** 55) *(and said)*

25:2

הַמְשֵׁל Hi. inf.abs. (**מָשַׁל** 605) *dominion*
וָפַחַד consec.-n.m.s. (I 808) *and fear*
עִמּוֹ prep.-3 m.s. sf. (767) *with him*
עֹשֶׂה Qal act.ptc. (**עָשָׂה** I 793; GK 116s) *he makes*
שָׁלוֹם n.m.s. (1022) *peace*
בִּמְרוֹמָיו prep.-n.m.p.-3 m.s. sf. (928) *in his high heaven*

25:3

הֲיֵשׁ interr.-subst. (441) *is there?*
מִסְפָּר n.m.s. (708) *any number*
לִגְדוּדָיו prep.-n.m.p.-3 m.s. sf. (151) *to his armies*
וְעַל־מִי conj.-prep.-interr. (566) *and upon whom*
לֹא־יָקוּם neg.-Qal impf. 3 m.s. (**קוּם** 877) *does not arise*
אוֹרֵהוּ n.m.s.-3 m.s. sf. (21; GK 91d; LXX ἔνεδρα παρ᾽ αὐτοῦ) *his light*

25:4

וּמַה־ conj.-interr. (552) *and how then*
יִצְדַּק Qal impf. 3 m.s. (**צָדַק** 842) *can be righteous*
אֱנוֹשׁ n.m.s. (60) *man*
עִם־אֵל prep. (767)-n.m.s. (42) *before God*
וּמַה־ v.supra *and how*
יִזְכֶּה Qal impf. 3 m.s. (**זָכָה** 269) *can be clean*

יְלוּד Qal pass.ptc. m.s. cstr. (יָלַד 408) *he who is born of*
אִשָּׁה n.f.s. (61) *woman*

25:5

הֵן interj. (243) *behold*
עַד־יָרֵחַ prep. (III 723)–n.m.s. (I 437; LXX σελήνῃ συντάσσει) *even the moon*
וְלֹא יַאֲהִיל conj.–neg.–Hi. impf. 3 m.s. (אָהַל II 14; LXX καὶ οὐκ ἐπιφαύσκει) *is not bright*
וְכוֹכָבִים conj.–n.m.p. (456) *and the stars*
לֹא־זַכּוּ neg.–Qal pf. 3 c.p. (זָכָה 269; GK 67ee) *are not clean*
בְעֵינָיו prep.–n.f.p.–3 m.s. sf. (744) *in his sight*

25:6

אַף כִּי־ conj. (64)–conj. (471) *how much less*
אֱנוֹשׁ n.m.s. (60) *man*
רִמָּה n.f.s. (942) *a maggot*
וּבֶן־אָדָם conj.–n.m.s. cstr. (118)–n.m.s. (9) *and a son of a man*
תּוֹלֵעָה n.f.s. (1069) *who is a worm*

26:1

וַיַּעַן consec.–Qal impf. 3 m.s. (עָנָה I 772) *then answered*
אִיּוֹב pr.n. (33) *Job*
וַיֹּאמַר consec.–Qal impf. 3 m.s. (אָמַר 55) *(and said)*

26:2

מֶה־עָזַרְתָּ interr. (552)–Qal pf. 2 m.s. (עָזַר 740) *how you have helped*
לְלֹא־כֹחַ prep.–neg.–n.m.s. (470; GK 152aN, 152u,v) *him who has no power*
הוֹשַׁעְתָּ Hi. pf. 2 m.s. (יָשַׁע 446) *how you have saved*
זְרוֹעַ n.f.s. (283) *the arm*
לֹא־עֹז neg.–n.m.s. (738) *that has no strength*

26:3

מַה־יָּעַצְתָּ interr. (552)–Qal pf. 2 m.s. (יָעַץ 419) *how you have counseled*
לְלֹא חָכְמָה prep.–neg.–n.f.s. (315; GK 152aN) *him who has no wisdom*
וְתוּשִׁיָּה conj.–n.f.s. (444) *and sound wisdom*
לָרֹב prep.–n.m.s. (913) *abundantly*
הוֹדָעְתָּ Hi. pf. 2 m.s. paus. (יָדַע 393) *you have caused to know*

26:4

אֶת־מִי prep. (II 85)–interr. (566) *with whom*
הִגַּדְתָּ Hi. pf. 2 m.s. (נָגַד 616; GK 117gg) *have you uttered*
מִלִּין n.f.p. (576) *words*
וְנִשְׁמַת־מִי conj.–n.f.s. cstr. (675)–interr. (566) *and whose spirit*
יָצְאָה Qal pf. 3 f.s. (יָצָא 422) *has come forth*
מִמֶּךָּ prep.–2 m.s. sf. *from you*

26:5 (LXX>vss.5–11)

הָרְפָאִים def.art.–n.m.p. (I 952) *the shades*
יְחוֹלָלוּ Polal impf. 3 m.p. paus. (חוּל I 296) *are made to writhe*
מִתַּחַת מַיִם prep.–prep. (1065)–n.m.p. (565; GK 119c) *(underneath) waters*
וְשֹׁכְנֵיהֶם conj.–Qal act.ptc. m.p.–3 m.p. sf. (שָׁכַן 1014) *and their inhabitants*

26:6

עָרוֹם adj. m.s. (736) *naked*
שְׁאוֹל pr.n. (982) *Sheol*
נֶגְדּוֹ prep.–3 m.s. sf. (617) *before him*
וְאֵין כְּסוּת conj.–subst. cstr. (II 34)–n.f.s. (492) *and there is no covering*
לָאֲבַדּוֹן prep.–pr.n. (2) *for Abaddon*

26:7

נֹטֶה Qal act.ptc. (נָטָה 639; GK 116s) *he stretches out*
צָפוֹן n.f.s. (860) *the north*
עַל־תֹּהוּ prep.–n.m.s. (1062) *over the void*
תֹּלֶה Qal act.ptc. (תָּלָה 1067) *he hangs*
אֶרֶץ n.f.s. (75) *earth*
עַל־בְּלִי־מָה prep.–neg. (115)–interr. (552; also see n.m.s. 116) *upon nothing(ness)*

26:8

צֹרֵר־ Qal act.ptc. (I 864) *he binds up*
מַיִם n.m.p. (565) *waters*
בְּעָבָיו prep.–n.m.p.–3 m.s. sf. (728) *in his thick clouds*
וְלֹא־נִבְקַע conj.–neg.–Ni. pf. 3 m.s. (בָּקַע 131) *and ... is not rent*
עָנָן n.m.s. (777) *cloud*
תַּחְתָּם prep.–3 m.p. sf. (1065) *under them*

26:9

מְאַחֵז Pi. ptc. (אָחַז 28) *he covers*
פְּנֵי־כִסֵּה n.m.p. cstr. (815)–n.m.s. (490) *the face of (his) throne*
פַּרְשֵׁז Pilel inf.abs. (פַּרְשֵׁז 831; GK 56) *he spreads*
עָלָיו prep.–3 m.s. sf. *over it*

עֲנָנוֹ n.m.s.-3 m.s. sf. (777) *his cloud*

26:10

חֹק־ n.m.s. (349) *a prescribed limit*
חָג Qal pf. 3 m.s. (חוּג 295) *he has drawn*
עַל־פְּנֵי־מָיִם prep.-n.m.p. cstr. (815)-n.m.p. paus. (565) *upon face of waters*
עַד־תַּכְלִית prep. (III 723)-n.f.s. cstr. (479) *at boundary between*
אוֹר n.m.s. (21) *light*
עִם־חֹשֶׁךְ prep. (767)-n.m.s. (365) *and darkness*

26:11

עַמּוּדֵי n.m.p. cstr. (765) *pillars of*
שָׁמַיִם n.m.p. (1029) *heaven*
יְרוֹפָפוּ Po'el impf. 3 m.p. paus. (רָפַף 952) *tremble*
וְיִתְמְהוּ conj.-Qal impf. 3 m.p. (תָּמַהּ 1069) *and are astounded*
מִגַּעֲרָתוֹ prep.-n.f.s.-3 m.s. sf. (172) *at his rebuke*

26:12

בְּכֹחוֹ prep.-n.m.s.-3 m.s. sf. (470) *by his power*
רָגַע Qal pf. 3 m.s. (I 920) *he disturbed*
הַיָּם def.art.-n.m.s. (410) *the sea*
וּבִתְבוּנָתוֹ conj.-prep.-n.f.s.-3 m.s. sf. (108) *and by his understanding*
מָחַץ Qal pf. 3 m.s. (563) *he smote*
רָהַב n.m.s. paus. (923) *Rahab* (lit. *storm, arrogance*)

26:13

בְּרוּחוֹ prep.-n.f.s.-3 m.s. sf. (924) *by his wind*
שָׁמַיִם n.m.p. (1029; LXX κλεῖθρα δὲ οὐρανοῦ δεδοίκασιν αὐτόν) *heavens*
שִׁפְרָה n.f.s. (1051) *(become) fair(ness)*
חֹלְלָה Po'el pf. 3 f.s. (חָלַל I 319) *pierced*
יָדוֹ n.f.s.-3 m.s. sf. (388) *his hand*
נָחָשׁ בָּרִחַ n.m.s. (638)-adj. m.s. (I 138) *fleeing serpent*

26:14

הֶן־אֵלֶּה interj. (243)-demons.adj. c.p. (41) *lo, these*
קְצוֹת n.f.p. cstr. (892) *the outskirts of*
דְּרָכָו n.m.p.-3 m.s. sf. (202; Q דְּרָכָיו) *his ways*
וּמַה־ conj.-interr. (552) *and how (small)*
שֵׁמֶץ n.m.s. cstr. (1036) *a whisper of*
דָּבָר n.m.s. (182) *a word*
נִשְׁמַע־בּוֹ Ni. pf. 3 m.s. (שָׁמַע 1033; or Qal impf. 1 c.p.; GK 119m)-prep.-3 m.s. sf. *is heard of him*

וְרַעַם conj.-n.m.s. cstr. (947) *but the thunder of*
גְּבוּרֹתָו n.f.p.-3 m.s. sf. (150) *his power*
מִי יִתְבּוֹנָן interr. (566)-Hithpolel impf. 3 m.s. paus. (בִּין 106; LXX ὁπότε ποιήσει) *who can understand*

27:1

וַיֹּסֶף consec.-Hi. impf. 3 m.s. (יָסַף 414) *and again (added)*
אִיּוֹב pr.n. (33) *Job*
שְׂאֵת Qal inf.cstr. (נָשָׂא 669) *took up*
מְשָׁלוֹ n.m.s.-3 m.s. sf. (605) *his discourse*
וַיֹּאמַר consec.-Qal impf. 3 m.s. (55) *and said*

27:2

חַי־אֵל adj. m.s. (I 311; GK 93aa)-n.m.s. (42) *as God lives*
הֵסִיר Hi. pf. 3 m.s. (סוּר 693) *who has taken away*
מִשְׁפָּטִי n.m.s.-1 c.s. sf. (1048) *my right*
וְשַׁדַּי conj.-pr.n. (994) *and the Almighty*
הֵמַר Hi. pf. 3 m.s. (מָרַר I 600) *who has made bitter*
נַפְשִׁי n.f.s.-1 c.s. sf. (659) *my soul*

27:3

כִּי־כָל־עוֹד conj. (471)-n.m.s. (481)-adv. (728; GK 128e) *for as long as*
נִשְׁמָתִי בִי n.f.s.-1 c.s. sf. (675)-prep.-1 c.s. sf. *my breath is in me*
וְרוּחַ conj.-n.f.s. cstr. (924) *and the spirit of*
אֱלוֹהַּ n.m.s. (42) *God*
בְּאַפִּי prep.-n.m.s.-1 c.s. sf. (I 60) *in my nostrils*

27:4

אִם־תְּדַבֵּרְנָה hypoth.part. (49)-Pi. impf. 3 f.p. (180 דָּבַר) *will not speak*
שְׂפָתַי n.f.p.-1 c.s. sf. (973) *my lips*
עַוְלָה n.f.s. (732) *falsehood*
וּלְשׁוֹנִי conj.-n.m.s.-1 c.s. sf. (546) *and my tongue*
אִם־יֶהְגֶּה hypoth.part. (49)-Qal impf. 3 m.s. (הָגָה I 211) *will not utter*
רְמִיָּה n.f.s. (I 941) *deceit*

27:5

חָלִילָה לִּי subst.-loc.he (321; GK 149a)-prep.-1 c.s. sf. *far be it from me*
אִם־אַצְדִּיק hypoth.part. (49)-Hi. impf. 1 c.s. (צָדַק 842) *that I would justify*
אֶתְכֶם dir.obj.-2 m.p. sf. *you*
עַד־אֶגְוָע prep. (III 723)-Qal impf. 1 c.s. paus. (157 גָּוַע) *till I die*

לֹא־אָסִיר neg.-Hi. impf. 1 c.s. (סוּר 693) *I will not put away*
תֻּמָּתִי n.f.s.-1 c.s. sf. (1070) *my integrity*
מִמֶּנִּי prep.-1 c.s. sf. *from me*

27:6

בְּצִדְקָתִי prep.-n.f.s.-1 c.s. sf. (842) *(to) my righteousness*
הֶחֱזַקְתִּי Hi. pf. 1 c.s. (חָזַק 304) *I hold fast*
וְלֹא אַרְפֶּהָ conj.-neg.-Hi. impf. 1 c.s.-3 f.s. sf. (רָפָה 951) *and will not let it go*
לֹא־יֶחֱרַף neg.-Qal impf. 3 m.s. (חָרַף 357) *does not reproach*
לְבָבִי n.m.s.-1 c.s. sf. (523) *my heart*
מִיָּמָי prep.-n.m.p.-1 c.s. sf. (398; GK 119wN) *for any of my days*

27:7

יְהִי Qal impf. 3 m.s. apoc.juss. (הָיָה 224) *let be*
כְרָשָׁע prep.-adj. m.s. (957; GK 118x) *as the wicked*
אֹיְבִי Qal act.ptc.-1 c.s. sf. (אָיַב 33) *my enemy*
וּמִתְקוֹמְמִי conj.-Hithpolel ptc. m.s.-1 c.s. sf. (קוּם 877) *and him that rises up against me*
כְעַוָּל prep.-n.m.s. (732; GK 118x) *as the unrighteous*

27:8

כִּי מַה־ conj. (471)-interr. (552) *for what*
תִּקְוַת n.f.s. cstr. (876) *the hope of*
חָנֵף adj. m.s. (338) *the godless*
כִּי יִבְצָע conj. (471)-Qal impf. 3 m.s. paus. (בָּצַע 130) *when he cuts (him) off*
כִּי יֵשֶׁל conj. (471)-Qal impf. 3 m.s. apoc. (שָׁלָה II 1017; GK 109k; LXX πεποιθὼς ἐπὶ κύριον ἆρα σωθήσεται) *when ... takes away*
אֱלוֹהַּ n.m.s. (42) *God*
נַפְשׁוֹ n.f.s.-3 m.s. sf. (659) *his life*

27:9

הֲצַעֲקָתוֹ interr.-n.f.s.-3 m.s. sf. (858) *his cry?*
יִשְׁמַע Qal impf. 3 m.s. (שָׁמַע 1033) *will ... hear?*
אֵל n.m.s. (42) *God*
כִּי־תָבוֹא conj. (471)-Qal pf. 3 f.s. (בּוֹא 97) *when comes*
עָלָיו prep.-3 m.s. sf. *upon him*
צָרָה n.f.s. (I 865) *trouble*

27:10

אִם־עַל־שַׁדַּי hypoth.part. (49)-prep.-pr.n. (994) *in the Almighty?*
יִתְעַנָּג Hith. impf. 3 m.s. paus. (עָנַג 772) *will he take delight?*
יִקְרָא Qal impf. 3 m.s. (קָרָא 894) *will he call*
אֱלוֹהַּ n.m.s. (42) *God*
בְּכָל־עֵת prep.-n.m.s. cstr. (481)-n.f.s. (773) *at all times*

27:11

אוֹרֶה Hi. impf. 1 c.s. (יָרָה 434) *I will teach*
אֶתְכֶם dir.obj.-2 m.p. sf. *you*
בְּיַד־אֵל prep.-n.f.s. cstr. (388)-n.m.s. (42) *concerning the hand of God*
אֲשֶׁר עִם־שַׁדַּי rel. (81)-prep. (767)-pr.n. (994) *what is with the Almighty*
לֹא אֲכַחֵד neg.-Pi. impf. 1 c.s. (כָּחַד 470) *I will not conceal*

27:12

הֵן־אַתֶּם interj. (243)-pers.pr. 2 m.p. (61) *behold, you*
כֻּלְּכֶם n.m.s.-2 m.p. sf. (481) *all of you*
חֲזִיתֶם Qal pf. 2 m.p. (חָזָה 302; GK 117q) *have seen (it)*
וְלָמָּה־זֶּה conj.-prep.-interr. (552)-demons.adj. m.s. (260) *why then*
הֶבֶל תֶּהְבָּלוּ n.m.s. (I 210)-Qal impf. 2 m.p. paus. (הָבַל 211) *have you become altogether vain*

27:13

זֶה demons.adj. m.s. (260) *this is*
חֵלֶק־ n.m.s. cstr. (324) *the portion of*
אָדָם רָשָׁע n.m.s. (9)-adj. m.s. (957) *a wicked man*
עִם־אֵל prep. (767)-n.m.s. (42) *with God*
וְנַחֲלַת conj.-n.f.s. cstr. (635) *and the heritage of*
עָרִיצִים adj. m.p. (792) *oppressors*
מִשַּׁדַּי prep.-pr.n. (994) *from the Almighty*
יִקָּחוּ Qal impf. 3 m.p. paus. (לָקַח 542) *which they receive*

27:14

אִם־יִרְבּוּ hypoth.part. (49)-Qal impf. 3 m.p. (רָבָה I 915) *if ... are multiplied*
בָנָיו n.m.p.-3 m.s. sf. (119) *his children*
לְמוֹ־חָרֶב prep.-3 m.p. sf.-n.f.s. paus. (352) *a sword for them*
וְצֶאֱצָאָיו conj.-n.m.p.-3 m.s. sf. (425) *and his offspring*
לֹא יִשְׂבְּעוּ־ neg.-Qal impf. 3 m.p. (שָׂבַע 959) *are not satisfied*
לָחֶם n.m.s. (536) *with bread*

27:15

שְׂרִידָו n.m.s. (Q rd. pl.)-3 m.s. sf. (975) *those who survive him*
בַּמָּוֶת prep.-def.art.-n.m.s. (560) *in the death*
יִקָּבֵרוּ Ni. impf. 3 m.p. (קָבַר 868) *will be buried*
וְאַלְמְנֹתָיו conj.-n.f.p.-3 m.s. sf. (48) *and their widows*
לֹא תִבְכֶּינָה neg.-Qal impf. 3 f.p. (בָּכָה 113; LXX οὐθεὶς ἐλεήσει) *make no lamentation*

27:16

אִם־יִצְבֹּר hypoth.part. (49)-Qal impf. 3 m.s. (840 צָבַר) *though he heap up*
כֶּעָפָר prep.-def.art.-n.m.s. (779) *like dust*
כָּסֶף n.m.s. paus. (494) *silver*
וְכַחֹמֶר conj.-prep.-def.art.-n.m.s. (I 330) *like clay*
יָכִין Hi. impf. 3 m.s. (כּוּן I 465) *pile up*
מַלְבּוּשׁ n.m.s. (528; LXX χρυσίον) *clothing*

27:17

יָכִין Hi. impf. 3 m.s. (I 465) *may pile it up*
וְצַדִּיק conj.-adj. m.s. (843) *but the just*
יִלְבָּשׁ Qal impf. 3 m.s. paus. (לָבַשׁ 527) *will wear it*
וְכֶסֶף conj.-n.m.s. (494) *and the silver*
נָקִי adj. m.s. (667) *the innocent*
יַחֲלֹק Qal impf. 3 m.s. (חָלַק 323) *will divide*

27:18

בָּנָה Qal pf. 3 m.s. (124) *he builds*
כָעָשׁ prep.-def.art.-n.m.s. (II 799) *like the moth*
בֵּיתוֹ n.m.s.-3 m.s. sf. (108) *his house*
וּכְסֻכָּה conj.-prep.-n.f.s. (697) *and like a booth*
עָשָׂה Qal pf. 3 m.s. (I 793) *which ... makes*
נֹצֵר Qal act.ptc. (נָצַר 665) *a watchman*

27:19

עָשִׁיר n.m.s. (799) *rich*
יִשְׁכַּב Qal impf. 3 m.s. (שָׁכַב 1011) *he goes to bed*
וְלֹא יֵאָסֵף conj.-neg.-Ni. impf. 3 m.s. (אָסַף 62; 1120-LXX, Syr., rd. יוֹסִף - προσθήσει *but will do so no more*; GK 68h,120dN) *he shall not be gathered*
עֵינָיו n.f. du.-3 m.s. sf. (744) *his eyes*
פָּקַח Qal pf. 3 m.s. (824) *he opens*
וְאֵינֶנּוּ conj.-subst.-3 m.s. sf. (II 34) *and it is gone*

27:20

תַּשִּׂיגֵהוּ Hi. impf. 3 f.s.-3 m.s. sf. (נָשַׂג 673) *overtake him*
כַמַּיִם prep.-def.art.-n.m.p. (565) *like a flood*
בַּלָּהוֹת n.f.p. (117) *terrors*
לַיְלָה n.m.s. (538) *in the night*
גְּנָבַתּוּ Qal pf. 3 f.s.-3 m.s. sf. (גָּנַב 170) *carries him off*
סוּפָה n.f.s. (I 693) *a whirlwind*

27:21

יִשָּׂאֵהוּ Qal impf. 3 m.s.-3 m.s. sf. (נָשָׂא 669) *lifts him up*
קָדִים n.m.s. (870) *the east wind*
וְיֵלַךְ conj.-Qal impf. 3 m.s. paus. (הָלַךְ 229) *and he departs*
וִישָׂעֲרֵהוּ conj.-Pi. impf. 3 m.s.-3 m.s. sf. (שָׂעַר 973) *and it sweeps him*
מִמְּקֹמוֹ prep.-n.m.s.-3 m.s. sf. (879) *out of his place*

27:22

וְיַשְׁלֵךְ conj.-Hi. impf. 3 m.s. apoc. (שָׁלַךְ 1020) *and he hurls*
עָלָיו prep.-3 m.s. sf. *at him*
וְלֹא יַחְמֹל conj.-neg.-Qal impf. 3 m.s. (חָמַל 328) *without pity*
מִיָּדוֹ prep.-n.f.s.-3 m.s. sf. (388) *from his power*
בָּרוֹחַ יִבְרָח Qal inf.abs. (137)-Qal impf. 3 m.s. (137) *he flees in headlong flight*

27:23

יִשְׂפֹּק Qal impf. 3 m.s. (שָׂפַק 706) *he claps*
עָלֵימוֹ prep.-3 m.p. sf. (GK 103fN) *at him*
כַפֵּימוֹ n.f.p.-3 m.s. sf. (496) *his hands*
וְיִשְׁרֹק conj.-Qal impf. 3 m.s. (שָׁרַק 1056) *and hisses*
עָלָיו prep.-3 m.s. sf. *at him*
מִמְּקֹמוֹ prep.-n.m.s.-3 m.s. sf. (879) *from his place*

28:1

כִּי יֵשׁ conj. (471)-subst. (441) *surely there is*
לַכֶּסֶף prep.-def.art.-n.m.s. (494) *for silver*
מוֹצָא n.m.s. (I 425) *a mine*
וּמָקוֹם conj.-n.m.s. (879) *and a place*
לַזָּהָב prep.-def.art.-n.m.s. (262) *for gold*
יָזֹקּוּ Qal impf. 3 m.p. (זָקַק I 279; GK 155h) *which they refine*

28:2

בַּרְזֶל n.m.s. (137) *iron*
מֵעָפָר prep.-n.m.s. (779) *from dry earth*
יֻקָּח Ho. impf. 3 m.s. paus. (לָקַח 542; GK 121d) *is taken*

וְאֶבֶן conj.-n.f.s. (6) *and ore*
יָצוּק Qal impf. 3 m.s. (צוק II 848; GK 117ii; LXX λατομεῖται) *(men) melt (it)*
נְחוּשָׁה n.f.s. (639) *(into) copper*

28:3

קֵץ n.m.s. (893) *an end*
שָׂם Qal pf. 3 m.s. or Qal act.ptc. m.s. (שִׂים I 962) *(men) put*
לַחֹשֶׁךְ prep.-def.art.-n.m.s. (365) *to darkness*
וּלְכָל־ conj.-prep.-n.m.s. cstr. (481) *and to every*
תַּכְלִית n.f.s. (479) *end (the farthest limit)*
הוּא חוֹקֵר pers.pr. 3 m.s. (214)-Qal act.ptc. (חָקַר 350) *they search out*
אֶבֶן n.f.s. (6) *the ore*
אֹפֶל n.m.s. (66) *in gloom*
וְצַלְמָוֶת conj.-n.m.s. (853) *and deep darkness*

28:4

פָּרַץ Qal pf. 3 m.s. (829) *(they) open shafts*
נַחַל n.m.s. (636) *in a valley*
מֵעִם־ prep.-prep. (769) *away from*
גָּר Qal act.ptc. m.s. (גור I 157) *sojourning (sojourner)*
הַנִּשְׁכָּחִים def.art.-Ni. ptc. m.p. (שָׁכַח 1013; GK 126b) *they are forgotten*
מִנִּי־רָגֶל prep. (577)-n.f.s. paus. (919) *from foot*
דַּלּוּ Qal pf. 3 c.p. (דָּלַל 195) *they hang (depend)*
מֵאֱנוֹשׁ prep.-n.m.s. (60) *from men*
נָעוּ Qal pf. 3 c.p. (נוע 631) *they swing to and fro*

28:5

אֶרֶץ מִמֶּנָּה n.f.s. (75)-prep.-3 f.s. sf. *as for the earth, out of it*
יֵצֵא Qal impf. 3 m.s. (יָצָא 422) *comes*
לָחֶם n.m.s. paus. (536) *bread*
וְתַחְתֶּיהָ conj.-prep.-3 f.s. sf. (1065) *but underneath it*
נֶהְפַּךְ Ni. pf. 3 m.s. (הָפַךְ 245) *it is turned up*
כְּמוֹ־אֵשׁ prep. (453)-n.f.s. (77; GK 118w) *as fire*

28:6

מְקוֹם־ n.m.s. cstr. (879) *the place of*
סַפִּיר n.m.s. (705) *sapphires*
אֲבָנֶיהָ n.f.p.-3 f.s. sf. (6) *its stones*
וְעַפְרֹת conj.-n.m.p. cstr. (779; GK 124,l) *and dust of*
זָהָב n.m.s. (262) *gold*
לוֹ prep.-3 m.s. sf. *it has (to him)*

28:7

נָתִיב n.m.s. (677) *that path*
לֹא־יְדָעוֹ neg.-Qal pf. 3 m.s.-3 m.s. sf. (יָדַע 393) *knows it not*
עַיִט n.m.s. paus. (743) *bird of prey*
וְלֹא שְׁזָפַתּוּ conj.-neg.-Qal pf. 3 f.s.-3 m.s. sf. (1004 שָׁזַף) *and has not seen it*
עֵין אַיָּה n.f.s. cstr. (744)-n.f.s. (I 17) *the falcon's eye*

28:8

לֹא־הִדְרִיכֻהוּ neg.-Hi. pf. 3 c.p.-3 m.s. sf. (דָּרַךְ 201) *have not trodden it*
בְנֵי־שָׁחַץ n.m.s. cstr. (119)-n.m.s. paus. (1006) *the proud beasts*
לֹא־עָדָה neg.-Qal pf. 3 m.s. (עָדָה I 723) *has not passed*
עָלָיו prep.-3 m.s. sf. *over it*
שָׁחַל n.m.s. paus. (1006) *the lion*

28:9

בַּחַלָּמִישׁ prep.-def.art.-n.m.s. (321) *to the flinty rock*
שָׁלַח Qal pf. 3 m.s. (1018) *man puts*
יָדוֹ n.f.s.-3 m.s. sf. (388) *his hand*
הָפַךְ Qal pf. 3 m.s. (245) *he overturns*
מִשֹּׁרֶשׁ prep.-n.m.s. (1057) *by the roots*
הָרִים n.m.p. (249) *mountains*

28:10

בַּצּוּרוֹת prep.-def.art.-n.m.p. (849) *in the rocks*
יְאֹרִים n.m.p. (384) *channels*
בִּקֵּעַ Pi. pf. 3 m.s. (בָּקַע 131) *he cuts out*
וְכָל־יְקָר conj.-n.m.s. cstr. (481)-n.m.s. (430) *and every precious thing*
רָאֲתָה Qal pf. 3 f.s. (רָאָה 906) *sees*
עֵינוֹ n.f.s.-3 m.s. sf. (744) *his eye*

28:11

מִבְּכִי prep.-n.m.s. (113; GK 119x) *so that they do not trickle (from weeping)*
נְהָרוֹת n.m.p. (625) *the streams*
חִבֵּשׁ Pi. pf. 3 m.s. (חָבַשׁ) *he binds up*
וְתַעֲלֻמָהּ conj.-n.f.s. (761) *and the thing that is hid*
יֹצִא Hi. impf. 3 m.s. (יָצָא 422) *he brings forth*
אוֹר n.m.s. (21) *to light*

28:12

וְהַחָכְמָה conj.-def.art.-n.f.s. (315) *and the wisdom*
מֵאַיִן prep.-adv. (32) *where*

תִּמָּצֵא Ni. impf. 3 f.s. (מָצָא 592) *shall be found*
וְאֵ זֶה conj.-interr.adv. cstr. (32)-demons.adj. m.s. (260; GK 119ff) *and where*
מְקוֹם n.m.s. cstr. (879) *the place of*
בִּינָה n.f.s. (108) *understanding*

28:13

לֹא־יָדַע neg.-Qal pf. 3 m.s. (393) *does not know*
אֱנוֹשׁ n.m.s. (60) *man*
עֶרְכָּהּ n.m.s.-3 f.s. sf. (789; LXX ὁδὸν αὐτῆς) *its price*
וְלֹא תִמָּצֵא conj.-neg.-Ni. impf. 3 f.s. (מָצָא 592) *and it is not found*
בְּאֶרֶץ prep.-n.f.s. cstr. (75) *in the land of*
הַחַיִּים def.art.-adj. m.p. (I 311) *the living*

28:14

תְּהוֹם n.m.s. (1062) *the deep*
אָמַר Qal pf. 3 m.s. (55) *says*
לֹא בִי־הִיא neg.-prep.-1 c.s. sf.-pers.pr. 3 f.s. (214) *it is not in me*
וְיָם conj.-n.m.s. (410) *and the sea*
אָמַר v.supra *says*
אֵין עִמָּדִי subst.cstr. (II 34)-prep.-1 c.s. sf. (767) *it is not with me*

28:15

לֹא־יֻתַּן neg.-Ho. impf. 3 m.s. (נָתַן 678) *it cannot be gotten*
סְגוֹר n.m.s. (689) *enclosure*
תַּחְתֶּיהָ prep.-3 f.s. sf. (1065) *for it*
וְלֹא יִשָּׁקֵל conj.-neg.-Ni. impf. 3 m.s. (שָׁקַל 1053) *and cannot be weighed*
כֶּסֶף n.m.s. (494) *silver*
מְחִירָהּ n.m.s.-3 f.s. sf. (I 564) *as its price*

28:16

לֹא־תְסֻלֶּה neg.-Pu. impf. 3 f.s. (סָלָה II 699) *it cannot be valued*
בְּכֶתֶם prep.-n.m.s. cstr. (508) *in the gold of*
אוֹפִיר pr.n. (20) *Ophir*
בְּשֹׁהַם יָקָר prep.-n.m.s. (I 995)-adj. m.s. (429) *in precious onyx*
וְסַפִּיר conj.-n.m.s. (705) *or sapphire*

28:17

לֹא־יַעַרְכֶנָּה neg.-Qal impf. 3 m.s.-3 f.s. sf. (עָרַךְ 789) *cannot equal it*
זָהָב n.m.s. (262) *gold*
וּזְכוֹכִית conj.-n.f.s. (269) *and glass*
וּתְמוּרָתָהּ conj.-n.f.s.-3 f.s. sf. (558; GK 152z) *nor its exchange*
כְּלִי־פָז n.m.s. cstr. (479)-n.m.s. paus. (808) *jewels of fine gold*

28:18

רָאמוֹת n.f.p. (910) *coral*
וְגָבִישׁ conj.-n.m.s. (150) *or crystal*
לֹא יִזָּכֵר neg.-Ni. impf. 3 m.s. (זָכַר 269) *shall not be mentioned*
וּמֶשֶׁךְ conj.-n.m.s. cstr. (I 604) *and the drawing up of*
חָכְמָה n.f.s. (315) *wisdom*
מִפְּנִינִים prep.-n.f.p. (819) *above pearls*

28:19

לֹא־יַעַרְכֶנָּה neg.-Qal impf. 3 m.s.-3 f.s. sf. (עָרַךְ 789) *cannot compare with it*
פִּטְדַת־ n.f.s. cstr. (809) *the topaz of*
כּוּשׁ pr.n. (I 468) *Ethiopia*
בְּכֶתֶם טָהוֹר prep.-n.m.s. (508)-adj. m.s. (373) *in pure gold*
לֹא תְסֻלֶּה neg.-Pu. impf. 3 f.s. (סָלָה II 699) *it cannot be valued*

28:20

וְהַחָכְמָה conj.-def.art.-n.f.s. (315) *then the wisdom*
מֵאַיִן prep.-adv. (32) *whence*
תָּבוֹא Qal impf. 3 f.s. (בּוֹא 97) *comes (the wisdom)*
וְאֵי זֶה conj.-interr.adv. cstr. (32)-demons.adj. m.s. (260) *and where is*
מְקוֹם n.m.s. cstr. (879) *the place of*
בִּינָה n.f.s. (108) *understanding*

28:21

וְנֶעֶלְמָה conj.-Ni. pf. 3 f.s. (עָלַם I 761) *for it is hid*
מֵעֵינֵי prep.-n.f. du. cstr. (744) *from eyes of*
כָל־חָי n.m.s. cstr. (481)-adj. m.s. (311) *all living*
וּמֵעוֹף conj.-prep.-n.m.s. cstr. (733) *and from the birds of*
הַשָּׁמַיִם def.art.-n.m.p. (1029) *the air*
נִסְתָּרָה Ni. pf. 3 f.s. paus. (סָתַר 711) *concealed*

28:22

אֲבַדּוֹן n.f.s. (2) *Abaddon*
וָמָוֶת conj.-n.m.s. (560) *and Death*
אָמְרוּ Qal pf. 3 c.p. (אָמַר 55) *say*
בְּאָזְנֵינוּ prep.-n.f. du.-1 c.p. sf. (23) *with our ears*
שָׁמַעְנוּ Qal pf. 1 c.p. (שָׁמַע 1033) *we have heard*
שִׁמְעָהּ n.m.s.-3 f.s. sf. (1034) *a report of it*

28:23

אֱלֹהִים n.m.p. (43) *God*
הֵבִין Hi. pf. 3 m.s. (בִּין 106; LXX εὖ συνέστησεν) *understands*
דַּרְכָּהּ n.m.s.-3 f.s. sf. (202) *the way to it*
וְהוּא יָדַע conj.-pers.pr. 3 m.s. (214)-Qal pf. 3 m.s. (393) *and he knows*
אֶת־מְקוֹמָהּ dir.obj.-n.m.s.-3 f.s. sf. (879) *its place*

28:24

כִּי־הוּא conj.-pers.pr. 3 m.s. (214) *for he*
לִקְצוֹת־ prep.-n.f.p. cstr. (892) *to the ends of*
הָאָרֶץ def.art.-n.f.s. (75) *the earth*
יַבִּיט Hi. impf. 3 m.s. (נָבַט 613) *looks*
תַּחַת כָּל־ prep. (1065)-n.m.s. cstr. (481) *under all of*
הַשָּׁמַיִם def.art.-n.m.p. (1029) *the heavens*
יִרְאֶה Qal impf. 3 m.s. (רָאָה 906) *he sees*

28:25

לַעֲשׂוֹת prep.-Qal inf.cstr. (עָשָׂה I 793; GK 114r) *to give (make)*
לָרוּחַ prep.-def.art.-n.f.s. (924) *to the wind*
מִשְׁקָל n.m.s. paus. (1054) *a weight*
וּמַיִם conj.-n.m.p. (565) *and waters*
תִּכֵּן Pi. pf. 3 m.s. (תָּכַן 1067; GK 114r) *he meted out*
בְמִדָּה prep.-n.f.s. (I 551) *by measure*

28:26

בַּעֲשֹׂתוֹ prep.-Qal inf.cstr.-3 m.s. sf. (עָשָׂה I 793) *when he made*
לַמָּטָר prep.-def.art.-n.m.s. (564) *for the rain*
חֹק n.m.s. (349) *a decree*
וְדֶרֶךְ conj.-n.m.s. (202) *and a way*
לַחֲזִיז prep.-n.m.s. cstr. (304) *for the lightning of*
קֹלוֹת n.m.p. (876) *the thunder*

28:27

אָז רָאָהּ adv. (23)-Qal pf. 3 m.s.-3 f.s. sf. (רָאָה 906) *then he saw it*
וַיְסַפְּרָהּ consec.-Pi. impf. 3 m.s.-3 f.s. sf. (סָפַר 707; GK 60d) *and declared it*
הֱכִינָהּ Hi. pf. 3 m.s.-3 f.s. sf. (כּוּן 465; LXX ἑτοιμάσας) *he established it*
וְגַם־ conj.-adv. (168) *and also*
חֲקָרָהּ Qal pf. 3 m.s.-3 f.s. sf. (חָקַר 350) *searched it out*

28:28

וַיֹּאמֶר consec.-Qal impf. 3 m.s. (אָמַר 55) *and he said*
לָאָדָם prep.-def.art.-n.m.s. (9) *to man*
הֵן interj. (243) *behold*
יִרְאַת n.f.s. cstr. (432) *the fear of*
אֲדֹנָי n.m.p.-1 c.s. sf. as pr.n. (10) *the Lord*
הִיא חָכְמָה pers.pr. 3 f.s. (214)-n.f.s. (315) *that is wisdom*
וְסוּר conj.-Qal inf.cstr. (סוּר 693) *and to depart*
מֵרָע prep.-n.m.s. (948) *from evil*
בִּינָה n.f.s. (108) *is understanding*

29:1

וַיֹּסֶף consec.-Hi. impf. 3 m.s. (יָסַף 414) *and again (added)*
אִיּוֹב pr.n. (33) *Job*
שְׂאֵת Qal inf.cstr. (נָשָׂא 669) *took up*
מְשָׁלוֹ n.m.s.-3 m.s. sf. (II 605) *his discourse*
וַיֹּאמַר consec.-Qal impf. 3 m.s. (אָמַר 55) *and said*

29:2

מִי־יִתְּנֵנִי interr. (566)-Qal impf. 3 m.s.-1 c.s. sf. (נָתַן 678) *Oh, that I were*
כְיַרְחֵי־ prep.-n.m.p. cstr. (I 437) *as in the months of*
קֶדֶם n.m.s. (869) *old*
כִּימֵי prep.-n.m.s. cstr. (398; GK 118u,130d,151b) *as in the days (when) of*
אֱלוֹהַּ n.m.s. (42) *God*
יִשְׁמְרֵנִי Qal impf. 3 m.s.-1 c.s. sf. (שָׁמַר 1036) *watched over me*

29:3

בְּהִלּוֹ prep.-Qal inf.cstr.-3 m.s. sf. (הָלַל I 237; GK 67p,131o) *when it shone*
נֵרוֹ n.m.s.-3 m.s. sf. (632; GK 118h) *his lamp*
עֲלֵי רֹאשִׁי prep. (II 752)-n.m.s.-1 c.s. sf. (910) *upon my head*
לְאוֹרוֹ prep.-n.m.s.-3 m.s. sf. (21) *by his light*
אֵלֶךְ Qal impf. 1 c.s. (הָלַךְ 229) *I walked*
חֹשֶׁךְ n.m.s. (365) *through darkness*

29:4

כַּאֲשֶׁר prep.-rel. (81) *as*
הָיִיתִי Qal pf. 1 c.s. (הָיָה 224) *I was*
בִּימֵי חָרְפִּי prep.-n.m.s. cstr. (398)-n.m.s.-1 c.s. sf. (358) *in my autumn days*
בְּסוֹד prep.-n.m.s. cstr. (691) *when the friendship of (secret counsel)*
אֱלוֹהַּ n.m.s. (42) *God*
עֲלֵי אָהֳלִי prep.-n.m.s.-1 c.s. sf. (13) *upon my tent*

29:5

בְּעוֹד prep.-adv. (728) *when yet*
שַׁדַּי pr.n. (994) *the Almighty*
עִמָּדִי prep.-1 c.s. sf. *with me*
סְבִיבוֹתַי subst. p. as prep. (686)-1 c.s. sf. *about me*
נְעָרָי n.m.p.-1 c.s. sf. (654) *my children*

29:6

בִּרְחֹץ prep.-Qal inf.cstr. (רָחַץ 934) *in the washing of*
הֲלִיכַי n.m.p.-1 c.s. sf. (237) *my steps*
בְּחֵמָה prep.-n.f.s. (328, 404; GK 23f; LXX, V., rd. בְּחֶמְאָה n.f.s. 326; *with milk*) *with wrath*
וְצוּר conj.-n.m.s. (849) *and rock*
יָצוּק Qal impf. 3 m.s. (צוק II 848) *poured out*
עִמָּדִי prep.-1 c.s. sf. (767) *for me*
פַּלְגֵי־שָׁמֶן n.m.p. cstr. (I 811)-n.m.s. paus. (1032) *streams of oil*

29:7

בְּצֵאתִי prep.-Qal inf.cstr.-1 c.s. sf. (יָצָא 422) *when I went out*
שַׁעַר n.m.s. (1044; LXX ὄρθριος) *(to) the gate*
עֲלֵי־קָרֶת prep.-n.f.s. paus. (900) *of the city*
בָּרְחוֹב prep.-def.art.-n.f.s. (932) *in the square*
אָכִין Hi. impf. 1 c.s. (כון 465) *I prepared*
מוֹשָׁבִי n.m.s.-1 c.s. sf. (444) *my seat*

29:8

רָאוּנִי Qal pf. 3 c.p.-1 c.s. sf. (רָאָה 906) *saw me*
נְעָרִים n.m.p. (654) *the young men*
וְנֶחְבָּאוּ conj.-Ni. pf. 3 c.p. paus. (חָבָא 285) *and withdrew*
וִישִׁישִׁים conj.-adj. m.p. (450) *and the aged*
קָמוּ Qal pf. 3 c.p. (קום 877) *rose*
עָמָדוּ Qal pf. 3 c.p. paus. (עָמַד 763; GK 120gN) *stood*

29:9

שָׂרִים n.m.p. (978) *princes*
עָצְרוּ Qal pf. 3 c.p. (עָצַר 783) *refrained*
בְמִלִּין prep.-n.f.p. (576) *from words*
וְכַף conj.-n.f.s. (496) *and (their) hand*
יָשִׂימוּ Qal impf. 3 m.p. (שִׂים 962) *they laid*
לְפִיהֶם prep.-n.m.s.-3 m.p. sf. (804) *on their mouth*

29:10

קוֹל־ n.m.s. cstr. (876) *(the) voice of*
נְגִידִים n.m.p. (617; GK 146a) *nobles*
נֶחְבָּאוּ Ni. pf. 3 c.p. paus. (חָבָא 285) *was hushed*
וּלְשׁוֹנָם conj.-n.f.s.-3 m.p. sf. (546) *and their tongue*
לְחִכָּם prep.-n.m.s.-3 m.p. sf. (335) *to the roof of their mouth*
דָּבֵקָה Qal pf. 3 f.s. paus. (דָּבַק 179; GK 44c) *cleaved*

29:11

כִּי אֹזֶן conj.-n.f.s. (23) *when (the) ear*
שָׁמְעָה Qal pf. 3 f.s. (1033) *heard*
וַתְּאַשְּׁרֵנִי consec.-Pi. impf. 3 f.s.-1 c.s. sf. (אָשַׁר 80) *it called me blessed*
וְעַיִן conj.-n.f.s. (744) *and when (the) eye*
רָאֲתָה Qal pf. 3 f.s. (רָאָה 906) *saw*
וַתְּעִידֵנִי consec.-Hi. impf. 3 f.s.-1 c.s. sf. (עוד 729) *it approved*

29:12

כִּי־אֲמַלֵּט conj.-Pi. impf. 1 c.s. (מָלַט 572) *because I delivered*
עָנִי adj. m.s. (776) *(the) poor*
מְשַׁוֵּעַ Pi. ptc. m.s. (שָׁוַע 1002; LXX ἐκ χειρὸς δυνάστου) *who cried*
וְיָתוֹם conj.-n.m.s. (450) *and (the) fatherless*
וְלֹא־עֹזֵר לוֹ conj.-neg.-Qal act.ptc. (740; GK 152u,155n)-prep.-3 m.s. sf. *who had none to help him*

29:13

בִּרְכַּת n.f.s. cstr. (139) *the blessing of*
אֹבֵד Qal act.ptc. m.s. (1) *him who was about to perish*
עָלַי prep.-1 c.s. sf. *upon me*
תָּבֹא Qal impf. 3 f.s. (בּוֹא 97) *came*
וְלֵב conj.-n.m.s. cstr. (524) *and heart of*
אַלְמָנָה n.f.s. (48) *widow*
אַרְנִן Hi. impf. 1 c.s. (רָנַן 943) *I caused to sing for joy*

29:14

צֶדֶק n.m.s. (841) *righteousness*
לָבַשְׁתִּי Qal pf. 1 c.s. (לָבַשׁ 527) *I put on*
וַיִּלְבָּשֵׁנִי consec.-Qal impf. 3 m.s.-1 c.s. sf. (לָבַשׁ 527) *and it clothed me*
כִּמְעִיל prep.-n.m.s. (591) *like a robe*
וְצָנִיף conj.-n.m.s. (857) *and a turban*
מִשְׁפָּטִי n.m.s.-1 c.s. sf. (1048; LXX> sf.) *my justice*

29:15

עֵינַיִם n.f. du. (744) *eyes*
הָיִיתִי Qal pf. 1 c.s. (הָיָה 224) *I was*

לַעִוֵּר prep.-def.art.-adj. m.s. (734; GK 141d) *to the blind*
וְרַגְלַיִם conj.-n.f. du. (919) *and feet*
לַפִּסֵּחַ prep.-def.art.-adj. m.s. (820; GK 141d) *to the lame*
אָנִי pers.pr. 1 c.s. paus. (58) *I*

29:16

אָב אָנֹכִי n.m.s. (3)-pers.pr. 1 c.s. (59) *I was a father*
לָאֶבְיוֹנִים prep.-def.art.-adj. m.p. (2) *to the poor*
וְרִב conj.-n.m.s. cstr. (936; GK 130d,155n) *and the cause of*
לֹא־יָדַעְתִּי neg.-Qal pf. 1 c.s. (393) *him whom I did not know*
אֶחְקְרֵהוּ Qal impf. 1 c.s.-3 m.s. sf. (חָקַר 350) *I searched (it) out*

29:17

וָאֲשַׁבְּרָה consec.-Pi. impf. 1 c.s.-coh.he (שָׁבַר 990; GK 108g) *I broke*
מְתַלְּעוֹת n.f.p. cstr. (1069) *fangs of*
עַוָּל n.m.s. (732) *unrighteous*
וּמִשִּׁנָּיו conj.-prep.-n.f.p.-3 m.s. sf. (1042) *and from his teeth*
אַשְׁלִיךְ Hi. impf. 1 c.s. (שָׁלַךְ 1020) *I made (him) drop*
טָרֶף n.m.s. paus. (383) *(his) prey*

29:18

וָאֹמַר consec.-Qal impf. 1 c.s. (אָמַר 55) *then I thought*
עִם־קִנִּי prep. (767)-n.m.s.-1 c.s. sf. (890; LXX ἡ ἡλικία μου) *in my nest*
אֶגְוָע Qal impf. 1 c.s. paus. (גָּוַע 157; LXX γηράσει) *I shall die*
וְכַחוֹל conj.-prep.-def.art.-n.m.s. (297; LXX ὥσπερ στέλεχος φοίνικος) *and as the sand*
אַרְבֶּה Hi. impf. 1 c.s. (רָבָה I 915) *I shall multiply*
יָמִים n.m.p. (398) *my days*

29:19

שָׁרְשִׁי n.m.s.-1 c.s. sf. (1057) *my roots*
פָּתוּחַ Qal pass.ptc. (פָּתַח 834) *spread out*
אֱלֵי־מָיִם prep. (39)-n.m.p. paus. (565) *to (the) waters*
וְטַל conj.-n.m.s. (378) *and (the) dew*
יָלִין Qal impf. 3 m.s. (לִין I 533) *remains all night*
בִּקְצִירִי prep.-n.m.s.-1 c.s. sf. (II 894) *on my branches*

29:20

כְּבוֹדִי n.m.s.-1 c.s. sf. (458) *my glory*
חָדָשׁ adj. m.s. (294) *fresh*
עִמָּדִי prep.-1 c.s. sf. (767) *with me*
וְקַשְׁתִּי conj.-n.f.s.-1 c.s. sf. (905) *and my bow*
בְּיָדִי prep.-n.f.s.-1 c.s. sf. (388) *in my hand*
תַחֲלִיף Hi. impf. 3 f.s. (חָלַף 322) *shows newness*

29:21

לִי־שָׁמְעוּ prep.-1 c.s. sf.-Qal pf. 3 c.p. (1033) *(men) listened to me*
וְיִחֵלּוּ conj.-Pi. pf. 3 c.p. (יָחַל 403; GK 20i,24e) *and waited*
וְיִדְּמוּ conj.-Qal impf. 3 m.p. (דָּמַם I 198; GK 67g) *and kept silence*
לְמוֹ עֲצָתִי prep. (518, 530)-n.f.s.-1 c.s. sf. (420; many mss. לְמוֹעֲצָתִי) *for my counsel*

29:22

אַחֲרֵי דְבָרִי prep. (29)-n.m.s.-1 c.s. sf. (182) *after my word*
לֹא יִשְׁנוּ neg.-Qal impf. 3 m.p. (שָׁנָה III 1040) *they did not speak again*
וְעָלֵימוֹ conj.-prep.-3 m.p. sf. *and upon them*
תִּטֹּף Qal impf. 3 f.s. (נָטַף 642) *dropped*
מִלָּתִי n.f.s.-1 c.s. sf. (576) *my word*

29:23

וְיִחֲלוּ conj.-Pi. pf. 3 c.p. (יָחַל 403) *and they waited*
כַמָּטָר prep.-def.art.-n.m.s. (564; GK 118w) *as for the rain*
לִי prep.-1 c.s. sf. *for me*
וּפִיהֶם conj.-n.m.s.-3 m.p. sf. (804) *and their mouths*
פָּעֲרוּ Qal pf. 3 c.p. (פָּעַר 822) *they opened*
לְמַלְקוֹשׁ prep.-n.m.s. (545) *as for spring rain*

29:24

אֶשְׂחַק Qal impf. 1 c.s. (שָׂחַק 965) *I smiled*
אֲלֵהֶם prep.-3 m.p. sf. *on them*
לֹא יַאֲמִינוּ neg.-Hi. impf. 3 m.p. (אָמַן 52) *when they had no confidence*
וְאוֹר conj.-n.m.s. cstr. (21) *and the light of*
פָּנַי n.m.p.-1 c.s. sf. (815) *my countenance*
לֹא יַפִּילוּן neg.-Hi. impf. 3 m.p. (נָפַל 656) *they did not cast down*

29:25

אֶבְחַר Qal impf. 1 c.s. (בָּחַר 103; GK 10g) *I chose*
דַּרְכָּם n.m.s.-3 m.p. sf. (202) *their way*

וָאֵשֵׁב conj.-Qal impf. 1 c.s. (יָשַׁב 442) *and sat*
רֹאשׁ n.m.p. (910; GK 126p) *as chief*
וְאֶשְׁכּוֹן conj.-Qal impf. 1 c.s. (שָׁכַן 1014) *and I dwelt*
כְּמֶלֶךְ prep.-n.m.s. (I 572) *like a king*
בַּגְּדוּד prep.-def.art.-n.m.s. (I 151) *among (his) troops*
כַּאֲשֶׁר prep.-rel. (81) *like*
אֲבֵלִים adj. m.p. (I 5) *mourners*
יְנַחֵם Pi. impf. 3 m.s. (נָחַם 636) *one who comforts*

30:1

וְעַתָּה conj.-adv. (773) *but now*
שָׂחֲקוּ Qal pf. 3 c.p. (שָׂחַק 965) *they make sport*
עָלַי prep.-1 c.s. sf. *of me*
צְעִירִים adj. m.p. (859) *young(er)*
מִמֶּנִּי prep.-1 c.s. sf. *than I*
לְיָמִים prep.-n.m.p. (398) *of days*
אֲשֶׁר־מָאַסְתִּי rel. (81)-Qal pf. 1 c.s. (מָאַס 549) *I would have disdained*
אֲבוֹתָם n.m.p.-3 m.p. sf. (3) *whose fathers*
לָשִׁית prep.-Qal inf.cstr. (שִׁית 1011) *to put*
עִם־כַּלְבֵי prep. (767)-n.m.p. cstr. (476) *the dogs of*
צֹאנִי n.f.s.-1 c.s. sf. (838) *my flock*

30:2

גַּם־כֹּחַ adv. (168)-n.m.s. cstr. (470) *also, the strength of*
יְדֵיהֶם n.f.p.-3 m.p. sf. (388) *their hands*
לָמָּה לִּי prep.-interr. (552)-prep.-1 c.s. sf. *what could I gain*
עָלֵימוֹ prep.-3 m.p. sf. *from them*
אָבַד Qal pf. 3 m.s. (1) *has gone*
כָּלַח n.m.s. paus. (480) *vigor*

30:3

בְּחֶסֶר prep.-n.m.s. (341) *through want*
וּבְכָפָן conj.-prep.-n.m.s. (495) *and hunger*
גַּלְמוּד adj. m.s. (166) *hard*
הַעֹרְקִים def.art.-Qal act.ptc. m.p. (עָרַק 792; GK 126b) *they who gnaw*
צִיָּה n.f.s. (851) *the dry ground*
אֶמֶשׁ adv. (57) *yesterday*
שׁוֹאָה n.f.s. (996) *waste*
וּמְשֹׁאָה conj.-n.f.s. (996; GK 133,l) *and desolation*

30:4

הַקֹּטְפִים def.art.-Qal act.ptc. m.p. (קָטַף 882) *they who pluck out*
מַלּוּחַ n.m.s. (572) *mallow*
עֲלֵי־שִׂיחַ prep. (755)-n.m.s. (967; or n.m.p. cstr. 750) *by (the leaves of) bushes*
וְשֹׁרֶשׁ conj.-n.m.s. cstr. (1057) *and roots of*
רְתָמִים n.m.p. (958) *broom*
לַחְמָם prep.-Qal inf.cstr.-3 m.p. sf. (חָמַם 328; others rd. n.m.s.-3 m.p. sf. 536-their food) *to warm themselves*

30:5

מִן־גֵּו prep.-n.m.s. (II 156) *from the midst (of men)*
יְגֹרָשׁוּ Pu. impf. 3 m.p. (גָּרַשׁ 176) *they are driven out*
יָרִיעוּ Hi. impf. 3 m.p. (רוּעַ 929) *they shout*
עָלֵימוֹ prep.-3 m.p. sf. *after them*
כַּגַּנָּב prep.-def.art.-n.m.s. (170) *as after a thief*

30:6

בַּעֲרוּץ prep.-adj. m.s. cstr. (792; GK 133h) *in the (most) dreadful of*
נְחָלִים n.m.p. (636) *torrents*
לִשְׁכֹּן prep.-Qal inf.cstr. (שָׁכַן 1014; GK 114k) *they must dwell*
חֹרֵי n.m.p. cstr. (III 359) *in holes of*
עָפָר n.m.s. (779) *earth*
וְכֵפִים conj.-n.m.p. (495) *and rocks*

30:7

בֵּין־שִׂיחִים prep. (107)-n.m.p. (967) *among the bushes*
יִנְהָקוּ Qal impf. 3 m.p. paus. (נָהַק 625) *they bray*
תַּחַת חָרוּל prep. (1065)-n.m.s. (355) *under nettles*
יְסֻפָּחוּ Pu. impf. 3 m.p. paus. (סָפַח I 705) *they huddle together*

30:8

בְּנֵי־נָבָל n.m.p. cstr. (119)-adj. m.s. (614) *a senseless brood*
גַּם־בְּנֵי adv. (168)-v.supra *also a brood of*
בְלִי־שֵׁם subst. as neg. (115)-n.m.s. (1027) *disreputable ones*
נִכְּאוּ Ni. pf. 3 c.p. (נָכָא 644) *they have been whipped out*
מִן־הָאָרֶץ prep.-def.art.-n.f.s. (75) *of the land*

30:9

וְעַתָּה conj.-adv. (773) *and now*
נְגִינָתָם n.f.s.-3 m.p. sf. (618) *their song*
הָיִיתִי Qal pf. 1 c.s. (הָיָה 224) *I have become*
וָאֱהִי consec.-Qal impf. 1 c.s. (הָיָה 224) *I am*
לָהֶם prep.-3 m.p. sf. *to them*

לְמָשָׁל prep.-n.f.s. (576) *a byword*

30:10

תִּעֲבוּנִי Pi. pf. 3 c.p.-1 c.s. sf. (תָּעַב 1073) *they abhor me*
רָחֲקוּ Qal pf. 3 c.p. (רָחַק 934; GK 106g) *they keep aloof*
מֶנִּי prep.-1 c.s. sf. *from me*
וּמִפָּנַי conj.-prep.-n.m.p.-1 c.s. sf. (815) *and at the sight of me*
לֹא־חָשְׂכוּ neg.-Qal pf. 3 c.p. (חָשַׂךְ 362) *they do not hesitate to*
רֹק n.m.s. (956) *spit*

30:11

כִּי־יִתְרוֹ conj. (471)-n.m.s.-3 m.s. sf. (452; Q-1 c.s. sf.; LXX αὐτοῦ) *because my cord*
פִּתַּח Pi. pf. 3 m.s. (פָּתַח I 834) *he has loosed*
וַיְעַנֵּנִי consec.-Pi. impf. 3 m.s.-1 c.s. sf. (עָנָה III 776) *and humbled me*
וְרֶסֶן conj.-n.m.s. (I 943) *and restraint*
מִפָּנַי prep.-n.m.p.-1 c.s. sf. (815) *in my presence*
שִׁלֵּחוּ Pi. pf. 3 c.p. paus. (שָׁלַח 1018) *they have cast off*

30:12

עַל־יָמִין prep.-n.f.s. (I 411) *on (my) right hand*
פִּרְחַח n.m. coll. (827) *rabble (brood)*
יָקוּמוּ Qal impf. 3 m.p. (קוּם 877) *rise*
רַגְלַי n.f. du.-1 c.s. sf. (919) *my feet*
שִׁלֵּחוּ Pi. pf. 3 c.p. paus. (שָׁלַח 1018) *they drive forth*
וַיָּסֹלּוּ consec.-Qal impf. 3 m.p. (סָלַל I 699) *and they cast up*
עָלַי prep.-1 c.s. sf. *against me*
אָרְחוֹת אֵידָם n.m.p. cstr. (73)-n.m.s.-3 m.p. sf. (15) *their ways of destruction*

30:13

נָתְסוּ Qal impf. 3 c.p. (נָתַס 683) *they break up*
נְתִיבָתִי n.f.s.-1 c.s. sf. (677; LXX τρίβοι μου) *my path*
לְהַוָּתִי־ prep.-n.f.s.-1 c.s. sf. (217) *my calamity*
יֹעִילוּ Hi. impf. 3 m.p. (יָעַל I 418) *they promote (profit)*
לֹא עֹזֵר לָמוֹ neg.-Qal act.ptc. (עָזַר 740; GK 152u,155n)-prep.-3 m.p. sf. *no one helps them*

30:14

כְּפֶרֶץ רָחָב prep.-n.m.s. (I 829)-adj. m.s. (I 932) *like a wide breach*

יֶאֱתָיוּ Qal impf. 3 m.p. (אָתָה 87; GK 75u) *they come*
תַּחַת שֹׁאָה prep. (1065)-n.f.s. (996) *amid crash*
הִתְגַּלְגָּלוּ Hithpalpel pf. 3 c.p. paus. (גָּלַל II 164) *they roll on*

30:15

הָהְפַּךְ Ho. pf. 3 m.s. (הָפַךְ 245; GK 121b) *are turned*
עָלַי prep.-1 c.s. sf. *upon me*
בַּלָּהוֹת n.f.p. (117) *terrors*
תִּרְדֹּף Qal impf. 3 f.s. (רָדַף 922) *is pursued*
כָּרוּחַ prep.-def.art.-n.f.s. (924) *as by the wind*
נְדִבָתִי n.f.s.-1 c.s. sf. (622; LXX μου ἡ ἐλπίς) *my honor*
וּכְעָב conj.-prep.-n.m.s. (728) *and like a cloud*
עָבְרָה Qal pf. 3 f.s. (עָבַר 716) *has passed away*
יְשֻׁעָתִי n.f.s.-1 c.s. sf. (447) *my prosperity*

30:16

וְעַתָּה conj.-adv. (773) *and now*
עָלַי prep.-1 c.s. sf. *within me*
תִּשְׁתַּפֵּךְ Hith. impf. 3 f.s. (שָׁפַךְ 1049) *is poured out*
נַפְשִׁי n.f.s.-1 c.s. sf. (659) *my soul*
יֹאחֲזוּנִי Qal impf. 3 m.p.-1 c.s. sf. (אָחַז 28) *have taken hold of me*
יְמֵי־עֹנִי n.m.p. cstr. (398)-n.m.s. paus. (777) *days of affliction*

30:17

לַיְלָה n.m.s. (538) *night*
עֲצָמַי n.f.p.-1 c.s. sf. (782) *my bones*
נִקַּר Pi. pf. 3 m.s. (נָקַר 669) *racks (bores)*
מֵעָלָי prep.-prep.-1 c.s. sf. paus. (758) *from off me*
וְעֹרְקַי conj.-Qal act.ptc. m.p.-1 c.s. sf. (עָרַק 792) *and the pains that gnaw me*
לֹא יִשְׁכָּבוּן neg.-Qal impf. 3 m.p. paus. (שָׁכַב 1011) *take no rest*

30:18

בְּרָב־כֹּחַ prep.-n.m.s. cstr. (913)-n.m.s. (470) *with abundance of strength*
יִתְחַפֵּשׂ Hith. impf. 3 m.s. (חָפַשׂ 344; LXX ἐπελάβετο) *is disguised*
לְבוּשִׁי n.m.s.-1 c.s. sf. (528) *my garment*
כְּפִי prep.-n.m.s. cstr. (804) *like the collar of*
כֻּתָּנְתִּי n.f.s.-1 c.s. sf. (509) *my tunic*
יַאַזְרֵנִי Qal impf. 3 m.s.-1 c.s. sf. (אָזַר 25) *it binds me*

30:19

הֹרָנִי Hi. pf. 3 m.s.–1 c.s. sf. (יָרָה 434; GK 59f) *he has cast me*

לַחֹמֶר prep.–def.art.–n.m.s. (I 330) *into the mire*

וָאֶתְמַשֵּׁל consec.–Hith. impf. 1 c.s. (מָשַׁל I 605) *and I have become like*

כֶּעָפָר prep.–def.art.–n.m.s. (779) *as the dust*

וָאֵפֶר conj.–n.m.s. (68) *and ashes*

30:20

אֲשַׁוַּע Pi. impf. 1 c.s. (שָׁוַע 1002) *I cry*

אֵלֶיךָ prep.–2 m.s. sf. *to thee*

וְלֹא תַעֲנֵנִי conj.–neg.–Qal impf. 2 m.s.–1 c.s. sf. (I 772 עָנָה; GK 75,ll) *and thou dost not answer me*

עָמַדְתִּי Qal pf. 1 c.s. (עָמַד 763) *I stand*

וַתִּתְבֹּנֶן בִּי consec.–Hithpolel impf. 2 m.s. (בִּין 106; GK 72bb)–prep.–1 c.s. sf. *and you consider me diligently*

30:21

תֵּהָפֵךְ Ni. impf. 2 m.s. (הָפַךְ 245) *thou hast turned*

לְאַכְזָר prep.–adj. m.s. as subst. (470) *cruel*

לִי prep.–1 c.s. sf. *to me*

בְּעֹצֶם prep.–n.m.s. cstr. (782) *with the might of*

יָדְךָ n.f.s.–2 m.s. sf. (388) *thy hand*

תִשְׂטְמֵנִי Qal impf. 2 m.s.–1 c.s. sf. (שָׂטַם 966; LXX με ἐμαστίγωσας) *thou dost persecute me*

30:22

תִּשָּׂאֵנִי Qal impf. 2 m.s.–1 c.s. sf. (נָשָׂא 669) *thou liftest me up*

אֶל־רוּחַ prep.–n.f.s. (924) *on wind*

תַּרְכִּיבֵנִי Hi. impf. 2 m.s.–1 c.s. sf. (רָכַב 938) *thou makest me ride on it*

וּתְמֹגְגֵנִי conj.–Polel impf. 2 m.s.–1 c.s. sf. (מוּג 556) *thou softenest me (dissipate)*

תְּשֻׁוָּה n.f.s. (444; some suggest n.f.s. 996 = into the roar of the storm) *with abiding success*

30:23

כִּי־יָדַעְתִּי conj. (471)–Qal pf. 1 c.s. (393) *yea, I know*

מָוֶת n.m.s. (560) *to death*

תְּשִׁיבֵנִי Hi. impf. 2 m.s.–1 c.s. sf. (שׁוּב 996) *thou wilt bring me*

וּבֵית conj.–n.m.s. cstr. (108) *and to house (of)*

מוֹעֵד n.m.s. (417) *appointed*

לְכָל־חָי prep.–n.m.s. cstr. (481)–adj. m.s. paus. (311) *for all living*

30:24

אַךְ adv. (36) *yet*

לֹא־בְעִי neg.–prep.–n.m.s. (730) *not in a heap of ruins*

יִשְׁלַח־ Qal impf. 3 m.s. (שָׁלַח 1018) *does one stretch out*

יָד n.f.s. paus. (388) *his hand*

אִם־בְּפִידוֹ hypoth.part. (49)–prep.–n.m.s.–3 m.s. sf. (810) *and in his disaster*

לָהֶן prep.–3 m.p. sf. (514 לָכֵן = therefore) *to them*

שׁוּעַ n.m.s. (1002) *a cry for help*

30:25

אִם־לֹא בָכִיתִי hypoth.part. (49)–neg.–Qal pf. 1 c.s. (בָּכָה 113) *did I not weep*

לִקְשֵׁה־יוֹם prep.–adj. m.s. cstr. (904)–n.m.s. (398) *for him whose day was hard?*

עָגְמָה Qal pf. 3 f.s. (עָגַם 723) *was (not) grieved?*

נַפְשִׁי n.f.s.–1 c.s. sf. (659) *my soul*

לָאֶבְיוֹן prep.–def.art.–adj. m.s. (2) *for the poor*

30:26

כִּי טוֹב conj.–n.m.s. (III 375) *but good*

קִוִּיתִי Pi. pf. 1 c.s. (קָוָה I 875) *I looked for*

וַיָּבֹא רָע consec.–Qal impf. 3 m.s. (בּוֹא 97)–n.m.s. (II 948) *but evil came*

וַאֲיַחֲלָה conj.–Pi. impf. 1 c.s.–coh.he (יָחַל 403; GK 49e,108e) *and when I waited*

לְאוֹר prep.–n.m.s. (21) *for light*

וַיָּבֹא consec.–Qal impf. 3 m.s. (בּוֹא 97) *then came*

אֹפֶל n.m.s. (66) *darkness*

30:27

מֵעַי n.m.p.–1 c.s. sf. (588) *my heart (inward parts)*

רֻתְּחוּ Pu. pf. 3 c.p. (958) *have been made to boil*

וְלֹא־דָמּוּ conj.–neg.–Qal pf. 3 c.p. paus. (דָּמַם I 198) *and is never still*

קִדְּמֻנִי Pi. pf. 3 c.p.–1 c.s. sf. (קָדַם 869) *come to meet me*

יְמֵי־עֹנִי n.m.p. cstr. (398)–n.m.s. paus. (777) *days of affliction*

30:28

קֹדֵר Qal act.ptc. (871) *being dark*

הִלַּכְתִּי Pi. pf. 1 c.s. (הָלַךְ 229) *I go about*

בְּלֹא חַמָּה prep.–neg.–n.f.s. (328; GK 118n) *but not by (the) sun*

קַמְתִּי Qal pf. 1 c.s. (קוּם 877) *I stand up*

בַקָּהָל prep.–def.art.–n.m.s. (874) *in the assembly*

אֲשַׁוֵּעַ Pi. impf. 1 c.s. (שָׁוַע 1002; GK 120c) *and cry for help*

30:29

אָח הָיִיתִי n.m.s. (26)–Qal pf. 1 c.s. (הָיָה 224) *I am a brother*
לְתַנִּים prep.–n.m.p. (1072; GK 87e) *of jackals*
וְרֵעַ conj.–n.m.s. (945) *and a companion*
לִבְנוֹת יַעֲנָה prep.–n.f.p. cstr. (I 123)–n.f.s. (419) *of ostriches*

30:30

עוֹרִי n.m.s.–1 c.s. sf. (736) *my skin*
שָׁחַר Qal pf. 3 m.s. (I 1007) *turns black*
מֵעָלָי prep.–prep.–1 c.s. sf. paus. *from me*
וְעַצְמִי־ conj.–n.f.s.–1 c.s. sf. (782) *and my bones*
חָרָה Qal pf. 3 f.s. (חָרַר I 359) *burn*
מִנִּי־חֹרֶב prep. (577)–n.m.s. (I 351) *with heat*

30:31

וַיְהִי consec.–Qal impf. 3 m.s. (הָיָה 224) *and turns (becomes)*
לְאֵבֶל prep.–n.m.s. (5) *to mourning*
כִּנֹּרִי n.m.s.–1 c.s. sf. (490) *my lyre*
וְעֻגָבִי conj.–n.m.s.–1 c.s. sf. (721) *and my pipe*
לְקוֹל prep.–n.m.s. cstr. (876) *to voice of*
בֹּכִים Qal act.ptc. m.p. (בָּכָה 113) *those who weep*

31:1

בְּרִית n.f.s. (136) *a covenant*
כָּרַתִּי Qal pf. 1 c.s. (כָּרַת 503) *I have made*
לְעֵינָי prep.–n.f. du.–1 c.s. sf. (744) *with my eyes*
וּמָה conj.–interr. (552; GK 148a) *how then?*
אֶתְבּוֹנֵן Hithpolel impf. 1 c.s. (בִּין 106) *could I look*
עַל־בְּתוּלָה prep.–n.f.s. (143) *upon a virgin*

31:2

וּמֶה חֵלֶק conj.–interr. (552)–n.m.s. (324) *what would be my portion*
אֱלוֹהַּ n.m.s. (42) *from God*
מִמָּעַל prep.–adv. (751) *above*
וְנַחֲלַת conj.–n.f.s. cstr. (635) *and my heritage from*
שַׁדַּי pr.n. (994) *the Almighty*
מִמְּרֹמִים prep.–n.m.p. (928) *on high*

31:3

הֲלֹא־אֵיד interr.–neg.–n.m.s. (15) *is not calamity?*
לְעַוָּל consec.–n.m.s. (732) *to the unrighteous*
וְנֵכֶר conj.–n.m.s. (648) *and disaster*

לְפֹעֲלֵי prep.–Qal act.ptc. m.p. cstr. (פָּעַל 821) *to workers of*
אָוֶן n.m.s. (19) *iniquity*

31:4

הֲלֹא־הוּא interr.–neg.–pers.pr. 3 m.s. (214) *does he not*
יִרְאֶה Qal impf. 3 m.s. (רָאָה 906) *see?*
דְרָכָי n.m.p.–1 c.s. sf. (202) *my ways*
וְכָל־ conj.–n.m.s. cstr. (481) *and all (of)*
צְעָדַי n.m.p.–1 c.s. sf. (857) *my steps*
יִסְפּוֹר Qal impf. 3 m.s. (סָפַר 707) *he numbers*

31:5

אִם־הָלַכְתִּי hypoth.part. (49)–Qal pf. 1 c.s. (הָלַךְ 229) *if I have walked*
עִם־שָׁוְא prep. (767)–n.m.s. (996; LXX μετὰ γελοιαστῶν) *with falsehood*
וַתַּחַשׁ consec.–Qal impf. 3 f.s. (חוּשׁ I 301; GK 72ff) *and has hastened*
עַל־מִרְמָה prep.–n.f.s. (941) *to deceit*
רַגְלִי n.f.s.–1 c.s. sf. (919) *my foot*

31:6

יִשְׁקְלֵנִי Qal impf. 3 m.s.–1 c.s. sf. (שָׁקַל 1053) *let him weigh me*
בְמֹאזְנֵי־צֶדֶק prep.–n.m. du. cstr. (24)–n.m.s. (841) *in a just balance*
וְיֵדַע אֱלוֹהַּ conj.–Qal impf. 3 m.s. (יָדַע 393) –n.m.s. (42) *and let God know*
תֻּמָּתִי n.f.s.–1 c.s. sf. (1070) *my integrity*

31:7

אִם תִּטֶּה hypoth.part. (49)–Qal impf. 3 f.s. (נָטָה 639; GK 108f) *if has turned aside*
אַשֻּׁרִי n.f.s.–1 c.s. sf. (81) *my step*
מִנִּי הַדָּרֶךְ prep. (577)–def.art.–n.m.s. (202) *from the way*
וְאַחַר עֵינַי conj.–prep. (29)–n.f. du.–1 c.s. sf. (744) *and after my eyes*
הָלַךְ לִבִּי Qal pf. 3 m.s. (229)–n.m.s.–1 c.s. sf. (524) *my heart has gone*
וּבְכַפַּי conj.–prep.–n.f. du.–1 c.s. sf. (496) *and to my hands*
דָּבַק Qal pf. 3 m.s. (179) *has cleaved*
מְאוּם n.m.s. (548; GK 23c) *any spot*

31:8

אֶזְרְעָה Qal impf. 1 c.s.–coh.he (זָרַע 281; GK 108f) *then let me sow*
וְאַחֵר conj.–adj. m.s. (I 29) *and another*
יֹאכֵל Qal impf. 3 m.s. (אָכַל 37) *eat*

וְצֶאֱצָאַי conj.-n.m.p.-1 c.s. sf. (425) *and what grows for me*
יְשֹׁרָשׁוּ Pu. impf. 3 m.p. (שָׁרַשׁ 1057; GK 108f) *let be rooted out*

31:9

אִם־נִפְתָּה hypoth.part. (49)-Ni. pf. 3 m.s. (פָּתָה 834; GK 159m) *if has been enticed*
לִבִּי n.m.s.-1 c.s. sf. (524) *my heart*
עַל־אִשָּׁה prep.-n.f.s. (61) *to a woman*
וְעַל־פֶּתַח conj.-prep.-n.m.s. cstr. (835) *and at the door of*
רֵעִי n.m.s.-1 c.s. sf. (945) *my neighbor*
אָרָבְתִּי Qal pf. 1 c.s. (אָרַב 70) *I have lain in wait*

31:10

תִּטְחַן Qal impf. 3 f.s. (טָחַן 377; GK 159m) *let ... grind*
לְאַחֵר prep.-adj. m.s. (29) *for another*
אִשְׁתִּי n.f.s.-1 c.s. sf. (61) *my wife*
וְעָלֶיהָ conj.-prep.-3 f.s. sf. *and upon her*
יִכְרְעוּן Qal impf. 3 m.p. (כָּרַע 502) *let ... bow down*
אֲחֵרִין adj. m.p. (29; GK 87e) *others*

31:11

כִּי־הוּא conj. (471)-demons.adj. f.s. (214) *for that (would be)*
זִמָּה n.f.s. (I 273) *a heinous crime (device, plan)*
וְהִיא conj.-demons.adj. f.s. (214; GK 32,l) *that (would be)*
עָוֹן n.m.s. (730; GK 131s) *an iniquity*
פְּלִילִים n.m.p. (813) *judges*

31:12

כִּי אֵשׁ הִיא conj. (471)-n.f.s. (77)-demons.adj. f.s. (214; GK 155f) *for that would be a fire*
עַד־אֲבַדּוֹן prep. (III 723)-pr.n. (2) *until Abaddon*
תֹּאכֵל Qal impf. 3 f.s. (אָכַל 37) *which consumes*
וּבְכָל־ conj.-prep.-n.m.s. cstr. (481) *and all of*
תְּבוּאָתִי n.f.s.-1 c.s. sf. (100) *my increase*
תְשָׁרֵשׁ Pi. impf. 3 f.s. (שָׁרַשׁ 1057) *it would burn to the root*

31:13

אִם־אֶמְאַס hypoth.part. (49)-Qal impf. 1 c.s. (549 מָאַס) *if I have rejected*
מִשְׁפַּט n.m.s. cstr. (1048) *the cause of*
עַבְדִּי n.m.s.-1 c.s. sf. (713) *my manservant*
וַאֲמָתִי conj.-n.f.s.-1 c.s. sf. (51) *or my maidservant*

בְּרִבָם prep.-Qal inf.cstr.-3 m.p. sf. (רִיב 936; or n.m.s.) *when they brought a complaint*
עִמָּדִי prep.-1 c.s. sf. (767) *against me*

31:14

וּמָה conj.-interr. (552) *what then*
אֶעֱשֶׂה Qal impf. 1 c.s. (עָשָׂה I 793) *shall I do*
כִּי־יָקוּם conj. (471)-Qal impf. 3 m.s. (877; LXX ἔτασίν μου ποιήσηται) *when ... rises up?*
אֵל n.m.s. (42) *God*
וְכִי־יִפְקֹד conj.-conj. (471)-Qal impf. 3 m.s. (פָּקַד 823) *and when he makes inquiry*
מָה אֲשִׁיבֶנּוּ interr. (552)-Hi. impf. 1 c.s.-3 m.s. sf. (שׁוּב 996) *what shall I answer him?*

31:15

הֲלֹא־בַבֶּטֶן interr.-neg.-prep.-def.art.-n.f.s. (105) *not in the womb?*
עֹשֵׂנִי Qal act.ptc. m.s.-1 c.s. sf. (עָשָׂה I 793) *he who made me*
עָשָׂהוּ Qal pf. 3 m.s.-3 m.s. sf. (I 793) *make him?*
וַיְכֻנֶנּוּ consec.-Polel impf. 3 m.s.-3 m.s. sf. (כּוּן I 465; GK 58k,72cc; or 1 c.p. sf.) *and did ... fashion him (us)*
בָּרֶחֶם prep.-def.art.-n.m.s. (933); LXX ἐν τῇ αὐτῇ κοιλίᾳ) *in the womb*
אֶחָד adj. m.s. (25) *one*

31:16

אִם־אֶמְנַע hypoth.part. (49)-Qal impf. 1 c.s. (מָנַע 586) *if I have withheld*
מֵחֵפֶץ prep.-n.m.s. cstr. (343) *from desire of*
דַּלִּים adj. m.p. (195) *poor*
וְעֵינֵי conj.-n.f. du. cstr. (744) *or eyes of*
אַלְמָנָה n.f.s. (48) *widow*
אֲכַלֶּה Pi. impf. 1 c.s. (כָּלָה I 477) *I have caused to fail*

31:17

וְאֹכַל conj.-Qal impf. 1 c.s. (אָכַל 37) *or have eaten*
פִּתִּי n.f.s.-1 c.s. sf. (837) *my morsel*
לְבַדִּי prep.-n.m.s.-1 c.s. sf. (II 94) *alone*
וְלֹא־אָכַל conj.-neg.-Qal pf. 3 m.s. (37) *and has not eaten*
יָתוֹם n.m.s. (450) *fatherless*
מִמֶּנָּה prep.-3 f.s. sf. *of it*

31:18

כִּי מִנְּעוּרַי conj. (471; GK 163b)-prep.-n.m.p.-1 c.s. sf. (655) *for from my youth*

גִּדֵּלַנִי Qal pf. 3 m.s.-1 c.s. sf. (גָּדַל 152; GK 117x) *he grew up to me*
כְאָב prep. (GK 126p)-n.m.s. (3) *as a father*
וּמִבֶּטֶן conj.-prep.-n.f.s. cstr. (105) *and from the womb of*
אִמִּי n.f.s.-1 c.s. sf. (51) *my mother*
אַנְחֶנָּה Hi. impf. 1 c.s.-3 f.s. sf. (נָחָה 634) *I guided her*

31:19

אִם־אֶרְאֶה hypoth.part. (49)-Qal impf. 1 c.s. (רָאָה 906) *if I have seen*
אוֹבֵד Qal act.ptc. (1) *any one perish*
מִבְּלִי לְבוּשׁ prep.-neg. (115)-n.m.s. (528) *for lack of clothing*
וְאֵין כְּסוּת conj.-subst. cstr. (II 34)-n.f.s. (492) *or there is no covering*
לָאֶבְיוֹן prep.-def.art.-adj. m.s. (2) *for the poor*

31:20

אִם־לֹא hypoth.part. (49)-neg. *if ... not*
בֵּרְכוּנִי Pi. pf. 3 c.p.-1 c.s. sf. (בָּרַךְ 138) *have blessed me*
חֲלָצָו n.f. du.-3 m.s. sf. (323) *his loins*
וּמִגֵּז conj.-prep.-n.m.s. cstr. (159) *and with the fleece of*
כְּבָשַׂי n.m.p.-1 c.s. sf. (461) *my sheep*
יִתְחַמָּם Hith. impf. 3 m.s. paus. (חָמַם 328) *he warmed himself*

31:21

אִם־הֲנִיפוֹתִי hypoth.part. (49)-Hi. pf. 1 c.s. (נוּף I 631) *if I have raised*
עַל־יָתוֹם prep.-n.m.s. (450) *against fatherless*
יָדִי n.f.s.-1 c.s. sf. (388) *my hand*
כִּי־אֶרְאֶה conj.-Qal impf. 1 c.s. (רָאָה 906) *because I saw*
בַשַּׁעַר prep.-def.art.-n.m.s. (1044) *in the gate*
עֶזְרָתִי n.f.s.-1 c.s. sf. (740) *my help*

31:22

כְּתֵפִי n.f.s.-1 c.s. sf. (509) *my shoulder-blade*
מִשִּׁכְמָה prep.-n.f.s. (1014; GK 91e) *from my shoulder*
תִפּוֹל Qal impf. 3 f.s. (נָפַל 656) *let fall*
וְאֶזְרֹעִי conj.-n.f.s.-1 c.s. sf. (284) *and my arm*
מִקָּנָה prep.-n.m.s.-3 f.s. sf. (889; GK 91e) *from its socket*
תִשָּׁבֵר Ni. impf. 3 f.s. (שָׁבַר 990) *let be broken*

31:23

כִּי פַחַד conj.-n.m.s. (808) *for terror*
אֵלַי prep.-1 c.s. sf. (LXX κυρίου συνέσχεν με) *unto me*
אֵיד אֵל n.m.s. cstr. (15)-n.m.s. (42) *calamity from God*
וּמִשְּׂאֵתוֹ conj.-prep.-n.f.s.-3 m.s. sf. (673) *and (from) his majesty*
לֹא אוּכָל neg.-Qal impf. 1 c.s. (יָכֹל 407) *I have no power*

31:24

אִם־שַׂמְתִּי hypoth.part. (49)-Qal pf. 1 c.s. (שִׂים 962) *if I have made*
זָהָב n.m.s. (262) *gold*
כִּסְלִי n.m.s.-1 c.s. sf. (492) *my trust*
וְלַכֶּתֶם conj.-prep.-def.art.-n.m.s. (508) *or fine gold*
אָמַרְתִּי Qal pf. 1 c.s. (55) *I called*
מִבְטַחִי n.m.s.-1 c.s. sf. (105) *my confidence*

31:25

אִם־אֶשְׂמַח hypoth.part. (49)-Qal impf. 1 c.s. (שָׂמַח 970) *if I have rejoiced*
כִּי־רַב conj. (471)-adj. m.s. (I 912) *because great*
חֵילִי n.m.s.-1 c.s. sf. (298) *my wealth*
וְכִי־כַבִּיר conj.-conj. (471)-adj. m.s. (460) *or because much*
מָצְאָה Qal pf. 3 f.s. (מָצָא 592) *had gotten*
יָדִי n.f.s.-1 c.s. sf. (388) *my hand*

31:26

אִם־אֶרְאֶה hypoth.part. (49)-Qal impf. 1 c.s. (רָאָה 906) *if I have looked at*
אוֹר n.m.s. (21) *sun (light)*
כִּי יָהֵל conj. (471)-Hi. impf. 3 m.s. (הָלַל I 237; GK 67p) *when it shone*
וְיָרֵחַ consec.-n.m.s.s (437) *or moon*
יָקָר adj. m.s. (429; GK 118sn) *in splendor*
הֹלֵךְ Qal act.ptc. (הָלַךְ 229; GK 118q) *moving*

31:27

וַיִּפְתְּ consec.-Qal impf. 3 m.s. (פָּתָה 834; GK 75q,111q; LXX ἠπατήθη) *and has been enticed*
בַּסֵּתֶר prep.-def.art.-n.m.s. (712) *secretly*
לִבִּי n.m.s.-1 c.s. sf. (524) *my heart*
וַתִּשַּׁק consec.-Qal impf. 3 f.s. (נָשַׁק I 676) *and ... has kissed*
יָדִי n.f.s.-1 c.s. sf. (388) *my hand*
לְפִי prep.-n.m.s.-1 c.s. sf. (804) *to my mouth*

31:28

גַּם־הוּא adv. (168)-demons.adj. m.s. (214) *this also*

עָוֺן n.m.s. (730) *(would be) an iniquity*
פְּלִילִי adj. m.s. (813) *to be punished by judges*
כִּי־כִחַשְׁתִּי conj.-Pi. pf. 1 c.s. (כָּחַשׁ 471; GK 159dd) *for I should have been false*
לָאֵל prep.-def.art.-n.m.s. (42) *to the God*
מִמָּעַל prep.-subst. (751) *above*

31:29

אִם־אֶשְׂמַח hypoth.part. (49)-Qal impf. 1 c.s. (970 שָׂמַח) *if I have rejoiced*
בְּפִיד prep.-n.m.s. cstr. (810) *at the ruin of*
מְשַׂנְאִי Pi. ptc. m.s.-1 c.s. sf. (שָׂנֵא 971) *him that hated me*
וְהִתְעֹרַרְתִּי conj.-Hithpolel pf. 1 c.s. (עוּר I 734; GK 112e) *or exulted*
כִּי־מְצָאוֹ conj. (471)-Qal pf. 3 m.s.-3 m.s. sf. (592 מָצָא) *when overtook him*
רָע n.m.s. paus. (II 948) *evil*

31:30

וְלֹא־נָתַתִּי conj.-neg.-Qal pf. 1 c.s. (נָתַן 678) *I have not let (given)*
לַחֲטֹא prep.-Qal inf.cstr. (חָטָא 306) *to sin*
חִכִּי n.m.s.-1 c.s. sf. (335) *my mouth*
לִשְׁאֹל prep.-Qal inf.cstr. (שָׁאַל 981) *by asking for*
בְּאָלָה prep.-n.f.s. (46) *with a curse*
נַפְשׁוֹ n.f.s.-1 c.s. sf. (659) *his life*

31:31

אִם־לֹא hypoth.part. (49)-neg. *if not*
אָמְרוּ Qal pf. 3 c.p. (55) *have said*
מְתֵי n.m.p. cstr. (607) *the men of*
אָהֳלִי n.m.s.-1 c.s. sf. (13) *my tent*
מִי־יִתֵּן interr. (566)-Qal impf. 3 m.s. (נָתַן 678; GK 151b) *who is there?*
מִבְּשָׂרוֹ prep.-n.m.s.-3 m.s. sf. (142) *with his meat*
לֹא נִשְׂבָּע neg.-Ni. ptc. (שָׂבַע 959) *has not been filled (sated)*

31:32

בַּחוּץ prep.-def.art.-n.m.s. (299) *in the street*
לֹא־יָלִין neg.-Qal impf. 3 m.s. (לִין I 533) *has not lodged*
גֵּר n.m.s. (158) *sojourner*
דְּלָתַי n.f.p.-1 c.s. sf. (195) *my doors*
לָאֹרַח prep.-def.art.-n.m.s. (73; LXX παντὶ ἐλθόντι) *to the wayfarer*
אֶפְתָּח Qal impf. 1 c.s. (I 834) *I have opened*

31:33

אִם־כִּסִּיתִי hypoth.part. (49)-Pi. pf. 1 c.s. (כָּסָה 491) *if I have concealed*
כְאָדָם prep.-n.m.s. (9) *like men (Adam)*
פְּשָׁעָי n.m.p.-1 c.s. sf. (833) *my transgressions*
לִטְמוֹן prep.-Qal inf.cstr. (380) *by hiding*
בְּחֻבִּי prep.-n.m.s.-1 c.s. sf. (285; 300) *in my bosom*
עֲוֺנִי n.m.s.-1 c.s. sf. (730) *my iniquity*

31:34

כִּי אֶעֱרוֹץ conj. (471)-Qal impf. 1 c.s. (עָרַץ 791) *because I stood in fear*
הָמוֹן רַבָּה n.f.s. (242)-adj. f.s. (I 912) *of the great multitude*
וּבוּז־ conj.-n.m.s. cstr. (II 100) *and contempt of*
מִשְׁפָּחוֹת n.f.p. (1046) *families*
יְחִתֵּנִי Hi. impf. 3 m.s.-1 c.s. sf. (חָתַת 369) *terrified me*
וָאֶדֹּם consec.-Qal impf. 1 c.s. (דָּמַם I 198; GK 111q) *so that I kept silence*
לֹא־אֵצֵא neg.-Qal impf. 1 c.s. (יָצָא 422; GK 156f) *and did not go out*
פָתַח n.m.s. paus. (835) *of doors*

31:35

מִי יִתֶּן־ interr. (566)-Qal impf. 3 m.s. (נָתַן 678) *oh, that*
לִי prep.-1 c.s. sf. *I had (to me)*
שֹׁמֵעַ לִי Qal act.ptc. (שָׁמַע 1033; GK 151b)-v.supra *one to hear me*
הֶן־תָּוִי interj. (243)-n.m.s.-1 c.s. sf. (1067) *here is my signature*
שַׁדַּי pr.n. (994) *the Almighty*
יַעֲנֵנִי Qal impf. 3 m.s.-1 c.s. sf. (עָנָה I 772) *let him answer me*
וְסֵפֶר conj.-n.m.s. (706) *and indictment*
כָּתַב Qal pf. 3 m.s. (507) *written by*
אִישׁ רִיבִי n.m.s. cstr. (35)-n.m.s.-1 c.s. sf. (936) *my adversary*

31:36

אִם־לֹא hypoth.part. (49)-neg. *surely*
עַל־שִׁכְמִי prep.-n.m.s.-1 c.s. sf. (I 1014) *on my shoulder*
אֶשָּׂאֶנּוּ Qal impf. 1 c.s.-3 m.s. sf. (נָשָׂא 669) *I would carry it*
אֶעֶנְדֶנּוּ Qal impf. 1 c.s.-3 m.s. sf. (עָנַד 772) *I would bind it*
עֲטָרוֹת n.f.p. (I 742) *as a crown*
לִי prep.-1 c.s. sf. *on me*

31:37

מִסְפַּר n.m.s. cstr. (708) *an account of all of*
צְעָדַי n.m.p.-1 c.s. sf. (857) *my steps*
אַגִּידֶנּוּ Hi. impf. 1 c.s.-3 m.s. sf. (נָגַד 616) *I would give*
כְּמוֹ־נָגִיד prep. (453)-n.m.s. (617) *like a prince*
אֲקָרְבֶנּוּ Pi. impf. 1 c.s.-3 m.s. sf. (קָרַב I 897) *I would approach him*

31:38

אִם־עָלַי hypoth.part. (49)-prep.-1 c.s. sf. *if against me*
אַדְמָתִי n.f.s.-1 c.s. sf. (9) *my land*
תִזְעָק Qal impf. 3 f.s. paus. (זָעַק 277) *has cried out*
וְיַחַד conj.-adv. (403) *and together*
תְּלָמֶיהָ n.m.p.-3 f.s. sf. (1068) *its furrows*
יִבְכָּיוּן Qal impf. 3 m.p. (בָּכָה 113) *have wept*

31:39

אִם־כֹּחָהּ hypoth.part. (49)-n.m.s.-3 f.s. sf. (470) *if its yield (strength)*
אָכַלְתִּי Qal pf. 1 c.s. (אָכַל 37) *I have eaten*
בְלִי־כָסֶף neg. (115)-n.m.s. paus. (494) *without payment*
וְנֶפֶשׁ conj.-n.f.s. cstr. (659) *and the life of*
בְּעָלֶיהָ n.m.p.-3 f.s. sf. (127) *its owners*
הִפָּחְתִּי Hi. pf. 1 c.s. (נָפַח 655) *I have caused (them) to breathe out*

31:40

תַּחַת חִטָּה prep. (1065)-n.f.s. (334) *instead of wheat*
יֵצֵא Qal impf. 3 m.s. (יָצָא 422) *let grow*
חוֹחַ n.m.s. (296) *thorns*
וְתַחַת־שְׂעֹרָה conj.-v.supra-n.f.s. (972) *and instead of barley*
בָאְשָׁה n.f.s. (93) *foul weeds*
תַּמּוּ Qal pf. 3 c.p. (תָּמַם 1070) *are ended*
דִּבְרֵי n.m.p. cstr. (182) *the words of*
אִיּוֹב pr.n. (33) *Job*

32:1

וַיִּשְׁבְּתוּ consec.-Qal impf. 3 m.p. (שָׁבַת 991) *so ceased*
שְׁלֹשֶׁת num. f. cstr. (1025; LXX οἱ τρεῖς φίλοι αὐτοῦ) *three of*
הָאֲנָשִׁים הָאֵלֶּה def.art.-n.m.p. (35)-def.art.-demons.adj. c.p. (41) *these men*
מֵעֲנוֹת prep.-Qal inf.cstr. (עָנָה I 772) *to answer*
אֶת־אִיּוֹב dir.obj.-pr.n. (33) *Job*
כִּי הוּא conj. (471)-pers.pr. 3 m.s. (214) *because he (was)*
צַדִּיק adj. m.s. (843) *righteous*
בְּעֵינָיו prep.-n.f. du.-3 m.s. sf. (744) *in his own eyes*

32:2

וַיִּחַר consec.-Qal impf. 3 m.s. (חָרָה 354) *then became kindled*
אַף n.m.s. cstr. (I 60) *the anger of*
אֱלִיהוּא pr.n. (45) *Elihu*
בֶן־בַּרַכְאֵל n.m.s. cstr. (119)-pr.n. (140) *the son of Barachel*
הַבּוּזִי def.art.-pr.n. gent. (100) *the Buzite*
מִמִּשְׁפַּחַת prep.-n.f.s. cstr. (1046) *of the family of*
רָם pr.n. (928) *Ram*
בְּאִיּוֹב prep.-pr.n. (33) *at Job*
חָרָה אַפּוֹ Qal pf. 3 m.s. (חָרָה 354)-n.m.s.-3 m.s. sf. (I 60) *he was angry*
עַל־צַדְּקוֹ prep. Pi. inf.cstr.-3 m.s. sf. (צָדַק 842) *because he justified*
נַפְשׁוֹ n.f.s.-3 m.s. sf. (659) *himself*
מֵאֱלֹהִים prep.-n.m.p. (43) *rather than God*

32:3

וּבִשְׁלֹשֶׁת conj.-prep.-num. f.s. cstr. (1025) *at three (of)*
רֵעָיו n.m.p.-3 m.s. sf. (945) *his friends*
חָרָה אַפּוֹ Qal pf. 3 m.s. (354)-n.m.s.-3 m.s. sf. (I 60) *he was angry*
עַל אֲשֶׁר prep.-rel. (81) *because*
לֹא־מָצְאוּ neg.-Qal pf. 3 c.p. (מָצָא 592) *they had not found*
מַעֲנֶה n.m.s. (775) *an answer*
וַיַּרְשִׁיעוּ consec.-Hi. impf. 3 m.p. (רָשַׁע 957) *although they had declared to be in the wrong*
אֶת־אִיּוֹב dir.obj.-pr.n. (33) *Job*

32:4

וֶאֱלִיהוּ conj.-pr.n. (45) *now Elihu*
חִכָּה Pi. pf. 3 m.s. (חָכָה 314) *had waited*
אֶת־אִיּוֹב dir.obj.-pr.n. (33) *on Job*
בִּדְבָרִים prep.-n.m.p. (182) *with words*
כִּי־זְקֵנִים־ conj. (471)-adj. m.p. (278) *old(er)*
הֵמָּה pers.pr. 3 m.p. (241) *they*
מִמֶּנּוּ prep.-3 m.s. sf. *than he*
לְיָמִים prep.-n.m.p. (398) *(in days)*

32:5

וַיַּרְא consec.-Qal impf. 3 m.s. (רָאָה 906) *and when saw*
אֱלִיהוּא pr.n. (45) *Elihu*
כִּי אֵין conj. (471)-subst. cstr. (II 34) *that there was no*
מַעֲנֶה n.m.s. (775) *answer*
בְּפִי prep.-n.m.s. cstr. (804) *in the mouth of*
שְׁלֹשֶׁת num. f.s. cstr. (1025) *the three (of)*
הָאֲנָשִׁים def.art.-n.m.p. (35, 60) *men*
וַיִּחַר אַפּוֹ consec.-Qal impf. 3 m.s. (חָרָה 354)-n.m.s.-3 m.s. sf. (I 60) *he became angry*

32:6

וַיַּעַן consec.-Qal impf. 3 m.s. (עָנָה I 772) *and answered*
אֱלִיהוּא pr.n. (45) *Elihu*
בֶּן־בַּרַכְאֵל n.m.s. cstr. (119)-pr.n. (140) *the son of Barachel*
הַבּוּזִי def.art.-pr.n. gent. (100) *the Buzite*
וַיֹּאמַר consec.-Qal impf. 3 m.s. (אָמַר 55; GK 68e) *(and said)*
צָעִיר אֲנִי adj. m.s. (I 859)-pers.pr. 1 c.s. (58) *I am young*
לְיָמִים prep.-n.m.p. (398) *in days (years)*
וְאַתֶּם conj.-pers.pr. 2 m.p. (61) *and you are*
יְשִׁישִׁים adj. m.p. (450) *aged*
עַל־כֵּן prep.-adv. (485) *therefore*
זָחַלְתִּי Qal pf. 1 c.s. (זָחַל II 267) *I was timid*
וָאִירָא consec.-Qal impf. 1 c.s. (יָרֵא 431) *and afraid*
מֵחַוֹּת prep.-Pi. inf.cstr. (חָוָה III 296) *to declare*
דֵּעִי n.m.s.-1 c.s. sf. (395; GK 69m) *my opinion*
אֶתְכֶם dir.obj.-2 m.p. sf. *to you*

32:7

אָמַרְתִּי Qal pf. 1 c.s. (אָמַר 55) *I said*
יָמִים יְדַבֵּרוּ n.m.p. (398)-Pi. impf. 3 m.p. (דָּבַר 180) *let days speak*
וְרֹב שָׁנִים conj.-n.m.s. cstr. (913)-n.f.p. (1040; GK 146a) *and many years*
יֹדִיעוּ Hi. impf. 3 m.p. (יָדַע 393) *let ... teach*
חָכְמָה n.f.s. (315) *wisdom*

32:8

אָכֵן adv. (38) *but indeed*
רוּחַ־הִיא n.f.s. (924)-demons.adj. f.s. (214) *it is the spirit*
בֶאֱנוֹשׁ prep.-n.m.s. (60) *in a man*
וְנִשְׁמַת conj.-n.f.s. cstr. (675) *and the breath of*
שַׁדַּי pr.n. (994) *the Almighty*
תְּבִינֵם Hi. impf. 3 f.s.-3 m.p. sf. (בִּין 106) *that makes him understand*

32:9

לֹא־רַבִּים neg.-adj. m.p. (I 912; LXX οὐχ οἱ πολυχρόνιοι) *it is not the many*
יֶחְכָּמוּ Qal impf. 3 m.p. (חָכַם 314) *that are wise*
וּזְקֵנִים conj.-adj. m.p. (278) *nor the aged*
יָבִינוּ Qal impf. 3 m.p. (בִּין 106) *that understand*
מִשְׁפָּט n.m.s. (1048) *what is right*

32:10

לָכֵן prep.-adv. (485) *therefore*
אָמַרְתִּי Qal pf. 1 c.s. (אָמַר 55) *I say*
שִׁמְעָה־לִּי Qal impv. 2 m.s.-vol.he (שָׁמַע 1033; LXX ἀκούσατέ μου)-prep.-1 c.s. sf. *listen to me*
אֲחַוֶּה Pi. impf. 1 c.s. (חָוָה III 296) *let me declare*
דֵעִי n.m.s.-1 c.s. sf. (395) *my opinion*
אַף־אָנִי conj. (II 64)-pers.pr. 1 c.s. (58) *even me*

32:11

הֵן interj. (243) *behold*
הוֹחַלְתִּי Hi. pf. 1 c.s. (יָחַל 403) *I waited*
לְדִבְרֵיכֶם prep.-n.m.p.-2 m.p. sf. (182) *for your words*
אָזִין (some mss. rd. אַאֲזִין) Hi. impf. 1 c.s. (אָזַן I 24; GK 68i) *I listened*
עַד־תְּבוּנֹתֵיכֶם prep. (III 723)-n.f.p.-2 m.p. sf. (108) *for your wise sayings*
עַד־תַּחְקְרוּן prep. (III 723)-Qal impf. 2 m.p. (חָקַר 350) *while you searched*
מִלִּין n.f.p. (576) *words*

32:12

וְעָדֵיכֶם prep.-2 m.p. sf. (III 723; GK 103o) *unto you*
אֶתְבּוֹנָן Hithpolel impf. 1 c.s. (בִּין 106) *I gave attention*
וְהִנֵּה conj.-interj. (243) *and behold*
אֵין לְאִיּוֹב subst. cstr. (II 34)-prep.-pr.n. (33) *there is not to Job*
מוֹכִיחַ Hi. ptc. m.s. (יָכַח 406) *any to confute*
עוֹנֶה Qal act.ptc. (עָנָה I 772) *or one to answer*
אֲמָרָיו n.m.p.-3 m.s. sf. (56) *his words*
מִכֶּם prep.-2 m.p. sf. *among you*

32:13

פֶּן־תֹּאמְרוּ conj. (814)-Qal impf. 2 m.p. (אָמַר 55) *beware lest you say*
מָצָאנוּ Qal pf. 1 c.p. (מָצָא 592) *we have found*

חָכְמָה n.f.s. (315) *wisdom*
אֵל n.m.s. (42) *God*
יִדְּפֶנּוּ Qal impf. 3 m.s.-3 m.s. sf. (juss.) (נָדַף 623) *may vanquish him*
לֹא־אִישׁ neg.-n.m.s. (35) *not man*

32:14

וְלֹא־עָרַךְ conj.-neg.-Qal pf. 3 m.s. (789) *he has not directed*
אֵלַי prep.-1 c.s. sf. *against me*
מִלִּין n.f.p. (576) *words*
וּבְאִמְרֵיכֶם conj.-prep.-n.m.p.-2 m.p. sf. (56) *and with your speeches*
לֹא אֲשִׁיבֶנּוּ neg.-Hi. impf. 1 c.s.-3 m.s. sf. (שׁוּב 996) *I will not answer him*

32:15

חַתּוּ Qal pf. 3 c.p. (חָתַת 369) *they are discomfited*
לֹא־עָנוּ עוֹד neg.-Qal pf. 3 c.p. (עָנָה I 772)-adv. (728) *they answer no more*
הֶעְתִּיקוּ Hi. pf. 3 c.p. (עָתַק 801) *have moved away*
מֵהֶם prep.-3 m.p. sf. *from them*
מִלִּים n.f.p. (576) *words*

32:16

וְהוֹחַלְתִּי conj.-Hi. pf. 1 c.s. (יָחַל 403) *and shall I wait*
כִּי־לֹא יְדַבֵּרוּ conj.-neg.-Pi. impf. 3 m.p. (דָּבַר 180) *because they do not speak*
כִּי עָמְדוּ conj.-Qal pf. 3 c.p. (763) *because they stand (there)*
לֹא־עָנוּ עוֹד neg.-Qal pf. 3 c.p. (עָנָה I 772)-adv. (728) *and answer no more*

32:17

אַעֲנֶה Qal impf. 1 c.s. (עָנָה I 772; GK 63f) *I give my answer*
אַף־אָנִי conj. (II 64)-pers.pr. 1 c.s. (58) *indeed I*
חֶלְקִי n.m.s.-1 c.s. sf. (I 324) *my portion*
אֲחַוֶּה Pi. impf. 1 c.s. (חָוָה III 296) *I will declare*
דֵעִי n.m.s.-1 c.s. sf. (395) *my opinion*
אַף־אָנִי v.supra-v.supra *indeed I*

32:18

כִּי מָלֵתִי conj. (471)-Qal pf. 1 c.s. (מָלֵא 569; GK 23f,74k) *for I am full of*
מִלִּים n.f.p. (576) *words*
הֱצִיקַתְנִי Hi. pf. 3 f.s.-1 c.s. sf. (צוּק I 847) *constrains me*
רוּחַ בִּטְנִי n.f.s. (924)-n.f.s.-1 c.s. sf. (I 105) *the spirit within me*

32:19

הִנֵּה־בִטְנִי interj. (243)-n.f.s.-1 c.s. sf. (I 105) *behold my heart (seat of intelligent faculties)*
כְּיַיִן prep.-n.m.s. (406) *like wine*
לֹא־יִפָּתֵחַ neg.-Ni. impf. 3 m.s. (פָּתַח I 834) *that has no vent*
כְּאֹבוֹת prep.-n.m.p. (15) *like wineskins*
חֲדָשִׁים adj. m.p. (294) *new*
יִבָּקֵעַ Ni. impf. 3 m.s. (בָּקַע 131) *it is ready to burst*

32:20

אֲדַבְּרָה Pi. impf. 1 c.s.-vol.he (דָּבַר 180) *I must speak*
וְיִרְוַח־לִי conj.-Qal impf. 3 m.s. (רָוַח 926) -prep.-1 c.s. sf. *that I may find relief*
אֶפְתַּח Qal impf. 1 c.s. (פָּתַח I 834) *I must open*
שְׂפָתַי n.f.p.-1 c.s. sf. (973) *my lips*
וְאֶעֱנֶה conj. Qal impf. 1 c.s. (עָנָה I 772) *and answer*

32:21

אַל־נָא אֶשָּׂא neg. (39)-part.of entreaty (609)-Qal impf. 1 c.s. (נָשָׂא 669) *I will not lift up*
פְּנֵי־אִישׁ n.m.p. cstr. (815)-n.m.s. (35) *the face of any person*
וְאֶל־אָדָם conj.-prep.-n.m.s. (9) *or toward any man*
לֹא אֲכַנֶּה neg.-Pi. impf. 1 c.s. (כָּנָה 487) *I do not intend to give flattering titles*

32:22

כִּי לֹא יָדַעְתִּי conj. (471)-neg.-Qal pf. 1 c.s. (יָדַע 393; GK 120c) *for I do not know how*
אֲכַנֶּה Pi. impf. 1 c.s. (487) *to give flattering titles*
כִּמְעַט prep.-subst. (589) *or quickly*
יִשָּׂאֵנִי Qal impf. 3 m.s.-1 c.s. sf. (נָשָׂא 669) *would put an end to me*
עֹשֵׂנִי Qal act.ptc. m.s.-1 c.s. sf. (עָשָׂה I 793) *my Maker*

33:1

וְאוּלָם conj.-adv. (III 19) *but now*
שְׁמַע־נָא Qal impv. 2 m.s. (1033)-part.of entreaty (609) *hear*
אִיּוֹב pr.n. (33) *O Job*
מִלָּי n.f.p.-1 c.s. sf. paus. (576) *my speech*

וְכָל־דְּבָרַי conj.-n.m.s. cstr. (481)-n.m.p.-1 c.s. sf. (182) *and all my words*
הַאֲזִינָה Hi. impv. 2 m.s.-vol.he (אָזַן 24) *listen to*

33:2

הִנֵּה־נָא interj. (243)-part.of entreaty (609) *behold*
פָּתַחְתִּי Qal pf. 1 c.s. (פָּתַח I 834) *I open*
פִי n.m.s.-1 c.s. sf. (804) *my mouth*
דִּבְּרָה Pi. pf. 3 f.s. (דָּבַר 180) *speaks*
לְשׁוֹנִי n.f.s.-1 c.s. sf. (546) *my tongue*
בְחִכִּי prep.-n.m.s.-1 c.s. sf. (335) *in my mouth*

33:3

יֹשֶׁר־ n.m.s. cstr. (449) *the uprightness of*
לִבִּי n.m.s.-1 c.s. sf. (524) *my heart*
אֲמָרָי n.m.p.-1 c.s. sf. (56) *my words*
וְדַעַת conj.-n.f.s. cstr. (395) *and the knowledge of*
שְׂפָתַי n.f.p.-1 c.s. sf. (973) *my lips*
בָּרוּר Qal pass.ptc. (בָּרַר 140) *in a pure, sincere manner*
מִלֵּלוּ Pi. pf. 3 c.p. paus. (מָלַל I 576) *they speak*

33:4

רוּחַ־אֵל n.f.s. cstr. (924)-n.m.s. (42; GK 16h) *the spirit of God*
עָשָׂתְנִי Qal pf. 3 f.s.-1 c.s. sf. (עָשָׂה I 793; GK 75mm) *has made me*
וְנִשְׁמַת conj.-n.f.s. cstr. (675) *and the breath of*
שַׁדַּי pr.n. (994) *the Almighty*
תְּחַיֵּנִי Pi. impf. 3 f.s.-1 c.s. sf. (חָיָה 310) *gives me life*

33:5

אִם־תּוּכַל hypoth.part. (49)-Qal impf. 2 m.s. (יָכֹל 407) *if you can*
הֲשִׁיבֵנִי Hi. impv. 2 m.s.-1 c.s. sf. (שׁוּב 996; LXX πρὸς ταῦτα) *answer me*
עֶרְכָה Qal impv. 2 m.s.-vol.he (עָרַךְ 789; GK 48i) *set in order*
לְפָנַי prep.-n.m.p.-1 c.s. sf. (815) *before me*
הִתְיַצָּבָה Hith. impv. 2 m.s.-vol.he (יָצַב 426; GK 54k) *take your stand*

33:6

הֶן־אֲנִי interj. (243)-pers.pr. 1 c.s. (58) *behold, I am*
כְפִיךָ prep.-n.m.s.-2 m.s. sf. (804) *(in proportion of thee) as you are*
לָאֵל prep.-def.art.-n.m.s. (42) *toward God*
מֵחֹמֶר prep.-n.m.s. (I 330) *from a piece of clay*
קֹרַצְתִּי Pu. pf. 1 c.s. (קָרַץ 902) *I was formed (nipped off)*
גַם־אָנִי adv. (168)-pers.pr. 1 c.s. paus. (58) *even I*

33:7

הִנֵּה interj. (243) *behold*
אֵמָתִי n.f.s.-1 c.s. sf. (33) *fear of me*
לֹא־תְבַעֲתֶךָּ neg.-Pi. impf. 3 f.s.-2 m.s. sf. (בָּעַת 129) *need not terrify you*
וְאַכְפִּי conj.-n.m.s.-1 c.s. sf. (38) *my pressure*
עָלֶיךָ prep.-2 m.s. sf. *upon you*
לֹא־יִכְבָּד neg.-Qal impf. 3 m.s. paus. (כָּבַד 457) *will not be heavy*

33:8

אַךְ אָמַרְתָּ adv. (36)-Qal pf. 2 m.s. (אָמַר 55) *surely, you have spoken*
בְאָזְנָי prep.-n.f. du.-1 c.s. sf. paus. (23) *in my hearing*
וְקוֹל conj.-n.m.s. cstr. (876) *and the sound of*
מִלִּין n.f.p. (576; LXX ῥημάτων σου) *words*
אֶשְׁמָע Qal impf. 1 c.s. paus. (שָׁמַע 1033) *I have heard*

33:9

זַךְ אֲנִי adj. m.s. (269)-pers.pr. 1 c.s. (58) *I am clean*
בְּלִי פָשַׁע neg. (115)-n.m.s. paus. (833) *without transgression*
חַף אָנֹכִי adj. m.s. (342)-pers.pr. 1 c.s. (59) *I am pure*
וְלֹא עָוֹן לִי conj.-neg.-n.m.s. (730)-prep.-1 c.s. sf. *and there is no iniquity in me*

33:10

הֵן interj. (243) *behold*
תְּנוּאוֹת n.f.p. (626) *occasions (oppositions)*
עָלַי prep.-1 c.s. sf. *against me*
יִמְצָא Qal impf. 3 m.s. (מָצָא 592) *he finds*
יַחְשְׁבֵנִי Qal impf. 3 m.s.-1 c.s. sf. (חָשַׁב 362) *he counts me*
לְאוֹיֵב לוֹ prep.-Qal act.ptc. as n.m.s. (33)-prep.-3 m.s. sf. *as his enemy*

33:11

יָשֵׂם Qal impf. 3 m.s. (שִׂים 962) *he puts*
בַּסַּד prep.-def.art.-n.m.s. (690) *in the stocks*
רַגְלָי n.f. du.-1 c.s. sf. (919) *my feet*
יִשְׁמֹר Qal impf. 3 m.s. (שָׁמַר 1036) *and watches*
כָּל־אָרְחֹתָי n.m.s. cstr. (481)-n.m.p.-1 c.s. sf. (73) *all my paths*

33:12

הֶן־זֹאת interj. (243)–demons.adj. f.s. (260) *behold, in this*

לֹא־צָדַקְתָּ neg.–Qal pf. 2 m.s. (842) *you are not right*

אֶעֱנֶךָּ Qal impf. 1 c.s.–2 m.s. sf. (עָנָה I 772) *I will answer you*

כִּי־יִרְבֶּה conj. (471)–Qal impf. 3 m.s. (רָבָה I 915) *for is great(er)*

אֱלוֹהַּ n.m.s. (42) *God*

מֵאֱנוֹשׁ prep.–n.m.s. (60) *than man*

33:13

מַדּוּעַ adv. (396) *why*

אֵלָיו prep.–3 m.s. sf. *against him*

רִיבוֹתָ Qal pf. 2 m.s. (רִיב 936) *do you contend*

כִּי כָל־דְּבָרָיו conj. (471)–n.m.s. cstr. (481)–n.m.p. –3 m.s. sf. (182) *that all of his words*

לֹא־יַעֲנֶה neg.–Qal impf. 3 m.s. (עָנָה I 772) *he will not answer*

33:14

כִּי־בְאַחַת conj. (471)–prep.–num. f.s. (25, 1120; GK 134r) *for in one way*

יְדַבֶּר־אֵל Pi. impf. 3 m.s. (180)–n.m.s. (42) *God speaks*

וּבִשְׁתַּיִם conj.–prep.–num. f.s. (1040) *and in two*

לֹא יְשׁוּרֶנָּה neg.–Qal impf. 3 m.s.–3 f.s. sf. (שׁוּר II 1003) *though man does not perceive it*

33:15

בַּחֲלוֹם prep.–n.m.s. (321) *in a dream*

חֶזְיוֹן n.m.s. cstr. (303; LXX ἢ ἐν μελέτῃ) *in a vision of*

לַיְלָה n.m.s. (538) *a night*

בִּנְפֹל prep.–Qal inf.cstr. (נָפַל 656) *when falls*

תַּרְדֵּמָה n.f.s. (922) *deep sleep*

עַל־אֲנָשִׁים prep.–n.m.p. (35) *upon men*

בִּתְנוּמוֹת prep.–n.f.p. (630) *while they slumber*

עֲלֵי מִשְׁכָּב prep.–n.m.s. (1012) *on (their) beds*

33:16

אָז יִגְלֶה adv. (23)–Qal impf. 3 m.s. (גָּלָה 162) *then he opens*

אֹזֶן n.f.s. cstr. (23) *ears of*

אֲנָשִׁים n.m.p. (35) *men*

וּבְמֹסָרָם conj.–prep.–n.m.s.–3 m.p. sf. (416) *and with (their) warnings (corrections)*

יַחְתֹּם Qal impf. 3 m.s. (חָתַם 367; LXX ἐξεφόβησεν) *he puts his seal (ratifies it)*

33:17

לְהָסִיר prep.–Hi. inf.cstr. (סוּר 693) *that he may turn aside*

אָדָם n.m.s. (9) *man*

מַעֲשֶׂה n.m.s. (795; LXX ἐξ ἀδικίας) *from his deed*

וְגֵוָה conj.–n.f.s. (145; LXX τὸ δὲ σῶμα αὐτοῦ) *and pride*

מִגֶּבֶר prep.–n.m.s. (149; LXX ἀπὸ πτώματος) *from man*

יְכַסֶּה Pi. impf. 3 m.s. (כָּסָה 491; LXX ἐρρύσατο) *he may hide*

33:18

יַחְשֹׂךְ Qal impf. 3 m.s. (חָשַׂךְ 362) *he keeps back*

נַפְשׁוֹ n.f.s.–3 m.s. sf. (659) *his soul*

מִנִּי־שָׁחַת prep. (577)–n.f.s. paus. (1001) *from the pit*

וְחַיָּתוֹ conj.–n.f.s.–3 m.s. sf. (I 312) *and his life*

מֵעֲבֹר prep.–Qal inf.cstr. (עָבַר 716) *from perishing*

בַּשָּׁלַח prep.–def.art.–n.m.s. paus. (1019) *by the sword*

33:19

וְהוּכַח conj.–Ho. pf. 3 m.s. (יָכַח 406; LXX πάλιν δὲ ἤλεγξεν αὐτὸν) *man is also chastened*

בְמַכְאוֹב prep.–n.m.s. (456) *with pain*

עַל־מִשְׁכָּבוֹ prep.–n.m.s.–3 m.s. sf. (1012) *upon his bed*

וְרִיב conj.–n.m.s. cstr. (936; Q וְרוֹב n.m.s. cstr. 914) *and strife of*

עֲצָמָיו n.f.p.–3 m.s. sf. (782) *his bones*

אֵתָן adj. m.s. (I 450; LXX ἐνάρκησεν) *continual*

33:20

וְזִהֲמַתּוּ conj.–Pi. pf. 3 f.s.–3 m.s. sf. (זָהַם 263) *so that loathes (it)*

חַיָּתוֹ n.f.s.–3 m.s. sf. (I 312) *his life*

לָחֶם n.m.s. paus. (536) *bread*

וְנַפְשׁוֹ conj.–n.f.s.–3 m.s. sf. (659) *and his appetite*

מַאֲכַל תַּאֲוָה n.m.s. cstr. (38)–n.f.s. (16) *dainty food*

33:21

יִכֶל Qal impf. 3 m.s. apoc. (כָּלָה I 477; GK 109k) *is so wasted away*

בְּשָׂרוֹ n.m.s.–3 m.s. sf. (142) *his flesh*

מֵרֹאִי prep.–n.m.s. paus. (909) *that it cannot be seen*

וְשֻׁפִּי conj.-n.m.s. cstr. (1046; Q וְשֻׁפּוּ Pu. pf. 3 c.p.; שָׁפָה I 1045; GK 14d=are laid bare) *and the bareness of*
עַצְמוֹתָיו n.f.p.-3 m.s. sf. (782) *his bones*
לֹא רֻאּוּ neg.-Pu. pf. 3 c.p. (רָאָה 906; GK 14d, 64e) *which were not seen*

33:22

וַתִּקְרַב consec.-Qal impf. 3 f.s. (קָרַב 897) *draws near*
לַשַּׁחַת prep.-def.art.-n.f.s. (1001) *to the pit*
נַפְשׁוֹ n.f.s.-3 m.s. sf. (659) *his soul*
וְחַיָּתוֹ conj.-n.f.s.-3 m.s. sf. (I 312) *and his life*
לַמְמִתִים prep.-def.art.-Hi. ptc. m.p. (מוּת 559; LXX ἐν ᾅδῃ) *to those who bring death*

33:23

אִם־יֵשׁ hypoth.part. (49)-subst. (441) *if there be*
עָלָיו prep.-3 m.s. sf. *for him*
מַלְאָךְ n.m.s. (521) *an angel*
מֵלִיץ Hi. ptc. (לִיץ 539) *a mediator*
אֶחָד num. m.s. (25) *one*
מִנִּי־אָלֶף prep. (577)-num. m.s. (48) *of the thousand*
לְהַגִּיד prep.-Hi. inf.cstr. (נָגַד 616) *to declare*
לְאָדָם prep.-n.m.s. (9) *to man*
יָשְׁרוֹ n.m.s.-3 m.s. sf. (449; LXX τὴν ἑαυτοῦ μέμψιν; LXX+τὴν δὲ ἄνοιαν αὐτοῦ δείξῃ) *what is right for him*

33:24

וַיְחֻנֶּנּוּ consec.-Qal impf. 3 m.s.-3 m.s. sf. (חָנַן I 335) *and he is gracious to him*
וַיֹּאמֶר consec.-Qal impf. 3 m.s. (אָמַר 55) *and says*
פְּדָעֵהוּ Qal impv. 2 m.s.-3 m.s. sf. (פָּדַע 804) *deliver him*
מֵרֶדֶת prep.-Qal inf.cstr. (יָרַד 432) *from going down*
שַׁחַת n.f.s. (1001) *into the pit*
מָצָאתִי Qal pf. 1 c.s. (מָצָא 592) *I have found*
כֹפֶר n.m.s. (I 497) *a ransom*

33:25

רֻטֲפַשׁ pass. pf. 3 m.s. (רֻטֲפַשׁ 936; GK 56) *let become fresh*
בְּשָׂרוֹ n.m.s.-3 m.s. sf. (142) *his flesh*
מִנֹּעַר prep.-n.m.s. (655) *with youth*
יָשׁוּב Qal impf. 3 m.s. (שׁוּב 996) *let him return*
לִימֵי prep.-n.m.p. cstr. (398) *to the days of*
עֲלוּמָיו n.m.p.-3 m.s. sf. (761) *his youthful vigor*

33:26

יֶעְתַּר Qal impf. 3 m.s. (עָתַר 801) *let him pray*
אֶל־אֱלוֹהַּ prep.-n.m.s. (42) *to God*
וַיִּרְצֵהוּ consec.-Qal impf. 3 m.s.-3 m.s. sf. (רָצָה 953) *and he accepts him*
וַיַּרְא consec.-Qal impf. 3 m.s. (רָאָה 906) *and he sees*
פָּנָיו n.m.p.-3 m.s. sf. (815) *his face*
בִּתְרוּעָה prep.-n.f.s. (929) *with a shout of joy*
וַיָּשֶׁב consec.-Hi impf. 3 m.s. (שׁוּב 996) *and he returns*
לֶאֱנוֹשׁ prep.-n.m.s. (60) *to men*
צִדְקָתוֹ n.f.s.-3 m.s. sf. (842) *his salvation*

33:27

יָשֹׁר Qal impf. 3 m.s. (שׁוּר II 1003; some rd. יָשִׁר as Qal impf. 3 m.s. שִׁיר 1010) *and he sings (he beholds)*
עַל־אֲנָשִׁים prep.-n.m.p. (35) *before men*
וַיֹּאמֶר consec.-Qal impf. 3 m.s. (אָמַר 55) *and says*
חָטָאתִי Qal pf. 1 c.s. (חָטָא 306) *I sinned*
וְיָשָׁר conj.-adj. m.s. (449) *and what was right*
הֶעֱוֵיתִי Hi. pf. 1 c.s. (עָוָה I 730) *I perverted*
וְלֹא־שָׁוָה לִי conj.-neg.-Qal pf. 3 m.s. (I 1000) -prep.-1 c.s. sf. *and it was not requited to me*

33:28

פָּדָה Qal pf. 3 m.s. (804) *he has redeemed*
נַפְשִׁי n.f.s.-1 c.s. sf. (659; Q נַפְשׁוֹ) *my soul*
מֵעֲבֹר prep.-Qal inf.cstr. (עָבַר 716) *from going down*
בַּשָּׁחַת prep.-def.art.-n.f.s. (1001) *into the pit*
וְחַיָּתִי conj.-n.f.s.-1 c.s. sf. (I 312) *and my life*
בָּאוֹר prep.-def.art.-n.m.s. (21) *the light*
תִּרְאֶה Qal impf. 3 f.s. (רָאָה 906) *shall see*

33:29

הֶן־ interj. (243) *behold*
כָּל־אֵלֶּה n.m.s. cstr. (481)-demons.adj. c.p. (41) *all these things*
יִפְעַל־ Qal impf. 3 m.s. (פָּעַל 821) *does*
אֵל n.m.s. (42) *God*
פַּעֲמַיִם n.f. du. (821) *two times*
שָׁלוֹשׁ num. m.s. (1025) *three*
עִם־גָּבֶר prep.-n.m.s. paus. (149) *with a man*

33:30

לְהָשִׁיב prep.-Hi. inf.cstr. (שׁוּב 996) *to bring back*
נַפְשׁוֹ n.f.s.-3 m.s. sf. (659) *his soul*

מִנִּי־שָׁחַת prep. (577)-n.f.s. paus. (1001) *from the pit*
לֵאוֹר Ni. inf.cstr. (אוֹר 21; GK 51,l;72v) *to be lighted*
בְּאוֹר prep.-n.m.s. cstr. (21) *with the light of*
הַחַיִּים def.art.-n.m.p. (I 311) *life*

33:31

הַקְשֵׁב Hi. impv. 2 m.s. (קָשַׁב 904) *give heed*
אִיּוֹב pr.n. (33) *O Job*
שְׁמַע־לִי Qal impv. 2 m.s. (1033)-prep.-1 c.s. st. *listen to me*
הַחֲרֵשׁ Hi. impv. 2 m.s. (חָרַשׁ II 361) *be silent*
וְאָנֹכִי conj.-pers.pr. 1 c.s. (59) *and I*
אֲדַבֵּר Pi. impf. 1 c.s. (180) *will speak*

33:32

אִם־יֵשׁ־ hypoth.part. (49)subst. (441) *if there are*
מִלִּין n.f.p. (576) *words*
הֲשִׁיבֵנִי Hi. impv. 2 m.s.-1 c.s. sf. (שׁוּב 906) *answer me*
דַּבֵּר Pi. impv. 2 m.s. (180) *speak*
כִּי־חָפַצְתִּי conj. (471)-Qal pf. 1 c.s. (חָפֵץ 342) *for I desire*
צַדְּקֶךָּ Pi. inf.cstr.-2 m.s. sf. (צָדֵק 842; GK 61d) *to justify you*

33:33

אִם־אַיִן hypoth.part. (49)-subst. neg. (II 34) *if not*
אַתָּה pers.pr. 2 m.s. (61) *you!*
שְׁמַע־לִי Qal impv. 2 m.s. (1033)-prep.-1 c.s. sf. *listen to me*
הַחֲרֵשׁ Hi. impv. 2 m.s. (חָרַשׁ II 361) *be silent*
וַאֲאַלֶּפְךָ conj.-Pi. impf. 1 c.s.-2 m.s. sf. (אָלַף 48) *and I will teach you*
חָכְמָה n.f.s. (315) *wisdom*

34:1

וַיַּעַן consec.-Qal impf. 3 m.s. (עָנָה I 772) *then answered*
אֱלִיהוּא pr.n. (45) *Elihu*
וַיֹּאמַר consec.-Qal impf. 3 m.s. (אָמַר 55) *and said*

34:2

שִׁמְעוּ Qal impv. 2 m.p. (שָׁמַע 1033) *hear*
חֲכָמִים adj. m.p. (314) *wise men*
מִלָּי n.f.p.-1 c.s. sf. paus. (576) *my words*
וְיֹדְעִים conj.-Qal act.ptc. m.p. (יָדַע 393) *and (you) who know*
הַאֲזִינוּ לִי Hi. impv. 2 m.p. (אָזַן 24)-prep.-1 c.s. sf. *give ear to me*

34:3

כִּי־אֹזֶן conj. (471)-n.f.s. (23) *for an ear*
מִלִּין n.f.p. (576) *words*
תִּבְחָן Qal impf. 3 f.s. paus. (בָּחַן 103) *tests*
וְחֵךְ conj.-n.m.s. (335) *as the palate*
יִטְעַם Qal impf. 3 m.s. (381) *tastes*
לֶאֱכֹל prep.-Qal inf.cstr. (37; LXX βρῶσιν) *to eat*

34:4

מִשְׁפָּט n.m.s. (1048) *what is right*
נִבְחֲרָה־לָּנוּ Qal impf. 1 c.p.-vol.he (בָּחַר 103) -prep.-1 c.p. sf. *let us choose for ourselves*
נֵדְעָה Qal impf. 1 c.p.-vol.he (יָדַע 393) *let us determine*
בֵינֵינוּ prep.-1 c.p. sf. (107) *among ourselves*
מַה־טּוֹב interr. (552)-adj. m.s. (II 373) *what is good*

34:5

כִּי־אָמַר conj. (471)-Qal pf. 3 m.s. (55) *for has said*
אִיּוֹב pr.n. (33) *Job*
צָדַקְתִּי Qal pf. 1 c.s. (צָדַק 842) *I am innocent*
וְאֵל conj.-n.m.s. (42) *and God*
הֵסִיר Hi. pf. 3 m.s. (סוּר 693) *has taken away*
מִשְׁפָּטִי n.m.s.-1 c.s. sf. (1048) *my right*

34:6

עַל־מִשְׁפָּטִי prep.-n.m.s.-1 c.s. sf. (1048) *in spite of my right*
אֲכַזֵּב Pi. impf. 1 c.s. (כָּזַב 469; LXX ἐψεύσατο) *I am counted a liar*
אָנוּשׁ Qal pass.ptc. (אָנַשׁ I 60) *incurable*
חִצִּי n.m.s.-1 c.s. sf. (346) *my wound (arrow)*
בְלִי־פָשַׁע neg. (115)-n.m.s. paus. (833) *without transgression*

34:7

מִי־גֶבֶר interr. (566)-n.m.s. (149) *what man is*
כְּאִיּוֹב prep.-pr.n. (33) *like Job*
יִשְׁתֶּה־ Qal impf. 3 m.s. (שָׁתָה 1059) *who drinks up*
לַעַג n.m.s. (541) *scoffing*
כַּמָּיִם prep.-def.art.-n.m.p. (565) *like water*

34:8

וְאָרַח conj.-Qal pf. 3 m.s. (72) *who goes*
לְחֶבְרָה prep.-n.f.s. (288) *in company*

עִם־פֹּעֲלֵי prep. (767)–Qal act.ptc. m.p. cstr. (פָּעַל 821) *with doers of*
אָוֶן n.m.s. (19) *evil*
וְלָלֶכֶת conj.–prep.–Qal inf.cstr. (הָלַךְ 229) *and walks*
עִם־אַנְשֵׁי־רֶשַׁע prep.–n.m.p. cstr. (35)–n.m.s. (957) *with wicked men*

34:9

כִּי־אָמַר conj. (471)–Qal pf. 3 m.s. (55) *for he has said*
לֹא יִסְכָּן־ neg.–Qal impf. 3 m.s. (סָכַן I 698) *it profits nothing*
גָּבֶר n.m.s. paus. (149) *man*
בִּרְצֹתוֹ prep.–Qal inf.cstr.–3 m.s. sf. (רָצָה 953) *that he should take delight*
עִם־אֱלֹהִים prep. (767)–n.m.p. (43) *in God*

34:10

לָכֵן prep.–adv. (485) *therefore*
אַנְשֵׁי לֵבָב n.m.p. cstr. (35)–n.m.s. (523) *men of understanding*
שִׁמְעוּ לִי Qal impv. 2 m.p. (1033)–prep.–1 c.s. sf. *hear me*
חָלִלָה subst.–loc.he (321) *far be it*
לָאֵל prep.–def.art.–n.m.s. (42) *from God*
מֵרֶשַׁע prep.–n.m.s. (957) *that he should do wickedness*
וְשַׁדַּי conj.–pr.n. (994) *and from the Almighty*
מֵעָוֶל prep.–n.m.s. (732; LXX ταράξαι τὸ δίκαιον) *that he should do wrong*

34:11

כִּי פֹעַל conj. (471)–n.m.s. cstr. (821) *for according to the work of*
אָדָם n.m.s. (9) *a man*
יְשַׁלֶּם־לוֹ Pi. impf. 3 m.s. (שָׁלֵם 1022)–prep.–3 m.s. sf. *he will requite him*
וּכְאֹרַח אִישׁ conj.–prep.–n.m.s. cstr. (73)–n.m.s. (35) *and according to man's ways*
יַמְצִאֶנּוּ Hi. impf. 3 m.s.–3 m.s. sf. (מָצָא 592) *he will make it befall him*

34:12

אַף־אָמְנָם conj. (II 64)–adv. (53) *of a truth*
אֵל לֹא־יַרְשִׁיעַ n.m.s. (42)–neg.–Hi. impf. 3 m.s. (957 רָשַׁע) *God will not do wickedly*
וְשַׁדַּי conj.–pr.n. (994) *and the Almighty*
לֹא־יְעַוֵּת neg.–Pi. impf. 3 m.s. (עָוַת 736) *will not pervert*
מִשְׁפָּט n.m.s. (1048) *justice*

34:13

מִי־פָקַד interr. (566)–Qal pf. 3 m.s. (823) *who gave charge*
עָלָיו prep.–3 m.s. sf. *unto him*
אַרְצָה n.f.s.–dir.he (75; GK 90f) *over the earth*
וּמִי שָׂם conj.–interr. (566)–Qal pf. 3 m.s. (שִׂים I 962) *and who laid*
תֵּבֵל n.f.s. (385) *the world*
כֻּלָּהּ n.m.s.–3 f.s. sf. (481) *all of it*

34:14

אִם־יָשִׂים hypoth.part. (49)–Qal impf. 3 m.s. (I 962 שִׂים; LXX εἰ γὰρ βούλοιτο συνέχειν) *if he should take back*
אֵלָיו prep.–3 m.s. sf. *to himself*
לִבּוֹ n.m.s.–3 m.s. sf. (524) *his heart*
רוּחוֹ n.f.s.–3 m.s. sf. (924) *his spirit*
וְנִשְׁמָתוֹ conj.–n.f.s.–3 m.s. sf. (675) *and his breath*
אֵלָיו v.supra *to himself*
יֶאֱסֹף Qal impf. 3 m.s. (אָסַף 62) *he should gather*

34:15

יִגְוַע Qal impf. 3 m.s. (גָּוַע 157) *would perish*
כָּל־בָּשָׂר n.m.s. cstr. (481)–n.m.s. (142) *all flesh*
יָחַד adv. paus. (403) *together*
וְאָדָם conj.–n.m.s. (9) *and man*
עַל־עָפָר prep.–n.m.s. (779) *to dust*
יָשׁוּב Qal impf. 3 m.s. (שׁוּב 996) *would return*

34:16

וְאִם־בִּינָה conj.–hypoth.part. (49)–n.f.s. (108; LXX εἰ δὲ μὴ νουθετῇ) *if you have understanding*
שִׁמְעָה־זֹּאת Qal impv. 2 m.s.–vol.he (שָׁמַע 1033)–demons.adj. f.s. (260) *hear this*
הַאֲזִינָה Hi. impv. 2 m.s.–vol.he (אָזַן 24) *listen*
לְקוֹל prep.–n.m.s. cstr. (876) *to the sound of*
מִלָּי n.f.p.–1 c.s. sf. paus. (576) *my words*

34:17

הַאַף שׂוֹנֵא interr.part.–conj. (II 64)–Qal act.ptc. (971 שָׂנֵא) *shall one who hates*
מִשְׁפָּט n.m.s. (1048) *justice*
יַחֲבוֹשׁ Qal impf. 3 m.s. (חָבַשׁ 289) *govern?*
וְאִם־צַדִּיק conj.–hypoth.part. (49)–adj. m.s. (843) *and will ... the righteous*
כַּבִּיר adj. m.s. (460) *the mighty*
תַּרְשִׁיעַ Hi. impf. 2 m.s. (רָשַׁע 957) *you condemn?*

34:18

הֶאָמֹר interr.part.-Qal inf.cstr. (אָמַר 55; GK 113eeN; LXX ὁ λέγων) *who says*
לְמֶלֶךְ prep.-n.m.s. (I 572) *to a king*
בְּלִיַּעַל n.m.s. (116) *worthless one*
רָשָׁע adj. m.s. (957) *wicked man*
אֶל־נְדִיבִים prep.-adj. m.p. (622) *to nobles*

34:19

אֲשֶׁר לֹא־נָשָׂא rel. (81)-neg.-Qal pf. 3 m.s. (669) *who does not lift up*
פְּנֵי שָׂרִים n.m.p. cstr. (815)-n.m.p. (978) *the face of princes*
וְלֹא נִכַּר־ conj.-neg.-Pi. pf. 3 m.s. (נָכַר I 647) *nor regards*
שׁוֹעַ adj. m.s. (447) *the noble*
לִפְנֵי־דָל prep.-n.m.p. cstr. (815)-adj. m.s. paus. (195) *more than the poor*
כִּי־מַעֲשֵׂה conj. (471)-n.m.s. cstr. (795) *for the work of*
יָדָיו n.f.p.-3 m.s. sf. (388) *his hands*
כֻּלָּם n.m.s.-3 m.p. sf. (481) *all of them*

34:20

רֶגַע adv. (921) *in a moment*
יָמֻתוּ Qal impf. 3 m.p. (מוּת 559) *they die*
וַחֲצוֹת לָיְלָה conj.-n.f.p. cstr. (345)-n.m.s. (538) *and at midnight*
יְגֹעֲשׁוּ Pu. impf. 3 m.p. (גָּעַשׁ 172) *are shaken*
עָם n.m.s. (I 766) *people*
וְיַעֲבֹרוּ conj.-Qal impf. 3 m.p. (עָבַר 716) *and pass away*
וְיָסִירוּ conj.-Hi. impf. 3 m.p. (סוּר 693) *and are taken away*
אַבִּיר adj. m.s. (7) *the mighty*
לֹא בְיָד neg.-prep.-n.f.s. (388) *by no human hand*

34:21

כִּי־עֵינָיו conj. (471)-n.f. du.-3 m.s. sf. (744) *for his eyes*
עַל־דַּרְכֵי־ prep.-n.m.p. cstr. (202) *upon the ways of*
אִישׁ n.m.s. (35) *a man*
וְכָל־צְעָדָיו conj.-n.m.s. cstr. (481)-n.m.p.-3 m.s. sf. (857) *and all his steps*
יִרְאֶה Qal impf. 3 m.s. (רָאָה 906) *he sees*

34:22

אֵין־חֹשֶׁךְ subst. cstr. (II 34)-n.m.s. (365) *there is no gloom*
וְאֵין צַלְמָוֶת conj.-v.supra-n.m.s. (853) *and no deep darkness*
לְהִסָּתֶר prep.-Ni. inf.cstr. (סָתַר 711; GK 115g) *to hide themselves*
שָׁם adv. (1027) *there*
פֹּעֲלֵי אָוֶן Qal act.ptc. m.p. cstr. (פָּעַל 821)-n.m.s. (19) *evildoers*

34:23

כִּי לֹא עַל־אִישׁ conj. (471)-neg.-prep.-n.m.s. (35) *for not for any man*
יָשִׂים Qal impf. 3 m.s. (שִׂים 962) *he has appointed*
עוֹד adv. (728) *yet*
לַהֲלֹךְ prep.-Qal inf.cstr. (הָלַךְ 229) *to walk*
אֶל־אֵל prep.-n.m.s. (42) *before God*
בַּמִּשְׁפָּט prep.-def.art.-n.m.s. (1048) *in judgment*

34:24

יָרֹעַ Qal impf. 3 m.s. (רָעַע II 949) *he shatters*
כַּבִּירִים prep.-def.art.-adj. m.p. (460) *the mighty*
לֹא־חֵקֶר neg.-n.m.s. (350) *without investigation*
וַיַּעֲמֵד consec.-Hi. impf. 3 m.s. (עָמַד 763) *and sets*
אֲחֵרִים adj. m.p. (29) *others*
תַּחְתָּם prep.-3 m.p. sf. (1065) *in their place*

34:25

לָכֵן prep.-adv. (485) *thus*
יַכִּיר Hi. impf. 3 m.s. (נָכַר 647) *he knows*
מַעְבָּדֵיהֶם n.m.p.-3 m.p. sf. (716) *their works*
וְהָפַךְ conj.-Qal pf. 3 m.s. (245) *and he overturns (them)*
לַיְלָה n.m.s. (538) *in the night*
וְיִדַּכָּאוּ conj.-Hith. impf. 3 m.p. paus. (דָּכָא 193) *and they are crushed*

34:26

תַּחַת־רְשָׁעִים prep. (1065)-adj. m.p. (957) *for their wickedness*
סְפָקָם Qal pf. 3 m.s.-3 m.p. sf. (סָפַק 706) *he strikes them*
בִּמְקוֹם רֹאִים prep.-n.m.s. cstr. (879)-Qal act.ptc. m.p. (רָאָה 906) *in the sight of men*

34:27

אֲשֶׁר עַל־כֵּן rel. (81)-prep.-adv. (485) *because*
סָרוּ Qal pf. 3 c.p. (סוּר 693) *they turned aside*
מֵאַחֲרָיו prep.-prep.-3 m.s. sf. (29) *from following him*
וְכָל־דְּרָכָיו conj.-n.m.s. cstr. (481)-n.m.p.-3 m.s. sf. (202) *and for any of his ways*

לֹא הִשְׂכִּילוּ neg.-Hi. pf. 3 c.p. (שָׂכַל 968) *had no regard*

34:28

לְהָבִיא prep.-Hi. inf.cstr. (בּוֹא 97) *so that they caused to come*
עָלָיו prep.-3 m.s. sf. *to him*
צַעֲקַת־ n.f.s. cstr. (858) *the cry of*
דָּל adj. m.s. paus. (195) *the poor*
וְצַעֲקַת conj.-v.supra *and the cry of*
עֲנִיִּים adj. m.p. (776) *the afflicted*
יִשְׁמָע Qal impf. 3 m.s. paus. (1033) *he heard*

34:29

וְהוּא יַשְׁקִט conj.-pers.pr. 3 m.s. (214)-Hi. impf. 3 m.s. (שָׁקַט 1052) *when he is quiet*
וּמִי יַרְשִׁעַ conj.-interr. (566)-Hi. impf. 3 m.s. (957 רָשַׁע) *who can condemn?*
וְיַסְתֵּר conj.-Hi. impf. 3 m.s. apoc. (סָתַר 711) *when he hides*
פָּנִים n.m.p. (815) *(his) face*
וּמִי v.supra *who*
יְשׁוּרֶנּוּ Qal impf. 3 m.s.-3 m.s. sf. (שׁוּר II 1003) *can behold him*
וְעַל־גּוֹי conj.-prep.-n.m.s. (156) *whether a nation*
וְעַל־אָדָם v.supra-n.m.s. (9) *or a man*
יָחַד adv. paus. (403) *together*

34:30

מִמְּלֹךְ prep.-Qal inf.cstr. (573) *that should not reign*
אָדָם חָנֵף n.m.s. (9)-adj. m.s. (338) *a godless man*
מִמֹּקְשֵׁי עָם prep.-Qal act.ptc. m.p. cstr. (as n.m.p. cstr. 430)-n.m.s. (I 766) *that he should not ensnare the people*

34:31

כִּי־אֶל־אֵל conj. (471)-prep.-n.m.s. (42) *for to God*
הֶאָמַר interr.part.-Qal pf. 3 m.s. (55) *has any one said?*
נָשָׂאתִי Qal pf. 1 c.s. (נָשָׂא 669) *I have borne (chastisement)*
לֹא אֶחְבֹּל neg.-Qal impf. 1 c.s. (II 287) *I will not offend any more*

34:32

בִּלְעֲדֵי אֶחֱזֶה neg.-prep. (116)-Qal impf. 1 c.s. (302 חָזָה) *what I do not see*
אַתָּה הֹרֵנִי pers.pr. 2 m.s. (61)-Hi. impv. 2 m.s.-1 c.s. sf. (יָרָה 434) *teach me*
אִם־עָוֶל hypoth.part. (49)-n.m.s. (732) *if iniquity*
פָּעַלְתִּי Qal pf. 1 c.s. (821) *I have done*
לֹא אֹסִיף neg.-Hi. impf. 1 c.s. (יָסַף 414) *I will do it no more*

34:33

הֲמֵעִמְּךָ interr.part.-prep.-prep. (768)-2 m.s. sf. *at thy judgment?*
יְשַׁלְמֶנָּה Pi. impf. 3 m.s.-3 f.s. sf. (שָׁלַם 1022) *will he make requital?*
כִּי־מָאַסְתָּ conj. (471)-Qal pf. 2 m.s. (מָאַס 549) *because you reject (it)*
כִּי־אַתָּה conj. (471)-pers.pr. 2 m.s. (61) *for you*
תִבְחַר Qal impf. 2 m.s. (בָּחַר 103) *must choose*
וְלֹא־אָנִי conj.-neg.-pers.pr. 1 c.s. paus. (58) *and not I*
וּמַה־ conj.-interr. (552) *and what*
יָדַעְתָּ Qal pf. 2 m.s. (יָדַע 393) *you know*
דַבֵּר Pi. impv. 2 m.s. (180) *declare*

34:34

אַנְשֵׁי לֵבָב n.m.p. cstr. (35)-n.m.s. (523) *men of understanding*
יֹאמְרוּ לִי Qal impf. 3 m.p. (55)-prep.-1 c.s. sf. *will say to me*
וְגֶבֶר חָכָם conj.-n.m.s. (149)-adj. m.s. (314) *and the wise man*
שֹׁמֵעַ לִי Qal act.ptc. (1033)-prep.-1 c.s. sf. *who hears me*

34:35

אִיּוֹב pr.n. (33) *Job*
לֹא־בְדַעַת neg.-prep.-n.f.s. (395) *without knowledge*
יְדַבֵּר Pi. impf. 3 m.s. (180) *speaks*
וּדְבָרָיו conj.-n.m.p.-3 m.s. sf. (182) *and his words*
לֹא בְהַשְׂכֵּיל neg.-prep.-Hi. inf.abs. (שָׂכַל I 968; GK 53k) *without insight*

34:36

אָבִי Qal impf. 1 c.s. (בָּיי 106; GK 159cc) *would that* (lit. *I entreat that*)
יִבָּחֵן Ni. impf. 3 m.s. (בָּחַן 103) *were tried*
אִיּוֹב pr.n. (33) *Job*
עַד־נֶצַח prep. (III 723)-n.m.s. (I 664) *to the end*
עַל־תְּשֻׁבֹת prep.-n.f.p. (1000) *because he answers*
בְּאַנְשֵׁי־אָוֶן prep.-n.m.p. cstr. (35)-n.m.s. (19) *like wicked men*

34:37

כִּי יֹסִיף conj. (471)-Hi. impf. 3 m.s. (יָסַף 414) *for he adds*

עַל־חַטָּאתוֹ prep.-n.f.s.-3 m.s. sf. (308) *to his sin*

פֶּשַׁע n.m.s. (833) *rebellion*

בֵּינֵינוּ prep.-1 c.p. sf. (107) *among us*

יִסְפּוֹק Qal impf. 3 m.s. (סָפַק 706) *he claps his hands*

וְיֶרֶב conj.-Qal impf. 3 m.s. (רָבָה 915) *and multiplies*

אֲמָרָיו n.m.p.-3 m.s. sf. (56) *his words*

לָאֵל prep.-def.art.-n.m.s. (42) *against God*

35:1

וַיַּעַן consec.-Qal impf. 3 m.s. (עָנָה I 772) *and answered*

אֱלִיהוּא pr.n. (45) *Elihu*

וַיֹּאמַר consec.-Qal impf. 3 m.s. (אָמַר 55) *(and said)*

35:2

הֲזֹאת interr.part.-demons.adj. f.s. (260) *this?*

חָשַׁבְתָּ Qal pf. 2 m.s. (חָשַׁב 362) *do you think*

לְמִשְׁפָּט prep.-n.m.s. (1048) *to be just*

אָמַרְתָּ Qal pf. 2 m.s. (55) *do you say*

צִדְקִי n.m.s.-1 c.s. sf. (841; LXX Δίκαιός εἰμι) *it is my right*

מֵאֵל prep.-n.m.s. (42) *before God*

35:3

כִּי־תֹאמַר conj. (471)-Qal impf. 2 m.s. (55) *that you ask*

מַה־יִּסְכָּן־ interr. (552)-Qal impf. 3 m.s. (סָכַן I 698) *what advantage*

לָךְ prep.-2 m.s. paus. *to you*

מָה־אֹעִיל interr. (552)-Hi. impf. 1 c.s. (יָעַל I 418) *how am I better off*

מֵחַטָּאתִי prep.-n.f.s.-1 c.s. sf. (308) *than if I had sinned*

35:4

אֲנִי אֲשִׁיבְךָ pers.pr. 1 c.s. (58)-Hi. impf. 1 c.s.-3 m.s. sf. (שׁוּב 996) *I will answer you*

מִלִּין n.f.p. (576) *with words*

וְאֶת־רֵעֶיךָ conj.-dir.obj.-n.m.p.-2 m.s. sf. (945; LXX+τρισίν) *and your friends*

עִמָּךְ prep.-2 m.s. sf. paus. (767) *with you*

35:5

הַבֵּט Hi. impv. 2 m.s. (נָבַט 613) *look*

שָׁמַיִם n.m.p. (1029) *at the heavens*

וּרְאֵה conj.-Qal impv. 2 m.s. (רָאָה 906) *and see*

וְשׁוּר conj.-Qal impv. 2 m.s. (שׁוּר II 1003) *and behold*

שְׁחָקִים n.m.p. (1007) *the clouds*

גָּבְהוּ Qal pf. 3 c.p. (גָּבַהּ 146) *which are higher*

מִמֶּךָּ prep.-2 m.s. sf. paus. *than you*

35:6

אִם־חָטָאתָ hypoth.part. (49)-Qal pf. 2 m.s. (חָטָא 306) *if you have sinned*

מַה־תִּפְעָל־ interr. (552)-Qal impf. 2 m.s. (פָּעַל 821) *what do you accomplish*

בּוֹ prep.-3 m.s. sf. *against him*

וְרַבּוּ conj.-Qal pf. 3 c.p. (רָבַב I 912) *and if are multiplied*

פְּשָׁעֶיךָ n.m.p.-2 m.s. sf. (833) *your transgressions*

מַה־תַּעֲשֶׂה־ interr. (552)-Qal impf. 2 m.s. (עָשָׂה I 793) *what do you do*

לוֹ prep.-3 m.s. sf. *to him*

35:7

אִם־צָדַקְתָּ hypoth.part. (49)-Qal pf. 2 m.s. (צָדַק 842) *if you are righteous*

מַה־תִּתֶּן־ interr. (552)-Qal impf. 2 m.s. (נָתַן 678) *what do you give*

לוֹ prep.-3 m.s. sf. *to him*

אוֹ מַה־ conj. (14)-interr. (552) *or what*

מִיָּדְךָ prep.-n.f.s.-2 m.s. sf. (388) *from your hand*

יִקָּח Qal impf. 3 m.s. paus. (לָקַח 542) *does he receive*

35:8

לְאִישׁ־ prep.-n.m.s. (35) *concerns a man*

כָּמוֹךָ prep.-2 m.s. sf. (453) *like yourself*

רִשְׁעֶךָ n.m.p.-2 m.s. sf. paus. (957) *your wickedness*

וּלְבֶן־אָדָם conj.-prep.-n.m.s. cstr. (119)-n.m.s. (9) *and a son of man*

צִדְקָתֶךָ n.f.s.-2 m.s. sf. (842) *your righteousness*

35:9

מֵרֹב prep.-n.m.s. cstr. (913) *because of the multitude of*

עֲשׁוּקִים n.m.p. (799) *oppressions*

יַזְעִיקוּ Hi. impf. 3 m.p. (זָעַק 277) *people cry out*

יְשַׁוְּעוּ Pi. impf. 3 m.p. (שָׁוַע 1002) *they call for help*

מִזְּרוֹעַ prep.-n.f.s. cstr. (283) *because of the arm of*

רַבִּים adj. m.p. (I 912) *the mighty*

35:10

וְלֹא־אָמַר conj.-neg.-Qal pf. 3 m.s. (55) *but none says*
אַיֵּה אֱלוֹהַּ adv. (32)-n.m.s. (42) *where is God*
עֹשָׂי Qal act.ptc. m.p.-1 c.s. sf. paus. (עָשָׂה I 793; GK 93ss,124k) *my Maker*
נֹתֵן Qal act.ptc. m.s. (נָתַן 678) *who gives*
זְמִרוֹת n.f.p. (I 274) *songs*
בַּלָּיְלָה prep.-def.art.-n.m.s. (538) *in the night*

35:11

מַלְּפֵנוּ Pi. ptc. m.s.-1 c.p. sf. (אָלַף I 48; GK 68k) *who teaches us*
מִבַּהֲמוֹת prep.-n.f.p. cstr. (96) *more than the beasts of*
אָרֶץ n.f.s. paus. (75) *the earth*
וּמֵעוֹף conj.-prep.-n.m.s. cstr. (733) *and than the birds of*
הַשָּׁמַיִם def.art.-n.m.p. (1029) *the air*
יְחַכְּמֵנוּ Pi. impf. 3 m.s.-1 c.p. sf. (חָכַם 314) *he makes us wise(r)*

35:12

שָׁם adv. (1027) *there*
יִצְעֲקוּ Qal impf. 3 m.p. (צָעַק 858) *they cry out*
וְלֹא יַעֲנֶה conj.-neg.-Qal impf. 3 m.s. (עָנָה I 772) *but he does not answer*
מִפְּנֵי גְּאוֹן prep.-n.m.p. cstr. (815)-n.m.s. cstr. (144) *because of the pride of*
רָעִים adj. m.p. (I 948) *evil men*

35:13

אַךְ־ adv. (36) *surely*
שָׁוְא n.m.s. (996) *an empty cry*
לֹא־יִשְׁמַע neg.-Qal impf. 3 m.s. (1033) *does not hear*
אֵל n.m.s. (42) *God*
וְשַׁדַּי conj.-pr.n. (994) *nor the Almighty*
לֹא יְשׁוּרֶנָּה neg.-Qal impf. 3 m.s.-3 f.s. sf. (שׁוּר 1003) *does regard it*

35:14

אַף כִּי־ conj. (64)-conj. (471) *how much less*
תֹאמַר Qal impf. 2 m.s. (55) *when you say*
לֹא תְשׁוּרֶנּוּ neg.-Qal impf. 2 m.s.-3 m.s. sf. (1003 שׁוּר) *that you do not see him*
דִּין n.m.s. (192) *that the case*
לְפָנָיו prep.-n.m.p.-3 m.s. sf. (815) *before him*
וּתְחוֹלֵל conj.-Polel impf. 2 m.s. (חוּל I 296) *and you are waiting*
לוֹ prep.-3 m.s. sf. *for him*

35:15

וְעַתָּה conj.-adv. (773) *and now*
כִּי־אַיִן פָּקַד conj. (471)-subst. II 34; GK 152k)-Qal pf. 3 m.s. (823) *because does not punish*
אַפּוֹ n.m.s.-3 m.s. sf. (I 60) *his anger*
וְלֹא־יָדַע conj.-neg.-Qal pf. 3 m.s. (393) *and he does not heed (know)*
בַּפַּשׁ prep.-def.art.-n.m.s. (832) LXX παραπτώματι *the folly*
מְאֹד adv. (547) *greatly*

35:16

וְאִיּוֹב conj.-pr.n. (33) *Job*
הֶבֶל n.m.s. as adv.acc. (I 210) *in empty talk*
יִפְצֶה־ Qal impf. 3 m.s. (פָּצָה 822) *opens*
פִּיהוּ n.m.s.-3 m.s. sf. (804) *his mouth*
בִּבְלִי־דַעַת prep.-neg. (115)-n.f.s. (395) *without knowledge*
מִלִּין n.f.p. (576) *words*
יַכְבִּר Hi. impf. 3 m.s. (כָּבַר I 460) *he multiplies*

36:1

וַיֹּסֶף consec.-Hi. impf. 3 m.s. (יָסַף 414) *and continued*
אֱלִיהוּא pr.n. (45) *Elihu*
וַיֹּאמַר consec.-Qal impf. 3 m.s. (55) *and said*

36:2

כַּתַּר־לִי Pi. impv. 2 m.s. (כָּתַר 509; GK 65e) -prep.-1 c.s. sf. *bear with me*
זְעֵיר n.m.s. (277) *a little*
וַאֲחַוֶּךָּ consec.-Pi. impf. 1 c.s.-2 m.s. sf. (חָוָה III 296) *and I will show you*
כִּי עוֹד conj. (471)-adv. (728) *for yet*
לֶאֱלוֹהַּ prep.-n.m.s. (42; LXX ἐν ἐμοί) *on God's behalf*
מִלִּים n.f.p. (576) *words*

36:3

אֶשָּׂא Qal impf. 1 c.s. (נָשָׂא 669) *I will fetch*
דֵעִי n.m.s.-1 c.s. sf. (395) *my knowledge*
לְמֵרָחוֹק prep.-prep.-adj. m.s. (935) *from afar*
וּלְפֹעֲלִי conj.-prep.-Qal act.ptc.-1 c.s. sf. (פָּעַל 821) *and to my Maker*
אֶתֵּן־ Qal impf. 1 c.s. (נָתַן 678) *I will ascribe*
צֶדֶק n.m.s. (841) *righteousness*

36:4

כִּי־אָמְנָם conj. (471)-adv. (53) *for truly*
לֹא־שֶׁקֶר neg.-n.m.s. (1055) *not false*
מִלָּי n.f.p.-1 c.s. sf. paus. (576) *my words*

תְּמִים adj. m.s. cstr. (1071) *one who is perfect in*
דֵּעוֹת n.f.p. (395) *knowledge*
עִמָּךְ prep.-2 m.s. sf. paus. (767) *with you*

36:5

הֶן־אֵל interj. (243)-n.m.s. (42) *behold, God is*
כַּבִּיר adj. m.s. (460) *mighty*
וְלֹא יִמְאָס conj.-neg.-Qal impf. 3 m.s. paus. (549 מָאַס) *and does not despise (any)*
כַּבִּיר v.supra *mighty*
כֹּחַ לֵב n.m.s. cstr. (470)-n.m.s. (524) *in strength of understanding*

36:6

לֹא־יְחַיֶּה neg.-Pi. impf. 3 m.s. (חָיָה 310) *he does not keep alive*
רָשָׁע adj. m.s. (957) *the wicked*
וּמִשְׁפַּט conj.-n.m.s. cstr. (1048) *and the right of*
עֲנִיִּים adj. m.p. (776) *the afflicted*
יִתֵּן Qal impf. 3 m.s. (נָתַן 678) *he gives*

36:7

לֹא־יִגְרַע neg.-Qal impf. 3 m.s. (גָּרַע 175) *he does not withdraw*
מִצַּדִּיק prep.-adj. m.s. (843) *from the righteous*
עֵינָיו n.f. du.-3 m.s. sf. (744) *his eyes*
וְאֶת־מְלָכִים conj.-dir.obj.-n.m.p. (I 572) *but with kings*
לַכִּסֵּא prep.-def.art.-n.m.s. (490) *upon the throne*
וַיֹּשִׁיבֵם consec.-Hi. impf. 3 m.s.-3 m.p. sf. (יָשַׁב 442) *he sets them*
לָנֶצַח prep.-n.m.s. (I 664) *for ever*
וַיִּגְבָּהוּ consec.-Qal impf. 3 m.p. paus. (גָּבַהּ 146; GK 111bN) *and they are exalted*

36:8

וְאִם־אֲסוּרִים conj.-hypoth.part. (49)-Qal pass.ptc. m.p. (אָסַר 63) *and if they are bound*
בַּזִּקִּים prep.-def.art.-n.m.p. (279) *in fetters*
יִלָּכְדוּן Ni. impf. 3 m.p. (לָכַד 539) *and caught*
בְּחַבְלֵי־עֹנִי prep.-n.m.p. cstr. (I 286)-n.m.s. (777) *in cords of affliction*

36:9

וַיַּגֵּד consec.-Hi. impf. 3 m.s. (נָגַד 616) *then he declares*
לָהֶם prep.-3 m.p. sf. *to them*
פָּעֳלָם n.m.s.-3 m.p. sf. (821) *their work*
וּפִשְׁעֵיהֶם conj.-n.m.p.-3 m.p. sf. (833) *and their transgressions*
כִּי יִתְגַּבָּרוּ conj.-Hith. impf. 3 m.p. paus. (גָּבַר 149) *that they are behaving arrogantly*

36:10

וַיִּגֶל consec.-Qal impf. 3 m.s. (גָּלָה 162) *he opens (uncovers)*
אָזְנָם n.f.s.-3 m.p. sf. (23) *their ears*
לַמּוּסָר prep.-def.art.-n.m.s. (416) *to instruction*
וַיֹּאמֶר consec.-Qal impf. 3 m.s. (55) *and commands*
כִּי־יְשֻׁבוּן conj. (471)-Qal impf. 3 m.p. (שׁוּב 996) *that they return*
מֵאָוֶן prep.-n.m.s. (19) *from iniquity*

36:11

אִם־יִשְׁמְעוּ hypoth.part. (49)-Qal impf. 3 m.p. (1033) *if they hearken*
וְיַעֲבֹדוּ conj.-Qal impf. 3 m.p. (עָבַד 712) *and serve (him)*
יְכַלּוּ Pi. impf. 3 m.p. (כָּלָה I 477) *they complete*
יְמֵיהֶם n.m.p.-3 m.p. sf. (398) *their days*
בַּטּוֹב prep.-def.art.-n.m.s. (III 375) *in prosperity*
וּשְׁנֵיהֶם conj.-n.f.p.-3 m.p. sf. (1040) *and their years*
בַּנְּעִימִים prep.-def.art.-adj. m.p. (653) *in pleasantness*

36:12

וְאִם־ conj.-hypoth.part. (49) *but if*
לֹא יִשְׁמְעוּ neg.-Qal impf. 3 m.p. (1033) *they do not hearken*
בְּשֶׁלַח prep.-n.m.s. (1019) *by sword*
יַעֲבֹרוּ Qal impf. 3 m.p. (עָבַר 716) *they perish*
וְיִגְוְעוּ conj.-Qal impf. 3 m.p. (גָּוַע 157) *and they die*
בִּבְלִי־דָעַת prep.-neg. (115)-n.f.s. paus. (395) *without knowledge*

36:13

וְחַנְפֵי־ conj.-adj. m.p. cstr. (338) *and godless of (in)*
לֵב n.m.s. (524) *heart*
יָשִׂימוּ Qal impf. 3 m.p. (שִׂים 962) *cherish*
אָף n.m.s. paus. (I 60) *anger*
לֹא יְשַׁוְּעוּ neg.-Pi. impf. 3 m.p. (שָׁוַע 1002) *they do not cry for help*
כִּי אֲסָרָם conj. (471)-Qal pf. 3 m.s.-3 m.p. sf. (63 אָסַר) *when he binds them*

36:14

תָּמֹת Qal impf. 3 f.s. (מוּת 559) ... *die*
בַּנֹּעַר prep.-def.art.-n.m.s. (655) *in youth*
נַפְשָׁם n.f.s.-3 m.p. sf. (659) *they (their life)*
וְחַיָּתָם conj.-n.f.s.-3 m.p. sf. (I 312) *and their life*

בַּקְּדֵשִׁים prep.-def.art.-n.m.p. (I 873) *among the cult prostitutes*

36:15

יְחַלֵּץ Pi. impf. 3 m.s. (חָלַץ I 322) *he delivers*
עָנִי adj. m.s. (776) *the afflicted*
בְעָנְיוֹ prep.-n.m.s.-3 m.s. sf. (777) *by their affliction*
וְיִגֶל conj.-Qal impf. 3 m.s. (גָּלָה 162) *and opens*
בַּלַּחַץ prep.-def.art.-n.m.s. (537) *by adversity*
אָזְנָם n.f.s.-3 m.p. sf. (23) *their ear*

36:16

וְאַף conj.-conj. (II 64) *also*
הֲסִיתְךָ Hi. pf. 3 m.s.-2 m.s. sf. (סוּת 694) *he allured you*
מִפִּי־צָר prep.-n.m.s. cstr. (804)-n.m.s. paus. (II 865) *out of distress*
רַחַב n.m.s. (931) *into a broad place*
לֹא־מוּצָק neg.-n.m.s. (II 848) *where there was no cramping*
תַּחְתֶּיהָ prep.-3 f.s. sf. (1065) *(instead of it)*
וְנַחַת conj.-n.f. (m.?) s. cstr. (629) *and the comfort of*
שֻׁלְחָנְךָ n.m.s.-2 m.s. sf. (1020) *your table*
מָלֵא Qal pf. 3 m.s. (569) *was full of*
דָשֶׁן n.m.s. (206) *fatness*

36:17

וְדִין־ conj.-n.m.s. cstr. (192) *but judgment on*
רָשָׁע adj. m.s. (957) *the wicked*
מָלֵאתָ Qal pf. 2 m.s. (מָלֵא 569) *you are full of*
דִּין n.m.s. (192) *judgment*
וּמִשְׁפָּט conj.-n.m.s. (1048) *and justice*
יִתְמֹכוּ Qal impf. 3 m.p. paus. (תָּמַךְ 1069) *seize (you)*

36:18

כִּי־חֵמָה conj. (471)-n.f.s. (404) *for wrath*
פֶּן־יְסִיתְךָ conj. (814)-Hi. impf. 3 m.s.-2 m.s. sf. (694 סוּת) *lest he entice you*
בְסָפֶק prep.-n.m.s. paus. (סָפַק 706) *into scoffing*
וְרָב־ conj.-n.m.s. cstr. (913) *and greatness of*
כֹּפֶר n.m.s. (I 497) *ransom*
אַל־יַטֶּךָּ neg.-Hi. impf. 3 m.s.-2 m.s. sf. (נָטָה 639: GK 145u) *let not ... turn you aside*

36:19

הֲיַעֲרֹךְ interr.part.-Qal impf. 3 m.s. (עָרַךְ 789) *will ... avail*
שׁוּעֲךָ n.m.s.-2 m.s. sf. (I 1002) *your cry for help*
לֹא בְצָר neg.-prep.-n.m.s. (865) *from distress*
וְכֹל conj.-n.m.s. cstr. (481) *and all (of)*
מַאֲמַצֵּי־ n.m.p. cstr. (55) *force of*
כֹחַ n.m.s. (470) *(your) strength*

36:20

אַל־תִּשְׁאַף neg.-Qal impf. 2 m.s. (שָׁאַף I 983) *do not long for*
הַלָּיְלָה def.art.-n.m.s. (538) *the night*
לַעֲלוֹת prep.-Qal inf.cstr. (עָלָה 748) *when ... go up*
עַמִּים n.m.p. (I 766) *peoples*
תַּחְתָּם prep.-3 m.p. sf. (1065) *in their place*

36:21

הִשָּׁמֶר Ni. impv. 2 m.s. (שָׁמַר 1036) *take heed*
אַל־תֵּפֶן neg.-Qal impf. 2 m.s. (פָּנָה 815) *do not turn*
אֶל־אָוֶן prep.-n.m.s. (19) *to iniquity*
כִּי־עַל־זֶה conj. (471)-prep.-demons.adj. m.s. (260) *for this*
בָּחַרְתָּ Qal pf. 2 m.s. (בָּחַר 103) *you have chosen*
מֵעֹנִי prep.-n.m.s. paus. (777) *rather than affliction*

36:22

הֶן־אֵל interj. (243)-n.m.s. (42) *behold, God*
יַשְׂגִּיב Hi. impf. 3 m.s. (שָׂגַב 960) *is exalted*
בְּכֹחוֹ prep.-n.m.s.-3 m.s. sf. (470) *in his power*
מִי interr. (566) *who is*
כָמֹהוּ prep.-3 m.s. sf. *like him*
מוֹרֶה n.m.s. (II 435; LXX δυνάστης) *a teacher*

36:23

מִי־פָקַד interr. (566)-Qal pf. 3 m.s. (823) *who has prescribed*
עָלָיו prep.-3 m.s. sf. *for him*
דַּרְכּוֹ n.m.s.-3 m.s. sf. (202) *his way*
וּמִי־אָמַר conj.-v.supra-Qal pf. 3 m.s. (55) *or who can say*
פָּעַלְתָּ Qal pf. 2 m.s. (821) *thou hast done*
עַוְלָה n.f.s. (732) *wrong*

36:24

זְכֹר Qal impv. 2 m.s. (269) *remember*
כִּי־תַשְׂגִּיא conj. (471)-Hi. impf. 2 m.s. (שָׂגָא 960) *that you extol*
פָעֳלוֹ n.m.s.-3 m.s. sf. (821) *his work*
אֲשֶׁר שֹׁרְרוּ rel. (81)-Polel pf. 3 c.p. (שִׁיר 1010) *of which have sung*
אֲנָשִׁים n.m.p. (35) *men*

36:25

כָּל־אָדָם n.m.s. cstr. (481)-n.m.s. (9) *all men*
חָזוּ־ Qal pf. 3 c.p. (חָזָה 302) *have looked*
בוֹ prep.-3 m.s. sf. *on it*
אֱנוֹשׁ n.m.s. (60) *man*
יַבִּיט Hi. impf. 3 m.s. (נָבַט 613) *beholds*
מֵרָחוֹק prep.-adj. m.s. (935) *from afar*

36:26

הֶן־אֵל interj. (243)-n.m.s. (42; GK 143d) *behold, God is*
שַׂגִּיא adj. m.s. (960) *great*
וְלֹא נֵדָע conj.-neg.-Qal impf. 1 c.p. (יָדַע 393) *and we know (him) not*
מִסְפַּר n.m.s. cstr. (708) *the number of*
שָׁנָיו n.f.p.-3 m.s. sf. (1040) *his years*
וְלֹא־חֵקֶר conj.-neg.-n.m.s. (350) *unsearchable*

36:27

כִּי יְגָרַע conj.-Pi. impf. 3 m.s. (גָּרַע 175) *for he draws up*
נִטְפֵי־מָיִם n.m.p. cstr. (643)-n.m.p. paus. (565) *drops of water*
יָזֹקּוּ Qal impf. 3 m.p. (זָקַק I 279) *he distils*
מָטָר n.m.s. (564) *in rain*
לְאֵדוֹ prep.-n.m.s.-3 m.s. sf. (15) *his mist*

36:28

אֲשֶׁר־יִזְּלוּ rel. (81)-Qal impf. 3 m.p. (נָזַל 633) *which ... pour down*
שְׁחָקִים n.m.p. (1007) *skies (clouds)*
יִרְעֲפוּ Qal impf. 3 m.p. (רָעַף 950) *they drop*
עֲלֵי אָדָם prep.-n.m.s. (9) *upon man*
רָב adj. m.s. as adv. (I 912) *abundantly*

36:29

אַף אִם־יָבִין conj. (II 64)-hypoth.part. (49)-Qal impf. 3 m.s. (בִּין 106) *can any one understand*
מִפְרְשֵׂי־ n.m.p. cstr. (831) *the spreading of*
עָב n.m.s. (728) *clouds*
תְּשֻׁאוֹת n.f.p. cstr. (996) *the thunderings of*
סֻכָּתוֹ n.f.s.-3 m.s. sf. (697) *his pavilion*

36:30

הֶן־פָּרַשׂ interj. (243)-Qal pf. 3 m.s. (831) *behold, he scatters*
עָלָיו prep.-3 m.s. sf. *about him*
אוֹרוֹ n.m.s.-3 m.s. sf. (21) *his lightning*
וְשָׁרְשֵׁי conj.-n.m.p. cstr. (1057) *and the roots of*
הַיָּם def.art.-n.m.s. (410) *the sea*
כִּסָּה Pi. pf. 3 m.s. (כָּסָה 491) *he covers*

36:31

כִּי־בָם conj. (471)-prep.-3 m.p. sf. *for by these*
יָדִין Qal impf. 3 m.s. (דִּין 192) *he judges*
עַמִּים n.m.p. (I 766) *peoples*
יִתֶּן־ Qal impf. 3 m.s. (נָתַן 678) *he gives*
אֹכֶל n.m.s. (38) *food*
לְמַכְבִּיר prep.-Hi. ptc. (כָּבַר I 460) *in abundance*

36:32

עַל־כַּפַּיִם prep.-n.f. du. (496) *with (his) hands*
כִּסָּה־ Pi. pf. 3 m.s. (כָּסָה 491) *he covers*
אוֹר n.m.s. (21; GK 122o) *lightning*
וַיְצַו consec.-Pi. impf. 3 m.s. (צָוָה 845) *and commands*
עָלֶיהָ prep.-3 f.s. sf. *it*
בְמַפְגִּיעַ prep.-Hi. ptc. (פָּגַע 803) *to make attack*

36:33

יַגִּיד Hi. impf. 3 m.s. (נָגַד 616) *declares*
עָלָיו prep.-3 m.s. sf. *concerning him*
רֵעוֹ n.m.s.-3 m.s. sf. (929) *its crashing*
מִקְנֶה n.m.s. (889) *cattle*
אַף n.m.s. (I 60) *with anger*
עַל־עוֹלֶה prep.-n.f.s. (732; if pointed עַוְלָה) *against iniquity*

37:1

אַף־לְזֹאת conj. (II 64)-prep.-demons.adj. f.s. (260) *at this also*
יֶחֱרַד Qal impf. 3 m.s. (חָרַד 353) *trembles*
לִבִּי n.m.s.-1 c.s. sf. (524) *my heart*
וְיִתַּר conj.-Qal impf. 3 m.s. (נָתַר I 684) *and leaps out*
מִמְּקוֹמוֹ prep.-n.m.s.-3 m.s. sf. (879) *of its place*

37:2

שִׁמְעוּ שָׁמוֹעַ Qal impv. 2 m.p. (1033)-Qal inf.abs. (1033) *hearken*
בְּרֹגֶז prep.-n.m.s. cstr. (919) *to the thunder of*
קֹלוֹ n.m.s.-3 m.s. sf. (876) *his voice*
וְהֶגֶה conj.-n.m.s. (211) *and rumbling*
מִפִּיו prep.-n.m.s.-3 m.s. sf. (804) *from his mouth*
יֵצֵא Qal impf. 3 m.s. (יָצָא 422) *that comes*

37:3

תַּחַת־כָּל־הַשָּׁמַיִם prep. (1065)-n.m.s. cstr. (481) -def.art.-n.m. du. (1029) *under the whole heaven*
יִשְׁרֵהוּ Pi. pf. 3 m.s.-3 m.s. sf. (יָשַׁר 448) *he lets it go*
וְאוֹרוֹ conj.-n.m.s.-3 m.s. sf. (21) *and his lightning*

עַל־כַּנְפוֹת prep.-n.f.p. cstr. (489) *to the corners of*
הָאָרֶץ def.art.-n.f.s. (75) *the earth*

37:4

אַחֲרָיו prep.-3 m.s. sf. (29) *after it*
יִשְׁאַג־ Qal impf. 3 m.s. (שָׁאַג 980) *roars*
קוֹל n.m.s. (876) *(his) voice*
יַרְעֵם Hi. impf. 3 m.s. apoc. (רָעַם 947) *he thunders*
בְּקוֹל גְּאוֹנוֹ prep.-n.m.s. cstr. (876)-n.m.s.-3 m.s. sf. (144) *with his majestic voice*
וְלֹא יְעַקְּבֵם conj.-neg.-Pi. impf. 3 m.s.-3 m.p. sf. (עָקַב 784) *and he does not restrain them*
כִּי־יִשָּׁמַע conj. (471)-Ni. impf. 3 m.s. (1033) *when is heard*
קוֹלוֹ n.m.s.-3 m.s. sf. (876) *his voice*

37:5

יַרְעֵם Hi. impf. 3 m.s. apoc. (רָעַם 947) *thunders*
אֵל n.m.s. (42) *God*
בְּקוֹלוֹ prep.-n.m.s.-3 m.s. sf. (876) *with his voice*
נִפְלָאוֹת Ni. ptc. f.p. (פָּלָא 810; GK 118p) *wondrously*
עֹשֶׂה Qal act.ptc. (I 793) *he does*
גְדֹלוֹת adj. f.p. as subst. (152) *great things*
וְלֹא נֵדָע conj.-neg.-Qal impf. 1 c.p. paus. (יָדַע 393) *which we cannot apprehend*

37:6

כִּי לַשֶּׁלֶג conj. (471)-prep.-def.art.-n.m.s. (1017) *for to the snow*
יֹאמַר Qal impf. 3 m.s. (אָמַר 55) *he says*
הֱוֵא Qal impv. 2 m.s. (הָוָא 216; GK 75hh) *fall*
אָרֶץ n.f.s. (75) *on the earth*
וְגֶשֶׁם conj.-n.m.s cstr. (II 177) *and to the shower of*
מָטָר n.m.s. (564) *rain*
וְגֶשֶׁם conj.-v.supra *and to the shower of*
מִטְרוֹת n.m.p. (564) *rains*
עֻזּוֹ n.m.s.-3 m.s. sf. (738) *his strength*

37:7

בְּיַד־ prep.-n.f.s. cstr. (388) *hand of*
כָּל־אָדָם n.m.s. cstr. (481)-n.m.s. (9) *every man*
יַחְתּוֹם Qal impf. 3 m.s. (חָתַם 367) *he seals up*
לָדַעַת prep.-Qal inf.cstr. (יָדַע 393) *that may know*
כָּל־אַנְשֵׁי n.m.s. cstr. (481)-n.m.p. cstr. (35) *all men whom*
מַעֲשֵׂהוּ n.m.s.-3 m.s. sf. (795) *he has made*

37:8

וַתָּבֹא consec.-Qal impf. 3 f.s. (בּוֹא 97) *then ... go*
חַיָּה n.f.s. (I 312) *beasts*
בְמוֹ־אָרֶב prep.-n.m.s. (70) *into lairs*
וּבִמְעוֹנֹתֶיהָ conj.-prep.-n.f.p.-3 f.s. sf. (733) *and in their dens*
תִשְׁכֹּן Qal impf. 3 f.s. (שָׁכַן 1014) *remain*

37:9

מִן־הַחֶדֶר prep.-def.art.-n.m.s. (293) *from its chamber*
תָּבוֹא Qal impf. 3 f.s. (בּוֹא 97) *comes*
סוּפָה n.f.s. (I 693) *whirlwind*
וּמִמְּזָרִים conj.-prep.-Pi. ptc. m.p. (זָרָה 279) *from scattering winds*
קָרָה n.f.s. (903) *cold*

37:10

מִנִּשְׁמַת־ prep.-n.f.s. cstr. (675) *by the breath of*
אֵל n.m.s. (42) *God*
יִתֶּן־ Qal impf. 3 m.s. (נָתַן 678) *is given*
קָרַח n.m.s. (901) *ice*
וְרֹחַב מַיִם conj.-n.m.s. cstr. (931)-n.m.p. (565) *and broad waters*
בְּמוּצָק prep.-n.m.s. (II 848) *in constraint (i.e. frozen)*

37:11

אַף־בְּרִי conj. (II 64)-prep.-n.m.s. (924) *surely with moisture*
יַטְרִיחַ Hi. impf. 3 m.s. (טָרַח 382) *he loads*
עָב n.m.s. (728) *thick cloud*
יָפִיץ Hi. impf. 3 m.s. (פּוּץ I 806) *he scatters*
עֲנַן אוֹרוֹ n.m.s. cstr. (I 777)-n.m.s.-3 m.s. sf. (21) *the clouds of his lightning*

37:12

וְהוּא conj.-pers.pr. 3 m.s. (214) *and he*
מְסִבּוֹת n.f.p. as adv. (687) *in all directions (on all sides)*
מִתְהַפֵּךְ Hith. ptc. m.s. (הָפַךְ 245) *turns*
בְּתַחְבּוּלֹתָו prep.-n.f.p.-3 m.s. sf. (287) *by his guidance*
לְפָעֳלָם prep.-Qal inf.cstr.-3 m.p. sf. (פָּעַל 821) *to accomplish*
כֹּל אֲשֶׁר n.m.s. (481)-rel. (81) *all that*
יְצַוֵּם Pi. impf. 3 m.s.-3 m.p. sf. (צָוָה 845) *he commands them*
עַל־פְּנֵי prep.-n.m.p. cstr. (815) *on the face of*
תֵבֵל n.f.s. cstr. (385) *the world of*
אַרְצָה n.f.s.-loc.he (75; GK 90f) *the earth*

37:13

אִם־לְשֵׁבֶט conj. (49)-prep.-n.m.s. (986) *whether for correction*

אִם־לְאַרְצוֹ v.supra-prep.-n.f.s.-3 m.s. sf. (75) *or for his land*

אִם־לְחֶסֶד v.supra-prep.-n.m.s. (338) *or for love*

יַמְצִאֵהוּ Hi. impf. 3 m.s.-3 m.s. sf. (מָצָא 592) *he causes it to happen*

37:14

הַאֲזִינָה Hi. impv. 2 m.s.-vol.he (אָזַן 24) *hear*

זֹאת demons.adj. f.s. (260) *this*

אִיּוֹב pr.n. (33) *Job*

עֲמֹד Qal impv. 2 m.s. (עָמַד 763) *stand (stop)*

וְהִתְבּוֹנֵן conj.-Hithpolel impv. 2 m.s. (בִּין 106; GK 117w) *and consider*

נִפְלְאוֹת Ni. ptc. f.p. cstr. (פָּלָא 810) *the wondrous works of*

אֵל n.m.s. (42) *God*

37:15

הֲתֵדַע interr.part.-Qal impf. 2 m.s. (יָדַע 393) *do you know*

בְּשׂוּם־אֱלוֹהַּ prep.-Qal inf.cstr. (שִׂים 962; LXX ὅτι ὁ θεὸς ἔθετο ἔργω αὐτοῦ) *how God lays his commands*

עֲלֵיהֶם prep.-3 m.p. sf. *upon them*

וְהוֹפִיעַ conj.-Hi. pf. 3 m.s. (יָפַע 422) *and causes to shine*

אוֹר n.m.s. cstr. (21) *the lightning of*

עֲנָנוֹ n.m.s.-3 m.s. sf. (777) *his cloud*

37:16

הֲתֵדַע interr.part.-Qal impf. 2 m.s. (יָדַע 393) *do you know*

עַל־מִפְלְשֵׂי־ prep.-n.m.p. cstr. (814) *balancings of*

עָב n.m.s. (728) *clouds*

מִפְלְאוֹת n.f.p. cstr. (811) *wondrous works of*

תְּמִים adj. m.s. cstr. (1071) *him who is perfect in*

דֵּעִים n.m.p. (395; GK 124e) *knowledge*

37:17

אֲשֶׁר־בְּגָדֶיךָ rel. (81)-n.m.p.-2 m.s. sf. (93) *you whose garments*

חַמִּים adj. m.p. (III 328) *are hot*

בְּהַשְׁקִט prep.-Hi. inf.cstr. (שָׁקַט 1052) *when ... is still*

אֶרֶץ n.f.s. (75) *earth*

מִדָּרוֹם prep.-n.m.s. (204) *because of the south wind*

37:18

תַּרְקִיעַ Hi. impf. 2 m.s. (רָקַע 955; GK 150b) *can you spread out*

עִמּוֹ prep.-3 m.s. sf. (767) *like him*

לִשְׁחָקִים prep.-n.m.p. (1007) *skies*

חֲזָקִים adj. m.p. (305) *hard*

כִּרְאִי מוּצָק prep.-n.m.s. (909)-Ho. ptc. m.s. (יָצַק 427) *as a molten mirror*

37:19

הוֹדִיעֵנוּ Hi. impv. 2 m.s.-1 c.p. sf. (יָדַע 393; LXX δίδαξόν με) *teach us*

מַה־נֹּאמַר לוֹ interr. (552)-Qal impf. 1 c.p. (אָמַר 55)-prep.-3 m.s. sf. *what we shall say to him*

לֹא־נַעֲרֹךְ neg.-Qal impf. 1 c.p. (עָרַךְ 789) *we cannot draw up our case*

מִפְּנֵי־חֹשֶׁךְ prep.-n.m.p. cstr. (815)-n.m.s. (365) *because of darkness*

37:20

הַיְסֻפַּר interr.part.-Pu. impf. 3 m.s. (סָפַר 707) *shall it be told*

לוֹ prep.-3 m.s. sf. *him*

כִּי אֲדַבֵּר conj.-Pi. impf. 1 c.s. (דָּבַר 180) *that I would speak*

אִם־אָמַר hypoth.part. (49)-Qal pf. 3 m.s. (55) *did ... ever wish*

אִישׁ n.m.s. (35) *a man*

כִּי יְבֻלָּע conj. (471)-Pu. impf. 3 m.s. paus. (בָּלַע 118) *that he would be swallowed up*

37:21

וְעַתָּה conj.-adv. (773) *and now*

לֹא רָאוּ neg.-Qal pf. 3 c.p. (רָאָה 906) *men cannot look*

אוֹר n.m.s. (21) *on the light*

בָּהִיר הוּא adj. m.s. (97)-pers.pr. 3 m.s. (214) *when it is bright*

בַּשְּׁחָקִים prep.-def.art.-n.m.p. (1007) *in the skies*

וְרוּחַ conj.-n.f.s. (924) *when wind*

עָבְרָה Qal pf. 3 f.s. (עָבַר 716) *has passed*

וַתְּטַהֲרֵם consec.-Pi. impf. 3 f.s.-3 m.p. sf. (טָהֵר 372) *and cleared them*

37:22

מִצָּפוֹן prep.-n.f.s. (860) *out of the north*

זָהָב n.m.s. (262) *golden splendor*

יֶאֱתֶה Qal impf. 3 m.s. (אָתָה 87) *comes*

עַל־אֱלוֹהַּ prep.-n.m.s. (42) *upon God*

נוֹרָא הוֹד Ni. ptc. m.s. (יָרֵא 431)-n.m.s. (I 217) *terrible majesty*

37:23

שַׁדַּי pr.n. (994) *the Almighty*
לֹא־מְצָאנֻהוּ neg.-Qal pf. 1 c.p.-3 m.s. sf. (מָצָא 592) *we cannot find him*
שַׂגִּיא־כֹחַ adj. m.s. cstr. (960)-n.m.s. (470) *great in power*
וּמִשְׁפָּט conj.-n.m.s. (1048) *and justice*
וְרֹב־צְדָקָה conj.-n.m.s. cstr. (913)-n.f.s. (842) *and abundant righteousness*
לֹא יְעַנֶּה neg.-Pi. impf. 3 m.s. (עָנָה III 776) *he will not violate*

37:24

לָכֵן prep.-adv. (485) *therefore*
יְרֵאוּהוּ Qal pf. 3 c.p.-3 m.s. sf. (יָרֵא 431; GK 59i) *fear him*
אֲנָשִׁים n.m.p. (35) *men*
לֹא־יִרְאֶה neg.-Qal impf. 3 m.s. (רָאָה 906) *he does not regard*
כָּל־חַכְמֵי־ n.m.s. cstr. (481)-adj. m.p. cstr. (314) *any who are wise of*
לֵב n.m.s. (524) *heart*

38:1

LXX+Μετὰ δὲ τὸ παύσασθαι Ελιουν τῆς λέξεως
וַיַּעַן־ consec.-Qal impf. 3 m.s. (עָנָה I 772) *then answered*
יהוה pr.n. (217) *Yahweh*
אֶת־אִיּוֹב dir.obj.-pr.n. (33) *Job*
מִנ הַסְּעָרָה prep.-def.art.-n.f.s. (704) *out of the whirlwind*
וַיֹּאמַר consec.-Qal impf. 3 m.s. (אָמַר 55) *(and said)*

38:2

מִי זֶה interr. (566)-demons.adj. m.s. (260; GK 136c) *who is this*
מַחְשִׁיךְ Hi. ptc. m.s. (חָשַׁךְ 364) *that darkens*
עֵצָה n.f.s. (420) *counsel*
בְמִלִּין prep.-n.f.p. (576) *by words*
בְּלִי־דָעַת neg. (115)-n.f.s. paus. (395) *without knowledge*

38:3

אֱזָר־ Qal impv. 2 m.s. (אָזַר 25) *gird up*
נָא part.of entreaty (609) *(I pray thee)*
כְגֶבֶר prep.-n.m.s. (149; GK 126p) *like a man*
חֲלָצֶיךָ n.f. du.-2 m.s. sf. (323) *your loins*
וְאֶשְׁאָלְךָ conj.-Qal impf. 1 c.s.-2 m.s. sf. (שָׁאַל 981) *I will question you*
וְהוֹדִיעֵנִי conj.-Hi. impv. 2 m.s.-1 c.s. sf. (יָדַע 393) *and you shall declare to me*

38:4

אֵיפֹה הָיִיתָ adv. (33)-Qal pf. 2 m.s. (הָיָה 224) *where were you*
בְּיָסְדִי־ prep.-Qal inf.cstr.-1 c.s. sf. (יָסַד 413) *when I laid the foundation of*
אָרֶץ n.f.s. paus. (75) *the earth*
הַגֵּד Hi. impv. 2 m.s. (נָגַד 616) *tell (me)*
אִם־יָדַעְתָּ hypoth.part. (49)-Qal pf. 2 m.s. (יָדַע 393) *if you have*
בִינָה n.f.s. (108) *understanding*

38:5

מִי־שָׂם interr. (566)-Qal pf. 3 m.s. (שִׂים 962) *who determined*
מְמַדֶּיהָ n.m.p.-3 f.s. sf. (551) *its measurements*
כִּי תֵדָע conj.-Qal impf. 2 m.s. paus. (יָדַע 393; GK 159dd) *surely you know*
אוֹ מִי־ conj. (14)-interr. (566) *or who*
נָטָה Qal pf. 3 m.s. (639) *stretched*
עָלֶיהָ prep.-3 f.s. sf. *upon it*
קָו n.m.s. paus. (876) *(the) line*

38:6

עַל־מָה prep.-interr. (552; GK 137b) *on what*
אֲדָנֶיהָ n.m.p.-3 f.s. sf. (10) *its bases*
הָטְבָּעוּ Ho. pf. 3 c.p. (טָבַע 371) *were sunk*
אוֹ מִי־ conj. (14)-interr. (566) *or who*
יָרָה Qal pf. 3 m.s. (יָרָה 434) *laid*
אֶבֶן n.f.s. cstr. (6) *the stone of*
פִּנָּתָהּ n.f.s.-3 f.s. sf. (819) *its corner*

38:7

בְּרָן־יַחַד prep.-Qal inf.cstr. (רָנַן 943; GK 67n, 114r)-adv. (403) *when sang together*
כּוֹכְבֵי n.m.p. cstr. (456) *the stars of*
בֹקֶר n.m.s. (133) *(the) morning*
וַיָּרִיעוּ consec.-Hi. impf. 3 m.p. (רוּעַ 929) *and shouted for joy*
כָּל־בְּנֵי n.m.s. cstr. (481)-n.m.p. cstr. (119; GK 128v) *all the sons of*
אֱלֹהִים n.m.p. (43) *God*

38:8

וַיָּסֶךְ consec.-Qal impf. 3 m.s. (סוּךְ II 692; LXX ἔφραξα) *or who shut*
בִּדְלָתַיִם prep.-n.f. du. (195) *with doors*
יָם n.m.s. (410) *the sea*
בְּגִיחוֹ prep.-Qal inf.cstr.-3 m.s. sf. (גִּיחַ 161) *when it burst forth*

מֵרֶחֶם prep.-n.m.s. (933) *from (the) womb*
יֵצֵא Qal impf. 3 m.s. (יָצָא 422) *who brings forth*

38:9

בְּשׂוּמִי prep.-Qal inf.cstr.-1 c.s. sf. (שִׂים 962; GK 114r) *when I made*
עָנָן n.m.s. (777) *clouds*
לְבֻשׁוֹ n.m.s.-3 m.s. sf. (528) *its garment*
וַעֲרָפֶל conj.-n.m.s. (791) *and thick darkness*
חֲתֻלָּתוֹ n.f.s.-3 m.s. sf. (367) *its swaddling band*

38:10

וָאֶשְׁבֹּר consec.-Qal impf. 1 c.s. (שָׁבַר 990; LXX ἐθέμην δὲ) *and I broke (prescribed)*
עָלָיו prep.-3 m.s. sf. *for it*
חֻקִּי n.m.s.-1 c.s. sf. (349; LXX ὅρια) *my bounds*
וָאָשִׂים consec.-Qal impf. 1 c.s. (שִׂים 962) *and set*
בְּרִיחַ n.m.s. (138) *bars*
וּדְלָתָיִם conj.-n.f. du. (195) *and doors*

38:11

וָאֹמַר consec.-Qal impf. 1 c.s. (אָמַר 55) *and I said*
עַד־פֹּה prep. (III 723)-adv. (805) *thus far*
תָבוֹא Qal impf. 2 m.s. (בּוֹא 97) *shall you come*
וְלֹא תֹסִיף conj.-neg.-Hi. impf. 2 m.s. (יָסַף 414) *and no farther*
וּפֹא־יָשִׁית conj.-adv. (805)-Qal impf. 3 m.s. (1011 שִׁית; LXX ἀλλ' ἐν σεαυτῇ) *and here shall be stayed*
בִּגְאוֹן גַּלֶּיךָ prep.-n.m.s. cstr. (144)-n.m.p.-2 m.s. sf. paus. (164; LXX συντριβήσεταί σου τὰ κύματα) *your proud waves*

38:12

הְמִיָּמֶיךָ interr.part.-prep.-n.m.p.-2 m.s. sf. (398; GK 119wN; LXX ἢ ἐπὶ σοῦ) *since your days (began)*
צִוִּיתָ Pi. pf. 2 m.s. (צָוָה 845; LXX συντέταχα φέγγος) *have you commanded*
בֹּקֶר n.m.s. (133) *(the) morning*
יִדַּעְתָּה Pi. pf. 2 m.s. (יָדַע 393) *have you caused to know*
שַׁחַר def.art.-n.m.s. (1007) *the dawn*
מְקֹמוֹ n.m.s.-3 m.s. sf. (879) *its place*

38:13

לֶאֱחֹז prep.-Qal inf.cstr. (אָחַז 28; GK 114r) *that it might take hold*
בְּכַנְפוֹת prep.-n.f.p. cstr. (489) *of the skirts of*
הָאָרֶץ def.art.-n.f.s. (75) *the earth*
וְיִנָּעֲרוּ conj.-Ni. impf. 3 m.p. (נָעַר II 654) *and might be shaken*
רְשָׁעִים adj. m.p. (957; GK 5n) *the wicked*
מִמֶּנָּה prep.- 3 f.s. sf. *out of it*

38:14

תִּתְהַפֵּךְ Hith. impf. 3 f.s. (הָפַךְ 245) *it is changed*
כְּחֹמֶר prep.-n.m.s. cstr. (I 330) *like clay of (under)*
חוֹתָם n.m.s. (I 368) *the seal*
וְיִתְיַצְּבוּ conj.-Hith. impf. 3 m.p. (יָצַב 426) *and they stand forth*
כְּמוֹ לְבוּשׁ prep. (453)-n.m.s. (528; GK 118w) *like a garment*

38:15

וְיִמָּנַע conj.-Ni. impf. 3 m.s. (מָנַע 586) *and is withheld*
מֵרְשָׁעִים prep.-adj. m.p. (957; GK 5n) *from (the) wicked*
אוֹרָם n.m.s.-3 m.p. sf. (21) *their light*
וּזְרוֹעַ רָמָה conj.-n.f.s. (283)-Qal pass.ptc. f.s. (926 רוּם) *and their uplifted arm*
תִּשָּׁבֵר Ni. impf. 3 f.s. (שָׁבַר 990) *is broken*

38:16

הֲבָאתָ interr.part.-Qal pf. 2 m.s. (בּוֹא 97) *have you entered*
עַד־נִבְכֵי־יָם prep. (III 723)-n.m.p. cstr. (614) -n.m.s. (410) *into (the) springs of (the) sea*
וּבְחֵקֶר conj.-prep.-n.m.s. cstr. (350; GK 150h) *or in (the) recesses of*
תְּהוֹם n.f.s. (1062) *(the) deep*
הִתְהַלָּכְתָּ Hith. pf. 2 m.s. (הָלַךְ 229) *have you walked*

38:17

הֲנִגְלוּ interr.part.-Ni. pf. 3 c.p. (גָּלָה 162) *have been revealed?*
לְךָ prep.-2 m.s. sf. *to you*
שַׁעֲרֵי־ n.m.p. cstr. (1044) *gates of*
מָוֶת n.m.s. (560) *death*
וְשַׁעֲרֵי conj.-v.supra (LXX πυλωροὶ δὲ ᾅδου) *or (the) gates of*
צַלְמָוֶת n.m.s. (853) *deep darkness*
תִּרְאֶה Qal impf. 2 m.s. (רָאָה 906) *have you seen*

38:18

הִתְבֹּנַנְתָּ Hithpolel pf. 2 m.s. (בִּין 106; GK 150b) *have you comprehended*

עַד־רַחֲבֵי־ prep. (III 723)–n.m.p. cstr. (931) *the expanse of*
אָרֶץ n.f.s. paus. (75) *(the) earth*
הַגֵּד Hi. impv. 2 m.s. (נָגַד 616) *declare*
אִם־יָדַעְתָּ hypoth.part. (49)–Qal pf. 2 m.s. (יָדַע 393) *if you know*
כֻּלָּהּ n.m.s.–3 f.s. sf. (481; GK 122q; LXX πόση τίς ἐστιν) *all this*

38:19

אֵי־זֶה adv. (32)–demons.adj. m.s. (260) *which is?*
הַדֶּרֶךְ def.art.–n.m.s. (202; GK 155k) *the way*
יִשְׁכָּן־אוֹר Qal impf. 3 m.s. (שָׁכַן 1014)–n.m.s. (21) *to the dwelling of light*
וְחֹשֶׁךְ conj.–n.m.s. (365) *and darkness*
אֵי־זֶה מְקֹמוֹ v.supra–n.m.s.–3 m.s. sf. (879) *where is its place?*

38:20

כִּי תִקָּחֶנּוּ conj. (471)–Qal impf. 2 m.s.–3 m.s. sf. (542 לָקַח) *that you may take it*
אֶל־גְּבוּלוֹ prep.–n.m.s.–3 m.s. sf. (147) *to its territory*
וְכִי תָבִין conj.–conj.–Qal impf. 2 m.s. (בִּין 106) *and that you may discern*
נְתִיבוֹת n.f.p. cstr. (677) *the paths to*
בֵּיתוֹ n.m.s.–3 m.s. sf. (108) *its home*

38:21

יָדַעְתָּ Qal pf. 2 m.s. (393) *you know*
כִּי־אָז conj.–adv. (23) *for then*
תִּוָּלֵד Ni. impf. 2 m.s. (יָלַד 408; GK 107c) *you were born*
וּמִסְפַּר conj.–n.m.s. cstr. (708) *and the number of*
יָמֶיךָ n.m.p.–2 m.s. sf. (398; GK 146a) *your days*
רַבִּים adj. m.p. (I 912) *is great*

38:22

הֲבָאתָ interr.part.–Qal pf. 2 m.s. (בּוֹא 97) *have you entered*
אֶל־אֹצְרוֹת prep.–n.m.p. cstr. (69) *the storehouses of*
שָׁלֶג n.m.s. paus. (1017) *snow*
וְאֹצְרוֹת conj.–v.supra (GK 150h) *or storehouses of*
בָּרָד n.m.s. (135) *hail*
תִּרְאֶה Qal impf. 2 m.s. (רָאָה 906) *have you seen*

38:23

אֲשֶׁר־חָשַׂכְתִּי rel. (81)–Qal pf. 1 c.s. (חָשַׂךְ 362) *which I have reserved*
לְעֶת־צָר prep.–n.f.s. cstr. (773)–n.m.s. paus. (II 865) *for time of trouble*
לְיוֹם prep.–n.m.s. cstr. (398) *for day of*
קְרָב n.m.s. (898) *battle*
וּמִלְחָמָה conj.–n.f.s. (536) *and war*

38:24

אֵי־זֶה adv. (32)–demons.adj. m.s. (260; LXX πόθεν δὲ) *what is*
הַדֶּרֶךְ def.art.–n.m.s. (202; LXX ἐκπορεύεται) *the way*
יֵחָלֶק Ni. impf. 3 m.s. (חָלַק 323; GK 165a) *where is distributed*
אוֹר n.m.s. (21; LXX πάχνη) *light*
יָפֵץ Hi. impf. 3 m.s. (פּוּץ I 806; LXX διασκεδάννυται νότος) *or is scattered*
קָדִים n.m.s. (870) *east wind*
עֲלֵי־אָרֶץ prep.–n.f.s. paus. (75) *upon earth*

38:25

מִי־פִלַּג interr. (566)–Pi. pf. 3 m.s. (פָּלַג 811) *who has cleft*
לַשֶּׁטֶף prep.–def.art.–n.m.s. (1009) *for the torrents of rain*
תְּעָלָה n.f.s. (752) *a channel*
וְדֶרֶךְ conj.–n.m.s. (202) *and a way*
לַחֲזִיז קֹלוֹת prep.–n.m.s. cstr. (304)–n.m.p. (876) *for (the) thunderbolt*

38:26

לְהַמְטִיר prep.–Hi. inf.cstr. (מָטַר 565) *to bring rain*
עַל־אֶרֶץ prep.–n.f.s. (75) *on a land*
לֹא־אִישׁ neg.–n.m.s. (35; GK 152u,155e) *where no man is*
מִדְבָּר n.m.s. (184) *on the desert*
לֹא־אָדָם בּוֹ neg.–n.m.s. (9)–prep.–3 m.s. sf. *in which there is no man*

38:27

לְהַשְׂבִּיעַ prep.–Hi. inf.cstr. (שָׂבַע 959) *to satisfy*
שֹׁאָה n.f.s. (996) *(the) waste land*
וּמְשֹׁאָה conj.–n.f.s. (996; GK 133,l) *and desolate*
וּלְהַצְמִיחַ conj.–prep.–Hi. inf.cstr. (צָמַח 855) *and to make put forth*
מֹצָא n.m.s. (I 425) *(the) ground (the growing-place)*
דֶּשֶׁא n.m.s. (206) *grass*

38:28

הֲיֵשׁ־ interr.part.–subst. (441; GK 150g) *is there?*
לַמָּטָר prep.–def.art.–n.m.s. (564) *for the rain*

אָב n.m.s. (3) *a father*
אוֹ מִי־הוֹלִיד conj. (14)–interr. (566)–Hi. pf. 3 m.s. (יָלַד 408; GK 150g) *or who has begotten*
אֶגְלֵי־טָל n.m.p. cstr. (8)–n.m.s. paus. (378) *drops of dew*

38:29

מִבֶּטֶן מִי prep.–n.f.s. cstr. (105)–interr. (566)` *from whose womb*
יָצָא Qal pf. 3 m.s. (422) *did come forth*
הַקָּרַח def.art.–n.m.s. (901) *ice*
וּכְפֹר conj.–n.m.s. cstr. (II 499) *and (the) hoarfrost of*
שָׁמַיִם n.m. du. (1029) *heaven*
מִי יְלָדוֹ interr. (566)–Qal pf. 3 m.s.–3 m.s. sf. (408) *who has given birth to it*

38:30

כָּאֶבֶן prep.–def.art.–n.f.s. (6; GK 118w) *like stone*
מַיִם n.m.p. (565) *(the) waters*
יִתְחַבָּאוּ Hith. impf. 3 m.p. paus. (חָבָא 285) *become hard*
וּפְנֵי תְהוֹם conj.–n.m.p. cstr. (815)–n.f.s. (1062) *and face of deep*
יִתְלַכָּדוּ Hith. impf. 3 m.p. paus. (לָכַד 539) *is frozen*

38:31

הַתְקַשֵּׁר interr.part.–Pi. impf. 2 m.s. (קָשַׁר 905) *can you bind?*
מַעֲדַנּוֹת n.f.p. cstr. (588) *chains of*
כִּימָה n.f.s. (465) *Pleiades*
אוֹ־מֹשְׁכוֹת conj. (14)–n.f.p. cstr. (604) *or cords of*
כְּסִיל n.m.s. (II 493) *Orion*
תְּפַתֵּחַ Pi. impf. 2 m.s. (פָּתַח I 834) *can you loose*

38:32

הֲתֹצִיא interr.part.–Hi. impf. 2 m.s. (יָצָא 422) *can you lead forth*
מַזָּרוֹת n.f.p. (561) *Mazzaroth (constellation?)*
בְּעִתּוֹ prep.–n.f.s.–3 m.s. sf. (773; GK 145m) *in their season*
וְעַיִשׁ conj.–n.f.s. (747; GK 150h) *or Bear*
עַל־בָּנֶיהָ prep.–n.m.p.–3 f.s. sf. (119) *with its children*
תַנְחֵם Hi. impf. 2 m.s.–3 m.p. sf. (נָחָם 634) *can you guide them?*

38:33

הֲיָדַעְתָּ interr.part.–Qal pf. 2 m.s. (393) *do you know?*
חֻקּוֹת n.f.p. cstr. (349) *ordinances of*
שָׁמָיִם n.m. du. paus. (1029) *heavens*
אִם־תָּשִׂים conj. (49)–Qal impf. 2 m.s. (שִׂים 962) *can you establish*
מִשְׁטָרוֹ n.m.s.–3 m.s. sf. (1009) *their rule*
בָאָרֶץ prep.–def.art.–n.f.s. (75) *on the earth*

38:34

הֲתָרִים interr.part.–Hi. impf. 2 m.s. (רוּם 926) *can you lift up*
לָעָב prep.–def.art.–n.m.s. (728) *to the clouds*
קוֹלֶךָ n.m.s.–2 m.s. sf. (876) *your voice*
וְשִׁפְעַת־ conj.–n.f.s. cstr. (1051) *that a flood of*
מַיִם n.m.p. (565) *waters*
תְּכַסֶּךָּ Pi. impf. 3 f.s.–2 m.s. sf. (כָּסָה 491; LXX ὑπακούσεταί σου) *may cover you*

38:35

הַתְשַׁלַּח interr.part.–Pi. impf. 2 m.s. (שָׁלַח 1018) *can you send forth*
בְּרָקִים n.m.p. (140) *lightnings*
וְיֵלֵכוּ conj.–Qal impf. 3 m.p. paus. (הָלַךְ 229) *that they may go*
וְיֹאמְרוּ לְךָ conj.–Qal impf. 3 m.p. (אָמַר 55) –prep.–2 m.s. sf. *and that they may say to you*
הִנֵּנוּ interj.–1 c.p. sf. (243) *here we are*

38:36

מִי־שָׁת interr. (566)–Qal pf. 3 m.s. (שִׁית 1011) *who has put*
בַּטֻּחוֹת prep.–def.art.–n.f.p. (376) *in the inward parts*
חָכְמָה n.f.s. (315) *wisdom*
אוֹ מִי־נָתַן conj. (14)–interr. (566)–Qal pf. 3 m.s. (678) *or has given*
לַשֶּׂכְוִי prep.–def.art.–n.m.s. (967) *a celestial appearance*
בִינָה n.f.s. (108) *understanding*

38:37

מִי־יְסַפֵּר interr. (566)–Pi. impf. 3 m.s. (סָפַר 707) *who can number*
שְׁחָקִים n.m.p. (1007) *(the) clouds*
בְּחָכְמָה prep.–n.f.s. (315) *by wisdom?*
וְנִבְלֵי conj.–n.m.p. cstr. (614) *or waterskins of*
שָׁמַיִם n.m. du. (1029) *heavens*
מִי יַשְׁכִּיב interr. (566)–Hi. impf. 3 m.s. (שָׁכַב 1011) *who can tilt*

38:38

בְּצֶקֶת prep.-Qal inf.cstr. (יָצַק 427) *when ... runs*
עָפָר n.m.s. (779) *dust*
לַמּוּצָק prep.-def.art.-n.m.s. (I 427) *into a mass*
וּרְגָבִים conj.-n.m.p. (918; LXX+ὥσπερ λίθῳ) *and clods*
יְדֻבָּקוּ Pu. impf. 3 m.p. paus. (דָּבַק 179) *cleave fast together*

38:39

הֲתָצוּד interr.part.-Qal impf. 2 m.s. (צוּד I 844) *can you hunt?*
לְלָבִיא prep.-n.m.s. (522) *for the lion*
טָרֶף n.m.s. paus. (383) *the prey*
וְחַיַּת conj.-n.f.s. cstr. (I 312; GK 150h) *or the appetite of*
כְּפִירִים n.m.p. (498) *young lions*
תְּמַלֵּא Pi. impf. 2 m.s. (מָלֵא 569) *can you satisfy?*

38:40

כִּי־יָשֹׁחוּ conj. (471)-Qal impf. 3 m.p. (שָׁחַח 1005) *when they crouch*
בַמְּעוֹנוֹת prep.-def.art.-n.f.p. (733) *in their dens*
יֵשְׁבוּ Qal impf. 3 m.p. (יָשַׁב 442) *or they remain*
בַסֻּכָּה prep.-def.art.-n.f.s. (697) *in their covert*
לְמוֹ־אָרֶב prep. (530)-n.m.s. (70) *for a lying-in-wait*

38:41

מִי יָכִין interr. (566)-Hi. impf. 3 m.s. (כּוּן I 465) *who provides*
לָעֹרֵב prep.-def.art.-n.m.s. (788) *for the raven*
צֵידוֹ n.m.s.-3 m.s. sf. (845) *its prey*
כִּי־יְלָדָו conj.-n.m.p.-3 m.s. sf. (409) *when its young ones*
אֶל־אֵל prep.-n.m.s. (42) *to God*
יְשַׁוֵּעוּ Pi. impf. 3 m.p. (שָׁוַע 1002) *cry*
יִתְעוּ Qal impf. 3 m.p. (תָּעָה 1073) *they wander about*
לִבְלִי־אֹכֶל prep.-neg. (115)-n.m.s. (38; LXX τὰ σῖτα ζητοῦντες) *for lack of food*

39:1

הֲיָדַעְתָּ interr.part.-Qal pf. 2 m.s. (יָדַע 393) *do you know*
עֵת n.f.s. cstr. (773) *when (the time of)*
לֶדֶת Qal inf.cstr. (יָלַד 408) *the bringing forth of*
יַעֲלֵי־ n.m.p. cstr. (I 418) *the mountain-goats of*
סָלַע n.m.s. paus. (I 700) *the cliff*
חֹלֵל Polel inf.cstr. (חוּל I 296; GK 64d) *the calving of*
אַיָּלוֹת n.f.p. (19) *the hinds*
תִּשְׁמֹר Qal impf. 2 m.s. (שָׁמַר 1036) *do you observe*

39:2

תִּסְפֹּר Qal impf. 2 m.s. (סָפַר 707; GK 150) *can you number*
יְרָחִים n.m.p. (I 437) *(the) months*
תְּמַלֶּאנָה Pi. impf. 3 f.p. (מָלֵא 569) *that they fulfil*
וְיָדַעְתָּ conj.-Qal pf. 2 m.s. (393) *and do you know*
עֵת n.f.s. cstr. (773) *the time when (of)*
לִדְתָּנָה Qal inf.cstr.-3 f.p. sf. (יָלַד 408; GK 91f) *they bring forth*

39:3

תִּכְרַעְנָה Qal impf. 3 f.p. (כָּרַע 502) *when they crouch*
יַלְדֵיהֶן n.m.p.-3 f.p. sf. (409) *their offspring*
תְּפַלַּחְנָה Pi. impf. 3 f.p. (פָּלַח 812) *when they bring forth*
חֶבְלֵיהֶם n.m.p.-3 m.p. sf. (286; GK 135o) *their young (pains of travail)*
תְּשַׁלַּחְנָה Pi. impf. 3 f.p. (שָׁלַח 1018) *when they are delivered of*

39:4

יַחְלְמוּ Qal impf. 3 m.p. (חָלַם I 321) *become strong*
בְנֵיהֶם n.m.p.-3 m.p. sf. (119) *their young ones*
יִרְבּוּ Qal impf. 3 m.p. (רָבָה I 915) *they grow up*
בַבָּר prep.-def.art.-n.m.s. (141) *in the open (field)*
יָצְאוּ Qal pf. 3 c.p. (יָצָא 422) *they go forth*
וְלֹא־שָׁבוּ conj.-neg.-Qal pf. 3 c.p. (שׁוּב 996) *and do not return*
לָמוֹ prep.-3 m.p. sf. *to them*

39:5

מִי־שִׁלַּח interr. (566)-Pi. pf. 3 m.s. (שָׁלַח 1018) *who has let go*
פֶּרֶא n.m.s. (825) *the wild ass*
חָפְשִׁי adj. m.s. (344) *free*
וּמֹסְרוֹת conj.-n.m.p. cstr. (64) *and the bonds of*
עָרוֹד n.m.s. (789) *the swift ass*
מִי פִתֵּחַ v.supra-Pi. pf. 3 m.s. (פָּתַח I 834) *who has loosed*

39:6

אֲשֶׁר־שַׂמְתִּי rel. (81)–Qal pf. 1 c.s. (שׂוּם 962) *to whom I have given*

עֲרָבָה n.f.s. (I 787) *the steppe*

בֵּיתוֹ n.m.s.–3 m.s. sf. (108) *for his home*

וּמִשְׁכְּנוֹתָיו conj.–n.f.p.–3 m.s. sf. (1015) *and for his dwelling place*

מְלֵחָה n.f.s. (572) *salt land*

39:7

יִשְׂחַק Qal impf. 3 m.s. (שָׂחַק 965) *he scorns*

לַהֲמוֹן prep.–n.m.s. cstr. (242) *tumult of*

קִרְיָה n.f.s. (900) *the city*

תְּשֻׁאוֹת n.f.p. cstr. (996) *the shouts of*

נוֹגֵשׂ Qal act.ptc. (נָגַשׂ 620) *the driver*

לֹא יִשְׁמָע neg.–Qal impf. 3 m.s. paus. (שָׁמַע 1033) *he hears not*

39:8

יְתוּר Qal impf. 3 m.s. (תּוּר 1064) *he ranges (explores)*

הָרִים n.m.p. (249) *the mountains*

מִרְעֵהוּ n.m.s.–3 m.s. sf. (945) *as his pasture*

וְאַחַר conj.–prep. (29) *and after*

כָּל־יָרוֹק n.m.s. cstr. (481)–n.m.s. (438) *every green thing*

יִדְרוֹשׁ Qal impf. 3 m.s. (דָּרַשׁ 205) *he searches*

39:9

הֲיֹאבֶה interr.part.–Qal impf. 3 m.s. (אָבָה 2) *is ... willing?*

רֵים n.m.s. (910) *the wild ox*

עָבְדֶךָ Qal inf.cstr.–2 m.s. sf. paus. (עָבַד 712) *to serve you*

אִם־יָלִין hypoth.part. (49)–Qal impf. 3 m.s. (533) *will he spend the night*

עַל־אֲבוּסֶךָ prep.–n.m.s.–2 m.s. sf. paus. (7) *at your crib*

39:10

הֲתִקְשָׁר־ interr.part.–Qal impf. 2 m.s. (קָשַׁר 905) *can you bind*

רֵים n.m.s. (910) *the wild ox*

בְּתֶלֶם prep.–n.m.s. (1068) *in the furrow*

עֲבֹתוֹ n.m.s.–3 m.s. sf. (721) *with (his) ropes*

אִם־יְשַׂדֵּד hypoth.part. (49)–Pi. impf. 3 m.s. (961 שָׂדַד) *or will he harrow*

עֲמָקִים n.m.p. (770) *the valleys*

אַחֲרֶיךָ prep.–2 m.s. sf. (29) *after you*

39:11

הֲתִבְטַח־ interr.part.–Qal impf. 2 m.s. (בָּטַח 105) *will you depend*

בּוֹ prep.–3 m.s. sf. *on him*

כִּי־רַב conj. (471)–adj. m.s. (I 912) *because ... is great*

כֹּחוֹ n.m.s.–3 m.s. sf. (470) *his strength*

וְתַעֲזֹב conj.–Qal impf. 2 m.s. (עָזַב I 736) *and will you leave*

אֵלָיו prep.–3 m.s. sf. *to him*

יְגִיעֶךָ n.m.s.–2 m.s. sf. paus. (388) *your labor*

39:12

הֲתַאֲמִין interr.part.–Hi. impf. 2 m.s. (אָמַן 52) *do you have faith*

בּוֹ prep.–3 m.s. sf. *in him*

כִּי־יָשׁוּב conj. (471)–Qal impf. 3 m.s. (שׁוּב 996; Q יָשִׁיב) *that he will return*

זַרְעֶךָ n.m.s.–2 m.s. sf. (282) *your (seed) grain*

וְגָרְנְךָ conj.–n.m.s.–2 m.s. sf. (175) *and to your threshing floor*

יֶאֱסֹף Qal impf. 3 m.s. (אָסַף 62) *he will bring*

39:13

כְּנַף־ n.f.s. cstr. (489) *the wings of*

רְנָנִים n.m.p. (943) *ostriches*

נֶעֱלָסָה Ni. pf. 3 f.s. (עָלַס 763) *wave proudly*

אִם־אֶבְרָה conj. (49)–n.f.s. (7; GK 150f) *if pinions*

חֲסִידָה adj. f.s. (339) *kind*

וְנֹצָה conj.–n.f.s. (663) *and plumage*

39:14

כִּי־תַעֲזֹב conj. (471)–Qal impf. 3 f.s. (עָזַב I 736) *for she leaves*

לָאָרֶץ prep.–def.art.–n.f.s. (75) *to the earth*

בֵּצֶיהָ n.f.p.–3 f.s. sf. (101) *her eggs*

וְעַל־עָפָר conj.–prep.–n.m.s. (779) *and on the ground*

תְּחַמֵּם Pi. impf. 3 f.s. (חָמַם 328; GK 135p) *she keeps (them) warm*

39:15

וַתִּשְׁכַּח consec.–Qal impf. 3 f.s. (1013; GK 135p) *forgetting*

כִּי־רֶגֶל conj. (471)–n.f.s. (919) *that a foot*

תְּזוּרֶהָ Qal impf. 3 f.s.–3 f.s. sf. (זוּר III 266) *may crush them*

וְחַיַּת conj.–n.f.s. cstr. (I 312) *and that the beast of*

הַשָּׂדֶה def.art.–n.m.s. (961) *the field*

תְּדוּשֶׁהָ Qal impf. 3 f.s.-3 f.s. sf. (דּוּשׁ 190) *may trample them*

39:16

הִקְשִׁיחַ Hi. pf. 3 m.s. (קָשַׁח 905) *she (the ostrich) deals cruelly*
בָּנֶיהָ n.m.p.-3 f.s. sf. (119) *with her young*
לְלֹא־לָהּ prep.-neg.-prep.-3 f.s. sf. *as if they were not hers*
לְרִיק prep.-n.m.s. (938) *in vain*
יְגִיעָהּ n.m.s.-3 f.s. sf. (388) *her labor*
בְּלִי־פָחַד neg. (115)-Qal pf. 3 m.s. (808) *yet she (he) has not fear*

39:17

כִּי־הִשָּׁהּ conj. (471)-Hi. pf. 3 m.s.-3 f.s. sf. (נָשָׁה II 674) *because ... has made her forget*
אֱלוֹהַּ n.m.s. (42) *God*
חָכְמָה n.f.s. (315) *wisdom*
וְלֹא־חָלַק conj.-neg.-Qal pf. 3 m.s. (323; GK 119m) *and has given no share*
לָהּ prep.-3 f.s. sf. *to her*
בַּבִּינָה prep.-def.art.-n.f.s. (108) *in understanding*

39:18

כָּעֵת prep.-def.art.-n.f.s. (773) *according to the time*
בַּמָּרוֹם prep.-def.art.-n.m.s. (928) *in a high place*
תַּמְרִיא Hi. impf. 3 f.s. (מָרָא I 597) *she flaps away*
תִּשְׂחַק Qal impf. 3 f.s. (שָׂחַק 965) *she laughs*
לַסּוּס prep.-def.art.-n.m.s. (692) *at the horse*
וּלְרֹכְבוֹ conj.-prep.-Qal act.ptc. m.s.-3 m.s. sf. (938 רָכַב) *and his rider*

39:19

הֲתִתֵּן interr.part.-Qal impf. 2 m.s. (נָתַן 678) *do you give*
לַסּוּס prep.-def.art.-n.m.s. (692) *to the horse*
גְּבוּרָה n.f.s. (150) *(his) might*
הֲתַלְבִּישׁ interr.part.-Hi. impf. 2 m.s. (לָבַשׁ 527) *do you clothe*
צַוָּארוֹ n.m.s.-3 m.s. sf. (848) *his neck*
רַעְמָה n.f.s. (947) *with quivering mane*

39:20

הֲתַרְעִישֶׁנּוּ interr.part.-Hi. impf. 2 m.s.-3 m.s. sf. (רָעַשׁ 950) *do you make him leap*
כָּאַרְבֶּה prep.-def.art.-n.m.s. (916) *like the locust*
הוֹד n.m.s. cstr. (I 217) *the majesty of*
נַחְרוֹ n.m.s.-3 m.s. sf. (637) *his snorting*
אֵימָה n.f.s. (33) *is terrible*

39:21

יַחְפְּרוּ Qal impf. 3 m.p. (חָפַר I 343) *they dig*
בָעֵמֶק prep.-def.art.-n.m.s. (770) *in the valley*
וְיָשִׂישׂ conj.-Qal impf. 3 m.s. (שׂוּשׂ 965) *and he exults*
בְּכֹחַ prep.-n.m.s. (470) *in (his) strength*
יֵצֵא Qal impf. 3 m.s. (יָצָא 422) *he goes out*
לִקְרַאת־ prep.-Qal inf.cstr. (קָרָא II 896) *to meet*
נָשֶׁק n.m.s. paus. (676) *(the) weapons*

39:22

יִשְׂחַק Qal impf. 3 m.s. (965) *he laughs*
לְפַחַד prep.-n.m.s. (808) *at fear*
וְלֹא יֵחָת conj.-neg.-Qal impf. 3 m.s. paus. (חָתַת 369) *and is not dismayed*
וְלֹא־יָשׁוּב conj.-neg.-Qal impf. 3 m.s. (שׁוּב 996) *and he does not turn back*
מִפְּנֵי־חָרֶב prep.-n.m.p. cstr. (815)-n.f.s. (352) *from the sword*

39:23

עָלָיו prep.-3 m.s. sf. *upon him*
תִּרְנֶה Qal impf. 3 f.s. (רָנָה 943) *rattles*
אַשְׁפָּה n.f.s. (80) *(the) quiver*
לַהַב חֲנִית n.m.s. cstr. (529)-n.f.s. (333) *(the) flashing spear*
וְכִידוֹן conj.-n.m.s. (475) *and (the) javelin*

39:24

בְּרַעַשׁ prep.-n.m.s. (950) *with fierceness*
וְרֹגֶז conj.-n.m.s. (919) *and rage*
יְגַמֶּא־ Pi. impf. 3 m.s. (גָּמָא 167; GK 75oo) *he swallows*
אָרֶץ n.f.s. paus. (75) *(the) ground*
וְלֹא־יַאֲמִין conj.-neg.-Hi. impf. 3 m.s. (אָמַן 52) *and he cannot stand still*
כִּי־קוֹל conj.-n.m.s. cstr. (876) *at the sound of*
שׁוֹפָר n.m.s. (1051) *the trumpet*

39:25

בְּדֵי שֹׁפָר prep.-subst. cstr. (191)-n.m.s. (1051) *in (the) abundance of (the) trumpet*
יֹאמַר Qal impf. 3 m.s. (55) *he says*
הֶאָח interj. (210) *Aha!*
וּמֵרָחוֹק conj.-prep.-adj. m.s. (935) *from afar*
יָרִיחַ Hi. impf. 3 m.s. (רִיחַ 926) *he smells*
מִלְחָמָה n.f.s. (536) *the battle*
רַעַם n.m.s. cstr. (947) *the thunder of*
שָׂרִים n.m.p. (978) *the captains*
וּתְרוּעָה conj.-n.f.s. (929) *and the shouting*

39:26

הֲמִבִּינָתְךָ interr.part.-prep.-n.f.s.-2 m.s. sf. (108) *is it by your wisdom*

יַאֲבֶר־ Hi. impf. 3 m.s. (אָבַר 7; GK 53n) *that soars*

נֵץ n.m.s. (II 665) *(the) hawk*

יִפְרֹשׂ Qal impf. 3 m.s. (831) *he spreads*

כְּנָפָו n.f. du.-3 m.s. sf. (489) *his wings*

לְתֵימָן prep.-n.f.s. (412) *toward (the) south*

39:27

אִם־עַל־פִּיךָ hypoth.part. (49)-prep.-n.m.s.-2 m.s. sf. (804) *is it at your command*

יַגְבִּיהַּ Hi. impf. 3 m.s. (גָּבַהּ 146) *that mounts up*

נָשֶׁר n.m.s. paus. (676) *(the) eagle*

וְכִי יָרִים conj.-conj. (471)-Hi. impf. 3 m.s. (רוּם 926) *and makes on high*

קִנּוֹ n.m.s.-3 m.s. sf. (890) *his nest*

39:28

סֶלַע n.m.s. (I 700) *on the rock*

יִשְׁכֹּן Qal impf. 3 m.s. (1014) *he dwells*

וְיִתְלֹנָן conj.-Hithpolel impf. 3 m.s. paus. (לוּן I 533) *and makes his home*

עַל־שֶׁן־ prep.-n.f.s. cstr. (1042) *on the tooth of*

סֶלַע v.supra *the crag*

וּמְצוּדָה conj.-n.f.s. (845) *and fastness (stronghold)*

39:29

מִשָּׁם prep.-adv. (1027) *from there*

חָפַר־ Qal pf. 3 m.s. (343) *he spies out*

אֹכֶל n.m.s. (38) *the prey (food)*

לְמֵרָחוֹק prep.-prep.-adj. (935) *afar off*

עֵינָיו n.f. du.-3 m.s. sf. (744) *his eyes*

יַבִּיטוּ Hi. impf. 3 m.p. (נָבַט 613) *behold (it)*

39:30

וְאֶפְרֹחָו conj.-n.m.p.-3 m.s. sf. (827) *and his young ones*

יְעַלְעוּ־ Pi. impf. 3 m.p. (עָלַע 763; v. לוּעַ I 534; GK 55f) *suck up*

דָם n.m.s. (196) *blood*

וּבַאֲשֶׁר conj.-prep.-rel. (81) *and where*

חֲלָלִים n.m.p. (319) *the slain are*

שָׁם הוּא adv. (1027)-pers.pr. 3 m.s. (214) *there is he*

40:1

וַיַּעַן consec.-Qal impf. 3 m.s. (עָנָה I 772) *and said*

יהוה pr.n. (217) *Yahweh*

אֶת־אִיּוֹב dir.obj.-pr.n. (33) *to Job*

וַיֹּאמַר consec.-Qal impf. 3 m.s. (אָמַר 55) *(and said)*

40:2

הֲרֹב interr.part.-Qal inf.abs. (רִיב 936; GK 113ee,gg) *shall contend?*

עִם־שַׁדַּי prep. (767)-pr.n. (994) *with the Almighty*

יִסּוֹר n.m.s. (416) *a faultfinder*

מוֹכִיחַ Hi. ptc. m.s. cstr. (יָכַח 406) *he who argues with*

אֱלוֹהַּ n.m.s. (42) *God*

יַעֲנֶנָּה Qal impf. 3 m.s.-3 f.s. sf. (עָנָה I 772) *let him answer it*

40:3

וַיַּעַן consec.-Qal impf. 3 m.s. (עָנָה I 772) *then answered*

אִיּוֹב pr.n. (33) *Job*

אֶת־יהוה dir.obj.-pr.n. (217) *Yahweh*

וַיֹּאמַר consec.-Qal impf. 3 m.s. (אָמַר 55) *(and said)*

40:4

הֵן interj. (243) *behold*

קַלֹּתִי Qal impf. 1 c.s. (קָלַל 886) *I am of small account*

מָה אֲשִׁיבֶךָּ interr. (552)-Hi. impf. 1 c.s.-2 m.s. sf. (שׁוּב 996) *what shall I answer thee?*

יָדִי n.f.s.-1 c.s. sf. (388) *my hand*

שַׂמְתִּי Qal pf. 1 c.s. (שׂוּם 962) *I lay*

לְמוֹ־פִי prep.-n.m.s.-1 c.s. sf. (804) *on my mouth*

40:5

אַחַת num. f.s. (25: GK 134r,s) *once*

דִּבַּרְתִּי Pi. pf. 1 c.s. *I have spoken*

וְלֹא אֶעֱנֶה conj.-neg.-Qal impf. 1 c.s. (עָנָה I 772) *and I will not answer*

וּשְׁתַּיִם conj.-n.f. du. (1040) *and twice*

וְלֹא אוֹסִיף conj.-neg.-Hi. impf. 1 c.s. (יָסַף 414) *but I will proceed no further*

40:6

וַיַּעַן־ consec.-Qal impf. 3 m.s. (I 772) *then answered*

יהוה pr.n. (217) *Yahweh*

אֶת־אִיּוֹב dir.obj.-pr.n. (33) *Job*

מִן סְעָרָה prep.-n.f.s. (704) *out of the whirlwind*

וַיֹּאמַר consec.-Qal impf. 3 m.s. (אָמַר 55) *(and said)*

40:7

אֱזָר־ Qal impv. 2 m.s. (אָזַר 25) *gird*
נָא part.of entreaty (609) *(I pray thee)*
כְגֶבֶר prep.-n.m.s. (149) *like a man*
חֲלָצֶיךָ n.f. du.-2 m.s. sf. (323) *your loins*
אֶשְׁאָלְךָ Qal impf. 1 c.s.-2 m.s. sf. (שָׁאַל 981) *I will question you*
וְהוֹדִיעֵנִי conj.-Hi. impv. 2 m.s.-1 c.s. sf. (יָדַע 393) *and you declare to me*

40:8

הַאַף interr.part.-conj. (64; GK 150g) *will ... even?*
תָּפֵר Hi. impf. 2 m.s. (פָּרַר I 830) *you ... make ineffectual*
מִשְׁפָּטִי n.m.s.-1 c.s. sf. (1048) *my judgment*
תַּרְשִׁיעֵנִי Hi. impf. 2 m.s.-1 c.s. sf. (רָשַׁע 957) *will you condemn me*
לְמַעַן תִּצְדָּק prep.-prep. (775)-Qal impf. 2 m.s. (842 צָדַק) *that you may be justified*

40:9

וְאִם־זְרוֹעַ conj.-hypoth.part. (49)-n.f.s. (283) *and an arm?*
כָּאֵל prep.-def.art.-n.m.s. (42) *like God*
לָךְ prep.-2 m.s. sf. paus. *to you*
וּבְקוֹל conj.-prep.-n.m.s. (876) *and with a voice*
כָּמֹהוּ prep.-3 m.s. sf. *like his*
תַּרְעֵם Hi. impf. 2 m.s. apoc. (רָעַם 947) *can you thunder*

40:10

עֲדֵה נָא Qal impv. 2 m.s. (עָדָה II 725)-part.of entreaty (609) *deck yourself*
גָאוֹן n.m.s. (144) *with majesty*
וָגֹבַהּ conj.-n.m.s. (147) *and dignity*
וְהוֹד conj.-n.m.s. (I 217) *with glory*
וְהָדָר conj.-n.m.s. (214) *and splendor*
תִּלְבָּשׁ Qal impf. 2 m.s. paus. (לָבַשׁ 527) *clothe yourself*

40:11

הָפֵץ Hi. impv. 2 m.s. (פּוּץ 806) *pour forth*
עֶבְרוֹת n.f.p. cstr. (720) *the overflowings of*
אַפֶּךָ n.m.s.-2 m.s. sf. (I 60) *your anger*
וּרְאֵה conj.-Qal impv. 2 m.s. (רָאָה 906; LXX>) *and look on*
כָל־גֵּאֶה n.m.s. cstr. (481)-adj. m.s. (144) *every one that is proud*
וְהַשְׁפִּילֵהוּ conj.-Hi. impv. 2 m.s.-3 m.s. sf. (שָׁפֵל 1050) *and abase him*

40:12

רְאֵה Qal impv. 2 m.s. (906; LXX>) *look on*
כָל־גֵּאֶה n.m.s. cstr. (481)-adj. m.s. (144) *every one that is proud*
הַכְנִיעֵהוּ Hi. impv. 2 m.s.-3 m.s. sf. (כָּנַע 488) *bring him low*
וַהֲדֹךְ conj.-Qal impv. 2 m.s. (הָדַךְ 213) *and tread down*
רְשָׁעִים adj. m.p. (957) *the wicked*
תַּחְתָּם prep.-3 m.p. sf. (1065; LXX παραχρῆμα) *where they stand*

40:13

טָמְנֵם Qal impv. 2 m.s.-3 m.p. sf. (טָמַן 380) *hide them*
בֶּעָפָר prep.-def.art.-n.m.s. (779) *in the dust*
יָחַד adv. paus. (403) *together*
פְּנֵיהֶם n.m.p.-3 m.p. sf. (815) *their faces*
חֲבֹשׁ Qal impv. 2 m.s. (חָבַשׁ 289) *bind*
בַּטָּמוּן prep.-def.art.-Qal pass.ptc. (380) *in the hidden place*

40:14

וְגַם־אֲנִי conj.-adv. (168)-pers.pr. 1 c.s. (58) *then also I*
אוֹדֶךָּ Hi. impf. 1 c.s.-2 m.s. sf. (יָדָה 392) *I will acknowledge to you*
כִּי־תוֹשִׁעַ conj. (471)-Hi. impf. 3 f.s. (יָשַׁע 446) *that ... can give victory*
לְךָ prep.-2 m.s. sf. *to you*
יְמִינֶךָ n.f.s.-2 m.s. sf. (411) *your own right hand*

40:15

הִנֵּה־נָא interj. (243)-part.of entreaty (609) *behold*
בְהֵמוֹת n.m.s. (97) *Behemoth (the hippopotamus)*
אֲשֶׁר־עָשִׂיתִי rel. (81)-Qal pf. 1 c.s. (עָשָׂה I 793; LXX>) *which I made*
עִמָּךְ prep.-2 m.s. sf. paus. (767) *as I made you*
חָצִיר n.m.s. (II 348) *green grass*
כַּבָּקָר prep.-def.art.-n.m.s. (133) *like the ox*
יֹאכֵל Qal impf. 3 m.s. (אָכַל 37) *he eats*

40:16

הִנֵּה־נָא interj. (243)-part.of entreaty (609) *behold*
כֹחוֹ n.m.s.-3 m.s. sf. (470) *his strength*
בְמָתְנָיו prep.-n.m. du.-3 m.s. sf. (608) *in his loins*
וְאֹנוֹ conj.-n.m.s.-3 m.s. sf. (I 20) *and his power*
בִּשְׁרִירֵי prep.-n.m.p. cstr. (1057) *in the muscles of*
בִטְנוֹ n.f.s.-3 m.s. sf. (I 105) *his belly*

40:17

יַחְפֹּץ Qal impf. 3 m.s. (חָפֵץ 343) *be bendeth down (extendeth down stiffly)*
זְנָבוֹ n.m.s.-3 m.s. sf. (275) *his tail*
כְמוֹ־אָרֶז prep.-n.m.s. paus. (72) *like a cedar*
גִּידֵי n.m.p. cstr. (161) *the sinews of*
פַחֲדָו n.m.s.-3 m.s. sf. (II 808; Q pl.) *his thighs*
יְשֹׂרָגוּ Pu. impf. 3 m.p. paus. (שָׂרַג 974) *are knit together*

40:18

עֲצָמָיו n.f.p.-3 m.s. sf. (782) *his bones*
אֲפִיקֵי n.m.p. cstr. (67) *tubes of*
נְחוּשָׁה n.f.s. (639) *bronze*
גְּרָמָיו n.m.p.-3 m.s. sf. (175) *his limbs*
כִּמְטִיל prep.-n.m.s. cstr. (564) *like bars of*
בַּרְזֶל n.m.s. (137) *iron*

40:19

הוּא pers.pr. 3 m.s. (214) *he is*
רֵאשִׁית n.f.s. cstr. (912) *the first of*
דַּרְכֵי־ n.m.p. cstr. (202) *the ways of*
אֵל n.m.s. (42) *God*
הָעֹשׂוֹ def.art.-Qal act.ptc.-3 m.s. sf. (עָשָׂה I 793; GK 116gN,127i; LXX πεποιημένον) *let him who made him*
יַגֵּשׁ Hi. impf. 3 m.s. apoc.juss. (נָגַשׁ 620) *let him bring near*
חַרְבּוֹ n.f.s.-3 m.s. sf. (352) *his sword*

40:20

כִּי־בוּל conj.-n.m.s. (385) *for food*
הָרִים n.m.p. (249) *mountains*
יִשְׂאוּ־ Qal impf. 3 m.p. (נָשָׂא 669) *yield*
לוֹ prep.-3 m.s. sf. *for him*
וְכָל־חַיַּת conj.-n.m.s. cstr. (481)-n.f.s. cstr. (I 312) *and all the beasts of*
הַשָּׂדֶה def.art.-n.m.s. (961) *the field*
יְשַׂחֲקוּ־ Pi. impf. 3 m.p. (שָׂחַק 965) *play*
שָׁם adv. (1027) *there*

40:21

תַּחַת־צֶאֱלִים prep. (1065)-n.m.p. (838) *under the lotus plants*
יִשְׁכָּב Qal impf. 3 m.s. (שָׁכַב 1011) *he lies*
בְּסֵתֶר prep.-n.m.s. cstr. (712) *in the covert of*
קָנֶה n.m.s. (889) *reeds*
וּבִצָּה conj.-n.f.s. (130) *and in the marsh*

40:22

יְסֻכֻּהוּ Qal impf. 3 m.p.-3 m.s. sf. (סָכָה I 696; GK 67n) *cover him*
צֶאֱלִים n.m.p. (838) *the lotus trees*
צִלְלוֹ n.m.s.-3 m.s. sf. (צֵל 853) *his shade*
יְסֻבּוּהוּ Qal impf. 3 m.p.-3 m.s. sf. (סָבַב 685) *surround him*
עַרְבֵי־ n.f.p. cstr. (II 788) *the willows of*
נָחַל n.m.s. cstr. (I 636) *the brook*

40:23

הֵן interj. (243; GK 159w; LXX ἐὰν) *behold*
יַעֲשֹׁק Qal impf. 3 m.s. (עָשַׁק 798; LXX γένηται πλήμμυρα) *is turbulent*
נָהָר n.m.s. (625) *the river*
לֹא יַחְפּוֹז neg.-Qal impf. 3 m.s. (חָפַז 342) *he is not frightened*
יִבְטַח Qal impf. 3 m.s. (105) *he is confident*
כִּי־יָגִיחַ conj. (471)-Qal impf. 3 m.s. (גִּיחַ 161) *though ... rushes*
יַרְדֵּן pr.n. (434) *Jordan*
אֶל־פִּיהוּ prep. (39)-n.m.s.-3 m.s. sf. (804) *against his mouth*

40:24

בְּעֵינָיו prep.-n.f. du.-3 m.s. sf. (744) *in his eyes*
יִקָּחֶנּוּ Qal impf. 3 m.s.-3 m.s. sf. (לָקַח 542; GK 66f) *can one take him*
בְּמוֹקְשִׁים prep.-n.m.p. (430) *with a snare*
יִנְקָב־ Qal impf. 3 m.s. (נָקַב 666) *can one pierce*
אָף n.m.s. paus. (I 60) *his nose*

40:25 (Eng.41:1)

תִּמְשֹׁךְ Qal impf. 2 m.s. (מָשַׁךְ 604; GK 150aN) *can you draw out*
לִוְיָתָן n.m.s. (531) *Leviathan (crocodile)*
בְּחַכָּה prep.-n.f.s. (335) *with a fishhook*
וּבְחֶבֶל conj.-prep.-n.m.s. (I 286) *or with a cord*
תַּשְׁקִיעַ Hi. impf. 2 m.s. (שָׁקַע 1054) *can you press down*
לְשֹׁנוֹ n.f.s.-3 m.s. sf. (546) *his tongue*

40:26 (Eng.41:2)

הֲתָשִׂים interr.part.-Qal impf. 2 m.s. (שִׂים 962) *can you put?*
אַגְמֹן n.m.s. (8; LXX κρίκον) *a rope*
בְּאַפּוֹ prep.-n.m.s.-3 m.s. sf. (I 60) *in his nose*
וּבְחוֹחַ conj.-prep.-n.m.s. (296) *or with a hook*
תִּקּוֹב Qal impf. 2 m.s. (נָקַב 666) *can you pierce*
לֶחֱיוֹ n.m.s.-3 m.s. sf. (I 534) *his jaw*

40:27 (Eng.41:3)

הֲיַרְבֶּה interr.part.-Hi. impf. 3 m.s. (רָבָה I 915) *will he make many*
אֵלֶיךָ prep.-2 m.s. sf. *to you*
תַּחֲנוּנִים n.m.p. (337) *supplications*
אִם־יְדַבֵּר conj. (49)-Pi. impf. 3 m.s. (180) *or will he speak*
אֵלֶיךָ prep.-2 m.s. sf. *to you*
רַכּוֹת adj. f.p. (940) *soft words*

40:28 (Eng.41:4)

הֲיִכְרֹת interr.part.-Qal impf. 3 m.s. (כָּרַת 503) *will he make*
בְּרִית n.f.s. (136) *a covenant*
עִמָּךְ prep.-2 m.s. sf. paus. (767) *with you*
תִּקָּחֶנּוּ Qal impf. 2 m.s.-3 m.s. sf. (לָקַח 542) *to take him*
לְעֶבֶד prep.-n.m.s. (713) *for a servant*
עוֹלָם n.m.s. (761) *for ever*

40:29 (Eng.41:5)

הַתְשַׂחֶק־ interr.part.-Pi. impf. 2 m.s. (שָׂחַק 965) *will you play*
בּוֹ prep.-3 m.s. sf. *with him*
כַּצִּפּוֹר prep.-def.art.-n.f.s. (861) *as with a bird*
וְתִקְשְׁרֶנּוּ conj.-Qal impf. 2 m.s.-3 m.s. sf. (קָשַׁר 905; LXX+ὥσπερ στρουθίον) *or will you put him on a leash*
לְנַעֲרוֹתֶיךָ prep.-n.f.p.-2 m.s. sf. (655) *for your maidens*

40:30 (Eng.41:6)

יִכְרוּ Qal impf. 3 m.p. (כָּרָה II 500; GK 150b) *will ... bargain*
עָלָיו prep.-3 m.s. sf. *over him*
חַבָּרִים n.m.p. (289) *traders*
יֶחֱצוּהוּ Qal impf. 3 m.p.-3 m.s. sf. (חָצָה 345) *will they divide him up*
בֵּין כְּנַעֲנִים prep. (107)-n.m.p. (II 489; LXX φοινίκων γένη) *among the merchants*

40:31 (Eng.41:7)

הַתְמַלֵּא interr.part.-Pi. impf. 2 m.s. (מָלֵא 569) *can you fill*
בְשֻׂכּוֹת prep.-n.f.p. (968; LXX πλωτὸν) *with harpoons*
עוֹרוֹ n.m.s.-3 m.s. sf. (736) *his skin*
וּבְצִלְצַל דָּגִים conj.-n.m.s. cstr. (852)-n.m.p. (185) *or with fishing spears*
רֹאשׁוֹ n.m.s.-3 m.s. sf. (910) *his head*

40:32 (Eng.41:8)

שִׂים Qal impv. 2 m.s. (שִׂים 962) *lay*
עָלָיו prep.-3 m.s. sf. *on him*
כַּפֶּךָ n.f.p.-2 m.s. sf. (496) *your hands*
זְכֹר Qal impv. 2 m.s. (269) *think of*
מִלְחָמָה n.f.s. (536) *the battle*
אַל־תּוֹסַף neg.-Hi. impf. 2 m.s. (יָסַף 414; GK 69v) *you will not do it again*

41:1 (41:9)

הֶן־תֹּחַלְתּוֹ interj. (243)-n.f.s.-3 f.s. sf. (404; GK 150aN) *behold, his hope*
נִכְזָבָה Ni. pf. 3 f.s. (כָּזַב 469) *is disappointed (has been made deceptive)*
הֲגַם interr.part. (209)-adv. (168) *even*
אֶל־מַרְאָיו prep.-n.m.p.-3 m.s. sf. (909; GK 93ss) *at the sight of him*
יֻטָל Ho. impf. 3 m.s. (טוּל 376) *he is laid low*

41:2 (Eng.41:10)

לֹא־אַכְזָר neg.-adj. m.s. (470) *no one is so fierce*
כִּי יְעוּרֶנּוּ conj. (471)-Qal impf. 3 m.s.-3 m.s. sf. (I 734 עוּר; GK 72cc) *that he dares to stir him up*
וּמִי conj.-interr. (566) *who then*
הוּא pers.pr. 3 m.s. (214) *he*
לְפָנַי prep.-n.m.p.-1 c.s. sf. (815) *before me*
יִתְיַצָּב Hith. impf. 3 m.s. paus. (יָצַב 426) *can stand*

41:3 Eng. 41:11)

מִי הִקְדִּימַנִי interr. (566)-Hi. pf. 3 m.s.-1 c.s. sf. (869 קָדַם) *who has anticipated me?*
וַאֲשַׁלֵּם conj.-Pi. impf. 1 c.s. (שָׁלַם 1022; LXX καὶ ὑπομενεῖ) *that I should repay him*
תַּחַת כָּל־הַשָּׁמַיִם prep. (1065)-n.m.s. cstr. (481) -def.art.-n.m.p. (1029) *under the whole heaven*
לִי־הוּא prep.-1 c.s. sf.-demons.adj. m.s. (214) *whatever ... is mine*

41:4 (Eng.41:12)

לֹא־אַחֲרִישׁ neg.-Hi. impf. 1 c.s. (חָרַשׁ II 361; GK 103g) *I will not keep silence*
בַּדָּיו n.m.p.-3 m.s. sf. (II 94) *concerning his limbs*
וּדְבַר־ conj.-n.m.s. cstr. (182) *or the story of*
גְּבוּרוֹת n.f.p. (150; GK 124e) *strength*
וְחִין conj.-n.m.s. cstr. (336) *or the grace of*
עֶרְכּוֹ n.m.s.-3 m.s. sf. (789) *his symmetry*

41:5 (Eng.41:13)

מִי־גִלָּה interr. (566)–Pi. pf. 3 m.s. (גָּלָה 162) *who can strip off*

פְּנֵי לְבוּשׁוֹ n.m.p. cstr. (915)–n.m.s.–3 m.s. sf. (528) *his outer garment*

בְּכֶפֶל prep.–n.m.s. cstr. (495) *within the double of*

רִסְנוֹ n.m.s.–3 m.s. sf. (943; LXX θώρακος αὐτοῦ) *his jaw*

מִי יָבוֹא interr. (566)–Qal impf. 3 m.s. (בּוֹא 97) *who can penetrate*

41:6 (Eng.41:14)

דַּלְתֵי n.f. du. cstr. (195) *the doors of*

פָנָיו n.m.p.–3 m.s. sf. (815) *his face*

מִי פִתֵּחַ interr. (566)–Pi. pf. 3 m.s. (פָּתַח I 834) *who can open*

סְבִיבוֹת subst. f.p. as prep. (686) *round about*

שִׁנָּיו n.f.p.–3 m.s. sf. (1042) *his teeth*

אֵימָה n.f.s. (33) *is terror*

41:7 (Eng.41:15)

גַּאֲוָה n.f.s. (144; LXX τὰ ἔγκατα αὐτοῦ) *pride (is made up of)*

אֲפִיקֵי n.m.p. cstr. (67) *rows of*

מָגִנִּים n.m.p. (171) *shields*

סָגוּר Qal pass.ptc. (I 688) *shut up*

חוֹתָם צָר n.m.s. (I 368)–adj. m.s. paus. (I 865; GK 118r) *as with a tight sealed signet*

41:8

אֶחָד בְּאֶחָד num. (25)–prep.–num. (25) *one to another*

יִגַּשׁוּ Qal impf. 3 m.p. (נָגַשׁ 620) *they draw near*

וְרוּחַ conj.–n.m.s. (924) *that air*

לֹא־יָבוֹא neg.–Qal impf. 3 m.s. (97) *cannot come*

בֵינֵיהֶם prep.–3 m.p. sf. (107) *between them*

41:9

אִישׁ־בְּאָחִיהוּ n.m.s. (35)–prep.–n.m.s.–3 m.s. sf. (26) *a man to his brother*

יְדֻבָּקוּ Pu. impf. 3 m.p. paus. (דָּבַק 179) *they are joined*

יִתְלַכְּדוּ Hith. impf. 3 m.p. (לָכַד 539) *they clasp each other*

וְלֹא יִתְפָּרָדוּ conj.–neg.–Hith. impf. 3 m.p. paus. (פָּרַד 825) *and cannot be separated*

41:10 (Eng.41:18)

עֲטִישֹׁתָיו n.f.p.–3 m.s. sf. (743) *his sneezings*

תָּהֶל Hi. impf. 3 f.s. (הָלַל I 237) *flash forth*

אוֹר n.m.s. (21) *light*

וְעֵינָיו conj.–n.f. du.–3 m.s. sf. (744) *and his eyes*

כְּעַפְעַפֵּי־ prep.–n.m.p. cstr. (733) *are like the eyelids of*

שָׁחַר n.m.s. paus. (1007) *the dawn*

41:11

מִפִּיו prep.–n.m.s.–3 m.s. sf. (804) *out of his mouth*

לַפִּידִים n.m.p. (542) *flaming torches*

יַהֲלֹכוּ Qal impf. 3 m.p. (הָלַךְ 229) *go*

כִּידוֹדֵי n.m.p. cstr. (461) *sparks of*

אֵשׁ n.f.s. (77) *fire*

יִתְמַלָּטוּ Hith. impf. 3 m.p. paus. (מָלַט 572) *leap forth*

41:12 (Eng.41:20)

מִנְּחִירָיו prep.–n.m. du.–3 m.s. sf. (638) *out of his nostrils*

יֵצֵא Qal impf. 3 m.s. (יָצָא 422) *comes forth*

עָשָׁן n.m.s. (I 798) *smoke*

כְּדוּד נָפוּחַ prep.–n.m.s. (188)–Qal pass.ptc. (נָפַח 655; LXX καμίνου καιομένης) *as from a boiling pot*

וְאַגְמֹן conj.–n.m.s. (8) *and burning rushes*

41:13

נַפְשׁוֹ n.f.s.–3 m.s. sf. (659) *his breath*

גֶּחָלִים n.f.p. (160) *coals*

תְּלַהֵט Pi. impf. 3 f.s. (לָהַט 529) *kindles*

וְלַהַב conj.–n.m.s. (529) *and a flame*

מִפִּיו prep.–n.m.s.–3 m.s. sf. (804) *from his mouth*

יֵצֵא Qal impf. 3 m.s. (יָצָא 422) *comes forth*

41:14 (Eng. 41:22)

בְּצַוָּארוֹ prep.–n.m.s.–3 m.s. sf. (848) *in his neck*

יָלִין Qal impf. 3 m.s. (לוּן I 533) *abides*

עֹז n.m.s. (738) *strength*

וּלְפָנָיו conj.–prep.–n.m.p.–3 m.s. sf. (815) *and before him*

תָּדוּץ Qal impf. 3 f.s. (דּוּץ 189; LXX τρέχει) *dances*

דְּאָבָה n.f.s. (178; LXX ἀπώλεια) *terror*

41:15

מַפְּלֵי n.m.p. cstr. (658) *the folds of*

בְשָׂרוֹ n.m.s.–3 m.s. sf. (142) *his flesh*

דָּבֵקוּ Qal pf. 3 c.p. (179) *cleave together*

יָצוּק Qal pass.ptc. (יָצַק 427) *firmly cast*

עָלָיו prep.–3 m.s. sf. *upon him*

בַּל־יִמּוֹט neg. (115)–Ni. impf. 3 m.s. (מוֹט 556; GK 156g) *and immovable*

41:16 (Eng.41:24)
לִבּוֹ n.m.s.-3 m.s. sf. (524) *his heart*
יָצוּק Qal pass.ptc. (יָצַק 427) *is hard*
כְּמוֹ־אָבֶן prep.-n.f.s. (6) *as a stone*
וְיָצוּק conj.-v.supra *and hard*
כְּפֶלַח prep.-n.f.s. (812) *as the millstone*
תַּחְתִּית adj. f.s. (1066) *nether*

41:17
מִשֵּׂתוֹ prep.-n.f.s.-3 m.s. sf. (673; GK 76b) *when he raises himself up*
יָגוּרוּ Qal impf. 3 m.p. (גּוּר III 158) *are afraid*
אֵלִים n.m.p. (42) *gods*
מִשְּׁבָרִים prep.-n.m.p. (I 991) *at the crashing*
יִתְחַטָּאוּ Hith. impf. 3 m.p. paus. (חָטָא 306) *they are beside themselves*

41:18 (Eng.41:26)
מַשִּׂיגֵהוּ Hi. ptc. m.s.-3 m.s. sf. (נָשַׂג 673) *though ... reaches him*
חֶרֶב n.f.s. (352) *the sword*
בְּלִי תָקוּם neg. (115)-Qal impf. 3 f.s. (קוּם 877) *it does not avail*
חֲנִית n.f.s. (333) *nor the spear*
מַסָּע n.m.s. (II 652) *the dart*
וְשִׁרְיָה conj.-n.f.s. (1056) *or the javelin*

41:19
יַחְשֹׁב Qal impf. 3 m.s. (חָשַׁב 362) *he counts*
לְתֶבֶן prep.-n.m.s. (1061) *as straw*
בַּרְזֶל n.m.s. (137) *iron*
לְעֵץ רִקָּבוֹן prep.-n.m.s. cstr. (781)-n.m.s. (955) *as rotten wood*
נְחוּשָׁה n.f.s. (639) *bronze*

41:20 (Eng.41:28)
לֹא־יַבְרִיחֶנּוּ neg.-Hi. impf. 3 m.s.-3 m.s. sf. (בָּרַח 137) *cannot make him flee*
בֶּן־קָשֶׁת n.m.s. cstr. (119)-n.f.s. paus. (905; GK 128v) *the arrow*
לְקַשׁ prep.-n.m.s. (905) *to stubble*
נֶהְפְּכוּ־לוֹ Ni. pf. 3 c.p. (הָפַךְ 245)-prep.-3 m.s. sf. *are turned for him*
אַבְנֵי־קָלַע n.f.p. cstr. (6)-n.m.s. paus. (I 887) *slingstones*

41:21
כְּקַשׁ prep.-n.m.s. (905) *as stubble*
נֶחְשְׁבוּ Ni. pf. 3 c.p. (חָשַׁב 362) *are counted*
תוֹתָח n.m.s. (450) *clubs*
וְיִשְׂחַק conj.-Qal impf. 3 m.s. (שָׂחַק 965) *he laughs*
לְרַעַשׁ כִּידוֹן prep.-n.m.s. cstr. (950)-n.m.s. (I 475) *at the rattle of javelins*

41:22
תַּחְתָּיו n.m.p.-3 m.s. sf. (1065) *his underparts*
חַדּוּדֵי חָרֶשׂ adj. m.p. cstr. as subst. (292)-n.m.s. paus. (360; GK 133h) *are like sharp potsherds*
יִרְפַּד Qal impf. 3 m.s. (רָפַד 951) *he spreads himself*
חָרוּץ adj. m.s. (I 358) *like a threshing sledge*
עֲלֵי־טִיט prep. (II 752)-n.m.s. (376) *on the mire*

41:23
יַרְתִּיחַ Hi. impf. 3 m.s. (רָתַח 958) *he makes ... boil*
כַּסִּיר prep.-def.art.-n.m.s. (I 696) *like a pot*
מְצוּלָה n.f.s. (846) *the deep*
יָם n.m.s. (410) *the sea*
יָשִׂים Qal impf. 3 m.s. (שִׂים 962) *he makes*
כַּמֶּרְקָחָה prep.-def.art.-n.f.s. (955) *like a pot of ointment*

41:24 (Eng.41:32)
אַחֲרָיו prep.-3 m.s. sf. (29; LXX τὸν δὲ τάρταρον τῆς ἀβύσσου) *behind him*
יָאִיר Hi. impf. 3 m.s. (אוֹר 21) *he leaves a shining*
נָתִיב n.m.s. (677) *wake (path)*
יַחְשֹׁב Qal impf. 3 m.s. (חָשַׁב 362) *one would think*
תְּהוֹם n.f.s. (1062) *the deep*
לְשֵׂיבָה prep.-n.f.s. (966; LXX εἰς περίπατον) *to be hoary*

41:25
אֵין־עַל־עָפָר subst. cstr. (II 34)-prep.-n.m.s. (779) *there is not upon the earth*
מָשְׁלוֹ n.m.s.-3 m.s. sf. (I 605) *his like*
הֶעָשׂוּ def.art.-Qal pass.ptc. (עָשָׂה I 793; GK 24b,75v,126b) *a creature*
לִבְלִי־חָת prep.-neg. (115)-n.m.s. (I 369) *without fear*

41:26 (Eng.41:34)
אֵת־כָּל־גָּבֹהַּ dir.obj.-n.m.s. cstr. (481)-adj. m.s. (147; GK 16f,117aN) *everything that is high*
יִרְאֶה Qal impf. 3 m.s. (רָאָה 906) *he beholds*
הוּא מֶלֶךְ pers.pr. 3 m.s. (214)-n.m.s. (I 572) *he is king*

עַל־כָּל־בְּנֵי־ prep.-n.m.s. cstr. (481)-n.m.p. cstr. (119; LXX πάντων τῶν ἐν τοῖς ὕδασιν) *over all the sons of*
שָׁחַץ n.m.s. paus. (1006) *pride*

42:1

וַיַּעַן consec.-Qal impf. 3 m.s. (עָנָה I 772) *then answered*
אִיּוֹב pr.n. (33) *Job*
אֶת־יהוה dir.obj.-pr.n. (217) *Yahweh*
וַיֹּאמַר consec.-Qal impf. 3 m.s. (אָמַר 55) *(and said)*

42:2

יָדַעְתָּ Qal pf. 1 c.s. (יָדַע 393; GK 44i) *I know*
כִּי־כֹל conj. (471)-n.m.s. (481) *that all things*
תּוּכָל Qal impf. 2 m.s. (יָכֹל 407) *thou canst do*
וְלֹא־יִבָּצֵר conj.-neg.-Ni. impf. 3 m.s. (בָּצַר 130) *and that no ... can be thwarted*
מִמְּךָ prep.-2 m.s. sf. *of thine*
מְזִמָּה n.f.s. (272; LXX οὐθέν) *purpose*

42:3

מִי זֶה interr. (566)-demons.adj. m.s. (260) *who is this*
מַעְלִים Hi. ptc. m.s. (עָלַם I 761) *that hides*
עֵצָה n.f.s. (420; LXX ῥημάτων) *counsel*
בְּלִי דָעַת neg. (115)-n.f.s. paus. (395) *without knowledge*
לָכֵן הִגַּדְתִּי prep.-adv. (485)-Hi. pf. 1 c.s. (נָגַר 616; LXX+μεγάλα) *therefore I have uttered*
וְלֹא אָבִין conj.-neg.-Qal impf. 1 c.s. (בִּין 106) *what I did not understand*
נִפְלָאוֹת מִמֶּנִּי Ni. ptc. f.p. (פָּלָא 810; GK 133d) -prep.-1 c.s. sf. *things too wonderful for me*
וְלֹא אֵדָע conj.-neg.-Qal impf. 1 c.s. paus. (יָדַע 393; GK 156f) *which I did not know*

42:4

שְׁמַע־נָא Qal impv. 2 m.s. (1033)-part.of entreaty (609) *hear (I pray thee)*
וְאָנֹכִי אֲדַבֵּר conj.-pers.pr. 1 c.s. (59)-Pi. impf. 1 c.s. (180) *and I will speak*
אֶשְׁאָלְךָ Qal impf. 1 c.s.-2 m.s. sf. (שָׁאַל 981) *I will question you*
וְהוֹדִיעֵנִי conj.-Hi. impv. 2 m.s.-1 c.s. sf. (יָדַע 393) *and you declare to me*

42:5

לְשֵׁמַע־ prep.-n.m.s. cstr. (1034) *by the hearing of*
אֹזֶן n.f.s. (23) *the ear*
שְׁמַעְתִּיךָ Qal pf. 1 c.s.-2 m.s. sf. (1033) *I had heard of thee*
וְעַתָּה conj.-adv. (773) *but now*
עֵינִי n.f.s.-1 c.s. sf. (744) *my eye*
רָאָתְךָ Qal pf. 3 f.s.-2 m.s. sf. (רָאָה 906; GK 75mm) *sees thee*

42:6

עַל־כֵּן prep. adv. (485) *therefore*
אֶמְאַס Qal impf. 1 c.s. (מָאַס 549) *I despise myself*
וְנִחַמְתִּי conj.-Ni. pf. 1 c.s. (נָחַם 636) *and repent*
עַל־עָפָר prep.-n.m.s. (779) *in dust*
וָאֵפֶר conj.-n.m.s. (68) *and ashes*

42:7

וַיְהִי consec.-Qal impf. 3 m.s. (הָיָה 224) *(and it was)*
אַחַר דִּבֶּר prep. (29)-Pi. pf. 3 m.s. (180; GK 164d) *after ... had spoken*
יהוה pr.n. (217) *Yahweh*
אֶת־הַדְּבָרִים dir.obj.-def.art.-n.m.s. (182) *words*
הָאֵלֶּה def.art.-demons.adj. c.p. (41) *these*
אֶל־אִיּוֹב prep.-pr.n. (33) *to Job*
וַיֹּאמֶר consec.-Qal impf. 3 m.s. (55) *and said*
יהוה v.supra *Yahweh*
אֶל־אֱלִיפַז prep.-pr.n. (45) *to Eliphaz*
הַתֵּימָנִי def.art.-pr.n. gent. (412) *the Temanite*
חָרָה Qal pf. 3 m.s. (354) *is kindled*
אַפִּי n.m.s.-1 c.s. sf. (I 60) *my wrath*
בְךָ prep.-2 m.s. sf. *against you*
וּבִשְׁנֵי conj.-prep.-num. cstr. (1040) *and against two of*
רֵעֶיךָ n.m.p.-2 m.s. sf. (945) *your friends*
כִּי לֹא דִבַּרְתֶּם conj.-neg.-Pi. pf. 2 m.p. (180) *for you have not spoken*
אֵלַי prep.-1 c.s. sf. *of me*
נְכוֹנָה Ni. ptc. f.s. (כּוּן I 465) *what is right*
כְּעַבְדִּי prep.-n.m.s.-1 c.s. sf. (713) *as my servant*
אִיּוֹב pr.n. (33) *Job*

42:8

וְעַתָּה conj.-adv. (773) *now therefore*
קְחוּ־לָכֶם Qal impv. 2 m.p. (לָקַח 542)-prep.-2 m.p. sf. *take (to you)*
שִׁבְעָה־פָרִים num. f.s. (988)-n.m.p. (830) *seven bulls*
וְשִׁבְעָה אֵילִים conj.-v.supra-n.m.p. (I 17) *and seven rams*
וּלְכוּ conj.-Qal impv. 2 m.p. (הָלַךְ 229) *and go*

אֶל־עַבְדִּי prep.-n.m.s.-1 c.s. sf. (713) *to my servant*
אִיּוֹב pr.n. (33) *Job*
וְהַעֲלִיתֶם conj.-Hi. pf. 2 m.p. (עָלָה 748) *and offer up*
עוֹלָה n.f.s. (I 750) *a burnt offering*
בַּעַדְכֶם prep.-2 m.p. sf. (126) *for yourselves*
וְאִיּוֹב conj.-pr.n. (33) *and Job*
עַבְדִּי v.supra *my servant*
יִתְפַּלֵּל Hith. impf. 3 m.s. (פָּלַל 813) *shall pray*
עֲלֵיכֶם prep.-2 m.p. sf. *for you*
כִּי אִם־פָּנָיו conj. (471)-hypoth.part. (49)-n.m.p.-3 m.s. sf. (815; GK 163d) *for his face*
אֶשָּׂא Qal impf. 1 c.s. (נָשָׂא 669) *I will lift up*
לְבִלְתִּי עֲשׂוֹת prep.-neg. (116)-Qal inf.cstr. (עָשָׂה I 793) *not to deal*
עִמָּכֶם prep.-2 m.p. sf. (767) *with you*
נְבָלָה n.f.s. (615) *according to your folly*
כִּי לֹא דִבַּרְתֶּם conj. (471)-neg.-Pi. pf. 2 m.p. (180) *for you have not spoken*
אֵלַי prep.-1 c.s. sf. *of me*
נְכוֹנָה Ni. ptc. f.s. (כּוּן 465) *what is right*
כְּעַבְדִּי prep.-n.m.s.-1 c.s. sf. (713; LXX κατὰ τοῦ θεράποντός μου) *as my servant*
אִיּוֹב pr.n. (33) *Job*

42:9

וַיֵּלְכוּ consec.-Qal impf. 3 m.p. (הָלַךְ 229) *so went*
אֱלִיפַז pr.n. (45) *Eliphaz*
הַתֵּמָנִי def.art.-adj.gent. pr.n. (412) *the Temanite*
וּבִלְדַּד conj.-pr.n. (115) *and Bildad*
הַשּׁוּחִי def.art.-adj.gent. pr.n. (1001) *the Shuhite*
צֹפַר pr.n. (862) *(and) Zophar*
הַנַּעֲמָתִי def.art.-adj.gent. pr.n. (654) *the Naamathite*
וַיַּעֲשׂוּ consec.-Qal impf. 3 m.p. (עָשָׂה I 793) *and did*
כַּאֲשֶׁר prep.-rel. (81) *what*
דִּבֶּר Pi. pf. 3 m.s. (180) *had told*
אֲלֵיהֶם prep.-3 m.p. sf. *them*
יהוה pr.n. (217) *Yahweh*
וַיִּשָּׂא consec.-Qal impf. 3 m.s. (נָשָׂא 669) *and lifted*
יהוה pr.n. 217) *Yahweh*
אֶת־פְּנֵי dir.obj.-n.m.p. cstr. (815) *the face of*
אִיּוֹב pr.n. (33) *Job*

42:10

וַיהוה conj.-pr.n. (217) *and Yahweh*
שָׁב Qal pf. 3 m.s. (שׁוּב 996) *restored*
אֶת־שְׁבִית dir.obj.-n.f.s. cstr. (986) *the fortunes of*
אִיּוֹב pr.n. (33) *Job*
בְּהִתְפַּלְלוֹ prep.-Hith. inf.cstr.-3 m.s. sf. (פָּלַל 813) *when he had prayed*
בְּעַד רֵעֵהוּ prep. (126)-n.m.s.-3 m.s. sf. (945; GK 91k) *for his friends*
וַיֹּסֶף consec.-Hi. impf. 3 m.s. (יָסַף 414) *and added*
יהוה pr.n. (217) *Yahweh*
אֶת־כָּל־אֲשֶׁר dir.obj.-n.m.s. cstr. (481)-rel. (81) *everything which*
לְאִיּוֹב prep.-pr.n. (33) *belonged to Job*
לְמִשְׁנֶה prep.-n.m.s. (1041) *twice (double)*

42:11

וַיָּבֹאוּ consec.-Qal impf. 3 m.p. (בּוֹא 97) *then came*
אֵלָיו prep.-3 m.s. sf. *to him*
כָּל־אֶחָיו n.m.s. cstr. (481)-n.m.p.-3 m.s. sf. (26) *all his brothers*
וְכָל־אַחְיֹתָיו conj.-v.supra-n.f.p.-3 m.s. sf. (27) *and all his sisters*
וְכָל־יֹדְעָיו v.supra-Qal act.ptc. m.p.-3 m.s. sf. (393 יָדַע) *and all who had known him*
לְפָנִים prep.-n.m.p. (815) *before*
וַיֹּאכְלוּ consec.-Qal impf. 3 m.p. (אָכַל 37; LXX+ καὶ πιόντες) *and ate*
עִמּוֹ prep.-3 m.s. sf. (767) *with him*
לֶחֶם n.m.s. (536) *bread*
בְּבֵיתוֹ prep.-n.m.s.-3 m.s. sf. (108) *in his house*
וַיָּנֻדוּ consec.-Qal impf. 3 m.p. (נוּד 626) *and they showed sympathy*
לוֹ prep.-3 m.s. sf. *to him*
וַיְנַחֲמוּ consec.-Pi. impf. 3 m.p. (נָחַם 636) *and comforted*
אֹתוֹ dir.obj.-3 m.s. sf. *him*
עַל כָּל־הָרָעָה prep.-n.m.s. cstr. (481)-def.art.-n.f.s. (949) *for all the evil*
אֲשֶׁר־הֵבִיא rel. (81)-Hi. pf. 3 m.s. (בּוֹא 97) *that had brought*
יהוה pr.n. (217) *Yahweh*
עָלָיו prep.-3 m.s. sf. *upon him*
וַיִּתְּנוּ־ consec.-Qal impf. 3 m.p. (נָתַן 678) *and gave*
לוֹ prep.-3 m.s. sf. *to him*
אִישׁ n.m.s. (35) *each*
קְשִׂיטָה אֶחָת n.f.s. (903)-num. f.s. (25) *a piece of money (qesitah)*
וְאִישׁ conj.-v.supra *and each*
נֶזֶם זָהָב n.m.s. cstr. (633)-n.m.s. (262) *a ring of gold*

אֶחָד num. m.s. (25) *one*

42:12

ויהוה conj.-pr.n. (217) *and Yahweh*
בֵּרַךְ Pi. pf. 3 m.s. (בָּרַךְ 138) *blessed*
אֶת־אַחֲרִית dir.obj.-n.f.s. cstr. (31) *the latter days of*
אִיּוֹב pr.n. (33) *Job*
מֵרֵאשִׁתוֹ prep.-n.f.s.-3 m.s. sf. (912) *more than his beginning*
וַיְהִי־לוֹ consec.-Qal impf. 3 m.s. (הָיָה 224) -prep.-3 m.s. sf. *and he had*
אַרְבָּעָה עָשָׂר num. f.s. (I 916)-num. (797) *fourteen*
אֶלֶף n.m.s. (II 48) *thousand*
צֹאן n.f.s. (838) *sheep*
וְשֵׁשֶׁת conj.-num. f. (995) *and six*
אֲלָפִים n.m.p. (II 48) *thousand*
גְּמַלִּים n.m.p. (168) *camels*
וְאֶלֶף־ conj.-n.m.s. cstr. (II 48) *and a thousand*
צֶמֶד n.m.s. cstr. (855) *yoke of*
בָּקָר n.m.s. (133) *oxen*
וְאֶלֶף v.supra-v.supra *and a thousand*
אֲתוֹנוֹת n.f.p. (87) *she-asses*

42:13

וַיְהִי־לוֹ consec.-Qal impf. 3 m.s. (הָיָה 224) -prep.-3 m.s. sf. *and he had*
שִׁבְעָנָה num. f.s. (I 987; GK 97c) *seven*
בָנִים n.m.p. (119) *sons*
וְשָׁלוֹשׁ conj.-num. (1025) *and three*
בָּנוֹת n.f.p. (I 123) *daughters*

42:14

וַיִּקְרָא consec.-Qal impf. 3 m.s. (קָרָא 894) *and he called*
שֵׁם־ n.m.s. cstr. (1027) *the name of*
הָאַחַת def.art.-num. f.s. (25) *the first*
יְמִימָה pr.n. f. (410) *Jemimah*
וְשֵׁם conj.-v.supra *and the name of*
הַשֵּׁנִית def.art.-adj. num.ord. f. (1041) *the second*
קְצִיעָה pr.n. f. (II 893) *Keziah*
וְשֵׁם v.supra *and the name of*
הַשְּׁלִישִׁית def.art.-adj. num.ord. f. (1026) *the third*

קֶרֶן הַפּוּךְ pr.n. f. (902) *Keren-happuch*

42:15

וְלֹא נִמְצָא conj.-neg.-Ni. pf. 3 m.s. (מָצָא 592; GK 145o) *and there were not found*
נָשִׁים n.f.p. (61) *women*
יָפוֹת adj. f.p. (421) *so fair*
כִּבְנוֹת prep.-n.f.p. cstr. (I 123) *as the daughters of*
אִיּוֹב pr.n. (33) *Job*
בְּכָל־הָאָרֶץ prep.-n.m.s. cstr. (481)-def.art.-n.f.s. (75) *in all the land*
וַיִּתֵּן consec.-Qal impf. 3 m.s. (נָתַן 678) *and ... gave*
לָהֶם prep.-3 m.p. sf. (GK 135o) *to them*
אֲבִיהֶם n.m.s.-3 m.p. sf. (33) *their father*
נַחֲלָה n.f.s. (635) *inheritance*
בְּתוֹךְ אֲחֵיהֶם prep.-n.m.s. cstr. (1063)-n.m.p.-3 m.p. sf. (26) *among their brothers*

42:16

וַיְחִי consec.-Qal impf. 3 m.s. (חָיָה 310) *and lived*
אִיּוֹב pr.n. (33) *Job*
אַחֲרֵי־זֹאת prep. (29)-demons.adj. f.s. (260) *after this*
מֵאָה n.f.s. (547; LXX ἔτη διακόσια τεσσαράκοντα ὀκτώ) *a hundred*
וְאַרְבָּעִים conj.-num. m.p. (917) *and forty*
שָׁנָה n.f.s. (1040) *years*
וַיַּרְא consec.-Qal impf. 3 m.s. (רָאָה 906; GK 75t; Q וַיִּרְאֶה) *and saw*
אֶת־בָּנָיו dir.obj.-n.m.p.-3 m.s. sf. (119) *his sons*
וְאֶת־בְּנֵי בָנָיו conj.-dir.obj.-n.m.p. cstr. (119) -v.supra *and his sons' sons*
אַרְבָּעָה num. f.s. (916) *four*
דֹּרוֹת n.m.p. (189) *generations*

42:17

וַיָּמָת consec.-Qal impf. 3 m.s. (מוּת 559) *and died*
אִיּוֹב pr.n. (33) *Job*
זָקֵן adj. m.s. (278) *an old man*
וּשְׂבַע conj.-adj. m.s. cstr. (960) *and full of*
יָמִים n.m.p. (398) *days*

Psalms

1:1

אַשְׁרֵי n.f.p. cstr. (80) ***blessed***
הָאִישׁ def.art.-n.m.s. (35) ***the man***
אֲשֶׁר rel. (81) ***who***
לֹא הָלַךְ Qal pf. 3 m.s. (229) ***walks not***
בַּעֲצַת prep.-n.f.s. cstr. (420) ***in the counsel of***
רְשָׁעִים adj. m.p. (957) ***the wicked***
וּבְדֶרֶךְ conj.-prep.-n.m.s. cstr. (202) ***and in the way of***
חַטָּאִים adj. m.p. (308) ***sinners***
לֹא עָמָד neg.-Qal pf. 3 m.s. paus. (עָמַד 763) ***stands not***
וּבְמוֹשַׁב conj.-prep.-n.m.s. cstr. (44) ***and in the seat of***
לֵצִים Qal act.ptc. m.p. (לִיץ 539) ***scoffers***
לֹא יָשָׁב neg.-Qal pf. 3 m.s. paus. (יָשַׁב 442) ***sits not***

1:2

כִּי אִם conj.-hypoth.part. (474; GK 163a) ***but (if)***
בְּתוֹרַת prep.-n.f.s. cstr. (435) ***in the law of***
יהוה pr.n. (217) ***Yahweh***
חֶפְצוֹ n.m.s.-3 m.s. sf. (343) ***his delight***
וּבְתוֹרָתוֹ conj.-prep.-n.f.s.-3 m.s. sf. (435) ***and on his law***
יֶהְגֶּה Qal impf. 3 m.s. (הָגָה 211) ***he meditates***
יוֹמָם adv. (401) ***day***
וָלָיְלָה conj.-n.m.s. paus. (538) ***and night***

1:3

וְהָיָה conj.-Qal pf. 3 m.s. (224; GK 16g) ***and he is***
כְּעֵץ prep.-n.m.s. (781) ***like a tree***
שָׁתוּל Qal pass.ptc. (שָׁתַל 1060) ***planted***
עַל־פַּלְגֵי prep. (GK 119cc)-n.m.p. cstr. (I 811) ***by streams of***
מָיִם n.m.p. paus. (565) ***water***
אֲשֶׁר פִּרְיוֹ rel. (81)-n.m.s.-3 m.s. sf. (826) ***that its fruit***
יִתֵּן Qal impf. 3 m.s. (נָתַן 678; GK 107g) ***yields***
בְּעִתּוֹ prep.-n.f.s.-3 m.s. sf. (773) ***in its season***
וְעָלֵהוּ conj.-n.m.s.-3 m.s. sf. (750) ***and its leaf***
לֹא־יִבּוֹל neg.-Qal impf. 3 m.s. (נָבֵל 615; GK 47h) ***does not wither***
וְכֹל אֲשֶׁר conj.-n.m.s. (481)-rel. (81) ***and all that***
יַעֲשֶׂה Qal impf. 3 m.s. (עָשָׂה I 793) ***he does***
יַצְלִיחַ Hi. impf. 3 m.s. (צָלַח II 852) ***he prospers***

1:4

לֹא־כֵן neg.-adv. (485) ***not so***
הָרְשָׁעִים def.art.-n.m.p. (957) ***the wicked***
כִּי אִם־ conj.-hypoth.part. (474) ***but***

כַּמֹּץ prep.-def.art.-n.m.s. (558) *like chaff*
אֲשֶׁר־תִּדְּפֶנּוּ rel. (81)-Qal impf. 3 f.s.-3 m.s. sf. (623 נָדַף) *which drives away*
רוּחַ n.f.s. (924) *the wind* (LXX+ἀπὸ προσώπου τῆς γῆς)

1:5

עַל־כֵּן prep.-adv. (485) *therefore*
לֹא־יָקֻמוּ neg.-Qal impf. 3 m.p. (קוּם 877) *will not stand*
רְשָׁעִים adj. m.p. (957) *the wicked*
בַּמִּשְׁפָּט prep.-def.art.-n.m.s. (1048) *in the judgment*
וְחַטָּאִים conj.-adj. m.p. (308) *nor sinners*
בַּעֲדַת prep.-n.f.s. cstr. (II 417; LXX ἐν βουλῇ) *in the congregation of*
צַדִּיקִים adj. m.p. (843) *the righteous*

1:6

כִּי־יוֹדֵעַ conj. (471)-Qal act.ptc. (יָדַע 393) *for knows*
יהוה pr.n. (217) *Yahweh*
דֶּרֶךְ n.m.s. cstr. (202) *the way of*
צַדִּיקִים adj. m.p. (843) *the righteous*
וְדֶרֶךְ conj.-v.supra *but the way of*
רְשָׁעִים adj. m.p. (957) *the wicked*
תֹּאבֵד Qal impf. 3 f.s. (אָבַד 1; GK 68c) *will perish*

2:1

לָמָּה prep.-interr. (552) *why*
רָגְשׁוּ Qal pf. 3 c.p. (רָגַשׁ 921; GK 106,l) *do conspire*
גוֹיִם n.m.p. (156) *nations*
וּלְאֻמִּים conj.-n.m.p. (522) *and the peoples*
יֶהְגּוּ־רִיק Qal impf. 3 m.p. (הָגָה 211)-n.m.s. (938) *plot in vain*

2:2

יִתְיַצְּבוּ Hith. impf. 3 m.p. (יָצַב 426) *set themselves*
מַלְכֵי־אֶרֶץ n.m.p. cstr. (I 572)-n.f.s. (75; GK 126h) *kings of earth*
וְרוֹזְנִים conj.-Qal act.ptc. m.p. (רָזַן 931) *and rulers*
נוֹסְדוּ־יָחַד Ni. pf. 3 c.p. (יָסַד 413)-adv. paus. (403) *take counsel together*
עַל־יהוה prep. (GK 119dd)-pr.n. (217) *against Yahweh*
וְעַל־מְשִׁיחוֹ conj.-prep.-n.m.s.-3 m.s. sf. (603; LXX+διάψαλμα) *and his anointed*

2:3

נְנַתְּקָה Pi. impf. 1 c.p.-coh.he (נָתַק 683; GK 108b) *let us burst asunder*
אֶת־מוֹסְרוֹתֵימוֹ dir.obj.-n.f.p.-3 m.p. sf. (64; GK 91,l) *their bonds*
וְנַשְׁלִיכָה conj.-Hi. impf.-coh.he (שָׁלַךְ 1020) *and let us cast*
מִמֶּנּוּ prep.-1 c.p. sf. *(from us)*
עֲבֹתֵימוֹ n.m.p.-3 m.p. sf. (721; GK 91,l) *their cords*

2:4

יוֹשֵׁב Qal act.ptc. (יָשַׁב 442) *he who sits*
בַּשָּׁמַיִם prep.-def.art.-n.m. du. (1029; GK 126h) *in the heavens*
יִשְׂחָק Qal impf. 3 m.s. (שָׂחַק 965) *laughs*
אֲדֹנָי n.m.p.-1 c.s. sf. (10) *the Lord*
יִלְעַג־ Qal impf. 3 m.s. (לָעַג 541) *has in derision*
לָמוֹ prep.-3 m.p. sf. *them*

2:5

אָז adv. (23) *then*
יְדַבֵּר Pi. impf. 3 m.s. (דָּבַר 180) *he will speak*
אֵלֵימוֹ prep.-3 m.p. sf. *to them*
בְאַפּוֹ prep.-n.m.s.-3 m.s. sf. (I 60) *in his wrath*
וּבַחֲרוֹנוֹ conj.-prep.-n.m.s.-3 m.s. sf. (354) *and in his fury*
יְבַהֲלֵמוֹ Pi. impf. 3 m.s.-3 m.p. sf. (בָּהַל 96) *he terrifies them*

2:6

וַאֲנִי conj.-pers.pr. 1 c.s. (58; GK 135a,154b) *and I*
נָסַכְתִּי Qal pf. 1 c.s. (נָסַךְ III 651) *have set*
מַלְכִּי n.m.s.-1 c.s. sf. (I 572) *my king*
עַל־צִיּוֹן prep.-pr.n. (851) *on Zion*
הַר־קָדְשִׁי n.m.s. cstr. (249)-adj. m.s.-1 c.s. sf. (872; GK 135n) *my holy hill*

2:7

אֲסַפְּרָה Pi. impf. 1 c.s.-coh.he (סָפַר 707) *I will tell*
אֶל חֹק יהוה prep.-n.m.s. cstr. (349)-pr.n. (217) *of the decree of Yahweh*
אָמַר אֵלַי Qal pf. 3 m.s. (55)-prep.-1 c.s. sf. *he said to me*
בְּנִי אַתָּה n.m.s.-1 c.s. sf. (119)-pers.pr. 2 m.s. (61) *you are my son*
אֲנִי הַיּוֹם pers.pr. 1 c.s. (58)-def.art.-n.m.s. (398) *today I*
יְלִדְתִּיךָ Qal pf. 1 c.s.-2 m.s. (יָלַד 408; GK 44d, 69s) *have begotten you*

2:8

שְׁאַל מִמֶּנִּי Qal impv. 2 m.s. (שָׁאַל 981)–prep.–1 c.s. sf. *ask of me*

וְאֶתְּנָה conj.–Qal impf. 1 c.s.–coh.he (נָתַן 678) *and I will make*

גוֹיִם n.m.p. (156) *nations*

נַחֲלָתֶךָ n.f.s.–2 m.s. sf. paus. (635) *your heritage*

וַאֲחֻזָּתְךָ conj.–n.f.s.–2 m.s. sf. (28) *and your possession*

אַפְסֵי־אָרֶץ n.m.p. cstr. (67)–n.f.s. paus. (75) *the ends of the earth*

2:9

תְּרֹעֵם Qal impf. 2 m.s.–3 m.p. sf. (רָעַע II 949; LXX ποιμανεῖς) *you shall break them*

בְּשֵׁבֶט prep.–n.m.s. cstr. (986) *with a rod of*

בַּרְזֶל n.m.s. (137) *iron*

כִּכְלִי יוֹצֵר prep.–n.m.s. cstr. (479)–Qal act.ptc. (427) *like a potter's vessel*

תְּנַפְּצֵם Pi. impf. 2 m.s.–3 m.p. sf. (נָפַץ I 658) *dash them in pieces*

2:10

וְעַתָּה conj. (GK 154b)–adv. (773) *now therefore*

מְלָכִים n.m.p. (I 572; GK 126h) *O kings*

הַשְׂכִּילוּ Hi. impv. 2 m.p. (שָׂכַל 968) *be wise*

הִוָּסְרוּ Ni. impv. 2 m.p. (יָסַר 415) *be warned*

שֹׁפְטֵי אָרֶץ Qal act.ptc. m.p. cstr. (שָׁפַט 1047) –n.f.s. paus. (75) *O rulers of earth*

2:11

עִבְדוּ Qal impv. 2 m.p. (עָבַד 712) *serve*

אֶת־יהוה dir.obj.–pr.n. (217) *Yahweh*

בְּיִרְאָה prep.–n.f.s. (432) *with fear*

וְגִילוּ conj.–Qal impv. 2 m.p. (גִּיל 162) *and rejoice*

בִּרְעָדָה prep.–n.f.s. (944) *with trembling*

2:12

נַשְּׁקוּ־ Pi. impv. 2 m.p. (נָשַׁק 676) *kiss*

בַר n.m.s. (135) *a son*

פֶּן־יֶאֱנַף hypoth.part. (814)–Qal impf. 3 m.s. (אָנַף 60) *lest he be angry*

וְתֹאבְדוּ conj.–Qal impf. 2 m.p. (אָבַד 1) *and you perish*

דֶרֶךְ n.m.s. (202; GK 118gN) *in the way*

כִּי־יִבְעַר conj.–Qal impf. 3 m.s. (בָּעַר 128) *for is kindled*

כִּמְעַט prep.–subst. (589) *quickly*

אַפּוֹ n.m.s.–3 m.s. sf. (I 60) *his wrath*

אַשְׁרֵי n.m.p. cstr. (80) *blessed*

כָּל־חוֹסֵי n.m.s. cstr. (481)–Qal act.ptc. m.p. cstr. (340 חָסָה; GK 130a) *all who take refuge*

בוֹ prep.–3 m.s. sf. *in him*

3:1

מִזְמוֹר n.m.s. (274) *a psalm*

לְדָוִד prep. (GK 129c)–pr.n. (187) *to David*

בְּבָרְחוֹ prep.–Qal inf.cstr.–3 m.s. sf. (בָּרַח 137) *when he fled*

מִפְּנֵי prep.–n.m.p. cstr. (815) *from*

אַבְשָׁלוֹם pr.n. (5) *Absalom*

בְּנוֹ n.m.s.–3 m.s. sf. (119) *his son*

3:2

יהוה pr.n. (217) *O Yahweh*

מָה־ interr. (552) *how*

רַבּוּ Qal pf. 3 c.p. (רָבַב I 912; GK 67ee) *many are*

צָרָי n.m.p.–1 c.s. sf. (III 865) *my foes*

רַבִּים adj. m.p. (I 912) *many*

קָמִים Qal act.ptc. m.p. (קוּם 877) *are rising*

עָלָי prep.–1 c.s. sf. paus. *against me*

3:3

רַבִּים adj. m.p. (I 912) *many*

אֹמְרִים Qal act.ptc. m.p. (55) *are saying*

לְנַפְשִׁי prep.–n.f.s.–1 c.s. sf. (659) *of me*

אֵין יְשׁוּעָתָה subst. cstr. (II 34; GK 152nN)–n.f.s. (447; GK 90g) *there is no help*

לּוֹ prep.–3 m.s. sf. *for him*

בֵאלֹהִים prep.–n.m.p. (43) *in God*

סֶלָה interj. from Qal impv. 2 m.s. (סָלַל 699) *Selah*

3:4

וְאַתָּה conj.–pers.pr. 2 m.s. (61) *but thou*

יהוה pr.n. (217) *O Yahweh*

מָגֵן n.m.s. (171) *a shield*

בַּעֲדִי prep.–1 c.s. sf. (126) *about me*

כְּבוֹדִי n.m.s.–1 c.s. sf. (458) *my glory*

וּמֵרִים conj.–Hi. ptc. (רוּם 926) *and the lifter*

רֹאשִׁי n.m.s.–1 c.s. sf. (910) *of my head*

3:5

קוֹלִי n.m.s.–1 c.s. sf. (876; GK 144m) *my voice*

אֶל־יהוה prep.–pr.n. (217) *to Yahweh*

אֶקְרָא Qal impf. 1 c.s. (קָרָא 894) *I will lift*

וַיַּעֲנֵנִי consec.–Qal impf. 3 m.s.–1 c.s. sf. (עָנָה I 772) *and he answers me*

מֵהַר קָדְשׁוֹ prep.–n.m.s. cstr. (249)–n.m.s.–3 m.s. sf. (871) *from his holy hill*

סֶלָה interj. (699) *Selah*

3:6

שָׁכַבְתִּי אֲנִי pers.pr. 1 c.s. (58)-Qal pf. 1 c.s. (שָׁכַב 1011) *I lie down*

וָאִישָׁנָה consec.-Qal impf. 1 c.s. (יָשֵׁן 445; GK 49e) *and sleep*

הֱקִיצוֹתִי Hi. pf. 1 c.s. (קִיץ 884) *I wake again*

כִּי יהוה conj. (471)-pr.n. (217) *for Yahweh*

יִסְמְכֵנִי Qal impf. 3 m.s.-1 c.s. sf. (סָמַךְ 701) *sustains me*

3:7

לֹא־אִירָא neg.-Qal impf. 1 c.s. (יָרֵא 431) *I am not afraid*

מֵרִבְבוֹת prep.-n.f.p. cstr. (914) *of ten thousands of*

עָם n.m.s. (I 766) *people*

אֲשֶׁר סָבִיב rel. (81)-subst. (686) *who round about*

שָׁתוּ Qal pf. 3 c.p. (1011) *have set themselves*

עָלָי prep.-1 c.s. sf. paus. *against me*

3:8

קוּמָה Qal impv. 2 m.s.-vol.he (קוּם 877; GK 72s) *arise*

יהוה pr.n. (217) *O Yahweh*

הוֹשִׁיעֵנִי Hi. impv. 2 m.s.-1 c.s. sf. (יָשַׁע 446) *deliver me*

אֱלֹהַי n.m.p.-1 c.s. sf. (43) *O my God*

כִּי־הִכִּיתָ conj. (471)-Hi. pf. 2 m.s. (נָכָה 645) *for thou dost smite*

אֶת־כָּל־ dir.obj.-n.m.s. cstr. (481) *all*

אֹיְבַי Qal act.ptc. m.p.-1 c.s. sf. (אָיַב 33) *my enemies*

לֶחִי n.m.s. paus. (I 534; GK 117,ll) *on the cheek*

שִׁנֵּי n.f. du. cstr. (I 1042) *the teeth of*

רְשָׁעִים adj. m.p. (957) *the wicked*

שִׁבַּרְתָּ Pi. pf. 2 m.s. (שָׁבַר 990) *thou dost break*

3:9

ליהוה prep.-pr.n. (217) *to Yahweh*

הַיְשׁוּעָה def.art.-n.f.s. (447) *deliverance*

עַל־עַמְּךָ prep.-n.m.s.-2 m.s. sf. (I 766) *upon thy people*

בִרְכָתֶךָ n.f.s.-2 m.s. sf. (139) *thy blessing*

סֶלָה interj. (699) *Selah*

4:1

לַמְנַצֵּחַ prep.-def.art.-Pi. ptc. (נָצַח I 663) *to the choirmaster*

בִּנְגִינוֹת prep.-n.f.p. (618; GK 124f) *with stringed instruments*

מִזְמוֹר n.m.s. (274) *a psalm*

לְדָוִד prep.-pr.n. (187) *to David*

4:2

בְּקָרְאִי prep.-Qal inf.cstr.-1 c.s. sf. (קָרָא I 894) *when I call*

עֲנֵנִי Qal impv. 2 m.s.-1 c.s. sf. (עָנָה I 772) *answer me*

אֱלֹהֵי צִדְקִי n.m.p. cstr. (43)-n.m.s.-1 c.s. sf. (841) *O God of my right*

בַּצָּר prep.-def.art.-n.m.s. (II 865) *in distress*

הִרְחַבְתָּ Hi. pf. 2 m.s. (רָחַב 931) *thou hast given room*

לִּי prep.-1 c.s. sf. *to me*

חָנֵּנִי Qal impv. 2 m.s.-1 c.s. sf. (חָנַן I 335) *be gracious to me*

וּשְׁמַע conj.-Qal impv. 2 m.s. (1033) *and hear*

תְּפִלָּתִי n.f.s.-1 c.s. sf. (813) *my prayer*

4:3

בְּנֵי אִישׁ n.m.p. cstr. (119)-n.m.s. (35) *O men*

עַד־מֶה prep. (III 723)-interr. (552; GK 37e) *how long*

כְבוֹדִי n.m.s.-1 c.s. sf. (458) *my honor*

לִכְלִמָּה prep.-n.f.s. (484) *to shame*

תֶּאֱהָבוּן Qal impf. 2 m.p. (אָהַב 12; GK 57m) *will you love*

רִיק n.m.s. (938) *vain words*

תְּבַקְשׁוּ Pi. impf. 2 m.p. (בָּקַשׁ 134; GK 156d) *seek*

כָזָב n.m.s. (469) *after lies*

סֶלָה interj. (699) *Selah*

4:4

וּדְעוּ conj. (GK 154b)-Qal impv. 2 m.p. (יָדַע 393) *but know*

הִפְלָה conj.-Hi. pf. 3 m.s. (פָּלָה 811) *that has set apart*

יהוה pr.n. (217) *Yahweh*

חָסִיד adj. m.s. (339) *the godly*

לוֹ prep.-3 m.s. sf. *for himself*

יהוה pr.n. (217) *Yahweh*

יִשְׁמַע Qal impf. 3 m.s. (שָׁמַע 1033) *hears*

בְּקָרְאִי prep.-Qal inf.cstr.-1 c.s. sf. (קָרָא I 894) *when I call*

אֵלָיו prep.-3 m.s. sf. *to him*

4:5

רִגְזוּ Qal impv. 2 m.p. (רָגַז 919) *be angry* (lit. *come quivering in fear, awe*)

וְאַל־תֶּחֱטָאוּ conj.-neg.-Qal impf. 2 m.p. (חָטָא 306) *but sin not*

אִמְרוּ Qal impv. 2 m.p. (55) *commune*

בִלְבַבְכֶם prep.-n.m.s.-2 m.p. sf. (523) *with your own hearts*

עַל־מִשְׁכַּבְכֶם prep.-n.m.s.-2 m.p. sf. (1012) *on your beds*
וְדֹמּוּ conj.-Qal impv. 2 m.p. (דָּמַם I 198) *and be silent*
סֶלָה interj. (699) *Selah*

4:6

זִבְחוּ Qal impv. 2 m.p. (זָבַח 256) *offer*
זִבְחֵי־צֶדֶק n.m.p. cstr. (257)-n.m.s. (841) *right sacrifices*
וּבִטְחוּ conj.-Qal impv. 2 m.p. (בָּטַח 105) *and put your trust*
אֶל־יהוה prep.-pr.n. (217) *in Yahweh*

4:7

רַבִּים adj. m.p. (I 912) *there are many*
אֹמְרִים Qal act.ptc. m.p. (אָמַר 55) *who say*
מִי־ interr. (566) *O that*
יַרְאֵנוּ Hi. impf. 1 c.p. (רָאָה 906) *we might see*
טוֹב adj. m.s. (II 373) *some good*
נְסָה־עָלֵינוּ Qal impv. 2 m.s. (נָשָׂא 669; GK 76b)-prep.-1 c.p. sf. *lift up upon us*
אוֹר פָּנֶיךָ n.m.s. cstr. (21)-n.m.p.-2 m.s. sf. (815) *the light of thy countenance*
יהוה pr.n. (217) *O Yahweh*

4:8

נָתַתָּה Qal pf. 2 m.s. (נָתַן 678) *thou hast put*
שִׂמְחָה n.f.s. (970) *joy*
בְלִבִּי prep.-n.m.s.-1 c.s. sf. (524) *in my heart*
מֵעֵת prep.-n.f.s. cstr. (773; GK 133eN;155,1) *beyond the time of*
דְּגָנָם n.m.s.-3 m.p. sf. (186) *their grain*
וְתִירוֹשָׁם conj.-n.m.s.-3 m.p. sf. (440) *and their wine*
רָבּוּ Qal pf. 3 c.p. (רָבַב I 912) *abound*

4:9

בְּשָׁלוֹם prep.-n.m.s. (1022) *in peace*
יַחְדָּו adv. (403) *both*
אֶשְׁכְּבָה Qal impf. 1 c.s.-coh.he (שָׁכַב 1011) *I will lie down*
וְאִישָׁן conj.-Qal impf. 1 c.s. (יָשֵׁן 445) *and sleep*
כִּי־אַתָּה conj. (471)-pers.pr. 2 m.s. (61) *for thou*
יהוה pr.n. (217) *Yahweh*
לְבָדָד prep.-n.m.s. (94) *alone*
לָבֶטַח prep.-n.m.s. (105) *in safety*
תּוֹשִׁיבֵנִי Hi. impf. 2 m.s.-1 c.s. sf. (יָשַׁב 442) *makes me dwell*

5:1

לַמְנַצֵּחַ prep.-def.art.-Pi. ptc. (663) *to the choirmaster*
אֶל־הַנְּחִילוֹת prep.-def.art.-n.f.p. (636) *for the flutes*
מִזְמוֹר n.m.s. (274) *a psalm*
לְדָוִד prep.-pr.n. (187) *to David*

5:2

אֲמָרַי n.m.p.-1 c.s. sf. (56) *my words*
הַאֲזִינָה Hi. impv. 2 m.s.-vol.he (אָזַן 24) *give ear to*
יהוה pr.n. (217) *O Yahweh*
בִּינָה Qal impv. 2 m.s.-vol.he (בִּין 106) *give heed to*
הֲגִיגִי n.m.s.-1 c.s. sf. (211) *my groaning*

5:3

הַקְשִׁיבָה Hi. impv. 2 m.s.-vol.he (קָשַׁב 904) *hearken*
לְקוֹל prep.-n.m.s. cstr. (876) *to the sound of*
שַׁוְעִי Pi. inf.cstr.-1 c.s. sf. (שָׁוַע 1002) *my cry*
מַלְכִּי n.m.s.-1 c.s. sf. (I 572) *my King*
וֵאלֹהָי conj.-n.m.p.-1 c.s. sf. paus. (43) *and my God*
כִּי־אֵלֶיךָ conj. (471)-prep.-2 m.s. sf. *for to thee*
אֶתְפַּלָּל Hith. impf. 1 c.s. (פָּלַל 813) *do I pray*

5:4

יהוה pr.n. (217) *O Yahweh*
בֹּקֶר n.m.s. (133; GK 118i) *in the morning*
תִּשְׁמַע Qal impf. 2 m.s. (שָׁמַע 1033) *thou dost hear*
קוֹלִי n.m.s.-1 c.s. sf. (876) *my voice*
בֹּקֶר v.supra *in the morning*
אֶעֱרָךְ־לְךָ Qal impf. 1 c.s. (עָרַךְ 789)-prep.-2 m.s. sf. *I prepare for thee*
וַאֲצַפֶּה conj.-Pi. impf. 1 c.s. (צָפָה I 859) *and watch*

5:5

כִּי לֹא אֵל־ conj. (471)-neg. n.m.s. (42) *for not a God*
חָפֵץ adj. m.s. (383; GK 116f) *who delights*
רֶשַׁע n.m.s. (957) *in wickedness*
אָתָּה pers.pr. 2 m.s. paus. (61) *thou*
לֹא יְגֻרְךָ neg.-Qal impf. 3 m.s.-2 m.s. sf. (גּוּר 157; GK 107s,117bb) *may not sojourn with thee*
רָע n.m.s. (949) *evil*

5:6

לֹא־יִתְיַצְּבוּ neg.-Hith. impf. 3 m.p. (יָצַב 426) *may not stand*

הוֹלְלִים Qal act.ptc. m.p. (הָלַל II 237) *the boastful*

לְנֶגֶד prep.-prep. (617) *before*

עֵינֶיךָ n.f. du.-2 m.s. sf. (744) *thy eyes*

שָׂנֵאתָ Qal pf. 2 m.s. (שָׂנֵא 971) *thou hatest*

כָּל־פֹּעֲלֵי n.m.s. cstr. (481)-Qal act.ptc. m.p. cstr. (821 פָּעַל) *all doers of*

אָוֶן n.m.s. (19) *evil*

5:7

תְּאַבֵּד Pi. impf. 2 m.s. (אָבַד 1) *thou destroyest*

דֹּבְרֵי Qal act.ptc. m.p. cstr. (דָּבַר 180) *those who speak*

כָזָב n.m.s. (469) *lies*

אִישׁ־דָּמִים n.m.s. cstr. (35; GK 128a,t)-n.m.p. (196) *bloodthirsty men*

וּמִרְמָה conj.-n.f.s. (941) *and deceitful*

יְתָעֵב Pi. impf. 3 m.s. (תָּעַב 1073) *abhors*

יהוה pr.n. (217) *Yahweh*

5:8

וַאֲנִי conj.-pers.pr. 1 c.s. (58) *but I*

בְּרֹב prep.-n.m.s. cstr. (913) *through the abundance of*

חַסְדְּךָ n.m.s.-2 m.s. sf. (338) *thy steadfast love*

אָבוֹא Qal impf. 1 c.s. (בּוֹא 97; GK 107s) *will enter*

בֵיתֶךָ n.m.s.-2 m.s. sf. (108) *thy house*

אֶשְׁתַּחֲוֶה Hithpalel impf. 1 c.s. (שָׁחָה 1005) *I will worship*

אֶל־הֵיכַל־ prep.-n.m.s. cstr. (228) *toward the temple of*

קָדְשְׁךָ n.m.s.-2 m.s. sf. (871) *thy holiness*

בְּיִרְאָתֶךָ prep.-n.f.s.-2 m.s. sf. (432) *in the fear of thee*

5:9

יהוה pr.n. (217) *O Yahweh*

נְחֵנִי Qal impv. 2 m.s.-1 c.s. sf. (נָחָה 634) *lead me*

בְצִדְקָתֶךָ prep.-n.f.s.-2 m.s. sf. (842) *in thy righteousness*

לְמַעַן prep. (775) *because of*

שׁוֹרְרָי n.m.p.-1 c.s. sf. (1004) *my enemies*

הַיְשַׁר Hi. impv. 2 m.s. (יָשַׁר 448; GK 24fN,70b) *make straight*

לְפָנַי prep.-n.m.p.-1 c.s. sf. (815) *before me*

דַּרְכֶּךָ n.m.s.-2 m.s. sf. paus. (202) *thy way*

5:10

כִּי אֵין conj. (471)-subst. cstr. (II 34; GK 152o) *for there is not*

בְּפִיהוּ prep.-n.m.s.-3 m.s. sf. (804; GK 145m) *in their mouth*

נְכוֹנָה Ni. ptc. f.s. (כּוּן I 465; GK 122q) *truth*

קִרְבָּם n.m.s.-3 m.p. sf. (899) *their heart*

הַוּוֹת n.f.p. (217; GK 124e) *destruction*

קֶבֶר־פָּתוּחַ n.m.s. (868)-Qal pass.ptc. (פָּתַח I 834) *an open sepulchre*

גְּרוֹנָם n.m.s.-3 m.p. sf. (173) *their throat*

לְשׁוֹנָם n.f.s.-3 m.p. sf. (546) *with their tongue*

יַחֲלִיקוּן Hi. impf. 3 m.p. (חָלַק II 325) *they flatter*

5:11

הַאֲשִׁימֵם Hi. impv. 2 m.s.-3 m.p. sf. (אָשַׁם 79) *make them bear their guilt*

אֱלֹהִים n.m.p. (43) *O God*

יִפְּלוּ Qal impf. 3 m.p. (נָפַל 656) *let them fall*

מִמֹּעֲצוֹתֵיהֶם prep.-n.f.p.-3 m.p. sf. (420) *by their own counsels*

בְּרֹב prep.-n.m.s. cstr. (913) *because of the multitude of*

פִּשְׁעֵיהֶם n.m.p.-3 m.p. sf. (833) *their transgressions*

הַדִּיחֵמוֹ Hi. impv. 2 m.s.-3 m.p. sf. (נָדַח 623) *cast them out*

כִּי־מָרוּ conj. (471)-Qal pf. 3 c.p. (מָרָה 598; GK 29e) *for they have rebelled*

בָךְ prep.-2 m.s. sf. paus. *against thee*

5:12

וְיִשְׂמְחוּ conj.-Qal impf. 3 m.p. (שָׂמַח 970) *but let rejoice*

כָל־חוֹסֵי n.m.s. cstr. (481)-Qal act.ptc. m.p. cstr. (340 חָסָה) *all who take refuge*

בָךְ prep.-2 m.s. sf. paus. *in thee*

לְעוֹלָם prep.-n.m.s. (761) *ever*

יְרַנֵּנוּ Pi. impf. 3 m.p. (רָנַן 943) *let them sing for joy*

וְתָסֵךְ conj.-Hi. impf. 2 m.s. (סָכַךְ I 696; GK 156d) *and do thou defend*

עָלֵימוֹ prep.-3 m.p. sf. *them*

וְיַעְלְצוּ conj.-Qal impf. 3 m.p. (עָלַץ 763) *that may exult*

בְךָ prep.-2 m.s. sf. *in thee*

אֹהֲבֵי Qal act.ptc. m.p. cstr. (אָהַב 12; GK 116g) *those who love*

שְׁמֶךָ n.m.s.-2 m.s. sf. (1027) *thy name*

5:13

כִּי־אַתָּה conj. (471)-pers.pr. 2 m.s. (61) *for thou*

תְּבָרֵךְ Pi. impf. 2 m.s. (בָּרַךְ 138) *dost bless*

צַדִּיק adj. m.s. (843) *the righteous*

יהוה pr.n. (217) *O Yahweh*

כַּצִּנָּה prep.-def.art.-n.f.s. (III 857) *as with a shield*

רָצוֹן n.m.s. (953) *with favor*

תַּעְטְרֶנּוּ Qal impf. 2 m.s.-3 m.s. sf. (עָטַר 742; GK 117ee) *thou dost cover him*

6:1

לַמְנַצֵּחַ prep.-def.art.-Pi. ptc. (I 663) *to the choirmaster*

בִּנְגִינוֹת prep.-n.f.p. (618) *with stringed instruments*

עַל־הַשְּׁמִינִית prep.-def.art.-adj. (1033) *according to the Sheminith*

מִזְמוֹר n.m.s. (274) *a psalm*

לְדָוִד prep.-pr.n. (187) *to (for) David*

6:2

יהוה pr.n. (217) *O Yahweh*

אַל־בְּאַפְּךָ neg. (GK 152h)-prep.-n.m.s.-3 m.s. sf. (I 60) *not in thy anger*

תוֹכִיחֵנִי Hi. impf. 2 m.s.-1 c.s. sf. (יָכַח 406) *rebuke me*

וְאַל־בַּחֲמָתְךָ conj.-neg.-prep.-n.f.s.-2 m.s. sf. (404) *nor in thy wrath*

תְיַסְּרֵנִי Pi. impf. 2 m.s.-1 c.s. sf. (יָסַר 415) *chasten me*

6:3

חָנֵּנִי Qal impv. 2 m.s.-1 c.s. sf. (חָנַן 335) *be gracious to me*

יהוה pr.n. (217) *O Yahweh*

כִּי אֻמְלַל אָנִי conj. (471)-adj. (51)-pers.pr. 1 c.s. (58) *for I am languishing*

רְפָאֵנִי Qal impv. 2 m.s.-1 c.s. sf. (רָפָא 950) *heal me*

יהוה pr.n. (217) *O Yahweh*

כִּי נִבְהֲלוּ conj. (471)-Ni. pf. 3 c.p. (בָּהַל 96) *for are troubled*

עֲצָמָי n.f.p.-1 c.s. sf. paus. (782) *my bones*

6:4

וְנַפְשִׁי conj.-n.f.s.-1 c.s. sf. (659) *my soul*

נִבְהֲלָה Ni. pf. 3 f.s. (בָּהַל 96) *is troubled*

מְאֹד adv. (547) *sorely*

וְאַתָּ conj.-pers.pr. 2 m.s. (61) *but thou*

יהוה pr.n. (217) *O Yahweh*

עַד־מָתָי prep. (III 723)-adv. (607; GK 147c) *how long?*

6:5

שׁוּבָה Qal impv. 2 m.s.-vol.he (שׁוּב 996) *turn*

יהוה pr.n. (217) *O Yahweh*

חַלְּצָה Pi. impv. 2 m.s.-vol.he (חָלַץ I 322) *save*

נַפְשִׁי n.f.s.-1 c.s. sf. (659) *my life*

הוֹשִׁיעֵנִי Hi. impv. 2 m.s.-1 c.s. sf. (יָשַׁע 446) *deliver me*

לְמַעַן חַסְדֶּךָ prep. (775)-n.m.s.-2 m.s. sf. (338) *for the sake of thy steadfast love*

6:6

כִּי אֵין conj. (471)-subst. (II 34; GK 152o) *for there is not*

בַּמָּוֶת prep.-def.art.-n.m.s. (560) *in death*

זִכְרֶךָ n.m.s.-2 m.s. sf. paus. (271) *remembrance of thee*

בִּשְׁאוֹל prep.-n.f.s. (982) *in Sheol*

מִי interr. (566) *who*

יוֹדֶה־לָּךְ Hi. impf. 3 m.s. (יָדָה 392)-prep.-2 m.s. sf. paus. *can give thee praise*

6:7

יָגַעְתִּי Qal pf. 1 c.s. (יָגַע 388; GK 106g) *I am weary*

בְּאַנְחָתִי prep.-n.f.s.-1 c.s. sf. (58) *with my moaning*

אַשְׂחֶה Hi. impf. 1 c.s. (שָׂחָה 965) *I flood (cause to swim)*

בְכָל־לַיְלָה prep.-n.m.s. cstr. (481)-n.m.s. (538) *every night*

מִטָּתִי n.f.s.-1 c.s. sf. (641) *my bed*

בְּדִמְעָתִי prep.-n.f.s.-1 c.s. sf. (199) *with my weeping*

עַרְשִׂי n.f.s.-1 c.s. sf. (793) *my couch*

אַמְסֶה Hi. impf. 1 c.s. (מָסָה 587) *I drench*

6:8

עָשְׁשָׁה Qal pf. 3 f.s. (עָשֵׁשׁ 799) *wastes away*

מִכַּעַס prep.-n.m.s. (495) *because of grief*

עֵינִי n.f.s.-1 c.s. sf. paus. (744) *my eye*

עָתְקָה Qal pf. 3 f.s. (עָתֵק 801) *it grows weak*

בְּכָל־ prep.-n.m.s. cstr. (481) *because of all*

צוֹרְרָי Qal act.ptc. m.p.-1 c.s. sf. (צָרַר III 865) *my foes*

6:9

סוּרוּ Qal impv. 2 m.p. (סוּר 693) *depart*

מִמֶּנִּי prep.-1 c.s. sf. *from me*

כָּל־פֹּעֲלֵי n.m.s. cstr. (481)-Qal act.ptc. m.p. cstr. (821 פָּעַל) *all workers of*
אָוֶן n.m.s. (19) *evil*
כִּי־שָׁמַע conj. (471)-Qal pf. 3 m.s. (1033) *for has heard*
יהוה pr.n. (217) *Yahweh*
קוֹל n.m.s. cstr. (876) *the sound of*
בִּכְיִי n.m.s.-1 c.s. sf. (113) *my weeping*

6:10

שָׁמַע Qal pf. 3 m.s. (1033) *has heard*
יהוה pr.n. (217) *Yahweh*
תְּחִנָּתִי n.f.s.-1 c.s. sf. (337) *my supplication*
יהוה pr.n. (217; GK 142f) *Yahweh*
תְּפִלָּתִי n.f.s.-1 c.s. sf. (813) *my prayer*
תִּקָּח Qal impf. 3 m.s. paus. (לָקַח 542) *accepts*

6:11

יֵבֹשׁוּ Qal impf. 3 m.p. (בּוֹשׁ 101) *shall be ashamed*
וְיִבָּהֲלוּ conj.-Ni. impf. 3 m.p. (בָּהַל 96) *and troubled*
מְאֹד adv. (547) *sorely*
כָּל־אֹיְבָי n.m.s. cstr. (481)-Qal act.ptc. m.p.-1 c.s. sf. (אָיַב 33) *all my enemies*
יָשֻׁבוּ Qal impf. 3 m.p. (שׁוּב 996) *they shall turn back*
יֵבֹשׁוּ v.supra *they shall be put to shame*
רָגַע n.m.s. as adv. (921; LXX σφόδρα διὰ τάχους) *in a moment*

7:1

שִׁגָּיוֹן n.m.s. (993) *a Shiggaion*
לְדָוִד prep.-pr.n. (187) *to (for) David*
אֲשֶׁר־שָׁר rel. (81)-Qal pf. 3 m.s. (שִׁיר 1010) *which he sang*
ליהוה prep.-pr.n. (217) *to Yahweh*
עַל־דִּבְרֵי־כוּשׁ prep.-n.m.p. cstr. (182)-pr.n. (II 469) *concerning Cush*
בֶּן־יְמִינִי n.m.s. cstr. (119)-adj.gent. (122) *a Benjaminite*

7:2

יהוה pr.n. (217) *O Yahweh*
אֱלֹהַי n.m.p.-1 c.s. sf. (43) *my God*
בְּךָ prep.-2 m.s. sf. *in thee*
חָסִיתִי Qal pf. 1 c.s. (חָסָה 340) *do I take refuge*
הוֹשִׁיעֵנִי Hi. impv. 2 m.s.-1 c.s. sf. (יָשַׁע 446) *save me*
מִכָּל־ prep.-n.m.s. cstr. (481) *from*
רֹדְפַי Qal act.ptc. m.p.-1 c.s. sf. (רָדַף 922) *my pursuers*
וְהַצִּילֵנִי conj.-Hi. impv. 2 m.s.-1 c.s. sf. (נָצַל 664) *and deliver me*

7:3

פֶּן־יִטְרֹף conj. (814)-Qal impf. 3 m.s. (טָרַף 382) *lest they rend*
כְּאַרְיֵה prep.-n.m.s. (71) *like a lion*
נַפְשִׁי n.f.s.-1 c.s. sf. (659) *me*
פֹּרֵק Qal act.ptc. (פָּרַק 830) *dragging me away*
וְאֵין מַצִּיל conj.-subst. (II 34; GK 152,l)-Hi. ptc. (664 נָצַל) *with none to rescue*

7:4

יהוה pr.n. (217) *O Yahweh*
אֱלֹהַי n.m.p.-1 c.s. sf. (43) *my God*
אִם־עָשִׂיתִי hypoth.part. (49; GK 159m)-Qal pf. 1 c.s. (עָשָׂה I 793) *if I have done*
זֹאת demons.adj. f.s. (260) *this*
אִם־יֶשׁ־ v.supra-subst. (441) *if there is*
עָוֶל n.m.s. (732) *wrong*
בְּכַפָּי prep.-n.f.p.-1 c.s. sf. (496) *in my hands*

7:5

אִם־גָּמַלְתִּי hypoth.part. (49)-Qal pf. 1 c.s. (גָּמַל 168) *if I have requited*
שׁוֹלְמִי Qal act.ptc.-1 c.s. sf. (שָׁלַם 1023) *my friend*
רָע n.m.s. (949) *with evil*
וָאֲחַלְּצָה consec.-Pi. impf. 1 c.s. (חָלַץ I 322; GK 49e) *or plundered*
צוֹרְרִי Qal act.ptc.-1 c.s. sf. (צָרַר II 865) *my enemy*
רֵיקָם adv. (938) *without cause*

7:6

יִרַדֹּף Qal impf. 3 m.s. (רָדַף 922; GK 63n) *let pursue*
אוֹיֵב Qal act.ptc. (אָיַב 33) *the enemy*
נַפְשִׁי n.f.s.-1 c.s. sf. (659) *me*
וְיַשֵּׂג conj.-Hi. impf. 3 m.s. (נָשַׂג 673) *and overtake*
וְיִרְמֹס conj.-Qal impf. 3 m.s. (רָמַס 942) *and let him trample*
לָאָרֶץ prep.-def.art.-n.f.s. (75) *to the ground*
חַיָּי n.m.p.-1 c.s. sf. (313) *my life*
וּכְבוֹדִי conj.-n.m.s.-1 c.s. sf. (458) *and my soul* (lit. *my honor*)
לֶעָפָר prep.-def.art.-n.m.s. (779) *in the dust*
יַשְׁכֵּן Hi. impf. 3 m.s. apoc. (שָׁכַן 1014) *lay*
סֶלָה interr. (699) *Selah*

7:7

קוּמָה Qal impv. 2 m.s.-vol.he (קוּם 877; GK 72s) *arise*

יהוה pr.n. (217) *O Yahweh*

בְּאַפֶּךָ prep.-n.m.s.-2 m.s. sf. (I 60) *in thy anger*

הִנָּשֵׂא Ni. impv. 2 m.s. (נָשָׂא 669) *lift thyself up*

בְּעַבְרוֹת prep. (GK 119gg)-n.f.p. cstr. (720) *against the fury of*

צוֹרְרָי Qal act.ptc. m.p.-1 c.s. sf. paus. (צָרַר II 865) *my enemies*

וְעוּרָה conj.-Qal impv. 2 m.s.-vol.he (עוּר I 734) *awake*

אֵלַי prep.-1 c.s. sf. *for me*

מִשְׁפָּט n.m.s. (1048; GK 156d) *a judgment*

צִוִּיתָ Pi. pf. 2 m.s. (צָוָה 845) *thou hast appointed*

7:8

וַעֲדַת conj.-n.f.s. cstr. (I 417) *and the assembly of*

לְאֻמִּים n.m.p. (522) *the peoples*

תְּסוֹבְבֶךָּ Po'el impf. 3 f.s.-2 m.s. sf. (סָבַב 685) *let be gathered about thee*

וְעָלֶיהָ conj.-prep.-3 f.s. sf. *and over it*

לַמָּרוֹם prep.-def.art.-n.m.s. (928) *on high*

שׁוּבָה Qal impv. 2 m.s.-vol.he (שׁוּב 996) *return*

7:9

יהוה pr.n. (217) *Yahweh*

יָדִין Qal impf. 3 m.s. (דִּין 192) *judges*

עַמִּים n.m.p. (I 766) *the peoples*

שָׁפְטֵנִי Qal impv. 2 m.s.-1 c.s. sf. (שָׁפַט 1047) *judge me*

יהוה pr.n. (217) *O Yahweh*

כְּצִדְקִי prep.-n.m.s.-1 c.s. sf. (841) *according to my righteousness*

וּכְתֻמִּי conj.-prep.-n.m.s.-1 c.s. sf. (1070) *and according to my integrity*

עָלָי prep.-1 c.s. sf. paus. *that is in me*

7:10

יִגְמָר־נָא Qal impf. 3 m.s. (גָּמַר 170)-part.of entreaty (609) *O let come to an end*

רַע adj. m.s. cstr. (948) *the evil of*

רְשָׁעִים adj. m.p. (957) *the wicked*

וּתְכוֹנֵן conj.-Polel impf. 2 m.s. (כּוּן I 465) *but establish thou*

צַדִּיק adj. m.s. (843) *the righteous*

וּבֹחֵן conj.-Qal act.ptc. (בָּחַן 103) *thou who triest*

לִבּוֹת n.m.p. (524) *the minds*

וּכְלָיוֹת conj. (GK 158a)-n.f.p. (480) *and hearts*

אֱלֹהִים צַדִּיק n.m.p. (43; GK 124g,132h)-adj. m.s. (843) *thou righteous God*

7:11

מָגִנִּי n.m.s.-1 c.s. sf. (171) *my shield*

עַל־אֱלֹהִים prep.-n.m.p. (43) *is with God*

מוֹשִׁיעַ Hi. ptc. (יָשַׁע 446) *who saves*

יִשְׁרֵי־ adj. m.p. cstr. (449) *the upright in*

לֵב n.m.s. (524) *heart*

7:12

אֱלֹהִים n.m.p. (43) *God*

שׁוֹפֵט צַדִּיק Qal act.ptc. (1047)-adj. (843) *a righteous judge*

וְאֵל conj.-n.m.s. (42) *and a God*

זֹעֵם Qal act.ptc. (זָעַם 276) *who has indignation*

בְּכָל־יוֹם prep.-n.m.s. cstr. (481)-n.m.s. (398; GK 127b) *every day*

7:13

אִם־לֹא יָשׁוּב hypoth.part. (49)-neg.-Qal impf. 3 m.s. (שׁוּב 996; GK 120g) *if he does not repent*

חַרְבּוֹ n.f.s.-3 m.s. sf. (352) *his sword*

יִלְטוֹשׁ Qal impf. 3 m.s. (לָטַשׁ 538) *he will whet*

קַשְׁתּוֹ n.f.s.-3 m.s. sf. (905) *his bow*

דָּרַךְ Qal pf. 3 m.s. (201) *he has bent*

וַיְכוֹנְנֶהָ consec.-Polel impf. 3 m.s.-3 f.s. sf. (כּוּן I 465) *and strung it*

7:14

וְלוֹ conj.-prep.-3 m.s. sf. *and for him*

הֵכִין Hi. pf. 3 m.s. (כּוּן I 465) *he has prepared*

כְּלֵי־מָוֶת n.m.p. cstr. (479)-n.m.s. (560) *his deadly weapons*

חִצָּיו n.m.p.-3 m.s. sf. (346) *his arrows*

לְדֹלְקִים prep.-Qal act.ptc. m.p. (דָּלַק 196) *fiery shafts*

יִפְעָל Qal impf. 3 m.s. paus. (פָּעַל 821) *making*

7:15

הִנֵּה demons.part. (243) *behold*

יְחַבֶּל־ Pi. impf. 3 m.s. (חָבַל I 286) *he conceives*

אָוֶן n.m.s. (19) *evil*

וְהָרָה conj.-Qal pf. 3 m.s. (הָרָה I 247) *and is pregnant*

עָמָל n.m.s. (765) *with mischief*

וְיָלַד conj.-Qal pf. 3 m.s. (408) *and brings forth*

שָׁקֶר n.m.s. paus. (1055) *lies*

7:16

בּוֹר n.m.s. (92) *a pit*

כָּרָה Qal pf. 3 m.s. (500) *he makes*

וַיַּחְפְּרֵהוּ consec.-Qal impf. 3 m.s.-3 m.s. sf. (חָפַר I 343) *digging it out*

וַיִּפֹּל consec.-Qal impf. 3 m.s. (נָפַל 656) *and falls*

בְּשַׁחַת prep.-n.f.s. cstr. (1001; GK 155h) *into the hole*

יִפְעָל Qal impf. 3 m.s. paus. (פָּעַל 821) *which he has made*

7:17

יָשׁוּב Qal impf. 3 m.s. (שׁוּב 996) *returns*

עֲמָלוֹ n.m.s.-3 m.s. sf. (765) *his mischief*

בְּרֹאשׁוֹ prep.-n.m.s.-3 m.s. sf. (910) *upon his own head*

וְעַל קָדְקֳדוֹ conj.-prep.-n.m.s.-3 m.s. sf. (869; GK 10h) *and on his own pate*

חֲמָסוֹ n.m.s.-3 m.s. sf. (329) *his violence*

יֵרֵד Qal impf. 3 m.s. (יָרַד 432) *descends*

7:18

אוֹדֶה Hi. impf. 1 c.s. (יָדָה 392) *I will give thanks*

יהוה pr.n. (217) *to Yahweh*

כְּצִדְקוֹ prep.-n.m.s.-3 m.s. sf. (841) *due to his righteousness*

וַאֲזַמְּרָה conj.-Pi. impf. 1 c.s. (זָמַר I 274) *and I will sing praise*

שֵׁם־יהוה n.m.s. cstr. (1027)-v.supra *to the name of Yahweh*

עֶלְיוֹן n.m.s. (II 751) *the Most High*

8:1

לַמְנַצֵּחַ prep.-def.art.-Pi. ptc. (663) *to the choirmaster*

עַל־הַגִּתִּית prep.-def.art.-n.f.p. (388) *according to the Gittith*

מִזְמוֹר n.m.s. (274) *a psalm*

לְדָוִד prep.-pr.n. (187) *to (for) David*

8:2

יהוה pr.n. (217) *Yahweh*

אֲדֹנֵינוּ n.f.p.-1 c.p. sf. (10) *our Lord*

מָה־אַדִּיר interr. (552)-n.m.s. (12) *how majestic*

שִׁמְךָ n.m.s.-2 m.s. sf. (1027) *thy name*

בְּכָל־הָאָרֶץ prep.-n.m.s. cstr. (481)-def.art.-n.f.s. (75) *in all the world*

אֲשֶׁר תְּנָה rel. (81)-Qal impv. 2 m.s.-coh.he (678; rd. prb. Qal pf. 3 f.s. GK 66h) *reaches up*

הוֹדְךָ n.m.s.-2 m.s. sf. (I 217) *your praise*

עַל־הַשָּׁמָיִם prep.-def.art.-n.m. du. paus. (1029) *to the heavens*

8:3

מִפִּי prep.-n.m.s. cstr. (804; GK 128a) *by the mouth of*

עוֹלְלִים n.m.p. (760) *babes*

וְיֹנְקִים conj.-Qal act.ptc. m.p. (413) *and infants (sucking ones)*

יִסַּדְתָּ עֹז Pi. pf. 2 m.s. (413)-n.m.s. (738) *you have built a fortress*

לְמַעַן prep. (775) *because of*

צוֹרְרֶיךָ Qal act.ptc. m.p.-2 m.s. sf. (II 865) *your foes*

לְהַשְׁבִּית prep.-Hi. inf.cstr. (991) *to stop*

אוֹיֵב Qal act.ptc. (33) *your enemies*

וּמִתְנַקֵּם conj.-Hith. ptc. (667) *and adversaries*

8:4

כִּי־אֶרְאֶה conj. (471)-Qal impf. 1 c.s. (906) *when I look at*

שָׁמֶיךָ n.m. du.-2 m.s. sf. (1029) *the sky*

מַעֲשֵׂי n.m.p. cstr. (795) *the works of*

אֶצְבְּעֹתֶיךָ n.f.p.-2 m.s. sf. (840) *your fingers*

יָרֵחַ n.m.s. (437) *the moon*

וְכוֹכָבִים conj.-n.m.p. (456) *and the stars*

אֲשֶׁר כּוֹנָנְתָּה rel. (81)-Polel pf. 2 m.s. paus. (465; GK 159dd) *which you set in their places*

8:5

מָה־אֱנוֹשׁ interr. (GK 150h)-n.m.s. (60) *what is man*

כִּי־תִזְכְּרֶנּוּ conj. (471; GK 111m)-Qal impf. 2 m.s.-3 m.s. sf. (269; GK 107v) *that you think of him*

וּבֶן־אָדָם conj.-n.m.s. cstr. (119)-n.m.s. (9) *and mere man*

כִּי תִפְקְדֶנּוּ conj. (471; GK 111m)-Qal impf. 2 m.s.-3 m.s. sf. (823; GK 107v) *that you care for him*

8:6

וַתְּחַסְּרֵהוּ consec.-Pi. impf. 2 m.s.-3 m.s. sf. (341) *yet you made him inferior*

מְּעַט מֵאֱלֹהִים adv. (589)-prep.-n.m.p. (43) *only to (God) yourself*

וְכָבוֹד וְהָדָר conj.-n.m.s. (458)-conj.-n.m.s. (214) *with glory and honor*

תְּעַטְּרֵהוּ Pi. impf. 2 m.s.-3 m.s. sf. (742; GK 117cc) *you crowned him*

8:7

תַּמְשִׁילֵהוּ Hi. impf. 2 m.s.-3 m.s. sf. (605) *you made him ruler over*

בְּמַעֲשֵׂי יָדֶיךָ prep.-n.m.p. cstr. (795)-n.f.p.-2 m.s. sf. (388) *all you have made*
כֹּל n.m.s. (481) *all things*
שַׁתָּה Qal pf. 2 m.s. (שִׁית 1011) *you placed*
תַחַת־רַגְלָיו prep. (1065)-n.f.p.-3 m.s. sf. (919) *under his feet*

8:8

צֹנֶה n.m.p. (856) *sheep*
וַאֲלָפִים כֻּלָּם conj.-n.m.p. (48)-n.m.s.-3 m.p. sf. (481) *and cattle (all of them)*
וְגַם conj.-adv. (168) *too*
בַּהֲמוֹת שָׂדָי n.f.p. cstr. (96)-n.m.s. paus. (961) *and wild animals*

8:9

צִפּוֹר שָׁמַיִם n.f.s. cstr. (861)-n.m.p. (1029) *the birds*
וּדְגֵי הַיָּם conj.-n.m.p. cstr. (185)-def.art.-n.m.s. (410) *and the fish*
עֹבֵר Qal act.ptc. (716) *passing through*
אָרְחוֹת יַמִּים n.f.p. cstr. (73)-n.m.p. (410) *the paths of the seas*

8:10

יהוה אֲדֹנֵינוּ pr.n. (217)-n.m.p.-1 c.p. sf. (10) *Yahweh, our Lord*
מָה־אַדִּיר שִׁמְךָ interr. (552)-n.m.s. (12)-n.m.s.-2 m.s. sf. paus. (1027) *how excellent thy name*
בְּכָל־הָאָרֶץ prep.-n.m.s. cstr. (481)-def.art.-n.f.s. (75) *in all the world*

9:1

לַמְנַצֵּחַ prep.-def.art.-Pi. ptc. (נָצַח I 663) *to the choirmaster*
עַלְמוּת לַבֵּן prb.rd. עַל מוּת לַבֵּן as prep.-n.f.p. (761)-prep.-def.art.-n.m.s. (119) *according to Muth-labben* (mng. *soprano voice of boys*)
מִזְמוֹר n.m.s. (274) *a psalm*
לְדָוִד prep.-pr.n. (187) *to David*

9:2

אוֹדֶה Hi. impf. 1 c.s. (יָדָה 392; GK 5h) *I will give thanks*
יהוה pr.n. (217) *to Yahweh*
בְּכָל־לִבִּי prep.-n.m.s. cstr. (481)-n.m.s.-1 c.s. sf. (524; GK 13c) *with my whole heart*
אֲסַפְּרָה Pi. impf. 1 c.s.-vol.he (סָפַר 707) *I will tell*
כָּל־נִפְלְאוֹתֶיךָ n.m.s. cstr. (481)-Ni. ptc. f.p.-2 m.s. sf. (פָּלָא 810) *of all thy wonderful deeds*

9:3

אֶשְׂמְחָה Qal impf. 1 c.s.-vol.he (שָׂמַח 970) *I will be glad*
וְאֶעֶלְצָה conj.-Qal impf. 1 c.s.-vol.he (עָלַץ 763) *and exult*
בָךְ prep.-2 m.s. sf. paus. *in thee*
אֲזַמְּרָה Pi. impf. 1 c.s.-vol.he (זָמַר I 274) *I will sing praise*
שִׁמְךָ n.m.s.-2 m.s. sf. (1027) *to thy name*
עֶלְיוֹן n.m.s. (II 751) *O Most High*

9:4

בְּשׁוּב־ prep.-Qal inf.cstr. (שׁוּב 996) *when ... turned back*
אוֹיְבַי Qal act.ptc. m.p.-1 c.s. sf. (אָיַב 33) *my enemies*
אָחוֹר subst. (30) *back*
יִכָּשְׁלוּ Ni. impf. 3 m.p. (כָּשַׁל 505) *they stumbled*
וְיֹאבְדוּ conj.-Qal impf. 3 m.p. (אָבַד 1) *and perished*
מִפָּנֶיךָ prep.-n.m.p.-2 m.p. sf. (815) *before thee*

9:5

כִּי־עָשִׂיתָ conj. (471)-Qal pf. 2 m.s. (עָשָׂה I 793) *for thou hast maintained*
מִשְׁפָּטִי n.m.s.-1 c.s. sf. (1048) *my justice*
וְדִינִי conj.-n.m.s.-1 c.s. sf. (192) *and my judgment*
יָשַׁבְתָּ Qal pf. 2 m.s. (יָשַׁב 442) *thou hast sat*
לְכִסֵּא prep.-n.m.s. (490) *on a throne*
שׁוֹפֵט Qal act.ptc. (שָׁפַט 1047) *giving ... judgment*
צֶדֶק n.m.s. (841) *righteous*

9:6

גָּעַרְתָּ Qal pf. 2 m.s. (גָּעַר 172) *thou hast rebuked*
גוֹיִם n.m.p. (156) *the nations*
אִבַּדְתָּ Pi. pf. 2 m.s. (אָבַד 1) *thou hast destroyed*
רָשָׁע adj. m.s. (957) *wicked*
שְׁמָם n.m.s.-3 m.p. sf. (1027) *their name*
מָחִיתָ Qal pf. 2 m.s. (מָחָה 562) *thou hast blotted out*
לְעוֹלָם prep.-n.m.s. (761) *for ever*
וָעֶד conj.-n.m.s. (I 723) *and ever*

9:7

הָאוֹיֵב def.art.-Qal act.ptc. (אָיַב 33) *the enemy*
תַּמּוּ Qal pf. 3 c.p. (תָּמַם 1070) *have vanished* (some rd. דַּמּוּ = *are destroyed*)
חֳרָבוֹת n.f.p. (352) *ruins*
לָנֶצַח prep.-n.m.s. (I 664) *for ever*
וְעָרִים conj.-n.f.p. (746) *and cities*

נָתַשְׁתָּ Qal pf. 2 m.s. (נָתַשׁ 684) *thou hast rooted out*
אָבַד Qal pf. 3 m.s. (1) *has perished*
זִכְרָם n.m.s.-3 m.p. sf. (271) *the very memory of them*
הֵמָּה pers.pr. 3 m.p. (241; GK 135f) *(they)*

9:8

ויהוה conj.-pr.n. (217) *but Yahweh*
לְעוֹלָם prep.-n.m.s. (761) *for ever*
יֵשֵׁב Qal impf. 3 m.s. (יָשַׁב 442) *sits enthroned*
כּוֹנֵן Polel pf. 3 m.s. (כּוּן I 465) *he has established*
לַמִּשְׁפָּט prep.-def.art.-n.m.s. (1048) *for judgment*
כִּסְאוֹ n.m.s.-3 m.s. sf. (490) *his throne*

9:9

וְהוּא יִשְׁפֹּט־ conj.-pers.pr. 3 m.s. (214)-Qal impf. 3 m.s. (שָׁפַט 1047) *and he judges*
תֵּבֵל n.f.s. (385) *the world*
בְּצֶדֶק prep.-n.m.s. (841) *with righteousness*
יָדִין Qal impf. 3 m.s. (דִּין 192) *he judges*
לְאֻמִּים n.m.p. (522) *the peoples*
בְּמֵישָׁרִים prep.-n.m.p. (449) *with equity*

9:10

וִיהִי conj.-Qal impf. 3 m.s. (הָיָה 224) *and is*
יהוה pr.n. (217) *Yahweh*
מִשְׂגָּב n.m.s. (I 960) *a stronghold*
לַדָּךְ prep.-def.art.-adj. m.s. (194) *for the oppressed*
מִשְׂגָּב v.supra *a stronghold*
לְעִתּוֹת prep.-n.f.p. cstr. (773) *in times of*
בַּצָּרָה n.f.s. (131) *trouble*

9:11

וְיִבְטְחוּ conj.-Qal impf. 3 m.p. (בָּטַח 105) *and put their trust*
בְךָ prep.-2 m.s. sf. *in thee*
יוֹדְעֵי Qal act.ptc. m.p. cstr. (יָדַע 393) *those who know*
שְׁמֶךָ n.m.s.-2 m.s. sf. (1027) *thy name*
כִּי לֹא־עָזַבְתָּ conj. (471)-neg.-Qal pf. 2 m.s. (עָזַב I 736; GK 106k) *for thou hast not forsaken*
דֹּרְשֶׁיךָ Qal act.ptc. m.p.-2 m.s. sf. (דָּרַשׁ 205) *those who seek thee*
יהוה pr.n. (217) *O Yahweh*

9:12

זַמְּרוּ Pi. impv. 2 m.p. (זָמַר I 274) *sing praises*
ליהוה prep.-pr.n. (217) *to Yahweh*
יֹשֵׁב Qal act.ptc. (יָשַׁב 442) *who dwells in*
צִיּוֹן pr.n. (851) *Zion*
הַגִּידוּ Hi. impv. 2 m.p. (נָגַד 616) *tell*
בָעַמִּים prep.-def.art.-n.m.p. (I 766) *among the peoples*
עֲלִילוֹתָיו n.f.p.-3 m.s. sf. (760) *his deeds*

9:13

כִּי־דֹרֵשׁ conj. (471)-Qal act.ptc. (205) *for he who avenges*
דָּמִים n.m.p. (196) *blood*
אוֹתָם dir.obj.-3 m.p. sf. *them*
זָכָר Qal pf. 3 m.s. paus. (269) *is mindful of*
לֹא־שָׁכַח neg.-Qal pf. 3 m.s. (1013) *he does not forget*
צַעֲקַת n.f.s. cstr. (858) *the cry of*
עֲנָיִים adj. m.p. paus. (776) *the afflicted*

9:14

חָנְנֵנִי Qal impv. 2 m.s.-1 c.s. sf. (חָנַן 335; GK 20b;63,l) *be gracious to me*
יהוה pr.n. (217) *O Yahweh*
רְאֵה Qal impv. 2 m.s. (רָאָה 906) *behold*
עָנְיִי adj. m.s.-1 c.s. sf. (776) *what I suffer*
מִשֹּׂנְאָי prep.-Qal act.ptc. m.p.-1 c.s. sf. (שָׂנֵא 971) *from those who hate me*
מְרוֹמְמִי Polel ptc. m.s.-1 c.s. sf. (רוּם 926) *O thou who liftest me up*
מִשַּׁעֲרֵי prep.-n.m.p. cstr. (1044) *from the gates of*
מָוֶת n.m.s. (560) *death*

9:15

לְמַעַן אֲסַפְּרָה conj. (775)-Pi. impf. 1 c.s.-vol.he (707 סָפַר) *that I may recount*
כָּל־תְּהִלָּתֶיךָ n.m.s. cstr. (481)-n.f.p.-2 m.s. sf. (239) *all thy praises*
בְּשַׁעֲרֵי prep.-n.m.p. cstr. (1044) *in the gates of*
בַת־צִיּוֹן n.f.s. cstr. (I 123)-pr.n. (851) *the daughter of Zion*
אָגִילָה Qal impf. 1 c.s.-vol.he (162) *I may rejoice*
בִּישׁוּעָתֶךָ prep.-n.f.s.-2 m.s. sf. paus. (447) *in thy deliverance*

9:16

טָבְעוּ Qal pf. 3 c.p. (371) *have sunk*
גוֹיִם n.m.p. (156) *nations*
בְּשַׁחַת prep.-n.f.s. (1001) *in the pit*
עָשׂוּ Qal pf. 3 c.p. (עָשָׂה I 793) *they made*
בְּרֶשֶׁת־ prep.-n.f.s. (440) *in the net*
זוּ rel. (262; GK 138g) *which*
טָמָנוּ Qal pf. 3 c.p. paus. (טָמַן 380) *they hid*

נִלְכְּדָה Ni. pf. 3 f.s. (לָכַד 539) *has been caught*
רַגְלָם n.f.s.-3 m.p. sf. (919) *their own foot*

9:17

נוֹדַע Ni. pf. 3 m.s. (יָדַע 393) *has made himself known*
יהוה pr.n. (217) *Yahweh*
מִשְׁפָּט n.m.s. (1048) *judgment*
עָשָׂה Qal pf. 3 m.s. (I 793) *he has executed*
בְּפֹעַל prep.-n.m.s. cstr. (821) *in the work of*
כַּפָּיו n.f.p.-3 m.s. sf. (496) *their own hands*
נוֹקֵשׁ Qal act.ptc. (נָקַשׁ 669) *he striketh down* (some rd. נוֹקַשׁ Ni. pf. 3 m.s. from יָקֹשׁ 430 = *are snared)*
רָשָׁע adj. m.s. (957) *the wicked*
הִגָּיוֹן n.m.s. (212) *Higgaion;* mng. *meditation*
סֶלָה interj. (699) *Selah*

9:18

יָשׁוּבוּ Qal impf. 3 m.p. (שׁוּב 996) *shall depart*
רְשָׁעִים adj. m.p. (957) *the wicked*
לִשְׁאוֹלָה prep.-n.f.s.-dir.he (982) *to Sheol*
כָּל־גּוֹיִם n.m.s. cstr. (481)-n.m.p. (156) *all the nations*
שְׁכֵחֵי adj. m.p. cstr. (1013) *that forget*
אֱלֹהִים n.m.p. (43) *God*

9:19

כִּי לֹא לָנֶצַח conj. (471)-neg.-prep.-n.m.s. (664) *for not always*
יִשָּׁכַח Ni. impf. 3 m.s. (שָׁכַח 1013) *shall be forgotten*
אֶבְיוֹן adj. m.s. (2) *the needy*
תִּקְוַת n.f.s. cstr. (876) *the hope of*
עֲנִוִּים adj. m.p. (776) *the poor*
תֹּאבַד Qal impf. 3 f.s. (אָבַד 1, GK 152z) *shall perish*
לָעַד prep.-n.m.s. (I 723) *for ever*

9:20

קוּמָה Qal impv. 2 m.s.-vol.he (קוּם 877) *arise*
יהוה pr.n. (217) *O Yahweh*
אַל־יָעֹז neg.-Qal impf. 3 m.s. (עָזַז 738) *let not prevail*
אֱנוֹשׁ n.m.s. (60) *man*
יִשָּׁפְטוּ Ni. impf. 3 m.p. (שָׁפַט 1047) *let be judged*
גוֹיִם n.m.p. (156) *nations*
עַל־פָּנֶיךָ prep.-n.m.p.-2 m.s. sf. (815) *before thee*

9:21

שִׁיתָה Qal impv. 2 m.s.-coh.he (שִׁית 1011) *put*
יהוה pr.n. (217) *O Yahweh*
מוֹרָה n.m.s. (I 432) *in fear*
לָהֶם prep.-3 m.p. sf. *them*
יֵדְעוּ Qal impf. 3 m.p. (יָדַע 393) *let know*
גוֹיִם n.m.p. (156) *nations*
אֱנוֹשׁ n.m.s. (60, GK 157a) *men*
הֵמָּה pers.pr. 3 m.p. (241) *they*
סֶלָה interj. (699) *Selah*

10:1

לָמָה interr. (552; GK 5h) *why*
יהוה pr.n. (217) *O Yahweh*
תַּעֲמֹד Qal impf. 2 m.s. (עָמַד 763) *dost thou stand*
בְּרָחוֹק prep.-adj. (935) *afar off*
תַּעְלִים Hi. impf. 2 m.s. (עָלַם I 761) *dost thou hide thyself*
לְעִתּוֹת prep.-n.f.p. cstr. (773) *in times of*
בַּצָּרָה n.f.s. (131) *trouble*

10:2

בְּגַאֲוַת prep.-n.f.s. cstr. (144) *in arrogance of*
רָשָׁע adj. m.s. (957) *the wicked*
יִדְלַק Qal impf. 3 m.s. (דָּלַק 196) *he pursues hotly*
עָנִי adj. (776) *the poor*
יִתָּפְשׂוּ Ni. impf. 3 m.p. (תָּפַשׂ 1074) *let them be caught*
בִּמְזִמּוֹת prep.-n.f.p. (273) *in the schemes*
זוּ rel. (262) *which*
חָשָׁבוּ Qal pf. 3 c.p. paus. (362) *they have devised*

10:3

כִּי־הִלֵּל conj. (471)-Pi. pf. 3 m.s. (הָלַל II 237) *for boasts*
רָשָׁע adj. m.s. (957) *the wicked*
עַל־תַּאֲוַת prep.-n.f.s. cstr. (16) *of the desires of*
נַפְשׁוֹ n.f.s.-3 m.s. sf. (659) *his heart*
וּבֹצֵעַ conj.-Qal act.ptc. (בָּצַע 130) *and the man greedy for gain*
בֵּרֵךְ Pi. pf. 3 m.s. (בָּרַךְ 138) *curses*
נִאֵץ Pi. pf. 3 m.s. (נָאַץ 610) *renounces*
יהוה pr.n. (217) *Yahweh*

10:4

רָשָׁע adj. (957) *the wicked*
כְּגֹבַהּ prep.-n.m.s. cstr. (147) *in the pride of*
אַפּוֹ n.m.s.-3 m.s. sf. (I 60) *his countenance*
בַּל־יִדְרֹשׁ neg. (115)-Qal impf. 3 m.s. (דָּרַשׁ 205) *does not seek him*

אֵין אֱלֹהִים neg. (II 34)–n.m.p. (43) *there is no God*
כָּל־מְזִמּוֹתָיו n.m.s. cstr. (481)–n.f.p.–3 m.s. sf. (273) *all his thoughts*

10:5

יָחִילוּ Qal impf. 3 m.p. (חִיל II 298) *prosper (are firm)*
דְרָכָיו n.m.p.–3 m.s. sf. (202) *his ways*
בְּכָל־עֵת prep.–n.m.s. cstr. (481)–n.f.s. (773) *at all times*
מָרוֹם n.m.s. (928) *are on high*
מִשְׁפָּטֶיךָ n.m.p.–2 m.s. sf. (1048; GK 141c) *thy judgments*
מִנֶּגְדּוֹ prep.–subst.–3 m.s. sf. (617) *out of his sight*
כָּל־צוֹרְרָיו n.m.s. cstr. (481)–Qal act.ptc. m.p.–3 m.s. sf. (צָרַר 865) *as for all his foes*
יָפִיחַ Hi. impf. 3 m.s. (פּוּחַ 806) *he puffs*
בָּהֶם prep.–3 m.p. sf. *at them*

10:6

אָמַר Qal pf. 3 m.s. (55) *he thinks*
בְּלִבּוֹ prep.–n.m.s.–3 m.s. sf. (524) *in his heart*
בַּל־אֶמּוֹט neg. (115)–Ni. impf. 1 c.s. (מוֹט 556) *I shall not be moved*
לְדֹר וָדֹר prep.–n.m.s. (189)–conj.–v.supra *throughout all generations*
אֲשֶׁר לֹא־בְרָע rel. (81)–neg.–prep.–n.m.s. paus. (II 948) *I shall not meet adversity*

10:7

אָלָה n.f.s. (46) *with cursing*
פִּיהוּ n.m.s.–3 m.s. sf. (804) *his mouth*
מָלֵא Qal pf. 3 m.s. (569) *is filled*
וּמִרְמוֹת conj.–n.f.p. (941) *and deceit*
וָתֹךְ conj.–n.m.s. (1067) *and oppression*
תַּחַת prep. (1065) *under*
לְשׁוֹנוֹ n.f.s.–3 m.s. sf. (546) *his tongue*
עָמָל n.m.s. (765) *mischief*
וָאָוֶן conj.–n.m.s. (19) *and iniquity*

10:8

יֵשֵׁב Qal impf. 3 m.s. (יָשַׁב 442) *he sits*
בְּמַאְרַב prep.–n.m.s. cstr. (70) *in ambush in*
חֲצֵרִים n.m.p. (II 347) *villages*
בַּמִּסְתָּרִים prep.–def.art.–n.m.p. (712) *in hiding places*
יַהֲרֹג Qal impf. 3 m.s. (הָרַג 246) *he murders*
נָקִי adj. m.s. (667) *the innocent*
עֵינָיו n.f.p.–3 m.s. sf. (744) *his eyes*
לְחֵלְכָה prep.–adj. (319) *for the hapless*

יִצְפֹּנוּ Qal impf. 3 m.p. (צָפַן 860) *stealthily watch (lurk)*

10:9

יֶאֱרֹב Qal impf. 3 m.s. (אָרַב 70) *he lurks*
בַּמִּסְתָּר prep.–def.art.–n.m.s. (712) *in secret*
כְּאַרְיֵה prep.–n.m.s. (71) *like a lion*
בְסֻכֹּה prep.–n.m.s.–3 m.s. sf. (697; GK 91e) *in his covert*
יֶאֱרֹב v.supra *he lurks*
לַחֲטוֹף prep.–Qal inf.cstr. (חָטַף 310) *that he may seize*
עָנִי adj. paus. (776) *the poor*
יַחְטֹף Qal impf. 3 m.s. (חָטַף 310) *he seizes*
עָנִי v.supra *the poor*
בְּמָשְׁכוֹ prep.–Qal inf.cstr.–3 m.s. sf. (מָשַׁךְ 604) *when he draws him*
בְרִשְׁתּוֹ prep.–n.f.s.–3 m.s. sf. (440) *into his net*

10:10

וְדְכֶה some rd. as וְדָכָה Qal pf. 3 m.s. (194); others rd. יִדְּכֶה as Ni. impf. 3 m.s. (194) *is crushed*
יָשֹׁחַ Qal impf. 3 m.s. (שָׁחַח 1005; GK 154N) *sinks down (is bowed down)*
וְנָפַל conj.–Qal pf. 3 m.s. (656) *and falls*
בַּעֲצוּמָיו prep.–adj. m.p.–3 m.s. sf. (783) *by his might*
חֵלְכָּאִים adj. m.p. (319; GK 93x) *the hapless*

10:11

אָמַר Qal pf. 3 m.s. (55) *he thinks*
בְּלִבּוֹ prep.–n.m.s.–3 m.s. sf. (524) *in his heart*
שָׁכַח Qal pf. 3 m.s. (1013) *has forgotten*
אֵל n.m.s. (42) *God*
הִסְתִּיר Hi. pf. 3 m.s. (סָתַר 711; GK 106g) *he has hidden*
פָּנָיו n.m.p.–3 m.s. sf. (815) *his face*
בַּל־רָאָה neg. (115)–Qal pf. 3 m.s. (906) *he will not see it*
לָנֶצַח prep.–n.m.s. (664) *ever*

10:12

קוּמָה Qal impv. 2 m.s.–vol.he (קוּם 877) *arise*
יהוה pr.n. (217) *O Yahweh*
אֵל n.m.s. (42) *O God*
נְשָׂא Qal impv. 2 m.s. (נָשָׂא 669; GK 66c,76b) *lift up*
יָדֶךָ n.f.s.–2 m.s. sf. paus. (388) *thy hand*
אַל־תִּשְׁכַּח neg.–Qal impf. 2 m.s. (שָׁכַח 1013) *forget not*
עֲנָיִים adj. m.p. (776) *the afflicted*

10:13
עַל־מֶה prep.-interr. (552) *why*
נִאֵץ Pi. pf. 3 m.s. (נָאַץ 610) *does renounce*
רָשָׁע adj. m.s. (957) *the wicked*
אֱלֹהִים n.m.p. (43) *God*
אָמַר Qal pf. 3 m.s. (55) *and say*
בְּלִבּוֹ prep.-n.m.s.-3 m.s. sf. (524) *in his heart*
לֹא תִּדְרֹשׁ neg.-Qal impf. 2 m.s. (דָּרַשׁ 205) *thou wilt not call to account*

10:14
רָאִתָה Qal pf. 2 m.s. (רָאָה 906) *thou dost see*
כִּי־ conj. (I 471) *yea*
אַתָּה pers.pr. 2 m.s. (61) *thou*
עָמָל n.m.s. (765) *trouble*
וָכַעַס conj.-n.m.s. (495) *and vexation*
תַּבִּיט Hi. impf. 2 m.s. (נָבַט 613) *dost note*
לָתֵת prep.-Qal inf.cstr. (נָתַן 678) *that thou mayest take it*
בְּיָדֶךָ prep.-n.f.s.-2 m.s. sf. paus. (388) *into thy hands*
עָלֶיךָ prep.-2 m.s. sf. *to thee*
יַעֲזֹב Qal impf. 3 m.s. (עָזַב I 736) *commits himself*
חֵלְכָה adj. paus. (319) *the hapless*
יָתוֹם n.m.s. (450) *of the fatherless*
אַתָּה הָיִיתָ pers.pr. 2 m.s. (61)-Qal pf. 2 m.s. (הָיָה 224) *thou hast been*
עוֹזֵר Qal act.ptc. (עָזַר 740) *the helper*

10:15
שְׁבֹר Qal impv. 2 m.s. (שָׁבַר 990) *break thou*
זְרוֹעַ n.f.s. cstr. (283) *the arm of*
רָשָׁע adj. m.s. (957) *the wicked*
וָרָע conj.-adj. paus. (948) *and evildoer*
תִּדְרוֹשׁ־ Qal impf. 2 m.s. (דָּרַשׁ 205) *seek out*
רִשְׁעוֹ n.m.s.-3 m.s. sf. (957) *his wickedness*
בַל־תִּמְצָא neg. (115)-Qal impf. 2 m.s. (מָצָא 592) *till thou find none*

10:16
יהוה pr.n. (217) *Yahweh*
מֶלֶךְ n.m.s. (I 572) *is king*
עוֹלָם n.m.s. (761) *for ever*
וָעֶד conj.-n.m.s. (I 723) *and ever*
אָבְדוּ Qal pf. 3 c.p. (אָבַד 1) *shall perish*
גוֹיִם n.m.p. (156) *the nations*
מֵאַרְצוֹ prep.-n.f.s.-3 m.s. sf. (75) *from his land*

10:17
תַּאֲוַת n.f.s. cstr. (16) *the desire of*
עֲנָוִים adj. m.p. (776) *the meek*
שָׁמַעְתָּ Qal pf. 2 m.s. (שָׁמַע 1033) *thou wilt hear*
יהוה pr.n. (217) *O Yahweh*
תָּכִין Hi. impf. 2 m.s. (כּוּן 465) *thou wilt strengthen*
לִבָּם n.m.s.-3 m.p. sf. (524) *their heart*
תַּקְשִׁיב Hi. impf. 2 m.s. (קָשַׁב 904) *thou wilt incline*
אָזְנֶךָ n.f.s.-2 m.s. sf. paus. (23) *thy ear*

10:18
לִשְׁפֹּט prep.-Qal inf.cstr. (1047) *to do justice*
יָתוֹם n.m.s. (450) *to the fatherless*
וָדָךְ conj.-adj. paus. (194) *and the oppressed*
בַּל־יוֹסִיף neg. (115)-Hi. impf. 3 m.s. (יָסַף 414) *that there may not be*
עוֹד adv. (728) *any more*
לַעֲרֹץ prep.-Qal inf.cstr. (עָרַץ 791) *a striking of terror*
אֱנוֹשׁ n.m.s. (60) *man*
מִן־הָאָרֶץ prep.-def.art.-n.f.s. (75) *of the earth*

11:1
לַמְנַצֵּחַ prep.-def.art.-Pi. ptc. (I 663) *to the choirmaster*
לְדָוִד prep.-pr.n. (187; GK 129c) *to David*
בַּיהוה prep.-pr.n. (217) *in Yahweh*
חָסִיתִי Qal pf. 1 c.s. (חָסָה 340) *I take refuge*
אֵיךְ adv. (32; GK 148b) *how*
תֹּאמְרוּ Qal impf. 2 m.p. (אָמַר 55) *can you say*
לְנַפְשִׁי prep.-n.f.s.-1 c.s. sf. (659) *to me*
נוּדִי Qal impv. 2 f.s. (נוּד 626; K נוּדוּ 2 m.p.) *flee*
הַרְכֶם n.m.s.-2 m.p. sf. (249) *to your mountain*
צִפּוֹר n.f.s. (861; GK 118r) *like a bird*

11:2
כִּי הִנֵּה conj. (471)-demons.part. (243) *for lo*
הָרְשָׁעִים def.art.-adj. m.p. (957) *the wicked*
יִדְרְכוּן Qal impf. 3 m.p. (דָּרַךְ 201; GK 47m) *bend*
קֶשֶׁת n.f.s. (905) *the bow*
כּוֹנְנוּ Polel pf. 3 c.p. (כּוּן I 465) *they have fitted*
חִצָּם n.m.s.-3 m.p. sf. (346) *their arrow*
עַל־יֶתֶר prep.-n.m.s. (II 452) *to the string*
לִירוֹת prep.-Qal inf.cstr. (יָרָה 434) *to shoot*
בְּמוֹ־אֹפֶל prep. (91)-n.m.s. (66) *in the dark*
לְיִשְׁרֵי־ prep.-adj. m.p. cstr. (449) *at the upright in*
לֵב n.m.s. (524) *heart*

11:3

כִּי הַשָּׁתוֹת conj. (471)-def.art.-n.m.p. (1011) *if the foundations*

יֵהָרֵסוּן Ni. impf. 3 m.p. (הָרַס 248) *are destroyed*

צַדִּיק adj. m.s. (843) *the righteous*

מַה־פָּעָל interr. (552)-Qal pf. 3 m.s. paus. (821) *what can do*

11:4

יהוה pr.n. (217) *Yahweh*

בְּהֵיכַל prep.-n.m.s. cstr. (228) *in the temple of*

קָדְשׁוֹ n.m.s.-3 m.s. sf. (871) *his holiness*

יהוה v.supra *Yahweh*

בַּשָּׁמַיִם prep.-def.art.-n.m. du. (1029; GK 155e) *in heaven*

כִּסְאוֹ n.m.s.-3 m.s. sf. (490) *his throne*

עֵינָיו n.f.p.-3 m.s. sf. (744) *his eyes*

יֶחֱזוּ Qal impf. 3 m.p. (חָזָה 302; GK 145u) *behold*

עַפְעַפָּיו n.m. du.-3 m.s. sf. (733) *his eyelids*

יִבְחֲנוּ Qal impf. 3 m.p. (בָּחַן 103) *test*

בְּנֵי אָדָם n.m.p. cstr. (119)-n.m.s. (9) *the children of men*

11:5

יהוה pr.n. (217) *Yahweh*

צַדִּיק adj. m.s. (843) *the righteous*

יִבְחָן Qal impf. 3 m.s. (בָּחַן 103) *tests*

וְרָשָׁע conj.-adj. m.s. (957) *and the wicked*

וְאֹהֵב conj.-Qal act.ptc. (אָהֵב 12) *and him that loves*

חָמָס n.m.s. paus. (329) *violence*

שָׂנְאָה Qal pf. 3 f.s. (שָׂנֵא 971) *hates*

נַפְשׁוֹ n.f.s.-3 m.s. sf. (659) *his soul*

11:6

יַמְטֵר Hi. impf. 3 m.s. (מָטַר 565; GK 109k) *he will rain*

עַל־רְשָׁעִים prep.-adj. m.p. (957) *on the wicked*

פַּחִים n.m.s. cstr. (rd. פַּחַם from פֶּחָם 809) *coals of*

אֵשׁ n.f.s. (77) *fire*

וְגָפְרִית conj.-n.f.s. (172) *and brimstone*

וְרוּחַ זִלְעָפוֹת conj.-n.f.s. cstr. (924)-n.f.p. (273) *and a scorching wind*

מְנָת n.f.s. cstr. (584) *the portion of*

כּוֹסָם n.f.s.-3 m.p. sf. (468) *their cup*

11:7

כִּי־צַדִּיק conj. (471)-adj. (843) *for is righteous*

יהוה pr.n. (217) *Yahweh*

צְדָקוֹת n.f.p. (842) *righteous deeds*

אָהֵב Qal pf. 3 m.s. (12) *he loves*

יָשָׁר adj. (449) *the upright*

יֶחֱזוּ Qal impf. 3 m.p. (חָזָה 302) *shall behold*

פָנֵימוֹ n.m.p.-3 m.s. sf. (815; GK 103f) *his face*

12:1

לַמְנַצֵּחַ prep.-def.art.-Pi. ptc. (I 663) *to the choirmaster*

עַל־הַשְּׁמִינִית prep.-def.art.-adj. num. (1033) *according to the Sheminith*

מִזְמוֹר n.m.s. (274) *a Psalm*

לְדָוִד prep.-pr.n. (187) *to David*

12:2

הוֹשִׁיעָה Hi. impv. 2 m.s.-vol.he (יָשַׁע 446) *Help*

יהוה pr.n. (217) *Yahweh*

כִּי־גָמַר conj.-Qal pf. 3 m.s. (170) *for there is no longer*

חָסִיד adj. (339; GK 123b) *any that is godly*

כִּי־פַסּוּ conj. (471)-Qal pf. 3 c.p. (פָּסַס II 821) *for have vanished*

אֱמוּנִים Qal pass.ptc. m.p. (אָמַן I 52) *the faithful*

מִבְּנֵי אָדָם prep.-n.m.p. cstr. (119)-n.m.s. (9) *among the sons of men*

12:3

שָׁוְא n.m.s. (996) *lies*

יְדַבְּרוּ Pi. impf. 3 m.p. (דָּבַר 180) *utters*

אִישׁ n.m.s. (35) *every one*

אֶת־רֵעֵהוּ dir.obj.-n.m.s.-3 m.s. sf. (945) *to his neighbor*

שְׂפַת חֲלָקוֹת n.f.s. cstr. (973)-n.f.p. (II 325) *with flattering lips*

בְּלֵב וָלֵב prep. (GK 117t,123f)-n.m.s. cstr. (524) -conj.-v.supra *and a double heart*

יְדַבֵּרוּ v.supra paus. *they speak*

12:4

יַכְרֵת Hi. impf. 3 m.s. apoc. (כָּרַת 503) *may ... cut off*

יהוה pr.n. (217) *Yahweh*

כָּל־שִׂפְתֵי n.m.s. cstr. (481)-n.f.p. cstr. (973) *all ... lips*

חֲלָקוֹת n.f.p. (II 325) *flattering*

לָשׁוֹן n.f.s. (546) *the tongue*

מְדַבֶּרֶת Pi. ptc. f.s. (דָּבַר 180) *that makes boasts*

גְּדֹלוֹת adj. f.p. (152; GK 122q) *great*

12:5

אֲשֶׁר אָמְרוּ rel. (81)-Qal pf. 3 c.p. (55) *those who say*

לִלְשֹׁנֵנוּ prep.-n.f.s.-1 c.p. sf. (546) *with our tongue*
נַגְבִּיר Hi. impf. 1 c.p. (גָּבַר 149) *we will prevail*
שְׂפָתֵינוּ n.f.p.-1 c.p. sf. (973) *our lips*
אִתָּנוּ prep.-1 c.p. sf. (II 85) *with us*
מִי אָדוֹן interr. (566)-n.m.s. (10) *who is master*
לָנוּ prep.-1 c.p. sf. *of us*

12:6

מִשֹּׁד עֲנִיִּים prep.-n.m.s. cstr. (I 994)-adj. m.p. (776) *because the poor are despoiled*
מֵאַנְקַת אֶבְיוֹנִים prep.-n.f.s. cstr. (I 60)-adj. m.p. (2) *because the needy groan*
עַתָּה אָקוּם adv. (773)-Qal impf. 1 c.s. (קוּם 877) *I will now arise*
יֹאמַר יהוה Qal impf. 3 m.s. (אָמַר 55)-pr.n. (217) *says Yahweh*
אָשִׁית Qal impf. 1 c.s. (שִׁית 1011) *I will place*
בְּיֵשַׁע prep.-n.m.s. (447) *in the safety*
יָפִיחַ לוֹ Hi. impf. 3 m.s. (פּוּחַ 806)-prep.-3 m.s. sf. *for which he longs*

12:7

אִמְרוֹת n.f.p. cstr. (57; GK 10g) *the promises of*
יהוה pr.n. (217) *Yahweh*
אֲמָרוֹת n.f.p. (57) *promises*
טְהֹרוֹת adj. f.p. (373) *pure*
כֶּסֶף n.m.s. (494) *silver*
צָרוּף Qal pass.ptc. (צָרַף 864) *refined*
בַּעֲלִיל prep.-n.m.s. (760) *in a furnace*
לָאָרֶץ prep.-def.art.-n.f.s. (75) *on the ground*
מְזֻקָּק Pu. ptc. (I 279) *purified*
שִׁבְעָתָיִם n.f. du. paus. (988; GK 97h) *seven times*

12:8

אַתָּה־ pers.pr. 2 m.s. (61) *do thou*
יהוה pr.n. (217) *O Yahweh*
תִּשְׁמְרֵם Qal impf. 2 m.s.-3 m.p. sf. (שָׁמַר 1036) *protect us* (Heb. *them*)
תִּצְּרֶנּוּ Qal impf. 2 m.s.-1 c.p. sf. (נָצַר I 665) *guard us*
מִן־הַדּוֹר prep.-def.art.-n.m.s. (189) *from ... generation*
זוּ rel. (262; GK 126y) *this*
לְעוֹלָם prep.-n.m.s. (761) *ever*

12:9

סָבִיב subst. (686) *on every side*
רְשָׁעִים adj. m.p. (957) *the wicked*
יִתְהַלָּכוּן Hith. impf. 3 m.p. paus. (הָלַךְ 229; GK 54k) *prowl*
כְּרֻם prep.-Qal inf.cstr. (רוּם 926) *as is exalted*
זֻלּוּת n.f.s. (273) *vileness*
לִבְנֵי prep.-n.m.p. cstr. (119) *among the sons of*
אָדָם n.m.s. (9) *men*

13:1

לַמְנַצֵּחַ prep.-def.art.-Pi. ptc. (I 663) *to the choirmaster*
מִזְמוֹר n.m.s. (274) *a Psalm*
לְדָוִד prep.-pr.n. (187) *to David*

13:2

עַד־אָנָה prep. (III 723)-adv. (33) *how long*
יהוה pr.n. (217) *O Yahweh*
תִּשְׁכָּחֵנִי Qal impf. 2 m.s.-1 c.s. sf. (שָׁכַח 1013) *wilt thou forget me*
נֶצַח n.m.s. (664) *for ever*
עַד־אָנָה v.supra *how long*
תַּסְתִּיר Hi. impf. 2 m.s. (סָתַר 711) *wilt thou hide*
אֶת־פָּנֶיךָ dir.obj.-n.m.p.-2 m.s. sf. (815) *thy face*
מִמֶּנִּי prep.-1 c.s. sf. *from me*

13:3

עַד־אָנָה prep. (III 723)-adv. (33) *how long*
אָשִׁית Qal impf. 1 c.s. (שִׁית 1011) *shall I hold*
עֵצוֹת n.f.p. (420) *counsels*
בְּנַפְשִׁי prep.-n.f.s.-1 c.s. sf. (659) *in my soul*
יָגוֹן n.m.s. (387) *and sorrow*
בִּלְבָבִי prep.-n.m.s.-1 c.s. sf. (523) *in my heart*
יוֹמָם adv. (401) *all the day*
עַד־אָנָה v.supra *how long*
יָרוּם Qal impf. 3 m.s. (רוּם 926) *shall be exalted*
אֹיְבִי Qal act.ptc.-1 c.s. sf. (אָיַב 33) *my enemy*
עָלָי prep.-1 c.s. sf. *over me*

13:4

הַבִּיטָה Hi. impv. 2 m.s.-vol.he (נָבַט 613) *consider*
עֲנֵנִי Qal impv. 2 m.s.-1 c.s. sf. (עָנָה I 772) *answer me*
יהוה pr.n. (217) *Yahweh*
אֱלֹהָי n.m.p.-1 c.s. sf. paus. (43) *my God*
הָאִירָה Hi. impv. 2 m.s.-vol.he (אוֹר 21) *lighten*
עֵינַי n.f. du.-1 c.s. sf. (744) *my eyes*
פֶּן־אִישַׁן conj. (814)-Qal impf. 1 c.s. (יָשֵׁן 445) *lest I sleep*
הַמָּוֶת def.art.-n.m.s. (560; GK 117rN) *the death*

13:5

פֶּן־יֹאמַר conj. (814)-Qal impf. 3 m.s. (55) *lest ... say*
אֹיְבִי Qal act.ptc.-1 c.s. sf. (אָיַב 33) *my enemy*

יְכָלְתִּיו Qal pf. 1 c.s.-3 m.s. sf. (יָכֹל 407; GK 44e,59i) *I have prevailed over him*

צָרַי n.m.p.-1 c.s. sf. (III 865) *my foes*

יָגִילוּ Qal impf. 3 m.p. (גִּיל 162; GK 152z) *rejoice*

כִּי אֶמּוֹט conj.-Ni. impf. 1 c.s. (מוֹט 556) *because I am shaken*

13:6

וַאֲנִי conj.-pers.pr. 1 c.s. (58) *but I*

בְּחַסְדְּךָ prep.-n.m.s.-2 m.s. sf. (338) *in thy steadfast love*

בָטַחְתִּי Qal pf. 1 c.s. (בָּטַח 105) *have trusted*

יָגֵל Qal impf. 3 m.s. (גִּיל 162) *shall rejoice*

לִבִּי n.m.s.-1 c.s. sf. (524) *my heart*

בִּישׁוּעָתֶךָ prep.-n.f.s.-2 m.s. sf. (447) *in thy salvation*

אָשִׁירָה Qal impf. 1 c.s.-vol.he (שִׁיר 1010) *I will sing*

ליהוה prep.-pr.n. (217) *to Yahweh*

כִּי גָמַל conj. (471)-Qal pf. 3 m.s. (168) *because he has dealt bountifully*

עָלָי prep.-1 c.s. sf. paus. *with me*

14:1

לַמְנַצֵּחַ prep.-def.art.-Pi. ptc. (נָצַח I 663) *to the choirmaster*

לְדָוִד prep.-pr.n. (187) *to David*

אָמַר נָבָל Qal pf. 3 m.s. (55)-adj. m.s. (I 614) *a fool says*

בְּלִבּוֹ prep.-n.m.s.-3 m.s. sf. (524) *in his heart*

אֵין אֱלֹהִים neg. (II 34)-n.m.p. (43) *there is no God*

הִשְׁחִיתוּ Hi. pf. 3 c.p. (שָׁחַת 1007; GK 154aN) *they are corrupt*

הִתְעִיבוּ Hi. pf. 3 c.p. (תָּעַב 1073; GK 154aN) *they do abominable*

עֲלִילָה n.f.s. (760) *deeds*

אֵין־עֹשֵׂה־טוֹב neg. (II 34)-Qal act.ptc. (I 793) -adj. (II 373) *there is none that does good*

14:2

יהוה pr.n. (217) *Yahweh*

מִשָּׁמַיִם prep.-n.m. du. (1029) *from heaven*

הִשְׁקִיף Hi. pf. 3 m.s. (שָׁקַף I 1054) *looks down*

עַל־בְּנֵי־אָדָם prep.-n.m.p. cstr. (119)-n.m.s. (9) *upon the children of men*

לִרְאוֹת prep.-Qal inf.cstr. (רָאָה 906) *to see*

הֲיֵשׁ מַשְׂכִּיל interr.part.-subst. (441)-Hi. ptc. (968 שָׂכַל) *if there are any that act wisely*

דֹּרֵשׁ Qal act.ptc. (205) *that seek*

אֶת־אֱלֹהִים dir.obj.-n.m.p. (43) *after God*

14:3

הַכֹּל def.art.-n.m.s. (481) *they all*

סָר Qal pf. 3 m.s. (סוּר 693) *have gone astray*

יַחְדָּו adv. (403) *together*

נֶאֱלָחוּ Ni. pf. 3 c.p. paus. (47) *they are corrupt*

אֵין עֹשֵׂה־טוֹב neg. (II 34)-Qal act.ptc. (I 793) -adj. (373) *there is none that does good*

אֵין גַּם־אֶחָד v.supra-adv. (168)-num. 25; GK 152o) *no, not one*

14:4

הֲלֹא יָדְעוּ interr.part.-neg.-Qal pf. 3 c.p. (393) *have they no knowledge?*

כָּל־פֹּעֲלֵי n.m.s. cstr. (481)-Qal act.ptc. m.p. cstr. (821 פָּעַל) *all the ... doers*

אָוֶן n.m.s. (19) *evil*

אֹכְלֵי עַמִּי Qal act.ptc. m.p. cstr. (37)-n.m.s.-1 c.s. sf. (I 766) *who eat up my people*

אָכְלוּ Qal pf. 3 c.p. (37) *as they eat*

לֶחֶם n.m.s. (536) *bread*

יהוה pr.n. (217) *upon Yahweh*

לֹא קָרָאוּ neg.-Qal pf. 3 c.p. paus. (קָרָא 894) *they do not call*

14:5

שָׁם adv. (1027) *there*

פָּחֲדוּ פָחַד Qal pf. 3 c.p. (808)-n.m.s. paus. (808; GK 117p) *they shall be in great terror*

כִּי־אֱלֹהִים conj.-pr.n. (43) *for God*

בְּדוֹר צַדִּיק prep.-n.m.s. (189)-adj. m.s. (843) *with the generation of the righteous*

14:6

עֲצַת־עָנִי n.f.s. cstr. (420)-n.m.s. (776) *the plans of the poor*

תָבִישׁוּ Hi. impf. 2 m.p. (בּוֹשׁ 101) *you would confound*

כִּי יהוה conj. (471)-pr.n. (217) *but Yahweh*

מַחְסֵהוּ n.m.s.-3 m.s. sf. (340) *his refuge*

14:7

מִי יִתֵּן interr. (566)-Qal impf. 3 m.s. (נָתַן 678; GK 151b) *Oh that*

מִצִּיּוֹן prep.-pr.n. (851) *out of Zion*

יְשׁוּעַת יִשְׂרָאֵל n.f.s. cstr. (447)-pr.n. (975) *deliverance for Israel*

בְּשׁוּב יהוה prep.-Qal inf.cstr. (996)-pr.n. (217) *when Yahweh restores*

שְׁבוּת עַמּוֹ n.f.s. cstr. (986)-n.m.s.-3 m.s. sf. (I 766) *the fortunes of his people*

יָגֵל Qal impf. 3 m.s. apoc. (גִּיל 162) *let rejoice*

יַעֲקֹב pr.n. (784) *Jacob*

יִשְׂמַח Qal impf. 3 m.s. (שָׂמַח 970) *let be glad*
יִשְׂרָאֵל pr.n. (975) *Israel*

15:1

מִזְמוֹר n.m.s. (274) *a Psalm*
לְדָוִד prep.-pr.n. (187) *to David*
יהוה pr.n. (217) *Yahweh*
מִי־יָגוּר interr. (566)-Qal impf. 3 m.s. (157) *who may live*
בְּאָהֳלֶךָ prep.-n.m.s.-2 m.s. sf. paus. (13) *in your temple*
מִי־יִשְׁכֹּן interr. (566)-Qal impf. 3 m.s. (1014) *who may stay*
בְּהַר קָדְשֶׁךָ prep.-n.m.s. cstr. (249)-n.m.s.-2 m.s. sf. paus. (871) *on Zion, your sacred hill*

15:2

הוֹלֵךְ Qal act.ptc. (הָלַךְ 229) *the man who walks*
תָּמִים adj. (1071; GK 118n) *perfectly*
וּפֹעֵל conj.-Qal act.ptc. (פָּעַל 821) *and who does*
צֶדֶק n.m.s. (841) *what is right*
וְדֹבֵר conj.-Qal act.ptc. (180) *and speaks*
אֱמֶת n.f.s. (54) *truth*
בִּלְבָבוֹ prep.-n.m.s.-3 m.s. sf. (523) *in his heart*

15:3

לֹא־רָגַל neg.-Qal pf. 3 m.s. (920) *and who does not slander*
עַל־לְשֹׁנוֹ prep.-n.m.s.-3 m.s. sf. (546) *with his tongue*
לֹא־עָשָׂה neg.-Qal pf. 3 m.s. (I 793) *and he does not do*
לְרֵעֵהוּ prep.-n.m.s.-3 m.s. sf. (945) *to his friend*
רָעָה n.f.s. (948) *wrong*
וְחֶרְפָּה conj.-n.f.s. (357) *and reproach*
לֹא־נָשָׂא neg.-Qal pf. 3 m.s. (669) *he does not lift up*
עַל־קְרֹבוֹ prep.-adj.-3 m.s. sf. (898) *against his neighbors*

15:4

נִבְזֶה Ni. ptc. (בָּזָה 102) *he despises*
בְּעֵינָיו prep.-n.f.p.-3 m.s. sf. (744) *in his own eyes*
נִמְאָס Ni. ptc. (549) *those rejected*
וְאֶת־יִרְאֵי יהוה conj.-dir.obj.-Qal act.ptc. m.p. cstr. (יָרֵא 431)-pr.n. (217) *but those who obey Yahweh*
יְכַבֵּד Pi. impf. 3 m.s. (457) *he honors*
נִשְׁבַּע Ni. pf. 3 m.s. (989) *he swears himself*
לְהָרַע prep.-Hi. inf.cstr. (949) *to his own hurt*
וְלֹא יָמִר conj.-neg.-Hi. impf. 3 m.s. defective (558 מוּר) *and he does not change*

15:5

כַּסְפּוֹ n.m.s.-3 m.s. sf. (494) *his money*
לֹא־נָתַן neg.-Qal pf. 3 m.s. (678) *he does not give*
בְּנֶשֶׁךְ prep.-n.m.s. (675) *for interest*
וְשֹׁחַד conj.-n.m.s. (1005) *and a bribe*
עַל־נָקִי prep.-adj. (667) *against the innocent*
לֹא לָקָח neg.-Qal pf. 3 m.s. paus. (542) *he does not accept*
עֹשֵׂה־אֵלֶּה Qal act.ptc. cstr. (עָשָׂה I 793) -demons.adj. c.p. (41) *he who does these things*
לֹא יִמּוֹט neg.-Ni. impf. 3 m.s. (מוֹט 556) *he shall not be moved*
לְעוֹלָם prep.-n.m.s. (761) *for ever*

16:1

מִכְתָּם n.m.s. (508) *a Miktam*
לְדָוִד prep.-pr.n. (187) *to David*
שָׁמְרֵנִי Qal impv. 2 m.s.-1 c.s. sf. (שָׁמַר I 1036; GK 48i,61f) *preserve me*
אֵל n.m.s. (42) *O God*
כִּי־חָסִיתִי conj. (471)-Qal pf. 1 c.s. (חָסָה 340) *for I take refuge*
בָךְ prep.-2 m.s. sf. paus. *in thee*

16:2

אָמַרְתְּ Qal pf. 2 f.s. (55; GK 44i) *you say* (some rd. אָמַרְתִּי *I say*)
לַיהוה prep.-pr.n. (217) *to Yahweh*
אֲדֹנָי n.m.p.-1 c.s. sf. (10) *my lord*
אָתָּה pers.pr. 2 m.s. (61) *thou art*
טוֹבָתִי n.f.s.-1 c.s. sf. (375) *my good*
בַּל־עָלֶיךָ neg. (115; GK 152t)-prep.-2 m.s. sf. *not apart from thee*

16:3

לִקְדוֹשִׁים prep.-adj. m.p. (872; GK 143e) *as for the saints*
אֲשֶׁר־בָּאָרֶץ rel. (81)-prep.-def.art.-n.f.s. (75) *in the land*
הֵמָּה pers.pr. 3 m.p. (241) *they*
וְאַדִּירֵי conj.-adj. m.p. cstr. (12; GK 130d) *and the noble ones (of)*
כָּל־חֶפְצִי־ n.m.s. cstr. (481)-n.m.s.-1 c.s. sf. (343) *all my delight*
בָם prep.-3 m.p. sf. *in them*

16:4

יִרְבּוּ Qal impf. 3 m.p. (רָבָה I 915; GK 145p) *they multiply*

עַצְּבוֹתָם n.f.p.-3 m.p. sf. (781) *their pains*

אַחֵר adj. (I 29) *another*

מָהָרוּ Qal pf. 3 c.p. paus. (מָהַר III 555; txt. dubious) *they obtained in exchange*

בַּל־אַסִּיךְ neg. (115)-Hi. impf. 1 c.s. (נָסַךְ 650) *I will not pour out*

נִסְכֵּיהֶם n.m.p.-3 m.p. sf. (651; GK 93m) *their libations*

מִדָּם prep.-n.m.s. (196) *of blood*

וּבַל־אֶשָּׂא conj.-neg. (115)-Qal impf. 1 c.s. (נָשָׂא 669) *or I will not take*

אֶת־שְׁמוֹתָם dir.obj.-n.m.p.-3 m.p. sf. (1027) *their names*

עַל־שְׂפָתָי prep.-n.f. du.-1 c.s. sf. (973) *upon my lips*

16:5

יהוה pr.n. (217) *Yahweh*

מְנָת־חֶלְקִי n.f.s. cstr. (584)-n.m.s.-1 c.s. sf. (324) *my chosen portion*

וְכוֹסִי conj.-n.f.s.-1 c.s. sf. (468) *and my cup*

אַתָּה תּוֹמִיךְ pers.pr. 2 m.s. (61)-Qal act.ptc. (תָּמַךְ 1069; GK 50e) *thou holdest*

גּוֹרָלִי n.m.s.-1 c.s. sf. (174) *my lot*

16:6

חֲבָלִים n.m.p. (286) *the lines*

נָפְלוּ־לִי Qal pf. 3 c.p. (נָפַל 656)-prep.-1 c.s. sf. *have fallen for me*

בַּנְּעִמִים prep.-def.art.-adj. m.p. (I 653; GK 122q) *in pleasant places*

אַף־ conj. (II 64) *yea*

נַחֲלָת n.f.s. (635; GK 80g) *a heritage*

שָׁפְרָה Qal pf. 3 f.s. (שָׁפַר 1051) *is beautiful*

עָלָי prep.-1 c.s. sf. paus. *for me*

16:7

אֲבָרֵךְ Pi. impf. 1 c.s. (בָּרַךְ 138) *I bless*

אֶת־יהוה dir.obj.-pr.n. (217) *Yahweh*

אֲשֶׁר יְעָצָנִי rel. (81)-Qal pf. 3 m.s.-1 c.s. sf. paus. (יָעַץ 419) *who gives me counsel*

אַף־לֵילוֹת conj. (II 64)-n.m.p. (538) *in the night also*

יִסְּרוּנִי Pi. pf. 3 c.p.-1 c.s. sf. (יָסַר 415) *instructs me*

כִלְיוֹתָי n.f.p.-1 c.s. sf. paus. (480) *my heart*

16:8

שִׁוִּיתִי Pi. pf. 1 c.s. (שָׁוָה I 1000) *I keep*

יהוה pr.n. (217) *Yahweh*

לְנֶגְדִּי prep.-prep.-1 c.s. sf. (617) *before me*

תָמִיד n.m.s. (556; GK 116s) *always*

כִּי מִימִינִי conj. (471)-prep.-n.f.s.-1 c.s. sf. (411) *because at my right hand*

בַּל־אֶמּוֹט neg. (115)-Ni. impf. 1 c.s. (מוֹט 556) *I shall not be moved*

16:9

לָכֵן prep.-adv. (485) *therefore*

שָׂמַח Qal pf. 3 m.s. (שָׂמַח 970; GK 111r) *is glad*

לִבִּי n.m.s.-1 c.s. sf. (524) *my heart*

וַיָּגֶל consec.-Qal impf. 3 m.s. (גִּיל 162) *and rejoices*

כְבוֹדִי n.m.s.-1 c.s. sf. (II 458) *my soul*

אַף־בְּשָׂרִי conj. (II 64)-n.m.s.-1 c.s. sf. (142) *my body also*

יִשְׁכֹּן Qal impf. 3 m.s. (שָׁכַן 1014) *dwells*

לָבֶטַח prep.-n.m.s. (105) *secure*

16:10

כִּי לֹא־תַעֲזֹב conj. (471)-neg.-Qal impf. 2 m.s. (I 736 עָזַב) *for thou dost not give up*

נַפְשִׁי n.f.s.-1 c.s. sf. (659) *me*

לִשְׁאוֹל prep.-n.f.s. (982) *to Sheol*

לֹא־תִתֵּן neg.-Qal impf. 2 m.s. (נָתַן 678; GK 114m) *or let* (lit. *you will not give*)

חֲסִידְךָ adj.-2 m.s. sf. (339) *thy godly one*

לִרְאוֹת prep.-Qal inf.cstr. (רָאָה 906) *to see*

שָׁחַת n.f.s. (1001) *the Pit*

16:11

תּוֹדִיעֵנִי Hi. impf. 2 m.s.-1 c.s. sf. (יָדַע 393; GK 114m) *thou dost show me*

אֹרַח n.m.s. cstr. (73) *the path of*

חַיִּים n.m.p. (313) *life*

שֹׂבַע n.m.s. cstr. (959) *fulness of*

שְׂמָחוֹת n.f.p. (970; GK 124e) *joy*

אֶת־פָּנֶיךָ dir.obj.-n.m.p.-2 m.s. sf. (815) *in thy presence*

נְעִמוֹת adj. f.p. (653; GK 122q) *pleasures*

בִּימִינְךָ prep.-n.f.s.-2 m.s. sf. (411) *in thy right hand*

נֶצַח n.m.s. (664) *for evermore*

17:1

תְּפִלָּה n.f.s. (813) *a Prayer*

לְדָוִד prep.-pr.n. (187) *to David*

שִׁמְעָה Qal impv. 2 m.s.-vol.he (שָׁמַע 1033) *hear*

יהוה pr.n. (217) *O Yahweh*

צֶדֶק n.m.s. (841) *a just cause*

הַקְשִׁיבָה Hi. impv. 2 m.s.-vol.he (קָשַׁב 904) *attend*

רִנָּתִי n.f.s.-1 c.s. sf. (943) *my cry*

הַאֲזִינָה Hi. impv. 2 m.s.-vol.he (אָזַן 24) *give ear*

תְּפִלָּתִי n.f.s.-1 c.s. sf. (813) *to my prayer*

בְּלֹא שִׂפְתֵי prep.-neg.-n.f.p. cstr. (973) *from lips free of*

מִרְמָה n.f.s. (941) *deceit*

17:2

מִלְּפָנֶיךָ prep.-prep.-n.m.p.-2 m.s. sf. (815) *from thee*

מִשְׁפָּטִי n.m.s.-1 c.s. sf. (1048) *my vindication*

יֵצֵא Qal impf. 3 m.s. (יָצָא 422) *let come*

עֵינֶיךָ n.f. du.-2 m.s. sf. (744) *thy eyes*

תֶּחֱזֶינָה Qal impf. 3 f.p. (חָזָה 302) *let see*

מֵישָׁרִים n.m.p. (449) *the right*

17:3

בָּחַנְתָּ Qal pf. 2 m.s. (בָּחַן 103) *if thou triest*

לִבִּי n.m.s.-1 c.s. sf. (524) *my heart*

פָּקַדְתָּ Qal pf. 2 m.s. (פָּקַד 823) *if thou visitest*

לַּיְלָה n.m.s. (538) *by night*

צְרַפְתַּנִי Qal pf. 2 m.s.-1 c.s. sf. (צָרַף 864; GK 59h) *if thou testest me*

בַל־תִּמְצָא neg. (115)-Qal impf. 2 m.s. (מָצָא 592) *thou wilt find no*

זַמֹּתִי Qal pf. 1 c.s. (זָמַם 273) *wickedness in me* if rd. as זַמֹּתִי (lit. *I have considered*)

בַּל־יַעֲבָר־ neg. (115)-Qal impf. 3 m.s. (עָבַר 716) *does not transgress*

פִּי n.m.s.-1 c.s. sf. (804) *my mouth*

17:4

לִפְעֻלּוֹת prep. (GK 143e)-n.f.p. cstr. (821) *with regard to the works of*

אָדָם n.m.s. (9) *men*

בִּדְבַר prep.-n.m.s. cstr. (182) *by the word of*

שְׂפָתֶיךָ n.f. du.-2 m.s. sf. (973) *thy lips*

אֲנִי שָׁמַרְתִּי pers.pr. 1 c.s. (58)-Qal pf. 1 c.s. (שָׁמַר 1036) *I have avoided*

אָרְחוֹת n.m.p. cstr. (73) *the ways of*

פָּרִיץ n.m.s. (829) *the violent*

17:5

תָּמֹךְ Qal inf.abs. (תָּמַךְ 1069; GK 113gg) *have held fast*

אֲשֻׁרַי n.f.p.-1 c.s. sf. (81) *my steps*

בְּמַעְגְּלוֹתֶיךָ prep.-n.m.p.-2 m.s. sf. (722) *to thy paths*

בַּל־נָמוֹטּוּ neg. (115)-Ni. pf. 3 c.p. (מוֹט 556) *have not slipped*

פְּעָמָי n.f.p.-1 c.s. sf. paus. (821) *my feet*

17:6

אֲנִי־קְרָאתִיךָ pers.pr. 1 c.s. (58)-Qal pf. 1 c.s.-2 m.s. sf. (קָרָא 894) *I call upon thee*

כִּי־תַעֲנֵנִי conj. (471)-Qal impf. 2 m.s.-1 c.s. sf. (I 772 עָנָה) *for thou wilt answer me*

אֵל n.m.s. (42) *O God*

הַט־אָזְנְךָ Hi. impv. 2 m.s. (נָטָה 639)-n.f.s.-2 m.s. sf. (23) *incline thy ear*

לִי prep.-1 c.s. sf. *to me*

שְׁמַע Qal impv. 2 m.s. (שָׁמַע 1033) *hear*

אִמְרָתִי n.f.s.-1 c.s. sf. (57) *my words*

17:7

הַפְלֵה Hi. impv. 2 m.s. (פָּלָה 811) *wondrously show*

חֲסָדֶיךָ n.m.p.-2 m.s. sf. (338) *thy steadfast love*

מוֹשִׁיעַ Hi. ptc. (יָשַׁע 446) *O Savior*

חוֹסִים Qal act.ptc. m.p. (חָסָה 340) *of those who seek refuge*

מִמִּתְקוֹמְמִים prep.-Hithpolel ptc. m.p. (קוּם 877) *from their adversaries*

בִּימִינֶךָ prep.-n.f.s.-2 m.s. sf. paus. (411) *at thy right hand*

17:8

שָׁמְרֵנִי Qal impv. 2 m.s.-1 c.s. sf. (שָׁמַר 1036) *keep me*

כְּאִישׁוֹן prep.-n.m.s. cstr. (36) *as the apple of*

בַּת־עָיִן n.f.s. cstr. (I 123)-n.f.s. paus. (744) *the eye*

בְּצֵל prep.-n.m.s. cstr. (853) *in the shadow of*

כְּנָפֶיךָ n.f.p.-2 m.s. sf. (489) *thy wings*

תַּסְתִּירֵנִי Hi. impf. 2 m.s.-1 c.s. sf. (סָתַר 711) *hide me*

17:9

מִפְּנֵי prep.-n.m.p. cstr. (815) *from*

רְשָׁעִים adj. m.p. (957) *the wicked*

זוּ שַׁדּוּנִי rel. (262; GK 138g)-Qal pf. 3 c.p.-1 c.s. sf. (שָׁדַד 994) *who despoil me*

אֹיְבַי Qal act.ptc. m.p.-1 c.s. sf. (אָיַב 33) *my enemies*

בְּנֶפֶשׁ prep.-n.f.s. (659) *deadly*

יַקִּיפוּ Hi. impf. 3 m.p. (נָקַף II 668) *who surround*

עָלָי prep.-1 c.s. sf. paus. *me*

17:10

חֶלְבָּמוֹ n.m.s.-3 m.p. sf. (316; GK 91f) *their hearts*

סָּגְרוּ Qal pf. 3 c.p. (סָגַר 688) *they close to pity*

פִּימוֹ n.m.s.-3 m.p. sf. (804) *with their mouths*
דִּבְּרוּ Pi. pf. 3 c.p. (דָּבַר 180) *they speak*
בְגֵאוּת prep.-n.f.s. (145) *arrogantly*

17:11

אַשֻּׁרֵינוּ n.f.p.-1 c.p. sf. (81) *our steps*
עַתָּה סְבָבוּנִי adv. (773)-Qal pf. 3 c.p.-1 c.s. sf. (685 סָבַב) *now they surround me*
עֵינֵיהֶם n.f. du.-3 m.p. sf. (744) *their eyes*
יָשִׁיתוּ Qal pf. 3 c.p. (שִׁית 1011) *they set*
לִנְטוֹת prep.-Qal inf.cstr. (נָטָה 639) *to cast me*
בָּאָרֶץ prep.-def.art.-n.f.s. (75) *to the ground*

17:12

דִּמְיֹנוֹ n.m.s.-3 m.s. sf. (198) *his likeness*
כְּאַרְיֵה prep.-n.m.s. (71) *as a lion*
יִכְסוֹף Qal impf. 3 m.s. (כָּסַף 493) *eager*
לִטְרוֹף prep.-Qal inf.cstr. (טָרַף 382) *to tear*
וְכִכְפִיר conj.-prep.-n.m.s. (498; GK 126p) *and as a young lion*
יֹשֵׁב Qal act.ptc. (יָשַׁב 442) *lurking*
בְּמִסְתָּרִים prep.-n.m.p. (712) *in ambush*

17:13

קוּמָה Qal impv. 2 m.s.-vol.he (877) *arise*
יהוה pr.n. (217) *O Yahweh*
קַדְּמָה פָנָיו Pi. impv. 2 m.s.-vol.he (קָדַם 869)-n.m.p.-3 m.s. sf. (815) *confront them*
הַכְרִיעֵהוּ Hi. impv. 2 m.s.-3 m.s. sf. (כָּרַע 502) *overthrow them*
פַּלְּטָה Pi. impv. 2 m.s.-vol.he (פָּלַט 812) *deliver*
נַפְשִׁי n.f.s.-1 c.s. sf. (659) *my life*
מֵרָשָׁע prep.-adj. m.s. (957) *from the wicked*
חַרְבֶּךָ n.f.s.-2 m.s. sf. (352; GK 144m) *by thy sword*

17:14

מִמְתִים prep.-n.m.p. (607) *from men*
יָדְךָ n.f.s.-2 m.s. sf. (388) *by thy hand*
יהוה pr.n. (217) *O Yahweh*
מִמְתִים v.supra *from men*
מֵחֶלֶד prep.-n.m.s. (317) *of the world*
חֶלְקָם n.m.s.-3 m.p. sf. (324) *whose portion*
בַּחַיִּים prep.-def.art.-n.m.p. (313) *in life*
וּצְפִינְךָ conj.-Qal pass.ptc.-2 m.s. sf. (צָפַן 860) *and with what thou hast stored up*
תְּמַלֵּא Pi. impf. 3 f.s. (מָלֵא 569) *may be filled*
בִטְנָם n.f.s.-3 m.p. sf. (105) *their belly*
יִשְׂבְּעוּ Qal impf. 3 m.p. (שָׂבֵעַ 959) *may have more than enough*
בָנִים n.m.p. (119) *their children*
וְהִנִּיחוּ conj.-Hi. pf. 3 c.p. (נוּחַ 628) *may they leave*
יִתְרָם n.m.s.-3 m.p. sf. (451) *something over*
לְעוֹלְלֵיהֶם prep.-n.m.p.-3 m.p. sf. (760) *to their babes*

17:15

אֲנִי pers.pr. 1 c.s. (58) *as for me*
בְּצֶדֶק prep.-n.m.s. (841) *in righteousness*
אֶחֱזֶה Qal impf. 1 c.s. (חָזָה 302) *I shall behold*
פָנֶיךָ n.m.p.-2 m.s. sf. (815) *thy face*
אֶשְׂבְּעָה Qal impf. 1 c.s.-vol.he (שָׂבֵעַ 959) *I shall be satisfied*
בְהָקִיץ prep.-Hi. inf.cstr. (קִיץ I 884) *when I awake*
תְּמוּנָתֶךָ n.f.s.-2 m.s. sf. (568) *thy form*

18:1

לַמְנַצֵּחַ prep.-def.art.-Pi. ptc. (I 663) *to the choirmaster*
לְעֶבֶד יהוה prep.-n.m.s. cstr. (713)-pr.n. (217) *to the servant of Yahweh*
לְדָוִד prep.-pr.n. (187) *to David*
אֲשֶׁר דִּבֶּר rel. (81)-Pi. pf. 3 m.s. (דָּבַר (180) *who addressed*
ליהוה prep.-pr.n. (217) *to Yahweh*
אֶת־דִּבְרֵי dir.obj.-n.m.p. cstr. (182) *the words of*
הַשִּׁירָה הַזֹּאת def.art.-n.f.s. (1010)-def.art. -demons.adj. f.s. (260) *this song*
בְּיוֹם prep.-n.m.s. cstr. (398; GK 130d) *on the day when*
הִצִּיל־יהוה Hi. pf. 3 m.s. (נָצַל 664; GK 53,l) -pr.n. (217) *Yahweh delivered*
אוֹתוֹ dir.obj.-3 m.s. sf. *him*
מִכַּף prep.-n.f.s. cstr. (496) *from the hand of*
כָּל־אֹיְבָיו n.m.s. cstr. (481)-Qal act.ptc. m.p.-3 m.s. sf. (אָיַב 33) *all his enemies*
וּמִיַּד conj. (GK 154aN)-prep.-n.f.s. cstr. (388) *and from the hand of*
שָׁאוּל pr.n. (982) *Saul*

18:2

וַיֹּאמַר consec.-Qal impf. 3 m.s. (55; GK 2r) *he said*
אֶרְחָמְךָ Qal impf. 1 c.s.-2 m.s. sf. (רָחַם 933) *I love thee*
יהוה pr.n. (217) *O Yahweh*
חִזְקִי n.m.s.-1 c.s. sf. (305) *my strength*

18:3

יהוה pr.n. (217) *Yahweh*
סַלְעִי n.m.s.-1 c.s. sf. (I 700) *my rock*

וּמְצוּדָתִי conj.-n.f.s.-1 c.s. sf. (II 845) *and my fortress*
וּמְפַלְטִי conj.-Pi. ptc.-1 c.s. sf. (פָּלַט 812) *and my deliverer*
אֵלִי n.m.s.-1 c.s. sf. (42) *my God*
צוּרִי n.m.s.-1 c.s. sf. (849) *my rock*
אֶחֱסֶה־בּוֹ Qal impf. 1 c.s. (חָסָה 340; GK 155i) -prep.-3 m.s. sf. *in whom I take refuge*
מָגִנִּי n.m.s.-1 c.s. sf. (171) *my shield*
וְקֶרֶן־ conj.-n.f.s. cstr. (901) *and the horn of*
יִשְׁעִי n.m.s.-1 c.s. sf. (447) *my salvation*
מִשְׂגַּבִּי n.m.s.-1 c.s. sf. (960; GK 93pp) *my stronghold*

18:4

מְהֻלָּל Pu. ptc. (הָלַל II 237; GK 116e,132b) *who is worthy to be praised*
אֶקְרָא Qal impf. 1 c.s. (קָרָא 894; GK 10gN) *I call upon*
יהוה pr.n. (217) *Yahweh*
וּמִן־אֹיְבַי conj.-prep.-Qal act.ptc. m.p.-1 c.s. sf. (33 אָיַב) *and from my enemies*
אִוָּשֵׁעַ Ni. impf. 1 c.s. (יָשַׁע 442) *I am saved*

18:5

אֲפָפוּנִי Qal pf. 3 c.p.-1 c.s. sf. (אָפַף 67) *encompassed me*
חֶבְלֵי־מָוֶת n.m.p. cstr. (286)-n.m.s. (560) *the cords of death*
וְנַחֲלֵי conj.-n.m.p. cstr. (636) *and the torrents of*
בְלִיַּעַל n.m.s. (116) *perdition*
יְבַעֲתוּנִי Pi. impf. 3 m.p.-1 c.s. sf. (בָּעַת 129) *assailed me*

18:6

חֶבְלֵי n.m.p. cstr. (286) *the cords of*
שְׁאוֹל n.f.s. (982) *Sheol*
סְבָבוּנִי Qal pf. 3 c.p.-1 c.s. sf. (סָבַב 685) *entangled me*
קִדְּמוּנִי Pi. pf. 3 c.p.-1 c.s. sf. (קָדַם 869) *confronted me*
מוֹקְשֵׁי n.m.p. cstr. (430) *the snares of*
מָוֶת n.m.s. (560) *death*

18:7

בַּצַּר־לִי prep.-def.art.-n.m.s. (II 865)-prep.-1 c.s. sf. *in my distress*
אֶקְרָא Qal impf. 1 c.s. (קָרָא 894; GK 107b) *I called upon*
יהוה pr.n. (217) *Yahweh*
וְאֶת־אֱלֹהַי conj.-prep.-n.m.p.-1 c.s. sf. (43) *to my God*
אֲשַׁוֵּעַ Pi. impf. 1 c.s. (שָׁוַע 1002) *I cried for help*
יִשְׁמַע Qal impf. 3 m.s. (שָׁמַע 1033) *he heard*
מֵהֵיכָלוֹ prep.-n.m.s.-3 m.s. sf. (228) *from his temple*
קוֹלִי n.m.s.-1 c.s. sf. (876) *my voice*
וְשַׁוְעָתִי conj.-n.f.s.-1 c.s. sf. (1003) *and my cry*
לְפָנָיו prep.-n.m.p.-3 m.s. sf. (815) *to him*
תָּבוֹא Qal impf. 3 f.s. (בּוֹא 97) *reached*
בְאָזְנָיו prep.-n.f. du.-3 m.s. sf. (23) *his ears*

18:8

וַתִּגְעַשׁ consec.-Qal impf. 3 f.s. (גָּעַשׁ 172) *then reeled*
וַתִּרְעַשׁ consec.-Qal impf. 3 f.s. (רָעַשׁ 950) *and rocked*
הָאָרֶץ def.art.-n.f.s. (75) *the earth*
וּמוֹסְדֵי conj.-n.m.p. cstr. (414) *the foundations also*
הָרִים n.m.p. (249) *the mountains*
יִרְגָּזוּ Qal impf. 3 m.p. paus. (רָגַז 919) *trembled*
וַיִּתְגָּעֲשׁוּ consec.-Hith. impf. 3 m.p. (גָּעַשׁ 172) *and quaked*
כִּי־חָרָה לוֹ conj. (471)-Qal pf. 3 m.s. (354) -prep.-3 m.s. sf. *because he was angry*

18:9

עָלָה Qal pf. 3 m.s. (748) *went up*
עָשָׁן n.m.s. (I 798) *smoke*
בְּאַפּוֹ prep.-n.m.s.-3 m.s. sf. (I 60) *from his nostrils*
וְאֵשׁ־מִפִּיו conj.-n.f.s. (77)-prep.-n.m.p.-3 m.s. sf. (804) *and fire from his mouth*
תֹּאכֵל Qal impf. 3 f.s. (אָכַל 37) *devouring*
גֶּחָלִים n.f.p. (160) *glowing coals*
בָּעֲרוּ Qal pf. 3 c.p. (בָּעַר 128) *flamed forth*
מִמֶּנּוּ prep.-3 m.s. sf. *from him*

18:10

וַיֵּט consec.-Qal impf. 3 m.s. (נָטָה 639) *he bowed*
שָׁמַיִם n.m. du. (1029) *the heavens*
וַיֵּרַד consec.-Qal impf. 3 m.s. (יָרַד 432; GK 69p) *and came down*
וַעֲרָפֶל conj.-n.m.s. (791) *and thick darkness*
תַּחַת רַגְלָיו prep. (1065)-n.f. du.-3 m.s. sf. (919) *under his feet*

18:11

וַיִּרְכַּב consec.-Qal impf. 3 m.s. (רָכַב 938) *he rode*
עַל־כְּרוּב prep.-n.m.s. (II 500) *on a cherub*

וַיָּעֹף consec.-Qal impf. 3 m.s. (עוּף I 733) *and flew*

וַיֵּדֶא consec.-Qal impf. 3 m.s. (דָּאָה 178) *he came swiftly*

עַל־כַּנְפֵי־ prep.-n.f.p. cstr. (489) *upon the wings of*

רוּחַ n.f.s. (924) *the wind*

18:12

יָשֶׁת Qal impf. 3 m.s. (שִׁית 1011; GK 109k) *he made*

חֹשֶׁךְ n.m.s. (365) *darkness*

סִתְרוֹ n.m.s.-3 m.s. sf. (712) *his covering*

סְבִיבוֹתָיו subst.p.-3 m.s. sf. (686) *around him*

סֻכָּתוֹ n.f.s.-3 m.s. sf. (697) *his canopy*

חֶשְׁכַת־מַיִם n.f.s. cstr. (365)-n.m.p. (565) *dark with water*

עָבֵי שְׁחָקִים n.f.p. cstr. (II 728)-n.m.p. (1007) *thick clouds*

18:13

מִנֹּגַהּ prep.-n.f.s. (I 618) *out of the brightness*

נֶגְדּוֹ subst.-3 m.s. sf. (617) *before him*

עָבָיו n.m.p.-3 m.s. sf. (II 728) *his clouds*

עָבְרוּ Qal pf. 3 c.p. (עָבַר 716) *there broke through*

בָּרָד n.m.s. (135) *hailstones*

וְגַחֲלֵי־אֵשׁ conj.-n.f.p. cstr. (160)-n.f.s. (77) *and coals of fire*

18:14

וַיַּרְעֵם consec.-Hi. impf. 3 m.s. (רָעַם 947) *also thundered*

בַּשָּׁמַיִם prep.-def.art.-n.m. du. (1029) *in the heavens*

יהוה pr.n. (217) *Yahweh*

וְעֶלְיוֹן conj.-n.m.s. (751) *and the Most High*

יִתֵּן Qal impf. 3 m.s. (נָתַן 678) *uttered*

קֹלוֹ n.m.s.-3 m.s. sf. (876) *his voice*

בָּרָד n.m.s. (135) *hailstones*

וְגַחֲלֵי־אֵשׁ conj.-n.f.p. cstr. (160)-n.f.s. (77) *and coals of fire*

18:15

וַיִּשְׁלַח consec.-Qal impf. 3 m.s. (שָׁלַח 1018) *and he sent out*

חִצָּיו n.m.p.-3 m.s. sf. (346) *his arrows*

וַיְפִיצֵם consec.-Hi. impf. 3 m.s.-3 m.p. sf. (פּוּץ I 806) *and scattered them*

וּבְרָקִים conj.-n.m.p. (140) *and lightnings*

רָב Qal pf. 3 m.s. (רָבַב II 914) *he flashed forth*

וַיְהֻמֵּם consec.-Qal impf. 3 m.s.-3 m.p. sf. (הָמַם 243) *and routed them*

18:16

וַיֵּרָאוּ consec.-Ni. impf. 3 m.p. (רָאָה 906) *then were seen*

אֲפִיקֵי n.m.p. cstr. (67) *the channels of*

מַיִם n.m.p. (565) *the sea*

וַיִּגָּלוּ consec.-Ni. impf. 3 m.p. (גָּלָה 162) *and were laid bare*

מוֹסְדוֹת n.m.p. cstr. (414) *the foundations of*

תֵּבֵל n.f.s. (385) *the world*

מִגַּעֲרָתְךָ prep.-n.f.s.-2 m.s. sf. (172) *at thy rebuke*

יהוה pr.n. (217) *O Yahweh*

מִנִּשְׁמַת prep.-n.f.s. cstr. (675) *at the blast of*

רוּחַ n.f.s. cstr. (924) *the breath of*

אַפֶּךָ n.m.s.-2 m.s. sf. (I 60) *thy nostrils*

18:17

יִשְׁלַח Qal impf. 3 m.s. (שָׁלַח 1018; GK 117g) *he reached*

מִמָּרוֹם prep.-n.m.s. (928) *from on high*

יִקָּחֵנִי Qal impf. 3 m.s.-1 c.s. sf. (לָקַח 542) *he took me*

יַמְשֵׁנִי Hi. impf. 3 m.s.-1 c.s. sf. (מָשָׁה 602) *he drew me*

מִמַּיִם רַבִּים prep.-n.m.p. (565)-adj. m.p. (I 912) *out of many waters*

18:18

יַצִּילֵנִי Hi. impf. 3 m.s.-1 c.s. sf. (נָצַל 664) *he delivered me*

מֵאֹיְבִי prep.-Qal act.ptc.-1 c.s. sf. (אָיַב 33) *from my enemy*

עָז adj. m.s. paus. (738; GK 126z) *strong*

וּמִשֹּׂנְאַי conj.-prep.-Qal act.ptc. m.p.-1 c.s. sf. (971 שָׂנֵא) *and from those who hated me*

כִּי־אָמְצוּ conj.-Qal pf. 3 c.p. (אָמֵץ 54) *for they were mighty*

מִמֶּנִּי prep.-1 c.s. sf. *from me*

18:19

יְקַדְּמוּנִי Pi. impf. 3 m.p.-1 c.s. sf. (קָדַם 869) *they came upon me*

בְיוֹם־ prep.-n.m.s. cstr. (398) *in the day of*

אֵידִי n.m.s.-1 c.s. sf. (15) *my calamity*

וַיְהִי־ consec.-Qal impf. 3 m.s. (הָיָה 224) *but was*

יהוה pr.n. (217) *Yahweh*

לְמִשְׁעָן לִי prep.-n.m.s. (1044)-prep.-1 c.s. sf. *my stay*

18:20

וַיּוֹצִיאֵנִי consec.-Hi. impf. 3 m.s.-1 c.s. sf. (יָצָא 422) *and he brought me forth*

לַמֶּרְחָב prep.-def.art.-n.m.s. (932) *into a broad place*

יְחַלְּצֵנִי Pi. impf. 3 m.s.-1 c.s. sf. (חָלַץ I 322) *and he delivered me*

כִּי חָפֵץ בִּי conj. (471)-Qal pf. 3 m.s. (342) -prep.-1 c.s. sf. *because he delighted in me*

18:21

יִגְמְלֵנִי Qal impf. 3 m.s.-1 c.s. sf. (גָּמַל 168) *rewarded me*

יהוה pr.n. (217) *Yahweh*

כְּצִדְקִי prep.-n.m.s.-1 c.s. sf. (841) *according to my righteousness*

כְּבֹר prep.-n.m.s. cstr. (II 141) *according to the cleanness of*

יָדַי n.f. du.-1 c.s. sf. (388) *my hands*

יָשִׁיב לִי Hi. impf. 3 m.s. (שׁוּב 996)-prep.-1 c.s. sf. *he recompensed me*

18:22

כִּי־שָׁמַרְתִּי conj. (471)-Qal pf. 1 c.s. (שָׁמַר 1036) *for I have kept*

דַּרְכֵי n.m.p. cstr. (202) *the ways of*

יהוה pr.n. (217) *Yahweh*

וְלֹא־רָשַׁעְתִּי conj.-neg.-Qal pf. 1 c.s. (רָשַׁע 957) *and have not wickedly departed*

מֵאֱלֹהָי prep. (GK 119ff)-n.m.p.-1 c.s. sf. paus. (43) *from my God*

18:23

כִּי כָל־מִשְׁפָּטָיו conj. (471)-n.m.s. cstr. (481) -n.m.p.-3 m.s. sf. (1048) *for all his ordinances*

לְנֶגְדִּי prep.-subst.-1 c.s. sf. (617) *before me*

וְחֻקֹּתָיו conj.-n.f.p.-3 m.s. sf. (349) *and his statutes*

לֹא־אָסִיר מֶנִּי neg.-Hi. impf. 1 c.s. (סוּר 693) -prep.-1 c.s. sf. *I did not put away from me*

18:24

וָאֱהִי consec.-Qal impf. 1 c.s. (הָיָה 224) *and I was*

תָמִים adj. (1071) *blameless*

עִמּוֹ prep.-3 m.s. sf. *before him*

וָאֶשְׁתַּמֵּר consec.-Hith. impf. 1 c.s. (שָׁמַר 1036) *and I kept myself*

מֵעֲוֹנִי prep.-n.m.s.-1 c.s. sf. (730) *from my guilt*

18:25

וַיָּשֶׁב־יהוה consec.-Hi. impf. 3 m.s. (שׁוּב 996) -pr.n. (217) *therefore Yahweh has recompensed*

לִי prep.-1 c.s. sf. *me*

כְּצִדְקִי prep.-n.m.s.-1 c.s. sf. (841) *according to my righteousness*

כְּבֹר יָדַי prep.-n.m.s. cstr. (II 141)-n.f. du.-1 c.s. sf. (388) *according to the cleanness of my hands*

לְנֶגֶד עֵינָיו prep.-subst. (617)-n.f. du.-3 m.s. sf. (744) *in his sight*

18:26

עִם־חָסִיד prep.-adj. (339) *with the loyal*

תִּתְחַסָּד Hith. impf. 2 m.s. paus. (חָסַד I 338) *thou dost show thyself loyal*

עִם־גְּבַר תָּמִים prep.-n.m.s. cstr. (I 149; GK 93h,s)-adj. (1071) *with the blameless man*

תִּתַּמָּם Hith. impf. 2 m.s. (תָּמַם 1070) *thou dost show thyself blameless*

18:27

עִם־נָבָר prep.-Ni. ptc. (בָּרַר 140) *with the pure*

תִּתְבָּרָר Hith. impf. 2 m.s. paus. (בָּרַר 140) *thou dost show thyself pure*

וְעִם־עִקֵּשׁ conj.-prep.-adj. (I 786) *and with the crooked*

תִּתְפַּתָּל Hith. impf. 2 m.s. paus. (פָּתַל 836) *thou dost show thyself perverse*

18:28

כִּי־אַתָּה conj. (471)-pers.pr. 2 m.s. (61) *for thou*

עַם־עָנִי n.m.s. (I 766)-adj. (776) *a humble people*

תוֹשִׁיעַ Hi. impf. 2 m.s. (יָשַׁע 446) *dost deliver*

וְעֵינַיִם רָמוֹת conj.-n.f. du. (744)-Qal act.ptc. f.p. (רוּם 926; GK 132f) *but the haughty eyes*

תַּשְׁפִּיל Hi. impf. 2 m.s. (שָׁפֵל 1050) *thou dost bring down*

18:29

כִּי־אַתָּה conj. (471)-pers.pr. 2 m.s. (61) *yea, thou*

תָּאִיר Hi. impf. 2 m.s. (אוֹר 21) *dost light*

נֵרִי n.m.s.-1 c.s. sf. (632) *my lamp*

יהוה אֱלֹהַי pr.n. (217)-n.m.p.-1 c.s. sf. (43) *Yahweh my God*

יַגִּיהַּ Hi. impf. 3 m.s. (נָגַהּ 618) *lightens*

חָשְׁכִּי n.m.s.-1 c.s. sf. (365) *my darkness*

18:30

כִּי־בְךָ conj. (471)-prep.-2 m.s. sf. (GK 119o) *yea, by thee*

אָרֻץ Qal impf. 1 c.s. (רָצַץ 954; GK 67q) *I can crush*
גְּדוּד n.m.s. (I 151) *a troop*
וּבֵאלֹהַי conj.-prep.-n.m.p.-1 c.s. sf. (43) *and by my God*
אֲדַלֶּג־ Pi. impf. 1 c.s. (דָּלַג 194) *I can leap over*
שׁוּר n.m.s. (II 1004) *a wall*

18:31

הָאֵל def.art.-n.m.s. (42; GK 140d,143a) *this God*
תָּמִים adj. (1071) *perfect*
דַּרְכּוֹ n.m.s.-3 m.s. sf. (202; GK 126c) *his way*
אִמְרַת־יהוה n.f.s. cstr. (57)-pr.n. (217) *the promise of Yahweh*
צְרוּפָה Qal pass.ptc. f.s. (צָרַף 864) *proves true*
מָגֵן n.m.s. (171) *a shield*
הוּא pers.pr. 3 m.s. (214) *he is*
לְכֹל prep.-n.m.s. cstr. (481) *for all*
הַחֹסִים def.art.-Qal act.ptc. m.p. (חָסָה 340) *those who take refuge*
בּוֹ prep.-3 m.s. sf. *in him*

18:32

כִּי מִי conj. (471)-interr. (566) *for who*
אֱלוֹהַּ n.m.s. (42) *God*
מִבַּלְעֲדֵי יהוה prep.-prep. (116)-pr.n. (217) *but Yahweh*
וּמִי conj.-interr. (566) *and who*
צוּר n.m.s. (849) *a rock*
זוּלָתִי prep. cstr. (265) *except*
אֱלֹהֵינוּ n.m.p.-1 c.p. sf. (43) *our God*

18:33

הָאֵל def.art.-n.m.s. (42) *the God*
הַמְאַזְּרֵנִי def.art.-Pi. ptc.-1 c.s. sf. (אָזַר 25; GK 116f,117cc) *who girded me*
חָיִל n.m.s. paus. (298) *with strength*
וַיִּתֵּן consec.-Qal impf. 3 m.s. (נָתַן 678; GK 116x) *and made*
תָּמִים subst. (1071) *safe*
דַּרְכִּי n.m.s.-1 c.s. sf. (202) *my way*

18:34

מְשַׁוֶּה Pi. ptc. (שָׁוָה II 1001) *he made*
רַגְלַי n.f. du.-1 c.s. sf. (919) *my feet*
כָּאַיָּלוֹת prep.-def.art.-n.f.p. (19) *like hinds' feet*
וְעַל בָּמֹתַי conj.-prep.-n.f.p.-1 c.s. sf. (119) *on the (my) heights*
יַעֲמִידֵנִי Hi. impf. 3 m.s.-1 c.s. sf. (עָמַד 763) *he set me secure*

18:35

מְלַמֵּד Pi. ptc. (540) *he trains*
יָדַי n.f. du.-1 c.s. sf. (388) *my hands*
לַמִּלְחָמָה prep.-def.art.-n.f.s. (536) *for war*
וְנִחֲתָה conj.-Pi. pf. 3 f.s. (נָחַת 639) *so that can bend*
קֶשֶׁת־נְחוּשָׁה n.f.s. cstr. (905)-n.f.s. (639) *a bow of bronze*
זְרוֹעֹתָי n.f.p.-1 c.s. sf. paus. (283; GK 145k) *my arms*

18:36

וַתִּתֶּן־לִי consec.-Qal impf. 2 m.s. (נָתַן 678) -prep.-1 c.s. sf. *thou hast given me*
מָגֵן n.m.s. cstr. (171) *the shield of*
יִשְׁעֶךָ n.m.s.-2 m.s. sf. (447) *thy salvation*
וִימִינְךָ conj.-n.f.s.-2 m.s. sf. (411) *and thy right hand*
תִסְעָדֵנִי Qal impf. 3 f.s.-1 c.s. sf. (סָעַד 703) *supported me*
וְעַנְוַתְךָ conj.-n.f.s.-2 m.s. sf. (776) *and thy condescension*
תַרְבֵּנִי Hi. impf. 3 f.s.-1 c.s. sf. (רָבָה I 915) *made me great*

18:37

תַּרְחִיב Hi. impf. 2 m.s. (רָחַב 931) *thou didst give a wide place*
צַעֲדִי n.m.s.-1 c.s. sf. (857) *my step*
תַחְתָּי prep.-1 c.s. sf. paus. (1065) *under me*
וְלֹא מָעֲדוּ conj.-neg.-Qal pf. 3 c.p. (מָעַד 588) *and did not slip*
קַרְסֻלָּי n.f.p.-1 c.s. sf. paus. (902) *my ankles*

18:38

אֶרְדּוֹף Qal impf. 1 c.s. (רָדַף 922) *I pursued*
אוֹיְבַי Qal act.ptc. m.p.-1 c.s. sf. (אָיַב 33) *my enemies*
וְאַשִּׂיגֵם conj. (GK 107bN)-Hi. impf. 1 c.s.-3 m.p. sf. (נָשַׂג 673) *and overtook them*
וְלֹא־אָשׁוּב conj.-neg.-Qal impf. 1 c.s. (שׁוּב 996) *and did not turn back*
עַד־כַּלּוֹתָם adv. (III 723)-Pi. inf.cstr.-3 m.p. sf. (477 כָּלָה) *until they were consumed*

18:39

אֶמְחָצֵם Qal impf. 1 c.s.-3 m.p. sf. (מָחַץ 563) *I thrust them through*
וְלֹא־יֻכְלוּ conj.-neg.-Qal impf. 3 m.p. (יָכֹל 407) *so that they were not able*
קוּם Qal inf.cstr. (877) *to rise*
יִפְּלוּ Qal impf. 3 m.p. (נָפַל 656) *they fell*

תַּחַת רַגְלָי prep. (1065)–n.f. du.–1 c.s. sf. paus. (919) *under my feet*

18:40

וַתְּאַזְּרֵנִי consec.–Pi. impf. 2 m.s.–1 c.s. sf. (אָזַר 25) *for thou didst gird me*
חַיִל n.m.s. (298) *with strength*
לַמִּלְחָמָה prep.–def.art.–n.f.s. (536) *for the battle*
תַּכְרִיעַ Hi. impf. 2 m.s. (כָּרַע 502) *thou didst make sink*
קָמַי Qal act.ptc. m.p.–1 c.s. sf. (קוּם 877; GK 116i) *my assailants*
תַּחְתָּי prep.–1 c.s. sf. paus. (1065) *under me*

18:41

וְאֹיְבַי conj.–Qal act.ptc. m.p.–1 c.s. sf. (אָיַב 33) *and my enemies*
נָתַתָּה לִּי Qal pf. 2 m.s. (נָתַן 678; GK 117iiN) –prep.–1 c.s. sf. *thou didst make turn to me*
עֹרֶף n.m.s. (791) *their backs*
וּמְשַׂנְאַי conj.–Pi. ptc. m.p.–1 c.s. sf. (שָׂנֵא 971) *and those who hated me*
אַצְמִיתֵם Hi. impf. 1 c.s.–3 m.p. sf. (צָמַת 856) *I destroyed*

18:42

יְשַׁוְּעוּ Pi. impf. 3 m.p. (שָׁוַע 1002) *they cried for help*
וְאֵין־מוֹשִׁיעַ conj.–subst. cstr. (II 34)–Hi. ptc. (446 יָשַׁע) *but there was none to save*
עַל־יהוה prep.–pr.n. (217) *to Yahweh*
וְלֹא עָנָם conj.–neg.–Qal pf. 3 m.s.–3 m.p. sf. (I 772 עָנָה) *but he did not answer them*

18:43

וְאֶשְׁחָקֵם conj.–Qal impf. 1 c.s.–3 m.p. sf. (שָׁחַק 1006) *I beat them fine*
כְּעָפָר prep.–n.m.s. (779) *as dust*
עַל־פְּנֵי־רוּחַ prep.–n.m.p. cstr. (815)–n.f.s. (924) *before the wind*
כְּטִיט prep.–n.m.s. cstr. (376) *like the mire of*
חוּצוֹת n.m.p. (299) *the streets*
אֲרִיקֵם Hi. impf. 1 c.s.–3 m.p. sf. (ריק 937; but some rd. אֲדִקֵם as Hi. impf. 1 c.s.–3 m.p. sf. of דָּקַק 200; cf. II Sam. 22:43) *I cast them out*

18:44

תְּפַלְּטֵנִי Pi. impf. 2 m.s.–1 c.s. sf. (פָּלַט 812) *thou didst deliver me*
מֵרִיבֵי prep.–n.m.p. cstr. (936) *from strife with*
עָם n.m.s. (I 766) *people*
תְּשִׂימֵנִי Qal impf. 2 m.s.–1 c.s. sf. (שׂוּם 962) *thou didst make me*
לְרֹאשׁ prep.–n.m.s. cstr. (910) *the head of*
גּוֹיִם n.m.p. (156) *the nations*
עַם n.m.s. (I 766) *people*
לֹא־יָדַעְתִּי neg.–Qal pf. 1 c.s. (יָדַע 393) *whom I had not known*
יַעַבְדוּנִי Qal impf. 3 m.p.–1 c.s. sf. (עָבַד 712) *served me*

18:45

לְשֵׁמַע אֹזֶן prep.–n.m.s. cstr. (1034)–n.f.s. (23) *as soon as they heard*
יִשָּׁמְעוּ לִי Ni. impf. 3 m.p. (שָׁמַע 1033)–prep.–1 c.s. sf. *they obeyed me*
בְּנֵי־נֵכָר n.m.p. cstr. (119)–n.m.s. (648) *foreigners*
יְכַחֲשׁוּ Pi. impf. 3 m.p. (כָּחַשׁ 471) *came cringing*
לִי prep.–1 c.s. sf. *to me*

18:46

בְּנֵי־נֵכָר n.m.p. cstr. (119)–n.m.s. (648) *foreigners*
יִבֹּלוּ Qal impf. 3 m.p. (נָבֵל 615) *lost heart*
וְיַחְרְגוּ conj.–Qal impf. 3 m.p. (חָרַג 353) *and came trembling*
מִמִּסְגְּרוֹתֵיהֶם prep.–n.f.p.–3 m.p. sf. (689) *out of their fastnesses*

18:47

חַי־יהוה adj. (311)–pr.n. (217) *Yahweh lives*
וּבָרוּךְ conj.–Qal pass.ptc. (בָּרַךְ 138) *and blessed be*
צוּרִי n.m.s.–1 c.s. sf. (849) *my rock*
וְיָרוּם conj.–Qal impf. 3 m.s. (רוּם 926) *and exalted be*
אֱלוֹהֵי n.m.p. cstr. (43) *the God of*
יִשְׁעִי n.m.s.–1 c.s. sf. (447) *my salvation*

18:48

הָאֵל def.art.–n.m.s. (42) *the God*
הַנּוֹתֵן def.art.–Qal act.ptc. (נָתַן 678) *who gave*
נְקָמוֹת n.f.p. (668) *vengeance*
לִי prep.–1 c.s. sf. *to me*
וַיַּדְבֵּר consec.–Hi. impf. 3 m.s. (דָּבַר 180) *and subdued*
עַמִּים n.m.p. (I 766) *peoples*
תַּחְתָּי prep.–1 c.s. sf. paus. (1065) *under me*

18:49

מְפַלְּטִי Pi. ptc.–1 c.s. sf. (פָּלַט 812) *who delivered me*

מֵאֹיְבָי prep.-Qal act.ptc. m.p.-1 c.s. sf. (אָיַב 33) *from my enemies*
אַף מִן־קָמַי conj. (II 64)-prep.-Qal act.ptc. m.p.-1 c.s. sf. (קוּם 877; GK 116i) *yea, above my adversaries*
תְּרוֹמְמֵנִי Polel impf. 2 m.s.-1 c.s. sf. (רוּם 926) *thou didst exalt me*
מֵאִישׁ prep.-n.m.s. cstr. (35) *from men of*
חָמָס n.m.s. (329) *violence*
תַּצִּילֵנִי Hi. impf. 2 m.s.-1 c.s. sf. (נָצַל 664) *thou didst deliver me*

18:50

עַל־כֵּן prep.-adv. (485) *for this*
אוֹדְךָ Hi. impf. 1 c.s.-2 m.s. sf. (יָדָה 392) *I will extol thee*
בַגּוֹיִם prep.-def.art.-n.m.p. (156) *among the nations*
יהוה pr.n. (217) *O Yahweh*
וּלְשִׁמְךָ conj.-prep.-n.m.s.-2 m.s. sf. (1027) *and to thy name*
אֲזַמֵּרָה Pi. impf. 1 c.s.-vol.he (זָמַר I 274) *I will sing praises*

18:51

מַגְדִּל Hi. ptc. (גָּדַל 152) *making great*
יְשׁוּעוֹת n.f.p. cstr. (447) *the triumphs of*
מַלְכּוֹ n.m.s.-3 m.s. sf. (I 572) *his king*
וְעֹשֶׂה conj.-Qal act.ptc. (עָשָׂה I 793) *and shows*
חֶסֶד n.m.s. (338) *steadfast love*
לִמְשִׁיחוֹ prep.-n.m.s.-3 m.s. sf. (603) *to his anointed*
לְדָוִד prep.-pr.n. (187) *to David*
וּלְזַרְעוֹ conj.-prep.-n.m.s.-3 m.s. sf. (282) *and to his descendants*
עַד־עוֹלָם prep. (III 723)-n.m.s. (761) *for ever*

19:1

לַמְנַצֵּחַ prep.-Pi. ptc. (663) *to the choirmaster*
מִזְמוֹר n.m.s. (274) *a Psalm*
לְדָוִד prep.-pr.n. (187) *to David*

19:2

הַשָּׁמַיִם def.art.-n.m. du. (1029) *the heavens*
מְסַפְּרִים Pi. ptc. m.p. (סָפַר 707) *are telling*
כְּבוֹד־אֵל n.m.s. cstr. (458)-n.m.s. (42) *the glory of God*
וּמַעֲשֵׂה יָדָיו conj.-n.m.s. cstr. (795)-n.f.p.-3 m.s. sf. (388) *and his handiwork*
מַגִּיד Hi. ptc. (נָגַד 616) *proclaims*
הָרָקִיעַ def.art.-n.m.s. (956) *the firmament*

19:3

יוֹם לְיוֹם n.m.s. (398)-prep.-v.supra *day to day*
יַבִּיעַ Hi. impf. 3 m.s. (נָבַע 615) *pours forth*
אֹמֶר n.m.s. (56) *speech*
וְלַיְלָה לְּלַיְלָה conj.-n.m.s. (538)-prep.-v.supra (GK 20f) *and night to night*
יְחַוֶּה־דָּעַת Pi. impf. 3 m.s. (חָוָה III 296)-n.f.s. paus. (395) *declares knowledge*

19:4

אֵין־אֹמֶר subst.s. cstr. (II 34)-n.m.s. (56) *there is no speech*
וְאֵין דְּבָרִים conj.-v.supra-n.m.p. (182) *nor are there words*
בְּלִי נִשְׁמָע neg. (115); GK 152t)-Ni. ptc. (1033) *is not heard*
קוֹלָם n.m.s.-3 m.p. sf. (876) *their voice*

19:5

בְּכָל־הָאָרֶץ prep.-n.m.s. cstr. (481)-def.art.-n.f.s. (75) *through all the earth*
יָצָא קַוָּם Qal pf. 3 m.s. (422)-n.m.s.-3 m.p. sf. (II 876; some rd. קוֹלָם = *their voice*) *their line goes out*
וּבִקְצֵה תֵבֵל conj.-n.m.s. cstr. (892)-n.f.s. (385) *and to the end of the world*
מִלֵּיהֶם n.f.p.-3 m.p. sf. (576) *their words*
לַשֶּׁמֶשׁ prep.-def.art.-n.f.s. (1039) *for the sun*
שָׂם־אֹהֶל Qal pf. 3 m.s. (שׂוּם I 962)-n.m.s. (13) *he has set a tent*
בָּהֶם prep.-3 m.p. sf. (GK 135p) *in them*

19:6

וְהוּא כְּחָתָן conj.-pers.pr. 3 m.s. (214; GK 122o) -prep.-n.m.s. (368) *and he like a bridegroom*
יֹצֵא Qal act.ptc. (יָצָא 422) *leaving*
מֵחֻפָּתוֹ prep.-n.f.s.-3 m.s. sf. (I 342) *his chamber*
יָשִׂישׂ Qal impf. 3 m.s. (שׂוּשׂ 965) *he rejoices*
כְּגִבּוֹר prep.-n.m.s. (150) *like a strong man*
לָרוּץ אֹרַח prep.-Qal inf.cstr. (930)-n.m.s. (73) *runs its course*

19:7

מִקְצֵה הַשָּׁמַיִם prep.-n.m.s. cstr. (892)-def.art. -n.m. du. (1029) *from the end of the heavens*
מוֹצָאוֹ n.m.s.-3 m.s. sf. (425) *its rising*
וּתְקוּפָתוֹ conj.-n.f.s.-3 m.s. sf. (880) *and its circuit*
עַל־קְצוֹתָם prep.-n.f.p.-3 m.p. sf. (892) *to the end of them*

וְאֵין נִסְתָּר conj.-subst. cstr. (II 34)-Ni. ptc. (סָתַר 711) *and there is nothing hid*
מֵחַמָּתוֹ prep.-n.f.s.-3 m.s. sf. (328) *from its heat*

19:8

תּוֹרַת יהוה n.f.s. cstr. (435)-pr.n. (217) *the law of Yahweh*
תְּמִימָה adj. f.s. (1071) *is perfect*
מְשִׁיבַת Hi. ptc. f.s. cstr. (שׁוּב 996; GK 116g) *reviving*
נָפֶשׁ n.f.s. paus. (659) *the soul*
עֵדוּת יהוה n.f.s. cstr. (730)-v.supra *the testimony of Yahweh*
נֶאֱמָנָה Ni. ptc. f.s. (אָמֵן 52) *is sure*
מַחְכִּימַת Hi. ptc. f.s. cstr. (חָכַם 314) *making wise*
פֶּתִי adj. (834) *the simple*

19:9

פִּקּוּדֵי יהוה n.m.p. cstr. (824; GK 116g)-pr.n. (217) *the precepts of Yahweh*
יְשָׁרִים adj. m.p. (449) *are right*
מְשַׂמְּחֵי־לֵב Pi. ptc. m.p. cstr. (שָׂמַח 970)-n.m.s. (523) *rejoicing the heart*
מִצְוַת יהוה n.f.s. cstr. (846)-v.supra *the commandment of Yahweh*
בָּרָה adj. f.s. (II 141) *is pure*
מְאִירַת Hi. ptc. f.s. cstr. (21) *enlightening*
עֵינָיִם n.f. du. paus. (744) *the eyes*

19:10

יִרְאַת יהוה n.f.s. cstr. (432)-pr.n. (217) *the fear of Yahweh*
טְהוֹרָה adj. f.s. (373) *is clean*
עוֹמֶדֶת Qal act.ptc. f.s. segh. (עָמַד 763) *enduring*
לָעַד prep.-n.m.s. (723) *for ever*
מִשְׁפְּטֵי־יהוה n.m.p. cstr. (1048)-v.supra *the ordinances of Yahweh*
אֱמֶת n.f.s. (54; GK 141c) *are true*
צָדְקוּ Qal pf. 3 c.p. (צָדַק 842) *are righteous*
יַחְדָּו adv. (403) *altogether*

19:11

הַנֶּחֱמָדִים def.art.-Ni. ptc. m.p. (חָמַד 326; GK 116e) *more to be desired*
מִזָּהָב prep.-n.m.s. (262) *than gold*
וּמִפַּז רָב conj.-prep.-n.m.s. (808)-adj. m.s. paus. (I 912) *and even much fine gold*
וּמְתוּקִים conj.-adj. m.p. (608) *and sweeter*
מִדְּבַשׁ prep.-n.m.s. (185) *than honey*
וְנֹפֶת צוּפִים conj.-n.m.s. cstr. (661)-n.m.p. (I 847) *and drippings of the honeycomb*

19:12

גַּם־עַבְדְּךָ adv. (168)-n.m.s.-2 m.s. sf. (712) *moreover thy servant*
נִזְהָר בָּהֶם Ni. ptc. (II 264)-prep.-3 m.p. sf. *is warned by them*
בְּשָׁמְרָם prep.-Qal inf.cstr.-3 m.p. sf. (שָׁמַר 1036) *in keeping them*
עֵקֶב רָב n.m.s. (784)-adj. m.s. paus. (I 912) *great reward*

19:13

שְׁגִיאוֹת n.f.p. (993) *(his) errors*
מִי־יָבִין interr. (566)-Qal impf. 3 m.s. (בִּין 106) *who can discern*
מִנִּסְתָּרוֹת prep.-Ni. ptc. f.p. (סָתַר 711) *from hidden faults*
נַקֵּנִי Pi. impv. 2 m.s.-1 c.s. sf. (נָקָה 667) *clear thou me*

19:14

גַּם מִזֵּדִים adv. (168)-prep.-adj. m.p. (267) *also from presumptuous sins*
חֲשֹׂךְ עַבְדֶּךָ Qal impv. 2 m.s. (חָשַׂךְ 362) -n.m.s.-2 m.s. sf. (713) *keep back thy servant*
אַל־יִמְשְׁלוּ־בִי neg.-Qal impf. 3 m.p. (605) -prep.-1 c.s. sf. *let them not have dominion over me*
אָז אֵיתָם adv. (23)-Qal impf. 1 c.s. (תָּמַם 1070; GK 67p) *then I shall be blameless*
וְנִקֵּיתִי conj.-Pi. pf. 1 c.s. (נָקָה 667; GK 49k) *and innocent*
מִפֶּשַׁע רָב prep.-n.m.s. (833)-adj. m.s. paus. (I 912) *of great transgression*

19:15

יִהְיוּ Qal impf. 3 m.p. juss. (הָיָה 224) *let be*
לְרָצוֹן prep.-n.m.s. (953) *acceptable*
אִמְרֵי־פִי n.m.p. cstr. (56)-n.m.s.-1 c.s. sf. (804) *the words of my mouth*
וְהֶגְיוֹן לִבִּי conj.-n.m.s. cstr. (212)-n.m.s.-1 c.s. sf. (523) *and the meditation of my heart*
לְפָנֶיךָ prep.-n.m.p.-2 m.s. sf. (815) *in thy sight*
יהוה pr.n. (217) *O Yahweh*
צוּרִי n.m.s.-1 c.s. sf. (I 849) *my rock*
וְגֹאֲלִי conj.-Qal act.ptc.-1 c.s. sf. (I 145) *and my redeemer*

20:1

לַמְנַצֵּחַ prep.-Pi. ptc. (663) *to the choirmaster*
מִזְמוֹר n.m.s. (274) *a Psalm*
לְדָוִד prep.-pr.n. (187) *to David*

20:2

יַעַנְךָ יהוה Qal impf. 3 m.s.-2 m.s. sf. (עָנָה I 772)-pr.n. (217) *Yahweh answer you*
בְּיוֹם צָרָה prep.-n.m.s. cstr. (398)-n.f.s. (865) *in the day of trouble*
יְשַׂגֶּבְךָ Pi. impf. 3 m.s.-2 m.s. sf. (שָׂגַב 960) *may ... protect you*
שֵׁם n.m.s. cstr. (1027) *the name of*
אֱלֹהֵי יַעֲקֹב n.m.p. cstr. (43)-pr.n. (784) *the God of Jacob*

20:3

יִשְׁלַח Qal impf. 3 m.s. (שָׁלַח 1018) *may he send*
עֶזְרְךָ n.m.s.-2 m.s. sf. (740; GK 135m) *you help*
מִקֹּדֶשׁ prep.-n.m.s. (871) *from the sanctuary*
וּמִצִּיּוֹן conj.-prep.-pr.n. (851) *and from Zion*
יִסְעָדֶךָּ Qal impf. 3 m.s.-2 m.s. sf. paus. (סָעַד 703) *give you support*

20:4

יִזְכֹּר Qal impf. 3 m.s. (269) *may he remember*
כָּל־מִנְחֹתֶךָ n.m.s. cstr. (481)-n.f.p.-2 m.s. sf. (585) *all your offerings*
וְעוֹלָתְךָ conj.-n.f.p.-2 m.s. sf. (750) *and your burnt sacrifices*
יְדַשְּׁנֶה Pi. impf. 3 m.s. vol. (דָּשֵׁן 206; GK 48d) *regard with favor*
סֶלָה interj. (699) *Selah*

20:5

יִתֶּן־לְךָ Qal impf. 3 m.s. (נָתַן 678)-prep.-2 m.s. sf. *may he grant you*
כִלְבָבֶךָ prep.-n.m.s.-2 m.s. sf. (523) *your heart's desire*
וְכָל־עֲצָתְךָ conj.-n.m.s. cstr. (481)-n.f.s.-2 m.s. sf. (420) *and all your plans*
יְמַלֵּא Pi. impf. 3 m.s. (569) *fulfil*

20:6

נְרַנְּנָה Pi. impf. 1 c.p. coh. (רָנַן 943) *may we shout for joy*
בִּישׁוּעָתֶךָ prep.-n.f.s.-2 m.s. sf. paus. (447) *over your victory*
וּבְשֵׁם־אֱלֹהֵינוּ conj.-prep.-n.m.s. cstr. (1027) -n.m.p.-1 c.p. sf. (43) *and in the name of our God*
נִדְגֹּל Qal impf. 1 c.p. (דָּגַל 186) *set up our banners*
יְמַלֵּא יהוה Pi. impf. 3 m.s. (569)-pr.n. (217) *may Yahweh fulfil*
כָּל־מִשְׁאֲלוֹתֶיךָ n.m.s. cstr. (481)-n.f.p.-2 m.s. sf. (982) *all your petitions*

20:7

עַתָּה יָדַעְתִּי adv. (773)-Qal pf. 1 c.s. (393) *now I know*
כִּי הוֹשִׁיעַ יהוה conj. (471)-Hi. pf. 3 m.s. (יָשַׁע 446)-pr.n. (217) *that Yahweh will help*
מְשִׁיחוֹ n.m.s.-3 m.s. sf. (603) *his anointed*
יַעֲנֵהוּ Qal impf. 3 m.s.-3 m.s. sf. (עָנָה I 772) *he will answer him*
מִשְּׁמֵי קָדְשׁוֹ prep.-n.m. du. cstr. (1029)-n.m.s.-3 m.s. sf. (871) *from his holy heaven*
בִּגְבֻרוֹת prep.-n.f.p. (150) *with mighty victories*
יֵשַׁע יְמִינוֹ Qal impf. 3 m.s. (יָשַׁע 446)-n.m.s.-3 m.s. sf. (411) *he will save by his right hand*

20:8

אֵלֶּה בָרֶכֶב demons.adj. c.p. (41)-prep.-def. art.-n.m.s. (939) *these of chariots*
וְאֵלֶּה בַסּוּסִים conj.-v.supra-prep.-def.art.-n.m.p. (692) *and these of horses*
וַאֲנַחְנוּ בְּשֵׁם־ conj.-pers.pr. 1 c.p. (59)-prep. -n.m.s. cstr. (1027) *but we of the name of*
יהוה אֱלֹהֵינוּ pr.n. (217)-n.m.p.-1 c.p. sf. (43) *Yahweh our God*
נַזְכִּיר Hi. impf. 1 c.p. (זָכַר 269) *boast*

20:9

הֵמָּה כָּרְעוּ pers.pr. 3 m.p. (241)-Qal pf. 3 c.p. (502) *they will collapse*
וְנָפָלוּ conj.-Qal pf. 3 c.p. paus. (656) *and fall*
וַאֲנַחְנוּ קַּמְנוּ conj.-pers.pr. 1 c.p. (59)-Qal pf. 1 c.p. (קוּם 877) *but we shall rise*
וַנִּתְעוֹדָד consec.-Hithpo'el impf. 1 c.p. (עוּד 728) *and stand upright*

20:10

יהוה הוֹשִׁיעָה pr.n. (217)-Hi. impv. 2 m.s. coh. (446 יָשַׁע) *O Yahweh give victory*
הַמֶּלֶךְ def.art.-n.m.s. (I 572) *to the king*
יַעֲנֵנוּ Qal impf. 3 m.s.-1 c.p. sf. (עָנָה I 772) *let him answer us*
בְיוֹם־קָרְאֵנוּ prep.-n.m.s. cstr. (398)-Qal inf.cstr.-1 c.p. sf. (קָרָא 894) *when we call*

21:1

לַמְנַצֵּחַ prep.-Pi. ptc. (663) *to the choirmaster*
מִזְמוֹר n.m.s. (274) *a Psalm*
לְדָוִד prep.-pr.n. (187) *to David*

21:2

יהוה בְּעָזְּךָ pr.n. (217)-prep.-n.m.s.-2 m.s. sf. (738) *O Yahweh, in thy strength*

יִשְׂמַח־מֶלֶךְ Qal impf. 3 m.s. (שָׂמַח 970)-n.m.s. (I 572: GK 126h) *the king rejoices*

וּבִישׁוּעָתְךָ conj.-prep.-n.f.s.-2 m.s. sf. (447) *and in thy help*

מַה־יָּגִיל interr. (GK 148b)-Qal impf. 3 m.s. (162; GK 109k) *how he exults*

מְאֹד adv/ (547) *greatly*

21:3

תַּאֲוַת לִבּוֹ n.f.s. cstr. (16)-n.m.s.-3 m.s. sf. (524) *his heart's desire*

נָתַתָּה לּוֹ Qal pf. 2 m.s. (נָתַן 678)-prep.-3 m.s. sf. *thou hast given him*

וַאֲרֶשֶׁת שְׂפָתָיו conj.-n.f.s. cstr. (77)-n.f.s.-3 m.s. sf. (973) *and the request of his lips*

בַּל־מָנַעְתָּ neg. (115)-Qal pf. 2 m.s. (586) *hast not withheld*

סֶלָה interj. (699) *Selah*

21:4

כִּי־תְקַדְּמֶנּוּ conj. (471)-Pi. impf. 2 m.s.-3 m.s. sf. (קָדַם 869; GK 117ff) *for thou dost meet him*

בִּרְכוֹת טוֹב n.f.p. cstr. (139)-n.m.s. (II 375) *with goodly blessings*

תָּשִׁית Qal impf. 2 m.s. (שִׁית 1011) *thou dost set*

לְרֹאשׁוֹ prep.-n.m.s.-3 m.s. sf. (910) *on his head*

עֲטֶרֶת פָּז n.f.s. cstr. (742)-n.m.s. paus. (808) *a gold crown*

21:5

חַיִּים שָׁאַל n.m.p. (313)-Qal pf. 3 m.s. (981) *he asked life*

מִמְּךָ prep.-2 m.s. sf. *of thee*

נָתַתָּה לּוֹ Qal impf. 2 m.s. (נָתַן 678)-prep.-3 m.s. sf. *thou gavest it to him*

אֹרֶךְ יָמִים n.m.s. cstr. (73)-n.m.p. (398) *length of days*

עוֹלָם וָעֶד n.m.s. (761)-conj.-n.m.s. paus. (I 723) *for ever and ever*

21:6

גָּדוֹל כְּבוֹדוֹ adj. m.s. (152)-n.m.s.-3 m.s. sf. (458) *his glory is great*

בִּישׁוּעָתֶךָ prep.-n.f.s.-2 m.s. sf. paus. (447) *through thy help*

הוֹד וְהָדָר n.m.s. (217)-conj.-n.m.s. (214) *splendor and majesty*

תְּשַׁוֶּה עָלָיו Pi. impf. 2 m.s. (II 1001)-prep.-3 m.s. sf. *thou dost bestow upon him*

21:7

כִּי־תְשִׁיתֵהוּ conj. (471)-Qal impf. 2 m.s.-3 m.s. sf. (1011; GK 117ii) *yea, thou dost make him*

בְרָכוֹת n.f.p. (139) *most blessed*

לָעַד prep.-n.m.s. (I 723) *for ever*

תְּחַדֵּהוּ Pi. impf. 2 m.s.-3 m.s. sf. (חָדָה II 292) *thou dost make him glad*

בְשִׂמְחָה prep.-n.f.s. (970) *with the joy*

אֶת־פָּנֶיךָ dir.obj.-n.m.p.-2 m.s. sf. (815) *of thy presence*

21:8

כִּי־הַמֶּלֶךְ conj. (471)-def.art.-n.m.s. (I 572) *for the king*

בֹּטֵחַ בַּיהוה Qal act.ptc. (בָּטַח 105)-prep.-pr.n. (217) *trusts in Yahweh*

וּבְחֶסֶד עֶלְיוֹן conj.-prep.-n.m.s. cstr. (338)-n.m.s. (751) *and through the steadfast love of the Most High*

בַּל־יִמּוֹט neg. (115)-Ni. impf. 3 m.s. (מוֹט 556) *he shall not be moved*

21:9

תִּמְצָא יָדְךָ Qal impf. 3 f.s. (592)-n.f.s.-2 m.s. sf. (388) *your hand will find out*

לְכָל־אֹיְבֶיךָ prep.-n.m.s. cstr. (481)-Qal act.ptc. m.p.-2 m.s. sf. (אָיַב 33) *all your enemies*

יְמִינְךָ תִּמְצָא n.f.s.-2 m.s. sf. (411)-Qal impf. 3 f.s. (מָצָא 592) *your right hand will find out*

שֹׂנְאֶיךָ Qal act.ptc. m.p.-2 m.s. sf. (שָׂנֵא 971) *those who hate you*

21:10

תְּשִׁיתֵמוֹ Qal impf. 2 m.s.-3 m.p. sf. (1011) *you will make them*

כְּתַנּוּר אֵשׁ prep.-n.m.s. cstr. (1072)-n.f.s. (77) *as a blazing oven*

לְעֵת פָּנֶיךָ prep.-n.f.s. cstr. (773)-n.m.p.-2 m.s. sf. (815) *when you appear*

יהוה בְּאַפּוֹ pr.n. (217)-prep.-n.m.s.-3 m.s. sf. (60) *Yahweh in his wrath*

יְבַלְּעֵם Pi. impf. 3 m.s.-3 m.p. sf. (118) *will swallow them up*

וְתֹאכְלֵם אֵשׁ conj.-Qal impf. 3 f.s.-3 m.p. sf. (37 אָכַל)-n.f.s. (77) *and fire will consume them*

21:11

פִּרְיָמוֹ מֵאֶרֶץ n.m.s.-3 m.p. sf. (826)-prep.-n.f.s. (75) *their offspring from the earth*

תְּאַבֵּד Pi. impf. 2 m.s. (אָבַד 1) *will kill*

וְזַרְעָם conj.-n.m.s.-3 m.p. sf. (282) *and their children*

מִבְּנֵי אָדָם prep.-n.m.p. cstr. (119)-n.m.s. (9) *from among the sons of men*

21:12

כִּי־נָטוּ conj. (471)-Qal pf. 3 c.p. (נָטָה 639) *if they plan*
עָלֶיךָ prep.-2 m.s. sf. *against you*
רָעָה n.f.s. (948) *evil*
חָשְׁבוּ Qal pf. 3 c.p. (חָשַׁב *362) if they devise*
מְזִמָּה n.f.s. (273) *mischief*
בַּל־יוּכָלוּ neg. (115)-Qal impf. 3 m.p. paus. (יָכֹל 407) *they will not succeed*

21:13

כִּי תְּשִׁיתֵמוֹ conj. (471)-Qal impf. 2 m.s.-3 m.p. sf. (1011; GK 117iiN) *for you put them*
שֶׁכֶם n.m.s. (I 1014) *to flight*
בְּמֵיתָרֶיךָ prep.-n.m.p.-2 m.s. sf. (452) *with your bows*
תְּכוֹנֵן Polel impf. 2 m.s. (כּוּן 465) *you will aim*
עַל־פְּנֵיהֶם prep.-n.m.p.-3 m.p. sf. (815) *at their faces*

21:14

רוּמָה יהוה Qal impv. 2 m.s.-coh.he (רוּם 926) -pr.n. (217) *be exalted, O Yahweh,*
בְעֻזֶּךָ prep.-n.m.s.-2 m.s. sf. (738) *in thy strength*
נָשִׁירָה Qal impf. 1 c.p.-coh.he (שִׁיר 1010) *we will sing*
וּנְזַמְּרָה conj.-Pi. impf. 1 c.p.-coh.he (זָמַר I 274) *and praise*
גְּבוּרָתֶךָ n.f.s.-2 m.s. sf. paus. (150) *thy power*

22:1

לַמְנַצֵּחַ prep.-Pi. ptc. (663) *to the choirmaster*
עַל־אַיֶּלֶת prep.-n.f.s. cstr. (19) *according to the Hind of*
הַשַּׁחַר def.art.-n.m.s. (1007) *the Dawn*
מִזְמוֹר n.m.s. (274) *a Psalm*
לְדָוִד prep.-pr.n. (187) *to David*

22:2

אֵלִי אֵלִי n.m.s.-1 c.s. sf. (42)-v.supra *My God, My God*
לָמָה prep.-interr. (552) *why*
עֲזַבְתָּנִי Qal pf. 2 m.s.-1 c.s. sf. (I 736; GK 59h) *hast thou forsaken me?*
רָחוֹק adj. (935) *far*
מִישׁוּעָתִי prep.-n.f.s.-1 c.s. sf. (447) *from helping me*
דִּבְרֵי n.m.p. cstr. (182) *the words of*
שַׁאֲגָתִי n.f.s.-1 c.s. sf. (980) *my groaning*

22:3

אֱלֹהַי n.m.p.-1 c.s. sf. (43) *O my God*
אֶקְרָא Qal impf. 1 c.s. (894) *I cry*
יוֹמָם adv. (401) *by day*
וְלֹא תַעֲנֶה conj.-neg.-Qal impf. 2 m.s. (עָנָה I 772) *but thou dost not answer*
וְלַיְלָה conj.-n.m.s. (538) *and by night*
וְלֹא־דוּמִיָּה לִי conj.-neg.-n.f.s. (189; GK 152d)-prep.-1 c.s. sf. *but find no rest*

22:4

וְאַתָּה קָדוֹשׁ conj.-pers.pr. 2 m.s. (61)-n.m.s. (871) *Yet thou art holy*
יוֹשֵׁב Qal act.ptc. (יָשַׁב 442; GK 117bb) *enthroned*
תְּהִלּוֹת יִשְׂרָאֵל n.f.p. cstr. (239)-pr.n. (975) *on the praises of Israel*

22:5

בְּךָ בָּטְחוּ prep.-2 m.s. sf.-Qal pf. 3 c.p. (בָּטַח 105) *in thee ... trusted*
אֲבֹתֵינוּ n.m.p.-1 c.p. sf. (3) *our fathers*
בָּטְחוּ v.supra *they trusted*
וַתְּפַלְּטֵמוֹ consec.-Pi. impf. 2 m.s.-3 m.p. sf. (פָּלַט 812) *and thou didst deliver them*

22:6

אֵלֶיךָ זָעֲקוּ prep.-2 m.s. sf.-Qal pf. 3 c.p. (זָעַק 277) *to thee they cried*
וְנִמְלָטוּ conj.-Ni. pf. 3 c.p. (מָלַט 572; GK 112h) *and were saved*
בְּךָ בָטְחוּ prep.-2 m.s. sf.-Qal pf. 3 c.p. (בָּטַח 105) *in thee they trusted*
וְלֹא־בוֹשׁוּ conj.-neg.-Qal pf. 3 c.p. (בּוֹשׁ 101) *and were not dissappointed*

22:7

וְאָנֹכִי תוֹלַעַת conj.-pers.pr. 1 c.s. (59)-n.f.s. (1069) *but I am a worm*
וְלֹא־אִישׁ conj.-neg.-n.m.s. (35) *and no man*
חֶרְפַּת אָדָם n.f.s. cstr. (357)-n.m.s. (9) *scorned by men*
וּבְזוּי עָם conj.-Qal pass.ptc. cstr. (בָּזָה 102)-n.m.s. (I 766) *and despised by the people*

22:8

כָּל־רֹאַי n.m.s. cstr. (481)-Qal act.ptc. m.p.-1 c.s. sf. (רָאָה 906) *all who see me*
יַלְעִגוּ לִי Hi. impf. 3 m.p. (לָעַג 541)-prep.-1 c.s. sf. *mock at me*

יַפְטִירוּ בְשָׂפָה Hi. impf. 3 m.p. (פָּטַר 809)–prep. (GK 119q)–n.f.s. (973) *they make mouths at me*
יָנִיעוּ Hi. impf. 3 m.p. (נוּעַ 631) *they wag*
רֹאשׁ n.m.s. (910) *their heads*

22:9

גֹּל Qal impv. 2 m.s. (גָּלַל II 164) *roll*
אֶל־יהוה prep.–pr.n. (217) *on Yahweh*
יְפַלְּטֵהוּ Pi. impf. 3 m.s.–3 m.s. sf. (812; GK 144p) *let him deliver him*
יַצִּילֵהוּ Hi. impf. 3 m.s.–3 m.s. sf. (נָצַל 664) *let him rescue him*
כִּי חָפֵץ בּוֹ conj. (471)–Qal pf. 3 m.s. (342) –prep.–3 m.s. sf. *for he delights in him*

22:10

כִּי־אַתָּה conj. (471)–pers.pr. 2 m.s. (61) *yet thou art*
גֹחִי Qal act.ptc.–1 c.s. sf. (גִּיחַ 161) *he who took me*
מִבָּטֶן prep.–n.f.s. paus. (105) *from the womb*
מַבְטִיחִי Hi. ptc.–1 c.s. sf. (בָּטַח 105) *thou didst keep me safe*
עַל־שְׁדֵי אִמִּי prep.–n.m. du. cstr. (994)–n.f.s.–1 c.s. sf. (51) *upon my mother's breasts*

22:11

עָלֶיךָ prep.–2 m.s. sf. *upon thee*
הָשְׁלַכְתִּי Ho. pf. 1 c.s. (שָׁלַךְ 1020) *was I cast*
מֵרָחֶם prep.–n.m.s. paus. (933) *from the womb*
מִבֶּטֶן אִמִּי prep.–n.f.s. cstr. (105)–n.m.s.–1 c.s. sf. (51) *from the womb of my mother*
אֵלִי אָתָּה n.m.s.–1 c.s. sf. (42)–pers.pr. 2 m.s. paus. *(61) thou hast been my God*

22:12

אַל־תִּרְחַק neg.vol.–Qal impf. 2 m.s. (934) *be not far*
מִמֶּנִּי prep.–1 c.s. sf. *from me*
כִּי־צָרָה conj. (471)–n.f.s. (865) *for trouble*
קְרוֹבָה adj. f.s. (898) *is near*
כִּי־אֵין עוֹזֵר conj. (471)–neg. cstr. (II 34)–Qal act.ptc. (740) *and there is none to help*

22:13

סְבָבוּנִי Qal pf. 3 c.p.–1 c.s. sf. (סָבַב 685) *encompass me*
פָּרִים רַבִּים n.m.p. (830)–adj. m.p. (I 912) *many bulls*
אַבִּירֵי בָשָׁן adj. m.p. cstr. (7)–pr.n. (143) *strong bulls of Bashan*

כִּתְּרוּנִי Pi. pf. 3 c.p.–1 c.s. sf. (509) *surround me*

22:14

פָּצוּ עָלַי Qal pf. 3 c.p. (פָּצָה 822)–prep.–1 c.s. sf. *they open wide at me*
פִּיהֶם n.m.s.–3 m.p. sf. (804) *their mouths*
אַרְיֵה n.m.s. (71; GK 118r) *like a lion*
טֹרֵף Qal act.ptc. (382) *ravening*
וְשֹׁאֵג conj.–Qal act.ptc. (980) *and roaring*

22:15

כַּמַּיִם prep.–def.art.–n.m.p. (565) *like water*
נִשְׁפַּכְתִּי Ni. pf. 1 c.s. (שָׁפַךְ 1049) *I am poured out*
וְהִתְפָּרְדוּ conj.–Hith. pf. 3 c.p. (פָּרַד 825) *and are out of joint*
כָּל־עַצְמוֹתָי n.m.s. cstr. (481)–n.f.p.–1 c.s. sf. (782) *all my bones*
הָיָה Qal pf. 3 m.s. (224) *is*
לִבִּי n.m.s.–1 c.s. sf. (524) *my heart*
כַּדּוֹנָג prep.–def.art.–n.m.s. (200) *like wax*
נָמֵס Ni. ptc. (מָסַס 587) *it is melted*
בְּתוֹךְ מֵעָי prep.–n.m.s. cstr. (1063)–n.m.p.–1 c.s. sf. (588) *within my breast*

22:16

יָבֵשׁ Qal pf. 3 m.s. (386) *is dried up*
כַּחֶרֶשׂ prep.–def.art.–n.m.s. (360) *like a potsherd*
כֹּחִי prep.––1 c.s. sf. (470) *my strength*
וּלְשׁוֹנִי conj.–n.m.s.–1 c.s. sf. (546; GK 122n) *and my tongue*
מֻדְבָּק Ho. ptc. (דָּבַק 179; GK 121c) *cleaves*
מַלְקוֹחָי n.m. du.–1 c.s. sf. paus. (II 544) *to my jaws*
וְלַעֲפַר־מָוֶת conj.–prep.–n.m.s. cstr. (779)–n.m.s. (560) *and in the dust of death*
תִּשְׁפְּתֵנִי Qal impf. 2 m.s.–1 c.s. sf. (1046) *thou dost lay me*

22:17

כִּי סְבָבוּנִי conj. (471)–Qal pf. 3 c.p.–1 c.s. sf. (685) *yea, are round about me*
כְּלָבִים n.m.p. (476) *dogs*
עֲדַת מְרֵעִים n.f.s. cstr. (II 417)–Hi. ptc. m.p. (רָעַע 949) *a company of evildoers*
הִקִּיפוּנִי Hi. pf. 3 c.p.–1 c.s. sf. (נָקַף II 668) *encircle me*
כָּאֲרִי prep.–def.art.–n.m.s. (71; some rd. כָּאֲרוּ and others rd. כָּרוּ; LXX ὤρυξαν) *like the lion*
יָדַי n.f. du.–1 c.s. sf. (388) *my hands*
וְרַגְלָי conj.–n.f. du.–1 c.s. sf. paus. (919) *and my feet*

22:18

אֲסַפֵּר Pi. impf. 1 c.s. (707; GK 107s) *I can count*
כָּל־עַצְמוֹתָי n.m.s. cstr. (481)–n.f.p.–1 c.s. sf. (782) *all my bones*
הֵמָּה יַבִּיטוּ pers.pr. 3 m.p. (241)–Hi. impf. 3 m.p. (נָבַט 613) *they stare*
יִרְאוּ־בִי Qal impf. 3 m.p. (רָאָה 906)–prep.–1 c.s. sf. *and gloat over me*

22:19

יְחַלְּקוּ Pi. impf. 3 m.p. (חָלַק 323) *they divide*
בְגָדַי n.m.s.–1 c.s. sf. (93) *my garments*
לָהֶם prep.–3 m.p. sf. *among them*
וְעַל־לְבוּשִׁי conj.–prep.–n.m.s.–1 c.s. sf. (528) *and for my raiment*
יַפִּילוּ גוֹרָל Hi. impf. 3 m.p. (נָפַל 656)–n.m.s. (174) *they cast lots*

22:20

וְאַתָּה יהוה conj.–pers.pr. 2 m.s. (61)–pr.n. (217) *but thou, O Yahweh,*
אַל־תִּרְחָק neg.coh.–Qal impf. 2 m.s. paus. (רָחַק 934) *be not far off*
אֱיָלוּתִי n.f.s.–1 c.s. sf. (33) *my help*
לְעֶזְרָתִי prep.–n.f.s.–1 c.s. sf. (740) *to my aid*
חוּשָׁה Qal impv. 2 m.s.–coh.he (חוּשׁ I 301) *hasten*

22:21

הַצִּילָה Hi. impv. 2 m.s.–coh.he (נָצַל 664) *deliver*
מֵחֶרֶב prep.–n.f.s. (352) *from the sword*
נַפְשִׁי n.f.s.–1 c.s. sf. (659) *my soul*
מִיַּד־כֶּלֶב prep.–n.f.s. cstr. (388)–n.m.s. (476) *from the power of the dog*
יְחִידָתִי n.f.s.–1 c.s. sf. (402) *my only one* (poet. for *my life*)

22:22

הוֹשִׁיעֵנִי Hi. impv. 2 m.s.–1 c.s. sf. (יָשַׁע 446) *save me*
מִפִּי אַרְיֵה prep.–n.m.s. cstr. (804)–n.m.s. (71) *from the mouth of the lion*
וּמִקַּרְנֵי רֵמִים conj.–prep.–n.f.p. cstr. (901; GK 119ff)–n.m.p. (910; GK 23f) *from the horns of the wild ox*
עֲנִיתָנִי Qal pf. 2 m.s.–1 c.s. sf. (עָנָה I 772; LXX τὴν ταπείνωσίν μου) *thou hast answered me*

22:23

אֲסַפְּרָה Pi. impf. 1 c.s.–coh.he (707) *I will tell*
שִׁמְךָ לְאֶחָי n.m.s.–2 m.s. sf. (1027)–prep.–n.m.p.–1 c.s. sf. (26) *of thy name to my brethren*
בְּתוֹךְ קָהָל prep.–n.m.s. cstr. (1063)–n.m.s. (874) *in the midst of the congregation*
אֲהַלְלֶךָּ Pi. impf. 1 c.s.–2 m.s. sf. (הָלַל II 237) *I will praise thee*

22:24

יִרְאֵי יהוה Qal act.ptc. m.p. cstr. (431)–pr.n. (217) *you who fear Yahweh*
הַלְלוּהוּ Pi. impv. 2 m.p.–3 m.s. sf. (הָלַל II 237) *praise him*
כָּל־זֶרַע יַעֲקֹב n.m.s. cstr. (481)–n.m.s. cstr. (282) –pr.n. (784) *all you sons of Jacob*
כַּבְּדוּהוּ Pi. impv. 2 m.p.–3 m.s. sf. (457) *glorify him*
וְגוּרוּ מִמֶּנּוּ conj.–Qal impv. 2 m.p. (גּוּר III 158) –prep.–3 m.s. sf. *and stand in awe of him*
כָּל־זֶרַע יִשְׂרָאֵל v.supra–v.supra–pr.n. (975) *all you sons of Israel*

22:25

כִּי לֹא־בָזָה conj. (471)–neg.–Qal pf. 3 m.s. (102) *for he has not despised*
וְלֹא שִׁקַּץ conj.–neg.–Pi. pf. 3 m.s. (1055) *or abhorred*
עֱנוּת עָנִי n.f.s. cstr. (776)–adj. (776) *the affliction of the afflicted*
וְלֹא הִסְתִּיר conj.–neg.–Hi. pf. 3 m.s. (711) *and he has not hid*
פָּנָיו n.m.p.–3 m.s. sf. (815) *his face*
מִמֶּנּוּ prep.–3 m.s. sf. *from him*
וּבְשַׁוְּעוֹ אֵלָיו conj.–prep.–Pi. inf.cstr. (שָׁוַע 1002)–prep.–3 m.s. sf. *when he cried to him*
שָׁמֵעַ Qal pf. 3 m.s. (1033) *but he has heard*

22:26

מֵאִתְּךָ תְּהִלָּתִי prep.–prep.–2 m.s. sf.–n.f.s.–1 c.s. sf. (239) *from thee comes my praise*
בְּקָהָל רָב prep.–n.m.s. (874)–adj. m.s. (I 912) *in the great congregation*
נְדָרַי n.m.p.–1 c.s. sf. (623) *my vows*
אֲשַׁלֵּם Pi. impf. 1 c.s. (1022) *I will pay*
נֶגֶד יְרֵאָיו prep. (617)–n.m.p.–3 m.s. sf. (431) *before those who fear him*

22:27

יֹאכְלוּ Qal impf. 3 m.p. (אָכַל 37) *shall eat*
עֲנָוִים n.m.p. (776) *the poor*
וְיִשְׂבָּעוּ conj.–Qal impf. 3 m.p. (959) *and be satisfied*

יְהַלְלוּ יהוה Pi. impf. 3 m.p. (II 237)-pr.n. (217) *shall praise Yahweh*
דֹּרְשָׁיו Qal act.ptc. m.p.-3 m.s. sf. (205) *those who seek him*
יְחִי Qal impf. 3 m.s. apoc. (חָיָה 310) *may live*
לְבַבְכֶם n.m.s.-2 m.p. sf. (523) *your hearts*
לָעַד prep.-n.m.s. (I 723) *for ever*

22:28

יִזְכְּרוּ Qal impf. 3 m.p. (269) *shall remember*
וְיָשֻׁבוּ conj.-Qal impf. 3 m.p. (שׁוּב 996) *and turn*
אֶל־יהוה prep.-pr.n. (217) *to Yahweh*
כָּל־אַפְסֵי־אָרֶץ n.m.s. cstr. (481)-n.m.p. cstr. (67) -n.f.s. paus. (75) *all the ends of the earth*
וְיִשְׁתַּחֲווּ conj.-Hithpalel impf. 3 m.p. (1005) *and shall worship*
לְפָנֶיךָ prep.-n.m.p.-2 m.s. sf. (815) *before (thee) him*
כָּל־מִשְׁפְּחוֹת n.m.s. cstr. (481)-n.f.p. cstr. (1046) *all the families of*
גוֹיִם n.m.p. (156) *the nations*

22:29

כִּי לַיהוה conj. (471)-prep.-pr.n. (217) *for to Yahweh*
הַמְּלוּכָה def.art.-n.f.s. (574) *dominion*
וּמֹשֵׁל conj. (GK 116s)-Qal act.ptc. (605) *and he rules*
בַּגּוֹיִם prep.-def.art.-n.m.p. (156) *over the nations*

22:30

אָכְלוּ Qal pf. 3 c.p. (אָכַל 37) *they have eaten*
וַיִּשְׁתַּחֲווּ consec.-Hithpalel impf. 3 m.p. (1005) *shall bow down*
כָּל־דִּשְׁנֵי־ n.m.s. cstr. (481)-adj. m.p. cstr. (206) *all the proud of*
אֶרֶץ n.f.s. (75) *the earth*
לְפָנָיו prep.-n.m.p.-3 m.s. sf. (815) *before him*
יִכְרְעוּ כָּל־יוֹרְדֵי Qal impf. 3 m.p. (502)-v.supra -Qal act.ptc. m.p. cstr. (432) *shall bow all who go down to*
עָפָר n.m.s. (779) *the dust*
וְנַפְשׁוֹ conj.-n.f.s.-3 m.s. sf. (659) *and he himself*
לֹא חִיָּה neg.-Pi. pf. 3 m.s. (חָיָה 310) *cannot keep alive*

22:31

זֶרַע n.m.s. (282) *posterity*
יַעַבְדֶנּוּ Qal impf. 3 m.s.-3 m.s. sf. (עָבַד 712) *shall serve him*
יְסֻפַּר Pu. impf. 3 m.s. (707) *men shall tell*
לַאדֹנָי prep.-n.m.p.-1 c.s. sf. (10) *of the Lord*
לַדּוֹר prep.-def.art.-n.m.s. (189) *to the coming generation*

22:32

יָבֹאוּ Qal impf. 3 m.p. (בּוֹא 97) *they shall come*
וְיַגִּידוּ conj.-Hi. impf. 3 m.p. (נָגַד 616) *and proclaim*
צִדְקָתוֹ n.f.s.-3 m.s. sf. (842) *his deliverance*
לְעַם נוֹלָד prep.-n.m.s. (I 766)-Ni. ptc. (יָלַד 408; GK 116e) *to a people yet unborn*
כִּי עָשָׂה conj. (471)-Qal pf. 3 m.s. (I 793) *that he has wrought it*

23:1

מִזְמוֹר n.m.s. (274) *a Psalm*
לְדָוִד prep.-pr.n. (187) *to David*
יהוה רֹעִי pr.n. (217)-Qal act.ptc.-1 c.s. sf. (רָעָה I 944) *Yahweh is my shepherd*
לֹא אֶחְסָר neg.-Qal impf. 1 c.s. paus. (חָסֵר 341) *I shall not lack*

23:2

בִּנְאוֹת דֶּשֶׁא prep.-n.f.p. cstr. (II 627; GK 128p)-n.m.s. (206) *in green pastures*
יַרְבִּיצֵנִי Hi. impf. 3 m.s.-1 c.s. sf. (רָבַץ 918) *he makes me lie down*
עַל־מֵי מְנֻחוֹת prep.-n.m.p. cstr. (565)-n.f.p. (629; GK 124e,128p) *beside still waters*
יְנַהֲלֵנִי Pi. impf. 3 m.s.-1 c.s. sf. (624) *he leads me*

23:3

נַפְשִׁי n.f.s.-1 c.s. sf. (659) *my soul*
יְשׁוֹבֵב Polel impf. 3 m.s. (שׁוּב 996) *he restores*
יַנְחֵנִי Hi. impf. 3 m.s.-1 c.s. sf. (נָחָה 634) *he leads me*
בְמַעְגְּלֵי־צֶדֶק prep.-n.m.p. cstr. (722)-n.m.s. (841) *in paths of righteousness*
לְמַעַן שְׁמוֹ prep. (775)-n.m.s.-3 m.s. sf. (1027) *for his name's sake*

23:4

גַּם כִּי־אֵלֵךְ adv. (168)-conj. (471)-Qal impf. 1 c.s. (הָלַךְ 229; GK 107x,159bb) *even though I walk*
בְּגֵיא צַלְמָוֶת prep.-n.m.s. cstr. (161)-n.m.s. (853) *through the shadow of death (deep darkness)*
לֹא־אִירָא neg.-Qal impf. 1 c.s. (יָרֵא 431) *I fear no*
רָע n.m.s. (948) *evil*

כִּי־אַתָּה conj. (471)-pers.pr. 2 m.s. (61) *for thou art*
עִמָּדִי prep.-1 c.s. sf. (767) *with me*
שִׁבְטְךָ n.m.s.-2 m.s. sf. (986) *thy rod*
וּמִשְׁעַנְתֶּךָ conj.-n.f.s.-2 m.s. sf. (1044) *and thy staff*
הֵמָּה יְנַחֲמֻנִי pers.pr. 3 m.p. (241)-Pi. impf. 3 m.p.-1 c.s. sf. (נָחַם 636) *they comfort me*

23:5

תַּעֲרֹךְ Qal impf. 2 m.s. (עָרַךְ 789) *thou preparest*
לְפָנַי prep.-n.m.p.-1 c.s. sf. (815) *before me*
שֻׁלְחָן n.m.s. (1020) *a table*
נֶגֶד צֹרְרָי prep. (617)-Qal act.ptc. m.p.-1 c.s. sf. paus. (III 865) *in the presence of my enemies*
דִּשַּׁנְתָּ Pi. pf. 2 m.s. (206) *thou anointest*
בַשֶּׁמֶן prep.-def.art.-n.m.s. (1032; GK 126n) *with oil*
רֹאשִׁי n.m.s.-1 c.s. sf. (910) *my head*
כּוֹסִי n.f.s.-1 c.s. sf. (468) *my cup*
רְוָיָה n.f.s. (924; GK 141c,d) *overflows*

23:6

אַךְ טוֹב adv. (36)-n.m.s. (III 375) *surely goodness*
וָחֶסֶד conj.-n.m.s. (338) *and mercy*
יִרְדְּפוּנִי Qal impf. 3 m.p.-1 c.s. sf. (922) *shall follow me*
כָּל־יְמֵי חַיָּי n.m.s. cstr. (481)-n.m.p. cstr. (398) -n.m.p.-1 c.s. sf. paus. (313) *all the days of my life*
וְשַׁבְתִּי conj.-Qal pf. 1 c.s. (שׁוּב 996; GK 69mN) or n.f.s.-1 c.s. sf. (I 443) *and I shall dwell*
בְּבֵית יהוה prep.-n.m.s. cstr. (108)-pr.n. (217) *in the house of Yahweh*
לְאֹרֶךְ יָמִים prep.-n.m.s. cstr. (73)-n.m.p. (398) *for ever*

24:1

לְדָוִד prep.-pr.n. (187; GK 129c) *to David*
מִזְמוֹר n.m.s. (274) *a Psalm*
לַיהוה prep.-pr.n. (217) *to Yahweh*
הָאָרֶץ def.art.-n.f.s. (75) *the earth*
וּמְלוֹאָהּ conj.-n.m.s.-3 f.s. sf. (571) *and the fulness thereof*
תֵּבֵל n.f.s. (385) *the world*
וְיֹשְׁבֵי בָהּ conj.-Qal act.ptc. m.p. cstr. (יָשַׁב 442; GK 130a)-prep.-3 f.s. sf. *and those who dwell therein*

24:2

כִּי־הוּא conj. (471)-pers.pr. 3 m.s. (214) *for he*
עַל־יַמִּים prep.-n.m.p. (410) *upon the seas*
יְסָדָהּ Qal pf. 3 m.s.-3 f.s. sf. (יָסַד 413) *has founded it*
וְעַל־נְהָרוֹת conj.-prep.-n.f.p. (625; GK 124e) *and upon the rivers*
יְכוֹנְנֶהָ Polel impf. 3 m.s.-3 f.s. sf. (465; GK 107b) *established it*

24:3

מִי־יַעֲלֶה interr. (566)-Qal impf. 3 m.s. (עָלָה 748) *who shall ascend*
בְהַר־יהוה prep.-n.m.s. cstr. (249)-pr.n. (217) *the hill of Yahweh?*
וּמִי־יָקוּם conj.-v.supra-Qal impf. 3 m.s. (קוּם 877) *and who shall stand*
בִּמְקוֹם קָדְשׁוֹ prep.-n.m.s. cstr. (879)-n.m.s.-3 m.s. sf. (871) *in his holy place?*

24:4

נְקִי כַפַּיִם adj. cstr. (667; GK 128y)-n.f. du. (496) *clean hands*
וּבַר־לֵבָב conj.-adj. cstr. (II 141)-n.m.s. (523) *and a pure heart*
אֲשֶׁר לֹא־נָשָׂא rel. (81)-neg.-Qal pf. 3 m.s. (669) *who does not lift up*
לַשָּׁוְא prep.-def.art.-n.m.s. (996) *to what is false*
נַפְשִׁי n.f.s.-1 c.s. sf. (659; some rd. נַפְשׁוֹ) *my (his) soul*
וְלֹא נִשְׁבַּע conj.-neg.-Ni. pf. 3 m.s. (שָׁבַע 989) *and does not swear*
לְמִרְמָה prep.-n.f.s. (941) *deceitfully*

24:5

יִשָּׂא Qal impf. 3 m.s. (נָשָׂא 669) *he will receive*
בְרָכָה n.f.s. (139) *blessing*
מֵאֵת יהוה prep.-prep. (II 85)-pr.n. (217) *from Yahweh*
וּצְדָקָה conj.-n.f.s. (842) *and vindication*
מֵאֱלֹהֵי יִשְׁעוֹ prep.-n.m.p. cstr. (43)-n.m.s.-3 m.s. sf. (447) *from the God of his salvation*

24:6

זֶה דּוֹר demons.adj. m.s. (260)-n.m.s. cstr. (189) *such is the generation of*
דֹּרְשָׁו Qal act.ptc. m.p.-3 m.s. sf. paus. (דָּרַשׁ 205) *those who seek him*
מְבַקְשֵׁי Pi. ptc. m.p. cstr. (בָּקַשׁ 134) *who seek*
פָנֶיךָ n.m.p.-2 m.s. sf. (815) *thy face*
יַעֲקֹב pr.n. (784) *O Jacob*
סֶלָה interj. (699) *Selah*

24:7

שְׂאוּ Qal impv. 2 m.p. (נָשָׂא 669) *lift up*
שְׁעָרִים n.m.p. (1044) *O gates*
רָאשֵׁיכֶם n.m.p.-2 m.p. sf. (910) *your heads*
וְהִנָּשְׂאוּ conj.-Ni. impv. 2 m.p. (נָשָׂא 669) *and be lifted up*
פִּתְחֵי עוֹלָם n.m.p. cstr. (835)-n.m.s. (761) *O ancient doors*
וְיָבוֹא conj.-Qal impf. 3 m.s. (בּוֹא 97) *that may come in*
מֶלֶךְ הַכָּבוֹד n.m.s. cstr. (I 572)-def.art.-n.m.s. (458) *the King of glory*

24:8

מִי זֶה interr. (566)-demons.adj. m.s. (260; GK 136c) *who is this?*
מֶלֶךְ הַכָּבוֹד n.m.s. cstr. (I 572)-def.art.-n.m.s. (458) *the King of glory?*
יהוה pr.n. (217) *Yahweh*
עִזּוּז adj. m.s. (739) *strong*
וְגִבּוֹר conj.-adj. m.s. (150) *and mighty*
יהוה pr.n. (217) *Yahweh*
גִּבּוֹר מִלְחָמָה n.m.s. cstr. (150)-n.f.s. (536) *mighty in battle*

24:9

שְׂאוּ Qal impv. 2 m.p. (נָשָׂא 669) *lift up*
שְׁעָרִים n.m.p. (1044) *O gates*
רָאשֵׁיכֶם n.m.p.-2 m.p. sf. (910) *your heads*
וּשְׂאוּ conj.-v.supra *and lift up*
פִּתְחֵי עוֹלָם n.m.p. cstr. (835)-n.m.s. (761) *O ancient doors*
וְיָבֹא conj.-Qal impf. 3 m.s. (בּוֹא 97) *that may come in*
מֶלֶךְ הַכָּבוֹד n.m.s. cstr. (I 572)-def.art.-n.m.s. (458) *the King of glory*

24:10

מִי הוּא זֶה interr. (566)-pers.pr. 3 m.s. (214) -demons.adj. m.s. (260) *who is this*
מֶלֶךְ הַכָּבוֹד n.m.s. cstr. (I 572)-def.art.-n.m.s. (458) *the King of glory?*
יהוה צְבָאוֹת pr.n. (217)-n.f.p. (838) *Yahweh of hosts*
הוּא pers.pr. 3 m.s. (214) *he is*
מֶלֶךְ הַכָּבוֹד v.supra-v.supra *the King of glory*
סֶלָה interj. (699) *Selah*

25:1

לְדָוִד prep.-pr.n. (187; GK 5h) *to David*
אֵלֶיךָ prep.-2 m.s. sf. *to thee*
יהוה pr.n. (217) *O Yahweh*
נַפְשִׁי n.f.s.-1 c.s. sf. (659) *my soul*
אֶשָּׂא Qal impf. 1 c.s. (נָשָׂא 669) *I lift up*

25:2

אֱלֹהַי בְּךָ n.m.p.-1 c.s. sf. (43)-prep.-2 m.s. sf. *O my God, in thee*
בָטַחְתִּי Qal pf. 1 c.s. (בָּטַח 105) *I trust*
אַל־אֵבוֹשָׁה neg.juss.-Qal impf. 1 c.s.-coh.he (בּוֹשׁ 101) *let me not be put to shame*
אַל־יַעַלְצוּ neg.juss.-Qal impf. 3 m.p. (עָלַץ 763) *let not exult*
אֹיְבַי לִי Qal act.ptc. m.p.-1 c.s. sf. (אָיַב 33) -prep.-1 c.s. sf. *my enemies over me*

25:3

גַּם כָּל־קֹוֶיךָ adv. (168)-n.m.s. cstr. (481)-Qal act.ptc. m.p.-2 m.s. sf. (קָוָה I 875) *yea, let ... that wait for thee*
לֹא יֵבֹשׁוּ neg.-Qal impf. 3 m.s. (בּוֹשׁ 101) *not be put to shame*
יֵבֹשׁוּ v.supra *let them be ashamed*
הַבּוֹגְדִים def.art.-Qal act.ptc. m.p. (בָּגַד 93) *who are treacherous*
רֵיקָם adv. (938) *wantonly*

25:4

דְּרָכֶיךָ יהוה n.m.p.-2 m.s. sf. (202)-pr.n. (217) *thy ways, O Yahweh*
הוֹדִיעֵנִי Hi. impv. 2 m.s.-1 c.s. sf. (יָדַע 393) *make me to know*
אֹרְחוֹתֶיךָ n.f.p.-2 m.s. sf. (73) *thy paths*
לַמְּדֵנִי Pi. impv. 2 m.s.-1 c.s. sf. (540) *teach me*

25:5

הַדְרִיכֵנִי Hi. impv. 2 m.s.-1 c.s. sf. (דָּרַךְ 201) *lead me*
בַאֲמִתֶּךָ prep.-n.f.s.-2 m.s. sf. (54) *in thy truth*
וְלַמְּדֵנִי conj.-Pi. impv. 2 m.s.-1 c.s. sf. (540) *and teach me*
כִּי־אַתָּה conj. (471)-pers.pr. 2 m.s. (61) *for thou art*
אֱלֹהֵי יִשְׁעִי n.m.p. cstr. (43)-n.m.s.-1 c.s. sf. (447) *the God of my salvation*
אוֹתְךָ dir.obj.-2 m.s. sf. *for thee*
קִוִּיתִי Pi. pf. 1 c.s. (קָוָה I 875) *I wait*
כָּל־הַיּוֹם n.m.s. cstr. (481)-def.art.-n.m.s. (398) *all the day long*

25:6

זְכֹר־ Qal impv. 2 m.s. (זָכַר 269) *be mindful*
רַחֲמֶיךָ n.m.p.-2 m.s. sf. (933) *of thy mercy*
יהוה pr.n. (217) *O Yahweh*

וַחֲסָדֶיךָ conj.-n.m.p.-2 m.s. sf. (338) *and of thy steadfast love*

כִּי מֵעוֹלָם conj. (471)-prep.-n.m.s. (761) *for ... from of old*

הֵמָּה pers.pr. 3 m.p. (241) *they have been*

25:7

חַטֹּאות נְעוּרַי n.f.p. cstr. (308)-n.m.p.-1 c.s. sf. (655) *the sins of my youth*

וּפְשָׁעַי conj.-n.m.p.-1 c.s. sf. (833) *or my transgressions*

אַל־תִּזְכֹּר neg.juss.-Qal impf. 2 m.s. (269) *remember not*

כְּחַסְדְּךָ prep.-n.m.s.-2 m.s. sf. (338) *according to thy steadfast love*

זְכָר־לִי־אַתָּה Qal impv. 2 m.s. (269)-prep.-1 c.s. sf.-pers.pr. 2 m.s. (61) *remember me*

לְמַעַן טוּבְךָ prep. (775)-n.m.s.-2 m.s. sf. (375) *for thy goodness' sake*

יהוה pr.n. (217) *O Yahweh*

25:8

טוֹב־וְיָשָׁר adj. m.s. (I 373)-conj.-adj. m.s. (449) *good and upright*

יהוה pr.n. (217) *is Yahweh*

עַל־כֵּן יוֹרֶה prep.-adv. (485)-Hi. impf. 3 m.s. (434 יָרָה) *therefore he instructs*

חַטָּאִים n.m.p. (308) *sinners*

בַּדָּרֶךְ prep.-def.art.-n.m.s. (202) *in the way*

25:9

יַדְרֵךְ Hi. impf. 3 m.s. apoc. (דָּרַךְ 201) *he leads*

עֲנָוִים n.m.p. (776) *the humble*

בַּמִּשְׁפָּט prep.-def.art.-n.m.s. (1048) *in what is right*

וִילַמֵּד conj.-Pi. impf. 3 m.s. (540) *and teaches*

עֲנָוִים v.supra *the humble*

דַּרְכּוֹ n.m.s.-3 m.s. sf. (202) *his way*

25:10

כָּל־אָרְחוֹת n.m.s. cstr. (481)-n.f.p. cstr. (73) *all the paths of*

יהוה pr.n. (217) *Yahweh*

חֶסֶד n.m.s. (338; GK 141c) *are steadfast love*

וֶאֱמֶת conj.-n.f.s. (54) *and faithfulness*

לְנֹצְרֵי prep.-Qal act.ptc. m.p. cstr. (נָצַר 665) *for those who keep*

בְּרִיתוֹ n.f.s.-3 m.s. sf. (136) *his covenant*

וְעֵדֹתָיו conj.-n.f.p.-3 m.s. sf. (730) *and his testimonies*

25:11

לְמַעַן־שִׁמְךָ prep. (775)-n.m.s.-2 m.s. sf. (1027) *for thy name's sake*

יהוה pr.n. (217) *O Yahweh*

וְסָלַחְתָּ conj.-Qal pf. 2 m.s. (סָלַח 699; GK 112nn) *and pardon*

לַעֲוֹנִי prep.-n.m.s.-1 c.s. sf. (730) *my guilt*

כִּי רַב־הוּא conj. (471)-adj. m.s. (I 912)-demons. adj. m.s. (214) *for it is great*

25:12

מִי־זֶה interr. (566)-demons.adj. m.s. (260) *who is this*

הָאִישׁ def.art.-n.m.s. (35) *the man*

יְרֵא יהוה Qal act.ptc. m.s. cstr. (יָרֵא 431)-pr.n. (217) *that fears Yahweh*

יוֹרֶנּוּ Hi. impf. 3 m.s.-3 m.s. sf. (יָרָה 434) *Him will he instruct*

בְּדֶרֶךְ prep.-n.m.s. (202) *in the way*

יִבְחָר Qal impf. 3 m.s. (בָּחַר 103) *he should choose*

25:13

נַפְשׁוֹ n.f.s.-3 m.s. sf. (659) *he himself*

בְּטוֹב prep.-adj. m.s. (I 373) *in prosperity*

תָּלִין Qal impf. 3 f.s. (לוּן I 533) *shall abide*

וְזַרְעוֹ conj.-n.m.s.-3 m.s. sf. (282) *and his children*

יִירַשׁ Qal impf. 3 m.s. (יָרַשׁ 439) *shall possess*

אָרֶץ n.f.s. paus. (75) *the land*

25:14

סוֹד יהוה n.m.s. cstr. (691)-pr.n. (217) *the friendship of Yahweh*

לִירֵאָיו prep.-Qal act.ptc. m.p.-3 m.s. sf. (יָרֵא 431) *for those who fear him*

וּבְרִיתוֹ conj.-n.f.s.-3 m.s. sf. (136) *and his covenant*

לְהוֹדִיעָם prep.-Hi. inf.cstr.-3 m.p. sf. (יָדַע 393) *he makes known to them*

25:15

עֵינַי תָּמִיד n.f.p.-1 c.s. sf. (744)-adv. (556) *my eyes are ever*

אֶל־יהוה prep.-pr.n. (217) *toward Yahweh*

כִּי הוּא־ conj. (471)-pers.pr. 3 m.s. (214) *for he*

יוֹצִיא Hi. impf. 3 m.s. (יָצָא 422) *will pluck*

מֵרֶשֶׁת prep.-n.f.s. (440) *out of the net*

רַגְלָי n.f.p.-1 c.s. sf. paus. (919) *my feet*

25:16

פְּנֵה־אֵלַי Qal impv. 2 m.s. (פָּנָה 815)-prep.-1 c.s. sf. *turn thou to me*

וְחָנֵּנִי conj.-Qal impv. 2 m.s.-1 c.s. sf. (חָנַן I 335) *and be gracious to me*

כִּי־יָחִיד conj. (471)-adj. m.s. (402) *for ... lonely*

וְעָנִי conj.-adj. m.s. (776) *and afflicted*

אָנִי pers.pr. 1 c.s. (58) *I am*

25:17

צָרוֹת לְבָבִי n.f.p. cstr. (865)-n.m.s.-1 c.s. sf. (523) *the troubles of my heart*

הִרְחִיבוּ Hi. pf. 3 c.p. (רָחַב 931) *relieve*

מִמְּצוּקוֹתַי prep.-n.f.p.-1 c.s. sf. (848) *out of my distresses*

הוֹצִיאֵנִי Hi. impv. 2 m.s.-1 c.s. sf. (יָצָא 422) *bring me out*

25:18

רְאֵה Qal impv. 2 m.s. (רָאָה 906) *consider*

עָנְיִי n.m.s.-1 c.s. sf. (777) *my affliction*

וַעֲמָלִי conj.-n.m.s.-1 c.s. sf. (765) *and my trouble*

וְשָׂא conj.-Qal impv. 2 m.s. (נָשָׂא 669) *and forgive*

לְכָל־חַטֹּאותָי prep.-n.m.s. cstr. (481)-n.f.p.-1 c.s. sf. (308) *all my sins*

25:19

רְאֵה Qal impv. 2 m.s. (רָאָה 906) *consider*

אוֹיְבַי Qal act.ptc. m.p.-1 c.s. sf. (אָיַב 33) *my foes*

כִּי־רָבּוּ conj. (471)-Qal pf. 3 c.p. (רָבַב I 912) *how many are*

וְשִׂנְאַת חָמָס conj.-n.f.s. cstr. (971)-n.m.s. (329) *and with what violent hatred*

שְׂנֵאוּנִי Qal pf. 3 c.p.-1 c.s. sf. (שָׂנֵא 971) *they hate me*

25:20

שָׁמְרָה Qal impv. 2 m.s.-coh.he (שָׁמַר I 1036) *Oh guard*

נַפְשִׁי n.f.s.-1 c.s. sf. (659) *my life*

וְהַצִּילֵנִי conj.-Hi. impv. 2 m.s.-1 c.s. sf. (נָצַל 664) *and deliver me*

אַל־אֵבוֹשׁ neg.coh.-Qal impf. 1 c.s. (בּוֹשׁ 101) *let me not be put to shame*

כִּי־חָסִיתִי בָךְ conj. (471)-Qal pf. 1 c.s. (חָסָה 340) -prep.-2 m.s. sf. paus. *for I take refuge in thee*

25:21

תֹּם וָיֹשֶׁר n.m.s. (1070)-conj.-n.m.s. (449) *integrity and uprightness*

יִצְּרוּנִי Qal impf. 3 m.p.-1 c.s. sf. (נָצַר I 665) *may ... preserve me*

כִּי קִוִּיתִיךָ conj. (471)-Pi. pf. 1 c.s.-2 m.s. sf. (קָוָה I 875) *for I wait for thee*

25:22

פְּדֵה Qal impv. 2 m.s. (פָּדָה 804) *redeem*

אֱלֹהִים n.m.p. (43) *O God*

אֶת־יִשְׂרָאֵל dir.obj.-pr.n. (975) *Israel*

מִכֹּל צָרוֹתָיו prep.-n.m.s. cstr. (481)-n.f.p.-3 m.s. sf. (865) *out of all his troubles*

26:1

לְדָוִד prep.-pr.n. (187) *to David*

שָׁפְטֵנִי Qal impv. 2 m.s.-1 c.s. sf. (שָׁפַט 1047) *vindicate me*

יהוה pr.n. (217) *O Yahweh*

כִּי־אֲנִי conj. (471)-pers.pr. 1 c.s. (58) *for I*

בְּתֻמִּי prep.-n.m.s.-1 c.s. sf. (1070) *in my integrity*

הָלַכְתִּי Qal pf. 1 c.s. (הָלַךְ 229) *have walked*

וּביהוה conj.-prep.-pr.n. (217) *and in Yahweh*

בָּטַחְתִּי Qal pf. 1 c.s. (בָּטַח 105) *I have trusted*

לֹא אֶמְעָד neg. Qal impf. 1 c.s. (מָעַד 588) *without wavering*

26:2

בְּחָנֵנִי Qal impv. 2 m.s.-1 c.s. sf. (בָּחַן 103) *prove me*

יהוה pr.n. (217) *O Yahweh*

וְנַסֵּנִי conj.-Pi. impv. 2 m.s.-1 c.s. sf. (נָסָה 650) *and try me*

צָרְופָה Qal impv. 2 m.s.-coh.he (צָרַף 864; GK 48i) *test*

כִלְיוֹתַי n.f.p.-1 c.s. sf. (480) *my kidneys (*as seat of emotions*)*

וְלִבִּי conj.-n.m.s.-1 c.s. sf. (524) *and my mind*

26:3

כִּי־חַסְדְּךָ conj. (471)-n.m.s.-2 m.s. sf. (338) *for thy steadfast love*

לְנֶגֶד עֵינָי prep.-prep. (617)-n.f.p.-1 c.s. sf. (744) *is before my eyes*

וְהִתְהַלַּכְתִּי conj.-Hith. pf. 1 c.s. (הָלַךְ 229; GK 112rr) *and I walk*

בַּאֲמִתֶּךָ prep.-n.f.s.-2 m.s. sf. paus. (54) *in thy faithfulness*

26:4

לֹא־יָשַׁבְתִּי neg.-Qal pf. 1 c.s. (יָשַׁב 442) *I do not sit*

עִם־מְתֵי־שָׁוְא prep.-n.m.p. cstr. (607; GK 128t)-n.m.s. (996) *with false men*

וְעִם נַעֲלָמִים conj.-prep.-Ni. ptc. m.p. (עָלַם I 761) *nor with dissemblers*
לֹא אָבוֹא neg.-Qal impf. 1 c.s. (בּוֹא 97) *do I consort*

26:5
שָׂנֵאתִי Qal pf. 1 c.s. (שָׂנֵא 971) *I hate*
קְהַל מְרֵעִים n.m.s. cstr. (874)-Hi. ptc. m.p. (רָעַע 949) *the company of evildoers*
וְעִם־רְשָׁעִים conj.-prep.-n.m.p. (957) *and with the wicked*
לֹא אֵשֵׁב neg.-Qal impf. 1 c.s. (יָשַׁב 442) *I will not sit*

26:6
אֶרְחַץ Qal impf. 1 c.s. (רָחַץ 934) *I wash*
בְּנִקָּיוֹן prep.-n.m.s. (667) *in innocence*
כַּפָּי n.f.p.-1 c.s. sf. paus. (496) *my hands*
וַאֲסֹבְבָה conj.-Po'el impf. 1 c.s.-coh.he (סָבַב 685) *and go about*
אֶת־מִזְבַּחֲךָ dir.obj.-n.m.s.-2 m.s. sf. (258) *thy altar*
יהוה pr.n. (217) *O Yahweh*

26:7
לַשְׁמִעַ prep.-Hi. inf.cstr. (שָׁמַע 1033) *singing aloud*
בְּקוֹל תּוֹדָה prep.-n.m.s. cstr. (876)-n.f.s. (392) *with a voice of thanksgiving*
וּלְסַפֵּר conj.-prep.-Pi. inf.cstr. (707) *and telling*
כָּל־נִפְלְאוֹתֶיךָ n.m.s. cstr. (481)-Ni. ptc. f.p.-2 m.s. sf. (810) *all thy wondrous deeds*

26:8
יהוה pr.n. (217) *O Yahweh*
אָהַבְתִּי Qal pf. 1 c.s. (אָהֵב 12) *I love*
מְעוֹן בֵּיתֶךָ n.m.s. cstr. (732)-n.m.s.-2 m.s. sf. (108) *the habitation of thy house*
וּמְקוֹם מִשְׁכַּן conj.-n.m.s. cstr. (879)-n.m.s. cstr. (1015) *and the place where dwells*
כְּבוֹדֶךָ n.m.s.-2 m.s. sf. (458) *thy glory*

26:9
אַל־תֶּאֱסֹף neg.juss.-Qal impf. 2 m.s. (אָסַף 62) *sweep not away*
עִם־חַטָּאִים prep.-n.m.p. (308) *with sinners*
נַפְשִׁי n.f.s.-1 c.s. sf. (659) *me*
וְעִם־אַנְשֵׁי דָמִים conj.-prep.-n.m.p. cstr. (60)-n.m.p. (196) *nor with bloodthirsty men*
חַיָּי n.m.p.-1 c.s. sf. (313) *my life*

26:10
אֲשֶׁר־בִּידֵיהֶם rel. (81)-prep.-n.f.p.-3 m.p. sf. (388) *men in whose hands*
זִמָּה n.f.s. (273) *are evil devices*
וִימִינָם conj.-n.f.s.-3 m.p. sf. (411) *and whose right hands*
מָלְאָה Qal pf. 3 f.s. (מָלֵא 570; GK 20f) *are full of*
שֹּׁחַד n.m.s. (1005) *bribes*

26:11
וַאֲנִי conj.-pers.pr. 1 c.s. (58) *but as for me*
בְּתֻמִּי prep.-n.m.s.-1 c.s. sf. (1070) *in my integrity*
אֵלֵךְ Qal impf. 1 c.s. (הָלַךְ 229) *I walk*
פְּדֵנִי Qal impv. 2 m.s.-1 c.s. sf. (פָּדָה 804) *redeem me*
וְחָנֵּנִי conj.-Qal impv. 2 m.s.-1 c.s. sf. (חָנַן I 335) *and be gracious to me*

26:12
רַגְלִי n.f.s.-1 c.s. sf. (919) *my foot*
עָמְדָה Qal pf. 3 f.s. (עָמַד 763) *stands*
בְמִישׁוֹר prep.-n.m.s. (449) *on level ground*
בְּמַקְהֵלִים prep.-n.m.p. (875; GK 93qq) *in the great congregation*
אֲבָרֵךְ יהוה Pi. impf. 1 c.s. (בָּרַךְ 138)-pr.n. (217) *I will bless Yahweh*

27:1
לְדָוִד prep.-pr.n. (187) *to David*
יהוה אוֹרִי pr.n. (217)-n.m.s.-1 c.s. sf. (21) *Yahweh is my light*
וְיִשְׁעִי conj.-n.m.s.-1 c.s. sf. (447) *and my salvation*
מִמִּי prep.-interr. (566) *whom*
אִירָא Qal impf. 1 c.s. paus. (יָרֵא 431) *shall I fear*
יהוה pr.n. (217) *Yahweh is*
מָעוֹז־חַיַּי n.m.s. cstr. (731)-n.m.p.-1 c.s. sf. (313) *the stronghold of my life*
מִמִּי v.supra *of whom*
אֶפְחָד Qal impf. 1 c.s. paus. (פָּחַד 808) *shall I be afraid*

27:2
בִּקְרֹב עָלַי prep.-Qal inf.cstr. (897)-prep.-1 c.s. sf. *when ... assail me*
מְרֵעִים Hi. ptc. m.p. (רָעַע 949) *evildoers*
לֶאֱכֹל אֶת־בְּשָׂרִי prep.-Qal inf.cstr. (אָכַל 37)-dir. obj.-n.m.s.-1 c.s. sf. (142) *to eat up my flesh*
צָרַי n.m.p.-1 c.s. sf. (III 865) *my adversaries*

וְאֹיְבַי לִי conj.-Qal act.ptc. m.p.-1 c.s. sf. (אֹיֵב 33)-prep.-1 c.s. sf. *and my foes (against me)*
הֵמָּה כָשְׁלוּ pers.pr. 3 c.p. (241)-Qal pf. 3 c.p. (505 כָּשַׁל) *they shall stumble*
וְנָפָלוּ conj.-Qal pf. 3 c.p. paus. (נָפַל 656) *and fall*

27:3

אִם־תַּחֲנֶה hypoth.part. (49)-Qal impf. 3 f.s. (חָנָה 333) *though ... encamp*
עָלַי prep.-1 c.s. sf. *against me*
מַחֲנֶה n.m.s. (334) *a host*
לֹא־יִירָא neg.-Qal impf. 3 m.s. (יָרֵא 431) *shall not fear*
לִבִּי n.m.s.-1 c.s. sf. (524) *my heart*
אִם־תָּקוּם hypoth.part. (49)-Qal impf. 3 f.s. (קוּם 877) *though arise*
עָלַי prep.-1 c.s. sf. *against me*
מִלְחָמָה n.f.s. (536) *war*
בְּזֹאת prep.-demons.adj. f.s. (260) *yet (in this)*
אֲנִי בוֹטֵחַ pers.pr. 1 c.s. (58)-Qal act.ptc. (בָּטַח 105) *I will be confident*

27:4

אַחַת num.adj. f.s. (25) *one thing*
שָׁאַלְתִּי Qal pf. 1 c.s. (שָׁאַל 981) *have I asked*
מֵאֵת־יהוה prep.-dir.obj.-pr.n. (217) *of Yahweh*
אוֹתָהּ אֲבַקֵּשׁ dir.obj.-3 f.s. sf.-Pi. impf. 1 c.s. (134 בָּקַשׁ) *that will I seek after*
שִׁבְתִּי Qal inf.cstr.-1 c.s. sf. (יָשַׁב 442) *that I may dwell*
בְּבֵית־יהוה prep.-n.m.s. cstr. (108)-pr.n. (217) *in the house of Yahweh*
כָּל־יְמֵי חַיַּי n.m.s. cstr. (481)-n.m.p. cstr. (398) -n.m.p.-1 c.s. sf. (313) *all the days of my life*
לַחֲזוֹת prep.-Qal inf.cstr. (חָזָה 302) *to behold*
בְּנֹעַם־יהוה prep.-n.m.s. cstr. (653)-pr.n. (217) *the beauty of Yahweh*
וּלְבַקֵּר conj.-prep.-Pi. inf.cstr. (בָּקַר 133) *and to inquire*
בְּהֵיכָלוֹ prep.-n.m.s.-3 m.s. sf. (228) *in his temple*

27:5

כִּי יִצְפְּנֵנִי conj. (471)-Qal impf. 3 m.s.-1 c.s. sf. (860 צָפַן) *for he will hide me*
בְּסֻכֹּה prep.-n.m.s.-3 m.s. sf. (697) *in his shelter*
בְּיוֹם רָעָה prep.-n.m.s. cstr. (398)-n.f.s. (948) *in the day of trouble*
יַסְתִּרֵנִי Hi. impf. 3 m.s.-1 c.s. sf. (סָתַר 711) *he will conceal me*
בְּסֵתֶר אָהֳלוֹ prep.-n.m.s. cstr. (712)-n.m.s.-3 m.s. sf. (13) *under the cover of his tent*
בְּצוּר prep.-n.m.s. (849) *upon a rock*
יְרוֹמְמֵנִי Polel impf. 3 m.s.-1 c.s. sf. (רום 926) *he will set me high*

27:6

וְעַתָּה conj.-adv. (773) *and now*
יָרוּם רֹאשִׁי Qal impf. 3 m.s. (רום 926)-n.m.s.-1 c.s. sf. (910) *my head shall be lifted up*
עַל אֹיְבַי prep.-Qal act.ptc. m.p.-1 c.s. sf. (אֹיֵב 33) *above my enemies*
סְבִיבוֹתַי prep.-1 c.s. sf. (686) *round about me*
וְאֶזְבְּחָה conj.-Qal impf. 1 c.s.-coh.he (זָבַח 256) *and I will offer*
בְאָהֳלוֹ prep.-n.m.s.-3 m.s. sf. (13) *in his tent*
זִבְחֵי תְרוּעָה n.m.p. cstr. (257)-n.f.p. (929) *sacrifices with shouts of joy*
אָשִׁירָה Qal impf. 1 c.s.-coh.he (שִׁיר 1010) *I will sing*
וַאֲזַמְּרָה conj.-Pi. impf. 1 c.s.-coh.he (זָמַר I 274) *and make melody*
ליהוה prep.-pr.n. (217) *to Yahweh*

27:7

שְׁמַע־יהוה Qal impv. 2 m.s. (1033)-pr.n. (217) *hear, O Yahweh*
קוֹלִי n.m.s.-1 c.s. sf. (876; GK 144m) *my voice*
אֶקְרָא Qal impf. 1 c.s. (קָרָא 894) *when I call*
וְחָנֵּנִי conj.-Qal impv. 2 m.s.-1 c.s. sf. (חָנַן I 335) *be gracious to me*
וַעֲנֵנִי conj.-Qal impv. 2 m.s.-1 c.s. sf. (עָנָה I 772) *and answer me*

27:8

לְךָ אָמַר prep.-2 m.s. sf.-Qal pf. 3 m.s. (55) *says to thee*
לִבִּי n.m.s.-1 c.s. sf. (524) *my heart*
בַּקְּשׁוּ פָנָי Pi. impv. 2 m.s. (בָּקַשׁ 134)-n.m.p.-1 c.s. sf. *seek my face*
אֶת־פָּנֶיךָ dir.obj.-n.m.p.-2 m.s. sf. (815) *thy face*
יהוה pr.n. (217) *Yahweh*
אֲבַקֵּשׁ Pi. impf. 1 c.s. (134) *do I seek*

27:9

אַל־תַּסְתֵּר neg.juss.-Hi. impf. 2 m.s. apoc. (סָתַר 711) *hide not*
פָּנֶיךָ מִמֶּנִּי n.m.p.-2 m.s. sf. (815)-prep.-1 c.s. sf. *thy face from me*
אַל־תַּט־ neg.-juss.-Hi. impf. 2 m.s. apoc. (נָטָה 639) *turn not*
בְּאַף prep.-n.m.s. (60) *in anger*
עַבְדֶּךָ n.m.s.-2 m.s. sf. (712) *thy servant*
עֶזְרָתִי n.f.s.-1 c.s. sf. (740) *my help*

הָיִיתָ Qal pf. 2 m.s. (הָיָה 224) *you have been*
אַל־תִּטְּשֵׁנִי neg.-juss.-Qal impf. 2 m.s.-1 c.s. sf. (643 נָטַשׁ) *cast me not off*
וְאַל־תַּעַזְבֵנִי conj.-neg.juss.-Qal impf. 2 m.s.-1 c.s. sf. (I 736) *forsake me not*
אֱלֹהֵי יִשְׁעִי n.m.p. cstr. (43)-n.m.s.-1 c.s. sf. (447) *O God of my salvation*

27:10

כִּי־אָבִי conj. (471)-n.m.s.-1 c.s. sf. (3) *for my father*
וְאִמִּי conj.-n.f.s.-1 c.s. sf. (51) *and my mother*
עֲזָבוּנִי Qal pf. 3 c.p.-1 c.s. sf. (I 736) *have forsaken me*
ויהוה conj.-pr.n. (217) *but Yahweh*
יַאַסְפֵנִי Qal impf. 3 m.s.-1 c.s. sf. (אָסַף 62) *will take me up*

27:11

הוֹרֵנִי יהוה Hi. impv. 2 m.s.-1 c.s. sf. (יָרָה 434) -pr.n. (217) *teach me, O Yahweh*
דַּרְכֶּךָ n.m.s.-2 m.s. sf. (202) *thy way*
וּנְחֵנִי conj.-Qal impv. 2 m.s.-1 c.s. sf. (נָחָה 634) *and lead me*
בְּאֹרַח מִישׁוֹר prep.-n.m.s. cstr. (73)-n.m.s. (449) *on a level path*
לְמַעַן שׁוֹרְרָי prep. (775)-n.m.p.-1 c.s. sf. (1004) *because of my enemies*

27:12

אַל־תִּתְּנֵנִי neg.juss.-Qal impf. 2 m.s.-1 c.s. sf. (נָתַן 678) *give me not up*
בְּנֶפֶשׁ צָרָי prep.-n.f.s. cstr. (659)-n.m.p.-1 c.s. sf. (III 865) *to the will of my adversaries*
כִּי קָמוּ־בִי conj. (471)-Qal pf. 3 c.p. (רוּם 977) -prep.-1 c.s. sf. *for have risen against me*
עֵדֵי־שֶׁקֶר n.m.p. cstr. (729)-n.m.s. (1055) *false witnesses*
וִיפֵחַ חָמָס conj.-adj. m.s. cstr. (422)-n.m.s. (329) *and they breathe out violence*

27:13

לוּלֵא הֶאֱמַנְתִּי conj. (530; GK 5n,159dd,167a)-Hi. pf. 1 c.s. (אָמַן 52) *I believe*
לִרְאוֹת prep.-Qal inf.cstr. (רָאָה 906) *that I shall see*
בְּטוּב־יהוה prep.-n.m.s. cstr. (375)-pr.n. (217) *the goodness of Yahweh*
בְּאֶרֶץ חַיִּים prep.-n.f.s. cstr. (75)-n.m.p. (313) *in the land of the living*

27:14

קַוֵּה Pi. impv. 2 m.s. (קָוָה I 875) *wait*
אֶל־יהוה prep.-pr.n. (217) *for Yahweh*
חֲזַק Qal impv. 2 m.s. (304) *be strong*
וְיַאֲמֵץ לִבֶּךָ conj.-Hi. impf. 3 m.s. apoc. (אָמֵן 54)-n.m.s.-2 m.s. sf. (524) *and let your heart take courage*
וְקַוֵּה conj.-v.supra *yea, wait*
אֶל־יהוה v.supra-v.supra *for Yahweh*

28:1

לְדָוִד prep.-pr.n. (187) *to David*
אֵלֶיךָ יהוה prep.-2 m.s. sf.-pr.n. (217) *to thee, O Yahweh*
אֶקְרָא Qal impf. 1 cv.s. (894) *I call*
צוּרִי n.m.s.-1 c.s. sf. (849) *my rock*
אַל־תֶּחֱרַשׁ neg.juss.-Qal impf. 2 m.s. (חָרַשׁ II 361) *be not deaf*
מִמֶּנִּי prep.-1 c.s. sf. *to me*
פֶּן־תֶּחֱשֶׁה conj. (814)-Qal impf. 2 m.s. (חָשָׁה 364) *lest, if thou be silent*
מִמֶּנִּי v.supra *to me*
וְנִמְשַׁלְתִּי conj.-Ni. pf. 1 c.s. (מָשַׁל I 605) *I become like*
עִם־יוֹרְדֵי בוֹר prep.-Qal act.ptc. m.p. cstr. (יָרַד 432)-n.m.s. (92) *those who go down to the Pit*

28:2

שְׁמַע Qal impv. 2 m.s. (1033) *hear*
קוֹל תַּחֲנוּנַי n.m.s. cstr. (876)-n.m.p.-1 c.s. sf. (337) *the voice of my supplication*
בְּשַׁוְּעִי prep.-Pi. inf.cstr.-1 c.s. sf. (שָׁוַע 1002) *as I cry for help*
אֵלֶיךָ prep.-2 m.s. sf. *to thee*
בְּנָשְׂאִי prep.-Qal inf.cstr.-1 c.s. sf. (נָשָׂא 669) *as I lift up*
יָדַי n.f. du.-1 c.s. sf. (388) *my hands*
אֶל־דְּבִיר קָדְשֶׁךָ prep.-n.m.s. cstr. (I 184)-n.m.s.-2 m.s. sf. (871) *toward thy innermost sanctuary*

28:3

אַל־תִּמְשְׁכֵנִי neg.juss.-Qal impf. 2 m.s.-1 c.s. sf. (604 מָשַׁךְ) *take me not off*
עִם־רְשָׁעִים prep.-n.m.p. (957) *with the wicked*
וְעִם־פֹּעֲלֵי אָוֶן conj.-prep.-Qal act.ptc. m.p. cstr. (פָּעַל 821)-n.m.s. (19) *with those who are workers of evil*
דֹּבְרֵי שָׁלוֹם Qal act.ptc. m.p. cstr. (180)-n.m.s. (1022) *who speak peace*

עִם־רֵעֵיהֶם prep.-n.m.p.-3 m.p. sf. (945) *with their neighbors*
וְרָעָה conj.-n.f.s. (948) *while mischief*
בִּלְבָבָם prep.-n.m.s.-3 m.p. sf. (523) *in their hearts*

28:4

תֶּן־לָהֶם Qal impv. 2 m.s. (נָתַן 678)-prep.-3 m.p. sf. *requite them*
כְּפָעֳלָם prep.-n.m.s.-3 m.s. sf. (821) *according to their work*
וּכְרֹעַ מַעַלְלֵיהֶם conj.-prep.-n.m.s. cstr. (947) -n.m.p.-3 m.p. sf. (760) *and according to the evil of their deeds*
כְּמַעֲשֵׂה יְדֵיהֶם prep.-n.m.s. cstr. (795)-n.f.p.-3 m.p. sf. (388) *according to the work of their hands*
תֵּן לָהֶם Qal impv. 2 m.s. (נָתַן 678)-prep.-3 m.p. sf. *requite them*
הָשֵׁב Hi. impv. 2 m.s. (שׁוּב 996) *render*
גְּמוּלָם לָהֶם n.m.s.-3 m.p. sf. (168)-prep.-3 m.p. sf. *their due reward*

28:5

כִּי לֹא יָבִינוּ conj. (471)-neg.-Qal impf. 3 m.p. (בִּין 106) *because they do not regard*
אֶל־פְּעֻלֹּת יהוה prep.-n.f.p. cstr. (821)-pr.n. (217) *the works of Yahweh*
וְאֶל־מַעֲשֵׂה conj.-prep.-n.m.s. cstr. (795) *or the work of*
יָדָיו n.f.p.-3 m.s. sf. (388) *his hands*
יֶהֶרְסֵם Qal impf. 3 m.s.-3 m.p. sf. (הָרַס 248) *he will break them down*
וְלֹא יִבְנֵם conj.-neg.-Qal impf. 3 m.s.-3 m.p. sf. (בָּנָה 124) *and build them up no more*

28:6

בָּרוּךְ יהוה Qal pass.ptc. (בָּרַךְ 138)-pr.n. (217) *Blessed be Yahweh*
כִּי־שָׁמַע conj. (471)-Qal pf. 3 m.s. (1033) *for he has heard*
קוֹל תַּחֲנוּנָי n.m.s. cstr. (876)-n.m.p.-1 c.s. sf. (337) *the voice of my supplications*

28:7

יהוה עֻזִּי pr.n. (217)-n.m.s.-1 c.s. sf. (738) *Yahweh is my strength*
וּמָגִנִּי conj.-n.m.s.-1 c.s. sf. (171) *and my shield*
בּוֹ בָטַח prep.-3 m.s. sf.-Qal pf. 3 m.s. (105) *in him ... trusts*
לִבִּי n.m.s.-1 c.s. sf. (524) *my heart*
וְנֶעֱזָרְתִּי conj.-Ni. pf. 1 c.s. (עָזַר 740) *so I am helped*
וַיַּעֲלֹז consec.-Qal impf. 3 m.s. (עָלַז 759) *and exults*
לִבִּי v.supra *my heart*
וּמִשִּׁירִי conj.-prep.-n.m.s.-1 c.s. sf. (1010) *and with my song*
אֲהוֹדֶנּוּ Hi. impf. 1 c.s.-3 m.s. sf. (392; GK 53q) *I give thanks to him*

28:8

יהוה עֹז־ pr.n. (217)-n.m.s. (738) *Yahweh is the strength*
לָמוֹ prep.-3 m.p. sf. *of them (his people)*
וּמָעוֹז conj.-n.m.s. (731) ... *the refuge*
יְשׁוּעוֹת מְשִׁיחוֹ n.f.p. cstr. (447)-n.m.s.-3 m.s. sf. (603) *victories of his anointed*
הוּא pers.pr. 3 m.s. (214) *he is*

28:9

הוֹשִׁיעָה Hi. impv. 2 m.s.-coh.he (יָשַׁע 446) *O save*
אֶת־עַמֶּךָ dir.obj.-n.m.s.-2 m.s. sf. (I 766) *thy people*
וּבָרֵךְ conj.-Pi. impv. 2 m.s. (138) *and bless*
אֶת־נַחֲלָתֶךָ dir.obj.-n.f.s.-2 m.s. sf. (635) *thy heritage*
וּרְעֵם conj.-Qal impv. 2 m.s.-3 m.p. sf. (רָעָה I 944; GK 10g) *be thou their shepherd*
וְנַשְּׂאֵם conj.-Pi. impv. 2 m.s.-3 m.p. sf. (נָשָׂא 669) *and carry them*
עַד־הָעוֹלָם prep. (III 723)-def.art.-n.m.s. (761) *for ever*

29:1

מִזְמוֹר n.m.s. (274) *a Psalm*
לְדָוִד prep.-pr.n. (187) *to David*
הָבוּ ליהוה Qal impv. 2 m.p. (יָהַב 396)-prep. -pr.n. (217) *ascribe to Yahweh*
בְּנֵי אֵלִים n.m.p. cstr. (119; GK 124q,128v)-n.m.p. (42) *sons of gods*
הָבוּ ליהוה v.supra-v.supra *ascribe to Yahweh*
כָּבוֹד n.m.s. (458) *glory*
וָעֹז conj.-n.m.s. (738) *and strength*

29:2

הָבוּ ליהוה Qal impv. 2 m.p. (יָהַב 396)-prep. -pr.n. (217) *ascribe to Yahweh*
כְּבוֹד שְׁמוֹ n.m.s. cstr. (458)-n.m.s.-3 m.s. sf. (1027) *the glory of his name*
הִשְׁתַּחֲווּ Hithpalel impv. 2 m.p. (שָׁחָה 1005) *worship*

ליהוה v.supra–v.supra *Yahweh*
בְּהַדְרַת־קֹדֶשׁ prep.–n.f.s. cstr. (214)–n.m.s. (871) *in holy array*

29:3

קוֹל יהוה n.m.s. cstr. (876)–pr.n. (217) *the voice of Yahweh*
עַל־הַמָּיִם prep.–def.art.–n.m.p. (565) *upon the waters*
אֵל־הַכָּבוֹד n.m.s. cstr. (42)–def.art.–n.m.s. (458) *the God of glory*
הִרְעִים Hi. pf. 3 m.s. (רָעַם 947) *thunders*
יהוה v.supra *Yahweh*
עַל־מַיִם רַבִּים prep.–n.m.p. (565)–adj. m.p. (I 912) *upon many waters*

29:4

קוֹל־יהוה n.m.s. cstr. (876)–pr.n. (217) *the voice of Yahweh*
בַּכֹּחַ prep.–def.art.–n.m.s. (470) *is powerful*
קוֹל יהוה v.supra–v.supra *the voice of Yahweh*
בֶּהָדָר prep.–def.art.–n.m.s. (214) *is full of majesty*

29:5

קוֹל יהוה n.m.s. cstr. (876)–pr.n. (217) *the voice of Yahweh*
שֹׁבֵר אֲרָזִים Qal act.ptc. (שָׁבַר 990)–n.m.p. (72) *breaks the cedars*
וַיְשַׁבֵּר יהוה consec.–Pi. impf. 3 m.s. (990)–pr.n. (217) *Yahweh breaks*
אֶת־אַרְזֵי dir.obj.–n.m.p. cstr. (72) *the cedars of*
הַלְּבָנוֹן def.art.–pr.n. (526) *Lebanon*

29:6

וַיַּרְקִידֵם consec.–Hi. impf. 3 m.s.–3 m.p. sf. (רָקַד 955) *he makes ... to skip*
כְּמוֹ־עֵגֶל prep.–n.m.s. (722) *like a calf*
לְבָנוֹן pr.n. (526) *Lebanon*
וְשִׂרְיֹן conj.–pr.n. (976) *and Sirion*
כְּמוֹ בֶן־רְאֵמִים prep.–n.m.s. cstr. (119)–n.m.p. (910) *like a young wild ox*

29:7

קוֹל־יהוה n.m.s. cstr. (876)–pr.n. (217) *the voice of Yahweh*
חֹצֵב Qal act.ptc. (חָצַב 345) *flashes forth*
לַהֲבוֹת אֵשׁ n.f.p. cstr. (529)–n.f.s. (77) *flames of fire*

29:8

קוֹל יהוה n.m.s. cstr. (876)–pr.n. (217) *the voice of Yahweh*
יָחִיל Hi. impf. 3 m.s. (חוּל I 296) *shakes*
מִדְבָּר n.m.s. (184) *the wilderness*
יָחִיל יהוה v.supra–v.supra *Yahweh shakes*
מִדְבַּר קָדֵשׁ n.m.s. cstr. (184)–pr.n. (II 873) *the wilderness of Kadesh*

29:9

קוֹל יהוה n.m.s. cstr. (876)–pr.n. (217) *the voice of Yahweh*
יְחוֹלֵל Polel impf. 3 m.s. (חוּל I 296) *makes to whirl*
אַיָּלוֹת n.f.p. (19) *the hinds*
וַיֶּחֱשֹׂף consec.–Qal impf. 3 m.s. (חָשַׂף 362) *and strips*
יְעָרוֹת n.f.p. (I 420) *the forests*
וּבְהֵיכָלוֹ conj.–prep.–n.m.s.–3 m.s. sf. (228) *and in his temple*
כֻּלּוֹ אֹמֵר n.m.s.–3 m.s. sf. (481)–Qal act.ptc. (55) *all cry*
כָּבוֹד n.m.s. (458) *Glory*

29:10

יהוה pr.n. (217) *Yahweh*
לַמַּבּוּל prep.–def.art.–n.m.s. (550) *over the flood*
יָשָׁב Qal pf. 3 m.s. paus. (יָשַׁב 442) *sits enthroned*
וַיֵּשֶׁב יהוה consec.–Qal impf. 3 m.s. (יָשַׁב 442; GK 111r)–pr.n. (217) *Yahweh sits enthroned*
מֶלֶךְ n.m.s. (I 572) *as king*
לְעוֹלָם prep.–n.m.s. (761) *for ever*

29:11

יהוה pr.n. (217) *Yahweh*
עֹז n.m.s. (738) *strength*
לְעַמּוֹ prep.–n.m.s.–3 m.s. sf. (I 766) *to his people*
יִתֵּן Qal impf. 3 m.s. (נָתַן 678) *may give*
יהוה v.supra *Yahweh*
יְבָרֵךְ Pi. impf. 3 m.s. (בָּרַךְ 138) *may bless*
אֶת־עַמּוֹ dir.obj.–n.m.s.–3 m.s. sf. (I 766) *his people*
בַשָּׁלוֹם prep.–def.art.–n.m.s. (1022) *with peace*

30:1

מִזְמוֹר n.m.s. (274) *a Psalm*
שִׁיר־חֲנֻכַּת n.m.s. cstr. (1010)–n.f.s. cstr. (335) *a song at the dedication of*
הַבַּיִת def.art.–n.m.s. (108) *the Temple*
לְדָוִד prep.–pr.n. (187) *to David*

30:2

אֲרוֹמִמְךָ Polel impf. 1 c.s.-2 m.s. sf. (רום 926; GK 60f) *I will extol thee*

יהוה pr.n. (217) *O Yahweh*

כִּי דִלִּיתָנִי conj. (471)-Pi. pf. 2 m.s.-1 c.s. sf. (194) *for thou hast drawn me up*

וְלֹא־שִׂמַּחְתָּ conj.-neg.-Pi. pf. 2 m.s. (שָׂמַח 970) *and hast not let rejoice*

אֹיְבַי לִי Qal act.ptc. m.p.-1 c.s. sf. (אָיַב 33)-prep. -1 c.s. sf. *my foes over me*

30:3

יהוה אֱלֹהָי pr.n. (217)-n.m.p.-1 c.s. sf. paus. (43) *O Yahweh my God*

שִׁוַּעְתִּי אֵלֶיךָ Pi. pf. 1 c.s. (שָׁוַע 1002)-prep.-2 m.s. sf. *I cried to thee for help*

וַתִּרְפָּאֵנִי consec.-Qal impf. 2 m.s.-1 c.s. sf. (950) *and thou hast healed me*

30:4

יהוה pr.n. (217) *O Yahweh*

הֶעֱלִיתָ Hi. pf. 2 m.s. (עָלָה 748) *thou hast brought up*

מִן־שְׁאוֹל prep.-n.f.s. (982) *from Sheol*

נַפְשִׁי n.f.s.-1 c.s. sf. (659) *my soul*

חִיִּיתַנִי Pi. pf. 2 m.s.-1 c.s. sf. (חָיָה 310) *restored me to life*

מִיָּרְדִי־ rd.prb. מִיּוֹרְדֵי prep.-Qal act.ptc. m.p. cstr. (יָרַד 432; GK 69m) *from among those gone down to*

בוֹר n.m.s. (92) *the Pit*

30:5

זַמְּרוּ לַיהוה Pi. impv. 2 m.p. (זָמַר I 274)-prep. -pr.n. (217) *sing praises to Yahweh*

חֲסִידָיו adj. m.p.-3 m.s. sf. (339) *his saints*

וְהוֹדוּ conj.-Hi. impv. 2 m.p. (יָדָה 392) *and give thanks*

לְזֵכֶר קָדְשׁוֹ prep.-n.m.s. cstr. (271)-n.m.s.-3 m.s. sf. (871) *to his holy name*

30:6

כִּי רֶגַע conj. (471)-n.m.s. (921) *for ... for a moment*

בְּאַפּוֹ prep.-n.m.s.-3 m.s. sf. (60) *his anger*

חַיִּים n.m.p. (313) *for a lifetime*

בִּרְצוֹנוֹ prep.-n.m.s.-3 m.s. sf. (953) *his favor*

בָּעֶרֶב prep.-def.art.-n.m.s. (787) *for the night*

יָלִין בֶּכִי Qal impf. 3 m.s. (I 533)-n.m.s. (113) *weeping may tarry*

וְלַבֹּקֶר conj.-prep.-def.art.-n.m.s. (133) *but with the morning*

רִנָּה n.f.s. (943) *joy*

30:7

וַאֲנִי conj.-pers.pr. 1 c.s. (58) *as for me*

אָמַרְתִּי Qal pf. 1 c.s. (55) *I said*

בְשַׁלְוִי prep.-n.m.s.-1 c.s. sf. (1017) *in my prosperity*

בַּל־אֶמּוֹט neg. (115)-Ni. impf. 1 c.s. (מוֹט 556) *I shall not be moved*

לְעוֹלָם prep.-n.m.s. (761) *for ever*

30:8

יהוה pr.n. (217) *O Yahweh*

בִּרְצוֹנְךָ prep.-n.m.s.-2 m.s. sf. (953) *by thy favor*

הֶעֱמַדְתָּה Hi. pf. 2 m.s. (עָמַד 763) *thou hadst established me*

לְהַרְרִי עֹז prep.-n.m.s.-1 c.s. sf. (249; GK 90n, 93aa)-n.m.s. (738) *as a strong mountain*

הִסְתַּרְתָּ Hi. pf. 2 m.s. (סָתַר 711) *thou didst hide*

פָנֶיךָ n.m.p.-2 m.s. sf. (815) *thy face*

הָיִיתִי נִבְהָל Qal pf. 1 c.s. (הָיָה 224)-Ni. ptc. (96 בָּהַל) *I was dismayed*

30:9

אֵלֶיךָ יהוה prep.-2 m.s. sf.-pr.n. (217) *to thee O Yahweh*

אֶקְרָא Qal impf. 1 c.s. (894) *I cried*

וְאֶל־אֲדֹנָי conj.-prep.-n.m.p.-1 c.s. sf. (10) *and to the Lord*

אֶתְחַנָּן Hith. impf. 1 c.s. (I 335) *I made supplication*

30:10

מַה־בֶּצַע interr. (552)-n.m.s. (130) *what profit*

בְּדָמִי prep.-n.m.s.-1 c.s. sf. (196) *in my death*

בְּרִדְתִּי prep.-Qal inf.cstr.-1 c.s. sf. (יָרַד 432) *if I go down*

אֶל־שָׁחַת prep.-n.f.p. (1001) *to the Pit*

הֲיוֹדְךָ עָפָר interr.part.-Hi. impf. 3 m.s.-2 m.s. sf. (יָדָה 392)-n.m.s. (779) *will the dust praise thee?*

הֲיַגִּיד interr.part.-Hi. impf. 3 m.s. (נָגַד 616) *will it tell of*

אֲמִתֶּךָ n.f.s.-2 m.s. sf. (54) *thy faithfulness*

30:11

שְׁמַע־יהוה Qal impv. 2 m.s. (1033)-pr.n. (217) *Hear O Yahweh*

וְחָנֵּנִי conj.-Qal impv. 2 m.s.-1 c.s. sf. (I 335) *and be gracious to me*

יהוה pr.n. (217) *O Yahweh*

הֱיֵה־ Qal impv. 2 m.s. (חָיָה 224) *be thou*

עֹזֵר לִי Qal act.ptc. (740)–prep.–1 c.s. sf. *my helper*

30:12

הָפַכְתָּ Qal pf. 2 m.s. (245) *thou hast turned*
מִסְפְּדִי n.m.s.–1 c.s. sf. (704) *my mourning*
לְמָחוֹל לִי prep.–n.m.s. (298)–prep.–1 c.s. sf. *into dancing*
פִּתַּחְתָּ Pi. pf. 2 m.s. (פָּתַח I 864) *thou hast loosed*
שַׂקִּי n.m.s.–1 c.s. sf. (974) *my sackcloth*
וַתְּאַזְּרֵנִי consec.–Pi. impf. 2 m.s.–1 c.s. sf. (אָזַר 25) *and girded me*
שִׂמְחָה n.f.s. (970) *with gladness*

30:13

לְמַעַן יְזַמֶּרְךָ prep. (775)–Pi. impf. 3 m.s.–2 m.s. sf. (I 274) *that (my soul) may praise thee*
כָבוֹד n.m.s. (458) *with glory*
וְלֹא יִדֹּם conj.–neg.–Qal impf. 3 m.s. (I 198) *and not be silent*
יהוה אֱלֹהַי pr.n. (217)–n.m.p.–1 c.s. sf. (43) *O Yahweh my God*
לְעוֹלָם prep.–n.m.s. (761) *for ever*
אוֹדֶךָּ Hi. impf. 1 c.s.–2 m.s. sf. (יָדָה 392) *I will give thanks to thee*

31:1

לַמְנַצֵּחַ prep.–def.art.–Pi. ptc. (663) *to the choirmaster*
מִזְמוֹר n.m.s. (274) *a Psalm*
לְדָוִד prep.–pr.n. (187) *to David*

31:2

בְּךָ יהוה prep.–2 m.s. sf.–pr.n. (217) *in thee, O Yahweh*
חָסִיתִי Qal pf. 1 c.s. (חָסָה 340) *do I seek refuge*
אַל־אֵבוֹשָׁה neg.–Qal impf. 1 c.s.–coh.he (בּוֹשׁ 101; GK 108c) *let me not be put to shame*
לְעוֹלָם prep.–n.m.s. (761) *forever*
בְּצִדְקָתְךָ prep.–n.f.s.–2 m.s. sf. (842) *in thy righteousness*
פַּלְּטֵנִי Pi. impv. 2 m.s.–1 c.s. sf. (פָּלַט 812) *deliver me*

31:3

הַטֵּה Hi. impv. 2 m.s. (נָטָה 639) *incline*
אֵלַי prep.–1 c.s. sf. *to me*
אָזְנְךָ n.f.s.–2 m.s. sf. (23) *thy ear*
מְהֵרָה adv. (555) *speedily*
הַצִּילֵנִי Hi. impv. 2 m.s.–1 c.s. sf. (נָצַל 664) *rescue me*
הֱיֵה לִי Qal impv. 2 m.s. (הָיָה 224)–prep.–1 c.s. sf. *be thou for me*
לְצוּר־מָעוֹז prep.–n.m.s. cstr. (849)–n.m.s. (731) *a rock of refuge*
לְבֵית מְצוּדוֹת prep.–n.m.s. cstr. (108)–n.f.p. (II 845) *a strong fortress*
לְהוֹשִׁיעֵנִי prep.–Hi. inf.cstr.–1 c.s. sf. (יָשַׁע 446) *to save me*

31:4

כִּי־סַלְעִי conj. (471)–n.m.s.–1 c.s. sf. (700) *yea, my rock*
וּמְצוּדָתִי conj.–n.f.s.–1 c.s. sf. (II 845) *and my fortress*
אָתָּה pers.pr. 2 m.s. (61) *thou art*
וּלְמַעַן שִׁמְךָ conj.–prep. (775)–n.m.s.–2 m.s. sf. (1027) *for thy name's sake*
תַּנְחֵנִי Hi. impf. 2 m.s.–1 c.s. sf. (נָחָה 634) *lead me*
וּתְנַהֲלֵנִי conj.–Pi. impf. 2 m.s.–1 c.s. sf. (נָהַל 624) *and guide me*

31:5

תּוֹצִיאֵנִי Hi. impf. 2 m.s.–2 m.s. sf. (יָצָא 422) *take me out*
מֵרֶשֶׁת prep.–n.f.s. (440) *of the net*
זוּ טָמְנוּ לִי rel. (262)–Qal pf. 3 c.p. (טָמַן 380)–prep.–1 c.s. sf. *which is hidden for me*
כִּי־אַתָּה conj. (471)–pers.pr. 2 m.s. (61) *for thou art*
מָעוּזִּי n.m.s.–1 c.s. sf. (731) *my refuge*

31:6

בְּיָדְךָ prep.–n.f.s.–2 m.s. sf. (388) *into thy hand*
אַפְקִיד Hi. impf. 1 c.s. (פָּקַד 823) *I commit*
רוּחִי n.f.s.–1 c.s. sf. (924) *my spirit*
פָּדִיתָה Qal pf. 2 m.s. (פָּדָה 804) *thou hast redeemed*
אוֹתִי יהוה dir.obj.–1 c.s. sf.–pr.n. (217) *me, O Yahweh*
אֵל אֱמֶת n.m.s. cstr. (42)–n.f.s. (54) *faithful God*

31:7

שָׂנֵאתִי Qal pf. 1 c.s. (שָׂנֵא 971) *I hate*
הַשֹּׁמְרִים def.art.–Qal act.ptc. m.p. (שָׁמַר 1036) *those who pay regard*
הַבְלֵי־שָׁוְא n.m.p. cstr. (I 210)–n.m.s. (996) *to vain idols*
וַאֲנִי conj.–pers.pr. 1 c.s. (58) *but I*
אֶל־יהוה prep.–pr.n. (217) *in Yahweh*
בָּטָחְתִּי Qal pf. 1 c.s. paus. (בָּטַח 105) *I trust*

31:8

אָגִילָה Qal impf. 1 c.s.-coh.he (גִּיל 162) *I will rejoice*
וְאֶשְׂמְחָה conj.-Qal impf. 1 c.s.-coh.he (970) *and be glad*
בְּחַסְדֶּךָ prep.-n.m.s.-2 m.s. sf. (338) *for thy steadfast love*
אֲשֶׁר רָאִיתָ rel. (81)-Qal pf. 2 m.s. (רָאָה 906) *because thou hast seen*
אֶת־עָנְיִי dir.obj.-n.m.s.-1 c.s. sf. (777) *my affliction*
יָדַעְתָּ Qal pf. 2 m.s. (יָדַע 393) *thou hast taken heed*
בְּצָרוֹת נַפְשִׁי prep.-n.f.p. cstr. (865)-n.f.s.-1 c.s. sf. (659) *my adversities*

31:9

וְלֹא הִסְגַּרְתַּנִי conj.-neg.-Hi. pf. 2 m.s.-1 c.s. sf. (688) *and thou hast not delivered me*
בְּיַד־אוֹיֵב prep.-n.f.s. cstr. (388)-Qal act.ptc. (אָיַב 33) *into the hand of the enemy*
הֶעֱמַדְתָּ Hi. pf. 2 m.s. (763) *thou hast set*
בַמֶּרְחָב prep.-def.art.-n.m.s. (932) *in a broad place*
רַגְלָי n.f.s.-1 c.s. sf. paus. (919) *my feet*

31:10

חָנֵּנִי יהוה Qal impv. 2 m.s.-1 c.s. sf. (חָנַן I 335) -pr.n. (217) *be gracious to me, O Yahweh*
כִּי צַר־לִי conj. (471)-n.m.s. (II 865)-prep.-1 c.s. sf. *for I am in distress*
עָשְׁשָׁה Qal pf. 3 f.s. (עָשֵׁשׁ 799) *is wasted*
בְכַעַס prep.-n.m.s. (495) *from grief*
עֵינִי n.f.s.-1 c.s. sf. (744) *my eye*
נַפְשִׁי n.f.s.-1 c.s. sf. (659) *my soul*
וּבִטְנִי conj.-n.f.s.-1 c.s. sf. (105) *and my body*

31:11

כִּי כָלוּ conj. (471)-Qal pf. 3 c.p. (כָּלָה I 477) *for is spent*
בְיָגוֹן prep.-n.m.s. (387) *with sorrow*
חַיַּי n.m.p.-1 c.s. sf. (313) *my life*
וּשְׁנוֹתַי conj.-n.f.p.-1 c.s. sf. (1040) *and my years*
בַּאֲנָחָה prep.-n.f.s. (58) *with sighing*
כָּשַׁל Qal pf. 3 m.s. (505) *fails*
בַּעֲוֹנִי prep.-n.m.s.-1 c.s. sf. (730) *because of my iniquity*
כֹּחִי n.m.s.-1 c.s. sf. (470) *my strength*
וַעֲצָמַי conj.-n.f.p.-1 c.s. sf. (782) *and my bones*
עָשֵׁשׁוּ Qal pf. 3 c.p. paus. (799) *waste away*

31:12

מִכָּל־צֹרְרַי prep.-n.m.s. cstr. (481)-Qal act.ptc. m.p.-1 c.s. sf. (III 865) *of all my adversaries*
הָיִיתִי Qal pf. 1 c.s. (הָיָה 224) *I am*
חֶרְפָּה n.f.s. (357) *the scorn*
וְלִשְׁכֵנַי conj.-prep.-n.m.p.-1 c.s. sf. (1015) *and to my neighbors*
מְאֹד adv. (547) *exceedingly*
וּפַחַד conj.-n.m.s. (808) *and an object of dread*
לִמְיֻדָּעָי prep.-Pu. ptc. m.p.-1 c.s. sf. (יָדַע 393) *to my acquaintances*
רֹאַי Qal act.ptc. m.p.-1 c.s. sf. (רָאָה 906) *those who see me*
בַּחוּץ prep.-def.art.-n.m.s. (299) *in the street*
נָדְדוּ מִמֶּנִּי Qal pf. 3 c.p. (622)-prep.-1 c.s. sf. *flee from me*

31:13

נִשְׁכַּחְתִּי Ni. pf. 1 c.s. (שָׁכַח 1013) *I have passed out*
כְּמֵת prep.-Qal act.ptc. (מוּת 559) *like one who is dead*
מִלֵּב prep.-n.m.s. (524) *out of mind*
הָיִיתִי Qal pf. 1 c.s. (הָיָה 224) *I have become*
כִּכְלִי prep.-n.m.s. (479) *like a vessel*
אֹבֵד Qal act.ptc. (אָבַד 1) *broken*

31:14

כִּי שָׁמַעְתִּי conj. (471)-Qal pf. 1 c.s. (1033) *yea, I hear*
דִּבַּת רַבִּים n.f.s. cstr. (179)-adj. m.p. (I 912) *the whispering of many*
מָגוֹר n.m.s. (II 159) *terror*
מִסָּבִיב prep.-prep. (686) *on every side*
בְּהִוָּסְדָם prep.-Ni. inf.cstr.-3 m.p. sf. (יָסַד 413) *as they scheme*
יַחַד עָלַי adv. (403)-prep.-1 c.s. sf. *together against me*
לָקַחַת prep.-Qal inf.cstr. (לָקַח 542) *to take*
נַפְשִׁי n.f.s.-1 c.s. sf. (659) *my life*
זָמָמוּ Qal pf. 3 c.p. paus. (זָמַם 273) *they plot*

31:15

וַאֲנִי conj.-pers.pr. 1 c.s. (58) *but I*
עָלֶיךָ בָטַחְתִּי prep.-2 m.s. sf.-Qal pf. 1 c.s. (105) *in thee, I trust*
יהוה pr.n. (217) *O Yahweh*
אָמַרְתִּי Qal pf. 1 c.s. (55) *I say*
אֱלֹהַי n.m.p.-1 c.s. sf. (43) *my God*
אָתָּה pers.pr. 2 m.s. paus. (61) *thou art*

31:16

בְּיָדְךָ prep.-n.f.s.-2 m.s. sf. (388) *in thy hand*

עִתֹּתָי n.f.p.-1 c.s. sf. (773) *my times*

הַצִּילֵנִי Hi. impv. 2 m.s.-1 c.s. sf. (נָצַל 664) *deliver me*

מִיַּד־אוֹיְבַי prep.-n.f.s. cstr. (388)-Qal act.ptc. m.p.-1 c.s. sf. (אָיַב 33) *from the hand of my enemies*

וּמֵרֹדְפָי conj.-prep.-Qal act.ptc. m.p.-1 c.s. sf. (922 רָדַף) *and from my persecutors*

31:17

הָאִירָה Hi. impv. 2 m.s.-coh.he (21) *let shine*

פָּנֶיךָ n.m.p.-2 m.s. sf. (815) *thy face*

עַל־עַבְדֶּךָ prep.-n.m.s.-2 m.s. sf. (712) *on thy servant*

הוֹשִׁיעֵנִי Hi. impv. 2 m.s.-1 c.s. sf. (יָשַׁע 446) *save me*

בְחַסְדֶּךָ prep.-n.m.s.-2 m.s. sf. paus. (338) *in thy steadfast love*

31:18

יהוה pr.n. (217) *O Yahweh*

אַל־אֵבוֹשָׁה neg.-Qal impf. 1 c.s.-coh.he (בּוֹשׁ 101) *let me not be put to shame*

כִּי קְרָאתִיךָ conj. (471)-Qal pf. 1 c.s.-2 m.s. sf. (894) *for I call on thee*

יֵבֹשׁוּ Qal impf. 3 m.p. (101) *let be put to shame*

רְשָׁעִים adj. m.p. (957) *the wicked*

יִדְּמוּ Qal impf. 3 m.p. (דָּמַם I 198) *let them go dumbfounded*

לִשְׁאוֹל prep.-n.f.s. (982) *to Sheol*

31:19

תֵּאָלַמְנָה Ni. impf. 3 f.p. (אָלַם 47) *let be dumb*

שִׂפְתֵי שָׁקֶר n.f.p. cstr. (973)-n.m.s. (1055) *the lying lips*

הַדֹּבְרוֹת def.art.-Qal act.ptc. f.p. (180) *which speak*

עַל־צַדִּיק prep.-adj. m.s. (843) *against the righteous*

עָתָק adj. m.s. (801) *insolently*

בְּגַאֲוָה prep.-n.f.s. (144) *in pride*

וָבוּז conj.-n.m.s. (II 100) *and contempt*

31:20

מָה רַב־טוּבְךָ interr. (552)-adj. m.s. cstr. (I 912) -n.m.s.-2 m.s. sf. (375) *O how abundant is thy goodness*

אֲשֶׁר־צָפַנְתָּ rel. (81)-Qal pf. 2 m.s. (860) *which thou hast laid up*

לִּירֵאֶיךָ prep.-Qal act.ptc. m.p.-2 m.s. sf. (יָרֵא 431) *for those who fear thee*

פָּעַלְתָּ Qal pf. 2 m.s. (פָּעַל 821) *and wrought*

לַחֹסִים בָּךְ prep.-def.art.-Qal act.ptc. m.p. (340)-prep.-2 m.s. sf. *for those who take refuge in thee*

נֶגֶד prep. 617) *in the sight of*

בְּנֵי אָדָם n.m.p. cstr. (119)-n.m.s. (9) *the sons of men*

31:21

תַּסְתִּירֵם Hi. impf. 2 m.s.-3 m.p. sf. (סָתַר 711) *thou hidest them*

בְּסֵתֶר פָּנֶיךָ prep.-n.m.s. cstr. (712)-n.m.p.-2 m.s. sf. (815) *in the covert of thy presence*

מֵרֻכְסֵי אִישׁ prep.-n.m.p. cstr. (940; GK 93r) -n.m.s. (35) *from the plots of men*

תִּצְפְּנֵם Qal impf. 2 m.s.-3 m.p. sf. (צָפַן 860) *thou holdest them safe*

בְּסֻכָּה prep.-n.f.s. (697) *under shelter*

מֵרִיב לְשֹׁנוֹת prep.-n.m.s. cstr. (936)-n.f.p. (546) *from the strife of tongues*

31:22

בָּרוּךְ יהוה Qal pass.ptc. (138)-pr.n. (217) *blessed be Yahweh*

כִּי הִפְלִיא conj. (471)-Hi. pf. 3 m.s. (פָּלָא 810) *for he has wondrously shown*

חַסְדּוֹ לִי n.m.s.-3 m.s. sf. (338)-prep.-1 c.s. sf. *his steadfast love to me*

בְּעִיר מָצוֹר prep.-n.f.s. cstr. (746)-n.m.s. (848) *in a besieged city*

31:23

וַאֲנִי אָמַרְתִּי conj.-pers.pr. 1 c.s. (58)-Qal pf. 1 c.s. (55) *I had said*

בְחָפְזִי prep.-Qal inf.cstr.-1 c.s. sf. (342) *in my alarm*

נִגְרַזְתִּי Ni. pf. 1 c.s. (גָּרַז 173) *I am cut off*

מִנֶּגֶד עֵינֶיךָ prep.-prep. (617)-n.f.p.-2 m.s. sf. (744) *from thy sight*

אָכֵן שָׁמַעְתָּ adv. (38)-Qal pf. 2 m.s. (1033) *but thou didst hear*

קוֹל תַּחֲנוּנַי n.m.s. cstr. (876)-n.f.p.-1 c.s. sf. (337) *my supplications*

בְּשַׁוְּעִי prep.-Pi. inf.cstr.-1 c.s. sf. (1002) *when I cried for help*

אֵלֶיךָ prep.-2 m.s. sf. *to thee*

31:24

אֶהֱבוּ Qal impv. 2 m.p. (12) *love*

אֶת־יהוה dir.obj.-pr.n. (217) *Yahweh*

כָּל־חֲסִידָיו n.m.s. cstr. (481)-adj. m.p.-3 m.s. sf. (339) *all you his saints*

אֱמוּנִים Qal pass.ptc. m.p. (I 52) *the faithful*

נֹצֵר יהוה Qal act.ptc. (665)-pr.n. (217) *Yahweh preserves*

וּמְשַׁלֵּם conj.-Pi. ptc. (1022) *but requites them*

עַל־יֶתֶר prep.-n.m.s. cstr. (451) *abundantly*

עֹשֵׂה גַאֲוָה Qal act.ptc. cstr. (I 793)-n.f.s. (144) *him who acts haughtily*

31:25

חִזְקוּ Qal impv. 2 m.p. (304) *be strong*

וְיַאֲמֵץ conj.-Hi. impf. 3 m.s. juss. (אָמֵץ 54) *and let take courage*

לְבַבְכֶם n.m.s.-2 m.p. sf. (523) *your heart*

כָּל־הַמְיַחֲלִים n.m.s. cstr. (481)-def.art.-Pi. ptc. m.p. (יָחַל 403) *all you who wait*

לַיהוה prep.-pr.n. (217) *for Yahweh*

32:1

לְדָוִד prep.-pr.n. (187) *to David*

מַשְׂכִּיל n.m.s. (968) *a Maskil*

אַשְׁרֵי n.m.p. cstr. (80) *blessed is*

נְשׂוּי־פֶּשַׁע Qal pass.ptc. cstr. (נָשָׂא 669; GK 75qq,116k)-n.m.s. (833) *he whose transgression is forgiven*

כְּסוּי חֲטָאָה Qal pass.ptc. cstr. (491)-n.f.s. (308) *whose sin is covered*

32:2

אַשְׁרֵי אָדָם n.m.p. cstr. (80)-n.m.s. (9) *blessed is the man*

לֹא יַחְשֹׁב neg.-Qal impf. 3 m.s. (362) *does not impute*

יהוה לוֹ pr.n. (217)-prep.-3 m.s. sf. *Yahweh ... to him*

עָוֹן n.m.s. (730) *iniquity*

וְאֵין בְּרוּחוֹ conj.-subst. cstr. (II 34)-prep.-n.f.s.-3 m.s. sf. (924) *and there is no ... in his spirit*

רְמִיָּה n.f.s. (941; GK 155i) *deceit*

32:3

כִּי־הֶחֱרַשְׁתִּי conj. (471)-Hi. pf. 1 c.s. (II 361) *when I was silent*

בָּלוּ עֲצָמָי Qal pf. 3 c.p. (בָּלָה 115)-n.m.p.-1 c.s. sf. (782) *my body wasted away*

בְּשַׁאֲגָתִי prep.-n.f.s.-1 c.s. sf. (980) *through my groaning*

כָּל־הַיּוֹם n.m.s. cstr. (481)-def.art.-n.m.s. (398) *all day long*

32:4

כִּי יוֹמָם conj. (471)-adv. (401) *for day*

וָלַיְלָה conj.-n.m.s. (538) *and night*

תִּכְבַּד עָלַי Qal impf. 3 f.s. (457)-prep.-1 c.s. sf. *was heavy upon me*

יָדֶךָ n.f.s.-2 m.s. sf. (388) *thy hand*

נֶהְפַּךְ Ni. pf. 3 m.s. (הָפַךְ 245) *was overturned*

לְשַׁדִּי n.m.s.-1 c.s. sf. (545) *my strength (juice)*

בְּחַרְבֹנֵי קַיִץ prep.-n.m.p. cstr. (351)-n.m.s. (884) *by the heat of summer*

סֶלָה interj. (699) *Selah*

32:5

חַטָּאתִי n.f.s.-1 c.s. sf. (308) *my sin*

אוֹדִיעֲךָ Hi. impf. 1 c.s.-2 m.s. sf. (יָדַע 393) *I acknowledged*

וַעֲוֹנִי conj.-n.m.s.-1 c.s. sf. (730) *and my iniquity*

לֹא־כִסִּיתִי neg.-Pi. pf. 1 c.s. (כָּסָה 491) *I did not hide*

אָמַרְתִּי Qal pf. 1 c.s. (55) *I said*

אוֹדֶה Hi. impf. 1 c.s. (יָדָה 392) *I will confess*

עֲלֵי פְשָׁעַי prep. (752)-n.m.p.-1 c.s. sf. (833) *my transgressions*

לַיהוה prep.-pr.n. (217) *to Yahweh*

וְאַתָּה נָשָׂאתָ conj.-pers.pr. 2 m.s. (61)-Qal pf. 2 m.s. (669) *then thou didst forgive*

עֲוֹן חַטָּאתִי n.m.s. cstr. (730)-n.f.s.-1 c.s. sf. (308) *the guilt of my sin*

סֶלָה interj. (699) *Selah*

32:6

עַל־זֹאת prep.-demons.adj. f.s. (260) *therefore*

יִתְפַּלֵּל Hith. impf. 3 m.s. (פָּלַל 813) *let ... offer prayer*

כָּל־חָסִיד n.m.s. cstr. (481)-adj. m.s. (339) *every one who is godly*

אֵלֶיךָ prep.-2 m.s. sf. *to thee*

לְעֵת מְצֹא prep.-n.f.s. cstr. (773)-Qal inf.cstr. (592) *at a time of finding*

רַק adv. (956; GK 153) *only*

לְשֵׁטֶף מַיִם prep. (GK 143e)-n.m.s. cstr. (1009) -n.m.p. (565) *in the rush of ... waters*

רַבִּים adj. m.p. (I 912) *great*

אֵלָיו prep.-3 m.s. sf. *him*

לֹא יַגִּיעוּ neg.-Hi. impf. 3 m.p. (נָגַע 619) *they shall not reach*

32:7

אַתָּה pers.pr. 2 m.s. (61) *thou art*

סֵתֶר לִי n.m.s. (712)-prep.-1 c.s. sf. *a hiding place for me*

מִצַּר prep.-n.m.s. (II 865) *from trouble*

תִּצְּרֵנִי Qal impf. 2 m.s.–1 c.s. sf. (נָצַר 665) *thou preservest me*
רָנֵּי פַלֵּט n.m.p. cstr. (943)–n.m.s. (812) *shouts of deliverance*
תְּסוֹבְבֵנִי Polel impf. 2 m.s.–1 c.s. sf. (סָבַב 685) *thou dost encompass me with*
סֶלָה interj. (699) *Selah*

32:8

אַשְׂכִּילְךָ Hi. impf. 1 c.s.–2 m.s. sf. (968) *I will instruct you*
וְאוֹרְךָ conj.–Hi. impf. 1 c.s.–2 m.s. sf. (יָרָה 434) *and teach you*
בְּדֶרֶךְ־ prep.–n.m.s. (202) *the way*
זוּ תֵלֵךְ rel. (262; GK 107q,138g,156c)–Qal impf. 2 m.s. (הָלַךְ 229) *you should go*
אִיעֲצָה Qal impf. 1 c.s.–coh.he (יָעַץ 419) *I will counsel*
עָלֶיךָ prep.–2 m.s. sf. *upon you*
עֵינִי n.f.s.–1 c.s. sf. (I 744) *with my eye*

32:9

אַל־תִּהְיוּ neg.–Qal impf. 2 m.p. (הָיָה 224) *be not*
כְּסוּס prep.–n.m.s. (692) *like a horse*
כְּפֶרֶד prep.–n.m.s. (825) *or a mule*
אֵין הָבִין subst. cstr. (II 34)–Hi. inf.cstr. (בִּין 106; GK 114a) *without understanding*
בְּמֶתֶג־ prep.–n.m.s. (607) *with bit*
וָרֶסֶן conj.–n.m.s. (I 943) *and bridle*
עֶדְיוֹ n.m.s.–3 m.s. sf. (725) *his trappings*
לִבְלוֹם prep.–Qal inf.cstr. (117; GK 114k) *which must be curbed*
בַּל קְרֹב אֵלֶיךָ neg. (GK 114s)–Qal inf.cstr. (897) -prep.–2 m.s. sf. *else it will not keep you*

32:10

רַבִּים adj. m.p. (I 912) *many are*
מַכְאוֹבִים n.m.p. (456) *the pangs*
לָרָשָׁע prep.–def.art.–n.m.s. (957) *of the wicked*
וְהַבּוֹטֵחַ conj.–def.art.–Qal act.ptc. (105) *but ... who trusts*
בַּיהוה prep.–pr.n. (217) *in Yahweh*
חֶסֶד n.m.s. (338) *steadfast love*
יְסוֹבְבֶנּוּ Po'el impf. 3 m.s.–3 m.s. sf. (סָבַב 685) *surrounds him*

32:11

שִׂמְחוּ Qal impv. 2 m.p. (970) *be glad*
בַּיהוה prep.–pr.n. (217) *in Yahweh*
וְגִילוּ conj.–Qal impv. 2 m.p. (גִּיל 162) *and rejoice*
צַדִּיקִים n.m.p. (843) *O righteous*
וְהַרְנִינוּ conj.–Hi. impv. 2 m.p. (רָנַן 943) *and shout for joy*
כָּל־יִשְׁרֵי־לֵב n.m.s. cstr. (481)–adj. m.p. cstr. (449)–n.m.s. (524) *all you upright in heart*

33:1

רַנְּנוּ Pi. impv. 2 m.p. (רָנַן 943) *rejoice*
צַדִּיקִים adj. m.p. (843) *O righteous*
בַּיהוה prep.–pr.n. (217) *in Yahweh*
לַיְשָׁרִים prep.–def.art.–adj. m.p. (449) *the upright*
נָאוָה adj. f.s. (610) *befits*
תְהִלָּה n.f.s. (239) *praise*

33:2

הוֹדוּ Hi. impv. 2 m.s. (יָדָה 392) *praise*
לַיהוה prep.–pr.n. (217) *Yahweh*
בְּכִנּוֹר prep.–n.m.s. (490) *with the lyre*
בְּנֵבֶל prep.–n.m.s. cstr. (614) *with the harp of*
עָשׂוֹר n.m.s. (797) *ten strings*
זַמְּרוּ־ Pi. impv. 2 m.p. (זָמַר I 274) *make melody*
לוֹ prep.–3 m.s. sf. *to him*

33:3

שִׁירוּ־לוֹ Qal impv. 2 m.p. (שִׁיר 1010)–prep.–3 m.s. sf. *sing to him*
שִׁיר חָדָשׁ n.m.s. (1010)–adj. m.s. (I 294) *a new song*
הֵיטִיבוּ נַגֵּן Hi. impv. 2 m.p. (יָטַב 405)–Pi. inf.cstr. (נָגַן 618) *play skillfully on the strings*
בִּתְרוּעָה prep.–n.f.s. (929) *with loud shouts*

33:4

כִּי־יָשָׁר conj. (471)–adj. m.s. (449) *for is upright*
דְּבַר־יהוה n.m.s. cstr. (182)–pr.n. (217) *the word of Yahweh*
וְכָל־מַעֲשֵׂהוּ conj.–n.m.s. cstr. (481)–n.m.s.–3 m.s. sf. (795) *and all his work*
בֶּאֱמוּנָה prep.–n.f.s. (53) *in faithfulness*

33:5

אֹהֵב Qal act.ptc. (אָהֵב 12; GK 116s) *he loves*
צְדָקָה n.f.s. (842) *righteousness*
וּמִשְׁפָּט conj.–n.m.s. (1048) *and justice*
חֶסֶד יהוה n.m.s. cstr. (338)–pr.n. (217) *the steadfast love of Yahweh*
מָלְאָה Qal pf. 3 f.s. (מָלֵא 569) *is full*
הָאָרֶץ def.art.–n.f.s. (75) *the earth*

33:6

בִּדְבַר יהוה prep.–n.m.s. cstr. (182)–pr.n. (217) *by the word of Yahweh*

שָׁמַיִם n.m. du. (1029) *the heavens*
נַעֲשׂוּ Ni. pf. 3 c.p. (עָשָׂה I 793) *were made*
וּבְרוּחַ פִּיו conj.-prep.-n.f.s. cstr. (924)-n.m.s.-3 m.s. sf. (804) *and by the breath of his mouth*
כָּל־צְבָאָם n.m.s. cstr. (481)-n.m.s.-3 m.p. sf. (838) *all their host*

33:7

כֹּנֵס Qal act.ptc. (כָּנַס 488) *he gathered*
כַּנֵּד prep.-def.art.-n.m.s. (622; GK 118w) *as in a heap*
מֵי הַיָּם n.m.p. cstr. (565)-def.art.-n.m.s. (410) *the waters of the sea*
נֹתֵן Qal act.ptc. (נָתַן 678) *he put*
בְּאֹצָרוֹת prep.-n.m.p. (69) *in storehouses*
תְּהוֹמוֹת n.f.p. (1062) *the deeps*

33:8

יִירְאוּ Qal impf. 3 m.p. (יָרֵא 431) *let fear*
מֵיהוה prep.-pr.n. (217) *Yahweh*
כָּל־הָאָרֶץ n.m.s. cstr. (481)-def.art.-n.f.s. (75; GK 145e) *all the earth*
מִמֶּנּוּ prep.-3 m.s. sf. *of him*
יָגוּרוּ Qal impf. 3 m.p. (גּוּר III 158) *let stand in awe*
כָּל־יֹשְׁבֵי n.m.s. cstr. (481)-Qal act.ptc. m.p. cstr. (442 יָשַׁב) *all the inhabitants of*
תֵבֵל n.f.s. (385) *the world*

33:9

כִּי הוּא conj. (471)-pers.pr. 3 m.s. (214) *for he*
אָמַר Qal pf. 3 m.s. (55) *spoke*
וַיֶּהִי consec.-Qal impf. 3 m.s. (הָיָה 224) *and it came to be*
הוּא־צִוָּה v.supra-Pi. pf. 3 m.s. (צָוָה 845) *he commanded*
וַיַּעֲמֹד consec.-Qal impf. 3 m.s. (עָמַד 763) *and it stood forth*

33:10

יהוה pr.n. (217) *Yahweh*
הֵפִיר Hi. pf. 3 m.s. (פָּרַר I 830; GK 67v) *brings to nought*
עֲצַת־ n.f.s. cstr. (420) *the counsel of*
גּוֹיִם n.m.p. (156) *the nations*
הֵנִיא Hi. pf. 3 m.s. (נוּא 626) *he frustrates*
מַחְשְׁבוֹת n.f.p. cstr. (364) *the plans of*
עַמִּים n.m.p. (I 766) *the peoples*

33:11

עֲצַת n.f.s. cstr. (420) *the counsel of*
יהוה pr.n. (217) *Yahweh*
לְעוֹלָם prep.-n.m.s. (761) *for ever*
תַּעֲמֹד Qal impf. 3 f.s. (עָמַד 763) *stands*
מַחְשְׁבוֹת n.f.p. cstr. (364) *the thoughts of*
לִבּוֹ n.m.s.-3 m.s. sf. (524) *his heart*
לְדֹר וָדֹר prep.-n.m.s. (189)-conj.-v.supra *to all generations*

33:12

אַשְׁרֵי הַגּוֹי n.m.p. cstr. (80)-def.art.-n.m.s. (156) *blessed is the nation*
אֲשֶׁר־יהוה rel. (81; GK 155h)-pr.n. (217) *which Yahweh*
אֱלֹהָיו n.m.p.-3 m.s. sf. (43) *his God*
הָעָם def.art.-n.m.s. (I 766) *the people*
בָּחַר Qal pf. 3 m.s. (103) *he has chosen*
לְנַחֲלָה לוֹ prep.-n.f.s. (635)-prep.-3 m.s. sf. *as his heritage*

33:13

מִשָּׁמַיִם prep.-n.m. du. (1029) *from heaven*
הִבִּיט Hi. pf. 3 m.s. (נָבַט 613) *looks down*
יהוה pr.n. (217) *Yahweh*
רָאָה Qal pf. 3 m.s. (906) *he sees*
אֶת־כָּל־ dir.obj.-n.m.s. cstr. (481) *all*
בְּנֵי הָאָדָם n.m.p. cstr. (119)-def.art.-n.m.s. (9) *the sons of men*

33:14

מִמְּכוֹן־שִׁבְתּוֹ prep.-n.m.s. cstr. (467)-Qal inf.cstr. -3 m.s. sf. (יָשַׁב 442) *from where he sits enthroned*
הִשְׁגִּיחַ Hi. pf. 3 m.s. (שָׁגַח 993) *he looks forth*
אֶל כָּל־ prep.-n.m.s. cstr. (481) *on all*
יֹשְׁבֵי הָאָרֶץ Qal act.ptc. m.p. cstr. (יָשַׁב 442) -def.art.-n.f.s. (75) *the inhabitants of the earth*

33:15

הַיֹּצֵר def.art.-Qal act.ptc. (427) *he who fashions*
יַחַד adv. (403) *altogether*
לִבָּם n.m.s.-3 m.p. sf. (524) *the hearts of them*
הַמֵּבִין def.art. (GK 126b)-Hi. ptc. (בִּין 106) *and observes*
אֶל־כָּל־ prep.-n.m.s. cstr. (481) *all*
מַעֲשֵׂיהֶם n.m.p.-3 m.p. sf. (795) *their deeds*

33:16

אֵין הַמֶּלֶךְ subst.neg. (II 34)-def.art.-n.m.s. (I 572) *a king is not*
נוֹשָׁע Ni. ptc. (יָשַׁע 446) *saved*
בְּרָב־חָיִל prep.-n.m.s. cstr. (913)-n.m.s. paus. (298) *by his great army*

גִּבּוֹר n.m.s. (150) *a warrior*
לֹא־יִנָּצֵל neg.-Ni. impf. 3 m.s. (נָצַל 664) *is not delivered*
בְּרָב־כֹּחַ v.supra-n.m.s. (470) *by his great strength*

33:17

שֶׁקֶר הַסּוּס n.m.s. (1055)-def.art.-n.m.s. (692) *the war horse is a vain hope*
לִתְשׁוּעָה prep.-n.f.s. (448) *for victory*
וּבְרֹב חֵילוֹ conj.-prep.-n.m.s. cstr. (913)-n.m.s.-3 m.s. sf. (298) *and by its great might*
לֹא יְמַלֵּט neg.-Pi. impf. 3 m.s. (מָלַט 572) *it cannot save*

33:18

הִנֵּה demons.part. (243) *behold*
עֵין יהוה n.f.s. cstr. (744)-pr.n. (217) *the eye of Yahweh*
אֶל־יְרֵאָיו prep.-Qal act.ptc. m.p.-3 m.s. sf. (יָרֵא 431) *on those who fear him*
לַמְיַחֲלִים prep.-def.art.-Pi. ptc. m.p. (403) *on those who hope*
לְחַסְדּוֹ prep.-n.m.s.-3 m.s. sf. (338) *in his steadfast love*

33:19

לְהַצִּיל prep.-Hi. inf.cstr. (נָצַל 664) *that he may deliver*
מִמָּוֶת prep.-n.m.s. (560) *from death*
נַפְשָׁם n.f.s.-3 m.p. sf. (659) *their soul*
וּלְחַיּוֹתָם conj.-prep.-Pi. inf.cstr.-3 m.p. sf. (חָיָה 310) *and keep them alive*
בָּרָעָב prep.-def.art.-n.m.s. (944) *in famine*

33:20

נַפְשֵׁנוּ n.f.s.-1 c.p. sf. (659) *our soul*
חִכְּתָה Pi. pf. 3 f.s. (חָכָה 314) *waits*
לַיהוה prep.-pr.n. (217) *for Yahweh*
עֶזְרֵנוּ n.m.s.-1 c.p. sf. (740) *our help*
וּמָגִנֵּנוּ conj.-n.m.s.-1 c.p. sf. (171) *and our shield*
הוּא pers.pr. 3 m.s. (214) *he is*

33:21

כִּי־בוֹ conj. (471)-prep.-3 m.s. sf. *yea, in him*
יִשְׂמַח Qal impf. 3 m.s. (שָׂמַח 970) *is glad*
לִבֵּנוּ n.m.s.-1 c.p. sf. (524) *our heart*
כִּי בְשֵׁם קָדְשׁוֹ conj.-prep.-n.m.s. cstr. (1027)-n.m.s.-3 m.s. sf. (871) *because in his holy name*
בָטָחְנוּ Qal pf. 1 c.p. paus. (בָּטַח 105) *we trust*

33:22

יְהִי־ Qal impf. 3 m.s. apoc. (הָיָה 224) *let be*
חַסְדְּךָ n.m.s.-2 m.s. sf. (338) *thy steadfast love*
יהוה pr.n. (217) *O Yahweh*
עָלֵינוּ prep.-1 c.p. sf. *upon us*
כַּאֲשֶׁר prep.-rel. (81) *even as*
יִחַלְנוּ Pi. pf. 1 c.p. (יָחַל 403) *we hope*
לָךְ prep.-2 m.s. sf. paus. *in thee*

34:1

לְדָוִד prep.-pr.n. (187; GK 5h) *to David*
בְּשַׁנּוֹתוֹ prep.-Pi. inf.cstr.-3 m.s. sf. (שָׁנָה 1039) *when he feigned* (lit. *changed*)
אֶת־טַעְמוֹ dir.obj.-n.m.s.-3 m.s. sf. (381) *madness (his judgment)*
לִפְנֵי prep.-n.m.p. cstr. (815) *before*
אֲבִימֶלֶךְ pr.n. (4) *Abimelech* (cf. 1 Sam. 21:11f.)
וַיְגָרֲשֵׁהוּ consec.-Pi. impf. 3 m.s.-3 m.s. sf. (גָּרַשׁ 176) *so that he drove him out*
וַיֵּלַךְ consec.-Qal impf. 3 m.s. (הָלַךְ 229) *and he went away*

34:2

אֲבָרְכָה Pi. impf. 1 c.s.-vol.he (בָּרַךְ 138) *I will bless*
אֶת־יהוה dir.obj.-pr.n. (217) *Yahweh*
בְּכָל־עֵת prep.-n.m.s. cstr. (481)-n.f.s. (773) *at all times*
תָּמִיד adv. (556) *continually*
תְּהִלָּתוֹ n.f.s.-3 m.s. sf. (239) *his praise*
בְּפִי prep.-n.m.s.-1 c.s. sf. (804; GK 21d) *in my mouth*

34:3

בַּיהוה prep.-pr.n. (217) *in Yahweh*
תִּתְהַלֵּל Hith. impf. 3 f.s. (הָלַל II 237) *makes its boast*
נַפְשִׁי n.f.s.-1 c.s. sf. (659) *my soul*
יִשְׁמְעוּ Qal impf. 3 m.p. (שָׁמַע 1033) *let ... hear*
עֲנָוִים n.m.p. (776) *the afflicted*
וְיִשְׂמָחוּ conj.-Qal impf. 3 m.p. paus. (שָׂמַח 970) *and be glad*

34:4

גַּדְּלוּ Pi. impv. 2 m.p. (גָּדַל 152) *O magnify*
לַיהוה prep.-pr.n. (217) *Yahweh*
אִתִּי prep.-1 c.s. sf. (II 85) *with me*
וּנְרוֹמְמָה conj.-Polel impf. 1 c.p.-vol.he (רוּם 926) *let us exalt*
שְׁמוֹ n.m.s.-3 m.s. sf. (1027) *his name*
יַחְדָּו adv. (403) *together*

34:5

דָּרַשְׁתִּי Qal pf. 1 c.s. (דָּרַשׁ 205) *I sought*
אֶת־יהוה dir.obj.-pr.n. (217) *Yahweh*
וְעָנָנִי conj.-Qal pf. 3 m.s.-1 c.s. sf. (עָנָה I 772) *and he answered me*
וּמִכָּל־ conj.-prep.-n.m.s. cstr. (481) *and from all*
מְגוּרוֹתַי n.f.p.-1 c.s. sf. (159) *my fears*
הִצִּילָנִי Hi. pf. 3 m.s.-1 c.s. sf. paus. (נָצַל 664) *he delivered me*

34:6

הִבִּיטוּ Hi. pf. 3 c.p. (נָבַט 613; some הַבִּיטוּ Hi. impv. 2 m.p.) *they look*
אֵלָיו prep.-3 m.s. sf. *to him*
וְנָהָרוּ conj.-Qal pf. 3 c.p. paus. (נָהַר II 626) *and are radiant*
וּפְנֵיהֶם conj.-n.m.p.-3 m.p. sf. (815) *so their faces*
אַל־יֶחְפָּרוּ neg.-Qal impf. 3 m.p. paus. (חָפֵר II 344; GK 109e) *shall never be ashamed*

34:7

זֶה עָנִי demons.adj. m.s. (260)-n.m.s. (776) *this poor man*
קָרָא Qal pf. 3 m.s. (894) *cried*
ויהוה conj.-pr.n. (217) *and Yahweh*
שָׁמֵעַ Qal pf. 3 m.s. paus. (שָׁמַע 1033) *heard*
וּמִכָּל־ conj.-prep.-n.m.s. cstr. (481) *and out of all*
צָרוֹתָיו n.f.p.-3 m.s. sf. (865) *his troubles*
הוֹשִׁיעוֹ Hi. pf. 3 m.s.-3 m.s. sf. (יָשַׁע 446) *saved him*

34:8

חֹנֶה Qal act.ptc. (חָנָה 333) *encamps*
מַלְאַךְ־ n.m.s. cstr. (521) *the angel of*
יהוה pr.n. (217) *Yahweh*
סָבִיב subst. (686) *around*
לִירֵאָיו prep.-Qal act.ptc. m.p.-3 m.s. sf. (יָרֵא 431) *those who fear him*
וַיְחַלְּצֵם consec.-Pi. impf. 3 m.s.-3 m.p. sf. (חָלַץ I 322) *and delivers them*

34:9

טַעֲמוּ Qal impv. 2 m.p. (טָעַם 380) *taste*
וּרְאוּ conj.-Qal impv. 2 m.p. (רָאָה 906) *and see*
כִּי־טוֹב conj. (471)-adj. m.s. (II 373) *that is good*
יהוה pr.n. (217) *Yahweh*
אַשְׁרֵי n.m.p. cstr. (80) *happy is*
הַגֶּבֶר def.art.-n.m.s. (149) *the man*
יֶחֱסֶה־בּוֹ Qal impf. 3 m.s. (חָסָה 340; GK 155f) -prep.-3 m.s. sf. *who takes refuge in him*

34:10

יְראוּ Qal impv. 2 m.p. (יָרֵא 431) *fear*
אֶת־יהוה dir.obj.-pr.n. (217) *Yahweh*
קְדֹשָׁיו adj. m.p.-3 m.s. sf. (872) *his saints*
כִּי־אֵין מַחְסוֹר conj. (471)-neg. (II 34)-n.m.s. (341) *for have no want*
לִירֵאָיו prep.-Qal act.ptc. m.p.-3 m.s. sf. (יָרֵא 431) *those who fear him*

34:11

כְּפִירִים n.m.p. (498) *the young lions*
רָשׁוּ Qal pf. 3 c.p. (רוּשׁ 930) *suffer want*
וְרָעֵבוּ conj.-Qal pf. 3 c.p. paus. (רָעֵב 944) *and hunger*
וְדֹרְשֵׁי conj.-Qal act.ptc. m.p. cstr. (דָּרַשׁ 205) *but those who seek*
יהוה pr.n. (217) *Yahweh*
לֹא־יַחְסְרוּ neg.-Qal impf. 3 m.p. (חָסֵר 341) *do not lack*
כָל־טוֹב n.m.s. cstr. (481)-n.m.s. (375) *any good thing*

34:12

לְכוּ־ Qal impv. 2 m.p. (הָלַךְ 229) *come*
בָנִים n.m.p. (119) *O sons*
שִׁמְעוּ־לִי Qal impv. 2 m.p. (שָׁמַע 1033)-prep.-1 c.s. sf. *listen to me*
יִרְאַת יהוה n.f.s. cstr. (432)-pr.n. (217) *the fear of Yahweh*
אֲלַמֶּדְכֶם Pi. impf. 1 c.s.-2 m.p. sf. (לָמַד 540; GK 60f) *I will teach you*

34:13

מִי־הָאִישׁ interr. (566)-def.art.-n.m.s. (35) *what man*
הֶחָפֵץ def.art.-adj. m.s. (343) *who desires*
חַיִּים adj. m.p. (313) *life*
אֹהֵב Qal act.ptc. (אָהֵב 12) *and covets*
יָמִים n.m.p. (398) *days*
לִרְאוֹת prep.-Qal inf.cstr. (רָאָה 906) *that he may enjoy*
טוֹב adj. m.s. (373) *good*

34:14

נְצֹר Qal impv. 2 m.s. (נָצַר 665) *keep*
לְשׁוֹנְךָ n.f.s.-2 m.s. sf. (546) *your tongue*
מֵרָע prep.-n.m.s. (949) *from evil*
וּשְׂפָתֶיךָ conj.-n.f.p.-2 m.s. sf. (973) *and your lips*
מִדַּבֵּר prep.-Pi. inf.cstr. (180) *from speaking*
מִרְמָה n.f.s. (941) *deceit*

34:15

סוּר Qal impv. 2 m.s. (סוּר 693) *depart*

מֵרָע prep.-n.m.s. (949) *from evil*

וַעֲשֵׂה־טוֹב conj.-Qal impv. 2 m.s. (עָשָׂה I 793)-n.m.s. (373) *and do good*

בַּקֵּשׁ Pi. impv. 2 m.s. (בָּקַשׁ 134) *seek*

שָׁלוֹם n.m.s. (1022) *peace*

וְרָדְפֵהוּ conj.-Qal impv. 2 m.s.-3 m.s. sf. (רָדַף 922) *and pursue it*

34:16

עֵינֵי n.f. du. cstr. (744) *the eyes of*

יהוה pr.n. (217) *Yahweh*

אֶל־צַדִּיקִים prep.-adj. m.p. (843) *toward the righteous*

וְאָזְנָיו conj.-n.f. du.-3 m.s. sf. (23) *and his ears*

אֶל־שַׁוְעָתָם prep.-n.f.s.-3 m.p. sf. (1003) *toward their cry*

34:17

פְּנֵי יהוה n.m.p. cstr. (815)-pr.n. (217) *the face of Yahweh*

בְּעֹשֵׂי רָע prep.-Qal act.ptc. m.p. cstr. (עָשָׂה I 793)-n.m.s. (949) *against evildoers*

לְהַכְרִית prep.-Hi. inf.cstr. (כָּרַת 503) *to cut off*

מֵאֶרֶץ prep.-n.f.s. (75) *from the earth*

זִכְרָם n.m.s.-3 m.p. sf. (271) *the remembrance of them*

34:18

צָעֲקוּ Qal pf. 3 c.p. (צָעַק 858) *they cry for help*

וַיהוה conj.-pr.n. (217) *and Yahweh*

שָׁמֵעַ Qal pf. 3 m.s. paus. (1033) *hears*

וּמִכָּל־ conj.-prep.-n.m.s. cstr. (481) *and out of all*

צָרוֹתָם n.f.p.-3 m.p. sf. (865) *their troubles*

הִצִּילָם Hi. pf. 3 m.s.-3 m.p. sf. (נָצַל 664) *he delivers them*

34:19

קָרוֹב adj. (898) *is near*

יהוה pr.n. (217) *Yahweh*

לְנִשְׁבְּרֵי־לֵב prep.-Ni. ptc. m.p. cstr. (שָׁבַר 990)-n.m.s. (524) *to the brokenhearted*

וְאֶת־דַּכְּאֵי־רוּחַ conj.-dir.obj.-adj. m.p. cstr. (194)-n.f.s. (924) *and the crushed in spirit*

יוֹשִׁיעַ Hi. impf. 3 m.s. (יָשַׁע 446) *saves*

34:20

רַבּוֹת adj. f.p. (I 912) *many are*

רָעוֹת צַדִּיק n.f.p. cstr. (949)-adj. (843) *the afflictions of the righteous*

וּמִכֻּלָּם conj.-prep.-n.m.s.-3 m.p. sf. (481) *but out of them all*

יַצִּילֶנּוּ Hi. impf. 3 m.s.-3 m.s. sf. (נָצַל 664) *delivers him*

יהוה pr.n. (217) *Yahweh*

34:21

שֹׁמֵר Qal act.ptc. (שָׁמַר 1036) *he keeps*

כָּל־ n.m.s. cstr. (481) *all*

עַצְמוֹתָיו n.f.p.-3 m.s. sf. (782) *his bones*

אַחַת מֵהֵנָּה num. f. cstr. (25)-prep.-pers.pr. 3 f.p. (241) *one of them*

לֹא נִשְׁבָּרָה neg.-Ni. pf. 3 f.s. (שָׁבַר 990) *is not broken*

34:22

תְּמוֹתֵת Polel impf. 3 f.s. (מוּת 559) *shall slay*

רָשָׁע adj. m.s. (957) *the wicked*

רָעָה n.f.s. (949) *evil*

וְשֹׂנְאֵי conj.-Qal act.ptc. m.p. cstr. (שָׂנֵא 971) *and those who hate*

צַדִּיק adj. m.s. (843) *the righteous*

יֶאְשָׁמוּ Qal impf. 3 m.p. paus. (אָשַׁם 79) *will be condemned*

34:23

פּוֹדֶה Qal act.ptc. (פָּדָה 804) *redeems*

יהוה pr.n. (217) *Yahweh*

נֶפֶשׁ n.f.s. cstr. (659) *the life of*

עֲבָדָיו n.m.p.-3 m.s. sf. (713) *his servants*

וְלֹא יֶאְשְׁמוּ conj.-neg.-Qal impf. 3 m.p. (אָשַׁם 79) *and will not be condemned*

כָּל־ n.m.s. cstr. (481) *all of*

הַחֹסִים בּוֹ def.art.-Qal act.ptc. m.p. (חָסָה 340) -prep.-3 m.s. sf. *those who take refuge in him*

35:1

לְדָוִד prep.-pr.n. (187) *to David*

רִיבָה Qal impv. 2 m.s.-vol.he (רִיב 936; GK 73d) *contend*

יהוה pr.n. (217) *O Yahweh*

אֶת־יְרִיבַי dir.obj.-n.m.p.-1 c.s. sf. (937) *with those who contend with me*

לְחַם Qal impv. 2 m.s. (לָחַם 535) *fight*

אֶת־לֹחֲמָי dir.obj.-Qal act.ptc. m.p.-1 c.s. sf. paus. (לָחַם 535) *against those who fight against me*

35:2

הַחֲזֵק Hi. impv. 2 m.s. (חָזַק 304) *take hold of*

מָגֵן n.m.s. (171) *shield*

וְצִנָּה conj.-n.f.s. (857) *and buckler*
וְקוּמָה conj.-Qal impv. 2 m.s.-vol.he (קוּם 877) *and rise*
בְּעֶזְרָתִי prep.-n.f.s.-1 c.s. sf. (740) *for my help*

35:3

וְהָרֵק conj.-Hi. impv. 2 m.s. (רִיק 937) *and draw (make empty)*
חֲנִית n.f.s. (333) *the spear*
וּסְגֹר conj.-Qal inf.cstr. (סָגַר I 688) *and close up* (v. BDB p.689, 2b; some rd. *battle-axe*)
לִקְרַאת prep.-Qal inf.cstr. (קָרָא 894) *to call*
רֹדְפָי Qal act.ptc. m.p.-1 c.s. sf. paus. (רָדַף 922) *my pursuers*
אֱמֹר Qal impv. 2 m.s. (55) *say*
לְנַפְשִׁי prep.-n.f.s.-1 c.s. sf. (659) *to my soul*
יְשֻׁעָתֵךְ n.f.s.-2 f.s. sf. (447) *your deliverance*
אָנִי pers.pr. 1 c.s. (58) *I am*

35:4

יֵבֹשׁוּ Qal impf. 3 m.p. (בּוֹשׁ 101) *let them be put to shame*
וְיִכָּלְמוּ conj.-Ni. impf. 3 m.p. (כָּלַם 483) *and dishonor*
מְבַקְשֵׁי Pi. ptc. m.p. cstr. (בָּקַשׁ 134) *who seek after*
נַפְשִׁי n.f.s.-1 c.s. sf. (659) *my life*
יִסֹּגוּ Ni. impf. 3 m.p. (סוּג I 690) *let them be turned*
אָחוֹר subst. (30) *back*
וְיַחְפְּרוּ conj.-Qal impf. 3 m.p. (חָפֵר II 344) *and confounded*
חֹשְׁבֵי Qal act.ptc. m.p. cstr. (חָשַׁב 362) *who devise*
רָעָתִי n.f.s.-1 c.s. sf. (949) *evil against me*

35:5

יִהְיוּ Qal impf. 3 m.p. (הָיָה 224) *let them be*
כְּמֹץ prep.-n.m.s. (558) *like chaff*
לִפְנֵי־רוּחַ prep.-n.m.p. cstr. (815)-n.f.s. (924) *before the wind*
וּמַלְאַךְ conj.-n.m.s. cstr. (521) *with the angel of*
יהוה pr.n. (217) *Yahweh*
דּוֹחֶה Qal act.ptc. (דָּחָה 190) *driving them on*

35:6

יְהִי־ Qal impf. 3 m.s. apoc. (הָיָה 224) *let be*
דַּרְכָּם n.m.s.-3 m.p. sf. (202) *their way*
חֹשֶׁךְ n.m.s. (365) *dark*
וַחֲלַקְלַקּוֹת conj.-n.f.p. (325) *and slippery*
וּמַלְאַךְ conj.-n.m.s. cstr. (521) *with the angel of*
יהוה pr.n. (217) *Yahweh*

רֹדְפָם Qal act.ptc.-3 m.p. sf. (רָדַף 922) *pursuing them*

35:7

כִּי־חִנָּם conj. (471)-subst. (336) *for without cause*
טָמְנוּ־לִי Qal pf. 3 c.p. (טָמַן 380)-prep.-1 c.s. sf. *they hid for me*
שַׁחַת n.f.s. cstr. (1001) *the pit of*
רִשְׁתָּם n.f.s.-3 m.p. sf. (440) *their net*
חִנָּם v.supra *without cause*
חָפְרוּ Qal pf. 3 c.p. (חָפַר I 343) *they dug*
לְנַפְשִׁי prep.-n.f.s.-1 c.s. sf. (659) *for my life*

35:8

תְּבוֹאֵהוּ Qal impf. 3 f.s.-3 m.s. sf. (בּוֹא 97) *let come upon them*
שׁוֹאָה n.f.s. (996) *ruin*
לֹא־יֵדָע neg.-Qal impf. 3 m.s. (יָדַע 393; GK 156g) *unawares (he does not know)*
וְרִשְׁתּוֹ conj.-n.f.s.-3 m.s. sf. (440) *and their net*
אֲשֶׁר־טָמַן rel. (81)-Qal pf. 3 m.s. (טָמַן 380) *which they hid*
תִּלְכְּדוֹ Qal impf. 3 f.s.-3 m.s. sf. (לָכַד 539) *let ... ensnare them*
בְּשׁוֹאָה prep.-n.f.s. (996) *to ruin*
יִפָּל־בָּהּ Qal impf. 3 m.s. (נָפַל 656)-prep.-3 f.s. sf. *let them fall therein*

35:9

וְנַפְשִׁי conj.-n.f.s.-1 c.s. sf. (659) *then my soul*
תָּגִיל Qal impf. 3 f.s. (גִּיל 162) *shall rejoice*
בַּיהוה prep.-pr.n. (217) *in Yahweh*
תָּשִׂישׂ Qal impf. 3 f.s. (שׂוּשׂ 965) *exulting*
בִּישׁוּעָתוֹ prep.-n.f.s.-3 m.s. sf. (447) *in his deliverance*

35:10

כָּל n.m.s. cstr. (481; GK 9u) *all*
עַצְמוֹתַי n.f.p.-1 c.s. sf. (782) *my bones*
תֹּאמַרְנָה Qal impf. 3 f.p. (אָמַר 55) *shall say*
יהוה pr.n. (217) *O Yahweh*
מִי כָמוֹךָ interr. (566)-prep.-2 m.s. sf. *who is like thee*
מַצִּיל Hi. ptc. (נָצַל 664) *thou who deliverest*
עָנִי n.m.s. (776) *the weak*
מֵחָזָק prep.-adj. m.s. (305) *from him who is too strong*
מִמֶּנּוּ prep.-3 m.s. sf. *for him*
וְעָנִי conj.-v.supra *and the weak*
וְאֶבְיוֹן conj.-adj. m.s. (2) *and needy*

מִגֹּזְלוֹ prep.-Qal act.ptc.-3 m.s. sf. (גָּזַל 159) *from him who despoils him*

35:11

יְקוּמוּן Qal impf. 3 m.p. (קוּם 877) *shall rise up*
עֵדֵי חָמָס n.m.p. cstr. (729)-n.m.s. (329) *malicious witnesses*
אֲשֶׁר לֹא־יָדַעְתִּי rel. (81)-neg.-Qal pf. 1 c.s. (יָדַע 393) *that I know not*
יִשְׁאָלוּנִי Qal impf. 3 m.p.-1 c.s. sf. (שָׁאַל 981) *they ask me*

35:12

יְשַׁלְּמוּנִי Pi. impf. 3 m.p.-1 c.s. sf. (שָׁלֵם 1022) *they requite me*
רָעָה n.f.s. (949) *evil*
תַּחַת טוֹבָה prep. (1065)-n.f.s. (375) *for good*
שְׁכוֹל n.m.s. (1013) *bereavement*
לְנַפְשִׁי prep.-n.f.s.-1 c.s. sf. (659) *to my soul*

35:13

וַאֲנִי conj.-pers.pr. 1 c.s. (58) *but I*
בַּחֲלוֹתָם prep.-Qal inf.cstr.-3 m.p. sf. (חָלָה I 317) *when they were sick*
לְבוּשִׁי n.m.s.-1 c.s. sf. (528) *my garment*
שָׂק n.m.s. (974) *sackcloth*
עִנֵּיתִי Pi. pf. 1 c.s. (עָנָה III 776) *I afflicted*
בַצּוֹם prep.-def.art.-n.m.s. (847) *with fasting*
נַפְשִׁי n.f.s.-1 c.s. sf. (659) *myself*
וּתְפִלָּתִי conj.-n.f.s.-1 c.s. sf. (813) *and my prayer*
עַל־חֵיקִי prep.-n.m.s.-1 c.s. sf. (300) *on my bosom*
תָשׁוּב Qal impf. 3 f.s. (שׁוּב 996) *turned back*

35:14

כְּרֵעַ prep.-n.m.s. (945) *as a friend*
כְּאָח לִי prep.-n.m.s. (26)-prep.-1 c.s. sf. *as a brother to me*
הִתְהַלָּכְתִּי Hith. pf. 1 c.s. (הָלַךְ 229) *I walked about*
כַּאֲבֶל־ prep.-adj. m.s. cstr. (5; GK 93hh) *as the mourning of*
אֵם n.f.s. (51) *a mother*
קֹדֵר Qal act.ptc. (קָדַר 871) *mourning*
שַׁחוֹתִי Qal pf. 1 c.s. (שָׁחָה 1005) *I was bowed down*

35:15

וּבְצַלְעִי conj.-prep.-n.m.s.-1 c.s. sf. (854) *but at my stumbling*
שָׂמְחוּ Qal pf. 3 c.p. (שָׂמַח 970) *they rejoiced*
וְנֶאֱסָפוּ conj.-Ni. pf. 3 c.p. (אָסַף 62) *and gathered*
נֶאֶסְפוּ עָלַי Ni. pf. 3 c.p. (אָסַף 62)-prep.-1 c.s. sf. *they gathered together against me*
נֵכִים adj. m.p. (646) *smitten ones*
וְלֹא יָדַעְתִּי conj.-neg.-Qal pf. 1 c.s. (יָדַע 393) *whom I knew not*
קָרְעוּ Qal pf. 3 c.p. (קָרַע 902) *they tear*
וְלֹא־דָמּוּ conj.-neg.-Qal pf. 3 c.p. (דָּמַם I 198) *without ceasing* (lit. *and they are silent*)

35:16

בְּחַנְפֵי prep.-adj. m.p. cstr. (338) *as profane men*
לַעֲגֵי מָעוֹג n.m.p. cstr. (541)-n.m.s. (728) *mockers of a cake*
חָרֹק Qal inf.abs. (חָרַק 359; GK 113h) *gnashing*
עָלַי prep.-1 c.s. sf. *at me*
שִׁנֵּימוֹ n.f. du.-3 m.p. sf. (1042) *with their teeth*

35:17

אֲדֹנָי n.m.p.-1 c.s. sf. (10) *O Lord*
כַּמָּה prep.-def.art.-interr. (552) *how long*
תִּרְאֶה Qal impf. 2 m.s. (רָאָה 906) *wilt thou look on*
הָשִׁיבָה נַפְשִׁי Hi. impf. 2 m.s. (שׁוּב 996)-n.f.s.-1 c.s. sf. (659) *rescue me*
מִשֹּׁאֵיהֶם prep.-n.m.p.-3 m.p. sf. (996) *from their ravages*
מִכְּפִירִים prep.-n.m.p. (498) *from lions*
יְחִידָתִי adj. f.s.-1 c.s. sf. (402) *my life*

35:18

אוֹדְךָ Hi. impf. 1 c.s.-2 m.s. sf. (יָדָה 392) *I will thank thee*
בְּקָהָל רָב prep.-n.m.s. (874)-adj. m.s. (I 912) *in the great congregation*
בְּעָם עָצוּם prep.-n.m.s. (I 766)-adj. m.s. (783) *in the mighty throng*
אֲהַלְלֶךָּ Pi. impf. 1 c.s.-2 m.s. sf. (הָלַל II 237) *I will praise thee*

35:19

אַל־יִשְׂמְחוּ־לִי neg.-Qal impf. 3 m.p. (שָׂמַח 970)-prep.-1 c.s. sf. *let not rejoice over me*
אֹיְבַי שֶׁקֶר Qal act.ptc. m.p.-1 c.s. sf. (אָיַב 33)-n.m.s. (1055; GK 131qN) *who are wrongfully my foes*
שֹׂנְאַי Qal act.ptc. m.p.-1 c.s. sf. (שָׂנֵא 971) *who hate me*
חִנָּם subst. (336) *without cause*
יִקְרְצוּ־עָיִן Qal impf. 3 m.p. (קָרַץ 902)-n.f.s. paus. (744) *let not those wink the eye*

35:20

כִּי לֹא שָׁלוֹם conj. (471)-neg.-n.m.s. (1022) *for not peace*

יְדַבֵּרוּ Pi. impf. 3 m.p. (דָּבַר 180) *they speak*

וְעַל רִגְעֵי־ conj.-prep.-adj. m.p. cstr. (921) *but against those who are quiet in*

אֶרֶץ n.f.s. (75) *the land*

דִּבְרֵי n.m.p. cstr. (182) *words of*

מִרְמוֹת n.f.p. (941) *deceit*

יַחֲשֹׁבוּן Qal impf. 3 m.p. (חָשַׁב 362) *they conceive*

35:21

וַיַּרְחִיבוּ consec.-Hi. impf. 3 m.p. (רָחַב 931) *they open wide*

עָלַי prep.-1 c.s. sf. *against me*

פִּיהֶם n.m.s.-3 m.p. sf. (804) *their mouths*

אָמְרוּ Qal pf. 3 c.p. (אָמַר 55) *they say*

הֶאָח הֶאָח interj. (210)-v.supra *Aha, Aha*

רָאֲתָה Qal pf. 3 f.s. (רָאָה 906) *have seen*

עֵינֵינוּ n.f. du.-1 c.p. sf. (744) *our eyes*

35:22

רָאִיתָה Qal pf. 2 m.s. (רָאָה 906) *thou hast seen*

יהוה pr.n. (217) *O Yahweh*

אַל־תֶּחֱרַשׁ neg.-Qal impf. 2 m.s. (חָרֵשׁ II 361) *be not silent*

אֲדֹנָי n.m.p.-1 c.s. sf. (10) *O Lord*

אַל־תִּרְחַק neg.-Qal impf. 2 m.s. (רָחַק 934) *be not far*

מִמֶּנִּי prep.-1 c.s. sf. *from me*

35:23

הָעִירָה Hi. impv. 2 m.s. (עוּר 734) *bestir thyself*

וְהָקִיצָה conj.-Hi. impv. 2 m.s. (קִיץ I 884) *and awake*

לְמִשְׁפָּטִי prep.-n.m.s.-1 c.s. sf. (1048) *for my right*

אֱלֹהַי n.m.p.-1 c.s. sf. (43) *my God*

וַאדֹנָי conj.-n.m.p.-1 c.s. sf. (10) *and my Lord*

לְרִיבִי prep.-n.m.s.-1 c.s. sf. (936) *for my cause*

35:24

שָׁפְטֵנִי Qal impv. 2 m.s.-1 c.s. sf. (שָׁפַט 1047) *vindicate me*

כְצִדְקְךָ prep.-n.m.s.-2 m.s. sf. (841) *according to thy righteousness*

יהוה pr.n. (217) *O Yahweh*

אֱלֹהָי n.m.p.-1 c.s. sf. paus. (43) *my God*

וְאַל־יִשְׂמְחוּ־לִי conj.-neg.-Qal impf. 3 m.p. (970 שָׂמַח)-prep.-1 c.s. sf. *and let them not rejoice over me*

35:25

אַל־יֹאמְרוּ neg.-Qal impf. 3 m.p. (אָמַר 55) *let them not say*

בְלִבָּם prep.-n.m.s.-3 m.p. sf. (524) *to themselves*

הֶאָח interj. (210) *Aha*

נַפְשֵׁנוּ n.f.s.-1 c.p. sf. (659) *our desire*

אַל־יֹאמְרוּ v.supra-v.supra *let them not say*

בִּלַּעֲנוּהוּ Pi. pf. 1 c.p.-3 m.s. sf. (בָּלַע 118) *we have swallowed him up*

35:26

יֵבֹשׁוּ Qal impf. 3 m.p. (בּוֹשׁ 101) *let them be put to shame*

וְיַחְפְּרוּ conj.-Qal impf. 3 m.p. (חָפֵר II 344) *and confusion*

יַחְדָּו adv. (403) *altogether*

שְׂמֵחֵי רָעָתִי adj. m.p. cstr. (970)-n.f.s.-1 c.s. sf. (949) *who rejoice at my calamity*

יִלְבְּשׁוּ־בֹשֶׁת Qal impf. 3 m.p. (לָבֵשׁ 527)-n.f.s. (102) *let them be clothed with shame*

וּכְלִמָּה conj.-n.f.s. (484) *and dishonor*

הַמַּגְדִּילִים def.art.-Hi. ptc. m.p. (גָּדַל 152) *who magnify themselves*

עָלָי prep.-1 c.s. sf. paus. *against me*

35:27

יָרֹנּוּ Qal impf. 3 m.p. (רָנַן 943) *let shout for joy*

וְיִשְׂמְחוּ conj.-Qal impf. 3 m.p. (שָׂמַח 970) *and be glad*

חֲפֵצֵי adj. m.p. cstr. (343) *those who desire*

צִדְקִי n.m.s.-1 c.s. sf. (841) *my vindication*

וְיֹאמְרוּ conj.-Qal impf. 3 m.p. (אָמַר 55) *and say*

תָמִיד adv. (556) *evermore*

יִגְדַּל Qal impf. 3 m.s. (גָּדַל 152) *is great*

יהוה pr.n. (217) *Yahweh*

הֶחָפֵץ def.art.-adj. m.s. (343) *who delights*

שְׁלוֹם n.m.s. cstr. (1022) *in the welfare of*

עַבְדּוֹ n.m.s.-3 m.s. sf. (713) *his servant*

35:28

וּלְשׁוֹנִי conj.-n.f.s.-1 c.s. sf. (546) *then my tongue*

תֶּהְגֶּה Qal impf. 3 f.s. (הָגָה I 211) *shall tell of*

צִדְקֶךָ n.m.s.-2 m.s. sf. (841) *thy righteousness*

כָּל־הַיּוֹם n.m.s. cstr. (481)-def.art.-n.m.s. (398) *all the day long*

תְּהִלָּתֶךָ n.f.s.-2 m.s. sf. (239) *of thy praise*

36:1

לַמְנַצֵּחַ prep.-def.art.-Pi. ptc. (I 663) *to the choirmaster*

לְעֶבֶד־ prep.-n.m.s. cstr. (713) *to the servant of*

יהוה pr.n. (217) *Yahweh*

לְדָוִד prep.-pr.n. (187) *to David*

36:2

נְאֻם־פֶּשַׁע n.m.s. cstr. (610)-n.m.s. (833) *an utterance of transgression*
לָרָשָׁע prep.-def.art.-adj. m.s. (957) *to the wicked*
בְּקֶרֶב לִבִּי prep.-n.m.s. cstr. (899)-n.m.s.-1 c.s. sf. (524) *deep in his* (lit. *my*) *heart*
אֵין־פַּחַד subst. cstr. (II 34)-n.m.s. cstr. (808) *there is no fear of*
אֱלֹהִים n.m.p. (43) *God*
לְנֶגֶד עֵינָיו prep.-prep. (617)-n.f. du.-3 m.s. sf. (744) *before his eyes*

36:3

כִּי־הֶחֱלִיק conj. (471)-Hi. pf. 3 m.s. (חָלַק II 325) *for he flatters*
אֵלָיו prep.-3 m.s. sf. *himself*
בְּעֵינָיו prep.-n.f. du.-3 m.s. sf. (744) *in his own eyes*
לִמְצֹא prep.-Qal inf.cstr. (592) *about finding*
עֲוֹנוֹ n.m.s.-3 m.s. sf. (730) *his iniquity*
לִשְׂנֹא prep.-Qal inf.cstr. (שָׂנֵא 971) *about hating*

36:4

דִּבְרֵי־ n.m.p. cstr. (182) *the words of*
פִיו n.m.s.-3 m.s. sf. (804) *his mouth*
אָוֶן n.m.s. (19) *mischief*
וּמִרְמָה conj.-n.f.s. (941) *and deceit*
חָדַל Qal pf. 3 m.s. (292) *he has ceased*
לְהַשְׂכִּיל prep.-Hi. inf.cstr. (שָׂכַל 968) *to act wisely*
לְהֵיטִיב prep.-Hi. inf.cstr. (יָטַב 405) *and do good*

36:5

אָוֶן n.m.s. (19) *mischief*
יַחְשֹׁב Qal impf. 3 m.s. (חָשַׁב 362) *he plots*
עַל־מִשְׁכָּבוֹ prep.-n.m.s.-3 m.s. sf. (1012) *while on his bed*
יִתְיַצֵּב Hith. impf. 3 m.s. (יָצַב 426) *he sets himself*
עַל־דֶּרֶךְ prep.-n.m.s. (202) *in a way*
לֹא־טוֹב neg.-adj. m.s. (II 373) *not good*
רָע adj. m.s. (948) *evil*
לֹא יִמְאָס neg.-Qal impf. 3 m.s. paus. (מָאַס 549) *he spurns not*

36:6

יהוה pr.n. (217) *O Yahweh*
בְּהַשָּׁמַיִם prep.-def.art.-n.m. du. (1029; GK 35n) *to the heavens*
חַסְדֶּךָ n.m.s.-2 m.s. sf. (338) *thy steadfast love*
אֱמוּנָתְךָ n.f.s.-2 m.s. sf. (53) *thy faithfulness*
עַד־שְׁחָקִים prep.-n.m.p. (1007) *to the clouds*

36:7

צִדְקָתְךָ n.f.s.-2 m.s. sf. (842) *thy righteousness*
כְּהַרְרֵי־ prep.-n.m.p. cstr. (249) *like the mountains of*
אֵל n.m.s. (42) *God*
מִשְׁפָּטְךָ n.m.s.-2 m.s. sf. (1048) *thy judgments*
תְּהוֹם רַבָּה n.f.s. (1062)-adj. f.s. (912) *like the great deep*
אָדָם־ n.m.s. (9) *man*
וּבְהֵמָה conj.-n.f.s. (96) *and beast*
תוֹשִׁיעַ Hi. impf. 2 m.s. (יָשַׁע 446) *thou savest*
יהוה pr.n. (217) *O Yahweh*

36:8

מַה־יָּקָר interr. (552)-n.m.s. (429) *how precious*
חַסְדְּךָ n.m.s.-2 m.s. sf. (338) *thy steadfast love*
אֱלֹהִים n.m.p. (43) *O God*
וּבְנֵי אָדָם conj.-n.m.p. cstr. (119)-n.m.s. (9) *and the children of men*
בְּצֵל prep.-n.m.s. cstr. (853) *in the shadow of*
כְּנָפֶיךָ n.f.p.-2 m.s. sf. (489) *thy wings*
יֶחֱסָיוּן Qal impf. 3 m.p. (חָסָה 340; GK 75u) *take refuge*

36:9

יִרְוְיֻן Qal impf. 3 m.p. (רָוָה 924; GK 75u) *they feast*
מִדֶּשֶׁן prep.-n.m.s. cstr. (206) *on the abundance of*
בֵּיתֶךָ n.m.s.-2 m.s. sf. (108) *thy house*
וְנַחַל conj.-n.m.s. cstr. (636) *from the river of*
עֲדָנֶיךָ n.m.p.-2 m.p. sf. (I 726) *thy delights*
תַשְׁקֵם Hi. impf. 2 m.s.-3 m.p. sf. (שָׁקָה 1052) *thou givest them drink*

36:10

כִּי־עִמְּךָ conj. (471)-prep.-2 m.s. sf. *for with thee*
מְקוֹר n.m.s. cstr. (881) *the fountain of*
חַיִּים n.m.p. (313) *life*
בְּאוֹרְךָ prep.-n.m.s.-2 m.s. sf. (21) *in thy light*
נִרְאֶה־ Qal impf. 1 c.p. (רָאָה 906) *do we see*
אוֹר n.m.s. (21) *light*

36:11

מְשֹׁךְ Qal impv. 2 m.s. (מָשַׁךְ 604) *continue*
חַסְדְּךָ n.m.s.-2 m.s. sf. (338) *thy steadfast love*

לְיֹדְעֶיךָ prep.-Qal act.ptc. m.p.-2 m.s. sf. (יָדַע 393) *to those who know thee*
וְצִדְקָתְךָ conj.-n.f.s.-2 m.s. sf. (842) *and thy salvation*
לְיִשְׁרֵי־ prep.-adj. m.p. cstr. (449) *to the upright of*
לֵב n.m.s. (524) *heart*

36:12

אַל־תְּבוֹאֵנִי neg.-Qal impf. 3 f.s.-1 c.s. sf. (בּוֹא 97) *let not come upon me*
רֶגֶל n.f.s. cstr. (919) *the foot of*
גַּאֲוָה n.f.s. (144) *arrogance*
וְיַד־ conj.-n.f.s. cstr. (388) *nor the hand of*
רְשָׁעִים adj. m.p. (957) *the wicked*
אַל־תְּנִדֵנִי neg.-Hi. impf. 3 f.s.-1 c.s. sf. (נוּד 626) *let drive me away*

36:13

שָׁם adv. (1027) *there*
נָפְלוּ Qal pf. 3 c.p. (נָפַל 656) *lie prostrate*
פֹּעֲלֵי־אָוֶן Qal act.ptc. m.p. cstr. (פָּעַל 821)-n.m.s. (19) *the evildoers*
דֹּחוּ Pu. pf. 3 c.p. (דָּחָה 190; GK 64d) *they are thrust down*
וְלֹא־יָכְלוּ conj.-neg.-Qal pf. 3 c.p. (יָכֹל 407) *they are not able*
קוּם Qal inf.cstr. (877) *to rise*

37:1

לְדָוִד prep.-pr.n. (187; GK 5h) *to David*
אַל־תִּתְחַר neg.-Hith. impf. 2 m.s. apoc. (חָרָה 354; GK 75bb) *fret not yourself*
בַּמְּרֵעִים prep.-def.art.-Hi. ptc. m.p. (949; GK 35b) *because of the wicked*
אַל־תְּקַנֵּא neg.-Pi. impf. 2 m.s. (888) *be not envious*
בְּעֹשֵׂי prep.-Qal act.ptc. m.p. cstr. (I 793) *of ... doers*
עַוְלָה n.f.s. (732) *wrong*

37:2

כִּי conj. (471) *for*
כֶּחָצִיר prep.-def.art.-n.m.s. (II 348) *like the grass*
מְהֵרָה n.f.s. as adv. (555) *soon*
יִמָּלוּ Qal impf. 3 m.p. (מָלַל III 576) *they will fade*
וּכְיֶרֶק conj.-prep.-n.m.s. (438) *and like the green*
דֶּשֶׁא n.m.s. (206) *herb*
יִבּוֹלוּן Qal impf. 3 m.p. (נָבֵל 615) *wither*

37:3

בְּטַח Qal impv. 2 m.s. (105) *trust*
בַּיהוה prep.-pr.n. (217) *in Yahweh*
וַעֲשֵׂה־ conj.-Qal impv. 2 m.s. (עָשָׂה I 793) *and do*
טוֹב adj. m.s. (I 373) *good*
שְׁכָן־ Qal impv. 2 m.s. (1014) *so you will dwell*
אֶרֶץ n.f.s. (75) *in the land*
וּרְעֵה conj.-Qal impv. 2 m.s. (II 945) *and enjoy*
אֱמוּנָה n.f.s. (53) *security*

37:4

וְהִתְעַנַּג conj.-Hith. impv. 2 m.s. (עָנַג 772) *take delight*
עַל־יהוה prep.-pr.n. (217) *in Yahweh*
וְיִתֶּן־ conj.-Qal impf. 3 m.s. (נָתַן 678) *and he will give*
לְךָ prep.-2 m.s. sf. *you*
מִשְׁאֲלֹת n.f.p. cstr. (982) *the desires of*
לִבֶּךָ n.m.s.-2 m.s. sf. (524) *your heart*

37:5

גּוֹל Qal impv. 2 m.s. (גָּלַל II 164; GK 67n) *commit*
עַל־יהוה prep.-pr.n. (217) *to Yahweh*
דַּרְכֶּךָ n.m.s.-2 m.s. sf. paus. (202) *your way*
וּבְטַח conj.-Qal impv. 2 m.s. (105) *trust*
עָלָיו prep.-3 m.s. sf. *in him*
וְהוּא conj.-pers.pr. 3 m.s. (214) *and he*
יַעֲשֶׂה Qal impf. 3 m.s. (I 793) *will act*

37:6

וְהוֹצִיא conj.-Hi. pf. 3 m.s. (יָצָא 422) *he will bring forth*
כָאוֹר prep.-def.art.-n.m.s. (21) *as the light*
צִדְקֶךָ n.m.s.-2 m.s. sf. (841) *your vindication*
וּמִשְׁפָּטֶךָ conj.-n.m.s.-2 m.s. sf. (1048) *and your right*
כַּצָּהֳרָיִם prep.-def.art.-n.m.p. (I 843) *as the noonday*

37:7

דּוֹם Qal impv. 2 m.s. (דָּמַם I 198) *be still*
לַיהוה prep.-pr.n. (217) *before Yahweh*
וְהִתְחוֹלֵל conj.-Hithpolel impv. 2 m.s. (I 296) *and wait patiently*
לוֹ prep.-3 m.s. sf. *for him*
אַל־תִּתְחַר cf. 37:1 neg.-Hith. impf. 2 m.s. apoc. (354 חָרָה) *fret not yourself*
בְּמַצְלִיחַ prep.-Hi. ptc. (II 852) *over him who prospers*
דַּרְכּוֹ n.m.s.-3 m.s. sf. (202) *in his way*

בְּאִישׁ prep.-n.m.s. (35) *over the man*
עֹשֶׂה Qal act.ptc. (I 793) *who carries out*
מְזִמּוֹת n.f.p. (273) *evil devices*

37:8

הֶרֶף Hi. impv. 2 m.s. (רָפָה 951) *refrain*
מֵאַף prep.-n.m.s. (I 60) *from anger*
וַעֲזֹב conj.-Qal impv. 2 m.s. (I 736) *and forsake*
חֵמָה n.f.s. (404) *wrath*
אַל־תִּתְחַר cf. 37:1,7 neg.-Hith. impf. 2 m.s. apoc. (354) *fret not yourself*
אַךְ־לְהָרֵעַ adv. (36)-prep.-Hi. inf.cstr. (949) *only to evil*

37:9

כִּי־ conj. (471) *for*
מְרֵעִים Hi. ptc. m.p. (רָעַע 949) *the wicked*
יִכָּרֵתוּן Ni. impf. 3 m.p. (503) *shall be cut off*
וְקֹוֵי conj.-Qal act.ptc. m.p. cstr. (I 875) *but those who wait for*
יהוה pr.n. (217) *Yahweh*
הֵמָּה pers.pr. 3 m.s. (241; GK 20f) *(they)*
יִירְשׁוּ־ Qal impf. 3 m.p. (יָרַשׁ 439) *shall possess*
אָרֶץ n.f.s. paus. (75) *the land*

37:10

וְעוֹד conj.-adv. (728) *yet*
מְעַט subst. (589) *a little while*
וְאֵין conj.-neg. cstr. (II 34) *and will be no more*
רָשָׁע adj. m.s. (957) *the wicked*
וְהִתְבּוֹנַנְתָּ conj.-Hithpolel pf. 2 m.s. (בִּין 106) *though you look well*
עַל־מְקוֹמוֹ prep.-n.m.s.-3 m.s. sf. (879) *at his place*
וְאֵינֶנּוּ conj.-neg. cstr.-3 m.s. sf. (II 34) *he will not be there*

37:11

וַעֲנָוִים conj.-n.m.p. (776) *but the meek*
יִירְשׁוּ־ Qal impf. 3 m.p. (יָרַשׁ 439) *shall possess*
אָרֶץ n.f.s. paus. (75) *the land*
וְהִתְעַנְּגוּ conj.-Hith. pf. 3 c.p. (772) *and delight themselves*
עַל־רֹב prep.-n.m.s. (913) *in abundant*
שָׁלוֹם n.m.s. (1022) *prosperity*

37:12

זֹמֵם Qal act.ptc. (273) *plots*
רָשָׁע adj. m.s. (957) *the wicked*
לַצַּדִּיק prep.-def.art.-adj. m.s. (843) *against the righteous*
וְחֹרֵק conj.-Qal act.ptc. (I 357) *and gnashes*
עָלָיו prep.-3 m.s. sf. *at him*
שִׁנָּיו n.f.p.-3 m.s. sf. (I 1042) *his teeth*

37:13

אֲדֹנָי n.m.p.-1 c.s. sf. (10) *the Lord*
יִשְׂחַק־לוֹ Qal impf. 3 m.s. (965)-prep.-3 m.s. sf. *laughs at the wicked (at him)*
כִּי־רָאָה conj. (471)-Qal pf. 3 m.s. (906) *for he sees*
כִּי־יָבֹא conj. (471)-Qal impf. 3 m.s. (בּוֹא 97) *that is coming*
יוֹמוֹ n.m.s.-3 m.s. sf. (398) *his day*

37:14

חֶרֶב n.f.s. (352) *the sword*
פָּתְחוּ Qal pf. 3 c.p. (I 834) *draw*
רְשָׁעִים adj. m.p. (957) *the wicked*
וְדָרְכוּ conj.-Qal pf. 3 c.p. (201) *and bend*
קַשְׁתָּם n.f.s.-3 m.p. sf. (905) *their bows*
לְהַפִּיל prep.-Hi. inf.cstr. (656) *to bring down*
עָנִי n.m.s. (776) *the poor*
וְאֶבְיוֹן conj.-n.m.s. (2) *and needy*
לִטְבוֹחַ prep.-Qal inf.cstr. (370; GK 45g) *to slay*
יִשְׁרֵי־דָרֶךְ adj. m.p. cstr. (449)-n.m.s. (202) *those who walk uprightly*

37:15

חַרְבָּם n.f.s.-3 m.p. sf. (352) *their sword*
תָּבוֹא Qal impf. 3 f.s. (בּוֹא 97) *shall enter*
בְלִבָּם prep.-n.m.s.-3 m.p. sf. (524) *their own heart*
וְקַשְּׁתוֹתָם conj.-n.f.p.-3 m.p. sf. (905; GK 20h) *and their bows*
תִּשָּׁבַרְנָה Ni. impf. 3 f.p. (990) *shall be broken*

37:16

טוֹב־ adj. m.s. (I 373) *better is*
מְעַט subst. (589) *a little*
לַצַּדִּיק prep.-def.art.-adj. m.s. (843; GK 129b) *that the righteous has*
מֵהֲמוֹן prep.-n.m.s. cstr. (242) *than the abundance of*
רְשָׁעִים רַבִּים n.m.p. (957)-adj. m.p. (I 912) *many wicked*

37:17

כִּי conj. (471) *for*
זְרוֹעוֹת n.f.p. cstr. (283) *the arms of*
רְשָׁעִים n.m.p. (957) *the wicked*

תִּשָּׁבַרְנָה Ni. impf. 3 f.p. (990) *shall be broken*
וְסוֹמֵךְ conj.-Qal act.ptc. (701) *but ... upholds*
צַדִּיקִים adj. m.p. (843) *the righteous*
יהוה pr.n. (217) *Yahweh*

37:18

יוֹדֵעַ Qal act.ptc. (יָדַע 393) *knows*
יהוה pr.n. (217) *Yahweh*
יְמֵי n.m.p. cstr. (398) *the days of*
תְמִימִם adj. m.p. (1071) *the blameless*
וְנַחֲלָתָם conj.-n.f.s.-3 m.p. sf. (635) *and their heritage*
לְעוֹלָם prep.-n.m.s. (761) *for ever*
תִּהְיֶה Qal impf. 3 f.s. (הָיָה 224) *will abide*

37:19

לֹא־יֵבֹשׁוּ neg.-Qal impf. 3 m.s. (בּוֹשׁ 101) *they are not put to shame*
בְּעֵת רָעָה prep.-n.f.s. (773)-adj. f.s. (948) *in evil times*
וּבִימֵי conj.-prep.-n.m.p. cstr. (398) *in the days of*
רְעָבוֹן n.m.s. (944) *famine*
יִשְׂבָּעוּ Qal impf. 3 m.p. paus. (959) *they have abundance*

37:20

כִּי conj. (471) *but*
רְשָׁעִים n.m.p. (957) *the wicked*
יֹאבֵדוּ Qal impf. 3 m.p. (1) *perish*
וְאֹיְבֵי conj.-Qal act.ptc. m.p. cstr. (אֵיב 33) *the enemies of*
יהוה pr.n. (217) *Yahweh*
כִּיקַר prep.-adj. m.s. cstr. (429) *like the glory of*
כָּרִים n.m.p. (II 499) *the pastures*
כָּלוּ Qal pf. 3 c.p. (I 477; GK 29o,75m) *they vanish*
בֶעָשָׁן prep.-def.art.-n.m.s. (I 798) *like smoke*
כָּלוּ v.supra *they vanish away*

37:21

לֹוֶה Qal act.ptc. (II 531) *borrows*
רָשָׁע n.m.s. (957) *the wicked*
וְלֹא יְשַׁלֵּם conj.-neg.-Pi. impf. 3 m.s. (1022) *and cannot pay back*
וְצַדִּיק conj.-adj. m.s. (843) *but the righteous*
חוֹנֵן Qal act.ptc. (I 335) *is generous*
וְנוֹתֵן conj.-Qal act.ptc. (678) *and gives*

37:22

כִּי conj. (471) *for*
מְבֹרָכָיו Pu. ptc. m.p.-3 m.s. sf. (138) *those blessed by him*
יִירְשׁוּ Qal impf. 3 m.p. (יָרַשׁ 439) *shall possess*
אָרֶץ n.f.s. paus. (75) *the land*
וּמְקֻלָּלָיו conj.-Pu. ptc. m.p.-3 m.s. sf. (886) *but those cursed by him*
יִכָּרֵתוּ Ni. impf. 3 m.p. (503) *shall be cut off*

37:23

מֵיהוה prep.-pr.n. (217) *from Yahweh*
מִצְעֲדֵי־ n.m.p. cstr. (857) *the steps of*
גֶבֶר n.m.s. (149) *a man*
כּוֹנָנוּ Polal pf. 3 c.p. (כּוּן I 465; GK 121f) *and he establishes* (a man's steps are established)
וְדַרְכּוֹ conj.-n.m.s.-3 m.s. sf. (202) *(and) in whose way*
יֶחְפָּץ Qal impf. 3 m.s. (342) *he delights*

37:24

כִּי־ conj. (471; GK 159bb) *though*
יִפֹּל Qal impf. 3 m.s. (נָפַל 656) *he fall*
לֹא־יוּטָל neg.-Ho. impf. 3 m.s. (376) *he shall not be cast headlong*
כִּי־יהוה conj. (471)-pr.n. (217) *for Yahweh is*
סוֹמֵךְ Qal act.ptc. (701) *the stay of*
יָדוֹ n.f.s.-3 m.s. sf. (388) *his hand*

37:25

נַעַר n.m.s. (654) *young*
הָיִיתִי Qal pf. 1 c.s. (הָיָה 224) *I have been*
גַּם־זָקַנְתִּי adv. (168)-Qal pf. 1 c.s. (278) *and now am old*
וְלֹא־רָאִיתִי conj.-neg.-Qal pf. 1 c.s. (רָאָה 906) *yet I have not seen*
צַדִּיק adj. m.s. (843) *the righteous*
נֶעֱזָב Ni. ptc. (I 736) *forsaken*
וְזַרְעוֹ conj.-n.m.s.-3 m.s. sf. (282) *or his children*
מְבַקֶּשׁ־ Pi. ptc. (134) *begging*
לָחֶם n.m.s. paus. (536) *bread*

37:26

כָּל־הַיּוֹם n.m.s. cstr. (481)-def.art.-n.m.s. (398) *ever (all the day)*
חוֹנֵן Qal act.ptc. (I 335) *he is giving liberally*
וּמַלְוֶה conj.-Hi. ptc. (II 531) *and lending*
וְזַרְעוֹ cf. 37:25 conj.-n.m.s.-3 m.s. sf. (282) *and his children*
לִבְרָכָה prep.-n.f.s. (139) *become a blessing*

37:27

סוּר Qal impv. 2 m.s. (693) *depart*
מֵרָע prep.-n.m.s. (948) *from evil*

וַעֲשֵׂה־ conj.-Qal impv. 2 m.s. (I 793) *and do*
טוֹב adj. m.s. (I 373) *good*
וּשְׁכֹן conj.-Qal impv. 2 m.s. (1014) *so shall you abide*
לְעוֹלָם prep.-n.m.s. (761) *for ever*

37:28

כִּי יהוה conj. (471)-pr.n. (217) *for Yahweh*
אֹהֵב Qal act.ptc. (12) *loves*
מִשְׁפָּט n.m.s. (1048) *justice*
וְלֹא־יַעֲזֹב conj.-neg.-Qal impf. 3 m.s. (I 736) *he will not forsake*
אֶת־חֲסִידָיו dir.obj.-n.m.p.-3 m.s. sf. (339) *his saints*
לְעוֹלָם prep.-n.m.s. (761) *for ever*
נִשְׁמָרוּ Ni. pf. 3 c.p. (1036) *(the righteous) shall be preserved*
וְזֶרַע conj.-n.m.s. cstr. (282) *but the children of*
רְשָׁעִים n.m.p. (957) *the wicked*
נִכְרָת Ni. pf. 3 m.s. paus. (503) *shall be cut off*

37:29

צַדִּיקִים adj. m.p. (843) *the righteous*
יִירְשׁוּ־ Qal impf. 3 m.p. (יָרַשׁ 439) *shall possess*
אָרֶץ n.f.s. paus. (75) *the land*
וְיִשְׁכְּנוּ conj.-Qal impf. 3 m.p. (שָׁכַן 1014) *and dwell*
לָעַד prep.-n.m.s. (I 723) *for ever*
עָלֶיהָ prep.-3 f.s. sf. *upon it*

37:30

פִּי־ n.m.s. cstr. (804) *the mouth of*
צַדִּיק adj. m.s. (843) *the righteous*
יֶהְגֶּה Qal impf. 3 m.s. (I 211) *utters*
חָכְמָה n.f.s. (315) *wisdom*
וּלְשׁוֹנוֹ conj.-n.f.s.-3 m.s. sf. (546) *and his tongue*
תְּדַבֵּר Pi. impf. 3 f.s. (180) *speaks*
מִשְׁפָּט n.m.s. (1048) *justice*

37:31

תּוֹרַת n.f.s. cstr. (435) *the law of*
אֱלֹהָיו n.m.p.-3 m.s. sf. (43) *his God*
בְּלִבּוֹ prep.-n.m.s.-3 m.s. sf. (524) *is in his heart*
לֹא תִמְעַד neg.-Qal impf. 3 f.s. (588) *do not slip*
אֲשֻׁרָיו n.f.p.-3 m.s. sf. (81; GK 145k) *his steps*

37:32

צוֹפֶה Qal act.ptc. (I 859) *watches*
רָשָׁע adj. m.s. (957) *the wicked*
לַצַּדִּיק prep.-def.art.-adj. m.s. (843) *the righteous*
וּמְבַקֵּשׁ conj.-Pi. ptc. (134) *and seeks*
לַהֲמִיתוֹ prep.-Hi. inf.cstr.-3 m.s. sf. (559) *to slay him*

37:33

יהוה pr.n. (217) *Yahweh*
לֹא־יַעַזְבֶנּוּ neg.-Qal impf. 3 m.s.-3 m.s. sf. (I 736) *will not abandon*
בְיָדוֹ prep.-n.f.s.-3 m.s. sf. (388) *to his power*
וְלֹא יַרְשִׁיעֶנּוּ conj.-neg.-Hi. impf. 3 m.s.-3 m.s. sf. (957) *or let him be condemned*
בְּהִשָּׁפְטוֹ prep.-Ni. inf.cstr.-3 m.s. sf. (1047) *when he is brought to trial*

37:34

קַוֵּה Pi. impv. 2 m.s. (I 875) *wait*
אֶל־יהוה prep.-pr.n. (217) *for Yahweh*
וּשְׁמֹר conj.-Qal impv. 2 m.s. (1036) *and keep*
דַּרְכּוֹ n.m.s.-3 m.s. sf. (202) *to his way*
וִירוֹמִמְךָ conj.-Polel impf. 3 m.s.-2 m.s. sf. (926) *and he will exalt you*
לָרֶשֶׁת prep.-Qal inf.cstr. (יָרַשׁ 439) *to possess*
אָרֶץ n.f.s. paus. (75) *the land*
בְּהִכָּרֵת prep.-Ni. inf.cstr. (503) *on the destruction of*
רְשָׁעִים adj. m.p. (957) *the wicked*
תִּרְאֶה Qal impf. 2 m.s. (906) *you will look*

37:35

רָאִיתִי Qal pf. 1 c.s. (906) *I have seen*
רָשָׁע n.m.s. (957) *a wicked man*
עָרִיץ adj. m.s. (792) *overbearing*
וּמִתְעָרֶה conj.-Hith. ptc. (788) *and towering*
כְּאֶזְרָח prep.-n.m.s. (280) *like a cedar of*
רַעֲנָן adj. m.s. (947) *Lebanon (luxuriant)*

37:36

וַיַּעֲבֹר consec.-Qal impf. 3 m.s. (716) *again I (he) passed by*
וְהִנֵּה conj.-interj. (243) *and lo*
אֵינֶנּוּ neg.-3 m.s. sf. (II 34) *he was no more*
וָאֲבַקְשֵׁהוּ consec.-Pi. impf. 1 c.s.-3 m.s. sf. (134) *though I sought him*
וְלֹא נִמְצָא conj.-neg.-Ni. ptc. (592) *he could not be found*

37:37

שְׁמָר־ Qal impv. 2 m.s. (1036) *mark*
תָּם adj. m.s. (1070) *the blameless man*
וּרְאֵה conj.-Qal impv. 2 m.s. (906) *and behold*
יָשָׁר adj. m.s. (449) *the upright*
כִּי־ conj. (471) *for*
אַחֲרִית n.f.s. (31) *there is posterity*

לְאִישׁ prep.-n.m.s. cstr. (35) *for the man of*
שָׁלוֹם n.m.s. (1022) *peace*

37:38

וּפֹשְׁעִים conj.-Qal act.ptc. m.p. (833) *but transgressors*
נִשְׁמְדוּ Ni. pf. 3 c.p. (1029) *shall be destroyed*
יַחְדָּו adv. (403) *altogether*
אַחֲרִית cf. 37:37 n.f.s. cstr. (31) *the posterity of*
רְשָׁעִים adj. m.p. (957) *the wicked*
נִכְרָתָה Ni. pf. 3 f.s. (503) *shall be cut off*

37:39

וּתְשׁוּעַת conj.-n.f.s. cstr. (448) *the salvation of*
צַדִּיקִים adj. m.p. (843) *the righteous*
מֵיְהוָה prep.-pr.n. (217) *is from Yahweh*
מָעוּזָּם n.m.s.-3 m.p. sf. (731) *their refuge*
בְּעֵת prep.-n.f.s. cstr. (773) *in the time of*
צָרָה n.f.s. (865) *trouble*

37:40

וַיַּעְזְרֵם consec.-Qal impf. 3 m.s.-3 m.p. sf. (740) *helps them*
יהוה pr.n. (217) *Yahweh*
וַיְפַלְּטֵם consec.-Pi. impf. 3 m.s.-3 m.p. sf. (812) *and delivers them*
יְפַלְּטֵם Pi. impf. 3 m.s.-3 m.p. sf. (812) *he delivers them*
מֵרְשָׁעִים prep.-n.m.p. (957) *from the wicked*
וְיוֹשִׁיעֵם conj.-Hi. impf. 3 m.s.-3 m.p. sf. (יָשַׁע 446) *and saves them*
כִּי־ conj. (471) *because*
חָסוּ בוֹ Qal pf. 3 c.p. (חָסָה 340)-prep.-3 m.s. sf. *they take refuge in him*

38:1

מִזְמוֹר n.m.s. (274) *a Psalm*
לְדָוִד prep.-pr.n. (187) *to David*
לְהַזְכִּיר prep.-Hi. inf.cstr. (זָכַר 269) *for the memorial offering*

38:2

יהוה pr.n. (217) *O Yahweh*
אַל־בְּקֶצְפְּךָ neg.-prep.-n.m.s.-2 m.s. sf. (893) *not in thy anger*
תוֹכִיחֵנִי Hi. impf. 2 m.s.-1 c.s. sf. (יָכַח 406) *rebuke me*
וּבַחֲמָתְךָ conj.-prep.-n.f.s.-2 m.s. sf. (404) *and in thy wrath*
תְיַסְּרֵנִי Pi. impf. 2 m.s.-1 c.s. sf. (יָסַר 415) *chasten me*

38:3

כִּי־חִצֶּיךָ conj. (471)-n.m.p.-2 m.s. sf. (346) *for thy arrows*
נִחֲתוּ Ni. pf. 3 c.p. (נָחֵת 639) *have sunk*
בִי prep.-1 c.s. sf. *into me*
וַתִּנְחַת consec.-Qal impf. 3 f.s. (נָחֵת 639) *and has come down*
עָלַי prep.-1 c.s. sf. *on me*
יָדֶךָ n.f.s.-2 m.s. sf. (388) *thy hand*

38:4

אֵין־מְתֹם neg. cstr. (II 34)-n.m.s. (1071) *there is no soundness*
בִּבְשָׂרִי prep.-n.m.s.-1 c.s. sf. (142) *in my flesh*
מִפְּנֵי prep.-n.m.p. cstr. (815) *because of*
זַעְמֶךָ n.m.s.-2 m.s. sf. (276) *thy indignation*
אֵין־שָׁלוֹם v.supra-n.m.s. (1022) *there is no health*
בַּעֲצָמַי prep.-n.f.p.-1 c.s. sf. (782) *in my bones*
מִפְּנֵי חַטָּאתִי v.supra-n.f.s.-1 c.s. sf. (308) *because of my sin*

38:5

כִּי עֲוֹנֹתַי conj. (471)-n.m.p.-1 c.s. sf. (730) *for my iniquities*
עָבְרוּ Qal pf. 3 c.p. (עָבַר 716) *have gone over*
רֹאשִׁי n.m.s.-1 c.s. sf. (910) *my head*
כְּמַשָּׂא prep.-n.m.s. (I 672) *like a burden*
כָּבֵד adj. m.s. (458) *too heavy*
יִכְבְּדוּ Qal impf. 3 m.p. (כָּבֵד 457) *they weigh*
מִמֶּנִּי prep.-1 c.s. sf. *for me*

38:6

הִבְאִישׁוּ Hi. pf. 3 c.p. (בָּאַשׁ 92) *grow foul*
נָמַקּוּ Ni. pf. 3 c.p. (מָקַק 596) *they fester*
חַבּוּרֹתָי n.f.p.-1 c.s. sf. paus. (289) *my wounds*
מִפְּנֵי אִוַּלְתִּי prep.-n.m.p. cstr. (815)-n.f.s.-1 c.s. sf. (17) *because of my foolishness*

38:7

נַעֲוֵיתִי Ni. pf. 1 c.s. (עָוָה I 730) *I am bowed down*
שַׁחֹתִי Qal pf. 1 c.s. (שָׁחָה 1005) *I am prostrate*
עַד־מְאֹד prep.-adv. (547) *utterly*
כָּל־הַיּוֹם n.m.s. cstr. (481)-def.art.-n.m.s. (398) *all the day*
קֹדֵר Qal act.ptc. (קָדַר 871) *mourning*
הִלָּכְתִּי Pi. pf. 1 c.s. paus. (הָלַךְ 229) *I go about*

38:8

כִּי־כְסָלַי conj. (471)-n.m.p.-1 c.s. sf. (492) *for my loins*

מָלְאוּ Qal pf. 3 c.p. (מָלֵא 569) *are filled with*
נִקְלֶה Ni. ptc. (קָלָה I 885) *burning*
וְאֵין מְתֹם conj.-neg. cstr. (II 34)-n.m.s. (1071) *and there is no soundness*
בִּבְשָׂרִי prep.-n.m.s.-1 c.s. sf. (142) *in my flesh*

38:9

נְפוּגוֹתִי Ni. pf. 1 c.s. (פוּג 806) *I am spent*
וְנִדְכֵּיתִי conj.-Ni. pf. 1 c.s. (דָּכָה 194) *and crushed*
עַד־מְאֹד prep.-adv. (547) *utterly*
שָׁאַגְתִּי Qal pf. 1 c.s. (שָׁאַג 980) *I groan*
מִנַּהֲמַת prep.-n.f.s. cstr. (625) *because of the tumult of*
לִבִּי n.m.s.-1 c.s. sf. (524) *my heart*

38:10

אֲדֹנָי n.m.p.-1 c.s. sf. (10) *my Lord*
נֶגְדְּךָ prep.-2 m.s. sf. (617) *is known to thee*
כָל־תַּאֲוָתִי n.m.s. cstr. (481)-n.f.s.-1 c.s. sf. (16) *all my longings*
וְאַנְחָתִי conj.-n.f.s.-1 c.s. sf. (58) *and my sighing*
מִמְּךָ prep.-2 m.s. sf. *from thee*
לֹא־נִסְתָּרָה neg.-Ni. pf. 3 f.s. (סָתַר 711) *is not hidden*

38:11

לִבִּי n.m.s.-1 c.s. sf. (524) *my heart*
סְחַרְחַר Pe'al'al pf. 3 m.s. (סָחַר 695; GK 55e) *throbs*
עֲזָבַנִי Qal pf. 3 m.s.-1 c.s. sf. (עָזַב I 736) *fails me*
כֹחִי n.m.s.-1 c.s. sf. (470) *my strength*
וְאוֹר־עֵינַי conj.-n.m.s. cstr. (21)-n.f. du.-1 c.s. sf. (744) *and the light of my eyes*
גַּם־הֵם adv. (168)-pers.pr. 3 m.p. (241) *it also*
אֵין אִתִּי neg. cstr. (II 34)-prep.-1 c.s. sf. (II 85) *has gone from me*

38:12

אֹהֲבַי Qal act.ptc. m.p.-1 c.s. sf. (אָהֵב 12) *my friends*
וְרֵעַי conj.-n.m.p.-1 c.s. sf. (945) *and companions*
מִנֶּגֶד נִגְעִי prep.-prep. (617)-n.m.s.-1 c.s. sf. (619) *from my plague*
יַעֲמֹדוּ Qal impf. 3 m.p. (עָמַד 763) *stand aloof*
וּקְרוֹבַי conj.-adj. m.p.-1 c.s. sf. (898) *and my kinsmen*
מֵרָחֹק prep.-adj. (935) *afar off*
עָמָדוּ Qal pf. 3 c.p. paus. (עָמַד 763) *stand*

38:13

וַיְנַקְשׁוּ consec.-Pi. impf. 3 m.p. (נָקַשׁ 669) *lay their snares*
מְבַקְשֵׁי Pi. ptc. m.p. cstr. (בָּקַשׁ 134) *those who seek*
נַפְשִׁי n.f.s.-1 c.s. sf. (659) *my life*
וְדֹרְשֵׁי conj.-Qal act.ptc. m.p. cstr. (דָּרַשׁ 205) *those who seek*
רָעָתִי n.f.s.-1 c.s. sf. (949) *my hurt*
דִּבְּרוּ Pi. pf. 3 c.p. (דָּבַר 180) *speak of*
הַוּוֹת n.f.p. (217) *ruin*
וּמִרְמוֹת conj.-n.f.p. (941; GK 124e) *and treachery*
כָּל־הַיּוֹם n.m.s. cstr. (481)-def.art.-n.m.s. (398) *all the day long*
יֶהְגּוּ Qal impf. 3 m.p. (הָגָה I 211) *they meditate*

38:14

וַאֲנִי conj.-pers.pr. 1 c.s. (58) *but I*
כְחֵרֵשׁ prep.-adj. m.s. (361) *like a deaf man*
לֹא אֶשְׁמָע neg.-Qal impf. 1 c.s. paus. (שָׁמַע 1033) *I do not hear*
וּכְאִלֵּם conj.-prep.-adj. m.s. (48) *and like a dumb man*
לֹא יִפְתַּח־ neg.-Qal impf. 3 m.s. (פָּתַח I 834) *who does not open*
פִּיו n.m.s.-3 m.s. sf. (804) *his mouth*

38:15

וָאֱהִי consec.-Qal impf. 1 c.s. (הָיָה 224) *yea, I am*
כְּאִישׁ prep.-n.m.s. (35) *like a man*
אֲשֶׁר לֹא־שֹׁמֵעַ rel. (81)-neg.-Qal act.ptc. (שָׁמַע 1033) *who does not hear*
וְאֵין בְּפִיו conj.-neg. cstr. (II 34)-prep.-n.m.s.-3 m.s. sf. (804) *and in whose mouth are no*
תּוֹכָחוֹת n.f.p. (407) *rebukes*

38:16

כִּי־לְךָ conj.-prep.-2 m.s. sf. *but for thee*
יהוה pr.n. (217) *O Yahweh*
הוֹחָלְתִּי Hi. pf. 1 c.s. paus. (יָחַל 403) *do I wait*
אַתָּה pers.pr. 2 m.s. (61) *it is thou*
תַעֲנֶה Qal impf. 2 m.s. (עָנָה I 772) *who wilt answer*
אֲדֹנָי n.m.p.-1 c.s. sf. (10) *Lord*
אֱלֹהָי n.m.p.-1 c.s. sf. paus. (43) *my God*

38:17

כִּי־אָמַרְתִּי conj. (471)-Qal pf. 1 c.s. (אָמַר 55) *for I pray*

פֶּן־יִשְׂמְחוּ־ conj. (814)–Qal impf. 3 m.p. (שָׂמַח 970) *only let them not rejoice*
לִי prep.–1 c.s. sf. *over me*
בְּמוֹט prep.–Qal inf.cstr. (מוֹט 556) *when slips*
רַגְלִי n.f.s.–1 c.s. sf. (919) *my foot*
עָלַי prep.–1 c.s. sf. *against me*
הִגְדִּילוּ Hi. pf. 3 c.p. (גָּדַל 152) *who boast*

38:18

כִּי־אֲנִי conj. (471)–pers.pr. 1 c.s. (58) *for I*
לְצֶלַע prep.–n.m.s. (854) *for falling*
נָכוֹן Ni. ptc. (כּוּן I 465) *am ready*
וּמַכְאוֹבִי conj.–n.m.s.–1 c.s. sf. (456) *and my pain*
נֶגְדִּי prep.–1 c.s. sf. (617) *with me*
תָמִיד adv. (556) *ever*

38:19

כִּי־עֲוֹנִי conj. (471)–n.m.s.–1 c.s. sf. (730) *for my iniquity*
אַגִּיד Hi. impf. 1 c.s. (נָגַד 616) *I confess*
אֶדְאַג Qal impf. 1 c.s. (דָּאַג 178) *I am sorry*
מֵחַטָּאתִי prep.–n.f.s.–1 c.s. sf. (308) *for my sin*

38:20

וְאֹיְבַי conj.–Qal act.ptc. m.p.–1 c.s. sf. (אָיַב 33) *and those who are my foes*
חַיִּים n.m.p. (313) *living*
עָצֵמוּ Qal pf. 3 c.p. paus. (עָצַם I 782) *are mighty*
וְרַבּוּ conj.–Qal pf. 3 c.p. (רָבַב I 912) *and are many*
שֹׂנְאַי Qal act.ptc. m.p.–1 c.s. sf. (שָׂנֵא 971) *those who hate me*
שָׁקֶר n.m.s. paus. (1055) *wrongfully*

38:21

וּמְשַׁלְּמֵי conj.–Pi. ptc. m.p. cstr. (שָׁלֵם 1022) *and those who render*
רָעָה n.f.s. (949) *evil*
תַּחַת טוֹבָה prep. (1065)–n.f.s. (375) *for good*
יִשְׂטְנוּנִי Qal impf. 3 m.p.–1 c.s. sf. (שָׂטַן 966) *are my adversaries*
תַּחַת רָדְופִי־ prep. (1065)–Qal inf.cstr.–1 c.s. sf. (922 רָדַף; GK 61c) *because I follow after*
טוֹב adj. m.s. (II 373) *good*

38:22

אַל־תַּעַזְבֵנִי neg.–Qal impf. 2 m.s.–1 c.s. sf. (עָזַב I 736) *do not forsake me*
יהוה pr.n. (217) *O Yahweh*
אֱלֹהַי n.m.p.–1 c.s. sf. (43) *O my God*

אַל־תִּרְחַק neg.–Qal impf. 2 m.s. (רָחַק 934) *be not far*
מִמֶּנִּי prep.–1 c.s. sf. *from me*

38:23

חוּשָׁה Qal impv. 2 m.s.–vol.he (חוּשׁ 301) *make haste*
לְעֶזְרָתִי prep.–n.f.s.–1 c.s. sf. (I 740) *to help me*
אֲדֹנָי n.m.p.–1 c.s. sf. (10) *O Lord*
תְּשׁוּעָתִי n.f.s.–1 c.s. sf. (448) *my salvation*

39:1

לַמְנַצֵּחַ prep.–def.art.–Pi. ptc. (I 663) *to the choirmaster*
לִידִיתוּן prep.–pr.n. (393) *to Jeduthun*
מִזְמוֹר n.m.s. (274) *a Psalm*
לְדָוִד prep.–pr.n. (187) *to David*

39:2

אָמַרְתִּי Qal pf. 1 c.s. (אָמַר 55) *I said*
אֶשְׁמְרָה Qal impf. 1 c.s.–vol.he (שָׁמַר 1036) *I will guard*
דְרָכַי n.m.p.–1 c.s. sf. (202) *my ways*
מֵחֲטוֹא prep.–Qal inf.cstr. (חָטָא 306) *that I may not sin*
בִלְשׁוֹנִי prep.–n.f.s.–1 c.s. sf. (546) *with my tongue*
אֶשְׁמְרָה v.supra *I will bridle (guard)*
לְפִי prep.–n.m.s.–1 c.s. sf. (804) *my mouth*
מַחְסוֹם n.m.s. (340) *a muzzle*
בְּעֹד prep.–adv. (728) *so long as*
רָשָׁע adj. m.s. (957) *the wicked*
לְנֶגְדִּי prep.–prep.–1 c.s. sf. (617) *in my presence*

39:3

נֶאֱלַמְתִּי Ni. pf. 1 c.s. (אָלַם 47) *I was dumb*
דוּמִיָּה n.f.s. (189) *silence*
הֶחֱשֵׁיתִי Hi. pf. 1 c.s. (חָשָׁה 364) *I held my peace*
מִטּוֹב prep.–adj. m.s. (II 373) *to no avail*
וּכְאֵבִי conj.–n.m.s.–1 c.s. sf. (456) *and my distress*
נֶעְכָּר Ni. pf. 3 m.s. paus. (עָכַר 747) *grew worse*

39:4

חַם־ Qal pf. 3 m.s. (חָמַם 328) *became hot*
לִבִּי n.m.s.–1 c.s. sf. (524) *my heart*
בְּקִרְבִּי prep.–n.m.s.–1 c.s. sf. (899) *within me*
בַּהֲגִיגִי prep.–n.m.s.–1 c.s. sf. (211) *as I mused*
תִבְעַר־ Qal impf. 3 f.s. (בָּעַר 128) *burned*
אֵשׁ n.f.s. (77) *the fire*
דִּבַּרְתִּי Pi. pf. 1 c.s. (דָּבַר 180) *then I spoke*
בִּלְשׁוֹנִי prep.–n.f.s.–1 c.s. sf. (546) *with my tongue*

39:5

הוֹדִיעֵנִי Hi. impv. 2 m.s.-1 c.s. sf. (יָדַע 393) *let me know*

יהוה pr.n. (217) *O Yahweh*

קִצִּי n.m.s.-1 c.s. sf. (893) *my end*

וּמִדַּת conj.-n.f.s. cstr. (551) *and the measure of*

יָמַי n.m.p.-1 c.s. sf. (398) *my days*

מַה־הִיא interr. (552)-demons.adj. f.s. (214) *what is*

אֵדְעָה Qal impf. 1 c.s.-vol.he (יָדַע 393) *let me know*

מֶה־חָדֵל interr. (552)-adj. m.s. (293) *how fleeting*

אָנִי pers.pr. 1 c.s. (58) *my life*

39:6

הִנֵּה demons.part. (243) *behold*

טְפָחוֹת n.m.p. (381) *a few handbreadths*

נָתַתָּה Qal pf. 2 m.s. (נָתַן 678) *thou hast made*

יָמַי n.m.p.-1 c.s. sf. (398) *my days*

וְחֶלְדִּי conj.-n.m.s.-1 c.s. sf. (317) *and my lifetime*

כְאַיִן prep.-subst. (II 34) *as nothing*

נֶגְדֶּךָ prep.-2 m.s. sf. (617) *in thy sight*

אַךְ adv. (36) *surely*

כָּל־הֶבֶל n.m.s. cstr. (481)-n.m.s. (I 210) *as a mere breath*

כָּל־אָדָם v.supra-n.m.s. (9) *every man*

נִצָּב Ni. ptc. (נָצַב 662) *stands*

סֶלָה interj. (699) *Selah*

39:7

אַךְ adv. (36) *surely*

בְּצֶלֶם prep.-n.m.s. (853) *as a shadow*

יִתְהַלֶּךְ־ Hith. impf. 3 m.s. (הָלַךְ 229) *goes about*

אִישׁ n.m.s. (35) *man*

אַךְ־הֶבֶל v.supra-n.m.s. (I 210) *surely for nought*

יֶהֱמָיוּן Qal impf. 3 m.p. (הָמָה 242) *are they in turmoil*

יִצְבֹּר Qal impf. 3 m.s. (צָבַר 840) *man heaps up*

וְלֹא־יֵדַע conj.-neg.-Qal impf. 3 m.s. (יָדַע 393) *and knows not*

מִי־אֹסְפָם interr. (566)-Qal act.ptc.-3 m.p. sf. (62 אָסַף) *who will gather (them)*

39:8

וְעַתָּה conj.-adv. (773) *and now*

מַה־קִּוִּיתִי interr. (552)-Pi. pf. 1 c.s. (קָוָה I 875) *for what do I wait*

אֲדֹנָי n.m.p.-1 c.s. sf. (10) *Lord*

תּוֹחַלְתִּי n.f.s.-1 c.s. sf. (404) *my hope*

לְךָ הִיא prep.-2 m.s. sf.-pers.pr. 3 f.s. (214) *is in thee*

39:9

מִכָּל־פְּשָׁעַי prep.-n.m.s. cstr. (481)-n.m.p.-1 c.s. sf. (833) *from all my transgressions*

הַצִּילֵנִי Hi. impv. 2 m.s.-1 c.s. sf. (נָצַל 664) *deliver me*

חֶרְפַּת n.f.s. cstr. (357) *the scorn of*

נָבָל adj. m.s. (I 614) *the fool*

אַל־תְּשִׂימֵנִי neg.-Qal impf. 2 m.s.-1 c.s. sf. (שׂוּם 962) *make me not*

39:10

נֶאֱלַמְתִּי Ni. pf. 1 c.s. (אָלַם 47) *I am dumb*

לֹא אֶפְתַּח־ neg.-Qal impf. 1 c.s. (פָּתַח I 834) *I do not open*

פִּי n.m.s.-1 c.s. sf. (804) *my mouth*

כִּי אַתָּה conj. (471)-pers.pr. 2 m.s. (61) *for it is thou*

עָשִׂיתָ Qal pf. 2 m.s. (עָשָׂה I 793) *who hast done it*

39:11

הָסֵר Hi. impv. 2 m.s. (סוּר 693) *remove*

מֵעָלַי prep.-prep.-1 c.s. sf. *from me*

נִגְעֶךָ n.m.s.-2 m.s. sf. (619) *thy stroke*

מִתִּגְרַת prep.-n.f.s. cstr. (173) *by the hostility of*

יָדְךָ n.f.s.-2 m.s. sf. (388) *thy hand*

אֲנִי כָלִיתִי pers.pr. 1 c.s. (58)-Qal pf. 1 c.s. (כָּלָה 477) *I am spent*

39:12

בְּתוֹכָחוֹת prep.-n.f.p. (407) *with rebukes*

עַל־עָוֹן prep.-n.m.s. (730) *for sin*

יִסַּרְתָּ Pi. pf. 2 m.s. (יָסַר 415) *thou dost chasten*

אִישׁ n.m.s. (35) *man*

וַתֶּמֶס consec.-Hi. impf. 2 m.s. (מָסָה 587) *thou dost consume*

כָּעָשׁ prep.-def.art.-n.m.s. (II 799) *like a moth*

חֲמוּדוֹ Qal pass.ptc.-3 m.s. sf. (חָמַד 326) *what is dear to him*

אַךְ הֶבֶל adv. (36)-n.m.s. (210) *surely a mere breath*

כָּל־אָדָם n.m.s. cstr. (481)-n.m.s. (9) *every man*

סֶלָה interj. (699) *Selah*

39:13

שִׁמְעָה־ Qal impv. 2 m.s.-vol.he (שָׁמַע 1033; GK 10h) *hear*

תְפִלָּתִי n.f.s.-1 c.s. sf. (813) *my prayer*

יהוה pr.n. (217) *O Yahweh*

וְשַׁוְעָתִי conj.-n.f.s.-1 c.s. sf. (1003) *and my cry*

הַאֲזִינָה Hi. impv. 2 m.s.-vol.he (אָזַן 24) *give ear to*

אֶל־דִּמְעָתִי prep.-n.f.s.-1 c.s. sf. (199) *at my tears*
אַל־תֶּחֱרַשׁ neg.-Qal impf. 2 m.s. (חָרַשׁ II 361) *hold not thy peace*
כִּי גֵר conj. (471)-n.m.s. (158) *for a passing guest*
אָנֹכִי pers.pr. 1 c.s. (59) *I am*
עִמָּךְ prep.-2 m.s. sf. paus. *with you*
תּוֹשָׁב n.m.s. (444) *a sojourner*
כְּכָל־אֲבוֹתָי prep.-n.m.s. cstr. (481)-n.m.p.-1 c.s. sf. paus. (3) *like all my fathers*

39:14

הָשַׁע Hi. impv. 2 m.s. (שָׁעָה 1043; GK 75gg) *look away*
מִמֶּנִּי prep.-1 c.s. sf. *from me*
וְאַבְלִיגָה conj.-Hi. impf. 1 c.s.-vol.he (בָּלַג 114) *that I may know gladness*
בְּטֶרֶם אֵלֵךְ prep.-adv. (382)-Qal impf. 1 c.s. (הָלַךְ 229) *before I depart*
וְאֵינֶנִּי conj.-neg.-1 c.s. sf. (II 34) *and be no more*

40:1

לַמְנַצֵּחַ prep.-def.art.-Pi. ptc. (I 663) *to the choirmaster*
לְדָוִד prep.-pr.n. (187) *to David*
מִזְמוֹר n.m.s. (274) *a Psalm*

40:2

קַוֺּה קִוִּיתִי Pi. inf.abs. (קָוָה I 875; GK 75aa)-Pi. pf. 1 c.s. (I 875) *I waited patiently*
יהוה pr.n. (217) *for Yahweh*
וַיֵּט consec.-Qal impf. 3 m.s. (נָטָה 639) *and he inclined*
אֵלַי prep.-1 c.s. sf. *to me*
וַיִּשְׁמַע consec.-Qal impf. 3 m.s. (שָׁמַע 1033) *and he heard*
שַׁוְעָתִי n.f.s.-1 c.s. sf. (1003) *my cry*

40:3

וַיַּעֲלֵנִי consec.-Hi. impf.3 m.s.-1 c.s. sf. (עָלָה 748) *and he drew me up*
מִבּוֹר שָׁאוֹן prep.-n.m.s. cstr. (92)-n.m.s. (981) *from a pit of tumult*
מִטִּיט הַיָּוֵן prep.-n.m.s. cstr. (376)-def.art.-n.m.s. (401) *out of the miry bog*
וַיָּקֶם consec.-Hi. impf. 3 m.s. (קוּם 877) *and he set*
עַל־סֶלַע prep.-n.m.s. (700) *upon a rock*
רַגְלַי n.f.p.-1 c.s. sf. (919) *my feet*
כּוֹנֵן Polel pf. 3 m.s. (כּוּן 465) *making secure*
אֲשֻׁרָי n.f.p.-1 c.s. sf. paus. (81) *my steps*

40:4

וַיִּתֵּן consec.-Qal impf. 3 m.s. (נָתַן 678) *and he put*
בְּפִי prep.-n.m.s.-1 c.s. sf. (804) *in my mouth*
שִׁיר חָדָשׁ n.m.s. (1010)-adj. m.s. (I 294) *a new song*
תְּהִלָּה n.f.s. (239) *praise*
לֵאלֹהֵינוּ prep.-n.m.p.-1 c.p. sf. (43) *to our God*
יִרְאוּ רַבִּים Qal impf. 3 m.p. (רָאָה 906)-adj. m.p. (I 912) *many will see*
וְיִירָאוּ conj.-Qal impf. 3 m.p. paus. (יָרֵא 431) *and fear*
וְיִבְטְחוּ conj.-Qal impf. 3 m.p. (בָּטַח 105) *and put their trust*
בַּיהוה prep.-pr.n. (217) *in Yahweh*

40:5

אַשְׁרֵי n.m.p. cstr. (80) *Oh, the happinesses of*
הַגֶּבֶר def.art.-n.m.s. (149) *the man*
אֲשֶׁר־שָׂם rel. (81)-Qal pf. 3 m.s. (שִׂים 962) *who makes*
יהוה pr.n. (217) *Yahweh*
מִבְטַחוֹ n.m.s.-3 m.s. sf. (105; GK 93oo) *his trust*
וְלֹא־פָנָה conj.-neg.-Qal pf. 3 m.s. (815) *and who does not turn*
אֶל־רְהָבִים prep.-adj. m.p. (923) *to the proud*
וְשָׂטֵי conj.-Qal act.ptc. m.p. cstr. (שׂוּט 962) *to those who go astray*
כָזָב n.m.s. (469) *after false gods*

40:6

רַבּוֹת עָשִׂיתָ adj. f.p. (I 912)-Qal pf. 2 m.s. (עָשָׂה I 793) *thou hast multiplied*
אַתָּה pers.pr. 2 m.s. (61) *(thou)*
יהוה אֱלֹהַי pr.n. (217)-n.m.p.-1 c.s. sf. (43) *O Yahweh my God*
נִפְלְאֹתֶיךָ Ni. ptc. f.p.-2 m.s. sf. (פָּלָא 810) *thy wondrous deeds*
וּמַחְשְׁבֹתֶיךָ conj.-n.f.p.-2 m.s. sf. (364) *and thy thoughts*
אֵלֵינוּ prep.-1 c.p. sf. *toward us*
אֵין עֲרֹךְ neg. cstr. (II 34)-Qal inf.cstr. (עָרַךְ 789) *none can compare*
אֵלֶיךָ prep.-2 m.s. sf. *with thee*
אַגִּידָה Hi. impf. 1 c.s.-vol.he (נָגַד 616; GK 108f) *were I to proclaim*
וַאֲדַבֵּרָה conj.-Pi. impf. 1 c.s.-vol.he (דָּבַר 180) *and tell*
עָצְמוּ Qal pf. 3 c.p. (עָצַם I 782) *they would be more*
מִסַּפֵּר prep.-Pi. inf.cstr. (סָפַר 707) *than can be numbered*

40:7

זֶבַח n.m.s. (257) *sacrifice*
וּמִנְחָה conj.-n.f.s. (585) *and offering*
לֹא־חָפַצְתָּ neg.-Qal pf. 2 m.s. (חָפֵץ 342) *thou dost not desire*
אָזְנַיִם n.f. du. (23) *ears*
כָּרִיתָ Qal pf. 2 m.s. (כָּרָה I 500) *thou hast dug*
לִּי prep.-1 c.s. sf. *for me*
עוֹלָה n.f.s. (II 750) *burnt offering*
וַחֲטָאָה conj.-n.f.s. (308) *and sin offering*
לֹא שָׁאָלְתָּ neg.-Qal pf. 2 m.s. paus. (שָׁאַל 981) *thou hast not required*

40:8

אָז adv. (23) *then*
אָמַרְתִּי Qal pf. 1 c.s. (55) *I said*
הִנֵּה־בָאתִי demons.part. (243)-Qal pf. 1 c.s. (בּוֹא 97) *lo, I come*
בִּמְגִלַּת־ prep.-n.f.s. cstr. (166) *in the roll of*
סֵפֶר n.m.s. (706) *the book*
כָּתוּב Qal pass.ptc. (כָּתַב 507) *it is written*
עָלָי prep.-1 c.s. sf. paus. *of me*

40:9

לַעֲשׂוֹת־ prep.-Qal inf.cstr. (עָשָׂה I 793) *to do*
רְצוֹנְךָ n.m.s.-2 m.s. sf. (953) *thy will*
אֱלֹהַי n.m.p.-1 c.s. sf. (43) *my God*
חָפָצְתִּי Qal pf. 1 c.s. paus. (חָפֵץ 342) *I delight*
וְתוֹרָתְךָ conj.-n.f.s.-2 m.s. sf. (435) *and thy law*
בְּתוֹךְ prep.-n.m.s. cstr. (1063) *within*
מֵעָי n.m.p.-1 c.s. sf. paus. (588) *my heart*

40:10

בִּשַּׂרְתִּי Pi. pf. 1 c.s. (בָּשַׂר 142) *I have told the glad news*
צֶדֶק n.m.s. (841) *of deliverance*
בְּקָהָל רָב prep.-n.m.s. (874)-adj. m.s. paus. (I 912) *in the great congregation*
הִנֵּה שְׂפָתַי demons.part. (243)-n.f. du.-1 c.s. sf. (973) *lo, my lips*
לֹא אֶכְלָא neg.-Qal impf. 1 c.s. (כָּלָא 476) *I have not restrained*
יהוה pr.n. (217) *Yahweh*
אַתָּה יָדָעְתָּ pers.pr. 2 m.s. (61)-Qal pf. 2 m.s. paus. (יָדַע 393) *thou knowest*

40:11

צִדְקָתְךָ n.f.s.-2 m.s. sf. (842) *thy saving help*
לֹא־כִסִּיתִי neg.-Pi. pf. 1 c.s. (כָּסָה 491) *I have not hid*
בְּתוֹךְ לִבִּי prep.-n.m.s. cstr. (1063)-n.m.s.-1 c.s. sf. (524) *within my heart*
אֱמוּנָתְךָ n.f.s.-2 m.s. sf. (53) *thy faithfulness*
וּתְשׁוּעָתְךָ conj.-n.f.s.-2 m.s. sf. (448) *and thy salvation*
אָמָרְתִּי Qal pf. 1 c.s. paus. (55) *I have spoken of*
לֹא־כִחַדְתִּי neg.-Pi. pf. 1 c.s. (כָּחַד 470) *I have not concealed*
חַסְדְּךָ n.m.s.-2 m.s. sf. (338) *thy steadfast love*
וַאֲמִתְּךָ conj.-n.f.s.-2 m.s. sf. (54) *and thy faithfulness*
לְקָהָל רָב prep.-n.m.s. (874)-adj. m.s. (I 912) *from the great congregation*

40:12

אַתָּה pers.pr. 2 m.s. (61) *thou*
יהוה pr.n. (217) *O Yahweh*
לֹא־תִכְלָא neg.-Qal impf. 2 m.s. (כָּלָא 476) *do not withhold*
רַחֲמֶיךָ n.m.p.-2 m.s. sf. (933) *thy mercy*
מִמֶּנִּי prep.-1 c.s. sf. *from me*
חַסְדְּךָ n.m.s.-2 m.s. sf. (338) *thy steadfast love*
וַאֲמִתְּךָ conj.-n.f.s.-2 m.s. sf. (54) *and thy faithfulness*
תָּמִיד adv. (556) *ever*
יִצְּרוּנִי Qal impf. 3 m.p.-1 c.s. sf. (נָצַר I 665) *preserve me*

40:13

כִּי אָפְפוּ־ conj. (471)-Qal pf. 3 c.p. (אָפַף 67) *for have encompassed*
עָלַי prep.-1 c.s. sf. *me*
רָעוֹת n.f.p. (949) *evil*
עַד־אֵין prep. (III 723)-neg. cstr. (II 34) *without*
מִסְפָּר n.m.s. (708) *number*
הִשִּׂיגוּנִי Hi. pf. 3 c.p.-1 c.s. sf. (נָשַׂג 673) *have overtaken me*
עֲוֹנֹתַי n.m.p.-1 c.s. sf. (730) *my iniquities*
וְלֹא־יָכֹלְתִּי conj.-neg.-Qal pf. 1 c.s. (יָכֹל 407) *till I cannot*
לִרְאוֹת prep.-Qal inf.cstr. (רָאָה 906) *see*
עָצְמוּ Qal pf. 3 c.p. (עָצַם I 782) *they are more*
מִשַּׂעֲרוֹת prep.-n.f.p. cstr. (972) *than the hairs of*
רֹאשִׁי n.m.s.-1 c.s. sf. (910) *my head*
וְלִבִּי conj.-n.m.s.-1 c.s. sf. (524) *and my heart*
עֲזָבָנִי Qal pf. 3 m.s.-1 c.s. sf. (עָזַב I 736) *fails me*

40:14

רְצֵה Qal impv. 2 m.s. (רָצָה 953) *be pleased*
יהוה pr.n. (217) *O Yahweh*
לְהַצִּילֵנִי prep.-Hi. inf.cstr.-1 c.s. sf. (נָצַל 664) *to deliver me*

יהוה pr.n. (217) *O Yahweh*

לְעֶזְרָתִי prep.-n.f.s.-1 c.s. sf. (I 740) *to help me*

חוּשָׁה Qal impv. 2 m.s.-vol.he (חוּשׁ I 301) *make haste*

40:15

יֵבֹשׁוּ Qal impf. 3 m.p. (בּוֹשׁ 101) *let them be put to shame*

וְיַחְפְּרוּ conj.-Qal impf. 3 m.p. (חָפֵר II 344) *and confusion*

יַחַד adv. (403) *altogether*

מְבַקְשֵׁי Pi. ptc. m.p. cstr. (בָּקַשׁ 134) *who seek*

נַפְשִׁי n.f.s.-1 c.s. sf. (659) *my life*

לִסְפּוֹתָהּ prep.-Qal inf.cstr.-3 f.s. sf. (סָפָה 705) *to snatch away (it)*

יִסֹּגוּ Ni. impf. 3 m.p. (סוּג I 690) *let them be turned*

אָחוֹר subst. (30) *back*

וְיִכָּלְמוּ conj.-Ni. impf. 3 m.p. (כָּלַם 483; GK 29oN) *and brought to dishonor*

חֲפֵצֵי adj. m.p. cstr. (343) *who desire*

רָעָתִי n.f.s.-1 c.s. sf. (949) *my hurt*

40:16

יָשֹׁמּוּ Qal impf. 3 m.p. (שָׁמֵם 1030) *let them be appalled*

עַל־עֵקֶב prep.-adv. (784) *because of*

בָּשְׁתָּם n.f.p.-3 m.p. sf. (102) *their shame*

הָאֹמְרִים def.art.-Qal act.ptc. m.p. (אָמַר 55) *who say*

לִי prep.-1 c.s. sf. *to me*

הֶאָח הֶאָח interj. (210)—v.supra *Aha, Aha*

40:17

יָשִׂישׂוּ Qal impf. 3 m.p. (שׂוּשׂ 965) *may ... rejoice*

וְיִשְׂמְחוּ conj.-Qal impf. 3 m.p. (שָׂמַח 970) *and be glad*

בְּךָ prep.-2 m.s. sf. *in thee*

כָּל־מְבַקְשֶׁיךָ n.m.s. cstr. (481)-Pi. ptc. m.p.-2 m.s. sf. (בָּקַשׁ 134) *all who seek thee*

יֹאמְרוּ Qal impf. 3 m.p. (אָמַר 55) *may ... say*

תָּמִיד adv. (556) *continually*

יִגְדַּל Qal impf. 3 m.s. (גָּדַל 152) *great is*

יהוה pr.n. (217) *Yahweh*

אֹהֲבֵי Qal act.ptc. m.p. cstr. (אָהֵב 12) *those who love*

תְּשׁוּעָתֶךָ n.f.s.-2 m.s. sf. paus. (448) *thy salvation*

40:18

וַאֲנִי conj.-pers.pr. 1 c.s. (58) *as for me*

עָנִי adj. m.s. (776) *poor*

וְאֶבְיוֹן conj.-adj. m.s. (2) *and needy*

אֲדֹנָי n.m.p.-1 c.s. sf. (10) *the Lord*

יַחֲשָׁב Qal impf. 3 m.s. (חָשַׁב 362) *takes thought*

לִי prep.-1 c.s. sf. *for me*

עֶזְרָתִי n.f.s.-1 c.s. sf. (I 740) *my help*

וּמְפַלְטִי conj.-Pi. ptc.-1 c.s. sf. (פָּלַט 812) *and my deliverer*

אַתָּה pers.pr. 2 m.s. (61) *thou*

אֱלֹהַי n.m.p.-1 c.s. sf. (43) *O my God*

אַל־תְּאַחַר neg.-Pi. impf. 2 m.s. (אָחַר 29; GK 29q) *do not tarry*

41:1

לַמְנַצֵּחַ prep.-def.art.-Pi. ptc. (I 663) *to the choirmaster*

מִזְמוֹר n.m.s. (274) *a Psalm*

לְדָוִד prep.-pr.n. (187) *to David*

41:2

אַשְׁרֵי n.m.p. cstr. (80) *blessed is*

מַשְׂכִּיל Hi. ptc. (שָׂכַל 968) *he who considers*

אֶל־דָּל prep.-adj. m.s. paus. (195) *the poor*

בְּיוֹם prep.-n.m.s. cstr. (398) *in the day of*

רָעָה n.f.s. (949) *trouble*

יְמַלְּטֵהוּ Pi. impf. 3 m.s.-3 m.s. sf. (פָּלַט 812) *delivers him*

יהוה pr.n. (217) *Yahweh*

41:3

יהוה pr.n. (217) *Yahweh*

יִשְׁמְרֵהוּ Qal impf. 3 m.s.-3 m.s. sf. (שָׁמַר 1036) *protects him*

וִיחַיֵּהוּ conj.-Pi. impf. 3 m.s.-3 m.s. sf. (חָיָה 310) *and keeps him alive*

יְאֻשַּׁר Pu. impf. 3 m.s. (אָשַׁר 80) *he is called blessed*

בָּאָרֶץ prep.-def.art.-n.f.s. (75) *in the land*

וְאַל־תִּתְּנֵהוּ conj.-neg.-Qal impf. 2 m.s.-3 m.s. sf. (נָתַן 678; GK 109e) *thou dost not give him up*

בְּנֶפֶשׁ prep.-n.f.s. cstr. (659) *to the will of*

אֹיְבָיו Qal act.ptc. m.p.-3 m.s. sf. (אָיַב 33) *his enemies*

41:4

יהוה pr.n. (217) *Yahweh*

יִסְעָדֶנּוּ Qal impf. 3 m.s.-3 m.s. sf. (סָעַד 703) *sustains him*

עַל־עֶרֶשׂ דְּוָי prep.-n.f.s. cstr. (793)-n.m.s. paus. (188) *on his sickbed*

כָּל־מִשְׁכָּבוֹ n.m.s. cstr. (481)–n.m.s.–3 m.s. sf. (1012) *all his bed*

הָפַכְתָּ Qal pf. 2 m.s. (הָפַךְ 245) *thou changest*

בְחָלְיוֹ prep.–n.m.s.–3 m.s. sf. (318) *in his illness*

41:5

אֲנִי־ pers.pr. 1 c.s. (58) *as for me*

אָמַרְתִּי Qal pf. 1 c.s. (55) *I said*

יהוה pr.n. (217) *O Yahweh*

חָנֵּנִי Qal impv. 2 m.s.–1 c.s. sf. (חָנַן I 335) *be gracious to me*

רְפָאָה Qal impv. 2 m.s.–vol.he (רָפָא 950; GK 74h) *heal*

נַפְשִׁי n.f.s.–1 c.s. sf. (659) *me*

כִּי־חָטָאתִי conj. (471)–Qal pf. 1 c.s. (חָטָא 306) *for I have sinned*

לָךְ prep.–2 m.s. sf. paus. *against thee*

41:6

אוֹיְבַי Qal act.ptc. m.p.–1 c.s. sf. (אָיַב 33) *my enemies*

יֹאמְרוּ Qal impf. 3 m.p. (אָמַר 55) *say*

רַע n.m.s. (II 948) *in malice*

לִי prep.–1 c.s. sf. *of me*

מָתַי adv. (607) *when*

יָמוּת Qal impf. 3 m.s. (מוּת 559) *will he die*

וְאָבַד conj.–Qal pf. 3 m.s. (1) *and perish*

שְׁמוֹ n.m.s.–3 m.s. sf. (1027) *his name*

41:7

וְאִם־ conj.–hypoth.part. (49) *and when*

בָּא Qal pf. 3 m.s. (בּוֹא 97) *one comes*

לִרְאוֹת prep.–Qal inf.cstr. (רָאָה 9060) *to see*

שָׁוְא n.m.s. (996) *empty words*

יְדַבֵּר Pi. impf. 3 m.s. (דָּבַר 180) *he utters*

לִבּוֹ n.m.s.–3 m.s. sf. (524) *his heart*

יִקְבָּץ־ Qal impf. 3 m.s. (קָבַץ 867) *gathers*

אָוֶן n.m.s. (19) *mischief*

לוֹ prep.–3 m.s. sf. *(for him)*

יֵצֵא Qal impf. 3 m.s. (יָצָא 422) *he goes out*

לַחוּץ prep.–def.art.–n.m.s. (299) *abroad*

יְדַבֵּר Pi. impf. 3 m.s. (דָּבַר 180) *he tells it*

41:8

יַחַד adv. (403) *together*

עָלַי prep.–1 c.s. sf. *about me*

יִתְלַחֲשׁוּ Hith. impf. 3 m.p. (לָחַשׁ 538; GK 54h) *whisper*

כָּל־שֹׂנְאָי n.m.s. cstr. (481)–Qal act.ptc. m.p.–1 c.s. sf. paus. (שָׂנֵא 971) *all who hate me*

עָלַי v.supra *for me*

יַחְשְׁבוּ Qal impf. 3 m.p. (חָשַׁב 362) *they imagine*

רָעָה n.f.s. (949) *the worst*

לִי prep.–1 c.s. sf. *for me*

41:9

דְּבַר־בְּלִיַּעַל n.m.s. cstr. (182)–n.m.s. (116) *a deadly thing*

יָצוּק Qal pass.ptc. (יָצַק 427) *has fastened*

בּוֹ prep.–3 m.s. sf. *upon him*

וַאֲשֶׁר conj.–rel. (81) *and from where*

שָׁכַב Qal pf. 3 m.s. (1011) *he lies*

לֹא־יוֹסִיף neg.–Hi. impf. 3 m.s. (יָסַף 414) *he will not again*

לָקוּם prep.–Qal inf.cstr. (קוּם 877) *rise*

41:10

גַּם־ adv. (168) *even*

אִישׁ שְׁלוֹמִי n.m.s. cstr. (35)–n.m.s.–1 c.s. sf. (שָׁלֵם 1022) *my bosom friend*

אֲשֶׁר־בָּטַחְתִּי rel. (81)–Qal pf. 1 c.s. (בָּטַח 105) *in whom I trusted*

בּוֹ prep.–3 m.s. sf. *(in him)*

אוֹכֵל Qal act.ptc. (אָכַל 37) *who ate*

לַחְמִי n.m.s.–1 c.s. sf. (536) *my bread*

הִגְדִּיל Hi. pf. 3 m.s. (גָּדַל 152) *has lifted*

עָלַי prep.–1 c.s. sf. *against me*

עָקֵב n.m.s. (I 784) *his heel*

41:11

וְאַתָּה conj.–pers.pr. 2 m.s. (61) *but thou*

יהוה pr.n. (217) *O Yahweh*

חָנֵּנִי Qal impv. 2 m.s.–1 c.s. sf. (חָנַן I 335) *be gracious to me*

וַהֲקִימֵנִי conj.–Hi. impv. 2 m.s.–1 c.s. sf. (קוּם 877) *and raise me up*

וַאֲשַׁלְּמָה conj.–Pi. impf. 1 c.s.–vol.he (שָׁלֵם 1022) *that I may requite*

לָהֶם prep.–3 m.p. sf. *them*

41:12

בְּזֹאת prep.–demons.adj. f.s. (260) *by this*

יָדַעְתִּי Qal pf. 1 c.s. (יָדַע 393) *I know*

כִּי־חָפַצְתָּ conj. (471)–Qal pf. 2 m.s. (חָפֵץ 342) *that thou art pleased*

בִּי prep.–1 c.s. sf. *with me*

כִּי לֹא־יָרִיעַ conj. (471)–neg.–Hi. impf. 3 m.s. (רוּעַ 929) *in that has not triumphed*

אֹיְבִי Qal act.ptc.–1 c.s. sf. (אָיַב 33) *my enemy*

עָלָי prep.–1 c.s. sf. paus. *over me*

41:13

וַאֲנִי conj.–pers.pr. 1 c.s. (58) *but as for me*

בְּתֻמִּי prep.-n.m.s.-1 c.s. sf. (1070) *because of my integrity*
תָּמַכְתָּ Qal pf. 2 m.s. (תָּמַךְ 1069) *thou hast upheld*
בִּי prep.-1 c.s. sf. *me*
וַתַּצִּיבֵנִי consec.-Hi. impf. 2 m.s.-1 c.s. sf. (נָצַב 662) *and set me*
לְפָנֶיךָ prep.-n.m.p.-2 m.s. sf. (815) *in thy presence*
לְעוֹלָם prep.-n.m.s. (761) *for ever*

41:14

בָּרוּךְ Qal pass.ptc. (בָּרַךְ 138) *blessed*
יהוה pr.n. (217) *Yahweh*
אֱלֹהֵי n.m.p. cstr. (43) *the God of*
יִשְׂרָאֵל pr.n. (975) *Israel*
מֵהָעוֹלָם prep.-def.art.-n.m.s. (761) *from everlasting*
וְעַד conj.-prep. (III 723) *to*
הָעוֹלָם def.art.-n.m.s. (761) *everlasting*
אָמֵן וְאָמֵן adv. (53)-conj.-v.supra *Amen and Amen*

42:1

לַמְנַצֵּחַ prep.-def.art.-Pi. ptc. (I 663) *to the choirmaster*
מַשְׂכִּיל n.m.s. (968) *a Maskil*
לִבְנֵי־קֹרַח prep.-n.m.p. cstr. (119)-pr.n. (901) *to the Sons of Korah*

42:2

כְּאַיָּל prep.-n.f.s. (19; GK 122f,155g) *as a hart*
תַּעֲרֹג Qal impf. 3 f.s. (עָרַג 788) *longs*
עַל־אֲפִיקֵי־מָיִם prep.-n.m.p. cstr. (67)-n.m.p. paus. (565) *for flowing streams*
כֵּן נַפְשִׁי adv. (485)-n.f.s.-1 c.s. sf. (659) *so my soul*
תַּעֲרֹג v.supra *longs*
אֵלֶיךָ prep.-2 m.s. sf. paus. *for thee*
אֱלֹהִים n.m.p. (43) *O God*

42:3

צָמְאָה Qal pf. 3 f.s. (צָמֵא 854) *thirsts*
נַפְשִׁי n.f.s.-1 c.s. sf. (659) *my soul*
לֵאלֹהִים prep.-n.m.p. (43) *for God*
לְאֵל חָי prep.-n.m.s. (42)-adj. m.s. paus. (I 311) *for the living God*
מָתַי adv. (607) *when*
אָבוֹא Qal impf. 1 c.s. (בּוֹא 97) *shall I come*
וְאֵרָאֶה conj.-Ni. impf. 1 c.s. (רָאָה 906) *and behold (appear)*

פְּנֵי אֱלֹהִים n.m.p. cstr. (815)-n.m.p. (43) *the face of God*

42:4

הָיְתָה־לִּי Qal pf. 3 f.s. (הָיָה 224)-prep.-1 c.s. sf. *have been for me*
דִמְעָתִי n.f.s.-1 c.s. sf. (199) *my tears*
לֶחֶם n.m.s. (536) *my food*
יוֹמָם adv. (401) *day*
וָלָיְלָה conj.-n.m.s. paus. (538) *and night*
בֶּאֱמֹר prep.-Qal inf.cstr. (55; GK 115eN) *while men say*
אֵלַי prep.-1 c.s. sf. *to me*
כָּל־הַיּוֹם n.m.s. cstr. (481)-def.art.-n.m.s. (398) *continually*
אַיֵּה adv. (32) *where*
אֱלֹהֶיךָ n.m.p.-2 m.s. sf. (43) *your God*

42:5

אֵלֶּה demons.adj. c.p. (41) *these things*
אֶזְכְּרָה Qal impf. 1 c.s.-vol.he (זָכַר 269) *I remember*
וְאֶשְׁפְּכָה conj.-Qal impf. 1 c.s.-vol.he (שָׁפַךְ 1049) *as I pour out*
עָלַי prep.-1 c.s. sf. *(upon me)*
נַפְשִׁי n.f.s.-1 c.s. sf. (659) *my soul*
כִּי אֶעֱבֹר conj. (471)-Qal impf. 1 c.s. (עָבַר 716) *how I went*
בַּסָּךְ prep.-def.art.-n.m.s. (697) *with the throng*
אֶדַּדֵּם Pi. impf. 1 c.s.-3 m.p. sf. (דָּדָה 186; GK 117x) *and led them in procession*
עַד־בֵּית prep. (III 723)-n.m.s. cstr. (108) *to the house of*
אֱלֹהִים n.m.p. (43) *God*
בְּקוֹל־ prep.-n.m.s. cstr. (876) *with shouts of*
רִנָּה n.f.s. (943) *joy*
וְתוֹדָה conj.-n.f.s. (392) *and thanksgiving*
הָמוֹן n.m.s. (242) *a multitude*
חוֹגֵג Qal act.ptc. (חָגַג 290) *keeping festival*

42:6

מַה־תִּשְׁתּוֹחֲחִי interr. (552)-Hithpo'el impf. 2 f.s. (שָׁחַח 1005) *why are you cast down*
נַפְשִׁי n.f.s.-1 c.s. sf. (659) *O my soul*
וַתֶּהֱמִי consec.-Qal impf. 2 f.s. (הָמָה 242; GK 111t) *and why are you disquieted*
עָלָי prep.-1 c.s. sf. paus. *within me*
הוֹחִילִי Hi. impv. 2 f.s. (יָחַל 403) *hope*
לֵאלֹהִים prep.-n.m.p. (43) *in God*
כִּי־עוֹד conj. (471)-adv. (728) *for again*
אוֹדֶנּוּ Hi. impf. 1 c.s.-3 m.s. sf. (יָדָה 392) *I shall praise him*

יְשׁוּעוֹת n.f.p. (447) *help*
פָּנָיו n.m.p.-3 m.s. sf. (815) *before him*

42:7

אֱלֹהַי n.m.p.-1 c.s. sf. (43) *my God*
עָלַי prep.-1 c.s. sf. *within me*
נַפְשִׁי n.f.s.-1 c.s. sf. (659) *my soul*
תִשְׁתּוֹחָח Hithpo'el impf. 3 f.s. (שָׁחַח 1005) *is cast down*
עַל־כֵּן prep.-adv. (485) *therefore*
אֶזְכָּרְךָ Qal impf. 1 c.s.-2 m.s. sf. (זָכַר 269) *I remember thee*
מֵאֶרֶץ prep.-n.f.s. cstr. (75) *from the land of*
יַרְדֵּן pr.n. (434) *Jordan*
וְחֶרְמוֹנִים conj.-pr.n. p. (356) *and Hermon*
מֵהַר מִצְעָר prep.-n.m.s. cstr. (249)-pr.n. (II 859) *and from Mizar*

42:8

תְּהוֹם־אֶל־תְּהוֹם n.f.s. (1062)-prep.-v.supra *deep to deep*
קוֹרֵא Qal act.ptc. (קָרָא 894) *calls*
לְקוֹל prep.-n.m.s. cstr. (876) *at the thunder of*
צִנּוֹרֶיךָ n.m.p.-2 m.s. sf. (857) *thy waterspouts*
כָּל־מִשְׁבָּרֶיךָ n.m.s. cstr. (481)-n.m.p.-2 m.s. sf. (991) *all thy waves*
וְגַלֶּיךָ conj.-n.m.p.-2 m.s. sf. (164) *and thy billows*
עָלַי prep.-1 c.s. sf. *over me*
עָבָרוּ Qal pf. 3 c.p. paus. (עָבַר 716) *have gone*

42:9

יוֹמָם adv. (401) *by day*
יְצַוֶּה Pi. impf. 3 m.s. (צָוָה 845) *commands*
יהוה pr.n. (217) *Yahweh*
חַסְדּוֹ n.m.s.-3 m.s. sf. (338) *his steadfast love*
וּבַלַּיְלָה conj.-prep.-def.art.-n.m.s. (538) *and at night*
שִׁירֹה n.m.s.-3 m.s. sf. (1010) *his song*
עִמִּי prep.-1 c.s. sf. *with me*
תְּפִלָּה n.f.s. (813) *a prayer*
לְאֵל prep.-n.m.s. cstr. (42) *to the God of*
חַיָּי adj. m.p.-1 c.s. sf. paus. (I 311) *my life*

42:10

אוֹמְרָה Qal impf. 1 c.s.-vol.he (אָמַר 55; GK 68g) *I say*
לְאֵל prep.-n.m.s. (42) *to God*
סַלְעִי n.m.s.-1 c.s. sf. (700) *my rock*
לָמָה interr. (552) *why*
שְׁכַחְתָּנִי Qal pf. 2 m.s.-1 c.s. sf. (שָׁכַח 1013) *hast thou forgotten me*
לָמָּה־ interr. (552; GK 102,l) *why*
קֹדֵר Qal act.ptc. (871) *mourning*
אֵלֵךְ Qal impf. 1 c.s. (הָלַךְ 229) *go I*
בְּלַחַץ prep.-n.m.s. cstr. (537) *because of the oppression of*
אוֹיֵב Qal act.ptc. (אָיַב 33) *the enemy*

42:11

בְּרֶצַח prep.-n.m.s. (954) *with a deadly wound*
בְּעַצְמוֹתַי prep.-n.f.p.-1 c.s. sf. (782) *in my body*
חֵרְפוּנִי Pi. pf. 3 c.p.-1 c.s. sf. (357) *taunt me*
צוֹרְרָי Qal act.ptc. m.p.-1 c.s. sf. (צָרַר III 865) *my adversaries*
בְּאָמְרָם prep.-Qal inf.cstr.-3 m.p. sf. (אָמַר 55) *while they say*
אֵלַי prep.-1 c.s. sf. *to me*
כָּל־הַיּוֹם n.m.s. cstr. (481)-def.art.-n.m.s. (398) *continually*
אַיֵּה adv. (32) *where*
אֱלֹהֶיךָ n.m.p.-2 m.s. sf. (43) *your God*

42:12

מַה־תִּשְׁתּוֹחֲחִי interr. (552)-Hithpo'el impf. 2 f.s. (שָׁחַח 1005) *why are you cast down*
נַפְשִׁי n.f.s.-1 c.s. sf. (659) *O my soul*
וּמַה־תֶּהֱמִי conj.-interr. (552)-Qal impf. 2 f.s. (242 הָמָה) *and why are you disquieted*
עָלָי prep.-1 c.s. sf. paus. *within me*
הוֹחִילִי Hi. impv. 2 f.s. (יָחַל 403) *hope*
לֵאלֹהִים prep.-n.m.p. (43) *in God*
כִּי־עוֹד conj. (471)-adv. (728) *for again*
אוֹדֶנּוּ Hi. impf. 1 c.s.-3 m.s. sf. (יָדָה 392) *I shall praise him*
יְשׁוּעֹת פָּנַי n.f.p. cstr. (447)-n.m.p.-1 c.s. sf. (815) *help of my face*
וֵאלֹהָי conj.-n.m.p.-1 c.s. sf. paus. (43) *and my God*

43:1

שָׁפְטֵנִי Qal impv. 2 m.s.-1 c.s. sf. (שָׁפַט 1047) *vindicate me*
אֱלֹהִים n.m.p. (43) *O God*
וְרִיבָה conj.-Qal impv. 2 m.s.-vol.he (רִיב 936; GK 72s) *and defend*
רִיבִי n.m.s.-1 c.s. sf. (936) *my cause*
מִגּוֹי prep.-n.m.s. (156) *against a people*
לֹא־חָסִיד neg.-adj. (339) *ungodly*
מֵאִישׁ־ prep.-n.m.s. cstr. (35) *from a man of*
מִרְמָה n.f.s. (941) *deceit*
וְעַוְלָה conj.-n.f.s. (732) *and injustice*
תְפַלְּטֵנִי Pi. impf. 2 m.s.-1 c.s. sf. (פָּלַט 812) *deliver me*

43:2

כִּי־אַתָּה conj.-pers.pr. 2 m.s. (61) *for thou art*
אֱלֹהֵי n.m.p. cstr. (43) *the God of*
מָעוּזִּי n.m.s.-1 c.s. sf. (731) *my protection*
לָמָה interr. (552; GK 102,l) *why*
זְנַחְתָּנִי Qal pf. 2 m.s.-1 c.s. sf. (זָנַח I 276) *hast thou cast me off*
לָמָּה־קֹדֵר interr. (552)-Qal act.ptc. (קָדַר 871) *why mourning*
אֶתְהַלֵּךְ Hith. impf. 1 c.s. (הָלַךְ 229) *go I*
בְּלַחַץ prep.-n.m.s. cstr. (537) *because of the oppression of*
אוֹיֵב Qal act.ptc. (אָיַב 33) *the enemy*

43:3

שְׁלַח־ Qal impv. 2 m.s. (שָׁלַח 1018) *send out*
אוֹרְךָ n.m.s.-2 m.s. sf. (21) *thy light*
וַאֲמִתְּךָ conj.-n.f.s.-2 m.s. sf. (54) *and thy truth*
הֵמָּה pers.pr. 3 m.p. (241) *them*
יַנְחוּנִי Hi. impf. 3 m.p.-1 c.s. sf. (נָחָה 634) *let them lead me*
יְבִיאוּנִי Hi. impf. 3 m.p.-1 c.s. sf. (בּוֹא 97) *let them bring me*
אֶל־הַר־ prep.-n.m.s. cstr. (249) *to the mount of*
קָדְשְׁךָ n.m.s.-2 m.s. sf. (871) *thy holiness*
וְאֶל־מִשְׁכְּנוֹתֶיךָ conj.-prep.-n.m.p.-2 m.s. sf. (1015; GK 124b) *and to thy dwelling*

43:4

וְאָבוֹאָה conj.-Qal impf. 1 c.s.-vol.he (בּוֹא 97) *then I will go*
אֶל־מִזְבַּח prep.-n.m.s. cstr. (258) *to the altar of*
אֱלֹהִים n.m.p. (43) *God*
אֶל־אֵל prep.-n.m.s. (42) *to God*
שִׂמְחַת גִּילִי n.f.s. cstr. (970)-n.m.s.-1 c.s. sf. (I 162) *my exceeding joy*
וְאוֹדְךָ conj.-Hi. impf. 1 c.s.-2 m.s. sf. (יָדָה 392) *and I will praise thee*
בְכִנּוֹר prep.-n.m.s. (490) *with a lyre*
אֱלֹהִים n.m.p. (43) *O God*
אֱלֹהָי n.m.p.-1 c.s. sf. (43) *my God*

43:5

מַה־תִּשְׁתּוֹחֲחִי interr. (552)-Hithpo'el impf. 2 f.s. (שָׁחַח 1005) *why are you cast down*
נַפְשִׁי n.f.s.-1 c.s. sf. (659) *O my soul*
וּמַה־תֶּהֱמִי conj.-interr. (552)-Qal impf. 2 f.s. (242 הָמָה) *and why are you disquieted*
עָלָי prep.-1 c.s. sf. paus. *within me*
הוֹחִילִי Hi. impv. 2 f.s. (יָחַל 403) *hope*
לֵאלֹהִים prep.-n.m.p. (43) *in God*

כִּי־עוֹד conj. (471)-adv. (728) *for again*
אוֹדֶנּוּ Hi. impf. 1 c.s.-3 m.s. sf. (יָדָה 392) *I shall praise him*
יְשׁוּעֹת פָּנַי n.f.p. cstr. (447)-n.m.p.-1 c.s. sf. (815) *the help of my face*
וֵאלֹהָי conj.-n.m.p.-1 c.s. sf. paus. (43) *and my God*

44:1

לַמְנַצֵּחַ prep.-def.art.-Pi. ptc. (I 663) *to the choirmaster*
לִבְנֵי־קֹרַח prep.-n.m.p. cstr. (119)-pr.n. (901) *to the sons of Korah*
מַשְׂכִּיל n.m.s. (968) *a Maskil*

44:2

אֱלֹהִים n.m.p. (43) *O God*
בְּאָזְנֵינוּ prep.-n.f. du.-1 c.p. sf. (23) *with our ears*
שָׁמַעְנוּ Qal pf. 1 c.p. (שָׁמַע 1033) *we have heard*
אֲבוֹתֵינוּ n.m.p.-1 c.p. sf. (3) *our fathers*
סִפְּרוּ־ Pi. pf. 3 c.p. (סָפַר 707) *have told*
לָנוּ prep.-1 c.p. sf. *us*
פֹּעַל n.m.s. (821) *deed*
פָּעַלְתָּ Qal pf. 2 m.s. (פָּעַל 821) *thou didst perform*
בִימֵיהֶם prep.-n.m.p.-3 m.p. sf. (398) *in their days*
בִּימֵי prep.-n.m.p. cstr. (398) *in the days of*
קֶדֶם n.m.s. (869) *old*

44:3

אַתָּה pers.pr. 2 m.s. (61; GK 144m) *thou*
יָדְךָ n.f.s.-2 m.s. sf. (388) *with thy own hand*
גּוֹיִם n.m.p. (156) *nations*
הוֹרַשְׁתָּ Hi. pf. 2 m.s. (יָרַשׁ 439) *didst drive out*
וַתִּטָּעֵם consec.-Qal impf. 2 m.s.-3 m.p. sf. (נָטַע 642) *but them thou didst plant*
תָּרַע Hi. impf. 2 m.s. (רָעַע 949) *thou didst afflict*
לְאֻמִּים n.m.p. (522) *peoples*
וַתְּשַׁלְּחֵם consec.-Pi. impf. 2 m.s.-3 m.p. sf. (1018 שָׁלַח) *but them thou didst set free*

44:4

כִּי לֹא בְחַרְבָּם conj.-neg.-prep.-n.f.s.-3 m.p. sf. (352) *for not by their own sword*
יָרְשׁוּ Qal pf. 3 c.p. (ירשׁ 439) *did they win*
אָרֶץ n.f.s. paus. (75) *the land*
וּזְרוֹעָם conj.-n.f.s.-3 m.p. sf. (283) *nor did their own arm*
לֹא־הוֹשִׁיעָה neg.-Hi. pf. 3 f.s. (יָשַׁע 446) *give victory*

לָמוֹ prep.-3 m.p. sf. *them*
כִּי־יְמִינְךָ conj. (471)-n.f.s.-2 m.s. sf. (411) *but thy right hand*
וּזְרוֹעֲךָ conj.-n.f.s.-2 m.s. sf. (283) *and thy arm*
וְאוֹר conj.-n.m.s. cstr. (21) *and the light of*
פָּנֶיךָ n.m.p.-2 m.s. sf. (815) *thy countenance*
כִּי רְצִיתָם conj.-Qal pf. 2 m.s.-3 m.p. sf. (רָצָה 953) *for thou didst delight in them*

44:5

אַתָּה־הוּא pers.pr. 2 m.s. (61)-demons.adj. m.s. (214) *thou art he*
מַלְכִּי n.m.s.-1 c.s. sf. (I 572) *my King*
אֱלֹהִים n.m.p. (43) *God*
צַוֵּה Pi. impv. 2 m.s. (צָוָה 845) *ordain*
יְשׁוּעוֹת n.f.p. cstr. (447) *victories for*
יַעֲקֹב pr.n. (784) *Jacob*

44:6

בְּךָ prep.-2 m.s. sf. (GK 119o) *through thee*
צָרֵינוּ n.m.p.-1 c.p. sf. (III 865) *our foes*
נְנַגֵּחַ Pi. impf. 1 c.p. (נָגַח 618) *we push down*
בְּשִׁמְךָ prep.-n.m.s.-2 m.s. sf. (1027) *through thy name*
נָבוּס Qal impf. 1 c.p. (בּוּס 100) *we tread down*
קָמֵינוּ Qal act.ptc. m.p.-1 c.p. sf. (קוּם 877) *our assailants*

44:7

כִּי לֹא בְקַשְׁתִּי conj. (471)-neg.-n.f.s.-1 c.s. sf. (905) *for not in my bow*
אֶבְטָח Qal impf. 1 c.s. (בָּטַח 105) *do I trust*
וְחַרְבִּי conj.-n.f.s.-1 c.s. sf. (352) *nor my sword*
לֹא תוֹשִׁיעֵנִי neg.-Hi. impf. 3 f.s.-1 c.s. sf. (יָשַׁע 446) *can save me*

44:8

כִּי הוֹשַׁעְתָּנוּ conj.-Hi. pf. 2 m.s.-1 c.p. sf. (יָשַׁע 446) *but thou hast saved us*
מִצָּרֵינוּ prep.-n.m.p.-1 c.p. sf. (III 865) *from our foes*
וּמְשַׂנְאֵינוּ conj.-Pi. ptc. m.p.-1 c.p. sf. (שָׂנֵא 971) *and those who hate us*
הֱבִישׁוֹתָ Hi. pf. 2 m.s. (בּוֹשׁ 101) *thou hast put to confusion*

44:9

בֵּאלֹהִים prep.-n.m.p. (43) *in God*
הִלַּלְנוּ Pi. pf. 1 c.p. (הָלַל II 237) *we have boasted*
כָּל־הַיּוֹם n.m.s. cstr. (481)-def.art.-n.m.s. (398) *continually*
וְשִׁמְךָ conj.-n.m.s.-2 m.s. sf. (1027) *and thy name*
לְעוֹלָם prep.-n.m.s. (761) *for ever*
נוֹדֶה Hi. impf. 1 c.p. (יָדָה 392) *we will give thanks*
סֶלָה interj. (699) *Selah*

44:10

אַף־זָנַחְתָּ conj. (II 64)-Qal pf. 2 m.s. (זָנַח I 276) *yet thou hast cast off*
וַתַּכְלִימֵנוּ consec.-Hi. impf. 2 m.s.-1 c.p. sf. (כָּלַם 483) *and abased us*
וְלֹא־תֵצֵא conj.-neg.-Qal impf. 2 m.s. (יָצָא 422) *and hast not gone out*
בְּצִבְאוֹתֵינוּ prep.-n.m.p.-1 c.p. sf. (838) *with our armies*

44:11

תְּשִׁיבֵנוּ Hi. impf. 2 m.s.-1 c.p. sf. (שׁוּב 996) *thou hast made us turn*
אָחוֹר adv. (30) *back*
מִנִּי־צָר prep. (577; GK 90,3a)-n.m.s. paus. (III 865) *from the foe*
וּמְשַׂנְאֵינוּ conj.-Pi. ptc. m.p.-1 c.p. sf. (שָׂנֵא 971) *and those who hate us*
שָׁסוּ לָמוֹ Qal pf. 3 c.p. (שָׁסָה 1042)-prep.-3 m.p. sf. *have plundered for themselves*

44:12

תִּתְּנֵנוּ Qal impf. 2 m.s.-1 c.p. sf. (נָתַן 678) *thou hast made us*
כְּצֹאן prep.-n.f.s. (838) *like sheep*
מַאֲכָל n.m.s. (38) *food*
וּבַגּוֹיִם conj.-prep.-def.art.-n.m.p. (156) *and among the nations*
זֵרִיתָנוּ Pi. pf. 2 m.s.-1 c.p. sf. (זָרָה 279) *thou hast scattered us*

44:13

תִּמְכֹּר־ Qal impf. 2 m.s. (מָכַר 569) *thou hast sold*
עַמְּךָ n.m.s.-2 m.s. sf. (I 766) *thy people*
בְלֹא־הוֹן prep.-neg.-n.m.s. (223) *for a trifle* (lit. *for not wealth*)
וְלֹא־רִבִּיתָ conj.-neg.-Pi. pf. 2 m.s. (רָבָה I 915) *and thou hast not made great*
בִּמְחִירֵיהֶם prep.-n.m.p.-3 m.p. sf. (I 564) *with their price*

44:14

תְּשִׂימֵנוּ Qal impf. 2 m.s.-1 c.p. sf. (שׂוּם 962) *thou hast made us*
חֶרְפָּה n.f.s. (357) *a taunt*

לִשְׁכֵנֵינוּ prep.-adj. m.p.-1 c.p. sf. (1015) *of our neighbors*
לַעַג n.m.s. (541) *derision*
וָקֶלֶס conj.-n.m.s. (887) *and scorn*
לִסְבִיבוֹתֵינוּ prep.-subst. p.-1 c.p. sf. (686) *of those about us*

44:15

תְּשִׂימֵנוּ Qal impf. 2 m.s.-1 c.p. sf. (שׂוּם 962) *thou hast made us*
מָשָׁל n.m.s. (605) *a byword*
בַּגּוֹיִם prep.-def.art.-n.m.p. (156) *among the nations*
מְנוֹד־רֹאשׁ n.m.s. cstr. (627)-n.m.s. (910) *a shaking of the head*
בַּל־אֻמִּים rd. as prep.-n.m.p. (522 בַּלְאֻמִּים) *among the peoples*

44:16

כָּל־הַיּוֹם n.m.s. cstr. (481)-def.art.-n.m.s. (398) *all day long*
כְּלִמָּתִי n.f.s.-1 c.s. sf. (484) *my disgrace*
נֶגְדִּי prep.-1 c.s. sf. (617) *before me*
וּבֹשֶׁת conj.-n.f.s. (102) *and shame*
פָּנַי n.m.p.-1 c.s. sf. (815) *my face*
כִּסָּתְנִי Pi. pf. 3 f.s.-1 c.s. sf. (כָּסָה I 491) *has covered (me)*

44:17

מִקּוֹל prep.-n.m.s. cstr. (876) *at the words of*
מְחָרֵף Pi. ptc. (חָרַף 357) *the taunters*
וּמְגַדֵּף conj.-Pi. ptc. (154) *and revilers*
מִפְּנֵי prep.-n.m.p. cstr. (815) *at the sight of*
אוֹיֵב Qal act.ptc. (אָיַב 33) *the enemy*
וּמִתְנַקֵּם conj.-Hith. ptc. (נָקַם 667) *and the avenger*

44:18

כָּל־זֹאת n.m.s. cstr. (481)-demons.adj. f.s. (260) *all this*
בָּאַתְנוּ Qal pf. 3 f.s.-1 c.p. sf. (בּוֹא 97) *has come upon us*
וְלֹא שְׁכַחֲנוּךָ conj.-neg.-Qal pf. 1 c.p.-2 m.s. sf. (1013 שָׁכַח) *though we have not forgotten thee*
וְלֹא־שִׁקַּרְנוּ conj.-neg.-Pi. pf. 1 c.p. (שָׁקַר 1055; GK 156f) *or been false*
בִּבְרִיתֶךָ prep.-n.f.s.-2 m.s. sf. (136) *to thy covenant*

44:19

לֹא־נָסוֹג neg.-Ni. pf. 3 m.s. (סוּג I 690) *has not been turned*
אָחוֹר adv. (30) *back*
לִבֵּנוּ n.m.s.-1 c.p. sf. (524) *our heart*
וַתֵּט consec.-Qal impf. 3 f.s. (נָטָה 639) *nor have departed*
אֲשֻׁרֵינוּ n.f.p.-1 c.p. sf. (81) *our steps*
מִנִּי אָרְחֶךָ prep. (poetic 577)-n.m.s.-2 m.s. sf. (73) *from thy way*

44:20

כִּי דִכִּיתָנוּ conj.-Pi. pf. 2 m.s.-1 c.p. sf. (דָּכָה 194) *that thou shouldst have broken us*
בִּמְקוֹם prep.-n.m.s. cstr. (879) *in the place of*
תַּנִּים n.m.p. (1072) *jackals*
וַתְּכַס consec.-Pi. impf. 2 m.s. (כָּסָה 491) *and covered*
עָלֵינוּ prep.-1 c.p. sf. *us*
בְצַלְמָוֶת prep. (GK 119q)-n.m.s. (853) *with deep darkness*

44:21

אִם־שָׁכַחְנוּ hypoth.part. (49)-Qal pf. 1 c.p. (שָׁכַח 1013) *if we had forgotten*
שֵׁם n.m.s. cstr. (1027) *the name of*
אֱלֹהֵינוּ n.m.p.-1 c.p. sf. (43) *our God*
וַנִּפְרֹשׂ consec.-Qal impf. 1 c.p. (פָּרַשׂ 831) *or spread forth*
כַּפֵּינוּ n.f.p.-1 c.p. sf. (496) *our hands*
לְאֵל זָר prep.-n.m.s. (42)-Qal act.ptc. as adj. (זוּר I 266) *to a strange god*

44:22

הֲלֹא אֱלֹהִים interr.-neg.-n.m.p. (43) *would not God*
יַחֲקָר־ Qal impf. 3 m.s. (350) *discover*
זֹאת demons.adj. f.s. (260) *this*
כִּי־הוּא conj. (471)-pers.pr. 3 m.s. (214) *for he*
יֹדֵעַ Qal act.ptc. (יָדַע 393) *knows*
תַּעֲלֻמוֹת n.f.p. cstr. (761) *the secrets of*
לֵב n.m.s. (524) *the heart*

44:23

כִּי־עָלֶיךָ conj. (471)-prep.-2 m.s. sf. *nay, for thy sake*
הֹרַגְנוּ Pu. pf. 1 c.p. (הָרַג 246) *we are slain*
כָל־הַיּוֹם n.m.s. cstr. (481)-def.art.-n.m.s. (398) *all the day long*
נֶחְשַׁבְנוּ Ni. pf. 1 c.p. (חָשַׁב 362) *and accounted*
כְּצֹאן prep.-n.f.s. cstr. (838; GK 128q) *as sheep*
טִבְחָה n.f.s. (370) *for the slaughter*

44:24

עוּרָה Qal impv. 2 m.s.-vol.he (עוּר 734) *rouse thyself*

לָמָּה תִישַׁן interr. (552)-Qal impf. 2 m.s. (יָשֵׁן 445) *why sleepest thou*

אֲדֹנָי n.m.p.-1 c.s. sf. (10) *O Lord*

הָקִיצָה Hi. impv. 2 m.s.-vol.he (קִיץ I 884) *awake*

אַל־תִּזְנַח neg.-Qal impf. 2 m.s. (זָנַח I 276) *do not cast off*

לָנֶצַח prep.-n.m.s. paus. (664) *for ever*

44:25

לָמָּה־פָנֶיךָ interr. (552)-n.m.p.-2 m.s. sf. (815) *why thy face*

תַסְתִּיר Hi. impf. 2 m.s. (סָתַר 711) *dost thou hide*

תִּשְׁכַּח Qal impf. 2 m.s. (שָׁכַח 1013) *dost thou forget*

עָנְיֵנוּ n.m.s.-1 c.p. sf. (777) *our affliction*

וְלַחֲצֵנוּ conj.-n.m.s.-1 c.p. sf. (537) *and our oppression*

44:26

כִּי שָׁחָה conj. (471)-Qal pf. 3 f.s. (שׁוּחַ 1001; GK 67k) *for is bowed down*

לֶעָפָר prep.-def.art.-n.m.s. (779) *to the dust*

נַפְשֵׁנוּ n.f.s.-1 c.p. sf. (659) *our soul*

דָּבְקָה Qal pf. 3 f.s. (דָּבַק 179) *cleaves*

לָאָרֶץ prep.-def.art.-n.f.s. (75) *to the ground*

בִּטְנֵנוּ n.f.s.-1 c.p. sf. (105) *our body*

44:27

קוּמָה Qal impv. 2 m.s.-vol.he (קוּם 877; GK 72s) *rise up*

עֶזְרָתָה n.f.s. (I 740) *help*

לָּנוּ prep.-1 c.p. sf. *for us*

וּפְדֵנוּ conj.-Qal impv. 2 m.s.-1 c.p. sf. (פָּדָה 804) *and deliver us*

לְמַעַן חַסְדֶּךָ prep. (775)-n.m.s.-2 m.s. sf. (338) *for the sake of thy steadfast love*

45:1

לַמְנַצֵּחַ prep.-def.art.-Pi. ptc. (I 663) *to the choirmaster*

עַל־שֹׁשַׁנִּים prep.-n.m.p. (I 1004) *according to Lilies*

לִבְנֵי־קֹרַח prep.-n.m.p. cstr. (119)-pr.n. (901) *to the sons of Korah*

מַשְׂכִּיל n.m.s. (968) *a Maskil*

שִׁיר יְדִידֹת n.m.s. cstr. (1010)-adj. f.p. (391; GK 124e) *a love song*

45:2

רָחַשׁ Qal pf. 3 m.s. (935) *overflows (is astir)*

לִבִּי n.m.s.-1 c.s. sf. (524) *my heart*

דָּבָר טוֹב n.m.s. (182)-adj. m.s. (II 373) *with a goodly theme*

אֹמֵר אָנִי Qal act.ptc. (55)-pers.pr. 1 c.s. (58) *I address*

מַעֲשַׂי n.m.p.-1 c.s. sf. (795) *my verses*

לְמֶלֶךְ prep.-n.m.s. (I 572) *to the king*

לְשׁוֹנִי n.f.s.-1 c.s. sf. (546) *my tongue*

עֵט n.m.s. cstr. (741) *like a pen of*

סוֹפֵר מָהִיר n.m.s. (708)-adj. m.s. (555) *a ready scribe*

45:3

יָפְיָפִיתָ Pe'al'al pf. 2 m.s. (יָפָה 421; GK 55e) *you are the fairest*

מִבְּנֵי אָדָם prep.-n.m.p. cstr. (119)-n.m.s. (9) *of the sons of men*

הוּצַק Ho. pf. 3 m.s. (יָצַק 427) *is poured*

חֵן n.m.s. (336) *grace*

בְּשְׂפְתוֹתֶיךָ prep.-n.f.p.-2 m.s. sf. (973) *upon your lips*

עַל־כֵּן prep.-adv. (485) *therefore*

בֵּרַכְךָ Pi. pf. 3 m.s.-2 m.s. sf. (בָּרַךְ 138) *has blessed you*

אֱלֹהִים n.m.p. (43) *God*

לְעוֹלָם prep.-n.m.s. (761) *for ever*

45:4

חֲגוֹר־ Qal impv. 2 m.s. (חָגַר 291) *gird*

חַרְבְּךָ n.f.s.-2 m.s. sf. (352) *your sword*

עַל־יָרֵךְ prep.-n.f.s. (437) *upon thigh*

גִּבּוֹר adj. m.s. (150) *O mighty one*

הוֹדְךָ n.m.s.-2 m.s. sf. (I 217) *your glory*

וַהֲדָרֶךָ conj.-n.m.s.-2 m.s. sf. (214) *and your majesty*

45:5

וַהֲדָרְךָ conj.-n.m.s.-2 m.s. sf. (214) *and your majesty*

צְלַח Qal impv. 2 m.s. (צָלַח II 852) *be successful*

רְכַב Qal impv. 2 m.s. (רָכַב 938) *ride forth*

עַל־דְּבַר־ prep.-n.m.s. cstr. (182) *for the cause of*

אֱמֶת n.f.s. (54) *truth*

וְעַנְוָה־ conj. (GK 154aN)-n.f.s. (776) *and meekness*

צֶדֶק n.m.s. (841; GK 131c) *righteousness*

וְתוֹרְךָ conj.-Hi. impf. 3 f.s.-2 m.s. sf. (יָרָה 434) *let ... teach you*

נוֹרָאוֹת Ni. ptc. f.p. (יָרֵא 431) *dread deeds*
יְמִינֶךָ n.f.s.-2 m.s. sf. (411) *your right hand*

45:6
חִצֶּיךָ n.m.p.-2 m.s. sf. (346) *your arrows*
שְׁנוּנִים Qal pass.ptc. m.p. (שָׁנַן 1041) *are sharp*
עַמִּים n.m.p. (I 766) *peoples*
תַּחְתֶּיךָ prep.-2 m.s. sf. (1065) *under you*
יִפְּלוּ Qal impf. 3 m.p. (נָפַל 656; GK 15o,29oN) *fall*
בְּלֵב prep.-n.m.s. cstr. (524) *in the heart of*
אוֹיְבֵי Qal act.ptc. m.p. cstr. (אָיַב 33) *the enemies of*
הַמֶּלֶךְ def.art.-n.m.s. (I 572) *the king*

45:7
כִּסְאֲךָ n.m.s.-2 m.s. sf. (490) *your throne*
אֱלֹהִים n.m.p. (43; GK 128d) *O God*
עוֹלָם n.m.s. (761) *for ever*
וָעֶד conj.-n.m.s. paus. (I 723) *and ever*
שֵׁבֶט n.m.s. cstr. (986) *scepter of*
מִישֹׁר n.m.s. (449) *uprightness*
שֵׁבֶט v.supra *a scepter of*
מַלְכוּתֶךָ n.f.s.-2 m.s. sf. (574) *your royal power*

45:8
אָהַבְתָּ Qal pf. 2 m.s. (אָהַב 12) *you love*
צֶּדֶק n.m.s. (841) *righteousness*
וַתִּשְׂנָא consec.-Qal impf. 2 m.s. (שָׂנֵא 971) *and hate*
רֶשַׁע n.m.s. (957) *wickedness*
עַל־כֵּן prep.-adv. (485) *therefore*
מְשָׁחֲךָ Qal pf. 3 m.s.-2 m.s. sf. (מָשַׁח 602; GK 117ee) *has anointed you*
אֱלֹהִים n.m.p. (43) *God*
אֱלֹהֶיךָ n.m.p.-2 m.s. sf. (43) *your God*
שֶׁמֶן n.m.s. cstr. (1032) *oil of*
שָׂשׂוֹן n.m.s. (965) *gladness*
מֵחֲבֵרֶיךָ prep.-n.m.p.-2 m.s. sf. (288) *above your fellows*

45:9
מֹר־ n.m.s. (600) *myrrh*
וַאֲהָלוֹת conj. (GK 154aN)-n.m.p. (III 14) *and aloes*
קְצִיעוֹת n.f.p. (I 893) *and cassia*
כָּל־בִּגְדֹתֶיךָ n.m.s. cstr. (481)-n.m.p.-2 m.s. sf. (93) *all your robes*
מִן־הֵיכְלֵי prep.-n.m.p. cstr. (228) *from palaces of*
שֵׁן n.f.s. (I 1042) *ivory*
מִנִּי n.m.p. (rd. מִנִּים I 577) *stringed instruments*

שִׂמְּחוּךָ Pi. pf. 3 c.p.-2 m.s. sf. (שָׂמַח 970) *make you glad*

45:10
בְּנוֹת n.f.p. cstr. (I 123) *daughters of*
מְלָכִים n.m.p. (I 572) *kings*
בְּיִקְּרוֹתֶיךָ prep.-adj. f.p.-2 m.s. sf. (429; GK 20hN) *among your ladies of honor*
נִצְּבָה Ni. pf. 3 f.s. (נָצַב 662) *stands*
שֵׁגַל n.f.s. (993) *queen*
לִימִינְךָ prep.-n.f.s.-2 m.s. sf. (411) *at your right hand*
בְּכֶתֶם אוֹפִיר prep.-n.m.s. cstr. (508)-pr.n. (20) *in gold of Ophir*

45:11
שִׁמְעִי־ Qal impv. 2 f.s. (שָׁמַע 1033) *hear*
בַת n.f.s. (I 123) *O daughter*
וּרְאִי conj.-Qal impv. 2 f.s. (רָאָה 906) *and consider*
וְהַטִּי conj.-Hi. impv. 2 f.s. (נָטָה 639) *and incline*
אָזְנֵךְ n.f.s.-2 f.s. sf. (23) *your ear*
וְשִׁכְחִי conj.-Qal impv. 2 f.s. (שָׁכַח 1013) *and forget*
עַמֵּךְ n.m.s.-2 f.s. sf. (I 766) *your people*
וּבֵית conj.-n.m.s. cstr. (108) *and the house of*
אָבִיךְ n.m.s.-2 f.s. sf. paus. (3) *your father*

45:12
וְיִתְאָו conj.-Hith. impf. 3 m.s. apoc. (אָוָה I 16; GK 75bb,109h) *and will desire*
הַמֶּלֶךְ def.art.-n.m.s. (I 572) *the king*
יָפְיֵךְ n.m.s.-2 f.s. sf. (421) *your beauty*
כִּי־הוּא conj. (471)-pers.pr. 3 m.s. (214) *since he is*
אֲדֹנַיִךְ n.m.p.-2 f.s. sf. (10; GK 124i) *your lord*
וְהִשְׁתַּחֲוִי־ conj.-Hithpalel impv. 2 f.s. (שָׁחָה 1005) *bow*
לוֹ prep.-3 m.s. sf. *to him*

45:13
וּבַת־צֹר conj.-n.f.s. cstr. (I 123)-pr.n. (I 862) *and the daughter of Tyre*
בְּמִנְחָה prep.-n.f.s. (585) *with gifts*
פָּנַיִךְ n.m.p.-2 f.s. sf. (815) *your face*
יְחַלּוּ Pi. impf. 3 m.p. (חָלָה II 318) *will sue your favor*
עֲשִׁירֵי adj. m.p. cstr. (799) *the richest of*
עָם n.m.s. paus. (I 766) *people*

45:14

כָּל־כְּבוּדָּה n.m.s. cstr. (481)–adj. f.s. (458) *all glorious*

בַת־מֶלֶךְ n.f.s. cstr. (I 123)–n.m.s. (I 572) *the princess*

פְּנִימָה adv. (819) *in her chamber* (lit. *towards the inside*)

מִמִּשְׁבְּצוֹת זָהָב prep.–n.f.p. cstr. (990)–n.m.s. (262) *with gold-woven robes*

לְבוּשָׁהּ n.m.s.–3 f.s. sf. (528) *her raiment*

45:15

לִרְקָמוֹת prep.–n.f.p. (955) *in many-colored robes*

תּוּבַל Ho. impf. 3 f.s. (יָבַל 384) *she is led*

לַמֶּלֶךְ prep.–def.art.–n.m.s. (I 572) *to the king*

בְּתוּלוֹת n.f.p. (143) *virgins*

אַחֲרֶיהָ prep.–3 f.s. sf. (29) *after her*

רֵעוֹתֶיהָ n.f.p.–3 f.s. sf. (946) *her companions*

מוּבָאוֹת לָךְ Ho. ptc. f.p. (בּוֹא 97)–prep.–2 f.s. sf. *those brought to you*

45:16

תּוּבַלְנָה Ho. impf. 3 f.p. (יָבַל 384) *they are led along*

בִּשְׂמָחֹת prep.–n.f.p. (970) *with joy*

וָגִיל conj.–n.m.s. (I 162) *and gladness*

תְּבֹאֶינָה Qal impf. 3 f.p. (בּוֹא 97; GK 76g) *as they enter*

בְּהֵיכַל prep.–n.m.s. cstr. (228) *the palace of*

מֶלֶךְ n.m.s. (I 572) *the king*

45:17

תַּחַת prep. (1065) *instead of*

אֲבֹתֶיךָ n.m.p.–2 m.s. sf. (3) *your fathers*

יִהְיוּ Qal impf. 3 m.p. (הָיָה 224) *shall be*

בָנֶיךָ n.m.p.–2 m.p. sf. (119) *your sons*

תְּשִׁיתֵמוֹ Qal impf. 2 m.s.–3 m.p. sf. (שִׁית 1011) *you will make them*

לְשָׂרִים prep.–n.m.p. (978) *princes*

בְּכָל־הָאָרֶץ prep.–n.m.s. cstr. (481)–def.art.–n.f.s. (75) *in all the earth*

45:18

אַזְכִּירָה Hi. impf. 1 c.s.–coh.he (זָכַר 269) *I will cause to be celebrated*

שִׁמְךָ n.m.s.–2 m.s. sf. (1027) *your name*

בְּכָל־דֹּר prep.–n.m.s. cstr. (481)–n.m.s. (189) *in all generation*

וָדֹר conj.–v.supra (GK 123c) *and generation*

עַל־כֵּן prep.–adv. (485) *therefore*

עַמִּים n.m.p. (I 766) *the peoples*

יְהוֹדֻךָ Hi. impf. 3 m.p.–2 m.s. sf. (יָדָה 392; GK 53q) *will praise you*

לְעֹלָם prep.–n.m.s. (761) *for ever*

וָעֶד conj.–n.m.s. paus. (I 723) *and ever*

46:1

לַמְנַצֵּחַ prep.–def.art.–Pi. ptc. (I 663) *to the choirmaster*

לִבְנֵי־קֹרַח prep.–n.m.p. cstr. (119)–pr.n. (901) *to the Sons of Korah*

עַל־עֲלָמוֹת prep.–n.f.p. (761) *according to Alamoth*

שִׁיר n.m.s. (1010) *a song*

46:2

אֱלֹהִים n.m.p. (43) *God*

לָנוּ prep.–1 c.p. sf. *to us*

מַחֲסֶה n.m.s. (340) *refuge*

וָעֹז conj.–n.m.s. (738) *and strength*

עֶזְרָה n.f.s. (740) *help*

בְצָרוֹת prep.–n.f.p. (I 865) *in trouble*

נִמְצָא מְאֹד Ni. ptc. (מָצָא 592)–adv. (547) *well proved*

46:3

עַל־כֵּן prep.–adv. (485) *therefore*

לֹא־נִירָא neg.–Qal impf. 1 c.p. (יָרֵא 431) *we will not fear*

בְּהָמִיר prep.–Hi. inf.cstr. (מוּר 558; GK 115g) *though ... should change*

אָרֶץ n.f.s. paus. (75) *the earth*

וּבְמוֹט conj.–prep.–Qal inf.cstr. (מוֹט 556) *though shake*

הָרִים n.m.p. (249) *mountains*

בְּלֵב prep.–n.m.s. cstr. (524) *in the heart of*

יַמִּים n.m.p. (410) *the seas*

46:4

יֶהֱמוּ Qal impf. 3 m.p. (הָמָה 242) *though roar*

יֶחְמְרוּ Qal impf. 3 m.p. (חָמַר I 330) *and foam*

מֵימָיו n.m.p.–3 m.s. sf. (565; GK 132hN) *its waters*

יִרְעֲשׁוּ Qal impf. 3 m.p. (רָעַשׁ 950) *though tremble*

הָרִים n.m.p. (249) *mountains*

בְּגַאֲוָתוֹ prep.–n.f.s.–3 m.s. sf. (144) *with its tumult*

סֶלָה interj. (699) *Selah*

46:5

נָהָר n.m.s. (625) *a river*

פְּלָגָיו n.m.p.–3 m.s. sf. (I 811) *whose streams*

יְשַׂמְּחוּ Pi. impf. 3 m.p. (שָׂמַח 970) *make glad*
עִיר־ n.f.s. cstr. (746) *the city of*
אֱלֹהִים n.m.p. (43) *God*
קְדֹשׁ מִשְׁכְּנֵי adj. m.s. cstr. (872)–n.m.p. cstr. (1015; GK 124b) *the holy habitation of*
עֶלְיוֹן n.m.s. (II 751; GK 132c) *the Most High*

46:6

אֱלֹהִים n.m.p. (43) *God*
בְּקִרְבָּהּ prep.–n.m.s.–3 f.s. sf. (899) *in the midst of her*
בַּל־תִּמּוֹט neg. (115)–Ni. impf. 3 f.s. (מוֹט 556) *she shall not be moved*
יַעְזְרֶהָ Qal impf. 3 m.s.–3 f.s. sf. (עָזַר 740) *will help her*
אֱלֹהִים n.m.p. (43) *God*
לִפְנוֹת בֹּקֶר prep.–Qal inf.cstr. (פָּנָה 815)–n.m.s. (133) *right early* (lit. *to turn the morning)*

46:7

הָמוּ Qal pf. 3 c.p. (הָמָה 242) *rage*
גוֹיִם n.m.p. (156) *nations*
מָטוּ Qal pf. 3 c.p. (מוֹט 556) *totter*
מַמְלָכוֹת n.f.p. (575) *kingdoms*
נָתַן Qal pf. 3 m.s. (678) *he utters*
בְּקוֹלוֹ prep. (GK 119q)–n.m.s.–3 m.s. sf. (876) *his voice*
תָּמוּג Qal impf. 3 f.s. (מוּג 556) *melts*
אָרֶץ n.f.s. paus. *(75) the earth*

46:8

יהוה צְבָאוֹת pr.n. (217)–pr.n. (838) *Yahweh of hosts*
עִמָּנוּ prep.–1 c.p. sf. *with us*
מִשְׂגָּב־לָנוּ n.m.s. (960)–prep.–1 c.p. sf. *our refuge*
אֱלֹהֵי יַעֲקֹב n.m.p. cstr. (43)–pr.n. (784) *the God of Jacob*
סֶלָה interj. (699) *Selah*

46:9

לְכוּ־ Qal impv. 2 m.p. (הָלַךְ 229) *come*
חֲזוּ Qal impv. 2 m.p. (חָזָה 302) *behold*
מִפְעֲלוֹת n.f.p. cstr. (821) *the works of*
יהוה pr.n. (217) *Yahweh*
אֲשֶׁר־שָׂם rel. (81)–Qal pf. 3 m.s. (שׂוּם I 962) *how he has wrought*
שַׁמּוֹת n.f.p. (I 1031) *desolations*
בָּאָרֶץ prep.–def.art.–n.f.s. (75) *in the earth*

46:10

מַשְׁבִּית Hi. ptc. (שָׁבַת 991) *he makes cease*
מִלְחָמוֹת n.f.p. (536) *wars*
עַד־קְצֵה prep. (III 723)–n.m.s. cstr. (892) *to the ends of*
הָאָרֶץ def.art.–n.f.s. (75) *the earth*
קֶשֶׁת n.f.s. (905) *a bow*
יְשַׁבֵּר Pi. impf. 3 m.s. (שָׁבַר 990) *he breaks*
וְקִצֵּץ conj.–Pi. pf. 3 m.s. (קָצַץ 893) *and shatters*
חֲנִית n.f.s. (333) *a spear*
עֲגָלוֹת n.f.p. (722) *chariots*
יִשְׂרֹף Qal impf. 3 m.s. (שָׂרַף 976) *he burns*
בָּאֵשׁ prep.–def.art.–n.f.s. (77) *with fire*

46:11

הַרְפּוּ Hi. impv. 2 m.p. (רָפָה 951) *be still*
וּדְעוּ conj.–Qal impv. 2 m.p. (יָדַע 393) *and know*
כִּי־אָנֹכִי conj. (471)–pers.pr. 1 c.s. (59) *that I*
אֱלֹהִים n.m.p. (43) *God*
אָרוּם Qal impf. 1 c.s. (רוּם 926) *I am exalted*
בַּגּוֹיִם prep.–def.art.–n.m.p. (156) *among the nations*
אָרוּם v.supra *I am exalted*
בָּאָרֶץ prep.–def.art.–n.f.s. (75) *in the earth*

46:12

יהוה צְבָאוֹת pr.n. (217)–pr.n. (838) *Yahweh of hosts*
עִמָּנוּ prep.–1 c.p. sf. *with us*
מִשְׂגָּב־לָנוּ n.m.s. (I 960)–prep.–1 c.p. sf. *our refuge*
אֱלֹהֵי n.m.p. cstr. (43) *the God of*
יַעֲקֹב pr.n. (784) *Jacob*
סֶלָה interj. (699) *Selah*

47:1

לַמְנַצֵּחַ prep.–def.art.–Pi. ptc. (I 663) *to the choirmaster*
לִבְנֵי־קֹרַח prep.–n.m.p. cstr. (119)–pr.n. (901) *to the sons of Korah*
מִזְמוֹר n.m.s. (274) *a Psalm*

47:2

כָּל־הָעַמִּים n.m.s. cstr. (481)–def.art.–n.m.p. (I 766) *all peoples*
תִּקְעוּ־ Qal impv. 2 m.p. (תָּקַע 1075) *clap*
כָף n.f.s. (496) *your hands*
הָרִיעוּ Hi. impv. 2 m.p. (רוּעַ 929) *shout*
לֵאלֹהִים prep.–n.m.p. (43) *to God*
בְּקוֹל רִנָּה prep.–n.m.s. cstr. (876)–n.f.s. (943) *with loud songs of joy*

47:3

כִּי־יהוה conj. (471)–pr.n. (217) *for Yahweh*
עֶלְיוֹן n.m.s. (751) *the Most High*

נוֹרָא Ni. ptc. (יָרֵא 431) *is terrible*
מֶלֶךְ גָּדוֹל n.m.s. (I 572)–adj. m.s. (152) *a great king*
עַל־כָּל־הָאָרֶץ prep.–n.m.s. cstr. (481)–def.art. –n.f.s. (75) *over all the earth*

47:4

יַדְבֵּר Hi. impf. 3 m.s. apoc. (דָּבַר 180) *he subdued*
עַמִּים n.m.p. (I 766) *peoples*
תַּחְתֵּינוּ prep.–1 c.p. sf. (1065) *under us*
וּלְאֻמִּים conj.–n.m.p. (522) *and nations*
תַּחַת רַגְלֵינוּ prep. (1065)–n.f. du.–1 c.p. sf. (919) *under our feet*

47:5

יִבְחַר־ Qal impf. 3 m.s. (בָּחַר 103) *he chose*
לָנוּ prep.–1 c.p. sf. *for us*
אֶת־נַחֲלָתֵנוּ dir.obj.–n.f.s.–1 c.p. sf. (635) *our heritage*
אֶת גְּאוֹן יַעֲקֹב dir.obj.–n.m.s. cstr. (144)–pr.n. (784) *the pride of Jacob*
אֲשֶׁר־אָהֵב rel. (81)–Qal pf. 3 m.s. (12) *whom he loves*
סֶלָה interj. (699) *Selah*

47:6

עָלָה Qal pf. 3 m.s. (748) *has gone up*
אֱלֹהִים n.m.p. (43) *God*
בִּתְרוּעָה prep.–n.f.s. (929) *with a shout*
יהוה pr.n. (217) *Yahweh*
בְּקוֹל prep.–n.m.s. cstr. (876) *with sound of*
שׁוֹפָר n.m.s. (1051) *a trumpet*

47:7

זַמְּרוּ Pi. impv. 2 m.p. (I 274) *sing praises*
אֱלֹהִים n.m.p. (43) *to God*
זַמֵּרוּ Pi. impv. 2 m.p. paus. I 274) *sing praises*
זַמְּרוּ v.supra *sing praises*
לְמַלְכֵּנוּ prep.–n.m.s.–1 c.p. sf. (I 572) *to our King*
זַמֵּרוּ v.supra *sing praises*

47:8

כִּי מֶלֶךְ conj. (471)–n.m.s. cstr. (I 572) *for the king of*
כָּל־הָאָרֶץ n.m.s. cstr. (481)–def.art.–n.f.s. (75) *all the earth*
אֱלֹהִים n.m.p. (43) *God*
זַמְּרוּ Pi. impv. 2 m.p. (I 274) *sing praises*
מַשְׂכִּיל n.m.s. (968) *a maskil*

47:9

מָלַךְ Qal pf. 3 m.s. (573) *reigns*
אֱלֹהִים n.m.p. (43) *God*
עַל־גּוֹיִם prep.–n.m.p. (156) *over nations*
אֱלֹהִים v.supra *God*
יָשַׁב Qal pf. 3 m.s. (442) *sits*
עַל־כִּסֵּא prep.–n.m.s. cstr. (490) *on the throne of*
קָדְשׁוֹ n.m.s.–3 m.s. sf. (871) *his holiness*

47:10

נְדִיבֵי adj. m.p. cstr. (622) *princes of*
עַמִּים n.m.p. (I 766) *peoples*
נֶאֱסָפוּ Ni. pf. 3 c.p. paus. (אָסַף 62) *gather*
עַם n.m.s. cstr. (I 766) *people of*
אֱלֹהֵי n.m.p. cstr. (43) *the God of*
אַבְרָהָם pr.n. (4) *Abraham*
כִּי לֵאלֹהִים conj. (471)–prep.–n.m.p. (43) *for to God*
מָגִנֵּי־אֶרֶץ n.m.p. cstr. (171)–n.f.s. (75) *shields of earth*
מְאֹד נַעֲלָה adv. (547)–Ni. pf. 3 m.s. (עָלָה 748) *he is highly exalted*

48:1

שִׁיר n.m.s. (1010) *a song*
מִזְמוֹר n.m.s. (274) *a Psalm*
לִבְנֵי־קֹרַח prep.–n.m.p. cstr. (119)–pr.n. (901) *to the sons of Korah*

48:2

גָּדוֹל adj. m.s. (152) *great*
יהוה pr.n. (217) *Yahweh*
וּמְהֻלָּל conj.–Pu. ptc. (הָלַל II 237) *and to be praised*
מְאֹד adv. (547) *greatly*
בְּעִיר prep.–n.f.s. cstr. (746) *in the city of*
אֱלֹהֵינוּ n.m.p.–1 c.p. sf. (43) *our God*
הַר־ n.m.s. cstr. (249) *the mountain of*
קָדְשׁוֹ n.m.s.–3 m.s. sf. (871) *his holiness*

48:3

יְפֵה נוֹף adj. m.s. cstr. (421)–n.m.s. (632) *beautiful in elevation*
מְשׂוֹשׂ n.m.s. cstr. (965) *the joy of*
כָּל־הָאָרֶץ n.m.s. cstr. (481)–def.art.–n.f.s. (75) *all the earth*
הַר־צִיּוֹן n.m.s. cstr. (249)–pr.n. (851) *Mount Zion*
יַרְכְּתֵי צָפוֹן n.f. du. cstr. (438)–n.m.s. (860) *in the far north*
קִרְיַת n.f.s. cstr. (900) *city of*
מֶלֶךְ רָב n.m.s. (I 572)–adj. m.s. (I 912) *a great king*

48:4

אֱלֹהִים n.m.p. (43) *God*

בְּאַרְמְנוֹתֶיהָ prep.-n.f.p.-3 f.s. sf. (74) *within her citadels*

נוֹדַע Ni. pf. 3 m.s. (יָדַע 393) *has shown himself*

לְמִשְׂגָּב prep.-n.m.s. (I 960) *a sure defense*

48:5

כִּי־הִנֵּה conj. (471)-demons.part. (243) *for lo*

הַמְּלָכִים def.art.-n.m.p. (I 572) *the kings*

נוֹעֲדוּ Ni. pf. 3 c.p. (יָעַד 416) *assembled*

עָבְרוּ Qal pf. 3 c.p. (עָבַר 716) *they came on*

יַחְדָּו adv. (403) *together*

48:6

הֵמָּה רָאוּ pers.pr. 3 m.p. (241)-Qal pf. 3 c.p. (906 רָאָה) *they saw*

כֵּן תָּמָהוּ adv. (485; GK 164bN)-Qal pf. 3 c.p. paus. (תָּמַהּ 1069) *thus they were astounded*

נִבְהֲלוּ Ni. pf. 3 c.p. (בָּהַל 96) *they were in panic*

נֶחְפָּזוּ Ni. pf. 3 c.p. paus. (חָפַז 342) *they took to flight*

48:7

רְעָדָה n.f.s. (944) *trembling*

אֲחָזָתַם Qal pf. 3 f.s.-3 m.p. sf. (אָחַז 28) *took hold of them*

שָׁם adv. (1027) *there*

חִיל n.m.s. (297) *anguish*

כַּיּוֹלֵדָה prep.-def.art.-Qal act.ptc. f.s. (יָלַד 408) *as of a woman in travail*

48:8

בְּרוּחַ קָדִים prep.-n.f.s. cstr. (924)-n.m.s. (870) *by the east wind*

תְּשַׁבֵּר Pi. impf. 2 m.s. (שָׁבַר 990) *thou didst shatter*

אֳנִיּוֹת n.f.p. cstr. (58) *the ships of*

תַּרְשִׁישׁ pr.n. (II 1076) *Tarshish*

48:9

כַּאֲשֶׁר שָׁמַעְנוּ prep.-rel. (81)-Qal pf. 1 c.p. (שָׁמַע 1033) *as we have heard*

כֵּן רָאִינוּ adv. (485)-Qal pf. 1 c.p. (רָאָה 906) *so have we seen*

בְּעִיר־ prep.-n.f.s. cstr. (746) *in the city of*

יהוה צְבָאוֹת pr.n. (217)-pr.n. (838) *Yahweh of hosts*

בְּעִיר v.supra *in the city of*

אֱלֹהֵינוּ n.m.p.-1 c.p. sf. (43) *our God*

אֱלֹהִים n.m.p. (43) *God*

יְכוֹנְנֶהָ Polel impf. 3 m.s.-3 f.s. sf. (כּוּן I 465) *establishes it*

עַד־עוֹלָם prep. (III 723)-n.m.s. (761) *for ever*

סֶלָה interj. (699) *Selah*

48:10

דִּמִּינוּ Pi. pf. 1 c.p. (דָּמָה I 197) *we have thought*

אֱלֹהִים n.m.p. (43) *O God*

חַסְדֶּךָ n.m.s.-2 m.s. sf. (338) *on thy steadfast love*

בְּקֶרֶב prep.-n.m.s. cstr. (899) *in the midst of*

הֵיכָלֶךָ n.m.s.-2 m.s. sf. paus. (228) *thy temple*

48:11

כְּשִׁמְךָ prep.-n.m.s.-2 m.s. sf. (1027) *as thy name*

אֱלֹהִים n.m.p. (43) *O God*

כֵּן תְּהִלָּתְךָ adv. (485)-n.f.s.-2 m.s. sf. (239) *so thy praise*

עַל־קַצְוֵי־ prep.-n.m.p. cstr. (892; GK 93x) *to the ends of*

אֶרֶץ n.f.s. (75; GK 93g) *the earth*

צֶדֶק n.m.s. (841) *with victory*

מָלְאָה Qal pf. 3 f.s. (מָלֵא 569) *is filled*

יְמִינֶךָ n.f.s.-2 m.s. sf. (411) *thy right hand*

48:12

יִשְׂמַח Qal impf. 3 m.s. (שָׂמַח 970) *let be glad*

הַר־צִיּוֹן n.m.s. cstr. (249)-pr.n. (851) *Mount Zion*

תָּגֵלְנָה Qal impf. 3 f.p. (גִּיל 162) *let rejoice*

בְּנוֹת יְהוּדָה n.f.p. cstr. (I 123)-pr.n. (397) *the daughters of Judah*

לְמַעַן מִשְׁפָּטֶיךָ prep. (775)-n.m.p.-2 m.s. sf. (1048) *because of thy judgments*

48:13

סֹבּוּ Qal impv. 2 m.p. (סָבַב 685) *walk about*

צִיּוֹן pr.n. (851) *Zion*

וְהַקִּיפוּהָ conj.-Hi. impv. 2 m.p.-3 f.s. sf. (נָקַף II 668) *go round about her*

סִפְרוּ Qal impv. 2 m.p. (סָפַר 707) *number*

מִגְדָּלֶיהָ n.m.p.-3 f.s. sf. (153) *her towers*

48:14

שִׁיתוּ לִבְּכֶם Qal impv. 2 m.p. (שִׁית 1011) -n.m.s.-2 m.p. sf. (524) *consider well*

לְחֵילָה prep.-n.m.s.-3 f.s. sf. (298) *her ramparts*

פַּסְּגוּ Pi. impv. 2 m.p. (פָּסַג 819) *pass through*

אַרְמְנוֹתֶיהָ n.m.p.-3 f.s. sf. (74) *her citadels*

לְמַעַן תְּסַפְּרוּ prep. (775)-Pi. impf. 2 m.p. (סָפַר 707) *that you may tell*

לְדוֹר אַחֲרוֹן prep.-n.m.s. (189)-adj. m.s. (30) *the next generation*

48:15

כִּי זֶה conj. (471)–demons.adj. m.s. (260) *that this*
אֱלֹהִים n.m.p. (43; GK 126aa) *God*
אֱלֹהֵינוּ n.m.p.–1 c.p. sf. (43) *our God*
עוֹלָם n.m.s. (761) *for ever*
וָעֶד conj.–n.m.s. paus. (I 723) *and ever*
הוּא יְנַהֲגֵנוּ pers.pr. 3 m.s. (214)–Pi. impf. 3 m.s.–1 c.p. sf. (נָהַג 624) *he will be our guide*
עַל־מוּת prep.–Qal inf.cstr. (559) *until death*

49:1

לַמְנַצֵּחַ prep.–def.art.–Pi. ptc. (I 663) *to the choirmaster*
לִבְנֵי־קֹרַח prep.–n.m.p. cstr. (119)–pr.n. (901) *to the sons of Korah*
מִזְמוֹר n.m.s. (274) *a Psalm*

49:2

שִׁמְעוּ־זֹאת Qal impv. 2 m.p. (1033)–demons.adj. f.s. (260) *hear this*
כָּל־הָעַמִּים n.m.s. cstr. (481)–def.art.–n.m.p. (I 766) *all peoples*
הַאֲזִינוּ Hi. impv. 2 m.p. (אָזַן 24) *give ear*
כָּל־יֹשְׁבֵי n.m.s. cstr. (481)–Qal act.ptc. m.p. cstr. (442 יָשַׁב) *all inhabitants of*
חָלֶד n.m.s. paus. (317) *the world*

49:3

גַּם־בְּנֵי אָדָם adv. (168)–n.m.p. cstr. (119)–n.m.s. (9) *both high*
גַּם־בְּנֵי־אִישׁ v.supra–v.supra–n.m.s. (35) *and low*
יַחַד adv. (403) *together*
עָשִׁיר adj. (799) *rich*
וְאֶבְיוֹן conj.–adj. (2) *and poor*

49:4

פִּי n.m.s.–1 c.s. sf. (804) *my mouth*
יְדַבֵּר Pi. impf. 3 m.s. (180) *shall speak*
חָכְמוֹת n.f.p. (315) *wisdom*
וְהָגוּת conj.–n.f.s. cstr. (212) *and the meditation of*
לִבִּי n.m.s.–1 c.s. sf. (524) *my heart*
תְבוּנוֹת n.f.p. (108) *understanding*

49:5

אַטֶּה Hi. impf. 1 c.s. (נָטָה 639) *I will incline*
לְמָשָׁל prep.–n.m.s. (605) *to a proverb*
אָזְנִי n.f.s.–1 c.s. sf. (23) *my ear*
אֶפְתַּח Qal impf. 1 c.s. (פָּתַח I 834) *I will solve*
בְּכִנּוֹר prep.–n.m.s. (490) *to the music of the lyre*
חִידָתִי n.f.s.–1 c.s. sf. (295) *my riddle*

49:6

לָמָּה אִירָא prep.–interr. (552; GK 102,l)–Qal impf. 1 c.s. (יָרֵא 431) *why should I fear*
בִּימֵי רָע prep.–n.m.p. cstr. (398)–n.m.s. (948) *in times of trouble*
עֲוֹן n.m.s. cstr. (730) *the iniquity of*
עֲקֵבַי vb.adj. m.p.–1 c.s. sf. (784) *my persecutors*
יְסוּבֵּנִי Qal impf. 3 m.s.–1 c.s. sf. (סָבַב 685) *surrounds me*

49:7

הַבֹּטְחִים def.art.–Qal act.ptc. m.p. (בָּטַח 105; GK 126b) *men who trust*
עַל־חֵילָם prep.–n.m.s.–3 m.p. sf. (298) *in their wealth*
וּבְרֹב conj.–prep.–n.m.s. cstr. (913) *and of the abundance of*
עָשְׁרָם n.m.s.–3 m.p. sf. (799) *their riches*
יִתְהַלָּלוּ Hith. impf. 3 m.p. paus. (הָלַל II 237) *boast*

49:8

אָח n.m.s. (26; some rd. אַךְ adv. 36 = *truly*) *a brother*
לֹא־פָדֹה יִפְדֶּה neg.–Qal inf.abs. (פָּדָה 804; GK 113v)–Qal impf. 3 m.s. (804) *cannot ransom*
אִישׁ n.m.s. (35) *a man*
לֹא־יִתֵּן neg.–Qal impf. 3 m.s. (נָתַן 678) *or not give*
לֵאלֹהִים prep.–n.m.p. (43) *to God*
כָּפְרוֹ n.m.s.–3 m.s. sf. (I 497) *the price of his life*

49:9

וְיֵקַר conj.–Qal impf. 3 m.s. (יָקַר 429) *for is costly*
פִּדְיוֹן n.m.s. cstr. (804) *the ransom of*
נַפְשָׁם n.f.s.–3 m.p. sf. (659) *their life*
וְחָדַל conj.–Qal pf. 3 m.s. (292) *and he ceases* (*or it ceases*)
לְעוֹלָם prep.–n.m.s. (761) *for ever*

49:10

וִיחִי conj.–Qal impf. 3 m.s. apoc. (חָיָה 310) *that he should continue to live*
עוֹד לָנֶצַח adv. (728)–prep.–n.m.s. (664) *for ever*
לֹא יִרְאֶה neg.–Qal impf. 3 m.s. (רָאָה 906) *and never see*
הַשָּׁחַת def.art.–n.f.s. paus. (1001) *the Pit*

49:11

כִּי יִרְאֶה conj. (471)-Qal impf. 3 m.s. (רָאָה 906) *yea, he shall see*

חֲכָמִים adj. m.p. (314) *the wise*

יָמוּתוּ Qal impf. 3 m.p. (מוּת 559) *die*

יַחַד adv. (403) *alike*

כְּסִיל n.m.s. (493) *the fool*

וָבַעַל conj.-n.m.s. (129) *and the stupid*

יֹאבֵדוּ Qal impf. 3 m.p. paus. (אָבַד 1) *must perish*

וְעָזְבוּ conj.-Qal pf. 3 c.p. (עָזַב I 736) *and leave*

לַאֲחֵרִים prep.-adj. m.p. (29) *to others*

חֵילָם n.m.s.-3 m.p. sf. (298) *their wealth*

49:12

קִרְבָּם n.m.s.-3 m.p. sf. (899) *their inward thought* (some rd. קִבְרָם 868; *their graves)*

בָּתֵּימוֹ n.m.p.-3 m.p. sf. (108) *their homes*

לְעוֹלָם prep.-n.m.s. (761) *for ever*

מִשְׁכְּנֹתָם n.m.p.-3 m.p. sf. (1015) *their dwelling places*

לְדֹר וָדֹר prep.-n.m.s. (189)-conj.-v.supra *to all generations*

קָרְאוּ Qal pf. 3 c.p. (קָרָא 894) *though they named (called)*

בִשְׁמוֹתָם prep.-n.m.p.-3 m.p. sf. (1027) *(by their names)*

עֲלֵי אֲדָמוֹת prep. (752)-n.f.p. (9) *upon lands*

49:13

וְאָדָם conj.-n.m.s. (9) *man*

בִּיקָר prep.-n.m.s. (430) *in his pomp*

בַּל־יָלִין neg. (115)-Qal impf. 3 m.s. (לוּן I 533) *cannot abide*

נִמְשַׁל Ni. pf. 3 m.s. (מָשַׁל I 605) *he is like*

כַּבְּהֵמוֹת prep.-def.art.-n.f.p. (96) *the beasts*

נִדְמוּ Ni. pf. 3 c.p. (דָּמָה II 198) *that perish*

49:14

זֶה demons.adj. m.s. (260) *this*

דַרְכָּם n.m.s.-3 m.p. sf. (202) *their fate*

כֵּסֶל n.m.s. (492; GK 155e) *stupidity*

לָמוֹ prep.-3 m.p. sf. *to them*

וְאַחֲרֵיהֶם conj.-prep.-3 m.p. sf. (29) *and after them*

בְּפִיהֶם prep.-n.m.s.-3 m.p. sf. (804) *with their portion*

יִרְצוּ Qal impf. 3 m.p. (רָצָה 953) *they are pleased*

סֶלָה interj. (699) *Selah*

49:15

כַּצֹּאן prep.-def.art.-n.f.s. (838) *like sheep*

לִשְׁאוֹל prep.-n.f.s. (982; GK 10g) *for Sheol*

שַׁתּוּ Qal pf. 3 c.p. (שִׁית 1011; GK 67ee) *they are appointed*

מָוֶת n.m.s. (560) *death*

יִרְעֵם Qal impf. 3 m.s.-3 m.p. sf. (רָעָה I 944) *will shepherd them*

וַיִּרְדּוּ consec.-Qal impf. 3 m.p. (רָדָה I 921) *and shall have dominion*

בָם prep.-3 m.p. sf. *over them*

יְשָׁרִים adj. m.p. (449) *the upright*

לַבֹּקֶר prep.-def.art.-n.m.s. (133) *in the morning*

וְצִירָם conj.-n.m.s.-3 m.p. sf. (I 849) *and their form*

לְבַלּוֹת prep.-Pi. inf.cstr. (בָּלָה 115; GK 114kN) *shall waste away*

שְׁאוֹל n.f.s. (982) *Sheol*

מִזְּבֻל לוֹ prep.-n.m.s. (I 259)-prep.-3 m.s. sf. *their home*

49:16

אַךְ־אֱלֹהִים adv. (36)-n.m.p. (43) *but God*

יִפְדֶּה Qal impf. 3 m.s. (פָּדָה 804) *will ransom*

נַפְשִׁי n.f.s.-1 c.s. sf. (659) *my soul*

מִיַּד־ prep.-n.f.s. cstr. (388) *from the power of*

שְׁאוֹל n.f.s. (982) *Sheol*

כִּי יִקָּחֵנִי conj.-Qal impf. 3 m.s.-1 c.s. sf. (לָקַח 542) *for he will receive me*

סֶלָה interj. (699) *Selah*

49:17

אַל־תִּירָא neg.-Qal impf. 2 m.s. (יָרֵא 431) *be not afraid*

כִּי־יַעֲשִׁר conj. (471)-Hi. impf. 3 m.s. (עָשַׁר 799) *when becomes rich*

אִישׁ n.m.s. (35) *one*

כִּי־יִרְבֶּה conj. (471)-Qal impf. 3 m.s. (רָבָה I 915) *when increases*

כְּבוֹד בֵּיתוֹ n.m.s. cstr. (II 458)-n.m.s.-3 m.s. sf. (108) *the glory of his house*

49:18

כִּי לֹא בְמוֹתוֹ conj. (471)-neg.-prep.-n.m.s.-3 m.s. sf. (560) *for not in his dying*

יִקַּח Qal impf. 3 m.s. (לָקַח 542) *he will carry away*

הַכֹּל def.art.-n.m.s. (481) *the whole*

לֹא־יֵרֵד neg.-Qal impf. 3 m.s. (יָרַד 432) *will not go down*

אַחֲרָיו prep.-3 m.s. sf. (29) *after him*

כְּבוֹדוֹ n.m.s.-3 m.s. sf. (II 458) *his glory*

49:19

כִּי־נַפְשׁוֹ conj. (471)–n.f.s.–3 m.s. sf. (659) *though himself*

בְּחַיָּיו prep.–adj. m.p.–3 m.s. sf. (313) *while he lives*

יְבָרֵךְ Pi. impf. 3 m.s. (בָּרַךְ 138) *he counts happy*

וְיוֹדֻךָ conj.–Hi. impf. 3 m.p.–2 m.s. sf. (יָדָה 392) *and though they praise you*

כִּי־תֵיטִיב לָךְ conj. (471)–Hi. impf. 2 m.s. (יָטַב 405)–prep.–2 m.s. sf. paus. *when you do well for yourself*

49:20

תָּבוֹא Qal impf. 2 m.s. (בּוֹא 97) *you will go*

עַד־דּוֹר prep. (III 723)–n.m.s. (189) *to the generation of*

אֲבוֹתָיו n.m.p.–3 m.s. sf. (3) *his fathers*

עַד־נֵצַח v.supra–n.m.s. (664) *for ever*

לֹא־יִרְאוּ neg.–Qal impf. 3 m.p. (רָאָה 906) *they will not see*

אוֹר n.m.s. (21) *light*

49:21

אָדָם n.m.s. (9) *man*

בִּיקָר prep.–n.m.s. (430) *in his pomp*

וְלֹא יָבִין conj.–neg.–Qal impf. 3 m.s. (בִּין 106) *and he will not discern*

נִמְשַׁל Ni. pf. 3 m.s. (I 605) *he is like*

כַּבְּהֵמוֹת prep.–def.art.–n.f.p. (96) *the beasts*

נִדְמוּ Ni. pf. 3 c.p. (דָּמָה II 198) *that perish*

50:1

מִזְמוֹר n.m.s. (274) *a Psalm*

לְאָסָף prep.–pr.n. (63) *to Asaph*

אֵל n.m.s. (42) *God*

אֱלֹהִים n.m.p. (43) *God*

יהוה pr.n. (217) *Yahweh*

דִּבֶּר Pi. pf. 3 m.s. (180) *speaks*

וַיִּקְרָא־ consec.–Qal impf. 3 m.s. (קָרָא 894) *and summons*

אָרֶץ n.f.s. paus. (75) *the earth*

מִמִּזְרַח־שֶׁמֶשׁ prep.–n.m.s. cstr. (280)–n.f.s. (1039) *from the rising of the sun*

עַד־מְבֹאוֹ prep. (III 723)–n.m.s.–3 m.s. sf. (99) *to its setting*

50:2

מִצִּיּוֹן prep.–pr.n. (851) *out of Zion*

מִכְלַל־יֹפִי n.m.s. cstr. (483)–n.m.s. (421) *the perfection of beauty*

אֱלֹהִים n.m.p. (43) *God*

הוֹפִיעַ Hi. pf. 3 m.s. (יָפַע 422) *shines forth*

50:3

יָבֹא Qal impf. 3 m.s. (בּוֹא 97) *comes*

אֱלֹהֵינוּ n.m.p.–1 c.p. sf. (43) *our God*

וְאַל־יֶחֱרַשׁ conj.–neg. (GK 109e)–Qal impf. 3 m.s. (II 361) *he does not keep silence*

אֵשׁ־לְפָנָיו n.f.s. (77)–prep.–n.m.p.–3 m.s. sf. (815) *fire before him*

תֹּאכֵל Qal impf. 3 f.s. (אָכַל 37) *devours*

וּסְבִיבָיו conj.–subst. m.p.–3 m.s. sf. (686) *round about him*

נִשְׂעֲרָה Ni. pf. 3 f.s. (שָׂעַר 973; GK 144c) *it is tempestuous*

מְאֹד adv. (547) *exceedingly*

50:4

יִקְרָא Qal impf. 3 m.s. (894) *he calls*

אֶל־הַשָּׁמַיִם prep.–def.art.–n.m. du. (1029) *to the heavens*

מֵעָל prep.–prep. (758) *above*

וְאֶל־הָאָרֶץ conj.–prep.–def.art.–n.f.s. (75) *and to the earth*

לָדִין prep. (GK 115b)–Qal inf.cstr. (192) *that he may judge*

עַמּוֹ n.m.s.–3 m.s. sf. (I 766) *his people*

50:5

אִסְפוּ־ Qal impv. 2 m.p. (אָסַף 62) *gather*

לִי prep.–1 c.s. sf. *to me*

חֲסִידָי adj. m.p.–1 c.s. sf. paus. (339) *my faithful ones*

כֹּרְתֵי Qal act.ptc. m.p. cstr. (503) *who made*

בְרִיתִי n.f.s.–1 c.s. sf. (136) *my covenant*

עֲלֵי־זָבַח prep. (752)–n.m.s. paus. (257) *by sacrifice*

50:6

וַיַּגִּידוּ consec.–Hi. impf. 3 m.p. (נָגַד 616) *and declare*

שָׁמַיִם n.m. du. (1029) *heavens*

צִדְקוֹ n.m.s.–3 m.s. sf. (841) *his righteousness*

כִּי־אֱלֹהִים conj. (471)–n.m.p. (43) *for God*

שֹׁפֵט Qal act.ptc. (1047) *is judge*

הוּא pers.pr. 3 m.s. (214) *himself*

סֶלָה interj. (699) *Selah*

50:7

שִׁמְעָה Qal impv. 2 m.s.–vol.he (1033) *hear*

עַמִּי n.m.s.–1 c.s. sf. (I 766) *O my people*

וַאֲדַבֵּרָה conj.–Pi. impf. 1 c.s.–vol.he (דָּבַר 180) *and I will speak*

יִשְׂרָאֵל pr.n. (975) *O Israel*

וְאָעִידָה conj.-Hi. impf. 1 c.s.-vol.he (עוּד 729) *I will testify*

בָּךְ prep.-2 m.s. sf. paus. *against you*

אֱלֹהִים n.m.p. (43) *God*

אֱלֹהֶיךָ n.m.p.-2 m.s. sf. (43) *your God*

אָנֹכִי pers.pr. 1 c.s. (59) *I am*

50:8

לֹא עַל־זְבָחֶיךָ neg.-prep.-n.m.p.-2 m.s. sf. (256) *not for your sacrifices*

אוֹכִיחֶךָ Hi. impf. 1 c.s.-2 m.s. sf. (יָכַח 406) *I do reprove you*

וְעוֹלֹתֶיךָ conj.-n.f.p.-2 m.s. sf. (750) *and your burnt offerings*

לְנֶגְדִּי prep.-prep.-1 c.s. sf. (617) *before me*

תָמִיד n.m.s. (556) *continually*

50:9

לֹא־אֶקַּח neg.-Qal impf. 1 c.s. (לָקַח 542) *I will not accept*

מִבֵּיתְךָ prep.-n.m.s.-2 m.s. sf. (108) *from your house*

פָר n.m.s. (830) *a bull*

מִמִּכְלְאֹתֶיךָ prep.-n.m.p.-2 m.s. sf. (I 476) *from your folds*

עַתּוּדִים n.m.p. (800) *he-goats*

50:10

כִּי־לִי conj. (471)-prep.-1 c.s. sf. *for is mine*

כָל־חַיְתוֹ־ n.m.s. cstr. (481)-n.f.s. cstr. (I 312) *every beast of*

יָעַר n.m.s. paus. (420) *the forest*

בְּהֵמוֹת n.f.p. (96) *cattle*

בְּהַרְרֵי־אָלֶף prep.-n.m.p. cstr. (249; GK 90n)-n.m.s. (II 48) *on a thousand hills*

50:11

יָדַעְתִּי Qal pf. 1 c.s. (393) *I know*

כָּל־עוֹף n.m.s. cstr. (481)-n.m.s. cstr. (733) *all the birds of*

הָרִים n.m.p. (249) *the mountains*

וְזִיז שָׂדַי conj.-n.m.s. cstr. (I 265)-n.m.s. (961) *and all that moves in the field*

עִמָּדִי prep.-1 c.s. sf. *mine*

50:12

אִם־אֶרְעַב hypoth.part. (49; GK 159m,r)-Qal impf. 1 c.s. (944) *if I were hungry*

לֹא־אֹמַר לָךְ neg.-Qal impf. 1 c.s. (55)-prep.-2 m.s. sf. paus. *I would not tell you*

כִּי־לִי conj. (471)-prep.-1 c.s. sf. *for is mine*

תֵּבֵל n.f.s. (385) *the world*

וּמְלֹאָהּ conj.-n.m.s.-3 f.s. sf. (571) *and all that is in it*

50:13

הַאוֹכַל interr.-Qal impf. 1 c.s. (אָכַל 37) *do I eat*

בְּשַׂר אַבִּירִים n.m.s. cstr. (142)-adj. m.p. (7) *the flesh of bulls*

וְדַם conj.-n.m.s. cstr. (196) *or the blood of*

עַתּוּדִים n.m.p. (800) *goats*

אֶשְׁתֶּה Qal impf. 1 c.s. (שָׁתָה 1059) *do I drink*

50:14

זְבַח Qal impv. 2 m.s. (זָבַח 256) *make sacrifice*

לֵאלֹהִים prep.-n.m.p. (43) *to God*

תּוֹדָה n.f.s. (392) *thanksgiving*

וְשַׁלֵּם conj.-Pi. impv. 2 m.s. (1022) *and pay*

לְעֶלְיוֹן prep.-n.m.s. (751) *to the Most High*

נְדָרֶיךָ n.m.p.-2 m.s. sf. (623) *your vows*

50:15

וּקְרָאֵנִי conj.-Qal impv. 2 m.s.-1 c.s. sf. (894) *and call upon me*

בְּיוֹם prep.-n.m.s. cstr. (398) *in the day of*

צָרָה n.f.s. (I 865) *trouble*

אֲחַלֶּצְךָ Pi. impf. 1 c.s.-2 m.s. sf. (חָלַץ 323) *I will deliver you*

וּתְכַבְּדֵנִי conj.-Pi. impf. 2 m.s.-1 c.s. sf. (כָּבֵד 457) *and you shall glorify me*

50:16

וְלָרָשָׁע conj.-prep.-def.art.-adj. m.s. (957) *but to the wicked*

אָמַר Qal pf. 3 m.s. (55) *says*

אֱלֹהִים n.m.p. (43) *God*

מַה־לְּךָ interr. (552)-prep.-2 m.s. sf. *what right have you*

לְסַפֵּר prep.-Pi. inf.cstr. (707) *to recite*

חֻקָּי n.m.p.-1 c.s. sf. paus. *my statutes*

וַתִּשָּׂא consec.-Qal impf. 2 m.s. (נָשָׂא 669) *or take*

בְרִיתִי n.f.s.-1 c.s. sf. (136) *my covenant*

עֲלֵי־פִיךָ prep. (752)-n.m.s.-2 m.s. sf. (804) *on your lips*

50:17

וְאַתָּה conj. (GK 142d)-pers.pr. 2 m.s. (61) *for you*

שָׂנֵאתָ Qal pf. 2 m.s. (971) *hate*

מוּסָר n.m.s. (416) *discipline*

וַתַּשְׁלֵךְ consec.-Hi. impf. 2 m.s. (1020) *and you cast*

דְּבָרַי n.m.p.-1 c.s. sf. (182) *my words*

אַחֲרֶיךָ prep.-2 m.s. sf. (29) *behind you*

50:18

אִם־רָאִיתָ hypoth.part. (49)-Qal pf. 2 m.s. (רָאָה 906) *if you see*

גַנָּב n.m.s. (170) *a thief*

וַתִּרֶץ עִמּוֹ consec.-Qal impf. 2 m.s. (רָצָה 953)-prep.-3 m.s. sf. *and you accept him*

וְעִם מְנָאֲפִים conj.-prep.-Pi. ptc. m.p. (נָאַף 610) *and with adulterers*

חֶלְקֶךָ n.m.s.-2 m.s. sf. (324) *your portion*

50:19

פִּיךָ n.m.s.-2 m.s. sf. (804) *your mouth*

שָׁלַחְתָּ Qal pf. 2 m.s. (1018) *you give free rein*

בְרָעָה prep.-n.f.s. (949) *for evil*

וּלְשׁוֹנְךָ conj.-n.f.s.-2 m.s. sf. (546) *and your tongue*

תַּצְמִיד Hi. impf. 3 f.s. (855) *frames*

מִרְמָה n.f.s. (941) *deceit*

50:20

תֵּשֵׁב Qal impf. 2 m.s. (יָשַׁב 442) *you sit*

בְּאָחִיךָ prep.-n.m.s.-2 m.s. sf. (26) *against your brother*

תְדַבֵּר Pi. impf. 2 m.s. (180) *you speak*

בְּבֶן־אִמְּךָ prep.-n.m.s. cstr. (119)-n.f.s.-2 m.s. sf. (51) *your own mother's son*

תִּתֶּן־דֹּפִי Qal impf. 2 m.s. (נָתַן 678)-n.m.s. paus. (200) *you slander*

50:21

אֵלֶּה demons.adj. c.p. (41) *these things*

עָשִׂיתָ Qal pf. 2 m.s. (עָשָׂה I 793) *you have done*

וְהֶחֱרַשְׁתִּי conj.-Hi. pf. 1 c.s. (חָרַשׁ II 361; GK 112cc) *and I have been silent*

דִּמִּיתָ Pi. pf. 2 m.s. (דָּמָה I 197) *you thought*

הֱיוֹת־אֶהְיֶה Qal inf.cstr. (הָיָה 224; GK 113x, 157a)-Qal impf. 1 c.s. (224) *I was*

כָמוֹךָ prep.-2 m.s. sf. *like yourself*

אוֹכִיחֲךָ Hi. impf. 1 c.s.-2 m.s. sf. (יָכַח 406) *I rebuke you*

וְאֶעֶרְכָה conj.-Qal impf. 1 c.s.-vol.he (עָרַךְ 789) *and lay the charge*

לְעֵינֶיךָ prep.-n.f. du.-2 m.s. sf. (744) *before you*

50:22

בִּינוּ־ Qal impv. 2 m.p. (בִּין 106) *mark*

נָא part.of entreaty (609) *then*

זֹאת demons.adj. f.s. (260) *this*

שֹׁכְחֵי Qal act.ptc. m.p. cstr. (1013; GK 116b) *you who forget*

אֱלוֹהַּ n.m.s. (42) *God*

פֶּן־ conj. (814) *lest*

אֶטְרֹף Qal impf. 1 c.s. (382) *I rend*

וְאֵין מַצִּיל conj.-neg. cstr. (II 34)-Hi. ptc. (נָצַל 664) *and there be none to deliver*

50:23

זֹבֵחַ תּוֹדָה Qal act.ptc. (256)-n.f.s. (392) *he who brings thanksgiving as his sacrifice*

יְכַבְּדָנְנִי Pi. impf. 3 m.s.-1 c.s. sf. (כָּבֵד 457; GK 58i) *honors me*

וְשָׂם conj.-Qal act.ptc. (שׂוּם 962) *to him who orders aright*

דֶּרֶךְ n.m.s. (202) *his way*

אַרְאֶנּוּ Hi. impf. 1 c.s.-3 m.s. sf. (רָאָה 906) *I will show him*

בְּיֵשַׁע prep.-n.m.s. cstr. (447) *the salvation of*

אֱלֹהִים n.m.p. (43) *God*

51:1

לַמְנַצֵּחַ prep.-def.art.-Pi. ptc. (I 663) *to the choirmaster*

מִזְמוֹר n.m.s. (274) *a Psalm*

לְדָוִד prep.-pr.n. (187) *to David*

51:2

בְּבוֹא־אֵלָיו prep.-Qal inf.cstr. (97)-prep.-3 m.s. sf. *in coming to him*

נָתָן pr.n. (681) *Nathan*

הַנָּבִיא def.art.-n.m.s. (611) *the prophet*

כַּאֲשֶׁר־בָּא prep.-rel. (81)-Qal pf. 3 m.s. (בּוֹא 97) *as he had gone*

אֶל־בַּת־שָׁבַע prep.-pr.n. (124) *to Bathsheba*

51:3

חָנֵּנִי Qal impv. 2 m.s.-1 c.s. sf. (חָנַן I 335) *have mercy on me*

אֱלֹהִים n.m.p. (43) *O God*

כְּחַסְדֶּךָ prep.-n.m.s.-2 m.s. sf. (338) *according to thy steadfast love*

כְּרֹב רַחֲמֶיךָ prep.-n.m.s. cstr. (913)-n.m.p.-2 m.s. sf. (933) *according to thy abundant mercy*

מְחֵה Qal impv. 2 m.s. (מָחָה 562) *blot out*

פְּשָׁעָי n.m.p.-1 c.s. sf. (833) *my transgressions*

51:4

הֶרֶבה Hi. impv. 2 m.s. (רָבָה I 915; K הַרְבֵּה Hi. inf.abs. GK 75gg) *thoroughly*

כַּבְּסֵנִי Pi. impv. 2 m.s.-1 c.s. sf. (כָּבַס 460; GK 120g) *wash me*

מֵעֲוֹנִי prep.-n.m.s.-1 c.s. sf. (730) *from my iniquity*

וּמֵחַטָּאתִי conj.-prep.-n.f.s.-1 c.s. sf. (308) *and from my sin*

טַהֲרֵנִי Pi. impv. 2 m.s.-1 c.s. sf. (טָהֵר 372) *cleanse me*

51:5

כִּי־פְשָׁעַי conj.-n.m.p.-1 c.s. sf. (833; GK 142f) *for my transgressions*

אֲנִי אֵדָע pers.pr. 1 c.s. (58)-Qal impf. 1 c.s. (יָדַע 393) *I know*

וְחַטָּאתִי conj.-n.f.s.-1 c.s. sf. (308) *and my sin*

נֶגְדִּי prep.-1 c.s. sf. (617) *before me*

תָמִיד n.m.s. (556) *ever*

51:6

לְךָ prep.-2 m.s. sf. *against thee*

לְבַדְּךָ prep.-n.m.s.-2 m.s. sf. (II 94; cf. Gen. 43:32) *against thee separately*

חָטָאתִי Qal pf. 1 c.s. (חָטָא 306) *have I sinned*

וְהָרַע conj.-def.art.-n.m.s. (II 948) *and that which is evil*

בְּעֵינֶיךָ prep.-n.f. du.-2 m.s. sf. (744) *in thy sight*

עָשִׂיתִי Qal pf. 1 c.s. (עָשָׂה I 793) *I have done*

לְמַעַן prep. (775) *so that*

תִּצְדַּק Qal impf. 2 m.s. (842) *thou art just*

בְּדָבְרֶךָ prep.-Qal inf.cstr.-2 m.s. sf. (דָּבַר 180) *in thy sentence*

תִּזְכֶּה Qal impf. 2 m.s. (זָכָה 269) *and blameless*

בְשָׁפְטֶךָ prep.-Qal inf.cstr.-2 m.s. sf. (שָׁפַט 1047) *in thy judgment*

51:7

הֵן־בְּעָווֹן demons.part. (243)-prep.-n.m.s. (730) *behold, in iniquity*

חוֹלָלְתִּי Polal pf. 1 c.s. (חוּל I 296) *I was brought forth*

וּבְחֵטְא conj.-prep.-n.m.s. (307) *and in sin*

יֶחֱמַתְנִי Pi. pf. 3 f.s.-1 c.s. sf. (יָחַם 404; GK 64h) *did conceive me*

אִמִּי n.f.s.-1 c.s. sf. (51) *my mother*

51:8

הֵן־אֱמֶת demons.part. (243)-n.f.s. (54) *behold, truth*

חָפַצְתָּ Qal pf. 2 m.s. (חָפֵץ 342) *thou desirest*

בַטֻּחוֹת prep.-def.art.-n.f.p. (376) *in the inward being*

וּבְסָתֻם conj.-prep.-Qal pass.ptc. (סָתַם 711) *and in my secret heart*

חָכְמָה n.f.s. (315) *wisdom*

תוֹדִיעֵנִי Hi. impf. 2 m.s.-1 c.s. sf. (יָדַע 393) *teach me*

51:9

תְּחַטְּאֵנִי Pi. impf. 2 m.s.-1 c.s. sf. (חָטָא 306) *purge me*

בְאֵזוֹב prep.-n.m.s. (23) *with hyssop*

וְאֶטְהָר conj.-Qal impf. 1 c.s. (טָהֵר 372; GK 165a) *and I shall be clean*

תְּכַבְּסֵנִי Pi. impf. 2 m.s.-1 c.s. sf. (כָּבַס 460) *wash me*

וּמִשֶּׁלֶג conj.-prep.-n.m.s. (1017) *and than snow*

אַלְבִּין Hi. impf. 1 c.s. (לָבֵן 526) *I shall be whiter*

51:10

תַּשְׁמִיעֵנִי Hi. impf. 2 m.s.-1 c.s. sf. (שָׁמַע 1033) *make me to hear*

שָׂשׂוֹן n.m.s. (965) *joy*

וְשִׂמְחָה conj.-n.f.s. (970) *and gladness*

תָּגֵלְנָה Qal impf. 3 f.p. apoc. (גִּיל 162) *let rejoice*

עֲצָמוֹת n.f.p. cstr. (782; GK 155h) *the bones*

דִּכִּיתָ Pi. pf. 2 m.s. (דָּכָה 194) *thou hast broken*

51:11

הַסְתֵּר Hi. impv. 2 m.s. (סָתַר 711) *hide*

פָּנֶיךָ n.m.p.-2 m.s. sf. (815) *thy face*

מֵחֲטָאָי prep.-n.m.p.-1 c.s. sf. paus. (307) *from my sins*

וְכָל־עֲוֹנֹתַי conj.-n.m.s. cstr. (481)-n.m.p.-1 c.s. sf. (730) *and all my iniquities*

מְחֵה Qal impv. 2 m.s. (מָחָה 562) *blot out*

51:12

לֵב טָהוֹר n.m.s. (524)-adj. m.s. (373) *a clean heart*

בְּרָא־לִי Qal impv. 2 m.s. (בָּרָא 135)-prep.-1 c.s. sf. *create in me*

אֱלֹהִים n.m.p. (43) *O God*

וְרוּחַ נָכוֹן conj.-n.f.s. cstr. (924)-Ni. ptc. (כּוּן I 465) *and a spirit of steadfastness*

חַדֵּשׁ Pi. impv. 2 m.s. (293) *renew*

בְּקִרְבִּי prep.-n.m.s.-1 c.s. sf. (899) *within me*

51:13

אַל־תַּשְׁלִיכֵנִי neg.-Hi. impf. 2 m.s.-1 c.s. sf. (שָׁלַךְ 1020) *cast me not away*

מִלְּפָנֶיךָ prep.-prep.-n.m.p.-2 m.s. sf. (815) *from thy presence*

וְרוּחַ קָדְשְׁךָ conj.-n.f.s. cstr. (924)-n.m.s.-2 m.s. sf. (871) *and the spirit of thy holiness*

אַל־תִּקַּח neg.-Qal impf. 2 m.s. (לָקַח 542) *take not*

מִמֶּנִּי prep.-1 c.s. sf. *from me*

51:14

הָשִׁיבָה לִּי Hi. impv. 2 m.s.-vol.he (שׁוּב 996) -prep.-1 c.s. sf. *restore to me*

שְׂשׂוֹן יִשְׁעֶךָ n.m.s. cstr. (965)-n.m.s.-2 m.s. sf. (447) *the joy of thy salvation*

וְרוּחַ נְדִיבָה conj.-n.f.s. cstr. (924)-n.f.s. (622) *and with a spirit of willingness (nobility)*

תִסְמְכֵנִי Qal impf. 2 m.s.-1 c.s. sf. (סָמַךְ 701; GK 117ff) *uphold me*

51:15

אֲלַמְּדָה Pi. impf. 1 c.s.-vol.he (לָמַד 540) *I will teach*

פֹשְׁעִים Qal act.ptc. m.p. (833) *transgressors*

דְּרָכֶיךָ n.m.p.-2 m.s. sf. (202) *thy ways*

וְחַטָּאִים conj.-n.m.p. (308) *and sinners*

אֵלֶיךָ prep.-2 m.s. sf. *to thee*

יָשׁוּבוּ Qal impf. 3 m.p. (996) *will return*

51:16

הַצִּילֵנִי Hi. impv. 2 m.s.-1 c.s. sf. (נָצַל 664) *deliver me*

מִדָּמִים prep.-n.m.p. (196) *from bloodguiltiness*

אֱלֹהִים n.m.p. (43) *O God*

אֱלֹהֵי n.m.p. cstr. (43) *the God of*

תְּשׁוּעָתִי n.f.s.-1 c.s. sf. (448) *my salvation*

תְּרַנֵּן Pi. impf. 3 f.s. (רָנַן 943) *will sing aloud*

לְשׁוֹנִי n.f.s.-1 c.s. sf. (546) *my tongue*

צִדְקָתֶךָ n.f.s.-2 m.s. sf. (842) *of thy deliverance*

51:17

אֲדֹנָי n.m.p.-1 c.s. sf. (10) *O Lord*

שְׂפָתַי n.f.p.-1 c.s. sf. (973) *my lips*

תִּפְתָּח Qal impf. 2 m.s. paus. (פָּתַח I 834) *open thou*

וּפִי conj.-n.m.s.-1 c.s. sf. (804) *and my mouth*

יַגִּיד Hi. impf. 3 m.s. (נָגַד 616) *shall show forth*

תְּהִלָּתֶךָ n.f.s.-2 m.s. sf. (239) *thy praise*

51:18

כִּי לֹא־תַחְפֹּץ conj. (471)-neg.-Qal impf. 2 m.s. (342 חָפֵץ) *for thou hast no delight*

זֶבַח n.m.s. (257) *in sacrifice*

וְאֶתֵּנָה conj.-Qal impf. 1 c.s.-coh.he (נָתַן 678; GK 108f) *were I to give*

עוֹלָה n.f.s. (750) *a burnt offering*

לֹא תִרְצֶה neg.-Qal impf. 2 m.s. (953) *thou wouldst not be pleased*

51:19

זִבְחֵי n.m.p. cstr. (257; GK 128h) *the sacrifice acceptable to*

אֱלֹהִים n.m.p. (43) *God*

רוּחַ נִשְׁבָּרָה n.f.s. cstr. (924)-Ni. ptc. f.s. (שָׁבַר 990) *a spirit of brokenness*

לֵב־נִשְׁבָּר n.m.s. (524)-Ni. ptc. (990) *a broken heart*

וְנִדְכֶּה conj.-Ni. ptc. (דָּכָה 194) *and contrite*

אֱלֹהִים n.m.p. (43) *God*

לֹא תִבְזֶה neg.-Qal impf. 2 m.s. (בָּזָה 102) *thou wilt not despise*

51:20

הֵיטִיבָה Hi. impv. 2 m.s.-vol.he (יָטַב 405) *do good*

בִרְצוֹנְךָ prep.-n.m.s.-2 m.s. sf. (953) *in thy good pleasure*

אֶת־צִיּוֹן dir.obj.-pr.n. (851) *to Zion*

תִּבְנֶה Qal impf. 2 m.s. (בָּנָה 124) *rebuild*

חוֹמוֹת n.f.p. cstr. (327) *the walls of*

יְרוּשָׁלָ͏ִם pr.n. paus. (436) *Jerusalem*

51:21

אָז adv. (23) *then*

תַּחְפֹּץ Qal impf. 2 m.s. (342) *wilt thou delight in*

זִבְחֵי־צֶדֶק n.m.p. cstr. (257)-n.m.s. (841) *right sacrifices*

עוֹלָה n.f.s. (750) *in burnt offerings*

וְכָלִיל conj.-subst. m.s. (483) *and whole burnt offerings*

אָז v.supra *then*

יַעֲלוּ Qal impf. 3 m.p. (עָלָה 748) *will be offered*

עַל־מִזְבַּחֲךָ prep.-n.m.s.-2 m.s. sf. (258) *on thy altar*

פָרִים n.m.p. (830) *bulls*

52:1

לַמְנַצֵּחַ prep.-def.art.-Pi. ptc. (I 663) *to the choirmaster*

מַשְׂכִּיל n.m.s. (968) *a Maskil*

לְדָוִד prep.-pr.n. (187) *to David*

52:2

בְּבוֹא prep.-Qal inf.cstr. (97) *when came*

דּוֹאֵג pr.n. (178) *Doeg*

הָאֲדֹמִי def.art.-adj.gent. (10) *the Edomite*

וַיַּגֵּד consec.-Hi. impf. 3 m.s. (נָגַד 616) *and told*

לְשָׁאוּל prep.-pr.n. (982) *to Saul*

וַיֹּאמֶר לוֹ consec.-Qal impf. 3 m.s. (55)-prep.-3 m.s. sf. *and said to him*

בָּא דָוִד Qal pf. 3 m.s. (בּוֹא 97)-pr.n. (187) *David has come*

אֶל־בֵּית prep.-n.m.s. cstr. (108) *to the house of*

אֲחִימֶלֶךְ pr.n. (27) *Ahimelech*

52:3

מַה־תִּתְהַלֵּל interr. (552)-Hith. impf. 2 m.s. (הָלַל I 237) *why do you boast*

בְּרָעָה prep.-n.f.s. (949) *of mischief*

הַגִּבּוֹר def.art.-adj. m.s. (150) *O mighty man*

חֶסֶד אֵל n.m.s. cstr. (338)-n.m.s. (42) *the kindness of God*

כָּל־הַיּוֹם n.m.s. cstr. (481)-def.art.-n.m.s. (398) *all the day*

52:4

הַוּוֹת n.f.p. (217) *destruction*

תַּחְשֹׁב Qal impf. 2 m.s. (362) *you are plotting*

לְשׁוֹנֶךָ n.f.s.-2 m.s. sf. (546) *your tongue*

כְּתַעַר מְלֻטָּשׁ prep.-n.m.s. (789)-Pu. ptc. (לָטַשׁ 538) *like a sharp razor*

עֹשֵׂה Qal act.ptc. m.s. cstr. (עָשָׂה I 793) *worker of*

רְמִיָּה n.f.s. (I 941) *treachery*

52:5

אָהַבְתָּ Qal pf. 2 m.s. (אָהֵב 12) *you love*

רָע n.m.s. (948) *evil*

מִטּוֹב prep.-adj. m.s. (II 373) *than good*

שֶׁקֶר n.m.s. (1055) *lying*

מִדַּבֵּר צֶדֶק prep.-Pi. inf.cstr. (180)-n.m.s. (841) *more than speaking the truth*

סֶלָה interj. (699) *Selah*

52:6

אָהַבְתָּ Qal pf. 2 m.s. (12) *you love*

כָל־דִּבְרֵי־ n.m.s. cstr. (481)-n.m.p. cstr. (182) *all words that*

בָלַע n.m.s. paus. (I 118) *devour*

לְשׁוֹן מִרְמָה n.f.s. cstr. (546)-n.f.s. (941) *O deceitful tongue*

52:7

גַּם־אֵל adv. (168)-n.m.s. (42) *but God*

יִתָּצְךָ Qal impf. 3 m.s.-2 m.s. sf. (נָתַץ 683) *will break you down*

לָנֶצַח prep.-n.m.s. (664) *for ever*

יַחְתְּךָ Qal impf. 3 m.s.-2 m.s. sf. (חָתָה 367) *he will snatch you*

וְיִסָּחֲךָ conj.-Qal impf. 3 m.s.-2 m.s. sf. (נָסַח 650) *and tear you*

מֵאֹהֶל prep.-n.m.s. (13) *from a tent*

וְשֵׁרֶשְׁךָ conj.-Pi. pf. 3 m.s.-2 m.s. sf. (שָׁרַשׁ 1057) *and he will uproot you*

מֵאֶרֶץ prep.-n.f.s. cstr. (75) *from the land of*

חַיִּים adj. m.p. (313) *the living*

סֶלָה interj. (699) *Selah*

52:8

וְיִרְאוּ conj.-Qal impf. 3 m.p. (רָאָה 906) *and shall see*

צַדִּיקִים adj. m.p. (843) *the righteous*

וְיִירָאוּ conj.-Qal impf. 3 m.p. (יָרֵא 431) *and fear*

וְעָלָיו conj.-prep.-3 m.s. sf. *at him*

יִשְׂחָקוּ Qal impf. 3 m.p. paus. (שָׂחַק 965) *shall laugh*

52:9

הִנֵּה demons.part. (243) *behold*

הַגֶּבֶר def.art.-n.m.s. (149) *the man*

לֹא יָשִׂים neg.-Qal impf. 3 m.s. (שִׂים 962) *who would not make*

אֱלֹהִים n.m.p. (43) *God*

מָעוּזּוֹ n.m.s.-3 m.s. sf. (731) *his refuge*

וַיִּבְטַח consec.-Qal impf. 3 m.s. (105) *but trusted*

בְּרֹב prep.-n.m.s. cstr. (913) *in the abundance of*

עָשְׁרוֹ n.m.s.-3 m.s. sf. (799) *his riches*

יָעֹז Qal impf. 3 m.s. (עָזַז 738) *and sought refuge*

בְּהַוָּתוֹ prep.-n.f.s.-3 m.s. sf. (217) *in his wealth*

52:10

וַאֲנִי conj.-pers.pr. 1 c.s. (58) *but I*

כְּזַיִת רַעֲנָן prep.-n.m.s. (268)-adj. m.s. (947) *like a green olive tree*

בְּבֵית prep.-n.m.s. cstr. (108) *in the house of*

אֱלֹהִים n.m.p. (43) *God*

בָּטַחְתִּי Qal pf. 1 c.s. (105) *I trust*

בְּחֶסֶד־ prep.-n.m.s. cstr. (338) *in the steadfast love of*

אֱלֹהִים n.m.p. (43) *God*

עוֹלָם n.m.s. (761) *for ever*

וָעֶד conj.-n.m.s. paus. (I 723) *and ever*

52:11

אוֹדְךָ Hi. impf. 1 c.s.-2 m.s. sf. (יָדָה 392) *I will thank thee*

לְעוֹלָם prep.-n.m.s. (761) *for ever*

כִּי עָשִׂיתָ conj.-Qal pf. 2 m.s. (עָשָׂה I 793) *because thou hast done it*

וַאֲקַוֶּה conj.-Pi. impf. 1 c.s. (קָוָה I 875) *and I will wait for*

שִׁמְךָ n.m.s.-2 m.s. sf. (1027) *thy name*

כִּי־טוֹב conj. (471)-adj. m.s. (II 373) *for it is good*

נֶגֶד חֲסִידֶיךָ prep. (617)-adj. m.p.-2 m.s. sf. (339) *in the presence of thy godly*

53:1

לַמְנַצֵּחַ prep.-def.art.-Pi. ptc. (I 663) *to the choirmaster*

עַל־מָחֲלַת prep.-n.f.s. (I 318) *according to Mahalath*

מַשְׂכִּיל n.m.s. (968) *a Maskil*

לְדָוִד prep.-pr.n. (187) *to David*

53:2

אָמַר נָבָל Qal pf. 3 m.s. (55)-adj. m.s. (I 614) *a fool says*

בְּלִבּוֹ prep.-n.m.s.-3 m.s. sf. (524) *in his heart*

אֵין אֱלֹהִים neg. cstr. (II 34)-n.m.p. (43) *there is no God*

הִשְׁחִיתוּ Hi. pf. 3 c.p. (שָׁחַת 1007) *they are corrupt*

וְהִתְעִיבוּ conj.-Hi. pf. 3 c.p. (תָּעַב 1073) *doing abominable*

עָוֶל n.m.s. (732) *iniquity*

אֵין עֹשֵׂה־ v.supra-Qal act.ptc. m.s. cstr. (עָשָׂה I 793) *there is none that does*

טוֹב adj. m.s. (II 373) *good*

53:3

אֱלֹהִים n.m.p. (43) *God*

מִשָּׁמַיִם prep.-n.m. du. (1029) *from heaven*

הִשְׁקִיף Hi. pf. 3 m.s. (שָׁקַף I 1054) *looks down*

עַל־בְּנֵי אָדָם prep.-n.m.p. cstr. (119)-n.m.s. (9) *upon the sons of men*

לִרְאוֹת prep.-Qal inf.cstr. (רָאָה 906) *to see*

הֲיֵשׁ interr.-subst. (441) *if there are any that*

מַשְׂכִּיל Hi. ptc. (שָׂכַל 968) *are wise*

דֹּרֵשׁ Qal act.ptc. (205) *that seek*

אֶת־אֱלֹהִים dir.obj.-n.m.p. (43) *after God*

53:4

כֻּלּוֹ n.m.s.-3 m.s. sf. (481) *all of them*

סָג Qal pf. 3 m.s. (סוּג I 690) *have fallen away*

יַחְדָּו adv. (403) *alike*

נֶאֱלָחוּ Ni. pf. 3 c.p. paus. (אָלַח 47) *they are depraved*

אֵין עֹשֵׂה־ neg. cstr. (II 34)-Qal act.ptc. m.s. cstr. (I 793) *there is none that does*

טוֹב adj. m.s. (II 373) *good*

אֵין גַּם־אֶחָד v.supra-adv. (168)-num. paus. (25) *there is not even one*

53:5

הֲלֹא יָדְעוּ interr.-neg.-Qal pf. 3 c.p. (יָדַע 393) *have no understanding?*

פֹּעֲלֵי אָוֶן Qal act.ptc. m.p. cstr. (821)-n.m.s. (19) *those who work evil*

אֹכְלֵי עַמִּי Qal act.ptc. m.p. cstr. (37)-n.m.s.-1 c.s. sf. (I 766) *who eat up my people*

אָכְלוּ לֶחֶם Qal pf. 3 c.p. (37)-n.m.s. (536) *as they eat bread*

אֱלֹהִים n.m.p. (43) *upon God*

לֹא קָרָאוּ neg.-Qal pf. 3 c.p. paus. (894) *they do not call*

53:6

שָׁם adv. (1027) *there*

פָּחֲדוּ־פַחַד Qal pf. 3 c.p. (808)-n.m.s. (808) *they are in great terror*

לֹא־הָיָה neg.-Qal pf. 3 m.s. (224) *such as has not been*

פָּחַד Qal pf. 3 m.s. (808) *they are in terror*

כִּי־אֱלֹהִים conj.-n.m.p. (43) *for God*

פִּזַּר Pi. pf. 3 m.s. (808) *will scatter*

עַצְמוֹת n.f.p. cstr. (782) *the bones of*

חֹנָךְ Qal act.ptc.-2 m.s. sf. paus. (חָנָה 333; GK 91e,116i) *him who encamps against you*

הֱבִשֹׁתָה Hi. pf. 2 m.s. (בּוֹשׁ 101) *you will put to shame*

כִּי־אֱלֹהִים conj.-v.supra *for God*

מְאָסָם Qal pf. 3 m.s.-3 m.p. sf. (מָאַס 549) *has rejected them*

53:7

מִי יִתֵּן interr. (566)-Qal impf. 3 m.s. (נָתַן 678) *O that*

מִצִּיּוֹן prep.-pr.n. (851) *from Zion*

יְשֻׁעוֹת n.f.p. cstr. (447) *deliverance for*

יִשְׂרָאֵל pr.n. (975) *Israel*

בְּשׁוּב prep.-Qal inf.cstr. (996) *when returns*

אֱלֹהִים n.m.p. (43) *God*

שְׁבוּת n.f.s. cstr. (986) *the fortunes of*

עַמּוֹ n.m.s.-3 m.s. sf. (I 766) *my people*

יָגֵל Qal impf. 3 m.s. (גִּיל 162) *will rejoice*

יַעֲקֹב pr.n. (784) *Jacob*

יִשְׂמַח Qal impf. 3 m.s. (970) *will be glad*

יִשְׂרָאֵל v.supra *Israel*

54:1

לַמְנַצֵּחַ prep.-def.art.-Pi. ptc. (I 663) *to the choirmaster*

בִּנְגִינֹת prep.-n.f.p. (618) *with stringed instruments*

מַשְׂכִּיל n.m.s. (968) *a Maskil*

לְדָוִד prep.-pr.n. (187) *to David*

54:2

בְּבוֹא prep.-Qal inf.cstr. (בּוֹא 97) *when went*
הַזִּיפִים def.art.-adj.gent. m.p. (268) *the Ziphites*
וַיֹּאמְרוּ consec.-Qal impf. 3 m.p. (55) *and told*
לְשָׁאוּל prep.-pr.n. (982) *Saul*
הֲלֹא דָוִד interr.-neg.-pr.n. (187) *is not David?*
מִסְתַּתֵּר Hith. ptc. (סָתַר 711) *hiding*
עִמָּנוּ prep.-1 c.p. sf. *among us*

54:3

אֱלֹהִים n.m.p. (43) *O God*
בְּשִׁמְךָ prep.-n.m.s.-2 m.s. sf. (1027) *by thy name*
הוֹשִׁיעֵנִי Hi. impv. 2 m.s.-1 c.s. sf. (יָשַׁע 446) *save me*
וּבִגְבוּרָתְךָ conj.-prep.-n.f.s.-2 m.s. sf. (150) *and by thy might*
תְדִינֵנִי Qal impf. 2 m.s.-1 c.s. sf. (דִּין 192) *vindicate me*

54:4

אֱלֹהִים n.m.p. (43) *O God*
שְׁמַע Qal impv. 2 m.s. (1033) *hear*
תְּפִלָּתִי n.f.s.-1 c.s. sf. (813) *my prayer*
הַאֲזִינָה Hi. impv. 2 m.s.-vol.he (אָזַן 24) *give ear*
לְאִמְרֵי־ prep.-n.m.p. cstr. (56) *to the words of*
פִי n.m.s.-1 c.s. sf. (804) *my mouth*

54:5

כִּי זָרִים conj. (471)-Qal act.ptc. m.p. (זוּר I 266) *for strangers*
קָמוּ Qal pf. 3 c.p. (קוּם 877) *have risen*
עָלַי prep.-1 c.s. sf. *against me*
וְעָרִיצִים conj.-adj. m.p. (792) *and ruthless men*
בִּקְשׁוּ Pi. pf. 3 c.p. (134) *seek*
נַפְשִׁי n.f.s.-1 c.s. sf. (659) *my life*
לֹא שָׂמוּ neg.-Qal pf. 3 c.p. (שִׂים 962) *they do not set*
אֱלֹהִים n.m.p. (43) *God*
לְנֶגְדָּם prep.-prep.-3 m.p. sf. (617) *before them*
סֶלָה interj. (699) *Selah*

54:6

הִנֵּה demons.part. (243) *behold*
אֱלֹהִים n.m.p. (43) *God*
עֹזֵר לִי Qal act.ptc. (740)-prep.-1 c.s. sf. *my helper*
אֲדֹנָי n.m.p.-1 c.s. sf. (10) *the Lord*
בְּסֹמְכֵי prep. (GK 119i)-Qal act.ptc. m.p. cstr. (701 סָמַךְ) *with those who uphold*
נַפְשִׁי n.f.s.-1 c.s. sf. (659) *my life*

54:7

יָשׁוּב Hi. impf. 3 m.s. (שׁוּב 996) *he will requite*
הָרַע def.art.-n.m.s. (949) *with evil*
לְשֹׁרְרָי prep.-n.m.p.-1 c.s. sf. paus. (1004) *my enemies*
בַּאֲמִתְּךָ prep.-n.f.s.-2 m.s. sf. (54) *in thy faithfulness*
הַצְמִיתֵם Hi. impv. 2 m.s.-3 m.p. sf. (צָמַת 856) *put an end to them*

54:8

בִּנְדָבָה prep.-n.f.s. (621) *with a freewill offering*
אֶזְבְּחָה־לָּךְ Qal impf. 1 c.s.-vol.he (זָבַח 256) -prep.-2 m.s. sf. paus. *I will sacrifice to thee*
אוֹדֶה Hi. impf. 1 c.s. (יָדָה 392) *I will give thanks*
שִׁמְךָ n.m.s.-2 m.s. sf. (1027) *to thy name*
יהוה pr.n. (217) *O Yahweh*
כִּי־טוֹב conj. (471)-adj. m.s. (II 373) *for it is good*

54:9

כִּי מִכָּל־צָרָה conj. (471)-prep.-n.m.s. cstr. (481) -n.f.s. (865) *for from every trouble*
הִצִּילָנִי Hi. pf. 3 m.s.-1 c.s. sf. (נָצַל 664) *he has delivered me*
וּבְאֹיְבַי conj.-prep.-Qal act.ptc. m.p.-1 c.s. sf. (אָיַב 33) *and on my enemies*
רָאֲתָה Qal pf. 3 f.s. (רָאָה 906) *has looked*
עֵינִי n.f.s.-1 c.s. sf. (744) *my eye*

55:1

לַמְנַצֵּחַ prep.-def.art.-Pi. ptc. (I 663) *to the choirmaster*
בִּנְגִינֹת prep.-n.f.p. (618) *with stringed instruments*
מַשְׂכִּיל n.m.s. (968) *a Maskil*
לְדָוִד prep.-pr.n. (187) *to David*

55:2

הַאֲזִינָה Hi. impv. 2 m.s.-vol.he (אָזַן 24) *give ear*
אֱלֹהִים n.m.p. (43) *O God*
תְּפִלָּתִי n.f.s.-1 c.s. sf. (813) *to my prayer*
וְאַל־תִּתְעַלַּם conj.-neg.-Hith. impf. 2 m.s. (עָלַם I 761) *and hide not thyself*
מִתְּחִנָּתִי prep.-n.f.s.-1 c.s. sf. (337) *from my supplication*

55:3

הַקְשִׁיבָה Hi. impv. 2 m.s.-vol.he (קָשַׁב 904; GK 108g) *attend*

לִּי prep.-1 c.s. sf. *to me*

וַעֲנֵנִי conj.-Qal impv. 2 m.s.-1 c.s. sf. (עָנָה I 772) *and answer me*

אָרִיד Hi. impf. 1 c.s. (רוּד 923) *I am overcome (I show restlessness)*

בְּשִׂיחִי prep.-n.m.s.-1 c.s. sf. (I 967) *by my trouble*

וְאָהִימָה conj.-Hi. impf. 1 c.s. (הוּם 223) *and I am distraught*

55:4

מִקּוֹל prep.-n.m.s. cstr. (876) *by the noise of*

אוֹיֵב Qal act.ptc. (33) *the enemy*

מִפְּנֵי prep.-n.m.p. cstr. (815) *because of*

עָקַת n.f.s. cstr. (734) *the oppression of*

רָשָׁע adj. m.s. (957) *the wicked*

כִּי־יָמִיטוּ conj. (471)-Hi. impf. 3 m.p. (מוֹט 556) *for they cause to totter*

עָלַי prep.-1 c.s. sf. *over me*

אָוֶן n.m.s. (19) *trouble*

וּבְאַף conj.-prep.-n.m.s. (I 60) *and in anger*

יִשְׂטְמוּנִי Qal impf. 3 m.p.-1 c.s. sf. (שָׂטַם 966) *they cherish enmity against me*

55:5

לִבִּי n.m.s.-1 c.s. sf. (524) *my heart*

יָחִיל Qal impf. 3 m.s. (חוּל I 296) *is in anguish*

בְּקִרְבִּי prep.-n.m.s.-1 c.s. sf. (899) *within me*

וְאֵימוֹת conj.-n.f.p. cstr. (33) *and terrors of*

מָוֶת n.m.s. (560) *death*

נָפְלוּ Qal pf. 3 c.p. (656) *have fallen*

עָלָי prep.-1 c.s. sf. paus. *upon me*

55:6

יִרְאָה n.f.s. (432) *fear*

וָרַעַד conj.-n.m.s. (944) *and trembling*

יָבֹא בִי Qal impf. 3 m.s. (בּוֹא 97)-prep.-1 c.s. sf. *come upon me*

וַתְּכַסֵּנִי consec.-Pi. impf. 3 f.s.-1 c.s. sf. (כָּסָה 491) *and overwhelms me*

פַּלָּצוּת n.f.s. (814) *horror*

55:7

וָאֹמַר consec.-Qal impf. 1 c.s. (אָמַר 55) *and I say*

מִי־יִתֶּן־ interr. (566)-Qal impf. 3 m.s. (נָתַן 678) *O that*

לִי prep.-1 c.s. sf. *I had*

אֵבֶר n.m.s. (7) *wings*

כַּיּוֹנָה prep.-def.art.-n.f.s. (401) *like the dove*

אָעוּפָה Qal impf. 1 c.s.-vol.he (עוּף 733; GK 108f) *I would fly away*

וְאֶשְׁכֹּנָה conj.-Qal impf. 1 c.s.-vol.he (שָׁכַן 1014) *and be at rest*

55:8

הִנֵּה demons.part. (243) *behold*

אַרְחִיק נְדֹד Hi. impf. 1 c.s. (רָחַק 934)-Qal inf.cstr. (נָדַד I 622) *I would wander afar*

אָלִין Qal impf. 1 c.s. (לוּן I 533) *I would lodge*

בַּמִּדְבָּר prep.-def.art.-n.m.s. (184) *in the wilderness*

סֶלָה interj. (699) *Selah*

55:9

אָחִישָׁה Hi. impf. 1 c.s.-vol.he (חוּשׁ I 301) *I would haste*

מִפְלָט n.m.s. (812) *a shelter*

לִי prep.-1 c.s. sf. *for me*

מֵרוּחַ סֹעָה prep.-n.f.s. (924)-Qal act.ptc. f.s. (703 סָעָה) *from the raging wind*

מִסָּעַר prep.-n.m.s. paus. (704) *and from tempest*

55:10

בַּלַּע Pi. impv. 2 m.s. (118) *destroy*

אֲדֹנָי n.m.p.-1 c.s. sf. (10) *O Lord*

פַּלַּג Pi. impv. 2 m.s. (811; GK 52n) *confuse*

לְשׁוֹנָם n.f.s.-3 m.p. sf. (546) *their tongues*

כִּי־רָאִיתִי conj. (471)-Qal pf. 1 c.s. (רָאָה 906) *for I see*

חָמָס n.m.s. (329) *violence*

וְרִיב conj.-n.m.s. (936) *and strife*

בָּעִיר prep.-def.art.-n.f.s. (746) *in the city*

55:11

יוֹמָם subst. (401) *day*

וָלַיְלָה conj.-n.m.s. (538) *and night*

יְסוֹבְבֻהָ Po'el impf. 3 m.p.-3 f.s. sf. (סָבַב 685) *they go around it*

עַל־חוֹמֹתֶיהָ prep.-n.f.p.-3 f.s. sf. (327) *on its walls*

וְאָוֶן conj.-n.m.s. (19) *and mischief*

וְעָמָל conj.-n.m.s. (765) *and trouble*

בְּקִרְבָּהּ prep.-n.m.s.-3 f.s. sf. (899) *within it*

55:12

הַוּוֹת n.f.p. (217) *ruin*

בְּקִרְבָּהּ prep.-n.m.s.-3 f.s. sf. (899) *in its midst*

וְלֹא־יָמִישׁ conj.-neg.-Hi. impf. 3 m.s. (מוּשׁ I 559) *and do not depart*

מֵרְחֹבָהּ prep.-n.f.s.-3 f.s. sf. (932) *from its market place*
תֹּךְ n.m.s. (1067) *oppression*
וּמִרְמָה conj.-n.f.s. (941) *and fraud*

55:13

כִּי לֹא־אוֹיֵב consec. (471)-neg.-Qal act.ptc. (אָיַב 33) *for it is not an enemy*
יְחָרְפֵנִי Pi. impf. 3 m.s.-1 c.s. sf. (חָרַף 357) *who taunts me*
וְאֶשָּׂא conj.-Qal impf. 1 c.s. (נָשָׂא 669) *then I could bear it*
לֹא־מְשַׂנְאִי neg.-Pi. ptc.-1 c.s. sf. (שָׂנֵא 971) *it is not one who hates me*
עָלַי prep.-1 c.s. sf. *with me*
הִגְדִּיל Hi. pf. 3 m.s. (גָּדַל 152) *who deals insolently*
וְאֶסָּתֵר conj.-Ni. impf. 1 c.s. (סָתַר 711) *then I could hide myself*
מִמֶּנּוּ prep.-3 m.s. sf. *from him*

55:14

וְאַתָּה conj.-pers.pr. 2 m.s. (61) *but it is you*
אֱנוֹשׁ n.m.s. (60) *a man*
כְּעֶרְכִּי prep.-n.m.s.-1 c.s. sf. (789) *my equal*
אַלּוּפִי n.m.s.-1 c.s. sf. (I 48) *my companion*
וּמְיֻדָּעִי conj.-Pu. ptc.-1 c.s. sf. (יָדַע 393) *and my familiar friend*

55:15

אֲשֶׁר יַחְדָּו rel. (81)-adv. (403) *together*
נַמְתִּיק Hi. impf. 1 c.p. (מָתַק 608) *we used to hold sweet*
סוֹד n.m.s. (691) *converse*
בְּבֵית prep.-n.m.s. cstr. (108) *within the house of*
אֱלֹהִים n.m.p. (43) *God*
נְהַלֵּךְ Pi. impf. 1 c.p. (הָלַךְ 229) *we walked*
בְּרָגֶשׁ prep.-n.m.s. paus. (921) *in the throng*

55:16

יַשִּׁימָוֶת rd. יַשִּׁיא מָוֶת Hi. impf. 3 m.s. נָשָׁא II 674)-n.m.s. (560; GK 74k) *let death beguile*
עָלֵימוֹ prep.-3 m.p. sf. *them*
יֵרְדוּ Qal impf. 3 m.p. (יָרַד 432) *let them go down*
שְׁאוֹל pr.n. or n.f.s. (982) *to Sheol*
חַיִּים adj. m.p. (313) *alive*
כִּי־רָעוֹת conj. (471)-n.f.p. (949) *for evils*
בִּמְגוּרָם prep.-n.m.s.-3 m.p. sf. (158) *in their habitation*
בְּקִרְבָּם prep.-n.m.s.-3 m.p. sf. (899) *in their midst*

55:17

אֲנִי pers.pr. 1 c.s. (58) *but I*
אֶל־אֱלֹהִים prep.-n.m.p. (43) *upon God*
אֶקְרָא Qal impf. 1 c.s. (894) *I call*
וַיהוה conj.-pr.n. (217) *and Yahweh*
יוֹשִׁיעֵנִי Hi. impf. 3 m.s.-1 c.s. sf. (יָשַׁע 446) *will save me*

55:18

עֶרֶב n.m.s. (787) *evening*
וָבֹקֶר conj.-n.m.s. (133) *and morning*
וְצָהֳרַיִם conj.-n.m.p. (I 843) *and at noon*
אָשִׂיחָה Qal impf. 1 c.s.-vol.he (שִׂיחַ 967; GK 108g) *I utter my complaint*
וְאֶהֱמֶה conj.-Qal impf. 1 c.s. (הָמָה 242) *and moan*
וַיִּשְׁמַע consec.-Qal impf. 3 m.s. (1033) *and he will hear*
קוֹלִי n.m.s.-1 c.s. sf. (876) *my voice*

55:19

פָּדָה Qal pf. 3 m.s. (804) *he will deliver*
בְשָׁלוֹם prep.-n.m.s. (1022; GK 119gg) *in safety*
נַפְשִׁי n.f.s.-1 c.s. sf. (659) *my soul*
מִקְּרָב־לִי prep.-Qal inf.cstr. (קָרַב I 897)-prep.-1 c.s. sf. *from the battle that I wage*
כִּי־בְרַבִּים conj.-prep.-adj. m.p. (I 912) *for many*
הָיוּ Qal pf. 3 c.p. (הָיָה 224) *as are arrayed*
עִמָּדִי prep.-1 c.s. sf. *against me*

55:20

יִשְׁמַע Qal impf. 3 m.s. (1033) *will give ear*
אֵל n.m.s. (42) *God*
וְיַעֲנֵם conj.-Hi. impf. 3 m.s.-3 m.p. sf. (עָנָה III 776) *and humble them*
וְיֹשֵׁב conj.-Qal act.ptc. (442) *and he who is enthroned*
קֶדֶם n.m.s. (869) *from of old*
סֶלָה interj. (699) *Selah*
אֲשֶׁר אֵין rel. (81)-neg. cstr. (II 34) *for there is no*
חֲלִיפוֹת n.f.p. (322) *change*
לָמוֹ prep.-3 m.p. sf. *to them*
וְלֹא יָרְאוּ conj.-neg.-Qal pf. 3 c.p. (יָרֵא 431) *and they do not fear*
אֱלֹהִים n.m.p. (43) *God*

55:21

שָׁלַח Qal pf. 3 m.s. (1018) *he stretched out*
יָדָיו n.f.p.-3 m.s. sf. (388) *his hands*

בִּשְׁלֹמָיו prep.-adj. m.p.-3 m.s. sf. (1022) *against those at peace with him*
חִלֵּל Pi. pf. 3 m.s. (III 320) *he violated*
בְּרִיתוֹ n.f.s.-3 m.s. sf. (136) *his covenant*

55:22

חָלְקוּ Qal pf. 3 c.p. (II 325) *was smooth*
מַחְמָאֹת פִּיו n.f.p. cstr. (563)-n.m.s.-3 m.s. sf. (804) *the butter-words of his mouth*
וּקֲרָב־ conj.-n.m.s. (898; GK 10h) *and war*
לִבּוֹ n.m.s.-3 m.s. sf. (524) *his heart*
רַכּוּ Qal pf. 3 c.p. (רָכַךְ 939) *were softer*
דְבָרָיו n.m.p.-3 m.s. sf. (182) *his words*
מִשֶּׁמֶן prep.-n.m.s. (1032) *than oil*
וְהֵמָּה conj.-pers.pr. 3 m.p. (241) *yet they*
פְתִחוֹת n.f.p. (836) *were drawn swords*

55:23

הַשְׁלֵךְ Hi. impv. 2 m.s. (שָׁלַךְ 1020) *cast*
עַל־יהוה prep.-pr.n. (217) *upon Yahweh*
יְהָבְךָ n.m.s.-2 m.s. sf. (396; GK 117x) *your lot*
וְהוּא conj.-pers.pr. 3 m.s. (214) *and he*
יְכַלְכְּלֶךָ Pilpel impf. 3 m.s.-2 m.s. sf. (כּוּל 465) *will sustain you*
לֹא־יִתֵּן neg.-Qal impf. 3 m.s. (נָתַן 678) *he will not permit*
לְעוֹלָם prep.-n.m.s. (761) *for ever*
מוֹט n.m.s. (557) *a shaking*
לַצַּדִּיק prep.-def.art.-adj. m.s. (843) *to the righteous*

55:24

וְאַתָּה conj.-pers.pr. 2 m.s. (61) *but thou*
אֱלֹהִים n.m.p. (43) *O God*
תּוֹרִדֵם Hi. impf. 2 m.s.-3 m.p. sf. (יָרַד 432) *wilt cast them down*
לִבְאֵר prep.-n.f.s. cstr. (91) *into a well of*
שַׁחַת n.f.s. (1001) *a pit*
אַנְשֵׁי n.m.p. cstr. (35) *men of*
דָמִים n.m.p. (196) *blood*
וּמִרְמָה conj.-n.f.s. (941) *and treachery*
לֹא־יֶחֱצוּ neg.-Qal impf. 3 m.p. (חָצָה 345) *shall not live out half*
יְמֵיהֶם n.m.p.-3 m.p. sf. (398) *their days*
וַאֲנִי conj.-pers.pr. 1 c.s. (58) *but I*
אֶבְטַח־בָּךְ Qal impf. 1 c.s. (105)-prep.-2 m.s. sf. paus. *will trust in thee*

56:1

לַמְנַצֵּחַ prep.-def.art.-Pi. ptc. (I 663) *to the choirmaster*
עַל־יוֹנַת prep.-n.f.s. cstr. (401) *according to the dove of*
אֵלֶם n.m.s. (48) *silence* (some rd. אֵלִים n.m.p. IV 18 = *terebinths*)
רְחֹקִים adj. m.p. (935) *far-off*
לְדָוִד prep.-pr.n. (187) *to David*
מִכְתָּם n.m.s. (508) *a Miktam*
בֶּאֱחֹז prep.-Qal inf.cstr. (אָחַז 28) *when seized*
אֹתוֹ dir.obj.-3 m.s. sf. *him*
פְלִשְׁתִּים pr.n. gent. p. (814) *the Philistines*
בְּגַת prep.-pr.n. (II 387) *in Gath*

56:2

חָנֵּנִי Qal impv. 2 m.s.-1 c.s. sf. (חָנַן I 335) *be gracious to me*
אֱלֹהִים n.m.p. (43) *O God*
כִּי־שְׁאָפַנִי conj. (471)-Qal pf. 3 m.s.-1 c.s. sf. (II 983 שָׁאַף) *for trample upon me*
אֱנוֹשׁ n.m.s. (60) *men*
כָּל־הַיּוֹם n.m.s. cstr. (481)-def.art.-n.m.s. (398) *all day long*
לֹחֵם Qal act.ptc. (535) *foemen*
יִלְחָצֵנִי Qal impf. 3 m.s.-1 c.s. sf. (לָחַץ 537) *oppress me*

56:3

שָׁאֲפוּ Qal pf. 3 c.p. (II 983) *trample*
שׁוֹרְרַי n.m.p.-1 c.s. sf. (1004) *my enemies*
כָּל־הַיּוֹם n.m.s. cstr. (481)-def.art.-n.m.s. (398) *all day long*
כִּי־רַבִּים conj. (471)-adj. m.p. (I 912) *for many*
לֹחֲמִים Qal act.ptc. m.p. (535) *fight*
לִי prep.-1 c.s. sf. *against me*
מָרוֹם n.m.s. as adv. (928) *proudly*

56:4

יוֹם אִירָא n.m.s. (398; GK 155,l)-Qal impf. 1 c.s. (431 יָרֵא) *when I am afraid*
אֲנִי אֵלֶיךָ pers.pr. 1 c.s. (58)-prep.-2 m.s. sf. *I in thee*
אֶבְטָח Qal impf. 1 c.s. (105) *put my trust*

56:5

בֵּאלֹהִים prep.-n.m.p. (43) *in God*
אֲהַלֵּל Pi. impf. 1 c.s. (II 237) *I praise*
דְּבָרוֹ n.m.s.-3 m.s. sf. (182) *his word*
בֵּאלֹהִים v.supra *in God*
בָּטַחְתִּי Qal pf. 1 c.s. (105) *I trust*
לֹא אִירָא neg.-Qal impf. 1 c.s. (יָרֵא 431) *I do not fear*
מַה־יַּעֲשֶׂה interr. (552)-Qal impf. 3 m.s. (עָשָׂה I 793) *what can ... do?*

בָּשָׂר n.m.s. (142) *flesh*
לִי prep.-1 c.s. sf. *to me*

56:6

כָּל־הַיּוֹם n.m.s. cstr. (481)-def.art.-n.m.s. (398) *all day long*
דְּבָרַי n.m.p.-1 c.s. sf. (182) *my cause*
יְעַצֵּבוּ Pi. impf. 3 m.p. paus. (עָצַב I 780) *they seek to injure*
עָלַי prep.-1 c.s. sf. *against me*
כָּל־מַחְשְׁבֹתָם n.m.s. cstr. (481)-n.f.p.-3 m.p. sf. (364) *all their thoughts*
לָרָע prep.-n.m.s. paus. (948) *for evil*

56:7

יָגוּרוּ Qal impf. 3 m.p. (II 158) *they stir up strife*
יִצְפּוֹנוּ Qal impf. 3 m.p. (צָפַן 860) *they hide*
הֵמָּה pers.pr. 3 m.p. (241) *they*
עֲקֵבַי n.m.p.-1 c.s. sf. (I 784) *my steps*
יִשְׁמֹרוּ Qal impf. 3 m.p. paus. (1036) *watch*
כַּאֲשֶׁר קִוּוּ prep.-rel. (81)-Pi. pf. 3 c.p. (קָוָה I 875) *as they have waited for*
נַפְשִׁי n.f.s.-1 c.s. sf. (659) *my life*

56:8

עַל־אָוֶן prep.-n.m.s. (19) *for crime*
פַּלֶּט־לָמוֹ n.m.s. (812)-prep.-3 m.p. sf. *deliverance for them*
בְּאַף prep.-n.m.s. (I 60) *in wrath*
עַמִּים n.m.p. (I 766) *peoples*
הוֹרֵד Hi. impv. 2 m.s. (יָרַד 432) *cast down*
אֱלֹהִים n.m.p. (43) *O God*

56:9

נֹדִי n.m.s.-1 c.s. sf. (I 627) *my tossings*
סָפַרְתָּה Qal pf. 2 m.s. (707) *thou hast kept count of*
אָתָּה pers.pr. 2 m.s. paus. (61) *(thou)*
שִׂימָה Qal impv. 2 m.s.-vol.he (שׂוּם 962) *put thou*
דִמְעָתִי n.f.s.-1 c.s. sf. (199) *my tears*
בְנֹאדֶךָ prep.-n.m.s.-2 m.s. sf. (609) *in thy bottle*
הֲלֹא interr.part.-neg. *are they not?*
בְּסִפְרָתֶךָ prep.-n.f.s.-2 m.s. sf. (707) *in thy book*

56:10

אָז יָשׁוּבוּ adv. (23)-Qal impf. 3 m.p. (996) *then will be turned*
אוֹיְבַי Qal act.ptc. m.p.-1 c.s. sf. (אָיַב 33) *my enemies*
אָחוֹר adv. (30) *back*
בְּיוֹם prep.-n.m.s. (398; GK 155,l) *in the day*
אֶקְרָא Qal impf. 1 c.s. (894) *I call*
זֶה־יָדַעְתִּי demons.adj. m.s. (260)-Qal pf. 1 c.s. (393) *this I know*
כִּי־אֱלֹהִים לִי conj. (471)-n.m.p. (43)-prep.-1 c.s. sf. *that God is for me*

56:11

בֵּאלֹהִים prep.-n.m.p. (43) *in God*
אֲהַלֵּל Pi. impf. 1 c.s. (II 237) *I praise*
דָּבָר n.m.s. (182) *a word*
בַּיהוה prep.-pr.n. (217) *in Yahweh*
אֲהַלֵּל v.supra *I praise*
דָּבָר v.supra *a word*

56:12

בֵּאלֹהִים prep.-n.m.p. (43) *in God*
בָּטַחְתִּי Qal pf. 1 c.s. (105) *I trust*
לֹא אִירָא neg.-Qal impf. 1 c.s. (יָרֵא 431) *I do not fear*
מַה־יַּעֲשֶׂה interr. (552)-Qal impf. 3 m.s. (I 793) *what can do*
אָדָם n.m.s. (9) *man*
לִי prep.-1 c.s. sf. *to me*

56:13

עָלַי prep.-1 c.s. sf. *to me*
אֱלֹהִים n.m.p. (43) *O God*
נְדָרֶיךָ n.m.p.-2 m.s. sf. (623) *thy vows*
אֲשַׁלֵּם Pi. impf. 1 c.s. (1022) *I will render*
תּוֹדֹת n.f.p. (392) *thank offerings*
לָךְ prep.-2 m.s. sf. paus. *to thee*

56:14

כִּי הִצַּלְתָּ conj. (471)-Hi. pf. 2 m.s. (נָצַל 664) *for thou hast delivered*
נַפְשִׁי n.f.s.-1 c.s. sf. (659) *my soul*
מִמָּוֶת prep.-n.m.s. (560) *from death*
הֲלֹא רַגְלַי interr.part.-neg.-n.f. du.-1 c.s. sf. (919) *yea, my feet*
מִדֶּחִי prep.-n.m.s. (191) *from falling*
לְהִתְהַלֵּךְ prep.-Hith. inf.cstr. (הָלַךְ 229) *that I may walk*
לִפְנֵי prep.-n.m.p. cstr. (815) *before*
אֱלֹהִים n.m.p. (43) *God*
בְּאוֹר prep.-n.m.s. cstr. (21) *in the light of*
הַחַיִּים def.art.-n.m.p. (313) *life*

57:1

לַמְנַצֵּחַ prep.-def.art.-Pi. ptc. (I 663) *to the choirmaster*
אַל־תַּשְׁחֵת neg.-Hi. impf. 2 m.s. apoc. (שָׁחַת 1007) *do not destroy*

לְדָוִד prep.-pr.n. (187) *to David*
מִכְתָּם n.m.s. (508) *a Miktam*
בְּבָרְחוֹ prep.-Qal inf.cstr.-3 m.s. sf. (בָּרַח 137) *when he fled*
מִפְּנֵי־שָׁאוּל prep.-n.m.p. cstr. (815)-pr.n. (982) *from Saul*
בַּמְּעָרָה prep.-def.art.-n.f.s. (792) *in the cave*

57:2

חָנֵּנִי Qal impv. 2 m.s.-1 c.s. sf. (חָנַן I 335) *be merciful to me*
אֱלֹהִים n.m.p. (43) *O God*
חָנֵּנִי v.supra *be merciful to me*
כִּי בְךָ conj. (471)-prep.-2 m.s. sf. *for in thee*
חָסָיָה Qal pf. 3 f.s. paus. (חָסָה 340, GK 75u) *takes refuge*
נַפְשִׁי n.f.s.-1 c.s. sf. (659) *my soul*
וּבְצֵל־ conj.-prep.-n.m.s. cstr. (853) *and in the shadow of*
כְּנָפֶיךָ n.f.p.-2 m.s. sf. (489) *thy wings*
אֶחְסֶה Qal impf. 1 c.s. (340) *I will take refuge*
עַד יַעֲבֹר prep. (III 723)-Qal impf. 3 m.s. (716) *till pass by*
הַוּוֹת n.f.p. (217) *storms of destruction*

57:3

אֶקְרָא Qal impf. 1 c.s. (894) *I cry*
לֵאלֹהִים prep.-n.m.p. (43) *to God*
עֶלְיוֹן adj. m.s. (I 751) *Most High*
לָאֵל prep.-def.art.-n.m.s. (42) *to the God*
גֹּמֵר Qal act.ptc. (170) *who fulfils his purpose*
עָלָי prep.-1 c.s. sf. paus. *for me*

57:4

יִשְׁלַח Qal impf. 3 m.s. (1018) *he will send*
מִשָּׁמַיִם prep.-n.m. du. (1029) *from heaven*
וְיוֹשִׁיעֵנִי conj.-Hi. impf. 3 m.s.-1 c.s. sf. (יָשַׁע 446) *and save me*
חֵרֵף Pi. pf. 3 m.s. (I 357) *he will put to shame*
שֹׁאֲפִי Qal act.ptc. m.s.-1 c.s. sf. (II 983) *those who trample upon me*
סֶלָה interj. (699) *Selah*
יִשְׁלַח v.supra *will send forth*
אֱלֹהִים n.m.p. (43) *God*
חַסְדּוֹ n.m.s.-3 m.s. sf. (338) *his steadfast love*
וַאֲמִתּוֹ conj.-n.f.s.-3 m.s. sf. (54) *and his faithfulness*

57:5

נַפְשִׁי n.f.s.-1 c.s. sf. (659; GK 144m) *my soul*
בְּתוֹךְ prep.-n.m.s. cstr. (1063) *in the midst of*
לְבָאִם n.m.p. (522) *lions*
אֶשְׁכְּבָה Qal impf. 1 c.s.-vol.he (שָׁכַב 1011; GK 117bb) *I lie*
לֹהֲטִים Qal act.ptc. m.p. (529) *that are aflame*
בְּנֵי־אָדָם n.m.p. cstr. (119)-n.m.s. (9) *the sons of men*
שִׁנֵּיהֶם n.f. du.-3 m.p. sf. (I 1042) *their teeth*
חֲנִית n.f.s. (333) *spears*
וְחִצִּים conj.-n.m.p. (346) *and arrows*
וּלְשׁוֹנָם conj.-n.f.s.-3 m.p. sf. (546) *and their tongues*
חֶרֶב חַדָּה n.f.s. (352)-adj. f.s. (II 292) *sharp swords*

57:6

רוּמָה Qal impv. 2 m.s.-vol.he (רוּם 926) *be exalted*
עַל־הַשָּׁמַיִם prep.-def.art.-n.m. du. (1029) *above the heavens*
אֱלֹהִים n.m.p. (43) *O God*
עַל כָּל־הָאָרֶץ prep.-n.m.s. cstr. (481)-def.art.-n.f.s. (75) *over all the earth*
כְּבוֹדֶךָ n.m.s.-2 m.s. sf. (458) *thy glory*

57:7

רֶשֶׁת n.f.s. (440) *a net*
הֵכִינוּ Hi. pf. 3 c.p. (כּוּן 465) *they set*
לִפְעָמַי prep.-n.f.p.-1 c.s. sf. (821) *for my steps*
כָּפַף Qal pf. 3 m.s. (496) *was bowed down*
נַפְשִׁי n.f.s.-1 c.s. sf. (659) *my soul*
כָּרוּ Qal pf. 3 c.p. (כָּרָה I 500) *they dug*
לְפָנַי prep.-n.m.p.-1 c.s. sf. (815) *in my way*
שִׁיחָה n.f.s. (1001) *a pit*
נָפְלוּ Qal pf. 3 c.p. (656) *but they have fallen*
בְתוֹכָהּ prep.-n.m.s.-3 f.s. sf. (1063) *into it*
סֶלָה interj. (699) *Selah*

57:8

נָכוֹן Ni. ptc. (כּוּן I 465) *is steadfast*
לִבִּי n.m.s.-1 c.s. sf. (524) *my heart*
אֱלֹהִים n.m.p. (43) *O God*
נָכוֹן v.supra *is steadfast*
לִבִּי v.supra *my heart*
אָשִׁירָה Qal impf. 1 c.s.-vol.he (שִׁיר 1010) *I will sing*
וַאֲזַמֵּרָה conj.-Pi. impf. 1 c.s.-vol.he (I 274) *and make melody*

57:9

עוּרָה Qal impv. 2 m.s.-vol.he (734) *awake*
כְבוֹדִי n.m.s.-1 c.s. sf. (458) *my soul*
עוּרָה v.supra *awake*
הַנֵּבֶל def.art.-n.m.s. (614) *O harp*

וְכִנּוֹר conj.-n.m.s. (490) *and lyre*
אָעִירָה Hi. impf. 1 c.s.-vol.he (734) *I will awake*
שָׁחַר n.m.s. paus. *(1007) the dawn*

57:10

אוֹדְךָ Hi. impf. 1 c.s.-2 m.s. sf. (יָדָה 392) *I will give thanks to thee*
בָעַמִּים prep.-def.art.-n.m.p. (I 766) *among the peoples*
אֲדֹנָי n.m.p.-1 c.s. sf. (10) *O Lord*
אֲזַמֶּרְךָ Pi. impf. 1 c.s.-2 m.s. sf. (זָמַר I 274) *I will sing praises*
בַּל־אֻמִּים neg. (115)-n.m.p. (52) *not people* (some rd. בַּלְאֻמִּים prep.-def.art.-n.m.p. 522 - *among the nations)*

57:11

כִּי־גָדֹל conj. (471)-adj. m.s. (152) *for great*
עַד־שָׁמַיִם prep. (III 723)-n.m. du. (1029) *to the heavens*
חַסְדֶּךָ n.m.s.-2 m.s. sf. (338) *thy steadfast love*
וְעַד־שְׁחָקִים conj.-v.supra-n.m.p. (1007) *and to the clouds*
אֲמִתֶּךָ n.f.s.-2 m.s. sf. (54) *thy faithfulness*

57:12

רוּמָה Qal impv. 2 m.s.-vol.he (926) *be exalted*
עַל־שָׁמַיִם prep.-n.m. du. (1029) *above the heavens*
אֱלֹהִים n.m.p. (43) *O God*
עַל כָּל־הָאָרֶץ prep.-n.m.s. cstr. (481)-def.art. -n.f.s. (75) *over all the earth*
כְּבוֹדֶךָ n.m.s.-2 m.s. sf. (458) *thy glory*

58:1

לַמְנַצֵּחַ prep.-def.art.-Pi. ptc. (I 663) *to the choirmaster*
אַל־תַּשְׁחֵת neg.-Hi. impf. 2 m.s. apoc. (שָׁחַת 1007) *do not destroy*
לְדָוִד prep.-pr.n. (187) *to David*
מִכְתָּם n.m.s. (508) *a Miktam*

58:2

הַאֻמְנָם interr.part.-adv. (53) *indeed?*
אֵלֶם adv. (48) *in silence (*some אֵלִים n.m.p. III 18 *mighty lords)*
צֶדֶק n.m.s. (841) *what is right*
תְּדַבֵּרוּן Pi. impf. 2 m.p. (180; GK 52n) *do you decree*
מֵישָׁרִים n.m.p. (449) *uprightly*
תִּשְׁפְּטוּ Qal impf. 2 m.p. (1047) *do you judge*

בְּנֵי אָדָם n.m.p. cstr. (119)-n.m.s. (9) *the sons of men*

58:3

אַף־ conj. (II 64) *nay*
בְּלֵב prep.-n.m.s. (524) *in your hearts*
עוֹלֹת n.f.p. (732) *wrongs*
תִּפְעָלוּן Qal impf. 2 m.p. paus. (821) *you work*
בָּאָרֶץ prep.-def.art.-n.f.s. (75) *on the earth*
חֲמַס n.m.s. cstr. (329) *the violence of*
יְדֵיכֶם n.f. du.-2 m.p. sf. (388) *your hands*
תְּפַלֵּסוּן Pi. impf. 2 m.p. (פָּלַס 814) *you weigh out*

58:4

זֹרוּ Qal pf. 3 c.p. (זור I 266) *go astray*
רְשָׁעִים adj. m.p. (957) *the wicked*
מֵרָחֶם prep.-n.m.s. (933) *from the womb*
תָּעוּ Qal pf. 3 c.p. (תָּעָה 1073) *they err*
מִבֶּטֶן prep.-n.f.s. (105) *from their birth*
דֹּבְרֵי Qal act.ptc. m.p. cstr. (180) *speaking*
כָזָב n.m.s. (469) *lies*

58:5

חֲמַת־לָמוֹ n.f.s. cstr. (404)-prep.-3 m.p. sf. *they have venom*
כִּדְמוּת prep.-n.f.s. cstr. (198) *like*
חֲמַת־נָחָשׁ v.supra-n.m.s. (638) *the venom of a serpent*
כְּמוֹ־פֶתֶן חֵרֵשׁ conj. (455)-n.m.s. (837)-adj. m.s. (361) *like the deaf adder*
יַאְטֵם Hi. impf. 3 m.s. apoc. (אָטַם 31; GK 63n) *that stops*
אָזְנוֹ n.f.s.-3 m.s. sf. (23) *his ear*

58:6

אֲשֶׁר לֹא־יִשְׁמַע rel. (81)-neg.-Qal impf. 3 m.s. (1033) *so that it does not hear*
לְקוֹל prep.-n.m.s. cstr. (876) *the voice of*
מְלַחֲשִׁים Pi. ptc. m.p. (538) *charmers*
חוֹבֵר חֲבָרִים Qal act.ptc. (חָבַר 287)-n.m.p. (288) *or the enchanter*
מְחֻכָּם Pu. ptc. (חָכַם 314) *cunning*

58:7

אֱלֹהִים n.m.p. (43) *O God*
הֲרָס־ Qal impv. 2 m.s. (248) *break*
שִׁנֵּימוֹ n.f. du.-3 m.p. sf. (1042) *their teeth*
בְּפִימוֹ prep.-n.m.s.-3 m.p. sf. (804) *in their mouth*
מַלְתְּעוֹת n.f.p. cstr. (1069) *the fangs of*
כְּפִירִים n.m.p. (498) *the young lions*
נְתֹץ Qal impv. 2 m.s. (683) *tear out*

יהוה pr.n. (217) *O Yahweh*

58:8

יִמָּאֲסוּ Ni. impf. 3 m.p. (549) *let them vanish*

כְמוֹ־מַיִם prep. (455)-n.m.p. (565) *like water*

יִתְהַלְּכוּ־ Hith. impf. 3 m.p. (הָלַךְ 229) *that runs away*

לָמוֹ prep.-3 m.p. sf. *(them)*

יִדְרֹךְ Qal impf. 3 m.s. (201) *he treads*

חִצָּו n.m.p.-3 m.s. sf. (346) *his arrows*

כְּמוֹ יִתְמֹלָלוּ conj. (455)-Hithpolel impf. 3 m.p. paus. (מוּל 557) *and they are made blunt (cut off)*

58:9

כְּמוֹ שַׁבְּלוּל conj. (455)-n.m.s. (117) *like the snail*

תֶּמֶס n.m.s. (588) *into melting (leaving a slimy track)*

יַהֲלֹךְ Qal impf. 3 m.s. (229; GK 69x) *it goes*

נֵפֶל אֵשֶׁת n.m.s. cstr. (658; GK 118r)-n.f.s. cstr. (61; GK 96) *like the untimely birth that*

בַּל־חָזוּ neg. (115)-Qal pf. 3 c.p. (302) *never sees*

שָׁמֶשׁ n.f.s. paus. (1039) *the sun*

58:10

בְּטֶרֶם prep.-adv. (382) *sooner than*

יָבִינוּ Qal impf. 3 m.p. (בִּין 106) *can feel*

סִּירֹתֵיכֶם n.m.p.-2 m.p. sf. (I 696) *your pots*

אָטָד n.m.s. (31) *thorns*

כְּמוֹ־חַי conj. (455)-adj. m.s. (311) *whether alive*

כְּמוֹ־חָרוֹן conj. (455)-n.m.s. (354) *or burning*

יִשְׂעָרֶנּוּ Qal impf. 3 m.s.-3 m.s. sf. (שָׂעַר II 973) *may he sweep them away*

58:11

יִשְׂמַח Qal impf. 3 m.s. (970) *will rejoice*

צַדִּיק adj. m.s. (843) *the righteous*

כִּי־חָזָה conj. (471)-Qal pf. 3 m.s. (302) *when he sees*

נָקָם n.m.s. paus. (668) *vengeance*

פְּעָמָיו n.f.p.-3 m.s. sf. (821) *his feet*

יִרְחַץ Qal impf. 3 m.s. (934) *he will bathe*

בְּדַם prep.-n.m.s. cstr. (196) *in the blood of*

הָרָשָׁע def.art.-n.m.s. (957) *the wicked*

58:12

וְיֹאמַר conj.-Qal impf. 3 m.s. (55) *will say*

אָדָם n.m.s. (9) *men*

אַךְ־פְּרִי adv. (36)-n.m.s. (826) *surely a reward*

לַצַּדִּיק prep.-def.art.-adj. m.s. (843) *for the righteous*

אַךְ יֵשׁ־ adv. (36)-subst. (441) *surely there is*

אֱלֹהִים n.m.p. (43) *a God*

שֹׁפְטִים Qal act.ptc. m.p. (1047) *who judges*

בָּאָרֶץ prep.-def.art.-n.f.s. (75) *on earth*

59:1

לַמְנַצֵּחַ prep.-def.art.-Pi. ptc. (I 663) *to the choirmaster*

אַל־תַּשְׁחֵת neg.-Hi. impf. 2 m.s. apoc. (1007) *according to "do not destroy"*

לְדָוִד prep.-pr.n. (187) *to David*

מִכְתָּם n.m.s. (508) *a Miktam*

בִּשְׁלֹחַ prep.-Qal inf.cstr. (1018) *when sent*

שָׁאוּל pr.n. (982) *Saul*

וַיִּשְׁמְרוּ consec.-Qal impf. 3 m.p. (1036) *to watch*

אֶת־הַבַּיִת dir.obj.-def.art.-n.m.s. (108) *his house*

לַהֲמִיתוֹ prep.-Hi. inf.cstr.-3 m.s. sf. (מוּת 559) *to kill him*

59:2

הַצִּילֵנִי Hi. impv. 2 m.s.-1 c.s. sf. (נָצַל 664) *deliver me*

מֵאֹיְבַי prep.-Qal act.ptc. m.p.-1 c.s. sf. (אָיַב 33) *from my enemies*

אֱלֹהָי n.m.p.-1 c.s. sf. (43) *O my God*

מִמִּתְקוֹמְמַי prep.-Hithpolel ptc. m.p.-1 c.s. sf. (877 קוּם) *from those who rise up against me*

תְּשַׂגְּבֵנִי Pi. impf. 2 m.s.-1 c.s. sf. (שָׂגַב 960) *protect me*

59:3

הַצִּילֵנִי Hi. impv. 2 m.s.-1 c.s. sf. (נָצַל 664) *deliver me*

מִפֹּעֲלֵי prep.-Qal act.ptc. m.p. cstr. (821) *from those who work*

אָוֶן n.m.s. (19) *evil*

וּמֵאַנְשֵׁי conj.-prep.-n.m.p. cstr. (35) *and from men of*

דָמִים n.m.p. (196) *blood*

הוֹשִׁיעֵנִי Hi. impv. 2 m.s.-1 c.s. sf. (יָשַׁע 447) *save me*

59:4

כִּי הִנֵּה conj. (471)-demons.part. (243) *for lo*

אָרְבוּ Qal pf. 3 c.p. (70) *they lie in wait*

לְנַפְשִׁי prep.-n.f.s.-1 c.s. sf. (659) *for my life*

יָגוּרוּ Qal impf. 3 m.p. (II 158) *band themselves*

עָלַי prep.-1 c.s. sf. *against me*

עַזִּים adj. m.p. (738) *fierce men*

לֹא־פִשְׁעִי neg.-n.m.s.1 c.s. sf. (833) *for not my transgression*

וְלֹא־חַטָּאתִי conj.-neg.-n.f.s.-1 c.s. sf. (308) *and not my sin*
יהוה pr.n. (217) *O Yahweh*

59:5

בְּלִי־עָוֹן neg. (115)-n.m.s. (730) *for no fault of mine*
יְרוּצוּן Qal impf. 3 m.p. (רוּץ 930) *they run*
וְיִכּוֹנָנוּ conj.-Hithpolel impf. 3 m.p. (כּוּן I 465) *and make ready*
עוּרָה Qal impv. 2 m.s.-vol.he (734) *rouse thyself*
לִקְרָאתִי prep.-Qal inf.cstr.-1 c.s. sf. (II 896) *come to my help*
וּרְאֵה conj.-Qal impv. 2 m.s. (906) *and see*

59:6

וְאַתָּה conj.-pers.pr. 2 m.s. (61) *and thou*
יהוה־ pr.n. (217; GK 131s) *Yahweh*
אֱלֹהִים n.m.p. (43; GK 125h) *God*
צְבָאוֹת n.m.p. (838) *of hosts*
אֱלֹהֵי יִשְׂרָאֵל n.m.p. cstr. (43)-pr.n. (975) *God of Israel*
הָקִיצָה Hi. impv. 2 m.s.-vol.he (קִיץ I 884) *awake*
לִפְקֹד prep.-Qal inf.cstr. (823) *to punish*
כָּל־הַגּוֹיִם n.m.s. cstr. (481)-def.art.-n.m.p. (156) *all the nations*
אַל־תָּחֹן neg.-Qal impf. 2 m.s. (חָנַן I 335) *spare none*
כָּל־בֹּגְדֵי n.m.s. cstr. (481)-Qal act.ptc. m.p. cstr. (93; GK 128x) *of those who treacherously plot*
אָוֶן n.m.s. (19) *evil*
סֶלָה interj. (699) *Selah*

59:7

יָשׁוּבוּ Qal impf. 3 m.p. (996) *they come back*
לָעֶרֶב prep.-def.art.-n.m.s. (787) *every evening*
יֶהֱמוּ Qal impf. 3 m.p. (הָמָה 242) *howling*
כַכָּלֶב prep.-def.art.-n.m.s. (476) *like dogs*
וִיסוֹבְבוּ conj.-Po'el impf. 3 m.p. (סָבַב 685) *and prowling about*
עִיר n.f.s. (746) *the city*

59:8

הִנֵּה demons.part. (243) *behold*
יַבִּיעוּן Hi. impf. 3 m.p. (נָבַע 615) *bellowing*
בְּפִיהֶם prep.-n.m.s.-3 m.p. sf. (804) *with their mouths*
חֲרָבוֹת n.f.p. (352) *swords*

בְּשִׂפְתוֹתֵיהֶם prep.-n.f.p.-3 m.p. sf. (973) *in their lips*
כִּי־מִי conj. (471)-interr. (566) *for who*
שֹׁמֵעַ Qal act.ptc. (1033; GK 151a) *will hear*

59:9

וְאַתָּה conj.-pers.pr. 2 m.s. (61) *but thou*
יהוה pr.n. (217) *O Yahweh*
תִּשְׂחַק־ Qal impf. 2 m.s. (965) *dost laugh*
לָמוֹ prep.-3 m.p. sf. *at them*
תִּלְעַג Qal impf. 2 m.s. (541) *thou dost hold in derision*
לְכָל־גּוֹיִם prep.-n.m.s. cstr. (481)-n.m.p. (156) *all nations*

59:10

עֻזּוֹ n.m.s.-3 m.s. sf. (738) *O his strength*
אֵלֶיךָ prep.-2 m.s. sf. *for thee*
אֶשְׁמֹרָה Qal impf. 1 c.s.-vol.he (1036) *I will watch*
כִּי־אֱלֹהִים conj. (471)-n.m.p. (43) *for God*
מִשְׂגַּבִּי n.m.s.-1 c.s. sf. (I 960) *my fortress*

59:11

אֱלֹהֵי חַסְדִּו n.m.p. cstr. (43)-n.m.s.-1 c.s. sf. (338) *God of my steadfast love*
יְקַדְּמֵנִי Pi. impf. 3 m.s.-1 c.s. sf. (קָדַם 869) *will meet me*
אֱלֹהִים n.m.p. (43) *God*
יַרְאֵנִי Hi. impf. 3 m.s.-1 c.s. sf. (רָאָה 906) *will let me look*
בְשֹׁרְרָי prep.-n.m.p.-1 c.s. sf. paus. (1004) *on my enemies*

59:12

אַל־תַּהַרְגֵם neg.-Qal impf. 2 m.s.-3 m.p. sf. (הָרַג 246) *slay them not*
פֶּן־יִשְׁכְּחוּ adv. (814)-Qal impf. 3 m.p. (1013) *lest forget*
עַמִּי n.m.s.-1 c.s. sf. (I 766) *my people*
הֲנִיעֵמוֹ Hi. impv. 2 m.s.-3 m.p. sf. (נוּעַ 631) *make them totter*
בְחֵילְךָ prep.-n.m.s.-2 m.s. sf. (298) *by thy power*
וְהוֹרִידֵמוֹ conj.-Hi. impv. 2 m.s.-3 m.p. sf. (יָרַד 432) *and bring them down*
מָגִנֵּנוּ n.m.s.-1 c.p. sf. (171) *our shield*
אֲדֹנָי n.m.p.-1 c.s. sf. (10) *O Lord*

59:13

חַטַּאת־ n.f.s. cstr. (308) *the sin of*
פִּימוֹ n.m.s.-3 m.p. sf. (804) *their mouths*
דְּבַר־ n.m.s. cstr. (182) *the word of*

שִׂפְתֵימוֹ n.f.p.-3 m.p. sf. (973) *their lips*
וְיִלָּכְדוּ conj.-Ni. impf. 3 m.p. (539) *let them be trapped*
בִגְאוֹנָם prep.-n.m.s.-3 m.p. sf. (144) *in their pride*
וּמֵאָלָה conj.-prep.-n.f.s. (46) *and cursing*
וּמִכַּחַשׁ conj.-prep.-n.m.s. (471) *and lies*
יְסַפֵּרוּ Pi. impf. 3 m.p. paus. (סָפַר 707) *they utter*

59:14

כַּלֵּה Pi. impv. 2 m.s. (כָּלָה I 477) *consume*
בְחֵמָה prep.-n.f.s. (404) *in wrath*
כַּלֵּה v.supra *consume*
וְאֵינֵמוֹ conj.-neg.-3 m.p. sf. (II 34) *till they are no more*
וְיֵדְעוּ conj.-Qal impf. 3 m.p. (393) *that men may know*
כִּי־אֱלֹהִים conj. (471)-n.m.p. (43) *that God*
מֹשֵׁל Qal act.ptc. (605) *rules*
בְּיַעֲקֹב prep.-pr.n. (784) *over Jacob*
לְאַפְסֵי prep.-n.m.p. cstr. (67) *to the ends of*
הָאָרֶץ def.art.-n.f.s. (75) *the earth*
סֶלָה interj. (699) *Selah*

59:15

וְיָשׁוּבוּ conj.-Qal impf. 3 m.p. (996) *they come back*
לָעֶרֶב prep.-def.art.-n.m.s. (787) *each evening*
יֶהֱמוּ Qal impf. 3 m.p. (הָמָה 242) *howling*
כַכָּלֶב prep.-def.art.-n.m.s. (476) *like dogs*
וִיסוֹבְבוּ conj.-Po'el impf. 3 m.p. (סָבַב 685) *and prowling about*
עִיר n.f.s. (746) *the city*

59:16

הֵמָּה יְנוּעוּן pers.pr. 3 m.p. (241)-Hi. impf. 3 m.p. (נוּעַ 631) *they roam about*
לֶאֱכֹל prep.-Qal inf.cstr. (37) *to eat*
אִם־לֹא יִשְׂבְּעוּ hypoth.part. (49)-neg.-Qal impf. 3 m.p. (959) *and if they do not get their fill*
וַיָּלִינוּ consec.-Hi. impf. 3 m.p. (לוּן II 534; GK 159s) *and they growl*

59:17

וַאֲנִי conj.-pers.pr. 1 c.s. (58) *but I*
אָשִׁיר Qal impf. 1 c.s. (1010) *will sing*
עֻזֶּךָ n.m.s.-2 m.s. sf. (738) *of thy might*
וַאֲרַנֵּן conj.-Pi. impf. 1 c.s. (943) *and I will sing aloud*
לַבֹּקֶר prep.-def.art.-n.m.s. (133) *in the morning*
חַסְדֶּךָ n.m.s.-2 m.s. sf. (338) *of thy steadfast love*
כִּי־הָיִיתָ conj. (471)-Qal pf. 2 m.s. (הָיָה 224) *for thou hast been*
מִשְׂגָּב n.m.s. (I 960) *a fortress*
לִי prep.-1 c.s. sf. *to me*
וּמָנוֹס conj.-n.m.s. (631) *and a refuge*
בְּיוֹם prep.-n.m.s. cstr. (398) *in the day of*
צַר־ n.m.s. (II 865) *distress*
לִי v.supra *to me*

59:18

עֻזִּי n.m.s.-1 c.s. sf. (738) *O my Strength*
אֵלֶיךָ prep.-2 m.s. sf. *to thee*
אֲזַמֵּרָה Pi. impf. 1 c.s.-vol.he (זָמַר I 274) *I will sing praises*
כִּי־אֱלֹהִים conj. (471)-n.m.p. (43) *for O God*
מִשְׂגַּבִּי n.m.s.-1 c.s. sf. (I 960) *my fortress*
אֱלֹהֵי חַסְדִּי n.m.p. cstr. (43)-n.m.s.-1 c.s. sf. (338) *the God who shows me steadfast love*

60:1

לַמְנַצֵּחַ prep.-def.art.-Pi. ptc. (I 663) *to the choirmaster*
עַל־שׁוּשַׁן עֵדוּת prep.-n.m.s. (I 1004)-n.f.s. (730) *according to Shushan Eduth*
מִכְתָּם n.m.s. (508) *a Miktam*
לְדָוִד prep.-pr.n. (187) *to David*
לְלַמֵּד prep.-Pi. inf.cstr. (540) *for instruction*

60:2

בְּהַצּוֹתוֹ prep.-Hi. inf.cstr.-3 m.s. sf. (נָצָה II 663) *when he strove with*
אֶת אֲרַם נַהֲרַיִם dir.obj.-pr.n. (74)-n.m. du. (625) *Aram-naharaim*
וְאֶת־אֲרַם צוֹבָה conj.-dir.obj.-v.supra-pr.n. (844) *and with Aram-zobah*
וַיָּשָׁב consec.-Qal impf. 3 m.s. (שׁוּב 996) *and returned*
יוֹאָב pr.n. (222) *Joab*
וַיַּךְ consec.-Hi. impf. 3 m.s. (נָכָה 645) *and killed*
אֶת־אֱדוֹם dir.obj.-pr.n. (10) *Edom*
בְּגֵיא־ prep.-n.m.s. cstr. (161) *in the Valley of*
מֶלַח n.m.s. (571) *Salt*
שְׁנֵים עָשָׂר num. (1040)-num. (796) *twelve*
אָלֶף n.m.s. paus. (48) *thousand*

60:3

אֱלֹהִים n.m.p. (43) *O God*
זְנַחְתָּנוּ Qal pf. 2 m.s.-1 c.p. sf. (I 276) *thou hast rejected us*

פְּרַצְתָּנוּ Qal pf. 2 m.s.-1 c.p. sf. (I 829) *thou hast broken us*

אָנַפְתָּ Qal pf. 2 m.s. (60) *thou hast been angry*

תְּשׁוֹבֵב לָנוּ Polel impf. 2 m.s. (שׁוּב 996)-prep.-1 c.p. sf. *oh, restore us*

60:4

הִרְעַשְׁתָּה Hi. pf. 2 m.s. (רָעַשׁ 950) *thou hast made to quake*

אֶרֶץ n.f.s. (75) *the land*

פְּצַמְתָּהּ Qal pf. 2 m.s.-3 f.s. sf. (822) *thou hast rent it open*

רְפָה Qal impv. 2 m.s. (951; GK 75pp) *repair*

שְׁבָרֶיהָ n.m.p.-3 f.s. sf. (I 991) *its breaches*

כִּי־מָטָה conj. (471)-Qal pf. 3 f.s. (מוֹט 556) *for it totters*

60:5

הִרְאִיתָה Hi. pf. 2 m.s. (רָאָה 906) *thou hast made ... see*

עַמְּךָ n.m.s.-2 m.s. sf. (I 766) *thy people*

קָשָׁה adj. f.s. (904) *hard things*

הִשְׁקִיתָנוּ Hi. pf. 2 m.s.-1 c.p. sf. (שָׁקָה 1052) *thou hast given us to drink*

יַיִן n.m.s. cstr. (406; GK 131c) *wine of*

תַּרְעֵלָה n.f.s. (947) *reeling*

60:6

נָתַתָּה Qal pf. 2 m.s. (נָתַן 678) *thou hast set up*

לִּירֵאֶיךָ prep.-Qal act.ptc. m.p.-2 m.s. sf. (יָרֵא 431) *for those who fear thee*

נֵּס n.m.s. (651) *a banner*

לְהִתְנוֹסֵס prep.-Hithpo'el inf.cstr. (נָסַס II 651) *that it may be displayed*

מִפְּנֵי קֹשֶׁט prep.-n.m.p. cstr. (815)-n.m.s. (905) *from the bow*

סֶלָה interj. (699) *Selah*

60:7

לְמַעַן יֵחָלְצוּן prep. (775)-Ni. impf. 3 m.p. (חָלַץ I 322) *that may be delivered*

יְדִידֶיךָ adj. m.p.-2 m.s. sf. (391) *thy beloved*

הוֹשִׁיעָה Hi. impv. 2 m.s.-vol.he (יָשַׁע 446) *give victory*

יְמִינְךָ n.f.s.-2 m.s. sf. (411) *by thy right hand*

וַעֲנֵנוּ conj.-Qal impv. 2 m.s.-1 c.p. sf. (עָנָה I 772) *and answer us*

60:8

אֱלֹהִים n.m.s. (43) *God*

דִּבֶּר Pi. pf. 3 m.s. (180) *has spoken*

בְּקָדְשׁוֹ prep.-n.m.s.-3 m.s. sf. (871) *by his holiness*

אֶעְלֹזָה Qal impf. 1 c.s.-vol.he (עָלַז 759) *I will exult*

אֲחַלְּקָה Pi. impf. 1 c.s.-vol.he (חָלַק 323) *I will divide*

שְׁכֶם pr.n. (II 1014) *Shechem*

וְעֵמֶק conj.-n.m.s. cstr. (770) *and the Vale of*

סֻכּוֹת pr.n. (697) *Succoth*

אֲמַדֵּד Pi. impf. 1 c.s. (מָדַד 551) *I will portion out*

60:9

לִי prep.-1 c.s. sf. *is mine*

גִלְעָד pr.n. (166) *Gilead*

וְלִי conj.-v.supra *and is mine*

מְנַשֶּׁה pr.n. (586) *Manasseh*

וְאֶפְרַיִם conj.-pr.n. (68) *and Ephraim*

מָעוֹז רֹאשִׁי n.m.s. cstr. (731)-n.m.s.-1 c.s. sf. (910) *my helmet*

יְהוּדָה pr.n. (397) *Judah*

מְחֹקְקִי Po'el ptc.-1 c.s. sf. (חָקַק 349) *my scepter (commander's staff)*

60:10

מוֹאָב pr.n. (555) *Moab*

סִיר רַחְצִי n.m.s. cstr. (I 696)-n.m.s.-1 c.s. sf. (934) *my washbasin*

עַל־אֱדוֹם prep.-pr.n. (10) *upon Edom*

אַשְׁלִיךְ Hi. impf. 1 c.s. (1020) *I cast*

נַעֲלִי n.f.s.-1 c.s. sf. (653) *my shoe*

עָלַי פְּלֶשֶׁת prep.-pr.n. (814) *over Philistia*

הִתְרֹעָעִי Hithpolel impv. 2 f.s. (רוּעַ 929) *shout*

60:11

מִי יֹבִלֵנִי interr. (566)-Hi. impf. 3 m.s.-1 c.s. sf. (יָבַל 384) *who will bring me*

עִיר מָצוֹר n.f.s. cstr. (746)-n.m.s. (I 848) *the fortified city*

מִי נָחַנִי v.supra-Qal pf. 3 m.s.-1 c.s. sf. (נָחָה 634) *who will lead me*

עַד־אֱדוֹם prep. (III 723)-pr.n. (10) *to Edom*

60:12

הֲלֹא־אַתָּה interr.part.-neg.-pers.pr. 2 m.s. (61) *hast thou not*

אֱלֹהִים n.m.p. (43) *O God*

זְנַחְתָּנוּ Qal pf. 2 m.s.-1 c.p. sf. (זָנַח I 276) *rejected us*

וְלֹא־תֵצֵא conj.-neg.-Qal impf. 2 m.s. (יָצָא 422) *thou dost not go forth*

אֱלֹהִים n.m.p. (43) *O God*
בְּצִבְאוֹתֵינוּ prep.-n.m.p.-1 c.p. sf. (838) *with our armies*

60:13

הָבָה־ Qal impv. 2 m.s.-vol.he (יָהַב 396) *O grant*
לָּנוּ prep.-1 c.p. sf. *us*
עֶזְרָת n.f.s. (I 740; GK 80g) *help*
מִצָּר prep.-n.m.s. (III 865) *against the foe*
וְשָׁוְא conj. (GK 158a)-n.m.s. (996) *for vain*
תְּשׁוּעַת n.f.s. cstr. (448) *the help of*
אָדָם n.m.s. (9) *man*

60:14

בֵּאלֹהִים prep.-n.m.p. (43) *with God*
נַעֲשֶׂה־ Qal impf. 1 c.p. (I 793) *we shall do*
חָיִל n.m.s. paus. (298) *valiantly*
וְהוּא conj.-pers.pr. 3 m.s. (214) *it is he*
יָבוּס Qal impf. 3 m.s. (100) *who will tread down*
צָרֵינוּ n.m.p.-1 c.p. sf. (III 865) *our foes*

61:1

לַמְנַצֵּחַ prep.-def.art.-Pi. ptc. (I 663) *to the choirmaster*
עַל־נְגִינַת prep.-n.f.s. (618; GK 80f) *with stringed instruments*
לְדָוִד prep.-pr.n. (187) *to David*

61:2

שִׁמְעָה Qal impv. 2 m.s.-vol.he (1033) *hear*
אֱלֹהִים n.m.p. (43) *O God*
רִנָּתִי n.f.s.-1 c.s. sf. (943) *my cry*
הַקְשִׁיבָה Hi. impv. 2 m.s.-vol.he (904) *listen to*
תְּפִלָּתִי n.f.s.-1 c.s. sf. (813) *my prayer*

61:3

מִקְצֵה prep.-n.m.s. cstr. (892) *from the end of*
הָאָרֶץ def.art.-n.f.s. (75) *the earth*
אֵלֶיךָ prep.-2 m.s. sf. *to thee*
אֶקְרָא Qal impf. 1 c.s. (894) *I call*
בַּעֲטֹף prep.-Qal inf.cstr. (III 742) *when is faint*
לִבִּי n.m.s.-1 c.s. sf. (524) *my heart*
בְּצוּר־ prep.-n.m.s. (849) *to the rock*
יָרוּם מִמֶּנִּי Qal impf. 3 m.s. (926)-prep.-1 c.s. sf. *that is higher than I*
תַנְחֵנִי Hi. impf. 2 m.s.-1 c.s. sf. (נָחָה 634) *lead thou me*

61:4

כִּי־הָיִיתָ conj. (471)-Qal pf. 2 m.s. (הָיָה 224) *for thou art*
מַחְסֶה לִי n.m.s. (340)-prep.-1 c.s. sf. *my refuge*
מִגְדַּל־עֹז n.m.s. cstr. (153)-n.m.s. (738) *a strong tower*
מִפְּנֵי אוֹיֵב prep.-n.m.p. cstr. (815)-Qal act.ptc. (33 אָיַב) *against the enemy*

61:5

אָגוּרָה Qal impf. 1 c.s.-vol.he (גּוּר 157) *let me dwell*
בְאָהָלְךָ prep.-n.m.s.-2 m.s. sf. (13) *in thy tent*
עוֹלָמִים n.m.p. (761) *for ever*
אֶחֱסֶה Qal impf. 1 c.s. (חָסָה 340) *let me seek refuge*
בְסֵתֶר prep.-n.m.s. cstr. (712) *under the shelter of*
כְּנָפֶיךָ n.f.p.-2 m.s. sf. (489) *thy wings*
סֶלָה interj. (699) *Selah*

61:6

כִּי־אַתָּה conj. (471)-pers.pr. 2 m.s. (61) *for thou*
אֱלֹהִים n.m.p. (43) *O God*
שָׁמַעְתָּ Qal pf. 2 m.s. (1033) *hast heard*
לִנְדָרָי prep.-n.m.p.-1 c.s. sf. paus. (623) *my vows*
נָתַתָּ Qal pf. 2 m.s. (נָתַן 678) *thou hast given*
יְרֻשַּׁת n.f.s. cstr. (440) *the heritage of*
יִרְאֵי Qal act.ptc. m.p. cstr. (431) *those who fear*
שְׁמֶךָ n.m.s.-2 m.s. sf. (1027) *thy name*

61:7

יָמִים n.m.p. (398) *days*
עַל־יְמֵי prep.-n.m.p. cstr. (398) *to the days of*
מֶלֶךְ n.m.s. (I 572) *the king*
תּוֹסִיף Hi. impf. 2 m.s. (יָסַף 414) *add*
שְׁנוֹתָיו n.f.p.-3 m.s. sf. (1040) *his years*
כְּמוֹ־דֹר prep. (455)-n.m.s. (189) *to generation*
וָדֹר conj.-v.supra *to generation*

61:8

יֵשֵׁב Qal impf. 3 m.s. (יָשַׁב 442) *may he be enthroned*
עוֹלָם n.m.s. (761) *for ever*
לִפְנֵי prep.-n.m.p. cstr. (815) *before*
אֱלֹהִים n.m.p. (43) *God*
חֶסֶד n.m.s. (338) *steadfast love*
וֶאֱמֶת conj.-n.f.s. (54) *and faithfulness*
מַן Pi. impv. 2 m.s. (מָנָה 584; GK 75cc) *bid*
יִנְצְרֻהוּ Qal impf. 3 m.p.-3 m.s. sf. (נָצַר 665) *watch over him*

61:9

כֵּן אֲזַמְּרָה adv. (485)-Pi. impf. 1 c.s.-vol.he (I 274) *so will I sing praises*
שִׁמְךָ n.m.s.-2 m.s. sf. (1027) *to thy name*

לָעַד prep.-n.m.s. (I 723) *ever*
לְשַׁלְּמִי prep.-Pi. inf.cstr.-1 c.s. sf. (1022) *as I pay*
נְדָרַי n.m.p.-1 c.s. sf. (623) *my vows*
יוֹם יוֹם n.m.s. (398)-v.supra *day after day*

62:1

לַמְנַצֵּחַ prep.-def.art.-Pi. ptc. (I 663) *to the choirmaster*
עַל־יְדוּתוּן prep.-pr.n. (393) *according to Jeduthun*
מִזְמוֹר n.m.s. (274) *a Psalm*
לְדָוִד prep.-pr.n. (187) *to David*

62:2

אַךְ adv. (36) *alone*
אֶל־אֱלֹהִים prep.-n.m.p. (43) *for God*
דּוּמִיָּה n.f.s. (189) *in silence*
נַפְשִׁי n.f.s.-1 c.s. sf. (659) *my soul*
מִמֶּנּוּ prep.-3 m.s. sf. *from him*
יְשׁוּעָתִי n.f.s.-1 c.s. sf. (447) *my salvation*

62:3

אַךְ־הוּא adv. (36)-pers.pr. 3 m.s. (214) *he only*
צוּרִי n.m.s.-1 c.s. sf. (849) *my rock*
וִישׁוּעָתִי conj.-n.f.s.-1 c.s. sf. (447) *and my salvation*
מִשְׂגַּבִּי n.m.s.-1 c.s. sf. (I 960) *my fortress*
לֹא־אֶמּוֹט neg.-Ni. impf. 1 c.s. (מוֹט 556) *I shall not be moved*
רַבָּה adj. f.s. as adv. (I 912) *greatly*

62:4

עַד־אָנָה prep. (III 723)-adv.-loc.he (33) *how long*
תְּהוֹתְתוּ Polel impf. 2 m.p. (הות 223) *will you set*
עַל אִישׁ prep.-n.m.s. (35) *upon a man*
תְּרָצְּחוּ Pu. impf. 2 m.p. (רָצַח 953; GK 52q) *to shatter*
כֻּלְּכֶם n.m.s.-2 m.p. sf. (481) *all of you*
כְּקִיר prep.-n.m.s. (885) *as a wall*
נָטוּי Qal pass.ptc. (נָטָה 639) *leaning*
גָּדֵר n.m.s. (154) *a fence*
הַדְּחוּיָה def.art.-Qal pass.ptc. f.s. (דָּחָה 190) *tottering (pushed in)*

62:5

אַךְ adv. (36) *only*
מִשְּׂאֵתוֹ prep.-n.f.s.-3 m.s. sf. (673; GK 145m) *from his eminence*
יָעֲצוּ Qal pf. 3 c.p. (יָעַץ 419) *they plan*
לְהַדִּיחַ prep.-Hi. inf.cstr. (נָדַח 623) *to thrust (him) down*
יִרְצוּ Qal impf. 3 m.p. (רָצָה 953) *they take pleasure in*
כָזָב n.m.s. (469) *falsehood*
בְּפִיו prep.-n.m.s.-3 m.s. sf. (804) *with their mouths*
יְבָרֵכוּ Pi. impf. 3 m.p. paus. (138) *they bless*
וּבְקִרְבָּם conj.-prep.-n.m.s.-3 m.p. sf. (899) *but inwardly*
יְקַלְלוּ־ Pi. impf. 3 m.p. (886) *they curse*
סֶלָה interj. (699) *Selah*

62:6

אַךְ לֵאלֹהִים adv. (36)-prep.-n.m.p. (43) *only to God*
דּוֹמִּי Qal inf.cstr.-1 c.s. sf. (דָּמַם I 198) *my silence*
נַפְשִׁי n.f.s.-1 c.s. sf. (659) *my soul*
כִּי־מִמֶּנּוּ conj. (471)-prep.-3 m.s. sf. *for from him*
תִּקְוָתִי n.f.s.-1 c.s. sf. (876) *my hope*

62:7

אַךְ־הוּא adv. (36)-pers.pr. 3 m.s. (214) *he only*
צוּרִי n.m.s.-1 c.s. sf. (849) *my rock*
וִישׁוּעָתִי conj.-n.f.s.-1 c.s. sf. (447) *and my salvation*
מִשְׂגַּבִּי n.m.s.-1 c.s. sf. (I 960) *my fortress*
לֹא אֶמּוֹט neg.-Ni. impf. 1 c.s. (556) *I shall not be shaken*

62:8

עַל־אֱלֹהִים prep.-n.m.p. (43) *on God*
יִשְׁעִי n.m.s.-1 c.s. sf. (447) *my deliverance*
וּכְבוֹדִי conj.-n.m.s.-1 c.s. sf. (458) *and my honor*
צוּר־עֻזִּי n.m.s. cstr. (849)-n.m.s.-1 c.s. sf. (738) *my mighty rock*
מַחְסִי n.m.s.-1 c.s. sf. (340; GK 13c) *my refuge*
בֵּאלֹהִים prep.-n.m.p. (43) *in God*

62:9

בִּטְחוּ Qal impv. 2 m.p. (105) *trust*
בוֹ prep.-3 m.s. sf. *in him*
בְּכָל־עֵת prep.-n.m.s. cstr. (481)-n.f.s. (773) *at all times*
עָם n.m.s. (I 766) *O people*
שִׁפְכוּ־ Qal impv. 2 m.p. (1049) *pour out*
לְפָנָיו prep.-n.m.p.-3 m.s. sf. (815) *before him*
לְבַבְכֶם n.m.s.-2 m.p. sf. (523) *your heart*
אֱלֹהִים n.m.p. (43) *God*

מַחֲסֶה־לָּנוּ n.m.s. (340)-prep.-1 c.p. sf. *a refuge for us*
סֶלָה interj. (699) *Selah*

62:10

אַךְ הֶבֶל adv. (36)-n.m.s. (I 210) *but a breath*
בְּנֵי־אָדָם n.m.p. cstr. (119)-n.m.s. (9) *sons of men*
כָּזָב n.m.s. (469) *a delusion*
בְּנֵי אִישׁ v.supra-n.m.s. (35) *sons of men*
בְּמֹאזְנַיִם prep.-n.m. du. (24) *in balances*
לַעֲלוֹת prep.-Qal inf.cstr. (עָלָה 748) *they go up*
הֵמָּה pers.pr. 3 m.p. (241) *they*
מֵהֶבֶל prep.-n.m.s. (I 210) *than a breath*
יָחַד adv. paus. (403) *together*

62:11

אַל־תִּבְטְחוּ neg.-Qal impf. 2 m.p. (בָּטַח 105) *put no confidence*
בְעֹשֶׁק prep.-n.m.s. (799) *in extortion*
וּבְגָזֵל conj.-prep.-n.m.s. (160) *and on robbery*
אַל־תֶּהְבָּלוּ neg.-Qal impf. 2 m.p. paus. (הָבַל 211) *set no vain hopes*
חַיִל n.m.s. (298) *riches*
כִּי־יָנוּב conj. (471)-Qal impf. 3 m.s. (626) *if they bear fruit*
אַל־תָּשִׁיתוּ neg.-Qal impf. 2 m.p. (1011) *set not*
לֵב n.m.s. (524) *your heart*

62:12

אַחַת adj. f.s. (25) *once*
דִּבֶּר Pi. pf. 3 m.s. (180) *has spoken*
אֱלֹהִים n.m.p. (43) *God*
שְׁתַּיִם־ num. f. du. (1040) *twice*
זוּ demons.pron. (262) *this*
שָׁמָעְתִּי Qal pf. 1 c.s. paus. (1033) *have I heard*
כִּי עֹז conj. (471)-n.m.s. (738) *that power*
לֵאלֹהִים prep.-n.m.p. (43) *to God*

62:13

וּלְךָ־ conj.-prep.-2 m.s. sf. *and to thee*
אֲדֹנָי n.m.p.-1 c.s. sf. (10) *O Lord*
חָסֶד n.m.s. paus. (338) *steadfast love*
כִּי־אַתָּה conj. (471)-pers.pr. 2 m.s. (61) *for thou*
תְשַׁלֵּם Pi. impf. 2 m.s. (1023) *dost requite*
לְאִישׁ prep.-n.m.s. (35) *a man*
כְּמַעֲשֵׂהוּ prep.-n.m.s.-3 m.s. sf. (795) *according to his work*

63:1

מִזְמוֹר n.m.s. (274) *a Psalm*
לְדָוִד prep.-pr.n. (187) *to David*

בִּהְיוֹתוֹ prep.-Qal inf.cstr.-3 m.s. sf. (הָיָה 224) *when he was*
בְּמִדְבַּר prep.-n.m.s. cstr. (184) *in the wilderness of*
יְהוּדָה pr.n. (397) *Judah*

63:2

אֱלֹהִים n.m.p. (43) *O God*
אֵלִי n.m.s.-1 c.s. sf. (42) *my God*
אַתָּה pers.pr. 2 m.s. (61) *thou*
אֲשַׁחֲרֶךָּ Pi. impf. 1 c.s.-2 m.s. sf. (שָׁחַר 1007) *I seek thee*
צָמְאָה Qal pf. 3 f.s. (854) *thirsts*
לְךָ prep.-2 m.s. sf. *for thee*
נַפְשִׁי n.f.s.-1 c.s. sf. (659) *my soul*
כָּמַהּ Qal pf. 3 m.s. (484) *faints*
לְךָ prep.-2 m.s. sf. *for thee*
בְשָׂרִי n.m.s.-1 c.s. sf. (142) *my flesh*
בְּאֶרֶץ־צִיָּה prep.-n.f.s. (75)-adj. f.s. (851) *in a dry land*
וְעָיֵף conj.-adj. m.s. (746; GK 132d) *and weary*
בְּלִי־מָיִם neg. (115)-n.m.p. paus. (565) *where no water is*

63:3

כֵּן בַּקֹּדֶשׁ adv. (485)-prep.-def.art.-n.m.s. (871) *so in holiness*
חֲזִיתִיךָ Qal pf. 1 c.s.-2 m.s. sf. (חָזָה 302) *I have looked upon thee*
לִרְאוֹת prep.-Qal inf.cstr. (רָאָה 906) *beholding*
עֻזְּךָ n.m.s.-2 m.s. sf. (738) *thy power*
וּכְבוֹדֶךָ conj.-n.m.s.-2 m.s. sf. (458) *and glory*

63:4

כִּי־טוֹב conj. (471)-adj. m.s. (II 373) *because better*
חַסְדְּךָ n.m.s.-2 m.s. sf. (338) *thy steadfast love*
מֵחַיִּים prep.-n.m.p. (313) *than life*
שְׂפָתַי n.f. du.-1 c.s. sf. (973) *my lips*
יְשַׁבְּחוּנְךָ Pi. impf. 3 m.p.-2 m.s. sf. (שָׁבַח II 986; GK 60e) *will praise thee*

63:5

כֵּן אֲבָרֶכְךָ adv. (485)-Pi. impf. 1 c.s.-2 m.s. sf. (138 בָּרַךְ) *so I will bless thee*
בְחַיָּי prep.-n.m.p.-1 c.s. sf. (313) *as long as I live*
בְּשִׁמְךָ prep.-n.m.s.-2 m.s. sf. (1027) *on thy name*
אֶשָּׂא Qal impf. 1 c.s. (נָשָׂא 669) *I will lift up*
כַפָּי n.f. du.-1 c.s. sf. paus. (496) *my hands*

63:6

כְּמוֹ חֵלֶב conj. (455)-n.m.s. (316) *as with marrow*

וְדֶשֶׁן conj.-n.m.s. (206) *and fat*
תִּשְׂבַּע Qal impf. 3 f.s. (שָׂבַע 959) *is feasted*
נַפְשִׁי n.f.s.-1 c.s. sf. (659) *my soul*
וְשִׂפְתֵי רְנָנוֹת conj.-n.f. du. cstr. (973; GK 117t)-n.f.p. (943) *and with joyful lips*
יְהַלֶּל־ Pi. impf. 3 m.s. (הָלַל II 237) *praises*
פִּי n.m.s.-1 c.s. sf. (804) *my mouth*

63:7

אִם־זְכַרְתִּיךָ hypoth.part. (49)-Qal pf. 1 c.s.-2 m.s. sf. (זָכַר 269) *when I think of thee*
עַל־יְצוּעָי prep.-n.m.p.-1 c.s. sf. (426) *upon my bed*
בְּאַשְׁמֻרוֹת prep.-n.f.p. (1038) *in the watches of the night*
אֶהְגֶּה־ Qal impf. 1 c.s. (הָגָה I 211) *I meditate*
בָּךְ prep.-2 m.s. sf. paus. *on thee*

63:8

כִּי־הָיִיתָ conj. (471)-Qal pf. 2 m.s. (הָיָה 224) *for thou hast been*
עֶזְרָתָה n.f.s. (I 740) *help*
לִּי prep.-1 c.s. sf. *my*
וּבְצֵל conj.-prep.-n.m.s. cstr. (853) *and in the shadow of*
כְּנָפֶיךָ n.f. du.-2 m.s. sf. (489) *thy wings*
אֲרַנֵּן Pi. impf. 1 c.s. (943) *I sing for joy*

63:9

דָּבְקָה Qal pf. 3 f.s. (179) *clings*
נַפְשִׁי n.f.s.-1 c.s. sf. (659) *my soul*
אַחֲרֶיךָ prep.-2 m.s. sf. (29) *to thee*
בִּי תָּמְכָה prep.-1 c.s. sf.-Qal pf. 3 f.s. (תָּמַךְ 1069) *upholds me*
יְמִינֶךָ n.f.s.-2 m.s. sf. (411) *thy right hand*

63:10

וְהֵמָּה conj.-pers.pr. 3 m.p. (241) *but they*
לְשׁוֹאָה prep.-n.f.s. (996) *destruction*
יְבַקְשׁוּ Pi. impf. 3 m.p. (134) *seek*
נַפְשִׁי n.f.s.-1 c.s. sf. (659) *my life*
יָבֹאוּ Qal impf. 3 m.p. (בּוֹא 97) *shall go down*
בְּתַחְתִּיּוֹת prep.-adj. f.p. cstr. (1066) *into the depths of*
הָאָרֶץ def.art.-n.f.s. (75) *the earth*

63:11

יַגִּירֻהוּ Hi. impf. 3 m.p.-3 m.s. sf. (נָגַר 620) *they shall be given over*
עַל־יְדֵי prep.-n.f. du. cstr. (388) *to the power of*
חָרֶב n.f.s. paus. (352) *the sword*
מְנָת n.f.s. cstr. (584) *prey for*
שֻׁעָלִים n.m.p. (I 1043) *jackals*
יִהְיוּ Qal impf. 3 m.p. (הָיָה 224) *they shall be*

63:12

וְהַמֶּלֶךְ conj.-def.art.-n.m.s. (I 572) *but the king*
יִשְׂמַח Qal impf. 3 m.s. (970) *shall rejoice*
בֵּאלֹהִים prep.-n.m.p. (43) *in God*
יִתְהַלֵּל Hith. impf. 3 m.s. (II 237) *shall glory*
כָּל־הַנִּשְׁבָּע n.m.s. cstr. (481)-def.art.-Ni. ptc. (989) *all who swear*
בּוֹ prep.-3 m.s. sf. *by him*
כִּי יִסָּכֵר conj. (471)-Ni. impf. 3 m.s. (I 698) *for will be stopped*
פִּי n.m.s. cstr. (804) *the mouths of*
דוֹבְרֵי־שָׁקֶר Qal act.ptc. m.p. cstr. (180)-n.m.s. paus. (1055) *liars*

64:1

לַמְנַצֵּחַ prep.-def.art.-Pi. ptc. (I 663) *to the choirmaster*
מִזְמוֹר n.m.s. (274) *a Psalm*
לְדָוִד prep.-pr.n. (187) *to David*

64:2

שְׁמַע־ Qal impv. 2 m.s. (1033) *hear*
אֱלֹהִים n.m.p. (43) *O God*
קוֹלִי n.m.s.-1 c.s. sf. (876) *my voice*
בְשִׂיחִי prep.-n.m.s.-1 c.s. sf. (I 967) *in my complaint*
מִפַּחַד prep.-n.m.s. cstr. (808) *from dread of*
אוֹיֵב Qal act.ptc. (אָיַב 33) *an enemy*
תִּצֹּר Qal impf. 2 m.s. (נָצַר I 665) *preserve*
חַיָּי n.m.p.-1 c.s. sf. (313) *my life*

64:3

תַּסְתִּירֵנִי Hi. impf. 2 m.s.-1 c.s. sf. (711) *hide me*
מִסּוֹד prep.-n.m.s. cstr. (691) *from secret plots*
מְרֵעִים Hi. ptc. m.p. (רָעַע 949) *wicked ones*
מֵרִגְשַׁת prep.-n.f.s. cstr. (921) *from the throng of*
פֹּעֲלֵי אָוֶן Qal act.ptc. m.p. cstr. (פָּעַל 821)-n.m.s. (19) *evildoers*

64:4

אֲשֶׁר שָׁנְנוּ rel. (81)-Qal pf. 3 c.p. (שָׁנַן 1041) *who whet*
כַחֶרֶב prep.-def.art.-n.f.s. (352) *like swords*
לְשׁוֹנָם n.f.s.-3 m.p. sf. (546) *their tongues*
דָּרְכוּ Qal pf. 3 c.p. (201) *who aim*
חִצָּם n.m.s.-3 m.p. sf. (346) *their arrows*
דָּבָר מָר n.m.s. (182)-adj. m.s. paus. (I 600) *bitter words*

64:5

לִירוֹת prep.-Qal inf.cstr. (יָרָה 434) *shooting*
בַּמִּסְתָּרִים prep.-def.art.-n.m.p. (712) *from ambush*
תָּם n.m.s. (1070) *at the blameless*
פִּתְאֹם adv. (837) *suddenly*
יֹרֻהוּ Hi. impf. 3 m.p.-3 m.s. sf. (יָרָה 434; GK 69r) *shooting at him*
וְלֹא יִירָאוּ conj.-neg.-Qal impf. 3 m.p. paus. (יָרֵא 431) *without fear*

64:6

יְחַזְּקוּ־ Pi. impf. 3 m.p. (304) *they hold fast*
לָמוֹ prep.-3 m.p. sf. *to themselves*
דָּבָר רָע n.m.s. (182)-adj. m.s. (II 948) *evil purpose*
יְסַפְּרוּ Pi. impf. 3 m.p. (707) *they talk*
לִטְמוֹן prep.-Qal inf.cstr. (טָמַן 380) *of laying secretly*
מוֹקְשִׁים n.m.p. (430) *snares*
אָמְרוּ Qal pf. 3 c.p. (55) *thinking*
מִי יִרְאֶה־ interr. (566)-Qal impf. 3 m.s. (רָאָה 906) *who can see*
לָמוֹ prep.-3 m.p. sf. *them*

64:7

יַחְפְּשׂוּ־ Qal impf. 3 m.p. (344) *they search out*
עוֹלֹת n.f.p. (732) *crimes*
תַּמְנוּ Qal pf. 3 c.p. (תָּמַם 1070; GK 67dd) *we have thought out*
חֵפֶשׂ n.m.s. (344) *a plot*
מְחֻפָּשׂ Pu. ptc. (חָפַשׂ 344) *cunningly conceived*
וְקֶרֶב אִישׁ conj.-n.m.s. cstr. (899)-n.m.s. (35) *for the inward mind*
וְלֵב conj.-n.m.s. (524) *and heart*
עָמֹק adj. m.s. (771) *are deep*

64:8

וַיֹּרֵם consec.-Hi. impf. 3 m.s.-3 m.p. sf. (יָרָה 434) *but will shoot at them*
אֱלֹהִים n.m.p. (43) *God*
חֵץ n.m.s. (346; GK 117ff) *an arrow*
פִּתְאוֹם adv. (837) *suddenly*
הָיוּ Qal pf. 3 c.p. (הָיָה 224) *will be*
מַכּוֹתָם n.f.p.-3 m.p. sf. (646) *their wounds*

64:9

וַיַּכְשִׁילוּהוּ consec.-Hi. impf. 3 m.p.-3 m.s. sf. (505 כָּשַׁל) *they will bring to ruin him*
עָלֵימוֹ prep.-3 m.p. sf. *against them*
לְשׁוֹנָם n.f.s.-3 m.p. sf. (546) *their tongue*
יִתְנֹדְדוּ Hithpo'el impf. 3 m.p. (נָדַד I 622; or 626 נוּד) *will wag their heads (will flee away)*
כָּל־רֹאֵה n.m.s. cstr. (481)-Qal act.ptc. (? cstr.) (906; GK 130a) *all who see*
בָם prep.-3 m.p. sf. *them*

64:10

וַיִּירְאוּ consec.-Qal impf. 3 m.p. (יָרֵא 431) *then will fear*
כָּל־אָדָם n.m.s. cstr. (481)-n.m.s. (9) *all men*
וַיַּגִּידוּ consec.-Hi. impf. 3 m.p. (נָגַד 616) *they will tell*
פֹּעַל אֱלֹהִים n.m.s. cstr. (821)-n.m.p. (43) *the deed of God*
וּמַעֲשֵׂהוּ conj.-n.m.s.-3 m.s. sf. (795) *and what he has done*
הִשְׂכִּילוּ Hi. pf. 3 c.p. (968) *they ponder*

64:11

יִשְׂמַח Qal impf. 3 m.s. (970) *let rejoice*
צַדִּיק adj. m.s. (843) *the righteous*
בַּיהוה prep.-pr.n. (217) *in Yahweh*
וְחָסָה conj.-Qal pf. 3 m.s. (340) *and take refuge*
בוֹ prep.-3 m.s. sf. *in him*
וְיִתְהַלְלוּ conj.-Hith. impf. 3 m.p. (הָלַל II 237) *let glory*
כָּל־יִשְׁרֵי־ n.m.s. cstr. (481)-adj. m.p. cstr. (449) *all the upright in*
לֵב n.m.s. (524) *heart*

65:1

לַמְנַצֵּחַ prep.-def.art.-Pi. ptc. (I 663) *to the choirmaster*
מִזְמוֹר n.m.s. (274) *a Psalm*
לְדָוִד prep.-pr.n. (187) *to David*
שִׁיר n.m.s. (1010) *a Song*

65:2

לְךָ prep.-2 m.s. sf. *to thee*
דֻמִיָּה n.f.s. (189) *still waiting*
תְהִלָּה n.f.s. (239) *praise*
אֱלֹהִים n.m.p. (43) *O God*
בְּצִיּוֹן prep.-pr.n. (851) *in Zion*
וּלְךָ conj.-v.supra *and to thee*
יְשֻׁלַּם־ Pu. impf. 3 m.s. (1022) *shall be performed*
נֶדֶר n.m.s. (623) *vows*

65:3

שֹׁמֵעַ Qal act.ptc. (1033) *O one hearing*
תְּפִלָּה n.f.s. (813) *prayer*

עָדֶיךָ prep.-2 m.s. sf. (III 723) *to thee*
כָּל־בָּשָׂר n.m.s. cstr. (481)-n.m.s. (142) *all flesh*
יָבֹאוּ Qal impf. 3 m.p. (בּוֹא 97) *shall come*

65:4

דִּבְרֵי עֲוֹנֹת n.m.p. cstr. (182)-n.f.p. (730) *on account of sins*
גָּבְרוּ Qal pf. 3 c.p. (149) *prevail*
מֶנִּי prep.-1 c.s. sf. *over me*
פְּשָׁעֵינוּ n.m.p.-1 c.p. sf. (833) *our transgressions*
אַתָּה pers.pr. 2 m.s. (61) *thou*
תְכַפְּרֵם Pi. impf. 2 m.s.-3 m.p. sf. (כָּפַר 497) *dost forgive them*

65:5

אַשְׁרֵי n.m.p. cstr. (80) *blessed is*
תִּבְחַר Qal impf. 2 m.s. (103) *(he whom) thou dost choose*
וּתְקָרֵב conj.-Pi. impf. 2 m.s. (קָרַב 897) *and bring near*
יִשְׁכֹּן Qal impf. 3 m.s. (1014) *that he may dwell*
חֲצֵרֶיךָ n.m.p.-2 m.s. sf. (I 346) *thy courts*
נִשְׂבְּעָה Qal impf. 1 c.p.-vol.he (שָׂבַע 959) *we shall be satisfied*
בְּטוּב prep.-n.m.s. cstr. (375) *with the goodness of*
בֵּיתֶךָ n.m.s.-2 m.s. sf. (108) *thy house*
קְדֹשׁ הֵיכָלֶךָ adj. m.s. cstr. (872)-n.m.s.-2 m.s. sf. (228) *thy holy temple*

65:6

נוֹרָאוֹת Ni. ptc. f.p. (יָרֵא 431) *by dread deeds*
בְּצֶדֶק prep.-n.m.s. (841) *with deliverance*
תַּעֲנֵנוּ Qal impf. 2 m.s.-1 c.p. sf. (עָנָה I 772) *thou dost answer us*
אֱלֹהֵי n.m.p. cstr. (43) *O God of*
יִשְׁעֵנוּ n.m.s.-1 c.p. sf. (447) *our salvation*
מִבְטָח n.m.s. cstr. (105; GK 92g) *the hope of*
כָּל־קַצְוֵי־ n.m.s. cstr. (481)-n.m.p. cstr. (892) *all the ends of*
אֶרֶץ n.f.s. (75) *the earth*
וְיָם רְחֹקִים conj.-n.m.s. (410)-adj. m.p. (935) *and of the farthest seas*

65:7

מֵכִין Hi. ptc. (כּוּן I 465) *who hast established*
הָרִים n.m.p. (249) *mountains*
בְּכֹחוֹ prep.-n.m.s.-3 m.s. sf. (470) *by his strength*
נֶאְזָר Ni. ptc. (25) *being girded*
בִּגְבוּרָה prep.-n.f.s. (150) *with might*

65:8

מַשְׁבִּיחַ Hi. ptc. (I 986) *who dost still*
שְׁאוֹן n.m.s. cstr. (981) *the roaring of*
יַמִּים n.m.p. (410) *the seas*
שְׁאוֹן v.supra *the roaring of*
גַּלֵּיהֶם n.m.p.-3 m.p. sf. (164) *their waves*
וַהֲמוֹן conj.-n.m.s. cstr. (242) *and the tumult of*
לְאֻמִּים n.m.p. (522) *the peoples*

65:9

וַיִּירְאוּ consec.-Qal impf. 3 m.p. (יָרֵא 431) *that ... are afraid*
יֹשְׁבֵי Qal act.ptc. m.p. cstr. (יָשַׁב 442) *those who dwell at*
קְצָוֹת n.f.p. (892) *the boundaries*
מֵאוֹתֹתֶיךָ prep.-n.f.p.-2 m.s. sf. (16) *at thy signs*
מוֹצָאֵי־ n.m.p. cstr. (I 425) *the outgoings of*
בֹקֶר n.m.s. (133) *the morning*
וָעֶרֶב conj.-n.m.s. (787) *and the evening*
תַּרְנִין Hi. impf. 2 m.s. (רָנַן 943) *thou makest to shout for joy*

65:10

פָּקַדְתָּ Qal pf. 2 m.s. (823) *thou visitest*
הָאָרֶץ def.art.-n.f.s. (75) *the earth*
וַתְּשֹׁקְקֶהָ consec.-Polel impf. 2 m.s.-3 f.s. sf. (II 1003 שׁוּק) *and givest it abundance*
רַבַּת adj. f.s. (I 912; an Aramaism) as adv. *greatly*
תַּעְשְׁרֶנָּה Hi. impf. 2 m.s.-3 f.s. sf. (עָשַׁר 799; GK 53n,60g) *thou enrichest it*
פֶּלֶג n.m.s. cstr. (I 811) *the river of*
אֱלֹהִים n.m.p. (43) *God*
מָלֵא Qal pf. 3 m.s. (569) *is full of*
מָיִם n.m.p. paus. (565) *water*
תָּכִין Hi. impf. 2 m.s. (כּוּן I 465) *thou providest*
דְּגָנָם n.m.s.-3 m.p. sf. (186) *their grain*
כִּי־כֵן conj. (471)-adv. (485) *for so*
תְּכִינֶהָ Hi. impf. 2 m.s.-3 f.s. sf. (כּוּן I 465) *thou hast prepared it*

65:11

תְּלָמֶיהָ n.m.p.-3 f.s. sf. (1068) *its furrows*
רַוֵּה Pi. impv. 2 m.s. (רָוָה 924; or inf.) *thou waterest*
נַחֵת Pi. inf.abs. (נָחַת 639) *settling*
גְּדוּדֶיהָ n.m.p.-3 f.s. sf. (151) *its ridges*
בִּרְבִיבִים prep.-n.m.p. (914) *with showers*
תְּמֹגְגֶנָּה Polel impf. 2 m.s.-3 f.s. sf. (מוּג 556) *softening it*
צִמְחָהּ n.m.s.-3 f.s. sf. (855) *its growth*
תְּבָרֵךְ Pi. impf. 2 m.s. (138) *you bless*

65:12
עִטַּרְתָּ Pi. pf. 2 m.s. (742) *thou crownest*
שְׁנַת n.f.s. cstr. (1040) *the year with*
טוֹבָתֶךָ n.f.s.-2 m.s. sf. (375) *thy bounty*
וּמַעְגָּלֶיךָ conj.-n.m.p.-2 m.s. sf. (722) *and the tracks of thy chariot*
יִרְעֲפוּן Qal impf. 3 m.p. (50) *drip*
דָּשֶׁן n.m.s. paus. (206) *with fatness*

65:13
יִרְעֲפוּ Qal impf. 3 m.p. (950) *drip*
נְאוֹת n.f.p. cstr. (II 627) *the pastures of*
מִדְבָּר n.m.s. (184) *the wilderness*
וְגִיל conj.-n.m.s. (I 162) *and with joy*
גְּבָעוֹת n.f.p. (148) *the hills*
תַּחְגֹּרְנָה Qal impf. 3 f.p. (291) *gird themselves*

65:14
לָבְשׁוּ Qal pf. 3 c.p. (527; GK 117y) *clothe themselves*
כָרִים n.m.p. (II 499) *the meadows*
הַצֹּאן def.art.-n.f.s. (838) *with flocks*
וַעֲמָקִים conj.-n.m.p. (770) *and the valleys*
יַעַטְפוּ־ Qal impf. 3 m.p. (II 742; GK 117y) *deck themselves*
בָר n.m.s. (III 141) *with grain*
יִתְרוֹעֲעוּ Hithpolel impf. 3 m.p. (רוּעַ 929) *they shout for joy*
אַף־יָשִׁירוּ conj. (64)-Qal impf. 3 m.p. (1010) *and sing*

66:1
לַמְנַצֵּחַ prep.-def.art.-Pi. ptc. (I 663) *to the choirmaster*
שִׁיר n.m.s. (1010) *a Song*
מִזְמוֹר n.m.s. (274) *a Psalm*
הָרִיעוּ Hi. impv. 2 m.p. (רוּעַ 929) *make a joyful noise*
לֵאלֹהִים prep.-n.m.p. (43) *to God*
כָּל־הָאָרֶץ n.m.s. cstr. (481)-def.art.-n.f.s. (75) *all the earth*

66:2
זַמְּרוּ Pi. impv. 2 m.p. (I 274) *sing*
כְבוֹד־ n.m.s. cstr. (458) *the glory of*
שְׁמוֹ n.m.s.-3 m.s. sf. (1027) *his name*
שִׂימוּ Qal impv. 2 m.p. (962) *give*
כָבוֹד n.m.s. (458) *glory*
תְּהִלָּתוֹ n.f.s.-3 m.s. sf. (239) *his praise*

66:3
אִמְרוּ Qal impv. 2 m.p. (55) *say*
לֵאלֹהִים prep.-n.m.p. (43) *to God*
מַה־נּוֹרָא interr. (552)-Ni. ptc. (יָרֵא 431) *how terrible*
מַעֲשֶׂיךָ n.m.p.-2 m.s. sf. (795) *thy deeds*
בְּרֹב prep.-n.m.s. cstr. (913) *so great*
עֻזְּךָ n.m.s.-2 m.s. sf. (738) *thy power*
יְכַחֲשׁוּ Pi. impf. 3 m.p. (471) *cringe*
לְךָ prep.-2 m.s. sf. *before thee*
אֹיְבֶיךָ Qal act.ptc. m.p.-2 m.s. sf. (אָיַב 33) *thy enemies*

66:4
כָּל־הָאָרֶץ n.m.s. cstr. (481)-def.art.-n.f.s. (75) *all the earth*
יִשְׁתַּחֲווּ Hithpalel impf. 3 m.p. (שָׁחָה 1005) *worships*
לְךָ prep.-2 m.s. sf. *thee*
וִיזַמְּרוּ־ conj.-Pi. impf. 3 m.p. (I 274) *and they sing praises*
לָךְ prep.-2 m.s. sf. paus. *to thee*
יְזַמְּרוּ Pi. impf. 3 m.p. (I 274) *they sing praises*
שִׁמְךָ n.m.s.-2 m.s. sf. (1027) *to thy name*
סֶלָה interj. (699) *Selah*

66:5
לְכוּ Qal impv. 2 m.p. (הָלַךְ 229) *come*
וּרְאוּ conj.-Qal impv. 2 m.p. (רָאָה 906) *and see*
מִפְעֲלוֹת n.f.p. cstr. (821) *the deeds of*
אֱלֹהִים n.m.p. (43) *God*
נוֹרָא Ni. ptc. (יָרֵא 431) *terrible*
עֲלִילָה n.f.s. (760) *in his deeds*
עַל־בְּנֵי אָדָם prep.-n.m.p. cstr. (119)-n.m.s. (9) *among men*

66:6
הָפַךְ Qal pf. 3 m.s. (245) *he turned*
יָם n.m.s. (410) *the sea*
לְיַבָּשָׁה prep.-n.f.s. (387) *into dry land*
בַּנָּהָר prep.-def.art.-n.m.s. (625) *through the river*
יַעַבְרוּ Qal impf. 3 m.p. (716) *men passed*
בְרָגֶל prep.-n.f.s. paus. (919) *on foot*
שָׁם adv. (1027) *there*
נִשְׂמְחָה־ Qal impf. 1 c.p.-coh.he (שָׂמַח 970; GK 108g) *did we rejoice*
בּוֹ prep.-3 m.s. sf. *in him*

66:7
מֹשֵׁל Qal act.ptc. (605) *who rules*
בִּגְבוּרָתוֹ prep.-n.f.s.-3 m.s. sf. (150) *by his might*
עוֹלָם n.m.s. (761) *for ever*
עֵינָיו n.f. du.-3 m.s. sf. (744) *whose eyes*
בַּגּוֹיִם prep.-def.art.-n.m.p. (156) *on the nations*

תִּצְפֶּינָה Qal impf. 3 f.p. (צָפָה I 859) *keep watch*
הַסּוֹרְרִים def.art.-Qal act.ptc. m.p. (710) *the rebellious*
אַל־יָרִימוּ neg.-Qal impf. 3 m.p. (רוּם 926) *let not ... exalt*
לָמוֹ prep.-3 m.p. sf. *themselves*
סֶלָה interj. (699) *Selah*

66:8

בָּרְכוּ Pi. impv. 2 m.p. (138) *bless*
עַמִּים n.m.p. (I 766) *O peoples*
אֱלֹהֵינוּ n.m.p.-1 c.p. sf. (43) *our God*
וְהַשְׁמִיעוּ conj.-Hi. impv. 2 m.p. (1033) *let ... be heard*
קוֹל n.m.s. cstr. (876) *the sound of*
תְּהִלָּתוֹ n.f.s.-3 m.s. sf. (239) *his praise*

66:9

הַשָּׂם def.art.-Qal act.ptc. (שׂוּם 962) *who has kept*
נַפְשֵׁנוּ n.f.s.-1 c.p. sf. (659) *us*
בַּחַיִּים prep.-def.art.-n.m.p. (313) *among the living*
וְלֹא־נָתַן conj.-neg.-Qal pf. 3 m.s. (678) *and has not let*
לַמּוֹט prep.-def.art.-n.m.s. (557) *slip*
רַגְלֵנוּ n.f.s.-1 c.p. sf. (919) *our feet*

66:10

כִּי־בְחַנְתָּנוּ conj. (471)-Qal pf. 2 m.s.-1 c.p. sf. (בָּחַן 103) *for thou hast tested us*
אֱלֹהִים n.m.p. (43) *O God*
צְרַפְתָּנוּ Qal pf. 2 m.s.-1 c.p. sf. (864) *thou hast tried us*
כִּצְרָף־ prep.-Qal inf.cstr. (864) *as trying of*
כָּסֶף n.m.s. paus. (494) *silver*

66:11

הֲבֵאתָנוּ Hi. pf. 2 m.s.-1 c.p. sf. (בּוֹא 97) *thou didst bring us*
בַמְּצוּדָה prep.-def.art.-n.f.s. (845) *into the net*
שַׂמְתָּ Qal pf. 2 m.s. (שׂוּם 962) *thou didst lay*
מוּעָקָה n.f.s. (734) *affliction*
בְמָתְנֵינוּ prep.-n.m. du.-1 c.p. sf. (608) *on our loins*

66:12

הִרְכַּבְתָּ Hi. pf. 2 m.s. (רָכַב 938) *thou didst let ride*
אֱנוֹשׁ n.m.s. (60) *men*
לְרֹאשֵׁנוּ prep.-n.m.s.-1 c.p. sf. (910) *over our heads*
בָּאנוּ־ Qal pf. 1 c.p. (בּוֹא 97) *we went*
בָאֵשׁ prep.-def.art.-n.f.s. (77) *through fire*
וּבַמַּיִם conj.-prep.-def.art.-n.m.p. (565) *and through water*
וַתּוֹצִיאֵנוּ consec.-Hi. impf. 2 m.s.-1 c.p. sf. (יָצָא 422) *yet thou hast brought us forth*
לָרְוָיָה prep.-def.art.-n.f.s. (924) *to saturation*

66:13

אָבוֹא Qal impf. 1 c.s. (97; GK 119n) *I will come*
בֵיתְךָ n.m.s.-2 m.s. sf. (108) *into thy house*
בְעוֹלוֹת prep.-n.f.p. (750) *with burnt offerings*
אֲשַׁלֵּם Pi. impf. 1 c.s. (1022) *I will pay*
לְךָ prep.-2 m.s. sf. *thee*
נְדָרָי n.m.p.-1 c.s. sf. paus. (623) *my vows*

66:14

אֲשֶׁר־פָּצוּ rel. (81)-Qal pf. 3 c.p. (פָּצָה 822) *that which uttered*
שְׂפָתָי n.f. du.-1 c.s. sf. paus. (973) *my lips*
וְדִבֶּר־פִּי conj.-Pi. pf. 3 m.s. (180)-n.m.s.-1 c.s. sf. (804) *and my mouth promised*
בַּצַּר־לִי prep.-def.art.-n.m.s. (II 865)-prep.-1 c.s. sf. *when I was in trouble*

66:15

עֹלוֹת n.f.p. cstr. (750) *burnt offerings of*
מֵחִים n.m.p. (562) *fatlings*
אַעֲלֶה־לָּךְ Hi. impf. 1 c.s. (748)-prep.-2 m.s. sf. paus. *I will offer to thee*
עִם־קְטֹרֶת prep.-n.f.s. cstr. (882) *with the smoke of*
אֵילִים n.m.p. (I 17) *rams*
אֶעֱשֶׂה Qal impf. 1 c.s. (I 793) *I will make an offering of*
בָקָר n.m.s. (133) *bulls*
עִם־עַתּוּדִים prep. (767)-n.m.p. (800) *and goats*
סֶלָה interj. (699) *Selah*

66:16

לְכוּ־ Qal impv. 2 m.p. (הָלַךְ 229) *come*
שִׁמְעוּ Qal impv. 2 m.p. (1033) *hear*
וַאֲסַפְּרָה conj.-Pi. impf. 1 c.s.-vol.he (סָפַר 707) *and I will tell*
כָּל־יִרְאֵי n.m.s. cstr. (481)-Qal act.ptc. m.p. cstr. (יָרֵא 431) *all who fear*
אֱלֹהִים n.m.p. (43) *God*
אֲשֶׁר עָשָׂה rel. (81)-Qal pf. 3 m.s. (I 793) *what he has done*
לְנַפְשִׁי prep.-n.f.s.-1 c.s. sf. (659) *for me*

66:17

אֵלָיו prep.-3 m.s. sf. *to him*

פִּי־קָרָאתִי n.m.s.-1 c.s. sf. (804; GK 144m)-Qal pf. 1 c.s. paus. (894) *I cried aloud*

וְרוֹמַם conj.-Polal pf. 3 m.s. (רוּם 926) *and he was extolled*

תַּחַת לְשׁוֹנִי prep. (1065)-n.f.s.-1 c.s. sf. (546) *with my tongue*

66:18

אָוֶן n.m.s. (19) *iniquity*

אִם־רָאִיתִי hypoth.part. (49)-Qal pf. 1 c.s. (רָאָה 906) *if I had cherished*

בְלִבִּי prep.-n.m.s.-1 c.s. sf. (524) *in my heart*

לֹא יִשְׁמַע neg.-Qal impf. 3 m.s. (1033) *would not have listened*

אֲדֹנָי n.m.p.-1 c.s. sf. (10) *the Lord*

66:19

אָכֵן adv. (38) *truly*

שָׁמַע Qal pf. 3 m.s. (1033) *has listened*

אֱלֹהִים n.m.p. (43) *God*

הִקְשִׁיב Hi. pf. 3 m.s. (קָשַׁב 904) *he has given heed*

בְּקוֹל prep.-n.m.s. cstr. (876) *to the voice of*

תְּפִלָּתִי n.f.s.-1 c.s. sf. (813) *my prayer*

66:20

בָּרוּךְ Qal pass.ptc. (138) *blessed be*

אֱלֹהִים n.m.p. (43) *God*

אֲשֶׁר לֹא־הֵסִיר rel. (81)-neg.-Hi. pf. 3 m.s. (סוּר 693) *because he has not rejected (removed)*

תְּפִלָּתִי n.f.s.-1 c.s. sf. (813) *my prayer*

וְחַסְדּוֹ conj.-n.m.s.-3 m.s. sf. (338) *or his steadfast love*

מֵאִתִּי prep.-prep.-1 c.s. sf. (II 85) *from me*

67:1

לַמְנַצֵּחַ prep.-def.art.-Pi. ptc. (I 669) *to the choirmaster*

בִּנְגִינֹת prep.-n.f.p. (618) *with stringed instruments*

מִזְמוֹר n.m.s. (274) *a Psalm*

שִׁיר n.m.s. (1010) *a Song*

67:2

אֱלֹהִים n.m.p. (43) *God*

יְחָנֵּנוּ Pi. impf. 3 m.s.-1 c.p. sf. (חָנַן I 335) *may ... be gracious to us*

וִיבָרְכֵנוּ conj.-Pi. impf. 3 m.s.-1 c.p. sf. (138) *and bless us*

יָאֵר Hi. impf. 3 m.s. apoc. (אוֹר 21) *and make to shine*

פָּנָיו n.m.p.-3 m.s. sf. (815) *his face*

אִתָּנוּ prep.-1 c.p. sf. (II 85) *upon us*

סֶלָה interj. (699) *Selah*

67:3

לָדַעַת prep.-Qal inf.cstr. (יָדַע 393) *that may be known*

בָּאָרֶץ prep.-def.art.-n.f.s. (75) *upon earth*

דַּרְכֶּךָ n.m.s.-2 m.s. sf. paus. (202) *thy way*

בְּכָל־גּוֹיִם prep.-n.m.s. cstr. (481)-n.m.p. (156) *among all nations*

יְשׁוּעָתֶךָ n.f.s.-2 m.s. sf. (447) *thy saving power*

67:4

יוֹדוּךָ Hi. impf. 3 m.s.-2 m.s. sf. (יָדָה 392) *let praise thee*

עַמִּים n.m.p. (I 766) *peoples*

אֱלֹהִים n.m.p. (43) *O God*

יוֹדוּךָ v.supra *let praise thee*

עַמִּים v.supra *peoples*

כֻּלָּם n.m.s.-3 m.p. sf. (481) *all of them*

67:5

יִשְׂמְחוּ Qal impf. 3 m.p. (970) *let ... be glad*

וִירַנְּנוּ conj.-Pi. impf. 3 m.p. (רָנַן 943) *and sing for joy*

לְאֻמִּים n.m.p. (522) *nations*

כִּי־תִשְׁפֹּט conj. (471)-Qal impf. 2 m.s. (1047) *for thou dost judge*

עַמִּים n.m.p. (I 766) *peoples*

מִישׁוֹר n.m.s. (449) *with equity*

וּלְאֻמִּים conj.-v.supra *and nations*

בָּאָרֶץ prep.-def.art.-n.f.s. (75) *upon earth*

תַּנְחֵם Hi. impf. 2 m.s. apoc. (נָחַם 636) *guide*

סֶלָה interj. (699) *Selah*

67:6

יוֹדוּךָ Hi. impf. 3 m.p.-2 m.s. sf. (יָדָה 392) *let ... praise thee*

עַמִּים n.m.p. (I 766) *peoples*

אֱלֹהִים n.m.p. (43) *O God*

יוֹדוּךָ v.supra *let praise thee*

עַמִּים v.supra *peoples*

כֻּלָּם n.m.s.-3 m.p. sf. (481) *all of them*

67:7

אֶרֶץ n.f.s. (75) *earth*

נָתְנָה Qal pf. 3 f.s. (678) *has yielded*

יְבוּלָהּ n.m.s.-3 f.s. sf. (385) *its increase*

יְבָרְכֵנוּ Pi. impf. 3 m.s.-1 c.p. sf. (בָּרַךְ 138) *has blessed us*
אֱלֹהִים n.m.p. (43) *God*
אֱלֹהֵינוּ n.m.p.-1 c.p. sf. (43) *our God*

67:8

יְבָרְכֵנוּ Pi. impf. 3 m.s.-1 c.p. sf. (בָּרַךְ 138) *has blessed us*
אֱלֹהִים n.m.p. (43) *God*
וְיִירְאוּ conj.-Qal impf. 3 m.p. (יָרֵא 431) *let ... fear*
אֹתוֹ dir.obj.-3 m.s. sf. *him*
כָּל־אַפְסֵי־ n.m.s. cstr. (481)-n.m.p. cstr. (67) *all the ends of*
אָרֶץ n.f.s. paus. (75) *the earth*

68:1

לַמְנַצֵּחַ prep.-def.art.-Pi. ptc. (I 669) *to the choirmaster*
לְדָוִד prep.-pr.n. (187) *to David*
מִזְמוֹר n.m.s. (274) *a Psalm*
שִׁיר n.m.s. (1010) *a Song*

68:2

יָקוּם Qal impf. 3 m.s. (קוּם 877) *let arise*
אֱלֹהִים n.m.p. (43) *God*
יָפוּצוּ Qal impf. 3 m.p. (פּוּץ 806) *let be scattered*
אוֹיְבָיו Qal act.ptc. m.p.-3 m.s. sf. (אָיַב 33) *his enemies*
וְיָנוּסוּ conj.-Qal impf. 3 m.p. (630) *and let flee*
מְשַׂנְאָיו Pi. ptc. m.p.-3 m.s. sf. (שָׂנֵא 971) *those who hate him*
מִפָּנָיו prep.-n.m.p.-3 m.s. sf. (815) *before him*

68:3

כְּהִנְדֹּף prep.-Ni. inf.cstr. (נָדַף 623; GK 19c,51k) *as is driven away*
עָשָׁן n.m.s. (798) *smoke*
תִּנְדֹּף Qal impf. 2 m.s. (623) *so drive them away*
כְּהִמֵּס prep.-Ni. inf.cstr. (מָסַס 587; GK 67t) *as melts*
דּוֹנַג n.m.s. (200) *wax*
מִפְּנֵי־אֵשׁ prep.-n.m.p. cstr. (815)-n.f.s. (77) *before fire*
יֹאבְדוּ Qal impf. 3 m.p. (1) *let ... perish*
רְשָׁעִים adj. m.p. (957) *the wicked*
מִפְּנֵי אֱלֹהִים v.supra-n.m.p. (43) *before God*

68:4

וְצַדִּיקִים conj.-adj. m.p. (843) *but the righteous*
יִשְׂמְחוּ Qal impf. 3 m.p. (970) *let be joyful*
יַעַלְצוּ Qal impf. 3 m.p. (עָלַץ 763) *let them exult*
לִפְנֵי אֱלֹהִים prep.-n.m.p. cstr. (815)-n.m.p. (43) *before God*
וְיָשִׂישׂוּ conj.-Qal impf. 3 m.p. (שׂוּשׂ 965) *let them be jubilant*
בְשִׂמְחָה prep.-n.f.s. (970) *with joy*

68:5

שִׁירוּ Qal impv. 2 m.p. (1010) *sing*
לֵאלֹהִים prep.-n.m.p. (43) *to God*
זַמְּרוּ Pi. impv. 2 m.p. (I 274) *sing praises to*
שְׁמוֹ n.m.s.-3 m.s. sf. (1027) *his name*
סֹלּוּ Qal impv. 2 m.p. (סָלַל 699) *cast up a highway*
לָרֹכֵב prep.-def.art.-Qal act.ptc. (938) *for him who rides*
בָּעֲרָבוֹת prep.-def.art.-n.f.p. (787) *through the deserts*
בְּיָהּ prep.-pr.n. (219; GK 119iN) *in Yah*
שְׁמוֹ n.m.s.-3 m.s. sf. (1027) *his name*
וְעִלְזוּ Qal impv. 2 m.p. (עָלַז 759) *exult*
לְפָנָיו prep.-n.m.p.-3 m.s. sf. (815) *before him*

68:6

אֲבִי n.m.s. cstr. (3) *father of*
יְתוֹמִים n.m.p. (450) *fatherless*
וְדַיַּן conj.-n.m.s. cstr. (193) *and protector of*
אַלְמָנוֹת n.f.p. (48) *widows*
אֱלֹהִים n.m.p. (43) *God*
בִּמְעוֹן קָדְשׁוֹ prep.-n.m.s. cstr. (732)-n.m.s.-3 m.s. sf. (871) *in his holy habitation*

68:7

אֱלֹהִים n.m.p. (43) *God*
מוֹשִׁיב Hi. ptc. (יָשַׁב 442) *gives to dwell in*
יְחִידִים adj. m.p. (402) *the desolate*
בַּיְתָה n.m.s.-dir.he (108) *a home*
מוֹצִיא Hi. ptc. (יָצָא 422) *he leads out*
אֲסִירִים n.m.p. (64) *prisoners*
בַּכּוֹשָׁרוֹת prep.-def.art.-n.f.p. (507; GK 124e) *to prosperity*
אַךְ adv. (36) *but*
סוֹרְרִים Qal act.ptc. m.p. (710; GK 10g) *rebellious*
שָׁכְנוּ Qal pf. 3 c.p. (1014; GK 117bb) *dwell*
צְחִיחָה n.f.s. (850) *in a parched land*

68:8

אֱלֹהִים (43) *O God*
בְּצֵאתְךָ prep.-Qal inf.cstr.-2 m.s. sf. (יָצָא 422) *when thou didst go forth*
לִפְנֵי עַמֶּךָ prep.-n.m.p. cstr. (815)-n.m.s.-2 m.s. sf. (I 766) *before thy people*

בְּצַעְדְּךָ prep.-Qal inf.cstr.-2 m.s. sf. (צָעַד 857) *when thou didst march*
בִישִׁימוֹן prep.-n.m.s. (445) *through the wilderness*
סֶלָה interj. (699) *Selah*

68:9

אֶרֶץ n.f.s. (75) *earth*
רָעָשָׁה Qal pf. 3 f.s. (רָעַשׁ 950) *quaked*
אַף־שָׁמַיִם adv. (II 64)-n.m. du. (1029) *yea, heavens*
נָטְפוּ Qal pf. 3 c.p. (642) *poured down rain*
מִפְּנֵי אֱלֹהִים prep.-n.m.p. cstr. (815)-n.m.p. (43) *at the presence of God*
זֶה סִינַי demons.adj. m.s. (260)-pr.n. (696; GK 136dN) *yon Sinai*
מִפְּנֵי אֱלֹהִים v.supra-v.supra *at the presence of God*
אֱלֹהֵי n.m.p. cstr. (43) *the God of*
יִשְׂרָאֵל pr.n. (975) *Israel*

68:10

גֶּשֶׁם n.m.s. (177) *rain*
נְדָבוֹת n.f.p. (621) *in abundance*
תָּנִיף Hi. impf. 2 m.s. (נוּף 631) *thou didst shed abroad*
אֱלֹהִים n.m.p. (43) *O God*
נַחֲלָתְךָ n.f.s.-2 m.s. sf. (635) *thy heritage*
וְנִלְאָה conj.-Ni. pf. 3 m.s. (לָאָה 521) *as it languished*
אַתָּה כוֹנַנְתָּהּ pers.pr. 2 m.s. (61)-Polel pf. 2 m.s.-3 f.s. sf. (כּוּן 465) *thou didst restore (it)*

68:11

חַיָּתְךָ n.f.s.-2 m.s. sf. (312) *thy flock*
יָשְׁבוּ־ Qal pf. 3 c.p. (442) *they found a dwelling*
בָהּ prep.-3 f.s. sf. *in it*
תָּכִין Hi. impf. 2 m.s. (כּוּן 465) *thou didst provide*
בְּטוֹבָתְךָ prep.-n.f.s.-2 m.s. sf. (375) *in thy goodness*
לֶעָנִי prep.-def.art.-n.m.s. (776) *for the needy*
אֱלֹהִים n.m.p. (43) *O God*

68:12

אֲדֹנָי n.m.p.-1 c.s. sf. (10) *the Lord*
יִתֶּן־ Qal impf. 3 m.s. (נָתַן 678) *gives*
אֹמֶר n.m.s. (56) *the command*
הַמְבַשְּׂרוֹת def.art.-Pi. ptc. f.p. (בָּשַׂר 142) *those who bore the tidings*
צָבָא n.m.s. (838) *the host*
רָב adj. m.s. (I 912) *great*

68:13

מַלְכֵי n.m.p. cstr. (I 572) *kings of*
צְבָאוֹת n.m.p. (838) *armies*
יִדֹּדוּן Qal impf. 3 m.p. (נָדַד 622) *they flee*
יִדֹּדוּן v.supra *they flee*
וּנְוַת conj.-adj. f.s. cstr. (627) *the women at*
בַּיִת n.m.s. (108) *home*
תְּחַלֵּק Pi. impf. 3 f.s. (חָלַק 323) *divide*
שָׁלָל n.m.s. paus. (1021) *spoil*

68:14

אִם־תִּשְׁכְּבוּן hypoth.part. (49)-Qal impf. 2 m.p. (1014 שָׁכַב) *though you stay*
בֵּין שְׁפַתָּיִם prep. (107)-n.f. du. (1046) *among the sheepfolds*
כַּנְפֵי n.f.p. cstr. (489) *the wings of*
יוֹנָה n.f.s. (401) *a dove*
נֶחְפָּה Ni. pf. 3 m.s. (חָפָה 341) *covered*
בַכֶּסֶף prep.-def.art.-n.m.s. (494) *with silver*
וְאֶבְרוֹתֶיהָ conj.-n.f.p.-3 f.s. sf. (7) *and its pinions*
בִּירַקְרַק חָרוּץ prep.-adj. m.s. (439)-n.m.s. (359) *with green gold*

68:15

בְּפָרֵשׂ prep.-Pi. inf.cstr. (831) *when ... scattered*
שַׁדַּי pr.n. (994) *the Almighty*
מְלָכִים n.m.p. (I 572) *kings*
בָּהּ prep.-3 f.s. sf. *there*
תַּשְׁלֵג Hi. impf. 2 m.s. apoc. (שָׁלַג 1017) *thou didst cause snow to fall*
בְּצַלְמוֹן prep.-pr.n. (854) *on Zalmon*

68:16

הַר־אֱלֹהִים n.m.s. cstr. (249)-n.m.p. (43) *O mountain of God*
הַר־בָּשָׁן v.supra-pr.n. (143) *mountain of Bashan*
הַר גַּבְנֻנִּים v.supra-n.m.p. (148) *O many-peaked mountain*
הַר־בָּשָׁן v.supra-v.supra *mountain of Bashan*

68:17

לָמָּה interr. (552) *why*
תְּרַצְּדוּן Pi. impf. 2 m.p. (רָצַד 952) *look you with envy*
הָרִים גַּבְנֻנִּים n.m.p. (249)-n.m.p. (148) *O many-peaked mountain*
הָהָר def.art.-n.m.s. (249) *at the mount*
חָמַד Qal pf. 3 m.s. (326; GK 131c) *desired*

אֱלֹהִים n.m.p. (43) *God*
לְשִׁבְתּוֹ prep.-n.f.s.-3 m.s. sf. (443) *for his abode*
אַף־יְהוָה adv. (II 64)-pr.n. (217) *yea, Yahweh*
יִשְׁכֹּן Qal impf. 3 m.s. (1014) *will dwell*
לָנֶצַח prep.-n.m.s. paus. (664) *for ever*

68:18

רֶכֶב אֱלֹהִים n.m.s. cstr. (939)-n.m.p. (43) *chariot of God*
רִבֹּתַיִם n.f. du. (914; GK 97h) *twice ten thousand*
אַלְפֵי שִׁנְאָן n.m.p. cstr. (48)-n.m.s. (1041) *thousands upon thousands*
אֲדֹנָי n.m.p.-1 c.s. sf. (10) *the Lord*
בָם prep.-3 m.p. sf. (GK 21c) *among them*
סִינַי pr.n. (696) *Sinai*
בַּקֹּדֶשׁ prep.-def.art.-n.m.s. (871) *in the holy place*

68:19

עָלִיתָ Qal pf. 2 m.s. (עָלָה 748) *thou didst ascend*
לַמָּרוֹם prep.-def.art.-n.m.s. (928) *the high mount*
שָׁבִיתָ שֶּׁבִי Qal pf. 2 m.s. (שָׁבָה 985; GK 20f)-n.m.s. paus. (985) *leading captives in thy train*
לָקַחְתָּ Qal pf. 2 m.s. (542) *thou receivest*
מַתָּנוֹת n.f.p. (682) *gifts*
בָּאָדָם prep.-def.art.-n.m.s. (9) *among men*
וְאַף conj.-adv. (II 64) *even*
סוֹרְרִים Qal act.ptc. m.p. (710) *the rebellious*
לִשְׁכֹּן prep.-Qal inf.cstr. (1014; GK 117bb) *that may dwell*
יָהּ אֱלֹהִים pr.n. (219)-n.m.p. (43) *Yahweh God*

68:20

בָּרוּךְ Qal pass.ptc. (138) *blessed*
אֲדֹנָי n.m.p.-1 c.s. sf. (10) *the Lord*
יוֹם יוֹם n.m.s. (398)-v.supra *daily*
יַעֲמָס־לָנוּ Qal impf. 3 m.s. (770)-prep.-1 c.p. sf. *bears us up*
הָאֵל def.art.-n.m.s. (42) *God*
יְשׁוּעָתֵנוּ n.f.s.-1 c.p. sf. (447) *our salvation*
סֶלָה interj. (699) *Selah*

68:21

הָאֵל לָנוּ def.art.-n.m.s. (42)-prep.-1 c.p. sf. *our God*
אֵל n.m.s. (42) *a God*
לְמוֹשָׁעוֹת prep.-n.f.p. (448) *of salvation*
וְלֵיהוִה conj.-prep.-pr.n. (217) *and to Yahweh*
אֲדֹנָי n.m.p.-1 c.s. sf. (10) *the Lord*
לַמָּוֶת prep.-def.art.-n.m.s. (560) *from death*

תּוֹצָאוֹת n.f.p. (426) *belongs escape*

68:22

אַךְ־אֱלֹהִים adv. (36)-n.m.p. (43) *but God*
יִמְחַץ Qal impf. 3 m.s. (563) *will shatter*
רֹאשׁ n.m.s. cstr. (910) *the heads of*
אֹיְבָיו Qal act.ptc. m.p.-3 m.s. sf. (אָיַב 33) *his enemies*
קָדְקֹד שֵׂעָר n.m.s. (869)-n.m.s. (972; GK 128c) *hairy crown*
מִתְהַלֵּךְ Hith. ptc. (229) *of him who walks*
בַּאֲשָׁמָיו prep.-n.m.p.-3 m.s. sf. (79) *in his guilty ways*

68:23

אָמַר Qal pf. 3 m.s. (55) *said*
אֲדֹנָי n.m.p.-1 c.s. sf. (10) *the Lord*
מִבָּשָׁן prep.-pr.n. (143) *from Bashan*
אָשִׁיב Hi. impf. 1 c.s. (שׁוּב 996) *I will bring them back*
אָשִׁיב v.supra *I will bring them back*
מִמְּצֻלוֹת יָם prep.-n.f.p. cstr. (846)-n.m.s. (410) *from the depths of the sea*

68:24

לְמַעַן prep. (775) *that*
תִּמְחַץ Qal impf. 2 m.s. (563) *you may shatter*
רַגְלְךָ n.f.s.-2 m.s. sf. (919) *your feet*
בְּדָם prep.-n.m.s. (196) *in blood*
לְשׁוֹן n.f.s. cstr. (546) *the tongues of*
כְּלָבֶיךָ n.m.p.-2 m.s. sf. (476) *your dogs*
מֵאֹיְבִים prep.-Qal act.ptc. m.p. (33) *from the foe*
מִנֵּהוּ n.m.s.-3 m.s. sf. (585; GK 103m) *their portion*

68:25

רָאוּ Qal pf. 3 c.p. (רָאָה 906) *they have seen*
הֲלִיכוֹתֶיךָ n.f.p.-2 m.s. sf. (237) *thy solemn processions*
אֱלֹהִים n.m.p. (43) *O God*
הֲלִיכוֹת n.f.p. cstr. (237) *the processions of*
אֵלִי n.m.s.-1 c.s. sf. (42) *my God*
מַלְכִּי n.m.s.-1 c.s. sf. (I 572) *my King*
בַקֹּדֶשׁ prep.-def.art.-n.m.s. (871) *into the sanctuary*

68:26

קִדְּמוּ Pi. pf. 3 c.p. (869) *are in front*
שָׁרִים Qal act.ptc. m.p. (שִׁיר 1010) *singers*
אַחַר נֹגְנִים prep. (29)-Qal act.ptc. m.p. (נָגַן 618) *the minstrels last*

בְּתוֹךְ עֲלָמוֹת prep.-n.m.s. cstr. (1063)-n.f.p. (761) *between them maidens*
תּוֹפֵפוֹת Qal act.ptc. f.p. (תָּפַף 1074) *playing timbrels*

68:27

בְּמַקְהֵלוֹת prep.-n.f.p. (875) *in the great congregation*
בָּרְכוּ Pi. impv. 2 m.p. (138) *bless*
אֱלֹהִים n.m.p. (43) *God*
יהוה pr.n. (217) *Yahweh*
מִמְּקוֹר prep.-n.m.s. cstr. (881) *from the fountain of*
יִשְׂרָאֵל pr.n. (975) *Israel*

68:28

שָׁם adv. (1027) *there*
בִּנְיָמִן pr.n. (122) *Benjamin*
צָעִיר adv. (I 859) *the least of them*
רֹדֵם Qal act.ptc.-3 m.p. sf. (רָדָה I 921) *in the lead*
שָׂרֵי n.m.p. cstr. (978) *princes of*
יְהוּדָה pr.n. (397) *Judah*
רִגְמָתָם n.f.s.-3 m.p. sf. (920) *in their throng*
שָׂרֵי v.supra *princes of*
זְבֻלוּן pr.n. (259) *Zebulun*
שָׂרֵי v.supra *princes of*
נַפְתָּלִי pr.n. (836) *Naphtali*

68:29

צִוָּה Pi. pf. 3 m.s. (845) *summoned*
אֱלֹהֶיךָ n.m.p.-2 m.s. sf. (43) *thy God*
עֻזֶּךָ n.m.s.-2 m.s. sf. (738) *thy strength*
עוּזָּה Qal impv. 2 m.s.-vol.he (עָזַז 738) *show thy strength*
אֱלֹהִים n.m.p. (43) *O God*
זוּ rel. (262) *that*
פָּעַלְתָּ Qal pf. 2 m.s. (821) *thou hast wrought*
לָּנוּ prep.-1 c.p. sf. *for us*

68:30

מֵהֵיכָלֶךָ prep.-n.m.s.-2 m.s. sf. (228) *because of thy temple*
עַל־יְרוּשָׁלָםִ prep.-pr.n. (436) *at Jerusalem*
לְךָ prep.-2 m.s. sf. *to thee*
יוֹבִילוּ Hi. impf. 3 m.p. (יָבַל 384) *bear*
מְלָכִים n.m.p. (I 572) *kings*
שָׁי n.m.s. paus. (1009) *gifts*

68:31

גְּעַר Qal impv. 2 m.s. (172) *rebuke*
חַיַּת n.f.s. cstr. (312) *the beasts of*
קָנֶה n.m.s. (889) *the reeds*
עֲדַת n.f.s. cstr. (417) *herd of*
אַבִּירִים n.m.p. (7) *bulls*
בְּעֶגְלֵי prep.-n.m.p. cstr. (722) *with calves of*
עַמִּים n.m.p. (I 766) *peoples*
מִתְרַפֵּס Hith. ptc. (רָפַס 952) *trampling*
בְּרַצֵּי־ prep.-n.m.p. cstr. (954) *after pieces of*
כָסֶף n.m.s. paus. (494) *silver*
בִּזַּר Pi. pf. 3 m.s. (בָּזַר 103; rd. prb. בַּזֵּר Pi. impv. 2 m.s.) *scatter*
עַמִּים n.m.p. (I 766) *peoples*
קְרָבוֹת n.f.p. (899) *nearness (?)*
יֶחְפָּצוּ Qal impf. 3 m.p. (חָפֵץ 342) *they delight in*

68:32

יֶאֱתָיוּ Qal impf. 3 m.p. (אָתָה 87; GK 75u) *let be brought*
חַשְׁמַנִּים n.m.p. (365) *bronze (?)*
מִנִּי מִצְרָיִם prep. (577)-pr.n. paus. (595) *from Egypt*
כּוּשׁ pr.n. (468) *Ethiopia (Cush)*
תָּרִיץ Hi. impf. 3 f.s. (רוּץ 930) *let hasten to stretch out*
יָדָיו n.f.p.-3 m.s. sf. (388) *her hands (his hands)*
לֵאלֹהִים prep.-n.m.p. (43) *to God*

68:33

מַמְלְכוֹת n.f.p. cstr. (575) *O kingdoms of*
הָאָרֶץ def.art.-n.f.s. (75) *the earth*
שִׁירוּ Qal impv. 2 m.p. (1010) *sing*
לֵאלֹהִים prep.-n.m.p. (43) *to God*
זַמְּרוּ Pi. impv. 2 m.p. (I 274) *sing praises*
אֲדֹנָי n.m.p.-1 c.s. sf. (10) *to the Lord*
סֶלָה interj. (699) *Selah*

68:34

לָרֹכֵב prep.-def.art.-Qal act.ptc. (רָכַב 938) *to him who rides*
בִּשְׁמֵי prep.-n.m. du. cstr. (1029) *in the heavens*
שְׁמֵי־קֶדֶם v.supra-n.m.s. (869) *the ancient heavens*
הֵן demons.part. (243) *lo*
יִתֵּן Qal impf. 3 m.s. (נָתַן 678; GK 119q) *he sends forth*
בְּקוֹלוֹ prep.-n.m.s.-3 m.s. sf. (876) *his voice*
קוֹל עֹז n.m.s. cstr. (876)-n.m.s. (738) *his mighty voice*

68:35

תְּנוּ Qal impv. 2 m.p. (נָתַן 678) *ascribe*
עֹז n.m.s. (738) *power*

לֵאלֹהִים prep.-n.m.p. (43) *to God*
עַל־יִשְׂרָאֵל prep.-pr.n. (975) *over Israel*
גַּאֲוָתוֹ n.f.s.-3 m.s. sf. (144) *his majesty*
וְעֻזּוֹ conj.-n.m.s.-3 m.s. sf. (738) *and his power*
בַּשְּׁחָקִים prep.-def.art.-n.m.p. (1007) *in the skies*

68:36

נוֹרָא Ni. ptc. (יָרֵא 431) *terrible*
אֱלֹהִים n.m.p. (43) *God*
מִמִּקְדָּשֶׁיךָ prep.-n.m.p.-2 m.s. sf. (874) *from thy sanctuary*
אֵל יִשְׂרָאֵל n.m.s. cstr. (42)-pr.n. (975) *the God of Israel*
הוּא נֹתֵן pers.pr. 3 m.s. (214)-Qal act.ptc. (678) *he gives*
עֹז n.m.s. (738) *power*
וְתַעֲצֻמוֹת conj.-n.f.p. (783) *and strength*
לָעָם prep.-def.art.-n.m.s. (I 766) *to the people*
בָּרוּךְ Qal pass.ptc. (138) *blessed*
אֱלֹהִים n.m.p. (43) *God*

69:1

לַמְנַצֵּחַ prep.-def.art.-Pi. ptc. (I 669) *to the choirmaster*
עַל־שׁוֹשַׁנִּים prep.-n.m.p. (1004) *according to Lilies*
לְדָוִד prep.-pr.n. (187) *to David*

69:2

הוֹשִׁיעֵנִי Hi. impv. 2 m.s.-1 c.s. sf. (יָשַׁע 446) *save me*
אֱלֹהִים n.m.p. (43) *O God*
כִּי בָאוּ conj. (471)-Qal pf. 3 c.p. (בּוֹא 97) *for have come*
מַיִם n.m.p. (565) *waters*
עַד־נָפֶשׁ prep. (III 723)-n.f.s. (659) *up to my neck*

69:3

טָבַעְתִּי Qal pf. 1 c.s. (371) *I sink*
בִּיוֵן מְצוּלָה prep.-n.m.s. cstr. (401)-n.f.s. (846) *in deep mire*
וְאֵין מָעֳמָד conj.-neg. cstr. (II 34)-n.m.s. (765) *where there is no foothold*
בָּאתִי Qal pf. 1 c.s. (בּוֹא 97) *I have come*
בְמַעֲמַקֵּי־מַיִם prep.-n.m.p. cstr. (771)-n.m.p. (565) *into deep waters*
וְשִׁבֹּלֶת conj.-n.f.s. (987) *and the flood*
שְׁטָפָתְנִי Qal pf. 3 f.s.-1 c.s. sf. (שָׁטַף 1009) *sweeps over me*

69:4

יָגַעְתִּי Qal pf. 1 c.s. (יָגַע 388) *I am weary*
בְקָרְאִי prep.-Qal inf.cstr.-1 c.s. sf. (894) *with my crying*
נִחַר Ni. pf. 3 m.s. (חָרַר 359) *is parched*
גְּרוֹנִי n.m.s.-1 c.s. sf. (173) *my throat*
כָּלוּ Qal pf. 3 c.p. (כָּלָה 477) *grow dim*
עֵינַי n.f. du.-1 c.s. sf. (744) *my eyes*
מְיַחֵל Pi. ptc. (יָחַל 403; GK 118p) *with waiting*
לֵאלֹהָי prep.-n.m.p.-1 c.s. sf. paus. *(43) for my God*

69:5

רַבּוּ Qal pf. 3 c.p. (רָבַב 912) *are more in number*
מִשַּׂעֲרוֹת prep.-n.f.p. cstr. (972; GK 122t) *than the hairs of*
רֹאשִׁי n.m.s.-1 c.s. sf. (910) *my head*
שֹׂנְאַי Qal act.ptc. m.p.-1 c.s. sf. (שָׂנֵא 971) *those who hate me*
חִנָּם adv. (336; GK 131qN) *without cause*
עָצְמוּ Qal pf. 3 c.p. (782) *are mighty*
מַצְמִיתַי Hi. ptc. m.p.-1 c.s. sf. (צָמַת 856) *those who would destroy me*
אֹיְבַי Qal act.ptc. m.p.-1 c.s. sf. (אָיַב 33) *those who attack me*
שֶׁקֶר n.m.s. (1055) *with lies*
אֲשֶׁר לֹא־גָזַלְתִּי rel. (81)-neg.-Qal pf. 1 c.s. (159) *what I did not steal*
אָז אָשִׁיב adv. (23)-Hi. impf. 1 c.s. (שׁוּב 996) *must I now restore?*

69:6

אֱלֹהִים n.m.p. (43) *O God*
אַתָּה pers.pr. 2 m.s. (61) *thou*
יָדַעְתָּ Qal pf. 2 m.s. (393) *knowest*
לְאִוַּלְתִּי prep.-n.f.s.-1 c.s. sf. (17) *my folly*
וְאַשְׁמוֹתַי conj.-n.f.p.-1 c.s. sf. (80) *and the wrongs I have done*
מִמְּךָ prep.-2 m.s. sf. *from thee*
לֹא־נִכְחָדוּ neg.-Ni. pf. 3 c.p. paus. (כָּחַד 470) *are not hidden*

69:7

אַל־יֵבֹשׁוּ neg.-Qal impf. 3 m.p. (בּוֹשׁ 101) *let not be put to shame*
בִי prep.-1 c.s. sf. *through me*
קֹוֶיךָ Qal act.ptc. m.p.-2 m.s. sf. (קָוָה I 875) *those who hope in thee*
אֲדֹנָי n.m.p.-1 c.s. sf. (10) *O Lord*
יהוה צְבָאוֹת pr.n. (217)-pr.n. (838) *Yahweh of hosts*

אַל־יֵבֹשׁוּ neg.-Ni. impf. 3 m.p. (483) *let not be brought to dishonor*
בִּי v.supra *through me*
מְבַקְשֶׁיךָ Pi. ptc. m.p.-2 m.s. sf. (134) *those who seek thee*
אֱלֹהֵי יִשְׂרָאֵל n.m.p. cstr. (43)-pr.n. (975) *O God of Israel*

69:8

כִּי־עָלֶיךָ conj. (471)-prep.-2 m.s. sf. *for for thy sake*
נָשָׂאתִי Qal pf. 1 c.s. (669) *I have borne*
חֶרְפָּה n.f.s. (357) *reproach*
כִּסְּתָה Pi. pf. 3 f.s. (כָּסָה 491) *has covered*
כְלִמָּה n.f.s. (484) *shame*
פָנָי n.m.p.-1 c.s. sf. paus. (815) *my face*

69:9

מוּזָר Ho. ptc. (זור I 266) *estranged*
הָיִיתִי Qal pf. 1 c.s. (הָיָה 224) *I have become*
לְאֶחָי prep.-n.m.p.-1 c.s. sf. paus. (26) *to my brethren*
וְנָכְרִי conj.-n.m.s. (648) *and an alien*
לִבְנֵי prep.-n.m.p. cstr. (119) *to the sons of*
אִמִּי n.f.s.-1 c.s. sf. (51) *my mother*

69:10

כִּי־קִנְאַת conj. (471)-n.f.s. cstr. (888) *for zeal for*
בֵּיתְךָ n.m.s.-2 m.s. sf. (108) *thy house*
אֲכָלָתְנִי Qal pf. 3 f.s.-1 c.s. sf. (37) *has consumed me*
וְחֶרְפּוֹת conj.-n.f.p. cstr. (357; GK 95bN) *and the insults of*
חוֹרְפֶיךָ Qal act.ptc. m.p.-2 m.s. sf. (חָרַף 357) *those who insult thee*
נָפְלוּ Qal pf. 3 c.p. (656) *have fallen*
עָלָי prep.-1 c.s. sf. paus. *on me*

69:11

וָאֶבְכֶּה consec.-Qal impf. 1 c.s. (בָּכָה 113; GK 144,lN) *and I wept*
בַצּוֹם prep.-def.art.-n.m.s. (847) *with fasting*
נַפְשִׁי n.f.s.-1 c.s. sf. (659) *my soul*
וַתְּהִי consec.-Qal impf. 3 f.s. (הָיָה 224) *and it became*
לַחֲרָפוֹת לִי prep.-n.f.p. (357)-prep.-1 c.s. sf. *my reproach*

69:12

וָאֶתְּנָה consec.-Qal impf. 1 c.s. (נָתַן 678) *when I made*
לְבוּשִׁי n.m.s.-1 c.s. sf. (528) *my clothing*
שָׂק n.m.s. (974) *sackcloth*
וָאֱהִי consec.-Qal impf. 1 c.s. (הָיָה 224) *then I became*
לָהֶם prep.-3 m.p. sf. *to them*
לְמָשָׁל prep.-n.m.s. (605) *a byword*

69:13

יָשִׂיחוּ Qal impf. 3 m.p. (שִׂיחַ 967) *I am the talk (?)* (lit. *they talk about)*
בִי prep.-1 c.s. sf. *at me*
יֹשְׁבֵי Qal act.ptc. m.p. cstr. (442) *those who sit*
שָׁעַר n.m.s. paus. (1044) *in the gate*
וּנְגִינוֹת conj.-n.f.p. (618) *and make songs*
שׁוֹתֵי שֵׁכָר Qal act.ptc. m.p. cstr. (שָׁתָה 1059) -n.m.s. paus. (1016) *the drunkards*

69:14

וַאֲנִי conj.-pers.pr. 1 c.s. (58) *but as for me*
תְפִלָּתִי־ n.f.s.-1 c.s. sf. (813) *my prayer*
לְךָ prep.-2 m.s. sf. *to thee*
יהוה pr.n. (217) *O Yahweh*
עֵת רָצוֹן n.f.s. cstr. (773)-n.m.s. (953) *at an acceptable time*
אֱלֹהִים n.m.p. (43) *O God*
בְּרָב־חַסְדֶּךָ prep.-n.m.s. cstr. (913)-n.m.s.-2 m.s. sf. paus. (338) *in the abundance of thy steadfast love*
עֲנֵנִי Qal impv. 2 m.s.-1 c.s. sf. (עָנָה I 772) *answer me*
בֶּאֱמֶת יִשְׁעֶךָ prep.-n.f.s. cstr. (54)-n.m.s.-2 m.s. sf. (447) *with thy faithful help*

69:15

הַצִּילֵנִי Hi. impv. 2 m.s.-1 c.s. sf. (נָצַל 664) *rescue me*
מִטִּיט prep.-n.m.s. (376) *from mire*
וְאַל־אֶטְבָּעָה conj.-neg.-Qal impv. 1 c.s.-vol.he (371 טָבַע) *that I may not sink*
אִנָּצְלָה Ni. impf. 1 c.s.-vol.he (664) *let me be delivered*
מִשֹּׂנְאַי prep.-Qal act.ptc. m.p.-1 c.s. sf. (שָׂנֵא 971) *from my enemies*
וּמִמַּעֲמַקֵּי־מָיִם conj.-prep.-n.m.p. cstr. (771) -n.m.p. paus. (565) *and from the deep waters*

69:16

אַל־תִּשְׁטְפֵנִי neg.-Qal impf. 3 f.s.-1 c.s. sf. (1009) *let not sweep over me*
שִׁבֹּלֶת מַיִם n.f.s. cstr. (987)-n.m.p. (565) *the flood*

וְאַל־תִּבְלָעֵנִי conj.-neg.-Qal impf. 3 f.s.-1 c.s. sf. (118 בָּלַע) *or let not swallow me*
מְצוּלָה n.f.s. (846) *the deep*
וְאַל־תֶּאְטַר־ conj.-neg.-Qal impf. 3 f.s. (אָטַר 32) *or let not close*
עָלַי prep.-1 c.s. sf. *over me*
בְּאֵר n.f.s. (91) *the pit*
פִּיהָ n.m.s.-3 f.s. sf. (804) *its mouth*

69:17

עֲנֵנִי Qal impv. 2 m.s.-1 c.s. sf. (עָנָה I 772) *answer me*
יהוה pr.n. (217) *O Yahweh*
כִּי־טוֹב conj. (471)-adj. m.s. (II 373) *for is good*
חַסְדֶּךָ n.m.s.-2 m.s. sf. (338) *thy steadfast love*
כְּרֹב prep.-n.m.s. cstr. (913) *according to the abundance of*
רַחֲמֶיךָ n.m.p.-2 m.s. sf. (933) *thy mercies*
פְּנֵה Qal impv. 2 m.s. (815) *turn*
אֵלָי prep.-1 c.s. sf. paus. *to me*

69:18

וְאַל־תַּסְתֵּר conj.-neg.-Hi. impf. 2 m.s. apoc. (711 סָתַר) *hide not*
פָּנֶיךָ n.m.p.-2 m.s. sf. (815) *thy face*
מֵעַבְדֶּךָ prep.-n.m.s.-2 m.s. sf. (713) *from thy servant*
כִּי־צַר־לִי conj. (471)-n.m.s. (865)-prep.-1 c.s. sf. *for I am in distress*
מַהֵר Pi. impv. 2 m.s. (I 554) *make haste*
עֲנֵנִי Qal impv. 2 m.s.-1 c.s. sf. (עָנָה I 772) *answer me*

69:19

קָרְבָה Qal impv. 2 m.s.-vol.he (897; GK 48i) *draw near*
אֶל־נַפְשִׁי prep.-n.f.s.-1 c.s. sf. (659) *to me*
גְאָלָהּ Qal impv. 2 m.s.-3 f.s. sf. (I 145) *redeem me (my life)*
לְמַעַן אֹיְבַי prep. (775)-Qal act.ptc. m.p.-1 c.s. sf. (אָיַב 33) *because of my enemies*
פְּדֵנִי Qal impv. 2 m.s.-1 c.s. sf. (פָּדָה 804) *set me free*

69:20

אַתָּה יָדַעְתָּ pers.pr. 2 m.s. (61)-Qal pf. 2 m.s. (393) *thou knowest*
חֶרְפָּתִי n.f.s.-1 c.s. sf. (357) *my reproach*
וּבָשְׁתִּי conj.-n.f.s.-1 c.s. sf. (102) *and my shame*
וּכְלִמָּתִי conj.-n.f.s.-1 c.s. sf. (484) *and my dishonor*
נֶגְדְּךָ prep.-2 m.s. sf. (617) *known to thee*

כָּל־צוֹרְרָי n.m.s. cstr. (481)-Qal act.ptc. m.p.-1 c.s. sf. paus. (III 865) *all my foes*

69:21

חֶרְפָּה n.f.s. (357) *insults*
שָׁבְרָה Qal pf. 3 f.s. (990) *have broken*
לִבִּי n.m.s.-1 c.s. sf. (524) *my heart*
וָאָנוּשָׁה consec.-Qal impf. 1 c.s. (נוּשׁ 633) *so that I am in despair*
וָאֲקַוֶּה consec.-Pi. impf. 1 c.s. (קָוָה I 875) *so I looked*
לָנוּד prep.-Qal inf.cstr. (626) *for pity*
וָאַיִן conj.-neg. (II 34) *but there was none*
וְלַמְנַחֲמִים conj.-prep.-def.art.-Pi. ptc. m.p. (נָחַם 636) *and for comforters*
וְלֹא מָצָאתִי conj.-neg.-Qal pf. 1 c.s. (מָצָא 592) *but I found none*

69:22

וַיִּתְּנוּ consec.-Qal impf. 3 m.p. (נָתַן 678) *and they gave*
בְּבָרוּתִי prep.-n.f.s.-1 c.s. sf. (136) *for my food*
רֹאשׁ n.m.s. (II 912) *poison*
וְלִצְמָאִי conj.-prep.-n.m.s.-1 c.s. sf. (854) *and for my thirst*
יַשְׁקוּנִי Hi. impf. 3 m.p.-1 c.s. sf. (שָׁקָה 1052) *and they gave me to drink*
חֹמֶץ n.m.s. (330) *vinegar*

69:23

יְהִי־ Qal impf. 3 m.s. apoc. (הָיָה 224) *let become*
שֻׁלְחָנָם n.m.s.-3 m.p. sf. (1020) *their own table*
לִפְנֵיהֶם prep.-n.m.p.-3 m.p. sf. (815) *before them*
לְפָח prep.-n.m.s. paus. (809) *a snare*
וְלִשְׁלוֹמִים conj.-prep.-n.m.p. (1022) *and for security*
לְמוֹקֵשׁ prep.-n.m.s. (430) *a trap*

69:24

תֶּחְשַׁכְנָה Qal impf. 3 f.p. (חָשַׁךְ 364) *let be darkened*
עֵינֵיהֶם n.f.p.-3 m.p. sf. (744) *their eyes*
מֵרְאוֹת prep.-Qal inf.cstr. (רָאָה 906) *so that they cannot see*
וּמָתְנֵיהֶם conj.-n.m. du.-3 m.p. sf. (608) *and their loins*
תָּמִיד adv. (556) *continually*
הַמְעַד Hi. impv. 2 m.s. (מָעַד 588; GK 64h) *tremble*

69:25

שְׁפָךְ Qal impv. 2 m.s. (1049) *pour out*

עֲלֵיהֶם prep.-3 m.p. sf. *upon them*

זַעְמֶךָ n.m.s.-2 m.s. sf. (276) *thy indignation*

וַחֲרוֹן אַפְּךָ conj.-n.m.s. cstr. (354)-n.m.s.-2 m.s. sf. (I 60) *and thy burning anger*

יַשִּׂיגֵם Hi. impf. 3 m.s.-3 m.p. sf. (נָשַׂג 673) *let overtake them*

69:26

תְּהִי־ Qal impf. 3 f.s. apoc. (הָיָה 224) *may be*

טִירָתָם n.f.s.-3 m.p. sf. (377) *their camp*

נְשַׁמָּה Ni. ptc. f.s. (שָׁמֵם 1030) *a desolation*

בְּאָהֳלֵיהֶם prep.-n.m.p.-3 m.p. sf. (13) *in their tents*

אַל־יְהִי neg.-Qal impf. 3 m.s. apoc. (הָיָה 224) *let not be*

יֹשֵׁב Qal act.ptc. (יָשַׁב 442) *a dweller*

69:27

כִּי־אַתָּה conj. (471)-pers.pr. 2 m.s. (61) *for thou*

אֲשֶׁר־הִכִּיתָ rel. (81)-Hi. pf. 2 m.s. (נָכָה 645) *whom thou hast smitten*

רָדָפוּ Qal pf. 3 c.p. paus. (922) *they persecuted*

וְאֶל־מַכְאוֹב חֲלָלֶיךָ conj.-prep.-n.m.s. cstr. (456) -n.m.p.-2 m.s. sf. (319) *and the pain of thy wounded ones*

יְסַפֵּרוּ Pi. impf. 3 m.p. paus. (707) *they recount*

69:28

תְּנָה־ Qal impv. 2 m.s.-vol.he (נָתַן 678) *add*

עָוֹן n.m.s. (730) *punishment*

עַל־עֲוֹנָם prep.-n.m.s.-3 m.p. sf. (730) *upon their punishment*

וְאַל־יָבֹאוּ conj.-neg.-Qal impf. 3 m.p. (בּוֹא 97) *and may they not come*

בְּצִדְקָתֶךָ prep.-n.f.s.-2 m.s. sf. (842) *into thy acquittal*

69:29

יִמָּחוּ Ni. impf. 3 m.p. (מָחָה 562) *let them be blotted out*

מִסֵּפֶר prep.-n.m.s. cstr. (706) *out of the book of*

חַיִּים adj. m.p. (313) *the living*

וְעִם צַדִּיקִים conj.-prep.-adj. m.p. (843) *and among the righteous*

אַל־יִכָּתֵבוּ neg.-Ni. impf. 3 m.p. paus. (כָּתַב 507) *let them not be enrolled*

69:30

וַאֲנִי conj.-pers.pr. 1 c.s. (58) *but I*

עָנִי adj. m.s. (776) *afflicted*

וְכוֹאֵב conj.-Qal act.ptc. (כָּאַב 456) *and in pain*

יְשׁוּעָתְךָ n.f.s.-2 m.s. sf. (447) *thy salvation*

אֱלֹהִים n.m.p. (43) *O God*

תְּשַׂגְּבֵנִי Pi. impf. 2 m.s.-1 c.s. sf. (שָׂגַב 960) *let set me on high*

69:31

אֲהַלְלָה Pi. impf. 1 c.s.-vol.he (הָלַל II 237) *I will praise*

שֵׁם־אֱלֹהִים n.m.s. cstr. (1027)-n.m.p. (43) *the name of God*

בְּשִׁיר prep.-n.m.s. (1010) *with a song*

וַאֲגַדְּלֶנּוּ conj.-Pi. impf. 1 c.s.-3 m.s. sf. (גָּדַל 152) *and I will magnify him*

בְתוֹדָה prep.-n.f.s. (392) *with thanksgiving*

69:32

וְתִיטַב conj.-Qal impf. 3 f.s. (יָטַב 405) *and let this please*

לַיהוה prep.-pr.n. (217) *Yahweh*

מִשּׁוֹר prep.-n.m.s. (1004) *more than an ox*

פָּר n.m.s. (830) *or a bull*

מַקְרִן Hi. ptc. (קָרַן 902) *with horns*

מַפְרִיס Hi. ptc. (פָּרַס 828) *and hoofs*

69:33

רָאוּ Qal pf. 3 c.p. (רָאָה 906) *have seen*

עֲנָוִים n.m.p. (776) *the oppressed*

יִשְׂמָחוּ Qal impf. 3 m.p. paus. (970) *let them be glad*

דֹּרְשֵׁי Qal act.ptc. m.p. cstr. (205) *those who seek*

אֱלֹהִים n.m.p. (43) *God*

וִיחִי conj.-Qal impf. 3 m.s. apoc. (חָיָה 310) *and let revive*

לְבַבְכֶם n.m.s.-2 m.p. sf. (523) *your hearts*

69:34

כִּי־שֹׁמֵעַ conj. (471)-Qal act.ptc. (1033) *for hears*

אֶל־אֶבְיוֹנִים prep.-adj. m.p. (2) *the needy*

יהוה pr.n. (217) *Yahweh*

וְאֶת־אֲסִירָיו conj.-dir.obj.-n.m.p.-3 m.s. sf. (64) *and his own that are in bonds*

לֹא בָזָה neg.-Qal pf. 3 m.s. (102) *he does not despise*

69:35

יְהַלְלוּהוּ Pi. impf. 3 m.p.-3 m.s. sf. (הָלַל II 237) *let praise him*

שָׁמַיִם n.m. du. (1029) *heaven*

וָאָרֶץ conj.-n.f.s. (75) *and earth*

יַמִּים n.m.p. (410) *seas*

וְכָל־ conj.-n.m.s. cstr. (481) *and everything*

רֹמֵשׂ Qal act.ptc. (942) *that moves*
בָּם prep.-3 m.p. sf. *therein*

69:36

כִּי אֱלֹהִים conj. (471)-pr.n. (43) *for God*
יוֹשִׁיעַ Hi. impf. 3 m.s. (יָשַׁע 446) *will save*
צִיּוֹן pr.n. (851) *Zion*
וְיִבְנֶה conj.-Qal impf. 3 m.s. (124) *and rebuild*
עָרֵי n.f.p. cstr. (746) *the cities of*
יְהוּדָה pr.n. (397) *Judah*
וְיָשְׁבוּ conj.-Qal pf. 3 c.p. (442) *and they shall dwell*
שָׁם adv. (1027) *there*
וִירֵשׁוּהָ conj.-Qal impf. 3 m.p.-3 f.s. sf. (יָרַשׁ 439; GK 69s) *and possess it*

69:37

וְזֶרַע conj.-n.m.s. cstr. (282) *and the children of*
עֲבָדָיו n.m.p.-3 m.s. sf. (713) *his servants*
יִנְחָלוּהָ Qal impf. 3 m.p.-3 f.s. sf. (נָחַל 635) *shall inherit it*
וְאֹהֲבֵי conj.-Qal act.ptc. m.p. cstr. (אָהַב 12) *and those who love*
שְׁמוֹ n.m.s.-3 m.s. sf. (1027) *his name*
יִשְׁכְּנוּ־ Qal impf. 3 m.p. (1014) *shall dwell*
בָהּ prep.-3 f.s. sf. *in it*

70:1

לַמְנַצֵּחַ prep.-def.art.-Pi. ptc. (I 663) *to the choirmaster*
לְדָוִד prep.-pr.n. (187) *to David*
לְהַזְכִּיר prep.-Hi. inf.cstr. (269) *for the memorial offering*

70:2

אֱלֹהִים n.m.p. (43) *O God*
לְהַצִּילֵנִי prep.-Hi. inf.cstr.-1 c.s. sf. (נָצַל 664) *to deliver me*
יהוה pr.n. (217) *O Yahweh*
לְעֶזְרָתִי prep.-n.f.s.-1 c.s. sf. (740) *and for my help*
חוּשָׁה Qal impv. 2 m.s.-vol.he (חוּשׁ I 301) *make haste*

70:3

יֵבֹשׁוּ Qal impf. 3 m.s. (בּוֹשׁ 101) *let them be put to shame*
וְיַחְפְּרוּ conj.-Qal impf. 3 m.p. (II 344) *and be put to confusion*
מְבַקְשֵׁי Pi. ptc. m.p. cstr. (134) *those who seek*
נַפְשִׁי n.f.s.-1 c.s. sf. (659) *my life*
יִסֹּגוּ Ni. impf. 3 m.p. (נָסַג I 690) *let them be turned back*
אָחוֹר adv. (30) *back*
וְיִכָּלְמוּ conj.-Ni. impf. 3 m.p. (483) *and brought to dishonor*
חֲפֵצֵי adj. m.p. cstr. (343) *those who desire*
רָעָתִי n.f.s.-1 c.s. sf. (949) *my hurt*

70:4

יָשׁוּבוּ Qal impf. 3 m.p. (996) *let them turn*
עַל־עֵקֶב prep.-n.m.s. cstr. (784) *because of*
בָּשְׁתָּם n.f.s.-3 m.p. sf. (102) *their shame*
הָאֹמְרִים def.art.-Qal act.ptc. m.p. (55) *who say*
הֶאָח הֶאָח interj. (210)-v.supra *Aha, Aha*

70:5

יָשִׂישׂוּ Qal impf. 3 m.p. (שׂוּשׂ 965) *may they rejoice*
וְיִשְׂמְחוּ conj.-Qal impf. 3 m.p. (970) *and be glad*
בְּךָ prep.-2 m.s. sf. *in thee*
כָּל־מְבַקְשֶׁיךָ n.m.s. cstr. (481)-Pi. ptc. m.p.-2 m.s. sf. (134) *all who seek thee*
וְיֹאמְרוּ conj.-Qal impf. 3 m.p. (55) *may they say*
תָמִיד adv. (556) *evermore*
יִגְדַּל Qal impf. 3 m.s. (152) *is great*
אֱלֹהִים n.m.p. (43) *God*
אֹהֲבֵי Qal act.ptc. m.p. cstr. (12) *those who love*
יְשׁוּעָתֶךָ n.f.s.-2 m.s. sf. (447) *thy salvation*

70:6

וַאֲנִי conj.-pers.pr. 1 c.s. (58) *but I*
עָנִי adj. m.s. (776) *am poor*
וְאֶבְיוֹן conj.-adj. m.s. (2) *and needy*
אֱלֹהִים n.m.p. (43) *O God*
חוּשָׁה־לִּי Qal impv. 2 m.s.-vol.he (חוּשׁ I 301)-prep.-1 c.s. sf. *hasten to me*
עֶזְרִי n.m.s.-1 c.s. sf. (I 740) *my help*
וּמְפַלְטִי conj.-Pi. ptc.-1 c.s. sf. (פָּלַט 812) *and my deliverer*
אַתָּה pers.pr. 2 m.s. (61) *thou art*
יהוה pr.n. (217) *O Yahweh*
אַל־תְּאַחַר neg.-Pi. impf. 2 m.s. (29) *do not tarry*

71:1

בְּךָ־יהוה prep.-2 m.s. sf.-pr.n. (217) *in thee, O Yahweh*
חָסִיתִי Qal pf. 1 c.s. (חָסָה 340) *do I take refuge*
אַל־אֵבוֹשָׁה neg.-Qal impf. 1 c.s.-coh.he (בּוֹשׁ 101; GK 108c) *let me not be put to shame*
לְעוֹלָם prep.-n.m.s. (761) *for ever*

71:2

בְּצִדְקָתְךָ prep.-n.f.s.-2 m.s. sf. (842) *in thy righteousness*

תַּצִּילֵנִי Hi. impf. 2 m.p.-1 c.s. sf. (נָצַל 664) *deliver me*

וּתְפַלְּטֵנִי conj.-Pi. impf. 2 m.s.-1 c.s. sf. (פָּלַט 812) *and rescue me*

הַטֵּה־אֵלַי Hi. impv. 2 m.s. (נָטָה 639)-prep.-1 c.s. sf. *incline to me*

אָזְנְךָ n.f.s.-2 m.s. sf. (23) *thy ear*

וְהוֹשִׁיעֵנִי conj.-Hi. impv. 2 m.s.-1 c.s. sf. (יָשַׁע 446) *and save me*

71:3

הֱיֵה לִי Qal impv. 2 m.s. (224)-prep.-1 c.s. sf. *be thou to me*

לְצוּר מָעוֹן prep.-n.m.s. cstr. (849)-n.m.s. (I 732) *a rock of dwelling*

לָבוֹא prep.-Qal inf.cstr. (בּוֹא 97) *to come*

תָּמִיד adv. (556) *continually*

צִוִּיתָ Pi. pf. 2 m.s. (צָוָה 845) *thou hast commanded*

לְהוֹשִׁיעֵנִי prep.-Hi. inf.cstr.-1 c.s. sf. (יָשַׁע 446) *to save me*

כִּי־סַלְעִי conj. (471)-n.m.s.-1 c.s. sf. (700) *for my rock*

וּמְצוּדָתִי conj.-n.f.s.-1 c.s. sf. (II 845) *and my fortress*

אָתָּה pers.pr. 2 m.s. paus. (61) *thou art*

71:4

אֱלֹהַי n.m.p.-1 c.s. sf. (43) *O my God*

פַּלְּטֵנִי Pi. impv. 2 m.s.-1 c.s. sf. (פָּלַט 812) *rescue me*

מִיַּד prep.-n.f.s. cstr. (388) *from the hand of*

רָשָׁע adj. m.s. (957) *the wicked*

מִכַּף prep.-n.f.s. cstr. (496) *from the grasp of*

מְעַוֵּל Pi. ptc. (עָוַל 732) *the unjust*

וְחוֹמֵץ conj.-Qal act.ptc. (III 330) *and ruthless*

71:5

כִּי־אַתָּה conj. (471)-pers.pr. 2 m.s. (61) *for thou*

תִקְוָתִי n.f.s.-1 c.s. sf. (876) *my hope*

אֲדֹנָי n.m.p.-1 c.s. sf. (10) *O Lord*

יהוה pr.n. (217) *Yahweh*

מִבְטַחִי n.m.s.-1 c.s. sf. (105) *my trust*

מִנְּעוּרָי prep.-n.m.p.-1 c.s. sf. paus. (655) *from my youth*

71:6

עָלֶיךָ prep.-2 m.s. sf. *upon thee*

נִסְמַכְתִּי Ni. pf. 1 c.s. (סָמַךְ 701) *I have leaned*

מִבֶּטֶן prep.-n.f.s. (105) *from birth*

מִמְּעֵי אִמִּי prep.-n.m.p. cstr. (588)-n.f.s.-1 c.s. sf. (51) *from my mother's womb*

אַתָּה גוֹזִי pers.pr. 2 m.s. (61)-Qal act.ptc.-1 c.s. sf. (גָּזָה 159) *thou art he who took me*

בְּךָ prep.-2 m.s. sf. *of thee*

תְהִלָּתִי n.f.s.-1 c.s. sf. (239) *my praise*

תָמִיד adv. (556) *continually*

71:7

כְּמוֹפֵת prep.-n.m.s. (68) *as a portent*

הָיִיתִי Qal pf. 1 c.s. (הָיָה 224) *I have been*

לְרַבִּים prep.-adj. m.p. (I 912) *to many*

וְאַתָּה conj.-pers.pr. 2 m.s. (61) *but thou*

מַחֲסִי־עֹז n.m.s.-1 c.s. sf. (349)-n.m.s. (738; GK 131r) *my strong refuge*

71:8

יִמָּלֵא Ni. impf. 3 m.s. (569) *is filled*

פִי n.m.s.-1 c.s. sf. (804) *my mouth*

תְּהִלָּתֶךָ n.f.s.-2 m.s. sf. (239) *with thy praise*

כָּל־הַיּוֹם n.m.s. cstr. (481)-def.art.-n.m.s. (398) *all the day*

תִּפְאַרְתֶּךָ n.f.s.-2 m.s. sf. (802) *with thy glory*

71:9

אַל־תַּשְׁלִיכֵנִי neg.-Hi. impf. 2 m.s.-1 c.s. sf. (שָׁלַךְ 1020) *do not cast me off*

לְעֵת זִקְנָה prep.-n.f.s. cstr. (773)-n.f.s. (279) *in the time of old age*

כִּכְלוֹת prep.-Qal inf.cstr. (כָּלָה 477) *when is spent*

כֹּחִי n.m.s.-1 c.s. sf. (470) *my strength*

אַל־תַּעַזְבֵנִי neg.-Qal impf. 2 m.s.-1 c.s. sf. (עָזַב I 736) *forsake me not*

71:10

כִּי־אָמְרוּ conj. (471)-Qal pf. 3 c.p. (55) *for speak*

אוֹיְבַי Qal act.ptc. m.p.-1 c.s. sf. (אָיַב 33) *my enemies*

לִי prep.-1 c.s. sf. *concerning me*

וְשֹׁמְרֵי conj.-Qal act.ptc. m.p. cstr. (1036) *those who watch for*

נַפְשִׁי n.f.s.-1 c.s. sf. (659) *my life*

נוֹעֲצוּ Ni. pf. 3 c.p. (יָעַץ 419) *consult*

יַחְדָּו adv. (403) *together*

71:11

לֵאמֹר prep.-Qal inf.cstr. (55) *and say*

אֱלֹהִים n.m.p. (43) *God*

עֲזָבוֹ Qal pf. 3 m.s.-3 m.s. sf. (I 736) *has forsaken him*

רִדְפוּ Qal impv. 2 m.p. (922) *pursue*
וְתִפְשׂוּהוּ conj.-Qal impv. 2 m.p.-3 m.s. sf. (תָּפַשׂ 1074) *and seize him*
כִּי־אֵין מַצִּיל conj. (471)-neg. cstr. (II 34)-Hi. ptc. (נָצַל 664) *for there is none to deliver him*

71:12

אֱלֹהִים n.m.p. (43) *O God*
אַל־תִּרְחַק neg.-Qal impf. 2 m.s. (934) *be not far*
מִמֶּנִּי prep.-1 c.s. sf. *from me*
אֱלֹהַי n.m.p.-1 c.s. sf. (43) *O my God*
לְעֶזְרָתִי prep.-n.f.s.-1 c.s. sf. (740) *to help me*
חִישָׁה Qal impv. 2 m.s.-vol.he (חוּשׁ I 301) *make haste*

71:13

יֵבֹשׁוּ Qal impf. 3 m.p. (בּוֹשׁ 101) *may be put to shame*
יִכְלוּ Qal impf. 3 m.p. (כָּלָה 477) *and consumed*
שֹׂטְנֵי Qal act.ptc. m.p. cstr. (966) *the ones accusing of*
נַפְשִׁי n.f.s.-1 c.s. sf. (659) *my life*
יַעֲטוּ Qal impf. 3 m.p. (עָטָה I 741) *may they be covered*
חֶרְפָּה n.f.s. (357) *with reproach*
וּכְלִמָּה conj.-n.f.s. (484) *and disgrace*
מְבַקְשֵׁי Pi. ptc. m.p. cstr. (134) *who seek*
רָעָתִי n.f.s.-1 c.s. sf. (949) *my hurt*

71:14

וַאֲנִי conj.-pers.pr. 1 c.s. (58) *but I*
תָּמִיד adv. (556) *continually*
אֲיַחֵל Pi. impf. 1 c.s. (יָחַל 403) *hope*
וְהוֹסַפְתִּי conj.-Hi. pf. 1 c.s. (יָסַף 414) *and I add*
עַל־כָּל־ prep.-n.m.s. cstr. (481) *to all*
תְּהִלָּתֶךָ n.f.s.-2 m.s. sf. (239) *thy praise*

71:15

פִּי n.m.s.-1 c.s. sf. (804) *my mouth*
יְסַפֵּר Pi. impf. 3 m.s. (707) *will tell*
צִדְקָתֶךָ n.f.s.-2 m.s. sf. (842) *of thy righteousness*
כָּל־הַיּוֹם n.m.s. cstr. (481)-def.art.-n.m.s. (398) *all the day*
תְּשׁוּעָתֶךָ n.f.s.-2 m.s. sf. (448) *of thy deeds of salvation*
כִּי לֹא יָדַעְתִּי conj. (471)-neg.-Qal pf. 1 c.s. (393) *for I do not know*
סְפֹרוֹת n.f.p. (708) *their number*

71:16

אָבוֹא Qal impf. 1 c.s. (97) *I will come*
בִּגְבֻרוֹת prep.-n.f.p. cstr. (150) *with the mighty deeds of*
אֲדֹנָי n.m.p.-1 c.s. sf. (10) *the Lord*
יהוה pr.n. (217) *Yahweh*
אַזְכִּיר Hi. impf. 1 c.s. (269) *I will cause to remember*
צִדְקָתְךָ n.f.s.-2 m.s. sf. (842) *thy righteousness*
לְבַדֶּךָ prep.-n.m.s.-2 m.s. sf. (94) *thine alone*

71:17

אֱלֹהִים n.m.p. (43) *O God*
לִמַּדְתַּנִי Pi. pf. 2 m.s.-1 c.s. sf. (540) *thou hast taught me*
מִנְּעוּרָי prep.-n.m.p.-1 c.s. sf. (655) *from my youth*
וְעַד־הֵנָּה conj.-prep. (III 723)-adv. (I 244) *and still*
אַגִּיד Hi. impf. 1 c.s. (נָגַד 616) *I proclaim*
נִפְלְאוֹתֶיךָ n.f.p.-2 m.s. sf. (Ni. ptc. f.p. - פָּלָא 810) *thy wondrous deeds*

71:18

וְגַם conj.-adv. (168) *so even*
עַד־זִקְנָה prep. (III 723)-n.f.s. (279) *to old age*
וְשֵׂיבָה conj.-n.f.s. (966) *and gray hairs*
אֱלֹהִים n.m.p. (43) *O God*
אַל־תַּעַזְבֵנִי neg.-Qal impf. 2 m.s.-1 c.s. sf. (עָזַב I 736) *do not forsake me*
עַד־אַגִּיד prep. (III 723)-Hi. impf. 1 c.s. (נָגַד 616) *till I proclaim*
זְרוֹעֲךָ n.f.s.-2 m.s. sf. (283) *thy might*
לְדוֹר prep.-n.m.s. (189) *to a generation*
לְכָל־יָבוֹא prep.-n.m.s. (481)-Qal impf. 3 m.s. (97) *to all that come*
גְּבוּרָתֶךָ n.f.s.-2 m.s. sf. (150) *thy power*

71:19

וְצִדְקָתְךָ n.f.s.-2 m.s. sf. (842) *thy righteousness*
אֱלֹהִים n.m.p. (43) *O God*
עַד־מָרוֹם prep. (III 723)-n.m.s. (928) *to heights*
אֲשֶׁר־עָשִׂיתָ rel. (81)-Qal pf. 2 m.s. (I 793) *thou who hast done*
גְדֹלוֹת adj. f.p. (152) *great things*
אֱלֹהִים n.m.p. (43) *O God*
מִי כָמוֹךָ interr. (566)-prep.-2 m.s. sf. *who is like thee?*

71:20

אֲשֶׁר הִרְאִיתַנוּ rel. (81)-Hi. pf. 2 m.s.-1 c.s. sf. (רָאָה 906) *thou who hast made me see*
צָרוֹת n.f.p. (865) *troubles*
רַבּוֹת adj. f.p. (I 912) *many*

וְרָעוֹת conj.-adj. f.p. (I 948) *and sore*
תָּשׁוּב Qal impf. 2 m.s. (996) *thou wilt return*
תְּחַיֵּינִי Pi. impf. 2 m.s.-1 c.s. sf. (חָיָה 310) *thou wilt revive me*
וּמִתְּהֹמוֹת conj.-prep.-n.f.p. cstr. (1062) *and from the depths of*
הָאָרֶץ def.art.-n.f.s. (75) *the earth*
תָּשׁוּב v.supra *thou wilt return (again)*
תַּעֲלֵנִי Hi. impf. 2 m.s.-1 c.s. sf. (עָלָה 748) *thou wilt bring me up*

71:21
תֶּרֶב Hi. impf. 2 m.s. (רָבָה I 915) *thou wilt increase*
גְּדֻלָּתִי n.f.s.-1 c.s. sf. (153) *my honor*
וְתִסֹּב conj.-Qal impf. 2 m.s. (סָבַב 685) *thou wilt turn about (again)*
תְּנַחֲמֵנִי Pi. impf. 2 m.s.-1 c.s. sf. (נָחַם 636) *thou wilt comfort me*

71:22
גַּם־אֲנִי adv. (168)-pers.pr. 1 c.s. (58) *also I*
אוֹדְךָ Hi. impf. 1 c.s.-2 m.s. sf. (יָדָה 392) *will praise thee*
בִכְלִי־נֶבֶל prep.-n.m.s. cstr. (479)-n.m.s. (614) *with the harp (vessel of music)*
אֲמִתְּךָ n.f.s.-2 m.s. sf. (54) *for thy faithfulness*
אֱלֹהָי n.m.p.-1 c.s. sf. (43) *O my God*
אֲזַמְּרָה Pi. impf. 1 c.s.-vol.he (זָמַר I 274) *I will sing praises*
לְךָ prep.-2 m.s. sf. *to thee*
בְכִנּוֹר prep.-n.m.s. (490) *with the lyre*
קְדוֹשׁ adj. m.s. cstr. (972) *O Holy One of*
יִשְׂרָאֵל pr.n. (975) *Israel*

71:23
תְּרַנֵּנָּה Pi. impf. 3 f.p. (רָנַן 943; GK 44o) *will shout for joy*
שְׂפָתַי n.f. du.-1 c.s. sf. (973) *my lips*
כִּי אֲזַמְּרָה־ conj.-Pi. impf. 1 c.s.-vol.he (I 274) *when I sing praises*
לָּךְ prep.-2 m.s. sf. paus. *to thee*
וְנַפְשִׁי conj.-n.f.p.-1 c.s. sf. (659) *my soul also*
אֲשֶׁר פָּדִיתָ rel. (81)-Qal pf. 2 m.s. (פָּדָה 804) *which thou hast rescued*

71:24
גַּם־לְשׁוֹנִי adv. (168)-n.f.s.-1 c.s. sf. (546) *also my tongue*
כָּל־הַיּוֹם n.m.s. cstr. (481)-def.art.-n.m.s. (398) *all the day long*
תֶּהְגֶּה Qal impf. 3 f.s. (הָגָה I 211) *will talk of*
צִדְקָתֶךָ n.f.s.-2 m.s. sf. (842) *thy righteous help*
כִּי־בֹשׁוּ conj.-Qal pf. 3 c.p. (בּוֹשׁ 101) *for they have been put to shame*
כִּי־חָפְרוּ conj. (471)-Qal pf. 3 c.p. (II 344) *and disgraced*
מְבַקְשֵׁי Pi. ptc. m.p. cstr. (134) *who sought*
רָעָתִי n.f.s.-1 c.s. sf. (949) *my hurt*

72:1
לִשְׁלֹמֹה prep.-pr.n. (1024) *to Solomon*
אֱלֹהִים n.m.p. (43) *O God*
מִשְׁפָּטֶיךָ n.m.p.-2 m.s. sf. (1048) *thy justice*
לְמֶלֶךְ prep.-n.m.s. (I 572) *to the king*
תֵּן Qal impv. 2 m.s. (נָתַן 678) *give*
וְצִדְקָתְךָ conj.-n.f.s.-2 m.s. sf. (842) *and thy righteousness*
לְבֶן־מֶלֶךְ prep.-n.m.s. cstr. (119)-n.m.s. (I 572) *to the royal son*

72:2
יָדִין Qal impf. 3 m.s. (דִּין 192; GK 107n) *may he judge*
עַמְּךָ n.m.s.-2 m.s. sf. (I 766) *thy people*
בְצֶדֶק prep.-n.m.s. (841) *with righteousness*
וַעֲנִיֶּיךָ conj.-n.m.p.-2 m.s. sf. (776) *and thy poor*
בְמִשְׁפָּט prep.-n.m.s. (1048) *with justice*

72:3
יִשְׂאוּ Qal impf. 3 m.p. (נָשָׂא 669) *let bear*
הָרִים n.m.p. (249) *mountains*
שָׁלוֹם n.m.s. (1022) *prosperity*
לָעָם prep.-def.art.-n.m.s. (I 766) *for the people*
וּגְבָעוֹת conj.-n.f.p. (148) *and hills*
בִּצְדָקָה prep.-n.f.s. (842) *in righteousness*

72:4
יִשְׁפֹּט Qal impf. 3 m.s. (1047) *may he defend the cause*
עֲנִיֵּי־עָם n.m.p. cstr. (776)-n.m.s. (I 766) *the poor of the people*
יוֹשִׁיעַ Hi. impf. 3 m.s. (יָשַׁע 446) *may he give deliverance*
לִבְנֵי אֶבְיוֹן prep.-n.m.p. cstr. (119)-adj. m.s. (2) *to the needy*
וִידַכֵּא conj.-Pi. impf. 3 m.s. (193) *and crush*
עוֹשֵׁק Qal act.ptc. (798) *the oppressor*

72:5
יִירָאוּךָ Qal impf. 3 m.p.-2 m.s. sf. (יָרֵא 431) *may they fear thee*
עִם־שָׁמֶשׁ prep.-n.f.s. paus. (1039) *with the sun*

וְלִפְנֵי יָרֵחַ conj.-prep.-n.m.p. cstr. (815)-n.m.s. (437) *and as long as the moon*
דּוֹר דּוֹרִים n.m.s. cstr. (189)-n.m.p. (189) *throughout all generations*

72:6

יֵרֵד Qal impf. 3 m.s. (יָרַד 432) *may he come down*
כְּמָטָר prep.-n.m.s. (564) *like rain*
עַל־גֵּז prep.-n.m.s. (159) *on the mown grass*
כִּרְבִיבִים prep.-n.m.p. (914) *like showers*
זַרְזִיף n.m.s. cstr. (284) *that water*
אָרֶץ n.f.s. paus. (75) *the earth*

72:7

יִפְרַח Qal impf. 3 m.s. (827) *may flourish*
בְּיָמָיו prep.-n.m.p.-3 m.s. sf. (398) *in his days*
צַדִּיק adj. m.s. (843) *righteousness*
וְרֹב שָׁלוֹם conj.-n.m.s. cstr. (913)-n.m.s. (1022) *and peace abound*
עַד־בְּלִי יָרֵחַ prep. (III 723)-neg. (115)-n.m.s. (437) *till the moon be no more*

72:8

וְיֵרְדְּ conj.-Qal impf. 3 m.s. juss. (רָדָה I 921) *may he have dominion*
מִיָּם עַד־יָם prep.-n.m.s. (410)-prep. (III 723)-v.supra *from sea to sea*
וּמִנָּהָר conj.-prep.-n.m.s. (625) *and from the River*
עַד־אַפְסֵי־אָרֶץ prep. (III 723)-n.m.p. cstr. (67) -n.f.s. paus. (75) *to the ends of the earth*

72:9

לְפָנָיו prep.-n.m.p.-3 m.s. sf. (815) *before him*
יִכְרְעוּ Qal impf. 3 m.p. (502) *may bow down*
צִיִּים n.m.p. (II 850) *those that dwell in the wilderness*
וְאֹיְבָיו conj.-Qal act.ptc. m.p.-3 m.s. sf. (אָיַב 33) *and his enemies*
עָפָר n.m.s. (779) *the dust*
יְלַחֵכוּ Pi. impf. 3 m.p. paus. (לָחַךְ 535) *may lick*

72:10

מַלְכֵי n.m.p. cstr. (I 572) *the kings of*
תַּרְשִׁישׁ pr.n. (II 1076) *Tarshish*
וְאִיִּים conj.-n.m.p. (I 15) *and the isles*
מִנְחָה n.f.s. (585) *tribute*
יָשִׁיבוּ Hi. impf. 3 m.p. (שׁוּב 996) *may render*
מַלְכֵי v.supra *kings of*
שְׁבָא pr.n. (985) *Sheba*
וּסְבָא conj.-pr.n. (685) *and Seba*

אֶשְׁכָּר n.m.s. (1016) *gifts*
יַקְרִיבוּ Hi. impf. 3 m.p. (897) *may bring*

72:11

וְיִשְׁתַּחֲווּ־ conj.-Hith. impf. 3 m.p. (שָׁחָה 1005) *may fall down*
לוֹ prep.-3 m.s. sf. *before him*
כָל־מְלָכִים n.m.s. cstr. (481)-n.m.p. (I 572) *all kings*
כָּל־גּוֹיִם v.supra-n.m.p. (156) *all nations*
יַעַבְדוּהוּ Qal impf. 3 m.p.-3 m.s. sf. (עָבַד 712) *may serve him*

72:12

כִּי־יַצִּיל conj. (471)-Hi. impf. 3 m.s. (נָצַל 664) *for he delivers*
אֶבְיוֹן adj. m.s. (2) *the needy*
מְשַׁוֵּעַ Pi. ptc. (שָׁוַע 1002) *when he calls*
וְעָנִי conj.-adj. m.s. (776) *and the poor*
וְאֵין־עֹזֵר conj.-neg. cstr. (II 34)-Qal act.ptc. (740) *and there is no helper*
לוֹ prep.-3 m.s. sf. *for him*

72:13

יָחֹס Qal impf. 3 m.s. (חוּס 299; GK 72r,109k) *he has pity*
עַל־דַּל prep.-n.m.s. (195) *on the weak*
וְאֶבְיוֹן conj.-adj. m.s. (2) *and the needy*
וְנַפְשׁוֹת conj.-n.f.p. cstr. (659) *and the lives of*
אֶבְיוֹנִים adj. m.p. (2) *the needy*
יוֹשִׁיעַ Hi. impf. 3 m.s. (446) *he will save*

72:14

מִתּוֹךְ prep.-n.m.s. (1067) *from oppression*
וּמֵחָמָס conj.-prep.-n.m.s. (329) *and from violence*
יִגְאַל Qal impf. 3 m.s. (I 145) *he redeems*
נַפְשָׁם n.f.s.-3 m.p. sf. (659) *their life*
וְיֵיקַר conj.-Qal impf. 3 m.s. (429; GK 69f) *and is precious*
דָּמָם n.m.s.-3 m.p. sf. (196) *their blood*
בְּעֵינָיו prep.-n.f. du.-3 m.s. sf. (744) *in his sight*

72:15

וִיחִי conj.-Qal impf. 3 m.s. apoc. (חָיָה 310) *and may he live*
וְיִתֶּן־לוֹ conj.-Qal impf. 3 m.s. (נָתַן 678)-prep.-3 m.s. sf. *and may he give to him*
מִזְּהַב prep.-n.m.s. cstr. (262) *gold of*
שְׁבָא pr.n. (985) *Sheba*
וְיִתְפַּלֵּל conj.-Hith. impf. 3 m.s. (813) *may prayer be made*

בַּעֲדוֹ prep.-3 m.s. sf. (126) *for him*
תָּמִיד adv. (556) *continually*
כָּל־הַיּוֹם n.m.s. cstr. (481)-def.art.-n.m.s. (398) *all the day*
יְבָרֲכֶנְהוּ Pi. impf. 3 m.s.-3 m.s. sf. (בָּרַךְ 138; GK 58i) *may blessings be invoked for him*

72:16

יְהִי Qal impf. 3 m.s. apoc. (הָיָה 224) *may there be*
פִּסַּת־ n.f.s. cstr. (821) *abundance of*
בַּר n.m.s. (III 141) *grain*
בָּאָרֶץ prep.-def.art.-n.f.s. (75) *in the land*
בְּרֹאשׁ prep.-n.m.s. cstr. (910) *on the tops of*
הָרִים n.m.p. (249) *the mountains*
יִרְעַשׁ Qal impf. 3 m.s. (950) *may it wave*
כַּלְּבָנוֹן prep.-def.art.-pr.n. (526) *like Lebanon*
פִּרְיוֹ n.m.s.-3 m.s. sf. (826) *his fruit*
וְיָצִיצוּ conj.-Qal impf. 3 m.p. (צוּץ I 847) *and may men blossom forth*
מֵעִיר prep.-n.f.s. (746) *from cities*
כְּעֵשֶׂב prep.-n.m.s. cstr. (793) *like the grass of*
הָאָרֶץ def.art.-n.f.s. (75) *the field*

72:17

יְהִי Qal impf. 3 m.s. apoc. (הָיָה 224) *may endure*
שְׁמוֹ n.m.s.-3 m.s. sf. (1027) *his name*
לְעוֹלָם prep.-n.m.s. (761) *for ever*
לִפְנֵי־שֶׁמֶשׁ prep.-n.m.p. cstr. (815)-n.f.s. (1039) *as long as the sun*
יִנּוֹן Qal impf. 3 m.s. (נוּן 630) *may continue*
שְׁמוֹ n.m.s.-3 m.s. sf. (1027) *his fame*
וְיִתְבָּרְכוּ בוֹ conj.-Hith. impf. 3 m.p. (בָּרַךְ 138; GK 10g)-prep.-3 m.s. sf. *may men bless themselves by him*
כָּל־גּוֹיִם n.m.s. cstr. (481)-n.m.p. (156) *all nations*
יְאַשְּׁרוּהוּ Pi. impf. 3 m.p.-3 m.s. sf. (אָשַׁר 80) *call him blessed*

72:18

בָּרוּךְ Qal pass.ptc. (156) *blessed be*
יהוה pr.n. (217) *Yahweh*
אֱלֹהִים n.m.p. (43) *God*
אֱלֹהֵי n.m.p. cstr. (43) *the God of*
יִשְׂרָאֵל pr.n. (975) *Israel*
עֹשֵׂה Qal act.ptc. (I 793) *who does*
נִפְלָאוֹת Ni. ptc. f.p. (פָּלָא 810) *wondrous things*
לְבַדּוֹ prep.-n.m.s.-3 m.s. sf. (94) *alone*

72:19

וּבָרוּךְ conj.-Qal pass.ptc. (156) *and blessed be*
שֵׁם כְּבוֹדוֹ n.m.s. cstr. (1027)-n.m.s.-3 m.s. sf. (458) *his glorious name*
לְעוֹלָם prep.-n.m.s. (761) *for ever*
וְיִמָּלֵא conj.-Ni. impf. 3 m.s. (569) *may fill*
כְבוֹדוֹ n.m.s.-3 m.s. sf. (458) *his glory*
אֶת־כֹּל הָאָרֶץ dir.obj.-n.m.s. cstr. (481)-def. art.-n.f.s. (75) *the whole earth*
אָמֵן וְאָמֵן adv. (53)-conj.-v.supra *Amen and Amen*

72:20

כָּלּוּ Pu. pf. 3 c.p. (כָּלָה I 477; GK 52q) *are ended*
תְּפִלּוֹת n.f.p. cstr. (813) *the prayers of*
דָּוִד pr.n. (187) *David*
בֶּן־יִשָׁי n.m.s. cstr. (119)-pr.n. (445) *the son of Jesse*

73:1

מִזְמוֹר n.m.s. (274) *a Psalm*
לְאָסָף prep.-pr.n. (63) *to Asaph*
אַךְ adv. (36) *truly*
טוֹב adj. m.s. (II 373) *is good*
לְיִשְׂרָאֵל prep.-pr.n. (975) *to Israel*
אֱלֹהִים n.m.p. (43) *God*
לְבָרֵי prep.-adj. m.p. cstr. (II 141) *to those who are pure in*
לֵבָב n.m.s. (523) *heart*

73:2

וַאֲנִי conj.-pers.pr. 1 c.s. (58) *but as for me*
כִּמְעַט prep.-adv. (589) *almost*
נָטָיוּ Qal pass.ptc. (נָטָה 639; Q - נָטָיוּ as Qal pf. 3 c.p.; GK 75u) *had stumbled*
רַגְלָי n.f.p.-1 c.s. sf. paus. (919) *my feet*
כְּאַיִן prep.-neg. (II 34) *well nigh*
שֻׁפְּכָה Pu. pf. 3 c.p. (שָׁפַךְ 1049) *had slipped*
אֲשֻׁרָי n.f.p.-1 c.s. sf. (81) *my steps*

73:3

כִּי־קִנֵּאתִי conj. (471)-Pi. pf. 1 c.s. (888) *for I was envious*
בַּהוֹלְלִים prep.-def.art.-Qal act.ptc. m.p. (II 237) *of the arrogant*
שְׁלוֹם רְשָׁעִים n.m.s. cstr. (1022)-adj. m.p. (957) *the prosperity of the wicked*
אֶרְאֶה Qal impf. 1 c.s. (906) *when I saw*

73:4

כִּי אֵין conj. (471)-neg. cstr. (II 34) *for they have no*
חַרְצֻבּוֹת n.f.p. (359) *pangs*

לְמוֹתָם rd.prb. לָמוֹ תָּם prep.-3 m.p. sf.-adj. m.s. (1070) *to them, are sound*
וּבָרִיא conj.-adj. m.s. (135) *and fat*
אוּלָם n.m.s.-3 m.p. sf. (I 17) *their bodies*

73:5
בַּעֲמַל prep.-n.m.s. cstr. (765) *in trouble of*
אֱנוֹשׁ n.m.s. (60) *man*
אֵינֵמוֹ neg.-3 m.p. sf. *there is not of them*
וְעִם־אָדָם conj.-prep.-n.m.s. (9) *and among men*
לֹא יְנֻגָּעוּ neg.-Pu. impf. 3 m.p. paus. (נָגַע 619) *they are not stricken*

73:6
לָכֵן prep.-adv. (485) *therefore*
עֲנָקַתְמוֹ Qal pf. 3 f.s.-3 m.p. sf. (עָנַק 778) *their necklace*
גַאֲוָה n.f.s. (144) *pride*
יַעֲטָף־ Qal impf. 3 m.s. (עָטַף II 742) *covers*
שִׁית n.m.s. (1011) *as a garment*
חָמָס n.m.s. (329) *violence*
לָמוֹ prep.-3 m.p. sf. *them*

73:7
יָצָא Qal pf. 3 m.s. (422) *swell out*
מֵחֵלֶב prep.-n.m.s. (316) *with fatness*
עֵינֵמוֹ n.f. du.-3 m.p. sf. (744; GK 145o) *their eyes*
עָבְרוּ Qal pf. 3 c.p. (716) *overflow*
מַשְׂכִּיּוֹת n.f.p. (967) *with follies*
לֵבָב n.m.s. paus. (523) *their hearts*

73:8
יָמִיקוּ Qal impf. 3 m.p. (מוּק 558) *they scoff*
וִידַבְּרוּ conj.-Pi. impf. 3 m.p. (180) *and speak*
בְרָע prep.-n.m.s. (948) *with malice*
עֹשֶׁק n.m.s. (799) *oppression*
מִמָּרוֹם prep.-n.m.s. (928) *loftily*
יְדַבֵּרוּ Pi. impf. 3 m.p. (180) *they threaten*

73:9
שַׁתּוּ Qal pf. 3 c.p. (שִׁית 1011) *they set*
בַשָּׁמַיִם prep.-def.art.-n.m. du. (1029) *against the heaven*
פִּיהֶם n.m.s.-3 m.p. sf. (804) *their mouths*
וּלְשׁוֹנָם conj.-n.f.s.-3 m.p. sf. (546) *and their tongue*
תִּהֲלַךְ Qal impf. 3 f.s. (הָלַךְ 229; GK 63n,69x) *struts*
בָּאָרֶץ prep.-def.art.-n.f.s. (75) *through the earth*

73:10
לָכֵן prep.-adv. (485) *therefore*
יָשִׁיב Qal impf. 3 m.s. (שׁוּב 996) *return*
עַמּוֹ n.m.s.-3 m.s. sf. (I 766) *his people*
הֲלֹם adv. (240) *hither*
וּמֵי מָלֵא conj.-n.m.p. cstr. (565)-n.m.s. (570) *and abundant waters*
יִמָּצוּ Ni. impf. 3 m.p. (מָצָה 594) *are drained*
לָמוֹ prep.-3 m.p. sf. *by them*

73:11
וְאָמְרוּ conj.-Qal pf. 3 c.p. (55) *and they say*
אֵיכָה adv. (32) *how*
יָדַע־ Qal pf. 3 m.s. (393) *can know*
אֵל n.m.s. (42) *God*
וְיֵשׁ conj.-subst. (441) *and is there*
דֵעָה n.f.s. (395) *knowledge*
בְעֶלְיוֹן prep.-n.m.s. (751) *in the Most High*

73:12
הִנֵּה־ demons.part. (243) *behold*
אֵלֶּה demons.adj. c.p. (41) *these*
רְשָׁעִים adj. m.p. (957) *the wicked*
וְשַׁלְוֵי עוֹלָם conj.-adj. m.p. cstr. (1017)-n.m.s. (761) *always at ease*
הִשְׂגּוּ־ Hi. pf. 3 c.p. (שָׂגָה 960) *they increase*
חָיִל n.m.s. paus. (298) *in riches*

73:13
אַךְ־רִיק adv. (36)-n.m.s. as adv. (938) *all in vain*
זִכִּיתִי Pi. pf. 1 c.s. (זָכָה 269) *I kept clean*
לְבָבִי n.m.s.-1 c.s. sf. (523) *my heart*
וָאֶרְחַץ consec.-Qal impf. 1 c.s. (934) *and I washed*
בְּנִקָּיוֹן prep.-n.m.s. (667) *in innocence*
כַּפָּי n.f.p.-1 c.s. sf. (496) *my hands*

73:14
וָאֱהִי consec.-Qal impf. 1 c.s. (הָיָה 224) *for I have been*
נָגוּעַ Qal pass.ptc. (619) *stricken*
כָּל־הַיּוֹם n.m.s. cstr. (481)-def.art.-n.m.s. (398) *all the day long*
וְתוֹכַחְתִּי conj.-n.f.s.-1 c.s. sf. (407) *and chastened*
לַבְּקָרִים prep.-def.art.-n.m.p. (133; GK 123c) *every morning*

73:15
אִם־אָמַרְתִּי hypoth.part. (49)-Qal pf. 1 c.s. (55) *if I had said*

אֲסַפְּרָה Pi. impf. 1 c.s.-vol.he (סָפַר 707) *I will speak*
כְמוֹ prep.-3 m.p. sf. *thus*
הִנֵּה demons.part. (243) *behold*
דּוֹר בָּנֶיךָ n.m.s. cstr. (189)-n.m.p.-2 m.s. sf. (119) *the generation of thy children*
בָגָדְתִּי Qal pf. 1 c.s. paus. (93) *I would have been untrue*

73:16

וָאֲחַשְּׁבָה consec.-Pi. impf. 1 c.s.-vol.he (362; GK 49e,108e) *but when I thought*
לָדַעַת prep.-Qal inf.cstr. (יָדַע 393) *to understand*
זֹאת demons.adj. f.s. (260) *this*
עָמָל n.m.s. (765) *a wearisome task*
הִיא demons.adj. f.s. (214) *it*
בְעֵינָי prep.-n.f. du.-1 c.s. sf. (744) *in my eyes*

73:17

עַד־אָבוֹא adv. (III 723; GK 108h)-Qal impf. 1 c.s. (בּוֹא 97) *until I went*
אֶל־מִקְדְּשֵׁי־אֵל prep.-n.m.p. cstr. (874)-n.m.s. (42) *into the sanctuaries of God*
אָבִינָה Qal impf. 1 c.s.-vol.he (בִּין 106) *then I perceived*
לְאַחֲרִיתָם prep.-n.f.s.-3 m.p. sf. (31) *their end*

73:18

אַךְ adv. (36) *truly*
בַּחֲלָקוֹת prep.-n.f.p. (II 325) *in slippery places*
תָּשִׁית Qal impf. 2 m.s. (שִׁית 1011) *thou dost set*
לָמוֹ prep.-3 m.p. sf. *them*
הִפַּלְתָּם Hi. pf. 2 m.s.-3 m.p. sf. (נָפַל 656) *thou dost make them fall*
לְמַשּׁוּאוֹת prep.-n.f.p. (996) *to ruin*

73:19

אֵיךְ adv. (32) *how*
הָיוּ Qal pf. 3 c.p. (הָיָה 224) *they are*
לְשַׁמָּה prep.-n.f.s. (I 103) *destroyed*
כְרָגַע prep.-n.m.s. paus. (921) *in a moment*
סָפוּ Qal pf. 3 c.p. (סוּף 692) *they are swept away (cease)*
תַּמּוּ Qal pf. 3 c.p. (תָּמַם 1070) *utterly*
מִן־בַּלָּהוֹת prep.-n.f.p. (117) *by terrors*

73:20

כַּחֲלוֹם prep.-n.m.s. (321) *like a dream*
מֵהָקִיץ prep.-Hi. inf.cstr. (קִיץ I 884; GK 119yN) *when one awakes*
אֲדֹנָי n.m.p.-1 c.s. sf. (10) *Lord*
בָּעִיר prep.-Hi. inf.cstr. (עוּר I 734; בְּהָעִיר GK 53q) *on awaking*
צַלְמָם n.m.s.-3 m.p. sf. (853) *their phantoms*
תִּבְזֶה Qal impf. 2 m.s. (102) *you despise*

73:21

כִּי יִתְחַמֵּץ conj. (471)-Hith. impf. 3 m.s. (חָמֵץ I 329) *when was embittered*
לְבָבִי n.m.s.-1 c.s. sf. (523) *my soul*
וְכִלְיוֹתַי conj.-n.f.p.-1 c.s. sf. (480) *when in heart*
אֶשְׁתּוֹנָן Hithpo'el impf. 1 c.s. (שָׁנַן 1041) *I was pricked*

73:22

וַאֲנִי־ conj.-pers.pr. 1 c.s. (58) *I was*
בַעַר n.m.s. (129) *stupid*
וְלֹא אֵדָע conj.-neg.-Qal impf. 1 c.s. paus. (יָדַע 393) *and I did not know*
בְּהֵמוֹת n.f.p. (96) *like beasts*
הָיִיתִי Qal pf. 1 c.s. (הָיָה 224) *I was*
עִמָּךְ prep.-2 m.s. sf. paus. *toward thee*

73:23

וַאֲנִי conj.-pers.pr. 1 c.s. (58) *nevertheless I*
תָמִיד adv. (556) *continually*
עִמָּךְ prep.-2 m.s. sf. paus. *with thee*
אָחַזְתָּ Qal pf. 2 m.s. (אָחַז 28) *thou dost hold*
בְּיַד־יְמִינִי prep.-n.f.s. cstr. (388)-n.f.s.-1 c.s. sf. (411) *my right hand*

73:24

בַּעֲצָתְךָ prep.-n.f.s.-2 m.s. sf. (420) *with thy counsel*
תַנְחֵנִי Hi. impf. 2 m.s.-1 c.s. sf. (נָחָה 634) *thou dost guide me*
וְאַחַר conj.-adv. (29) *and afterward*
כָּבוֹד n.m.s. (458) *honor*
תִּקָּחֵנִי Qal impf. 2 m.s.-1 c.s. sf. (לָקַח 542) *thou wilt receive me*

73:25

מִי־לִי interr. (566)-prep.-1 c.s. sf. *whom have I*
בַשָּׁמָיִם prep.-def.art.-n.m. du. paus. (1029) *in heaven*
וְעִמְּךָ conj.-prep.-2 m.s. sf. *but thee*
לֹא־חָפַצְתִּי neg.-Qal pf. 1 c.s. (342) *I do not desire*
בָאָרֶץ prep.-def.art.-n.f.s. (75) *upon earth*

73:26

כָּלָה Qal pf. 3 m.s. (477) *may fail*
שְׁאֵרִי n.m.s.-1 c.s. sf. (984) *my flesh*

וּלְבָבִי conj.-n.m.s.-1 c.s. sf. (523) *and my heart*
צוּר־לְבָבִי n.m.s. cstr. (849)-n.m.s.-1 c.s. sf. (523) *the rock of my heart*
וְחֶלְקִי conj.-n.m.s.-1 c.s. sf. (324) *and my portion*
אֱלֹהִים n.m.p. (43) *God*
לְעוֹלָם prep.-n.m.s. (761) *for ever*

73:27

כִּי־הִנֵּה conj. (471)-demons.part. (243) *for lo*
רְחֵקֶיךָ adj. m.p.-2 m.s. sf. (935) *those who are far from thee*
יֹאבֵדוּ Qal impf. 3 m.p. paus. (אָבַד 1) *shall perish*
הִצְמַתָּה Hi. pf. 2 m.s. (צָמַת 856) *thou dost put an end*
כָּל־זוֹנֶה n.m.s. cstr. (481)-Qal act.ptc. (275; GK 119ff) *to all those who are false*
מִמֶּךָּ prep.-2 m.s. sf. *to thee*

73:28

וַאֲנִי conj.-pers.pr. 1 c.s. (58) *but for me*
קִרֲבַת אֱלֹהִים n.f.s. cstr. (898)-n.m.p. (43) *near God*
לִי־טוֹב prep.-1 c.s. sf.-adj. m.s. (II 373) *it is good*
שַׁתִּי Qal pf. 1 c.s. (שִׁית 1011; GK 73d) *I have made*
בַּאדֹנָי prep.-n.m.p.-1 c.s. sf. (10) *the Lord*
יהוה pr.n. (217) *Yahweh*
מַחְסִי n.m.s.-1 c.s. sf. (340) *my refuge*
לְסַפֵּר prep.-Pi. inf.cstr. (707) *that I may tell of*
כָּל־ n.m.s. cstr. (481) *all*
מַלְאֲכוֹתֶיךָ n.f.p.-2 m.s. sf. (521) *thy works*

74:1

מַשְׂכִּיל n.m.s. (968) *a Maskil*
לְאָסָף prep.-pr.n. (63) *to Asaph*
לָמָה interr. (552) *why*
אֱלֹהִים n.m.p. (43) *O God*
זָנַחְתָּ Qal pf. 2 m.s. (I 276) *dost thou cast us off*
לָנֶצַח prep.-n.m.s. (664) *for ever*
יֶעְשַׁן Qal impf. 3 m.s. (798) *does smoke*
אַפְּךָ n.m.s.-2 m.s. sf. (I 60) *thy anger*
בְּצֹאן prep.-n.f.s. cstr. (838) *against the sheep of*
מַרְעִיתֶךָ n.f.s.-2 m.s. sf. (945) *thy pasture*

74:2

זְכֹר Qal impv. 2 m.s. (269) *remember*
עֲדָתְךָ n.f.s.-2 m.s. sf. (II 417) *thy congregation*
קָנִיתָ Qal pf. 2 m.s. (קָנָה 888) *which thou hast gotten*
קֶּדֶם n.m.s. (869) *of old*
גָּאַלְתָּ Qal pf. 2 m.s. (I 145) *which thou hast redeemed*
שֵׁבֶט n.m.s. cstr. (986) *the tribe of*
נַחֲלָתֶךָ n.f.s.-2 m.s. sf. (635) *thy heritage*
הַר־צִיּוֹן n.m.s. cstr. (249)-pr.n. (851) *Mount Zion*
זֶה demons.adj. m.s. (260) *this*
שָׁכַנְתָּ Qal pf. 2 m.s. (1014) *thou hast dwelt*
בּוֹ prep.-3 m.s. sf. *in it*

74:3

הָרִימָה Hi. impv. 2 m.s.-coh.he (רוּם 926) *direct*
פְעָמֶיךָ n.f.p.-2 m.s. sf. (821) *thy steps*
לְמַשֻּׁאוֹת prep.-n.f.p. cstr. (674) *to the ruins of*
נֶצַח n.m.s. (664) *perpetuity*
כָּל־ n.m.s. (481) *everything*
הֵרַע Hi. pf. 3 m.s. (רָעַע 949) *has destroyed*
אוֹיֵב Qal act.ptc. (אָיַב 33) *enemy*
בַּקֹּדֶשׁ prep.-def.art.-n.m.s. (871) *in the sanctuary*

74:4

שָׁאֲגוּ Qal pf. 3 c.p. (980) *have roared*
צֹרְרֶיךָ Qal act.ptc. m.p.-2 m.s. sf. (צָרַר III 865) *thy foes*
בְּקֶרֶב prep.-n.m.s. cstr. (899) *in the midst of*
מוֹעֲדֶךָ n.m.s.-2 m.s. sf. (417) *thy holy place*
שָׂמוּ Qal pf. 3 c.p. (שׂוּם 962) *they set up*
אוֹתֹתָם n.m.p.-3 m.p. sf. (16) *their own signs*
אֹתוֹת n.m.p. (16) *for signs*

74:5

יִוָּדַע Ni. impf. 3 m.s. (יָדַע 393) *it is known*
כְּמֵבִיא prep.-Hi. ptc. (בּוֹא 97) *as coming*
לְמָעְלָה prep.-n.f.s. *to the step*
בִּסֲבָךְ־ prep.-n.m.s. cstr. (687) *on the trellis of*
עֵץ n.m.s. (781) *wood*
קַרְדֻּמּוֹת n.f.p. (899) *with axes*

74:6

וְעַתָּ conj.-adv. (773) *and then*
פִּתּוּחֶיהָ n.m.p.-3 f.s. sf. (836) *its carved wood*
יָּחַד adv. paus. (403) *together*
בְּכַשִּׁיל prep.-n.m.s. (506) *with hatchets*
וְכֵילַפֹּת conj.-n.f.p. (476) *and hammers*
יַהֲלֹמוּן Qal impf. 3 m.p. (240) *they broke down*

74:7

שִׁלְחוּ Pi. pf. 3 c.p. (1018) *they set*
בָאֵשׁ prep.-def.art.-n.f.s. (77) *on fire*
מִקְדָּשֶׁךָ n.m.s.-2 m.s. sf. (874) *thy sanctuary*
לָאָרֶץ prep. (GK 119gg)-def.art.-n.f.s. (75) *to the ground*

חִלְּלוּ Pi. pf. 3 c.p. (III 320) *they desecrated*
מִשְׁכַּן־שְׁמֶךָ n.m.s. cstr. (1015)-n.m.s.-2 m.s. sf. (1027) *the dwelling place of thy name*

74:8
אָמְרוּ Qal pf. 3 c.p. (55) *they said*
בְלִבָּם prep.-n.m.s.-3 m.p. sf. (524) *to themselves*
נִינָם Qal impf. 1 c.p.-3 m.p. sf. (יָנָה 413; GK 76f) *we will subdue them*
יָחַד adv. paus. (403) *utterly*
שָׂרְפוּ Qal pf. 3 c.p. (976) *they burned*
כָל־מוֹעֲדֵי־ n.m.s. cstr. (481)-n.m.p. cstr. (417) *all the meeting places of*
אֵל n.m.s. (42) *God*
בָּאָרֶץ prep.-def.art.-n.f.s. (75) *in the land*

74:9
אוֹתֹתֵינוּ n.m.p.-1 c.p. sf. (16) *our signs*
לֹא רָאִינוּ neg.-Qal pf. 1 c.p. (רָאָה 906) *we do not see*
אֵין־עוֹד neg. cstr. (II 34)-adv. (728) *there is no longer*
נָבִיא n.m.s. (611) *any prophet*
וְלֹא־אִתָּנוּ conj.-neg.-prep.-1 c.p. sf. (II 85) *and there is none among us*
יֹדֵעַ Qal act.ptc. (יָדַע 393) *who knows*
עַד־מָה prep. (III 723)-interr. (552) *how long*

74:10
עַד־מָתַי prep. (III 723)-adv. (607) *how long*
אֱלֹהִים n.m.p. (42) *O God*
יְחָרֶף Pi. impf. 3 m.s. (357) *is to scoff*
צָר n.m.s. (III 865) *the foe*
יְנָאֵץ Pi. impf. 3 m.s. (610; GK 64e) *is to revile*
אוֹיֵב Qal act.ptc. (אָיַב 33) *the enemy*
שִׁמְךָ n.m.s.-2 m.s. sf. (1027) *thy name*
לָנֶצַח prep.-n.m.s. paus. (664) *for ever*

74:11
לָמָּה תָשִׁיב prep.-interr. (552)-Hi. impf. 2 m.s. (996 שׁוּב) *why dost thou hold back*
יָדְךָ n.f.s.-2 m.s. sf. (388) *thy hand*
וִימִינֶךָ conj.-n.f.s.-2 m.s. (411) *and thy right hand*
מִקֶּרֶב prep.-n.m.s. cstr. (899) *from*
חוֹקְךָ n.m.s.-2 m.s. sf. (300) *thy bosom*
כַלֵּה Pi. impv. 2 m.s. (477) *consume*

74:12
וֵאלֹהִים conj.-n.m.p. (43) *yet God*
מַלְכִּי n.m.s.-1 c.s. sf. (I 572) *my King*
מִקֶּדֶם prep.-n.m.s. (869) *from of old*
פֹּעֵל Qal act.ptc. (821) *working*
יְשׁוּעוֹת n.f.p. (447) *salvation*
בְּקֶרֶב prep.-n.m.s. cstr. (899) *in the midst of*
הָאָרֶץ def.art.-n.f.s. (75) *the earth*

74:13
אַתָּה pers.pr. 2 m.s. (61) *thou*
פוֹרַרְתָּ Po. pf. 2 m.s. (פָּרַר II 830) *didst divide*
בְעָזְּךָ prep.-n.m.s.-2 m.s. sf. (738) *by thy might*
יָם n.m.s. (410) *the sea*
שִׁבַּרְתָּ Pi. pf. 2 m.s. (990) *thou didst break*
רָאשֵׁי n.m.p. cstr. (910) *the heads of*
תַנִּינִים n.m.p. (1072) *the dragons*
עַל־הַמָּיִם prep.-def.art.-n.m.p. paus. (565) *on the waters*

74:14
אַתָּה pers.pr. 2 m.s. (61) *thou*
רִצַּצְתָּ Pi. pf. 2 m.s. (954) *didst crush*
רָאשֵׁי n.m.p. cstr. (910) *the heads of*
לִוְיָתָן pr.n. (531) *Leviathan*
תִּתְּנֶנּוּ Qal impf. 2 m.s.-3 m.s. sf. (נָתַן 678) *thou didst give him*
מַאֲכָל n.m.s. (38) *food*
לְעָם prep.-n.m.s. (I 766) *for people*
לְצִיִּים prep.-n.m.p. (II 850) *for the creatures of the wilderness*

74:15
אַתָּה pers.pr. 2 m.s. (61) *thou*
בָקַעְתָּ Qal pf. 2 m.s. (131) *didst cleave open*
מַעְיָן n.m.s. (745) *springs*
וָנָחַל conj.-n.m.s. (636) *and brooks*
אַתָּה v.supra *thou*
הוֹבַשְׁתָּ Hi. pf. 2 m.s. (יָבֵשׁ 386) *didst dry up*
נַהֲרוֹת אֵיתָן n.f.p. cstr. (625)-adj. m.s. (I 450) *ever-flowing streams*

74:16
לְךָ יוֹם prep.-2 m.s. sf.-n.m.s. (398) *thine is the day*
אַף־ conj. (II 64) *also*
לְךָ לָיְלָה v.supra-n.m.s. (538) *thine the night*
אַתָּה pers.pr. 2 m.s. (61) *thou*
הֲכִינוֹתָ Hi. pf. 2 m.s. (כּוּן 465) *hast established*
מָאוֹר n.m.s. (22) *the luminaries*
וָשָׁמֶשׁ conj.-n.f.s. paus. (1039) *and the sun*

74:17
אַתָּה pers.pr. 2 m.s. (61) *thou*
הִצַּבְתָּ Hi. pf. 2 m.s. (נָצַב 662) *hast fixed*

כָּל־גְּבוּלוֹת n.m.s. cstr. (481)–n.f.p. cstr. (148) *all the bounds of*
אָרֶץ n.f.s. paus. (75) *the earth*
קַיִץ n.m.s. (884) *summer*
וָחֹרֶף conj.–n.m.s. (358) *and autumn*
אַתָּה v.supra *thou*
יְצַרְתָּם Qal pf. 2 m.s.–3 m.p. sf. (יָצַר 427) *hast made*

74:18

זְכָר־זֹאת Qal impv. 2 m.s. (269)–demons.adj. f.s. (260) *remember this*
אוֹיֵב Qal act.ptc. (אָיַב 33) *an enemy*
חֵרֵף Pi. pf. 3 m.s. (I 357) *scoffs*
יהוה pr.n. (217) *O Yahweh*
וְעַם נָבָל conj.–n.m.s. (I 766)–adj. m.s. (I 614) *and an impious people*
נִאֲצוּ Pi. pf. 3 c.p. (610) *reviles*
שְׁמֶךָ n.m.s.–2 m.s. sf. (1027) *thy name*

74:19

אַל־תִּתֵּן neg.–Qal impf. 2 m.s. (נָתַן 678) *do not deliver*
לְחַיַּת prep.–n.f.s. cstr. (312) *to life*
נֶפֶשׁ n.f.s. cstr. (659) *the soul of*
תּוֹרֶךָ n.f.s.–2 m.s. sf. (II 1076) *thy dove*
חַיַּת n.f.s. cstr. (312; GK 80f) *the life of*
עֲנִיֶּיךָ adj. m.p.–2 m.s. sf. (776) *thy poor*
אַל־תִּשְׁכַּח neg.–Qal impf. 2 m.s. (1013) *do not forget*
לָנֶצַח prep.–n.m.s. (664) *for ever*

74:20

הַבֵּט Hi. impv. 2 m.s. (נָבַט 613) *have regard*
לַבְּרִית prep.–def.art.–n.f.s. (136) *for the covenant*
כִּי מָלְאוּ conj.–Qal pf. 3 c.p. (569) *for are full*
מַחֲשַׁכֵּי־ n.m.p. cstr. (365) *the dark places of*
אֶרֶץ n.f.s. (75) *the land*
נְאוֹת n.f.p. cstr. (נָוָה II 627) *of the habitations of*
חָמָס n.m.s. (329) *violence*

74:21

אַל־יָשֹׁב neg.–Qal impf.s 3 m.s. juss. (שׁוּב 996) *let not turn*
דַּךְ adj. m.s. (194) *the downtrodden*
נִכְלָם Ni. ptc. (כָּלַם 483) *shame*
עָנִי adj. m.s. (776) *the poor*
וְאֶבְיוֹן conj.–adj. m.s. (2) *and needy*
יְהַלְלוּ Pi. impf. 3 m.p. (II 237) *let praise*
שְׁמֶךָ n.m.s.–2 m.s. sf. (1027) *thy name*

74:22

קוּמָה Qal impv. 2 m.s.–vol.he (877) *arise*
אֱלֹהִים n.m.p. (43) *O God*
רִיבָה Qal impv. 2 m.s.–vol.he (רִיב 936) *plead*
רִיבֶךָ n.m.s.–2 m.s. sf. (936) *thy cause*
זְכֹר Qal impv. 2 m.s. (269) *remember*
חֶרְפָּתְךָ n.f.s.–2 m.s. sf. (357) *thy reproach*
מִנִּי־נָבָל prep.poet. (577)–adj. (I 614) *from the impious*
כָּל־הַיּוֹם n.m.s. cstr. (481)–def.art.–n.m.s. (398) *all the day*

74:23

אַל־תִּשְׁכַּח neg.–Qal impf. 2 m.s. (1013) *do not forget*
קוֹל n.m.s. cstr. (876) *the clamor of*
צֹרְרֶיךָ Qal act.ptc. m.p.–2 m.s. sf. (צָרַר III 865) *thy foes*
שְׁאוֹן n.m.s. cstr. (981) *the uproar of*
קָמֶיךָ Qal act.ptc. m.p.–2 m.s. sf. (קוּם 877) *thy adversaries*
עֹלֶה Qal act.ptc. (עָלָה 748) *which goes up*
תָמִיד adv. (556) *continually*

75:1

לַמְנַצֵּחַ prep.–def.art.–Pi. ptc. (I 663) *to the choirmaster*
אַל־תַּשְׁחֵת neg.–Hi. impf. 2 m.s. apoc. (1007) *do not destroy*
מִזְמוֹר n.m.s. (274) *a Psalm*
לְאָסָף prep.–pr.n. (63) *to Asaph*
שִׁיר n.m.s. (1010) *a Song*

75:2

הוֹדִינוּ Hi. pf. 1 c.p. (יָדָה 392) *we give thanks*
לְּךָ prep.–2 m.s. sf. *to thee*
אֱלֹהִים n.m.p. (43) *O God*
הוֹדִינוּ v.supra *we give thanks*
וְקָרוֹב conj.–adj. (898) *and near*
שְׁמֶךָ n.m.s.–2 m.s. sf. (1027) *thy name*
סִפְּרוּ Pi. pf. 3 c.p. (707) *they recount*
נִפְלְאוֹתֶיךָ Ni. ptc. f.p.–2 m.s. sf. (פָּלָא 810) *thy wondrous deeds*

75:3

כִּי אֶקַּח conj. (471)–Qal impf. 1 c.s. (לָקַח 542) *when I appoint*
מוֹעֵד n.m.s. (417) *the set time*
אֲנִי pers.pr. 1 c.s. (58) *I*
מֵישָׁרִים n.m.p. (449) *with equity*
אֶשְׁפֹּט Qal impf. 1 c.s. (1047) *will judge*

75:4

נְמֹגִים Ni. ptc. m.p. (מוג 556; GK 116w,146g) *when melts*
אֶרֶץ n.f.s. (75) *the earth*
וְכָל־יֹשְׁבֶיהָ conj.-n.m.s. cstr. (481)-Qal act.ptc. m.p.-3 f.s. sf. (442) *and all its inhabitants*
אָנֹכִי pers.pr. 1 c.s. (59) *it is I*
תִכַּנְתִּי Pi. pf. 1 c.s. (תָּכַן 1067) *who keep steady*
עַמּוּדֶיהָ n.m.p.-3 f.s. sf. (765) *its pillars*
סֶלָה interj. (699) *Selah*

75:5

אָמַרְתִּי Qal pf. 1 c.s. (55) *I say*
לַהוֹלְלִים prep.-def.art.-Qal act.ptc. m.p. (II 237) *to the boastful*
אַל־תָּהֹלּוּ neg.-Qal impf. 2 m.p. (הָלַל II 237) *do not boast*
וְלָרְשָׁעִים conj.-prep.-def.art.-adj. m.p. (957) *and to the wicked*
אַל־תָּרִימוּ neg.-Hi. impf. 2 m.p. (רוּם 926) *do not lift up*
קָרֶן n.f.s. (901) *your horn*

75:6

אַל־תָּרִימוּ neg.-Hi. impf. 2 m.p. (רוּם 926) *do not lift up*
לַמָּרוֹם prep.-def.art.-n.m.s. (928) *on high*
קַרְנְכֶם n.f.s.-2 m.p. sf. (901) *your horn*
תְּדַבְּרוּ Pi. impf. 2 m.p. (180) *or speak*
בְצַוָּאר prep.-n.m.s. (848) *with ... neck*
עָתָק adj. m.s. (801) *insolent*

75:7

כִּי לֹא conj. (471)-neg. *for not*
מִמּוֹצָא prep.-n.m.s. (I 425) *from east*
וּמִמַּעֲרָב conj.-prep.-n.m.s. (II 788) *or from west*
וְלֹא conj.-neg. *and not*
מִמִּדְבַּר prep.-n.m.s. (184) *from wilderness*
הָרִים Hi. inf.cstr. (רוּם 926) *lifting up*

75:8

כִּי־אֱלֹהִים conj. (471)-n.m.p. (43) *but it is God*
שֹׁפֵט Qal act.ptc. (1047) *who executes judgment*
זֶה demons.adj. m.s. (260) *one*
יַשְׁפִּיל Hi. impf. 3 m.s. (1050) *he puts down*
וְזֶה conj.-v.supra *and another*
יָרִים Hi. impf. 3 m.s. (רוּם 926) *he lifts up*

75:9

כִּי כוֹס conj. (471)-n.f.s. (468) *for there is a cup*
בְּיַד־יהוה prep.-n.f.s. cstr. (388)-pr.n. (217) *in the hand of Yahweh*
וְיַיִן conj.-n.m.s. (406) *with wine*
חָמַר Qal pf. 3 m.s. (330) *which foams*
מָלֵא מֶסֶךְ adj. m.s. (570)-n.m.s. (587) *a full mixture*
וַיַּגֵּר consec.-Hi. impf. 3 m.s. (נָגַר 620) *and he will pour*
מִזֶּה prep.-demons.adj. m.s. (260) *from it*
אַךְ־שְׁמָרֶיהָ adv. (36)-n.m.p.-3 f.s. sf. (1038) *surely its dregs*
יִמְצוּ Qal impf. 3 m.p. (מָצָה 594) *they drain*
יִשְׁתּוּ Qal impf. 3 m.p. (שָׁתָה 1059) *they drink*
כֹּל רִשְׁעֵי־ n.m.s. cstr. (481)-adj. m.p. cstr. (957) *all the wicked of*
אָרֶץ n.f.s. paus. (75) *the earth*

75:10

וַאֲנִי אַגִּיד conj.-pers.pr. 1 c.s. (58)-Hi. impf. 1 c.s. (נָגַד 616) *but I will declare*
לְעֹלָם prep.-n.m.s. (761) *for ever*
אֲזַמְּרָה Pi. impf. 1 c.s.-vol.he (זָמַר I 274) *I will sing praises*
לֵאלֹהֵי prep.-n.m.p. cstr. (43) *to the God of*
יַעֲקֹב pr.n. (784) *Jacob*

75:11

וְכָל־קַרְנֵי conj.-n.m.s. cstr. (481)-n.f.p. cstr. (901) *and all the horns of*
רְשָׁעִים adj. m.p. (957) *the wicked*
אֲגַדֵּעַ Pi. impf. 1 c.s. (154) *I will cut off*
תְּרוֹמַמְנָה Polal impf. 3 f.p. (רוּם 926) *shall be exalted*
קַרְנוֹת n.f.p. cstr. (901) *the horns of*
צַדִּיק adj. m.s. (843) *the righteous*

76:1

לַמְנַצֵּחַ prep.-def.art.-Pi. ptc. (I 663) *to the choirmaster*
בִּנְגִינֹת prep.-n.f.p. (618) *with stringed instruments*
מִזְמוֹר n.m.s. (274) *a Psalm*
לְאָסָף prep.-pr.n. (63) *to Asaph*
שִׁיר n.m.s. (1010) *a song*

76:2

נוֹדָע Ni. ptc. (יָדַע 393) *is known*
בִּיהוּדָה prep.-pr.n. (397) *in Judah*
אֱלֹהִים n.m.p. (43) *God*
בְּיִשְׂרָאֵל prep.-pr.n. (975) *in Israel*
גָּדוֹל adj. m.s. (152) *is great*
שְׁמוֹ n.m.s.-3 m.s. sf. (1027) *his name*

76:3

וַיְהִי consec.-Qal impf. 3 m.s. (הָיָה 224) *and has been established*

בְשָׁלֵם prep.-pr.n. (II 1024) *in Salem*

סֻכּוֹ n.m.s.-3 m.s. sf. (697) *his abode*

וּמְעוֹנָתוֹ conj.-n.f.s.-3 m.s. sf. (733) *and his dwelling place*

בְצִיּוֹן prep.-pr.n. (851) *in Zion*

76:4

שָׁמָּה adv.-dir.he (1027) *there*

שִׁבַּר Pi. pf. 3 m.s. (990) *he broke*

רִשְׁפֵי־קָשֶׁת n.m.p. cstr. (958)-n.f.s. (905) *the flashing arrows*

מָגֵן n.m.s. (171) *shield*

וְחֶרֶב conj.-n.f.s. (352) *sword*

וּמִלְחָמָה conj.-n.f.s. (536) *and weapons of war*

סֶלָה interj. (699) *Selah*

76:5

נָאוֹר Ni. ptc. (אוֹר 21) *lighted up (glorious)*

אַתָּה pers.pr. 2 m.s. (61) *art thou*

אַדִּיר adj. (12) *(more) majestic*

מֵהַרְרֵי־טָרֶף prep.-n.m.p. cstr. (249)-n.m.s. paus. (383) *than the mountains of prey*

76:6

אֶשְׁתּוֹלְלוּ Hithpo'el pf. 3 c.p. (שָׁלַל II 1021; GK 53k,54aN) *were stripped of their spoil*

אַבִּירֵי לֵב adj. m.p. cstr. (7)-n.m.s. (524) *the stouthearted*

נָמוּ Qal pf. 3 c.p. (נוּם 630) *they slumbered*

שְׁנָתָם n.f.s.-3 m.p. sf. (446) *their sleep*

וְלֹא־מָצְאוּ conj.-neg.-Qal pf. 3 c.p. (592) *and ... were unable to use*

כָל־אַנְשֵׁי־ n.m.s. cstr. (481)-n.m.p. cstr. (35) *all the men of*

חַיִל n.m.s. (298) *war*

יְדֵיהֶם n.f. du.-3 m.p. sf. (388) *their hands*

76:7

מִגַּעֲרָתְךָ prep.-n.f.s.-2 m.s. sf. (172) *at thy rebuke*

אֱלֹהֵי n.m.p. cstr. (43) *O God of*

יַעֲקֹב pr.n. (784) *Jacob*

נִרְדָּם Ni. ptc. (רָדַם 922) *lay stunned*

וְרֶכֶב conj.-n.m.s. (939) *both rider*

וָסוּס conj.-n.m.s. (692) *and horse*

76:8

אַתָּה pers.pr. 2 m.s. (61) *but thou*

נוֹרָא Ni. ptc. (יָרֵא 431) *terrible*

אַתָּה v.supra *thou*

וּמִי־ conj.-interr. (566) *and who*

יַעֲמֹד Qal impf. 3 m.s. (763) *can stand*

לְפָנֶיךָ prep.-n.m.p.-2 m.s. sf. (815) *before thee*

מֵאָז adv. (23) *from time of*

אַפֶּךָ n.m.s.-2 m.s. sf. (I 60) *thy anger*

76:9

מִשָּׁמַיִם prep.-n.m. du. (1029) *from heaven*

הִשְׁמַעְתָּ Hi. pf. 2 m.s. (1033) *thou didst utter*

דִּין n.m.s. (192) *judgment*

אֶרֶץ n.f.s. (75) *earth*

יָרְאָה Qal pf. 3 f.s. (יָרֵא 431) *feared*

וְשָׁקָטָה conj.-Qal pf. 3 f.s. paus. (1052) *and was still*

76:10

בְּקוּם־ prep.-Qal inf.cstr. (877) *when arose*

לַמִּשְׁפָּט prep.-def.art.-n.m.s. (1048) *to judgment*

אֱלֹהִים n.m.p. (43) *God*

לְהוֹשִׁיעַ prep.-Hi. inf.cstr. (יָשַׁע 446) *to save*

כָּל־עַנְוֵי־ n.m.s. cstr. (481)-n.m.p. cstr. (776) *all the oppressed of*

אָרֶץ n.f.s. paus. (75) *earth*

סֶלָה interj. (699) *Selah*

76:11

כִּי־חֲמַת conj. (471)-n.f.s. cstr. (404) *surely wrath of*

אָדָם n.m.s. (9) *man*

תּוֹדֶךָּ Hi. impf. 3 f.s.-2 m.s. sf. (יָדָה 392) *shall praise thee*

שְׁאֵרִית n.f.s. cstr. (984) *the residue of*

חֵמֹת n.f.p. (404; GK 124e) *wrath*

תַּחְגֹּר Qal impf. 2 m.s. (חָגַר 291) *thou wilt gird upon thee*

76:12

נִדְרוּ Qal impv. 2 m.p. (623) *make your vows*

וְשַׁלְּמוּ conj.-Pi. impv. 2 m.p. (1022) *and perform them*

לַיהוה prep.-pr.n. (217) *to Yahweh*

אֱלֹהֵיכֶם n.m.p.-2 m.p. sf. (43) *your God*

כָּל־סְבִיבָיו n.m.s. cstr. (481)-n.m.p.-3 m.s. sf. (686) *all around him*

יוֹבִילוּ Hi. impf. 3 m.p. (יָבַל 384) *let bring*

שַׁי n.m.s. (1009) *gifts*

לַמּוֹרָא prep.-def.art.-n.m.s. (432) *to him who is to be feared*

76:13

יִבְצֹר Qal impf. 3 m.s. (130) *who cuts off*

רוּחַ n.f.s. cstr. (924) *the spirit of*
נְגִידִים n.m.p. (617) *princes*
נוֹרָא Ni. ptc. (יָרֵא 431) *who is terrible*
לְמַלְכֵי־ prep.-n.m.p. cstr. (I 572) *to the kings of*
אָרֶץ n.f.s. paus. (75) *the earth*

77:1

לַמְנַצֵּחַ prep.-def.art.-Pi. ptc. (I 663) *to the choirmaster*
עַל־יְדִיתוּן prep.-pr.n. (393) *according to Jeduthun*
לְאָסָף prep.-pr.n. (63) *to Asaph*
מִזְמוֹר n.m.s. (274) *a Psalm*

77:2

קוֹלִי n.m.s.-1 c.s. sf. (876) *my voice*
אֶל־אֱלֹהִים prep.-n.m.p. (43) *to God*
וְאֶצְעָקָה conj.-Qal impf. 1 c.s.-vol.he (צָעַק 858) *I cry aloud*
קוֹלִי v.supra *my voice*
אֶל־אֱלֹהִים v.supra-v.supra *to God*
וְהַאֲזִין conj.-Hi. pf. 3 m.s. (אָזַן I 24; or Hi. impv. 2 m.s.; GK 63o) *that he may hear*
אֵלָי prep.-1 c.s. sf. paus. *me*

77:3

בְּיוֹם prep.-n.m.s. cstr. (398) *in the day of*
צָרָתִי n.f.s.-1 c.s. sf. (865) *my trouble*
אֲדֹנָי n.m.p.-1 c.s. sf. (10) *the Lord*
דָּרָשְׁתִּי Qal pf. 1 c.s. paus. (205) *I seek*
יָדִי n.f.s.-1 c.s. sf. (388) *my hand*
לַיְלָה n.m.s. (538) *in the night*
נִגְּרָה Ni. pf. 3 f.s. (נָגַר 620) *is stretched out*
וְלֹא תָפוּג conj.-neg.-Qal impf. 3 f.s. (פוּג 806) *without wearying*
מֵאֲנָה Pi. pf. 3 f.s. (549) *refuses*
הִנָּחֵם Ni. inf.cstr. (636) *to be comforted*
נַפְשִׁי n.f.s.-1 c.s. sf. (659) *my soul*

77:4

אֶזְכְּרָה Qal impf. 1 c.s.-vol.he (זָכַר 269) *I think of*
אֱלֹהִים n.m.p. (43) *God*
וְאֶהֱמָיָה conj.-Qal impf. 1 c.s.-vol.he (הָמָה 242; GK 75,l;75u) *and I moan*
אָשִׂיחָה Qal impf. 1 c.s.-vol.he (שִׂיחַ 967) *I meditate*
וְתִתְעַטֵּף conj.-Hith. impf. 3 f.s. (עָטַף III 742) *and faints*
רוּחִי n.f.s.-1 c.s. sf. (924) *my spirit*
סֶלָה interj. (699) *Selah*

77:5

אָחַזְתָּ Qal pf. 2 m.s. (אָחַז 28) *thou dost hold*
שְׁמֻרוֹת עֵינָי n.f.p. cstr. (1037)-n.f. du.-1 c.s. sf. paus. (744) *my eyelids*
נִפְעַמְתִּי Ni. pf. 1 c.s. (פָּעַם 821) *I am so troubled*
וְלֹא אֲדַבֵּר conj.-neg.-Pi. impf. 1 c.s. (180) *that I cannot speak*

77:6

חִשַּׁבְתִּי Pi. pf. 1 c.s. (362) *I consider*
יָמִים n.m.p. (398) *the days*
מִקֶּדֶם prep.-n.m.s. (869) *of old*
שְׁנוֹת n.f.p. cstr. (1040) *years*
עוֹלָמִים n.m.p. (761) *long ago*

77:7

אֶזְכְּרָה Qal impf. 1 c.s.-vol.he (269) *I remember*
נְגִינָתִי n.f.s.-1 c.s. sf. (618) *my music*
בַּלָּיְלָה prep.-def.art.-n.m.s. (538) *in the night*
עִם־לְבָבִי prep.-n.m.s.-1 c.s. sf. (523) *with my heart*
אָשִׂיחָה Qal impf. 1 c.s.-vol.he (967) *I meditate*
וַיְחַפֵּשׂ consec.-Pi. impf. 3 m.s. (344) *and searches*
רוּחִי n.m.s.-1 c.s. sf. (924) *my spirit*

77:8

הַלְעוֹלָמִים interr.part.-prep.-n.m.p. (761) *for ever?*
יִזְנַח Qal impf. 3 m.s. (276) *will spurn*
אֲדֹנָי n.m.p.-1 c.s. sf. (10) *the Lord*
וְלֹא־יֹסִיף conj.-neg.-Hi. impf. 3 m.s. (יָסַף 414) *and never*
לִרְצוֹת prep.-Qal inf.cstr. (רָצָה 953) *be favorable*
עוֹד adv. (728) *again?*

77:9

הֶאָפֵס interr.part.-Qal pf. 3 m.s. (67) *has ceased?*
לָנֶצַח prep.-n.m.s. (664) *for ever*
חַסְדּוֹ n.m.s.-3 m.s. sf. (338) *his steadfast love*
גָּמַר Qal pf. 3 m.s. (170) *are at an end*
אֹמֶר n.m.s. (56) *his promises*
לְדֹר וָדֹר prep.-n.m.s. (189)-conj.-n.m.s. (189) *for all time*

77:10

הֲשָׁכַח interr.part.-Qal pf. 3 m.s. (1013) *has forgotten?*
חַנּוֹת Qal inf.cstr. (חָנַן I 335; GK 67r) *to be gracious*
אֵל n.m.s. (42) *God*

אִם־קָפַץ interr. (50)-Qal pf. 3 m.s. (891) *has he shut up?*
בְּאַף prep.-n.m.s. (I 60) *in anger*
רַחֲמָיו n.m.p.-3 m.s. sf. (933) *his compassion*
סֶלָה interj. (699) *Selah*

77:11

וָאֹמַר consec.-Qal impf. 1 c.s. (אָמַר 55) *and I say*
חַלּוֹתִי Pi. inf.cstr.-1 c.s. sf. (חָלָה I 317; GK 67r) *my grief*
הִיא demons.adj. f.s. (214) *it is*
שְׁנוֹת Qal inf.cstr. (שָׁנָה 1039) *that has changed*
יְמִין n.f.s. cstr. (411) *the right hand of*
עֶלְיוֹן n.m.s. (751) *the Most High*

77:12

אֶזְכִּיר Qal impf. 1 c.s. (269) *I will call to mind*
מַעַלְלֵי־ n.m.p. cstr. (760) *the deeds of*
יָהּ pr.n. (219) *Yah*
כִּי־אֶזְכְּרָה conj. (471)-Qal impf. 1 c.s.-vol.he (269) *yea, I will remember*
מִקֶּדֶם prep.-n.m.s. (869) *of old*
פִּלְאֶךָ n.m.s.-2 m.s. sf. (810) *thy wonders*

77:13

וְהָגִיתִי conj.-Qal pf. 1 c.s. (הָגָה I 211) *I will meditate*
בְכָל־ prep.-n.m.s. cstr. (481) *on all*
פָּעֳלֶךָ n.m.s.-2 m.s. sf. (821) *thy work*
וּבַעֲלִילוֹתֶיךָ conj.-prep.-n.f.p.-2 m.s. sf. (760) *and on thy mighty deeds*
אָשִׂיחָה Qal impf. 1 c.s.-vol.he (967) *I will muse*

77:14

אֱלֹהִים n.m.p. (43) *O God*
בַּקֹּדֶשׁ prep.-def.art.-n.m.s. (871) *in the holiness*
דַּרְכֶּךָ n.m.s.-2 m.s. sf. (202) *thy way*
מִי־ interr. (566) *who is*
אֵל גָּדוֹל n.m.s. (42)-adj. m.s. (152) *a great God*
כֵּאלֹהִים prep.-n.m.p. (43) *like God*

77:15

אַתָּה pers.pr. 2 m.s. (61) *thou*
הָאֵל def.art.-n.m.s. (42) *the God*
עֹשֵׂה Qal act.ptc. m.s. cstr. (עָשָׂה I 793) *who workest*
פֶלֶא n.m.s. (810) *wonders*
הוֹדַעְתָּ Hi. pf. 2 m.s. (יָדַע 393) *thou hast manifested*
בָעַמִּים prep.-def.art.-n.m.p. (I 766) *among the peoples*

עֻזֶּךָ n.m.s.-2 m.s. sf. (738) *thy might*

77:16

גָּאַלְתָּ Qal pf. 2 m.s. (I 145) *thou didst redeem*
בִּזְרוֹעַ prep.-n.f.s. (283; GK 20g,125c) *with thy arm*
עַמֶּךָ n.m.s.-2 m.s. sf. (I 766) *thy people*
בְּנֵי־ n.m.p. cstr. (119) *the sons of*
יַעֲקֹב pr.n. (784) *Jacob*
וְיוֹסֵף conj.-pr.n. (415) *and Joseph*
סֶלָה interj. (699) *Selah*

77:17

רָאוּךָ Qal pf. 3 c.p.-2 m.s. sf. (רָאָה 906) *when saw thee*
מַּיִם n.m.p. (565) *the waters*
אֱלֹהִים n.m.p. (43) *O God*
רָאוּךָ v.supra *when saw thee*
מַּיִם v.supra *the waters*
יָחִילוּ Qal impf. 3 m.p. (חוּל I 296) *they were afraid (in anguish)*
אַף conj. (II 64) *yea*
יִרְגְּזוּ Qal impf. 3 m.p. (919) *trembled*
תְהֹמוֹת n.f.p. (1062) *the deep*

77:18

זֹרְמוּ Pu. pf. 3 c.p. (זָרַם 281; GK 55b) *poured out*
מַיִם n.m.p. (565) *water*
עָבוֹת n.m.p. (II 728) *the clouds*
קוֹל n.m.s. (876) *thunder*
נָתְנוּ Qal pf. 3 c.p. (678) *gave forth*
שְׁחָקִים n.m.p. (1007) *the clouds*
אַף־ conj. (II 64) *yea*
חֲצָצֶיךָ n.m.p.-2 m.p. sf. (346; GK 93bb) *thy arrows*
יִתְהַלָּכוּ Hith. impf. 3 m.p. paus. (229) *flashed on every side*

77:19

קוֹל n.m.s. cstr. (876) *the crash of*
רַעַמְךָ n.m.s.-2 m.s. sf. (947) *thy thunder*
בַּגַּלְגַּל prep.-def.art.-n.m.s. (165) *in the whirlwind*
הֵאִירוּ Hi. pf. 3 c.p. (אוֹר 21) *lighted up*
בְרָקִים n.m.p. (140) *lightnings*
תֵּבֵל n.f.s. (385) *the world*
רָגְזָה Qal pf. 3 f.s. (919) *trembled*
וַתִּרְעַשׁ consec.-Qal impf. 3 f.s. (950) *and shook*
הָאָרֶץ def.art.-n.f.s. (75) *the earth*

77:20

בַּיָּם prep.-def.art.-n.m.s. (410) *through the sea*
דַּרְכֶּךָ n.m.s.-2 m.s. sf. (202) *thy way*

וּשְׁבִילְךָ conj.-n.m.p.-2 m.s. sf. (987) *and thy paths*

בְּמַיִם רַבִּים prep.-n.m.p. (565)-adj. m.p. (I 912) *through the great waters*

וְעִקְּבוֹתֶיךָ conj.-n.m.p.-2 m.s. sf. (I 784; GK 20h) *yet thy footprints*

לֹא נֹדָעוּ neg.-Ni. pf. 3 c.p. paus. (יָדַע 393) *were unseen*

77:21

נָחִיתָ Qal pf. 2 m.s. (נָחָה 634) *thou didst lead*

כַּצֹּאן prep.-def.art.-n.f.s. (838) *like a flock*

עַמֶּךָ n.m.s.-2 m.s. sf. (I 766) *thy people*

בְּיַד־ prep.-n.f.s. cstr. (388) *by the hand of*

מֹשֶׁה pr.n. (602) *Moses*

וְאַהֲרֹן conj.-pr.n. (14) *and Aaron*

78:1

מַשְׂכִּיל n.m.s. (968) *a Maskil*

לְאָסָף prep.-pr.n. (63) *to Asaph*

הַאֲזִינָה Hi. impv. 2 m.s.-vol.he (אָזַן 24) *give ear*

עַמִּי n.m.s.-1 c.s. sf. (I 766) *O my people*

תּוֹרָתִי n.f.s.-1 c.s. sf. (435) *to my teaching*

הַטּוּ Hi. impv. 2 m.p. (נָטָה 639) *incline*

אָזְנְכֶם n.f.s.-2 m.p. sf. (23) *your ear*

לְאִמְרֵי־פִי prep.-n.m.p. cstr. (56)-n.m.s.-1 c.s. sf. (804) *to the words of my mouth*

78:2

אֶפְתְּחָה Qal impf. 1 c.s.-vol.he (פָּתַח I 834) *I will open*

בְמָשָׁל prep.-n.m.s. (605) *in a parable*

פִּי n.m.s.-1 c.s. sf. (804) *my mouth*

אַבִּיעָה Hi. impf. 1 c.s.-vol.he (נָבַע 615) *I will utter*

חִידוֹת n.f.p. (295) *dark sayings*

מִנִּי־קֶדֶם prep. (577)-n.m.s. (869) *from of old*

78:3

אֲשֶׁר שָׁמַעְנוּ rel. (81)-Qal pf. 1 c.p. (1033) *things that we have heard*

וַנֵּדָעֵם consec.-Qal impf. 1 c.p.-3 m.p. sf. (יָדַע 393) *and known them*

וַאֲבוֹתֵינוּ conj.-n.m.p.-1 c.p. sf. (3) *that our fathers*

סִפְּרוּ־לָנוּ Pi. pf. 3 c.p. (707)-prep.-1 c.p. sf. *have told us*

78:4

לֹא נְכַחֵד neg.-Pi. impf. 1 c.p. (470) *we will not hide*

מִבְּנֵיהֶם prep.-n.m.p.-3 m.p. sf. (119) *from their children*

לְדוֹר אַחֲרוֹן prep.-n.m.s. (189)-adj. m.s. (30) *to the coming generation*

מְסַפְּרִים Pi. ptc. m.p. (707) *telling*

תְּהִלּוֹת n.f.p. cstr. (239) *the glorious deeds of*

יהוה pr.n. (217) *Yahweh*

וֶעֱזוּזוֹ conj.-n.m.s.-3 m.s. sf. (739) *and his might*

וְנִפְלְאוֹתָיו conj.-Ni. ptc. f.p.-3 m.s. sf. (810) *and his wonders*

אֲשֶׁר עָשָׂה rel. (81)-Qal pf. 3 m.s. (I 793) *which he has wrought*

78:5

וַיָּקֶם consec.-Hi. impf. 3 m.s. (קוּם 877) *and he established*

עֵדוּת n.f.s. (730) *a testimony*

בְּיַעֲקֹב prep.-pr.n. (784) *in Jacob*

וְתוֹרָה conj.-n.f.s. (435) *and a law*

שָׂם Qal pf. 3 m.s. (שִׂים 962) *he appointed*

בְּיִשְׂרָאֵל prep.-pr.n. (975) *in Israel*

אֲשֶׁר צִוָּה rel. (81)-Pi. pf. 3 m.s. (צָוָה 845) *which he commanded*

אֶת־אֲבוֹתֵינוּ dir.obj.-n.m.p.-1 c.p. sf. (3) *our fathers*

לְהוֹדִיעָם prep.-Hi. inf.cstr.-3 m.p. sf. (יָדַע 393) *to teach them*

לִבְנֵיהֶם prep.-n.m.p.-3 m.p. sf. (119) *to their children*

78:6

לְמַעַן יֵדְעוּ prep. (775; GK 107k)-Qal impf. 3 m.p. (יָדַע 393) *that might know*

דּוֹר אַחֲרוֹן n.m.s. (189)-adj. m.s. (30) *the next generation*

בָּנִים n.m.p. (119) *the children*

יִוָּלֵדוּ Ni. impf. 3 m.p. paus. (יָלַד 408) *yet unborn*

יָקֻמוּ Qal impf. 3 m.p. (קוּם 877) *they might arise*

וִיסַפְּרוּ conj.-Pi. impf. 3 m.p. (707) *and tell*

לִבְנֵיהֶם prep.-n.m.p.-3 m.p. sf. (119) *to their children*

78:7

וְיָשִׂימוּ conj.-Qal impf. 3 m.p. (שִׂים 962) *so that they should set*

בֵּאלֹהִים prep.-n.m.p. (43) *in God*

כִּסְלָם n.m.s.-3 m.p. sf. (492) *their hope*

וְלֹא יִשְׁכְּחוּ conj.-neg.-Qal impf. 3 m.p. (1013) *and not forget*

מַעַלְלֵי־אֵל n.m.p. cstr. (760)-n.m.s. (42) *the works of God*

וּמִצְוֺתָיו conj.-n.f.p.-3 m.s. sf. (846) *but his commandments*
יִנְצֹרוּ Qal impf. 3 m.p. paus. (נָצַר 665) *keep*

78:8
וְלֹא יִהְיוּ conj.-neg.-Qal impf. 3 m.p. (224) *and they should not be*
כַּאֲבוֹתָם prep.-n.m.p.-3 m.p. sf. (3) *like their fathers*
דּוֹר n.m.s. (189) *a generation*
סוֹרֵר Qal act.ptc. (710) *stubborn*
וּמֹרֶה conj.-Qal act.ptc. (598) *and rebellious*
דּוֹר v.supra *a generation*
לֹא־הֵכִין neg.-Hi. pf. 3 m.s. (כּוּן 465) *was not steadfast*
לִבּוֹ n.m.s.-3 m.s. sf. (524) *whose heart*
וְלֹא־נֶאֶמְנָה conj.-neg.-Ni. pf. 3 f.s. (אָמַן 52) *was not faithful*
אֶת־אֵל dir.obj.-n.m.s. (42) *to God*
רוּחוֹ n.f.s.-3 m.s. sf. (924) *whose spirit*

78:9
בְּנֵי־ n.m.p. cstr. (119) *the sons of*
אֶפְרַיִם pr.n. (68) *Ephraim*
נוֹשְׁקֵי Qal act.ptc. m.p. cstr. (II 676) *being armed with*
רוֹמֵי־ Qal act.ptc. m.p. cstr. (רָמָה I 941) *shooting of*
קָשֶׁת n.f.s. paus. (905) *a bow*
הָפְכוּ Qal pf. 3 c.p. (הָפַךְ 245) *they turned back*
בְּיוֹם prep.-n.m.s. cstr. (398) *on the day of*
קְרָב n.m.s. (898) *battle*

78:10
לֹא שָׁמְרוּ neg.-Qal pf. 3 c.p. (1036) *they did not keep*
בְּרִית n.f.s. cstr. (136) *the covenant of*
אֱלֹהִים n.m.p. (43) *God*
וּבְתוֹרָתוֹ conj.-prep.-n.f.s.-3 m.s. sf. (435) *but according to his law*
מֵאֲנוּ Pi. pf. 3 c.p. (549) *they refused*
לָלֶכֶת prep.-Qal inf.cstr. (הָלַךְ 229) *to walk*

78:11
וַיִּשְׁכְּחוּ consec.-Qal impf. 3 m.p. (1013) *and they forgot*
עֲלִילוֹתָיו n.f.p.-3 m.s. sf. (760) *what he had done*
וְנִפְלְאוֹתָיו conj.-Ni. ptc. f.p.-3 m.s. sf. (פָּלָא 810) *and the miracles*
אֲשֶׁר הֶרְאָם rel. (81)-Hi. pf. 3 m.s.-3 m.p. sf. (906 רָאָה) *that he had shown them*

78:12
נֶגֶד אֲבוֹתָם prep. (617)-n.m.p.-3 m.p. sf. (3) *in the sight of their fathers*
עָשָׂה Qal pf. 3 m.s. (I 793) *he wrought*
פֶלֶא n.m.s. (810) *marvels*
בְּאֶרֶץ prep.-n.f.s. cstr. (75) *in the land of*
מִצְרַיִם pr.n. (595) *Egypt*
שְׂדֵה־ n.m.s. cstr. (961) *in the field of*
צֹעַן pr.n. (858) *Zoan*

78:13
בָּקַע Qal pf. 3 m.s. (131) *he divided*
יָם n.m.s. (410) *the sea*
וַיַּעֲבִירֵם consec.-Hi. impf. 3 m.s.-3 m.p. sf. (עָבַר 716) *and let them pass through it*
וַיַּצֶּב־ consec.-Hi. impf. 3 m.s. (נָצַב 662) *and made stand*
מַיִם n.m.p. (565) *the waters*
כְּמוֹ־נֵד adv. (455)-n.m.s. (622) *like a heap*

78:14
וַיַּנְחֵם consec.-Hi. impf. 3 m.s.-3 m.p. sf. (נָחָה 634) *and he led them*
בֶּעָנָן prep.-def.art.-n.m.s. (777) *with a cloud*
יוֹמָם adv. (401) *in the daytime*
וְכָל־הַלַּיְלָה conj.-n.m.s. cstr. (481)-def.art.-n.m.s. (538) *and all the night*
בְּאוֹר אֵשׁ prep.-n.m.s. cstr. (21)-n.f.s. (77) *with a fiery light*

78:15
יְבַקַּע Pi. impf. 3 m.s. (131) *and he cleft*
צֻרִים n.m.p. (849) *rocks*
בַּמִּדְבָּר prep.-def.art.-n.m.s. (184) *in the wilderness*
וַיַּשְׁקְ consec.-Hi. impf. 3 m.s. (שָׁקָה 1052) *and gave them drink*
כִּתְהֹמוֹת prep.-n.f.p. (1062) *from the deep*
רַבָּה adj. f.s. as adv. (I 912; GK 132hN) *abundantly*

78:16
וַיּוֹצִא consec.-Hi. impf. 3 m.s. (יָצָא 422; GK 74,l) *and he made come out*
נוֹזְלִים Qal act.ptc. m.p. (633) *streams*
מִסָּלַע prep.-n.m.s. paus. (700) *out of the rock*
וַיּוֹרֶד consec.-Hi. impf. 3 m.s. (יָרַד 432) *and caused to flow down*
כַּנְּהָרוֹת prep.-def.art.-n.m.p. (625) *like rivers*
מָיִם n.m.p. paus. (565) *waters*

78:17

וַיּוֹסִיפוּ consec.-Hi. impf. 3 m.p. (יָסַף 414) *and they added*

עוֹד adv. (728) *still*

לַחֲטֹא־ prep.-Qal inf.cstr. (307) *to sin*

לוֹ prep.-3 m.s. sf. *against him*

לַמְרוֹת prep.-Hi. inf.cstr. (מָרָה 598) *rebelling against*

עֶלְיוֹן n.m.s. (751) *the Most High*

בַּצִּיָּה prep.-def.art.-n.f.s. (851) *in the desert*

78:18

וַיְנַסּוּ־ consec.-Pi. impf. 3 m.p. (נָסָה 650) *and they tested*

אֵל n.m.s. (42) *God*

בִּלְבָבָם prep.-n.m.s.-3 m.p. sf. (523) *in their heart*

לִשְׁאָל־ prep.-Qal inf.cstr. (981) *by demanding*

אֹכֶל n.m.s. (38) *food*

לְנַפְשָׁם prep.-n.f.s.-3 m.p. sf. (659) *for their appetite*

78:19

וַיְדַבְּרוּ consec.-Pi. impf. 3 m.p. (180) *and they spoke*

בֵּאלֹהִים prep.-n.m.p. (43) *against God*

אָמְרוּ Qal pf. 3 c.p. (55) *they said*

הֲיוּכַל interr.part.-Qal impf. 3 m.s. (יָכֹל 407) *can?*

אֵל n.m.s. (42) *God*

לַעֲרֹךְ prep.-Qal inf.cstr. (789) *spread*

שֻׁלְחָן n.m.s. (1020) *a table*

בַּמִּדְבָּר prep.-def.art.-n.m.s. (184) *in the wilderness*

78:20

הֵן interj. (243) *lo*

הִכָּה־ Hi. pf. 3 m.s. (נָכָה 645) *he smote*

צוּר n.m.s. (849) *a rock*

וַיָּזוּבוּ consec.-Qal impf. 3 m.p. (זוּב 264) *so that gushed out*

מַיִם n.m.p. (565) *water*

וּנְחָלִים conj.-n.m.p. (636) *and streams*

יִשְׁטֹפוּ Qal impf. 3 m.p. (1009) *overflowed*

הֲגַם־לֶחֶם interr.part.-adv. (168)-n.m.s. (536) *also bread?*

יוּכַל Qal impf. 3 m.s. (יָכֹל 407) *can he*

תֵּת Qal inf.cstr. (נָתַן 678) *give*

אִם־יָכִין interr. (50)-Hi. impf. 3 m.s. (כּוּן 465) *or can he provide*

שְׁאֵר n.m.s. (984) *meat*

לְעַמּוֹ prep.-n.m.s.-3 m.s. sf. (I 766) *for his people*

78:21

לָכֵן prep.-adv. (485) *therefore*

שָׁמַע Qal pf. 3 m.s. (1033) *when heard*

יהוה pr.n. (217) *Yahweh*

וַיִּתְעַבָּר consec.-Hith. impf. 3 m.s. (עָבַר 720) *he was full of wrath*

וְאֵשׁ conj.-n.f.s. (77) *and a fire*

נִשְּׂקָה Ni. pf. 3 f.s. (שָׂלַק 969; GK 66e) *was kindled*

בְיַעֲקֹב prep.-pr.n. (784) *against Jacob*

וְגַם־אַף conj.-adv. (168)-n.m.s. (I 60) *and also anger*

עָלָה Qal pf. 3 m.s. (748) *mounted*

בְיִשְׂרָאֵל prep.-pr.n. (975) *against Israel*

78:22

כִּי לֹא הֶאֱמִינוּ conj. (471)-neg.-Hi. pf. 3 c.p. (52 אָמַן) *because they had no faith*

בֵּאלֹהִים prep.-n.m.p. (43) *in God*

וְלֹא בָטְחוּ conj.-neg.-Qal pf. 3 c.p. (105) *and did not trust*

בִּישׁוּעָתוֹ prep.-n.f.s.-3 m.s. sf. (447) *his saving power*

78:23

וַיְצַו consec.-Pi. impf. 3 m.s. (צָוָה 845) *yet he commanded*

שְׁחָקִים n.m.p. (1007) *the skies*

מִמָּעַל prep.-subst. (II 751) *above*

וְדַלְתֵי conj.-n.f.p. cstr. (195) *and doors of*

שָׁמַיִם n.m. du. (1029) *heavens*

פָּתָח Qal pf. 3 m.s. paus. (I 834) *opened*

78:24

וַיַּמְטֵר consec.-Hi. impf. 3 m.s. (565) *and he rained down*

עֲלֵיהֶם prep.-3 m.p. sf. *upon them*

מָן n.m.s. (I 577) *manna*

לֶאֱכֹל prep.-Qal inf.cstr. (37) *to eat*

וּדְגַן־ conj.-n.m.s. cstr. (186) *and the grain of*

שָׁמַיִם n.m. du. (1029) *heaven*

נָתַן לָמוֹ Qal pf. 3 m.s. (678)-prep.-3 m.p. sf. *he gave them*

78:25

לֶחֶם n.m.s. cstr. (536) *bread of*

אַבִּירִים adj. m.p. (7) *angels*

אָכַל אִישׁ Qal pf. 3 m.s. (37)-n.m.s. (35) *man ate*

צֵידָה n.f.s. (845) *food*

שָׁלַח Qal pf. 3 m.s. (1018) *he sent*
לָהֶם prep.-3 m.p. sf. *them*
לָשֹׂבַע prep.-n.m.s. (959) *in abundance*

78:26

יַסַּע Hi. impf. 3 m.s. (נָסַע I 652) *he caused to blow*
קָדִים n.m.s. (870) *the east wind*
בַּשָּׁמָיִם prep.-def.art.-n.m. du. (1029) *in the heavens*
וַיְנַהֵג consec.-Pi. impf. 3 m.s. (624) *and he led out*
בְּעֻזּוֹ prep.-n.m.s.-3 m.s. sf. (738) *by his power*
תֵימָן n.f.s. paus. (I 412) *the south wind*

78:27

וַיַּמְטֵר consec.-Hi. impf. 3 m.s. (565) *and he rained*
עֲלֵיהֶם prep.-3 m.p. sf. *upon them*
כֶּעָפָר prep.-def.art.-n.m.s. (779) *like dust*
שְׁאֵר n.m.s. (984) *flesh*
וּכְחוֹל conj.-prep.-n.m.s. cstr. (297) *and like the sand of*
יַמִּים n.m.p. (410) *the seas*
עוֹף כָּנָף n.m.s. cstr. (733)-n.f.s. (489) *winged birds*

78:28

וַיַּפֵּל consec.-Hi. impf. 3 m.s. (נָפַל 656) *he let them fall*
בְּקֶרֶב prep.-n.m.s. cstr. (899) *in the midst of*
מַחֲנֵהוּ n.m.s.-3 m.s. sf. (334) *their camp*
סָבִיב adv. (686) *all around*
לְמִשְׁכְּנֹתָיו prep.-n.f.p.-3 m.s. sf. (1015) *their habitations*

78:29

וַיֹּאכְלוּ consec.-Qal impf. 3 m.p. (37) *and they ate*
וַיִּשְׂבְּעוּ consec.-Qal impf. 3 m.p. (959) *and were filled*
מְאֹד adv. (547) *well*
וְתַאֲוָתָם conj.-n.f.s.-3 m.p. sf. (16) *for what they craved*
יָבִא Hi. impf. 3 m.s. (בּוֹא 97) *he gave*
לָהֶם prep.-3 m.p. sf. *them*

78:30

לֹא־זָרוּ neg.-Qal pf. 3 c.p. (זוּר I 266) *but before they had sated*
מִתַּאֲוָתָם prep.-n.f.s.-3 m.p. sf. (16) *their craving*
עוֹד adv. (728) *still*
אָכְלָם n.m.s.-3 m.p. sf. (38) *their food*
בְּפִיהֶם prep.-n.m.s.-3 m.p. sf. (804) *in their mouths*

78:31

וְאַף conj.-n.m.s. cstr. (I 60) *and anger of*
אֱלֹהִים n.m.p. (43) *God*
עָלָה Qal pf. 3 m.s. (748) *rose*
בָהֶם prep.-3 m.p. sf. *against them*
וַיַּהֲרֹג consec.-Qal impf. 3 m.s. (246) *and he slew*
בְּמִשְׁמַנֵּיהֶם prep.-n.m.p.-3 m.p. sf. (1032) *the strongest of them*
וּבַחוּרֵי conj.-n.m.p. cstr. (104) *and the picked men of*
יִשְׂרָאֵל pr.n. (975) *Israel*
הִכְרִיעַ Hi. pf. 3 m.s. (502) *laid low*

78:32

בְּכָל־זֹאת prep.-n.m.s. cstr. (481)-demons.adj. f.s. (260) *in spite of all this*
חָטְאוּ־עוֹד Qal pf. 3 c.p. (307)-adv. (728) *they still sinned*
וְלֹא־הֶאֱמִינוּ conj.-neg.-Hi. pf. 3 c.p. (אָמַן 52) *and they did not believe*
בְּנִפְלְאוֹתָיו prep.-Ni. ptc. f.p.-3 m.s. sf. (פָּלָא 810) *despite his wonders*

78:33

וַיְכַל־ consec.-Pi. impf. 3 m.s. (כָּלָה I 477) *so he made vanish*
בַּהֶבֶל prep.-def.art.-n.m.s. (I 210) *like a breath*
יְמֵיהֶם n.m.p.-3 m.p. sf. (398) *their days*
וּשְׁנוֹתָם conj.-n.f.p.-3 m.p. sf. (1040) *and their years*
בַּבֶּהָלָה prep.-def.art.-n.f.s. (96) *in terror*

78:34

אִם־הֲרָגָם interr. (49)-Qal pf. 3 m.s.-3 m.p. sf. (246 הָרַג) *when he slew them*
וּדְרָשׁוּהוּ conj.-Qal pf. 3 c.p.-3 m.s. sf. (דָּרַשׁ 205) *they sought for him*
וְשָׁבוּ conj.-Qal pf. 3 c.p. (שׁוּב 996) *they repented*
וְשִׁחֲרוּ־אֵל conj.-Pi. pf. 3 c.p. (1007)-n.m.s. (42) *and sought God earnestly*

78:35

וַיִּזְכְּרוּ consec.-Qal impf. 3 m.p. (269) *they remembered*
כִּי־אֱלֹהִים conj. (471)-n.m.p. (43) *that God*
צוּרָם n.m.s.-3 m.p. sf. (849) *their rock*

וְאֵל conj.-n.m.s. (42) *and God*
עֶלְיוֹן n.m.s. (751) *Most High*
גֹּאֲלָם Qal act.ptc.-3 m.p. sf. (I 145) *their redeemer*

78:36

וַיְפַתּוּהוּ consec.-Pi. impf. 3 m.p.-3 m.s. sf. (פָּתָה 834) *but they flattered him*
בְּפִיהֶם prep.-n.m.s.-3 m.p. sf. (804) *with their mouths*
וּבִלְשׁוֹנָם conj.-prep.-n.f.s.-3 m.p. sf. (546) *and with their tongues*
יְכַזְּבוּ־ Pi. impf. 3 m.p. (469) *they lied*
לוֹ prep.-3 m.s. sf. *to him*

78:37

וְלִבָּם conj.-n.m.s.-3 m.p. sf. (524) *and their heart*
לֹא־נָכוֹן neg.-Ni. ptc. (כּוּן I 465) *was not steadfast*
עִמּוֹ prep.-3 m.s. sf. *toward him*
וְלֹא נֶאֶמְנוּ conj.-neg.-Ni. pf. 3 c.p. (אָמַן 52) *and they were not true*
בִּבְרִיתוֹ prep.-n.f.s.-3 m.s. sf. (136) *to his covenant*

78:38

וְהוּא conj.-pers.pr. 3 m.s. (214) *yet he*
רַחוּם adj. m.s. (933) *being compassionate*
יְכַפֵּר Pi. impf. 3 m.s. (497) *forgave*
עָוֹן n.m.s. (730) *iniquity*
וְלֹא־יַשְׁחִית conj.-neg.-Hi. impf. 3 m.s. (שָׁחַת 1007) *and did not destroy them*
וְהִרְבָּה לְהָשִׁיב conj.-Hi. pf. 3 m.s. (רָבָה I 915) -prep.-Hi. inf.cstr. (שׁוּב 996) *he restrained often*
אַפּוֹ n.m.s.-3 m.s. sf. (I 60) *his anger*
וְלֹא־יָעִיר conj.-neg.-Hi. impf. 3 m.s. (עוּר I 734) *and did not stir up*
כָּל־חֲמָתוֹ n.m.s. cstr. (481)-n.f.s.-3 m.s. sf. (404) *all his wrath*

78:39

וַיִּזְכֹּר consec.-Qal impf. 3 m.s. (269) *he remembered*
כִּי־בָשָׂר conj. (471)-n.m.s. (142) *that flesh*
הֵמָּה pers.pr. 3 m.p. (241) *they were*
רוּחַ n.m.s. (924) *a wind*
הוֹלֵךְ Qal act.ptc. (הָלַךְ 229) *that passes*
וְלֹא יָשׁוּב conj.-neg.-Qal impf. 3 m.s. (996) *and comes not again*

78:40

כַּמָּה prep.-def.art.-interr. (553) *how often*
יַמְרוּהוּ Hi. impf. 3 m.p.-3 m.s. sf. (מָרָה 598) *they rebelled against him*
בַמִּדְבָּר prep.-def.art.-n.m.s. (184) *in the wilderness*
יַעֲצִיבוּהוּ Hi. impf. 3 m.p.-3 m.s. sf. (I 780) *and grieved him*
בִּישִׁימוֹן prep.-n.m.s. (445) *in the desert*

78:41

וַיָּשׁוּבוּ consec.-Qal impf. 3 m.p. (996) *and again (they turned)*
וַיְנַסּוּ consec.-Pi. impf. 3 m.p. (נָסָה 650) *they tested*
אֵל n.m.s. (42) *God*
וּקְדוֹשׁ conj.-adj. m.s. cstr. (872) *and the Holy One of*
יִשְׂרָאֵל pr.n. (975) *Israel*
הִתְווּ Hi. pf. 3 c.p. (תָּוָה II 1063) *they provoked (pained)*

78:42

לֹא־זָכְרוּ neg.-Qal pf. 3 c.p. (269) *they did not keep in mind*
אֶת־יָדוֹ dir.obj.-n.f.s.-3 m.s. sf. (388) *his power*
יוֹם n.m.s. (398) *the day*
אֲשֶׁר־פָּדָם rel. (81)-Qal pf. 3 m.s.-3 m.p. sf. (פָּדָה 804) *when he redeemed them*
מִנִּי־צָר prep. (577)-n.m.s. paus. (III 865) *from the foe*

78:43

אֲשֶׁר־שָׂם rel. (81)-Qal pf. 3 m.s. (שׂוּם 962) *when he wrought*
בְּמִצְרַיִם prep.-pr.n. (595) *in Egypt*
אֹתוֹתָיו n.m.p.-3 m.s. sf. (16) *his signs*
וּמוֹפְתָיו conj.-n.m.p.-3 m.s. sf. (68) *and his miracles*
בִּשְׂדֵה־ prep.-n.m.s. cstr. (961) *in the fields of*
צֹעַן pr.n. (858) *Zoan*

78:44

וַיַּהֲפֹךְ consec.-Qal impf. 3 m.s. (245) *he turned*
לְדָם prep.-n.m.s. (196) *to blood*
יְאֹרֵיהֶם n.m.p.-3 m.p. sf. (384; GK 124e) *their rivers*
וְנֹזְלֵיהֶם conj.-Qal act.ptc. m.p.-3 m.p. sf. (נָזַל 633) *so that of their streams*
בַּל־יִשְׁתָּיוּן neg. (115)-Qal impf. 3 m.p. paus. (1059 שָׁתָה; GK 75u) *they could not drink*

78:45

יְשַׁלַּח Pi. impf. 3 m.s. (1018) *he sent*
בָּהֶם prep.-3 m.p. sf. *among them*
עָרֹב n.m.s. (786) *swarms of flies*
וַיֹּאכְלֵם consec.-Qal impf. 3 m.s.-3 m.p. sf. (אָכַל 37) *which devoured them*
וּצְפַרְדֵּעַ conj.-n.f.s. (862) *and frogs*
וַתַּשְׁחִיתֵם consec.-Hi. impf. 3 f.s.-3 m.p. sf. (1007 שָׁחַת) *which destroyed them*

78:46

וַיִּתֵּן consec.-Qal impf. 3 m.s. (נָתַן 678) *he gave*
לֶחָסִיל prep.-def.art.-n.m.s. (340) *to the caterpillar*
יְבוּלָם n.m.s.-3 m.p. sf. (385) *their crops*
וִיגִיעָם conj.-n.m.s.-3 m.p. sf. (388) *and the fruit of their labor*
לָאַרְבֶּה prep.-def.art.-n.m.s. (916) *to the locust*

78:47

יַהֲרֹג Qal impf. 3 m.s. (246) *he destroyed*
בַּבָּרָד prep.-def.art.-n.m.s. (135) *with hail*
גַּפְנָם n.f.s.-3 m.p. sf. (172) *their vines*
וְשִׁקְמוֹתָם conj.-n.f.p.-3 m.p. sf. (1054) *and their sycomores*
בַּחֲנָמַל prep.-def.art.-n.m.s. (335) *with frost*

78:48

וַיַּסְגֵּר consec.-Hi. impf. 3 m.s. (סָגַר 688) *he gave over*
לַבָּרָד prep.-def.art.-n.m.s. (135) *to the hail*
בְּעִירָם n.m.s.-3 m.p. sf. (129) *their cattle*
וּמִקְנֵיהֶם conj.-n.m.p.-3 m.p. sf. (889) *and their flocks*
לָרְשָׁפִים prep.-def.art.-n.m.p. (958) *to thunderbolts*

78:49

יְשַׁלַּח־ Pi. impf. 3 m.s. (1018) *he let loose*
בָּם prep.-3 m.p. sf. *on them*
חֲרוֹן אַפּוֹ n.m.s. cstr. (354)-n.m.s.-3 m.s. sf. (I 60) *his fierce anger*
עֶבְרָה n.f.s. (720) *wrath*
וָזַעַם conj.-n.m.s. (276) *indignation*
וְצָרָה conj.-n.f.s. (865) *and distress*
מִשְׁלַחַת n.f.s. cstr. (1020) *a company of*
מַלְאֲכֵי n.m.p. cstr. (521) *angels of*
רָעִים adj. m.p. (I 948) *destruction*

78:50

יְפַלֵּס Pi. impf. 3 m.s. (814) *he made (level)*
נָתִיב n.m.s. (677) *a path*
לְאַפּוֹ prep.-n.m.s.-3 m.s. sf. (I 60) *for his anger*
לֹא־חָשַׂךְ neg.-Qal pf. 3 m.s. (362) *he did not spare*
מִמָּוֶת prep.-n.m.s. (560) *from death*
נַפְשָׁם n.f.s.-3 m.p. sf. (659) *them*
וְחַיָּתָם conj.-n.f.s.-3 m.p. sf. (I 312) *but their lives*
לַדֶּבֶר prep.-def.art.-n.m.s. (184) *to the plague*
הִסְגִּיר Hi. pf. 3 m.s. (688) *he gave over*

78:51

וַיַּךְ consec.-Hi. impf. 3 m.s. (נָכָה 645) *he smote*
כָּל־בְּכוֹר n.m.s. cstr. (481)-n.m.s. (114) *all the first-born*
בְּמִצְרָיִם prep.-pr.n. paus. (595) *in Egypt*
רֵאשִׁית n.f.s. cstr. (912) *the first issue of*
אוֹנִים n.m.p. (I 20) *strength*
בְּאָהֳלֵי prep.-n.m.p. cstr. (13) *in the tents of*
חָם pr.n. (I 325) *Ham*

78:52

וַיַּסַּע consec.-Hi. impf. 3 m.s. (נָסַע I 652) *then he led forth*
כַּצֹּאן prep.-def.art.-n.f.s. (838) *like sheep*
עַמּוֹ n.m.s.-3 m.s. sf. (I 766) *his people*
וַיְנַהֲגֵם consec.-Pi. impf. 3 m.s.-3 m.p. sf. (נָהַג I 624) *he guided them*
כַּעֵדֶר prep.-def.art.-n.m.s. (727) *like a flock*
בַּמִּדְבָּר prep.-def.art.-n.m.s. (184) *in the wilderness*

78:53

וַיַּנְחֵם consec.-Hi. impf. 3 m.s.-3 m.p. sf. (נָחָה 634) *he led them*
לָבֶטַח prep.-n.m.s. (105) *in safety*
וְלֹא פָחָדוּ conj.-neg.-Qal pf. 3 c.p. paus. (808) *so that they were not afraid*
וְאֶת־אוֹיְבֵיהֶם conj.-dir.obj.-Qal act.ptc. m.p.-3 m.p. sf. (אָיַב 33) *but their enemies*
כִּסָּה Pi. pf. 3 m.s. (491) *overwhelmed*
הַיָּם def.art.-n.m.s. (410) *the sea*

78:54

וַיְבִיאֵם consec.-Hi. impf. 3 m.s.-3 m.p. sf. (בּוֹא 97) *and he brought them*
אֶל־גְּבוּל prep.-n.m.s. cstr. (147) *to the border of*
קָדְשׁוֹ n.m.s.-3 m.s. sf. (871) *holiness*
הַר־ n.m.s. (249; GK 138g) *to the mountain*
זֶה demons. as. rel. (261) *which*
קָנְתָה Qal pf. 3 f.s. (888) *had won*
יְמִינוֹ n.f.s.-3 m.s. sf. (411) *his right hand*

78:55

וַיְגָרֶשׁ consec.-Pi. impf. 3 m.s. (176) *he drove out*
מִפְּנֵיהֶם prep.-n.m.p.-3 m.p. sf. (815) *before them*
גּוֹיִם n.m.p. (156) *nations*
וַיַּפִּילֵם consec.-Hi. impf. 3 m.s.-3 m.p. sf. (נָפַל 656) *and he apportioned them*
בְּחֶבֶל prep.-n.m.s. (I 286) *by a measuring cord*
נַחֲלָה n.f.s. (635) *for a possession*
וַיַּשְׁכֵּן consec.-Hi. impf. 3 m.s. (1014) *and settled*
בְּאָהֳלֵיהֶם prep.-n.m.p.-3 m.p. sf. (13) *in their tents*
שִׁבְטֵי n.m.p. cstr. (986) *the tribes of*
יִשְׂרָאֵל pr.n. (975) *Israel*

78:56

וַיְנַסּוּ consec.-Pi. impf. 3 m.p. (נָסָה 650) *yet they tested*
וַיַּמְרוּ consec.-Hi. impf. 3 m.p. (מָרָה 598) *and rebelled*
אֶת־אֱלֹהִים dir.obj.-n.m.p. (43) *against God*
עֶלְיוֹן n.m.s. (II 751) *Most High*
וְעֵדוֹתָיו conj.-n.f.p.-3 m.s. sf. (I 729) *and his testimonies*
לֹא שָׁמָרוּ neg.-Qal pf. 3 c.p. paus. (1036) *did not deserve*

78:57

וַיִּסֹּגוּ consec.-Ni. impf. 3 m.p. (סוּג I 690) *but turned away*
וַיִּבְגְּדוּ consec.-Qal impf. 3 m.p. (בָּגַד 93) *and acted treacherously*
כַּאֲבוֹתָם prep.-n.m.p.-3 m.p. sf. (3) *like their fathers*
נֶהְפְּכוּ Ni. pf. 3 c.p. (245) *they twisted*
כְּקֶשֶׁת prep.-n.f.s. cstr. (905) *like a bow*
רְמִיָּה n.f.s. (941) *deceitful*

78:58

וַיַּכְעִיסוּהוּ consec.-Hi. impf. 3 m.p.-3 m.s. sf. (494 כָּעַס) *for they provoked him to anger*
בְּבָמוֹתָם prep.-n.f.p.-3 m.p. sf. (119) *with their high places*
וּבִפְסִילֵיהֶם conj.-prep.-n.m.p.-3 m.p. sf. (820) *and with their graven images*
יַקְנִיאוּהוּ Hi. impf. 3 m.p.-3 m.s. sf. (קָנָא 888) *they moved him to jealousy*

78:59

שָׁמַע Qal pf. 3 m.s. (1033) *when heard*
אֱלֹהִים n.m.p. (55) *God*
וַיִּתְעַבָּר consec.-Hith. impf. 3 m.s. (עָבַר 720) *he was full of wrath*
וַיִּמְאַס consec.-Qal impf. 3 m.s. (549) *and he rejected*
מְאֹד adv. (547) *utterly*
בְּיִשְׂרָאֵל prep.-pr.n. (975) *Israel*

78:60

וַיִּטֹּשׁ consec.-Qal impf. 3 m.s. (נָטַשׁ 643) *he forsook*
מִשְׁכַּן n.m.s. cstr. (1015) *his dwelling at*
שִׁלוֹ pr.n. (1017) *Shiloh*
אֹהֶל n.m.s. (13) *the tent*
שִׁכֵּן Pi. pf. 3 m.s. (1014) *where he dwelt*
בָּאָדָם prep.-def.art.-n.m.s. (9) *among men*

78:61

וַיִּתֵּן consec.-Qal impf. 3 m.s. (נָתַן 678) *and he delivered*
לַשְּׁבִי prep.-def.art.-n.m.s. (985) *to captivity*
עֻזּוֹ n.m.s.-3 m.s. sf. (738) *his power*
וְתִפְאַרְתּוֹ conj.-n.f.s.-3 m.s. sf. (802) *and his glory*
בְּיַד־ prep.-n.f.s. cstr. (388) *to the hand of*
צָר n.m.s. paus. (III 865) *the foe*

78:62

וַיַּסְגֵּר consec.-Hi. impf. 3 m.s. (688) *he gave over*
לַחֶרֶב prep.-def.art.-n.f.s. (352) *to the sword*
עַמּוֹ n.m.s.-3 m.s. sf. (I 766) *his people*
וּבְנַחֲלָתוֹ conj.-prep.-n.f.s.-3 m.s. sf. (635) *on his heritage*
הִתְעַבָּר Hith. impf. 3 m.s. (720) *vented his wrath*

78:63

בַּחוּרָיו n.m.p.-3 m.s. sf. (104) *their young men*
אָכְלָה־אֵשׁ Qal pf. 3 f.s. (37)-n.f.s. (77) *fire devoured*
וּבְתוּלֹתָיו conj.-n.f.p.-3 m.s. sf. (143) *and their maidens*
לֹא הוּלָּלוּ neg.-Pu. pf. 3 c.p. paus. (הָלַל II 237) *had no marriage song*

78:64

כֹּהֲנָיו n.m.p.-3 m.s. sf. (463) *their priests*
בַּחֶרֶב prep.-def.art.-n.f.s. (352) *by the sword*
נָפָלוּ Qal pf. 3 c.p. paus. (656) *fell*
וְאַלְמְנֹתָיו conj.-n.f.p.-3 m.s. sf. (48) *and their widows*
לֹא תִבְכֶּינָה neg.-Qal impf. 3 f.p. (בָּכָה 113) *made no lamentation*

78:65

וַיִּקַץ consec.-Qal impf. 3 m.s. (יָקַץ 429) *then awoke*
כְּיָשֵׁן prep.-adj. m.s. (445) *as from sleep*
אֲדֹנָי n.m.p.-1 c.s. sf. (10) *the Lord*
כְּגִבּוֹר prep.-adj. m.s. (150) *like a strong man*
מִתְרוֹנֵן Hithpo'el ptc. (רָנַן 943) *shouting*
מִיָּיִן prep.-n.m.s. paus. (406) *because of wine*

78:66

וַיַּךְ־ consec.-Hi. impf. 3 m.s. (נָכָה 645) *and he smote*
צָרָיו n.m.p.-3 m.s. sf. (III 865) *his adversaries*
אָחוֹר adv. (30) *backward*
חֶרְפַּת n.f.s. cstr. (357) *shame of*
עוֹלָם n.m.s. (761) *everlasting*
נָתַן לָמוֹ Qal pf. 3 m.s. (678)-prep.-3 m.p. sf. *he put them*

78:67

וַיִּמְאַס consec.-Qal impf. 3 m.s. (549) *he rejected*
בְּאֹהֶל prep.-n.m.s. cstr. (13) *the tent of*
יוֹסֵף pr.n. (415) *Joseph*
וּבְשֵׁבֶט conj.-prep.-n.m.s. cstr. (986) *and the tribe of*
אֶפְרַיִם pr.n. (68) *Ephraim*
לֹא בָחָר neg.-Qal pf. 3 m.s. paus. (103) *he did not choose*

78:68

וַיִּבְחַר consec.-Qal impf. 3 m.s. (103) *but he chose*
אֶת־שֵׁבֶט dir.obj.-n.m.s. cstr. (986) *the tribe of*
יְהוּדָה pr.n. (397) *Judah*
אֶת־הַר def.art.-n.m.s. cstr. (249) *the mountain of*
צִיּוֹן pr.n. (851) *Zion*
אֲשֶׁר אָהֵב rel. (81)-Qal pf. 3 m.s. (12) *which he loves*

78:69

וַיִּבֶן consec.-Qal impf. 3 m.s. (בָּנָה 124) *he built*
כְּמוֹ־רָמִים conj. (455)-Qal act.ptc. m.p. (רוּם 926) *like the high heavens*
מִקְדָּשׁוֹ n.m.s.-3 m.s. sf. (874) *his sanctuary*
כְּאֶרֶץ prep.-n.f.s. (75) *like the earth*
יְסָדָהּ Qal pf. 3 m.s.-3 f.s. sf. (413) *which he has founded*
לְעוֹלָם prep.-n.m.s. (761) *for ever*

78:70

וַיִּבְחַר consec.-Qal impf. 3 m.s. (103) *he chose*
בְּדָוִד prep.-pr.n. (187) *David*
עַבְדּוֹ n.m.s.-3 m.s. sf. (713) *his servant*
וַיִּקָּחֵהוּ consec.-Qal impf. 3 m.s.-3 m.s. sf. (לָקַח 542) *and took him*
מִמִּכְלְאֹת צֹאן prep.-n.m.p. cstr. (476)-n.f.s. (838) *from the sheepfolds*

78:71

מֵאַחַר עָלוֹת prep.-prep. (29)-Qal act.ptc. f.p. (I 732 עוּל) *from after the ewes*
הֱבִיאוֹ Hi. pf. 3 m.s.-3 m.s. sf. (בּוֹא 97) *he brought him*
לִרְעוֹת prep.-Qal inf.cstr. (רָעָה I 944) *to be the shepherd*
בְּיַעֲקֹב prep.-pr.n. (784) *of Jacob*
עַמּוֹ n.m.s.-3 m.s. sf. (I 766) *his people*
וּבְיִשְׂרָאֵל conj.-prep.-pr.n. (975) *and of Israel*
נַחֲלָתוֹ n.f.s.-3 m.s. sf. (635) *his inheritance*

78:72

וַיִּרְעֵם consec.-Qal impf. 3 m.s.-3 m.p. sf. (רָעָה I 944) *and he tended them*
כְּתֹם לְבָבוֹ prep.-n.m.s. cstr. (1070)-n.m.s.-3 m.s. sf. (523) *with upright heart*
וּבִתְבוּנוֹת כַּפָּיו n.m.p.prep.-n.f.p. cstr. (108) -n.f.p.-3 m.s. sf. (496) *and with skilful hand*
יַנְחֵם Hi. impf. 3 m.s.-3 m.p. sf. (נָחָה 634) *guided them*

79:1

מִזְמוֹר n.m.s. (274) *a Psalm*
לְאָסָף prep.-pr.n. (63) *to Asaph*
אֱלֹהִים n.m.p. (43) *O God*
בָּאוּ Qal pf. 3 c.p. (בּוֹא 97) *have come*
גוֹיִם n.m.p. (156) *the heathen*
בְּנַחֲלָתֶךָ prep.-n.f.s.-2 m.s. sf. (635) *into thy inheritance*
טִמְּאוּ Pi. pf. 3 c.p. (379) *they have defiled*
אֶת־הֵיכַל dir.obj.-n.m.s. cstr. (228) *the temple of*
קָדְשֶׁךָ n.m.s.-2 m.s. sf. (871) *thy holiness*
שָׂמוּ Qal pf. 3 c.p. (שׂוּם 962) *they have laid*
אֶת־יְרוּשָׁלַםִ dir.obj.-pr.n. (436) *Jerusalem*
לְעִיִּים prep.-n.m.p. (730) *in ruins*

79:2

נָתְנוּ Qal pf. 3 c.p. (678) *they have given*
אֶת־נִבְלַת dir.obj.-n.f.s. cstr. (615) *the bodies of*
עֲבָדֶיךָ n.m.p.-2 m.s. sf. (713) *thy servants*
מַאֲכָל n.m.s. (38) *for food*
לְעוֹף prep.-n.m.s. cstr. (733) *to the birds of*
הַשָּׁמַיִם def.art.-n.m. du. (1029) *the air*
בְּשַׂר n.m.s. cstr. (142) *the flesh of*

חֲסִידֶיךָ adj. m.p.-2 m.s. sf. (339) *thy saints*
לְחַיְתוֹ־ prep.-n.f.s. cstr. (I 312) *to the beasts of*
אָרֶץ n.f.s. paus. (75) *the earth*

79:3

שָׁפְכוּ Qal pf. 3 c.p. (1049) *they have poured out*
דָמָם n.m.s.-3 m.p. sf. (196) *their blood*
כַּמַּיִם prep.-def.art.-n.m.p. (565) *like water*
סְבִיבוֹת subst. p. cstr. (686) *round about*
יְרוּשָׁלָם pr.n. paus. (436) *Jerusalem*
וְאֵין conj.-neg. cstr. (II 34) *and there was none*
קוֹבֵר Qal act.ptc. (868) *to bury*

79:4

הָיִינוּ Qal pf. 1 c.p. (הָיָה 224) *we have become*
חֶרְפָּה n.f.s. (357) *a taunt*
לִשְׁכֵנֵינוּ prep.-adj. m.p.-1 c.p. sf. (1015) *to our neighbors*
לַעַג n.m.s. (541) *mocked*
וָקֶלֶס conj.-n.m.s. (887) *and derided*
לִסְבִיבוֹתֵינוּ prep.-subst. p.-1 c.p. sf. (686) *by those round about us*

79:5

עַד־מָה prep. (III 723)-interr. (552) *how long*
יהוה pr.n. (217) *O Yahweh*
תֶּאֱנַף Qal impf. 2 m.s. (60) *wilt thou be angry*
לָנֶצַח prep.-n.m.s. (664) *for ever*
תִּבְעַר Qal impf. 3 f.s. (128) *will burn*
כְּמוֹ־אֵשׁ prep. (455)-n.f.s. (77) *like fire*
קִנְאָתֶךָ n.f.s.-2 m.s. sf. (888) *thy jealous wrath*

79:6

שְׁפֹךְ Qal impv. 2 m.s. (1049) *pour out*
חֲמָתְךָ n.f.s.-2 m.s. sf. (404) *thy anger*
אֶל־הַגּוֹיִם prep.-def.art.-n.m.p. (156) *on the nations*
אֲשֶׁר לֹא־יְדָעוּךָ rel. (81)-neg.-Qal pf. 3 c.p.-2 m.s. sf. (יָדַע 393) *that do not know thee*
וְעַל מַמְלָכוֹת conj.-prep.-n.f.p. (575) *and on the kingdoms*
אֲשֶׁר בְּשִׁמְךָ rel. (81)-prep.-n.m.s.-2 m.s. sf. (1027) *that on thy name*
לֹא קָרָאוּ neg.-Qal pf. 3 c.p. paus. (894) *they do not call*

79:7

כִּי אָכַל conj. (471)-Qal pf. 3 m.s. (37) *for he has devoured*
אֶת־יַעֲקֹב dir.obj.-pr.n. (784) *Jacob*
וְאֶת־נָוֵהוּ conj.-dir.obj.-n.m.s.-3 m.s. sf. (627) *and his habitation*
הֵשַׁמּוּ Hi. pf. 3 c.p. (שָׁמֵם 1030) *they laid waste*

79:8

אַל־תִּזְכָּר neg.-Qal pf. 2 m.s. (269) *do not remember*
לָנוּ prep.-1 c.p. sf. *against us*
עֲוֹנֹת n.m.p. cstr. (730) *the iniquities of*
רִאשֹׁנִים adj. m.p. (911) *forefathers*
מַהֵר adv. (II 555) *speedily*
יְקַדְּמוּנוּ Pi. impf. 3 m.p.-1 c.p. sf. (869) *let come to meet us*
רַחֲמֶיךָ n.m.p.-2 m.s. sf. (933) *thy compassion*
כִּי דַלּוֹנוּ conj. (471)-Qal pf. 1 c.p. (דָּלַל 195) *for we are brought low*
מְאֹד adv. (547) *very*

79:9

עָזְרֵנוּ Qal impv. 2 m.s.-1 c.p. sf. (עָזַר I 740) *help us*
אֱלֹהֵי n.m.p. cstr. (43) *O God of*
יִשְׁעֵנוּ n.m.s.-1 c.p. sf. (447) *our salvation*
עַל־דְּבַר prep.-n.m.s. cstr. (182) *for the word of*
כְּבוֹד־ n.m.s. cstr. (458) *the glory of*
שְׁמֶךָ n.m.s.-2 m.s. sf. (1027) *thy name*
וְהַצִּילֵנוּ conj.-Hi. impv. 2 m.s.-1 c.p. sf. (נָצַל 664) *and deliver us*
וְכַפֵּר conj.-Pi. impv. 2 m.s. (497) *and forgive*
עַל־חַטֹּאתֵינוּ prep.-n.f.p.-1 c.p. sf. (308) *our sins*
לְמַעַן שְׁמֶךָ prep. (775)-n.m.s.-2 m.s. sf. (1027) *for thy name's sake*

79:10

לָמָּה prep.-interr. (552) *why*
יֹאמְרוּ Qal impf. 3 m.p. (55) *should say*
הַגּוֹיִם def.art.-n.m.p. (156) *the nations*
אַיֵּה adv. (32) *where*
אֱלֹהֵיהֶם n.m.p.-3 m.p. sf. (43) *their God*
יִוָּדַע Ni. impf. 3 m.s. (יָדַע 393) *let be known*
בַּגּוֹיִם prep.-def.art.-n.m.p. (156) *among the nations*
לְעֵינֵינוּ prep.-n.f. du.-1 c.p. sf. (744) *before our eyes*
נִקְמַת n.f.s. cstr. (668) *the avenging of*
דַּם־ n.m.s. cstr. (196) *the blood of*
עֲבָדֶיךָ n.m.p.-2 m.s. sf. (713) *thy servants*
הַשָּׁפוּךְ def.art.-Qal pass.ptc. (1049) *the outpoured*

79:11

תָּבוֹא Qal impf. 3 f.s. (בּוֹא 97) *let come*
לְפָנֶיךָ prep.-n.m.p.-2 m.s. sf. (815) *before thee*
אֶנְקַת n.f.s. cstr. (I 60) *the groans of*

אָסִיר n.m.s. (64) *the prisoners*
כְּגֹדֶל prep.-n.m.s. cstr. (152) *according to the greatness of*
זְרוֹעֲךָ n.f.s.-2 m.s. sf. (283) *thy power*
הוֹתֵר Hi. impv. 2 m.s. (יָתַר 451) *preserve*
בְּנֵי תְמוּתָה n.m.p. cstr. (119)-n.f.s. (560) *those doomed to die*

79:12

וְהָשֵׁב conj.-Hi. impv. 2 m.s. (שׁוּב 996) *return*
לִשְׁכֵנֵינוּ prep.-adj. m.p.-1 c.p. sf. (1015) *to our neighbors*
שִׁבְעָתַיִם n.f. du. (988) *sevenfold*
אֶל־חֵיקָם prep.-n.m.s.-3 m.p. sf. (300) *into their bosom*
חֶרְפָּתָם n.f.s.-3 m.p. sf. (357) *their taunts*
אֲשֶׁר חֵרְפוּךָ rel. (81)-Pi. pf. 3 c.p.-2 m.s. sf. (חָרַף 357) *which they have taunted thee*
אֲדֹנָי n.m.p.-1 c.s. sf. (10) *O Lord*

79:13

וַאֲנַחְנוּ conj.-pers.pr. 1 c.p. (59) *then we*
עַמְּךָ n.m.s.-2 m.s. sf. (I 766) *thy people*
וְצֹאן conj.-n.f.s. cstr. (838) *and the flock of*
מַרְעִיתֶךָ n.f.s.-2 m.s. sf. (945) *thy pasture*
נוֹדֶה Hi. impf. 1 c.p. (יָדָה 392) *will give thanks*
לְךָ prep.-2 m.s. sf. *to thee*
לְעוֹלָם prep.-n.m.s. (761) *for ever*
לְדֹר prep.-n.m.s. (189) *from generation*
וָדֹר conj.-v.supra *to generation*
נְסַפֵּר Pi. impf. 1 c.p. (סָפַר 707) *we will recount*
תְּהִלָּתֶךָ n.f.s.-2 m.s. sf. (239) *thy praise*

80:1

לַמְנַצֵּחַ prep.-def.art.-Pi. ptc. (I 663) *to the choirmaster*
אֶל־שֹׁשַׁנִּים prep.-n.m.p. (1004) *according to Lilies*
עֵדוּת n.f.s. (730) *a testimony*
לְאָסָף prep.-pr.n. (63) *to Asaph*
מִזְמוֹר n.m.s. (274) *a Psalm*

80:2

רֹעֵה Qal act.ptc. m.s. cstr. (רָעָה I 944) *O Shepherd of*
יִשְׂרָאֵל pr.n. (975) *Israel*
הַאֲזִינָה Hi. impv. 2 m.s.-vol.he (24) *give ear*
נֹהֵג Qal act.ptc. (624) *thou who leadest*
כַּצֹּאן prep.-def.art.-n.f.s. (838) *like the flock*
יוֹסֵף pr.n. (415) *Joseph*
יֹשֵׁב Qal act.ptc. (יָשַׁב 442) *thou who art enthroned*
הַכְּרוּבִים def.art.-n.m.p. (500) *upon the cherubim*
הוֹפִיעָה Hi. impv. 2 m.s.-vol.he (יָפַע 422) *shine forth*

80:3

לִפְנֵי prep.-n.m.p. cstr. (815) *before*
אֶפְרַיִם pr.n. (68) *Ephraim*
וּבִנְיָמִן conj.-pr.n. (122) *and Benjamin*
וּמְנַשֶּׁה conj.-pr.n. (586) *and Manasseh*
עוֹרְרָה Polel impv. 2 m.s.-vol.he (עוּר I 734) *stir up*
אֶת־גְּבוּרָתֶךָ dir.obj.-n.f.s.-2 m.s. sf. (150) *thy might*
וּלְכָה conj.-Qal impv. 2 m.s.-vol.he (הָלַךְ 229) *and come*
לִישֻׁעָתָה prep.-n.f.s. (447) *for salvation*
לָנוּ prep.-1 c.p. sf. *for us*

80:4

אֱלֹהִים n.m.p. (43) *O God*
הֲשִׁיבֵנוּ Hi. impv. 2 m.s.-1 c.p. sf. (996) *restore us*
וְהָאֵר conj.-Hi. impv. 2 m.s. (אוֹר 21) *and let shine*
פָּנֶיךָ n.m.p.-2 m.s. sf. (815) *thy face*
וְנִוָּשֵׁעָה conj.-Ni. impf. 1 c.p.-vol.he (יָשַׁע 446) *that we may be saved*

80:5

יהוה pr.n. (217) *O Yahweh*
אֱלֹהִים צְבָאוֹת n.m.p. (43)-pr.n. (838) *God of hosts*
עַד־מָתַי prep. (III 723)-interr. (607) *how long*
עָשַׁנְתָּ Qal pf. 2 m.s. (798) *wilt thou be angry*
בִּתְפִלַּת prep.-n.f.s. cstr. (813) *with the prayers of*
עַמֶּךָ n.m.s.-2 m.s. sf. (I 766) *thy people*

80:6

הֶאֱכַלְתָּם Hi. pf. 2 m.s.-3 m.p. sf. (אָכַל 37) *thou hast fed them*
לֶחֶם n.m.s. cstr. (536) *with the bread of*
דִּמְעָה n.f.s. (199) *tears*
וַתַּשְׁקֵמוֹ consec.-Hi. impf. 2 m.s.-3 m.p. sf. (שָׁקָה 1052) *and given them to drink*
בִּדְמָעוֹת prep.-n.f.p. (199) *tears*
שָׁלִישׁ n.m.s. (I 1026) *in full measure*

80:7

תְּשִׂימֵנוּ Qal impf. 2 m.s.-1 c.p. sf. (שׂוּם 962) *thou dost make us*
מָדוֹן n.m.s. (I 193) *strife*

לִשְׁכֵנֵינוּ prep.-adj. m.p.-1 c.p. sf. (1015) *of our neighbors*
וְאֹיְבֵינוּ conj.-Qal act.ptc. m.p.-1 c.p. sf. (אֵיב 33) *and our enemies*
יִלְעֲגוּ־ Qal impf. 3 m.p. (541) *laugh*
לָמוֹ prep.-3 m.p. sf. *among themselves*

80:8

אֱלֹהִים n.m.p. (43) *O God*
צְבָאוֹת pr.n. (838; GK 131s) *of hosts*
הֲשִׁיבֵנוּ Hi. impv. 2 m.s.-1 c.p. sf. (שׁוּב 996) *restore us*
וְהָאֵר conj.-Hi. impv. 2 m.s. (אוֹר 21) *let shine*
פָּנֶיךָ n.m.p.-2 m.s. sf. (815) *thy face*
וְנִוָּשֵׁעָה conj.-Ni. impf. 1 c.p.-vol.he (יָשַׁע 446) *that we may be saved*

80:9

גֶּפֶן n.f.s. (172) *a vine*
מִמִּצְרַיִם prep.-pr.n. (595) *out of Egypt*
תַּסִּיעַ Hi. impf. 2 m.s. (נָסַע 652) *thou didst bring*
תְּגָרֵשׁ Pi. impf. 2 m.s. (גָּרַשׁ 176) *thou didst drive out*
גּוֹיִם n.m.p. (156) *the nations*
וַתִּטָּעֶהָ consec.-Qal impf. 2 m.s.-3 f.s. sf. (נָטַע 642) *and plant it*

80:10

פִּנִּיתָ Pi. pf. 2 m.s. (פָּנָה 815) *thou didst clear*
לְפָנֶיהָ prep.-n.m.p.-3 f.s. sf. (815) *before it*
וַתַּשְׁרֵשׁ consec.-Hi. impf. 2 m.s. (שָׁרַשׁ 1057) *and it took root*
שָׁרָשֶׁיהָ n.m.p.-3 f.s. sf. (1057) *its root*
וַתְּמַלֵּא־ consec.-Pi. impf. 2 m.s. (מָלֵא 569) *and filled*
אָרֶץ n.f.s. paus. (75) *the land*

80:11

כָּסּוּ Pu. pf. 3 c.p. (כָּסָה I 491; GK 52q,121d) *were covered*
הָרִים n.m.p. (249) *the mountains*
צִלָּהּ n.m.s.-3 f.s. sf. (853) *with its shade*
וַעֲנָפֶיהָ conj.-n.m.p.-3 f.s. sf. (778) *and its branches*
אַרְזֵי־אֵל n.m.p. cstr. (72)-n.m.s. (43) *the mighty cedars*

80:12

תְּשַׁלַּח Pi. impf. 3 f.s. (1018) *it sent out*
קְצִירֶהָ n.m.p.-3 f.s. sf. (II 894) *its branches*
עַד־יָם prep. (III 723)-n.m.s. (410) *to the sea*
וְאֶל־נָהָר conj.-prep.-n.m.s. (625) *and to the river*
יוֹנְקוֹתֶיהָ n.f.p.-3 f.s. sf. (413) *its shoots*

80:13

לָמָּה prep.-interr. (552) *why then*
פָּרַצְתָּ Qal pf. 2 m.s. (I 829) *hast thou broken down*
גְדֵרֶיהָ n.m.p.-3 f.s. sf. (154) *its walls*
וְאָרוּהָ conj.-Qal pf. 3 c.p.-3 f.s. sf. (אָרָה I 71) *so that ... pluck its fruit*
כָּל־עֹבְרֵי n.m.s. cstr. (481)-Qal act.ptc. m.p. cstr. (716) *all who pass along*
דָרֶךְ n.m.s. paus. (202) *the way*

80:14

יְכַרְסְמֶנָּה Pi. impf. 3 m.s.-3 f.s. sf. (כִּרְסֵם 493; GK 56) *ravages it*
חֲזִיר n.m.s. (306) *the boar*
מִיָּעַר prep.-n.m.s. (420; GK 5n) *from the forest*
וְזִיז conj.-n.m.s. cstr. (I 265) *and all that move in*
שָׂדַי n.m.s. (961) *the field*
יִרְעֶנָּה Qal impf. 3 m.s.-3 f.s. sf. (רָעָה I 944) *feed on it*

80:15

אֱלֹהִים n.m.p. (43) *God*
צְבָאוֹת pr.n. (838; GK 125h) *of hosts*
שׁוּב־נָא Qal impv. 2 m.s. (996)-part.of entreaty (609) *turn again*
הַבֵּט Hi. impv. 2 m.s. (נָבַט 613) *look down*
מִשָּׁמַיִם prep.-n.m. du. (1029) *from heaven*
וּרְאֵה conj.-Qal impv. 2 m.s. (906) *and see*
וּפְקֹד conj.-Qal impv. 2 m.s. (823) *and have regard for*
גֶּפֶן זֹאת n.f.s. (172)-demons.adj. f.s. (260) *this vine*

80:16

וְכַנָּה conj.-n.f.s. (488) *and the stock*
אֲשֶׁר־נָטְעָה rel. (81)-Qal pf. 3 f.s. (642) *which has planted*
יְמִינֶךָ n.f.s.-2 m.s. sf. (411) *thy right hand*
וְעַל־בֵּן conj.-prep.-n.m.s. (119) *and upon the son*
אִמַּצְתָּה Pi. pf. 2 m.s. (אָמֵץ 54) *whom thou hast reared*
לָּךְ prep.-2 m.s. sf. paus. *for thyself*

80:17

שְׂרֻפָה Qal pass.ptc. f.s. (שָׂרַף 976) *they have burned it*
בָאֵשׁ prep.-def.art.-n.f.s. (77) *with fire*

כְּסוּחָה Qal pass.ptc. f.s. (כָּסַח 492) *they have cut it down*
מִגַּעֲרַת prep.-n.f.s. cstr. (172) *at the rebuke of*
פָּנֶיךָ n.m.p.-2 m.s. sf. (815) *thy countenance*
יֹאבֵדוּ Qal impf. 3 m.p. paus. (1) *may they perish*

80:18

תְּהִי־ Qal impf. 3 f.s. apoc. (הָיָה 224) *let be*
יָדְךָ n.f.s.-2 m.s. sf. (388) *thy hand*
עַל־אִישׁ prep.-n.m.s. cstr. (35) *upon the man of*
יְמִינֶךָ n.f.s.-2 m.s. sf. (411) *thy right hand*
עַל־בֶּן־אָדָם prep.-n.m.s. cstr. (119)-n.m.s. (9) *the son of man*
אִמַּצְתָּ לָּךְ Pi. pf. 2 m.s. (54)-prep.-2 m.s. sf. paus. *whom thou hast made strong for thyself*

80:19

וְלֹא־נָסוֹג conj.-neg.-Qal impf. 1 c.p. (סוג I 690; GK 72t) *then we will never turn back*
מִמֶּךָּ prep.-2 m.s. sf. *from thee*
תְּחַיֵּנוּ Pi. impf. 2 m.s.-1 c.p. sf. (חָיָה 310) *give us life*
וּבְשִׁמְךָ conj.-prep.-n.m.s.-2 m.s. sf. (1027) *and on thy name*
נִקְרָא Qal impf. 1 c.p. (894) *we will call*

80:20

יהוה pr.n. (217) *O Yahweh*
אֱלֹהִים n.m.p. (43) *God*
צְבָאוֹת pr.n. (838; GK 131s) *of hosts*
הֲשִׁיבֵנוּ Hi. impv. 2 m.s.-1 c.p. sf. (שׁוּב 996) *restore us*
הָאֵר Hi. impv. 2 m.s. (אוֹר 21) *let shine*
פָּנֶיךָ n.m.p.-2 m.s. sf. (815) *thy face*
וְנִוָּשֵׁעָה conj.-Ni. impf. 1 c.p.-vol.he (יָשַׁע 446) *that we may be saved*

81:1

לַמְנַצֵּחַ prep.-def.art.-Pi. ptc. (I 663) *to the choirmaster*
עַל־הַגִּתִּית prep.-def.art.-n.f.s. (388) *according to the Gittith*
לְאָסָף prep.-pr.n. (63) *to Asaph*

81:2

הַרְנִינוּ Hi. impv. 2 m.p. (רָנַן 943) *sing aloud*
לֵאלֹהִים prep.-n.m.p. (43) *to God*
עוּזֵּנוּ n.m.s.-1 c.p. sf. (738) *our strength*
הָרִיעוּ Hi. impv. 2 m.p. (רוּעַ 929) *shout for joy*
לֵאלֹהֵי prep.-n.m.p. cstr. (43) *to the God of*
יַעֲקֹב pr.n. (784) *Jacob*

81:3

שְׂאוּ־ Qal impv. 2 m.p. (נָשָׂא 669) *raise*
זִמְרָה n.f.s. (I 274) *a song*
וּתְנוּ־ conj.-Qal impv. 2 m.p. (נָתַן 678) *sound*
תֹף n.m.s. (1074) *the timbrel*
כִּנּוֹר נָעִים n.m.s. (490)-adj. m.s. (II 654) *the sweet lyre*
עִם־נָבֶל prep.-n.m.s. (614) *with the harp*

81:4

תִּקְעוּ Qal impv. 2 m.p. (תָּקַע 1075) *blow*
בַחֹדֶשׁ prep.-def.art.-n.m.s. (II 294) *at the new moon*
שׁוֹפָר n.m.s. (1051) *the trumpet*
בַּכֶּסֶה prep.-def.art.-n.m.s. (490) *at the full moon*
לְיוֹם prep.-n.m.s. cstr. (398) *on the day of*
חַגֵּנוּ n.m.s.-1 c.p. sf. (290) *our feast*

81:5

כִּי חֹק conj.-n.m.s. (349) *for a statute*
לְיִשְׂרָאֵל prep.-pr.n. (975) *for Israel*
הוּא pers.pr. 3 m.s. (214) *it is*
מִשְׁפָּט n.m.s. (1048) *an ordinance*
לֵאלֹהֵי prep.-n.m.p. cstr. (43) *of the God of*
יַעֲקֹב pr.n. (784) *Jacob*

81:6

עֵדוּת n.f.s. (730) *a decree*
בִּיהוֹסֵף prep.-pr.n. (415) *in Joseph*
שָׂמוֹ Qal pf. 3 m.s.-3 m.s. sf. (962) *he made it*
בְּצֵאתוֹ prep.-Qal inf.cstr.-3 m.s. sf. (יָצָא 422) *when he went out*
עַל־אֶרֶץ prep.-n.f.s. cstr. (75) *against the land of*
מִצְרָיִם pr.n. paus. (595) *Egypt*
שְׂפַת n.f.s. cstr. (973) *a voice which*
לֹא־יָדַעְתִּי neg.-Qal pf. 1 c.s. (393) *I had not known*
אֶשְׁמָע Qal impf. 1 c.s. paus. (1033) *I hear*

81:7

הֲסִירוֹתִי Hi. pf. 1 c.s. (סוּר 693) *I relieved*
מִסֵּבֶל prep.-n.m.s. (687) *of the burden*
שִׁכְמוֹ n.m.s.-3 m.s. sf. (1014) *his shoulder*
כַּפָּיו n.f.p.-3 m.s. sf. (496) *his hands*
מִדּוּד prep.-n.m.s. (188) *from the basket*
תַּעֲבֹרְנָה Qal impf. 3 f.p. (עָבַר 716) *were freed*

81:8

בַּצָּרָה prep.-def.art.-n.f.s. (865) *in distress*
קָרָאתָ Qal pf. 2 m.s. (894) *you called*

וָאֲחַלֶּצְךָ consec.-Pi. impf. 1 c.s.-2 m.s. sf. (חָלַץ 323) *and I delivered you*
אֶעֶנְךָ Qal impf. 1 c.s.-2 m.s. sf. (עָנָה 772) *I answered you*
בְּסֵתֶר prep.-n.m.s. cstr. (712) *in the secret place of*
רַעַם n.m.s. (947) *thunder*
אֶבְחָנְךָ Qal impf. 1 c.s.-2 m.s. sf. (בָּחַן 103) *I tested you*
עַל־מֵי prep.-n.m.p. cstr. (565) *at the waters of*
מְרִיבָה pr.n. (II 937) *Meribah*
סֶלָה interj. (699) *Selah*

81:9

שְׁמַע Qal impv. 2 m.s. (1033) *hear*
עַמִּי n.m.s.-1 c.s. sf. (I 766) *O my people*
וְאָעִידָה conj.-Hi. impf. 1 c.s.-vol.he (עוּד 729) *while I àdmonish*
בָּךְ prep.-2 m.s. sf. paus. *you*
יִשְׂרָאֵל pr.n. (975) *O Israel*
אִם־תִּשְׁמַע־ hypoth.part. (49)-Qal impf. 2 m.s. (1033; GK 109b) *if you would but listen*
לִי prep.-1 c.s. sf. *to me*

81:10

לֹא־יִהְיֶה neg.-Qal impf. 3 m.s. (224) *there shall be no*
בְךָ prep.-2 m.s. sf. *among you*
אֵל זָר n.m.s. (42)-Qal act.ptc. (זוּר I 266) *strange god*
וְלֹא תִשְׁתַּחֲוֶה conj.-neg.-Hith. impf. 2 m.s. (1005 שָׁחָה) *you shall not bow down*
לְאֵל נֵכָר prep.-n.m.s. (42)-adj. m.s. (648) *to a foreign god*

81:11

אָנֹכִי pers.pr. 1 c.s. (59) *I am*
יהוה pr.n. (217) *Yahweh*
אֱלֹהֶיךָ n.m.p.-2 m.s. sf. (43) *your God*
הַמַּעַלְךָ def.art.-Hi. ptc.-2 m.s. sf. (עָלָה 748; GK 116f) *who brought you up*
מֵאֶרֶץ prep.-n.f.s. cstr. (75) *out of the land of*
מִצְרָיִם pr.n. paus. (595) *Egypt*
הַרְחֶב־פִּיךָ Hi. impv. 2 m.s. (רָחַב 931)-n.m.s.-2 m.s. sf. (804) *open your mouth wide*
וַאֲמַלְאֵהוּ conj.-Pi. impf. 1 c.s.-3 m.s. sf. (מָלֵא 569) *and I will fill it*

81:12

וְלֹא־שָׁמַע conj.-neg.-Qal pf. 3 m.s. (1033) *but did not listen*
עַמִּי n.m.s.-1 c.s. sf. (I 766) *my people*
לְקוֹלִי prep.-n.m.s.-1 c.s. sf. (876) *to my voice*
וְיִשְׂרָאֵל conj.-pr.n. (975) *and Israel*
לֹא־אָבָה neg.-Qal pf. 3 m.s. (2) *would have none*
לִי prep.-1 c.s. sf. *of me*

81:13

וָאֲשַׁלְּחֵהוּ consec.-Pi. impf. 1 c.s.-3 m.s. sf. (שָׁלַח 1018) *so I gave them over*
בִּשְׁרִירוּת prep.-n.f.s. cstr. (1057) *to the stubbornness of*
לִבָּם n.m.s.-3 m.p. sf. (524) *their heart*
יֵלְכוּ Qal impf. 3 m.p. (הָלַךְ 229) *to follow*
בְּמוֹעֲצוֹתֵיהֶם prep.-n.f.p.-3 m.p. sf. (420) *their own counsels*

81:14

לוּ עַמִּי conj. (530)-n.m.s.-1 c.s. sf. (I 766) *O that my people*
שֹׁמֵעַ לִי Qal act.ptc. (1033)-prep.-1 c.s. sf. *would listen to me*
יִשְׂרָאֵל pr.n. (975) *that Israel*
בִּדְרָכַי prep.-n.m.p.-1 c.s. sf. (202) *in my ways*
יְהַלֵּכוּ Pi. impf. 3 m.p. paus. (229) *would walk*

81:15

כִּמְעַט prep.-adv. (589) *soon*
אוֹיְבֵיהֶם Qal act.ptc. m.p.-3 m.p. sf. (אָיַב 33) *their enemies*
אַכְנִיעַ Hi. impf. 1 c.s. (488) *I would subdue*
וְעַל צָרֵיהֶם conj.-prep.-n.m.p.-3 m.p. sf. (III 865) *and against their foes*
אָשִׁיב Hi. impf. 1 c.s. (שׁוּב 996) *I would turn*
יָדִי n.f.s.-1 c.s. sf. (388) *my hand*

81:16

מְשַׂנְאֵי Pi. ptc. m.p. cstr. (971) *those who hate*
יהוה pr.n. (217) *Yahweh*
יְכַחֲשׁוּ־ Pi. impf. 3 m.p. (471) *would cringe*
לוֹ prep.-3 m.s. sf. *toward him*
וִיהִי conj.-Qal impf. 3 m.s. apoc. (הָיָה 224) *and would last*
עִתָּם n.f.s.-3 m.p. sf. (773) *their fate*
לְעוֹלָם prep.-n.m.s. (761) *for ever*

81:17

וַיַּאֲכִילֵהוּ consec.-Hi. impf. 3 m.s.-3 m.s. sf. (אָכַל 37) *and he would feed him*
מֵחֵלֶב חִטָּה prep.-n.m.s. cstr. (I 316)-n.f.s. (334) *with the finest of the wheat*
וּמִצּוּר conj.-prep.-n.m.s. (849) *and from the rock*

דְּבַשׁ n.m.s. (185) *with honey*
אַשְׂבִּיעֶךָ Hi. impf. 1 c.s.-2 m.s. sf. (שָׂבַע 959) *I would satisfy you*

82:1

מִזְמוֹר n.m.s. (274) *a Psalm*
לְאָסָף prep.-pr.n. (63) *to Asaph*
אֱלֹהִים n.m.p. (43) *God*
נִצָּב Ni. ptc. (נָצַב 662) *has taken his place*
בַּעֲדַת־אֵל prep.-n.f.s. cstr. (I 417)-n.m.s. (42) *in the council of El*
בְּקֶרֶב prep.-n.m.s. cstr. (899) *in the midst of*
אֱלֹהִים n.m.p. (43) *gods*
יִשְׁפֹּט Qal impf. 3 m.s. (1047) *he holds judgment*

82:2

עַד־מָתַי prep. (III 723)-interr. (607) *how long*
תִּשְׁפְּטוּ־ Qal impf. 2 m.p. (1047) *will you judge*
עָוֶל n.m.s. (732) *unjustly*
וּפְנֵי רְשָׁעִים conj.-n.m.s. cstr. (815)-adj. m.p. (957) *and to the wicked*
תִּשְׂאוּ־ Qal impf. 2 m.p. (נָשָׂא 669) *you show partiality*
סֶלָה interj. (699) *Selah*

82:3

שִׁפְטוּ־ Qal impv. 2 m.p. (1047) *give justice*
דָל n.m.s. (195) *to the weak*
וְיָתוֹם conj.-n.m.s. (450) *and the fatherless*
עָנִי n.m.s. (776) *the afflicted*
וָרָשׁ conj.-Qal act.ptc. (רוּשׁ 930) *and the destitute*
הַצְדִּיקוּ Hi. impv. 2 m.p. (842) *maintain the right*

82:4

פַּלְּטוּ־ Pi. impv. 2 m.p. (812) *rescue*
דַל n.m.s. (195) *the weak*
וְאֶבְיוֹן conj.-adj. m.s. (2) *and the needy*
מִיַּד prep.-n.f.s. cstr. (388) *from the hand of*
רְשָׁעִים adj. m.p. (957) *the wicked*
הַצִּילוּ Hi. impv. 2 m.p. (נָצַל 664) *deliver*

82:5

לֹא יָדְעוּ neg.-Qal pf. 3 c.p. (393) *they have neither knowledge*
וְלֹא יָבִינוּ conj.-neg.-Qal impf. 3 m.p. (בִּין 106) *nor have understanding*
בַּחֲשֵׁכָה prep.-def.art.-n.f.s. (365) *in darkness*
יִתְהַלָּכוּ Hith. impf. 3 m.p. paus. (229) *they walk about*
יִמּוֹטוּ Ni. impf. 3 m.p. (מוֹט 556) *are shaken*
כָּל־מוֹסְדֵי n.m.s. cstr. (481)-n.m.p. cstr. (414) *all the foundations of*
אָרֶץ n.f.s. paus. (75) *the earth*

82:6

אֲנִי־אָמַרְתִּי pers.pr. 1 c.s. (58)-Qal pf. 1 c.s. (55) *I say*
אֱלֹהִים n.m.p. (43) *gods*
אַתֶּם pers.pr. 2 m.p. (61) *you are*
וּבְנֵי conj.-n.m.p. cstr. (119) *sons of*
עֶלְיוֹן n.m.s. (751) *the Most High*
כֻּלְּכֶם n.m.s.-2 m.p. sf. (481) *all of you*

82:7

אָכֵן adv. (38) *nevertheless*
כְּאָדָם prep.-n.m.s. (9) *like men*
תְּמוּתוּן Qal impf. 2 m.p. (מוּת 559) *you shall die*
וּכְאַחַד conj.-prep.-adj. num. cstr. (25) *and as one of*
הַשָּׂרִים def.art.-n.m.p. (978) *the princes*
תִּפֹּלוּ Qal impf. 2 m.p. (נָפַל 656) *you shall fall*

82:8

קוּמָה Qal impv. 2 m.s.-vol.he (877) *arise*
אֱלֹהִים n.m.p. (43) *O God*
שָׁפְטָה Qal impv. 2 m.s.-vol.he (1047) *judge*
הָאָרֶץ def.art.-n.f.s. (75) *the earth*
כִּי־אַתָּה conj. (471)-pers.pr. 2 m.s. (61) *for you*
תִנְחַל Qal impf. 2 m.s. (635) *possess*
בְּכָל־ prep.-n.m.s. cstr. (481) *all*
הַגּוֹיִם def.art.-n.m.p. (156) *the nations*

83:1

שִׁיר n.m.s. (1010) *a song*
מִזְמוֹר n.m.s. (274) *a Psalm*
לְאָסָף prep.-pr.n. (63) *to Asaph*

83:2

אֱלֹהִים n.m.p. (43) *O God*
אַל־דֳּמִי־לָךְ neg.-n.m.s. (198)-prep.-2 m.s. sf. paus. *do not keep silence*
אַל־תֶּחֱרַשׁ neg.-Qal impf. 2 m.s. (חָרַשׁ II 361) *do not hold thy peace*
וְאַל־תִּשְׁקֹט conj.-neg.-Qal impf. 2 m.s. (1052) *or be still*
אֵל n.m.s. (42) *O God*

83:3

כִּי־הִנֵּה conj. (471)-demons.part. (243) *for lo*
אוֹיְבֶיךָ Qal act.ptc. m.p.-2 m.s. sf. (אָיַב 33) *thy enemies*

יֶהֱמָיוּן Qal impf. 3 m.p. (הָמָה 242) *are in tumult*
וּמְשַׂנְאֶיךָ conj.-Pi. ptc. m.p.-2 m.s. sf. (שָׂנֵא 971) *those who hate thee*
נָשְׂאוּ Qal pf. 3 c.p. (669) *have raised*
רֹאשׁ n.m.s. (910) *their heads*

83:4

עַל־עַמְּךָ prep.-n.m.s.-2 m.s. sf. (I 766) *against thy people*
יַעֲרִימוּ סוֹד Hi. impf. 3 m.p. (791)-n.m.s. (691) *they lay crafty plans*
וְיִתְיָעֲצוּ conj.-Hith. impf. 3 m.p. (יָעַץ 419) *and they consult together*
עַל־צְפוּנֶיךָ prep.-Qal pass.ptc. m.p.-2 m.s. sf. (860 צָפַן) *against thy protected ones*

83:5

אָמְרוּ Qal pf. 3 c.p. (55) *they say*
לְכוּ Qal impv. 2 m.p. (הָלַךְ 229) *come*
וְנַכְחִידֵם conj.-Hi. impf. 1 c.p.-3 m.p. sf. (כָּחַד 470) *and let us wipe them out*
מִגּוֹי prep.-n.m.s. (156) *as a nation*
וְלֹא־יִזָּכֵר conj.-neg.-Ni. impf. 3 m.s. (269) *and let not be remembered*
שֵׁם־ n.m.s. cstr. (1027) *the name of*
יִשְׂרָאֵל pr.n. (975) *Israel*
עוֹד adv. (728) *any more*

83:6

כִּי נוֹעֲצוּ conj. (471)-Ni. pf. 3 c.p. (יָעַץ 419) *yea, they conspire*
לֵב יַחְדָּו n.m.s. (524)-adv. (403) *with one accord*
עָלֶיךָ prep.-2 m.s. sf. *against thee*
בְּרִית n.f.s. (136) *a coverant*
יִכְרֹתוּ Qal impf. 3 m.p. paus. (503) *they make*

83:7

אָהֳלֵי n.m.p. cstr. (13) *the tents of*
אֱדוֹם pr.n. (10) *Edom*
וְיִשְׁמְעֵאלִים conj.-adj. gent. p. (1035) *and the Ishmaelites*
מוֹאָב pr.n. (555) *Moab*
וְהַגְרִים conj.-pr.n. gent. p. (212) *and Hagrites*

83:8

גְּבָל pr.n. (148) *Gebal*
וְעַמּוֹן conj.-pr.n. (769) *and Ammon*
וַעֲמָלֵק conj.-pr.n. (766) *and Amalek*
פְּלֶשֶׁת pr.n. (814) *Philistia*
עִם־יֹשְׁבֵי prep.-Qal act.ptc. m.p. cstr. (יָשַׁב 442) *with the inhabitants of*
צוֹר pr.n. (I 862) *Tyre*

83:9

גַּם־אַשּׁוּר adv. (168)-pr.n. (78) *Assyria also*
נִלְוָה Ni. pf. 3 m.s. (לָוָה I 530) *has joined*
עִמָּם prep.-3 m.p. sf. *them*
הָיוּ Qal pf. 3 c.p. (הָיָה 224) *they are*
זְרוֹעַ n.f.s. (283) *the arm*
לִבְנֵי־ prep.-n.m.p. cstr. (119) *of the children of*
לוֹט pr.n. (II 532) *Lot*
סֶלָה interj. (699) *Selah*

83:10

עֲשֵׂה־ Qal impv. 2 m.s. (I 793) *do*
לָהֶם prep.-3 m.p. sf. *to them*
כְּמִדְיָן prep.-pr.n. (193) *as Midian*
כְּסִיסְרָא prep.-pr.n. (696) *as to Sisera*
כְּיָבִין prep.-pr.n. (108) *as Jabin*
בְּנַחַל prep.-n.m.s. cstr. (636) *at the river*
קִישׁוֹן pr.n. (885) *Kishon*

83:11

נִשְׁמְדוּ Ni. pf. 3 c.p. (שָׁמַד 1029) *who were destroyed*
בְעֵין־דֹּאר prep.-pr.n. (745) *at En-dor*
הָיוּ Qal pf. 3 c.p. (הָיָה 224) *who became*
דֹּמֶן n.m.s. (199) *dung*
לָאֲדָמָה prep.-def.art.-n.f.s. (9) *for the ground*

83:12

שִׁיתֵמוֹ Qal impv. 2 m.s.-3 m.p. sf. (שִׁית 1011) *make them*
נְדִיבֵמוֹ n.m.s.-3 m.p. sf. (622; GK 131o) *their nobles*
כְּעֹרֵב prep.-pr.n. (788) *like Oreb*
וְכִזְאֵב conj.-prep.-pr.n. (II 255) *and like Zeeb*
וּכְזֶבַח conj.-prep.-pr.n. (II 258) *and like Zebah*
וּכְצַלְמֻנָּע conj.-prep.-pr.n. (854) *and like Zalmunna*
כָּל־נְסִיכֵמוֹ n.m.s. cstr. (481)-n.m.p.-3 m.p. sf. (651) *all their princes*

83:13

אֲשֶׁר אָמְרוּ rel. (81)-Qal pf. 3 c.p. (55) *who said*
נִירְשָׁה Qal impf. 1 c.p.-vol.he (יָרַשׁ 439) *let us take possession*
לָנוּ prep.-1 c.p. sf. *for ourselves*
אֵת נְאוֹת dir.obj.-n.f.p. cstr. (II 627) *of the pastures of*
אֱלֹהִים n.m.p. (43) *God*

83:14

אֱלֹהַי n.m.p.-1 c.s. sf. (43) *O my God*

שִׁיתֵמוֹ Qal impv. 2 m.s.-3 m.p. sf. (1011) *make them*

כַגַּלְגַּל prep.-def.art.-n.m.s. (165) *like whirling dust*

כְּקַשׁ prep.-n.m.s. (905) *like chaff*

לִפְנֵי־רוּחַ prep.-n.m.p. cstr. (815)-n.f.s. (924) *before the wind*

83:15

כְּאֵשׁ prep.-n.f.s. (77) *as fire*

תִּבְעַר־ Qal impf. 3 f.s. (128) *consumes*

יָעַר n.m.s. paus. (420) *the forest*

וּכְלֶהָבָה conj.-prep.-n.f.s. (529) *as the flame*

תְּלַהֵט Pi. impf. 3 f.s. (529) *sets ablaze*

הָרִים n.m.p. (249) *the mountains*

83:16

כֵּן תִּרְדְּפֵם adv. (485)-Qal impf. 2 m.s.-3 m.p. sf. (רָדַף 922) *so do thou pursue them*

בְּסַעֲרֶךָ prep.-n.m.s.-2 m.s. sf. (704) *with thy tempest*

וּבְסוּפָתְךָ conj.-prep.-n.f.s.-2 m.s. sf. (I 693) *and with thy hurricane*

תְבַהֲלֵם Pi. impf. 2 m.s.-3 m.p. sf. (בָּהַל 96) *you terrify them*

83:17

מַלֵּא Pi. impv. 2 m.s. (569) *fill*

פְנֵיהֶם n.m.p.-3 m.p. sf. (815) *their faces*

קָלוֹן n.m.s. (885) *with shame*

וִיבַקְשׁוּ conj.-Pi. impf. 3 m.p. (בָּקַשׁ 134) *that they may seek*

שִׁמְךָ n.m.s.-2 m.s. sf. (1027) *thy name*

יהוה pr.n. (217) *O Yahweh*

83:18

יֵבֹשׁוּ Qal impf. 3 m.p. (בּוֹשׁ 101) *let them be put to shame*

וְיִבָּהֲלוּ conj.-Ni. impf. 3 m.p. (בָּהַל 96) *and be dismayed*

עֲדֵי־עַד prep. (III 723)-prep. (III 723) *for ever*

וְיַחְפְּרוּ conj.-Qal impf. 3 m.p. (חָפֵר II 344) *and let them be ashamed*

וְיֹאבֵדוּ conj.-Qal impf. 3 m.p. (אָבַד 1) *and let them perish*

83:19

וְיֵדְעוּ conj.-Qal impf. 3 m.p. (יָדַע 393) *and let them know*

כִּי־אַתָּה conj. (4871)-pers.pr. 2 m.s. (61) *that thou art*

שִׁמְךָ n.m.s.-2 m.s. sf. (1027) *whose name*

יהוה pr.n. (217) *is Yahweh*

לְבַדֶּךָ prep.-n.m.s.-2 m.s. sf. (II 94) *alone*

עֶלְיוֹן n.m.s. (751; GK 144,lN) *the Most High*

עַל־כָּל prep.-n.m.s. cstr. (481) *over all*

הָאָרֶץ def.art.-n.f.s. paus. (75) *the earth*

84:1

לַמְנַצֵּחַ prep.-def.art.-Pi. ptc. (663) *to the choirmaster*

עַל־הַגִּתִּית prep.-def.art.-n.f.s. (388) *upon the lyre*

לִבְנֵי־ prep.-n.m.p. cstr. (119) *for the sons of*

קֹרַח pr.n. (901) *Korah*

מִזְמוֹר n.m.s. (274) *a Psalm*

84:2

מַה־יְּדִידוֹת interr. (552)-adj. f.p. (391) *how beloved (are)*

מִשְׁכְּנוֹתֶיךָ n.m.p.-2 m.s. sf. (1015) *your dwelling places*

יהוה pr.n. (217) *Yahweh*

צְבָאוֹת pr.n. (838) *of hosts*

84:3

נִכְסְפָה Ni. pf. 3 f.s. (493) *longs*

וְגַם־כָּלְתָה conj.-adv. (168)-Qal pf. 3 f.s. (כָּלָה 477) *yea, faints*

נַפְשִׁי n.f.s.-1 c.s. sf. (659) *my soul*

לְחַצְרוֹת prep.-n.f.p. cstr. (I 346) *for the courts of*

יהוה pr.n. (217) *Yahweh*

לִבִּי n.m.s.-1 c.s. sf. (524) *my heart*

וּבְשָׂרִי conj.-n.m.s.-1 c.s. sf. (142) *and my flesh*

יְרַנְּנוּ Pi. impf. 3 c.p. (943) *sing for joy*

אֶל אֵל־חָי prep. (39)-n.m.s. (42)-adj. m.s. (I 311) *to the living God*

84:4

גַּם־צִפּוֹר adv. (168)-n.f.s. (861) *even the sparrow*

מָצְאָה Qal pf. 3 f.s. (592) *finds*

בַיִת n.m.s. (108) *a home*

וּדְרוֹר conj.-n.f.s. (204) *and the swallow*

קֵן n.m.s. (890) *a nest*

לָהּ prep.-3 f.s. sf. *for herself*

אֲשֶׁר־שָׁתָה rel. (81)-Qal pf. 3 f.s. (שִׁית 1011) *where she may lay*

אֶפְרֹחֶיהָ n.m.p.-3 f.s. sf. (827) *her young*

אֶת־מִזְבְּחוֹתֶיךָ dir.obj.-n.f.p.-2 m.s. sf. (84) *at thy altars*

יהוה pr.n. (217) *O Yahweh*
צְבָאוֹת pr.n. (838) *of hosts*
מַלְכִּי n.m.s.-1 c.s. sf. (I 572) *my king*
וֵאלֹהָי conj.-n.m.p.-1 c.s. sf. paus. (43) *and my God*

84:5

אַשְׁרֵי n.m.p. cstr. (80) *blessed (are)*
יוֹשְׁבֵי Qal act.ptc. m.p. cstr. (442) *those who dwell in*
בֵיתֶךָ n.m.s.-2 m.s. sf. (108) *thy house*
עוֹד adv. (728) *ever*
יְהַלְלוּךָ Pi. impf. 3 m.p.-2 m.s. sf. (II 237) *singing thy praise*
סֶלָה interj. (699) *Selah*

84:6

אַשְׁרֵי n.m.p. cstr. (80) *blessed (are)*
אָדָם n.m.s. (9) *the men*
עוֹז־לוֹ n.m.s. (738)-prep.-3 m.s. sf. *whose strength*
בָךְ prep.-2 m.s. sf. paus. *in thee*
מְסִלּוֹת n.f.p. (700) *the highways*
בִּלְבָבָם prep.-n.m.s.-3 m.p. sf. (523) *in their heart*

84:7

עֹבְרֵי Qal act.ptc. m.p. cstr. (716) *as they go*
בְּעֵמֶק prep.-n.m.s. cstr. (770) *through the valley of*
הַבָּכָא def.art.-n.m.s. (113) *Baca (balsam)*
מַעְיָן n.m.s. (745) *a place of springs*
יְשִׁיתוּהוּ Qal impf. 3 m.p.-3 m.s. sf. (שִׁית 1011) *they make it*
גַּם־בְּרָכוֹת adv. (168)-n.f.p. (139) *also blessings* (if בְּרֵכוֹת n.f.p. 140=*even pools*)
יַעְטֶה Hi. impf. 3 m.s. (or Qal; 741) *enwrappeth*
מוֹרֶה n.m.s. (435) *the early rain*

84:8

יֵלְכוּ Qal impf. 3 m.p. (הָלַךְ 229) *they go*
מֵחַיִל prep.-n.m.s. (298) *from strength*
אֶל־חָיִל prep.-v.supra *to strength*
יֵרָאֶה Ni. impf. 3 m.s. (רָאָה 906) *will be seen*
אֶל־אֱלֹהִים prep.-n.m.p. (43) *God (of gods)*
בְּצִיּוֹן prep.-pr.n. (851) *in Zion*

84:9

יהוה pr.n. (217) *Yahweh*
אֱלֹהִים n.m.p. (43; GK 125h) *God*
צְבָאוֹת pr.n. (838) *of hosts*
שִׁמְעָה Qal impv. 2 m.s.-vol.he (1033; GK 48i) *hear*
תְּפִלָּתִי n.f.s.-1 c.s. sf. (813) *my prayer*
הַאֲזִינָה Hi. impv. 2 m.s.-vol.he (24; GK 48i) *give ear*
אֱלֹהֵי n.m.p. cstr. (43) *O God of*
יַעֲקֹב pr.n. (784) *Jacob*
סֶלָה interj. (699) *Selah*

84:10

מָגִנֵּנוּ n.m.s.-1 c.p. sf. (171) *our shield*
רְאֵה Qal impv. 2 m.s. (רָאָה 906) *behold*
אֱלֹהִים n.m.p. (43) *O God*
וְהַבֵּט conj.-Hi. impv. 2 m.s. (נָבַט 613) *and look*
פְּנֵי n.m.p. cstr. (815) *the face of*
מְשִׁיחֶךָ n.m.s.-2 m.s. sf. (603) *thine anointed*

84:11

כִּי conj. (471) *for*
טוֹב־ adj. m.s. (I 373) *is better*
יוֹם n.m.s. (398) *a day*
בַּחֲצֵרֶיךָ prep.-n.m.p.-2 m.s. sf. (I 346) *in thy courts*
מֵאָלֶף prep.-n.m.s. (48) *than a thousand*
בָּחַרְתִּי Qal pf. 1 c.s. (103) *I have chosen*
הִסְתּוֹפֵף Hithpo'el inf.cstr. (ספף 706) *to stand at the threshhold*
בְּבֵית prep.-n.m.s. cstr. (108) *in the house of*
אֱלֹהַי n.m.p.-1 c.s. sf. (43) *my God*
מִדּוּר prep.-Qal inf.cstr. (דור 189) *rather than dwell*
בְּאָהֳלֵי־ prep.-n.m.p. cstr. (13) *in tents of*
רֶשַׁע n.m.s. (957) *wickedness*

84:12

כִּי שֶׁמֶשׁ conj. (471)-n.f.s. (1039) *for a sun*
וּמָגֵן conj.-n.m.s. (171) *and a shield*
יהוה pr.n. (217) *Yahweh*
אֱלֹהִים n.m.p. (43) *God*
חֵן n.m.s. (336) *favor*
וְכָבוֹד conj.-n.m.s. (458) *and honor*
יִתֵּן Qal impf. 3 m.s. (נָתַן 678) *he bestows*
יהוה pr.n. (217) *Yahweh*
לֹא יִמְנַע־ neg.-Qal impf. 3 m.s. (586) *he does not withhold*
טוֹב n.m.s. (III 375) *a good thing*
לַהֹלְכִים prep.-def.art.-Qal act.ptc. m.p. (הָלַךְ 229) *from those who walk*
בְּתָמִים prep.-n.m.p. (1071) *uprightly*

84:13

יהוה pr.n. (217) *O Yahweh*

צְבָאוֹת pr.n. (838) *of hosts*
אַשְׁרֵי n.m.p. cstr. (80) *blessed (is)*
אָדָם n.m.s. (9) *the man*
בֹּטֵחַ בָּךְ Qal act.ptc. m.s. (105)-prep.-2 m.s. sf. paus. *who trusts in thee*

85:1

לַמְנַצֵּחַ prep.-def.art.-Pi. ptc. (I 663) *to the choirmaster*
לִבְנֵי־קֹרַח prep.-n.m.p. cstr. (119)-pr.n. (901) *to the sons of Korah*
מִזְמוֹר n.m.s. (274) *a Psalm*

85:2

רָצִיתָ Qal pf. 2 m.s. (רָצָה 953) *thou wast favorable*
יהוה pr.n. (217) *Yahweh*
אַרְצֶךָ n.f.s.-2 m.s. sf. (75) *to thy land*
שַׁבְתָּ Qal pf. 2 m.s. (שׁוּב 996) *thou didst restore*
שְׁבוּת n.f.s. cstr. (986) *the fortunes of*
יַעֲקֹב pr.n. (784) *Jacob*

85:3

נָשָׂאתָ Qal pf. 2 m.s. (נָשָׂא 669) *thou didst forgive*
עֲוֹן n.m.s. cstr. (730) *the iniquity of*
עַמֶּךָ n.m.s.-2 m.s. sf. (I 766) *thy people*
כִּסִּיתָ Pi. pf. 2 m.s. (כָּסָה 491) *thou didst pardon*
כָל־חַטָּאתָם n.m.s. cstr. (481)-n.f.s.-3 m.p. sf. (308) *all their sin*
סֶלָה interj. (699) *Selah*

85:4

אָסַפְתָּ Qal pf. 2 m.s. (אָסַף 62) *thou didst withdraw*
כָל־עֶבְרָתֶךָ n.m.s. cstr. (481)-n.f.s.-2 m.s. sf. (720) *all thy wrath*
הֱשִׁיבוֹתָ Hi. pf. 2 m.s. (שׁוּב 996) *thou didst turn*
מֵחֲרוֹן אַפֶּךָ prep.-n.m.s. cstr. (354)-n.m.s.-2 m.s. sf. (I 60) *from thy hot anger*

85:5

שׁוּבֵנוּ Qal impv. 2 m.s.-1 c.p. sf. (996) *restore us*
אֱלֹהֵי n.m.p. cstr. (43) *O God of*
יִשְׁעֵנוּ n.m.s.-1 c.p. sf. (447) *our salvation*
וְהָפֵר conj.-Hi. impv. 2 m.s. (פָּרַר I 830) *and put away (frustrate)*
כַּעַסְךָ n.m.s.-2 m.s. sf. (495) *thy indignation*
עִמָּנוּ prep.-1 c.p. sf. *toward us*

85:6

הַלְעוֹלָם interr.-prep.-n.m.s. (761) *for ever?*
תֶּאֱנַף־ Qal impf. 2 m.s. (אָנַף 60) *wilt thou be angry*
בָּנוּ prep.-1 c.p. sf. *with us*
תִּמְשֹׁךְ Qal impf. 2 m.s. (מָשַׁךְ 604) *wilt thou prolong*
אַפְּךָ n.m.s.-2 m.s. sf. (I 60) *thy anger*
לְדֹר וָדֹר prep.-n.m.s. (189)-conj.-v.supra *to all generations*

85:7

הֲלֹא־אַתָּה interr.-neg.-pers.pr. 2 m.s. (61) *wilt thou not?*
תָּשׁוּב Qal impf. 2 m.s. (שׁוּב 996) *again*
תְּחַיֵּנוּ Pi. impf. 2 m.s.-1 c.p. sf. (חָיָה 310) *revive us*
וְעַמְּךָ conj.-n.m.s.-2 m.s. sf. (I 766) *that thy people*
יִשְׂמְחוּ־ Qal impf. 3 m.p. (970) *may rejoice*
בָךְ prep.-2 m.s. sf. paus. *in thee*

85:8

הַרְאֵנוּ Hi. impv. 2 m.s.-1 c.p. sf. (רָאָה 906) *show us*
יהוה pr.n. (217) *O Yahweh*
חַסְדֶּךָ n.m.s.-2 m.s. sf. (338) *thy steadfast love*
וְיֶשְׁעֲךָ conj.-n.m.s.-2 m.s. sf. (447) *and thy salvation*
תִּתֶּן־לָנוּ Qal impf. 2 m.s. (נָתַן 678)-prep.-1 c.p. sf. *grant us*

85:9

אֶשְׁמְעָה Qal impf. 1 c.s.-vol.he (1033) *let me hear*
מַה־יְדַבֵּר interr. (552)-Pi. impf. 3 m.s. (180) *what will speak*
הָאֵל def.art.-n.m.s. (42) *the God*
יהוה pr.n. (217) *Yahweh*
כִּי יְדַבֵּר conj.-v.supra *for he will speak*
שָׁלוֹם n.m.s. (1022) *peace*
אֶל־עַמּוֹ prep.-n.m.s.-3 m.s. sf. (I 766) *to his people*
וְאֶל־חֲסִידָיו conj.-prep.-adj. m.p.-3 m.s. sf. (339) *and to his saints*
וְאַל־יָשׁוּבוּ conj.-neg.-Qal impf. 3 m.p. (שׁוּב 996) *but let them not turn back*
לְכִסְלָה prep.-n.f.s. (493) *to folly*

85:10

אַךְ קָרוֹב adv. (36)-adj. m.s. (898) *surely at hand*
לִירֵאָיו prep.-Qal act.ptc. m.p.-3 m.s. sf. (יָרֵא 431) *for those who fear him*
יִשְׁעוֹ n.m.s.-3 m.s. sf. (447) *his salvation*

לִשְׁכֹּן prep.-Qal inf.cstr. (1014) *that may dwell*
כָּבוֹד n.m.s. (458) *glory*
בְּאַרְצֵנוּ prep.-n.f.s.-1 c.p. sf. (75) *in our land*

85:11

חֶסֶד־ n.m.s. (338) *steadfast love*
וֶאֱמֶת conj.-n.f.s. (54) *and faithfulness*
נִפְגָּשׁוּ Ni. pf. 3 c.p. (פָּגַשׁ 803) *will meet*
צֶדֶק n.m.s. (841) *righteousness*
וְשָׁלוֹם conj.-n.m.s. (1022) *and peace*
נָשָׁקוּ Qal pf. 3 c.p. paus. (I 676) *will kiss each other*

85:12

אֱמֶת n.f.s. (54) *faithfulness*
מֵאֶרֶץ prep.-n.f.s. (75) *from the ground*
תִּצְמָח Qal impf. 3 f.s. (855) *will spring up*
וְצֶדֶק conj.-n.m.s. (841) *and righteousness*
מִשָּׁמַיִם prep.-n.m. du. (1029) *from the sky*
נִשְׁקָף Ni. ptc. (שָׁקַף I 1054) *will look down*

85:13

גַּם־יהוה adv. (168)-pr.n. (217) *yea, Yahweh*
יִתֵּן Qal impf. 3 m.s. (נָתַן 678) *will give*
הַטּוֹב def.art.-n.m.s. (375) *what is good*
וְאַרְצֵנוּ conj.-n.f.s.-1 c.p. sf. (75) *and our land*
תִּתֵּן Qal impf. 3 f.s. (נָתַן 678) *will yield*
יְבוּלָהּ n.m.s.-3 f.s. sf. (385) *its increase*

85:14

צֶדֶק n.m.s. (841) *righteousness*
לְפָנָיו prep.-n.m.p.-3 m.s. sf. (815) *before him*
יְהַלֵּךְ Pi. impf. 3 m.s. (229) *will go*
וְיָשֵׂם conj.-Qal impf. 3 m.s. (שׂוּם I 962) *and make*
לְדֶרֶךְ prep.-n.m.s. (202) *a way*
פְּעָמָיו n.f.p.-3 m.s. sf. (821) *his footsteps*

86:1

תְּפִלָּה n.f.s. (813) *a prayer*
לְדָוִד prep.-pr.n. (187) *to David*
הַטֵּה־ Hi. impv. 2 m.s. (נָטָה 639) *incline*
יהוה pr.n. (217) *O Yahweh*
אָזְנְךָ n.f.s.-2 m.s. sf. (23) *thy ear*
עֲנֵנִי Qal impv. 2 m.s.-1 c.s. sf. (עָנָה I 772) *answer me*
כִּי־עָנִי conj. (471)-adj. m.s. (776) *for poor*
וְאֶבְיוֹן conj.-adj. m.s. (2) *and needy*
אָנִי pers.pr. 1 c.s. paus. (58) *I am*

86:2

שָׁמְרָה Qal impv. 2 m.s.-vol.he (שָׁמַר I 1036; GK 9v,48iN,61fN) *preserve*
נַפְשִׁי n.f.s.-1 c.s. sf. (659) *my life*
כִּי־חָסִיד conj. (471)-adj. m.s. (339) *for godly*
אָנִי pers.pr. 1 c.s. (58) *I am*
הוֹשַׁע Hi. impv. 2 m.s. (יָשַׁע 446) *save*
עַבְדְּךָ n.m.s.-2 m.s. sf. (713) *thy servant*
אַתָּה pers.pr. 2 m.s. (61) *thou art*
אֱלֹהַי n.m.p.-1 c.s. sf. (43) *my God*
הַבּוֹטֵחַ def.art.-Qal act.ptc. (בָּטַח 105) *who trusts*
אֵלֶיךָ prep.-2 m.s. sf. *in thee*

86:3

חָנֵּנִי Pi. impv. 2 m.s.-1 c.s. sf. (חָנַן I 335) *be gracious to me*
אֲדֹנָי n.m.p.-1 c.s. sf. (10) *O Lord*
כִּי אֵלֶיךָ conj. (471)-prep.-2 m.s. sf. *for to thee*
אֶקְרָא Qal impf. 1 c.s. (894) *do I cry*
כָּל־הַיּוֹם n.m.s. cstr. (481)-def.art.-n.m.s. (398) *all the day*

86:4

שַׂמֵּחַ Pi. impv. 2 m.s. (970) *gladden*
נֶפֶשׁ n.f.s. cstr. (659) *the soul of*
עַבְדֶּךָ n.m.s.-2 m.s. sf. (713) *thy servant*
כִּי אֵלֶיךָ conj. (471)-prep.-2 m.s. sf. *for to thee*
אֲדֹנָי n.m.p.-1 c.s. sf. (10) *O Lord*
נַפְשִׁי n.f.s.-1 c.s. sf. (659) *my soul*
אֶשָּׂא Qal impf. 1 c.s. (נָשָׂא 669) *do I lift up*

86:5

כִּי־אַתָּה conj. (471)-pers.pr. 2 m.s. (61) *for thou*
אֲדֹנָי n.m.p.-1 c.s. sf. (10) *O Lord*
טוֹב adj. m.s. (II 373) *art good*
וְסַלָּח conj.-adj. m.s. (699) *and forgiving*
וְרַב־חֶסֶד conj.-adj. m.s. cstr. (I 912)-n.m.s. (338) *abounding in steadfast love*
לְכָל־קֹרְאֶיךָ prep.-n.m.s. cstr. (481)-Qal act.ptc. m.p.-2 m.s. sf. (894) *to all who call on thee*

86:6

הַאֲזִינָה Hi. impv. 2 m.s.-vol.he (אָזַן 24) *give ear*
יהוה pr.n. (217) *O Yahweh*
תְּפִלָּתִי n.f.s.-1 c.s. sf. (813) *to my prayer*
וְהַקְשִׁיבָה conj.-Hi. impv. 2 m.s.-vol.he (904) *and hearken*
בְּקוֹל prep.-n.m.s. cstr. (876) *to the cry of*
תַּחֲנוּנוֹתָי n.m.p.-1 c.s. sf. paus. (337) *my supplications*

86:7

בְּיוֹם prep.-n.m.s. cstr. (398) *in the day of*
צָרָתִי n.f.s.-1 c.s. sf. (865) *my trouble*
אֶקְרָאֶךָּ Qal impf. 1 c.s.-2 m.s. sf. (894) *I call on thee*
כִּי תַעֲנֵנִי conj. (471)-Qal impf. 2 m.s.-1 c.s. sf. (I 772 עָנָה) *for thou dost answer me*

86:8

אֵין־כָּמוֹךָ neg. cstr. (II 34)-prep.-2 m.s. sf. *there is none like thee*
בָאֱלֹהִים prep.-def.art.-n.m.p. (43) *among the gods*
אֲדֹנָי n.m.p.-1 c.s. sf. (10) *O Lord*
וְאֵין conj.-v.supra *nor are there*
כְּמַעֲשֶׂיךָ prep.-n.m.p.-2 m.s. sf. (795) *any works like thine*

86:9

כָּל־גּוֹיִם n.m.s. cstr. (481)-n.m.p. (156) *all the nations*
אֲשֶׁר עָשִׂיתָ rel. (81)-Qal pf. 2 m.s. (I 793) *thou hast made*
יָבוֹאוּ Qal impf. 3 m.p. (בּוֹא 97) *shall come*
וְיִשְׁתַּחֲווּ conj.-Hith. impf. 3 m.p. (שָׁחָה 1005) *and bow down*
לְפָנֶיךָ prep.-n.m.p.-2 m.s. sf. *before thee*
אֲדֹנָי n.m.p.-1 c.s. sf. (10) *O Lord*
וִיכַבְּדוּ conj.-Pi. impf. 3 m.p. (457; GK 117n) *and shall glorify*
לִשְׁמֶךָ prep.-n.m.s.-2 m.s. sf. (1027) *thy name*

86:10

כִּי־גָדוֹל conj. (471)-adj. m.s. (152) *for great*
אַתָּה pers.pr. 2 m.s. (61) *thou art*
וְעֹשֵׂה conj.-Qal act.ptc. m.s. cstr. (עָשָׂה I 793) *and doest*
נִפְלָאוֹת Ni. ptc. f.p. (פָּלָא 810) *wondrous things*
אַתָּה v.supra *thou art*
אֱלֹהִים n.m.p. (43) *God*
לְבַדֶּךָ prep.-n.m.s.-2 m.s. sf. (94) *alone*

86:11

הוֹרֵנִי Hi. impv. 2 m.s.-1 c.s. sf. (יָרָה 434) *teach me*
יהוה pr.n. (217) *O Yahweh*
דַּרְכֶּךָ n.m.p.-2 m.s. sf. (202) *thy ways*
אֲהַלֵּךְ Pi. impf. 1 c.s. (הָלַךְ 229) *that I may walk*
בַּאֲמִתֶּךָ prep.-n.f.s.-2 m.s. sf. (54) *in thy truth*
יַחֵד Pi. impv. 2 m.s. (יָחַד 402) *unite*
לְבָבִי n.m.s.-1 c.s. sf. (523) *my heart*
לְיִרְאָה prep.-Qal inf.cstr. (יָרֵא 431) *to fear*
שְׁמֶךָ n.m.s.-2 m.s. sf. (1027) *thy name*

86:12

אוֹדְךָ Hi. impf. 1 c.s.-2 m.s. sf. (יָדָה 392) *I give thanks to thee*
אֲדֹנָי n.m.p.-1 c.s. sf. (10) *O Lord*
אֱלֹהַי n.m.p.-1 c.s. sf. (43) *my God*
בְּכָל־לְבָבִי prep.-n.m.s. cstr. (481)-n.m.s.-1 c.s. sf. (523) *with all my heart*
וַאֲכַבְּדָה conj.-Pi. impf. 1 c.s.-vol.he (כָּבֵד 457) *and I will glorify*
שִׁמְךָ n.m.s.-2 m.s. sf. (1027) *thy name*
לְעוֹלָם prep.-n.m.s. (761) *for ever*

86:13

כִּי־חַסְדְּךָ conj. (471)-n.m.s.-2 m.s. sf. (338) *for thy steadfast love*
גָּדוֹל adj. m.s. (152) *great*
עָלָי prep.-1 c.s. sf. paus. *toward me*
וְהִצַּלְתָּ conj.-Hi. pf. 2 m.s. (נָצַל 664) *and thou hast delivered*
נַפְשִׁי n.f.s.-1 c.s. sf. (659) *my soul*
מִשְּׁאוֹל prep.-n.m.s. (982) *from Sheol*
תַּחְתִּיָּה adj. f.s. (1066) *lowest*

86:14

אֱלֹהִים n.m.p. (43) *O God*
זֵדִים adj. m.p. (267) *insolent men*
קָמוּ־ Qal pf. 3 c.p. (קוּם 877) *have risen up*
עָלַי prep.-1 c.s. sf. *against me*
וַעֲדַת conj.-n.f.s. cstr. (I 417) *and a band of*
עָרִיצִים adj. m.p. (792) *ruthless men*
בִּקְשׁוּ Pi. pf. 3 c.p. (134) *seek*
נַפְשִׁי n.f.s.-1 c.s. sf. (659) *my life*
וְלֹא שָׂמוּךָ conj.-neg.-Qal pf. 3 c.p.-2 m.s. sf. (962 שׂוּם) *and they do not set thee*
לְנֶגְדָּם prep.-n.m.s.-3 m.p. sf. (617) *before them*

86:15

וְאַתָּה conj.-pers.pr. 2 m.s. (61) *but thou*
אֲדֹנָי n.m.p.-1 c.s. sf. (10) *O Lord*
אֵל־רַחוּם n.m.s. (42)-adj. m.s. (933) *a merciful God*
וְחַנּוּן conj.-adj. m.s. (337) *and gracious*
אֶרֶךְ אַפַּיִם adj. m.s. cstr. (74)-n.m. du. (I 60) *slow to anger*
וְרַב־חֶסֶד conj.-adj. m.s. cstr. (I 912)-n.m.s. (338) *and abounding in steadfast love*
וֶאֱמֶת conj.-n.f.s. (54) *and faithfulness*

86:16

פְּנֵה Qal impv. 2 m.s. (815) *turn*

אֵלַי prep.-1 c.s. sf. *to me*
וְחָנֵּנִי conj.-Qal impv. 2 m.s.-1 c.s. sf. (חָנַן I 335) *and take pity on me*
תְּנָה־עֻזְּךָ Qal impv. 2 m.s.-vol.he (נָתַן 678) -n.m.s.-2 m.s. sf. (738) *give thy strength*
לְעַבְדֶּךָ prep.-n.m.s.-2 m.s. sf. (713) *to thy servant*
וְהוֹשִׁיעָה conj.-Hi. impv. 2 m.s.-vol.he (יָשַׁע 446) *and save*
לְבֶן־ prep.-n.m.s. cstr. (119) *the son of*
אֲמָתֶךָ n.f.s.-2 m.s. sf. (51) *thy handmaid*

86:17

עֲשֵׂה־עִמִּי Qal impv. 2 m.s. (I 793)-prep.-1 c.s. sf. *do with me (show)*
אוֹת n.m.s. (16) *a sign*
לְטוֹבָה prep.-n.f.s. (375) *of thy favor*
וְיִרְאוּ conj.-Qal impf. 3 m.p. (רָאָה 906) *that may see*
שֹׂנְאַי Qal act.ptc. m.p.-1 c.s. sf. (שָׂנֵא 971) *those who hate me*
וְיֵבֹשׁוּ conj.-Qal impf. 3 m.p. (בּוֹשׁ 101) *and be put to shame*
כִּי־אַתָּה conj. (471)-pers.pr. 2 m.s. (61) *because thou*
יהוה pr.n. (217) *O Yahweh*
עֲזַרְתַּנִי Qal pf. 2 m.s.-1 c.s. sf. (עָזַר 740) *hast helped me*
וְנִחַמְתָּנִי conj.-Pi. pf. 2 m.s.-1 c.s. sf. paus. (נָחַם 636) *and comforted me*

87:1

לִבְנֵי־קֹרַח prep.-n.m.p. cstr. (119)-pr.n. (901) *to the sons of Korah*
מִזְמוֹר n.m.s. (274) *a Psalm*
שִׁיר n.m.s. (1010) *a song*
יְסוּדָתוֹ n.f.s.-3 m.s. sf. (414) *his city founded*
בְּהַרְרֵי־קֹדֶשׁ prep.-n.m.p. cstr. (249)-n.m.s. (871) *on the holy mountains*

87:2

אֹהֵב Qal act.ptc. (אָהֵב 12) *loves*
יהוה pr.n. (217) *Yahweh*
שַׁעֲרֵי צִיּוֹן n.m.p. cstr. (1044)-pr.n. (851) *the gates of Zion*
מִכֹּל prep.-n.m.s. cstr. (481) *more than all*
מִשְׁכְּנוֹת n.m.p. cstr. (1015) *the dwelling places of*
יַעֲקֹב pr.n. (784) *Jacob*

87:3

נִכְבָּדוֹת Ni. ptc. f.p. (כָּבֵד 457; GK 121dN) *glorious things*
מְדֻבָּר Pu. ptc. (דָּבַר 180; GK 145u) *are spoken*
בָּךְ prep.-2 m.s. sf. paus. *of you*
עִיר n.f.s. cstr. (746) *O city of*
הָאֱלֹהִים def.art.-n.m.p. (43) *God*
סֶלָה interj. (699) *Selah*

87:4

אַזְכִּיר Hi. impf. 1 c.s. (זָכַר 269) *I mention*
רַהַב pr.n. (923) *Rahab*
וּבָבֶל conj.-pr.n. (93) *and Babylon*
לְיֹדְעָי prep.-Qal act.ptc. m.p.-1 c.s. sf. (ydi 393) *among those who know me*
הִנֵּה demons.part. (243) *behold*
פְלֶשֶׁת pr.n. (814) *Philistia*
וְצוֹר conj.-pr.n. (I 862) *and Tyre*
עִם־כּוּשׁ prep.-pr.n. (I 468) *with Cush*
זֶה demons.adj. m.s. (260) *this one*
יֻלַּד־ Pu. pf. 3 m.s. (יָלַד 408) *was born*
שָׁם adv. (1027) *there*

87:5

וּלְצִיּוֹן conj.-prep.-pr.n. (851) *and of Zion*
יֵאָמַר Ni. impf. 3 m.s. (אָמַר 55) *it shall be said*
אִישׁ n.m.s. (35; GK 123c) *this one*
וְאִישׁ conj.-v.supra *and that one*
יֻלַּד־ Pu. pf. 3 m.s. (יָלַד 408) *were born*
בָּהּ prep.-3 f.s. sf. *in her*
וְהוּא conj.-pers.pr. 3 m.s. (214) *for he himself*
יְכוֹנְנֶהָ Polel impf. 3 m.s.-3 f.s. sf. (כּוּן 465) *will establish her*
עֶלְיוֹן n.m.s. (751) *the Most High*

87:6

יהוה pr.n. (217) *Yahweh*
יִסְפֹּר Qal impf. 3 m.s. (707) *records*
בִּכְתוֹב prep.-Qal inf.cstr. (507) *as he registers*
עַמִּים n.m.p. (I 766) *the peoples*
זֶה demons.adj. m.s. (260) *this one*
יֻלַּד־ Pu. pf. 3 m.s. (408) *was born*
שָׁם adv. (1027) *there*
סֶלָה interj. (699) *Selah*

87:7

וְשָׁרִים conj.-Qal act.ptc. m.p. (שִׁיר 1010) *and singers*
כְּחֹלְלִים prep.-Qal act.ptc. m.p. (חָלַל II 320) *as the pipe-players*
כָּל־ n.m.s. cstr. (481) *all*
מַעְיָנַי n.m.p.-1 c.s. sf. (745) *my springs*
בָּךְ prep.-2 m.s. sf. paus. *in you*

88:1

שִׁיר n.m.s. (1010) *a song*
מִזְמוֹר n.m.s. (274) *a Psalm*
לִבְנֵי prep.-n.m.p. cstr. (119) *to the sons of*
קֹרַח pr.n. (901) *Korah*
לַמְנַצֵּחַ prep.-def.art.-Pi. ptc. (I 663) *to the choirmaster*
עַל־מָחֲלַת prep.-n.f.s. cstr. (I 318) *according to Mahalath*
לְעַנּוֹת prep.-Pi. inf.cstr. (עָנָה IV 777) *Leannoth*
מַשְׂכִּיל n.m.s. (968) *a maskil*
לְהֵימָן prep.-pr.n. (54) *to Heman*
הָאֶזְרָחִי def.art.-adj. gent. (280) *the Ezrahite*

88:2

יהוה pr.n. (217) *O Yahweh*
אֱלֹהֵי n.m.p. cstr. (43) *the God of*
יְשׁוּעָתִי n.f.s.-1 c.s. sf. (447) *my salvation*
יוֹם־ n.m.s. (398) *by day*
צָעַקְתִּי Qal pf. 1 c.s. (858) *I cry out*
בַלַּיְלָה prep.-def.art.-n.m.s. (538) *in the night*
נֶגְדֶּךָ prep.-2 m.s. sf. (617) *before thee*

88:3

תָּבוֹא Qal impf. 3 f.s. (בּוֹא 97) *let come*
לְפָנֶיךָ prep.-n.m.p.-2 m.s. sf. (815) *before thee*
תְּפִלָּתִי n.f.s.-1 c.s. sf. (813) *my prayer*
הַטֵּה־ Hi. impv. 2 m.s. (נָטָה 639) *incline*
אָזְנְךָ n.f.s.-2 m.s. sf. (23) *thy ear*
לְרִנָּתִי prep.-n.f.s.-1 c.s. sf. (943) *to my cry*

88:4

כִּי־שָׂבְעָה conj. (471)-Qal pf. 3 f.s. (959) *for is full*
בְרָעוֹת prep.-n.f.p. (949) *of troubles*
נַפְשִׁי n.f.s.-1 c.s. sf. (659) *my soul*
וְחַיַּי conj.-n.m.p.-1 c.s. sf. (313) *and my life*
לִשְׁאוֹל prep.-n.f.s. (982) *to Sheol*
הִגִּיעוּ Hi. pf. 3 m.s. (נָגַע 619) *draws near*

88:5

נֶחְשַׁבְתִּי Ni. pf. 1 c.s. (חָשַׁב 362) *I am reckoned*
עִם־יוֹרְדֵי prep.-Qal act.ptc. m.p. cstr. (יָרַד 432) *among those who go down to*
בוֹר n.m.s. (I 92) *the Pit*
הָיִיתִי Qal pf. 1 c.s. (הָיָה 224) *I am*
כְּגֶבֶר prep.-n.m.s. (149) *as a man*
אֵין־אֱיָל neg. cstr. (II 34; GK 152u)-n.m.s. paus. (33) *who has no strength (help)*

88:6

בַּמֵּתִים prep.-def.art.-Qal act.ptc. m.p. (מוּת 559) *among the dead*
חָפְשִׁי adj. m.s. (344) *free*
כְּמוֹ חֲלָלִים conj. (455)-n.m.p. (I 319) *like the slain*
שֹׁכְבֵי Qal act.ptc. m.p. cstr. (1011; GK 116h) *that lie in*
קֶבֶר n.m.s. (868) *the grave*
אֲשֶׁר לֹא זְכַרְתָּם rel. (81)-neg.-Qal pf. 2 m.s.-3 m.p. sf. (269) *whom thou dost not remember (them)*
עוֹד adv. (728) *any more*
וְהֵמָּה conj.-pers.pr. 3 m.p. (241) *for they*
מִיָּדְךָ prep.-n.f.s.-2 m.s. sf. (388) *from thy hand*
נִגְזָרוּ Ni. pf. 3 c.p. paus. (160) *they are cut off*

88:7

שַׁתַּנִי Qal pf. 2 m.s.-1 c.s. sf. (שִׁית 1011) *thou hast put me*
בְּבוֹר תַּחְתִּיּוֹת prep.-n.m.s. cstr. (92)-adj. f.p. (1066) *in the depths of the Pit*
בְּמַחֲשַׁכִּים prep.-n.m.p. (365) *in the dark regions*
בִּמְצֹלוֹת prep.-n.f.p. (846) *in the deep regions*

88:8

עָלַי prep.-1 c.s. sf. *upon me*
סָמְכָה Qal pf. 3 f.s. (701) *lies heavy*
חֲמָתֶךָ n.f.s.-2 m.s. sf. paus. (404) *thy wrath*
וְכָל־מִשְׁבָּרֶיךָ conj.-n.m.s. cstr. (481)-n.m.p.-2 m.s. sf. (991) *and with all thy waves*
עִנִּיתָ Pi. pf. 2 m.s. (עָנָה III 776) *thou dost overwhelm (afflict)*
סֶּלָה interj. (699) *Selah*

88:9

הִרְחַקְתָּ Hi. pf. 2 m.s. (רָחַק 934) *thou hast caused to be far*
מְיֻדָּעַי Pu. ptc. m.p.-1 c.s. sf. (יָדַע 393) *my companions*
מִמֶּנִּי prep.-1 c.s. sf. *from me*
שַׁתַּנִי Qal pf. 2 m.s.-1 c.s. sf. (שִׁית 1011) *thou hast made me*
תוֹעֵבוֹת n.f.p. (1072) *a thing of horror*
לָמוֹ prep.-3 m.p. sf. *to them*
כָּלֻא Qal pass.ptc. (כָּלָא 476) *am shut in*
וְלֹא אֵצֵא conj.-neg.-Qal impf. 1 c.s. (יָצָא 422) *so that I cannot escape*

88:10

עֵינִי n.f.s.-1 c.s. sf. (744) *my eye*
דָאֲבָה Qal pf. 3 f.s. (דָּאַב 178) *grows dim*

מִנִּי עֹנִי prep. (577)-n.m.s. (777) *through sorrow*
קְרָאתִיךָ Qal pf. 1 c.s.-2 m.s. sf. (894) *I call upon thee*
יהוה pr.n. (217) *O Yahweh*
בְּכָל־יוֹם prep.-n.m.s. cstr. (481)-n.m.s. (398) *every day*
שִׁטַּחְתִּי Pi. pf. 1 c.s. (1008) *I spread out*
אֵלֶיךָ prep.-2 m.s. sf. *to thee*
כַפָּי n.f. du.-1 c.s. sf. (496) *my hands*

88:11

הֲלַמֵּתִים interr.-prep.-def.art.-Qal act.ptc. m.p. (559 מוּת) *for the dead?*
תַּעֲשֶׂה־ Qal impf. 2 m.s. (I 793) *dost thou work*
פֶּלֶא n.m.s. (810) *wonders*
אִם־רְפָאִים conj. (49)-n.m.p. (I 952) *or the shades*
יָקוּמוּ Qal impf. 3 m.p. (קוּם 877) *rise up?*
יוֹדוּךָ Hi. impf. 3 m.p.-2 m.s. sf. (יָדָה 392) *let them praise thee*
סֶּלָה interj. (699) *Selah*

88:12

הַיְסֻפַּר interr.-Pu. impf. 3 m.s. (707) *is declared?*
בַּקֶּבֶר prep.-def.art.-n.m.s. (868) *in the grave*
חַסְדֶּךָ n.m.s.-2 m.s. sf. (338) *thy steadfast love*
אֱמוּנָתְךָ n.f.s.-2 m.s. sf. (53) *or thy faithfulness*
בָּאֲבַדּוֹן prep.-def.art.-n.f.p. as pr.n. (2) *in Abaddon*

88:13

הֲיִוָּדַע interr.-Ni. impf. 3 m.s. (יָדַע 393) *are known?*
בַּחֹשֶׁךְ prep.-def.art.-n.m.s. (365) *in the darkness*
פִּלְאֶךָ n.m.s.-2 m.s. sf. (810) *thy wonders*
וְצִדְקָתְךָ conj.-n.f.s.-2 m.s. sf. (842) *or thy saving help (righteousness)*
בְּאֶרֶץ prep.-n.f.s. cstr. (75) *in the land of*
נְשִׁיָּה n.f.s. (674) *forgetfulness*

88:14

וַאֲנִי conj.-pers.pr. 1 c.s. (58) *but I*
אֵלֶיךָ prep.-2 m.s. sf. *to thee*
יהוה pr.n. (217) *O Yahweh*
שִׁוַּעְתִּי Pi. pf. 1 c.s. (שָׁוַע 1002) *I cry*
וּבַבֹּקֶר conj.-prep.-def.art.-n.m.s. (133) *and in the morning*
תְּפִלָּתִי n.f.s.-1 c.s. sf. (813) *my prayer*
תְקַדְּמֶךָּ Pi. impf. 3 f.s.-2 m.s. sf. (קָדַם 869) *comes before thee*

88:15

לָמָה יהוה prep.-interr. (552)-pr.n. (217) *why O Yahweh*
תִּזְנַח Qal impf. 2 m.s. (I 276) *dost thou cast off*
נַפְשִׁי n.f.s.-1 c.s. sf. (659) *me*
תַּסְתִּיר Hi. impf. 2 m.s. (סָתַר 711) *dost thou hide*
פָּנֶיךָ n.m.p.-2 m.s. sf. (815) *thy face*
מִמֶּנִּי prep.-1 c.s. sf. *from me*

88:16

עָנִי adj. m.s. (776) *afflicted*
אֲנִי pers.pr. 1 c.s. (58) *am I*
וְגֹוֵעַ conj.-Qal act.ptc. (גָּוַע 157) *and close to death*
מִנֹּעַר prep.-n.m.s. (655) *from my youth*
נָשָׂאתִי Qal pf. 1 c.s. (669) *I suffer*
אֵמֶיךָ n.f.p.-2 m.s. sf. (33) *thy terrors*
אָפוּנָה Qal impf. 1 c.s.-vol.he (פּוּן 806; but prb. rd. אָפוּגָה from פּוּג 806) *I am helpless*

88:17

עָלַי prep.-1 c.s. sf. *over me*
עָבְרוּ Qal pf. 3 c.p. (716) *has swept over*
חֲרוֹנֶיךָ n.m.p.-2 m.s. sf. (354) *thy wrath*
בִּעוּתֶיךָ n.m.p.-2 m.s. sf. (130) *thy dread assaults*
צִמְּתוּתֻנִי Pi'lel pf. 3 c.p.-1 c.s. sf. (צָמַת 856; prb. rd. צִמְּתוּנִי GK 55d or צִמְּתָתְנִי GK 145k) *destroys me*

88:18

סַבּוּנִי Qal pf. 3 c.p.-1 c.s. sf. (סָבַב 685) *they surround me*
כַמַּיִם prep.-def.art.-n.m.p. (565) *like a flood*
כָּל־הַיּוֹם n.m.s. cstr. (481)-def.art.-n.m.s. (398) *all day long*
הִקִּיפוּ Hi. pf. 3 c.p. (נָקַף II 668) *they close in*
עָלַי prep.-1 c.s. sf. *upon me*
יָחַד adv. (403) *together*

88:19

הִרְחַקְתָּ Hi. pf. 2 m.s. (934) *thou hast caused to shun*
מִמֶּנִּי prep.-1 c.s. sf. *me*
אֹהֵב Qal act.ptc. (12) *lover*
וָרֵעַ conj.-n.m.s. (945) *and friend*
מְיֻדָּעַי Pu. ptc. m.p.-1 c.s. sf. (יָדַע 393) *my companions*
מַחְשָׁךְ n.m.s. (365) *in a dark place*

89:1

מַשְׂכִּיל n.m.s. (68) *a Maskil*
לְאֵיתָן prep.-pr.n. (II 451) *to Ethan*

הָאֶזְרָחִי def.art.-adj. gent. (280) *the Ezrahite*

89:2

חַסְדֵי יהוה n.m.p. cstr. (338)-pr.n. (217) *the steadfast loves of Yahweh*
עוֹלָם n.m.s. (761) *for ever*
אָשִׁירָה Qal impf. 1 c.s.-vol.he (שִׁיר 1010) *I will sing*
לְדֹר וָדֹר prep.-n.m.s. (189)-conj.-v.supra *to all generations*
אוֹדִיעַ Hi. impf. 1 c.s. (יָדַע 393) *I will proclaim*
אֱמוּנָתְךָ n.f.s.-2 m.s. sf. (53) *thy faithfulness*
בְּפִי prep.-n.m.s.-1 c.s. sf. (804) *with my mouth*

89:3

כִּי־אָמַרְתִּי conj. (471)-Qal pf. 1 c.s. (55) *for I said*
עוֹלָם n.m.s. (761) *for ever*
חֶסֶד n.m.s. (338) *steadfast love*
יִבָּנֶה Ni. impf. 3 m.s. (בָּנָה 124) *was established*
שָׁמַיִם n.m. du. (1029) *as the heavens*
תָּכִין Hi. impf. 2 m.s. (כּוּן I 465) *you make firm*
אֱמוּנָתְךָ n.f.s.-2 m.s. sf. (53) *thy faithfulness*
בָהֶם prep.-3 m.p. sf. *in them*

89:4

כָּרַתִּי Qal pf. 1 c.s. (כָּרַת 503) *I have made*
בְרִית n.f.s. (136) *a covenant*
לִבְחִירִי prep.-n.m.s.-1 c.s. sf. (104) *with my chosen one*
נִשְׁבַּעְתִּי Ni. pf. 1 c.s. (שָׁבַע 989) *I have sworn*
לְדָוִד prep.-pr.n. (187) *to David*
עַבְדִּי n.m.s.-1 c.s. sf. (713) *my servant*

89:5

עַד־עוֹלָם prep. (III 723)-n.m.s. (761) *for ever*
אָכִין Hi. impf. 1 c.s. (כּוּן I 465) *I will establish*
זַרְעֶךָ n.m.s.-2 m.s. sf. (282) *your descendants*
וּבָנִיתִי conj.-Qal pf. 1 c.s. (בָּנָה 124) *and build*
לְדֹר־וָדוֹר prep.-n.m.s. (189)-conj.-v.supra *for all generations*
כִּסְאֲךָ n.m.s.-2 m.s. sf. (490) *your throne*
סֶלָה interj. (699) *Selah*

89:6

וְיוֹדוּ conj.-Hi. impf. 3 m.p. (יָדָה 392) *let praise*
שָׁמַיִם n.m. du. (1029) *the heavens*
פִּלְאֲךָ n.m.s.-2 m.s. sf. (810) *thy wonders*
יהוה pr.n. (217) *O Yahweh*
אַף־אֱמוּנָתְךָ conj. (II 64)-n.f.s.-2 m.s. sf. (53) *thy faithfulness*
בִּקְהַל prep.-n.m.s. cstr. (874) *in the assembly of*
קְדֹשִׁים adj. m.p. (872) *the holy ones*

89:7

כִּי מִי conj. (471)-interr. (566) *for who*
בַשַּׁחַק prep.-def.art.-n.m.s. (1007) *in the skies*
יַעֲרֹךְ Qal impf. 3 m.s. (עָרַךְ 789) *can be compared*
לַיהוה prep.-pr.n. (217) *to Yahweh*
יִדְמֶה Qal impf. 3 m.s. (דָּמָה 197) *is like*
לַיהוה prep.-pr.n. (217) *to Yahweh*
בִּבְנֵי אֵלִים prep.-n.m.p. cstr. (119; GK 124q, 128v)-n.m.p. (42) *among the sons of gods*

89:8

אֵל n.m.s. (42) *a God*
נַעֲרָץ Ni. ptc. (עָרַץ 791) *feared*
בְּסוֹד־ prep.-n.m.s. cstr. (691) *in the council of*
קְדֹשִׁים adj. m.p. (872) *the holy ones*
רַבָּה adj. f.s. (I 912) *great*
וְנוֹרָא conj.-Ni. ptc. (יָרֵא 431) *and terrible*
עַל־כָּל־ prep.-n.m.s. cstr. (481) *above all*
סְבִיבָיו subst. m.p.-3 m.s. sf. (686) *round about him*

89:9

יהוה pr.n. (217) *O Yahweh*
אֱלֹהֵי צְבָאוֹת n.m.p. cstr. (43)-pr.n. (838) *God of hosts*
מִי־כָמוֹךָ interr. (566)-prep.-2 m.s. sf. *who is as thou art*
חֲסִין adj. m.s. (340) *mighty*
יָהּ pr.n. (219) *O Yah*
וֶאֱמוּנָתְךָ conj.-n.f.s.-2 m.s. sf. (53) *with thy faithfulness*
סְבִיבוֹתֶיךָ subst. f.p.-2 m.s. sf. (686) *round about thee*

89:10

אַתָּה מוֹשֵׁל pers.pr. 2 m.s. (61)-Qal act.ptc. (605) *thou dost rule*
בְּגֵאוּת prep.-n.f.s. cstr. (145) *the raging of (swelling of)*
הַיָּם def.art.-n.m.s. (410) *the sea*
בְּשׂוֹא prep.-Qal inf.cstr. (נָשָׂא 669; GK 76b; LXX τὸν δὲ σάλον) *when rise*
גַלָּיו n.m.p.-3 m.s. sf. (164) *its waves*
אַתָּה תְשַׁבְּחֵם pers.pr. 2 m.s. (61)-Pi. impf. 2 m.s.-3 m.p. sf. (שָׁבַח I 986) *thou stillest them*

89:11

אַתָּה דִכִּאתָ pers.pr. 2 m.s. (61)-Pi. pf. 2 m.s. (193 דָּכָא) *thou didst crush*

כֶּחָלָל prep.-def.art.-n.m.s. (I 319) *like a carcass*
רָהַב pr.n. paus. (923) *Rahab*
בִּזְרוֹעַ עֻזְּךָ prep.-n.f.s. cstr. (283)-n.m.s.-2 m.s. sf. (738) *with thy mighty arm*
פִּזַּרְתָּ Pi. pf. 2 m.s. (808) *thou didst scatter*
אוֹיְבֶיךָ Qal act.ptc. m.p.-2 m.s. sf. (אָיַב 33) *thy enemies*

89:12

לְךָ prep.-2 m.s. sf. *are thine*
שָׁמַיִם n.m. du. (1029) *heavens*
אַף־לְךָ conj. (II 64)-v.supra *also is thine*
אָרֶץ n.f.s. paus. (75) *earth*
תֵּבֵל n.f.s. (385) *the world*
וּמְלֹאָהּ conj.-n.m.s.-3 f.s. sf. (571) *and all that is in it*
אַתָּה pers.pr. 2 m.s. (61) *thou*
יְסַדְתָּם Qal pf. 2 m.s.-3 m.p. sf. (יָסַד 413) *hast founded them*

89:13

צָפוֹן n.f.s. (860) *the north*
וְיָמִין conj.-n.f.s. (I 411) *and the south*
אַתָּה pers.pr. 2 m.s. (61) *thou*
בְרָאתָם Qal pf. 2 m.s.-3 m.p. sf. (בָּרָא 135) *hast created them*
תָּבוֹר pr.n. (1061) *Tabor*
וְחֶרְמוֹן conj.-pr.n. (356) *and Hermon*
בְּשִׁמְךָ prep.-n.m.s.-2 m.s. sf. (1027) *thy name*
יְרַנֵּנוּ Pi. impf. 3 m.p. (רָנַן 943) *joyously praise*

89:14

לְךָ זְרוֹעַ prep.-2 m.s. sf.-n.f.s. (283) *thou hast a ... arm*
עִם־גְּבוּרָה prep.-adj. f.s. (150) *mighty*
תָּעֹז Qal impf. 3 f.s. (עָזַז 738) *is strong*
יָדְךָ n.f.s.-2 m.s. sf. (388) *thy hand*
תָּרוּם Qal impf. 3 f.s. (רוּם 926) *is high*
יְמִינֶךָ n.f.s.-2 m.s. sf. (411) *thy right hand*

89:15

צֶדֶק n.m.s. (841) *righteousness*
וּמִשְׁפָּט conj.-n.m.s. (1048) *and justice*
מְכוֹן n.m.s. cstr. (467) *the foundation of*
כִּסְאֶךָ n.m.s.-2 m.s. sf. (490) *thy throne*
חֶסֶד n.m.s. (338) *steadfast love*
וֶאֱמֶת conj.-n.f.s. (54) *and faithfulness*
יְקַדְּמוּ Pi. impf. 3 m.p. (869) *go before*
פָנֶיךָ n.m.p.-2 m.s. sf. (815) *thee*

89:16

אַשְׁרֵי n.m.p. cstr. (80) *blessed*
הָעָם def.art.-n.m.s. (I 766) *the people*
יוֹדְעֵי Qal act.ptc. m.p. cstr. (יָדַע 393) *who know*
תְרוּעָה n.f.s. (929) *the festal shout*
יהוה pr.n. (217) *O Yahweh*
בְּאוֹר־ prep.-n.m.s. cstr. (21) *in the light of*
פָּנֶיךָ n.m.p.-2 m.s. sf. (815) *thy countenance*
יְהַלֵּכוּן Pi. impf. 3 m.p. (הָלַךְ 229) *they walk*

89:17

בְּשִׁמְךָ prep.-n.m.s.-2 m.s. sf. (1027) *in thy name*
יְגִילוּן Qal impf. 3 m.p. (גִּיל 162) *who exult*
כָּל־הַיּוֹם n.m.s. cstr. (481)-def.art.-n.m.s. (398) *all the day*
וּבְצִדְקָתְךָ conj.-prep.-n.f.s.-2 m.s. sf. (842) *and thy righteousness*
יָרוּמוּ Qal impf. 3 m.p. (רוּם 926) *they extol*

89:18

כִּי־תִפְאֶרֶת conj. (471)-n.f.s. cstr. (802) *for the glory of*
עֻזָּמוֹ n.m.s.-3 m.p. sf. (738) *their strength*
אָתָּה pers.pr. 2 m.s. paus. (61) *thou art*
וּבִרְצֹנְךָ conj.-prep.-n.m.s.-2 m.s. sf. (953) *and by thy favor*
תָּרִים Qal impf. 3 f.s. (רוּם 926) *is exalted*
קַרְנֵנוּ n.f.s.-1 c.p. sf. (901) *our horn*

89:19

כִּי לַיהוה conj. (471)-prep.-pr.n. (217) *for to Yahweh*
מָגִנֵּנוּ n.m.s.-1 c.p. sf. (171) *our shield*
וְלִקְדוֹשׁ conj.-prep.-adj. m.s. cstr. (872) *and to the Holy One of*
יִשְׂרָאֵל pr.n. (975) *Israel*
מַלְכֵּנוּ n.m.s.-1 c.p. sf. (I 572) *our king*

89:20

אָז adv. (23) *of old*
דִּבַּרְתָּ־ Pi. pf. 2 m.s. (180) *thou didst speak*
בְחָזוֹן prep.-n.m.s. (302) *in a vision*
לַחֲסִידֶיךָ prep.-adj. m.p.-2 m.s. sf. (339) *to thy faithful ones*
וַתֹּאמֶר consec.-Qal impf. 2 m.s. (55) *and say*
שִׁוִּיתִי Pi. pf. 1 c.s. (שָׁוָה II 1001) *I have set*
עֵזֶר n.m.s. (I 740) *help*
עַל־גִּבּוֹר prep.-adj. m.s. (150) *upon one who is mighty*
הֲרִימוֹתִי Hi. pf. 1 c.s. (רוּם 926) *I have exalted*
בָחוּר Qal pass.ptc. (103) *one chosen*
מֵעָם prep.-n.m.s. (I 766) *from the people*

89:21

מָצָאתִי Qal pf. 1 c.s. (592) *I have found*
דָּוִד pr.n. (187) *David*
עַבְדִּי n.m.s.-1 c.s. sf. (713) *my servant*
בְּשֶׁמֶן prep.-n.m.s. cstr. (1032) *with the oil of*
קָדְשִׁי n.m.s.-1 c.s. sf. (871) *my holiness*
מְשַׁחְתִּיו Qal pf. 1 c.s.-3 m.s. sf. (מָשַׁח 602) *I have anointed him*

89:22

אֲשֶׁר יָדִי rel. (81)-n.f.s.-1 c.s. sf. (388) *so that my hand*
תִּכּוֹן Ni. impf. 3 f.s. (כּוּן I 465) *shall ever abide*
עִמּוֹ prep.-3 m.s. sf. *with him*
אַף־זְרוֹעִי conj. (II 64)-n.f.s.-1 c.s. sf. (283) *my arm also*
תְאַמְּצֶנּוּ Pi. impf. 3 f.s.-3 m.s. sf. (אָמֵץ 54) *shall strengthen him*

89:23

לֹא־יַשִּׁא neg.-Hi. impf. 3 m.s. (נָשָׁא I 673) *shall not act as the creditor*
אוֹיֵב Qal act.ptc. (אָיַב 33) *the enemy*
בּוֹ prep.-3 m.s. sf. *against him*
וּבֶן־עַוְלָה conj.-n.m.s. cstr. (119)-n.f.s. (732) *and the wicked*
לֹא יְעַנֶּנּוּ neg.-Pi. impf. 3 m.s.-3 m.s. sf. (עָנָה III 776) *shall not humble him*

89:24

וְכַתּוֹתִי conj.-Qal pf. 1 c.s. (כָּתַת 510) *I will crush*
מִפָּנָיו prep.-n.m.p.-3 m.s. sf. (815) *before him*
צָרָיו n.m.p.-3 m.s. sf. (III 865) *his foes*
וּמְשַׂנְאָיו conj.-Pi. ptc. m.p.-3 m.s. sf. (שָׂנֵא 971) *and those who hate him*
אֶגּוֹף Qal impf. 1 c.s. (נָגַף 619) *I will strike down*

89:25

וֶאֱמוּנָתִי conj.-n.f.s.-1 c.s. sf. (53) *and my faithfulness*
וְחַסְדִּי conj.-n.m.s.-1 c.s. sf. (338) *and my steadfast love*
עִמּוֹ prep.-3 m.s. sf. *with him*
וּבִשְׁמִי conj.-prep.-n.m.s.-1 c.s. sf. (1027) *and in my name*
תָּרוּם Qal impf. 3 f.s. (רוּם 926) *shall be exalted*
קַרְנוֹ n.f.s.-3 m.s. sf. (901) *his horn*

89:26

וְשַׂמְתִּי conj.-Qal pf. 1 c.s. (שׂוּם 962) *I will set*
בַּיָּם prep.-def.art.-n.m.s. (410) *on the sea*
יָדוֹ n.f.s.-3 m.s. sf. (388) *his hand*
וּבַנְּהָרוֹת conj.-prep.-def.art.-n.m.p. (625) *and on the rivers*
יְמִינוֹ n.f.s.-3 m.s. sf. (411) *his right hand*

89:27

הוּא pers.pr. 3 m.s. (214) *he*
יִקְרָאֵנִי Qal impf. 3 m.s.-1 c.s. sf. (894) *shall cry to me*
אָבִי n.m.s.-1 c.s. sf. (3) *my father*
אָתָּה pers.pr. 2 m.s. paus. (61) *thou art*
אֵלִי n.m.s.-1 c.s. sf. (42) *my God*
וְצוּר conj.-n.m.s. cstr. (849) *and the rock of*
יְשׁוּעָתִי n.f.s.-1 c.s. sf. (447) *my salvation*

89:28

אַף־אָנִי conj. (II 64)-pers.pr. 1 c.s. (58) *also I*
בְּכוֹר n.m.s. (114) *the first-born*
אֶתְּנֵהוּ Qal impf. 1 c.s.-3 m.s. sf. (נָתַן 678) *I will make him*
עֶלְיוֹן n.m.s. (751) *the highest*
לְמַלְכֵי־ prep.-n.m.p. cstr. (I 572) *of the kings of*
אָרֶץ n.f.s. paus. (75) *the earth*

89:29

לְעוֹלָם prep.-n.m.s. (761) *for ever*
אֶשְׁמוֹר־לוֹ Qal impf. 1 c.s. (שָׁמַר 1036)-prep.-3 m.s. sf. *I will keep for him*
חַסְדִּי n.m.s.-1 c.s. sf. (338) *my steadfast love*
וּבְרִיתִי conj.-n.f.s.-1 c.s. sf. (136) *and my covenant*
נֶאֱמֶנֶת Ni. ptc. f.s. (אָמַן I 52) *will stand firm*
לוֹ prep.-3 m.s. sf. *for him*

89:30

וְשַׂמְתִּי conj.-Qal pf. 1 c.s. (שׂוּם 962) *and I will establish*
לָעַד prep.-def.art.-n.m.s. (I 723) *for ever*
זַרְעוֹ n.m.s.-3 m.s. sf. (282) *his line*
וְכִסְאוֹ conj.-n.m.s.-3 m.s. sf. (490) *and his throne*
כִּימֵי prep.-n.m.p. cstr. (398) *as the days of*
שָׁמָיִם n.m. du. paus. (1029) *the heavens*

89:31

אִם־יַעַזְבוּ hypoth.part. (49)-Qal impf. 3 m.p. (I עָזַב 736) *if forsake*
בָנָיו n.m.p.-3 m.s. sf. (119) *his children*
תּוֹרָתִי n.f.s.-1 c.s. sf. (435) *my law*
וּבְמִשְׁפָּטַי conj.-prep.-n.m.p.-1 c.s. sf. (1048) *and according to my ordinances*
לֹא יֵלֵכוּן neg.-Qal impf. 3 m.p. (הָלַךְ 229) *they do not walk*

89:32

אִם־חֻקֹּתַי hypoth.part. (49)-n.f.p.-1 c.s. sf. (349) *if my statutes*

יְחַלֵּלוּ Pi. impf. 3 m.p. (חָלַל III 320) *they violate*

וּמִצְוֹתַי conj.-n.f.p.-1 c.s. sf. (846) *and my commandments*

לֹא יִשְׁמֹרוּ neg.-Qal impf. 3 m.p. paus. (שָׁמַר 1036) *they do not keep*

89:33

וּפָקַדְתִּי conj.-Qal pf. 1 c.s. (823) *then I will punish*

בְשֵׁבֶט prep.-n.m.s. (986) *with a rod*

פִּשְׁעָם n.m.s.-3 m.p. sf. (833) *their transgression*

וּבִנְגָעִים conj.-prep.-n.m.p. (619) *and with scourges*

עֲוֹנָם n.m.s.-3 m.p. sf. (730) *their iniquity*

89:34

וְחַסְדִּי conj.-n.m.s.-1 c.s. sf. (338) *but my steadfast love*

לֹא־אָפִיר neg.-Hi. impf. 1 c.s. (פָּרַר I 830) *I will not remove*

מֵעִמּוֹ prep.-prep.-3 m.s. sf. *from him*

וְלֹא־אֲשַׁקֵּר conj.-neg.-Pi. impf. 1 c.s. (שָׁקַר 1055) *or be false*

בֶּאֱמוּנָתִי prep.-n.f.s.-1 c.s. sf. (53) *to my faithfulness*

89:35

לֹא־אֲחַלֵּל neg.-Pi. impf. 1 c.s. (III 320) *I will not violate*

בְּרִיתִי n.f.s.-1 c.s. sf. (136) *my covenant*

וּמוֹצָא conj.-n.m.s. cstr. (425) *or that went forth from*

שְׂפָתַי n.f. du.-1 c.s. sf. (973) *my lips*

לֹא אֲשַׁנֶּה neg.-Pi. impf. 1 c.s. (שָׁנָה I 1039) *I will not alter*

89:36

אַחַת adj. f.s. (25) *once for all*

נִשְׁבַּעְתִּי Ni. pf. 1 c.s. (שָׁבַע 989) *I have sworn*

בְקָדְשִׁי prep.-n.m.s.-1 c.s. sf. (871) *by my holiness*

אִם־לְדָוִד conj. (49)-prep.-pr.n. (187) *to David*

אֲכַזֵּב Pi. impf. 1 c.s. (469) *I will not lie*

89:37

זַרְעוֹ n.m.s.-3 m.s. sf. (282) *his line*

לְעוֹלָם prep.-n.m.s. (761) *for ever*

יִהְיֶה Qal impf. 3 m.s. (224) *shall endure*

וְכִסְאוֹ conj.-n.m.s.03 m.s. sf. (490) *and his throne*

כַשֶּׁמֶשׁ prep.-def.art.-n.f.s. (1039) *as the sun*

נֶגְדִּי prep.-1 c.s. sf. (617) *before me*

89:38

כְּיָרֵחַ prep.-n.m.s. (437) *like the moon*

יִכּוֹן Ni. impf. 3 m.s. (כּוּן 465) *it shall be established*

עוֹלָם n.m.s. (761) *for ever*

וְעֵד conj.-n.m.s. (729) *and the witness*

בַּשַּׁחַק prep.-def.art.-n.m.s. (1007) *in the skies*

נֶאֱמָן Ni. ptc. paus. (אָמַן 52) *is sure*

סֶלָה interj. (699) *Selah*

89:39

וְאַתָּה conj.-pers.pr. 2 m.s. (61) *but thou*

זָנַחְתָּ Qal pf. 2 m.s. (I 276) *hast cast off*

וַתִּמְאָס consec.-Qal impf. 2 m.s. (מָאַס 549) *and rejected*

הִתְעַבַּרְתָּ Hith. pf. 2 m.s. (עָבַר 720) *thou art full of wrath*

עִם־מְשִׁיחֶךָ prep.-n.m.s.-2 m.s. sf. (603) *against thy anointed*

89:40

נֵאַרְתָּה Pi. pf. 2 m.s. (נָאַר 611; GK 64e) *thou hast renounced*

בְּרִית n.f.s. cstr. (136) *the covenant with*

עַבְדֶּךָ n.m.s.-2 m.s. sf. (713) *thy servant*

חִלַּלְתָּ Pi. pf. 2 m.s. (חָלַל III 320) *thou hast defiled*

לָאָרֶץ prep.-def.art.-n.f.s. (75) *in the dust*

נִזְרוֹ n.m.s.-3 m.s. sf. (634) *his crown*

89:41

פָּרַצְתָּ Qal pf. 2 m.s. (I 829) *thou hast breached*

כָל־גְּדֵרֹתָיו n.m.s. cstr. (481)-n.f.p.-3 m.s. sf. (155) *all his walls*

שַׂמְתָּ Qal pf. 2 m.s. (שׂוּם 962) *thou hast laid*

מִבְצָרָיו n.m.p.-3 m.s. sf. (131) *his strongholds*

מְחִתָּה n.f.s. (369) *in ruins*

89:42

שַׁסֻּהוּ Qal pf. 3 c.p.-3 m.s. sf. (שָׁסַס 1042) *they despoil him*

כָּל־עֹבְרֵי n.m.s. cstr. (481)-Qal act.ptc. m.p. cstr. (716) *all that pass by*

דָרֶךְ n.m.s. paus. (202) *(the way)*

הָיָה Qal pf. 3 m.s. (224) *he has become*

חֶרְפָּה n.f.s. (357) *the scorn*

לִשְׁכֵנָיו prep.-adj. m.p.-3 m.s. sf. (1015) *of his neighbors*

89:43

הֲרִימוֹתָ Hi. pf. 2 m.s. (רוּם 926) *thou hast exalted*

יְמִין n.f.s. cstr. (411) *the right hand of*

צָרָיו n.m.p.-3 m.s. sf. (III 865) *his foes*

הִשְׂמַחְתָּ Hi. pf. 2 m.s. (שָׂמַח 970) *thou hast made rejoice*

כָּל־אוֹיְבָיו n.m.s. cstr. (481)-Qal act.ptc. m.p.-3 m.s. sf. (אָיַב 33) *all his enemies*

89:44

אַף־ conj. (II 64) *yea*

תָּשִׁיב Hi. impf. 2 m.s. (שׁוּב 996) *thou hast turned back*

צוּר n.m.s. cstr. (I 849) *edge of* (or some rd. צֹר II 866) *flint of*

חַרְבּוֹ n.f.s.-3 m.s. sf. (352) *his sword*

וְלֹא הֲקֵימֹתוֹ conj.-neg.-Hi. pf. 2 m.s.-3 m.s. sf. (877 קוּם) *and thou hast made him stand*

בַּמִּלְחָמָה prep.-def.art.-n.f.s. (536) *in battle*

89:45

הִשְׁבַּתָּ Hi. pf. 2 m.s. (שָׁבַת 991) *thou hast removed*

מִטְּהָרוֹ prep.-n.m.s.-3 m.s. sf. (372) *his cleanness*

וְכִסְאוֹ conj.-n.m.s.-3 m.s. sf. (490) *and his throne*

לָאָרֶץ prep.-def.art.-n.f.s. (75) *to the ground*

מִגַּרְתָּה Pi. pf. 2 m.s. (מָגַר 550) *thou hast cast*

89:46

הִקְצַרְתָּ Hi. pf. 2 m.s. (קָצַר 894) *thou hast cut short*

יְמֵי n.m.p. cstr. (398) *the days of*

עֲלוּמָיו n.m.p.-3 m.s. sf. (761) *his youth*

הֶעֱטִיתָ Hi. pf. 2 m.s. (עָטָה I 741) *thou hast covered*

עָלָיו prep.-3 m.s. sf. *him*

בּוּשָׁה n.f.s. (102) *with shame*

סֶלָה interj. (699) *Selah*

89:47

עַד־מָה prep. (III 723)-interr. (552) *how long*

יהוה pr.n. (217) *O Yahweh*

תִּסָּתֵר Ni. impf. 2 m.s. (711) *wilt thou hide thyself*

לָנֶצַח prep.-n.m.s. paus. (664) *for ever*

תִּבְעַר Qal impf. 3 f.s. (128) *will burn*

כְּמוֹ־אֵשׁ prep. (455)-n.f.s. (77) *like fire*

חֲמָתֶךָ n.f.s.-2 m.s. sf. (404) *thy wrath*

89:48

זְכָר־ Qal impv. 2 m.s. (269) *remember*

אֲנִי pers.pr. 1 c.s. (58; GK 135f) *I*

מֶה־חָלֶד interr. (552)-n.m.s. paus. (317) *of what duration*

עַל־מַה־שָּׁוְא prep.-interr. (552)-n.m.s. (996) *for what vanity*

בָּרָאתָ Qal pf. 2 m.s. (135) *thou hast created*

כָל־בְּנֵי־ n.m.s. cstr. (481)-n.m.p. cstr. (119) *all the sons of*

אָדָם n.m.s. (9) *men*

89:49

מִי גֶבֶר interr. (566)-n.m.s. (149) *what man*

יִחְיֶה Qal impf. 3 m.s. (חָיָה 310) *can live*

וְלֹא יִרְאֶה־ conj.-neg.-Qal impf. 3 m.s. (906) *and never see*

מָּוֶת n.m.s. (560) *death*

יְמַלֵּט Pi. impf. 3 m.s. (572) *who can deliver*

נַפְשׁוֹ n.f.s.-3 m.s. sf. (659) *his soul*

מִיַּד־שְׁאוֹל prep.-n.f.s. cstr. (388)-n.f.s. (982) *from the power of Sheol*

סֶלָה interj. (699) *Selah*

89:50

אַיֵּה adv. (32) *where*

חֲסָדֶיךָ n.m.p.-2 m.s. sf. (338) *thy steadfast love*

הָרִאשֹׁנִים def.art.-adj. m.p. (911) *of old*

אֲדֹנָי n.m.p.-1 c.s. sf. (10) *Lord*

נִשְׁבַּעְתָּ Ni. pf. 2 m.s. (שָׁבַע 989) *thou didst swear*

לְדָוִד prep.-pr.n. (187) *to David*

בֶּאֱמוּנָתֶךָ prep.-n.f.s.-2 m.s. sf. (53) *by thy faithfulness*

89:51

זְכֹר Qal impv. 2 m.s. (269) *remember*

אֲדֹנָי n.m.p.-1 c.s. sf. (10) *Lord*

חֶרְפַּת עֲבָדֶיךָ n.f.s. cstr. (357)-n.m.p.-2 m.s. sf. (713) *the scorn of thy servant*

שְׂאֵתִי Qal inf.cstr.-1 c.s. sf. (נָשָׂא 669) *how I bear*

בְחֵיקִי prep.-n.m.s.-1 c.s. sf. (300) *in my bosom*

כָּל־רַבִּים עַמִּים n.m.s. cstr. (481)-adj. m.p. (I 912)-n.m.p. (I 766) *all of many peoples*

89:52

אֲשֶׁר חֵרְפוּ rel. (81)-Pi. pf. 3 c.p. (חָרַף I 357) *with which ... taunt*

אוֹיְבֶיךָ Qal act.ptc. m.p.-2 m.s. sf. (אָיַב 33) *thy enemies*

יהוה pr.n. (217) *O Yahweh*

אֲשֶׁר חֵרְפוּ v.supra-v.supra *with which they mock*

עִקְּבוֹת n.m.p. cstr. (784) *the footsteps of*
מְשִׁיחֶךָ n.m.s.-2 m.s. sf. (603) *thy anointed*

89:53

בָּרוּךְ Qal pass. ptc. (138) *blessed be*
יהוה pr.n. (217) *Yahweh*
לְעוֹלָם prep.-n.m.s. (761) *for ever*
אָמֵן וְאָמֵן adv. (53)-conj.-v.supra *Amen and Amen*

90:1

תְּפִלָּה n.f.s. (813) *a prayer*
לְמֹשֶׁה prep.-pr.n. (602) *to Moses*
אִישׁ־ n.m.s. cstr. (35) *the man of*
הָאֱלֹהִים def.art.-n.m.p. (43) *God*
אֲדֹנָי n.m.p.-1 c.s. sf. (10) *Lord*
מָעוֹן n.m.s. (I 732) *dwelling place*
אַתָּה הָיִיתָ pers.pr. 2 m.s. (61)-Qal pf. 2 m.s. (הָיָה 224) *thou hast been*
לָּנוּ prep.-1 c.p. sf. *to us*
בְּדֹר וָדֹר prep.-n.m.s. (189)-conj.-v.supra *in all generations*

90:2

בְּטֶרֶם prep.-adv. (382) *before*
הָרִים n.m.p. (249) *mountains*
יֻלָּדוּ Pu. pf. 3 c.p. (יָלַד 408; GK 107c,152r) *were brought forth*
וַתְּחוֹלֵל consec.-Polel impf. 2 m.s. (חוּל I 296) *or thou hadst formed (writhed in travail with)*
אֶרֶץ n.f.s. (75) *the earth*
וְתֵבֵל conj.-n.f.s. (385) *and the world*
וּמֵעוֹלָם conj.-prep.-n.m.s. (761) *and from everlasting*
עַד־עוֹלָם prep. (III 723)-n.m.s. (761) *to everlasting*
אַתָּה אֵל pers.pr. 2 m.s. (61)-n.m.s. (42) *thou art God*

90:3

תָּשֵׁב Hi. impf. 2 m.s. (שׁוּב 996; GK 109k) *thou turnest back*
אֱנוֹשׁ n.m.s. (60) *man*
עַד־דַּכָּא prep. (III 723)-n.m.s. (194) *to dust*
וַתֹּאמֶר consec.-Qal impf. 2 m.s. (55; GK 111t) *and thou sayest*
שׁוּבוּ Qal impv. 2 m.p. (996) *turn back*
בְנֵי־אָדָם n.m.p. cstr. (119)-n.m.s. (9) *O children of men*

90:4

כִּי אֶלֶף conj. (471)-n.m.s. cstr. (48) *for a thousand of*
שָׁנִים n.f.p. (1040) *years*
בְּעֵינֶיךָ prep.-n.f. du.-2 m.s. sf. (744) *in thy sight*
כְּיוֹם prep.-n.m.s. cstr. (398) *as a day of*
אֶתְמוֹל subst. (1069) *yesterday*
כִּי יַעֲבֹר conj. (471)-Qal impf. 3 m.s. (716) *when it is past*
וְאַשְׁמוּרָה conj.-n.f.s. (1038; GK 118r) *or a watch*
בַלָּיְלָה prep.-def.art.-n.m.s. paus. (538) *in the night*

90:5

זְרַמְתָּם Qal pf. 2 m.s.-3 m.p. sf. (281) *thou dost sweep them away* (lit. *floodest them with rain*)
שֵׁנָה n.f.s. (446) *sleep*
יִהְיוּ Qal impf. 3 m.p. (הָיָה 224) *they are*
בַּבֹּקֶר prep.-def.art.-n.m.s. (133) *in the morning*
כֶּחָצִיר prep. (GK 155g)-def.art.-n.m.s. (II 348) *like the grass*
יַחֲלֹף Qal impf. 3 m.s. (322) *which is renewed*

90:6

בַּבֹּקֶר prep.-def.art.-n.m.s. (133) *in the morning*
יָצִיץ Qal impf. 3 m.s. (צוּץ I 847) *it flourishes*
וְחָלָף conj.-Qal pf. 3 m.s. paus. (322) *and is renewed*
לָעֶרֶב prep.-def.art.-n.m.s. (787) *in the evening*
יְמוֹלֵל Po'el impf. 3 m.s. (מָלַל III 576) *it fades*
וְיָבֵשׁ conj. (GK 112m)-Qal pf. 3 m.s. (386) *and withers*

90:7

כִּי־כָלִינוּ conj. (471)-Qal pf. 1 c.p. (כָּלָה 477) *for we are consumed*
בְאַפֶּךָ prep.-n.m.s.-2 m.s. sf. (I 60) *by thy anger*
וּבַחֲמָתְךָ conj.-prep.-n.f.s.-2 m.s. sf. (404) *and by thy wrath*
נִבְהָלְנוּ Ni. pf. 1 c.p. paus. (בָּהַל 96) *we are overwhelmed*

90:8

שַׁתָּ Qal pf. 2 m.s. (שִׁית 1011; GK 73d) *thou hast set*
עֲוֹנֹתֵינוּ n.m.p.-1 c.p. sf. (730) *our iniquities*
לְנֶגְדֶּךָ prep.-n.m.s.-2 m.s. sf. (617) *before thee*
עֲלֻמֵנוּ Qal pass.ptc.-1 c.p. sf. (עָלַם I 761) *our secret sins*
לִמְאוֹר prep.-n.m.s. cstr. (22) *in the light of*
פָּנֶיךָ n.m.p.-2 m.s. sf. (815) *thy countenance*

90:9

כִּי כָל־ conj. (471)–n.m.s. cstr. (481) *for all*
יָמֵינוּ n.m.p.–1 c.p. sf. (398) *our days*
פָּנוּ Qal pf. 3 c.p. (פָּנָה 815) *pass away*
בְעֶבְרָתֶךָ prep.–n.f.s.–2 m.s. sf. (720) *under thy wrath*
כִּלִּינוּ Pi. pf. 1 c.p. (כָּלָה 477) *we bring to an end*
שָׁנֵינוּ n.f.p.–1 c.p. sf. (1040) *our years*
כְמוֹ־הֶגֶה prep. (455)–n.m.s. (211) *like a sigh*

90:10

יְמֵי n.m.p. cstr. (398) *the days of*
שְׁנוֹתֵינוּ n.f.p.–1 c.p. sf. (1040) *our years*
בָהֶם prep.–3 m.p. sf. *in them*
שִׁבְעִים num. p. (988) *seventy*
שָׁנָה n.f.s. (1040) *years*
וְאִם בִּגְבוּרֹת conj.–hypoth.part. (49)–prep.–n.f.p. (150) *or even by reason of strength*
שְׁמוֹנִים num. p. (1033) *eighty*
שָׁנָה n.f.s. (1040) *years*
וְרָהְבָּם conj.–n.m.s.–3 m.p. sf. (923) *yet their pride*
עָמָל n.m.s. (765) *toil*
וָאָוֶן conj.–n.m.s. (19) *and trouble*
כִּי־גָז conj. (471)–Qal pf. 3 m.s. (גּוּז I 156) *they are gone away*
חִישׁ adv. (301) *soon*
וַנָּעֻפָה consec.–Qal impf. 1 c.p. (עוּף I 733; GK 49e) *and we fly away*

90:11

מִי־יוֹדֵעַ interr. (566)–Qal act.ptc. (393) *who considers*
עֹז n.m.s. cstr. (738) *the power of*
אַפֶּךָ n.m.s.–2 m.s. sf. (I 60) *thy anger*
וּכְיִרְאָתְךָ conj.–prep.–n.f.s.–2 m.s. sf. (432) *and according to the fear of thee*
עֶבְרָתֶךָ n.f.s.–2 m.s. sf. (720) *thy wrath*

90:12

לִמְנוֹת prep.–Qal inf.cstr. (מָנָה 584) *to number*
יָמֵינוּ n.m.p.–1 c.p. sf. (398) *our days*
כֵּן הוֹדַע adv. (485)–Hi. impv. 2 m.s. (יָדַע 393) *so teach us*
וְנָבִא conj.–Hi. impf. 1 c.p. (בּוֹא 97) *that we may get*
לְבַב n.m.s. cstr. (523) *a heart of*
חָכְמָה n.f.s. (315) *wisdom*

90:13

שׁוּבָה Qal impv. 2 m.s.–vol.he (996) *return*
יהוה (217) *O Yahweh*
עַד־מָתָי prep. (III 723)–interr.adv. (607; GK 147c) *how long?*
וְהִנָּחֵם conj.–Ni. impv. 2 m.s. (נָחַם 636) *have pity*
עַל־עֲבָדֶיךָ prep.–n.m.p.–2 m.s. sf. (713) *on thy servants*

90:14

שַׂבְּעֵנוּ Pi. impv. 2 m.s.–1 c.p. sf. (שָׂבַע 959) *satisfy us*
בַבֹּקֶר prep.–def.art.–n.m.s. (133) *in the morning*
חַסְדֶּךָ n.m.s.–2 m.s. sf. (338) *with thy steadfast love*
וּנְרַנְּנָה conj.–Pi. impf. 1 c.p.–vol.he (רָנַן 943) *that we may rejoice*
וְנִשְׂמְחָה conj.–Qal impf. 1 c.p.–vol.he (שָׂמַח 970) *and be glad*
בְּכָל־יָמֵינוּ prep.–n.m.s. cstr. (481)–n.m.p.–1 c.p. sf. (398) *all our days*

90:15

שַׂמְּחֵנוּ Pi. impv. 2 m.s.–1 c.p. sf. (970) *make us glad*
כִּימוֹת prep.–n.m.p. (398) *as days*
עִנִּיתָנוּ Pi. pf. 2 m.s.–1 c.p. sf. (עָנָה III 776) *as thou hast afflicted us*
שְׁנוֹת n.m.p. cstr. (1040; GK 87n) *years*
רָאִינוּ Qal pf. 1 c.p. (רָאָה 906; GK 130d) *we have seen*
רָעָה n.f.s. (949) *evil*

90:16

יֵרָאֶה Ni. impf. 3 m.s. (906) *let be manifest*
אֶל־עֲבָדֶיךָ prep.–n.m.p.–2 m.s. sf. (713) *to thy servants*
פָעֳלֶךָ n.m.s.–2 m.s. sf. (821) *thy work*
וַהֲדָרְךָ conj.–n.m.s.–2 m.s. sf. (214) *and thy glorious power*
עַל־בְּנֵיהֶם prep.–n.m.p.–3 m.p. sf. (119) *to their children*

90:17

וִיהִי conj.–Qal impf. 3 m.s. apoc. (הָיָה 224) *let be*
נֹעַם n.m.s. cstr. (653) *the favor of*
אֲדֹנָי n.m.p.–1 c.s. sf. (10) *the Lord*
אֱלֹהֵינוּ n.m.p.–1 c.p. sf. (43) *our God*
עָלֵינוּ prep.–1 c.p. sf. *upon us*
וּמַעֲשֵׂה conj.–n.m.s. cstr. (795) *and the work of*
יָדֵינוּ n.f. du.–1 c.p. sf. (388) *our hands*

כּוֹנְנָה Polel impv. 2 m.s.-vol.he (כּוּן I 465) *establish thou*
עָלֵינוּ prep.-1 c.p. sf. *upon us*
וּמַעֲשֵׂה v.supra *yea, the work of*
יָדֵינוּ v.supra *our hands*
כּוֹנְנֵהוּ Polel impv. 2 m.s.-3 m.s. sf. (כּוּן I 465) *establish thou it*

91:1

יֹשֵׁב Qal act.ptc. (442) *he who dwells*
בְּסֵתֶר prep.-n.m.s. cstr. (712) *in the shelter of*
עֶלְיוֹן n.m.s. (751) *the Most High*
בְּצֵל prep.-n.m.s. cstr. (853) *in the shadow of*
שַׁדַּי n.m.s. (994) *the Almighty*
יִתְלוֹנָן Hithpolel impf. 3 m.s. paus. (לוּן I 533) *who abides*

91:2

אֹמַר Qal impf. 1 c.s. (55; LXX ἐρεῖ) *will say*
לַיהוה prep.-pr.n. (217) *to Yahweh*
מַחְסִי n.m.s.-1 c.s. sf. (340) *my refuge*
וּמְצוּדָתִי conj.-n.f.s.-1 c.s. sf. (II 845) *and my fortress*
אֱלֹהַי n.m.p.-1 c.s. sf. (43) *my God*
אֶבְטַח־בּוֹ Qal impf. 1 c.s. (105)-prep.-3 m.s. sf. *in whom I trust*

91:3

כִּי הוּא conj. (471)-pers.pr. 3 m.s. (214) *for he*
יַצִּילְךָ Hi. impf. 3 m.s.-2 m.s. sf. (נָצַל 664) *will deliver you*
מִפַּח prep.-n.m.s. cstr. (809) *from the snare of*
יָקוּשׁ n.m.s. (430) *the fowler*
מִדֶּבֶר prep.-n.m.s. cstr. (184) *from the pestilence of*
הַוּוֹת n.f.p. (217) *destruction*

91:4

בְּאֶבְרָתוֹ prep.-n.f.s.-3 m.s. sf. (7) *with his pinions*
יָסֶךְ לָךְ Hi. impf. 3 m.s. (סָכַךְ I 696; GK 67p, 109k)-prep.-2 m.s. sf. paus. *he will cover you*
וְתַחַת־כְּנָפָיו conj.-prep. (1065)-n.f.p.-3 m.s. sf. (489) *and under his wings*
תֶּחְסֶה Qal impf. 2 m.s. (חָסָה 340) *you will find refuge*
צִנָּה n.f.s. (III 857) *a shield*
וְסֹחֵרָה conj.-n.f.s. (695) *and buckler*
אֲמִתּוֹ n.f.s.-3 m.s. sf. (54) *his faithfulness*

91:5

לֹא־תִירָא neg.-Qal impf. 2 m.s. (יָרֵא 431) *you will not fear*
מִפַּחַד prep.-n.m.s. cstr. (808) *the terror of*
לָיְלָה n.m.s. paus. (538) *the night*
מֵחֵץ prep.-n.m.s. (346) *nor the arrow*
יָעוּף Qal impf. 3 m.s. (עוּף 733) *that flies*
יוֹמָם adv. (401) *by day*

91:6

מִדֶּבֶר prep.-n.m.s. (184) *nor the pestilence*
בָּאֹפֶל prep.-def.art.-n.m.s. (66) *in darkness*
יַהֲלֹךְ Qal impf. 3 m.s. (הָלַךְ 229) *that stalks*
מִקֶּטֶב prep.-n.m.s. (881) *nor the destruction*
יָשׁוּד Qal impf. 3 m.s. (שָׁדַד 994; GK 67q) *that wastes*
צָהֳרָיִם n.m.p. paus. (843; GK 118i) *at noonday*

91:7

יִפֹּל Qal impf. 3 m.s. (נָפַל 656) *may fall*
מִצִּדְּךָ prep.-n.m.s.-2 m.s. sf. (841) *at your side*
אֶלֶף n.m.s. (48) *a thousand*
וּרְבָבָה conj.-n.f.s. (914) *and ten thousand*
מִימִינֶךָ prep.-n.f.s.-2 m.s. sf. (411) *at your right hand*
אֵלֶיךָ prep.-2 m.s. sf. *near you*
לֹא יִגָּשׁ neg.-Qal impf. 3 m.s. paus. (נָגַשׁ 621) *it will not come near*

91:8

רַק adv. (956) *only*
בְּעֵינֶיךָ prep.-n.f. du.-2 m.s. sf. (744) *with your eyes*
תַבִּיט Hi. impf. 2 m.s. (נָבַט 613) *you will look*
וְשִׁלֻּמַת conj.-n.f.s. cstr. (1024) *and the recompense of*
רְשָׁעִים adj. m.p. (957) *the wicked*
תִּרְאֶה Qal impf. 2 m.s. (רָאָה 906) *you will see*

91:9

כִּי־אַתָּה conj. (471)-pers.pr. 2 m.s. (61) *because thou*
יהוה pr.n. (217) *O Yahweh*
מַחְסִי n.m.s.-1 c.s. sf. (340) *art my refuge*
עֶלְיוֹן n.m.s. (751) *the Most High*
שַׂמְתָּ Qal pf. 2 m.s. (שׂוּם 962; GK 117ii) *you have made*
מְעוֹנֶךָ n.m.s.-2 m.s. sf. (I 732) *your habitation*

91:10

לֹא־תְאֻנֶּה neg.-Pu. impf. 3 f.s. (III 58) *shall befall not*

אֵלֶיךָ prep.-2 m.s. sf. *you*
רָעָה n.f.s. (949) *evil*
וְנֶגַע conj.-n.m.s. (619) *and a scourge*
לֹא־יִקְרַב neg.-Qal impf. 3 m.s. (897) *shall not come near*
בְּאָהֳלֶךָ prep.-n.m.s.-2 m.s. sf. (13) *your tent*

91:11

כִּי מַלְאָכָיו conj.-n.m.p.-3 m.s. sf. (521) *for his angels*
יְצַוֶּה־ Pi. impf. 3 m.s. (צָוָה 845) *he will give charge*
לָּךְ prep.-2 m.s. sf. paus. (GK 20c) *of you*
לִשְׁמָרְךָ prep.-Qal inf.cstr.-2 m.s. sf. (שָׁמַר 1036) *to guard you*
בְּכָל־דְּרָכֶיךָ prep.-n.m.s. cstr. (481)-n.m.p.-2 m.s. sf. (202) *in all your ways*

91:12

עַל־כַּפַּיִם prep.-n.f. du. (496) *on their hands*
יִשָּׂאוּנְךָ Qal impf. 3 m.p.-2 m.s. sf. (נָשָׂא 669; GK 60e) *they will bear you up*
פֶּן־תִּגֹּף conj. (814)-Qal impf. 2 m.s. (נָגַף 619) *lest you dash*
בָּאֶבֶן prep.-def.art.-n.f.s. (6) *against the stone*
רַגְלֶךָ n.f.s.-2 m.s. sf. (919) *your foot*

91:13

עַל־שַׁחַל prep.-n.m.s. (1006) *on the lion*
וָפֶתֶן conj.-n.m.s. (837) *and the adder*
תִּדְרֹךְ Qal impf. 2 m.s. (דָּרַךְ 201) *you will tread*
תִּרְמֹס Qal impf. 2 m.s. (רָמַס 942) *you will trample*
כְּפִיר n.m.s. (498) *the young lion*
וְתַנִּין conj.-n.m.s. (1072) *and the serpent*

91:14

כִּי בִי conj. (471)-prep.-1 c.s. sf. *because to me*
חָשַׁק Qal pf. 3 m.s. (I 365) *he cleaves in love*
וַאֲפַלְּטֵהוּ conj.-Pi. impf. 1 c.s.-3 m.s. sf. (פָּלַט 812) *I will deliver him*
אֲשַׂגְּבֵהוּ Pi. impf. 1 c.s.-3 m.s. sf. (שָׂגַב 960) *I will protect him*
כִּי־יָדַע conj. (471)-Qal pf. 3 m.s. (393) *because he knows*
שְׁמִי n.m.s.-1 c.s. sf. (1027) *my name*

91:15

יִקְרָאֵנִי Qal impf. 3 m.s.-1 c.s. sf. (894) *he calls me*
וְאֶעֱנֵהוּ conj.-Qal impf. 1 c.s.-3 m.s. sf. (עָנָה I 772) *I will answer him*
עִמּוֹ־ prep.-3 m.s. sf. *with him*
אָנֹכִי pers.pr. 1 c.s. (59) *I will be*
בְצָרָה prep.-n.f.s. (865) *in trouble*
אֲחַלְּצֵהוּ Pi. impf. 1 c.s.-3 m.s. sf. (חָלַץ 323) *I will rescue him*
וַאֲכַבְּדֵהוּ conj.-Pi. impf. 1 c.s.-3 m.s. sf. (כָּבֵד 457) *and I will honor him*

91:16

אֹרֶךְ יָמִים n.m.s. cstr. (73)-n.m.p. (398) *with long days*
אַשְׂבִּיעֵהוּ Hi. impf. 1 c.s.-3 m.s. sf. (שָׂבַע 959) *I will satisfy him*
וְאַרְאֵהוּ conj.-Hi. impf. 1 c.s.-3 m.s. sf. (רָאָה 906) *and I will show him*
בִּישׁוּעָתִי prep.-n.f.s.-1 c.s. sf. (447) *my salvation*

92:1

מִזְמוֹר n.m.s. (274) *a Psalm*
שִׁיר n.m.s. (1010) *a song*
לְיוֹם הַשַּׁבָּת prep.-n.m.s. cstr. (398)-def.art.-n.f.s. (992) *for the Sabbath day*

92:2

טוֹב adj. m.s. (II 373) *it is good*
לְהֹדוֹת prep.-Hi. inf.cstr. (יָדָה 392) *to give thanks*
ליהוה prep.-pr.n. (217) *to Yahweh*
וּלְזַמֵּר conj.-prep.-Pi. inf.cstr. (I 274) *to sing praises*
לְשִׁמְךָ prep.-n.m.s.-2 m.s. sf. (1027) *to thy name*
עֶלְיוֹן n.m.s. (751) *O Most High*

92:3

לְהַגִּיד prep.-Hi. inf.cstr. (נָגַד 616) *to declare*
בַּבֹּקֶר prep.-def.art.-n.m.s. (133) *in the morning*
חַסְדֶּךָ n.m.s.-2 m.s. sf. (338) *thy steadfast love*
וֶאֱמוּנָתְךָ conj.-n.f.s.-2 m.s. sf. (53) *and thy faithfulness*
בַּלֵּילוֹת prep.-def.art.-n.m.p. (538) *by night*

92:4

עֲלֵי־עָשׂוֹר prep. (752)-n.m.s. (797) *to the music of the lute (a ten-stringed instrument)*
וַעֲלֵי־נָבֶל conj.-v.supra-n.m.s. paus. (II 614) *and the harp*
עֲלֵי הִגָּיוֹן v.supra-n.m.s. (212) *to the melody*
בְּכִנּוֹר prep.-n.m.s. (490) *of the lyre*

92:5

כִּי שִׂמַּחְתַּנִי conj.-Pi. pf. 2 m.s.-1 c.s. sf. (שָׂמַח 970) *for thou hast me glad*

יהוה pr.n. (217) *O Yahweh*
בְּפָעֳלֶךָ prep.-n.m.s.-2 m.s. sf. (821) *by thy work*
בְּמַעֲשֵׂי prep.-n.m.p. cstr. (795) *at the works of*
יָדֶיךָ n.f. du.-2 m.s. sf. (388) *thy hands*
אֲרַנֵּן Pi. impf. 1 c.s. (רָנַן 943) *I sing for joy*

92:6

מַה־גָּדְלוּ interr. (552)-Qal pf. 3 c.p. (152) *how great are*
מַעֲשֶׂיךָ n.m.p.-2 m.s. sf. (795) *thy works*
יהוה pr.n. (217) *O Yahweh*
מְאֹד עָמְקוּ adv. (547)-Qal pf. 3 c.p. (770) *are very deep*
מַחְשְׁבֹתֶיךָ n.f.p.-2 m.s. sf. (364) *thy thoughts*

92:7

אִישׁ־בַּעַר n.m.s. cstr. (35)-n.m.s. (129) *the dull man*
לֹא יֵדָע neg.-Qal impf. 3 m.s. (יָדַע 393) *cannot know*
וּכְסִיל conj.-n.m.s. (493) *and the stupid*
לֹא־יָבִין neg.-Qal impf. 3 m.s. (בִּין 106) *cannot understand*
אֶת־זֹאת dir.obj.-demons.adj. f.s. (260) *this*

92:8

בִּפְרֹחַ prep.-Qal inf.cstr. (I 827) *though ... sprout*
רְשָׁעִים adj. m.p. (957) *the wicked*
כְּמוֹ עֵשֶׂב prep. (455)-n.m.s. (793) *like grass*
וַיָּצִיצוּ consec.-Qal impf. 3 m.p. (צוּץ I 847) *and flourish*
כָּל־פֹּעֲלֵי n.m.s. cstr. (481)-Qal act.ptc. m.p. cstr. (821) *all doers of*
אָוֶן n.m.s. (19) *evil*
לְהִשָּׁמְדָם prep.-Ni. inf.cstr.-3 m.p. sf. (שָׁמַד 1029) *to be destroyed*
עֲדֵי־עַד prep. (III 723)-n.m.s. (I 723) *for ever*

92:9

וְאַתָּה conj.-pers.pr. 2 m.s. (61) *but thou*
מָרוֹם n.m.s. (928) *art on high*
לְעֹלָם prep.-n.m.s. (761) *for ever*
יהוה pr.n. (217) *O Yahweh*

92:10

כִּי הִנֵּה conj. (471)-demons.part. (243) *for lo*
אֹיְבֶיךָ Qal act.ptc. m.p.-2 m.s. sf. (אָיַב 33) *thy enemies*
יהוה pr.n. (217) *O Yahweh*
כִּי־הִנֵּה v.supra-v.supra *for lo*
אֹיְבֶיךָ v.supra *thy enemies*
יֹאבֵדוּ Qal impf. 3 m.p. (1) *shall perish*
יִתְפָּרְדוּ Hith. impf. 3 m.p. (פָּרַד 825) *shall be scattered*
כָּל־פֹּעֲלֵי n.m.s. cstr. (481)-Qal act.ptc. m.p. cstr. (821) *all workers of*
אָוֶן n.m.s. (19) *evil*

92:11

וַתָּרֶם consec.-Hi. impf. 2 m.s. (רוּם 926) *but thou hast exalted*
כִּרְאֵים prep.-n.m.s. (910) *like that of the wild ox*
קַרְנִי n.f.s.-1 c.s. sf. (901) *my horn*
בַּלֹּתִי Qal pf. 1 c.s. (בָּלַל I 117) *I shall be anointed* (or Pi. inf.cstr.-1 c.s. sf. בָּלָה 115 *I shall use to the full)*
בְּשֶׁמֶן רַעֲנָן prep.-n.m.s. cstr. (1032)-adj. m.s. (947) *fresh oil*

92:12

וַתַּבֵּט consec.-Hi. impf. 3 f.s. (נָבַט 613) *have seen*
עֵינִי n.f.s.-1 c.s. sf. (744) *my eyes*
בְּשׁוּרָי prep.-n.m.p.-1 c.s. sf. (prb.rd. בְּשׁוֹרְרָי 1004) *my insidious watchers*
בַּקָּמִים prep.-def.art.-Qal act.ptc. m.p. (קוּם 877) *in the rising*
עָלַי prep.-1 c.s. sf. *against me*
מְרֵעִים Hi. ptc. m.p. (רָעַע 949) *my evil assailants*
תִּשְׁמַעְנָה Qal impf. 3 f.p. (שָׁמַע 1033; GK 132b) *have heard*
אָזְנָי n.f. du.-1 c.s. sf. (23) *my ears*

92:13

צַדִּיק adj. m.s. (843) *the righteous*
כַּתָּמָר prep.-def.art.-n.m.s. (I 1071) *like the palm tree*
יִפְרָח Qal impf. 3 m.s. paus. (I 827) *flourish*
כְּאֶרֶז prep.-n.m.s. (72) *like a cedar*
בַּלְּבָנוֹן prep.-def.art.-pr.n. (526) *in Lebanon*
יִשְׂגֶּה Qal impf. 3 m.s. (960) *grow*

92:14

שְׁתוּלִים Qal pass.ptc. m.p. (1060) *they are planted*
בְּבֵית יהוה prep.-n.m.s. cstr. (108)-pr.n. (217) *in the house of Yahweh*
בְּחַצְרוֹת prep.-n.f.p. cstr. (I 346) *in the courts of*
אֱלֹהֵינוּ n.m.p.-1 c.p. sf. (43) *our God*
יַפְרִיחוּ Hi. impf. 3 m.p. (I 827) *they flourish*

92:15

עוֹד adv. (728) *still*

יְנוּבוּן Qal impf. 3 m.p. (נוב 626) *they bring forth fruit*
בְּשֵׂיבָה prep.-n.f.s. (966) *in old age*
דְּשֵׁנִים adj. m.p. (206) *full of sap (fat)*
וְרַעֲנַנִּים conj.-adj. m.p. (947) *and green*
יִהְיוּ Qal impf. 3 m.p. (הָיָה 224) *they are*

92:16

לְהַגִּיד prep.-Hi. inf.cstr. (נָגַד 616) *to show*
כִּי־יָשָׁר conj. (471)-adj. m.s. (449) *is upright*
יהוה pr.n. (217) *Yahweh*
צוּרִי n.m.s.-1 c.s. sf. (849) *my rock*
וְלֹא־עַלְתָה conj.-neg.-n.f.s. (732) *and there is no unrighteousness*
בּוֹ prep.-3 m.s. sf. *in him*

93:1

יהוה pr.n. (217) *Yahweh*
מָלָךְ Qal pf. 3 m.s.? (573) *reigns*
גֵּאוּת n.f.s. (145) *in majesty*
לָבֵשׁ Qal pf. 3 m.s. (527) *he is robed*
לָבֵשׁ v.supra *he is robed*
יהוה v.supra *Yahweh*
עֹז n.m.s. (738) *with strength*
הִתְאַזָּר Hith. pf. 3 m.s. paus. (אָזַר 25) *he is girded*
אַף־תִּכּוֹן conj. (64)-Ni. impf. 3 f.s. (כּוּן 465) *yea, is established*
תֵּבֵל n.f.s. (385) *the world*
בַּל־תִּמּוֹט neg. (115)-Ni. impf. 3 f.s. (מוֹט 556) *it shall never be moved*

93:2

נָכוֹן Ni. ptc. (כּוּן 465) *is established*
כִּסְאֲךָ n.m.s.-2 m.s. sf. (490) *thy throne*
מֵאָז prep.-adv. (23) *from of old*
מֵעוֹלָם prep.-n.m.s. (761) *from everlasting*
אָתָּה pers.pr. 2 m.s. paus. (61) *thou art*

93:3

נָשְׂאוּ Qal pf. 3 c.p. (669) *have lifted up*
נְהָרוֹת n.m.p. (625) *the floods*
יהוה pr.n. (217) *O Yahweh*
נָשְׂאוּ v.supra *have lifted up*
נְהָרוֹת v.supra *the floods*
קוֹלָם n.m.s.-3 m.p. sf. (876) *their voice*
יִשְׂאוּ־ Qal impf. 3 m.p. (נָשָׂא 669) *lift up*
נְהָרוֹת v.supra *the floods*
דָּכְיָם n.m.s.-3 m.p. sf. (194) *their roaring*

93:4

מִקֹּלוֹת prep.-n.m.p. cstr. (876) *than the thunders of*
מַיִם n.m.p. (565) *waters*
רַבִּים adj. m.p. (I 912) *mightier*
אַדִּירִים adj. m.p. (12) *mightier*
מִשְׁבְּרֵי־ n.m.p. cstr. (991) *the waves of*
יָם n.m.s. (410) *the sea*
אַדִּיר adj. m.s. (12) *mighty*
בַּמָּרוֹם prep.-def.art.-n.m.s. (928) *on high*
יהוה pr.n. (217) *Yahweh*

93:5

עֵדֹתֶיךָ n.f.p. (III 730) *thy decrees*
נֶאֶמְנוּ Ni. pf. 3 c.p. (אָמַן 52) *are sure*
מְאֹד adv. (547) *very*
לְבֵיתְךָ prep.-n.m.s.-2 m.s. sf. (108) *to thy house*
נַאֲוָה־ adj. f.s. (610; GK 75x) *befits (is seemly)*
קֹדֶשׁ n.m.s. (871) *holiness*
יהוה pr.n. (217) *Yahweh*
לְאֹרֶךְ יָמִים prep.-n.m.s. cstr. (73)-n.m.p. (398) *for evermore*

94:1

אֵל־נְקָמוֹת n.m.s. cstr. (42)-n.f.p. (668) *God of vengeance*
יהוה pr.n. (217) *Yahweh*
אֵל נְקָמוֹת v.supra-v.supra *God of vengeance*
הוֹפִיעַ Hi. impv. 2 m.s. paus. (יָפַע 422; GK 53m,69v) *shine forth*

94:2

הִנָּשֵׂא Ni. impv. 2 m.s. (669) *rise up*
שֹׁפֵט הָאָרֶץ Qal act.ptc. (1047)-def.art.-n.f.s. (75) *O judge of the earth*
הָשֵׁב Hi. impv. 2 m.s. (שׁוּב 996) *render*
גְּמוּל n.m.s. (168) *their deserts*
עַל־גֵּאִים prep.-adj. m.p. (144) *to the proud*

94:3

עַד־מָתַי prep. (III 723)-interr. (607) *how long*
רְשָׁעִים adj. m.p. (957) *the wicked*
יהוה pr.n. (217) *O Yahweh*
עַד־מָתַי v.supra-v.supra *how long*
רְשָׁעִים v.supra *the wicked*
יַעֲלֹזוּ Qal impf. 3 m.p. (עָלַז 759) *shall exult*

94:4

יַבִּיעוּ Hi. impf. 3 m.s. (נָבַע 615) *they pour out*
יְדַבְּרוּ Pi. impf. 3 m.p. (180) *they speak*
עָתָק adj. m.s. (801) *arrogance*
יִתְאַמְּרוּ Hith. impf. 3 m.p. (אָמַר 55) *they boast*

כָּל־פֹּעֲלֵי n.m.s. cstr. (481)-Qal act.ptc. m.p. cstr. (821) *all the workers of*
אָוֶן n.m.s. (19) *evil*

94:5

עַמְּךָ n.m.s.-2 m.s. sf. (I 766) *thy people*
יהוה pr.n. (217) *O Yahweh*
יְדַכְּאוּ Pi. impf. 3 m.p. (193) *they crush*
וְנַחֲלָתְךָ conj.-n.f.s.-2 m.s. sf. (635) *and thy heritage*
יְעַנּוּ Pi. impf. 3 m.p. (עָנָה III 776) *they afflict*

94:6

אַלְמָנָה n.f.s. (48) *the widow*
וְגֵר conj.-n.m.s. (158) *and the sojourner*
יַהֲרֹגוּ Qal impf. 3 m.p. (הָרַג 246) *they slay*
וִיתוֹמִים conj.-n.m.p. (450) *and the fatherless*
יְרַצֵּחוּ Pi. impf. 3 m.p. (רָצַח 953) *they murder*

94:7

וַיֹּאמְרוּ consec.-Qal impf. 3 m.p. (55) *and they say*
לֹא יִרְאֶה־ neg.-Qal impf. 3 m.s. (רָאָה 906) *does not see*
יָּהּ pr.n. (219) *Yah*
וְלֹא־יָבִין conj.-neg.-Qal impf. 3 m.s. (106) *and does not perceive*
אֱלֹהֵי n.m.p. cstr. (43) *the God of*
יַעֲקֹב pr.n. (784) *Jacob*

94:8

בִּינוּ Qal impv. 2 m.p. (בִּין 106) *understand*
בֹּעֲרִים Qal act.ptc. m.p. (בָּעַר II 129) *dull-hearted ones*
בָּעָם prep.-def.art.-n.m.s. (I 766) *of the people*
וּכְסִילִים conj.-n.m.p. (493) *and fools*
מָתַי interr. (607) *when*
תַּשְׂכִּילוּ Hi. impf. 2 m.p. (שָׂכַל 968) *will you be wise*

94:9

הֲנֹטַע interr.-Qal act.ptc. (642; GK 93qq) *he who planted*
אֹזֶן n.f.s. (23) *the ear*
הֲלֹא יִשְׁמָע interr.-neg.-Qal impf. 3 m.s. paus. (1033) *does he not hear?*
אִם־יֹצֵר hypoth.part. (49)-Qal act.ptc. (יָצַר 427) *he who formed*
עַיִן n.f.s. (744) *the eye*
הֲלֹא יַבִּיט interr.-neg.-Hi. impf. 3 m.s. (נָבַט 613) *does he not see?*

94:10

הֲיֹסֵר interr.-Qal act.ptc. (יָסַר 415) *he who chastens*
גּוֹיִם n.m.p. (156) *the nations*
הֲלֹא יוֹכִיחַ interr.-neg.-Hi. impf. 3 m.s. (יָכַח 406) *does he not judge*
הַמְלַמֵּד interr.-Pi. ptc. (540) *he who teaches*
אָדָם n.m.s. (9) *man*
דָּעַת n.f.s. paus. (395) *knowledge*

94:11

יהוה pr.n. (217) *Yahweh*
יֹדֵעַ Qal act.ptc. (393) *knows*
מַחְשְׁבוֹת n.f.p. cstr. (364) *the thoughts of*
אָדָם n.m.s. (9) *man*
כִּי־הֵמָּה conj. (471)-pers.pr. 3 m.p. (241) *that they are*
הָבֶל n.m.s. paus. (I 210) *a breath*

94:12

אַשְׁרֵי n.m.p. cstr. (80) *blessed is*
הַגֶּבֶר def.art.-n.m.s. (149) *the man*
אֲשֶׁר־תְּיַסְּרֶנּוּ rel. (81)-Pi. impf. 2 m.s.-3 m.s. sf. (415 יָסַר) *whom thou dost chasten (him)*
יָּהּ pr.n. (219; GK 20g) *O Yah*
וּמִתּוֹרָתְךָ conj.-prep.-n.f.s.-2 m.s. sf. (435) *and out of thy law*
תְלַמְּדֶנּוּ Pi. impf. 2 m.s.-3 m.s. sf. (לָמַד 540) *thou dost teach him*

94:13

לְהַשְׁקִיט לוֹ prep.-Hi. inf.cstr. (1052)-prep.-3 m.s. sf. *to give him respite*
מִימֵי prep.-n.m.p. cstr. (398) *from days of*
רָע n.m.s. paus. (II 948) *evil*
עַד יִכָּרֶה prep. (III 723)-Ni. impf. 3 m.s. (כָּרָה I 500) *until is dug*
לָרָשָׁע prep.-def.art.-adj. m.s. (957) *for the wicked*
שָׁחַת n.f.s. (1001) *a pit*

94:14

כִּי לֹא־יִטֹּשׁ conj. (471)-neg.-Qal impf. 3 m.s. (643 נָטַשׁ) *for will not forsake*
יהוה pr.n. (217) *Yahweh*
עַמּוֹ n.m.s.-3 m.s. sf. (I 766) *his people*
וְנַחֲלָתוֹ conj.-n.f.s.-3 m.s. sf. (635) *and his heritage*
לֹא יַעֲזֹב neg.-Qal impf. 3 m.s. (עָזַב I 736) *he will not abandon*

94:15

כִּי־עַד־צֶדֶק conj. (471)–prep. (III 723)–n.m.s. (841) *for to the righteous*
יָשׁוּב Qal impf. 3 m.s. (996) *will return*
מִשְׁפָּט n.m.s. (1048) *justice*
וְאַחֲרָיו conj.–prep.–3 m.s. sf. (29) *and after him*
כָּל־יִשְׁרֵי־ n.m.s. cstr. (481)–adj. m.p. cstr. (449) *all the upright in*
לֵב n.m.s. (524) *heart*

94:16

מִי־יָקוּם interr. (566)–Qal impf. 3 m.s. (קוּם 877) *who rises up*
לִי prep.–1 c.s. sf. *for me*
עִם־מְרֵעִים prep.–Hi. ptc. m.p. (רָעַע I 949) *against evildoers*
מִי־יִתְיַצֵּב v.supra–Hith. impf. 3 m.s. (יָצַב 426) *who stands up*
לִי v.supra *for me*
עִם־פֹּעֲלֵי prep.–Qal act.ptc. m.p. cstr. (פָּעַל 821) *against workers of*
אָוֶן n.m.s. (19) *evil*

94:17

לוּלֵי conj. (530) *unless*
יהוה pr.n. (217) *Yahweh*
עֶזְרָתָה n.f.s. (740) *a help*
לִּי prep.–1 c.s. sf. *to me*
כִּמְעַט prep.–adv. (589) *soon*
שָׁכְנָה Qal pf. 3 f.s. (שָׁכַן 1014) *would have dwelt*
דוּמָה n.f.s. (I 189) *in silence*
נַפְשִׁי n.f.s.–1 c.s. sf. (659) *my soul*

94:18

אִם־אָמַרְתִּי conj. (49)–Qal pf. 1 c.s. (55) *when I thought*
מָטָה Qal pf. 3 f.s. (מוּט 556) *slips*
רַגְלִי n.f.s.–1 c.s. sf. (919) *my foot*
חַסְדְּךָ n.m.s.–2 m.s. sf. (338) *thy steadfast love*
יהוה pr.n. (217) *O Yahweh*
יִסְעָדֵנִי Qal impf. 3 m.s.–1 c.s. sf. (סָעַד 703) *help me up*

94:19

בְּרֹב שַׂרְעַפַּי prep.–n.m.s. cstr. (913)–n.m.p.–1 c.s. sf. (972) *when my disquieting thoughts are many*
בְּקִרְבִּי prep.–n.m.s.–1 c.s. sf. (899) *within me*
תַּנְחוּמֶיךָ n.m.p.–2 m.s. sf. (637) *thy consolations*
יְשַׁעַשְׁעוּ Pilpel impf. 3 m.p. (שָׁעַע II 1044) *cheer*
נַפְשִׁי n.f.s.–1 c.s. sf. (659) *my soul*

94:20

הַיְחָבְרְךָ interr.–Pu. impf. 3 m.s.–2 m.s. sf. (חָבַר 287; GK 60b,63m) *can be allied with thee*
כִּסֵּא הַוּוֹת n.m.s. cstr. (490)–n.f.p. (217) *the seat of destruction*
יֹצֵר Qal act.ptc. (יָצַר 427) *who frame*
עָמָל n.m.s. (765) *mischief*
עֲלֵי־חֹק prep.–n.m.s. (349) *by statute*

94:21

יָגוֹדּוּ Qal impf. 3 m.p. (גָּדַד 151) *they band together*
עַל־נֶפֶשׁ prep.–n.f.s. cstr. (659) *against the life of*
צַדִּיק adj. m.s. (843) *the righteous*
וְדָם נָקִי conj.–n.m.s. (196)–adj. m.s. (667) *and innocent blood*
יַרְשִׁיעוּ Hi. impf. 3 m.p. (957) *they condemn*

94:22

וַיְהִי consec.–Qal impf. 3 m.s. (הָיָה 224) *but has become*
יהוה pr.n. (217) *Yahweh*
לִי prep.–1 c.s. sf. *to me*
לְמִשְׂגָּב prep.–n.m.s. (I 960) *a stronghold*
וֵאלֹהַי conj.–n.m.s.–1 c.s. sf. (43) *and my God*
לְצוּר prep.–n.m.s. cstr. (849) *the rock of*
מַחְסִי n.m.s.–1 c.s. sf. (340) *my refuge*

94:23

וַיָּשֶׁב consec.–Hi. impf. 3 m.s. (שׁוּב 996) *he will bring back*
עֲלֵיהֶם prep.–3 m.p. sf. *on them*
אֶת־אוֹנָם dir.obj.–n.m.s.–3 m.p. sf. (19) *their iniquity*
וּבְרָעָתָם conj.–prep.–n.f.s.–3 m.p. sf. (949) *and for their wickedness*
יַצְמִיתֵם Hi. impf. 3 m.s.–3 m.p. sf. (צָמַת 856) *he will wipe them out*
יַצְמִיתֵם v.supra *will wipe them out*
יהוה pr.n. (217) *Yahweh*
אֱלֹהֵינוּ n.m.p.–1 c.p. sf. (43) *our God*

95:1

לְכוּ Qal impv. 2 m.p. (הָלַךְ 229) *come*
נְרַנְּנָה Pi. impf. 1 c.p.–vol.he (רָנַן 943) *let us sing*
לַיהוה prep.–pr.n. (217) *to Yahweh*
נָרִיעָה Hi. impf. 1 c.p.–vol.he (רוּעַ 929) *let us make a joyful noise*
לְצוּר prep.–n.m.s. cstr. (849) *to the rock of*
יִשְׁעֵנוּ n.m.s.–1 c.p. sf. (447) *our salvation*

95:2

נְקַדְּמָה Pi. impf. 1 c.p.-vol.he (קָדַם 869) *let us come*

פָנָיו n.m.p.-3 m.s. sf. (815) *into his presence*

בְּתוֹדָה prep.-n.f.s. (392) *with thanksgiving*

בִּזְמִרוֹת prep.-n.m.p. (I 274) *with songs of praise*

נָרִיעַ Hi. impf. 1 c.p. (רוּעַ 929) *let us make a joyful noise*

לוֹ prep.-3 m.s. sf. *to him*

95:3

כִּי אֵל גָּדוֹל conj. (471)-n.m.s. (42)-adj. m.s. (152) *for a great God*

יהוה pr.n. (217) *is Yahweh*

וּמֶלֶךְ גָּדוֹל conj.-n.m.s. (I 572)-v.supra *and a great king*

עַל־כָּל־ prep.-n.m.s. cstr. (481) *above all*

אֱלֹהִים n.m.p. (43) *gods*

95:4

אֲשֶׁר בְּיָדוֹ rel. (81)-prep.-n.f.s.-3 m.s. sf. (388) *in his hand*

מֶחְקְרֵי־ n.m.p. cstr. (350) *the depths of*

אָרֶץ n.f.s. paus. (75) *the earth*

וְתוֹעֲפוֹת conj.-n.f.p. cstr. (419) *and heights of*

הָרִים n.m.p. (249) *mountains*

לוֹ prep.-3 m.s. sf. *are his also*

95:5

אֲשֶׁר־לוֹ rel. (81)-prep.-3 m.s. sf. *is his*

הַיָּם def.art.-n.m.s. (410) *the sea*

וְהוּא עָשָׂהוּ conj.-pers.pr. 3 m.s. (214)-Qal pf. 3 m.s.-3 m.s. sf. (I 793) *for he made it*

וְיַבֶּשֶׁת conj.-n.f.s. (387) *for the dry land*

יָדָיו n.f.p.-3 m.s. sf. (388) *his hands*

יָצָרוּ Qal pf. 3 c.p. paus. (427) *formed*

95:6

בֹּאוּ Qal impv. 2 m.p. (בּוֹא 97) *come*

נִשְׁתַּחֲוֶה Hith. impf. 1 c.p. (שָׁחָה 1005) *let us worship*

וְנִכְרָעָה conj.-Qal impf. 1 c.p.-vol.he (502) *and let us bow down*

נִבְרְכָה Qal impf. 1 c.p.-vol.he (בָּרַךְ 138) *let us kneel*

לִפְנֵי־יהוה prep.-n.m.p. cstr. (815)-pr.n. (217) *before Yahweh*

עֹשֵׂנוּ Qal act.ptc. m.s.-1 c.p. sf. (I 793) *our Maker*

95:7

כִּי הוּא conj. (471)-pers.pr. 3 m.s. (214) *for he*

אֱלֹהֵינוּ n.m.p.-1 c.p. sf. (43) *our God*

וַאֲנַחְנוּ conj.-pers.pr. 1 c.p. (59) *and we*

עַם n.m.s. cstr. (I 766) *the people of*

מַרְעִיתוֹ n.f.s.-3 m.s. sf. (945) *his pasture*

וְצֹאן conj.-n.f.s. cstr. (838) *and the sheep of*

יָדוֹ n.f.s.-3 m.s. sf. (388) *his hand*

הַיּוֹם def.art.-n.m.s. (398) *today*

אִם־ hypoth.part. (49) *O that*

בְּקֹלוֹ prep.-n.m.s.-3 m.s. sf. (876) *to his voice*

תִשְׁמָעוּ Qal impf. 2 m.p. paus. (1033) *you would hearken*

95:8

אַל־תַּקְשׁוּ neg.-Hi. impf. 2 m.p. (קָשָׁה I 904) *harden not*

לְבַבְכֶם n.m.s.-2 m.p. sf. (524) *your hearts*

כִּמְרִיבָה prep.-pr.n. paus. (II 937) *as at Meribah*

כְּיוֹם prep.-n.m.s. cstr. (398) *as on the day at*

מַסָּה pr.n. (III 950) *Massah*

בַּמִּדְבָּר prep.-def.art.-n.m.s. (184) *in the wilderness*

95:9

אֲשֶׁר נִסּוּנִי rel. (81)-Pi. pf. 3 c.p.-1 c.s. sf. (נָסָה 650) *when tested me*

אֲבוֹתֵיכֶם n.m.p.-2 m.p. sf. (3) *your fathers*

בְּחָנוּנִי Qal pf. 3 c.p.-1 c.s. sf. (בָּחַן 103) *they put me to the proof*

גַּם־ adv. (168) *though*

רָאוּ Qal pf. 3 c.p. (רָאָה 906) *they had seen*

פָעֳלִי n.m.s.-1 c.s. sf. (821) *my work*

95:10

אַרְבָּעִים num. p. (917) *forty*

שָׁנָה n.f.s. (1040) *years*

אָקוּט Qal impf. 1 c.s. (קוּט 876) *I loathed*

בְּדוֹר prep.-n.m.s. (189) *that generation*

וָאֹמַר consec.-Qal impf. 1 c.s. (55) *and I said*

עַם n.m.s. cstr. (I 766) *a people who*

תֹּעֵי Qal act.ptc. m.p. cstr. (תָּעָה 1073) *err in*

לֵבָב n.m.s. (523) *heart*

הֵם pers.pr. 3 m.p. (241) *they are*

וְהֵם conj.-v.supra *and they*

לֹא־יָדְעוּ neg.-Qal pf. 3 c.p. (393) *do not regard*

דְרָכָי n.m.p.-1 c.s. sf. paus. (202) *my ways*

95:11

אֲשֶׁר־נִשְׁבַּעְתִּי rel. (81)-Ni. pf. 1 c.s. (שָׁבַע 989) *therefore I swore*

בְאַפִּי prep.-n.m.s.-1 c.s. sf. (I 60) *in my anger*

אִם־יְבֹאוּן emphatic neg. (50)–Qal impf. 3 m.p. (בּוֹא 97) *that they should not enter*
אֶל־מְנוּחָתִי prep.–n.f.s.–1 c.s. sf. (629) *my rest*

96:1

שִׁירוּ Qal impv. 2 m.p. (1010) *O sing*
לַיהוה prep.–pr.n. (217) *to Yahweh*
שִׁיר חָדָשׁ n.m.s. (1010)–adj. m.s. (I 294) *a new song*
שִׁירוּ v.supra *sing*
לַיהוה v.supra *to Yahweh*
כָּל־הָאָרֶץ n.m.s. cstr. (481)–def.art.–n.f.s. (75) *all the earth*

96:2

שִׁירוּ Qal impv. 2 m.p. (1010) *sing*
לַיהוה prep.–pr.n. (217) *to Yahweh*
בָּרְכוּ Pi. impv. 2 m.p. (138) *bless*
שְׁמוֹ n.m.s.–3 m.s. sf. (1027) *his name*
בַּשְּׂרוּ Pi. impv. 2 m.p. (142) *tell*
מִיּוֹם־ prep.–n.m.s. (398) *from day*
לְיוֹם prep.–v.supra *to day*
יְשׁוּעָתוֹ n.f.s.–3 m.s. sf. (447) *of his salvation*

96:3

סַפְּרוּ Pi. impv. 2 m.p. (707) *declare*
בַגּוֹיִם prep.–def.art.–n.m.p. (156) *among the nations*
כְּבוֹדוֹ n.m.s.–3 m.s. sf. (458) *his glory*
בְּכָל־ prep.–n.m.s. cstr. (481) *among all*
הָעַמִּים def.art.–n.m.p. (I 766) *the peoples*
נִפְלְאוֹתָיו Ni. ptc. f.p.–3 m.s. sf. (פָּלָא 810) *his marvelous works*

96:4

כִּי גָדוֹל conj. (471)–adj. m.s. (152) *for great is*
יהוה pr.n. (217) *Yahweh*
וּמְהֻלָּל מְאֹד conj.–Pu. ptc. (II 237)–adv. (547) *and greatly to be praised*
נוֹרָא Ni. ptc. (יָרֵא 431) *to be feared*
הוּא pers.pr. 3 m.s. (214) *he is*
עַל־כָּל־אֱלֹהִים prep.–n.m.s. cstr. (481)–n.m.p. (43) *above all gods*

96:5

כִּי כָּל־ conj. (471)–n.m.s. cstr. (481) *for all*
אֱלֹהֵי n.m.p. cstr. (43) *the gods of*
הָעַמִּים def.art.–n.m.s. (I 766) *the peoples*
אֱלִילִים adj. m.p. (47) *are idols*
וַיהוה conj.–pr.n. (217) *but Yahweh*
שָׁמַיִם n.m. du. (1029) *the heavens*
עָשָׂה Qal pf. 3 m.s. (I 793) *made*

96:6

הוֹד־ n.m.s. (I 217) *honor*
וְהָדָר conj.–n.m.s. (214) *and majesty*
לְפָנָיו prep.–n.m.p.–3 m.s. sf. (815) *before him*
עֹז n.m.s. (738) *strength*
וְתִפְאֶרֶת conj.–n.f.s. (802) *and beauty*
בְּמִקְדָּשׁוֹ prep.–n.m.s.–3 m.s. sf. (874) *in his sanctuary*

96:7

הָבוּ Qal impv. 2 m.p. (יָהַב 396) *ascribe*
לַיהוה prep.–pr.n. (217) *to Yahweh*
מִשְׁפְּחוֹת n.f.p. cstr. (1046) *O families of*
עַמִּים n.m.p. (I 766) *the peoples*
הָבוּ v.supra *ascribe*
לַיהוה v.supra *to Yahweh*
כָּבוֹד n.m.s. (458) *glory*
וָעֹז conj.–n.m.s. (738) *and strength*

96:8

הָבוּ Qal impv. 2 m.p. (יָהַב 396) *ascribe*
לַיהוה prep.–pr.n. (217) *to Yahweh*
כְּבוֹד n.m.s. cstr. (458) *the glory due*
שְׁמוֹ n.m.s.–3 m.s. sf. (1027) *his name*
שְׂאוּ־ Qal impv. 2 m.p. (נָשָׂא 669) *bring*
מִנְחָה n.f.s. (585) *an offering*
וּבֹאוּ conj.–Qal impv. 2 m.p. (בּוֹא 97) *and come*
לְחַצְרוֹתָיו prep.–n.f.p.–3 m.s. sf. (I 346) *into his courts*

96:9

הִשְׁתַּחֲווּ Hith. impv. 2 m.p. (שָׁחָה 1005) *worship*
לַיהוה prep.–pr.n. (217) *Yahweh*
בְּהַדְרַת־קֹדֶשׁ prep.–n.f.s. cstr. (214)–n.m.s. (871) *in holy array*
חִילוּ Qal impv. 2 m.p. (חוּל I 296) *tremble*
מִפָּנָיו prep.–n.m.p.–3 m.s. sf. (815) *before him*
כָּל־הָאָרֶץ n.m.s. cstr. (481)–def.art.–n.f.s. (75) *all the earth*

96:10

אִמְרוּ Qal impv. 2 m.p. (55) *say*
בַגּוֹיִם prep.–def.art.–n.m.p. (156) *among the nations*
יהוה pr.n. (217) *Yahweh*
מָלָךְ Qal pf. 3 m.s.? (573) *reigns*
אַף־תִּכּוֹן adv. (II 64)–Ni. impf. 3 f.s. (כּוּן I 465) *yea, is established*
תֵּבֵל n.f.s. (385) *the world*
בַּל־תִּמּוֹט neg. (115)–Ni. impf. 3 f.s. (מוֹט 556) *it shall never be moved*

יָדִין Qal impf. 3 m.s. (דִּין 192) *he will judge*
עַמִּים n.m.p. (I 766) *peoples*
בְּמֵישָׁרִים prep.-n.m.p. (449) *with equity*

96:11

יִשְׂמְחוּ Qal impf. 3 m.p. (970) *let be glad*
הַשָּׁמַיִם def.art.-n.m. du. (1029) *the heavens*
וְתָגֵל conj.-Qal impf. 3 f.s. apoc. (גִּיל 162) *and let rejoice*
הָאָרֶץ def.art.-n.f.s. (75) *the earth*
יִרְעַם Qal impf. 3 m.s. (947) *let roar*
הַיָּם def.art.-n.m.s. (410) *the sea*
וּמְלֹאוֹ conj.-n.m.s.-3 m.s. sf. (571) *and all that fills it*

96:12

יַעֲלֹז Qal impf. 3 m.s. (759) *let exult*
שָׂדַי n.m.s. (961) *the field*
וְכָל־אֲשֶׁר־בּוֹ conj.-n.m.s. (481)-rel. (81)-prep.-3 m.s. sf. *and everything in it*
אָז adv. (23) *then*
יְרַנְּנוּ Pi. impf. 3 m.p. (רָנַן 943) *shall sing for joy*
כָּל־עֲצֵי־ n.m.s. cstr. (481)-n.m.p. cstr. (781) *all the trees of*
יָעַר n.m.s. paus. (420) *the wood*

96:13

לִפְנֵי prep.-n.m.p. cstr. (815) *before*
יהוה pr.n. (217) *Yahweh*
כִּי־בָא conj. (471)-Qal pf. 3 m.s. (בּוֹא 97) *for he comes*
כִּי בָא v.supra-v.supra *for he comes*
לִשְׁפֹּט prep.-Qal inf.cstr. (1047) *to judge*
הָאָרֶץ def.art.-n.f.s. (75) *the earth*
יִשְׁפֹּט־ Qal impf. 3 m.s. (1047) *he will judge*
תֵּבֵל n.f.s. (385) *the world*
בְּצֶדֶק prep.-n.m.s. (841) *with righteousness*
וְעַמִּים conj.-n.m.p. (I 766) *and the peoples*
בֶּאֱמוּנָתוֹ prep.-n.f.s.-3 m.s. sf. (53) *with his truth*

97:1

יהוה pr.n. (217) *Yahweh*
מָלָךְ Qal pf. 3 m.s.? (573) *reigns*
תָּגֵל Qal impf. 3 f.s. apoc. (גִּיל 162) *let rejoice*
הָאָרֶץ def.art.-n.f.s. (75) *the earth*
יִשְׂמְחוּ Qal impf. 3 m.p. (970) *let be glad*
אִיִּים רַבִּים n.m.p. (I 15)-adj. m.p. (I 912) *the many coastlands*

97:2

עָנָן n.m.s. (777) *clouds*
וַעֲרָפֶל conj.-n.m.s. (791) *and thick darkness*
סְבִיבָיו adv.-3 m.s. sf. (686) *round about him*
צֶדֶק n.m.s. (841) *righteousness*
וּמִשְׁפָּט conj.-n.m.s. (1048) *and justice*
מְכוֹן n.m.s. cstr. (467) *the foundation of*
כִּסְאוֹ n.m.s.-3 m.s. sf. (490) *his throne*

97:3

אֵשׁ n.f.s. (77) *fire*
לְפָנָיו prep.-n.m.p.-3 m.s. sf. (815) *before him*
תֵּלֵךְ Qal impf. 3 f.s. (הָלַךְ 229) *goes*
וּתְלַהֵט conj.-Pi. impf. 3 f.s. (529) *and burns up*
סָבִיב adv. (686) *round about*
צָרָיו n.m.p.-3 m.s. sf. (III 865) *his adversaries*

97:4

הֵאִירוּ Hi. pf. 3 c.p. (אוֹר 21) *lighten*
בְרָקָיו n.m.p.-3 m.s. sf. (140) *his lightnings*
תֵּבֵל n.f.s. (385) *the world*
רָאֲתָה Qal pf. 3 f.s. (רָאָה 906) *sees*
וַתָּחֵל consec.-Hi. impf. 3 f.s. (חוּל I 296) *and trembles*
הָאָרֶץ def.art.-n.f.s. (75) *the earth*

97:5

הָרִים n.m.p. (249) *mountains*
כַּדּוֹנַג prep.-def.art.-n.m.s. (200) *like wax*
נָמַסּוּ Ni. pf. 3 c.p. (מָסַס 587) *melt*
מִלִּפְנֵי prep.-n.m.p. cstr. (815) *before*
יהוה pr.n. (217) *Yahweh*
מִלִּפְנֵי v.supra *before*
אֲדוֹן n.m.s. cstr. (10) *the Lord of*
כָּל־הָאָרֶץ n.m.s. cstr. (481)-def.art.-n.f.s. (75) *all the earth*

97:6

הִגִּידוּ Hi. pf. 3 c.p. (נָגַד 616) *declare*
הַשָּׁמַיִם def.art.-n.m. du. (1029) *the heavens*
צִדְקוֹ n.m.s.-3 m.s. sf. (41) *his righteousness*
וְרָאוּ conj.-Qal pf. 3 c.p. (רָאָה 906) *and behold*
כָל־הָעַמִּים n.m.s. cstr. (481)-def.art.-n.m.p. (I 766) *all the peoples*
כְּבוֹדוֹ n.m.s.-3 m.s. sf. (458) *his glory*

97:7

יֵבֹשׁוּ Qal impf. 3 m.p. (בּוֹשׁ 101) *are put to shame*
כָּל־עֹבְדֵי n.m.s. cstr. (481)-Qal act.ptc. m.p. cstr. (712) *all worshipers of*
פֶסֶל n.m.s. (820) *images*
הַמִּתְהַלְלִים def.art.-Hith. ptc. m.p. (II 237) *who make their boast*

בָּאֱלִילִים prep.-def.art.-n.m.p. (47) *in worthless idols*
הִשְׁתַּחֲווּ־ Hith. pf. 3 c.p. (שָׁחָה 1005) *bow down*
לוֹ prep.-3 m.s. sf. *before him*
כָּל־אֱלֹהִים n.m.s. cstr. (481)-n.m.p. (43) *all gods*

97:8

שָׁמְעָה Qal pf. 3 f.s. (1033) *hears*
וַתִּשְׂמַח consec.-Qal impf. 3 f.s. (970) *and is glad*
צִיּוֹן pr.n. (851) *Zion*
וַתָּגֵלְנָה consec.-Qal impf. 3 f.p. (גִּיל 162) *and rejoice*
בְּנוֹת n.f.p. cstr. (I 123) *the daughters of*
יְהוּדָה pr.n. (397) *Judah*
לְמַעַן prep. (775) *because of*
מִשְׁפָּטֶיךָ n.m.p.-2 m.s. sf. (1048) *thy judgments*
יהוה pr.n. (217) *O Yahweh*

97:9

כִּי־אַתָּה conj.-pers.pr. 2 m.s. (61) *for thou*
יהוה pr.n. (217) *O Yahweh*
עֶלְיוֹן adj. m.s. (751) *art most high*
עַל־כָּל־ prep.-n.m.s. cstr. (481) *over all*
הָאָרֶץ def.art.-n.f.s. (75) *the earth*
מְאֹד adv. (547) *far*
נַעֲלֵיתָ Ni. pf. 2 m.s. (עָלָה 748) *thou art exalted*
עַל־כָּל־ v.supra-v.supra *above all*
אֱלֹהִים n.m.p. (43) *gods*

97:10

אֹהֲבֵי Qal act.ptc. m.p. cstr. (12) *you who love*
יהוה pr.n. (217) *Yahweh*
שִׂנְאוּ Qal impv. 2 m.p. (971) *hate*
רָע n.m.s. (949) *evil*
שֹׁמֵר Qal act.ptc. m.s. (1036) *he preserves*
נַפְשׁוֹת n.f.p. cstr. (659) *the lives of*
חֲסִידָיו adj. m.p.-3 m.s. sf. (339) *his saints*
מִיַּד prep.-n.f.s. cstr. (388) *from the hand of*
רְשָׁעִים adj. m.p. (957) *the wicked*
יַצִּילֵם Hi. impf. 3 m.s.-3 m.p. sf. (נָצַל 664) *he delivers them*

97:11

אוֹר n.m.s. (21) *light*
זָרֻעַ Qal pass.ptc. (281) *is sown*
לַצַּדִּיק prep.-def.art.-adj. m.s. (843) *for the righteous*
וּלְיִשְׁרֵי־ conj.-prep.-n.m.p. cstr. (449) *and for the upright in*
לֵב n.m.s. (524) *heart*
שִׂמְחָה n.f.s. (970) *joy*

97:12

שִׂמְחוּ Qal impv. 2 m.p. (970) *rejoice*
צַדִּיקִים adj. m.p. (843) *O you righteous*
בַּיהוה prep.-pr.n. (217) *in Yahweh*
וְהוֹדוּ conj.-Hi. impv. 2 m.p. (יָדָה 392) *and give thanks*
לְזֵכֶר קָדְשׁוֹ prep.-n.m.s. cstr. (271)-n.m.s.-3 m.s. sf. (871) *to his holy name*

98:1

מִזְמוֹר n.m.s. (274) *a Psalm*
שִׁירוּ Qal impv. 2 m.p. (שִׁיר 1010) *sing*
לַיהוה prep.-pr.n. (217) *to Yahweh*
שִׁיר חָדָשׁ n.m.s. (1010)-adj. m.s. (I 294) *a new song*
כִּי־נִפְלָאוֹת conj. (471)-Ni. ptc. f.p. (פָּלָא 810) *for marvelous things*
עָשָׂה Qal pf. 3 m.s. (I 793) *he has done*
הוֹשִׁיעָה־ Hi. pf. 3 f.s. (יָשַׁע 446) *have gotten victory*
לוֹ prep.-3 m.s. sf. *for him*
יְמִינוֹ n.f.s.-3 m.s. sf. (411) *his right hand*
וּזְרוֹעַ conj.-n.f.s. cstr. (283) *and the arm of*
קָדְשׁוֹ n.m.s.-3 m.s. sf. (871) *his holiness*

98:2

הוֹדִיעַ Hi. pf. 3 m.s. (יָדַע 393) *has made known*
יהוה pr.n. (217) *Yahweh*
יְשׁוּעָתוֹ n.f.s.-3 m.s. sf. (447) *his victory*
לְעֵינֵי prep.-n.f. du. cstr. (744) *in the sight of*
הַגּוֹיִם def.art.-n.m.p. (156) *the nations*
גִּלָּה Pi. pf. 3 m.s. (162) *he has revealed*
צִדְקָתוֹ n.f.s.-3 m.s. sf. (842) *his vindication*

98:3

זָכַר Qal pf. 3 m.s. (269) *he has remembered*
חַסְדּוֹ n.m.s.-3 m.s. sf. (338) *his steadfast love*
וֶאֱמוּנָתוֹ conj.-n.f.s.-3 m.s. sf. (53) *and his faithfulness*
לְבֵית prep.-n.m.s. cstr. (108) *to the house of*
יִשְׂרָאֵל pr.n. (975) *Israel*
רָאוּ Qal pf. 3 c.p. (רָאָה 906) *have seen*
כָל־אַפְסֵי־ n.m.s. cstr. (481)-n.m.p. cstr. (67) *all the ends of*
אָרֶץ n.f.s. paus. (75) *the earth*
אֵת יְשׁוּעַת dir.obj.-n.f.s. cstr. (447) *the victory of*
אֱלֹהֵינוּ n.m.p.-1 c.p. sf. (43) *our God*

98:4

הָרִיעוּ Hi. impv. 2 m.p. (רוּעַ 929) *make a joyful noise*

לַיהוה prep.-pr.n. (217) *to Yahweh*
כָּל־הָאָרֶץ n.m.s. cstr. (481)-def.art.-n.f.s. (75) *all the earth*
פִּצְחוּ Qal impv. 2 m.p. (822) *break forth*
וְרַנְּנוּ conj.-Pi. impv. 2 m.p. (רָנַן 943) *give a ringing cry*
וְזַמֵּרוּ conj.-Pi. impv. 2 m.p. paus. (I 274) *and sing praises*

98:5

זַמְּרוּ Pi. impv. 2 m.p. (I 274) *sing praises*
לַיהוה prep.-pr.n. (217) *to Yahweh*
בְּכִנּוֹר prep.-n.m.s. (490) *with the lyre*
בְּכִנּוֹר v.supra *with the lyre*
וְקוֹל conj.-n.m.s. cstr. (876) *and the sound of*
זִמְרָה n.f.s. (I 271) *melody*

98:6

בַּחֲצֹצְרוֹת prep.-def.art.-n.f.p. (348) *with trumpets*
וְקוֹל conj.-n.m.s. cstr. (876) *and the sound of*
שׁוֹפָר n.m.s. (1051) *the horn*
הָרִיעוּ Hi. impv. 2 m.p. (רוּעַ 929) *make a joyful noise*
לִפְנֵי prep.-n.m.p. cstr. (815) *before*
הַמֶּלֶךְ def.art.-n.m.s. (I 572) *the king*
יהוה pr.n. (217) *Yahweh*

98:7

יִרְעַם Qal impf. 3 m.s. (רָעַם 947) *let roar*
הַיָּם def.art.-n.m.s. (410) *the sea*
וּמְלֹאוֹ conj.-n.m.s.-3 m.s. sf. (571) *and all that fills it*
תֵּבֵל n.f.s. (385) *the world*
וְיֹשְׁבֵי בָהּ conj.-Qal act.ptc. m.p. cstr. (יָשַׁב 442) -prep.-3 f.s. sf. *and those who dwell in it*

98:8

נְהָרוֹת n.m.p. (625) *the floods*
יִמְחֲאוּ־ Qal impf. 3 m.p. (מָחָא 561) *let clap*
כָף n.f.s. paus. (496) *their hands*
יַחַד adv. (403) *together*
הָרִים n.m.p. (249) *the hills*
יְרַנֵּנוּ Pi. impf. 3 m.p. paus. (רָנַן 943) *let sing for joy*

98:9

לִפְנֵי־ prep.-n.m.p. cstr. (815) *before*
יהוה pr.n. (217) *Yahweh*
כִּי בָא conj. (471)-Qal pf. 3 m.s. (בּוֹא 97) *for he comes*
לִשְׁפֹּט prep.-Qal inf.cstr. (1047) *to judge*
הָאָרֶץ def.art.-n.f.s. (75) *the earth*
יִשְׁפֹּט־ Qal impf. 3 m.s. (1047) *he will judge*
תֵּבֵל n.f.s. (385) *the world*
בְּצֶדֶק prep.-n.m.s. (841) *with righteousness*
וְעַמִּים conj.-n.m.p. (I 766) *and the peoples*
בְּמֵישָׁרִים prep.-n.m.p. (449) *with equity*

99:1

יהוה pr.n. (217) *Yahweh*
מָלָךְ Qal pf. 3 m.s.? (573) *reigns*
יִרְגְּזוּ Qal impf. 3 m.p. (919) *let tremble*
עַמִּים n.m.p. (I 766) *peoples*
יֹשֵׁב Qal act.ptc. (442) *he sits enthroned upon*
כְּרוּבִים adj. m.p. (500) *the cherubim*
תָּנוּט Qal impf. 3 f.s. (נוּט 630) *let quake*
הָאָרֶץ def.art.-n.f.s. (75) *the earth*

99:2

יהוה pr.n. (217) *Yahweh*
בְּצִיּוֹן prep.-pr.n. (851) *in Zion*
גָּדוֹל adj. m.s. (152) *is great*
וְרָם conj.-Qal act.ptc. (רוּם 926) *and is exalted*
הוּא pers.pr. 3 m.s. (214) *he*
עַל־כָּל־ prep.-n.m.s. cstr. (481) *over all*
הָעַמִּים def.art.-n.m.p. (I 766) *the peoples*

99:3

יוֹדוּ Hi. impf. 3 m.p. (יָדָה 392) *let them praise*
שִׁמְךָ n.m.s.-2 m.s. sf. (1027) *thy name*
גָּדוֹל adj. m.s. (152) *great*
וְנוֹרָא conj.-Ni. ptc. (יָרֵא 431) *and terrible*
קָדוֹשׁ adj. m.s. (872) *holy*
הוּא pers.pr. 3 m.s. (214) *is he*

99:4

וְעֹז מֶלֶךְ conj.-n.m.s. cstr. (738)-n.m.s. (I 572) *and the king's strength*
מִשְׁפָּט n.m.s. (1048) *justice*
אָהֵב Qal pf. 3 m.s. (12) *he loves*
אַתָּה כּוֹנַנְתָּ pers.pr. 2 m.s. (61)-Polel pf. 2 m.s. (465 כּוּן) *thou hast established*
מֵישָׁרִים n.m.p. (449) *uprightness*
מִשְׁפָּט v.supra *justice*
וּצְדָקָה conj.-n.f.s. (842) *and righteousness*
בְּיַעֲקֹב prep.-pr.n. (784) *in Jacob*
אַתָּה עָשִׂיתָ v.supra-Qal pf. 2 m.s. (עָשָׂה I 793) *thou hast executed*

99:5

רוֹמְמוּ Polel impv. 2 m.p. (רוּם 926) *extol*
יהוה pr.n. (217) *Yahweh*
אֱלֹהֵינוּ n.m.p.-1 c.p. sf. (43) *our God*

וְהִשְׁתַּחֲווּ conj.-Hith. impv. 2 m.p. (שָׁחָה 1005) *and worship*
לַהֲדֹם רַגְלָיו prep.-n.m.s. cstr. (213)-n.f. du.-3 m.s. sf. (919) *at his footstool*
קָדוֹשׁ adj. (872) *holy*
הוּא pers.pr. 3 m.s. (214) *is he*

99:6

מֹשֶׁה pr.n. (602) *Moses*
וְאַהֲרֹן conj.-pr.n. (14) *and Aaron*
בְּכֹהֲנָיו prep.-n.m.p.-3 m.s. sf. (463) *among his priests*
וּשְׁמוּאֵל conj.-pr.n. (1028) *Samuel also*
בְּקֹרְאֵי prep.-Qal act.ptc. m.p. cstr. (894) *among those who called on*
שְׁמוֹ n.m.s.-3 m.s. sf. (1027) *his name*
קֹרְאִים Qal act.ptc. m.p. (894; GK 74i,75oo,119i) *crying*
אֶל־יהוה prep.-pr.n. (217) *to Yahweh*
וְהוּא conj.-pers.pr. 3 m.s. (214) *and he*
יַעֲנֵם Qal impf. 3 m.s.-3 m.p. sf. (עָנָה I 772) *answered them*

99:7

בְּעַמּוּד prep.-n.m.s. cstr. (765) *in the pillar of*
עָנָן n.m.s. (777) *cloud*
יְדַבֵּר Pi. impf. 3 m.s. (180) *he spoke*
אֲלֵיהֶם prep.-3 m.p. sf. *to them*
שָׁמְרוּ Qal pf. 3 c.p. (1036) *they kept*
עֵדֹתָיו n.f.p.-3 m.s. sf. (I 729) *his testimonies*
וְחֹק conj.-n.m.s. (349) *and the statutes*
נָתַן־לָמוֹ Qal pf. 3 m.s. (678)-prep.-3 m.p. sf. *that he gave them*

99:8

יהוה pr.n. (217) *Yahweh*
אֱלֹהֵינוּ n.m.p.-1 c.p. sf. (43) *our God*
אַתָּה pers.pr. 2 m.s. (61) *thou*
עֲנִיתָם Qal pf. 2 m.s.-3 m.p. sf. (עָנָה I 772) *thou didst answer them*
אֵל נֹשֵׂא n.m.s. (42)-Qal act.ptc. (669) *a forgiving God*
הָיִיתָ לָהֶם Qal pf. 2 m.s. (הָיָה 224)-prep.-3 m.p. sf. *thou wast to them*
וְנֹקֵם conj.-Qal act.ptc. (667) *but an avenger*
עַל־עֲלִילוֹתָם prep.-n.f.p.-3 m.p. sf. (760) *of their wrongdoings*

99:9

רוֹמְמוּ Polel impv. 2 m.p. (רוּם 926) *extol*
יהוה pr.n. (217) *Yahweh*
אֱלֹהֵינוּ n.m.p.-1 c.p. sf. (43) *our God*
וְהִשְׁתַּחֲווּ conj.-Hith. impv. 2 m.p. (שָׁחָה 1005) *and worship*
לְהַר קָדְשׁוֹ prep.-n.m.s. cstr. (249)-n.m.s.-3 m.s. sf. (871) *at his holy mountain*
כִּי־קָדוֹשׁ conj.-adj. (872) *for is holy*
יהוה pr.n. (217) *Yahweh*
אֱלֹהֵינוּ v.supra *our God*

100:1

מִזְמוֹר n.m.s. (274) *a Psalm*
לְתוֹדָה prep.-n.f.s. (392) *for the thank offering*
הָרִיעוּ Hi. impv. 2 m.p. (רוּעַ 929) *make a joyful noise*
לַיהוה prep.-pr.n. (217) *to Yahweh*
כָּל־הָאָרֶץ n.m.s. cstr. (481)-def.art.-n.f.s. (75) *all the earth*

100:2

עִבְדוּ -Qal impv. 2 m.p. (712) *serve*
אֶת־יהוה dir.obj.-pr.n. (217) *Yahweh*
בְּשִׂמְחָה prep.-n.f.s. (970) *with gladness*
בֹּאוּ Qal impv. 2 m.p. (בּוֹא 97) *come*
לְפָנָיו prep.-n.m.p.-3 m.s. sf. (815) *into his presence*
בִּרְנָנָה prep.-n.f.s. (943) *with singing*

100:3

דְּעוּ Qal impv. 2 m.p. (יָדַע 393) *know*
כִּי־יהוה conj. (471)-pr.n. (217) *that Yahweh*
הוּא pers.pr. 3 m.s. (214) *he is*
אֱלֹהִים n.m.p. (43) *God*
הוּא עָשָׂנוּ v.supra-Qal pf. 3 m.s.-1 c.p. sf. (עָשָׂה I 793) *it is he that made us*
וְלֹא אֲנַחְנוּ conj.-neg. (GK 103g)-pers.pr. 1 c.p. (59) *and not we ourselves*
עַמּוֹ n.m.s.-3 m.s. sf. (I 766) *his people*
וְצֹאן conj.-n.f.s. cstr. (838) *and the sheep of*
מַרְעִיתוֹ n.f.s.-3 m.s. sf. (945) *his pasture*

100:4

בֹּאוּ Qal impv. 2 m.p. (בּוֹא 97) *enter*
שְׁעָרָיו n.m.p.-3 m.s. sf. (1044) *his gates*
בְּתוֹדָה prep.-n.f.s. (392) *with thanksgiving*
חֲצֵרֹתָיו n.f.p.-3 m.s. sf. (I 346) *and his courts*
בִּתְהִלָּה prep.-n.f.s. (239) *with praise*
הוֹדוּ־ Hi. impv. 2 m.p. (יָדָה 392) *give thanks*
לוֹ prep.-3 m.s. sf. *to him*
בָּרְכוּ Pi. impv. 2 m.p. (בָּרַךְ 138) *bless*
שְׁמוֹ n.m.s.-3 m.s. sf. (1027) *his name*

100:5

כִּי־טוֹב conj.-adj. (II 373) *for is good*

יהוה pr.n. (217) *Yahweh*
לְעוֹלָם prep.-n.m.s. (761) *for ever*
חַסְדּוֹ n.m.s.-3 m.s. sf. (338) *his steadfast love*
וְעַד־דֹּר וָדֹר conj.-prep. (III 723)-n.m.s. (189)-conj.-v.supra *and to all generations*
אֱמוּנָתוֹ n.f.s.-3 m.s. sf. (53) *his faithfulness*

101:1

לְדָוִד prep.-pr.n. (187) *to David*
מִזְמוֹר n.m.s. (274) *a Psalm*
חֶסֶד־ n.m.s. (338) *of loyalty*
וּמִשְׁפָּט conj.-n.m.s. (1048) *and of justice*
אָשִׁירָה Qal impf. 1 c.s.-vol.he (שִׁיר 1010) *I will sing*
לְךָ prep.-2 m.s. sf. *to thee*
יהוה pr.n. (217) *O Yahweh*
אֲזַמֵּרָה Pi. impf. 1 c.s.-vol.he (זָמַר I 274) *I will sing*

101:2

אַשְׂכִּילָה Hi. impf. 1 c.s.-vol.he (שָׂכַל 968) *I will give heed*
בְּדֶרֶךְ prep.-n.m.s. cstr. (202) *to the way that*
תָּמִים adj. m.p. (1071) *is blameless*
מָתַי interr. (607) *when*
תָּבוֹא Qal impf. 2 m.s. (בּוֹא 97) *wilt thou come*
אֵלָי prep.-1 c.s. sf. paus. *to me*
אֶתְהַלֵּךְ Hith. impf. 1 c.s. (הָלַךְ 229) *I will walk*
בְּתָם־ prep.-n.m.s. cstr. (1070) *with integrity of*
לְבָבִי n.m.s.-1 c.s. sf. (523) *my heart*
בְּקֶרֶב בֵּיתִי prep.-n.m.s. cstr. (899)-n.m.s.-1 c.s. sf. (108) *within my house*

101:3

לֹא־אָשִׁית neg.-Qal impf. 1 c.s. (שִׁית 1011) *I will not set*
לְנֶגֶד עֵינַי prep.-n.m.s. cstr. (617)-n.f.p.-1 c.s. sf. (744) *before my eyes*
דְּבַר־ n.m.s. cstr. (182) *anything that*
בְּלִיָּעַל n.m.s. paus. (116) *is base*
עֲשֹׂה־ Qal inf.cstr. (עָשָׂה I 793) *the work of those who*
סֵטִים n.m.p. (962) *fall away*
שָׂנֵאתִי Qal pf. 1 c.s. (971) *I hate*
לֹא יִדְבַּק neg.-Qal impf. 3 m.s. (179) *it shall not cleave*
בִּי prep.-1 c.s. sf. *to me*

101:4

לֵבָב עִקֵּשׁ n.m.s. (523)-adj. m.s. (I 786) *a twisted heart*
יָסוּר Qal impf. 3 m.s. (סוּר 693) *shall be far*
מִמֶּנִּי prep.-1 c.s. sf. *from me*
רָע n.m.s. (II 948) *evil*
לֹא אֵדָע neg.-Qal impf. 1 c.s. (יָדַע 393) *I will know not*

101:5

מְלוֹשְׁנִי Po'el ptc. (לָשַׁן 546; GK 55b,64i,90m) *him who slanders*
בַסֵּתֶר prep.-def.art.-n.m.s. (712) *in secret*
רֵעֵהוּ n.m.s.-3 m.s. sf. (945) *his neighbor*
אוֹתוֹ dir.obj.-3 m.s. sf. *him*
אַצְמִית Hi. impf. 1 c.s. (צָמַת 856) *I will destroy*
גְּבַהּ־עֵינַיִם adj. m.s. cstr. (147)-n.f. du. (744) *haughty of eyes*
וּרְחַב לֵבָב conj.-adj. m.s. cstr. (I 932)-n.m.s. (523) *and arrogant of heart*
אֹתוֹ dir.obj.-3 m.s. sf. *him*
לֹא אוּכָל neg.-Qal impf. 1 c.s. (יָכֹל 407) *I will not endure (I cannot)*

101:6

עֵינַי n.f. du.-1 c.s. sf. (744) *my eyes*
בְּנֶאֶמְנֵי־אֶרֶץ prep.-Ni. ptc. m.p. cstr. (אָמַן I 52)-n.f.s. (75) *on the faithful of the land*
לָשֶׁבֶת prep.-Qal inf.cstr. (יָשַׁב 442) *that they may dwell*
עִמָּדִי prep.-1 c.s. sf. (767) *with me*
הֹלֵךְ Qal act.ptc. (הָלַךְ 229) *he who walks*
בְּדֶרֶךְ תָּמִים prep.-n.m.s. (202)-adj. (1071) *in the way that is blameless*
הוּא יְשָׁרְתֵנִי pers.pr. 3 m.s. (214)-Pi. impf. 3 m.s. -1 c.s. sf. (שָׁרַת 1058) *he shall minister to me*

101:7

לֹא־יֵשֵׁב neg.-Qal impf. 3 m.s. (יָשַׁב 442) *shall not dwell*
בְּקֶרֶב בֵּיתִי prep.-n.m.s. cstr. (899)-n.m.s.-1 c.s. sf. (108) *in my house*
עֹשֵׂה רְמִיָּה Qal act.ptc. m.s. cstr. (עָשָׂה I 793) -n.f.s. (I 941) *he who practices deceit*
דֹּבֵר שְׁקָרִים Qal act.ptc. m.s. cstr. (דָּבַר 180) -n.m.p. (1055) *he who utters lies*
לֹא־יִכּוֹן neg.-Ni. impf. 3 m.s. (כּוּן 465) *shall not continue*
לְנֶגֶד עֵינָי prep.-n.m.s. cstr. (617)-n.f. du.-1 c.s. sf. paus. (744) *in my presence*

101:8

לַבְּקָרִים prep.-def.art.-n.m.p. (133) *in the mornings*
אַצְמִית Hi. impf. 1 c.s. (צָמַת 856) *I will destroy*

כָּל־רִשְׁעֵי־ n.m.s. cstr. (481)-adj. m.p. cstr. (957) *all the wicked of*
אָרֶץ n.f.s. paus. (75) *the land*
לְהַכְרִית prep.-Hi. inf.cstr. (כָּרַת 503) *cutting off*
מֵעִיר־יהוה prep.-n.f.s. cstr. (746)-pr.n. (217) *from the city of Yahweh*
כָּל־פֹּעֲלֵי n.m.s. cstr. (481)-Qal act.ptc. m.p. cstr. (821 פָּעַל) *all the doers of*
אָוֶן n.m.s. (19) *evil*

102:1

תְּפִלָּה n.f.s. (813) *a prayer*
לְעָנִי prep.-adj. m.s. (776) *of one afflicted*
כִּי־יַעֲטֹף conj. (471)-Qal impf. 3 m.s. (III 742) *when he is faint*
וְלִפְנֵי יהוה conj.-prep.-n.m.p. cstr. (815)-pr.n. (217) *and before Yahweh*
יִשְׁפֹּךְ Qal impf. 3 m.s. (1049) *he pours out*
שִׂיחוֹ n.m.s.-3 m.s. sf. (I 967) *his complaint*

102:2

יהוה pr.n. (217) *O Yahweh*
שִׁמְעָה Qal impv. 2 m.s.-vol.he (1033) *hear*
תְפִלָּתִי n.f.s.-1 c.s. sf. (813) *my prayer*
וְשַׁוְעָתִי conj.-n.f.s.-1 c.s. sf. (1003) *and my cry*
אֵלֶיךָ prep.-2 m.s. sf. *to thee*
תָבוֹא Qal impf. 3 f.s. (בּוֹא 97) *let come*

102:3

אַל־תַּסְתֵּר neg.-Hi. impf. 2 m.s. (711) *do not hide*
פָּנֶיךָ n.m.p.-2 m.s. sf. (815) *thy face*
מִמֶּנִּי prep.-1 c.s. sf. *from me*
בְּיוֹם prep.-n.m.s. cstr. (398) *in the day of*
צַר n.m.s. (II 865) *distress*
לִי prep.-1 c.s. sf. *to me*
הַטֵּה־אֵלַי Hi. impv. 2 m.s. (נָטָה 639)-prep.-1 c.s. sf. *incline to me*
אָזְנֶךָ n.f.s.-2 m.s. sf. (23) *thy ear*
בְּיוֹם v.supra *in the day when*
אֶקְרָא Qal impf. 1 c.s. (894) *I call*
מַהֵר adv. (II 555) *speedily*
עֲנֵנִי Qal impv. 2 m.s.-1 c.s. sf. (עָנָה I 772) *answer me*

102:4

כִּי־כָלוּ conj. (471)-Qal pf. 3 c.p. (כָּלָה 477) *for pass away*
בְעָשָׁן prep.-n.m.s. (I 798) *like smoke*
יָמָי n.m.p.-1 c.s. sf. paus. (398) *my days*
וְעַצְמוֹתַי conj.-n.f.p.-1 c.s. sf. (782) *and my bones*
כְּמוֹ־קֵד prep. (455)-unknown word (prb. כְּמוֹקֵד n.m.s. 428) *like a burning mass*
נִחָרוּ Ni. pf. 3 c.p. paus. (חָרַר I 359; GK 67u) *burn*

102:5

הוּכָּה־ Ho. pf. 3 m.s. (נָכָה 645) *is smitten*
כָעֵשֶׂב prep.-def.art.-n.m.s. (793) *like grass*
וַיִּבַשׁ consec.-Qal impf. 3 m.s. (יָבֵשׁ I 386) *and withered*
לִבִּי n.m.s.-1 c.s. sf. (524) *my heart*
כִּי־שָׁכַחְתִּי conj. (471)-Qal pf. 1 c.s. (1013) *for I forget*
מֵאֲכֹל prep.-Qal inf.cstr. (37) *to eat*
לַחְמִי n.m.s.-1 c.s. sf. (536) *my bread*

102:6

מִקּוֹל אַנְחָתִי prep.-n.m.s. cstr. (876)-n.f.s.-1 c.s. sf. (58) *because of my loud groaning*
דָּבְקָה Qal pf. 3 f.s. (179) *cleave*
עַצְמִי n.f.s.-1 c.s. sf. (782) *my bones*
לִבְשָׂרִי prep.-n.m.s.-1 c.s. sf. (142) *to my flesh*

102:7

דָּמִיתִי Qal pf. 1 c.s. (דָּמָה 197) *I am like*
לִקְאַת מִדְבָּר prep.-n.f.s. cstr. (866)-n.m.s. (II 184) *to a bird of the wilderness*
הָיִיתִי Qal pf. 1 c.s. (הָיָה 224) *I am*
כְּכוֹס prep.-n.m.s. cstr. (II 468) *like an owl of*
חֳרָבוֹת n.f.p. (352) *waste places*

102:8

שָׁקַדְתִּי Qal pf. 1 c.s. (1052) *I lie awake*
וָאֶהְיֶה consec.-Qal impf. 1 c.s. (הָיָה 224) *and I am*
כְּצִפּוֹר prep.-n.f.s. (861) *like a bird*
בּוֹדֵד Qal act.ptc. (I 94) *lonely*
עַל־גָּג prep.-n.m.s. (150) *on the housetop*

102:9

כָּל־הַיּוֹם n.m.s. cstr. (481)-def.art.-n.m.s. (398) *all the day*
חֵרְפוּנִי Pi. pf. 3 c.p.-1 c.s. sf. (חָרַף 357) *taunt me*
אוֹיְבָי Qal act.ptc. m.p.-1 c.s. sf. (אָיַב 33) *my enemies*
מְהוֹלָלַי Po'al ptc. m.p.-1 c.s. sf. (הָלַל II 237; GK 116i) *those who deride me*
בִּי prep.-1 c.s. sf. *at me*
נִשְׁבָּעוּ Ni. pf. 3 c.p. paus. (989) *swear*

102:10

כִּי־אֵפֶר conj. (471)-n.m.s. (68) *for ashes*

כַּלֶּחֶם prep.-def.art.-n.m.s. (536) *like bread*
אָכָלְתִּי Qal pf. 1 c.s. paus. (37) *I eat*
וְשִׁקֻּוַי conj.-n.m.p.-1 c.s. sf. (1052) *and my drink*
בִּבְכִי prep.-n.m.s. (113) *with tears*
מָסָכְתִּי Qal pf. 1 c.s. paus. (587) *I mingle*

102:11

מִפְּנֵי־זַעַמְךָ prep.-n.m.p. cstr. (815)-n.m.s.-2 m.s. sf. (276) *because of thy indignation*
וְקִצְפֶּךָ conj.-n.m.s.-2 m.s. sf. (893) *and anger*
כִּי נְשָׂאתַנִי conj. (471)-Qal pf. 2 m.s.-1 c.s. sf. (669 נָשָׂא) *for thou hast taken me up*
וַתַּשְׁלִיכֵנִי consec.-Hi. impf. 2 m.s.-1 c.s. sf. (שָׁלַךְ 1020) *and thrown me away*

102:12

יָמַי n.m.p.-1 c.s. sf. (398) *my days*
כְּצֵל נָטוּי prep.-n.m.s. (853)-Qal pass.ptc. (נָטָה 639) *like an evening shadow*
וַאֲנִי conj.-pers.pr. 1 c.s. (58) *and I*
כָּעֵשֶׂב prep.-def.art.-n.m.s. (793) *like grass*
אִיבָשׁ Qal impf. 1 c.s. (יָבֵשׁ 386) *I wither*

102:13

וְאַתָּה conj.-pers.pr. 2 m.s. (61) *but thou*
יהוה pr.n. (217) *O Yahweh*
לְעוֹלָם prep.-n.m.s. (761) *for ever*
תֵּשֵׁב Qal impf. 2 m.s. (יָשַׁב 442) *art enthroned*
וְזִכְרְךָ conj.-n.m.s.-2 m.s. sf. (271) *and thy remembrance*
לְדֹר וָדֹר prep.-n.m.s. (189)-conj.-v.supra *to all generations*

102:14

אַתָּה תָקוּם pers.pr. 2 m.s. (61)-Qal impf. 2 m.s. (877 קוּם) *thou wilt arise*
תְּרַחֵם Pi. impf. 2 m.s. (רָחַם 933) *and have pity*
צִיּוֹן pr.n. (851) *on Zion*
כִּי־עֵת conj. (471)-n.f.s. (773) *for a time*
לְחֶנְנָהּ prep.-Qal inf.cstr.-3 f.s. sf. (חָנַן I 335; GK 67cc) *to favor her*
כִּי־בָא conj. (471)-Qal pf. 3 m.s. (בּוֹא 97) *for has come*
מוֹעֵד n.m.s. (417) *the time*

102:15

כִּי־רָצוּ conj. (471)-Qal pf. 3 c.p. (רָצָה 953) *for hold dear*
עֲבָדֶיךָ n.m.p.-2 m.s. sf. (713) *thy servants*
אֶת־אֲבָנֶיהָ dir.obj.-n.f.p.-3 f.s. sf. (6) *her stones*
וְאֶת־עֲפָרָהּ conj.-dir.obj.-n.m.s.-3 f.s. sf. (779) *and her dust*

יְחֹנֵנוּ Po'el impf. 3 m.p. (חָנַן I 335) *they have pity on*

102:16

וְיִירְאוּ conj.-Qal impf. 3 m.p. (יָרֵא 431) *and will fear*
גוֹיִם n.m.p. (156) *nations*
אֶת־שֵׁם dir.obj.-n.m.s. cstr. (1027) *the name of*
יהוה pr.n. (217) *Yahweh*
וְכָל־מַלְכֵי conj.-n.m.s. cstr. (481)-n.m.p. cstr. (I 572) *and all the kings of*
הָאָרֶץ def.art.-n.f.s. (75) *the earth*
אֶת־כְּבוֹדֶךָ dir.obj.-n.m.s.-2 m.s. sf. (II 458) *thy glory*

102:17

כִּי־בָנָה conj. (471)-Qal pf. 3 m.s. (124) *for will build up*
יהוה pr.n. (217) *Yahweh*
צִיּוֹן pr.n. (851) *Zion*
נִרְאָה Ni. pf. 3 m.s. (רָאָה 906) *he will appear*
בִּכְבוֹדוֹ prep.-n.m.s.-3 m.s. sf. (458) *in his glory*

102:18

פָּנָה Qal pf. 3 m.s. (815) *he will regard*
אֶל־תְּפִלַּת prep.-n.f.s. cstr. (813) *the prayer of*
הָעַרְעָר def.art.-adj. m.s. paus. (792) *the destitute*
וְלֹא־בָזָה conj.-neg.-Qal pf. 3 m.s. (102) *and will not despise*
אֶת־תְּפִלָּתָם dir.obj.-n.f.s.-3 m.p. sf. (813) *their supplication*

102:19

תִּכָּתֶב Ni. impf. 3 f.s. (כָּתַב 507) *let be recorded*
זֹאת demons.adj. f.s. (260) *this*
לְדוֹר prep.-n.m.s. (189) *for a generation*
אַחֲרוֹן adj. m.s. (30) *to come*
וְעַם נִבְרָא conj.-n.m.s. (I 766)-Ni. ptc. (I 135; GK 116e) *so that a people yet unborn*
יְהַלֶּל־ Pi. impf. 3 m.s. (הָלַל II 237) *may praise*
יָהּ pr.n. (219) *Yah*

102:20

כִּי־הִשְׁקִיף conj. (471)-Hi. pf. 3 m.s. (I 1054) *that he looked down*
מִמְּרוֹם prep.-n.m.s. cstr. (928) *from the height of*
קָדְשׁוֹ n.m.s.-3 m.s. sf. (871) *his holiness*
יהוה pr.n. (217) *Yahweh*
מִשָּׁמַיִם prep.-n.m. du. (1029) *from heaven*
אֶל־אֶרֶץ prep.-n.f.s. (75) *at earth*
הִבִּיט Hi. pf. 3 m.s. (נָבַט 613) *looked*

102:21
לִשְׁמֹעַ prep.-Qal inf.cstr. (1033) *to hear*
אֶנְקַת n.f.s. cstr. (60) *the groans of*
אָסִיר n.m.s. (64) *the prisoners*
לְפַתֵּחַ prep.-Pi. inf.cstr. (פָּתַח I 834) *to set free*
בְּנֵי תְמוּתָה n.m.p. cstr. (119)-n.f.s. (560) *those who were doomed to die*

102:22
לְסַפֵּר prep.-Pi. inf.cstr. (707) *that men may declare*
בְּצִיּוֹן prep.-pr.n. (851) *in Zion*
שֵׁם יהוה n.m.s. cstr. (1027)-pr.n. (217) *the name of Yahweh*
וּתְהִלָּתוֹ conj.-n.f.s.-3 m.s. sf. (239) *and his praise*
בִּירוּשָׁלָ͏ִם prep.-pr.n. paus. (436) *in Jerusalem*

102:23
בְּהִקָּבֵץ prep.-Ni. inf.cstr. (867) *when gather*
עַמִּים n.m.p. (I 766) *peoples*
יַחְדָּו adv. (403) *together*
וּמַמְלָכוֹת conj.-n.f.p. (575) *and kingdoms*
לַעֲבֹד prep.-Qal inf.cstr. (712) *to worship*
אֶת־יהוה dir.obj.-pr.n. (217) *Yahweh*

102:24
עִנָּה Pi. pf. 3 m.s. (III 776) *he has broken*
בַדֶּרֶךְ prep.-def.art.-n.m.s. (202) *in mid-course*
כֹּחוֹ n.m.s.-1 c.s. sf. (470) *my strength*
קִצַּר Pi. pf. 3 m.s. (894) *he has shortened*
יָמָי n.m.p.-1 c.s. sf. paus. *(398) my days*

102:25
אֹמַר Qal impf. 1 c.s. (55) *I say*
אֵלִי n.m.s.-1 c.s. sf. (42) *O my God*
אַל־תַּעֲלֵנִי neg.-Hi. impf. 2 m.s.-1 c.s. sf. (עָלָה 748) *take me not hence*
בַּחֲצִי יָמָי prep.-n.m.s. cstr. (345)-n.m.p.-1 c.s. sf. (398) *in the midst of my days*
בְּדוֹר דּוֹרִים prep.-n.m.s. cstr. (189)-n.m.p. (189) *throughout all generations*
שְׁנוֹתֶיךָ n.f.p.-2 m.s. sf. (1040) *thy years*

102:26
לְפָנִים prep.-n.m.p. (815) *of old*
הָאָרֶץ def.art.-n.f.s. (75) *the earth*
יָסַדְתָּ Qal pf. 2 m.s. (יָסַד 413) *thou didst lay the foundation of*
וּמַעֲשֵׂה conj.-n.m.s. cstr. (795) *and the work of*
יָדֶיךָ n.f.p.-2 m.s. sf. (388) *thy hands*
שָׁמָיִם n.m. du. paus. (1029) *the heavens*

102:27
הֵמָּה יֹאבֵדוּ pers.pr. 3 m.p. (241)-Qal impf. 3 m.p. (1) *they will perish*
וְאַתָּה תַעֲמֹד conj.-pers.pr. 2 m.s. (61)-Qal impf. 2 m.s. (763) *but thou dost endure*
וְכֻלָּם conj.-n.m.s.-3 m.p. sf. (481) *and all of them*
כַּבֶּגֶד prep.-def.art.-n.m.s. (93) *like a garment*
יִבְלוּ Qal impf. 3 m.p. (בָּלָה 115) *will wear out*
כַּלְּבוּשׁ prep.-def.art.-n.m.s. (528) *like raiment*
תַּחֲלִיפֵם Hi. impf. 2 m.s.-3 m.p. sf. (חָלַף 322) *thou changest them*
וְיַחֲלֹפוּ conj.-Qal impf. 3 m.p. (322) *and they pass away*

102:28
וְאַתָּה־הוּא conj.-pers.pr. 2 m.s. (61; GK 135aN) -demons.adj. m.s. (214) *but thou art the same*
וּשְׁנוֹתֶיךָ conj.-n.f.p.-2 m.s. sf. (1040) *and thy years*
לֹא יִתָּמּוּ neg.-Qal impf. 3 m.p. (תָּמַם 1070; GK 67g) *have no end*

102:29
בְּנֵי־עֲבָדֶיךָ n.m.p. cstr. (119)-n.m.p.-2 m.s. sf. (713) *the children of thy servants*
יִשְׁכּוֹנוּ Qal impf. 3 m.p. paus. (שָׁכַן 1014) *shall dwell secure*
וְזַרְעָם conj.-n.m.s.-3 m.p. sf. (282) *and their posterity*
לְפָנֶיךָ prep.-n.m.p.-2 m.s. sf. (815) *before thee*
יִכּוֹן Ni. impf. 3 m.s. (כּוּן 465) *shall be established*

103:1
לְדָוִד prep.-pr.n. (187) *to David*
בָּרְכִי Pi. impv. 2 f.s. (138; GK 10g) *bless thou*
נַפְשִׁי n.f.s.-1 c.s. sf. (659) *O my soul*
אֶת־יהוה dir.obj.-pr.n. (217) *Yahweh*
וְכָל־קְרָבַי conj.-n.m.s. cstr. (481)-n.m.p.-1 c.s. sf. (899) *and all that is within me*
אֶת־שֵׁם dir.obj.-n.m.s. cstr. (1027) *the name of*
קָדְשׁוֹ n.m.s.-3 m.s. sf. (871) *his holiness*

103:2
בָּרְכִי Pi. impv. 2 f.s. (138) *bless*
נַפְשִׁי n.f.s.-1 c.s. sf. (659) *O my soul*
אֶת־יהוה dir.obj.-pr.n. (217) *Yahweh*
וְאַל־תִּשְׁכְּחִי conj.-neg.-Qal impf. 2 f.s. (1013) *and forget not*
כָּל־גְּמוּלָיו n.m.s. cstr. (481)-n.m.p.-3 m.s. sf. (168) *all his benefits*

103:3

הַסֹּלֵחַ def.art.-Qal act.ptc. (699) *who forgives*
לְכָל־עֲוֹנֵכִי prep.-n.m.s. cstr. (481)-n.m.s.-2 f.s. sf. (730; GK 91e,l) *all your iniquity*
הָרֹפֵא def.art.-Qal act.ptc. (950) *who heals*
לְכָל־תַּחֲלֻאָיְכִי prep.-n.m.s. cstr. (481)-n.m.p.-2 f.s. sf. (316; GK 91,l) *all your diseases*

103:4

הַגּוֹאֵל def.art.-Qal act.ptc. (I 145) *who redeems*
מִשַּׁחַת prep.-n.f.s. (1001) *from the Pit*
חַיָּיְכִי n.m.p.-2 f.s. sf. (313) *your life*
הַמְעַטְּרֵכִי def.art.-Pi. ptc. m.s.-2 f.s. sf. (742; GK 58g) *who crowns you*
חֶסֶד n.m.s. (338) *with steadfast love*
וְרַחֲמִים conj.-n.m.p. (933) *and mercy*

103:5

הַמַּשְׂבִּיעַ def.art.-Hi. ptc. (959) *who satisfies*
בַּטּוֹב prep.-def.art.-n.m.s. (III 375) *with good*
עֶדְיֵךְ n.m.s.-2 f.s. sf. (725) *your ornaments*
תִּתְחַדֵּשׁ Hith. impf. 2 m.s. (293; GK 145k,156d) *so that you renew*
כַּנֶּשֶׁר prep.-def.art.-n.m.s. (676) *like the eagle*
נְעוּרָיְכִי n.f.p.-2 f.s. sf. (655) *your youth*

103:6

עֹשֵׂה Qal act.ptc. m.s. cstr. (I 793) *works*
צְדָקוֹת n.f.p. (842) *vindication*
יהוה pr.n. (217) *Yahweh*
וּמִשְׁפָּטִים conj.-n.m.p. (1048) *and justice*
לְכָל־עֲשׁוּקִים prep.-n.m.s. cstr. (481)-Qal pass.ptc. m.p. (798) *for all who are oppressed*

103:7

יוֹדִיעַ Hi. impf. 3 m.s. (יָדַע 393) *he made known*
דְּרָכָיו n.m.p.-3 m.s. sf. (202) *his ways*
לְמֹשֶׁה prep.-pr.n. (602) *to Moses*
לִבְנֵי יִשְׂרָאֵל prep.-n.m.p. cstr. (119)-pr.n. (975) *to the people of Israel*
עֲלִילוֹתָיו n.f.p.-3 m.s. sf. (760) *his acts*

103:8

רַחוּם adj. (933) *merciful*
וְחַנּוּן conj.-adj. (337) *and gracious*
יהוה pr.n. (217) *Yahweh*
אֶרֶךְ אַפַּיִם adj. m.s. cstr. (74)-n.m. du. (I 60) *slow to anger*
וְרַב־חָסֶד conj.-adj. m.s. cstr. (I 912)-n.m.s. (338) *and abounding in steadfast love*

103:9

לֹא־לָנֶצַח neg.-prep.-n.m.s. (664) *not always*
יָרִיב Qal impf. 3 m.s. (רִיב 936) *he will chide*
וְלֹא לְעוֹלָם conj.-neg.-prep.-n.m.s. (761) *and not for ever*
יִטּוֹר Qal impf. 3 m.s. (נָטַר 643; GK 117g) *will he keep*

103:10

לֹא כַחֲטָאֵינוּ neg.-prep.-n.m.p.-1 c.p. sf. (307) *not according to our sins*
עָשָׂה לָנוּ Qal pf. 3 m.s. (I 793)-prep.-1 c.p. sf. *he deals with us*
וְלֹא כַעֲוֹנֹתֵינוּ conj.-neg.-prep.-n.m.p.-1 c.p. sf. (730) *and not according to our iniquities*
גָּמַל עָלֵינוּ Qal pf. 3 m.s. (168)-prep.-1 c.p. sf. *does he requite us*

103:11

כִּי כִגְבֹהַּ conj. (471)-prep.-adj. cstr. (147) *for the height of*
שָׁמַיִם n.m. du. (1029) *the heavens*
עַל־הָאָרֶץ prep.-def.art.-n.f.s. (75) *above the earth*
גָּבַר Qal pf. 3 m.s. (149) *so great is*
חַסְדּוֹ n.m.s.-3 m.s. sf. (338) *his steadfast love*
עַל־יְרֵאָיו prep.-Qal act.ptc. m.p.-3 m.s. sf. (יָרֵא 431) *those who fear him*

103:12

כִּרְחֹק prep.-Qal inf.cstr. (934) *as far as*
מִזְרָח n.m.s. (280) *the east*
מִמַּעֲרָב prep.-n.m.s. (II 788) *from the west*
הִרְחִיק Hi. pf. 3 m.s. (934) *so far does he remove*
מִמֶּנּוּ prep.-1 c.p. sf. *from us*
אֶת־פְּשָׁעֵינוּ dir.obj.-n.m.p.-1 c.p. sf. (833) *our transgressions*

103:13

כְּרַחֵם prep.-Pi. inf.cstr. (933) *as pities*
אָב n.m.s. (3) *a father*
עַל־בָּנִים prep.-n.m.p. (119) *his children*
רִחַם יהוה Pi. pf. 3 m.s. (933)-pr.n. (217) *so Yahweh pities*
עַל־יְרֵאָיו prep.-Qal act.ptc. m.p.-3 m.s. sf. (יָרֵא 431) *those who fear him*

103:14

כִּי־הוּא יָדַע conj. (471)-pers.pr. 3 m.s. (214)-Qal pf. 3 m.s. (393) *for he knows*
יִצְרֵנוּ n.m.s.-1 c.p. sf. (428) *our frame*

זָכוּר Qal pass.ptc. (269) *he remembers*
כִּי־עָפָר conj. (471)-n.m.s. (779) *that dust*
אֲנָחְנוּ pers.pr. 1 c.p. paus. *(59) we are*

103:15

אֱנוֹשׁ n.m.s. (60) *as for man*
כֶּחָצִיר prep.-def.art.-n.m.s. (II 348) *like grass*
יָמָיו n.m.p.-3 m.s. sf. (398) *his days*
כְּצִיץ prep.-n.m.s. cstr. (I 847) *like a flower of*
הַשָּׂדֶה def.art.-n.m.s. (961) *the field*
כֵּן יָצִיץ adv. (485)-Qal impf. 3 m.s. (צוּץ I 847) *thus he flourishes*

103:16

כִּי רוּחַ conj. (471)-n.f.s. (924) *for the wind*
עָבְרָה־בּוֹ Qal pf. 3 f.s. (716)-prep.-3 m.s. sf. *passes over it*
וְאֵינֶנּוּ conj.-neg.-3 m.s. sf. (II 34) *and it is gone*
וְלֹא־יַכִּירֶנּוּ conj.-neg.-Hi. impf. 3 m.s.-3 m.s. sf. (נָכַר 647) *and knows it not*
עוֹד adv. (728) *any more*
מְקוֹמוֹ n.m.s.-3 m.s. sf. (879) *its place*

103:17

וְחֶסֶד יהוה conj.-n.m.s. cstr. (338)-pr.n. (217) *but the steadfast love of Yahweh*
מֵעוֹלָם prep.-n.m.s. (761) *from everlasting*
וְעַד־עוֹלָם conj.-prep. (III 723)-v.supra *to everlasting*
עַל־יְרֵאָיו prep.-Qal act.ptc. m.p.-3 m.s. sf. (יָרֵא 431) *upon those who fear him*
וְצִדְקָתוֹ conj.-n.f.s.-3 m.s. sf. (842) *and his righteousness*
לִבְנֵי בָנִים prep.-n.m.p. cstr. (119)-n.m.p. (119) *to children's children*

103:18

לְשֹׁמְרֵי prep.-Qal act.ptc. m.p. cstr. (1036) *to those who keep*
בְרִיתוֹ n.f.s.-3 m.s. sf. (136) *his covenant*
וּלְזֹכְרֵי conj.-prep.-Qal act.ptc. m.p. cstr. (269) *and remember*
פִקֻּדָיו n.m.p.-3 m.s. sf. (824) *his commandments*
לַעֲשׂוֹתָם prep.-Qal inf.cstr.-3 m.p. sf. (עָשָׂה I 793) *to do them*

103:19

יהוה pr.n. (217) *Yahweh*
בַּשָּׁמַיִם prep.-def.art.-n.m. du. (1029) *in the heavens*
הֵכִין Hi. pf. 3 m.s. (כּוּן 465) *has established*
כִּסְאוֹ n.m.s.-3 m.s. sf. (490) *his throne*
וּמַלְכוּתוֹ conj.-n.f.s.-3 m.s. sf. (574) *and his kingdom*
בַּכֹּל prep.-def.art.-n.m.s. (481) *over all*
מָשָׁלָה Qal pf. 3 f.s. paus. (מָשַׁל 605) *rules*

103:20

בָּרְכוּ Pi. impv. 2 m.p. (138) *bless you*
יהוה pr.n. (217) *Yahweh*
מַלְאָכָיו n.m.p.-3 m.s. sf. (521) *O his angels*
גִּבֹּרֵי כֹחַ adj. m.p. cstr. (150)-n.m.s. (470) *mighty ones*
עֹשֵׂי Qal act.ptc. m.p. cstr. (עָשָׂה I 793) *who do*
דְבָרוֹ n.m.s.-3 m.s. sf. (182) *his word*
לִשְׁמֹעַ prep.-Qal inf.cstr. (1033) *hearkening*
בְּקוֹל דְּבָרוֹ prep.-n.m.s. cstr. (876)-v.supra *to the voice of his word*

103:21

בָּרְכוּ Pi. impv. 2 m.p. (138) *bless*
יהוה pr.n. (217) *Yahweh*
כָּל־צְבָאָיו n.m.s. cstr. (481)-n.m.p.-3 m.s. sf. (838) *all his hosts*
מְשָׁרְתָיו Pi. ptc. m.p.-3 m.s. sf. (שָׁרַת 1058) *his ministers*
עֹשֵׂי Qal act.ptc. m.p. cstr. (עָשָׂה I 793) *that do*
רְצוֹנוֹ n.m.s.-3 m.s. sf. (953) *his will*

103:22

בָּרְכוּ Pi. impv. 2 m.p. (138) *bless*
יהוה pr.n. (217) *Yahweh*
כָּל־מַעֲשָׂיו n.m.s. cstr. (481)-n.m.p.-3 m.s. sf. (795) *all his works*
בְּכָל־מְקֹמוֹת prep.-v.supra-n.m.p. cstr. (879) *in all places of*
מֶמְשַׁלְתּוֹ n.f.s.-3 m.s. sf. (606) *his dominion*
בָּרְכוּ Pi. impv. 2 m.p. (138) *bless*
נַפְשִׁי n.f.s.-1 c.s. sf. (659) *O my soul*
אֶת־יהוה dir.obj.-pr.n. (217) *Yahweh*

104:1

בָּרְכִי Pi. impv. 2 f.s. (138) *bless*
נַפְשִׁי n.f.s.-1 c.s. sf. (659) *O my soul*
אֶת־יהוה dir.obj.-pr.n. (217) *Yahweh*
יהוה v.supra *O Yahweh*
אֱלֹהַי n.m.p.-1 c.s. sf. (43) *my God*
גָּדַלְתָּ Qal pf. 2 m.s. (152; GK 106g) *thou art ... great*
מְאֹד adv. (547) *very*
הוֹד וְהָדָר n.m.s. (217)-conj.-n.m.s. (214) *honor and majesty*
לָבָשְׁתָּ Qal pf. 2 m.s. paus. (לָבַשׁ 527) *thou art clothed with*

104:2

עֹטֶה־ Qal act.ptc. (עָטָה I 741) *who coverest thyself with*
אוֹר n.m.p. (21) *light*
כַּשַּׂלְמָה prep.-def.art.-n.f.s. (II 971) *as with a garment*
נוֹטֶה Qal act.ptc. (639) *who hast stretched out*
שָׁמַיִם n.m. du. (1029) *the heavens*
כַּיְרִיעָה prep.-def.art.-n.f.s. (438) *like a tent*

104:3

הַמְקָרֶה def.art.-Pi. ptc. (קָרָה 900; GK 20mN) *who has laid the beams*
בַמַּיִם prep.-def.art.-n.m.p. (565) *on the waters*
עֲלִיּוֹתָיו n.f.p.-3 m.s. sf. (751) *his chambers*
הַשָּׂם־ def.art.-Qal act.ptc. (שׂוּם 962) *who makest*
עָבִים n.m.p. (728) *clouds*
רְכוּבוֹ n.m.s.-3 m.s. sf. (939) *his chariot*
הַמְהַלֵּךְ def.art.-Pi. ptc. (הָלַךְ 229; GK 35b,126b) *who walkest*
עַל־כַּנְפֵי־רוּחַ prep.-n.f.p. cstr. (489)-n.f.s. (924) *on the wings of the wind*

104:4

עֹשֶׂה Qal act.ptc. (I 793) *who makest*
מַלְאָכָיו n.m.p.-3 m.s. sf. (521) *his messengers*
רוּחוֹת n.f.p. (924) *the winds*
מְשָׁרְתָיו Pi. ptc. m.p.-3 m.s. sf. (שָׁרַת 1058) *his ministers*
אֵשׁ לֹהֵט n.f.s. (77)-Qal act.ptc. (529) *a flaming fire*

104:5

יָסַד־ Qal pf. 3 m.s. (413) *he did set*
אֶרֶץ n.f.s. (75) *the earth*
עַל־מְכוֹנֶיהָ prep.-n.m.p.-3 f.s. sf. (467) *on its foundations*
בַּל־תִּמּוֹט neg. (115)-Ni. impf. 3 f.s. (מוֹט 556) *so that it should not be shaken*
עוֹלָם וָעֶד n.m.s. (761)-conj.-n.m.s. (I 723) *ever and ever*

104:6

תְּהוֹם n.f.s. (1062) *the deep*
כַּלְּבוּשׁ prep.-def.art.-n.m.s. (528) *as with the garment*
כִּסִּיתוֹ Pi. pf. 2 f.s.-3 m.s. sf. (כָּסָה 491) *thou didst cover it*
עַל־הָרִים prep.-n.m.p. (249) *above the mountains*
יַעַמְדוּ־ Qal impf. 3 m.p. (763) *stood*
מָיִם n.m.p. paus. (565) *the waters*

104:7

מִן־גַּעֲרָתְךָ prep.-n.f.s.-2 m.s. sf. (172) *at thy rebuke*
יְנוּסוּן Qal impf. 3 m.p. (נוּס 630) *they fled*
מִן־קוֹל רַעַמְךָ prep.-n.m.s. cstr. (876)-n.m.s.-2 m.s. sf. (947) *at the sound of thy thunder*
יֵחָפֵזוּן Ni. impf. 3 m.p. paus. (חָפַז 342) *they took to flight*

104:8

יַעֲלוּ Qal impf. 3 m.p. (עָלָה 748) *rose*
הָרִים n.m.p. (249) *the mountains*
יֵרְדוּ Qal impf. 3 m.p. (יָרַד 432) *sank down*
בְקָעוֹת n.f.p. (132) *the valleys*
אֶל־מְקוֹם זֶה prep.-n.m.s. cstr. (879)-demons.adj. m.s. as rel. (260; GK 138g) *to the place which*
יָסַדְתָּ Qal pf. 2 m.s. (יָסַד 413) *thou didst appoint*
לָהֶם prep.-3 m.p. sf. *for them*

104:9

גְּבוּל־שַׂמְתָּ n.m.s. (147)-Qal pf. 2 m.s. (שׂוּם 962) *a bound thou didst set*
בַּל־יַעֲבֹרוּן neg. (115)-Qal impf. 3 m.p. (716) *which they should not pass*
בַּל־יְשׁוּבוּן לְכַסּוֹת v.supra-Qal impf. 3 m.p. (שׁוּב 996)-prep.-Pi. inf.cstr. (כָּסָה 491) *so that they might not again cover*
הָאָרֶץ def.art.-n.f.s. (75) *the earth*

104:10

הַמְשַׁלֵּחַ def.art.-Pi. ptc. (1018) *who sends forth*
מַעְיָנִים n.m.p. (745) *springs*
בַּנְּחָלִים prep.-def.art.-n.m.p. (636) *in the valleys*
בֵּין הָרִים prep. (107)-n.m.p. (249) *between the hills*
יְהַלֵּכוּן Pi. impf. 3 m.p. (הָלַךְ 229) *they flow*

104:11

יַשְׁקוּ Hi. impf. 3 m.p. (שָׁקָה 1052) *they give drink*
כָּל־חַיְתוֹ n.m.s. cstr. (481)-n.f.s. cstr. (312; GK 90o) *to every beast of*
שָׂדָי n.m.s. paus. (961) *the field*
יִשְׁבְּרוּ Qal impf. 3 m.p. (990) *quench*
פְרָאִים n.m.p. (825) *the wild asses*
צְמָאָם n.m.s.-3 m.p. sf. (854) *their thirst*

104:12

עֲלֵיהֶם prep.-3 m.p. sf. *by them*

עוֹף־ n.m.s. cstr. (733) *the birds of*

הַשָּׁמַיִם def.art.-n.m. du. (1029) *the air*

יִשְׁכּוֹן Qal impf. 3 m.s. (שָׁכַן 1014) *have their habitation*

מִבֵּין עֳפָאיִם prep.-prep. (107)-n.m.p. (779; GK 93z) *among the branches*

יִתְּנוּ־קוֹל Qal impf. 3 m.p. (נָתַן 678)-n.m.s. (876) *they sing*

104:13

מַשְׁקֶה הָרִים Hi. ptc. (שָׁקָה 1052)-n.m.p. (249) *one watering the mountains*

מֵעֲלִיּוֹתָיו prep.-n.f.p.-3 m.s. sf. (751) *from his lofty abode*

מִפְּרִי prep.-n.m.s. cstr. (826) *with the fruit of*

מַעֲשֶׂיךָ n.m.p.-2 m.s. sf. (795) *thy work*

תִּשְׂבַּע Qal impf. 3 f.s. (959) *is satisfied*

הָאָרֶץ def.art.-n.f.s. (75) *the earth*

104:14

מַצְמִיחַ Hi. ptc. (צָמַח 855) *one causing to grow*

חָצִיר n.m.s. (II 348) *the grass*

לַבְּהֵמָה prep.-def.art.-n.f.s. (96) *for the cattle*

וְעֵשֶׂב conj.-n.m.s. (793) *and plants*

לַעֲבֹדַת prep.-n.f.s. cstr. (715) *for the labor of*

הָאָדָם def.art.-n.m.s. (9) *the man*

לְהוֹצִיא prep.-Hi. inf.cstr. (יָצָא 422) *that he may bring forth*

לֶחֶם n.m.s. (536) *food*

מִן־הָאָרֶץ prep.-def.art.-n.f.s. (75) *from the earth*

104:15

וְיַיִן conj.-n.m.s. (406) *and wine*

יְשַׂמַּח Pi. impf. 3 m.s. (970) *to gladden*

לְבַב־אֱנוֹשׁ n.m.s. cstr. (523)-n.m.s. (60) *the heart of man*

לְהַצְהִיל prep.-Hi. inf.cstr. (צָהַל II 843) *to make shine*

פָּנִים n.m.p. (815) *his face*

מִשָּׁמֶן prep.-n.m.s. paus. (1032) *from oil*

וְלֶחֶם conj.-n.m.s. (536) *and bread*

לְבַב־אֱנוֹשׁ v.supra-v.supra *man's heart*

יִסְעָד Qal impf. 3 m.s. paus. (703) *to strengthen*

104:16

יִשְׂבְּעוּ Qal impf. 3 m.p. (959) *are watered abundantly*

עֲצֵי יהוה n.m.p. cstr. (781)-pr.n. (217) *the trees of Yahweh*

אַרְזֵי לְבָנוֹן n.m.p. cstr. (72)-pr.n. (526) *the cedars of Lebanon*

אֲשֶׁר נָטָע rel. (81)-Qal pf. 3 m.s. paus. (642) *which he planted*

104:17

אֲשֶׁר־שָׁם rel. (81)-1027) *which there*

צִפֳּרִים n.m.p. (861) *the birds*

יְקַנֵּנוּ Pi. impf. 3 m.p. (קָנַן 890) *build their nests*

חֲסִידָה n.f.s. (339) *the stork*

בְּרוֹשִׁים n.m.p. (141) *in the fir trees*

בֵּיתָהּ n.m.s.-3 f.s. sf. (108) *her home*

104:18

הָרִים n.m.p. (249; GK 126x) *mountains*

הַגְּבֹהִים def.art.-adj. m.p. (147) *the high ones*

לַיְּעֵלִים prep.-def.art.-n.m.p. (418) *for the wild goats*

סְלָעִים n.m.p. (700) *the rocks*

מַחְסֶה n.m.s. (340) *a refuge*

לַשְׁפַנִּים prep.-def.art.-n.m.p. (I 1050; GK 20m) *for the badgers*

104:19

עָשָׂה Qal pf. 3 m.s. (I 793) *he made*

יָרֵחַ n.m.s. (437) *the moon*

לְמוֹעֲדִים prep.-n.m.p. (417) *for seasons*

שֶׁמֶשׁ n.f.s. (1039) *the sun*

יָדַע Qal pf. 3 m.s. (393) *he knew*

מְבוֹאוֹ n.m.s.-3 m.s. sf. (99) *his time for setting*

104:20

תָּשֶׁת־ Qal impf. 2 m.s. (1011) *thou makest*

חֹשֶׁךְ n.m.s. (365) *darkness*

וִיהִי conj.-Qal impf. 3 m.s. apoc. (הָיָה 224; GK 109h,159d) *and it is*

לָיְלָה n.m.s. (538) *night*

בּוֹ־תִרְמֹשׂ prep.-3 m.s. sf.-Qal impf. 3 f.s. (רָמַשׂ 942) *when creep forth*

כָּל־חַיְתוֹ־ n.m.s. cstr. (481)-n.f.s. cstr. (I 312; GK 90o) *all the beasts of*

יָעַר n.m.s. paus. (420) *the forest*

104:21

הַכְּפִירִים def.art.-n.m.p. (498) *the young lions*

שֹׁאֲגִים Qal act.ptc. m.p. (980) *roar*

לַטָּרֶף prep.-def.art.-n.m.s. paus. (383) *for their prey*

וּלְבַקֵּשׁ conj.-prep.-Pi. inf.cstr. (134; GK 114p) *seeking*

מֵאֵל prep.-n.m.s. (42) *from God*

אָכְלָם n.m.s.-3 m.p. sf. (38) *their food*

104:22

תִּזְרַח Qal impf. 3 f.s. (280) *rises*
הַשֶּׁמֶשׁ def.art.-n.f.s. (1039) *the sun*
יֵאָסֵפוּן Ni. impf. 3 m.p. paus. (אָסַף 62) *they get them away*
וְאֶל־מְעוֹנֹתָם conj.-prep.-n.m.p.-3 m.p. sf. (I 732) *and in their dens*
יִרְבָּצוּן Qal impf. 3 m.p. paus. (רָבַץ 918) *they lie down*

104:23

יֵצֵא Qal impf. 3 m.s. (יָצָא 422) *goes forth*
אָדָם n.m.s. (9) *man*
לְפָעֳלוֹ prep.-n.m.s.-3 m.s. sf. (821) *to his work*
וְלַעֲבֹדָתוֹ conj.-prep.-n.f.s.-3 m.s. sf. (715) *and to his labor*
עֲדֵי־עָרֶב prep. (III 723)-n.m.s. (787) *until evening*

104:24

מָה־רַבּוּ interr. (552)-Qal pf. 3 c.p. (רָבַב I 912) *how manifold are*
מַעֲשֶׂיךָ n.m.p.-2 m.s. sf. (795) *thy works*
יהוה pr.n. (217) *O Yahweh*
כֻּלָּם n.m.s.-3 m.p. sf. (481) *them all*
בְּחָכְמָה prep.-n.f.s. (315) *in wisdom*
עָשִׂיתָ Qal pf. 2 m.s. (עָשָׂה I 793) *thou hast made*
מָלְאָה Qal pf. 3 f.s. (569) *is full of*
הָאָרֶץ def.art.-n.f.s. (75) *the earth*
קִנְיָנֶךָ n.m.s.-2 m.s. sf. paus. (889) *thy creatures*

104:25

זֶה הַיָּם demons.adj. m.s. (260; GK 136dN)-def. art.-n.m.s. (410) *yonder is the sea*
גָּדוֹל adj. m.s. (152) *great*
וּרְחַב יָדָיִם conj.-adj. m.s. cstr. (932)-n.f. du. paus. (388) *and wide*
שָׁם־רֶמֶשׂ adv. (1027)-n.m.s. (943) *which teems*
וְאֵין מִסְפָּר conj.-neg. cstr. (II 34)-n.m.s. (708) *innumerable*
חַיּוֹת n.f.p. (312) *living things*
קְטַנּוֹת adj. f.p. (I 881) *small*
עִם־גְּדֹלוֹת prep. (767)-adj. f.p. (152) *and great*

104:26

שָׁם adv. (1027) *there*
אֳנִיּוֹת n.f.p. (58) *ships*
יְהַלֵּכוּן Pi. impf. 3 m.p. paus. (הָלַךְ 229) *go*
לִוְיָתָן n.m.s. (531) *Leviathan*
זֶה־יָצַרְתָּ demons.adj. as rel. (260; GK 138g)-Qal pf. 2 m.s. (יָצַר 427) *which thou didst form*
לְשַׂחֶק־בּוֹ prep.-Pi. inf.cstr. (שָׂחַק 965)-prep.-3 m.s. sf. *to sport in it*

104:27

כֻּלָּם n.m.s.-3 m.p. sf. (481) *these all*
אֵלֶיךָ prep.-2 m.s. sf. *to thee*
יְשַׂבֵּרוּן Pi. impf. 3 m.p. paus. (שָׂבַר II 960) *look*
לָתֵת prep.-Qal inf.cstr. (נָתַן 678) *to give*
אָכְלָם n.m.s.-3 m.p. sf. (38) *their food*
בְּעִתּוֹ prep.-n.f.s.-3 m.s. sf. (773) *in due season*

104:28

תִּתֵּן Qal impf. 2 m.s. (נָתַן 678; GK 159c) *when thou givest*
לָהֶם prep.-3 m.p. sf. *to them*
יִלְקֹטוּן Qal impf. 3 m.p. paus. (544; GK 47m) *they gather it up*
תִּפְתַּח Qal impf. 2 m.s. (פָּתַח I 834) *when thou openest*
יָדְךָ n.f.s.-2 m.s. sf. (388) *thy hand*
יִשְׂבְּעוּן Qal impf. 3 m.p. (959) *they are filled with*
טוֹב n.m.s. (III 375) *good things*

104:29

תַּסְתִּיר Hi. impf. 2 m.s. (סָתַר 711) *when thou hidest*
פָּנֶיךָ n.m.p.-2 m.s. sf. (815) *thy face*
יִבָּהֵלוּן Ni. impf. 3 m.p. paus. (בָּהַל 96) *they are dismayed*
תֹּסֵף Qal impf. 2 m.s. (אָסַף 62) *when thou takest away*
רוּחָם n.f.s.-3 m.p. sf. (924) *their breath*
יִגְוָעוּן Qal impf. 3 m.p. paus. (גָּוַע 157) *they die*
וְאֶל־עֲפָרָם conj.-prep.-n.m.s.-3 m.p. sf. (779) *and to their dust*
יְשׁוּבוּן Qal impf. 3 m.p. (שׁוּב 996) *they return*

104:30

תְּשַׁלַּח Pi. impf. 2 m.s. (1018) *when thou sendest forth*
רוּחֲךָ n.f.s.-2 m.s. sf. (924) *thy Spirit* (or *breath*)
יִבָּרֵאוּן Ni. impf. 3 m.p. paus. (בָּרָא 135) *they are created*
וּתְחַדֵּשׁ conj.-Pi. impf. 2 m.s. (293) *and thou renewest*
פְּנֵי אֲדָמָה n.m.p. cstr. (815)-n.f.s. (9) *the face of the ground*

104:31

יְהִי Qal impf. 3 m.s. apoc. (הָיָה 224) *may be*

כְּבוֹד יהוה n.m.s. cstr. (458)-pr.n. (217) *the glory of Yahweh*
לְעוֹלָם prep.-n.m.s. (761) *for ever*
יִשְׂמַח Qal impf. 3 m.s. (970) *may rejoice*
יהוה v.supra *Yahweh*
בְּמַעֲשָׂיו prep.-n.m.p.-3 m.s. sf. (795) *in his works*

104:32
הַמַּבִּיט def.art.-Hi. ptc. (נָבַט 613) *who looks*
לָאָרֶץ prep.-def.art.-n.f.s. (75) *on the earth*
וַתִּרְעָד consec.-Qal impf. 3 f.s. paus. (רָעַד 944) *and it trembles*
יִגַּע Qal impf. 3 m.s. (נָגַע 619) *he touches*
בֶּהָרִים prep.-def.art.-n.m.p. (249) *the mountains*
וְיֶעֱשָׁנוּ conj.-Qal impf. 3 m.p. paus. (עָשַׁן 798) *and they smoke*

104:33
אָשִׁירָה Qal impf. 1 c.s.-vol.he (שִׁיר 1010) *I will sing*
לַיהוה prep.-pr.n. (217) *to Yahweh*
בְּחַיָּי prep.-n.m.p.-1 c.s. sf. (313) *as long as I live*
אֲזַמְּרָה Pi. impf. 1 c.s.-vol.he (I 274) *I will sing praise*
לֵאלֹהַי prep.-n.m.p.-1 c.s. sf. (43) *to my God*
בְּעוֹדִי prep.-subst.-1 c.s. sf. (728) *while I have being*

104:34
יֶעֱרַב Qal impf. 3 m.s. (III 787) *may be pleasing*
עָלָיו prep.-3 m.s. sf. *to him*
שִׂיחִי n.m.s.-1 c.s. sf. (I 967) *my meditation*
אָנֹכִי אֶשְׂמַח pers.pr. 1 c.s. (59)-Qal impf. 1 c.s. (970) *for I rejoice*
בַּיהוה prep.-pr.n. (217) *in Yahweh*

104:35
יִתַּמּוּ Qal impf. 3 m.p. (תָּמַם 1070) *let be consumed*
חַטָּאִים adj. m.p. (308) *sinners*
מִן־הָאָרֶץ prep.-def.art.-n.f.s. (75) *from the earth*
וּרְשָׁעִים conj.-adj. m.p. (957) *and the wicked*
עוֹד אֵינָם adv. (728)-neg.-3 m.p. sf. (II 34) *let be no more (of them)*
בָּרְכִי Pi. impv. 2 f.s. (138) *bless*
נַפְשִׁי n.f.s.-1 c.s. sf. (659) *O my soul*
אֶת־יהוה dir.obj.-pr.n. (217) *Yahweh*
הַלְלוּ־יָהּ Pi. impv. 2 m.p. (II 237)-pr.n. (219) *Praise Yah*

105:1
הוֹדוּ Hi. impv. 2 m.p. (יָדָה 392) *O give thanks*
לַיהוה prep.-pr.n. (217) *to Yahweh*
קִרְאוּ Qal impv. 2 m.p. (894) *call*
בִּשְׁמוֹ prep.-n.m.s.-3 m.s. sf. (1027) *on his name*
הוֹדִיעוּ Hi. impv. 2 m.p. (יָדַע 393) *make known*
בָעַמִּים prep.-def.art.-n.m.p. (I 766) *among the peoples*
עֲלִילוֹתָיו n.f.p.-3 m.s. sf. (760) *his deeds*

105:2
שִׁירוּ־לוֹ Qal impv. 2 m.p. (1010)-prep.-3 m.s. sf. *sing to him*
זַמְּרוּ־לוֹ Pi. impv. 2 m.p. (I 274)-v.supra *sing praises to him*
שִׂיחוּ Qal impv. 2 m.p. (967) *tell*
בְּכָל־נִפְלְאוֹתָיו prep.-n.m.s. cstr. (481)-Ni. ptc. f.p. -3 m.s. sf. (פָּלָא 810) *of all his wonderful works*

105:3
הִתְהַלְלוּ Hith. impv. 2 m.p. (הָלַל II 237) *glory*
בְּשֵׁם קָדְשׁוֹ prep.-n.m.s. cstr. (1027)-n.m.s.-3 m.s. sf. (871) *in his holy name*
יִשְׂמַח Qal impf. 3 m.s. (970) *let rejoice*
לֵב n.m.s. cstr. (524) *the hearts of*
מְבַקְשֵׁי Pi. ptc. m.p. cstr. (134) *those who seek*
יהוה pr.n. (217) *Yahweh*

105:4
דִּרְשׁוּ Qal impv. 2 m.p. (205) *seek*
יהוה pr.n. (217) *Yahweh*
וְעֻזּוֹ conj.-n.m.s.-3 m.s. sf. (738) *and his strength*
בַּקְּשׁוּ Pi. impv. 2 m.p. (134) *seek*
פָנָיו n.m.p.-3 m.s. sf. (815) *his presence*
תָּמִיד adv. (556) *continually*

105:5
זִכְרוּ Qal impv. 2 m.p. (269) *remember*
נִפְלְאוֹתָיו Ni. ptc. f.p.-3 m.s. sf. (810) *the wonderful works (of him)*
אֲשֶׁר־עָשָׂה rel. (81)-Qal pf. 3 m.s. (I 793) *that he has done*
מֹפְתָיו n.m.p.-3 m.s. sf. (68) *his miracles*
וּמִשְׁפְּטֵי־ conj.-n.m.p. cstr. (1048) *and the judgments of*
פִיו n.m.s.-3 m.s. sf. (804) *he uttered* (lit. *his mouth*)

105:6
זֶרַע n.m.s. cstr. (282) *O offspring of*
אַבְרָהָם pr.n. (4) *Abraham*

עַבְדּוֹ n.m.s.-3 m.s. sf. (713) *his servant*
בְּנֵי יַעֲקֹב n.m.p. cstr. (119)-pr.n. (784) *sons of Jacob*
בְּחִירָיו n.m.p.-3 m.s. sf. (104) *his chosen ones*

105:7

הוּא יהוה pers.pr. 3 m.s. (214)-pr.n. (217) *he is Yahweh*
אֱלֹהֵינוּ n.m.p.-1 c.p. sf. (43) *our God*
בְּכָל־הָאָרֶץ prep.-n.m.s. cstr. (481)-def.art.-n.f.s. (75) *in all the earth*
מִשְׁפָּטָיו n.m.p.-3 m.s. sf. (1048) *his judgments*

105:8

זָכַר Qal pf. 3 m.s. (269) *he is mindful*
לְעוֹלָם prep.-n.m.s. (761) *for ever*
בְּרִיתוֹ n.f.s.-3 m.s. sf. (136) *his covenant*
דָּבָר n.m.s. (182) *of the word*
צִוָּה Pi. pf. 3 m.s. (צָוָה 845) *that he commanded*
לְאֶלֶף דּוֹר prep.-n.m.s. cstr. (II 48)-n.m.s. (189) *for a thousand generations*

105:9

אֲשֶׁר כָּרַת rel. (81)-Qal pf. 3 m.s. (503) *that he made*
אֶת־אַבְרָהָם dir.obj.-pr.n. (4) *with Abraham*
וּשְׁבוּעָתוֹ conj.-n.f.s.-3 m.s. sf. (989) *and his sworn promise*
לְיִשְׂחָק prep.-pr.n. (850) *to Isaac*

105:10

וַיַּעֲמִידֶהָ consec.-Hi. impf. 3 m.s.-3 f.s. sf. (עָמַד 763) *which he confirmed*
לְיַעֲקֹב prep.-pr.n. (784) *to Jacob*
לְחֹק prep.-n.m.s. (349) *as a statute*
לְיִשְׂרָאֵל prep.-pr.n. (975) *to Israel*
בְּרִית עוֹלָם n.f.s. cstr. (136)-n.m.s. (761) *as an everlasting covenant*

105:11

לֵאמֹר prep.-Qal inf.cstr. (55) *saying*
לְךָ prep.-2 m.s. sf. *to you*
אֶתֵּן Qal impf. 1 c.s. (נָתַן 678) *I will give*
אֶת־אֶרֶץ־ dir.obj.-n.f.s. cstr. (75) *the land of*
כְּנָעַן pr.n. paus. (488) *Canaan*
חֶבֶל נַחֲלַתְכֶם n.m.s. cstr. (286)-n.f.s.-2 m.p. sf. (635) *your portion for an inheritance*

105:12

בִּהְיוֹתָם prep.-Qal inf.cstr.-3 m.p. sf. (הָיָה 224) *when they were*
מְתֵי n.m.p. cstr. (607) *men of*
מִסְפָּר n.m.s. (708) *number*
כִּמְעַט prep.-subst. (589; GK 118x) *of little account*
וְגָרִים בָּהּ conj.-Qal act.ptc. m.p. (גּוּר 157) -prep.-3 f.s. sf. *and sojourners in it*

105:13

וַיִּתְהַלְּכוּ consec.-Hith. impf. 3 m.p. (הָלַךְ 229) *wandering*
מִגּוֹי prep.-n.m.s. (156) *from nation*
אֶל־גּוֹי prep.-v.supra *to nation*
מִמַּמְלָכָה prep.-n.f.s. (575) *from one kingdom*
אֶל־עַם אַחֵר prep.-n.m.s. (I 766)-adj. m.s. (29) *to another people*

105:14

לֹא־הִנִּיחַ neg.-Hi. pf. 3 m.s. (נוּחַ 628) *he allowed not*
אָדָם n.m.s. (9) *a man*
לְעָשְׁקָם prep.-Qal inf.cstr.-3 m.p. sf. (עָשַׁק 798) *to oppress them*
וַיּוֹכַח consec.-Hi. impf. 3 m.s. (יָכַח 406) *and he rebuked*
עֲלֵיהֶם prep.-3 m.p. sf. *on their account*
מְלָכִים n.m.p. (I 572) *kings*

105:15

אַל־תִּגְּעוּ neg.-Qal impf. 2 m.p. (נָגַע 619) *touch not*
בִמְשִׁיחָי prep.-n.m.p.-1 c.s. sf. (603) *my anointed ones*
וְלִנְבִיאַי conj.-prep.-n.m.p.-1 c.s. sf. (611) *and my prophets*
אַל־תָּרֵעוּ neg.-Hi. impf. 2 m.p. (רָעַע 949) *do no harm*

105:16

וַיִּקְרָא consec.-Qal impf. 3 m.s. (894) *when he summoned*
רָעָב n.m.s. (944) *a famine*
עַל־הָאָרֶץ prep.-def.art.-n.f.s. (75) *on the land*
כָּל־מַטֵּה־ n.m.s. cstr. (481)-n.m.s. cstr. (641) *every staff of*
לֶחֶם n.m.s. (536) *bread*
שָׁבָר Qal pf. 3 m.s. paus. (990) *he broke*

105:17

שָׁלַח Qal pf. 3 m.s. (1018) *he had sent*
לִפְנֵיהֶם prep.-n.m.p.-3 m.p. sf. (815) *ahead of them*
אִישׁ n.m.s. (35) *a man*
לְעֶבֶד prep.-n.m.s. (713) *as a slave*

נִמְכַּר Ni. pf. 3 m.s. (מָכַר 569) *was sold*
יוֹסֵף pr.n. (415) *Joseph*

105:18
עִנּוּ Pi. pf. 3 c.p. (עָנָה III 776) *were hurt*
בַכֶּבֶל prep.-def.art.-n.m.s. (459) *with fetters*
רַגְלָיו n.f.p.-3 m.s. sf. (919) *his feet*
בַּרְזֶל n.m.s. (137) *iron*
בָּאָה Qal pf. 3 f.s. (בּוֹא 97) *was put*
נַפְשׁוֹ n.f.s.-3 m.s. sf. (659) *his neck*

105:19
עַד־עֵת prep. (III 723)-n.f.s. (773) *until the time*
בֹּא־ Qal inf.cstr. (בּוֹא 97) *the coming to pass of*
דְבָרוֹ n.m.s.-3 m.s. sf. (182) *his word*
אִמְרַת n.f.s. cstr. (57) *the word of*
יהוה pr.n. (217) *Yahweh*
צְרָפָתְהוּ Qal pf. 3 f.s.-3 m.s. sf. (צָרַף 864) *tested him*

105:20
שָׁלַח Qal pf. 3 m.s. (1018) *sent*
מֶלֶךְ n.m.s. (I 572) *the king*
וַיַּתִּירֵהוּ consec.-Hi. impf. 3 m.s.-3 m.s. sf. (נָתַר II 684) *and released him*
מֹשֵׁל Qal act.ptc. m.s. cstr. (605) *a ruler of*
עַמִּים n.m.p. (I 766) *peoples*
וַיְפַתְּחֵהוּ consec.-Pi. impf. 3 m.s.-3 m.s. sf. (פָּתַח I 834) *set him free*

105:21
שָׂמוֹ Qal pf. 3 m.s.-3 m.s. sf. (שׂוּם 962) *he made him*
אָדוֹן n.m.s. (10) *Lord*
לְבֵיתוֹ prep.-n.m.s.-3 m.s. sf. (108) *of his house*
וּמֹשֵׁל conj.-Qal act.ptc. (605) *and ruler*
בְּכָל־קִנְיָנוֹ prep.-n.m.s. cstr. (481)-n.m.s.-3 m.s. sf. (889) *of all his possessions*

105:22
לֶאְסֹר prep.-Qal inf.cstr. (אָסַר 63) *to bind*
שָׂרָיו n.m.p.-3 m.s. sf. (978) *his princes*
בְּנַפְשׁוֹ prep.-n.f.s.-3 m.s. sf. (659) *at his pleasure* (or *to himself*)
וּזְקֵנָיו conj.-adj. m.p.-3 m.s. sf. (278) *and his elders*
יְחַכֵּם Pi. impf. 3 m.s. (חָכַם 314) *he teaches wisdom*

105:23
וַיָּבֹא consec.-Qal impf. 3 m.s. (בּוֹא 97) *then came*
יִשְׂרָאֵל pr.n. (975) *Israel*
מִצְרָיִם pr.n. paus. (595) *to Egypt*
וְיַעֲקֹב conj.-pr.n. (784) *and Jacob*
גָּר Qal pf. 3 m.s. (גּוּר 157) *sojourned*
בְּאֶרֶץ־חָם prep.-n.f.s. cstr. (75)-pr.n. (I 325) *in the land of Ham*

105:24
וַיֶּפֶר consec.-Hi. impf. 3 m.s. (פָּרָה 826) *and he made fruitful*
אֶת־עַמּוֹ dir.obj.-n.m.s.-3 m.s. sf. (I 766) *his people*
מְאֹד adv. (547) *very*
וַיַּעֲצִמֵהוּ consec.-Hi. impf. 3 m.s.-3 m.s. sf. (עָצַם I 782) *and made them stronger*
מִצָּרָיו prep.-n.m.p.-3 m.s. sf. (III 865) *than their foes*

105:25
הָפַךְ Qal pf. 3 m.s. (245) *he turned*
לִבָּם n.m.s.-3 m.p. sf. (524) *their hearts*
לִשְׂנֹא prep.-Qal inf.cstr. (שָׂנֵא 971) *to hate*
עַמּוֹ n.m.s.-3 m.s. sf. (I 766) *his people*
לְהִתְנַכֵּל prep.-Hith. inf.cstr. (נָכַל 647) *to deal craftily*
בַּעֲבָדָיו prep.-n.m.p.-3 m.s. sf. (713) *with his servants*

105:26
שָׁלַח Qal pf. 3 m.s. (1018) *he sent*
מֹשֶׁה pr.n. (602) *Moses*
עַבְדּוֹ n.m.s.-3 m.s. sf. (713) *his servant*
אַהֲרֹן pr.n. (14) *Aaron*
אֲשֶׁר בָּחַר־בּוֹ rel. (81)-Qal pf. 3 m.s. (103) -prep.-3 m.s. sf. *whom he had chosen*

105:27
שָׂמוּ־ Qal pf. 3 c.p. (שׂוּם 962) *they wrought*
בָם prep.-3 m.p. sf. *among them*
דִּבְרֵי אֹתוֹתָיו n.m.p. cstr. (182)-n.m.p.-3 m.s. sf. (16) *his signs* (lit. *the words of his signs*)
וּמֹפְתִים conj.-n.m.p. (68) *and miracles*
בְּאֶרֶץ חָם prep.-n.f.s. cstr. (75)-pr.n. (I 325) *in the land of Ham*

105:28
שָׁלַח Qal pf. 3 m.s. (1018) *he sent*
חֹשֶׁךְ n.m.s. (365) *darkness*

וַיַּחְשִׁךְ consec.-Hi. impf. 3 m.s. (חָשַׁךְ 364; GK 53n) *and made (the land) dark*
וְלֹא־מָרוּ conj.-neg.-Qal pf. 3 c.p. (מָרָה 598) *and they did not rebel against*
אֶת־דְּבָרוֹ dir.obj.-n.m.s.-3 m.s. sf. (182; many rd. דְּבָרָיו n.m.p.-3 m.s. sf.) *his words*

105:29

הָפַךְ Qal pf. 3 m.s. (245) *he turned*
אֶת־מֵימֵיהֶם dir.obj.-n.m.p.-3 m.p. sf. (565) *his waters*
לְדָם prep.-n.m.s. (196) *into blood*
וַיָּמֶת consec.-Hi. impf. 3 m.s. (מוּת 559) *and caused to die*
אֶת־דְּגָתָם dir.obj.-n.f.s.-3 m.p. sf. (185) *their fish*

105:30

שָׁרַץ Qal pf. 3 m.s. (1056) *swarmed with*
אַרְצָם n.f.s.-3 m.p. sf. (75) *their land*
צְפַרְדְּעִים n.f.p. (862) *frogs*
בְּחַדְרֵי prep.-n.m.p. cstr. (293) *in the chambers of*
מַלְכֵיהֶם n.m.p.-3 m.p. sf. (I 572) *their kings*

105:31

אָמַר Qal pf. 3 m.s. (55) *he spoke*
וַיָּבֹא consec.-Qal impf. 3 m.s. (בּוֹא 97) *and there came*
עָרֹב n.m.s. (786) *swarms of flies*
כִּנִּים n.m.p. (IV 487) *gnats*
בְּכָל־גְּבוּלָם prep.-n.m.s. cstr. (481)-n.m.s.-3 m.p. sf. (147) *in all their borders*

105:32

נָתַן Qal pf. 3 m.s. (678) *he gave*
גִּשְׁמֵיהֶם n.m.p.-3 m.p. sf. (II 177) *for rain*
בָּרָד n.m.s. (135) *hail*
אֵשׁ n.f.s. (77) *lightning*
לֶהָבוֹת n.f.p. (529) *flames*
בְּאַרְצָם prep.-n.f.s.-3 m.p. sf. (75) *through their land*

105:33

וַיַּךְ consec.-Hi. impf. 3 m.s. (נָכָה 645) *and he smote*
גַּפְנָם n.f.s.-3 m.p. sf. (172) *their vines*
וּתְאֵנָתָם conj.-n.f.s.-3 m.p. sf. (1061) *and their fig trees*
וַיְשַׁבֵּר consec.-Pi. impf. 3 m.s. (990) *and shattered*
עֵץ גְּבוּלָם n.m.s. cstr. (781)-n.m.s.-3 m.p. sf. (147) *the trees of their country*

105:34

אָמַר Qal pf. 3 m.s. (55) *he spoke*
וַיָּבֹא consec.-Qal impf. 3 m.s. (בּוֹא 97) *and came*
אַרְבֶּה n.m.s. (916) *locusts*
וְיֶלֶק conj.-n.m.s. (410) *and young locusts*
וְאֵין מִסְפָּר conj.-neg. cstr. (II 34)-n.m.s. (708) *without number*

105:35

וַיֹּאכַל consec.-Qal impf. 3 m.s. (37) *which devoured*
כָּל־עֵשֶׂב n.m.s. cstr. (481)-n.m.s. (793) *all the vegetation*
בְּאַרְצָם prep.-n.f.s.-3 m.p. sf. (75) *in their land*
וַיֹּאכַל v.supra *and ate up*
פְּרִי n.m.s. cstr. (826) *the fruit of*
אַדְמָתָם n.f.s.-3 m.p. sf. (9) *their ground*

105:36

וַיַּךְ consec.-Hi. impf. 3 m.s. (נָכָה 645) *and he smote*
כָּל־בְּכוֹר n.m.s. cstr. (481)-n.m.s. (114) *all the first-born*
בְּאַרְצָם prep.-n.f.s.-3 m.p. sf. (75) *in their land*
רֵאשִׁית n.f.s. (912) *the first issue*
לְכָל־אוֹנָם prep.-n.m.s. cstr. (481)-n.m.s.-3 m.p. sf. (I 20) *of all their strength*

105:37

וַיּוֹצִיאֵם consec.-Hi. impf. 3 m.s.-3 m.s. sf. (יָצָא 422) *then he led forth (them)*
בְּכֶסֶף prep.-n.m.s. (494) *with silver*
וְזָהָב conj.-n.m.s. (262) *and gold*
וְאֵין בִּשְׁבָטָיו conj.-neg. cstr. (II 34)-prep.-n.m.p.-3 m.s. sf. (986) *and there was none among his tribes*
כּוֹשֵׁל Qal act.ptc. (505) *who stumbled*

105:38

שָׂמַח Qal pf. 3 m.s. (970) *was glad*
מִצְרַיִם pr.n. (595) *Egypt*
בְּצֵאתָם prep.-Qal inf.cstr.-3 m.p. sf. (יָצָא 422) *when they departed*
כִּי־נָפַל conj. (471)-Qal pf. 3 m.s. (656) *for had fallen*
פַּחְדָּם n.m.s.-3 m.p. sf. (808) *dread of them*
עֲלֵיהֶם prep.-3 m.p. sf. *upon it (them)*

105:39

פָּרַשׂ Qal pf. 3 m.s. (831) *he spread*

עָנָן n.m.s. (777) *a cloud*
לְמָסָךְ prep.-n.m.s. (697) *for a covering*
וְאֵשׁ conj.-n.f.s. (77) *and fire*
לְהָאִיר prep.-Hi. inf.cstr. (אוֹר 21) *to give light*
לָיְלָה n.m.s. (538) *by night*

105:40

שָׁאַל Qal pf. 3 m.s. (981) *they asked*
וַיָּבֵא consec.-Hi. impf. 3 m.s. (בּוֹא 97) *and he brought*
שְׂלָו n.f.s. (969) *quails*
וְלֶחֶם conj.-n.m.s. (536) *and bread*
שָׁמַיִם n.m. du. (1029) *from heaven*
יַשְׂבִּיעֵם Hi. impf. 3 m.s.-3 m.p. sf. (שָׂבַע 959) *he gave them in abundance*

105:41

פָּתַח Qal pf. 3 m.s. (I 834) *he opened*
צוּר n.m.s. (849) *the rock*
וַיָּזוּבוּ consec.-Qal impf. 3 m.p. (זוּב 264) *and gushed forth*
מָיִם n.m.p. paus. (565) *water*
הָלְכוּ Qal pf. 3 c.p. (הָלַךְ 229) *it flowed*
בַּצִּיּוֹת prep.-def.art.-n.f.p. (851) *through the desert*
נָהָר n.m.s. (625) *like a river*

105:42

כִּי־זָכַר conj. (471)-Qal pf. 3 m.s. (269) *for he remembered*
אֶת־דְּבַר קָדְשׁוֹ dir.obj.-n.m.s. cstr. (182)-n.m.s.-3 m.s. sf. (871) *his holy promise*
אֶת־אַבְרָהָם dir.obj.-pr.n. (4) *Abraham*
עַבְדּוֹ n.m.s.-3 m.s. sf. (713) *his servant*

105:43

וַיּוֹצִא consec.-Hi. impf. 3 m.s. (יָצָא 422; GK 74,l) *so he led forth*
עַמּוֹ n.m.s.-3 m.s. sf. (I 766) *his people*
בְּשָׂשׂוֹן prep.-n.m.s. (965) *with joy*
בְּרִנָּה prep.-n.f.s. (943) *with singing*
אֶת־בְּחִירָיו dir.obj.-n.m.p.-3 m.s. sf. (104) *his chosen ones*

105:44

וַיִּתֵּן consec.-Qal impf. 3 m.s. (נָתַן 678) *and he gave*
לָהֶם prep.-3 m.p. sf. *them*
אַרְצוֹת n.f.p. cstr. (75) *the lands of*
גּוֹיִם n.m.p. (156) *the nations*
וַעֲמַל conj.-n.m.s. cstr. (765) *and the toil of*
לְאֻמִּים n.m.p. (522) *peoples*

יִירָשׁוּ Qal impf. 3 m.p. paus. (יָרַשׁ 439) *they took possession of*

105:45

בַּעֲבוּר prep.-prep. (721) *to the end that*
יִשְׁמְרוּ Qal impf. 3 m.p. (1036) *they should keep*
חֻקָּיו n.m.p.-3 m.s. sf. (349) *his statutes*
וְתוֹרֹתָיו conj.-n.f.p.-3 m.s. sf. (435) *and his laws*
יִנְצֹרוּ Qal impf. 3 m.p. paus. (נָצַר 665) *observe*
הַלְלוּ־יָהּ Pi. impv. 2 m.p. (II 237)-pr.n. (219) *praise Yah*

106:1

הַלְלוּיָהּ Pi. impv. 2 m.p. (II 237)-pr.n. (219) *praise Yah* (rd. הַלְלוּ יָהּ)
הוֹדוּ Hi. impv. 2 m.p. (יָדָה 392) *O give thanks*
לַיהוה prep.-pr.n. (217) *to Yahweh*
כִּי־טוֹב conj. (471)-adj. (II 373) *for he is good*
כִּי לְעוֹלָם conj. (471)-prep.-n.m.s. (761) *for for ever*
חַסְדּוֹ n.m.s.-3 m.s. sf. (338) *his steadfast love*

106:2

מִי יְמַלֵּל interr. (566)-Pi. impf. 3 m.s. (מָלַל I 576) *who can utter*
גְּבוּרוֹת n.f.p. cstr. (150) *the mighty doings of*
יהוה pr.n. (217) *Yahweh*
יַשְׁמִיעַ Hi. impf. 3 m.s. (1033) *or show forth*
כָּל־תְּהִלָּתוֹ n.m.s. cstr. (481)-n.f.s.-3 m.s. sf. (239) *all his praise*

106:3

אַשְׁרֵי n.m.p. cstr. (80) *blessed are*
שֹׁמְרֵי Qal act.ptc. m.p. cstr. (1036) *they who observe*
מִשְׁפָּט n.m.s. (1048) *justice*
עֹשֵׂה Qal act.ptc. m.s. cstr. (I 793) *who do*
צְדָקָה n.f.s. (842) *righteousness*
בְּכָל־עֵת prep.-n.m.s. cstr. (481)-n.f.s. (773) *at all times*

106:4

זָכְרֵנִי Qal impv. 2 m.s.-1 c.s. sf. (זָכַר 269) *remember me*
יהוה pr.n. (217) *O Yahweh*
בִּרְצוֹן prep.-n.m.s. cstr. (953) *when thou showest favor to*
עַמֶּךָ n.m.s.-2 m.s. sf. (I 766) *thy people*
פָּקְדֵנִי Qal impv. 2 m.s.-1 c.s. sf. (פָּקַד 823) *help me*
בִּישׁוּעָתֶךָ prep.-n.f.s.-2 m.s. sf. (447) *when thou deliverest them*

106:5

לִרְאוֹת prep.-Qal inf.cstr. (רָאָה 906) *that I may see*

בְּטוֹבַת prep.-n.f.s. cstr. (375) *the prosperity of*

בְּחִירֶיךָ n.m.p.-2 m.s. sf. (104) *thy chosen ones*

לִשְׂמֹחַ prep.-Qal inf.cstr. (970) *that I may rejoice*

בְּשִׂמְחַת prep.-n.f.s. cstr. (970) *in the gladness of*

גּוֹיֶךָ n.m.p.-2 m.s. sf. (156) *thy nation*

לְהִתְהַלֵּל prep.-Hith. inf.cstr. (הָלַל II 237) *that I may glory*

עִם־נַחֲלָתֶךָ prep.-n.f.s.-2 m.s. sf. (635) *with thy heritage*

106:6

חָטָאנוּ Qal pf. 1 c.p. (306) *we have sinned*

עִם־אֲבוֹתֵינוּ prep.-n.m.p.-1 c.p. sf. (3) *with our fathers*

הֶעֱוִינוּ Hi. pf. 1 c.p. (עָוָה 731) *we have committed iniquity*

הִרְשָׁעְנוּ Hi. pf. 1 c.p. (רָשַׁע 957) *we have done wickedly*

106:7

אֲבוֹתֵינוּ n.m.p.-1 c.p. sf. (3) *our fathers*

בְמִצְרַיִם prep.-pr.n. (595) *in Egypt*

לֹא־הִשְׂכִּילוּ neg.-Hi. pf. 3 c.p. (968) *did not consider*

נִפְלְאוֹתֶיךָ Ni. ptc. f.p.-2 m.s. sf. (פָּלָא 810) *thy wonderful works*

לֹא זָכְרוּ neg.-Qal pf. 3 c.p. (269) *they did not remember*

אֶת־רֹב dir.obj.-n.m.s. cstr. (913) *the abundance of*

חֲסָדֶיךָ n.m.p.-2 m.s. sf. (I 338) *thy steadfast love*

וַיַּמְרוּ consec.-Hi. impf. 3 m.p. (מָרָה 598) *but rebelled*

עַל־יָם prep.-n.m.s. (410) *at the sea*

בְּיַם־סוּף prep.-n.m.s. cstr. (410)-n.m.s. (I 693) *at the Red Sea* (lit. *the sea of reeds*)

106:8

וַיּוֹשִׁיעֵם consec.-Hi. impf. 3 m.s.-3 m.p. sf. (יָשַׁע 446) *yet he saved them*

לְמַעַן שְׁמוֹ prep. (775)-n.m.s.-3 m.s. sf. (1027) *for his name's sake*

לְהוֹדִיעַ prep.-Hi. inf.cstr. (יָדַע 393) *that he might make known*

אֶת־גְּבוּרָתוֹ dir.obj.-n.f.s.-3 m.s. sf. (150) *his mighty power*

106:9

וַיִּגְעַר consec.-Qal impf. 3 m.s. (גָּעַר 172) *he rebuked*

בְּיַם־סוּף prep.-n.m.s. cstr. (410)-n.m.s. (I 693) *the Red Sea*

וַיֶּחֱרָב consec.-Qal impf. 3 m.s. (חָרֵב I 351) *and it became dry*

וַיּוֹלִיכֵם consec.-Hi. impf. 3 m.s.-3 m.p. sf. (הָלַךְ 229) *and he led them*

בַּתְּהֹמוֹת prep.-def.art.-n.f.p. (1062) *through the deep*

כַּמִּדְבָּר prep.-def.art.-n.m.s. (II 184) *as through a desert*

106:10

וַיּוֹשִׁיעֵם consec.-Hi. impf. 3 m.s.-3 m.s. sf. (יָשַׁע 446) *so he saved them*

מִיַּד prep.-n.f.s. cstr. (388) *from the hand of*

שׂוֹנֵא Qal act.ptc. (971) *the foe*

וַיִּגְאָלֵם consec.-Qal impf. 3 m.s.-3 m.p. sf. (גָּאַל I 145) *and delivered them*

מִיַּד v.supra *from the power of*

אוֹיֵב Qal act.ptc. (אָיַב 33) *the enemy*

106:11

וַיְכַסּוּ־ consec.-Pi. impf. 3 m.p. (כָּסָה 491) *and covered*

מַיִם n.m.p. (565) *waters*

צָרֵיהֶם n.m.p.-3 m.p. sf. (III 865) *their adversaries*

אֶחָד מֵהֶם num. (25)-prep.-3 m.p. sf. *one of them*

לֹא נוֹתָר neg.-Ni. pf. 3 m.s. paus. (יָתַר 451) *was not left*

106:12

וַיַּאֲמִינוּ consec.-Hi. impf. 3 m.p. (אָמַן 52) *then they believed*

בִדְבָרָיו prep.-n.m.p.-3 m.s. sf. (182) *on his words*

יָשִׁירוּ Qal impf. 3 m.p. (1010) *they sang*

תְּהִלָּתוֹ n.f.s.-3 m.s. sf. (239) *his praise*

106:13

מִהֲרוּ שָׁכְחוּ Pi. pf. 3 c.p. (I 554)-Qal pf. 3 c.p. (1013) *but they soon forgot*

מַעֲשָׂיו n.m.p.-3 m.s. sf. (795) *his works*

לֹא־חִכּוּ neg.-Pi. pf. 3 c.p. (חָכָה 314) *they did not wait*

לַעֲצָתוֹ prep.-n.f.s.-3 m.s. sf. (420) *for his counsel*

106:14

וַיִּתְאַוּוּ תַאֲוָה consec.-Hith. impf. 3 m.p. (אָוָה I 16)-n.f.s. (16) *but they had a wanton craving*
בַּמִּדְבָּר prep.-def.art.-n.m.s. (II 1184) *in the wilderness*
וַיְנַסּוּ־אֵל consec.-Pi. impf. 3 m.p. (נָסָה 650) -n.m.s. (42) *and put God to the test*
בִּישִׁימוֹן prep.-n.m.s. (445) *in the desert*

106:15

וַיִּתֵּן consec.-Qal impf. 3 m.s. (נָתַן 678) *and he gave*
לָהֶם prep.-3 m.p. sf. *them*
שֶׁאֱלָתָם n.f.s.-3 m.p. sf. (982) *what they asked*
וַיְשַׁלַּח consec.-Pi. impf. 3 m.s. (1018) *but sent*
רָזוֹן n.m.s. (I 931) *a wasting disease*
בְּנַפְשָׁם prep.-n.f.s.-3 m.p. sf. (659) *among them*

106:16

וַיְקַנְאוּ consec.-Pi. impf. 3 m.p. (קָנָא 888) *when men were jealous*
לְמֹשֶׁה prep.-pr.n. (602) *of Moses*
בַּמַּחֲנֶה prep.-def.art.-n.m.s. (334) *in the camp*
לְאַהֲרֹן prep.-pr.n. (14) *of Aaron*
קְדוֹשׁ יהוה adj. m.s. cstr. (872)-pr.n. (217) *the holy one of Yahweh*

106:17

תִּפְתַּח־ Qal impf. 3 f.s. (I 834) *opened*
אֶרֶץ n.f.s. (75) *the earth*
וַתִּבְלַע consec.-Qal impf. 3 f.s. (בָּלַע 118) *and swallowed up*
דָּתָן pr.n. (206) *Dathan*
וַתְּכַס consec.-Pi. impf. 3 f.s. (כָּסָה 491) *and covered*
עַל־עֲדַת prep.-n.f.s. cstr. (I 417) *the company of*
אֲבִירָם pr.n. (4) *Abiram*

106:18

וַתִּבְעַר־אֵשׁ consec.-Qal impf. 3 f.s. (בָּעַר 128)-n.f.s. (77) *fire also broke out*
בַּעֲדָתָם prep.-n.f.s.-3 m.p. sf. (I 417) *in their company*
לֶהָבָה n.f.s. (529) *flame*
תְּלַהֵט Pi. impf. 3 f.s. (לָהַט 529) *burned up*
רְשָׁעִים adj. m.p. (957) *the wicked*

106:19

יַעֲשׂוּ־ Qal impf. 3 m.p. (עָשָׂה I 793) *they made*
עֵגֶל n.m.s. (722) *a calf*
בְּחֹרֵב prep.-pr.n. (352) *in Horeb*
וַיִּשְׁתַּחֲווּ consec.-Hithpalel impf. 3 m.p. (שָׁחָה 1005) *and worshiped*
לְמַסֵּכָה prep.-n.f.s. (651) *a molten image*

106:20

וַיָּמִירוּ consec.-Hi. impf. 3 m.p. (מוּר 558) *and they exchanged*
אֶת־כְּבוֹדָם dir.obj.-adj. m.s.-3 m.p. sf. (458) *their glory*
בְּתַבְנִית prep.-n.f.s. cstr. (125) *for the image of*
שׁוֹר n.m.s. (1004) *an ox*
אֹכֵל Qal act.ptc. (37) *that eats*
עֵשֶׂב n.m.s. (793) *grass*

106:21

שָׁכְחוּ Qal pf. 3 c.p. (1013) *they forgot*
אֵל n.m.s. (42) *God*
מוֹשִׁיעָם Hi. ptc.-3 m.p. sf. (יָשַׁע 446) *their Savior*
עֹשֶׂה Qal act.ptc. (I 793) *who had done*
גְדֹלוֹת adj. f.p. (152) *great things*
בְּמִצְרָיִם prep.-pr.n. paus. (595) *in Egypt*

106:22

נִפְלָאוֹת Ni. ptc. f.p. (פָּלָא 810) *wondrous works*
בְּאֶרֶץ prep.-n.f.s. cstr. (75) *in the land of*
חָם pr.n. (I 325) *Ham*
נוֹרָאוֹת Ni. ptc. f.p. (יָרֵא 431) *terrible things*
עַל־יַם־סוּף prep.-n.m.s. cstr. (410)-n.m.s. (I 693) *by the Red Sea* (lit. *by the sea of reeds*)

106:23

וַיֹּאמֶר consec.-Qal impf. 3 m.s. (55) *therefore he said*
לְהַשְׁמִידָם prep.-Hi. inf.cstr.-3 m.p. sf. (שָׁמַד 1029) *that he would destroy them*
לוּלֵי מֹשֶׁה conj. (530)-pr.n. (602) *had not Moses*
בְּחִירוֹ n.m.s.-3 m.s. sf. (104) *his chosen one*
עָמַד Qal pf. 3 m.s. (763) *stood*
בַּפֶּרֶץ prep.-def.art.-n.m.s. (I 829) *in the breach*
לְפָנָיו prep.-n.m.p.-3 m.s. sf. (815) *before him*
לְהָשִׁיב prep.-Hi. inf.cstr. (שׁוּב 996) *to turn away*
חֲמָתוֹ n.f.s.-3 m.s. sf. (404) *his wrath*
מֵהַשְׁחִית prep.-Hi. inf.cstr. (שָׁחַת 1007) *from destroying them*

106:24

וַיִּמְאֲסוּ consec.-Qal impf. 3 m.p. (מָאַס 549) *then they despised*

בְּאֶרֶץ חֶמְדָּה prep.-n.m.s. cstr. (75)-n.f.s. (326) *the pleasant land*
לֹא־הֶאֱמִינוּ neg.-Hi. pf. 3 c.p. (אָמַן 52) *having no faith*
לִדְבָרוֹ prep.-n.m.s.-3 m.s. sf. (182) *in his promise*

106:25

וַיֵּרָגְנוּ consec.-Ni. impf. 3 m.p. (רָגַן 920) *and they murmured*
בְאָהֳלֵיהֶם prep.-n.m.p.-3 m.p. sf. (13) *in their tents*
לֹא שָׁמְעוּ neg.-Qal pf. 3 c.p. (1033) *and did not obey*
בְּקוֹל יהוה prep.-n.m.s. cstr. (876)-pr.n. (217) *the voice of Yahweh*

106:26

וַיִּשָּׂא consec.-Qal impf. 3 m.s. (נָשָׂא 669) *therefore he raised*
יָדוֹ n.f.s.-3 m.s. sf. (388) *his hand*
לָהֶם prep.-3 m.p. sf. *to them*
לְהַפִּיל prep.-Hi. inf.cstr. (נָפַל 656) *that he would make fall*
אוֹתָם dir.obj.-3 m.p. sf. *them*
בַּמִּדְבָּר prep.-def.art.-n.m.s. (II 184) *in the wilderness*

106:27

וּלְהַפִּיל conj.-prep.-Hi. inf.cstr. (נָפַל 656) *and would cause to fall*
זַרְעָם n.m.s.-3 m.p. sf. (282) *their descendants*
בַּגּוֹיִם prep.-def.art.-n.m.p. (156) *among the nations*
וּלְזָרוֹתָם conj.-prep.-Pi. inf.cstr.-3 m.p. sf. (זָרָה 279) *scattering them*
בָּאֲרָצוֹת prep.-def.art.-n.f.p. (75) *over the lands*

106:28

וַיִּצָּמְדוּ consec.-Ni. impf. 3 m.p. (צָמַד 855) *then they attached themselves*
לְבַעַל prep.-n.m.s. cstr. (127) *to the Baal of*
פְּעוֹר pr.n. (128) *Peor*
וַיֹּאכְלוּ consec.-Qal impf. 3 m.p. (אָכַל 37) *and ate*
זִבְחֵי n.m.p. cstr. (257) *sacrifices of*
מֵתִים Qal act.ptc. m.p. (מוּת 559) *dead*

106:29

וַיַּכְעִיסוּ consec.-Hi. impf. 3 m.p. (כָּעַס 494) *and they provoked*
בְּמַעַלְלֵיהֶם prep.-n.m.p.-3 m.p. sf. (760) *with their doings*

וַתִּפְרָץ־ consec.-Qal impf. 3 f.s. (פָּרַץ I 829) *and broke out*
בָּם prep.-3 m.p. sf. *among them*
מַגֵּפָה n.f.s. (620) *a plague*

106:30

וַיַּעֲמֹד consec.-Qal impf. 3 m.s. (763) *then stood up*
פִּינְחָס pr.n. (810) *Phinehas*
וַיְפַלֵּל consec.-Pi. impf. 3 m.s. (פָּלַל 813) *and interposed*
וַתֵּעָצַר consec.-Ni. impf. 3 f.s. (עָצַר 783) *and was stayed*
הַמַּגֵּפָה def.art.-n.f.s. (620) *the plague*

106:31

וַתֵּחָשֶׁב consec.-Ni. impf. 3 f.s. (חָשַׁב 362) *and that has been reckoned*
לוֹ prep.-3 m.s. sf. *to him*
לִצְדָקָה prep.-n.f.s. (842) *as righteousness*
לְדֹר וָדֹר prep.-n.m.s. (189)-conj.-v.supra *from generation to generation*
עַד־עוֹלָם prep. (III 723)-n.m.s. (761) *for ever*

106:32

וַיַּקְצִיפוּ consec.-Hi. impf. 3 m.p. (קָצַף 893) *and they angered*
עַל־מֵי prep.-n.m.p. cstr. (565) *at the waters of*
מְרִיבָה pr.n. (II 937) *Meribah*
וַיֵּרַע consec.-Qal impf. 3 m.s. (רָעַע 949) *and it went ill*
לְמֹשֶׁה prep.-pr.n. (602) *with Moses*
בַּעֲבוּרָם prep.-prep.-3 m.p. sf. (721) *on their account*

106:33

כִּי־הִמְרוּ conj. (471)-Hi. pf. 3 c.p. (מָרָה 598) *for they made bitter*
אֶת־רוּחוֹ dir.obj.-n.f.s.-3 m.s. sf. (924) *his spirit*
וַיְבַטֵּא consec.-Pi. impf. 3 m.s. (בָּטָה 104) *for he spoke rashly*
בִּשְׂפָתָיו prep.-n.f.s.-3 m.s. sf. (973) *with his lips*

106:34

לֹא־הִשְׁמִידוּ neg.-Hi. pf. 3 c.p. (שָׁמַד 1029) *they did not destroy*
אֶת־הָעַמִּים dir.obj.-def.art.-n.m.p. (I 766) *the peoples*
אֲשֶׁר אָמַר rel. (81)-Qal pf. 3 m.s. (55) *as had commanded*
יהוה pr.n. (217) *Yahweh*
לָהֶם prep.-3 m.p. sf. *them*

106:35

וַיִּתְעָרְבוּ consec.-Hith. impf. 3 m.p. (עָרַב II 786) *but they mingled*
בַגּוֹיִם prep.-def.art.-n.m.p. (156) *with the nations*
וַיִּלְמְדוּ consec.-Qal impf. 3 m.p. (540) *and learned*
מַעֲשֵׂיהֶם n.m.p.-3 m.p. sf. (795) *their works*

106:36

וַיַּעַבְדוּ consec.-Qal impf. 3 m.p. (712) *and they served*
אֶת־עֲצַבֵּיהֶם dir.obj.-n.m.p.-3 m.p. sf. (781) *their idols*
וַיִּהְיוּ consec.-Qal impf. 3 m.p. (הָיָה 224) *which became*
לָהֶם prep.-3 m.p. sf. *to them*
לְמוֹקֵשׁ prep.-n.m.s. (430) *a snare*

106:37

וַיִּזְבְּחוּ consec.-Qal impf. 3 m.p. (זָבַח 256) *and they sacrificed*
אֶת־בְּנֵיהֶם dir.obj.-n.m.p.-3 m.p. sf. (119) *their sons*
וְאֶת־בְּנוֹתֵיהֶם conj.-dir.obj.-n.f.p.-3 m.p. sf. (I 123) *and their daughters*
לַשֵּׁדִים prep.-def.art.-n.m.p. (993) *to the demons*

106:38

וַיִּשְׁפְּכוּ consec.-Qal impf. 3 m.p. (שָׁפַךְ 1049) *and they poured out*
דָם נָקִי n.m.s. (196)-adj. m.s. (667) *innocent blood*
דַּם־בְּנֵיהֶם n.m.s. cstr. (196)-n.m.p.-3 m.p. sf. (119) *the blood of their sons*
וּבְנוֹתֵיהֶם conj.-n.f.p.-3 m.p. sf. (I 123) *and their daughters*
אֲשֶׁר זִבְּחוּ rel. (81)-Pi. pf. 3 c.p. (256) *whom they sacrificed*
לַעֲצַבֵּי prep.-n.m.p. cstr. (781) *to the idols of*
כְנָעַן pr.n. (488) *Canaan*
וַתֶּחֱנַף consec.-Qal impf. 3 f.s. (חָנֵף 337) *and was polluted*
הָאָרֶץ def.art.-n.f.s. (75) *the land*
בַּדָּמִים prep.-def.art.-n.m.p. (196) *with blood*

106:39

וַיִּטְמְאוּ consec.-Qal impf. 3 m.p. (379) *thus they became unclean*
בְמַעֲשֵׂיהֶם prep.-n.m.p.-3 m.p. sf. (795) *by their acts*
וַיִּזְנוּ consec.-Qal impf. 3 m.p. (זָנָה 275) *and played the harlot*
בְּמַעַלְלֵיהֶם prep.-n.m.p.-3 m.p. sf. (760) *in their doings*

106:40

וַיִּחַר consec.-Qal impf. 3 m.s. (חָרָה 354) *then was kindled*
אַף־יהוה n.m.s. cstr. (I 60)-pr.n. (217) *the anger of Yahweh*
בְּעַמּוֹ prep.-n.m.s.-3 m.s. sf. (I 766) *against his people*
וַיְתָעֵב consec.-Pi. impf. 3 m.s. (תָּעַב 1073) *and he abhorred*
אֶת־נַחֲלָתוֹ dir.obj.-n.f.s.-3 m.s. sf. (635) *his heritage*

106:41

וַיִּתְּנֵם consec.-Qal impf. 3 m.s.-3 m.p. sf. (נָתַן 678) *and he gave them*
בְּיַד־גּוֹיִם prep.-n.f.s. cstr. (388)-n.m.p. (156) *into the hand of the nations*
וַיִּמְשְׁלוּ consec.-Qal impf. 3 m.p. (605) *so that ruled*
בָהֶם prep.-3 m.p. sf. *over them*
שֹׂנְאֵיהֶם Qal act.ptc. m.p.-3 m.p. sf. (שָׂנֵא 971) *those who hated them*

106:42

וַיִּלְחָצוּם consec.-Qal impf. 3 m.p.-3 m.p. sf. (537 לָחַץ) *and oppressed them*
אוֹיְבֵיהֶם Qal act.ptc. m.p.-3 m.p. sf. (אָיַב 33) *their enemies*
וַיִּכָּנְעוּ consec.-Ni. impf. 3 m.p. (כָּנַע 488) *and they were brought into subjection*
תַּחַת יָדָם prep. (1065)-n.f.s.-3 m.p. sf. (388) *under their power*

106:43

פְּעָמִים רַבּוֹת n.f.p. (821)-adj. f.p. (I 912) *many times*
יַצִּילֵם Hi. impf. 3 m.s.-3 m.p. sf. (נָצַל 664) *he delivered them*
וְהֵמָּה conj.-pers.pr. 3 m.p. (241) *but they*
יַמְרוּ Hi. impf. 3 m.p. (מָרָה 598) *were rebellious*
בַעֲצָתָם prep.-n.f.s.-3 m.p. sf. (I 420) *in their purposes*
וַיָּמֹכּוּ consec.-Qal impf. 3 m.p. (מָכַךְ 568) *and were brought low*
בַּעֲוֹנָם prep.-n.m.s.-3 m.p. sf. (730) *through their iniquity*

106:44

וַיַּרְא consec.-Qal impf. 3 m.s. (רָאָה 906) *nevertheless he regarded*

בַּצַּר לָהֶם prep.-def.art.-n.m.s. (II 865)-prep.-3 m.p. sf. *their distress*

בְּשָׁמְעוֹ prep.-Qal inf.cstr.-3 m.s. sf. (1033) *when he heard*

אֶת־רִנָּתָם dir.obj.-n.f.s.-3 m.p. sf. (943) *their cry*

106:45

וַיִּזְכֹּר consec.-Qal impf. 3 m.s. (269) *and he remembered*

לָהֶם prep.-3 m.p. sf. *for their sake*

בְּרִיתוֹ n.f.s.-3 m.s. sf. (136) *his covenant*

וַיִּנָּחֵם consec.-Ni. impf. 3 m.s. (נָחַם 636) *and relented*

כְּרֹב prep.-n.m.s. cstr. (913) *according to the abundance of*

חֲסָדָו n.m.p.-3 m.s. sf. (338) *his steadfast love*

106:46

וַיִּתֵּן consec.-Qal impf. 3 m.s. (נָתַן 678) *and he gave*

אוֹתָם dir.obj.-3 m.p. sf. *them*

לְרַחֲמִים prep.-n.m.p. (933) *to compassion*

לִפְנֵי prep.-n.m.p. cstr. (815) *before*

כָּל־שׁוֹבֵיהֶם n.m.s. cstr. (481)-Qal act.ptc. m.p.-3 m.p. sf. (שָׁבָה 985) *those who held them captive*

106:47

הוֹשִׁיעֵנוּ Hi. impv. 2 m.s.-1 c.p. sf. (יָשַׁע 446) *save us*

יהוה pr.n. (217) *O Yahweh*

אֱלֹהֵינוּ n.m.p.-1 c.p. sf. (43) *our God*

וְקַבְּצֵנוּ conj.-Pi. impv. 2 m.s.-1 c.p. sf. (קָבַץ 867) *and gather us*

מִן־הַגּוֹיִם prep.-def.art.-n.m.p. (156) *from among the nations*

לְהֹדוֹת prep.-Hi. inf.cstr. (יָדָה 392) *that we may give thanks*

לְשֵׁם prep.-n.m.s. cstr. (1027) *to the name of*

קָדְשֶׁךָ n.m.s.-2 m.s. sf. (871) *thy holiness*

לְהִשְׁתַּבֵּחַ prep.-Hith. inf.cstr. (שָׁבַח II 986) *and glory*

בִּתְהִלָּתֶךָ prep.-n.f.s.-2 m.s. sf. (239) *in thy praise*

106:48

בָּרוּךְ Qal pass.ptc. (138) *blessed be*

יהוה pr.n. (217) *Yahweh*

אֱלֹהֵי יִשְׂרָאֵל n.m.p. cstr. (43)-pr.n. (975) *the God of Israel*

מִן־הָעוֹלָם prep.-def.art.-n.m.s. (761) *from everlasting*

וְעַד הָעוֹלָם conj.-prep. (III 723)-v.supra *to everlasting*

וְאָמַר conj.-Qal pf. 3 m.s. (55) *and said*

כָּל־הָעָם n.m.s. cstr. (481)-def.art.-n.m.s. (I 766) *all the people*

אָמֵן adv. (53) *Amen*

הַלְלוּ־יָהּ Pi. impv. 2 m.p. (II 237)-pr.n. (219) *Praise Yah*

107:1

הֹדוּ Hi. impv. 2 m.p. (יָדָה 392) *O give thanks*

ליהוה prep.-pr.n. (217) *to Yahweh*

כִּי־טוֹב conj.-adv. m.s. (II 373) *for he is good*

כִּי לְעוֹלָם conj. (471)-prep.-n.m.s. (761) *for for ever*

חַסְדּוֹ n.m.s.-3 m.s. sf. (338) *his steadfast love*

107:2

יֹאמְרוּ Qal impf. 3 m.p. (55) *let say*

גְּאוּלֵי Qal pass.ptc. m.p. cstr. (גָּאַל I 145) *the redeemed of*

יהוה pr.n. (217) *Yahweh*

אֲשֶׁר גְּאָלָם rel. (81)-Qal pf. 3 m.s.-3 m.p. sf. (I 145) *whom he has redeemed*

מִיַּד־צָר prep.-n.f.s. cstr. (388)-n.m.s. paus. (III 865) *from trouble* (lit. *from the hand of the adversary*)

107:3

וּמֵאֲרָצוֹת conj.-prep.-n.f.p. (75) *and from the lands*

קִבְּצָם Pi. pf. 3 m.s.-3 m.p. sf. (קָבַץ 867) *gathered them in*

מִמִּזְרָח prep.-n.m.s. (280) *from the east*

וּמִמַּעֲרָב conj.-prep.-n.m.s. (II 788) *and from the west*

מִצָּפוֹן prep.-n.f.s. (860) *from the north*

וּמִיָּם conj.-prep.-n.m.s. (410; some rd. וּמִיָּמִין) *and from the west*

107:4

תָּעוּ Qal pf. 3 c.p. (תָּעָה 1073) *some wandered*

בַמִּדְבָּר prep.-def.art.-n.m.s. (II 184) *in the desert*

בִּישִׁימוֹן דָּרֶךְ prep.-n.m.s. cstr. (445)-n.m.s. paus. (202) *in the waste of a way*

עִיר מוֹשָׁב n.f.s. cstr. (746)-n.m.s. (444) *a city to dwell in*

לֹא מָצָאוּ neg.-Qal pf. 3 c.p. paus. (592) *finding not*

107:5

רְעֵבִים adj. m.p. (944) *hungry*
גַּם־צְמֵאִים adv. (168)-adj. m.p. (854) *and thirsty*
נַפְשָׁם n.f.s.-3 m.p. sf. (659) *their soul*
בָּהֶם prep.-3 m.p. sf. *within them*
תִּתְעַטָּף Hith. impf. 3 f.s. paus. (עָטַף III 742) *fainted*

107:6

וַיִּצְעֲקוּ consec.-Qal impf. 3 m.p. (858) *then they cried*
אֶל־יהוה prep.-pr.n. (217) *to Yahweh*
בַּצַּר לָהֶם prep.-def.art.-n.m.s. (II 865)-prep.-3 m.p. sf. *in their trouble*
מִמְּצוּקוֹתֵיהֶם prep.-n.f.p.-3 m.p. sf. (848) *from their distresses*
יַצִּילֵם Hi. impf. 3 m.s.-3 m.p. sf. (נָצַל 664) *he delivered them*

107:7

וַיַּדְרִיכֵם consec.-Hi. impf. 3 m.s.-3 m.p. sf. (דָּרַךְ 201) *he led them*
בְּדֶרֶךְ יְשָׁרָה prep.-n.m.s. cstr. (202)-adj. f.s. (449) *by a straight way*
לָלֶכֶת prep.-Qal inf.cstr. (הָלַךְ 229) *till they reached*
אֶל־עִיר מוֹשָׁב prep.-n.f.s. cstr. (746)-n.m.s. (444) *a city to dwell in*

107:8

יוֹדוּ Hi. impf. 3 m.p. (יָדָה 392) *let them thank*
לַיהוה prep.-pr.n. (217) *Yahweh*
חַסְדּוֹ n.m.s.-3 m.s. sf. (338) *for his steadfast love*
וְנִפְלְאוֹתָיו conj.-Ni. ptc. f.p.-3 m.s. sf. (פָּלָא 810) *for his wonderful works*
לִבְנֵי אָדָם prep.-n.m.p. cstr. (119)-n.m.s. (9) *to the sons of men*

107:9

כִּי־הִשְׂבִּיעַ conj.-Hi. pf. 3 m.s. (שָׂבַע 959) *for he satisfies*
נֶפֶשׁ שֹׁקֵקָה n.f.s. (659)-Qal act.ptc. f.s. (שָׁקַק 1055) *him who is thirsty*
וְנֶפֶשׁ רְעֵבָה conj.-n.f.s. (659)-adj. f.s. (944) *and the hungry*
מִלֵּא־ Pi. pf. 3 m.s. (569) *he fills*
טוֹב n.m.s. (375) *with good things*

107:10

יֹשְׁבֵי Qal act.ptc. m.p. cstr. (יָשַׁב 442) *some sat in*
חֹשֶׁךְ n.m.s. (365) *darkness*
וְצַלְמָוֶת conj.-n.m.s. (853) *and in gloom*
אֲסִירֵי n.m.p. cstr. (64) *prisoners in*
עֳנִי n.m.s. (777) *affliction*
וּבַרְזֶל conj.-n.m.s. (137) *and in irons*

107:11

כִּי־הִמְרוּ conj. (471)-Hi. pf. 3 c.p. (מָרָה 598) *for they had rebelled*
אִמְרֵי־ n.m.p. cstr. (56) *against the words of*
אֵל n.m.s. (42) *God*
וַעֲצַת conj.-n.f.s. cstr. (420) *and the counsel of*
עֶלְיוֹן n.m.s. (751) *the Most High*
נָאָצוּ Qal pf. 3 c.p. paus. (נָאַץ 610) *they spurned*

107:12

וַיַּכְנַע consec.-Hi. impf. 3 m.s. (כָּנַע 488) *was bowed down*
בֶּעָמָל prep.-def.art.-n.m.s. (765) *with hard labor*
לִבָּם n.m.s.-3 m.p. sf. (524) *their heart*
כָּשְׁלוּ Qal pf. 3 c.p. (505) *they fell down*
וְאֵין עֹזֵר conj.-neg. cstr. (II 34)-Qal act.ptc. (740) *and none to help*

107:13

וַיִּזְעֲקוּ consec.-Qal impf. 3 m.p. (277) *then they cried*
אֶל־יהוה prep.-pr.n. (217) *to Yahweh*
בַּצַּר לָהֶם prep.-def.art.-n.m.s. (II 865)-prep.-3 m.p. sf. *in their trouble*
מִמְּצֻקוֹתֵיהֶם prep.-n.f.p.-3 m.p. sf. (848) *and from their distress*
יוֹשִׁיעֵם Hi. impf. 3 m.s.-3 m.p. sf. (יָשַׁע 446) *he delivered them*

107:14

יוֹצִיאֵם Hi. impf. 3 m.s.-3 m.p. sf. (יָצָא 422) *he brought them out*
מֵחֹשֶׁךְ prep.-n.m.s. (365) *of darkness*
וְצַלְמָוֶת conj.-n.m.s. (853) *and gloom*
וּמוֹסְרוֹתֵיהֶם conj.-n.m.p.-3 m.p. sf. (64) *and their bonds*
יְנַתֵּק Pi. impf. 3 m.s. (נָתַק 683) *he broke asunder*

107:15

יוֹדוּ Hi. impf. 3 m.p. (יָדָה 392) *let them thank*
לַיהוה prep.-pr.n. (217) *Yahweh*

חַסְדּוֹ n.m.s.-3 m.s. sf. (338) *for his steadfast love*
וְנִפְלְאוֹתָיו conj.-Ni. ptc. f.p.-3 m.s. sf. (פָּלָא 810) *for his wonderful works*
לִבְנֵי אָדָם prep.-n.m.p. cstr. (119)-n.m.s. (9) *to the sons of men*

107:16

כִּי־שִׁבַּר conj. (471)-Pi. pf. 3 m.s. (990) *for he shatters*
דַּלְתוֹת n.f.p. cstr. (195) *the doors of*
נְחֹשֶׁת n.f.s. (I 638) *bronze*
וּבְרִיחֵי conj.-n.m.p. cstr. (138) *and the bars of*
בַרְזֶל n.m.s. (187) *iron*
גִּדֵּעַ Pi. pf. 3 m.s. (154) *cuts in two*

107:17

אֱוִלִים adj. m.p. (17) *some were fools*
מִדֶּרֶךְ prep.-n.m.s. cstr. (202) *through the way of*
פִּשְׁעָם n.m.s.-3 m.p. sf. (833) *their sin*
וּמֵעֲוֹנֹתֵיהֶם conj.-prep.-n.m.p.-3 m.p. sf. (עָוֹן 730) *and because of their iniquities*
יִתְעַנּוּ Hith. impf. 3 m.p. (עָנָה III 776) *they suffered affliction*

107:18

כָּל־אֹכֶל n.m.s. cstr. (481)-n.m.s. (38) *any kind of food*
תְּתַעֵב Pi. impf. 3 f.s. (תָּעַב 1073) *loathed*
נַפְשָׁם n.f.s.-3 m.p. sf. (659) *they themselves*
וַיַּגִּיעוּ consec.-Hi. impf. 3 m.p. (נָגַע 619) *and they drew near*
עַד־שַׁעֲרֵי prep. (III 723)-n.m.p. cstr. (1044) *to the gates of*
מָוֶת n.m.s. (560) *death*

107:19

וַיִּזְעֲקוּ consec.-Qal impf. 3 m.p. (277) *then they cried*
אֶל־יהוה prep.-pr.n. (217) *to Yahweh*
בַּצַּר לָהֶם prep.-def.art.-n.m.s. (II 865)-prep.-3 m.p. sf. *in their trouble*
מִמְּצֻקוֹתֵיהֶם prep.-n.f.p.-3 m.p. sf. (848) *from their distress*
יוֹשִׁיעֵם Hi. impf. 3 m.s.-3 m.p. sf. (יָשַׁע 446) *he delivered them*

107:20

יִשְׁלַח Qal impf. 3 m.s. (1018) *he sent forth*
דְּבָרוֹ n.m.s.-3 m.s. sf. (182) *his word*
וְיִרְפָּאֵם conj.-Qal impf. 3 m.s.-3 m.p. sf. (950) *and healed them*
וִימַלֵּא conj.-Pi. impf. 3 m.s. (572) *and delivered them*
מִשְּׁחִיתוֹתָם prep.-n.f.p.-3 m.p. sf. (1005) *from destruction*

107:21

יוֹדוּ Hi. impf. 3 m.p. (יָדָה 392) *let them thank*
לַיהוה prep.-pr.n. (217) *Yahweh*
חַסְדּוֹ n.m.s.-3 m.s. sf. (338) *for his steadfast love*
וְנִפְלְאוֹתָיו conj.-Ni. ptc. f.p.-3 m.s. sf. (פָּלָא 810) *and for his wonderful works*
לִבְנֵי אָדָם prep.-n.m.p. cstr. (119)-n.m.s. (9) *to the sons of men*

107:22

וְיִזְבְּחוּ conj.-Qal impf. 3 m.p. (256) *and let them offer sacrifices*
זִבְחֵי n.m.p. cstr. (257) *sacrifices of*
תוֹדָה n.f.s. (392) *thanksgiving*
וִיסַפְּרוּ conj.-Pi. impf. 3 m.p. (707) *and tell of*
מַעֲשָׂיו n.m.p.-3 m.s. sf. (795) *his deeds*
בְּרִנָּה prep.-n.f.s. (943) *in songs of joy*

107:23

יוֹרְדֵי Qal act.ptc. m.p. cstr. (יָרַד 432; GK 5n,17e) *some went down*
הַיָּם def.art.-n.m.s. (410) *to the sea*
בָּאֳנִיּוֹת prep.-n.f.p. (58) *in ships*
עֹשֵׂי Qal act.ptc. m.p. cstr. (עָשָׂה I 793) *doing*
מְלָאכָה n.f.s. (521) *business*
בְּמַיִם רַבִּים prep.-n.m.p. (565)-adj. m.p. (I 912) *on the great waters*

107:24

הֵמָּה רָאוּ pers.pr 3 m.p. (241)-Qal pf. 3 c.p. (רָאָה 906) *they saw*
מַעֲשֵׂי n.m.p. cstr. (795) *the deeds of*
יהוה pr.n. (217) *Yahweh*
וְנִפְלְאוֹתָיו conj.-Ni. ptc. f.p.-3 m.s. sf. (פָּלָא 810) *and his wondrous works*
בִּמְצוּלָה prep.-n.f.s. (846) *in the deep*

107:25

וַיֹּאמֶר consec.-Qal impf. 3 m.s. (55) *for he commanded*
וַיַּעֲמֵד consec.-Hi. impf. 3 m.s. (עָמַד 763) *and raised (caused to stand)*
רוּחַ סְעָרָה n.f.s. (924)-adj. f.s. (704) *the stormy wind*
וַתְּרוֹמֵם consec.-Polel impf. 3 f.s. (רוּם 926) *which lifted up*

גַּלָּיו n.m.p.-3 m.s. sf. (164) *the waves of the sea*

107:26

יַעֲלוּ Qal impf. 3 m.p. (עָלָה 748) *they mounted up*
שָׁמַיִם n.m. du. (1029) *to heaven*
יֵרְדוּ Qal impf. 4 m.p. (יָרַד 432) *they went down*
תְהוֹמוֹת n.f.p. (1062) *to the depths*
נַפְשָׁם n.f.s.-3 m.p. sf. (659) *their courage*
בְּרָעָה prep.-n.f.s. (949) *in their evil plight*
תִתְמוֹגָג Hith. impf. 3 f.s. (מוג 556) *melted away*

107:27

יָחוֹגּוּ Qal impf. 3 m.p. (חָגַג 290) *they reeled*
וְיָנוּעוּ conj.-Qal impf. 3 m.p. (נוּעַ 631) *and staggered*
כַּשִּׁכּוֹר prep.-def.art.-adj. m.s. (1016) *like drunken men*
וְכָל־חָכְמָתָם conj.-n.m.s. cstr. (481)-n.f.s.-3 m.p. sf. (315) *and all their wisdom*
תִּתְבַּלָּע Hith. impf. 3 f.s. (בָּלַע 118) *is swallowed up*

107:28

וַיִּצְעֲקוּ consec.-Qal impf. 3 m.p. (858) *then they cried*
אֶל־יהוה prep.-pr.n. (217) *to Yahweh*
בַּצַּר לָהֶם prep.-def.art.-n.m.s. (II 865)-prep.-3 m.p. sf. *in their trouble*
וּמִמְּצוּקֹתֵיהֶם conj.-prep.-n.f.p.-3 m.p. sf. (848) *and from their distress*
יוֹצִיאֵם Hi. impf. 3 m.s.-3 m.p. sf. (422) *he delivered them*

107:29

יָקֵם Hi. impf. 3 m.s. apoc. (קוּם 877) *he made*
סְעָרָה n.f.s. (704) *the storm*
לִדְמָמָה prep.-n.f.s. (199) *be still*
וַיֶּחֱשׁוּ consec.-Qal impf. 3 m.p. (חָשָׁה 364) *and were hushed*
גַּלֵּיהֶם n.m.p.-3 m.p. sf. (164) *their waves*

107:30

וַיִּשְׂמְחוּ consec.-Qal impf. 3 m.p. (970) *then they were glad*
כִּי־יִשְׁתֹּקוּ conj. (471)-Qal impf. 3 m.p. paus. (1060) *because they had quiet*
וַיַּנְחֵם consec.-Hi. impf. 3 m.s.-3 m.p. sf. (נָחָה 634) *and he brought them*
אֶל־מְחוֹז prep.-n.m.s. cstr. (562) *to the city of*
חֶפְצָם n.m.s.-3 m.p. sf. (343) *their delight*

107:31

יוֹדוּ Hi. impf. 3 m.p. (יָדָה 392) *let them thank*
לַיהוה prep.-pr.n. (217) *Yahweh*
חַסְדּוֹ n.m.s.-3 m.s. sf. (338) *for his steadfast love*
וְנִפְלְאוֹתָיו conj.-Ni. ptc. f.p.-3 m.s. sf. (פָּלָא 810) *and for his wonderful works*
לִבְנֵי אָדָם prep.-n.m.p. cstr. (119)-n.m.s. (9) *to the sons of men*

107:32

וִירֹמְמוּהוּ conj.-Polel impf. 3 m.p.-3 m.s. sf. (רוּם 926) *and let them extol him*
בִּקְהַל־ prep.-n.m.s. cstr. (874) *in the congregation of*
עָם n.m.s. (I 766) *the people*
וּבְמוֹשַׁב conj.-prep.-n.m.s. cstr. (444) *and in the assembly of*
זְקֵנִים adj. m.p. (278) *the elders*
יְהַלְלוּהוּ Pi. impf. 3 m.p.-3 m.s. sf. (הָלַל II 237) *praise him*

107:33

יָשֵׂם Qal impf. 3 m.s. apoc. (שׂוּם I 962) *he turns*
נְהָרוֹת n.m.p. (625) *rivers*
לְמִדְבָּר prep.-n.m.s. (II 184) *into a desert*
וּמֹצָאֵי conj.-n.m.p. cstr. (I 425) *and springs of*
מַיִם n.m.p. (565) *water*
לְצִמָּאוֹן prep.-n.m.s. (855) *into thirsty ground*

107:34

אֶרֶץ פְּרִי n.f.s. cstr. (75)-n.m.s. (826) *a fruitful land*
לִמְלֵחָה prep.-n.f.s. (572) *into a salty waste*
מֵרָעַת prep.-n.f.s. cstr. (949) *because of the wickedness of*
יֹשְׁבֵי Qal act.ptc. m.p. cstr. (442) *the inhabitants of*
בָהּ prep.-3 f.s. sf. *it*

107:35

יָשֵׂם Qal impf. 3 m.s. apoc. (שׂוּם I 962) *he turns*
מִדְבָּר n.m.s. (II 184) *a desert*
לַאֲגַם־מַיִם prep.-n.m.s. cstr. (8)-n.m.p. (565) *into pools of water*
וְאֶרֶץ צִיָּה conj.-n.f.s. (75)-adj. f.s. (851) *a parched land*
לְמֹצָאֵי prep.-n.m.p. cstr. (I 425) *into springs of*
מָיִם n.m.p. paus. (565) *water*

107:36

וַיּוֹשֶׁב consec.-Hi. impf. 3 m.s. (יָשַׁב 442) *and he lets dwell*
שָׁם adv. (1027) *there*
רְעֵבִים adj. m.p. (944) *the hungry*
וַיְכוֹנְנוּ consec.-Polel impf. 3 m.p. (כּוּן I 465) *and they establish*
עִיר n.f.s. (746) *a city*
מוֹשָׁב n.m.s. (444) *to live in*

107:37

וַיִּזְרְעוּ consec.-Qal impf. 3 m.p. (281) *and they sow*
שָׂדוֹת n.m.p. (961) *fields*
וַיִּטְּעוּ consec.-Qal impf. 3 m.p. (נָטַע 642) *and plant*
כְרָמִים n.m.p. (501) *vineyards*
וַיַּעֲשׂוּ consec.-Qal impf. 3 m.p. (עָשָׂה I 793) *and get*
פְּרִי תְבוּאָה n.m.s. cstr. (826)-n.f.s. (100) *a fruitful yield*

107:38

וַיְבָרֲכֵם consec.-Pi. impf. 3 m.s.-3 m.p. sf. (בָּרַךְ 138) *by his blessing*
וַיִּרְבּוּ consec.-Qal impf. 3 m.p. (רָבָה I 915) *and they multiply*
מְאֹד adv. (547) *greatly*
וּבְהֶמְתָּם conj.-n.f.s.-3 m.p. sf. (96) *and their cattle*
לֹא יַמְעִיט neg.-Hi. impf. 3 m.s. (מָעַט 589) *he does not let diminish*

107:39

וַיִּמְעֲטוּ consec.-Qal impf. 3 m.p. (589) *when they are diminished*
וַיָּשֹׁחוּ consec.-Qal impf. 3 m.p. (שָׁחַח 1005) *and brought low*
מֵעֹצֶר prep.-n.m.s. (783) *through oppression*
רָעָה n.f.s. (949) *trouble*
וְיָגוֹן conj.-n.m.s. (387) *and sorrow*

107:40

שֹׁפֵךְ Qal act.ptc. (1049; GK 5n) *he pours*
בּוּז n.m.s. (II 100) *contempt*
עַל־נְדִיבִים prep.-n.m.p. (622) *upon princes*
וַיַּתְעֵם consec.-Hi. impf. 3 m.s.-3 m.p. sf. (תָּעָה 1073) *and makes them wander*
בְּתֹהוּ prep.-n.m.s. (1062) *in wastes*
לֹא־דָרֶךְ neg.-n.m.s. paus. (202) *trackless*

107:41

וַיְשַׂגֵּב consec.-Pi. impf. 3 m.s. (שָׂגַב 960) *but he raises up*
אֶבְיוֹן adj. m.s. (2) *the needy*
מֵעוֹנִי prep.-n.m.s. paus. (777) *out of affliction*
וַיָּשֶׂם consec.-Qal impf. 3 m.s. (שׂוּם I 962) *and makes*
כַּצֹּאן prep.-def.art.-n.f.s. (838) *like flocks*
מִשְׁפָּחוֹת n.f.p. (1046) *their families*

107:42

יִרְאוּ Qal impf. 3 m.p. (רָאָה 906) *see it*
יְשָׁרִים adj. m.p. (449) *the upright*
וְיִשְׂמָחוּ conj.-Qal impf. 3 m.p. paus. (970) *and are glad*
וְכָל־עַוְלָה conj.-n.m.s. cstr. (481)-n.f.s. (732) *and all wickedness*
קָפְצָה Qal pf. 3 f.s. (קָפַץ 891) *stops*
פִּיהָ n.m.s.-3 f.s. sf. (804) *its mouth*

107:43

מִי־חָכָם interr. (566)-adj. m.s. (314) *whoever is wise*
וְיִשְׁמָר־ conj.-Qal impf. 3 m.s. (1036) *let him give heed to*
אֵלֶּה demons.adj. c.p. (41) *these things*
וְיִתְבּוֹנְנוּ conj.-Hithpolel impf. 3 m.p. (בִּין 106) *let men consider*
חַסְדֵי n.m.p. cstr. (338; GK 93m) *the steadfast love of*
יהוה pr.n. (217) *Yahweh*

108:1

שִׁיר n.m.s. (1010) *a song*
מִזְמוֹר n.m.s. (274) *a Psalm*
לְדָוִד prep.-pr.n. (187) *to David*

108:2

נָכוֹן Ni. ptc. (כּוּן I 465) *is steadfast*
לִבִּי n.m.s.-1 c.s. sf. (524) *my heart*
אֱלֹהִים n.m.p. (43) *O God*
אָשִׁירָה Qal impf. 1 c.s.-vol.he (שִׁיר 1010) *I will sing*
וַאֲזַמְּרָה conj.-Pi. impf. 1 c.s.-vol.he (זָמַר I 274) *and make melody*
אַף־כְּבוֹדִי conj. (II 64)-n.m.s.-1 c.s. sf. (II 458) *indeed my glory*

108:3

עוּרָה Qal impv. 2 m.s.-vol.he (עוּר I 734) *awake*
הַנֵּבֶל def.art.-n.m.s. (II 614) *O harp*
וְכִנּוֹר conj.-n.m.s. (490) *and lyre*

אָעִירָה Hi. impf. 1 c.s.-vol.he (עוּר I 734) *I will awake*

שָׁחַר n.m.s. paus. (1007) *the dawn*

108:4

אוֹדְךָ Hi. impf. 1 c.s.-2 m.s. sf. (יָדָה 392) *I will give thanks to thee*

בָעַמִּים prep.-def.art.-n.m.p. (I 766) *among the peoples*

יהוה pr.n. (217) *O Yahweh*

וַאֲזַמֶּרְךָ conj.-Pi. impf. 1 c.s.-2 m.s. sf. (זָמַר I 274) *I will sing praises to thee*

בַּל־אֻמִּים neg. (115)-n.f.p. (52) *not peoples* (but many rd. בַּלְאֻמִּים as prep.-n.m.p. (522) *among the peoples*)

108:5

כִּי־גָדוֹל conj. (471)-adj. m.s. (152) *for is great*

מֵעַל־שָׁמַיִם prep. (758)-n.m. du. (1029) *above the heavens*

חַסְדֶּךָ n.m.s.-2 m.s. sf. paus. (338) *thy steadfast love*

וְעַד־שְׁחָקִים conj.-prep. (III 723)-n.m.p. (1007) *reaches to the clouds*

אֲמִתֶּךָ n.f.s.-2 m.s. sf. paus. (54) *thy faithfulness*

108:6

רוּמָה Qal impv. 2 m.s.-vol.he (רוּם 926) *be exalted*

עַל־שָׁמַיִם prep.-n.m. du. (1029) *above the heavens*

אֱלֹהִים n.m.p. (43) *O God*

וְעַל כָּל־הָאָרֶץ conj.-prep.-n.m.s. cstr. (481)-def. art.-n.f.s. (75) *and over all the earth*

כְּבוֹדֶךָ adj. m.s.-2 m.s. sf. paus. (458) *thy glory*

108:7

לְמַעַן יֵחָלְצוּן prep. (775)-Ni. impf. 3 m.p. (חָלַץ I 322) *that may be delivered*

יְדִידֶיךָ adj. m.p.-2 m.s. sf. (391) *thy beloved*

הוֹשִׁיעָה Hi. impv. 2 m.s.-vol.he (יָשַׁע 446) *give help by*

יְמִינְךָ n.f.s.-2 m.s. sf. (411; GK 144m) *thy right hand*

וַעֲנֵנִי conj.-Qal impv. 2 m.s.-1 c.s. sf. (עָנָה I 772) *and answer me*

108:8

אֱלֹהִים n.m.p. (43) *God*

דִּבֶּר Pi. pf. 3 m.s. (180) *has promised*

בְּקָדְשׁוֹ prep.-n.m.s.-3 m.s. sf. (871) *in his holiness*

אֶעְלֹזָה Qal impf. 1 c.s.-vol.he (עָלַז 759) *with exultation*

אֲחַלְּקָה Pi. impf. 1 c.s.-vol.he (חָלַק 323) *I will divide up*

שְׁכֶם pr.n. (II 1014) *Shechem*

וְעֵמֶק conj.-n.m.s. cstr. (770) *and the Vale of*

סֻכּוֹת pr.n. (697) *Succoth*

אֲמַדֵּד Pi. impf. 1 c.s. (מָדַד 551) *I will portion out*

108:9

לִי prep.-1 c.s. sf. *is mine*

גִלְעָד pr.n. (166) *Gilead*

לִי v.supra *is mine*

מְנַשֶּׁה pr.n. (586) *Manasseh*

וְאֶפְרַיִם conj.-pr.n. (68) *and Ephraim*

מָעוֹז רֹאשִׁי n.m.s. cstr. (731)-n.m.s.-1 c.s. sf. (910) *my helmet*

יְהוּדָה pr.n. (397) *Judah*

מְחֹקְקִי Po. ptc.-1 c.s. sf. (חָקַק 349) *my scepter*

108:10

מוֹאָב pr.n. (555) *Moab*

סִיר רַחְצִי n.m.s. cstr. (I 696)-n.m.s.-1 c.s. sf. (934) *my washbasin*

עַל־אֱדוֹם prep.-pr.n. (10) *upon Edom*

אַשְׁלִיךְ Hi. impf. 1 c.s. (שָׁלַךְ 1020) *I cast*

נַעֲלִי n.f.s.-1 c.s. sf. (653) *my shoe*

עֲלֵי־פְלֶשֶׁת prep. (752)-pr.n. (814) *over Philistia*

אֶתְרוֹעָע Hithpolel impf. 1 c.s. (רוּעַ 929) *I shout in triumph*

108:11

מִי יֹבִלֵנִי interr. (566)-Hi. impf. 3 m.s.-1 c.s. sf. (384 יָבַל) *who will bring me*

עִיר מִבְצָר n.f.s. cstr. (746)-n.m.s. (131) *to the fortified city*

מִי נָחַנִי v.supra-Qal pf. 3 m.s.-1 c.s. sf. (נָחָה 634) *who will lead me*

עַד־אֱדוֹם prep. (III 723)-pr.n. (10) *to Edom*

108:12

הֲלֹא־אֱלֹהִים interr.-neg.-n.m.p. (43) *hast not God*

זְנַחְתָּנוּ Qal pf. 2 m.s.-1 c.p. sf. (זָנַח I 276) *thou rejected us?*

וְלֹא־תֵצֵא conj.-neg.-Qal impf. 2 m.s. (יָצָא 422) *thou dost not go forth*

אֱלֹהִים v.supra *O God*

בְּצִבְאוֹתֵינוּ prep.-n.m.p.-1 c.p. sf. (838) *with our armies*

108:13

הָבָה־לָּנוּ Qal impv. 2 m.s.-vol.he (יָהַב 396) -prep.-1 c.p. sf. *O grant us*
עֶזְרָת n.f.s. (740) *help*
מִצָּר prep.-n.m.s. paus. (III 865) *against the foe*
וְשָׁוְא conj.-n.m.s. (996) *for vain*
תְּשׁוּעַת n.f.s. cstr. (448) *the help of*
אָדָם n.m.s. (9) *man*

108:14

בֵּאלֹהִים prep.-n.m.p. (43) *with God*
נַעֲשֶׂה־ Qal impf. 1 c.p. (עָשָׂה I 793) *we shall do*
חָיִל n.m.s. paus. (298) *valiantly*
וְהוּא conj.-pers.pr. 3 m.s. (214) *it is he*
יָבוּס Qal impf. 3 m.s. (בּוּס 100) *who will tread down*
צָרֵינוּ n.m.p.-1 c.p. sf. (III 865) *our foes*

109:1

לַמְנַצֵּחַ prep.-def.art.-Pi. ptc. (I 663) *to the choirmaster*
לְדָוִד prep.-pr.n. (187) *to David*
מִזְמוֹר n.m.s. (274) *a Psalm*
אֱלֹהֵי n.m.p. cstr. (43) *O God of*
תְהִלָּתִי n.f.s.-1 c.s. sf. (239) *my praise*
אַל־תֶּחֱרַשׁ neg.-Qal impf. 2 m.s. (חָרַשׁ II 361) *be not silent*

109:2

כִּי פִי conj. (471)-n.m.s. cstr. (804) *for the mouth of*
רָשָׁע adj. m.s. (957) *the wicked*
וּפִי־ conj.-v.supra *and the mouth of*
מִרְמָה n.f.s. (941) *deceit*
עָלַי prep.-1 c.s. sf. *against me*
פָּתָחוּ Qal pf. 3 c.p. paus. (פָּתַח I 834) *are opened*
דִּבְּרוּ Pi. pf. 3 c.p. (180) *speaking*
אִתִּי prep.-1 c.s. sf. (II 85) *against me*
לְשׁוֹן שָׁקֶר n.f.s. cstr. (546; GK 117t)-n.m.s. paus. (1055) *with lying tongues*

109:3

וְדִבְרֵי שִׂנְאָה conj.-n.m.s. cstr. (182)-n.f.s. (971) *with words of hate*
סְבָבוּנִי Qal pf. 3 c.p.-1 c.s. sf. (סָבַב 685) *they beset me*
וַיִּלָּחֲמוּנִי consec.-Ni. impf. 3 m.p.-1 c.s. sf. (לָחַם 535; GK 57N) *and attack me*
חִנָּם adv. (336) *without cause*

109:4

תַּחַת־אַהֲבָתִי prep. (1065)-n.f.s.-1 c.s. sf. (13) *in return for my love*
יִשְׂטְנוּנִי Qal impf. 3 m.p.-1 c.s. sf. (שָׂטַן 966) *they accuse me*
וַאֲנִי conj.-pers.pr. 1 c.s. (58) *and I*
תְפִלָּה n.f.s. (813) *a prayer*

109:5

וַיָּשִׂימוּ consec.-Qal impf. 3 m.p. (שׂוּם 962) *so they reward*
עָלַי prep.-1 c.s. sf. *me*
רָעָה n.f.s. (949) *evil*
תַּחַת טוֹבָה prep. (1065)-n.f.s. (375) *for good*
וְשִׂנְאָה conj.-n.f.s. (971) *and hatred*
תַּחַת אַהֲבָתִי prep. (1065)-n.f.s.-1 c.s. sf. (13) *for my love*

109:6

הַפְקֵד Hi. impv. 2 m.s. (פָּקַד 823) *appoint*
עָלָיו prep.-3 m.s. sf. *against him*
רָשָׁע adj. m.s. (957) *a wicked man*
וְשָׂטָן conj.-n.m.s. (966) *and an accuser*
יַעֲמֹד Qal impf. 3 m.s. (763) *let stand*
עַל־יְמִינוֹ prep.-n.f.s.-3 m.s. sf. (411) *at his right hand*

109:7

בְּהִשָּׁפְטוֹ prep.-Ni. inf.cstr.-3 m.s. sf. (שָׁפַט 1047) *when he is tried*
יֵצֵא Qal impf. 3 m.s. (יָצָא 422) *let him come forth*
רָשָׁע adj. m.s. (957) *guilty*
וּתְפִלָּתוֹ conj.-n.f.s.-3 m.s. sf. (813) *and his prayer*
תִּהְיֶה Qal impf. 3 f.s. (הָיָה 224) *let be counted*
לַחֲטָאָה prep.-n.f.s. (308) *as sin*

109:8

יִהְיוּ־ Qal impf. 3 m.p. (הָיָה 224) *may be*
יָמָיו n.m.p.-3 m.s. sf. (398) *his days*
מְעַטִּים subst. p. (589) *few*
פְּקֻדָּתוֹ n.f.s.-3 m.s. sf. (824) *his goods*
יִקַּח Qal impf. 3 m.s. (לָקַח 542) *may seize*
אַחֵר adj. (I 29) *another*

109:9

יִהְיוּ־ Qal impf. 3 m.p. (הָיָה 224) *may be*
בָנָיו n.m.p.-3 m.s. sf. (119) *his children*
יְתוֹמִים n.m.p. (450) *fatherless*

וְאִשְׁתּוֹ conj.-n.f.s.-3 m.s. sf. (61) *and his wife*
אַלְמָנָה n.f.s. (48) *a widow*

109:10

וְנוֹעַ יָנוּעוּ conj.-Qal inf.abs. (נוּעַ 631)-Qal impf. 3 m.p. (631) *and may wander about*
בָנָיו n.m.p.-3 m.s. sf. (119) *his children*
וְשִׁאֵלוּ conj.-Pi. pf. 3 c.p. (שָׁאַל 981; GK 64e) *and beg*
וְדָרְשׁוּ conj.-Qal pf. 3 c.p. (דָּרַשׁ 205) *and seek*
מֵחָרְבוֹתֵיהֶם prep.-n.f.p.-3 m.p. sf. (352) *out of the ruins*

109:11

יְנַקֵּשׁ Pi. impf. 3 m.s. (נָקַשׁ 669) *may seize*
נוֹשֶׁה Qal act.ptc. (נָשָׁה I 674) *the creditor*
לְכָל־אֲשֶׁר־לוֹ prep.-n.m.s. (481)-rel. (81)-prep.-3 m.s. sf. *all that he has*
וְיָבֹזּוּ conj.-Qal impf. 3 m.p. (בָּזַז 102) *may plunder*
זָרִים Qal act.ptc. m.p. (זוּר I 266) *strangers*
יְגִיעוֹ n.m.s.-3 m.s. sf. (388) *the fruits of his toil*

109:12

אַל־יְהִי־לוֹ neg.-Qal impf. 3 m.s. apoc. (הָיָה 224) -prep.-3 m.s. sf. *let there be none to him*
מֹשֵׁךְ Qal act.ptc. (מָשַׁךְ 604) *to extend*
חָסֶד n.m.s. paus. (338) *kindness*
וְאַל־יְהִי conj.-neg.-v.supra *nor any*
חוֹנֵן Qal act.ptc. (חָנַן I 335) *to pity*
לִיתוֹמָיו prep.-n.m.p.-3 m.s. sf. (450) *his fatherless children*

109:13

יְהִי־ Qal impf. 3 m.s. apoc. (הָיָה 224) *may be*
אַחֲרִיתוֹ n.f.s.-3 m.s. sf. (31) *his posterity*
לְהַכְרִית prep.-Hi. inf.cstr. (כָּרַת 503) *cut off*
בְּדוֹר אַחֵר prep.-n.m.s. (189)-adj. m.s. (29) *in the second generation*
יִמַּח Ni. impf. 3 m.s. (מָחָה I 562; GK 75y) *may be blotted out*
שְׁמָם n.m.s.-3 m.p. sf. (1027) *their name*

109:14

יִזָּכֵר Ni. impf. 3 m.s. (זָכַר 269) *may be remembered*
עֲוֹן n.m.s. cstr. (730) *the iniquity of*
אֲבֹתָיו n.m.p.-3 m.s. sf. (3) *his fathers*
אֶל־יהוה prep.-pr.n. (217) *before Yahweh*
וְחַטַּאת conj.-n.f.s. cstr. (308) *and the sin of*
אִמּוֹ n.f.s.-3 m.s. sf. (51) *his mother*

אַל־תִּמָּח neg.-Ni. impf. 3 f.s. paus. (מָחָה I 562) *let not be blotted out*

109:15

יִהְיוּ Qal impf. 3 m.p. (הָיָה 224) *let them be*
נֶגֶד־יהוה prep. (617)-pr.n. (217) *before Yahweh*
תָּמִיד adv. (556) *continually*
וְיַכְרֵת conj.-Hi. impf. 3 m.s. apoc. (כָּרַת 503) *and may be cut off*
מֵאֶרֶץ prep.-n.f.s. (75) *from the earth*
זִכְרָם n.m.s.-3 m.p. sf. (271) *their memory*

109:16

יַעַן אֲשֶׁר conj. (774)-rel. (81) *for*
לֹא זָכַר neg.-Qal pf. 3 m.s. (269) *he did not remember*
עֲשׂוֹת חָסֶד Qal inf.cstr. (עָשָׂה I 793)-n.m.s. paus. (338) *to show kindness*
וַיִּרְדֹּף consec.-Qal impf. 3 m.s. (922) *but pursued*
אִישׁ־ n.m.s. (35) *a man*
עָנִי adj. m.s. (776) *poor*
וְאֶבְיוֹן conj.-adj. m.s. (2) *and needy*
וְנִכְאֵה לֵבָב conj.-Ni. ptc. m.s. cstr. (כָּאָה 456) -n.m.s. (523) *and the broken hearted*
לְמוֹתֵת prep.-Polel inf.cstr. (מוּת 559) *to their death*

109:17

וַיֶּאֱהַב consec.-Qal impf. 3 m.s. (אָהַב 12) *he loved*
קְלָלָה n.f.s. (887) *to curse*
וַתְּבוֹאֵהוּ consec.-Qal impf. 3 f.s.-3 m.s. sf. (בּוֹא 97) *and it came on him*
וְלֹא־חָפֵץ conj.-neg.-Qal pf. 3 m.s. (342) *he did not like*
בִּבְרָכָה prep.-n.f.s. (139) *blessing*
וַתִּרְחַק consec.-Qal impf. 3 f.s. (934) *may it be far (or it was far)*
מִמֶּנּוּ prep.-3 m.s. sf. *from him*

109:18

וַיִּלְבַּשׁ consec.-Qal impf. 3 m.s. (527) *and he clothed himself*
קְלָלָה n.f.s. (887) *with cursing*
כְּמַדּוֹ prep.-n.m.s.-3 m.s. sf. (551) *as his coat*
וַתָּבֹא consec.-Qal impf. 3 f.s. (97) *may it soak*
כַמַּיִם prep.-def.art.-n.m.p. (565) *like water*
בְּקִרְבּוֹ prep.-n.m.s.-3 m.s. sf. (899) *into his body*
וְכַשֶּׁמֶן conj.-prep.-def.art.-n.m.s. (1032) *and like oil*

בְּעַצְמוֹתָיו prep.-n.f.p.-3 m.s. sf. (782) *into his bones*

109:19

תְּהִי־לוֹ Qal impf. 3 f.s. apoc. (הָיָה 224)-prep.-3 m.s. sf. *may it be to him*
כְּבֶגֶד prep.-n.m.s. (93) *like a garment*
יַעְטֶה Qal impf. 3 m.s. (עָטָה I 741) *which he wraps round him*
וּלְמֵזַח conj.-prep.-n.m.s. (561) *and like a belt*
תָּמִיד adv. (556) *continually*
יַחְגְּרֶהָ Qal impf. 3 m.s.-3 f.s. sf. (חָגַר 291) *with which he girds himself*

109:20

זֹאת demons.adj. f.s. (260) *this*
פְּעֻלַּת n.f.s. cstr. (821) *the reward of*
שֹׂטְנַי Qal act.ptc. m.p.-1 c.s. sf. (שָׂטַן 966) *my accusers*
מֵאֵת יהוה prep.-prep. (II 85)-pr.n. (217) *from Yahweh*
וְהַדֹּבְרִים conj.-def.art.-Qal act.ptc. m.p. (180) *of those who speak*
רָע n.m.s. (948) *evil*
עַל־נַפְשִׁי prep.-n.f.s.-1 c.s. sf. (659) *against my life*

109:21

וְאַתָּה conj.-pers.pr. 2 m.s. (61) *but thou*
יהוה pr.n. (217) *Yahweh*
אֲדֹנָי n.m.p.-1 c.s. sf. (10) *my Lord*
עֲשֵׂה־אִתִּי Qal impv. 2 m.s. (I 793)-prep.-1 c.s. sf. (II 85) *deal on my behalf*
לְמַעַן שְׁמֶךָ prep. (775)-n.m.s.-2 m.s. sf. (1027) *for thy name's sake*
כִּי־טוֹב conj. (471)-adj. m.s. (II 373) *because is good*
חַסְדְּךָ n.m.s.-2 m.s. sf. (338) *thy steadfast love*
הַצִּילֵנִי Hi. impv. 2 m.s.-1 c.s. sf. (נָצַל 664) *deliver me*

109:22

כִּי־עָנִי conj. (471)-adj. m.s. (776) *for poor*
וְאֶבְיוֹן conj.-adj. m.s. (2) *and needy*
אָנֹכִי pers.pr. 1 c.s. (59) *I am*
וְלִבִּי conj.-n.m.s.-1 c.s. sf. (524) *and my heart*
חָלַל Qal pf. 3 m.s. (I 319) *is stricken*
בְּקִרְבִּי prep.-n.m.s.-1 c.s. sf. (899) *within me*

109:23

כְּצֵל־ prep.-n.m.s. (853) *like a shadow*
כִּנְטוֹתוֹ prep.-Qal inf.cstr.-3 m.s. sf. (נָטָה 639) *at evening*
נֶהֱלָכְתִּי Ni. pf. 1 c.s. paus. (הָלַךְ 229) *I am gone*
נִנְעַרְתִּי Ni. pf. 1 c.s. (נָעַר II 654) *I am shaken off*
כָּאַרְבֶּה prep.-def.art.-n.m.s. (916) *like a locust*

109:24

בִּרְכַּי n.f.p.-1 c.s. sf. (139) *my knees*
כָּשְׁלוּ Qal pf. 3 c.p. (505) *are weak*
מִצּוֹם prep.-n.m.s. (847) *through fasting*
וּבְשָׂרִי conj.-n.m.s.-1 c.s. sf. (142) *and my body*
כָּחַשׁ מִשָּׁמֶן Qal pf. 3 m.s. (471)-prep.-n.m.s. paus. (1032) *has become gaunt*

109:25

וַאֲנִי conj.-pers.pr. 1 c.s. (58) *and I*
הָיִיתִי Qal pf. 1 c.s. (הָיָה 224) *am*
חֶרְפָּה n.f.s. (357) *an object of scorn*
לָהֶם prep.-3 m.p. sf. *to them*
יִרְאוּנִי Qal impf. 3 m.p.-1 c.s. sf. (רָאָה 906) *when they see me*
יְנִיעוּן Hi. impf. 3 m.p. (נוּעַ 631) *they wag*
רֹאשָׁם n.m.s.-3 m.p. sf. (910) *their heads*

109:26

עָזְרֵנִי Qal impv. 2 m.s.-1 c.s. sf. (עָזַר I 740) *help me*
יהוה pr.n. (217) *O Yahweh*
אֱלֹהָי n.m.p.-1 c.s. sf. paus. (43) *my God*
הוֹשִׁיעֵנִי Hi. impv. 2 m.s.-1 c.s. sf. (יָשַׁע 446) *save me*
כְּחַסְדֶּךָ prep.-n.m.s.-2 m.s. sf. paus. (338) *according to thy steadfast love*

109:27

וְיֵדְעוּ conj.-Qal impf. 3 m.p. (יָדַע 393) *and let them know*
כִּי־יָדְךָ conj. (471)-n.f.s.-2 m.s. sf. (388) *that thy hand*
זֹאת demons.adj. f.s. (260) *this*
אַתָּה pers.pr. 2 m.s. (61) *thou*
יהוה pr.n. (217) *O Yahweh*
עֲשִׂיתָהּ Qal pf. 2 m.s.-3 f.s. sf. (עָשָׂה I 793) *hast done it*

109:28

יְקַלְלוּ־ Pi. impf. 3 m.p. (886) *let them curse*
הֵמָּה pers.pr. 3 m.p. (241) *them*
וְאַתָּה conj.-pers.pr. 2 m.s. (61) *but do thou*
תְּבָרֵךְ Pi. impf. 3 f.s. (בָּרַךְ 138) *bless*
קָמוּ Qal pf. 3 c.p. (קוּם 877) *they have arisen*

וַיֵּבֹשׁוּ consec.-Qal impf. 3 m.p. (בּוֹשׁ 101) *and have been put to shame*
וְעַבְדְּךָ conj.-n.m.s.-2 m.s. sf. (713) *and thy servant*
יִשְׂמָח Qal impf. 3 m.s. paus. (970) *may be glad*

109:29

יִלְבְּשׁוּ Qal impf. 3 m.p. (527) *may be clothed*
שׂוֹטְנַי Qal act.ptc. m.p.-1 c.s. sf. (שָׂטַן 966) *my accusers*
כְּלִמָּה n.f.s. (484) *with dishonor*
וְיַעֲטוּ conj.-Qal impf. 3 m.p. (עָטָה I 741) *may they be wrapped*
כַמְעִיל prep.-def.art.-n.m.s. (591) *as in a mantle*
בָּשְׁתָּם n.f.s.-3 m.p. sf. (102) *in their own shame*

109:30

אוֹדֶה Hi. impf. 1 c.s. (יָדָה 392) *I will give thanks*
יהוה pr.n. (217) *to Yahweh*
מְאֹד adv. (547) *great*
בְּפִי prep.-n.m.s.-1 c.s. sf. (804) *with my mouth*
וּבְתוֹךְ conj.-prep.-n.m.s. cstr. (1063) *and in the midst of*
רַבִּים adj. m.p. (I 912) *the throng*
אֲהַלְלֶנּוּ Pi. impf. 1 c.s.-3 m.s. sf. (הָלַל II 273) *I will praise him*

109:31

כִּי־יַעֲמֹד conj. (471)-Qal impf. 3 m.s. (763) *for he stands*
לִימִין prep.-n.f.s. cstr. (411) *at the right hand of*
אֶבְיוֹן adj. m.s. (2) *the needy*
לְהוֹשִׁיעַ prep.-Hi. inf.cstr. (יָשַׁע 446) *to save*
מִשֹּׁפְטֵי prep.-Qal act.ptc. m.p. cstr. (1047) *from those who condemn*
נַפְשׁוֹ n.f.s.-3 m.s. sf. (659) *him*

110:1

לְדָוִד prep.-pr.n. (187) *to David*
מִזְמוֹר n.m.s. (274) *a Psalm*
נְאֻם יהוה n.m.s. cstr. (610)-pr.n. (217) *Yahweh says*
לַאדֹנִי prep.-n.m.s.-1 c.s. sf. (10) *to my lord*
שֵׁב Qal impv. 2 m.s. (יָשַׁב 442) *sit*
לִימִינִי prep.-n.f.s.-1 c.s. sf. (411) *at my right hand*
עַד־אָשִׁית prep.-Qal impf. 1 c.s. (שִׁית 1011; GK 164f) *till I make*
אֹיְבֶיךָ Qal act.ptc. m.p.-2 m.s. sf. (אָיַב 33) *your enemies*
הֲדֹם n.m.s. (213) *(stool)*
לְרַגְלֶיךָ n.f.p.-2 m.s. sf. (919) *your footstool*

110:2

מַטֵּה־ n.m.s. cstr. (641) *scepter (of)*
עֻזְּךָ n.m.s.-2 m.s. sf. (738) *your mighty*
יִשְׁלַח Qal impf. 3 m.s. (1018) *sends forth*
יהוה pr.n. (217) *Yahweh*
מִצִּיּוֹן prep.-pr.n. (851) *from Zion*
רְדֵה Qal impv. 2 m.s. (רָדָה I 921; GK 110c) *rule*
בְּקֶרֶב prep.-n.m.s. cstr. (899) *in the midst of*
אֹיְבֶיךָ v.supra *your foes*

110:3

עַמְּךָ n.m.s.-2 m.s. sf. (I 766) *your people*
נְדָבֹת n.f.p. (621; GK 141c) *will offer themselves*
בְּיוֹם prep.-n.m.s. cstr. (398) *on the day (of)*
חֵילֶךָ n.m.s.-2 m.s. sf. (298) *your host*
בְּהַדְרֵי־ prep.-n.m.p. cstr. (214) *in splendor* (or array); some rd. בְּהַרְרֵי *upon mountains*
קֹדֶשׁ n.m.s. (871) *holy*
מֵרֶחֶם prep.-n.m.s. cstr. (933) *from the womb of*
מִשְׁחָר n.m.s. (1007) *the morning*
לְךָ prep.-2 m.s. sf. *to you*
טַל n.m.s. (378) *like dew*
יַלְדֻתֶיךָ n.f.p.-2 m.s. sf. (409) *your youth*

110:4

נִשְׁבַּע Ni. pf. 3 m.s. (989) *has sworn*
יהוה pr.n. (217) *Yahweh*
וְלֹא יִנָּחֵם conj.-neg.-Ni. impf. 3 m.s. (636) *and will not change his mind*
אַתָּה־ pers.pr. 2 m.s. (61) *you*
כֹהֵן n.m.s. (463) *a priest*
לְעוֹלָם prep.-n.m.s. (761) *for ever*
עַל־דִּבְרָתִי prep.-n.f.s. cstr. (184; ancient genitive ending; GK 90,l) *after the order of*
מַלְכִּי־צֶדֶק pr.n. (575) *Melchizedek*

110:5

אֲדֹנָי n.m.p.-1 c.s. sf. (10) *the Lord*
עַל־יְמִינְךָ prep.-n.f.s.-2 m.s. sf. (411) *at your right hand*
מָחַץ Qal pf. 3 m.s. (563) *he will shatter*
בְּיוֹם־ prep.-n.m.s. cstr. (398) *on the day of*
אַפּוֹ n.m.s.-3 m.s. sf. (I 60) *his wrath*
מְלָכִים n.m.p. (I 572) *kings*

110:6

יָדִין Qal impf. 3 m.s. (דִּין 192) *he will execute judgment*
בַּגּוֹיִם prep.-def.art.-n.m.p. (156) *among the nations*

מְלֵא Qal act.ptc. (569) *filling* (them)
גְוִיּוֹת n.f.p. (156) *with corpses*
מָחַץ Qal pf. 3 m.s. (563) *he will shatter*
רֹאשׁ n.m.s. (910) *chiefs (head)*
עַל־אֶרֶץ prep.-n.f.s. (75) *over the earth*
רַבָּה adj. f.s. (I 912) *wide*

110:7

מִנַּחַל prep.-n.m.s. (636) *from the brook*
בַּדֶּרֶךְ prep.-def.art.-n.m.s. (202) *by the way*
יִשְׁתֶּה Qal impf. 3 m.s. (1059) *he will drink*
עַל־כֵּן prep.-adv. (I 485) *therefore*
יָרִים Hi. impf. 3 m.s. (רוּם 926) *he will lift up*
רֹאשׁ n.m.s. (910) *his head*

111:1

הַלְלוּ יָהּ Pi. impv. 2 m.p. (II 237)-pr.n. (219) *praise Yah*
אוֹדֶה Hi. impf. 1 c.s. (יָדָה 392; GK 5h) *I will give thanks*
יהוה pr.n. (217) *to Yahweh*
בְּכָל־לֵבָב prep.-n.m.s. cstr. (481)-n.m.s. (523) *with my whole heart*
בְּסוֹד prep.-n.m.s. cstr. (691) *in the company of*
יְשָׁרִים adj. m.p. (449) *the upright*
וְעֵדָה conj.-n.f.s. (730) *and the congregation*

111:2

גְּדֹלִים adj. m.p. (152) *great are*
מַעֲשֵׂי n.m.p. cstr. (795) *the works of*
יהוה pr.n. (217) *Yahweh*
דְּרוּשִׁים Qal pass.ptc. m.p. (205) *studied by*
לְכָל־חֶפְצֵיהֶם prep.-n.m.s. cstr. (481)-n.m.p.-3 m.p. sf. (343) *all who have pleasure in them*

111:3

הוֹד־ n.m.s. (I 217) *majesty*
וְהָדָר conj.-n.m.s. (214) *and honor*
פָּעֳלוֹ n.m.s.-3 m.s. sf. (821) *his work*
וְצִדְקָתוֹ conj.-n.f.s.-3 m.s. sf. (842) *and his righteousness*
עֹמֶדֶת Qal act.ptc. f.s. (עָמַד 763) *endures*
לָעַד prep.-n.m.s. paus. (I 723) *for ever*

111:4

זֵכֶר עָשָׂה n.m.s. (271)-Qal pf. 3 m.s. (I 793) *a memorial he has made*
לְנִפְלְאֹתָיו prep.-Ni. ptc. f.p.-3 m.s. sf. (פָּלָא 810) *to his wonderful works*
חַנּוּן adj. m.s. (337) *gracious*
וְרַחוּם conj.-adj. m.s. (933) *and merciful*
יהוה pr.n. (217) *Yahweh*

111:5

טֶרֶף n.m.s. (383) *food*
נָתַן Qal pf. 3 m.s. (678) *he provides*
לִירֵאָיו prep.-Qal act.ptc. m.p.-3 m.s. sf. (יָרֵא 431) *for those who fear him*
יִזְכֹּר Qal impf. 3 m.s. (269) *he is mindful*
לְעוֹלָם prep.-n.m.s. (761) *ever*
בְּרִיתוֹ n.f.s.-3 m.s. sf. (136) *of his covenant*

111:6

כֹּחַ n.m.s. cstr. (470) *the power of*
מַעֲשָׂיו n.m.p.-3 m.s. sf. (795) *his works*
הִגִּיד Hi. pf. 3 m.s. (נָגַד 616) *he has shown*
לְעַמּוֹ prep.-n.m.s.-3 m.s. sf. (I 766) *to his people*
לָתֵת לָהֶם prep.-Qal inf.cstr. (נָתַן 678)-prep.-3 m.p. sf. *in giving them*
נַחֲלַת n.f.s. cstr. (635) *the heritage of*
גּוֹיִם n.m.p. (156) *the nations*

111:7

מַעֲשֵׂי n.m.p. cstr. (795) *the works of*
יָדָיו n.f.p.-3 m.s. sf. (388) *his hands*
אֱמֶת n.f.s. (54) *faithful*
וּמִשְׁפָּט conj.-n.m.s. (1048) *and just*
נֶאֱמָנִים Ni. ptc. m.p. (אָמַן 52) *are trustworthy*
כָּל־פִּקּוּדָיו n.m.s. cstr. (481)-n.m.p.-3 m.s. sf. (824) *all his precepts*

111:8

סְמוּכִים Qal pass.ptc. m.p. (סָמַךְ 701) *they are established*
לָעַד prep.-n.m.s. (I 723) *for ever*
לְעוֹלָם prep.-n.m.s. (761) *and ever*
עֲשׂוּיִם Qal pass.ptc. m.p. (I 793) *to be performed*
בֶּאֱמֶת prep.-n.f.s. (54) *with faithfulness*
וְיָשָׁר conj.-adj. m.s. (449) *and uprightness*

111:9

פְּדוּת n.f.s. (804) *redemption*
שָׁלַח Qal pf. 3 m.s. (1018) *he sent*
לְעַמּוֹ prep.-n.m.s.-3 m.s. sf. (I 766) *to his people*
צִוָּה־ Pi. pf. 3 m.s. (צָוָה 845) *he has commanded*
לְעוֹלָם prep.-n.m.s. (761) *for ever*
בְּרִיתוֹ n.f.s.-3 m.s. sf. (136) *his covenant*
קָדוֹשׁ adj. m.s. (872) *holy*
וְנוֹרָא conj.-Ni. ptc. (יָרֵא 431) *and terrible*
שְׁמוֹ n.m.s.-3 m.s. sf. (1027) *his name*

111:10

רֵאשִׁית n.f.s. cstr. (912) *the beginning of*

חָכְמָה n.f.s. (315) *wisdom*
יִרְאַת n.f.s. cstr. (432) *the fear of*
יהוה pr.n. (217) *Yahweh*
שֵׂכֶל טוֹב n.m.s. (968)-adj. m.s. (II 373) *a good understanding*
לְכָל־עֹשֵׂיהֶם prep.-n.m.s. cstr. (481)-Qal act.ptc. m.p.-3 m.p. sf. (I 793) *to all those who practice it*
תְּהִלָּתוֹ n.f.s.-3 m.s. sf. (239) *his praise*
עֹמֶדֶת Qal act.ptc. f.s. (763) *endures*
לָעַד prep.-n.m.s. (I 723) *for ever*

112:1

הַלְלוּ יָהּ Pi. impv. 2 m.p. (II 237)-pr.n. (219) *praise Yah*
אַשְׁרֵי־ n.m.p. cstr. (80; GK 5h) *blessed is*
אִישׁ n.m.s. (35) *the man*
יָרֵא Qal act.ptc. (431) *who fears*
אֶת־יהוה dir.obj.-pr.n. (217) *Yahweh*
בְּמִצְוֹתָיו prep.-n.f.p.-3 m.s. sf. (846) *in his commandments*
חָפֵץ Qal act.ptc. (I 342) *who delights*
מְאֹד adv. (547) *greatly*

112:2

גִּבּוֹר adj. m.s. (150) *mighty*
בָּאָרֶץ prep.-def.art.-n.f.s. (75) *in the land*
יִהְיֶה Qal impf. 3 m.s. (224) *will be*
זַרְעוֹ n.m.s.-3 m.s. sf. (282) *his descendants*
דּוֹר n.m.s. cstr. (189) *the generation of*
יְשָׁרִים adj. m.p. (449) *the upright*
יְבֹרָךְ Pu. impf. 3 m.s. (בָּרַךְ 138) *will be blessed*

112:3

הוֹן־ n.m.s. (223) *wealth*
וָעֹשֶׁר conj.-n.m.s. (799) *and riches*
בְּבֵיתוֹ prep.-n.m.s.-3 m.s. sf. (108) *in his house*
וְצִדְקָתוֹ conj.-n.f.s.-3 m.s. sf. (842) *and his righteousness*
עֹמֶדֶת Qal act.ptc. f.s. (עָמַד 763) *endures*
לָעַד prep.-n.m.s. (I 723) *for ever*

112:4

זָרַח Qal pf. 3 m.s. (280) *rises*
בַּחֹשֶׁךְ prep.-def.art.-n.m.s. (365) *in the darkness*
אוֹר n.m.s. (21) *light*
לַיְשָׁרִים prep.-def.art.-adj. m.p. (449) *for the upright*
חַנּוּן adj. m.s. (337) *gracious*
וְרַחוּם conj.-adj. m.s. (933) *and merciful*
וְצַדִּיק conj.-adj. m.s. (843) *and righteous*

112:5

טוֹב־אִישׁ adj. m.s. (II 373)-n.m.s. (35) *it is well with the man*
חוֹנֵן Qal act.ptc. (I 335) *who deals generously*
וּמַלְוֶה conj.-Hi. ptc. (II 531) *and lends*
יְכַלְכֵּל Pilpel impf. 3 m.s. (כּוּל 465) *who conducts*
דְּבָרָיו n.m.p.-3 m.s. sf. (182) *his affairs*
בְּמִשְׁפָּט prep.-n.m.s. (1048) *with justice*

112:6

כִּי־לְעוֹלָם conj. (471)-prep.-n.m.s. (761) *for for ever*
לֹא־יִמּוֹט neg.-Ni. impf. 3 m.s. (מוֹט 556) *will not be moved*
לְזֵכֶר prep.-n.m.s. (271) *for remembrance*
עוֹלָם n.m.s. (761) *for ever*
יִהְיֶה Qal impf. 3 m.s. (224) *he will be*
צַדִּיק adj. m.s. (843) *the righteous*

112:7

מִשְּׁמוּעָה רָעָה prep.-n.f.s. (1035)-adj. f.s. (948) *of evil tidings*
לֹא יִירָא neg.-Qal impf. 3 m.s. (יָרֵא 431) *he is not afraid*
נָכוֹן Ni. ptc. (כּוּן 465) *is firm*
לִבּוֹ n.m.s.-3 m.s. sf. (524) *his heart*
בָּטֻחַ Qal pass.ptc. (I 105) *trusting*
בַּיהוה prep.-pr.n. (217) *in Yahweh*

112:8

סָמוּךְ Qal pass.ptc. (701) *is steady*
לִבּוֹ n.m.s.-3 m.s. sf. (524) *his heart*
לֹא יִירָא neg.-Qal impf. 3 m.s. (431) *he will not be afraid*
עַד אֲשֶׁר־ prep. (III 723)-rel. (81) *until*
יִרְאֶה Qal impf. 3 m.s. (906; GK 164f) *he sees*
בְצָרָיו prep.-n.m.p.-3 m.s. sf. (III 865) *on his adversaries*

112:9

פִּזַּר Pi. pf. 3 m.s. (808; GK 120g) *he has scattered*
נָתַן Qal pf. 3 m.s. (678) *he has given*
לָאֶבְיוֹנִים prep.-def.art.-adj. m.p. (2) *to the poor*
צִדְקָתוֹ n.f.s.-3 m.s. sf. (842) *his righteousness*
עֹמֶדֶת Qal act.ptc. f.s. (763) *endureth*
לָעַד prep.-n.m.s. paus. (I 723) *for ever*
קַרְנוֹ n.f.s.-3 m.s. sf. (901) *his horn*
תָּרוּם Qal impf. 3 f.s. (926) *is exalted*
בְּכָבוֹד prep.-adj. m.s. (458) *in honor*

112:10

רָשָׁע adj. m.s. (957) *the wicked man*
יִרְאֶה Qal impf. 3 m.s. (906) *sees*
וְכָעָס conj.-Qal pf. 3 m.s. paus. (494) *and is angry*
שִׁנָּיו n.f.p.-3 m.s. sf. (1042) *his teeth*
יַחֲרֹק Qal impf. 3 m.s. (359) *he gnashes*
וְנָמָס conj.-Ni. pf. 3 m.s. paus. (מָסַס 587) *and melts away*
תַּאֲוַת n.f.s. cstr. (16) *the desire of*
רְשָׁעִים adj. m.p. (957) *the wicked men*
תֹּאבֵד Qal impf. 3 f.s. (אָבַד 1) *comes to nought*

113:1

הַלְלוּ יָהּ Pi. impv. 2 m.p. (II 237)-pr.n. (219) *praise Yah*
הַלְלוּ v.supra *praise*
עַבְדֵי n.m.p. cstr. (713) *O servants of*
יהוה pr.n. (217) *Yahweh*
הַלְלוּ v.supra *praise*
אֶת־שֵׁם dir.obj.-n.m.s. cstr. (1027) *the name of*
יהוה v.supra *Yahweh*

113:2

יְהִי Qal impf. 3 m.s. apoc. (הָיָה 224) *let be*
שֵׁם n.m.s. cstr. (1027) *the name of*
יהוה pr.n. (217) *Yahweh*
מְבֹרָךְ Pu. ptc. (בָּרַךְ 138) *blessed*
מֵעַתָּה prep.-adv. (773) *from now*
וְעַד־עוֹלָם conj.-prep. (III 723)-n.m.s. (761) *and for evermore*

113:3

מִמִּזְרַח־ prep.-n.m.s. cstr. (280) *from the rising of*
שֶׁמֶשׁ n.f.s. (1039) *the sun*
עַד־מְבוֹאוֹ prep. (III 723)-n.m.s.-3 m.s. sf. (99) *to its setting*
מְהֻלָּל Pu. ptc. (II 237) *is to be praised*
שֵׁם יהוה n.m.s. cstr. (1027)-pr.n. (217) *the name of Yahweh*

113:4

רָם Qal pf. 3 m.s. (רוּם 926) *is high*
עַל־כָּל־גּוֹיִם prep.-n.m.s. cstr. (481)-n.m.p. (156) *above all nations*
יהוה pr.n. (217) *Yahweh*
עַל הַשָּׁמַיִם prep.-def.art.-n.m. du. (1029) *above the heavens*
כְּבוֹדוֹ n.m.s.-3 m.s. sf. (458) *his glory*

113:5

מִי interr. (566) *who is*
כַּיהוה prep.-pr.n. (217) *like Yahweh*
אֱלֹהֵינוּ n.m.p.-1 c.p. sf. (43) *our God*
הַמַּגְבִּיהִי def.art.-Hi. ptc. gent. (גָּבַהּ 146; GK 90m) *who is on high*
לָשָׁבֶת prep.-Qal inf.cstr. paus. (יָשַׁב 442) *seated*

113:6

הַמַּשְׁפִּילִי def.art.-Hi. ptc. gent. (1050; GK 90m) *who far down*
לִרְאוֹת prep.-Qal inf.cstr. (רָאָה 906) *looks*
בַּשָּׁמַיִם prep.-def.art.-n.m. du. (1029) *upon the heavens*
וּבָאָרֶץ conj.-prep.-def.art.-n.f.s. (75) *and the earth*

113:7

מְקִימִי Hi. ptc. gent. (קוּם 877; GK 90m) *he raises*
מֵעָפָר prep.-n.m.s. (779) *from the dust*
דָּל adj. m.s. paus. (195) *the poor*
מֵאַשְׁפֹּת prep.-n.m.s. (1046) *from the ash heap*
יָרִים Hi. impf. 3 m.s. (רוּם 926) *he lifts*
אֶבְיוֹן adj. m.s. (2) *the needy*

113:8

לְהוֹשִׁיבִי prep.-Hi. inf.cstr. (יָשַׁב 442; GK 90n) *to make them sit*
עִם־נְדִיבִים prep.-adj. m.p. (622) *with princes*
עִם נְדִיבֵי prep.-adj. m.p. cstr. (622) *with the princes of*
עַמּוֹ n.m.s.-3 m.s. sf. (I 766) *his people*

113:9

מוֹשִׁיבִי Hi. ptc. (יָשַׁב 442; GK 90m) *he gives*
עֲקֶרֶת הַבַּיִת adj. f.s. cstr. (785)-def.art.-n.m.s. (108) *the barren woman of the house*
אֵם־הַבָּנִים n.f.s. cstr. (51)-def.art.-n.m.p. (119) *the mother of the children*
שְׂמֵחָה adj. f.s. (970) *joyful*
הַלְלוּ־יָהּ Pi. impv. 2 m.p. (II 237)-pr.n. (219) *praise Yah*

114:1

בְּצֵאת prep.-Qal inf.cstr. (יָצָא 422) *when went forth*
יִשְׂרָאֵל pr.n. (975) *Israel*
מִמִּצְרָיִם prep.-pr.n. paus. (595) *from Egypt*
בֵּית n.m.s. cstr. (108; GK 128aN) *the house of*
יַעֲקֹב pr.n. (784) *Jacob*
מֵעַם prep.-n.m.s. (I 766) *from a people*

לֹעֵז Qal act.ptc. (541) *talking unintelligibly*

114:2

הָיְתָה Qal pf. 3 f.s. (הָיָה 224) *became*
יְהוּדָה pr.n. (397) *Judah*
לְקָדְשׁוֹ prep.-n.m.s.-3 m.s. sf. (871) *his sanctuary*
יִשְׂרָאֵל pr.n. (975) *Israel*
מַמְשְׁלוֹתָיו n.f.p.-3 m.s. sf. (606) *his dominion*

114:3

הַיָּם def.art.-n.m.s. (410) *the sea*
רָאָה Qal pf. 3 m.s. (906) *looked*
וַיָּנֹס consec.-Qal impf. 3 m.s. (נוּס 630) *and fled*
הַיַּרְדֵּן def.art.-pr.n. (434) *Jordan*
יִסֹּב Qal impf. 3 m.s. (סָבַב 685) *turned*
לְאָחוֹר prep.-subst. (30) *back*

114:4

הֶהָרִים def.art.-n.m.p. (249) *the mountains*
רָקְדוּ Qal pf. 3 c.p. (955) *skipped*
כְאֵילִים prep.-n.m.p. (I 17) *like rams*
גְּבָעוֹת n.f.p. (148) *the hills*
כִּבְנֵי־צֹאן prep.-n.m.p. cstr. (119)-n.f.s. (838) *like lambs*

114:5

מַה־לְּךָ interr. (552)-prep.-2 m.s. sf. *what ails you*
הַיָּם def.art.-n.m.s. (410) *O sea*
כִּי תָנוּס conj.-Qal impf. 2 m.s. (נוּס 630) *that you flee*
הַיַּרְדֵּן def.art.-pr.n. (434) *O Jordan*
תִּסֹּב Qal impf. 2 m.s. (685) *that you turn*
לְאָחוֹר prep.-subst. (30) *back*

114:6

הֶהָרִים def.art.-n.m.p. (249) *O mountains*
תִּרְקְדוּ Qal impf. 2 m.s. (955) *that you skip*
כְאֵילִים prep.-n.m.p. (I 17) *like rams*
גְּבָעוֹת n.f.p. (148) *O hills*
כִּבְנֵי־צֹאן prep.-n.m.p. cstr. (119)-n.f.s. (838) *like lambs*

114:7

מִלִּפְנֵי prep.-prep.-n.m.p. cstr. (815) *at the presence of*
אָדוֹן n.m.s. (10) *the Lord*
חוּלִי Qal impv. 2 f.s. (חוּל I 296) *tremble*
אָרֶץ n.f.s. paus. (75) *O earth*
מִלִּפְנֵי v.supra *at the presence of*
אֱלוֹהַּ n.m.s. cstr. (42) *the God of*
יַעֲקֹב pr.n. (784) *Jacob*

114:8

הַהֹפְכִי def.art.-Qal act.ptc. (הָפַךְ 245; GK 90m) *who turns*
הַצּוּר def.art.-n.m.s. (849) *the rock*
אֲגַם־מָיִם n.m.s. cstr. (8)-n.m.p. paus. (565) *into a pool of water*
חַלָּמִישׁ n.m.s. (321) *the flint*
לְמַעְיְנוֹ־ prep.-n.m.s. cstr. (745; GK 90o) *into a spring of*
מָיִם n.m.p. paus. (565) *water*

115:1

לֹא לָנוּ neg.-prep.-1 c.p. sf. *not to us*
יהוה pr.n. (217) *O Yahweh*
לֹא לָנוּ v.supra-v.supra *not to us*
כִּי־לְשִׁמְךָ conj. (471)-prep.-n.m.s.-2 m.s. sf. (1027) *but to thy name*
תֵּן כָּבוֹד Qal impv. 2 m.s. (נָתַן 678)-n.m.s. (458) *give glory*
עַל־חַסְדְּךָ prep.-n.m.s.-2 m.s. sf. (338) *for the sake of thy steadfast love*
עַל־אֲמִתֶּךָ prep.-n.f.s.-2 m.s. sf. (54) *and thy faithfulness*

115:2

לָמָּה interr. (552) *why*
יֹאמְרוּ Qal impf. 3 m.p. (55) *should say*
הַגּוֹיִם def.art.-n.m.p. (156) *the nations*
אַיֵּה־ interr. (32) *where*
נָא part.of entreaty (609) *(I pray thee)*
אֱלֹהֵיהֶם n.m.p.-3 m.p. sf. (43) *their God*

115:3

וֵאלֹהֵינוּ conj.-n.m.p.-1 c.p. sf. (43) *and our God*
בַשָּׁמָיִם prep.-def.art.-n.m. du. paus. (1029) *in the heavens*
כֹּל אֲשֶׁר־ n.m.s. (481)-rel. (81) *whatever*
חָפֵץ Qal pf. 3 m.s. (342) *he pleases*
עָשָׂה Qal pf. 3 m.s. (I 793) *he does*

115:4

עֲצַבֵּיהֶם n.m.p.-3 m.p. sf. (781) *their idols*
כֶּסֶף n.m.s. (494) *silver*
וְזָהָב conj.-n.m.s. (262) *and gold*
מַעֲשֵׂה n.m.s. cstr. (795) *the work of*
יְדֵי אָדָם n.f. du. cstr. (388)-n.m.s. (9) *men's hands*

115:5

פֶּה־לָהֶם n.m.s. (804)-prep.-3 m.p. sf. *they have mouths*

וְלֹא יְדַבֵּרוּ conj.-neg.-Pi. impf. 3 m.p. paus. (180) *but do not speak*

עֵינַיִם לָהֶם n.f. du. (744)-v.supra *eyes to them*

וְלֹא יִרְאוּ conj.-neg.-Qal impf. 3 m.p. (רָאָה 906) *but do not see*

115:6

אָזְנַיִם לָהֶם n.f. du. (23)-prep.-3 m.p. sf. *they have ears*

וְלֹא יִשְׁמָעוּ conj.-neg.-Qal impf. 3 m.p. paus. (1033) *but do not hear*

אַף לָהֶם n.m.s. (I 60)-v.supra *noses to them*

וְלֹא יְרִיחוּן conj.-neg.-Hi. impf. 3 m.p. (רִיחַ 926) *but do not smell*

115:7

יְדֵיהֶם n.f. du.-3 m.p. sf. (388; GK 147e) *they have hands*

וְלֹא יְמִישׁוּן conj. (GK 143d)-neg.-Hi. impf. 3 m.p. (מוּשׁ II 559) *but do not feel*

רַגְלֵיהֶם n.f. du.-3 m.p. sf. (919; GK 147e) *their feet*

וְלֹא יְהַלֵּכוּ conj. (GK 143d)-neg.-Pi. impf. 3 m.p. paus. (229) *but do not walk*

לֹא־יֶהְגּוּ neg.-Qal impf. 3 m.p. (הָגָה I 211) *and they do not make a sound*

בִּגְרוֹנָם prep.-n.m.s.-3 m.p. sf. (173) *in their throat*

115:8

כְּמוֹהֶם יִהְיוּ prep.-3 m.p. sf.-Qal impf. 3 m.p. (224 הָיָה) *are like them*

עֹשֵׂיהֶם Qal act.ptc. m.p.-3 m.p. sf. (עָשָׂה I 793) *those who make them*

כֹּל אֲשֶׁר־ n.m.s. (481)-rel. (81) *all who*

בֹּטֵחַ Qal act.ptc. (105) *trust*

בָּהֶם prep.-3 m.p. sf. *in them*

115:9

יִשְׂרָאֵל pr.n. (975) *O Israel*

בְּטַח Qal impv. 2 m.s. (105) *trust*

בַּיהוה prep.-pr.n. (217) *in Yahweh*

עֶזְרָם n.m.s.-3 m.p. sf. (I 740) *their help*

וּמָגִנָּם conj.-n.m.s.-3 m.p. sf. (171) *and their shield*

הוּא pers.pr. 3 m.s. (214) *he is*

115:10

בֵּית אַהֲרֹן n.m.s. cstr. (108)-pr.n. (14) *O house of Aaron*

בִּטְחוּ Qal impv. 2 m.p. (105) *trust*

בַּיהוה prep.-pr.n. (217) *in Yahweh*

עֶזְרָם n.m.s.-3 m.p. sf. (I 740) *their help*

וּמָגִנָּם conj.-n.m.s.-3 m.p. sf. (171) *and their shield*

הוּא pers.pr. 3 m.s. (214) *he is*

115:11

יִרְאֵי Qal act.ptc. m.p. cstr. (431) *you who fear*

יהוה pr.n. (217) *Yahweh*

בִּטְחוּ Qal impv. 2 m.p. (105) *trust*

בַּיהוה prep.-pr.n. (217) *in Yahweh*

עֶזְרָם n.m.s.-3 m.p. sf. (I 740) *their help*

וּמָגִנָּם conj.-n.m.s.-3 m.p. sf. (171) *and their shield*

הוּא pers.pr. 3 m.s. (214) *he is*

115:12

יהוה pr.n. (217) *Yahweh*

זְכָרָנוּ Qal pf. 3 m.s.-1 c.p. sf. (269) *has been mindful of us*

יְבָרֵךְ Pi. impf. 3 m.s. (138) *he will bless*

יְבָרֵךְ v.supra *he will bless*

אֶת־בֵּית יִשְׂרָאֵל dir.obj.-n.m.s. cstr. (108)-pr.n. (975) *the house of Israel*

יְבָרֵךְ v.supra *he will bless*

אֶת־בֵּית אַהֲרֹן dir.obj.-v.supra-pr.n. (14) *the house of Aaron*

115:13

יְבָרֵךְ Pi. impf. 3 m.s. (138) *he will bless*

יִרְאֵי יהוה Qal act.ptc. m.p. cstr. (431)-pr.n. (217) *those who fear Yahweh*

הַקְּטַנִּים def.art.-adj. m.p. (I 881) *both small*

עִם־הַגְּדֹלִים prep.-def.art.-adj. m.p. (152) *and great*

115:14

יֹסֵף Hi. impf. 3 m.s. apoc. (יָסַף 414) *may give increase*

יהוה pr.n. (217) *Yahweh*

עֲלֵיכֶם prep.-2 m.p. sf. *(to) you*

עֲלֵיכֶם v.supra *you*

וְעַל־בְּנֵיכֶם conj.-prep.-n.m.p.-2 m.p. sf. (119) *and your children*

115:15

בְּרוּכִים Qal pass.ptc. m.p. (138) *blessed*

אַתֶּם pers.pr. 2 m.p. (61) *be you*

לַיהוה prep.-pr.n. (217) *by Yahweh*
עֹשֵׂה Qal act.ptc. m.s. cstr. (I 793) *who made*
שָׁמַיִם n.m. du. (1029) *heaven*
וָאָרֶץ conj.-n.f.s. paus. (75) *and earth*

115:16

הַשָּׁמַיִם def.art.-n.m. du. (1029) *the heavens*
שָׁמַיִם n.m. du. (1029) *heavens*
לַיהוה prep.-pr.n. (217) *to Yahweh*
וְהָאָרֶץ conj.-def.art.-n.f.s. (75) *but the earth*
נָתַן Qal pf. 3 m.s. (678) *he has given*
לִבְנֵי־אָדָם prep.-n.m.p. cstr. (119)-n.m.s. (9) *to the sons of men*

115:17

לֹא הַמֵּתִים neg.-def.art.-Qal act.ptc. m.p. (מוּת 559) *not the dead*
יְהַלְלוּ־ Pi. impf. 3 m.p. (II 237) *praise*
יָהּ pr.n. (219) *Yah*
וְלֹא כָּל־ conj.-neg.-n.m.s. cstr. (481) *nor do any*
יֹרְדֵי Qal act.ptc. m.p. cstr. (432) *that go down*
דוּמָה n.f.s. (I 189) *in silence*

115:18

וַאֲנַחְנוּ conj.-pers.pr. 1 c.p. (59) *but we*
נְבָרֵךְ Pi. impf. 1 c.p. (בָּרַךְ 138) *will bless*
יָהּ pr.n. (29) *Yah*
מֵעַתָּה prep.-adv. (773) *from this time*
וְעַד־עוֹלָם conj.-prep. (III 723)-n.m.s. (761) *and for evermore*
הַלְלוּ־יָהּ Pi. impv. 2 m.p. (II 237)-pr.n. (219) *Praise Yah*

116:1

אָהַבְתִּי Qal pf. 1 c.s. (אָהֵב 12) *I love*
כִּי־יִשְׁמַע conj. (471)-Qal impf. 3 m.s. (שָׁמַע 1033) *because he has heard*
יהוה pr.n. (217) *Yahweh*
אֶת־קוֹלִי dir.obj.-n.m.s.-1 c.s. sf. (876; GK 90n) *my voice*
תַּחֲנוּנָי n.m.p.-1 c.s. sf. (337) *my supplications*

116:2

כִּי־הִטָּה conj. (471)-Hi. pf. 3 m.s. (נָטָה 639) *because he inclined*
אָזְנוֹ n.f.s.-3 m.s. sf. (23) *his ear*
לִי prep.-1 c.s. sf. *to me*
וּבְיָמַי conj.-prep.-n.m.p.-1 c.s. sf. (398) *and in my days*
אֶקְרָא Qal impf. 1 c.s. (894) *I will call*

116:3

אֲפָפוּנִי Qal pf. 3 c.p.-1 c.s. sf. (אָפַף 67) *encompassed me*
חֶבְלֵי־ n.m.p. cstr. (286) *the snares of*
מָוֶת n.m.s. (560) *death*
וּמְצָרֵי conj.-n.m.p. cstr. (865) *and the pangs of*
שְׁאוֹל pr.n. (982) *Sheol*
מְצָאוּנִי Qal pf. 3 c.p.-1 c.s. sf. (592) *laid hold on me*
צָרָה n.f.s. (865) *distress*
וְיָגוֹן conj.-n.m.s. (387) *and anguish*
אֶמְצָא Qal impf. 1 c.s. (592) *I suffered*

116:4

וּבְשֵׁם־ conj.-prep.-n.m.s. cstr. (1027) *then on the name of*
יהוה pr.n. (217) *Yahweh*
אֶקְרָא Qal impf. 1 c.s. (894) *I called*
אָנָּה interj. (58; GK 16fN) *I beseech thee*
יהוה v.supra *O Yahweh*
מַלְּטָה Pi. impv. 2 m.s.-vol.he (מָלַט 571) *save*
נַפְשִׁי n.f.s.-1 c.s. sf. (659) *my life*

116:5

חַנּוּן adj. (337) *gracious is*
יהוה pr.n. (217) *Yahweh*
וְצַדִּיק conj.-adj. m.s. (843) *and righteous*
וֵאלֹהֵינוּ conj.-n.m.p.-1 c.p. sf. (43) *and our God*
מְרַחֵם Pi. ptc. (רָחַם 933) *is merciful*

116:6

שֹׁמֵר Qal act.ptc. (1036) *preserves*
פְּתָאִים adj. m.p. (834) *the simple*
יהוה pr.n. (217) *Yahweh*
דַּלּוֹתִי Qal pf. 1 c.s. (דָּלַל 195) *when I was brought low*
וְלִי conj.-prep.-1 c.s. sf. *and me*
יְהוֹשִׁיעַ Hi. impf. 3 m.s. (יָשַׁע 446; GK 53q) *he saved*

116:7

שׁוּבִי Qal impv. 2 f.s. (996; GK 72s) *return*
נַפְשִׁי n.f.s.-1 c.s. sf. (659) *O my soul*
לִמְנוּחָיְכִי prep.-n.m.p.-2 f.s. sf. (629) *to your rest*
כִּי־יהוה conj. (471)-pr.n. (217) *for Yahweh*
גָּמַל Qal pf. 3 m.s. (168) *has dealt bountifully*
עָלָיְכִי prep.-2 f.s. sf. (GK 91,l) *with you*

116:8

כִּי חִלַּצְתָּ conj. (471)-Pi. pf. 2 m.s. (323) *for thou hast delivered*
נַפְשִׁי n.f.s.-1 c.s. sf. (659) *my soul*

מִמָּוֶת prep.-n.m.s. (560) *from death*
אֶת־עֵינִי dir.obj.-n.f.s.-1 c.s. sf. (744) *my eyes*
מִן־דִּמְעָה prep.-n.f.s. (199) *from tears*
אֶת־רַגְלִי dir.obj.-n.f.s.-1 c.s. sf. (919) *my feet*
מִדֶּחִי prep.-n.m.s. (191) *from stumbling*

116:9

אֶתְהַלֵּךְ Hith. impf. 1 c.s. (הָלַךְ 229) *I walk*
לִפְנֵי יהוה prep.-n.m.p. cstr. (815)-pr.n. (217) *before Yahweh*
בְּאַרְצוֹת prep.-n.f.p. cstr. (75) *in the land of*
הַחַיִּים def.art.-n.m.p. (313) *the living*

116:10

הֶאֱמַנְתִּי Hi. pf. 1 c.s. (אָמַן 52) *I kept my faith*
כִּי אֲדַבֵּר conj. (471)-Pi. impf. 1 c.s. (180) *even when I said*
אֲנִי עָנִיתִי pers.pr. 1 c.s. (58)-Qal pf. 1 c.s. (עָנָה III 776) *I am afflicted*
מְאֹד adv. (547) *greatly*

116:11

אֲנִי אָמַרְתִּי pers.pr. 1 c.s. (58)-Qal pf. 1 c.s. (55) *I said*
בְחָפְזִי prep.-Qal inf.cstr.-1 c.s. sf. (חָפַז 342) *in my consternation*
כָּל־הָאָדָם n.m.s. cstr. (481)-def.art.-n.m.s. (9) *men are all*
כֹּזֵב Qal act.ptc. (כָּזַב 469) *a vain hope*

116:12

מָה־ interr. (552) *what*
אָשִׁיב Hi. impf. 1 c.s. (שׁוּב 996) *shall I render*
לַיהוה prep.-pr.n. (217) *to Yahweh*
כָּל־תַּגְמוּלוֹהִי n.m.s. cstr. (481)-n.m.p.-3 m.s. sf. (168; GK 91,l) *for all his bounty*
עָלָי prep.-1 c.s. sf. paus. *to me*

116:13

כּוֹס־ n.f.s. cstr. (468) *the cup of*
יְשׁוּעוֹת n.f.p. (447) *salvation*
אֶשָּׂא Qal impf. 1 c.s. (נָשָׂא 669) *I will lift up*
וּבְשֵׁם יהוה conj.-prep.-n.m.s. cstr. (1027)-pr.n. (217) *and on the name of Yahweh*
אֶקְרָא Qal impf. 1 c.s. (894) *I will call*

116:14

נְדָרַי n.m.p.-1 c.s. sf. (623) *my vows*
לַיהוה prep.-pr.n. (217) *to Yahweh*
אֲשַׁלֵּם Pi. impf. 1 c.s. (שָׁלֵם 1022) *I will pay*
נֶגְדָה־נָּא prep.-loc.he (617; GK 90f)-part.of entreaty (609) *in the presence of*

לְכָל־עַמּוֹ prep.-n.m.s. cstr. (481)-n.m.s.-3 m.s. sf. (I 766) *all his people*

116:15

יָקָר adj. m.s. (429) *precious*
בְּעֵינֵי prep.-n.f. du. cstr. (744) *in the sight of*
יהוה pr.n. (217) *Yahweh*
הַמָּוְתָה def.art.-n.m.s. (560) *the death*
לַחֲסִידָיו prep.-adj. m.p.-3 m.s. sf. (339) *of his saints*

116:16

אָנָּה יהוה interj. (58)-pr.n. (217) *O Yahweh*
כִּי־אֲנִי conj. (471)-pers.pr. 1 c.s. (58) *for I am*
עַבְדֶּךָ n.m.s.-2 m.s. sf. (713) *thy servant*
אֲנִי־עַבְדְּךָ v.supra-n.m.s.-2 m.s. sf. (713) *I am thy servant*
בֶּן־אֲמָתֶךָ n.m.s. cstr. (119)-n.f.s.-2 m.s. sf. (51) *the son of thy handmaid*
פִּתַּחְתָּ Pi. pf. 2 m.s. (פָּתַח I 834) *thou hast loosed*
לְמוֹסֵרָי prep.-n.m.p.-1 c.s. sf. paus. (64) *my bonds*

116:17

לְךָ־אֶזְבַּח prep.-2 m.s. sf.-Qal impf. 1 c.s. (זָבַח 256) *I will offer to thee*
זֶבַח n.m.s. cstr. (257) *the sacrifice of*
תּוֹדָה n.f.s. (392) *thanksgiving*
וּבְשֵׁם conj.-prep.-n.m.s. cstr. (1027) *and on the name of*
יהוה pr.n. (217) *Yahweh*
אֶקְרָא Qal impf. 1 c.s. (894) *I will call*

116:18

נְדָרַי n.m.p.-1 c.s. sf. (623) *my vows*
לַיהוה prep.-pr.n. (217) *to Yahweh*
אֲשַׁלֵּם Pi. impf. 1 c.s. (שָׁלֵם 1022) *I will pay*
נֶגְדָה־נָּא prep.-loc.he (617)-part.of entreaty (609) *in the presence of*
לְכָל־עַמּוֹ prep.-n.m.s. cstr. (481)-n.m.s.-3 m.s. sf. (I 766) *all his people*

116:19

בְּחַצְרוֹת prep.-n.f.p. cstr. (I 346) *in the courts of*
בֵּית יהוה n.m.s. cstr. (108)-pr.n. (217) *the house of Yahweh*
בְּתוֹכֵכִי prep.-n.m.s.-2 f.s. sf. (1063) *in your midst*
יְרוּשָׁלָםִ pr.n. paus. (436) *O Jerusalem*
הַלְלוּ־יָהּ Pi. impv. 2 m.p. (II 237)-pr.n. (219) *Praise Yah*

117:1

הַלְלוּ Pi. impv. 2 m.p. (II 237) *praise*

אֶת־יהוה dir.obj.-pr.n. (217) *Yahweh*

כָּל־גּוֹיִם n.m.s. cstr. (481)-n.m.p. (156) *all nations*

שַׁבְּחוּהוּ Pi. impv. 2 m.p.-3 m.s. sf. (שָׁבַח II 986) *extol him*

כָּל־הָאֻמִּים n.m.s. cstr. (481)-def.art.-n.f.p. (52) *all peoples*

117:2

כִּי גָבַר conj. (471)-Qal pf. 3 m.s. (149) *for great is*

עָלֵינוּ prep.-1 c.p. sf. *toward us*

חַסְדּוֹ n.m.s.-3 m.s. sf. (338) *his steadfast love*

וֶאֱמֶת־ conj.-n.f.s. cstr. (54) *and the faithfulness of*

יהוה pr.n. (217) *Yahweh*

לְעוֹלָם prep.-n.m.s. (761) *for ever*

הַלְלוּ־יָהּ Pi. impv. 2 m.p. (II 237)-pr.n. (219) *Praise Yah*

118:1

הוֹדוּ Hi. impv. 2 m.p. (יָדָה 392) *O give thanks*

לַיהוה prep.-pr.n. (217) *to Yahweh*

כִּי־טוֹב conj. (471)-adj. m.s. (II 373) *for he is good*

כִּי לְעוֹלָם conj. (471)-prep.-n.m.s. (761) *for ever*

חַסְדּוֹ n.m.s.-3 m.s. sf. (338) *his steadfast love*

118:2

יֹאמַר־נָא Qal impf. 3 m.s. (55)-part.of entreaty (609) *let say*

יִשְׂרָאֵל pr.n. (975) *Israel*

כִּי לְעוֹלָם conj. (471)-prep.-n.m.s. (761) *for ever*

חַסְדּוֹ n.m.s.-3 m.s. sf. (338) *his steadfast love*

118:3

יֹאמְרוּ־נָא Qal impf. 3 m.p. (55)-part.of entreaty (609) *let say*

בֵית־אַהֲרֹן n.m.s. cstr. (108)-pr.n. (14) *the house of Aaron*

כִּי לְעוֹלָם conj. (471)-prep.-n.m.s. (761) *for ever*

חַסְדּוֹ n.m.s.-3 m.s. sf. (338) *his steadfast love*

118:4

יֹאמְרוּ־נָא Qal impf. 3 m.s. (55)-part.of entreaty (609) *let say*

יִרְאֵי יהוה Qal act.ptc. m.p. cstr. (יָרֵא 431)-pr.n. (217) *those who fear Yahweh*

כִּי לְעוֹלָם conj. (471)-prep.-n.m.s. (761) *for ever*

חַסְדּוֹ n.m.s.-3 m.s. sf. (338) *his steadfast love*

118:5

מִן־הַמֵּצַר prep.-def.art.-n.m.s. (865) *out of distress*

קָרָאתִי Qal pf. 1 c.s. (894) *I called on*

יָּהּ pr.n. (219; GK 20g) *Yah*

עָנָנִי Qal pf. 3 m.s.-1 c.s. sf. (עָנָה I 772; GK 59f) *answered me*

בַמֶּרְחָב prep.-def.art.-n.m.s. (932; GK 119gg) *in the spacious place*

יָהּ pr.n. (219) *Yah*

118:6

יהוה לִי pr.n. (217)-prep.-1 c.s. sf. *Yahweh on my side*

לֹא אִירָא neg.-Qal impf. 1 c.s. (יָרֵא 431) *I do not fear*

מַה־יַּעֲשֶׂה interr. (552)-Qal impf. 3 m.s. (I 793) *what can do?*

לִי prep.-1 c.s. sf. *to me*

אָדָם n.m.s. (9) *man*

118:7

יהוה לִי pr.n. (217)-prep.-1 c.s. sf. *Yahweh on my side*

בְּעֹזְרָי prep. (GK 119i)-Qal act.ptc. m.p.-1 c.s. sf. (I 740 עָזַר) *to help me*

וַאֲנִי conj.-pers.pr. 1 c.s. (58) *and I*

אֶרְאֶה Qal impf. 1 c.s. (רָאָה 906) *shall look*

בְשֹׂנְאָי prep.-Qal act.ptc. m.p.-1 c.s. sf. (שָׂנֵא 971) *on those who hate me*

118:8

טוֹב adj. m.s. (II 373) *better*

לַחֲסוֹת prep.-Qal inf.cstr. (חָסָה 340) *to take refuge*

בַּיהוה prep.-pr.n. (217) *in Yahweh*

מִבְּטֹחַ prep.-Qal inf.cstr. (105) *than to put confidence*

בָּאָדָם prep.-def.art.-n.m.s. (9) *in man*

118:9

טוֹב לַחֲסוֹת adj. m.s. (II 373)-prep.-Qal inf.cstr. (340 חָסָה) *better to take refuge*

בַּיהוה prep.-pr.n. (217) *in Yahweh*

מִבְּטֹחַ prep.-Qal inf.cstr. (105) *than to put confidence*

בִּנְדִיבִים prep.-adj. m.p. (622) *in princes*

118:10

כָּל־גּוֹיִם n.m.s. cstr. (481)-n.m.p. (156) *all nations*

סְבָבוּנִי Qal pf. 3 c.p. (סָבַב 685)-1 c.s. sf. *surrounded me*

בְּשֵׁם יהוה prep.-n.m.s. cstr. (1027)-pr.n. (217) *in the name of Yahweh*
כִּי אֲמִילַם conj.-Hi. impf. 1 c.s.-3 m.p. sf. paus. (557 מוּל; GK 60d) *I cut them off*

118:11

סַבּוּנִי Qal pf. 3 c.p.-1 c.s. sf. (סָבַב 685) *they surrounded me*
גַּם־סְבָבוּנִי adv. (168)-Qal pf. 3 c.p.-1 c.s. sf. (סָבַב 685; GK 67cc) *surrounded me*
בְּשֵׁם יהוה prep.-n.m.s. cstr. (1027)-pr.n. (217) *in the name of Yahweh*
כִּי אֲמִילַם conj. (471)-Hi. impf. 1 c.s.-3 m.p. sf. paus. (מוּל 557) *I cut them off*

118:12

סַבּוּנִי Qal pf. 3 c.p.-1 c.s. sf. (סָבַב 685) *they surrounded me*
כִדְבוֹרִים prep.-n.f.p. (II 184) *like bees*
דֹּעֲכוּ Pu. pf. 3 c.p. (דָּעַךְ 200) *they were extinguished*
כְּאֵשׁ prep.-n.f.s. cstr. (77) *like a fire of*
קוֹצִים n.m.p. (I 881) *thorns*
בְּשֵׁם יהוה prep.-n.m.s. cstr. (1027)-pr.n. (217) *in the name of Yahweh*
כִּי אֲמִילַם v.supra *I cut them off*

118:13

דַּחֹה דְחִיתַנִי Qal inf.abs. (דָּחָה 190; GK 113p) -Qal pf. 2 m.s.-1 c.s. sf. (190) *thou didst push me hard*
לִנְפֹּל prep.-Qal inf.cstr. (656) *so that I was falling*
וַיהוה conj.-pr.n. (217) *but Yahweh*
עֲזָרָנִי Qal pf. 3 m.s.-1 c.s. sf. (740) *helped me*

118:14

עָזִּי n.m.s.-1 c.s. sf. (738) *my strength*
וְזִמְרָת conj.-n.f.s. (274; GK 80g; prb.rd. וְזִמְרָתִי +1 c.s. sf.) *and my song*
יָהּ pr.n. (219) *Yah*
וַיְהִי־לִי consec.-Qal impf. 3 m.s. (הָיָה 224) -prep.-1 c.s. sf. *he has become to me*
לִישׁוּעָה prep.-n.f.s. (447) *salvation*

118:15

קוֹל n.m.s. (876) *hark*
רִנָּה n.f.s. (943) *songs*
וִישׁוּעָה conj.-n.f.s. (447) *and victory*
בְּאָהֳלֵי prep.-n.m.p. cstr. (13) *in the tents of*
צַדִּיקִים adj. m.p. (843) *the righteous*
יְמִין n.f.s. cstr. (411) *the right hand of*
יהוה pr.n. (217) *Yahweh*
עֹשָׂה Qal act.ptc. f.s. (עָשָׂה I 793) *does*
חָיִל n.m.s. paus. (298) *valiantly*

118:16

יְמִין יהוה n.f.s. cstr. (411)-pr.n. (217) *the right hand of Yahweh*
רוֹמֵמָה Polel pf. 3 f.s. paus. (רוּם 926) *is exalted*
יְמִין יהוה v.supra-v.supra *the right hand of Yahweh*
עֹשָׂה חָיִל v.supra-v.supra *does valiantly*

118:17

לֹא אָמוּת neg.-Qal impf. 1 c.s. (559) *I shall not die*
כִּי־אֶחְיֶה conj. (471)-Qal impf. 1 c.s. (חָיָה 310) *but I shall live*
וַאֲסַפֵּר conj.-Pi. impf. 1 c.s. (סָפַר 707) *and recount*
מַעֲשֵׂי יָהּ n.m.p. cstr. (795)-pr.n. (219) *the deeds of Yah*

118:18

יַסֹּר יִסְּרַנִּי Pi. inf.abs. (יָסַר 415; GK 113p)-Pi. pf. 3 m.s.-1 c.s. sf. (יָסַר 415; GK 59f) *has chastened me sorely*
יָּהּ pr.n. (219; GK 20g) *Yah*
וְלַמָּוֶת conj.-prep.-def.art.-n.m.s. (560) *but to death*
לֹא נְתָנָנִי neg.-Qal pf. 3 m.s.-1 c.s. sf. (נָתַן 678) *he has not given me over*

118:19

פִּתְחוּ־לִי Qal impv. 2 m.p. (I 834)-prep.-1 c.s. sf. *open to me*
שַׁעֲרֵי־צֶדֶק n.m.p. cstr. (1044)-n.m.s. (841) *the gates of righteousness*
אָבֹא־בָם Qal impf. 1 c.s. (בּוֹא 97)-prep.-3 m.p. sf. *that I may enter through them*
אוֹדֶה יָהּ Hi. impf. 1 c.s. (יָדָה 392)-pr.n. (219) *give thanks to Yah*

118:20

זֶה־הַשַּׁעַר demons.adj. m.s. (260)-def.art.-n.m.s. (1044) *this is the gate*
לַיהוה prep.-pr.n. (217) *of Yahweh*
צַדִּיקִים adj. m.p. (843) *the righteous*
יָבֹאוּ בוֹ Qal impf. 3 m.p. (בּוֹא 97)-prep.-3 m.s. sf. *shall enter through it*

118:21

אוֹדְךָ Hi. impf. 1 c.s.-2 m.s. sf. (יָדָה 392) *I thank thee*

כִּי עֲנִיתָנִי conj. (471)-Qal pf. 2 m.s.-1 c.s. sf. (עָנָה I 772) *that thou hast answered me*

וַתְּהִי־לִי consec.-Qal impf. 2 m.s. (הָיָה 224) -prep.-1 c.s. sf. *and hast become to me*

לִישׁוּעָה prep.-n.f.s. (447) *salvation*

118:22

אֶבֶן n.f.s. (6) *the stone which*

מָאֲסוּ Qal pf. 3 c.p. (549) *rejected*

הַבּוֹנִים def.art.-Qal act.ptc. m.p. (בָּנָה 124) *the builders*

הָיְתָה Qal pf. 3 f.s. (הָיָה 224) *has become*

לְרֹאשׁ פִּנָּה prep.-n.m.s. cstr. (910)-n.f.s. (819) *the head of the corner*

118:23

מֵאֵת יהוה prep.-prep. (II 85)-pr.n. (217) *from Yahweh*

הָיְתָה זֹּאת Qal pf. 3 f.s. (הָיָה 224)-demons.adj. f.s. (260) *this has become*

הִיא נִפְלָאת demons.adj. f.s. (214)-Ni. ptc. f.s. (810 פָּלָא; GK 74g) *it is marvelous*

בְּעֵינֵינוּ prep.-n.f. du.-1 c.p. sf. (744) *in our eyes*

118:24

זֶה־הַיּוֹם demons.adj. m.s. (260)-def.art.-n.m.s. (398) *this is the day*

עָשָׂה יהוה Qal pf. 3 m.s. (I 793)-pr.n. (217) *which Yahweh has made*

נָגִילָה Qal impf. 1 c.p.-vol.he (גִּיל 162) *let us rejoice*

וְנִשְׂמְחָה בוֹ conj.-Qal impf. 1 c.p.-vol.he (שָׂמַח 970)-prep.-3 m.s. sf. *and be glad in it*

118:25

אָנָּה interj. (58) *we beseech thee*

יהוה pr.n. (217) *O Yahweh*

הוֹשִׁיעָה Hi. impv. 2 m.s.-vol.he (יָשַׁע 446; GK 53m) *save us*

נָא part.of entreaty (609) *(we pray thee)*

אָנָּא יהוה interj. (58)-pr.n. (217) *we beseech thee, Yahweh*

הַצְלִיחָה Hi. impv. 2 m.s.-vol.he (צָלַח II 852) *give us success*

נָא part.of entreaty (609) *(we pray thee)*

118:26

בָּרוּךְ Qal pass.ptc. (בָּרַךְ 138) *blessed*

הַבָּא def.art.-Qal act.ptc. (בּוֹא 97) *he who enters*

בְּשֵׁם יהוה prep.-n.m.s. cstr. (1027)-pr.n. (217) *in the name of Yahweh*

בֵּרַכְנוּכֶם Pi. pf. 1 c.p.-2 m.p. sf. (בָּרַךְ 138; GK 59e) *we bless you*

מִבֵּית יהוה prep.-n.m.s. cstr. (108)-pr.n. (217) *from the house of Yahweh*

118:27

אֵל n.m.s. (42) *is God*

יהוה pr.n. (217) *Yahweh*

וַיָּאֶר לָנוּ consec.-Hi. impf. 3 m.s. (אוֹר 21) -prep.-1 c.p. sf. *and he has given us light*

אִסְרוּ־ Qal impv. 2 m.p. (63) *bind*

חַג n.m.s. (290) *the festal procession*

בַּעֲבֹתִים prep.-n.m.p. (721) *with branches*

עַד־קַרְנוֹת prep. (III 723)-n.f.p. cstr. (901) *up to the horns of*

הַמִּזְבֵּחַ def.art.-n.m.s. (258) *the altar*

118:28

אֵלִי n.m.s.-1 c.s. sf. (42) *my God*

אַתָּה pers.pr. 2 m.s. (61) *thou art*

וְאוֹדֶךָּ conj.-Hi. impf. 1 c.s.-2 m.s. sf. (יָדָה 392) *and I will give thanks to thee*

אֱלֹהַי n.m.p.-1 c.s. sf. (43) *my God*

אֲרוֹמְמֶךָּ Polel impf. 1 c.s.-2 m.s. sf. (רוּם 926) *I will extol thee*

118:29

הוֹדוּ Hi. impv. 2 m.p. (יָדָה 392) *O give thanks*

לַיהוה prep.-pr.n. (217) *to Yahweh*

כִּי־טוֹב conj. (471)-adj. m.s. (II 373) *for he is good*

כִּי לְעוֹלָם conj. (471)-prep.-n.m.s. (761) *for for ever*

חַסְדּוֹ n.m.s.-3 m.s. sf. (338) *his steadfast love*

119:1

אַשְׁרֵי n.m.p. cstr. (80; GK 5h) *blessed are*

תְמִימֵי־דָרֶךְ adj. m.p. cstr. (1071)-n.m.s. paus. (202) *those whose way is blameless*

הַהֹלְכִים def.art.-Qal act.ptc. m.p. (הָלַךְ 229) *who walk*

בְּתוֹרַת יהוה prep.-n.f.s. cstr. (435)-pr.n. (217) *in the law of Yahweh*

119:2

אַשְׁרֵי n.m.p. cstr. (80) *blessed are*

נֹצְרֵי Qal act.ptc. m.p. cstr. (נָצַר 665) *those who keep*

עֵדֹתָיו n.f.p.-3 m.s. sf. (730) *his testimonies*

בְּכָל־לֵב prep.-n.m.s. cstr. (481)-n.m.s. (524) *with their whole heart*
יִדְרְשׁוּהוּ Qal impf. 3 m.p.-3 m.s. sf. (205) *who seek him*

119:3

אַף לֹא פָעֲלוּ conj. (II 64)-neg.-Qal pf. 3 c.p. (821) *also they do not do*
עַוְלָה n.f.s. (732) *wrong*
בִּדְרָכָיו prep.-n.m.p.-3 m.s. sf. (202) *in his ways*
הָלָכוּ Qal pf. 3 c.p. paus. (229) *they walk*

119:4

אַתָּה צִוִּיתָה pers.pr. 2 m.s. (61)-Pi. pf. 2 m.s. (845 צָוָה) *thou hast commanded*
פִקֻּדֶיךָ n.m.p.-2 m.s. sf. (824) *thy precepts*
לִשְׁמֹר מְאֹד prep.-Qal inf.cstr. (1036)-adv. (547) *to be kept diligently*

119:5

אַחֲלַי subst. (25) *O that*
יִכֹּנוּ Ni. impf. 3 m.p. (כּוּן I 465) *may be steadfast*
דְרָכָי n.m.p.-1 c.s. sf. paus. (202) *my ways*
לִשְׁמֹר prep.-Qal inf.cstr. (1036) *in keeping*
חֻקֶּיךָ n.m.p.-2 m.s. sf. (349) *thy statutes*

119:6

אָז לֹא־אֵבוֹשׁ adv. (23)-neg.-Qal impf. 1 c.s. (101 בּוֹשׁ) *then I shall not be put to shame*
בְּהַבִּיטִי prep.-Hi. inf.cstr.-1 c.s. sf. (נָבַט 613) *having my eyes fixed*
אֶל־כָּל־מִצְוֹתֶיךָ prep.-n.m.s. cstr. (481)-n.f.p.-2 m.s. sf. (846) *on all thy commandments*

119:7

אוֹדְךָ Hi. impf. 1 c.s.-2 m.s. sf. (יָדָה 392) *I will praise thee*
בְּיֹשֶׁר לֵבָב prep.-n.m.s. cstr. (449)-n.m.s. (523) *with an upright heart*
בְּלָמְדִי prep.-Qal inf.cstr.-1 c.s. sf. (לָמַד 540) *when I learn*
מִשְׁפְּטֵי צִדְקֶךָ n.m.p. cstr. (1048)-n.m.s.-2 m.s. sf. (841) *thy righteous ordinances*

119:8

אֶת־חֻקֶּיךָ dir.obj.-n.m.p.-2 m.s. sf. (349) *thy statutes*
אֶשְׁמֹר Qal impf. 1 c.s. (1036) *I will observe*
אַל־תַּעַזְבֵנִי neg.-Qal impf. 2 m.s.-1 c.s. sf. (I 736) *O forsake me not*
עַד־מְאֹד prep. (III 723)-adv. (547) *utterly*

119:9

בַּמֶּה prep.-def.art.-interr. (552) *how*
יְזַכֶּה־ Pi. impf. 3 m.s. (זָכָה 269) *can keep pure*
נַּעַר n.m.s. (654) *a young man*
אֶת־אָרְחוֹ dir.obj.-n.m.s.-3 m.s. sf. (73) *his way*
לִשְׁמֹר prep.-Qal inf.cstr. (1036) *by guarding it*
כִּדְבָרֶךָ prep.-n.m.s.-2 m.s. sf. paus. (182) *according to thy word*

119:10

בְּכָל־לִבִּי prep.-n.m.s. cstr. (481)-n.m.s.-1 c.s. sf. (524) *with my whole heart*
דְרַשְׁתִּיךָ Qal pf. 1 c.s.-2 m.s. sf. (205) *I seek thee*
אַל־תַּשְׁגֵּנִי neg.-Hi. impf. 2 m.s.-1 c.s. sf. (שָׁגָה 993) *let me not wander*
מִמִּצְוֹתֶיךָ prep.-n.f.p.-2 m.s. sf. (846) *from thy commandments*

119:11

בְּלִבִּי prep.-n.m.s.-1 c.s. sf. (524) *in my heart*
צָפַנְתִּי Qal pf. 1 c.s. (860) *I have laid up*
אִמְרָתֶךָ n.f.s.-2 m.s. sf. (57) *thy word*
לְמַעַן prep. (775) *that*
לֹא אֶחֱטָא־לָךְ neg.-Qal impf. 1 c.s. (306)-prep. -2 m.s. sf. paus. *I might not sin against thee*

119:12

בָּרוּךְ Qal pass.ptc. (138) *blessed be*
אַתָּה pers.pr. 2 m.s. (61) *thou*
יהוה pr.n. (217) *O Yahweh*
לַמְּדֵנִי Pi. impv. 2 m.s.-1 c.s. sf. (540) *teach me*
חֻקֶּיךָ n.m.p.-2 m.s. sf. (349) *thy statutes*

119:13

בִּשְׂפָתַי prep.-n.f.p.-1 c.s. sf. (973) *with my lips*
סִפַּרְתִּי Pi. pf. 1 c.s. (707) *I declare*
כֹּל n.m.s. cstr. (481) *all*
מִשְׁפְּטֵי־ n.m.p. cstr. (1048) *the ordinances of*
פִיךָ n.m.s.-2 m.s. sf. (804) *thy mouth*

119:14

בְּדֶרֶךְ prep.-n.m.s. cstr. (202) *in the way of*
עֵדְוֹתֶיךָ n.f.p.-2 m.s. sf. (730) *thy testimonies*
שַׂשְׂתִּי Qal pf. 1 c.s. (שׂוּשׂ 965) *I delight*
כְּעַל כָּל־ prep.-prep.-n.m.s. cstr. (481) *as much as in all*
הוֹן n.m.s. (223) *riches*

119:15

בְּפִקֻּדֶיךָ prep.-n.m.p.-2 m.s. sf. (824) *on thy precepts*

אָשִׂיחָה Qal impf. 1 c.s.-vol.he (שִׂיחַ 967) *I will meditate*
וְאַבִּיטָה conj.-Hi. impf. 1 c.s.-vol.he (נָבַט 613) *and I will fix my eyes*
אֹרְחֹתֶיךָ n.m.p.-2 m.s. sf. (73) *on thy ways*

119:16

בְּחֻקֹּתֶיךָ prep.-n.f.p.-2 m.s. sf. (349) *in thy statutes*
אֶשְׁתַּעֲשָׁע Hithpalpel impf. 1 c.s. (שָׁעַע II 1044) *I will delight*
לֹא אֶשְׁכַּח neg.-Qal impf. 1 c.s. (1013) *I will not forget*
דְּבָרֶךָ n.m.s.-2 m.s. sf. (182) *thy word*

119:17

גְּמֹל Qal impv. 2 m.s. (168) *deal bountifully*
עַל־עַבְדְּךָ prep.-n.m.s.-2 m.s. sf. (713) *with thy servant*
אֶחְיֶה Qal impf. 1 c.s. (חָיָה 310) *that I may live*
וְאֶשְׁמְרָה conj.-Qal impf. 1 c.s.-vol.he (1036) *and observe*
דְבָרֶךָ n.m.s.-2 m.s. sf. (182) *thy word*

119:18

גַּל־ Pi. impv. 2 m.s. (גָּלָה 162; GK 75cc) *open*
עֵינַי n.f. du.-1 c.s. sf. (744) *my eyes*
וְאַבִּיטָה conj.-Hi. impf. 1 c.s.-vol.he (נָבַט 613) *that I may behold*
נִפְלָאוֹת Ni. ptc. f.p. (פָּלָא 810) *wondrous things*
מִתּוֹרָתֶךָ prep.-n.f.s.-2 m.s. sf. (435) *out of thy law*

119:19

גֵּר אָנֹכִי n.m.s. (158)-pers.pr. 1 c.s. (59) *I am a sojourner*
בָאָרֶץ prep.-def.art.-n.f.s. (65) *on earth*
אַל־תַּסְתֵּר neg.-Hi. impf. 2 m.s. (סָתַר 711) *hide not*
מִמֶּנִּי prep.-1 c.s. sf. *from me*
מִצְוֹתֶיךָ n.f.p.-2 m.s. sf. (846) *thy commandments*

119:20

גָּרְסָה Qal pf. 3 f.s. (גָּרַס 176) *is consumed*
נַפְשִׁי n.f.s.-1 c.s. sf. (659) *my soul*
לְתַאֲבָה prep.-n.f.s. (1060) *with longing*
אֶל־מִשְׁפָּטֶיךָ prep.-n.m.p.-2 m.s. sf. (1048) *for thy ordinances*
בְכָל־עֵת prep.-n.m.s. cstr. (481)-n.f.s. (773) *at all times*

119:21

גָּעַרְתָּ Qal pf. 2 m.s. (גָּעַר 172) *thou dost rebuke*
זֵדִים adj. m.p. (267) *the insolent*
אֲרוּרִים Qal pass.ptc. m.p. (אָרַר 76) *accursed ones*
הַשֹּׁגִים def.art.-Qal act.ptc. m.p. (שָׁגָה 993) *who wander*
מִמִּצְוֹתֶיךָ prep.-n.f.p.-2 m.s. sf. (846) *from thy commandments*

119:22

גַּל Qal impv. 2 m.s. (גָּלָה II 164; GK 75cc) *take away*
מֵעָלַי prep.-prep.-1 c.s. sf. *from me*
חֶרְפָּה n.f.s. (357) *scorn*
וָבוּז conj.-n.m.s. (II 100) *and contempt*
כִּי עֵדֹתֶיךָ conj.-n.f.p.-2 m.s. sf. (730) *for thy testimonies*
נָצָרְתִּי Qal pf. 1 c.s. paus. (665) *I have kept*

119:23

גַּם יָשְׁבוּ adv. (168)-Qal pf. 3 c.p. (442) *even though ... sit*
שָׂרִים n.m.p. (978) *princes*
בִּי prep.-1 c.s. sf. *against me*
נִדְבָּרוּ Ni. pf. 3 c.p. (דָּבַר 180) *plotting*
עַבְדְּךָ n.m.s.-2 m.s. sf. (713) *thy servant*
יָשִׂיחַ Qal impf. 3 m.s. (שִׂיחַ 967) *will meditate*
בְּחֻקֶּיךָ prep.-n.m.p.-2 m.s. sf. (349) *on thy statutes*

119:24

גַּם־עֵדֹתֶיךָ adv. (168)-n.f.p.-2 m.s. sf. (730) *indeed, thy testimonies*
שַׁעֲשֻׁעָי n.m.p.-1 c.s. sf. paus. (1044) *my delight*
אַנְשֵׁי עֲצָתִי n.m.p. cstr. (35)-n.f.s.-1 c.s. sf. (420) *they are my counselors*

119:25

דָּבְקָה Qal pf. 3 f.s. (179) *cleaves*
לֶעָפָר prep.-def.art.-n.m.s. (779) *to the dust*
נַפְשִׁי n.f.s.-1 c.s. sf. (659) *my soul*
חַיֵּנִי Pi. impv. 2 m.s.-1 c.s. sf. (חָיָה 310) *revive me*
כִּדְבָרֶךָ prep.-n.m.s.-2 m.s. sf. (182) *according to thy word*

119:26

דְּרָכַי n.m.p.-1 c.s. sf. (202) *my ways*
סִפַּרְתִּי Pi. pf. 1 c.s. (707) *I told*
וַתַּעֲנֵנִי consec.-Qal impf. 2 m.s.-1 c.s. sf. (עָנָה I 772) *and thou didst answer me*

לַמְּדֵנִי Pi. impv. 2 m.s.-1 c.s. sf. (540) *teach me*
חֻקֶּיךָ n.m.p.-2 m.s. sf. (349) *thy statutes*

119:27

דֶּרֶךְ־ n.m.s. cstr. (202) *the way of*
פִּקּוּדֶיךָ n.m.p.-2 m.s. sf. (824) *thy precepts*
הֲבִינֵנִי Hi. impv. 2 m.s.-1 c.s. sf. (בִּין 106) *make me understand*
וְאָשִׂיחָה conj.-Qal impf. 1 c.s.-vol.he (שִׂיחַ 967) *and I will meditate*
בְּנִפְלְאוֹתֶיךָ prep.-Ni. ptc. f.p.-2 m.s. sf. (פָּלָא 810) *on thy wondrous works*

119:28

דָּלְפָה Qal pf. 3 f.s. (196) *melts away*
נַפְשִׁי n.f.s.-1 c.s. sf. (659) *my soul*
מִתּוּגָה prep.-n.f.s. (387) *for sorrow*
קַיְּמֵנִי Pi. impv. 2 m.s.-1 c.s. sf. (קוּם 877) *strengthen me*
כִּדְבָרֶךָ prep.-n.m.s.-2 m.s. sf. (182) *according to thy word*

119:29

דֶּרֶךְ־שֶׁקֶר n.m.s. cstr. (202)-n.m.s. (1055) *false ways*
הָסֵר Hi. impv. 2 m.s. (סוּר 693) *put far*
מִמֶּנִּי prep.-1 c.s. sf. *from me*
וְתוֹרָתְךָ conj.-n.f.s.-2 m.s. sf. (435) *and thy law*
חָנֵּנִי Qal impv. 2 m.s.-1 c.s. sf. (חָנַן 335) *be gracious to me*

119:30

דֶּרֶךְ־ n.m.s. cstr. (202) *the way of*
אֱמוּנָה n.f.s. (53) *faithfulness*
בָחָרְתִּי Qal pf. 1 c.s. paus. (103) *I have chosen*
מִשְׁפָּטֶיךָ n.m.p.-2 m.s. sf. (1048) *thy ordinances*
שִׁוִּיתִי Pi. pf. 1 c.s. (שָׁוָה I 1000-*accounted suitable*; II 1001-*I set*)

119:31

דָּבַקְתִּי Qal pf. 1 c.s. (179) *I cleave*
בְעֵדְוֹתֶיךָ prep.-n.f.p.-2 m.s. sf. (730) *to thy testimonies*
יהוה pr.n. (217) *O Yahweh*
אַל־תְּבִישֵׁנִי neg.-Hi. impf. 2 m.s.-1 c.s. sf. (בּוֹשׁ 101) *let me not be put to shame*

119:32

דֶּרֶךְ־ n.m.s. cstr. (202) *the way of*
מִצְוֹתֶיךָ n.f.p.-2 m.s. sf. (846) *thy commandments*
אָרוּץ Qal impf. 1 c.s. (רוּץ 930) *I will run*
כִּי תַרְחִיב conj. (471)-Hi. impf. 2 m.s. (רָחַב 931) *when thou enlargest*
לִבִּי n.m.s.-1 c.s. sf. (524) *my understanding*

119:33

הוֹרֵנִי Hi. impv. 2 m.s.-1 c.s. sf. (יָרָה 434) *teach me*
יהוה pr.n. (217) *O Yahweh*
דֶּרֶךְ חֻקֶּיךָ n.m.s. cstr. (202)-n.m.p.-2 m.s. sf. (349) *the way of thy statutes*
וְאֶצְּרֶנָּה conj.-Qal impf. 1 c.s.-3 f.s. sf. (נָצַר 665) *and I will keep it*
עֵקֶב adv. (784) *to the end*

119:34

הֲבִינֵנִי Hi. impv. 2 m.s.-1 c.s. sf. (בִּין 106) *give me understanding*
וְאֶצְּרָה conj.-eQal impf. 1 c.s.-vol.he (נָצַר 665) *that I may keep*
תוֹרָתֶךָ n.f.s.-2 m.s. sf. (435) *thy law*
וְאֶשְׁמְרֶנָּה conj.-Qal impf. 1 c.s.-3 f.s. sf. (1036) *and observe it*
בְכָל־לֵב prep.-n.m.s. cstr. (481)-n.m.s. (524) *with my whole heart*

119:35

הַדְרִיכֵנִי Hi. impv. 2 m.s.-1 c.s. sf. (דָּרַךְ 201) *lead me*
בִּנְתִיב prep.-n.m.s. cstr. (677) *in the path of*
מִצְוֹתֶיךָ n.f.p.-2 m.s. sf. (846) *thy commandments*
כִּי־בוֹ conj.-prep.-3 m.s. sf. *for in it*
חָפָצְתִּי Qal pf. 1 c.s. paus. (342) *I delight*

119:36

הַט־לִבִּי Hi. impv. 2 m.s. (נָטָה 639)-n.m.s.-1 c.s. sf. (524) *incline my heart*
אֶל־עֵדְוֹתֶיךָ prep.-n.f.p.-2 m.s. sf. (730) *to thy testimonies*
וְאַל conj.-neg. *and not*
אֶל־בָּצַע prep.-n.m.s. paus. (130) *to gain*

119:37

הַעֲבֵר Hi. impv. 2 m.s. (716) *turn*
עֵינַי n.f.p.-1 c.s. sf. (744) *my eyes*
מֵרְאוֹת prep.-Qal inf.cstr. (רָאָה 906) *from looking*
שָׁוְא n.m.s. (996) *at vanities*
בִּדְרָכֶךָ prep.-n.m.p.-2 m.s. sf. (202) *and in thy ways*
חַיֵּנִי Pi. impv. 2 m.s.-1 c.s. sf. (חָיָה 310) *give me life*

119:38

הָקֵם Hi. impv. 2 m.s. (קוּם 877) *confirm*
לְעַבְדְּךָ prep.-n.m.s.-2 m.s. sf. (713) *to thy servant*
אִמְרָתֶךָ n.f.s.-2 m.s. sf. (57) *thy promise*
אֲשֶׁר לְיִרְאָתֶךָ rel. (81)-prep.-n.f.s.-2 m.s. sf. (432) *which is for those who fear thee*

119:39

הַעֲבֵר Hi. impv. 2 m.s. (716) *turn away*
חֶרְפָּתִי n.f.s.-1 c.s. sf. (357) *my reproach*
אֲשֶׁר יָגֹרְתִּי rel. (81)-Qal pf. 1 c.s. (יָגֹר 388) *which I dread*
כִּי מִשְׁפָּטֶיךָ conj. (471)-n.m.p.-2 m.s. sf. (1048) *for thy ordinances*
טוֹבִים adj. m.p. (II 373) *are good*

119:40

הִנֵּה interj. (243) *behold*
תָּאַבְתִּי Qal pf. 1 c.s. (1060) *I long*
לְפִקֻּדֶיךָ prep.-n.m.p.-2 m.s. sf. (824) *for thy precepts*
בְּצִדְקָתְךָ prep.-n.f.s.-2 m.s. sf. (842) *in thy righteousness*
חַיֵּנִי Pi. impv. 2 m.s.-1 c.s. sf. (חָיָה 310) *give me life*

119:41

וִיבֹאֻנִי conj.-Qal impf. 3 m.p.-1 c.s. sf. (בּוֹא 97) *and let come to me*
חֲסָדֶךָ n.m.p.-2 m.s. sf. (338) *thy steadfast love*
יהוה pr.n. (217) *O Yahweh*
תְּשׁוּעָתְךָ n.f.s.-2 m.s. sf. (448) *thy salvation*
כְּאִמְרָתֶךָ prep.-n.f.s.-2 m.s. sf. paus. (57) *according to thy promise*

119:42

וְאֶעֱנֶה conj.-Qal impf. 1 c.s. (I 772) *then shall I have an answer*
חֹרְפִי Qal act.ptc.-1 c.s. sf. (357) *for those who taunt me*
דָבָר n.m.s. (182) *(an answer)*
כִּי־בָטַחְתִּי conj. (471)-Qal pf. 1 c.s. (105) *for I trust*
בִּדְבָרֶךָ prep.-n.m.s.-2 m.s. sf. (182) *in thy word*

119:43

וְאַל־תַּצֵּל conj.-neg.-Hi. impf. 2 m.s. (נָצַל 664) *and take not*
מִפִּי prep.-n.m.s.-1 c.s. sf. (804) *out of my mouth*
דְבַר־אֱמֶת n.m.s. cstr. (182)-n.f.s. (54) *the word of truth*
עַד־מְאֹד prep. (III 723)-adv. (547) *utterly*
כִּי לְמִשְׁפָּטֶךָ conj. (471)-prep.-n.m.s.-2 m.s. sf. (1048) *for in thy ordinances*
יִחָלְתִּי Pi. pf. 1 c.s. paus. (יָחַל 403) *I hope*

119:44

וְאֶשְׁמְרָה conj.-Qal impf. 1 c.s.-vol.he (שָׁמַר 1036) *and I will keep*
תוֹרָתְךָ n.f.s.-2 m.s. sf. (435) *thy law*
תָמִיד adv. (556) *continually*
לְעוֹלָם prep.-n.m.s. (761) *for ever*
וָעֶד conj.-n.m.s. (I 723) *and ever*

119:45

וְאֶתְהַלְּכָה conj.-Hith. impf. 1 c.s.-vol.he (הָלַךְ 229) *and I shall walk*
בָרְחָבָה prep.-def.art.-adj. f.s. (I 932) *at liberty*
כִּי פִקֻּדֶיךָ conj. (471)-n.m.p.-2 m.s. sf. (824) *for thy precepts*
דָרָשְׁתִּי Qal pf. 1 c.s. paus. (205) *I have sought*

119:46

וַאֲדַבְּרָה conj.-Pi. impf. 1 c.s.-vol.he (דָּבַר 180) *I will also speak*
בְעֵדֹתֶיךָ prep.-n.f.p.-2 m.s. sf. (730) *of thy testimonies*
נֶגֶד מְלָכִים prep. (617)-n.m.p. (I 572) *before kings*
וְלֹא אֵבוֹשׁ conj.-neg.-Qal impf. 1 c.s. (בּוֹשׁ 101) *and shall not be put to shame*

119:47

וְאֶשְׁתַּעֲשַׁע conj.-Hithpalpel impf. 1 c.s. (שָׁעַע II 1044) *for I find delight*
בְּמִצְוֹתֶיךָ prep.-n.f.p.-2 m.s. sf. (846) *in thy commandments*
אֲשֶׁר אָהָבְתִּי rel. (81)-Qal pf. 1 c.s. paus. (12) *which I love*

119:48

וְאֶשָּׂא־כַפַּי conj.-Qal impf. 1 c.s. (נָשָׂא 669)-n.f. du.-1 c.s. sf. (496) *and I lift my hands*
אֶל־מִצְוֹתֶיךָ prep.-n.f.p.-2 m.s. sf. (846) *unto thy commandments*
אֲשֶׁר אָהָבְתִּי rel. (81)-Qal pf. 1 c.s. (12) *which I love*
וְאָשִׂיחָה conj.-Qal impf. 1 c.s.-vol.he (967) *and I will meditate*
בְחֻקֶּיךָ prep.-n.m.p.-2 m.s. sf. (349) *on thy statutes*

119:49

זְכֹר־דָּבָר Qal impv. 2 m.s. (269)-n.m.s. (182) *remember a word*
לְעַבְדֶּךָ prep.-n.m.s.-2 m.s. sf. (713) *to thy servant*
עַל אֲשֶׁר prep.-rel. (81) *in which*
יִחַלְתָּנִי Pi. pf. 2 m.s.-1 c.s. sf. (יָחַל 403) *thou hast made me hope*

119:50

זֹאת demons.adj. f.s. (260) *this is*
נֶחָמָתִי n.f.s.-1 c.s. sf. (637) *my comfort*
בְעָנְיִי prep.-n.m.s.-1 c.s. sf. (777) *in my affliction*
כִּי אִמְרָתְךָ conj. (471)-n.f.s.-2 m.s. sf. (57) *that thy promise*
חִיָּתְנִי Pi. pf. 3 f.s.-1 c.s. sf. (חָיָה 310) *gives me life*

119:51

זֵדִים adj. m.p. (267) *godless men*
הֱלִיצֻנִי Hi. pf. 3 c.p.-1 c.s. sf. (לִיץ 539) *deride me*
עַד־מְאֹד prep. (III 723)-adv. (547) *utterly*
מִתּוֹרָתְךָ prep.-n.f.s.-2 m.s. sf. (4 35) *from thy law*
לֹא נָטִיתִי neg.-Qal pf. 1 c.s. (נָטָה 639) *I do not turn away*

119:52

זָכַרְתִּי Qal pf. 1 c.s. (269) *I remember*
מִשְׁפָּטֶיךָ n.m.p.-2 m.s. sf. (1048) *thy ordinances*
מֵעוֹלָם prep.-n.m.s. (761) *from of old*
יהוה pr.n. (217) *O Yahweh*
וָאֶתְנֶחָם consec.-Hith. impf. 1 c.s. (נָחַם 636) *I take comfort*

119:53

זַלְעָפָה n.f.s. (273) *hot indignation*
אֲחָזַתְנִי Qal pf. 3 f.s.-1 c.s. sf. (אָחַז 28) *seizes me*
מֵרְשָׁעִים prep.-adj. m.p. (957) *because of the wicked*
עֹזְבֵי Qal act.ptc. m.p. cstr. (I 736) *who forsake*
תּוֹרָתֶךָ n.f.s.-2 m.s. sf. (435) *thy law*

119:54

זְמִרוֹת n.m.p. (I 274) *songs*
הָיוּ־לִי Qal pf. 3 c.p. (הָיָה 224)-prep.-1 c.s. sf. *have been to me*
חֻקֶּיךָ n.m.p.-2 m.s. sf. (349) *thy statutes*
בְּבֵית מְגוּרָי prep.-n.m.s. cstr. (108)-n.m.p.-1 c.s. sf. (158) *in the house of my pilgrimage*

119:55

זָכַרְתִּי Qal pf. 1 c.s. (269) *I remember*
בַלַּיְלָה prep.-def.art.-n.m.s. (538) *in the night*
שִׁמְךָ n.m.s.-2 m.s. sf. (1027) *thy name*
יהוה pr.n. (217) *O Yahweh*
וָאֶשְׁמְרָה consec.-Qal impf. 1 c.s.-vol.he (שָׁמַר 1036) *and keep*
תּוֹרָתֶךָ n.f.s.-2 m.s. sf. (435) *thy law*

119:56

זֹאת demons.adj. f.s. (260) *this*
הָיְתָה־לִּי Qal pf. 3 f.s. (הָיָה 224)-prep.-1 c.s. sf. *has fallen to me*
כִּי פִקֻּדֶיךָ conj. (471)-n.m.p.-2 m.s. sf. (824) *that thy precepts*
נָצָרְתִּי Qal pf. 1 c.s. paus. (665) *I have kept*

119:57

חֶלְקִי n.m.s.-1 c.s. sf. (324) *my portion*
יהוה pr.n. (217) *Yahweh*
אָמַרְתִּי Qal pf. 1 c.s. (55) *I promise*
לִשְׁמֹר prep.-Qal inf.cstr. (1036) *to keep*
דְּבָרֶיךָ n.m.p.-2 m.s. sf. (182) *thy words*

119:58

חִלִּיתִי Pi. pf. 1 c.s. (חָלָה II 318) *I entreat*
פָנֶיךָ n.m.p.-2 m.s. sf. (815) *thy favor*
בְכָל־לֵב prep.-n.m.s. cstr. (481)-n.m.s. (524) *with all my heart*
חָנֵּנִי Qal impv. 2 m.s.-1 c.s. sf. (חָנַן I 335) *be gracious to me*
כְּאִמְרָתֶךָ prep.-n.f.s.-2 m.s. sf. (57) *according to thy promise*

119:59

חִשַּׁבְתִּי Pi. pf. 1 c.s. (362) *I think*
דְרָכָי n.m.p.-1 c.s. sf. paus. (202) *of thy (my) ways*
וָאָשִׁיבָה consec.-Hi. impf. 1 c.s.-vol.he (שׁוּב 996) *I turn*
רַגְלַי n.f.p.-1 c.s. sf. (919) *my feet*
אֶל־עֵדֹתֶיךָ prep.-n.f.p.-2 m.s. sf. (730) *to thy testimonies*

119:60

חַשְׁתִּי Qal pf. 1 c.s. (חוּשׁ I 301) *I hasten*
וְלֹא הִתְמַהְמָהְתִּי conj.-neg.-Hithpalpel impf. 1 c.s. (מָהַהּ 554) *and I do not delay*
לִשְׁמֹר prep.-Qal inf.cstr. (1036) *to keep*
מִצְוֹתֶיךָ n.f.p.-2 m.s. sf. (846) *thy commandments*

119:61

חַבְלֵי n.m.p. cstr. (286) *the cords of*
רְשָׁעִים adj. m.p. (957) *the wicked*
עִוְּדֻנִי Pi. pf. 3 c.p.-1 c.s. sf. (עוּד 728) *surround me*
תּוֹרָתְךָ n.f.s.-2 m.s. sf. (435) *thy law*
לֹא שָׁכָחְתִּי neg.-Qal pf. 1 c.s. paus. (1013) *I do not forget*

119:62

חֲצוֹת־לַיְלָה n.f.p. cstr. (354)-n.m.s. (538) *at midnight*
אָקוּם Qal impf. 1 c.s. (קוּם 877) *I rise*
לְהוֹדוֹת prep.-Hi. inf.cstr. (יָדָה 392) *to praise*
לָךְ prep.-2 m.s. sf. paus. *thee*
עַל מִשְׁפְּטֵי prep.-n.m.p. cstr. (1048) *because of the ordinances of*
צִדְקֶךָ n.m.s.-2 m.s. sf. (841) *thy righteousness*

119:63

חָבֵר אָנִי adj. m.s. (288)-pers.pr. 1 c.s. (58) *I am a companion*
לְכָל־אֲשֶׁר prep.-n.m.s. (481)-rel. (81) *of all who*
יְרֵאוּךָ Qal pf. 3 c.p.-2 m.s. sf. (יָרֵא 431) *fear thee*
וּלְשֹׁמְרֵי conj.-prep.-Qal act.ptc. m.p. cstr. (1036) *of those who keep*
פִּקּוּדֶיךָ n.m.p.-2 m.s. sf. (824) *thy precepts*

119:64

חַסְדְּךָ n.m.s.-2 m.s. sf. (338) *thy steadfast love*
יהוה pr.n. (217) *O Yahweh*
מָלְאָה Qal pf. 3 f.s. (569) *is full*
הָאָרֶץ def.art.-n.f.s. (75) *the earth*
חֻקֶּיךָ n.m.p.-2 m.s. sf. (349) *thy statutes*
לַמְּדֵנִי Pi. impv. 2 m.s.-1 c.s. sf. (540) *teach me*

119:65

טוֹב adj. m.s. (II 373) *well*
עָשִׂיתָ Qal pf. 2 m.s. (עָשָׂה I 793) *thou hast dealt*
עִם־עַבְדְּךָ prep.-n.m.s.-2 m.s. sf. (713) *with thy servant*
יהוה pr.n. (217) *O Yahweh*
כִּדְבָרֶךָ prep.-n.m.s.-2 m.s. sf. paus. (182) *according to thy word*

119:66

טוּב טַעַם n.m.s. cstr. (375)-n.m.s. (381) *good judgment*
וָדַעַת conj.-n.f.s. (395) *and knowledge*
לַמְּדֵנִי Pi. impv. 2 m.s.-1 c.s. sf. (540) *teach me*
כִּי בְמִצְוֹתֶיךָ conj. (471)-prep.-n.f.p.-2 m.s. sf. (846) *for in thy commandments*
הֶאֱמָנְתִּי Hi. pf. 1 c.s. paus. (אָמַן 52) *I believe*

119:67

טֶרֶם adv. (382) *before*
אֶעֱנֶה Qal impf. 1 c.s. (עָנָה III 776) *I was afflicted*
אֲנִי שֹׁגֵג pers.pr. 1 c.s. (58)-Qal act.ptc. (שָׁגַג 992) *I went astray*
וְעַתָּה conj.-adv. (773) *but now*
אִמְרָתְךָ n.f.s.-2 m.s. sf. (57) *thy word*
שָׁמָרְתִּי Qal pf. 1 c.s. paus. (1036) *I keep*

119:68

טוֹב־אַתָּה adj. m.s. (II 373)-pers.pr. 2 m.s. (61) *thou art good*
וּמֵטִיב conj.-Hi. ptc. (יָטַב 405) *and doest good*
לַמְּדֵנִי Pi. impv. 2 m.s.-1 c.s. sf. (540) *teach me*
חֻקֶּיךָ n.m.p.-2 m.s. sf. (349) *thy statutes*

119:69

טָפְלוּ Qal pf. 3 c.p. (381) *besmear*
עָלַי prep.-1 c.s. sf. *me*
שֶׁקֶר n.m.s. (1055) *with lies*
זֵדִים adj. m.p. (267) *the godless ones*
אֲנִי pers.pr. 1 c.s. (58) *I*
בְּכָל־לֵב prep.-n.m.s. cstr. (481)-n.m.s. (524) *with my whole heart*
אֶצֹּר Qal impf. 1 c.s. (נָצַר 665) *keep*
פִּקּוּדֶיךָ n.m.p.-2 m.s. sf. (824) *thy precepts*

119:70

טָפַשׁ Qal pf. 3 m.s. (382) *is gross*
כַּחֵלֶב prep.-def.art.-n.m.s. (316) *like fat*
לִבָּם n.m.s.-3 m.p. sf. (524) *their heart*
אֲנִי pers.pr. 1 c.s. (58) *I*
תּוֹרָתְךָ n.f.s.-2 m.s. sf. (435) *in thy law*
שִׁעֲשָׁעְתִּי Pilpel pf. 1 c.s. paus. (שָׁעַע II 1044) *I delight*

119:71

טוֹב־לִי adj. m.s. (II 373)-prep.-1 c.s. sf. *it is good for me*
כִּי־עֻנֵּיתִי conj. (471)-Pu. pf. 1 c.s. (עָנָה III 776) *that I was afflicted*
לְמַעַן prep. (775) *that*
אֶלְמַד Qal impf. 1 c.s. (540) *I might learn*
חֻקֶּיךָ n.m.p.-2 m.s. sf. (349) *thy statutes*

119:72

טוֹב־לִי adj. m.s. (II 373)-prep.-1 c.s. sf. *is better to me*

תּוֹרַת־ n.f.s. cstr. (435) *the law of*

פִּיךָ n.m.s.-2 m.s. sf. (804) *thy mouth*

מֵאַלְפֵי prep.-n.m.p. cstr. (48) *than thousands of*

זָהָב n.m.s. (262) *gold*

וָכָסֶף conj.-n.m.s. paus. (494) *and silver*

119:73

יָדֶיךָ n.f.p.-2 m.s. sf. (388) *thy hands*

עָשׂוּנִי Qal pf. 3 c.p.-1 c.s. sf. (עָשָׂה I 793) *have made me*

וַיְכוֹנְנוּנִי consec.-Polel impf. 3 m.p.-1 c.s. sf. (כּוּן I 465) *fashioned me*

הֲבִינֵנִי Hi. impv. 2 m.s.-1 c.s. sf. (בִּין 106) *give me understanding*

וְאֶלְמְדָה conj.-Qal impf. 1 c.s.-vol.he (540) *that I may learn*

מִצְוֹתֶיךָ n.f.p.-2 m.s. sf. (846) *thy commandments*

119:74

יְרֵאֶיךָ Qal act.ptc. m.p.-2 m.s. sf. (יָרֵא 431) *those who fear thee*

יִרְאוּנִי Qal impf. 3 m.p.-1 c.s. sf. (רָאָה 906) *shall see me*

וְיִשְׂמָחוּ conj.-Qal impf. 3 m.p. paus. (970) *and rejoice*

כִּי לִדְבָרְךָ conj. (471)-prep.-n.m.s.-2 m.s. sf. (182) *because in thy word*

יִחָלְתִּי Pi. pf. 1 c.s. paus. (יָחַל 403) *I have hoped*

119:75

יָדַעְתִּי Qal pf. 1 c.s. (393) *I know*

יהוה pr.n. (217) *O Yahweh*

כִּי־צֶדֶק conj. (471)-n.m.s. cstr. (841) *that are right*

מִשְׁפָּטֶיךָ n.m.p.-2 m.s. sf. (1048) *thy judgments*

וֶאֱמוּנָה conj.-n.f.s. (53) *and that in faithfulness*

עִנִּיתָנִי Pi. pf. 2 m.s.-1 c.s. sf. (עָנָה III 776) *thou hast afflicted me*

119:76

יְהִי־נָא Qal impf. 3 m.s. apoc. (הָיָה 224)-part.of entreaty (609) *let be*

חַסְדְּךָ n.m.s.-2 m.s. sf. (338) *thy steadfast love*

לְנַחֲמֵנִי prep.-Pi. inf.cstr.-1 c.s. sf. (נָחַם 636) *to comfort me*

כְּאִמְרָתְךָ prep.-n.f.s.-2 m.s. sf. (57) *according to thy promise*

לְעַבְדֶּךָ prep.-n.m.s.-2 m.s. sf. paus. (713) *to thy servant*

119:77

יְבֹאוּנִי Qal impf. 3 m.p.-1 c.s. sf. (בּוֹא 97) *let come*

רַחֲמֶיךָ n.m.p.-2 m.s. sf. (933) *thy mercy*

וְאֶחְיֶה conj.-Qal impf. 1 c.s. (חָיָה 310) *that I may live*

כִּי־תוֹרָתְךָ conj.-n.f.s.-2 m.s. sf. (435) *for thy law*

שַׁעֲשֻׁעָי n.m.p.-1 c.s. sf. paus. (1044) *my delight*

119:78

יֵבֹשׁוּ Qal impf. 3 m.p. (בּוֹשׁ 101) *let be put to shame*

זֵדִים adj. m.p. (267) *the godless ones*

כִּי־שֶׁקֶר conj.-n.m.s. (1055) *because with guile*

עִוְּתוּנִי Pi. pf. 3 c.p.-1 c.s. sf. (עָוַת 736) *they have subverted me*

אֲנִי אָשִׂיחַ pers.pr. 1 c.s. (58)-Qal impf. 1 c.s. (967 שִׂיחַ) *as for me, I will meditate*

בְּפִקּוּדֶיךָ prep.-n.m.p.-2 m.s. sf. (824) *on thy precepts*

119:79

יָשׁוּבוּ לִי Qal impf. 3 m.p. (שׁוּב 996)-prep.-1 c.s. sf. *let turn to me*

יְרֵאֶיךָ Qal act.ptc. m.p.-2 m.s. sf. (יָרֵא 431) *those who fear thee*

וְיֹדְעוּ conj.-Qal act.ptc. m.p. cstr. (יָדַע 393; some rd. וְיֵדְעוּ conj.-Qal impf. 3 m.p.) *that they may know*

עֵדֹתֶיךָ n.f.p.-2 m.s. sf. (730) *thy testimonies*

119:80

יְהִי־לִבִּי Qal impf. 3 m.s. apoc. (הָיָה 224) -n.m.s.-1 c.s. sf. (524) *may my heart be*

תָמִים adj. (1071) *blameless*

בְּחֻקֶּיךָ prep.-n.m.p.-2 m.s. sf. (349) *in thy statutes*

לְמַעַן לֹא אֵבוֹשׁ prep. (775)-neg.-Qal impf. 1 c.s. (בּוֹשׁ 101) *that I may not be put to shame*

119:81

כָּלְתָה Qal pf. 3 f.s. (כָּלָה I 477) *languishes*

לִתְשׁוּעָתְךָ prep.-n.f.s.-2 m.s. sf. (448) *for thy salvation*

נַפְשִׁי n.f.s.-1 c.s. sf. (659) *my soul*

לִדְבָרְךָ prep.-n.m.s.-2 m.s. sf. (182) *in thy word*

יִחָלְתִּי Pi. pf. 1 c.s. paus. (יָחַל 403) *I hope*

119:82

כָּלוּ Qal pf. 3 c.p. (כָּלָה I 477) *fail*
עֵינַי n.f.p.-1 c.s. sf. (744) *my eyes*
לְאִמְרָתֶךָ prep.-n.f.s.-2 m.s. sf. (57) *for thy promise*
לֵאמֹר prep.-Qal inf.cstr. (55) *I ask*
מָתַי interr.adv. (607) *when*
תְּנַחֲמֵנִי Pi. impf. 2 m.s.-1 c.s. sf. (נָחַם 636) *wilt thou comfort me*

119:83

כִּי־הָיִיתִי conj. (471)-Qal pf. 1 c.s. (הָיָה 224) *for I have become*
כְּנֹאד prep.-n.m.s. (609) *like a wineskin*
בְּקִיטוֹר prep.-n.m.s. (882) *in the smoke*
חֻקֶּיךָ n.m.p.-2 m.s. sf. (349) *thy statutes*
לֹא שָׁכָחְתִּי neg.-Qal pf. 1 c.s. paus. (1013) *I have not forgotten*

119:84

כַּמָּה prep.-def.art.-interr. (552) *how long*
יְמֵי־עַבְדֶּךָ n.m.p. cstr. (398)-n.m.s.-2 m.s. sf. (713) *the days of thy servant*
מָתַי interr.adv. (607) *when*
תַּעֲשֶׂה Qal impf. 2 m.s. (I 793) *wilt thou make*
בְרֹדְפַי prep.-Qal act.ptc. m.p.-1 c.s. sf. (922) *for those who persecute me*
מִשְׁפָּט n.m.s. (1048) *judgment*

119:85

כָּרוּ־לִי Qal pf. 3 c.p. (כָּרָה I 500)-prep.-1 c.s. sf. *have dug for me*
זֵדִים adj. m.p. (267) *godless men*
שִׁיחוֹת n.f.p. (1001) *pitfalls*
אֲשֶׁר לֹא כְתוֹרָתֶךָ rel. (81)-neg.-prep.-n.f.s.-2 m.s. sf. (435) *men who do not conform to thy law*

119:86

כָּל־מִצְוֹתֶיךָ n.m.s. cstr. (481)-n.f.p.-2 m.s. sf. (846) *all thy commandments*
אֱמוּנָה n.f.s. (53) *are sure*
שֶׁקֶר n.m.s. (1055) *with falsehood*
רְדָפוּנִי Qal pf.3 c.p.-1 c.s. sf. (רָדַף 922) *they persecute me*
עָזְרֵנִי Pi. impv. 2 m.s.-1 c.s. sf. (עָזַר 740) *help me*

119:87

כִּמְעַט prep.-adv. (589) *almost*
כִּלּוּנִי Pi. pf. 3 c.p.-1 c.s. sf. (כָּלָה 477) *they have made an end of me*
בָאָרֶץ prep.-def.art.-n.f.s. (75) *on earth*
וַאֲנִי conj.-pers.pr. 1 c.s. (58) *but I*
לֹא־עָזַבְתִּי neg.-Qal pf. 1 c.s. (I 736) *have not forsaken*
פִקֻּדֶיךָ n.m.p.-2 m.s. sf. (824) *thy precepts*

119:88

כְּחַסְדְּךָ prep.-n.m.s.-2 m.s. sf. (338) *in thy steadfast love*
חַיֵּנִי Pi. impv. 2 m.s.-1 c.s. sf. (חָיָה 310) *spare my life*
וְאֶשְׁמְרָה conj.-Qal impf. 1 c.s.-vol.he (1036) *that I may keep*
עֵדוּת פִּיךָ n.f.s. cstr. (730)-n.m.s.-2 m.s. sf. (804) *the testimonies of thy mouth*

119:89

לְעוֹלָם prep.-n.m.s. (761) *for ever*
יהוה pr.n. (217) *O Yahweh*
דְּבָרְךָ n.m.s.-2 m.s. sf. (182) *thy word*
נִצָּב Ni. ptc. (נָצַב 662) *is firmly fixed*
בַּשָּׁמָיִם prep.-def.art.-n.m. du. paus. (1029) *in the heavens*

119:90

לְדֹר וָדֹר prep.-n.m.s. (189)-conj.-n.m.s. (189) *to all generations*
אֱמוּנָתֶךָ n.f.s.-2 m.s. sf. (53) *thy faithfulness*
כּוֹנַנְתָּ Polel pf. 2 m.s. (כּוּן 465) *thou hast established*
אֶרֶץ n.f.s. (75) *the earth*
וַתַּעֲמֹד consec.-Qal impf. 3 f.s. (763) *and it stands fast*

119:91

לְמִשְׁפָּטֶיךָ prep.-n.m.p.-2 m.s. sf. (1048) *by thy appointment*
עָמְדוּ Qal pf. 3 c.p. (763) *they stand*
הַיּוֹם def.art.-n.m.s. (398) *this day*
כִּי הַכֹּל conj. (471)-def.art.-n.m.s. (481) *for all things*
עֲבָדֶיךָ n.m.p.-2 m.s. sf. (713) *thy servants*

119:92

לוּלֵי תוֹרָתְךָ conj. (530)-n.f.s.-2 m.s. sf. (435) *if thy law*
שַׁעֲשֻׁעָי n.m.p.-1 c.s. sf. paus. (1044) *my delight*
אָז אָבַדְתִּי adv. (23)-Qal pf. 1 c.s. (אָבַד 1) *then I should have perished*
בְעָנְיִי prep.-n.m.s.-1 c.s. sf. (776) *in my affliction*

119:93

לְעוֹלָם prep.-n.m.s. (761) *for ever*
לֹא־אֶשְׁכַּח neg.-Qal impf. 1 c.s. (1013) *I will not forget*
פִּקּוּדֶיךָ n.m.p.-2 m.s. sf. (824) *thy precepts*
כִּי בָם conj. (471)-prep.-3 m.p. sf. *for by them*
חִיִּיתָנִי Pi. pf. 2 m.s.-1 c.s. sf. (חָיָה 310) *thou hast given me life*

119:94

לְךָ־אֲנִי prep.-2 m.s. sf.-pers.pr. 1 c.s. (58) *I am thine*
הוֹשִׁיעֵנִי Hi. impv. 2 m.s.-1 c.s. sf. (יָשַׁע 446) *save me*
כִּי פִקּוּדֶיךָ conj. (471)-n.m.p.-2 m.s. sf. (824) *for thy precepts*
דָרָשְׁתִּי Qal pf. 1 c.s. paus. (205) *I have sought*

119:95

לִי קִוּוּ prep.-1 c.s. sf.-Pi. pf. 3 c.p. (קָוָה I 875) *lie in wait for me*
רְשָׁעִים adj. m.p. (957) *the wicked*
לְאַבְּדֵנִי prep.-Pi. inf.cstr.-1 c.s. sf. (אָבַד 1) *to destroy me*
עֵדֹתֶיךָ n.f.p.-2 m.s. sf. (730) *thy testimonies*
אֶתְבּוֹנָן Hithpolel impf. 1 c.s. (בִּין 106) *I consider*

119:96

לְכָל תִּכְלָה prep.-n.m.s. cstr. (481)-n.f.s. (479) *to all perfection*
רָאִיתִי Qal pf. 1 c.s. (רָאָה 906) *I have seen*
קֵץ n.m.s. (893) *a limit*
רְחָבָה adj. f.s. (I 932) *is broad*
מִצְוָתְךָ n.f.s.-2 m.s. sf. (846) *thy commandment*
מְאֹד adv. (547) *exceedingly*

119:97

מָה־אָהַבְתִּי interr. (552)-Qal pf. 1 c.s. (אָהַב 12) *how I love*
תוֹרָתֶךָ n.f.s.-2 m.s. sf. (435) *thy law*
כָּל־הַיּוֹם n.m.s. cstr. (481)-def.art.-n.m.s. (398) *all the day*
הִיא שִׂיחָתִי demons.adj. f.s. (214)-n.f.s.-1 c.s. sf. (967) *it is my meditation*

119:98

מֵאֹיְבַי prep.-Qal act.ptc. m.p.-1 c.s. sf. (אָיַב 33) *than my enemies*
תְּחַכְּמֵנִי Pi. impf. 3 f.s.-1 c.s. sf. (חָכַם 314) *makes me wiser*
מִצְוֹתֶךָ n.f.p.-2 m.s. sf. (846; GK 91n) *thy commandments*
כִּי לְעוֹלָם conj. (471)-prep.-n.m.s. (761) *for ever*
הִיא־לִי demons.adj. f.s. (214)-prep.-1 c.s. sf. *it is with me*

119:99

מִכָּל־מְלַמְּדַי prep.-n.m.s. cstr. (481)-Pi. ptc. m.p.-1 c.s. sf. (לָמַד 540) *than all my teachers*
הִשְׂכַּלְתִּי Hi. pf. 1 c.s. (968) *I have more understanding*
כִּי עֵדְוֹתֶיךָ conj.-n.f.p.-2 m.s. sf. (730) *for thy testimonies*
שִׂיחָה לִי n.f.s. (967)-prep.-1 c.s. sf. *are my meditation*

119:100

מִזְּקֵנִים prep.-adj. m.p. (278) *than the aged*
אֶתְבּוֹנָן Hithpolel impf. 1 c.s. (בִּין 106) *I understand*
כִּי פִקּוּדֶיךָ conj.-n.m.p.-2 m.s. sf. (824) *for thy precepts*
נָצָרְתִּי Qal pf. 1 c.s. paus. (665) *I keep*

119:101

מִכָּל־אֹרַח רָע prep.-n.m.s. cstr. (481)-n.m.s. (73)-adj. m.s. (I 948) *from every evil way*
כָּלָאתִי Qal pf. 1 c.s. (כָּלָא 476; GK 75oo) *I hold back*
רַגְלָי n.f.p.-1 c.s. sf. (919) *my feet*
לְמַעַן אֶשְׁמֹר prep. (775)-Qal impf. 1 c.s. (1036) *in order to keep*
דְּבָרֶךָ n.m.s.-2 m.s. sf. (182) *thy word*

119:102

מִמִּשְׁפָּטֶיךָ prep.-n.m.p.-2 m.s. sf. (1048) *from thy ordinances*
לֹא־סָרְתִּי neg.-Qal pf. 1 c.s. (סוּר 693) *I do not turn aside*
כִּי־אַתָּה conj. (471)-pers.pr. 2 m.s. (61) *for thou*
הוֹרֵתָנִי Hi. pf. 2 m.s.-1 c.s. sf. (יָרָה 434) *hast taught me*

119:103

מַה־ interr. (552) *how*
נִּמְלְצוּ Ni. pf. 3 c.p. (576) *sweet are*
לְחִכִּי prep.-n.m.s.-1 c.s. sf. (335) *to my taste*
אִמְרָתֶךָ n.f.s.-2 m.s. sf. (57) *thy words*
מִדְּבַשׁ prep.-n.m.s. (185) *than honey*
לְפִי prep.-n.m.s.-1 c.s. sf. (804) *to my mouth*

119:104

מִפִּקּוּדֶיךָ prep.-n.m.p.-2 m.s. sf. (824) *through thy precepts*

אֶתְבּוֹנָן Hithpolel impf. 1 c.s. (בִּין 106) *I get understanding*

עַל־כֵּן prep.-adv. (485) *therefore*

שָׂנֵאתִי Qal pf. 1 c.s. (971) *I hate*

כָּל־אֹרַח שָׁקֶר n.m.s. cstr. (481)-n.m.s. cstr. (73)-n.m.s. paus. (1055) *every false way*

119:105

נֵר־ n.m.s. (632) *a lamp*

לְרַגְלִי prep.-n.f.s.-1 c.s. sf. (919) *to my feet*

דְבָרֶךָ n.m.s.-2 m.s. sf. paus. (182) *thy word*

וְאוֹר conj.-n.m.s. (21) *and a light*

לִנְתִיבָתִי prep.-n.f.s.-1 c.s. sf. (677) *to my path*

119:106

נִשְׁבַּעְתִּי Ni. pf. 1 c.s. (שָׁבַע 989) *I have sworn an oath*

וָאֲקַיֵּמָה consec.-Pi. impf. 1 c.s. paus. (קוּם 877) *and confirmed it*

לִשְׁמֹר prep.-Qal inf.cstr. (1036) *to observe*

מִשְׁפְּטֵי n.m.p. cstr. (1048) *the ordinances of*

צִדְקֶךָ n.m.s.-2 m.s. sf. (841) *thy righteousness*

119:107

נַעֲנֵיתִי Ni. pf. 1 c.s. (עָנָה III 776) *I am afflicted*

עַד־מְאֹד prep. (III 723)-adv. (547) *sorely*

יהוה pr.n. (217) *O Yahweh*

חַיֵּנִי Pi. impv. 2 m.s.-1 c.s. sf. (חָיָה 310) *give me life*

כִדְבָרֶךָ prep.-n.m.s.-2 m.s. sf. (182) *according to thy word*

119:108

נִדְבוֹת n.f.p. cstr. (621) *offerings of*

פִּי n.m.s.-1 c.s. sf. (804) *my mouth*

רְצֵה־נָא Qal impv. 2 m.s. (953)-part.of entreaty (609) *accept*

יהוה pr.n. (217) *O Yahweh*

וּמִשְׁפָּטֶיךָ conj.-n.m.p.-2 m.s. sf. (1048) *and thy ordinances*

לַמְּדֵנִי Pi. impv. 2 m.s.-1 c.s. sf. (לָמַד 540) *teach me*

119:109

נַפְשִׁי n.f.s.-1 c.s. sf. (659) *my life*

בְכַפִּי prep.-n.f.s.-1 c.s. sf. (496) *in my hand*

תָמִיד adv. (556) *continually*

וְתוֹרָתְךָ conj.-n.f.s.-2 m.s. sf. (435) *but thy law*

לֹא שָׁכָחְתִּי neg.-Qal pf. 1 c.s. paus. (1013) *I do not forget*

119:110

נָתְנוּ Qal pf. 3 c.p. (נָתַן 678) *laid*

רְשָׁעִים adj. m.p. (957) *the wicked*

פַּח n.m.s. (809) *a snare*

לִי prep.-1 c.s. sf. *for me*

וּמִפִּקּוּדֶיךָ conj.-prep.-n.m.p.-2 m.s. sf. (824) *but from thy precepts*

לֹא תָעִיתִי neg.-Qal pf. 1 c.s. (תָּעָה 1073) *I do not stray*

119:111

נָחַלְתִּי Qal pf. 1 c.s. (נָחַל 635) *I have as a possession (inheritance)*

עֵדְוֹתֶיךָ n.f.p.-2 m.s. sf. (730) *thy testimonies*

לְעוֹלָם prep.-n.m.s. (761) *for ever*

כִּי־שְׂשׂוֹן conj. (471)-n.m.s. cstr. (965) *yea, the joy of*

לִבִּי n.m.s.-1 c.s. sf. (524) *my heart*

הֵמָּה demons.adj. (241) *they are*

119:112

נָטִיתִי Qal pf. 1 c.s. (נָטָה 639) *I incline*

לִבִּי n.m.s.-1 c.s. sf. (524) *my heart*

לַעֲשׂוֹת prep.-Qal inf.cstr. (עָשָׂה I 793) *to perform*

חֻקֶּיךָ n.m.p.-2 m.s. sf. (349) *thy statutes*

לְעוֹלָם prep.-n.m.s. (761) *for ever*

עֵקֶב adv.acc. (784) *to the end*

119:113

סֵעֲפִים adj. m.p. (II 704) *double-minded men*

שָׂנֵאתִי Qal pf. 1 c.s. (971) *I hate*

וְתוֹרָתְךָ conj.-n.f.s.-2 m.s. sf. (435) *but thy law*

אָהָבְתִּי Qal pf. 1 c.s. paus. (אָהַב 12) *I love*

119:114

סִתְרִי n.m.s.-1 c.s. sf. (712) *my hiding place*

וּמָגִנִּי conj.-n.m.s.-1 c.s. sf. (171) *and my shield*

אָתָּה pers.pr. 2 m.s. paus. (61) *thou art*

לִדְבָרְךָ prep.-n.m.s.-2 m.s. sf. (182) *in thy word*

יִחָלְתִּי Pi. pf. 1 c.s. paus. (יָחַל 403) *I hope*

119:115

סוּרוּ־ Qal impv. 2 m.p. (סוּר 693) *depart*

מִמֶּנִּי prep.-1 c.s. sf. *from me*

מְרֵעִים Hi. ptc. m.p. (רָעַע 949) *evildoers*

וְאֶצְּרָה conj.-Qal impf. 1 c.s.-vol.he (נָצַר 665) *that I may keep*

מִצְוֹת n.f.p. cstr. (846) *the commandments of*

אֱלֹהָי n.m.p.-1 c.s. sf. paus. (43) *my God*

119:116

סָמְכֵנִי Qal impv. 2 m.s.-1 c.s. sf. (סָמַךְ 701) *uphold me*

כְאִמְרָתְךָ prep.-n.f.s.-2 m.s. sf. (57) *according to thy promise*

וְאֶחְיֶה conj.-Qal impf. 1 c.s. (חָיָה 310) *that I may live*

וְאַל־תְּבִישֵׁנִי conj.-neg.-Hi. impf. 2 m.s.-1 c.s. sf. (בּוֹשׁ 101) *and let me not be put to shame*

מִשִּׂבְרִי prep.-n.m.s.-1 c.s. sf. (960) *in my hope*

119:117

סְעָדֵנִי Qal impv. 2 m.s.-1 c.s. sf. (סָעַד 703) *hold me up*

וְאִוָּשֵׁעָה conj.-Ni. impf. 1 c.s.-vol.he (יָשַׁע 446) *that I may be safe*

וְאֶשְׁעָה conj.-Qal impf. 1 c.s.-vol.he (שָׁעָה 1043; GK 75,l) *and I may have regard*

בְחֻקֶּיךָ prep.-n.m.p.-2 m.s. sf. (349) *for thy statutes*

תָמִיד adv. (556) *continually*

119:118

סָלִיתָ Qal pf. 2 m.s. (סָלָה I 699) *thou dost spurn*

כָּל־שׁוֹגִים n.m.s. cstr. (481)-Qal act.ptc. m.p. (שָׁגָה 993) *all who go astray*

מֵחֻקֶּיךָ prep.-n.m.p.-2 m.s. sf. (349) *from thy statutes*

כִּי־שֶׁקֶר conj. (471)-n.m.s. (1055) *yea, in vain*

תַּרְמִיתָם n.f.s.-3 m.p. sf. (941) *their cunning*

119:119

סִגִים n.m.p. (691) *as dross*

הִשְׁבַּתָּ Hi. pf. 2 m.s. (שָׁבַת 991) *you destroy*

כָל־רִשְׁעֵי־ n.m.s. cstr. (481)-adj. m.p. cstr. (957) *all the wicked of*

אָרֶץ n.f.s. paus. (75) *the earth*

לָכֵן prep.-adv. (485) *therefore*

אָהַבְתִּי Qal pf. 1 c.s. (אָהַב 12) *I love*

עֵדֹתֶיךָ n.f.p.-2 m.s. sf. (730) *thy testimonies*

119:120

סָמַר Qal pf. 3 m.s. (702) *trembles*

מִפַּחְדְּךָ prep.-n.m.s.-2 m.s. sf. (808) *for fear of thee*

בְשָׂרִי n.m.s.-1 c.s. sf. (142) *my flesh*

וּמִמִּשְׁפָּטֶיךָ conj.-prep.-n.m.p.-2 m.s. sf. (1048) *and of thy judgments*

יָרֵאתִי Qal pf. 1 c.s. (431) *I am afraid*

119:121

עָשִׂיתִי Qal pf. 1 c.s. (עָשָׂה I 793) *I have done*

מִשְׁפָּט n.m.s. (1048) *what is just*

וָצֶדֶק conj.-n.m.s. (841) *and right*

בַּל־תַּנִּיחֵנִי neg. (115)-Hi. impf. 2 m.s.-1 c.s. sf. (628 נוּחַ) *do not leave me*

לְעֹשְׁקָי prep.-Qal act.ptc. m.p.-1 c.s. sf. paus. (798 עָשַׁק) *to my oppressors*

119:122

עֲרֹב Qal impv. 2 m.s. (II 786) *be surety for*

עַבְדְּךָ n.m.s.-2 m.s. sf. (713) *thy servant*

לְטוֹב prep.-adj. m.s. (II 373) *for good*

אַל־יַעַשְׁקֻנִי neg.-Qal impf. 3 m.p.-1 c.s. sf. (עָשַׁק 798) *let not oppress me*

זֵדִים adj. m.p. (267) *the godless*

119:123

עֵינַי n.f. du.-1 c.s. sf. (744) *my eyes*

כָּלוּ Qal pf. 3 c.p. (כָּלָה 477) *fail*

לִישׁוּעָתֶךָ prep.-n.f.s.-2 m.s. sf. (448) *for thy salvation*

וּלְאִמְרַת conj.-prep.-n.f.s. cstr. (57) *and for the fulfilment of*

צִדְקֶךָ n.m.s.-2 m.s. sf. (841) *thy righteousness*

119:124

עֲשֵׂה Qal impv. 2 m.s. (עָשָׂה I 793) *deal*

עִם־עַבְדְּךָ prep.-n.m.s.-2 m.s. sf. (713) *with thy servant*

כְחַסְדֶּךָ prep.-n.m.s.-2 m.s. sf. (338) *according to thy steadfast love*

וְחֻקֶּיךָ conj.-n.m.p.-2 m.s. sf. (349) *and thy statutes*

לַמְּדֵנִי Pi. impv. 2 m.s.-1 c.s. sf. (540) *teach me*

119:125

עַבְדְּךָ־ n.m.s.-2 m.s. sf. (713) *thy servant*

אָנִי pers.pr. 1 c.s. (58) *I am*

הֲבִינֵנִי Hi. impv. 2 m.s.-1 c.s. sf. (בִּין 106) *give me understanding*

וְאֵדְעָה conj.-Qal impf. 1 c.s.-vol.he (יָדַע 393) *that I may know*

עֵדֹתֶיךָ n.f.p.-2 m.s. sf. (730) *thy testimonies*

119:126

עֵת n.f.s. (773) *it is time*

לַעֲשׂוֹת prep.-Qal inf.cstr. (עָשָׂה I 793) *to act*

לַיהוה prep.-pr.n. (217) *for Yahweh*

הֵפֵרוּ Hi. pf. 3 c.p. (פָּרַר I 830) *they have broken*

תּוֹרָתֶךָ n.f.s.-2 m.s. sf. (435) *thy law*

119:127

עַל־כֵּן prep.-adv. (485) *therefore*

אָהַבְתִּי Qal pf. 1 c.s. (אָהֵב 12) *I love*

מִצְוֺתֶיךָ n.f.p.-2 m.s. sf. (846) *thy commandments*

מִזָּהָב prep.-n.m.s. (262) *above gold*

וּמִפָּז conj.-prep.-n.m.s. (808) *and above fine gold*

119:128

עַל־כֵּן prep.-adv. (485) *therefore*

כָּל־פִּקּוּדֵי כֹל n.m.s. cstr. (481)-n.m.p. cstr. (824) -n.m.s. (481; GK 130fN) *all the precepts of all*

יִשָּׁרְתִּי Pi. pf. 1 c.s. paus. (יָשַׁר 448) *I direct my steps*

כָּל־אֹרַח שֶׁקֶר n.m.s. cstr. (481)-n.m.s. cstr. (73) -n.m.s. (1055) *every false way*

שָׂנֵאתִי Qal pf. 1 c.s. (971) *I hate*

119:129

פְּלָאוֹת n.f.p. (810) *are wonderful*

עֵדְוֺתֶיךָ n.f.p.-2 m.s. sf. (730) *thy testimonies*

עַל־כֵּן prep.-adv. (485) *therefore*

נְצָרָתַם Qal pf. 3 f.s.-3 m.p. sf. (נָצַר 665) *keeps them*

נַפְשִׁי n.f.s.-1 c.s. sf. (659) *my soul*

119:130

פֵּתַח n.m.s. cstr. (836) *the unfolding of*

דְּבָרֶיךָ n.m.p.-2 m.s. sf. (182) *thy words*

יָאִיר Hi. impf. 3 m.s. (אוֹר 21) *gives light*

מֵבִין Hi. ptc. (בִּין 106) *it imparts understanding*

פְּתָיִים adj. m.p. (834) *to the simple*

119:131

פִּי־ n.m.s.-1 c.s. sf. (804) *with my mouth*

פָעַרְתִּי Qal pf. 1 c.s. (822) *I make open*

וָאֶשְׁאָפָה consec.-Qal impf. 1 c.s.-vol.he (שָׁאַף I 983) *and I pant*

כִּי לְמִצְוֺתֶיךָ conj. (471)-prep.-n.f.p.-2 m.s. sf. (846) *because for thy commandments*

יָאָבְתִּי Qal pf. 1 c.s. paus. (יָאַב 383) *I long*

119:132

פְּנֵה־ Qal impv. 2 m.s. (815) *turn*

אֵלַי prep.-1 c.s. sf. *to me*

וְחָנֵּנִי conj.-Qal impv. 2 m.s.-1 c.s. sf. (חָנַן I 335) *and be gracious to me*

כְּמִשְׁפָּט prep.-n.m.s. (1048) *as judgment*

לְאֹהֲבֵי prep.-Qal act.ptc. m.p. cstr. (אָהַב 12) *toward those who love*

שְׁמֶךָ n.m.s.-2 m.s. sf. (1027) *thy name*

119:133

פְּעָמַי n.f.p.-1 c.s. sf. (821) *my steps*

הָכֵן Hi. impv. 2 m.s. (כּוּן 465) *keep steady*

בְּאִמְרָתֶךָ prep.-n.f.s.-2 m.s. sf. (57) *according to thy promise*

וְאַל־תַּשְׁלֶט־ conj.-neg.-Hi. impf. 3 f.s. juss. (1020 שָׁלַט) *and let not get dominion*

בִּי prep.-1 c.s. sf. *over me*

כָל־אָוֶן n.m.s. cstr. (481)-n.m.s. (19) *any iniquity*

119:134

פְּדֵנִי Qal impv. 2 m.s.-1 c.s. sf. (פָּדָה 804) *redeem me*

מֵעֹשֶׁק prep.-n.m.s. cstr. (799) *from oppression of*

אָדָם n.m.s. (9) *man*

וְאֶשְׁמְרָה conj.-Qal impf. 1 c.s.-vol.he (שָׁמַר 1036) *that I may keep*

פִּקּוּדֶיךָ n.m.p.-2 m.s. sf. (824) *thy precepts*

119:135

פָּנֶיךָ n.m.p.-2 m.s. sf. (815) *thy face*

הָאֵר Hi. impv. 2 m.s. (אוֹר 21) *make shine*

בְּעַבְדֶּךָ prep.-n.m.s.-2 m.s. sf. (713) *upon thy servant*

וְלַמְּדֵנִי conj.-Pi. impv. 2 m.s.-1 c.s. sf. (540) *and teach me*

אֶת־חֻקֶּיךָ dir.obj.-n.m.p.-2 m.s. sf. (349) *thy statutes*

119:136

פַּלְגֵי־מַיִם n.m.p. cstr. (811)-n.m.p. (565) *streams of tears*

יָרְדוּ Qal pf. 3 c.p. (יָרַד 432) *shed*

עֵינָי n.f. du.-1 c.s. sf. (744) *my eyes*

עַל לֹא־שָׁמְרוּ prep.-neg. (GK 155n)-Qal pf. 3 c.p. (1036) *because do not keep*

תוֹרָתֶךָ n.f.s.-2 m.s. sf. (435) *thy law*

119:137

צַדִּיק adj. m.s. (843) *righteous*

אַתָּה pers.pr. 2 m.s. (61) *art thou*

יהוה pr.n. (217) *O Yahweh*

וְיָשָׁר conj.-adj. (449) *and right*

מִשְׁפָּטֶיךָ n.m.p.-2 m.s. sf. (1048; GK 145r) *thy judgments*

119:138

צִוִּיתָ Pi. pf. 2 m.s. (צָוָה 845) *thou hast appointed*

צֶדֶק n.m.s. (841) *in righteousness*
עֵדֹתֶיךָ n.f.p.-2 m.s. sf. (730) *thy testimonies*
וֶאֱמוּנָה מְאֹד conj.-n.f.s. (53)-adv. (547) *and in all faithfulness*

119:139

צִמְּתַתְנִי Pi. pf. 3 f.s.-1 c.s. sf. (צָמַת 856) *consumes me*
קִנְאָתִי n.f.s.-1 c.s. sf. (888) *my zeal*
כִּי־שָׁכְחוּ conj. (471)-Qal pf. 3 c.p. (1013) *because forget*
דְבָרֶיךָ n.m.p.-2 m.s. sf. (182) *thy words*
צָרָי n.m.p.-1 c.s. sf. (III 865) *my foes*

119:140

צְרוּפָה Qal pass.ptc. f.s. (צָרַף 864) *is tried*
אִמְרָתְךָ n.f.s.-2 m.s. sf. (57) *thy promise*
מְאֹד adv. (547) *well*
וְעַבְדְּךָ conj.-n.m.s.-2 m.s. sf. (713) *and thy servant*
אֲהֵבָהּ Qal pf. 3 m.s.-3 f.s. sf. (אָהֵב 12) *loves it*

119:141

צָעִיר adj. m.s. (I 859) *small*
אָנֹכִי pers.pr. 1 c.s. (59) *I am*
וְנִבְזֶה conj.-Ni. ptc. (בָּזָה 102) *despised*
פִּקֻּדֶיךָ n.m.p.-2 m.s. sf. (824) *thy precepts*
לֹא שָׁכָחְתִּי neg.-Qal pf. 1 c.s. paus. (1013) *I do not forget*

119:142

צִדְקָתְךָ n.f.s.-2 m.s. sf. (842) *thy righteousness*
צֶדֶק n.m.s. (841) *is righteous*
לְעוֹלָם prep.-n.m.s. (761) *for ever*
וְתוֹרָתְךָ conj.-n.f.s.-2 m.s. sf. (435) *and thy law*
אֱמֶת n.f.s. (54) *is true*

119:143

צַר־ n.m.s. (II 865) *trouble*
וּמָצוֹק conj.-n.m.s. (848) *and anguish*
מְצָאוּנִי Qal pf. 3 c.p.-1 c.s. sf. (מָצָא 592) *have come upon me*
מִצְוֹתֶיךָ n.f.p.-2 m.s. sf. (846) *thy commandments*
שַׁעֲשֻׁעָי n.m.p.-1 c.s. sf. paus. (1044) *are my delight*

119:144

צֶדֶק n.m.s. (841) *are righteous*
עֵדְוֹתֶיךָ n.f.p.-2 m.s. sf. (730) *thy testimonies*
לְעוֹלָם prep.-n.m.s. (761) *for ever*
הֲבִינֵנִי Hi. impv. 2 m.s.-1 c.s. sf. (בִּין 106) *give me understanding*
וְאֶחְיֶה conj.-Qal impf. 1 c.s. (310) *that I may live*

119:145

קָרָאתִי Qal pf. 1 c.s. (894) *I cry*
בְכָל־לֵב prep.-n.m.s. cstr. (481)-n.m.s. (524) *with my whole heart*
עֲנֵנִי Qal impv. 2 m.s.-1 c.s. sf. (עָנָה I 772) *answer me*
יהוה pr.n. (217) *O Yahweh*
חֻקֶּיךָ n.m.p.-2 m.s. sf. (349) *thy statutes*
אֶצֹּרָה Qal impf. 1 c.s.-vol.he (נָצַר 665) *I will keep*

119:146

קְרָאתִיךָ Qal pf. 1 c.s.-2 m.s. sf. (894) *I cry to thee*
הוֹשִׁיעֵנִי Hi. impv. 2 m.s.-1 c.s. sf. (יָשַׁע 446) *save me*
וְאֶשְׁמְרָה conj.-Qal impf. 1 c.s.-vol.he (1036) *that I may observe*
עֵדֹתֶיךָ n.f.p.-2 m.s. sf. (730) *thy testimonies*

119:147

קִדַּמְתִּי Pi. pf. 1 c.s. (קָדַם 869) *I rise*
בַנֶּשֶׁף prep.-def.art.-n.m.s. (676) *in the morning twilight*
וָאֲשַׁוֵּעָה consec.-Pi. impf. 1 c.s.-vol.he (שָׁוַע 1002) *and cry for help*
לִדְבָרְיךָ prep.-n.m.p.-2 m.p. sf. (182) *in thy words*
יִחָלְתִּי Pi. pf. 1 c.s. (יָחַל 403) *I hope*

119:148

קִדְּמוּ Pi. pf. 3 c.p. (קָדַם 869) *are awake before*
עֵינַי n.f. du.-1 c.s. sf. (744) *my eyes*
אַשְׁמֻרוֹת n.f.p. (1038) *the watches of the night*
לָשִׂיחַ prep.-Qal inf.cstr. (967) *that I may meditate*
בְּאִמְרָתֶךָ prep.-n.f.s.-2 m.s. sf. (57) *upon thy promise*

119:149

קוֹלִי n.m.s.-1 c.s. sf. (876) *my voice*
שִׁמְעָה Qal impv. 2 m.s.-vol.he (1033) *hear*
כְּחַסְדֶּךָ prep.-n.m.s.-2 m.s. sf. (338) *in thy steadfast love*
יהוה pr.n. (217) *O Yahweh*
כְּמִשְׁפָּטֶךָ prep.-n.m.s.-2 m.s. sf. (1048) *in thy justice*

חַיֵּנִי Pi. impv. 2 m.s.-1 c.s. sf. (חָיָה 310) *preserve me*

119:150

קָרְבוּ Qal pf. 3 c.p. (897) *they draw near*
רֹדְפֵי Qal act.ptc. m.p. cstr. (922) *who persecute*
זִמָּה n.f.s. (I 273) *with evil purpose*
מִתּוֹרָתְךָ prep.-n.f.s.-2 m.s. sf. (435) *from thy law*
רָחָקוּ Qal pf. 3 c.p. paus. (934) *they are far*

119:151

קָרוֹב adj. (898) *near*
אַתָּה pers.pr. 2 m.s. (61) *thou art*
יהוה pr.n. (217) *O Yahweh*
וְכָל־ conj.-n.m.s. cstr. (481) *and all*
מִצְוֹתֶיךָ n.f.p.-2 m.s. sf. (846) *thy commandments*
אֱמֶת n.f.s. (54) *are true*

119:152

קֶדֶם n.m.s. (869) *long*
יָדַעְתִּי Qal pf. 1 c.s. (393) *I have known*
מֵעֵדֹתֶיךָ prep.-n.f.p.-2 m.s. sf. (730) *from thy testimonies*
כִּי לְעוֹלָם conj. (471)-prep.-n.m.s. (761) *that for ever*
יְסַדְתָּם Qal pf. 2 m.s.-3 m.p. sf. (יָסַד 413) *thou hast founded them*

119:153

רְאֵה־ Qal impv. 2 m.s. (906) *look on*
עָנְיִי n.m.s.-1 c.s. sf. (777) *my affliction*
וְחַלְּצֵנִי conj.-Pi. impv. 2 m.s.-1 c.s. sf. (חָלַץ I 322) *and deliver me*
כִּי־תוֹרָתְךָ conj. (471)-n.f.s.-2 m.s. sf. (435) *for thy law*
לֹא שָׁכָחְתִּי neg.-Qal pf. 1 c.s. paus. (1013) *I do not forget*

119:154

רִיבָה Qal impv. 2 m.s.-vol.he (רִיב 936) *plead*
רִיבִי n.m.s.-1 c.s. sf. (936) *my cause*
וּגְאָלֵנִי conj.-Qal impv. 2 m.s.-1 c.s. sf. (גָּאַל I 145) *and redeem me*
לְאִמְרָתְךָ prep.-n.f.s.-2 m.s. sf. (57) *according to thy promise*
חַיֵּנִי Pi. impv. 2 m.s.-1 c.s. sf. (310) *give me life*

119:155

רָחוֹק adj. m.s. (935) *far*
מֵרְשָׁעִים prep.-adj. m.p. (957) *from the wicked*
יְשׁוּעָה n.f.s. (447) *salvation*
כִּי־חֻקֶּיךָ conj.-n.m.p.-2 m.s. sf. (349) *for thy statutes*
לֹא דָרָשׁוּ neg.-Qal pf. 3 c.p. paus. (205) *they do not seek*

119:156

רַחֲמֶיךָ n.m.p.-2 m.s. sf. (933) *thy mercy*
רַבִּים adj. m.p. (I 912) *great*
יהוה pr.n. (217) *O Yahweh*
כְּמִשְׁפָּטֶיךָ prep.-n.m.p.-2 m.s. sf. (1048) *according to thy justice*
חַיֵּנִי Pi. impv. 2 m.s.-1 c.s. sf. (310) *give me life*

119:157

רַבִּים adj. m.p. (I 912) *many are*
רֹדְפַי Qal act.ptc. m.p.-1 c.s. sf. (922) *my persecutors*
וְצָרָי conj.-n.m.p.-1 c.s. sf. (III 865) *and my adversaries*
מֵעֵדְוֹתֶיךָ prep.-n.f.p.-2 m.s. sf. (730) *but from thy testimonies*
לֹא נָטִיתִי neg.-Qal pf. 1 c.s. (נָטָה 639) *I do not swerve*

119:158

רָאִיתִי Qal pf. 1 c.s. (רָאָה 906) *I look at*
בֹגְדִים Qal act.ptc. m.p. (93) *the faithless*
וָאֶתְקוֹטָטָה consec.-Hithpolel impf. 1 c.s. paus. (876 קוט) *and I felt a loathing*
אֲשֶׁר אִמְרָתְךָ rel. (81)-n.f.s.-2 m.s. sf. (57) *because thy commands*
לֹא שָׁמָרוּ neg.-Qal pf. 3 c.p. paus. (1036) *they do not keep*

119:159

רְאֵה Qal impv. 2 m.s. (906) *consider*
כִּי־פִקּוּדֶיךָ conj. (471)-n.m.p.-2 m.s. sf. (824) *how thy precepts*
אָהָבְתִּי Qal pf. 1 c.s. paus. (אָהַב 12) *I love*
יהוה pr.n. (217) *O Yahweh*
כְּחַסְדְּךָ prep.-n.m.s.-2 m.s. sf. (338) *according to thy steadfast love*
חַיֵּנִי Pi. impv. 2 m.s.-1 c.s. sf. (310) *preserve my life*

119:160

רֹאשׁ־ n.m.s. cstr. (I 910) *the sum of*
דְּבָרְךָ n.m.s.-2 m.s. sf. (182) *thy word*
אֱמֶת n.f.s. (54) *is truth*
וּלְעוֹלָם conj.-prep.-n.m.s. (761) *and for ever*

כָּל־מִשְׁפַּט n.m.s. cstr. (481)–n.m.s. cstr. (1048) *every one of the ordinances of*
צִדְקֶךָ n.m.s.–2 m.s. sf. (841) *thy righteousness*

119:161
שָׂרִים n.m.p. (978) *princes*
רְדָפוּנִי Qal pf. 3 c.p.–1 c.s. sf. (922) *persecute me*
חִנָּם adv. (336) *without cause*
וּמִדְּבָרֶיךָ conj.–prep.–n.m.p.–2 m.s. sf. (182) *but of thy words*
פָּחַד Qal pf. 3 m.s. (808) *stands in awe*
לִבִּי n.m.s.–1 c.s. sf. (524) *my heart*

119:162
שָׂשׂ Qal act.ptc. (שׂוּשׂ 965) *rejoice*
אָנֹכִי pers.pr. 1 c.s. (59) *I*
עַל־אִמְרָתֶךָ prep.–n.f.s.–2 m.s. sf. (57) *at thy word*
כְּמוֹצֵא prep.–Qal act.ptc. m.s. (592) *like one who finds*
שָׁלָל רָב n.m.s. (1021)–adj. m.s. paus. (I 912) *great spoil*

119:163
שֶׁקֶר n.m.s. (1055) *falsehood*
שָׂנֵאתִי Qal pf. 1 c.s. (971) *I hate*
וַאֲתַעֵבָה conj.–Pi. impf. 1 c.s.–vol.he paus. (תָּעַב 1073) *and abhor*
תּוֹרָתְךָ n.f.s.–2 m.s. sf. (435) *but thy law*
אָהָבְתִּי Qal pf. 1 c.s. paus. (12) *I love*

119:164
שֶׁבַע num. (988) *seven*
בַּיּוֹם prep.–def.art.–n.m.s. (398) *in the day*
הִלַּלְתִּיךָ Pi. pf. 1 c.s.–2 m.s. sf. (II 237) *I praise thee*
עַל מִשְׁפְּטֵי prep.–n.m.p. cstr. (1048) *for the ordinances of*
צִדְקֶךָ n.m.s.–2 m.s. sf. (841) *thy righteousness*

119:165
שָׁלוֹם רָב n.m.s. (1022)–adj. m.s. (I 912) *great peace*
לְאֹהֲבֵי prep.–Qal act.ptc. m.p. cstr. (12) *those who love*
תוֹרָתֶךָ n.f.s.–2 m.s. sf. (435) *thy law*
וְאֵין־לָמוֹ conj.–neg. cstr. (II 34)–prep.–3 m.p. sf. *and there is not to them*
מִכְשׁוֹל n.m.s. (506) *stumbling*

119:166
שִׂבַּרְתִּי Pi. pf. 1 c.s. (שָׂבַר II 960) *I hope*
לִישׁוּעָתְךָ prep.–n.f.s.–2 m.s. sf. (447) *for thy salvation*
יהוה pr.n. (217) *O Yahweh*
וּמִצְוֺתֶיךָ conj.–n.f.p.–2 m.s. sf. (846) *and thy commandments*
עָשִׂיתִי Qal pf. 1 c.s. (עָשָׂה I 793) *I do*

119:167
שָׁמְרָה Qal pf. 3 f.s. (1036) *keeps*
נַפְשִׁי n.f.s.–1 c.s. sf. (659) *my soul*
עֵדֹתֶיךָ n.f.p.–2 m.s. sf. (730) *thy testimonies*
וָאֹהֲבֵם consec.–Qal impf. 1 c.s.–3 m.p. sf. (אָהַב 12) *and I love them*
מְאֹד adv. (547) *exceedingly*

119:168
שָׁמַרְתִּי Qal pf. 1 c.s. (1036) *I keep*
פִקּוּדֶיךָ n.m.p.–2 m.s. sf. (824) *thy precepts*
וְעֵדֹתֶיךָ conj.–n.f.p.–2 m.s. sf. (730) *and thy testimonies*
כִּי כָל־ conj. (471)–n.m.s. cstr. (481) *for all*
דְּרָכַי n.m.p.–1 c.s. sf. (202) *my ways*
נֶגְדֶּךָ prep.–2 m.s. sf. (617) *before thee*

119:169
תִּקְרַב Qal impf. 3 f.s. (קָרַב 897) *let come near*
רִנָּתִי n.f.s.–1 c.s. sf. (943) *my cry*
לְפָנֶיךָ prep.–n.m.p.–2 m.s. sf. (815) *before thee*
יהוה pr.n. (217) *O Yahweh*
כִּדְבָרְךָ prep.–n.m.s.–2 m.s. sf. (182) *according to thy word*
הֲבִינֵנִי Hi. impv. 2 m.s.–1 c.s. sf. (בִּין 107) *give me understanding*

119:170
תָּבוֹא Qal impf. 3 f.s. (בּוֹא 97) *let come*
תְּחִנָּתִי n.f.s.–1 c.s. sf. (337) *my supplication*
לְפָנֶיךָ prep.–n.m.p.–2 m.s. sf. (815) *before thee*
כְּאִמְרָתְךָ prep.–n.f.s.–2 m.s. sf. (57) *according to thy word*
הַצִּילֵנִי Hi. impv. 2 m.s.–1 c.s. sf. (נָצַל 665) *deliver me*

119:171
תַּבַּעְנָה Hi. impf. 3 f.p. (נָבַע 615) *will pour forth*
שְׂפָתַי n.f. du.–1 c.s. sf. (973) *my lips*
תְּהִלָּה n.f.s. (239) *praise*
כִּי תְלַמְּדֵנִי conj. (471)–Pi. impf. 2 m.s.–1 c.s. sf. (540 לָמַד) *that thou dost teach me*
חֻקֶּיךָ n.m.p.–2 m.s. sf. (349) *thy statutes*

119:172

תַּעַן Qal impf. 3 f.s. apoc. (עָנָה IV 777) *will sing (let sing)*
לְשׁוֹנִי n.f.s.-1 c.s. sf. (546) *my tongue*
אִמְרָתֶךָ n.f.s.-2 m.s. sf. (57) *of thy word*
כִּי כָל־ conj. (471)-n.m.s. cstr. (481) *for all*
מִצְוֹתֶיךָ n.f.p.-2 m.s. sf. (846) *thy commandments*
צֶּדֶק n.m.s. (841) *are right*

119:173

תְּהִי־ Qal impf. 3 f.s. apoc. (הָיָה 224) *let be*
יָדְךָ n.f.s.-2 m.s. sf. (388) *thy hand*
לְעָזְרֵנִי prep.-Qal inf.cstr.-1 c.s. sf. (עָזַר I 740) *to help me*
כִּי פִקּוּדֶיךָ conj. (471)-n.m.p.-2 m.s. sf. (824) *for thy precepts*
בָחָרְתִּי Qal pf. 1 c.s. paus. (103) *I have chosen*

119:174

תָּאַבְתִּי Qal pf. 1 c.s. (תָּאַב I 1060) *I long for*
לִישׁוּעָתְךָ prep.-n.f.s.-2 m.s. sf. (447) *thy salvation*
יהוה pr.n. (217) *O Yahweh*
וְתוֹרָתְךָ conj.-n.f.s.-2 m.s. sf. (435) *and thy law*
שַׁעֲשֻׁעָי n.m.p.-1 c.s. sf. paus. (1044) *my delight*

119:175

תְּחִי־ Qal impf. 3 f.s. (חָיָה 310) *let live*
נַפְשִׁי n.f.s.-1 c.s. sf. (659) *me (my soul)*
וּתְהַלְלֶךָּ conj.-Pi. impf. 3 f.s.-2 m.s. sf. (הָלַל II 237) *that it may praise thee*
וּמִשְׁפָּטֶךָ conj.-n.m.p.-2 m.s. sf. (1048) *and thy ordinances*
יַעֲזְרֻנִי Qal impf. 3 m.p.-1 c.s. sf. (עָזַר 740) *let help me*

119:176

תָּעִיתִי Qal pf. 1 c.s. (תָּעָה 1073) *I have gone astray*
כְּשֶׂה אֹבֵד prep.-n.m.s. (961)-Qal act.ptc. (אָבַד 1) *like a lost sheep*
בַּקֵּשׁ Pi. impv. 2 m.s. (134) *seek*
עַבְדֶּךָ n.m.s.-2 m.s. sf. paus. (713) *thy servant*
כִּי מִצְוֹתֶיךָ conj. (471)-n.f.p.-2 m.s. sf. (846) *for thy commandments*
לֹא שָׁכָחְתִּי neg.-Qal pf. 1 c.s. paus. (1013) *I do not forget*

120:1

שִׁיר הַמַּעֲלוֹת n.m.s. cstr. (1010; GK 127e)-def. art.-n.f.p. (II 752) *a song of ascents*
אֶל־יהוה prep.-pr.n. (217) *to Yahweh*
בַּצָּרָתָה prep.-def.art.-n.f.s. (I 865; GK 90g) *in distress*
לִּי prep.-1 c.s. sf. *to me*
קָרָאתִי Qal pf. 1 c.s. (894) *I cry*
וַיַּעֲנֵנִי consec.-Qal impf. 3 m.s.-1 c.s. sf. (עָנָה I 772) *that he may answer me*

120:2

יהוה pr.n. (217) *O Yahweh*
הַצִּילָה Hi. impv. 2 m.s.-vol.he (נָצַל 664) *deliver*
נַפְשִׁי n.f.s.-1 c.s. sf. (659) *me (my soul)*
מִשְּׂפַת־שֶׁקֶר prep.-n.f.s. cstr. (973)-n.m.s. (1055) *from lying lips*
מִלָּשׁוֹן רְמִיָּה prep.-n.f.s. (546)-n.f.s. (I 941) *from a deceitful tongue*

120:3

מַה־יִּתֵּן interr. (552)-Qal impf. 3 m.s. (נָתַן 678) *what shall be given*
לְךָ prep.-2 m.s. sf. *to you*
וּמַה־יֹּסִיף conj.-v.supra-Hi. impf. 3 m.s. (יָסַף 414) *and what more (shall be added)*
לָךְ prep.-2 m.s. sf. paus. *to you*
לָשׁוֹן רְמִיָּה n.f.s. (546)-n.f.s. (I 941) *deceitful tongue*

120:4

חִצֵּי גִבּוֹר n.m.p. cstr. (346)-adj. m.s. (150) *a warrior's arrows*
שְׁנוּנִים Qal pass.ptc. m.p. (שָׁנַן 1041) *sharpened*
עִם גַּחֲלֵי prep.-n.f.p. cstr. (160) *with glowing coals of*
רְתָמִים n.m.p. (958) *the broom tree*

120:5

אוֹיָה־לִי interj. (17)-prep.-1 c.s. sf. *woe is me*
כִּי־גַרְתִּי conj. (471)-Qal pf. 1 c.s. (גּוּר 157; GK 117bb) *that I sojourn*
מֶשֶׁךְ pr.n. (II 604) *in Meshech*
שָׁכַנְתִּי Qal pf. 1 c.s. (1014) *that I dwell*
עִם־אָהֳלֵי prep.-n.m.p. cstr. (13) *among the tents of*
קֵדָר pr.n. (871) *Kedar*

120:6

רַבַּת adj. f.s. cstr. as adv. (I 912; an Aramaism) *too long*
שָׁכְנָה־לָּהּ Qal pf. 3 f.s. (1014)-prep.-3 f.s. sf. (GK 119s) *have dwelled*
נַפְשִׁי n.f.s.-1 c.s. sf. (659) *I (myself)*

עִם שׂוֹנֵא prep.-Qal act.ptc. (971) *among those who hate*
שָׁלוֹם n.m.s. (1022) *peace*

120:7

אֲנִי־ pers.pr. 1 c.s. (58) *I am for*
שָׁלוֹם n.m.s. (1022; GK 141cN) *peace*
וְכִי אֲדַבֵּר conj.-conj. (471)-Pi. impf. 1 c.s. (180) *but when I speak*
הֵמָּה pers.pr. 3 m.p. (241) *they are*
לַמִּלְחָמָה prep.-def.art.-n.f.s. (536) *for war*

121:1

שִׁיר n.m.s. (1010; GK 127e) *a song*
לַמַּעֲלוֹת prep.-def.art.-n.f.p. (II 752) *of ascents*
אֶשָּׂא Qal impf. 1 c.s. (נָשָׂא 669) *I lift up*
עֵינַי n.f.p.-1 c.s. sf. (744) *my eyes*
אֶל־הֶהָרִים prep.-def.art.-n.m.p. (249) *to the hills*
מֵאַיִן prep.-adv. (I 32) *from whence*
יָבֹא Qal impf. 3 m.s. (בּוֹא 97) *does come*
עֶזְרִי n.m.s.-1 c.s. sf. (740) *my help*

121:2

עֶזְרִי n.m.s.-1 c.s. sf. (740) *my help*
מֵעִם יהוה prep.-prep.-pr.n. (217) *from Yahweh*
עֹשֵׂה Qal act.ptc. m.s. cstr. (עָשָׂה I 793) *who made*
שָׁמַיִם n.m. du. (1029) *heaven*
וָאָרֶץ conj.-n.f.s. (75) *and earth*

121:3

אַל־יִתֵּן neg.-Qal impf. 3 m.s. (נָתַן 678; GK 107p,109e) *he will not let*
לַמּוֹט prep.-def.art.-n.m.s. (557) *be moved*
רַגְלֶךָ n.f.s.-2 m.s. sf. (919) *your foot*
אַל־יָנוּם neg.-Qal impf. 3 m.s. (נוּם 630; GK 107p) *he will not slumber*
שֹׁמְרֶךָ Qal act.ptc.-2 m.s. sf. (1036) *who keeps you*

121:4

הִנֵּה interj. (243) *behold*
לֹא־יָנוּם neg.-Qal impf. 3 m.s. (630) *he will not slumber*
וְלֹא יִישָׁן conj.-neg.-Qal impf. 3 m.s. paus. (יָשֵׁן 445) *and will not sleep*
שׁוֹמֵר Qal act.ptc. cstr. (1036) *who keeps*
יִשְׂרָאֵל pr.n. (975) *Israel*

121:5

יהוה pr.n. (217) *Yahweh*
שֹׁמְרֶךָ Qal act.ptc.-2 m.s. sf. (1036; GK 124k) *your keeper*
יהוה v.supra *Yahweh*
צִלְּךָ n.m.s.-2 m.s. sf. (853) *your shade*
עַל־יַד יְמִינֶךָ prep.-n.f.s. cstr. (388)-n.f.s.-2 m.s. sf. (411) *on your right hand*

121:6

יוֹמָם adv. (401) *by day*
הַשֶּׁמֶשׁ def.art.-n.m.s. (1039) *the sun*
לֹא־יַכֶּכָּה neg.-Hi. impf. 3 m.s.-2 m.s. sf. (נָכָה 645) *shall not smite you*
וְיָרֵחַ conj.-n.m.s. (437) *nor the moon*
בַּלָּיְלָה prep.-def.art.-n.m.s. (538) *by night*

121:7

יהוה pr.n. (217) *Yahweh*
יִשְׁמָרְךָ Qal impf. 3 m.s.-2 m.s. sf. (1036) *will keep you*
מִכָּל־ prep.-n.m.s. cstr. (481) *from all*
רָע n.m.s. (947) *evil*
יִשְׁמֹר Qal impf. 3 m.s. (1036) *he will keep*
אֶת־נַפְשֶׁךָ dir.obj.-n.f.s.-2 m.s. sf. (659) *your life*

121:8

יהוה pr.n. (217) *Yahweh*
יִשְׁמָר־ Qal impf. 3 m.s. (1036) *will keep*
צֵאתְךָ Qal inf.cstr.-2 m.s. sf. (יָצָא 422) *your going out*
וּבוֹאֶךָ conj.-Qal inf.cstr.-2 m.s. sf. (בּוֹא 97) *and your coming in*
מֵעַתָּה prep.-adv. (773) *from this time forth*
וְעַד־עוֹלָם conj.-prep. (III 723)-n.m.s. (761) *and for evermore*

122:1

שִׁיר n.m.s. cstr. (1010) *a song of*
הַמַּעֲלוֹת def.art.-n.f.p. (II 752) *ascents*
לְדָוִד prep.-pr.n. (187) *to David*
שָׂמַחְתִּי Qal pf. 1 c.s. (970) *I was glad*
בְּאֹמְרִים prep.-Qal act.ptc. m.p. (55) *when they said*
לִי prep.-1 c.s. sf. *to me*
בֵּית יהוה n.m.s. cstr. (108)-pr.n. (217) *to the house of Yahweh*
נֵלֵךְ Qal impf. 1 c.p. (הָלַךְ 229) *let us go*

122:2

עֹמְדוֹת הָיוּ Qal act.ptc. f.p. (763)-Qal pf. 3 c.p. (224 הָיָה) *have been standing*
רַגְלֵינוּ n.f. du.-1 c.p. sf. (919) *our feet*

בִּשְׁעָרַיִךְ prep.-n.f.p.-2 f.s. sf. (1044) *within your gates*
יְרוּשָׁלָ͏ִם pr.n. paus. (436) *O Jerusalem*

122:3
יְרוּשָׁלַ͏ִם pr.n. (436) *Jerusalem*
הַבְּנוּיָה def.art.-Qal pass.ptc. f.s. (בָּנָה 124) *built*
כְּעִיר prep.-n.f.s. (746) *as a city*
שֶׁחֻבְּרָה־לָּהּ rel. (81)-Pu. pf. 3 f.s. (287)-prep.-3 f.s. sf. *which is bound firmly*
יַחְדָּו adv. (403) *together*

122:4
שֶׁשָּׁם rel. (81)-adv. (1027) *to which*
עָלוּ Qal pf. 3 c.p. (עָלָה 748) *go up*
שְׁבָטִים n.m.p. (986) *the tribes*
שִׁבְטֵי־יָהּ n.m.p. cstr. (986)-pr.n. (219) *the tribes of Yah*
עֵדוּת n.f.s. (730) *as was decreed*
לְיִשְׂרָאֵל prep.-pr.n. (975) *for Israel*
לְהֹדוֹת prep.-Hi. inf.cstr. (יָדָה 392) *to give thanks*
לְשֵׁם יהוה prep.-n.m.s. cstr. (1027)-pr.n. (217) *to the name of Yahweh*

122:5
כִּי שָׁמָּה conj. (471)-adv.-dir.he (1027) *for there*
יָשְׁבוּ Qal pf. 3 c.p. (442) *were set*
כִסְאוֹת n.m.p. (490) *thrones*
לְמִשְׁפָּט prep.-n.m.s. (1048) *for judgment*
כִּסְאוֹת v.supra *the thrones*
לְבֵית דָּוִיד prep.-n.m.s. cstr. (108)-pr.n. (187) *of the house of David*

122:6
שַׁאֲלוּ Qal impv. 2 m.p. (981) *pray for*
שְׁלוֹם n.m.s. cstr. (1022) *the peace of*
יְרוּשָׁלָ͏ִם pr.n. (436) *Jerusalem*
יִשְׁלָיוּ Qal impf. 3 m.p. (שָׁלָה 1017; GK 75u) *may they prosper*
אֹהֲבָיִךְ Qal act.ptc. m.p.-2 f.s. sf. paus. (12) *those who love you*

122:7
יְהִי־ Qal impf. 3 m.s. apoc. (הָיָה 224) *let be*
שָׁלוֹם n.m.s. (1022) *peace*
בְּחֵילֵךְ prep.-n.m.p.-2 f.s. sf. (298) *within your walls*
שַׁלְוָה n.f.s. (1017) *security*
בְּאַרְמְנוֹתָיִךְ prep.-n.f.p.-2 f.s. sf. (74) *within your towers*

122:8
לְמַעַן אַחַי prep. (775)-n.m.p.-1 c.s. sf. (26) *for my brethren*
וְרֵעָי conj.-n.m.p.-1 c.s. sf. paus. (945) *and companions*
אֲדַבְּרָה־נָּא Pi. impf. 1 c.s.-vol.he (180)-part.of entreaty (609) *I will say*
שָׁלוֹם בָּךְ n.m.s. (1022)-prep.-2 f.s. sf. *peace within you*

122:9
לְמַעַן prep. (775) *for the sake of*
בֵּית־יהוה אֱלֹהֵינוּ n.m.s. cstr. (108)-pr.n. (217) -n.m.p.-1 c.p. sf. *the house of Yahweh our God*
אֲבַקְשָׁה Pi. impf. 1 c.s.-vol.he (134) *I will seek*
טוֹב לָךְ adj. m.s. (II 373)-prep.-2 f.s. sf. *your good*

123:1
שִׁיר n.m.s. cstr. (1010) *a song of*
הַמַּעֲלוֹת def.art.-n.f.p. (II 752) *ascents*
אֵלֶיךָ prep.-2 m.s. sf. *to thee*
נָשָׂאתִי Qal pf. 1 c.s. (669) *I lift up*
אֶת־עֵינַי dir.obj.-n.f. du.-1 c.s. sf. (744) *my eyes*
הַיֹּשְׁבִי def.art.-Qal act.ptc. gent. (יָשַׁב 442; GK 90m) *O thou who art enthroned*
בַּשָּׁמָיִם prep.-def.art.-n.m. du. paus. (1029) *in the heavens*

123:2
הִנֵּה interj. (243) *behold*
כְעֵינֵי prep.-n.f. du. cstr. (744) *as the eyes of*
עֲבָדִים n.m.p. (713) *servants*
אֶל־יַד prep.-n.f.s. cstr. (388) *to the hand of*
אֲדוֹנֵיהֶם n.m.p.-3 m.p. sf. (10) *their master*
כְּעֵינֵי v.supra *as the eyes of*
שִׁפְחָה n.f.s. (1046) *a maid*
אֶל־יַד v.supra-v.supra *to the hand of*
גְּבִרְתָּהּ n.f.s.-3 f.s. sf. (150) *her mistress*
כֵּן adv. (485) *so*
עֵינֵינוּ n.f. du.-1 c.p. sf. (744) *our eyes*
אֶל־יהוה prep.-pr.n. 217) *to Yahweh*
אֱלֹהֵינוּ n.m.p.-1 c.p. sf. (43) *our God*
עַד שֶׁיְּחָנֵּנוּ prep. (III 723)-rel. (979)-Qal impf. 3 m.s.-1 c.p. sf. (חָנַן I 335) *till he have mercy upon us*

123:3
חָנֵּנוּ Qal impv. 2 m.s.-1 c.p. sf. (חָנַן I 335) *have mercy upon us*
יהוה pr.n. (217) *O Yahweh*

חָנֵּנוּ v.supra *have mercy upon us*
כִּי־רַב conj. (471)-adj. m.s. (I 912) *for great*
שָׂבַעְנוּ Qal pf. 1 c.p. (959) *we have had enough*
בוּז n.m.s. (100) *contempt*

123:4

רַבַּת adj. f.s. cstr. as adv. (I 912) *too long*
שָׂבְעָה־לָּהּ Qal pf. 3 f.s. (שָׂבַע 959)-prep.-3 f.s. sf. (GK 119s) *has been sated*
נַפְשֵׁנוּ n.f.s.-1 c.p. sf. (659) *our soul*
הַלַּעַג def.art.-n.m.s. (541) *with the scorn*
הַשַּׁאֲנַנִּים def.art.-adj. m.p. (983) *those who art at ease*
הַבּוּז def.art.-n.m.s. (100) *the contempt*
לִגְאֵיוֹנִים Q rds. prep. (GK 127g)-adj. m.p. cstr. (144)-n.f.p. (I 401) *of the proud doves*

124:1

שִׁיר n.m.s. cstr. (1010) *a song of*
הַמַּעֲלוֹת def.art.-n.f.p. (II 752) *ascents*
לְדָוִד prep.-pr.n. (187) *to David*
לוּלֵי יהוה conj. (530)-pr.n. (217) *if it had not been for Yahweh*
שֶׁהָיָה לָנוּ rel. (979)-Qal pf. 3 m.s. (224)-prep.-1 c.p. sf. *who was on our side*
יֹאמַר־נָא Qal impf. 3 m.s. (55)-part.of entreaty (609) *let now say*
יִשְׂרָאֵל pr.n. (975) *Israel*

124:2

לוּלֵי יהוה conj. (530)-pr.n. (217) *if it had not been for Yahweh*
שֶׁהָיָה לָנוּ rel. (979)-Qal pf. 3 m.s. (224)-prep.-1 c.p. sf. *who was on our side*
בְּקוּם prep.-Qal inf.cstr. (877) *when rose up*
עָלֵינוּ prep.-1 c.p. sf. *against us*
אָדָם n.m.s. (9) *men*

124:3

אֲזַי חַיִּים adv. (23)-n.m.p. (313) *then alive*
בְּלָעוּנוּ Qal pf. 3 c.p.-1 c.p. sf. (בָּלַע 118) *they would have swallowed us*
בַּחֲרוֹת prep.-Qal inf.cstr. (חָרָה 354) *when was kindled*
אַפָּם n.m.s.-3 m.p. sf. (I 60) *their anger*
בָּנוּ prep.-1 c.p. sf. *against us*

124:4

אֲזַי הַמַּיִם adv. (23)-def.art.-n.m.p. (565) *then the flood*
שְׁטָפוּנוּ Qal pf. 3 c.p.-1 c.p. sf. (שָׁטַף 1009) *would have swept us away*
נַחְלָה n.f.s. (I 636; GK 90f) *the torrent*
עָבַר Qal pf. 3 m.s. (716) *would have gone*
עַל־נַפְשֵׁנוּ prep.-n.f.s.-1 c.p. sf. (659) *over us*

124:5

אֲזַי עָבַר adv. (23)-Qal pf. 3 m.s. (716) *then would have gone*
עַל־נַפְשֵׁנוּ prep.-n.f.s.-1 c.p. sf. (659) *over us*
הַמַּיִם הַזֵּידוֹנִים def.art.-n.m.p. (565)-def.art.-adj. m.p. (268) *the raging waters*

124:6

בָּרוּךְ Qal pass.ptc. (138) *blessed be*
יהוה pr.n. (217) *Yahweh*
שֶׁלֹּא נְתָנָנוּ rel. (979)-neg.-Qal pf. 3 m.s.-1 c.p. sf. (נָתַן 678) *who has not given us*
טֶרֶף n.m.s. (383) *as prey*
לְשִׁנֵּיהֶם prep.-n.f.p.-3 m.p. sf. (1042) *to their teeth*

124:7

נַפְשֵׁנוּ n.f.s.-1 c.p. sf. (659) *we*
כְּצִפּוֹר prep.-n.f.s. (861) *as a bird*
נִמְלְטָה Ni. pf. 3 f.s. (מָלַט 572) *have escaped*
מִפַּח prep.-n.m.s. cstr. (809) *from the snare of*
יוֹקְשִׁים Qal act.ptc. m.p. (יָקֹשׁ 430) *the fowlers*
הַפַּח def.art.-n.m.s. (809) *the snare*
נִשְׁבָּר Ni. ptc. (990) *is broken*
וַאֲנַחְנוּ conj.-pers.pr. 1 c.p. (59) *and we*
נִמְלָטְנוּ Ni. pf. 1 c.p. paus. (מָלַט 572) *have escaped*

124:8

עֶזְרֵנוּ n.m.s.-1 c.p. sf. (I 740) *our help*
בְּשֵׁם יהוה prep.-n.m.s. cstr. (1027)-pr.n. (217) *in the name of Yahweh*
עֹשֵׂה Qal act.ptc. (I 793) *who made*
שָׁמַיִם n.m. du. (1029) *heaven*
וָאָרֶץ conj.-n.f.s. paus. (75) *and earth*

125:1

שִׁיר n.m.s. cstr. (1010) *a song of*
הַמַּעֲלוֹת def.art.-n.f.p. (II 752) *ascents*
הַבֹּטְחִים def.art.-Qal act.ptc. m.p. (105) *those who trust*
בַּיהוה prep.-pr.n. (217) *in Yahweh*
כְּהַר־צִיּוֹן prep.-n.m.s. cstr. (249)-pr.n. (851) *like Mount Zion*
לֹא־יִמּוֹט neg.-Ni. impf. 3 m.s. (556; GK 155g) *which cannot be moved*
לְעוֹלָם prep.-n.m.s. (761) *but for ever*
יֵשֵׁב Qal impf. 3 m.s. (יָשַׁב 442) *abides*

125:2

יְרוּשָׁלַםִ pr.n. (436) *Jerusalem*
הָרִים n.m.p. (249) *mountains*
סָבִיב לָהּ adv. (686)-prep.-3 f.s. sf. *round about her*
וַיהוה conj.-pr.n. (217) *and Yahweh*
סָבִיב לְעַמּוֹ adv. (686)-prep.-n.m.s.-3 m.s. sf. (I 766) *round about his people*
מֵעַתָּה prep.-adv. (773) *from this time forth*
וְעַד־עוֹלָם conj.-prep. (III 723)-n.m.s. (761) *and for evermore*

125:3

כִּי לֹא יָנוּחַ conj. (471)-neg.-Qal impf. 3 m.s. (628 נוּחַ) *for shall not rest*
שֵׁבֶט n.m.s. cstr. (986) *the scepter of*
הָרֶשַׁע def.art.-n.m.s. (957) *wickedness*
עַל גּוֹרַל prep.-n.m.s. cstr. (174) *upon the land allotted to*
הַצַּדִּיקִים def.art.-adj. m.p. (843) *the righteous*
לְמַעַן לֹא־יִשְׁלְחוּ conj. (775)-neg.-Qal impf. 3 m.p. (שָׁלַח 1018) *lest put forth*
הַצַּדִּיקִים v.supra *the righteous*
בְּעַוְלָתָה prep.-n.f.s. (732) *to unrighteousness*
יְדֵיהֶם n.f.p.-3 m.p. sf. (388) *their hands*

125:4

הֵיטִיבָה Hi. impv. 2 m.s.-vol.he (יָטַב 405) *do good*
יהוה pr.n. (217) *O Yahweh*
לַטּוֹבִים prep.-def.art.-adj. m.p. (II 373) *to those who are good*
וְלִישָׁרִים conj.-prep.-adj. m.p. (449) *and to those who are upright*
בְּלִבּוֹתָם prep.-n.m.p.-3 m.p. sf. (524) *in their hearts*

125:5

וְהַמַּטִּים conj.-def.art.-Hi. ptc. m.p. (נָטָה 639) *those who turn aside*
עֲקַלְקַלּוֹתָם adj. f.p.-3 m.p. sf. (785) *their crooked ways*
יוֹלִיכֵם Hi. impf. 3 m.s.-3 m.p. sf. (הָלַךְ 229) *will lead away (them)*
יהוה pr.n. (217) *Yahweh*
אֶת־פֹּעֲלֵי prep. (II 85)-Qal act.ptc. m.p. cstr. (821) *with workers of*
הָאָוֶן def.art.-n.m.s. (19) *evil*
שָׁלוֹם n.m.s. (1022) *peace*
עַל־יִשְׂרָאֵל prep.-pr.n. (975) *in Israel*

126:1

שִׁיר n.m.s. cstr. (1010) *a song of*
הַמַּעֲלוֹת def.art.-n.f.p. (II 752) *ascents*
בְּשׁוּב prep.-Qal inf.cstr. (996) *when restored*
יהוה pr.n. (217) *Yahweh*
אֶת־שִׁיבַת dir.obj.-n.f.s. cstr. (II 1000 *those who returned to*; some rd. שְׁבוּת n.f.s. cstr. 986) *the fortunes of*
צִיּוֹן pr.n. (851) *Zion*
הָיִינוּ Qal pf. 1 c.p. (הָיָה 224) *we were*
כְּחֹלְמִים prep.-Qal act.ptc. m.p. (חָלַם 321) *like those who dream*

126:2

אָז יִמָּלֵא adv. (23)-Ni. impf. 3 m.s. (569) *then was filled*
שְׂחוֹק n.m.s. (966) *with laughter*
פִּינוּ n.m.s.-1 c.p. sf. (804) *our mouth*
וּלְשׁוֹנֵנוּ conj.-n.f.s.-1 c.p. sf. (546) *and our tongue*
רִנָּה n.f.s. (943) *with shouts of joy*
אָז יֹאמְרוּ v.supra-Qal impf. 3 m.p. (55) *then they said*
בַגּוֹיִם prep.-def.art.-n.m.p. (156) *among the nations*
הִגְדִּיל Hi. pf. 3 m.s. (גָּדַל 152) *has done great things*
יהוה pr.n. (217) *Yahweh*
לַעֲשׂוֹת prep.-Qal inf.cstr. (עָשָׂה I 793) *to do*
עִם־אֵלֶּה prep.-demons.adj. c.p. (41) *for them*

126:3

הִגְדִּיל יהוה Hi. pf. 3 m.s. (גָּדַל 152)-pr.n. (217) *Yahweh has done great things*
לַעֲשׂוֹת prep.-Qal inf.cstr. (עָשָׂה I 793) *to do*
עִמָּנוּ prep.-1 c.p. sf. *for us*
הָיִינוּ Qal pf. 1 c.p. (הָיָה 224) *we are*
שְׂמֵחִים adj. m.p. (970) *glad*

126:4

שׁוּבָה Qal impv. 2 m.s.-vol.he (996) *restore*
יהוה pr.n. (217) *O Yahweh*
אֶת־שְׁבוּתֵנוּ dir.obj.-n.f.s.-1 c.p. sf. (986) *our fortunes*
כַּאֲפִיקִים prep.-n.m.p. (67) *like the watercourses*
בַּנֶּגֶב prep.-def.art.-n.m.s. (616) *in the Negeb*

126:5

הַזֹּרְעִים def.art.-Qal act.ptc. m.p. (281) *those who sow*
בְּדִמְעָה prep.-n.f.s. (199) *in tears*
בְּרִנָּה prep.-n.f.s. (943) *with shouts of joy*

יִקְצֹרוּ Qal impf. 3 m.p. (II 894) *may reap*

126:6

הָלוֹךְ יֵלֵךְ Qal inf.abs. (229; GK 113u)-Qal impf. 3 m.s. (229) *he that goes forth*

וּבָכֹה conj.-Qal inf.abs. (113; GK 113p) *weeping*

נֹשֵׂא Qal act.ptc. (נָשָׂא 669) *bearing*

מֶשֶׁךְ־ n.m.s. cstr. (I 604) *a trail of*

הַזָּרַע def.art.-n.m.s. paus. (282) *seed*

בֹּא־יָבוֹא Qal inf.abs. (97)-Qal impf. 3 m.s. (בּוֹא 97) *shall come home*

בְרִנָּה prep.-n.f.s. (943) *with shouts of joy*

נֹשֵׂא Qal act.ptc. (669) *bringing*

אֲלֻמֹּתָיו n.f.p.-3 m.s. sf. (48) *his sheaves*

127:1

שִׁיר n.m.s. cstr. (1010) *a song of*

הַמַּעֲלוֹת def.art.-n.f.p. (II 752) *ascents*

לִשְׁלֹמֹה prep.-pr.n. (1024) *to Solomon*

אִם־יהוה hypoth.part. (49)-pr.n. (217) *unless (if) Yahweh*

לֹא־יִבְנֶה neg.-Qal impf. 3 m.s. (בָּנָה 124) *does (not) build*

בַיִת n.m.s. (108) *the house*

שָׁוְא n.m.s. (996) *in vain*

עָמְלוּ Qal pf. 3 c.p. (765) *they labor*

בוֹנָיו בּוֹ Qal act.ptc. m.p.-3 m.s. sf. (בָּנָה 124) -prep.-3 m.s. sf. *those who build it*

אִם־יהוה v.supra-v.supra *if Yahweh*

לֹא־יִשְׁמָר־ neg.-Qal impf. 3 m.s. (1036) *does not watch over*

עִיר n.f.s. (746) *the city*

שָׁוְא v.supra *in vain*

שָׁקַד Qal pf. 3 m.s. (1052) *stays awake*

שׁוֹמֵר Qal act.ptc. (1036) *the watchman*

127:2

שָׁוְא לָכֶם n.m.s. (996)-prep.-2 m.p. sf. *it is in vain that you*

מַשְׁכִּימֵי קוּם Hi. ptc. m.p. cstr. (1014; GK 114n) -Qal inf.cstr. (877) *you rise up early*

מְאַחֲרֵי־שֶׁבֶת Pi. ptc. m.p. cstr. (אָחַר 29)-Qal inf.cstr. (יָשַׁב 442) *and go late to rest*

אֹכְלֵי Qal act.ptc. m.p. cstr. (37) *eating*

לֶחֶם n.m.s. cstr. (536) *the bread of*

הָעֲצָבִים def.art.-n.m.p. (I 780) *anxious toil*

כֵּן יִתֵּן adv. (485)-Qal impf. 3 m.s. (נָתַן 678) *so he gives*

לִידִידוֹ prep.-adj. m.s.-3 m.s. sf. (391) *to his beloved*

שֵׁנָא n.f.s. (446; GK 23,l;80h;118i) *sleep*

127:3

הִנֵּה interj. (243) *lo*

נַחֲלַת יהוה n.f.s. cstr. (635)-pr.n. (217) *a heritage from Yahweh*

בָּנִים n.m.p. (119) *sons*

שָׂכָר n.m.s. (I 969) *a reward*

פְּרִי הַבָּטֶן n.m.s. cstr. (826)-def.art.-n.f.s. paus. (105) *the fruit of the womb*

127:4

כְּחִצִּים prep.-n.m.p. (346) *like arrows*

בְּיַד־גִּבּוֹר prep.-n.f.s. cstr. (388)-adj. m.s. (150) *in the hand of a warrior*

כֵּן בְּנֵי adv. (485)-n.m.p. cstr. (119) *so the sons of*

הַנְּעוּרִים def.art.-adj. m.p. (655) *one's youth*

127:5

אַשְׁרֵי n.m.p. cstr. (80) *happy is*

הַגֶּבֶר def.art.-n.m.s. (149) *the man*

אֲשֶׁר מִלֵּא rel. (81)-Pi. pf. 3 m.s. (569) *which is full*

אֶת־אַשְׁפָּתוֹ dir.obj.-n.f.s.-3 m.s. sf. (80) *his quiver*

מֵהֶם prep.-3 m.p. sf. *of them*

לֹא־יֵבֹשׁוּ neg.-Qal impf. 3 m.p. (בּוֹשׁ 101) *he shall not be put to shame*

כִּי־יְדַבְּרוּ conj. (471)-Pi. impf. 3 m.p. (180) *when he speaks*

אֶת־אוֹיְבִים prep. (II 85)-Qal act.ptc. m.p. (אָיַב 33) *with his enemies*

בַּשָּׁעַר prep.-def.art.-n.m.s. paus. (1044) *in the gate*

128:1

שִׁיר n.m.s. cstr. (1010) *a song of*

הַמַּעֲלוֹת def.art.-n.f.p. (II 752) *ascents*

אַשְׁרֵי n.m.p. cstr. (80) *blessed*

כָּל־יְרֵא n.m.s. cstr. (481)-Qal act.ptc. m.s. cstr. 431) *every one who fears*

יהוה pr.n. (217) *Yahweh*

הַהֹלֵךְ def.art.-Qal act.ptc. (229) *who walks*

בִּדְרָכָיו prep.-n.m.p.-3 m.s. sf. (202) *in his ways*

128:2

יְגִיעַ כַּפֶּיךָ n.m.s. cstr. (388)-n.f.p.-2 m.s. sf. (496) *the fruit of the labor of your hands*

כִּי תֹאכֵל conj. (471)-Qal impf. 2 m.s. (אָכַל 37) *you shall eat*

אַשְׁרֶיךָ n.m.p.-2 m.s. sf. (80) *you shall be happy*

וְטוֹב לָךְ conj.-adj. m.s. (II 373)-prep.-2 m.s. sf. *and it shall be well with you*

128:3

אֶשְׁתְּךָ n.f.s.-2 m.s. sf. (61; GK 96) *your wife*
כְּגֶפֶן פֹּרִיָּה prep.-n.f.s. (172)-Qal act.ptc. f.s. (פָּרָה 826) *like a fruitful vine*
בְּיַרְכְּתֵי prep.-n.m.p. cstr. (438) *within*
בֵיתֶךָ n.m.s.-2 m.s. sf. (108) *your house*
בָּנֶיךָ n.m.p.-2 m.s. sf. (119) *your children*
כִּשְׁתִלֵי זֵיתִים prep.-n.m.p. cstr. (1060)-n.m.p. (268) *like olive shoots*
סָבִיב adv. (686) *around*
לְשֻׁלְחָנֶךָ prep.-n.m.s.-2 m.s. sf. (1020) *your table*

128:4

הִנֵּה demons.part. (243) *lo*
כִּי־כֵן conj. (471)-adv. (485) *thus*
יְבֹרַךְ Pu. impf. 3 m.s. (138) *shall be blessed*
גָּבֶר n.m.s. paus. (149) *the man*
יְרֵא יהוה Qal act.ptc. m.s. cstr. (431)-pr.n. (217) *who fears Yahweh*

128:5

יְבָרֶכְךָ Pi. impf. 3 m.s.-2 m.s. sf. (138) *bless you*
יהוה pr.n. (217) *Yahweh*
מִצִּיּוֹן prep.-pr.n. (851) *from Zion*
וּרְאֵה conj.-Qal impv. 2 m.s. (906; GK 110i) *and may you see*
בְּטוּב prep.-n.m.s. cstr. (375) *the prosperity of*
יְרוּשָׁלָם pr.n. paus. (436) *Jerusalem*
כֹּל יְמֵי n.m.s. cstr. (481)-n.m.p. cstr. (398) *all the days of*
חַיֶּיךָ n.m.p.-2 m.s. sf. (313) *your life*

128:6

וּרְאֵה־ conj.-Qal impv. 2 m.s. (906) *and may you see*
בָנִים לְבָנֶיךָ n.m.p. (119)-prep.-n.m.p.-2 m.s. sf. (119) *your children's children*
שָׁלוֹם n.m.s. (1022) *peace*
עַל־יִשְׂרָאֵל prep.-pr.n. (975) *upon Israel*

129:1

שִׁיר n.m.s. cstr. (1010) *a song*
הַמַּעֲלוֹת def.art.-n.f.p. (II 752) *of ascents*
רַבַּת adj. f.s. as adv. (I 912) *sorely*
צְרָרוּנִי Qal pf. 3 c.p.-1 c.s. sf. (צָרַר III 865) *have they afflicted me*
מִנְּעוּרַי prep.-n.m.p.-1 c.s. sf. (655) *from my youth*
יֹאמַר־נָא Qal impf. 3 m.s. (55)-part.of entreaty (609) *let now say*
יִשְׂרָאֵל pr.n. (975) *Israel*

129:2

רַבַּת adj. f.s. as. adv. (I 912) *sorely*
צְרָרוּנִי Qal pf. 3 c.p.-1 c.s. sf. (צָרַר III 865) *have they afflicted me*
מִנְּעוּרָי prep.-n.m.p.-1 c.s. sf. paus. (655) *from my youth*
גַּם adv. (168) *yet*
לֹא־יָכְלוּ לִי neg.-Qal pf. 3 c.p. (יָכֹל 407)-prep.-1 c.s. sf. *they have not prevailed against me*

129:3

עַל־גַּבִּי prep.-n.m.s.-1 c.s. sf. (146) *upon my back*
חָרְשׁוּ Qal pf. 3 c.p. (I 360) *plowed*
חֹרְשִׁים Qal act.ptc. m.p. (I 360) *the plowers*
הֶאֱרִיכוּ Hi. pf. 3 c.p. (אָרַךְ 73) *they made long*
לְמַעֲנוֹתָם prep.-n.f.p.-3 m.p. sf. (776) *their furrows*

129:4

יהוה pr.n. (217) *Yahweh*
צַדִּיק adj. m.s. (843) *is righteous*
קִצֵּץ Pi. pf. 3 m.s. (893) *he has cut*
עֲבוֹת n.m.s. cstr. (721) *the cords of*
רְשָׁעִים adj. m.p. (957) *the wicked*

129:5

יֵבֹשׁוּ Qal impf. 3 m.p. (בּוֹשׁ 101) *may be put to shame*
וְיִסֹּגוּ conj.-Ni. impf. 3 m.p. (סוּג I 690) *and may be turned*
אָחוֹר adv. (30) *backward*
כֹּל שֹׂנְאֵי n.m.s. cstr. (481)-Qal act.ptc. m.p. cstr. (971 שָׂנֵא) *all who hate*
צִיּוֹן pr.n. (851) *Zion*

129:6

יִהְיוּ Qal impf. 3 m.p. (הָיָה 224) *let them be*
כַּחֲצִיר prep.-n.m.s. cstr. (II 348) *like the grass on*
גַּגּוֹת n.m.p. (150) *the housetops*
שֶׁקַּדְמַת rel. (979)-n.f.s. cstr. as conj. (870) *which before*
שָׁלַף Qal pf. 3 m.s. (1025) *it grows up*
יָבֵשׁ Qal pf. 3 m.s. (386) *it withers*

129:7

שֶׁלֹּא מִלֵּא rel. (979) neg.-Pi. pf. 3 m.s. (569) *with which does not fill*
כַפּוֹ n.f.s.-3 m.s. sf. (496) *his hand*
קוֹצֵר Qal act.ptc. (II 894) *the reaper*
וְחִצְנוֹ conj.-n.m.s.-3 m.s. sf. (346) *or his bosom*
מְעַמֵּר Pi. ptc. (771) *the binder of sheaves*

129:8

וְלֹא אָמְרוּ conj.-neg.-Qal pf. 3 c.p. (55) *while they do not say*

הָעֹבְרִים def.art.-Qal act.ptc. m.p. (716) *those who pass by*

בִּרְכַּת־יהוה n.f.s. cstr. (139)-pr.n. (217) *the blessing of Yahweh*

אֲלֵיכֶם prep.-2 m.p. sf. *be upon you*

בֵּרַכְנוּ Pi. pf. 1 c.p. (בָּרַךְ 138) *we bless*

אֶתְכֶם dir.obj.-2 m.p. sf. *you*

בְּשֵׁם prep.-n.m.s. cstr. (1027) *in the name of*

יהוה pr.n. (217) *Yahweh*

130:1

שִׁיר n.m.s. cstr. (1010) *a song of*

הַמַּעֲלוֹת def.art.-n.f.p. (II 752) *ascents*

מִמַּעֲמַקִּים prep.-n.m.p. (771) *out of the depths*

קְרָאתִיךָ Qal pf. 1 c.s.-2 m.s. sf. (894) *I cry to thee*

יהוה pr.n. (217) *O Yahweh*

130:2

אֲדֹנָי n.m.p.-1 c.s. sf. (10) *Lord*

שִׁמְעָה Qal impv. 2 m.s.-vol.he (1033) *hear*

בְקוֹלִי prep.-n.m.s.-1 c.s. sf. (876) *my voice*

תִּהְיֶינָה Qal impf. 3 f.p. (הָיָה 224) *let be*

אָזְנֶיךָ n.f. du.-2 m.s. sf. (23) *thy ears*

קַשֻּׁבוֹת adj. f.p. (904) *attentive*

לְקוֹל prep.-n.m.s. cstr. (876) *to the voice of*

תַּחֲנוּנָי n.m.p.-1 c.s. sf. (337) *my supplications*

130:3

אִם־עֲוֺנוֹת hypoth.part. (49)-n.f.p. (730) *if iniquities*

תִּשְׁמָר־ Qal impf. 2 m.s. (1036) *thou shouldst mark*

יָהּ pr.n. (219) *O Yah*

אֲדֹנָי n.m.p.-1 c.s. sf. (10) *Lord*

מִי יַעֲמֹד interr. (566)-Qal impf. 3 m.s. (763) *who could stand*

130:4

כִּי־עִמְּךָ conj. (471)-prep.-2 m.s. sf. *but with thee*

הַסְּלִיחָה def.art.-n.f.s. (699) *forgiveness*

לְמַעַן תִּוָּרֵא prep. (775)-Ni. impf. 2 m.s. (יָרֵא 431) *that thou mayest be feared*

130:5

קִוִּיתִי Pi. pf. 1 c.s. (קָוָה I 875) *I wait for*

יהוה pr.n. (217) *Yahweh*

קִוְּתָה Pi. pf. 3 f.s. (קָוָה I 875) *waits*

נַפְשִׁי n.f.s.-1 c.s. sf. (659) *my soul*

וְלִדְבָרוֹ conj.-prep.-n.m.s.-3 m.s. sf. (182) *and in his word*

הוֹחָלְתִּי Hi. pf. 1 c.s. paus. (יָחַל 403) *I hope*

130:6

נַפְשִׁי n.f.s.-1 c.s. sf. (659) *my soul*

לַאדֹנָי prep.-n.m.p.-1 c.s. sf. (10) *for the Lord*

מִשֹּׁמְרִים prep.-Qal act.ptc. m.p. (1036) *more than watchmen*

לַבֹּקֶר prep.-def.art.-n.m.s. (133) *for the morning*

שֹׁמְרִים Qal act.ptc. m.p. (1036) *more than watchmen*

לַבֹּקֶר v.supra *for the morning*

130:7

יַחֵל Pi. impv. 2 m.s. (יָחַל 403) *hope*

יִשְׂרָאֵל pr.n. (975) *O Israel*

אֶל־יהוה prep.-pr.n. (217) *in Yahweh*

כִּי־עִם־יהוה conj. (471)-prep.-pr.n. (217) *for with Yahweh*

הַחֶסֶד def.art.-n.m.s. (338) *there is steadfast love*

וְהַרְבֵּה conj.-Hi. inf.abs. as adv. (רָבָה I 915) *and plenteous*

עִמּוֹ prep.-3 m.s. sf. *with him*

פְדוּת n.f.s. (804) *redemption*

130:8

וְהוּא conj.-pers.pr. 3 m.s. (214) *and he*

יִפְדֶּה Qal impf. 3 m.s. (804) *will redeem*

אֶת־יִשְׂרָאֵל dir.obj.-pr.n. (975) *Israel*

מִכֹּל prep.-n.m.s. cstr. (481) *from all*

עֲוֺנֹתָיו n.f.p.-3 m.s. sf. (730) *his iniquities*

131:1

שִׁיר n.m.s. cstr. (1010) *a song of*

הַמַּעֲלוֹת def.art.-n.f.p. (II 752) *ascents*

לְדָוִד prep.-pr.n. (187) *to David*

יהוה pr.n. (217) *O Yahweh*

לֹא־גָבַהּ neg.-Qal pf. 3 m.s. (146) *is not lifted up*

לִבִּי n.m.s.-1 c.s. sf. (524) *my heart*

וְלֹא־רָמוּ conj.-neg.-Qal pf. 3 c.p. (רוּם 926; GK 72,l) *and are not raised*

עֵינַי n.f. du.-1 c.s. sf. (744) *my eyes*

וְלֹא־הִלַּכְתִּי conj.-neg.-Pi. pf. 1 c.s. (הָלַךְ 229) *I do not occupy myself*

בִּגְדֹלוֹת prep.-adj. f.p. (152) *with things too great*

וּבְנִפְלָאוֹת conj.-prep.-Ni. ptc. f.p. (פָּלָא 810) *and too marvelous*

מִמֶּנִּי prep.-1 c.s. sf. *for me*

131:2

אִם־לֹא שִׁוִּיתִי hypoth.part. (49)-neg.-Pi. pf. 1 c.s. (שָׁוָה I 1000) *but I have calmed*
וְדוֹמַמְתִּי conj.-Po'el pf. 1 c.s. (דָּמַם I 198) *and quieted*
נַפְשִׁי n.f.s.-1 c.s. sf. (659) *my soul*
כְּגָמֻל prep.-Qal pass.ptc. (168) *as a weaned child*
עֲלֵי אִמּוֹ prep.-n.f.s.-3 m.s. sf. (51) *at its mother's breast*
כַּגָּמֻל prep.-def.art.-v.supra *like a child*
עָלַי נַפְשִׁי prep.-1 c.s. sf.-n.f.s.-1 c.s. sf. (659) *my soul*

131:3

יַחֵל Pi. impv. 2 m.s. (יָחַל 403) *hope*
יִשְׂרָאֵל pr.n. (975) *O Israel*
אֶל־יהוה prep.-pr.n. (217) *in Yahweh*
מֵעַתָּה prep.-adv. (773) *from this time forth*
וְעַד־עוֹלָם conj.-prep. (III 723)-n.m.s. (761) *and for evermore*

132:1

שִׁיר n.m.s. cstr. (1010) *a song of*
הַמַּעֲלוֹת def.art.-n.f.p. (II 752) *ascents*
זְכוֹר־ Qal impv. 2 m.s. (269) *remember*
יהוה pr.n. (217) *O Yahweh*
לְדָוִד prep.-pr.n. (187) *in David's favor*
אֵת כָּל־ dir.obj.-n.m.s. cstr. (481) *all*
עֻנּוֹתוֹ Pu. inf.cstr.-3 m.s. sf. (עָנָה III 776; GK 52r) *his hardships*

132:2

אֲשֶׁר rel. (81) *how*
נִשְׁבַּע Ni. pf. 3 m.s. (989) *he swore*
לַיהוה prep.-pr.n. (217) *to Yahweh*
נָדַר Qal pf. 3 m.s. (623) *he vowed*
לַאֲבִיר prep.-adj. m.s. cstr. (7) *to the Mighty One of*
יַעֲקֹב pr.n. (784) *Jacob*

132:3

אִם־אָבֹא hypoth.part. (49)-Qal impf. 1 c.s. (בּוֹא 97) *I will not enter*
בְּאֹהֶל בֵּיתִי prep.-n.m.s. cstr. (13)-n.m.s.-1 c.s. sf. (108; GK 128m) *the tent of my house*
אִם־אֶעֱלֶה v.supra-Qal impf. 1 c.s. (עָלָה 748) *or I will not get*
עַל־עֶרֶשׂ prep.-n.f.s. cstr. (793) *into the couch of*
יְצוּעָי n.m.p.-1 c.s. sf. (426) *my bed*

132:4

אִם־אֶתֵּן hypoth.part. (49)-Qal impf. 1 c.s. (נָתַן 678) *I will not give*
שְׁנַת n.f.s. (cstr.?) (446; GK 80g,h; many שְׁנָת) *sleep*
לְעֵינָי prep.-n.f. du.-1 c.s. sf. (744) *to my eyes*
לְעַפְעַפַּי prep.-n.m. du.-1 c.s. sf. (733) *to my eyelids*
תְּנוּמָה n.f.s. (630) *slumber*

132:5

עַד־אֶמְצָא prep. (III 723)-Qal impf. 1 c.s. (592) *until I find*
מָקוֹם n.m.s. (879) *a place*
לַיהוה prep.-pr.n. (217) *for Yahweh*
מִשְׁכָּנוֹת n.m.p. (1015) *a dwelling place*
לַאֲבִיר prep.-adj. m.s. cstr. (7) *for the Mighty One of*
יַעֲקֹב pr.n. (784) *Jacob*

132:6

הִנֵּה interj. (243) *lo*
שְׁמַעֲנוּהָ Qal pf. 1 c.p.-3 f.s. sf. (1033) *we heard of it*
בְאֶפְרָתָה prep.-pr.n. (68) *in Ephrathah*
מְצָאנוּהָ Qal pf. 3 c.p.-3 f.s. sf. (592) *we found it*
בִּשְׂדֵי־ prep.-n.m.p. cstr. (961) *in the fields of*
יָעַר n.m.s. paus. as pr.n. (I 420) *Jaar*

132:7

נָבוֹאָה Qal impf. 1 c.p.-vol.he (בּוֹא 97) *let us go*
לְמִשְׁכְּנוֹתָיו prep.-n.m.p.-3 m.s. sf. (1015) *to his dwelling place*
נִשְׁתַּחֲוֶה Hith. impf. 1 c.p.-vol.he (שָׁחָה 1005) *let us worship*
לַהֲדֹם רַגְלָיו prep.-n.m.s. cstr. (213)-n.f. du.-3 m.s. sf. (919) *at his footstool*

132:8

קוּמָה Qal impv. 2 m.s.-vol.he (877) *arise*
יהוה pr.n. (217) *O Yahweh*
לִמְנוּחָתֶךָ prep.-n.f.s.-2 m.s. sf. (629) *to thy resting place*
אַתָּה pers.pr. 2 m.s. (61) *thou*
וַאֲרוֹן conj.-n.m.s. cstr. (75) *and the ark of*
עֻזֶּךָ n.m.s.-2 m.s. sf. (738) *thy might*

132:9

כֹּהֲנֶיךָ n.m.p.-2 m.s. sf. (463) *thy priests*
יִלְבְּשׁוּ־ Qal impf. 3 m.p. (527) *let be clothed with*
צֶדֶק n.m.s. (841) *righteousness*

וַחֲסִידֶיךָ conj.-adj. m.p.-2 m.s. sf. (339) *and thy saints*

יְרַנֵּנוּ Pi. impf. 3 m.p. (רָנַן 943) *let shout for joy*

132:10

בַּעֲבוּר דָּוִד prep.-prep. (II 720)-pr.n. (187) *for David's sake*

עַבְדֶּךָ n.m.s.-2 m.s. sf. (713) *thy servant*

אַל־תָּשֵׁב neg.-Hi. impf. 2 m.s. apoc. (שׁוּב 996) *do not turn away*

פְּנֵי n.m.p. cstr. (815) *the face of*

מְשִׁיחֶךָ n.m.s.-2 m.s. sf. (603) *thy anointed one*

132:11

נִשְׁבַּע־ Ni. pf. 3 m.s. (989) *swore*

יהוה pr.n. (217) *Yahweh*

לְדָוִד prep.-pr.n. (187) *to David*

אֱמֶת n.f.s. (54) *a sure oath*

לֹא־יָשׁוּב neg.-Qal impf. 3 m.s. (996) *he will not turn back*

מִמֶּנָּה prep.-3 f.s. sf. *from it*

מִפְּרִי prep.-n.m.s. cstr. (826) *from the fruit of*

בִטְנְךָ n.f.s.-2 m.s. sf. (105) *thy womb*

אָשִׁית Qal impf. 1 c.s. (1011) *I will set*

לְכִסֵּא־לָךְ prep.-n.m.s. (490)-prep.-2 m.s. sf. paus. *on your throne*

132:12

אִם־יִשְׁמְרוּ hypoth.part. (49)-Qal impf. 3 m.p. (1036) *if ... keep*

בָנֶיךָ n.m.p.-2 m.s. sf. (119) *your sons*

בְּרִיתִי n.f.s.-1 c.s. sf. (136) *my covenant*

וְעֵדֹתִי conj.-n.f.p.-1 c.s. sf. (730; GK 91n) *and my testimonies*

זוֹ אֲלַמְּדֵם rel. (262; GK 34b,138g)-Pi. impf. 1 c.s.-3 m.p. sf. (540) *which I shall teach them*

גַּם־בְּנֵיהֶם conj. (168)-n.m.p.-3 m.p. sf. (119) *also their sons*

עֲדֵי־עַד prep. (III 723)-prep. (III 723) *for ever*

יֵשְׁבוּ Qal impf. 3 m.p. (יָשַׁב 442) *shall sit*

לְכִסֵּא־לָךְ prep.-n.m.s. (490)-prep.-2 m.s. sf. paus. *upon your throne*

132:13

כִּי־בָחַר conj. (471)-Qal pf. 3 m.s. (103) *for has chosen*

יהוה pr.n. (217) *Yahweh*

בְּצִיּוֹן prep.-pr.n. (851) *Zion*

אִוָּהּ Pi. pf. 3 m.s.-3 f.s. sf. (אָוָה I 16) *he has desired it*

לְמוֹשָׁב לוֹ prep.-n.m.s. (444)-prep.-3 m.s. sf. *for his habitation*

132:14

זֹאת־מְנוּחָתִי demons.adj. f.s. (260)-n.f.s.-1 c.s. sf. (629) *this is my resting place*

עֲדֵי־עַד prep. (III 723)-prep. (III 723) *for ever*

פֹּה־אֵשֵׁב adv. (805)-Qal impf. 1 c.s. (יָשַׁב 442) *here I will dwell*

כִּי אִוִּתִיהָ conj. (471)-Pi. pf. 1 c.s.-3 f.s. sf. (אָוָה I 16) *for I have desired it*

132:15

צֵידָהּ n.m.s.-3 f.s. sf. (II 845) *her provisions*

בָּרֵךְ אֲבָרֵךְ Pi. inf.abs. (138)-Pi. impf. 1 c.s. (138) *I will abundantly bless*

אֶבְיוֹנֶיהָ adj. m.p.-3 f.s. sf. (2) *her poor*

אַשְׂבִּיעַ Hi. impf. 1 c.s. (959) *I will satisfy*

לָחֶם n.m.s. paus. (536) *with bread*

132:16

וְכֹהֲנֶיהָ conj.-n.m.p.-3 f.s. sf. (463) *her priests*

אַלְבִּישׁ Hi. impf. 1 c.s. (527) *I will clothe*

יֶשַׁע n.m.s. (447) *with salvation*

וַחֲסִידֶיהָ conj.-adj. m.p.-3 f.s. sf. (339) *and her saints*

רַנֵּן יְרַנֵּנוּ Pi. inf.abs. (943)-Pi. impf. 3 m.p. (943) *will shout for joy*

132:17

שָׁם adv. (1027) *there*

אַצְמִיחַ Hi. impf. 1 c.s. (855) *I will make to sprout*

קֶרֶן n.f.s. (901) *a horn*

לְדָוִד prep.-pr.n. (187) *for David*

עָרַכְתִּי Qal pf. 1 c.s. (789) *I have prepared*

נֵר n.m.s. (632) *a lamp*

לִמְשִׁיחִי prep.-n.m.s.-1 c.s. sf. (603) *for my anointed*

132:18

אוֹיְבָיו Qal act.ptc. m.p.-3 m.s. sf. (אָיַב 33) *his enemies*

אַלְבִּישׁ Hi. impf. 1 c.s. (527) *I will clothe*

בֹּשֶׁת n.f.s. (102) *with shame*

וְעָלָיו conj.-prep.-3 m.s. sf. *but upon himself*

יָצִיץ Qal impf. 3 m.s. (צוּץ I 847) *will shed its luster (shine)*

נִזְרוֹ n.m.s.-3 m.s. sf. (634) *his crown*

133:1

שִׁיר n.m.s. cstr. (1010) *a song of*

הַמַּעֲלוֹת def.art.-n.f.p. (II 752) *ascents*

לְדָוִד prep.-pr.n. (187) *to David*

הִנֵּה interj. (243) *behold*

מַה־טּוֹב interr. (552)-adj. m.s. (II 373) *how good*
וּמַה־נָּעִים conj.-v.supra-adj. m.s. (I 653) *and pleasant*
שֶׁבֶת אַחִים n.f.s. cstr. (I 443)-n.m.p. (26) *dwelling of brothers*
גַּם־יָחַד adv. (168)-adv. (403) *also together*

133:2

כַּשֶּׁמֶן הַטּוֹב prep.-def.art.-n.m.s. (1032; GK 126x)-def.art.-adj. m.s. (II 373) *like the precious oil*
עַל־הָרֹאשׁ prep.-def.art.-n.m.s. (910) *upon the head*
יֹרֵד Qal act.ptc. (432) *running down*
עַל־הַזָּקָן prep.-def.art.-n.m.s. (278) *upon the beard*
זְקַן־אַהֲרֹן n.m.s. cstr. (278)-pr.n. (14) *the beard of Aaron*
שֶׁיֹּרֵד rel. (979)-v.supra (432) *which running down*
עַל־פִּי prep.-n.m.s. cstr. (804) *on the collar of*
מִדּוֹתָיו n.f.p.-3 m.s. sf. (551) *his robes*

133:3

כְּטַל־ prep.-n.m.s. cstr. (378) *like dew of*
חֶרְמוֹן pr.n. (356) *Hermon*
שֶׁיֹּרֵד rel. (979)-Qal act.ptc. (יָרַד 432) *which falls*
עַל־הַרְרֵי prep.-n.m.p. cstr. (249) *on the mountains of*
צִיּוֹן pr.n. (851) *Zion*
כִּי שָׁם conj. (471)-adv. (1027) *for there*
צִוָּה Pi. pf. 3 m.s. (845) *has commanded*
יהוה pr.n. (217) *Yahweh*
אֶת־הַבְּרָכָה dir.obj.-def.art.-n.f.s. (139) *the blessing*
חַיִּים n.m.p. (313) *life*
עַד־הָעוֹלָם prep. (III 723)-def.art.-n.m.s. (761) *for evermore*

134:1

שִׁיר n.m.s. cstr. (1010) *a song of*
הַמַּעֲלוֹת def.art.-n.f.p. (II 752) *ascents*
הִנֵּה interj. (243) *come*
בָּרְכוּ Pi. impv. 2 m.p. (138) *bless*
אֶת־יהוה dir.obj.-pr.n. (217) *Yahweh*
כָּל־עַבְדֵי n.m.s. cstr. (481)-n.m.p. cstr. (713) *all servants of*
יהוה pr.n. (217) *Yahweh*
הָעֹמְדִים def.art.-Qal act.ptc. m.p. (763) *who stand*
בְּבֵית־ prep.-n.m.s. cstr. (108) *in the house of*
יהוה v.supra *Yahweh*
בַּלֵּילוֹת prep.-def.art.-n.m.p. (538) *by night*

134:2

שְׂאוּ־ Qal impv. 2 m.p. (נָשָׂא 669) *lift up*
יְדֵכֶם n.f. du.-2 m.p. sf. (388) *your hands*
קֹדֶשׁ n.m.s. (871) *to the holy place*
וּבָרְכוּ conj.-Pi. impv. 2 m.p. (138) *and bless*
אֶת־יהוה dir.obj.-pr.n. (217) *Yahweh*

134:3

יְבָרֶכְךָ Pi. impf. 3 m.s.-2 m.s. sf. (138) *may bless you*
יהוה pr.n. (217) *Yahweh*
מִצִּיּוֹן prep.-pr.n. (851) *from Zion*
עֹשֵׂה Qal act.ptc. m.s. cstr. (I 793) *he who made*
שָׁמַיִם n.m. du. (1029) *heaven*
וָאָרֶץ conj.-n.f.s. paus. (75) *and earth*

135:1

הַלְלוּ יָהּ Pi. impv. 2 m.p. (II 237)-pr.n. (219) *praise Yah*
הַלְלוּ v.supra *praise*
אֶת־שֵׁם יהוה dir.obj.-n.m.s. cstr. (1027)-pr.n. (217) *the name of Yahweh*
הַלְלוּ v.supra *praise*
עַבְדֵי יהוה n.m.p. cstr. (713)-pr.n. (217) *O servants of Yahweh*

135:2

שֶׁעֹמְדִים rel. (979)-Qal act.ptc. m.p. (763) *that stand*
בְּבֵית יהוה prep.-n.m.s. cstr. (108)-pr.n. (217) *in the house of Yahweh*
בְּחַצְרוֹת prep.-n.f.p. cstr. (I 346) *in the courts of*
בֵּית n.m.s. cstr. (108) *the house of*
אֱלֹהֵינוּ n.m.p.-1 c.p. sf. (43) *our God*

135:3

הַלְלוּ־ Pi. impv. 2 m.p. (II 237) *praise*
יָהּ pr.n. (219) *Yahweh*
כִּי־טוֹב conj. (471)-adj. m.s. (II 373) *for is good*
יהוה pr.n. (217) *Yahweh*
זַמְּרוּ Pi. impv. 2 m.p. (I 274) *sing*
לִשְׁמוֹ prep.-n.m.s.-3 m.s. sf. (1027) *to his name*
כִּי נָעִים conj. (471)-adj. m.s. (I 653) *for he is gracious*

135:4

כִּי־יַעֲקֹב conj. (471)-pr.n. (784) *for Jacob*
בָּחַר לוֹ Qal pf. 3 m.s. (103)-prep.-3 m.s. sf. *has chosen for himself*

יָהּ pr.n. (219) *Yah*
יִשְׂרָאֵל pr.n. (975) *Israel*
לִסְגֻלָּתוֹ prep.-n.f.s.-3 m.s. sf. (688) *as his own possession*

135:5

כִּי אֲנִי conj. (471)-pers.pr. 1 c.s. (58) *for I*
יָדַעְתִּי Qal pf. 1 c.s. (393) *know*
כִּי־גָדוֹל conj.-adj. m.s. (152) *that is great*
יהוה pr.n. (217) *Yahweh*
וַאֲדֹנֵינוּ conj.-n.m.p.-1 c.p. sf. (10) *and that our Lord*
מִכָּל־ prep.-n.m.s. cstr. (481) *above all*
אֱלֹהִים n.m.p. (43) *gods*

135:6

כֹּל אֲשֶׁר־ n.m.s. (481)-rel. (81) *whatever*
חָפֵץ יהוה Qal pf. 3 m.s. (342)-pr.n. (217) *Yahweh pleases*
עָשָׂה Qal pf. 3 m.s. (I 793) *he does*
בַּשָּׁמַיִם prep.-def.art.-n.m. du. (1029) *in heaven*
וּבָאָרֶץ conj.-prep.-def.art.-n.f.s. (75) *and on earth*
בַּיַּמִּים prep.-consec.-rn.m.p. (410) *in the seas*
וְכָל־תְּהוֹמוֹת conj.-n.m.s. cstr. (481)-n.f.p. (1062) *and all deeps*

135:7

מַעֲלֶה Hi. ptc. m.s. cstr. (I 793) *he it is who makes*
נְשִׂאִים n.m.p. (II 672) *rise*
מִקְצֵה prep.-n.m.s. cstr. (892) *at the end of*
הָאָרֶץ def.art.-n.f.s. (75) *the earth*
בְּרָקִים n.m.p. (140) *lightnings*
לַמָּטָר prep.-def.art.-n.m.s. (564) *for the rain*
עָשָׂה Qal pf. 3 m.s. (I 793) *who makes*
מוֹצֵא־ Hi. ptc. m.s. cstr. (יָצָא 422; GK 53o) *who brings forth*
רוּחַ n.f.s. (924) *the wind*
מֵאוֹצְרוֹתָיו prep.-n.m.p.-3 m.s. sf. (69) *for his storehouses*

135:8

שֶׁהִכָּה rel. (979)-Hi. pf. 3 m.s. (נָכָה 645) *he it was who smote*
בְּכוֹרֵי n.m.p. cstr. (114) *the first-born of*
מִצְרָיִם pr.n. paus. (595) *Egypt*
מֵאָדָם prep.-n.m.s. (9) *both of man*
עַד־בְּהֵמָה prep. (III 723)-n.f.s. (96) *and of beast*

135:9

שָׁלַח Qal pf. 3 m.s. (1018) *who sent*
אֹתוֹת n.m.p. (16) *signs*
וּמֹפְתִים conj.-n.m.p. (68) *and wonders*
בְּתוֹכֵכִי prep.-subst.-2 f.s. sf. (1063) *into thy midst*
מִצְרָיִם pr.n. paus. (595) *Egypt*
בְּפַרְעֹה prep.-pr.n. (829) *against Pharaoh*
וּבְכָל־ conj.-prep.-n.m.s. cstr. (481) *and all*
עֲבָדָיו n.m.p.-3 m.s. sf. (713) *his servants*

135:10

שֶׁהִכָּה rel. (979)-Hi. pf. 3 m.s. (נָכָה 645) *who smote*
גּוֹיִם רַבִּים n.m.p. (156)-adj. m.p. (I 912) *many nations*
וְהָרַג conj.-Qal pf. 3 m.s. (246) *and slew*
מְלָכִים n.m.p. (I 572) *kings*
עֲצוּמִים adj. m.p. (783) *mighty*

135:11

לְסִיחוֹן prep.-pr.n. (695) *Sihon*
מֶלֶךְ n.m.s. cstr. (I 572) *king of*
הָאֱמֹרִי def.art.-pr.n. gent. (57) *the Amorites*
וּלְעוֹג conj.-prep.-pr.n. (728) *and Og*
מֶלֶךְ v.supra *king of*
הַבָּשָׁן def.art.-pr.n. (143) *Bashan*
וּלְכֹל conj.-prep.-n.m.s. cstr. (481) *and all*
מַמְלְכוֹת n.f.p. cstr. (575) *the kingdoms of*
כְּנָעַן pr.n. (488) *Canaan*

135:12

וְנָתַן conj.-Qal pf. 3 m.s. (678) *and gave*
אַרְצָם n.f.s.-3 m.p. sf. (75) *their land*
נַחֲלָה n.f.s. (635) *as a heritage*
נַחֲלָה v.supra *a heritage*
לְיִשְׂרָאֵל prep.-pr.n. (975) *to Israel*
עַמּוֹ n.m.s.-3 m.s. sf. (I 766) *his people*

135:13

יהוה pr.n. (217) *O Yahweh*
שִׁמְךָ n.m.s.-2 m.s. sf. (1027) *thy name*
לְעוֹלָם prep.-n.m.s. (761) *for ever*
יהוה v.supra *O Yahweh*
זִכְרְךָ n.m.s.-2 m.s. sf. (271) *thy renown*
לְדֹר־וָדֹר prep.-n.m.s. (189)-conj.-n.m.s. (189) *throughout all ages*

135:14

כִּי־יָדִין conj. (471)-Qal impf. 3 m.s. (דִּין 192) *for will vindicate*
יהוה pr.n. (217) *Yahweh*
עַמּוֹ n.m.s.-3 m.s. sf. (I 766) *his people*

וְעַל־עֲבָדָיו conj.-prep.-n.m.p.-3 m.s. sf. (713) *and on his servants*
יִתְנֶחָם Hith. impf. 3 m.s. (נָחַם 636) *have compassion*

135:15

עֲצַבֵּי n.m.p. cstr. (781) *the idols of*
הַגּוֹיִם def.art.-n.m.p. (156) *the nations*
כֶּסֶף n.m.s. (494) *silver*
וְזָהָב conj.-n.m.s. (262) *and gold*
מַעֲשֵׂה n.m.s. cstr. (795) *the work of*
יְדֵי אָדָם n.f. du. cstr. (388)-n.m.s. (9) *men's hands*

135:16

פֶּה־ n.m.s. (804) *mouths*
לָהֶם prep.-3 m.p. sf. *they have*
וְלֹא יְדַבֵּרוּ conj.-neg.-Pi. impf. 3 m.p. (180) *but they speak not*
עֵינַיִם n.f. du. (744) *eyes*
לָהֶם v.supra *they have*
וְלֹא יִרְאוּ conj.-neg.-Qal impf. 3 m.p. (רָאָה 906) *but they see not*

135:17

אָזְנַיִם n.f. du. (23) *ears*
לָהֶם prep.-3 m.p. sf. *they have*
וְלֹא יַאֲזִינוּ conj.-neg.-Hi. impf. 3 m.p. (24) *but they hear not*
אַף אֵין־יֶשׁ־ conj. (II 64)-subst. cstr. (II 34) -subst. cstr. (441) *nor is there any*
רוּחַ n.f.s. (524) *breath*
בְּפִיהֶם prep.-n.m.s.-3 m.p. sf. (804) *in their mouths*

135:18

כְּמוֹהֶם prep.-3 m.p. sf. *like them*
יִהְיוּ Qal impf. 3 m.p. (הָיָה 224) *be*
עֹשֵׂיהֶם Qal act.ptc. m.p.-3 m.p. sf. (עָשָׂה I 793) *those who make them*
כֹּל אֲשֶׁר־ n.m.s. (481)-rel. (81) *every one*
בֹּטֵחַ Qal act.ptc. (105) *who trusts*
בָּהֶם prep.-3 m.p. sf. *in them*

135:19

בֵּית יִשְׂרָאֵל n.m.s. cstr. (108)-pr.n. (975) *O house of Israel*
בָּרְכוּ Pi. impv. 2 m.p. (138) *bless*
אֶת־יהוה dir.obj.-pr.n. (217) *Yahweh*
בֵּית אַהֲרֹן v.supra-pr.n. (14) *O house of Aaron*
בָּרְכוּ v.supra *bless*
אֶת־יהוה v.supra-v.supra *Yahweh*

135:20

בֵּית הַלֵּוִי n.m.s. cstr. (108)-def.art.-pr.n. (I 532) *O house of Levi*
בָּרְכוּ Pi. impv. 2 m.p. (138) *bless*
אֶת־יהוה dir.obj.-pr.n. (217) *Yahweh*
יִרְאֵי Qal act.ptc. m.p. cstr. (יָרֵא 431) *you that fear*
יהוה pr.n. (217) *Yahweh*
בָּרְכוּ v.supra *bless*
אֶת־יהוה v.supra-v.supra *Yahweh*

135:21

בָּרוּךְ Qal pass.ptc. (138) *blessed*
יהוה pr.n. (217) *Yahweh*
מִצִּיּוֹן prep.-pr.n. (851) *from Zion*
שֹׁכֵן Qal act.ptc. (1014) *he who dwells*
יְרוּשָׁלָם pr.n. paus. (436) *in Jerusalem*
הַלְלוּ־ Pi. impv. 2 m.p. (II 237) *praise*
יָהּ pr.n. (219) *Yah*

136:1

הוֹדוּ Hi. impv. 2 m.p. (יָדָה 392; GK 2r) *O give thanks*
לַיהוה prep.-pr.n. (217) *to Yahweh*
כִּי־טוֹב conj. (471)-adj. (II 373) *for he is good*
כִּי לְעוֹלָם conj.-prep.-n.m.s. (761) *for for ever*
חַסְדּוֹ n.m.s.-3 m.s. sf. (338) *his steadfast love*

136:2

הוֹדוּ Hi. impv. 2 m.p. (יָדָה 392) *O give thanks*
לֵאלֹהֵי prep.-n.m.p. cstr. (43) *to the God of*
הָאֱלֹהִים def.art.-n.m.p. (43) *gods*
כִּי לְעוֹלָם conj. (471)-prep.-n.m.s. (761) *for for ever*
חַסְדּוֹ n.m.s.-3 m.s. sf. (338) *his steadfast love*

136:3

הוֹדוּ Hi. impv. 2 m.p. (יָדָה 392) *O give thanks*
לַאֲדֹנֵי prep.-n.m.p. cstr. (10) *to the Lord of*
הָאֲדֹנִים def.art.-n.m.p. (10; GK 102m) *lords*
כִּי לְעֹלָם conj. (471)-prep.-n.m.s. (761) *for for ever*
חַסְדּוֹ n.m.s.-3 m.s. sf. (338) *his steadfast love*

136:4

לְעֹשֵׂה prep.-Qal act.ptc. m.s. cstr. (I 793) *to him who does*
נִפְלָאוֹת Ni. ptc. f.p. (פָּלָא 810) *wonders*
גְּדֹלוֹת adj. f.p. (152) *great*
לְבַדּוֹ prep.-n.m.s.-3 m.s. sf. (II 94) *alone*
כִּי לְעוֹלָם conj. (471)-prep.-n.m.s. (761) *for for ever*

חַסְדּוֹ n.m.s.-3 m.s. sf. (338) *his steadfast love*

136:5

לְעֹשֵׂה prep.-Qal act.ptc. (עָשָׂה I 793) *to him who made*
הַשָּׁמַיִם def.art.-n.m. du. (1029) *the heavens*
בִּתְבוּנָה prep.-n.f.s. (108) *by understanding*
כִּי לְעוֹלָם v.supra *for for ever*
חַסְדּוֹ v.supra *his steadfast love*

136:6

לְרֹקַע prep.-Qal act.ptc. m.s. cstr. (955; GK 65d) *to him who spread out*
הָאָרֶץ def.art.-n.f.s. (75) *the earth*
עַל־הַמָּיִם prep.-def.art.-n.m.p. paus. (565) *upon the waters*
כִּי לְעוֹלָם v.supra-v.supra *for for ever*
חַסְדּוֹ v.supra *his steadfast love*

136:7

לְעֹשֵׂה prep.-Qal act.ptc. m.s. cstr. (I 793) *to him who made*
אוֹרִים גְּדֹלִים n.m.p. (21)-adj. m.p. (152) *the great lights*
כִּי לְעוֹלָם conj. (471)-prep.-n.m.s. (761) *for for ever*
חַסְדּוֹ n.m.s.-3 m.s. sf. (338) *his steadfast love*

136:8

אֶת־הַשֶּׁמֶשׁ dir.obj.-def.art.-n.f.s. (1039) *the sun*
לְמֶמְשֶׁלֶת prep.-n.f.s. cstr. (606) *to rule*
בַּיּוֹם prep.-def.art.-n.m.s. (398) *the day*
כִּי לְעוֹלָם conj. (471)-prep.-n.m.s. (761) *for for ever*
חַסְדּוֹ n.m.s.-3 m.s. sf. (338) *his steadfast love*

136:9

אֶת־הַיָּרֵחַ dir.obj.-def.art.-n.m.s. (437) *the moon*
וְכוֹכָבִים conj.-n.m.p. (456) *and stars*
לְמֶמְשְׁלוֹת prep.-n.f.p. (606) *to rule*
בַּלָּיְלָה prep.-def.art.-n.m.s. (538) *over the night*
כִּי לְעוֹלָם conj. (471)-prep.-n.m.s. (761) *for for ever*
חַסְדּוֹ n.m.s.-3 m.s. sf. (338) *his steadfast love*

136:10

לְמַכֵּה prep.-Hi. ptc. m.s. cstr. (נָכָה 645) *to him who smote*
מִצְרַיִם pr.n. (595) *Egypt*
בִּבְכוֹרֵיהֶם prep.-n.m.p.-3 m.p. sf. (114) *the first-born of them*
כִּי לְעוֹלָם v.supra-v.supra *for for ever*
חַסְדּוֹ v.supra *his steadfast love*

136:11

וַיּוֹצֵא consec.-Hi. impf. 3 m.s. (יָצָא 422) *and brought out*
יִשְׂרָאֵל pr.n. (975) *Israel*
מִתּוֹכָם prep.-n.m.s.-3 m.p. sf. (1063) *from among them*
כִּי לְעוֹלָם v.supra-v.supra *for for ever*
חַסְדּוֹ v.supra *his steadfast love*

136:12

בְּיָד חֲזָקָה prep.-n.f.s. (388)-adj. f.s. (305) *with a strong hand*
וּבִזְרוֹעַ נְטוּיָה conj.-prep.-n.f.s. (283)-Qal pass. ptc. f.s. as adj. (נָטָה 639) *and with an outstretched arm*
כִּי לְעוֹלָם v.supra-v.supra *for for ever*
חַסְדּוֹ v.supra *his steadfast love*

136:13

לְגֹזֵר prep.-Qal act.ptc. m.s. cstr. (160) *to him who divided*
יַם־סוּף n.m.s. cstr. (410)-n.m.s. (I 693) *the Red Sea (sea of rushes)*
לִגְזָרִים prep.-n.m.p. (I 160) *in sunder*
כִּי לְעוֹלָם conj. (471)-prep.-n.m.s. (761) *for for ever*
חַסְדּוֹ n.m.s.-3 m.s. sf. (338) *his steadfast love*

136:14

וְהֶעֱבִיר conj.-Hi. pf. 3 m.s. (716) *and made pass*
יִשְׂרָאֵל pr.n. (975) *Israel*
בְּתוֹכוֹ prep.-n.m.s.-3 m.s. sf. (1063) *through the midst of it*
כִּי לְעוֹלָם conj. (471)-prep.-n.m.s. (761) *for for ever*
חַסְדּוֹ n.m.s.-3 m.s. sf. (338) *his steadfast love*

136:15

וְנִעֵר conj.-Pi. pf. 3 m.s. (II 654) *but overthrew*
פַּרְעֹה pr.n. (829) *Pharaoh*
וְחֵילוֹ conj.-n.m.s.-3 m.s. sf. (298) *and his host*
בְיַם־סוּף prep.-n.m.s. cstr. (410)-n.m.s. (I 693) *in the Red Sea (sea of reeds)*
כִּי לְעוֹלָם v.supra-v.supra *for for ever*
חַסְדּוֹ v.supra *his steadfast love*

136:16

לְמוֹלִיךְ prep.-Hi. ptc. (הָלַךְ 229) *to him who led*
עַמּוֹ n.m.s.-3 m.s. sf. (I 766) *his people*

בַּמִּדְבָּר prep.-def.art.-n.m.s. (II 184) *through the wilderness*
כִּי לְעוֹלָם conj. (471)-prep.-n.m.s. (761) *for for ever*
חַסְדּוֹ n.m.s.-3 m.s. sf. (338) *his steadfast love*

136:17

לְמַכֵּה prep.-Hi. ptc. m.s. cstr. (נָכָה 645) *to him who smote*
מְלָכִים גְּדֹלִים n.m.p. (I 572)-adj. m.p. (152) *great kings*
כִּי לְעוֹלָם conj. (471)-prep.-n.m.s. (761) *for for ever*
חַסְדּוֹ n.m.s.-3 m.s. sf. (338) *his steadfast love*

136:18

וַיַּהֲרֹג consec.-Qal impf. 3 m.s. (הָרַג 246) *and slew*
מְלָכִים אַדִּירִים n.m.p. (I 572)-adj. m.p. (12) *famous kings*
כִּי לְעוֹלָם v.supra-v.supra *for for ever*
חַסְדּוֹ v.supra *his steadfast love*

136:19

לְסִיחוֹן prep.-pr.n. (695) *Sihon*
מֶלֶךְ הָאֱמֹרִי n.m.s. cstr. (I 572)-def.art.-pr.n. gent. (57) *king of the Amorites*
כִּי לְעוֹלָם conj. (471)-prep.-n.m.s. (761) *for for ever*
חַסְדּוֹ n.m.s.-3 m.s. sf. (338) *his steadfast love*

136:20

וּלְעוֹג conj.-prep.-pr.n. (728) *and Og*
מֶלֶךְ n.m.s. cstr. (I 572) *king of*
הַבָּשָׁן def.art.-pr.n. (143) *Bashan*
כִּי לְעוֹלָם conj. (471)-prep.-n.m.s. (761) *for for ever*
חַסְדּוֹ n.m.s.-3 m.s. sf. (338) *his steadfast love*

136:21

וְנָתַן conj.-Qal pf. 3 m.s. (678) *and gave*
אַרְצָם n.f.s.-3 m.p. sf. (75) *their land*
לְנַחֲלָה prep.-n.f.s. (635) *as a heritage*
כִּי לְעוֹלָם conj. (471)-prep.-n.m.s. (761) *for for ever*
חַסְדּוֹ n.m.s.-3 m.s. sf. (338) *his steadfast love*

136:22

נַחֲלָה n.f.s. (635) *a heritage*
לְיִשְׂרָאֵל prep.-pr.n. (975) *to Israel*
עַבְדּוֹ n.m.s.-3 m.s. sf. (713) *his servant*
כִּי לְעוֹלָם v.supra-v.supra *for for ever*
חַסְדּוֹ v.supra *his steadfast love*

136:23

שֶׁבְּשִׁפְלֵנוּ rel. (979)-prep.-n.m.s.-1 c.p. sf. (1050) *who in our low estate*
זָכַר לָנוּ Qal pf. 3 m.s. (269)-prep.-1 c.p. sf. *remembered us*
כִּי לְעוֹלָם conj. (471)-prep.-n.m.s. (761) *for for ever*
חַסְדּוֹ n.m.s.-3 m.s. sf. (338) *his steadfast love*

136:24

וַיִּפְרְקֵנוּ consec.-Qal impf. 3 m.s.-1 c.p. sf. (פָּרַק 830) *and rescued us*
מִצָּרֵינוּ prep.-n.m.p.-1 c.p. sf. (III 865) *from our foes*
כִּי לְעוֹלָם v.supra-v.supra *for for ever*
חַסְדּוֹ v.supra *his steadfast love*

136:25

נֹתֵן Qal act.ptc. (678) *he who gives*
לֶחֶם n.m.s. (536) *food*
לְכָל־בָּשָׂר prep.-n.m.s. cstr. (481)-n.m.s. (142) *to all flesh*
כִּי לְעוֹלָם conj. (471)-prep.-n.m.s. (761) *for for ever*
חַסְדּוֹ n.m.s.-3 m.s. sf. (338) *his steadfast love*

136:26

הוֹדוּ Hi. impv. 2 m.p. (יָדָה 392) *O give thanks*
לְאֵל prep.-n.m.s. cstr. (42) *to the God of*
הַשָּׁמָיִם def.art.-n.m. du. paus. (1029) *heaven*
כִּי לְעוֹלָם conj. (471)-prep.-n.m.s. (761) *for for ever*
חַסְדּוֹ n.m.s.-3 m.s. sf. (338) *his steadfast love*

137:1

עַל נַהֲרוֹת prep.-n.m.p. (625; GK 124e) *by the streams of*
בָּבֶל pr.n. (93) *Babylon*
שָׁם adv. (1027) *there*
יָשַׁבְנוּ Qal pf. 1 c.p. (יָשַׁב 442) *we sat down*
גַּם־בָּכִינוּ adv. (168)-Qal pf. 1 c.p. (בָּכָה 113) *and wept*
בְּזָכְרֵנוּ prep.-Qal inf.cstr.-1 c.p. sf. (זָכַר 269) *when we remembered*
אֶת־צִיּוֹן dir.obj.-pr.n. (851) *Zion*

137:2

עַל־עֲרָבִים prep.-n.f.p. (II 788) *on the poplars*
בְּתוֹכָהּ prep.-n.m.s.-3 f.s. sf. (1063) *there (in its midst)*

תָּלִינוּ Qal pf. 1 c.p. (תָּלָה 1067) *we hung up*
כִּנֹּרוֹתֵינוּ n.m.p.-1 c.p. sf. (490) *our lyres*

137:3
כִּי שָׁם conj. (471)-adv. (1027) *for there*
שְׁאֵלוּנוּ Qal pf. 3 c.p.-1 c.p. sf. (שָׁאַל 981; GK 117gg) *required of us*
שׁוֹבֵינוּ Qal act.ptc. m.p.-1 c.p. sf. (שָׁבָה 985) *our captors*
דִּבְרֵי־שִׁיר n.m.p. cstr. (182)-n.m.s. (1010) *songs*
וְתוֹלָלֵינוּ conj.-n.m.p.-1 c.p. sf. (1064) *and our tormentors*
שִׂמְחָה n.f.s. (970) *mirth*
שִׁירוּ Qal impv. 2 m.p. (1010) *sing*
לָנוּ prep.-1 c.p. sf. *us*
מִשִּׁיר צִיּוֹן prep.-n.m.s. cstr. (1010)-pr.n. (851) *one of the songs of Zion*

137:4
אֵיךְ נָשִׁיר adv. (32)-Qal impf. 1 c.p. (שִׁיר 1010) *how shall we sing?*
אֶת־שִׁיר־ dir.obj.-n.m.s. cstr. (1010) *the song of*
יהוה pr.n. (217) *Yahweh*
עַל אַדְמַת נֵכָר prep.-n.f.s. cstr. (9)-n.m.s. (648) *in a foreign land*

137:5
אִם־אֶשְׁכָּחֵךְ hypoth.part. (49; GK 159m)-Qal impf. 1 c.s.-2 f.s. sf. (שָׁכַח 1013) *if I forget you*
יְרוּשָׁלָםִ pr.n. paus. (436) *O Jerusalem*
תִּשְׁכַּח Qal impf. 3 f.s. (1013) *let wither (forget)*
יְמִינִי n.f.s.-1 c.s. sf. (411) *my right hand*

137:6
תִּדְבַּק־ Qal impf. 3 f.s. (179) *let cleave*
לְשׁוֹנִי n.f.s.-1 c.s. sf. (546) *my tongue*
לְחִכִּי prep.-n.m.s.-1 c.s. sf. (335) *to the roof of my mouth*
אִם־לֹא אֶזְכְּרֵכִי hypoth.part. (49)-neg.-Qal impf. 1 c.s.-2 f.s. sf. (זָכַר 269; GK 58g) *if I do not remember you*
אִם־לֹא אַעֲלֶה v.supra-neg.-Qal impf. 1 c.s. (עָלָה 748) *if I do not set*
אֶת־יְרוּשָׁלַםִ dir.obj.-pr.n. (436) *Jerusalem*
עַל רֹאשׁ prep.-n.m.s. cstr. (910) *above the top of*
שִׂמְחָתִי n.f.s.-1 c.s. sf. (970) *my joy*

137:7
זְכֹר Qal impv. 2 m.s. (269) *remember*
יהוה pr.n. (217) *Yahweh*
לִבְנֵי אֱדוֹם prep.-n.m.p. cstr. (119)-pr.n. (10) *against the Edomites*
אֵת יוֹם dir.obj.-n.m.s. cstr. (398) *the day of*
יְרוּשָׁלָםִ v.supra paus. (436) *Jerusalem*
הָאֹמְרִים def.art.-Qal act.ptc. m.p. (55; GK 116d) *how they said*
עָרוּ Pi. impv. 2 m.p. (עָרָה 788; GK 75cc) *rase it*
עָרוּ v.supra *rase it*
עַד הַיְסוֹד בָּהּ prep. (III 723)-dir.obj.-n.f.s. (414) -prep.-3 f.s. sf. *down to its foundations*

137:8
בַּת־בָּבֶל n.f.s. cstr. (I 123)-pr.n. (93) *O daughter of Babylon*
הַשְּׁדוּדָה def.art.-Qal pass.ptc. f.s. (שָׁדַד 994) *who are devastated*
אַשְׁרֵי n.m.p. cstr. (80) *happy*
שֶׁיְשַׁלֶּם־לָךְ rel. (979)-Pi. impf. 3 m.s. (שָׁלֵם 1022)-prep.-2 f.s. sf. *who requites you*
אֶת־גְּמוּלֵךְ prep. (II 85)-n.m.s.-2 f.s. sf. (168) *with what (with your recompense)*
שֶׁגָּמַלְתְּ לָנוּ rel. (979)-Qal pf. 2 f.s. (גָּמַל 168) -prep.-1 c.p. sf. *which you have done to us*

137:9
אַשְׁרֵי n.m.p. cstr. (80) *happy shall be*
שֶׁיֹּאחֵז rel. (979)-Qal impf. 3 m.s. (אָחַז 28) *who takes*
וְנִפֵּץ conj.-Pi. pf. 3 m.s. (נָפַץ I 658) *and dashes*
אֶת־עֹלָלַיִךְ dir.obj.-n.m.p.-2 f.s. sf. (760) *your little ones*
אֶל־הַסָּלַע prep.-def.art.-n.m.s. paus. (700) *against the rock*

138:1
לְדָוִד prep.-pr.n. (187) *to David*
אוֹדְךָ Hi. impf. 1 c.s.-2 m.s. sf. (יָדָה 392) *I give thee thanks*
בְכָל־לִבִּי prep.-n.m.s. cstr. (481)-n.m.s.-1 c.s. sf. (524) *with my whole heart*
נֶגֶד אֱלֹהִים prep. (617)-n.m.p. (43) *before the gods*
אֲזַמְּרֶךָּ Pi. impf. 1 c.s.-2 m.s. sf. (זָמַר I 274) *I will sing thy praise*

138:2
אֶשְׁתַּחֲוֶה Hith. impf. 1 c.s. (שָׁחָה 1005) *I bow down*
אֶל־הֵיכַל prep.-n.m.s. cstr. (228) *toward the temple of*
קָדְשְׁךָ n.m.s.-2 m.s. sf. (871) *thy holiness*
וְאוֹדֶה conj.-Hi. impf. 1 c.s. (יָדָה 392) *and give*

thanks
אֶת־שְׁמֶךָ dir.obj.-n.m.s.-2 m.s. sf. (1027) *to thy name*
עַל־חַסְדְּךָ prep.-n.m.s.-2 m.s. sf. (338) *for thy steadfast love*
וְעַל־אֲמִתֶּךָ conj.-prep.-n.f.s.-2 m.s. sf. (54) *and thy faithfulness*
כִּי־הִגְדַּלְתָּ conj. (471)-Hi. pf. 2 m.s. (152) *for thou hast exalted*
עַל־כָּל־שִׁמְךָ prep.-n.m.s. cstr. (481; GK 16f) -n.m.s.-2 m.s. sf. (1027) *above all thy name*
אִמְרָתֶךָ n.f.s.-2 m.s. sf. (57) *thy word*

138:3

בְּיוֹם prep.-n.m.s. (398) *on the day*
קָרָאתִי Qal pf. 1 c.s. (894) *I called*
וַתַּעֲנֵנִי consec.-Qal impf. 2 m.s.-1 c.s. sf. (עָנָה I 772) *and thou didst answer me*
תַּרְהִבֵנִי Hi. impf. 2 m.s.-1 c.s. sf. (רָהַב 923) *thou didst make me arrogant*
בְנַפְשִׁי prep.-n.f.s.-1 c.s. sf. (659) *in my soul*
עֹז n.m.s. (738) *with strength*

138:4

יוֹדוּךָ Hi. impf. 3 m.p.-2 m.s. sf. (יָדָה 392) *shall praise thee*
יהוה pr.n. (217) *O Yahweh*
כָּל־מַלְכֵי־ n.m.s. cstr. (481)-n.m.p. cstr. (I 572) *all the kings of*
אָרֶץ n.f.s. paus. (75) *the earth*
כִּי שָׁמְעוּ conj. (471)-Qal pf. 3 c.p. (1033) *for they have heard*
אִמְרֵי־ n.m.p. cstr. (56) *the words of*
פִּיךָ n.m.s.-2 m.s. sf. (804) *thy mouth*

138:5

וְיָשִׁירוּ conj.-Qal impf. 3 m.p. (1010) *and they shall sing*
בְּדַרְכֵי prep.-n.m.p. cstr. (202) *of the ways of*
יהוה pr.n. (217) *Yahweh*
כִּי גָדוֹל conj. (471)-adj. m.s. (152) *for great is*
כְּבוֹד n.m.s. cstr. (458) *the glory of*
יהוה pr.n. (217) *Yahweh*

138:6

כִּי־רָם conj. (471)-Qal pf. 3 m.s. (רוּם 926) *for is high*
יהוה pr.n. (217) *Yahweh*
וְשָׁפָל conj.-adj. m.s. (1050) *but the lowly*
יִרְאֶה Qal impf. 3 m.s. (906) *he regards*
וְגָבֹהַּ conj.-adj. (147) *but the haughty*
מִמֶּרְחָק prep.-n.m.s. (935) *from afar*
יְיֵדָע Qal impf. 3 m.s. (יָדַע 393; GK 69bN,69p) *he knows*

138:7

אִם־אֵלֵךְ hypoth.part. (49)-Qal impf. 1 c.s. (הָלַךְ 229) *though I walk*
בְּקֶרֶב prep.-n.m.s. cstr. (899) *in the midst of*
צָרָה n.f.s. (I 865) *trouble*
תְּחַיֵּנִי Pi. impf. 2 m.s.-1 c.s. sf. (חָיָה 310) *thou dost preserve my life*
עַל אַף prep.-n.m.s. cstr. (I 60) *against the wrath of*
אֹיְבַי Qal act.ptc. m.p.-1 c.s. sf. (אָיַב 33) *my enemies*
תִּשְׁלַח Qal impf. 2 m.s. (1018) *thou dost stretch out*
יָדֶךָ n.f.s.-2 m.s. sf. (388) *thy hand*
וְתוֹשִׁיעֵנִי conj.-Hi. impf. 3 f.s.-1 c.s. sf. (יָשַׁע 446) *and delivers me*
יְמִינֶךָ n.f.s.-2 m.s. sf. (411) *thy right hand*

138:8

יהוה pr.n. (217) *Yahweh*
יִגְמֹל Qal impf. 3 m.s. (170) *will fulfil his purpose*
בַּעֲדִי prep.-1 c.s. sf. (126) *for me*
יהוה pr.n. (217) *O Yahweh*
חַסְדְּךָ n.m.s.-2 m.s. sf. (338) *thy steadfast love*
לְעוֹלָם prep.-n.m.s. (761) *for ever*
מַעֲשֵׂי n.m.p. cstr. (795) *the work of*
יָדֶיךָ n.f. du.-2 m.s. sf. (388) *thy hands*
אַל־תֶּרֶף neg.-Hi. impf. 2 m.s. apoc. (רָפָה 951) *do not forsake*

139:1

לַמְנַצֵּחַ prep.-def.art.-Pi. ptc. (I 663) *to the choirmaster*
לְדָוִד prep.-pr.n. (187) *to David*
מִזְמוֹר n.m.s. (274) *a Psalm*
יהוה pr.n. (217) *O Yahweh*
חֲקַרְתַּנִי Qal pf. 2 m.s.-1 c.s. sf. (חָקַר 350; GK 59h) *thou hast searched me*
וַתֵּדָע consec.-Qal impf. 2 m.s. (יָדַע 393) *and known me*

139:2

אַתָּה יָדַעְתָּ pers.pr. 2 m.s. (393) *thou knowest*
שִׁבְתִּי Qal inf.cstr.-1 c.s. sf. (יָשַׁב 442) *when I sit down*
וְקוּמִי conj.-Qal inf.cstr.-1 c.s. sf. (877) *and when I rise up*

בַּנְתָּה Qal pf. 2 m.s. (בִּין 106; GK 73aN) *thou discernest*
לְרֵעִי prep.-n.m.s.-1 c.s. sf. (III 946) *my thoughts*
מֵרָחוֹק prep.-adv. (935) *from afar*

139:3

אָרְחִי n.m.s.-1 c.s. sf. (73) *my path*
וְרִבְעִי conj.-Qal inf.cstr.-1 c.s. sf. (רָבַע II 918) *and my lying down*
זֵרִיתָ Pi. pf. 2 m.s. (זָרָה 279=scatter) *thou searchest out*
וְכָל־דְּרָכַי conj.-n.m.s. cstr. (481)-n.m.p.-1 c.s. sf. (202) *and all my ways*
הִסְכַּנְתָּה Hi. pf. 2 m.s. (סָכַן I 698) *thou art acquainted with*

139:4

כִּי אֵין מִלָּה conj. (471)-neg. cstr. (II 34)-n.f.s. (576) *even before a word*
בִּלְשׁוֹנִי prep.-n.f.s.-1 c.s. sf. (546) *on my tongue*
הֵן demons.part. (243) *lo*
יהוה pr.n. (217) *O Yahweh*
יָדַעְתָּ Qal pf. 2 m.s. (393) *thou knowest*
כֻלָּהּ n.m.s.-3 f.s. sf. (481) *it altogether*

139:5

אָחוֹר adv. (30) *behind*
וָקֶדֶם conj.-adv. (869) *and before*
צַרְתָּנִי Qal pf. 2 m.s.-1 c.s. sf. (צוּר II 848) *thou dost beset me*
וַתָּשֶׁת consec.-Qal impf. 2 m.s. (1011) *and layest*
עָלַי prep.-1 c.s. sf. *upon me*
כַּפֶּכָה n.f.s.-2 m.s. sf. (496; GK 91e) *thy hand*

139:6

פְּלִאיָה adj. f.s. (811) *wonderful*
דַעַת n.f.s. (395) *knowledge*
מִמֶּנִּי prep.-1 c.s. sf. *too ... for me*
נִשְׂגְּבָה Ni. pf. 3 f.s. (960) *it is high*
לֹא־אוּכַל לָהּ neg.-Qal impf. 1 c.s. (יָכֹל 407)-prep.-3 f.s. sf. *I cannot attain it*

139:7

אָנָה adv.-loc.he (33) *whither*
אֵלֵךְ Qal impf. 1 c.s. (הָלַךְ 229) *shall I go*
מֵרוּחֶךָ prep.-n.f.s.-2 m.s. sf. (924) *from thy spirit*
וְאָנָה conj.-v.supra *or whither*
מִפָּנֶיךָ prep.-n.m.p.-2 m.s. sf. (815) *from thy presence*
אֶבְרָח Qal impf. 1 c.s. (137) *shall I flee*

139:8

אִם־אֶסַּק hypoth.part. (49; GK 159m)-Qal impf. 1 c.s. (סָלַק 701; GK 66e) *I ascend*
שָׁמַיִם n.m. du. (1029) *to heaven*
שָׁם adv. (1027) *there*
אָתָּה pers.pr. 2 m.s. paus. (61) *thou art*
וְאַצִּיעָה conj.-Hi. impf. 1 c.s.-dir.he (יָצַע 426; GK 71) *and if I make my bed*
שְׁאוֹל n.f.s. (982) *in Sheol*
הִנֶּךָּ demons.part.-2 m.s. sf. (243) *thou art there*

139:9

אֶשָּׂא Qal impf. 1 c.s. (נָשָׂא 669) *if I take*
כַנְפֵי־ n.f. du. cstr. (489) *the wings of*
שָׁחַר n.m.s. paus. (1007) *the morning*
אֶשְׁכְּנָה Qal impf. 1 c.s.-vol.he (1014) *and dwell*
בְּאַחֲרִית prep.-n.f.s. cstr. (31) *in the uttermost parts of*
יָם n.m.s. (410) *the sea*

139:10

גַּם־שָׁם adv. (168)-adv. (1027) *even there*
יָדְךָ n.f.s.-2 m.s. sf. (388) *thy hand*
תַנְחֵנִי Hi. impf. 3 f.s.-1 c.s. sf. (נָחָה 634) *shall lead me*
וְתֹאחֲזֵנִי conj.-Qal impf. 3 f.s.-1 c.s. sf. (אָחַז 28) *and shall hold me*
יְמִינֶךָ n.f.s.-2 m.s. sf. (411) *thy right hand*

139:11

וָאֹמַר consec.-Qal impf. 1 c.s. (55; GK 111x,159f) *if I say*
אַךְ־חֹשֶׁךְ adv. (36)-n.m.s. (365) *only darkness*
יְשׁוּפֵנִי Qal impf. 3 m.s.-1 c.s. sf. (שׁוּף 1003) *let cover me* (lit. *bruise*) (prb.rd. יְשׂוּכֵּנִי=*let hedge me about*)
וְלַיְלָה conj.-n.m.s. (538) *and night*
אוֹר n.m.s. (21) *light*
בַּעֲדֵנִי prep.-1 c.s. sf. (126; GK 103d) *about me*

139:12

גַּם־חֹשֶׁךְ adv. (168)-n.m.s. (365) *even the darkness*
לֹא־יַחְשִׁיךְ neg.-Hi. impf. 3 m.s. (364) *is not dark (does not hide)*
מִמֶּךָ prep. (GK 133bN)-2 m.s. sf. *to thee*
וְלַיְלָה conj.-n.m.s. (538) *and the night*
כַּיּוֹם prep.-def.art.-n.m.s. (398) *as the day*
יָאִיר Hi. impf. 3 m.s. (אוֹר 21) *is bright*
כַּחֲשֵׁיכָה prep.-def.art.-n.f.s. (365) *as the darkness*
כָּאוֹרָה prep.-def.art.-n.f.s. (I 21) *as the light*

139:13

כִּי־אַתָּה conj. (471)-pers.pr. 2 m.s. (61) *for thou*
קָנִיתָ Qal pf. 2 m.s. (קָנָה 888) *didst form*
כִלְיֹתָי n.f.p.-1 c.s. sf. (480) *my inward parts*
תְּסֻכֵּנִי Qal impf. 2 m.s.-1 c.s. sf. (סָכַךְ II 697) *thou didst knit me*
בְּבֶטֶן prep.-n.f.s. cstr. (105) *in the womb of*
אִמִּי n.f.s.-1 c.s. sf. (51) *my mother*

139:14

אוֹדְךָ Hi. impf. 1 c.s.-2 m.s. sf. (יָדָה 392) *I praise thee*
עַל כִּי נוֹרָאוֹת prep.-conj. (471)-Ni. ptc. f.p. (יָרֵא 431; GK 118p) *for fearful things*
נִפְלֵיתִי Ni. pf. 1 c.s. (פָּלָה 811; GK 75qq) *I am wonderful*
נִפְלָאִים Ni. ptc. m.p. (810) *are wonderful*
מַעֲשֶׂיךָ n.m.p.-2 m.s. sf. (795) *thy works*
וְנַפְשִׁי conj.-n.f.s.-1 c.s. sf. (659) *and me*
יֹדַעַת Qal act.ptc. f.s. (יָדַע 393) *thou knowest*
מְאֹד adv. (547) *right well*

139:15

לֹא־נִכְחַד neg.-Ni. pf. 3 m.s. (470) *was not hidden*
עָצְמִי n.m.s.-1 c.s. sf. (782) *my frame*
מִמֶּךָּ prep.-2 m.s. sf. *from thee*
אֲשֶׁר־עֻשֵּׂיתִי rel. (81)-Pu. pf. 1 c.s. (עָשָׂה I 793) *when I was being made*
בַסֵּתֶר prep.-def.art.-n.m.s. (712) *in secret*
רֻקַּמְתִּי Pu. pf. 1 c.s. (955) *I was intricately wrought*
בְּתַחְתִּיּוֹת prep.-adj. f.p. cstr. (1066) *in the depths of*
אָרֶץ n.f.s. paus. (75) *the earth*

139:16

גָּלְמִי n.m.s.-1 c.s. sf. (166) *my unformed substance*
רָאוּ Qal pf. 3 c.p. (רָאָה 906) *beheld*
עֵינֶיךָ n.f. du.-2 m.s. sf. (744) *thy eyes*
וְעַל־סִפְרְךָ conj.-prep.-n.m.s.-2 m.s. sf. (706) *and in thy book*
כֻּלָּם n.m.s.-3 m.p. sf. (481) *every one of them*
יִכָּתֵבוּ Ni. impf. 3 m.p. paus. (507) *were written*
יָמִים n.m.p. (398) *days*
יֻצָּרוּ Pu. pf. 3 c.p. paus. (יָצַר 427) *that were formed*
וְלֹא אֶחָד conj.-neg.-num. (25) *and not one*
בָּהֶם prep.-3 m.p. sf. *of them*

139:17

וְלִי conj.-prep.-1 c.s. sf. *and to me*
מַה־יָּקְרוּ interr. (552)-Qal pf. 3 c.p. (יָקַר 429) *how precious are*
רֵעֶיךָ n.m.p.-2 m.s. sf. (III 946) *thy thoughts*
אֵל n.m.s. (42) *O God*
מֶה עָצְמוּ interr. (552)-Qal pf. 3 c.p. (I 782) *how vast is*
רָאשֵׁיהֶם n.m.p.-3 m.p. sf. (I 910) *the sum of them*

139:18

אֶסְפְּרֵם Qal impf. 1 c.s.-3 m.p. sf. (סָפַר 707) *if I would count them*
מֵחוֹל prep.-n.m.s. (297) *than the sand*
יִרְבּוּן Qal impf. 3 m.p. (רָבָה I 915; GK 159cN) *they are more*
הֱקִיצֹתִי Hi. pf. 1 c.s. (קִיץ I 884) *when I awake*
וְעוֹדִי conj.-adv.-1 c.s. sf. (728) *and I am still*
עִמָּךְ prep.-2 m.s. sf. paus. *with thee*

139:19

אִם־תִּקְטֹל hypoth.part. (49)-Qal impf. 2 m.s. (881) *O that thou wouldst slay*
אֱלוֹהַּ n.m.s. (42) *O God*
רָשָׁע adj. m.s. (957) *the wicked*
וְאַנְשֵׁי conj.-n.m.p. cstr. (35) *and men of*
דָמִים n.m.p. (196) *blood*
סוּרוּ Qal impv. 2 m.p. (some rd. סָרוּ or יָסוּרוּ 693) *would depart*
מֶנִּי prep.-1 c.s. sf. *from me*

139:20

אֲשֶׁר יֹאמְרֻךָ rel. (81)-Qal impf. 3 m.p.-2 m.s. sf. (55; GK 68h) *who say of thee*
לִמְזִמָּה prep.-n.f.s. (273) *wickedly*
נָשֻׂא Qal pass.ptc. (669; GK 23i,75oo) *who lift themselves*
לַשָּׁוְא prep.-def.art.-n.m.s. (996) *for evil*
עָרֶיךָ n.f.p.-2 m.s. sf. (746 or 786 *enemies*) *thy cities*

139:21

הֲלוֹא־מְשַׂנְאֶיךָ interr.-neg.-Pi. ptc. m.p.-2 m.s. sf. (971) *not them that hate thee?*
יהוה pr.n. (217) *O Yahweh*
אֶשְׂנָא Qal impf. 1 c.s. (971) *I hate*
וּבִתְקוֹמְמֶיךָ conj.-prep.-Hithpolel ptc. m.p.-2 m.s. sf. (קוּם 877; GK 72cc) *and them that rise up against thee*
אֶתְקוֹטָט Hithpolel impf. 1 c.s. (קוּט 876) *I loathe*

139:22

תַּכְלִית שִׂנְאָה n.f.s. cstr. (479)-n.f.s. (971; GK 117q,128r) *with perfect hatred*

שְׂנֵאתִים Qal pf. 1 c.s.-3 m.p. sf. (971) *I hate them*

לְאוֹיְבִים prep.-Qal act.ptc. m.p. (אָיַב 33) *for enemies*

הָיוּ לִי Qal pf. 3 c.p. (הָיָה 224)-prep.-1 c.s. sf. *they are to me*

139:23

חָקְרֵנִי Qal impv. 2 m.s.-1 c.s. sf. (350) *search me*

אֵל n.m.s. (42) *O God*

וְדַע conj.-Qal impv. 2 m.s. (יָדַע 393) *and know*

לְבָבִי n.m.s.-1 c.s. sf. (523) *my heart*

בְּחָנֵנִי Qal impv. 2 m.s.-1 c.s. sf. (בָּחַן 103) *try me*

וְדַע v.supra *and know*

שַׂרְעַפָּי n.m.p.-1 c.s. sf. (972; GK 85w) *my thoughts*

139:24

וּרְאֵה conj.-Qal impv. 2 m.s. (906) *and see*

אִם־ hypoth.part. (49) *if*

דֶּרֶךְ־עֹצֶב n.m.s. cstr. (202)-n.m.s. (I 780) *any hurtful way*

בִּי prep.-1 c.s. sf. *in me*

וּנְחֵנִי conj.-Qal impv. 2 m.s.-1 c.s. sf. (נָחָה 634) *and lead me*

בְּדֶרֶךְ עוֹלָם prep.-n.m.s. cstr. (202)-n.m.s. (761) *in the way everlasting*

140:1

לַמְנַצֵּחַ prep.-def.art.-Pi. ptc. (I 663) *to the choirmaster*

מִזְמוֹר n.m.s. (274) *a Psalm*

לְדָוִד prep.-pr.n. (187) *to David*

140:2

חַלְּצֵנִי Pi. impv. 2 m.s.-1 c.s. sf. (חָלַץ 322) *deliver me*

יהוה pr.n. (217) *O Yahweh*

מֵאָדָם רָע prep.-n.m.s. (9)-adj. m.s. (948) *from evil men*

מֵאִישׁ חֲמָסִים prep.-n.m.s. cstr. (35)-n.m.p. (329) *from men of violence*

תִּנְצְרֵנִי Qal impf. 2 m.s.-1 c.s. sf. (נָצַר 665) *preserve me*

140:3

אֲשֶׁר חָשְׁבוּ rel. (81)-Qal pf. 3 c.p. (362) *who plan*

רָעוֹת adj. f.p. (I 948) *evil things*

בְּלֵב prep.-n.m.s. (524) *in their heart*

כָּל־יוֹם n.m.s. cstr. (481)-n.m.s. (398) *continually*

יָגוּרוּ Qal impf. 3 m.p. (גּוּר II 158) *they stir up*

מִלְחָמוֹת n.f.p. (536) *wars*

140:4

שָׁנְנוּ Qal pf. 3 c.p. (1041) *they make sharp*

לְשׁוֹנָם n.f.s.-3 m.p. sf. (546) *their tongue*

כְּמוֹ־נָחָשׁ adv. (455)-n.m.s. (638) *as a serpent*

חֲמַת n.f.s. cstr. (404) *the poison of*

עַכְשׁוּב n.m.s. (747) *vipers*

תַּחַת prep. (1065) *under*

שְׂפָתֵימוֹ n.f.p.-3 m.p. sf. (973; GK 91,l) *their lips*

סֶלָה interj. (699) *Selah*

140:5

שָׁמְרֵנִי Qal impv. 2 m.s.-1 c.s. sf. (1036) *guard me*

יהוה pr.n. (217) *O Yahweh*

מִידֵי prep.-n.f. du. cstr. (388) *from the hands of*

רָשָׁע adj. m.s. (957) *the wicked*

מֵאִישׁ prep.-n.m.s. cstr. (35) *from men of*

חֲמָסִים n.m.p. (329) *violence*

תִּנְצְרֵנִי Qal impf. 2 m.s.-1 c.s. sf. (נָצַר 665) *preserve me*

אֲשֶׁר חָשְׁבוּ rel. (81)-Qal pf. 3 c.p. (362) *who have planned*

לִדְחוֹת prep.-Qal inf.cstr. (דָּחָה 190) *to trip up*

פְּעָמָי n.f.p.-1 c.s. sf. (821) *my feet*

140:6

טָמְנוּ־ Qal pf. 3 c.p. (380) *have hidden*

גֵאִים adj. m.p. (144) *arrogant men*

פַּח לִי n.m.s. (809)-prep.-1 c.s. sf. *a trap for me*

וַחֲבָלִים conj.-n.m.p. (286) *and with cords*

פָּרְשׂוּ Qal pf. 3 c.p. (831) *they have spread*

רֶשֶׁת n.f.s. (440) *a net*

לְיַד־מַעְגָּל prep.-n.f.s. cstr. (388)-n.m.s. (722) *by the wayside*

מֹקְשִׁים n.m.p. (430) *snares*

שָׁתוּ־ Qal pf. 3 c.p. (שִׁית 1011) *they have set*

לִי prep.-1 c.s. sf. *for me*

סֶלָה interj. (699) *Selah*

140:7

אָמַרְתִּי Qal pf. 1 c.s. (55) *I say*

לַיהוה prep.-pr.n. (217) *to Yahweh*

אֵלִי n.m.s.-1 c.s. sf. (42) *my God*

אָתָּה pers.pr. 2 m.s. paus. (61) *thou art*

הַאֲזִינָה Hi. impv. 2 m.s.-vol.he (אָזַן 24) *give ear*

יהוה pr.n. (217) *O Yahweh*

קוֹל n.m.s. cstr. (876) *to the voice of*

תַּחֲנוּנָי n.m.p.-1 c.s. sf. paus. (337) *my supplications*

140:8

יהוה pr.n. (217) *O Yahweh*
אֲדֹנָי n.m.p.-1 c.s. sf. (10) *my Lord*
עֹז n.m.s. cstr. (738) *strength of*
יְשׁוּעָתִי n.f.s.-1 c.s. sf. (447) *my deliverance*
סַכֹּתָה Qal pf. 2 m.s. (סָכַךְ I 696) *thou hast covered*
לְרֹאשִׁי prep.-n.m.s.-1 c.s. sf. (910) *my head*
בְּיוֹם prep.-n.m.s. cstr. (398) *in the day of*
נָשֶׁק n.m.s. paus. (676) *battle*

140:9

אַל־תִּתֵּן neg.-Qal impf. 2 m.s. (נָתַן 678) *grant not*
יהוה pr.n. (217) *O Yahweh*
מַאֲוַיֵּי n.m.p. cstr. (16) *the desires of*
רָשָׁע adj. m.s. (957) *the wicked*
זְמָמוֹ n.m.s.-3 m.s. sf. (273) *his evil plot*
אַל־תָּפֵק neg.-Hi. impf. 2 m.s. apoc. (פוק II 807) *do not further*
יָרוּמוּ Qal impf. 3 m.p. (רום 926) *they lift up*
סֶלָה interj. (699) *Selah*

140:10

רֹאשׁ n.m.s. (910) *their head*
מְסִבָּי Hi. ptc. m.p.-1 c.s. sf. paus. (סָבַב 685) *those who surround me*
עֲמַל n.m.s. cstr. (765) *the mischief of*
שְׂפָתֵימוֹ n.f.p.-3 m.p. sf. (973; GK 91,l) *their lips*
יְכַסֵּומוֹ Pi. impf. 3 m.s.-3 m.p. sf. (כָּסָה 491; GK 75mm) *let overwhelm them*

140:11

יִמִּיטוּ Ni. impf. 3 m.p. (מוט 556) *let fall* (lit. *let be shaken*)
עֲלֵיהֶם prep.-3 m.p. sf. *upon them*
גֶּחָלִים n.f.p. (160) *coals*
בָּאֵשׁ prep.-def.art.-n.f.s. (77) *in the fire*
יַפִּלֵם Hi. impf. 3 m.s.-3 m.p. sf. apoc. (נָפַל 656) *let them be cast*
בְּמַהֲמֹרוֹת prep.-n.f.p. (243) *into pits*
בַּל־יָקוּמוּ neg.-Qal impf. 3 m.p. (877) *no more to rise*

140:12

אִישׁ לָשׁוֹן n.m.s. cstr. (35)-n.f.s. (546) *a man of a tongue*
בַּל־יִכּוֹן neg.-Ni. impf. 3 m.s. (כּוּן I 465) *let not be established*
בָּאָרֶץ prep.-def.art.-n.f.s. (75) *in the land*
אִישׁ־חָמָס n.m.s. cstr. (35)-n.m.s. (329) *a man of violence*
רָע n.m.s. (949) *evil*
יְצוּדֶנּוּ Qal impf. 3 m.s.-3 m.s. sf. (צוּד I 844) *let hunt him down*
לְמַדְחֵפֹת prep.-n.f.p. (191) *speedily* (lit. *with thrusts*)

140:13

יָדַעְתִּ Qal pf. 1 c.s. (393; GK 44i) *I know*
כִּי־יַעֲשֶׂה conj. (471)-Qal impf. 3 m.s. (I 793) *that maintains*
יהוה pr.n. (217) *Yahweh*
דִּין n.m.s. cstr. (192) *the cause of*
עָנִי adj. m.s. (776) *the afflicted*
מִשְׁפַּט n.m.s. cstr. (1048) *justice for*
אֶבְיֹנִים adj. m.p. (2) *the needy*

140:14

אַךְ adv. (32) *surely*
צַדִּיקִים adj. m.p. (843) *the righteous*
יוֹדוּ Hi. impf. 3 m.p. (יָדָה 392) *shall give thanks*
לִשְׁמֶךָ prep.-n.m.s.-2 m.s. sf. (1027) *to thy name*
יֵשְׁבוּ Qal impf. 3 m.p. (יָשַׁב 442) *shall dwell*
יְשָׁרִים adj. m.p. (449) *the upright*
אֶת־פָּנֶיךָ dir.obj.-n.m.p.-2 m.s. sf. (815) *in thy presence*

141:1

מִזְמוֹר n.m.s. (274) *a Psalm*
לְדָוִד prep.-pr.n. (187) *to David*
יהוה pr.n. (217) *O Yahweh*
קְרָאתִיךָ Qal pf. 1 c.s.-2 m.s. sf. (894) *I call upon thee*
חוּשָׁה לִּי Qal impv. 2 m.s.-vol.he (חוּשׁ I 301) -prep.-1 c.s. sf. *make haste to me*
הַאֲזִינָה Hi. impv. 2 m.s.-vol.he (אָזַן 24) *give ear*
קוֹלִי n.m.s.-1 c.s. sf. (876) *to my voice*
בְּקָרְאִי־ prep.-Qal inf.cstr.-1 c.s. sf. (I 894) *when I call*
לָךְ prep.-2 m.s. sf. paus. *to thee*

141:2

תִּכּוֹן Ni. impf. 3 f.s. (כּוּן I 465) *let be counted*
תְּפִלָּתִי n.f.s.-1 c.s. sf. (813) *my prayer*
קְטֹרֶת n.f.s. (882) *as incense*
לְפָנֶיךָ prep.-n.m.p.-2 m.s. sf. (815) *before thee*
מַשְׂאַת n.f.s. cstr. (673) *the lifting of*
כַּפַּי n.f. du.-1 c.s. sf. (496) *my hands*
מִנְחַת־עָרֶב n.f.s. cstr. (585)-n.m.s. paus. (787) *as an evening sacrifice*

141:3

שִׁיתָה Qal impv. 2 m.s.-vol.he (שִׁית 1011) *set*
יהוה pr.n. (217) *O Yahweh*
שָׁמְרָה n.f.s. (1037) *a guard*
לְפִי prep.-n.m.s.-1 c.s. sf. (804) *over my mouth*
נִצְּרָה Qal impv. 2 m.s.-vol.he (נָצַר I 665; GK 20h,48i) *keep watch*
עַל־דַּל prep.-n.m.s. cstr. (194) *over the door of*
שְׂפָתָי n.f. du.-1 c.s. sf. (973) *my lips*

141:4

אַל־תַּט־ neg.-Hi. impf. 2 m.s. apoc. (נָטָה 639) *incline not*
לִבִּי n.m.s.-1 c.s. sf. (524) *my heart*
לְדָבָר רָע prep.-n.m.s. (182)-adj. m.s. (948) *to any evil*
לְהִתְעוֹלֵל prep.-Hithpo'el inf.cstr. (עָלַל I 759) *to busy myself*
עֲלִלוֹת n.f.p. (760) *deeds*
בְּרֶשַׁע prep.-n.m.s. (957) *with wickedness*
אֶת־אִישִׁים prep. (II 85)-n.m.p. (35; GK 96) *in company with men*
פֹּעֲלֵי־ Qal act.ptc. m.p. cstr. (821) *who work*
אָוֶן n.m.s. (19) *iniquity*
וּבַל־אֶלְחַם conj.-neg. (115)-Qal impf. 1 c.s. (לָחַם II 536) *and let me not eat*
בְּמַנְעַמֵּיהֶם prep.-n.m.p.-3 m.p. sf. (654) *of their dainties*

141:5

יֶהֶלְמֵנִי־ Qal impf. 3 m.s.-1 c.s. sf. (הָלַם 240) *let strike me*
צַדִּיק adj. m.s. (843) *a good man*
חֶסֶד n.m.s. (338) *in kindness*
וְיוֹכִיחֵנִי conj.-Hi. impf. 3 m.s.-1 c.s. sf. (יָכַח 406) *or rebuke me*
שֶׁמֶן רֹאשׁ n.m.s. cstr. (1032)-n.m.s. (I 910) *the oil of the chief* (LXX ἁμαρτωλοῦ = רָשָׁע *wicked*)
אַל־יָנִי neg.-Hi. impf. 3 m.s. apoc. (נוא 626; some rd. יָנִיא GK 74k) *let not refuse*
רֹאשִׁי n.m.s.-1 c.s. sf. (910) *my head*
כִּי־עוֹד conj. (471)-adv. (728) *for continually*
וּתְפִלָּתִי conj.-n.f.s.-1 c.s. sf. (813) *my prayer*
בְּרָעוֹתֵיהֶם prep.-n.f.p.-3 m.p. sf. (949) *against their wicked deeds*

141:6

נִשְׁמְטוּ Ni. pf. 3 c.p. (שָׁמַט 1030) *have been thrown down*
בִידֵי־סֶלַע prep.-n.f. du. cstr. (388)-n.m.s. (I 700) *on the rocks*
שֹׁפְטֵיהֶם Qal act.ptc. m.p.-3 m.p. sf. (1047) *those who shall condemn them*
וְשָׁמְעוּ conj.-Qal pf. 3 c.p. (1033) *then they shall hear*
אֲמָרַי n.m.p.-1 c.s. sf. (56) *my words*
כִּי נָעֵמוּ conj. (471)-Qal pf. 3 c.p. paus. (I 653) *that they are true*

141:7

כְּמוֹ פֹלֵחַ adv. (455)-Qal act.ptc. (812) *as one cleaves*
וּבֹקֵעַ conj.-Qal act.ptc. (131) *and shatters*
בָּאָרֶץ prep.-def.art.-n.f.s. (75) *on the land*
נִפְזְרוּ Ni. pf. 3 c.p. (808) *are scattered*
עֲצָמֵינוּ n.f.p.-1 c.p. sf. (782) *our bones*
לְפִי שְׁאוֹל prep.-n.m.s. cstr. (804)-n.f.s. (982) *at the mouth of Sheol*

141:8

כִּי אֵלֶיךָ conj. (471)-prep.-2 m.s. sf. *but toward thee*
יהוה pr.n. (217) *O Yahweh*
אֲדֹנָי n.m.p.-1 c.s. sf. (10) *Lord*
עֵינָי n.f. du.-1 c.s. sf. (744) *my eyes*
בְּכָה prep.-2 m.s. sf. *in thee*
חָסִיתִי Qal pf. 1 c.s. (חָסָה 340) *I seek refuge*
אַל־תְּעַר neg.-Pi. impf. 2 m.s. apoc. (עָרָה 788; GK 75bb) *leave not defenseless*
נַפְשִׁי n.f.s.-1 c.s. sf. (659) *me*

141:9

שָׁמְרֵנִי Qal impv. 2 m.s.-1 c.s. sf. (1036) *keep me*
מִידֵי פַח prep.-n.f. du. cstr. (388)-n.m.s. (809) *from the trap*
יָקְשׁוּ Qal pf. 3 c.p. (יָקֹשׁ 430) *they have laid*
לִי prep.-1 c.s. sf. *for me*
וּמֹקְשׁוֹת conj.-n.f.p. (430) *and the snares of*
פֹּעֲלֵי אָוֶן Qal act.ptc. m.p. cstr. (821)-n.m.s. (19) *evildoers*

141:10

יִפְּלוּ Qal impf. 3 m.p. (נָפַל 656) *let fall*
בְמַכְמֹרָיו prep.-n.m.p.-3 m.s. sf. (485; GK 145m) *into their own nets*
רְשָׁעִים adj. m.p. (957) *the wicked*
יַחַד adv. (403) *together*
אָנֹכִי pers.pr. 1 c.s. (59) *I*
עַד־אֶעֱבוֹר prep. (III 723)-Qal impf. 1 c.s. (716) *while I escape*

142:1

מַשְׂכִּיל n.m.s. (968) *a maskil*
לְדָוִד prep.-pr.n. (187) *to David*
בִּהְיוֹתוֹ prep.-Qal inf.cstr.-3 m.s. sf. (הָיָה 224) *when he was*
בַמְּעָרָה prep.-def.art.-n.f.s. (792) *in the cave*
תְפִלָּה n.f.s. (813) *a prayer*

142:2

קוֹלִי n.m.s.-1 c.s. sf. (876) *my voice*
אֶל־יהוה prep.-pr.n. (217) *to Yahweh*
אֶזְעָק Qal impf. 1 c.s. (277) *I cry*
קוֹלִי v.supra *with my voice*
אֶל־יהוה v.supra-v.supra *to Yahweh*
אֶתְחַנָּן Hith. impf. 1 c.s. (I 335) *I make supplication*

142:3

אֶשְׁפֹּךְ Qal impf. 1 c.s. (1049) *I pour out*
לְפָנָיו prep.-n.m.p.-3 m.s. sf. (815) *before him*
שִׂיחִי n.m.s.-1 c.s. sf. (I 967) *my complaint*
צָרָתִי n.f.s.-1 c.s. sf. (865) *my trouble*
לְפָנָיו prep.-n.m.p.-3 m.s. sf. (815) *before him*
אַגִּיד Hi. impf. 1 c.s. (נָגַד 616) *I tell*

142:4

בְּהִתְעַטֵּף prep.-Hith. inf.cstr. (III 742) *when is faint*
עָלַי prep.-1 c.s. sf. *upon me*
רוּחִי n.f.s.-1 c.s. sf. (924) *my spirit*
וְאַתָּה יָדַעְתָּ conj.-pers.pr. 2 m.s. (61)-Qal pf. 2 m.s. (393) *thou knowest*
נְתִיבָתִי n.f.s.-1 c.s. sf. (677) *my way*
בְּאֹרַח־ prep.-n.m.s. (73) *in the path*
זוּ אֲהַלֵּךְ rel. (262)-Pi. impf. 1 c.s. (הָלַךְ 229) *where I walk*
טָמְנוּ Qal pf. 3 c.p. (380) *they have hidden*
פַח לִי n.m.s. (809)-prep.-1 c.s. sf. *a trap for me*

142:5

הַבֵּיט Hi. impv. 2 m.s. (נָבַט 613; GK 113bb) *look*
יָמִין n.f.p. (411) *to the right*
וּרְאֵה conj.-Qal impv. 2 m.s. (906) *and watch*
וְאֵין־לִי conj.-neg. (II 34)-prep.-1 c.s. sf. *but there is none ... of me*
מַכִּיר Hi. ptc. (נָכַר 647) *who takes notice*
אָבַד Qal pf. 3 m.s. (1) *has vanished*
מָנוֹס n.m.s. (631) *refuge*
מִמֶּנִּי prep.-1 c.s. sf. *from me*
אֵין דּוֹרֵשׁ neg. cstr. (II 34)-Qal act.ptc. (205) *no man seeks*
לְנַפְשִׁי prep.-n.f.s.-1 c.s. sf. (659) *for me*

142:6

זָעַקְתִּי Qal pf. 1 c.s. (277) *I cry*
אֵלֶיךָ prep.-2 m.s. sf. *to thee*
יהוה pr.n. (217) *O Yahweh*
אָמַרְתִּי Qal pf. 1 c.s. (55) *I say*
אַתָּה מַחְסִי pers.pr. 2 m.s. (61)-n.m.s.-1 c.s. sf. (340) *thou art my refuge*
חֶלְקִי n.m.s.-1 c.s. sf. (324) *my portion*
בְּאֶרֶץ prep.-n.f.s. cstr. (75) *in the land of*
הַחַיִּים def.art.-n.m.p. (313) *the living*

142:7

הַקְשִׁיבָה Hi. impv. 2 m.s.-vol.he (קָשַׁב 904) *give heed*
אֶל־רִנָּתִי prep.-n.f.s.-1 c.s. sf. (943) *to my cry*
כִּי־דַלּוֹתִי מְאֹד conj. (471)-Qal pf. 1 c.s. (דָּלַל 195)-adv. (547) *for I am brought very low*
הַצִּילֵנִי Hi. impv. 2 m.s.-1 c.s. sf. (נָצַל 664) *deliver me*
מֵרֹדְפַי prep.-Qal act.ptc. m.p.-1 c.s. sf. (רָדַף 922) *from my persecutors*
כִּי אָמְצוּ conj. (471)-Qal pf. 3 c.p. (אָמֵץ 54) *for they are stronger*
מִמֶּנִּי prep.-1 c.s. sf. *than I*

142:8

הוֹצִיאָה Hi. impv. 2 m.s.-vol.he (יָצָא 422) *bring out*
מִמַּסְגֵּר prep.-n.m.s. (689) *out of prison*
נַפְשִׁי n.f.s.-1 c.s. sf. (659) *me*
לְהוֹדוֹת prep.-Hi. inf.cstr. (יָדָה 392) *that I may give thanks*
אֶת־שְׁמֶךָ dir.obj.-n.m.s.-2 m.s. sf. (1027) *to thy name*
בִּי יַכְתִּרוּ prep.-1 c.s. sf.-Hi. impf. 3 m.p. (כָּתַר 509) *will surround me*
צַדִּיקִים adj. m.p. (843) *righteous ones*
כִּי תִגְמֹל conj. (471)-Qal impf. 2 m.s. (168) *for thou wilt deal bountifully*
עָלָי prep.-1 c.s. sf. paus. *with me*

143:1

מִזְמוֹר n.m.s. (274) *a Psalm*
לְדָוִד prep.-pr.n. (187) *to David*
יהוה pr.n. (217) *O Yahweh*
שְׁמַע Qal impv. 2 m.s. (1033) *hear*
תְּפִלָּתִי n.f.s.-1 c.s. sf. (813) *my prayer*
הַאֲזִינָה Hi. impv. 2 m.s.-vol.he (אָזַן 24) *give ear*
אֶל־תַּחֲנוּנַי prep.-n.m.p.-1 c.s. sf. (337) *to my supplications*
בֶּאֱמֻנָתְךָ prep.-n.f.s.-2 m.s. sf. (53) *in thy faithfulness*

עֲנֵנִי Qal impv. 2 m.s.-1 c.s. sf. (עָנָה I 772) *answer me*
בְּצִדְקָתֶךָ prep.-n.f.s.-2 m.s. sf. (842) *in thy righteousness*

143:2

וְאַל־תָּבוֹא conj.-neg.-Qal impf. 2 m.s. (בּוֹא 97) *enter not*
בְמִשְׁפָּט prep.-n.m.s. (1048) *into judgment*
אֶת־עַבְדֶּךָ prep. (II 85)-n.m.s.-2 m.s. sf. (713) *with thy servant*
כִּי לֹא־יִצְדַּק conj. (471)-neg.-Qal impf. 3 m.s. (842) *for is not righteous*
לְפָנֶיךָ prep.-n.m.p.-2 m.s. sf. (815) *before thee*
כָל־חָי n.m.s. cstr. (481)-adj. m.s. (311) *any man living*

143:3

כִּי רָדַף conj.-Qal pf. 3 m.s. (922) *for has pursued*
אוֹיֵב Qal act.ptc. (33) *the enemy*
נַפְשִׁי n.f.s.-1 c.s. sf. (659) *me*
דִּכָּא Pi. pf. 3 m.s. (דָּכָא 193) *he has crushed*
לָאָרֶץ prep.-def.art.-n.f.s. (75) *to the ground*
חַיָּתִי n.f.s.-1 c.s. sf. (I 312) *my life*
הוֹשִׁיבַנִי Hi. pf. 3 m.s.-1 c.s. sf. (יָשַׁב 442) *he has made me sit*
בְמַחֲשַׁכִּים prep.-n.m.p. (365) *in darkness*
כְּמֵתֵי עוֹלָם prep.-Qal act.ptc. m.p. cstr. (מוּת 559)-n.m.s. (761) *like those long dead*

143:4

וַתִּתְעַטֵּף consec.-Hith. impf. 3 f.s. (עָטַף III 742) *therefore faints*
עָלַי prep.-1 c.s. sf. *within me*
רוּחִי n.f.s.-1 c.s. sf. (924) *my spirit*
בְּתוֹכִי prep.-n.m.s.-1 c.s. sf. (1063) *within me*
יִשְׁתּוֹמֵם Hithpo'el impf. 3 m.s. (שָׁמֵם 1030) *is appalled*
לִבִּי n.m.s.-1 c.s. sf. (524) *my heart*

143:5

זָכַרְתִּי Qal pf. 1 c.s. (269) *I remember*
יָמִים n.m.p. (398) *the days*
מִקֶּדֶם prep.-n.m.s. (869) *of old*
הָגִיתִי Qal pf. 1 c.s. (הָגָה I 211) *I meditate*
בְכָל־פָּעֳלֶךָ prep.-n.m.s. cstr. (481)-n.m.s.-2 m.s. sf. (821) *on all that thou hast done*
בְּמַעֲשֵׂה prep.-n.m.s. cstr. (795) *on the work of*
יָדֶיךָ n.f. du.-2 m.s. sf. (388) *thy hands*
אֲשׂוֹחֵחַ Polel impf. 1 c.s. (שִׂיחַ 967) *I muse*

143:6

פֵּרַשְׂתִּי Pi. pf. 1 c.s. (831; GK 106g) *I stretch out*
יָדַי n.f. du.-1 c.s. sf. (388) *my hands*
אֵלֶיךָ prep.-2 m.s. sf. *to thee*
נַפְשִׁי n.f.s.-1 c.s. sf. (659) *my soul*
כְּאֶרֶץ־עֲיֵפָה prep.-n.f.s. (75)-adj. f.s. (746) *like a parched land*
לְךָ prep.-2 m.s. sf. *for thee*
סֶלָה interj. (699) *Selah*

143:7

מַהֵר Pi. impv. 2 m.s. (I 554) *make haste*
עֲנֵנִי Qal impv. 2 m.s.-1 c.s. sf. (עָנָה I 772) *answer me*
יהוה pr.n. (217) *O Yahweh*
כָּלְתָה Qal pf. 3 f.s. (477) *fails*
רוּחִי n.f.s.-1 c.s. sf. (924) *my spirit*
אַל־תַּסְתֵּר neg.-Hi. impf. 2 m.s. apoc. (סָתַר 711) *hide not*
פָּנֶיךָ n.m.p.-2 m.s. sf. (815) *thy face*
מִמֶּנִּי prep.-1 c.s. sf. *from me*
וְנִמְשַׁלְתִּי conj.-Ni. pf. 1 c.s. (I 605) *lest I be like*
עִם־יֹרְדֵי prep.-Qal act.ptc. m.p. cstr. (432) *those who go down*
בוֹר n.m.s. (92) *to the Pit*

143:8

הַשְׁמִיעֵנִי Hi. impv. 2 m.s.-1 c.s. sf. (1033) *let me hear*
בַבֹּקֶר prep.-def.art.-n.m.s. (133) *in the morning*
חַסְדֶּךָ n.f.s.-2 m.s. sf. (338) *thy steadfast love*
כִּי־בְךָ conj. (471)-prep.-2 m.s. sf. *for in thee*
בָטָחְתִּי Qal pf. 1 c.s. paus. (105) *I put my trust*
הוֹדִיעֵנִי Hi. impv. 2 m.s.-1 c.s. sf. (יָדַע 393) *teach me*
דֶּרֶךְ־ n.m.s. (202) *the way*
זוּ אֵלֵךְ rel. (262)-Qal impf. 1 c.s. (הָלַךְ 229) *in which I should go*
כִּי־אֵלֶיךָ conj. (471)-prep.-2 m.s. sf. *for to thee*
נָשָׂאתִי Qal pf. 1 c.s. (669) *I lift up*
נַפְשִׁי n.f.s.-1 c.s. sf. (659) *my soul*

143:9

הַצִּילֵנִי Hi. impv. 2 m.s.-1 c.s. sf. (נָצַל 664) *deliver me*
מֵאֹיְבַי prep.-Qal act.ptc. m.p.-1 c.s. sf. (אָיַב 33) *from my enemies*
יהוה pr.n. (217) *O Yahweh*
אֵלֶיךָ prep.-2 m.s. sf. *to thee*
כִסִּתִי Pi. pf. 1 c.s. (כָּסָה 491) *I have fled for refuge*

143:10

לַמְּדֵנִי Pi. impv. 2 m.s.-1 c.s. sf. (540) *teach me*
לַעֲשׂוֹת prep.-Qal inf.cstr. (עָשָׂה I 793) *to do*
רְצוֹנֶךָ n.m.s.-2 m.s. sf. (953) *thy will*
כִּי־אַתָּה conj. (471)-pers.pr. 2 m.s. (61) *for thou*
אֱלוֹהָי n.m.p.-1 c.s. sf. paus. (43) *my God*
רוּחֲךָ n.f.s.-2 m.s. sf. (924) *thy spirit*
טוֹבָה adj. f.s. (II 373) *good*
תַּנְחֵנִי Hi. impf. 2 m.s.-1 c.s. sf. (נָחָה 634) *let lead me*
בְּאֶרֶץ מִישׁוֹר prep.-n.f.s. cstr. (75)-n.m.s. (449) *on a level path*

143:11

לְמַעַן־שִׁמְךָ prep. (775)-n.m.s.-2 m.s. sf. (1027) *for thy name's sake*
יהוה pr.n. (217) *O Yahweh*
תְּחַיֵּנִי Pi. impf. 2 m.s.-1 c.s. sf. (חָיָה 310) *preserve me*
בְּצִדְקָתְךָ prep.-n.f.s.-2 m.s. sf. (942) *in thy righteousness*
תוֹצִיא Hi. impf. 2 m.s. (יָצָא 422) *bring out*
מִצָּרָה prep.-n.f.s. (865) *out of trouble*
נַפְשִׁי n.f.s.-1 c.s. sf. (659) *my soul*

143:12

וּבְחַסְדְּךָ conj.-prep.-n.m.s.-2 m.s. sf. (338) *and in thy steadfast love*
תַּצְמִית Hi. impf. 2 m.s. (צָמַת 856) *cut off*
אֹיְבָי Qal act.ptc. m.p.-1 c.s. sf. paus. (אָיַב 33) *my enemies*
וְהַאֲבַדְתָּ conj.-Hi. pf. 2 m.s. (אָבַד 1) *and destroy*
כָּל־צֹרְרֵי n.m.s. cstr. (481)-Qal act.ptc. m.p. cstr. (III 865 צָרַר) *all the adversaries of*
נַפְשִׁי n.f.s.-1 c.s. sf. (659) *my soul*
כִּי אֲנִי conj. (471)-pers.pr. 1 c.s. (58) *for I am*
עַבְדֶּךָ n.m.s.-2 m.s. sf. (713) *thy servant*

144:1

לְדָוִד prep.-pr.n. (187) *to David*
בָּרוּךְ Qal pass.ptc. (138) *blessed*
יהוה pr.n. (217) *Yahweh*
צוּרִי n.m.s.-1 c.s. sf. (849) *my rock*
הַמְלַמֵּד def.art.-Pi. ptc. (לָמַד 540) *who trains*
יָדַי n.f. du.-1 c.s. sf. (388) *my hands*
לַקְרָב prep.-def.art.-n.m.s. (898) *for war*
אֶצְבְּעוֹתַי n.f.p.-1 c.s. sf. (840) *my fingers*
לַמִּלְחָמָה prep.-def.art.-n.f.s. (536) *for battle*

144:2

חַסְדִּי n.m.s.-1 c.s. sf. (338) *my steadfast love*
וּמְצוּדָתִי conj.-n.f.s.-1 c.s. sf. (II 845) *and my fortress*
מִשְׂגַּבִּי n.m.s.-1 c.s. sf. (I 960) *my stronghold*
וּמְפַלְטִי conj.-Pi. ptc.-1 c.s. sf. (פָּלַט 812) *and my deliverer*
לִי prep.-1 c.s. sf. *(to me)*
מָגִנִּי n.m.s.-1 c.s. sf. (171) *my shield*
וּבוֹ conj.-prep.-3 m.s. sf. *and in whom*
חָסִיתִי Qal pf. 1 c.s. (חָסָה 340) *I take refuge*
הָרוֹדֵד def.art.-Qal act.ptc. (רָדַד 921) *who subdues*
עַמִּי n.m.s.-1 c.s. sf. (I 766; GK 87f) *my people*
תַחְתָּי prep.-1 c.s. paus. (1065) *under me*

144:3

יהוה pr.n. (217) *O Yahweh*
מָה־אָדָם interr. (552)-n.m.s. (9) *what is man*
וַתֵּדָעֵהוּ consec.-Qal impf. 2 m.s.-3 m.s. sf. (יָדַע 393) *that thou dost regard him (know him)*
בֶּן־אֱנוֹשׁ n.m.s. cstr. (119)-n.m.s. (60) *or the son of man*
וַתְּחַשְּׁבֵהוּ consec.-Pi. impf. 2 m.s.-3 m.s. sf. (362 חָשַׁב) *that thou dost think of him*

144:4

אָדָם n.m.s. (9) *man*
לַהֶבֶל prep.-def.art.-n.m.s. (I 210) *to breath*
דָּמָה Qal pf. 3 m.s. (197) *is like*
יָמָיו n.m.p.-3 m.s. sf. (398) *his days*
כְּצֵל עוֹבֵר prep.-n.m.s. (853)-Qal act.ptc. (716) *like a passing shadow*

144:5

יהוה pr.n. (217) *O Yahweh*
הַט־ Hi. impv. 2 m.s. apoc. (נָטָה 639) *bow*
שָׁמֶיךָ n.m. du.-2 m.s. sf. (1029) *thy heavens*
וְתֵרֵד conj.-Qal impf. 2 m.s. (יָרַד 432) *and come down*
גַּע Qal impv. 2 m.s. (נָגַע 619) *touch*
בֶּהָרִים prep.-def.art.-n.m.p. (249) *the mountains*
וְיֶעֱשָׁנוּ conj.-Qal impf. 3 m.p. paus. (עָשַׁן 798) *that they smoke*

144:6

בְּרוֹק Qal impv. 2 m.s. (140) *flash forth*
בָּרָק n.m.s. (140) *the lightning*
וּתְפִיצֵם conj.-Hi. impf. 2 m.s.-3 m.p. sf. (פוּץ I 806) *and scatter them*
שְׁלַח Qal impv. 2 m.s. (1018) *send out*
חִצֶּיךָ n.m.p.-2 m.s. sf. (346) *thy arrows*
וּתְהֻמֵּם conj.-Qal impf. 2 m.s.-3 m.p. sf. (הָמַם 243) *and rout them*

144:7

שְׁלַח Qal impv. 2 m.s. (1018) *stretch forth*
יָדֶיךָ n.f. du.-2 m.s. sf. (388) *thy hand*
מִמָּרוֹם prep.-n.m.s. (928) *from on high*
פְּצֵנִי Qal impv. 2 m.s.-1 c.s. sf. (פָּצָה 822) *rescue me*
וְהַצִּילֵנִי conj.-Hi. impv. 2 m.s.-1 c.s. sf. (נָצַל 664) *and deliver me*
מִמַּיִם רַבִּים prep.-n.m.p. (565)-adj. m.p. (I 912) *from the many waters*
מִיַּד prep.-n.f.s. cstr. (388) *from the hand of*
בְּנֵי נֵכָר n.m.p. cstr. (119)-n.m.s. (648) *aliens*

144:8

אֲשֶׁר פִּיהֶם rel. (81)-n.m.s.-3 m.p. sf. (804) *whose mouth*
דִּבֶּר־ Pi. pf. 3 m.s. (180) *speaks*
שָׁוְא n.m.s. (996) *lies*
וִימִינָם conj.-n.f.s.-3 m.p. sf. (411) *and whose right hand*
יְמִין שָׁקֶר n.f.s. cstr. (411)-n.m.s. (1055) *a right hand of falsehood*

144:9

אֱלֹהִים n.m.p. (43) *O God*
שִׁיר חָדָשׁ n.m.s. (1010)-adj. m.s. (I 294) *a new song*
אָשִׁירָה Qal impf. 1 c.s.-vol.he (1010) *I will sing*
לָּךְ prep.-2 m.s. sf. paus. *to thee*
בְּנֵבֶל עָשׂוֹר prep.-n.m.s. (614)-n.m.s. (797) *upon a ten-stringed harp*
אֲזַמְּרָה־ Pi. impf. 1 c.s.-vol.he (I 274) *I will play*
לָּךְ v.supra *to thee*

144:10

הַנּוֹתֵן def.art.-Qal act.ptc. (נָתַן 678) *who gives*
תְּשׁוּעָה n.f.s. (448) *victory*
לַמְּלָכִים prep.-def.art.-n.m.p. (I 572) *to kings*
הַפּוֹצֶה def.art.-Qal act.ptc. (פָּצָה 822) *who rescuest*
אֶת־דָּוִד dir.obj.-pr.n. (187) *David*
עַבְדּוֹ n.m.s.-3 m.s. sf. (713) *his servant*
מֵחֶרֶב רָעָה prep.-n.f.s. (352)-adj. f.s. (I 948) *from the cruel sword*

144:11

פְּצֵנִי Qal impv. 2 m.s.-1 c.s. sf. (פָּצָה 822) *rescue me*
וְהַצִּילֵנִי conj.-Hi. impv. 2 m.s.-1 c.s. sf. (נָצַל 664) *and deliver me*
מִיַּד prep.-n.f.s. cstr. (388) *from the hand of*
בְּנֵי־נֵכָר n.m.p. cstr. (119)-n.m.s. (648) *aliens*
אֲשֶׁר פִּיהֶם rel. (81)-n.m.s.-3 m.p. sf. (804) *whose mouth*
דִּבֶּר־ Pi. pf. 3 m.s. (180) *speaks*
שָׁוְא n.m.s. (996) *lies*
וִימִינָם conj.-n.f.s.-3 m.p. sf. (411) *and whose right hand*
יְמִין שָׁקֶר n.f.s. cstr. (411)-n.m.s. paus. (1055) *a right hand of falsehood*

144:12

אֲשֶׁר בָּנֵינוּ rel. (81)-n.m.p.-1 c.p. sf. (119) *may our sons*
כִּנְטִעִים prep.-n.m.p. (642) *like plants*
מְגֻדָּלִים Pu. ptc. m.p. (152) *full grown*
בִּנְעוּרֵיהֶם prep.-n.m.p.-3 m.p. sf. (655) *in their youth*
בְּנוֹתֵינוּ n.f.p.-1 c.p. sf. (I 123) *our daughters*
כְזָוִיֹּת prep.-n.f.p. (265) *like corner pillars*
מְחֻטָּבוֹת Pu. ptc. f.p. (310) *cut*
תַּבְנִית n.f.s. cstr. (125) *the structure of*
הֵיכָל n.m.s. (228) *a palace*

144:13

מְזָוֵינוּ n.m.p.-1 c.p. sf. (265) *our garners*
מְלֵאִים Qal act.ptc. m.p. (569) *be full*
מְפִיקִים Hi. ptc. m.p. (פוק II 807) *providing*
מִזַּן אֶל־זַן prep.-n.m.s. (275)-prep.-v.supra *all manner of store*
צֹאונֵנוּ n.f.s.-1 c.p. sf. (838) *may our sheep*
מַאֲלִיפוֹת Hi. ptc. f.p. (1120; cf. אֶלֶף II 48) *bring forth thousands*
מְרֻבָּבוֹת Pu. ptc. f.p. (1127; cf. רָבַב I 912) *and ten thousands*
בְּחוּצוֹתֵינוּ prep.-n.m.p.-1 c.p. sf. (299) *in our fields*

144:14

אַלּוּפֵינוּ n.m.p.-1 c.p. sf. (I 48; GK 122e) *may our cattle*
מְסֻבָּלִים Pu. ptc. m.p. (סָבַל 687) *be heavy with young*
אֵין־פֶּרֶץ neg. cstr. (II 34)-n.m.s. (829) *suffering no mischance*
וְאֵין יוֹצֵאת conj.-v.supra-Qal act.ptc. f.s. (422) *or failure in bearing*
וְאֵין צְוָחָה v.supra-n.f.s. (846) *may there be no cry of distress*
בִּרְחֹבֹתֵינוּ prep.-n.f.p.-1 c.p. sf. (I 932) *in our streets*

144:15

אַשְׁרֵי n.m.p. cstr. (80) *happy*
הָעָם def.art.-n.m.s. (I 766) *the people*
שֶׁכָּכָה rel. (979)-adv. (462) *to which it is thus*
לּוֹ prep.-3 m.s. sf. *(to them)*
אַשְׁרֵי v.supra *happy*
הָעָם v.supra *the people*
שֶׁיהוה rel. (979)-pr.n. (217) *which Yahweh*
אֱלֹהָיו n.m.p.-3 m.s. sf. (43) *his God*

145:1

תְּהִלָּה n.f.s. (239; GK 5h) *praise*
לְדָוִד prep.-pr.n. (187) *to David*
אֲרוֹמִמְךָ Polel impf. 1 c.s. (רום 926)-2 m.s. sf. *I will extol thee*
אֱלוֹהַי n.m.p.-1 c.s. sf. (43) *my God*
הַמֶּלֶךְ def.art.-n.m.s. (I 572) *the King*
וַאֲבָרְכָה conj.-Pi. impf. 1 c.s.-vol.he (בָּרַךְ 138) *and I will bless*
שִׁמְךָ n.m.s.-2 m.s. sf. (1027) *thy name*
לְעוֹלָם prep.-n.m.s. (761) *for ever*
וָעֶד conj.-n.m.s. (I 723) *and ever*

145:2

בְּכָל־יוֹם prep.-n.m.s. cstr. (481)-n.m.s. (398) *every day*
אֲבָרְכֶךָּ Pi. impf. 1 c.s.-2 m.s. sf. (בָּרַךְ 138) *I will bless thee*
וַאֲהַלְלָה conj.-Pi. impf. 1 c.s.-vol.he (הָלַל II 237) *and praise*
שִׁמְךָ n.m.s.-2 m.s. sf. (1027) *thy name*
לְעוֹלָם prep.-n.m.s. (761) *for ever*
וָעֶד conj.-n.m.s. (I 723) *and ever*

145:3

גָּדוֹל adj.m.s. (152) *great is*
יהוה pr.n. (217) *Yahweh*
וּמְהֻלָּל conj.-Pu. ptc. (הָלַל II 237) *and to be praised*
מְאֹד adv. (547) *greatly*
וְלִגְדֻלָּתוֹ conj.-prep.-n.f.s.-3 m.s. sf. (153) *and to his greatness*
אֵין חֵקֶר neg. cstr. (II 34)-n.m.s. (350) *there is no searching*

145:4

דּוֹר לְדוֹר n.m.s. (189)-prep.-v.supra *generation to generation*
יְשַׁבַּח Pi. impf. 3 m.s. (שָׁבַח II 986) *shall laud*
מַעֲשֶׂיךָ n.m.p.-2 m.s. sf. (795) *thy works*
וּגְבוּרֹתֶיךָ conj.-n.f.p.-2 m.s. sf. (150) *and thy mighty acts*
יַגִּידוּ Hi. impf. 3 m.p. (נָגַד 616) *shall declare*

145:5

הֲדַר כְּבוֹד n.m.s. cstr. (214)-n.m.s. cstr. (II 458) *the splendor of the glory of*
הוֹדֶךָ n.m.s.-2 m.s. sf. (I 217) *thy majesty*
וְדִבְרֵי נִפְלְאוֹתֶיךָ conj.-n.m.p. cstr. (182)-Ni. ptc. f.p.-2 m.s. sf. (פָּלָא 810) *and on thy wondrous works*
אָשִׂיחָה Qal impf. 1 c.s.-vol.he (שִׂיחַ 967) *I will meditate*

145:6

וֶעֱזוּז conj.-n.m.s. cstr. (739) *and the might of*
נוֹרְאֹתֶיךָ Ni. ptc. f.p.-2 m.s. sf. (יָרֵא 431) *thy terrible acts*
יֹאמֵרוּ Qal impf. 3 m.p. paus. (55) *men shall proclaim*
וּגְדוּלָּתְךָ conj.-n.f.s.-2 m.s. sf. (153) *and thy greatness*
אֲסַפְּרֶנָּה Pi. impf. 1 c.s.-3 f.s. sf. (סָפַר 707) *I will declare (it)*

145:7

זֵכֶר n.m.s. cstr. (271) *the fame of*
רַב־ adj. m.s. cstr. (I 912; GK 132b) *the abundance of*
טוּבְךָ n.m.s.-2 m.s. sf. (375) *thy goodness*
יַבִּיעוּ Hi. impf. 3 m.p. (נָבַע 615) *they shall pour forth*
וְצִדְקָתְךָ conj.-n.f.s.-2 m.s. sf. (842) *and of thy righteousness*
יְרַנֵּנוּ Pi. impf. 3 m.p. (רָנַן 943) *they shall sing aloud*

145:8

חַנּוּן adj. m.s. (337) *gracious*
וְרַחוּם conj.-adj. m.s. (933) *and merciful*
יהוה pr.n. (217) *Yahweh*
אֶרֶךְ adj. m.s. cstr. (74) *slow to*
אַפַּיִם n.m. du. (I 60) *anger*
וּגְדָל־ conj.-adj. m.s. cstr. (152) *and abounding in*
חָסֶד n.m.s. paus. (338) *steadfast love*

145:9

טוֹב־ adj. m.s. (II 373) *is good*
יהוה pr.n. (217) *Yahweh*
לַכֹּל prep.-def.art.-n.m.s. (481) *to all*
וְרַחֲמָיו conj.-n.m.p.-3 m.s. sf. (933) *and his compassion*
עַל־כָּל־ prep.-n.m.s. cstr. (481) *over all that*
מַעֲשָׂיו n.m.p.-3 m.s. sf. (795) *he has made*

145:10

יוֹדוּךָ Hi. impf. 3 m.p.-2 m.s. sf. (יָדָה 392) *shall give thanks to thee*

יהוה pr.n. (217) *O Yahweh*

כָּל־מַעֲשֶׂיךָ n.m.s. cstr. (481)-n.m.p.-2 m.s. sf. (795) *all thy works*

וַחֲסִידֶיךָ conj.-adj. m.p.-2 m.s. sf. (339) *and thy saints*

יְבָרְכוּכָה Pi. impf. 3 m.p.-2 m.s. sf. (בָּרַךְ 138) *shall bless thee*

145:11

כְּבוֹד n.m.s. cstr. (458) *the glory of*

מַלְכוּתְךָ n.f.s.-2 m.s. sf. (574) *thy kingdom*

יֹאמֵרוּ Qal impf. 3 m.p. paus. (55) *they shall speak*

וּגְבוּרָתְךָ conj.-n.f.s.-2 m.s. sf. (150) *and of thy power*

יְדַבֵּרוּ Pi. impf. 3 m.p. (180) *they shall tell*

145:12

לְהוֹדִיעַ prep.-Hi. inf.cstr. (יָדַע 393) *to make known*

לִבְנֵי הָאָדָם prep.-n.m.p. cstr. (119)-def.art.-n.m.s. (9) *to the sons of men*

גְּבוּרֹתָיו n.f.p.-3 m.s. sf. (150) *his mighty deeds*

וּכְבוֹד conj.-n.m.s. cstr. (458) *and the glory of*

הֲדַר n.m.s. cstr. (214) *the splendor of*

מַלְכוּתוֹ n.f.s.-3 m.s. sf. (574) *his kingdom*

145:13

מַלְכוּתְךָ n.f.s.-2 m.s. sf. (574) *thy kingdom*

מַלְכוּת n.f.s. cstr. (574) *a kingdom of*

כָּל־עֹלָמִים n.m.s. cstr. (481; GK 123c)-n.m.p. (761) *all antiquities*

וּמֶמְשַׁלְתְּךָ conj.-n.f.s.-2 m.s. sf. (606) *and thy dominion*

בְּכָל־דּוֹר וָדוֹר prep.-n.m.s. cstr. (481)-n.m.s. (189)-conj.-n.m.s. (189) *throughout all generations*

145:14

סוֹמֵךְ Qal act.ptc. (סָמַךְ 701) *upholds*

יהוה pr.n. (217) *Yahweh*

לְכָל־הַנֹּפְלִים prep.-n.m.s. cstr. (481)-def.art.-Qal act.ptc. m.p. (656) *all who are falling*

וְזוֹקֵף conj.-Qal act.ptc. (זָקַף 279) *and raises up*

לְכָל־הַכְּפוּפִים v.supra-def.art.-Qal pass.ptc. m.p. (496 כָּפַף) *all who are bowed down*

145:15

עֵינֵי־כֹל n.f. du. cstr. (744)-n.m.s. (481) *the eyes of all*

אֵלֶיךָ prep.-2 m.s. sf. *to thee*

יְשַׂבֵּרוּ Pi. impf. 3 m.p. paus. (II 960) *shall hope*

וְאַתָּה conj.-pers.pr. 2 m.s. (61) *and thou*

נוֹתֵן־ Qal act.ptc. (678) *givest*

לָהֶם prep.-3 m.p. sf. *them*

אֶת־אָכְלָם dir.obj.-n.m.s.-3 m.p. sf. (38) *their food*

בְּעִתּוֹ prep.-n.f.s.-3 m.s. sf. (773) *in due season*

145:16

פּוֹתֵחַ Qal act.ptc. (פָּתַח I 834) *thou openest*

אֶת־יָדֶךָ dir.obj.-n.f.s.-2 m.s. sf. (388) *thy hand*

וּמַשְׂבִּיעַ conj.-Hi. ptc. (שָׂבַע 959) *and satisfiest*

לְכָל־חַי prep.-n.m.s. cstr. (481)-adj. m.s. (311) *of every living thing*

רָצוֹן n.m.s. (953) *the desire*

145:17

צַדִּיק adj. m.s. (843) *is just*

יהוה pr.n. (217) *Yahweh*

בְּכָל־דְּרָכָיו prep.-n.m.s. cstr. (481)-n.m.p.-3 m.s. sf. (202) *in all his ways*

וְחָסִיד conj.-adj. m.s. (339) *and kind*

בְּכָל־מַעֲשָׂיו v.supra-n.m.p.-3 m.s. sf. (795) *in all his doings*

145:18

קָרוֹב adj. m.s. (898) *is near*

יהוה pr.n. (217) *Yahweh*

לְכָל־קֹרְאָיו prep.-n.m.s. cstr. (481)-Qal act.ptc. m.p.-3 m.s. sf. (894) *to all who call upon him*

לְכֹל אֲשֶׁר prep.-n.m.s. (481)-rel. (81) *to all who*

יִקְרָאֻהוּ Qal impf. 3 m.p.-3 m.s. sf. (קָרָא 894) *(they) call upon him*

בֶאֱמֶת prep.-n.f.s. (54) *in truth*

145:19

רְצוֹן־ n.m.s. cstr. (953) *the desire of*

יְרֵאָיו Qal act.ptc. m.p.-3 m.s. sf. (יָרֵא 431) *those who fear him*

יַעֲשֶׂה Qal impf. 3 m.s. (עָשָׂה I 793) *he fulfils*

וְאֶת־שַׁוְעָתָם conj.-dir.obj.-n.f.s.-3 m.p. sf. (1003) *and their cry*

יִשְׁמַע Qal impf. 3 m.s. (1033) *he hears*

וְיוֹשִׁיעֵם conj.-Hi. impf. 3 m.s.-3 m.p. sf. (יָשַׁע 446) *and saves them*

145:20

שׁוֹמֵר Qal act.ptc. (1036) *preserves*

יהוה pr.n. (217) *Yahweh*
אֶת־כָּל־אֹהֲבָיו dir.obj.-n.m.s. cstr. (481)-Qal act. ptc. m.p.-3 m.s. sf. (אָהַב 12) *all who love him*
וְאֵת כָּל־הָרְשָׁעִים conj.-dir.obj.-n.m.s. cstr. (481) -def.art.-adj. m.p. (957) *but all the wicked*
יַשְׁמִיד Hi. impf. 3 m.s. (1029) *he will destroy*

145:21

תְּהִלַּת n.f.s. cstr. (239) *the praise of*
יהוה pr.n. (217) *Yahweh*
יְדַבֶּר־ Pi. impf. 3 m.s. (180) *will speak*
פִּי n.m.s.-1 c.s. sf. (804) *my mouth*
וִיבָרֵךְ conj.-Pi. impf. 3 m.s. (138) *and let bless*
כָּל־בָּשָׂר n.m.s. cstr. (481)-n.m.s. (142) *all flesh*
שֵׁם קָדְשׁוֹ n.m.s. cstr. (1027)-n.m.s.-3 m.s. sf. (871) *the name of his holiness*
לְעוֹלָם prep.-n.m.s. (761) *for ever*
וָעֶד conj.-n.m.s. paus. (I 723) *and ever*

146:1

הַלְלוּ־יָהּ Pi. impv. 2 m.p. (II 237)-pr.n. (219) *Praise Yah*
הַלְלִי Pi. impv. 2 f.s. (II 237) *praise*
נַפְשִׁי n.f.s.-1 c.s. sf. (659) *O my soul*
אֶת־יהוה dir.obj.-pr.n. (217) *Yahweh*

146:2

אֲהַלְלָה Pi. impf. 1 c.s.-vol.he (II 237) *I will praise*
יהוה pr.n. (217) *Yahweh*
בְּחַיָּי prep.-n.m.p.-1 c.s. sf. paus. (313) *as long as I live*
אֲזַמְּרָה Pi. impf. 1 c.s.-vol.he (I 274) *I will sing praises*
לֵאלֹהַי prep.-n.m.p.-1 c.s. sf. (43) *to my God*
בְּעוֹדִי prep.-subst.-1 c.s. sf. (728) *while I have being*

146:3

אַל־תִּבְטְחוּ neg.-Qal impf. 2 m.p. (105) *put not your trust*
בִנְדִיבִים prep.-adj. m.p. (622) *in princes*
בְּבֶן־אָדָם prep.-n.m.s. cstr. (119)-n.m.s. (9) *in a son of man*
שֶׁאֵין לוֹ rel. (979)-neg. (II 34)-prep.-3 m.s. sf. *in whom there is no*
תְשׁוּעָה n.f.s. (448) *help*

146:4

תֵּצֵא Qal impf. 3 f.s. (יָצָא 422) *departs*
רוּחוֹ n.f.s.-3 m.s. sf. (924) *his breath*
יָשֻׁב Qal impf. 3 m.s. (שׁוּב 996) *he returns*
לְאַדְמָתוֹ prep.-n.f.s.-3 m.s. sf. (9) *to his earth*
בַּיּוֹם הַהוּא prep.-def.art.-n.m.s. (398)-def.art. -demons.adj. m.s. (214) *on that very day*
אָבְדוּ Qal pf. 3 c.p. (1) *perish*
עֶשְׁתֹּנֹתָיו n.f.p.-3 m.s. sf. (799) *his plans*

146:5

אַשְׁרֵי n.m.p. cstr. (80) *happy is he*
שֶׁאֵל יַעֲקֹב rel. (979)-n.m.s. (42)-pr.n. (784) *which the God of Jacob*
בְּעֶזְרוֹ prep.-n.m.s.-3 m.s. sf. (I 740) *his help*
שִׂבְרוֹ n.m.s.-3 m.s. sf. (960) *whose help*
עַל־יהוה prep.-pr.n. (217) *Yahweh*
אֱלֹהָיו n.m.p.-3 m.s. sf. (43) *his God*

146:6

עֹשֶׂה Qal act.ptc. (I 793) *who made*
שָׁמַיִם n.m. du. (1029) *heaven*
וָאָרֶץ conj.-n.f.s. paus. (75) *and earth*
אֶת־הַיָּם dir.obj.-def.art.-n.m.s. (410) *the sea*
וְאֶת־כָּל־ conj.-dir.obj.-n.m.s. (481) *and all*
אֲשֶׁר־בָּם rel. (81)-prep.-3 m.p. sf. *that is in them*
הַשֹּׁמֵר def.art.-Qal act.ptc. (1036) *who keeps*
אֱמֶת n.f.s. (54) *faith*
לְעוֹלָם prep.-n.m.s. (761) *for ever*

146:7

עֹשֶׂה Qal act.ptc. (I 793) *who executes*
מִשְׁפָּט n.m.s. (1048) *justice*
לָעֲשׁוּקִים prep.-def.art.-Qal pass.ptc. m.p. (עָשַׁק 798) *for the oppressed*
נֹתֵן Qal act.ptc. (678) *who gives*
לֶחֶם n.m.s. (536) *food*
לָרְעֵבִים prep.-def.art.-adj. m.p. (944) *to the hungry*
יהוה pr.n. (217) *Yahweh*
מַתִּיר Hi. ptc. (נָתַר II 684) *sets free*
אֲסוּרִים Qal pass.ptc. m.p. (אָסַר 63) *the prisoners*

146:8

יהוה pr.n. (217) *Yahweh*
פֹּקֵחַ Qal act.ptc. (824) *opens the eyes of*
עִוְרִים adj. m.p. (734) *the blind*
יהוה v.supra *Yahweh*
זֹקֵף Qal act.ptc. (279) *lifts up*
כְּפוּפִים Qal pass.ptc. m.p. (496) *those who are bowed down*
יהוה v.supra *Yahweh*
אֹהֵב Qal act.ptc. (12) *loves*
צַדִּיקִים adj. m.p. (843) *the righteous*

146:9

יהוה pr.n. (217) *Yahweh*
שֹׁמֵר Qal act.ptc. (1036) *watches over*
אֶת־גֵּרִים dir.obj.-n.m.p. (158) *the sojourners*
יָתוֹם n.m.s. (450) *the fatherless*
וְאַלְמָנָה conj.-n.f.s. (48) *and the widow*
יְעוֹדֵד Polel impf. 3 m.s. (עוּד 728) *he upholds*
וְדֶרֶךְ conj.-n.m.s. cstr. (202) *but the way of*
רְשָׁעִים adj. m.p. (957) *the wicked*
יְעַוֵּת Pi. impf. 3 m.s. (עָוַת 736) *he brings to ruin*

146:10

יִמְלֹךְ Qal impf. 3 m.s. (573) *will reign*
יהוה pr.n. (217) *Yahweh*
לְעוֹלָם prep.-n.m.s. (761) *for ever*
אֱלֹהַיִךְ n.m.p.-2 f.s. sf. (43) *thy God*
צִיּוֹן pr.n. (851) *O Zion*
לְדֹר וָדֹר prep.-n.m.s. (189)-conj.-n.m.s. (189) *to all generations*
הַלְלוּ־יָהּ Pi. impv. 2 m.p. (II 237)-pr.n. (219) *Praise Yah*

147:1

הַלְלוּ יָהּ Pi. impv. 2 m.p. (II 237)-pr.n. (219) *Praise Yah*
כִּי־טוֹב conj. (471)-adj. m.s. (II 373) *for it is good*
זַמְּרָה Pi. inf.cstr. (זָמַר I 274; GK 52p) *to sing praises*
אֱלֹהֵינוּ n.m.p.-1 c.p. sf. (43) *to our God*
כִּי־נָעִים conj. (471)-adj. (I 653) *for he is gracious*
נָאוָה adj. f.s. (610) *is seemly*
תְהִלָּה n.f.s. (239) *a song of praise*

147:2

בּוֹנֵה Qal act.ptc. (בָּנָה 124) *builds up*
יְרוּשָׁלַםִ pr.n. (436) *Jerusalem*
יהוה pr.n. (217) *Yahweh*
נִדְחֵי Ni. ptc. m.p. cstr. (623; GK 20m) *the outcasts of*
יִשְׂרָאֵל pr.n. (975) *Israel*
יְכַנֵּס Pi. impf. 3 m.s. (כָּנַס 488) *he gathers*

147:3

הָרֹפֵא def.art.-Qal act.ptc. (רָפָא 950) *he heals*
לִשְׁבוּרֵי לֵב prep.-Qal pass.ptc. m.p. cstr. (שָׁבַר 990)-n.m.s. (524) *the brokenhearted*
וּמְחַבֵּשׁ conj.-Pi. ptc. (חָבַשׁ 289) *and binds up*
לְעַצְּבוֹתָם prep.-n.f.p.-3 m.p. sf. (781) *their wounds*

147:4

מוֹנֶה Qal act.ptc. (584) *he determines*
מִסְפָּר n.m.s. (708) *the number*
לַכּוֹכָבִים prep.-def.art.-n.m.p. (456) *of the stars*
לְכֻלָּם prep.-n.m.s.-3 m.p. sf. (481) *to all of them*
שֵׁמוֹת n.m.p. (1027) *names*
יִקְרָא Qal impf. 3 m.s. (894) *he gives*

147:5

גָּדוֹל adj. m.s. (152) *great is*
אֲדוֹנֵינוּ n.m.p.-1 c.p. sf. (10) *our Lord*
וְרַב־כֹּחַ conj.-adj. m.s. cstr. (I 912)-n.m.s. (470) *and abundant in power*
לִתְבוּנָתוֹ prep.-n.f.s.-3 m.s. sf. (108) *to his understanding*
אֵין מִסְפָּר neg. (II 34)-n.m.s. (708) *there is no measure*

147:6

מְעוֹדֵד Polel ptc. (עוּד 728) *lifts up*
עֲנָוִים n.m.p. (776) *the downtrodden*
יהוה pr.n. (217) *Yahweh*
מַשְׁפִּיל Hi. ptc. (1050) *he casts*
רְשָׁעִים adj. m.p. (957) *the wicked*
עֲדֵי־אָרֶץ prep. (III 723)-n.f.s. (75) *to the ground*

147:7

עֱנוּ Qal impv. 2 m.p. (עָנָה IV 777) *sing*
לַיהוה prep.-pr.n. (217) *to Yahweh*
בְּתוֹדָה prep.-n.f.s. (392) *with thanksgiving*
זַמְּרוּ Pi. impv. 2 m.p. (I 274) *make melody*
לֵאלֹהֵינוּ prep.-n.m.p.-1 c.p. sf. (43) *to our God*
בְכִנּוֹר prep.-n.m.s. (490) *upon the lyre*

147:8

הַמְכַסֶּה def.art.-Pi. ptc. (כָּסָה 491) *he covers*
שָׁמַיִם n.m. du. (1029) *the heavens*
בְּעָבִים prep.-n.m.p. (728) *with clouds*
הַמֵּכִין def.art.-Hi. ptc. (כּוּן I 465) *he prepares*
לָאָרֶץ prep.-def.art.-n.f.s. (75) *for the earth*
מָטָר n.m.s. (564) *rain*
הַמַּצְמִיחַ def.art.-Hi. ptc. (855) *he makes grow*
הָרִים n.m.p. (249) *upon the hills*
חָצִיר n.m.s. (II 348) *grass*

147:9

נוֹתֵן Qal act.ptc. (678) *he gives*
לִבְהֵמָה prep.-n.f.s. (96) *to the beasts*
לַחְמָהּ n.m.s.-3 f.s. sf. (536) *their food*
לִבְנֵי עֹרֵב prep.-n.m.p. cstr. (119)-n.m.s. (788) *to the young ravens*

אֲשֶׁר יִקְרָאוּ rel. (81)-Qal impf. 3 m.p. (894) *which cry*

147:10

לֹא בִגְבוּרַת neg.-prep.-n.f.s. cstr. (150) *not in the strength of*
הַסּוּס def.art.-n.m.s. (692) *the horse*
יֶחְפָּץ Qal impf. 3 m.s. (חָפֵץ 342) *he delights*
לֹא־בְשׁוֹקֵי neg.-prep.-n.f. du. cstr. (1003) *not in the legs of*
הָאִישׁ def.art.-n.m.s. (35) *the man*
יִרְצֶה Qal impf. 3 m.s. (רָצָה 953) *he is pleased*

147:11

רוֹצֶה Qal act.ptc. (953) *takes pleasure*
יהוה pr.n. (217) *Yahweh*
אֶת־יְרֵאָיו dir.obj.-Qal act.ptc. m.p.-3 m.s. sf. (יָרֵא 431) *in those who fear him*
אֶת־הַמְיַחֲלִים dir.obj.-def.art.-Pi. ptc. m.p. (יָחַל 403) *in those who hope*
לְחַסְדּוֹ prep.-n.m.s.-3 m.s. sf. (338) *in his steadfast love*

147:12

שַׁבְּחִי Pi. impv. 2 f.s. (שָׁבַח II 986) *praise*
יְרוּשָׁלַםִ pr.n. (436) *O Jerusalem*
אֶת־יהוה dir.obj.-pr.n. (217) *Yahweh*
הַלְלִי Pi. impv. 2 f.s. (II 237) *praise*
אֱלֹהַיִךְ n.m.p.-2 f.s. sf. (43) *your God*
צִיּוֹן pr.n. (851) *O Zion*

147:13

כִּי־חִזַּק conj. (471)-Pi. pf. 3 m.s. (304) *for he strengthens*
בְּרִיחֵי n.m.p. cstr. (138) *the bars of*
שְׁעָרָיִךְ n.m.p.-2 f.s. sf. (1044) *your gates*
בֵּרַךְ Pi. pf. 3 m.s. (138) *he blesses*
בָּנַיִךְ n.m.p.-2 f.s. sf. (119) *your sons*
בְּקִרְבֵּךְ prep.-n.m.s.-2 f.s. sf. (899) *within you*

147:14

הַשָּׂם־ def.art.-Qal act.ptc. (שׂוּם 962) *he makes*
גְּבוּלֵךְ n.m.s.-2 f.s. sf. (147) *in your borders*
שָׁלוֹם n.m.s. (1022) *peace*
חֵלֶב n.m.s. cstr. (I 316) *the finest of*
חִטִּים n.f.p. (334) *wheat*
יַשְׂבִּיעֵךְ Hi. impf. 3 m.s.-2 f.s. sf. (שָׂבַע 959) *he fills you with*

147:15

הַשֹּׁלֵחַ def.art.-Qal act.ptc. (1018) *he sends forth*
אִמְרָתוֹ n.f.s.-3 m.s. sf. (57) *his command*
אָרֶץ n.f.s. paus. (75) *to the earth*
עַד־מְהֵרָה prep. (III 723)-n.f.s. (555) *swiftly*
יָרוּץ Qal impf. 3 m.s. (רוּץ 930) *runs*
דְּבָרוֹ n.m.s.-3 m.s. sf. (182) *his word*

147:16

הַנֹּתֵן def.art.-Qal act.ptc. (678) *he gives*
שֶׁלֶג n.m.s. (1017) *snow*
כַּצָּמֶר prep.-def.art.-n.m.s. paus. (856) *like wool*
כְּפוֹר n.m.s. (II 499) *hoarfrost*
כָּאֵפֶר prep.-def.art.-n.m.s. (68) *like ashes*
יְפַזֵּר Pi. impf. 3 m.s. (808) *he scatters*

147:17

מַשְׁלִיךְ Hi. ptc. (1020) *he casts forth*
קַרְחוֹ n.m.s.-3 m.s. sf. (901) *his ice*
כְפִתִּים prep.-n.f.p. (837) *like morsels*
לִפְנֵי קָרָתוֹ prep.-n.m.p. cstr. (815)-n.f.s. (903) *before his cold*
מִי יַעֲמֹד interr. (566)-Qal impf. 3 m.s. (עָמַד 763) *who can stand*

147:18

יִשְׁלַח Qal impf. 3 m.s. (1018) *he sends forth*
דְּבָרוֹ n.m.s.-3 m.s. sf. (182) *his word*
וְיַמְסֵם conj.-Hi. impf. 3 m.s.-3 m.p. sf. (מָסָה 587) *and melts them*
יַשֵּׁב Hi. impf. 3 m.s. apoc. (נָשַׁב 674) *he makes blow*
רוּחוֹ n.f.s.-3 m.s. sf. (924) *his wind*
יִזְּלוּ־ Qal impf. 3 m.p. (נָזַל 633) *flow*
מָיִם n.m.p. paus. (565) *waters*

147:19

מַגִּיד Hi. ptc. (נָגַד 616) *he declares*
דְּבָרָו n.m.s.-3 m.s. sf. (182) *his word*
לְיַעֲקֹב prep.-pr.n. (784) *to Jacob*
חֻקָּיו n.m.p.-3 m.s. sf. (349) *his statutes*
וּמִשְׁפָּטָיו conj.-n.m.p.-3 m.s. sf. (1048) *and his ordinances*
לְיִשְׂרָאֵל prep.-pr.n. (975) *to Israel*

147:20

לֹא עָשָׂה neg.-Qal pf. 3 m.s. (I 793) *he has not dealt*
כֵן adv. (485) *thus*
לְכָל־גּוֹי prep.-n.m.s. cstr. (481)-n.m.s. (156) *with any other nation*
וּמִשְׁפָּטִים conj.-n.m.p. (1048) *and ordinances*
בַּל־יְדָעוּם neg. (115)-Qal pf. 3 c.p.-3 m.p. sf. (יָדַע 393) *they do not know (them)*

הַלְלוּ־יָהּ Pi. impv. 2 m.p. (II 237)-pr.n. (219) *Praise Yah*

148:1

הַלְלוּ יָהּ Pi. impv. 2 m.p. (II 237)-pr.n. (219) *Praise Yah*

הַלְלוּ v.supra *praise*

אֶת־יהוה dir.obj.-pr.n. (217) *Yahweh*

מִן־הַשָּׁמַיִם prep.-def.art.-n.m. du. (1029) *from the heavens*

הַלְלוּהוּ Pi. impv. 2 m.p.-3 m.s. sf. (II 237) *praise him*

בַּמְּרוֹמִים prep.-def.art.-n.m.p. (928) *in the heights*

148:2

הַלְלוּהוּ Pi. impv. 2 m.p.-3 m.s. sf. (II 237) *praise him*

כָל־מַלְאָכָיו n.m.s. cstr. (481)-n.m.p.-3 m.s. sf. (521) *all his angels*

הַלְלוּהוּ v.supra *praise him*

כָּל־צְבָאָו v.supra-n.m.p.-3 m.s. sf. paus. (838) *all his hosts*

148:3

הַלְלוּהוּ Pi. impv. 2 m.p.-3 m.s. sf. (II 237) *praise him*

שֶׁמֶשׁ n.f.s. (1029) *sun*

וְיָרֵחַ conj.-n.m.s. (437) *and moon*

הַלְלוּהוּ v.supra *praise him*

כָּל־כּוֹכְבֵי אוֹר n.m.s. cstr. (481)-n.m.p. cstr. (456) -n.m.s. (21) *all of the stars of light*

148:4

הַלְלוּהוּ Pi. impv. 2 m.p.-3 m.s. sf. (II 237) *praise him*

שְׁמֵי הַשָּׁמָיִם n.m. du. cstr. (1029)-def.art.-n.m. du. paus. (1029) *heavens of heavens*

וְהַמַּיִם conj.-def.art.-n.m.p. (565) *and waters*

אֲשֶׁר מֵעַל rel. (81)-prep.-prep. *above*

הַשָּׁמָיִם v.supra *the heavens*

148:5

יְהַלְלוּ Pi. impf. 3 m.p. (II 237) *let them praise*

אֶת־שֵׁם dir.obj.-n.m.s. cstr. (1027) *the name of*

יהוה pr.n. (217) *Yahweh*

כִּי הוּא conj. (471)-pers.pr. 3 m.s. (214) *for he*

צִוָּה Pi. pf. 3 m.s. (צָוָה 845) *commanded*

וְנִבְרָאוּ conj.-Ni. pf. 3 c.p. (בָּרָא 135) *and they were created*

148:6

וַיַּעֲמִידֵם consec.-Hi. impf. 3 m.s.-3 m.p. sf. (עָמַד 763) *and he established them*

לָעַד לְעוֹלָם prep.-def.art.-n.m.s. (I 723)-prep. -n.m.s. (761) *for ever and ever*

חָק־נָתַן n.m.s. (349)-Qal pf. 3 m.s. (678) *he fixed their bounds*

וְלֹא יַעֲבוֹר conj.-neg.-Qal impf. 3 m.s. (716) *and he did not pass*

148:7

הַלְלוּ Pi. impv. 2 m.p. (II 237) *praise*

אֶת־יהוה dir.obj.-pr.n. (217) *Yahweh*

מִן־הָאָרֶץ prep.-def.art.-n.f.s. (75) *from the earth*

תַּנִּינִים n.m.p. (1072) *sea monsters*

וְכָל־תְּהֹמוֹת conj.-n.m.s. cstr. (481)-n.f.p. (1062) *and all deeps*

148:8

אֵשׁ n.f.s. (77) *fire*

וּבָרָד conj.-n.m.s. (135) *and hail*

שֶׁלֶג n.m.s. (1017) *snow*

וְקִיטוֹר conj.-n.m.s. (882) *and thick smoke*

רוּחַ סְעָרָה n.f.s. (924)-n.f.s. (704) *stormy wind*

עֹשָׂה Qal act.ptc. f.s. (I 793) *fulfilling*

דְבָרוֹ n.m.s.-3 m.s. sf. (182) *his command*

148:9

הֶהָרִים def.art.-n.m.p. (249) *mountains*

וְכָל־גְּבָעוֹת conj.-n.m.s. cstr. (481)-n.f.p. (148) *and all hills*

עֵץ פְּרִי n.m.s. cstr. (781)-n.m.s. (826) *fruit trees*

וְכָל־אֲרָזִים conj.-v.supra-n.m.p. (72) *and all cedars*

148:10

הַחַיָּה def.art.-n.f.s. (I 312) *beasts*

וְכָל־בְּהֵמָה conj.-n.m.s. cstr. (481)-n.f.s. (96) *and all cattle*

רֶמֶשׂ n.m.s. (943) *creeping things*

וְצִפּוֹר כָּנָף conj.-n.f.s. cstr. (861)-n.f.s. (489) *and flying birds*

148:11

מַלְכֵי־ n.m.p. cstr. (I 572) *kings of*

אֶרֶץ n.f.s. (75) *earth*

וְכָל־לְאֻמִּים conj.-n.m.s. cstr. (481)-n.m.p. (522) *and all peoples*

שָׂרִים n.m.p. (978) *princes*

וְכָל־שֹׁפְטֵי v.supra-Qal act.ptc. m.p. cstr. (1047) *and all rulers of*

אָרֶץ n.f.s. paus. (75) *earth*

148:12

בַּחוּרִים n.m.p. (104) *young men*
וְגַם־בְּתוּלוֹת conj.-adv. (168)-n.f.p. (143) *and maidens together*
זְקֵנִים adj. m.p. (278) *old men*
עִם־נְעָרִים prep.-n.m.p. (654) *and children*

148:13

יְהַלְלוּ Pi. impf. 3 m.p. (II 237) *let them praise*
אֶת־שֵׁם dir.obj.-n.m.s. cstr. (1027) *the name of*
יהוה pr.n. (217) *Yahweh*
כִּי־נִשְׂגָּב conj.-Ni. ptc. (שָׂגַב 960) *for is exalted*
שְׁמוֹ n.m.s.-3 m.s. sf. (1027) *his name*
לְבַדּוֹ prep.-n.m.s.-3 m.s. sf. (94) *alone*
הוֹדוֹ n.m.s.-3 m.s. sf. (I 217) *his glory*
עַל־אֶרֶץ prep.-n.f.s. (75) *above earth*
וְשָׁמָיִם conj.-n.m. du. paus. (1029) *and heaven*

148:14

וַיָּרֶם consec.-Hi. impf. 3 m.s. (רום 926) *he has raised up*
קֶרֶן n.f.s. (901) *a horn*
לְעַמּוֹ prep.-n.m.s.-3 m.s. sf. (I 766) *for his people*
תְּהִלָּה n.f.s. (239) *praise*
לְכָל־חֲסִידָיו prep.-n.m.s. cstr. (481)-adj. m.p.-3 m.s. sf. (339) *for all his saints*
לִבְנֵי יִשְׂרָאֵל prep.-n.m.p. cstr. (119)-pr.n. (975) *for the people of Israel*
עַם־קְרֹבוֹ n.m.s. cstr. (I 766)-adj. m.s.-3 m.s. sf. (898) *who are near to him*
הַלְלוּ־יָהּ Pi. impv. 2 m.p. (II 237)-pr.n. (219) *Praise Yah*

149:1

הַלְלוּ יָהּ Pi. impv. 2 m.p. (II 237)-pr.n. (219) *Praise Yah*
שִׁירוּ Qal impv. 2 m.p. (1010) *sing*
לַיהוה prep.-pr.n. (217) *to Yahweh*
שִׁיר חָדָשׁ n.m.s. (1010)-adj. m.s. (I 294) *a new song*
תְּהִלָּתוֹ n.f.s.-3 m.s. sf. (239) *his praise*
בִּקְהַל prep.-n.m.s. cstr. (874) *in the assembly of*
חֲסִידִים adj. m.p. (339) *the faithful*

149:2

יִשְׂמַח Qal impf. 3 m.s. (970) *let be glad*
יִשְׂרָאֵל pr.n. (975) *Israel*
בְּעֹשָׂיו prep.-Qal act.ptc. m.p.-3 m.s. sf. (עָשָׂה I 793; GK 124k) *in his Maker*
בְּנֵי־צִיּוֹן n.m.p. cstr. (119)-pr.n. (851) *the sons of Zion*
יָגִילוּ Qal impf. 3 m.p. (גִּיל 162) *let rejoice*
בְמַלְכָּם prep.-n.m.s.-3 m.p. sf. (I 572) *in their King*

149:3

יְהַלְלוּ Pi. impf. 3 m.p. (II 237) *let them praise*
שְׁמוֹ n.m.s.-3 m.s. sf. (1027) *his name*
בְמָחוֹל prep.-n.m.s. (I 298) *with dancing*
בְּתֹף prep.-n.m.s. (1074) *with timbrel*
וְכִנּוֹר conj.-n.m.s. (490) *and lyre*
יְזַמְּרוּ־לוֹ Pi. impf. 3 m.p. (I 274)-prep.-3 m.s. sf. *making melody to him*

149:4

כִּי־רוֹצֶה conj.-Qal act.ptc. (953) *for takes pleasure*
יהוה pr.n. (217) *Yahweh*
בְּעַמּוֹ prep.-n.m.s.-3 m.s. sf. (I 766) *in his people*
יְפָאֵר Pi. impf. 3 m.s. (פָּאַר I 802) *he adorns*
עֲנָוִים n.m.p. (776) *the humble*
בִּישׁוּעָה prep.-n.f.s. (447) *with victory*

149:5

יַעְלְזוּ Qal impf. 3 m.p. (759) *let exult*
חֲסִידִים adj. m.p. (339) *the faithful*
בְּכָבוֹד prep.-n.m.s. (458) *in glory*
יְרַנְּנוּ Pi. impf. 3 m.p. (943) *let them sing for joy*
עַל־מִשְׁכְּבוֹתָם prep.-n.m.p.-3 m.p. sf. (1012) *on their couches*

149:6

רוֹמְמוֹת אֵל n.m.p. cstr. (928)-n.m.s. (42) *the high praises of God*
בִּגְרוֹנָם prep.-n.m.s.-3 m.p. sf. (173) *in their throats*
וְחֶרֶב פִּיפִיּוֹת conj.-n.f.s. cstr. (352)-n.m.p. (804; GK 96) *and two-edged swords*
בְּיָדָם prep.-n.f.s.-3 m.p. sf. (388) *in their hands*

149:7

לַעֲשׂוֹת prep.-Qal inf.cstr. (ïēh I 793) *to wreak*
נְקָמָה n.f.s. (668) *vengeance*
בַּגּוֹיִם prep.-def.art.-n.m.p. (156) *on the nations*
תּוֹכֵחֹת n.f.p. (407) *chastisements*
בַּל־אֻמִּים neg. (115)-n.f.p. (52; lit. *not peoples*; cf. 44:15; many rd. בַּלְאֻמִּים prep.-n.m.p. 552) *on the peoples*

149:8

לֶאְסֹר prep.-Qal inf.cstr. (63) *to bind*

מַלְכֵיהֶם n.m.p.-3 m.p. sf. (I 572) *their kings*
בְּזִקִּים prep.-n.m.p. (II 279) *with chains*
וְנִכְבְּדֵיהֶם conj.-Ni. ptc. m.p.-3 m.p. sf. (כָּבֵד 457) *and their nobles*
בְּכַבְלֵי בַרְזֶל prep.-n.m.p. cstr. (459)-n.m.s. (137) *with fetters of iron*

149:9

לַעֲשׂוֹת prep.-Qal inf.cstr. (עָשָׂה I 793) *to execute*
בָּהֶם prep.-3 m.p. sf. *on them*
מִשְׁפָּט n.m.s. (1048) *the judgment*
כָּתוּב Qal pass.ptc. (כָּתַב 507) *written*
הָדָר הוּא n.m.s. (214)-demons.adj. m.s. (214) *this is glory*
לְכָל־חֲסִידָיו prep.-n.m.s. cstr. (481)-adj. m.p.-3 m.s. sf. (339) *for all his faithful ones*
הַלְלוּ־יָהּ Pi. impv. 2 m.p. (הָלַל II 237)-pr.n. (219) *praise Yah*

150:1

הַלְלוּ Pi. impv. 2 m.p. (הָלַל II 237) *praise*
יָהּ pr.n. (219) *Yah*
הַלְלוּ־אֵל v.supra-n.m.s. (42) *praise God*
בְּקָדְשׁוֹ prep.-n.m.s.-3 m.s. sf. (871) *in his sanctuary*
הַלְלוּהוּ Pi. impv. 2 m.p.-3 m.s. sf. (II 237) *praise him*
בִּרְקִיעַ prep.-n.m.s. cstr. (956) *in the firmament of*
עֻזּוֹ n.m.s.-3 m.s. sf. (738) *his might*

150:2

הַלְלוּהוּ Pi. impv. 2 m.p.-3 m.s. sf. (II 237) *praise him*
בִגְבוּרֹתָיו prep.-n.f.p.-3 m.s. sf. (150) *for his mighty deeds*
הַלְלוּהוּ v.supra *praise him*
כְּרֹב prep.-n.m.s. cstr. (913) *according to the abundance of*
גֻּדְלוֹ n.m.s.-3 m.s. sf. (152) *his greatness*

150:3

הַלְלוּהוּ Pi. impv. 2 m.p.-3 m.s. sf. (II 237) *praise him*
בְּתֵקַע prep.-n.m.s. cstr. (1075) *with sound of*
שׁוֹפָר n.m.s. (1051) *trumpet*
הַלְלוּהוּ v.supra *praise him*
בְּנֵבֶל prep.-n.m.s. (614) *with lute*
וְכִנּוֹר conj.-n.m.s. (490) *and harp*

150:4

הַלְלוּהוּ Pi. impv. 2 m.p.-3 m.s. sf. (II 237) *praise him*
בְתֹף prep.-n.m.s. (1074) *with timbrel*
וּמָחוֹל conj.-n.m.s. (I 298) *and dance*
הַלְלוּהוּ v.supra *praise him*
בְּמִנִּים prep.-n.m.p. (I 577) *with strings*
וְעוּגָב conj.-n.m.s. (721) *and pipe*

150:5

הַלְלוּהוּ Pi. impv. 2 m.p.-3 m.s. sf. (II 237) *praise him*
בְּצִלְצְלֵי־ prep.-n.m.p. cstr. (852) *with cymbals of*
שָׁמַע n.m.s. paus. (1034) *sound*
הַלְלוּהוּ v.supra *praise him*
בְּצִלְצְלֵי v.supra *with cymbals of*
תְרוּעָה n.f.s. (929) *alarm*

150:6

כֹּל הַנְּשָׁמָה n.m.s. cstr. (481)-def.art.-n.f.s. (675) *everything that breathes*
תְּהַלֵּל Pi. impf. 3 f.s. (II 237) *let praise*
יָהּ pr.n. (219) *Yah*
הַלְלוּ־יָהּ Pi. impv. 2 m.p. (II 237)-pr.n. (219) *praise Yah*

Proverbs

1:1

מִשְׁלֵי n.m.p. cstr. 605) *the proverbs of*
שְׁלֹמֹה pr.n. (1024) *Solomon*
בֶן־דָּוִד n.m.s. cstr. (119)-pr.n. (187) *son of David*
מֶלֶךְ n.m.s. cstr. (I 572) *king of*
יִשְׂרָאֵל pr.n. (975) *Israel*

1:2

לָדַעַת prep.-Qal inf.cstr. (יָדַע 393) *that men may know*
חָכְמָה n.f.s. (315) *wisdom*
וּמוּסָר conj.-n.m.s. (416) *and instruction*
לְהָבִין prep.-Hi. inf.cstr. (בִּין 106) *may understand*
אִמְרֵי n.m.p. cstr. (56) *words of*
בִינָה n.f.s. (108) *insight*

1:3

לָקַחַת prep.-Qal inf.cstr. (לָקַח 542) *may receive*
מוּסַר n.m.s. cstr. (416) *instruction in*
הַשְׂכֵּל Hi. inf.abs. as subst (שָׂכַל I 968) *wise dealing*
צֶדֶק n.m.s. (841) *righteousness*
וּמִשְׁפָּט conj.-n.m.s. (1048) *and justice*
וּמֵישָׁרִים conj.-n.m.p. (449) *and equity*

1:4

לָתֵת prep.-Qal inf.cstr. (נָתַן 678) *that may be given*
לִפְתָאיִם prep.-adj. m.p. (834) *to the simple*
עָרְמָה n.f.s. (791) *prudence*
לְנַעַר prep.-n.m.s. (II 654) *to the youth*
דַּעַת n.f.s. (395) *knowledge*
וּמְזִמָּה conj.-n.f.s. (273) *and discretion*

1:5

יִשְׁמַע Qal impf. 3 m.s. (1033) *may hear*
חָכָם adj. m.s. (314) *the wise man*
וְיוֹסֶף conj.-Hi. impf. 3 m.s. apoc. (יָסַף 414) *and increase*
לֶקַח n.m.s. (544) *in learning*
וְנָבוֹן conj.-Ni. ptc. m.s. (בִּין 106) *and the man of understanding*
תַּחְבֻּלוֹת n.f.p. (287) *skill*
יִקְנֶה Qal impf. 3 m.s. (קָנָה I 888) *may acquire*

1:6

לְהָבִין prep.-Hi. inf.cstr. (בִּין 106) *to understand*
מָשָׁל n.m.s. (605) *a proverb*
וּמְלִיצָה conj.-n.f.s. (539) *and a figure*
דִּבְרֵי חֲכָמִים n.m.p. cstr. (182)-adj. m.p. (314) *the words of the wise*

וְחִידֹתָם conj.-n.f.p.-3 m.p. sf. (295) *and their riddles*

1:7

יִרְאַת יהוה n.f.s. cstr. (432)-pr.n. (217) *the fear of Yahweh*
רֵאשִׁית דָּעַת n.f.s. cstr. (912)-n.f.s. paus. (395) *the beginning of knowledge*
חָכְמָה n.f.s. (315) *wisdom*
וּמוּסָר conj.-n.m.s. (416) *and instruction*
אֱוִילִים n.m.p. (17) *fools*
בָּזוּ Qal pf. 3 c.p. (בּוּז 100) *despise*

1:8

שְׁמַע Qal impv. 2 m.s. (1033) *hear*
בְּנִי n.m.s.-1 c.s. sf. (119) *my son*
מוּסַר אָבִיךָ n.m.s. cstr. (416)-n.m.s.-2 m.s. sf. (3) *your father's instruction*
וְאַל־תִּטֹּשׁ conj.-neg.-Qal impf. 2 m.s. (נָטַשׁ 643) *and reject not*
תּוֹרַת אִמֶּךָ n.f.s. cstr. 435)-n.f.s.-2 m.s. sf. (51) *your mother's teaching*

1:9

כִּי לִוְיַת חֵן conj. (471)-n.f.s. cstr. (531)-n.m.s. (I 336) *for a fair garland*
הֵם pers.pr. 3 m.p. (241) *they (are)*
לְרֹאשֶׁךָ prep.-n.m.s.-2 m.s. sf. (910) *for your head*
וַעֲנָקִים conj.-n.m.p. (II 778) *and pendants*
לְגַרְגְּרֹתֶיךָ prep.-n.f.p.-2 m.s. sf. (176) *for your neck*

1:10

בְּנִי n.m.s.-1 c.s. sf. (119) *my son*
אִם־יְפַתּוּךָ hypoth.part. (49)-Pi. impf. 3 m.p.-2 m.s. sf. (פָּתָה 834) *if ... entice you*
חַטָּאִים adj.m.p. (308) *sinners*
אַל־תֹּבֵא neg.-Qal impf. 2 m.s. juss. (אָבָה I 2; many mss. rd. אַל־תָּאבֶה) *do not consent*

1:11

אִם־יֹאמְרוּ hypoth.part. (49)-Qal impf. 3 m.p. (55) *if they say*
לְכָה אִתָּנוּ Qal impv. 2 m.s.-vol.he (הָלַךְ 229) -prep.-1 c.p. sf. (II 85) *come with us*
נֶאֶרְבָה Qal impf. 1 c.p.-vol.he (אָרַב 70) *let us lie in wait*
לְדָם prep.-n.m.s. (196) *for blood*
נִצְפְּנָה Qal impf. 1 c.p.-vol.he (צָפַן 860) *let us ambush*
לְנָקִי prep.-adj. m.s. (667) *the innocent*
חִנָּם adv. (336) *wantonly*

1:12

נִבְלָעֵם Qal impf. 1 c.p.-3 m.p. sf. (בָּלַע 118) *let us swallow them*
כִּשְׁאוֹל prep.-n.f.s. (982) *like Sheol*
חַיִּים adj. m.p. (311) *alive*
וּתְמִימִים conj.-adj. m.p. (1071) *and whole*
כְּיוֹרְדֵי בוֹר prep.-Qal act.ptc. m.p. cstr. (יָרַד 432)-n.m.s. (92) *like those who go down to the Pit*

1:13

כָּל־הוֹן יָקָר n.m.s. cstr. (481)-n.m.s. (223)-adj. m.s. (429) *all precious goods*
נִמְצָא Qal impf. 1 c.p. (מָצָא 592) *we shall find*
נְמַלֵּא Pi. impf. 1 c.p. (מָלֵא 569) *we shall fill*
בָתֵּינוּ n.m.p.-1 c.p. sf. (108) *our houses*
שָׁלָל n.m.s. (1021) *with spoil*

1:14

גּוֹרָלְךָ n.m.s.-2 m.s. sf. (174) *your lot*
תַּפִּיל Hi. impf. 2 m.s. (נָפַל 656) *throw in*
בְּתוֹכֵנוּ prep.-n.m.s.-1 c.p. sf. (1063) *among us*
כִּיס אֶחָד n.m.s. (476)-num. (25) *one purse*
יִהְיֶה לְכֻלָּנוּ Qal impf. 3 m.s. (הָיָה 224)-prep. -n.m.s.-1 c.p. sf. (481) *we will all have*

1:15

בְּנִי n.m.s.-1 c.s. sf. (119) *my son*
אַל־תֵּלֵךְ neg.-Qal impf. 2 m.s. (הָלַךְ 229) *do not walk*
בְּדֶרֶךְ prep.-n.m.s. (202) *in the way*
אִתָּם prep.-3 m.p. sf. (II 85) *with them*
מְנַע Qal impv. 2 m.s. (מָנַע 586) *hold back*
רַגְלְךָ n.f.s.-2 m.s. sf. (919) *your foot*
מִנְּתִיבָתָם prep.-n.f.s.-3 m.p. sf. (677) *from their paths*

1:16

כִּי רַגְלֵיהֶם conj. (471)-n.f. du.-3 m.p. sf. (919) *for with their feet*
לָרַע prep.-def.art.-n.m.s. (948) *to evil*
יָרוּצוּ Qal impf. 3 m.p. (רוּץ 930) *they run*
וִימַהֲרוּ conj.-Qal impf. 3 m.p. (מָהַר I 554) *and they make haste*
לִשְׁפָּךְ־דָּם prep.-Qal inf.cstr. (שָׁפַךְ 1049)-n.m.s. (196) *to shed blood*

1:17

כִּי־חִנָּם conj. (471)-adv. (336) *for in vain*
מְזֹרָה Pu. ptc. (זָרָה 279) *is spread*

הָרָֽשֶׁת def.art.-n.f.s. paus. (440) *the net*
בְּעֵינֵי כָּל־ prep.-n.f. du. cstr. (744)-n.m.s. cstr. (481) *in the sight of any*
בַּעַל כָּנָף n.m.s. cstr. (127; some omit)-n.f.s. (489) *bird*

1:18

וְהֵם conj.-demons.adj. m.p. (241) *but these men*
לְדָמָם prep.-n.m.s.-3 m.p. sf. (196) *for their own blood*
יֶאֱרֹבוּ Qal impf. 3 m.p. (אָרַב 70) *lie in wait*
יִצְפְּנוּ Qal impf. 3 m.p. (צָפַן 860) *they set an ambush*
לְנַפְשֹׁתָם prep.-n.f.p.-3 m.p. sf. (659) *for their own lives*

1:19

כֵּן adv. (485) *such (are)*
אָרְחוֹת n.m.p. cstr. (73) *the ways*
כָּל־בֹּצֵעַ n.m.s. cstr. (481)-Qal act.ptc. (בָּצַע 130) *all who get gain*
בָּצַע n.m.s. paus. (130) *by violence*
אֶת־נֶפֶשׁ dir.obj.-n.f.s. cstr. (659) *the life of*
בְּעָלָיו n.m.p.-3 m.s. sf. (127) *of its possessors*
יִקָּח Qal impf. 3 m.s. paus. (לָקַח 542) *it takes away*

1:20

חָכְמוֹת n.f.p. (315) *wisdom*
בַּחוּץ prep.-def.art.-n.m.s. (299) *in the street*
תָּרֹנָּה Qal impf. 3 f.p. (רָנַן 943) *cries aloud*
בָּרְחֹבוֹת prep.-def.art.-n.f.p. (932) *in the markets*
תִּתֵּן Qal impf. 3 f.s. (נָתַן 678) *she raises*
קוֹלָהּ n.m.s.-3 f.s. sf. (876) *her voice*

1:21

בְּרֹאשׁ prep.-n.m.s. cstr. (910) *on the top of*
הֹמִיּוֹת Qal act.ptc. f.p. (הָמָה 242; *stirring (bustling) streets*) LXX τειχέων = חֹמוֹת *walls*
תִּקְרָא Qal impf. 3 f.s. (קָרָא 894) *she cries out*
בְּפִתְחֵי prep.-n.m.p. cstr. (835) *at the entrance of*
שְׁעָרִים בָּעִיר n.m.p.-prep.-def.art.-n.f.s. (746) *the city gates*
אֲמָרֶיהָ תֹאמֵר n.m.p.-3 f.s. sf. (56)-Qal impf. 3 f.s. (55) *she speaks (her words)*

1:22

עַד־מָתַי prep. (III 723)-adv. (607) *how long*
פְּתָיִם adj. m.p. (834) *O simple ones*
תְּאֵהֲבוּ Qal impf. 2 m.p. (אָהֵב 12) *will you love*
פֶתִי adj. m.s. (834) *being simple*

וְלֵצִים conj.-Qal act.ptc. m.p. (לִיץ 539) *and scoffers*
לָצוֹן n.m.s. (539) *in their scoffing*
חָמְדוּ Qal pf. 3 c.p. (חָמַד 326) *delight in*
לָהֶם prep.-3 m.p. sf. *(they)*
וּכְסִילִים conj.-n.m.p. (493) *and fools*
יִשְׂנְאוּ־ Qal impf. 3 m.p. (שָׂנֵא 971) *hate*
דָעַת n.f.s. paus. (395) *knowledge*

1:23

תָּשׁוּבוּ Qal impf. 2 m.p. (שׁוּב 996) *turn*
לְתוֹכַחְתִּי prep.-n.f.s.-1 c.s. sf. (407) *to my reproof*
הִנֵּה demons.part. (243) *behold*
אַבִּיעָה Hi. impf. 1 c.s.-dir.he (נָבַע 615) *I will pour out*
לָכֶם prep.-2 m.p. sf. *to you*
רוּחִי n.f.s.-1 c.s. sf. (924) *my spirit*
אוֹדִיעָה Hi. impf. 1 c.s.-dir.he (יָדַע 393) *I will make known*
דְבָרַי n.m.p.-1 c.s. sf. (182) *my words*
אֶתְכֶם dir.obj.-2 m.p. sf. *to you*

1:24

יַעַן קָרָאתִי conj. (774)-Qal pf. 1 c.s. (894) *because I have called*
וַתְּמָאֵנוּ consec.-Pi. impf. 2 m.p. (מָאֵן 549) *and you refused (to listen)*
נָטִיתִי Qal pf. 1 c.s. (נָטָה 639) *I have stretched out*
יָדִי n.f.s.-1 c.s. sf. (388) *my hand*
וְאֵין מַקְשִׁיב conj.-neg. cstr. (II 34)-Hi. ptc. (קָשַׁב 904) *and no one has heeded*

1:25

וַתִּפְרְעוּ consec.-Qal impf. 2 m.p. (פָּרַע III 828) *and you have ignored*
כָּל־עֲצָתִי n.m.s. cstr. (481)-n.f.s.-1 c.s. sf. (420) *all my counsel*
וְתוֹכַחְתִּי conj.-n.f.s.-1 c.s. sf. (407) *and my reproof*
לֹא אֲבִיתֶם neg.-Qal pf. 2 m.p. (אָבָה 2) *you would have not*

1:26

גַּם־אֲנִי adv. (168)-pers.pr. 1 c.s. (58) *I also*
בְּאֵידְכֶם prep.-n.m.s.-2 m.p. sf. (15) *at your calamity*
אֶשְׂחָק Qal impf. 1 c.s. (שָׂחַק 965) *I will laugh*
אֶלְעַג Qal impf. 1 c.s. (לָעַג 541) *I will mock*
בְּבֹא prep.-Qal inf.cstr. (בּוֹא 97) *when ...strikes*
פַחְדְּכֶם n.m.s.-2 m.p. sf. (808) *panic ... you*

1:27

בְּבֹא prep.-Qal inf.cstr. (בּוֹא 97) *when ... strikes*
כְשֹׁאָוָה prep.-n.f.s. (981) *like a storm*
פַּחְדְּכֶם n.m.s.-2 m.p. sf. (808) *panic ... you*
וְאֵידְכֶם conj.-n.m.s.-2 m.p. sf. (15) *and your calamity*
כְּסוּפָה prep.-n.f.s. (I 693) *like a whirlwind*
יֶאֱתֶה Qal impf. 3 m.s. (אָתָה 87) *comes*
בְּבֹא v.supra *when come*
עֲלֵיכֶם prep.-2 m.p. sf. *upon you*
צָרָה n.f.s. (I 865) *distress*
וְצוּקָה conj.-n.f.s. (848) *and anguish*

1:28

אָז יִקְרָאֻנְנִי adv. (23)-Qal impf. 3 m.p.-1 c.s. sf. (894 קָרָא) *then they will call upon me*
וְלֹא אֶעֱנֶה conj.-neg.-Qal impf. 1 c.s. (עָנָה I 772) *but I will not answer*
יְשַׁחֲרֻנְנִי Pi. impf. 3 m.p.-1 c.s. sf. (שָׁחַר 1007) *they will seek me diligently*
וְלֹא יִמְצָאֻנְנִי conj.-neg.-Qal impf. 3 c.p.-1 c.s. sf. (מָצָא 592) *but they will not find me*

1:29

תַּחַת prep. (1065) *because*
כִּי־שָׂנְאוּ conj. (471)-Qal pf. 3 c.p. (שָׂנֵא 971) *they hated*
דָעַת n.f.s. paus. (395) *knowledge*
וְיִרְאַת יהוה conj.-n.f.s. cstr. (432)-pr.n. (217) *and the fear of Yahweh*
לֹא בָחָרוּ neg.-Qal pf. 3 c.p. paus. (בָּחַר 103) *they did not choose*

1:30

לֹא אָבוּ neg.-Qal pf. 3 c.p. (אָבָה 2) *they would have none*
לַעֲצָתִי prep.-n.f.s.-1 c.s. sf. (420) *of my counsel*
נָאֲצוּ Qal pf. 3 c.p. (נָאַץ 610) *they despised*
כָּל־תּוֹכַחְתִּי n.m.s. cstr. (481)-n.f.s.-1 c.s. sf. (407) *all my reproof*

1:31

וְיֹאכְלוּ conj.-Qal impf. 3 m.p. (אָכַל 37) *therefore they shall eat*
מִפְּרִי דַרְכָּם prep.-n.m.s. cstr. (826)-n.m.s.-3 m.p. sf. (202) *the fruit of their way*
וּמִמֹּעֲצֹתֵיהֶם conj.-prep.-n.f.p.-3 m.p. sf. (420) *and with their own devices*
יִשְׂבָּעוּ Qal impf. 3 m.p. paus. (שָׂבַע 959) *they shall be sated*

1:32

כִּי conj. (471) *for*
מְשׁוּבַת פְּתָיִם n.f.s. cstr. (1000)-adj. m.p. (834) *(by) the turning away of the simple*
תַּהַרְגֵם Qal impf. 3 f.s.-3 m.p. sf. (הָרַג 246) *shall kill them*
וְשַׁלְוַת כְּסִילִים conj.-n.f.s. cstr. (1017)-adj. m.p. (I 493) *and the complacence of fools*
תְּאַבְּדֵם Pi. impf. 3 f.s.-3 m.p. sf. (אָבַד 1) *destroys them*

1:33

וְשֹׁמֵעַ לִי conj.-Qal act.ptc. (1033)-prep.-1 c.s. sf. *but he who listens to me*
יִשְׁכָּן־בֶּטַח Qal impf. 3 m.s. (שָׁכַן 1014)-n.m.s. as adv. (105) *will dwell secure*
וְשַׁאֲנַן conj.-Palel pf. 3 m.s. (שָׁאַן 983) *and will be at ease*
מִפַּחַד רָעָה prep.-n.m.s. cstr. (I 808)-n.f.s. (949) *without dread of evil*

2:1

בְּנִי n.m.s.-1 c.s. sf. (119) *my son*
אִם־תִּקַּח hypoth.part. (49)-Qal impf. 2 m.s. (לָקַח 542) *if you receive*
אֲמָרָי n.m.p.-1 c.s. sf. paus. (56) *my words*
וּמִצְוֹתַי conj.-n.f.p.-1 c.s. sf. (846) *and my commandments*
תִּצְפֹּן אִתָּךְ Qal impf. 2 m.s. (צָפַן 860)-prep.-2 m.s. sf. paus. (II 85) *you treasure up with you*

2:2

לְהַקְשִׁיב prep.-Hi. inf.cstr. (קָשַׁב 904) *making attentive*
לַחָכְמָה prep.-n.f.s. (315) *to wisdom*
אָזְנֶךָ n.f.s.-2 m.s. sf. (23) *your ear*
תַּטֶּה Hi. impf. 2 m.s. (נָטָה 639) *and inclining*
לִבְּךָ n.m.s.-2 m.s. sf. (524) *your heart*
לַתְּבוּנָה prep.-def.art.-n.f.s. (108) *to understanding*

2:3

כִּי אִם conj. (471)-hypoth.part. (49) *yes, if*
לַבִּינָה prep.-def.art.-n.f.s. (108) *for insight*
תִקְרָא Qal impf. 2 m.s. (קָרָא 894) *you cry out*
לַתְּבוּנָה prep.-def.art.-n.f.s. (108) *and for understanding*
תִּתֵּן קוֹלֶךָ Qal impf. 2 m.s. (נָתַן 678)-n.m.s.-2 m.s. sf. (876) *you raise your voice*

2:4

אִם־תְּבַקְשֶׁנָּה hypoth.part. (49)-Pi. impf. 2 m.s.-3 f.s. sf. (בָּקַשׁ 134) *if you seek it*
כַּכָּסֶף prep.-def.art.-n.m.s. paus. (494) *like silver*
וְכַמַּטְמוֹנִים conj.-prep.-def.art.-n.m.p. (380) *and as for hidden treasures*
תַּחְפְּשֶׂנָּה Qal impf. 2 m.s.-3 f.s. sf. (חָפַשׂ 344) *you search for it*

2:5

אָז תָּבִין adv. (23)-Qal impf. 2 m.s. (בִּין 106) *then you will understand*
יִרְאַת יהוה n.f.s. cstr. (432)-pr.n. (217) *the fear of Yahweh*
וְדַעַת אֱלֹהִים conj.-n.f.s. cstr. (395)-n.m.p. (43) *and the knowledge of God*
תִּמְצָא Qal impf. 2 m.s. (מָצָא 592) *find*

2:6

כִּי־יהוה conj. (471)-pr.n.(217) *for Yahweh*
יִתֵּן חָכְמָה Qal impf. 3 m.s. (נָתַן 678)-n.f.s. (315) *gives wisdom*
מִפִּיו prep.-n.m.s.-3 m.s. sf. (804) *from his mouth*
דַּעַת n.f.s. (395) *knowledge*
וּתְבוּנָה conj.-n.f.s. (108) *and understanding*

2:7

וְצְפֹּן conj.-Qal impv. 2 m.s. (צָפַן 860; LXX θησαυρίζει; Q יצפן Qal impf. 3 m.s.) *he stores up*
לַיְשָׁרִים prep.-def.art.-n.m.p. (449) *for the upright*
תּוּשִׁיָּה n.f.s. (444) *sound wisdom*
מָגֵן n.m.s. (171) *a shield*
לְהֹלְכֵי תֹם prep.-Qal act.ptc. m.p. cstr. (הָלַךְ 229)-n.m.s. (1070) *to those who walk in integrity*

2:8

לִנְצֹר prep.-Qal inf.cstr. (נָצַר 665) *guarding*
אָרְחוֹת מִשְׁפָּט n.m.p. cstr. (73)-n.m.s. (1048) *the paths of justice*
וְדֶרֶךְ חֲסִידָו conj.-n.m.s. cstr. (202)-adj. m.p.-3 m.s. sf. (339; Q חסידיו; LXX εὐλαβουμένων αὐτόν) *and the way of his saints*
יִשְׁמֹר Qal impf. 3 m.s. (1036) *preserving*

2:9

אָז תָּבִין adv. (23)-Qal impf. 2 m.s. (בִּין 106) *then you will understand*
צֶדֶק n.m.s. (841) *righteousness*
וּמִשְׁפָּט conj.-n.m.s. (1048) *and justice*
וּמֵישָׁרִים conj.-n.m.p. (449) *and equity*
כָּל־מַעְגַּל־טוֹב n.m.s. cstr. (481)-n.m.s. cstr. (722)-n.m.s. (III 375) *every good path*

2:10

כִּי־תָבוֹא conj. (471)-Qal impf. 3 f.s. (בּוֹא 97) *for will come*
חָכְמָה n.f.s. (315) *wisdom*
בְלִבֶּךָ prep.-n.m.s.-2 m.s. sf. paus. (524) *into your heart*
וְדַעַת conj.-n.f.s. (395) *and knowledge*
לְנַפְשְׁךָ prep.-n.f.s.-2 m.s. sf. (659) *to your soul*
יִנְעָם Qal impf. 3 m.s. (נָעֵם I 653) *will be pleasant*

2:11

מְזִמָּה n.f.s. (273) *discretion*
תִּשְׁמֹר Qal impf. 3 f.s. (שָׁמַר 1036) *will watch*
עָלֶיךָ prep.-2 m.s. sf. *over you*
תְּבוּנָה n.f.s. (108) *understanding*
תִנְצְרֶכָּה Qal impf. 3 f.s.-2 m.s. sf. (נָצַר 665) *will guard you*

2:12

לְהַצִּילְךָ prep.-Hi. inf.cstr.-2 m.s. sf. (נָצַל 664) *delivering you*
מִדֶּרֶךְ רָע prep.-n.m.s. cstr. (202)-n.m.s. paus. (II 948) *from the way of evil*
מֵאִישׁ prep.-n.m.s. (35) *from men*
מְדַבֵּר Pi. ptc. (180) *speaking*
תַּהְפֻּכוֹת n.f.p. (246) *perversity*

2:13

הַעֹזְבִים def.art.-Qal act.ptc. m.p. (עָזַב I 736) *who forsake*
אָרְחוֹת יֹשֶׁר n.m.p. cstr. (73)-n.m.s. (449) *the paths of uprightness*
לָלֶכֶת prep.-Qal inf.cstr. (הָלַךְ 229) *to walk*
בְּדַרְכֵי־חֹשֶׁךְ prep.-n.m.p. cstr. (202)-n.m.s. (365) *in the ways of darkness*

2:14

הַשְּׂמֵחִים def.art.-Qal act.ptc. m.p. (שָׂמַח 970) *who rejoice*
לַעֲשׂוֹת רָע prep.-Qal inf.cstr. (עָשָׂה I 793) -n.m.s. paus. (II 948) *in doing evil*
יָגִילוּ Qal impf. 3 m.p. (גִּיל 162) *and delight*
בְּתַהְפֻּכוֹת רָע prep.-n.f.p. cstr. (246)-v.supra *in the perverseness of evil*

2:15

אֲשֶׁר אָרְחֹתֵיהֶם rel. (81)–n.m.p.–3 m.p. sf. (73) *men whose paths*

עִקְּשִׁים adj. m.p. (786) *(are) crooked*

וּנְלוֹזִים conj.–Ni. ptc. m.p. (לוז 531) *and who are devious*

בְּמַעְגְּלוֹתָם prep.–n.m.p.–3 m.p. sf. (722) *in their ways*

2:16

לְהַצִּילְךָ prep.–Hi. inf.cstr.–2 m.s. sf. (נָצַל 664) *you will be saved*

מֵאִשָּׁה זָרָה prep.–n.f.s. (61)–Qal act.ptc. f.s. (זור I 266) *from the strange woman*

מִנָּכְרִיָּה prep.–adj. f.s. (648) *from the adventuress (foreign woman)*

אֲמָרֶיהָ n.m.p.–3 f.s. sf. (56) *her words*

הֶחֱלִיקָה Hi. pf. 3 f.s. (חָלַק II 325) *she has made smooth*

2:17

הַעֹזֶבֶת def.art.–Qal act.ptc. f.s. (עָזַב I 736) *who forsakes*

אַלּוּף adj. m.s. cstr. (I 48) *the companion of*

נְעוּרֶיהָ n.m.p.–3 f.s. sf. (655) *her youth*

וְאֶת־בְּרִית אֱלֹהֶיהָ conj.–dir.obj.–n.f.s. cstr. (136)–n.m.p.–3 f.s. sf. (43) *and the covenant of her God*

שָׁכֵחָה Qal act.ptc. f.s. paus. (שָׁכַח 1013) *she forgets*

2:18

כִּי שָׁחָה conj. (471)–Qal pf. 3 f.s. (שׁוּחַ 1001) *for ... sinks down*

אֶל־מָוֶת prep.–n.m.s. (560) *to death*

בֵּיתָהּ n.m.s.–3 f.s. sf. (108) *her house*

וְאֶל־רְפָאִים conj.–prep.–n.m.p. (I 952) *to the shades*

מַעְגְּלֹתֶיהָ n.m.p.–3 f.s. sf. (722) *her paths*

2:19

כָּל־בָּאֶיהָ n.m.s. cstr. (481)–Qal act.ptc. m.p.–3 f.s. sf. (בּוֹא 97) *all who go to her*

לֹא יְשׁוּבוּן neg.–Qal impf. 3 m.p. (שׁוּב 996) *none will come back*

וְלֹא־יַשִּׂיגוּ conj.–neg.–Hi. impf. 3 m.p. (נָשַׂג 673) *and they will not regain*

אָרְחוֹת חַיִּים n.m.p. (73)–n.m.p. (313) *the paths of life*

2:20

לְמַעַן תֵּלֵךְ conj. (775)–Qal impf. 2 m.s. (הָלַךְ 229) *so you will walk*

בְּדֶרֶךְ טוֹבִים prep.–n.m.s. cstr. (202)–adj. m.p. (II 373) *in the way of good men*

וְאָרְחוֹת צַדִּיקִים conj.–n.m.p. cstr. (73)–adj. m.p. (843) *and to the paths of the righteous*

תִּשְׁמֹר Qal impf. 2 m.s. (שָׁמַר 1036) *you will keep*

2:21

כִּי־יְשָׁרִים conj. (471)–adj. m.p. (449) *for the upright*

יִשְׁכְּנוּ־ Qal impf. 3 m.p. (שָׁכַן 1014) *will inhabit*

אָרֶץ n.f.s. paus. (75) *the land*

וּתְמִימִים conj.–adj. m.p. (1071) *and men of integrity*

יִוָּתְרוּ בָהּ Ni. impf. 3 m.p. (יָתַר 451)–prep.–3 f.s. sf. *will remain in it*

2:22

וּרְשָׁעִים conj.–adj. m.p. (957) *but the wicked*

מֵאֶרֶץ prep.–n.f.s. (75) *from the land*

יִכָּרֵתוּ Ni. impf. 3 m.p. paus. (כָּרַת 503) *will be cut off*

וּבוֹגְדִים conj.–Qal act.ptc. m.p. (בָּגַד 93) *and the treacherous*

יִסְּחוּ Qal impf. 3 m.p. (נָסַח 650) *will be rooted*

מִמֶּנָּה prep.–3 f.s. sf. *out of it*

3:1

בְּנִי n.m.s.–1 c.s. sf. (119) *my son*

תּוֹרָתִי n.f.s.–1 c.s. sf. (435) *my teaching*

אַל־תִּשְׁכָּח neg.–Qal impf. 2 m.s. paus. (שָׁכַח 1013) *do not forget*

וּמִצְוֹתַי conj.–n.f.p.–1 c.s. sf. (846) *but my commandments*

יִצֹּר לִבֶּךָ Qal impf. 3 m.s. (נָצַר I 665)–n.m.s.–2 m.s. sf. (524) *let your heart keep*

3:2

כִּי אֹרֶךְ יָמִים conj. (471)–n.m.s. cstr. (73)–n.m.p. (398) *for length of days*

וּשְׁנוֹת חַיִּים conj.–n.f.p. cstr. (1040)–n.m.p. (313) *and years of life*

וְשָׁלוֹם conj.–n.m.s. (1022) *and abundant welfare*

יוֹסִיפוּ לָךְ Hi. impf. 3 m.p. (יָסַף 414)–prep.–2 m.s. sf. paus. *will they give you*

3:3

חֶסֶד n.m.s. (338) *loyalty*

וֶאֱמֶת conj.–n.f.s. (54) *and faithfulness*

אַל־יַעַזְבֻךָ neg.-Qal impf. 3 m.s.-2 m.s. sf. (עָזַב I 736) *let not ... forsake you*
קָשְׁרֵם Qal impv. 2 m.s.-3 m.p. sf. (קָשַׁר 905) *bind them*
עַל־גַּרְגְּרוֹתֶיךָ n.f.p.-2 m.s. sf. (176) *about your neck*
כָּתְבֵם Qal impv. 2 m.s.-3 m.p. sf. (כָּתַב 507) *write them*
עַל־לוּחַ לִבֶּךָ prep.-n.m.s. cstr. (531)-n.m.s.-2 m.s. sf. paus. (524) *on the tablet of your heart*

3:4

וּמְצָא־חֵן conj.-Qal impv. 2 m.s. (מָצָא 592) -n.m.s. (336) *so you will find favor*
וְשֵׂכֶל־טוֹב conj.-n.m.s. (968)-adj. m.s. (II 373) *and good repute*
בְּעֵינֵי prep.-n.f.p. cstr. (744) *in the sight of*
אֱלֹהִים n.m.p. (43) *God*
וְאָדָם conj.-n.m.s. (9) *and man*

3:5

בְּטַח אֶל־יהוה Qal impv. 2 m.s. (בָּטַח 105)-prep. -pr.n. (217) *trust in Yahweh*
בְּכָל־לִבֶּךָ prep.-n.m.s. cstr. (481)-n.m.s.-2 m.s. sf. paus. (524) *with all your heart*
וְאֶל־בִּינָתְךָ conj.-prep.-n.f.s.-2 m.s. sf. (108) *and on your own insight*
אַל־תִּשָּׁעֵן neg.-Ni. impf. 2 m.s. (שָׁעַן 1043) *do not rely*

3:6

בְּכָל־דְּרָכֶיךָ prep.-n.m.s. cstr. (481)-n.m.p.-2 m.s. sf. (202) *in all your ways*
דָעֵהוּ Qal impv. 2 m.s.-3 m.s. sf. (יָדַע 393) *acknowledge him*
וְהוּא יְיַשֵּׁר conj.-pers.pr. 3 m.s. (214)-Pi. impf. 3 m.s. (יָשַׁר 448) *and he will make straight*
אֹרְחֹתֶיךָ n.m.p.-2 m.s. sf. (73) *your paths*

3:7

אַל־תְּהִי חָכָם neg.-Qal impf. 2 m.s. (הָיָה 224)-adj. m.s. (314) *be not wise*
בְּעֵינֶיךָ prep.-n.f.p.-2 m.s. sf. (744) *in your own eyes*
יְרָא Qal impv. 2 m.s. (יָרֵא 431) *fear*
אֶת־יהוה dir.obj.-pr.n. (217) *Yahweh*
וְסוּר conj.-Qal impv. 2 m.s. (סוּר 693) *and turn away*
מֵרָע prep.-n.m.s. (II 948) *from evil*

3:8

רִפְאוּת n.f.s. (951) *healing*
תְּהִי Qal impf. 2 m.s. (הָיָה 224) *it will be*
לְשָׁרֶּךָ n.m.s.-2 m.s. sf. (1057) *to your navel-string*
וְשִׁקּוּי conj.-n.m.s. (1052) *and refreshment*
לְעַצְמוֹתֶיךָ prep.-n.f.p.-2 m.s. sf. (I 782) *to your bones*

3:9

כַּבֵּד Pi. impv. 2 m.s. (כָּבֵד 457) *honor*
אֶת־יהוה dir.obj.-pr.n. (217) *Yahweh*
מֵהוֹנֶךָ prep.-n.m.s.-2 m.s. sf. (223) *with your substance*
וּמֵרֵאשִׁית conj.-prep.-n.f.s. cstr. (912) *and with the first fruits of*
כָּל־תְּבוּאָתֶךָ n.m.s. cstr. (481)-n.f.s.-2 m.s. sf. (100) *all your produce*

3:10

וְיִמָּלְאוּ conj.-Ni. impf. 3 m.p. (מָלֵא 569) *then will be filled*
אֲסָמֶיךָ n.m.p.-2 m.s. sf. (62) *your barns*
שָׂבָע n.m.s. (960) *with plenty*
וְתִירוֹשׁ conj.-n.m.s. (440) *and with wine*
יְקָבֶיךָ n.m.p.-2 m.s. sf. (428) *your vats*
יִפְרֹצוּ Qal impf. 3 m.p. (פָּרַץ I 829) *will be bursting*

3:11

מוּסַר יהוה n.m.s. cstr. (416)-pr.n. (217) *Yahweh's discipline*
בְּנִי n.m.s.-1 c.s. sf. (119) *my son*
אַל־תִּמְאָס neg.-Qal impf. 2 m.s. (מָאַס 549) *do not despise*
וְאַל־תָּקֹץ conj.-neg.-Qal impf. 2 m.s. juss. (קוּץ I 880) *or be not weary*
בְּתוֹכַחְתּוֹ prep.-n.f.s.-3 m.s. sf. (407) *of his reproof*

3:12

כִּי אֶת אֲשֶׁר conj. (471)-dir.obj.-rel. (81) *for whom*
יֶאֱהַב Qal impf. 3 m.s. (אָהַב 12) *he loves*
יהוה יוֹכִיחַ pr.n. (217)-Hi. impf. 3 m.s. (יָכַח 406) *Yahweh reproves*
וּכְאָב conj.-prep.-n.m.s. (3) *as a father*
אֶת־בֵּן dir.obj.-n.m.s. (119) *the son*
יִרְצֶה Qal impf. 3 m.s. (רָצָה 953) *in whom he delights*

3:13

אַשְׁרֵי אָדָם n.m.p. cstr. (80)-n.m.s. (9) *happy is the man*

מָצָא חָכְמָה Qal pf. 3 m.s. (592)-n.f.s. (315) *who finds wisdom*
וְאָדָם conj.-n.m.s. (9) *and the man*
יָפִיק תְּבוּנָה Hi. impf. 3 m.s. (פּוּק II 807)-n.f.s. (108) *who gets understanding*

3:14

כִּי טוֹב conj. (471)-adj. m.s. (II 373) *for is better*
סַחְרָהּ n.m.s.-3 f.s. sf. (695) *the gain from it*
מִסְּחַר־כֶּסֶף prep.-n.m.s. cstr. (695)-n.m.s. paus. (494) *than gain from silver*
וּמֵחָרוּץ conj.-prep.-n.m.s. (359) *than gold*
תְּבוּאָתָהּ n.f.s.-3 f.s. sf. (100) *its profit*

3:15

יְקָרָה הִיא adj. f.s. (יָקָר 429)-pers.pr. 3 f.s. (214) *she is more precious*
מִפְּנִיִּים prep.-n.f.p. (819) *than jewels*
וְכָל־חֲפָצֶיךָ conj.-n.m.s. cstr. (481)-n.m.p.-2 m.s. sf. (343) *and all things to be desired*
לֹא יִשְׁווּ־בָהּ neg.-Qal impf. 3 m.p. (שָׁוָה I 1000)-prep.-3 f.s. sf. *cannot compare with her*

3:16

אֹרֶךְ יָמִים n.m.s. cstr. (73)-n.m.p. (398) *long life*
בִּימִינָהּ prep.-n.f.s.-3 f.s. sf. (I 411) *in her right hand*
בִּשְׂמֹאולָהּ prep.-n.m.s.-3 f.s. sf. (969) *in her left hand*
עֹשֶׁר n.m.s. (799) *riches*
וְכָבוֹד conj.-n.m.s. (II 458) *and honor*

3:17

דְּרָכֶיהָ n.m.p.-3 f.s. sf. (202) *her ways*
דַרְכֵי־נֹעַם n.m.p. cstr. (202)-n.m.s. (653) *ways of pleasantness*
וְכָל־נְתִיבוֹתֶיהָ conj.-n.m.s. cstr. (481)-n.f.p.-3 f.s. sf. (677) *and all her paths*
שָׁלוֹם n.m.s. (1022) *peace*

3:18

עֵץ־חַיִּים n.m.s. cstr. (781)-n.m.p. (313) *a tree of life*
הִיא pers.pr. 3 f.s. (214) *she (is)*
לַמַּחֲזִיקִים בָּהּ prep.-def.art.-Hi. ptc. m.p. (חָזַק 304)-prep.-3 f.s. sf. *to those who lay hold of her*
וְתֹמְכֶיהָ conj.-Qal act.ptc. m.p.-3 f.s. sf. (תָּמַךְ 1069) *those who hold her fast*
מְאֻשָּׁר Pu. ptc. (אָשַׁר 80) *are called happy*

3:19

יהוה pr.n. (217) *Yahweh*
בְּחָכְמָה prep.-n.f.s. (315) *by wisdom*
יָסַד־אָרֶץ Qal pf. 3 m.s. (413)-n.f.s. paus. (75) *founded the earth*
כּוֹנֵן Polel pf. 3 m.s. (כּוּן I 465) *he established*
שָׁמַיִם n.m. du. (1029) *the heavens*
בִּתְבוּנָה prep.-n.f.s. (108) *by understanding*

3:20

בְּדַעְתּוֹ prep.-n.f.s.-3 m.s. sf. (395) *by his knowledge*
תְּהוֹמוֹת n.f.p. (1062) *the deeps*
נִבְקָעוּ Ni. pf. 3 c.p. (בָּקַע 131) *broke forth*
וּשְׁחָקִים conj.-n.m.p. (1007) *and the clouds*
יִרְעֲפוּ־טָל Qal impf. 3 m.p. (רָעַף 950)-n.m.s. paus. (378) *drop down the dew*

3:21

בְּנִי n.m.s.-1 c.s. sf. (119) *my son*
אַל־יָלֻזוּ neg.-Qal impf. 3 m.p. (לוּז 531) *let them not depart*
מֵעֵינֶיךָ prep.-n.f.p.-2 m.s. sf. (744) *from your sight*
נְצֹר Qal impv. 2 m.s. (נָצַר 665) *keep*
תֻּשִׁיָּה n.f.s. (444) *sound wisdom*
וּמְזִמָּה conj.-n.f.s. (273) *and discretion*

3:22

וְיִהְיוּ חַיִּים conj.-Qal impf. 3 m.p. (הָיָה 224) -n.m.p. (313) *and they will be life*
לְנַפְשֶׁךָ prep.-n.f.s.-2 m.s. sf. (659) *for your soul*
וְחֵן conj.-n.m.s. (336) *and adornment*
לְגַרְגְּרֹתֶיךָ prep.-n.f.p.-2 m.s. sf. (176) *for your neck*

3:23

אָז תֵּלֵךְ adv. (23)-Qal impf. 2 m.s. (הָלַךְ 229) *then you will walk*
לָבֶטַח prep.-n.m.s. (I 105) *securely*
דַּרְכֶּךָ n.m.s.-2 m.s. sf. paus. (202) *on your way*
וְרַגְלְךָ conj.-n.f.s.-2 m.s. sf. (919) *and your foot*
לֹא תִגּוֹף neg.-Qal impf. 2 m.s. (נָגַף 619) *will not stumble*

3:24

אִם־תִּשְׁכַּב hypoth.part. (49)-Qal impf. 2 m.s. (1011 שָׁכַב) *if you lie down*
לֹא תִפְחָד neg.-Qal impf. 2 m.s. (פָּחַד 808) *you will not be afraid*
וְשָׁכַבְתָּ conj.-Qal pf. 2 m.s. (שָׁכַב 1011) *when you lie down*

וְעָרְבָה conj.-Qal pf. 3 f.s. (עָרֵב III 787) *and will be sweet*
שְׁנָתֶךָ n.f.s.-2 m.s. sf. (446) *your sleep*

3:25

אַל־תִּירָא neg.-Qal impf. 2 m.s. (יָרֵא 431) *do not be afraid*
מִפַּחַד פִּתְאֹם prep.-n.m.s. cstr. (808)-subst. (837) *of sudden panic*
וּמִשֹּׁאַת רְשָׁעִים conj.-prep.-n.f.s. cstr. (996)-adj. m.p. (957) *or of the ruin of the wicked*
כִּי תָבֹא conj. (471)-Qal impf. 3 f.s. (בּוֹא 97) *when it comes*

3:26

כִּי־יהוה conj. (471)-pr.n. (217) *for Yahweh*
יִהְיֶה Qal impf. 3 m.s. (הָיָה 224) *will be*
בְכִסְלֶךָ prep.-n.m.s.-2 m.s. sf. (492) *your confidence*
וְשָׁמַר conj.-Qal pf. 3 m.s. (1036) *and will keep*
רַגְלְךָ n.f.s.-2 m.s. sf. (919) *your foot*
מִלָּכֶד prep.-n.m.s. paus. (540) *from being caught*

3:27

אַל־תִּמְנַע־טוֹב neg.-Qal impf. 2 m.s. (מָנַע 586)-n.m.s. (III 375) *do not withhold good*
מִבְּעָלָיו prep.-n.m.p.-3 m.s. sf. (I 127) *from those to whom it is due*
בִּהְיוֹת prep.-Qal inf.cstr. (הָיָה 224) *when it is*
לְאֵל יָדֶיךָ prep.-n.m.s. cstr. (43)-n.f.s.-2 m.s. sf. (388) *in the power of your hand*
לַעֲשׂוֹת prep.-Qal inf.cstr. (עָשָׂה I 793) *to do*

3:28

אַל־תֹּאמַר neg.-Qal impf. 2 m.s. (אָמַר 55) *do not say*
לְרֵעֶיךָ prep.-n.m.s.-2 m.s. sf. (945) *to your neighbor*
לֵךְ Qal impv. 2 m.s. (הָלַךְ 229) *go*
וָשׁוּב conj.-Qal impv. 2 m.s. (שׁוּב 996) *and come again*
וּמָחָר conj.-adv. (563) *and tomorrow*
אֶתֵּן Qal impf. 1 c.s. (נָתַן 678) *I will give*
וְיֵשׁ אִתָּךְ conj.-subst. (441)-prep.-2 m.s. sf. paus. (II 85) *when you have it with you*

3:29

אַל־תַּחֲרֹשׁ neg.-Qal impf. 2 m.s. (חָרַשׁ I 360) *do not plan*
עַל־רֵעֲךָ prep.-n.m.s.-2 m.s. sf. (945) *against your neighbor*
רָעָה n.f.s. (949) *evil*

וְהוּא־יוֹשֵׁב conj.-pers.pr. 3 m.s. (214)-Qal act.ptc. (יָשַׁב 442) *who dwells*
לָבֶטַח prep.-n.m.s. (105) *trustingly*
אִתָּךְ prep.-2 m.s. sf. paus. (II 85) *beside you*

3:30

אַל־תָּרוֹב neg.-Qal impf. 2 m.s. (רִיב 936) *do not contend*
עִם־אָדָם prep. (767)-n.m.s. (9) *with a man*
חִנָּם adv. (336) *for no reason*
אִם־לֹא גְמָלְךָ hypoth.part. (49)-neg.-Qal pf. 3 m.s.-2 m.s. sf. (גָּמַל 168) *when he has done you no*
רָעָה n.f.s. (949) *harm*

3:31

אַל־תְּקַנֵּא neg.-Pi. impf. 2 m.s. (קָנָא 888) *do not envy*
בְּאִישׁ חָמָס prep.-n.m.s. cstr. (35)-n.m.s. (329) *a man of violence*
וְאַל־תִּבְחַר conj.-neg.-Qal impf. 2 m.s. (בָּחַר 103) *and do not choose*
בְּכָל־דְּרָכָיו prep.-n.m.s. cstr. (481)-n.m.p.-3 m.s. sf. (202) *any of his ways*

3:32

כִּי תוֹעֲבַת conj. (481)-n.f.s. cstr. (1072) *for an abomination to*
יהוה pr.n. (217) *Yahweh*
נָלוֹז Ni. ptc. (לוּז 531) *the perverse man*
וְאֶת־יְשָׁרִים conj.-dir.obj.-adj. m.p. (449) *with the upright*
סוֹדוֹ n.m.s.-3 m.s. sf. (691) *is his intimacy*

3:33

מְאֵרַת יהוה n.f.s. cstr. (76)-pr.n. (217) *Yahweh's curse*
בְּבֵית רָשָׁע prep.-n.m.s. cstr. (108)-adj. m.s. (957) *on the house of the wicked*
וּנְוֵה צַדִּיקִים conj.-n.m.s. cstr. (I 627)-adj. m.p. (843) *but the abode of the righteous*
יְבָרֵךְ Pi. impf. 3 m.s. (בָּרַךְ 138) *he blesses*

3:34

אִם־לַלֵּצִים hypoth.part. (49)-prep.-def.art.-Qal act.ptc. m.p. (לִיץ 539) *toward the scorners*
הוּא־יָלִיץ pers.pr. 3 m.s. (214)-Qal impf. 3 m.s. (539 לִיץ) *he is scornful*
וְלַעֲנָיִים conj.-prep.-def.art.-adj. m.p. (776) *but to the humble*
יִתֶּן־חֵן Qal impf. 3 m.s. (נָתַן 678)-n.m.s. (336) *he shows favor*

3:35

כָּבוֹד n.m.s. (458) *honor*
חֲכָמִים adj. m.p. (314) *the wise*
יִנְחָלוּ Qal impf. 3 m.p. paus. (נָחַל 635) *will inherit*
וּכְסִילִים conj.-n.m.p. (493) *but fools*
מֵרִים Hi. ptc. (רום 926) *get (exalt)*
קָלוֹן n.m.s. (885) *disgrace*

4:1

שִׁמְעוּ Qal impv. 2 m.p. (1033) *hear*
בָנִים n.m.p. (119) *O sons*
מוּסַר אָב n.m.s. cstr. (416)-n.m.s. (3) *a father's instruction*
וְהַקְשִׁיבוּ conj.-Hi. impv. 2 m.p. (קָשַׁב 904) *and be attentive*
לָדַעַת prep.-Qal inf.cstr. (יָדַע 393) *that you may gain (know)*
בִּינָה n.f.s. (108) *insight*

4:2

כִּי לֶקַח טוֹב conj. (471)-n.m.s. (544)-adj. m.s. (II 373) *for good precepts*
נָתַתִּי לָכֶם Qal pf. 1 c.s. (נָתַן 678)-prep.-2 m.p. sf. *I give you*
תּוֹרָתִי n.f.s.-1 c.s. sf. (435) *my teaching*
אַל־תַּעֲזֹבוּ neg.-Qal impf. 2 m.p. (עָזַב I 736) *do not forsake*

4:3

כִּי־בֵן conj. (471)-n.m.s. (119) *when a son*
הָיִיתִי Qal pf. 1 c.s. (הָיָה 224) *I was*
לְאָבִי prep.-n.m.s.-1 c.s. sf. (3) *with my father*
רַךְ וְיָחִיד adj. m.s. (940)-conj.-adj. m.s. (402) *tender and the only one*
לִפְנֵי אִמִּי prep.-n.m.p. cstr. (815)-n.f.s.-1 c.s. sf. (51) *in the sight of my mother*

4:4

וַיֹּרֵנִי consec.-Hi. impf. 3 m.s.-1 c.s. sf. (יָרָה 434) *and he taught me*
וַיֹּאמֶר לִי consec.-Qal impf. 3 m.s. (אָמַר 55) -prep.-1 c.s. sf. *and said to me*
יִתְמָךְ־ Qal impf. 3 m.s. (תָּמַךְ 1069) *let ... hold fast*
דְּבָרַי n.m.p.-1 c.s. sf. (182) *my words*
לִבֶּךָ n.m.s.-2 m.s. sf. (524) *your heart*
שְׁמֹר מִצְוֹתַי Qal impv. 2 m.s. (1036)-n.f.p.-1 c.s. sf. (846) *keep my commandments*
וֶחְיֵה conj.-Qal impv. 2 m.s. (חָיָה 310) *and live*

4:5

קְנֵה חָכְמָה Qal impv. 2 m.s. (קָנָה 888)-n.f.s. (315) *get wisdom*
קְנֵה בִינָה v.supra-n.f.s. (108) *get insight*
אַל־תִּשְׁכַּח neg.-Qal impf. 2 m.s. (שָׁכַח 1013) *do not forget*
וְאַל־תֵּט conj.-neg.-Qal impf. 2 m.s. juss. (נָטָה 639) *and do not turn away*
מֵאִמְרֵי־פִי prep.-n.m.p. cstr. (56)-n.m.s.-1 c.s. sf. (804) *from the words of my mouth*

4:6

אַל־תַּעַזְבֶהָ neg.-Qal impf. 2 m.s.-3 f.s. sf. (עָזַב I 736) *do not forsake her*
וְתִשְׁמְרֶךָּ conj.-Qal impf. 3 f.s.-2 m.s. sf. (שָׁמַר 1036) *and she will keep you*
אֱהָבֶהָ Qal impv. 2 m.s.-3 f.s. sf. (אָהַב 12) *love her*
וְתִצְּרֶךָּ conj.-Qal impf. 3 f.s.-2 m.s. sf. (נָצַר 665) *and she will guard you*

4:7

רֵאשִׁית חָכְמָה n.f.s. cstr. (912)-n.f.s. (315) *the beginning of wisdom*
קְנֵה חָכְמָה Qal impv. 2 m.s. (קָנָה 888)-n.f.s. (315) *get wisdom*
וּבְכָל־קִנְיָנְךָ conj.-prep.-n.m.s. cstr. (481)-n.m.s.-2 m.s. sf. (889) *and whatever you get*
קְנֵה בִינָה v.supra-n.f.s. (108) *get insight*

4:8

סַלְסְלֶהָ Pilpel impv. 2 m.s.-3 f.s. sf. (סָלַל 699) *exalt her*
וּתְרוֹמְמֶךָּ conj.-Polel impf. 3 f.s.-2 m.s. sf. (רום 926) *and she will exalt you*
תְּכַבֵּדְךָ Pi. impf. 3 f.s.-2 m.s. sf. (כָּבֵד 457) *she will honor you*
כִּי תְחַבְּקֶנָּה conj. (471)-Pi. impf. 2 m.s.-3 f.s. sf. (חָבַק 287) *if you embrace her*

4:9

תִּתֵּן Qal impf. 3 f.s. (נָתַן 678) *she will place*
לְרֹאשְׁךָ prep.-n.m.s.-2 m.s. sf. (910) *on your head*
לִוְיַת־חֵן n.f.s. cstr. (531)-n.m.s. (336) *a fair garland*
עֲטֶרֶת תִּפְאֶרֶת n.f.s. cstr. (742)-n.f.s. (802) *a beautiful crown*
תְּמַגְּנֶךָּ Pi. impf. 3 f.s.-2 m.s. sf. (מָגַן 171) *she will bestow on you*

4:10

שְׁמַע בְּנִי Qal impv. 2 m.s. (1033)-n.m.s.-1 c.s. sf. (119) *hear, my son*

וְקַח אֲמָרָי conj.-Qal impv. 2 m.s. (לָקַח 542) -n.m.p.-1 c.s. sf. (56) *and accept my words*

וְיִרְבּוּ לְךָ conj.-Qal impf. 3 m.p. (רָבָה I 915) -prep.-2 m.s. sf. *that may be many for you*

שְׁנוֹת חַיִּים n.f.p. cstr. (1040)-n.m.p. (313) *the years of life*

4:11

בְּדֶרֶךְ חָכְמָה prep.-n.m.s. cstr. (202)-n.f.s. (315) *in the way of wisdom*

הֹרֵתִיךָ Hi. pf. 1 c.s.-2 m.s. sf. (יָרָה 434) *I have taught you*

הִדְרַכְתִּיךָ Hi. pf. 1 c.s.-2 m.s. sf. (דָּרַךְ 201) *I have led you*

בְּמַעְגְּלֵי־יֹשֶׁר prep.-n.m.p. cstr. (722)-n.m.s. (449) *in the paths of uprightness*

4:12

בְּלֶכְתְּךָ neg.-Qal inf.cstr.-2 m.s. sf. (הָלַךְ 229) *when you walk*

לֹא־יֵצַר neg.-Qal impf. 3 m.s. (צָרַר I 864B) *will not be hampered*

צַעֲדֶךָ n.m.s.-2 m.s. sf. (857) *your step*

וְאִם־תָּרוּץ conj.-hypoth.part. (49)-Qal impf. 2 m.s. (רוּץ 930) *and if you run*

לֹא תִכָּשֵׁל neg.-Ni. impf. 2 m.s. (כָּשַׁל 505) *you will not stumble*

4:13

הַחֲזֵק Hi. impv. 2 m.s. (חָזַק 304) *keep hold*

בַּמּוּסָר prep.-def.art.-n.m.s. (416) *of instruction*

אַל־תֶּרֶף neg.-Hi. impf. 2 m.s. juss. (רָפָה 951) *do not let go*

נִצְּרֶהָ Qal impv. 2 m.s.-3 f.s. sf. (נָצַר I 665) *guard her*

כִּי־הִיא חַיֶּיךָ conj. (471)-pers.pr. 3 f.s. (214) -n.m.p.-2 m.s. sf. (313) *for she is your life*

4:14

בְּאֹרַח רְשָׁעִים prep.-n.m.s. cstr. (73)-adj. m.p. (957) *the path of the wicked*

אַל־תָּבֹא neg.-Qal impf. 2 m.s. (בּוֹא 97) *do not enter*

וְאַל־תְּאַשֵּׁר conj.-neg.-Pi. impf. 2 m.s. (אָשַׁר 80) *and do not walk*

בְּדֶרֶךְ רָעִים prep.-n.m.s. cstr. (202)-adj. m.p. (948) *in the way of evil men*

4:15

פְּרָעֵהוּ Qal impv. 2 m.s.-3 m.s. sf. (פָּרַע III 828) *avoid it*

אַל־תַּעֲבָר־בּוֹ neg.-Qal impf. 2 m.s. (716)-prep.-3 m.s. sf. *do not go on it*

שְׂטֵה מֵעָלָיו Qal impv. 2 m.s. (שָׂטָה 966)-prep. -prep.-3 m.s. sf. *turn away from it*

וַעֲבוֹר conj.-Qal impv. 2 m.s. (716) *and pass on*

4:16

כִּי לֹא יִשְׁנוּ conj. (471)-neg.-Qal impf. 3 m.p. (445 יָשֵׁן) *for they cannot sleep*

אִם־לֹא יָרֵעוּ hypoth.part. (49)-neg.-Hi. impf. 3 m.p. (רָעַע 949) *unless they have done wrong*

וְנִגְזְלָה שְׁנָתָם conj.-Ni. pf. 3 f.s. (גָּזַל 159)-n.f.s.-3 m.p. sf. (446) *they are robbed of sleep*

אִם־לֹא יַכְשׁוֹלוּ v.supra-Hi. impf. 3 m.p. (כָּשַׁל 505) *unless they have made some one stumble*

4:17

כִּי לָחֲמוּ conj. (471)-Qal pf. 3 c.p. (לָחַם II 536) *for they eat*

לֶחֶם רֶשַׁע n.m.s. cstr. (536)-n.m.s. (957) *the bread of wickedness*

וְיֵין חֲמָסִים conj.-n.m.s. cstr. (406)-n.m.p. (329) *and the wine of violence*

יִשְׁתּוּ Qal impf. 3 m.p. (שָׁתָה 1059) *they drink*

4:18

וְאֹרַח צַדִּיקִים conj.-n.m.s. cstr. (73)-adj. m.p. (843) *but the path of the righteous*

כְּאוֹר נֹגַהּ prep.-n.m.s. cstr. (21)-n.f.s. (618) *is like the light of brightness*

הוֹלֵךְ וָאוֹר Qal act.ptc. (הָלַךְ 229)-conj.-Qal act.ptc. (אוֹר 21; GK 72R) *which shines brighter and brighter*

עַד־נְכוֹן הַיּוֹם prep. (III 723)-Ni. ptc. cstr. (כּוּן I 465)-def.art.-n.m.s. (398) *until full day*

4:19

דֶּרֶךְ רְשָׁעִים n.m.s. cstr. (202)-adj. m.p. (957) *the way of the wicked*

כָּאֲפֵלָה prep.-def.art.-n.f.s. (66) *is like deep darkness*

לֹא יָדְעוּ neg.-Qal pf. 3 c.p. (יָדַע 393) *they do not know*

בַּמֶּה יִכָּשֵׁלוּ prep.-def.art.-interr. (552)-Ni. impf. 3 m.p. paus. (כָּשַׁל 505) *over what they stumble*

4:20

בְּנִי n.m.s.-1 c.s. sf. (119) *my son*
לִדְבָרַי prep.-n.m.p.-1 c.s. sf. (182) *to my words*
הַקְשִׁיבָה Hi. impv. 2 m.s.-vol.he (קָשַׁב 904) *be attentive*
לַאֲמָרַי prep.-n.m.p.-1 c.s. sf. (56) *to my sayings*
הַט־אָזְנֶךָ Hi. impv. 2 m.s. (נָטָה 639)-n.f.s.-2 m.s. sf. (23) *incline your ear*

4:21

אַל־יַלִּיזוּ neg.-Hi. impf. 3 m.p. (לוז 531; GK 72ee) *let them not escape*
מֵעֵינֶיךָ prep.-n.f.p.-2 m.s. sf. (744) *from your sight*
שָׁמְרֵם Qal impv. 2 m.s.-3 m.p. sf. (שָׁמַר 1036) *keep them*
בְּתוֹךְ לְבָבֶךָ prep.-n.m.s. cstr. (1063)-n.m.s.-2 m.s. sf. (524) *within your heart*

4:22

כִּי־חַיִּים הֵם conj. (471)-n.m.p. (313)-pers.pr. 3 m.p. (241) *for they are life*
לְמֹצְאֵיהֶם prep.-Qal act.ptc. m.p.-3 m.p. sf. (מָצָא 592) *to him who finds them*
וּלְכָל־בְּשָׂרוֹ conj.-prep.-n.m.s. cstr. (481)-n.m.s.-3 m.s. sf. (142) *and to all his flesh*
מַרְפֵּא n.m.s. (951) *healing*

4:23

מִכָּל־מִשְׁמָר prep.-n.m.s. cstr. (481)-n.m.s. (1038) *with all vigilance*
נְצֹר לִבֶּךָ Qal impv. 2 m.s. (נָצַר 665)-n.m.s.-2 m.s. sf. (524) *keep your heart*
כִּי־מִמֶּנּוּ conj. (471)-prep.-3 m.s. sf. *for from it*
תּוֹצְאוֹת n.f.p. cstr. (426) *sources of*
חַיִּים n.m.p. (313) *life*

4:24

הָסֵר מִמְּךָ Hi. impv. 2 m.s. (סוּר 693)-prep.-2 m.s. sf. *put away from you*
עִקְּשׁוּת פֶּה n.f.s. cstr. (786)-n.m.s. (804) *crooked speech*
וּלְזוּת שְׂפָתַיִם conj.-n.f.s. cstr. (631)-n.f. du. (973) *and devious talk*
הַרְחֵק Hi. impv. 2 m.s. (רָחַק 934) *put far*
מִמֶּךָּ prep.-2 m.s. sf. *from you*

4:25

עֵינֶיךָ n.f.p.-2 m.s. sf. (744) *your eyes*
לְנֹכַח prep.-adv. (647) *directly forward*
יַבִּיטוּ Hi. impf. 3 m.p. (נָבַט 613) *let ... look*
וְעַפְעַפֶּיךָ conj.-n.m.p.-2 m.s. sf. (733) *and your gaze*
יַיְשִׁרוּ Hi. impf. 3 m.p. (יָשַׁר 448) *be straight*
נֶגְדֶּךָ prep.-2 m.s. sf. (617) *before you*

4:26

פַּלֵּס Pi. impv. 2 m.s. (פָּלַס 814) *make level*
מַעְגַּל רַגְלֶךָ n.m.s. cstr. (722)-n.f.s.-2 m.s. sf. (919) *the path of your feet*
וְכָל־דְּרָכֶיךָ conj.-n.m.s. cstr. (481)-n.m.p.-2 m.s. sf. (202) *then all your ways*
יִכֹּנוּ Ni. impf. 3 m.p. (כּוּן I 465) *will be sure*

4:27

אַל־תֵּט־יָמִין neg.-Qal impf. 2 m.s. juss. (נָטָה 639)-n.f.s. (411) *do not swerve to the right*
וּשְׂמֹאול conj.-n.m.s. (969) *or to the left*
הָסֵר רַגְלְךָ Hi. impv. 2 m.s. (סוּר 693)-n.f.s.-2 m.s. sf. (919) *turn your foot away*
מֵרָע prep.-n.m.s. paus. (948) *from evil*

5:1

בְּנִי n.m.s.-1 c.s. sf. (119) *my son*
לְחָכְמָתִי prep.-n.f.s.-1 c.s. sf. (315) *to my wisdom*
הַקְשִׁיבָה Hi. impv. 2 m.s.-vol.he (קָשַׁב 904) *be attentive*
לִתְבוּנָתִי prep.-n.f.s.-1 c.s. sf. (108) *to my understanding*
הַט־אָזְנֶךָ Hi. impv. 2 m.s. (נָטָה 639)-n.f.s.-2 m.s. sf. (23) *incline your ear*

5:2

לִשְׁמֹר prep.-Qal inf.cstr. (1036) *that you may keep*
מְזִמּוֹת n.f.p. (273) *discretion*
וְדַעַת conj.-n.f.s. (395) *and knowledge*
שְׂפָתֶיךָ n.f.p.-2 m.s. sf. (973) *your lips*
יִנְצֹרוּ Qal impf. 3 m.p. paus. (נָצַר 665) *may guard*

5:3

כִּי נֹפֶת conj. (471)-n.m.s. (661) *for honey*
תִּטֹּפְנָה Qal impf. 3 f.p. (נָטַף 642) *drip*
שִׂפְתֵי זָרָה n.f.p. cstr. (973)-Qal act.ptc. f.s. (זוּר I 266) *the lips of a loose woman*
וְחָלָק conj.-adj. m.s. (325) *and is smooth(er)*
מִשֶּׁמֶן prep.-n.m.s. (1032) *than oil*
חִכָּהּ n.m.s.-3 f.s. sf. (335) *her palate*

5:4

וְאַחֲרִיתָהּ conj.-n.f.s.-3 f.s. sf. (31) *but in the end*
מָרָה adj. f.s. (I 600) *she is bitter*

כַּלַּעֲנָה prep.-def.art.-n.f.s. (542) *as wormwood*
חַדָּה adj. f.s. (II 292) *sharp*
כְּחֶרֶב פִּיּוֹת prep.-n.f.s. cstr. (352)-n.m.p. (804) *as a two-edged sword*

5:5

רַגְלֶיהָ n.f.p.-3 f.s. sf. (919) *her feet*
יֹרְדוֹת Qal act.ptc. f.p. (יָרַד 432) *go down*
מָוֶת n.m.s. paus. (560) *to death*
שְׁאוֹל n.f.s. (982) *to Sheol*
צְעָדֶיהָ n.m.p.-3 f.s. sf. (857) *her steps*
יִתְמֹכוּ Qal impf. 3 m.p. paus. (תָּמַךְ 1069) *follow*

5:6

אֹרַח חַיִּים n.m.s. cstr. (73)-n.m.p. (313) *the path of life*
פֶּן־תְּפַלֵּס conj. (814)-Pi. impf. 3 f.s. (פָּלַס 814) *lest she make level*
נָעוּ מַעְגְּלֹתֶיהָ Qal pf. 3 c.p. (נוּעַ 631)-n.m.p.-3 f.s. sf. (722) *her ways wander*
לֹא תֵדָע neg.-Qal impf. 3 f.s. (יָדַע 393) *she does not know (it)*

5:7

וְעַתָּה conj.-adv. (773) *and now*
בָנִים n.m.p. (119) *O sons*
שִׁמְעוּ־לִי Qal impv. 2 m.s. (1033)-prep.-1 c.s. sf. *listen to me*
וְאַל־תָּסוּרוּ conj.-neg.-Qal impf. 2 m.p. (סוּר 693) *and do not depart*
מֵאִמְרֵי־פִי prep.-n.m.p. cstr. (56)-n.m.s.-1 c.s. sf. (804) *from the words of my mouth*

5:8

הַרְחֵק Hi. impv. 2 m.s. (רָחַק 934) *keep far*
מֵעָלֶיהָ prep.-prep.-3 f.s. sf. *from her*
דַּרְכֶּךָ n.m.s.-2 m.s. sf. (202) *your way*
וְאַל־תִּקְרַב conj.-neg.-Qal impf. 2 m.s. (קָרַב 897) *and do not go near*
אֶל־פֶּתַח בֵּיתָהּ prep.-n.m.s. cstr. (835)-n.m.s.-3 f.s. sf. (108) *the door of her house*

5:9

פֶּן־תִּתֵּן conj. (814)-Qal impf. 2 m.s. (נָתַן 678) *lest you give*
לַאֲחֵרִים prep.-adj. m.p. (I 29) *to others*
הוֹדֶךָ n.m.s.-2 m.s. sf. (I 217) *your honor*
וּשְׁנֹתֶיךָ conj.-n.f.p.-2 m.s. sf. (1040) *and your years*
לְאַכְזָרִי prep.-adj. m.s. (470) *to the merciless*

5:10

פֶּן־יִשְׂבְּעוּ conj. (814)-Qal impf. 3 m.p. (שָׂבַע 959) *lest ... take their fill*
זָרִים Qal act.ptc. m.p. (זוּר I 266) *strangers*
כֹּחֶךָ n.m.s.-2 m.s. sf. (470) *of your strength*
וַעֲצָבֶיךָ conj.-n.m.p.-2 m.s. sf. (I 780) *and your labors*
בְּבֵית נָכְרִי prep.-n.m.s. cstr. (108)-adj. m.s. (648) *to the house of an alien*

5:11

וְנָהַמְתָּ conj.-Qal pf. 2 m.s. (נָהַם 625) *and you groan*
בְאַחֲרִיתֶךָ prep.-n.f.s.-2 m.s. sf. (31) *at the end of your life*
בִּכְלוֹת prep.-Qal inf.cstr. (כָּלָה I 477) *when are consumed*
בְּשָׂרְךָ n.m.s.-2 m.s. sf. (142) *your flesh*
וּשְׁאֵרֶךָ conj.-n.m.s.-2 m.s. sf. (984) *and your body*

5:12

וְאָמַרְתָּ conj.-Qal pf. 2 m.s. (55) *and you say*
אֵיךְ שָׂנֵאתִי interr.adv. (32)-Qal pf. 1 c.s. (שָׂנֵא 971) *how I hated*
מוּסָר n.m.s. (416) *discipline*
וְתוֹכַחַת conj.-n.f.s. (407) *and reproof*
נָאַץ לִבִּי Qal pf. 3 m.s. (610)-n.m.s.-1 c.s. sf. (514) *my heart despised*

5:13

וְלֹא־שָׁמַעְתִּי conj.-neg.-Qal pf. 1 c.s. (שָׁמַע 1033) *and I did not listen*
בְּקוֹל מוֹרָי prep.-n.m.s. cstr. (876)-n.m.p.-1 c.s. sf. paus. (435) *to the voice of my teachers*
וְלִמְלַמְּדַי conj.-prep.-Pi. ptc. m.p.-1 c.s. sf. (לָמַד 540) *or to my instructors*
לֹא־הִטִּיתִי אָזְנִי neg.-Hi. pf. 1 c.s. (נָטָה 639) -n.f.s.-1 c.s. sf. (23) *I did not incline my ear*

5:14

כִּמְעַט prep.-subst. (589) *almost*
הָיִיתִי Qal pf. 1 c.s. (הָיָה 224) *I was*
בְכָל־רָע prep.-n.m.s. cstr. (481)-n.m.s. paus. (948) *in utter ruin*
בְּתוֹךְ קָהָל prep.-n.m.s. cstr. (1063)-n.m.s. (874) *in the assembly*
וְעֵדָה conj.-n.f.s. (417) *and congregation*

5:15

שְׁתֵה־מַיִם Qal impv. 2 m.s. (שָׁתָה 1059)-n.m.p. (565) *drink water*

מִבּוֹרֶךָ prep.-n.m.s.-2 m.s. sf. paus. (92) *from your own cistern*
וְנֹזְלִים conj.-Qal act.ptc. m.p. (נָזַל 633) *flowing water*
מִתּוֹךְ בְּאֵרֶךָ prep.-n.m.s.-2 m.s. sf. (1063) -n.f.s.-2 m.s. sf. (91) *from your own well*

5:16

יָפוּצוּ Qal impf. 3 m.p. (פּוּץ 806) *should be scattered*
מַעְיְנֹתֶיךָ n.m.p.-2 m.s. sf. (745) *your springs*
חוּצָה n.m.s.-loc.he (299) *abroad*
בָּרְחֹבוֹת prep.-def.art.-n.f.p. (I 932) *in the streets*
פַּלְגֵי־מָיִם n.m.p. cstr. (I 811)-n.m.p. paus. (565) *streams of water*

5:17

יִהְיוּ־לְךָ Qal impf. 3 m.p. (הָיָה 224)-prep.-2 m.s. sf. *let them be for yourself*
לְבַדֶּךָ prep.-n.m.s.-2 m.s. sf. paus. (94) *alone*
וְאֵין לְזָרִים conj.-neg. (II 34)-prep.-Qal act.ptc. m.p. (זוּר 266) *and not for strangers*
אִתָּךְ prep.-2 m.s. sf. paus. (II 85) *with you*

5:18

יְהִי־מְקוֹרְךָ Qal impf. 3 m.s. apoc.juss. (הָיָה 224) -n.m.s.-2 m.s. sf. (881) *let your fountain be*
בָרוּךְ Qal pass.ptc. (בָּרַךְ 138) *blessed*
וּשְׂמַח conj.-Qal impv. 2 m.s. (שָׂמַח 970) *and rejoice*
מֵאֵשֶׁת prep.-n.f.s. cstr. (61) *in the wife of*
נְעוּרֶךָ n.m.p.-2 m.s. sf. (655) *your youth*

5:19

אַיֶּלֶת אֲהָבִים n.f.s. cstr. (19)-n.m.p. (13) *a lovely hind*
וְיַעֲלַת־חֵן conj.-n.f.s. cstr. (I 418)-n.m.s. (336) *a graceful doe*
דַּדֶּיהָ n.m. du.-3 f.s. sf. (186) *her affection (breasts)*
יְרַוֻּךָ Pi. impf. 3 m.p.-2 m.s. sf. (רָוָה 924) *let ... fill you with delight*
בְכָל־עֵת prep.-n.m.s. cstr. (481)-n.f.s. (773) *at all times*
בְּאַהֲבָתָהּ prep.-n.f.s.-3 f.s. sf. (13) *with her love*
תִּשְׁגֶּה Qal impf. 2 m.s. (שָׁגָה 993) *be infatuated*
תָמִיד adv. (556) *always*

5:20

וְלָמָּה conj.-interr. (552) *and why*
תִשְׁגֶּה Qal impf. 2 m.s. (שָׁגָה 993) *should you be infatuated*

בְנִי n.m.s.-1 c.s. sf. (119) *my son*
בְזָרָה prep.-Qal act.ptc. f.s. (זוּר 266) *with a loose woman*
וּתְחַבֵּק conj.-Pi. impf. 2 m.s. (חָבַק 287) *and embrace*
חֵק נָכְרִיָּה n.m.s. cstr. (300)-adj. f.s. (648) *the bosom of an adventuress*

5:21

כִּי נֹכַח conj. (471)-prep. (647) *for before*
עֵינֵי יהוה n.f.p. cstr. (744)-pr.n. (217) *the eyes of Yahweh*
דַּרְכֵי־אִישׁ n.m.p. cstr. (202)-n.m.s. (35) *a man's ways*
וְכָל־מַעְגְּלֹתָיו conj.-n.m.s. cstr. (481)-n.m.p.-3 m.s. sf. (722) *and all his paths*
מְפַלֵּס Pi. ptc. (פָּלַס 814) *he makes level*

5:22

עֲווֹנוֹתָיו n.m.p.-3 m.s. sf. (730) *his iniquities*
יִלְכְּדֻנוֹ Qal impf. 3 m.s.-3 m.s. sf. (לָכַד 539) *ensnare him*
אֶת־הָרָשָׁע dir.obj.-def.art.-adj. m.s. (957; many omit) *even the wicked*
וּבְחַבְלֵי חַטָּאתוֹ conj.-prep.-n.m.p. cstr. (I 286) -n.f.s.-3 m.s. sf. (308) *and in the cords of his sin*
יִתָּמֵךְ Ni. impf. 3 m.s. (תָּמַךְ 1069) *he is caught*

5:23

הוּא יָמוּת pers.pr. 3 m.s. (214)-Qal impf. 3 m.s. (מוּת 559) *he dies*
בְּאֵין מוּסָר prep.-neg. (II 34)-n.m.s. (416) *for lack of discipline*
וּבְרֹב אִוַּלְתּוֹ conj.-prep.-n.m.s. cstr. (913)-n.f.s.-3 m.s. sf. (17) *and because of his great folly*
יִשְׁגֶּה Qal impf. 3 m.s. (שָׁגָה 993) *he is lost*

6:1

בְּנִי n.m.s.-1 c.s. sf. (119) *my son*
אִם־עָרַבְתָּ hypoth.part. (49)-Qal pf. 2 m.s. (עָרַב II 786) *if you have become surety*
לְרֵעֶךָ prep.-n.m.s.-2 m.s. sf. (945) *for your neighbor*
תָּקַעְתָּ Qal pf. 2 m.s. (תָּקַע 1075) *(if you) have given in pledge*
לַזָּר prep.-def.art.-Qal act.ptc. m.s. (זוּר 266) *for a stranger*
כַּפֶּיךָ n.f.p.-2 m.s. sf. (496) *your hand*

6:2

נוֹקַשְׁתָּ Ni. pf. 2 m.s. (יָקֹשׁ 430) *if you are snared*

בְאִמְרֵי־פִיךָ prep.-n.m.p. cstr. (56)-n.m.s.-2 m.s. sf. (804) *in the words of your mouth*

נִלְכַּדְתָּ Ni. pf. 2 m.s. (לָכַד 539) *caught*

בְּאִמְרֵי־פִיךָ v.supra-v.supra *in the words of your mouth*

6:3

עֲשֵׂה זֹאת אֵפוֹא Qal impv. 2 m.s. (עָשָׂה I 793)-demons.adj. f.s. (260)-enclitic part. (66) *then do this*

בְּנִי n.m.s.-1 c.s. sf. (119) *my son*

וְהִנָּצֵל conj.-Ni. impv. 2 m.s. (נָצַל 664) *and save yourself*

כִּי בָאתָ conj. (471)-Qal pf. 2 m.s. (בּוֹא 97) *for you have come*

בְכַף־רֵעֶךָ prep.-n.f.s. cstr. (496)-n.m.s.-2 m.s. sf. (945) *into your neighbor's power*

לֵךְ הִתְרַפֵּס Qal impv. 2 m.s. (הָלַךְ 229)-Hith. impv. 2 m.s. (רָפַס 952) *go, humble yourself*

וּרְהַב רֵעֶיךָ conj.-Qal impv. 2 m.s. (רָהַב 923) -n.m.p.-2 m.s. sf. (945) *and importune your neighbor*

6:4

אַל־תִּתֵּן neg.-Qal impf. 2 m.s. (נָתַן 678) *do not give*

שֵׁנָה n.f.s. (446) *sleep*

לְעֵינֶיךָ prep.-n.f.p.-2 m.s. sf. (744) *to your eyes*

וּתְנוּמָה conj.-n.f.s. (630) *and slumber*

לְעַפְעַפֶּיךָ prep.-n.m.p.-2 m.s. sf. (733) *to your eyelids*

6:5

הִנָּצֵל Ni. impv. 2 m.s. (נָצַל 664) *save yourself*

כִּצְבִי prep.-n.m.s. (II 840) *like a gazelle*

מִיָּד prep.-n.f.s. (388) *from a hand*

וּכְצִפּוֹר conj.-prep.-n.f.s. (861) *and like a bird*

מִיַּד יָקוּשׁ prep.-n.f.s. cstr. (388)-n.m.s. (430) *from the hand of the fowler*

6:6

לֵךְ־אֶל־נְמָלָה Qal impv. 2 m.s. (הָלַךְ 229) -prep.-n.f.s. (649) *go to the ant*

עָצֵל adj. m.s. (782) *O sluggard*

רְאֵה דְרָכֶיהָ Qal impv. 2 m.s. (906)-n.m.p.-3 f.s. sf. (202) *consider her ways*

וַחֲכָם conj.-Qal impv. 2 m.s. paus. (חָכַם 314) *and be wise*

6:7

אֲשֶׁר אֵין־לָהּ rel. (81)-neg. (II 34)-prep.-3 f.s. sf. *without having*

קָצִין n.m.s. (892) *a chief*

שֹׁטֵר n.m.s. (1009) *officer*

וּמֹשֵׁל conj.-Qal act.ptc. (605) *or ruler*

6:8

תָּכִין Hi. impf. 3 f.s. (כּוּן I 465) *she prepares*

בַּקַּיִץ prep.-def.art.-n.m.s. (884) *in the summer*

לַחְמָהּ n.m.s.-3 f.s. sf. (536) *her food*

אָגְרָה Qal pf. 3 f.s. (אָגַר I 8) *she gathers*

בַקָּצִיר prep.-def.art.-n.m.s. (894) *in the harvest*

מַאֲכָלָהּ n.m.s.-3 f.s. sf. (38) *her food*

6:9

עַד־מָתַי prep. (III 723)-adv. (607) *how long*

עָצֵל adj. m.s. (782) *O sluggard*

תִּשְׁכָּב Qal impf. 2 m.s. paus. (שָׁכַב 1011) *will you lie there*

מָתַי v.supra *when*

תָּקוּם Qal impf. 2 m.s. (קוּם 877) *will you arise*

מִשְּׁנָתֶךָ prep.-n.f.s.-2 m.s. sf. (446) *from your sleep?*

6:10

מְעַט שֵׁנוֹת subst. cstr. (589)-n.f.p. (446) *a little sleep*

מְעַט תְּנוּמוֹת v.supra-n.f.p. (630) *a little slumber*

מְעַט חִבֻּק יָדַיִם v.supra-n.m.s. cstr. (287)-n.f. du. (388) *a little folding of the hands*

לִשְׁכָּב prep.-Qal inf.cstr. paus. (שָׁכַב 1011) *to rest*

6:11

וּבָא־כִמְהַלֵּךְ conj.-Qal pf. 3 m.s. (בּוֹא 97) -prep.-Pi. ptc. (הָלַךְ 229) *and will come like a vagabond*

רֵאשֶׁךָ n.m.s.-2 m.s. sf. (רִישׁ 930) *poverty upon you*

וּמַחְסֹרְךָ conj.-n.m.s.-2 m.s. sf. (341) *and your want*

כְּאִישׁ מָגֵן prep.-n.m.s. cstr. (35)-n.m.s. (171) *like an armed man*

6:12

אָדָם בְּלִיַּעַל n.m.s. cstr. (9)-n.m.s. (116) *a worthless person*

אִישׁ אָוֶן n.m.s. cstr. (35)-n.m.s. (19) *a wicked man*

הוֹלֵךְ Qal act.ptc. (הָלַךְ 229) *goes about*

עִקְּשׁוּת פֶּה n.f.s. cstr. (786)-n.m.s. (804) *with crooked speech*

6:13

קֹרֵץ -Qal act.ptc. (902) *winks*

בְּעֵינָו prep.-n.f.s.-3 m.s. sf. (744; Q בְּעֵינָיו) *with his eyes*

מֹלֵל בְּרַגְלָו Qal act.ptc. (מָלַל II 576)-prep.-n.f.s.-3 m.s. sf. (919) *scrapes with his feet*

מֹרֶה Hi. ptc. (יָרָה 434) *points*

בְּאֶצְבְּעֹתָיו prep.-n.f.p.-3 m.s. sf. (840) *with his fingers*

6:14

תַּהְפֻּכוֹת n.f.p. (246) *with perversity*

בְּלִבּוֹ prep.-n.m.s.-3 m.s. sf. (524) *in his heart*

חֹרֵשׁ רָע Qal act.ptc. (I 360)-n.m.s. paus. (II 948) *he devises evil*

בְּכָל־עֵת prep.-n.m.s. cstr. (481)-n.f.s. (773) *continually*

מִדְ֯נִים n.m.p. (מָדוֹן I 193; K מְדָנִים; Q מִדְיָנִים) *discord*

יְשַׁלֵּחַ Pi. impf. 3 m.s. (שָׁלַח 1018) *he sows*

6:15

עַל־כֵּן פִּתְאֹם prep.-adv. (485)-adv. (837) *therefore suddenly*

יָבוֹא אֵידוֹ Qal impf. 3 m.s. (בּוֹא 97)-n.m.s.-3 m.s. sf. (15) *calamity will come upon him*

פֶּתַע adv. (837) *in a moment*

יִשָּׁבֵר Ni. impf. 3 m.s. (990) *he will be broken*

וְאֵין מַרְפֵּא conj.-neg. (II 34)-n.m.s. (951) *beyond healing*

6:16

שֶׁשׁ־הֵנָּה num. (995)-pers.pr. 3 f.p. (241) *there are six things*

שָׂנֵא יהוה Qal pf. 3 m.s. (971)-pr.n. (217) *which Yahweh hates*

וְשֶׁבַע conj.-num. (I 987) *and seven which*

תּוֹעֲבוֹת נַפְשׁוֹ n.f.s. cstr. (1072)-n.f.s.-3 m.s. sf. (659) *an abomination to him*

6:17

עֵינַיִם רָמוֹת n.f. du. (744)-Qal act.ptc. f.p. (רוּם 926) *haughty eyes*

לְשׁוֹן שָׁקֶר n.f.s. cstr. (546)-n.m.s. paus. (1055) *a lying tongue*

וְיָדַיִם conj.-n.f. du. (388) *and hands*

שֹׁפְכוֹת Qal act.ptc. f.p. (שָׁפַךְ 1049) *that shed*

דָּם־נָקִי n.m.s. (196)-adj. m.s. (667) *innocent blood*

6:18

לֵב חֹרֵשׁ n.m.s. (524)-Qal act.ptc. (I 360) *a heart that devises*

מַחְשְׁבוֹת אָוֶן n.f.p. cstr. (364)-n.m.s. (19) *wicked plans*

רַגְלַיִם n.f. du. (919) *feet*

מְמַהֲרוֹת Pi. ptc. f.p. (מָהַר I 554) *that make haste*

לָרוּץ prep.-Qal inf.cstr. (רוּץ 930) *to run*

לָרָעָה prep.-def.art.-n.f.s. (949) *to evil*

6:19

יָפִיחַ Hi. impf. 3 m.s. (פּוּחַ 806) *who breathes out*

כְּזָבִים n.m.p. (469) *lies*

עֵד שָׁקֶר n.m.s. cstr. (729)-n.m.s. paus. (1055) *a false witness*

וּמְשַׁלֵּחַ conj.-Pi. ptc. (שָׁלַח 1018) *and a man who sows*

מְדָנִים n.m.p. (I 193) *discord*

בֵּין אַחִים prep. (107)-n.m.p. (26) *among brothers*

6:20

נְצֹר Qal impv. 2 m.s. (נָצַר 665) *keep*

בְּנִי n.m.s.-1 c.s. sf. (119) *my son*

מִצְוַת אָבִיךָ n.f.s. cstr. (846)-n.m.s.-2 m.s. sf. (3) *your father's commandment*

וְאַל־תִּטֹּשׁ conj.-prep.-Qal impf. 2 m.s. (נָטַשׁ 643) *and forsake not*

תּוֹרַת אִמֶּךָ n.f.s. cstr. (435)-n.f.s.-2 m.s. sf. (51) *your mother's teaching*

6:21

קָשְׁרֵם Qal impv. 2 m.s.-3 m.p. sf. (קָשַׁר 905) *bind them*

עַל־לִבְּךָ prep.-n.m.s.-2 m.s. sf. (524) *upon your heart*

תָמִיד subst. as adv. (556) *always*

עָנְדֵם Qal impv. 2 m.s.-3 m.p. sf. (עָנַד 772) *tie them*

עַל־גַּרְגְּרֹתֶךָ prep.-n.f.p.-2 m.s. sf. (176) *about your neck*

6:22

בְּהִתְהַלֶּכְךָ prep.-Hith. inf.cstr.-2 m.s. sf. (הָלַךְ 229) *when you walk*

תַּנְחֶה אֹתָךְ Hi. impf. 3 f.s. (נָחָה 634)-dir.obj.-2 m.s. sf. paus. *it will lead you*

בְּשָׁכְבְּךָ prep.-Qal inf.cstr.-2 m.s. sf. (שָׁכַב 1011) *when you lie down*

תִּשְׁמֹר עָלֶיךָ Qal impf. 2 m.s. (שָׁמַר 1036) -prep.-2 m.s. sf. *it will watch over you*

וַהֲקִיצוֹתָ conj.-Hi. pf. 2 m.s. (קִיץ I 884) *and when you awake*
הִיא תְשִׂיחֶךָ pers.pr. 3 f.s. (214)-Qal impf. 3 f.s.-2 m.s. sf. (שִׂיחַ 967) *it will talk with you*

6:23
כִּי נֵר מִצְוָה conj. (471)-n.m.s. (632)-n.f.s. (846) *for the commandment is a lamp*
וְתוֹרָה אוֹר conj.-n.f.s. (435)-n.m.s. (21) *and the teaching a light*
וְדֶרֶךְ חַיִּים conj.-n.m.s. cstr. (202)-n.m.p. (313) *and the way of life*
תּוֹכְחוֹת מוּסָר n.f.p. cstr. (407)-n.m.s. paus. (416) *the reproofs of discipline*

6:24
לִשְׁמָרְךָ prep.-Qal inf.cstr.-2 m.s. sf. (שָׁמַר 1036) *to preserve you*
מֵאֵשֶׁת רָע prep.-n.f.s. cstr. (61)-n.m.s. paus. (948) *from the evil woman*
מֵחֶלְקַת לָשׁוֹן prep.-n.f.s. cstr. (325)-n.f.s. (546) *from the smooth tongue*
נָכְרִיָּה adj. f.s. (648) *the adventuress (foreign woman)*

6:25
אַל־תַּחְמֹד neg.-Qal impf. 2 m.s. juss. (חָמַד 326) *do not desire*
יָפְיָהּ n.m.s.-3 f.s. sf. (יֳפִי 421) *her beauty*
בִּלְבָבֶךָ prep.-n.m.s.-2 m.s. sf. (523) *in your heart*
וְאַל־תִּקָּחֲךָ conj.-neg.-Qal impf. 3 f.s.-2 m.s. sf. (542 לָקַח) *and do not let her capture you*
בְּעַפְעַפֶּיהָ prep.-n.m.p.-3 f.s. sf. (733) *with her eyelashes*

6:26
כִּי בְעַד־אִשָּׁה זוֹנָה conj. (471)-prep. (126)-n.f.s. (61)-Qal act.ptc. f.s. (זָנָה 275) *for because of a harlot*
עַד־כִּכַּר prep. (III 723)-n.f.s. cstr. (503) *to a loaf of*
לָחֶם n.m.s. paus. (536) *bread*
וְאֵשֶׁת אִישׁ conj.-n.f.s. cstr. (61)-n.m.s. (35) *but a man's wife*
נֶפֶשׁ יְקָרָה n.f.s. (659)-adj. f.s. (429) *a man's very life*
תָצוּד Qal impf. 3 f.s. (צוּד I 844) *stalks*

6:27
הֲיַחְתֶּה אִישׁ interr.-Qal impf. 3 m.s. (חָתָה 367)-n.m.s. (35) *can a man carry*
אֵשׁ n.f.s. (77) *fire*
בְּחֵיקוֹ prep.-n.m.s.-3 m.s. sf. (300) *in his bosom*
וּבְגָדָיו conj.-n.m.p.-3 m.s. sf. (93) *and his clothes*
לֹא תִשָּׂרַפְנָה neg.-Ni. impf. 3 f.p. (שָׂרַף 976) *not be burned*

6:28
אִם־יְהַלֵּךְ אִישׁ hypoth.part. (49)-Pi. impf. 3 m.s. (הָלַךְ 229)-n.m.s. (35) *or can one walk*
עַל־הַגֶּחָלִים prep.-def.art.-n.f.p. (160) *upon hot coals*
וְרַגְלָיו conj.-n.f.p.-3 m.s. sf. (919) *and his feet*
לֹא תִכָּוֶינָה neg.-Ni. impf. 3 f.p. (כָּוָה 464) *not be scorched*

6:29
כֵּן הַבָּא adv. (485)-def.art.-Qal act.ptc. m.s. (בּוֹא 97) *so is he who goes in*
אֶל־אֵשֶׁת רֵעֵהוּ prep.-n.f.s. cstr. (61)-n.m.s.-3 m.s. sf. (945; GK 84a,i) *to his neighbor's wife*
לֹא יִנָּקֶה neg.-Ni. impf. 3 m.s. (נָקָה 667) *will not go unpunished*
כָּל־הַנֹּגֵעַ בָּהּ n.m.s. cstr. (481)-def.art.-Qal act.ptc. (נָגַע 619)-prep.-3 f.s. sf. *any one who touches her*

6:30
לֹא־יָבוּזוּ neg.-Qal impf. 3 m.p. (בּוּז I 100) *do not men despise*
לַגַּנָּב prep.-def.art.-n.m.s. (170) *a thief*
כִּי יִגְנוֹב conj. (471)-Qal impf. 3 m.s. (גָּנַב 170) *if he steals*
לְמַלֵּא נַפְשׁוֹ prep.-Pi. inf.cstr. (מָלֵא 569)-n.f.s.-3 m.s. sf. (659) *to satisfy his appetite*
כִּי יִרְעָב conj. (471)-Qal impf. 3 m.s. (רָעֵב 944) *when he is hungry*

6:31
וְנִמְצָא conj.-Ni. pf. 3 m.s. (מָצָא 592) *and if he is caught*
יְשַׁלֵּם Pi. impf. 3 m.s. (שָׁלֵם 1023) *he will pay*
שִׁבְעָתָיִם n.f. du. paus. (988) *sevenfold*
אֶת־כָּל־ dir.obj.-n.m.s. cstr. (481) *and all (of)*
הוֹן־בֵּיתוֹ n.m.s. cstr. (223)-n.m.s.-3 m.s. sf. (108) *the goods of his house*
יִתֵּן Qal impf. 3 m.s. (נָתַן 678) *he will give*

6:32
נֹאֵף אִשָּׁה Qal act.ptc. (610)-n.f.s. (61) *he who commits adultery*
חֲסַר־לֵב adj. m.s. cstr. (341)-n.m.s. (524) *has no sense*

מַשְׁחִית נַפְשׁוֹ Hi ptc. (שָׁחַת 1007)–n.f.s.–3 m.s. sf. (659) *destroys himself*
הוּא יַעֲשֶׂנָּה pers.pr. 3 m.s. (214)–Qal impf. 3 m.s.–3 f.s. sf. (עָשָׂה I 793) *he who does it*

6:33
נֶגַע־וְקָלוֹן n.m.s. (619)–conj.–n.m.s. (885) *wounds and dishonor*
יִמְצָא Qal impf. 3 m.s. (מָצָא 592) *will he get*
וְחֶרְפָּתוֹ conj.–n.f.s.–3 m.s. sf. (357) *and his disgrace*
לֹא תִמָּחֶה neg.–Ni. impf. 3 f.s. (מָחָה 562) *will not be wiped away*

6:34
כִּי־קִנְאָה conj. (471)–n.f.s. (888) *for jealousy*
חֲמַת־גָּבֶר n.f.s. cstr. (404)–n.m.s. paus. (149) *makes a man furious*
וְלֹא־יַחְמוֹל conj.–neg.–Qal impf. 3 m.s. (חָמַל 328) *and he will not spare*
בְּיוֹם נָקָם prep.–n.m.s. cstr. (398)–n.m.s. (668) *when he takes revenge*

6:35
לֹא־יִשָּׂא neg.–Qal impf. 3 m.s. (נָשָׂא 669) *he will not accept*
פְּנֵי כָל־כֹּפֶר n.m.p. cstr. (815)–n.m.s. cstr. (481) –n.m.s. (I 497) *any compensation*
וְלֹא־יֹאבֶה conj.–neg.–Qal impf. 3 m.s. (אָבָה 2) *nor be appeased*
כִּי תַרְבֶּה־ conj. (471)–Hi. impf. 2 m.s. (רָבָה I 915) *though you multiply*
שֹׁחַד n.m.s. (1005) *gifts*

7:1
בְּנִי n.m.s.–1 c.s. sf. (119) *my son*
שְׁמֹר אֲמָרָי Qal impv. 2 m.s. (1036)–n.m.p.–1 c.s. sf. (56) *keep my words*
וּמִצְוֹתַי conj.–n.f.p.–1 c.s. sf. (846) *and my commandments*
תִּצְפֹּן Qal impf. 2 m.s. (צָפַן 860) *treasure up*
אִתָּךְ prep.–2 m.s. sf. paus. (II 85) *with you*

7:2
שְׁמֹר מִצְוֹתַי Qal impv. 2 m.s. (1036)–n.f.p.–1 c.s. sf. (846) *keep my commandments*
וֶחְיֵה conj.–Qal impv. 2 m.s. (חָיָה 310) *and live*
וְתוֹרָתִי conj.–n.f.s.–1 c.s. sf. (435) *and my teachings*
כְּאִישׁוֹן עֵינֶיךָ prep.–n.m.s. cstr. (36)–n.f. du.–2 m.s. sf. (744) *as the apple of your eye*

7:3
קָשְׁרֵם Qal impv. 2 m.s.–3 m.p. sf. (קָשַׁר 905) *bind them*
עַל־אֶצְבְּעֹתֶיךָ prep.–n.f.p.–2 m.s. sf. (840) *on your fingers*
כָּתְבֵם Qal impv. 2 m.s.–3 m.p. sf. (כָּתַב 507) *write them*
עַל־לוּחַ לִבֶּךָ prep.–n.m.s. cstr. (531)–n.m.s.–2 m.s. sf. (524) *on the tablet of your heart*

7:4
אֱמֹר Qal impv. 2 m.s. (55) *say*
לַחָכְמָה prep.–def.art.–n.f.s. (315) *to wisdom*
אֲחֹתִי אָתְּ n.f.s.–1 c.s. sf. (27)–pers.pr. 2 f.s. paus. (61) *you are my sister*
וּמֹדָע conj.–n.m.s. (396) *a kinsman*
לַבִּינָה prep.–def.art.–n.f.s. (108) *to insight*
תִקְרָא Qal impf. 2 m.s. (קָרָא 894) *call*

7:5
לִשְׁמָרְךָ prep.–Qal inf.cstr.–2 m.s. sf. (שָׁמַר 1036) *to preserve you*
מֵאִשָּׁה זָרָה prep.–n.f.s. (61)–Qal act.ptc. f.s. (זוּר 266) *from the loose woman*
מִנָּכְרִיָּה prep.–adj. f.s. (648) *from the adventuress*
אֲמָרֶיהָ n.m.p.–3 f.s. sf. (56) *her words*
הֶחֱלִיקָה Hi. pf. 3 f.s. (חָלַק 325) *deal smoothly*

7:6
כִּי בְּחַלּוֹן conj. (471)–prep.–n.m.s. cstr. (319) *for at the window of*
בֵּיתִי n.m.s.–1 c.s. sf. (108) *my house*
בְּעַד אֶשְׁנַבִּי prep. (126)–n.m.s.–1 c.s. sf. (1039) *through my lattice*
נִשְׁקָפְתִּי Ni. pf. 1 c.s. (שָׁקַף I 1054) *I have looked out*

7:7
וָאֵרֶא consec.–Qal impf. 1 c.s. (רָאָה 906) *and I have seen*
בַפְּתָאִים prep.–def.art.–adj. m.p. (834; GK 93x) *among the simple*
אָבִינָה Qal impf. 1 c.s. (בִּין 106) *I have perceived*
בַבָּנִים prep.–def.art.–n.m.p. (119) *among the youths*
נַעַר חֲסַר־לֵב n.m.s. (654)–adj. m.s. cstr. (341) –n.m.s. (524) *a young man without sense*

7:8
עֹבֵר בַּשּׁוּק Qal act.ptc. (716)–prep.–def.art.–n.m.s. (1003) *passing along the street*

אֵצֶל פִּנָּהּ prep. (69)-n.f.s.-3 f.s. sf. (819) *near her corner*
וְדֶרֶךְ בֵּיתָהּ conj.-n.m.s. cstr. (202)-n.m.s.-3 f.s. sf. (108) *the road to her house*
יִצְעָד Qal impf. 3 m.s. (צָעַד 857) *taking (he steps)*

7:9

בְּנֶשֶׁף־ prep.-n.m.s. (676) *in the twilight*
בְּעֶרֶב prep.-n.m.s. (787) *in the evening*
יוֹם n.m.s. (398) *(a day)*
בְּאִישׁוֹן prep.-n.m.s. cstr. (36) *in the midst of*
לַיְלָה n.m.s. (538) *night*
וַאֲפֵלָה conj.-n.f.s. (66) *and darkness*

7:10

וְהִנֵּה אִשָּׁה conj.-interj. (243)-n.f.s. (61) *and lo, a woman*
לִקְרָאתוֹ prep.-Qal inf.cstr.-3 m.s. sf. (קָרָא II 896) *meets him*
שִׁית זוֹנָה n.m.s. cstr. (1011)-Qal act.ptc. f.s. (זָנָה 275) *dressed as a harlot*
וּנְצֻרַת לֵב conj.-Qal pass.ptc. f.s. cstr. (נצר I 665)-n.m.s. (524) *wily of heart*

7:11

הֹמִיָּה הִיא Qal act.ptc. f.s. (הָמָה 242)-pers.pr. 3 f.s. (214) *she is loud*
וְסֹרָרֶת conj.-Qal act.ptc. f.s. (סָרַר 710) *and wayward*
בְּבֵיתָהּ prep.-n.m.s.-3 f.s. sf. (108) *at home*
לֹא־יִשְׁכְּנוּ רַגְלֶיהָ neg.-Qal impf. 3 m.p. (שָׁכַן 1014)-n.f.p.-3 f.s. sf. (919) *her feet do not stay*

7:12

פַּעַם בַּחוּץ n.f.s. (821)-prep.-def.art.-n.m.s. (299) *now in the street*
פַּעַם בָּרְחֹבוֹת v.supra-prep.-def.art.-n.f.p. (932) *now in the market*
וְאֵצֶל כָּל־פִּנָּה conj.-prep. (I 69)-n.m.s. cstr. (481)-n.f.s. (819) *and at every corner*
תֶאֱרֹב Qal impf. 3 f.s. (אָרַב 70) *she lies in wait*

7:13

וְהֶחֱזִיקָה בּוֹ conj.-Hi. pf. 3 f.s. (חָזַק 304)-prep.-3 m.s. sf. *she seizes him*
וְנָשְׁקָה־לּוֹ conj.-Qal pf. 3 f.s. (נָשַׁק I 676) -prep.-3 m.s. sf. *and kisses him*
הֵעֵזָה פָנֶיהָ Hi. pf. 3 f.s. (עָזַז 738)-n.m.p.-3 f.s. sf. (815) *she maketh bold her face*

וַתֹּאמַר לוֹ consec.-Qal impf. 3 f.s. (אָמַר 55) -prep.-3 m.s. sf. *and says to him*

7:14

זִבְחֵי שְׁלָמִים n.m.p. cstr. (257)-n.m.p. (1023) *sacrifices of peace*
עָלָי prep.-1 c.s. sf. paus. *upon me*
הַיּוֹם def.art.-n.m.s. (398) *today*
שִׁלַּמְתִּי Pi. pf. 1 c.s. (שָׁלֵם 1022) *I have paid*
נְדָרָי n.m.p.-1 c.s. sf. (623) *my vows*

7:15

עַל־כֵּן יָצָאתִי prep.-adv. (485)-Qal pf. 1 c.s. (יָצָא 422) *so now I have come out*
לִקְרָאתֶךָ prep.-Qal inf.cstr.-2 m.s. sf. (קָרָא II 896) *to meet you*
לְשַׁחֵר פָּנֶיךָ prep.-Pi. inf.cstr. (שָׁחַר 1007)-n.m.p. -2 m.s. sf. (815) *to seek you eagerly*
וָאֶמְצָאֶךָּ consec.-Qal impf. 1 c.s.-2 m.s. sf. (מָצָא 592) *and I have found you*

7:16

מַרְבַדִּים n.m.p. (915) *with coverings*
רָבַדְתִּי Qal pf. 1 c.s. (רָבַד II 914) *I have decked*
עַרְשִׂי n.f.s.-1 c.s. sf. (793) *my couch*
חֲטֻבוֹת n.f.p. cstr. (310) *colored spreads of*
אֵטוּן n.m.s. cstr. (32) *linen (yarn) of*
מִצְרָיִם pr.n. paus. (595) *Egypt*

7:17

נַפְתִּי Qal pf. 1 c.s. (נוּף I 631) *I have perfumed*
מִשְׁכָּבִי n.m.s.-1 c.s. sf. (1012) *my bed*
מֹר n.m.s. (600) *with myrrh*
אֲהָלִים n.m.p. (III 14) *aloes*
וְקִנָּמוֹן conj.-n.m.s. (890) *and cinnamon*

7:18

לְכָה Qal impv. 2 m.s.-vol.he (הָלַךְ 229) *come*
נִרְוֶה Qal impf. 1 c.p. (רָוָה 924) *let us take our fill*
דֹדִים n.m.p. (187) *of love*
עַד־הַבֹּקֶר prep. (III 723)-def.art.-n.m.s. (133) *till morning*
נִתְעַלְּסָה Hith. impf. 1 c.p.-vol.he (עָלַס 763) *let us delight ourselves*
בָּאֳהָבִים prep.-def.art.-n.m.p. (13) *with love*

7:19

כִּי אֵין הָאִישׁ conj. (471)-neg. (II 34)-def.art. -n.m.s. (35) *for my husband is not*
בְּבֵיתוֹ prep.-n.m.s.-3 m.s. sf. (108) *at home*
הָלַךְ Qal pf. 3 m.s. (229) *he has gone*

בְּדֶרֶךְ prep.-n.m.s. (202) *on a journey*
מֵרָחוֹק prep.-adj. m.s. (935) *long (to a distance)*

7:20

צְרוֹר־הַכֶּסֶף n.m.s. cstr. (I 865)-def.art.-n.m.s. (494) *a bag of money*
לָקַח בְּיָדוֹ Qal pf. 3 m.s. (542)-prep.-n.f.s.-3 m.s. sf. (388) *he took with him (in his hand)*
לְיוֹם הַכֵּסֶא prep.-n.m.s. cstr. (398)-def.art.-n.m.s. (490) *at full moon*
יָבֹא בֵיתוֹ Qal impf. 3 m.s. (בּוֹא 97)-n.m.s.-3 m.s. sf. (108) *he will come home*

7:21

הִטַּתּוּ Hi. pf. 3 f.s.-3 m.s. sf. (נָטָה 639) *she persuades him*
בְּרֹב לִקְחָהּ prep.-n.m.s. cstr. (913)-n.m.s.-3 f.s. sf. (544) *with much seductive speech*
בְּחֵלֶק שְׂפָתֶיהָ prep.-n.m.s. cstr. (325)-n.f.p.-3 f.s. sf. (973) *with the seductiveness of her lips*
תַּדִּיחֶנּוּ Hi. impf. 3 f.s.-3 m.s. sf. (נָדַח 623) *she compels him*

7:22

הוֹלֵךְ אַחֲרֶיהָ Qal act.ptc. (הָלַךְ 229)-prep.-3 f.s. sf. (29) *he follows her*
פִּתְאֹם adv. (837) *all at once*
כְּשׁוֹר prep.-n.m.s. (1004) *as an ox*
אֶל־טָבַח prep.-n.m.s. (I 370) *to the slaughter*
יָבוֹא Qal impf. 3 m.s. (בּוֹא 97) *goes*
וּכְעֶכֶס conj.-prep.-n.m.s. (747) *or as anklets*
אֶל־מוּסַר prep.-n.m.s. cstr. (416) *until the chastisement of*
אֱוִיל adj. m.s. (17) *a fool*

7:23

עַד יְפַלַּח חֵץ prep. (III 723)-Pi. impf. 3 m.s. (812 פָּלַח)-n.m.s. (346) *till an arrow pierces*
כְּבֵדוֹ n.m.s.-3 m.s. sf. (458) *its liver*
כְּמַהֵר prep.-Pi. inf.cstr. (מָהַר I 554) *as ... rushes*
צִפּוֹר n.f.s. (861) *a bird*
אֶל־פָּח prep.-n.m.s. paus. (I 809) *into a snare*
וְלֹא־יָדַע conj.-neg.-Qal pf. 3 m.s. (393) *and he does not know*
כִּי־בְנַפְשׁוֹ הוּא conj. (471)-prep.-n.f.s.-3 m.s. sf. (659)-pers.pr. 3 m.s. (214) *that it for his life*

7:24

וְעַתָּה בָנִים conj.-adv. (773)-n.m.p. (119) *and now, O sons*
שִׁמְעוּ־לִי Qal impv. 2 m.p. (1033)-prep.-1 c.s. sf. *listen to me*
וְהַקְשִׁיבוּ conj.-Hi. impv. 2 m.p. (קָשַׁב 904) *and be attentive*
לְאִמְרֵי־פִי prep.-n.m.p. cstr. (56)-n.m.s.-1 c.s. sf. (804) *to the words of my mouth*

7:25

אַל־יֵשְׂטְ neg.-Qal impf. 3 m.s. apoc. (שָׂטָה 966) *let not ... turn aside*
אֶל־דְּרָכֶיהָ prep.-n.m.p.-3 f.s. sf. (202) *to her ways*
לִבֶּךָ n.m.s.-2 m.s. sf. (524) *your heart*
אַל־תֵּתַע neg.-Qal impf. 2 m.s. (תָּעָה 1073) *do not stray*
בִּנְתִיבוֹתֶיהָ prep.-n.f.p.-3 f.s. sf. (677) *into her paths*

7:26

כִּי־רַבִּים חֲלָלִים conj. (471)-adj. m.p. (I 912)-adj. m.p. (321) *for many a victim*
הִפִּילָה Hi. pf. 3 f.s. (נָפַל 656) *has she laid low*
וַעֲצֻמִים conj.-adj. m.p. (783) *and a mighty host*
כָּל־הֲרֻגֶיהָ n.m.s. cstr. (481)-Qal pass.ptc. m.p.-3 f.s. sf. (הָרַג 246) *all her slain*

7:27

דַּרְכֵי שְׁאוֹל n.m.p. cstr. (202)-n.f.s. (982) *the ways to Sheol*
בֵּיתָהּ n.m.s.-3 f.s. sf. (108) *her house*
יֹרְדוֹת Qal act.ptc. f.p. (יָרַד 432) *going down*
אֶל־חַדְרֵי־מָוֶת prep.-n.m.p. cstr. (293)-n.m.s. (560) *to the chambers of death*

8:1

הֲלֹא־חָכְמָה interr.-neg.-n.f.s. (315) *does not wisdom*
תִקְרָא Qal impf. 3 f.s. (קָרָא 894) *call*
וּתְבוּנָה conj.-n.f.s. (108) *and understanding*
תִּתֵּן קוֹלָהּ Qal impf. 3 f.s. (נָתַן 678)-n.m.s.-3 f.s. sf. (876) *does (not) raise her voice*

8:2

בְּרֹאשׁ־מְרוֹמִים prep.-n.m.s. cstr. (910)-n.m.p. (928) *on the heights*
עֲלֵי־דָרֶךְ prep. (752)-n.m.s. paus. (202) *beside the way*
בֵּית נְתִיבוֹת n.m.s. cstr. or prep. (108)-n.f.p. (677) *in the paths*
נִצָּבָה Ni. pf. 3 f.s. (נָצַב 662) *she takes her stand*

8:3

לְיַד־שְׁעָרִים prep.-n.f.s. cstr. (388)-n.m.p. (1044) *beside the gates*

לְפִי־קָרֶת prep.-n.m.s. cstr. (804)-n.f.s. paus. (900) *in front of the town*

מְבוֹא פְתָחִים n.m.s. cstr. (99)-n.m.p. (835) *at the entrance of the portals*

תָּרֹנָּה Qal impf. 3 f.p. (רָנַן 943) *she cries aloud*

8:4

אֲלֵיכֶם prep.-2 m.p. sf. *to you*

אִישִׁים n.m.p. (35) *O men*

אֶקְרָא Qal impf. 1 c.s. (קָרָא 894) *I call*

וְקוֹלִי conj.-n.m.s.-1 c.s. sf. (876) *and my cry*

אֶל־בְּנֵי אָדָם prep.-n.m.p. cstr. (119)-n.m.s. (9) *to the sons of men*

8:5

הָבִינוּ Hi. impv. 2 m.p. (בִּין 106) *learn*

פְתָאִים adj. m.p. (834; GK 93x) *O simple ones*

עָרְמָה n.f.s. (791) *prudence*

וּכְסִילִים conj.-n.m.p. (I 493) *and O foolish men*

הָבִינוּ לֵב v.supra (LXX ἔνθεσθε)-n.m.s. (524) *learn heart (pay attention)*

8:6

שִׁמְעוּ Qal impv. 2 m.p. (1033) *hear*

כִּי־נְגִידִים conj. (471)-n.m.p. (617) *for ... noble things*

אֲדַבֵּר Pi. impf. 1 c.s. (180) *I will speak*

וּמִפְתַּח שְׂפָתַי conj.-n.m.s. cstr. (836)-n.f.p.-1 c.s. sf. (973) *and from my lips*

מֵישָׁרִים n.m.p. (449) *what is right*

8:7

כִּי־אֱמֶת conj. (471)-n.f.s. (54) *for truth*

יֶהְגֶּה חִכִּי Qal impf. 3 m.s. (הָגָה I 211)-n.m.s.-1 c.s. sf. (335) *my mouth will utter*

וְתוֹעֲבַת שְׂפָתַי conj.-n.f.s. cstr. (1072)-n.f.p.-1 c.s. sf. (973) *an abomination to my lips*

רֶשַׁע n.m.s. (957) *wickedness*

8:8

בְּצֶדֶק prep.-n.m.s. (841) *righteous*

כָּל־אִמְרֵי־פִי n.m.s. cstr. (481)-n.m.p. cstr. (56) -n.m.s.-1 c.s. sf. (804) *all the words of my mouth*

אֵין בָּהֶם neg. (II 34)-prep.-3 m.p. sf. *there is nothing ... in them*

נִפְתָּל Ni. ptc. (פָּתַל 836) *twisted*

וְעִקֵּשׁ conj.-adj. m.s. (I 786) *or crooked*

8:9

כֻּלָּם n.m.s.-3 m.p. sf. (481) *they all*

נְכֹחִים adj. m.p. (647) *are straight*

לַמֵּבִין prep.-def.art.-Hi. ptc. m.s. (בִּין 106) *to him who understands*

וִישָׁרִים conj.-adj. m.p. (449) *and right*

לְמֹצְאֵי דָעַת prep.-Qal act.ptc. m.p. cstr. (מָצָא 592)-n.f.s. paus. (395) *to those who find knowledge*

8:10

קְחוּ־מוּסָרִי Qal impv. 2 m.p. (לָקַח 542)-n.m.s.-1 c.s. sf. (416) *take my instruction*

וְאַל־כָּסֶף conj.-neg.-n.m.s. paus. (494) *instead of silver*

וְדַעַת conj.-n.f.s. (395) *and knowledge*

מֵחָרוּץ נִבְחָר prep.-n.m.s. (359)-Ni. ptc. m.s. (בָּחַר 103) *rather than choice gold*

8:11

כִּי־טוֹבָה חָכְמָה conj. (471)-adj. f.s. (II 373)-n.f.s. (315) *for wisdom is better*

מִפְּנִינִים prep.-n.f.p. (819) *than jewels*

וְכָל־חֲפָצִים conj.-n.m.s. cstr. (481)-n.m.p. (343) *and all that you may desire*

לֹא יִשְׁווּ־בָהּ neg.-Qal impf. 3 m.p. (שָׁוָה I 1000)-prep.-3 f.s. sf. *cannot compare with her*

8:12

אֲנִי־חָכְמָה pers.pr. 1 c.s. (58)-n.f.s. (315) *I wisdom*

שָׁכַנְתִּי Qal pf. 1 c.s. (שָׁכַן 1014) *dwell*

עָרְמָה n.f.s. (791) *in prudence*

וְדַעַת conj.-n.f.s. (395) *and knowledge*

מְזִמּוֹת n.f.p. (273) *discretion*

אֶמְצָא Qal impf. 1 c.s. (מָצָא 592) *I find*

8:13

יִרְאַת יהוה n.f.s. cstr. (432)-pr.n. (217) *the fear of Yahweh*

שְׂנֹאת רָע Qal inf.cstr. (שָׂנֵא 971)-n.m.s. paus. (II 948) *hatred of evil*

גֵּאָה n.f.s. (144) *pride*

וְגָאוֹן conj.-n.m.s. (144) *and arrogance*

וְדֶרֶךְ רָע conj.-n.m.s. cstr. (202)-v.supra *and the way of evil*

וּפִי תַהְפֻּכוֹת conj.-n.m.s. cstr. (804)-n.f.p. (246) *and perverted speech*

שָׂנֵאתִי Qal pf. 1 c.s. (שָׂנֵא 971) *I hate*

8:14

לִי־עֵצָה prep.-1 c.s. sf.-n.f.s. (420) *I have counsel*

וְתוּשִׁיָּה conj.-n.f.s. (444) *and sound wisdom*

אֲנִי בִינָה pers.pr. 1 c.s. (58)-n.f.s. (108) *I have insight*

לִי גְבוּרָה v.supra-n.f.s. (150) *I have strength*

8:15

בִּי מְלָכִים prep.-1 c.s. sf.-n.m.p. (I 572) *by me kings*

יִמְלֹכוּ Qal impf. 3 m.p. (מָלַךְ 573) *reign*

וְרוֹזְנִים Qal act.ptc. m.p. as n.m.p. (רָזַן 931) *and rulers*

יְחֹקְקוּ Po'el impf. 3 m.p. (חָקַק 349) *decree*

צֶדֶק n.m.s. (841) *what is just*

8:16

בִּי שָׂרִים prep.-1 c.s. sf.-n.m.p. (978) *by me princes*

יָשֹׂרוּ Qal impf. 3 m.p. (שָׂרַר 979) *rule*

וּנְדִיבִים conj.-n.m.p. (622) *and nobles*

כָּל־שֹׁפְטֵי צֶדֶק n.m.s. cstr. (481)-Qal act.ptc. m.p. cstr. (1047; LXX γρατοῦσι)-n.m.s. (841; LXX γῆς) *all the governors of righteousness*

8:17

אֲנִי אֹהֲבֶיהָ pers.pr. 1 c.s. (58)-Qal act.ptc. m.p.-3 f.s. sf. (אָהֵב 12; Q אֹהֲבַי; LXX τοὺς ἐμὲ φιλοῦντας) *I those who love me*

אֵהָב Qal impf. 1 c.s. (אָהֵב 12) *love*

וּמְשַׁחֲרַי conj.-Pi. ptc. m.p.-1 c.s. sf. (שָׁחַר 1007) *and those who seek me diligently*

יִמְצָאֻנְנִי Qal impf. 3 m.p.-1 c.s. sf. (מָצָא 592) *find me*

8:18

עֹשֶׁר־וְכָבוֹד n.m.s. (799)-conj.-n.m.s. (458) *riches and honor*

אִתִּי prep.-1 c.s. sf. (II 85) *are with me*

הוֹן עָתֵק n.m.s. (223)-adj. m.s. (801) *eminent wealth*

וּצְדָקָה conj.-n.f.s. (842) *and prosperity*

8:19

טוֹב פִּרְיִי adj. m.s. (II 373)-n.m.s.-1 c.s. sf. (826) *my fruit is better*

מֵחָרוּץ prep.-n.m.s. (359) *than gold*

וּמִפָּז conj.-prep.-n.m.s. paus. (808) *even fine gold*

וּתְבוּאָתִי conj.-n.f.s.-1 c.s. sf. (100) *and my yield*

מִכֶּסֶף נִבְחָר prep.-n.m.s. (494)-Ni. ptc. m.s. (בָּחַר 103) *than choice silver*

8:20

בְּאֹרַח־צְדָקָה prep.-n.m.s. cstr. (73)-n.f.s. (842) *in the way of righteousness*

אֲהַלֵּךְ Pi. impf. 1 c.s. (הָלַךְ 229) *I walk*

בְּתוֹךְ נְתִיבוֹת prep.-n.m.s. cstr. (1063)-n.f.p. cstr. (677) *in the paths of*

מִשְׁפָּט n.m.s. (1048) *justice*

8:21

לְהַנְחִיל prep.-Hi. inf.cstr. (נָחַל 635) *endowing*

אֹהֲבַי Qal act.ptc. m.p.-1 c.s. sf. (אָהֵב 12) *those who love me*

יֵשׁ subst. (441) *with wealth*

וְאֹצְרֹתֵיהֶם conj.-n.m.p.-3 m.p. sf. (69) *and their treasuries*

אֲמַלֵּא Pi. impf. 1 c.s. (מָלֵא 569) *I will fill*

8:22

יהוה קָנָנִי pr.n. (217)-Qal pf. 3 m.s.-1 c.s. sf. (קָנָה 888) *Yahweh created me*

רֵאשִׁית דַּרְכּוֹ n.f.s. cstr. (912)-n.m.s.-3 m.s. sf. (202) *at the beginning of his way*

קֶדֶם מִפְעָלָיו n.m.s. cstr. (869)-n.m.p.-3 m.s. sf. (821) *the first of his acts*

מֵאָז adv. (23) *of old*

8:23

מֵעוֹלָם prep.-n.m.s. (761) *ages ago*

נִסַּכְתִּי Ni. pf. 1 c.s. (נָסַךְ III 651) *I was set up*

מֵרֹאשׁ prep.-n.m.s. (910) *at the first*

מִקַּדְמֵי־אָרֶץ prep.-n.m.p. cstr. (869)-n.f.s. paus. (75) *before the beginning of the earth*

8:24

בְּאֵין־תְּהֹמוֹת prep.-neg. (II 34)-n.f.p. (1062) *when there were no depths*

חוֹלָלְתִּי Po'lal pf. 1 c.s. (חוּל I 296) *I was brought forth*

בְּאֵין מַעְיָנוֹת v.supra-n.m.p. (745) *when there were no springs*

נִכְבַּדֵּי־מָיִם Ni. ptc. m.p. cstr. (כָּבֵד 457)-n.m.p. paus. (565) *abounding with water*

8:25

בְּטֶרֶם הָרִים prep.-adv. (382)-n.m.p. (249) *before the mountains*

הָטְבָּעוּ Ho. pf. 3 c.p. (טָבַע 371) *had been shaped (sunk)*

לִפְנֵי גְבָעוֹת prep.-n.m.p. cstr. (815)-n.f.p. (148) *before the hills*
חוֹלָלְתִּי Po'lal pf. 1 c.s. (חוּל I 296) *I was brought forth*

8:26

עַד־לֹא עָשָׂה adv. (III 723)-neg.-Qal pf. 3 m.s. (I 793) *before he had made*
אֶרֶץ n.f.s. (75) *the earth*
וְחוּצוֹת conj.-n.m.p. (299) *and the open spaces*
וְרֹאשׁ עַפְרוֹת conj.-n.m.s. cstr. (910)-n.m.p. cstr. (779) *or the first of the dust of*
תֵּבֵל n.f.s. (385) *the world*

8:27

בַּהֲכִינוֹ שָׁמַיִם prep.-Hi. inf.cstr.-3 m.s. sf. (כּוּן 465)-n.m. du. (1029) *when he established the heavens*
שָׁם אָנִי adv. (1027)-pers.pr. 1 c.s. (58) *I was there*
בְּחוּקוֹ חוּג prep.-Qal inf.cstr.-3 m.s. sf. (חָקַק 349)-n.m.s. (295) *when he drew a circle*
עַל־פְּנֵי תְהוֹם prep.-n.m.p. cstr. (815)-n.f.s. (1062) *on the face of the deep*

8:28

בְּאַמְּצוֹ prep.-Pi. inf.cstr.-3 m.s. sf. (אָמֵץ 54) *when he made firm*
שְׁחָקִים n.m.p. (1007) *the clouds (the skies)*
מִמָּעַל prep.-adv. (751) *above*
בַּעֲזוֹז prep.-Qal inf.cstr. (עָזַז 738) *when he established*
עִינוֹת תְּהוֹם n.f.p. cstr. (745; GK 93v)-n.f.s. (1062) *the fountains of the deep*

8:29

בְּשׂוּמוֹ לַיָּם prep.-Qal inf.cstr.-3 m.s. sf. (שׂוּם 962)-prep.-def.art.-n.m.s. (410) *when he assigned to the sea*
חֻקּוֹ n.m.s.-3 m.s. sf. (349) *its limit*
וּמַיִם conj.-n.m.p. (565) *so that the waters*
לֹא יַעַבְרוּ־פִיו neg.-Qal impf. 3 m.p. (עָבַר 716)-n.m.s.-3 m.s. sf. (804) *might not transgress his command*
בְּחוּקוֹ prep.-Qal inf.cstr.-3 m.s. sf. (חָקַק 349) *when he marked out*
מוֹסְדֵי אָרֶץ n.m.p. cstr. (414)-n.f.s. paus. (75) *the foundations of the earth*

8:30

וָאֶהְיֶה consec.-Qal impf. 1 c.s. (הָיָה 224) *then I was*
אֶצְלוֹ prep.-3 m.s. sf. (I 69) *before him*
אָמוֹן n.m.s. (II 54; LXX ἁρμόζουσα) *like a master workman*
וָאֶהְיֶה v.supra *and I was*
שַׁעֲשֻׁעִים n.m.p. (1044) *delight*
יוֹם יוֹם n.m.s. (398)-v.supra *daily*
מְשַׂחֶקֶת Pi. ptc. f.s. (שָׂחַק 965) *rejoicing*
לְפָנָיו prep.-n.m.p.-3 m.s. sf. (815) *before him*
בְּכָל־עֵת prep.-n.m.s. cstr. (481)-n.f.s. (773) *always*

8:31

מְשַׂחֶקֶת Pi. ptc. f.s. (שָׂחַק 965) *rejoicing*
בְּתֵבֵל אַרְצוֹ prep.-n.f.s. cstr. (385)-n.f.s.-3 m.s. sf. (75) *in his inhabited world*
וְשַׁעֲשֻׁעַי consec.-n.m.p.-1 c.s. sf. (1044) *and (my) delighting*
אֶת־בְּנֵי אָדָם dir.obj.-n.m.p. cstr. (119)-n.m.s. (9) *in the sons of men*

8:32

וְעַתָּה בָנִים conj.-adv. (773)-n.m.p. (119) *and now my sons*
שִׁמְעוּ־לִי Qal impv. 2 m.p. (1033)-prep.-1 c.s. sf. *listen to me*
וְאַשְׁרֵי conj.-n.m.p. cstr. (81) *and happy*
דְּרָכַי n.m.p.-1 c.s. sf. (202) *my ways*
יִשְׁמֹרוּ Qal impf. 3 m.p. paus. (1036) *those who keep*

8:33

שִׁמְעוּ Qal impv. 2 m.p. (1033) *hear*
מוּסָר n.m.s. (416) *instruction*
וַחֲכָמוּ conj.-Qal impv. 2 m.p. (חָכַם 314) *and be wise*
וְאַל־תִּפְרָעוּ conj.-neg.-Qal impf. 2 m.p. paus. (III 828 פָּרַע) *and do not neglect it*

8:34

אַשְׁרֵי אָדָם n.m.p. cstr. (81)-n.m.s. (9) *happy is the man*
שֹׁמֵעַ לִי Qal act.ptc. (1033)-prep.-1 c.s. sf. *who listens to me*
לִשְׁקֹד prep.-Qal inf.cstr. (שָׁקַד 1052) *watching*
עַל־דַּלְתֹתַי prep.-n.f.p.-1 c.s. sf. (195) *at my gates*
יוֹם יוֹם n.m.s. (398)-v.supra *daily*
לִשְׁמֹר prep.-Qal inf.cstr. (1036) *waiting*
מְזוּזֹת פְּתָחָי n.f.p. cstr. (265)-n.m.p.-1 c.s. sf. paus. (835) *beside my doors*

8:35

כִּי מֹצְאִי conj. (471)–Qal act.ptc.–1 c.s. sf. (מָצָא 592) *for he who finds me*

מָצָאי חַיִּים Qal pf. 3 m.s. (rd. מָצָא; 592)–n.m.p. (313) *finds life*

וַיָּפֶק consec.–Hi. impf. 3 m.s. (פּוּק II 807) *and obtains*

רָצוֹן n.m.s. (953) *favor*

מֵיהוה prep.–pr.n. (217) *from Yahweh*

8:36

וְחֹטְאִי conj.–Qal act.ptc.–1 c.s. sf. (חָטָא 306) *but he who misses me*

חֹמֵס נַפְשׁוֹ Qal act.ptc. (329)–n.f.s.–3 m.s. sf. (659) *injures himself*

כָּל־מְשַׂנְאַי n.m.s. cstr. (481)–Pi. ptc. m.p.–1 c.s. sf. (שָׂנֵא 971) *all who hate me*

אָהֲבוּ מָוֶת Qal pf. 3 c.p. (אָהֵב 12)–n.m.s. (560) *love death*

9:1

חָכְמוֹת n.f.p. (315) *wisdom*

בָּנְתָה Qal pf. 3 f.s. (בָּנָה 124) *builds*

בֵיתָהּ n.m.s.–3 f.s. sf. (108) *her house*

חָצְבָה Qal pf. 3 f.s. (חָצַב 345) *she has hewn*

עַמּוּדֶיהָ שִׁבְעָה n.m.p.–3 f.s. sf. (765)–num. f. (I 987) *her seven pillars*

9:2

טָבְחָה Qal pf. 3 f.s. (טָבַח 370) *she has slaughtered*

טִבְחָהּ n.m.s.–3 f.s. sf. (I 370) *her beasts*

מָסְכָה Qal pf. 3 f.s. (מָסַךְ 587) *she has mixed*

יֵינָהּ n.m.s.–3 f.s. sf. (406) *her wine*

אַף עָרְכָה conj. II 64)–Qal pf. 3 f.s. (עָרַךְ 789) *she has also set*

שֻׁלְחָנָהּ n.m.s.–3 f.s. sf. (1020) *her table*

9:3

שָׁלְחָה Qal pf. 3 f.s. (שָׁלַח 1018) *she has sent out*

נַעֲרֹתֶיהָ n.f.p.–3 f.s. sf. (655) *her maids*

תִקְרָא Qal impf. 3 f.s. (קָרָא 894) *to call*

עַל־גַּפֵּי מְרֹמֵי prep.–n.m.p. cstr. (172)–n.m.p. cstr. (928) *from the highest places in*

קָרֶת n.f.s. paus. (900) *the town*

9:4

מִי־פֶתִי interr. (566)–adj. m.s. (834) *whoever is simple*

יָסֻר הֵנָּה Qal impf. 3 m.s. apoc.juss. (סוּר 693)–adv. (I 244) *let him turn in here*

חֲסַר־לֵב adj. m.s. cstr. (341)–n.m.s. (524) *who is without sense*

אָמְרָה לוֹ Qal pf. 3 f.s. (אָמַר 55)–prep.–3 m.s. sf. *she says to him*

9:5

לְכוּ Qal impv. 2 m.p. (הָלַךְ 229) *come*

לַחֲמוּ Qal impv. 2 m.p. (לָחַם II 536) *eat*

בְלַחֲמִי prep.–n.m.s.–1 c.s. sf. (536) *of my bread*

וּשְׁתוּ בְּיַיִן conj.–Qal impv. 2 m.p. (שָׁתָה 1059) –prep.–n.m.s. (406) *and drink of the wine*

מָסָכְתִּי Qal pf. 1 c.s. paus. (מָסַךְ 587) *I have mixed*

9:6

עִזְבוּ פְתָאִים Qal impv. 2 m.p. (עָזַב I 736)–adj. m.p. (834; GK 93x) *leave simple ones*

וִחְיוּ conj.–Qal impv. 2 m.p. (חָיָה 310) *and live*

וְאִשְׁרוּ conj.–Qal impv. 2 m.p. (אָשַׁר 80) *and walk*

בְּדֶרֶךְ בִּינָה prep.–n.m.s. cstr. (202)–n.f.s. (108) *in the way of insight*

9:7

יֹסֵר לֵץ Qal act.ptc. (יָסַר 415)–Qal act.ptc. (לִיץ 539) *he who corrects a scoffer*

לֹקֵחַ לוֹ קָלוֹן Qal act.ptc. (לָקַח 542)–prep.–3 m.s. sf.–n.m.s. (885) *gets himself abuse*

וּמוֹכִיחַ לְרָשָׁע conj.–Hi. ptc. m.s. (יָכַח 406) –prep.–adj. m.s. (957) *and he who reproves a wicked man*

מוּמוֹ n.m.s.–3 m.s. sf. (548) *incurs blemish*

9:8

אַל־תּוֹכַח לֵץ neg.–Hi. impf. 2 m.s. (יָכַח 406) –Qal act.ptc. (לִיץ 539) *do not reprove a scoffer*

פֶּן־יִשְׂנָאֶךָּ conj. 814)–Qal impf. 3 m.s.–2 m.s. sf. (971 שָׂנֵא) *or he will hate you*

הוֹכַח לְחָכָם Hi. impv. 2 m.s. (יָכַח 406)–prep. –adj. m.s. (314) *reprove a wise man*

וְיֶאֱהָבֶךָּ conj.–Qal impf. 3 m.s.–2 m.s. sf. (אָהֵב 12) *and he will love you*

9:9

תֵּן לְחָכָם Qal impv. 2 m.s. (נָתַן 678)–prep.–adj. m.s. (314) *give to a wise man*

וְיֶחְכַּם־עוֹד conj.–Qal impf. 3 m.s. (חָכַם 314) –adv. (728) *and he will be still wiser*

הוֹדַע Hi. impv. 2 m.s. (יָדַע 393) *teach*

לְצַדִּיק prep.–adj. m.s. (843) *a righteous man*

וְיוֹסֶף conj.-Hi. impf. 3 m.s. (יָסַף 414) *and he will increase*
לֶקַח n.m.s. (544) *in learning*

9:10

תְּחִלַּת חָכְמָה n.f.s. cstr. (321)-n.f.s. (315) *the beginning of wisdom*
יִרְאַת יהוה n.f.s. cstr. (432)-pr.n. (217) *the fear of Yahweh*
וְדַעַת קְדֹשִׁים conj.-n.f.s. cstr. (395)-adj. m.p. (872) *and the knowledge of the Holy One*
בִּינָה n.f.s. (108) *insight*

9:11

כִּי־בִי conj. (471)-prep.-1 c.s. sf. *for by me*
יִרְבּוּ יָמֶיךָ Qal impf. 3 m.p. (רָבָה I 915)-n.m.p.-2 m.s. sf. (398) *your days will be multiplied*
וְיוֹסִיפוּ conj.-Hi. impf. 3 m.p. (יָסַף 414; LXX προστεθήσεται) *and will be added*
לְּךָ prep.-2 m.s. sf. *to you*
שְׁנוֹת חַיִּים n.f.p. cstr. (1040)-n.m.p. (313) *years of life*

9:12

אִם־חָכַמְתָּ hypoth.part. (49)-Qal pf. 2 m.s. (חָכַם 314) *if you are wise*
חָכַמְתָּ לָּךְ v.supra-prep.-2 m.s. sf. paus. *you are wise for yourself*
וְלַצְתָּ conj.-Qal pf. 2 m.s. (לִיץ 539) *if you scoff*
לְבַדְּךָ תִשָּׂא prep.-n.m.s.-2 m.s. sf. (II 94)-Qal impf. 2 m.s. (נָשָׂא 669) *you alone will bear it*

9:13

אֵשֶׁת כְּסִילוּת n.f.s. cstr. (61)-n.f.s. (493) *a foolish woman*
הֹמִיָּה Qal act.ptc. f.s. (הָמָה 242) *is noisy*
פְּתַיּוּת n.f.s. (834) *is wanton*
וּבַל־יָדְעָה מָּה conj.-neg.-Qal pf. 3 f.s. (יָדַע 393)-interr. (552) *and does not know anything*

9:14

וְיָשְׁבָה conj.-Qal pf. 3 f.s. (יָשַׁב 442) *she sits*
לְפֶתַח בֵּיתָהּ prep.-n.m.s. cstr. (835)-n.m.s.-2 m.s. sf. (108) *at the door of her house*
עַל־כִּסֵּא prep.-n.m.s. cstr. (490) *on a seat on*
מְרֹמֵי קָרֶת n.m.p. cstr. (928)-n.f.s. paus. (900) *the high places of the town*

9:15

לִקְרֹא prep.-Qal inf.cstr. (קָרָא 894) *calling*
לְעֹבְרֵי־דָרֶךְ prep.-Qal act.ptc. m.p. cstr. (עָבַר 716)-n.m.s. paus. (202) *to those who pass by*
הַמְיַשְּׁרִים def.art.-Pi. ptc. m.p. (יָשַׁר 448) *who are going straight*
אֹרְחוֹתָם n.m.p.-3 m.p. sf. (73) *on their way*

9:16

מִי־פֶתִי interr. (566)-adj. m.s. (834) *whoever is simple*
יָסֻר הֵנָּה Qal impf. 3 m.s. apoc. (סוּר 693)-adv. (I 244) *let him turn in here*
וַחֲסַר־לֵב conj.-adj. m.s. cstr. (341)-n.m.s. (524) *and to him who is without sense*
וְאָמְרָה לּוֹ conj.-Qal pf. 3 f.s. (55)-prep.-3 m.s. sf. *she says*

9:17

מַיִם־גְּנוּבִים n.m.p. (565)-Qal pass.ptc. m.p. (גָּנַב 170) *stolen water*
יִמְתָּקוּ Qal impf. 3 m.p. paus. (מָתֹק 608) *is sweet*
וְלֶחֶם conj.-n.m.s. (536) *and bread*
סְתָרִים n.m.p. (712) *in secret*
יִנְעָם Qal impf. 3 m.s. (נָעֵם 653) *is pleasant*

9:18

וְלֹא־יָדַע conj.-neg.-Qal pf. 3 m.s. (393) *but he does not know*
כִּי־רְפָאִים שָׁם conj. (471)-n.m.p. I 952)-adv. (1027) *that shades are there*
בְּעִמְקֵי שְׁאוֹל prep.-n.m.p. cstr. (771)-n.f.s. (982) *in the depths of Sheol*
קְרֻאֶיהָ Qal pass.ptc. m.p.-3 f.s. sf. (קָרָא I 894) *her guests*

10:1

מִשְׁלֵי שְׁלֹמֹה n.m.p. cstr. (605)-pr.n. (1024) *the proverbs of Solomon*
בֵּן חָכָם n.m.s. (119)-adj. m.s. (314) *a wise son*
יְשַׂמַּח־אָב Pi. impf. 3 m.s. (שָׂמַח 970)-n.m.s. (3) *makes a glad father*
וּבֵן כְּסִיל conj.-n.m.s. (119)-adj. m.s. (I 493) *but a foolish son*
תּוּגַת אִמּוֹ n.f.s. cstr. (387)-n.f.s.-3 m.s. sf. (51) *is a sorrow to his mother*

10:2

לֹא־יוֹעִילוּ neg.-Hi. impf. 3 m.p. (יָעַל I 418) *do not profit*
אוֹצְרוֹת רֶשַׁע n.m.p. cstr. (69)-n.m.s. (957) *treasures gained by wickedness*

וּצְדָקָה conj.-n.f.s. (842) *but righteousness*
תַּצִּיל Hi. impf. 3 f.s. (נָצַל 665) *delivers*
מִמָּוֶת prep.-n.m.s. (560) *from death*

10:3

לֹא־יַרְעִיב neg.-Hi. impf. 3 m.s. (רָעֵב 944) *does not let ... go hungry*
יהוה pr.n. (217) *Yahweh*
נֶפֶשׁ צַדִּיק n.f.s. cstr. (659)-adj. m.s. (843) *the righteous*
וְהַוַּת רְשָׁעִים conj.-n.f.s. cstr. 217)-adj. m.p. (957) *the craving of the wicked*
יֶהְדֹּף Qal impf. 3 m.s. (הָדַף 213) *he thwarts*

10:4

רָאשׁ עֹשָׂה n.m.s. (930; LXX πενία; v. רִישׁ)-Qal act.ptc. (I 793) *causes poverty*
כַּף־רְמִיָּה n.f.s. cstr. (496)-n.f.s. (II 941) *a slack hand*
וְיַד חָרוּצִים conj.-n.f.s. cstr. (388)-adj. m.p. (I 358) *but the hand of the diligent*
תַּעֲשִׁיר Hi. impf. 3 f.s. (עָשַׁר 799) *makes rich*

10:5

אֹגֵר בַּקַּיִץ Qal act.ptc. (אָגַר 8)-prep.-def.art. -n.m.s. (884) *who gathers in summer*
בֵּן n.m.s. (119) *a son*
מַשְׂכִּיל Hi. ptc. (שָׂכַל I 968) *is prudent*
נִרְדָּם בַּקָּצִיר Ni. ptc. (רָדַם 922)-prep.-def.art. -n.m.s. (894) *who sleeps in harvest*
בֵּן v.supra *a son*
מֵבִישׁ Hi. ptc. (בּוֹשׁ 101) *brings shame*

10:6

בְּרָכוֹת n.f.p. (139) *blessings*
לְרֹאשׁ צַדִּיק prep.-n.m.s. cstr. (910)-adj. m.s. (843) *on the head of the righteous*
וּפִי רְשָׁעִים conj.-n.m.s. cstr. (804)-adj.m.p. (957) *but the mouth of the wicked*
יְכַסֶּה Pi. impf. 3 m.s. (כָּסָה 491) *covers*
חָמָס n.m.s. (329) *violence*

10:7

זֵכֶר צַדִּיק n.m.s. cstr. (271)-adj. m.s. (843) *the memory of the righteous*
לִבְרָכָה prep.-n.f.s. (139) *is a blessing*
וְשֵׁם רְשָׁעִים conj.-n.m.s. cstr. (1027)-adj. m.p. (957) *but the name of the wicked*
יִרְקָב Qal impf. 3 m.s. (רָקֵב 955) *will rot*

10:8

חֲכַם־לֵב adj. m.s. (314)-n.m.s. (524) *the wise of heart*
יִקַּח מִצְוֹת Qal impf. 3 m.s. (לָקַח 542)-n.f.p. (846) *will heed commandments*
וֶאֱוִיל שְׂפָתַיִם conj.-adj. m.s. cstr. (17)-n.f. du. (973) *but a prating fool*
יִלָּבֵט Ni. impf. 3 m.s. (לָבַט 526) *will come to ruin*

10:9

הוֹלֵךְ בַּתֹּם Qal act.ptc. (הָלַךְ 229)-prep.-def. art.-n.m.s. (1070) *he who walks in integrity*
יֵלֶךְ בֶּטַח Qal impf. 3 m.s. (הָלַךְ 229)-n.m.s. as adv. (105) *walks securely*
וּמְעַקֵּשׁ conj.-Pi. ptc. (עָקַשׁ 786) *but he who perverts*
דְּרָכָיו n.m.p.-3 m.s. sf. (202) *his ways*
יִוָּדֵעַ Ni. impf. 3 m.s. (יָדַע 393) *will be found out*

10:10

קֹרֵץ עַיִן Qal act.ptc. (קָרַץ 902)-n.f.s. (744) *he who winks the eye*
יִתֵּן עַצָּבֶת Qal impf. 3 m.s. (נָתַן 678)-n.f.s. paus. (781) *causes trouble*
וֶאֱוִיל שְׂפָתַיִם conj.-adj. m.s. cstr. (17)-n.f. du. (973) *but a prating fool*
יִלָּבֵט cf. 10:8b Ni. impf. 3 m.s. (לָבַט 526) *will come to ruin*

10:11

מְקוֹר חַיִּים n.m.s. cstr. (881)-n.m.p. (313) *a fountain of life*
פִּי צַדִּיק n.m.s. cstr. (804)-adj. m.s. (843) *the mouth of the righteous*
וּפִי רְשָׁעִים conj.-v.supra-adj. m.p. (957) *but the mouth of the wicked*
יְכַסֶּה cf. 10:6b Pi. impf. 3 m.s. (כָּסָה 491) *conceals*
חָמָס n.m.s. (329) *violence*

10:12

שִׂנְאָה n.f.s. (971) *hatred*
תְּעוֹרֵר Polel impf. 3 f.s. (עוּר I 734) *stirs up*
מְדָנִים n.m.p. (I 193) *strife*
וְעַל כָּל־פְּשָׁעִים conj.-prep.-n.m.s. cstr. (481) -n.m.p. (833) *but all offenses*
תְּכַסֶּה Pi. impf. 3 f.s. (כָּסָה 491) *covers*
אַהֲבָה n.f.s. (13) *love*

10:13

בְּשִׂפְתֵי נָבוֹן prep.-n.f. du. cstr. (973)-Ni. ptc. (בִּין 106) *on the lips of him who has understanding*

תִּמָּצֵא Ni. impf. 3 f.s. (מָצָא 592) *is found*

חָכְמָה n.f.s. (315) *wisdom*

וְשֵׁבֶט conj.-n.m.s. (986) *but a rod*

לְגֵו prep.-n.m.s. cstr. (I 156) *for the back of*

חֲסַר־לֵב adj. m.s. cstr. (341)-n.m.s. (524) *him who lacks sense*

10:14

חֲכָמִים adj. m.s. (314) *wise men*

יִצְפְּנוּ־דָעַת Qal impf. 3 m.p. (צָפַן 860)-n.f.s. paus. (395) *lay up knowledge*

וּפִי־אֱוִיל conj.-n.m.s. cstr. (804)-adj. m.s. (17) *but the babbling of a fool*

מְחִתָּה קְרֹבָה n.f.s. (369)-adj. f.s. (898) *imminent ruin*

10:15

הוֹן עָשִׁיר n.m.s. cstr. (223)-adj. m.s. (799) *a rich man's wealth*

קִרְיַת עֻזּוֹ n.f.s. cstr. (900)-n.m.s.-3 m.s. sf. (738) *his strong city*

מְחִתַּת דַּלִּים n.f.s. cstr. (369)-adj. m.p. (195) *the ruin of the poor*

רֵישָׁם n.m.s.-3 m.p. sf. (930) *their poverty*

10:16

פְּעֻלַּת צַדִּיק n.f.s. cstr. (821)-adj. m.s. (843) *the wage of the righteous*

לְחַיִּים prep.-n.m.p. (313) *leads to life*

תְּבוּאַת רָשָׁע n.f.s. cstr. (100)-adj. m.s. (957) *the gain of the wicked*

לְחַטָּאת prep.-n.f.s. paus. (308) *to sin*

10:17

אֹרַח n.m.s. (73) *on the path*

לְחַיִּים prep.-n.m.p. (313) *to life*

שׁוֹמֵר מוּסָר Qal act.ptc. (שָׁמַר 1036)-n.m.s. (416) *he who heeds instruction*

וְעוֹזֵב תּוֹכַחַת conj.-Qal act.ptc. (עָזַב I 736)-n.f.s. (407) *but he who rejects reproof*

מַתְעֶה Hi. ptc. (תָּעָה 1073) *goes astray*

10:18

מְכַסֶּה Pi. ptc. (כָּסָה 491) *he who conceals*

שִׂנְאָה n.f.s. (971) *hatred*

שִׂפְתֵי־שָׁקֶר n.f.p. cstr. (973)-n.m.s. paus. (1055) *lying lips*

וּמוֹצִא דִבָּה conj.-Hi. ptc. (יָצָא 422)-n.f.s. (179) *and he who utters slander*

הוּא כְסִיל pers.pr. 3 m.s. (214)-n.m.s. (493) *he is a fool*

10:19

בְּרֹב דְּבָרִים prep.-n.m.s. cstr. (913)-n.m.p. (182) *when words are many*

לֹא־יֶחְדַּל־פָּשַׁע neg.-Qal impf. 3 m.s. (חָדַל 292) -n.m.s. (833) *transgression is not lacking*

וְחֹשֵׂךְ שְׂפָתָיו conj.-Qal act.ptc. (חָשַׂךְ 362) -n.f.p.-3 m.s. sf. (973) *but he who restrains his lips*

מַשְׂכִּיל Hi. ptc. m.s. (שָׂכַל I 968) *is prudent*

10:20

כֶּסֶף נִבְחָר n.m.s. (494)-Ni. ptc. m.s. (בָּחַר 103) *choice silver*

לְשׁוֹן צַדִּיק n.f.s. cstr. (546)-adj. m.s. (843) *the tongue of the righteous*

לֵב רְשָׁעִים n.m.s. cstr. (524)-adj. m.p. (957) *the mind of the wicked*

כִּמְעָט prep.-subst. (589) *of little worth*

10:21

שִׂפְתֵי צַדִּיק n.f.p. cstr. (973)-adj. m.s. (843) *the lips of the righteous*

יִרְעוּ רַבִּים Qal impf. 3 m.p. (רָעָה I 944)-adj. m.p. (I 912) *feed many*

וֶאֱוִילִים conj.-n.m.p. (17) *but fools*

בַּחֲסַר־לֵב prep.-Qal inf.cstr. (חָסֵר 341)-n.m.s. (524) *for lack of sense*

יָמוּתוּ Qal impf. 3 m.p. (מוּת 559) *die*

10:22

בִּרְכַּת יהוה n.f.s. cstr. (139)-pr.n. (217) *the blessing of Yahweh*

הִיא תַעֲשִׁיר demons.adj. f.s. (214)-Hi. impf. 3 f.s. (עָשַׁר 799) *makes rich*

וְלֹא־יוֹסִף conj.-neg.-Hi. impf. 3 m.s. (יָסַף 414) *and he adds no*

עֶצֶב n.m.s. (I 780) *sorrow*

עִמָּהּ prep.-3 f.s. sf. *with it*

10:23

כִּשְׂחוֹק prep.-n.m.s. (966) *like sport*

לִכְסִיל prep.-n.m.s. (493) *to a fool*

עֲשׂוֹת זִמָּה Qal inf.cstr. (עָשָׂה I 793)-n.f.s. (I 273) *to do wrong*

וְחָכְמָה conj.-n.f.s. (315) *but wisdom*

לְאִישׁ תְּבוּנָה prep.-n.m.s. cstr. (35)-n.f.s. (108) *to a man of understanding*

10:24

מְגוֹרַת רָשָׁע n.f.s. cstr. (159)-adj. m.s. (957) *what the wicked dreads*

הִיא תְבוֹאֶנּוּ demons.adj. f.s. (214)-Qal impf. 3 f.s.-3 m.s. sf. (בּוֹא 97) *will come upon him*

וְתַאֲוַת צַדִּיקִים conj.-n.f.s. cstr. (16)-adj. m.p. (843) *but the desire of the righteous*

יִתֵּן Qal impf. 3 m.s. (נָתַן 678) *will be granted*

10:25

כַּעֲבוֹר סוּפָה prep.-Qal inf.cstr. (עָבַר 716)-n.f.s. (I 693) *when the tempest passes*

וְאֵין רָשָׁע conj.-neg. (II 34)-adj. m.s. (957) *the wicked is no more*

וְצַדִּיק conj.-adj. m.s. (843) *but the righteous*

יְסוֹד n.f.s. (414) *is established*

עוֹלָם n.m.s. (761) *for ever*

10:26

כַּחֹמֶץ prep.-def.art.-n.m.s. (330) *like vinegar*

לַשִּׁנַּיִם prep.-def.art.-n.f. du. (1042) *to the teeth*

וְכֶעָשָׁן conj.-prep.-n.m.s. (I 798) *and smoke*

לָעֵינָיִם prep.-def.art.-n.f. du. paus. (744) *to the eyes*

כֵּן הֶעָצֵל adv. (485)-def.art.-adj. m.s. (782) *so is the sluggard*

לְשֹׁלְחָיו prep.-Qal act.ptc. m.p.-3 m.s. sf. (שָׁלַח 1018) *to those who send him*

10:27

יִרְאַת יהוה n.f.s. cstr. (432)-pr.n. (217) *the fear of Yahweh*

תּוֹסִיף יָמִים Hi. impf. 3 f.s. (יָסַף 414)-n.m.p. (398) *prolongs life*

וּשְׁנוֹת רְשָׁעִים conj.-n.f.p. cstr. (1040)-adj. m.p. (957) *but the years of the wicked*

תִּקְצֹרְנָה Qal impf. 3 f.p. (קָצַר 894) *will be short*

10:28

תּוֹחֶלֶת צַדִּיקִים n.f.p. cstr. (404)-adj. m.p. (843) *the hope of the righteous*

שִׂמְחָה n.f.s. (970) *ends in gladness*

וְתִקְוַת רְשָׁעִים conj.-n.f.s. cstr. (II 876)-adj. m.p. (957) *but the expectation of the wicked*

תֹּאבֵד Qal impf. 3 f.s. (אָבַד 1) *comes to nought*

10:29

מָעוֹז n.m.s. (731) *a stronghold*

לַתֹּם דֶּרֶךְ prep.-def.art.-n.m.s. (1070)-m.s. (202) *to him whose way is upright*

יהוה pr.n. (217) *Yahweh*

וּמְחִתָּה conj.-n.f.s. (369) *but destruction*

לְפֹעֲלֵי אָוֶן prep.-Qal act.ptc. m.p. cstr. (פָּעַל 821)-n.m.s. (19) *to evildoers*

10:30

צַדִּיק adj. m.s. (843) *the righteous*

לְעוֹלָם prep.-n.m.s. (761) *for ever*

בַּל־יִמּוֹט neg. (115)-Ni. impf. 3 m.s. (מוֹט 556) *will not be moved*

וּרְשָׁעִים conj.-adj. m.p. (957) *but the wicked*

לֹא־יִשְׁכְּנוּ־אָרֶץ neg.-Qal impf. 3 m.p. (שָׁכַן 1014)-n.f.s. paus. (75) *will not dwell in the land*

10:31

פִּי־צַדִּיק n.m.s. cstr. (804)-adj. m.s. (843) *the mouth of the righteous*

יָנוּב Qal impf. 3 m.s. (נוּב 626) *brings forth*

חָכְמָה n.f.s. (315) *wisdom*

וּלְשׁוֹן תַּהְפֻּכוֹת conj.-n.f.s. cstr. (546)-n.f.p. (246) *but the perverse tongue*

תִּכָּרֵת Ni. impf. 3 f.s. (כָּרַת 503) *will be cut off*

10:32

שִׂפְתֵי צַדִּיק n.f.p. cstr. (973)-adj. m.s. (843) *the lips of the righteous*

יֵדְעוּן Qal impf. 3 m.p. (יָדַע 393) *know*

רָצוֹן n.m.s. (953) *what is acceptable*

וּפִי רְשָׁעִים conj.-n.m.s. cstr. (804)-adj. m.p. (957) *but the mouth of the wicked*

תַּהְפֻּכוֹת n.f.p. (246) *is perverse*

11:1

מֹאזְנֵי מִרְמָה n.m. du. cstr. (24)-n.f.s. (941) *a false balance*

תּוֹעֲבַת יהוה n.f.s. cstr. (1072)-pr.n. (217) *an abomination to Yahweh*

וְאֶבֶן שְׁלֵמָה conj.-n.f.s. (6)-adj. f.s. (I 1023) *but a just weight*

רְצוֹנוֹ n.m.s.-3 m.s. sf. (953) *his delight*

11:2

בָּא־זָדוֹן Qal pf. 3 m.s. (בּוֹא 97)-n.m.s. (268) *when pride comes*

וַיָּבֹא קָלוֹן consec.-Qal impf. 3 m.s. (בּוֹא 97)-n.m.s. (885) *then comes disgrace*

וְאֶת־צְנוּעִים conj.-prep. (II 85)-adj. m.p. (857) *but with the humble*

חָכְמָה n.f.s. (315) *wisdom*

11:3

תֻּמַּת יְשָׁרִים n.f.s. cstr. (1070)–adj. m.p. (449) *the integrity of the upright*

תַּנְחֵם Hi. impf. 3 f.s.–3 m.p. sf. (נָחָה 634) *guides them*

וְסֶלֶף בּוֹגְדִים conj.–n.m.s. cstr. (701)–Qal act.ptc. m.p. (בָּגַד 93) *but the crookedness of the treacherous*

וְשָׁדֵּם conj.–Qal impf. 3 m.s.–3 m.p. sf. (שָׁדַד 994; Q יְשָׁדֵּם; GK 67n) *destroys them*

11:4

לֹא־יוֹעִיל הוֹן neg.–Hi. impf. 3 m.s. (יָעַל I 418)–n.m.s. (223) *riches do not profit*

בְּיוֹם עֶבְרָה prep.–n.m.s. cstr. (398)–n.f.s. (720) *in the day of wrath*

וּצְדָקָה conj.–n.f.s. (842) *but righteousness*

תַּצִּיל Hi. impf. 3 f.s. (נָצַל 664) *delivers*

מִמָּוֶת prep.–n.m.s. (560) *from death*

11:5

צִדְקַת תָּמִים n.f.s. cstr. (842)–adj. m.s. (1071) *the righteousness of the blameless*

תְּיַשֵּׁר Pi. impf. 3 f.s. (יָשַׁר 448) *keeps straight*

דַּרְכּוֹ n.m.s.–3 m.s. sf. (202) *his way*

וּבְרִשְׁעָתוֹ conj.–prep.–n.f.s.–3 m.s. sf. (958) *but by his own wickedness*

יִפֹּל רָשָׁע Qal impf. 3 m.s. (נָפַל 656)–adj. m.s. (957) *the wicked falls*

11:6

צִדְקַת יְשָׁרִים n.f.s. cstr. (842)–adj. m.p. (449) *the righteousness of the upright*

תַּצִּילֵם Hi. impf. 3 f.s.–3 m.p. sf. (נָצַל 664) *delivers them*

וּבְהַוַּת בֹּגְדִים conj.–prep.–n.f.s. cstr. (217)–Qal act.ptc. m.p. (בָּגַד 93) *but the desire of the treacherous*

יִלָּכֵדוּ Ni. impf. 3 m.p. (לָכַד 539) *are taken captive*

11:7

בְּמוֹת אָדָם רָשָׁע prep.–n.m.s. cstr. (560)–n.m.s. (9)–adj. m.s. (957) *when the wicked man dies*

תֹּאבַד תִּקְוָה Qal impf. 3 f.s. (אָבַד 1)–n.f.s. (876) *his hope perishes*

וְתוֹחֶלֶת אוֹנִים conj.–n.f.s. cstr. (404)–n.m.p. (19 or I 20) *and the expectation of the godless* (or *in strength*)

אָבָדָה Qal pf. 3 f.s. paus. (אָבַד 1) *comes to nought*

11:8

צַדִּיק adj. m.s. (843) *the righteous*

מִצָּרָה prep.–n.f.s. (865) *from trouble*

נֶחֱלָץ Ni. pf. 3 m.s. paus. (חָלַץ I 322) *is delivered*

וַיָּבֹא רָשָׁע consec.–Qal impf. 3 m.s. (בּוֹא 97)–adj. m.s. (957) *and the wicked gets into*

תַּחְתָּיו prep.–3 m.s. sf. (1065) *instead of it*

11:9

בְּפֶה prep.–n.m.s. (804) *with his mouth*

חָנֵף adj. m.s. (338) *the godless man*

יַשְׁחִת Hi. impf. 3 m.s. (שָׁחַת 1007) *would destroy*

רֵעֵהוּ n.m.s.–3 m.s. sf. (945) *his neighbor*

וּבְדַעַת conj.–prep.–n.f.s. (395) *but by knowledge*

צַדִּיקִים adj. m.p. (843) *the righteous*

יֵחָלֵצוּ Ni. pf. 3 m.p. (חָלַץ I 322) *are delivered*

11:10

בְּטוּב צַדִּיקִים prep.–n.m.s. cstr. (375)–adj. m.p. (843) *when it goes well with the righteous*

תַּעֲלֹץ קִרְיָה Qal impf. 3 f.s. (עָלַץ 763) n.f.s. (900) *the city rejoices*

וּבַאֲבֹד רְשָׁעִים conj.–prep.–Qal inf.cstr. (אָבַד 1)–adj. m.p. (957) *and when the wicked perish*

רִנָּה n.f.s. (943) *shouts of gladness*

11:11

בְּבִרְכַּת יְשָׁרִים prep.–n.f.s. cstr. (139)–adj. m.p. (449) *by the blessing of the upright*

תָּרוּם קָרֶת Qal impf. 3 f.s. (רוּם 926)–n.f.s. paus. (900) *a city is exalted*

וּבְפִי רְשָׁעִים conj.–prep.–n.m.s. cstr. (804)–adj. m.p. (957) *but by the mouth of the wicked*

תֵּהָרֵס Ni. impf. 3 f.s. (הָרַס 248) *it is overthrown*

11:12

בָּז־לְרֵעֵהוּ Qal act.ptc. (בּוּז I 100)–prep.–n.m.s.–3 m.s. sf. (945) *he who belittles his neighbor*

חֲסַר־לֵב adj. m.s. cstr. (341)–n.m.s. (524) *lacks sense*

וְאִישׁ תְּבוּנוֹת conj.–n.m.s. cstr. (35)–n.f.p. (108) *but a man of understanding*

יַחֲרִישׁ Hi. impf. 3 m.s. (חָרַשׁ II 361) *remains silent*

11:13

הוֹלֵךְ Qal act.ptc. (הָלַךְ 229) *he who goes about*

רָכִיל n.m.s. (940) *as a talebearer*

מְגַלֶּה־סּוֹד Pi. ptc. (גָּלָה 162)-n.m.s. (691) *reveals secrets*

וְנֶאֱמַן־רוּחַ conj.-Ni. ptc. m.s. cstr. (אָמַן I 52) -n.f.s. (924) *but he who is trustworthy in spirit*

מְכַסֶּה דָבָר Pi. ptc. (כָּסָה 491)-n.m.s. (182) *keeps a thing hidden*

11:14

בְּאֵין תַּחְבֻּלוֹת prep.-neg. cstr. (II 34)-n.f.p. (287) *when there is no guidance*

יִפָּל־עָם Qal impf. 3 m.s. (נָפַל 656)-n.m.s. (I 766) *a people falls*

וּתְשׁוּעָה conj.-n.f.s. (448) *but safety*

בְּרֹב יוֹעֵץ prep.-n.m.s. cstr. (913)-Qal act.ptc. (419 יָעַץ) *in an abundance of counselors*

11:15

רַע־יֵרוֹעַ n.m.s. (II 948)-Ni. impf. 3 m.s. (רָעַע 949) *he suffers hurt*

כִּי־עָרַב זָר conj. (471)-Qal pf. 3 m.s. (II 786)-Qal act.ptc. (זוּר I 266) *when he gives surety for a stranger*

וְשֹׂנֵא תֹקְעִים conj.-Qal act.ptc. (שָׂנֵא 971)-Qal act.ptc. m.p. (תָּקַע 1075) *but he who hates suretyship*

בוֹטֵחַ Qal act.ptc. (בָּטַח I 105) *is secure*

11:16

אֵשֶׁת־חֵן n.f.s. cstr. (61)-n.m.s. (I 336) *a gracious woman*

תִּתְמֹךְ כָּבוֹד Qal impf. 3 f.s. (תָּמַךְ 1069)-n.m.s. (II 458) *gets honor*

וְעָרִיצִים conj.-adj. m.p. (792) *and violent men*

יִתְמְכוּ־עֹשֶׁר Qal impf. 3 m.p. (תָּמַךְ 1069)-n.m.s. (799) *get riches*

11:17

גֹּמֵל נַפְשׁוֹ Qal act.ptc. (גָּמַל 168)-n.f.s.-3 m.s. sf. (659) *benefits himself*

אִישׁ חָסֶד n.m.s. cstr. (35)-n.m.s. paus. (I 338) *a man who is kind*

וְעֹכֵר שְׁאֵרוֹ conj.-Qal act.ptc. (עָכַר 747)-n.m.s.-3 m.s. sf. (984) *but hurts himself*

אַכְזָרִי adj. m.s. (470) *a cruel man*

11:18

רָשָׁע עֹשֶׂה adj. m.s. (957)-Qal act.ptc. (עָשָׂה I 793) *a wicked man earns*

פְּעֻלַּת־שָׁקֶר n.f.s. cstr. (821)-n.m.s. paus. (1055) *deceptive wages*

וְזֹרֵעַ צְדָקָה conj.-Qal act.ptc. (281)-n.f.s. (842) *but one who sows righteousness*

שֶׂכֶר אֱמֶת n.m.s. cstr. (969)-n.f.s. (54) *a sure reward*

11:19

כֵּן־צְדָקָה adj. m.s. cstr. (I 467)-n.f.s. (842) *he who is steadfast in righteousness*

לְחַיִּים prep.-n.m.p. (313) *will live*

וּמְרַדֵּף רָעָה conj.-Pi. ptc. (רָדַף 922)-n.f.s. (949) *but he who pursues evil*

לְמוֹתוֹ prep.-n.m.s.-3 m.s. sf. (560) *will die*

11:20

תּוֹעֲבַת יהוה n.f.s. cstr. (1072)-pr.n. (217) *an abomination to Yahweh*

עִקְּשֵׁי־לֵב adj. m.p. cstr. (786)-n.m.s. (524) *men of perverse mind*

וּרְצוֹנוֹ conj.-n.m.s.-3 m.s. sf. (953) *but his delight*

תְּמִימֵי דָרֶךְ adj. m.p. cstr. (1071)-n.m.s. paus. (202) *those of blameless ways*

11:21

יָד לְיָד n.f.s. (388)-prep.-v.supra *hand to hand*

לֹא־יִנָּקֶה neg.-Ni. impf. 3 m.s. (נָקָה 667) *will not go unpunished*

רָע adj. m.s. (I 948) *an evil man*

וְזֶרַע צַדִּיקִים conj.-n.m.s. cstr. (282)-adj. m.p. (843) *but those who are righteous*

נִמְלָט Ni. pf. 3 m.s. (מָלַט 572) *will be delivered*

11:22

נֶזֶם זָהָב n.m.s. cstr. (633)-n.m.s. (262) *like a gold ring*

בְּאַף חֲזִיר prep.-n.m.s. cstr. (I 60)-n.m.s. (306) *in a swine's snout*

אִשָּׁה יָפָה n.f.s. (61)-adj. f.s. (421) *a beautiful woman*

וְסָרַת טָעַם conj.-Qal act.ptc. f.s. cstr. (סוּר 693)-n.m.s. paus. (381) *without discretion*

11:23

תַּאֲוַת צַדִּיקִים n.f.s. cstr. (16)-adj. m.p. (843) *the desire of the righteous*

אַךְ־טוֹב adv. (36)-n.m.s. (III 375) *only in good*

תִּקְוַת רְשָׁעִים n.f.s. cstr. (876)-adj. m.p. (957) *the expectation of the wicked*

עֶבְרָה n.f.s. (720) *in wrath*

11:24

יֵשׁ מְפַזֵּר subst. (441)-Pi. ptc. (פָּזַר 808) *one man scatters freely*

וְנוֹסָף עוֹד conj.-Ni. ptc. (יָסַף 414)-adv. (728) *yet grows all the richer*
וְחוֹשֵׂךְ מִיֹּשֶׁר conj.-Qal act.ptc. (חָשַׂךְ 362) -prep.-n.m.s. (449) *another withholds what he should give*
אַךְ־לְמַחְסוֹר adv. (36)-prep.-n.m.s. (341) *only suffers want*

11:25

נֶפֶשׁ־בְּרָכָה n.f.s. cstr. (659)-n.f.s. (I 139) *a liberal man*
תְדֻשָּׁן Pu. impf. 3 f.s. (דָּשֵׁן 206) *will be enriched*
וּמַרְוֶה conj.-Hi. ptc. (רָוָה 924) *and one who waters*
גַּם־הוּא יוֹרֶא adv. (168)-pers.pr. 3 m.s. (214)-Ho. impf. 3 m.s. (רָוָה 924) *will himself be watered*

11:26

מֹנֵעַ בָּר Qal act.ptc. (מָנַע 586)-n.m.s. (III 141) *who holds back grain*
יִקְּבֻהוּ לְאוֹם Qal impf. 3 m.p.-3 m.s. sf.-n.m.s. (522) *the people curse him*
וּבְרָכָה conj.-n.f.s. (139) *but a blessing*
לְרֹאשׁ מַשְׁבִּיר prep.-n.m.s. cstr. (910)-Hi. ptc. (שָׁבַר 991) *on the head of him who sells it*

11:27

שֹׁחֵר טוֹב Qal act.ptc. (שָׁחַר 1007)-n.m.s. (III 375) *he who seeks good*
יְבַקֵּשׁ רָצוֹן Pi. impf. 3 m.s. (בָּקַשׁ 134)-n.m.s. (953) *seeks favor*
וְדֹרֵשׁ רָעָה conj.-Qal act.ptc. (דָּרַשׁ 205)-n.f.s. (949) *but to him who searches for evil*
תְבוֹאֶנּוּ Qal impf. 3 f.s.-3 m.s. sf. (בּוֹא 97) *it will come to him*

11:28

בּוֹטֵחַ בְּעָשְׁרוֹ Qal act.ptc. (בָּטַח 105)-prep. -n.m.s.-3 m.s. sf. (799) *he who trusts in his riches*
הוּא יִפֹּל pers.pr. 3 m.s. (214)-Qal impf. 3 m.s. (נָפַל 656) *will fall*
וְכֶעָלֶה conj.-prep.-def.art.-n.m.s. (750) *but like a green leaf*
צַדִּיקִים יִפְרָחוּ adj. m.p. (843)-Qal impf. 3 m.p. paus. (פָּרַח I 827) *the righteous will flourish*

11:29

עוֹכֵר בֵּיתוֹ Qal act.ptc. (עָכַר 747)-n.m.s.-3 m.s. sf. (108) *he who troubles his household*
יִנְחַל־רוּחַ Qal impf. 3 m.s. (נָחַל 635)-n.f.s. (924) *will inherit wind*
וְעֶבֶד אֱוִיל conj.-n.m.s. (713)-adj. m.s. (17) *and the fool will be servant*
לַחֲכַם־לֵב prep.-adj. m.s. cstr. (314)-n.m.s. (524) *to the wise*

11:30

פְּרִי־צַדִּיק n.m.s. cstr. (826)-adj. m.s. (843) *the fruit of the righteous*
עֵץ חַיִּים n.m.s. cstr. (781)-n.m.p. (313) *a tree of life*
וְלֹקֵחַ נְפָשׁוֹת conj.-Qal act.ptc. (לָקַח 542)-n.f.p. (659) *but takes away lives*
חָכָם adj. m.s. (314) *a wise man*

11:31

הֵן צַדִּיק demons.adv. (II 243)-adj. m.s. (843) *if the righteous*
בָּאָרֶץ prep.-def.art.-n.f.s. (75) *on earth*
יְשֻׁלָּם Pu. impf. 3 m.s. (שָׁלֵם 1022) *is requited*
אַף כִּי־רָשָׁע conj. (64)-conj. (471)-adj. m.s. (957) *how much more the wicked*
וְחוֹטֵא conj.-Qal act.ptc. (חָטָא 306) *and the sinner*

12:1

אֹהֵב מוּסָר Qal act.ptc. (אָהַב 12)-n.m.s. (416) *whoever loves discipline*
אֹהֵב דָּעַת v.supra-n.f.s. paus. (395) *loves knowledge*
וְשֹׂנֵא תוֹכַחַת conj.-Qal act.ptc. (שָׂנֵא 971)-n.f.s. (407) *but he who hates reproof*
בָעַר n.m.s. paus. (129) *is stupid*

12:2

טוֹב adj. m.s. (II 373) *a good man*
יָפִיק רָצוֹן Hi. impf. 3 m.s. (פוק II 807)-n.m.s. (953) *obtains favor*
מֵיהוה prep.-pr.n. (217) *from Yahweh*
וְאִישׁ מְזִמּוֹת conj.-n.m.s. cstr. (35)-n.f.p. (273) *but a man of evil devices*
יַרְשִׁיעַ Hi. impf. 3 m.s. (רָשַׁע 957) *he condemns*

12:3

לֹא־יִכּוֹן neg.-Ni. impf. 3 m.s. (כּוּן I 465) *is not established*
אָדָם n.m.s. (9) *a man*
בְּרֶשַׁע prep.-n.m.s. (957) *by wickedness*
וְשֹׁרֶשׁ צַדִּיקִים conj.-n.m.s. cstr. (1057)-adj. m.p. (843) *but the root of the righteous*

בַּל־יִמּוֹט neg. (115)-Ni. impf. 3 m.s. (מוֹט 556) *will never be moved*

12:4

אֵשֶׁת־חַיִל n.f.s. cstr. (61)-n.m.s. (298) *a good wife*

עֲטֶרֶת בַּעְלָהּ n.f.s. cstr. (I 742)-n.m.s.-3 f.s. sf. (127) *the crown of her husband*

וּכְרָקָב conj.-prep.-n.m.s. (955) *but like rottenness*

בְּעַצְמוֹתָיו prep.-n.f.p.-3 m.s. sf. (782) *in his bones*

מְבִישָׁה Hi. ptc. f.s. (בּוֹשׁ 101) *she who brings shame*

12:5

מַחְשְׁבוֹת n.f.p. cstr. (364) *the thoughts of*

צַדִּיקִים adj. m.p. (843) *the righteous*

מִשְׁפָּט n.m.s. (1048) *are just*

תַּחְבֻּלוֹת n.f.p. cstr. (287) *the counsels of*

רְשָׁעִים adj. m.p. (957) *the wicked*

מִרְמָה n.f.s. (I 941) *are treacherous*

12:6

דִּבְרֵי רְשָׁעִים n.m.p. cstr. (182)-adj. m.p. (957) *the words of the wicked*

אֱרָב־דָּם Qal inf.cstr. (אָרַב 70)-n.m.s. (196) *lie in wait for blood*

וּפִי יְשָׁרִים conj.-n.m.s. cstr. (804)-adj. m.p. (449) *but the mouth of the upright*

יַצִּילֵם Hi. impf. 3 m.s.-3 m.p. sf. (נָצַל 664) *delivers them*

12:7

הָפוֹךְ Qal inf.abs. (הָפַךְ 245) *are overthrown*

רְשָׁעִים adj. m.p. (957) *the wicked*

וְאֵינָם conj.-neg.-3 m.p. sf. (II 34) *and are no more*

וּבֵית צַדִּיקִים conj.-n.m.s. cstr. (108)-adj. m.p. (843) *but the house of the righteous*

יַעֲמֹד Qal impf. 3 m.s. (עָמַד 763) *will stand*

12:8

לְפִי־שִׂכְלוֹ prep.-n.m.s. cstr. (804)-n.m.s.-3 m.s. sf. (968) *according to his good sense*

יְהֻלַּל־אִישׁ Pu. impf. 3 m.s. (הָלַל II 237)-n.m.s. (35) *a man is commended*

וְנַעֲוֵה־לֵב conj.-Ni. ptc. m.s. cstr. (עָוָה I 730) -n.m.s. (524) *but one of perverse mind*

יִהְיֶה לָבוּז Qal impf. 3 m.s. (הָיָה 224)-prep. -n.m.s. paus. (II 100) *is despised*

12:9

טוֹב נִקְלֶה adj. m.s. (II 373)-Ni. ptc. m.s. (קָלָה II 885) *better is a man of humble standing*

וְעֶבֶד לוֹ conj.-n.m.s. (713)-prep.-3 m.s. sf. *who works for himself*

מִמְּתַכַּבֵּד prep.-Hith. ptc. m.s. (כָּבֵד 457) *than one who plays the great man*

וַחֲסַר־לָחֶם conj.-adj. m.s. cstr. (341)-n.m.s. paus. (536) *but lacks bread*

12:10

יוֹדֵעַ Qal act.ptc. (יָדַע 393) *has regard for*

צַדִּיק adj. m.s. (843) *a righteous man*

נֶפֶשׁ n.f.s. cstr. (659) *for the life of*

בְּהֶמְתּוֹ n.f.s.-3 m.s. sf. (96) *his beast*

וְרַחֲמֵי רְשָׁעִים conj.-n.m.p. cstr. (933)-adj. m.p. (957) *but the mercy of the wicked*

אַכְזָרִי adj. m.s. (470) *is cruel*

12:11

עֹבֵד אַדְמָתוֹ Qal act.ptc. (712)-n.f.s.-3 m.s. sf. (9) *he who tills his land*

יִשְׂבַּע־לָחֶם Qal impf. 3 m.s. (שָׂבַע 959)-n.m.s. paus. (536) *will have plenty of bread*

וּמְרַדֵּף רֵיקִים conj.-Pi. ptc. (רָדַף 922)-adj. m.p. (938) *but he who follows worthless pursuits*

חֲסַר־לֵב adj. m.s. cstr. (341)-n.m.s. (524) *has no sense*

12:12

חָמַד Qal pf. 3 m.s. (326) *desires* (in bad sense)

רָשָׁע adj. m.s. (957) *the wicked*

מְצוֹד רָעִים n.m.s. cstr. (II 844)-adj. m.p. (I 948) *the implements of evil*

וְשֹׁרֶשׁ צַדִּיקִים conj.-n.m.s. cstr. (1057)-adj. m.p. (843) *but the root of the righteous*

יִתֵּן Qal impf. 3 m.s. (נָתַן 678) *stands firm*

12:13

בְּפֶשַׁע שְׂפָתַיִם prep.-n.m.s. cstr. (833)-n.f. du. (973) *by the transgression of his lips*

מוֹקֵשׁ רָע n.m.s. (430)-adj. m.s. (I 948) *an evil man is ensnared*

וַיֵּצֵא מִצָּרָה consec.-Qal impf. 3 m.s. (יָצָא 422) -prep.-n.f.s. (I 865) *but ... escapes from trouble*

צַדִּיק adj. m.s. (843) *the righteous*

12:14

מִפְּרִי פִי־אִישׁ prep.-n.m.s. cstr. (826)-n.m.s. cstr. (804)-n.m.s. (35) *from the fruit of a man's words*

יִשְׂבַּע־טוֹב Qal impf. 3 m.s. (שָׂבַע 959)-n.m.s. (III 375) *he is satisfied with good*

וּגְמוּל יְדֵי־אָדָם conj.-n.m.s. cstr. (168)-n.f.p. cstr. (388)-n.m.s. (9) *and the work of a man's hands*

יָשׁוּב לוֹ Qal impf. 3 m.s. (שׁוּב 996; Q יָשִׁיב) -prep.-3 m.s. sf. *comes back to him*

12:15

דֶּרֶךְ אֱוִיל n.m.s. cstr. (202)-adj. m.s. (17) *the way of a fool*

יָשָׁר adj. m.s. (449) *is right*

בְּעֵינָיו prep.-n.f.p.-3 m.s. sf. (744) *in his own eyes*

וְשֹׁמֵעַ conj.-Qal act.ptc. (1033) *but listens*

לְעֵצָה prep.-n.f.s. (420) *to advice*

חָכָם adj. m.s. (314) *a wise man*

12:16

אֱוִיל adj. m.s. (17) *a fool*

בַּיּוֹם prep.-def.art.-n.m.s. (398) *at once*

יִוָּדַע כַּעְסוֹ Ni. impf. 3 m.s. (יָדַע 393)-n.m.s.-3 m.s. sf. (495) *his vexation is known*

וְכֹסֶה conj.-Qal act.ptc. (כָּסָה I 491) *but ignores*

קָלוֹן n.m.s. (885) *an insult*

עָרוּם adj. m.s. (791) *the prudent man*

12:17

יָפִיחַ אֱמוּנָה Hi. impf. 3 m.s. (פּוּחַ 806)-n.f.s. (53) *he breathes out faithfulness*

יַגִּיד צֶדֶק Hi. impf. 3 m.s. (נָגַד 616)-n.m.s. (841) *shows forth righteousness*

וְעֵד שְׁקָרִים conj.-n.m.s. cstr. (729)-n.m.p. (1055) *but a false witness*

מִרְמָה n.f.s. (941) *deceit*

12:18

יֵשׁ בּוֹטֶה subst. (441)-Qal act.ptc. (בָּטָה 104) *there is one whose rash words*

כְּמַדְקְרוֹת חָרֶב prep.-n.f.p. cstr. (201)-n.f.s. paus. (352) *like sword thrusts*

וּלְשׁוֹן חֲכָמִים conj.-n.f.s. cstr. (546)-adj. m.p. (314) *but the tongue of the wise*

מַרְפֵּא n.m.s. (951) *healing*

12:19

שְׂפַת־אֱמֶת n.f.s. cstr. (973)-n.f.s. (54) *truthful lips*

תִּכּוֹן Ni. impf. 3 f.s. (כּוּן I 465) *endure*

לָעַד prep.-n.m.s. (I 723) *for ever*

וְעַד־אַרְגִּיעָה conj.-prep. (III 723)-Hi. impf. 1 c.s.-coh.he (רָגַע I 920) *but while I would twinkle (only for a moment)*

לְשׁוֹן שָׁקֶר n.f.s. cstr. (546)-n.m.s. paus. (1055) *a lying tongue*

12:20

מִרְמָה n.f.s. (941) *deceit*

בְּלֶב־ prep.-n.m.s. cstr. (524) *in the heart of*

חֹרְשֵׁי רָע Qal act.ptc. m.p. cstr. (חָרַשׁ I 360) -n.m.s. paus. (II 948) *those who devise evil*

וּלְיֹעֲצֵי שָׁלוֹם conj.-prep.-Qal act.ptc. m.p. cstr. (419 יָעַץ)-n.m.s. (1022) *but those who plan good*

שִׂמְחָה n.f.s. (970) *have joy*

12:21

לֹא־יְאֻנֶּה neg.-Pu. impf. 3 m.s. (אָנָה III 58) *does not befall*

לַצַּדִּיק prep.-def.art.-adj. m.s. (843) *to the righteous*

כָּל־אָוֶן n.m.s. cstr. (481)-n.m.s. (19) *any ill*

וּרְשָׁעִים conj.-adj. m.p. (957) *but the wicked*

מָלְאוּ רָע Qal pf. 3 c.p. (מָלֵא 569)-n.m.s. (II 948) *are filled with trouble*

12:22

תּוֹעֲבַת יהוה n.f.s. cstr. (1072)-pr.n. (217) *an abomination to Yahweh*

שִׂפְתֵי־שָׁקֶר n.f.p. cstr. (973)-n.m.s. paus. (1055) *lying lips*

וְעֹשֵׂי אֱמוּנָה conj.-Qal act.ptc. m.p. cstr. (עָשָׂה I 793)-n.f.s. (53) *but those who act faithfully*

רְצוֹנוֹ n.m.s.-3 m.s. sf. (953) *his delight*

12:23

אָדָם עָרוּם n.m.s. (9)-adj. m.s. (791) *a prudent man*

כֹּסֶה דָּעַת Qal act.ptc. (כָּסָה 491)-n.f.s. paus. (395) *conceals his knowledge*

וְלֵב כְּסִילִים conj.-n.m.s. cstr. (524)-n.m.p. (I 493) *but the heart of fools*

יִקְרָא אִוֶּלֶת Qal impf. 3 m.s. (894)-n.f.s. (17) *proclaim folly*

12:24

יַד־חָרוּצִים n.f.s. cstr. (388)-adj. m.p. (I 358) *the hand of the diligent*

תִּמְשׁוֹל Qal impf. 3 f.s. (מָשַׁל 605) *will rule*

וּרְמִיָּה conj.-n.f.s. (941) *while the slothful*

תִּהְיֶה לָמַס Qal impf. 3 f.s. (הָיָה 224)-prep.-n.m.s. paus. (I 586) *will be put to forced labor*

12:25

דְּאָגָה n.f.s. (178) *anxiety*

בְלֶב־אִישׁ prep.-n.m.s. cstr. (524)-n.m.s. (35) *in a man's heart*

יַשְׁחֶנָּה Hi. impf. 3 m.s.-3 f.s. sf. (שָׁחַח 1005) *weighs him (it) down*

וְדָבָר טוֹב conj.-n.m.s. (182)-adj. m.s. (II 373) *but a good word*

יְשַׂמְּחֶנָּה Pi. impf. 3 m.s.-3 f.s. sf. (שָׂמַח 970) *makes him (it) glad*

12:26

יָתֵר Hi. impf. 3 m.s. apoc. (תּוּר 1064) *searches out (spies out)*

מֵרֵעֵהוּ prep.-n.m.s.-3 m.s. sf. (II 945; or n.m.s.-3 m.s. sf. מֵרֵעַ 946) *his friend*

צַדִּיק adj. m.s. (843) *a righteous man*

וְדֶרֶךְ רְשָׁעִים conj.-n.f.s. cstr. (202)-adj. m.p. (957) *but the way of the wicked*

תַּתְעֵם Hi. impf. 3 f.s.-3 m.p. sf. (תָּעָה 1073) *leads them astray*

12:27

לֹא־יַחֲרֹךְ neg.-Qal impf. 3 m.s. (חָרַךְ I 355; LXX ἐπιτεύξεται) *does not start*

רְמִיָּה n.f.s. (II 941) *slackness*

צֵידוֹ n.m.s.-3 m.s. sf. (844) *his prey*

וְהוֹן־אָדָם conj.-n.m.s. (223)-n.m.s. (9) *but the diligent man*

יָקָר חָרוּץ adj. m.s. (429)-subst. m.s. (I 358) *precious wealth*

12:28

בְּאֹרַח־צְדָקָה prep.-n.m.s. cstr. (73)-n.f.s. (842) *in the path of righteousness*

חַיִּים n.m.p. (313) *is life*

וְדֶרֶךְ נְתִיבָה conj.-n.m.s. cstr. (202)-n.f.s. (677) *but the way of error*

אַל־מָוֶת neg. (rd.prb. אֶל)-n.m.s. (560) *leads to death*

13:1

בֵּן חָכָם n.m.s. (119)-adj. m.s. (314) *a wise son*

מוּסַר אָב n.m.s. cstr. (416)-n.m.s. (3) *his father's instruction*

וְלֵץ conj.-Qal act.ptc. (לוּץ 539) *but a scoffer*

לֹא־שָׁמַע neg.-Qal pf. 3 m.s. (1033) *does not listen*

גְּעָרָה n.f.s. (172) *rebuke*

13:2

מִפְּרִי prep.-n.m.s. cstr. (826) *from the fruit of*

פִי־אִישׁ n.m.s. cstr. (804)-n.m.s. (35) *of a man's mouth*

יֹאכַל טוֹב Qal impf. 3 m.s. (אָכַל 37)-n.m.s. (III 375) *eats good*

וְנֶפֶשׁ בֹּגְדִים conj.-n.f.s. cstr. (659)-Qal act.ptc. m.p. (בָּגַד 93) *but the desire of the treacherous*

חָמָס n.m.s. (329) *violence*

13:3

נֹצֵר פִּיו Qal act.ptc. (נָצַר 665)-n.m.s.-3 m.s. sf. (804) *he who guards his mouth*

שֹׁמֵר נַפְשׁוֹ Qal act.ptc. (שָׁמַר 1036)-n.f.s.-3 m.s. sf. (659) *preserves his life*

פֹּשֵׂק שְׂפָתָיו Qal act.ptc. (פָּשַׂק 832)-n.f.p.-3 m.s. sf. (973) *he who opens wide his lips*

מְחִתָּה־לוֹ n.f.s. (369)-prep.-3 m.s. sf. *comes to ruin*

13:4

מִתְאַוָּה Hith. ptc. f.s. (אָוָה 16) *craves*

וָאַיִן conj.-neg. (II 34) *and gets nothing*

נַפְשׁוֹ עָצֵל n.f.s.-3 m.s. sf. (659)-adj. m.s. (782) *the soul of the sluggard*

וְנֶפֶשׁ חָרֻצִים conj.-n.f.s. cstr. (659)-adj. m.p. (I 358) *while the soul of the diligent*

תְּדֻשָּׁן Pu. impf. 3 f.s. (דָּשֵׁן 206) *is richly supplied*

13:5

דְּבַר־שֶׁקֶר n.m.s. cstr. (182)-n.m.s. (1055) *falsehood*

יִשְׂנָא Qal impf. 3 m.s. (שָׂנֵא 971) *hates*

צַדִּיק adj. m.s. (843) *a righteous man*

וְרָשָׁע conj.-adj. m.s. (957) *but a wicked man*

יַבְאִישׁ Hi. impf. 3 m.s. (92) *acts shamefully*

וְיַחְפִּיר conj.-Hi. impf. 3 m.s. (חָפֵר II 344) *and disgracefully*

13:6

צְדָקָה n.f.s. (842) *righteousness*

תִּצֹּר Qal impf. 3 f.s. (נָצַר I 665) *guards*

תָּם־דָּרֶךְ n.m.s. cstr. (1070)-n.m.s. paus. (202) *him whose way is upright*

וְרִשְׁעָה conj.-n.f.s. (958) *but the wicked*

תְּסַלֵּף Pi. impf. 3 f.s. (סָלַף 701) *overthrows*

חַטָּאת n.f.s. (308) *sin*

13:7

יֵשׁ מִתְעַשֵּׁר subst. (441)–Hith. ptc. (עָשַׁר 799) *one man pretends to be rich*

וְאֵין כֹּל conj.–neg. (II 34)–n.m.s. (481) *yet has nothing*

מִתְרוֹשֵׁשׁ Hithpolel ptc. (רוּשׁ 930) *another pretends to be poor*

וְהוֹן רָב conj.–n.m.s. (223)–adj. m.s. paus. (I 912) *yet has great wealth*

13:8

כֹּפֶר n.m.s. cstr. (I 497) *the ransom of*

נֶפֶשׁ־אִישׁ n.f.s. cstr. (659)–n.m.s. (35) *a man's life*

עָשְׁרוֹ n.m.s.–3 m.s. sf. (799) *his wealth*

וְרָשׁ conj.–Qal act.ptc. m.s. (רוּשׁ 930) *but a poor man*

לֹא־שָׁמַע neg.–Qal pf. 3 m.s. (1033) *does not hear*

גְּעָרָה n.f.s. (172) *rebuke*

13:9

אוֹר־צַדִּיקִים n.m.s. cstr. (21)–adj. m.p. (843) *the light of the righteous*

יִשְׂמָח Qal impf. 3 m.s. (שָׂמַח 970) *rejoices*

וְנֵר רְשָׁעִים conj.–n.m.s. cstr. (632)–adj. m.p. (957) *but the lamp of the wicked*

יִדְעָךְ Qal impf. 3 m.s. (דָּעַךְ 200) *will be put out*

13:10

רַק־בְּזָדוֹן adv. (956)–prep.–n.m.s. (268) *only by insolence*

יִתֵּן מַצָּה Qal impf. 3 m.s. (נָתַן 678)–n.f.s. (II 663) *he makes strife*

וְאֶת־נוֹעָצִים conj.–prep. (II 85)–Ni. ptc. m.p. (יָעַץ 419) *but with those who take advice*

חָכְמָה n.f.s. (315) *is wisdom*

13:11

הוֹן מֵהֶבֶל n.m.s. (223)–prep.–n.m.s. (I 210) *wealth from vanity*

יִמְעָט Qal impf. 3 m.s. (מָעַט 589) *will dwindle*

וְקֹבֵץ conj.–Qal act.ptc. m.s. (קָבַץ 867) *but he who gathers*

עַל־יָד prep.–n.f.s. (388) *little by little*

יַרְבֶּה Hi. impf. 3 m.s. (רָבָה I 915) *will increase*

13:12

תּוֹחֶלֶת מְמֻשָּׁכָה n.f.s. (404)–Pu. ptc. f.s. (מָשַׁךְ 604) *hope deferred*

מַחֲלָה־לֵב Hi. ptc. f.s. (חָלָה I 317)–n.m.s. (524) *makes the heart sick*

וְעֵץ חַיִּים conj.–n.m.s. cstr. (781)–n.m.p. (313) *but a tree of life*

תַּאֲוָה בָאָה n.f.s. (16)–Qal act.ptc. f.s. (בּוֹא 97) *a desire fulfilled*

13:13

בָּז לְדָבָר Qal act.ptc. (בּוּז I 100)–prep.–n.m.s. (182) *he who despises the word*

יֵחָבֶל לוֹ Ni. impf. 3 m.s. (חָבַל I 286)–prep.–3 m.s. sf. *brings destruction on himself*

וִירֵא מִצְוָה conj.–Qal act.ptc. m.s. cstr. (יָרֵא 431)–n.f.s. (846) *but he who respects the commandment*

הוּא יְשֻׁלָּם pers.pr. 3 m.s. (214)–Pu. impf. 3 m.s. (1022 שָׁלֵם) *will be rewarded*

13:14

תּוֹרַת חָכָם n.f.s. cstr. (435)–adj. m.s. (314) *the teaching of the wise*

מְקוֹר חַיִּים n.m.s. cstr. (881)–n.m.p. (313) *a fountain of life*

לָסוּר prep.–Qal inf.cstr. (סוּר 693) *that one may avoid*

מִמֹּקְשֵׁי מָוֶת prep.–n.m.p. cstr. (430)–n.m.s. (560) *the snares of death*

13:15

שֵׂכֶל־טוֹב n.m.s. (968)–adj. m.s. (II 373) *good sense*

יִתֶּן־חֵן Qal impf. 3 m.s. (נָתַן 678)–n.m.s. (336) *wins favor*

וְדֶרֶךְ בֹּגְדִים conj.–n.m.s. cstr. (202)–Qal act.ptc. m.p. (בָּגַד 93) *but the way of the faithless*

אֵיתָן adj. m.s. (I 450; LXX ἐν ἀπωλείᾳ) *is enduring*

13:16

כָּל־עָרוּם n.m.s. (481)–adj. m.s. (791) *in everything a prudent man*

יַעֲשֶׂה בְדָעַת Qal impf. 3 m.s. (עָשָׂה I 793) –prep.–n.f.s. paus. (395) *acts with knowledge*

וּכְסִיל conj.–n.m.s. (I 493) *but a fool*

יִפְרֹשׂ Qal impf. 3 m.s. (פָּרַשׂ 831) *flaunts*

אִוֶּלֶת n.f.s. (17) *folly*

13:17

מַלְאָךְ רָשָׁע n.m.s. (521)–adj. m.s. (957) *a bad messenger*

יִפֹּל בְּרָע Qal impf. 3 m.s. (נָפַל 656)–prep.–n.m.s. (II 948) *plunges into trouble*

וְצִיר אֱמוּנִים conj.–n.m.s. cstr. (851)–n.m.p. (53) *but a faithful envoy*

מַרְפֵּא n.m.s. (951) *brings healing*

13:18

רֵישׁ וְקָלוֹן n.m.s. (930)–conj.–n.m.s. (885) *poverty and disgrace*

פּוֹרֵעַ מוּסָר Qal act.ptc. (פָּרַע III 828)–n.m.s. (416) *to him who ignores instruction*

וְשׁוֹמֵר תּוֹכַחַת conj.–Qal act.ptc. (1036)–n.f.s. (407) *but he who heeds reproof*

יְכֻבָּד Pu. impf. 3 m.s. paus. (כָּבֵד 457) *is honored*

13:19

תַּאֲוָה נִהְיָה n.f.s. (16)–Ni. ptc. f.s. (הָיָה 224) *a desire fulfilled*

תֶּעֱרַב Qal impf. 3 f.s. (עָרֵב III 787) *is sweet*

לְנָפֶשׁ prep.–n.f.s. paus. (659) *to the soul*

וְתוֹעֲבַת כְּסִילִים conj.–n.f.s. cstr. (1072)–n.m.p. (I 493) *but an abomination to fools*

סוּר מֵרָע Qal inf.cstr. (693)–prep.–n.m.s. (II 948) *to turn away from evil*

13:20

הָלוֹךְ Qal act.ptc. (הָלַךְ 229) *he who walks*

אֶת־חֲכָמִים prep. (II 85)–adj. m.p. (314) *with wise men*

וֶחְכָּם conj.–Qal impv. 2 m.s. paus. (314; Q יֶחְכָּם) *becomes wise*

וְרֹעֶה כְסִילִים conj.–Qal act.ptc. (רָעָה II 945) –n.m.p. (493) *but the companion of fools*

יֵרוֹעַ Ni. impf. 3 m.s. (רָעַע 949) *will suffer harm*

13:21

חַטָּאִים adj. m.p. (308) *sinners*

תְּרַדֵּף רָעָה Pi. impf. 3 f.s. (רָדַף 922)–n.f.s. (949) *misfortune pursues*

וְאֶת־צַדִּיקִים conj.–dir.obj.–adj. m.p. (843) *but the righteous*

יְשַׁלֶּם־טוֹב Pi. impf. 3 m.s. (שָׁלֵם 1022)–n.m.s. (375) *prosperity rewards*

13:22

טוֹב adj. m.s. (II 374) *a good man*

יַנְחִיל Hi. impf. 3 m.s. (נָחַל 635) *leaves an inheritance*

בְּנֵי־בָנִים n.m.p. cstr. (119)–n.m.p. (119) *to his children's children*

וְצָפוּן conj.–Qal pass.ptc. (צָפַן 860) *but is laid up*

לַצַּדִּיק prep.–def.art.–adj. m.s. (843) *for the righteous*

חֵיל חוֹטֵא n.m.s. cstr. (298)–Qal act.ptc. (חָטָא 306) *the sinner's wealth*

13:23

רָב־אֹכֶל adj. m.s. (I 912)–n.m.s. (38) *much food*

נִיר רָאשִׁים n.m.s. cstr. (644)–Qal act.ptc. m.p. (930 רוּשׁ; LXX δίκαιοι) *the fallow ground of the poor*

וְיֵשׁ נִסְפֶּה conj.–subst. (441)–Ni. ptc. (סָפָה 705) *but it is swept away*

בְּלֹא מִשְׁפָּט prep.–neg.–n.m.s. (1048) *through injustice*

13:24

חוֹשֵׂךְ שִׁבְטוֹ Qal act.ptc. (חָשַׂךְ 362)–n.m.s.–3 m.s. sf. (986) *he who spares the rod*

שׂוֹנֵא בְנוֹ Qal act.ptc. (שָׂנֵא 971)–n.m.s.–3 m.s. sf. (119) *hates his son*

וְאֹהֲבוֹ conj.–Qal act.ptc.–3 m.s. sf. (אָהַב 12) *but he who loves him*

שִׁחֲרוֹ מוּסָר Pi. pf. 3 m.s.–3 m.s. sf. (שָׁחַר 1007) –n.m.s. (416) *is diligent to discipline him*

13:25

צַדִּיק adj. m.s. (843) *the righteous*

אֹכֵל n.m.s. (38) *food*

לְשֹׂבַע נַפְשׁוֹ prep.–n.m.s. cstr. (959)–n.f.s.–3 m.s. sf. (659) *has enough to satisfy his appetite*

וּבֶטֶן רְשָׁעִים conj.–n.f.s. cstr. (105)–adj. m.p. (957) *but the belly of the wicked*

תֶּחְסָר Qal impf. 3 f.s. (חָסֵר 341) *suffers want*

14:1

חַכְמוֹת נָשִׁים n.f.p. cstr. (315)–n.f.p. (61) *wisdom of women*

בָּנְתָה בֵיתָהּ Qal pf. 3 f.s. (בָּנָה 124)–n.m.s.–3 f.s. sf. (108) *builds her house*

וְאִוֶּלֶת conj.–n.f.s. (17) *but folly*

בְּיָדֶיהָ prep.–n.f.p.–3 f.s. sf. (388) *with her own hands*

תֶּהֶרְסֶנּוּ Qal impf. 3 f.s.–3 m.s. sf. (הָרַס 248) *tears it down*

14:2

הוֹלֵךְ בְּיָשְׁרוֹ Qal act.ptc. (הָלַךְ 229)–prep. –n.m.s.–3 m.s. sf. (449) *he who walks in uprightness*

יְרֵא יהוה Qal act.ptc. m.s. cstr. (יָרֵא 431)–pr.n. (217) *fears Yahweh*

וּנְלוֹז דְּרָכָיו conj.–Ni. ptc. m.s. cstr. (לוּז 531) –n.m.p.–3 m.s. sf. (202) *but he who is devious in his ways*

בּוֹזֵהוּ Qal act.ptc.-3 m.s. sf. (בָּזָה 102) *despises him*

14:3

בְּפִי־אֱוִיל prep.-n.m.s. cstr. (804)-adj. m.s. (17) *the talk of a fool*

חֹטֶר גַּאֲוָה n.m.s. cstr. (310)-n.f.s. (144) *a rod of pride*

וְשִׂפְתֵי חֲכָמִים conj.-n.f.p. cstr. (973)-adj. m.p. (314) *but the lips of the wise*

תִּשְׁמוּרֵם Qal impf. 3 f.s.-3 m.p. sf. (שָׁמַר 1036; GK 47g) *will preserve them*

14:4

בְּאֵין אֲלָפִים prep.-neg. (II 34)-n.m.p. (I 48) *where there are no oxen*

אֵבוּס בָּר n.m.s. (7)-adj. m.s. paus. (II 141; or n.m.s. paus. III 141) *crib is clean*

וְרָב־תְּבוּאוֹת conj.-adj. m.s. cstr. (I 912)-n.f.p. (100) *but abundant crops*

בְּכֹחַ שׁוֹר prep.-n.m.s. cstr. (470)-n.m.s. (1004) *by the strength of the ox*

14:5

עֵד אֱמוּנִים n.m.s. cstr. (729)-n.m.p. (53) *a faithful witness*

לֹא יְכַזֵּב neg.-Pi. impf. 3 m.s. (כָּזַב 469) *does not lie*

וְיָפִיחַ conj.-Hi. impf. 3 m.s. (פּוּחַ 806) *but breathes out*

כְּזָבִים n.m.p. (469) *lies*

עֵד שָׁקֶר n.m.s. cstr. (729)-n.m.s. paus. (1055) *a false witness*

14:6

בִּקֶּשׁ־לֵץ Pi. pf. 3 m.s. (בָּקַשׁ 134)-Qal act.ptc. (לוּץ 539) *a scoffer seeks*

חָכְמָה n.f.s. (315) *wisdom*

וָאָיִן conj.-neg. paus. (II 34) *in vain*

וְדַעַת conj.-n.f.s. (395) *but knowledge*

לְנָבוֹן prep.-Ni. ptc. m.s. (בִּין 106) *for a man of understanding*

נָקָל Ni. pf. 3 m.s. paus. (קָלַל 886) *is easy*

14:7

לֵךְ Qal impv. 2 m.s. (הָלַךְ 229) *leave*

מִנֶּגֶד prep.-prep. (617) *the presence*

לְאִישׁ כְּסִיל prep.-n.m.s. (35)-n.m.s. (I 493) *of a fool*

וּבַל־יָדַעְתָּ conj.-neg.-Qal pf. 2 m.s. (יָדַע 393; LXX ὅπλα δὲ αἰσθήσεως) *for you do not know*

שִׂפְתֵי־דָעַת n.f.p. cstr. (973)-n.f.s. paus. (395) *words of knowledge*

14:8

חָכְמַת עָרוּם n.f.s. cstr. (315)-adj. m.s. (791) *the wisdom of a prudent man*

הָבִין דַּרְכּוֹ Hi. inf.cstr. (בִּין 106)-n.m.s.-3 m.s. sf. (202) *is to discern his way*

וְאִוֶּלֶת כְּסִילִים conj.-n.f.s. cstr. (17)-n.m.p. (493) *but the folly of fools*

מִרְמָה n.f.s. (I 941) *is deceiving*

14:9

אֱוִלִים יָלִיץ adj. m.p. (17)-Qal impf. 3 m.s. (לוּץ 539; LXX οἰκίαι παρανόμων) *scorns the wicked*

אָשָׁם n.m.s. (79) *guilt*

וּבֵין יְשָׁרִים conj.-subst. (107; LXX οἰκίαι δέ)-adj. m.p. (449) *but the interval of the upright*

רָצוֹן n.m.s. (953) *his favor*

14:10

לֵב יוֹדֵעַ n.m.s. (524)-Qal act.ptc. (יָדַע 393) *the heart knows*

מָרַּת נַפְשׁוֹ n.f.s. cstr. (601)-n.f.s.-3 m.s. sf. (659) *its own bitterness*

וּבְשִׂמְחָתוֹ conj.-prep.-n.f.s.-3 m.s. (970) *and in its joy*

לֹא־יִתְעָרַב neg.-Hith. impf. 3 m.s. (עָרַב II 786) *does not share*

זָר Qal act.ptc. (זוּר I 266) *a stranger*

14:11

בֵּית רְשָׁעִים n.m.s. cstr. (108)-adj. m.p. (957) *the house of the wicked*

יִשָּׁמֵד Ni. impf. 3 m.s. (שָׁמַד 1029) *will be destroyed*

וְאֹהֶל יְשָׁרִים conj.-n.m.s. cstr. (13)-adj. m.p. (449) *but the tent of the upright*

יַפְרִיחַ Hi. impf. 3 m.s. (פָּרַח I 827) *will flourish*

14:12

יֵשׁ דֶּרֶךְ subst. (441)-n.m.s. (202) *there is a way*

יָשָׁר adj. m.s. (449) *which is straight*

לִפְנֵי־אִישׁ prep.-n.m.p. cstr. (815)-n.m.s. (35) *before a man*

וְאַחֲרִיתָהּ conj.-n.f.s.-3 f.s. sf. (31) *but its end*

דַּרְכֵי־מָוֶת n.m.p. cstr. (202)-n.m.s. (560) *ways of death*

14:13

גַּם־בִּשְׂחוֹק adv. (168)-prep.-n.m.s. (966) *even in laughter*
יִכְאַב־לֵב Qal impf. 3 m.s. (כָּאַב 456)-n.m.s. (524) *the heart is sad*
וְאַחֲרִיתָהּ conj.-n.f.s.-3 f.s. sf. (31) *and its end*
שִׂמְחָה n.f.s. (970) *joy*
תוּגָה n.f.s. (387) *grief*

14:14

מִדְּרָכָיו prep.-n.m.p.-3 m.s. sf. (202) *with his deeds*
יִשְׂבַּע Qal impf. 3 m.s. (שָׂבַע 959) *will be filled*
סוּג לֵב Qal act.ptc. cstr. (סוּג I 690)-n.m.s. (524) *a perverse man*
וּמֵעָלָיו conj.-prep.-prep.-3 m.s. sf. *and from upon him*
אִישׁ טוֹב n.m.s. (35)-adj. m.s. (II 373) *a good man*

14:15

פֶּתִי adj. m.s. (834) *the simple*
יַאֲמִין Hi. impf. 3 m.s. (אָמַן 52) *believes*
לְכָל־דָּבָר prep.-n.m.s. cstr. (481)-n.m.s. (182) *everything*
וְעָרוּם conj.-adj. m.s. (791) *but the prudent*
יָבִין Qal impf. 3 m.s. (בִּין 106) *looks*
לַאֲשֻׁרוֹ prep.-n.f.s.-3 m.s. sf. (81) *where he is going*

14:16

חָכָם adj. m.s. (314) *a wise man*
יָרֵא Qal act.ptc. (יָרֵא 431; or Qal pf. 3 m.s.) *is cautious*
וְסָר מֵרָע conj.-Qal act.ptc. (סוּר 693; or Qal pf. 3 m.s.)-prep.-n.m.s. paus. (II 948) *and turns away from evil*
וּכְסִיל conj.-n.m.s. (493) *but a fool*
מִתְעַבֵּר Hith. ptc. (עָבַר 720) *throws off restraint*
וּבוֹטֵחַ conj.-Qal act.ptc. (בָּטַח I 105) *and is careless*

14:17

קְצַר־אַפַּיִם adj. m.s. cstr. (894)-n.m. du. (I 60) *a man of quick temper*
יַעֲשֶׂה אִוֶּלֶת Qal impf. 3 m.s. (עָשָׂה I 793)-n.f.s. (17) *acts foolishly*
וְאִישׁ מְזִמּוֹת conj.-n.m.s. cstr. (35)-n.f.p. (273) *but a man of discretion*
יִשָּׂנֵא Ni. impf. 3 m.s. (שָׂנֵא 971; LXX ὑποφέρει) *is hated*

14:18

נָחֲלוּ Qal pf. 3 c.p. (נָחַל 635) *acquire*
פְתָאִים adj. m.p. (834; GK 93x) *the simple*
אִוֶּלֶת n.f.s. (17) *folly*
וַעֲרוּמִים conj.-adj. m.p. (791) *but the prudent*
יַכְתִּרוּ Hi. impf. 3 m.p. (כָּתַר 509) *are crowned with*
דָעַת n.f.s. paus. (395) *knowledge*

14:19

שַׁחוּ רָעִים Qal pf. 3 c.p. (שָׁחַח 1005)-adj. m.p. (I 948) *the evil bow down*
לִפְנֵי טוֹבִים prep.-n.m.p. cstr. (815)-adj. m.p. (II 373) *before the good*
וּרְשָׁעִים conj.-adj. m.p. (957) *and the wicked*
עַל־שַׁעֲרֵי צַדִּיק prep.-n.m.p. cstr. (1044)-adj. m.s. (843) *at the gates of the righteous*

14:20

גַּם־לְרֵעֵהוּ adv. (168)-prep.-n.m.s.-3 m.s. sf. (945) *even by his neighbor*
יִשָּׂנֵא רָשׁ Ni. impf. 3 m.s. (שָׂנֵא 971)-Qal act.ptc. (רוּשׁ 930) *the poor is disliked*
וְאֹהֲבֵי עָשִׁיר conj.-Qal act.ptc. m.p. cstr. (אָהַב 12)-adj. m.s. (799) *but the lovers of the rich*
רַבִּים adj. m.p. (I 912) *are many*

14:21

בָּז־לְרֵעֵהוּ Qal act.ptc. (בּוּז 100)-prep.-n.m.s.-3 m.s. sf. (945) *he who despises his neighbor*
חוֹטֵא Qal act.ptc. (חָטָא 306) *is a sinner*
וּמְחוֹנֵן עֲנָיִים conj.-Po'el ptc. (חָנַן I 355)-n.m.p. (776) *but he who is kind to the poor*
אַשְׁרָיו n.m.p.-3 m.s. sf. (80) *his happiness*

14:22

הֲלוֹא־יִתְעוּ interr.-neg.-Qal impf. 3 m.p. (תָּעָה 1073) *do not err*
חֹרְשֵׁי רָע Qal act.ptc. m.p. cstr. (חָרַשׁ I 360) -n.m.s. paus. (II 948) *they that devise evil*
וְחֶסֶד conj.-n.m.s. (338) *and meet loyalty*
וֶאֱמֶת conj.-n.f.s. (54) *and faithfulness*
חֹרְשֵׁי טוֹב v.supra-n.m.s. (III 375) *those who devise good*

14:23

בְּכָל־עֶצֶב prep.-n.m.s. cstr. (481)-n.m.s. (I 780) *in all toil*
יִהְיֶה מוֹתָר Qal impf. 3 m.s. (הָיָה 224)-n.m.s. (452) *there is profit (abundance)*

וּדְבַר־שְׂפָתַיִם conj.-n.m.s. cstr. (182)-n.f. du. (973) *but mere talk*

אַךְ־לְמַחְסוֹר adv. (36)-prep.-n.m.s. (341) *tends only to want*

14:24

עֲטֶרֶת חֲכָמִים n.f.s. cstr. (I 742)-adj. m.p. (314) *the crown of the wise*

עָשְׁרָם n.m.s.-3 m.p. sf. (799) *their riches*

אִוֶּלֶת כְּסִילִים n.f.s. cstr. (17)-n.m.p. (I 493) *the folly of fools*

אִוֶּלֶת n.f.s. (17) *folly*

14:25

מַצִּיל נְפָשׁוֹת Hi. ptc. (נָצַל 664)-n.f.p. (659) *saves lives*

עֵד אֱמֶת n.m.s. cstr. (729)-n.f.s. (54) *a truthful witness*

וְיָפִחַ כְּזָבִים conj.-Hi. impf. 3 m.s. (פּוּחַ 806) -n.m.p. (469) *but one who utters lies*

מִרְמָה n.f.s. (941) *is a betrayer (deceit)*

14:26

בְּיִרְאַת יהוה prep.-n.f.s. cstr. (432)-pr.n. (217) *in the fear of Yahweh*

מִבְטַח־עֹז n.m.s. cstr. (105)-n.m.s. (738) *strong confidence*

וּלְבָנָיו conj.-prep.-n.m.p.-3 m.s. sf. (119) *and his children*

יִהְיֶה מַחְסֶה Qal impf. 3 m.s. (הָיָה 224)-n.m.s. (340) *will have a refuge*

14:27

יִרְאַת יהוה n.f.s. cstr. (432)-pr.n. (217) *the fear of Yahweh*

מְקוֹר חַיִּים n.m.s. cstr. (881)-n.m.p. (313) *a fountain of life*

לָסוּר prep.-Qal inf.cstr. (סוּר 693) *that one may avoid*

מִמֹּקְשֵׁי מָוֶת prep.-n.m.p. cstr. (430)-n.m.s. (560) *the snares of death*

14:28

בְּרָב־עָם prep.-n.m.s. cstr. (913)-n.m.s. (I 766) *in a multitude of people*

הַדְרַת־מֶלֶךְ n.f.s. cstr. (214)-n.m.s. (I 572) *the glory of a king*

וּבְאֶפֶס לְאֹם conj.-prep.-n.m.s. cstr. (67)-n.m.s. (522) *but without people*

מְחִתַּת רָזוֹן n.f.s. cstr. (369)-n.m.s. (II 931) *a prince is ruined*

14:29

אֶרֶךְ אַפַּיִם adj. m.s. cstr. (74)-n.m. du. (I 60) *he who is slow to anger*

רַב־תְּבוּנָה adj. m.s. cstr. (913)-n.f.s. (108) *has great understanding*

וּקְצַר־רוּחַ conj.-adj. m.s. cstr. (894)-n.f.s. (924) *but he who has a hasty temper*

מֵרִים אִוֶּלֶת Hi. ptc. (רוּם 926)-n.f.s. (17) *exalts folly*

14:30

חַיֵּי בְשָׂרִים n.m.p. cstr. (313)-n.m.p. (142) *gives life to the flesh*

לֵב מַרְפֵּא n.m.s. cstr. (524)-n.m.s. (951) *a tranquil mind*

וּרְקַב עֲצָמוֹת conj.-n.m.s. cstr. (955)-n.f.p. (782) *but makes the bones rot*

קִנְאָה n.f.s. (888) *passion*

14:31

עֹשֵׁק־דָּל Qal act.ptc. (עָשַׁק 798)-adj. m.s. (195) *he who oppresses a poor man*

חֵרֵף עֹשֵׂהוּ Pi. pf. 3 m.s. (חָרַף I 357)-Qal act. ptc.-3 m.s. sf. (עָשָׂה I 793) *insults his maker*

וּמְכַבְּדוֹ conj.-Pi. ptc. m.s.-3 m.s. sf. (כָּבֵד 457) *but honors him*

חֹנֵן אֶבְיוֹן Qal act.ptc. (חָנַן I 335)-adj. m.s. (2) *he who is kind to the needy*

14:32

בְּרָעָתוֹ prep.-n.f.s.-3 m.s. sf. (949) *through his evil-doing*

יִדָּחֶה רָשָׁע Ni. impf. 3 m.s. (דָּחָה 190)-adj. m.s. (957) *the wicked is overthrown*

וְחֹסֶה conj.-Qal act.ptc. (חָסָה 340) *but finds refuge*

בְמוֹתוֹ prep.-n.m.s.-3 m.s. sf. (560) *in his death*

צַדִּיק adj. m.s. (843) *the righteous*

14:33

בְּלֵב נָבוֹן prep.-n.m.s. cstr. (524)-Ni. ptc. m.s. (בִּין 106) *in the mind of a man of understanding*

תָּנוּחַ חָכְמָה Qal impf. 3 f.s. (נוּחַ 628)-n.f.s. (315) *wisdom abides*

וּבְקֶרֶב כְּסִילִים conj.-prep.-n.m.s. cstr. (899) -n.m.p. (493) *but in the heart of fools*

תִּוָּדֵעַ Ni. impf. 3 f.s. (יָדַע 393) *is known*

14:34

צְדָקָה n.f.s. (842) *righteousness*

תְּרוֹמֵם־גּוֹי Polel impf. 3 f.s. (רוּם 926)-n.m.s. (156) *exalts a nation*

וְחֶסֶד conj.–n.m.s. (II 340; LXX ἐλασσονοῦσι δὲ) *but a reproach*
לְאֻמִּים n.m.p. (522) *to any people*
חַטָּאת n.f.s. (308) *sin*

14:35

רְצוֹן־מֶלֶךְ n.m.s. cstr. (953)–n.m.s. (I 572) *the king's favor*
לְעֶבֶד prep.–n.m.s. (713) *to a servant*
מַשְׂכִּיל Hi. ptc. (שָׂכַל 968) *who deals wisely*
וְעֶבְרָתוֹ conj.–n.f.s.–3 m.s. sf. (720) *but his wrath*
תִּהְיֶה מֵבִישׁ Qal impf. 3 f.s. (הָיָה 224)–Hi. ptc. (בּוֹשׁ 101) *falls on one who acts shamefully*

15:1

מַעֲנֶה־רַּךְ n.m.s. (775)–adj. m.s. (940) *a soft answer*
יָשִׁיב חֵמָה Hi. impf. 3 m.s. (שׁוּב 996)–n.f.s. (404) *turns away wrath*
וּדְבַר־עֶצֶב conj.–n.m.s. cstr. (182)–n.m.s. (I 780) *but a harsh word*
יַעֲלֶה־אָף Hi. impf. 3 m.s. (עָלָה 748)–n.m.s. paus. (I 60) *stirs up anger*

15:2

לְשׁוֹן חֲכָמִים n.f.s. cstr. (546)–adj. m.p. (314) *the tongue of the wise*
תֵּיטִיב דָּעַת Hi. impf. 3 f.s. (יָטַב 405)–n.f.s. paus. (395) *makes knowledge good*
וּפִי כְסִילִים conj.–n.m.s. cstr. (804)–n.m.p. (493) *but the mouths of fools*
יַבִּיעַ אִוֶּלֶת Hi. impf. 3 m.s. (נָבַע 615)–n.f.s. (17) *pour out folly*

15:3

בְּכָל־מָקוֹם prep.–n.m.s. cstr. (481)–n.m.s. (879) *in every place*
עֵינֵי יהוה n.f.p. cstr. (744)–pr.n. (217) *the eyes of Yahweh*
צֹפוֹת Qal act.ptc. f.p. (צָפָה 859) *keeping watch on*
רָעִים adj. m.p. (948) *the evil*
וטוֹבִים conj.–adj. m.p. (373) *and the good*

15:4

מַרְפֵּא לָשׁוֹן n.m.s. cstr. (951)–n.f.s. (546) *a gentle tongue*
עֵץ חַיִּים n.m.s. cstr. (781)–n.m.p. (313) *a tree of life*
וְסֶלֶף בָּהּ conj.–n.m.s. (701)–prep.–3 f.s. sf. *but perverseness in it*

שֶׁבֶר בְּרוּחַ n.m.s. (I 991)–prep.–n.f.s. (924) *breaks the spirit*

15:5

אֱוִיל n.m.s. (17) *a fool*
יִנְאַץ Qal impf. 3 m.s. (נָאַץ 610) *despises*
מוּסַר אָבִיו n.m.s. cstr. (416)–n.m.s.–3 m.s. sf. (3) *his father's instruction*
וְשֹׁמֵר תּוֹכַחַת conj.–Qal act.ptc. (שָׁמַר 1036) –n.f.s. (407) *but he who heeds admonition*
יַעְרִם Qal impf. 3 m.s. (עָרַם 791; GK 63n) *is prudent*

15:6

בֵּית צַדִּיק n.m.s. cstr. (108)–adj. m.s. (843) *in the house of the righteous*
חֹסֶן רָב n.m.s. (340)–adj. m.s. (I 912) *much treasure*
וּבִתְבוּאַת רָשָׁע conj.–prep.–n.f.s. cstr. (100)–adj. m.s. (957) *but the income of the wicked*
נֶעְכָּרֶת Ni. ptc. f.s. paus. (עָכַר 747) *trouble befalls*

15:7

שִׂפְתֵי חֲכָמִים n.f.p. cstr. (973)–adj. m.p. (314) *the lips of the wise*
יְזָרוּ דָעַת Pi. impf. 3 m.p. (זָרָה 279)–n.f.s. paus. (395) *spread knowledge*
וְלֵב כְּסִילִים conj.–n.m.s. cstr. (524)–n.m.p. (493) *but the minds of fools*
לֹא־כֵן neg.–adv. (485) *not so*

15:8

זֶבַח רְשָׁעִים n.m.s. cstr. (257)–adj. m.p. (957) *the sacrifice of the wicked*
תּוֹעֲבַת יהוה n.f.s. cstr. (1072)–pr.n. (217) *an abomination to Yahweh*
וּתְפִלַּת יְשָׁרִים conj.–n.f.s. cstr. (813)–adj. m.p. (449) *but the prayer of the upright*
רְצוֹנוֹ n.m.s.–3 m.s. sf. (953) *his delight*

15:9

תּוֹעֲבַת יהוה n.f.s. cstr. (1072)–pr.n. (217) *an abomination to Yahweh*
דֶּרֶךְ רָשָׁע n.m.p. cstr. (202)–adj. m.s. (957) *the way of the wicked*
וּמְרַדֵּף צְדָקָה conj.–Pi. ptc. (רָדַף 922)–n.f.s. (842) *but him who pursues righteousness*
יֶאֱהָב Qal impf. 3 m.s. (אָהַב 12) *he loves*

15:10

מוּסָר רָע n.m.s. (416)-adj. m.s. (I 948) *severe discipline*

לְעֹזֵב אֹרַח prep.-Qal act.ptc. (עָזַב I 736)-n.m.s. (73) *him who forsakes the way*

שׂוֹנֵא תוֹכַחַת Qal act.ptc. (שָׂנֵא 971)-n.f.s. (407) *he who hates reproof*

יָמוּת Qal impf. 3 m.s. (מוּת 559) *will die*

15:11

שְׁאוֹל n.f.s. (982) *Sheol*

וַאֲבַדּוֹן conj.-n.f.s. (2) *and Abaddon*

נֶגֶד יהוה prep. (617)-pr.n. (217) *lie open before Yahweh*

אַף כִּי־ conj. (II 64)-conj. (471) *how much more*

לִבּוֹת בְּנֵי־אָדָם n.m.p. cstr. (524)-n.m.p. cstr. (119)-n.m.s. (9) *the hearts of men*

15:12

לֹא יֶאֱהַב־לֵץ neg.-Qal impf. 3 m.s. (אָהַב 12) -Qal act.ptc. (לוּץ 539) *a scoffer does not like*

הוֹכֵחַ לוֹ Hi. inf.abs. (יָכַח 406)-prep.-3 m.s. sf. *to be reproved*

אֶל־חֲכָמִים prep.--adj. m.p. (314) *to the wise*

לֹא יֵלֵךְ neg.-Qal impf. 3 m.s. (הָלַךְ 229) *he will not go*

15:13

לֵב שָׂמֵחַ n.m.s. (524)-adj. m.s. (970) *a glad heart*

יֵיטִב פָּנִים Hi. impf. 3 m.s. (יָטַב 405)-n.m.p. (815) *makes glad faces*

וּבְעַצְּבַת־לֵב conj.-prep.-n.f.s. cstr. (781)-v.supra *but by sorrow of heart*

רוּחַ נְכֵאָה n.f.s. (924)-adj. f.s. (644) *the spirit is broken*

15:14

לֵב נָבוֹן n.m.s. (524)-Ni. ptc. m.s. (בִּין 106) *the mind of him who has understanding*

יְבַקֶּשׁ־דָּעַת Pi. impf. 3 m.s. (134)-n.f.s. paus. (395) *seeks knowledge*

וּפִי כְסִילִים conj.-n.m.p. cstr. (815; וּפְנֵי; Q וּפִי) -n.m.p. (493) *but the mouths of fools*

יִרְעֶה אִוֶּלֶת Qal impf. 3 m.s. (רָעָה I 944)-n.f.s. (17) *feeds on folly*

15:15

כָּל־יְמֵי עָנִי n.m.s. cstr. (481)-n.m.p. cstr. (398) -adj. m.s. (776) *all the days of the afflicted*

רָעִים adj. m.p. (948) *are evil*

וְטוֹב־לֵב conj.-adj. m.s. cstr. (II 373)-n.m.s. (524) *but a cheerful heart*

מִשְׁתֶּה תָמִיד n.m.s. cstr. (1059)-n.m.s. (556) *a continual feast*

15:16

טוֹב־מְעַט adj. m.s. (II 373)-subst. (589) *better is a little*

בְּיִרְאַת יהוה prep.-n.f.s. cstr. (432)-pr.n. (217) *with the fear of Yahweh*

מֵאוֹצָר רָב prep.-n.m.s. (69)-adj. m.s. (I 912) *than great treasure*

וּמְהוּמָה בוֹ conj.-n.f.s. (223)-prep.-3 m.s. sf. *and trouble with it*

15:17

טוֹב אֲרֻחַת adj. m.s. (II 373)-n.f.s. cstr. (73) *better is a dinner of*

יָרָק n.m.s. (438) *herbs*

וְאַהֲבָה־שָׁם conj.-n.f.s. (13)-adv. (1027) *where love is*

מִשּׁוֹר אָבוּס prep.-n.m.s. (1004)-Qal pass.ptc. (7 אָבַס) *than a fatted ox*

וְשִׂנְאָה־בוֹ conj.-n.f.s. (971)-prep.-3 m.s. sf. *and hatred with it*

15:18

אִישׁ חֵמָה n.m.s. cstr. (35)-n.f.s. (404) *a hot-tempered man*

יְגָרֶה מָדוֹן Pi. impf. 3 m.s. (גָּרָה 173)-n.m.s. (I 193) *stirs up strife*

וְאֶרֶךְ אַפַּיִם conj.-n.m.s. cstr. (73)-n.m. du. (60) *but he who is slow to anger*

יַשְׁקִיט רִיב Hi. impf. 3 m.s. (שָׁקַט 1052)-n.m.s. (936) *quiets contention*

15:19

דֶּרֶךְ עָצֵל n.m.s. cstr. (202)-adj. m.s. (782) *the way of a sluggard*

כִּמְשֻׂכַת חָדֶק n.f.s. cstr. (962, 968)-n.m.s. paus. 293) *is overgrown with thorns*

וְאֹרַח יְשָׁרִים conj.-n.m.s. cstr. (73)-adj. m.p. (449) *but the path of the upright*

סְלֻלָה Qal pass.ptc. f.s. (סָלַל 699) *a level highway*

15:20

בֵּן חָכָם n.m.s. (119)-adj. m.s. (314) *a wise son*

יְשַׂמַּח־אָב Pi. impf. 3 m.s. (שָׂמַח 970)-n.m.s. (3) *makes a glad father*

וּכְסִיל אָדָם conj. n.m.s. cstr. (493)-n.m.s. (9) *but a foolish man*

בּוֹזֶה אִמּוֹ Qal act.ptc. (בָּזָה 102)-n.f.s.-3 m.s. sf. (51) *despises his mother*

15:21

אִוֶּלֶת n.f.s. (17) *folly is*
שִׂמְחָה n.f.s. (970) *a joy*
לַחֲסַר־לֵב prep.-adj. m.s. cstr. (341)-n.m.s. (524) *to him who has no sense*
וְאִישׁ תְּבוּנָה conj.-n.m.s. cstr. (35)-n.f.s. (108) *but a man of understanding*
יְיַשֶּׁר־לָכֶת Pi. impf. 3 m.s. (יָשַׁר 448)-Qal inf.cstr. paus. (הָלַךְ 229) *walks aright*

15:22

הָפֵר מַחֲשָׁבוֹת Hi. inf.abs. (פָּרַר 830)-n.f.p. (364) *plans go wrong*
בְּאֵין סוֹד prep.-neg. (II 34)-n.m.s. (691) *without counsel*
וּבְרֹב יוֹעֲצִים conj.-prep.-n.m.s. cstr. (913)-Qal act.ptc. m.p. (יָעַץ 419) *but with many advisors*
תָּקוּם Qal impf. 3 f.s. (קוּם 877; LXX+βουλή) *they succeed*

15:23

שִׂמְחָה לָאִישׁ n.f.s. (970)-prep.-def.art.-n.m.s. (35) *a joy to a man*
בְּמַעֲנֵה־פִיו prep.-n.m.s. cstr. (775)-n.m.s.-3 m.s. sf. (804) *to make an apt answer*
וְדָבָר conj.-n.m.s. (182) *and a word*
בְּעִתּוֹ prep.-n.f.s.-3 m.s. sf. (773) *in season*
מַה־טּוֹב interr. (552)-adj. m.s. (II 373) *how good*

15:24

אֹרַח חַיִּים n.m.s. cstr. (73)-n.m.p. (313) *a path to life*
לְמַעְלָה prep.-subst.-loc.he (751) *upward*
לְמַשְׂכִּיל prep.-Hi. ptc. (שָׂכַל I 968) *for the wise man*
לְמַעַן סוּר prep. (775)-Qal inf.cstr. (סוּר 693) *that he may avoid*
מִשְּׁאוֹל prep.-n.f.s. (982) *Sheol*
מָטָּה adv. paus. (641) *beneath*

15:25

בֵּית גֵּאִים n.m.s. cstr. (108)-adj. m.p. (144) *the house of the proud*
יִסַּח יהוה Qal impf. 3 m.s. (נָסַח 650)-pr.n. (217) *Yahweh tears down*
וְיַצֵּב conj.-Hi. impf. 3 m.s. (נָצַב 662) *but maintains*

גְּבוּל אַלְמָנָה n.m.s. cstr. (147)-n.f.s. (48) *the widow's boundaries*

15:26

תּוֹעֲבַת יהוה n.f.s. cstr. (1072)-pr.n. (217) *an abomination to Yahweh*
מַחְשְׁבוֹת רָע n.f.p. cstr. (364)-n.m.s. paus. (948) *the thoughts of the wicked*
וּטְהֹרִים conj.-adj. m.p. (373) *are pure*
אִמְרֵי־נֹעַם n.m.p. cstr. (56)-n.m.s. (653) *pleasant words*

15:27

עֹכֵר בֵּיתוֹ Qal act.ptc. (עָכַר 747)-n.m.s.-3 m.s. sf. (108) *makes trouble for his household*
בּוֹצֵעַ בָּצַע Qal act.ptc. (בָּצַע 130)-n.m.s. paus. (130) *he who is greedy for unjust gain*
וְשׂוֹנֵא מַתָּנֹת conj.-Qal act.ptc. (971)-n.f.p. (I 682) *but he who hates bribes*
יִחְיֶה Qal impf. 3 m.s. (חָיָה 310) *will live*

15:28

לֵב צַדִּיק n.m.s. cstr. (524)-adj. m.s. (843) *the mind of the righteous*
יֶהְגֶּה לַעֲנוֹת Qal impf. 3 m.s. (הָגָה I 211)-prep. -Qal inf.cstr. (עָנָה I 772) *ponders how to answer*
וּפִי רְשָׁעִים conj.-n.m.s. cstr. (804)-adj. m.p. (957) *but the mouth of the wicked*
יַבִּיעַ רָעוֹת Hi. impf. 3 m.s. (נָבַע 615)-adj. f.p. (I 948) *pours out evil things*

15:29

רָחוֹק יהוה adj. m.s. (935)-pr.n. (217) *Yahweh is far*
מֵרְשָׁעִים prep.-adj. m.p. (957) *from the wicked*
וּתְפִלַּת צַדִּיקִים conj.-n.f.s. cstr. (813)-adj. m.p. (843) *but the prayer of the righteous*
יִשְׁמָע Qal impf. 3 m.s. (שָׁמַע 1033) *he hears*

15:30

מְאוֹר־עֵינַיִם n.m.s. cstr. (22)-n.f. du. (744) *the light of the eyes*
יְשַׂמַּח־לֵב Pi. impf. 3 m.s. (שָׂמַח 970)-n.m.s. (524) *rejoices the heart*
שְׁמוּעָה טוֹבָה n.f.s. (1035)-adj. f.s. (II 373) *and good news*
תְּדַשֶּׁן־עָצֶם Pi. impf. 3 f.s. (דָּשֵׁן 206)-n.f.s. paus. (782) *makes fat the bones*

15:31

שֹׁמַעַת אֹזֶן n.f.s. (25)-Qal act.ptc. f.s. cstr. (שָׁמַע 1033) *he whose ear heeds*

תּוֹכַחַת חַיִּים n.f.s. cstr. (407)-n.m.p. (313) *wholesome admonition*

בְּקֶרֶב חֲכָמִים prep.-n.m.s. cstr. (899)-adj. m.p. (314) *among the wise*

תָּלִין Qal impf. 3 f.s. (לוּן I 533) *will abide*

15:32

פּוֹרֵעַ מוּסָר Qal act.ptc. (פָּרַע III 828)-n.m.s. (416) *he who ignores instruction*

מוֹאֵס נַפְשׁוֹ Qal act.ptc. (מָאַס 549)-n.f.s.-3 m.s. sf. (659) *despises himself*

וְשׁוֹמֵעַ תּוֹכַחַת conj.-Qal act.ptc. (שָׁמַע 1033) -n.f.s. (407) *but he who heeds admonition*

קוֹנֶה לֵּב Qal act.ptc. (קָנָה 888)-n.m.s. (524) *gains understanding*

15:33

יִרְאַת יהוה n.f.s. cstr. (432)-pr.n. (217) *the fear of Yahweh*

מוּסַר חָכְמָה n.m.s. cstr. (416)-n.f.s. (315) *instruction in wisdom*

וְלִפְנֵי כָבוֹד conj.-prep.-n.m.p. cstr. (815)-n.m.s. (458) *and before honor*

עֲנָוָה n.f.s. (776) *humility*

16:1

לְאָדָם prep.-n.m.s. (9) *to man*

מַעַרְכֵי־לֵב n.m.p. cstr. (790)-n.m.s. (524) *the plans of the mind*

וּמֵיהוה conj.-prep.-pr.n. (217) *but from Yahweh*

מַעֲנֵה לָשׁוֹן n.m.s. cstr. (775)-n.f.s. (546) *the answer of the tongue*

16:2

כָּל־דַּרְכֵי־אִישׁ n.m.s. cstr. (481)-n.m.p. cstr. (202)-n.m.s. (35) *all the ways of a man*

זַךְ בְּעֵינָיו adj. m.s. (269)-prep.-n.f.p.-3 m.s. sf. (744) *pure in his own eyes*

וְתֹכֵן conj.-Qal act.ptc. (תָּכַן 1067) *but weighs*

רוּחוֹת n.f.p. (924) *the spirit*

יהוה pr.n. (217) *Yahweh*

16:3

גֹּל Qal impv. 2 m.s. (גָּלַל II 164) *commit*

אֶל יהוה prep.-pr.n. (217) *to Yahweh*

מַעֲשֶׂיךָ n.m.p.-2 m.s. sf. (795) *your work*

וְיִכֹּנוּ conj.-Ni. impf. 3 m.p. (כּוּן I 465) *and will be established*

מַחְשְׁבֹתֶיךָ n.f.p.-2 m.s. sf. (364) *your plans*

16:4

כֹּל n.m.s. (481) *everything*

פָּעַל יהוה Qal pf. 3 m.s. (821)-pr.n. (217) *Yahweh has made*

לַמַּעֲנֵהוּ prep.-def.art.-n.m.s.-3 m.s. sf. (775) *for its purpose*

וְגַם־רָשָׁע conj.-adv. (168)-adj. m.s. (957) *even the wicked*

לְיוֹם רָעָה prep.-n.m.s. cstr. (398)-n.f.s. (949) *for the day of trouble*

16:5

תּוֹעֲבַת יהוה n.f.s. cstr. (1072)-pr.n. (217) *an abomination to Yahweh*

כָּל־גְּבַהּ־לֵב n.m.s. cstr. (481)-adj. m.s. cstr. (147) -n.m.s. (524) *every one who is arrogant*

יָד לְיָד n.f.s. (388)-prep.-v.supra *be assured* (lit. *hand to hand)*

לֹא יִנָּקֶה neg.-Ni. impf. 3 m.s. (נָקָה 667) *he will not go unpunished*

16:6

בְּחֶסֶד prep.-n.m.s. (338) *by loyalty*

וֶאֱמֶת conj.-n.f.s. (54) *and faithfulness*

יְכֻפַּר עָוֹן Pu. impf. 3 m.s. (כָּפַר 497)-n.m.s. (730) *iniquity is atoned for*

וּבְיִרְאַת יהוה conj.-prep.-n.f.s. cstr. (432)-pr.n. (217) *and by the fear of Yahweh*

סוּר מֵרָע Qal inf.cstr. (סוּר 693)-prep.-n.m.s. paus. (II 948) *a man avoids evil*

16:7

בִּרְצוֹת יהוה prep.-Qal inf.cstr. (רָצָה 953)-pr.n. (217) *when ... please Yahweh*

דַּרְכֵי־אִישׁ n.m.p. cstr. (202)-n.m.s. (35) *a man's ways*

גַּם־אוֹיְבָיו adv. (168)-Qal act.ptc. m.p.-3 m.s. sf. (אָיַב 33) *even his enemies*

יַשְׁלִם אִתּוֹ Hi. impf. 3 m.s. (שָׁלֵם 1022)-prep.-3 m.s. sf. (II 85) *he makes ... to be at peace with him*

16:8

טוֹב־מְעַט adj. m.s. (II 373)-adv. (589) *better is a little*

בִּצְדָקָה prep.-n.f.s. (842) *with righteousness*

מֵרֹב תְּבוּאוֹת prep.-n.m.s. cstr. (913)-n.f.p. (100) *than great revenues*

בְּלֹא מִשְׁפָּט prep.-neg.-n.m.s. (1048) *with injustice*

16:9

לֵב אָדָם n.m.s. cstr. (524)-n.m.s. (9) *a man's mind*

יְחַשֵּׁב דַּרְכּוֹ Pi. impf. 3 m.s. (חָשַׁב 362)-n.m.s.-3 m.s. sf. (202) *plans his way*

ויהוה conj.-pr.n. (217) *but Yahweh*

יָכִין צַעֲדוֹ Hi. impf. 3 m.s. (כּוּן 465)-n.m.s.-3 m.s. sf. (857) *directs his steps*

16:10

קֶסֶם n.m.s. (890) *inspired decisions*

עַל־שִׂפְתֵי־מֶלֶךְ prep.-n.f.p. cstr. (973)-n.m.s. (I 572) *on the lips of a king*

בְּמִשְׁפָּט prep.-n.m.s. (1048) *in judgment*

לֹא יִמְעַל־פִּיו neg.-Qal impf. 3 m.s. (מָעַל 591) -n.m.s.-3 m.s. sf. (804) *his mouth does not sin*

16:11

פֶּלֶס n.m.s. (813) *a balance*

וּמֹאזְנֵי מִשְׁפָּט conj.-n.m. du. cstr. (24)-n.m.s. (1048) *and scales of justice*

ליהוה prep.-pr.n. (217) *are Yahweh's*

מַעֲשֵׂהוּ n.m.s.-3 m.s. sf. (795) *his work*

כָּל־אַבְנֵי־כִיס n.m.s. cstr. (481)-n.f.p. cstr. (6) -n.m.s. (476) *all the weights in the bag*

16:12

תּוֹעֲבַת מְלָכִים n.f.s. cstr. (1072)-n.m.p. (I 572) *an abomination to kings*

עֲשׂוֹת רֶשַׁע Qal inf.cstr. (עָשָׂה I 793)-n.m.s. (957) *to do evil*

כִּי בִצְדָקָה conj. (471)-prep.-n.f.s. (842) *for by righteousness*

יִכּוֹן כִּסֵּא Ni. impf. 3 m.s. (כּוּן I 465)-n.m.s. (490) *the throne is established*

16:13

רְצוֹן מְלָכִים n.m.s. cstr. (953)-n.m.p. (I 572) *the delight of a king*

שִׂפְתֵי־צֶדֶק n.f.p. cstr. (973)-n.m.s. (841) *righteous lips*

וְדֹבֵר יְשָׁרִים conj.-Qal act.ptc. (180)-adj. m.p. (449) *and him who speaks what is right*

יֶאֱהָב Qal impf. 3 m.s. paus. (אָהֵב 12) *he loves*

16:14

חֲמַת־מֶלֶךְ n.f.s. cstr. (404)-n.m.s. (I 572) *a king's wrath*

מַלְאֲכֵי־מָוֶת n.m.p. cstr. (521)-n.m.s. (560) *a messenger of death*

וְאִישׁ חָכָם conj.-n.m.s. (35)-adj. m.s. (314) *and a wise man*

יְכַפְּרֶנָּה Pi. impf. 3 m.s.-3 f.s. sf. (כָּפַר 497) *will appease it*

16:15

בְּאוֹר־פְּנֵי־מֶלֶךְ prep.-n.m.s. cstr. 21)-n.m.p. cstr. (815)-n.m.s. (I 572) *in the light of a king's face*

חַיִּים n.m.p. (313) *life*

וּרְצוֹנוֹ conj.-n.m.s.-3 m.s. sf. (953) *and his favor*

כְּעָב prep.-n.m.s. cstr. (728) *like the clouds of*

מַלְקוֹשׁ n.m.s. (545) *a spring rain*

16:16

קְנֹה־חָכְמָה Qal inf.cstr. (קָנָה 888)-n.f.s. (315) *to get wisdom*

מַה־טּוֹב interr. (552)-adj. m.s. (II 373) *how much better*

מֵחָרוּץ prep.-n.m.s. (359) *than gold*

וּקְנוֹת בִּינָה conj.-Qal inf.cstr. (קָנָה 888)-n.f.s. (108) *and to get understanding*

נִבְחָר Ni. ptc. (בָּחַר 103) *is to be chosen*

מִכָּסֶף prep.-n.m.s. paus. (494) *than silver*

16:17

מְסִלַּת יְשָׁרִים n.f.s. cstr. (700)-adj. m.p. (449) *the highway of the upright*

סוּר מֵרָע Qal inf.cstr. (סוּר 693)-prep.-adj. m.s. (948) *turns aside from evil*

שֹׁמֵר נַפְשׁוֹ Qal act.ptc. (1036)-n.f.s.-3 m.s. sf. (659) *preserves his life*

נֹצֵר דַּרְכּוֹ Qal act.ptc. (נָצַר 665)-n.m.s.-3 m.s. sf. (202) *he who guards his way*

16:18

לִפְנֵי־שֶׁבֶר prep.-n.m.p. cstr. (815)-n.m.s. (I 991) *before destruction*

גָּאוֹן n.m.s. (144) *pride*

וְלִפְנֵי כִשָּׁלוֹן conj.-v.supra-n.m.s. (506) *and before a fall*

גֹּבַהּ רוּחַ n.m.s. cstr. (147)-n.f.s. (924) *a haughty spirit*

16:19

טוֹב שְׁפַל־רוּחַ adj. (373)-adj. m.s. cstr. (1050) -n.f.s. (924) *it is better to be of a lowly spirit*

אֶת־עֲנָיִים prep. (II 85)-adj. m.p. (776) *with the poor*

מֵחַלֵּק שָׁלָל prep.-Pi. inf.cstr. (חָלַק 323)-n.m.s. (1021) *than to divide the spoil*

אֶת־גֵּאִים prep. (II 85)-adj. m.p. (144) *with the proud*

16:20

מַשְׂכִּיל Hi. ptc. (שָׂכַל 968) *he who gives heed*
עַל־דָּבָר prep.-n.m.s. (182) *to the word*
יִמְצָא־טוֹב Qal impf. 3 m.s. (מָצָא 592)-n.m.s. (III 375) *will prosper*
וּבוֹטֵחַ בַּיהוה conj.-Qal act.ptc. (בָּטַח 105)-prep. -pr.n. (217) *and he who trusts in Yahweh*
אַשְׁרָיו n.m.p.-3 m.s. sf. (80) *is happy*

16:21

לַחֲכַם־לֵב prep.-adj. m.s. cstr. (314)-n.m.s. (524) *the wise of heart*
יִקָּרֵא Ni. impf. 3 m.s. (קָרָא 894) *is called*
נָבוֹן Ni. ptc. (בִּין 106) *a man of discernment*
וּמֶתֶק שְׂפָתַיִם conj.-n.m.s. cstr. (608)-n.f. du. (973) *and pleasant speech*
יֹסִיף לֶקַח Hi. impf. 3 m.s. (יָסַף 414)-n.m.s. (544) *increases persuasiveness*

16:22

מְקוֹר חַיִּים n.m.s. cstr. (881)-n.m.p. (313) *a fountain of life*
שֵׂכֶל n.m.s. (968) *wisdom*
בְּעָלָיו n.m.p.-3 m.s. sf. (127) *to him who has it*
וּמוּסַר אֱוִלִים conj.-n.m.s. cstr. (416)-adj. m.p. (17) *the chastisement of fools*
אִוֶּלֶת n.f.s. (17) *folly*

16:23

לֵב חָכָם n.m.s. cstr. (524)-adj. m.s. (314) *the mind of the wise*
יַשְׂכִּיל פִּיהוּ Hi. impf. 3 m.s. (שָׂכַל 968)-n.m.s.-3 m.s. sf. (804) *makes his speech judicious*
וְעַל־שְׂפָתָיו conj.-prep.-n.f. du.-3 m.s. sf. (973) *and to his lips*
יֹסִיף לֶקַח Hi. impf. 3 m.s. (יָסַף 414)-n.m.s. (544) *adds persuasiveness*

16:24

צוּף־דְּבַשׁ n.m.s. cstr. (I 847)-n.m.s. (185) *like a honeycomb*
אִמְרֵי־נֹעַם n.m.p. cstr. (56)-n.m.s. (653) *pleasant words*
מָתוֹק n.m.s. (608) *sweetness*
לַנֶּפֶשׁ prep.-def.art.-n.f.s. (659) *to the soul*
וּמַרְפֵּא conj.-n.m.s. (951) *and health*
לָעֶצֶם prep.-def.art.-n.f.s. (782) *to the body*

16:25

יֵשׁ דֶּרֶךְ subst. (441)-n.m.s. (202) *there is a way*
יָשָׁר adj. m.s. (449) *right*
לִפְנֵי־אִישׁ prep.-n.m.p. cstr. (815)-n.m.s. (35) *to a man*
וְאַחֲרִיתָהּ conj.-n.f.s.-3 f.s. sf. (31) *but its end*
דַּרְכֵי־מָוֶת n.m.p. cstr. (202)-n.m.s. (560) *is the way(s) to death*

16:26

נֶפֶשׁ עָמֵל n.f.s. cstr. (659)-n.m.s. (I 766) *a worker's appetite*
עָמְלָה לּוֹ Qal pf. 3 f.s. (עָמַל 765)-prep.-3 m.s. sf. *works for him*
כִּי־אָכַף עָלָיו conj. (471)-Qal pf. 3 m.s. (38) -prep.-3 m.s. sf. *but urges him on*
פִּיהוּ n.m.s.-3 m.s. sf. (804) *his mouth*

16:27

אִישׁ בְּלִיַּעַל n.m.s. cstr. (35)-n.m.s. (116) *a worthless man*
כֹּרֶה רָעָה Qal act.ptc. (כָּרָה I 500)-n.f.s. (949) *plots evil*
וְעַל־שְׂפָתָיו conj.-prep.-n.f. du.-3 m.s. sf. (973; Q שְׂפָתוֹ) *and his speech*
כְּאֵשׁ צָרָבֶת prep.-n.f.s. (77)-adj. f.s. paus. (863) *like a scorching fire*

16:28

אִישׁ תַּהְפֻּכוֹת n.m.s. cstr. (35)-n.f.s. (246) *a perverse man*
יְשַׁלַּח מָדוֹן Pi. impf. 3 m.s. (שָׁלַח 1018)-n.m.s. (I 193) *spreads strife*
וְנִרְגָּן conj.-Ni. ptc. (רָגַן 920) *and a whisperer*
מַפְרִיד אַלּוּף Hi. ptc. (פָּרַד 825)-n.m.s. (I 48) *separates close friends*

16:29

אִישׁ חָמָס n.m.s. cstr. (35)-n.m.s. (329) *a man of violence*
יְפַתֶּה רֵעֵהוּ Pi. impf. 3 m.s. (פָּתָה 834)-n.m.s.-3 m.s. sf. (945) *entices his neighbor*
וְהוֹלִיכוֹ conj.-Hi. pf. 3 m.s.-3 m.s. sf. (הָלַךְ 229) *and leads him*
בְּדֶרֶךְ prep.-n.m.s. (202) *in a way*
לֹא־טוֹב neg.-adj. m.s. (373) *that is not good*

16:30

עֹצֶה עֵינָיו Qal act.ptc. (עָצָה I 781)-n.f.p.-3 m.s. sf. (744) *he who winks his eyes*
לַחְשֹׁב תַּהְפֻּכוֹת prep.-Qal inf.cstr. (חָשַׁב 362) -n.f.p. (246) *to plan perverse things*

קֹרֵץ שְׂפָתָיו Qal act.ptc. (קָרַץ 902)-n.f. du.-3 m.s. sf. (973) *he who compresses his lips*

כִּלָּה רָעָה Pi. pf. 3 m.s. (כָּלָה I 477)-n.f.s. (949) *brings evil to pass*

16:31

עֲטֶרֶת תִּפְאֶרֶת n.f.s. cstr. (742)-n.f.s. (802) *a crown of glory*

שֵׂיבָה n.f.s. (966) *a hoary head*

בְּדֶרֶךְ צְדָקָה prep.-n.m.s. cstr. (202)-n.f.s. (842) *in a righteous life*

תִּמָּצֵא Ni. impf. 3 f.s. (מָצָא 592) *it is gained*

16:32

טוֹב אֶרֶךְ אַפַּיִם adj. m.s. (II 373)-adj. m.s. cstr. (74)-n.m. du. (I 60) *he who is slow to anger is better*

מִגִּבּוֹר prep.-adj. m.s. (150) *than the mighty*

וּמֹשֵׁל בְּרוּחוֹ conj.-Qal act.ptc. (605)-prep.-n.f.s.-3 m.s. sf. (924) *and he who rules his spirit*

מִלֹּכֵד עִיר prep.-Qal act.ptc. (לָכַד 539)-n.f.s. (746) *than he who takes a city*

16:33

בַּחֵיק prep.-def.art.-n.m.s. (300) *into the lap*

יוּטַל Ho. impf. 3 m.s. (טוּל 376) *is cast*

אֶת־הַגּוֹרָל dir.obj.-def.art.-n.m.s. (174) *the lot*

וּמֵיהוה conj.-prep.-pr.n. (217) *but from Yahweh*

כָּל־מִשְׁפָּטוֹ n.m.s. cstr. (481)-n.m.s.-3 m.s. sf. (1048) *all of his decision*

17:1

טוֹב פַּת חֲרֵבָה adj. m.s. (II 373)-n.f.s. (837)-adj. f.s. (351) *better is a dry morsel*

וְשַׁלְוָה־בָהּ conj.-n.f.s. (1017)-prep.-3 f.s. sf. *with quiet*

מִבַּיִת prep.-n.f.s. (108) *than a house*

מָלֵא adj. m.s. (570) *full*

זִבְחֵי־רִיב n.m.p. cstr. (257)-n.m.s. (936) *of feasting with strife*

17:2

עֶבֶד־מַשְׂכִּיל n.m.s. (713)-Hi. ptc. (שָׂכַל 968) *a slave who deals wisely*

יִמְשֹׁל Qal impf. 3 m.s. (מָשַׁל 605) *will rule*

בְּבֵן מֵבִישׁ prep.-n.m.s. (119)-Hi. ptc. (בּוֹשׁ 101) *over a son who acts shamefully*

וּבְתוֹךְ אַחִים conj.-prep.-n.m.s. cstr. (1063)-n.m.p. (26) *and in the midst of brothers*

יַחֲלֹק נַחֲלָה Qal impf. 3 m.s. (חָלַק 323)-n.f.s. (635) *will share the inheritance*

17:3

מַצְרֵף לַכֶּסֶף n.m.s. (864)-prep.-def.art.-n.m.s. (494) *the crucible is for silver*

וְכוּר לַזָּהָב conj.-n.m.s. (468)-prep.-def.art.-n.m.s. (262) *and the furnace for gold*

וּבֹחֵן לִבּוֹת conj.-Qal act.ptc. (בָּחַן 103)-n.m.p. (524) *and tries hearts*

יהוה pr.n. (217) *Yahweh*

17:4

מֵרַע Hi. ptc. (רָעַע 949) *an evildoer*

מַקְשִׁיב Hi. ptc. (קָשַׁב 904) *listens*

עַל־שְׂפַת־אָוֶן prep.-n.f.s. cstr. (973)-n.m.s. (19) *to wicked lips*

שֶׁקֶר n.m.s. (1055) *a liar*

מֵזִין Hi. ptc. (אָזַן I 24) *listens*

עַל־לְשׁוֹן הַוֺּת prep.-n.f.s. cstr. (546)-n.f.p. (217) *to a mischievous tongue*

17:5

לֹעֵג לָרָשׁ Qal act.ptc. (לָעַג 541)-prep.-def.art.-Qal act.ptc. (רוּשׁ 930) *he who mocks the poor*

חֵרֵף Pi. pf. 3 m.s. (חָרַף 357) *insults*

עֹשֵׂהוּ Qal act.ptc.-3 m.s. sf. (עָשָׂה I 793) *his Maker*

שָׂמֵחַ לְאֵיד adj. m.s. (970)-prep.-n.m.s. (15) *he who is glad at calamity*

לֹא יִנָּקֶה neg.-Ni. impf. 3 m.s. (נָקָה 667) *will not go unpunished*

17:6

עֲטֶרֶת זְקֵנִים n.f.s. cstr. (I 742)-adj. m.p. (278) *the crown of the aged*

בְּנֵי בָנִים n.m.p. cstr. (119)-n.m.p. (119) *grandchildren*

וְתִפְאֶרֶת בָּנִים conj.-n.f.s. cstr. (802)-n.m.p. (119) *and the glory of sons*

אֲבוֹתָם n.m.p.-3 m.p. sf. (3) *is their fathers*

17:7

לֹא־נָאוָה neg.-adj. m.s. (610) *not becoming*

לְנָבָל prep.-adj. m.s. (614) *to a fool*

שְׂפַת־יֶתֶר n.f.s. cstr. (973)-n.m.s. (I 451) *fine speech* (lit. *a lip of excess*)

אַף כִּי־לְנָדִיב conj. (II 64)-conj. (471)-prep.-n.m.s. (622) *still less to a prince*

שְׂפַת־שָׁקֶר n.f.s. cstr. (973)-n.m.s. paus. (1055) *false speech*

17:8

אֶבֶן־חֵן n.f.s. cstr. (6)-n.m.s. (I 336) *a magic stone*

הַשֹּׁחַד def.art.-n.m.s. (1005) *a bribe*

בְּעֵינֵי בְעָלָיו prep.-n.f.p. cstr. (744)-n.m.p.-3 m.s. sf. (127) *in the eyes of him who gives it*

אֶל־כָּל־אֲשֶׁר prep. (39)-n.m.s. (481)-rel. (81) *wherever*

יִפְנֶה Qal impf. 3 m.s. (פָּנָה 815) *he turns*

יַשְׂכִּיל Hi. impf. 3 m.s. (שָׂכַל 968) *he prospers*

17:9

מְכַסֶּה־פֶּשַׁע Pi. ptc. (כָּסָה 491)-n.m.s. (833) *he who forgives an offense*

מְבַקֵּשׁ Pi. ptc. (בָּקַשׁ 134) *seeks*

אַהֲבָה n.f.s. (13) *love*

וְשֹׁנֶה בְדָבָר conj.-Qal act.ptc. (שָׁנָה III 1040) -prep.-n.m.s. (182) *but he who repeats a matter*

מַפְרִיד Hi. ptc. (פָּרַד 825) *alienates*

אַלּוּף n.m.s. (48) *a friend*

17:10

תֵּחַת גְּעָרָה Qal impf. 3 f.s. (נָחַת 639)-n.f.s. (172) *a rebuke goes deeper*

בְּמֵבִין prep.-Hi. ptc. (בִּין 106) *into a man of understanding*

מֵהַכּוֹת כְּסִיל prep.-Hi. inf.cstr. (נָכָה 645)-n.m.s. (493) *than ... blows into a fool*

מֵאָה n.f.s. (547) *a hundred*

17:11

אַךְ־מְרִי adv. (36)-n.m.s. (598) *only rebellion*

יְבַקֶּשׁ־רָע Pi. impf. 3 m.s. (בָּקַשׁ 134)-n.m.s. (948) *an evil man seeks*

וּמַלְאָךְ אַכְזָרִי conj.-n.m.s. (521)-adj. m.s. (470) *and a cruel messenger*

יְשֻׁלַּח־בּוֹ Pu. impf. 3 m.s. (שָׁלַח 1018)-prep.-3 m.s. sf. *will be sent against him*

17:12

פָּגוֹשׁ Qal inf.abs. (פָּגַשׁ 803) *let ... meet*

דֹּב שַׁכּוּל n.m.s. (179)-adj. m.s. (1014) *a she-bear robbed of her cubs*

בְּאִישׁ prep.-n.m.s. (35) *a man*

וְאַל־כְּסִיל conj.-neg.-n.m.s. (493) *rather than a fool*

בְּאִוַּלְתּוֹ prep.-n.f.s.-3 m.s. sf. (17) *in his folly*

17:13

מֵשִׁיב רָעָה Hi. ptc. (שׁוּב 996)-n.f.s. (949) *if a man returns evil*

תַּחַת טוֹבָה prep. (1065)-n.f.s. (375) *for good*

לֹא־תָמִישׁ neg.-Qal (or Hi.) impf. 3 f.s. (מוּשׁ 559) *will not depart*

רָעָה v.supra *evil*

מִבֵּיתוֹ prep.-n.m.s.-3 m.s. sf. (108) *from his house*

17:14

פּוֹטֵר מַיִם Qal act.ptc. (פָּטַר 809-n.m.p. (565) *letting out water*

רֵאשִׁית מָדוֹן n.f.s. cstr. (912)-n.m.s. (I 193) *the beginning of strife*

וְלִפְנֵי הִתְגַּלַּע conj.-prep.-n.m.p. cstr. (815)-Hith. pf. 3 m.s. (גָּלַע 166) *so ... before breaks out*

הָרִיב def.art.-n.m.s. (936) *the quarrel*

נְטוֹשׁ Qal impv. 2 m.s. (נָטַשׁ 643) *quit*

17:15

מַצְדִּיק רָשָׁע Hi. ptc. (צָדַק 842)-adj. m.s. (957) *he who justifies the wicked*

וּמַרְשִׁיעַ צַדִּיק conj.-Hi. ptc. (רָשַׁע 957)-adj. m.s. (843) *and he who condemns the righteous*

תּוֹעֲבַת יהוה n.f.s. cstr. (1072)-pr.n. (217) *an abomination to Yahweh*

גַּם־שְׁנֵיהֶם adv. (168)-n.m.p.-3 m.p. sf. (1040) *are both alike*

17:16

לָמָּה־זֶּה מְחִיר interr. (552)-demons.adj. m.s. (260)-n.m.s. (I 564) *why should ... have a price*

בְּיַד־כְּסִיל prep.-n.f.s. cstr. (388)-n.m.s. (493) *in the hand of a fool*

לִקְנוֹת חָכְמָה prep.-Qal inf.cstr. (קָנָה 888)-n.f.s. (315) *to buy wisdom*

וְלֶב־אָיִן conj.-n.m.s. (524)-neg. (II 34) *when he has no mind*

17:17

בְּכָל־עֵת prep.-n.m.s. cstr. (481)-n.f.s. (773) *at all times*

אֹהֵב הָרֵעַ Qal act.ptc. (אָהֵב 12)-def.art.-n.m.s. (945) *a friend loves*

וְאָח conj.-n.m.s. (26) *and a brother*

לְצָרָה prep.-n.f.s. (865) *for adversity*

יִוָּלֵד Ni. impf. 3 m.s. (יָלַד 408) *is born*

17:18

אָדָם n.m.s. (9) *a man*

חֲסַר־לֵב adj. m.s. cstr. (341)-n.m.s. (524) *without sense*

תּוֹקֵעַ כָּף Qal act.ptc. (תָּקַע 1075)-n.f.s. paus. (496) *gives a pledge*
עֹרֵב עֲרֻבָּה Qal act.ptc. (עָרַב II 786)-n.f.s. (786) *and becomes surety*
לִפְנֵי רֵעֵהוּ prep.-n.m.p. cstr. (815)-n.m.s.-3 m.s. sf. (945) *in the presence of his neighbor*

17:19

אֹהֵב פֶּשַׁע Qal act.ptc. (אָהַב 12)-n.m.s. (833) *he who loves transgression*
אֹהֵב מַצָּה v.supra-n.f.s. (II 663) *loves strife*
מַגְבִּיהַּ פִּתְחוֹ Hi. ptc. (גָּבַהּ 146)-n.m.s.-3 m.s. sf. (835) *he who makes his door high*
מְבַקֶּשׁ־שָׁבֶר Pi. ptc. (בָּקַשׁ 134)-n.m.s. paus. (991) *seeks destruction*

17:20

עִקֶּשׁ־לֵב adj. m.s. cstr. (786)-n.m.s. (524) *a man of crooked mind*
לֹא־יִמְצָא־טוֹב neg.-Qal impf. 3 m.s. (מָצָא 592)-n.m.s. (III 375) *does not find a good thing*
וְנֶהְפָּךְ בִּלְשׁוֹנוֹ conj.-Ni. ptc. (הָפַךְ 245)-prep. -n.f.s.-3 m.s. sf. (546) *and one with a perverse tongue*
יִפּוֹל בְּרָעָה Qal impf. 3 m.s. (נָפַל 656)-prep. -n.f.s. (949) *falls into calamity*

17:21

יֹלֵד כְּסִיל Qal act.ptc. (יָלַד 408)-n.m.s. (493) *the one begetting a fool*
לְתוּגָה לוֹ prep.-n.f.s. (387)-prep.-3 m.s. sf. *for grief to him*
וְלֹא־יִשְׂמַח conj.-neg.-Qal impf. 3 m.s. (שָׂמַח 970) *and has no joy*
אֲבִי נָבָל n.m.s. cstr. (3)-adj. m.s. (I 614) *the father of a fool*

17:22

לֵב שָׂמֵחַ n.m.s. (524)-adj. m.s. (970) *a cheerful heart*
יֵיטִב גֵּהָה Hi. impf. 3 m.s. (יָטַב 405)-n.f.s. (155) *is a good medicine*
וְרוּחַ נְכֵאָה conj.-n.f.s. (924)-adj. f.s. (644) *but a downcast spirit*
תְּיַבֶּשׁ־גָּרֶם Pi. impf. 3 f.s. (יָבֵשׁ I 386)-n.m.s. paus. (175) *dries up the bones*

17:23

שֹׁחַד מֵחֵיק n.m.s. (1005)-prep.-n.m.s. (300) *a bribe from the bosom*
רָשָׁע יִקָּח adj. m.s. (957)-Qal impf. 3 m.s. paus. (542 לָקַח) *a wicked man accepts*
לְהַטּוֹת prep.-Hi. inf.cstr. (נָטָה 639) *to pervert*
אָרְחוֹת מִשְׁפָּט n.m.p. cstr. (73)-n.m.s. (1048) *the ways of justice*

17:24

אֶת־פְּנֵי מֵבִין dir.obj.-n.m.p. cstr. (815)-Hi. ptc. (106 בִּין) *the face of the man of understanding*
חָכְמָה n.f.s. (315) *wisdom*
וְעֵינֵי כְסִיל conj.-n.f. du. cstr. (744)-n.m.s. (493) *but the eyes of a fool*
בִּקְצֵה־אָרֶץ prep.-n.m.s. cstr. (8992)-n.f.s. paus. (75) *on the ends of the earth*

17:25

כַּעַס לְאָבִיו n.m.s. (495)-prep.-n.m.s.-3 m.s. sf. (3) *a grief to his father*
בֵּן כְּסִיל n.m.s. (119)-adj. m.s. (493) *a stupid son*
וּמֶמֶר conj.-n.m.s. (601) *and bitterness*
לְיוֹלַדְתּוֹ prep.-Qal act.ptc. f.s.-3 m.s. sf. (יָלַד 408) *to her who bore him*

17:26

גַּם עֲנוֹשׁ adv. (168)-Qal inf.cstr. (עָנַשׁ 778) *also to impose a fine*
לַצַּדִּיק prep.-def.art.-adj. m.s. (843) *on a righteous man*
לֹא־טוֹב neg.-adj. m.s. (II 373) *is not good*
לְהַכּוֹת נְדִיבִים prep.-Hi. inf.cstr. (נָכָה 645)-adj. m.p. (622) *to flog noble men*
עַל־יֹשֶׁר prep.-n.m.s. (449) *is wrong*

17:27

חוֹשֵׂךְ אֲמָרָיו Qal act.ptc. (חָשַׂךְ 362)-n.m.p.-3 m.s. sf. (56) *he who restrains his words*
יוֹדֵעַ דָּעַת Qal act.ptc. (יָדַע 393)-n.f.s. paus. (395) *has knowledge*
וְקַר־רוּחַ conj.-adj. m.s. cstr. (903)-n.f.s. (924) *and he who has a cool spirit*
אִישׁ תְּבוּנָה n.m.s. cstr. (35)-n.f.s. (108) *a man of understanding*

17:28

גַּם אֱוִיל adv. (168)-adj. m.s. (17) *even a fool*
מַחֲרִישׁ Hi. ptc. (חָרַשׁ II 361) *who keeps silent*
חָכָם יֵחָשֵׁב adj. m.s. (314)-Ni. impf. 3 m.s. (חָשַׁב 362) *is considered wise*
אֹטֵם שְׂפָתָיו Qal act.ptc. (אטם 31)-n.f. du.-3 m.s. sf. (973) *when he closes his lips*
נָבוֹן Ni. ptc. (בִּין 106) *he is deemed intelligent*

18:1

לְתַאֲוָה יְבַקֵּשׁ prep.-n.f.s. (16)-Pi. impf. 3 m.s. (134 בָּקַשׁ) *seeks desire*

נִפְרָד Ni. ptc. (פָּרַד 825) *he who is separated*

בְּכָל־תּוּשִׁיָּה prep.-n.m.s. cstr. (481)-n.f.s. (444) *against all sound judgment*

יִתְגַּלָּע Hith. impf. 3 m.s. (גָּלַע 166) *to break out*

18:2

לֹא־יַחְפֹּץ neg.-Qal impf. 3 m.s. (חָפֵץ 342) *takes no pleasure*

כְּסִיל n.m.s. (493) *a fool*

בִּתְבוּנָה prep.-n.f.s. (108) *in understanding*

כִּי אִם־בְּהִתְגַּלּוֹת conj. (471)-conj. (49; 474)-Hith. inf.cstr. (גָּלָה 162) *that may reveal itself*

לִבּוֹ n.m.s.-3 m.s. sf. (524) *his heart*

18:3

בְּבוֹא־רָשָׁע prep.-Qal inf.cstr. (בּוֹא 97)-adj. m.s. (957) *when wickedness comes*

בָּא גַם־בּוּז Qal pf. 3 m.s. (בּוֹא 97)-adv. (168) -n.m.s. (II 100) *contempt comes also*

וְעִם־קָלוֹן conj.-prep. (767)-n.m.s. (885) *and with dishonor*

חֶרְפָּה n.f.s. (357) *disgrace*

18:4

מַיִם עֲמֻקִּים n.m.p. (565)-adj. m.p. (771) *deep waters*

דִּבְרֵי פִי־אִישׁ n.m.p. cstr. (182)-n.m.s. cstr. (804) -n.m.s. (35) *the words of a man's mouth*

נַחַל נֹבֵעַ n.m.s. (636)-Qal act.ptc. (נָבַע 615) *a gushing stream*

מְקוֹר חָכְמָה n.m.s. cstr. (881)-n.f.s. (315) *the fountain of wisdom*

18:5

שְׂאֵת פְּנֵי־רָשָׁע Qal inf.cstr. (נָשָׂא 669)-n.m.p. cstr. (815)-adj. m.s. (957) *to be partial to a wicked man*

לֹא־טוֹב neg.-adj. m.s. (II 373) *it is not good*

לְהַטּוֹת צַדִּיק prep.-Hi. inf.cstr. (נָטָה 639)-adj. m.s. (843) *to deprive a righteous man*

בַּמִּשְׁפָּט prep.-def.art.-n.m.s. (1048) *of justice*

18:6

שִׂפְתֵי כְסִיל n.f. du. cstr. (973)-n.m.s. (493) *a fool's lips*

יָבֹאוּ בְרִיב Qal impf. 3 m.p. (בּוֹא 97)-prep. -n.m.s. (936) *bring strife*

וּפִיו conj.-n.m.s.-3 m.s. sf. (804) *and his mouth*

לְמַהֲלֻמוֹת prep.-n.f.p. (240) *a flogging*

יִקְרָא Qal impf. 3 m.s. (קָרָא 894) *invites*

18:7

פִּי־כְסִיל n.m.s. cstr. (804)-n.m.s. (493) *a fool's mouth*

מְחִתָּה־לוֹ n.f.s. (369)-prep.-3 m.s. sf. *is his ruin*

וּשְׂפָתָיו conj.-n.f. du.-3 m.s. sf. (973) *and his lips*

מוֹקֵשׁ נַפְשׁוֹ n.m.s. cstr. (430)-n.f.s.-3 m.s. sf. (659) *are a snare to himself*

18:8

דִּבְרֵי נִרְגָּן n.m.p. cstr. (182)-Ni. ptc. (רָגַן 920) *the words of a whisperer*

כְּמִתְלַהֲמִים prep.-Hith. ptc. m.p. (לָהַם 529) *are like delicious morsels*

וְהֵם יָרְדוּ conj.-pers.pr. 3 m.p. (241)-Qal pf. 3 c.p. (יָרַד 432) *they go down*

חַדְרֵי־בָטֶן n.m.p. cstr. (293)-n.f.s. paus. (105) *into the inner parts of the body*

18:9

גַּם מִתְרַפֶּה adv. (168)-Hi. ptc. (רָפָה 951) *he who is slack*

בִמְלַאכְתּוֹ prep.-n.f.s.-3 m.s. sf. (521) *in his work*

אָח הוּא n.m.s. (26)-pers.pr. 3 m.s. (214) *he is a brother*

לְבַעַל מַשְׁחִית prep.-n.m.s. cstr. (127)-n.m.s. (1008) *to him who destroys*

18:10

מִגְדַּל־עֹז n.m.s. cstr. (153)-n.m.s. (738) *a strong tower*

שֵׁם יהוה n.m.s. cstr. (1027)-pr.n. (217) *the name of Yahweh*

בּוֹ־יָרוּץ צַדִּיק prep.-3 m.s. sf.-Qal impf. 3 m.s. (930 רוּץ)-adj. m.s. (843) *the righteous man runs into it*

וְנִשְׂגָּב conj.-Ni. pf. 3 m.s. paus. (שָׂגַב 960) *and is safe*

18:11

הוֹן עָשִׁיר n.m.s. cstr. (223)-adj. m.s. (799) *a rich man's wealth*

קִרְיַת עֻזּוֹ n.f.s. cstr. (900)-n.m.s.-3 m.s. sf. (738) *his strong city*

וּכְחוֹמָה נִשְׂגָּבָה conj.-prep.-n.f.s. (327)-Ni. ptc. f.s. (שָׂגַב 960) *and like a high wall*

בְּמַשְׂכִּיתוֹ prep.-n.f.s.-3 m.s. sf. (967) *in his imagination*

18:12

לִפְנֵי־שֶׁבֶר prep.-n.m.p. cstr. (815)-n.m.s. (I 991) *before destruction*

יִגְבַּהּ Qal impf. 3 m.s. (גָּבַהּ 147) *is haughty*

לֵב־אִישׁ n.m.s. cstr. (524)-n.m.s. (35) *a man's heart*

וְלִפְנֵי כָבוֹד conj.-prep.-n.m.p. cstr. (815)-n.m.s. (458) *but before honor*

עֲנָוָה n.f.s. (776) *humility*

18:13

מֵשִׁיב דָּבָר Hi. ptc. (שׁוּב 996)-n.m.s. (182) *if one gives answer*

בְּטֶרֶם יִשְׁמָע prep.-adv. (382)-Qal impf. 3 m.s. paus. (שָׁמַע 1033) *before he hears*

אִוֶּלֶת n.f.s. (17) *folly*

הִיא־לוֹ pers.pr. 3 f.s. (214)-prep.-3 m.s. sf. *it is to him*

וּכְלִמָּה conj.-n.f.s. (484) *and shame*

18:14

רוּחַ־אִישׁ n.f.s. cstr. (924)-n.m.s. (35) *a man's spirit*

יְכַלְכֵּל Pilpel impf. 3 m.s. (כּוּל I 465) *will endure*

מַחֲלֵהוּ n.m.s.-3 m.s. sf. (318) *his sickness*

וְרוּחַ נְכֵאָה conj.-n.f.s. (924)-adj. f.s. (644) *but a broken spirit*

מִי יִשָּׂאֶנָּה interr. (566)-Qal impf. 3 m.s.-3 f.s. sf. (נָשָׂא 669) *who can bear*

18:15

לֵב נָבוֹן n.m.s. (524)-Ni. ptc. (בִּין 106) *an intelligent mind*

יִקְנֶה־דָּעַת Qal impf. 3 m.s. (קָנָה 888)-n.f.s. paus. (395) *acquires knowledge*

וְאֹזֶן חֲכָמִים conj.-n.f.s. cstr. (23)-adj. m.p. (314) *and the ear of the wise*

תְּבַקֶּשׁ־דָּעַת Pi. impf. 3 f.s. (בָּקַשׁ 134)-v.supra *seeks knowledge*

18:16

מַתָּן אָדָם n.m.s. cstr. (682)-n.m.s. (9) *a man's gift*

יַרְחִיב לוֹ Hi. impf. 3 m.s. (רָחַב 931)-prep.-3 m.s. sf. *makes room for him*

וְלִפְנֵי גְדֹלִים conj.-prep.-n.m.p. cstr. (815)-adj. m.p. (152) *and before great men*

יַנְחֶנּוּ Hi. impf. 3 m.s.-3 m.s. sf. (נָחָה 634) *brings him*

18:17

צַדִּיק adj. m.s. (843) *seems right*

הָרִאשׁוֹן def.art.-adj. m.s. (911) *the first*

בְּרִיבוֹ prep.-n.m.s.-3 m.s. sf. (936) *in his case*

יּבָא־רֵעֵהוּ conj.-Qal pf. 3 m.s. (בּוֹא 97)-n.m.s.-3 m.s. sf. (945) *until the other comes*

וַחֲקָרוֹ conj.-Qal pf. 3 m.s.-3 m.s. sf. (חָקַר 350) *and examines him*

18:18

מִדְיָנִים n.m.p. (I 193) *disputes*

יַשְׁבִּית הַגּוֹרָל Hi. impf. 3 m.s. (שָׁבַת 991)-def. art.-n.m.s. (174) *the lot puts an end to*

וּבֵין עֲצוּמִים conj.-prep. (107)-adj. m.p. (783) *and between powerful contenders*

יַפְרִיד Hi. impf. 3 m.s. (פָּרַד 825) *decides*

18:19

אָח נִפְשָׁע n.m.s. (26)-Ni. ptc. (פָּשַׁע 833; LXX βοηθούμενος) *a brother offended*

מִקִּרְיַת־עֹז prep.-n.f.s. cstr. (900)-n.m.s. (738) *from a strong city*

וּמִדְוָנִים conj.-n.m.p. (I 193) *but quarreling*

כִּבְרִיחַ אַרְמוֹן prep.-n.m.s. (138)-n.m.s. (74) *like the bars of a castle*

18:20

מִפְּרִי פִי־אִישׁ prep.-n.m.s. cstr. (826)-n.m.s. cstr. (804)-n.m.s. (35) *from the fruit of a man's mouth*

תִּשְׂבַּע בִּטְנוֹ Qal impf. 3 f.s. (שָׂבַע 959)-n.f.s.-3 m.s. sf. (105) *his body is satisfied*

תְּבוּאַת שְׂפָתָיו n.f.s. cstr. (100)-n.f. du.-3 m.s. sf. (973) *by the yield of his lips*

יִשְׂבָּע Qal impf. 3 m.s. paus. (שָׂבַע 959) *he is satisfied*

18:21

מָוֶת n.m.s. (560) *death*

וְחַיִּים conj.-n.m.p. (313) *and life*

בְּיַד־לָשׁוֹן prep.-n.f.s. cstr. (388)-n.f.s. (546) *in the power of the tongue*

וְאֹהֲבֶיהָ conj.-Qal act.ptc. m.p.-3 f.s. sf. (אָהֵב 12) *and those who love it*

יֹאכַל פִּרְיָהּ Qal impf. 3 m.s. (אָכַל 37)-n.m.s.-3 f.s. sf. (826) *will eat its fruits*

18:22

מָצָא אִשָּׁה Qal pf. 3 m.s. (592)-n.f.s. (61) *he who finds a wife*

מָצָא טוֹב v.supra-n.m.s. (III 375) *finds a good thing*

וַיָּפֶק רָצוֹן consec.-Hi. impf. 3 m.s. (פּוּק II 807) -n.m.s. (953) *and obtains favor*
מֵיהוה prep.-pr.n. (217) *from Yahweh*

18:23

תַּחֲנוּנִים n.m.p. (337) *entreaties*
יְדַבֶּר־רָשׁ Pi. impf. 3 m.s. (180)-Qal act.ptc. (רוּשׁ 930) *the poor use*
וְעָשִׁיר conj.-adj. m.s. (799) *but the rich*
יַעֲנֶה עַזּוֹת Qal impf. 3 m.s. (עָנָה I 772)-adj. f.p. (738) *answer roughly*

18:24

אִישׁ רֵעִים n.m.s. cstr. (35)-n.m.p. (945) *a man of friends*
לְהִתְרֹעֵעַ prep.-Hithpo'el inf.cstr. (רָעַע II 949) *to be broken*
וְיֵשׁ אֹהֵב conj.-subst. (441)-Qal act.ptc. (אָהַב 12) *but there is a friend*
דָּבֵק adj. m.s. (180) *who sticks closer*
מֵאָח prep.-n.m.s. (26) *than a brother*

19:1

טוֹב־רָשׁ adj. m.s. (II 373)-Qal act.ptc. (רוּשׁ 930) *a poor man is better*
הוֹלֵךְ בְּתֻמּוֹ Qal act.ptc. (הָלַךְ 229)-prep.-n.m.s.-3 m.s. sf. (1070) *who walks in his integrity*
מֵעִקֵּשׁ שְׂפָתָיו prep.-adj. m.s. cstr. (I 786)-n.f. du.-3 m.s. sf. (973) *than a man who is perverse in speech*
וְהוּא כְסִיל conj.-pers.pr. 3 m.s. (214)-n.m.s. (493) *and is a fool*

19:2

גַּם בְּלֹא־דַעַת נֶפֶשׁ adv. (168)-prep.-neg.-n.f.s. (395)-n.f.s. (659) *also for a man to be without knowledge*
לֹא־טוֹב neg.-adj. m.s. (II 373) *it is not good*
וְאָץ בְּרַגְלַיִם conj.-Qal act.ptc. (אוּץ 21)-prep.-n.f. du. (919) *and he who makes haste with his feet*
חוֹטֵא Qal act.ptc. (חָטָא 306) *misses his way*

19:3

אִוֶּלֶת אָדָם n.f.s. cstr. (17)-n.m.s. (9) *a man's folly*
תְּסַלֵּף דַּרְכּוֹ Pi. impf. 3 f.s. (סָלַף 701)-n.m.s.-3 m.s. sf. (202) *brings his way to ruin*
וְעַל־יהוה conj.-prep.-pr.n. (217) *and against Yahweh*
יִזְעַף לִבּוֹ Qal impf. 3 m.s. (זָעַף 277)-n.m.s.-3 m.s. sf. (524) *his heart rages*

19:4

הוֹן יֹסִיף n.m.s. (223)-Hi. impf. 3 m.s. (יָסַף 414) *wealth brings*
רֵעִים רַבִּים n.m.p. (945)-adj. m.p. (I 912) *many friends*
וְדָל conj.-adj. m.s. (195) *but a poor man*
מֵרֵעֵהוּ prep.-n.m.s.-3 m.s. sf. (945) *from his friend*
יִפָּרֵד Ni. impf. 3 m.s. (פָּרַד 825) *is separated*

19:5

עֵד שְׁקָרִים n.m.s. cstr. (729)-n.m.p. (1055) *a false witness*
לֹא יִנָּקֶה neg.-Ni. impf. 3 m.s. (נָקָה 667) *will not go unpunished*
וְיָפִיחַ כְּזָבִים conj.-Hi. impf. 3 m.s. (פּוּחַ 806) -n.m.p. (469) *and he who utters lies*
לֹא יִמָּלֵט neg.-Ni. impf. 3 m.s. (מָלַט 572) *will not escape*

19:6

רַבִּים יְחַלּוּ adj. m.p. (I 912)-Pi. impf. (חָלָה II 318) *many seek the favor*
פְנֵי־נָדִיב n.m.p. cstr. (815)-adj. m.s. (622) *of a generous man*
וְכָל־הָרֵעַ conj.-n.m.s. (481)-def.art.-n.m.s. (945) *and every one is a friend*
לְאִישׁ מַתָּן prep.-n.m.s. (35)-n.m. coll. (682) *a man who gives gifts*

19:7

כָּל אֲחֵי־רָשׁ n.m.s. cstr. (481)-n.m.p. cstr. (26) -Qal act.ptc. (רוּשׁ 930) *all a poor man's brothers*
שְׂנֵאֻהוּ Qal pf. 3 c.p.-3 m.s. sf. (שָׂנֵא 971) *hate him*
אַף כִּי מְרֵעֵהוּ conj. (64)-conj. (471)-n.m.s.-3 m.s. sf. (946) *how much more do his friends*
רָחֲקוּ מִמֶּנּוּ Qal pf. 3 c.p. (רָחַק 934)-prep.-3 m.s. sf. *go far from him*
מְרַדֵּף אֲמָרִים Pi. ptc. (רָדַף 922)-n.m.p. (56) *he pursues them with words*
לֹא־הֵמָּה neg.-pr. 3 m.p. (241) *does not have them*

19:8

קֹנֶה־לֵּב Qal act.ptc. (קָנָה 888)-n.m.s. (524) *he who gets wisdom*
אֹהֵב נַפְשׁוֹ Qal act.ptc. (אָהַב 12)-n.f.s.-3 m.s. sf. (659) *loves himself*

שֹׁמֵר תְּבוּנָה Qal act.ptc. (שָׁמַר 1036)–n.f.s. (108) *he who keeps understanding*

לִמְצֹא־טוֹב prep.–Qal inf.cstr. (מָצָא 592)–n.m.s. (III 375) *will prosper*

19:9

עֵד שְׁקָרִים n.m.s. cstr. (729)–n.m.p. (1055) *a false witness*

לֹא יִנָּקֶה neg.–Ni. impf. 3 m.s. (נָקָה 667) *will not go unpunished*

וְיָפִיחַ כְּזָבִים conj.–Hi. impf. 3 m.s. (פּוּחַ 806) –n.m.p. (469) *and he who utters lies*

יֹאבֵד Qal impf. 3 m.s. (אָבַד 1) *will perish*

19:10

לֹא־נָאוֶה neg.–adj. m.s. (610) *it is not fitting*

לִכְסִיל prep.–n.m.s. (493) *for a fool*

תַּעֲנוּג n.m.s. (772) *to live in luxury*

אַף כִּי־לְעֶבֶד conj. (II 64)–conj. (471)–prep.–n.m.s. (713) *much less for a slave*

מְשֹׁל בְּשָׂרִים Qal inf.cstr. (מָשַׁל 605)–prep. –n.m.p. (978) *to rule over princes*

19:11

שֵׂכֶל אָדָם n.m.s. cstr. (968)–n.m.s. (9) *good sense ... a man*

הֶאֱרִיךְ אַפּוֹ Hi. pf. 3 m.s. (אָרַךְ 73)–n.m.s.–3 m.s. sf. (60) *makes ... slow to anger*

וְתִפְאַרְתּוֹ conj.–n.f.s.–3 m.s. sf. (802) *and it is his glory*

עֲבֹר עַל־פָּשַׁע Qal inf.cstr. (עָבַר 716)–prep. –n.m.s. paus. (833) *to overlook an offense*

19:12

נַהַם כַּכְּפִיר n.m.s. (625)–prep.–def.art.–n.m.s. (498) *like the growling of a lion*

זַעַף מֶלֶךְ n.m.s. cstr. (277)–n.m.s. (I 572) *a king's wrath*

וּכְטַל עַל־עֵשֶׂב conj.–prep.–n.m.s. (378)–prep. –n.m.s. (793) *but like dew upon the grass*

רְצוֹנוֹ n.m.s.–3 m.s. sf. (953) *his favor*

19:13

הַוֹּת לְאָבִיו n.f.p. (217)–prep.–n.m.s.–3 m.s. sf. (3) *ruin to his father*

בֵּן כְּסִיל n.m.s. (119)–n.m.s. (493) *a foolish son*

וְדֶלֶף טֹרֵד conj.–n.m.s. (196)–Qal act.ptc. (טָרַד 382) *a continual dripping of rain*

מִדְיְנֵי אִשָּׁה n.m.p. cstr. (193)–n.f.s. (61) *a wife's quarreling*

19:14

בַּיִת וָהוֹן n.m.s. (108)–conj.–n.m.s. (223) *house and wealth*

נַחֲלַת אָבוֹת n.f.s. cstr. (635)–n.m.p. (3) *are inherited from fathers*

וּמֵיהוה conj.–prep.–pr.n. (217) *but from Yahweh*

אִשָּׁה מַשְׂכָּלֶת n.f.s. (61)–Hi. ptc. f.s. paus. (שָׂכַל I 968) *a prudent wife*

19:15

עַצְלָה n.f.s. (782) *slothfulness*

תַּפִּיל Hi. impf. 3 f.s. (נָפַל 656) *casts*

תַּרְדֵּמָה n.f.s. (922) *a deep sleep*

וְנֶפֶשׁ רְמִיָּה conj.–n.f.s. cstr. (659)–n.f.s. (941) *and an idle person*

תִרְעָב Qal impf. 3 f.s. (רָעֵב 914) *will suffer hunger*

19:16

שֹׁמֵר מִצְוָה Qal act.ptc. (שָׁמַר 1036)–n.f.s. (846) *he who keeps the commandment*

שֹׁמֵר נַפְשׁוֹ v.supra–n.f.s.–3 m.s. sf. (659) *keeps his life*

בּוֹזֵה דְרָכָיו Qal act.ptc. cstr. (בָּזָה 102)–n.m.p.–3 m.s. sf. (202) *he who despises his ways*

יוּמָת Qal impf. 3 m.s. (מוּת 559) *will die*

19:17

מַלְוֵה יהוה Hi. ptc. cstr. (לָוָה II 531)–pr.n. (217) *lends to Yahweh*

חוֹנֵן דָּל Qal act.ptc. (חָנַן I 335)–adj. m.s. paus. (195) *he who is kind to the poor*

וּגְמֻלוֹ conj.–n.m.s.–3 m.s.sf. (168) *and for his deed*

יְשַׁלֶּם־לוֹ Pi. impf. 3 m.s. (שָׁלֵם 1022)–prep.–3 m.s. sf. *he will repay him*

19:18

יַסֵּר בִּנְךָ Pi. impv. 2 m.s. (יָסַר 415)–n.m.s.–2 m.s. sf. (119) *discipline your son*

כִּי־יֵשׁ תִּקְוָה conj. (471)–subst. (441)–n.f.s. (876) *while there is hope*

וְאֶל־הֲמִיתוֹ conj.–prep.–Hi. inf.cstr.–3 m.s. sf. (559 מוּת) *on his destruction*

אַל־תִּשָּׂא נַפְשֶׁךָ neg.–Qal impf. 2 m.s. (נָשָׂא 669)–n.f.s.–2 m.s. sf. (659) *do not set your heart*

19:19

גְּרָל־חֵמָה adj. m.s. cstr. (175; Q גְּדָל; LXX ἀνὴρ) –n.f.s. (404) *a man of great wrath*

נֹשֵׂא עֹנֶשׁ Qal act.ptc. (נָשָׂא 669)–n.m.s. (778) *will pay the penalty*

כִּי אִם־תַּצִּיל conj. (471)–hypoth.part. (49; 475) –Hi. impf. 2 m.s. (נָצַל 664) *for if you deliver him*

וְעוֹד תּוֹסִף conj.–adv. (728)–Hi. impf. 2 m.s. (יָסַף 414) *and yet you will add*

19:20

שְׁמַע עֵצָה Qal impv. 2 m.s. (1033)–n.f.s. (420) *listen to advice*

וְקַבֵּל מוּסָר conj.–Pi. impv. 2 m.s. (קָבַל 867) –n.m.s. (416) *and accept instruction*

לְמַעַן תֶּחְכַּם conj. (775)–Qal impf. 2 m.s. (חָכַם 314) *that you may gain wisdom*

בְּאַחֲרִיתֶךָ prep.–n.f.s.–2 m.s. sf. (31) *for the future*

19:21

רַבּוֹת מַחֲשָׁבוֹת adj. f.p. cstr. (I 912)–n.f.p. (364) *many are the plans*

בְּלֶב־אִישׁ prep.–n.m.s. cstr. (524)–n.m.s. (35) *in the mind of a man*

וַעֲצַת יהוה conj.–n.f.s. cstr. (420)–pr.n. (217) *but it is the purpose of Yahweh*

הִיא תָקוּם demons.adj. f.s. (214)–Qal impf. 3 f.s. (877 קוּם) *that will be established*

19:22

תַּאֲוַת אָדָם n.f.s. cstr. (16)–n.m.s. (9) *what is desired in a man*

חַסְדּוֹ n.m.s.–3 m.s. sf. (338) *is loyalty*

וְטוֹב־רָשׁ conj.–adj. m.s. (II 373)–Qal act.ptc. (930 רוּשׁ) *and a poor man is better*

מֵאִישׁ כָּזָב prep.–n.m.s. cstr. (35)–n.m.s. (469) *than a liar*

19:23

יִרְאַת יהוה n.f.s. cstr. (432)–pr.n. (217) *the fear of Yahweh*

לְחַיִּים prep.–n.m.p. (313) *to life*

וְשָׂבֵעַ יָלִין conj.–adj. m.s. (960)–Qal impf. 3 m.s. (I 533 לִין) *he shall continue satisfied*

בַּל־יִפָּקֶד רָע neg.–Ni. impf. 3 m.s. (פָּקַד 823) –n.m.s. paus. (948) *he will not be visited by harm*

19:24

טָמַן Qal pf. 3 m.s. (380) *buries*

עָצֵל adj. m.s. (782) *the sluggard*

יָדוֹ n.f.s.–3 m.s. sf. (388) *his hand*

בַּצַּלָּחַת prep.–def.art.–n.f.s. paus. (852) *in the dish*

גַּם־אֶל־פִּיהוּ adv. (168)–prep.–n.m.s.–3 m.s. sf. (804) *and even to his mouth*

לֹא יְשִׁיבֶנָּה neg.–Hi. impf. 3 m.s.–3 f.s. sf. (שׁוּב 996) *he will not bring it back*

19:25

לֵץ תַּכֶּה Qal act.ptc. (לִיץ 539)–Hi. impf. 2 m.s. (645 נָכָה) *strike a scoffer*

וּפֶתִי יַעְרִם conj.–adj. m.s. (834)–Hi. impf. 3 m.s. (791 עָרַם) *and the simple will learn prudence*

וְהוֹכִיחַ conj.–Hi. inf.cstr. (יָכַח 406) *and reprove*

לְנָבוֹן prep.–Ni. ptc. (בִּין 106) *a man of understanding*

יָבִין דָּעַת Qal impf. 3 m.s. (בִּין 106)–n.f.s. paus. (395) *and he will gain knowledge*

19:26

מְשַׁדֶּד־אָב Pi. ptc. (שָׁדַד 994)–n.m.s. (3) *he who does violence to his father*

יַבְרִיחַ אֵם Hi. impf. 3 m.s. (בָּרַח 137)–n.f.s. (51) *and chases away his mother*

בֵּן מֵבִישׁ n.m.s. (119)–Hi. ptc. (בּוֹשׁ 101) *a son who causes shame*

וּמַחְפִּיר conj.–Hi. ptc. (חָפֵר II 344) *and brings reproach*

19:27

חֲדַל־בְּנִי Qal impv. 2 m.s. (292)–n.m.s.–1 c.s. sf. (119) *cease, my son*

לִשְׁמֹעַ מוּסָר prep.–Qal inf.cstr. (שָׁמַע 1033) –n.m.s. (416) *to hear instruction*

לִשְׁגוֹת prep.–Qal inf.cstr. (שָׁגָה 993) *to stray*

מֵאִמְרֵי־דָעַת prep.–n.m.p. cstr. (56)–n.f.s. paus. (395) *from the words of knowledge*

19:28

עֵד בְּלִיַּעַל n.m.s. (729)–n.m.s. (116) *a worthless witness*

יָלִיץ Qal impf. 3 m.s. (לוּץ 539) *mocks at*

מִשְׁפָּט n.m.s. (1048) *justice*

וּפִי רְשָׁעִים conj. n.m.s. cstr. (804)–adj. m.p. (957) *and the mouth of the wicked*

יְבַלַּע־אָוֶן Pi. impf. 3 m.s. (בָּלַע 118)–n.m.s. (19) *devours iniquity*

19:29

נָכוֹנוּ Ni. pf. 3 c.p. (כּוּן I 465) *is ready*

לַלֵּצִים prep.–def.art.–Qal act.ptc. m.p. (לוּץ 539) *for scoffers*

שְׁפָטִים n.m.p. (1048) *condemnation*
וּמַהֲלֻמוֹת conj.-n.f.p. (240) *and flogging*
לְגֵו כְּסִילִים prep.-n.m.s. cstr. (156)-n.m.p. (493) *for the backs of fools*

20:1

לֵץ הַיַּיִן Qal act.ptc. (לוּץ 539)-def.art.-n.m.s. (406) *wine is a mocker*
הֹמֶה שֵׁכָר Qal act.ptc. (הָמָה 242)-n.m.s. (1016) *strong drink is a brawler*
וְכָל־שֹׁגֶה בּוֹ conj.-n.m.s. cstr. (481)-Qal act.ptc. (993 שָׁגָה)-prep.-3 m.s. sf. *and whoever is led astray by it*
לֹא יֶחְכָּם neg.-Qal impf. 3 m.s. (חָכַם 314) *is not wise*

20:2

נַהַם כַּכְּפִיר n.m.s. (625)-prep.-def.art.-n.m.s. (498) *like the growling of a lion*
אֵימַת מֶלֶךְ n.f.s. cstr. (33; LXX ἀπειλή)-n.m.s. (I 572) *the dread wrath of a king*
מִתְעַבְּרוֹ Hith. ptc.-3 m.s. sf. (עָבַר 720) *he who provokes him to anger*
חוֹטֵא נַפְשׁוֹ Qal act.ptc. (חָטָא 306)-n.f.s.-3 m.s. sf. (659) *forfeits his life*

20:3

כָּבוֹד לָאִישׁ n.m.s. (458)-prep.-def.art.-n.m.s. (35) *it is an honor for the man*
שֶׁבֶת מֵרִיב n.f.s. (992)-prep.-n.m.s. (936) *to keep aloof from strife*
וְכָל־אֱוִיל conj.-n.m.s. cstr. (481)-adj. m.s. (17) *but every fool*
יִתְגַּלָּע Hith. impf. 3 m.s. (גָּלַע 166) *will be quarreling*

20:4

מֵחֹרֶף prep.-n.m.s. (358) *in the autumn*
עָצֵל adj. m.s. (782) *the sluggard*
לֹא־יַחֲרֹשׁ neg.-Qal impf. 3 m.s. (חָרַשׁ I 360) *does not plow*
יְשָׁאַל Pi. impf. 3 m.s. (שָׁאַל 981) *he will seek*
בַּקָּצִיר prep.-def.art.-n.m.s. (I 894) *at harvest*
וָאָיִן conj.-neg. paus. (II 34) *and have nothing*

20:5

מַיִם עֲמֻקִּים n.m.p. (565)-adj. m.p. (771) *like deep water*
עֵצָה n.f.s. (420) *the purpose*
בְלֶב־אִישׁ prep.-n.m.s. cstr. (524)-n.m.s. (35) *in a man's mind*
וְאִישׁ תְּבוּנָה conj.-n.m.s. cstr. (35)-n.f.s. (108) *but a man of understanding*
יִדְלֶנָּה Qal impf. 3 m.s.-3 f.s. sf. (דָּלָה 194) *will draw it out*

20:6

רָב־אָדָם n.m.s. cstr. (913)-n.m.s. (9) *many a man*
יִקְרָא Qal impf. 3 m.s. (קָרָא 894) *proclaims*
אִישׁ חַסְדּוֹ n.m.s. (35)-n.m.s.-3 m.s. sf. (338) *a man his loyalty*
וְאִישׁ אֱמוּנִים conj.-n.m.s. cstr. (35)-n.m.p. (53) *but a faithful man*
מִי יִמְצָא interr. (566)-Qal impf. 3 m.s. (מָצָא 592) *who can find?*

20:7

מִתְהַלֵּךְ Hith. ptc. (הָלַךְ 229) *who walks*
בְּתֻמּוֹ prep.-n.m.s.-3 m.s. sf. (1070) *in his integrity*
צַדִּיק adj. m.s. (843) *a righteous man*
אַשְׁרֵי בָנָיו n.m.p. cstr. (80)-n.m.p.-3 m.s. sf. (119) *blessed are his sons*
אַחֲרָיו prep.-3 m.s. sf. (29) *after him*

20:8

מֶלֶךְ יוֹשֵׁב n.m.s. (I 572)-Qal act.ptc. (442) *a king who sits*
עַל־כִּסֵּא־דִין prep.-n.m.s. cstr. (490)-n.m.s. (192) *on the throne of judgment*
מְזָרֶה Pi. ptc. (זָרָה 279) *winnows*
בְעֵינָיו prep.-n.f.p.-3 m.s. sf. (744) *with his eyes*
כָּל־רָע n.m.s. cstr. (481)-n.m.s. paus. (II 948) *all evil*

20:9

מִי־יֹאמַר interr. (566)-Qal impf. 3 m.s. (55) *who can say*
זִכִּיתִי לִבִּי Pi. pf. 1 c.s. (זָכָה 269)-n.m.s.-1 c.s. sf. (524) *I have made my heart clean*
טָהַרְתִּי Qal pf. 1 c.s. (טָהֵר 372) *I am pure*
מֵחַטָּאתִי prep.-n.f.s.-1 c.s. sf. (308) *from my sin*

20:10

אֶבֶן וָאֶבֶן n.f.s. (6)-conj.-v.supra *diverse weights*
אֵיפָה וְאֵיפָה n.f.s. (35)-conj.-v.supra *and diverse measures*
תּוֹעֲבַת יהוה n.f.s. cstr. (1072)-pr.n. (217) *an abomination to Yahweh*
גַּם־שְׁנֵיהֶם adv. (168)-n.m. du.-3 m.p. sf. (1040) *both alike*

20:11

גַּם בְּמַעֲלָלָיו adv. (168)-prep.-n.m.p.-3 m.s. sf. (760) *even by his acts*

יִתְנַכֶּר־נָעַר Hith. impf. 3 m.s. (נָכַר 647)-n.m.s. paus. (654) *a child makes himself known*

אִם־זַךְ hypoth.part. (49)-adj. m.s. (269) *whether pure*

וְאִם־יָשָׁר conj.-v.supra-adj. m.s. (449) *and right*

פָּעֳלוֹ n.m.s.-3 m.s. sf. (821) *what he does*

20:12

אֹזֶן שֹׁמַעַת n.f.s. (23)-Qal act.ptc. f.s. (שָׁמַע 1033) *the hearing ear*

וְעַיִן רֹאָה conj.-n.f.s. (744)-Qal act.ptc. f.s. (רָאָה 906) *and the seeing eye*

יהוה עָשָׂה pr.n. (217)-Qal pf. 3 m.s. (I 793) *Yahweh has made*

גַּם־שְׁנֵיהֶם adv. (168)-n.m. du.-3 m.p. sf. (1040) *them both*

20:13

אַל־תֶּאֱהַב neg.-Qal impf. 2 m.s. (אָהֵב 12) *love not*

שֵׁנָה n.f.s. (446) *sleep*

פֶּן־תִּוָּרֵשׁ conj. (814)-Ni. impf. 2 m.s. (יָרַשׁ 439) *lest you come to poverty*

פְּקַח עֵינֶיךָ Qal impv. 2 m.s. (פָּקַח 824)-n.f.p.-2 m.s. sf. (744) *open your eyes*

שְׂבַע־לָחֶם Qal impv. 2 m.s. (שָׂבַע 959)-n.m.s. paus. (536) *have plenty of bread*

20:14

רַע רַע adj. m.s. (948)-v.supra *it is bad, it is bad*

יֹאמַר הַקּוֹנֶה Qal impf. 3 m.s. (55)-def.art.-Qal act.ptc. (קָנָה 888) *says the buyer*

וְאֹזֵל לוֹ conj.-Qal act.ptc. (אָזַל 23)-prep.-3 m.s. sf. *but when he goes away*

אָז יִתְהַלָּל adv. (23)-Hith. impf. 3 m.s. paus. (הָלַל II 237) *then he boasts*

20:15

יֵשׁ זָהָב subst. (441)-n.m.s. (262) *there is gold*

וְרָב־פְּנִינִים conj.-n.m.s. cstr. (913)-n.f.p. (819) *and abundance of costly stones*

וּכְלִי יְקָר conj.-n.m.s. cstr. (479)-n.m.s. (430) *but a precious jewel*

שִׂפְתֵי־דָעַת n.f.p. cstr. (973)-n.f.s. paus. (395) *the lips of knowledge*

20:16

לְקַח־בִּגְדוֹ Qal impv. 2 m.s. (לָקַח 542)-n.m.s.-3 m.s. sf. (93) *take a man's garment*

כִּי־עָרַב זָר conj. (471)-Qal pf. 3 m.s. (עָרַב II 786)-Qal act.ptc. (זוּר I 266) *when he has given surety for a stranger*

וּבְעַד נָכְרִיִּם conj.-prep. (126)-adj. m.p. (Q נָכְרִיָּה; 648) *and when he gives surety for foreigners*

חַבְלֵהוּ Qal impv. 2 m.s.-3 m.s. sf. (חָבַל I 286) *hold him in pledge*

20:17

עָרֵב לָאִישׁ adj. m.s. (787)-prep.-def.art.-n.m.s. (35) *sweet to the man*

לֶחֶם שָׁקֶר n.m.s. (536)-n.m.s. paus. (1055) *bread gained by deceit*

וְאַחַר conj.-adv. (29) *and afterward*

יִמָּלֵא־פִיהוּ Ni. impf. 3 m.s. (מָלֵא 569)-n.m.s.-3 m.s. sf. (804) *his mouth will be full of*

חָצָץ n.m.s. (346) *gravel*

20:18

מַחֲשָׁבוֹת n.f.p. (364) *plans*

בְּעֵצָה prep.-n.f.s. (420) *by counsel*

תִכּוֹן Ni. impf. 3 f.s. (כּוּן I 465) *are established*

וּבְתַחְבֻּלוֹת conj.-prep.-n.f.p. (287) *and by wise guidance*

עֲשֵׂה מִלְחָמָה Qal impv. 2 m.s. (עָשָׂה I 793) -n.f.s. (536) *wage war*

20:19

גּוֹלֶה־סּוֹד Qal act.ptc. (גָּלָה 162)-n.m.s. (691) *reveals secrets*

הוֹלֵךְ רָכִיל Qal act.ptc. (הָלַךְ 229)-n.m.s. (940) *he who goes about gossiping*

וּלְפֹתֶה שְׂפָתָיו conj.-prep.-Qal act.ptc. (פָּתָה 834)-n.f.p.-3 m.s. sf. (973) *with one who speaks foolishly* (either *one open as to lips* or *one foolish as to his lips*)

לֹא תִתְעָרָב neg.-Hith. impf. 2 m.s. (עָרַב II 786) *do not associate*

20:20

מְקַלֵּל אָבִיו Pi. ptc. (קָלַל 886)-prep.-3 m.s. sf. (3) *if one curses his father*

וְאִמּוֹ conj.-n.f.s.-3 m.s. sf. (51) *or his mother*

יִדְעַךְ נֵרוֹ Qal impf. 3 m.s. (דָּעַךְ 200)-n.m.s.-3 m.s. sf. (632) *his lamp will be put out*

בֶּאֱשׁוּן חֹשֶׁךְ prep.-n.m.s. cstr. (36)-n.m.s. (365) *in utter darkness*

20:21

נַחֲלָה מְבֹחֶלֶת n.f.s. (635)-Pu. ptc. f.s. (בָּהַל 96; II בָּחַל 103) *an inheritance gotten hastily*

בְּרֵאשֹׁנָה prep.-adj. f.s. (911) *in the beginning*
וְאַחֲרִיתָהּ conj.-n.f.s.-3 f.s. sf. (31) *in the end*
לֹא תְבֹרָךְ neg.-Pu. impf. 3 f.s. paus. (בָּרַךְ 138) *will not be blessed*

20:22

אַל־תֹּאמַר neg.-Qal impf. 2 m.s. (אָמַר 55) *do not say*
אֲשַׁלְּמָה־רָע Pi. impf. 1 c.s.-vol.he (שָׁלֵם 1022)-n.m.s. (II 948) *I will repay evil*
קַוֵּה לַיהוה Pi. impv. 2 m.s. (קָוָה I 875) -prep.-pr.n. (217) *wait for Yahweh*
וְיֹשַׁע לָךְ conj.-Hi. impf. 3 m.s. juss. (יָשַׁע 446) -prep.-2 m.s. sf. paus. *and he will help you*

20:23

תּוֹעֲבַת יהוה n.f.s. cstr. (1072)-pr.n. (217) *an abomination to Yahweh*
אֶבֶן וָאָבֶן n.f.s. (6)-conj.-n.f.s. paus. (6) *diverse weights*
וּמֹאזְנֵי מִרְמָה conj.-n.m. du. cstr. (24)-n.f.s. (941) *and false scales*
לֹא־טוֹב neg.-adj. m.s. (II 373) *are not good*

20:24

מֵיהוה prep.-pr.n. (217) *by Yahweh*
מִצְעֲדֵי־גָבֶר n.m.p. cstr. (857)-n.m.s. paus. (149) *a man's steps*
וְאָדָם conj.-n.m.s. (9) *and man*
מַה־יָּבִין interr. (552)-Qal impf. 3 m.s. (בִּין 106) *how can understand*
דַּרְכּוֹ n.m.s.-3 m.s. sf. (202) *his way*

20:25

מוֹקֵשׁ אָדָם n.m.s. cstr. (430)-n.m.s. (9) *a snare for a man*
יָלַע קֹדֶשׁ Qal impf. 3 m.s. (לוּעַ II 534)-n.m.s. (871) *to say rashly, it is holy*
וְאַחַר נְדָרִים conj.-prep. (29)-n.m.p. (623) *and after making his vows*
לְבַקֵּר prep.-Pi. inf.cstr. (בָּקַר 133) *to reflect*

20:26

מְזָרֶה רְשָׁעִים Pi. ptc. (זָרָה 279)-adj. m.p. (957) *winnows the wicked*
מֶלֶךְ חָכָם n.m.s. (I 572)-adj. m.s. (314) *a wise king*
וַיָּשֶׁב consec.-Hi. impf. 3 m.s. (שׁוּב 996; LXX καὶ ἐπιβαλεῖ) *and drives*
עֲלֵיהֶם prep.-3 m.p. sf. *over them*
אוֹפָן n.m.s. paus. (66) *a wheel*

20:27

נֵר יהוה n.m.s. cstr. (632)-pr.n. (217) *the lamp of Yahweh*
נִשְׁמַת אָדָם n.f.s. cstr. (675)-n.m.s. (9) *the spirit of man*
חֹפֵשׂ Qal act.ptc. (חָפַשׂ 344) *searching*
כָּל־חַדְרֵי־בָטֶן n.m.s. cstr. (481)-n.m.p. cstr. (293)-n.f.s. paus. (105) *all his innermost parts*

20:28

חֶסֶד וֶאֱמֶת n.m.s. (338)-conj.-n.f.s. (54) *loyalty and faithfulness*
יִצְּרוּ־מֶלֶךְ Qal impf. 3 m.p. (נָצַר I 665)-n.m.s. (I 572) *preserve the king*
וְסָעַד conj.-Qal pf. 3 m.s. (סָעַד 703) *and is upheld*
בַּחֶסֶד prep.-def.art.-n.m.s. (338) *by loyalty*
כִּסְאוֹ n.m.s.-3 m.s. sf. (490) *his throne*

20:29

תִּפְאֶרֶת בַּחוּרִים n.f.s. cstr. (802)-n.m.p. (104) *the glory of young men*
כֹּחָם n.m.s.-3 m.p. sf. (II 470) *their strength*
וַהֲדַר זְקֵנִים conj.-n.m.s. cstr. (214)-adj. m.p. (278) *but the beauty of old men*
שֵׂיבָה n.f.s. (966) *gray hair*

20:30

חַבֻּרוֹת פֶּצַע n.f.p. cstr. (289)-n.m.s. (822) *blows that wound*
תַּמְרִיק n.m.s. (600) *would cleanse away*
בְּרָע prep.-n.m.s. paus. (II 948) *evil*
וּמַכּוֹת conj.-n.f.p. (646) *strokes*
חַדְרֵי־בָטֶן n.m.p. cstr. (293)-n.f.s. paus. (105) *the innermost parts*

21:1

פַּלְגֵי־מַיִם n.m.p. cstr. (I 811)-n.m.p. (565) *streams of water*
לֶב־מֶלֶךְ n.m.s. cstr. (524)-n.m.s. (I 572) *the king's heart*
בְּיַד־יהוה prep.-n.f.s. cstr. (388)-pr.n. (217) *in the hand of Yahweh*
עַל־כָּל־אֲשֶׁר prep.-n.m.s. (481)-rel. (81) *wherever*
יַחְפֹּץ Qal impf. 3 m.s. (חָפֵץ 342) *he will*
יַטֶּנּוּ Hi. impf. 3 m.s.-3 m.s. sf. (נָטָה 639) *he turns it*

21:2

כָּל־דֶּרֶךְ־אִישׁ n.m.s. cstr. (481)-n.m.s. cstr. (202) -n.m.s. (35) *every way of a man*

יָשָׁר בְּעֵינָיו adj. m.s. (449)-prep.-n.f.p.-3 m.s. sf. (744) *right in his own eyes*
וְתֹכֵן לִבּוֹת conj.-Qal act.ptc. (תָּכַן 1067)-n.m.p. (524) *but weighs the heart*
יהוה pr.n. (217) *Yahweh*

21:3

עֲשֹׂה צְדָקָה Qal inf.cstr. (עָשָׂה I 793)-n.f.s. (842) *to do righteousness*
וּמִשְׁפָּט conj.-n.m.s. (1048) *and justice*
נִבְחָר לַיהוה Ni. ptc. (בָּחַר 103)-prep.-pr.n. (217) *is more acceptable to Yahweh*
מִזָּבַח prep.-n.m.s. paus. (257) *than sacrifice*

21:4

רוּם־עֵינַיִם n.m.s. cstr. (927)-n.f. du. (744) *haughty eyes*
וּרְחַב־לֵב conj.-adj. m.s. cstr. (932)-n.m.s. (524) *and a proud heart*
נֵר רְשָׁעִים n.m.s. cstr. (632)-adj. m.p. (957) *the lamp of the wicked*
חַטָּאת n.f.s. (308) *are sin*

21:5

מַחְשְׁבוֹת חָרוּץ n.f.p. cstr. (364)-adj. m.s. (I 358) *the plans of the diligent*
אַךְ־לְמוֹתָר adv. (36)-prep.-n.m.s. (452) *surely to abundance*
וְכָל־אָץ conj.-n.m.s. (481)-Qal act.ptc. (אוּץ 21) *but every one who is hasty*
אַךְ־לְמַחְסוֹר adv. (36)-prep.-n.m.s. (341) *only to want*

21:6

פֹּעַל אוֹצָרוֹת n.m.s. cstr. (821)-n.m.p. (69) *the getting of treasures*
בִּלְשׁוֹן שָׁקֶר prep.-n.f.s. cstr. (546)-n.m.s. paus. (1055) *by a lying tongue*
הֶבֶל נִדָּף n.m.s. cstr. (I 210)-Ni. ptc. (נָדַף 623) *a fleeting vapor*
מְבַקְשֵׁי־מָוֶת Pi. ptc. m.p. cstr. (בָּקַשׁ 134)-n.m.s. (560) *and a snare of death*

21:7

שֹׁד־רְשָׁעִים n.m.s. cstr. (994)-adj. m.p. (957) *the violence of the wicked*
יְגוֹרֵם Qal impf. 3 m.s.-3 m.p. sf. (גָּרַר 176) *will sweep them away*
כִּי מֵאֲנוּ conj. (471)-Pi. pf. 3 c.p. (מָאַן 549) *because they refuse*
לַעֲשׂוֹת prep.-Qal inf.cstr. (עָשָׂה I 793) *to do*
מִשְׁפָּט n.m.s. (1048) *what is just*

21:8

הֲפַכְפַּךְ adj. m.s. (246) *is crooked*
דֶּרֶךְ אִישׁ n.m.s. cstr. (202)-n.m.s. (35) *the way of the ... man*
וָזָר adj. m.s. (255) *guilty*
וְזַךְ conj.-adj. m.s. (269) *but the pure*
יָשָׁר adj. m.s. (449) *is right*
פָּעֳלוֹ n.m.s.-3 m.s. sf. (821) *his conduct*

21:9

טוֹב לָשֶׁבֶת adj. m.s. (II 373)-prep.-Qal inf.cstr. (442 יָשַׁב) *it is better to live*
עַל־פִּנַּת־גָּג prep.-n.f.s. cstr. (819)-n.m.s. (150) *in a corner of the housetop*
מֵאֵשֶׁת מִדְיָנִים prep.-n.f.s. cstr. (61)-n.m.p. (193) *than with a contentious woman*
וּבֵית חָבֶר conj.-n.m.s. cstr. (108)-n.m.s. paus. (288) *and a house of association*

21:10

נֶפֶשׁ רָשָׁע n.f.s. cstr. (659)-adj. m.s. (957) *the soul of the wicked*
אִוְּתָה־רָע Pi. pf. 3 f.s. (אָוָה 16)-n.m.s. (II 948) *desires evil*
לֹא־יֻחַן neg.-Ho. impf. 3 m.s. (חָנַן I 335) *finds no mercy*
בְּעֵינָיו prep.-n.f.p.-3 m.s. sf. (744) *in his eyes*
רֵעֵהוּ n.m.s.-3 m.s. sf. (945) *his neighbor*

21:11

בַּעְנָשׁ־לֵץ prep.-Qal inf.cstr. (עָנַשׁ 778)-Qal act.ptc. (לִיץ 539) *when a scoffer is punished*
יֶחְכַּם־פֶּתִי Qal impf. 3 m.s. (חָכַם 314)-adj. m.s. (834) *the simple becomes wise*
וּבְהַשְׂכִּיל conj.-prep.-Hi. inf.cstr. (שָׂכַל 968) *and when is instructed*
לְחָכָם prep.-adj. m.s. (314) *the wise man*
יִקַּח־דָּעַת Qal impf. 3 m.s. (לָקַח 542)-n.f.s. paus. (395) *he gains knowledge*

21:12

מַשְׂכִּיל Hi. ptc. (שָׂכַל 968) *observes*
צַדִּיק adj. m.s. (843) *the righteous*
לְבֵית רָשָׁע prep.-n.m.s. cstr. (108)-adj. m.s. (957) *the house of the wicked*
מְסַלֵּף Pi. ptc. (סָלַף 701) *are cast down*
רְשָׁעִים adj. m.p. (957) *the wicked*
לָרָע prep.-n.m.s. (II 948) *to ruin*

21:13

אֹטֵם אָזְנוֹ Qal act.ptc. (אָטַם 31)-n.f.s.-3 m.s. sf. (23) *he who closes his ear*

מִזַּעֲקַת־דָּל prep.-n.f.s. cstr. (277)-adj. m.s. paus. (195) *to the cry of the poor*

גַּם־הוּא יִקְרָא adv. (168)-pers.pr. 3 m.s. (214)-Qal impf. 3 m.s. (קָרָא 894) *will himself cry out*

וְלֹא יֵעָנֶה conj.-neg.-Ni. impf. 3 m.s. (עָנָה I 772) *and not be heard*

21:14

מַתָּן בַּסֵּתֶר n.m. coll. (682)-prep.-def.art.-n.m.s. (712) *a gift in secret*

יִכְפֶּה־אָף Qal impf. 3 m.s. (כָּפָה 495)-n.m.s. paus. (I 60) *averts anger*

וְשֹׁחַד בַּחֵק conj.-n.m.s. (1005)-prep.-def.art. -n.m.s. (300) *and a bribe in the bosom*

חֵמָה עַזָּה n.f.s. (404)-adj. f.s. (738) *strong wrath*

21:15

שִׂמְחָה לַצַּדִּיק n.f.s. (970)-prep.-def.art.-adj. m.s. (843) *a joy to the righteous*

עֲשׂוֹת מִשְׁפָּט Qal inf.cstr. (עָשָׂה I 793)-n.m.s. (1048) *when justice is done*

וּמְחִתָּה conj.-n.f.s. (369) *but dismay*

לְפֹעֲלֵי אָוֶן prep.-Qal act.ptc. m.p. cstr. (פָּעַל 821)-n.m.s. (19) *to evildoers*

21:16

אָדָם תּוֹעֶה n.m.s. (9)-Qal act.ptc. (תָּעָה 1073) *a man who wanders*

מִדֶּרֶךְ הַשְׂכֵּל prep.-n.m.s. cstr. (202)-Hi. inf.abs. (שָׂכַל 968) *from the way of understanding*

בִּקְהַל רְפָאִים prep.-n.m.s. cstr. (874)-n.m.p. (I 952) *in the assembly of the dead*

יָנוּחַ Qal impf. 3 m.s. (נוּחַ 628) *will rest*

21:17

אִישׁ מַחְסוֹר n.m.s. cstr. (35)-n.m.s. (341) *a man of poverty*

אֹהֵב שִׂמְחָה Qal act.ptc. (אָהַב 12)-n.f.s. (970) *he who loves pleasure*

אֹהֵב יַיִן־וָשֶׁמֶן v.supra-n.m.s. (406)-conj.-n.f.s. (1032) *he who loves wine and oil*

לֹא יַעֲשִׁיר neg.-Hi. impf. 3 m.s. (עָשַׁר 799) *will not be rich*

21:18

כֹּפֶר לַצַּדִּיק Qal act.ptc. (כָּפַר 497)-prep.-def.art. -adj. m.s. (843) *a ransom for the righteous*

רָשָׁע adj. m.s. (957) *the wicked*

וְתַחַת יְשָׁרִים conj.-prep. (1065)-adj. m.p. (449) *and for the upright*

בּוֹגֵד Qal act.ptc. (בָּגַד 93) *the faithless*

21:19

טוֹב adj. m.s. (II 373) *it is better*

שֶׁבֶת בְּאֶרֶץ־מִדְבָּר Qal inf.cstr. (יָשַׁב 442)-prep. -n.f.s. cstr. (75)-n.m.s. (II 184) *to live in a desert land*

מֵאֵשֶׁת מִדְוָנִים prep.-n.f.s. cstr. (61)-n.m.p. (I 193) *than with a contentious woman*

וָכָעַס conj.-n.m.s. paus. (495) *and fretful*

21:20

אוֹצָר נֶחְמָד n.m.s. (69)-Ni. ptc. (326) *precious treasure*

וָשֶׁמֶן בִּנְוֵה conj.-n.m.s. (1032)-prep.-n.m.s. cstr. (I 627; LXX ἀναπαύσεται ἐπὶ στόματος) *and oil in the dwelling of*

חָכָם adj. m.s. (314) *a wise man*

וּכְסִיל אָדָם conj.-n.m.s. cstr. (493)-n.m.s. (9) *but a foolish man*

יְבַלְּעֶנּוּ Pi. impf. 3 m.s.-3 m.s. sf. (בָּלַע 118) *devours it*

21:21

רֹדֵף צְדָקָה Qal act.ptc. (רָדַף 922)-n.f.s. (842) *he who pursues righteousness*

וָחָסֶד conj.-n.m.s. paus. (338) *and kindness*

יִמְצָא חַיִּים Qal impf. 3 m.s. (מָצָא 592)-n.m.p. (313) *will find life*

צְדָקָה וְכָבוֹד n.f.s. (842)-conj.-n.m.s. (458) *righteousness and honor*

21:22

עִיר גִּבֹּרִים n.f.s. cstr. (746)-adj. m.p. (150) *the city of the mighty*

עָלָה חָכָם Qal pf. 3 m.s. (748)-adj. m.s. (314) *a wise man scales*

וַיֹּרֶד עֹז consec.-Hi. impf. 3 m.s. (יָרַד 432) -n.m.s. cstr. (738) *and brings down the stronghold of*

מִבְטֶחָה n.m.s.-3 f.s. sf.? (105) *their trust*

21:23

שֹׁמֵר פִּיו Qal act.ptc. (1036)-n.m.s.-3 m.s. sf. (804) *he who keeps his mouth*

וּלְשׁוֹנוֹ conj.-n.f.s.-3 m.s. sf. (546) *and his tongue*

שֹׁמֵר מִצָּרוֹת v.supra-prep.-n.f.p. (I 865) *keeps out of trouble*

נַפְשׁוֹ n.f.s.-3 m.s. sf. (659) *himself*

21:24

זֵד יָהִיר adj. m.s. (267)–adj. m.s. (397) *a haughty man*

לֵץ שְׁמוֹ Qal act.ptc. (ליץ 539)–n.m.s.–3 m.s. sf. (1027) *scoffer is his name*

עוֹשֶׂה Qal act.ptc. (עָשָׂה I 793) *who acts*

בְּעֶבְרַת זָדוֹן prep.–n.f.s. cstr. (720)–n.m.s. (268) *with arrogant pride*

21:25

תַּאֲוַת עָצֵל n.f.s. cstr. (16)–adj. m.s. (782) *the desire of the sluggard*

תְּמִיתֶנּוּ Hi. impf. 3 f.s.–3 m.s. sf. (מות 559) *kills him*

כִּי־מֵאֲנוּ יָדָיו conj. (471)–Pi. pf. 3 c.p. (מָאֵן 549) –n.f.p.–3 m.s. sf. (388) *for his hands refuse*

לַעֲשׂוֹת prep.–Qal inf.cstr. (עָשָׂה I 793) *to labor*

21:26

כָּל־הַיּוֹם n.m.s. cstr. (481)–def.art.–n.m.s. (398) *all day long*

הִתְאַוָּה תַאֲוָה Hith. impf. 3 m.s. (אָוָה 16)–n.f.s. (16) *he covets covetously*

וְצַדִּיק יִתֵּן conj.–adj. m.s. (843)–Qal impf. 3 m.s. (678 נָתַן) *but the righteous gives*

וְלֹא יַחְשֹׂךְ conj.–neg.–Qal impf. 3 m.s. (חָשַׂךְ 362) *and does not hold back*

21:27

זֶבַח רְשָׁעִים n.m.s. cstr. (257)–adj. m.p. (957) *the sacrifice of the wicked*

תּוֹעֵבָה n.f.s. (1072) *an abomination*

אַף כִּי־בְזִמָּה conj. (II 64)–conj. (471)–prep.–n.f.s. (I 273) *how much more with evil intent*

יְבִיאֶנּוּ Hi. impf. 3 m.s.–3 m.s. sf. (בּוֹא 97) *he brings it*

21:28

עֵד־כְּזָבִים n.m.s. cstr. (729)–n.m.p. (469) *a false witness*

יֹאבֵד Qal impf. 3 m.s. (אָבַד 1) *will perish*

וְאִישׁ שׁוֹמֵעַ conj.–n.m.s. cstr. (35)–Qal act.ptc. (1033 שָׁמַע) *but a man who hears*

לָנֶצַח prep.–n.m.s. (664) *for ever*

יְדַבֵּר Pi. impf. 3 m.s. (דָּבַר 180) *will speak*

21:29

הֵעֵז Hi. pf. 3 m.s. (עָזַז 738) *makes firm*

אִישׁ רָשָׁע n.m.s. (35)–adj. m.s. (957) *a wicked man*

בְּפָנָיו prep.–n.m.p.–3 m.s. sf. (815) *his face*

וְיָשָׁר conj.–adj. m.s. (449) *but an upright man*

הוּא יָכִין pers.pr. 3 m.s. (214)–Hi. impf. 3 m.s. (I 465 כּוּן some rd. יָבִין *considers*) *establishes*

דַּרְכּוֹ n.m.s.–3 m.s. sf. (202; K דְּרָכָיו; Q דַּרְכּוֹ) *his ways*

21:30

אֵין חָכְמָה prep. (II 34)–n.f.s. (315) *no wisdom*

וְאֵין תְּבוּנָה conj.–v.supra–n.f.s. (108) *no understanding*

וְאֵין עֵצָה v.supra–n.f.s. (420) *no counsel*

לְנֶגֶד יהוה prep.–prep. (617)–pr.n. (217) *before Yahweh*

21:31

סוּס מוּכָן n.m.s. (692)–Ho. ptc. (כּוּן I 465) *the horse is made ready*

לְיוֹם מִלְחָמָה prep.–n.m.s. cstr. (398)–n.f.s. (536) *for the day of battle*

וְליהוה conj.–prep.–pr.n. (217) *but to Yahweh*

הַתְּשׁוּעָה def.art.–n.f.s. (448) *the victory*

22:1

נִבְחָר שֵׁם Ni. ptc. (בָּחַר 103)–n.m.s. (1027; LXX+ καλόν) *a name is to be chosen*

מֵעֹשֶׁר רָב prep.–n.m.s. (799)–adj. m.s. paus. (I 912) *rather than great riches*

מִכֶּסֶף prep.–n.m.s. (494) *than silver*

וּמִזָּהָב conj.–prep.–n.m.s. (262) *or gold*

חֵן טוֹב n.m.s. (336)–adj. m.s. (II 373) *favor is better*

22:2

עָשִׁיר וָרָשׁ adj. m.s. (799)–conj.–Qal act.ptc. (רוּשׁ 930) *the rich and the poor*

נִפְגָּשׁוּ Ni. pf. 3 c.p. paus. (פָּגַשׁ 803) *meet together*

עֹשֵׂה כֻלָּם Qal act.ptc. cstr. (עָשָׂה I 793)–n.m.s. –3 m.p. sf. (481) *the maker of them all*

יהוה pr.n. (217) *Yahweh*

22:3

עָרוּם adj. m.s. (791) *a prudent man*

רָאָה רָעָה Qal pf. 3 m.s. (906)–n.f.s. (949) *sees danger*

וְיִסָּתֵר conj.–Qal impf. 3 m.s. (סָתַר 711) *and hides himself*

וּפְתָיִים conj.–adj. m.p. (834) *but the simple*

עָבְרוּ Qal pf. 3 c.p. (עָבַר 716) *go on*

וְנֶעֱנָשׁוּ conj.–Ni. pf. 3 c.p. (עָנַשׁ 778) *and suffer for it*

22:4

עֵקֶב עֲנָוָה n.m.s. cstr. (784)-n.f.s. (776) *the reward for humility*

יִרְאַת יהוה n.f.s. cstr. (432)-pr.n. (217) *the fear of Yahweh*

עֹשֶׁר n.m.s. (799) *riches*

וְכָבוֹד conj.-n.m.s. (458) *and honor*

וְחַיִּים conj.-n.m.p. (313) *and life*

22:5

צִנִּים פַּחִים n.m.p. (856)-n.m.p. (809) *thorns (and) snares*

בְּדֶרֶךְ עִקֵּשׁ prep.-n.m.s. cstr. (202)-adj. m.s. (I 786) *in the way of the perverse*

שׁוֹמֵר נַפְשׁוֹ Qal act.ptc. (1036)-n.f.s.-3 m.s. sf. (659) *he who guards himself*

יִרְחַק מֵהֶם Qal impf. 3 m.s. (רָחַק 934)-prep.-3 m.p. sf. *will keep far from them*

22:6

חֲנֹךְ לַנַּעַר Qal impv. 2 m.s. (חָנַךְ II 335)-prep.-def.art.-n.m.s. (654) *train up a child*

עַל־פִּי דַרְכּוֹ prep.-n.m.s. cstr. (804)-n.m.s.-3 m.s. sf. (202) *in the way he should go*

גַּם כִּי־יַזְקִין adv. (168)-conj. (471)-Hi. impf. 3 m.s. (זָקֵן 278) *and when he is old*

לֹא־יָסוּר מִמֶּנָּה neg.-Qal impf. 3 m.s. (סוּר 693)-prep.-3 f.s. sf. *he will not depart from it*

22:7

עָשִׁיר בְּרָשִׁים adj. m.s. (799)-prep.-Qal act.ptc. m.p. (רוּשׁ 930) *the rich over the poor*

יִמְשׁוֹל Qal impf. 3 m.s. (מָשַׁל 605) *rules*

וְעֶבֶד לֹוֶה conj.-n.m.s. cstr. (713)-Qal act.ptc. (II 531 לָוָה) *a borrower is slave*

לְאִישׁ מַלְוֶה prep.-n.m.s. (35)-Hi. ptc. (לָוָה II 531) *to a man who lends*

22:8

זוֹרֵעַ עַוְלָה Qal act.ptc. (זָרַע 281)-n.f.s. (732) *he who sows injustice*

יִקְצָור־אָוֶן Qal impf. 3 m.s. (קָצַר 894)-n.m.s. (19) *will reap calamity*

וְשֵׁבֶט עֶבְרָתוֹ conj.-n.m.s. cstr. (986)-n.f.s.-3 m.s. sf. (720) *and the rod of his fury*

יִכְלֶה Qal impf. 3 m.s. (כָּלָה I 477) *will fail*

22:9

טוֹב־עַיִן adj. m.s. cstr. (II 373)-n.f.s. (744) *he who has a bountiful eye*

הוּא יְבֹרָךְ pers.pr. 3 m.s. (214)-Pu. impf. 3 m.s. (138 בָּרַךְ) *will be blessed*

כִּי־נָתַן מִלַּחְמוֹ conj. (471)-Qal pf. 3 m.s. (678)-prep.-n.m.s.-3 m.s. sf. (536) *for he shares his bread*

לַדָּל prep.-def.art.-adj. m.s. paus. (195) *with the poor*

22:10

גָּרֵשׁ לֵץ Pi. impv. 2 m.s. (גָּרַשׁ 176)-Qal act.ptc. m.s. (לִיץ 539) *drive out a scoffer*

וְיֵצֵא מָדוֹן conj.-Qal impf. 3 m.s. (יָצָא 422)-n.m.s. (I 193) *and strife will go out*

וְיִשְׁבֹּת conj.-Qal impf. 3 m.s. (שָׁבַת 991) *and will cease*

דִּין וְקָלוֹן n.m.s. (192)-conj.-n.m.s. (885) *quarreling and abuse*

22:11

אֹהֵב Qal act.ptc. (אָהֵב 12) *he who loves*

טְהָור־לֵב adj. m.s. cstr. (373)-n.m.s. (524) *purity of heart*

חֵן שְׂפָתָיו n.m.s. (336)-n.f.p.-3 m.s. sf. (973) *whose speech is gracious*

רֵעֵהוּ מֶלֶךְ n.m.s.-3 m.s. sf. (945)-n.m.s. (I 572) *will have a king as his friend*

22:12

עֵינֵי יהוה n.f.p. cstr. (744)-pr.n. (217) *the eyes of Yahweh*

נָצְרוּ דָעַת Qal pf. 3 c.p. (נָצַר 665)-n.f.s. paus. (395) *keep watch over knowledge*

וַיְסַלֵּף consec.-Pi. impf. 3 m.s. (סָלַף 701) *but he overthrows*

דִּבְרֵי בֹגֵד n.m.p. cstr. (182)-Qal act.ptc. (בָּגַד 93) *the words of the faithless*

22:13

אָמַר עָצֵל Qal pf. 3 m.s. (55)-adj. m.s. (782) *the sluggard says*

אֲרִי בַחוּץ n.m.s. (71)-prep.-def.art.-n.m.s. (299) *there is a lion outside*

בְּתוֹךְ רְחֹבוֹת prep.-n.m.s. cstr. (1063)-n.f.p. (I 932) *in the streets*

אֵרָצֵחַ Ni. impf. 1 c.s. (רָצַח 953) *I shall be slain*

22:14

שׁוּחָה עֲמֻקָּה n.f.s. (1001)-adj. f.s. (771) *a deep pit*

פִּי זָרוֹת n.m.s. cstr. (804)-Qal act.ptc. f.p. (זוּר I 266) *the mouth of a loose woman*

זְעוּם יהוה Qal pass.ptc. cstr. (זָעַם 276)-pr.n. (217) *he with whom Yahweh is angry*

יִפָּול־שָׁם Qal impf. 3 m.s. (נָפַל 656)-adv. (1027) *will fall into it*

22:15

אִוֶּלֶת n.f.s. (17) *folly*

קְשׁוּרָה Qal pass.ptc. f.s. (קָשַׁר 905) *is bound up*

בְלֶב־נָעַר prep.-n.m.s. cstr. (524)-n.m.s. paus. (654) *in the heart of a child*

שֵׁבֶט מוּסָר n.m.s. cstr. (986)-n.m.s. (416) *but the rod of discipline*

יַרְחִיקֶנָּה מִמֶּנּוּ Hi. impf. 3 m.s.-3 f.s. sf. (רָחַק 934)-prep.-3 m.s. sf. *drives it far from him*

22:16

עֹשֵׁק דָּל Qal act.ptc. (עָשַׁק 798)-adj. m.s. (195) *he who oppresses the poor*

לְהַרְבּוֹת לוֹ prep.-Hi. inf.cstr. (רָבָה I 915)-prep. -3 m.s. sf. *to increase his (own wealth)*

נֹתֵן לְעָשִׁיר Qal act.ptc. (נָתַן 678)-prep.-adj. m.s. (799) *gives to the rich*

אַךְ־לְמַחְסוֹר adv. (36)-prep.-n.m.s. (341) *will only come to want*

22:17

הַט אָזְנְךָ Hi. impv. 2 m.s. (נָטָה 639)-n.f.s.-2 m.s. sf. (23) *incline your ear*

וּשְׁמַע conj.-Qal impv. 2 m.s. (שָׁמַע 1033) *and hear*

דִּבְרֵי חֲכָמִים n.m.p. cstr. (182)-adj. m.p. (314) *the words of the wise*

וְלִבְּךָ תָּשִׁית conj.-n.m.s.-2 m.s. sf. (524)-Qal impf. 2 m.s. (שִׁית 1011) *and apply your mind*

לְדַעְתִּי prep.-n.f.s.-1 c.s. sf. (395) *to my knowledge*

22:18

כִּי־נָעִים conj. (471)-adj. m.s. (I 653) *for it will be pleasant*

כִּי־תִשְׁמְרֵם v.supra-Qal impf. 2 m.s.-3 m.p. sf. (1036 שָׁמַר) *if you keep them*

בְּבִטְנֶךָ prep.-n.f.s.-2 m.s. sf. (105) *within you*

יִכֹּנוּ יַחְדָּו Ni. impf. 3 m.p. (כּוּן I 465)-adv. (403) *if all of them are ready*

עַל־שְׂפָתֶיךָ prep.-n.f.p.-2 m.s. sf. (973) *on your lips*

22:19

לִהְיוֹת בַּיהוה prep.-Qal inf.cstr. (הָיָה 224)-prep. -pr.n. (217) *that may be in Yahweh*

מִבְטַחֶךָ n.m.s.-2 m.s. sf. (105) *your trust*

הוֹדַעְתִּיךָ Hi. pf. 1 c.s.-2 m.s. sf. (יָדַע 393) *I have made them known to you*

הַיּוֹם def.art.-n.m.s. (398) *today*

אַף־אָתָּה adv. (II 64)-pers.pr. 2 m.s. paus. (61) *even to you*

22:20

הֲלֹא כָתַבְתִּי לְךָ interr.-neg.-Qal pf. 1 c.s. (כָּתַב 507)-prep.-2 m.s. sf. *have I not written for you*

שָׁלְשׁוֹם adv. (1026; Q שָׁלִישִׁים n.m.p. III 1026; LXX τρισσῶς) *thirty sayings (three days ago)*

בְּמוֹעֵצוֹת prep.-n.f.p. (420) *of admonitions*

וָדָעַת conj.-n.f.s. paus. (395) *and knowledge*

22:21

לְהוֹדִיעֲךָ קֹשְׁטְ prep.-Hi. inf.cstr.-2 m.s. sf. (יָדַע 393)-n.m.s. (905) *to show you what is right*

אִמְרֵי אֱמֶת n.m.p. cstr. (182)-n.f.s. (54) *words of truth*

לְהָשִׁיב אֲמָרִים prep.-Hi. inf.cstr. (שׁוּב 996) -n.m.p. (56) *to return words*

אֱמֶת v.supra *truth*

לְשֹׁלְחֶיךָ prep.-Qal act.ptc. m.p.-2 m.s. sf. (שָׁלַח 1018) *to those who sent you*

22:22

אַל־תִּגְזָל־דָּל prep.-Qal impf. 2 m.s. (גָּזַל 159)-adj. m.s. (195) *do not rob the poor*

כִּי דַל־הוּא conj. (471)-adj. m.s. (195)-pers.pr. 3 m.s. (214) *because he is poor*

וְאַל־תְּדַכֵּא עָנִי conj.-neg.-Pi. impf. 2 m.s. (דָּכָא 193)-adj. m.s. (776) *or do not crush the afflicted*

בַשָּׁעַר prep.-def.art.-n.m.s. paus. (1044) *in the gate*

22:23

כִּי־יהוה conj. (471)-pr.n. (217) *for Yahweh*

יָרִיב רִיבָם Qal impf. 3 m.s. (רִיב 936)-n.m.s.-3 m.p. sf. (936) *will plead their cause*

וְקָבַע conj.-Qal pf. 3 m.s. (קָבַע 867) *and despoil*

אֶת־קֹבְעֵיהֶם dir.obj.-Qal act.ptc. m.p.-3 m.p. sf. (867 קָבַע) *those who despoil them*

נָפֶשׁ n.f.s. paus. (659) *of life*

22:24

אַל־תִּתְרַע neg.-Hith. impf. 2 m.s. (רָעָה II 945) *make no friendship*

אֶת־בַּעַל prep. (II 85)-n.m.s. cstr. (127) *with a man given to*

אָף n.m.s. paus. (I 60) *anger*

וְאֶת־אִישׁ חֵמוֹת conj.-prep. (II 85)-n.m.s. cstr. (35)-n.f.p. (404) *nor with a wrathful man*

לֹא תָבוֹא neg.-Qal impf. 2 m.s. (בּוֹא 97) *go*

22:25

פֶּן־תֶּאֱלַף adv. (814)-Qal impf. 2 m.s. (אָלַף I 48) *lest you learn*

אֹרְחֹתָו n.m.p.-3 m.s. sf. (73) *his ways*

וְלָקַחְתָּ conj.-Qal pf. 2 m.s. (לָקַח 542) *and entangle*

מוֹקֵשׁ n.m.s. (430) *in a snare*

לְנַפְשֶׁךָ prep.-n.f.s.-2 m.s. sf. (659) *yourself*

22:26

אַל־תְּהִי neg.-Qal impf. 2 m.s. (הָיָה 224) *be not*

בְתֹקְעֵי־כָף prep.-Qal act.ptc. m.p. cstr. (תָּקַע 1075)-n.f.s. paus. (496) *one of those who give pledges (strike the hand)*

בַּעֹרְבִים מַשָּׁאוֹת prep.-def.art.-Qal act.ptc. m.p. (II 786 עָרַב)-n.f.p. (673) *who become surety for debts*

22:27

אִם־אֵין־לְךָ hypoth.part. (49)-neg. (II 34)-prep.-2 m.s. sf. *if you have nothing*

לְשַׁלֵּם prep.-Pi. inf.cstr. (שָׁלֵם 1022) *with which to pay*

לָמָּה יִקַּח prep.-interr. (552)-Qal impf. 3 m.s. (542 לָקַח) *why should ... be taken*

מִשְׁכָּבְךָ n.m.s.-2 m.s. sf. (1012) *your bed*

מִתַּחְתֶּיךָ prep.-prep.-2 m.s. sf. (1065) *from under you*

22:28

אַל־תַּסֵּג neg.-Hi. impf. 2 m.s. juss. (סוּג I 690) *remove not*

גְּבוּל עוֹלָם n.m.s. cstr. (147)-n.m.s. (761) *the ancient landmark*

אֲשֶׁר עָשׂוּ rel. (81)-Qal pf. 3 c.p. (עָשָׂה I 793) *which ... have set*

אֲבוֹתֶיךָ n.m.p.-2 m.s. sf. (3) *your fathers*

22:29

חָזִיתָ Qal pf. 2 m.s. (חָזָה 302) *do you see*

אִישׁ מָהִיר n.m.s. (35)-adj. m.s. (555) *a man skilful*

בִּמְלַאכְתּוֹ prep.-n.f.s.-3 m.s. sf. (521) *in his work*

לִפְנֵי־מְלָכִים prep.-n.m.p. cstr. (815)-n.m.p. (I 572) *before kings*

יִתְיַצָּב Hith. impf. 3 m.s. paus. (יָצַב 426) *he will stand*

בַּל־יִתְיַצֵּב neg. (115)-Hith. impf. 3 m.s. (יָצַב 426) *he will not stand*

לִפְנֵי חֲשֻׁכִּים v.supra-adj. m.p. (365) *before obscure men*

23:1

כִּי־תֵשֵׁב conj. (471)-Qal impf. 2 m.s. (יָשַׁב 442) *when you sit down*

לִלְחוֹם prep.-Qal inf.cstr. (לָחַם II 536) *to eat*

אֶת־מוֹשֵׁל prep. (II 85)-Qal act.ptc. (מָשַׁל 605) *with a ruler*

בִּין תָּבִין Qal inf.abs. (בִּין 106)-Qal impf. 2 m.s. (106 בִּין) *observe carefully*

אֶת־אֲשֶׁר לְפָנֶיךָ dir.obj.-rel. (81)-prep.-n.m.p.-2 m.s. sf. (815) *what is before you*

23:2

וְשַׂמְתָּ שַׂכִּין Qal pf. 2 m.s. (שִׂים 962)-n.m.s. (967) *and you put a knife*

בְּלֹעֶךָ prep.-n.m.s.-2 m.s. sf. (534) *to your throat*

אִם־בַּעַל hypoth.part. (49)-n.m.s. (127) *if a man*

נֶפֶשׁ אָתָּה n.f.s. (659)-pers.pr. 2 m.s. paus. (61) *given to appetite you are*

23:3

אַל־תִּתְאָו neg.-Hith. impf. 2 m.s. apoc. (אָוָה 16) *do not desire*

לְמַטְעַמּוֹתָיו prep.-n.m.p.-3 m.s. sf. (381) *his delicacies*

וְהוּא לֶחֶם כְּזָבִים conj.-pers.pr. 3 m.s. (214)-n.m.s. cstr. (536)-n.m.p. (469) *for they are deceptive food*

23:4

אַל־תִּיגַע neg.-Qal impf. 2 m.s. (יָגַע 388) *do not toil*

לְהַעֲשִׁיר prep.-Hi. inf.cstr. (עָשַׁר 799) *to acquire wealth*

מִבִּינָתְךָ prep.-n.f.s.-2 m.s. sf. (108) *be wise enough*

חֲדָל Qal inf.cstr. (חָדַל 292) *to desist*

23:5

הֲתָעוּף עֵינֶיךָ בּוֹ interr.-Hi. impf. 3 f.s. (עוּף I 733)-n.f.p.-2 m.s. (744)-prep.-3 m.s. sf. *when your eyes light upon it*

וְאֵינֶנּוּ conj.-neg.-3 m.s. sf. (II 34) *it is gone*

כִּי עָשֹׂה יַעֲשֶׂה־לּוֹ conj. (471)-Qal inf.abs. (עָשָׂה I 793)-Qal impf. 3 m.s. (I 793)-prep.-3 m.s. sf. *for it takes to itself (suddenly)*

כְנָפַיִם n.f.p. (489) *wings*

כְּנֶשֶׁר prep.-n.m.s. (676) *like an eagle*

וְעָיף conj.-Qal impf. 3 m.s. (עוּף I 733; Q יָעוּף) *flying*

הַשָּׁמָיִם def.art.-n.m. du. paus. (1029) *toward heaven*

23:6

אַל־תִּלְחַם neg.-Qal impf. 2 m.s. (לָחַם II 536) *do not eat*
אֶת־לֶחֶם dir.obj.-n.m.s. cstr. (536) *the bread of*
רַע עָיִן adj. m.s. (948)-n.f.s. paus. *a niggardly one*
וְאַל־תִּתְאָו conj.-neg.-Hith. impf. 2 m.s. apoc. (16 אָוָה) *do not desire*
לְמַטְעַמֹּתָיו prep.-n.m.p.-3 m.s. sf. (381) *his delicacies*

23:7

כִּי כְּמוֹ־שָׁעַר conj. (471)-conj. (455)-Qal pf. 3 m.s. (II 1045; LXX τρίχα) *for he is like one who is reckoning*
בְּנַפְשׁוֹ prep.-n.f.s.-3 m.s. sf. (659) *inwardly*
כֶּן־הוּא adv. (485)-pers.pr. 3 m.s. (214) *so is he*
אֱכֹל וּשְׁתֵה Qal impv. 2 m.s. (אָכַל 37)-conj.-Qal impv. 2 m.s. (שָׁתָה 1059) *eat and drink*
יֹאמַר לָךְ Qal impf. 3 m.s. (55)-prep.-2 m.s. sf. paus. *he says to you*
וְלִבּוֹ conj.-n.m.s.-3 m.s. sf. (524) *but his heart*
בַּל־עִמָּךְ neg.-prep.-2 m.s. sf. paus. *is not with you*

23:8

פִּתְּךָ־אָכַלְתָּ n.f.s.-2 m.s. sf. (837)-Qal pf. 2 m.s. (37 אָכַל) *the morsels which you have eaten*
תְקִיאֶנָּה Qal impf. 2 m.s.-3 f.s. sf. (קִיא 883) *you will vomit up*
וְשִׁחַתָּ conj.-Pi. pf. 2 m.s. (שָׁחַת 1008) *and waste*
דְּבָרֶיךָ הַנְּעִימִים n.m.p.-2 m.s. sf. (182)-def.art.-adj. m.p. (653) *your pleasant words*

23:9

בְּאָזְנֵי כְסִיל prep.-n.f.p. cstr. (23)-n.m.s. (493) *in the hearing of a fool*
אַל־תְּדַבֵּר neg.-Pi. impf. 2 m.s. (דָּבַר 180) *do not speak*
כִּי־יָבוּז conj. (471)-Qal impf. 3 m.s. (בּוּז I 100) *for he will despise*
לְשֵׂכֶל מִלֶּיךָ prep.-n.m.s. cstr. (968)-n.f.p.-2 m.s. sf. (576) *the wisdom of your words*

23:10

אַל־תַּסֵּג neg.-Hi. impf. 2 m.s. juss. (סוּג I 690) *do not remove*
גְּבוּל עוֹלָם n.m.s. cstr. (147)-n.m.s. (761) *an ancient landmark*
וּבִשְׂדֵי יְתוֹמִים conj.-prep.-n.m.p. cstr. (961)-n.m.p. (450) *or the fields of the fatherless*
אַל־תָּבֹא neg.-Qal impf. 2 m.s. (בּוֹא 97) *do not enter*

23:11

כִּי־גֹאֲלָם conj. (471)-Qal act.ptc.-3 m.p. sf. (גָּאַל I 145) *for their Redeemer*
חָזָק adj. m.s. (305) *is strong*
הוּא־יָרִיב pers.pr. 3 m.s. (214)-Qal impf. 3 m.s. (936 רִיב) *he will plead*
אֶת־רִיבָם dir.obj.-n.m.s.-3 m.p. sf. (936) *their cause*
אִתָּךְ prep. (II 85)-2 m.s. sf. paus. *against you*

23:12

הָבִיאָה Hi. impv. 2 m.s.-vol.he (בּוֹא 97) *apply*
לַמּוּסָר prep.-def.art.-n.m.s. (416) *to instruction*
לִבֶּךָ n.m.s.-2 m.s. sf. (524) *your mind*
וְאָזְנֶךָ conj.-n.f.s.-2 m.s. sf. (23) *and your ear*
לְאִמְרֵי־דָעַת prep.-n.m.p. cstr. (56)-n.f.s. paus. (395) *to words of knowledge*

23:13

אַל־תִּמְנַע neg.-Qal impf. 2 m.s. (מָנַע 586) *do not withhold*
מִנַּעַר prep.-n.m.s. (654) *from a child*
מוּסָר n.m.s. (416) *discipline*
כִּי־תַכֶּנּוּ conj. (471)-Hi. impf. 2 m.s.-3 m.s. sf. (645 נָכָה) *if you beat him*
בַּשֵּׁבֶט prep.-def.art.-n.m.s. (986) *with a rod*
לֹא יָמוּת neg.-Qal impf. 3 m.s. (מוּת 559) *he will not die*

23:14

אַתָּה pers.pr. 2 m.s. (61) *if you*
בַּשֵּׁבֶט prep.-def.art.-n.m.s. (986) *with the rod*
תַּכֶּנּוּ Hi. impf. 2 m.s.-3 m.s. sf. (נָכָה 645) *you beat him*
וְנַפְשׁוֹ conj.-n.f.s.-3 m.s. sf. (659) *his life*
מִשְּׁאוֹל prep.-n.f.s. (982) *from Sheol*
תַּצִּיל Hi. impf. 2 m.s. (נָצַל 664) *you will save*

23:15

בְּנִי n.m.s.-1 c.s. sf. (119) *my son*
אִם־חָכַם hypoth.part. (49)-adj. m.s. *if is wise*
לִבֶּךָ n.m.s.-2 m.s. sf. (524) *your heart*
יִשְׂמַח לִבִּי Qal impf. 3 m.s. (שָׂמַח 970)-n.m.s.-1 c.s. sf. (524) *my heart will be glad*
גַם־אָנִי adv. (168)-pers.pr. 1 c.s. paus. (58) *I too*

23:16

וְתַעֲלֹזְנָה conj.-Qal impf. 3 f.p. (עָלַז 759) *and will rejoice*
כִלְיוֹתָי n.f.p.-1 c.s. sf. (480) *my soul*
בְּדַבֵּר שְׂפָתֶיךָ prep.-Pi. inf.cstr. (דָּבַר 180)-n.f.p.-2 m.s. sf. (973) *when your lips speak*
מֵישָׁרִים n.m.p. (449) *what is right*

23:17

אַל־יְקַנֵּא neg.-Pi. impf. 3 m.s. (קָנָא 888) *let not ... envy*
לִבְּךָ n.m.s.-2 m.s. sf. (524) *your heart*
בַּחַטָּאִים prep.-def.art.-adj. m.p. (308) *sinners*
כִּי אִם־בְּיִרְאַת־יהוה conj. (471)-hypoth.part. (49)-prep.-n.f.s. cstr. (432)-pr.n. (217) *but in the fear of Yahweh*
כָּל־הַיּוֹם n.m.s. cstr. (481)-def.art.-n.m.s. (398) *all the day*

23:18

כִּי אִם־יֵשׁ conj.-hypoth. (474)-subst. (441) *surely there is*
אַחֲרִית n.f.s. (31) *a future*
וְתִקְוָתְךָ conj.-n.f.s.-2 m.s. sf. (876) *and your hope*
לֹא תִכָּרֵת neg.-Ni. impf. 3 f.s. (כָּרַת 503) *will not be cut off*

23:19

שְׁמַע־אַתָּה Qal impv. 2 m.s. (שָׁמַע 1033)-pers.pr. 2 m.s. (61) *hear*
בְּנִי n.m.s.-1 c.s. sf. (119) *my son*
וַחֲכָם conj.-Qal impv. 2 m.s. (חָכַם 314) *and be wise*
וְאַשֵּׁר conj.-Pi. impv. 2 m.s. (אָשַׁר 80) *and direct*
בַּדֶּרֶךְ neg.-def.art.-n.m.s. (202) *in the way*
לִבֶּךָ n.m.s.-2 m.s. sf. paus. (524) *your mind*

23:20

אַל־תְּהִי neg.-Qal impf. 2 m.s. juss. (הָיָה 224) *be not*
בְסֹבְאֵי־יָיִן prep.-Qal act.ptc. m.p. cstr. (סָבָא 684)-n.m.s. paus. (406) *among winebibbers*
בְּזֹלֲלֵי בָשָׂר לָמוֹ prep.-Qal act.ptc. m.p. cstr. (זָלַל II 272)-n.m.s. (142)-prep.-3 m.p. sf. paus. *or among gluttonous eaters of meat*

23:21

כִּי־סֹבֵא conj. (471)-Qal act.ptc. (סָבָא 684) *for the drunkard*
וְזוֹלֵל conj.-Qal act.ptc. (זָלַל II 272) *and the glutton*
יִוָּרֵשׁ Ni. impf. 3 m.s. (יָרַשׁ 439) *will come to poverty*
וּקְרָעִים conj.-n.m.p. (902) *and with rags*
תַּלְבִּישׁ Hi. impf. 3 f.s. (לָבַשׁ 527) *will clothe*
נוּמָה n.f.s. (630) *drowsiness*

23:22

שְׁמַע לְאָבִיךָ Qal impv. 2 m.s. (1033)-prep.-n.m.s.-2 m.s. sf. (3) *hearken to your father*
זֶה יְלָדֶךָ demons.adj. m.s. (260)-Qal pf. 3 m.s.-2 m.s. sf. (408) *who begot you*
וְאַל־תָּבוּז conj.-neg.-Qal impf. 2 m.s. juss. (בּוּז 100) *and do not despise*
כִּי־זָקְנָה conj. (471)-Qal pf. 3 f.s. (זָקֵן 278) *when she is old*
אִמֶּךָ n.f.s.-2 m.s. sf. (51) *your mother*

23:23

אֱמֶת קְנֵה n.f.s. (54)-Qal impv. 2 m.s. (קָנָה 888) *buy truth*
וְאַל־תִּמְכֹּר conj.-neg.-Qal impf. 2 m.s. (מָכַר 569) *and do not sell it*
חָכְמָה n.f.s. (315) *wisdom*
וּמוּסָר conj.-n.m.s. (416) *instruction*
וּבִינָה conj.-n.f.s. (108) *and understanding*

23:24

גּוֹל יָגוֹל Qal inf.abs. (גִּיל 162)-Qal impf. 3 m.s. (גִּיל 162; Q גִּיל יָגִיל) *will greatly rejoice*
אֲבִי צַדִּיק n.m.s. cstr. (3)-adj. m.s. (843) *the father of the righteous*
יוֹלֵד Qal act.ptc. (יָלַד 408) *he who begets*
חָכָם adj. m.s. (314) *a wise son*
וְיִשְׂמַח־בּוֹ conj.-Qal impf. 3 m.s. (שָׂמַח 970)-prep.-3 m.s. sf. *will be glad in him*

23:25

יִשְׂמַח־אָבִיךָ Qal impf. 3 m.s. (שָׂמַח 970)-n.m.s.-2 m.s. sf. (3) *let your father be glad*
וְאִמֶּךָ conj.-n.f.s.-2 m.s. sf. (51) *and your mother*
וְתָגֵל conj.-Qal impf. 3 f.s. apoc. (גִּיל 162) *let ... rejoice*
יוֹלַדְתֶּךָ Qal act.ptc. f.s.-2 m.s. sf. (יָלַד 408) *her who bore you*

23:26

תְּנָה־בְנִי Qal impv. 2 m.s.-vol.he (נָתַן 678)-n.m.s.-1 c.s. sf. (119) *give my son*
לִבְּךָ לִי n.m.s.-2 m.s. sf. (524)-prep.-1 c.s. sf. *your heart to me*

וְעֵינֶיךָ conj.-n.f.p.-2 m.s. sf. (744) *and your eyes*
דְּרָכַי n.m.p.-1 c.s. sf. (202) *my ways*
תִּרֹצְנָה Qal impf. 3 f.p. (רָצָה 953) *let delight in*

23:27

כִּי־שׁוּחָה עֲמֻקָּה conj. (471)-n.f.s. (1001)-adj. f.s. (771) *for a deep pit*
זוֹנָה Qal act.ptc. f.s. (זָנָה 275) *a harlot*
וּבְאֵר צָרָה conj.-n.f.s. (91)-adj. f.s. (865) *and a narrow well*
נָכְרִיָּה adj. f.s. (648) *an adventuress*

23:28

אַף־הִיא adv. (II 64)-pers.pr. 3 f.s. (214) *indeed she*
כְּחֶתֶף prep.-n.m.s. (369) *like a robber*
תֶּאֱרֹב Qal impf. 3 f.s. (אָרַב 70) *lies in wait*
וּבוֹגְדִים conj.-Qal act.ptc. m.p. (בָּגַד 93) *and the faithless*
בְּאָדָם prep.-n.m.s. (9) *among men*
תּוֹסִף Hi. impf. 3 f.s. (יָסַף 414) *she increases*

23:29

לְמִי אוֹי prep.-interr. (566)-subst. (17) *who has woe?*
לְמִי אֲבוֹי v.supra-interj. (5) *who has sorrow?*
לְמִי מִדְוָנִים v.supra-n.m.p. (I 193) *who has strife?*
לְמִי שִׂיחַ v.supra-n.m.s. (967) *who has complaining?*
לְמִי פְּצָעִים v.supra-n.m.p. (822) *who has wounds*
חִנָּם adv. (336) *without cause?*
לְמִי חַכְלִלוּת עֵינָיִם v.supra-n.f.s. cstr. (314)-n.f. du. paus. (744) *who has redness of eyes?*

23:30

לַמְאַחֲרִים prep.-def.art.-Pi. ptc. m.p. (אָחַר 29) *those who tarry long*
עַל־הַיָּיִן prep.-def.art.-n.m.s. paus. (406) *over wine*
לַבָּאִים prep.-def.art.-Qal act.ptc. m.p. (בּוֹא 97) *those who go*
לַחְקֹר prep.-Qal inf.cstr. (חָקַר 350) *to try*
מִמְסָךְ n.m.s. (587) *mixed wine*

23:31

אַל־תֵּרֶא יַיִן neg.-Qal impf. 2 m.s. apoc. (רָאָה 906)-n.m.s. (406) *do not look at wine*
כִּי יִתְאַדָּם conj. (471) Hith. impf. 3 m.s. (אָדֹם 10) *when it is red*
כִּי־יִתֵּן בַּכִּיס v.supra-Qal impf. 3 m.s. (נָתַן 678)-prep.-def.art.-n.f.s. (468) *when it sparkles (gives) in the cup*
עֵינוֹ n.f.s.-3 m.s. (744) *his eye*
יִתְהַלֵּךְ בְּמֵישָׁרִים Hith. impf. 3 m.s. (הָלַךְ 229)-prep.-n.m.p. (449) *and goes down smoothly*

23:32

אַחֲרִיתוֹ n.f.s.-3 m.s. sf. (31) *at the last*
כְּנָחָשׁ prep.-n.m.s. (638) *like a serpent*
יִשָּׁךְ Qal impf. 3 m.s. paus. (נָשַׁךְ 675) *it bites*
וּכְצִפְעֹנִי conj.-prep.-n.m.s. (861) *and like an adder*
יַפְרִשׁ Hi. impf. 3 m.s. (פָּרַשׁ II 831) *it stings*

23:33

עֵינֶיךָ n.f.p.-2 m.s. sf. (744) *your eyes*
יִרְאוּ Qal impf. 3 m.p. (רָאָה 906) *will see*
זָרוֹת Qal act.ptc. f.p. (זוּר I 266) *strange things*
וְלִבְּךָ conj.-n.m.s.-2 m.s. sf. (524) *and your mind*
יְדַבֵּר Pi. impf. 3 m.s. (דָּבַר 180) *will utter*
תַּהְפֻּכוֹת n.f.p. (246) *perverse things*

23:34

וְהָיִיתָ conj.-Qal pf. 2 m.s. (הָיָה 224) *you will be*
כְּשֹׁכֵב prep.-Qal act.ptc. (שָׁכַב 1011) *like one who lies down*
בְּלֶב־יָם prep.-n.m.s. cstr. (524)-n.m.s. (410) *in the midst of the sea*
וּכְשֹׁכֵב conj.-prep.-v.supra *and like one who lies*
בְּרֹאשׁ חִבֵּל prep.-n.m.s. cstr. (910)-n.m.s. (287) *on the top of a mast*

23:35

הִכּוּנִי Hi. pf. 3 c.p.-1 c.s. sf. (נָכָה 645) *they struck me*
בַּל־חָלִיתִי neg.-Qal pf. 1 c.s. (חָלָה I 317) *but I was not hurt*
הֲלָמוּנִי Qal pf. 3 c.p.-1 c.s. sf. (הָלַם 240) *they beat me*
בַּל־יָדָעְתִּי neg.-Qal pf. 1 c.s. paus. (יָדַע 393) *but I did not feel it*
מָתַי אָקִיץ adv. (607)-Hi. impf. 1 c.s. (קִיץ I 884) *when shall I awake?*
אוֹסִיף אֲבַקְשֶׁנּוּ Hi. impf. 1 c.s. (יָסַף 414)-Pi. impf. 1 c.s.-3 m.s. sf. (בָּקַשׁ 134) *I will seek another*
עוֹד adv. (728) *again*

24:1

אַל־תְּקַנֵּא neg.-Pi. impf. 2 m.s. (קָנָא 888) *be not envious*

בְּאַנְשֵׁי רָעָה prep.-n.m.p. cstr. (35)-n.f.s. (949) *of evil men*

וְאַל־תִּתְאָו conj.-neg.-Qal impf. 2 m.s. (אָוָה 16) *nor desire*

לִהְיוֹת אִתָּם prep.-Qal inf.cstr. (הָיָה 224) -prep.-3 m.p. sf. (II 85) *to be with them*

24:2

כִּי־שֹׁד conj. (471)-n.m.s. (994) *for violence*

יֶהְגֶּה לִבָּם Qal impf. 3 m.s. (הָגָה I 211)-n.m.s.-3 m.p. sf. (524) *their minds devise*

וְעָמָל conj.-n.m.s. (I 765) *and of mischief*

שִׂפְתֵיהֶם תְּדַבֵּרְנָה n.f.p.-3 m.p. sf. (973)-Pi. impf. 3 f.p. (דָּבַר 180) *their lips talk*

24:3

בְּחָכְמָה prep.-n.f.s. (315) *by wisdom*

יִבָּנֶה בָּיִת Ni. impf. 3 m.s. (בָּנָה 124)-n.m.s. paus. (108) *a house is built*

וּבִתְבוּנָה conj.-prep.-n.f.s. (108) *and by understanding*

יִתְכּוֹנָן Hithpolal impf. 3 m.s. paus. (כּוּן I 465) *it is established*

24:4

וּבְדַעַת conj.-prep.-n.f.s. (395) *by knowledge*

חֲדָרִים יִמָּלְאוּ n.m.p. (293)-Ni. impf. 3 m.p. (מָלֵא 569) *the rooms are filled*

כָּל־הוֹן יָקָר n.m.s. cstr. (481)-n.m.s. (223)-adj. m.s. (429) *with all precious riches*

וְנָעִים conj.-adj. m.s. (I 653) *and pleasant*

24:5

גֶּבֶר־חָכָם n.m.s. (149; LXX κρείσσων)-adj. m.s. (314) *a wise man is mightier*

בַּעוֹז prep.-def.art.-n.m.s. (738) *in strength*

וְאִישׁ־דַּעַת conj.-n.m.s. cstr. (35)-n.f.s. (395) *and a man of knowledge*

מְאַמֶּץ־כֹּחַ Pi. ptc. (אָמֵץ 54)-n.m.s. (470; LXX γεωργίου μεγάλου) *than he who has strength*

24:6

כִּי בְתַחְבֻּלוֹת conj. (471)-prep.-n.f.p. (287) *for by wise guidance*

תַּעֲשֶׂה־לְּךָ Qal impf. 2 m.s. (עָשָׂה I 793)-prep. -2 m.s. sf. *you can wage (make for yourself)*

מִלְחָמָה n.f.s. (536) *war*

וּתְשׁוּעָה conj.-n.f.s. (448) *and there is victory*

בְּרֹב יוֹעֵץ prep.-n.m.s. cstr. (913)-Qal act.ptc. (419 יָעַץ) *in abundance of counselors*

24:7

רָאמוֹת n.f.p. (910; ? רָמוֹת Qal act.ptc. f.p. רוּם 926) *corals*

לֶאֱוִיל prep.-adj. m.s. (17) *for a fool*

חָכְמוֹת adj. f.p. (314) *wisdom*

בַּשַּׁעַר prep.-def.art.-n.m.s. (1044) *in the gate*

לֹא־יִפְתַּח־פִּיהוּ neg.-Qal impf. 3 m.s. (פָּתַח I 834)-n.m.s.-3 m.s. sf. (804) *he does not open his mouth*

24:8

מְחַשֵּׁב Pi. ptc. (חָשַׁב 362) *he who plans*

לְהָרֵעַ prep.-Hi. inf.cstr. (רָעַע 949) *to do evil*

לוֹ בַּעַל־מְזִמּוֹת prep.-3 m.s. sf.-n.m.s. cstr. (127) -n.f.p. (273) *to him ... a mischief-maker*

יִקְרָאוּ Qal impf. 3 m.p. (קָרָא 894) *will be called*

24:9

זִמַּת אִוֶּלֶת n.f.s. cstr. (273)-n.f.s. (17) *the devising of folly*

חַטָּאת n.f.s. (308) *is sin*

וְתוֹעֲבַת conj.-n.f.s. cstr. (1072) *and an abomination*

לְאָדָם prep.-n.m.s. (9) *to men*

לֵץ Qal act.ptc. (לִיץ 539) *the scoffer*

24:10

הִתְרַפִּיתָ Hith. pf. 2 m.s. (רָפָה 951) *if you faint*

בְּיוֹם צָרָה prep.-n.m.s. cstr. (398)-n.f.s. (865) *in the day of adversity*

צַר כֹּחֶכָה adj. m.s. (865)-n.m.s.-2 m.s. sf. (470) *your strength is small*

24:11

הַצֵּל Hi. impv. 2 m.s. (נָצַל 664) *rescue*

לְקֻחִים לַמָּוֶת Qal pass.ptc. m.p. (לָקַח 542)-prep. -def.art.-n.m.s. (560) *those who are being taken away to death*

וּמָטִים לַהֶרֶג conj.-Qal act.ptc. m.p. (מוֹט 556)-prep.-def.art.-n.m.s. (247) *those who are stumbling to the slaughter*

אִם־תַּחְשׂוֹךְ hypoth.part. (49; LXX μή)-Qal impf. 2 m.s. (חָשַׂךְ 362) *hold back*

24:12

כִּי־תֹאמַר conj. (471)-Qal impf. 2 m.s. (אָמַר 55) *if you say*

הֵן לֹא־יָדַעְנוּ interj. (243)-neg.-Qal pf. 1 c.p. (393 יָדַע) *behold, we did not know*

זֶה demons.adj. m.s. (260) *this*
הֲלֹא־תֹכֵן interr.-neg.-Qal act.ptc. (תָּכַן 1067) *does not he who weighs*
לִבּוֹת n.m.p. (524) *hearts*
הוּא־יָבִין pers.pr. 3 m.s. (214)-Qal impf. 3 m.s. (106 בִּין) *perceive it?*
וְנֹצֵר נַפְשְׁךָ conj.-Qal act.ptc. (נָצַר 665)-n.f.s.-2 m.s. sf. (659) *does not he who keeps watch over your soul*
הוּא יֵדָע v.supra-Qal impf. 3 m.s. (יָדַע 393) *know it*
וְהֵשִׁיב לְאָדָם conj.-Hi. pf. 3 m.s. (שׁוּב 996) -prep.-n.m.s. (9) *and will he not requite man*
כְּפָעֳלוֹ prep.-n.m.s.-3 m.s. sf. (821) *according to his work?*

24:13
אֱכָל־בְּנִי Qal impv. 2 m.s. (אָכַל 37)-n.m.s.-1 c.s. sf. (119) *eat my son*
דְבַשׁ n.m.s. (185) *honey*
כִּי־טוֹב conj. (471)-adj. m.s. (373) *for it is good*
וְנֹפֶת conj.-n.m.s. (661) *and the drippings of the honeycomb*
מָתוֹק adj. m.s. (608) *are sweet*
עַל־חִכֶּךָ prep.-n.m.s.-2 m.s. sf. (335) *to your taste*

24:14
כֵּן דְּעֶה adv. (485)-Qal impv. 2 m.s. (יָדַע 393) *know that*
חָכְמָה n.f.s. (315) *wisdom*
לְנַפְשֶׁךָ prep.-n.f.s.-2 m.s. sf. (659) *to your soul*
אִם־מָצָאתָ hypoth.part. (49)-Qal pf. 2 m.s. (מָצָא 592) *if you find it*
וְיֵשׁ אַחֲרִית conj.-subst. (441)-n.f.s. (31) *there will be a future*
וְתִקְוָתְךָ conj.-n.f.s.-2 m.s. sf. (876) *and your hope*
לֹא תִכָּרֵת neg.-Ni. impf. 3 f.s. (כָּרַת 503) *will not be cut off*

24:15
אַל־תֶּאֱרֹב neg.-Qal impf. 2 m.s. (אָרַב 70) *lie not in wait*
רָשָׁע adj. m.s. (957) *as a wicked man*
לִנְוֵה צַדִּיק prep.-n.m.s. cstr. (627)-adj. m.s. (843) *against the dwelling of the righteous*
אַל־תְּשַׁדֵּד neg.-Pi. impf. 2 m.s. (שָׁדַד 994) *do not violence*
רִבְצוֹ n.m.s.-3 m.s. sf. (918) *to his home*

24:16
כִּי שֶׁבַע conj. (471)-num. (I 987) *for seven times*
יִפּוֹל צַדִּיק Qal impf. 3 m.s. (נָפַל 656)-adj. m.s. (843) *a righteous man falls*
וָקָם conj.-Qal pf. 3 m.s. (קוּם 877) *and rises again*
וּרְשָׁעִים conj.-adj. m.p. (957) *but the wicked*
יִכָּשְׁלוּ Ni. impf. 3 m.p. (כָּשַׁל 505) *are overthrown*
בְרָעָה prep.-n.f.s. (949) *by calamity*

24:17
בִּנְפֹל אוֹיִבְךָ prep.-Qal inf.cstr. (נָפַל 656)-Qal act.ptc. m.p.-2 m.s. sf. (אָיַב 33) *when your enemy falls*
אַל־תִּשְׂמָח neg.-Qal impf. 2 m.s. paus. (שָׂמַח 970) *do not rejoice*
וּבִכָּשְׁלוֹ conj.-prep.-Qal act.ptc.-3 m.s. sf. (כָּשַׁל 505) *and when he stumbles*
אַל־יָגֵל לִבֶּךָ neg.-Qal impf. 2 m.s. apoc. (גִּיל 162)-n.m.s.-2 m.s. sf. (524) *let not your heart be glad*

24:18
פֶּן־יִרְאֶה יהוה conj. (814)-Qal impf. 3 m.s. (רָאָה 906)-pr.n. (217) *lest Yahweh see it*
וְרַע בְּעֵינָיו conj.-Qal pf. 3 m.s. (רָעַע 949) -prep.-n.f.p.-3 m.s. sf. (744) *and be displeased*
וְהֵשִׁיב מֵעָלָיו conj.-Hi. pf. 3 m.s. (שׁוּב (996) -prep.-prep.-3 m.s. sf. *and turn away from him*
אַפּוֹ n.m.s.-3 m.s. sf. (I 60) *his anger*

24:19
אַל־תִּתְחַר neg.-Hith. impf. 2 m.s. (חָרָה 354) *fret not yourself*
בַּמְּרֵעִים prep.-def.art.-Hi. ptc. m.p. (רָעַע 949) *because of evildoers*
אַל־תְּקַנֵּא neg.-Pi. impf. 2 m.s. (קָנָא 888) *and be not envious*
בָּרְשָׁעִים prep.-def.art.-adj. m.p. (957) *of the wicked*

24:20
כִּי לֹא־תִהְיֶה conj. (471)-neg.-Qal impf. 2 m.s. (224 הָיָה) *for there is no*
אַחֲרִית n.f.s. (31) *future*
לָרָע prep.-def.art.-adj. m.s. (I 948) *for the evil man*
נֵר רְשָׁעִים n.m.s. cstr. (632)-adj. m.p. (957) *the lamp of the wicked*

יִדְעָךְ Qal impf. 3 m.s. paus. (דָּעַךְ 200) *will be put out*

24:21

יְרָא־אֶת־יהוה Qal impv. 2 m.s. (יָרֵא 431) -dir.obj.-pr.n. (217) *fear Yahweh*
בְּנִי n.m.s.-1 c.s. sf. (119) *my son*
וָמֶלֶךְ conj.-n.m.s. (I 572) *and the king*
עִם־שׁוֹנִים prep. (767)-Qal act.ptc. m.p. (שָׁנָה I 1039) *with those who change*
אַל־תִּתְעָרָב neg.-Hith. impf. 2 m.s. paus. (עָרַב 786) *do not associate*

24:22

כִּי־פִתְאֹם conj. (471)-adv.acc. (837) *for suddenly*
יָקוּם Qal impf. 3 m.s. (קוּם 877) *will rise*
אֵידָם n.m.s.-3 m.p. sf. (15) *disaster from them*
וּפִיד שְׁנֵיהֶם conj.-n.m.s. (810)-n.m. du.-3 m.p. sf. (1040) *and the ruin from them both*
מִי יוֹדֵעַ interr. (566)-Qal act.ptc. (יָדַע 393) *who knows*

24:23

גַּם־אֵלֶּה adv. (168)-demons.adj. c.p. (41) *these also*
לַחֲכָמִים prep.-def.art.-adj. m.p. (314) *to the wise*
הַכֵּר־פָּנִים Hi. inf.abs. (נָכַר I 647)-n.m.p. (815) *partiality*
בְּמִשְׁפָּט prep.-n.m.s. (1048) *in judging*
בַּל־טוֹב neg.-adj. m.s. (II 373) *is not good*

24:24

אֹמֵר לְרָשָׁע Qal act.ptc. (אָמַר 55)-prep.-adj. m.s. (957) *he who says to the wicked*
צַדִּיק אָתָּה adj. m.s. (843)-pers.pr. 2 m.s. paus. (61) *you are innocent*
יִקְּבֻהוּ עַמִּים Qal impf. 3 m.p.-3 m.s. sf. (קָבַב II 866)-n.m.p. (I 766) *will be cursed by peoples*
יִזְעָמוּהוּ לְאֻמִּים Qal impf. 3 m.p.-3 m.s. sf. (זָעַם 276)-n.m.p. (522) *abhorred by nations*

24:25

וְלַמּוֹכִיחִים conj.-prep.-def.art.-Hi. ptc. m.p. (יָכַח 406) *but those who rebuke*
יִנְעָם Qal impf. 3 m.s. paus. (נָעֵם I 653) *will have delight*
וַעֲלֵיהֶם תָּבוֹא conj.-prep.-3 m.p. sf.-Qal impf. 3 f.s. (בּוֹא 97) *and will come upon them*
בִּרְכַּת־טוֹב n.f.s. cstr. (139)-n.m.s. (III 375) *a good blessing*

24:26

שְׂפָתַיִם יִשָּׁק n.f. du. (973)-Qal impf. 3 m.s. paus. (נָשַׁק I 676) *he kisses the lips*
מֵשִׁיב דְּבָרִים Hi. ptc. (שׁוּב 996)-n.m.p. (182) *he who gives ... words*
נְכֹחִים adj. m.p. (647) *right*

24:27

הָכֵן בַּחוּץ Hi. impv. 2 m.s. (כּוּן I 465)-prep. -def.art.-n.m.s. (299) *prepare outside*
מְלַאכְתֶּךָ n.f.s.-2 m.s. paus. (521) *your work*
וְעַתְּדָהּ conj.-Pi. impv. 2 m.s.-3 f.s. sf. (עָתַד I 800) *and get it ready*
בַּשָּׂדֶה לָךְ prep.-def.art.-n.m.s. (961)-prep.-2 m.s. sf. paus. *for you in the field*
אַחַר adv. (29) *and after that*
וּבָנִיתָ בֵיתֶךָ conj.-Qal pf. 2 m.s. (בָּנָה 124) -n.m.s.-2 m.s. sf. (108) *build your house*

24:28

אַל־תְּהִי neg.-Qal impf. 2 m.s. apoc. (הָיָה 224) *be not*
עֵד־חִנָּם n.m.s. (729)-adv. (336) *a witness without cause*
בְּרֵעֶךָ prep.-n.m.s.-2 m.s. sf. (945) *against your neighbor*
וַהֲפִתִּיתָ conj.-Hi. pf. 2 m.s.? (פָּתָה 834) *and make wide*
בִּשְׂפָתֶיךָ prep.-n.f.p.-2 m.s. sf. (973) *with your lips*

24:29

אַל־תֹּאמַר neg.-Qal impf. 2 m.s. (אָמַר 55) *do not say*
כַּאֲשֶׁר עָשָׂה־לִי prep.-rel. (81)-Qal pf. 3 m.s. (I 793 עָשָׂה)-prep.-1 c.s. sf. *as he has done to me*
כֵּן אֶעֱשֶׂה־לּוֹ adv. (485)-Qal impf. 1 c.s. (עָשָׂה I 793)-prep.-3 m.s. sf. *thus I will do to him*
אָשִׁיב לָאִישׁ Hi. impf. 1 c.s. (שׁוּב 996)-prep. -def.art.-n.m.s. (35) *I will pay the man back*
כְּפָעֳלוֹ prep.-n.m.s.-3 m.s. sf. (821) *for what he has done*

24:30

עַל־שְׂדֵה אִישׁ־עָצֵל prep.-n.m.s. cstr. (961)-n.m.s. (35)-adj. m.s. (782) *by the field of a sluggard*
עָבַרְתִּי Qal pf. 1 c.s. (עָבַר 716) *I passed*
וְעַל־כֶּרֶם אָדָם conj.-prep.-n.m.s. cstr. (501)-n.m.s. (9) *and by the vineyard of a man*

חֲסַר־לֵב adj. m.s. cstr. (341)-n.m.s. (524) *without sense*

24:31

וְהִנֵּה conj.-interj. (243) *and lo*
עָלָה כֻלּוֹ Qal pf. 3 m.s. (עָלָה 748)-n.m.s.-3 m.s. sf. (481) *it was all overgrown*
קִמְּשֹׂנִים n.m. coll. (888) *with thorns*
כָּסּוּ פָנָיו Pu. pf. 3 c.p. (כָּסָה I 491)-n.m.p.-3 m.s. sf. (815) *and its face was covered*
חֲרֻלִּים n.m.p. (355) *with nettles*
וְגֶדֶר אֲבָנָיו conj.-n.m.s. cstr. (154)-n.f.p.-3 m.s. sf. (6) *and its stone wall*
נֶהֱרָסָה Ni. pf. 3 f.s. (הָרַס 248) *was broken down*

24:32

וָאֶחֱזֶה אָנֹכִי consec.-Qal impf. 1 c.s. (חָזָה 302)-pers.pr. 1 c.s. (59) *then I saw*
אָשִׁית לִבִּי Qal impf. 1 c.s. (שִׁית 1011)-n.m.s.-1 c.s. sf. (524) *and considered it*
רָאִיתִי Qal pf. 1 c.s. (רָאָה 906) *I looked*
לָקַחְתִּי מוּסָר Qal pf. 1 c.s. (לקח 542)-n.m.s. (416) *and received instruction*

24:33

מְעַט שֵׁנוֹת subst. cstr. (589)-n.f.p. (446) *a little sleep*
מְעַט תְּנוּמוֹת v.supra-n.f.p. (630) *a little slumber*
מְעַט חִבֻּק יָדַיִם v.supra-n.m.s. cstr. (287)-n.f. du. (388) *a little folding of the hands*
לִשְׁכָּב prep.-Qal inf.cstr. paus. (שָׁכַב 1011) *to rest*

24:34

וּבָא־מִתְהַלֵּךְ conj.-Qal pf. 3 m.s. (בּוֹא 97)-Hith. ptc. (הָלַךְ 229) *and will come marching*
רֵישֶׁךָ n.m.s.-2 m.s. sf. (930) *your poverty*
וּמַחְסֹרֶיךָ conj.-n.m.p.-2 m.s. sf. (341) *and your wants*
כְּאִישׁ מָגֵן prep.-n.m.s. cstr. (35)-n.m.s. (171) *like an armed man*

25:1

גַּם־אֵלֶּה adv. (168)-demons.adj. c.p. (41) *these also*
מִשְׁלֵי שְׁלֹמֹה n.m.p. cstr. (605)-pr.n. (1024) *proverbs of Solomon*
אֲשֶׁר הֶעְתִּיקוּ rel. (81)-Hi. pf. 3 c.p. (עָתַק 801) *which copied*
אַנְשֵׁי חִזְקִיָּה n.m.p. cstr. (35)-pr.n. (306) *the men of Hezekiah*

מֶלֶךְ־יְהוּדָה n.m.s. cstr. (I 572)-pr.n. (397) *king of Judah*

25:2

כְּבֹד אֱלֹהִים n.m.s. cstr. (II 458)-n.m.p. (43) *the glory of God*
הַסְתֵּר דָּבָר Hi. inf.cstr. (סָתַר 711)-n.m.s. (182) *to conceal things*
וּכְבֹד מְלָכִים conj.-v.supra-n.m.p. (I 572) *but the glory of kings*
חֲקֹר דָּבָר Qal inf.cstr. (חָקַר 350)-v.supra *to search things out*

25:3

שָׁמַיִם לָרוּם n.m. du. (1029)-prep.-def.art.-n.m.s. (927) *as the heavens for height*
וָאָרֶץ לָעֹמֶק conj.-n.f.s. (75)-prep.-def.art.-n.m.s. (771) *and the earth for depth*
וְלֵב מְלָכִים conj.-n.m.s. cstr. (524)-n.m.p. (I 572) *so the mind of kings*
אֵין חֵקֶר neg. (II 34)-n.m.s. (350) *is unsearchable*

25:4

הָגוֹ סִיגִים Qal inf.abs. (הָגָה II 212)-n.m.p. (691) *take away the dross*
מִכָּסֶף prep.-n.m.s. paus. (494) *from the silver*
וַיֵּצֵא consec.-Qal impf. 3 m.s. (יָצָא 422) *and there goes out*
לַצֹּרֵף prep.-def.art.-Qal act.ptc. (צָרַף 864) *for the smith*
כֶּלִי n.m.s. paus. (479) *a vessel*

25:5

הָגוֹ רָשָׁע Qal inf.abs. (הָגָה II 212)-adj. m.s. (957) *take away the wicked*
לִפְנֵי־מֶלֶךְ prep.-n.m.p. cstr. (815)-n.m.s. (I 572) *from the presence of the king*
וְיִכּוֹן conj.-Ni. impf. 3 m.s. (כּוּן I 465) *and will be established*
בַּצֶּדֶק prep.-def.art.-n.m.s. (841) *in righteousness*
כִּסְאוֹ n.m.s.-3 m.s. sf. (490) *his throne*

25:6

אַל־תִּתְהַדַּר neg.-Hith. impf. 2 m.s. (הָדַר 213) *do not put yourself forward*
לִפְנֵי־מֶלֶךְ prep.-n.m.p. cstr. (815)-n.m.s. (I 572) *in the king's presence*
וּבִמְקוֹם גְּדֹלִים conj.-prep.-n.m.s. cstr. (879)-adj. m.p. (152) *or in the place of the great*
אַל־תַּעֲמֹד neg.-Qal impf. 2 m.s. (עָמַד 763) *do not stand*

25:7

כִּי טוֹב conj. (471)-adj. m.s. (II 373) *for it is better*

אֲמָר־לְךָ Qal inf.cstr. (אָמַר 55)-prep.-2 m.s. sf. *to be told*

עֲלֵה הֵנָּה Qal impv. 2 m.s. (עָלָה 748)-adv. (I 244) *come up here*

מֵהַשְׁפִּילְךָ prep.-Hi. inf.cstr.-2 m.s. sf. (שָׁפֵל 1050) *than to be put lower*

לִפְנֵי נָדִיב prep.-n.m.p. cstr. (815)-adj. m.s. (622) *in the presence of the prince*

אֲשֶׁר רָאוּ עֵינֶיךָ rel. (81)-Qal pf. 3 c.p. (רָאָה 906)-n.f.p.-2 m.s. sf. (744) *what your eyes have seen*

25:8

אַל־תֵּצֵא לָרִב neg.-Qal impf. 2 m.s. (יָצָא 422)-prep.-Qal inf.cstr. (רִיב 936) *do not bring into court*

מַהֵר adv. (II 555) *hastily*

פֶּן מַה־תַּעֲשֶׂה conj. (814)-interr. (552)-Qal impf. 2 m.s. (עָשָׂה I 793) *lest what will you do*

בְּאַחֲרִיתָהּ prep.-n.f.s.-3 f.s. sf. (31) *in the end*

בְּהַכְלִים אֹתְךָ prep.-Hi. inf.cstr. (כָּלַם 483)-dir. obj.-2 m.s. sf. *when ... puts you to shame*

רֵעֶךָ n.m.s.-2 m.s. sf. (945) *your neighbor*

25:9

רִיבְךָ רִיב Qal inf.cstr.-2 m.s. sf. (רִיב 936)-n.m.s. (936) *argue your case*

אֶת־רֵעֶךָ prep. (II 85)-n.m.s.-2 m.s. sf. (945) *with your neighbor*

וְסוֹד אַחֵר conj.-n.m.s. cstr. (691)-adj. m.s. (I 29) *and another's secret*

אַל־תְּגָל neg.-Pi. impf. 2 m.s. paus. (גָּלָה 162) *do not disclose*

25:10

פֶּן־יְחַסֶּדְךָ conj. (814)-Pi. impf. 3 m.s.-2 m.s. sf. (II 340 חָסַד) *lest ... bring shame upon you*

שֹׁמֵעַ Qal act.ptc. (שָׁמַע 1033) *he who hears (you)*

וְדִבָּתְךָ conj.-n.f.s.-2 m.s. sf. (179) *and your ill repute*

לֹא תָשׁוּב neg.-Qal impf. 2 m.s. (שׁוּב 996) *have no end*

25:11

תַּפּוּחֵי זָהָב n.m.p. cstr. (656)-n.m.s. (262) *apples of gold*

בְּמַשְׂכִּיּוֹת כָּסֶף prep.-n.f.p. cstr. (967)-n.m.s. paus. (494) *in a setting of silver*

דָּבָר דָּבֻר n.m.s. (182)-Qal pass.ptc. (דָּבַר 180) *a word spoken*

עַל־אָפְנָיו prep.-n.m.p.-3 m.s. sf. (67) *fitly*

25:12

נֶזֶם זָהָב n.m.s. cstr. (634)-n.m.s. (262) *like a gold ring*

וַחֲלִי־כָתֶם conj.-n.m.s. cstr. 318)-n.m.s. paus. (508) *or an ornament of gold*

מוֹכִיחַ חָכָם Hi. ptc. (יָכַח 406)-adj. m.s. (314) *a wise reprover*

עַל־אֹזֶן שֹׁמָעַת prep.-n.f.s. (23)-Qal act.ptc. f.s. (1033 שָׁמַע) *to a listening ear*

25:13

כְּצִנַּת־שֶׁלֶג prep.-n.f.s. cstr. (II 856)-n.m.s. (1017) *like the cold of snow*

בְּיוֹם קָצִיר prep.-n.m.s. cstr. (398)-n.m.s. (894) *in the time of harvest*

צִיר נֶאֱמָן n.m.s. (II 851)-Ni. ptc. m.s. (אָמַן I 52) *a faithful messenger*

לְשֹׁלְחָיו prep.-Qal act.ptc. m.p.-3 m.s. sf. (שָׁלַח 1018) *to those who send him*

וְנֶפֶשׁ אֲדֹנָיו conj.-n.f.s. cstr. (659)-n.m.p.-3 m.s. sf. (10) *the spirit of his masters*

יָשִׁיב Hi. impf. 3 m.s. (שׁוּב 996) *he refeshes*

25:14

נְשִׂיאִים n.m.p. (II 672) *like clouds*

וְרוּחַ conj.-n.f.s. (924) *and wind*

וְגֶשֶׁם אָיִן conj.-n.m.s. (II 177)-neg. paus. (II 34) *without rain*

אִישׁ מִתְהַלֵּל n.m.s. (35)-Hith. ptc. (הָלַל II 237) *a man who boasts*

בְּמַתַּת־שָׁקֶר prep.-n.f.s. cstr. (682)-n.m.s. paus. (1055) *of a gift he does not give*

25:15

בְּאֹרֶךְ אַפַּיִם prep.-n.m.s. cstr. (73)-n.m. du. (I 60) *with patience*

יְפֻתֶּה קָצִין Pu. impf. 3 m.s. (פָּתָה 834)-n.m.s. (892) *a ruler may be persuaded*

וְלָשׁוֹן רַכָּה conj.-n.f.s. (546)-adj. f.s. (940) *and a soft tongue*

תִּשְׁבָּר־גָּרֶם Qal impf. 3 f.s. (שָׁבַר 990)-n.m.s. paus. (175) *will break a bone*

25:16

דְּבַשׁ מָצָאתָ n.m.s. (185)-Qal pf. 2 m.s. (מָצָא 592) *if you have found honey*

אֱכֹל דַּיֶּךָּ Qal impv. 2 m.s. (אָכַל 37)-subst.-2 m.s. sf. (191) *eat only enough for you*

פֶּן־תִּשְׂבָּעֶנּוּ conj. (814)-Qal impf. 2 m.s.-3 m.s. sf. (שָׂבַע 959) *lest you be sated with it*
וַהֲקֵאתוֹ conj.-Hi. pf. 2 m.s.-3 m.s. sf. (קִיא 883) *and vomit it*

25:17

הֹקַר רַגְלְךָ Hi. impv. 2 m.s. (יָקַר 429)-n.f.s.-2 m.s. sf. (919) *let your foot be seldom*
מִבֵּית רֵעֶךָ prep.-n.m.s. cstr. (108)-n.m.s.-2 m.s. sf. (945) *in your neighbor's house*
פֶּן־יִשְׂבָּעֲךָ conj. (814)-Qal impf. 3 m.s.-2 m.s. sf. (שָׂבַע 959) *lest he become weary of you*
וּשְׂנֵאֶךָ conj.-Qal pf. 3 m.s.-2 m.s. sf. (שָׂנֵא 971) *and hate you*

25:18

מֵפִיץ n.m.s. (807; rd. מַפֵּץ; LXX ῥόπαλον) *a scatterer*
וְחֶרֶב conj.-n.f.s. (352) *or a sword*
וְחֵץ שָׁנוּן conj.-n.m.s. (346)-Qal pass.ptc. (שָׁנַן 1041) *or a sharp arrow*
אִישׁ עֹנֶה n.m.s. (35)-Qal act.ptc. (עָנָה I 772) *a man who bears*
בְרֵעֵהוּ prep.-n.m.s.-3 m.s. sf. (945) *against his neighbor*
עֵד שָׁקֶר n.m.s. cstr. (729)-n.m.s. paus. (1055) *false witness*

25:19

שֵׁן רֹעָה n.f.s. (1042)-Qal act.ptc. f.s. (רָעַע II 949) *a bad tooth*
וְרֶגֶל מוּעָדֶת conj.-n.f.s. (919)-Pu. ptc. f.s. (מָעַד 588) *or a foot that slips*
מִבְטָח בּוֹגֵד n.m.s. (105)-Qal act.ptc. (בָּגַד 93) *trust in a faithless man*
בְּיוֹם צָרָה prep.-n.m.s. cstr. (398)-n.f.s. (865) *in time of trouble*

25:20

מַעֲדֶה בֶּגֶד Hi. ptc. (עָדָה I 723)-n.m.s. (93) *like one who takes off a garment*
בְּיוֹם קָרָה prep.-n.m.s. cstr. (398)-n.f.s. (903) *on a cold day*
חֹמֶץ n.m.s. (330) *like vinegar*
עַל־נָתֶר prep.-n.m.s. paus. (684) *on lye*
וְשָׁר בַּשִּׁרִים conj.-Qal act.ptc. (שִׁיר 1010)-prep.-def.art.-n.m.p. (1010) *he who sings songs*
עַל לֶב־רָע prep.-n.m.s. (524)-adj. m.s. (948) *to a heavy heart*

25:21

אִם־רָעֵב שֹׂנַאֲךָ hypoth.part. (49)-adj. m.s. (944)-Qal act.ptc. m.s.-2 m.s. sf. (שָׂנֵא 971) *if your enemy is hungry*
הַאֲכִלֵהוּ לָחֶם Hi. impv. 2 m.s.-3 m.s. sf. (אָכַל 37)-n.m.s. paus. (536) *give him bread to eat*
וְאִם־צָמֵא conj.-v.supra-adj. m.s. (854) *and if he is thirsty*
הַשְׁקֵהוּ מָיִם Hi. impv. 2 m.s.-3 m.s. sf. (שָׁקָה 1052)-n.m.p. paus. (565) *give him water to drink*

25:22

כִּי גֶחָלִים conj. (471)-n.f.p. (160) *for coals of fire*
אַתָּה חֹתֶה pers.pr. 2 m.s. (61)-Qal act.ptc. (חָתָה 367) *you will heap*
עַל־רֹאשׁוֹ prep.-n.m.s.-3 m.s. sf. (910) *on his head*
וַיהוה conj.-pr.n. (217) *and Yahweh*
יְשַׁלֶּם־לָךְ Pi. impf. 3 m.s. (שָׁלֵם 1023)-prep.-2 m.s. sf. paus. *will reward you*

25:23

רוּחַ צָפוֹן n.f.s. cstr. (924)-n.f.s. (I 860) *the north wind*
תְּחוֹלֵל גָּשֶׁם Polel impf. 3 f.s. (חוּל I 296)-n.m.s. paus. (II 177) *brings forth rain*
וּפָנִים נִזְעָמִים conj.-n.m.p. (815)-Ni. ptc. m.p. (276 זָעַם) *face stirred with indignation*
לְשׁוֹן סָתֶר n.f.s. cstr. (546)-n.m.s. paus. (712) *a backbiting tongue*

25:24

טוֹב שֶׁבֶת adj. m.s. (II 373)-Qal inf.cstr. (יָשַׁב 442) *it is better to live*
עַל־פִּנַּת־גָּג prep.-n.f.s. cstr. (819)-n.m.s. (150) *in a corner of the housetop*
מֵאֵשֶׁת מִדְוָנִים prep.-n.f.s. cstr. (61)-n.m.p. (I 193) *than with a contentious woman*
וּבֵית חָבֶר conj.-n.m.s. cstr. (108)-n.m.s. paus. (I 288) *in a house shared*

25:25

מַיִם קָרִים n.m.p. (565)-adj. m.p. (903) *like cold water*
עַל־נֶפֶשׁ עֲיֵפָה prep.-n.f.s. (659)-adj. f.s. (746) *to a thirsty soul*
וּשְׁמוּעָה טוֹבָה conj.-n.f.s. (1035)-adj. f.s. (II 373) *also good news*
מֵאֶרֶץ מֶרְחָק prep.-n.f.s. cstr. (75)-n.m.s. (935) *from a far country*

25:26

מַעְיָן נִרְפָּשׂ n.m.s. (745)–Ni. ptc. (רָפַס 952) *like a muddied spring*

וּמָקוֹר מָשְׁחָת conj.–n.m.s. (881)–Ho. ptc. (שָׁחַת 1007) *or a polluted fountain*

צַדִּיק adj. m.s. (843) *a righteous man*

מָט Qal act.ptc. (מוֹט 556) *who gives way*

לִפְנֵי־רָשָׁע prep.–n.m.p. cstr. (815)–adj. m.s. (957) *before the wicked*

25:27

אָכֹל דְּבַשׁ Qal inf.abs. (אָכַל 37)–n.m.s. (185) *eating honey*

הַרְבּוֹת Hi. inf.cstr. (רָבָה I 915) *much*

לֹא־טוֹב neg.–adj. m.s. (II 373) *it is not good*

וְחֵקֶר כְּבֹדָם conj.–n.m.s. cstr. (350)–n.m.s.–3 m.p. sf. (458) *searching out their glory*

כָּבוֹד n.m.s. (458) *is glory*

25:28

עִיר פְּרוּצָה n.f.s. (746)–Qal pass.ptc. f.s. (פָּרַץ I 829) *like a city broken into*

אֵין חוֹמָה neg. (II 34)–n.f.s. (327) *and left without walls*

אִישׁ אֲשֶׁר n.m.s. (35)–rel. (81) *a man*

אֵין מַעְצָר לְרוּחוֹ neg. (II 34)–n.m.s. (784)–prep. –n.f.s.–3 m.s. sf. (924) *without self control*

26:1

כַּשֶּׁלֶג prep.–def.art.–n.m.s. (1017) *like snow*

בַּקַּיִץ prep.–def.art.–n.m.s. (884) *in summer*

וְכַמָּטָר conj.–prep.–def.art.–n.m.s. (564) *or like rain*

בַּקָּצִיר prep.–def.art.–n.m.s. (894) *in harvest*

כֵּן לֹא־נָאוֶה adv. (485)–neg.–adj. m.s. (610) *so is not fitting*

לִכְסִיל prep.–n.m.s. (493) *for a fool*

כָּבוֹד n.m.s. (458) *honor*

26:2

כַּצִּפּוֹר prep.–def.art.–n.f.s. (861) *like a sparrow*

לָנוּד prep.–Qal inf.cstr. (נוּד 626) *in its flitting*

כַּדְּרוֹר prep.–def.art.–n.f.s. (II 204) *like a swallow*

לָעוּף prep.–Qal inf.cstr. (עוּף 733) *in its flying*

כֵּן קִלְלַת adv. (485)–n.f.s. cstr. (887) *so a curse*

חִנָּם adv. (336) *that is causeless*

לֹא תָבֹא neg.–Qal impf. 3 f.s. (בּוֹא 97) *does not alight*

26:3

שׁוֹט לַסּוּס n.m.s. (1002)–prep.–def.art.–n.m.s. (692) *a whip for the horse*

מֶתֶג לַחֲמוֹר n.m.s. (607)–prep.–def.art.–n.m.s. (331) *a bridle for the ass*

וְשֵׁבֶט conj.–n.m.s. (986) *and a rod*

לְגֵו כְּסִילִים prep.–n.m.s. cstr. (I 156)–n.m.p. (493) *for the back of fools*

26:4

אַל־תַּעַן neg.–Qal impf. 2 m.s. apoc. (עָנָה I 772) *answer not*

כְּסִיל n.m.s. (493) *a fool*

כְּאִוַּלְתּוֹ prep.–n.f.s.–3 m.s. sf. (17) *according to his folly*

פֶּן־תִּשְׁוֶה־לּוֹ conj. (814)–Qal impf. 2 m.s. (שָׁוָה I 1000)–prep.–3 m.s. sf. *lest you be like him*

גַם־אָתָּה adv. (168)–pers.pr. 2 m.s. paus. (61) *yourself*

26:5

עֲנֵה כְסִיל Qal impv. 2 m.s. (עָנָה I 772)–n.m.s. (493) *answer a fool*

כְּאִוַּלְתּוֹ prep.–n.f.s.–3 m.s. sf. (17) *according to his folly*

פֶּן־יִהְיֶה conj. (814)–Qal impf. 3 m.s. (הָיָה 224) *lest he be*

חָכָם adj. m.s. (314) *wise*

בְּעֵינָיו prep.–n.f.p.–3 m.s. sf. (744) *in his own eyes*

26:6

מְקַצֶּה רַגְלַיִם Pi. ptc. (קָצָה I 891)–n.f. du. (919) *cuts off his own feet*

חָמָס שֹׁתֶה n.m.s. (329)–Qal act.ptc. (שָׁתָה 1059) *drinks violence*

שֹׁלֵחַ דְּבָרִים Qal act.ptc. (שָׁלַח 1018)–n.m.p. (182) *he who sends a message*

בְּיַד־כְּסִיל prep.–n.f.s. cstr. (388)–n.m.s. (493) *by the hand of a fool*

26:7

דַּלְיוּ שֹׁקַיִם Qal pf. 3 c.p.? (דָּלָה 194; some rd. דַּלּוּ as Qal pf. 3 c.p. דָּלַל 195)–n.f. du. (1003) *legs, which hang useless*

מִפִּסֵּחַ prep.–adj. m.s. (820) *like a lame man's*

וּמָשָׁל conj.–n.m.s. (605) *is a proverb*

בְּפִי כְסִילִים prep.–n.m.s. cstr. (804)–n.m.p. (493) *in the mouth of fools*

26:8

כִּצְרוֹר אֶבֶן prep.–Qal inf.cstr. (צָרַר I 864)–n.f.s. (6) *like one who binds the stone*

בְּמַרְגֵּמָה prep.–n.f.s. (920) *in the sling*

כֵּן־נוֹתֵן adv. (485)-Qal act.ptc. (נָתַן 678) *so is he who gives*
לִכְסִיל prep.-n.m.s. (493) *to a fool*
כָּבוֹד n.m.s. (458) *honor*

26:9

חוֹחַ עָלָה n.m.s. (296)-Qal pf. 3 m.s. (748) *like a thorn that goes up*
בְיַד־שִׁכּוֹר prep.-n.f.s. cstr. (388)-adj. m.s. (1016) *into the hand of a drunkard*
וּמָשָׁל conj.-n.m.s. (605) *is a proverb*
בְּפִי כְסִילִים prep.-n.m.s. cstr. (804)-n.m.p. (493) *in the mouth of fools*

26:10

רַב adj. m.s. (I 912) *great (?)*
מְחוֹלֵל־כֹּל Polel ptc. (חול I 296)-n.m.s. (481) *who wounds everybody*
וְשֹׂכֵר כְּסִיל conj.-Qal act.ptc. (שָׂכַר 968)-n.m.s. (493) *is he who hires a fool*
וְשֹׂכֵר עֹבְרִים v.supra-Qal act.ptc. m.p. (עָבַר 716) *and hires ones passing*

26:11

כְּכֶלֶב prep.-n.m.s. (476) *like a dog*
שָׁב עַל־קֵאוֹ Qal act.ptc. (שׁוּב 996)-prep.-n.m.s. -3 m.s. sf. (883) *that returns to his vomit*
כְּסִיל n.m.s. (493) *is a fool*
שׁוֹנֶה Qal act.ptc. (שָׁנָה III 1040) *that repeats*
בְאִוַּלְתּוֹ prep.-n.f.s.-3 m.s. sf. (17) *his folly*

26:12

רָאִיתָ אִישׁ Qal pf. 2 m.s. (רָאָה 906)-n.m.s. (35) *do you see a man*
חָכָם בְּעֵינָיו adj. m.s. (314)-prep.-n.f. du.-3 m.s. sf. (744) *wise in his own eyes*
תִּקְוָה n.f.s. (876) *there is more hope*
לִכְסִיל prep.-n.m.s. (493) *for a fool*
מִמֶּנּוּ prep.-3 m.s. sf. *than for him*

26:13

אָמַר עָצֵל Qal pf. 3 m.s. (55)-adj. m.s. (782) *the sluggard says*
שַׁחַל בַּדָּרֶךְ n.m.s. (1006)-prep.-def.art.-n.m.s. paus. (202) *there is a lion in the road*
אֲרִי n.m.s. (71) *there is a lion*
בֵּין הָרְחֹבוֹת prep. (107)-def.art.-n.f.p. (932) *in the streets*

26:14

הַדֶּלֶת תִּסּוֹב def.art.-n.f.s. (195)-Qal impf. 3 f.s. (685 סָבַב) *as a door turns*
עַל־צִירָהּ prep.-n.m.s.-3 f.s. sf. (III 852) *on its hinges*
וְעָצֵל conj.-adj. m.s. (782) *so does a sluggard*
עַל־מִטָּתוֹ prep.-n.f.s.-3 m.s. sf. (641) *on his bed*

26:15

טָמַן עָצֵל Qal pf. 3 m.s. (380)-adj. m.s. (782) *the sluggard buries*
יָדוֹ n.f.s.-3 m.s. sf. (388) *his hand*
בַּצַּלָּחַת prep.-def.art.-n.f.s. (852) *in the dish*
נִלְאָה Ni. pf. 3 m.s. (לָאָה 521) *it wears him out*
לַהֲשִׁיבָהּ prep.-Hi. inf.cstr.-3 f.s. sf. (שׁוּב 996) *to bring it back*
אֶל־פִּיו prep.-n.m.s.-3 m.s. sf. (804) *to his mouth*

26:16

חָכָם עָצֵל adj. m.s. (314)-adj. m.s. (782) *the sluggard is wiser*
בְּעֵינָיו prep.-n.f. du.-3 m.s. sf. (744) *in his own eyes*
מִשִּׁבְעָה prep.-n.f.s. (I 987) *than seven men*
מְשִׁיבֵי טָעַם Hi. ptc. m.p. cstr. (שׁוּב 996)-n.m.s. paus. (1094) *who can answer discreetly*

26:17

מַחֲזִיק Hi. ptc. (חָזַק 304) *is like one who takes*
בְּאָזְנֵי־כָלֶב prep.-n.f. du. cstr. (23)-n.m.s. paus. (476) *by the ears of a dog*
עֹבֵר Qal act.ptc. (716) *passing*
מִתְעַבֵּר Hith. ptc. (עָבַר 720) *he who becomes furious*
עַל־רִיב לֹּא־לוֹ prep.-n.m.s. (936)-neg.-prep.-3 m.s. sf. *in a quarrel not his own*

26:18

כְּמִתְלַהְלֵהַּ prep.-Hithpalpel ptc. (לָהַהּ 529) *like a madman*
הַיֹּרֶה זִקִּים def.art.-Qal ptc. (יָרָה 434)-n.m.p. (I 278) *who throws firebrands*
חִצִּים n.m.p. (346) *arrows*
וָמָוֶת conj.-n.m.s. (560) *and death*

26:19

כֵּן־אִישׁ adv. (485)-n.m.s. (35) *so is the man*
רִמָּה אֶת־רֵעֵהוּ Pi. pf. 3 m.s. (רָמָה II 941)-dir. obj.-n.m.s.-3 m.s. sf. (945) *who deceives his neighbor*
וְאָמַר conj.-Qal pf. 3 m.s. (55) *and says*
הֲלֹא־מְשַׂחֵק אָנִי interr.-neg.-Pi. ptc. (שָׂחַק 965)-pers.pr. 1 c.s. paus. (58) *I am only joking*

26:20

בְּאֶפֶס עֵצִים prep.-n.m.s. (67)-n.m.p. (781) *for lack of wood*

תִּכְבֶּה־אֵשׁ Qal impf. 3 f.s. (כָּבָה 459)-n.f.s. (77) *the fire goes out*

וּבְאֵין נִרְגָּן conj.-prep.-neg. (II 34)-Ni. ptc. (רָגַן 920) *and where there is no whisperer*

יִשְׁתֹּק מָדוֹן Qal impf. 3 m.s. (שָׁתַק 1060)-n.m.s. (I 193) *quarreling ceases*

26:21

פֶּחָם n.m.s. (809) *as charcoal*

לְגֶחָלִים prep.-n.f.p. (160) *to hot embers*

וְעֵצִים לְאֵשׁ conj.-n.m.p. (781)-prep.-n.f.s. (77) *and wood to fire*

וְאִישׁ מִדְיָנִים conj.-n.m.s. cstr. (35)-n.m.p. (I 193) *so is a quarrelsome man*

לְחַרְחַר־רִיב prep.-Pilpel inf.cstr. (חָרַר I 359) -n.m.s. (936) *for kindling strife*

26:22

דִּבְרֵי נִרְגָּן n.m.p. cstr. (182)-Ni. ptc. (רָגַן 920) *the words of a whisperer*

כְּמִתְלַהֲמִים prep.-Hithpa'el ptc. m.p. (לָהַם 529) *like delicious morsels*

וְהֵם יָרְדוּ conj.-pers.pr. 3 m.p. (241)-Qal pf. 3 c.p. (יָרַד 432) *they go down*

חַדְרֵי־בָטֶן n.m.p. cstr. (293)-n.f.s. paus. (105) *into the inner parts of the body*

26:23

כֶּסֶף סִיגִים n.m.s. cstr. (494)-n.m.p. (691) *silver of dross*

מְצֻפֶּה Pu. ptc. (צָפָה II 860) *covering*

עַל־חָרֶשׂ prep.-n.m.s. paus. (360) *an earthen vessel*

שְׂפָתַיִם דֹּלְקִים n.f. du. (973)-Qal act.ptc. m.p. (196 דָּלַק) *burning lips*

וְלֶב־רָע n.m.s. (524)-adj. m.s. (I 948) *with an evil heart*

26:24

בִּשְׂפָתָו prep.-n.f. du.-3 m.s. sf. (973) *with his lips*

יִנָּכֵר Ni. impf. 3 m.s. (נָכַר 649) *dissembles*

שׂוֹנֵא Qal act.ptc. (שָׂנֵא 971) *he who hates*

וּבְקִרְבּוֹ conj.-prep.-n.m.s.-3 m.s. sf. (899) *and in his heart*

יָשִׁית מִרְמָה Qal impf. 3 m.s. (שִׁית 1011)-n.f.s. (941) *harbors deceit*

26:25

כִּי־יְחַנֵּן קוֹלוֹ conj. (471)-Pi. impf. 3 m.s. (חָנַן I 335)-n.m.s.-3 m.s. sf. (876) *when he speaks graciously*

אַל־תַּאֲמֶן־בּוֹ neg.-Hi. impf. 2 m.s. (אָמַן 52) -prep.-3 m.s. sf. *believe him not*

כִּי שֶׁבַע תּוֹעֵבוֹת conj. (471)-num. (I 987)-n.f.p. (1072) *for there are seven abominations*

בְּלִבּוֹ prep.-n.m.s.-3 m.s. sf. (524) *in his heart*

26:26

תִּכַּסֶּה שִׂנְאָה Hith. impf. 3 f.s. (כָּסָה I 491; LXX ὁ κρύπτων)-n.f.s. (971) *though his hatred be covered*

בְּמַשָּׁאוֹן prep.-n.m.s. (674) *with guile*

תִּגָּלֶה רָעָתוֹ Ni. impf. 3 f.s. (גָּלָה 162)-n.f.s.-3 m.s. sf. (949) *his wickedness will be exposed*

בְקָהָל prep.-n.m.s. (874) *in the assembly*

26:27

כֹּרֶה־שַׁחַת Qal act.ptc. (כָּרָה I 500)-n.f.s. (1001) *he who digs a pit*

בָּהּ יִפֹּל prep.-3 f.s. sf.-Qal impf. 3 m.s. (נָפַל 656) *will fall into it*

וְגֹלֵל אֶבֶן conj.-Qal act.ptc. (גָּלַל II 164)-n.f.s. (6) *and he who starts a stone rolling*

אֵלָיו תָּשׁוּב prep.-3 m.s. sf.-Qal impf. 3 f.s. (שׁוּב 996) *it will come back upon him*

26:28

לְשׁוֹן־שֶׁקֶר n.f.s. cstr. (546)-n.m.s. (1055) *a lying tongue*

יִשְׂנָא Qal impf. 3 m.s. (שָׂנֵא 971) *hates*

דַּכָּיו adj. m.p.-3 m.s. sf. (194) *its victims*

וּפֶה חָלָק conj.-n.m.s. (804)-adj. m.s. (325) *and a flattering mouth*

יַעֲשֶׂה מִדְחֶה Qal impf. 3 m.s. (עָשָׂה I 793) -n.m.s. (191) *works ruin*

27:1

אַל־תִּתְהַלֵּל neg.-Hith. impf. 2 m.s. (הָלַל II 237) *do not boast*

בְּיוֹם מָחָר prep.-n.m.s. (398)-n.m.s. (563) *about tomorrow*

כִּי לֹא־תֵדַע conj. (471)-neg.-Qal impf. 2 m.s. (393 יָדַע) *for you do not know*

מַה־יֵּלֶד יוֹם interr. (552)-Qal impf. 3 m.s. (יָלַד 408)-n.m.s. (398) *what a day may bring forth*

27:2

יְהַלֶּלְךָ זָר Pi. impf. 3 m.s.-2 m.s. sf. (הָלַל II 237)-Qal act.ptc. (זוּר I 266) *let another praise you*

וְלֹא־פִיךָ conj.-neg.-n.m.s.-2 m.s. sf. (804) *and not your own mouth*

נָכְרִי adj. m.s. (648) *a stranger*

וְאַל־שְׂפָתֶיךָ conj.-neg.-n.f. du.-2 m.s. sf. (973) *and not your own lips*

27:3

כֹּבֶד־אֶבֶן n.m.s. (458)-n.f.s. (6) *a stone is heavy*

וְנֵטֶל הַחוֹל conj.-n.m.s. (642)-def.art.-n.m.s. (297) *and sand is weighty*

וְכַעַס אֱוִיל conj.-n.m.s. cstr. (495)-adj. m.s. (17) *but a fool's provocation*

כָּבֵד adj. m.s. (458) *is heavier*

מִשְּׁנֵיהֶם prep.-num.-3 m.p. sf. (1040) *than both*

27:4

אַכְזְרִיּוּת חֵמָה n.f.s. (470)-n.f.s. (404) *wrath is cruel*

וְשֶׁטֶף אָף conj.-n.m.s. cstr. (1009)-n.m.s. paus. (I 60) *a flood of anger*

וּמִי יַעֲמֹד conj.-interr. (566)-Qal impf. 3 m.s. (763 עָמַד) *but who can stand*

לִפְנֵי קִנְאָה prep.-n.m.p. cstr. (815)-n.f.s. (888) *before jealousy*

27:5

טוֹבָה adj. f.s. (II 373) *better is*

תּוֹכַחַת מְגֻלָּה n.f.s. (407)-Pu. ptc. (גָּלָה 162) *open rebuke*

מֵאַהֲבָה מְסֻתָּרֶת prep.-n.f.s. (13)-Pu. ptc. f.s. (711 סָתַר) *than hidden love*

27:6

נֶאֱמָנִים Ni. ptc. m.p. (אָמַן 52) *faithful*

פִּצְעֵי אוֹהֵב n.m.p. cstr. (822)-Qal act.ptc. (אָהַב 12) *the wounds of a friend*

וְנַעְתָּרוֹת conj.-Ni. ptc. f.p. (עָתַר II 801) *profuse*

נְשִׁיקוֹת שׂוֹנֵא n.f.p. cstr. (676)-Qal act.ptc. (שָׂנֵא 971) *the kisses of an enemy*

27:7

נֶפֶשׁ שְׂבֵעָה n.f.s. (659)-adj. f.s. (960) *he who is sated*

תָּבוּס נֹפֶת Qal impf. 3 f.s. (בּוּס 100)-n.m.s. (661) *loathes honey*

וְנֶפֶשׁ רְעֵבָה conj.-v.supra-adj. f.s. (944) *but to one who is hungry*

כָּל־מַר מָתוֹק n.m.s. cstr. (481)-adj. m.s. (I 600) -adj. m.s. (608) *everything bitter is sweet*

27:8

כְּצִפּוֹר prep.-n.f.s. (861) *like a bird*

נוֹדֶדֶת Qal act.ptc. f.s. (נָדַד I 622) *that strays*

מִן־קִנָּהּ prep.-n.m.s.-3 f.s. sf. (890) *from its nest*

כֵּן־אִישׁ adv. (485)-n.m.s. (35) *so is a man*

נוֹדֵד Qal act.ptc. (נָדַד I 622) *who strays*

מִמְּקוֹמוֹ prep.-n.m.s.-3 m.s. sf. (879) *from his home*

27:9

שֶׁמֶן וּקְטֹרֶת n.m.p. (1032)-conj.-n.f.s. (882) *oil and perfume*

יְשַׂמַּח־לֵב Pi. impf. 3 m.s. (שָׂמַח 970)-n.m.s. (524) *make the heart glad*

וּמֶתֶק רֵעֵהוּ conj.-n.m.s. cstr. (608)-n.m.s.-3 m.s. sf. (945) *the sweetness of his friend*

מֵעֲצַת־נָפֶשׁ prep.-n.f.s. cstr. (420)-n.f.s. paus. (659) *from hearty counsel*

27:10

רֵעֲךָ n.m.s.-2 m.s. sf. (945) *your friend*

וְרֵעַ אָבִיךָ conj.-n.m.s. cstr. (946)-n.m.s.-2 m.s. sf. (3) *and your father's friend*

אַל־תַּעֲזֹב neg.-Qal impf. 2 m.s. (עָזַב I 736) *do not forsake*

וּבֵית אָחִיךָ conj.-n.m.s. cstr. (108)-n.m.s.-2 m.s. sf. (26) *and to your brother's house*

אַל־תָּבוֹא neg.-Qal impf. 2 m.s. (בּוֹא 97) *do not go*

בְּיוֹם אֵידֶךָ prep.-n.m.s. cstr. (398)-n.m.s.-2 m.s. sf. (15) *in the day of your calamity*

טוֹב שָׁכֵן adj. m.s. (II 373)-adj. m.s. (1015) *better is a neighbor*

קָרוֹב adj. m.s. (898) *who is near*

מֵאָח prep.-n.m.s. (26) *than a brother*

רָחוֹק adj. m.s. (935) *who is far away*

27:11

חֲכַם בְּנִי Qal impv. 2 m.s. (חָכַם 314)-n.m.s.-1 c.s. sf. (119) *be wise, my son,*

וְשַׂמַּח לִבִּי conj.-Pi. impv. 2 m.s. (שָׂמַח 970) -n.m.s.-1 c.s. sf. (524) *and make my heart glad*

וְאָשִׁיבָה conj.-Hi. impf. 1 c.s.-coh.he (שׁוּב 996) *that I may answer*

חֹרְפִי Qal act.ptc.-1 c.s. sf. (חָרַף 357) *him who reproaches me*

דָבָר n.m.s. (182) *(with a word)*

27:12

עָרוּם adj. m.s. (791) *a prudent man*

רָאָה רָעָה Qal pf. 3 m.s. (906)–n.f.s. (949) *sees danger*

נִסְתָּר Ni. ptc. (סָתַר 711) *and hides himself*

פְּתָאִים adj. m.p. (834; GK 93x) *but the simple*

עָבְרוּ Qal pf. 3 c.p. (עָבַר 716) *go on*

נֶעֱנָשׁוּ Ni. pf. 3 c.p. (עָנַשׁ 778) *and suffer for it*

27:13

קַח־בִּגְדוֹ Qal impv. 2 m.s. (לָקַח 542)–n.m.s.–3 m.s. sf. (93) *take a man's garment*

כִּי־עָרַב זָר conj. (471)–Qal pf. 3 m.s. (עָרַב II 786)–Qal act.ptc. (זוּר I 266) *when he has given surety for a stranger*

וּבְעַד נָכְרִיָּה conj.–prep. (126)–adj. f.s. (648) *and on behalf of a foreign woman*

חַבְלֵהוּ Qal impv. 2 m.s.–3 m.s. sf. (חָבַל I 286) *hold him in pledge*

27:14

מְבָרֵךְ רֵעֵהוּ Pi. ptc. (בָּרַךְ 138)–n.m.s.–3 m.s. sf. (945) *he who blesses his neighbor*

בְּקוֹל גָּדוֹל prep.–n.m.s. (876)–adj. m.s. (152) *with a loud voice*

בַּבֹּקֶר הַשְׁכֵּים prep.–def.art.–n.m.s. (133)–Hi. inf.abs. (שָׁכַם 1014) *rising early in the morning*

קְלָלָה n.f.s. (887) *as cursing*

תֵּחָשֶׁב לוֹ Ni. impf. 3 f.s. (חָשַׁב 362)–prep.–3 m.s. sf. *will be counted*

27:15

דֶּלֶף טוֹרֵד n.m.s. (196)–Qal act.ptc. (טָרַד 382) *a continual dripping*

בְּיוֹם סַגְרִיר prep.–n.m.s. cstr. (398)–n.m.s. (690) *on a rainy day*

וְאֵשֶׁת מִדְוָנִים conj.–n.f.s. cstr. (61)–n.m.p. (I 193) *and a contentious woman*

נִשְׁתָּוָה Nithpael pf. 3 f.s. (שָׁוָה I 1000; GK 75x) *are alike*

27:16

צֹפְנֶיהָ Qal act.ptc. m.p.–3 f.s. sf. (צָפַן 860) *to restrain her*

צָפַן־רוּחַ Qal pf. 3 m.s. (860)–n.f.s. (924) *is to restrain the wind*

וְשֶׁמֶן יְמִינוֹ conj.–n.m.s. (1032)–n.f.s.–3 m.s. sf. (411) *oil in his right hand*

יִקְרָא Qal impf. 3 m.s. (קָרָא I 894) *he will call for* (a corrupt verse; LXX βορέας σκληρὸς ἄνεμος, ὀνόματι δὲ ἐπιδέξιος καλεῖται)

27:17

בַּרְזֶל בְּבַרְזֶל יָחַד n.m.s. (137)–prep.–v.supra –Qal impf. 3 m.s. apoc. (חָדָה I 292) *iron sharpens iron*

וְאִישׁ יַחַד conj.–n.m.s. (35)–Hi. impf. 3 m.s. apoc. (חָדָה I 292) *and one man sharpens*

פְּנֵי־רֵעֵהוּ n.m.p. cstr. (815)–n.m.s.–3 m.s. sf. (945) *another*

27:18

נֹצֵר תְּאֵנָה Qal act.ptc. (נָצַר 665)–n.f.s. (1061) *he who tends a fig tree*

יֹאכַל פִּרְיָהּ Qal impf. 3 m.s. (אָכַל 37)–n.m.s.–3 f.s. sf. (826) *will eat its fruit*

וְשֹׁמֵר אֲדֹנָיו conj.–Qal act.ptc. (שָׁמַר 1036) –n.m.p.–3 m.s. sf. (10) *and he who guards his master*

יְכֻבָּד Pu. impf. 3 m.s. paus. (כָּבֵד 457) *will be honored*

27:19

כַּמַּיִם prep.–def.art.–n.m.p. (565) *as in water*

הַפָּנִים לַפָּנִים def.art.–n.m.p. (815)–prep. –def.art.–v.supra *face answers to face*

כֵּן לֵב־הָאָדָם adv. (485)–n.m.s. cstr. (524)–def. art.–n.m.s. (9) *so the mind of man*

לָאָדָם prep.–def.art.–n.m.s. (9) *reflects the man*

27:20

שְׁאוֹל וַאֲבַדֹּה n.f.s. (982)–conj.–n.f.s. (2; אֲבַדּוֹן) *Sheol and Abaddon*

לֹא תִשְׂבַּעְנָה neg.–Qal impf. 3 f.p. (שָׂבַע 959) *are never satisfied*

וְעֵינֵי הָאָדָם conj.–n.f.p. cstr. (744)–def.art.–n.m.s. (9) *and the eyes of man*

לֹא תִשְׂבַּעְנָה v.supra–v.supra *are never satisfied*

27:21

מַצְרֵף n.m.s. (864) *the crucible*

לַכֶּסֶף prep.–def.art.–n.m.s. (494) *for silver*

וְכוּר conj.–n.m.s. (468) *and the furnace*

לַזָּהָב prep.–def.art.–n.m.s. (262) *for gold*

וְאִישׁ conj.–n.m.s. (35) *and a man*

לְפִי מַהֲלָלוֹ prep.–n.m.s. cstr. (804)–n.m.s.–3 m.s. sf. (239) *is judged by his praise*

27:22

אִם תִּכְתּוֹשׁ־אֶת־הָאֱוִיל hypoth.part. (49)–Qal impf. 2 m.s. (כָּתַשׁ 509)–dir.obj.–def.art.–adj. m.s. (17) *crush a fool*

בַּמַּכְתֵּשׁ prep.–def.art.–n.m.s. (509) *in a mortar*

בְּתוֹךְ הָרִיפוֹת prep.–n.m.s. cstr. (1063)–def.art. –n.f.p. (937) *along with crushed grain*

בַּעֱלִי prep.–def.art.–n.m.s. (750) *with a pestle*

לֹא־תָסוּר neg.–Qal impf. 3 f.s. (סוּר 693) *yet will not depart*

מֵעָלָיו prep.–prep.–3 m.s. sf. *from him*

אִוַּלְתּוֹ n.f.s.–3 m.s. sf. (17) *his folly*

27:23

יָדֹעַ תֵּדַע Qal inf.abs. (יָדַע 393)–Qal impf. 2 m.s. (יָדַע 393) *know well*

פְּנֵי צֹאנֶךָ n.m.p. cstr. (815)–n.f.s.–2 m.s. sf. (838) *the condition of your flocks*

שִׁית לִבְּךָ Qal impv. 2 m.s. (שִׁית 1011)–n.m.s.–2 m.s. sf. (524) *give attention*

לַעֲדָרִים prep.–def.art.–n.m.p. (727) *to the herds*

27:24

כִּי לֹא לְעוֹלָם conj. (471)–neg.–prep.–n.m.s. (761) *for not for ever*

חֹסֶן n.m.s. (340) *riches*

וְאִם־נֵזֶר conj.–hypoth.part. (49)–n.m.s. (634) *and a crown*

לְדוֹר דוֹר prep.–n.m.s. (189)–conj.–v.supra *to all generations*

27:25

גָּלָה חָצִיר Qal pf. 3 m.s. (162)–n.m.s. (II 348) *when grass is gone*

וְנִרְאָה־דֶשֶׁא conj.–Ni. pf. 3 m.s. (רָאָה 906)–n.m.s. (206) *and the new growth appears*

וְנֶאֶסְפוּ conj.–Ni. pf. 3 c.p. (אָסַף 62) *and is gathered*

עִשְּׂבוֹת הָרִים n.m.p. cstr. (793)–n.m.p. (249) *the herbage of the mountains*

27:26

כְּבָשִׂים n.m.p. (461) *lambs*

לִלְבוּשֶׁךָ prep.–n.m.s.–2 m.s. sf. (528) *for your clothing*

וּמְחִיר שָׂדֶה conj.–n.m.s. cstr. (I 564)–n.m.s. (961) *and the price of a field*

עַתּוּדִים n.m.p. (800) *goats*

27:27

וְדֵי חֲלֵב עִזִּים conj.–subst. cstr. (191)–n.m.s. cstr. (316)–n.f.p. (777) *there will be enough goats' milk*

לְלַחְמְךָ prep.–n.m.s.–2 m.s. sf. (536) *for your food*

לְלֶחֶם בֵּיתֶךָ conj.–n.m.s. cstr. (536)–n.m.s.–2 m.s. sf. (108) *for the food of your household*

וְחַיִּים conj.–n.m.p. (313) *and life*

לְנַעֲרוֹתֶיךָ prep.–n.f.p.–2 m.s. sf. (655) *for your maidens*

28:1

נָסוּ Qal pf. 3 c.p. (נוּס 630) *flee*

וְאֵין רֹדֵף conj.–neg. (II 34)–Qal act.ptc. (רָדַף 922) *when no one pursues*

רָשָׁע adj. m.s. (957) *the wicked*

וְצַדִּיקִים conj.–adj. m.p. (843) *but the righteous*

כִּכְפִיר prep.–n.m.s. (498) *as a lion*

יִבְטָח Qal impf. 3 m.s. (בָּטַח 105 II) *are bold*

28:2

בְּפֶשַׁע אֶרֶץ prep.–n.m.s. cstr. (833)–n.f.s. (75) *when a land transgresses*

רַבִּים שָׂרֶיהָ adj. m.p. (I 912)–n.m.p.–3 f.s. sf. (978) *it has many rulers*

וּבְאָדָם conj.–prep.–n.m.s. (9) *but with men*

מֵבִין יֹדֵעַ Hi. ptc. (בִּין 106)–Qal act.ptc. (יָדַע 393) *understanding and knowledge*

כֵּן יַאֲרִיךְ adv. (485)–Hi. impf. 3 m.s. (אָרַךְ 73) *thus it will long continue*

28:3

גֶּבֶר רָשׁ n.m.s. (149)–Qal act.ptc. (רוּשׁ 930) *a poor man*

וְעֹשֵׁק דַּלִּים conj.–Qal act.ptc. (עָשַׁק 798)–adj. m.p. (195) *who oppresses the poor*

מָטָר סֹחֵף n.m.s. (564)–Qal act.ptc. (סָחַף 695) *a beating rain*

וְאֵין לָחֶם conj.–neg. (II 34)–n.m.s. paus. (536) *that leaves no food*

28:4

עֹזְבֵי תוֹרָה Qal act.ptc. m.p. cstr. (עָזַב I 736) –n.f.s. (435) *those who forsake the law*

יְהַלְלוּ רָשָׁע Pi. impf. 3 m.p. (הָלַל II 237)–adj. m.s. (957) *praise the wicked*

וְשֹׁמְרֵי תוֹרָה conj.–Qal act.ptc. m.p. cstr. (שָׁמַר 1036)–v.supra *but those who keep the law*

יִתְגָּרוּ בָם Hith. impf. 3 m.p. (גָּרָה 173)–prep.–3 m.p. sf. *are at strife with them*

28:5

אַנְשֵׁי־רָע n.m.p. cstr. (36)–n.m.s. (948) *evil men*

לֹא־יָבִינוּ neg.–Qal impf. 3 m.p. (בִּין 106) *do not understand*

מִשְׁפָּט n.m.s. (1048) *justice*

וּמְבַקְשֵׁי יהוה conj.–Pi. ptc. m.p. cstr. (בָּקַשׁ 134)–pr.n. (217) *but those who seek Yahweh*

יָבִינוּ כֹל v.supra–n.m.s. (481) *understand it completely*

28:6

טוֹב־רָשׁ adj. m.s. (II 373)–Qal act.ptc. (רוּשׁ 930) *better is a poor man*

הוֹלֵךְ בְּתֻמּוֹ Qal act.ptc. (הָלַךְ 229)–prep.–n.m.s.–3 m.s. sf. (1070) *who walks in his integrity*

מֵעִקֵּשׁ דְּרָכַיִם prep.–adj. m.s. cstr. (786)–n.m. du. (202) *than ... who is perverse in his ways*

וְהוּא עָשִׁיר conj.–pers.pr. 3 m.s. (214)–adj. m.s. (799) *and he is rich*

28:7

נוֹצֵר תּוֹרָה Qal act.ptc. (נָצַר 665)–n.f.s. (435) *he who keeps the law*

בֵּן מֵבִין n.m.s. (119)–Hi. ptc. (בִּין 106) *is a wise son*

וְרֹעֶה זוֹלְלִים conj.–Qal act.ptc. (רָעָה II 945)–Qal act.ptc. m.p. (זָלַל II 272) *but a companion of gluttons*

יַכְלִים אָבִיו Hi. impf. 3 m.s. (כָּלַם 483)–n.m.s.–3 m.s. sf. (3) *shames his father*

28:8

מַרְבֶּה הוֹנוֹ Hi. ptc. (רָבָה I 915)–n.m.s.–3 m.s. sf. (223) *he who augments his wealth*

בְּנֶשֶׁךְ prep.–n.m.s. (675) *by interest*

וּבְתַרְבִּית conj.–prep.–n.f.s. (916) *and increase*

לְחוֹנֵן דַּלִּים prep.–Qal act.ptc. (חָנַן I 335)–adj. m.p. (195) *for him who is kind to the poor*

יִקְבְּצֶנּוּ Qal impf. 3 m.s.–3 m.s. sf. (קָבַץ 867) *gathers it*

28:9

מֵסִיר אָזְנוֹ Hi. ptc. (סוּר 693)–n.f.s.–3 m.s. sf. (23) *if one turns away his ear*

מִשְּׁמֹעַ תּוֹרָה prep.–Qal inf.cstr. (1033)–n.f.s. (435) *from hearing the law*

גַּם־תְּפִלָּתוֹ adv. (168)–n.f.s.–3 m.s. sf. (813) *even his prayer*

תּוֹעֵבָה n.f.s. (1072) *is an abomination*

28:10

מַשְׁגֶּה יְשָׁרִים Hi. ptc. (שָׁגָה 993)–adj. m.p. (449) *he who misleads the upright*

בְּדֶרֶךְ רָע prep.–n.m.s. (202)–adj. m.s. (I 948) *into an evil way*

בִּשְׁחוּתוֹ prep.–n.f.s.–3 m.s. sf. (1005) *into his own pit*

הוּא־יִפּוֹל pers.pr. 3 m.s. (214)–Qal impf. 3 m.s. (נָפַל 656) *he will fall*

וּתְמִימִים conj.–adj. m.p. (1071) *but the blameless*

יִנְחֲלוּ־טוֹב Qal impf. 3 m.p. (נָחַל 635)–n.m.s. (III 375) *will have a goodly inheritance*

28:11

חָכָם בְּעֵינָיו adj. m.s. (314)–prep.–nf. du.–3 m.s. sf. (744) *is wise in his own eyes*

אִישׁ עָשִׁיר n.m.s. (35)–adj. m.s. (799) *a rich man*

וְדַל מֵבִין conj.–adj. m.s. (195)–Hi. ptc. (בִּין 106) *but a poor man who has understanding*

יַחְקְרֶנּוּ Qal impf. 3 m.s.–3 m.s. sf. (חָקַר 350) *will find him out*

28:12

בַּעֲלֹץ צַדִּיקִים prep.–Qal inf.cstr. (עָלַץ 763)–adj. m.p. (843) *when the righteous triumph*

רַבָּה תִפְאָרֶת adj. f.s. (I 912)–n.f.s. paus. (802) *great glory*

וּבְקוּם רְשָׁעִים conj.–prep.–Qal inf.cstr. (קוּם 877)–adj. m.p. (957) *but when the wicked rise*

יְחֻפַּשׂ אָדָם Pu. impf. 3 m.s. (חָפַשׂ 344)–n.m.s. (9) *men hide themselves*

28:13

מְכַסֶּה פְשָׁעָיו Pi. ptc. (כָּסָה 491)–n.m.p.–3 m.s. sf. (833) *he who conceals his transgressions*

לֹא יַצְלִיחַ neg.–Hi. impf. 3 m.s. (צָלַח II 852) *will not prosper*

וּמוֹדֶה וְעֹזֵב conj.–Hi. ptc. (יָדָה 392)–conj.–Qal act.ptc. (I 736) *but he who confesses and forsakes them*

יְרֻחָם Pu. impf. 3 m.s. (רָחַם 933) *will obtain mercy*

28:14

אַשְׁרֵי אָדָם n.m.p. cstr. (80)–n.m.s. (9) *blessed is the man*

מְפַחֵד תָּמִיד Pi. ptc. (פָּחַד 808)–n.m.s. (556) *who fears always*

וּמַקְשֶׁה לִבּוֹ conj.–Hi. ptc. (קָשָׁה 904)–n.m.s.–3 m.s. sf. (524) *but he who hardens his heart*

יִפּוֹל בְּרָעָה Qal impf. 3 m.s. (נָפַל 656)–prep.–n.f.s. (949) *will fall into calamity*

28:15

אֲרִי־נֹהֵם n.m.s. (71)-Qal act.ptc. (נָהַם 625) *like a roaring lion*

וְדֹב שׁוֹקֵק conj.-n.m.s. (179)-Qal act.ptc. (שָׁקַק 1055) *or a charging bear*

מֹשֵׁל רָשָׁע Qal act.ptc. (605)-adj. m.s. (957) *a wicked ruler*

עַל עַם־דָּל prep.-n.m.s. (I 766)-adj. m.s. paus. (195) *over a poor people*

28:16

נָגִיד n.m.s. (617) *a ruler*

חֲסַר תְּבוּנוֹת adj. m.s. cstr. (341)-n.f.p. (108) *who lacks understanding*

וְרַב מַעֲשַׁקּוֹת conj.-adj. m.s. cstr. (I 912)-n.f.p. (799) *and great in extortions*

שֹׂנֵאי בֶצַע Qal act.ptc. (שָׂנֵא 971)-n.m.s. (130) *but he who hates unjust gain*

יַאֲרִיךְ יָמִים Hi. impf. 3 m.s. (אָרַךְ 73)-n.m.p. (398) *will prolong his days*

28:17

אָדָם עָשֻׁק n.m.s. (9)-Qal pass.ptc. (עָשַׁק 798) *if a man is burdened*

בְּדַם־נָפֶשׁ prep.-n.m.s. cstr. (196)-n.f.s. paus. ()659) *with the blood of another*

עַד־בּוֹר יָנוּס prep. (III 723)-n.m.s. (92)-Qal impf. 3 m.s. (נוּס 630) *let him be a fugitive until the pit*

אַל־יִתְמְכוּ־בוֹ neg.-Qal impf. 3 m.p. (תָּמַךְ 1069)-prep.-3 m.s. sf. *let no one help him*

28:18

הוֹלֵךְ תָּמִים Qal act.ptc. (הָלַךְ 229)-adj. m.s. (1071) *he who walks in integrity*

יִוָּשֵׁעַ Ni. impf. 3 m.s. (יָשַׁע 446) *will be delivered*

וְנֶעְקַשׁ דְּרָכַיִם conj.-Ni. ptc. cstr. (עָקַשׁ 786)-n.m. du. (202) *but he who is perverse in his ways*

יִפּוֹל בְּאֶחָת Qal impf. 3 m.s. (נָפַל 656)-prep.-adj. f.s. paus. (25; some rd. בַּשָּׁחַת 1120) *will fall into one*

28:19

עֹבֵד אַדְמָתוֹ Qal act.ptc. (עָבַד 712)-n.f.s.-3 m.s. sf. (9) *he who tills his land*

יִשְׂבַּע־לָחֶם Qal impf. 3 m.s. (שָׂבַע 959)-n.m.s. paus. (536) *will have plenty of bread*

וּמְרַדֵּף רֵקִים conj.-Pi. ptc. (רָדַף 922)-adj. m.p. (938) *but he who follows worthless pursuits*

יִשְׂבַּע־רִישׁ v.supra-n.m.s. (930) *will have plenty of poverty*

28:20

אִישׁ אֱמוּנוֹת n.m.s. cstr. (35)-n.f.p. (53) *a faithful man*

רַב־בְּרָכוֹת adj. m.s. cstr. (I 912)-n.f.p. (139) *will abound with blessings*

וְאָץ לְהַעֲשִׁיר conj.-Qal act.ptc. (אוּץ 21)-prep. -Hi. inf.cstr. (עָשַׁר 799) *but he who hastens to be rich*

לֹא יִנָּקֶה neg.-Ni. impf. 3 m.s. (נָקָה 667) *will not go unpunished*

28:21

הַכֵּר־פָּנִים Hi. inf.abs. (נָכַר I 647)-n.m.p. (815) *to show partiality*

לֹא־טוֹב neg.-adj. m.s. (II 373) *is not good*

וְעַל־פַּת־לֶחֶם conj.-prep.-n.f.s. cstr. (837)-n.m.s. (536) *but for a piece of bread*

יִפְשַׁע־גָּבֶר Qal impf. 3 m.s. (פָּשַׁע 833)-n.m.s. paus. (149) *a man will do wrong*

28:22

נִבְהָל לַהוֹן Ni. ptc. (בָּהַל 96)-prep.-def.art.-n.m.s. (223) *hastens after wealth*

אִישׁ רַע עָיִן n.m.s. (35)-adj. m.s. cstr. (I 948) -n.f.s. (744) *a man evil of eye*

וְלֹא־יֵדַע conj.-neg.-Qal impf. 3 m.s. (יָדַע 393) *and does not know*

כִּי־חֶסֶר conj. (471)-n.m.s. (341) *that want*

יְבֹאֶנּוּ Qal impf. 3 m.s.-3 m.s. sf. (בּוֹא 97) *will come upon him*

28:23

מוֹכִיחַ אָדָם Hi. ptc. (יָכַח 406)-n.m.s. (9) *he who rebukes a man*

אַחֲרַי adj. (30) *afterward*

חֵן יִמְצָא n.m.s. (336)-Qal impf. 3 m.s. (מָצָא 592) *will find more favor*

מִמַּחֲלִיק לָשׁוֹן prep.-Hi. ptc. (חָלַק II 325)-n.f.s. (546) *than he who flatters with his tongue*

28:24

גּוֹזֵל Qal act.ptc. (גָּזַל 159) *he who robs*

אָבִיו וְאִמּוֹ n.m.s.-3 m.s. sf. (3)-conj.-n.f.s.-3 m.s. sf. (51) *his father or his mother*

וְאֹמֵר conj.-Qal act.ptc. (55) *and says*

אֵין־פָּשַׁע neg. (II 34)-n.m.s. paus. (833) *that is no transgression*

חָבֵר הוּא n.m.s. (288)-pers.pr. 3 m.s. (214) *he is the companion*

לְאִישׁ מַשְׁחִית prep.-n.m.s. (35)-Hi. ptc. (שָׁחַת 1007) *of a man who destroys*

28:25

רְחַב־נֶפֶשׁ adj. m.s. cstr. (932)-n.f.s. (659) *a greedy man*

יְגָרֶה מָדוֹן Pi. impf. 3 m.s. (גָּרָה 173)-n.m.s. (I 193) *stirs up strife*

וּבוֹטֵחַ עַל־יהוה conj.-Qal act.ptc. (בָּטַח 105) -prep.-pr.n. (217) *but he who trusts in Yahweh*

יְדֻשָּׁן Pu. impf. 3 m.s. paus. (דָּשֵׁן 206) *will be enriched*

28:26

בּוֹטֵחַ בְּלִבּוֹ Qal act.ptc. (בָּטַח 105)-prep.-n.m.s.-3 m.s. sf. (524) *he who trusts in his own mind*

הוּא כְסִיל pers.pr. 3 m.s. (214)-n.m.s. (493) *is a fool*

וְהוֹלֵךְ בְּחָכְמָה conj.-Qal act.ptc. (הָלַךְ 229)-prep. -n.f.s. (315) *but he who walks in wisdom*

הוּא יִמָּלֵט v.supra-Ni. impf. 3 m.s. (מָלַט 572) *will be delivered*

28:27

נוֹתֵן לָרָשׁ Qal act.ptc. (נָתַן 678)-prep.-def.art. -Qal act.ptc. (רוּשׁ 930) *he who gives to the poor*

אֵין מַחְסוֹר neg. (II 34)-n.m.s. (341) *will not want*

וּמַעְלִים עֵינָיו conj.-Hi. ptc. (עָלַם I 761)-n.f. du. -3 m.s. sf. (744) *but he who hides his eyes*

רַב־מְאֵרוֹת adj. m.s. cstr. (I 912)-n.f.p. (76) *will get many a curse*

28:28

בְּקוּם רְשָׁעִים prep.-Qal inf.cstr. (קוּם 877)-adj. m.p. (957) *when the wicked rise*

יִסָּתֵר אָדָם Ni. impf. 3 m.s. (סָתַר 711)-n.m.s. (9) *men hide themselves*

וּבְאָבְדָם conj.-prep.-Qal inf.cstr.-3 m.p. sf. (אָבַד 1) *but when they perish*

יִרְבּוּ צַדִּיקִים Qal impf. 3 m.p. (רָבָה 915)-adj. m.p. (843) *the righteous increase*

29:1

אִישׁ תּוֹכָחוֹת n.m.s. cstr. (35)-n.f.p. (407) *he who is often reproved*

מַקְשֶׁה־עֹרֶף Hi. ptc. (קָשָׁה 904)-n.m.s. (791) *yet stiffens his neck*

פֶּתַע יִשָּׁבֵר adv. (837)-Ni. impf. 3 m.s. (שָׁבַר 990) *will suddenly be broken*

וְאֵין מַרְפֵּא conj.-neg. (II 34)-n.m.s. (951) *beyond healing*

29:2

בִּרְבוֹת צַדִּיקִים prep.-Qal inf.cstr. (רָבָה I 915) -adj. m.p. (843) *when the righteous are in authority*

יִשְׂמַח הָעָם Qal impf. 3 m.s. (שָׂמַח 970)-def. art.-n.m.s. (I 766) *the people rejoice*

וּבִמְשֹׁל רָשָׁע conj.-prep.-Qal inf.cstr. (מָשַׁל 605)-adj. m.s. (957) *but when the wicked rule*

יֵאָנַח עָם Ni. impf. 3 m.s. (אָנַח 58)-n.m.s. (I 766) *the people groan*

29:3

אִישׁ־אֹהֵב חָכְמָה n.m.s. (35)-Qal act.ptc. (אָהַב 12)-n.f.s. (315) *he who loves wisdom*

יְשַׂמַּח אָבִיו Pi. impf. 3 m.s. (שָׂמַח 970)-n.m.s.-3 m.s. sf. (3) *makes his father glad*

וְרֹעֶה זוֹנוֹת conj.-Qal act.ptc. (רָעָה II 945)-Qal act.ptc. f.p. (זָנָה 275) *but one who keeps company with harlots*

יְאַבֶּד־הוֹן Pi. impf. 3 m.s. (אָבַד 1)-n.m.s. (223) *squanders his substance*

29:4

מֶלֶךְ בְּמִשְׁפָּט n.m.s. (I 572)-prep.-n.m.s. (1048) *a king by justice*

יַעֲמִיד אָרֶץ Hi. impf. 3 m.s. (עָמַד 763)-n.f.s. paus. (75) *gives stability to the land*

וְאִישׁ תְּרוּמוֹת conj.-n.m.s. cstr. (35)-n.f.p. (929) *but one who exacts gifts*

יֶהֶרְסֶנָּה Qal impf. 3 m.s.-3 f.s. sf. (הָרַס 248) *ruins it*

29:5

גֶּבֶר מַחֲלִיק n.m.s. (149)-Hi. ptc. (חָלַק II 325) *a man who flatters*

עַל־רֵעֵהוּ prep.-n.m.s.-3 m.s. sf. (945) *his neighbor*

רֶשֶׁת פּוֹרֵשׂ n.f.s. (440)-Qal act.ptc. (פָּרַשׂ 831) *spreads a net*

עַל־פְּעָמָיו prep.-n.f.p.-3 m.s. sf. (821) *for his feet*

29:6

בְּפֶשַׁע prep.-n.m.s. (833) *in his transgression*

אִישׁ רָע n.m.s. cstr. (35)-n.m.s. (II 948) *en evil man*

מוֹקֵשׁ n.m.s. (430) *a snare*

וְצַדִּיק conj.-adj. m.s. (843) *but a righteous man*

יָרוּן Qal impf. 3 m.s. (רָנַן 943; GK 67q) *sings*

וְשָׂמֵחַ conj.-Qal pf. 3 m.s. (שָׂמַח 970) *and rejoices*

29:7

יֹדֵעַ צַדִּיק Qal act.ptc. (יָדַע 393)-adj. m.s. (843) *a righteous man knows*
דִּין דַּלִּים n.m.s. cstr. (192)-adj. m.p. (195) *the rights of the poor*
רָשָׁע adj. m.s. (957) *a wicked man*
לֹא־יָבִין neg.-Qal impf. 3 m.s. (בִּין 106) *does not understand*
דָּעַת n.f.s. paus. (395) *such knowledge*

29:8

אַנְשֵׁי לָצוֹן n.m.p. cstr. (35)-n.m.s. (539) *scoffers*
יָפִיחוּ קִרְיָה Hi. impf. 3 m.s. (פּוּחַ 806)-n.f.s. (900) *set a city aflame*
וַחֲכָמִים conj.-adj. m.p. (314) *but wise men*
יָשִׁיבוּ אָף Hi. impf. 3 m.p. (שׁוּב 996)-n.m.s. paus. (I 60) *turn away wrath*

29:9

אִישׁ־חָכָם n.m.s. (35)-adj. m.s. (314) *if a wise man*
נִשְׁפָּט Ni. ptc. (שָׁפַט 1047) *has an argument*
אֶת־אִישׁ אֱוִיל prep. (II 85)-n.m.s. (35)-adj. m.s. (17) *with a fool*
וְרָגַז conj.-Qal pf. 3 m.s. (919) *only rages*
וְשָׂחַק conj.-Qal pf. 3 m.s. (965) *and laughs*
וְאֵין נָחַת conj.-neg. (II 34)-n.f.s. paus. (I 629) *and there is no quiet*

29:10

אַנְשֵׁי דָמִים n.m.p. cstr. (35)-n.m.p. (196) *bloodthirsty men*
יִשְׂנְאוּ־תָם Qal impf. 3 m.p. (שָׂנֵא 971)-adj. m.s. (1070) *hate one who is blameless*
וִישָׁרִים conj.-adj. m.p. (449; some rd. וּרְשָׁעִים 957) *and upright ones*
יְבַקְשׁוּ נַפְשׁוֹ Pi. impf. 3 m.p. (בָּקַשׁ 134)-n.f.s.-3 m.s. sf. (659) *seek his life*

29:11

כָּל־רוּחוֹ n.m.s. cstr. (481)-n.f.s.-3 m.s. sf. (924) *all his anger*
יוֹצִיא כְסִיל Hi. impf. 3 m.s. (יָצָא 422)-n.m.s. (493) *a fool gives full vent to*
וְחָכָם conj.-adj. m.s. (314) *but a wise man*
בְּאָחוֹר יְשַׁבְּחֶנָּה prep.-subst. (30)-Pi. impf. 3 m.s.-3 f.s. sf. (שָׁבַח I 986) *quietly holds it back*

29:12

מֹשֵׁל מַקְשִׁיב Qal act.ptc. (605)-Hi. ptc. (קָשַׁב 904) *if a ruler listens*
עַל־דְּבַר־שָׁקֶר prep.-n.m.s. cstr. (182)-n.m.s. paus. (1055) *to falsehood*
כָּל־מְשָׁרְתָיו n.m.s. cstr. (481)-Pi. ptc. m.p.-3 m.s. sf. (שָׁרַת 1058) *all his officials*
רְשָׁעִים adj. m.p. (957) *will be wicked*

29:13

רָשׁ Qal act.ptc. m.s. (רוּשׁ 930) *the poor man*
וְאִישׁ תְּכָכִים conj.-n.m.s. cstr. (35)-n.m.p. (1067) *and the oppressor*
נִפְגָּשׁוּ Ni. pf. 3 c.p. paus. (פָּגַשׁ 803) *meet together*
מֵאִיר־עֵינֵי שְׁנֵיהֶם Hi. ptc. (אוֹר 21)-n.f.p. cstr. (744)-num.-2 m.p. sf. (1040) *gives light to the eyes of both*
יהוה pr.n. (217) *Yahweh*

29:14

מֶלֶךְ שׁוֹפֵט n.m.s. (I 572)-Qal act.ptc. (שָׁפַט 1047) *if a king judges*
בֶּאֱמֶת prep.-n.f.s. (54) *with equity*
דַּלִּים adj. m.p. (195) *the poor*
כִּסְאוֹ n.m.s.-3 m.s. sf. (490) *his throne*
לָעַד יִכּוֹן prep.-def.art.-n.m.s. (I 723)-Ni. impf. 3 m.s. (כּוּן 465) *will be established for ever*

29:15

שֵׁבֶט וְתוֹכַחַת n.m.s. (986)-conj.-n.f.s. (407) *the rod and reproof*
יִתֵּן חָכְמָה Qal impf. 3 m.s. (נָתַן 678)-n.f.s. (315) *give wisdom*
וְנַעַר conj.-n.m.s. (654) *but a child*
מְשֻׁלָּח Pu. ptc. (שָׁלַח 1018) *left to himself*
מֵבִישׁ אִמּוֹ Hi. ptc. (בּוֹשׁ 101)-n.f.s.-3 m.s. sf. (51) *brings shame to his mother*

29:16

בִּרְבוֹת רְשָׁעִים prep.-Qal inf.cstr. (רָבָה I 915) -adj. m.p. (957) *when the wicked are in authority*
יִרְבֶּה־פָּשַׁע Qal impf. 3 m.s. (רָבָה I 915)-n.m.s. paus. (833) *transgression increases*
וְצַדִּיקִים conj.-adj. m.p. (843) *but the righteous*
בְּמַפַּלְתָּם prep.-n.f.s.-3 m.p. sf. (658) *upon their downfall*
יִרְאוּ Qal impf. 3 m.p. (רָאָה 906) *will look upon*

29:17

יַסֵּר בִּנְךָ Pi. impv. 2 m.s. (יָסַר 415)-n.m.s.-2 m.s. sf. (119) *discipline your son*

וִינִיחֶךָ conj.-Hi. impf. 3 m.p.-2 m.s. sf. *and he will give you rest*

וְיִתֵּן conj.-Qal impf. 3 m.s. (נָתַן 678) *and he will give*

מַעֲדַנִּים n.m.p. (726) *delight*

לְנַפְשֶׁךָ prep.-n.f.s.-2 m.s. sf. (659) *to your heart*

29:18

בְּאֵין חָזוֹן prep.-neg. (II 34)-n.m.s. (302) *where there is no prophecy*

יִפָּרַע עָם Ni. impf. 3 m.s. (פָּרַע III 828)-n.m.s. paus. (I 766) *the people cast off restraint*

וְשֹׁמֵר תּוֹרָה conj.-Qal act.ptc. (1036)-n.f.s. (435) *but he who keeps the law*

אַשְׁרֵהוּ n.m.p.-3 m.s. sf. (80) *blessed is he*

29:19

בִּדְבָרִים prep.-n.m.p. (182) *by words*

לֹא־יִוָּסֶר prep.-Ni. impf. 3 m.s. (יָסַר 415) *is not disciplined*

עָבֶד n.m.s. paus. (713) *a servant*

כִּי־יָבִין conj. (471)-Qal impf. 3 m.s. (בִּין 106) *for though he understands*

וְאֵין מַעֲנֶה conj.-neg. (II 34)-n.m.s. (775) *he will not give heed*

29:20

חָזִיתָ Qal pf. 2 m.s. (חָזָה 302) *do you see*

אִישׁ אָץ n.m.s. (35)-Qal act.ptc. (אוּץ 21) *a man who is hasty*

בִּדְבָרָיו prep.-n.m.p.-3 m.s. sf. (182) *in his words*

תִּקְוָה n.f.s. (876) *there is more hope*

לִכְסִיל prep.-n.m.s. (493) *for a fool*

מִמֶּנּוּ prep.-3 m.s. sf. *than for him*

29:21

מְפַנֵּק Pi. ptc. (פָּנַק 819) *he who pampers*

מִנֹּעַר prep.-n.m.s. (655) *from childhood*

עַבְדּוֹ n.m.s.-3 m.s. sf. (713) *his servant*

וְאַחֲרִיתוֹ conj.-n.f.s.-3 m.s. sf. (31) *in the end*

יִהְיֶה Qal impf. 3 m.s. (הָיָה 224) *will find him*

מָנוֹן n.m.s. (584) *his heir(?)*

29:22

אִישׁ־אַף n.m.s. cstr. (35)-n.m.s. (I 60) *a man of wrath*

יְגָרֶה מָדוֹן Pi. impf. 3 m.s. (גָּרָה 173)-n.m.s. (I 193) *stirs up strife*

וּבַעַל חֵמָה conj.-n.m.s. cstr. (127)-n.f.s. (404) *and a man given to anger*

רַב־פָּשַׁע adj. m.s. cstr. (913)-n.m.s. paus. (833) *causes much transgression*

29:23

גַּאֲוַת אָדָם n.f.s. cstr. (144)-n.m.s. (9) *a man's pride*

תַּשְׁפִּילֶנּוּ Hi. impf. 3 f.s.-3 m.s. sf. (1050) *will bring him low*

וּשְׁפַל־רוּחַ conj.-adj. m.s. cstr. (1050)-n.f.s. (924) *but he who is lowly in spirit*

יִתְמֹךְ כָּבוֹד Qal impf. 3 m.s. (תָּמַךְ 1069)-n.m.s. (458) *will obtain honor*

29:24

חוֹלֵק עִם־גַּנָּב Qal act.ptc. (חָלַק I 323)-prep. (767)-n.m.s. (170) *the partner of a thief*

שׂוֹנֵא נַפְשׁוֹ Qal act.ptc. (שָׂנֵא 971)-n.f.s.-3 m.s. sf. (659) *hates his own life*

אָלָה יִשְׁמַע n.f.s. (46)-Qal impf. 3 m.s. (שָׁמַע 1033) *he hears the curse*

וְלֹא יַגִּיד conj.-neg.-Hi. impf. 3 m.s. (נָגַד 616) *but discloses nothing*

29:25

חֶרְדַּת אָדָם n.f.s. cstr. (I 353)-n.m.s. (9) *the fear of man*

יִתֵּן מוֹקֵשׁ Qal impf. 3 m.s. (נָתַן 678)-n.m.s. (430) *lays a snare*

וּבוֹטֵחַ בַּיהוה conj.-Qal act.ptc. (בָּטַח 105)-prep. -pr.n. (217) *but he who trusts in Yahweh*

יְשֻׂגָּב Pu. impf. 3 m.s. paus. (שָׂגַב 960) *is safe*

29:26

רַבִּים מְבַקְשִׁים adj. m.p. (I 912)-Pi. ptc. m.p. (134 בָּקַשׁ) *many seek*

פְּנֵי־מוֹשֵׁל n.m.p. cstr. (815)-Qal act.ptc. (מָשַׁל 605) *the favor of a ruler*

וּמֵיהוה conj.-prep.-pr.n. (217) *but from Yahweh*

מִשְׁפַּט־אִישׁ n.m.s. cstr. (1048)-n.m.s. (35) *a man gets justice*

29:27

תּוֹעֲבַת צַדִּיקִים n.f.s. cstr. (1072)-adj. m.p. (843) *an abomination to the righteous*

אִישׁ עָוֶל n.m.s. cstr. (35)-n.m.s. (732) *an unjust man*

וְתוֹעֲבַת רָשָׁע conj.-n.f.s. cstr. (1072)-adj. m.s. (957) *but an abomination to the wicked*

יְשַׁר־דָּרֶךְ adj. m.s. cstr. (449)-n.m.s. paus. (202) *he whose way is straight*

30:1

דִּבְרֵי אָגוּר n.m.p. cstr. (182)-pr.n. (8) *the words of Agur*

בִּן־יָקֶה הַמַּשָּׂא n.m.s. cstr. (119)-pr.n. (429)-def. art.-pr.n. (601; or def.art.-n.m.s. III 672; LXX μετανόει) *son of Jakeh of Massa*

נְאֻם הַגֶּבֶר n.m.s. cstr. (610)-def.art.-n.m.s. (149) *the man says*

לְאִיתִיאֵל prep.-pr.n. (87) *to Ithiel*

לְאִיתִיאֵל v.supra *to Ithiel*

וְאֻכָל conj.-pr.n. (38, 87) *and Ucal*

30:2

כִּי בַעַר conj. (471)-n.m.s. (129) *for ... stupid*

אָנֹכִי מֵאִישׁ pers.pr. 1 c.s. (59)-prep.-n.m.s. (35) *I am ... to be a man*

וְלֹא־בִינַת אָדָם לִי conj.-neg.-n.f.s. cstr. (108) -n.m.s. (9)-prep.-1 c.s. sf. *I have not the understanding of a man*

30:3

וְלֹא־לָמַדְתִּי conj.-neg.-Qal pf. 1 c.s. (לָמַד 540) *I have not learned*

חָכְמָה n.f.s. (315) *wisdom*

וְדַעַת קְדֹשִׁים conj.-n.f.s. cstr. (395)-adj. m.p. (872) *and knowledge of the Holy One*

אֵדָע Qal impf. 1 c.s. paus. (יָדַע 393) *I have knowledge*

30:4

מִי עָלָה־שָׁמַיִם interr. (566)-Qal pf. 3 m.s. (748)-n.m. du. (1029) *who has ascended to heaven*

וַיֵּרַד consec.-Qal impf. 3 m.s. (יָרַד 432) *and come down?*

מִי אָסַף־רוּחַ v.supra-Qal pf. 3 m.s. (62)-n.f.s. (924) *who has gathered the wind*

בְּחָפְנָיו prep.-n.m.p.-3 m.s. sf. (342) *in his fists?*

מִי צָרַר־מַיִם v.supra-Qal pf. 3 m.s. (צָרַר I 864)-n.m.p. (565) *who has wrapped up the waters*

בַּשִּׂמְלָה prep.-def.art.-n.f.s. (971) *in a garment?*

מִי הֵקִים v.supra-Hi. pf. 3 m.s. (קוּם 877) *who has established*

כָּל־אַפְסֵי־אָרֶץ n.m.s. cstr. (481)-n.m.p. cstr. (67) -n.f.s. paus. (75) *all the ends of the earth?*

מַה־שְּׁמוֹ interr. (552)-n.m.s.-3 m.s. sf. (1027) *what is his name*

וּמַה־שֶּׁם־בְּנוֹ conj.-v.supra-n.m.s. cstr. (1027) -n.m.s.-3 m.s. sf. (119) *and what is his son's name?*

כִּי תֵדָע conj. (471)-Qal impf. 2 m.s. (יָדַע 393) *surely you know*

30:5

כָּל־אִמְרַת אֱלוֹהַּ n.m.s. cstr. (481)-n.f.s. cstr. (57)-n.m.s. (42) *every word of God*

צְרוּפָה Qal pass.ptc. f.s. (צָרַף 864) *proves true*

מָגֵן הוּא n.m.s. (171)-pers.pr. 3 m.s. (214) *he is a shield*

לַחֹסִים בּוֹ prep.-def.art.-Qal act.ptc. m.p. (חָסָה 340)-prep.-3 m.s. sf. *to those who take refuge in him*

30:6

אַל־תּוֹסְףְּ neg.-Hi. impf. 2 m.s. (יָסַף 414) *do not add*

עַל־דְּבָרָיו prep.-n.m.p.-3 m.s. sf. (182) *to his words*

פֶּן־יוֹכִיחַ בְּךָ conj. (814)-Hi. impf. 3 m.s. (יָכַח 406)-prep.-2 m.s. sf. *lest he rebuke you*

וְנִכְזָבְתָּ conj.-Ni. pf. 2 m.s. (כָּזַב 469) *and you be found a liar*

30:7

שְׁתַּיִם n.f. du. (1040) *two things*

שָׁאַלְתִּי Qal pf. 1 c.s. (שָׁאַל 981) *I ask*

מֵאִתָּךְ prep.-prep.-2 m.s. paus. (II 85) *of thee*

אַל־תִּמְנַע מִמֶּנִּי neg.-Qal impf. 2 m.s. (מָנַע 586)-prep.-1 c.s. sf. *deny them not to me*

בְּטֶרֶם אָמוּת prep.-adv. (382)-Qal impf. 1 c.s. (559 מוּת) *before I die*

30:8

שָׁוְא וּדְבַר־כָּזָב n.m.s. (996)-conj.-n.m.s. cstr. (182)-n.m.s. (469) *falsehood and lying*

הַרְחֵק מִמֶּנִּי Hi. impv. 2 m.s. (רָחַק 934)-prep.-1 c.s. sf. *remove far from me*

רֵאשׁ וָעֹשֶׁר n.m.s. (930)-conj.-n.m.s. (799) *poverty and riches*

אַל־תִּתֶּן־לִי neg.-Qal impf. 2 m.s. (נָתַן 678) -prep.-1 c.s. sf. *do not give me*

הַטְרִיפֵנִי Hi. impv. 2 m.s.-1 c.s. sf. (טָרַף 382) *feed me*

לֶחֶם n.m.s. cstr. (536) *with the food*

חֻקִּי n.m.s.-1 c.s. sf. (349) *that is needful for me*

30:9

פֶּן אֶשְׂבַּע conj. (814)-Qal impf. 1 c.s. (שָׂבַע 959) *lest I be full*

וְכִחַשְׁתִּי conj.-Pi. pf. 1 c.s. (כָּחַשׁ 471) *and deny thee*

וְאָמַרְתִּי conj.-Qal pf. 1 c.s. (אָמַר 55) *and I say*

מִי יהוה interr. (566)–pr.n. (217) *who is Yahweh?*
וּפֶן־אִוָּרֵשׁ conj.–conj. (814)–Ni. impf. 1 c.s. (יָרַשׁ 439) *or lest I be poor*
וְגָנַבְתִּי conj.–Qal pf. 1 c.s. (גָּנַב 170) *and steal*
וְתָפַשְׂתִּי conj.–Qal pf. 1 c.s. (תָּפַשׂ 1074) *and profane*
שֵׁם אֱלֹהָי n.m.s. cstr. (1027)–n.m.p.–1 c.s. sf. (43) *the name of my God*

30:10

אַל־תַּלְשֵׁן neg.–Hi. impf. 2 m.s. juss. (לָשַׁן 546) *do not slander*
עֶבֶד n.m.s. (713) *a servant*
אֶל־אֲדֹנָו prep.–n.m.p.–3 m.s. sf. (10) *to his master*
פֶּן־יְקַלֶּלְךָ conj. (814)–Pi. impf. 3 m.s.–2 m.s. sf. (886 קָלַל) *lest he curse you*
וְאָשָׁמְתָּ conj.–Qal pf. 2 m.s. (אָשַׁם 79) *and you be held guilty*

30:11

דּוֹר אָבִיו n.m.s. cstr. (189)–n.m.s.–3 m.s. sf. (3) *their fathers*
יְקַלֵּל Pi. impf. 3 m.s. (קָלַל 886) *there are those who curse*
וְאֶת־אִמּוֹ conj.–dir.obj.–n.f.s.–3 m.s. sf. (51) *and their mothers*
לֹא יְבָרֵךְ neg.–Pi. impf. 3 m.s. (בָּרַךְ 138) *do not bless*

30:12

דּוֹר טָהוֹר n.m.s. cstr. (189)–adj. m.s. (373) *there are those who are pure*
בְּעֵינָיו prep.–n.f.p.–3 m.s. sf. (744) *in their own eyes*
וּמִצֹּאָתוֹ conj.–prep.–n.f.s.–3 m.s. sf. (844) *but of their filth*
לֹא רֻחָץ neg.–Pu. pf. 3 m.s. (רָחַץ 934) *are not cleansed*

30:13

דּוֹר n.m.s. (189) *there are those*
מָה־רָמוּ interr. (552)–Qal pf. 3 c.p. (רוּם 926) *how lofty*
עֵינָיו n.f.p.–3 m.s. sf. (744) *their eyes*
וְעַפְעַפָּיו conj.–n.m.p.–3 m.s. sf. (733) *and their eyelids*
יִנָּשֵׂאוּ Ni. impf. 3 m.p. paus. (נָשָׂא 669) *are lifted up*

30:14

דּוֹר n.m.s. (189) *there are those*
חֲרָבוֹת n.f.p. (352) *are swords*
שִׁנָּיו n.f.p.–3 m.s. sf. (1042) *their teeth*
וּמַאֲכָלוֹת conj.–n.f.p. (38) *and knives*
מְתַלְּעֹתָיו n.f.p.–3 m.s. sf. (1069) *their teeth*
לֶאֱכֹל עֲנִיִּים prep.–Qal inf.cstr. (אָכַל 37)–adj. m.p. (776) *to devour the poor*
מֵאֶרֶץ prep.–n.f.s. (75) *from off the earth*
וְאֶבְיוֹנִים conj.–adj. m.p. (2) *and the needy*
מֵאָדָם prep.–n.m.s. (9) *from among men*

30:15

לַעֲלוּקָה prep.–n.f.s. (763) *the leech*
שְׁתֵּי בָנוֹת n.f.p. cstr. (1040)–n.f.p. (123) *has two daughters*
הַב הַב Qal impv. 2 m.s. (יָהַב 396)–v.supra *give, give*
שָׁלוֹשׁ הֵנָּה n.m.s. (1025)–pers.pr. 3 f.p. (241) *three things*
לֹא תִשְׂבַּעְנָה neg.–Qal impf. 3 f.p. (שָׂבַע 959) *are never satisfied*
אַרְבַּע לֹא־אָמְרוּ n.m.s. (916)–neg.–Qal pf. 3 c.p. (55) *four never say*
הוֹן n.m.s. (223) *enough*

30:16

שְׁאוֹל n.f.s. (982) *Sheol*
וְעֹצֶר רָחַם conj.–n.m.s. cstr. (783)–n.m.s. (933) *and restraint of womb*
אֶרֶץ n.f.s. (75) *the earth*
לֹא־שָׂבְעָה neg.–Qal pf. 3 f.s. (שָׂבַע 959) *ever thirsty*
מַּיִם n.m.p. (565) *for water*
וְאֵשׁ conj.–n.f.s. (77) *and the fire*
לֹא־אָמְרָה neg.–Qal pf. 3 f.s. (55) *which never says*
הוֹן n.m.s. (223) *enough*

30:17

עַיִן n.f.s. (744) *the eye*
תִּלְעַג לְאָב Qal impf. 3 f.s. (לָעַג 541)–prep.–n.m.s. (3) *mocks a father*
וְתָבוּז conj.–Qal impf. 3 f.s. (בּוּז I 100) *and scorns*
לִיקֲּהַת־אֵם prep.–n.f.s. cstr. (429)–n.f.s. (51) *to obey a mother*
יִקְּרוּהָ Qal impf. 3 m.p.–3 f.s. sf. (נָקַר 669) *will be picked out*
עֹרְבֵי־נַחַל n.m.p. cstr. (788)–n.m.s. (I 636) *by the ravens of the valley*
וְיֹאכְלוּהָ conj.–Qal impf. 3 m.p.–3 f.s. sf. (אָכַל 37) *and eaten*

בְּנֵי־נָשֶׁר n.m.p. cstr. (119)–n.m.s. paus. (676) *by the vultures*

30:18

שְׁלֹשָׁה n.f.s. (1025) *three things*
הֵמָּה נִפְלְאוּ pers.pr. 3 m.p. (241)–Ni. pf. 3 c.p. (810 פָּלָא) *they are two wonderful*
מִמֶּנִּי prep.–3 m.s. (1 c.s.) sf. *for me*
וְאַרְבָּעָ conj.–n.f.s. (916) *and four*
לֹא יְדַעְתִּים neg.–Qal pf. 1 c.s. (יָדַע 393) *I do not understand (them)*

30:19

דֶּרֶךְ הַנֶּשֶׁר n.m.s. cstr. (202)–def.art.–n.m.s. (676) *the way of an eagle*
בַּשָּׁמַיִם prep.–def.art.–n.m. du. (1029) *in the sky*
דֶּרֶךְ נָחָשׁ v.supra–n.m.s. (I 638) *the way of a serpent*
עֲלֵי צוּר prep. (752)–n.m.s. (849) *on a rock*
דֶּרֶךְ־אֳנִיָּה v.supra–n.f.s. (58) *the way of a ship*
בְלֶב־יָם prep.–n.m.s. cstr. (524)–n.m.s. (410) *on the high seas*
וְדֶרֶךְ גֶּבֶר conj.–v.supra–n.m.s. (149) *and the way of a man*
בְּעַלְמָה prep.–n.f.s. (761) *with a maiden*

30:20

כֵּן דֶּרֶךְ adv. (485)–n.m.s. cstr. (202) *this is the way of*
אִשָּׁה מְנָאָפֶת n.f.s. (61)–Pi. ptc. f.s. (נָאַף 610) *an adulteress*
אָכְלָה Qal pf. 3 f.s. (אָכַל 37) *she eats*
וּמָחֲתָה פִיהָ conj.–Qal pf. 3 f.s. (מָחָה 562) –n.m.s.–3 f.s. sf. (804) *and wipes her mouth*
וְאָמְרָה conj.–Qal pf. 3 f.s. (55) *and says*
לֹא־פָעַלְתִּי אָוֶן neg.–Qal pf. 1 c.s. (פָּעַל 821)–n.m.s. (19) *I have done no wrong*

30:21

תַּחַת שָׁלוֹשׁ prep. (1065)–n.m.s. (1025) *under three things*
רָגְזָה אֶרֶץ Qal pf. 3 f.s. (רָגַז 919)–n.f.s. (75) *the earth trembles*
וְתַחַת אַרְבַּע conj.–v.supra–n.m.s. (916) *and under four*
לֹא־תוּכַל שְׂאֵת neg.–Qal impf. 3 f.s. (יָכֹל 407) –Qal inf.cstr. (נָשָׂא 669) *it cannot bear up*

30:22

תַּחַת־עֶבֶד prep. (1065)–n.m.s. (713) *under a slave*
כִּי־יִמְלוֹךְ conj. (471)–Qal impf. 3 m.s. (מָלַךְ 573) *when he becomes king*
וְנָבָל conj.–adj. m.s. (614) *and a fool*
כִּי־יִשְׂבַּע־לָחֶם conj. (471)–Qal impf. 3 m.s. (שָׂבַע 959)–n.m.s. paus. (536) *when he is filled with food*

30:23

תַּחַת שְׂנוּאָה prep. (1065)–Qal pass.ptc. f.s. (שָׂנֵא 971) *under a hated woman*
כִּי תִבָּעֵל conj. (471)–Ni. impf. 3 f.s. (בָּעַל 127) *when she gets a husband*
וְשִׁפְחָה conj.–n.f.s. (1046) *and a maid*
כִּי־תִירַשׁ conj. (471)–Qal impf. 3 f.s. (יָרַשׁ 439) *when she succeeds*
גְּבִרְתָּהּ n.f.s.–3 f.s. sf. (150) *her mistress*

30:24

אַרְבָּעָה הֵם n.f.s. (916)–pers.pr. 3 m.p. (241) *four things*
קְטַנֵּי־אָרֶץ adj. m.p. cstr. (881)–n.f.s. paus. (75) *on earth are small*
וְהֵמָּה conj.–pers.pr. 3 m.p. (241) *but they*
חֲכָמִים מְחֻכָּמִים adj. m.p. (314)–Pu. ptc. m.p. (314 חָכַם) *exceedingly wise*

30:25

הַנְּמָלִים def.art.–n.f.p. ((649) *the ants*
עַם לֹא־עָז n.m.s. (I 766)–neg.–adj. m.s. (738) *a people not strong*
וַיָּכִינוּ consec.–Hi. impf. 3 m.p. (כּוּן I 465) *they provide*
בַקַּיִץ prep.–def.art.–n.m.s. (884) *in the summer*
לַחְמָם n.m.s.–3 m.p. sf. (536) *their food*

30:26

שְׁפַנִּים n.m.p. (I 1050) *the badgers*
עַם לֹא־עָצוּם n.m.s. (I 766)–neg.–adj. m.s. (783) *a people not mighty*
וַיָּשִׂימוּ consec.–Qal impf. 3 m.p. (שִׂים 962) *yet they make*
בַסֶּלַע prep.–def.art.–n.m.s. (700) *in the rocks*
בֵּיתָם n.m.s.–3 m.p. sf. (108) *their homes*

30:27

מֶלֶךְ אֵין n.m.s. (I 572)–neg. (II 34) *have no king*
לָאַרְבֶּה prep.–def.art.–n.m.s. (916) *the locusts*
וַיֵּצֵא חֹצֵץ consec.–Qal impf. 3 m.s. (יָצָא 422) –Qal act.ptc. (חָצַץ I 346) *yet they march in rank*
כֻּלּוֹ n.m.s.–3 m.s. sf. (481) *all of them*

30:28

שְׂמָמִית n.f.s. (971) *the lizard*

בְּיָדַיִם prep.-n.f. du. (388) *in your hands*
תְּתַפֵּשׂ Pi. impf. 2 m.s. (תָּפַשׂ 1074) *you can take*
וְהִיא conj.-pers.pr. 3 f.s. (214) *yet it*
בְּהֵיכְלֵי מֶלֶךְ prep.-n.m.p. cstr. (228)-n.m.s. (I 572) *in king's palaces*

30:29

שְׁלֹשָׁה הֵמָּה n.f.s. (1025)-pers.pr. 3 f.p. (241) *three things*
מֵיטִבֵי צָעַד Hi. ptc. m.p. cstr. (יָטַב 405)-n.m.s. paus. (857) *are stately in their march*
וְאַרְבָּעָה conj.-n.f.s. (916) *and four*
מֵיטִבֵי לָכֶת v.supra-Qal inf.cstr. paus. (הָלַךְ 229) *stately in their stride*

30:30

לַיִשׁ n.m.s. (I 539) *the lion*
גִּבּוֹר בַּבְּהֵמָה adj. m.s. (150)-prep.-def.art.-n.f.s. (96) *which is mightiest among beasts*
וְלֹא־יָשׁוּב conj.-neg.-Qal impf. 3 m.s. (שׁוּב 996) *and does not turn back*
מִפְּנֵי־כֹל prep.-n.m.p. cstr. (815)-n.m.s. (481) *before any*

30:31

זַרְזִיר adj. m.s. (267) *the strutting cock?*
מָתְנַיִם n.m. du. (608) *girt in the loins*
אוֹ־תַיִשׁ conj. (14)-n.m.s. paus. (1067) *or a he-goat*
וּמֶלֶךְ conj.-n.m.s. (I 572) *and a king*
אַלְקוּם עִמּוֹ n.m.s. (39)-prep.-3 m.s. sf. (767) *a band of soldiers with him*

30:32

אִם־נָבַלְתָּ hypoth.part. (49)-Qal pf. 2 m.s. (נָבַל II 614) *if you have been foolish*
בְהִתְנַשֵּׂא prep.-Hith. inf.cstr. (נָשָׂא 669) *exalting yourself*
וְאִם־זַמּוֹתָ conj.-v.supra-Qal pf. 2 m.s. (זָמַם 273) *or if you have been devising evil*
יָד לְפֶה n.f.s. (388)-prep.-n.m.s. (804) *put your hand on your mouth*

30:33

כִּי מִיץ חָלָב conj. (471)-n.m.s. cstr. (568)-n.m.s. (316) *for pressing milk*
יוֹצִיא חֶמְאָה Hi. impf. 3 m.s. (יָצָא 422)-n.f.s. (326) *produces curds*
וּמִיץ־אַף conj.-v.supra-n.m.s. (I 60) *and pressing the nose*
יוֹצִיא דָם v.supra-n.m.s. (196) *produces blood*
וּמִיץ אַפַּיִם v.supra-n.m. du. (I 60) *and pressing anger*
יוֹצִיא רִיב v.supra-n.m.s. (936) *produces strife*

31:1

דִּבְרֵי לְמוּאֵל n.m.p. cstr. (182)-pr.n. (541) *the words of Lemuel*
מֶלֶךְ מַשָּׂא n.m.s. cstr. (I 572)-pr.n. (I 601; or n.m.s. III 672) *king of Massa* or *king, an oracle*
אֲשֶׁר־יִסְּרַתּוּ אִמּוֹ rel. (81)-Pi. pf. 3 f.s.-3 m.s. sf. (415 יָסַר)-n.f.s.-3 m.s. sf. (51) *which his mother taught him*

31:2

מַה־בְּרִי interr. (552)-n.m.s.-1 c.s. sf. (135) *what, my son?*
LXX+ τί; ῥήσεις θεοῦ, πρωτογενές, σοὶ λέγω, υἱέ
וּמַה־בַּר־בִּטְנִי conj.-v.supra-n.m.s. cstr. (135)-n.f.s.-1 c.s. sf. (105) *what, son of my womb?*
וּמֶה בַּר־נְדָרָי conj.-interr. (552)-v.supra-n.m.p.-1 c.s. sf. (623) *what, son of my vows?*

31:3

אַל־תִּתֵּן neg.-Qal impf. 2 m.s. (נָתַן 678) *give not*
לַנָּשִׁים prep.-def.art.-n.f.p. (61) *to women*
חֵילֶךָ n.m.s.-2 m.s. sf. (298) *your strength*
וּדְרָכֶיךָ conj.-n.m.p.-2 m.s. sf. (202) *your ways*
לַמְחוֹת מְלָכִין prep.-Qal act.ptc. f.p. (מָחָה I 562)-n.m.p. (I 572) *to those who destroy kings*

31:4

אַל לַמְּלָכִים neg.-prep.-def.art.-n.m.p. (I 572) *it is not for kings*
לְמוֹאֵל pr.n. (541) *O Lemuel*
אַל לַמְּלָכִים v.supra-v.supra *it is not for kings*
שְׁתוֹ־יָיִן Qal inf.cstr. (שָׁתָה 1059)-n.m.s. paus. (406) *to drink wine*
וּלְרוֹזְנִים conj.-prep.-Qal act.ptc. m.p. (רָזַן 931) *or for rulers*
אֵו שֵׁכָר n.m.s. cstr. (16)-n.m.s. (1016) *to desire strong drink*

31:5

פֶּן־יִשְׁתֶּה conj. (814)-Qal impf. 3 m.s. (שָׁתָה 1059) *lest they drink*
וְיִשְׁכַּח conj.-Qal impf. 3 m.s. (שָׁכַח 1013) *and forget*
מְחֻקָּק Pu. ptc. (חָקַק 349) *what has been decreed*
וִישַׁנֶּה conj.-Pi. impf. 3 m.s. (שָׁנָה 1040) *and pervert*

דִּין כָּל־בְּנֵי־עֹנִי n.m.s. cstr. (192)-n.m.s. cstr. (481) -n.m.p. cstr. (119)-n.m.s. (777) *the rights of all the afflicted*

31:6

תְּנוּ־שֵׁכָר Qal impv. 2 m.p. (נָתַן 678)-n.m.s. (1016) *give strong drink*

לְאוֹבֵד prep.-Qal act.ptc. (אָבַד 1) *to him who is perishing*

וְיַיִן conj.-n.m.s. (406) *and wine*

לְמָרֵי נָפֶשׁ prep.-adj. m.p. cstr. (600)-n.f.s. paus. (659) *to those in bitter distress*

31:7

יִשְׁתֶּה Qal impf. 3 m.s. (שָׁתָה 1059) *let them drink*

וְיִשְׁכַּח conj.-Qal impf. 3 m.s. (שָׁכַח 1013) *and forget*

רִישׁוֹ n.m.s.-3 m.s. sf. (930) *their poverty*

וַעֲמָלוֹ conj.-n.m.s.-3 m.s. sf. (I 765) *and their misery*

לֹא יִזְכָּר־עוֹד neg.-Qal impf. 3 m.s. (זָכַר 269)-adv. (728) *remember no more*

31:8

פְּתַח־פִּיךָ Qal impv. 2 m.s. (פָּתַח I 834)-n.m.s.-2 m.s. sf. (804) *open your mouth*

לְאִלֵּם prep.-adj. m.s. (48) *for the dumb*

אֶל־דִּין prep.-n.m.s. cstr. (192) *for the rights of*

כָּל־בְּנֵי־חֲלוֹף n.m.s. cstr. (481)-n.m.p. cstr. (119) -n.m.s. (322) *all who are sons of passing away*

31:9

פְּתַח־פִּיךָ Qal impv. 2 m.s. (I 834)-n.m.s.-2 m.s. sf. (804) *open your mouth*

שְׁפָט־צֶדֶק Qal impv. 2 m.s. (1047)-n.m.s. (841) *judge righteously*

וְדִין conj.-Qal impv. 2 m.s. (דִּין 192) *maintain the rights of*

עָנִי adj. m.s. (776) *the poor*

וְאֶבְיוֹן conj.-adj. m.s. (2) *and needy*

31:10

אֵשֶׁת־חַיִל n.f.s. cstr. (61)-n.m.s. (298) *a good wife*

מִי יִמְצָא interr. (566)-Qal impf. 3 m.s. (מָצָא 592) *who can find*

וְרָחֹק conj.-adj. m.s. (935) *and more*

מִפְּנִינִים prep.-n.f.p. (819) *than jewels*

מִכְרָהּ n.m.s.-3 f.s. sf. (569) *her value*

31:11

בָּטַח בָּהּ Qal pf. 3 m.s. (105)-prep.-3 f.s. sf. *trusts in her*

לֵב בַּעְלָהּ n.m.s. cstr. (524)-n.m.s.-3 f.s. sf. (127) *the heart of her husband*

וְשָׁלָל conj.-n.m.s. (1021) *and gain*

לֹא יֶחְסָר neg.-Qal impf. 3 m.s. (חָסֵר 341) *he will have no lack*

31:12

גְּמָלַתְהוּ Qal pf. 3 f.s.-3 m.s. sf. (גָּמַל 168) *she does him*

טוֹב וְלֹא־רָע n.m.s. (III 375)-conj.-neg.-n.m.s. paus. (948) *good and not harm*

כֹּל יְמֵי חַיֶּיהָ n.m.s. cstr. (481)-n.m.p. cstr. (398) -n.m.p.-3 f.s. sf. (313) *all the days of her life*

31:13

דָּרְשָׁה Qal pf. 3 f.s. (דָּרַשׁ 205) *she seeks*

צֶמֶר וּפִשְׁתִּים n.m.s. (856)-conj.-n.m.p. (833) *wool and flax*

וַתַּעַשׂ consec.-Qal impf. 3 f.s. (עָשָׂה I 793) *and works*

בְּחֵפֶץ כַּפֶּיהָ prep.-n.m.s. cstr. (343)-n.f.p.-3 f.s. sf. (496) *with willing hands*

31:14

הָיְתָה Qal pf. 3 f.s. (הָיָה 224) *she is*

כָּאֳנִיּוֹת סוֹחֵר prep.-n.f.p. cstr. (58)-Qal act.ptc. (695 סָחַר) *like the ships of the merchant*

מִמֶּרְחָק prep.-n.m.s. (935) *from afar*

תָּבִיא לַחְמָהּ Hi. impf. 3 f.s. (בּוֹא 97)-n.m.s.-3 f.s. sf. (536) *she brings her food*

31:15

וַתָּקָם consec.-Qal impf. 3 f.s. (קוּם 877) *she rises*

בְּעוֹד לַיְלָה prep.-adv. (728)-n.m.s. (538) *while it is yet night*

וַתִּתֵּן טֶרֶף consec.-Qal impf. 3 f.s. (נָתַן 678) -n.m.s. (383) *and provides food*

לְבֵיתָהּ prep.-n.m.s.-3 f.s. sf. (108) *for her household*

וְחֹק conj.-n.m.s. (349) *and tasks*

לְנַעֲרֹתֶיהָ prep.-n.f.p.-3 f.s. sf. (655) *for her maidens*

31:16

זָמְמָה שָׂדֶה Qal pf. 3 f.s. (זָמַם 273)-n.m.s. (961) *she considers a field*

וַתִּקָּחֵהוּ consec.-Qal impf. 3 f.s.-3 m.s. sf. (לָקַח 542) ***and buys it***

מִפְּרִי כַפֶּיהָ prep.-n.m.s. cstr. (826)-n.f.p.-3 f.s. sf. (496) ***with the fruit of her hands***

נָטְעָ כָּרֶם Qal pf. 3 f.s. (נָטַע 642)-n.m.s. paus. (501) ***she plants a vineyard***

31:17

חָגְרָה Qal pf. 3 f.s. (חָגַר 291) ***she girds***

בְעוֹז prep.-n.m.s. (738) ***with strength***

מָתְנֶיהָ n.m. du.-3 f.s. sf. (608) ***her loins***

וַתְּאַמֵּץ consec.-Pi. impf. 3 f.s. (אָמֵץ 54) ***and makes strong***

זְרֹעוֹתֶיהָ n.f.p.-3 f.s. sf. (283) ***her arms***

31:18

טָעֲמָה Qal pf. 3 f.s. (טָעַם 380) ***she perceives***

כִּי־טוֹב conj. (471)-adj. m.s. (II 373) ***that is profitable***

סַחְרָהּ n.m.s.-3 f.s. sf. (695) ***her merchandise***

לֹא־יִכְבֶּה neg.-Qal impf. 3 m.s. (כָּבָה 459) ***does not go out***

בַלַּיְלָ prep.-def.art.-n.m.s. (538) ***at night***

נֵרָהּ n.m.s.-3 f.s. sf. (632) ***her lamp***

31:19

יָדֶיהָ n.f.p.-3 f.s. sf. (388) ***her hands***

שִׁלְּחָה Pi. pf. 3 f.s. (שָׁלַח 1018) ***she puts***

בַכִּישׁוֹר prep.-def.art.-n.m.s. (507) ***to the distaff***

וְכַפֶּיהָ conj.-n.f.p.-3 f.s. sf. (496) ***and her hands***

תָּמְכוּ פָלֶךְ Qal pf. 3 c.p. (תָּמַךְ 1069)-n.m.s. paus. (813) ***hold the spindle***

31:20

כַּפָּהּ פָּרְשָׂה n.f.s.-3 f.s. sf. (496)-Qal pf. 3 f.s. (831 פָּרַשׂ) ***she opens her hand***

לֶעָנִי prep.-def.art.-adj. m.s. (776) ***to the poor***

וְיָדֶיהָ שִׁלְּחָה conj.-n.f.p.-3 f.s. sf. (388)-Pi. pf. 3 f.s. (שָׁלַח 1018) ***and reaches out her hands***

לָאֶבְיוֹן prep.-def.art.-adj. m.s. (2) ***to the needy***

31:21

לֹא־תִירָא neg.-Qal impf. 3 f.s. (יָרֵא 431) ***she is not afraid***

לְבֵיתָהּ prep.-n.m.s.-3 f.s. sf. (108) ***for her household***

מִשָּׁלֶג prep.-n.m.s. (1017) ***of snow***

כִּי כָל־בֵּיתָהּ conj. (471)-n.m.s. cstr. (481)-n.m.s.-3 f.s. sf. (108) ***for all her household***

לָבֻשׁ שָׁנִים Qal pass.ptc. (לָבֵשׁ 527)-n.m.p. (1040) ***are clothed in scarlet***

31:22

מַרְבַדִּים n.m.p. (915) ***coverings***

עָשְׂתָה־לָּהּ Qal pf. 3 f.s. (עָשָׂה I 793)-prep.-3 f.s. sf. ***she makes herself***

שֵׁשׁ וְאַרְגָּמָן n.m.s. (1058)-conj.-n.m.s. (71) ***fine linen and purple***

לְבוּשָׁהּ n.m.s.-3 f.s. sf. (528) ***her clothing***

31:23

נוֹדָע Ni. ptc. (יָדַע 393) ***is known***

בַּשְּׁעָרִים prep.-def.art.-n.m.p. (1044) ***in the gates***

בַּעְלָהּ n.m.s.-3 f.s. sf. (127) ***her husband***

בְּשִׁבְתּוֹ prep.-Qal inf.cstr.-3 m.s. sf. (יָשַׁב 442) ***when he sits***

עִם־זִקְנֵי־אָרֶץ prep. (767)-adj. m.p. cstr. (278)-n.f.s. paus. (75) ***among the elders of the land***

31:24

סָדִין n.m.s. (690) ***linen garments***

עָשְׂתָה Qal pf. 3 f.s. (עָשָׂה I 793) ***she makes***

וַתִּמְכֹּר consec.-Qal impf. 3 f.s. (מָכַר 569) ***and sells (them)***

וַחֲגוֹר conj.-n.m.s. (292) ***girdles***

נָתְנָה לַכְּנַעֲנִי Qal pf. 3 f.s. (נָתַן 678)-prep.-def.art.-n.m.s. (II 489) ***she delivers to the merchant***

31:25

עֹז־וְהָדָר n.m.s. (738)-conj.-n.m.s. (214) ***strength and dignity***

לְבוּשָׁהּ n.m.s.-3 f.s. sf. (528) ***her clothing***

וַתִּשְׂחַק consec.-Qal impf. 3 f.s. (שָׂחַק 965) ***and she laughs***

לְיוֹם אַחֲרוֹן prep.-n.m.s. (398)-adj. m.s. (30) ***at the time to come***

31:26

פִּיהָ פָּתְחָה n.m.s.-3 f.s. sf. (804)-Qal pf. 3 f.s. (I 834 פָּתַח) ***she opens her mouth***

בְחָכְמָה prep.-n.f.s. (315) ***with wisdom***

וְתוֹרַת־חֶסֶד conj.-n.f.s. cstr. (435)-n.m.s. (338) ***and the teaching of kindness***

עַל־לְשׁוֹנָהּ prep.-n.f.s.-3 f.s. sf. (546) ***on her tongue***

31:27

צוֹפִיָּה Qal act.ptc. f.s. (צָפָה I 859) ***she looks well***

הֲלִיכוֹת בֵּיתָהּ n.f.p. cstr. (237)-n.m.s.-3 f.s. sf. (108) ***to the ways of her household***

וְלֶחֶם עַצְלוּת conj.-n.m.s. cstr. (536)-n.f.s. (782) ***and the bread of idleness***

לֹא תֹאכֵל neg.-Qal impf. 3 f.s. (אָכַל 37) *she does not eat*

31:28

קָמוּ בָנֶיהָ Qal pf. 3 c.p. (קוּם 877)-n.m.p.-3 f.s. (119) *her children rise up*

וַיְאַשְּׁרוּהָ consec.-Pi. impf. 3 m.p.-3 f.s. sf. (אָשַׁר 80) *and call her blessed*

בַּעְלָהּ n.m.s.-3 f.s. sf. (127) *her husband*

וַיְהַלְלָהּ consec.-Pi. impf. 3 m.s.-3 f.s. sf. (הלל II 237) *and he praises her*

31:29

רַבּוֹת בָּנוֹת adj. f.p. (I 912)-n.f.p. (I 123) *many women*

עָשׂוּ חָיִל Qal pf. 3 c.p. (עָשָׂה I 793)-n.m.s. paus. (298) *have done excellently*

וְאַתְּ עָלִית conj.-pers.pr. 2 f.s. (61)-Qal pf. 2 f.s. (748 עָלָה) *but you surpass*

עַל־כֻּלָּנָה prep.-n.m.s.-3 f.p. sf. (481) *them all*

31:30

שֶׁקֶר הַחֵן n.m.s. (1055)-def.art.-n.m.s. (336) *charm is deceitful*

וְהֶבֶל הַיֹּפִי conj.-n.m.s. (I 210)-def.art.-n.m.s. (421) *and beauty is vain*

אִשָּׁה n.f.s. (61) *a woman*

יִרְאַת־יהוה n.f.s. cstr. (432)-pr.n. (217; LXX γὰρ συνετή) *the fear of Yahweh*

הִיא תִתְהַלָּל pers.pr. 3 f.s. (214)-Hith. impf. 3 f.s. (הָלַל II 237) *is to be praised*

31:31

תְּנוּ־לָהּ Qal impf. 2 m.p. (נָתַן 678)-prep.-3 f.s. sf. *give her*

מִפְּרִי יָדֶיהָ prep.-n.m.s. cstr. (826)-n.f.p.-3 f.s. sf. (388) *of the fruit of her hands*

וִיהַלְלוּהָ conj.-Pi. impf. 3 m.p.-3 f.s. sf. (II 237) *and let ... praise her*

בַשְּׁעָרִים prep.-def.art.-n.m.p. (1044) *in the gates*

מַעֲשֶׂיהָ n.m.p.-3 f.s. sf. (795) *her works*

Ecclesiastes

1:1

דִּבְרֵי קֹהֶלֶת n.m.p. cstr. (182)-n.m.s. (875; GK 122r) ***the words of the Preacher***

בֶּן־דָּוִד n.m.s. cstr. (119)-pr.n. (187) ***the son of David***

מֶלֶךְ בִּירוּשָׁלָםִ n.m.s. (I 572)-prep.-pr.n. paus. (436) ***king in Jerusalem***

1:2

הֲבֵל הֲבָלִים n.m.s. cstr. (I 210; GK 133i)-n.m.p. (I 210) ***vanity of vanities***

אָמַר Qal pf. 3 m.s. (55) ***says***

קֹהֶלֶת n.m.s. (875) ***the Preacher***

הֲבֵל הֲבָלִים v.supra-v.supra ***vanity of vanities***

הַכֹּל הָבֶל def.art.-n.m.s. (481)-n.m.s. (I 210) ***all is vanity***

1:3

מַה־יִּתְרוֹן interr. (552)-n.m.s. (452) ***what gain***

לָאָדָם prep.-def.art.-n.m.s. (9) ***to man***

בְּכָל־עֲמָלוֹ prep.-n.m.s. cstr. (481)-n.m.s.-3 m.s. sf. (765) ***by all the toil***

שֶׁיַּעֲמֹל rel. (979)-Qal impf. 3 m.s. (765) ***at which he toils***

תַּחַת הַשָּׁמֶשׁ prep. (1065)-def.art.-n.f.s. (1039) ***under the sun***

1:4

דּוֹר הֹלֵךְ n.m.s. (189)-Qal act.ptc. (הָלַךְ 229; GK 116n) ***a generation goes***

וְדוֹר בָּא conj.-v.supra-Qal act.ptc. (בּוֹא 97) ***and a generation comes***

וְהָאָרֶץ conj.-def.art.-n.f.s. (75) ***but the earth***

לְעוֹלָם prep.-n.m.s. (761) ***for ever***

עֹמָדֶת Qal act.ptc. f.s. paus. (עָמַד 763) ***remains***

1:5

וְזָרַח conj.-Qal pf. 3 m.s. (280) ***rises***

הַשֶּׁמֶשׁ def.art.-n.f.s. (1039) ***the sun***

וּבָא conj.-Qal pf. 3 m.s. (בּוֹא 97) ***and goes down***

הַשָּׁמֶשׁ v.supra paus. ***the sun***

וְאֶל־מְקוֹמוֹ conj.-prep.-n.m.s.-3 m.s. sf. (879) ***and to the (its) place***

שׁוֹאֵף Qal act.ptc. (שָׁאַף I 983) ***hastens (he panteth)***

זוֹרֵחַ הוּא שָׁם Qal act.ptc. (280)-pers.pr. 3 m.s. (214)-adv. (1027) ***where it rises***

1:6

הוֹלֵךְ Qal act.ptc. (הָלַךְ 229; GK 113u) ***it goes***

אֶל־דָּרוֹם prep.-n.m.s. (204) ***to the south***

וְסוֹבֵב conj.-Qal act.ptc. (סָבַב 685) *and goes round*
אֶל־צָפוֹן prep.-n.f.s. (I 860) *to the north*
סוֹבֵב סֹבֵב v.supra-v.supra *round and round*
הוֹלֵךְ v.supra *goes*
הָרוּחַ def.art.-n.f.s. (924) *the wind*
וְעַל־סְבִיבֹתָיו conj.-prep.-subst. p.-3 m.s. sf. (686) *and on its circuits*
שָׁב הָרוּחַ Qal act.ptc. (שׁוּב 996)-v.supra *the wind returns*

1:7

כָּל־הַנְּחָלִים n.m.s. cstr. (481)-def.art.-n.m.p. (636) *all streams*
הֹלְכִים Qal act.ptc. m.p. (הָלַךְ 229) *run*
אֶל־הַיָּם prep.-def.art.-n.m.s. (410) *to the sea*
וְהַיָּם conj.-v.supra *but the sea*
אֵינֶנּוּ מָלֵא neg.-3 m.s. sf. (II 34)-adj. (570) *is not full*
אֶל־מְקוֹם prep.-n.m.s. cstr. (879) *to the place*
שֶׁהַנְּחָלִים rel. (979)-def.art.-n.m.p. (636) *where the streams*
הֹלְכִים Qal act.ptc. m.p. (הָלַךְ 229) *flow*
שָׁם הֵם adv. (1027)-pers.pr. 3 m.p. (241) *there they*
שָׁבִים לָלָכֶת Qal act.ptc. m.p. (שׁוּב 996)-prep.-Qal inf.cstr. (הָלַךְ 229) *flow again*

1:8

כָּל־הַדְּבָרִים n.m.s. cstr. (481)-def.art.-n.m.p. (182) *all things*
יְגֵעִים adj. m.p. (388) *are wearisome*
לֹא־יוּכַל neg.-Qal impf. 3 m.s. (יָכֹל 407) *cannot*
אִישׁ n.m.s. (35) *a man*
לְדַבֵּר prep.-Pi. inf.cstr. (180) *utter it*
לֹא־תִשְׂבַּע neg.-Qal impf. 3 f.s. (959) *is not satisfied*
עַיִן n.f.s. (744) *the eye*
לִרְאוֹת prep.-Qal inf.cstr. (רָאָה 906) *with seeing*
וְלֹא־תִמָּלֵא conj.-neg.-Ni. impf. 3 f.s. (מָלֵא 569) *nor filled*
אֹזֶן n.f.s. (23) *the ear*
מִשְּׁמֹעַ prep.-Qal inf.cstr. (1033) *with hearing*

1:9

מַה־שֶּׁהָיָה interr. (552)-rel. (979)-Qal pf. 3 m.s. (224) *what has been*
הוּא שֶׁיִּהְיֶה demons.adj. m.s. (214)-rel. (979)-Qal impf. 3 m.s. (224) *is what will be*
וּמַה־שֶּׁנַּעֲשָׂה conj.-v.supra-rel. (979; GK 137c)-Ni. pf. 3 m.s. (עָשָׂה I 793) *and what has been done*
הוּא שֶׁיֵּעָשֶׂה v.supra-v.supra-Ni. impf. 3 m.s. (793) *is what will be done*
וְאֵין כָּל־חָדָשׁ conj.-neg. cstr. (II 34)-n.m.s. cstr. (481)-adj. m.s. (294) *and there is nothing new*
תַּחַת הַשָּׁמֶשׁ prep. (1065)-def.art.-n.m.s. paus. (1039) *under the sun*

1:10

יֵשׁ דָּבָר subst. (441)-n.m.s. (182) *is there a thing*
שֶׁיֹּאמַר rel. (979)-Qal impf. 3 m.s. (55) *of which it is said*
רְאֵה־ Qal impv. 2 m.s. (רָאָה 906) *see*
זֶה חָדָשׁ הוּא demons.adj. m.s. (260)-v.supra-v.supra *this is new*
כְּבָר הָיָה adv. (I 460)-Qal pf. 3 m.s. (224) *it has been already*
לְעֹלָמִים prep.-n.m.p. (761) *in the ages*
אֲשֶׁר הָיָה מִלְּפָנֵנוּ rel. (81)-v.supra-prep.-prep.-n.m.p.-1 c.p. sf. (815) *before us*

1:11

אֵין זִכְרוֹן neg. cstr. (II 34)-n.m.s. cstr. (272) *there is no remembrance of*
לָרִאשֹׁנִים prep.-def.art.-adj. m.p. (911) *former things*
וְגַם לָאַחֲרֹנִים conj.-adv. (168)-prep.-def.art.-adj. m.p. (30) *and also of later things*
שֶׁיִּהְיוּ rel. (979)-Qal impf. 3 m.p. (הָיָה 224) *yet to happen*
לֹא־יִהְיֶה neg.-Qal impf. 3 m.s. (הָיָה 224) *there will not be*
לָהֶם prep.-3 m.p. sf. *for them*
זִכָּרוֹן n.m.s. (272) *any remembrance*
עִם שֶׁיִּהְיוּ prep.-rel. (979)-Qal impf. 3 m.p. (הָיָה 224) *among those who come*
לָאַחֲרֹנָה prep.-def.art.-adj. f.s. (30) *after*

1:12

אֲנִי קֹהֶלֶת pers.pr. 1 c.s. (58)-n.m.s. (875) *I the Preacher*
הָיִיתִי Qal pf. 1 c.s. (הָיָה 224) *have been*
מֶלֶךְ n.m.s. (I 572) *king*
עַל־יִשְׂרָאֵל prep.-pr.n. (975) *over Israel*
בִּירוּשָׁלָם prep.-pr.n. (436) *in Jerusalem*

1:13

וְנָתַתִּי conj. (GK 112ppN)-Qal pf. 1 c.s. (נָתַן 678) *and I applied*

אֶת־לִבִּי dir.obj.-n.m.s.-1 c.s. sf. (524) *my mind*
לִדְרוֹשׁ prep.-Qal inf.cstr. (205) *to seek*
וְלָתוּר conj.-prep.-Qal inf.cstr. (תּוּר 1064) *and to search out*
בַּחָכְמָה prep.-def.art.-n.f.s. (315) *by wisdom*
עַל כָּל־אֲשֶׁר prep.-n.m.s. cstr. (481)-rel. (81) *all that*
נַעֲשָׂה Ni. pf. 3 m.s. (עָשָׂה I 793) *is done*
תַּחַת הַשָּׁמָיִם prep. (1065)-def.art.-n.m. du. paus. (1029) *under heaven*
הוּא עִנְיַן רָע demons.adj. m.s. (214)-n.m.s. (cstr.?) (775)-adj. m.s. (948) *an unhappy business*
נָתַן אֱלֹהִים Qal pf. 3 m.s. (678)-n.m.p. (43) *that God has given*
לִבְנֵי prep.-n.m.p. cstr. (119) *to the sons of*
הָאָדָם def.art.-n.m.s. (9) *men*
לַעֲנוֹת בּוֹ prep.-Qal inf.cstr. (עָנָה II 775)-prep.-3 m.s. sf. *to be busy with*

1:14

רָאִיתִי Qal pf. 1 c.s. (רָאָה 906) *I have seen*
אֶת־כָּל־הַמַּעֲשִׂים dir.obj.-n.m.s. cstr. (481)-def. art.-n.m.p. (795) *everything*
שֶׁנַּעֲשׂוּ rel. (979)-Ni. pf. 3 c.p. (עָשָׂה I 793) *that is done*
תַּחַת הַשָּׁמֶשׁ prep. (1065)-def.art.-n.f.s. paus. (1039) *under the sun*
וְהִנֵּה conj.-interj. (243) *and behold*
הַכֹּל def.art.-n.m.s. (481) *all*
הֶבֶל n.m.s. (I 210) *is vanity*
וּרְעוּת רוּחַ conj.-n.f.s. cstr. (II 946)-n.f.s. (924) *and a striving after wind*

1:15

מְעֻוָּת Pu. ptc. (עָוַת 736) *what is crooked*
לֹא־יוּכַל neg.-Qal impf. 3 m.s. (יָכֹל 407) *cannot be made*
לִתְקֹן prep.-Qal inf.cstr. (תָּקַן 1075) *straight*
וְחֶסְרוֹן conj.-n.m.s. (341) *and what is lacking*
לֹא־יוּכַל v.supra-v.supra *cannot be*
לְהִמָּנוֹת prep.-Ni. inf.cstr. (מָנָה 584) *numbered*

1:16

דִּבַּרְתִּי אֲנִי Pi. pf. 1 c.s. (דָּבַר 180)-pers.pr. 1 c.s. (58; GK 135b) *I said*
עִם־לִבִּי prep. (767)-n.m.s.-1 c.s. sf. (524) *to myself*
לֵאמֹר prep.-Qal inf.cstr. (אָמַר 55) *(saying)*
אֲנִי הִנֵּה v.supra-demons.part. (243) *I*
הִגְדַּלְתִּי Hi. pf. 1 c.s. (גָּדַל 152) *have made great*
וְהוֹסַפְתִּי conj.-Hi. pf. 1 c.s. (יָסַף 414) *and increased*
חָכְמָה n.f.s. (315) *wisdom*
עַל כָּל־אֲשֶׁר־ prep.-n.m.s. (481)-rel. (81) *surpassing all who*
הָיָה לְפָנַי Qal pf. 3 m.s. (224)-prep.-n.m.p.-1 c.s. sf. (815) *were before me*
עַל־יְרוּשָׁלָם prep.-pr.n. paus. (436) *over Jerusalem*
וְלִבִּי conj.-n.m.s.-1 c.s. sf. (524) *and my mind*
רָאָה הַרְבֵּה Qal pf. 3 m.s. (906)-Hi. inf.abs. as adv. (רָבָה I 915) *has had great experience of*
חָכְמָה וָדָעַת n.f.s. (315)-conj.-n.f.s. (395) *wisdom and knowledge*

1:17

וָאֶתְּנָה consec. (GK 112ppN)-Qal impf. 1 c.s. (נָתַן 678) *and I applied*
לִבִּי n.m.s.-1 c.s. sf. (524) *my mind*
לָדַעַת prep.-Qal inf.cstr. (יָדַע 393) *to know*
חָכְמָה n.f.s. (315) *wisdom*
וְדַעַת conj.-Qal inf.cstr. (יָדַע 393) *and to know*
הוֹלֵלוֹת n.f.p. (239; GK 86,l) *madness*
וְשִׂכְלוּת conj.-n.f.s. (698) *and folly*
יָדַעְתִּי Qal pf. 1 c.s. (393) *I perceived*
שֶׁגַּם־זֶה rel. (979)-adv. (168)-demons.adj. m.s. (260) *that this also*
הוּא pers.pr. 3 m.s. (214) *is*
רַעְיוֹן רוּחַ n.m.s. cstr. (946)-n.f.s. (924) *a striving after wind*

1:18

כִּי בְּרֹב חָכְמָה conj. (471)-prep.-n.m.s. cstr. (913)-n.f.s. (315) *for in much wisdom*
רָב־כָּעַס n.m.s. cstr. (913)-n.m.s. paus. (495) *is much vexation*
וְיוֹסִיף דַּעַת conj.-Hi. impf. 3 m.s. (יָסַף 414) -n.f.s. (395) *and he who increases knowledge*
יוֹסִיף מַכְאוֹב v.supra-n.m.s. (456) *increases sorrow*

2:1

אָמַרְתִּי אֲנִי Qal pf. 1 c.s. (אָמַר 55)-pers.pr. 1 c.s. (58; GK 135b) *I said*
בְּלִבִּי prep.-n.m.s.-1 c.s. sf. (524) *to myself*
לְכָה־נָּא Qal impv. 2 m.s.-vol. he (הָלַךְ 229) -part.of entreaty (609) *come now*
אֲנַסְּכָה Pi. impf. 1 c.s.-2 m.s. sf. (?)(נָסָה 650) *I will make a test*
בְשִׂמְחָה prep.-n.f.s. (970) *of pleasure*
וּרְאֵה בְטוֹב conj.-Qal impv. 2 m.s. (רָאָה 906) -prep.-adj. m.s. (II 373) *enjoy yourself* (lit. *and look on goodness*)

וְהִנֵּה conj.-interj. (243) *but behold*
גַּם־הוּא adv. (168)-demons.adj. m.s. (214) *this also*
הָבֶל n.m.s. paus. (I 210) *was vanity*

2:2

לִשְׂחוֹק prep.-n.m.s. (966) *of laughter*
אָמַרְתִּי Qal pf. 1 c.s. (אָמַר 55) *I said*
מְהוֹלָל Po'al ptc. (הָלַל II 237) *it is mad*
וּלְשִׂמְחָה conj.-prep.-n.f.s. (970) *and of pleasure*
מַה־זֹּה עֹשָׂה interr. (552)-demons.adj. f.s. (262) -Qal act.ptc. f.s. (עָשָׂה I 793) *what use is it?*

2:3

תַּרְתִּי Qal pf. 1 c.s. (תּוּר 1064) *I searched*
בְלִבִּי prep.-n.m.s.-1 c.s. sf. (524) *with my mind*
לִמְשׁוֹךְ prep.-Qal inf.cstr. (מָשַׁךְ 604) *how to cheer* (lit. *to draw, lead*)
בַּיַּיִן prep.-def.art.-n.m.s. (406) *with wine*
אֶת־בְּשָׂרִי dir.obj.-n.m.s.-1 c.s. sf. (142) *my body*
וְלִבִּי conj.-n.m.s.-1 c.s. sf. (524) *and my mind*
נֹהֵג Qal act.ptc. (נָהַג 624) *guiding*
בַּחָכְמָה prep.-def.art.-n.f.s. (315) *with wisdom*
וְלֶאֱחֹז conj.-prep.-Qal inf.cstr. (אָחַז 28) *and how to lay hold*
בְּסִכְלוּת prep.-n.f.s. (698) *on folly*
עַד אֲשֶׁר־ prep. (III 723)-rel. (81) *till*
אֶרְאֶה Qal impf. 1 c.s. (רָאָה 906) *I might see*
אֵי־זֶה טוֹב interr.adv. (32)-demons.pr. (260)-adj. m.s. (II 373) *what was good*
לִבְנֵי prep.-n.m.p. cstr. (119) *for the sons of*
הָאָדָם def.art.-n.m.s. (9) *men*
אֲשֶׁר יַעֲשׂוּ rel. (81)-Qal impf. 3 m.p. (עָשָׂה I 793) *to do*
תַּחַת הַשָּׁמַיִם prep. (1065)-def.art.-n.m. du. (1029) *under heaven*
מִסְפַּר יְמֵי n.m.s. cstr. (708)-n.m.p. cstr. (398) *the number of the days of*
חַיֵּיהֶם n.m.p.-3 m.p. sf. (313) *their life*

2:4

הִגְדַּלְתִּי מַעֲשָׂי Hi. pf. 1 c.s. (גָּדַל 152)-n.m.p.-1 c.s. sf. (795) *I increased my works*
בָּנִיתִי לִי Qal pf. 1 c.s. (בָּנָה 124)-prep.-1 c.s. sf. *I built for myself*
בָּתִּים n.m.p. (108) *houses*
נָטַעְתִּי Qal pf. 1 c.s. (642) *I planted*
לִי v.supra *for myself*
כְּרָמִים n.m.p. (501) *vineyards*

2:5

עָשִׂיתִי לִי Qal pf. 1 c.s. (עָשָׂה I 793)-prep.-1 c.s. sf. *I made myself*
גַּנּוֹת n.f.p. (171) *gardens*
וּפַרְדֵּסִים conj.-n.m.p. (825) *and parks*
וְנָטַעְתִּי conj. (GK 112ppN)-Qal pf. 1 c.s. (642) *and I planted*
בָהֶם prep.-3 m.p. sf. *in them*
עֵץ n.m.s. (781) *trees*
כָּל־פֶּרִי n.m.s. cstr. (481)-n.m.s. paus. (826) *all kinds of fruit*

2:6

עָשִׂיתִי לִי Qal pf. 1 c.s. (עָשָׂה I 793)-prep.-1 c.s. sf. *I made myself*
בְּרֵכוֹת מָיִם n.f.p. cstr. (140)-n.m.p. paus. (565) *pools of water*
לְהַשְׁקוֹת prep.-Hi. inf.cstr. (שָׁקָה 1052) *to water*
מֵהֶם prep.-3 m.p. sf. *from them*
יַעַר n.m.s. (I 420) *the forest*
צוֹמֵחַ עֵצִים Qal act.ptc. (855)-n.m.p. (781) *growing of trees*

2:7

קָנִיתִי Qal pf. 1 c.s. (קָנָה 888) *I bought*
עֲבָדִים n.m.p. (713) *male slaves*
וּשְׁפָחוֹת conj.-n.f.p. (1046) *and female slaves*
וּבְנֵי־בַיִת conj.-n.m.p. cstr. (119)-n.m.s. (108) *and sons of the house*
הָיָה לִי Qal pf. 3 m.s. (224)-prep.-1 c.s. sf. *there were to me*
גַּם מִקְנֶה adv. (168)-n.m.s. (889) *also cattle*
בָקָר n.m.s. (133) *cattle*
וָצֹאן conj.-n.f.s. (838) *and flocks*
הַרְבֵּה Hi. inf.abs. as adv. (רָבָה I 915) *abundantly*
הָיָה לִי v.supra-v.supra (GK 145u) *I had*
מִכֹּל prep.-n.m.s. (481) *more than any*
שֶׁהָיוּ rel. (979)-Qal pf. 3 c.p. (הָיָה 224) *who had been*
לְפָנַי prep.-n.m.p.-1 c.s. sf. (815) *before me*
בִּירוּשָׁלָםִ prep.-pr.n. paus. (436) *in Jerusalem*

2:8

כָּנַסְתִּי לִי Qal pf. 1 c.s. (488)-prep.-1 c.s. sf. *I gathered for myself*
גַּם־כֶּסֶף adv. (168)-n.m.s. (494) *also silver*
וְזָהָב conj.-n.m.s. (262) *and gold*
וּסְגֻלַּת מְלָכִים conj.-n.f.s. cstr. (688)-n.m.p. (I 572) *and the treasure of kings*
וְהַמְּדִינוֹת conj.-def.art.-n.f.p. (193) *and the provinces*

עָשִׂיתִי לִי Qal pf. 1 c.s. (עָשָׂה I 793)-prep.-1 c.s. sf. *I got for myself*

שָׁרִים Qal act.ptc. m.p. (שִׁיר 1010) *men singers*

וְשָׁרוֹת conj.-Qal act.ptc. f .p. (שִׁיר 1010) *and women singers*

וְתַעֲנוּגֹת conj.-n.m.p. cstr. (772) *and the delights of*

בְּנֵי הָאָדָם n.m.p. cstr. (119)-def.art.-n.m.s. (9) *the sons of man*

שִׁדָּה וְשִׁדּוֹת n.f.s. (994)-conj.-n.f.p. (994; GK 122v)(meaning uncertain)(Koehler-Baumgartner 950 *lady*)

2:9

וְגָדַלְתִּי conj.-Qal pf. 1 c.s. (גָּדַל 152) *so I became great*

וְהוֹסַפְתִּי conj.-Hi. pf. 1 c.s. (יָסַף 414) *and surpassed*

מִכֹּל prep.-n.m.s. (481) *all*

שֶׁהָיָה rel. (979)-Qal pf. 3 m.s. (224) *who were*

לְפָנַי prep.-n.m.p.-1 c.s. sf. (815) *before me*

בִּירוּשָׁלָ͏ִם prep.-pr.n. paus. (436) *in Jerusalem*

אַף חָכְמָתִי conj. (II 64)-n.f.s.-1 c.s. sf. (315) *also my wisdom*

עָמְדָה לִּי Qal pf. 3 f.s. (763)-prep.-1 c.s. sf. *remained with me*

2:10

וְכֹל אֲשֶׁר conj.-n.m.s. (481)-rel. (81) *and whatever*

שָׁאֲלוּ עֵינַי Qal pf. 3 c.p. (שָׁאַל 981)-n.f. du.-1 c.s. sf. (744) *my eyes desired*

לֹא אָצַלְתִּי neg.-Qal pf. 1 c.s. (69) *I did not keep*

מֵהֶם prep.-3 m.p. sf. *from them*

לֹא־מָנַעְתִּי neg.-Qal pf. 1 c.s. (מָנַע 586) *I kept not*

אֶת־לִבִּי dir.obj.-n.m.s.-1 c.s. sf. (524) *my heart*

מִכָּל־שִׂמְחָה prep.-n.m.s. cstr. (481)-n.f.s. (970) *from any pleasure*

כִּי־לִבִּי conj. (471)-v.supra *for my heart*

שָׂמֵחַ Qal pf. 3 m.s. (970) *found pleasure*

מִכָּל־עֲמָלִי prep.-v.supra-n.m.s.-1 c.s. sf. (765) *in all my toil*

וְזֶה־הָיָה conj.-demons.pr. (260)-Qal pf. 3 m.s. (224) *and this was*

חֶלְקִי n.m.s.-1 c.s. sf. (324) *my reward*

מִכָּל־עֲמָלִי v.supra-v.supra *for all my toil*

2:11

וּפָנִיתִי אֲנִי conj.-Qal pf. 1 c.s. (פָּנָה 815)-pers.pr. 1 c.s. (58) *then I considered*

בְּכָל־מַעֲשַׂי prep.-n.m.s. cstr. (481)-n.m.p.-1 c.s. sf. (795) *all my works*

שֶׁעָשׂוּ rel. (979)-Qal pf. 3 c.p. (עָשָׂה I 793) *which had done*

יָדַי n.f. du.-1 c.s. sf. (388) *my hands*

וּבֶעָמָל conj.-prep.-def.art.-n.m.s. (765) *and the toil*

שֶׁעָמַלְתִּי rel. (979)-Qal pf. 1 c.s. (765) *which I had toiled*

לַעֲשׂוֹת prep.-Qal inf.cstr. (עָשָׂה I 793) *in doing it*

וְהִנֵּה conj.-demons.part. (243) *and behold*

הַכֹּל def.art.-n.m.s. (481) *all*

הֶבֶל n.m.s. (I 210) *was vanity*

וּרְעוּת רוּחַ conj.-n.f.s. cstr. (II 946)-n.f.s. (924) *and a striving after wind*

וְאֵין יִתְרוֹן conj.-neg. (II 34)-n.m.s. (452) *and there was nothing to be gained*

תַּחַת הַשָּׁמֶשׁ prep. (1065)-def.art.-n.f.s. paus. (1039) *under the sun*

2:12

וּפָנִיתִי אֲנִי conj.-Qal pf. 1 c.s. (פָּנָה 815)-pers.pr. 1 c.s. (58) *so I turned*

לִרְאוֹת prep.-Qal inf.cstr. (רָאָה 906) *to consider*

חָכְמָה n.f.s. (315) *wisdom*

וְהוֹלֵלוֹת conj.-n.f.p. (239) *and madness*

וְסִכְלוּת conj.-n.f.s. (698) *and folly*

כִּי מֶה הָאָדָם conj. (471)-interr. (552)-def.art.-n.m.s. (9) *for what the man*

שֶׁיָּבוֹא rel. (979)-Qal impf. 3 m.s. (בּוֹא 97) *who comes*

אַחֲרֵי הַמֶּלֶךְ prep. (29)-def.art.-n.m.s. (I 572) *after the king*

אֵת אֲשֶׁר־כְּבָר dir.obj.-rel. (81)-adv. (I 460) *what already*

עָשׂוּהוּ Qal pf. 3 c.p.-3 m.s. sf. (עָשָׂה I 793) *he has done it*

2:13

וְרָאִיתִי אָנִי conj.-Qal pf. 1 c.s. (רָאָה 906)-pers.pr. 1 c.s. (58) *then I saw*

שֶׁיֵּשׁ יִתְרוֹן rel. (979)-subst. (441)-n.m.s. (452) *that there is advantage*

לַחָכְמָה prep.-def.art.-n.f.s. (315) *to wisdom*

מִן־הַסִּכְלוּת prep. (GK 133b)-def.art.-n.f.s. (698) *over folly*

כִּיתְרוֹן prep.-n.m.s. cstr. (452; GK 24e) *as the advantage of*

הָאוֹר def.art.-n.m.s. (21) *the light*

מִן־הַחֹשֶׁךְ prep.-def.art.-n.m.s. (365) *over the darkness*

2:14

הֶחָכָם def.art.-adj. m.s. (314) *the wise man*
עֵינָיו n.f. du.-3 m.s. sf. (744) *his eyes*
בְּרֹאשׁוֹ prep.-n.m.s.-3 m.s. sf. (910) *in his head*
וְהַכְּסִיל conj.-def.art.-n.m.s. (I 493) *but the fool*
בַּחֹשֶׁךְ prep.-def.art.-n.m.s. (365) *in darkness*
הוֹלֵךְ Qal act.ptc. (הָלַךְ 229) *walks*
וְיָדַעְתִּי גַם־אָנִי conj.-Qal pf. 1 c.s. (יָדַע 393)-adv. (168)-pers.pr. 1 c.s. (58) *and yet I perceived*
שֶׁמִּקְרֶה אֶחָד rel. (979)-n.m.s. (899)-num. (25) *that one fate*
יִקְרֶה Qal impf. 3 m.s. (קָרָה 899) *comes to*
אֶת־כֻּלָּם dir.obj.-n.m.s.-3 m.p. sf. (481) *all of them*

2:15

וְאָמַרְתִּי אֲנִי conj.-Qal pf. 1 c.s. (אָמַר 55)-pers.pr. 1 c.s. (58) *and I said*
בְּלִבִּי prep.-n.m.s.-1 c.s. sf. (524) *to myself*
כְּמִקְרֵה prep.-n.m.s. cstr. (899; GK 93rr) *as the fate of*
הַכְּסִיל def.art.-n.m.s. (I 493) *the fool*
גַּם־אֲנִי adv. (168)-v.supra (GK 135e) *also me*
יִקְרֵנִי Qal impf. 3 m.s.-1 c.s. sf. (קָרָה (899) *will befall me*
וְלָמָּה conj.-prep.-interr. (552) *why then*
חָכַמְתִּי Qal pf. 1 c.s. (314) *have I been wise*
אֲנִי אָז יוֹתֵר v.supra-adv. (23)-Qal act.ptc. or n.m.s. (452) as adv. *so very*
וְדִבַּרְתִּי conj.-Pi. pf. 1 c.s. (דָּבַר 180) *and I said*
בְלִבִּי prep.-n.m.s.-1 c.s. sf. (524) *to myself*
שֶׁגַּם־זֶה rel. (979)-adv. (168)-demons.pron. (260) *that this also*
הָבֶל n.m.s. paus. (I 210) *is vanity*

2:16

כִּי אֵין זִכְרוֹן conj. (471)-neg. (II 34)-n.m.s. cstr. (272) *for there is no remembrance*
לֶחָכָם prep.-def.art.-adj. m.s. (314) *of the wise man*
עִם־הַכְּסִיל prep.-def.art.-n.m.s. (I 493) *as of the fool*
לְעוֹלָם prep.-n.m.s. (761) *enduring*
בְּשֶׁכְּבָר prep.-rel. (979)-adv. (I 460) *seeing that (in that already)*
הַיָּמִים הַבָּאִים dir.obj.-n.m.p. (398)-def.art.-Qal act.ptc. m.p. (בּוֹא 97) *in the days to come*
הַכֹּל נִשְׁכָּח def.art.-n.m.s. (481)-Ni. ptc. (שָׁכַח 1013) *all will have been forgotten*
וְאֵיךְ יָמוּת conj.-adv. (32)-Qal impf. 3 m.s. (מוּת 559) *and how dies*
הֶחָכָם def.art.-adj. m.s. (314) *the wise man*
עִם־הַכְּסִיל prep. (767)-def.art.-n.m.s. (I 493) *with the fool*

2:17

וְשָׂנֵאתִי conj.-Qal pf. 1 c.s. (שָׂנֵא 971) *so I hated*
אֶת־הַחַיִּים dir.obj.-def.art.-n.m.p. (313) *life*
כִּי רַע conj. (471)-adj. m.s. (I 948) *because was grievous*
עָלַי prep.-1 c.s. sf. *to me*
הַמַּעֲשֶׂה dir.obj.-n.m.s. (795) *the deed*
שֶׁנַּעֲשָׂה rel. (979)-Ni. pf. 3 m.s. (עָשָׂה I 793) *that was done*
תַּחַת הַשָּׁמֶשׁ prep. (1065)-def.art.-n.f.s. (1039) *under the sun*
כִּי־הַכֹּל conj. (471)-def.art.-n.m.s. (481) *for all*
הֶבֶל n.m.s. (I 210) *is vanity*
וּרְעוּת רוּחַ conj.-n.f.s. cstr. (II 946)-n.f.s. (924) *and a striving after wind*

2:18

וְשָׂנֵאתִי conj.-Qal pf. 1 c.s. (שָׂנֵא 971) *I hated*
אֲנִי pers.pr. 1 c.s. (58) *I*
אֶת־כָּל־עֲמָלִי dir.obj.-n.m.s. cstr. (481)-n.m.s.-1 c.s. sf. (765) *all my toil*
שֶׁאֲנִי עָמֵל rel. (979)-v.supra-adj. m.s. (II 766) *in which I have toiled*
תַּחַת הַשָּׁמֶשׁ prep. (1065)-def.art.-n.f.s. paus. (1039) *under the sun*
שֶׁאַנִּיחֶנּוּ v.supra-Hi. impf. 1 c.s.-3 m.s. sf. (נוּחַ B 628) *seeing that I must leave it*
לָאָדָם prep.-def.art.-n.m.s. (9) *to the man*
שֶׁיִּהְיֶה v.supra-Qal impf. 3 m.s. (הָיָה 224) *who will come*
אַחֲרָי prep.-1 c.s. sf. (29) *after me*

2:19

וּמִי יוֹדֵעַ conj.-interr. (566)-Qal act.ptc. (393) *and who knows*
הֶחָכָם def.art.-adj. m.s. (314) *whether a wise man*
יִהְיֶה Qal impf. 3 m.s. (הָיָה 224) *he will be*
אוֹ סָכָל conj. (14; GK 150g)-n.m.s. (698) *or a fool*
וְיִשְׁלַט conj.-Qal impf. 3 m.s. (שָׁלַט I 1020) *yet he will be master*
בְּכָל־עֲמָלִי prep.-n.m.s. cstr. (481)-n.m.s.-1 c.s. sf. (765) *of all my labor*
שֶׁעָמַלְתִּי rel. (979)-Qal pf. 1 c.s. (765) *which I toiled*
וְשֶׁחָכַמְתִּי conj.-rel. (979)-Qal pf. 1 c.s. (314) *and used my wisdom*
תַּחַת הַשָּׁמֶשׁ prep. (1065)-def.art.-n.f.s. paus. (1039) *under the sun*

גַּם־זֶה adv. (168)-demons.pron. (260) *this also*
הָבֶל n.m.s. paus. (I 210) *is vanity*

2:20

וְסַבּוֹתִי אֲנִי conj.-Qal pf. 1 c.s. (סָבַב 685)-pers.pr. 1 c.s. (58) *so I turned about*
לְיַאֵשׁ prep.-Pi. inf.cstr. (יָאַשׁ 384; GK 64e) *to make ... despair*
אֶת־לִבִּי dir.obj.-n.m.s.-1 c.s. sf. (524) *my heart*
עַל כָּל־הֶעָמָל prep.-n.m.s. cstr. (481)-def.art. -n.m.s. (675) *over all the toil*
שֶׁעָמַלְתִּי rel. (979)-Qal pf. 1 c.s. (765) *which I toiled*
תַּחַת הַשָּׁמֶשׁ prep. (1065)-def.art.-n.f.s. paus. (1039) *under the sun*

2:21

כִּי־יֵשׁ אָדָם conj. (471)-subst. (441)-n.m.s. (9) *because (there is) a man*
שֶׁעֲמָלוֹ rel. (979)-n.m.s.-3 m.s. sf. (765) *whose work*
בְּחָכְמָה prep.-n.f.s. (315) *with wisdom*
וּבְדַעַת conj.-prep.-n.f.s. (395) *and with knowledge*
וּבְכִשְׁרוֹן conj.-prep.-n.m.s. (507) *and with skill*
וּלְאָדָם conj.-prep.-n.m.s. (9) *and to a man*
שֶׁלֹּא עָמַל־בּוֹ rel. (979)-neg.-Qal pf. 3 m.s. (765)-prep.-3 m.s. sf. *who did not toil for it*
יִתְּנֶנּוּ חֶלְקוֹ Qal impf. 3 m.s.-3 m.s. (נָתַן 678) -n.m.s.-3 m.s. sf. (324) *he will give it his inheritance*
גַּם־זֶה adv. (168)-demons.pron. (260) *this also*
הֶבֶל n.m.s. (I 210; GK 131m) *is vanity*
וְרָעָה רַבָּה conj.-n.f.s. (949)-adj. f.s. (I 912) *and a great evil*

2:22

כִּי מֶה־הֹוֶה conj. (471)-interr. (552)-Qal act.ptc. (הָוָה 217) *what has*
לָאָדָם prep.-def.art.-n.m.s. (9) *a man*
בְּכָל־עֲמָלוֹ prep.-n.m.s. cstr. (481)-n.m.s.-3 m.s. sf. (765) *from all the (his) toil*
וּבְרַעְיוֹן לִבּוֹ conj.-prep.-n.m.s. cstr. (946)-n.m.s.-3 m.s. sf. (524) *and from the striving of his mind*
שֶׁהוּא עָמֵל rel. (979; GK 36)-pers.pr. 3 m.s. (214)-adj. m.s. (765) *with which he toils*
תַּחַת הַשָּׁמֶשׁ prep. (1065)-def.art.-n.f.s. paus. (1039) *under the sun*

2:23

כִּי כָל־יָמָיו conj. (481)-n.m.s. cstr. (481)-n.m.p.-3 m.s. sf. (398) *for all his days*
מַכְאֹבִים n.m.p. (456) *are pain*
וָכַעַס conj.-n.m.s. (495) *and a vexation*
עִנְיָנוֹ n.m.s.-3 m.s. sf. (775) *his work*
גַּם־בַּלַּיְלָה adv. (168)-prep.-def.art.-n.m.s. (538) *even in the night*
לֹא־שָׁכַב לִבּוֹ neg.-Qal pf. 3 m.s. (1011)-n.m.s.-3 m.s. sf. (524) *his mind does not rest*
גַּם־זֶה adv. (168)-demons.pr. m.s. (260) *this also*
הֶבֶל הוּא n.m.s. (I 210)-pers.pr. 3 m.s. (214) *is vanity*

2:24

אֵין־טוֹב neg. cstr. (II 34)-adj. m.s. (II 373) *there is nothing better*
בָּאָדָם prep.-def.art.-n.m.s. (9) *for a man*
שֶׁיֹּאכַל rel. (979)-Qal impf. 3 m.s. (אָכַל 37) *than that he should eat*
וְשָׁתָה conj.-Qal pf. 3 m.s. (1059) *and drink*
וְהֶרְאָה conj.-Hi. pf. 3 m.s. (רָאָה 906) *and should see*
אֶת־נַפְשׁוֹ dir.obj.-n.f.s.-3 m.s. sf. (659) *for himself*
טוֹב adj. m.s. (II 373) *good*
בַּעֲמָלוֹ prep.-n.m.s.-3 m.s. sf. (765) *in his toil*
גַּם־זֹה adv. (168)-demons.pr. (260) *this also*
רָאִיתִי אָנִי Qal pf. 1 c.s. (רָאָה 906)-pers.pr. 1 c.s. (58) *I saw*
כִּי מִיַּד conj. (471)-prep.-n.f.s. cstr. (388) *that from the hand of*
הָאֱלֹהִים def.art.-n.m.p. (43) *God*
הִיא pers.pr. 3 f.s. (214) *it is*

2:25

כִּי מִי יֹאכַל conj. (471)-interr. (566)-Qal impf. 3 m.s. (אָכַל 37) *for who can eat*
וּמִי יָחוּשׁ conj.-v.supra-Qal impf. 3 m.s. (חוּשׁ II 301) *or who can have enjoyment*
חוּץ מִמֶּנִּי n.m.s. (299)-prep.-1 c.s. sf. *apart from me*

2:26

כִּי לְאָדָם conj. (471)-prep.-n.m.s. (9) *for to man*
שֶׁטּוֹב rel. (979)-adj. m.s. (II 373) *who pleases*
לְפָנָיו prep.-n.m.p.-3 m.s. sf. (815) *him*
נָתַן Qal pf. 3 m.s. (678) *he gives*
חָכְמָה n.f.s. (315) *wisdom*
וְדַעַת conj.-n.f.s. (395) *and knowledge*
וְשִׂמְחָה conj.-n.f.s. (970) *and joy*

וְלַחוֹטֶא conj.-prep.-def.art.-Qal act.ptc. (306; GK 75oo) *but to the sinner*

נָתַן v.supra *he gives*

עִנְיָן n.m.s. (775) *the work*

לֶאֱסוֹף prep.-Qal inf.cstr. (אָסַף 62) *of gathering*

וְלִכְנוֹס conj.-prep.-Qal inf.cstr. (כָּנַס 488) *and heaping*

לָתֵת prep.-Qal inf.cstr. (נָתַן 678) *only to give*

לְטוֹב prep.-adj. m.s. (II 373) *to one who pleases*

לִפְנֵי הָאֱלֹהִים prep.-n.m.p. cstr. (815)-def.art. -n.m.p. (43) *God*

גַּם־זֶה adv. (168)-demons.pr. (260) *this also*

הֶבֶל n.m.s. (I 210) *is vanity*

וּרְעוּת רוּחַ conj.-n.f.s. cstr. (946)-n.f.s. (924) *and a striving after wind*

3:1

לַכֹּל prep.-def.art.-n.m.s. (481) *for everything*

זְמָן n.m.s. (273) *a season*

וְעֵת conj.-n.f.s. (773) *and a time*

לְכָל־חֵפֶץ prep.-n.m.s. cstr. (481)-n.m.s. (343) *for every matter*

תַּחַת הַשָּׁמָיִם prep. (1065)-def.art.-n.m. du. paus. (1029) *under heaven*

3:2

עֵת n.f.s. (773) *a time*

לָלֶדֶת prep.-Qal inf.cstr. (יָלַד 408) *to be born*

וְעֵת לָמוּת conj. (GK 2r)-v.supra-prep.-Qal inf.cstr. (מוּת 559) *and a time to die*

עֵת לָטַעַת v.supra-prep.-Qal inf.cstr. (נָטַע 642) *a time to plant*

וְעֵת לַעֲקוֹר conj.-v.supra-prep.-Qal inf.cstr. (עָקַר 785) *and a time to pluck up*

נָטוּעַ Qal pass.ptc. (נָטַע 642) *what is planted*

3:3

עֵת לַהֲרוֹג n.f.s. (773)-prep.-Qal inf.cstr. (הָרַג 246) *a time to kill*

וְעֵת לִרְפּוֹא conj.-v.supra-prep.-Qal inf.cstr. (רָפָא 950) *and a time to heal*

עֵת לִפְרוֹץ v.supra-prep.-Qal inf.cstr. (פָּרַץ I 829) *a time to break down*

וְעֵת לִבְנוֹת conj.-v.supra-prep.--Qal inf.cstr. (124 בָּנָה) *and a time to build up*

3:4

עֵת לִבְכּוֹת n.f.s. (773)-prep.-Qal inf.cstr. (בָּכָה 113; GK 114b) *a time to weep*

וְעֵת לִשְׂחוֹק conj.-v.supra-prep.-Qal inf.cstr. (965 שָׂחַק) *and a time to laugh*

עֵת סְפוֹד v.supra-Qal inf.cstr. (סָפַד 704) *a time to mourn*

וְעֵת רְקוֹד conj.-v.supra-Qal inf.cstr. (רָקַד 955) *and a time to dance*

3:5

עֵת לְהַשְׁלִיךְ n.f.s. (773)-prep.-Hi. inf.cstr. (שָׁלַךְ 1020) *a time to cast away*

אֲבָנִים n.f.p. (6) *stones*

וְעֵת כְּנוֹס conj.-v.supra-Qal inf.cstr. (כָּנַס 488) *and a time to gather*

אֲבָנִים v.supra *stones*

עֵת לַחֲבוֹק v.supra-Qal inf.cstr. (287) *a time to embrace*

וְעֵת לִרְחֹק v.supra-prep.-Qal inf.cstr. (רָחַק 934) *and a time to refrain*

מֵחַבֵּק prep.-Pi. inf.cstr. (287) *from embracing*

3:6

עֵת לְבַקֵּשׁ n.f.s. (773)-prep.-Pi. inf.cstr. (בָּקַשׁ 134) *a time to seek*

וְעֵת לְאַבֵּד conj.-v.supra-Pi. inf.cstr. (אָבַד 1) *and a time to lose*

עֵת לִשְׁמוֹר v.supra-prep.-Qal inf.cstr. (שָׁמַר 1036) *a time to keep*

וְעֵת לְהַשְׁלִיךְ conj.-v.supra-prep.-Hi. inf.cstr. (1020 שָׁלַךְ) *and a time to cast away*

3:7

עֵת לִקְרוֹעַ n.f.s. (773)-prep.-Qal inf.cstr. (קָרַע 902) *a time to rend*

וְעֵת לִתְפּוֹר conj.-v.supra-prep.-Qal inf.cstr. (תָּפַר 1074) *and a time to sew*

עֵת לַחֲשׁוֹת v.supra-prep.-Qal inf.cstr. (חָשָׁה 364) *a time to keep silence*

וְעֵת לְדַבֵּר conj.-v.supra-prep.-Pi. inf.cstr. (דָּבַר 180) *and a time to speak*

3:8

עֵת לֶאֱהֹב n.f.s. (773)-prep.-Qal inf.cstr. (אָהַב 12) *a time to love*

וְעֵת לִשְׂנֹא conj.-v.supra-prep.-Qal inf.cstr. (שָׂנֵא 971) *and a time to hate*

עֵת מִלְחָמָה n.f.s. cstr. (773)-n.f.s. (536) *a time for war*

וְעֵת שָׁלוֹם conj.-v.supra-n.m.s. (1022) *and a time for peace*

3:9

מַה־יִּתְרוֹן interr. (552)-n.m.s. (452) *what gain*

הָעוֹשֶׂה def.art.-Qal act.ptc. (עָשָׂה I 793) *the worker*

בַּאֲשֶׁר הוּא עָמֵל prep.-rel. (81)-pers.pr. 3 m.s. (214)-adj. m.s. (II 766) *from his toil*

3:10

רָאִיתִי Qal pf. 1 c.s. (רָאָה 906) *I have seen*

אֶת־הָעִנְיָן dir.obj.-def.art.-n.m.s. (775) *the business*

אֲשֶׁר נָתַן אֱלֹהִים rel. (81)-Qal pf. 3 m.s. (678)-n.m.p. (43) *that God has given*

לִבְנֵי הָאָדָם prep.-n.m.p. cstr. (119)-def.art.-n.m.s. (9) *to the sons of men*

לַעֲנוֹת בּוֹ prep.-Qal inf.cstr. (עָנָה II 775)-prep.-3 m.s. sf. *to be busy with (it)*

3:11

אֶת־הַכֹּל dir.obj.-def.art.-n.m.s. (481) *everything*

עָשָׂה Qal pf. 3 m.s. (I 793) *he has made*

יָפֶה adj. m.s. (421) *beautiful*

בְעִתּוֹ prep.-n.f.s.-3 m.s. sf. (773) *in its time*

גַּם אֶת־הָעֹלָם adv. (168)-dir.obj.-def.art.-n.m.s. (761) *also eternity*

נָתַן Qal pf. 3 m.s. (678) *he has put*

בְּלִבָּם prep.-n.m.s.-3 m.p. sf. (524) *into their mind*

מִבְּלִי אֲשֶׁר prep.-subst. (115; GK 152y)-rel. (81) *yet so that*

לֹא־יִמְצָא neg.-Qal impf. 3 m.s. (592) *cannot find out*

הָאָדָם def.art.-n.m.s. (9) *the man*

אֶת־הַמַּעֲשֶׂה dir.obj.-def.art.-n.m.s. (795) *the work*

אֲשֶׁר־עָשָׂה rel. (81)-Qal pf. 3 m.s. (I 793) *which has done*

הָאֱלֹהִים def.art.-n.m.p. (43) *God*

מֵרֹאשׁ prep.-n.m.s. (910) *from the beginning*

וְעַד־סוֹף conj.-prep. (III 723)-n.m.s. (693) *to the end*

3:12

יָדַעְתִּי Qal pf. 1 c.s. (393) *I know*

כִּי אֵין טוֹב conj. (471)-neg. (II 34)-adj. m.s. (II 373) *that there is nothing better*

בָּם prep.-3 m.p. sf. *for them*

כִּי אִם־לִשְׂמוֹחַ conj. (471)-hypoth.part. (49)-prep.-Qal inf.cstr. (שָׂמַח 970) *than to be happy*

וְלַעֲשׂוֹת טוֹב inf.cstr.prep.-Qal inf.cstr. (עָשָׂה I 793)-adj. m.s. (373) *and enjoy themselves*

בְּחַיָּיו prep.-n.m.p.-3 m.s. sf. (313) *as long as they live*

3:13

וְגַם כָּל־הָאָדָם conj.-adv. (168)-n.m.s. cstr. (481)-def.art.-n.m.s. (9) *and also every one*

שֶׁיֹּאכַל rel. (979)-Qal impf. 3 m.s. (אָכַל 37) *that he should eat*

וְשָׁתָה conj.-Qal pf. 3 m.s. (1059) *and drink*

וְרָאָה טוֹב conj.-Qal pf. 3 m.s. (906)-adj. m.s. (II 373) *and take pleasure*

בְּכָל־עֲמָלוֹ prep.-n.m.s. cstr. (481)-n.m.s.-3 m.s. sf. (765) *in all his toil*

מַתַּת אֱלֹהִים הִיא n.f.s. cstr. (682)-n.m.p. (43)-demons.adj. f.s. (214) *it is God's gift*

3:14

יָדַעְתִּי Qal pf. 1 c.s. (יָדַע 393) *I know*

כִּי כָּל־אֲשֶׁר conj. (471)-n.m.s. (481)-rel. (81) *that whatever*

יַעֲשֶׂה הָאֱלֹהִים Qal impf. 3 m.s. (I 793)-def.art.-n.m.p. (43) *God does*

הוּא יִהְיֶה לְעוֹלָם pers.pr. 3 m.s. (214)-Qal impf. 3 m.s. (הָיָה 224)-prep.-n.m.s. (761) *endured for ever*

עָלָיו אֵין לְהוֹסִיף prep.-3 m.s. sf.-neg. cstr. (II 34)-prep.-Hi. inf.cstr. (יָסַף 414) *nothing can be added to it*

וּמִמֶּנּוּ אֵין לִגְרֹעַ conj.-prep.-3 m.s. sf.-v.supra-prep.-Qal inf.cstr. (גָּרַע 175) *nor anything taken from it*

וְהָאֱלֹהִים עָשָׂה conj.-def.art.-n.m.p. (43)-Qal pf. 3 m.s. (I 793) *God has made it so*

שֶׁיִּרְאוּ rel. (979; GK 165b)-Qal impf. 3 m.p. (יָרֵא 431) *in order that men should fear*

מִלְּפָנָיו prep.-prep.-n.m.p.-3 m.s. sf. (815) *before him*

3:15

מַה־שֶּׁהָיָה interr. (552)-rel. (979)-Qal pf. 3 m.s. (224) *that which is*

כְּבָר הוּא adv. (I 460)-demons.adj. m.s. (214) *already has been*

וַאֲשֶׁר לִהְיוֹת conj.-rel. (81)-prep.-Qal inf.cstr. (224 הָיָה; GK 114i) *that which is to be*

כְּבָר הָיָה v.supra-v.supra *already has been*

וְהָאֱלֹהִים conj.-def.art.-n.m.p. (43) *and God*

יְבַקֵּשׁ Pi. impf. 3 m.s. (בָּקַשׁ 134) *seeks*

אֶת־נִרְדָּף dir.obj.-Ni. ptc. (רָדַף 922) *what has been driven away*

3:16

וְעוֹד רָאִיתִי conj.-adv. (728)-Qal pf. 1 c.s. (רָאָה 906) *moreover I saw*

תַּחַת הַשָּׁמֶשׁ prep. (1065)-def.art.-n.f.s. paus. (1039) *under the sun*
מְקוֹם n.m.s. cstr. (879) *in the place of*
הַמִּשְׁפָּט def.art.-n.m.s. (1048) *justice*
שָׁמָּה הָרֶשַׁע adv.-loc.he (1027)-def.art.-n.m.s. (957) *there was wickedness*
וּמְקוֹם conj.-v.supra *and in the place of*
הַצֶּדֶק def.art.-n.m.s. (841) *righteousness*
שָׁמָּה הָרָשַׁע v.supra-v.supra paus. *there was wickedness*

3:17

אָמַרְתִּי אֲנִי Qal pf. 1 c.s. (55)-pers.pr. 1 c.s. (58) *I said*
בְּלִבִּי prep.-n.m.s.-1 c.s. sf. (524) *in my heart*
אֶת־הַצַּדִּיק dir.obj.-def.art.-adj. m.s. (843) *the righteous*
וְאֶת־הָרָשָׁע conj.-dir.obj.-def.art.-adj. m.s. (957) *and the wicked*
יִשְׁפֹּט Qal impf. 3 m.s. (1047) *will judge*
הָאֱלֹהִים def.art.-n.m.p. (43) *God*
כִּי־עֵת conj. (471)-n.f.s. (773) *for a time*
לְכָל־חֵפֶץ prep.-n.m.s. cstr. (481)-n.m.s. (343) *for every matter*
וְעַל כָּל־הַמַּעֲשֶׂה conj.-prep.-v.supra-def.art. -n.m.s. (795) *and for every work*
שָׁם adv. (1027) *(there)*

3:18

אָמַרְתִּי אֲנִי Qal pf. 1 c.s. (55)-pers.pr. 1 c.s. (58) *I said*
בְּלִבִּי prep.-n.m.s.-1 c.s. sf. (524) *in my heart*
עַל־דִּבְרַת prep.-n.f.s. cstr. (184) *with regard to*
בְּנֵי הָאָדָם n.m.p. cstr. (119)-def.art.-n.m.s. (9) *the sons of men*
לְבָרָם prep.-Qal inf.cstr.-3 m.p. sf. (בָּרַר 140; GK 67p) *to purify them*
הָאֱלֹהִים def.art.-n.m.p. (43) *God*
וְלִרְאוֹת conj.-prep.-Qal inf.cstr. (רָאָה 906) *to show them*
שְׁהֶם־בְּהֵמָה rel. (979; GK 36)-3 m.p. sf.-n.f.s. (96) *they are beasts*
הֵמָּה לָהֶם pers.pr. 3 m.p. (241)-prep.-3 m.p. sf. *they indeed*

3:19

כִּי מִקְרֶה conj. (471)-n.m.s. (899) *for the fate*
בְנֵי־הָאָדָם n.m.p. cstr. (119)-def.art.-n.m.s. (9) *the sons of men*
וּמִקְרֶה conj.-v.supra *and the fate*
הַבְּהֵמָה def.art.-n.f.s. (96) *beasts*
וּמִקְרֶה אֶחָד conj.-v.supra (GK 93rr)-adj. m.s. (25) *also one fate*
לָהֶם prep.-3 m.p. sf. *for them*
כְּמוֹת זֶה prep.-Qal inf.cstr. (מוּת 559) -demons.adj. m.s. (260) *as one dies*
כֵּן מוֹת זֶה adv. (485)-v.supra-v.supra *so dies the other*
וְרוּחַ אֶחָד conj.-n.f.s. cstr. (924)-adj. m.s. (25) *the same breath*
לַכֹּל prep.-def.art.-n.m.s. (481) *to all*
וּמוֹתַר conj.-n.m.s. cstr. (452) *and the advantage of*
הָאָדָם def.art.-n.m.s. (9) *the man*
מִן־הַבְּהֵמָה prep.-def.art.-n.f.s. (96) *over the beasts*
אָיִן neg. (II 34) *there is none*
כִּי הַכֹּל conj. (471)-def.art.-n.m.s. (481) *for all*
הָבֶל n.m.s. paus. (I 210) *is vanity*

3:20

הַכֹּל def.art.-n.m.s. (481) *all*
הוֹלֵךְ Qal act.ptc. (הָלַךְ 229) *go*
אֶל־מָקוֹם אֶחָד prep.-n.m.s. (879)-adj. m.s. (25) *to one place*
הַכֹּל הָיָה v.supra-Qal pf. 3 m.s. (224) *all are*
מִן־הֶעָפָר prep.-def.art.-n.m.s. (779) *from the dust*
וְהַכֹּל conj.-v.supra *and all*
שָׁב Qal act.ptc. (שׁוּב 996) *turn again*
אֶל־הֶעָפָר prep.-def.art.-n.m.s. (779) *to dust*

3:21

מִי יוֹדֵעַ interr. (566)-Qal act.ptc. (יָדַע 393) *who knows*
רוּחַ n.f.s. cstr. (924) *the spirit of*
בְּנֵי הָאָדָם n.m.p. cstr. (119)-def.art.-n.m.s. (9) *man*
הָעֹלָה הִיא def.art. (GK 100m,150iN)-Qal act.ptc. f.s. (עָלָה 748)-pers.pr. 3 f.s. (214) *goes up*
לְמָעְלָה prep.-adv.-loc.he (751) *upward*
וְרוּחַ conj.-v.supra *and the spirit of*
הַבְּהֵמָה def.art.-n.f.s. (96) *the beast*
הַיֹּרֶדֶת הִיא def.art. (GK 100m,150iN)-Qal act.ptc. f.s. (יָרַד 432)-v.supra *goes down*
לְמַטָּה prep.-adv.-loc.he (641) *downward*
לָאָרֶץ prep.-def.art.-n.f.s. (75) *to the earth*

3:22

וְרָאִיתִי conj.-Qal pf. 1 c.s. (רָאָה 906) *so I saw*
כִּי אֵין טוֹב conj. (471)-neg. cstr. (II 34)-adj. m.s. (II 373) *that there is nothing better*

מֵאֲשֶׁר יִשְׂמַח prep.-rel. (81)-Qal impf. 3 m.s. (970 שָׂמַח) *than that should enjoy*
הָאָדָם def.art.-n.m.s. (9) *a man*
בְּמַעֲשָׂיו prep.-n.m.p.-3 m.s. sf. (795) *his work*
כִּי־הוּא חֶלְקוֹ conj. (471)-demons.adj. m.s. (214) -n.m.s.-3 m.s. sf. (324) *for that is his lot*
כִּי מִי conj. (471)-interr. (566) *for who*
יְבִיאֶנּוּ Hi. impf. 3 m.s.-3 m.s. sf. (בּוֹא 97) *can bring him*
לִרְאוֹת prep.-Qal inf.cstr. (רָאָה 906) *to see*
בְּמֶה שֶּׁיִּהְיֶה prep. (GK 102k)-interr. (552)-rel. (979)-Qal impf. 3 m.s. (הָיָה 224) *what will be*
אַחֲרָיו prep.-3 m.s. sf. (29) *after him*

4:1

וְשַׁבְתִּי אֲנִי conj.-Qal pf. 1 c.s. (שׁוּב 996)-pers.pr. 1 c.s. (58) *again I*
וָאֶרְאֶה consec.-Qal impf. 1 c.s. (רָאָה 906) *saw*
אֶת־כָּל־הָעֲשֻׁקִים dir.obj.-n.m.s. cstr. (481)-def.art. -n.m.p. (799) *all the oppressions*
אֲשֶׁר נַעֲשִׂים rel. (81)-Ni. ptc. m.p. (עָשָׂה I 793) *that are practiced*
תַּחַת הַשָּׁמֶשׁ prep. (1065)-def.art.-n.f.s. paus. (1039) *under the sun*
וְהִנֵּה conj.-interj. (243) *and behold*
דִּמְעַת n.f.s. cstr. (199) *the tears of*
הָעֲשֻׁקִים def.art.-Qal pass.ptc. m.p. (עָשַׁק 798) *the oppressed*
וְאֵין לָהֶם conj.-neg. cstr. (II 34)-prep.-3 m.p. sf. *and they had no one ... them*
מְנַחֵם Pi. ptc. (נָחַם 636) *to comfort*
וּמִיַּד conj.-prep.-n.f.s. cstr. (388) *and on the side of*
עֹשְׁקֵיהֶם Qal act.ptc. m.p.-3 m.p. sf. (עָשַׁק 798) *their oppressors*
כֹּחַ n.m.s. (470) *power*
וְאֵין לָהֶם מְנַחֵם v.supra-v.supra-v.supra *and there was no one to comfort them*

4:2

וְשַׁבֵּחַ אֲנִי conj.-Pi. inf.abs. (שָׁבַח 986; GK 113gg)-pers.pr. 1 c.s. (58) *and I thought more fortunate*
אֶת־הַמֵּתִים dir.obj.-def.art.-Qal act.ptc. m.p. (559 מוּת) *the dead*
שֶׁכְּבָר rel. (979)-adv. (I 460) *who already*
מֵתוּ Qal pf. 3 c.p. paus. (מוּת 559) *are dead*
מִן־הַחַיִּים prep.-def.art.-adj. m.p. (I 311) *than the living*
אֲשֶׁר הֵמָּה חַיִּים rel. (81)-pers.pr. 3 m.p. (241) -adj. m.p. (I 311) *who are alive*
עֲדֶנָה adv. (725) *still*

4:3

וְטוֹב מִשְּׁנֵיהֶם conj.-adj. m.s. (II 373)-prep.-n.m. du.-3 m.p. sf. (1040) *better than both of them*
אֵת אֲשֶׁר־עֲדֶן dir.obj.-rel. (81)-adv. (725; abbrev. from עַד־הֵן; GK 117,l) *who yet*
לֹא הָיָה neg.-Qal pf. 3 m.s. (224) *has not been*
אֲשֶׁר לֹא־רָאָה v.supra-neg.-Qal pf. 3 m.s. (906) *who has not seen*
אֶת־הַמַּעֲשֶׂה הָרָע dir.obj.-def.art.-n.m.s. (795) -def.art.-adj. m.s. paus. (I 948) *the evil deeds*
אֲשֶׁר נַעֲשָׂה v.supra-Ni. pf. 3 m.s. (עָשָׂה I 793) *that are done*
תַּחַת הַשָּׁמֶשׁ prep. (1065)-def.art.-n.f.s. paus. (1039) *under the sun*

4:4

וְרָאִיתִי אֲנִי conj.-Qal pf. 1 c.s. (רָאָה 906)-pers.pr. 1 c.s. (58) *and I saw*
אֶת־כָּל־עָמָל dir.obj.-n.m.s. cstr. (481)-n.m.s. (765) *all toil*
וְאֵת כָּל־כִּשְׁרוֹן הַמַּעֲשֶׂה conj.-dir.obj.-v.supra -n.m.s. cstr. (507)-def.art.-n.m.s. (795) *all skill in work*
כִּי הִיא conj. (471)-demons.adj. f.s. (214) *for is*
קִנְאַת־אִישׁ n.f.s. cstr. (888)-n.m.s. (35) *man's envy*
מֵרֵעֵהוּ prep.-n.m.s.-3 m.s. sf. (945) *of his neighbor*
גַּם־זֶה adv. (168)-demons.adj. m.s. (260) *this also*
הֶבֶל n.m.s. (I 210) *vanity*
וּרְעוּת רוּחַ conj.-n.f.s. cstr. (II 946)-n.f.s. (924) *and a striving after wind*

4:5

הַכְּסִיל def.art.-n.m.s. (493) *the fool*
חֹבֵק Qal act.ptc. (287) *folds*
אֶת־יָדָיו dir.obj.-n.f.p.-3 m.s. sf. (388) *his hands*
וְאֹכֵל conj.-Qal act.ptc. (37) *and eats*
אֶת־בְּשָׂרוֹ dir.obj.-n.m.s.-3 m.s. sf. (142) *his own flesh*

4:6

טוֹב adj. m.s. (II 373) *better is*
מְלֹא כַף נָחַת n.m.s. cstr. (571)-n.f.s. cstr. (496) -n.f.s. paus. (I 629) *a handful of quietness*
מִמְּלֹא חָפְנַיִם prep.-v.supra-n.m. du. (342) *than two hands full*
עָמָל n.m.s. (765) *toil*
וּרְעוּת רוּחַ conj.-n.f.s. cstr. (II 946)-n.f.s. (924) *and a striving after wind*

4:7

וְשַׁבְתִּי אֲנִי conj. (GK 112ppN)–Qal pf. 1 c.s. (שׁוּב 996)–pers.pr. 1 c.s. (58) *again* (lit. *and I turned*)

וָאֶרְאֶה consec.–Qal impf. 1 c.s. (רָאָה 906) *I saw*

הֶבֶל n.m.s. (I 210) *vanity*

תַּחַת הַשָּׁמֶשׁ prep. (1065)–def.art.–n.f.s. paus. (1039) *under the sun*

4:8

יֵשׁ אֶחָד subst. (441)–num. (25) *there is one*

וְאֵין שֵׁנִי conj.–neg. (II 34)–num. adj. m. (1041) *and there is not a second*

גַּם בֵּן adv. (168)–n.m.s. (119) *also a son*

וָאָח conj.–n.m.s. (26) *and a brother*

אֵין־לוֹ v.supra–prep.–3 m.s. *there is not to him*

וְאֵין קֵץ conj.–v.supra–n.m.s. (893) *yet there is no end*

לְכָל־עֲמָלוֹ prep.–n.m.s. cstr. (481)–n.m.s.–3 m.s. sf. (765) *to all his toil*

גַּם־עֵינָיו adv. (168)–n.f.s.–3 m.s. sf. (I 744) *and his eye*

לֹא־יִשְׂבַּע neg.–Qal impf. 3 f.s. (959) *is not satisfied*

עֹשֶׁר n.m.s. (799) *riches*

וּלְמִי conj.–prep.–interr. (566) *and for whom*

אֲנִי עָמֵל pers.pr. 1 c.s. (58)–adj. m.s. (II 766) *I am toiling*

וּמְחַסֵּר conj.–Pi. ptc. (חָסֵר 341) *and am depriving*

אֶת־נַפְשִׁי dir.obj.–n.f.s.–1 c.s. sf. (659) *myself*

מִטּוֹבָה prep.–n.f.s. (375) *of pleasure*

גַּם־זֶה adv. (168)–demons.adj. m.s. (260) *this also*

הֶבֶל n.m.s. (I 210) *vanity*

וְעִנְיַן רָע conj.–n.m.s. cstr. (775)–adj. paus. (I 948) *and an unhappy business*

הוּא demons.adj. m.s. (214) *(it is)*

4:9

טוֹבִים adj. m.p. (II 373) *better*

הַשְּׁנַיִם def.art.–n.m. du. (1040) *two*

מִן־הָאֶחָד prep.–def.art.–num. (25) *than one*

אֲשֶׁר יֵשׁ־לָהֶם rel. (81)–subst. (441)–prep.–3 m.p. sf. *because they have*

שָׂכָר טוֹב n.m.s. (I 969)–adj. m.s. (II 373) *a good reward*

בַּעֲמָלָם prep.–n.m.s.–3 m.p. sf. (765) *for their toil*

4:10

כִּי אִם־יִפֹּלוּ conj. (471)–hypoth.part. (49)–Qal impf. 3 m.p. (נָפַל 656; GK 124o) *for if they fall*

הָאֶחָד def.art.–num. (25) *one*

יָקִים Hi. impf. 3 m.s. (קוּם 877) *will lift up*

אֶת־חֲבֵרוֹ dir.obj.–adj. m.s.–3 m.s. sf. (288) *his fellow*

וְאִילוֹ conj.–interj.–prep.–3 m.s. sf. (III 33; rd. וְאִי לוֹ; GK 131n) *but woe to him*

הָאֶחָד v.supra *the one*

שֶׁיִּפּוֹל rel. (979)–Qal impf. 3 m.s. (נָפַל 656) *who falls*

וְאֵין שֵׁנִי conj.–neg. (II 34)–adj. m.s. (1041) *and there is not another*

לַהֲקִימוֹ prep.–Hi. inf.cstr.–3 m.s. sf. (קוּם 877) *to lift him up*

4:11

גַּם adv. (168) *again*

אִם־יִשְׁכְּבוּ hypoth.part. (49)–Qal impf. 3 m.p. (1011 שָׁכַב) *if lie together*

שְׁנַיִם n.m. du. (1040) *two*

וְחַם לָהֶם conj.–Qal pf. 3 m.s. (חָמַם 328)–prep.–3 m.p. sf. *they are warm*

וּלְאֶחָד conj.–prep.–num. (25) *but for one*

אֵיךְ יֵחָם adv. (32)–Qal impf. 3 m.s. paus. (חָמַם 328) *how can be warm*

4:12

וְאִם־יִתְקְפוֹ conj.–hypoth.part. (49)–Qal impf. 3 m.s.–3 m.s. sf. (תָּקַף 1075; GK 60d) *and though ... might prevail against him*

הָאֶחָד def.art.–num. (25) *one*

הַשְּׁנַיִם def.art.–n.m. du. (1040) *two*

יַעַמְדוּ נֶגְדּוֹ Qal impf. 3 m.p. (עָמַד 763)–prep.–3 m.s. sf. (617) *will withstand him*

וְהַחוּט הַמְשֻׁלָּשׁ conj.–def.art.–n.m.s. (296)–def. art.–Pu. ptc. (שָׁלַשׁ I 1026) *and a threefold cord*

לֹא בִמְהֵרָה neg.–prep.–n.f.s. (555) *not quickly*

יִנָּתֵק Ni. impf. 3 m.s. (נָתַק 683) *is broken*

4:13

טוֹב adj. m.s. (II 373) *better is*

יֶלֶד מִסְכֵּן וְחָכָם n.m.s. (409)–adj. m.s. (587) –conj.–adj. m.s. (314) *a poor and wise youth*

מִמֶּלֶךְ זָקֵן וּכְסִיל prep.–n.m.s. (I 572)–adj. m.s. (278)–conj.–adj. m.s. (I 493) *than an old and foolish king*

אֲשֶׁר לֹא־יָדַע rel. (81)–neg.–Qal pf. 3 m.s. (393) *who does not know*

לְהִזָּהֵר עוֹד prep.-Ni. inf.cstr. (זָהַר II 264)-adv. (728) *how to take admonition*

4:14

כִּי־מִבֵּית הָסוּרִים conj. (471)-prep.-n.m.s. cstr. (108)-def.art.-Qal pass.ptc. m.p. (אָסַר 63; GK 35d) *even though from prison*

יָצָא Qal pf. 3 m.s. (422) *he had gone*

לִמְלֹךְ prep.-Qal inf.cstr. (573) *to the throne* (lit. *to be king*)

כִּי גַּם בְּמַלְכוּתוֹ conj. (471)-adv. (168)-prep. -n.f.s.-3 m.s. sf. (574) *or in his own kingdom*

נוֹלַד רָשׁ Ni. pf. 3 m.s. (יָלַד 408)-Qal act.ptc. as adj. (רוּשׁ 930) *poor had been born*

4:15

רָאִיתִי Qal pf. 1 c.s. (רָאָה 906) *I saw*

אֶת־כָּל־הַחַיִּים dir.obj.-n.m.s. cstr. (481)-def. art.-adj. m.p. (I 311) *all the living*

הַמְהַלְּכִים def.art.-Pi. ptc. m.p. (הָלַךְ 229) *who move about*

תַּחַת הַשָּׁמֶשׁ prep. (1065)-def.art.-n.f.s. paus. (1039) *under the sun*

עִם הַיֶּלֶד הַשֵּׁנִי prep. (767)-def.art.-n.m.s. (409)-def.art.-adj. m.s. (1041) *as well as the second youth*

אֲשֶׁר יַעֲמֹד rel. (81)-Qal impf. 3 m.s. (763) *who was to stand*

תַּחְתָּיו prep.-3 m.s. sf. (1065) *in his place*

4:16

אֵין־קֵץ neg. cstr. (II 34)-n.m.s. (893) *there was no end*

לְכָל־הָעָם prep.-n.m.s. cstr. (481)-def.art.-n.m.s. (I 766) *of all the people*

לְכֹל אֲשֶׁר־הָיָה prep.-n.m.s. (481)-rel. (81)-Qal pf. 3 m.s. (224) *of all who were*

לִפְנֵיהֶם prep.-n.m.p.-3 m.p. sf. (815) *before them*

גַּם הָאַחֲרוֹנִים adv. (168)-def.art.-adj. m.p. (30) *yet those who come later*

לֹא יִשְׂמְחוּ־בוֹ neg.-Qal impf. 3 m.p. (970) -prep.-3 m.s. sf. *will not rejoice in him*

כִּי־גַם־זֶה conj.-adv. (168)-demons.adj. m.s. (260) *surely this also*

הֶבֶל n.m.s. (I 210) *vanity*

וְרַעְיוֹן רוּחַ conj.-n.m.s. cstr. (946)-n.f.s. (924) *and a striving after wind*

4:17

שְׁמֹר Qal impv. 2 m.s. (1036) *guard*

רַגְלְיךָ n.f. du.-2 m.s. sf. (919) *your steps*

כַּאֲשֶׁר תֵּלֵךְ prep.-rel. (81)-Qal impf. 2 m.s. (הָלַךְ 229) *when you go*

אֶל־בֵּית הָאֱלֹהִים prep.-n.m.s. cstr. (108)-def. art.-n.m.p. (43) *to the house of God*

וְקָרוֹב לִשְׁמֹעַ conj.-Qal inf.abs. (897)-prep.-Qal inf.cstr. (1033) *to draw near to listen*

מִתֵּת הַכְּסִילִים prep. (GK 133e)-Qal inf.cstr. (נָתַן 678)-def.art.-n.m.p. (493) *than the offering of fools*

זָבַח n.m.s. paus. (257; II,7) *sacrifice*

כִּי־אֵינָם conj. (471)-neg.-3 m.p. sf. (II 34) *for none of them*

יוֹדְעִים Qal act.ptc. m.p. (יָדַע 393) *know*

לַעֲשׂוֹת רָע prep.-Qal inf.cstr. (עָשָׂה I 793; 1124, 583b)-n.m.s. paus. (II 948) *that they are doing evil*

5:1 (Eng.5:2)

אַל־תְּבַהֵל prep.-Pi. impf. 2 m.s. (בָּהַל 96) *be not rash*

עַל־פִּיךָ prep.-n.m.s.-2 m.s. sf. (804) *with your mouth*

וְלִבְּךָ conj.-n.m.s.-2 m.s. sf. (524) *and your heart*

אַל־יְמַהֵר neg.-Pi. impf. 3 m.s. (I 554) *let not be hasty*

לְהוֹצִיא prep.-Hi. inf.cstr. (יָצָא 422) *to utter*

דָבָר n.m.s. (182) *a word*

לִפְנֵי הָאֱלֹהִים prep.-n.m.p. cstr. (815)-def.art. -n.m.p. (43) *before God*

כִּי הָאֱלֹהִים conj. (471)-v.supra *for God is*

בַשָּׁמַיִם prep.-def.art.-n.m. du. (1029) *in heaven*

וְאַתָּה conj.-pers.pr. 2 m.s. (61) *and you*

עַל־הָאָרֶץ prep.-def.art.-n.f.s. (75) *upon earth*

עַל־כֵּן prep.-adv. (485) *therefore*

יִהְיוּ Qal impf. 3 m.p. (הָיָה 224) *let be*

דְבָרֶיךָ n.m.p.-2 m.s. sf. (182) *your words*

מְעַטִּים subst. p. (589) *few*

5:2

כִּי בָּא conj. (471)-Qal pf. 3 m.s. (בּוֹא 97) *for comes*

הַחֲלוֹם def.art.-n.m.s. (321) *a dream*

בְּרֹב עִנְיָן prep.-n.m.s. cstr. (913)-n.m.s. (775) *with much business*

וְקוֹל כְּסִיל conj.-n.m.s. cstr. (876)-n.m.s. (493) *and a fool's voice*

בְּרֹב דְּבָרִים prep.-v.supra-n.m.p. (182) *with many words*

5:3

כַּאֲשֶׁר תִּדֹּר prep.-rel. (81)-Qal impf. 2 m.s. (נָדַר 623) *when you vow*

נֶדֶר n.m.s. (623) *a vow*
לֵאלֹהִים prep.-n.m.p. (43) *to God*
אַל־תְּאַחֵר neg.-Pi. impf. 2 m.s. (אָחַר 29) *do not delay*
לְשַׁלְּמוֹ prep.-Pi. inf.cstr.-3 m.s. sf. (1022) *paying it*
כִּי אֵין חֵפֶץ conj. (471)-neg. (II 34)-n.m.s. (343) *for he has no pleasure*
בַּכְּסִילִים prep.-def.art.-n.m.p. (493) *in fools*
אֵת אֲשֶׁר־תִּדֹּר dir.obj.-rel. (81)-Qal impf. 2 m.s. (נָדַר 623) *what you vow*
שַׁלֵּם Pi. impv. 2 m.s. (1022) *pay*

5:4

טוֹב אֲשֶׁר adj. m.s. (II 373)-rel. (81) *it is better that*
לֹא־תִדֹּר neg.-Qal impf. 2 m.s. (נָדַר 623) *you should not vow*
מִשֶּׁתִּדּוֹר prep.-rel. (979)-Qal impf. 2 m.s. (נָדַר 623) *than that you should vow*
וְלֹא תְשַׁלֵּם conj.-neg.-Pi. impf. 2 m.s. (שָׁלֵם 1022) *and not pay*

5:5

אַל־תִּתֵּן אֶת־פִּיךָ neg.-Qal impf. 2 m.s. (נָתַן 678)-dir.obj.-n.m.s.-2 m.s. sf. (804) *let not your mouth lead*
לַחֲטִיא prep.-Hi. inf.cstr. (חָטָא 306; GK 53q) *to sin (cause to sin)*
אֶת־בְּשָׂרֶךָ dir.obj.-n.m.p.-2 m.s. sf. (142) *(your flesh)*
וְאַל־תֹּאמַר conj.-neg.-Qal impf. 2 m.s. (55) *and do not say*
לִפְנֵי הַמַּלְאָךְ prep.-n.m.p. cstr. (815)-def.art. -n.m.s. (521) *before the messenger*
כִּי שְׁגָגָה הִיא conj. (471)-n.f.s. (993)-pers.pr. 3 f.s. (214) *that it was a mistake*
לָמָּה יִקְצֹף prep.-interr. (552)-Qal impf. 3 m.s. (893 קָצַף) *why should ... be angry*
הָאֱלֹהִים def.art.-n.m.p. (43) *God*
עַל־קוֹלֶךָ prep.-n.m.s.-2 m.s. sf. (876) *at your voice*
וְחִבֵּל conj.-Pi. pf. 3 m.s. (חָבַל II 287) *and destroy*
אֶת־מַעֲשֵׂה dir.obj.-n.m.s. cstr. (795) *the work of*
יָדֶיךָ n.f. du.-2 m.s. sf. (388) *your hands*

5:6

כִּי בְרֹב conj. (471)-prep.-n.m.s. cstr. (913) *for when ... increase*
חֲלֹמוֹת n.m.p. (321) *dreams*
וַהֲבָלִים conj. (GK 143d)-n.m.p. (I 210) *and futility*
וּדְבָרִים conj.-n.m.p. (182) *and words*
הַרְבֵּה Hi. inf.abs. (רָבָה I 915) *grow many*
כִּי אֶת־הָאֱלֹהִים conj. (471)-dir.obj. -def.art.-n.m.p. (43) *but God*
יְרָא Qal impv. 2 m.s. (יָרֵא 431) *you fear*

5:7

אִם־עֹשֶׁק hypoth.part. (49)-n.m.s. cstr. (799) *if oppression of*
רָשׁ Qal act.ptc. (רוּשׁ 930) *poor*
וְגֵזֶל conj.-n.m.s. cstr. (160) *and wresting of*
מִשְׁפָּט n.m.s. (1048) *justice*
וָצֶדֶק conj.-n.m.s. (841) *and right*
תִּרְאֶה Qal impf. 2 m.s. (רָאָה 906) *you see*
בַמְּדִינָה prep.-def.art.-n.f.s. (193) *in the province*
אַל־תִּתְמַהּ neg.-Qal impf. 2 m.s. (תָּמַהּ 1069) *do not be amazed*
עַל־הַחֵפֶץ prep.-def.art.-n.m.s. (343) *at the matter*
כִּי גָבֹהַּ conj. (471)-adj. m.s. (147) *for the high official*
מֵעַל גָּבֹהַּ prep.-prep.-v.supra *by a higher*
שֹׁמֵר Qal act.ptc. (1036) *is watched*
וּגְבֹהִים conj.-adj. m.p. (147; GK 124h) *and there are higher ones*
עֲלֵיהֶם prep.-3 m.p. sf. *over them*

5:8

וְיִתְרוֹן אֶרֶץ conj.-n.m.s. cstr. (452)-n.f.s. (75) *but the profit of the land*
בַּכֹּל היא prep.-def.art.-n.m.s. (481)-pers.pr. 3 m.s. (214; K הִיא 3 f.s.; GK 32,l) *is among all*
מֶלֶךְ n.m.s. (I 572) *a king*
לְשָׂדֶה נֶעֱבָד prep.-n.m.s. (961)-Ni. ptc. (עָבַד 712) *to a cultivated field*

5:9

אֹהֵב כֶּסֶף Qal act.ptc. (אָהֵב 12)-n.m.s. (494) *he who loves money*
לֹא־יִשְׂבַּע neg.-Qal impf. 3 m.s. (שָׂבֵעַ 959) *will not be satisfied with*
כֶּסֶף v.supra *money*
וּמִי־אֹהֵב conj.-interr. (566)-v.supra *nor he who loves*
בֶּהָמוֹן prep.-def.art.-n.m.s. (242) *with gain*
לֹא תְבוּאָה neg.-n.f.s. (100) *wealth*
גַּם־זֶה adv. (168)-demons.adj. m.s. (260) *this also*
הָבֶל n.m.s. paus. (I 210) *vanity*

5:10

בִּרְבוֹת הַטּוֹבָה prep.-Qal inf.cstr. (רָבָה I 915) -def.art.-n.f.s. (375) *when goods increase*

רַבּוּ Qal pf. 3 c.p. (רָבַב I 912) *they increase*

אוֹכְלֶיהָ Qal act.ptc. m.p.-3 f.s. (אָכַל 37) *who eat them*

וּמַה־כִּשְׁרוֹן conj.-interr. (552)-n.m.s. (507) *and what gain*

לִבְעָלֶיהָ prep.-n.m.p.-3 f.s. sf. (127) *to their owners*

כִּי אִם־רְאִיַּת conj. (471)-hypoth.part. (49)-Qal inf.cstr. (רָאָה 906; rd. רְאוֹת) *but to see*

עֵינָיו n.f. du.-3 m.s. sf. (744) *with his eyes*

5:11

מְתוּקָה adj. f.s. (608) *sweet is*

שְׁנַת n.f.p. cstr. (446) *the sleep of*

הָעֹבֵד def.art.-Qal act.ptc. (712) *the laborer*

אִם־מְעַט hypoth.part. (49)-subst. (589) *whether little*

וְאִם־הַרְבֵּה conj.-v.supra-Hi. inf.abs. as n. (רָבָה I 915) *or much*

יֹאכֵל Qal impf. 3 m.s. (37) *he eats*

וְהַשָּׂבָע conj.-def.art.-n.m.s. (960) *but the surfeit*

לֶעָשִׁיר prep.-def.art.-n.m.s. (799) *of the rich*

אֵינֶנּוּ מַנִּיחַ neg.-3 m.s. sf. (II 34)-Hi. ptc. (נוּחַ 628) *will not permit*

לוֹ לִישׁוֹן prep.-3 m.s. sf.-prep.-Qal inf.cstr. (יָשֵׁן 445; GK 69n) *him to sleep*

5:12

יֵשׁ רָעָה חוֹלָה subst. (441)-n.f.s. (949)-Qal act.ptc. f.s. as adj. f.s. (חָלָה I 317) *there is a grievous evil*

רָאִיתִי Qal pf. 1 c.s. (רָאָה 906) *I have seen*

תַּחַת הַשָּׁמֶשׁ prep. (1065)-def.art.-n.f.s. paus. (1039) *under the sun*

עֹשֶׁר n.m.s. (799) *riches*

שָׁמוּר Qal pass.ptc. (שָׁמַר 1036) *were kept*

לִבְעָלָיו prep.-n.m.p.-3 m.s. sf. (127) *by their owner*

לְרָעָתוֹ prep.-n.f.s.-3 m.s. sf. (949) *to his hurt*

5:13

וְאָבַד conj.-Qal pf. 3 m.s. (1) *and were lost*

הָעֹשֶׁר הַהוּא def.art.-n.m.s. (799)-def.art. -demons.adj. m.s. (214) *those riches*

בְּעִנְיַן רָע prep.-n.m.s. cstr. (775)-adj. m.s. (I 948) *in a bad venture*

וְהוֹלִיד conj.-Hi. pf. 3 m.s. (יָלַד 408) *and he is father of*

בֵּן n.m.s. (119) *a son*

וְאֵין בְּיָדוֹ conj.-neg. cstr. (II 34)-prep.-n.f.s.-3 m.s. sf. (388) *but he does not have in his hand*

מְאוּמָה pr. indef. (548) *anything*

5:14

כַּאֲשֶׁר יָצָא prep.-rel. (81)-Qal pf. 3 m.s. (422) *as he came*

מִבֶּטֶן אִמּוֹ prep.-n.f.s. cstr. (105)-n.f.s.-3 m.s. sf. (51) *from his mother's womb*

עָרוֹם יָשׁוּב adj. m.s. (736)-Qal impf. 3 m.s. (שׁוּב 996) *naked he shall again*

לָלֶכֶת prep.-Qal inf.cstr. (הָלַךְ 229) *go*

כְּשֶׁבָּא prep.-rel. (979)-Qal pf. 3 m.s. (בּוֹא 97) *as he came*

וּמְאוּמָה לֹא־יִשָּׂא conj.-pr. indef. (548)-neg.-Qal impf. 3 m.s. (נָשָׂא 669; GK 109i) *and shall take nothing*

בַעֲמָלוֹ prep.-n.m.s.-3 m.s. sf. (765) *for his toil*

שֶׁיֹּלֵךְ rel. (979)-Hi. impf. 3 m.s. apoc. (הָלַךְ 229) *which he may carry away*

בְּיָדוֹ prep.-n.f.s.-3 m.s. sf. (388) *in his hand*

5:15

וְגַם־זֹה conj.-adv. (168)-demons.adj. f.s. (260) *this also*

רָעָה חוֹלָה n.f.s. (949)-Qal act.ptc. f.s. as adj. f.s. (חָלָה I 317) *a grievous evil*

כָּל־עֻמַּת שֶׁבָּא n.m.s. cstr. (481)-n.f.s. (I 769)-rel. (979; GK 161b)-Qal pf. 3 m.s. (בּוֹא 97) *just as he came*

כֵּן יֵלֵךְ adv. (485)-Qal impf. 3 m.s. (הָלַךְ 229) *so shall he go*

וּמַה־יִּתְרוֹן conj.-interr. (552)-n.m.s. (452) *and what gain*

לוֹ prep.-3 m.s. sf. *has he*

שֶׁיַּעֲמֹל rel. (979)-Qal impf. 3 m.s. (765) *that he toiled*

לָרוּחַ prep.-def.art.-n.f.s. (924) *for the wind*

5:16

גַּם כָּל־יָמָיו adv. (168)-n.m.s. cstr. (481)-n.m.p.-3 m.s. sf. (398) *also all his days*

בַּחֹשֶׁךְ prep.-def.art.-n.m.s. (365) *in darkness*

יֹאכֵל Qal impf. 3 m.s. (אָכַל 37) *he eats*

וְכָעַס conj.-Qal pf. 3 m.s. (494) *and he is vexed*

הַרְבֵּה Hi. inf.abs. (רָבָה I 915) *exceedingly*

וְחָלְיוֹ conj.-n.m.s.-3 m.s. sf. (318; GK GK 147e) *and sickness*

וָקָצֶף conj.-n.m.s. paus. (I 893) *and wrath*

5:17

הִנֵּה interj. (243) *behold*

אֲשֶׁר־רָאִיתִי rel. (81)-Qal pf. 1 c.s. (רָאָה 906) *what I have seen*

אָנִי pers.pr. 1 c.s. (58) *myself*

טוֹב adj. m.s. (II 373) *to be good*

אֲשֶׁר־יָפֶה rel. (81)-adj. m.s. (421) *which is fitting*

לֶאֱכוֹל־ prep.-Qal inf.cstr. (אָכַל 37) *is to eat*

וְלִשְׁתּוֹת conj.-prep.-Qal inf.cstr. (שָׁתָה 1059) *and drink*

וְלִרְאוֹת טוֹבָה conj.-prep.-Qal inf.cstr. (רָאָה 906)-n.f.s. (375) *and find enjoyment*

בְּכָל־עֲמָלוֹ prep.-n.m.s. cstr. (481)-n.m.s.-3 m.s. sf. (765) *in all the toil*

שֶׁיַּעֲמֹל rel. (979)-Qal impf. 3 m.s. (עָמַל 765) *with which one toils*

תַּחַת־הַשֶּׁמֶשׁ prep. (1065)-def.art.-n.f.s. (1039) *under the sun*

מִסְפַּר יְמֵי־חַיָּו n.m.s. cstr. (708)-n.m.p. cstr. (398)-n.m.p.-3 m.s. sf. (313) *the few days of his life*

אֲשֶׁר־נָתַן־לוֹ rel. (81)-Qal pf. 3 m.s. (678)-prep.-3 m.s. sf. *which has given him*

הָאֱלֹהִים def.art.-n.m.p. (43) *God*

כִּי־הוּא conj. (471)-demons.adj. m.s. (214) *for this is*

חֶלְקוֹ n.m.s.-3 m.s. sf. (324) *his lot*

5:18

גַּם כָּל־הָאָדָם adv. (168)-n.m.s. cstr. (481)-def.art. -n.m.s. (9) *also every man*

אֲשֶׁר נָתַן־לוֹ rel. (81)-Qal pf. 3 m.s. (678)-prep.-3 m.s. sf. *to whom ... has given*

הָאֱלֹהִים def.art.-n.m.p. (43) *God*

עֹשֶׁר n.m.s. (799) *wealth*

וּנְכָסִים conj.-n.m.p. (647) *and possessions*

וְהִשְׁלִיטוֹ conj.-Hi. pf. 3 m.s.-3 m.s. sf. (שָׁלַט I 1020; GK 112ppN) *and given him power*

לֶאֱכֹל prep.-Qal inf.cstr. (אָכַל 37) *to eat*

מִמֶּנּוּ prep.-3 m.s. sf. *them*

וְלָשֵׂאת אֶת־חֶלְקוֹ conj.-prep.-Qal inf.cstr. (נָשָׂא 669)-dir.obj.-n.m.s.-3 m.s. sf. (324) *and to accept his lot*

וְלִשְׂמֹחַ conj.-prep.-Qal inf.cstr. (שָׂמַח 970) *and find enjoyment*

בַּעֲמָלוֹ prep.-n.m.s.-3 m.s. sf. (765) *in his toil*

זֹה demons.adj. f.s. (260; GK 141h) *this*

מַתַּת אֱלֹהִים n.f.s. cstr. (682)-n.m.p. (43) *the gift of God*

הִיא demons.adj. f.s. (214) *(is)*

5:19

כִּי לֹא הַרְבֵּה conj.-neg.-Hi. inf.abs. (רָבָה I 915) *for not much*

יִזְכֹּר Qal impf. 3 m.s. (269) *he will remember*

אֶת־יְמֵי חַיָּיו dir.obj.-n.m.p. cstr. (398)-n.m.p.-3 m.s. sf. (313) *the days of his life*

כִּי הָאֱלֹהִים conj. (471)-def.art.-n.m.p. (43) *because God*

מַעֲנֶה Hi. ptc. (עָנָה I 772) *keeps him occupied*

בְּשִׂמְחַת לִבּוֹ prep.-n.f.s. cstr. (970)-n.m.s.-3 m.s. sf. (524) *with joy in his heart*

6:1

יֵשׁ רָעָה subst. (441)-n.f.s. (949) *there is an evil*

אֲשֶׁר רָאִיתִי rel. (81)-Qal pf. 1 c.s. (רָאָה 906; GK 155h) *which I have seen*

תַּחַת הַשָּׁמֶשׁ prep. (1065)-def.art.-n.f.s. paus. (1039) *under the sun*

וְרַבָּה הִיא conj.-adj. f.s. (I 912)-demons.adj. f.s. (214) *and it lies heavy*

עַל־הָאָדָם prep.-def.art.-n.m.s. (9) *upon men*

6:2

אִישׁ n.m.s. (35) *a man*

אֲשֶׁר יִתֶּן־לוֹ rel. (81)-Qal impf. 3 m.s. (נָתַן 678)-prep.-3 m.s. sf. *to whom ... gives*

הָאֱלֹהִים def.art.-n.m.p. (43) *God*

עֹשֶׁר n.m.s. (799) *wealth*

וּנְכָסִים conj.-n.m.p. (647) *and possessions*

וְכָבוֹד conj.-n.m.s. (458) *and honor*

וְאֵינֶנּוּ חָסֵר conj.-neg.-3 m.s. sf. (II 34)-adj. m.s. (341) *so that there is not lacking*

לְנַפְשׁוֹ prep.-n.f.s.-3 m.s. sf. (659) *to his life*

מִכֹּל אֲשֶׁר־יִתְאַוֶּה prep.-n.m.s. (481)-rel. (81) -Hith. impf. 3 m.s. (אָוָה I 16) *of all that he desires*

וְלֹא־יַשְׁלִיטֶנּוּ conj.-neg.-Hi. impf. 3 m.s.-3 m.s. sf. (שָׁלַט I 1020) *and ... does not give him power*

הָאֱלֹהִים def.art.-n.m.p. (43) *God*

לֶאֱכֹל מִמֶּנּוּ prep.-Qal inf.cstr. (אָכַל 37)-prep.-3 m.s. sf. *to enjoy them*

כִּי אִישׁ נָכְרִי conj. (471)-n.m.s. (35)-adj. m.s. (648) *but a stranger*

יֹאכְלֶנּוּ Qal impf. 3 m.s.-3 m.s. sf. (אָכַל 37) *enjoys them*

זֶה הֶבֶל demons.adj. m.s. (260)-n.m.s. (I 210) *this is vanity*

וָחֳלִי רָע conj.-n.m.s. (318)-adj. m.s. (I 948) *a sore affliction*

הוּא pers.pr. 3 m.s. (214) *it is*

6:3

אִם־יוֹלִיד hypoth.part. (49)–Hi. impf. 3 m.s. (יָלַד 408) *if ... begets*
אִישׁ n.m.s. (35) *a man*
מֵאָה n.f.s. (547) *a hundred*
וְשָׁנִים רַבּוֹת conj.–n.f.p. (1040)–adj. f.p. (I 912) *and many years*
יִחְיֶה Qal impf. 3 m.s. (חָיָה 310) *lives*
וְרַב שֶׁיִּהְיוּ conj.–adj. m.s. (I 912)–rel. (979)–Qal impf. 3 m.s. (הָיָה 224) *so that are many*
יְמֵי־שָׁנָיו n.m.p. cstr. (398)–n.f.p.–3 m.s. sf. (1040) *the days of his years*
וְנַפְשׁוֹ conj.–n.f.s.–3 m.s. sf. (659) *so that he himself*
לֹא־תִשְׂבַּע neg.–Qal impf. 3 f.s. (שָׂבַע 959) *does not enjoy*
מִן־הַטּוֹבָה prep.–def.art.–adj. f.s. (II 373) *life's good things*
וְגַם־ conj.–adv. (168) *and also*
קְבוּרָה n.f.s. (869) *a burial*
לֹא־הָיְתָה לּוֹ neg.–Qal pf. 3 f.s. (224)–prep.–3 m.s. sf. *there is not to him*
אָמַרְתִּי Qal pf. 1 c.s. (אָמַר 55) *I say*
טוֹב מִמֶּנּוּ הַנָּפֶל adj. m.s. (II 373)–prep.–3 m.s. sf.–def.art.–n.m.s. paus. (658) *an untimely birth is better off than he*

6:4

כִּי־בַהֶבֶל conj. (471)–prep.–def.art.–n.m.s. (I 210) *for into vanity*
בָּא Qal pf. 3 m.s. (בּוֹא 97) *it comes*
וּבַחֹשֶׁךְ conj.–prep.–def.art.–n.m.s. (365) *and in darkness*
יֵלֵךְ Qal impf. 3 m.s. (הָלַךְ 229) *goes*
וּבַחֹשֶׁךְ v.supra *and in darkness*
שְׁמוֹ n.m.s.–3 m.s. sf. (1027) *its name*
יְכֻסֶּה Pu. impf. 3 m.s. (כָּסָה 491) *is covered*

6:5

גַּם־שֶׁמֶשׁ adv. (168)–n.f.s. (1039) *moreover the sun*
לֹא־רָאָה neg.–Qal pf. 3 m.s. (906) *it has not seen*
וְלֹא יָדָע conj.–prep.–Qal pf. 3 m.s. paus. (393) *or known anything*
נַחַת לָזֶה מִזֶּה n.f.s. (I 629)–prep.–demons.adj. m.s. (260)–prep.–v.supra *yet it finds rest rather than he*

6:6

וְאִלּוּ חָיָה conj.–conj. (47)–Qal pf. 3 m.s. (310) *even though he should live*
אֶלֶף שָׁנִים num. cstr. (48)–n.f.p. (1040) *a thousand years*
פַּעֲמַיִם n.f. du. (821) *twice told*
וְטוֹבָה לֹא רָאָה conj.–n.f.s. (375)–neg.–Qal pf. 3 m.s. (906) *yet enjoy no good*
הֲלֹא אֶל־מָקוֹם אֶחָד interr.–neg.–prep.–n.m.s. (879)–num. adj. (25) *do not to one place*
הַכֹּל הוֹלֵךְ def.art.–n.m.s. (481)–Qal act.ptc. (הָלַךְ 229) *all go*

6:7

כָּל־עֲמַל n.m.s. cstr. (481)–n.m.s. cstr. (765) *all the toil of*
הָאָדָם def.art.–n.m.s. (9) *man*
לְפִיהוּ prep.–n.m.s.–3 m.s. sf. (804) *for his mouth*
וְגַם־הַנֶּפֶשׁ conj.–adv. (168)–def.art.–n.f.s. (659) *yet his appetite*
לֹא תִמָּלֵא neg.–Ni. impf. 3 f.s. (מָלֵא 569) *is not satisfied*

6:8

כִּי מַה־יּוֹתֵר conj.–interr. (552)–n.m.s. (452) *for what advantage*
לֶחָכָם prep.–def.art.–adj. m.s. (314) *to the wise man*
מִן־הַכְּסִיל prep.–def.art.–n.m.s. (I 493) *over the fool*
מַה־לֶּעָנִי v.supra–prep.–def.art.–adj. m.s. (776) *and what to the poor man*
יוֹדֵעַ Qal act.ptc. (יָדַע 393) *who knows how*
לַהֲלֹךְ prep.–Qal inf.cstr. (הָלַךְ 229) *to conduct himself*
נֶגֶד הַחַיִּים prep. (617)–def.art.–adj. m.p. (I 311) *before the living*

6:9

טוֹב adj. m.s. (II 373) *better is*
מַרְאֵה עֵינַיִם n.m.s. cstr. (909)–n.f. du. (744) *the sight of the eyes*
מֵהֲלָךְ־נָפֶשׁ prep.–Qal inf.cstr. (הָלַךְ 229)–n.f.s. paus. (659) *than the wandering of desire*
גַּם־זֶה הֶבֶל adv. (168)–demons.adj. m.s. (260)–n.m.s. (I 210) *this also is vanity*
וּרְעוּת רוּחַ conj.–n.f.s. cstr. (II 946)–n.f.s. (924) *and a striving after wind*

6:10

מַה־שֶּׁהָיָה interr. (552)–rel. (979)–Qal pf. 3 m.s. (224) *whatever has come to be*
כְּבָר adv. (I 460) *already*
נִקְרָא שְׁמוֹ Ni. pf. 3 m.s. (or ptc.)(קָרָא 894)–n.m.s.–3 m.s. sf. (1027) *has been named*

וְנוֹדָע conj.-Ni. ptc. (יָדַע 393) *and it is known*
אֲשֶׁר־הוּא אָדָם rel. (81)-pers.pr. 3 m.s. (214) -n.m.s. (9) *what man is*
וְלֹא־יוּכַל conj.-neg.-Qal impf. 3 m.s. (יָכֹל 407) *and that he is not able*
לָדִין prep.-Qal inf.cstr. (דִּין 192) *to dispute*
עִם שֶׁהַתַּקִּיף prep. (767)-rel. (979)-adj. m.s. (1076) *with one stronger*
מִמֶּנּוּ prep.-3 m.s. sf. *than he*

6:11

כִּי יֵשׁ־דְּבָרִים conj. (471)-subst. (441)-n.m.p. (182) *when there are words*
הַרְבֵּה Hi. inf.abs. (רָבָה I 915) *more*
מַרְבִּים הָבֶל Hi. ptc. m.p. (רָבָה I 915)-n.m.s. (I 210) *the more vanity*
מַה־יֹּתֵר interr. (552)-n.m.s. (452) *what advantage*
לָאָדָם prep.-def.art.-n.m.s. (9) *to the man*

6:12

כִּי מִי־יוֹדֵעַ conj. (471)-interr. (566)-Qal act.ptc. (393 יָדַע) *for who knows*
מַה־טּוֹב interr. (552)-adj. m.s. (II 373) *what is good*
לָאָדָם prep.-def.art.-n.m.s. (9) *for man*
בַּחַיִּים prep.-def.art.-n.m.p. (313) *while he lives*
מִסְפַּר יְמֵי־חַיֵּי הֶבְלוֹ n.m.s. cstr. (708)-n.m.p. cstr. (398)-n.m.p. cstr. (313)-n.m.s.-3 m.s. sf. (I 210) *the few days of his vain life*
וְיַעֲשֵׂם conj.-Qal impf. 3 m.s.-3 m.p. sf. (עָשָׂה I 793) *which he passes (them)*
כַּצֵּל prep.-def.art.-n.m.s. (853) *like a shadow*
אֲשֶׁר מִי־יַגִּיד rel. (81)-interr. (566)-Hi. impf. 3 m.s. (נָגַד 616) *for who can tell*
לָאָדָם prep.-def.art.-n.m.s. (9) *man*
מַה־יִּהְיֶה v.supra-Qal impf. 3 m.s. (הָיָה 224) *what will be*
אַחֲרָיו prep.-3 m.s. sf. (29) *after him*
תַּחַת הַשָּׁמֶשׁ prep. (1065)-def.art.-n.f.s. paus. (1039) *under the sun*

7:1

טוֹב שֵׁם adj. m.s. (II 373)-n.m.s. (1027) *a good name*
מִשֶּׁמֶן prep.-n.m.s. (1032) *than ointment*
טוֹב adj. m.s. (II 373) *is better*
וְיוֹם הַמָּוֶת conj.-n.m.s. cstr. (398)-def.art.-n.m.s. (560) *and the day of death*
מִיּוֹם הִוָּלְדוֹ prep.-v.supra-Ni. inf.cstr.-3 m.s. sf. (יָלַד 408) *than the day of his birth*

7:2

טוֹב adj. m.s. (II 373) *it is better*
לָלֶכֶת prep.-Qal inf.cstr. (הָלַךְ 229) *to go*
אֶל־בֵּית אֵבֶל prep.-n.m.s. cstr. (108)-n.m.s. (5) *to the house of mourning*
מִלֶּכֶת prep.-v.supra *than to go*
אֶל־בֵּית מִשְׁתֶּה v.supra-v.supra-n.m.s. (1059) *to the house of feasting*
בַּאֲשֶׁר הוּא prep.-rel. (81)-demons.adj. m.s. (214) *for this is*
סוֹף n.m.s. cstr. (693) *the end of*
כָּל־הָאָדָם n.m.s. cstr. (481)-def.art.-n.m.s. (9) *all men*
וְהַחַי conj.-def.art.-adj. m.s. (I 311) *and the living*
יִתֵּן אֶל־לִבּוֹ Qal impf. 3 m.s. (נָתַן 678)-prep. -n.m.s.-3 m.s. sf. (524) *will lay it to heart*

7:3

טוֹב adj. m.s. (II 373) *is better*
כַּעַס n.m.s. (495) *sorrow*
מִשְּׂחֹק prep.-n.m.s. (966) *than laughter*
כִּי־בְרֹעַ פָּנִים conj.-prep.-n.m.s. cstr. (947)-n.m.p. (815) *for by sadness of countenance*
יִיטַב לֵב Qal impf. 3 m.s. (יָטַב 405)-n.m.s. (524) *the heart is made glad*

7:4

לֵב חֲכָמִים n.m.s. cstr. (524)-adj. m.p. (314) *the heart of the wise*
בְּבֵית אֵבֶל prep.-n.m.s. cstr. (108)-n.m.s. (5) *is in the house of mourning*
וְלֵב כְּסִילִים conj.-v.supra-n.m.p. (I 493) *but the heart of fools*
בְּבֵית שִׂמְחָה v.supra-n.f.s. (970) *is in the house of mirth*

7:5

טוֹב adj. m.s. (II 373) *is better*
לִשְׁמֹעַ prep.-Qal inf.cstr. (1033) *to hear*
גַּעֲרַת חָכָם n.f.s. cstr. (172)-adj. m.s. (314) *the rebuke of the wise*
מֵאִישׁ prep.-n.m.s. (35) *than a man*
שֹׁמֵעַ Qal act.ptc. (1033) *to hear*
שִׁיר כְּסִילִים n.m.s. cstr. (1010)-n.m.p. (I 493) *the song of fools*

7:6

כִּי כְקוֹל conj. (471)-prep.-n.m.s. cstr. (876) *for as the crackling of*
הַסִּירִים def.art.-n.m.p. (II 696) *thorns*
תַּחַת הַסִּיר prep. (1065)-def.art.-n.m.s. (I 696) *under a pot*

כֵּן שְׂחֹק adv. (485)-n.m.s. cstr. (966) *so is the laughter of*
הַכְּסִיל def.art.-n.m.s. (493) *the fools*
וְגַם־זֶה conj.-adv. (168)-demons.adj. m.s. (260) *this also*
הָבֶל n.m.s. (I 210) *vanity*

7:7

כִּי הָעֹשֶׁק conj. (471)-def.art.-n.m.s. (799) *surely oppression*
יְהוֹלֵל Po'el impf. 3 m.s. (הָלַל II 237) *makes foolish*
חָכָם adj. m.s. (314) *the wise man*
וִיאַבֵּד conj.-Pi. impf. 3 m.s. (אָבַד 1) *and corrupts*
אֶת־לֵב dir.obj. (GK 117c)-n.m.s. (524) *the mind*
מַתָּנָה n.f.s. (682) *a bribe*

7:8

טוֹב adj. m.s. (II 373) *better is*
אַחֲרִית n.f.s. cstr. (31) *the end of*
דָּבָר n.m.s. (182) *a thing*
מֵרֵאשִׁיתוֹ prep.-n.f.s.-3 m.s. sf. (912) *than its beginning*
טוֹב v.supra *is better*
אֶרֶךְ־רוּחַ adj. m.s. cstr. (74)-n.f.s. (924) *the patient in spirit*
מִגְּבַהּ־רוּחַ prep.-adj. m.s. cstr. (147)-v.supra *than the proud in spirit*

7:9

אַל־תְּבַהֵל neg.-Pi. impf. 2 m.s. (בָּהַל 96) *be not quick*
בְּרוּחֲךָ prep.-n.f.s.-2 m.s. sf. (924) *(in your spirit)*
לִכְעוֹס prep.-Qal inf.cstr. (כָּעַס 494) *to anger*
כִּי כַעַס conj. (471)-n.m.s. (495) *for anger*
בְּחֵיק prep.-n.m.s. cstr. (300) *in the bosom of*
כְּסִילִים n.m.p. (I 493) *fools*
יָנוּחַ Qal impf. 3 m.s. (נוּחַ 628) *lodges*

7:10

אַל־תֹּאמַר neg.-Qal impf. 2 m.s. (אָמַר 55) *say not*
מֶה הָיָה interr. (552)-Qal pf. 3 m.s. (224) *why is it*
שֶׁהַיָּמִים הָרִאשֹׁנִים rel. (979)-def.art.-n.m.p. (398) -def.art.-adj. m.p. (911) *that the former days*
הָיוּ טוֹבִים Qal pf. 3 c.p. (הָיָה 224)-adj. m.p. (II 373) *were better*
מֵאֵלֶּה prep.-demons.adj. c.p. (41) *than these*

כִּי לֹא מֵחָכְמָה conj. (471)-neg.-prep.-n.f.s. (315) *for it is not from wisdom*
שָׁאַלְתָּ Qal pf. 2 m.s. (שָׁאַל 981) *that you ask*
עַל־זֶה prep.-demons.adj. m.s. (260) *this*

7:11

טוֹבָה adj. f.s. (II 373) *is good*
חָכְמָה n.f.s. (315) *wisdom*
עִם־נַחֲלָה prep. (767)-n.f.s. (635) *with an inheritance*
וְיֹתֵר conj.-n.m.s. (452) *and an advantage*
לְרֹאֵי prep.-Qal act.ptc. m.p. cstr. (רָאָה 906) *to those who see*
הַשָּׁמֶשׁ def.art.-n.f.s. paus. (1039) *the sun*

7:12

כִּי בְּצֵל conj. (471)-prep.-n.m.s. cstr. (853; some rd. כְּצֵל) *for in the protection of*
הַחָכְמָה def.art.-n.f.s. (315) *wisdom*
בְּצֵל v.supra (LXX כְּצֵל) *like the protection of*
הַכָּסֶף def.art.-n.m.s. paus. (494) *money*
וְיִתְרוֹן conj.-n.m.s. cstr. (452) *and the advantage of*
דַּעַת n.f.s. (395) *knowledge*
הַחָכְמָה v.supra *wisdom*
תְּחַיֶּה Pi. impf. 3 f.s. (חָיָה 310) *preserves the life of*
בְעָלֶיהָ n.m.p.-3 f.s. sf. (I 127) *him who has it*

7:13

רְאֵה Qal impv. 2 m.s. (רָאָה 906) *consider*
אֶת־מַעֲשֵׂה dir.obj.-n.m.s. cstr. (795) *the work of*
הָאֱלֹהִים def.art.-n.m.p. (43) *God*
כִּי מִי יוּכַל conj. (471)-interr. (566)-Qal impf. 3 m.s. (יָכֹל 407) *for who can*
לְתַקֵּן prep.-Pi. inf.cstr. (תָּקַן 1075) *make straight*
אֵת אֲשֶׁר עִוְּתוֹ dir.obj.-rel. (81)-Pi. pf. 3 m.s.-3 m.s. sf. (עָוָה 736) *what he has made crooked*

7:14

בְּיוֹם טוֹבָה prep.-n.m.s. cstr. (398)-n.f.s. (375) *in the day of prosperity*
הֱיֵה בְטוֹב Qal impv. 2 m.s. (הָיָה 224)-prep. -n.m.s. (III 375) *be in prosperity*
וּבְיוֹם conj.-v.supra *and in the day of*
רָעָה n.f.s. (949) *adversity*
רְאֵה Qal impv. 2 m.s. (רָאָה 906) *consider*
גַּם אֶת־זֶה adv. (168)-dir.obj.-demons.adj. m.s. (260) *also the one*
לְעֻמַּת־זֶה prep.-n.f.s. cstr. as prep. (I 769) -v.supra *as well as the other*

עָשָׂה הָאֱלֹהִים Qal pf. 3 m.s. (I 793)-def.art.-n.m.p. (43) *God has made*
עַל־דִּבְרַת prep.-n.f.s. cstr. (184) *so that (because of)*
שֶׁלֹּא יִמְצָא rel. (979; GK 165b)-neg.-Qal impf. 3 m.s. (מָצָא 592) *may not find out*
הָאָדָם def.art.-n.m.s. (9) *man*
אַחֲרָיו prep.-3 m.s. sf. (29) *after him*
מְאוּמָה pr.indef. (548) *anything*

7:15

אֶת־הַכֹּל dir.obj.-def.art.-n.m.s. (481) *everything*
רָאִיתִי Qal pf. 1 c.s. (רָאָה 906) *I have seen*
בִּימֵי הֶבְלִי prep.-n.m.p. cstr. (398)-n.m.s.-1 c.s. sf. (I 210) *in my vain life*
יֵשׁ צַדִּיק subst. (441)-adj. m.s. (843) *there is a righteous man*
אֹבֵד Qal act.ptc. (אָבַד 1) *who perishes*
בְּצִדְקוֹ prep.-n.m.s.-3 m.s. sf. (841) *in his righteousness*
וְיֵשׁ רָשָׁע conj.-v.supra-adj. m.s. (957) *and there is a wicked man*
מַאֲרִיךְ Hi. ptc. (אָרַךְ 73) *who prolongs his life*
בְּרָעָתוֹ prep.-n.f.s.-3 m.s. sf. (949) *in his evil-doing*

7:16

אַל־תְּהִי צַדִּיק prep.-Qal impf. 2 m.s. (הָיָה 224) -adj. m.s. (843) *be not righteous*
הַרְבֵּה Hi. inf.abs. as adv. (רָבָה I 915; GK 131q) *overmuch*
וְאַל־תִּתְחַכַּם conj.-neg.-Hith. impf. 2 m.s. (חָכַם 314; GK 54k) *do not make yourself wise*
יוֹתֵר n.m.s. as adv. (452) *to excess*
לָמָּה תִּשּׁוֹמֵם prep.-interr. (552)-Hithpol'el impf. 2 m.s. (שָׁמֵם 1031; rd. תִּשְׁתּוֹמֵם GK 54c) *why should you destroy yourself*

7:17

אַל־תִּרְשַׁע neg.-Qal impf. 2 m.s. (רָשַׁע 957) *be not wicked*
הַרְבֵּה Hi. inf.abs. as adv. (רָבָה I 915) *overmuch*
וְאַל־תְּהִי conj.-neg.-Qal impf. 2 m.s. (הָיָה 224) *and be not*
סָכָל n.m.s. (698) *a fool*
לָמָּה תָמוּת prep.-interr. (552)-Qal impf. 2 m.s. (559 מוּת) *why should you die*
בְּלֹא עִתֶּךָ prep.-neg.-n.f.s.-2 m.s. sf. (773) *before your time*

7:18

טוֹב adj. m.s. (II 373) *it is good*
אֲשֶׁר תֶּאֱחֹז rel. (81)-Qal impf. 2 m.s. (אָחַז 28) *that you take hold*
בָּזֶה prep.-demons.adj. m.s. (260) *of this*
וְגַם־מִזֶּה conj.-adv. (168)-prep.-demons.adj. m.s. (260) *and from that*
אַל־תַּנַּח neg.-Hi. (B) impf. 2 m.s. juss. (נוּחַ 628) *withhold not*
אֶת־יָדֶךָ dir.obj.-n.f.s.-2 m.s. sf. (388) *your hand*
כִּי־יְרֵא conj. (471)-Qal act.ptc. m.s. cstr. (יָרֵא 431) *for he who fears*
אֱלֹהִים n.m.p. (43) *God*
יֵצֵא Qal impf. 3 m.s. (יָצָא 422) *shall come forth*
אֶת־כֻּלָּם dir.obj.-n.m.s.-3 m.p. sf. (481) *from them all*

7:19

הַחָכְמָה def.art.-n.f.s. (315) *wisdom*
תָּעֹז Qal impf. 3 f.s. (עָזַז 738) *gives strength*
לֶחָכָם prep.-def.art.-adj. m.s. (314) *to the wise man*
מֵעֲשָׂרָה שַׁלִּיטִים prep.-num. f. (796)-adj. m.p. (1020) *more than ten rulers*
אֲשֶׁר הָיוּ rel. (81)-Qal pf. 3 c.p. (הָיָה 224) *that are*
בָּעִיר prep.-def.art.-n.f.s. (746) *in a city*

7:20

כִּי אָדָם conj. (471)-n.m.s. (9) *surely a man*
אֵין צַדִּיק neg. (II 34)-adj. m.s. (843) *there is not a righteous one*
בָּאָרֶץ prep.-def.art.-n.f.s. (75) *on earth*
אֲשֶׁר יַעֲשֶׂה־טּוֹב rel. (81)-Qal impf. 3 m.s. (עָשָׂה I 793)-n.m.s. (III 375) *who does good*
וְלֹא יֶחֱטָא conj.-neg.-Qal impf. 3 m.s. (חָטָא 306) *and never sins*

7:21

גַּם לְכָל־הַדְּבָרִים adv. (168)-prep.-n.m.s. cstr. (481)-def.art.-n.m.p. (182) *also to all the things*
אֲשֶׁר יְדַבֵּרוּ rel. (81)-Pi. impf. 3 m.p. (דָּבַר 180) *that men say*
אַל־תִּתֵּן לִבֶּךָ neg.-Qal impf. 2 m.s. (נָתַן 678) -n.m.s.-2 m.s. sf. (524) *do not give heed*
אֲשֶׁר לֹא־תִשְׁמַע rel. (81)-neg.-Qal impf. 2 m.s. (1033 שָׁמַע) *lest you hear*
אֶת־עַבְדְּךָ dir.obj.-n.m.s.-2 m.s. sf. (713) *your servant*
מְקַלְלֶךָ Pi. ptc.-2 m.s. sf. (קָלַל 886) *cursing you*

7:22

כִּי גַּם־ conj. (471)–adv. (168) *for also*
פְּעָמִים רַבּוֹת n.f.p. (821)–adj. f.p. (I 912) *many times*
יָדַע לִבֶּךָ Qal pf. 3 m.s. (393)–n.m.s.–2 m.s. sf. (524) *your heart knows*
אֲשֶׁר גַּם־אַתָּ rel. (81)–v.supra–pers.pr. 2 m.s. (61) *that you yourself*
קִלַּלְתָּ Pi. pf. 2 m.s. (קָלַל 886) *have cursed*
אֲחֵרִים adj. m.p. (I 29) *others*

7:23

כָּל־זֹה n.m.s. cstr. (481)–demons.adj. (260) *all this*
נִסִּיתִי Pi. pf. 1 c.s. (נָסָה 650) *I have tested*
בַחָכְמָה prep.–def.art.–n.f.s. (315) *by wisdom*
אָמַרְתִּי Qal pf. 1 c.s. (אָמַר 55) *I said*
אֶחְכָּמָה Qal impf. 1 c.s.–vol.he (חָכַם 314) *I will be wise*
וְהִיא conj.–pers.pr. 3 f.s. (214) *but it*
רְחוֹקָה adj. f.s. (935) *was far*
מִמֶּנִּי prep.–1 c.s. sf. *from me*

7:24

רָחוֹק adj. m.s. (935) *far off*
מַה־שֶּׁהָיָה interr. (552)–rel. (979)–Qal pf. 3 m.s. (224) *that which is*
וְעָמֹק עָמֹק conj.–adj. m.s. (771; GK 133k)–v.supra *and deep, very deep*
מִי יִמְצָאֶנּוּ interr. (566)–Qal impf. 3 m.s.–3 m.s. sf. (מָצָא 592) *who can find it*

7:25

סַבּוֹתִי אֲנִי Qal pf. 1 c.s. (סָבַב 685)–pers.pr. 1 c.s. (58) *I myself turned*
וְלִבִּי conj.–n.m.s.–1 c.s. sf. (524) *my mind*
לָדַעַת prep.–Qal inf.cstr. (יָדַע 393) *to know*
וְלָתוּר conj.–prep.–Qal inf.cstr. (תּוּר 1064) *and to search out*
וּבַקֵּשׁ conj.–Pi. inf.cstr. (134) *and to seek*
חָכְמָה n.f.s. (315) *wisdom*
וְחֶשְׁבּוֹן conj.–n.m.s. (I 363) *and the sum of things*
וְלָדַעַת conj.–prep.–Qal inf.cstr. (יָדַע 393) *and to know*
רֶשַׁע כֶּסֶל n.m.s. cstr. (957)–n.m.s. (492) *the wickedness of folly*
וְהַסִּכְלוּת הוֹלֵלוֹת conj.–def.art.–n.f.s. cstr. (698)–n.f.p. (239; poss.rd. הוֹלֵלוּת cf. 10:13) *and the foolishness which is madness*

7:26

וּמוֹצֶא אֲנִי conj.–Qal act.ptc. (מָצָא 592; GK 75oo)–pers.pr. 1 c.s. (58) *and I found*
מַר מִמָּוֶת adj. m.s. (I 600)–prep.–n.m.s. (560) *more bitter than death*
אֶת־הָאִשָּׁה dir.obj.–def.art.–n.f.s. (61) *the woman*
אֲשֶׁר־הִיא מְצוֹדִים rel. (81)–pers.pr. 3 f.s. (214)–n.m.p. (II 844) *is snares*
וַחֲרָמִים conj.–n.m.p. (II 357) *and nets*
לִבָּהּ n.m.s.–3 f.s. sf. (524) *her heart*
אֲסוּרִים n.m.p. (64) *are fetters*
יָדֶיהָ n.f. du.–3 f.s. sf. (388) *whose hands*
טוֹב adj. m.s. (II 373) *he who pleases*
לִפְנֵי הָאֱלֹהִים prep.–n.m.p. cstr. (815)–def.art. –n.m.p. (43) *(before) God*
יִמָּלֵט מִמֶּנָּה Ni. impf. 3 m.s. (מָלַט 572)–prep.–3 f.s. sf. *escapes her*
וְחוֹטֵא conj.–Qal act.ptc. (חָטָא 306) *but the sinner*
יִלָּכֶד בָּהּ Ni. impf. 3 m.s. (לָכַד 539)–prep.–3 f.s. sf. *is taken by her*

7:27

רְאֵה Qal impv. 2 m.s. (רָאָה 906) *behold*
זֶה demons.adj. m.s. (260) *this*
מָצָאתִי Qal pf. 1 c.s. (מָצָא 592) *I found*
אָמְרָה Qal pf. 3 f.s. (אָמַר 55) *says* (prob. אָמַר הַקֹּהֶלֶת GK 122r)
קֹהֶלֶת n.m.s. (875) *the Preacher*
אַחַת לְאַחַת num. adj. f.s. (25)–prep.–v.supra *one thing to another*
לִמְצֹא prep.–Qal inf.cstr. (592) *to find*
חֶשְׁבּוֹן n.m.s. (I 363) *the sum*

7:28

אֲשֶׁר עוֹד־ rel. (81)–adv. (728) *which repeatedly*
בִּקְשָׁה Pi. pf. 3 f.s. (בָּקַשׁ 134) *has sought*
נַפְשִׁי n.f.s.–1 c.s. sf. (659) *my mind*
וְלֹא מָצָאתִי conj.–neg.–Qal pf. 1 c.s. (מָצָא 592) *but I have not found*
אָדָם אֶחָד n.m.s. (9)–num. adj. m.s. (25) *one man*
מֵאֶלֶף prep.–n.m.s. (48) *among a thousand*
מָצָאתִי v.supra *I have found*
וְאִשָּׁה conj.–n.f.s. (61) *but a woman*
בְכָל־אֵלֶּה prep.–n.m.s. cstr. (481)–demons.adj. c.p. (41) *among all these*
לֹא מָצָאתִי neg.–v.supra *I have not found*

7:29

לְבַד prep.–n.m.s. (II 94) *alone*
רְאֵה־זֶה Qal impv. 2 m.s. (רָאָה 906)–demons.adj. m.s. (260) *behold, this*

מָצָאתִי Qal pf. 1 c.s. (מָצָא 592) *I found*
אֲשֶׁר עָשָׂה rel. (81)-Qal pf. 3 m.s. (I 793) *that made*
הָאֱלֹהִים def.art.-n.m.p. (43) *God*
אֶת־הָאָדָם dir.obj.-def.art.-n.m.s. (9) *man*
יָשָׁר adj. m.s. (449) *upright*
וְהֵמָּה conj.-pers.pr. 3 m.p. (241) *but they*
בִקְשׁוּ Pi. pf. 3 c.p. (134) *have sought out*
חִשְּׁבֹנוֹת רַבִּים n.m.p. (364)-adj. m.p. (I 912) *many devices*

8:1

מִי כְּהֶחָכָם interr. (566)-prep.-def.art. (GK 35n)-adj. m.s. (314) *who is like the wise man*
וּמִי conj.-v.supra *and who*
יוֹדֵעַ Qal act.ptc. (393) *knows*
פֵּשֶׁר דָּבָר n.m.s. cstr. (833)-n.m.s. (182) *interpretation of a thing*
חָכְמַת אָדָם n.f.s. cstr. (315)-n.m.s. (9) *a man's wisdom*
תָּאִיר Hi. impf. 3 f.s. (אוֹר 21) *makes ... shine*
פָּנָיו n.m.p.-3 m.s. sf. (815) *his face*
וְעֹז פָּנָיו conj.-n.m.s. cstr. (738)-v.supra *and the hardness of his countenance*
יְשֻׁנֶּא Pu. impf. 3 m.s. (שָׁנָה I 1039; GK 75rr) *is changed*

8:2

אֲנִי pers.pr. 1 c.s. (58) *I*
פִּי־מֶלֶךְ n.m.s. cstr. (804)-n.m.s. (I 572) *the king's command*
שְׁמוֹר Qal impv. 2 m.s. (1036) *keep*
וְעַל דִּבְרַת conj.-prep.-n.f.s. cstr. (184) *and because of*
שְׁבוּעַת n.f.s. cstr. (989) *the oath of*
אֱלֹהִים n.m.p. (43) *God (sacred)*

8:3

אַל־תִּבָּהֵל neg.-Ni. impf. 2 m.s. (בָּהַל 96) *be not dismayed*
מִפָּנָיו prep.-n.m.p.-3 m.s. sf. (815) *from his presence*
תֵּלֵךְ Qal impf. 2 m.s. (הָלַךְ 229) *go*
אַל־תַּעֲמֹד neg.-Qal impf. 2 m.s. (763) *do not delay (stand)*
בְּדָבָר רָע prep.-n.m.s. (182)-adj. m.s. (948) *when the matter is unpleasant*
כִּי כָּל־אֲשֶׁר conj. (471)-n.m.s. (481)-rel. (81) *for whatever*
יַחְפֹּץ Qal impf. 3 m.s. (חָפֵץ 342) *he pleases*
יַעֲשֶׂה Qal impf. 3 m.s. (עָשָׂה I 793) *he does*

8:4

בַּאֲשֶׁר prep.-rel. (81; some rd. כַּאֲשֶׁר) *(accordingly)*
דְּבַר־מֶלֶךְ n.m.s. cstr. (182)-n.m.s. (I 572) *the word of the king*
שִׁלְטוֹן n.m.s. (1020) *is supreme*
וּמִי conj.-interr. (566) *and who*
יֹאמַר־לוֹ Qal impf. 3 m.s. (55)-prep.-3 m.s. sf. *may say to him*
מַה־תַּעֲשֶׂה interr. (552)-Qal impf. 2 m.s. (עָשָׂה I 793) *what are you doing*

8:5

שׁוֹמֵר Qal act.ptc. (1036) *he who obeys*
מִצְוָה n.f.s. (846) *a command*
לֹא יֵדַע neg.-Qal impf. 3 m.s. (יָדַע 393) *will not meet (know)*
דָּבָר רָע n.m.s. (182)-adj. m.s. (948) *harm*
וְעֵת וּמִשְׁפָּט conj.-n.f.s. (773)-conj.-n.m.s. (1048) *both the time and the way*
יֵדַע Qal impf. 3 m.s. (יָדַע 393) *will know*
לֵב חָכָם n.m.s. cstr. (524)-adj. m.s. (314) *the mind of a wise man*

8:6

כִּי לְכָל־חֵפֶץ conj. (471)-prep.-n.m.s. cstr. (481)-n.m.s. (343) *for every matter*
יֵשׁ עֵת subst. (441)-n.f.s. (773) *there is a time*
וּמִשְׁפָּט conj.-n.m.s. (1048) *and way*
כִּי־רָעַת הָאָדָם conj. (471)-n.f.s. cstr. (949)-def. art.-n.m.s. (9) *although man's trouble*
רַבָּה adj. f.s. (I 912) *lies heavy*
עָלָיו prep.-3 m.s. sf. *upon him*

8:7

כִּי־אֵינֶנּוּ יֹדֵעַ conj. (471)-neg.-3 m.s. sf. (II 34)-Qal act.ptc. (יָדַע 393) *for he does not know*
מַה־שֶּׁיִּהְיֶה interr. (552)-rel. (979)-Qal impf. 3 m.s. (הָיָה 224) *what is to be*
כִּי כַּאֲשֶׁר conj. (471)-prep.-rel. (81) *for how*
יִהְיֶה Qal impf. 3 m.s. (224) *it will be*
מִי יַגִּיד לוֹ interr. (566)-Hi. impf. 3 m.s. (נָגַד 616)-prep.-3 m.s. sf. *who can tell him*

8:8

אֵין אָדָם neg. cstr. (II 34)-n.m.s. (9) *there is no man*
שַׁלִּיט adj. m.s. (1020) *having mastery*
בָּרוּחַ prep.-def.art.-n.f.s. (924) *over the spirit*
לִכְלוֹא prep.-Qal inf.cstr. (כָּלָא 476) *to restrain*
אֶת־הָרוּחַ dir.obj.-def.art.-n.f.s. (924) *the spirit*

וְאֵין שִׁלְטוֹן conj.-v.supra-n.m.s. (1020) *and there is no mastery*
בְּיוֹם prep.-n.m.s. cstr. (398) *over the day of*
הַמָּוֶת def.art.-n.m.s. (560) *death*
וְאֵין מִשְׁלַחַת conj.-v.supra-n.f.s. (1020) *and there is no discharge*
בַּמִּלְחָמָה prep.-def.art.-n.f.s. (536) *from war*
וְלֹא־יְמַלֵּט conj.-neg.-Pi. impf. 3 m.s. (מָלַט 572) *nor will ... deliver*
רֶשַׁע n.m.s. (957) *wickedness*
אֶת בְּעָלָיו dir.obj.-n.m.p.-3 m.s. sf. (127) *those who are given to it*

8:9

אֶת־כָּל־זֶה dir.obj.-n.m.s. cstr. (481)-demons.adj. (260) *all this*
רָאִיתִי Qal pf. 1 c.s. (רָאָה 906) *I observed*
וְנָתוֹן conj.-Qal inf.abs. (נָתַן 678) *while applying*
אֶת־לִבִּי dir.obj.-n.m.s.-1 c.s. sf. (524) *my mind*
לְכָל־מַעֲשֶׂה prep.-n.m.s. cstr. (481)-n.m.s. (795) *to every work*
אֲשֶׁר נַעֲשָׂה rel. (81)-Ni. pf. 3 m.s. (עָשָׂה I 793) *that is done*
תַּחַת הַשָּׁמֶשׁ prep. (1065)-def.art.-n.f.s. paus. (1039) *under the sun*
עֵת אֲשֶׁר n.f.s. (773; some rd. אֵת)-rel. (81) *a time which*
שָׁלַט הָאָדָם Qal pf. 3 m.s. (I 1020)-def.art.-n.m.s. (9) *man lords it*
בְּאָדָם prep.-n.m.s. (9) *over man*
לְרַע לוֹ prep.-n.m.s. (II 948)-prep.-3 m.s. sf. *to his hurt*

8:10

וּבְכֵן רָאִיתִי conj.-prep.-adv. (486; GK 119ii)-Qal pf. 1 c.s. (רָאָה 906) *then I saw*
רְשָׁעִים adj. m.p. (957) *the wicked*
קְבֻרִים Qal pass.ptc. (קָבַר 868) *buried*
וָבָאוּ conj.-Qal pf. 3 c.p. (בּוֹא 97) *they used to go in*
וּמִמְּקוֹם קָדוֹשׁ conj.-prep.-n.m.s. cstr. (879)-adj. (872; GK 128wN) *and of the holy place*
יְהַלֵּכוּ Pi. impf. 3 m.p. (הָלַךְ 229) *go out*
וְיִשְׁתַּכְּחוּ conj.-Hith. impf. 3 m.p. (שָׁכַח 1013) *and they were forgotten* (many rd. וישתבחו as Hith. impf. 3 m.p. II 986; GK 54g *and were praised*)
בָעִיר prep.-def.art.-n.f.s. (746) *in the city*
אֲשֶׁר כֵּן־ rel. (81)-adv. (485) *where such things*
עָשׂוּ Qal pf. 3 c.p. (עָשָׂה I 793) *they had done*
גַּם־זֶה adv. (168)-demons.adj. m.s. (260) *this also*
הָבֶל n.m.s. paus. (I 210) *vanity*

8:11

אֲשֶׁר אֵין־נַעֲשָׂה rel. (81)-neg. cstr. (II 34)-Ni. pf. 3 m.s. (עָשָׂה I 793) *because it is not executed*
פִּתְגָם n.m.s. (834) *sentence*
מַעֲשֵׂה הָרָעָה n.m.s. cstr. (795)-def.art.-n.f.s. (949) *against an evil deed*
מְהֵרָה n.f.s. as adv. (555) *speedily*
עַל־כֵּן prep.-adv. (485) *therefore*
מָלֵא Qal pf. 3 m.s. (570) *is full*
לֵב n.m.s. cstr. (524) *the heart of*
בְּנֵי־הָאָדָם n.m.p. cstr. (119)-def.art.-n.m.s. (9) *the sons of men*
בָּהֶם prep.-3 m.p. sf. *(upon them)*
לַעֲשׂוֹת רָע prep.-Qal inf.cstr. (עָשָׂה I 793) -n.m.s. (II 948) *to do evil*

8:12

אֲשֶׁר חֹטֶא rel. (81)-Qal act.ptc. (306) *though a sinner*
עֹשֶׂה רָע Qal act.ptc. (עָשָׂה I 793)-n.m.s. (II 948) *does evil*
מְאַת n.f.s. cstr. (547; with word understood, see 1d) *a hundred times*
וּמַאֲרִיךְ conj.-Hi. ptc. (אָרַךְ 73) *and prolongs*
לוֹ prep.-3 m.s. sf. *his life*
כִּי גַּם־ conj. (471)-adv. (168) *yet*
יוֹדֵעַ אָנִי Qal act.ptc. (יָדַע 393)-pers.pr. 1 c.s. (58) *I know*
אֲשֶׁר יִהְיֶה־ rel. (81)-Qal impf. 3 m.s. (224) *that it will be*
טּוֹב adj. m.s. (II 373) *well*
לְיִרְאֵי prep.-Qal act.ptc. m.p. cstr. (יָרֵא 431) *with those who fear*
הָאֱלֹהִים def.art.-n.m.p. (43) *God*
אֲשֶׁר יִירְאוּ v.supra-Qal impf. 3 m.p. (יָרֵא 431) *because they fear*
מִלְּפָנָיו prep.-prep.-n.m.p.-3 m.s. sf. (815) *before him*

8:13

וְטוֹב לֹא־יִהְיֶה conj.-adj. m.s. (II 373)-neg.-Qal impf. 3 m.s. (הָיָה 224) *but it will not be well*
לָרָשָׁע prep.-def.art.-adj. m.s. (957) *with the wicked*
וְלֹא־יַאֲרִיךְ conj.-neg.-Hi. impf. 3 m.s. (אָרַךְ 73) *neither will he prolong*
יָמִים n.m.p. (398) *his days*
כַּצֵּל prep.-def.art.-n.m.s. (853) *like a shadow*

אֲשֶׁר אֵינֶנּוּ יָרֵא rel. (81)–neg.–3 m.s. sf. (II 34) –Qal act.ptc. (יָרֵא 431) *because he does not fear*

מִלִּפְנֵי אֱלֹהִים prep.–prep.–n.m.p. cstr. (815) –n.m.p. (43) *before God*

8:14

יֵשׁ־הֶבֶל subst. (441)–n.m.s. (I 210) *there is a vanity*

אֲשֶׁר נַעֲשָׂה rel. (81)–Ni. pf. 3 m.s. (עָשָׂה I 793) *which takes place*

עַל־הָאָרֶץ prep.–def.art.–n.f.s. (75) *on earth*

אֲשֶׁר יֵשׁ צַדִּיקִים rel. (81)–subst. (441)–adj. m.p. (843) *that there are righteous men*

אֲשֶׁר מַגִּיעַ אֲלֵהֶם rel. (81)–Hi. ptc. (נָגַע 619) –prep.–3 m.p. sf. *to whom it happens*

כְּמַעֲשֵׂה הָרְשָׁעִים prep.–n.m.s. cstr. (I 793)–def. art.–adj. m.p. (957) *according to the deeds of the wicked*

וְיֵשׁ רְשָׁעִים conj.–v.supra–v.supra *and there are wicked men*

שֶׁמַּגִּיעַ אֲלֵהֶם rel. (979)–v.supra–v.supra *to whom it happens*

כְּמַעֲשֵׂה הַצַּדִּיקִים v.supra–def.art.–adj. m.p. (843) *according to the deeds of the righteous*

אָמַרְתִּי Qal pf. 1 c.s. (55) *I said*

שֶׁגַּם־זֶה rel. (979)–adv. (168)–demons.adj. m.s. (260) *that this also*

הָבֶל n.m.s. paus. (I 210) *vanity*

8:15

וְשִׁבַּחְתִּי אֲנִי conj.–Pi. pf. 1 c.s. (II 986)–pers.pr. 1 c.s. (58) *and I commend*

אֶת־הַשִּׂמְחָה dir.obj.–def.art.–n.f.s. (970) *enjoyment*

אֲשֶׁר אֵין־טוֹב rel. (81)–neg. cstr. (II 34)–adj. m.s. (III 375) *for has no good thing*

לָאָדָם prep.–def.art.–n.m.s. (9) *man*

תַּחַת הַשֶּׁמֶשׁ prep. (1065)–def.art.–n.f.s. (1039) *under the sun*

כִּי אִם־לֶאֱכוֹל conj. (471)–hypoth.part. (49) –prep.–Qal inf.cstr. (אָכַל 37) *but to eat*

וְלִשְׁתּוֹת conj.–prep.–Qal inf.cstr. (שָׁתָה 1059) *and drink*

וְלִשְׂמוֹחַ conj.–prep.–Qal inf.cstr. (שָׂמַח 970) *and enjoy himself*

וְהוּא יִלְוֶנּוּ conj.–demons.adj. m.s. (214)–Qal impf. 3 m.s.–3 m.s. sf. (לָוָה I 530) *for this will go with him*

בַעֲמָלוֹ prep.–n.m.s.–3 m.s. sf. (765) *in his toil*

יְמֵי חַיָּיו n.m.p. cstr. (398)–n.m.p.–3 m.s. sf. (313) *through the days of his life*

אֲשֶׁר־נָתַן־לוֹ rel. (81)–Qal pf. 3 m.s. (678)–prep.–3 m.s. sf. *which ... gives him*

הָאֱלֹהִים def.art.–n.m.p. (43) *God*

תַּחַת הַשָּׁמֶשׁ prep. (1065)–v.supra paus. *under the sun*

8:16

כַּאֲשֶׁר נָתַתִּי prep.–rel. (81)–Qal pf. 1 c.s. (נָתַן 678) *when I applied*

אֶת־לִבִּי dir.obj.–n.m.s.–1 c.s. sf. (524) *my mind*

לָדַעַת prep.–Qal inf.cstr. (יָדַע 393) *to know*

חָכְמָה n.f.s. (315) *wisdom*

וְלִרְאוֹת conj.–prep.–Qal inf.cstr. (רָאָה 906) *and to see*

אֶת־הָעִנְיָן dir.obj.–def.art.–n.m.s. (775) *the business*

אֲשֶׁר נַעֲשָׂה rel. (81)–Ni. pf. 3 m.s. (עָשָׂה I 793) *that is done*

עַל־הָאָרֶץ prep.–def.art.–n.f.s. (75) *on earth*

כִּי גַם בַּיּוֹם conj. (471)–adv. (168)–prep.–def. art.–n.m.s. (398) *how in the day*

וּבַלַּיְלָה conj.–prep.–def.art.–n.m.s. (538) *and in the night*

שֵׁנָה בְּעֵינָיו n.f.s. (446)–prep.–n.f. du.–3 m.s. sf. (744) *sleep in his eyes*

אֵינֶנּוּ רֹאֶה neg.–3 m.s. sf. (II 34)–Qal act.ptc. (906 רָאָה) *he does not see*

8:17

וְרָאִיתִי conj.–Qal pf. 1 c.s. (רָאָה 906) *then I saw*

אֶת־כָּל־מַעֲשֵׂה dir.obj.–n.m.s. cstr. (481)–n.m.s. cstr. (795) *all the work of*

הָאֱלֹהִים def.art.–n.m.p. (43) *God*

כִּי לֹא יוּכַל הָאָדָם conj. (471)–neg.–Qal impf. 3 m.s. (יָכֹל 407)–def.art.–n.m.s. (9) *that man cannot*

לִמְצוֹא prep.–Qal inf.cstr. (מָצָא 592) *find out*

אֶת־הַמַּעֲשֶׂה dir.obj.–def.art.–n.m.s. (795) *the work*

אֲשֶׁר נַעֲשָׂה rel. (81)–Ni. pf. 3 m.s. (עָשָׂה I 793) *that is done*

תַחַת־הַשֶּׁמֶשׁ prep. (1065)–def.art.–n.f.s. (1039) *under the sun*

בְּשֶׁל אֲשֶׁר יַעֲמֹל prep.–rel. (979)–rel. (81)–Qal impf. 3 m.s. (765) *however much ... may toil*

הָאָדָם def.art.–n.m.s. (9) *man*

לְבַקֵּשׁ prep.–Pi. inf.cstr. (134) *in seeking*

וְלֹא יִמְצָא conj.–neg.–Qal impf. 3 m.s. (592) *he will not find*

וְגַם אִם־ conj.–adv. (168)–hypoth.part. (49) *even though*

יֹאמַר Qal impf. 3 m.s. (אָמַר 55) *claims*

הֶחָכָם def.art.–adj. m.s. (314) *a wise man*

לָדַעַת prep.-Qal inf.cstr. (יָדַע 393) *to know*
לֹא יוּכַל neg.-Qal impf. 3 m.s. (יָכֹל 407) *he cannot*
לִמְצֹא v.supra *find*

9:1

כִּי אֶת־כָּל־זֶה conj. (471)-dir.obj.-n.m.s. cstr. (481)-demons.adj. m.s. (260) *but all this*
נָתַתִּי Qal pf. 1 c.s. (נָתַן 678) *I laid*
אֶל־לִבִּי prep.-n.m.s.-1 c.s. sf. (524) *to my heart*
וְלָבוּר conj.-prep.-Qal inf.cstr. (בּוּר 101) *examining (making clear)*
אֶת־כָּל־זֶה dir.obj.-v.supra-v.supra *all this*
אֲשֶׁר הַצַּדִּיקִים rel. (81)-def.art.-adj. m.p. (843) *how the righteous*
וְהַחֲכָמִים conj.-def.art.-adj. m.p. (314) *and the wise*
וַעֲבָדֵיהֶם conj.-n.m.s.-3 m.p. sf. (714; GK 93ww) *and their deeds*
בְּיַד הָאֱלֹהִים prep.-n.f.s. cstr. (388)-def.art. -n.m.p. (43) *in the hand of God*
גַּם־אַהֲבָה adv. (168)-n.f.s. (13) *whether love*
גַּם־שִׂנְאָה v.supra-n.f.s. (971) *or hate*
אֵין יוֹדֵעַ הָאָדָם neg.- cstr. (II 34)-Qal act.ptc. (393 יָדַע)-def.art.-n.m.s. (9) *man does not know*
הַכֹּל לִפְנֵיהֶם def.art.-n.m.s. (481)-prep.-n.m.p.-3 m.p. sf. (815) *everything before them*

9:2

הַכֹּל כַּאֲשֶׁר לַכֹּל def.art.-n.m.s. (481)-prep.-rel. (81)-prep.-def.art.-n.m.s. (481) *everything just as to everything*
מִקְרֶה אֶחָד n.m.s. (899)-num. (25) *one fate*
לַצַּדִּיק prep.-def.art.-adj. m.s. (843) *to the righteous*
וְלָרָשָׁע conj.-prep.-def.art.-adj. m.s. (957) *and the wicked*
לַטּוֹב prep.-def.art.-adj. m.s. (II 373) *to the good*
וְלַטָּהוֹר conj.-prep.-def.art.-adj. m.s. (373) *to the clean*
וְלַטָּמֵא conj.-prep.-def.art.-adj. m.s. (II 379) *and the unclean*
וְלַזֹּבֵחַ conj.-prep.-def.art.-Qal act.ptc. m.s. (256) *to him who sacrifices*
וְלַאֲשֶׁר אֵינֶנּוּ זֹבֵחַ conj.-prep.-rel. (81)-neg.-3 m.s. sf. (II 34)-v.supra *and him who does not sacrifice*
כַּטּוֹב prep.-def.art.-adj. m.s. (II 373) *as is the good man*
כַּחֹטֶא prep.-def.art.-Qal act.ptc. (חָטָא 306) *so is the sinner*

הַנִּשְׁבָּע def.art.-Ni. ptc. m.s. (שָׁבַע 989) *and he who swears*
כַּאֲשֶׁר שְׁבוּעָה יָרֵא prep.-rel. (81)-n.f.s. (989)-Qal act.ptc. m.s. (יָרֵא 431) *as he who shuns an oath*

9:3

זֶה רָע demons.adj. m.s. (260)-adj. m.s. (948) *this is an evil*
בְּכֹל אֲשֶׁר־ prep.-n.m.s. (481)-rel. (81) *in all that*
נַעֲשָׂה Ni. pf. 3 m.s. (עָשָׂה I 793) *is done*
תַּחַת הַשָּׁמֶשׁ prep. (1065)-def.art.-n.f.s. (1039) *under the sun*
כִּי־מִקְרֶה אֶחָד conj.-n.m.s. (899)-num. (25) *that one fate*
לַכֹּל prep.-def.art.-n.m.s. (481) *to all*
וְגַם לֵב conj.-adv. (168) n.m.s. cstr. (524) *also the heart of*
בְּנֵי־הָאָדָם n.m.p. cstr. (119)-def.art.-n.m.s. (9) *men*
מָלֵא־ Qal pf. 3 m.s. or Qal act.ptc. (570) *is full of*
רָע adj. m.s. (948) *evil*
וְהוֹלֵלוֹת conj.-n.f.p. (239) *and madness*
בִּלְבָבָם prep.-n.m.s.-3 m.s. sf. (523) *in their heart*
בְּחַיֵּיהֶם prep.-n.m.p.-3 m.p. sf. (313) *while they live*
וְאַחֲרָיו conj.-prep.-3 m.s. sf. (29) *and after that*
אֶל־הַמֵּתִים prep.-def.art.-Qal act.ptc. m.p. (מוּת 559) *to the dead*

9:4

כִּי־מִי אֲשֶׁר conj. (471)-interr. (566)-rel. (81) *but he who*
יְבֻחַר Pu. impf. 3 m.s. (בָּחַר 103) *is chosen*
אֶל כָּל־הַחַיִּים prep.-n.m.s. cstr. (481)-def.art.-adj. m.p. (I 311) *with all the living*
יֵשׁ בִּטָּחוֹן subst. (441)-n.m.s. (105) *has hope*
כִּי־לְכֶלֶב חַי conj. (471)-prep. (GK 143e)-n.m.s. (476)-adj. m.s. (I 311) *for a living dog*
הוּא טוֹב demons.adj. m.s. (214)-adj. m.s. (II 373) *is better*
מִן־הָאַרְיֵה הַמֵּת prep.-def.art.-n.m.s. (71)-def. art.-Qal act.ptc. m.s. (מוּת 559) *than the dead lion*

9:5

כִּי הַחַיִּים conj. (471)-def.art.-adj. m.p. (311) *for the living*
יוֹדְעִים Qal act.ptc. m.p. (יָדַע 393) *know*
שֶׁיָּמֻתוּ rel. (979)-Qal impf. 3 m.p. (מוּת 559) *that they will die*

וְהַמֵּתִים conj.-def.art.-Qal act.ptc. m.p. (מוּת 559) *but the dead*
אֵינָם יוֹדְעִים neg.-3 m.p. sf. (II 34)-Qal act.ptc. m.p. (יָדַע 393) *do not know*
מְאוּמָה pr.indef. (548) *anything*
וְאֵין־עוֹד לָהֶם conj.-neg. (II 34)-adv. (728) -prep.-3 m.p. sf. *and they have no more*
שָׂכָר n.m.s. (I 969) *reward*
כִּי נִשְׁכַּח conj. (471)-Ni. pf. 3 m.s. (שָׁכַח 1013) *but is lost*
זִכְרָם n.m.s.-3 m.p. sf. (271) *the memory of them*

9:6

גַּם אַהֲבָתָם adv. (168)-n.f.s.-3 m.p. sf. (13) *their love*
גַּם־שִׂנְאָתָם v.supra-n.f.s.-3 m.p. sf. (971) *and their hate*
גַּם־קִנְאָתָם v.supra-n.f.s.-3 m.p. sf. (888) *and their envy*
כְּבָר adv. (I 460) *already*
אָבָדָה Qal pf. 3 f.s. paus. (אָבַד 1) *have perished*
וְחֵלֶק אֵין־לָהֶם conj.-n.m.s. (324)-neg. (II 34) -prep.-3 m.p. sf. *and they have no share*
עוֹד לְעוֹלָם adv. (728)-prep.-n.m.s. (761) *more for ever*
בְּכֹל אֲשֶׁר־ prep.-n.m.s. (481)-rel. (81) *in all that*
נַעֲשָׂה Ni. pf. 3 m.s. (עָשָׂה I 793) *is done*
תַּחַת הַשָּׁמֶשׁ prep. (1065)-def.art.-n.f.s. paus. (1039) *under the sun*

9:7

לֵךְ Qal impv. 2 m.s. (הָלַךְ 229) *go*
אֱכֹל Qal impv. 2 m.s. (אָכַל 37) *eat*
בְּשִׂמְחָה prep.-n.f.s. (970) *with enjoyment*
לַחְמֶךָ n.m.s.-2 m.s. sf. (536) *your bread*
וּשְׁתֵה conj.-Qal impv. 2 m.s. (שָׁתָה 1059) *and drink*
בְלֶב־טוֹב prep.-n.m.s. (524)-adj. m.s. (II 373) *with a merry heart*
יֵינֶךָ n.m.s.-2 m.s. sf. (406) *your wine*
כִּי כְבָר conj. (471)-adv. (I 460) *for already*
רָצָה Qal pf. 3 m.s. (953) *has approved*
הָאֱלֹהִים def.art.-n.m.p. (43) *God*
אֶת־מַעֲשֶׂיךָ dir.obj.-n.m.p.-2 m.s. sf. (795) *what you do*

9:8

בְּכָל־עֵת prep.-n.m.s. cstr. (481)-n.f.s. (773) *always*
יִהְיוּ Qal impf. 3 m.p. (הָיָה 224) *let be*
בְגָדֶיךָ n.m.p.-2 m.s. sf. (93) *your garments*
לְבָנִים adj. m.p. (I 526) *white*
וְשֶׁמֶן conj.-n.m.s. (1032) *and oil*
עַל־רֹאשְׁךָ prep.-n.m.s.-2 m.s. sf. (910) *on your head*
אַל־יֶחְסָר neg.-Qal impf. 3 m.s. (חָסֵר 341) *let not be lacking*

9:9

רְאֵה חַיִּים Qal impv. 2 m.s. (רָאָה 906)-n.m.p. (313) *enjoy life*
עִם־אִשָּׁה prep. (767)-n.f.s. (61) *with the wife*
אֲשֶׁר־אָהַבְתָּ rel. (81)-Qal pf. 2 m.s. (אָהַב 12) *whom you love*
כָּל־יְמֵי n.m.s. cstr. (481)-n.m.p. cstr. (398) *all the days of*
חַיֵּי הֶבְלֶךָ n.m.p. cstr. (313)-n.m.s.-2 m.s. sf. (I 210) *your vain life*
אֲשֶׁר נָתַן־לְךָ rel. (81)-Qal pf. 3 m.s. (678) -prep.-2 m.s. sf. *which he has given you*
תַּחַת הַשֶּׁמֶשׁ prep. (1065)-def.art.-n.f.s. (1039) *under the sun*
כֹּל יְמֵי הֶבְלֶךָ n.m.s. cstr. (481)-v.supra-v.supra *all the days of your vanity*
כִּי הוּא conj. (471)-demons.adj. m.s. (214) *because that is*
חֶלְקְךָ n.m.s.-2 m.s. sf. (324) *your portion*
בַּחַיִּים prep.-def.art.-n.m.p. (313) *in life*
וּבַעֲמָלְךָ conj.-prep.-n.m.s.-2 m.s. sf. (765) *and in your toil*
אֲשֶׁר־אַתָּה עָמֵל rel. (81)-pers.pr. 2 m.s. (61)-adj. m.s. (II 766) *at which you toil*
תַּחַת הַשָּׁמֶשׁ prep. (1065)-v.supra paus. *under the sun*

9:10

כֹּל אֲשֶׁר n.m.s. (481)-rel. (81) *whatever*
תִּמְצָא יָדְךָ Qal impf. 3 f.s. (מָצָא 592)-n.f.s.-2 m.s. sf. (388) *your hand finds*
לַעֲשׂוֹת prep.-Qal inf.cstr. (עָשָׂה I 793) *to do*
בְּכֹחֲךָ prep.-n.m.s.-2 m.s. sf. (470) *with your might*
עֲשֵׂה Qal impv. 2 m.s. (עָשָׂה I 793) *do it*
כִּי אֵין מַעֲשֶׂה conj. (471)-neg. cstr. (II 34)-n.m.s. (795) *for there is no work*
וְחֶשְׁבּוֹן conj.-n.m.s. (I 363) *or thought*
וְדַעַת conj.-n.f.s. (395) *or knowledge*
וְחָכְמָה conj.-n.f.s. (315) *or wisdom*
בִּשְׁאוֹל prep.-n.f.s. (982) *in Sheol*
אֲשֶׁר אַתָּה rel. (81)-pers.pr. 2 m.s. (61) *to which you*
הֹלֵךְ שָׁמָּה Qal act.ptc. (הָלַךְ 229)-adv.-dir.he (1027) *are going (there)*

9:11

שַׁבְתִּי וְרָאֹה Qal pf. 1 c.s. (שׁוּב 996)-conj.-Qal inf.abs. (רָאָה 906) *again I saw*

תַּחַת־הַשֶּׁמֶשׁ prep. (1065)-def.art.-n.f.s. (1039) *under the sun*

כִּי לֹא לַקַּלִּים conj.-neg.-prep.-def.art.-adj. m.p. (886) *that not to the swift*

הַמֵּרוֹץ def.art.-n.m.s. (930) *the race*

וְלֹא לַגִּבּוֹרִים conj.-neg.-prep.-def.art.-adj. m.p. (150) *nor to the strong*

הַמִּלְחָמָה def.art.-n.f.s. (536) *the battle*

וְגַם לֹא conj.-adv. (168)-neg. *nor*

לַחֲכָמִים prep.-def.art.-adj. m.p. (314) *to the wise*

לֶחֶם n.m.s. (536) *bread*

וְגַם לֹא v.supra-v.supra *nor*

לַנְּבֹנִים prep.-def.art.-Ni. ptc. m.p. (בִּין 106) *to the intelligent*

עֹשֶׁר n.m.s. (799) *riches*

וְגַם לֹא לַיֹּדְעִים v.supra-v.supra-prep.-def.art.-Qal act.ptc. m.p. (יָדַע 393) *nor to the men of skill*

חֵן n.m.s. (336) *favor*

כִּי־עֵת conj. (471)-n.f.s. (773) *but time*

וָפֶגַע conj.-n.m.s. (803) *and chance*

יִקְרֶה Qal impf. 3 m.s. (קָרָה 899) *happen*

אֶת־כֻּלָּם dir.obj.-n.m.s.-3 m.p. sf. (481) *to all of them*

9:12

כִּי גַּם conj. (471)-adv. (168) *for also*

לֹא־יֵדַע הָאָדָם neg.-Qal impf. 3 m.s. (יָדַע 393)-def.art.-n.m.s. (9) *man does not know*

אֶת־עִתּוֹ dir.obj.-n.f.s.-3 m.s. sf. (773) *his time*

כַּדָּגִים prep.-def.art.-n.m.p. (185) *like fish*

שֶׁנֶּאֱחָזִים rel. (979)-Ni. ptc. m.p. (אָחַז 28) *which are taken*

בִּמְצוֹדָה רָעָה prep.-n.f.s. (I 845)-adj. f.s. (948) *in an evil net*

וְכַצִּפֳּרִים conj.-prep.-def.art.-n.f.p. (I 861) *and like birds*

הָאֲחֻזוֹת def.art.-Qal pass.ptc. f.p. (אָחַז 28) *which are caught*

בַּפָּח prep.-def.art.-n.m.s. (I 809) *in a snare*

כָּהֵם prep.-3 m.p. sf. *so (like them)*

יוּקָשִׁים Pu. ptc. m.p. (יָקֹשׁ 430; GK 52s) *are snared*

בְּנֵי הָאָדָם n.m.p. cstr. (119)-def.art.-n.m.s. (9) *the sons of men*

לְעֵת רָעָה prep.-n.f.s. (773)-adj. f.s. (948) *at an evil time*

כְּשֶׁתִּפּוֹל prep.-rel. (979)-Qal impf. 3 f.s. (נָפַל 656) *when it falls*

עֲלֵיהֶם prep.-3 m.p. sf. *upon them*

פִּתְאֹם adv. (837) *suddenly*

9:13

גַּם־זֹה adv. (168)-demons.adj. f.s. (262) *also this*

רָאִיתִי Qal pf. 1 c.s. (רָאָה 906) *I have seen*

חָכְמָה n.f.s. (315) *wisdom*

תַּחַת הַשָּׁמֶשׁ prep. (1065)-def.art.-n.f.s. paus. (1039) *under the sun*

וּגְדוֹלָה conj.-adj. f.s. (152) *and great*

הִיא אֵלָי demons.adj. f.s. (214)-prep.-1 c.s. sf. *it to me*

9:14

עִיר קְטַנָּה n.f.s. (746)-adj. f.s. (I 881) *a little city*

וַאֲנָשִׁים conj.-n.m.p. (35) *with men*

בָּהּ prep.-3 f.s. sf. *in it*

מְעָט adv. (589) *few*

וּבָא־אֵלֶיהָ conj. (GK 112ppN)-Qal pf. 3 m.s. (בּוֹא 97)-prep.-3 f.s. sf. *and came against it*

מֶלֶךְ גָּדוֹל n.m.s. (I 572)-adj. m.s. (152) *a great king*

וְסָבַב אֹתָהּ conj.-Qal pf. 3 m.s. (685)-dir.obj.-3 f.s. sf. *and besieged it*

וּבָנָה conj.-Qal pf. 3 m.s. (בָּנָה 124) *and built*

עָלֶיהָ prep.-3 f.s. sf. *against it*

מְצוֹדִים גְּדֹלִים n.m.p. (I 844)-adj. m.p. (152) *great siegeworks*

9:15

וּמָצָא conj.-Qal pf. 3 m.s. (592) *but there was found*

בָהּ prep.-3 f.s. sf. *in it*

אִישׁ n.m.s. (35) *a man*

מִסְכֵּן adj. m.s. (587) *poor*

חָכָם adj. m.s. (314) *wise*

וּמִלַּט־הוּא conj.-Pi. pf. 3 m.s. (מָלַט 572)-pers. pr. 3 m.s. (214) *and he delivered*

אֶת־הָעִיר dir.obj.-def.art.-n.f.s. (746) *the city*

בְּחָכְמָתוֹ prep.-n.f.s.-3 m.s. sf. (315) *by his wisdom*

וְאָדָם לֹא זָכַר conj.-n.m.s. (9)-neg.-Qal pf. 3 m.s. (269) *yet no one remembered*

אֶת־הָאִישׁ dir.obj.-def.art.-n.m.s. (35) ... *man*

הַמִּסְכֵּן הַהוּא def.art.-adj. m.s. (587)-def.art. -demons.adj. m.s. (214) *that poor*

9:16

וְאָמַרְתִּי אָנִי conj.-Qal pf. 1 c.s. (55)-pers.pr. 1 c.s. (58) *but I say*

טוֹבָה adj. f.s. (II 373) *is better*

חָכְמָה n.f.s. (315) *wisdom*

מִגְּבוּרָה prep.-n.f.s. (150) *than might*

וְחָכְמַת הַמִּסְכֵּן conj.-n.f.s. cstr. (315)-def.art.-adj. m.s. (587) *though the poor man's wisdom*

בְּזוּיָה Qal pass.ptc. f.s. (בָּזָה 102) *is despised*

וּדְבָרָיו conj.-n.m.p.-3 m.s. sf. (182) *and his words*

אֵינָם נִשְׁמָעִים neg.-3 m.p. sf. (II 34)-Ni. ptc. m.p. (שָׁמַע 1033) *are not heeded*

9:17

דִּבְרֵי חֲכָמִים n.m.p. cstr. (182)-adj. m.p. (314) *the words of the wise*

בְּנַחַת prep.-n.f.s. (I 629) *in quiet*

נִשְׁמָעִים Ni. ptc. m.p. (שָׁמַע 1033) *heard*

מִזַּעֲקַת מוֹשֵׁל prep.-n.f.s. cstr. (277)-Qal act.ptc. m.s. (605) *than the shouting of a ruler*

בַּכְּסִילִים prep.-def.art.-n.m.p. (I 493) *among fools*

9:18

טוֹבָה adj. f.s. (II 373) *is better*

חָכְמָה n.f.s. (315) *wisdom*

מִכְּלֵי קְרָב prep.-n.m.p. cstr. (479)-n.m.s. (898) *than weapons of war*

וְחוֹטֶא אֶחָד conj.-Qal act.ptc. (חָטָא 306)-num. adj. (25) *but one sinner*

יְאַבֵּד Pi. impf. 3 m.s. (אָבַד 1) *destroys*

טוֹבָה הַרְבֵּה adj. f.s. (II 373)-Hi. inf.abs. as adv. (I 915 רָבָה) *much good*

10:1

זְבוּבֵי מָוֶת n.m.p. cstr. (256)-n.m.s. (560) *flies of death*

יַבְאִישׁ Hi. impf. 3 m.s. (בָּאַשׁ 92) *cause to stink*

יַבִּיעַ Hi. impf. 3 m.s. (נָבַע 615) *cause to bubble*

שֶׁמֶן רוֹקֵחַ n.m.s. cstr. (1032)-Qal act.ptc. (רָקַח 955) *the perfumer's ointment*

יָקָר adj. m.s. (429) *is weightier*

מֵחָכְמָה prep.-n.f.s. (315) *than wisdom*

מִכָּבוֹד prep.-n.m.s. (II 458) *than honor*

סִכְלוּת מְעָט n.f.s. (698)-subst. (589) *a little folly*

10:2

לֵב חָכָם n.m.s. cstr. (524)-adj. m.s. (314) *a wise man's heart*

לִימִינוֹ prep.-n.f.s.-3 m.s. sf. (411) *toward the right*

וְלֵב כְּסִיל conj.-v.supra-n.m.s. (I 493) *but a fool's heart*

לִשְׂמֹאלוֹ prep.-n.m.s.-3 m.s. sf. (969) *toward the left*

10:3

וְגַם־בַּדֶּרֶךְ conj.-adv. (168)-prep.-def.art.-n.m.s. (202) *even on the road*

כְּשֶׁהַסָּכָל prep.-rel. (979)-def.art.-n.m.s. (698) *when the fool*

הֹלֵךְ Qal act.ptc. (הָלַךְ 229) *walks*

לִבּוֹ חָסֵר n.m.s.-3 m.s. sf. (524)-Qal act.ptc. (חָסֵר 341) *he lacks sense*

וְאָמַר לַכֹּל conj.-Qal pf. 3 m.s. (55)-prep.-def. art.-n.m.s. (481) *and he says to every one*

סָכָל הוּא n.m.s. (698)-pers.pr. 3 m.s. (214) *he is a fool*

10:4

אִם־רוּחַ הַמּוֹשֵׁל hypoth.part. (49)-n.f.s. cstr. (924)-def.art.-Qal act.ptc. (III 605) *if the anger of the ruler*

תַּעֲלֶה עָלֶיךָ Qal impf. 3 f.s. (עָלָה 748)-prep.-2 m.s. sf. *rises against you*

מְקוֹמְךָ n.m.s.-2 m.s. sf. (879) *your place*

אַל־תַּנַּח neg.-Hi. impf. 2 m.s. apoc. (נוּחַ 628B) *do not leave*

כִּי מַרְפֵּא conj.-n.m.s. (951) *for deference*

יַנִּיחַ Hi. impf. 3 m.s. (נוּחַ 628B; rd.prob. נוּחַ 628A) *causeth to rest*

חֲטָאִים גְּדוֹלִים n.m.p. (307)-adj. m.p. (152) *great offenses*

10:5

יֵשׁ רָעָה subst. (441)-n.f.s. (949) *there is an evil*

רָאִיתִי Qal pf. 1 c.s. (רָאָה 906; GK 155h) *which I have seen*

תַּחַת הַשָּׁמֶשׁ prep. (1065)-def.art.-n.f.s. paus. (1039) *under the sun*

כִּשְׁגָגָה prep.-n.f.s. (993) *as it were an error*

שֶׁיֹּצָא rel. (979)-Qal act.ptc. f.s. (יָצָא 422; GK 75qq) *proceeding*

מִלִּפְנֵי הַשַּׁלִּיט prep.-prep.-n.m.p. cstr. (815)-def. art.-adj. m.s. as subst. (1020) *from the ruler*

10:6

נִתַּן Ni. pf. 3 m.s. (נָתַן 678) *is set*

הַסֶּכֶל def.art.-n.m.s. (698) *folly*

בַּמְּרוֹמִים רַבִּים prep.-def.art.-n.m.p. (928)-adj. m.p. (I 912) *in many high places*

וַעֲשִׁירִים conj.-adj. m.p. (799) *and the rich*

בַּשֵּׁפֶל prep.-def.art.-n.m.s. (1050) *in a low place (condition)*

יֵשֵׁבוּ Qal impf. 3 m.p. paus. (יָשַׁב 442) *sit*

10:7

רָאִיתִי Qal pf. 1 c.s. (רָאָה 906) *I have seen*

עֲבָדִים n.m.p. (713) *slaves*
עַל־סוּסִים prep.-n.m.p. (692) *on horses*
וְשָׂרִים conj.-n.m.p. (978) *and princes*
הֹלְכִים Qal act.ptc. m.p. (הָלַךְ 229) *walking*
כַּעֲבָדִים prep.-def.art.-n.m.p. (713) *like slaves*
עַל־הָאָרֶץ prep.-def.art.-n.f.s. (75) *on foot (upon the earth)*

10:8

חֹפֵר Qal act.ptc. (I 343) *he who digs*
גּוּמָּץ n.m.s. (170) *a pit*
בּוֹ יִפּוֹל prep.-3 m.s. sf.-Qal impf. 3 m.s. (נָפַל 656) *will fall into it*
וּפֹרֵץ גָּדֵר conj.-Qal act.ptc. (פָּרַץ I 829)-n.m.s. (154) *and him who breaks through a wall*
יִשְּׁכֶנּוּ Qal impf. 3 m.s.-3 m.s. sf. (נָשַׁךְ 675) *will bite him*
נָחָשׁ n.m.s. (638) *a serpent*

10:9

מַסִּיעַ אֲבָנִים Hi. ptc. m.s. (נָסַע I 652)-n.f.p. (6) *he who quarries stones*
יֵעָצֵב בָּהֶם Ni. impf. 3 m.s. (עָצַב I 780)-prep.-3 m.p. sf. *is hurt by them*
בּוֹקֵעַ עֵצִים Qal act.ptc. (בָּקַע 131)-n.m.p. (781) *he who splits logs*
יִסָּכֶן בָּם Ni. impf. 3 m.s. (סָכַן II 698)-prep.-3 m.p. sf. *is endangered by them*

10:10

אִם־קֵהָה הַבַּרְזֶל hypoth.part. (49)-Pi. pf. 3 m.s. (874 קָהָה)-def.art.-n.m.s. (137) *if the iron is blunt*
וְהוּא לֹא־פָנִים conj.-pers.pr. 3 m.s. (214)-neg. -n.m.p. (815) *and one not the edge*
קִלְקַל Pilpal pf. 3 m.s. (קָלַל 886) *does whet (move quickly to and fro)*
וַחֲיָלִים conj.-n.m.p. (298) *strength*
יְגַבֵּר Pi. impf. 3 m.s. (גָּבַר 149) *he must put forth*
וְיִתְרוֹן conj.-n.m.s. (452) *and profit*
הַכְשֵׁיר Hi. inf.cstr. (כָּשֵׁר 506) *for giving success*
חָכְמָה n.f.s. (315) *is wisdom*

10:11

אִם־יִשֹּׁךְ hypoth.part. (49)-Qal impf. 3 m.s. (נָשַׁךְ 675) *if bites*
הַנָּחָשׁ def.art.-n.m.s. (638) *the serpent*
בְּלוֹא־לָחַשׁ prep.-neg.-n.m.s. paus. (538) *without charming*
וְאֵין יִתְרוֹן conj.-neg. cstr. (II 34)-n.m.s. (452) *there is no advantage*
לְבַעַל הַלָּשׁוֹן prep.-n.m.s. cstr. (127)-def.art. -n.m.s. (546) *in a charmer (a master of the tongue)*

10:12

דִּבְרֵי n.m.p. cstr. (182) *the words of*
פִי־חָכָם n.m.s. cstr. (804)-adj. m.s. (314) *a wise man's mouth*
חֵן n.m.s. (I 336) *favor*
וְשִׂפְתוֹת conj.-n.f.p. cstr. (973) *but the lips of*
כְּסִיל n.m.s. (I 493) *a fool*
תְּבַלְּעֶנּוּ Pi. impf. 3 f.s.-3 m.s. sf. (בָּלַע 118) *consume him*

10:13

תְּחִלַּת n.f.s. cstr. (321) *the beginning of*
דִּבְרֵי n.m.p. cstr. (182) *the words of*
פִיהוּ n.m.s.-3 m.s. sf. (804) *his mouth*
סִכְלוּת n.f.s. (698) *is foolishness*
וְאַחֲרִית conj.-n.f.s. cstr. (31) *and the end of*
פִּיהוּ v.supra *his talk*
הוֹלֵלוּת רָעָה n.f.s. (239; GK 86,l)-adj. f.s. (I 948) *is wicked madness*

10:14

וְהַסָּכָל conj.-def.art.-n.m.s. (698) *a fool*
יַרְבֶּה Hi. impf. 3 m.s. (רָבָה I 915) *multiplies*
דְבָרִים n.m.p. (182) *words*
לֹא־יֵדַע הָאָדָם neg.-Qal impf. 3 m.s. (יָדַע 393)-def.art.-n.m.s. (9) *no man knows*
מַה־שֶׁיִּהְיֶה interr. (552)-rel. (979)-Qal impf. 3 m.s. (הָיָה 224) *what is to be*
וַאֲשֶׁר יִהְיֶה conj.-rel. (81)-v.supra *and what will be*
מֵאַחֲרָיו prep.-prep.--3 m.s. sf. (29) *after him*
מִי יַגִּיד לוֹ interr. (566)-Hi. impf. 3 m.s. (נָגַד 616)-prep.-3 m.s. sf. *who can tell him*

10:15

עֲמַל הַכְּסִילִים n.f.s. cstr. (765)-def.art.-n.m.p. (I 493; GK 145m) *the toil of a fool*
תְּיַגְּעֶנּוּ Pi. impf. 3 f.s.-3 m.s. sf. (יָגַע 388) *wearies him*
אֲשֶׁר לֹא־יָדַע rel. (81)-neg.-Qal pf. 3 m.s. (393) *so that he does not know*
לָלֶכֶת prep.-Qal inf.cstr. (הָלַךְ 229) *to go*
אֶל־עִיר prep.-n.f.s. (746) *to the city*

10:16

אִי־לָךְ interj. (III 33)-prep.-2 f.s. sf. *woe to you*

אֶרֶץ n.f.s. (75) *O land*
שֶׁמַּלְכֵּךְ rel. (979)–n.m.s.–2 f.s. sf. (I 572) *when your king*
נָעַר n.m.s. paus. (654) *is a child*
וְשָׂרַיִךְ conj.–n.m.p.–2 f.s. sf. (978) *and your princes*
בַּבֹּקֶר prep.–def.art.–n.m.s. (133) *in the morning*
יֹאכֵלוּ Qal impf. 3 m.p. paus. (אָכַל 37) *feast*

10:17

אַשְׁרֵיךְ n.m.p.–2 f.s. sf. (80; GK 91,l) *happy are you*
אֶרֶץ n.f.s. (75) *O land*
שֶׁמַּלְכֵּךְ rel. (979)–n.m.s.–2 f.s. sf. (I 572) *when your king*
בֶּן־חוֹרִים n.m.s. cstr. (119)–n.m.p. (II 359) *the son of free men*
וְשָׂרַיִךְ conj.–n.m.p.–2 f.s. sf. (978) *and your princes*
בָּעֵת prep.–def.art.–n.f.s. (773) *at the proper time*
יֹאכֵלוּ Qal impf. 3 m.s. (אָכַל 37) *feast*
בִּגְבוּרָה prep.–n.f.s. (150) *for strength*
וְלֹא בַשְּׁתִי conj.–neg.–prep.–def.art.–n.m.s. (I 1059) *and not for drunkenness*

10:18

בַּעֲצַלְתַּיִם prep.–n.f. du. (782; GK 88b) *through sloth*
יִמַּךְ Ni. impf. 3 m.s. (מָכַךְ 568) *sinks in*
הַמְּקָרֶה def.art.–n.m.s. (900) *the roof*
וּבְשִׁפְלוּת conj.–prep.–n.f.s. cstr. (1050) *and through the sinking of*
יָדַיִם n.f. du. (388) *hands*
יִדְלֹף Qal impf. 3 m.s. (דָּלַף 196) *leaks*
הַבָּיִת def.art.–n.m.s. paus. (108) *the house*

10:19

לִשְׂחוֹק prep.–n.m.s. (966) *for laughter*
עֹשִׂים Qal act.ptc. m.p. (עָשָׂה I 793) *they make*
לֶחֶם n.m.s. (536) *bread*
וְיַיִן conj.–n.m.s. (406) *and wine*
יְשַׂמַּח Pi. impf. 3 m.s. (שָׂמַח 970) *gladdens*
חַיִּים n.m.p. (313) *life*
וְהַכֶּסֶף conj.–def.art.–n.m.s. (494) *and money*
יַעֲנֶה Qal impf. 3 m.s. (עָנָה I 772) *answers*
אֶת־הַכֹּל dir.obj.–def.art.–n.m.s. (481) *everything*

10:20

גַּם בְּמַדָּעֲךָ adv. (168)–prep.–n.m.s.–2 m.s. sf. (396) *even in your thought*
מֶלֶךְ n.m.s. (I 572) *the king*
אַל־תְּקַלֵּל neg.–Pi. impf. 2 m.s. (קָלַל 886) *do not curse*
וּבְחַדְרֵי conj.–prep.–n.m.p. cstr. (293) *and in the chambers of*
מִשְׁכָּבְךָ n.m.s.–2 m.s. sf. (1012) *your bed*
אַל־תְּקַלֵּל neg.–v.supra *curse not*
עָשִׁיר adj. m.s. (799) *the rich*
כִּי עוֹף conj.–n.m.s. cstr. (733) *for the bird of*
הַשָּׁמַיִם def.art.–n.m. du. (1029) *the air (heavens)*
יוֹלִיךְ Hi. impf. 3 m.s. (הָלַךְ 229) *will carry*
אֶת־הַקּוֹל dir.obj.–def.art.–n.m.s. (876) *the voice*
וּבַעַל הַכְּנָפַיִם conj.–n.m.s. cstr. (I 127)–def.art.–n.f. du. (489) *or some winged creature*
יַגֵּיד Hi. impf. 3 m.s. (נָגַד 616; GK 53n) *will tell*
דָּבָר n.m.s. (182) *the matter*

11:1

שַׁלַּח Pi. impv. 2 m.s. (1018) *cast*
לַחְמְךָ n.m.s.–2 m.s. sf. (536) *your bread*
עַל־פְּנֵי הַמָּיִם prep.–n.m.p. cstr. (815)–def.art.–n.m.p. (565) *upon the waters*
כִּי־בְרֹב הַיָּמִים conj. (471)–prep.–n.m.s. cstr. (913)–def.art.–n.m.p. (398) *for after many days*
תִּמְצָאֶנּוּ Qal impf. 2 m.s.–3 m.s. sf. (מָצָא 592) *you will find it*

11:2

תֶּן־ Qal impv. 2 m.s. (נָתַן 678) *give*
חֵלֶק n.m.s. (324) *a portion*
לְשִׁבְעָה prep.–num. f.s. (988) *to seven*
וְגַם conj.–adv. (168) *or even*
לִשְׁמוֹנָה prep.–num. f.s. (1032; GK 134s) *to eight*
כִּי לֹא תֵדַע conj.–neg.–Qal impf. 2 m.s. (יָדַע 393) *for you know not*
מַה־יִּהְיֶה interr. (552)–Qal impf. 3 m.s. (הָיָה 224) *what ... may happen*
רָעָה n.f.s. (949) *evil*
עַל־הָאָרֶץ prep.–def.art.–n.f.s. (75) *on earth*

11:3

אִם־יִמָּלְאוּ hypoth.part. (49)–Ni. impf. 3 m.p. (569 מָלֵא) *if are full*
הֶעָבִים def.art.–n.m.p. (II 728) *the clouds*
גֶּשֶׁם n.m.s. (II 177) *rain*
עַל־הָאָרֶץ prep.–def.art.–n.f.s. (75) *on the earth*
יָרִיקוּ Hi. impf. 3 m.p. (רִיק 937) *they empty themselves*
וְאִם־יִפּוֹל conj.–v.supra–Qal impf. 3 m.s. (נָפַל 656) *and if ... falls*
עֵץ n.m.s. (781) *a tree*
בַּדָּרוֹם prep.–def.art.–n.m.s. (204) *to the south*

וְאִם בַּצָּפוֹן v.supra-prep.-def.art.-n.f.s. (860) *or to the north*

מְקוֹם n.m.s. cstr. (879) *the place*

שֶׁיִּפּוֹל הָעֵץ rel. (979)-v.supra-def.art.-n.m.s. (781) *where the tree falls*

שָׁם יְהוּא adv. (1027)-Qal impf. 3 m.s. apoc. (הָוָה 217; GK 23i,75s) *there it will lie*

11:4

שֹׁמֵר Qal act.ptc. (1036) *he who observes*

רוּחַ n.f.s. (924) *the wind*

לֹא יִזְרָע neg.-Qal impf. 3 m.s. (זָרַע 281) *will not sow*

וְרֹאֶה conj.-Qal act.ptc. (רָאָה 906) *and he who regards*

בֶּעָבִים prep.-def.art.-n.m.s. (II 728) *the clouds*

לֹא יִקְצוֹר neg.-Qal impf. 3 m.s. (קָצַר 894) *will not reap*

11:5

כַּאֲשֶׁר prep.-rel. (81) *as*

אֵינְךָ יוֹדֵעַ neg.-2 m.s. sf. (II 34)-Qal act.ptc. (393) *you do not know*

מַה־דֶּרֶךְ הָרוּחַ interr. (552)-n.m.s. cstr. (202) -def.art.-n.f.s. (924) *what is the way of the spirit*

כַּעֲצָמִים prep.-n.f.p. (782) *as bones*

בְּבֶטֶן prep.-n.f.s. cstr. (105) *in the womb of*

הַמְּלֵאָה def.art.-adj. f.s. (570) *the woman with child*

כָּכָה לֹא תֵדַע adv. (462)-neg.-Qal impf. 2 m.s. (393 יָדַע) *so you do not know*

אֶת־מַעֲשֵׂה dir.obj.-n.m.s. cstr. (795) *the work of*

הָאֱלֹהִים def.art.-n.m.p. (43) *God*

אֲשֶׁר יַעֲשֶׂה rel. (81)-Qal impf. 3 m.s. (עָשָׂה I 793) *who makes*

אֶת־הַכֹּל dir.obj.-def.art.-n.m.s. (481) *everything*

11:6

בַּבֹּקֶר prep.-def.art.-n.m.s. (133) *in the morning*

זְרַע Qal impv. 2 m.s. (281) *sow*

אֶת־זַרְעֶךָ dir.obj.-n.m.s.-2 m.s. sf. (282) *your seed*

וְלָעֶרֶב conj.-prep.-def.art.-n.m.s. (787) *and at evening*

אַל־תַּנַּח neg.-Hi. impf. (B) 2 m.s. (נוּחַ 628) *withhold not*

יָדֶךָ n.f.s.-2 m.s. sf. (388) *your hand*

כִּי אֵינְךָ יוֹדֵעַ conj. (471)-neg.--2 m.s. sf. (II 34)-Qal act.ptc. (יָדַע 393) *for you do not know*

אֵי זֶה interr.adv. (32)-demons.adj. m.s. (260) *which*

יִכְשַׁר Qal impf. 3 m.s. (506) *will prosper*

הֲזֶה interr.part.-v.supra *this*

אוֹ־זֶה conj. (14)-v.supra *or that*

וְאִם־שְׁנֵיהֶם conj.-hypoth.part. (49)-num.-3 m.p. sf. (1040) *or whether both*

כְּאֶחָד prep.-adj. num. (25) *alike*

טוֹבִים adj. m.p. (II 373) *will be good*

11:7

וּמָתוֹק conj.-adj. m.s. (608) *is sweet*

הָאוֹר def.art.-n.m.s. (21) *light*

וְטוֹב conj.-adj. m.s. (II 373) *and it is pleasant*

לַעֵינַיִם prep.-def.art.-n.f. du. (744) *for the eyes*

לִרְאוֹת prep.-Qal inf.cstr. (רָאָה 906) *to behold*

אֶת־הַשָּׁמֶשׁ dir.obj.-def.art.-n.f.s. paus. (1039) *the sun*

11:8

כִּי אִם־שָׁנִים הַרְבֵּה conj. (471)-hypoth.part. (49)-n.f.p. (1040)-Hi. inf.abs. as adv. (רָבָה I 915) *for if many years*

יִחְיֶה Qal impf. 3 m.s. (חָיָה 310) *lives*

הָאָדָם def.art.-n.m.s. (9) *a man*

בְּכֻלָּם prep.-n.m.s.-3 m.p. sf. (481) *in them all*

יִשְׂמָח Qal impf. 3 m.s. paus. (שָׂמַח 970) *let him rejoice*

וְיִזְכֹּר conj.-Qal impf. 3 m.s. (269) *but let him remember*

אֶת־יְמֵי הַחֹשֶׁךְ dir.obj.-n.m.p. cstr. (398)-def.art. -n.m.s. (365) *the days of darkness*

כִּי־הַרְבֵּה יִהְיוּ conj. (471)-Hi. inf.abs. as adv. (I 915 רָבָה)-Qal impf. 3 m.p. (הָיָה 224) *that they will be many*

כָּל־שֶׁבָּא n.m.s. (481)-rel. (979)-Qal act.ptc. or Qal pf. 3 m.s. (בּוֹא 97) *all that comes*

הָבֶל n.m.s. paus. (I 210) *is vanity*

11:9

שְׂמַח Qal impv. 2 m.s. (970) *rejoice*

בָּחוּר n.m.s. (104) *O young man*

בְּיַלְדוּתֶיךָ prep.-n.f.p.-2 m.s. sf. (409) *in your youth*

וִיטִיבְךָ conj.-Hi. impf. 3 m.s.-2 m.s. sf. (יָטַב 405) *and let ... cheer you*

לִבְּךָ n.m.s.-2 m.s. sf. (524) *your heart*

בִּימֵי בְחוּרוֹתֶךָ prep.-n.m.p. cstr. (398)-n.f.p.-2 m.s. sf. (104) *in the days of your youth*

וְהַלֵּךְ conj.-Pi. impv. 2 m.s. (הָלַךְ 229) *and walk*

בְּדַרְכֵי prep.-n.m.p. cstr. (202) *in the ways of*

לִבְּךָ n.m.s.-2 m.s. sf. (524) *your heart*

וּבְמַרְאֵי conj.-prep.-n.m.p. cstr. (909; GK 93ss) *and in the sight of*
עֵינֶיךָ n.f. du.-2 m.s. sf. (744) *your eyes*
וְדָע conj.-Qal impv. 2 m.s. (יָדַע 393) *but know*
כִּי עַל־כָּל־אֵלֶּה conj. (471)-prep.-n.m.s. cstr. (481)-demons.adj. c.p. (41) *that for all these things*
יְבִיאֲךָ Hi. impf. 3 m.s.-2 m.s. sf. (בּוֹא 97) *will bring you*
הָאֱלֹהִים def.art.-n.m.p. (43) *God*
בַּמִּשְׁפָּט prep.-def.art.-n.m.s. (1048) *into judgment*

11:10

וְהָסֵר conj.-Hi. impv. 2 m.s. (סוּר 693) *remove*
כַּעַס n.m.s. (495) *vexation*
מִלִּבֶּךָ prep.-n.m.s.-2 m.s. sf. (524) *from your mind*
וְהַעֲבֵר conj.-Hi. impv. 2 m.s. (עָבַר 716) *and put away*
רָעָה n.f.s. (949) *pain*
מִבְּשָׂרֶךָ prep.-n.m.s.-2 m.s. sf. (142) *from your body*
כִּי־הַיַּלְדוּת conj. (471)-def.art.-n.f.s. (409) *for youth*
וְהַשַּׁחֲרוּת conj.-def.art.-n.f.s. (1007) *and the dawn of life*
הָבֶל n.m.s. paus. (I 210) *are vanity*

12:1

וּזְכֹר conj.-Qal impv. 2 m.s. (269) *remember also*
אֶת־בּוֹרְאֶיךָ dir.obj.-Qal act.ptc. m.p.-2 m.s. sf. (I 135 בָּרָא; GK 124k) *your Creator*
בִּימֵי prep.-n.m.p. cstr. (398) *in the days of*
בְּחוּרֹתֶיךָ n.f.p.-2 m.s. sf. (104) *your youth*
עַד אֲשֶׁר לֹא־יָבֹאוּ prep. (III 723)-rel. (81)-neg.-Qal impf. 3 m.p. (בּוֹא 97) *before come*
יְמֵי הָרָעָה n.m.p. cstr. (398)-def.art.-n.f.s. (949) *the evil days*
וְהִגִּיעוּ conj.-Hi. pf. 3 c.p. (נָגַע 619) *and draw nigh*
שָׁנִים n.f.p. (1040) *the years*
אֲשֶׁר תֹּאמַר rel. (81)-Qal impf. 2 m.s. (אָמַר 55) *when you will say*
אֵין־לִי neg. cstr. (II 34)-prep.-1 c.s. sf. *I have no*
בָּהֶם prep.-3 m.p. sf. *in them*
חֵפֶץ n.m.s. (343) *pleasure*

12:2

עַד אֲשֶׁר לֹא־תֶחְשַׁךְ prep. (III 723)-rel. (81)-neg.-Qal impf. 3 f.s. (חָשַׁךְ 364) *before are darkened*
הַשֶּׁמֶשׁ def.art.-n.f.s. (1039) *the sun*
וְהָאוֹר conj.-def.art.-n.m.s. (21) *and the light*
וְהַיָּרֵחַ conj.-def.art.-n.m.s. (437) *and the moon*
וְהַכּוֹכָבִים conj.-def.art.-n.m.p. (456) *and the stars*
וְשָׁבוּ conj.-Qal pf. 3 c.p. (שׁוּב 996) *and return*
הֶעָבִים def.art.-n.m.p. (II 728) *the clouds*
אַחַר הַגָּשֶׁם prep. (29)-def.art.-n.m.s. paus. (II 177) *after the rain*

12:3

בַּיּוֹם prep.-def.art.-n.m.s. (398) *in the day*
שֶׁיָּזֻעוּ rel. (979)-Qal impf. 3 m.p. (זוּעַ 266) *when tremble*
שֹׁמְרֵי Qal act.ptc. m.p. cstr. (1036) *the keepers of*
הַבַּיִת def.art.-n.m.s. (108) *the house*
וְהִתְעַוְּתוּ conj.-Hith. pf. 3 c.p. (עָוַת 736) *and are bent*
אַנְשֵׁי הֶחָיִל n.m.p. cstr. (35)-def.art.-n.m.s. paus. (298) *the strong men*
וּבָטְלוּ conj.-Qal pf. 3 c.p. (בָּטַל 105) *and cease*
הַטֹּחֲנוֹת def.art.-Qal act.ptc. f.p. (טָחַן 377) *the grinders*
כִּי מִעֵטוּ conj. (471)-Pi. pf. 3 c.p. (מָעַט 589; GK 52k) *because they are few*
וְחָשְׁכוּ conj.-Qal pf. 3 c.p. (חָשַׁךְ 364) *and are dimmed*
הָרֹאוֹת def.art.-Qal act.ptc. f.p. (רָאָה 906) *those that look*
בָּאֲרֻבּוֹת prep.-def.art.-n.f.p. (70) *through the windows*

12:4

וְסֻגְּרוּ conj.-Pu. pf. 3 c.p. (סָגַר 688) *and are shut*
דְלָתַיִם n.f. du. (195; GK 93n) *the doors*
בַּשּׁוּק prep.-def.art.-n.m.s. (1003) *on the street*
בִּשְׁפַל prep.-Qal inf.cstr. (1050) *when is low*
קוֹל הַטַּחֲנָה n.m.s. cstr. (876)-def.art.-n.f.s. (377) *the sound of the grinding*
וְיָקוּם conj.-Qal impf. 3 m.s. (קוּם 877; GK 72t) *and one rises up*
לְקוֹל הַצִּפּוֹר prep.-n.m.s. cstr. (876)-def.art.-n.f.s. (861) *at the voice of a bird*
וְיִשַּׁחוּ conj.-Ni. impf. 3 m.p. (שָׁחַח 1005) *and are brought low*
כָּל־בְּנוֹת n.m.s. cstr. (481)-n.f.p. cstr. (I 123; GK 128v) *all the daughters of*
הַשִּׁיר def.art.-n.m.s. (1010) *song*

12:5

גַּם מִגָּבֹהַּ adv. (168)-prep.-adj. m.s. (147) *also of what is high*
יִרָאוּ Qal impf. 3 m.p. (יָרֵא 431) *they are afraid*
וְחַתְחַתִּים conj.-n.m.p. (369) *and terrors*
בַּדֶּרֶךְ prep.-def.art.-n.m.s. (202) *in the way*
וְיָנֵאץ conj.-Hi. impf. 3 m.s. (נָצַץ 665; GK 73g) *and wears blossoms*
הַשָּׁקֵד def.art.-n.m.s. (1052) *the almond*
וְיִסְתַּבֵּל conj.-Hith. impf. 3 m.s. (סָבַל 687) *and stuffs itself*
הֶחָגָב def.art.-n.m.s. (I 290) *the grasshopper*
וְתָפֵר conj.-Hi. impf. 3 f.s. (פָּרַר I 830) *and fails*
הָאֲבִיּוֹנָה def.art.-n.f.s. (2) *the caper-berry*
כִּי־הֹלֵךְ conj. (471)-Qal act.ptc. (הָלַךְ 229) *because ... goes*
הָאָדָם def.art.-n.m.s. (9) *man*
אֶל־בֵּית עוֹלָמוֹ prep.-n.m.s. cstr. (108)-n.m.s.-3 m.s. sf. (761) *to his eternal home*
וְסָבְבוּ conj.-Qal pf. 3 c.p. (סָבַב 685) *and go about*
בַשּׁוּק prep.-def.art.-n.m.s. (1003) *the streets*
הַסֹּפְדִים def.art.-Qal act.ptc. m.p. (סָפַד 704) *the mourners*

12:6

עַד אֲשֶׁר לֹא־יֵרָחֵק prep. (III 723)-rel. (81)-neg. -Ni. impf. 3 m.s. (רָחַק 934) *before is removed*
חֶבֶל הַכֶּסֶף n.m.s. cstr. (286)-def.art.-n.m.s. (494) *the silver cord*
וְתָרֻץ conj.-Qal impf. 3 f.s. (רָצַץ 954; GK 67q) *or is broken*
גֻּלַּת הַזָּהָב n.f.s. cstr. (165)-def.art.-n.m.s. (262) *the golden bowl*
וְתִשָּׁבֶר conj.-Ni. impf. 3 f.s. (שָׁבַר 990) *or is broken*
כַּד n.f.s. (461) *the pitcher (jar)*
עַל־הַמַּבּוּעַ prep.-def.art.-n.m.s. (616) *at the fountain*
וְנָרֹץ conj.-Ni. pf. 3 m.s. (רָצַץ 954; GK 67t) *or broken*
הַגַּלְגַּל def.art.-n.m.s. (165) *the wheel*
אֶל־הַבּוֹר prep.-def.art.-n.m.s. (I 92) *at the cistern*

12:7

וְיָשֹׁב conj.-Qal impf. 3 m.s. apoc. (שׁוּב 996; GK 109k) *and returns*
הֶעָפָר def.art.-n.m.s. (779) *the dust*
עַל־הָאָרֶץ prep.-def.art.-n.f.s. (75) *to the earth*
כְּשֶׁהָיָה prep.-rel. (979)-Qal pf. 3 m.s. (224) *as it was*
וְהָרוּחַ conj.-def.art.-n.f.s. (924) *and the spirit*
תָּשׁוּב Qal impf. 3 f.s. (996) *returns*
אֶל־הָאֱלֹהִים prep.-def.art.-n.m.p. (43) *to God*
אֲשֶׁר נְתָנָהּ rel. (81)-Qal pf. 3 m.s.-3 f.s. sf. (נָתַן 678) *who gave it*

12:8

הֲבֵל הֲבָלִים n.m.s. cstr. (I 210)-n.m.p. (I 210) *vanity of vanities*
אָמַר הַקּוֹהֶלֶת Qal pf. 3 m.s. (55)-def.art.-n.m.s. (875) *says the Preacher*
הַכֹּל def.art.-n.m.s. (481) *all is*
הָבֶל n.m.s. paus. (I 210) *vanity*

12:9

וְיֹתֵר שֶׁהָיָה conj.-n.m.s. (452)-rel. (979)-Qal pf. 3 m.s. (224) *besides that ... was*
קֹהֶלֶת n.m.s. (875) *the Preacher*
חָכָם adj. m.s. (314; GK 145h) *wise*
עוֹד לִמַּד־ adv. (728)-Pi. pf. 3 m.s. (540) *also taught*
דַּעַת n.f.s. (395) *knowledge*
אֶת־הָעָם dir.obj.-def.art.-n.m.s. (I 766) *the people*
וְאִזֵּן conj.-Pi. pf. 3 m.s. (אָזַן II 24) *weighing*
וְחִקֵּר conj.-Pi. pf. 3 m.s. (חָקַר *and studying*
תִּקֵּן מְשָׁלִים Pi. pf. 3 m.s. (תָּקַן 1075)-n.m.p. (605) *arranging proverbs*
הַרְבֵּה Hi. inf.abs. as adv. (רָבָה I 915) *with great care*

12:10

בִּקֵּשׁ Pi. pf. 3 m.s. (134) *sought*
קֹהֶלֶת n.m.s. (875) *the Preacher*
לִמְצֹא prep.-Qal inf.cstr. (592) *to find*
דִּבְרֵי־חֵפֶץ n.m.p. cstr. (182)-n.m.s. (343) *pleasing words*
וְכָתוּב conj.-Qal pass.ptc. (507) *and he wrote*
יֹשֶׁר n.m.s. (449) *uprightly*
דִּבְרֵי אֱמֶת n.m.p. cstr. (182)-n.f.s. (54) *words of truth*

12:11

דִּבְרֵי חֲכָמִים n.m.p. cstr. (182)-adj. m.p. (314) *the sayings of the wise*
כַּדָּרְבֹנוֹת prep.-def.art.-n.f.p. (201) *like goads*
וּכְמַשְׂמְרוֹת conj.-prep.-n.m.p. (971; 702) *and like nails* (rd.prb. מַסְמְרוֹת)
נְטוּעִים Qal pass.ptc. m.p. (נָטַע 642) *firmly fixed*

בַּעֲלֵי אֲסֻפּוֹת n.m.p. cstr. (127)–n.f.p. (63) ***the collected sayings***

נִתְּנוּ Ni. pf. 3 c.p. (נָתַן 678) ***which are given***

מֵרֹעֶה אֶחָד prep.–Qal act.ptc. (רָעָה I 944)–num. adj. (25) ***by one Shepherd***

12:12

וְיֹתֵר n.m.s. (452) ***and anything***

מֵהֵמָּה prep.–demons.adj. m.p. (241) ***beyond these***

בְּנִי n.m.s.–1 c.s. sf. (119) ***my son***

הִזָּהֵר Ni. impv. 2 m.s. (זָהַר 264) ***beware***

עֲשׂוֹת Qal inf.cstr. (עָשָׂה I 793) ***of making of***

סְפָרִים n.m.p. (706) ***books***

הַרְבֵּה Hi. inf.abs. as adv. (רָבָה I 915) ***many***

אֵין קֵץ neg. cstr. (II 34)–n.m.s. (893) ***there is no end***

וְלַהַג הַרְבֵּה conj.–n.m.s. (529)–v.supra ***and much study***

יְגִעַת בָּשָׂר n.f.s. cstr. (388)–n.m.s. (142) ***a weariness of the flesh***

12:13

סוֹף דָּבָר n.m.s. cstr. (683)–n.m.s. (182) ***the end of the matter***

הַכֹּל נִשְׁמָע def.art.–n.m.s. (481)–Ni. ptc. or pf. 3 m.s. paus. (שָׁמַע 1033) ***all has been heard***

אֶת־הָאֱלֹהִים dir.obj.–def.art.–n.m.p. (43) ***God***

יְרָא Qal impv. 2 m.s. (יָרֵא 431) ***fear***

וְאֶת־מִצְוֹתָיו conj.–dir.obj.–n.f.p.–3 m.s. sf. (846) ***and his commandments***

שְׁמוֹר Qal impv. 2 m.s. (1036) ***keep***

כִּי־זֶה conj. (471)–demons.adj. m.s. (260) ***for this is***

כָּל־הָאָדָם n.m.s. cstr. (481)–def.art.–n.m.s. (9) ***the wholeness of man***

12:14

כִּי אֶת־כָּל־מַעֲשֶׂה conj. (471)–dir.obj.–n.m.s. cstr. (481)–n.m.s. (795) ***for every deed***

הָאֱלֹהִים def.art.–n.m.p. (43) ***God***

יָבִא Hi. impf. 3 m.s. (בּוֹא 97) ***will bring***

בְמִשְׁפָּט prep.–n.m.s. (1048) ***into judgment***

עַל כָּל־נֶעְלָם prep.–v.supra–Ni. ptc. (עָלַם I 761) ***on every secret thing***

אִם־טוֹב hypoth.part. (49)–adj. m.s. (II 373) ***whether good***

וְאִם־רָע conj.–v.supra–adj. m.s. (I 948) ***or evil***

Song of Solomon

1:1

שִׁיר הַשִּׁירִים n.m.s. cstr. (1010)-def.art.-n.m.p. (1010; GK 133i) *the Song of Songs*

אֲשֶׁר לִשְׁלֹמֹה rel. (81)-prep.-pr.n. (1024) *which is Solomon's*

1:2

יִשָּׁקֵנִי Qal impf. 3 m.s.-1 c.s. sf. (נָשַׁק I 676) *O that he would kiss me*

מִנְּשִׁיקוֹת פִּיהוּ prep.-n.f.p. cstr. (676)-n.m.s.-3 m.s. sf. (804) *with the kisses of his mouth*

כִּי־טוֹבִים conj. (471)-adj. m.p. (II 373) *for better*

דֹדֶיךָ n.m.p.-3 m.s. sf. (187) *your love*

מִיָּיִן prep.-n.m.s. paus. (406) *than wine*

1:3

לְרֵיחַ שְׁמָנֶיךָ prep.-n.m.s. cstr. (926)-n.m.p.-2 m.s. sf. (1032) *the scent of your oils*

טוֹבִים adj. m.p. (II 373) *are fragrant*

שֶׁמֶן תּוּרַק n.f.s. (1032)-Ho. impf. 3 f.s. (ריק 937) *oil poured out*

שְׁמֶךָ neg.--2 m.s. sf. (1027) *your name*

עַל־כֵּן prep. (II 752)-adv. (485) *therefore*

עֲלָמוֹת n.f.p. (761) *the maidens*

אֲהֵבוּךָ Qal pf. 3 c.p. (אָהֵב 12)-2 m.s. sf. *love you*

1:4

מָשְׁכֵנִי Qal impv. 2 m.s.-1 c.s. sf. (מָשַׁךְ 604) *draw me*

אַחֲרֶיךָ prep.-2 m.s. sf. (29) *after you*

נָּרוּצָה Qal impf. 1 c.p.-vol.he (רוּץ 930) *let us make haste*

הֱבִיאַנִי Hi. pf. 3 m.s.-1 c.s. sf. (בּוֹא 97) *has brought me*

הַמֶּלֶךְ def.art.-n.m.s. (I 572) *the king*

חֲדָרָיו n.m.p.-3 m.s. sf. (293) *into his chambers*

נָגִילָה Qal impf. 1 c.p.-vol.he (גִּיל 160) *we will exult*

וְנִשְׂמְחָה בָּךְ conj.-Qal impf. 1 c.p.-vol.he (שָׂמַח 970)-prep.-2 m.s. sf. paus. *and rejoice in you*

נַזְכִּירָה Hi. impf. 1 c.p.-vol.he (זָכַר 269) *we will extol*

דֹדֶיךָ n.m.p.-2 m.s. sf. (187) *your love*

מִיַּיִן prep.-n.m.s. (406) *more than wine*

מֵישָׁרִים adv. of n.m.p. (449) *rightly*

אֲהֵבוּךָ Qal pf. 3 c.p.-2 m.s. sf. (אָהֵב 12) *do they love you*

1:5

שְׁחוֹרָה אֲנִי adj. f.s. (1007)-pers.pr. 1 c.s. (58) *I am very dark*

וְנָאוָה conj.-adj. f.s. (610) *but comely*

בְּנוֹת יְרוּשָׁלָ͏ִם n.f.p. cstr. (I 123)-pr.n. (436) *O daughters of Jerusalem*

כְּאָהֳלֵי קֵדָר prep.-n.m.p. cstr. (13)-pr.n. (871) *like the tents of Kedar*

כִּירִיעוֹת שְׁלֹמֹה prep.-n.f.p. cstr. (438)-pr.n. (1024) *like the curtains of Solomon*

1:6

אַל־תִּרְאוּנִי neg.-Qal impf. 2 m.p.-1 c.s. sf. (רָאָה 906; GK 60a) *do not gaze at me*

שֶׁאֲנִי שְׁחַרְחֹרֶת rel. (979)-adj. f.s. (1007) *because I am swarthy*

שֶׁשֱּׁזָפַתְנִי rel. (979)-Qal pf. 3 f.s.-1 c.s. sf. (שָׁזַף 1004) *because ... has scorched me*

הַשָּׁמֶשׁ def.art.-n.f.s. (1039) *the sun*

בְּנֵי אִמִּי n.m.p. cstr. (119)-n.f.s.-1 c.s. sf. (51) *my mother's sons*

נִחֲרוּ־בִי Ni. pf. 3 c.p. (חָרַר 359; GK 75x or חָרָה 354)-prep.-1 c.s. sf. *were angry with me*

שָׂמֻנִי Qal pf. 3 c.p.-1 c.s. sf. (שִׂים 962) *they made me*

נֹטֵרָה Qal act.ptc. f.s. (נָטַר 643) *keeper*

אֶת־הַכְּרָמִים dir.obj.-def.art.-n.m.p. (501) *of the vineyards*

כַּרְמִי שֶׁלִּי n.m.s.-1 c.s. sf. (501)-rel. (979)-prep.-1 c.s. sf. *my own vineyard*

לֹא נָטָרְתִּי neg.-Qal pf. 1 c.s. (נָטַר 643) *I have not kept*

1:7

הַגִּידָה לִּי Hi. impv. 2 m.s.-vol.he (נָגַד 616) -prep.-1 c.s. sf. *tell me*

שֶׁאָהֲבָה נַפְשִׁי rel. (979)-Qal pf. 3 f.s. (אָהַב 12)-n.f.s.-1 c.s. sf. (659) *whom my soul loves*

אֵיכָה תִרְעֶה adv. (32)-Qal impf. 2 m.s. (רָעָה I 944) *where you pasture your flock*

אֵיכָה תַּרְבִּיץ v.supra-Hi. impf. 2 m.s. (רָבַץ 918) *where you make it lie down*

בַּצָּהֳרָיִם prep.-def.art.-n.m.p. (I 843) *at noon*

שַׁלָּמָה אֶהְיֶה rel. (979; GK 36)-prep.-interr. (552)-Qal impf. 1 c.s. (224) *for why should I be*

כְּעֹטְיָה prep.-Qal act.ptc. f.s. (עָטָה I 741; GK 75v) *like one who wanders (one wrapping)*

עַל עֶדְרֵי חֲבֵרֶיךָ prep. (II 752)-n.m.p. cstr. (727)-adj. m.p.-2 m.s. sf. (288) *beside the flocks of your companions*

1:8

אִם־לֹא תֵדְעִי לָךְ hypoth.part. (49)-neg.-Qal impf. 2 f.s. (יָדַע 393)-prep.-2 f.s. sf. *if you do not know*

הַיָּפָה בַּנָּשִׁים def.art.-adj. f.s. (421)-prep. -def.art.-n.f.p. (61) *O fairest among women*

צְאִי־לָךְ Qal impv. 2 f.s. (יָצָא 422)-prep.-2 f.s. sf. *follow*

בְּעִקְבֵי הַצֹּאן prep.-n.m.p. cstr. (784; GK 20h) -def.art.-n.f.s. (83) *in the tracks of the flock*

וּרְעִי conj.-Qal impv. 2 f.s. (רָעָה I 944) *and pasture*

אֶת־גְּדִיֹּתַיִךְ dir.obj.-n.f.p.-2 f.s. sf. (152) *your kids*

עַל מִשְׁכְּנוֹת prep.-n.m.p. cstr. (1015) *beside the tents of*

הָרֹעִים def.art.-Qal act.ptc. m.p. (רָעָה I 944) *the shepherds*

1:9

לְסֻסָתִי prep.-n.f.s.-1 c.s. sf. (692) *to my mare*

בְּרִכְבֵי פַרְעֹה prep.-n.m.p. cstr. 939)-pr.n. (829) *of Pharaoh's chariots*

דִּמִּיתִיךְ Pi. pf. 1 c.s.-2 f.s. sf. (דָּמָהI 197) *I compare you*

רַעְיָתִי n.f.s.-1 c.s. sf. (946) *my love*

1:10

נָאווּ Pi'lel pf. 3 c.p. (נָאָה 610; GK 75x,141c) *are comely*

לְחָיַיִךְ n.m.p.-2 f.s. sf. (534) *your cheeks*

בַּתֹּרִים prep.-def.art.-n.m.p. (1064) *with ornaments*

צַוָּארֵךְ n.m.s.-2 f.s. sf. (848) *your neck*

בַּחֲרוּזִים prep.-def.art.-n.m.p. (354) *with strings of jewels*

1:11

תּוֹרֵי זָהָב n.m.p. cstr. (1064)-n.m.s. (262) *ornaments of gold*

נַעֲשֶׂה־לָּךְ Qal impf. 1 c.p. (עָשָׂה I 793)-prep.-2 f.s. sf. *we will make you*

עִם נְקֻדּוֹת הַכָּסֶף prep. (767)-n.f.p. cstr. (667) -def.art.-n.m.s. paus. (494) *studded with silver*

1:12

עַד־שֶׁהַמֶּלֶךְ prep. (III 723)-rel. (979)-def.art. -n.m.s. (I 572) *while the king*

בִּמְסִבּוֹ prep.-n.m.s.-3 m.s. sf. (687) *on his couch*

נִרְדִּי n.m.s.-1 c.s. sf. (669) *my nard*

נָתַן Qal pf. 3 m.s. (678) *gave forth*

רֵיחוֹ n.m.s.-3 m.s. sf. (926) *its fragrance*

1:13

צְרוֹר הַמֹּר n.m.s. cstr. (I 865)-def.art.-n.m.s. (600) *a bag of myrrh*
דּוֹדִי לִי n.m.s.-1 c.s. sf. (187)-prep.-1 c.s. sf. *my beloved is to me*
בֵּין שָׁדַי prep. (107)-n.m.p.-1 c.s. sf. (994) *between my breasts*
יָלִין Qal impf. 3 m.s. (לִין 533) *that lies*

1:14

אֶשְׁכֹּל הַכֹּפֶר n.m.s. cstr. (79)-def.art.-n.m.s. (III 499) *a cluster of henna blossoms*
דּוֹדִי לִי n.m.s.-1 c.s. sf. (187)-prep.-1 c.s. sf. *my beloved is to me*
בְּכַרְמֵי prep.-n.m.p. cstr. (501) *in the vineyards of*
עֵין גֶּדִי pr.n. (745) *En-gedi*

1:15

הִנָּךְ interj.-2 f.s. sf. (243) *behold you*
יָפָה adj. f.s. (421) *are beautiful*
רַעְיָתִי n.f.s.-1 c.s. sf. (946) *my love*
הִנָּךְ v.supra *behold you*
יָפָה v.supra *are beautiful*
עֵינַיִךְ n.f.p.-2 f.s. sf. (744; GK 141d) *your eyes*
יוֹנִים n.f.p. (I 401) *are doves*

1:16

הִנְּךָ interj.-2 m.s. sf. (243) *behold you*
יָפֶה adj. m.s. (421) *are beautiful*
דוֹדִי n.m.s.-1 c.s. sf. (187) *my beloved*
אַף נָעִים conj. (II 64)-adj. m.s. (I 653) *truly lovely*
אַף־עַרְשֵׂנוּ v.supra-n.f.s.-1 c.p. sf. (793) *our couch*
רַעֲנָנָה adj. f.s. (947) *is green (luxuriant)*

1:17

קֹרוֹת בָּתֵּינוּ n.f.p. cstr. (900)-n.m.p.-1 c.p. sf. (108) *the beams of our house*
אֲרָזִים n.m.p. (72) *are cedar*
רַחִיטֵנוּ n.m. coll.-1 c.p. sf. (923) *our rafters*
בְּרוֹתִים n.m.p. (141) *are pine*

2:1

אֲנִי pers.pr. 1 c.s. (58) *I am*
חֲבַצֶּלֶת הַשָּׁרוֹן n.f.s. cstr. (287)-def.art.-pr.n. (450) *a rose (crocus) of Sharon*
שׁוֹשַׁנַּת n.f.s. cstr. (1004) *a lily of*
הָעֲמָקִים def.art.-n.m.p. (770) *the valleys*

2:2

כְּשׁוֹשַׁנָּה prep.-n.f.s. (I 1004) *as a lily*
בֵּין הַחוֹחִים prep. (107)-def.art.-n.m.p. (296) *among brambles*
כֵּן רַעְיָתִי adv. (485)-n.f.s.-1 c.s. sf. (946) *so is my love*
בֵּין הַבָּנוֹת v.supra-def.art.-n.f.p. (I 123) *among maidens*

2:3

כְּתַפּוּחַ prep.-n.m.s. (I 656) *as an apple tree*
בַּעֲצֵי הַיַּעַר prep.-n.m.p. cstr. (781)-def.art.-n.m.s. (420) *among the trees of the wood*
כֵּן דּוֹדִי adv. (485)-n.m.s.-1 c.s. sf. (187) *so is my beloved*
בֵּין הַבָּנִים prep. (107)-def.art.-n.m.p. (119) *among young men*
בְּצִלּוֹ prep.-n.m.s.-3 m.s. sf. (853) *in his shadow*
חִמַּדְתִּי Pi. pf. 1 c.s. (חָמַד 326) *I delighted*
וְיָשַׁבְתִּי conj.-Qal pf. 1 c.s. (יָשַׁב 442) *and I sat*
וּפִרְיוֹ conj.-n.m.s.-3 m.s. sf. (826) *and his fruit*
מָתוֹק adj. m.s. (608) *was sweet*
לְחִכִּי prep.-n.m.s.-1 c.s. sf. (335) *to my taste*

2:4

הֱבִיאַנִי Hi. pf. 3 m.s.-1 c.s. sf. (בּוֹא 97) *he brought me*
אֶל־בֵּית הַיָּיִן prep.-n.m.s. cstr. (108)-def.art. -n.m.s. paus. (406) *to the banqueting house*
וְדִגְלוֹ conj.-n.m.s.-3 m.s. sf. (186) *and his banner*
עָלַי prep.-1 c.s. sf. (II 752) *over me*
אַהֲבָה n.f.s. (13) *was love*

2:5

סַמְּכוּנִי Pi. impv. 2 m.p.-1 c.s. sf. (סָמַךְ 701) *sustain me*
בָּאֲשִׁישׁוֹת prep.-def.art.-n.f.p. (84) *with raisins*
רַפְּדוּנִי Pi. impv. 2 m.p.-1 c.s. sf. (רָפַד 951) *refresh (support) me*
בַּתַּפּוּחִים prep.-def.art.-n.m.p. (I 656) *with apples*
כִּי־חוֹלַת conj. (471)-Qal act.ptc. f.s. (חָלָה I 317) *for ... sick with*
אַהֲבָה n.f.s. (13) *love*
אָנִי pers.pr. 1 c.s. paus. (58) *I am*

2:6

שְׂמֹאלוֹ n.m.s.-3 m.s. sf. (969) *his left hand*
תַּחַת לְרֹאשִׁי prep. (1065)-prep.-n.m.s.-1 c.s. sf. (910) *under my head*
וִימִינוֹ conj.-n.f.s.-3 m.s. sf. (411) *and his right hand*

תְּחַבְּקֵנִי Pi. impf. 3 f.s.-1 c.s. sf. (חָבַק 287) *embraced me*

2:7

הִשְׁבַּעְתִּי אֶתְכֶם Hi. pf. 1 c.s. (שָׁבַע 989)-dir. obj.-2 m.p. sf. (GK 144a) *I adjure you*

בְּנוֹת יְרוּשָׁלַםִ n.f.p. cstr. (I 123)-pr.n. (436) *O daughters of Jerusalem*

בִּצְבָאוֹת prep.-n.m.p. (II 840) *by the gazelles*

אוֹ בְּאַיְלוֹת conj. (14)-prep.-n.f.p. cstr. (19) *or the hinds of*

הַשָּׂדֶה def.art.-n.m.s. (961) *the field*

אִם־תָּעִירוּ hypoth.part. (49)-Hi. impf. 2 m.p. (I 734 עוּר) *that you stir not up*

וְאִם־תְּעוֹרְרוּ conj.-v.supra-Polel impf. 2 m.p. (I 734 עוּר) *nor awaken*

אֶת־הָאַהֲבָה dir.obj.-def.art.-n.f.s. (13) *love*

שֶׁתֶּחְפָּץ rel. (979)-Qal impf. 3 f.s. (חָפֵץ 342) *until it please*

2:8

קוֹל דּוֹדִי n.m.s. cstr. (876)-n.m.s.-1 c.s. sf. (187) *the voice of my beloved*

הִנֵּה־זֶה בָּא interj. (243)-demons.adj. m.s. (260) -Qal pf. 3 m.s. (בּוֹא 97) *behold, he comes*

מְדַלֵּג Pi. ptc. (דָּלַג 194) *leaping*

עַל־הֶהָרִים prep. (II 752)-def.art.-n.m.p. (249) *upon the mountains*

מְקַפֵּץ Pi. ptc. (קָפַץ 891) *bounding*

עַל־הַגְּבָעוֹת prep.-def.art.-n.f.p. (I 148) *over the hills*

2:9

דּוֹמֶה Qal act.ptc. (דָּמָה I 197) *is like*

דוֹדִי n.m.s.-1 c.s. sf. (187) *my beloved*

לִצְבִי prep.-n.m.s. (II 840) *like a gazelle*

אוֹ לְעֹפֶר הָאַיָּלִים conj. (14)-prep.-n.m.s. cstr. (780)-def.art.-n.m.p. (19) *or a young stag*

הִנֵּה־זֶה עוֹמֵד interj. (243)-demons.adj. m.s. (260)-Qal act.ptc. (עָמַד 763) *behold, there he stands*

אַחַר כָּתְלֵנוּ prep. (29)-n.m.s.-1 c.p. sf. (508) *our wall*

מַשְׁגִּיחַ Hi. ptc. (שָׁגַח 993) *gazing*

מִן־הַחַלֹּנוֹת prep.-def.art.-n.f.p. (319) *in at the windows*

מֵצִיץ Hi. ptc. (צוּץ II 847) *looking*

מִן־הַחֲרַכִּים prep.-def.art.-n.m.p. (355) *through the lattice*

2:10

עָנָה דוֹדִי Qal pf. 3 m.s. (I 772)-n.m.s.-1 c.s. sf. (187) *my beloved speaks*

וְאָמַר לִי conj.-Qal pf. 3 m.s. (55)-prep.-1 c.s. sf. *and says to me*

קוּמִי לָךְ Qal impv. 2 f.s. (קוּם 877)-prep.-2 f.s. sf. (GK 119s) *arise*

רַעְיָתִי n.f.s.-1 c.s. sf. (946) *my love*

יָפָתִי adj. f.s.-1 c.s. sf. (421) *my fair one*

וּלְכִי־לָךְ conj.-Qal impv. 2 f.s. (הָלַךְ 229) -v.supra *and come away*

2:11

כִּי־הִנֵּה conj. (471)-interj. (243) *for lo*

הַסְּתָו עָבָר def.art.-n.m.s. (711)-Qal pf. 3 m.s. paus. (716) *the winter is past*

הַגֶּשֶׁם def.art.-n.m.s. (II 177) *the rain*

חָלַף הָלַךְ לוֹ Qal pf. 3 m.s. (322)-Qal pf. 3 m.s. (229)-prep.-3 m.s. sf. *is over and gone*

2:12

הַנִּצָּנִים def.art.-n.m.p. (665; GK 85uN) *the flowers*

נִרְאוּ Ni. pf. 3 c.p. (רָאָה 906) *appear*

בָאָרֶץ prep.-def.art.-n.f.s. (75) *on the earth*

עֵת הַזָּמִיר n.f.s. cstr. (773)-def.art.-n.m.s. (I 274=song; II 274=pruning) *the time of singing*

הִגִּיעַ Hi. pf. 3 m.s. (נָגַע 619) *has come*

וְקוֹל הַתּוֹר conj.-n.m.s. cstr. (876)-def.art.-n.f.s. (II 1076) *and the voice of the turtledove*

נִשְׁמַע Ni. pf. 3 m.s. (שָׁמַע 1033) *is heard*

בְּאַרְצֵנוּ prep.-n.f.s.-1 c.p. sf. (75) *in our land*

2:13

הַתְּאֵנָה def.art.-n.f.s. (1061) *the fig tree*

חָנְטָה Qal pf. 3 f.s. (חָנַט 334) *puts forth*

פַגֶּיהָ n.f.p.-3 f.s. sf. (803) *its figs*

וְהַגְּפָנִים conj.-def.art.-n.f.p. (172; GK 141d) *and the vines*

סְמָדַר n.m.s. (701) *are in blossom*

נָתְנוּ רֵיחַ Qal pf. 3 c.p. (נָתַן 678)-n.m.s. (926) *they give forth fragrance*

קוּמִי לָכִי Qal impv. 2 f.s. (קוּם 877)-prep.-2 f.s. sf. (GK 119s) *arise*

רַעְיָתִי n.f.s.-1 c.s. sf. (946) *my love*

יָפָתִי adj. f.s.-1 c.s. sf. (421) *my fair one*

וּלְכִי־לָךְ conj.-Qal impv. 2 f.s. (הָלַךְ 229) -prep.-2 f.s. sf. *and come away*

2:14

יוֹנָתִי n.f.s.-1 c.s. sf. (I 401) *O my dove*

בְּחַגְוֵי הַסֶּלַע prep.-n.m.p. cstr. (291)-def.art. -n.m.s. (700) *in the clefts of the rock*
בְּסֵתֶר הַמַּדְרֵגָה prep.-n.m.s. cstr. (712)-def.art. -n.f.s. (201) *in the covert of the cliff*
הַרְאִינִי Hi. impv. 2 f.s.-1 c.s. sf. (רָאָה 906) *let me see*
אֶת־מַרְאַיִךְ dir.obj.-n.m.p.-2 f.s. sf. (909; GK 93ss) *your face*
הַשְׁמִיעִינִי Hi. impv. 2 f.s.-1 c.s. sf. (שָׁמַע 1033) *let me hear*
אֶת־קוֹלֵךְ dir.obj.-n.m.s.-2 f.s. sf. (876) *your voice*
כִּי־קוֹלֵךְ conj. (471)-v.supra *for your voice*
עָרֵב adj. m.s. (787) *is sweet*
וּמַרְאֵיךְ conj.-n.m.p.-2 f.s. sf. (909; GK 93ss) *and your face*
נָאוֶה adj. m.s. (610) *is comely*

2:15

אֶחֱזוּ־לָנוּ Qal impv. 2 m.p. (אָחַז 28)-prep.-1 c.p. sf. *catch us*
שׁוּעָלִים n.m.p. (1043) *the foxes*
שׁוּעָלִים קְטַנִּים v.supra-adj. m.p. (I 881) *the little foxes*
מְחַבְּלִים Pi. ptc. m.p. (חָבַל II 287) *that spoil*
כְּרָמִים n.m.p. (501) *the vineyards*
וּכְרָמֵינוּ conj.-n.m.p.-1 c.p. sf. (501) *for our vineyards*
סְמָדַר n.m.s. (701) *are in blossom*

2:16

דּוֹדִי לִי n.m.s.-1 c.s. sf. (187)-prep.-1 c.s. sf. *my beloved is mine*
וַאֲנִי לוֹ conj.-pers.pr. 1 c.s. (58)-prep.-3 m.s. sf. *and I am his*
הָרֹעֶה def.art.-Qal act.ptc. (רָעָה I 944) *he pastures his flock*
בַּשּׁוֹשַׁנִּים prep.-def.art.-n.m.p. (1004) *among the lilies*

2:17

עַד שֶׁיָּפוּחַ prep. (III 723)-rel. (979)-Qal impf. 3 m.s. (פּוּחַ 806) *until ... breathes*
הַיּוֹם def.art.-n.m.s. (398) *the day*
וְנָסוּ conj.-Qal pf. 3 c.p. (נוּס 630) *and ... flee*
הַצְּלָלִים def.art.-n.m.p. (853) *the shadows*
סֹב Qal impv. 2 m.s. (סָבַב 685) *turn*
דְּמֵה־לְךָ Qal impv. 2 m.s. (דָּמָה I 197)-prep.-2 m.s. sf. (GK 119s) *be like*
דוֹדִי n.m.s.-1 c.s. sf. (187) *my beloved*
לִצְבִי prep.-n.m.s. (II 840) *like a gazelle*
אוֹ לְעֹפֶר הָאַיָּלִים conj. (14)-prep.-n.m.s. cstr. (780)-def.art.-n.m.p. (19) *or a young stag*
עַל־הָרֵי בָתֶר prep.-n.m.p. cstr. (249)-n.m.s. paus. (144) *upon rugged mountains (mountains of cutting)*

3:1

עַל־מִשְׁכָּבִי prep. (II 752)-n.m.s.-1 c.s. sf. (1012) *upon my bed*
בַּלֵּילוֹת prep.-def.art.-n.m.p. (538) *by night*
בִּקַּשְׁתִּי Pi. pf. 1 c.s. (בָּקַשׁ 134) *I sought*
אֵת שֶׁאָהֲבָה dir.obj.-rel. (979)-Qal pf. 3 f.s. (אָהַב 12) *him whom ... loves*
נַפְשִׁי n.f.s.-1 c.s. sf. (659) *my soul*
בִּקַּשְׁתִּיו Pi. pf. 1 c.s.-3 m.s. sf. (בָּקַשׁ 134) *I sought him*
וְלֹא מְצָאתִיו conj.-neg.-Qal pf. 1 c.s.-3 m.s. sf. (592 מָצָא) *but found him not*
LXX+ ἐκάλεσα αὐτόν, καὶ οὐχ ὑπήκουσέν μου

3:2

אָקוּמָה נָּא Qal impf. 1 c.s.-vol.he (קוּם 877) -part.of entreaty (609) *I will rise now*
וַאֲסוֹבְבָה conj.-Po'el impf. 1 c.s.-vol.he (סָבַב 685) *and go about*
בָעִיר prep.-def.art.-n.f.s. (746) *the city*
בַּשְּׁוָקִים prep.-def.art.-n.m.p. (1003) *in the streets*
וּבָרְחֹבוֹת conj.-prep.-def.art.-n.f.p. (I 932) *and in the squares*
אֲבַקְשָׁה Pi. impf. 1 c.s.-vol.he (בָּקַשׁ 134) *I will seek*
שֶׁאָהֲבָה rel. (979)-Qal pf. 3 f.s. (אָהַב 12) *him whom ... loves*
נַפְשִׁי n.f.s.-1 c.s. sf. (659) *my soul*
בִּקַּשְׁתִּיו Pi. pf. 1 c.s.-3 m.s. sf. (בָּקַשׁ 134) *I sought him*
וְלֹא מְצָאתִיו conj.-neg.-Qal pf. 1 c.s.-3 m.s. sf. (592 מָצָא) *but found him not*

3:3

מְצָאוּנִי Qal pf. 3 c.p.-1 c.s. sf. (מָצָא 592) ... *found me*
הַשֹּׁמְרִים def.art.-Qal act.ptc. m.p. (שָׁמַר 1036) *the watchmen*
הַסֹּבְבִים def.art.-Qal act.ptc. m.p. (סָבַב 685) *as they went about*
בָּעִיר prep.-def.art.-n.f.s. (746) *in the city*
אֵת שֶׁאָהֲבָה dir.obj.-rel. (979)-Qal pf. 3 f.s. (אָהַב 12) *him whom ... loves*
נַפְשִׁי n.f.s.-1 c.s. sf. (659) *my soul*
רְאִיתֶם Qal pf. 2 m.p. (רָאָה 906) *have you seen*

3:4

כִּמְעַט prep.-subst. (589) *scarcely*

שֶׁעָבַרְתִּי מֵהֶם rel. (979)-Qal pf. 1 c.s. (עָבַר 716) -prep.-3 m.p. sf. *had I passed them*
עַד שֶׁמָּצָאתִי prep. (III 723)-rel. (979)-Qal pf. 1 c.s. (מָצָא 592) *when I found*
אֵת שֶׁאָהֲבָה dir.obj.-v.supra-Qal pf. 3 f.s. (אָהַב 12) *him whom ... loves*
נַפְשִׁי n.f.s.-1 c.s. sf. (659) *my soul*
אֲחַזְתִּיו Qal pf. 1 c.s.-3 m.s. sf. (אָחַז 28) *I held him*
וְלֹא אַרְפֶּנּוּ conj.-neg.-Hi. impf. 1 c.s.-3 m.s. sf. (951 רָפָה) *and would not let him go*
עַד־שֶׁהֲבֵיאתִיו prep. (III 723)-rel. (979)-Hi. pf. 1 c.s.-3 m.s. sf. (בּוֹא 97) *until I had brought him*
אֶל־בֵּית אִמִּי prep.-n.m.s. cstr. (108)-n.f.s.-1 c.s. sf. (51) *into my mother's house*
וְאֶל־חֶדֶר conj.-prep.-n.m.s. cstr. (293) *and into the chamber of*
הוֹרָתִי Qal act.ptc. f.s.-1 c.s. sf. (הָרָה 247) *her that conceived me*

3:5

הִשְׁבַּעְתִּי אֶתְכֶם Hi. pf. 1 c.s. (שָׁבַע 989)-dir. obj.-2 m.p. sf. *I adjure you*
בְּנוֹת יְרוּשָׁלַםִ n.f.p. cstr. (I 123)-pr.n. (436) *O daughters of Jerusalem*
בִּצְבָאוֹת prep.-n.m.p. (840) *by the gazelles*
אוֹ בְּאַיְלוֹת הַשָּׂדֶה conj. (14)-n.f.p. cstr. (19)-def. art.-n.m.s. (961) *or the hinds of the field*
אִם־תָּעִירוּ hypoth.part. (49)-Hi. impf. 2 m.p. (I 734 עוּר) *that you stir not up*
וְאִם־תְּעוֹרְרוּ conj.-v.supra-Polel impf. 2 m.p. (I 734 עוּר) *nor awaken*
אֶת־הָאַהֲבָה dir.obj.-def.art.-n.f.s. (13) *love*
עַד שֶׁתֶּחְפָּץ prep. (III 723)-rel. (979)-Qal impf. 3 f.s. (חָפֵץ 342) *until it please*

3:6

מִי זֹאת interr. (566)-demons.adj. f.s. (260) *what is that*
עֹלָה Qal act.ptc. f.s. (עָלָה 748) *coming up*
מִן־הַמִּדְבָּר prep.-def.art.-n.m.s. (184) *from the wilderness*
כְּתִימְרוֹת prep.-n.f.p. cstr. (1071) *like a column of*
עָשָׁן n.m.s. (798) *smoke*
מְקֻטֶּרֶת מוֹר Pu. ptc. f.s. (קָטַר 882)-n.m.s. (600) *perfumed with myrrh*
וּלְבוֹנָה conj.-n.f.s. (I 526) *and frankincense*
מִכֹּל אַבְקַת רוֹכֵל prep.-n.m.s. cstr. (481)-n.f.s. cstr. (7)-Qal act.ptc. (רָכַל 940) *with all the fragrant powders of the merchant*

3:7

הִנֵּה מִטָּתוֹ interj. (243)-n.f.s.-3 m.s. sf. (641) *behold, his litter*
שֶׁלִּשְׁלֹמֹה rel. (979; GK 131n)-prep.-pr.n. (1024) *of Solomon*
שִׁשִּׁים גִּבֹּרִים num. p. (995)-n.m.p. (150) *sixty mighty men*
סָבִיב לָהּ prep. (686)-prep.-3 f.s. sf. *about it*
מִגִּבֹּרֵי יִשְׂרָאֵל prep.-n.m.p. cstr. (150)-pr.n. (975) *of the mighty men of Israel*

3:8

כֻּלָּם n.m.s.-3 m.p. sf. (481) *all of them*
אֲחֻזֵי חֶרֶב Qal pass.ptc. m.p. cstr. (אָחַז 28; GK 60f)-n.f.s. (352) *girt with swords*
מְלֻמְּדֵי מִלְחָמָה Pu. ptc. m.p. cstr. (לָמַד 540) -n.f.s. (536) *expert in war*
אִישׁ n.m.s. (35) *each*
חַרְבּוֹ n.f.s.-3 m.s. sf. (352) *with his sword*
עַל־יְרֵכוֹ prep.-n.f.s.-3 m.s. sf. (437) *at his thigh*
מִפַּחַד prep.-n.m.s. (808) *against alarms*
בַּלֵּילוֹת prep.-def.art.-n.m.p. (538) *by night*

3:9

אַפִּרְיוֹן n.m.s. (68) *a palanquin*
עָשָׂה לוֹ Qal pf. 3 m.s. (I 793)-prep.-3 m.s. sf. *made himself*
הַמֶּלֶךְ def.art.-n.m.s. (I 572) *King*
שְׁלֹמֹה pr.n. (1024) *Solomon*
מֵעֲצֵי prep.-n.m.p. cstr. (781) *from the wood of*
הַלְּבָנוֹן def.art.-pr.n. (526) *Lebanon*

3:10

עַמּוּדָיו n.m.p.-3 m.s. sf. (765) *its posts*
עָשָׂה Qal pf. 3 m.s. (I 793) *he made*
כֶסֶף n.m.s. (494) *of silver*
רְפִידָתוֹ n.f.s.-3 m.s. sf. (951) *its back*
זָהָב n.m.s. (262) *of gold*
מֶרְכָּבוֹ n.m.s.-3 m.s. sf. (939) *its seat*
אַרְגָּמָן n.m.s. (71) *of purple*
תּוֹכוֹ n.m.s.-3 m.s. sf. (1063) *within (its midst)*
רָצוּף Qal pass.ptc. (רָצַף I 954) *it was wrought*
אַהֲבָה n.f.s. (13) *lovingly*
מִבְּנוֹת יְרוּשָׁלָםִ prep.-n.f.p. cstr. (I 123)-pr.n. paus. (436) *by the daughters of Jerusalem*

3:11

צְאֶינָה Qal impv. 2 f.p. (יָצָא 422) *go forth*
וּרְאֶינָה conj.-Qal impv. 2 f.p. (רָאָה 906; GK 75n) *and behold*
בְּנוֹת צִיּוֹן n.f.p. cstr. (I 123)-pr.n. (851) *O daughters of Zion*

בַּמֶּלֶךְ שְׁלֹמֹה prep.-def.art.-n.m.s. (I 572)-pr.n. (1024) *King Solomon*

בָּעֲטָרָה prep.-def.art.-n.f.s. (I 742) *with the crown*

שֶׁעִטְּרָה־לּוֹ rel. (979)-Pi. pf. 3 f.s. (עָטַר 742) -prep.-3 m.s. sf. *with which ... crowned him*

אִמּוֹ n.f.s.-3 m.s. sf. (51) *his mother*

בְּיוֹם חֲתֻנָּתוֹ prep.-n.m.s. cstr. (398)-n.f.s.-3 m.s. sf. (368) *on the day of his wedding*

וּבְיוֹם conj.-prep.-n.m.s. cstr. (398) *on the day of*

שִׂמְחַת לִבּוֹ n.f.s. cstr. (970)-n.m.s.-3 m.s. sf. (524) *the gladness of his heart*

4:1

הִנָּךְ interj.-2 f.s. sf. (243) *behold, you*

יָפָה adj. f.s. (421) *are beautiful*

רַעְיָתִי n.f.s.-1 c.s. sf. (946) *my love*

הִנָּךְ יָפָה v.supra-v.supra *behold, you are beautiful*

עֵינַיִךְ n.f.p.-2 f.s. sf. (744) *your eyes*

יוֹנִים n.f.p. (401) *are doves*

מִבַּעַד לְצַמָּתֵךְ prep.-prep. (126)-prep.-n.f.s.-2 f.s. sf. (855) *behind your veil*

שַׂעְרֵךְ n.m.s.-2 f.s. sf. (972) *your hair*

כְּעֵדֶר הָעִזִּים prep.-n.m.s. cstr. (727)-def.art. -n.f.p. (777) *like a flock of goats*

שֶׁגָּלְשׁוּ rel. (979)-Qal pf. 3 c.p. (גָּלַשׁ 167) *moving down the slopes*

מֵהַר גִּלְעָד prep.-n.m.s. cstr. (249)-pr.n. (166) *of Gilead*

4:2

שִׁנַּיִךְ n.f. du.-2 f.s. sf. (1042) *your teeth*

כְּעֵדֶר הַקְּצוּבוֹת prep.-n.m.s. cstr. (727)-def.art. -Qal pass.ptc. f.p. (קָצַב 891) *like a flock of shorn ewes*

שֶׁעָלוּ rel. (979)-Qal pf. 3 c.p. (עָלָה 748) *that have come up*

מִן־הָרַחְצָה prep.-def.art.-n.f.s. (934) *from the washing*

שֶׁכֻּלָּם rel. (979)-n.m.s.-3 m.p. sf. (481) *all of which*

מַתְאִימוֹת Hi. ptc. f.p. (תָּאַם 1060) *bear twins*

וְשַׁכֻּלָה conj.-adj. f.s. (1014) *and is bereaved*

אֵין בָּהֶם neg. (II 34)-prep.-3 m.p. sf. *not one among them*

4:3

כְּחוּט הַשָּׁנִי prep.-n.m.s. cstr. (296)-def.art.-n.m.s. (1040) *like a scarlet thread*

שִׂפְתֹתַיִךְ n.f.p.-2 f.s. sf. (973) *your lips*

וּמִדְבָּרֵיךְ conj.-n.m.s.-2 f.s. sf. (I 184) *and your mouth*

נָאוֶה adj. m.s. (610) *is lovely*

כְּפֶלַח הָרִמּוֹן prep.-n.f.s. cstr. (812)-def.art.-n.m.s. (I 941) *like halves of a pomegranate*

רַקָּתֵךְ n.f.s.-2 f.s. sf. (956) *your cheeks*

מִבַּעַד לְצַמָּתֵךְ prep.-prep. (126)-prep.-n.f.s.-2 f.s. sf. (855) *behind your veil*

4:4

כְּמִגְדַּל דָּוִיד prep.-n.m.s. cstr. (153)-pr.n. (187) *like the tower of David*

צַוָּארֵךְ n.m.s.-2 f.s. sf. (848) *your neck*

בָּנוּי Qal pass.ptc. (בָּנָה 124) *built*

לְתַלְפִּיּוֹת prep.-n.f.p. (1069; LXX εἰς θαλπιωθ) *for an arsenal*

אֶלֶף הַמָּגֵן n.m.s. cstr. (48)-def.art.-n.m.s. (171) *a thousand bucklers*

תָּלוּי עָלָיו Qal pass.ptc. (תָּלָה 1067)-prep.-3 m.s. sf. *whereon hang*

כֹּל שִׁלְטֵי הַגִּבּוֹרִים n.m.s. cstr. (481)-n.m.p. cstr. (1020)-def.art.-adj. m.p. (150) *all of them shields of warriors*

4:5

שְׁנֵי שָׁדַיִךְ num. cstr. (1040)-n.m. du.-2 f.s. sf. (994) *your two breasts*

כִּשְׁנֵי עֳפָרִים prep.-v.supra-n.m.p. (780) *like two fawns*

תְּאוֹמֵי צְבִיָּה n.m.p. cstr. (1060)-n.f.s. (I 840) *twins of a gazelle*

הָרוֹעִים def.art.-Qal act.ptc. m.p. (רָעָה I 944) *that feed*

בַּשּׁוֹשַׁנִּים prep.-def.art.-n.m.p. (1004) *among the lilies*

4:6

עַד שֶׁיָּפוּחַ prep. (III 723)-rel. (979)-Qal impf. 3 m.s. (פּוּחַ 806) *until ... breathes*

הַיּוֹם def.art.-n.m.s. (398) *the day*

וְנָסוּ conj.-Qal pf. 3 c.p. (נוּס 630) *and ... flee*

הַצְּלָלִים def.art.-n.m.p. (853) *the shadows*

אֵלֶךְ לִי Qal impf. 1 c.s. (הָלַךְ 229)-prep.-1 c.s. sf. *I will hie me*

אֶל־הַר הַמּוֹר prep.-n.m.s. cstr. (249)-def.art. -n.m.s. (600) *to the mountain of myrrh*

וְאֶל־גִּבְעַת הַלְּבוֹנָה conj.-prep.-n.f.s. cstr. (148) -def.art.-n.f.s. (I 526) *and the hill of frankincense*

4:7

כֻּלָּךְ n.m.s.-2 f.s. sf. (481) *you are all*

יָפָה adj. f.s. (421) *fair*
רַעְיָתִי n.f.s.-1 c.s. sf. (946) *my love*
וּמוּם conj.-n.m.s. (548) *and a flaw*
אֵין בָּךְ neg. (II 34)-prep.-2 f.s. sf. *there is not in you*

4:8

אִתִּי מִלְּבָנוֹן prep.-1 c.s. sf. (II 85; LXX Δεῦρο) -prep.-pr.n. (526) *with me from Lebanon*
כַּלָּה n.f.s. (483) *a bride*
אִתִּי מִלְּבָנוֹן v.supra-v.supra *with me from Lebanon*
תָּבוֹאִי Qal impf. 2 f.s. (בּוֹא 97) *come*
תָּשׁוּרִי Qal impf. 2 f.s. (שׁוּר II 1003) *depart (behold)*
מֵרֹאשׁ אֲמָנָה prep.-n.m.s. cstr. (910)-pr.n. (53) *from the peak of Amana*
מֵרֹאשׁ שְׂנִיר v.supra-pr.n. (972) *from the peak of Senir*
וְחֶרְמוֹן conj.-pr.n. (356) *and Hermon*
מִמְּעֹנוֹת אֲרָיוֹת prep.-n.f.p. cstr. (733)-n.m.p. (71) *from the dens of lions*
מֵהַרְרֵי נְמֵרִים prep.-n.m.p. cstr. (249)-n.m.p. (649) *from the mountains of leopards*

4:9

לִבַּבְתִּנִי Pi. pf. 2 f.s.-1 c.s. sf. (לבב 525; GK 59h) *you have ravished me (you have encouraged me)*
אֲחֹתִי n.f.s.-1 c.s. sf. (27) *my sister*
כַלָּה n.f.s. (483) *a bride*
לִבַּבְתִּינִי Pi. pf. 2 f.s.-1 c.s. sf. (לבב 525) *you have ravished my heart (you have encouraged me)*
בְּאַחַד מֵעֵינַיִךְ prep.-num. cstr. (25)-prep. -n.f.p.-2 f.s. sf. (744) *with a glance (one) of your eyes*
בְּאַחַד עֲנָק v.supra-n.m.s. (II 778) *with one neck-pendant*
מִצַּוְּרֹנָיִךְ prep.-n.m.p.-2 f.s. sf. (848) *of your necklace*

4:10

מַה־יָּפוּ interr. (552)-Qal pf. 3 c.p. (יָפָה 421) *how sweet is*
דֹדַיִךְ n.m.p.-2 f.s. sf. (187) *your love*
אֲחֹתִי n.f.s.-1 c.s. sf. (27) *my sister*
כַלָּה n.f.s. (483) *a bride*
מַה־טֹּבוּ v.supra-Qal pf. 3 c.p. (טוֹב I 373) *how much better is*
דֹדַיִךְ v.supra *your love*
מִיַּיִן prep.-n.m.s. (406) *than wine*
וְרֵיחַ שְׁמָנַיִךְ conj.-n.m.s. cstr. (926)-n.m.p.-2 f.s. sf. (1032) *and the fragrance of your oils*
מִכָּל־בְּשָׂמִים prep.-n.m.s. cstr. (481)-n.m.p. (141) *than any spice*

4:11

נֹפֶת תִּטֹּפְנָה n.m.s. (661)-Qal impf. 3 f.p. (נָטַף 642) ... *distil nectar*
שִׂפְתוֹתַיִךְ n.f.p.-2 f.s. sf. (973) *your lips*
כַּלָּה n.f.s. (483) *a bride*
דְּבַשׁ וְחָלָב n.m.s. (185)-conj.-n.m.s. (316) *honey and milk*
תַּחַת לְשׁוֹנֵךְ prep. (1065)-n.f.s.-2 f.s. sf. (546) *under your tongue*
וְרֵיחַ שַׂלְמֹתַיִךְ conj.-n.m.s. cstr. (926)-n.f.p.-2 f.s. sf. (971) *the scent of your garments*
כְּרֵיחַ לְבָנוֹן prep.-v.supra-pr.n. (526) *like the scent of Lebanon*

4:12

גַּן נָעוּל n.m.s. (171)-Qal pass.ptc. (נָעַל 653) *a garden locked*
אֲחֹתִי n.f.s.-1 c.s. sf. (27) *my sister*
כַלָּה n.f.s. (483) *a bride*
גַּל נָעוּל n.m.s. (164; LXX κῆπος)-v.supra *a garden (spring) locked*
מַעְיָן חָתוּם n.m.s. (745)-Qal pass.ptc. (חָתַם 367) *a fountain sealed*

4:13

שְׁלָחַיִךְ n.m.p.-2 f.s. sf. (1019) *your shoots*
פַּרְדֵּס רִמּוֹנִים n.m.s. cstr. (825)-n.m.p. (I 941) *an orchard of pomegranates*
עִם פְּרִי מְגָדִים prep. (767)-n.m.s. cstr. (826) -n.m.p. (550) *with all choicest fruits*
כְּפָרִים n.m.p. (III 499) *henna*
עִם־נְרָדִים prep. (767)-n.m.p. (669) *with nard*

4:14

נֵרְדְּ n.m.s. (669) *nard*
וְכַרְכֹּם conj.-n.m.s. (501) *and saffron*
קָנֶה n.m.s. (889) *calamus*
וְקִנָּמוֹן conj.-n.m.s. (890) *and cinnamon*
עִם כָּל־עֲצֵי prep. (767)-n.m.s. cstr. (481)-n.m.p. cstr. (781) *with all trees of*
לְבוֹנָה n.f.s. (I 526) *frankincense*
מֹר וַאֲהָלוֹת n.m.s. (600)-conj.-n.m.p. (III 14) *myrrh and aloes*
עִם כָּל־רָאשֵׁי prep. (767)-n.m.s. cstr. (481)-n.m.p. cstr. (910) *with all chief*
בְשָׂמִים n.m.p. (141) *spices*

4:15

מַעְיַן גַּנִּים n.m.s. cstr. (746)-n.m.p. (171) *a garden fountain*

בְּאֵר מַיִם חַיִּים n.f.s. cstr. (91)-n.m.p. (565)-adj. m.p. (I 311) *a well of living water*

וְנֹזְלִים conj.-Qal act.ptc. m.p. (נָזַל 633) *and flowing streams*

מִן־לְבָנוֹן prep.-pr.n. (526) *from Lebanon*

4:16

עוּרִי צָפוֹן Qal impv. 2 f.s. (עוּר 734)-n.f.s. (860) *awake, O north wind*

וּבוֹאִי תֵימָן conj.-Qal impv. 2 f.s. (בּוֹא 97)-n.f.s. (I 412) *and come, O south wind*

הָפִיחִי גַנִּי Hi. impv. 2 f.s. (פּוּחַ 806)-n.m.s.-1 c.s. sf. (171) *blow upon my garden*

יִזְּלוּ בְשָׂמָיו Qal impf. 3 m.p. (נָזַל 633)-n.m.p.-3 m.s. sf. (141) *let its fragrance be wafted abroad*

יָבֹא דוֹדִי Qal impf. 3 m.s. (בּוֹא 97)-n.m.s.-1 c.s. sf. (187) *let my beloved come*

לְגַנּוֹ prep.-n.m.s.-3 m.s. sf. (171) *to his garden*

וְיֹאכַל conj.-Qal impf. 3 m.s. (אָכַל 37) *and let eat*

פְּרִי מְגָדָיו n.m.s. cstr. (826)-n.m.p.-3 m.s. sf. (550) *its choicest fruits*

5:1

בָּאתִי Qal pf. 1 c.s. (בּוֹא 97) *I come*

לְגַנִּי prep.-n.m.s.-1 c.s. sf. (171) *to my garden*

אֲחֹתִי n.f.s.-1 c.s. sf. (27) *my sister*

כַלָּה n.f.s. (483) *a bride*

אָרִיתִי Qal pf. 1 c.s. (אָרָה I 71) *I gather*

מוֹרִי n.m.s.-1 c.s. sf. (600) *my myrrh*

עִם־בְּשָׂמִי prep. (767)-n.m.s.-1 c.s. sf. (141) *with my spice*

אָכַלְתִּי Qal pf. 1 c.s. (אָכַל 37) *I eat*

יַעְרִי n.m.s.-1 c.s. sf. (II 421) *my honeycomb*

עִם־דִּבְשִׁי prep. (767)-n.m.s.-1 c.s. sf. (185) *with my honey*

שָׁתִיתִי Qal pf. 1 c.s. (שָׁתָה 1059) *I drink*

יֵינִי n.m.s.-1 c.s. sf. (406) *my wine*

עִם־חֲלָבִי v.supra-n.m.s.-1 c.s. sf. (316) *with my milk*

אִכְלוּ רֵעִים Qal impv. 2 m.p. (אָכַל 37)-n.m.p. (945) *eat, O friends*

שְׁתוּ Qal impv. 2 m.p. (שָׁתָה 1059) *and drink*

וְשִׁכְרוּ conj.-Qal impv. 2 m.p. (שָׁכַר I 1016) *and drink deeply*

דּוֹדִים n.m.p. (187) *O lovers*

5:2

אֲנִי יְשֵׁנָה pers.pr. 1 c.s. (58)-adj. f.s. (I 445) *I slept*

וְלִבִּי עֵר conj.-n.m.s.-1 c.s. sf. (524)-Qal act.ptc. (I 734 עוּר) *but my heart was awake*

קוֹל n.m.s. (876) *hark*

דּוֹדִי דוֹפֵק n.m.s.-1 c.s. sf. (187)-Qal act.ptc. (דָּפַק 200) *my beloved is knocking*

פִּתְחִי־לִי Qal impv. 2 f.s. (פָּתַח 834)-prep.-1 c.s. sf. *open to me*

אֲחֹתִי n.f.s.-1 c.s. sf. (27) *my sister*

רַעְיָתִי n.f.s.-1 c.s. sf. (946) *my love*

יוֹנָתִי n.f.s.-1 c.s. sf. (I 401) *my dove*

תַמָּתִי adj. f.s.-1 c.s. sf. (1070) *my perfect one*

שֶׁרֹּאשִׁי rel. (979)-n.m.s.-1 c.s. sf. (910) *for my head*

נִמְלָא־טָל Ni. pf. 3 m.s. (מָלֵא 569)-n.m.s. paus. (378) *is wet (filled) with dew*

קְוֻצּוֹתַי n.f.p.-1 c.s. sf. (881) *my locks*

רְסִיסֵי לָיְלָה n.m.p. cstr. (944)-n.m.s. (538) *with the drops of the night*

5:3

פָּשַׁטְתִּי Qal pf. 1 c.s. (פָּשַׁט 832) *I had put off*

אֶת־כֻּתָּנְתִּי dir.obj.-n.f.s.-1 c.s. sf. (509) *my garment*

אֵיכָכָה adv. (32) *how*

אֶלְבָּשֶׁנָּה Qal impf. 1 c.s.-3 f.s. sf. (לָבַשׁ 527) *could I put it on*

רָחַצְתִּי Qal pf. 1 c.s. (רָחַץ 934) *I had bathed*

אֶת־רַגְלַי dir.obj.-n.f.p.-1 c.s. sf. (919) *my feet*

אֵיכָכָה v.supra *how*

אֲטַנְּפֵם Pi. impf. 1 c.s.-3 m.p. sf. (טָנַף 380) *could I soil them*

5:4

דּוֹדִי n.m.s.-1 c.s. sf. (187) *my beloved*

שָׁלַח יָדוֹ Qal pf. 3 m.s. (1018)-n.f.s.-3 m.s. sf. (388) *put his hand*

מִן־הַחֹר prep.-def.art.-n.m.s. (III 359) *to the latch*

וּמֵעַי conj.-n.m.p.-1 c.s. sf. (588) *and my heart*

הָמוּ עָלָיו Qal pf. 3 c.p. (הָמָה 242)-prep.-3 m.s. sf. (many rd. 1 c.s. sf.) *was thrilled within me*

5:5

קַמְתִּי אֲנִי Qal pf. 1 c.s. (קוּם 877)-pers.pr. 1 c.s. (58; GK 135b) *I arose*

לִפְתֹּחַ prep.-Qal inf.cstr. (פָּתַח I 834) *to open*

לְדוֹדִי prep.-n.m.s.-1 c.s. sf. (187) *to my beloved*

וְיָדַי conj.-n.f.p.-1 c.s. sf. (388) *and my hands*

נָטְפוּ־מוֹר Qal pf. 3 c.p. (נָטַף 642)-n.m.s. (600) *dripped with myrrh*

וְאֶצְבְּעֹתַי conj.-n.f.p.-1 c.s. sf. (840) *and my fingers*
מוֹר עֹבֵר v.supra-Qal act.ptc. (עָבַר 716) *with liquid myrrh*
עַל כַּפּוֹת הַמַּנְעוּל prep.-n.f.p. cstr. (496)-def.art. -n.m.s. (653) *upon the handles of the bolt*

5:6

פָּתַחְתִּי אֲנִי Qal pf. 1 c.s. (פָּתַח I 834)-pers.pr. 1 c.s. (58) *I opened*
לְדוֹדִי prep.-n.m.s.-1 c.s. sf. (187) *to my beloved*
וְדוֹדִי conj.-v.supra *but my beloved*
חָמַק Qal pf. 3 m.s. (330) *had turned*
עָבָר Qal pf. 3 m.s. paus. (716) *passed on*
נַפְשִׁי יָצְאָה n.f.s.-1 c.s. sf. (659)-Qal pf. 3 f.s. (422 יָצָא) *my soul failed me*
בְדַבְּרוֹ prep.-Pi. inf.cstr.-3 m.s. sf. (דָּבַר 180) *when he spoke*
בִּקַּשְׁתִּיהוּ Pi. pf. 1 c.s.-3 m.s. sf. (בָּקַשׁ 134) *I sought him*
וְלֹא מְצָאתִיהוּ conj.-neg.-Qal pf. 1 c.s.-3 m.s. sf. (מָצָא 592) *but found him not*
קְרָאתִיו Qal pf. 1 c.s.-3 m.s. sf. (קָרָא 894) *I called him*
וְלֹא עָנָנִי conj.-neg.-Qal pf. 3 m.s.-1 c.s. sf. (עָנָה I 772) *but he gave no answer*

5:7

מְצָאֻנִי Qal pf. 3 c.p.-1 c.s. sf. (מָצָא 592) *found me*
הַשֹּׁמְרִים def.art.-Qal act.ptc. m.p. (שָׁמַר 1036) *the watchmen*
הַסֹּבְבִים def.art.-Qal act.ptc. m.p. (סָבַב 685) *as they went about*
בָּעִיר prep.-def.art.-n.f.s. (746) *in the city*
הִכּוּנִי Hi. pf. 3 c.p.-1 c.s. sf. (נָכָה 645) *they beat me*
פְצָעוּנִי Qal pf. 3 c.p.-1 c.s. sf. (פָּצַע 822) *they wounded me*
נָשְׂאוּ Qal pf. 3 c.p. (נָשָׂא 669) *they took away*
אֶת־רְדִידִי dir.obj.-n.m.s.-1 c.s. sf. (921) *my mantle*
מֵעָלַי prep.-prep.-1 c.s. sf. *(from upon me)*
שֹׁמְרֵי הַחֹמוֹת Qal act.ptc. m.p. cstr. (שָׁמַר 1036)-def.art.-n.f.p. (327) *those watchmen of the walls*

5:8

הִשְׁבַּעְתִּי אֶתְכֶם Hi. pf. 1 c.s. (שָׁבַע 989)-dir. obj.-2 m.p. sf. *I adjure you*
בְּנוֹת יְרוּשָׁלָםִ n.f.p. cstr. (I 123)-pr.n. (436) *O daughters of Jerusalem*
אִם־תִּמְצְאוּ hypoth.part. (49)-Qal impf. 2 m.p. (592 מָצָא) *if you find*
אֶת־דּוֹדִי dir.obj.-n.m.s.-1 c.s. sf. (187) *my beloved*
מַה־תַּגִּידוּ לוֹ interr. (552; GK 137bN)-Hi. impf. 2 m.p. (נָגַד 616)-prep.-3 m.s. sf. *that you tell him*
שֶׁחוֹלַת אַהֲבָה rel. (979)-Qal act.ptc. f.s. cstr. (I 317 חָלָה)-n.f.s. (13) *sick with love*
אָנִי pers.pr. 1 c.s. paus. (58) *I am*

5:9

מַה־דּוֹדֵךְ interr. (552)-n.m.s.-2 f.s. sf. (187) *what is your beloved*
מִדּוֹד prep.-n.m.s. (187) *than another beloved*
הַיָּפָה def.art.-adj. f.s. (421) *O fairest*
בַּנָּשִׁים prep.-def.art.-n.f.p. (61) *among women*
מַה־דּוֹדֵךְ v.supra-v.supra *what is your beloved*
מִדּוֹד v.supra *more than another beloved*
שֶׁכָּכָה rel. (979)-adv. (462) *that thus*
הִשְׁבַּעְתָּנוּ Hi. pf. 2 m.s.-1 c.p. sf. (שָׁבַע 989; GK 59h) *you adjure us*

5:10

דּוֹדִי n.m.s.-1 c.s. sf. (187) *my beloved*
צַח וְאָדוֹם adj. m.s. (850)-adj. m.s. (10) *radiant and ruddy*
דָּגוּל Qal pass.ptc. (דָּגַל 186) *distinguished*
מֵרְבָבָה prep.-n.f.s. (914) *among ten thousand*

5:11

רֹאשׁוֹ n.m.s.-3 m.s. sf. (910) *his head*
כֶּתֶם פָּז n.m.s. cstr. (508)-n.m.s. paus. (808) *the finest gold*
קְוֻצּוֹתָיו n.f.p.-3 m.s. sf. (881) *his locks*
תַּלְתַּלִּים n.f.p. (1068) *wavy*
שְׁחֹרוֹת adj. f.p. (1007) *black*
כָּעוֹרֵב prep.-def.art.-n.m.s. (788) *as a raven*

5:12

עֵינָיו n.f.p.-3 m.s. sf. (744) *his eyes*
כְּיוֹנִים prep.-n.f.p. (I 401) *like doves*
עַל־אֲפִיקֵי מָיִם prep.-n.m.p. cstr. (67)-n.m.p. paus. (565) *beside springs of water*
רֹחֲצוֹת Qal act.ptc. f.p. (רָחַץ 934) *bathed*
בֶּחָלָב prep.-def.art.-n.m.s. (316) *in milk*
יֹשְׁבוֹת עַל־מִלֵּאת Qal act.ptc. f.p. (יָשַׁב 442)-prep.-n.f.s. (571) *fitly set*

5:13

לְחָיָו n.m.p.-3 m.s. sf. (534) *his cheeks*
כַּעֲרוּגַת הַבֹּשֶׂם prep.-n.f.s. cstr. (788)-def.art. -n.m.s. (141) *like beds of spices*

מִגְדְּלוֹת מֶרְקָחִים n.f.p. cstr. (153; LXX φύουσαι) -n.m.p. (955) *yielding (towers of) fragrance*
שִׂפְתוֹתָיו n.f.p.-3 m.s. sf. (973) *his lips*
שׁוֹשַׁנִּים n.m.p. (1004) *are lilies*
נֹטְפוֹת Qal act.ptc. f.p. (נָטַף 642) *distilling*
מוֹר עֹבֵר n.m.s. (600)-Qal act.ptc. (716) *liquid myrrh*

5:14

יָדָיו n.f.p.-3 m.s. sf. (388) *his arms*
גְּלִילֵי זָהָב n.m.p. cstr. (II 165)-n.m.s. (262) *rounded gold*
מְמֻלָּאִים Pu. ptc. m.p. (מָלֵא 569) *set*
בַּתַּרְשִׁישׁ prep.-def.art.-n.m.s. (I 1076) *with jewels*
מֵעָיו n.m.p.-3 m.s. sf. (588) *his body*
עֶשֶׁת שֵׁן n.m.s. cstr. (799)-n.f.s. (1042) *ivory work (plate of ivory)*
מְעֻלֶּפֶת סַפִּירִים Pu. ptc. f.s. cstr. (עָלַף 763) -n.m.p. (705) *encrusted with sapphires*

5:15

שׁוֹקָיו n.f.p.-3 m.s. sf. (1003) *his legs*
עַמּוּדֵי שֵׁשׁ n.m.p. cstr. (765)-n.m.s. (II 1010) *are alabaster columns*
מְיֻסָּדִים Pu. ptc. m.p. (יָסַד 413) *set*
עַל־אַדְנֵי־פָז prep.-n.m.p. cstr. (10)-n.m.s. paus. (808) *upon bases of gold*
מַרְאֵהוּ n.m.s.-3 m.s. sf. (909) *his appearance*
כַּלְּבָנוֹן prep.-def.art.-pr.n. (526) *like Lebanon*
בָּחוּר Qal pass.ptc. (בָּחַר 103) *choice*
כָּאֲרָזִים prep.-def.art.-n.m.p. (72) *as the cedars*

5:16

חִכּוֹ n.m.s.-3 m.s. sf. (335) *his speech*
מַמְתַקִּים n.m.p. (609; GK 85gN) *most sweet*
וְכֻלּוֹ conj.-n.m.s.-3 m.s. sf. (481) *and he is altogether*
מַחֲמַדִּים n.m.p. (326; GK 141c) *desirable*
זֶה דוֹדִי demons.adj. m.s. (260)-n.m.s.-1 c.s. sf. (187) *this is my beloved*
וְזֶה רֵעִי conj.-v.supra-n.m.s.-1 c.s. sf. (945) *and this is my friend*
בְּנוֹת יְרוּשָׁלָםִ n.f.p. cstr. (I 123)-pr.n. (436) *O daughters of Jerusalem*

6:1

אָנָה adv. (33) *whither*
הָלַךְ Qal pf. 3 m.s. (229) *has gone*
דּוֹדֵךְ n.m.s.-2 f.s. sf. (187) *your beloved*
הַיָּפָה def.art.-adj. f.s. (421) *O fairest*
בַּנָּשִׁים prep.-def.art.-n.f.p. (61) *among women*
אָנָה v.supra *whither*
פָּנָה Qal pf. 3 m.s. (815) *has turned*
דוֹדֵךְ v.supra *your beloved*
וּנְבַקְשֶׁנּוּ conj.-Pi. impf. 1 c.p.-3 m.s. sf. (בָּקַשׁ 134) *that we may seek him*
עִמָּךְ prep.-2 f.s. sf. (767) *with you*

6:2

דּוֹדִי יָרַד n.m.s.-1 c.s. sf. (187)-Qal pf. 3 m.s. (432) *my beloved has gone down*
לְגַנּוֹ prep.-n.m.s.-3 m.s. sf. (171) *to his garden*
לַעֲרוּגוֹת הַבֹּשֶׂם prep.-n.f.p. cstr. (788)-def. art.-n.m.s. (141) *to the beds of spices*
לִרְעוֹת prep.-Qal inf.cstr. (רָעָה I 944) *to pasture*
בַּגַּנִּים prep.-def.art.-n.m.p. (171) *in the gardens*
וְלִלְקֹט conj.-prep.-Qal inf.cstr. (לָקַט 544) *and to gather*
שׁוֹשַׁנִּים n.m.p. (I 1004) *lilies*

6:3

אֲנִי לְדוֹדִי pers.pr. 1 c.s. (58)-prep.-n.m.s.-1 c.s. sf. (187) *I am my beloved's*
וְדוֹדִי לִי conj.-v.supra-prep. 1 c.s. sf. *and my beloved is mine*
הָרֹעֶה def.art.-Qal act.ptc. (רָעָה I 944) *he pastures (his flock)*
בַּשּׁוֹשַׁנִּים prep.-def.art.-n.m.p. (I 1004) *among the lilies*

6:4

יָפָה אַתְּ adj. f.s. (421)-pers.pr. 2 f.s. (61) *you are beautiful*
רַעְיָתִי n.f.s.-1 c.s. sf. (946) *my love*
כְּתִרְצָה prep.-pr.n. (953) *as Tirzah*
נָאוָה adj. f.s. (610) *comely*
כִּירוּשָׁלָםִ prep.-pr.n. (436) *as Jerusalem*
אֲיֻמָּה adj. f.s. (33) *terrible*
כַּנִּדְגָּלוֹת prep.-def.art.-Ni. ptc. f.p. (דָּגַל 186) *as an army with banners*

6:5

הָסֵבִּי עֵינַיִךְ Hi. impv. 2 f.s. (סָבַב 685)-n.f.p.-2 f.s. sf. (744) *turn away your eyes*
מִנֶּגְדִּי prep.-prep.-1 c.s. sf. (617) *from me*
שֶׁהֵם הִרְהִיבֻנִי rel. (979)-pers.pr. 3 m.p. (241)-Hi. pf. 3 c.p.-1 c.s. sf. (רָהַב 923) *for they disturb me*
שַׂעְרֵךְ n.m.s.-2 f.s. sf. (972) *your hair*
כְּעֵדֶר הָעִזִּים prep.-n.m.s. cstr. (727)-def.art. -n.f.p. (777) *like a flock of goats*
שֶׁגָּלְשׁוּ rel. (979)-Qal pf. 3 c.p. (גָּלַשׁ 167) *moving down the slopes*

מִן־הַגִּלְעָד prep.-def.art.-pr.n. (166) *of Gilead*

6:6

שִׁנַּיִךְ n.f. du.-2 f.s. sf. (1042) *your teeth*
כְּעֵדֶר הָרְחֵלִים conj.-n.m.s. cstr. (I 727)-def. art.-n.f.p. (932) *like a flock of ewes*
שֶׁעָלוּ rel. (979)-Qal pf. 3 c.p. (עָלָה 748) *that have come up*
מִן־הָרַחְצָה prep.-def.art.-n.f.s. (934) *from the washing*
שֶׁכֻּלָּם rel. (979)-n.m.s.-3 m.p. sf. (481) *all of them*
מַתְאִימוֹת Hi. ptc. f.p. (תָּאַם 1060) *bear twins*
וְשַׁכֻּלָה conj.-adj. f.s. (1014) *and is bereaved*
אֵין בָּהֶם neg. (II 34)-prep.-3 m.p. sf. *not one among them*

6:7

כְּפֶלַח הָרִמּוֹן prep.-n.f.s. cstr. (812)-def.art.-n.m.s. (I 941) *like halves of a pomegranate*
רַקָּתֵךְ n.f.s.-2 f.s. sf. (956) *your cheeks*
מִבַּעַד לְצַמָּתֵךְ prep.-prep. (126)-n.f.s.-2 f.s. sf. (855) *behind your veil*

6:8

שִׁשִּׁים הֵמָּה num. p. (995)-pers.pr. 3 m.p. (241; GK 32n) *there are sixty*
מְלָכוֹת n.f.p. (573) *queens*
וּשְׁמֹנִים conj.-num. p. (1033) *and eighty*
פִּילַגְשִׁים n.f.p. (811) *concubines*
וַעֲלָמוֹת conj.-n.f.p. (761) *and maidens*
אֵין מִסְפָּר neg. (II 34)-n.m.s. paus. (708) *without number*

6:9

אַחַת הִיא num. f. (25)-pers.pr. 3 f.s. (214) *is only one*
יוֹנָתִי n.f.s.-1 c.s. sf. (401) *my dove*
תַמָּתִי adj. f.s.-1 c.s. sf. (1070) *my perfect one*
אַחַת הִיא v.supra-v.supra *the darling*
לְאִמָּהּ prep.-n.f.s.-3 f.s. sf. (51) *of her mother*
בָּרָה הִיא adj. f.s. (II 141)-v.supra *flawless*
לְיוֹלַדְתָּהּ prep.-Qal act.ptc. f.s.-3 f.s. sf. (יָלַד 408) *to her that bore her*
רָאוּהָ בָנוֹת Qal pf. 3 c.p.-3 f.s. sf. (רָאָה 906) -n.f.p. (I 123) *the maidens saw her*
וַיְאַשְּׁרוּהָ consec.-Pi. impf. 3 m.p.-3 f.s. sf. (אָשַׁר 80) *and called her happy*
מְלָכוֹת n.f.p. (573) *the queens*
וּפִילַגְשִׁים conj.-n.f.p. (811) *and concubines*
וַיְהַלְלוּהָ consec.-Pi. impf. 3 m.p.-3 f.s. sf. (הָלַל II 237) *and they praised her*

6:10

מִי־זֹאת interr. (566)-demons.adj. f.s. (260) *who is this*
הַנִּשְׁקָפָה def.art.-Ni. ptc. f.s. (שָׁקַף 1054) *that looks forth*
כְּמוֹ־שָׁחַר conj. (455)-n.m.s. paus. (1007) *like the dawn*
יָפָה adj. f.s. (421) *fair*
כַּלְּבָנָה prep.-def.art.-n.f.s. (I 526) *as the moon*
בָּרָה כַּחַמָּה adj. f.s. (II 141)-prep.-def.art.-n.f.s. (328) *bright as the sun*
אֲיֻמָּה adj. f.s. (33) *terrible*
כַּנִּדְגָּלוֹת prep.-def.art.-Ni. ptc. f.p. (דָּגַל 186) *as an army with banners*

6:11

אֶל־גִּנַּת אֱגוֹז prep.-n.f.p. cstr. (171)-n.m.s. (8) *to the nut orchard*
יָרַדְתִּי Qal pf. 1 c.s. (יָרַד 432) *I went down*
לִרְאוֹת prep.-Qal inf.cstr. (רָאָה 906) *to look*
בְּאִבֵּי הַנָּחַל prep.-n.m.p. cstr. (1)-def.art.-n.m.s. paus. (636) *at the blossoms of the valley*
לִרְאוֹת v.supra *to see*
הֲפָרְחָה הַגֶּפֶן interr.part.-Qal pf. 3 f.s. (פָּרַח I 827)-def.art.-n.f.s. (172) *whether the vines had budded*
הֵנֵצוּ הָרִמֹּנִים Hi. pf. 3 c.p. (נָצַץ 665; GK 67dd)-def.art.-n.m.p. (I 941) *the pomegranates were in bloom*

6:12

לֹא יָדַעְתִּי neg.-Qal pf. 1 c.s. (יָדַע 393) *I had not known*
נַפְשִׁי n.f.s.-1 c.s. sf. (659) *my fancy (my soul)*
שָׂמַתְנִי Qal pf. 3 f.s.-1 c.s. sf. (שִׂים 962) *set me*
מַרְכְּבוֹת n.f.p. (939) *in a chariot*
עַמִּי־נָדִיב n.m.s.-1 c.s. sf. (I 766)-adj. m.s. (622; LXX Αμιναδαβ) *beside my prince* (lit. *my people, noble*)

7:1 (Eng.6:13)

שׁוּבִי שׁוּבִי Qal impv. 2 f.s. (שׁוּב 996)-v.supra *return, return*
הַשּׁוּלַמִּית def.art.-adj. gent. f. (1002) *O Shulammite*
שׁוּבִי שׁוּבִי v.supra-v.supra *return, return*
וְנֶחֱזֶה־בָּךְ conj.-Qal impf. 1 c.p. (חָזָה 302) -prep.-2 f.s. sf. *that we may look upon you*
מַה־תֶּחֱזוּ interr. (552; GK 137bN)-Qal impf. 2 m.p. (חָזָה 302) *why should you look*
בַּשּׁוּלַמִּית prep.-def.art.-adj. gent. f. (1002) *upon the Shulammite*

כִּמְחֹלַת prep.-n.f.s. cstr. (298) *as upon a dance (of)*
הַמַּחֲנָיִם def.art.-pr.n. paus. (334; LXX τῶν παρεμβολῶν) *before two armies*

7:2

מַה־יָּפוּ interr. (552)-Qal pf. 3 c.p. (יָפָה 421) *how graceful are*
פְעָמַיִךְ n.f.p.-2 f.s. sf. (821) *your feet*
בַּנְּעָלִים prep.-def.art.-n.f.p. (653) *in sandals*
בַּת־נָדִיב n.f.s. cstr. (I 123)-adj. m.s. (622) *O queenly maiden*
חַמּוּקֵי יְרֵכַיִךְ n.m.p. cstr. (330)-n.f. du.-2 f.s. sf. (437) *your rounded thighs*
כְּמוֹ חֲלָאִים conj. (455)-n.m.p. (I 318; GK 93x) *are like jewels*
מַעֲשֵׂה יְדֵי אָמָּן n.m.s. cstr. (795)-n.f.p. cstr. (388)-n.m.s. (53) *the work of a master hand*

7:3

שָׁרְרֵךְ n.m.s.-2 f.s. sf. (שֹׁר 1057; LXX ὀμφαλός σου) *your navel*
אַגַּן הַסַּהַר n.m.s. cstr. (8)-def.art.-n.m.s. (690) *is a rounded bowl*
אַל־יֶחְסַר neg.-Qal impf. 3 m.s. (חָסֵר 341) *that never lacks*
הַמָּזֶג def.art.-n.m.s. (561) *mixed wine*
בִּטְנֵךְ n.f.s.-2 f.s. sf. (105) *your belly*
עֲרֵמַת חִטִּים n.f.s. cstr. (790)-n.f.p. (334) *a heap of wheat*
סוּגָה Qal pass.ptc. f. (סוג II 691) *encircled*
בַּשּׁוֹשַׁנִּים prep.-def.art.-n.f.p. (1004) *with lilies*

7:4

שְׁנֵי שָׁדַיִךְ num. p. cstr. (1040)-n.m. du.-2 f.s. sf. (994) *your two breasts*
כִּשְׁנֵי עֳפָרִים prep.-v.supra-n.m.p. (780) *are like two fawns*
תָּאֳמֵי צְבִיָּה n.m.p. cstr. (1060)-n.f.s. (I 840) *twins of a gazelle*

7:5

צַוָּארֵךְ n.m.s.-2 f.s. sf. (848) *your neck*
כְּמִגְדַּל הַשֵּׁן prep.-n.m.s. cstr. (153)-def.art.-n.f.s. (I 1042) *like an ivory tower*
עֵינַיִךְ n.f.p.-2 f.s. sf. (744) *your eyes*
בְּרֵכוֹת בְּחֶשְׁבּוֹן n.f.p. (140)-prep.-pr.n. (II 363) *pools in Heshbon*
עַל־שַׁעַר prep.-n.m.s. cstr. (1044) *by the gate of* (LXX ἐν πύλαις)
בַּת־רַבִּים pr.n. (123) *Bath-rabbim*
אַפֵּךְ n.m.s.-2 f.s. sf. (I 60) *your nose*
כְּמִגְדַּל הַלְּבָנוֹן v.supra-def.art.-pr.n. (526) *like a tower of Lebanon*
צוֹפֶה Qal act.ptc. (צָפָה I 859) *overlooking*
פְּנֵי דַמָּשֶׂק n.m.p. cstr. (815)-pr.n. (199) *Damascus*

7:6

רֹאשֵׁךְ n.m.s.-2 f.s. sf. (910) *your head*
עָלַיִךְ prep.-2 f.s. sf. (II 752) *crowns you (upon you)*
כַּכַּרְמֶל prep.-def.art.-pr.n. (II 502) *like Carmel*
וְדַלַּת רֹאשֵׁךְ conj.-n.f.s. cstr. (I 195)-v.supra *and your flowing locks*
כָּאַרְגָּמָן prep.-def.art.-n.m.s. (71) *like purple*
מֶלֶךְ אָסוּר n.m.s. (I 572)-Qal pass.ptc. (אָסַר 63) *a king is held captive*
בָּרְהָטִים prep.-def.art.-n.m.p. (923) *in the tresses*

7:7

מַה־יָּפִית interr. (552)-Qal pf. 2 f.s. (יָפָה 421) *how fair*
וּמַה־נָּעַמְתְּ conj.-v.supra-Qal pf. 2 f.s. (נָעֵם I 653) *and how pleasant*
אַהֲבָה n.f.s. (13) *O loved one*
בַּתַּעֲנוּגִים prep.-def.art.-n.m.p. (772) *delectable maiden (in delights)*

7:8

זֹאת קוֹמָתֵךְ demons.adj. f.s. (260)-n.f.s.-2 f.s. sf. (879) *this your stature*
דָּמְתָה Qal pf. 3 f.s. (דָּמָה I 197) *is like*
לְתָמָר prep.-n.m.s. (I 1071) *to a palm tree*
וְשָׁדַיִךְ conj.-n.m. du.-2 f.s. sf. (994) *and your breasts*
לְאַשְׁכֹּלוֹת prep.-n.m.p. (79) *to its clusters*

7:9

אָמַרְתִּי Qal pf. 1 c.s. (אָמַר 55) *I say*
אֶעֱלֶה בְתָמָר Qal impf. 1 c.s. (עָלָה 748)-prep.-n.m.s. (I 1071) *I will climb the palm tree*
אֹחֲזָה Qal impf. 1 c.s.-vol.he (אָחַז 28) *and I will lay hold*
בְּסַנְסִנָּיו prep.-n.m.p.-3 m.s. sf. (703) *of its branches (fruit-stalk)*
וְיִהְיוּ־נָא conj.-Qal impf. 3 m.p. (הָיָה 224)-part.of entreaty (609) *Oh, may ... be*
שָׁדַיִךְ n.m. du.-2 f.s. sf. (994) *your breasts*
כְּאֶשְׁכְּלוֹת הַגֶּפֶן prep.-n.m.p. cstr. (79)-def.art.-n.f.s. (172) *like clusters of the vine*
וְרֵיחַ אַפֵּךְ conj.-n.m.s. cstr. (926)-n.m.s.-2 f.s. sf. (I 60) *and the scent of your breath*
כַּתַּפּוּחִים prep.-def.art.-n.m.p. (I 656) *like apples*

7:10 (Eng.7:9)

וְחִכֵּךְ conj.-n.m.s.-2 f.s. sf. (335) *and your kisses*

כְּיֵין הַטּוֹב prep.-n.m.s. cstr. (406)-def.art.-adj. m.s. (373; GK 126x) *like the best wine*

הוֹלֵךְ לְדוֹדִי Qal act.ptc. (הָלַךְ 229)-prep.-n.m.s.-1 c.s. sf. (187) *goes down for my lover*

לְמֵישָׁרִים prep.-n.m.p. (449) *smoothly*

דּוֹבֵב Qal act.ptc. (דָּבַב 179) *gliding over*

שִׂפְתֵי יְשֵׁנִים n.f.p. cstr. (973)-adj. m.p. (I 445) *lips of sleepers*

7:11

אֲנִי לְדוֹדִי pers.pr. 1 c.s. (58)-prep.-n.m.s.-1 c.s. sf. (187) *I am my beloved's*

וְעָלַי conj.-prep.-1 c.s. sf. (II 752) *and for me*

תְּשׁוּקָתוֹ n.f.s.-3 m.s. sf. (1003) *his desire*

7:12

לְכָה דוֹדִי Qal impv. 2 m.s.-vol.he (הָלַךְ 229) -n.m.s.-1 c.s. sf. (187) *come my beloved*

נֵצֵא Qal impf. 1 c.p. (יָצָא 422) *let us go forth*

הַשָּׂדֶה def.art.-n.m.s. (961) *into the fields*

נָלִינָה Qal impf. 1 c.p.-vol.he (לוּן I 533) *and let us lodge*

בַּכְּפָרִים prep.-def.art.-n.m.p. (499) *in the villages*

7:13

נַשְׁכִּימָה Hi. impf. 1 c.p.-vol.he (שָׁכַם 1014) *let us go out early*

לַכְּרָמִים prep.-def.art.-n.m.p. (501) *to the vineyards*

נִרְאֶה Qal impf. 1 c.p. (רָאָה 906) *let us see*

אִם פָּרְחָה הַגֶּפֶן hypoth.part. (49)-Qal pf. 3 f.s. (I 827 פָּרַח)-def.art.-n.f.s. (172) *whether the vines have budded*

פִּתַּח הַסְּמָדַר Pi. pf. 3 m.s. (פָּתַח I 834)-def.art. -n.m.s. (701) *whether the grape blossoms have opened*

הֵנֵצוּ הָרִמּוֹנִים Hi. pf. 3 c.p. (נָצַץ 665)-def.art. -n.m.p. (I 941) *the pomegranates are in bloom*

שָׁם אֶתֵּן adv. (1027)-Qal impf. 1 c.s. (נָתַן 678) *there I will give*

אֶת־דֹּדַי לָךְ dir.obj.-n.m.p.-1 c.s. sf. (187)-prep.-2 f.s. sf. *you my love*

7:14 (Eng.7:13)

הַדּוּדָאִים def.art.-n.m.p. (188) *the mandrakes*

נָתְנוּ־רֵיחַ Qal pf. 3 c.p. (נָתַן 678)-n.m.s. (926) *give forth fragrance*

וְעַל־פְּתָחֵינוּ conj.-prep.-n.m.p.-1 c.p. sf. (835) *and over our doors*

כָּל־מְגָדִים n.m.s. cstr. (481)-n.m.p. (550) *all choice fruits*

חֲדָשִׁים adj. m.p. (294) *new*

גַּם־יְשָׁנִים adv. (168)-adj. m.p. (445) *as well as old*

דּוֹדִי n.m.s.-1 c.s. sf. (187) *my beloved*

צָפַנְתִּי לָךְ Qal pf. 1 c.s. (צָפַן 860)-prep.-2 f.s. sf. *which I have laid up for you*

8:1

מִי יִתֶּנְךָ interr. (566)-Qal impf. 3 m.s.-2 m.s. sf. (נָתַן 678) *O that you were*

כְּאָח לִי prep.-n.m.s. (26)-prep.-1 c.s. sf. *like a brother to me*

יוֹנֵק Qal act.ptc. (יָנַק 413) *nursing*

שְׁדֵי אִמִּי n.m.p. cstr. (994)-n.f.s.-1 c.s. sf. (51) *at my mother's breast*

אֶמְצָאֲךָ Qal impf. 1 c.s.-2 m.s. sf. (מָצָא 592) *if I met you*

בַחוּץ prep.-def.art.-n.m.s. (299) *outside*

אֶשָּׁקְךָ Qal impf. 1 c.s.-2 m.s. sf. (נָשַׁק I 676) *I would kiss you*

גַּם לֹא־יָבוּזוּ לִי adv. (168)-neg.-Qal impf. 3 m.p. (בּוּז 100)-prep.-1 c.s. sf. *and none would despise me*

8:2

אֶנְהָגֲךָ Qal impf. 1 c.s.-2 m.s. sf. (נָהַג I 624) *I would lead you*

אֲבִיאֲךָ Hi. impf. 1 c.s.-2 m.s. sf. (בּוֹא 97) *and bring you*

אֶל־בֵּית אִמִּי prep.-n.m.s. cstr. (108)-n.f.s.-1 c.s. sf. (51) *into the house of my mother*

תְּלַמְּדֵנִי Pi. impf. 3 f.s.-1 c.s. sf. (לָמַד 540) *she will teach me*

אַשְׁקְךָ Hi. impf. 1 c.s.-2 m.s. sf. (שָׁקָה 1052) *I would give you to drink*

מִיַּיִן הָרֶקַח prep.-n.m.s. cstr. (406)-def.art.-n.m.s. (955; GK 131cN) *spiced wine*

מֵעֲסִיס רִמֹּנִי prep.-n.m.s. cstr. (779)-n.m.s.-1 c.s. sf. (I 941; GK 87f) *the juice of my pomegranates*

8:3

שְׂמֹאלוֹ n.m.s.-3 m.s. sf. (969) *his left hand*

תַּחַת רֹאשִׁי prep. (1065)-n.m.s.-1 c.s. sf. (910) *under my head*

וִימִינוֹ conj.-n.f.s.-3 m.s. sf. (411) *and his right hand*

תְּחַבְּקֵנִי Pi. impf. 3 f.s.-1 c.s. sf. (חָבַק 287) *embraced me*

8:4

הִשְׁבַּעְתִּי אֶתְכֶם Hi. pf. 1 c.s. (שָׁבַע 989) -dir.obj.-2 m.p. sf. *I adjure you*

בְּנוֹת יְרוּשָׁלָ͏ִם n.f.p. cstr. (I 123)-pr.n. paus. (436) *O daughters of Jerusalem*

מַה־תָּעִירוּ interr. (552; GK 137bN)-Hi. impf. 2 m.p. (עוּר I 734) *why do you stir up*

וּמַה־תְּעֹרְרוּ conj.-v.supra-Polel impf. 2 m.p. (I 734 עוּר) *and why do you awaken*

אֶת־הָאַהֲבָה dir.obj.-def.art.-n.f.s. (13) *love*

עַד שֶׁתֶּחְפָּץ prep. (III 723)-rel. (81)-Qal impf. 3 f.s. (חָפֵץ 342) *until it please*

8:5

מִי זֹאת עֹלָה interr. (566)-demons.adj. f.s. (260) -Qal act.ptc. f.s. (עָלָה 748) *who is that coming up*

מִן־הַמִּדְבָּר prep.-def.art.-n.m.s. (184) *from the wilderness*

מִתְרַפֶּקֶת Hith. ptc. f.s. (רָפַק 952) *leaning*

עַל־דּוֹדָהּ prep.-n.m.s.-3 f.s. sf. (187) *upon her beloved*

תַּחַת הַתַּפּוּחַ prep. (1065)-def.art.-n.m.s. (I 656) *under the apple tree*

עוֹרַרְתִּיךָ Polel pf. 1 c.s.-2 m.s. sf. (עוּר 734) *I awakened you*

שָׁמָּה adv.-loc.he (1027) *there*

חִבְּלַתְךָ אִמֶּךָ Pi. pf. 3 f.s.-2 m.s. sf. (חָבַל I 286; GK 59gN)-n.f.s.-2 m.s. sf. (51) *your mother was in travail with you*

שָׁמָּה v.supra *there*

חִבְּלָה יְלָדַתְךָ Pi. pf. 3 f.s. (חָבַל I 286)-Qal act.ptc. f.s.-2 m.s. sf. (יָלַד 408; LXX ἡ τεκοῦσά σου) *she who bore you was in travail*

8:6

שִׂימֵנִי Qal impv. 2 m.s.-1 c.s. sf. (שִׂים 962) *set me*

כַחוֹתָם prep.-def.art.-n.m.s. (I 368) *as a seal*

עַל־לִבֶּךָ prep.-n.m.s.-2 m.s. sf. (524) *upon your heart*

כַּחוֹתָם v.supra *as a seal*

עַל־זְרוֹעֶךָ prep.-n.f.s.-2 m.s. sf. (283) *upon your arm*

כִּי־עַזָּה conj. (471)-adj. f.s. (738) *for is strong*

כַמָּוֶת prep.-def.art.-n.m.s. (560) *as death*

אַהֲבָה n.f.s. (13) *love*

קָשָׁה adj. f.s. (904) *is cruel*

כִשְׁאוֹל prep.-n.f.s. (982) *as the grave*

קִנְאָה n.f.s. (888) *jealousy*

רְשָׁפֶיהָ n.m.p.-3 f.s. sf. (958) *its flashes*

רִשְׁפֵּי אֵשׁ n.m.p. cstr. (958; GK 93m)-n.f.s. (77) *flashes of fire*

שַׁלְהֶבֶתְיָה n.f.s. (529) *a most vehement flame*

8:7

מַיִם רַבִּים n.m.p. (565)-adj. m.p. (I 912) *many waters*

לֹא יוּכְלוּ neg.-Qal impf. 3 m.p. (יָכֹל 407) *cannot*

לְכַבּוֹת prep.-Pi. inf.cstr. (כָּבָה 459) *quench*

אֶת־הָאַהֲבָה dir.obj.-def.art.-n.f.s. (13) *love*

וּנְהָרוֹת conj.-n.m.p. (625) *and floods*

לֹא יִשְׁטְפוּהָ neg.-Qal impf. 3 m.p.-3 f.s. sf. (1009 שָׁטַף) *cannot drown it*

אִם־יִתֵּן אִישׁ hypoth.part. (49)-Qal impf. 3 m.s. (678 נָתַן)-n.m.s. (35) *if a man offered*

אֶת־כָּל־הוֹן בֵּיתוֹ dir.obj.-n.m.s. cstr. (481)-n.m.s. cstr. (223)-n.m.s.-3 m.s. sf. (108) *all the wealth of his house*

בָּאַהֲבָה prep.-def.art.-n.f.s. (13) *for love*

בּוֹז יָבוּזוּ לוֹ Qal inf.abs. (בּוּז I 100)-Qal impf. 3 m.p. (בּוּז I 100)-prep.-3 m.s. sf. *it would be utterly scorned*

8:8

אָחוֹת לָנוּ n.f.s. (27)-prep.-1 c.p. sf. *we have a ... sister*

קְטַנָּה adj. f.s. (I 881) *little*

וְשָׁדַיִם conj.-n.m. du. (994) *and breasts*

אֵין לָהּ neg. (II 34)-prep.-3 f.s. sf. *she has no*

מַה־נַּעֲשֶׂה interr. (552)-Qal impf. 1 c.p. (עָשָׂה I 793) *what shall we do*

לַאֲחֹתֵנוּ prep.-n.f.s.-1 c.p. sf. (27) *for our sister*

בַּיּוֹם prep.-def.art.-n.m.s. (398) *on the day*

שֶׁיְּדֻבַּר־בָּהּ rel. (979)-Pu. impf. 3 m.s. (דָּבַר 180)-prep.-3 f.s. sf. *when she is spoken for*

8:9

אִם־חוֹמָה הִיא hypoth.part. (49)-n.f.s. (327) -pers.pr. 3 f.s. (214) *if she is a wall*

נִבְנֶה עָלֶיהָ Qal impf. 1 c.p. (בָּנָה 124)-prep.-3 f.s. sf. (II 752) *we will build upon her*

טִירַת כָּסֶף n.f.s. cstr. (377)-n.m.s. paus. (494) *a battlement of silver*

וְאִם־דֶּלֶת הִיא conj.-v.supra-n.f.s. (195)-v.supra *but if she is a door*

נָצוּר עָלֶיהָ Qal impf. 1 c.p. (צוּר II 848)-v.supra *we will enclose her*

לוּחַ אָרֶז n.m.s. cstr. (531)-n.m.s. paus. (72) *with boards of cedar*

8:10

אֲנִי חוֹמָה pers.pr. 1 c.s. (58)-n.f.s. (327) *I was a wall*

וְשָׁדַי conj.-n.m.p.-1 c.s. sf. (994) *and my breasts*

כַּמִּגְדָּלוֹת prep.-def.art.-n.f.p. (153) *were like towers*

אָז הָיִיתִי adv. (23)-Qal pf. 1 c.s. (הָיָה 224) *then I was*

בְעֵינָיו prep.-n.f.p.-3 m.s. sf. (744) *in his eyes*

כְּמוֹצְאֵת שָׁלוֹם conj.-Qal act.ptc. f.s. (מָצָא 592; GK 74i)-n.m.s. (1022) *as one who finds peace*

8:11

כֶּרֶם הָיָה n.m.s. (501)-Qal pf. 3 m.s. (224) *had a vineyard*

לִשְׁלֹמֹה prep.-pr.n. (1024) *Solomon*

בְּבַעַל הָמוֹן prep.-pr.n. (128) *at Baal-hamon*

נָתַן Qal pf. 3 m.s. (678) *he let out*

אֶת־הַכֶּרֶם dir.obj.-def.art.-n.m.s. (501) *the vineyard*

לַנֹּטְרִים prep.-def.art.-Qal act.ptc. m.p. (נָטַר 643) *to keepers*

אִישׁ יָבִא n.m.s. (35)-Hi. impf. 3 m.s. (בּוֹא 97) *each was to bring*

בְּפִרְיוֹ prep.-n.m.s.-3 m.s. sf. (826) *for its fruit*

אֶלֶף כָּסֶף n.m.s. cstr. (48)-n.m.s. paus. (494) *a thousand pieces of silver*

8:12

כַּרְמִי שֶׁלִּי n.m.s.-1 c.s. sf. (501)-rel. (979)-prep.-1 c.s. sf. *my vineyard, my very own*

לְפָנָי prep.-n.m.p.-1 c.s. sf. paus. (815) *is for myself*

הָאֶלֶף לְךָ def.art.-n.m.s. (48)-prep.-2 m.s. sf. *you may have the thousand*

שְׁלֹמֹה pr.n. (1024) *O Solomon*

וּמָאתַיִם conj.-n.f. du. (547) *and two hundred*

לְנֹטְרִים prep.-Qal act.ptc. m.p. (נָטַר 643) *to the keepers*

אֶת־פִּרְיוֹ dir.obj.-n.m.s.-3 m.s. sf. (826) *of the fruit*

8:13

הַיּוֹשֶׁבֶת def.art.-Qal act.ptc. f.s. (יָשַׁב 442) *O you who dwell*

בַּגַּנִּים prep.-def.art.-n.m.p. (171) *in the gardens*

חֲבֵרִים adj. m.p. (288) *companions*

מַקְשִׁיבִים Hi. ptc. m.p. (קָשַׁב 904) *are listening*

לְקוֹלֵךְ prep.-n.m.s.-2 f.s. sf. (876) *for your voice*

הַשְׁמִיעִנִי Hi. impv. 2 f.s.-1 c.s. sf. (שָׁמַע 1033) *let me hear it*

8:14

בְּרַח דּוֹדִי Qal impv. 2 m.s. (בָּרַח 137)-n.m.s.-1 c.s. sf. (187) *make haste, my beloved*

וּדְמֵה־לְךָ conj.-Qal impv. 2 m.s. (דָּמָה 197) -prep.-2 m.s. sf. (GK 119s) *and be (for yourself) like*

לִצְבִי prep.-n.m.s. (II 840) *a gazelle*

אוֹ לְעֹפֶר הָאַיָּלִים conj. (14)-prep.-n.m.s. cstr. (780)-def.art.-n.m.p. (19) *or a young stag*

עַל הָרֵי prep.-n.m.p. cstr. (249) *upon the mountains of*

בְשָׂמִים n.m.p. (141) *spices*

[redacted]
D0204222

[redacted]